Loring and Rounds: A Trustee's Handbook

by Charles E. Rounds, Jr. & Charles E. Rounds, III

Loring and Rounds: A Trustee's Handbook is an invaluable practical resource that addresses the rights, duties, and obligations of the parties once the trustee takes title to trust property. This Handbook steers you through this complex field, providing property owners with a mechanism for seeing to the needs of beneficiaries in cost-effective, creative, efficient, and flexible ways. *Loring and Rounds: A Trustee's Handbook* is a handy, ready reference and a gateway to the treatises, restatements, law review articles, uniform statutes, and cases you need to know.

Highlights of the 2016 Edition

This fully integrated and bound volume of the Handbook brings you up to date on the latest cases, statutes, and developments, as well as new sections and new or updated discussion of topics as follow:

- Attorneys' fees (§3.5.2.3; §5.6)
- Decanting (§3.5.3.2(a))
- Uniform Trust Code Section 1013 certification (§3.6; §7.2.9; §8.21; §9.6)
- New §4.1.4, Reserved General Inter Vivos Power of Appointment Opens Door to Settlor's Postmortem Creditors
- Expressly reserved beneficial interests and powers (§4.2)
- New §4.3, The Settlor-Brought Declaratory Judgment Action
- Any beneficiary's right to remedies for breaches of trust (§5.4.1.5)
- Renunciation or equitable interest or nonfiduciary power (§5.5)
- Beneficiary *qua* beneficiary is not an agent of the trustee (§5.6)
- Definition of the duty of loyalty and prudence in the trust context (§6.1.1)
- Trustee's duty of loyalty survives due assumption of trusteeship by successor (§6.1.3)

- 2015 Tax Rates for Trusts and 2016 Projected Tax Rate Schedule for Trusts (§10.4)

In addition, the 2016 Edition has approximately 215 more footnotes than did the 2015 Edition, and all tables and the index also have been completely updated.

12/15

For questions concerning this shipment, billing, or other customer service matters, call our Customer Service Department at 1-800-234-1660.

For toll-free ordering, please call 1-800-638-8437.

Loring and Rounds:
A Trustee's Handbook

2016 Edition

Charles E. Rounds, Jr.

Professor of Law
Suffolk University Law School

Member
Massachusetts Bar

and

Charles E. Rounds, III

Member
Colorado Bar

This is a new edition of *Loring and Rounds: A Trustee's Handbook*. Please discard all previous editions (including the 7th Edition).

 Wolters Kluwer

Copyright © 2016 CCH Incorporated. All Rights Reserved.

No part of this publication may be reproduced or transmitted in any form or by any means, including electronic, mechanical, photocopying, recording, or utilized by any information storage or retrieval system, without written permission from the publisher. For information about permissions or to request permissions online, visit us at *http://www.wklawbusiness.com/footer-pages/permissions*, or a written request may be faxed to our permissions department at 212-771-0803.

Published by Wolters Kluwer in New York.

Wolters Kluwer Legal & Regulatory Solutions U.S. serves customers worldwide with CCH, Aspen Publishers and Kluwer Law International products.

Printed in the United States of America

ISSN 1528-5219
ISBN 978-1-4548-5675-7

1 2 3 4 5 6 7 8 9 0

About Wolters Kluwer Legal & Regulatory Solutions U.S.

Wolters Kluwer Legal & Regulatory Solutions U.S. delivers expert content and solutions in the areas of law, corporate compliance, health compliance, reimbursement, and legal education. Its practical solutions help customers successfully navigate the demands of a changing environment to drive their daily activities, enhance decision quality and inspire confident outcomes.

Serving customers worldwide, its legal and regulatory solutions portfolio includes products under the Aspen Publishers, CCH Incorporated, Kluwer Law International, ftwilliam.com and MediRegs names. They are regarded as exceptional and trusted resources for general legal and practice-specific knowledge, compliance and risk management, dynamic workflow solutions, and expert commentary.

WOLTERS KLUWER SUPPLEMENT NOTICE

This product is updated on a periodic basis with supplements and/or new editions to reflect important changes in the subject matter.

If you would like information about enrolling this product in the update service, or wish to receive updates billed separately with a 30-day examination review, please contact our Customer Service Department at 1-800-234-1660 or e-mail us at: *customer.service@wolterskluwer.com*. You can also contact us at:

Wolters Kluwer
Distribution Center
7201 McKinney Circle
Frederick, MD 21704

Important Contact Information

- To order any title, go to *www.wklawbusiness.com* or call 1-800-638-8437.

- To reinstate your manual update service, call 1-800-638-8437.

- To contact Customer Service, e-mail *customer.service@wolterskluwer .com*, call 1-800-234-1660, fax 1-800-901-9075, or mail correspondence to: Order Department—Wolters Kluwer, PO Box 990, Frederick, MD 21705.

- To review your account history or pay an invoice online, visit *www.WKLawBusiness.com/payinvoices*.

Contents

(Internet addresses are provided as references in text for all primary source material.)

Preface to the First Edition (1898)

This little book is meant to state, simply and concisely, the rules which govern the management of trust estates, and the relationship existing between the trustee and beneficiary.

The lack of a Handbook of this kind has led me to complete and publish what were originally notes for personal use merely.

As the book is for general as well as professional readers, the citations are illustrative, with an approach to completeness only where the law is doubtful or conflicting. But pains has been taken to notice the peculiarities of local State Law, especially where dependent on statute.

I wish to acknowledge my obligation to the writers of the many admirable text books which bear on my subject, all of which I have used freely, and to which I have referred often for a fuller discussion of principles and a more complete citation of authorities; and I have to thank Mr. Edward A. Howes, Jr., for his valuable assistance in digesting cases and passing this volume through the press.

Augustus Peabody Loring

Foreword to the Centennial Edition (1998 Edition)

The first edition of *A Trustee's Handbook*, by Augustus Peabody Loring, appeared in 1898. Mr. Loring (1856-1938), who saw his brainchild through its fourth edition, was a practicing lawyer and a Boston trustee. In the forty years that passed before his death, his small, compact Handbook played an important role in the dramatic growth of trust administration in this country. It quickly became the trustee's text of first resort. In 1940 Professor Scott wrote that for more than three decades the Handbook had been on his desk or near at hand. Mayo Adams Shattuck, Esq. (1898-1952)[1] and James F. Farr, Esq. (1911-1993)[2] prepared the Handbook's fifth (1940) and sixth (1962) revisions respectively.

In 1994, the Handbook was given a new lease on life with the publication of the Seventh Edition in hardcover. That was followed by the 1996 Edition in softcover, and then the 1997 Edition also in softcover. The 1998 Edition in hardcover marks the passing of the publishing baton from Little, Brown & Company to Aspen Law & Business. The year 1998 also marks the 100th anniversary of the Handbook's existence.

I was fortunate to be Professor Rounds's chief student research assistant when he took on the challenge in 1992 of preparing the Seventh Edition. Times had changed since 1962. The state was now dispensing many more entitlements and regulating commercial activity far more intensely than had been the case thirty years earlier. In the late 1960s—perhaps in response to these developments—law schools had set about the process of downgrading courses

---

[1] Mayo Adams Shattuck, Esq. is buried in Chebeague Island Cemetery, Maine. His son, Mayo Adams Shattuck [Jr.] (1898-1952), was managing partner of State Street Research & Management Co., and at one time deputy treasurer of Harvard University. His son, Mayo Adams Shattuck, III (1954-), is a former investment banker and now CEO of Constellation Energy Group (2010). He was a finalist for the position of commissioner of the National Football League in 2006. His wife became an NFL cheerleader (Baltimore Ravens) at age 38.

[2] James F. Farr was for many years a partner in the Boston law firm of Haussermann, Davison & Shattuck.

in the law of trusts from required to elective status, so that by the early 1990s, while almost all law schools had made courses on state regulation mandatory, only a few (most notably Suffolk University Law School in Boston) were continuing to afford the law of trusts the status it had enjoyed in Mr. Loring's time. In most law schools, the law of trusts had become an afterthought, buried somewhere in an elective course on estate planning.[3] Professor Rounds and I, therefore, could not assume—as Mr. Loring could and surely did—that the young lawyers who would read the Seventh Edition had had any formal instruction in the law of trusts.

Moreover, much had happened in the field of trusts since 1962. The years since then had seen major developments in the area of creditors' rights, spousal rights, and Medicaid eligibility and recoupment. ERISA would not arrive on the scene until 1974. There was no such thing as an IRA or Keogh plan. RICO, CERCLA, and the consumer protection statutes had yet to be enacted. It would be many years before the social investment movement would come into its own. These are just some of the developments that had to be worked into the Seventh Edition.

The challenge of revamping and updating the Handbook proved a daunting task. Working off a table of contents that he had redesigned, Professor Rounds would compose the text, footnotes, and end matter on his word processor. As each chapter was completed, I would parcel various sections of it out to the other research assistants. They would then get to work tying up loose ends and cite checking. Processing and keeping track of the myriad drafts was perhaps the most rewarding of all the support tasks as I was the only one, besides Professor Rounds, who had a sense of the big picture. It was exciting to watch the Seventh Edition inexorably congeal. Professor Rounds set the pace for all of us by working nights, weekends, and holidays for months on end. He wanted the final product to be something of which we all could be proud. His energy, enthusiasm, and intellectual rigor were contagious.

The Seventh Edition was not to be a treatise. We wanted it to be a handy, ready reference: a gateway, as it were, to the treatises, restatements, law review articles, uniform statutes, and seminal cases. In 1898, Mr. Loring had succeeded in producing just such a book. Through the Seventh Edition we were endeavoring to revive and carry on the Loring tradition. In my opinion, we accomplished what we had set out to do. Now comes the 1998 Edition. Though it is much enhanced from earlier editions, Professor Rounds would be the first to admit that it stands on the shoulders of others. Much, of course, is owed to those who appear in the Acknowledgments. But much also is owed to those who participated in the Loring Project during the Loring, Shattuck, and Farr eras: Nathaniel Thayer, Herman Weisman, Frederick W. Doring, Samuel Vaughan, Arthur Drinkwater, Frank L. Wiegand, Jr., Stuart MacMillan, William M. Prest, Harold S. Davis, B. Devereux Barker, Levon Kasarjian, Jr., and Roger B. Hunt.

April 8, 1998   *George J. McElroy, Jr.*

---

[3] *See* §8.25 of this handbook (few American Law Schools still require agency, trusts, and equity).

HISTORY OF THE HANDBOOK'S EDITIONS

1898	A Trustee's Handbook, 1st ed., Augustus P. Loring
1900	A Trustee's Handbook, 1st ed., Augustus P. Loring
1907	A Trustee's Handbook, 2nd ed., Augustus P. Loring
1925	A Trustee's Handbook, 3rd ed., Augustus P. Loring
1928	A Trustee's Handbook, 4th ed., Augustus P. Loring
1935	A Trustee's Handbook, 4th ed., Augustus P. Loring
1940	Loring A Trustee's Handbook, 5th ed., Mayo Adams Shattuck
1962	Loring A Trustee's Handbook, 6th ed., James F. Farr
1994	Loring A Trustee's Handbook, 7th ed., Charles E. Rounds, Jr., et al.
1996	Loring A Trustee's Handbook, 1996 ed., Charles E. Rounds, Jr., et al.
1997	Loring A Trustee's Handbook, 1997 ed., Charles E. Rounds, Jr., et al.
1998	Loring A Trustee's Handbook, 1998 ed., Charles E. Rounds, Jr.
1999	Loring A Trustee's Handbook, 1999 ed., Charles E. Rounds, Jr.
2000	Loring A Trustee's Handbook, 2000 ed., Charles E. Rounds, Jr.
2001	Loring A Trustee's Handbook, 2001 ed., Charles E. Rounds, Jr.
2002	Loring A Trustee's Handbook, 2002 ed., Charles E. Rounds, Jr.
2003	Loring A Trustee's Handbook, 2003 ed., Charles E. Rounds, Jr.
2004	Loring A Trustee's Handbook, 2004 ed., Charles E. Rounds, Jr.
2005	Loring A Trustee's Handbook, 2005 ed., Charles E. Rounds, Jr.
2006	Loring A Trustee's Handbook, 2006 ed., Charles E. Rounds, Jr.
2007	Loring A Trustee's Handbook, 2007 ed., Charles E. Rounds, Jr.
2008	Loring A Trustee's Handbook, 2008 ed., Charles E. Rounds, Jr. & Charles E. Rounds, III
2009	Loring A Trustee's Handbook, 2009 ed., Charles E. Rounds, Jr. & Charles E. Rounds, III
2010 [binder]	Loring and Rounds: A Trustee's Handbook, Charles E. Rounds, Jr. & Charles E. Rounds, III
2011 [supplement]	Loring and Rounds: A Trustee's Handbook, Charles E. Rounds, Jr. & Charles E. Rounds, III

2012 [bound]	Loring and Rounds: A Trustee's Handbook, Charles E. Rounds, Jr. & Charles E. Rounds, III
2013 [bound]	Loring and Rounds: A Trustee's Handbook, Charles E. Rounds, Jr. & Charles E. Rounds, III
2014 [bound]	Loring and Rounds: A Trustee's Handbook, Charles E. Rounds, Jr. & Charles E. Rounds, III
2015 [bound]	Loring and Rounds: A Trustee's Handbook, Charles E. Rounds, Jr. & Charles E. Rounds, III
2016 [bound]	Loring and Rounds: A Trustee's Handbook, Charles E. Rounds, Jr. & Charles E. Rounds, III

Preface to the 2016 Edition of Loring and Rounds: A Trustee's Handbook
(117 Years Serving the Trust Community)

The fully integrated bound volume of the Handbook is back by popular demand. In the period from 1898 to 2009, 23 editions of *Loring: A Trustree's Handbook* were published. Each new edition was a single, fully integrated bound volume.

The failed experiment with the looseleaf binder and supplementation. In 2010, the Handbook's official title was changed to *Loring and Rounds: A Trustee's Handbook*. Also, the Handbook became a collection of small pages in a massive looseleaf ringed binder. The plan was that in subsequent years, the Handbook would be updated annually by supplementation. This experiment did not turn out well: The bulk and weight of the binder substantially diminished the Handbook's portability. Thumbing back and forth between the index and the sections was a physical challenge. Integrating the considerable 2011 supplementation into the binder—53 separate page-removal and page-insertion procedures to be exact—took far too much time and effort, particularly for those Handbook subscribers lacking secretarial support. It is likely that there are now many 2010 Handbooks in circulation that still have not been supplemented, and are unlikely ever to be, so much time now having passed. Accordingly, beginning with the 2012 edition, the hard-copy platform of the Handbook again became a fully integrated bound volume. It now has the feel of a serious desk reference.

Content that the 2011 supplementation to the now-retired looseleaf binder had brought into the Handbook. The 2011 supplementation had brought into the Handbook 170 pages of additional text; over 773 additional footnotes; 33 additional case citations; 28 additional law review citations; an eleventh chapter, *Tax Basis/Cost of Trust Property*; and 11 new sections, covering such topics as the trust entity doctrine, the doctrine of unjust enrichment, and the doctrine of allocation (marshalling). The 194 old footnotes had been reworked. We had substantially reworked, reorganized, and expanded the Handbook's coverage of jurisdiction and conflict of laws. We also had systematically combed the entire

Restatement of the Law of Restitution (1937) looking for trust-related material. Directly attributable to that exercise were 143 additional references to the Restatement of Restitution. We also had reworked, reorganized, and expanded the Handbook's sections on equitable remedies for breaches of trust.

The 2012 additions to the Handbook. Besides what had been added to the looseleaf Handbook by the 2011 supplementation, the 2012 bound volume contained approximately 77 pages of additional content. There were 482 additional footnotes, citations to 22 additional cases, and 13 new sections, covering such topics as the doctrine of equitable subrogation, the good-faith doctrine, the doctrine of equitable election, and the status of the chancery receiver. The 166 preexisting footnotes had been revised. For the 2012 edition, we systematically combed the relevant works of Prof. John Chipman Gray for useful trust-related material and wove what has been found into the fabric of Handbook.

The 2013 additions to the Handbook. The 2013 edition of the Handbook had approximately 100 more pages of main text (as well as approximately 500 more footnotes) than did the 2012 edition. Most of this new content was the byproduct of a careful textual analysis of the newly minted and profoundly flawed Restatement (Third) of Property, specifically those chapters dealing with powers of appointment, the rule against perpetuities, future interests, and class gifts. The 2013 edition also had nine more sections than did the 2012 edition.

The 2014 additions to the Handbook. The 2014 edition of the Handbook had approximately 55 more pages of main text (as well as approximately 260 more footnotes) than did the 2013 edition. Much new content was the byproduct of a careful textual analysis of the newly minted Restatement (Third) of Restitution and Unjust Enrichment. There were 40 additions to the Table of Cases, of which 11 were 2013 decisions. The 2014 edition had three new sections: (1) Section 8.15.91 (the direct-benefits estoppel doctrine in the context of trust arbitration clauses); (2) Section 8.15.92 (the rule in *Saunders v. Vautier*); and (3) Section 8.15.93 (the implied-gift-in-default doctrine in the context of expired non-general powers of appointment).

The 2015 additions to the Handbook. The 2015 edition of the Handbook had approximately 45 more pages of main text (as well as approximately 254 more footnotes) than did the 2014 edition. In addition, 111 preexisting footnotes were revised. There were 49 additions to the Table of Cases. Much of the new content was the byproduct of a careful textual analysis of the newly minted 4th and final volume of the Restatement (Third) of Trusts, which covers the following general topics (§§ 93—111):

- Remedying Breach of Trust: General Principles
- Trustee Liability to Beneficiaries
- Beneficiary Liability
- Liability of Trust or Trustee to Third Party
- Third-Party Liability to Trust
- Accounting for Principal and Income

The 2015 edition had three new sections: (1) Section 8.15.94 (Trust Repudiation Doctrine); (2) Section 8.47 (The President John Adams Trust for the Benefit of The Woodward School for Girls); and (3) Section 9.9.25 (whether the quiet or silent trust is a true trust). The content of preexisting Section 2.1.1 was augmented with an analysis of the newly minted Uniform Fiduciary Access to Digital Assets Act, which was approved July 16, 2014, by the Uniform Law Commission (ULC) at its 123rd Annual Meeting in Seattle.

The 2016 additions to the Handbook. There are 114 more case references in the 2016 Edition than the 2015 Edition. The Handbook's content has been substantially fleshed out and enriched by all this new material. Of the additional cases, 52 were decided in 2014 or later. Eleven of them are 2015 cases. There are also 214 more footnotes in the 2016 Edition, and 65 preexisting footnotes have been revised. We have made a concerted effort to flag where appropriate across the fabric of the Handbook the fact that Article VII of the Uniform Probate Code, which addressed selected issues of trust administration, including trust registration, the jurisdiction of the courts concerning trust, and the duties and liabilities of trustee, has been superseded by the Uniform Trust Code, which was approved in 2000. Article VII of the Uniform Probate Code was withdrawn in 2010. The new law review article by Rounds and Illes (*Is a Hungarian Trust a Clone of the Anglo-American Trust, or Just a Type of Contract? Parsing the Asset-Management Provisions of the New Hungarian Civil Code*, 6 Geo. Mason J. Int'l Com. L. 153 (2015)) was published in time to be cited where appropriate in the 2016 Edition.

In spite of all this new material, the 2016 edition of the Handbook is still lean and mean, all things considered. We have assiduously avoided frivolous footnoting and the mindless stringing of citations. Each footnote is either itself a wealth of useful information, or the gateway to it.

All that having been said, we must acknowledge that the ballooning of *Loring*, now *Loring and Rounds*, driven primarily by the Uniform Trust Code and other such trust-related codifications, is making it increasingly difficult for the student or busy trust practitioner to immediately extract from the Handbook information that is readily exploitable. In recent years we have received numerous e-mail and telephone communications from our readers requesting assistance. "We can't find it in *Loring*" is the typical refrain. In almost every case, we have managed to steer the reader to a paragraph or footnote that is directly on point. Accordingly, we are gratuitously inviting any reader of the book who is unable readily to locate that silver bullet to e-mail us for assistance at this address: *CRoundsJr@aol.com.*

The text of the e-mail should be brief, complete, and self-contained. While we ask that the identity, address, and contact telephone number of the sender be fully disclosed, the e-mail should contain absolutely no confidential information whatsoever. While we do not guarantee that this book will be helpful in every case, we expect that it will be in most. We reserve the right to revoke this gratuitous offer of assistance at any time. Under no circumstances should the offer be construed as part of the consideration for the purchase price of *Loring and Rounds: A Trustee's Handbook*. Nor should it be construed as practicing law. The offer is limited merely to informing the reader whether or not this handbook may have information useful to the reader and, if it does, to alerting the reader as to where in the book such information might be found.

Linkedin. We also invite our readers to join the *Loring and Rounds: A Trustee's Handbook* Linkedin closed Group and to participate in its discussions.

Charles E. Rounds, Jr.
Charles E. Rounds, III
December 1, 2015

<CRoundsJr@aol.com>
Web Page: <http://www.law.suffolk.edu>
<chadrounds@yahoo.com>
Web Page: <http://dwkpc.net/>

Acknowledgments

Our thanks go to Joel Bernstein, Esq. (MA); Amy K. Kanyuk, Esq. (NH); Courtney Maloney, Esq. (MA); and Christopher Webber, Esq. (VT); for supporting the Loring Project in 2015 with their advice and counsel; and to Steven B. Gorin, Esq. (MO); Donald D. Kozusko, Esq. (D.C.) and Robert G. Stewart, Esq. (MA) for their frequent and much-valued contributions to the discussions that are sponsored by the *Loring and Rounds: A Trustee's Handbook* LinkedIn Group.

Although we no longer employ research assistants on the Loring Project, and have not for several years, to complete the record, we note in alphabetical order past research assistants: Christopher J. Akeley, Linda E. Alsahili, Mark J. Alves, Renee M. Anckner, Ryan H. Bailey, Nina Bartush, Michelle D. Bazin, Adam R. Bemporad, Anne Bergstrom, Mark F. Bernard, Kelly Bierly, Mary-Jane Birdsey, Donald L. Blaszka, Jr., Joshua D. Blumen, Keith J. Bridgford, Alexis C. Brooks, John M. Brown, Stanley A. Bunner, Jr., Jennifer M. Callahan, Diana J. Cally, Christopher Carbone, Kristin M. Cataldo, Jessica E. Coccoli, Daniel Cocuzzo, Kimberly L. Collins, John Condon, James Francis Conway, III, Jeremy S. David, Lou DeMato, Antonio DiBenedetto, Phong T. Dinh, John L. Dolan, John Timothy Dynan, Dennis Ford Eagan, Christopher M. Falzone, Barry Faulkner, Jennifer A. Fazzi, Cherie L. Fineberg, Marie E. Finnerty, Robert E. Fitzpatrick, Marc Foley, Alison L. Forbes, Kevin Fulcher, Julia M. Gallagher, Lisa M. Glanvill, Suzanne Goldberg, Noah Benson Goodman, Kerry O'Shea Gorgone, Thomas Gormley, III, Ryan M. Gott, Ann Graglia-Kostos, Nicholas S. Gray, Ernst Guerrier, Keith S. Hanson, Shelley E. Harper, Justin Paul Hayes, Nathalie F. Hibble, Jennifer Hines, Michael F. Hogan, W. Todd Huston, Mark Iacono, Edward S. Jarmolowicz, Eric D. Karlberg, Celia M. Ketley, Steven C. Kiernan, Matthew D. Killeen, Polyxeny Angeliki Konandreas, Cynthia A. Korhonen, Brian Howard Kudish, John A. Laine, John P. Larochelle, Christine D. Lavallee, Jacob E. Lavin, Patrick J. Lavoie, Kathleen Leahy, Joel E. Lehrer, Brian Liberis, Emanuel J. Markis, Derek Massey, Katherine F. McCarthy, Michael McCormack, George J. McElroy, Jr., James J. McGhee, Colleen J. McHugh, Brian C. McManus, James A. Miller, Salina Millora, Nicole Miville, Reza Mollaaghababa, John B. Moretta, Paul J. Moura, Suzanne Marie Murray, Robert S. Nedder, Jr., Susan E. Neff, Renee Marie Northrop, Marjunette Nusbaum, Theresa A. O'Loughlin, Page Suzanne Ormond, Magdelena Parnell, Melanie Ann Patenaude, Randall Pratt, Michael J. Riley, Ashlie L. Ringel, Peter

Riordan, Andrea D. Roller, Gwendolyn Ann Rotter, Andrew Rubenstein, Julie Rubenstein, Robert Rudnick, Timothy J. Santoli, Jason M. Scally, Timothy R. Scannell, Anthony Sciaraffa, Robert D. Scolaro, Mark L. Seiden, Deanna Silva, Kenneth J. Simmons, Randy J. Spencer, Shannon Sprinkel, Kurt Steinkrauss, Christopher M. Tarrant, Stephanie M. Taverna, Jennifer L. Thompson, John D. Tuerck, Kristin Tyler, Alexei Tymoczko, Sara L. Uberman, Georgia N. Vagenas, Alina Vaisman, Stephen R. Warner, James Patrick Winston, Courtney B. Winter, David N. Wood, and Maryann Wood.

We acknowledge as well those who rendered assistance to the Loring Project during the Loring, Shattuck, and Farr eras: B. Devereux Barker, Harold S. Davies, Frederick W. Doring, Arthur Drinkwater, Edward A. Howes, Jr., Roger B. Hunt, Levon Kasarjian, Jr., Stuart MacMillan, William M. Prest, Nathaniel Thayer, Samuel Vaughan, Herman Weisman, and Frank L. Wiegand, Jr. Mr. Howes was the first, having rendered "valuable assistance" to Mr. Loring in "digesting cases" and "passing" the first edition (1898) "through the press."

Finally, thanks as always go to Alicia, wife of the senior author and mother of the junior author, for cheerfully working her schedule around the seasonal time demands of the Loring Project.

Charles E. Rounds, Jr.
Charles E. Rounds, III
December 1, 2015

<CRoundsJr@aol.com>
<http://www.law.suffolk.edu>

Special Notice

All tax forms and instructions can be downloaded from
<http://www.irs.gov/formspubs/index.html>.

The citations to the following books are thus abbreviated:

A. W. Scott & W. F. Fratcher, Scott on Trusts (4th ed. 1987), is cited as "Scott on Trusts."

A. W. Scott, W. F. Fratcher, & M. L. Ascher, Scott and Ascher on Trusts (5th ed. 2006), is cited as "Scott & Ascher."

G. G. Bogert & G. T. Bogert, The Law of Trusts and Trustees (2d ed., Revised, 1984), is cited as "Bogert."

J. Mowbray, L. Tucker, N. Le Poidevin, & E. Simpson, Lewin on Trusts (17th ed. 2000), is cited as "Lewin."

J. A. McGhee, Snell's Equity (31st ed. 2005) is cited as "Snell's Equity."

Uniform Trust Code is cited as "UTC."

Uniform Probate Code is cited as "UPC."

CHAPTER *1*
Introduction

Fiduciary relationships are children of the forced marriage of agency law and trust law, being respectively common law and equity ideas.[1]

Equity has added to our legal system, together with a number of detached doctrines, one novel and fertile institution, namely the trust; and three novel and fertile remedies, namely the decree for specific performance, the injunction, and the judicial administration of estates.[2]

The law of trusts in all fifty states, including Louisiana, "is based upon the system originally developed by the English Court of Chancery."[3] A trustee holds legal title to property for someone's benefit.[4] That is the essence of the trust, whose development from century to century is, in the opinion of Professor Maitland, the greatest achievement of English jurisprudence[5] and the largest and most important of equity's exploits.[6]

---

[1] Shepherd, *Towards a Unified Concept of Fiduciary Relationships*, 97 The L.Q. 51 (1981).

[2] Maitland, Equity 21–22 (Brunyate ed.). *But see* George L. Gretton, *Trusts Without Equity*, 49 Int'l & Comp. L.Q. 599, 618 (July 2000) (provocatively asserting that "[i]t is important that lawyers in the civil law tradition understand that the trust is not a 'unique institution' and has no necessary connection with equity").

[3] 7 Scott & Ascher §44.1.

[4] Albrecht v. Brais, 324 Ill. App. 3d 188, 191, 754 N.E.2d 396, 399 (2001).

[5] Maitland, Selected Essays 129 (1936), quoted in 1 Scott on Trusts §1. *See generally* §8.12.1 of this handbook (civil law alternatives to the trust).

[6] Maitland, Equity 23 (1936), quoted in 1 Scott & Ascher §1.1; 1 Scott on Trusts §1. Jurisdictions in Europe and the Americas tend to fall into two general categories: common law and code. France is now a code jurisdiction. England is and was a common law jurisdiction. By the fifteenth century, the English court system, however, had evolved into two sub-systems: the courts of the common law and the chancery courts. Equity is essentially a collection of principles that were first enunciated in decisions of the chancery courts. While it is said that equity affords relief when

The trust is a creature of equity. The trust relationship is a creature of Equity. "The trust owes its peculiar character to the more or less accidental circumstance that in England in the fifteenth century and for four hundred years thereafter there were separate courts of law and equity."[7] Whereas a judgment at law declares the plaintiff's rights, a decree in equity imposes duties on the defendant.[8] In other words, equity acts *in personam*.[9] An equitable interest is that kind of interest that has its origins in the principles, standards, and rules developed by courts of chancery. Thus, Equity should not be confused with *quitas* in Roman law, which was less a source of law and more a frame of mind in dealing with legal questions.[10]

The trust is a system of substantive rights with respect to property that evolved from a substantive equitable remedy for a wrong, a wrong that we would today call unjust enrichment.[11] The remedy was the specific enforcement order.[12] If A transferred the legal title to property to B for the benefit of C, B would have been unjustly enriched if B had assumed the beneficial interest for himself. As the common law was unsympathetic to the plight of C, Equity stepped in to enforce the entrustment. The rest is history:

> [I]n the rough days of the thirteenth century, a plaintiff was often unable to obtain a remedy in the common law courts, even when they should have had one for him, owing to the strength of the defendant, who would defy the court or intimidate the jury. Either deficiency of remedy or failure to administer it was a ground for petition to the King in Council to exercise his extraordinary judicial powers. A custom developed of referring certain classes of these petitions to the Chancellor, and this custom was confirmed by an order of Edward II in 1349. The Chancellor acted at first in the name of the King in Council, but in 1474 a decree was made on

---

there is no common law remedy, equity is still a creature of case law. It is far from a "code" as that term is understood in France and the other non-common law jurisdictions. *See generally* §8.12 of this handbook (where the trust is recognized outside the United States) for a discussion of the advantages and disadvantages of codification. "Just as the thirteen original states adopted substantially the entire common law of England, so they took over with little change the English system of equity jurisprudence, a part of which was the subject of trusts." Bogert §6. In some jurisdictions, however, it took a while before trusts were judicially enforced. It was not until 1877, for example, that "equity won full recognition as a complementary part of the judicial system of Massachusetts." Edwin H. Woodruff, *Chancery in Massachusetts*, XX The L.Q. Rev. 370, 383 (Oct. 1889). "In no other state in the Union was there such long and stubborn resistance made to the establishment of chancery." Edwin H. Woodruff, *Chancery in Massachusetts*, XX The L.Q. Rev. 370, 384 (Oct. 1889). Even today, the Uniform Trust Code (UTC), though comprehensive in scope, does not codify all aspects of the law of trusts. The National Conference of Commissioners on Uniform State Laws contemplated that the UTC would be supplemented by the common law of trusts and principles of equity. The UTC is available at <http://www.uniformlaws.org/Act.aspx?title=Trust%20Code>.

[7] 1 Scott & Ascher §1.1; 1 Scott on Trusts §1. *See also* Bogert §3.

[8] Bogert §3.

[9] 1 Scott & Ascher §1.1; 1 Scott on Trusts §1; Bogert §3.

[10] John Chipman Gray, The Nature and Sources of the Law 290–291 (1909).

[11] *See generally* §8.15.78 of this handbook (unjust enrichment).

[12] *See generally* §7.2.3.4 of this handbook (specific enforcement); Bogert §3.

his own authority, and this practice continued, so that there came to be a Court of Chancery as an institution independent of the King and his Council.[13]

The Lord Chancellor, usually a clergyman,[14] was the officer responsible for keeping the Great Seal of England, and was a close adviser of the monarch.[15] Under him served the chancery scribes who were responsible for the monarch's paperwork. It is said that "[t]he genealogy of modern Standard English goes back to Chancery, not Chaucer."[16]

As keeper of the King's (or Queen's) Conscience, the Lord Chancellor was once the chief judge of the court of chancery.[17] (In England, however, the High Court of Chancery was merged with the common law courts in 1873, and common law judges given the power to administer equity.) Only in 1362, well after the Norman invasion, did the Lord Chancellor begin addressing Parliament in English rather than in French.[18] He still outranks the Prime Minister in official precedence. Today he is *de facto* speaker of the House of Lords, head of the judiciary of the United Kingdom (as well as President of the Chancery division of the High Court), and a member of the Cabinet. The Lord Chancellor exercises a number of ecclesiastical functions as well. He also serves as Visitor of charitable organizations such as schools, colleges, and hospitals throughout the United Kingdom. In that capacity, he is responsible for resolving disputes, hearing appeals, and appointing persons to fill vacancies in the governing bodies of those institutions.

Figure 1–1. Lord Chancellors Since 1066[19]

Equity varies with the length of the Chancellor's foot—John Seldon[20]

I think it might be said that if the Court of Chancery saved the Trust, the Trust saved the Court of Chancery—Frederic William Maitland[21]

And hard by Temple Bar, in Lincoln's Inn Hall, at the very heart of the fog, sits the Lord High Chancellor in his High Court of Chancery.[22]

---

[13] P. V. Baker & P. St. J. Langan, Snell's Principles of Equity 8 (28th ed., 1982); *see also* Bogert §3.

[14] Bogert §3 n.7 ("In the Middle Ages the Chancellors were for the most part ecclesiastics and statesmen. It was only very rarely that they were lawyers").

[15] The Chancellor was a member of the monarch's private or "privy" council.

[16] David Crystal, The Cambridge Encyclopedia of the English Language (Cambridge University Press 41, 1995).

[17] *See generally* Bogert §3.

[18] *See generally* §8.15 of this handbook (discussing in part the phenomenon of "Law French").

[19] Some give the first chancellor of England as Angmendus, in 605.

[20] John Seldon, a seventeenth-century jurist, was expressing the historical criticism of equity that it allegedly lacks its own fixed rules, each Lord Chancellor allegedly giving judgment according to his own conscience.

[21] Maitland, Selected Essays 157 (1936).

[22] Charles Dickens, Bleak House, Chapter 1 (In Chancery) (noting also that "[n]ever can there come fog too thick, never can there come mud and mire too deep, to assort with the groping

- Herfast, 1068–1070
- Osmond, 1070–1078
- Maurice, Archdeacon of Le Mans, 1078–1085
- Gerard, Preceptor of Rouen, 1085–1092
- Robert Blouet, 1092–1093
- William Giffard, 1093–1101
- Roger, 1101–1102
- Waldric, 1102–1107
- Ranulf, 1107–1123
- Geoffrey Rufus, 1123–1133
- Robert de Sigillo, 1133–1135
- Roger le Poer, 1135–1139
- Philip de Harcourt, Dean of Lincoln, 1139–1140
- Robert of Ghent, Dean of York, 1140–1141
- William FitzGilbert, 1141–1142
- William de Vere, 1142
- Robert of Ghent, Dean of York, 1142–1154
- Thomas Becket, Archdeacon of Canterbury, 1155–1162
- Geoffrey Ridel, Archdeacon of Canterbury, 1162–1173
- Geoffrey, the Bastard, Plantagenet, 1181–1189
- William Longchamp, Bishop of Ely, 1189–1197
- Eustace, Dean of Salisbury, 1197–1198
- Eustace, Bishop of Ely, 1198–1199
- Hubert Walter, Archbishop of Canterbury, 1199–1205
- Walter de Gray, 1205–1214
- Richard Marsh, 1214–1226
- Ralph Neville, 1226–1240
- Richard le Gras, Abbot of Evesham, 1240–1242
- Ralph Neville, 1242–1244
- Silvester de Everdon, Archdeacon of Chester, 1244–1246
- John Mansel, Provost of Beverley, 1246–1247
- Sir John Lexington, 1247–1248
- John Mansel, 1248–1249
- Sir John Lexington, 1249–1250
- William of Kilkenny, 1250–1255
- Henry Wingham, 1255–1260
- Nicholas of Ely, Archdeacon of Ely, 1260–1261
- Walter de Merton, Archdeacon of Bath, 1261–1263
- Nicholas of Ely, Archdeacon of Ely, 1263
- John Chishull, Archdeacon of London, 1263–1264
- Thomas Cantilupe, Archdeacon of Stafford, 1264–1265
- Ralph Sandwich, 1265
- Walter Giffard, Bishop of Bath and Wells, 1265–1266
- Godfrey Giffard, Archdeacon of Wells, 1266–1268
- John Chishull, Dean of St. Pauls, 1268–1269
- Richard Middleton, Archdeacon of Northumberland, 1269–1272
- Walter de Merton, Archdeacon of Bath, 1272–1274
- Robert Burnell, Bishop of Bath, 1274–1292
- John Langton, Canon of Lincoln, 1292–1302
- William Greenfield, Dean of Chichester, 1302–1305
- William Hamilton, Dean of York, 1305–1307
- Ralph Baldock, Bishop of London, 1307
- John Langton, Bishop of Chichester, 1307–1310
- Walter Reynolds, Bishop of Worcester, 1310–1314

---

and floundering condition which this High Court of Chancery, most pestilent of hoary sinners, holds, this day, in the sight of heaven and earth.").

- John Sandall, Canon of Lincoln, 1314–1318
- John Hotham, Bishop of Ely, 1318–1320
- John Salmon, Bishop of Norwich, 1320–1323
- Robert Baldock, Archdeacon of Middlesex, 1323–1327
- William Airmyn, Bishop of Norwich, 1327–1328
- Henry Burghersh, Bishop of Lincoln, 1328–1330
- John de Stratford, Bishop of Winchester, 1330–1334
- Richard Bury, Bishop of Durham, 1334–1335
- John de Stratford, Archbishop of Canterbury, 1335–1337
- Robert de Stratford, Bishop of Chichester, 1337–1338
- Richard Bintworth, Bishop of London, 1338–1339
- John de Stratford, Archbishop of Canterbury, 1340
- Sir Robert Bourchier, 1340–1341
- Sir Robert Parving, 1341–1343
- John Offord, Dean of Lincoln, 1345–1349
- John Thoresby, Bishop of Worcester, 1349–1356
- William Edington, Bishop of Winchester, 1356–1363
- Simon Langham, Bishop of Ely, 1363–1367
- William of Wykeham, Bishop of Winchester, 1367–1371
- Sir Robert Thorp, 1371–1372
- Sir John Knyvet, 1372–1377
- Adam Houghton, Bishop of St. David's, 1377–1378
- Richard Scrope, Lord Scrope of Bolton, 1378–1380
- Simon Sudbury, Archbishop of Canterbury, 1380–1381
- Hugh Segrave, 1381

- William Courtenay, Bishop of London, 1381
- Robert Braybrook, Bishop of London, 1382–1383
- Michael de la Pole, 1st Earl of Suffolk, 1383–1386
- Thomas Arundel, Bishop of Ely, 1386–1389
- William of Wykeham, Bishop of Winchester, 1389–1391
- Thomas Arundel, Archbishop of York, 1391–1396
- Edmund Stafford, Bishop of Exeter, 1396–1399
- John Scarle, Archdeacon of Lincoln, 1399–1401
- Edmund Stafford, Bishop of Exeter, 1401–1403
- Henry Beaufort, Bishop of Lincoln, 1403–1405
- Thomas Langley, Dean of York, 1405
- Thomas Arundel, Archbishop of Canterbury, 1407–1410
- Sir Thomas Beaufort, 1410–1412
- Thomas Arundel, Archbishop of Canterbury, 1412–1413
- Henry Beaufort, Bishop of Winchester, 1413–1417
- Thomas Langley, Bishop of Durham, 1417–1424
- Henry Beaufort, Bishop of Winchester, 1424–1426
- John Kemp, Archbishop of York, 1426–1432
- John Stafford, Bishop of Bath (later Archbishop of Canterbury), 1432–1450
- John Kemp, Archbishop of York, 1450–1454
- Richard Neville, Earl of Salisbury, 1454–1455
- Thomas Bourchier, Archbishop of Canterbury, 1455–1456
- William Waynflete, Bishop of Winchester, 1456–1460

- George Neville, Bishop of Exeter, 1460–1467
- Richard Stillington, Bishop of Bath, 1467–1470
- George Neville, Archbishop of York, 1470–1471
- Richard Stillington, Bishop of Bath, 1471–1473
- Laurence Booth, Bishop of Durham, 1473–1475
- John Alcock, Bishop of Rochester, 1475
- Thomas Rotheram, Bishop of Lincoln, 1475–1483
- John Russell, Bishop of Lincoln, 1483–1485
- Thomas Rothram, Archbishop of York, 1485
- John Alcock, Bishop of Worcester, 1485–1487
- John Morton, Archbishop of Canterbury, 1487–1500
- Henry Deane, Archbishop of Canterbury, 1500–1502
- William Warham, Archbishop of Canterbury, 1502–1515
- Thomas Cardinal Wolsey, Archbishop of York, 1515–1529

- Sir Thomas More, 1529–1532[23]
- Thomas Audley, 1st Baron Audley of Walden, 1532–1544
- Thomas Wriothesley, 1st Baron of Wriothesley, 1544–1547
- William Paulet, 1st Baron St. John, 1547
- Richard Rich, 1st Baron Rich, 1547–1551
- Thomas Goodrich, Bishop of Ely, 1552–1553
- Stephen Gardiner, Bishop of Winchester, 1553–1555
- Nicholas Heath, Archbishop of York, 1555–1558
- Nicholas Bacon, 1558–1579
- Sir Thomas Bromley, 1579–1587
- Sir Christopher Hatton, 1587–1591
- In commission, 1591–1592
- Sir John Puckering, 1592
- Sir Thomas Egerton, 1596–1617
- Sir Francis Bacon, 1st Baron Verulam, 1617–1621[24]
- In commission, 1621
- John Williams Bishop of Lincoln, 1621–1625

---

[23] *See* 1 Scott & Ascher §1.2 (noting that although More, a trained lawyer, "held the great seal for only three years, equity made great strides under his administration"). Sir Thomas More, author of *Utopia* (published in Latin in 1516), is the hero of "A Man for All Seasons," a play by Robert Bolt. In 1535, More was sentenced to death for treason. His last words were "I die the king's good servant, and God's first." The king More referred to was Henry VIII. More was born in London in 1478.

[24] "Following his illustrious predecessor, Sir Thomas More, who also set himself a similar task,… [Chancellor Bacon]…was in the habit of summoning the common law judges to dinner, and then asking them to suggest instances where the process of chancery had appeared to them excessive. It is plain…that equity and English law generally gained a great deal more than has formerly been imagined from Bacon's administration of equity from 1617 until 1622…" Keeton, "Bacon as a Chancery Judge," 492, citing Potter, History of Equity, 49. "…[Bacon]…did much to restore harmony between the two jurisdictions, which Coke's ill-advised attack had broken." Keeton, "Bacon as a Chancery Judge," 492, citing Potter, History of Equity, 49. "In addition, there was a pressing need for Bacon's style of equity. 'Many Englishmen of that age were both unprincipled and litigious; and they thought nothing of starting simultaneous proceedings in different courts to vex their adversaries.' Bacon's decisions, by closely enforcing the *Ordinances* against vexatious litigants and following common law substantive rules wherever possible, greatly improved the situation." Daniel R. Coquillette, Francis Bacon 211(1992) (citing to Holdsworth, Francis Bacon's Decisions 62).

- Sir Thomas Coventry, 1st Baron Coventry, 1625–1640
- John Finch, 1st Baron Finch, 1640–1641
- Edward Littleton, 1st Baron Lyttleton of Mounslow, 1641–1642
- *In exile*
- Sir Richard Lane, 1645–1653
- Sir Edward Herbert, 1653–1658
- Sir Edward Hyde, 1658–1660
- *Restoration*
- Edward Hyde, 1st Earl of Calerendon, 1660–1667
- Sir Orlando Bridgeman (Lord Keeper), 1667–1672
- Anthony Ashley–Cooper, 1st Earl of Shaftesbury, 1672–1673
- Heneage Finch, 1st Earl of Nottingham (Lord Keeper to 1675), 1673–1682
- Francis North, 1st Baron Guilford (Lord Keeper), 1682–1685
- George Jeffreys, 1st Baron Jeffreys, 1685–1688
- In commission, 1689–1693
- John Somers, 1st Baron Somers (Lord Keeper to 1697), 1693–1700
- Sir Nathan Wright (Lord Keeper), 1700–1705
- William Cowper, 1st Baron Cowper (Lord Keeper), 1705–1707
- William Cowper, 1st Baron Cowper, 1707–1708
- In commission, 1708–1710
- Simon Harcourt, 1st Baron Harcourt (Lord Keeper to 1713), 1710–1714
- William Cowper, 1st Baron Cowper, 1714–1718

- Thomas Parker, 1st Earl of Macclesfield, 1718–1725
- In commission, 1725
- Peter King, 1st Baron King, 1725–1733
- Charles Talbot, 1st Baron Talbot of Hensol, 1733–1737
- Philip Yorke, 1st Earl of Hardwicke, 1737–1756
- In commission, 1756–1757
- Robert Henley, 1st Earl of Northington (Lord Keeper to 1761), 1757–1766
- Charles Pratt, 1st Baron Camden, 1766–1770
- Charles Yorke, 1770
- In commission, 1770–1771
- Henry Bathurst, 1st Baron Apsley, 1771–1778
- Edward Thurlow, 1st Baron Thurlow, 1778–1783
- In commission, 1783
- Edward Thurlow, 1st Baron Thurlow, 1783–1792
- In commission, 1792–1793
- Alexander Wedderburn, 1st Baron Loughborough, 1793–1801
- John Scott, 1st Baron Eldon, 1801–1806
- Thomas Erskine, 1st Baron Erskine, 1806–1807
- John Scott, 1st Earl of Eldon, 1807–1827
- John Singleton Copley, 1st Baron Lyndhurst, 1827–1830
- Henry Peter Brougham, 1st Baron Brougham and Vaux, 1830–1834[25]
- Robert Monsey Rolfe, 1st Baron Cranworth, 1852–1858

---

[25] Lord Brougham headed up a parliamentary commission that was charged with investigating the administration of charitable trusts in England. It found the charitable sector to be in a sorry state of affairs due to an absence of supervision. Much abuse was uncovered. "Thereafter, Parliament provided for the appointment of a permanent Charity Commission, responsible for the oversight of most charitable trusts." 5 Scott & Ascher §37.1.2.

- John Singleton Copley, 1st Baron Lyndhurst, 1834–1835
- In commission, 1835–1836
- Charles Pepys, 1st Baron Cottenham, 1836–1841
- John Singleton Copley, 1st Baron Lyndhurst, 1841–1846[26]
- Charles Pepys, 1st Baron Cottenham, 1846–1850
- Thomas Wilde, 1st Baron Truro, 1850–1852
- Edward Burtenshaw Sugden, 1st Baron St. Leonards, 1852
- Frederic Thesiger, 1st Baron Chelmsford, 1858–1859
- John Campbell, 1st Baron Campbell of St. Andrews, 1859–1861
- Richard Bethell, 1st Baron Westbury, 1861–1865
- Robert Monsey Rolfe, 1st Baron Cranworth, 1865–1866
- Frederic Thesiger, 1st Baron Chelmsford, 1866–1868
- Hugh McCalmont Cairns, 1st Baron Cairns, 1868
- William Page Wood, 1st Baron Hatherley, 1868–1872
- Roundell Palmer, 1st Baron Selborne, 1872–1874
- Hugh McCalmont Cairns, 1st Earl Cairns, 1874–1880
- Roundell Palmer, 1st Earl of Selborne, 1880–1885
- Hardinge Giffard, 1st Baron Halsbury, 1885–1886
- Farrer Herschell, 1st Baron Herschell, 1886
- Hardinge Giffard, 1st Baron Halsbury, 1886–1892
- Farrer Herschell, 1st Baron Herschell, 1892–1895
- Hardinge Giffard, 1st Earl of Halsbury, 1895–1905
- Robert Threshie Reid, 1st Earl of Loreburn, 1905–1912
- Richard Burdon Haldane, 1st Viscount Haldane, 1912–1915
- Stanley Buckmaster, 1st Baron Buckmaster, 1915–1916
- Robert Bannatyne Finlay, 1st Baron Finlay, 1916–1919
- Frederick Edwin Smith, 1st Baron Birkenhead, 1919–1922
- George Cave, 1st Viscount Cave, 1922–1924
- Richard Burdon Haldane, 1st Viscount Haldane, 1924
- George Cave, 1st Viscount Cave, 1924–1928
- Douglas Hogg, 1st Baron Hailsham, 1928–1929
- John Sankey, 1st Viscount Sankey, 1929–1935
- Douglas Hogg, 1st Viscount Hailsham, 1935–1938
- Frederick Maugham, 1st Baron Maugham, 1938–1939
- Thomas Inskip, 1st Viscount Caldecote, 1939–1940
- John Allsebrook Simon, 1st Viscount Simon, 1940–1945
- William Allen Jowitt, 1st Viscount Jowitt, 1945–1951
- Gavin Turnbull Simonds, 1st Baron Simonds, 1951–1954
- David Maxwell Fyfe, 1st Viscount Kilmuir, 1954–1962
- Reginald Manningham–Buller, 1st Viscount Dilhorne, 1962–1964

---

[26] Chancellor Copley was born May 21, 1772, in Boston, Massachusetts. At the age of two years, he was relocated with his family to England. His father, also John Singleton Copley, was the famous painter. In 1870, Edward Foss wrote: "...[The father's]...fame was soon established as a painter both in portraiture and history; and the high value at which his works are now estimated is proved by the large prices they produced in the recent sale of the late lord chancellor's collection." Edward Foss, Dictionary of Judges of England 189 (1870).

- Gerald Gardiner, Baron Gardiner, 1964–1970
- Quentin Hogg, Baron Hailsham of St. Marylebone, 1970–1974[27]
- Elwyn Jones, Baron Elwyn–Jones, 1974–1979
- Quentin Hogg, Baron Hailsham of St. Marylebone, 1979–1987
- Michael Havers, Baron Havers, 1987
- James Mackay, Baron Mackay of Clashfern, 1987–1997

- Derry Irvine, Baron Irvine of Lairg, 1997–2003
- Charles Falconer, Baron Falconer of Thoroton, 2003–2007[28]
- Jack Straw, 2007–2010[29]
- Kenneth Clarke, 2010–2012[30]
- Christopher Stephen Grayling, 2012–2015
- Michael Andrew Grove, 2015–

Prior to the American Revolution, it was typical for the governors of the thirteen colonies, aided by their councils, to exercise the powers of a chancellor.[31] "In New York in 1701, by an ordinance of governor and council, the governor was appointed chancellor."[32]

After the American Revolution, the thirteen original states adopted substantially the entire common law of England.[33] This included, with little change, its system of equity jurisprudence of which the institution of the trust was an integral part.[34] Massachusetts was the last hold-out, not fully recognizing equity as a complementary part of its judicial system until 1877.[35] Thus, for a while in some parts of the United States, trusts were being *enforced* in legal proceedings:

---

[27] "Infuriated by the high-church, high-Tory critiques of a British historian impertinent enough to suggest that the tercentenary of England's Glorious Revolution of 1688 was not worth celebrating, Mrs. Thatcher's then Lord Chancellor,…[Baron Hailsham of St. Marylebone]…jibed that 'academic historians never make their money by saying that the established truth is true.' " Andrew Stuttaford, *A Proper Revolution?* LXI National Review, No. 20, Nov. 2, 2009, at 59.

[28] In 2008, Lord Falconer joined the Los Angeles law firm of Gibson, Dunn & Crutcher as a senior counselor to advise on "dispute resolution, litigation and arbitration, and wider commercial and public issues, as well." Joe Parkinson, *Latest Recruit From Blair Days*, Wall St. J., July 9, 2008, at C2.

[29] Served as Foreign Secretary in the Cabinet of former Prime Minister Tony Blair.

[30] Chancellor of the Exchequer from 1993 to 1997.

[31] Bogert §6.

[32] Bogert §6 ("The legislature and people objected to this method of forming the new court and sought its abolition. This movement failed, but the court was thereafter unpopular and rarely patronized.").

[33] Bogert §6.

[34] Bogert §6 (listing in footnote 8 the citations to a number of cases involving trusts that were decided in Connecticut, Maryland, New Jersey, New York, Pennsylvania, South Carolina, and Virginia after the Revolution but before 1800).

[35] Edwin H. Woodruff, *Chancery in Massachusetts*, XX The L.Q. Rev. 370, 383 (Oct. 1889). *See also* 1 Scott & Ascher §1.9; Bogert §6.

It is true that...[actions for breach of contract by beneficiaries against trustees]...were once maintainable in Massachusetts and Pennsylvania, but that was because there was originally no equity jurisdiction in those states.[36]

In most states, with the notable exception of Delaware,[37] there are no longer separate courts of law and equity.[38] The consolidation, however, has left intact the substantive differences between legal interests and equitable interests.

The consolidation also has left intact the substantive differences between legal duties and equitable duties. "An equitable duty is a duty enforceable in a court of chancery or in a court having the powers of a court of chancery."[39] The duties of a trustee are equitable. In other words, "[a] trustee's obligation is based on equitable principles, whether enforced by a court having both legal or probate and equitable jurisdiction, or by a court having solely equitable functions."[40]

It is said that equity is not separate and apart from the *common law* as that term is understood in its broadest sense, but a gloss or a collection of appendices to the common law. "Equity without common law would have been a castle in the air, an impossibility."[41] By way of example, "[e]quity accepts the common law ownership of the trustee, but regards it as against conscience for him to exercise that legal ownership otherwise than for the benefit of the *cestui que trust*, and therefore engrafts the equitable obligation upon him."[42] But it would also not be correct to suggest that the procedural blending of law and equity, the consequence of a law reform movement that began on this side of the Atlantic in the middle of the nineteenth century,[43] has led to the elimination of the substantive distinctions between the two regimes. Had that happened, a whole-sale abolition of the law of trusts would have resulted.[44] It did not.

Common law defined. Because the trust is a "judge-made" institution, the reader will encounter numerous references to the *common law* in this handbook. The term has meant different things in different times, to include the following:

---

[36] 4 Scott & Ascher §24.1.2. *See also* Bogert §6.

[37] Arkansas, Tennessee, and Mississippi also have separate courts of chancery.

[38] Bogert §1.

[39] Restatement (Second) of Trusts §2 cmt. e.

[40] Bogert §1.

[41] Frederic William Maitland, Equity: Also the Forms of Action at Common Law 19 (Cambridge University Press, 1909) ("We ought not to think of common law and equity as of two rival systems. Equity was not a self-sufficient system; at every point it presupposed the existence of the common law.").

[42] G. W. Keeton, An Introduction to Equity (6th ed., 1965).

[43] Michael Lobban, *Preparing for Fusion: Reforming the Nineteenth Century Court of Chancery*, 22 Law & Hist. Rev. 565, 584 (2004) (noting that "the key political impetus for fusion came from America").

[44] *See* Maitland, Equity: Also the Forms of Action at Common Law, 16–18 (Cambridge University Press, 1909).

(1) The "law in force in all of the Kingdom of England, as distinguished from local customary law peculiar to a limited area, such as the custom of the county of Kent" during the medieval period;[45]

(2) "Judge–made law—judicial precedents—as distinguished from statutes enacted by Parliament or some other legislature";[46]

(3) "The law applied by the former royal courts of King's Bench, Common Pleas and Exchequer, as distinguished from the canon law applied by the ecclesiastical courts and the rules of equity administered by the High Court of Chancery";[47] and

(4) "The law of those areas which have systems of private law derived from and more or less resembling the law in force in the Kingdom of England when it merged in the Kingdom of Great Britain (1 May 1707)."[48]

When the term *common law* is employed in this handbook, it is usually employed in the broad fourth sense to distinguish the trust from analogous civil law institutions[49] on the Continent and elsewhere that are creatures of all-inclusive codification.[50] One is cautioned, therefore, not to read into the term *common law trust* and other such common law and equity juxtapositions any suggestion that the trust is somehow not a creature of equity. "There are, of course, both in England and in the United States many statutes that deal with rules of the law of trusts, but most of them deal with specific questions, such as what are proper trust investments."[51] Even those fiduciary duties articulated in the Employee Retirement Income Security Act (ERISA), however, are not exhaustive, Congress having deferred to traditional principles of equity to define the general scope of an ERISA trustee's fiduciary responsibility.[52]

Trust-related codifications. Since 1850, Parliament has been busy comprehensively tweaking English trust law.[53] In the United States, on the

---

[45] W. F. Fratcher, 6 Intl. Encyclopedia of Comp. Law 2–3 (F. H. Lawson ed., 1973).

[46] W. F. Fratcher, 6 Intl. Encyclopedia of Comp. Law 2–3 (F. H. Lawson ed., 1973).

[47] W. F. Fratcher, 6 Intl. Encyclopedia of Comp. Law 2–3 (F. H. Lawson ed., 1973).

[48] W. F. Fratcher, 6 Intl. Encyclopedia of Comp. Law 2–3 (F. H. Lawson ed., 1973). Such areas would include "the British Isles (except Scotland), the United States of America (except the State of Louisiana and the Commonwealth of Puerto Rico), Canada (except the Province of Quebec), Australia, New Zealand, the Republic of Liberia, and some of the present and former British colonies and possessions in Africa, the West Indies and elsewhere." W. F. Fratcher, 6 Intl. Encyclopedia of Comp. Law 2–3 (F. H. Lawson ed., 1973).

[49] *See generally* §8.12.1 of this handbook (civil law alternatives to the trust).

[50] *See, e.g.*, Charles E. Rounds, Jr. & Andreas Dehio, *Publicly-Traded Open End Mutual Funds in Common Law and Civil Law Jurisdictions: A Comparison of Legal Structures*, 3 N.Y.U. J. L. & Bus. 473 (2007).

[51] 1 Scott on Trusts §1.10. *See, e.g.*, Allen Trust Co. v. Cowlitz Bank, 210 Or. App. 648, 654, 152 P.3d 974, 977 (2007) (noting that Oregon statutes dealing with trusts "have not supplanted the common law and equitable principles pertaining to trusts in areas they do not address"). "In England, there was no general legislation about trusts until the Trustee Act of 1850; the Trustee Act 1893 saw a consolidation of existing enactments; and the Trustee Act 1925 was a further general statute." The Hon. Justice J.D. Heydon, A.C., *Does statutory reform stultify trusts law analysis?*, 6 Tr. Q. Rev. Issue 3, at 27 (2008) [a STEP publication].

[52] *See, e.g.*, Bixler v. Central Pa. Teamsters Health & Welfare Fund, 12 F.3d 1292 (1993).

[53] Bogert §7.

other hand, the various state legislatures, with the notable exceptions of New York and California, have generally been content to allow the law of trusts to evolve judicially, at least until relatively recently.[54] The Uniform Trust Code, the first comprehensive national codification of the law of trusts in the United States,[55] still makes no attempt to restrict the traditional and broad equitable jurisdiction that the courts have over trusts, and addresses only those portions of the law of express trusts that are amenable to codification.[56] The common law of trusts and principles of equity are intended to supplement the provisions of the Uniform *Probate* Code.[57] As to the Uniform *Trust* Code, however, notwith-standing the language of its Section 106, it is actually the other way around, the drafters having intentionally refrained from defining the trust relationship.[58] This is appropriate. "The common law of trusts is not static but includes the contemporary and evolving rules of decision developed by the courts in exercise of their power to adapt the law to new situations and changing conditions."[59] Or in the words of Chief Justice Lemuel Shaw, a former Chief Justice of the Massachusetts Supreme Judicial Court:

> It is one of the great merits and advantages of the common law, that instead of a series of detailed practical rules, established by positive provisions, and adapted to the precise circumstances of particular cases, which would become obsolete and fail, when the practice and course of business, to which they apply should cease or change, the common law consists of a few broad and comprehensive principles, founded on reason, natural justice, and enlightened public policy, modified and adapted to the circumstances of the particular cases which fall within it.[60]

Chief Justice Shaw penned those words in 1854. In 2008, Justice J.D. Heydon, of the High Court of Australia, in a paper delivered to the Sydney Branch of the Society of Trust and Estate Practitioners, similarly expressed the sentiment that codification has its limitations, at least when it comes to fine-tuning the law of trusts: "A system of judge-made law resting on principles of stare decisis has a degree of stability; but it teems with life, and is inherently capable of

---

[54] *See generally* Bogert §7. Probably the first model partial codification of the law of trusts was the Uniform Fiduciaries Act, which was promulgated in 1922. In 1931, the Uniform Principal and Income Act was promulgated. *Id.*

[55] The UTC (available at <http://www.uniformlaws.org/Act.aspx?title=Trust%20Code>) was drafted by the National Conference of Commissioners on Uniform State Laws. It approved and recommended the Code for enactment in all the states at its Annual Conference meeting in St. Augustine, Florida, July 28–August 4, 2000.

[56] UTC §106 cmt.

[57] UTC §1-103.

[58] *See* UTC §102, cmt. (available at <http://www.uniformlaws.org/Act.aspx?title=Trust%20Code>). ("The Code does not attempt to distinguish express trusts from other legal relation-ships with respect to property, such as agencies and contracts for the benefit of third parties.") Thus, §106 of the UTC has it backward when it suggests that the common law of trusts and principles of equity *supplement* the Code. It is the other way around.

[59] UTC §106 cmt. (available at <http://www.uniformlaws.org/Act.aspx?title=Trust%20Code>).

[60] Norway Plains Co. v. Boston & Me. R. R., 1 Gray 263, 267 (1854).

change in the light of experience," he said.[61] In other words, the law of trusts is best fine-tuned judicially though the application of general principles to doubtful problems. "The process revivifies the general principles: it enables them to be explored, understood afresh when looked at from the new angle, modified in the light of the new problem so that the general principles in turn can have slightly different applications in future."[62] Codification tends to "deaden and stultify" that process, at least for a time.[63] Still, over the long term, "[t]he silent waters of equity run deep—often too deep for legislation to obstruct."[64]

Again, the Uniform Trust Code (available at <http://www.uniformlaws. org/Act.aspx?title=Trust%20Code>), is not an all-inclusive codification of the civil law variety.[65] It is a model statute. The form and substance of its provisions, however, can become the law of a particular state by an act of its legislature. Or the substance of the Code can find its way piecemeal into the body of the state's decisional law. To the extent any provisions of the Code are in derogation of the common law or the principles of equity, they must be strictly construed.[66]

Trust doctrine is "a field where much depends on certainty and consistency as to the applicable rules of law."[67] Thus, it is regrettable that the wholesale enactment by the states in one form or another of the Uniform Trust Code, the Uniform Probate Code, the Uniform Prudent Investor Act, and other such codifications is not causing the law of trusts to become more uniform nationally, as many had hoped,[68] but less, as some had feared.[69] The reader is referred to Frances H. Foster's *Privacy and the Elusive Quest for Uniformity in the*

---

[61] The Hon. Justice J.D. Heydon, A.C., *Does statutory reform stultify trusts law analysis?*, 6 Tr. Q. Rev., Issue 3, at 28 (2008) [a STEP publication].

[62] The Hon. Justice J.D. Heydon, A.C., *Does statutory reform stultify trusts law analysis?*, 6 Tr. Q. Rev., Issue 3, at 28 (2008) [a STEP publication].

[63] The Hon. Justice J.D. Heydon, A.C., *Does statutory reform stultify trusts law analysis?*, 6 Tr. Q. Rev., Issue 3, at 28 (2008) [a STEP publication].

[64] The Hon. Justice J.D. Heydon, A.C., *Does statutory reform stultify trusts law analysis?*, 6 Tr. Q. Rev., Issue 3, at 28 (2008) [a STEP publication].

[65] Some states, most notably New York, have seen more legislative tampering with the decisional law applicable to trusts than others. Professor Scott, however, is unimpressed, particularly with the New York experience: "The provisions of the Revised Statutes of New York on uses and trusts have not worked well in many respects and have caused a great deal of litigation, and insofar as the code attempted to embody the common law, it is vague, inaccurate, and incomplete. 1 Scott on Trusts §1.10. In 1920, Louisiana legislatively incorporated the trust concept into its civil law jurisprudence. The Trust Act of 1920 was replaced by the Trust Estates Law of 1938. In 1964, a Trust Code was enacted in part to include certain important trust devices that are used at common law but were not expressly authorized by the Trust Estates Law." Leonard Oppenheim, Introductory Comments, Louisiana Trust Code, 3A La. Civ. Code Ann. 18 (West 1991). A settlor, for example, had not been able to create a trust for a class of children and grandchildren even though some of the beneficiaries might not be in being at the creation of the trust. That gap, among others, was closed by the 1964 legislation.

[66] Ladysmith Rescue Squad, Inc. v. Newlin, 694 S.E.2d 604, n.5 (2010).

[67] Beals v. State St. Bank & Trust Co., 326 N.E.2d 896 (Mass. 1975).

[68] *See, e.g.*, UPC §1-102(b)(5) (confirming that one underlying purpose and policy of the Code is "to make uniform the law among the various jurisdictions"). *See generally* Frances H. Foster, *Privacy and the Elusive Quest for Uniformity in the Law of Trusts*, 38 Ariz. St. L.J. 713 (2007).

Law of Trusts[70] and Trent S. Kiziah's *Remaining Heterogeneity in Trust Investment Law After Twenty-Five Years of Reform*.[71] Justice Heydon is another codification skeptic: "While the general principles of equity operated with substantial uniformity across all jurisdictions in periods where the role of statute was very limited, more general statutory development in some places but not others tends to reduce uniformity, not increase it."[72] In the United States, trust law is degrading inexorably into a state of legislatively induced incoherence.[73]

Another unintended consequence of codification in a common law environment is that it can foster more complexity and ambiguity in the law, and thus more litigation, not less.[74] Certainty is being sacrificed on the altar of flexibility.[75] A good example of how codification can fuel litigation is the New York legislature's well-intentioned but misguided meddling back in 1828 with the rule against perpetuities.[76] Prof. John Chipman Gray explains:

> Before the year 1828, the forty or fifty volumes of the New York Reports disclose but one case involving a question of remoteness. In that year the reviewers (clever men they were, too) undertook to remodel the Rule against Perpetuities, and what a mess they made of it! Between four and five hundred cases [as of 1886] have come before the New York Courts under the statute as to remoteness, an impressive warning on the danger of meddling with the subject.[77]

In any case, Chief Justice Shaw seems to have had it right in at least one respect: Codifications do tend to have a limited shelf life. After only thirty-five years, for example, the Uniform Management of Institutional Funds Act (UMIFA), which has been enacted in forty-seven jurisdictions, has now been superseded by the Uniform Prudent Management of Institutional Funds Act (UPMIFA).[78] This is because UMIFA is now apparently already "out of date."[79] While the prudence standards in UMIFA may have provided some "useful

---

[69] *See, e.g.*, Courtney J. Maloney & Charles E. Rounds, Jr., *The Massachusetts Uniform Trust Code: Context, Content, and Critique*, 96 Mass. L. Rev. 27 (Dec. 2014) [No. 2] (discussing the Massachusetts Uniform Trust Code's (MUTC's) myriad idiosyncrasies).

[70] 38 Ariz. St. L.J. 713 (2007).

[71] 37 ACTEC L.J. 317 (Fall 2011).

[72] The Hon. Justice J.D. Heydon, A.C., *Does statutory reform stultify trusts law analysis?*, 6 Tr. Q. Rev., Issue 3, at 27 (2008) [a STEP publication].

[73] *See, e.g.*, Turney P. Berry, David M. English, & Dana G. Fitzsimons, *Longmeyer* Exposes (or Creates) Uncertainty About the Duty to Inform Remainder Beneficiaries of a Revocable Trust, 35 ACTEC L.J. 125 (2009) (referring to J. P. Morgan Chase Bank, N.A. v. Longmeyer, 275 S.W.3d 697 (Ky. 2009)).

[74] *See generally* Frances H. Foster, *Privacy and the Elusive Quest for Uniformity in the Law of Trusts*, 38 Ariz. St. L.J. 713 (2007). *See also* Bogert §7 ("In some states, the law governing trusts is not collected in a single title of the state code and finding all of the provisions that are relevant to trusts can be quite difficult.").

[75] *See* Charles A. Redd, *Flexibility vs. Certainty—Has the Pendulum Swung Too Far?*, Trusts & Estates (Feb. 23, 2015).

[76] *See generally* §8.2.1 of this handbook (the rule against perpetuities).

[77] John Chipman Gray, The Rule Against Perpetuities, Appendix G, §871 (4th ed. 1942).

[78] Unif. Prudent Management Inst. Funds Act, Prefatory Note.

[79] Unif. Prudent Management Inst. Funds Act, Prefatory Note.

guidance," still "prudence norms evolve over time." These are the words of the National Conference of Commissioners on Uniform State Laws.[80] Unfortunately, "[a] culture of codification and regulation has so taken hold in the American law school that there is probably no turning back."[81]

Legal title is in the trustee. With the notable exception of certain trusts created under the Uniform Statutory Trust Entity Act, title to the property of a trust is in the trustee.[82] Title division and asset segregation are the keys to unlocking the secret of the trust. To the uninitiated in the common law jurisdictions, the trust is a vague, elusive, somewhat mysterious thing. On the Continent, even the lawyers are uncomfortable with the concept.[83] They find the trust to be incompatible with the civil law principle that "property is indivisible," that "not more than one person can have real rights with regard to the same object."[84] But title division and asset segregation are what enable the trust to work its magic. Title division and asset segregation are what give the trust its utility.

In England well into the seventeenth century, for example, one could not devise a freehold estate by will. It could only descend by intestacy. "The trust was a conveyancing device that defeated both the rigidities of intestacy (which still included primogeniture) and the burdensome taxes (called feudal incidents) that pertained when land passed on intestacy."[85] Today, land may pass by will, but the will also has its practical limitations. Because a will speaks only at death, for example, the revocable inter vivos trust offers the following advantages over a will, or a will with a testamentary trust provision:

- Lifetime property management;
- Guardianship avoidance;
- Probate avoidance;[86] and
- Privacy.[87]

---

[80] Unif. Prudent Management Inst. Funds Act, Prefatory Note.

[81] Charles E. Rounds, Jr., *Lawyer Codes Are Just about Licensure, the Lawyer's Relationship with the State: Recalling the Common Law Agency, Contract, Tort, Trust, and Property Principles the Regulate the Lawyer-Client Fiduciary Relationship*, 60 Baylor L. Rev. 771, 780 (2008).

[82] For more on the Uniform Statutory Trust Entity Act, *see* §9.6 of this handbook.

[83] *See generally* George L. Gretton, *Trusts Without Equity*, 49 Int'l & Comp. L.Q. 599 (2000).

[84] Pietro Supino & Andreas C. Limburg, *A Swiss Perspective on Trusts*, in Trusts in Prime Jurisdictions 383 (Alon Kaplan ed., 2000). *See generally* Charles E. Rounds, Jr. & Andreas Dehio, *Publicly-Traded Open End Mutual Funds in Common Law and Civil Law Jurisdictions: A Comparison of Legal Structures*, 3 N.Y.U. J. L. & Bus. 473 (2007).

[85] John H. Langbein, *Rise of the Management Trust*, Trusts & Estates 52 (Oct. 2004) .

[86] In a number of jurisdictions, including Massachusetts and Virginia, revocable inter vivos trusts are employed to avoid probate costs, particularly the costs of the probate accounting process for estates and testamentary trusts.

[87] *See* The New Massachusetts Uniform Probate Code: An Overview 535, MCLE (2009) ("It is believed that most Massachusetts settlors place great value on privacy. Since the trustee has a duty to keep the beneficiaries informed, there is no need to register a trust. Furthermore, creating a registry for trusts would place an undesirable administrative burden on the Registries of Probate"). *See also* Frances H. Foster, *Privacy and the Elusive Quest for Uniformity in the Law of Trusts*, 38 Ariz. St. L.J. 713 (2007).

Let us take the matter of probate avoidance.[88] As the legal title to the trust property is not in the beneficiary, the beneficiary's incapacity or death usually will not interrupt the continuity of the trust's administration.[89] On the other hand, because the trust property is segregated from the trustee's own assets, the trust property is not subject to the claims of the trustee's personal creditors.[90] Thus a single trust can substitute for the durable power of attorney, the conservatorship, the property guardianship, and the will.[91]

The trust is particularly suited to creating life estates, remainders, and other such limitations in personal property (chattels personal). In Appendix F of his treatise, The Rule Against Perpetuities,[92] Prof. John Chipman Gray discusses the profound obscurity of that corner of the common law that is reserved for legal future interests in chattels personal. There is also the perplexing practical issue of how to safeguard a legal remainder interest in a moveable chattel personal while physical possession is in the legal life tenant. Both as a legal matter and as a practical matter, vesting the full legal title to the chattel personal in a trustee, who in equity is bound to prudently look after, administer, and balance the equitable property interests of all parties, is generally the only way to go.

With legal title in someone other than the beneficiary, there is an added benefit: privacy.[93] Not everyone, however, thinks that that is such a good thing:

---

[88] "The term 'probate' originally applied only to the proceedings used to prove (probare) a will; it stood in contrast to 'administration,' which comprehended all subsequent proceedings winding up the estate." John H. Langbein, *The Non-probate Revolution and the Future of the Law of Succession*, 97 Harv. L. Rev. 1108 n.1 (1984). "In modern American usage, 'probate' embraces 'administration' and hence extends to the administration of both testate and intestate estates." John H. Langbein, *The Non-probate Revolution and the Future of the Law of Succession*, 97 Harv. L. Rev. 1108 n.1 (1984).

[89] Albrecht v. Brais, 324 Ill. App. 3d 188, 754 N.E.2d 396 (2001).

[90] "The exemption of the trust property from the personal obligations of the trustee is the most significant feature of Anglo-American trust law by comparison with the devices available in civil law countries." UTC §507 cmt. (available at <http://www.uniformlaws.org/Act.aspx?title=Trust%20Code>).

[91] "The validity of revocable inter vivos trusts as will substitutes is well established." Restatement (Third) of Property (Wills and Other Donative Transfers) §7.1 Reporter's Note 2 (Tentative Draft No. 3, Apr. 4, 2001). "Such trusts are not testamentary even if created with an intention to avoid probate, *see* National Shawmut Bank v. Joy, 53 N.E.2d 113 (Mass. 1944), and may be created without compliance with the requirements for the execution of a will." Restatement (Third) of Property (Wills and Other Donative Transfers) §7.1 Reporter's Note 2 (Tentative Draft No. 3, Apr. 4, 2001). "The traditional explanation for why a will substitute is not a will is that a will substitute transfers ownership during life—it effects a *present* transfer of a *nonpossessory future* interest or contract right, the time of possession or enjoyment being postponed until the donor's death." Restatement (Third) of Property (Wills and Other Donative Transfers) §7.1 cmt. a (Tentative Draft No. 3, Apr. 4, 2001). For a list of states that recognize the revocable inter vivos trust as a will substitute, *see* Jeffrey A. Schoenblum, 2000 Multistate Guide to Estate Planning 5-4 (2000). Relevant cases and statutes are cited. The Massachusetts Statutory Custodianship Trust is a conservatorship substitute but not a will substitute. *See* Mass. Gen. Laws ch. 190B, §§7-501, 7-502, and 7-503.

[92] John Chipman Gray, The Rule Against Perpetuities, Appendix F (4th ed. 1942).

[93] *See* UTC §201(b) (available at <http://www.uniformlaws.org/Act.aspx?title=Trust%20Code>) (providing that a trust is not subject to continuing judicial supervision unless ordered by

...[C]lear analysis shows why the trust, though immediately useful, is also dangerous. Legal systems have tended to agree that juristic personality, because of its dramatic consequences, should be subject to certain conditions, including (with some minor exceptions) the requirement of publicity. Yet the trust, which can be created by a private and even secret act, comes close to being a juristic person. Seen in that light, one can understand why many legal systems have traditionally been so reluctant to recognise special patrimonies. Legal systems contemplating the reception of the trust should be conscious of the implications of such a reception.[94]

It should be noted that Section 7-101 of the Uniform Probate Code, which was revoked/withdrawn in 2010, would have imposed on the trustee, even the trustee of a declaration of trust or oral trust, a duty to publicize the trust's existence. It provided that "[t]he trustee of a trust having its principal place of administration in...[a particular]...state shall register the trust in the Court of...[that]...state at the principal place of administration."[95] In the case of an oral trust, the trustee would even have had an obligation to publicly identify "the terms of the trust, including the subject matter, beneficiaries and time of performance."[96] The trust code of the People's Republic of China, which was enacted on April 28, 2001,[97] provides that a trust is void unless it is in writing and properly registered.[98]

As the economic interest, *i.e.*, the equitable title, is in the beneficiary and thus insulated from the claims of the trustee's personal creditors, the trust also has utility as an "instrument of commerce."[99] Pension trusts, U.S. and U.K. mutual funds,[100] U.S. real estate investment trusts (U.S.-REITs),[101] oil and gas

---

the court). "Contrary to the trust statutes in some States, the UTC does not create a system of routine or mandatory court supervision." UTC §201 cmt.

[94] George L. Gretton, *Trusts Without Equity*, 49 Int'l & Comp. L.Q. 599, 619 (2000). *See generally* §8.12.1 of this handbook (civil law alternatives to the trust) and §8.12.2 of this handbook (the Hague Convention on the law applicable to trusts and on their recognition). *See also* Francis H. Foster, *Trust Primacy*, 93 Cornell L. Rev. 555 (2008); Frances H. Foster, *Privacy and the Elusive Quest for Uniformity in the Law of Trusts*, 38 Ariz. St. L.J. 713 (2007).

[95] *See* UPC §7-102 (confirming that this duty to register applied to trustees of oral trusts as well as to trustees of other types of trust) (repealed/withdrawn in 2010).

[96] *See* UPC §7-102 (repealed/withdrawn in 2010).

[97] Xintuo Fa [Trust Law] (promulgated by the Standing Comm. Nat'l People's Cong., Apr. 28, 2001, effective Oct. 1, 2001).

[98] *See* Frances H. Foster, *American Trust Law in a Chinese Mirror*, 94 Minn. L. Rev. 602, 645–650 (2010) (the invisible trust).

[99] UTC §507 (available at <http://www.uniformlaws.org/Act.aspx?title=Trust%20Code>) (providing that the trust property is not subject to personal obligations of the trustee even if the trustee becomes insolvent or bankrupt). *See generally* John H. Langbein, *The Secret Life of the Trust: The Trust as an Instrument of Commerce*, 107 Yale L.J. 165 (1997).

[100] *See generally* Charles E. Rounds, Jr. & Andreas Dehio, *Publicly-Traded Open End Mutual Funds in Common Law and Civil Law Jurisdictions: A Comparison of Legal Structures*, 3 N.Y.U. J. L. & Bus. 473 (2007).

[101] A so-called UK-REIT, despite its name is not a trust. Neither is a German G-REIT. Each resembles a U.S. Subchapter S Corporation. *See generally* Charles E. Rounds, Jr. & Andreas Dehio, *Publicly-Traded Open End Mutual Funds in Common Law and Civil Law Jurisdictions: A Comparison of Legal Structures*, 3 N.Y.U. J. L. & Bus. 473, 479 (2007).

royalty trusts, asset securitization trusts, and indenture trusteeships that are incident to the sale of debt securities come to mind.[102]

This separation of the legal interest, *i.e.*, the legal title, from the economic interest, *i.e.*, the equitable title, coupled with the inability of the trustee's own creditors to get at the property, can be useful in a multi-jurisdictional setting as well. Why? Because chains of ownership can be collected in a locale that presumably affords some advantage or advantages to the beneficiary, *e.g.*, creditor protection, tax avoidance, secrecy, or simply convenience. "[I]f...[for example]...Caymanian corporation is used for one purpose, a Bahamian corporation for a second purpose, and a Channel Islands entity for a third, the shares can all be held and managed in a coordinated manner...."[103] The Bermuda trust that German industrialist and art collector Baron Hans Heinrich Thyssen-Bornemisza de Kászon established in 1983 as a business-management and estate-planning vehicle comes to mind. The "strands" of the Baron's "international network of 100 or so corporations," said to be worth billions at the time, were "drawn together" within the trust, of which the Baron's son (Georg) was both the designated protector and a beneficiary.[104] The Baron subsequently regretted the arrangement and commenced litigation in Bermuda to have the trust declared null and void. It is said that by the time the parties settled the matter out of court, they had collectively expended somewhere in the range of £40 Million (British) in litigation fees. The trial, which took eight months, had commenced in October 1999.

The trust distinguished from other legal relationships. *The pledge, agency, debt, and contract.* A trust is not a pledge,[105] agency,[106] debt, or contract for the benefit of a third party.[107] Nor is it a partnership,

---

[102] John H. Langbein, *The Secret Life of the Trust: The Trust as an Instrument of Commerce*, 107 Yale L.J. 165, 167–177 (1997). For the English perspective, *see* David Hayton, The Uses of Trusts in the Commercial Context, in Trusts in Prime Jurisdictions 431 (Alon Kaplan ed., 2000). *See also* Bogert §§248 (Investment Trusts and Real Estate Investment Trusts), 250 (Trusts to Secure or Pay Creditors).

[103] *See generally* Jeffrey A. Schoenblum, 1 Multistate and Multinational Estate Planning 40–41 (1999).

[104] John Harper, *The battle of the titans*, 22 STEP J. 29 (July 2014) [Issue 6]. The office of trust protector is discussed in §3.2.6 of this handbook.

[105] *See generally* 1 Scott & Ascher §2.3.5. Even when a pledgee wrongfully fails to return the pledged property after the underlying debt has been paid, it cannot be said that an express trust arises with respect to the unreturned property. 1 Scott & Ascher §2.3.5. This is because the fiduciary element inherent in an express trust is lacking. 1 Scott & Ascher §2.3.5. That is not to say, that the court could not declare the pledgee a constructive trustee of the property. A constructive trust, however, is an equitable relief, not to be confused with the express trust.

[106] *See generally* 1 Scott & Ascher §2.3.4. *See also* Albrecht v. Brais, 324 Ill. App. 3d 188, 191, 754 N.E.2d 396, 399 (2001) (noting that a trustee holds legal title to property for the welfare of the beneficiary, who holds equitable title, while an escrow agent is not vested with legal title to the property, though he may be entrusted with possession and he may have power to pass legal title).

[107] As noted, an agent also does not take title to the subject property. An agency is created by the consent of the principal and the agent; a trust may be created without the knowledge or consent of the beneficiary or the trustee. Restatement (Second) of Trusts §8 cmt. d. *See also* 1 Scott & Ascher §5.6. An agency can be terminated at the will of either the principal or the agent and is terminated by the death or incapacity of either. Restatement (Second) of Trusts §8 cmt. e. A trust

which is essentially a contract of mutual agency. It is actually not even an entity.[108]

The bailment. A trust is an equitable relationship while a bailment is a legal one.[109] A bailment, though sometimes confused with a trust,[110] is not a trust.[111] While a trustee generally takes the legal title to the subject property, a bailee generally does not.[112] Thus, a bailee may not transfer the property in his possession to a BFP (good-faith purchaser for value).[113] A trustee, on the other hand, can pass good title to a BFP.[114]

Only personalty may be made the subject of a bailment, whereas realty as well as personalty may be made the subject of a trust.[115] A bailee normally is under a duty to return to the bailor the specific bailed asset.[116] In the case of a trust, inception assets generally may be liquidated and the proceeds reinvested, unless the terms of the trust provide otherwise.[117]

---

is not ordinarily terminable at the will of either the beneficiary or the trustee or by the death or incapacity of either. Restatement (Second) of Trusts §8 cmt. e. *See generally* §9.9.2 of this handbook (agency arrangements). A debtor as such is not a fiduciary. A creditor as such has merely a personal claim against the debtor whereas the beneficiary of a trust has a beneficial interest in the trust property. Restatement (Second) of Trusts §12 cmt. a. *See generally* §9.9.4 of this handbook (bank accounts and other such debtor–creditor contractual arrangements are not trusts). The promisor of a third-party beneficiary contract is not in a fiduciary relation with the contract beneficiary. *See generally* §9.9.1 of this handbook (life insurance and third party beneficiary contracts generally); Restatement (Second) of Trusts §14. *See also* Joshua Getzler, *Legislative Incursions into Modern Trusts Doctrine in England: The Trustee Act 2000 and the Contracts (Rights of Third Parties) Act 1999,* 2 Global Jurist Topics, Issue 1, Art. 2 (2002) (suggesting that the analogy between the parties to a trust and the parties to a third-party-beneficiary contract breaks down when it comes to rights of enforcement); Restatement (Second) of Trusts §169 cmt. c (providing that although the trustee by accepting the office of trustee subjects himself to the duties of administration, his duties are not contractual in nature). *See, e.g.,* Schoneberger v. Oelze, 208 Ariz. 591, 595, 96 P.3d 1078, 1082 (2004) (a trust is not a contract).

[108] "Increasingly...[, however,]...modern common law and statutory concepts and terminology tacitly recognize the trust as a legal 'entity,' consisting of the trust estate and the associated fiduciary relation between the trustee and the beneficiaries." Restatement (Third) of Trusts §2 cmt. a.

[109] Restatement (Second) of Trusts §5 cmt. e; Bogert §11.

[110] *See* Doyle v. Burns, 123 Iowa 488, 497, 99 N.W. 195 (1904) (musing that the likes of Story and Kent have failed to sort out the differences between a trust and bailment); Bogert §11 ("Occasionally, a court treats a bailee as a strict trustee.... A bailment, however, is different from a trust in several legally significant ways.").

[111] 1 Scott & Ascher §1.8; Bogert §11.

[112] Bogert §11.

[113] Bogert §11; *see generally* §5.4.2 of this handbook (rights of the beneficiary as against transferees, including BFPs) and §8.15.63 of this handbook (doctrine of bona fide purchase; BFP).

[114] Bogert §11. The concept of the BFP is generally discussed in §8.15.63 of this handbook. For a comparison of the BFP, a creature of equity, with the holder in due course, a creature of law, the reader is referred to §8.15.68 of this handbook.

[115] Bogert §11.

[116] Bogert §11.

[117] Bogert §11.

There are differences related to procedure as well: The remedies against a recalcitrant bailee are generally legal, unless the subject property is unique, while those against a recalcitrant trustee are generally equitable.[118]

Unless the bailment is coupled with an agency or trust, it is not a fiduciary relationship.[119] "Although a few cases outside of the United States treat bailments as fiduciary relationships, that characterization has not been adopted by U.S. Courts."[120]

Had England not at one time had separate courts of law and equity, the evolution of the bailment and the trust might well have been synchronous:

> The differences between bailment and trust…grow largely out of the divergent history of the two institutions. Bailment arose in the common law courts before the use was recognized by chancery. Detinue was allowed to the bailor in courts of law before the subpoena in chancery was made available to the trust beneficiary. The law courts have attached certain incidents to the bailment, as it developed under their tutelage, and the courts of chancery have separately shaped the use and the trust.[121]

Formal definitions of the trust. Fashioning a definition of the trust relationship that is both comprehensive and exact is easier said than done.[122] The definition of a trust as set forth in the American Restatement (Second) of Trusts is a "fiduciary relationship with respect to property, subjecting the person by whom the title to the property is held to equitable duties to deal with the property for the benefit of another person, which arises as a result of a manifestation of an intention to create it."[123] The classic English definition is similar: "A trust is an equitable obligation, binding a person (who is called a trustee) to deal with property over which he has control (which is called the trust property), for the benefit of persons (who are called the beneficiaries or *cestuis que trust*), of whom he may himself be one, and any one of whom may enforce the obligation."[124] The definition in the American Restatement (Third) of Trusts is as follows:

> …[A] fiduciary relationship with respect to property, arising from a manifestation of intention to create that relationship and subjecting the person who holds title to

---

[118] Bogert §11; *see generally* §7.2.3 of this handbook (types of equitable relief for breaches of trust).

[119] 1 Scott & Ascher §2.3.1; Bogert §11.

[120] D. Gordon Smith, *The Critical Resource Theory of Fiduciary Duty*, 55 Vand. L. Rev. 1399, n.61 (2002).

[121] Bogert §11. The precursor of the modern trust is the "use," which is covered in §8.15.1 of this handbook. For a discussion of the now obsolete tort action of detinue, *see* Restatement of Restitution §4 cmt. c.

[122] *See* Bogert §1, n.1 (referencing W. J. Mowbray, Lewin 3 (16th ed. 1964).

[123] Restatement (Second) of Trusts §2. For a general discussion of the fiduciary obligation, *see* Bogert §481. Although the Restatement's current definition of a trust might suggest otherwise, a U.S. trustee personally may possess a beneficial interest in the trust property, provided that he shares the legal or the equitable interest with at least one other entity. *See generally* Restatement (Third) of Trusts §2 (confirming that a trustee also may be a beneficiary); §8.7 of this handbook (merger).

[124] Martyn Frost, *Overview of Trusts in England and Wales*, in Trusts in Prime Jurisdictions 13 (Alon Kaplan ed., 2000) (citing Underhill's Law of Trusts and Trustees, 11th ed., p. 3).

the property to duties to deal with it for the benefit of charity or for one or more persons, at least one of whom is not the sole trustee.[125]

Nonlawyers on both sides of the Atlantic tend to think of the trust not as a tangle of legal and equitable relationships but as some kind of incorporeal basket or receptacle.[126] How property gets into the basket and what role the trustee is supposed to play is a mystery to all but a select few.[127] For a discussion of the current trend of deeming the trust as an entity for some purposes, see Section 7.3.3 of this handbook.

Elements of a trust. *The black-letter law*. Thus, for a trust to arise, there needs to be property,[128] a present[129] intention to impress a trust on the property,[130] a purpose, beneficiaries that are ascertained or ascertainable

---

[125] Restatement (Third) of Trusts §2. For a trust to arise, the settlor need not know what a trust is. "The question in each case is whether the settlor has manifested the intention to create the kind of relationship that lawyers know as a trust." 1 Scott & Ascher §4.2.

[126] *See, e.g.*, Charles E. Rounds, Jr. & Andreas Dehio, *Publicly-Traded Open End Mutual Funds in Common Law and Civil Law Jurisdictions: A Comparison of Legal Structures*, 3 N.Y.U. J. L. & Bus. 473 (2007).

[127] *See generally* Charles E. Rounds, Jr. & Andreas Dehio, *Publicly-Traded Open End Mutual Funds in Common Law and Civil Law Jurisdictions: A Comparison of Legal Structures*, 3 N.Y.U. J. L. & Bus. 473 (2007).

[128] *See* Chapter 2 of this handbook. The term *trust property* denotes things or the interests in things that are held in trust. Restatement (Third) of Trusts §3 cmt. b. Synonyms for trust property are trust *estate*, trust *res*, trust *corpus*, trust *capital*, and "the *subject matter of the trust*." *See generally* Bogert §1. *See also* 1 Scott & Ascher §2.2.2 (noting that when differentiating the interest held by the trustee from the physical thing in which the interest exists, such as real or tangible personal property, the Restatements use "the subject matter of the trust" to refer to the thing itself).

[129] Bogert §46 ("Courts…usually hold that trust intent is lacking if the proof merely shows that the alleged settlor stated an intent to set apart a trust res later…"). While a gratuitous promise to create a trust in the future is unenforceable, rights under an enforceable contract may be made the subject of a present trust. 1 Scott & Ascher §4.4.4. Thus, one's promise to B, as trustee for C, may be made the subject of a present trust, provided there has been a present exchange of consideration. B, for example, may take title as trustee to his or someone else's nongratuitous promise to pay C's tuition bills. In the case of a testamentary trust, the present intent to impress a trust upon a portion or all of the probate estate is manifested in the terms of the will, which speaks at death.

[130] UTC §403 cmt. (available at <http://www.uniformlaws.org/Act.aspx?title=Trust%20 Code>). For an express trust to arise, the settlor must intend to impress a trust on his or her property. Such intent is a critical element of the express trust, whether or not the trust relationship itself is evidenced by a writing. *See Sarah v. Primarily Primates, Inc.*, 225 S.W.3d 132 (Tex. App. 2008) (a contract for the care of nine chimpanzees and three new world monkeys did not also create a trust relationship, there being no intent to impress a trust on the property that was the subject of the contract). It is not enough that the settlor secretly intends to create a trust. 1 Scott & Ascher §4.1 (noting that the settlor must outwardly express such an intention, *i.e.*, there must be a manifestation of intention). Conduct alone, however, may be a sufficient manifestation of intention, whereas use of the term *trust* or *trustee* may not necessarily be. 1 Scott & Ascher §4.2. The intention of the settlor which determines the terms of the trust is his intention at the time of the creation of the trust and not his subsequent intention. Restatement (Second) of Trusts §4 cmt. a. "The phrase 'terms of the trust' includes the manifestation of intention of the settlor at the time of the creation of the trust, whether expressed by written or spoken words or by conduct, to the extent that it is expressed in a manner which admits of its proof in judicial proceedings." Restatement (Second) of Trusts §4 cmt. a. "Thus, if the manifestation is inadmissible because of the Statute of

within the period of the rule against perpetuities,[131] title in the trustee,[132] and an absence of merger.[133] Thus, a trust may be created solely for the benefit of the settlor, provided the settlor is not also the sole trustee.[134] The Bogert treatise, however, would seem not to be in accord. It suggests that that one of the three requirements for the establishment of a valid private trust is "an expression of intent that property be held, at least in part, for the benefit of one other than the settlor."[135]

England. In England, it is said that for a valid private trust to arise there must be "three certainties": certainty of words (intent),[136] certainty of subject matter (property),[137] and certainty of objects (beneficiaries).[138]

Doctrinal exceptions and nuances. There are always exceptions, however. In some jurisdictions, an inter vivos trust with an associated pour-over will need not be token funded during the lifetime of the settlor.[139] A statutory trust may exist without the element of intent.[140] Charitable trusts generally cannot have

---

Wills, the Statute of Frauds, the parol evidence rule, or some rule of evidence, it is not a term of the trust." Restatement (Second) of Trusts §4 cmt. b. *See also* 1 Scott & Ascher §4.1. "The intention to create may be sufficiently manifested by a settlor without handing an instrument evidencing that intention or otherwise communicating the intention to the trustee, the beneficiary, or any other person." Restatement (Third) of Trusts §13. cmt. c. *See also* 1 Scott & Ascher §4.2.2. *See generally* §8.15.5 of this handbook (statute of frauds) and §8.15.6 of this handbook (parol evidence rule); 1 Scott on Trusts §23 (Requirement of Manifestation of Intention); Bogert §45 (settlor's expression of intent to have a trust). A declaration of trust or a transfer to a trustee is invalid if procured by undue influence, duress, or fraud. Restatement (Third) of Property (Wills and Other Donative Transfers) §8.3. Under the modern view, there is a presumption that mere expressions of desire on the part of a transferor of property as to what the transferee should do with the property, *i.e.*, precatory words, are insufficient to impose enforceable equitable duties on the transferee. 1 Scott & Ascher §4.3.2. *See generally* §8.15.58 of this handbook (precatory words).

[131] Restatement (Third) of Trusts §44; UTC §402(b) (available at <http://www.uniformlaws.org/Act.aspx?title=Trust%20Code>). *See also* Chapter 5 of this handbook (the beneficiary) and §8.2.1 of this handbook (rule against perpetuities).

[132] *See* §3.5.1 of this handbook (nature and extent of the trustee's estate). A guardian of someone's property, albeit a fiduciary, is not a trustee of the subject property in large part because title is not in the guardian. Title remains with the ward. The guardian has mere possession. *See generally* 1 Scott & Ascher §2.3.3.

[133] UTC §402(a)(5) (available at <http://www.uniformlaws.org/Act.aspx?title=Trust%20 Code>). *See also* §8.7 of this handbook (merger).

[134] UTC §402, cmt. (specifically the commentary on §402(a)(5)).

[135] Bogert §1 (citing as authority UTC §402(a)(3), although it does not appear that §402(a)(3) even addresses the settlor-as-sole-beneficiary question).

[136] *See* 1 Scott & Ascher §4.3.1 (precatory language may indicate a purpose too indefinite or uncertain to give rise to a trust). *See also* 1 Scott & Ascher §4.4.2; Bogert §§45 & 46.

[137] *See also* Scott & Ascher §§4.4.2, 10.3, 10.10.4, 13.3 (U.S.).

[138] Lewin ¶4-02 (England); 1 Scott & Ascher §4.4.2 (U.S.); Bogert §45 (U.S.). A gift from A to B for the benefit of B and B's "family," for example, might not give rise to a trust because of the uncertainty as to who the actual beneficiaries are, as well as their respective interests. B would take the property outright and free of trust, the reference to family being construed merely as an expression of motive. 1 Scott & Ascher §4.3.3. *See also* 2 Scott & Ascher §12.1 (Definite Beneficiary Necessary); 3 Scott & Ascher §13.3 (Definiteness of Extent of Beneficiary's Interest).

[139] *See* §2.2.1 of this handbook (the pour-over statute).

[140] *See* §9.16 of this handbook (statutory trusts). *See also* §3.3 of this handbook (involuntary trustees).

ascertained beneficiaries.[141] An attempted transfer in trust to someone who is incapable of taking title to the property due to age, incapacity, death, or otherwise may still give rise to a present trust.[142] "A trust does not fail at its inception or thereafter for lack of a trustee because the court will appoint a trustee to administer the trust property for the benefit of the beneficiary."[143] While it has been traditional doctrine that a dispositive power in a trustee to select from an indefinite class of persons is void,[144] under the Uniform Trust Code this would not necessarily be the case.[145]

Permissible evidence for determining settlor's intention. In the case of an irrevocable inter vivos trust, the settlor's intentions *at the time of funding* are what determine its terms.[146] That having been said, postfunding statements of the settlor might be admissible to clarify what those intentions were.[147] In the case of a testamentary trust, extrinsic evidence to contradict or add to the plain meaning of a relevant word in the will is generally not admissible, unless there is a latent ambiguity. We cover the parol evidence and plain meaning rules in Section 8.15.6 of this handbook.

Mental capacity required to establish a trust. If one has the mental capacity to make a will, one has the mental capacity to create a testamentary trust or a revocable inter vivos trust,[148] or to exercise a testamentary power of appointment in further trust.[149] "While the courts have differed as to the precise test for mental capacity, they are agreed that a testator is mentally deficient for the purpose of making a will if the testator lacks the ability to understand the general nature of the testamentary act, to know the nature and

---

[141] *See* §9.4 of this handbook (the charitable trust).

[142] 1 Scott & Ascher §4.4.3.

[143] Bogert §1.

[144] *See, e.g.,* Clark v. Campbell, 133 A. 166 (N.H. 1926). *See generally* §8.1.1 of this handbook (the fiduciary and nonfiduciary power of appointment).

[145] *See* UTC §402(c) (available at <http://www.uniformlaws.org/Act.aspx?title=Trust%20 Code>) ("A power in a trustee to select a beneficiary from an indefinite class is valid. If the power is not exercised within a reasonable time, the power fails and the property subject to the power passes to the persons who would have taken the property had the power not been conferred.") *See generally* §8.1.1 of this handbook (the fiduciary and nonfiduciary power of appointment).

[146] Restatement (Second) of Trusts §4 cmt. a. *See, e.g.,* Bilafer v. Bilafer, 161 Cal. App. 4th 363, 371 (2008) ("And we have confidence in the trial court's ability to distinguish between actual drafting errors and the mere claim of error disguising a new, postdrafting, dispositive intent.").

[147] Restatement (Third) of Property (Wills and Other Donative Transfers) §10.2 cmt. g.

[148] UTC §601 (available at <http://www.uniformlaws.org/Act.aspx?title=Trust%20Code>); 1 Scott & Ascher §3.2. *See, e.g.,* Anderson v. Hunt, 196 Cal. App. 4th 722, 126 Cal. Rptr. 3d 736 (2011); Bonady v. Bonady-Napier, 2005 WL 91252 (Cal. Ct. App. 2005). The grounds for contesting inter vivos trusts is touched on in the footnote accompanying §8.2.4 [item 2] of this handbook (trust termination checklist). In New Hampshire, a settlor during his or her life may commence a judicial proceeding to determine the validity of a trust, whether revocable or irrevocable, that he or she created. *See* RSA 564-B:4-406. Delaware has a similar statute. *See* Ravet v. Northern Trust Co. of Del. et al., C.A. No. 7743-VCG, Order of the Delaware Supreme Court (Feb. 12, 2015) ("This ruling, as affirmed by the Delaware Supreme Court, is the first Delaware case of its kind, upholding Delaware's pre-mortem validation statute, 12 Del. C. § 3546, which was enacted in 2000").

[149] 1 Scott & Ascher §3.2.

extent of the testator's property and the natural objects of his or her bounty, and to interrelate these factors."[150] The settlor of a trust possesses the mental capacity to exercise any reserved right of revocation if and when he or she possesses the mental capacity to make a will.[151]

The capacity standard for present irrevocable inter vivos transfers in trust (and for the exercise of inter vivos powers of appointment in further trust[152]) is either the higher contractual standard or the higher donative transfer standard.[153] The Restatement (Third) of Trusts is generally in accord.[154]

Execution formalities. A will traditionally must be in writing, signed by the testator, and "at least two individuals must sign the will, each of whom witnessed at least one of the following: the signing of the will; the testator's acknowledgment of the signature; or the testator's acknowledgment of the will."[155] Most jurisdictions do not require that an inter vivos trust instrument be executed with the same formality as a will.[156] Florida, Louisiana, and New York are notable exceptions. Each has formal execution requirements involving witnesses and/or a notary.[157] Of course any will that contains a testamentary trust provision must be executed with the same formalities applicable to wills

---

[150] Ritchie, Alford, Effland and Dobris, Cases and Materials on Decedents' Estates and Trusts 399 (1993). *See also* Restatement (Third) of Property (Wills and Other Donative Transfers) §8.1(b) (providing that "[i]f the donative transfer is in the form of a…revocable will substitute…the donor must be capable of knowing and understanding in a general way the nature and extent of his or her property, the natural objects of his or her bounty, and the disposition that he or she is making of that property, and must also be capable of relating these elements to one another and forming an orderly desire regarding the disposition of the property").

[151] Restatement (Third) of Property (Wills and Other Donative Transfers) §8.1(b).

[152] 1 Scott & Ascher §3.2.

[153] *See* Restatement (Third) of Property (Wills and Other Donative Transfers) §8.1, Reporter's Note 3 (Tentative Draft No. 3, Apr. 4, 2001) (suggesting a contractual standard). A person lacks capacity to contract if by reason of mental illness or defect he is unable to understand in a reasonable manner the nature and consequences of the transaction. Restatement (Second) of Contracts §15. *See, however,* 1 Scott & Ascher §3.2 (Endorsing a Gift Standard). *See also* UTC §402 cmt. (available at <http://www.uniformlaws.org/Act.aspx?title=Trust%20Code>) (suggesting that to create an irrevocable trust, the settlor must have capacity during lifetime to transfer the property free of trust). *See also* UTC §601 cmt.

[154] Restatement (Third) of Trusts §11.

[155] UPC §2-502 cmt.

[156] *See* Restatement (Third) of Property (Wills and Other Donative Transfers) §7.2 (providing that although a will substitute need not be executed in compliance with the statutory formalities required for a will, such an arrangement is, to the extent appropriate, subject to substantive restrictions on testation and to rules of construction and other rules applicable to testamentary disposition).

[157] **Florida:** Fla. Stat. Ann. §737.111(1) (West 1995), referencing the formalities of will execution in Fla. Stat. Ann. §732.502 (West 1995). The Florida statute of wills requires attestation by two witnesses. Florida, however, will recognize an inter vivos trust that was properly executed in another state in accordance with the laws of the other state. **Louisiana:** La. Rev. Stat. Ann. §9:1752. Louisiana requires the involvement of a notary and two witnesses or a signing by the settlor in the presence of two witnesses coupled with an acknowledgment by the settlor or one witness. **New York:** N.Y. Est. Powers & Trusts Law §7-1.17(a) (McKinney 2000). New York requires acknowledgment of the settlor and at least one trustee or attestation by two witnesses.

generally. The Uniform Probate Code would have the court uphold a defectively executed will when there is clear and convincing extrinsic evidence that the decedent intended the document in question to be his or her will.[158] The Restatement (Third) of Property is in accord.[159] This so-called harmless error rule is intended to unify the law of probate and nonprobate transfers, "extending to will formalities the harmless error principle that has long applied to defective compliance with the formal requirements for nonprobate transfers."[160]

At one time, the Uniform Probate Code had a requirement that inter vivos trusts, as well as testamentary trusts, be registered in an appropriate state court that had jurisdiction over the trust's principal place of administration.[161] The Code's concept of a " 'home base' court where optional proceedings—by and against trustees—could be conducted" had proven "too novel for some," particularly for those concerned that registration would lead to excessive court involvement in the administration of trusts.[162] There were also those who had privacy concerns.

Unifying the law of probate and nonprobate transfers. The Uniform Probate Code would even make dispositions under certain trusts subject to the antilapse and ademption rules that are applicable to wills, as well as the 120-hour survival requirement.[163] As a general rule, a bequest or devise to the spouse of a testator is revoked upon their divorce.[164] Under the Code, divorce also would extinguish the ex-spouse's equitable interest under the testator's revocable trust.[165] The Restatement (Third) of Property (Wills and Other Donative Transfers)'s muddled contributions to the unification of the law of wills and will substitutes, an obsession primarily of the nonpracticing academic, have rendered much of its power of appointment content either incoherent, or likely to be unworkable in practice, or both. We elaborate in Section 8.1.1 of this handbook.

Grounds for invalidating a trust. *Fraud, duress, and undue influence.* A trust is void to the extent its creation was induced by fraud, duress, or undue influence.[166] Or the purported settlor may have lacked the legal capacity to

---

[158] UPC §2-503 (harmless error).

[159] Restatement (Third) of Property (Wills and Other Donative Transfers) §3.3 (excusing harmless errors).

[160] UPC §2-503 cmt.

[161] UPC §7-101 (trustee's duty to register). [revoked/withdrawn in 2010].

[162] Bogert §7.

[163] *See generally* §8.15.55 of this handbook (antilapse [the trust application]), §8.15.54 of this handbook (ademption by extinction [the trust application]) and §8.15.56 of this handbook (120-hour survival requirement [the trust application]). *See also* Restatement (Third) of Property (Wills and Other Donative Transfers) §7.2 (application of will doctrines to will substitutes).

[164] *See, e.g.,* UPC §2-804.

[165] *See generally* UPC §2-804; Restatement (Third) of Property (Wills and Other Donative Transfers) §4.1 cmt. p; §5.3.4.1 of this handbook (spousal rights in common law states in the divorce context).

[166] 1 Scott & Ascher §§4.6.1 (Fraud), 4.6.2 (Undue Influence or Duress); UTC §406 (available at <http://www.uniformlaws.org/Act.aspx?title=Trust%20Code>); §8.2.2.1 of this handbook (fraud, duress, undue influence, or lack of mental incapacity as grounds for voidance);

impress a trust on property or the requisite intent to impress a trust on the particular property.[167] He or she may have failed to comply with certain formalities, such as the execution requirements of the statute of wills if the trust was to be testamentary or the writing requirement of the statute of frauds if it was to arise inter vivos.[168] A trust may be void if all of the designated equitable interests are contingent such that there is either a violation of the rule against perpetuities or the rule against accumulations.[169] A trust may be unenforceable *ab initio* for want of any designated beneficiary; or if intended to be charitable, the designated equitable interests may be too definite.[170] A trust is void *ab initio* if the contemplated purposes are illegal, capricious, or otherwise violate public policy.[171]

Mistake. A gratuitous transfer in trust may be set aside, rescinded, or reformed if occasioned by a material mistake,[172] as would be the case with an

---

Restatement of Restitution §166 ("Where the owner of property transfers it, being induced by fraud, duress or undue influence of the transferee, the transferee holds the property upon a constructive trust for the transferor"); Restatement (Third) of Restitution and Unjust Enrichment §13(2) ("A transfer induced by fraud is void if the transferor has neither knowledge of, nor reasonable opportunity to learn, the character of the resulting transfer or its essential terms. Otherwise the transferee obtains voidable title."); Restatement (Third) of Restitution and Unjust Enrichment §14(3) ("If the effect of duress is tantamount to physical compulsion, a transfer induced by duress is void. If not, a transfer induced by duress conveys voidable title."); Restatement (Third) of Restitution and Unjust Enrichment §15(2) ("A transfer induced by undue influence is subject to rescission and restitution. The transferee is liable in restitution as necessary to avoid unjust enrichment."). *Cf.* §8.2.2 of this handbook (when the trust may be modified or terminated). *See generally* Restatement (Third) of Trusts §12. "Where the owner of property receives consideration for making a declaration of trust or a transfer in trust, or for causing a transfer to be made in trust, the rules governing rescission, reformation, and the effects of wrongful conduct, mistake, and failure of consideration are the rules applicable to contracts or transfers for value, including rules concerning bona fide purchase." Restatement (Third) of Trusts §12 cmt. a. *Cf.* Restatement of Restitution §12 (unilateral mistake in bargains). An action for rescission may not lie, however, if the settlor by word or deed has ratified the trust or has unduly delayed in seeking its rescission. *See generally* 1 Scott & Ascher §4.6.4. *Cf.* §7.2.7 of this handbook (beneficiary consent, release, or ratification) and §7.2.10 of this handbook (limitations of actions by beneficiary against trustee: laches and statutes of limitation). While the trustee of a voidable trust is entitled to indemnity from the subject property for reasonable costs and expenses incurred before avoidance, a purported trustee of a purported trust that is held to be void ab initio may well not be. Lewin ¶21-23 (England).

[167] *See generally* Restatement (Third) of Restitution and Unjust Enrichment §16 (incapacity of transferor).

[168] *See generally* §8.15.1 of this handbook (statute of uses); §8.15.5 of this handbook (statute of frauds).

[169] *See generally* §8.2.1 of this handbook (rule against perpetuities); §8.15.8 of this handbook (rule against accumulations).

[170] *See* §9.4 of this handbook (for a trust to qualify as charitable, the beneficiary class needs to be sufficiently indefinite).

[171] *See generally* §8.15.39 of this handbook (capricious purposes); §9.24 of this handbook (public policy).

[172] Restatement (Third) of Trusts §12 cmt. a; 1 Scott & Ascher §4.6.3 (Mistake); Restatement of Restitution §163; Restatement (Third) of Restitution and Unjust Enrichment §5. *See also* §8.2.2.1 of this handbook.

outright gift.[173] This would include a mistake of law, as well as of fact.[174] The law of contracts generally applies, however, for transfers in trust that are supported by consideration:[175] "A person who confers a benefit upon another, manifesting that he does so as an offer of a bargain which the other accepts or as the acceptance of an offer which the other has made, is not entitled to restitution because of a mistake which the other does not share and the existence of which the other does not know or suspect."[176]

Entrustment incident to a breach of fiduciary duty. A transfer of property to a trustee in breach of some fiduciary duty to the legal or equitable owner of the property is subject to rescission and restitution.[177] Thus, if an agent in breach of a fiduciary duty to the principal transfers the principal's property to a trustee, the trustee is "liable in restitution" to the principal.[178] So also if a trustee in breach of trust decants to another trust with a different trustee and different beneficiaries, absent special facts.[179] The trustee of the other trust and, indirectly, the beneficiaries of the other trust are "liable in restitution" to the beneficiaries of the inception trust "as necessary to avoid unjust enrichment."[180]

Other grounds for voiding a trust. Some other grounds for calling into question the validity of a trust are the following:

---

[173] 1 Scott & Ascher §4.6.3. *See generally* Restatement (Third) of Restitution and Unjust Enrichment §11, cmt. a ("Because it is donative intent that gives legal justification (if not formal validity) to the donative transfer, the unintended and gratuitous transfer of something either greater than or different from what the donor intended results prima facie in the unjustified enrichment of the transferee."); §8.17 of this handbook (trust reformation to remedy mistakes; trust modification; tax objectives).

[174] Restatement of Restitution §49, cmt. a; Restatement (Third) of Restitution and Unjust Enrichment §5(2) ("An invalidating mistake may be a misapprehension of either fact or law.").

[175] *See generally* Restatement (Third) of Trusts §12. ("Where the owner of property receives consideration for making a declaration of trust or a transfer in trust, or for causing a transfer to be made in trust, the rules governing rescission, reformation, and the effects of wrongful conduct, mistake, and failure of consideration are the rules applicable to contracts or transfers for value, including rules concerning bona fide purchase."). *See generally* §8.15.63 of this handbook (doctrine of bona fide purchase).

[176] Restatement of Restitution §12 (unilateral mistake in bargains).

[177] *See* Restatement (Third) of Restitution and Unjust Enrichment §17 (lack of authority).

[178] *See, e.g.,* Gagnon v. Coombs, 39 Mass. App. Ct. 144, 654 N.E.2d 54 (1995). *See generally* Restatement (Third) of Restitution and Unjust Enrichment §17 (lack of authority); §3.4.1 of this handbook (whether an agent acting under a durable power of attorney can effectively transfer the principal's property in trust).

[179] *See generally* §3.5.3.2(a) of this handbook (decanting).

[180] *See* Restatement (Third) of Restitution and Unjust Enrichment §17 (lack of authority).

- The purported trust property was not owned by the settlor;[181]
- The purported trust property was not transferable;
- Uncertainty;[182]
- The trust is a noncharitable purpose trust;[183]
- The transfer of the purported trust property was in fraud of creditors;[184]
- The trust is a sham; and[185]
- The trust instrument is a testamentary document that violates the statute of wills.[186]

Pre-mortem trust validation. In New Hampshire, a *settlor* during his or her life may commence a judicial proceeding to determine the validity of a trust, whether revocable or irrevocable, that he or she has created.[187] This may be done in Delaware as well.[188]

The trust is a creature of state law. In the United States, the law of trusts, for the most part, is a creature of state law.[189] By state we mean "a State of the United States, the District of Columbia, Puerto Rico, the United States Virgin Islands, or any territory or insular possession subject to the jurisdiction of the United States."[190] The term also would include an Indian tribe or band recognized by federal law or formally acknowledged by a State.[191] While there is an Anglo-American system of trust law consisting of "legal concepts and principles and traditional techniques," there is no American law of trusts.[192]

It also must be said that after *Erie Railroad v. Tompkins*, there is no federal law of trusts, "except insofar as Congress creates one."[193] There has, for example, been some federal common law of trusts developing in the pension area. However, as the fiduciary duties articulated in the federal pension legislation known as ERISA are not exhaustive, the common law of the several states continues to define the general scope of the ERISA trustee's authority and

---

[181] Lewin ¶12-30 (England).

[182] Lewin ¶12-30 (England).

[183] Lewin ¶12-30 (England).

[184] Lewin ¶12-30 (England).

[185] Lewin ¶12-30 (England).

[186] Lewin ¶12-30 (England).

[187] *See* RSA 564-B:4-406 (N.H.).

[188] *See* Ravet v. Northern Trust Co. of Del. et al., C.A. No. 7743-VCG, Order of the Delaware Supreme Court (Feb. 12, 2015) ("This ruling, as affirmed by the Delaware Supreme Court, is the first Delaware case of its kind, upholding Delaware's pre-mortem validation statute, 12 Del. C. § 3546, which was enacted in 2000").

[189] 7 Scott & Ascher §44.1 (noting, however, that "the law of trusts in all fifty states, including Louisiana, is based upon the system originally developed by the English Court of Chancery").

[190] UTC §103(16) (available at <http://www.uniformlaws.org/Act.aspx?title=Trust%20 Code>).

[191] UTC §103(16) (available at <http://www.uniformlaws.org/Act.aspx?title=Trust%20 Code>).

[192] 7 Scott & Ascher, Epilogue.

[193] 7 Scott & Ascher, Epilogue.

responsibilities.[194] There is even less federal preemption in the mutual fund context.[195]

The trustee is a fiduciary. A trustee is a *fiduciary*.[196] What are the obligations of a fiduciary?[197] A *fiduciary* has a duty imposed by law to act solely for the benefit of another as to matters within the scope of the relation.[198] In other words, there is a duty of undivided loyalty.[199] A fiduciary who favors himself or herself in dealing with the property of others is quite likely to violate that duty.[200]

A fiduciary is generally saddled with a duty of care, though one need not be a fiduciary to owe someone a duty of care.[201] A fiduciary relationship in and of itself is not a contractual relationship,[202] although one may be incident to the other.[203] There is likely to be a compensation contract, for example, incident to a lawyer-client agent-fiduciary relationship,[204] while there is likely to be an agency-fiduciary relationship incident to a contract between a broker and his or her customer, provided the broker is vested with discretionary investment authority.

Again, a trustee is a fiduciary.[205] So is an agent with discretionary authority,[206] *e.g.*, an investment manager or an attorney-at-law.[207] An agent acting

---

[194] *See, e.g.*, Bixler v. Central Pa. Teamsters Health & Welfare Fund, 12 F.3d 1292 (1993).

[195] *See generally* Charles E. Rounds, Jr. & Andreas Dehio, *Publicly-Traded Open End Mutual Funds in Common Law and Civil Law Jurisdictions: A Comparison of Legal Structures*, 3 N.Y.U. J. L. & Bus. 473 (2007).

[196] *See* UPC §1-201(15).

[197] *See generally* Charles E. Rounds, Jr., *The Case for a Return to Mandatory Instruction in the Fiduciary Aspects of Agency and Trusts in the American Law School, Together with a Model Fiduciary Relations Course Syllabus*, 18 Regent U. L. Rev. 251 (2005–2006).

[198] *See generally* 1 Scott & Ascher §2.1.5; 1 Scott on Trusts §2.5. *See also* Scott, *The Fiduciary Principle*, 37 Cal. L. Rev. 539, 540 (1949).

[199] *See generally* Charles E. Rounds, Jr., *Lawyer Codes Are Just about Licensure, the Lawyer's Relationship with the State: Recalling the Common Law Agency, Contract, Tort, Trust, and Property Principles that Regulate the Lawyer-Client Fiduciary Relationship*, 60 Baylor L. Rev. 771 (2008).

[200] *See generally* 3 Scott & Ascher §17.2.10.

[201] *See generally* Charles E. Rounds, Jr., *Lawyer Codes Are Just about Licensure, the Lawyer's Relationship with the State: Recalling the Common Law Agency, Contract, Tort, Trust, and Property Principles that Regulate the Lawyer-Client Fiduciary Relationship*, 60 Baylor L. Rev. 771 (2008).

[202] *See* Scott Fitzgibbon, *Fiduciary Relationships Are Not Contracts*, 82 Marq. L. Rev. 303 (1999).

[203] *See generally* Charles E. Rounds, Jr., *Lawyer Codes Are Just about Licensure, the Lawyer's Relationship with the State: Recalling the Common Law Agency, Contract, Tort, Trust, and Property Principles that Regulate the Lawyer-Client Fiduciary Relationship*, 60 Baylor L. Rev. 771 (2008).

[204] *See generally* Charles E. Rounds, Jr., *Lawyer Codes Are Just about Licensure, the Lawyer's Relationship with the State: Recalling the Common Law Agency, Contract, Tort, Trust, and Property Principles that Regulate the Lawyer-Client Fiduciary Relationship*, 60 Baylor L. Rev. 771 (2008).

[205] Restatement (Third) of Trusts §78 cmt. a.

[206] *See generally* D. Gordon Smith, *The Critical Resource Theory of Fiduciary Duty*, 55 Vand. L. Rev. 1399 (2002) (suggesting that the allocation of discretion to a person who acts on behalf of another with respect to "critical resources" belonging to the other should determine whether a particular relationship should be treated as a fiduciary relationship).

[207] *See* Deborah A. DeMott, *The Lawyer as Agent*, 67 Fordham L. Rev. 301, 304–305 (1998) (suggesting that even a broad grant of discretion by the client to the lawyer does not negate the client's right under common law agency principles to be kept informed and to control the lawyer's

under a durable power of attorney, *i.e.*, an attorney-in-fact, is a fiduciary as a matter of law.[208] "The duty of loyalty is, for trustees," however, "particularly strict even by comparison to the standards of other fiduciary relationships."[209] Personal representatives (executors and administrators), guardians, and conservators are also fiduciaries.[210]

An equitable charge does not entail a fiduciary relationship.[211] Neither does a debt.[212] Generally the beneficiaries of a trust, unlike the members of a partnership, are not in a fiduciary relationship with one another. Having said that, "there is enough of a fiduciary element in their relationship to make it inequitable for one to seek to obtain an advantage over another."[213]

The priest-penitent, doctor-patient, professor-student, and parent-child relationships, in and of themselves, are confidential, not fiduciary.[214] (Regrettably, some courts have been employing the term *informal fiduciary relationship*[215] as a synonym for the term *confidential relationship*.) "A confidential relation exists between two persons when one has gained the confidence of the other and purports to act or advise with the other's interest in mind."[216] Thus, the execution of an antenuptial agreement could place the parties to it in a confidential relationship, depending upon the nature of the duties assumed and whether the element of reliance is present.[217] A key difference between the two relationships is reliance. In fact, for a confidential relationship to arise, there *must* be reliance on the part of the one reposing the confidence.[218] A fiduciary relationship, on the other hand, brings with it a duty of undivided

---

fiduciary activities). *See also* Patsos v. First Albany Corp., 433 Mass. 323, 333 (2001) (noting that in determining the scope of the broker's fiduciary obligations, courts typically look to the degree of discretion a customer entrusts to his broker); Leib v. Merrill Lynch, Pierce, Fenner & Smith, Inc., 461 F. Supp. 951, 953 (1978) (holding that unlike the broker who handles a nondiscretionary account, the broker handling a discretionary account becomes the fiduciary of his customer in a broad sense); 12 C.F.R. §9.2(e) (Regulation 9) (available at <www.gpo.gov/nara/cfr/index.html>) (deeming a bank that possesses investment *discretion* on behalf of another to be a fiduciary).

[208] Archbold v. Reifenrath, 274 Neb. 894, 900, 744 N.W.2d 701, 706 (2008); Vogt v. Warnock, 107 S.W.3d 778, 782 (Tex. 2003).

[209] Restatement (Third) of Trusts §78 cmt. a.

[210] UPC §1-201(15).

[211] 1 Scott & Ascher §2.3.6.4. *See generally* §9.9.10 of this handbook (an equitable charge is not a trust).

[212] 1 Scott & Ascher §2.3.8.

[213] 4 Scott & Ascher §25.3 (Beneficiary's Duty to Other Beneficiaries).

[214] 1 Scott on Trusts §2.5. *See generally* Charles E. Rounds, Jr., *The Common Law Is Not Just about Contracts: How Legal Education Has Been Short-Changing Feminism*, 43 U. Rich. L. Rev. 1185 (2009) (in part discussing the confidential relationship).

[215] *See generally* D. Gordon Smith, *The Critical Resource Theory of Fiduciary Duty*, 55 Vand. L. Rev. 1399, 1411–1416 (2002).

[216] Restatement (Second) of Trusts §2 cmt. b.

[217] *See, e.g.*, Estate of Draper v. Bank of Am., N.A. 288 Kan. 510, 205 P.3d 698 (2009) ("This inquiry fails to reflect the nature of this case, which is based on a confidential relationship between Clark and Ethel *because of the antenuptial agreement*.").

[218] "Whether a reliant relationship exists is a question of fact." Restatement (Third) of Property (Wills and Other Donative Transfers) §8.3 cmt. g (Tentative Draft No. 3, Apr. 4, 2001).

loyalty, whether or not there has been reliance.[219] Accordingly, a beneficiary in an action against a trustee for breach of fiduciary duty, absent special facts, need not plead reliance.

The Restatement (Third) of Restitution and Unjust Enrichment for certain purposes deems a mere confidential duty to be a fiduciary duty. To be specific, "[t]he distinction between a relation that is 'fiduciary' in a technical sense and one that is merely 'confidential' is without significance....Classified under either heading, a profitable breach of the special duties imposed by the relation gives rise to restitutionary claims and remedies...."[220]

Although the trustee-beneficiary relationship is a fiduciary relationship, it can also be one of confidence, depending on the facts and circumstances. In Section 6.1.3.5 of this handbook we consider the practical implications of a trustee being in a confidential relationship with a beneficiary.

Types of trusts covered in this handbook. This is a practical handbook that addresses the rights, duties, and obligations of the parties once the trustee takes title to the trust property, *i.e.*, once the property is in the basket. The focus is on trusts for personal purposes, although there is some discussion of trusts as instruments of commerce.[221] Trusts are everywhere. Mutual funds—even those that are packaged as corporations—are essentially trusts.[222] Much commercial real estate is held in trust. The trust is not merely an estate planning tool.[223] And then there are the trusts that are said to arise by operation of law, specifically the resulting trust and the constructive trust. These are covered herein as well.[224]

Some trust terminology. A trust is a fiduciary relationship with respect to property.[225] Thus it is no surprise that the subject of a trust is generally referred to as the trust *property*.[226] Synonyms for trust property are trust *res*, trust *corpus*, trust *capital*, and "the *subject matter of the trust*."[227] Another synonym is trust *estate*,

---

[219] Restatement (Third) of Property (Wills and Other Donative Transfers) §8.3 cmt. g (Tentative Draft No. 3, Apr. 4, 2001). *See* Sarah Worthington, *Fiduciaries: When Is Self-Denial Obligatory*, 58 Cambridge L.J. 500, 503 (1999) ("In short, fiduciary terminology should be used carefully and restrictively, so that fiduciary law operates only to exact loyalty; it does not concern itself with matters of contract, tort, unjust enrichment and other equitable obligations (such as breach of confidence)").

[220] Restatement (Third) of Restitution and Unjust Enrichment §43, cmt. f.

[221] *See* §9.6 of this handbook (trusts that resemble corporations or agencies).

[222] *See generally* Charles E. Rounds, Jr. & Andreas Dehio, *Publicly-Traded Open End Mutual Funds in Common Law and Civil Law Jurisdictions: A Comparison of Legal Structures*, 3 N.Y.U. J. L. & Bus. 473 (2007). As of December 2000, the aggregate value of participations in U.S. mutual funds was $7 trillion. Investment Company Institute <www.ici.org>. *See also* §8.10 of this handbook (fiduciary principles applicable to the mutual fund); Bogert §248 (Investment Trusts and Real Estate Investment Trusts).

[223] *See, e.g.*, Charles E. Rounds, Jr. & Andreas Dehio, *Publicly-Traded Open End Mutual Funds in Common Law and Civil Law Jurisdictions: A Comparison of Legal Structures*, 3 N.Y.U. J. L. & Bus. 473 (2007).

[224] *See* §3.3 of this handbook (the purchase money resulting trust and the constructive trust) and §4.1.1.1 of this handbook (the resulting trust).

[225] Bogert §1.

[226] Bogert §1.

[227] *See generally* Bogert §1.

although the term *estate* has an important second meaning in the trust context that is rooted in the ancient interactions of law and equity. This second meaning we take up in Section 3.5.1 of this handbook.[228]

Terms of the trust are the "manifestation of the intention of the settlor with respect to the trust provisions expressed in a manner that admits of its proof in judicial proceedings."[229] Thus, "it is not the language alone, but the language of the trust in its contextual circumstance, that comprises the terms of the trust."[230]

In this handbook, the term *settlor* encompasses any person who impresses a trust upon his own property,[231] whether by lifetime transfer to a trustee,[232] by declaring himself trustee (*i.e.*, by declaration), or by will.[233] Synonyms for settlor include *grantor, trustor, transferor, founder, creator, donor*, and, in the case of a testamentary trust, *testator*.[234] For purposes of taxation, creditor accessibility, and equitable division in the context of divorce, the deemed settlor will not necessarily be the person designated as such in the trust instrument, or even, for that matter, the person who nominally funded the trust.[235] It will be the person whose economic interest was actually made the subject of the trust by declaration, gift, contract, will, or otherwise.[236]

As a rule of thumb, an *express trust* is any trust other than a *resulting trust* or a *constructive trust*.[237] The purchase-money resulting trust and the constructive trust are covered in Section 3.3 of this handbook. The resulting trust that arises

---

[228] For its purposes, the UPC defines estate as "the property of the decedent, trust, or other person whose affairs are subject to this Code as originally constituted and as it exists from time to time during administration." UPC §1-201(13).

[229] Restatement (Third) of Trusts § 4.

[230] Fred Franke & Anna Katherine Moody, *The Terms of the Trust: Extrinsic Evidence of Settlor Intent*, 40 ACTEC L.J. 1, 2 (2014).

[231] *See generally* 3 Scott & Ascher §15.4.4 (Determining Who Is the Settlor); Bogert §41 (The Settlor); §8.43 of this handbook (who is the settlor of the trust?)

[232] Even in cases where the trust documentation suggests that the trustee is creating the trust, it is the one whose property is being transferred to the trustee who is the settlor. 1 Scott & Ascher §3.1. "This method of creating a trust may be appropriate when the settlor for some reason does not wish it to be known that he or she has created a trust." 1 Scott & Ascher §3.1. "One who furnishes the consideration necessary to induce another to create a trust is the settlor of the trust when it is created." Bogert §41.

[233] UTC §401 (available at <http://www.uniformlaws.org/Act.aspx?title=Trust%20Code>) (suggesting also that one who exercises a power of appointment in favor of a trustee is a settlor). "If more than one person creates or contributes property to a trust, each person is a settlor of the portion of the trust property attributable to that person's contribution except to the extent another person has the power to revoke or withdraw that portion." UTC §103(14). Thus, a contributor to a trust that is revocable by another person or over which another person has a power of withdrawal is not the settlor. It is actually the person with the right to revoke or the right of withdrawal who is the settlor. UTC §103 cmt. *Cf.* §9.3 of this handbook (the self-settled "special needs"/"supplemental needs" trust).

[234] *See generally* 1 Scott & Ascher §2.2.1; Bogert §§1 & 41.

[235] *See generally* 3 Scott & Ascher §15.4.4 (Determining Who Is the Settlor); Bogert §41.

[236] Restatement (Third) of Trusts §10, Reporter's Note to cmt. g, re: Clause (e); 3 Scott & Ascher §15.4.4; Bogert §41.

[237] Bogert §1.

upon the complete or partial failure of an express trust is discussed in Section 4.1.1.1 of this handbook. The long-standing custom of referring to resulting trusts and constructive trusts as *implied trusts* is not without its detractors.[238]

An express trust created by transfer, pursuant to the terms of a will, is referred to as a *testamentary* trust.[239] A trust that comes into existence by court decree is a *court trust*.[240] A trust created by lifetime transfer or declaration is referred to as an *inter vivos trust*, and in the noncommercial context, at least, "is essentially a gift, projected on the plane of time and so subjected to a management regime."[241] For an enforceable trust to arise, there need not be an exchange of consideration.[242] Although contractual rights may be the subject of a trust, the trust itself is not a contract.[243] The terms *inter vivos trust* and *living trust* are synonymous.[244] A trust also may be created by "an exercise of a power of appointment by appointing property to a person as trustee for one or more persons who are objects of the power; or...[by]...promise or beneficiary designation that creates enforceable rights in a person who immediately or later holds those rights as trustee, or who pursuant to those rights later receives property as trustee, for one or more persons."[245]

Some trusts are informally classified by purpose or objective. A *family trust* is a trust whose primary purpose is to benefit a class of relatives; a *business trust* is a trust whose purpose is to carry on a business or commercial enterprise, such as a mutual fund.[246] A trust *settlement* is a transfer of property to a trustee, such as by deed, to provide for the future needs of someone.[247] It should be noted that in England the term *settlement* is sometimes employed as a synonym for *inter vivos* trust.[248] A trust settlement is not to be confused with the settlement of a decedent's probate estate, which includes "the full process of administration, distribution, and closing."[249]

A *personal* trust takes its name not from how it is created or its purpose but from the nature of the particular equitable interest. The equitable interest of a beneficiary in a nonself-settled *personal* trust is so personal in character as to be unassignable by the beneficiary and unreachable by his or her creditors, even in

---

[238] Bogert §1.

[239] Bogert §1.

[240] Bogert §1.

[241] Bernard Rudden, Review, John P. Dawson, *Gifts and Promises*, 44 Mod. L. Rev. 610 (1981).

[242] Restatement (Third) of Trusts §15; 1 Scott & Ascher §3.3.

[243] On the other hand, a promise to create a trust in the future is enforceable only if the requirements for an enforceable contract are satisfied. Restatement (Third) of Trusts §15 cmt. b.

[244] Bogert §1.

[245] Restatement (Third) of Trusts §10(d) & (e). *See generally* §8.1.2 of this handbook (exercise of power of appointment in further trust). *See also* Lewin ¶3-03; 1 Scott & Ascher §3.1.

[246] *See* Bogert §1; §9.6 of this handbook (the business trust).

[247] *See, e.g.*, §9.30 of this handbook (marriage settlements (England)).

[248] Lewin ¶1-14 (England).

[249] *See* UPC §1-201(43).

the absence of a spendthrift provision.[250] The express right to occupy an entrusted residence comes to mind.

An *insurance trust* takes its name from how it is funded, namely, with contractual rights incident to a life insurance policy.[251] There is a brief discussion of insurance trusts in Section 9.2 of this handbook.

All trusts fall into either the active or passive category. A trust is *active* if the trustee has duties to perform apart from holding of legal title to the subject property and *passive* if holding legal title is all that the trustee is expected to do.[252] Whether a trust is active or passive may have practical implications, a topic that is taken up in Section 8.15.1 of this handbook.

As noted in Section 5.1 of this handbook, unless otherwise specified, the term *beneficiary* encompasses not only persons who during the life of the trust have some present vested or contingent interest in it but also the remaindermen.[253] It would include the holder of a nonfiduciary power of appointment as well, a topic we take up in Section 8.1 of this handbook.[254] "The beneficiary of a private trust ordinarily is an individual but the beneficiary can be an artificial legal entity such as a corporation."[255]

The term *beneficiary* captures not only those who receive their equitable interests under the express terms of a trust, but also those who receive their interests by other means, including assignment, exercise of a power of appointment, resulting trust, gap in a disposition, or operation of an antilapse statute.[256] While the public at large is said to be the beneficiary of a charitable

---

[250] *See generally* 2A Scott on Trusts §160. *See also* 3 Scott & Ascher §13.2.6 (discussing the extent of the beneficiary's interest under a personal trust).

[251] Bogert §1.

[252] Bogert §1.

[253] *See* §5.1 of this handbook (who can be a beneficiary). In §103(2) of the UTC (available at <http://www.uniformlaws.org/Act.aspx?title=Trust%20Code>), a beneficiary is defined not only as a person who has a present or future beneficial interest in a trust, whether vested or contingent, but also as someone who holds a power of appointment over trust property in a capacity other than that of trustee. The UPC is in accord. *See* UPC §1-201(3). Under the common law of trusts, the holder of a power of appointment would not be considered a trust beneficiary. *See, e.g.*, National Shawmut Bank v. Joy, 315 Mass. 457, 472, 53 N.E.2d 113, 123 (1944) (suggesting that under the common law of trusts a power of appointment is not considered property). The UTC also creates a category of beneficiary known as the qualified beneficiary. A qualified beneficiary has favored status, particularly when it comes to the right without solicitation to receive trust accountings and the right to receive advance notice of certain extraordinary actions that the trustee contemplates taking. *See* §103(12) of the UTC and §6.1.5 of this handbook (duty to account to the beneficiary). At a given point in time, a contingent remainderman would qualify for this special status, provided he or she is entitled to distributions of trust income or principal, whether or not in the discretion of the trustee, were the trust to terminate at that time. A terminating event might be the death of a beneficiary currently eligible to receive trust income. A remainderman who is not conceived at that time presumably would be a beneficiary but not a qualified beneficiary. In addition to the first-line remaindermen, those currently eligible to receive distributions of income or principal, whether or not in the discretion of the trustee, also would have qualified beneficiary status.

[254] *See* UPC §1-201(3) (providing that a "beneficiary designated in a governing instrument" includes a donee, appointee, or taker in default of a power of appointment).

[255] Bogert §1.

[256] UTC §103 cmt. (available at <http://www.uniformlaws.org/Act.aspx?title=Trust%20Code>); UPC §1-201(3). *See also* §8.15.55 of this handbook (antilapse applicable to trusts).

trust,[257] the Uniform Probate Code for its purposes defines the beneficiary of a charitable trust more narrowly as one who has standing to seek its enforcement in the courts, such as the state attorney general.[258] This interest of the beneficiary of an ongoing trust is known as an *equitable* or *beneficial* interest and is itself a property right.[259] A synonym for beneficiary is the Norman French *cestui que trust*.[260] "It is pronounced as if spelled 'cestwe kuh trust.'"[261]

In this handbook, unless otherwise specified, the term *revocable trust* is a trust whose property may be reacquired free of trust by the settlor during his or her lifetime.[262] The settlor is said to possess a reserved general inter vivos power of appointment.[263] The reader should understand, however, that a third party possessing a general inter vivos power of appointment would also possess the right to terminate, *i.e.*, revoke, the trust and directly or indirectly acquire the property free of trust.[264]

Unless the statute of wills or statute of frauds provides otherwise, neither the intention to create a trust nor its terms need be evidenced by a writing, although a writing is generally preferable.[265] A formal writing, which would actually be the will in the case of a testamentary trust, is called the *trust instrument*.[266] The statute of frauds is covered in Section 8.15.5 of this handbook.

Cross-reference. Scotland's trust analog (the "Tartan trust") is discussed generally in §8.12.1 of this handbook. In the case of a Tartan trust, "the settlor is the *truster*, a life tenant is a *liferenter*, and the capital beneficiary is the *fiar*."[267]

How trusts are enforced. "The Court has exclusive jurisdiction of proceedings initiated by interested parties concerning the internal affairs of trusts."[268] It generally falls to the beneficiary (or the state Attorney General in the case of a charitable trust), however, to keep the trustee on the straight and

---

[257] *See generally* Bogert §1.

[258] UPC §1-201(3). *See generally* §9.4.2 of this handbook (standing to enforce charitable trusts).

[259] Restatement of Property Introductory Note. *See* In re Catherwood's Trust, 173 A.2d 86, 91 (1961) (a gift of an equitable life estate in income or of a remainder does constitute a grant of a vested property right of which the recipients cannot be divested by legislative action).

[260] *See generally* §8.15 of this handbook (discussing in part the phenomenon of law French).

[261] Bogert §1, n.14.

[262] *See generally* UTC §103(13) (available at <http://www.uniformlaws.org/Act.aspx?title= Trust%20Code>) (defining the term *revocable trust*). *See also* §8.11 of this handbook (the duties of the trustee of a revocable inter vivos trust) and §5.3.3.1 of this handbook (access to a settlor's reserved beneficial interest by the settlor's creditors).

[263] *See generally* §8.1 of this handbook (powers of appointment).

[264] *See generally* §8.1 of this handbook (powers of appointment). *See also* 3 Scott & Ascher §16.6 (Effect of Presently Exercisable General Power of Appointment or Right of Withdrawal).

[265] *See, e.g.*, Jimenez v. Lee, 547 P.2d 126 (Or. 1976) ("The respective donors did not expressly direct defendant to hold the subject of the gift 'in trust' but this is not essential to create a trust relationship.").

[266] Bogert §1.

[267] Debbie King, *Tartan trusts*, 23 STEP J. 27 (Apr. 2015).

[268] UPC §7-201(a). *Cf.* §9.4.4 of this handbook (discussing whether the legislature may alter the terms of a charitable trust without violating the doctrine of separation of powers).

narrow. By that we mean that the court generally does not act on its own initiative in "protecting rights or enforcing duties."[269] On the other hand, once a matter involving the administration of a trust has been brought to a court, the court may well take it upon itself even after the matter has been resolved to maintain supervision,[270] a judicial practice, by the way, that the Uniform Probate Code would discourage on policy grounds.[271]

The trust beneficiary has standing to seek enforcement of the trust in the courts whether or not the beneficiary participated in the trust's creation and whether or not the trustee made any promises to the beneficiary.[272] "In this respect the law of trusts differs from the law of contracts where there have been some holdings that not all third party beneficiary contracts are enforceable."[273]

Tasks that trusts can perform. The trust is a complex legal organism that survives on private property. Its earlier forms predate even the Norman Conquest.[274] The trust as we know it today is the product of centuries of evolution:

> There are many landmarks, for example the development of the individual's rather than the Crown's, legal rights over land in Norman times; the first steps towards establishing equitable interests when a knight heading for the crusades would give property to a third party to hold for the benefit of the knight's spouse and children whilst he was away; and the 16th century practice of landholders transferring land to individuals, "cestuis que uses," during their lifetimes in order to prevent the land reverting to the owner of feudal rights.[275]

Professor Maitland saw the trust as "an 'institute' of great elasticity and generality; as elastic, as general as contract."[276] One Bermuda lawyer has recently echoed those sentiments: "Commercial lawyers are coming to realise what trust lawyers have always known, that the trust is incredibly flexible."[277] In

---

[269] 4 Scott & Ascher §24.4.4.

[270] 4 Scott & Ascher §24.4.4 (Court Acting on its Own Motion). *See, e.g.*, Quincy Trust Co. v. Taylor, 317 Mass. 195, 199, 57 N.E.2d 573, 576 (1944) ("...[[I]t would be a reproach to the law if the...court were compelled to remain inactive until some interested person should appear and file a petition for...[the fiduciary's]...removal").

[271] "Also, the general move of the Code away from the concept of supervisory jurisdiction over any fiduciary is compatible with the kinds of procedural provisions which are believed to be desirable for trustees." UPC, Part 4, Powers of Trustees, Comment.

[272] Bogert §1.

[273] Bogert §1.

[274] *See generally* §8.37 of this handbook (the origin of the English trust). *See also* W. F. Fratcher, Trusts, in VI Intl. Encyclopedia of Comp. Law, ch. 11, pp. 3, 8–20 (Frederick H. Lawson ed., 1973); Avisheh Avini, Comment, The Origins of the Modern Trust Revisited, 70 Tul. L. Rev. 1139 (1996) (suggesting the trust has its origins in Islamic Law). For related topics, *see generally* §8.12 of this handbook (where outside the United States the trust is recognized) and §8.15.1 of this handbook (statute of uses).

[275] Henry Beckwith, *The Trust—Your Flexible Friend*, Tr. & Est. L.J., No. 45, Apr. 2003, at i (pull-out). *See generally* §8.15.1 of this handbook (statute of uses) and §8.37 of this handbook (the origin of the English trust).

[276] Maitland, Equity (Brunyate ed.). Quotation also may be found in 1 Scott & Ascher §1.1.

[277] Randall Krebs, *Flexible friend*, 16(2) STEP J. 17 (Feb. 2008).

his view, "[t]he future development of new and innovative uses of trusts in commercial applications is limited only by the imagination of the lawyers designing the commercial or tax structures."[278]

In the noncommercial setting, the trust provides enlightened property owners and their lawyers with a mechanism for seeing to the needs of the young, the disabled, and the elderly far more efficiently, far more cost-effectively, far more creatively, far more flexibly, far more expeditiously, and with far more dignity than the state could ever do.[279] In this regard, even a public charitable trust is no match for the private trust. Only one's imagination limits the purposes for which such trusts may be created.[280] To be sure, the institution of the private personal trust can never accommodate the needs of everyone. Each person in need of assistance, however, who receives proper care pursuant to the institution's terms, is one less person who has to encounter—and be a burden to—the welfare bureaucracy. On the other hand, it is also said that a trust can dull the animal spirits of one's able-bodied children if one is not careful:

> Eventually, slowly, almost imperceptibly, something happened to Boston money, to its drive and daring. Fathers who doubted the mettle of their sons and heirs began tying up their fortunes in tightly drawn legacies, preserving them in the impenetrable amber of trusts. Trusteed money, in the hands of ever-so prudent conservators whose job it was to provide a sure and steady income for its beneficiaries, virtually withdrew from productive enterprise. By the 1930s, Boston money has gone to sleep, sustained by a steady 4 percent return and dreams of days long past. Once-bustling wharves and warehouses were rotting and falling into the harbor. Offices that had echoed to the springy stride of railroad builders and Canton sea captains now heard only the plodding of fiduciaries.[281]

A trust may be created only to the extent its purposes are lawful;[282] not contrary to public policy[283] or detrimental to the community;[284] and possible to

---

[278] Randall Krebs, *Flexible friend*, 16(2) STEP J. 17 (Feb. 2008).

[279] *See, e.g.*, The CJP Community Trust (a pooled trust for people with disabilities that is operated under the auspices of Combined Jewish Philanthropies and Jewish Family and Children's Service). Contact: Jewish Family and Children's Service, 1340 Centre Street, Newton, MA 02459. Phone: (617) 558-1278. Fax: (617) 558-5250. Governmental entities also tend not to be particularly good common law trustees. *See* §9.8.2 of this handbook (the city, the state, or the United States as trustee).

[280] "Private lawyers who counsel clients and draft their deeds and settlements are constantly adapting trusts to new ends, varying conventional trust structures to promote the commercial, tax, investment, family and succession interests of those clients." Joshua Getzler, *Legislative Incursions into Modern Trusts Doctrine in England: The Trustee Act 2000 and the Contracts (Rights of Third Parties) Act 1999*, 2 Global Jurist Topics, Issue 1, Art. 2 (2002) (noting that English trust law has always been shaped by "cautelary jurisprudence").

[281] Russell B. Adams, Jr., The Boston Money Tree x, xi (1977).

[282] *See* Restatement (Third) of Trusts §29(a); 2 Scott & Ascher §9.2 (noting that the mere fact that a trustee employs trust funds in an illegal business purpose does not relieve the trustee of accountability for the profits if the trust purposes are legitimate).

[283] Restatement (Third) of Trusts §29(c). *See generally* 2 Scott & Ascher §9.3; §9.24 of this handbook (public policy in the trust context).

[284] 2 Scott & Ascher §9.3.12.

achieve.[285] "A scheme to overthrow the government or to sell dope or to operate a bordello is no more enforceable as a trust than as a contract, a corporation, or a partnership."[286] Nor is a trust established for the purpose of defrauding creditors[287] or the government.[288]

The role that the private trust plays in lubricating the American capital markets has come to eclipse in significance the traditional role it has played in facilitating intrafamily wealth transfers.[289] On April 28, 2001, even the Peoples' Republic of China jumped on the global trust bandwagon:[290] "According to Chinese drafters and scholars, the initial impetus for the legislation was the urgent need to promote China's accession to the World Trade Organization and to address China's financial sector by adopting 'an important pillar of the modern financing industry in developed countries,' the trust."[291]

The trust having come into its own in the employee benefit, charitable, and commercial areas,[292] a relatively small number of institutional fiduciaries collectively now have the power to control much of corporate America. "This phenomenon has been labelled 'fiduciary capitalism.'"[293] Such a high

---

[285] UTC §404 (available at <http://www.uniformlaws.org/Act.aspx?title=Trust%20Code>). Generally, a trust has a purpose which is illegal if (1) its performance involves the commission of a criminal or tortious act by the trustee; (2) the settlor's purpose in creating the trust was to defraud creditors or others; or (3) the consideration for the creation of the trust was illegal. UTC §404 cmt. "Purposes violative of public policy include those that tend to encourage criminal or tortious conduct, that interfere with freedom to marry or encourage divorce, that limit religious freedom, or which are frivolous or capricious." UTC §404 cmt.

[286] John H. Langbein, *Mandatory Rules in the Law of Trusts*, 98 Nw. U. L. Rev. 1105, 1107 (2004). *See generally* 2 Scott & Ascher §9.4.2. *See also* 2 Scott & Ascher §§9.4.3 (When the Settlor Is Not the Beneficiary), 9.5 (When the Consideration Is Illegal); 9.5.1 (When the Beneficiary Is Innocent), 9.5.2 (When the Trust Property Has Been Acquired Illegally), 9.6 (Consequences of Provisions That Are Illegal or Contrary to Public Policy).

[287] 2 Scott & Ascher §§9.4 (Creditors of the Settlor), 9.4.2 (Creditors of the "Trustee").

[288] 2 Scott & Ascher §9.4.1.

[289] *See* Henry Hansmann & Ugo Mattei, *The Functions of Trust Law: A Comparative Legal and Economic Analysis*, 73 N.Y.U.L. Rev., 434, 436 (1998).

[290] Xintuo Fa [Trust Law] (promulgated by the Standing Comm. Nat'l People's Cong., Apr. 28, 2001, effective Oct. 1, 2001).

[291] Frances H. Foster, *American Trust Law in a Chinese Mirror*, 94 Minn. L. Rev. 602, 639–640 (2010).

[292] *See, e.g.*, §9.31 of this handbook (corporate trusts; trusts to secure creditors; the Trust Indenture Act of 1939; protecting bondholders).

[293] John H. Langbein & Bruce A. Wolk, Pension and Employee Benefit Law 803 (2000) (citing James P. Hawley & Andrew T. Williams, The Emergence of Fiduciary Capitalism, 5 Corp. Governance 206 (1997)). *See generally* Charles E. Rounds, Jr. & Andreas Dehio, *Publicly-Traded Open End Mutual Funds in Common Law and Civil Law Jurisdictions: A Comparison of Legal Structures*, 3 N.Y.U. J. L. & Bus. 473 (2007).

concentration of economic power[294] carries with it a danger that these fiduciaries could either become inappropriately engaged or inappropriately disengaged in matters that relate to the exercise of that power.[295] Some fear that this small cadre of trustees and agents might someday improperly exploit this power to control the economy in ways that are not in the interests of beneficial owners. Others fear that these fiduciaries will refrain altogether from monitoring the myriad enterprises over which they have voting control.[296] One learned commentator has written:

> Up to now, the larger pension funds have been reluctant to get...deeply involved in corporate governance; if they are unhappy with performance, they simply sell. However, the California Public Employees' Retirement System (Calpers) recently announced that it would vote against reappointing auditors at companies including Exxon Mobil, Home Depot, and McDonald's because they pay accountants for non–audit services...The logical continuation of this trend would be for the pension funds to nominate their own directors. It's in their interest to do so; after all, the collapse of Enron cost public pension funds about $3 billion.[297]

Despite the trust's elasticity and protean nature, its powers are not magical.[298] There are some problems that cannot be solved, even by the employment of a trust. H.G. Wells was not so sure. In 1920, he had occasion to interview Lenin at his offices in the Kremlin.[299] He came away with the view that as brutal and as incompetent as the Bolshevik regime was, it was preferable to whatever the counter-revolutionaries would be in a position to install.[300] In order to constructively engage the Bolsheviks with their "invincible prejudice" against

---

[294] "The mutual funds controlled by the 75 largest fund managers alone own $2.9 trillion of U.S. equities, equal to 20 percent of the $14.4 trillion market capitalization of the stock market at the beginning of 2001." John C. Bogle, *The 800-Pound Gorilla, Shareholders Arise!*, Am. Spectator, Mar./Apr. 2002, at 40.

[295] *See* John C. Bogle, *Individual Stockholder, R.I.P.*, Wall St. J., Oct. 3, 2005, at A16 (bemoaning the "rent-a-stock" mutual fund industry's lack of interest in how the corporations in which it invests are governed).

[296] *But see* Aaron Lucchetti, *A Mutual-Fund Giant Is Stalking Excessive Pay*, Wall St. J., June 12, 2002, at C1 (reporting that Fidelity mutual fund trustees may withhold votes for corporate directors who overcompensate their senior executives).

[297] Felix G. Rohatyn, *An Agenda for Corporate Reform*, Wall St. J., June 24, 2002, at A16. *See also* Tamar Frankel, *The Delaware Business Trust Act Failure as the New Corporate Law*, 23 Cardozo L. Rev. 325, 337 (2001) (confirming that when "dissatisfied with the corporate management of their investments, trustees–investment managers sell the shares, [*i.e.*,] they 'exit' rather than exercise 'voice'"). *But see* Yuka Hayashi, *Pension Funds Put Heads Together*, Wall St. J., Aug. 18, 2002, at D7 (reporting that representatives from some of the nation's largest pension funds are putting their heads together to find ways to mobilize their shareholder power); John C. Bogle, *The 800-Pound Gorilla: Shareholders Arise!*, Am. Spectator, Mar./Apr. 2002, at 40.

[298] That the U.S. State of Georgia (1776) was originally structured as a public charitable trust (1732/1733) is a dramatic example of the trust's elastic and protean nature.

[299] *See* H. G. Wells, Russia in the Shadows 128–129 (1920).

[300] *See* H. G. Wells, Russia in the Shadows 147–148 (1920).

individual businessmen, the intermediary of a trust would have to be employed.[301] This trust "should resemble in its general nature one of the big
buying and controlling trusts that were so necessary and effectual in the
European States during the Great War....This indeed is the only way in which a
capitalist State can hold commerce with a Communist State."[302] Wells observed
that "[t]he larger big business grows the more it approximates Collectivism."[303]
He feared that if his trust solution were not implemented there would be a "final
collapse of all that remains of modern civilization throughout what was formerly
the Russian Empire."[304] In his view, it was not beyond the realm of possibility
that all modern civilization ultimately could tumble into the abyss as well.[305]
Was H. G. Wells employing the term "trust" euphemistically, as the U.S.
Congress was to do later in the context of legislating its social security welfare
scheme, a topic we take up in Section 9.9.3 of this handbook? We do not think
that he was.

    The institution of the trust is principles-based. One commentator has
noted that "the concepts of the law of trusts are simple and easy to understand.
They are based not on technique but on broad human principles of conduct, on
a sense of justice and fair play."[306] Thus, for the institution of the trust to
survive, particularly in light of Equity's marginalization in the American legal
academy, there must be a bench and bar that achieves, whether by hook or by
crook, a proper appreciation of the concept of the trust, as well as a working
understanding of its infinite utility.[307] But without a corps of incorruptible and
conscientious trustees all is for naught. A principles-based regime, more so than
a rules-based one, can only work if administered by people with principles.
Thus the law has demanded—and must continue to demand—that the trustee
be absolutely loyal to the trust; that the trustee act solely in the interest of the
beneficiary, as that interest was perceived by the settlor, the one who originally
owned the subject property; and that any behavior on the trustee's part that
compromises the trust be subject to judicial sanction.[308] A trusteeship brings
with it "no small degree of trouble and anxiety," at least for the trustee who is
conscientious.[309]

---

[301] *See* H. G. Wells, Russia in the Shadows 149–153 (1920).

[302] *See* H. G. Wells, Russia in the Shadows 149–153 (1920).

[303] *See* H. G. Wells, Russia in the Shadows 149–153 (1920).

[304] *See* H. G. Wells, Russia in the Shadows 149–153 (1920).

[305] *See* H. G. Wells, Russia in the Shadows 149–153 (1920).

[306] 7 Scott & Ascher, Epilogue.

[307] *See generally* Charles E. Rounds, Jr., *The Case for a Return to Mandatory Instruction in the Fiduciary Aspects of Agency and Trusts in the American Law School*, 18 Regent Univ. L. Rev. 251 (2005–2006).

[308] *See, e.g.*, Charles E. Rounds, Jr. & Andreas Dehio, *Publicly-Traded Open End Mutual Funds in Common Law and Civil Law Jurisdictions: A Comparison of Legal Structures*, 3 N.Y.U. J. L. & Bus. 473 (2007).

[309] Knight v. Earl of Plymouth (1747), Dick. 120.

First consult the trust instrument. The fountainhead of the trustee's powers is the trust instrument.[310] "It is sometimes said that the trust instrument is the trustee's charter, and that the settlor's intention is the law of the trust."[311] The settlor has the right to include in the trust instrument any provision relating to the management of property or to the duties and powers of the trustee, provided it is not contrary to public policy or in derogation of the concept of the trust.[312] These provisions, unless varied by the court, are binding upon the trustee and will supersede much of the default law applicable to trustees that is threaded throughout this handbook.[313]

Accordingly, a contract to alter the terms of an irrevocable trust is generally unenforceable. The trustee has no authority to enter into a contract that would have the effect of altering the terms of the trust,[314] absent the consent of *all* the beneficiaries (and perhaps the settlor) or a court order (*e.g.*, a *cy pres* action).[315] Likewise, the donee of a nonfiduciary nongeneral power to appoint entrusted property may not by contract alter the terms of the power such that a benefit is conferred upon an impermissible appointee, a topic we take up in Section 8.15.26 of this handbook.[316]

---

[310] While a series of letters has given rise to a valid trust, an integrated formal writing that completely and unambiguously sets forth the rights and duties of the parties is, of course, preferable. *See* In re Trust Estate of Daoang, 87 Haw. 200, 204, 953 P.2d 959, 963 (1998).

[311] 2 Scott & Ascher §9.1.

[312] UTC §105(b) (available at <http://www.uniformlaws.org/Act.aspx?title=Trust%20 Code>) catalogs those provisions of the UTC that may not be overridden by the terms of a trust. *See also* UTC §802 cmt. (confirming that the settlor may override in the terms of the trust an otherwise applicable duty of loyalty). In §8.5 of this handbook, we note that the terms of a trust may even dictate which jurisdiction's laws are to be applied in determining the meaning and legal effect of those terms. Courts have even been known to surrender jurisdiction over their testamentary trusts in order to effectuate settlor intent, a topic we take up in §8.6 of this handbook.

[313] *See, e.g.*, Charles E. Rounds, Jr. & Andreas Dehio, *Publicly-Traded Open End Mutual Funds in Common Law and Civil Law Jurisdictions: A Comparison of Legal Structures*, 3 N.Y.U. J. L. & Bus. 473 (2007). In England, [t]he current approach, in professionally drafted deeds, is to confer on trustees such wider powers of administration as are appropriate to the size and purpose of the trust. Martyn Frost, *Overview of Trusts in England and Wales*, in Trusts in Prime Jurisdictions 15 (Alon Kaplan ed., 2000). In the United States, the practice is much the same. *See generally* §3.5.3.2 of this handbook (express powers granted to the trustee to engage in acts that might otherwise be breaches of trust).

[314] The terms of a trust include not just what lies within the four corners of the governing trust instrument but also the entire manifestation of the settlor's intention, whether in words or by conduct, as apparent from all of the circumstances at the creation of the trust, insofar as such evidence is admissible. 1 Scott & Ascher §2.2.4. "As to any matter expressly addressed in the governing instrument, the terms of the governing instrument ordinarily are the terms of the trust," unless the relevant provision is ambiguous. 1 Scott & Ascher §2.2.4. *See generally* §8.15.6 of this handbook (parol evidence rule).

[315] *See generally* Bogert §713. The *cy pres* doctrine is discussed in §9.4.3 of this handbook.

[316] *See also* §8.15.90 of this handbook (the power-in-trust doctrine). *See generally* Restatement (Third) of Property (Wills and Other Donative Transfers) §21.1(b) (when a contract to exercise a presently exercisable nongeneral power is unenforceable) & §21.2 (when a contract to exercise a power not presently exercisable is unenforceable).

Disclaiming fiduciary powers. Nor should the trustee be allowed to alter the terms of a trust by selectively disclaiming fiduciary powers.[317]

A trustee's ignorance of the terms of the trust is generally no excuse. "Lack of awareness or understanding of the terms of the trust normally will not protect a trustee from liability."[318] Mr. Loring would have been in accord, he in 1898 having penned these words in the first edition of this handbook: "THE FIRST AND MOST IMPORTANT DUTY OF THE TRUSTEE IS TO STUDY AND BECOME THOROUGHLY FAMILIAR WITH THE PROVISIONS OF THE TRUST INSTRUMENT,[319] AND THEREAFTER TO FOLLOW THEM OUT IMPLICITLY."[320] unless, we would add, to do so would be objectively stupid and imprudent or otherwise violate public policy.[321] It goes without saying that this cannot be done in a vacuum, *i.e.*, without all the relevant facts. "The trustee must know who the beneficiaries are and their ages, locations, sources of support apart from the trust (including, for instance, entitlement to social, medical and public benefits), and other circumstances relevant to their entitlement as beneficiaries; and [t]he trustee must regularly review and confirm the current accuracy and completeness of all such information...."[322]

When in reasonable doubt, the trustee should petition the court for instructions. When the current rights, duties, and obligations of the trustee are uncertain due to problems with the governing instrument or the terms of the trust generally,

---

[317] *Cf.* UPC §2-1105 cmt. ("As a policy matter, the creator of a trust or other arrangement creating a fiduciary relationship should be able to prevent a fiduciary accepting office under the arrangement from altering the parameters of the relationship").

[318] Restatement (Third) of Trusts §77 cmt. c.

[319] Restatement (Third) of Trusts §76 cmt. c. While the wording of a written trust instrument is almost always the most important determinant of a trust's terms, oral statements, "the situation of the beneficiaries, the purposes of the trust, the circumstances under which the trust is to be administered, and, to the extent the settlor was otherwise silent, rules of construction, all may have a bearing on determining a trust's meaning." UTC §103 cmt. (available at <http://www.uniformlaws.org/Act.aspx?title=Trust%20Code>). *See also* UTC §415 (providing that the court may reform the terms of a trust, even if unambiguous, to conform to the settlor's intention if it is proved by clear and convincing evidence that both the settlor's intent and the terms of the trust were affected by a mistake of fact or law, whether in expression or inducement).

[320] *See generally* Easterbrook and Fischel, *Contract and Fiduciary Duty*, 36 J.L. & Econ., 425, 429 (1993) (suggesting that nothing illustrates the contractual character of fiduciary law better than one of the cornerstones of trust law; an express provision in the trust instrument governs over the duty of loyalty in the event of conflict). *See also* Ritchie, *Reviewing Wills and Trust Agreements by Trust Legal Counsel*, 121 Tr. & Est. 35 (Nov. 1982). There are numerous trust document assembly programs on the market. A standard is Robert P. Wilkins, *Drafting Wills and Trust Agreements*, and its software, *Drafting Wills and Trust Agreements on CAPS* (West Group).

[321] 2 Scott & Ascher §9.3.14; 3 Scott & Ascher §§16.2 (Impossibility), 16.3 (Illegality).

[322] ACTEC Practice Committee, Fiduciary Matters Subcommittee, Guide for ACTEC Fellows Serving as Trustees, 26 ACTEC Notes 313, 322 (2001). *See also* Uniform Prudent Investor Act Section 2 (available at <http://www.uniformlaws.org/Act.aspx?title=Trust%20Code>) as Article 9 of the UTC) (providing that a trustee shall invest and manage trust assets as a prudent investor would, by considering the purposes, terms, distribution requirements, and other circumstances of the trust). Uniform Prudent Management of Institutional Funds Act (UPMIFA) §3(c)(2) expressly provides that the fiduciary shall make a reasonable effort to verify facts relevant to the management and investment of the fund. UPMIFA is intended to govern the investment activities of charitable corporations, as well as charitable trusts.

the trustee is entitled, at trust expense,[323] to initiate an action for instructions or declaratory judgment[324] in a court that has jurisdiction over the trust.[325] He is not obliged to rationalize conflicting provisions, resolve ambiguities, or supply missing terms on his own authority and at his own risk.[326] Trustees of business trusts are no exception.[327] "Beneficiaries, too, are entitled to seek judicial instructions regarding trust administration."[328] There must, however, be reasonable doubt.[329] Also, courts are generally not in the business of advising trustees on how to exercise their discretionary powers.[330] And, as a general matter, "[d]ecisions of questions which may arise upon the happening of events in the future must await those events."[331] That having been said, in New Hampshire, by statute, *a settlor* during his or her life may commence a judicial

---

[323] Restatement (Third) of Trusts §71 cmt. e.

[324] *See generally* §8.42 of this handbook (the complaint (petition) for instructions versus the complaint (petition) for declaratory judgment).

[325] *See* Restatement (Second) of Trusts §201 cmt. b (noting that if the trustee is in doubt as to the interpretation of the trust instrument, then he can protect himself by obtaining instructions from the court, the extent of his duties and powers being determined by the trust instrument and the rules of law which are applicable law, and not by his own interpretation of the instrument or his own belief as to the rules of law); UTC §201(c) (available at <http://www.uniformlaws.org/Act.aspx?title=Trust%20Code>) (Role of Court in Administration of Trust). For a catalog of other types of judicial proceedings involving trust administration that might be brought by a trustee or beneficiary, *see* UTC §112 cmt. (borrowing from California Probate Code §17200). In England, the courts exclusively have *inter alia* the power to vary the terms of trusts where they think fit (on the application of interested parties); the power to appoint trustees (when no other way of appointment can be used); the power to remove a trustee; the power to vary administrative provisions including investment powers; the power to determine the true construction of the terms of the trust; the power to enforce the terms of the trust; and the power to consider and award damages for breach of trust. Martyn Frost, *Overview of Trusts in England and Wales*, in Trusts in Prime Jurisdictions 19–20 (Alon Kaplan ed., 2000). *See generally* §9.4.4 of this handbook (may the legislature alter the terms of a charitable trust without violating the doctrine of separation of powers?).

[326] *See generally* 3 Scott & Ascher §16.8 (noting that "[t]rustees have received instructions on a wide range of questions, including the extent of their powers and duties, the identity of the trust beneficiaries and the extent of their interests, the proper allocation and apportionment of receipts or expenditures between income and principal, and the identity of those entitled to the trust property upon the termination of the trust"); Thomas H. Belknap, Newhall's Settlement of Estates and Fiduciary Law in Massachusetts §2:15 (1994).

[327] *See, e.g.,* Hauser v. Catlett, 197 Okla. 668, 173 P.2d 728 (1946) (a timely petition for instructions by the trustees of a business trust to resolve a trust termination issue).

[328] 3 Scott & Ascher §16.8.

[329] Restatement (Third) of Trusts §71; 3 Scott & Ascher §16.8.

[330] *See generally* 3 Scott & Ascher §16.8.

[331] Flye v. Jones, 283 Mass. 136, 138, 186 N.E. 64 (1933). *See also* In re Deed of Trust of McCargo, 652 A.2d 1330, 1337 (Pa. Super. 1994) (holding that an order of the lower court was improper because in part it purported to resolve a matter by declaratory judgment that was not based upon an event certain to occur); Dewire v. Haveles, 534 N.E.2d 782 (Mass. 1989) ("Although the gift over violates the rule against perpetuities [RAP] in its traditional form and in time may prove to violate it in actual fact," the RAP problem "need not be resolved at this time."). *See generally* Restatement (Third) of Trusts §71 cmt. d.

proceeding to determine the validity of a *revocable* inter vivos trust that he or she has created.[332]

Subject to the trustee's (or beneficiary's) right of appeal and provided all necessary parties[333] have properly been made parties to the proceeding, instructions issued by the court are binding on trustees and beneficiaries alike, unless the instructions were procured by fraud, duress, misrepresentation, concealment or, perhaps, as the result of manifest error.[334] "The court's determination of the questions involved marks them as res judicata."[335]

Concluding this introduction. We conclude this introduction with the final paragraph of the Epilogue to *Scott and Ascher on Trusts*, the "technicalities" referred to therein being the feudal forms of action that had so complicated the law of contracts and torts and that were so foreign to Equity and its child, the law of trusts:

> It is not to be wondered at that Lord Mansfield, who was not altogether successful in his attempts to slough off from the law of contracts some of these technicalities, looked at the achievements of the chancellors across the Hall and spoke of the "noble, rational, and uniform system" of the law of trusts. One cannot study the law of trusts without a profound feeling of admiration for the work of the courts of equity in creating and developing the concept of the trust and of the law of trusts. The evolution of the trust has been a great adventure in the field of jurisprudence. Nor has it ended. As long as the owner of property can dispose of it in accordance with his or legitimate wishes, the great adventure will go on. The law of trusts is living law.

---

[332] *See* RSA 564-B:4-406 (N.H.). The general rule has been that the ambulatory nature of a revocable inter vivos trust forecloses the bringing of such a declaratory judgment action while the settlor is alive. *See generally* Ullman v. Garcia, 645 So. 2d 168 (Fla. 3d DCA 1994).

[333] *Cf.* §5.7 of this handbook (the necessary parties to a suit brought by a trust beneficiary).

[334] Restatement (Third) of Trusts §71 cmt. b.

[335] 3 Scott & Ascher §16.8.

CHAPTER 2

The Property Requirement

§2.1   The Property Requirement

Equitable interests, as well as legal interests, can be held in trust.[1]

The attempt to define "property" is an elusive task. There is no cosmic synoptic definiens that can encompass its range. The word is at times more cognizable than recognizable. It is

---

§2.1   [1] Scott on Trusts §83. *See also* Bogert §1 ("A trustee's title usually is legal, but it may be equitable if the settlor expresses the intent to give such an interest and has the capacity to do so.").

not capable of anatomical or lexicographical definition or proof. It devolves upon the Court to fill in the definitional vacuum with the substance of the economics of our time.[2]

Property comprises, in large part, a category of illusory reference: it forms a conceptual mirage which slips elusively from sight just when it seems most attainably three-dimensional. Perhaps more accurately than any other legal notion it was "property" which deserved the Benthamite epithet, "rhetorical nonsense—nonsense upon stilts." "Property" remains ultimately an emotive phrase in search of a meaning.[3]

The property requirement. As a general rule, a trust cannot exist without property.[4] Moreover, the property must be ascertainable.[5] Declaring oneself trustee of the "bulk" of one's securities is not enough.[6] "Property denotes interests in things, not necessarily the things themselves, but necessarily things that are legally capable of being owned (and, ordinarily, transferred) and to which property interests can attach."[7]

Interests must be transferable to be entrustable. Any transferable[8] property interest, legal or equitable,[9] real or personal,[10] tangible or intangible,[11] vested[12] or contingent,[13] may be the subject of a trust.[14] In addition, the interest need not be full ownership of the property.[15] "Such limited interests as an estate

---

[2] First Victoria Bank v. United States, 620 F.2d 1096, 1102–1103 (5th Cir. 1980). For musings on how difficult it has been over the years for courts and legal scholars to develop an accurate and comprehensive definition of property, *see* Restatement (Third) of Trusts, Reporter's Notes on §40.

[3] K. Gray, Property in Thin Air, [1991] CLJ 253 at 305.

[4] *See generally* 1 Scott & Ascher §§2.1.6, 10.1; 1A Scott on Trusts §74. In §2.2.1 of this handbook (the pour-over statute), we note that the Uniform Testamentary Additions to Trusts Act (UTATA) allows for an *inter vivos trust* to be initially funded *postmortem* by a pour-over devise under the settlor's will. *See generally* Restatement (Third) of Property (Wills and Other Donative Transfers) §3.8 cmt. b. If the trust itself comes into existence before the settlor's death, then UTATA has carved out an exception to the property requirement. If the trust does not come into existence until the settlor's death, then UTATA has not carved out such an exception.

[5] 1 Scott & Ascher §10.3 (Indefinite Subject Matter). *See, e.g.*, Unthank v. Rippstein, 386 S.W.2d 134 (Tex. 1964) (purported declaration of trust unenforceable due to the lack of a discrete, specific, identifiable corpus).

[6] 1 Scott & Ascher §10.3 (Indefinite Subject Matter). *See, e.g.*, Palmer v. Simmonds, 2 Drew. 221 (1854).

[7] Restatement (Third) of Trusts §40 cmt. b.

[8] *See* Restatement (Third) of Trusts §40, cmts. c, d. "A nontransferable property interest. . . .[, however,]...may be held in trust when, as occasionally occurs, it is created in trust by act of the trustee or it accrues to a trustee of a trust that is already in existence." *See* Restatement (Third) of Trusts §40, cmts. c, d.

[9] 1 Scott & Ascher §10.7; Bogert §1 (entrusted equitable interests). There was a time when a "use on a use" was impermissible. *See* §8.15.1 of this handbook (statute of uses).

[10] *See generally* Bogert §43.

[11] 1 Scott & Ascher §10.6.

[12] Vested interests that are subject to a condition subsequent, *i.e.*, divestment, may also be the subject of a trust. *See* 1 Scott & Ascher §10.8.

[13] 1 Scott & Ascher §§10.8, 10.9.

[14] *See* §2.1.1 of this handbook for a discussion of what interests are and are not transferable.

[15] *See generally* Bogert §43.

for years, an estate for life, a future interest, a reversionary interest, a servitude, a mortgage or a share in common with others may be held in trust."[16]

What constitutes an effective transfer in trust. The effectiveness of a *donative transfer* in trust is determined by the laws relating to gifts.[17] (In the case of a declaration of trust, only the equitable interest is gifted, the legal title remaining with the settlor.[18]) Absent statute or special facts, the trust's enforceability *in equity* would *not* be contingent on notice of the transfer being given to third parties, such as to the transfer agent in the case of a block of stock or to the insurer in the case of an insurance contract, although for evidentiary purposes it is generally good practice to give such notice.[19] In the case of an ineffective donative transfer in trust where the intended beneficiaries have changed their position in reliance on the purported transfer such that it would be inequitable for the property owner to retain the property, equity may compel a transfer of the property upon the intended trust.[20] "If the owner of property attempts ineffectively to transfer it inter vivos to another as trustee but has received consideration for the purported transfer, the property owner is under a duty to complete the transfer similar to the duty that would exist if the property owner had made a contract to convey the property free of trust. . . In a proper case, specific performance may be had."[21] If all else fails, it is possible that an incomplete transfer in trust could be given effect through the judicial imposition of a constructive trust, a topic we take up in Section 3.3 of this handbook.[22]

The funding of a *testamentary trust* is governed by different rules. The effectiveness of a testamentary disposition in trust is determined by the law of wills.[23]

Interests that are not entrustable. On the other hand, a hope or an expectancy, not to be confused with a legal or an equitable future interest, is not

---

[16] W. F. Fratcher, 6 Intl. Encyclopedia of Comp. Law 33 (F. H. Lawson ed., 1973). *See also* 1 Scott & Ascher §10.4; Bogert §43.

[17] Restatement (Third) of Trusts §16 cmt. a.

[18] *See* Restatement (Third) of Trusts §16 cmt. d (noting that whether one is confronted with an incomplete gift in trust of the legal and equitable interests in an item of property or its enforceable entrustment by declaration is not all that easy to sort out when the facts are ambiguous as to what the property owner had intended). In §3.4.1 of this handbook we note that it is traditional property/trust doctrine that a declaration of trust may arise without a title-conveyance of the subject property from the settlor-declarant to the settlor-trustee. In the comment to Section 201 of the Uniform Powers of Appointment Act there is the assertion that a declaration of trust "necessarily entails a transfer of legal title from the owner-as-owner to the owner-as-trustee. . . ." No authority is supplied for this general proposition because there is none.

[19] Restatement (Third) of Trusts §16 cmt. b ("Unless the contrary is expressly provided in an applicable statute, or is necessarily implied from its provisions, formalities prescribed for the creation of a recordable document, or otherwise for protection of or from third parties, need not be satisfied in order to make a valid donative transfer, that is, one that is effective as between the transferor and the transferee(s).").

[20] Restatement (Third) of Trusts §16 cmt. b; Restatement of Restitution §16 cmt. b.

[21] Restatement (Third) of Trusts §16 cmt. b.

[22] *See also* Restatement (Third) of Trusts §16 cmt. c.

[23] Restatement (Third) of Trusts §16 cmt. a.

property and thus may not be the subject of a trust.[24] At common law, and under Florida law today, human remains are not property.[25] As to whether there may be a present transfer of future crops and unborn animals to a trustee, see Section 8.15.42 of this handbook.[26] At early common law one could not assign contractual rights incident to a debt, a topic we take up in Section 8.15.75 of this handbook. Time and the procedural merging of law and equity long ago washed away the proscription.

Title is generally in the trustee. Legal title to the property is in the trustee.[27] If the trustee sells an item of trust property, a trust is impressed upon the proceeds. "Where the relation of trustee and *cestui que trust* has once been established as to certain property in the hands of the trustee, no mere change of trust property from one form to another will destroy the relation."[28]

Unless the terms of the trust provide otherwise, the trustee takes the entire legal interest in personal property.[29] In other words, he takes an interest of unlimited duration that is a fee simple.[30] As to real property, the rule was that the trustee took "such an estate and only such an estate as was necessary to enable him to perform the trust by the exercise of such powers as were incident to ownership of the estate."[31] Thus, for example, it was possible that a passive trust of real estate for the life of a beneficiary caused the estate of the trustee to be cut back to a legal life estate, the measuring life being the life of the beneficiary.[32] The Restatement (Third) of Trusts has swept away once and for all the ancient distinctions between trusts of real property and trusts of personal property insofar as the nature and quality of the trustee's title is concerned:

> Unless a different intention is manifested, or the settlor owned only a lesser interest, the trustee takes a nonbeneficial interest of unlimited duration in the trust property and not an interest limited to the duration of the trust.[33]

---

[24] 1 Scott & Ascher §10.1.1.

[25] *See* Wilson v. Wilson, 138 So. 3d 1176 (Fla. Dist. Ct. App. 2014) ("Ashes are the decedent's remains. Common law, our supreme court, and this Court have always held that a decedent's remains are not property.").

[26] *See also* 1 Scott & Ascher §10.10.3.

[27] Bogert §1. When a trustee holds the beneficial interest in another trust, however, title to the underlying property is in the trustee of the other trust. *Cf.* Papale-Keefe v. Altomare, 38 Mass. App. Ct. 308 (1995) (involving an incomplete transfer of shares of beneficial interest to the trustee of an inter vivos trust).

[28] Bolton v. Stillwagon, 410 Pa. 618, 626, 190 A.2d 105, 109 (1963) (*citing to* 39 P.L.E. Trusts §387; O'Neill v. O'Neill, 227 Pa. 334, 76 A. 26; McLaughlin v. Fulton, 104 Pa. 161).

[29] 1 Scott & Ascher §10.12.

[30] 1 Scott & Ascher §10.12.

[31] *See* Restatement (Third) of Trusts, Reporter's Notes on §42.

[32] *See generally* §8.27 of this handbook (the difference between a legal life estate and an equitable life estate incident to a trust).

[33] Restatement (Third) of Trusts §42.

Consequences of the trustee possessing less than a full legal interest. Why might it have at one time made a difference whether the trustee possessed the full legal interest?[34] Professor Scott catalogued the reasons:

- If the remaindermen shared the legal title with the trustee, a conveyance of the trust property to them would not have been necessary upon the trust's termination;[35]
- If the remaindermen shared the legal title with the trustee, they might have been entitled to only legal remedies and not equitable remedies[36] as against the trustee or third parties;[37]
- If the remaindermen shared the legal title with the trustee, the statute of limitations for adverse possession of the trust property by a third person would not have begun to run against the remaindermen until the death of the life tenant;[38]
- If the remaindermen shared the legal title with the trustee, a conveyance in breach of trust to a good-faith purchaser for value or BFP would not have cut off the interests of the remaindermen;[39]
- If the remaindermen shared the legal estate with the trustee and the life tenant's interest was equitable, the Rule in Shelley's case, all other things being equal, would not have been applicable;[40]
- If the remaindermen shared the legal title with the trustee, the remaindermen would have been necessary parties to litigation with third parties with respect to the trust property;[41]
- If the remaindermen shared the legal interest with the trustee, the remaindermen and the trustee were not in a fiduciary relationship, and thus the remaindermen's "rights. . . [were]. . . only such as under the law of waste a remainderman. . . [had]. . . against a life tenant."[42]
- If the remaindermen shared the legal interest with the trustee, a spendthrift provision would be unenforceable as against the

---

[34] 1 Scott & Ascher §10.12.1.

[35] 1 Scott on Trusts §88.2 (1939 ed.). The beneficiary's title would still be subject to the trustee's powers and duties so far as necessary to satisfy obligations and wind up administration. *See* Restatement (Third) of Trusts §89 cmt. g. ("The trustee's duty of distribution is performed by surrendering possession of the subject matter of the trust within a reasonable time and taking steps that may be necessary to enable the beneficiaries readily to establish ownership.")

[36] *See generally* §7.2.3 of this handbook (types of equitable relief for a breach of trust).

[37] 1 Scott on Trusts §88.2 (1939 ed.).

[38] 1 Scott on Trusts §88.2 (1939 ed.).

[39] 1 Scott on Trusts §88.2 (1939 ed.). *See generally* §8.15.63 of this handbook (doctrine of bona fide purchase).

[40] 1 Scott on Trusts §88.2 (1939 ed.). *See generally* §8.15.3 of this handbook (rule in Shelley's Case).

[41] 1 Scott on Trusts §88.2 (1939 ed.). *See generally* §3.5.1 of this handbook (nature and extent of the trustee's estate).

[42] 1 Scott on Trusts §88.2 (1939 ed.). *See generally* §8.27 of this handbook (the difference between a legal life estate and an equitable life estate incident to a trust).

remaindermen, it being an impermissible restraint on the alienability of legal interests;[43] and

- If the remaindermen shared the legal interest with the trustee, a court could not have "authorize[d] a sale of a part of the property in order to make repairs upon another part."[44]

§2.1.1   The Inter Vivos Trust

We note at the outset that, as plaintiff contends, when an "owner of property declares himself trustee of property, a trust may be created without a transfer of title to the property.". . . Here, Peterson was both the settlor and the initial trustee. Consequently, so long as Peterson actually transferred the titled assets to the trust, it was unnecessary for him to take further action formally transferring title of those assets to the trust. As a matter of law, the conveyance of the property was sufficient.[45]

Must be a present transfer by the property owner for a classic inter vivos trust to arise. "If a property owner undertakes to make a donative inter vivos disposition in trust by transferring property to another as trustee, an express trust is not created if the property owner fails during life to complete the contemplated transfer of the property."[46] In other words, there must be a present transfer[47] of some property interest to the designated trustee.[48] If one gratuitously promises to transfer property in trust at some time in the future, a trust will not arise until the transfer is actually made, provided there is a manifestation of an intention to create a trust *at the time of the transfer.*[49]

Declarations of trust,[50] and, of course, testamentary trusts, are exempt from the present transfer requirement,[51] the former because legal title remains with the settlor,[52] the latter because a will speaks at death. In the case of declarations, however, there still must be the manifestation of an intention to

---

[43] 1 Scott on Trusts §88.2 (1939 ed.). *See generally* §8.15.40 of this handbook (the rule against direct restraints on alienation: the trust exception).

[44] 1 Scott on Trusts §88.2 (1939 ed.).

[45] Samuel v. King, 186 Or. App. 684, 692, 64 P.3d 1206, 1210 (2003).

[46] Restatement (Third) of Trusts §16(1). *See also* Bogert §43.

[47] 1 Scott & Ascher §4.4.

[48] 1 Scott & Ascher §3.3.3.

[49] 1 Scott & Ascher §4.4.5; Bogert §43.

[50] Note, also, that if a "property owner intends to make an outright gift inter vivos but fails to make the transfer that is required in order to do so, the gift intention will not be given effect by treating it as a declaration of trust." Restatement (Third) of Trusts §16(2).

[51] 1 Scott & Ascher §3.3.3.

[52] *See generally* Janet A. Lemons, *Trust Law: Creating a Trust by Declaration Does Not Require the Settlor to Transfer Legal Title of the Trust Property to Himself as Trustee [Taliaferro v. Taliaferro, 921 P.2d 803 (Kan. 1996)]*, 36 Washburn L.J. 511 (1997). There is, however, a present transfer of an equitable or beneficial interest. *See generally* 1 Scott & Ascher §3.3.3.

create a present trust.[53] Also, a promise to create a trust in the future, if supported by a present exchange of consideration, may be enforceable under contract principles.[54]

A will, on the other hand, speaks only at death. A will is a *testamentary* instrument (*i.e.*, it speaks only at death). An inter vivos trust is not a testamentary instrument. A revocable inter vivos trust may be a will substitute, but it is not a will.[55] Under the common law, an inter vivos trust arises when title to some interest in property passes to the trustee *during the lifetime of the settlor*.[56] Because a will is *ambulatory* (*i.e.*, it speaks only at death), the mere execution of a will that names a trustee as legatee or devisee under a so-called *pour-over provision*[57] will not give rise to an inter vivos trust. This is because no property interest passes at the time of the will's execution.[58] A will may be employed to add property postmortem to a trust that was established inter vivos[59] and, of course, to impress postmortem a testamentary trust upon probate property.[60] However, under the common law, pour-over provisions in wills cannot create inter vivos trusts and really have nothing to do with testamentary trusts.

---

[53] 1 Scott & Ascher §§4.4, 5.1; Bogert §43. *See also* 1 Scott & Ascher §5.1.1 (Stashes Found PostMortem).

[54] 1 Scott & Ascher §§3.3.3, 5.1.2; Bogert §43.

[55] Restatement (Third) of Property (Wills and Other Donative Transfers) §7.1 (Tentative Draft No. 3, Apr. 4, 2001).

[56] *See generally* Comment Note, *Creation of express trust in property to be acquired in the future*, 3 A.L.R.3d 1416 (1965); Restatement (Second) of Trusts §75.

[57] *See generally* Restatement (Third) of Trusts §19.

[58] 1 Scott & Ascher §§10.10 (After-Acquired Property) 10.10.1 (Expectancies). A will is validly executed if it is in writing and is signed by the testator and by a specified number of attesting witnesses under procedures provided by applicable law. Restatement (Third) of Property (Wills and Other Donative Transfers) §3.1.

[59] It is generally assumed that for a pour-over provision to be effective under the common law, the inter vivos trust must come into existence through a lifetime transfer of property to the trustee *prior* to the execution of the pour-over will. *See* Clark v. Citizens Nat'l Bank of Collingswood, 38 N.J. Super. 69, 118 A.2d 108 (1955). *But see* Bogert §106 (suggesting that even under the common law, a pour-over provision may be effective even though the inter vivos trust comes into existence through a lifetime transfer to the trustee after the will is executed). UPC §2-511 (Testamentary Additions to Trusts) would allow the inter vivos trust to come into existence *after or as of the settlor's death* when there is an associated pour-over will. *See* UPC §2-511 cmt. *See also* Restatement (Third) of Property (Wills and Other Donative Transfers) §3.8 cmt. a (suggesting that under the Revised Uniform Testamentary Additions to Trusts Act, the inter vivos "trust itself need not be established during the testator's lifetime, but can be established *by* the pour-over devise"). For more on the common law history of pour-over provisions, *see* §8.15.9 of this handbook (doctrine of independent legal significance).

[60] "In most cases, the major component of a decedent's probate estate consists of property that the decedent owned at death." Restatement (Third) of Property (Wills and Other Donative Transfers) §1.1 cmt. b. "Actual ownership, not ownership in substance, is required." Restatement (Third) of Property (Wills and Other Donative Transfers) §1.1 cmt. b. "The actual ownership must also be beneficial ownership." Restatement (Third) of Property (Wills and Other Donative Transfers) §1.1 cmt. b. "Nonbeneficial ownership, such as that held by a trustee, is not sufficient." Restatement (Third) of Property (Wills and Other Donative Transfers) §1.1 cmt. b.

The omitted-child (or pretermitted heir) statute. An omitted-child statute in a common law jurisdiction is designed to prevent unintentional disinheritance *by will* of the members of a designated class of individuals. At minimum, the class will comprise the children of the testator. In Section 8.15.89 of this handbook, we consider how the revocable inter vivos trust can be employed as an instrument of pretermission, specifically technical pretermission by pour-over devise and substantive pretermission by predeath funding.

When an agent may establish a trust of the principal's property. An agent acting under a durable power of attorney may impress an inter vivos trust upon the principal's property, provided the express language of the power of attorney authorizes the agent, *i.e.*, the attorney-in-fact, to create the trust.[61] Also, the principal must not have expressly or constructively revoked the agent's authority to do so prior to the purported entrustment.[62] On the other hand, the power to create a will is generally considered nondelegable.[63] Is the power to create a will substitute such as a revocable trust delegable? One court has held that it is:

> We do not agree. . . that delegation of authority to create a trust through a durable general power of attorney to serve the interests of the principal violates public policy as a matter of law, even when a trust's dispositive terms may serve a function similar to that of a will.[64]

Advantages of the inter vivos trust over the testamentary trust. There are few if any tax advantages to establishing a revocable inter vivos trust, at least any that can accrue to the settlor. There are, however, numerous possible nontax advantages to establishing and funding a revocable inter vivos trust. Property held in a revocable inter vivos trust during the lifetime of the settlor under normal circumstances would not be subject to judicial conservatorship/ guardianship proceedings in the event of the settlor's incapacity, title being in the trustee; nor would it be subject to judicial probate proceedings in the event of the settlor's death, again title being in the trustee. The attendant advantages are privacy,[65] cost savings, efficiency, and flexibility. The revocable inter vivos trust also can serve as a property management vehicle for someone who is alive and competent but unable or disinclined to manage a portion or all of his or her own property, *e.g.*, someone who is overseas for an extended period of time on business or with the military.

When a deceased settlor's estate is probated in one state and the designated trustee of his or her testamentary trust is domiciled in another state, the designated foreign trustee may have to qualify in a court of the settlor's domicil as a precondition to being appointed, a topic we take up in Section 3.1 of this handbook. Such multi-jurisdictional complications can easily be avoided at the

---

[61] Estate of Kurrelmeyer, 895 A.2d 207, 211 (Vt. 2006).
[62] Gagnon v. Coombs, 39 Mass. App. Ct. 144, 654 N.E.2d 54 (1995).
[63] Estate of Kurrelmeyer, 895 A.2d 207, 213 (Vt. 2006).
[64] Estate of Kurrelmeyer, 895 A.2d 207, 213 (Vt. 2006).
[65] For the public policy case against the privacy advantage, see Francis H. Foster, *Trust Primacy*, 93 Cornell L. Rev. 555 (2008).

estate planning stage if an inter vivos trust rather than a testamentary trust is employed. In the case of a probate pour-over to an out-of-state trustee of an inter vivos trust, it is generally unnecessary for the trustee to qualify in a court of the deceased settlor's domicil.[66]

The UPC and the inter vivos trust's privacy advantage. At one time, the Uniform Probate Code required that inter vivos trusts, as well as testamentary trusts, be registered in an appropriate state court having jurisdiction over the trust's principal place of administration.[67] The UPC still provides that before making a pour-over distribution of probate estate assets to the trustee of an inter vivos trust, the personal representative, *i.e.*, the executor or administrator of the probate estate, may require that the trustee register the trust "if the state in which . . . [the trust] . . . is to be administered provides for registration."[68] The formal registration requirement was a part of Article VII of the UPC. Article VII was superseded by various provisions of the Uniform *Trust* Code and "withdrawn" in 2010.

Other disadvantages of the inter vivos trust. The downside to a competent settlor funding his or her revocable inter vivos trust is some attendant administrative costs and inconvenience. In the past, a settlor who desired to put off funding his or her revocable inter vivos trust was advised to at least establish the legal relationship by token funding so that down the road the trust could be further funded, *e.g.*, by an agent acting under a durable power of attorney or by will.

In Kansas, a taxpayer may designate an "individual" as the postmortem beneficiary of his or her IRA account and in so doing insulate the IRA funds from the reach of the taxpayer's postmortem creditors.[69] Other states have similar statutes. In 2007, however, the Court of Appeals of Kansas ruled that Kansas's version of Uniform Trust Code (UTC) Section 505(a)(3) eliminated this spendthrift protection in cases where IRA funds are payable postmortem not to "individuals" but to trustees of self-settled revocable inter vivos trusts.[70] UTC Section 505(a)(3) provides that "[a]fter the death of a settlor. . . the property of a trust that was revocable at the settlor's death is subject to the claims of the settlor's creditors. . . to the extent the settlor's probate estate is inadequate to satisfy those claims. . . ."

Pouring over by will into a token funded inter vivos trust. Under the common law, for a will's pour-over provision to be effective, the trustee needed to have taken title to at least a nominal or token amount of property, *e.g.*, a cent or a peppercorn, *during the lifetime of the settlor*. Otherwise, the pour-over bequest or devise to the trustee would fail because of the nonexistence of a recipient inter vivos trust. Without property, there could be no trust, and without a trust, there could be no trustee to receive the bequest or devise. Moreover, "[a]n

---

[66] 7 Scott & Ascher §45.2.1.6.

[67] UPC §7-101 (trustee's duty to register) (now repealed).

[68] UPC §3-913(a).

[69] *See* Kan. Stat. Ann. 60-2308(b).

[70] *See* Commerce Bank, N.A. v. Bolander, 154 P.3d 1184, 2007 WL 1041760 (Kan. Ct. App. 2007).

expectation or hope of receiving property in the future, or an interest that has not come into existence or has ceased to exist, cannot be held in trust."[71]

The practice of token funding inter vivos trusts was an accommodation to the property requirement that is embedded in the common law of trusts, though to this day the practice has its skeptics, including the American Law Institute: "[I]f a nominal amount of property is included in the inter vivos trust, it is questionable whether it can be considered to have the independent significance necessary for the doctrine's application."[72]

The debate over the sufficiency of token funding in the context of the law of trusts is not to be confused with the debate over adequacy of consideration in the context of contract law, though down through the years the lowly peppercorn has figured prominently in each:

> The rule that market equivalence of consideration is not required. . . [for an enforceable contract]. . . , and that the value of the consideration is to be left solely to the free bargaining process of the parties, leads in extreme cases to seeming absurdities. When the consideration is only a "peppercorn" or a "tomtit" or a worthless piece of paper, the requirement of a consideration appeared to Holmes to be as much a mere formality as is a seal.[73]

In any case, the trustee should be aware that there are now statutes on the books in many states that create an exception to the common law requirement that for a pour-over to be effective the trustee of an inter vivos trust needs to take title to at least a nominal or token amount of property while the settlor is alive. The statutory exception generally applies only to "inter vivos" trusts that have associated pour-over wills.[74] Under Section 2-511(a) of the Uniform Probate Code, the trust instrument can even be prepared *after* the settlor's pour-over will has been executed. For more on these legislative intrusions into the common law of trusts the reader is referred to Section 2.2.1 of this handbook.

The pour-over will is probated in one state; the recipient trust is administered in another (conflict of laws issues). Assume a will with a pour-over provision. The testator's last domicil is State *X*. The formal validity of the will is governed by the laws of State *X*. Pursuant to the terms of the will, the residue pours over to a preexisting inter vivos trust that is sited in State *Y* and whose administration is governed by the laws of State *Y*. Whose laws regulate the testamentary addition? Here are the general rules: The validity of the residuary bequest itself is governed by the laws of State *X*. The recipient trustee, however,

---

[71] Restatement (Third) of Trusts §41. *See also* §8.15.42 of this handbook (the potential possession doctrine).

[72] Restatement (Third) of Trusts §19 cmt. b. For a discussion of the doctrine of independent legal significance, *see* §8.15.9 of this handbook. *See also* Restatement (Third) of Property (Wills and Other Donative Transfers) §3.8, cmt. d. ("The only requirement under the doctrine of independent significance is that the inter vivos trust must be *more than nominally funded* in order to give the trust document and any subsequent amendments independent significance.").

[73] Arthur Linton Corbin, 1 Corbin on Contracts §127 (1963) (citing to the opinion of Oliver Wendell Holmes in Krell v. Codman, 154 Mass. 454, 28 N.E. 578 (1891).

[74] *See* §2.2.1 of this handbook (the pour-over statute).

need not qualify in a State *X* court. Moreover, there is no segregation of the pour over such that there are now two trusts. If the bequest/devise is valid, the effect is merely to augment the trust estate. The administration of the trust estate continues to be governed exclusively by the laws of State *Y*, notwithstanding the fact that the addition came from State *X*, a foreign jurisdiction. The Restatement (Second) of Conflict of Laws is in accord.[75] The topic of conflict of laws is taken up generally in §8.5 of this handbook.

Postmortem additions may not be made by a deceased settlor's agents. In the context of postmortem additions to a trust in existence prior to the execution of the will, an *agency* is to be contrasted with a *will*, which speaks at death. An agency terminates upon the death of the principal.[76] Thus, an agent of the settlor acting under a durable power of attorney may not make postmortem additions of the settlor's property to a trust, or testamentary transfers of any kind for that matter.[77] Swiss law is generally in accord.[78] To effect a testamentary transfer there must be compliance with the statute of wills.

What may be made the subject of a trust. Any transferable[79] property interest may be used to establish an inter vivos trust.[80] Thus, one may not fund a trust with one's spouse or one's child, the settlor having no property rights in either. One's dog or a cat, however, could be made the subject of a trust.[81]

The mechanics of funding. All a settlor need do, for example, in order to make the settlor's fifty shares of stock the subject of a trust is to have the shares re-registered in the name of the trustee.[82] A simple phone call to a broker should set the re-registration process in motion. Rights under an insurance contract may be transferred during the insured's lifetime to a trust by assigning

---

[75] Restatement (Second) of Conflict of Laws §271, cmt. f.

[76] *But see* UPC §5-504:

> The death of a principal who has executed a written power of attorney, durable or otherwise, does not revoke or terminate the agency as to the attorney in fact or other person, who, without actual knowledge of the death of the principal, acts in good faith under the power. Any action so taken, unless otherwise invalid or unenforceable, binds successors in interest of the principal.

[77] *See generally* 1 Scott & Ascher §2.3.4 (noting that "if the owner of property hands it over to an agent with directions as to its disposition after the owner's death, the disposition may well be invalid under the statute of wills").

[78] *See* Tim Bennett, *Who is in control?*, STEP J. 31, 33 (Nov./Dec. 2005) (noting that "the Swiss courts have now confirmed that a post mortem power of attorney does not work: they give a power to administer assets after death, but they do not confer a power to transfer the title of property").

[79] 1 Scott & Ascher §§10.5; Bogert §43. *See also* 1 Scott & Ascher §§10.5.1 (Nontransferable Property); 10.5.2 (Limited Transferability); 10.5.3 (Seats on Exchanges); 10.5.4 (Property Nontransferable For Reasons Inapplicable to Declaration of Trust).

[80] *See generally* 1A Scott on Trusts §74.1; Bogert §43.

[81] Bogert §43. *See generally* §9.9.5 of this handbook (a pet-funded trust as an alternative to the UTC pet trust).

[82] Restatement (Third) of Trusts §16 cmt. b. ("Good practice certainly calls for the use of additional formalities and the taking of appropriate further steps, such as changes of registration, or the execution and recordation of deeds to land."); UTC §401 cmt. (available at <http://www.uniformlaws.org/Act.aspx?title=Trust%20Code>) ("However, such registration is not necessary to create the trust.").

the policy itself to the trustee or by merely filling out a form designating the trustee as recipient of the insurance proceeds. A bank account should be re-registered in the name of the trustee. All that having been said, "[e]ven when an owner of property surrenders possession of it or of a document of transfer in a manner that otherwise would be sufficient to transfer the property to a trustee, if the property owner does not intend to make a presently effective transfer there is no transfer of the title."[83]

Formal re-registration of title generally is not necessary in equity to impress a trust upon an item of intangible personal property.[84] "Thus, a delivery may be made in escrow or may be accomplished by acts of constructive or symbolic delivery performed with the requisite intention to make a present transfer."[85] A California court has enforced a declaration of trust of two parcels of real estate although the grant deeds had reflected that the deceased settlor had held each parcel in his individual capacity, not as trustee.[86] A North Carolina court has done much the same thing.[87] Courts even enforce oral trusts of cash.[88] Still, the lack of a formal paper trail invites litigation over whether there was the requisite intent to impress a trust upon the property.[89] It should be noted that in the case of a payable-on-death (POD) checking or savings account, a type of statutory will *substitute* grounded in contract, formal re-registration in the name of the trustee may be the only option.[90]

In some jurisdictions, a trust may not be impressed upon real property without the property being transferred to the trustee (or to the "trust") by a valid deed,[91] and preferably in a way that meets the writing requirements of the applicable statute of frauds.[92] A deed does not necessarily satisfy the Statute of Frauds, nor is a writing that satisfies the Statute of Frauds necessarily a deed.[93] Nowadays, the deed need not contain such words of inheritance as "to X and his heirs."[94] In California, on the other hand, a written declaration of trust of a certain parcel of real property has been enforced although there had never been a formal deeding of the property from the declarant to himself as

---

[83] Restatement (Third) of Trusts §16 cmt. b.

[84] 1 Scott & Ascher §5.1. *See, e.g.,* Bourgeois v. Hurley, 8 Mass. App. Ct. 213 (1979); Restatement (Third) of Trusts §16 cmt. b, illus. 4 (while one may not impress a trust upon an expectancy, one may by general assignment impress a trust upon whatever one is entitled to under the estate of someone who has died, even while legal title to the subject property is still lodged in the decedent's personal representative).

[85] Restatement (Third) of Trusts §16 cmt. b.

[86] *See* Ukkestad v. RBS Asset Fin., Inc., 185 Cal. Rptr. 3d 145 (Cal. App. 2015).

[87] *See* Nevitt v. Robotham, 762 S.E.2d 267 (N.C. App. Ct. 2014) (confirming that even in the case of the entrustment of real estate by declaration, the settlor and the trustee being the same person, "no transfer of legal title is required, since the trustee already holds legal title.").

[88] *See, e.g.,* Estate of Fournier, 902 A.2d 852 (Me. 2006).

[89] *See* UTC §401 cmt. (available at <http://www.uniformlaws.org/Act.aspx?title=Trust%20 Code>); Restatement (Third) of Trusts §16 cmt. b.

[90] *See, e.g.,* Estate of Moore, 209 Ariz. 3, 97 P.3d 103 (2004).

[91] *See, e.g.,* Schindler v. Pepple, 158 S.W.3d 784 (Mo. App. 2005).

[92] *See generally* §8.15.5 of this handbook (statute of frauds).

[93] *See generally* §8.15.5 of this handbook (statute of frauds).

[94] 3 Scott & Ascher §13.2.1.

trustee.[95] That the declarant had identified the parcel on an asset schedule attached to the written declaration was held sufficient for an enforceable trust of the parcel to arise. The trust instrument and the asset schedule, taken together, also satisfied the writing requirement of the Statute of Frauds. In another California case, a general assignment provision within the written declaration of trust of "all of the Grantor's right, title and interest in and to all of his real . . . property" satisfied the Statute of Frauds.[96] ". . . [I]t is a simple matter of referring to publicly available records to determine. . . [the Grantor's]. . . real estate holdings. . . ."[97]

In New York, by statute,[98] a trust may acquire property in the name of the trust as such name is designated in the trust instrument. It is not necessary that there be a conveyance to, or registration in the name of, the trustee. *Legal title as a matter of law, however, would still pass to the trustee.* Colorado has a similar statute (CSA §38-30-108.5(i)). The trustee records a "statement of authority" evidencing his legal authority to act with respect to the real estate.

For a more detailed discussion of funding procedures, see How to Fund a Revocable Living Trust Correctly.[99] For a discussion of the complex and time-sensitive mechanics of funding a trust with distributions from a qualified defined contribution plan account or IRA after the account owner's death, the reader is referred to Grassi and Welber.[100]

Impressing a revocable trust upon certain types of property can have unintended consequences. *Real estate.* A settlor contemplating an inter vivos transfer of title to his or her home to the trustee of a revocable inter vivos trust needs to understand that he or she, depending upon the jurisdiction, could lose one or more of the following as a result of the transfer: the personal/residential property tax exemption (statute), the homestead exemption from creditor access (statute), title insurance coverage (contract), and the right to have preexisting or future loans secured by the real estate (contract). Thus the prudent trustee should insist by written communication that the settlor seek legal advice on these and any other possible consequences of a transfer of title to the home out of the settlor's name.[101] It should be noted that federal law may

---

[95] *See* Heggstad v. Heggstad, 16 Cal. App. 4th 943 (1993).

[96] *See* Ukkestad v. RBS Asset Fin., Inc., 185 Cal. Rptr. 3d 145 (Cal. App. 2015).

[97] *See* Ukkestad v. RBS Asset Fin., Inc., 185 Cal. Rptr. 3d 145 (Cal. App. 2015).

[98] Estate Powers & Trusts Law §7-2.1. "To acquire the names of all the trustees and their signatures to sell or mortgage the property proved cumbersome." Margaret Valentine Turano, Practice Commentaries, 2002 Main Volume. "The legislature wanted to make these trusts parallel to partnerships, which can hold property in the partnership name. . . ." Margaret Valentine Turano, Practice Commentaries, 2002 Main Volume.

[99] For a more detailed discussion of funding procedures, *see* Schmidt, *How to Fund a Revocable Living Trust Correctly*, 20 Est. Plan. 67 (No. 2-1993). *See also* Bruce Fenton, *A Trust Is Only as Good as Its Funding*, 2002 LWUSA 164.

[100] Sebastian V. Grassi, Jr. & Nancy H. Welber, *Special Planning Is Needed for Retirement Benefits Payable to a Disabled Special-Needs Child*, J. Practical Estate Planning 51 (June–July 2010) ("Many of the concepts discussed in this article are also applicable where the beneficiary child is not a special-needs child").

[101] At one time in Florida, the transfer of a titled tangible personal property, *e.g.*, a motor vehicle, triggered a state sales tax liability.

well prohibit a bank from calling a loan secured by real estate, provided the only reason for calling the loan is that legal title to the real estate has been transferred by its owner to the trustee of a revocable inter vivos trust for the owner's benefit.[102] It goes without saying that a trustee should be wary of accepting title to a parcel of real estate without having in hand written assurance from counsel that there will be no title problems down the road stemming from the transfer.[103]

Interests in a closely held entity. If the owner of shares in a closely held entity is contemplating transferring them to the trustee of a revocable inter vivos trust for estate planning purposes, the settlor and the prospective trustee should check to see whether they are burdened by transfer restrictions, and if they are, whether in the face of those restrictions the transfer contemplated could cause problems down the road. While the type of transfer contemplated should not per se cause future complications, it being more a transfer in form than in substance, at least while the settlor is alive and competent, it is not to say that it won't. It has happened before.[104]

Individual Retirement Accounts. In Kansas, designating the trustee of a self-settled revocable inter vivos trust as the postmortem beneficiary of the settlor's IRA risks subjecting the IRA's assets to attachment postmortem by the settlor's creditors.[105]

Equitable property rights themselves may be made the subject of a trust. A transferable interest in one trust (perhaps an interest in a realty trust) may be held in another trust (perhaps a revocable inter vivos trust),[106] except if an effective spendthrift provision prevents a beneficiary from making such a transfer.[107] Thus, vested equitable life estates, vested equitable remainders, equitable remainders subject to divestment, and vested (transmissible) contingent remainders may themselves be the subject of trusts.[108] So also may reversionary interests.[109] "[B]ut an interest under a discretionary trust is future property, which cannot be settled except for value."[110]

An equitable property interest that is not incident to a trust relationship also may be made the subject of a trust. For example, "[i]f the settlor has merely contracted to buy land and has paid the purchase price,. . . and the settlor

---

[102] *See* 12 U.S.C.A. §1701j-3.

[103] *See generally* §6.2.2.2 of this handbook (the prudent investor's code of conduct).

[104] *See, e.g.,* Kesling v. Kesling, 967 N.E.2d 66 (Ind. Ct. App. 2012).

[105] *See* Commerce Bank, N.A. v. Bolander, 154 P.3d 1184, 2007 WL 1041760 (Kan. Ct. App. 2007) (the court citing in support Kansas's version of UTC §505(a)(3), which provides that "[a]fter the death of a settlor. . . the property of a trust that was revocable at the settlor's death is subject to the claims of the settlor's creditors. . . to the extent the settlor's probate estate is inadequate to satisfy those claims. . . ").

[106] 1A Scott on Trusts §83; 1 Scott & Ascher §10.4.

[107] *See generally* 2A Scott on Trusts §152.4.

[108] *See generally* Bogert §112 (What May Be the Trust Res?). *See also* §8.30 of this handbook (the difference between a vested equitable remainder subject to divestment and a vested (transmissible) contingent equitable remainder).

[109] *See generally* §4.1.1 of this handbook (the reversionary interest).

[110] Lewin ¶2-35 (England).

transfers that interest in the land to A in trust for B, A, the trustee, will hold merely the equitable title of the contract vendee of the land under a specifically enforceable contract."[111]

The anti-alienation provisions of ERISA should not extend to preventing an employee from making a present revocable transfer of any employee's remainder interest in a qualified employee benefit plan to the trustee of an inter vivos personal trust.[112] Such a transfer could be accomplished merely by the employee filling out a beneficiary designation form supplied by the employer's human resources office.

Impressing a trust upon a chose in action. While an assignee of a chose in action,[113] whether *ex contractu* (contract based) or *ex delicto* (tort based) is not *per se* a trustee,[114] as a general rule an assignable chose of action may be the subject of a trust.[115] On the other hand, just as "[a] trust cannot be declared of a peerage, which is by its very nature a personal possession,"[116] so a chose in action may be too "personal" to be assignable and thus may not be made the subject of a trust.

Impressing a trust upon digital assets. A digital asset has been defined as encompassing "electronic content; information or media; and the right to use that content, information, or media."[117] Here are some examples of digital assets:

- Email accounts.
- Smartphone.
- Tablets.
- Netbooks.
- Computers.
- Online sales accounts.
- Online purchasing accounts.
- Webpages.
- Domain names.
- Blogs.
- Social networking profiles.[118]

Transferable digital property ought to be entrustable under general common law principles. Absent a statute to the contrary, however, whether or not a particular digital asset is in fact transferable to a trustee, or to anyone else

---

[111] Bogert §1.

[112] Treas. Reg. §1.401-1(b)(4) (as amended in 1976).

[113] A chose of action is a "right to receive or recover a debt, demand, or damages on a cause of action *ex contractu* or for a tort or omission of a duty." Black's Law Dictionary (4th ed.).

[114] 1 Scott & Ascher §2.3.11.

[115] 1 Scott & Ascher §2.3.11.

[116] Lewin ¶2-36 (England).

[117] Prangley, Haller, & Coventry, *Web of Estate Planning Considerations for Digital Assets*, 40 Estate Planning No. 5 (May 2013), at 4.

[118] Prangley, Haller, & Coventry, *Web of Estate Planning Considerations for Digital Assets*, 40 Estate Planning No. 5 (May 2013), at 4.

for that matter, may depend upon the terms of the contract between the prospective settlor and the vendor of the digital platform.

Disposing of digital assets by will substitute, particularly via a revocable inter vivos declaration of trust, may not be a practical option, at least not until the applicable law sorts itself out a bit more. Here is why:

> Although the terms of service of a particular digital asset provider may permit non-individuals to own or operate the digital asset and may not specifically distinguish between trusts and corporate entities, ownership of digital assets by a trustee is far less common than ownership by a corporate entity. As a result, there may be a delay in processing trustee succession while the service provider's staff reviews legal documents that are unfamiliar to them and interprets (with very little, if any, reported case law or other legal guidance to go on) how stringent privacy laws should be applied in the context of a trust.[119]

On July 16, 2014, the Uniform Fiduciary Access to Digital Assets Act (UFADAA) was approved by the Uniform Law Commission (ULC) at its 123rd Annual Meeting in Seattle, Washington. For purposes of the Act, a fiduciary "means a person that is an original, additional, or successor personal representative, [conservator], agent, or trustee." A trustee with the right of access to a digital asset under Section 6 of the Act submits an access request to the custodian of the asset. Under Section 8(b)(4) of the Act, "the request must be accompanied by a certified copy of the trust instrument[, or a certification of the trust under [cite trust-certification statute, such as Uniform Trust Code 1010],] that authorizes the trustee to exercise authority over the digital asset." Delaware has enacted its own version of UFADAA (12 Del. C. §§ 5001-5007). Virginia, on the other hand, has signed on to the tech industry's alternative to UFADAA, namely, the Privacy Expectation Afterlife and Choices Act (Va. Code §§ 64.2-109, 64.2-110).

Property interests that may not be entrusted. One's contractual rights to the personal services of another, for example, are probably nontransferable under the terms of the contract and therefore cannot be the subject of a trust.[120] Future earnings under a preexisting employment contract, however, may well be assignable to a trustee.[121] As a matter of public policy, an unlitigated personal injury claim probably cannot be assigned to an inter vivos trustee,[122] although there would seem to be no public policy reason why such a claim should not be assignable for probate avoidance purposes to the trustee of a revocable inter vivos trust. Some courts have enforced assignments of legal

---

[119] Prangley, Haller, & Coventry, *Web of Estate Planning Considerations for Digital Assets*, 40 Estate Planning No. 5 (May 2013), at 7.

[120] *See generally* S. Williston, Contracts §421 (W. Jaeger ed., 3d ed. 1960).

[121] 1 Scott & Ascher §10.10.2.

[122] A claim to unliquidated damages for tortious injury to person or reputation is generally nonassignable, but once such a claim is reduced to judgment it becomes a money debt that is assignable. *See generally* 4A Corbin, Contracts §857 (1951); 1A Scott on Trusts §79. *See, e.g.,* Vittands v. Sudduth, 49 Mass. App. Ct. 401, 408, 730 N.E.2d 325, 333 (2000) (confirming that personal injury causes of action being nontransferable may not be made the subject of a trust).

malpractice claims and some have not.[123] Also, if a third party commits a tort *against the trust property itself*, the trustee holds the right of action in tort against the third party in trust, even if the right of action is ordinarily not assignable.[124] In any case, one's interest in freedom from harmful bodily contact, one's interest in one's child, and one's interest in one's spouse are definitely neither transferable nor property and thus may not be the subject of a trust.[125]

A stock option that is transferable as a matter of contract law may be the subject of a trust. As a matter of tax law, however, the transfer of an incentive stock option to a qualified blind trust or a charitable remainder trust before the expiration of the applicable holding period may trigger a realization of income by the transferor in the year the transfer was made.[126]

Transferable partial interests may be presently assigned to an inter vivos trustee. Thus, one's interest in property as a tenant in common may be so transferred.[127] Could an inter vivos trust be funded through a joint tenancy with right of survivorship? That is, could a nontrustee settlor hold property jointly with a trustee? Such an arrangement is probably not a viable way of effecting the funding of an inter vivos trust, not because there is no inter vivos transfer of a property interest associated with the creation of a joint interest—there is—but because there may not be a joint tenancy under such circumstances. The interests of the individual and the trustee, while perhaps concurrent, would not be *equal*,[128] for unlike the lifetime of an individual, that of the modern trust tends to be either fixed or perpetual, and not tied to the lifespan of the trustee.[129] On the other hand, it is settled law that a corporation and an individual may serve together as cotrustees and in their fiduciary capacities hold title jointly to the trust property.[130]

---

[123] *See* New Hampshire Ins. Co., Inc. v. McCann, 429 Mass. 202, 707 N.E.2d 332 (1999). *See generally* Restatement (Third) of Trusts, Reporter's Notes on §40, specifically on cmt. d thereof.

[124] 2 Scott & Ascher §11.14.

[125] 2 Scott & Ascher §10.1.

[126] Qualified Blind Trust: I.R.C. §424; Rev. Rul. 74-243, 1974-1 C.B. 107, 1974 WL 33580 (I.R.S.). *See generally* §9.19 of this handbook (the qualified blind trust). Charitable Remainder Trust: PLR 9308021, 1992 WL 443894 (I.R.S.). *See generally* §9.4.5.1 of this handbook (IRS-approved charitable remainder trusts).

[127] In a tenancy in common, each cotenant owns an interest, separate and distinct, that may be transferred at different times (independently of other cotenants). C. Moynihan, Introduction to the Law of Real Property 213–214 (2d ed. 1988).

[128] In a joint tenancy, cotenants have exactly the same rights in their individual proportional interests as the other cotenants have in theirs. C. Moynihan, Introduction to the Law of Real Property 207 (2d ed. 1988).

[129] Under the common law, a corporation and an individual or two corporations could not hold property as joint tenants but only as tenants in common. This is because a corporation might have a life of unlimited duration that would defeat the individual's right to survivorship. *See generally* 2 Scott on Trusts §103.1 n.1 and accompanying text. By analogy, this principle ought to apply to the trust as well as the corporation. *But see* 2 Scott on Trusts §103.1 on the related issue of whether an individual and a corporation may serve jointly as cotrustees.

[130] 2 Scott & Ascher §11.6.1.

One may not unilaterally entrust away one's contractual obligations.
One cannot extinguish one's obligation as a debtor by transferring the obligation away to a trustee.[131] Presumably, the right to extinguish the obligation (if
any) is lodged with the creditor or his transferee—the one who has the property
interest in the debt. Although some commentators disagree on the grounds that
one cannot be indebted to oneself,[132] a debtor—at the direction of the
creditor—ought to be able to hold the debt in trust for the benefit of another
without causing the trust to fail as to that property.[133] This is because in equity
the debtor essentially is indebted not to himself but to himself in a fiduciary
capacity—to the office of trustee as it were.[134] It should be noted that when a
bank trust department invests trust assets in the bank's commercial deposit
accounts, or in its bonds or other such debt instruments, for that matter, the
bank is acting as a trustee of its own obligations.[135] On the other hand, it is
settled law that a trust can be created by a promise that creates enforceable
rights in a person who immediately or later holds these rights as trustee.[136]

Establishing an inter vivos trust to defraud creditors. A transfer of
otherwise transferable property to a trustee for the purpose of hindering,
delaying, or defrauding *current* creditors of the transferor may be set aside by
the creditors.[137] Many states have adopted either the Uniform Fraudulent
Conveyance Act or the Uniform Fraudulent Transfer Act.[138] These acts apply to

---

[131] An individual must have an interest in property to make a present disposition. An obligor
has no property interest in that obligation that is capable of being transferred. 1A Scott on Trusts
§§74, 87.

[132] A "person cannot have a legal claim against himself, whether for his own benefit or for
the benefit of another." 1A Scott on Trusts §87. Where a debtor is indebted to himself there is no
longer an enforceable debt. 1A Scott on Trusts §87.4 (1987). *See also* Bogert §115.

[133] Restatement (Third) of Trusts §40 cmt. b.

[134] *See generally* Restatement (Third) of Trusts, Reporter's Notes on §2 cmt. i; 1 Scott &
Ascher §10.11.

[135] *See generally* 2A Scott on Trusts §170.18; Bogert §598.

[136] UTC §401 cmt. (available at <http://www.uniformlaws.org/Act.aspx?title=Trust%20
Code>). "A trust thus created is valid notwithstanding that the trustee may resign or die before the
promise is fulfilled." UTC §401 cmt. "Unless expressly made personal, the promise can be
enforced by a successor trustee." UTC Code §401 cmt. *See generally* §3.4.4.3 of this handbook
(successor trustees).

[137] *See generally* Bogert §211; Thomas Moers Mayer, *Will the Lawyers Pay? Counsel's Ethical,
Civil and Criminal Exposure for Creating Offshore Asset Protection Trusts*, submitted at the February 2002
Meeting of the American College of Trust and Estate Counsel, Feb. 27, 2002 (discussing in part the
1571 Statute of Elizabeth, the 1918 Uniform Fraudulent Conveyance Act, and the 1984 Uniform
Fraudulent Transfer Act).

[138] *See generally* Bogert §211; Thomas Moers Mayer, *Will the Lawyers Pay? Counsel's Ethical,
Civil and Criminal Exposure for Creating Offshore Asset Protection Trusts*, submitted at the February 2002
Meeting of the American College of Trust and Estate Counsel, Feb. 27, 2002 (discussing in part the
1571 Statute of Elizabeth, the 1918 Uniform Fraudulent Conveyance Act, and the 1984 Uniform
Fraudulent Transfer Act).

transfers in trust as well as outright transfers.[139] In many jurisdictions, the settlor's future creditors may reach property held in a self-settled trust.[140]

§2.1.2 The Testamentary Trust

When a will is the governing trust instrument. The provisions of an enforceable testamentary trust are set forth in a valid will.[141] The initial trustee is essentially just a devisee who happens to take title in a fiduciary capacity to a portion or all of the probate estate.[142] At minimum, therefore, there must have been compliance with the formal execution requirements applicable to wills generally.[143] The testator and the attesting witnesses, for example, must have signed the will. A testamentary trust arises when title to a portion or all of the decedent's probate estate is transferred from the executor or personal representative to the testamentary trustee. Thus, a testamentary trust cannot arise while the testator is alive. Only at death does the probate estate come into existence, because only then does the will speak. The term *pour-over* is generally not used in connection with a testamentary trust.[144] It refers to the transfer of probate assets to the trustee of an inter vivos trust.[145] Having said that, the Uniform Probate Code for purposes of the sub-section in which the word *distributee* is defined deems the trustee of an inter vivos trust to be a testamentary trustee of any assets that may have poured over to it from a probate estate.[146] While this narrowly focused conflation of the nomenclature may well contribute to the Code's internal coherence and logic, it is still somewhat unfortunate, particularly as not all trustees are lawyers and, nowadays, not all lawyers, and not all judges for that matter, have taken Trusts.[147]

Multi-jurisdictional complications. When a deceased settlor's estate is probated in one state and the designated trustee of his or her testamentary trust is domiciled in another state, the designated foreign trustee may have to qualify in a court of the settlor's domicil as a precondition to being appointed, a topic

---

[139] *See generally* Bogert §211; Thomas Moers Mayer, *Will the Lawyers Pay? Counsel's Ethical, Civil and Criminal Exposure for Creating Offshore Asset Protection Trusts*, submitted at the February 2002 Meeting of the American College of Trust and Estate Counsel, Feb. 27, 2002 (discussing in part the 1571 Statute of Elizabeth, the 1918 Uniform Fraudulent Conveyance Act, and the 1984 Uniform Fraudulent Transfer Act).

[140] *See generally* §5.3.3.1 of this handbook (whether the settlor's creditors may reach the settlor's reserved beneficial interest).

[141] *See generally* Restatement (Third) of Trusts §17(1); 1 Scott & Ascher §7.1.

[142] It should be noted, however, that under the UPC, "[a] beneficiary of a testamentary trust to whom the trustee has distributed property received from a personal representative is a distributee of the personal representative." UPC §1-201(12).

[143] 1 Scott & Ascher §7.1.

[144] *See generally* Polasky, *"Pour-Over" Wills and the Statutory Blessing*, 98 Tr. & Est. 949 (1959).

[145] *See generally* 1A Scott on Trusts §54.3; Restatement (Third) of Property (Wills and Other Donative Transfers) §3.8.

[146] UPC §1-201(12).

[147] *See generally* §8.25 of this handbook (supporting the assertion that few American law schools still require Agency, Trusts and Equity).

we take up in Section 3.1 of this handbook. Such multi-jurisdictional complications can easily be avoided at the estate planning stage if an inter vivos trust rather than a testamentary trust is employed. In the case of a probate pour-over to an out-of-state trustee of an inter vivos trust, it is generally unnecessary for the trustee to qualify in a court of the deceased settlor's domicil.[148]

When the designated testamentary trustee assumes fiduciary duties. One commentator has noted that "[w]here the same person is named executor and trustee. . . [of a testamentary trust]. . . it is not always easy to determine the exact point at which he ceases to act as executor and enters upon the performance of his duties as trustee."[149] It may be important to know this, for example, in cases where a *certain sum* is to be made the subject of the testamentary trust and the probate estate shrinks in value through no fault of the fiduciary. Who bears the loss? The nontrust residuary legatees and devisees or the trust beneficiaries? The residuary legatees and devisees will generally bear the loss if there has been no setting aside, segregation, or earmarking of estate property as trust property.[150] On the other hand, had the probate estate increased in value before segregation, the gain would have inured to the legatees and devisees.[151] To the extent the trust is to be funded with depreciated assets in lieu of cash or cash equivalents, the depreciated assets must be valued as of the time of funding.[152]

Pour-ups. A transfer from the trustee of an inter vivos trust to the trustee of a preexisting testamentary trust has been referred to as a "pour-up" transfer.[153] Such a transfer would not raise the statute-of-wills compliance issues that plagued the will pour-over (to an inter vivos trust) under the common law.[154] This is because the receptacle testamentary trust owes its very existence to the fact that its terms are in compliance with the statute of wills.[155]

A Massachusetts testamentary trust can now arise under a will not fully executed until an unspecified time after the testator's death. In Massachusetts before it enacted its version of the Uniform Probate Code, a will needed to be attested and subscribed by two witnesses in the conscious presence of the testator.[156] The model UPC's Section 2-502, instead, requires that the will be signed by at least two witnesses, each of whom signs within a reasonable time after he or she has observed the testator sign his name. Thus, under the model UPC a witness, if the circumstances were right, could actually sign after the testator had died. The Massachusetts version of UPC Section 2-502, however, has neither the old "conscious presence requirement" nor the model's "within a reasonable time" limitation, at least when it comes to signings by the

---

[148] 7 Scott & Ascher §45.2.1.6.

[149] 1 Scott on Trusts §6.

[150] 1 Scott & Ascher §2.3.2; 1 Scott on Trusts §6.

[151] 1 Scott & Ascher §2.3.2; 1 Scott on Trusts §6.

[152] 1 Scott & Ascher §2.3.2.

[153] Restatement (Third) of Property (Wills and Other Donative Transfers) §3.8, cmt. f.

[154] *See* §2.1.1 of this handbook (will pour-overs to inter vivos trusts).

[155] Restatement (Third) of Property (Wills and Other Donative Transfers) §3.8, cmt. f.

[156] *See* M.G.L.A. c. 191, §1 (now repealed).

witnesses.[157] (There is a conscious presence requirement, but only for one who signs "in the testator's name.") That being the case, it would seem that for some unspecified period of time after the testator has died, the witnesses can effectively complete the will's execution, at least if the new law is read literally and the omissions are taken as purposeful.[158] Should the will have a testamentary trust provision, one wonders what the status of the legal title to the subject property might be in the hiatus between the death of the testator/settlor and the time when the will is finally executed and begins to speak. Perhaps the legal title passes to the administrator of the intestate estate as of the time of death, subject to divestment in favor of the testamentary trustee should the will ever be executed.

§2.2 Funding Issues

In recent years, the revocable trust, the life insurance contract, and the employee benefit plan (including the Individual Retirement Account) have been transferring postmortem as much property as the will, and perhaps more.[1] These flexible, ambulatory, will-like devices have come to be known as will *substitutes*, and their proliferation has raised some trust-related funding issues.

§2.2.1 Uniform Testamentary Additions to Trust Act; the Uniform Real Property Transfer On Death Act

When the. . . [inter vivos]. . . "trust" —really, then, only a trust document—remains unfunded at the time of the testator's death, and does not control the disposition of property from any source other than the property of the testator's estate, the arrangement is not supportable under the doctrine of facts of independent legal significance.[2]

Will pour-over statutes. No property is passed at the time a will is executed. At common law, therefore, the execution of a will with a pour-over provision could not serve as the initial funding vehicle for an inter vivos trust. Something more was needed.

---

[157] *See* M.G.L.A. c. 190B, §2-502.

[158] In the commentary to M.G.L.A. §190B, §2-502, there is a reference to Healy v. Bartless, 73 N.H. 110, 59 A. 617 (1904), which is a witness-signing conscious-presence case, not a proxy-signing conscious-presence case. The contextually inappropriate reference to *Healy* suggests that Massachusetts' omission of the conscious-presence requirement when it comes to will-witness signing may have been a statute-drafting error.

§2.2 [1] *See generally* John Langbein, *The Nonprobate Revolution and the Future of the Law of Succession*, 97 Harv. L. Rev. 1108 (1984); John Langbein, *The Twentieth Century Revolution in Family Wealth Transmission*, 86 Mich. L. Rev. 722 (1988).

[2] Restatement (Third) of Trusts §19 cmt. a(3). *See generally* §8.15.9 of this handbook (doctrine of independent legal significance).

Thus, the practice evolved of funding inter vivos trusts with nominal amounts of property (*token funding*). It can be argued that if there is no inter vivos transfer of property, there is no inter vivos trust; if there is no inter vivos trust, the will's pour-over provision will lapse or fail. Many states have adopted in one form or another the Uniform Testamentary Additions to Trusts Act,[3] or Section 2-511(a) of the Uniform Probate Code, which essentially allows an inter vivos trust to arise without an inter vivos transfer of property, provided the trustee is named a beneficiary of a portion of the settlor's probate estate pursuant to a pour-over provision in the settlor's will.[4]

When then does the trust come into existence? Is it at the time the trust instrument is signed, at the time the will is executed, or at the death of the settlor? It would appear that it was contemplated that this inter vivos-testamentary hybrid would come into existence as of, or after, the settlor's death.[5] If that is the case, all we have is a signed instrument during the settlor's lifetime. Under Section 2-511(a) of the Uniform Probate Code, the instrument can even be prepared after the settlor's pour-over will has been executed.

---

[3] *See generally* 1 Scott & Ascher §7.1.3. The Uniform Testamentary Additions to Trusts Act is a freestanding model statute, promulgated in 1960 and revised in 1991, to track §2-511 of the UPC, which was promulgated in 1969 and revised in 1990. Of course it is the prerogative of each state wishing to adopt such a statute to adopt either model, with or without modification. *See* 1A Scott on Trusts §54.3 for a list of states adopting the Uniform Testamentary Additions to Trusts Act. *See also* UPC §2-511; Uniform Testamentary Additions to Trusts Act; Restatement (Third) of Property (Wills and Other Donative Transfers) §3.8 (pour-over devises); Restatement (Third) of Trusts §19 cmt. a(4).

[4] Earlier forms of the Uniform Testamentary Additions to Trusts Act and the UPC were somewhat ambiguous on the issue whether funding of an inter vivos trust was necessary during the lifetime of the settlor, provided there was a pour-over clause in the will. *See* Clymer v. Mayo, 393 Mass. 754, 473 N.E.2d 1084 (1985), involving a pour-over to an inter vivos trust that the court termed *unfunded*. The court suggested that the inter vivos trust was *unfunded* notwithstanding the fact that the trustee was a designated beneficiary of a life insurance policy. While it interpreted the Massachusetts Uniform Testamentary Additions to Trusts Act as not requiring that the inter vivos trust be funded at the time the will is executed, the court erred in characterizing the trust at issue as *unfunded*. The trust was in fact funded because the trustee had been designated the beneficiary of life insurance policies and beneficiary of the employee benefit plan and thus contained property in the form of contractual rights. *See* §2.2.2 of this handbook. In response to this confusion surrounding the term *unfunded*, the UPC and the Uniform Testamentary Additions to Trusts Act were revised to unequivocally provide that an inter vivos "trust" need not be funded during the lifetime of the settlor, provided there is an associated pour-over will. *See* UPC §2-511 cmt. *See also* 1991 Uniform Testamentary Additions to Trusts Act; Restatement (Third) of Property (Wills and Other Donative Transfers) §3.8 cmt. b. *See also* UTC §401 cmt. (available at <http://www.uniformlaws.org/Act.aspx?title=Trust%20Code>). Under §2-511(a) of the UPC, the trust instrument can even be prepared after the settlor's pour-over will has been executed.

[5] The comment to §3.8 of the Restatement (Third) of Property (Wills and Other Donative Transfers) is quite emphatic on this point. The trust does not come into existence when the settlor signs the trust instrument:

> The trust itself need not be established during the testator's lifetime, but can be established *by* the pour-over devise. (A trust is not established by executing a trust document; a trust is only established by transferring property to the trust.) *See* Restatement Second, Trusts §§31-32; Restatement (Third) of Trusts §41. *See also* Uniform Trust Code §401 cmt. (available on the internet at

As to the common law doctrine of independent legal significance as it applies to testamentary pour-overs to amendable inter vivos trusts, see Section 8.15.9 of this handbook. As to the limitations of the doctrine of incorporation by reference as a theory for validating pour-over devises to trustees of inter vivos trusts, see Section 8.15.17 of this handbook. As to the mechanics of administering a revocable inter vivos trust once the settlor has died but before all the trust property has been marshaled, the reader is referred to Section 9.9.14 of this handbook.[6]

Nonwill pour-over statutes. The Uniform Real Property Transfer on Death Act (the "model Act") was approved in 2009 by the National Conference of Commissioners on Uniform State Laws. The model Act would enable the owner of an interest in real property by means of a transfer on death deed (TODD) to convey the property at death to a beneficiary/grantee/transferee.[7] A TODD must contain the essential elements of a properly recordable inter vivos deed, except that it must include a statement that the transfer is to occur at the property owner's death.[8] A TODD, however, is effective without notice to, delivery to, or acceptance by the beneficiary/grantee/transferee during the property owner's life.[9] Still, a TODD must have been recorded inter vivos in an appropriate public registry to be effective.[10] Any instrument purporting to have revoked a TODD also would have to have been recorded inter vivos.[11] *Under the model Act, the trustee of a trust may be a beneficiary/grantee/transferee of a TODD.*[12]

A TODD is ambulatory, which means that it is fully revocable up until the death of the property owner.[13] Because it speaks at death, no legal and equitable rights in the subject property are altered merely by its inter vivos recording. In this regard, a TODD more closely resembles a will than the typical common law will substitute, which entails the inter vivos transfer of some property rights. The third-party beneficiary life insurance contract and the joint interest with right of survivorship come to mind in this regard.

While a trust may be funded by TODD, trust property may not be *conveyed out* by TODD.[14]

<http://www.uniformlaws.org/Act.aspx?title=Trust%20Code>) (suggesting that "[a] pourover devise to a previously unfunded trust is also valid and may constitute the property interest creating the trust"). The IRS has taken a different tack when it comes to trusts associated with Keogh plans. A trust will be deemed to have been in existence as of the last day of a particular tax year for purposes of deductions allowed under I.R.C. §404(a)(6) if the trust at the end of the tax year has all the requisite elements under local law except a corpus. *See* Rev. Rul. 81-114, 1981-1 C.B. 207.

[6] Discussing the administrative trust.

[7] Uniform Real Property Transfer on Death Act §5.

[8] Uniform Real Property Transfer on Death Act §9.

[9] Uniform Real Property Transfer on Death Act §10.

[10] Uniform Real Property Transfer on Death Act §9.

[11] Uniform Real Property Transfer on Death Act §11.

[12] Uniform Real Property Transfer on Death Act §2(4).

[13] Uniform Real Property Transfer on Death Act §6.

[14] Uniform Real Property Transfer on Death Act §2(7).

§2.2.2   *Life Insurance Beneficiary Designations*

Even though the insured reserves the right to change the beneficiary, the beneficiary immediately acquires a chose in action, a claim against the insurance company, although not enforceable until the death of the insured, and even though the insured, by changing the beneficiary, can divest this interest.[15]

It is a popular misconception that the revocable inter vivos designation of a trustee as a beneficiary of future life insurance proceeds is, alone, not enough to fund an inter vivos trust.[16] It is believed that something more is required, such as the present transfer of title to the contract itself or token funding. Some incorrectly refer to such trusts as *unfunded*.[17]

It is settled law, however, that even the revocable designation of a trustee as the recipient of life insurance proceeds, upon the future death of the insured, constitutes the present transfer of property to the trustee.[18] The inter vivos trustee is the third-party beneficiary of a contract under which there has been an inter vivos exchange of consideration between the insured and the insurance company, *i.e.,* the insured having transferred inter vivos a premium and the company having transferred inter vivos a promise to pay the proceeds upon the death of the insured.[19] The trustee has an enforceable claim against the insurance company in the event the designation remains unrevoked at the death of the insured.[20] In other words, "[a]n unfunded life-insurance trust is not a trust without a trust res; the trust res in an unfunded life-insurance trust is the contract right to the proceeds of the life-insurance policy conferred on the trustee by virtue of naming the trustee the beneficiary of the policy."[21]

The revocable life insurance beneficiary designation differs from a pour-over provision in a will in that under the common law there has been no inter vivos transfer of a property interest to anyone pursuant to the terms of the will

---

[15] 1 Scott & Ascher §10.8.1.

[16] *See generally* 1A Scott on Trusts §57.3.

[17] *See generally* 1A Scott on Trusts §57.3. *See also* UPC §2-511.

[18] *See generally* 1A Scott on Trusts §57.3. *See also* UTC §103(11) (available at <http://www.uniformlaws.org/Act.aspx?title=Trust%20Code>) (providing that the term *property* includes "a chose in action, a claim, and an interest created by a beneficiary designation under a policy of insurance, financial instrument, employees' trust, or deferred compensation or other retirement arrangement, whether revocable or irrevocable"). *See also* UTC §401 cmt. (noting that a revocable designation of the trustee as beneficiary of a life insurance policy or employee benefit plan has long been understood to be a property interest sufficient to create a trust).

[19] Restatement (Third) of Property (Wills and Other Donative Transfers) §7.1 cmt. c (Tentative Draft No. 3, Apr. 4, 2001).

[20] *See* Gordon v. Portland Trust Bank, 271 P.2d 653, 656 (Or. 1954) ("the beneficiary is the owner of a promise to pay the proceeds at the death of the insured, subject to insured's right of revocation").

[21] UPC §2-511 cmt. "Thus the term 'unfunded life-insurance trust' does not refer to an unfunded trust, but to a funded trust that has not received additional funding." UPC §2-511 cmt.

at the time the will is executed, whereas there *is* such a transfer at the time the insurance beneficiary designation is filled out.[22]

§2.2.3   The Custodial IRA

A taxpayer's individual retirement account (IRA) may be administered pursuant to what amounts under state law to an investment management agency agreement, known as a *custodial IRA*.[23] Because an agency terminates at the death of the principal, many jurisdictions have enacted statutes that provide that an IRA custodian may honor the postmortem dispositive provisions of the beneficiary designation form notwithstanding the requirements of the Statute of Wills.[24] In essence, these statutes extend the life of these IRA agency arrangements beyond the death of the taxpayer-principal. If such a statute has been enacted in the trustee's jurisdiction, do its terms provide that the designation of the trustee of an inter vivos trust as postmortem beneficiary of the taxpayer's custodial IRA, constitute an actual or constructive transfer of property that will cause the inter vivos trust to arise? If not, then something more may be needed, such as a token funding or the execution of a will with provisions that conform to the jurisdiction's pour-over statute.

§2.3   Wrongful Defunding Does Not Necessarily Terminate the Trust

Modern practices and their tacit acceptance in court—with no visible inconvenience or so much of an indication of an awareness of a contrary concept—support recognizing that a trustee's obligation to a trust constitutes an asset of the trust estate, whether that trustee continues administering the trust or is replaced by a successor trustee.[1]

If the trustee wrongfully makes off with all the trust property, the trust is not thereby extinguished, provided the property is susceptible of being followed or traced.[2] There is no defunding as the missing property has simply been transformed *inside the trust* into another type of property, namely, an

---

[22] 1 Scott & Ascher §8.2.3.

[23] I.R.C. §408(h) (1974) (effective for tax years beginning after December 31, 1974).

[24] *See, e.g.*, Mich. Comp. Laws Ann. §700.257 (West 1995); Mass. Gen. L. ch. 167D, §30 (1983); N.Y. Est. Powers & Trusts Law §13-3.2 (McKinney 1992); Conn. Gen. Stat. Ann. §45a-347 (West 1991); Tex. Prop. Code Ann. §121.052 (West 1995). *See generally* Bogert §255 n.11 and accompanying text (second note 11).

§2.3 [1] Restatement (Third) of Trusts §2, Reporter's Notes on cmt. i.

[2] *But see generally* 1A Scott on Trusts §74.2.

equitable claim against the trustee personally.[3] Moreover, an equitable action for restitution brought by the beneficiary to remedy the trustee's unjust enrichment may even be exempt from the reach of the Uniform Trust Code's five-year statute of ultimate repose, a topic we take up in Section 7.1.2 of this handbook. In the case of property that cannot be followed or traced, there is always the concern that the trustee's liability might be dischargeable in bankruptcy, a topic that is taken up in Section 7.4 of this handbook. The procedural equitable remedy of following *in specie* is taken up in Section 7.2.3.1.2 of this handbook. The procedural equitable remedy of tracing (following property into its product) is taken up in Section 7.2.3.1.3 of this handbook.

---

[3] *See generally* Restatement (Third) of Trusts §2 cmt. i; Restatement (Third) of Trusts at Reporter's Notes on §2 cmt. i. *See also* the Comment to §410 of the UTC (available at <http://www.uniformlaws.org/Act.aspx?title=Trust%20Code>) (suggesting that withdrawal of the trust property is not an event terminating a trust, the trust remaining in existence although the trustee has no duties to perform unless and until property is later contributed to the trust); 1 Scott & Ascher §10.1.2 (When the Trust Property Ceases to Exist). *But see generally* 1A Scott on Trusts §74.2.

CHAPTER *3*

The Trustee's Office

§3.1   Who Can Be a Trustee?

Legal capacity to take title. Legal capacity to receive, hold, and manage property in trust is one thing;[1] fitness to serve as trustee is another.[2] One with legal capacity to take title or hold property for oneself may do so as trustee.[3]

Minors and the insane. A minor has the capacity to hold title to property either in his or her own right or as trustee,[4] but because a minor's contracts and conveyances are voidable, a minor is unfit to administer a trust[5] and will be removed by the court. A conveyance by the minor to the successor trustee is generally not necessary.[6] A minor who misappropriates or embezzles trust property, sells it, and acquires other property with the proceeds, however, is chargeable as a constructive trustee of the other property.[7]

So too a trust estate may vest in an insane person, but, lacking the capacity to contract or make a conveyance, such an individual is unfit to administer a trust and will be removed.[8] As with the case of minors, a conveyance by the mentally incompetent person to the successor trustee is not necessary.[9]

A trust ordinarily does not fail because the individual or corporation named fails for whatever reason to serve or to continue to serve as trustee.[10] The court will appoint another trustee to serve in his place unless to do so would contravene the intentions of the settlor.[11] Thus, the transfer of property in trust to a minor or an insane person ordinarily will not prevent the trust from coming into being.[12]

Nonresidents. A nonresident individual generally may receive and administer trust property locally.[13] Some states have no qualification requirements for foreign individual testamentary trustees; others do.[14] Those that do may require that nonresident testamentary trustees appoint resident agents for the

---

§3.1 [1] 2 Scott & Ascher §11.1.

[2] Restatement (Third) of Trusts §32 cmt. a.

[3] UTC §103 cmt. (available at <http://www.uniformlaws.org/Act.aspx?title=Trust%20 Code>).

[4] *See generally* 2 Scott on Trusts §91.

[5] *See generally* 2 Scott on Trusts §91. *See also* Restatement (Third) of Property §8.2 cmt. f ; Restatement (Third) of Trusts §32 cmt. c.

[6] 2 Scott & Ascher §11.1.1.

[7] 4 Scott & Ascher §24.20 (Liability of Trustee Under Incapacity).

[8] 2 Scott on Trusts §92. *See also* Restatement (Third) of Property §8.1 cmt. n.

[9] 2 Scott & Ascher §11.1.2.

[10] UTC §401 cmt. (available at <http://www.uniformlaws.org/Act.aspx?title=Trust%20 Code>) (confirming that a trust can be created even though for a period of time no trustee is in office).

[11] *See* Restatement (Second) of Trusts §2 cmt. i.

[12] *See* Restatement (Second) of Trusts §2 cmt. i. *See also* 2 Scott & Ascher §11.1.

[13] *See generally* 2 Scott on Trusts §§94 (Nonresident Individuals), 96.6 (Nonresident Corporations); Bogert §132. *See also* 2 Scott & Ascher §11.1.4.

[14] *See generally* 7 Scott & Ascher §45.2.1.2 (Nonresident Individual Trustees).

purpose of accepting service of process.[15] A state that has adopted the Uniform Trust Code would not be among them, the Code providing that by accepting the trusteeship of a trust having its principal place of administration in the state or by moving the principal place of administration to the state, the trustee submits personally to the jurisdiction of the courts of the state regarding any matter involving the trust.[16]

It is highly doubtful whether one state may exclude altogether individual citizens from other states from serving as trustees of local inter vivos and testamentary trusts without running afoul of the privileges and immunities clause (Art. IV, Sect. 2, Clause 1) of the U.S. Constitution.[17] Just as a citizen of the United States cannot be denied the right to take and hold absolutely real and personal property in any particular state, so also a citizen cannot be denied the right to accept the conveyance of such property in trust.[18] This would certainly be the case if the foreign citizen took an equitable interest as well as the legal title.[19] The topic of limiting or regulating the right of a foreign trust company or charitable corporation to serve as a trustee of a trust that is locally established is taken up in Section 8.6 of this handbook.

In the case of either an individual testamentary trustee or a corporate testamentary trustee, if the settlor has manifested an intention in his or her will that the trust be administered in a state other than the settlor's domicil, then the trustee ought not to be required to qualify in a court of the state *of the settlor's domicil*.[20] The Uniform Probate Code was in accord,[21] although it would have required that the foreign trustee register the trust at its principal place of administration.[22] Likewise, increasingly, states are replacing continuing judicial supervision of trusts with "intervention on demand,"[23] a result that is achieved when a state enacts the Uniform Trust Code.[24]

In a case where a local probate court will not authorize an executor to transfer movables out-of-state to a foreign testamentary trustee until such time as the trustee has been qualified *in the state where the moveables are ultimately to be administered*, the usual procedure is for the designated testamentary trustee to file a copy of the will in an appropriate court in the state of administration and to request appointment as trustee under it.[25] In a case where a state statute precludes the judicial appointment of a local trustee of the moveables of a deceased nonresident testator, though the foreign will calls for such an appointment, the judicial authorities "are simply not clear" as to whether the foreign

[15] Bogert §132; 2 Scott & Ascher §11.2; 7 Scott & Ascher §45.2.1.2.
[16] UTC §202(a).
[17] *See generally* 7 Scott & Ascher §45.2.1.2.
[18] *See* Johnson v. Bowen, 85 N.J. Eq. 76, 82, 95 A. 370, 372 (1915) (in accord, albeit in dictum).
[19] *See* Robey v. Smith, 30 N.E. 1093, 1094 (Ind. 1892).
[20] *See* 7 Scott & Ascher §45.2.1.2.
[21] UPC §7-105. [Repealed.]
[22] UPC §7-101. [Repealed.]
[23] 7 Scott & Ascher §45.2.1.2.
[24] UTC §201(b).
[25] 7 Scott & Ascher §45.2.1.4.

executor will be permitted to transfer the movables to a trustee who cannot or will not qualify as such in the place of administration.[26] The problem is likely to arise if no property whatsoever of the foreign decedent was located in the proposed place of administration at the time of death.[27]

What if the settlor's movables happen to be situated at the time of death not where the settlor dies domiciled but in the very foreign jurisdiction which is to be the testamentary trust's principal place of administration? Presumably, the movables will be subject to an ancillary probate in the foreign jurisdiction. If that is the case, then it might well not be necessary for the individual or corporate testamentary trustee to be qualified in the state where the settlor died domiciled. Legal title to the subject property should pass directly from the ancillary administrator to the designated testamentary trustee.[28] In a case where some of the deceased settlor's movables are situated in the state where he or she died domiciled and some in the state where the testamentary trust is to be administered, we could end up with two testamentary trusts should qualification of the foreign trustee in a court of the domicil not be an option.[29] In jurisdictions that have adopted the Uniform Trust Code, testamentary trustees may appoint one another ancillary trustees for purposes of administering out-of-state assets.[30] The ancillary trusteeship is covered in Section 9.32 of this handbook.

Of course, such multi-jurisdictional probate-related complications can easily be avoided at the will drafting stage by employing an inter vivos trust rather than a testamentary trust.[31] In the case of a probate pour-over to an out-of-state trustee of an inter vivos trust, it is generally unnecessary for the trustee to qualify in a court of the deceased settlor's domicil.[32]

Aliens. The capacity of an alien to act as trustee may be limited in states where there are remnants of common law restrictions upon the capacity of an alien to hold property.[33] Courts, however, "have long found it unnecessary to require judicial qualification in the state of the testator's domicil in the case of a charitable trust that is to be administered in a foreign country, when the

---

[26] 7 Scott & Ascher §45.2.1.4.

[27] 7 Scott & Ascher §45.2.1.4.

[28] *See* 7 Scott & Ascher §45.2.1.5

[29] It may be possible to avoid multiple testamentary trusts if one executor is nominated in the will to administer movables situated in the settlor's domicil and another to administer movables situated in the state where the testamentary trust is to be administered; and if, pursuant to the terms of the will, the domiciliary executor is directed to transfer the net probate estate that is situated in the settlor's domicil to the foreign testamentary trustee via the other executor. *See* 7 Scott & Ascher §45.2.1.5 n.4.

[30] UTC §816(20).

[31] 7 Scott & Ascher §45.2.1.6 (Pouring Over by Will into Inter Vivos Trust).

[32] 7 Scott & Ascher §45.2.1.6.

[33] 2 Scott & Ascher §11.1.3; 2 Scott on Trusts §93; Restatement (Third) of Trusts §32, cmt. d. In Louisiana, notwithstanding its civil law roots, an alien who resides outside the United States may not serve as a trustee. La. Rev. Stat. Ann. §9:1783.

named trustees are citizens or subjects of the foreign country and the applicable law is that of the foreign country."[34]

Governmental entities. The United States, a state of the United States, or a municipality[35] may be a trustee, although principles of sovereign immunity may make the trust unenforceable absent a statute to the contrary.[36] For more on the governmental entity serving as a common law trustee, the reader is referred to Section 9.8.2 of this handbook.

Corporations. At early common law, a corporation could not serve as trustee.[37] This is no longer the case.[38] A corporation may act as trustee in furtherance of and as an adjunct to its corporate purpose.[39] A corporation may need statutory authority to have as its purpose the administration of trusts.[40] Thus, absent trust powers conferred by statute, an automobile manufacturing company, for example, could act as trustee of its own employee benefit plan but not as trustee of the plans of other companies.[41] Legislatures have traditionally conferred trust powers upon trust companies and banks,[42] although the culture of the lender is to some extent incompatible with that of the trust fiduciary.[43] It is not uncommon for state *X*, by statute, to prohibit a bank or trust company from another state from qualifying as a testamentary trustee, unless the other state allows state *X*'s institutions to qualify within its borders;[44] those states that place no restriction on the qualification rights of out-of-state institutions, however, will generally require the appointment of a local official as agent to accept service of process.[45] For more on qualifying a foreign trust company or foreign charitable corporation to serve as trustee of a testamentary trust established locally, the reader is referred to Section 8.6 of this handbook.

---

[34] 7 Scott & Ascher §45.2.1.2.

[35] 2 Scott & Ascher §11.1.6.1.

[36] *See generally* 2 Scott & Ascher §11.1.5; 2 Scott on Trusts §§95, 96.4; Hughes, *Can the Trustee Be Sued for Its Breach: The Sad Saga of United States v. Mitchell*, 26 S.D. L. Rev. 447 (1981) (discussing the fate of a breach of trust claim against the United States).

[37] *See* 2 Scott on Trusts §96.

[38] 2 Scott on Trusts §96. *See* The Trustees of Phillips Academy v. James King, Exec., 12 Mass. 545 (1815) (holding that a corporation is capable of taking and holding property as a trustee and suggesting that it was "unsettled" at the time of the passing of the statute of uses whether a corporation could take to any other use than its own). *See generally* §§8.15.1 of this handbook (statute of uses) and 8.6 of this handbook (the trustee who is not a human being). *See also* 2 Scott & Ascher §11.1.6.

[39] *See generally* 2 Scott on Trusts §96.3; Restatement (Second) of Trusts §96.

[40] *See generally* 2 Scott on Trusts §96.3; *but see* §8.6 of this handbook (the institutional trustee).

[41] *See generally* 2 Scott on Trusts §96.3; *but see* §8.6 of this handbook (the institutional trustee).

[42] 2 Scott & Ascher §11.1.6.2.

[43] *See generally* 2 Scott & Ascher §§96.5, 170.23A.

[44] 2 Scott & Ascher §11.1.6.3.

[45] *See generally* 5A Scott on Trusts §558 (containing in footnote 1 a catalog of state statutes that deal with the right of out-of-state banks and trust companies to serve as testamentary trustee); Bogert §132.

A corporation acting as trustee without express statutory authority would be well advised to have in its file a legal opinion that it has the authority to so act. For example, a corporation in the business of transacting in real estate should have such a letter to the extent it utilizes trusts in the conduct of its business. The same also could be said for the charitable corporation administering a trust with a noncharitable component (perhaps a provision for the benefit of a benefactor's spouse).[46]

A corporation acting as trustee under a statutory grant of authority—most often this will be a bank—should know the limits of its authority and the regulatory framework within which it must operate.[47] A national bank may be in danger that its commercial personnel may not be operating in compliance with "Regulation 9," the collection of federal regulations governing national bank fiduciary activities.[48] This could happen, for example, in the context of the marketing of trusteed individual retirement accounts (IRAs) and investment management agency services.[49] This could also happen when a bank enters into certain types of commercial relationships with a trust beneficiary or with the asset of one of its trusts.[50]

In Section 9.8.1 of this handbook, we take up the related issue of whether an inter vivos or testamentary transfer of property to a charitable corporation impresses a true trust upon that property, whether it actually can be said that the charitable corporation is a trustee of the subject property. One court has referred to the arrangement as a quasi trust.[51]

Unincorporated associations. An unincorporated association generally cannot take title to property for its own benefit, or in trust for others, absent enabling legislation.[52] A court, however, will see to it that a trust does not fail

---

[46] *See generally* 2 Scott on Trusts §96.3. *See, e.g.*, Ozee v. American Council on Gift Annuities, 888 F. Supp. 1318 (N.D. Tex. 1995) (a not-for-profit corporation acting as trustee of a charitable-remainder trust held to exceed the authority granted to it by its charter). *But see* In re Trust Created by Hormel, 282 Minn. 197, 163 N.W.2d 844 (1968) (holding that a charitable corporation may serve as trustee of a split-interest trust in which it had an interest).

[47] National banks must operate within the guidelines set out in Comptroller of the Currency Regulations, 12 C.F.R. Part 9 (as revised, effective Jan. 29, 1997) (known as "Regulation 9") (available at <www.gpoaccess.gov/cfr/index.html>), and are subject to the laws of the state in which they operate unless such laws conflict with federal laws or interfere with their purposes as defined by Congress. *See generally* 10 Am. Jur. 2d Banks §§15, 305 (1963); 2 Scott on Trusts §96.5; Melanie L. Fein, Securities Activities of Banks §11 (2d ed. Supp. 1998).

[48] 12 C.F.R. Part 9 (as revised, effective Jan. 29, 1997) (available at <www.gpoaccess.gov/cfr/index.html>). Revised Reg. 9, in part, defines "fiduciary capacity" as "any capacity in which the bank possesses investment discretion on behalf of another." 12 C.F.R. §9.2(e). *See generally* §8.18 of this handbook (Regulation 9 revised). *See generally* 2A Scott on Trusts §172.1.

[49] 2A Scott on Trusts §172.1.

[50] *See* §6.1.3 of this handbook (the trustee's duty of loyalty to the beneficiaries). *See also* 12 C.F.R. §9.5 (Revised Reg. 9) (available at <www.gpoaccess.gov/cfr/index.html>) (requiring that a national bank exercising fiduciary powers adopt and follow written policies and procedures that address methods for preventing self-dealing and conflicts of interest).

[51] American Institute of Architects v. Attorney General, 332 Mass. 619, 624, 127 N.E.2d 161, 164 (1955).

[52] 2 Scott & Ascher §11.1.7.

merely because an unincorporated association has been designated the trustee. If the governing instrument does not designate a suitable alternate trustee, the court will.

Partnerships. Absent statutory authority, a partnership may not take title to property for itself or as a trustee for others.[53] At common law, a partnership was not a legal entity.[54] When a partnership is involved in the administration of a trust, *e.g.*, a law firm, chances are it is the partners themselves who are the trustees, not the "partnership." Another possibility is that the "partnership" is acting as agent for a corporation or individual who is the actual trustee. A partnership can act as trustee if under state law it has the capacity to hold the legal title to property.[55]

Settlors and beneficiaries. One's capacity to be a trustee is not affected by the fact that one is also the settlor of the trust,[56] or a beneficiary for that matter.[57] Thus, a donor may make himself trustee of the gift such that the equitable interest only in the gifted property passes to the donee, not also the legal interest.[58] A donor of property, of course, may not be the donee as well. If they are one and the same, the gift is a nullity. Likewise, a person may not be the sole trustee and the sole beneficiary.[59] When there is a merger of the legal and equitable interests there is no trust.[60] One, however, may be sole trustee for oneself and others, or with others be trustee for oneself alone,[61] and, of course, may be trustee for himself for life with remainder for others or for others for life with remainder for himself.[62] In each of these situations, the trustee-beneficiary does not possess the *entire* legal and *entire* beneficial interest. For more on the doctrine of merger, the reader is referred to Section 8.7 of this handbook.

Cross references. For a discussion of when a trustee's appointment must be subject to court approval, the reader is referred to Sections 3.4.1 and 3.4.4.3 of this handbook. For more on whether a corporation may serve as a trustee, the reader is referred to Section 8.6 of this handbook.

---

[53] 2 Scott & Ascher §11.1.8.

[54] 2 Scott & Ascher §11.1.8.

[55] *See generally* 2 Scott on Trusts §98.

[56] UTC §103 cmt. (available at <http://www.uniformlaws.org/Act.aspx?title=Trust%20 Code>); Restatement (Third) of Trusts §32; 2 Scott & Ascher §11.3.

[57] UTC §103 cmt. (available at <http://www.uniformlaws.org/Act.aspx?title=Trust%20 Code>); Restatement (Third) of Trusts §32; 2 Scott & Ascher §11.3.

[58] Bogert §1, n.30.

[59] 2 Scott & Ascher §11.2.

[60] *See generally* Bogert §§129, 1003; 2 Scott on Trusts §99. *See also* §8.7 of this handbook (merger).

[61] 1 Scott & Ascher §11.2.4.

[62] Bogert §1.

§3.2   Who Is Fit to Be a Trustee?

For as a trust is an office necessary in the concerns between man and man, and which, if faithfully discharged, is attended with no small degree of trouble, and anxiety, it is an act of kindness to accept it.[1]

Trust administration is not for every personality and every ethic. It is not for the wheeler-dealer and the dabbler. A trust is a legally complicated relationship requiring sustained attention, often over a period of many years, with myriad tasks, of which some are clerical in nature (*e.g.*, keeping track of dividends) and some are not (*e.g.*, making discretionary distributions). Stewardship of another's property in and of itself is serious business, and yet it is only one of the trustee's many nondelegable functions.

Above all the trustee must act solely in the interest of the beneficiaries.[2] The trustee may not transact with the trust property for personal benefit, absent authority from the settlor, the court, or from all the beneficiaries. One of the hallmarks of the trust relationship is the trustee's duty of absolute loyalty to the trust. One should not accept the office of trustee if there are any doubts about one's ability to carry out the duty of loyalty.[3]

This does not mean that trust administration should be something other than a business. It *is* a business, and it should be. Compensation provides a trustee with the incentive to keep trust matters high on his list of priorities. However, trusteeship should not degrade to a state where it is merely an adjunct to other businesses such as brokerage, law, accounting, banking, or financial planning. Trust administration is a worthy profession in and of itself; it is a profession that thrives on regular attention over the long term, stability of personnel, the tried and true, and slow incremental changes for the better.

The court may appoint a trustee, or the governing trust instrument may empower an individual to appoint one.[4] In appointing a trustee, the court will have due regard for the wishes of the settlor but will decline to appoint an unfit person.[5] Thus, if someone authorized by the governing trust instrument selects an unfit or incapable person as trustee, the court may review the appointment. Ordinarily, one should not appoint oneself as trustee. The responsible individual should, giving due regard to the intentions of the settlor, consult the beneficiaries and appoint someone agreeable to them; this is what a court is expected to do.

Courts are reluctant to appoint nonresidents but, as a practical matter, they often do, particularly where some or all of the beneficiaries or property are

---

§3.2 [1] Lord Chancellor Hardwicke in Knight v. Earl of Plymouth, 21 Eng. Rep. 214, 216 (1747).

[2] Restatement (Third) of Trusts §170(1).

[3] *See* §6.1.3 of this handbook (duty to be loyal to the trust).

[4] *See generally* 2 Scott on Trusts §108.2 (Appointment by the Court), §108.3 (Noncourt Appointments).

[5] 2 Scott & Ascher §9.13.14.

out of state and especially if nominated by the testator.[6] In some states, the court may appoint a cotrustee to serve with a nonresident trustee.[7]

A substance abuser[8] or person of dishonest or bad character[9] will not be appointed since the property would not be in safe hands.[10] Unfitness would include mental incapacity.[11] It could also include a lack of "basic ability to administer the trust."[12] The entire matter of appointment and removal lies in the reasonable discretion of the court with due deference being given to reasonable provisions in the governing instrument.[13] "Before removing a trustee for unfitness the court should consider the extent to which the problem might be cured by a delegation of functions the trustee is personally incapable of performing."[14]

§3.2.1 The Professional Trustee and Single-Purpose Trust Company

A private trust company is an attractive option for many wealthy families because it allows a family to bundle and rebundle investment management, trust and custodial services according to family needs and desires. But such companies operate in the same legal framework as other trust institutions, and thus are no place for hobbyists.[15]

In an ideal world, only single-purpose trust companies[16] and individuals engaged full-time in the business of trust administration would serve as trustees. Experience in and knowledge of trust matters would be broad and deep.

---

[6] *See generally* Bogert §132.

[7] *See, e.g.,* 20 Pa. Cons. Stat. Ann. §7103 (Purdon 1975).

[8] *See, e.g.,* Ohio Rev. Code Ann. §2109.24 (Anderson 1953) (intoxication grounds for removing a trustee). The Pennsylvania fiduciary removal statute, however, has been amended to eliminate a reference to intoxication. 20 Pa. Cons. Stat. Ann. §3182 (Purdon 1992).

[9] *See, e.g.,* Parkman v. Hanna, 426 S.E.2d 743 (S.C. 1992) (holding that a disbarred attorney's past conduct was relevant in determining fitness to serve as a fiduciary).

[10] *See generally* 2 Scott on Trusts §107; Bogert §519 (The Court's Power to Remove Trustee).

[11] UTC §706 cmt. (available at <http://www.uniformlaws.org/Act.aspx?title=Trust%20 Code>).

[12] UTC §706 cmt. (available at <http://www.uniformlaws.org/Act.aspx?title=Trust%20 Code>).

[13] *See generally* 2 Scott on Trusts §108.2.

[14] UTC §706 cmt. (available at <http://www.uniformlaws.org/Act.aspx?title=Trust%20 Code>). *See also* §6.1.4 of this handbook (duty to give personal attention (not to delegate)).

[15] John P. C. Duncan, *Forming a Private Trust Company: Elements and Process*, 136 Tr. & Est. 36 (Aug. 1997). *See also* John P. C. Duncan, *The Private Trust Company: It Has Come of Age*, 142 Tr. & Est. 49 (Aug. 2003) (discussing the advantages of a state adopting the Conference of State Bank Supervisors' Model Multistate Trust Institutions Act).

[16] *See generally* John P. C. Duncan, *Forming a Private Trust Company: Elements and Process*, 136 Tr. & Est. 36 (Aug. 1997). *See also* John P. C. Duncan, *The Private Trust Company: It Has Come of Age*, 142 Tr. & Est. 49 (Aug. 2003) (discussing the advantages of a state adopting the Conference of State Bank Supervisors' Model Multistate Trust Institutions Act) and §8.6 of this handbook (the trustee

Attention to the welfare of the trust would be exclusive, focused, and sustained. Goods and services would be contracted for at arm's length on behalf of the trust.

Economic realities, however, are such that only a small percentage of the population has the wherewithal to purchase the services of trustees so single-mindedly committed. Moreover, there are those who feel that the professional trustee, no matter how competent, is unacceptable because of its inability to offer the personal attention that a family member or a family private trust company[17] ostensibly provides. In a less than ideal world, persons in other lines of work are called upon to serve as trustees. While their involvement is not *per se* undesirable, each category raises its own collection of red flags.

§3.2.2   The Lawyer

In an 1891 issue of Punch in an article entitled Taken Upon Trust a maiden laments that she has a lawyer for our trustee, who is most unobliging and expensive. . . . [Chantal Stebbing in her book The Private Trustee in Victorian England[18]] . . . states that by the end of the Victorian Period, a tenth of the large estates in England were in the hands of solicitor-trustees.[19]

The advantage of having a lawyer serve as trustee is that lawyers understand the equitable rights and obligations of the parties.[20] The disadvantage is that the lawyer who renders legal services to the trust for compensation over and above his or her reasonable trustee's fees brushes with a conflict of interest.[21] The lawyer-trustee is after all transacting with the trust "for his own

---

who is not a human being; corporate trustees; bank trustees; foreign trust companies) (discussing in part the common law and/or statutory authority of a corporation to act as trustee).

   [17] *See generally* John P. C. Duncan, *Forming a Private Trust Company: Elements and Process*, 136 Tr. & Est. 36 (Aug. 1997). *See also* John P. C. Duncan, *The Private Trust Company: It Has Come of Age*, 142 Tr. & Est. 49 (Aug. 2003) (discussing the advantages of a state adopting the Conference of State Bank Supervisors' Model Multistate Trust Institutions Act) and §8.6 of this handbook (the trustee who is not a human being; corporate trustees; bank trustees) (discussing in part the common law and/or statutory authority of a corporation to act as trustee).

   [18] Cambridge University Press, 2002.

   [19] Malcolm A. Moore, *The Joseph Trachtman Lecture—The Origin of Our Species: Trust and Estate Lawyers and How They Grew*, 32 ACTEC L.J. 159, 173 (2006).

   [20] *But see* Charles E. Rounds, Jr., *The Case for a Return to Mandatory Instruction in the Fiduciary Aspects of Agency and Trusts in the American Law School, Together With a Model Fiduciary Relations Course Syllabus*, 18 Regent U. L. Rev. 251 (2005–2006); §8.25 of this handbook (most American law schools no longer require Trusts, Agency and Equity).

   [21] *See* Blake v. Pegram, 109 Mass. 541, 553 (1872) (charges to the trust of legal fees by the lawyer/trustee are "open to serious question, because of the liability to abuse, or, at least, to the suspicion of abuse," this because the lawyer/trustee "is his own client"). *See also* Kentucky Nat'l Bank v. Stone, 93 Ky. 623, 20 S.W. 1040 (1893); Estate of Lankershim, 6 Cal. 2d 568, 58 P.2d 1282 (1936); Ontjes v. MacNider, 234 Iowa 208, 12 N.W.2d 284 (1943); Florida Bar v. Della-Donna, 583 So. 2d 307 (Fla. 1989); First Nat'l Bank of Boston v. Brink, 372 Mass. 257, 268, 361 N.E.2d 406, 412 (1977) (Liacos, J., concurring in part and dissenting in part) (commenting on the perceived or

account." It is not always clear when one is acting as trustee and when one is acting as counsel, nor is it clear what portion of the compensation is attributable to actions as trustee and what portion is attributable to the rendering of legal services. But perhaps the fundamental problem with administering a trust out of a multidisciplinary practice[22] is the loss to the trust of the independent perspective, of the checks and balances that operate when the functions are assumed by different entities.[23] It is a loss to the beneficiaries that cannot be mitigated or rationalized away by compensation adjustment. When functions are separated, the trustee to some extent monitors the lawyer and vice versa. When the functions coalesce in one person, there arises the danger that the lawyer as a practical matter is unaccountable as to performance and compensation.[24]

In any case, "a certain critical mass of trust business, and reasonable working capital, may be necessary before the practicing lawyer can afford to be equipped sufficiently to accept *any* trusteeship."[25] The practicing lawyer who intends to get into the business of serving as a trustee would do well to consult the Guide for ACTEC Fellows Serving as Trustees.[26]

§3.2.3 The Stockbroker

The trustee, under a duty to act solely in the interests of the beneficiaries, faces a built-in, structural incentive to violate that duty when he or she also serves as the trust's commissioned stockbroker. By selling when it is in the interest of the beneficiaries to hold and by buying when it is in the interests of the beneficiaries not to buy, the trustee-stockbroker personally benefits when the portfolio is "churned."[27]

---

actual conflicts of interest that can arise when an attorney and fiduciary are one and the same). *See generally* Krier, *The Attorney as Personal Representative or Trustee*, 65 Fla. B.J. 69 (1991). *See generally* §6.1.3.3 of this handbook (when the trustee benefits as a buyer or seller of trust property).

[22] *See generally* §6.1.3.3 of this handbook (when the trustee benefits as a buyer or seller of trust property) and §6.1.3.5 of this handbook (the trustee's duty of loyalty to the beneficiary in nontrust matters).

[23] *See* ACTEC Commentaries on the Model Rules of Professional Conduct (3d ed. 1999), at 59 (suggesting that "[a] lawyer undertaking to serve in both capacities should attempt to ameliorate any disadvantages that may come from dual service, including the potential loss of the benefits that are obtained by having a separate fiduciary and lawyer, such as the checks and balances that a separate fiduciary might provide upon the amount of fees sought by the lawyer and vice versa").

[24] *See generally* Gibbs v. Breed, Abbott and Morgan, 649 N.Y.S.2d 974, 170 Misc. 2d 493 (1996) (suggesting unacceptable stress is placed on a lawyer-executor's duty of undivided loyalty when his law firm requires that he remit to the firm (out of fiduciary commissions) any shortfall in his legal fees).

[25] ACTEC Practice Committee, *Fiduciary Matters Subcommittee, Guide for ACTEC Fellows Serving as Trustees*, 26 ACTEC Notes 313, 316 (2001).

[26] ACTEC Practice Committee, *Fiduciary Matters Subcommittee, Guide for ACTEC Fellows Serving as Trustees*, 26 ACTEC Notes 313, 316 (2001).

[27] *See, e.g.*, Armstrong v. McAlpin, 699 F.2d 79 (2d Cir. 1983).

One solution is for the trustee-stockbroker to place trades with another firm. This avoids the conflict inherent in placing trades with the trustee-stockbroker's firm, but it will not eliminate the indirect personal benefit—in goodwill and implied IOUs—that inevitably accrues to someone who parcels out business. Of course, this conflict is not confined to brokers of stock. It would also apply to brokers of insurance and real estate. If the trustee intends to operate the trust out of a brokerage facility, at the very least the facility's infrastructure should be capable of accommodating the trust's specialized operational requirements, particularly the separate accounting of income and principal.

§3.2.4   The Bank

It was perhaps something of an accident that the corporations which have obtained power to administer trusts are banking institutions. There is no necessary connection between the business of banking and the business of administering trusts. . . . In the first edition of Ames's Cases on Trusts there is only one case in which the trustee was a corporation, and in that case the trustee was the Massachusetts Hospital Life Insurance Company, which was the first corporation empowered to act as trustee, being incorporated in 1818.[28]

In the United States, however, from early on, certain corporations have been authorized to act as trustee. The first specific grant of such powers seems to have been to the Farmer's Fire Insurance & Loan Company, chartered in New York in 1822.[29]

A full-service bank is said to have two sides: the commercial side and the trust side. The trust side operates in the fiduciary's labor-intensive world, where beneficiaries are entitled to full disclosure, deference, and a degree of intimacy, while the commercial side operates in the world of the marketplace and by its rules. If a loan to a commercial customer goes bad, generally the lender is not bound by fiduciary ties and can take necessary steps to protect its interest. The bank in its role as creditor is different from the bank acting as trustee. As trustee, the bank is the legal owner of the property and as trustee, has a fiduciary duty to place the interest of the beneficiaries ahead of its own interests. "It is crucial that the trust department be a strong organization, so that it can exercise its own discretion, independent of the commercial banking department,"[30] the cultures being so different:

> . . . [A]mid financial-industry consolidation, many trusts are ending up under the purview of geographically remote managers who work for vast corporations. Customers complain of problems such as frequent turnover, relentless marketing

---

[28] Scott on Trusts §96.5 (1939) (referring to Durant v. Massachusetts Hosp. Life Ins. Co., 2 Lowell 575, Fed. Cas. No. 4188 (1877)). *See generally* §8.6 of this handbook (the trustee who is not a human being; corporate trustees; bank trustees).

[29] 1 Scott & Ascher §1.9.

[30] 3 Scott & Ascher §17.2.14.6.

and poor communications. . . .Big banks face more pressure "to sell the corporate product of the month," says Mike Carroll, president and chief executive of independent trust company Heritage Trust Co. in Oklahoma City. But, he says, it's tough business for large institutions: "It's too time-consuming, too much touch, too much relationship-driven."[31]

The commercial officers who run a full-service bank must strive to understand and adequately fund its trust function—a function that operates in a world that values, among other things, continuity of management and a smooth-running operational and administrative infrastructure.

In some situations, by state or federal law one or more of the trustees of a trust must be a bank or trust company. A so-called corporate trust established by a bond issuer to secure the contractual rights of its bondholders comes to mind.[32] For a discussion of the rights, duties, and obligations of the trustees of such trusts, known in the trade as "indenture trustees," see Section 9.31 of this handbook.

§3.2.5 *The Family Member*

Furthermore, when a beneficiary serves as trustee or when other conflict-of-interest situations exist, the conduct of the trustee in the administration of the trust will be subject to especially careful scrutiny.[33]

When the trustee is also a beneficiary, the general duty of loyalty,[34] as well as one its sub-duties, the duty of impartiality,[35] is squarely implicated: "The trustee who is also a beneficiary may not, in administering the trust, favor the trustee's own interest at the expense of the other beneficiaries, unless the terms of the trust so provide."[36] But apart from the legal considerations, there are personal ones as well: The seeds of family disharmony are all too often sown when a beneficiary is appointed trustee, particularly when the apparent default rule that a trustee-beneficiary may not participate in decisions regarding distributions of income and principal to himself is overridden by express

---

[31] Rachel Emma Silverman & Carrick Mollenkamp, *As Financial Services Consolidate, Trust Managers Come Under Fire*, Wall St. J., July 20, 2004, p. A1, col. 5.

[32] *See* The Barkley Trust Indenture Act of 1939, 15 U.S.C.A. §77jjj.

[33] Restatement (Third) of Trusts §37 cmt. f(I).

[34] *See generally* §6.1.3 of this handbook (the trustee's duty of loyalty to the beneficiaries or to the trust's charitable purposes).

[35] *See generally* §6.2.5 of this handbook (the trustee's duty of impartiality).

[36] 3 Scott & Ascher §17.15. *See, e.g.*, In re Benjamin F. Haddad Trust, 2013 WL 4081031 (Mich. Ct. App. Aug. 13, 2013) (The remainder beneficiary of the marital trust having brought an unsuccessful action against the trustees for allegedly making excessive distributions of principal to the widow, it would be inappropriate now for the court to appoint the very same remainder beneficiary as a successor trustee as he would have a strong incentive to approve only the minimum possible distributions to the widow.).

language in the governing instrument.[37] Take the appointment of a child of the settlor as trustee of a trust for the benefit of all the settlor's children and other issue.[38] Either the sibling-trustee is tempted to bend over backwards to his economic detriment or to the economic detriment of his issue in order to avoid even the appearance of impropriety and conflict of interest[39] (thus perhaps thwarting the settlor's wishes that all siblings and their issue be treated fairly) or the sibling-trustee is tempted to take unfair advantage of the office in furtherance of his economic interests to the exclusion of the interests of the other beneficiaries. Even under the best of circumstances, the sibling-trustee should expect to be regarded with suspicion by the other siblings and their spouses.[40] On the other hand, it can be a prescription for gridlock and deadlock if all the siblings are serving as cotrustees.[41] Moreover, the matter of trustee compensation can become a sensitive issue when the trustee is also a beneficiary.

The appointment of a beneficiary's near relation brings with it its own set of problems, although in the United States relations are more often appointed than strangers. Laxness of management, the overweening influence of beneficiaries, and condonations of misconduct too often are the price of these family arrangements.

There is no rule against making the spouse of a beneficiary a trustee. However, the risk does exist that the marriage will end in divorce before the trust terminates. In addition, it would be a tragedy if the spouse's appointment itself were to have a destabilizing effect on a marriage that until then had been solid.

---

[37] *See generally* Bogert §129; §3.5.3.2(a) of this handbook (the trustee's power to make discretionary payments of income and principal (the discretionary trust)). *See, e.g.*, Dana v. Gring, 374 Mass. 109, 371 N.E.2d 755 (1977). Presumably, the default rule that a trustee-beneficiary may not participate in decisions regarding distributions of principal to himself may be overridden by express language in the governing instrument. *See, e.g.*, Garfield v. United States, 47 A.F.T.R.2d ¶81-1583, 80-2 USTC ¶13,381 (D. Mass.).

[38] *See, e.g.*, Fletcher v. Fletcher, 480 S.E.2d 488 (Va. 1997) (involving an unsuccessful attempt on the part of the sibling trustee to deny a sibling beneficiary access to the entire trust document).

[39] *See* Restatement (Third) of Trusts §78 cmt. c(2) (suggesting that the "common situation in which one or more of a trust's beneficiaries are selected or authorized by the settlor to serve as trustee or co-trustee inevitably presents an array of conflicts between the trustee's interests as a beneficiary and the interests of other beneficiaries").

[40] "[T]here is . . . a general recognition that a trustee-beneficiary's conduct is to be closely scrutinized for abuse, including abuse by less than appropriate regard for the duty of impartiality." Restatement (Third) of Trusts §79 cmt. b(1).

[41] *See* UTC §706(b)(2) (available at <http://www.uniformlaws.org/Act.aspx?title=Trust%20 Code>) (providing that the court may remove a trustee if lack of cooperation among cotrustees substantially impairs the administration of the trust). "Removal is particularly appropriate if the naming of an even number of trustees, combined with their failure to agree, has resulted in deadlock requiring court resolution." UTC §706 cmt.

§3.2.6 Considerations in the Selection of a Trustee

A power to direct must be distinguished from a veto power. A power to direct involves action initiated and within the control of a third party. The trustee usually has no responsibility other than to carry out the direction when made. But if a third party holds a veto power, the trustee is responsible for initiating the decision, subject to the third party's approval. A trustee who administers a trust subject to a veto power occupies a position akin to that of a cotrustee and is responsible for taking appropriate action if the third party's refusal to consent would result in a serious breach of trust.[42]

Factors to consider in the selection of a trustee. The expected duration of the trust, the complexity of its assets, the needs of the beneficiaries, the level of administrative and investment expertise required, and the fees a professional trustee will charge must be considered in the selection of a trustee. The settlor should take the long view. A trust for a child with a mental disability or an orphaned grandchild, for example, could extend well beyond the settlor's lifetime, long after the settlor's close friends and relatives have died. In other words, the trust needs a spine. This could take the form of an institution in the first instance, an institution as a cotrustee, or an institution as a fall-back in default of named individuals.[43]

A trustee cannot be a guardian of the person. The settlor should not confuse the function of a *guardian* of the person[44] with the function of a *trustee*. The loving grandfather may be the perfect guardian of the orphaned grandchild's person, but he may be totally unsuited because of his age to act as trustee.[45]

Separation of fiduciary functions is advisable. Moreover, if different people hold both positions, the guardian benefits from the trustee's independent perspective and the child benefits from the checks and balances inherent in a separation of these responsibilities. A separation of responsibilities is also preferable if the settlor intends that the guardian of the person receive generous discretionary distributions of income and principal for domestic help, the

---

[42] UTC §808 cmt. (available at <http://www.uniformlaws.org/Act.aspx?title=Trust%20Code>).

[43] "One advantage of a corporate trustee is 'permanence.'" Restatement (Third) of Trusts, Reporter's Notes on §33. *See, e.g.*, In New England Mut. Nat'l Bank v. Centenary Methodist Church, 342 Mass. 360, 173 N.E.2d 294 (1961) (a trustee-bank having converted from a state bank to a national bank and merged with another bank, the new entity by statute succeeded to the trusteeship without reappointment or appointment).

[44] A "guardian" makes decisions with respect to personal care; a "conservator" manages property. UTC §103 cmt. (available at <http://www.uniformlaws.org/Act.aspx?title=Trust%20Code>). The terminology used is that employed in Article V of the UPC and its freestanding Uniform Guardianship and Protective Proceedings Act. UTC §103 cmt.

[45] In civil law jurisdictions, restricted transfers to minors are often made by means of a "guardianship." The civil law guardian or tutor, however, is likely to be charged with supervising both the child's person and the child's property. *See generally* Jeffrey A. Schoenblum, 1 Multistate and Multinational Estate Planning 1249 (1999). This linking of the personal and the financial makes the civil law guardianship a less than ideal as a trust substitute. *See generally* §8.12.1 of this handbook (civil law alternatives to the trust).

construction of an addition on the guardian's house, or such other purposes as will lessen the financial burden of the guardianship.[46] It is always awkward for trustees, even though duly authorized, to make discretionary distributions to themselves.[47] Even the possession of such a power could have tax implications for the trustee personally.[48]

There is more to a trusteeship than investment management. The settlor ought not to measure one's suitability to be a trustee solely by his or her investment successes. There is much more to a trusteeship than merely investing.

Declarations of trust and trustee succession. If the settlor intends to name himself as trustee in the first instance, he should make sure that matters of trustee succession are adequately addressed in the governing instrument. It is very important that the matter of the settlor's incapacity be addressed.

Trustee selection need not be an either/or choice between the bank or the lawyer or the family member. Many permutations and combinations of cotrusteeships[49] and orders of succession can exploit strengths and mitigate weaknesses. A trust need not be administered by a "traditional, plenipotent trustee" acting alone.[50] There can be co-actors, such as "co-trustees, directed trustees, trust advisors for investment and other functions, trust protectors, distribution advisors and committees, removers, and appointers."[51] The terms of a particular trust, for example, might provide for the appointment of a third party to "advise" the trustee,[52] or to designate new or successor trustees.[53] A

---

[46] *See* Restatement (Third) of Trusts §50 cmt. f, specifically the comments on illustration 14. *See generally* §3.5.3.2(a) of this handbook (the trustee's power to make discretionary payments of income and principal (the discretionary trust)).

[47] *See generally* 3 Scott & Ascher §18.2.5 (Trustee With Discretionary Power to Distribute to Self).

[48] *See generally* 3 Scott & Ascher §18.2.5 (Trustee With Discretionary Power to Distribute to Self). *See also* §8.9.3 of this handbook (tax-sensitive powers).

[49] "Cotrusteeship should not be called for without careful reflection." UTC §703 cmt. (available at <http://www.uniformlaws.org/Act.aspx?title=Trust%20Code>). To be sure, "[h]aving multiple decision-makers serves as a safeguard against eccentricity or misconduct." UTC §703 cmt. On the other hand, "[d]ivision of responsibility among cotrustees is often confused; the accountability of any individual trustee is uncertain; obtaining consent of all trustees can be burdensome; and, unless an odd number of trustees is named, deadlocks requiring court resolution can occur." UTC §703 cmt. *See generally* §§3.4.4.1 of this handbook (trustees) and 7.2.4 of this handbook (cofiduciary and predecessor liability and contribution in the trust context).

[50] *See* John P.C. Duncan & Anita M. Sarafa, *Achieve the Promise—and Limit the Risk—of Multi-Participant Trusts*, 36 ACTEC L.J. 769, 774 (Spring 2011).

[51] *See* John P.C. Duncan & Anita M. Sarafa, *Achieve the Promise—and Limit the Risk—of Multi-Participant Trusts*, 36 ACTEC L.J. 769, 774 (Spring 2011).

[52] *See* J. R. Kemper L.L.B, Annot., *Construction and operation of will or trust provision appointing advisors to trustee or executor*, 56 A.L.R.3d 1249 (1974). "'Advisers' have long been used for certain trustee functions, such as the power to direct investments or manage a closely-held business." UTC §808 cmt. (available at <http://www.uniformlaws.org/Act.aspx?title=Trust%20Code>). (Under Alaska's default law, a trustee is not required to follow the advice of the advisor; and the advisor is not liable as or considered to be a trustee of the trust or a fiduciary when acting as an advisor pursuant to the terms of the trust. *See* Alaska Stat. §13.36.370.) " 'Trust protector,' a term largely associated with offshore trust practice, is more recent, and usually connotes the grant of greater powers, sometimes including the power to amend or terminate the trust." UTC §808 cmt.

[53] 2 Scott & Ascher §11.11.3.

trust that has a constellation of fiduciaries and quasi-fiduciaries administering it has been referred to as a "multi-participant" trust.[54] For a discussion of how best to coordinate the activities of all these players such that critical fiduciary functions do not fall between the cracks, the reader is referred to Duncan and Sarafa, *Achieve the Promise—and Limit the Risk—of Multi-Participant Trusts*.[55] We now take up the mechanics of slicing and dicing the duties of a trustee and parceling out the pieces.

Trustee removal and replacement powers. For the settlor wishing to build in a measure of nonjudicial oversight, there are provisions for trustee removal and replacement that need not create tax problems if properly drafted.[56] However, care should be taken to draft any "donor control" provisions in a charitable trust in a way that neither jeopardizes the charitable tax deduction nor frustrates the intended use of the gift.[57]

The trust protector. *Defined.* Dr. Alexander A. Bove, Jr. defines the trust protector as a "party who has overriding discretionary powers with respect to the trust but who is not a trustee" and makes the case that the concept of the trust protector is nothing new.[58] It is essentially a form of trust advisor (not to be confused with someone whom the trustee is merely requested to consult but from whom the trustee is not required to take directions) whose powers could extend beyond asset management to include some form of nonjudicial oversight of the trustee's other activities:

> What may come as a surprise to many is the fact that the concept of trust protector, especially in the history of U.S. law, is not new at all; at best it is only the *term* that is new, as well as practitioners' recent "discovery" of what actually is an old concept in trust law . . . [T]rust attorneys in the U.S. and elsewhere have been employing the concept of trust "advisors" for decades, but unlike the "protector," it was more the *role* of the trust advisor than the name tag that was given formal recognition . . . Thus in earlier days it was not uncommon, for instance, for a settlor to name an "advisor" who had the power to direct and control all investments, or to remove and replace trustees. Although the term "advisor" is still customarily used when a

---

[54] *See* John P.C. Duncan & Anita M. Sarafa, *Achieve the Promise—and Limit the Risk—of Multi-Participant Trusts*, 36 ACTEC L.J. 769, 774 (Spring 2011).

[55] 36 ACTEC L.J. 769 (Spring 2011).

[56] UTC §705 cmt. (available at <http://www.uniformlaws.org/Act.aspx?title=Trust%20 Code>). *See generally* Estate of Wall v. Commissioner, 101 T.C. 300 (1993) (holding that the settlor's reserved power to remove and replace corporate trustees would not generate adverse estate-tax consequences upon the death of the settlor); Rev. Rul. 95-58, 1995-2 C.B. 191 (suggesting that a reserved power to remove and replace trustees will not bring adverse estate tax consequences upon death of settlor, provided the power does not extend to appointing an individual or corporate successor that is related or subordinate to the settlor within the meaning of §672(c) of the Internal Revenue Code). *See also* Berall, *New Ruling Provides More Flexibility in Removal of Trustees*, 23 Est. Planning 99 (Mar./Apr. 1996). *See generally* §§8.9.3 of this handbook (tax-sensitive powers) and 8.15.15 of this handbook (the ascertainable standard).

[57] *See generally* Alan F. Rothschild, Jr., *The Dos and Don'ts of Donor Control*, 30 ACTEC L.J. 261 (2005).

[58] *See* Alexander A. Bove, Jr., The Trust Protector: Friend, Foe, or Fiduciary? 34th Annual Notre Dame Tax and Estate Planning Institute, South Bend, Indiana, September 25–26, 2008.

power over only trust investments is granted, if the power extends beyond that, today that party is more likely to be called a "protector."[59]

In England and the offshore jurisdictions, nonjudicial third-party oversight of the trustee's activities is often effected through an express appointment in the governing instrument of a trust protector.[60] More and more this is the case in the United States as well.

Scope of trust protector's duties. Because the scope of a trust protector's duties tends to fall somewhere between the nonexistent or limited scope of duties of the holder of a special power of appointment and the broad scope of duties of a full-fledged trustee,[61] extreme caution should be exercised by anyone contemplating serving as a trustee or a trust protector of a trust *that provides for both offices* if that trust is to be subject to the jurisdiction of a state of the United States.[62] Before accepting either office pursuant to the terms of a particular trust instrument, the nominee would be well advised to obtain a written legal opinion spelling out the responsibilities of the trustee, if any, to monitor the activities of the trust protector; the duties and liabilities of the trustee protector, *e.g.*, whether or not he is a fiduciary; the rights of the trust protector, *e.g.*, whether or not he is entitled to be compensated for his services and indemnified for his liabilities; and the tax consequences for all concerned of the trust protector possessing and/or exercising his authority.[63]

When the protector is the de facto trustee. As noted in Section 8.12 of this handbook, equity looks to the intent (substance) of an arrangement rather than to its form. Thus, for example, "[w]here the trustee is not able to take any—or

---

[59] *See* Alexander A. Bove, Jr., The Trust Protector: Friend, Foe, or Fiduciary? 34th Annual Notre Dame Tax and Estate Planning Institute, South Bend, Indiana, September 25–26, 2008.

[60] *See generally* 1 Jeffrey A. Schoenblum, Multistate and Multinational Estate Planning 1372–1374 (1999); UTC §808 cmt. (available at <http://www.uniformlaws.org/Act.aspx?title=Trust%20Code>); 5 Scott & Ascher §33.1.3 n.1 (Termination or Modification by Third Person).

[61] Trust protectors have been given authority to do one or more of the following: remove and appoint trustees; review the trust administration and approve accounts; appoint auditors; agree to trustee compensation; approve self-dealing by trustees; petition the court on behalf of unborn or unascertained remaindermen; export the trust and change the governing law; trigger or cancel flight arrangements in flee clauses; withhold consent to investment, distributive, and administrative decisions of the trustees; direct trustees to exercise of investment, distributive, and/or administrative discretions; provide and obtain tax advice for the trustees; veto the settlor's exercise of reserved powers; decide whether the settlor is incapacitated so as to trigger suspension of reserved powers; and add members to or subtract members from a class of permissible discretionary beneficiaries. 1 Jeffrey A. Schoenblum, Multistate and Multinational Estate Planning 1372–1374 (1999). Prof. Schoenblum acknowledges Professor David Hayton for developing a comprehensive list of trust protector functions. David Hayton, *English Fiduciary Standards and Trust Law*, 32 Vand. J. Transnat'l L. 555, 583–584 (1999). That list is reproduced in §18.18[C][9] of Prof. Schoenblum's treatise. A slightly modified version of the list appears in this footnote. *See generally* 3 Scott & Ascher §16.7 (Effect of Power to Direct or Control Trustee).

[62] *See generally* James L. Dam, *More Estate Planners Are Using "Trust Protectors,"* 2001 LWUSA 854 (Oct. 29, 2001) (citing a Pennsylvania estate-planning attorney to the effect that in the United States settlors who designate trust protectors are venturing into "uncharted territory").

[63] *See generally* James L. Dam, *More Estate Planners Are Using "Trust Protectors,"* 2001 LWUSA 854 (Oct. 29, 2001) (suggesting that there is little "default law" addressing the powers and duties of protectors). *See generally* 3 Scott & Ascher §16.7 (Effect of Power to Direct or Control Trustee).

practically any—step in the . . . [trust] . . . administration without securing protector approval, the balance of power is so radically altered that it may be concluded that the trustee is no more than a custodian and the protector is, in reality, the trustee."[64]

Protectors are generally fiduciaries. It is the position of the Restatement (Third) of Trusts that "[a]bsent some clear indication of a settlor's contrary intent, powers granted to a protector . . . probably should be deemed to be held in a fiduciary capacity . . . , even if not strictly that of a trustee."[65] Dr. Bove is generally in accord.[66] Clearly indicating such a contrary intent, however, may be easier said than done. Take a trust with the following provision: "For the avoidance of doubt, it is hereby declared that no power is vested in the protector in a fiduciary capacity." In a case involving a trust with just such language the court ruled that because the express terms of the trust elsewhere in the instrument provided that the protector shall exercise his powers for the benefit of the beneficiaries, specifically the powers to appoint successor trustees and protectors, he was bound by fiduciary constraints in their exercise.[67] The only purpose of the exoneration language was to relieve the protector of any fiduciary duty to consider from time to time whether or not to exercise.[68] In other words, he had no fiduciary duty to be pro-active.

Protector liability. A lawyer practicing in the United States contemplating serving as a trust protector will want to ascertain whether his or her legal malpractice liability policy covers such activity.[69] It should be noted that in Alaska the stakes might not be as high as elsewhere. Alaska has by legislation clarified the default law relative to the protector's legal status: Subject to the terms of the governing instrument, a trust protector is *not* liable or accountable as a trustee or fiduciary because of an act or omission of the trust protector taken when performing the function of a trust protector under the trust instrument.[70]

Protector removal. Dr. Bove's dissertation (Universität Zürich) has a section on the power of the court to appoint and remove a protector.[71] On September 27, 2012, a court in the Bailiwick of Jersey (the British Crown dependency) removed a trust protector in part because of his "misconceived view of himself

---

[64] Dawn Goodman & Sarah Aughwane, *Who Holds the Gun?*, 21 STEP J. 51 (Oct. 2013) [Issue 8].

[65] Restatement (Third) of Trusts, Reporter's Notes on §64. *See also* 5 Scott & Ascher §33.1.3 (Termination or Modification by Third Person).

[66] *See* Alexander A. Bove, Jr., *The Development, Use, and Misuse of the Trust Protector and its Role in Trust Law and Practice* 2, Schulthess (2014); Alexander A. Bove, Jr., *The Trust Protector: Friend, Foe, or Fiduciary?*, 34th Annual Notre Dame Tax and Estate Planning Institute, South Bend, Indiana, September 25–26, 2008; Alexander A. Bove, Jr., *The Case Against the Trust Protector*, 37 ACTEC L.J. 77 (Summer 2011) (making the case that a trust protector cannot be the agent of either the settlor or the trustee).

[67] Centre Trustees v. Van Rooyen, [2010] WTLR 17 (decided by the Royal Court of Jersey).

[68] Centre Trustees v. Van Rooyen, [2010] WTLR 17 (decided by the Royal Court of Jersey).

[69] *See generally* §3.5.4.2 of this handbook (insuring the trustee against personal liability).

[70] Alaska Stat. §13.36.370.

[71] *See* Alexander A. Bove, Jr., *The Development, Use, and Misuse of the Trust Protector and its Role in Trust Law and Practice*, Schulthess (119–121) (2014).

as the living guardian and enforcer of the settlors' wishes."[72] Only selected "extracts" of the case were made public. As a result, it is not entirely clear what express limitations there were on the protector's powers. In any case, there is language in the materials that have been made available to the public suggesting that Jersey recognizes the benefit-of-the-beneficiaries-principle, the controversial policy centerpiece of the American (U.S.) Uniform Trust Code. The principle is taken up in Section 6.1.2 of this handbook. The Jersey court had this to say:

> It can be no part of the function of a protector with limited powers of the kind conferred on S by the trust instruments to ensure that a settlor's wishes are carried out any more than it is open to a settlor himself to insist on them being carried out. A trustee's duty as regards a letter of wishes is no more than to have due regard to such matters without any obligation to follow them. And a protector's duty can, correspondingly, be no higher than to do his best to see that trustees have due regard to the settlor's wishes (in whatever form they may have been imparted): From the moment of his acceptance of the office of protector his paramount duty is to the beneficiaries of the trust.[73]

Protector powers. It should also be noted here that Alaska has clarified by legislation[74] what powers a settlor may give to a trust protector. They are the following:

- To remove and appoint a trustee.
- To modify or amend the trust instrument to achieve favorable tax status or to respond to changes in 26 U.S.C. (Internal Revenue Code) or state law, or the ruling and regulations under those laws.
- To increase or decrease the interests of any beneficiary to the trusts but not to grant a beneficial interest to an individual or a class of individuals unless the individual or class of individuals is specifically provided for under the terms of the trust instrument.
- To modify the terms of a power of appointment granted by the trust.

A practice manual with forms (trust protectors). See generally Alexander A. Bove, Jr., Trust Protectors: A Practice Manual with Forms (Juris-2014).

Information surrogates. For a discussion of the duties and liabilities of the information surrogate, a type of trust protector, the reader is referred to Section 6.1.5.1 of this handbook.

The rights, duties, and obligations of the directed trustee. The Uniform Trust Code attempts to clear up some of the confusion in the default law that would govern those with the power to give directions, as well as those who are the recipients of those directions. The Code provides that if the terms of a trust confer upon a person other than the settlor of a revocable trust power to direct certain actions of the trustee, the trustee shall act in accordance with an exercise

---

[72] *See* In the matter of the A and B Trusts, [2012] JRC 169A.
[73] [2012] JRC 169A.
[74] Alaska Stat. §13.36.370.

of the power unless the attempted exercise is manifestly contrary to the terms of the trust or the trustee knows that the attempted exercise would constitute a serious breach of a fiduciary duty that the person holding the power owes to the beneficiaries of the trust.[75] The Restatement (Third) of Trusts is generally in accord.[76]

What is that duty? A person, other than a beneficiary, who holds a power to direct, is presumptively a fiduciary who, as such, is required to act in good faith with regard to the purposes of the trust and the interests of the beneficiaries.[77] The holder of a power to direct is liable for any loss that results from breach of a fiduciary duty.[78] In other words, the duties and liabilities of a fiduciary power holder generally are comparable to those of a trustee.[79]

The trustee has a fiduciary duty not to comply with the directions of a powerholder if the trustee knows that to do so would cause a violation of the *powerholder's* fiduciary duties.[80] The trustee even may have liability for complying with a direction that he knows, or should know, would violate the *powerholder's* fiduciary duties.[81] The New Hampshire legislature has addressed the issue squarely by providing that a directed trustee shall have no duty to review the actions of an exclusive *powerholder*.[82] It would insulate the directed trustee from liability for losses occasioned by following, pursuant to the terms of the trust, the *powerholder's* directions, or for the actions and inactions of the *powerholder* generally.[83] Whether a directed trustee who knowingly assists a powerholder in breaching the *powerholder's* fiduciary duties could escape liability altogether remains to be seen.

If proper administration of the trust depends upon directions and/or consents that have not been forthcoming, then the directed trustee would have a fiduciary duty to apply to the court for instructions.[84] This assumes that the powerholder has been informed of the problem, yet has chosen, for whatever reason, not to exercise the directory power. If all else fails, the directed trustee

---

[75] UTC §808(b) (available at <http://www.uniformlaws.org/Act.aspx?title=Trust%20Code>).

[76] Restatement (Third) of Trusts §74.

[77] UTC §808(d) (available at <http://www.uniformlaws.org/Act.aspx?title=Trust%20Code>); Restatement (Third) of Trusts §75 cmt. e.

[78] UTC §808(d) (available at <http://www.uniformlaws.org/Act.aspx?title=Trust%20Code>); Restatement (Third) of Trusts §75 cmt. f.

[79] Restatement (Third) of Trusts §75 cmt. f.

[80] Restatement (Third) of Trusts §75 cmt. e. *Cf.* §7.2.4 of this handbook (cofiduciary and predecessor liability and contribution). *See generally* 3 Scott & Ascher §16.7 (Effect of Power to Direct or Control Trustee).

[81] Restatement (Third) of Trusts §75 cmt. e. *Cf.* §7.2.4 of this handbook (cofiduciary and predecessor liability and contribution). *See generally* 3 Scott & Ascher §16.7 (Effect of Power to Direct or Control Trustee).

[82] RSA 564-B: 12-1204.

[83] RSA 564-B: 12-1205.

[84] Restatement (Third) of Trusts §75 cmt. g; 3 Scott & Ascher §16.7 (Effect of Power to Direct or Control Trustee).

might even have a duty to attempt to remove powerholders from the equation altogether by bringing a complaint for equitable deviation.[85]

The entrusted nongeneral power of appointment. In the case of a nongeneral power that may be exercised in further trust (Special Power #1), any grant of another nongeneral power of appointment incident to the exercise in further trust (Special Power #2) must be for the benefit of the permissible appointees of Special Power #1.[86] Under the Restatement (First) of Property, only a permissible appointee of Special Power #1 could be a grantee of Special Power #2.[87] The topic of exercising powers of appointment in further trust is taken up in Section 8.1.2 of this handbook. Powers of appointment generally are covered in Section 8.1.1 of this handbook.

Under the Restatement (Third) of Property (Wills and Other Donative Transfers), specifically Section 19.14, however, *an impermissible appointee of Special Power #1* may be a grantee as well.[88] The impermissible appointee, however, holds Special Power #2 in "confidence" for the benefit of the permissible appointees of Special Power #1. Unexplained in the commentary and reporter's notes to Section 19.14 is whether the impermissible appointee assumes any fiduciary duties incident to his stewardship of Special Power #2.

Here is the only guidance proffered, guidance that is fraught with ambiguity: "Because the donor has imposed confidence in the donee to select which permissible appointees to benefit by an appointment, the donee is authorized to grant the selection power to any other person."[89] Certainly the original donee is not a fiduciary, even under the logic of the guidance proffered. That is settled law.[90] The status of the donee's surrogate, however, is another matter. Loaded words like "confidence" and "benefit" suggest that the donee's surrogate may well be holding the Special Power #2 itself in trust for the benefit of the Special Power #1's permissible appointees. If that is the case, then it is not entirely clear how the fiduciary duties of the surrogate are to be coordinated with those of the trustee of the subject (appointive) property itself. Recall our discussion above of the ambiguous status of the trust protector, at least in certain situations. In any case, presumably, a breach of the surrogate's duty of confidence would constitute in the first instance and at minimum a fraud on Special Power #1. The fraud on a special power doctrine is taken up in Section 8.15.26 of this handbook.

A directory power held in a nonfiduciary capacity. One easily can conjure up situations where someone with a power to direct or otherwise control the actions of the trustee would not be a fiduciary. A power, for example, granted to a surviving spouse to invest in a residence or to prevent the sale of

---

[85] *See* §8.15.20 of this handbook (doctrine of equitable deviation).

[86] Restatement (Third) of Property (Wills and Other Donative Transfers) §19.14.

[87] Restatement (First) of Property §359(2) ("The donee of a special power can effectively exercise it by creating in an object an interest for life and a special power to appoint among persons all of whom are objects of the original power, unless the donor manifests a contrary intent.").

[88] Restatement (Third) of Property (Wills and Other Donative Transfers) §19.14, cmt. g(4).

[89] Restatement (Third) of Property (Wills and Other Donative Transfers) §19.14, cmt. g(4).

[90] *See* §8.1.1 of this handbook (powers of appointment).

entrusted real estate in which he or she is living would not be a power held in a fiduciary capacity.[91] Change the facts slightly, and we have a power of appointment, *e.g.*, the power to direct the trustee to distribute the real estate outright and free of trust to the power holder or someone else.[92] "Ultimately, the purposes of a power and the nature and extent of the rights, duties, and liabilities of the power holder, and thus also of the trustee, depend upon trust language and all relevant circumstances."[93] In any case, a power that is for the sole benefit of the powerholder is not a fiduciary power.[94] The trustee, however, has a fiduciary duty to make sure that the terms of the power, to the extent it is exercised, are honored.[95]

Information to which a powerholder is entitled. A prospective trustee of a trust under which a nonbeneficiary is to be granted a power to control certain actions of the trustee should insist that the governing instrument clearly spell out what the trustee's duties shall be when it comes to furnishing the power-holder with accountings and other information about the trust.[96] After all, under default law the trustee has a countervailing duty to the beneficiaries of confidentiality.[97] This should be done whether the exercise of the power is to be permissive or mandatory.[98] Presumably, when a power to control is mandatory and extensive, the powerholder's right to information about the trust is virtually absolute, as is the trustee's duty proactively to furnish the powerholder with that information.[99]

Death or incapacity of a powerholder. The governing instrument also should address the contingency of the incapacity or death of the powerholder before the trust's termination.[100] In the event of incapacity, is the power suspended?[101] May it be exercised by proxy?[102] In the event of death, does the directory or veto power terminate?[103] If not, what is the replacement mechanism? These are just some of the questions that need to be addressed in the governing instrument.[104] When they are not, there is always a risk that down the

---

[91] *See generally* 3 Scott & Ascher §16.7 (Effect of Power to Direct or Control Trustee).

[92] *See generally* §8.1 of this handbook (powers of appointment).

[93] Restatement (Third) of Trusts §75 cmt. c(1).

[94] Restatement (Third) of Trusts §75 cmt. d.

[95] Restatement (Third) of Trusts §75 cmt. d. *See generally* §8.15.26 of this handbook (fraud on the power doctrine).

[96] Restatement (Third) of Trusts §75 cmt. b(1).

[97] *See generally* §5.4.1.1 of this handbook (beneficiary's right to information and confidentiality) and §6.2.3 of this handbook (trustee's duty of confidentiality).

[98] *See generally* 3 Scott & Ascher §16.7 (Effect of Power to Direct or Control Trustee).

[99] *See generally* §5.4.1.1 of this handbook (trust beneficiary's right to information and confidentiality) and §6.2.3 of this handbook (trustee's duty of confidentiality); 3 Scott & Ascher §16.7 (Effect of Power to Direct or Control Trustee).

[100] For some default law, *see* Restatement (Third) of Trusts §75 cmt. g(1).

[101] *See generally* 3 Scott & Ascher §16.7 (Effect of Power to Direct or Control Trustee).

[102] *Cf.* §8.2.2.2 of this handbook (the revocable trust) (discussing the exercise of rights of revocation by conservators and agents acting under durable powers of attorney).

[103] *See generally* 3 Scott & Ascher §16.7 (Effect of Power to Direct or Control Trustee).

[104] *See generally* 3 Scott & Ascher §16.7 (Effect of Power to Direct or Control Trustee).

road the trustee will have a fiduciary duty to get the answers from a court,[105] as well as a right to deduct the attendant costs from the trust estate.[106] This is because the applicable default law is in a state of considerable flux, and is likely to remain so for some time:

> A number of older cases held that a trustee's power of sale that was subject to the consent of a third person terminated on the death of the third person. It would seem, however, that the result ought generally to differ these days, now that it is more widely understood that it is ordinarily better to empower, than to restrict, trustees' powers. The Restatement (Third) of Trusts takes the position that, upon the death or disability of the powerholder or the release of the power, the trustee is generally authorized to proceed with the administration of the trust as if the power had never existed.[107]

A trustee's power to delegate certain functions may expand the class of acceptable trustee candidates. There have been some recent developments on the delegation front[108] as well that a prospective settlor needs to take into account when looking for the right trustee. The Uniform Prudent Investor Act, versions of which have been adopted in a number of jurisdictions, has reversed the common law default rule that a trustee may not delegate investment *and management* functions.[109] The Act provides that a trustee will not be liable "to the beneficiaries or to the trust" for the decision or actions of his agents, provided the trustee exercises reasonable care, skill, and caution in selecting the agents, establishes the scope and terms of their responsibilities, and periodically monitors their activities.[110] The common law private trustees now have the same incentive to parcel out investment and management responsibilities to third parties that their ERISA counterparts have had since 1974.[111]

In language that tracks the spirit if not the letter of the Prudent Investor Rule, the Uniform Trust Code grants a trustee general authority to delegate "duties and powers that a prudent trustee of comparable skills could properly delegate under the circumstances."[112] In other words, whether there has been prudent delegation of a particular duty is dependent on the facts and circumstances of the particular trust relationship.[113] "For example, delegating some

---

[105] Restatement (Third) of Trusts §75 cmt. g(1).

[106] *See generally* §3.5.2.3 of this handbook (trustee's right in equity to exoneration and reimbursement from the trust estate to include the payment of the trustee's attorneys' fees).

[107] 3 Scott & Ascher §16.7 (Effect of Power to Direct or Control Trustee).

[108] *See generally* §6.1.4 of this handbook (trustee's duty not to delegate critical functions).

[109] Uniform Prudent Investor Act, *Prefatory Note*, 7B U.L.A. 280, 281 (2000). The Uniform Prudent Investor Act with the referenced prefatory note is available on the Internet at <http://www.uniformlaws.org/Act.aspx?title=Trust%20Code> as Article 9 of the UTC.

[110] Uniform Prudent Investor Act §9.

[111] ERISA §3(21)(A) (ERISA is the acronym for Employee Retirement Income Security Act of 1974, a topic we take up in §9.5.1 of this handbook).

[112] UTC §807(a) (available at <http://www.uniformlaws.org/Act.aspx?title=Trust%20Code>).

[113] UTC §807 cmt. (available at <http://www.uniformlaws.org/Act.aspx?title=Trust%20Code>).

administrative and reporting duties might be prudent for a family trustee but unnecessary for a corporate trustee."[114] A trustee who exercises reasonable care, skill, and caution in delegating his duties is not liable to the beneficiaries or the trust for an action of the agent to whom the function was delegated.[115] As between the trustee and the beneficiary, the beneficiary now would bear the loss.[116] The beneficiary's only recourse would be to the agent: "In performing a delegated function, an agent owes a duty to the trust to exercise reasonable care to comply with the terms of the delegation."[117]

From the perspective of the prospective settlor seeking the right trustee, this ability of a trustee to shift primary liability for failing to prudently carry out a particular investment or management function onto the shoulders of a third party, can be both a good thing and a bad thing. For the prospective settlor who has been coming up dry, it can open up the field of eligible trustee candidates to those who do not have investment or management expertise. On the other hand, the prospective settlor may not be entirely comfortable with the prospect of having important investment and management responsibilities shunted off to strangers. This is understandable. "The traditional prohibition on the delegation of discretionary duties, or the duties that trustees would be expected to perform themselves, was founded upon the belief that the typical trustee has been selected because of the settlor's confidence in the personal qualities and skills of the trustee."[118]

In any case, it is probably best that the prospective settlor and prospective trustee hammer out in advance what limitations, if any, are to be placed on the trustee's authority to delegate. The extent of the trustee's authority to delegate should then be set forth in the governing instrument. The prospective settlor may want to consider including in the governing instrument provisions that (1) limit or eliminate the trustee's authority to delegate specified functions; (2) expressly allocate responsibilities, such as investment management, to third parties;[119] and/or (3) establish criteria for the selection of the trustee's agents. A provision requiring that the trustee retain a particular lawyer to represent the trustee in trust matters, however, most likely would not be enforceable. Luckily, the Act's provisions are default rules.

---

[114] UTC §807 cmt. (available at <http://www.uniformlaws.org/Act.aspx?title=Trust%20Code>).

[115] UTC §807(c) (available at <http://www.uniformlaws.org/Act.aspx?title=Trust%20Code>).

[116] UTC §807(c) (available at <http://www.uniformlaws.org/Act.aspx?title=Trust%20Code>).

[117] Uniform Prudent Investor Act §9(b).

[118] Jerome J. Curtis, Jr., *The Transmogrification of the American Trust*, 3 Real Prop. Prob. & Tr. J. 251, 273 (1996).

[119] *See generally* 3 Scott & Ascher §16.7 (Effect of Power to Direct or Control Trustee).

For the public policy arguments in favor of the Act's delegation provisions, the reader is referred to John H. Langbein.[120] For the other view, the reader is referred to Jerome J. Curtis, Jr.[121]

When the scrivener has an affiliation with a prospective trustee. A final word of caution for trustee-seeking settlors and their lawyers: A prospective settlor would be well advised to shop around before selecting an individual or corporation with whom the settlor's lawyer has an informal or formal business referral relationship. As for the lawyer, he or she would be well advised not to "allow related business interests to affect representation, for example, by referring clients to an enterprise in which the lawyer has an undisclosed interest."[122]

§3.3   Involuntary Trustees: Constructive Trusts, Purchase Money Resulting Trusts, Trustee Succession, Deceased Trustees, Partnership Assets, Government Regulation of Property Ownership, and Other Such Matters

There are many synonyms for the constructive trust. It has frequently been called a trust ex maleficio or ex delicto because it is based on the wrongful conduct of the trustee. Other authorities lay emphasis on the lack of any intention on the part of the trustee to be such, and thus call it a trust in invitum, or an involuntary trust.[1]

In several states, statutes provide that anyone to whom property is transferred in violation of a trust holds as involuntary trustee under the trust, unless the transferee purchased in good faith and for a valuable consideration.[2]

---

[120] *The Uniform Prudent Investor Act and the Future of Trust Investing*, 81 Iowa L. Rev. 641 (1996).

[121] *The Transmogrification of the American Trust*, 31 Real Prop. Prob. & Tr. J. 251 (1996).

[122] Mass. Rules of Professional Conduct Rule 1.7 cmt. [6]. The lawyer making the referral would be an agent of the client who is shopping for trustees. This type of agency is a fiduciary relationship. As a fiduciary, the lawyer has a duty to the client of full disclosure. *See generally* Chapter 1 of this handbook (containing in part a definition of the term *fiduciary*). The lawyer has a duty to his client of undivided loyalty as well. If the lawyer is simultaneously in a de facto agency relationship with the individual or corporation to whom he is referring clients for trust services, the lawyer runs the risk of at best violating the duty of undivided loyalty and at worst engaging in self-dealing. *See generally* §6.1.3.3 of this handbook (discussing in part the multidisciplinary practice concept).

§3.3 [1] Bogert §471.

[2] 5 Scott & Ascher §29.1.5. *See generally* §8.15.63 of this handbook (doctrine of bona fide purchase).

With the following exceptions, one cannot be forced to serve as a trustee:

Absence of successor trustee. Once a trusteeship is voluntarily accepted, the law may require a sole trustee to remain in office until a qualified successor is in place.[3] Thus a trustee who at some point wants to resign may end up serving a portion of the trusteeship involuntarily. This is yet one more reason why the decision to serve as a trustee is not to be taken lightly.

Deceased trustee's personal representative. If the trustee dies and there is no provision for a successor, the trustee's personal representatives or those having an interest in the trustee's personal estate may find themselves de facto successor trustees until such time as qualified successors are in place.[4]

The constructive trust.[5] It is said that the "[c]onstructive trust is the principal device for vindicating equitable ownership against conflicting legal title."[6] A constructive trust arises "by operation of law" and thus can only be imposed by some court.[7] There are two broad categories of constructive trust, the institutional constructive trust, and the remedial constructive trust.[8] "Institutional constructive trusts are trusts which arise from some pre-existing fiduciary relationship before or apart from any breach of trust or duty, whereas remedial constructive trusts are imposed where no fiduciary relationship previously existed."[9] Each category of constructive trust has its own sub-categories.[10] Also there is the institutional/remedial constructive trust hybrid that is judicially imposed in response to the breach of an express trust, such as a breach of the trustee's critical duty not to engage in unauthorized self-dealing, a topic that we cover in Section 6.1.3 of this handbook.[11]

In Section 7.2.3.1 of this handbook, we consider whether the proprietary remedial constructive trust itself is an equitable remedy or whether it is merely a part of the process of laying the groundwork for such equitable remedies as restitution, injunction, and specific performance, in other words, merely a remedial device. Having allowed the person wronged to trace a particular item of property and having imposed a constructive trust upon it, the court then fashions whatever remedies are appropriate to make the beneficiary whole. Still, the imposition of a constructive trust on traceable property is a remedy in

---

[3] *See generally* Bogert §§511–512; 2 Scott on Trusts §106.1. *See also* UTC §707(a) (available at <http://www.uniformlaws.org/Act.aspx?title=Trust%20Code>) (providing that unless a cotrustee remains in office or the court otherwise orders, and until the trust property is delivered to a successor trustee or other person entitled to it, a trustee who has resigned or been removed has the duties of a trustee and the powers necessary to protect the trust property).

[4] *See generally* Bogert §529.

[5] The word *constructive* is derived from the verb *construe*, not from the word *construct*.

[6] Restatement (Third) of Restitution and Unjust Enrichment §55, cmt. a.

[7] Lewin ¶7-02.

[8] Lewin ¶7-11.

[9] Lewin ¶7-11.

[10] Lewin ¶7-12 (institutional constructive trust sub-categories); ¶7-13 (remedial constructive trust sub-categories).

[11] Lewin ¶7-12.

the sense that it freezes the status quo, *i.e.*, it prevents the transferee from consuming the property or passing it on to third parties.

The proprietary remedial constructive trustee's primary responsibility is to get title and possession safely into the hands of the rightful owner. "[I]f the trustee in breach of trust transfers trust property to a third person who knows of the breach, the third person holds the property on a constructive trust for the beneficiaries,"[12] the third person not being a BFP.[13] A proprietary remedial constructive trustee of property, though, may pass good title to a BFP. A proprietary remedial constructive trustee, however, may not in breach of trust enter into a specifically enforceable contract to sell the property to a third party or in breach of trust declare himself trustee of the property for the benefit of the third party.[14] Equity will not compel a trustee to commit or complete a breach of trust.[15]

But is the proprietary remedial constructive trust more than a remedy or remedial device? Is it also a true trust? Could it possibly be both? According to the Restatement of Restitution (1937) it is not a true trust.[16] This has come to be known as the American view.[17] The proprietary remedial constructive trust is an involuntary arrangement, or so the reasoning goes, whereas the express trust is the product of the voluntary reordering of rights, duties, and obligations with respect to property.[18] The trustee of an express trust, it is asserted, is a fiduciary; the trustee of a proprietary remedial constructive trust is not.[19] The proprietary remedial constructive trust, as is the case with the compensatory remedial constructive trust, is just a remedy, Equity's answer to the law's quasi contract.[20] 1937 marks the year when the constructive trust was formally "lopped off" from the Restatement of Trusts and "folded into" the Restatement of Restitution.[21]

The Restatement of Restitution's authors, however, did concede "that both in the case of an express trust and in that of a constructive trust one person holds the title to the property subject to an equitable duty to hold the property for or to convey it to another, and the latter has in each case some kind of an equitable interest in the property."[22] Moreover, they offered no explanation for why, as a matter of public policy or otherwise, the involuntariness of a proprietary remedial constructive trust should make it something other than a true

---

[12] 4 Scott on Trusts §282. *See generally* §5.4.1.8 of this handbook (right and standing of beneficiary to proceed instead of trustee against those with whom the trustee has contracted, against tortfeasors, and against the trustee's agents, *i.e.*, against third parties).

[13] *See generally* §8.15.63 of this handbook (doctrine of bona fide purchase; the BFP).

[14] 5 Scott & Ascher §29.1.3.

[15] 5 Scott & Ascher §29.1.3.

[16] Restatement of Restitution §160, cmt. a.

[17] Harold Greville Hanbury & Ronald Harling Maudsley, Modern Equity 310–311 (10th ed. 1976) (the American view); Lewin ¶7-13 (the "purely remedial" trust as a "North American" invention).

[18] Restatement of Restitution §160, cmt. a.

[19] Restatement of Restitution §160, cmt. a.

[20] Restatement of Restitution §160, cmt. a.

[21] Andrew Kull, *Restitution and Reform*, 32 S. Ill. U. L. J. 83, 92 (2007).

[22] Restatement of Restitution §160 cmt. a.

trust. Just because a duck has been artificially inseminated does not make it any less of a duck.[23] Can it really be said that the proprietary remedial constructive trustee of *X*'s property owes *X* no fiduciary duties? While it would go too far to suggest that a proprietary remedial constructive trustee without notice has a duty to invest the subject property, or should be held "to the usual standard of *exacta diligentia* which is required of express trustees in the performance of their duties," at minimum, the proprietary remedial constructive trustee will have a duty to get title and possession safely into the hands of its rightful owner, as would be the case with the trustee of an express trust that has terminated.[24]

The proprietary remedial constructive trust and the express trust share other critical characteristics as well. A proprietary remedial constructive trustee, for example, may be entitled to indemnity from the subject property, for the costs and expenses incurred in obtaining the property, or in effecting improvements that benefit the property.[25] He who seeks equity, in this case, the one who seeks imposition of a constructive trust, must do equity.[26]

And then there is the inconvenient issue of when the constructive trust is deemed to have come into existence, at the time of unjust enrichment or at the time of the equitable decree. As the Restatement (Third) of Restitution and Unjust Enrichment takes as a given that the constructive trust is not a true trust, that it is simply a "metaphor" for a composite of two equitable remedies, one procedural and one substantive, it would prefer not to take a stand either way.[27] The very question is inappropriate, or "artificial," its word.[28] The procedural remedy is simply a judicial declaration that B's title to property is subject to a superior equitable claim. The substantive remedy is simply a mandatory injunction directing B to surrender title to the equitable claimant. That's it. There is nothing more than that going on. But if the question must be answered, let it be answered by complementary metaphor: " . . . [T]he constructive trust 'exists' from the moment of the transaction on which restitution is based; or (if the court prefers) that the constructive trust arises on the date of judgment, but that the state of title it describes 'relates back' to the transaction between the parties."[29]

Since 1936 American academics have been having more than a little difficulty convincingly rationalizing away the inconvenient reality that the constructive trust straddles trust doctrine and unjust enrichment doctrine, that it is not susceptible to being entirely pigeon-holed into either's restatement. But so what? Aren't such loose ends what make the Anglo-American legal tradition

---

[23] The English would agree. *See generally* Lewin ¶7-13 ("Remedial constructive trusts can be subdivided into *proprietary* and *compensatory* remedial constructive trusts, to which may be added a transatlantic *purely remedial* trust, which has not yet reached . . . [England's] . . . shores").

[24] Harold Greville Hanbury & Ronald Harling Maudsley, Modern Equity 308–309 (10th ed. 1976).

[25] Lewin ¶21-21.

[26] *See generally* §8.12 of this handbook (where the trust is recognized outside the United States) which contains a catalog of equity maxims.

[27] Restatement (Third) of Restitution and Unjust Enrichment §55, cmt. b.

[28] Restatement (Third) of Restitution and Unjust Enrichment §55, cmt. e.

[29] Restatement (Third) of Restitution and Unjust Enrichment §55, cmt. e.

so jurisprudentially nimble and innovative? The very institution of the express trust, which essentially evolved from an equitable remedy, comes to mind in this regard.[30]

Certainly, English law is not in accord with the American view. Under English law, the proprietary remedial constructive trust still enjoys the status of a "substantive institution."[31] It has been asserted that since 1937 *no one* has considered any constructive trust a part of the law of trusts.[32] This may be the case, but only on this side of the Atlantic.

The pure institutional constructive trust sub-categories. The trustee *de son tort*, which is discussed in Section 8.15.35 of this handbook, is a sub-category of institutional constructive trust.[33] So is the quasi trust, which is discussed in Section 9.8.11 of this handbook.[34] Each relationship is voluntary on the part of the fiduciary.[35]

The pure remedial constructive trust and its sub-categories. The pure remedial constructive trust has two sub-categories, the proprietary remedial constructive trust, which involves identifiable property, and the compensatory remedial constructive trust, which does not.[36] Neither involves a preexisting trust relationship.[37]

A *pure proprietary remedial constructive trust* is imposed when equity determines that a nonfiduciary who has been unjustly enriched must transfer property *in specie* (in kind) to whoever is legally or equitably entitled to the property.[38] The parties are not in a preexisting trust or fiduciary relationship.[39] One who is unjustly enriched is unjustifiably enriched, that is to say there is no legal or equitable basis for the enrichment.[40] The proprietary remedial constructive trust is judicially imposed on the subject property to facilitate equitable remedies, the primary remedy being the remedy of restitution.[41]

---

[30] *See generally* §8.15.1 of this handbook.

[31] Harold Greville Hanbury & Ronald Harling Maudsley, Modern Equity 311 (10th ed. 1976)

[32] Andrew Kull, *Restitution and Reform*, 32 S. Ill. U. L. J. 83, 92 (2007).

[33] Lewin ¶7-15.

[34] Lewin ¶7-16.

[35] Lewin ¶7-12.

[36] Lewin ¶7-13.

[37] Lewin ¶7-13.

[38] Lewin ¶7-13 (England); Restatement of Restitution §163 (U.S.).

[39] Lewin ¶7-13.

[40] Restatement (Third) of Restitution and Unjust Enrichment §1, cmt. b (Discussion Draft, 2000).

[41] If, for example, "the owner of an interest in land transfers it to another upon an oral agreement for other land in exchange, and if the transferee relies on a statute of frauds in refusing to perform the agreement, the transferee holds the interest thereby acquired on a constructive trust for the transferor." Restatement (Third) of Trusts §24 cmt. d(1). Similar relief would be available to the settlor or the intended beneficiaries had the transfer been "in trust." Restatement (Third) of Trusts §24 cmt. g & h. In other words, the transferee may not retain the property for himself simply because the transferor has failed to comply with the statute of frauds. *See generally* §8.15.5 of this handbook (statute of frauds). *See generally* Restatement of Restitution §160.

If a person contractually or otherwise comes into possession of real or personal property as a result of fraud,[42] duress,[43] undue influence,[44] or some other such intentional wrong, he will hold the property not for himself or the perpetrator of the wrong but as a proprietary remedial constructive trustee for the person who, but for the wrong, would have received the property.[45] The proprietary remedial constructive trustee has an affirmative duty to transfer the legal title to the person wronged, and until that is accomplished a limited fiduciary duty not to harm, or allow others to harm, the property.[46] The fiduciary powers of a proprietary remedial constructive trustee are generally not disclaimable.[47] In the case of a wrongful transfer of property incident to a contract or otherwise, if the transferee occupies the dominant position in a confidential relationship with the transferor, then the element of fraud or undue influence need not be present for a proprietary remedial constructive trust to be imposed on the property, nor would the element of procurement for that matter.[48] The transferee need only have been unjustly enriched.[49] As the proprietary remedial constructive trust can arise even in the case of a transfer of land upon an oral trust,[50] the equitable device is said to be an exception to the

---

[42] 1 Scott & Ascher §6.11.1 (noting that "[i]f B, by a consciously false representation of fact, induces A to transfer land to B, who orally agrees to hold the land in trust or to reconvey it, it is clear that B may not keep the land"). *See also* 6 Scott & Ascher §43.1.1; Restatement of Restitution §166.

[43] Restatement of Restitution §166.

[44] Restatement of Restitution §166.

[45] 1 Scott & Ascher §6.11.1. *See, e.g.,* Nile v. Nile, 432 Mass. 390, 734 N.E.2d 1153 (2000) (upholding the imposition of a constructive trust on the assets of the decedent's revocable inter vivos trust in order to secure the decedent's obligations under a postdivorce settlement agreement between the decedent and his former wife); Lackey v. Lackey, 691 So. 2d 990 (Miss. 1997) (trust beneficiary entitled to have constructive trust imposed on proceeds of life insurance policy purchased with property embezzled from trust). *See generally* Bogert §§473 (Fraudulent Misrepresentation or Concealment), 474 (Mistake, Undue Influence, and Duress); Restatement of Restitution §166.

[46] Lewin ¶7-19.

[47] *Cf.* Uniform Probate Code §2-1102 cmt. (noting that the Uniform Disclaimer of Property Interests Act does not cover constructive trusts). *See generally* §3.5.3.4 of this handbook (the power of a trustee of an express trust to disclaim a fiduciary power).

[48] *See* 1 Scott & Ascher §6.11.2 (suggesting that the abuse of the confidential relationship can be merely the transferee's failure to do with the property what he said he would do). *See also* Restatement of Restitution §183, cmt. e.

[49] Restatement of Restitution §183, cmt. e.; 1 Scott & Ascher §6.11.2. If the payor of the part of the purchase price of a parcel of land *orally* agrees with the grantee that the payor shall have an interest in the land that is *greater* than the fractional interest in the land that corresponds to the fraction of the purchase price paid by the payor, then the payor is entitled either to the imposition of a purchase money resulting trust on just the fractional interest or a restitution of the amounts that were paid out, assuming the grantee refuses to perform the agreement. *See generally* 6 Scott & Ascher §43.7.1. If, however, the parties are in a fiduciary or confidential relationship in which the grantee is the dominant party and if the oral agreement is incident to an abuse of that relationship, then the payor may be entitled to the imposition of a constructive trust on the portion of the land that was orally agreed upon, or possibly even on the entire parcel. 6 Scott & Ascher §43.7.1.

[50] *See generally* Restatement of Restitution §183; 1 Scott & Ascher, ch. 6. Note that the trustee of an oral trust of land may pass good title to a personal creditor of the trustee who acts in good

statute of frauds.[51] We discuss the statute of frauds insofar as it may apply to trusts in Section 8.15.5 of this handbook. The Restatement of Restitution would impose certain limitations on the enforceability of oral trusts of land: "Where the owner of an interest in land transfers it inter vivos to another upon an oral trust in favor of a third person or upon an oral agreement to convey the land to a third person, and the trust or agreement is unenforceable because of the Statute of Frauds, and the transferee refuses to perform the trust or agreement, he holds the interest upon a . . . [proprietary remedial] . . . constructive trust for the third person, if, but only if, (a) the transferee by fraud, duress or undue influence induced the transferor not to create an enforceable interest in the third person, or (b) the transferee at the time of the transfer was in a confidential relation to the transferor, or (c) the transfer was made by the transferor in contemplation of death."[52]

Unjust enrichment occasioned by an innocent mistake also can give rise to a proprietary remedial constructive trust.[53] Here is an example:

> A, the owner of land, makes a gratuitous conveyance to B. By a mistake in the description in the deed, A transfers not only the tract which he intended to convey but also a second tract which he did not intend to include. B does not know of the mistake and believes that A intended to transfer both tracts. B holds the second tract upon a constructive trust for A.[54]

Courts also have imposed proprietary remedial constructive trusts to accommodate the intentions and purposes of settlors of secret and semi-secret trusts.[55] Such "trusts" are covered in Section 9.9.6 of this handbook.[56] The Restatement of Restitution explains: "Where a testator devises or bequeaths property to a person relying upon his agreement to hold the property in trust for or to convey it to a third person, the devisee or legatee holds the property upon a . . . [proprietary remedial] . . . constructive trust for the third person."[57] The reason for the rule is to prevent the devisee or legatee from being unjustly enriched.[58] Also, "[w]here a person dies intestate relying upon an agreement by

---

faith and gives value, provided the trust beneficiary by word or deed caused the creditor to reasonably rely on the trustee's apparent ownership. *See* 5 Scott & Ascher §29.5.1 (Rights of Creditors When Beneficiaries Are Estopped). *See generally* §§5.4.2 of this handbook (rights of the beneficiary as against transferees of the underlying property, including BFPs) and 8.15.63 of this handbook (doctrine of bona fide purchase; the BFP). Otherwise, "a creditor of the trustee ordinarily takes subject to the trust, even though the creditor has attached or levied on trust property without notice of the trust." 5 Scott & Ascher §29.5.1.

[51] *See* §8.15.5 of this handbook (statute of frauds); Restatement of Restitution §183.

[52] Restatement of Restitution §183.

[53] Restatement of Restitution §163, cmt. a.

[54] Restatement of Restitution §163 cmt. b, illus. 1.

[55] *See generally* §9.9.6 of this handbook (secret and semi-secret trusts); Restatement of Restitution §186, cmt. c.

[56] *See also* Restatement of Restitution §186 (Agreement by Person Taking under Will or by Intestacy).

[57] Restatement of Restitution §186.

[58] Restatement of Restitution §186. cmt. b.

his heir or next of kin to hold the property which he acquires by such intestacy in trust for or to convey it to a third person, the heir or next of kind holds the property upon a . . . [proprietary remedial] . . . constructive trust for the third person."[59]

The compensatory remedial constructive trust. In both the United States and England, a compensatory remedial constructive trust is not a true trust; it is a pure equitable remedy.[60] "The remedy here is merely personal. The defendant is misleadingly said to be compelled to 'account as constructive trustee,' but this only means that the defendant must account *as if he were*, or *in the same manner as*, a trustee, which he is not in any sense."[61] In the United States, the compensatory remedial constructive trust is the typical remedy for intellectual property rights infringement. For more on the subject of the intersection of intellectual property law and equity the reader is referred to Charles E. Rounds, Jr., Relief for IP Rights Is Primarily Equitable: How American Legal Education Is Short-Changing the 21st Century Corporate Litigator.[62]

The constructive trust that arises incident to a breach of fiduciary duty: an institutional/remedial hybrid. The institutional/remedial constructive trust hybrid is imposed to facilitate the equitable remedy of restitution for unjust enrichment in the context of a breach of a duty incident to an express trust or agency relationship, provided the breach relates somehow to the administration and/or disposition of identifiable property.[63] The panoply of equitable remedies that may be available to a beneficiary for a breach of trust is generally discussed in Section 7.2.3 of this handbook. One English commentator explains why such a constructive trust, which he ultimately elects to file in the institutional pigeon hole, is really an institutional/remedial hybrid:

> In a third category, institutional trusts are imposed by operation of law on someone who has accepted or assumed a fiduciary position in circumstances such that it would be unconscionable for the fiduciary to assert a personal beneficial interest in property acquired as fiduciary and deny the beneficial interest of those for whom the fiduciary undertook to act. In these cases the person on whom the trust is imposed is seeking to retain the trust property beneficially, which the law will not allow, so it would be possible to classify them as remedial, . . . but such trustees have accepted or assumed their fiduciary positions willingly and are therefore treated very much like ordinary express trustees, as with trustees *de son tort* and *quasi* trustees, so we include these among the institutional constructive trusts.[64]

---

[59] Restatement of Restitution §186.

[60] Lewin ¶7-13.

[61] Lewin ¶7-13.

[62] 26 Santa Clara Computer & High Tech. L. J. 313 (2010).

[63] Restatement of Restitution §190. *See, e.g.,* Gagnon v. Coombs, 39 Mass. App. Ct. 144, 654 N.E.2d 54 (1995) ("Gagnon, as a principal whose agent [Joan] violated her fiduciary duties, is entitled to a judgment ordering Joan, who stands as constructive trustee for his benefit with respect to the Shelburne property, to reconvey the property to him.").

[64] Lewin ¶7-12.

Thus, a fiduciary self-dealing transaction not only can result in an award of equitable damages, a topic that is covered in Section 7.3.3.2 of this handbook, but also simultaneously or in the alternative in the imposition of a constructive trust as a prelude to the issuing of a restitution, injunction, or specific performance order. The Restatement of Restitution explains: "Where a person in a fiduciary relation to another acquires property, and the acquisition or retention is in violation of his duty as fiduciary, he holds it upon a constructive trust for the other."[65] In the United States, a self-dealing indenture trustee could well suffer a similar fate.[66] Even a minor trustee who misappropriates trust property can be chargeable as a constructive trustee.[67] In Section 6.1.3 of this handbook we catalog some self-dealing transactions that would constitute a breach of the duty of loyalty if committed by a trustee, absent special facts, such as the beneficiary having given his or her informed consent.[68] Here are a few such transactions that might well warrant the imposition of a constructive trust:

- Purchase by fiduciary individually of property entrusted to him as fiduciary[69]
- Sale of fiduciary's individual property to himself as fiduciary[70]
- Purchase by fiduciary of property, which he should purchase for the beneficiary[71]
- Renewal of lease by fiduciary[72]
- Purchase by fiduciary of an encumbrance upon property held by him as fiduciary[73]
- Bonus or commission received by fiduciary[74]
- Profit made by the disposition of the beneficiary's property[75]
- Competition by fiduciary[76]
- Using confidential information[77]

As noted, profits incident to a breach of fiduciary duty can be the subject of a constructive trust. In England, if a trustee without authority profits from the trust estate, then a constructive trust may be imposed upon the profit, whether

[65] Restatement of Restitution §190.
[66] *See generally* §9.31 of this handbook (corporate trusts; trusts to secure creditors; The Trust Indenture Act of 1939; protecting bondholders).
[67] 4 Scott & Ascher §24.20 (Liability of Trustee Under Incapacity).
[68] Restatement of Restitution §191 (Effect of Consent of Beneficiary).
[69] Restatement of Restitution §192.
[70] Restatement of Restitution §193.
[71] Restatement of Restitution §194.
[72] Restatement of Restitution §195.
[73] Restatement of Restitution §196.
[74] Restatement of Restitution §197.
[75] Restatement of Restitution §198.
[76] Restatement of Restitution §199.
[77] Restatement of Restitution §200.

in cash or in kind, for the benefit of the beneficiaries,[78] subject to a possible offset for the value of the trustee's skill and labor.[79] So also in the United States.[80]

A breach of fiduciary duty in the agency context also can give rise to a constructive trust.[81] Take, for example, the situation in which X asks Y to purchase on X's behalf a certain parcel of land from an *independent vendor.* Y orally agrees to do so.[82] Y (the agent), however, in violation of his *fiduciary duty* to X (the principal), proceeds instead to purchase *with his own money*, not X's money, the land for himself. A court may order Y to hold the land upon a constructive trust for X, with an appropriate offset for what Y had paid.[83] Were the parties in neither a confidential nor a fiduciary relationship, Y might well be allowed to keep the land, unless the arrangement had somehow been incident to an enforceable contract.[84] Had X even indirectly furnished the consideration for the land transaction, then Y might be ordered to hold the land upon a purchase money resulting trust for X's benefit.[85]

The Restatement (Third) of Trusts' contribution to constructive trust jurisprudence. The Restatement (Third) of Trusts suggests that a settlor of an inter vivos trust *who has committed no wrong* would become a constructive trustee of the trust property if the designated trustee declined to accept the trust after having taken title to the trust property, provided the terms of the trust made no provision for an alternate trustee.[86]

It also suggests that in some circumstances, a constructive trust may be employed to effectuate a failed gratuitous inter vivos transfer of property to a trustee due to a violation of the statute of frauds, or otherwise.[87] The court would impose the constructive trust after the property owner's incapacity or death in order to "prevent unjust enrichment of the property owner's successors in interest,"[88] although "it is crucial to keep in mind that the great weight

---

[78] *See* Lewin ¶20-28. The advantages of the constructive trust remedy over mere personal accountability are as follows: (1) The profit—if in traceable form—may be traced into the hands of the trustee or non-BFP third parties, who themselves could become constructive trustees of the profit; (2) the profit may be recoverable in the event of the trustee's insolvency; (3) the appreciation as well as the initial monetary value of the profit may accrue to the trust estate should the trustee invest the profit in an appreciating asset. *See generally* Lewin ¶20-29.

[79] *See generally* Lewin ¶20-30.

[80] *See generally* §6.1.3 of this handbook (trustee's duty of undivided loyalty); Restatement of Restitution §198 (Profit Made by the Disposition of the Beneficiary's Property).

[81] *See generally* §9.9.2 of this handbook (agency arrangements); Restatement of Restitution §190, cmt. a.

[82] *See generally* §9.9.2 of this handbook (agency arrangements).

[83] 6 Scott & Ascher §43.1.1.

[84] 6 Scott & Ascher §43.1.1. *See generally* §9.9.11 of this handbook (contracts to convey land).

[85] 6 Scott & Ascher §43.1.1.

[86] Restatement (Third) of Trusts §14 cmt. d.

[87] 1 Scott & Ascher §6.11.

[88] Restatement (Third) of Trusts §16(1). *See generally* 1 Scott & Ascher §6.11.4.

of American authority is to the effect that the transferee . . . [, *if he has committed no wrong, . . .*] may keep the property."[89]

Finally, there is the situation where land is transferred to someone upon an oral trust, not for the benefit of the person who paid the purchase price but for the benefit of a third party. Should the trust fail for unenforceability due to a violation of the writing requirements of the statute of frauds, it would seem that the property ought to revert to the payor upon an ordinary resulting trust, a topic we cover in Section 4.1.1.1 of this handbook.[90] The payor, after all, is the true settlor of the express trust, not the transferor of the legal title, the so-called vendor.[91] The Restatement (Third) of Trusts, however, would seem to disagree. It provides that the property perhaps ought to accrue to the payor upon a constructive trust.[92] Its rationale apparently is that the imposition of a purchase money resulting trust would not be appropriate in that there was no intention to benefit the payor.[93] But why an ordinary resulting trust should not be imposed is not entirely clear. In the case of the imposition of an ordinary resulting trust upon the failure of an express trust, for the benefit of a third party, the issue is not whether there was an intention to benefit the third party but whether there was an intention to make an outright gift of the subject property to the transferee.[94] If there was no such intention, then we have an "operation of law" situation regardless of what the terms of the failed express trust might have been.[95]

The power-in-trust doctrine and the constructive trust. If the donee of a *nonfiduciary*, nongeneral power of appointment allows the power to expire unexercised, the power-in-trust doctrine may be implicated, a topic we take up in Section 8.15.90 of this handbook. If it is, title to the appointive property is held *by the donor* of the power (or by the personal representative of the donor if the donor has predeceased the power's expiration) upon a constructive trust for the benefit of the permissible appointees, title to the appointive property having passed to the donor or his personal representative pursuant to the imposition of a resulting trust.

The proprietary remedial constructive trust and purchase money resulting trust compared. As we have discussed elsewhere, the express trust is founded on the

---

[89] 1 Scott & Ascher §6.11 (noting that while an English court would be reluctant because of the statute of frauds to declare a constructive trust in favor of the beneficiaries of a gratuitous oral trust of land, it would be more willing than an American court to declare a constructive trust in favor of the transferor). *See also* Restatement of Restitution §183, cmt. a.

[90] *See also* §8.15.5 of this handbook (statute of frauds).

[91] *See generally* §4.1.1.1 of this handbook (the settlor of an express trust is not necessarily the person designated as such in the governing documentation).

[92] Restatement (Third) of Trusts §9 cmt. e. *See also* 6 Scott & Ascher §43.2.2 (Unenforceable Express Agreement by Grantee to Hold in Trust).

[93] Restatement (Third) of Trusts §9 cmt. e. *See also* 6 Scott & Ascher §43.2.2 (Unenforceable Express Agreement by Grantee to Hold in Trust).

[94] *See generally* §4.1.1.1 of this handbook (the imposition of a resulting trust upon the failure of an express trust).

[95] *See generally* §4.1.1.1 of this handbook (the imposition of a resulting trust upon the failure of an express trust).

express or inferred intention of the settlor.[96] The resulting trust, on the other hand, is founded on the presumed but rebuttable intention of the transferor (or of the furnisher of consideration in the case of a purchase money resulting trust) that the person who takes the legal title not also take the beneficial interest.[97] Thus, if A by will were to devise property to B "as trustee" without ever having designated a beneficiary, the property would revert upon a non-purchase-money resulting trust to A's probate estate, A not having intended to devise to B any beneficial interest in the property.[98]

As we have seen, "a constructive trust is imposed not because of the intention of the parties but because the person holding the title to property would profit by a wrong or would be unjustly enriched if he were permitted to keep the property."[99] Thus, as we shall see next, "[w]hen A purchases property in B's name, intending that B would hold the property in trust for A, and A is induced by B to do so by fraud or undue influence, there are grounds for imposing either a . . . [purchase money] . . . resulting trust or a . . . [proprietary remedial] . . . constructive trust."[100]

On the other hand, the imposition of neither would be appropriate were B merely to renege on an oral agreement with A that B purchase *with B's own money* a piece of land in which A has no present interest and then sell the land to A. First, the agreement would be unenforceable at law for want of consideration and for violating the statute of frauds.[101] Second, equity would lack a rationale for intervening. As B had not loaned the purchase price to A, the equitable imposition of a purchase money resulting trust would not be warranted.[102] The equitable imposition of a constructive trust would not be warranted either. This is because B had not had a fiduciary relationship with A;[103] nor could it be said that A had had a "preexisting interest in the property that A permitted B to acquire, while relying upon B's promise to reconvey the property to A."[104]

The purchase-money resulting trust.[105] The non-purchase-money resulting trust we take up in Section 4.1.1.1 of this handbook. The purchase-money resulting trust is a somewhat different animal. A purchase-money resulting trust[106] can arise when property is purchased and the purchase price is paid by one person and at his direction the seller (vendor) transfers the

---

[96] *See* Chapter 1 of this handbook (defining the express trust). *See also* Lewin ¶7-02.

[97] *See generally* §4.1.1.1 of this handbook (the resulting trust and the equitable reversionary interest); Lewin ¶7-02. The purchase money resulting trust is discussed further on in this section.

[98] *See generally* §4.1.1.1 of this handbook (the non-purchase-money resulting trust).

[99] Restatement of Restitution §160, cmt. b.

[100] 6 Scott & Ascher §43.1.1.

[101] *See* 6 Scott & Ascher §43.1.1.

[102] *See* 6 Scott & Ascher §43.1.1.

[103] *See* 6 Scott & Ascher §43.1.1; Restatement of Restitution §182.

[104] *See* 6 Scott & Ascher §43.1.1.; Restatement of Restitution §182.

[105] *See generally* 5 Scott on Trusts §440; Bogert §454; Lewin ¶9-16 through ¶9-47 (England).

[106] *See generally* 5 Scott on Trusts §440.1. If *A* purchases land and puts the legal title in *B*'s name, or *A* gives *B* money to purchase land on *A*'s behalf, and if there is no intention by *A* to make a gift to *B*, a *purchase money resulting trust* will arise.

property to another person.[107] If there is no intention that the transferee take
the beneficial interest, the titleholder (*i.e.*, the resulting trustee) must turn the
property over to the person who paid the consideration.[108] "In most states, the
courts have held that when a contributor has contributed a part of the purchase
price, without intending to make either a loan or a gift, there is a resulting trust
for the contributor of an interest proportional to his or her contribution,
whether or not it was an aliquot part of the total purchase price, in the absence
of any other evidence of the parties' intentions."[109] The payment of the

---

[107] *See generally* 5 Scott on Trusts §440.1; 6 Scott & Ascher §43.1. "A . . . [purchase-money] .
. . resulting trust does not arise in favor of someone who has paid nothing toward the purchase
price of land simply because he or she subsequently makes or pays for improvements on the
property," or for the discharge of outstanding encumbrances. *See generally* 6 Scott & Ascher §43.7.7
(Advances for Improvements or to Discharge Encumbrances). That is not to say that the payor
would not be entitled to an equitable lien on the property to secure any equitable right of
reimbursement the payor may have. *See generally* 6 Scott & Ascher §43.7.7.

[108] Restatement (Third) of Trusts §9(1). If *A* purchases land and puts the legal title in *B*'s
name, or *A* gives *B* money to purchase land on *A*'s behalf, and if there is no intention by *A* to make
a gift to *B*, a purchase money resulting trust will arise. Restatement (Third) of Trusts §9(1). So also
if *B* with money that *B* has loaned to *A* purchases property from a vendor and takes the legal title
in his own (*B*'s) name. A purchase money resulting trust arises in favor of A, subject to any security
interest *B* may have in the property. *See generally* 6 Scott & Ascher §43.6.4 (When Transferee Pays
Purchase Price as Loan to Another). The rationale for imposing a purchase money resulting trust
in this situation is that the loan to *A* and the payment to the vendor are a single transaction. *See
generally* 6 Scott & Ascher §43.6.4. A purchase money resulting trust also would arise in favor of *A*
if *B* discharges his debt to *A* by purchasing at *A*'s request property from a vendor and taking title
to it in his own (*B*'s) name. *See generally* 6 Scott & Ascher §43.6.5 (When Transferee Pays Purchase
Price in Discharge of Debt to Another). Had *B* (the transferee) made a gift of the purchase price to
A (the payor), *B* "presumptively" would hold the property upon a resulting trust for *A*. 6 Scott &
Ascher §43.6.6 (When Transferee Pays Purchase Price as Gift to Another). Had *A*'s payment of the
purchase price for the property been constructively a loan to a third party, the transferee would
hold the property upon a purchase money resulting trust *for the third party*. 6 Scott & Ascher §43.6.7
(When Payor Other Than Transferee Pays Full Purchase Price as Loan to Third Person). If a payor
satisfies the payor's debt to a third party by paying the vendor of certain property the purchase
price for it, the one who takes the title from the vendor (the transferee) may well hold the property
upon a purchase money resulting trust *for the third* party, provided the payment was made with the
third party's consent. 6 Scott & Ascher §43.6.8 (When Payor Other Than Transferee Pays Purchase
Price in Discharge of Debt to Third Person). *See also* 6 Scott & Ascher §43.7.8 (confirming that
when payor makes a part payment as a loan or debt discharge to a third party, a resulting trust
arises *pro tanto for the third party*). It has been suggested that a gratuitous express trust of property
for the benefit *of a third party* gives rise to a constructive trust, not a purchase money resulting trust,
for the benefit of the payor, the one who paid the purchase price, should the express trust fail for
noncompliance with the statute of frauds, or a resulting trust for the payor's benefit should the
failure be otherwise caused. 6 Scott & Ascher §43.6.9.

[109] 6 Scott & Ascher §43.7 (Payment of Part of Purchase Price). "Strictly speaking, an aliquot
part is one that is exactly contained in the whole without a remainder, i.e., a part that can be
expressed by a fraction that, when reduced to its lowest terms, has 1 in its numerator." 6 Scott &
Ascher §43.7. If the payor of the part of the purchase price of a parcel of land *orally* agrees with the
grantee that the payor shall have a portion of the land that is *greater* than the fraction of the land
that corresponds to the fraction of the purchase price paid by the payor, then the payor is entitled
either to the imposition of a purchase money resulting trust on just the fraction or a restitution of
the amounts that were paid out, assuming the grantee refuses to perform the agreement. *See
generally* 6 Scott & Ascher §43.7.1. If, however, the parties are in a fiduciary or confidential
relationship in which the grantee is the dominant party and if the oral agreement is incident to an

purchase may be made in cash or in kind, or partly in cash and partly in kind,[110] or on credit.[111] In order to raise a resulting trust, however, "someone other than the grantee must pay or assume an obligation to pay the purchase price, prior to or at the time of purchase."[112] The fiduciary powers of a purchase money resulting trustee are generally not disclaimable.[113]

Intention a critical element. A purchase-money resulting trust does not arise automatically.[114] It is essentially a form of express trust.[115] Thus, when there is an intention on the part of the person who paid the consideration to make a gift to the transferee, no purchase money resulting trust arises.[116] Likewise if there was an intention on the part of the payor to make a loan of the purchase price to the transferee,[117] or to discharge a prior debt that the payor owed the transferee.[118]

The purchase money resulting trust is actually an express trust. The purchase money resulting trust is actually a type of express trust rather than a true resulting trust.[119] The true resulting trust, such as one that is occasioned by the

---

abuse of that relationship, then the payor may be entitled to the imposition of a constructive trust on the fraction of the land that was orally agreed-upon, or possibly even on the entire parcel. *See generally* 6 Scott & Ascher §43.7.1. If the parties are not in a fiduciary relationship and have orally agreed that the payor of a portion of the purchase price shall receive less than his pro rata share of the land, then the payor is entitled only to the fraction that was orally agreed upon, parol evidence being admissible to rebut the presumption of a purchase money resulting trust, in this case the presumption with respect to the excess. *See generally* 6 Scott & Ascher §43.7.2 (Intention to Take Less Than Pro Rata Share). If the payor of a portion of the purchase price orally agrees with the grantee that the payor is to have a beneficial interest *in a particular part of a tract of land*, such as the part that fronts the lake, and the grantee reneges, then a purchase money resulting trust may be imposed upon the tract for the benefit of the payor, even if the *area* of the tract is greater than the area that would otherwise be attributable to the payor's monetary contribution. *See generally* 6 Scott & Ascher §43.7.3. While the area of the tract may not be commensurate with what was paid, its value may be. *See generally* 6 Scott & Ascher §43.7.3. So also when the oral understanding is that the payor is to take a limited estate in the land, such as an estate for life or a term of years. *See generally* 6 Scott & Ascher §43.7.4. Multiple payors presumptively share pro rata upon imposition of a purchase money resulting trust. *See generally* 6 Scott & Ascher §43.7.5.

[110] *See generally* 6 Scott & Ascher §43.8 (Payment Not in Money).

[111] *See generally* 6 Scott & Ascher §§43.9.1 (Purchase on Purchaser's Credit) and §43.9.2 (Purchase on Grantee's Credit, Purchaser Agreeing to Exonerate Grantee).

[112] 6 Scott & Ascher §43.10 (Payment Subsequent to Purchase).

[113] *Cf.* UPC §2-1102 cmt. (noting that the Uniform Disclaimer of Property Interests Act does not cover resulting trusts). *See generally* §3.5.3.4 of this handbook (the power of the trustee of an express trust to disclaim a fiduciary power).

[114] *See, e.g.,* Ravi Vajpeyi v. Shuaib Yusaf, [2003] EWHC 2339 (Ch) (England) (presumption of resulting trust rebutted by evidence that a loan of the property in question was intended).

[115] 6 Scott & Ascher §40.1.1 (Distinguishing Resulting Trusts From Express Trusts). *Cf.* 6 Scott & Ascher §43.2.1 (Unenforceable Express Agreement by Grantee to Hold in Trust).

[116] Restatement (Third) of Trusts §9(1)(a). *See generally* 6 Scott & Ascher §43.6.3 (When Payment is Gift to Transferee).

[117] 6 Scott & Ascher §43.6.1 (When Payment is Loan to Transferee). In the case of a loan, it is actually the transferee who is purchasing the land. *See also* §9.8.7 of this handbook (the Quistclose trust).

[118] 6 Scott & Ascher §43.6.2 (When Payment is in Discharge of Debt to Transferee).

[119] *Cf.* 6 Scott & Ascher §43.2.2 (Unenforceable Express Agreement by Grantee to Hold in Trust).

failure of an express trust, arises automatically in favor of those who took vested reversionary interests at the express trust's inception,[120] reversionary interests being vested at the outset.[121] The policy behind the purchase money resulting trust is to prevent the transferee from being unjustly enriched.[122] The Ohio Supreme Court appears to have lost sight of this critical difference between the two types of resulting trust in a case involving an express trust that failed for want of an equitable remainder;[123] the court then further confusing matters by mischaracterizing the nonexistent equitable remainder as a nonexistent "residue."[124] It is regrettable that American law schools no longer require Trusts, a problem we highlight in Section 8.25 of this handbook.

Historical antecedents. The origins of the concept of the purchase money resulting trust go back to fifteenth-century England, where and when it had become an almost universal custom to own land through an intermediary who would hold the actual legal title.[125] This trust-like arrangement was known as a *use*, which we explain more fully in Section 8.15.1 of this handbook. Back then there was a rebuttable presumption—now long abandoned—that a gratuitous transfer of land from *A* to *B* caused *B* to hold the land for the benefit of *A*.[126] There was a related presumption that if someone other than *A* had paid consideration for the land, *B* would hold the land upon a resulting *use* for the benefit of the one who had paid the consideration, not for the benefit of *A*.[127] The second presumption has survived more or less intact to this day incident to the enforcement of purchase money resulting trusts.[128] Personal property as well as land may be the subject of a purchase money resulting trust.[129] In a few U.S. states the purchase money resulting trust of land has been abolished by statute, such as in Kentucky, Michigan, New York, and Wisconsin.[130]

Illegal purposes. A purchase money resulting trust in furtherance of an illegal purpose, such as the defrauding of the payor's creditors, is generally

---

[120] *See generally* §4.1.1.1 of this handbook (discussing the resulting trust that arises due to the failure of an express trust). *See also* introductory quote to §4.1.1 of this handbook (the reversionary interest) (comparing a reversion with a remainder) and §8.26 of this handbook (will residue clauses).

[121] *See generally* §8.2.1.5 of this handbook (consequences of a violation of the common law rule).

[122] 6 Scott & Ascher §43.1.

[123] *See* Stevens v. Radey, 117 Ohio St. 3d 65, 881 N.E.2d 855 (2008).

[124] Stevens v. Radey, 117 Ohio St. 3d 65, 881 N.E.2d 855 (2008). *See* §8.15.2 of this handbook (remaindermen take "by purchase" from the trustee). *See also* introductory quote to §4.1.1 of this handbook (comparing a reversion with a remainder) and §8.26 of this handbook (will residue clauses).

[125] 6 Scott & Ascher §43.1.

[126] 6 Scott & Ascher §43.1.

[127] 6 Scott & Ascher §43.1.

[128] 6 Scott & Ascher §43.1.

[129] 6 Scott & Ascher §43.1.

[130] 6 Scott & Ascher §§43.1 and 43.1.2 (Statutes Abolishing Purchase Money Resulting Trusts). *See, however,* 6 Scott & Ascher §43.1.3 (Statutes Expressly Permitting Purchase Money Resulting Trusts).

unenforceable.[131] The transferee may keep the property, subject to any legitimate claims of third parties, such as of the payor's creditors.[132] He who comes into equity must come with clean hands.[133] "Although the illegality of the transaction precludes the enforcement of a resulting trust, if the trustee conveys the property to the payor, the payor can keep it."[134]

Legitimate reasons for not taking the legal title. Today there are some legitimate reasons why someone who pays consideration for an item of property might be motivated to have someone else take the legal title to it:

> One not uncommon motive is that of avoiding publicity; the purchaser does not want the vendor to know that the purchaser is purchasing, for fear that the vendor will raise the price, particularly if the purchaser is also trying to acquire adjoining properties. Not infrequently, such a purchase occurs in order to facilitate resale of the property, as when several persons contribute to the purchase price. Sometimes the purchase is in the name of another because the latter is believed to be more competent to undertake management responsibilities. On other occasions the arrangement is designed to provide the transferee with security for a debt already owed by the purchaser.[135]

Of course, the formal written express inter vivos trust is far better suited to accomplish such objectives.[136] There are not the uncertainties, inefficiencies, and costs attendant with the imposition of a purchase money resulting trust, which requires a court order.[137]

Burdens of proof. As to burdens of proof, a transferee of property for which a third party rather than the transferor has paid the purchase price is presumed to hold it upon a purchase money resulting trust for the third party.[138] Thus the third party's only initial burden is to prove that the purchase price had actually been paid by the third party.[139] It then falls to the transferee, assuming the transferee wishes to retain the property, to prove that the third party intended to make an outright gift of the property to the transferee.[140] If that burden

---

[131] 6 Scott & Ascher §43.5.

[132] 6 Scott & Ascher §43.5. "In these cases, the courts have recognized that public policy does not always require that the grantee be unjustly enriched at the expense of the purchaser, just because the purchaser's purpose was illegal, especially when the purchaser's conduct was not strongly reprehensible." 6 Scott & Ascher §43.5.

[133] *See generally* §8.12 of this handbook (equity's maxims).

[134] 6 Scott & Ascher §43.5.

[135] 6 Scott & Ascher §43.1. *See also* 6 Scott & Ascher §43.1.4.

[136] *See generally* 6 Scott & Ascher §43.1.4 (General Observations); 6 Scott & Ascher §43.2.1 (Enforceable Express Agreement by Grantee to Hold in Trust). *Cf.* 6 Scott & Ascher §43.2.2 (Unenforceable Express Agreement by Grantee to Hold in Trust).

[137] *See generally* 6 Scott & Ascher §§43.1.4 (General Observations) and 43.2.1 (Enforceable Express Agreement by Grantee to Hold in Trust).

[138] 6 Scott & Ascher §43.1.

[139] 6 Scott & Ascher §43.1.

[140] 6 Scott & Ascher §§43.1 and 43.2 (Rebutting the Purchase-Money Resulting Trust); 6 Scott & Ascher §43.2.3 (Rebutting Resulting Trust in Part); 6 Scott & Ascher §43.2.4 (Purchase in Name of Payor and Another); 6 Scott & Ascher §43.3 (Purchase in the Name of a Relative); 6 Scott & Ascher §43.4 (Rebutting Presumption of Gift to Relative).

cannot be met, then the court will order the transferee to convey the legal title to the property to the third party outright and free of trust, unless, in reliance on what was ostensibly a gift the transferee has so changed position that it would be inequitable to compel the transferee to surrender the property.[141] A conveyance to a close relative of the third party will raise an inference that an outright gift was intended, particularly if the relative is a natural object of the third party's bounty.[142]

Statute of frauds. A purchase money resulting trust of land need not comply with the memorandum requirements of statute of fraud to be enforceable.[143] In other words oral purchase money resulting trusts are enforceable, as they are said to arise by "operation" or "implication" of law, although, as we have seen, such trusts are actually more express-like than resulting-like. "The real reason, it would seem, that such trusts are valid without a writing is that, although they arise out of the parties' intention, the evidence of those intentions lies in the circumstances of the transaction rather than in testimony of the parties' discussions."[144] So also a purchase money resulting trust may be *rebutted* by parol evidence that a gift to the transferee was actually intended.[145] The statute of frauds applicable to trusts is covered in Section 8.15.5 of this handbook.

Title to land taken jointly. When two or more persons contribute to the purchase price of a parcel of land in unequal amounts and the legal title is taken by all jointly, there is a weak inference in some quarters that that a purchase money resulting trust is imposed on the land in favor of each payor, in proportion to what each had contributed.[146] This assumes that the rights, duties, and obligations of the parties have not been set forth in an appropriate writing and that the parties are at loggerheads.[147]

Passing title to a BFP. The trustee of a purchase money resulting trust of land may pass good title to a good-faith purchaser for value and in so doing cut off the rights of the payor *to the land*.[148] We discuss the concept of the BFP in Section 8.15.63 of this handbook. A creditor of the grantee, *i.e.*, of the trustee, generally will not qualify as a BFP of the property.[149] Having said that, one who has extended credit to the grantee in reliance on the grantee's apparent ownership of the property may well be able to obtain satisfaction from the

---

[141] 6 Scott & Ascher §43.1.

[142] 6 Scott & Ascher §43.2 (Rebutting the Purchase-Money Resulting Trust).

[143] 6 Scott & Ascher §43.1.

[144] 6 Scott & Ascher §43.1. "There is not, therefore, the same danger of perjured testimony." Scott & Ascher §43.1.

[145] 6 Scott & Ascher §43.2 (Rebutting the Resulting Trust). "In contrast, a resulting trust that arises because of the failure of an express trust declared in a will or other written instrument ordinarily cannot be rebutted by the settlor's oral statements." 6 Scott & Ascher §43.2.

[146] *See generally* 6 Scott & Ascher §43.7.6 (Transfer to Two or More Persons).

[147] *See* §8.15.5 of this handbook (statute of frauds).

[148] *See generally* 6 Scott & Ascher §43.13 (Rights of Creditors of Trustee When Beneficiary is Estopped). *See generally* §8.15.63 of this handbook (doctrine of bona fide purchase; the BFP).

[149] *See generally* 6 Scott & Ascher §43.13 (Rights of Creditors of Trustee When Beneficiary is Estopped).

property if the payor knew or should have known that the grantee was receiving credit because of the apparent ownership.[150]

The marital home. When a husband and wife take the legal title to their marital home jointly, they having contributed disproportionately to the purchase price and there being no written agreement as to the rights, duties, and obligations of the parties, the court may impose a purchase money resulting trust on the property in favor of each in proportion to his or her contribution, unless there is evidence of a different understanding at the time of purchase.[151] So also if the legal title had been taken in the name of only one spouse.[152] Unmarried cohabitants going their separate ways can be expected to be governed by similar rules.[153] As noted above, in order to benefit from the imposition of a purchase money resulting trust, one must have contributed to the purchase price *at the time of purchase.*[154] Marital home postpurchase mortgage payments and improvements may well be an exception, at least one commentator has so suggested.[155]

The imposition of a purchase money resulting trust is by no means the only equitable mechanism for sorting out a couple's proportional economic interests in the marital home, a problem that is likely in any case to surface only in the context of divorce or the postmortem disposition of property rights, nor is it likely the most utilized.[156] There also are the constructive trust and the equitable lien to prevent the unjust enrichment of one spouse at the expense of another.[157] Spousal agreements that are unenforceable at law may be enforceable in equity.[158] "Whatever the technical grounds, it would seem that, at bottom, the court is often simply enforcing a duty of fair dealing between spouses."[159] Unmarried cohabitants, of course, also may have contractual rights, duties, and obligations one to the other that are law-based.[160] For more on spousal rights in the context of divorce and the postmortem disposition of property interests, the reader is referred to Section 5.3.4.1 of this handbook.

Distinction between constructive trust and purchase money resulting trust. Take the situation where a transferee of land has not furnished the consideration for it. A third party has. The transferor of the legal title is merely the vendor. If the third party did not consent to his or her money being used in this way, or did not consent to the transfer itself, then a constructive trust, not a purchase money resulting trust, is imposed on the property for the benefit of the third party.[161]

---

[150] *See generally* 6 Scott & Ascher §43.13 (Rights of Creditors of Trustee When Beneficiary is Estopped).

[151] 6 Scott & Ascher §43.11 (Marital Home and Family Assets).

[152] 6 Scott & Ascher §43.11.

[153] *See generally* 6 Scott & Ascher §43.11.1 (Cohabitation Without Marriage).

[154] 6 Scott & Ascher §43.11.

[155] 6 Scott & Ascher §43.11.

[156] 6 Scott & Ascher §43.11.

[157] 6 Scott & Ascher §43.11.

[158] 6 Scott & Ascher §43.11.

[159] 6 Scott & Ascher §43.11.

[160] *See generally* 6 Scott & Ascher §43.11.1 (Cohabitation Without Marriage).

[161] 6 Scott & Ascher §43.1.1.

Had the third party, however, intended that the transferee take the legal title but not the beneficial interest, we would have a resulting trust fact pattern.[162] Had the third party been induced by fraud or undue influence to purchase the land in the name of the transferee with the understanding that the property would be held for the benefit of the third party, then there are grounds for imposing either a resulting trust or a constructive trust on the property for the third party's benefit.[163]

Equitable estoppel and the purchase money resulting trust. Now a word about equitable estoppel in the purchase-money resulting trust context: As we have seen elsewhere, if a trustee, in breach of trust, transfers trust property to a personal creditor of the trustee, the creditor-transferee is generally not a BFP.[164] The creditor-transferee takes subject to the trust beneficiary's equitable interest, unless the beneficiary by word or conduct has caused the creditor-transferee to believe that the property was not the subject of a trust.[165] Thus, "if the beneficiary of a . . . [purchase money] . . . resulting trust permits the . . . [purchase money] . . . trustee to continue to hold the property, although the . . . [purchase money trust] . . . beneficiary knows that the trustee is obtaining credit on the strength of the . . . [purchase money] . . . trustee's apparent ownership, the . . . [purchase money] . . . beneficiary cannot enforce the . . . [purchase money] . . . resulting trust as against a creditor who has extended credit on the faith of the trustee's apparent ownership."[166]

State-imposed ownership restrictions. It has long been the practice of federal, state, and local governments, in lieu of taking property for just compensation, to place restrictions on how certain types of properties may be used by their owners.[167] These restrictions are intended to further certain state interests, such as land and wildlife conservation, historic preservation, and

---

[162] 6 Scott & Ascher §43.1.1.

[163] 6 Scott & Ascher §43.1.1.

[164] *See* §5.4.2 of this handbook (rights of the beneficiary as against BFPs and other transferees of the underlying trust property) and §8.15.63 of this handbook (doctrine of bona fide purchase; the BFP).

[165] *See generally* §5.4.2 of this handbook (rights of the beneficiary as against BFPs and other transferees of the underlying trust property).

[166] 5 Scott & Ascher §29.5.1 (Rights of Creditors When Beneficiaries Are Estopped).

[167] *See, e.g.,* Penn Cent. Transp. Co. v. City of New York, 438 U.S. 104 (1978); Nollan v. California Coastal Comm'n, 483 U.S. 825 (1987); Dolan v. Tigard, 512 U.S. 374 (1994); Kmiec, *At Last the Supreme Court Solves the Takings Puzzle,* 19 Harv. J.L. & Pub. Pol'y 147 (1995). A point is reached, however, when a body of restrictions so circumscribes how an owner may use his property that he becomes a de facto trustee of the property for the benefit of the public. While the matter of restraints on coastal development has received considerable publicity because of the de facto takings cases, and while the spotted owl and the snail darter have brought public attention to matters of wildlife conservation, efforts to regulate the use of Native American burial sites discovered on private property or the interiors of historic homes in private hands perhaps show the trusteeship by restriction at its most intrusive. *See also* Rounds, *Protections Afforded to Massachusetts' Ancient Burial Grounds,* 73 Mass. L. Rev. 176 (1988). The better involuntary approach, both for the property owner and the public, is for the state to take a particular asset by eminent domain for just compensation and then irrevocably transfer it into a common law charitable trust, together with sufficient funds for its perpetual maintenance and for the adequate compensation of willing competent trustees.

residential zoning. In times when public treasuries are strapped for funds, trusteeships by restriction have a certain superficial appeal: They appear to be effective, cost-free mechanisms for limiting the use of property on behalf of the public. But one has to question the long-term effectiveness of such involuntary arrangements that require de facto trustees to serve without compensation and without reimbursement for expenses. The voluntary transfer of easements for conservation or preservation in trust to charitable organizations would seem the better way to go.[168] In the case of state-imposed restrictions on archaeological sites and the interiors of homes, there can be no credible enforcement of such trusts over the long-term without massive state expenditure and intrusion. Another problem is that the trusteeship by restriction is essentially a passive arrangement that neither makes provision for the perpetual maintenance of assets nor protects an asset in the event it is constructively abandoned (*e.g.*, due to the property owner's impoverishment).

Partner as trustee. Under the Uniform Partnership Act (1997), a partner has a duty to account to the partnership and hold as trustee for it any property, profit, or benefit derived by the partner in the conduct and winding up of the partnership business or derived from a use by the partner of partnership property, including the appropriation of partnership opportunity.[169] That the appropriation of a partnership opportunity may be the subject of a trust is a common law codification.[170]

§3.4   Avoiding, Assuming, and Vacating the Office

A trust arises as a result of the settlor's general intention to create it.[1] The transfer of title to the trustee is a legal consequence of that intention. A trust, however, will not fail for want of a trustee.[2] Thus, if property is transferred to

---

[168] "Even though not accompanied by the usual trappings of a trust, the creation and transfer of an easement for conservation or preservation will frequently create a charitable trust." UTC §414 cmt. (available at <http://www.uniformlaws.org/Act.aspx?title=Trust%20Code>). "The organization to whom the easement was conveyed will be deemed to be acting as trustee of what will ostensibly appear to be a contractual or property arrangement." Un UTC §414 cmt. "Because of the fiduciary obligation imposed, the termination or substantial modification of the easement by the 'trustee' could constitute a breach of trust." UTC §414 cmt.

[169] Uniform Partnership Act (1997) §404(b)(1). *Cf.* UTC §802 cmt. (available at <http://www.uniformlaws.org/Act.aspx?title=Trust%20Code>) (suggesting that although it is normally associated with corporations and with their directors and officers, what is usually referred to as the corporate opportunity doctrine also applies to trustees of express trusts).

[170] Meinhard v. Salmon, 249 N.Y. 458, 463, 164 N.E. 545, 546 (1928) (Cardozo, J.) (excerpted in §6.1.3 of this handbook (duty to be loyal to the trust)); Fouchek v. Janicek, 190 Or. 251, 225 P.2d 783 (1950).

§3.4 [1] UTC §402(a)(2) (available at <http://www.uniformlaws.org/Act.aspx?title=Trust%20Code>).

[2] UTC §401 cmt. (available at <http://www.uniformlaws.org/Act.aspx?title=Trust%20Code>).

one who cannot act, or if the one nominated disclaims, or if the trustee has died or is unable to act, the person in possession will hold the property until a proper trustee can be appointed. This was not always the case: "At first, the chancellors held that the use bound only the original feoffee," a situation that made the position of the beneficiary, to say the least, "quite precarious."[3]

A vacancy in a trusteeship occurs if a person designated as trustee rejects the trusteeship, a person designated as trustee cannot be identified or does not exist, a trustee resigns, a trustee is disqualified or removed, a trustee dies, or a guardian or conservator is appointed for an individual serving as trustee.[4] Under the Uniform Trust Code, if at least one trustee remains in office, a vacancy need not be filled.[5] The Code provides that a person designated in the terms of the trust to act as successor trustee shall fill a vacancy in a trusteeship required to be filled.[6] When there is no such designation, then the vacancy shall be filled by a person appointed by unanimous agreement of the qualified beneficiaries.[7] If all else fails, then a person appointed by the court shall fill the vacancy.[8] Of course, the court always possesses equitable powers to appoint an additional trustee or special fiduciary "whenever the court considers the appointment necessary for the administration of the trust."[9]

§3.4.1   Appointment

A trust does not fail because no trustee is designated or because the designated trustee declines, is unable, or ceases to act, unless the trust's creation or continuation depends on a specific person serving as trustee; a proper court will appoint a trustee as necessary and appropriate.[10]

The declaration of trust. A declaration of trust arises when the owner of an interest in property declares himself or herself to be a trustee of that interest for the benefit of someone. Declarations of trust were not enforceable in England until 1811.[11] "In any event, the rule is now settled, both in England and in the United States, that when the owner of property gratuitously declares himself or herself trustee for another, a trust arises, even if the declaration involves land."[12] Because a declaration of trust has no deed, delivery, or

---

[3] 3 Scott & Ascher §13.1.

[4] UTC §704(a) (available at <http://www.uniformlaws.org/Act.aspx?title=Trust%20Code>).

[5] UTC §704(b) (available at <http://www.uniformlaws.org/Act.aspx?title=Trust%20Code>).

[6] UTC §704(c) (available at <http://www.uniformlaws.org/Act.aspx?title=Trust%20Code>).

[7] Uniform Trust Code Qualified beneficiaries are essentially the current beneficiaries and the presumptive remaindermen. *See* UTC §103(12) (available at <http://www.uniformlaws.org/Act.aspx?title=Trust%20Code>) (defining the term *qualified beneficiary*).

[8] UTC §704(c) (available at <http://www.uniformlaws.org/Act.aspx?title=Trust%20Code>).

[9] UTC §704(d) (available at <http://www.uniformlaws.org/Act.aspx?title=Trust%20Code>).

[10] Restatement (Third) of Trusts §31.

[11] Ex parte Pye, 18 Ves. 140 (1811).

[12] 1 Scott & Ascher §3.3.1.

consideration requirement, it can be a useful fall-back theory for counsel struggling to prove the elements of a gift or a contract.[13]

The appointment of the trustee under a declaration of trust (*i.e.*, when the settlor and trustee are one and the same) requires no action by the court and no act of property transfer,[14] although Section 7-101 of the Uniform Probate Code, repealed/withdrawn in 2010, would have required that the trustee register the declaration of trust, whether oral or written, in the court upon assuming the trusteeship.[15] Any trustee of a declaration of trust who failed to duly register the trust would have been subject to removal and denial of compensation or to surcharge as the court may have directed.[16] Moreover, any trust term purporting to relieve the trustee of this duty to register would have been unenforceable.[17] The declarant becomes trustee simply by manifesting a present intention of impressing a trust upon his property.[18] In North Carolina, no transfer of legal title is required, even in the case of real estate, since the trustee already holds legal title.[19] However, the segregation of the property and the re-registration of securities and other such items of intangible personal property are advisable in order to generate factual evidence of the intent to impress a trust upon the property.[20] Thus, in the case of entrusted real estate, the formal

---

[13] 1 Scott & Ascher §3.3.1.

[14] *See* 1 Scott on Trusts §17.1; *see, e.g.*, Taliaferro v. Taliaferro, 921 P.2d 803, 809 (Kan. 1996) ("there is no requirement that a settlor who also serves as trustee of a trust established by declaration must transfer legal title to the trust property."). *See also*, Janet A. Lemons, *Trust Law: Creating a Trust by Declaration Does Not Require the Settlor to Transfer Legal Title of the Trust Property to Himself*, 36 Washburn L.J. 511 (1997); UTC §401 (available at <http://www.uniformlaws.org/Act.aspx?title=Trust%20Code>) ("A trust may be created by: . . . (2) declaration by the owner of property that the owner holds identifiable property as trustee . . . ").

[15] *See* UPC §7-101 (repealed/withdrawn). "The place of registration is related not to the place where the trust was created, which may lose its significance to the parties concerned, but is related to the place where the trust is primarily administered, which in turn is required (Section 7-305 (repealed/withdrawn)) to be at a location appropriate to the purposes of the trust and the interests of its beneficiaries." UPC Art. VII, Pt.1, Gen. Cmt. (repealed/withdrawn). "Registration shall be accomplished by filing a statement indicating the name and address of the trustee in which it acknowledges the trusteeship." UPC §7-101 (repealed/withdrawn).

[16] UPC §7-104 (repealed/withdrawn).

[17] UPC §7-104 (repealed/withdrawn).

[18] *See* 1 Scott on Trusts §17.1; *see, e.g.*, Taliaferro v. Taliaferro, 921 P.2d 803, 809 (Kan. 1996) ("there is no requirement that a settlor who also serves as trustee of a trust established by declaration must transfer legal title to the trust property."). *See also* UTC §401 (available at <http://www.uniformlaws.org/Act.aspx?title=Trust%20Code>) ("A trust may be created by: . . . (2) declaration by the owner of property that the owner holds identifiable property as trustee . . . ").

[19] *See* Nevitt v. Robotham, 762 S.E.2d 267 (N.C. App. Ct. 2014).

[20] UTC §401 cmt. (available at <http://www.uniformlaws.org/Act.aspx?title=Trust%20Code>) (recommending against funding a declaration of trust by attaching a schedule listing the assets in lieu of the formal execution of instruments of transfer, the absence of instruments of transfer making it difficult to later confirm title with third-party transferees). Absence of formal transfer documentation could also set up a conflict between the personal representative of the deceased declarant's estate and the successor trustee.

recordation of a deed is advisable. If real estate is involved, the statute of frauds may require a writing for the trust to be enforceable *as to the real estate*.[21] Again, for a declaration of trust to arise, there is no need of a conveyance from the owner to himself as trustee, or of a conveyance by the owner to a straw who in turn reconveys back to the owner as trustee.[22] In either case, title was already with the owner. Nor, as noted, is there need for some exchange of consideration.[23] In the Comment to Section 201 of the Uniform Powers of Appointment Act there is the assertion that a declaration of trust "necessarily entails a transfer of legal title from the owner-as-owner to the owner-as-trustee . . . ." No authority is supplied for this general proposition because there is none.

The inter vivos transfer in trust. A trust created by inter vivos transfer from *A* to *B* also requires no judicial act of appointment,[24] and no exchange of consideration,[25] although Section 7-101 of the Uniform Probate Code would have imposed on the trustee a duty to register the inter vivos trust, whether oral or written, in the appropriate court upon assuming the trusteeship.[26] Under the Uniform Probate Code any trustee of an inter vivos trust who failed to so register would have been subject to removal and denial of compensation or to surcharge as the court may direct.[27] Moreover, any trust term purporting to relieve the trustee of this duty to register would have been unenforceable.[28]

The completed-transfer requirement. A completed transfer of the trust property, however, must occur before such an inter vivos appointment is effective.[29] A transfer of possession alone will not suffice. Thus, a transfer of property from *A* to *B*, said property to be held on such trusts as *A* may set forth in *A*'s last will does not give rise to a trust at the time of the transfer of possession,[30] unless there was a valid incorporation by reference, a topic we cover in Section 8.15.17 of this handbook. *A* may compel *B* to return the property, at least up until *A*'s death.[31] On the other hand, if the property is to be held on such trusts the terms of which will be set forth in the next will that *A* executes, then at the time of the will's execution we might possibly have a valid inter vivos trust.[32] It would seem, however, that *A* would still have to have the requisite present intent to create a

---

[21] *See generally* §8.15.5 of this handbook (statute of frauds).

[22] 1 Scott & Ascher §3.1.1.

[23] 1 Scott & Ascher §3.1.1.

[24] 5A Scott on Trusts §557.

[25] 1 Scott & Ascher §3.3.2.

[26] *See* UPC §7-101. [Repealed.] "The place of registration is related not to the place where the trust was created, which may lose its significance to the parties concerned, but is related to the place where the trust is primarily administered, which in turn is required (Section 7-305) to be at a location appropriate to the purposes of the trust and the interests of its beneficiaries." UPC Art. VII, Pt.1, Gen. Cmt. "Registration shall be accomplished by filing a statement indicating the name and address of the trustee in which it acknowledges the trusteeship." UPC §7-101. [Repealed.]

[27] UPC §7-104. [Repealed.]

[28] UPC §7-104. [Repealed.]

[29] *See* 1 Scott on Trusts §§32.1–32.2.

[30] 5 Scott & Ascher §35.1.7 (When Creation of Trust Is Incomplete).

[31] 5 Scott & Ascher §35.1.7.

[32] 5 Scott & Ascher §35.1.7.

trust at the time the next will is executed.[33] Recall that a will is "executed" when it is signed and witnessed, not when it speaks, which is when the testator dies.

Notice to third parties. When the property is land, delivery of a deed completes the transfer; when the property is intangible personal property (*e.g.*, stocks and bonds), re-registration in the name of the trustee completes the transfer. However, what if the securities remain in the name of the original owner who, in lieu of re-registration, places them in the hands of the trustee with the present intention that they be held in trust? Has the appointment of a trustee been consummated? The better view is that it has. It is settled law, for example, that notice to an insurance company is not a requirement for impressing a trust in equity upon rights under an insurance contract.[34] Nor is notice to a bank required to impress a trust upon a bank account.[35] Likewise, no notice to a transfer agent is required to impress a trust in equity upon a block of securities.[36] Thus, it logically follows that the trustee's appointment can be effected in equity by the transfer of physical possession in lieu of re-registration, provided the act is coupled with the appropriate intent.[37]

Emergency general assignments. Of course, no rational person would intentionally forgo the formal re-registration of property intended to be entrusted, particularly securities, real estate, and the like, settling only for a transfer of physical possession, absent some emergency. The absence of a paper trail would hamper efforts to defend the trust against those who would attack the entrustment. But what if the to-be-entrusted items of property are physically inaccessible and their precise descriptions not readily ascertainable? Could an emergency entrustment be effected by the prospective settlor (or by his or her agent with entrustment authority under a durable power of attorney) executing and delivering a general unspecific present assignment of, say, all the securities he or she owns to the intended trustee? In this case, there is no re-registration *and* no physical transfer of the underlying paper. One court has enforced such a private general assignment, albeit of publicly recorded real property and in the context of a declaration of trust.[38] It is suggested that in cases of emergency, such as the imminent death of a would-be settlor, the transfer is sufficiently complete in equity to effect an entrustment because the property owner has done all that can be done under the circumstances to place the property in the hands of a trustee. There is at least one case with similar facts, but the holding is not particularly helpful.[39] A fall-back argument might be that the securities

---

[33] 5 Scott & Ascher §35.1.7.

[34] *See generally* 1A Scott on Trusts §57.3.

[35] *See generally* 1A Scott on Trusts §§58–58.6.

[36] *See generally* 2A Scott on Trusts §179.3.

[37] The reader is reminded that in a few jurisdictions, most notably Florida, Louisiana, and New York, the inter vivos trust instrument itself may have to have been executed with certain formalities. *See generally* Chapter 1 of this handbook.

[38] *See* Ukkestad v. RBS Asset Fin., Inc., 185 Cal. Rptr. 3d 145 (Cal. App. 2015) (statute of frauds not violated as the specific parcels of real property encompassed by the assignment were easily ascertainable from a perusal of the public record).

[39] *See* 3 Scott & Ascher §14.3.1 (Authorization to Receive Trust Property) (discussing Farmers' Loan & Trust Co. v. Winthrop, 144 N.E. 686 (N.Y. 1924). On the other hand, there is at

should be held upon a constructive trust for the benefit of the intended trust beneficiaries,[40] or even that there is a present declaration of trust, which is a type of trust that can arise without a formal transfer of title and physical possession.[41] The legal argument against an effective entrustment is that there is no completed gift, the element of delivery being lacking. Because equity will not enforce a gratuitous promise to make a gift, the property remains unentrusted.[42]

Holders of durable powers of attorney. Whether an agent acting under a durable power of attorney can effect the appointment of a trustee for the principal's property remains somewhat unsettled.[43] In some jurisdictions, the issue has been resolved by legislation.[44] However, if a particular appointment is in the interest of the principal and within the scope of the agent's express authority,[45] it ought to be upheld in equity.

On the other hand, a transfer of property to a trustee in breach of some fiduciary duty to the legal or equitable owner of the property is subject to rescission and restitution.[46] Thus, if an agent in breach of a fiduciary duty to the principal transfers the principal's property to a trustee, the trustee is "liable in restitution" to the principal.[47] So also if a trustee in breach of trust decants to another trust with a different trustee and different beneficiaries, absent special facts.[48] The trustee of the other trust and, indirectly, the beneficiaries of the other trust are "liable in restitution" to the beneficiaries of the inception trust "as necessary to avoid unjust enrichment."[49]

---

least one case to the effect that the *revocation* of a trust is effective upon the faxing of the instrument of revocation to the trustee, not when the trustee relinquishes possession of the subject property. *See* Estate of Noell v. Norwest Bank, 960 P.2d 499 (Wyo. 1998).

[40] *See* Restatement (Third) of Trusts §16 cmt. c, illus. 8; 1 Scott & Ascher §5.2.2.

[41] 1 Scott & Ascher §4.4.

[42] Farmers' Loan & Trust Co. v. Winthrop, 144 N.E. 686 (N.Y. 1924). *See generally* 1 Scott & Ascher §4.4. *See also* §8.12 of this handbook (where the trust is recognized outside the United States) (containing a catalog of equity maxims).

[43] *See generally* Hook, 859 T.M., *Durable Powers of Attorney* A-33 (2000) (confirming that the area is legally "murky" but providing suggested language authorizing the agent to execute a revocable inter vivos trust on behalf of the principal as well as a suggested preamble for the trust). *See also* Collin, *Gift Giving under Durable Powers of Attorney*, 20 Tax Mgmt., Est., Gifts & Tr. 63 (1995); Van Dolson & Whitaker, *Gifts by Agents under Durable Powers of Attorney*, 9 Prob. & Prop. 33, 38 (1995); McGovern, Trusts, *Custodianships, and Durable Powers of Attorney*, 27 Real Prop. Prob. & Tr. J. 1 (Spring 1992); 11 Institute on Estate Planning §305.2 (P. E. Heckerling ed., 1977).

[44] *See generally* Restatement (Third) of Trusts, Reporter's Notes on §11; 1 Scott & Ascher §3.2.

[45] *See, e.g.*, Stafford v. Crane, 382 F.3d 1175 (10th Cir. 2004) (finding the general weight of authority to suggest that the power to create, modify, or revoke a trust is personal and nondelegable to an attorney-in-fact unless expressly granted in the power of attorney).

[46] *See* Restatement (Third) of Restitution and Unjust Enrichment §17 (lack of authority).

[47] *See* Restatement (Third) of Restitution and Unjust Enrichment §17 (lack of authority).

[48] *See generally* §3.5.3.2(a) of this handbook (decanting).

[49] *See* Restatement (Third) of Restitution and Unjust Enrichment §17 (lack of authority).

Guardians. By statute, guardians generally with court approval may transfer the property of their wards to trustees.[50] "When asked for such approval, the court typically attempts to determine whether, under a very loosely grouped set of principles sometimes referred to as the 'substituted judgment' rule, the proposed action is reasonable, in light of the . . . [ward's] . . . overall personal, family, tax, and estate-planning objectives."[51]

The testamentary trust. In the case of testamentary trusts, the common requirement is that the trustee nominated must obtain appointment by the court,[52] as must any alternates or successors.[53] Some authorities describe this procedure as a mere confirmation of the appointment made by the will inasmuch as it is conceded that the trustee's powers, after appointment, mainly flow from the trust instrument and not from the court.[54] Under the Uniform Probate Code, the state court in which the will was probated would not retain continuing supervisory powers over the affairs of the testamentary trust.[55] If the trust's principal place of administration were to end up in another state, however, the trustee would have a duty to register the trust in an appropriate court of the other state.[56] Otherwise, the appointment and acceptance of a trusteeship or successor trusteeship "shall proceed expeditiously consistent with the terms of the trust, free of judicial intervention and without order, approval or other action of any court, subject to the jurisdiction of the Court as invoked by interested parties . . . ."[57] There is ample precedent for the Uniform Probate Code's hands-off approach, testamentary trustees at common law having been permitted to act without judicial confirmation: "An executor could fulfill his or her duty to account by showing a transfer of the assets to the trustee named in the will, and the trustee, like the trustee of an inter vivos trust, was required neither to qualify as trustee in any court nor to account in any particular court."[58] Qualifying a foreign trust company to serve as the trustee of a testamentary trust established locally is taken up in Section 8.6 of this handbook.

---

[50] 1 Scott & Ascher §3.2.

[51] 1 Scott & Ascher §3.2.

[52] *See generally* 5A Scott on Trusts §557. *See also* §3.5.4.3 of this handbook (bonds and sureties).

[53] 2 Scott & Ascher §11.11.2. *See, however,* James v. James, 260 Mass. 19, 156 N.E. 745 (1927), which seems to suggest that the terms of a testamentary trust may provide a nonjudicial process for the appointment of successor trustees, a process to which the court must defer. As a practical matter, however, third parties can be expected to be reluctant to transact or otherwise deal with a successor testamentary trustee who cannot present written evidence of a formal court appointment.

[54] Restatement (Third) of Trusts §34 cmt. a.

[55] UPC §7-201. *See generally* 7 Scott & Ascher §45.2.1.

[56] UPC §7-101.

[57] UPC §7-201(b).

[58] 7 Scott & Ascher §45.2.1.

Trustees who are appointed by decree of court may be required to give bond to the court for the faithful performance of their trust.[59] In testamentary trusts the trustee's bond ordinarily is required to be with sureties unless the testator expressly has excused the trustee from furnishing them or unless all persons beneficially interested join in requesting the exemption.[60] In many jurisdictions, corporate fiduciaries are exempt from providing sureties on their bonds.[61]

All trusts. Probate courts (usually by virtue of statute) and courts acting under statute or under their general equity jurisdiction have broad powers with regard to the appointment of trustees.[62] The court's power to appoint a trustee is exercised wherever circumstances make it necessary.[63] In case of need, such as the death of a sole trustee, the court will appoint a temporary trustee or receiver. In New York, apparently the court will undertake to administer the trust itself.[64] The cardinal principle is that a trust will not be allowed to fail for lack of a trustee.[65]

The trust instrument, whether testamentary or inter vivos, may specify a manner of appointment of an additional or successor trustee.[66] If so, the prescribed method should be followed strictly, whether or not the matter is before the court.[67] The beneficiaries cannot appoint a new trustee, unless they are authorized to do so by or because of the terms of the trust, or unless authorized by an applicable statute.[68] In England, the power in someone to appoint new trustees is a fiduciary power.[69] If the instrument does not provide for a successor trustee, only the court may appoint a successor when a vacancy occurs.[70] Some instruments bestow on trustees the power to appoint their own

---

[59] *See generally* Bogert §151; Restatement (Third) of Trusts §35 cmt. a(1); 7 Scott & Ascher §45.2.1. *See also* §3.5.4.3 of this handbook (bonds and sureties).

[60] *See generally* Bogert §151; Restatement (Third) of Trusts §35 cmt. a(1). *See also* §3.5.4.3 of this handbook (bonds and sureties).

[61] *See generally* Bogert §151; Restatement (Third) of Trusts §35 cmt. a(1). *See also* §3.5.4.3 of this handbook (bonds and sureties).

[62] *See generally* 2 Scott on Trusts §§108.2, 556; Bogert §151; Lewin ¶15-01 through ¶15-15 (England). *See, e.g.*, Reddick v. Suntrust Bank, E. Cent. Florida, 718 So. 2d 950 (Fla. App. 1998) (court denied petition to remove corporate trustee even though a successor was available who was prepared to serve for no compensation).

[63] 2 Scott on Trusts §108; Bogert §151.

[64] *See generally* Bogert §529 n.13 and accompanying text.

[65] *See* Restatement (Second) of Trusts §101 (1959). *But see* 2 Scott on Trusts §101.1 (discussing failure of the trust when the named trustee was deemed essential to the creation, purpose, and maintenance of the trust).

[66] 2 Scott & Ascher §11.11.

[67] *But see* W. E. Shipley, J.D., Annot., *Court's power to appoint additional trustees over number specified in trust instrument*, 59 A.L.R.3d 1129 (1974).

[68] 2 Scott & Ascher §11.11.4.

[69] Lewin ¶14-39 through ¶14-51.

[70] *See generally* 2 Scott on Trusts §108; Bogert §532 n.8 and accompanying text (suggesting that no power to appoint exists by implication in anyone other than the court).

cotrustees and successor trustees.[71] The rules that govern how new trustees are appointed in a given situation are generally the same, whether the trust is private or charitable.[72]

The carefully drawn trust instrument provides for the contingency of vacancy and succession in the office of trustee and commonly states that upon appointment the new trustee shall have title to the trust property. This sort of provision, if accurately followed, has been held sufficient to pass title.[73] Similarly, in cases where the new or successor trustee was appointed by the court, the decree has operated to vest title in him.[74] In many states today, doubt as to the vesting of title in the successor trustee pursuant to court appointment has been removed by statute.[75] "When the trust property consists of land outside the court's jurisdiction, the court lacks the power to vest title in a new trustee, and a transfer by the old trustee or other holder of legal title remains necessary."[76] In any case, where the court appoints a new trustee it is good practice to incorporate an order for conveyance in the decree. For the duties of the successor trustee, see Section 3.4.4.3 of this handbook.

Occasionally a trust contains a no-contest or *in terrorem* clause rescinding the appointment of a trustee who institutes a proceeding challenging the validity of all or a part of the trust. According to the Restatement (Third) of Property, such a provision would be enforceable, unless probable cause existed for instituting the proceeding.[77]

§3.4.2 Acceptance and Disclaimer

The author never forgets that the people who have as much to lose as any if a trust turns out to be a sham are the trustees. Indeed, much of the book seems to be written from the standpoint of innocent trustees who may, to their horror, find out that what they have accepted is not a trust, but a poisoned chalice.[78]

---

[71] *See* Annot., *Trustee's appointment of associate or successor trustee under powers of trust instrument*, 57 A.L.R.2d 887 (1958).

[72] *See generally* 5 Scott & Ascher §37.3.7 (The Charitable Trust).

[73] *See* 2 Scott on Trusts §110; 2 Scott & Ascher §11.13.

[74] *See* 2 Scott on Trusts §109.

[75] *See* 2 Scott on Trusts §109 nn.2–3 and accompanying text.

[76] 2 Scott & Ascher §11.2 (noting, however, that a number of states now have statutes that require a nonresident trustee to appoint a resident or public official as agent for service of process).

[77] *See generally* §5.5 of this handbook (involuntary or voluntary loss of the beneficiary's rights) (in part discussing no-contest/*in terrorem* provisions in trusts). Restatement (Third) of Property (Wills and Other Donative Transfers) §8.5.

[78] Adrian Wallace, *A Refreshing Read*, Tr. & Est. L.J., July/Aug. 2002, No. 38, at 14 (reviewing James Wadham, Willoughby's Misplaced Trust (2d ed. 2002)). Before accepting a trusteeship, a prospective trustee will want to consider the nature of the task he would be undertaking. For a list of "material considerations," the reader is referred to Lewin ¶12-28.

Apart from the exceptions discussed in Section 3.3 of this handbook, no one can be compelled to serve as a trustee.[79] Before acceptance, one who has been appointed a trustee may disclaim the office.[80] A disclaimer will generally preclude a subsequent acceptance, although on petition a court in the exercise of its equitable powers may allow the disclaimer to be withdrawn.[81] Partial disclaimers of trusteeships are generally not permitted.[82]

A testamentary trust can arise without notice to or acceptance by any trustee.[83] A person designated as a testamentary trustee, as noted, is free to decline to serve as such.[84] However, if he does and there is no provision in the will designating an alternate, an appropriate court will see to it that the vacancy is filled.[85]

On the other hand, no trust arises inter vivos, unless by declaration,[86] without a delivery of property to the prospective trustee that is coupled with the manifestation of an intent[87] on the part of the property owner to impress a trust upon the property.[88] A legal consequence of a trust arising is that title to the property shifts to the trustee.[89] Moreover, "[t]he courts . . . have held that if the settlor makes sufficient delivery of the subject matter of the trust or a deed of transfer, the trust arises at the time of the conveyance, even if the named trustee has no notice, and even though the named trustee disclaims upon learning of the trust."[90]

A trust once created will not fail for want of a trustee.[91] The trustee's disclaimer, however, could impose on those involved, particularly the poor settlor, a somewhat arcane sequence of legal and equitable obligations, assuming trustee succession is not addressed in the terms of the trust:

> When a trust is to be created by a property owner's inter vivos transfer to another as trustee (whether by delivery to the trustee or to a third person), the trustee may decline to act as trustee if he or she has not by words or conduct previously manifested consent to serve . . . .The effect of the intended trustee's disclaimer of the trusteeship *after delivery* is to vest the title in a successor trustee if any is named in the terms of the trust, and if not then to restore to the transferor the title that

---

[79] Lewin ¶12-07.

[80] Lewin ¶12-07; 2 Scott & Ascher §11.5.

[81] 2 Scott & Ascher §11.5.3.

[82] 2 Scott & Ascher §11.5.4.

[83] Restatement (Third) of Trusts §14; Scott & Ascher §§5.5, 11.5.2.

[84] Restatement (Third) of Trusts §35(2).

[85] 1 Scott & Ascher §5.3.

[86] A declaration of trust is a trust that arose when the settlor declared himself trustee of some or all of his own property.

[87] 1 Scott & Ascher §2.1.8 (noting that an express trust may arise even if the settlor has never called it a trust, and even if the settlor does not understand what a trust is). "It is sufficient if what the settlor appears to have in mind is in its essentials what the courts mean when they speak of a trust." 1 Scott & Ascher §2.1.8.

[88] 1 Scott & Ascher §5.5.1.

[89] 1 Scott & Ascher §5.5.

[90] 1 Scott & Ascher §5.5.

[91] 1 Scott & Ascher §5.2.3; Bogert §1.

had passed to the intended trustee, but not the beneficial interests. The transferor thereupon becomes constructive trustee of the property for the intended beneficiaries and purposes. As constructive trustee, unless the intended express trust was revocable, the transferor is under a duty either to make (expressly or impliedly) a declaration of trust or to transfer the property to a new trustee (to be selected by the transferor or, if necessary, by the court) upon the intended express trust.[92]

"Upon acceptance of the trust by the trustee, . . . [however,] . . . he is under a duty to the beneficiary to administer the trust."[93] A person designated as trustee accepts the trusteeship by substantially complying with a method of acceptance provided in the terms of the trust.[94] Acceptance of the duties of the trustee also may be shown by words or by conduct,[95] *e.g.*, by accepting delivery of the trust property, by exercising powers as trustee, or by performing duties as trustee.[96]

In the case of testamentary trusts, the intent to accept is ordinarily demonstrated by the filing of a petition of appointment, usually in the probate court.[97] In the case of a signed written declaration of trust that is coupled with a re-registration of the trust property, the existence of intent to act as trustee is obvious, since the owner declares himself trustee. There is always an intent issue, however, when a declaration of trust lacks a paper trail.

In the case of inter vivos transfers in trust, receipt of the property coupled with the transferee's failure to disclaim or reject within a reasonable time may amount to an acceptance-by-inaction[98] of the office.[99] In order to avoid a period of uncertainty, a nontestamentary trustee designee willing to serve should immediately and formally accept either by signing the trust instrument or an instrument of acceptance.[100] An instrument of acceptance need not be in any

---

[92] Restatement (Third) of Trusts §14, cmt. d. This is an example of how a settlor can become an involuntary trustee. *See generally* §3.3 of this handbook (involuntary trustees). *See also* Scott & Ascher §§5.5, 11.5.3.

[93] Restatement (Second) of Trusts §169. "Even though by the terms of the trust the trustee is to receive no compensation, he is under a duty if he has accepted the trust to administer it." Restatement (Second) of Trusts §169 cmt. b.

[94] UTC §701(a)(1) (available at <http://www.uniformlaws.org/Act.aspx?title=Trust%20 Code>).

[95] Restatement (Third) of Trusts §35(1).

[96] UTC §701(a)(2) (available at <http://www.uniformlaws.org/Act.aspx?title=Trust%20 Code>). *See* Restatement (Second) of Trusts §102. *See generally* 2 Scott on Trusts §102.1.

[97] *See, e.g.*, UPC §3-601 ("Prior to receiving letters, a personal representative shall qualify by filing with the appointing Court any required bond and a statement of acceptance of the duties of the office").

[98] 2 Scott & Ascher §11.5.2. On the other hand, one can incur liability by pro-actively taking on the administration of a trust in the absence of authority to do so, that is by "intermeddling." *See generally* §8.15.35 of this handbook (trustees *de son tort* and *de facto* trustees).

[99] *See generally* Bogert §150.

[100] Many instruments will specify procedures for acceptance, and it is good practice to follow these procedures to the letter. However, acceptance may be construed even in the absence of compliance with procedures set forth in the governing instrument. Thus, the nominee should not assume that mere noncompliance would suffice as a disclaimer. If a nominee wishes not to assume fiduciary responsibilities, he should take positive steps to disclaim. Bogert §150.

particular form; a letter will be sufficient. The instrument of acceptance should be affixed to the governing instrument so that there is a paper trail.

Upon acceptance of the trusteeship, it may be appropriate for the trustee to file a Notice Concerning Fiduciary Relationship (Form 56) with the Internal Revenue Service (IRS).[101] Trustees of administrative trusts, for example, are obliged to do this upon assuming office.[102]

Section 7-101 of the Uniform Probate Code would impose on a trustee the duty to register the trust in an appropriate state court at the trust's principal place of administration. This obligation to register would apply not only to trustees of testamentary trusts but also to trustees of inter vivos trusts, including trust declarations and oral trusts.[103] For more on the Uniform Probate Code's registration requirement, the reader is referred to Section 6.3.4 of this handbook. In 2008, Massachusetts adopted a gutted version of Section 7-101 that imposed no such duty to register on one who accepts a trusteeship.[104]

The Uniform Trust Code provides that by accepting the trusteeship, the trustee submits to the jurisdiction of the courts of the state where the trust has its principal place of administration.[105] The Uniform Probate Code is essentially in accord.[106]

"After a trustee has accepted the trust and qualified as required by the law of the state in question by filing an oath, giving bond, or taking such other steps as the statute, rule of court, or the trust instrument requires, it becomes his duty to carefully examine the terms of the trust and the trust assets in order to determine exactly what property forms the subject-matter of the trust, who are the beneficiaries, and what are the trustee's duties with respect to the trust property and the beneficiaries."[107] The trustee must then forthwith take reasonable steps to take control of all the property due the trust.[108]

Events triggering trust termination include the following: someone's death; a nondeath occurrence such as marriage of a beneficiary, loss of charitable standing with the IRS, or vacancy of entrusted real estate; passage of time; and revocation. Upon accepting the trusteeship, the prudent trustee establishes and maintains adequate internal controls to enable the trustee to identify promptly and respond appropriately to an event that triggers the particular trust's termination.[109]

As a general rule, a transaction affected by a conflict between the trustee's fiduciary and personal interests is voidable by a beneficiary who is affected by

---

[101] A copy of Form 56 may be found in Worksheet 16 (p. B-1601) of Acker, 852-2nd T.M., *Income Taxation of Trusts and Estates* (2000).
[102] *See generally* §9.9.14 of this handbook (the administrative trust).
[103] *See* UPC §7-102.
[104] *See* Mass. Gen. Laws ch. 190B, §7-101.
[105] UTC §202(a) (available at <http://www.uniformlaws.org/Act.aspx?title=Trust%20 Code>). *See generally* §8.40 of this handbook (judicial jurisdiction over the trustee).
[106] *See* UPC §§7-103, 7-104.
[107] Bogert §583.
[108] Bogert §583.
[109] *See generally* §8.2.4 of this handbook (trust termination checklist).

the transaction.[110] The Uniform Trust Code, however, would allow a trustee to implement a contract that the trustee had entered into before he contemplated becoming trustee.[111] Preexisting claims also could be pursued.[112] While such transactions may proceed without automatically being voidable by the beneficiary, they are "not necessarily free from scrutiny."[113] In Alaska, the trustee within thirty days after accepting the trust shall inform in writing current beneficiaries of the trustee's name and address.[114] The settlor, either by a provision in the governing instrument or by some other writing, may relieve the trustee of the obligation to so notify any beneficiary who is not entitled to a mandatory distribution of income or principal from the trust on an annual or more frequent basis.[115] This exemption from the notification requirement expires upon the first to occur—a judicial determination of the settlor's incapacity or the settlor's death.[116]

The Uniform Probate Code has similar but not identical postacceptance notification requirements: "Within 30 days after his acceptance of the trust, the trustee shall inform in writing the current beneficiaries and if possible, one or more persons who under Section 1-403 may represent beneficiaries with future interests, of the Court in which the trust is registered and of his name and address."[117] So does the Uniform Trust Code: "A trustee . . . within 60 days after accepting a trusteeship, shall notify the qualified beneficiaries of the acceptance and of the trustee's name, address, and telephone number . . . ."[118]

As a general rule and as noted above, no one need be a trustee involuntarily.[119] Usually the trustee nominated has the alternative of acceptance or disclaimer.[120] No particular form of disclaimer or rejection is necessary; it may

---

[110] UTC §802(b) (available at <http://www.uniformlaws.org/Act.aspx?title=Trust%20 Code>).

[111] UTC §802(b)(5) (available at <http://www.uniformlaws.org/Act.aspx?title=Trust%20 Code>).

[112] UTC §802(b)(5) (available at <http://www.uniformlaws.org/Act.aspx?title=Trust%20 Code>).

[113] UTC §802 cmt. (available at <http://www.uniformlaws.org/Act.aspx?title=Trust%20 Code>).

[114] Alaska Stat. §13.36.080. If possible, the trustee shall also so notify one or more persons who under Alaska Stat. §13.06.120 may represent beneficiaries with future interests.

[115] Alaska Stat. §13.36.080(b).

[116] Alaska Stat. §13.36.080(b).

[117] UPC §7-303(a).

[118] UTC §813(b)(2) (available at <http://www.uniformlaws.org/Act.aspx?title=Trust%20 Code>). "A trustee . . . within 60 days after the date the trustee acquires knowledge of the creation of an irrevocable trust, or the date the trustee acquires knowledge that a formerly revocable trust has become irrevocable, whether by death of the settlor or otherwise, shall notify the qualified beneficiaries of the trust's existence, of the identity of the settlor or settlors, of the right to request a copy of the trust instrument, and of the right to a trustee's report . . . ." UTC §813(a)(3).

[119] *See generally* Restatement (Second) of Trusts §102; 2 Scott on Trusts §102. *See, however,* §3.3 of this handbook (involuntary trustees) for a few exceptions.

[120] UTC §701(b) (available at <http://www.uniformlaws.org/Act.aspx?title=Trust%20 Code>).

be by words or by conduct.[121] The Uniform Trust Code provides that a designated trustee who does not accept the trusteeship within a reasonable time after knowing of the designation is deemed to have rejected the trusteeship.[122]

A designated trustee who wishes to disclaim or reject, however, wants to be certain of complete lack of responsibility from the outset. There is always the risk of an equitable acceptance by estoppel.[123] Accordingly, the disclaimer should be timely, in writing, and affirmative[124] and unequivocal. It should not be drafted in the form of a conveyance or assignment as that might imply prior acceptance.[125] It can be recorded in the place where the trust instrument is recorded or delivered to the person having custody of the instrument. It is also good practice to serve notice on cotrustees, if any, current beneficiaries, if any are known to the nominee, as well as to other parties having an equitable interest in the trust property, if known.[126] If the trust instrument is a will, a disclaimer filed in the probate court is appropriate and a printed form generally is used. As many states have enacted statutes establishing procedures and time frames for the filing of disclaimers, a person contemplating the disclaimer of a trusteeship would be well advised to search the annotated laws for any statutes that may apply.[127] In England, one's direct and incidental costs reasonably incurred in disclaiming are chargeable to the trust estate.[128]

Disclaimer is not allowable after acceptance of the office has taken place; resignation then becomes the only available option if a trustee no longer wishes to serve as such.[129] English law is in accord.[130] The problem with having to resort to resignation is that equity is disinclined to allow a trustee to resign—even when there is express authority to do so in the governing instrument—until there is a qualified successor in place.[131] In the interim, the unwilling trustee may be burdened with the fiduciary duties and subject to the

---

[121] *See generally* 2 Scott on Trusts §102.1; Restatement (Second) of Trusts §102 cmt. b; 2 Scott & Ascher §11.5.1.

[122] UTC §701(b) (available at <http://www.uniformlaws.org/Act.aspx?title=Trust%20 Code>). "To avoid an implied acceptance, a nominated testamentary trustee who is monitoring the actions of the personal representative but who has not yet made a final decision on acceptance should inform the beneficiaries that the nominated trustee has assumed only a limited role." UTC §401 cmt.

[123] *See generally* UTC §701 cmt. (available at <http://www.uniformlaws.org/Act.aspx?title= Trust%20Code>).

[124] *See* 2 Scott & Ascher §11.5.2 (Effect of Inaction).

[125] Lewin ¶12-08.

[126] "In the case of a person named as trustee of a revocable trust, it would be appropriate to communicate the rejection to the settlor." UTC §701 cmt. (available at <http://www. uniformlaws.org/Act.aspx?title=Trust%20Code>).

[127] For a list of statutes expressly providing that a person named as trustee may disclaim, *see* 2 Scott on Trusts §102 n.4.

[128] Lewin ¶12-22 (England).

[129] 2 Scott & Ascher §11.9. *See* §3.4.3 of this handbook (death of trustee; resignation of trustee; disqualification of trustee because of physical or mental ill health).

[130] Lewin ¶12-16 (England).

[131] UTC §707 cmt. (available at <http://www.uniformlaws.org/Act.aspx?title=Trust%20 Code>); Bogert §511; 2A Scott on Trusts §171.1.

fiduciary liabilities that are the subject of this handbook. Thus, as acceptance may be shown by actions as well as by words, it is important for the nominee to make up his, her, or its mind one way or the other speedily and unequivocally.[132]

If the nominee decides upon disclaimer, meticulous care should be taken to avoid any assumptions of authority or voluntary interference with or control of the trust property in a way that could be construed as constructive acceptance. Of course, one's actions are always open to reasonable explanations,[133] e.g., lack of interest or inconsistent conduct.[134]

It should be noted that the Uniform Trust Code would make it possible for a person designated as trustee to inspect or investigate trust property to determine potential liability, particularly under the environmental laws, without backing into an implied acceptance.[135] Likewise, the person designated as trustee also would be permitted to take actions to preserve the trust property, provided that within a reasonable time after taking such actions, the person sends a disclaimer or rejection of trusteeship to the settlor, if living.[136] If the settlor is dead or lacks capacity, the disclaimer or rejection should be sent to a qualified beneficiary.[137]

The effect of a disclaimer of one of several trustees is to vest the entire title in those who accept,[138] and it is said that in the case of a sole trustee who disclaims, the title is temporarily revested in the settlor or the settlor's successors as of the time of the transfer.[139] It is certain that the disclaiming trustee is relieved *ab initio* of any liability.[140] This does not mean destruction of the trust, however, because equity will not allow the trust to fail because of the failure of the individual trustee, except in the rare case where a particular trustee is

---

[132] "To avoid an implied acceptance, a nominated testamentary trustee who is monitoring the actions of the personal representative but who has not yet made a final decision on acceptance should inform the beneficiaries that it has assumed only a limited role." UTC §401 cmt. (available at <http://www.uniformlaws.org/Act.aspx?title=Trust%20Code>). "The failure so to inform the beneficiaries could result in liability if misleading conduct by the nominated trustee causes harm to the trust beneficiaries." UTC §401.

[133] If a person proceeds to administer the trust property, as would a trustee, such action may be construed as an acceptance. *See* Carter v. Carter, 321 Pa. 391, 184 A. 78 (1936) (acceptance indicated by collecting insurance proceeds due the trust); Lentz v. Lentz, 5 N.C. App. 309, 168 S.E.2d 437 (1969) (acceptance indicated by executing assignment of option to purchase real estate). However, if the nominee is merely protecting the property temporarily until a trustee is appointed, such action ought not to be construed as acceptance. *See generally* Bogert §150.

[134] Disclaimer has been implied under the following circumstances: lack of interest and inconsistent conduct; lack of acceptance; failure to give bond and to qualify as trustee; failure to act for a prolonged period. *See* 2 Scott on Trusts §102.2.

[135] UTC §701(c)(2) (available at <http://www.uniformlaws.org/Act.aspx?title=Trust%20Code>).

[136] UTC§701(c)(1) (available at <http://www.uniformlaws.org/Act.aspx?title=Trust%20Code>).

[137] UTC §701(c)(1) (available at <http://www.uniformlaws.org/Act.aspx?title=Trust%20Code>).

[138] *See* Bogert §150.

[139] *See* Restatement (Second) of Trusts §102 cmt. g; 2 Scott on Trusts §102.3.

[140] *See generally* 2 Scott on Trusts §102.3.

deemed essential to the whole trust purpose.[141] If for some reason the settlor has expressed an intent that the person nominated is to be the only trustee qualified, it can be said that the nominee's acceptance is necessary to the creation of the trust.[142] Once one has disclaimed, one cannot thereafter withdraw it except with the permission of the court.[143]

§3.4.3 Death of Trustee; Resignation of Trustee; Disqualification of Trustee Because of Physical or Mental Ill Health

The essential point of the foregoing cases is that a trustee should not leave the trust in the lurch by a resignation . . . .[144]

Trustees (where there is more than one) take a joint estate that is not subject to partition.[145] A conveyance out of the trust from one cotrustee acting alone is void.[146] This means that a contract that relates to the trust property between one of the cotrustees and a third party with notice of the trust is ineffective absent a statute to the contrary.[147] Of course, the trust instrument may permit action by fewer than all of the trustees. A conveyance to two trustees as tenants in common will have the effect of creating two separate trusts with each trustee holding an undivided interest.[148]

Death. When one trustee dies, the whole estate vests in the survivors.[149] Even in states in which there is a statutory presumption that multiple parties take title to property as tenants in common, cotrustees generally take as joint tenants.[150] If the trust instrument specifies a definite number of trustees and the death of one or more of them reduces the number below the required amount, the whole estate will still vest in the surviving trustees and will remain there until a successor or successors assume responsibility for the trust property, whether

---

[141] *See generally* 2 Scott on Trusts §101.1.

[142] *See generally* Bogert §150 n.22 and accompanying text.

[143] *See* 2 Scott on Trusts §102.3.

[144] Restatement (Third) of Trusts §36, cmt. a (referring to In Matter of Sherman B. Smith Family Trust, 167 Wis. 2d 196, 482 N.W.2d 118 (1992); Vale v. Union Bank, 88 Cal. App. 3d 330, 151 Cal. Rptr. 784 (1979)).

[145] The joint tenancy of trustees does not share all of the characteristics of the classic joint tenancy. The parties to a classic joint tenancy are entitled to convert the interest into a tenancy in common (*a petition to partition*). Cotrustees, however, have no power to partition the trust or extinguish the trust by a conveyance or other action. Their powers are confined to joining with their cotrustees in conveying the whole estate or a part of it. *See generally* Bogert §145.

[146] *See generally* Bogert §145. *See also* 3 Scott on Trusts §194.

[147] *See generally* 3 Scott on Trusts §194.

[148] 2 Scott & Ascher §11.6.

[149] *See* 2 Scott & Ascher §11.6; Restatement (Second) of Trusts §103.

[150] *See* Restatement (Second) of Trusts §103 cmt. a.

pursuant to court order or the terms of the governing instrument.[151] In certain situations where the trustees and the beneficiaries are one and the same, the fact that the trustees hold the legal title jointly with right of survivorship and the beneficiaries hold the equitable interest as tenants in common may prevent the destruction of the trust through merger.[152]

At common law, if a sole trustee died without leaving a will, the title to the trust property passed to the trustee's heirs in the case of real estate or to the trustee's personal representative in the case of personal property.[153] The heirs or personal representatives were not permitted to administer the trust unless authorized to do so by the terms of the trust.[154] Nor could they qualify as BFPs.[155] The trustee's legatees and devisees could not as well:[156] If a sole trustee died leaving a will, title to the trust property passed at common law to the general takers under the trustee's will, subject, of course, to the terms of the trust,[157] unless it happened that the testator-trustee expressed an intention to confine the testamentary disposition to that in which the testator-trustee had a personal beneficial interest.[158] Fortunately, in many jurisdictions statutes have been enacted to address the issue,[159] *e.g.*, depriving a sole trustee of the right to appoint a successor by will (absent express authority in the governing instrument) and imposing on the personal representative of a deceased sole trustee an obligation to account for the decedent's administration of the trust.[160] In New York, the executor of a deceased sole trustee of a trust can administer the trust until a qualified successor trustee is in place. Presumably, the executor in the interim would have the authority to sign and file any trust tax returns.

The Uniform Trust Code does not require that the trustee's personal representative wind up the deceased trustee's administration.[161] It would not, however, stand in the way of the personal representative's sending a final trust accounting or trustee's report to the trust's current beneficiaries and presumptive remaindermen and any other qualified beneficiaries.[162] In fact, the deceased trustee's personal representative would be well advised to prepare and obtain approval of the deceased trustee's final trust accounting or trustee's

---

[151] *See* §3.4.4.3 of this handbook (successor trustees).

[152] *See generally* 2 Scott on Trusts §99.5; First Ala. Bank of Tuscaloosa, N.A. v. Webb, 373 So. 2d 631 (Ala. 1979). *See also* §8.7 of this handbook (merger).

[153] 2 Scott & Ascher §§11.4, 11.7.

[154] *See generally* Bogert §529; 2 Scott on Trusts §104.

[155] *See generally* 5 Scott & Ascher §29.1.6.1 (Devolution on Death of Trustee); §8.15.63 of this handbook (doctrine of bona fide purchase).

[156] *See generally* 5 Scott & Ascher §29.1.6.1 (Devolution on Death of Trustee); §8.15.63 of this handbook (doctrine of bona fide purchase).

[157] 2 Scott & Ascher §11.8.

[158] *See generally* Bogert §529; 2 Scott on Trusts §104.

[159] *See generally* Bogert §529.

[160] 2 Scott & Ascher §11.8.

[161] UTC §707 cmt. (available at <http://www.uniformlaws.org/Act.aspx?title=Trust%20 Code>).

[162] UTC §813(c) (available at <http://www.uniformlaws.org/Act.aspx?title=Trust%20 Code>).

report. Otherwise, the estate would remain liable for actions taken during the trustee's term of office until liability is otherwise time barred.[163]

Some statutes provide that both title and the office of trusteeship pass to the takers under the will; others provide that the title and right to possession vest in the successor trustee.[164] In general, a clear distinction is made between the deceased trustee's own property and the property that is held in trust. Thus, the surviving spouse of the deceased trustee does not take an interest in the trust property as statutory heir or by dower or curtesy.[165]

Under the Uniform Trust Code, a judicial proceeding by a beneficiary against a trustee for breach of trust must be commenced within five years after the first occurrence of (1) the removal, resignation, or death of the trustee; (2) the termination of the beneficiary's interest in the trust; or (3) the termination of the trust.[166] "If a trusteeship terminates by reason of death, a claim against the trustee's estate for breach of fiduciary duty would, like other claims against the trustee's estate, be barred by a probate creditor's claim statute even though the statutory period prescribed by this section has not yet expired."[167]

What if the deceased trustee during his lifetime had sent the beneficiary a report that adequately disclosed the existence of a potential claim for breach of trust and had informed the beneficiary of the applicable statute of limitations for commencing a proceeding against the trustee? In that case, the beneficiary, pursuant to the provisions of the Uniform Trust Code, would be foreclosed from commencing a proceeding against the trustee for breach of trust more than one year after the date the beneficiary or an authorized representative of the beneficiary was sent the report.[168]

Resignation. One may not be relieved of one's obligations as trustee by mere transfer and abandonment.[169] Essentially the trustee will be held to have improperly delegated to the transferee—or the world at large in case of abandonment—responsibility for administering the trust.[170] A trustee of a revocable trust may resign with the consent of the settlor, provided the settlor is competent to give consent.[171] Otherwise, the trustee may resign upon

---

[163] UTC §707 cmt. (available at <http://www.uniformlaws.org/Act.aspx?title=Trust%20 Code>).

[164] *See generally* Bogert §529.

[165] *See generally* 2 Scott on Trusts §104 n.6 and accompanying text.

[166] UTC §1005(c) (available at <http://www.uniformlaws.org/Act.aspx?title=Trust%20 Code>).

[167] UTC §1005 cmt. (available at <http://www.uniformlaws.org/Act.aspx?title=Trust%20 Code>).

[168] UTC §1005(a) (available at <http://www.uniformlaws.org/Act.aspx?title=Trust%20 Code>). A report adequately discloses the existence of a potential claim for breach of trust if it provides sufficient information so that the beneficiary or representative knows of the potential claim or should have inquired into its existence. UTC §1005(b).

[169] *See generally* Bogert §§511, 512. *See also* UTC §705(c) and cmt. (available at <http://www.uniformlaws.org/Act.aspx?title=Trust%20Code>).

[170] *See generally* Bogert §512.

[171] *See* 2 Scott & Ascher §11.9.4.

permission of the court[172] or in accordance with the terms of the trust[173] or with the consent of all of the beneficiaries, including the remaindermen, be their interests vested or contingent.[174] The consent of the beneficiaries will not be a complete protection to the trustee, of course, unless every one of them is of full capacity and has joined in the consent.[175] More often than not, nonjudicial consent will not be a viable option as there are likely to be unrepresented unborn and unascertained individuals with beneficial interests under the trust.[176] Statutes in most states govern the resignation of trustees.[177]

The Uniform Trust Code rejects the common law rule that a trustee may resign only with permission of the court.[178] The Code would allow a trustee to resign upon at least thirty days' notice to all cotrustees and the qualified beneficiaries, *i.e.*, the current beneficiaries and the presumptive remaindermen.[179] It goes without saying that "[a]ny liability of a resigning trustee or of any sureties on the trustee's bond for acts or omissions of the trustee is not discharged or affected by the trustee's resignation."[180] Pending transfer of the trust property to a qualified successor trustee, "a . . . [sole] . . . trustee who has resigned or been removed has the duties of a trustee and the powers necessary to protect the trust property."[181]

The mere resignation and acceptance thereof may not, in the absence of statute or appropriate language in the governing instrument, operate to transfer the title to a successor trustee. Thus, the resigning sole trustee may need to execute suitable conveyances of the trust property to the successor in office.[182] The outgoing trustee will want to do so in any case to put others on notice of the succession.

---

[172] *See* 2 Scott & Ascher §11.9.3.

[173] *See* 2 Scott & Ascher §11.9.1.

[174] *See* 2 Scott on Trusts §106. *But see* UTC §705(a)(1) (available at <http://www.uniformlaws.org/Act.aspx?title=Trust%20Code>) (allowing for resignation upon at least 30 days' notice only to the qualified beneficiaries, *i.e.*, to the current beneficiaries and the presumptive remaindermen).

[175] *See* 2 Scott & Ascher §11.9.2; §5.5 of this handbook (voluntary or involuntary loss of the beneficiary's equitable rights).

[176] *See* §8.14 of this handbook (when a guardian ad litem or special representative is needed).

[177] *See* 2 Scott on Trusts §106 n.4 (A List of Statutes Governing the Resignation of Trustees).

[178] UTC §705 cmt. (available at <http://www.uniformlaws.org/Act.aspx?title=Trust%20Code>).

[179] UTC §705(a)(1) (available at <http://www.uniformlaws.org/Act.aspx?title=Trust%20Code>).

[180] UTC §705(c) (available at <http://www.uniformlaws.org/Act.aspx?title=Trust%20Code>).

[181] UTC §707(a) (available at <http://www.uniformlaws.org/Act.aspx?title=Trust%20Code>). *See, e.g.*, Wortman v. Hutaff, 2012 WL 379752 (N.C. Super.) (confirming that a resigning trustee retains residual affirmative fiduciary duties to protect the trust property until such time as the legal title thereto duly transfers to the successor trustee).

[182] Restatement (Second) of Trusts §106 cmt. b.

The resignation of a testamentary trustee will likely require court involvement. In inter vivos trust instruments, a nonjudicial method of resignation always should be provided. Absent an express provision, it is likely the trustee of an inter vivos trust will either need or want judicial approval to resign.[183] If the trust expressly provides a method for the trustee's resignation, then the trustee must follow these requirements.[184] Many trusts provide that upon written notice to the beneficiary or beneficiaries then entitled to receive income, the trustee may resign.[185] Often the instrument specifies that the resignation becomes effective after a period from the date notice is mailed. It bears repeating that in the interim, the resigning sole trustee remains responsible for the administration of the trust. Written notice should be sent by certified mail to ensure receipt by the beneficiary, and regardless of what the instrument may say, the prudent trustee should assume that he is not discharged unless there is a cotrustee in place or until the trust property has been transferred to a qualified and duly appointed successor.[186] The Uniform Trust Code would authorize the court to appoint a special fiduciary to hold the fort until a successor is in place.[187]

A trustee who has resigned shall proceed expeditiously to deliver the trust property within the trustee's possession to the cotrustee, successor trustee, or other person entitled to it.[188] Under the Uniform Trust Code, if a cotrustee remains in office, the former trustee need not submit a final trustee's report to the beneficiaries or the court.[189] Note, however, that submission of a report triggers the favorable one-year statute of limitations referred to above. Also, the departing cotrustee would still have a duty to account to the cotrustee remaining in office if the cotrustees had been acting independently. The governing instrument, for example, might have expressly allocated asset management responsibility to the departing cotrustee. In such a case, the remaining cotrustee would be well advised to obtain a formal written accounting or report from the departing cotrustee. It is important that this be done sooner, rather than later, as there is always the risk of cofiduciary liability, *e.g.*, should it later be revealed that the departing cotrustee had been in material breach of trust. As time elapses, memories fade and trails go cold.

---

[183] *See generally* 2 Scott on Trusts §106.1. *But see* UTC §705(a)(1) (available at <http://www.uniformlaws.org/Act.aspx?title=Trust%20Code>) (authorizing a trustee to resign upon at least thirty days' notice to the current beneficiaries, the presumptive remaindermen, and all the cotrustees).

[184] *See* 2 Scott on Trusts §106.2. *See* Croslow v. Croslow, 38 Ill. App. 3d 373, 347 N.E.2d 800 (1976) (holding ineffective a resignation not in accordance with the terms of the trust).

[185] *See* Bogert §1293 for examples of trustee resignation provisions.

[186] *See* §3.3 of this handbook (involuntary trustees). *See also* UTC §707(a) (available at <http://www.uniformlaws.org/Act.aspx?title=Trust%20Code>).

[187] UTC §707 cmt. (available at <http://www.uniformlaws.org/Act.aspx?title=Trust%20 Code>).

[188] UTC §707(b) (available at <http://www.uniformlaws.org/Act.aspx?title=Trust%20 Code>); Restatement (Third) of Trusts §36, cmt. e.

[189] UTC §707 cmt. (available at <http://www.uniformlaws.org/Act.aspx?title=Trust%20 Code>).

"Because significantly less work is normally involved . . . [in a transfer than in a termination,] . . . termination fees are less appropriate upon transfer to a successor trustee than upon termination of the trust."[190]

Disqualification because of physical or mental health condition. A trustee who is unable to properly continue to carry out his fiduciary responsibilities because of a physical or mental health condition needs to resign, be removed, or otherwise leave office. When resignation is not an option, then someone may well have to gain access to the trustee's health information. There may be a provision in the trust instrument that triggers removal in the event of mental or physical incapacity. The trustee may have to be involuntarily removed. The privacy provisions of the Health Insurance Portability and Accountability Act of 1996 (HIPAA) could pose a problem in this regard.[191] Two experienced practitioners have suggested some possible ways to address the HIPAA problem before a trustee becomes incapacitated:

- "Obtain a signed 508 . . . [HIPAA] . . . Authorization from the currently serving trustee, including the grantor,"[192]
- "Place HIPAA language in the trust agreement,"[193]
- "Condition continued service as Trustee upon providing a 508 Authorization when demanded by a named individual or a successor or cotrustee,"[194]
- "Condition the service of each Trustee (initial and successor) upon that person providing a 508 Authorization as a part of . . . [his] . . . initial qualification, and provide that such Trustee will automatically cease to serve if such authorization is ever revoked,"[195]
- "Condition continued service upon the affidavit of a family member or beneficiary rather than that of a physician, and"[196]
- "Use of a Trust Protector to Change Trustees When Appropriate."[197]

---

[190] UTC §708 cmt. (available at <http://www.uniformlaws.org/Act.aspx?title=Trust%20Code>).

[191] *See generally* Jacqueline Myles Crain, *HIPAA—A shield for Health Information and a Snag for Estate Planning and Corporate Documents*, 40 Real Prop. Prob. & Tr. J. 357 (Summer 2005).

[192] Michael L. Graham & Jonathan G. Blattmachr, *Planning for the HIPAA Privacy Rule*, 29 ACTEC L.J. 307, 310 (2004).

[193] Michael L. Graham & Jonathan G. Blattmachr, *Planning for the HIPAA Privacy Rule*, 29 ACTEC L.J. 307, 310 (2004).

[194] Michael L. Graham & Jonathan G. Blattmachr, *Planning for the HIPAA Privacy Rule*, 29 ACTEC L.J. 307, 310 (2004).

[195] Michael L. Graham & Jonathan G. Blattmachr, *Planning for the HIPAA Privacy Rule*, 29 ACTEC L.J. 307, 310 (2004).

[196] Michael L. Graham & Jonathan G. Blattmachr, *Planning for the HIPAA Privacy Rule*, 29 ACTEC L.J. 307, 310 (2004).

[197] Michael L. Graham & Jonathan G. Blattmachr, *Planning for the HIPAA Privacy Rule*, 29 ACTEC L.J. 307, 311 (2004). *See generally* §3.2.6 of this handbook (considerations in the selection of a trustee) (discussing in part the concept of the trust protector).

§3.4.4   Exercise and Devolution of Powers

Upon acceptance of the trusteeship, the trustee acquires the panoply of express and implied powers needed to carry out the terms of the trust.[198] If a power is not confined to the doing of a single act or restricted in point of time, it remains available throughout the trust and may be executed in part or in whole at any time.

§3.4.4.1   Multiple Trustees (Cotrustees)

Despite the general rule in the United States that a party to a lawsuit cannot require his opponent to pay his legal expenses therein, an errant fiduciary may be surcharged for the legal expenses incurred in establishing his wrongdoing and obtaining recoupment insofar as it appears that the services rendered were not solely for the defense of the co-fiduciary but were performed to establish the wrong committed by the errant fiduciary and to recoup from him the loss which he has caused to the estate.[199]

The office of cotrustee. There is no requirement in the default law that a trust have more than one trustee.[200] On the other hand, subject to the obvious constraints of feasibility and practicality, there is no limitation *per se* on the number of cotrustees a trust may have,[201] or how many additional trustees the court may appoint in the exercise of its inherent equitable powers.[202] The number of trustees is generally dictated by the terms of the trust and, on occasion, by the court.[203] "If the settlor transfers property to multiple trustees, one of whom is dead or otherwise incapable of taking title, title vests in the others."[204] If a cotrustee ceases for whatever reason to serve, the terms of the trust will generally dictate whether or not a replacement needs to be found.[205] Subject to the terms of the trust providing otherwise, a cotrustee not only has a right to participate in the administration of the trust,[206] he has a duty to do so,[207] unless the cotrustee is unavailable[208] to perform the function because of absence, illness, disqualification under law, or other temporary incapacity, or the cotrustee has properly delegated the performance of the function to

---

[198] *See* §3.5.3 of this handbook (the powers of the trustee in equity to manage the trust estate), which discusses the nature and scope of these powers.

[199] Parker v. Rogerson, 49 A.D.2d 689, 690, 370 N.Y.S.2d 753, 754–755 (1975).

[200] Lewin ¶12-01 (England).

[201] Lewin ¶12-01 (England).

[202] Matter of Ikuta's Estate, 64 Haw. 236, 247, 639 P.2d 400, 408 (1981).

[203] *See, e.g.,* Andris v. Biehl, 27 Ill. App. 2d 393, 169 N.E.2d 692 (1960) (number of trustees determined by trust's terms). As to the court's power to appoint additional trustees over number specified in instrument, see 59 A.L.R.3d 1129.

[204] 1 Scott & Ascher §5.4.

[205] 2 Scott & Ascher §11.11.1.

[206] Restatement (Third) of Trusts §81(1).

[207] Restatement (Third) of Trusts §81(1).

[208] Restatement (Third) of Trusts §81, cmt. c.

another trustee.[209] A trustee, however, may not delegate to a cotrustee the performance of a function the settlor reasonably expected the trustees to perform jointly.[210] Unless a delegation was irrevocable, a trustee may revoke a delegation previously made.[211] The Restatement (Third) of Trusts is in accord.[212] An action taken by one trustee with the consent or subsequent ratification of the other trustee(s) is valid.[213]

For more on the subject of the delegation of fiduciary functions between and among cotrustees, the reader is referred to Section 6.1.4 of this handbook. For a general discussion of cofiduciary liability, see Section 7.2.4 of this handbook.

Vacancies. If a vacancy occurs in a cotrusteeship, title vests in the remaining cotrustees[214] who may act for the trust.[215] Moreover, "[i]f several persons are named as co-trustees and one of them dies, becomes incapacitated, or otherwise ceases to serve as trustee, a replacement trustee is required only if the settlor manifested that intention or it is found conducive to the proper administration of the trust."[216] In other words, there is a default presumption that all trustee powers pass to and/or are exercisable by the remaining cotrustees.[217]

Title held jointly. As noted, at common law and by statute, trustees take title to trust property jointly.[218] Where there are several trustees, the powers, like the title, vest jointly.[219] Thus, with the exception of the charitable trust,[220] the traditional default law has been that trust powers may only be executed by the joint action of all trustees; an action by fewer than all, even though a majority, is void unless permitted by the instrument or by statute or by the court.[221] In England, it is said that "[w]here the administration of the trust is

---

[209] UTC §703(c) (available at <http://www.uniformlaws.org/Act.aspx?title=Trust%20Code>).

[210] UTC §703(e) (available at <http://www.uniformlaws.org/Act.aspx?title=Trust%20Code>).

[211] UTC §703(e) (available at <http://www.uniformlaws.org/Act.aspx?title=Trust%20Code>).

[212] Restatement (Third) of Trusts §81 cmt. c.

[213] Restatement (Third) of Trusts §39 cmt. b.

[214] 3 Scott & Ascher §18.4; 1 Scott & Ascher §5.4.

[215] UTC §703(b) (available at <http://www.uniformlaws.org/Act.aspx?title=Trust%20 Code>).

[216] Restatement (Third) of Trusts §85 cmt. e.

[217] Restatement (Third) of Trusts §85 cmt. e.

[218] Cornelius J. Moynihan, Introduction to the Law of Real Property 209 (2d ed. 1988). Lewin ¶13-01 (England).

[219] *See* Restatement (Second) of Trusts §194.

[220] Prof. Bogert suggests why trustees of charitable trusts traditionally have been allowed to act by majority vote: "In the case of charitable trusts numerous co-trustees are often used and the difficulties of getting all to unite in a decision . . . are greater than in the instance of the usual private trust where the employment of more than three trustees is rare." George T. Bogert, Trusts §91 (Hornbook, 6th ed. 1987). *See also* 5 Scott & Ascher §37.3.5 (Co-Trustees of a Charitable Trustee Have Long Been Permitted to Act by Majority Vote).

[221] Restatement (Third) of Trusts §81 cmt. c; Restatement (Second) of Trusts §194. *See also* 3 Scott & Ascher §18.3 (containing at note 4 a catalog of statutes authorizing action by a majority of a trust's cotrustees); 3 Scott on Trusts §194 (containing at notes 21 and 22 a catalog of statutes

vested in co-trustees, they all form as it were but one collective trustee and therefore must execute the duties of the office in their joint capacity."[222]

When there is deadlock. A theoretical result of this principle would be that refusal to concur on the part of one of several trustees would block all action. It has long been settled, however, that if a trustee unreasonably refuses to concur in the joint exercise of a power, the court may remove the trustee.[223] "If multiple trustees are deadlocked with regard to the exercise of a power, on application of a co-trustee or beneficiary a proper court may direct exercise of the power or take other action to break the deadlock."[224] If failure to exercise a power would constitute a breach of trust, the stymied trustees cannot just sit on their hands.[225] At minimum they would have a fiduciary duty to do what needs to be done to put the matter of the deadlock before the court, such as by a complaint or petition for instructions.[226] One trustee can, and may have a duty to, maintain a suit against a cotrustee to compel him to execute the trust, to enjoin him from committing a breach of trust, and/or to compel him to redress a breach of trust,[227] nor is he precluded from doing so because of unclean hands.[228] In an *emergency* one trustee may exercise joint powers without the concurrence of the others, and may have a duty to do so.[229]

When unanimity is not required. The law, however, has been trending for some time in the direction of majority action for charitable and noncharitable

---

authorizing action by a majority of a trust's cotrustees). UTC §703(a) (available at <http://www.uniformlaws.org/Act.aspx?title=Trust%20Code>) provides that "[c]otrustees who are unable to reach a unanimous decision may act by majority decision." Restatement (Third) of Trusts §39 provides: "Unless otherwise provided by the terms of the trust, if there are two trustees their powers may be exercised only by concurrence of both of them, absent an emergency or a proper delegation; but if there are three or more trustees their powers may be exercised by a majority." It should be noted that traditionally the unanimity requirement has not applied to coexecutors. *See generally* 1 Scott & Ascher §2.3.2.3; 3 Scott & Ascher §18.3 (When Powers are Exercisable by Several Trustees).

[222] Lewin 29-24 (England).

[223] *See generally* 3 Scott & Ascher §18.3; 3 Scott on Trusts §194. *See also* Restatement (Second) of Trusts §107(a) cmt. b.

[224] Restatement (Third) of Trusts §39, cmt. e. *See also* 3 Scott & Ascher §18.3.

[225] 3 Scott & Ascher §18.3.

[226] 3 Scott & Ascher §18.3.

[227] 4 Scott & Ascher §§24.29 (Liability for Co-Trustee's Breach of Trust) and 24.4.2 (The Settlor and the Settlor's Successors in Interest).

[228] 4 Scott & Ascher §24.4.2 (the purpose of the action being to protect the interests of the beneficiaries, not those of the trustee). *See generally* §8.12 of this handbook (where the trust is recognized outside the United States) (containing a catalog of equity maxims).

[229] *See* 3 Scott & Ascher §18.3; 3 Scott on Trusts §194. "If a co-trustee is unavailable to perform duties because of absence, illness, disqualification under other law, or other temporary incapacity, and prompt action is necessary to achieve the purposes of the trust or to avoid injury to the trust property, the remaining co-trustee or a majority of the remaining co-trustees may act for the trust." UTC §703(d) (available at <http://www.uniformlaws.org/Act.aspx?title=Trust%20Code>). *See also* Restatement (Third) of Trusts §81 cmt. c.

trusts alike.[230] The Uniform Trust Code, for example, provides that cotrustees who are unable to reach a unanimous decision may act by majority decision.[231] The Restatement (Third) of Trusts provides as follows:

> Unless otherwise provided by the terms of the trust, if there are two trustees their powers may be exercised only by concurrence of both of them, absent an emergency or a proper delegation; but if there are three or more trustees their powers may be exercised by a majority.[232]

Cotrustee removal. Under the Uniform Trust Code, grounds for judicial removal of a trustee would include lack of cooperation among cotrustees that substantially impairs the administration of the trust.[233] Each trustee, as well as the settlor and each beneficiary, would have standing to petition the court to remove a cotrustee.[234]

Suits against third parties. All of several trustees must join or be joined in any suit involving third parties, or to the settlement or compromise thereof, because trustees are joint tenants.[235] In one case, however, a trustee was permitted to bring an arbitration action against a third-party brokerage firm over the objections of her cotrustee, the cotrustee having allegedly used the firm to make "unsuitable" trades without her knowledge or approval. "Whenever a co-trustee determines that actions of the other trustee are dangerous to the interest of the trust beneficiary, the co-trustee must act to protect the beneficiary."[236] From the perspective of the third party, it is always safer to insist that receipts and other papers be signed by all of the trustees for, although payment received by one of them may amount to a good discharge at law, the validity of the receipt may well remain open to question in equity.[237]

---

[230] *See generally* 3 Scott & Ascher §18.3. *See generally* 5 Scott & Ascher §37.3.5 (". . . [I]n the case of charitable trusts, trustees have long been permitted to act by majority vote, unless the terms of the trust provide otherwise").

[231] UTC §703(a) (available at <http://www.uniformlaws.org/Act.aspx?title=Trust%20 Code>).

[232] Restatement (Third) of Trusts §39. *See also* 3 Scott & Ascher §18.3 (When Powers are Exercisable by Several Trustees).

[233] UTC §706(b)(2) (available at <http://www.uniformlaws.org/Act.aspx?title=Trust%20 Code>).

[234] UTC §706(a) (available at <http://www.uniformlaws.org/Act.aspx?title=Trust%20 Code>). *See generally* Lee R. Russ, *Award of Attorneys' Fees Out of Trust Estate in Action by Trustee Against Cotrustee*, 24 A.L.R.4th 624 (1983).

[235] *But see* Merrill Lynch Pierce Fenner & Smith Inc. v. Nora-Johnson, Tr., 797 A.2d 226 (N.J. Super. 2002) (ruling that a cotrustee could maintain an arbitration action against brokerage house though the other trustee opposed and did not participate in action).

[236] *See generally* 4 Scott & Ascher §24.29 (Liability for Co-Trustee's Breach of Trust); Merrill Lynch Pierce Fenner & Smith, Inc. v. Nora-Johnson, TTE, 351 N.J. Super. 177, 184, 797 A.2d 226, 230 (2002).

[237] As we have noted elsewhere, a third party who knowingly participates with a trustee in a breach of trust shares with the trustee liability for any loss caused by the breach. *See* §7.2.9 of this handbook (personal liability of third parties, including the trustee's agents, to the beneficiary; investment managers; directors and officers of trust companies; lawyers; brokers). Thus, if the trustee transfers trust property in breach of trust to a third-party purchaser who is aware of the

Disputes between/among cotrustees. Though cotrustees are expected to act jointly in their dealings with others, in their dealings with one another, unilateral action may be appropriate under certain circumstances. Each, for example, has a duty to use reasonable care to prevent the others from committing a breach of trust,[238] and to obtain redress if they do.[239] Thus, a cotrustee may have a duty to bring suit against his fellow cotrustees to remedy their breaches of trust.[240] This means that the cotrustee will have the requisite standing to maintain such an action. The cotrustee of a charitable trust is no exception.[241]

If he prevails, most likely his legal fees will be absorbed by the trust estate or by the defendants.[242] If he does not, it is in the discretion of the court whether reimbursement will be allowed.[243] Much will depend upon whether filing suit was a reasonable[244] thing to do at the time and whether the trust itself was in some way benefited by the action the minority or dissenting trustee took.[245]

A cotrustee's right to reimbursement for independent counsel fees. A cotrustee, of course, is entitled to retain independent counsel in a nonlitigation context, *e.g.*, to seek advice regarding his cofiduciary responsibilities.[246] Whether he will be entitled to reimbursement from the trust estate is another matter, *especially if there is already trust counsel in place receiving compensation from*

---

breach, the third-party purchaser holds the trust property subject to the terms of the trust. Otherwise, "such a purchaser is liable only if the trustee commits a breach of trust in making the transfer and the purchaser has notice that the trustee is doing so." 5 Scott & Ascher §30.1. At common law, however, it was doctrine that even the innocent third-party purchaser had a continuing obligation running to the trust beneficiaries to see to it that the trustee properly applied the purchase price. 5 Scott & Ascher §30.1. *See also* §8.15.69 of this handbook (third-party liability for trustee's misapplication of payments to trustee; the purchaser's duty to monitor the trustee's application of the purchase price). In the U.S., such an innocent third party either by case law or by statute has been relieved of such an obligation. *See* 5 Scott & Ascher §30.1. "In England, the old rule has been repudiated by statute." *See* 5 Scott & Ascher §30.1. Even today, however, paying the purchase price to a cotrustee without the consent of the other cotrustees would not be without its risks. If the cotrustee were then to misapply the purchase price, there is the remote chance that the purchaser might have to pay up a second time. *See* 5 Scott & Ascher §30.1.2.

[238] Restatement (Third) of Trusts §81(2); 4 Scott & Ascher §24.29 (Liability for Co-Trustee's Breach of Trust).

[239] Restatement (Third) of Trusts §81(2); 4 Scott & Ascher §24.29 (Liability for Co-Trustee's Breach of Trust).

[240] Restatement (Third) of Trusts §81 cmt. e; 4 Scott & Ascher §24.29 (Liability for Co-Trustee's Breach of Trust). *See generally* §6.1.4 of this handbook (trustee's duty not to delegate critical functions) and §7.2.4 of this handbook (cofiduciary and predecessor liability and contribution in the trust context). *See also* UTC §703(g) (available at <http://www.uniformlaws.org/Act.aspx?title=Trust%20Code>) (providing that each trustee shall exercise reasonable care to prevent a cotrustee from committing a serious breach of trust and compel a cotrustee to redress a serious breach of trust).

[241] *See* Restatement (Third) of Trusts §94 cmt. f.

[242] *See generally* 76 Am. Jur. 2d Trusts §738 (1992).

[243] *See generally* 76 Am. Jur. 2d Trusts §738 (1992).

[244] Restatement (Third) of Trusts §81 cmt. e.

[245] Restatement (Third) of Trusts §81 cmt. c.

[246] *See generally* §7.2.4 of this handbook (cofiduciary and predecessor liability and contribution in the trust context).

the trust estate. He will most likely be called upon to demonstrate to the satisfaction of his cotrustees and/or the court that the involvement of another lawyer has somehow furthered the interests of the trust beneficiaries.[247]

A cotrustee's right to contribution (breach-of-trust damages). The Uniform Trust Code provides (as does the Restatement of Trusts[248]) that if more than one trustee is liable to the beneficiaries for a breach of trust, a trustee is entitled to contribution from the other trustee or trustees.[249] A trustee is not entitled to contribution if the trustee was substantially more at fault than another trustee; or if the trustee committed the breach of trust in bad faith or with reckless indifference to the purposes of the trust or the interests of the beneficiaries; or if only the trustee benefited from the breach.[250] Joint and several liability may be imposed when there is joint participation.[251] It also may be imposed when a cotrustee acts alone, particularly in cases where the nonparticipating trustee fails to exercise reasonable care to prevent the active cotrustee from committing a serious breach of trust or to compel the active cotrustee to redress a serious breach of trust.[252] For more on cofiduciary liability in the trust context, see Section 7.2.4 of this handbook.

§3.4.4.2 Surviving Trustees

When for any reason one of several trustees ceases to hold his office, the trust powers ordinarily remain in the surviving trustees.[253] This may be the case even when a delay in filling vacancies occurs.[254] Only in cases where there are special reasons for believing that the settlor intended to limit discretion to all the trustees originally named, or to those times when all vacancies are filled, will the court conclude that the powers do not vest in the survivors.[255] This is in contrast to what was once the rule, namely, that transfers in trust to two or more

---

[247] *See generally* 76 Am. Jur. 2d Trusts §349 (1992); Restatement (Third) of Trusts §81 cmt. c.

[248] Restatement (Third) of Trusts §102; Restatement (Second) of Trusts §258.

[249] UTC §1002(b) (available at <http://www.uniformlaws.org/Act.aspx?title=Trust%20 Code>); Lewin ¶39-39 through ¶39-51 (England); 4 Scott & Ascher §24.32 (Contribution or Indemnity from Co-Trustee) (U.S.).

[250] UTC §1002(b) (available at <http://www.uniformlaws.org/Act.aspx?title=Trust%20 Code>). *See generally* 4 Scott & Ascher §§24.32.1 (Trustees Not Equally at Fault) (other trustees also entitled to be indemnified by the trustee), 24.32.3 (Breach of Trust Committed in Bad Faith) (trustee entitled to neither contribution nor indemnity under the equitable clean hands doctrine), and 24.32.2 (Benefit to One Trustee) (other trustees also entitled to be indemnified by trustee to the extent he has been benefited); Restatement (Third) of Trusts §102(2) ("A trustee who committed a breach in bad faith is not entitled to contribution unless the trustee or trustees from whom contribution is sought also acted in bad faith.").

[251] *See generally* 4 Scott & Ascher §24.29 (Liability for Co-Trustee's Breach of Trust).

[252] 4 Scott & Ascher §24.29 (Liability for Co-Trustee's Breach of Trust); UTC §1002 cmt. (available at <http://www.uniformlaws.org/Act.aspx?title=Trust%20Code>).

[253] *See* Restatement (Second) of Trusts §195. *See generally* 3 Scott & Ascher §18.4; 3 Scott on Trusts §195.

[254] *See* 3 Scott & Ascher §18.4; 3 Scott on Trusts §195 n.6 and accompanying text.

[255] *See generally* 3 Scott & Ascher §18.4; 3 Scott on Trusts §195.

individuals specified by name implied an intention that neither could exercise discretionary powers alone.[256]

§3.4.4.3 Successor Trustees

Our rule recognizes and endorses the long-held view that [i]n naming a trustee to fill a vacancy where the instrument does not prescribe a method, the court has a wide discretionary range.[257]

. . . Notwithstanding such discretion, our rule reflects the view that it would be folly for the judge not to pay attention to the judgment of the active trustees as to who their colleague should be.[258]

Devolution of trustee powers. It is an equitable maxim that a trust will not fail for want of a trustee.[259] Furthermore, the settlor is presumed to intend that the trust continue until its purposes are accomplished.[260] This leads to the general rule that all express and implied powers vested in the original trustee will pass to the successor trustees, unless the settlor expresses a contrary intention.[261] The Restatement (Third) of Trusts is in accord.[262]

Methods of filling a trusteeship vacancy. There are essentially three ways a prospective successor trustee can be appointed to fill a vacancy in the office of trustee:

- By being designated such in the governing instrument or pursuant to a nonjudicial process set forth in the governing instrument, *e.g.*, by a provision giving successor designation authority to the outgoing trustee;[263]
- By court order; or
- By unanimous agreement of the beneficiaries.[264]

In the case of a charitable trust, which will usually lack identified and/or identifiable individual beneficiaries, the Uniform Trust Code provides that absent an effective designation in the terms of the trust and in lieu of court

---

[256] *See, e.g.*, Weeks v. Frankel, 128 A.D. 223, 112 N.Y.S. 562 (1908).

[257] In re Crabtree, 2003 WL 22119871 (Mass.) (citing to Wilson, petitioner, 372 Mass. 325, 327 (1977)).

[258] In re Crabtree, 2003 WL 22119871 (Mass.) (citing to Wilson, petitioner, 372 Mass. 325, 329 (1977)).

[259] *See* Restatement (Third) of Trusts §31.

[260] 1 Scott & Ascher §5.3.1; 3 Scott & Ascher §18.5 (When Powers Are Exercisable by Successor Trustees).

[261] *See* Restatement (Second) of Trusts §196; 3 Scott & Ascher §18.5.

[262] Restatement (Third) of Trusts §85(2). *See generally* 3 Scott & Ascher §18.5.

[263] *See generally* Trustee's appointment of successor trustee under powers of trust instrument, 57 A.L.R.2d 887.

[264] UTC §704(a)(c)(2) (available at <http://www.uniformlaws.org/Act.aspx?title=Trust%20Code>).

involvement, charitable organizations entitled to receive trust distributions may, with the consent of the attorney general, make the appointment.[265]

What constitutes a trusteeship vacancy. A vacancy in a trusteeship occurs if a person designated as trustee rejects the trusteeship, a person designated as trustee cannot be identified or does not exist, a trustee re-signs, a trustee is disqualified or removed, a trustee dies, or a guardian or conservator is appointed for an individual serving as trustee.[266] Under the Uniform Trust Code, if at least one trustee remains in office, a vacancy need not be filled.[267]

Powers of successor. The cardinal principle, however, is that *the intention of the settlor as expressed in the trust instrument is controlling*.[268] A well-drawn trust will specify that successor trustees shall have all powers granted the original trustees.[269] In the absence of such specific language, however, the settlor's intentions on the matter must be inferred from the general terms of the instrument.[270] It has been said that the settlor who names a corporate trustee intends that discretionary powers will pass to the successor trustees.[271] On the other hand, the fact that discretionary powers are conferred on a named individual may be a slight indication that the powers were not intended to be exercised by anyone except the individual named.[272] The modern trend, however, is to disregard this distinction.[273] In the great bulk of cases, all powers, express and implied, have been found to be transmitted.[274] "Statutes now widely permit a successor trustee to exercise all of the original trustee's powers, unless the governing instrument provides otherwise."[275] The current aspira-tional law is in accord with what has been happening on the ground. The Restatement (Third) of Trusts, for example, endorses on policy grounds a default presumption of transmissibility:

> It should be noted that the occasional suggestion of a general distinction in this matter between powers that are ministerial and those that involve significant fiduciary judgment or discretion, or that affect the beneficiaries' rights to distri-butions, has not been accepted or reflected in the actual decisions of courts, and is rejected here. Such an approach to determining the authority and duties of successor trustees would undermine not only the effective managements of trusts

---

[265] UTC §704(a)(d) (available at <http://www.uniformlaws.org/Act.aspx?title=Trust%20Code>).

[266] UTC §704(a) (available at <http://www.uniformlaws.org/Act.aspx?title=Trust%20Code>).

[267] UTC §704(b) (available at <http://www.uniformlaws.org/Act.aspx?title=Trust%20Code>).

[268] *See* Restatement (Second) of Trusts §196.

[269] *See generally* 3 Scott & Ascher §18.5.

[270] *See generally* 3 Scott & Ascher §18.5; 3 Scott on Trusts §196.

[271] *See* Restatement (Second) of Trusts §196 cmt. f.

[272] Restatement (Second) of Trusts §196 cmt. a.

[273] 3 Scott & Ascher §18.5.

[274] *See generally* 3 Scott & Ascher §18.5; Restatement (Second) of Trusts §196 cmt. a.

[275] 3 Scott & Ascher §18.5 n.2 (containing list of citations to such statutes).

but also discretionary interests that are fundamental to the beneficial provisions of many trusts.[276]

Corporate trustee merges or consolidates. For the related issue of what happens when a bank trustee merges or consolidates, see Section 8.19 of this handbook.

When there is need for court involvement to effect trustee succession. The court generally must be involved in the process of replacing the trustee of a testamentary trust. Not so with an inter vivos trust, provided all contingencies are adequately addressed in the governing instrument.[277] That is enough of a reason for some prospective settlors to opt for the inter vivos trust and associated pour-over will.[278]

The Uniform Trust Code provides that a person designated in the terms of the trust to act as successor trustee shall fill a vacancy in a trusteeship required to be filled.[279] When there is no such designation, the vacancy shall be filled by a person appointed by unanimous agreement of the qualified beneficiaries.[280] If all else fails, a person appointed by the court shall fill the vacancy.[281] The Uniform Probate Code provides that the "[v]iews of adult beneficiaries shall be given weight in determining the suitability of the trustee and the place of administration."[282]

Of course, the court always possesses equitable powers to appoint an additional trustee or special fiduciary "whenever the court considers the appointment necessary for the administration of the trust."[283] "A person other than a beneficiary who in good faith assists a former trustee, or who in good faith and for value deals with a former trustee, without knowledge that the trusteeship has terminated, is protected from liability as if the former trustee were still a trustee."[284]

---

[276] Restatement (Third) of Trusts §85 cmt. d. *See also*, 3 Scott & Ascher §18.5 (When Powers Are Exercisable by Successor Trustees).

[277] *See, e.g.*, McNeil v. McNeil, 798 A.2d 503 (Del. 2002) (holding that the lower court should not have exercised its "residual" authority to appoint successor trustees in the face of an adequate trustee succession provision in the inter vivos trust's governing instrument).

[278] *See generally* §2.1.1 of this handbook (the inter vivos trust) (discussing the pour-over will). At least one individual successor trustee of an inter vivos trust has had the unfortunate experience of having to obtain from the court Letters of Appointment in order to satisfy a stock transfer agent. *See generally* §8.21 of this handbook (duty of third parties to investigate whether the trustee has power to act or if so whether he is properly exercising the power). Had a qualified bank been the custodian of the trust assets, there might not have been a need to invoke the court's jurisdiction. *See generally* §6.2.4.8 of this handbook (the operational aspects of keeping track of trust income and principal).

[279] UTC §704(c) (available at <http://www.uniformlaws.org/Act.aspx?title=Trust%20Code>).

[280] UTC §704(c) (available at <http://www.uniformlaws.org/Act.aspx?title=Trust%20Code>). *See* UTC §103(12) (defining the "qualified beneficiaries" as essentially the current beneficiaries and the presumptive remaindermen).

[281] UTC §704(c) (available at <http://www.uniformlaws.org/Act.aspx?title=Trust%20Code>).

[282] UPC §7-305. *See also* Mass. Gen. Laws ch. 190B, §7-305.

[283] UTC §704(d) (available at <http://www.uniformlaws.org/Act.aspx?title=Trust%20Code>).

[284] UTC §1012(d) (available at <http://www.uniformlaws.org/Act.aspx?title=Trust%20Code>).

Remedying a predecessor's breach of trust. A successor trustee can maintain a suit against a predecessor trustee to remedy a breach of trust, and may have a duty *to the beneficiaries* to do so.[285] "If the trustee is taking up the administration of a trust which has been administered by a predecessor trustee, he should demand a complete accounting and require that the predecessor deliver possession of all the trust property which the records show should have been available to the trust at the time . . . [; and] . . . [i]f there is any default by the predecessor in the performance of his duties in this regard, the successor trustee at the outset should bring whatever actions are necessary against the predecessor, his bondsman, or third persons, in order to repair the breach of trust by the predecessor."[286] The successor trustee, for example, may have a fiduciary duty to recapture any termination fees levied on the trust by the predecessor trustee.[287] This all means that the successor trustee will have the requisite standing to maintain a breach-of-trust action against his predecessor. The successor trustee of a charitable trust is no exception.[288]

The successor trustee has a duty to exercise due diligence in scrutinizing the accounts of the predecessor. The trustee is deemed to know about a predecessor's breach of trust if the trustee has actual knowledge of it; has received a notice or notification of it; or from all the facts and circumstances known to the trustee, has reason to know it.[289] Accordingly, anyone contemplating service as a successor trustee should obtain from the incumbent trustee accountings and tax filings for the prior three years.[290] This is standard practice no matter how reputable the incumbent. The documentation should be carefully scrutinized for irregularities and red flags, *e.g.*, tax returns not filed or real estate possibly infected with hazardous waste. All parcels of real estate should be visited and inspected.[291] Should the investigation reveal a material breach of trust, the prospective successor trustee will want to give serious consideration to

---

[285] 4 Scott & Ascher §§24.4.2 (Co-Trustees and Successor Trustees); 24.28 (Liability of Successor Trustee); 24.28.1 (When Successor Trustee Permits Continuation of Breach); 24.28.2 (When Successor Trustee Fails to Compel Predecessor to Deliver Trust Property); and 24.28.3 (When Successor Trustee Fails to Compel Predecessor to Redress Breach of Trust).

[286] Bogert §583. *See* UTC §812 (available at <http://www.uniformlaws.org/Act.aspx? title=Trust%20Code>) (requiring the trustee to take reasonable steps to compel a former trustee or other person to deliver trust property to the trustee and to redress a breach of trust known to the trustee to have been committed by a former trustee). *See also* UTC §705(c) (providing that any liability of a resigning trustee or of any sureties on the trustee's bond for acts or omissions of the trustee is not discharged or affected by the trustee's resignation); 4 Scott & Ascher §§24.4.2 (Co-Trustees and Successor Trustees); 24.28 (Liability of Successor Trustee); 24.28.1 (When Successor Trustee Permits Continuation of Breach); 24.28.2 (When Successor Trustee Fails to Compel Predecessor to Deliver Trust Property); and 24.28.3 (When Successor Trustee Fails to Compel Predecessor to Redress Breach of Trust).

[287] UTC §708 cmt. (available at <http://www.uniformlaws.org/Act.aspx?title=Trust%20Code>).

[288] *See* Restatement (Third) of Trusts §94 cmt. f.

[289] *See* UTC §§812, 104 (available at <http://www.uniformlaws.org/Act.aspx?title= Trust%20Code>).

[290] *See generally* 4 Scott & Ascher §24.28 (Liability of Successor Trustee).

[291] *See, e.g.*, Hamilton v. Mercantile Bank, 621 N.W.2d 401 (Iowa Sup. Ct. 2001) (assessing damages, including punitive damages, against a successor trustee for failing to inspect real estate that had fallen into disrepair during tenure of predecessor and for not remedying the situation).

conditioning his acceptance of the trusteeship on the incumbent having taken appropriate steps to remedy the breach.[292] In an English case, a trustee who resigned the trusteeship in consideration of the successor paying him a sum of money was held in breach of the duty of loyalty and ordered to turn the money over to the trust.[293]

The attorney-client privilege. In a suit by a successor trustee against a predecessor trustee, is the predecessor entitled to assert the attorney-client privilege against the successor? Courts have held that when the office of trustee passes from one person to another, the power to assert the attorney-client privilege passes as well.[294] This would include the power to assert the privilege with respect to confidential communications between a predecessor trustee and an attorney on matters of trust administration. Bottom line: The predecessor may not assert the privilege as against the successor. The predecessor, however, would still retain the right to claim the attorney-client privilege as to communications between the predecessor and his, her, or its personal attorney.[295]

Conflicts of interest. As a general rule, a transaction affected by a conflict between the trustee's fiduciary and personal interests is voidable by a beneficiary who is affected by the transaction.[296] The Uniform Trust Code, however, would allow the successor trustee to implement a contract that the successor trustee had entered into before he contemplated becoming a successor trustee.[297] Preexisting claims also could be pursued.[298] While such transactions may proceed without automatically being voidable by the beneficiary, they are "not necessarily free from scrutiny."[299]

Notice to beneficiaries and others of trustee succession. Under the Uniform Trust Code, within sixty days after accepting a trusteeship, the trustee shall notify the qualified beneficiaries, usually the current beneficiaries and presumptive remaindermen, of the acceptance and of the trustee's name, address, and telephone number.[300] In Alaska, within thirty days after acceptance of the trust, the trustee shall inform in writing the current beneficiaries of the following: the court in which the trust is registered and the trustee's name and address.[301] If possible, those who represent beneficiaries with future interests must also be so informed.[302] The settlor by express language in the governing instrument or in some other later writing may relieve the trustee of an obligation to so notify certain beneficiaries, namely, those not entitled to a

---

[292] *See generally* 4 Scott & Ascher §24.28.3 (When Successor Trustee Fails to Compel Predecessor to Redress Breach of Trust).

[293] Sugden v. Crossland (1856) 3 Sm. & G. 192.

[294] *See, e.g.*, In re Estate of Fedor and Catherine M. Fedor Revocable Trust, 356 N.J. Super. 218, 811 A.2d 970 (2001).

[295] *See generally* §8.8 of this handbook (whom trust counsel represents).

[296] UTC §802(b) (available at <http://www.uniformlaws.org/Act.aspx?title=Trust%20Code>).

[297] UTC §802(b)(5) (available at <http://www.uniformlaws.org/Act.aspx?title=Trust%20Code>).

[298] UTC §802(b)(5) (available at <http://www.uniformlaws.org/Act.aspx?title=Trust%20Code>).

[299] UTC §802 cmt. (available at <http://www.uniformlaws.org/Act.aspx?title=Trust%20Code>).

[300] UTC §813(b)(2) (available at <http://www.uniformlaws.org/Act.aspx?title=Trust%20Code>).

[301] Alaska Stat. §13.36.080.

[302] Alaska Stat. §13.36.080.

mandatory distribution of income or principal on an annual or more frequent basis[303] This limited exemption from Alaska's statutory notice requirement extinguishes upon the settlor's death.[304] An earlier judicial determination of the settlor's incapacity will also extinguish the exemption.[305]

Finally, it may be appropriate that the successor trustee upon assuming office file a Notice Concerning Fiduciary Relationship (Form 56) with the IRS.[306]

Cross references. In Section 7.2.4 of this handbook we take up the residual liabilities of a former trustee. In Section 7.1.2 of this handbook, we consider when a former trustee may avail himself of the laches defense against a beneficiary, as that defense may have been partially codified by a statute of limitations.

§3.5 Trustee's Relationship to the Trust Estate

The queen does not own the Royal Collection, but holds it in trust for her successors and the nation. She can't sell it, so it's pretty silly to count it as part of her wealth, though doing so makes royal stories more interesting.[1]

To be sure, "[i]n ordinary language the noun 'trust' is a person-word."[2] Professor Fratcher, however, reminds us that the trust—in contrast to the corporation—is really not a legal entity; rather it is "an aggregation of property," where the rights and duties associated with its ownership "are divided between the trustee and the beneficiary." In other words, it is a relationship or collection of relationships.[3] Thus, "the trust, as such, is incapable of owning property, acquiring claims or incurring liabilities."[4] Likewise, it cannot be said that trust counsel represents the "trust." Counsel represents the trustee, perhaps also the beneficiary in some jurisdictions,[5] but not the "trust."[6] Because the trust is not an entity, it is more legally accurate to say that "a trust has been

---

[303] Alaska Stat. §13.36.080.

[304] Alaska Stat. §13.36.080.

[305] Alaska Stat. §13.36.080.

[306] A copy of Form 56 may be found at http://www.irs.gov/pub/irs-pdf/f56.pdf.

§3.5 [1] Paul Levy, *Kings and Queens and the Art They Loved*, Wall St. J., July 16, 2002, at D6, col. 4.

[2] George L. Gretton, *Trusts Without Equity*, 49 Int'l & Comp. L.Q. 599, 617 (July 2000).

[3] *See generally* 1 Scott & Ascher §2.1.4.

[4] W. F. Fratcher, Trust §95, *in* VI Intl. Encyclopedia of Comp. Law ch. 11 (F. H. Lawson ed., 1973) (hereinafter "Fratcher"). *But see* Restatement (Third) of Trusts, Tentative Draft No. 1 (Apr. 5, 1996), Reporter's Notes on §2 cmt. i, at 39 (noting the tendency of modern law to treat trusts as distinct legal entities by distinguishing the trustee individually from the trustee in a fiduciary capacity, such as for purposes of the trustee's liability to third parties for trust obligations). *See also* Jerome J. Curtis, Jr., *The Transmogrification of the American Trust*, 31 Real Prop. Prob. & Tr. J. 251 (no. 2 1996) (suggesting that the "corporate paradigm" is not completely analogous to trusts).

[5] *See generally* §8.8 of this handbook (whom trust counsel represents).

impressed on Blackacre" or "Blackacre has been transferred to a trustee" than it is to say that "Blackacre has been put into a trust." Having said that, in recent years the law for certain purposes is beginning to treat the trust as a quasi-entity, specifically when it comes to limiting the trustee's liability for the acts of his agents[7] and the trustee's liability in tort to third parties.[8] In the tax area, of course, the trust has been treated as a juristic person for some time.[9]

In July 2009, the National Conference of Commissioners on Uniform State Laws approved the model Uniform Statutory Trust Entity Act. A trust created under the Act is intended to be a juridical entity, "separate from its trustees and beneficial owners, that has capacity to sue and be sued, own property, and transact in its own name."[10] A statutory trust created under the Act may not have "a predominantly donative purpose."[11] For whatever reason, the critical phrase *predominantly donative purpose* is not defined in the Act, although there is some murky and oblique commentary about excluding trusts established in an "estate planning or other donative context,"[12] commentary that is undermined by the fact that a statutory trust may have a charitable purpose,[13] and by the Reporter's own musings:

> Although the drafting committee contemplated that a statutory trust under this act will be used primarily as a mode of business organization, Section 603(a) confirms that a person may become a beneficial owner of a statutory trust without an exchange of consideration. It is therefore possible that a statutory trust could be used as a substitute for the common-law trust in noncommercial contexts.[14]

§3.5.1 *Nature and Extent of the Trustee's Estate*

In the 1990s, says Kevin Parke, president of MFS, America's tenth-largest and oldest mutual-fund company, based in Boston, some people in the fund-management industry forgot they are fiduciaries, and that the money they manage is not their own. When a portfolio manager at MFS in Boston says, I own Intel, or refers to my fund, he reminds them that the money actually belongs to the client.[15]

---

[6] *See, e.g.,* Huie v. DeShazo, 39 Tex. Sup. Ct. J. 288, 922 S.W.2d 920 (1996) (holding that the attorney-client privilege protects communications between a trustee and his or her attorney, the privilege extending neither to the beneficiary nor to the "trust," which is a relationship, not an entity).

[7] *See generally* 4 Scott & Ascher §22.4 (Tort Liability); §6.1.4 of this handbook (trustee's duty to give personal attention).

[8] *See generally* §7.3.3 of this handbook (trustee's liability as legal owner in tort to nonbeneficiaries); 4 Scott & Ascher §22.4 (Tort Liability).

[9] *See generally* Chapter 10 of this handbook (income taxation of trusts).

[10] Uniform Statutory Trust Entity Act, Prefatory Note.

[11] Uniform Statutory Trust Entity Act, §303.

[12] Uniform Statutory Trust Entity Act, §303, cmt.

[13] Uniform Statutory Trust Entity Act, §303, cmt.

[14] Uniform Statutory Trust Entity Act, Prefatory Note.

[15] The Law of Averages, 368 Economist No. 8331, July 5, 2003, at 8.

A trust is a fiduciary relationship with respect to property.[16] Thus it is no surprise that the subject of a trust is generally referred to as the trust property. Synonyms for trust property are trust *res* and trust *corpus*. Another synonym is *trust estate*.[17] The term *estate*, however, has an important second meaning in the trust context that is rooted in the ancient interactions of law and equity. The topic of this section is that other sense in which the term *estate* is employed. "The word estate is of feudal origin and is derived from the Latin word status."[18] In every trust there are two estates: the trustee's legal estate and the beneficiary's equitable estate.[19] Though these two estates are separate, they are bound together and tend to travel on parallel lines,[20] though not in every case. The law, for example, has generally frowned on the "overlapping of estates or a hiatus between them."[21] Not so with the equity courts, which early on began enforcing springing and shifting uses.[22]

Today, the trust is an important tool in the estate planner's kit, in large part because of such practical spin-offs from this law-equity divergence. The modern discretionary trust particularly comes to mind.[23] Essentially a vehicle for the creation and administration of springing and shifting equitable property interests, the discretionary trust has no serious equivalent in the pantheon of legal relationships.[24] The law-equity divergence also has positioned the trust as an instrument of law reform. In this regard, the reader is referred to Section 9.30 of this handbook, in which the English marriage settlement is discussed.

The trustee holds legal title to the trust property,[25] unless one of the following exceptions applies: it is a passive trust involving real estate;[26] the subject of the trust is an equitable interest; or the settlor expresses a contrary

---

[16] *See* Portico Mgmt. Grp., LLC v. Harrison, 202 Cal. App. 4th 464 (2011).

[17] For its purposes, the UPC defines estate as "the property of the decedent, trust, or other person whose affairs are subject to this Code as originally constituted and as it exists from time to time during administration." UPC §1-201(13).

[18] Cornelius J. Moynihan, Introduction to the Law of Real Property 24 (2d ed. 1988). "It speaks to us of a time when landholding was inseparably connected with a man's political and personal status in the community." Cornelius J. Moynihan, Introduction to the Law of Real Property 24 (2d ed. 1988).

[19] The *legal estate* is the whole estate, and the holder of the legal title is the sole owner. When the title is held for the benefit of another, as in a trust, the beneficial interest thus created is called an *equitable estate. See generally* Cornelius J. Moynihan, Introduction to the Law of Real Property §173 (2d ed. 1988). *See also* §8.27 of this handbook (what is the difference between a legal life estate and an equitable life estate under a trust?).

[20] *See generally* 2 Scott on Trusts §130.1; Bogert §181.

[21] 1 Scott & Ascher §1.1.

[22] 3 Scott & Ascher §13.1 (confirming that the chancellors early on began permitting springing and shifting uses in contravention of the legal rules requiring continuity in seisin).

[23] *See generally* §3.5.3.2(a) of this handbook (the discretionary trust).

[24] 2 Scott & Ascher §9.1.

[25] *See* Albrecht v. Brais, 324 Ill. App. 3d 188, 191, 754 N.E.2d 396, 399 (2001) (noting that title is in a trustee but not in an escrow agent, though an escrow agent "may have power to pass title").

[26] *See generally* 1A Scott on Trusts §88; §8.15.1 of this handbook (the statute of uses).

intent.[27] Thus it is said that the trustee owns the property.[28] Equity, however, can compel the trustee to yield rights incident to that legal ownership to the extent they interfere with the beneficiary's equitable interests.[29] Having said that, "[a]t common law, . . . the rule was that a court of equity acted in personam, and only in personam; thus although the property was within the state, a court of equity could not by its decree affect interests in the property."[30] Today, on the other hand, in an equitable action to remove a trustee, for example, the court may effect a vesting of legal title in the successor trustee if it has jurisdiction over the trust property.[31]

Contrast the trust with the civil law foundation. Title to its assets is in the entity itself, not in the members of its board or council.[32]

To the layman and the civil lawyer,[33] this splitting of interests is as mysterious as the Trinity.[34] How can it be that the trustee and the beneficiaries both own the property? We have here an "Athanasian mystery,"[35] or, as one learned commentator and wag has written: "Though the English do not lay exclusive claim to having discovered God, they do claim to have invented the trust with two natures in one."[36]

Perhaps it would be helpful to look at it this way: The trustee holds all rights to the trust property except the right to its benefit.[37] That right is given

---

[27] *See generally* 1A Scott on Trusts §88.1.

[28] *See* Portico Mgmt. Grp., LLC v. Harrison, 202 Cal. App. 4th 464 (2011).

[29] 1 Scott & Ascher §1.1.

[30] 7 Scott & Ascher §45.2.2.

[31] *See* 7 Scott & Ascher §45.2.2.

[32] *See generally* §8.12.1 of this handbook (the civil law foundation).

[33] *See generally* §8.12.1 of this handbook (civil law alternatives to the trust).

[34] Swiss civil law generally does not recognize the coexistence of equitable and legal rights in a single item of property. *See* Pietro Supino and Andreas C. Limburg, *A Swiss Perspective on Trusts*, in Trusts in Prime Jurisdictions 384 (Alon Kaplan ed., 2000) (noting that under Swiss law—subject to certain exceptions that are limited by the *numerus clausus* of real rights—the general rule is that "not more than one person can have real rights with regard to the same object" and further suggesting that under Swiss law, the fiduciary relationship is "of a purely contractual nature, with the consequence that the fiduciary holds the full property rights with regard to the objects transferred to him"). As to the Christian Trinity, one distinguished ecclesiastical scholar offers this explanation: "The Three Persons [Father, Son, and Holy Spirit] differ from one another not in Godhead for each one is wholly God; rather they differ in terms of their relations (not relationships!) with one another." Peter Toon, The Trinity as the Shield of Our Lives, 31 Mandate No. 3, at pg. 3 (May/June 2008).

[35] George L. Gretton, *Trusts Without Equity*, 49 Int'l & Comp. L.Q. 599, 600 (2000). The Athenasian Creed or Quicunque Vult, which was composed originally in Latin and later translated into Greek, had been widely employed in the West beginning in the early Middle Ages as an indispensable statement of the basic dogma of the Christian Trinity. It may be found in the English Book of Common Prayer of 1662 and the Canadian Book of Common Prayer of 1962. It is omitted from the American Book of Common Prayer of 1928.

[36] T. B. Smith, International Encyclopedia of Comparative Law, Vol. VI, ch. 2, ¶262.

[37] For a discussion of two limited exceptions to the general default rule that the trustee may not benefit from the trust property, one exception being archaic and the other current, *see* §4.1.1.1 of this handbook (the noncharitable trust; resulting trust defined).

to the beneficiary.[38] Thus, even absent a breach of trust, the trustee is accountable for any profit from the administration of the trust.[39] Of course, it is the prerogative of the settlor to withhold from the trustee other rights, such as the right to sell the trust property.[40] It would not, however, be accurate to say that the trustee "holds" all legal rights for the benefit of the beneficiary. In the words of Prof. Hohfeld: "One may literally 'hold' a physical object for another person without the destruction or alteration of the object. But how is it when a trustee 'holds' an aggregate of 'legal' relations for the benefit of another?"[41]

In England in earlier times, the beneficiary would look to the Lord Chancellor for help in protecting his beneficial interest, the Chancellor exercising his powers on the ground of conscience. "This appears to have been an importation from the canon law; almost all the medieval chancellors were ecclesiastics."[42] Today the beneficiary looks to the secular courts in the exercise of their equitable powers.[43]

What then is the practical difference between a trust and a contract, or between a trust and an agency such as a power of attorney, when it comes to the property that is the subject of these arrangements? By way of illustrating how the trust fits into the framework of fundamental common law legal relationships, let us take the village inn. Assume that one evening the building inspector is about in the village, and he notices that the fire escapes have fallen off the building. Whom then does he cite for an infraction of the building code? Certainly not the guests. The innkeeper is cited because he owns the inn. Now the guests may well find themselves out in the cold that evening. Their recourse however is a *legal* one against the innkeeper with whom they have a contractual relationship.[44] In earlier times, this would have been a legal matter for the secular courts. That is still the case today.

Let us now assume that the innkeeper is trustee of the inn and that the guests are beneficiaries, not parties to a contract with the innkeeper. Whom does the building inspector now cite? Again, the innkeeper is cited because, as far as the inspector is concerned, the innkeeper legally owns the inn.[45] Any complaint the guests may have against the innkeeper is not the inspector's

---

[38] *See* §5.1 of this handbook (who can be a trust beneficiary).

[39] Restatement (Third) of Trusts §99.

[40] *See generally* 3 Scott on Trusts §190. *See also* §3.5.3.1(a) of this handbook (trustee's power to sell).

[41] Wesley Hohfeld, *Supplemental Note on the Conflict of Equity and Law*, 26 Yale L. J. 767 (1917).

[42] Snell's Equity ¶ 1-09.

[43] *See generally* 3 Scott on Trusts §197.

[44] A breach of contract gives the injured party a right to damages (usually a sum of money based on an expectation interest) against the party in breach. Restatement (Second) of Contracts §§346–347.

[45] *See* 4 Scott & Ascher §26.4.4 (referring to Chicago v. Pielet, 95 N.E.2d 528 (Ill. App. 1950), a case where a trustee was held personally liable to a city for maintaining a dangerous fence on the trust premises in violation of the building code); 4 Scott & Ascher §26.1 (The Trustee's Liability—In General); Maine Shipyard & Marine Ry. v. Lilley, 2000 Me. 9, 743 A.2d 1264 (2000) (citing to this handbook).

problem. In earlier times, the beneficiary, not being in a contractual relationship with his trustee, would have had recourse against the innkeeper only to the
ecclesiastical courts for any breach of trust; today the beneficiary must invoke
the *equitable* powers of the secular courts. It always should be kept in mind that
even though the innkeeper receives the citation as legal owner of the trust
property, the equitable or beneficial interests of the guests are very much
interests in property as well.[46] A beneficiary's equitable right of enjoyment, for
example, may not be seized by the *trustee's* personal creditors or by the *trustee's*
spouse.[47]

It is out of more than mere historical interest that we ponder the nature of
the trustee's estate. As one can see, rights are affected. For example, what about
the ironmonger who improperly installed the fire escapes? If the innkeeper
owns the inn in his individual nonfiduciary capacity, it is the innkeeper who sues
the ironmonger in contract. Even if the innkeeper were under guardianship,
suit would still be brought in his name. Why? Because title would have remained
in the innkeeper.[48] The inn would merely be in the guardian's possession.

If, on the other hand, the inn were the subject of a trust, who brings suit
against the ironmonger, the trustee or the beneficiaries? Under the common
law, the trustee is the plaintiff because, as legal owner of the property,[49] the
trustee is in a contractual relationship with the ironmonger.[50] Note, however,
that should the matter reach the federal courts, the trustee, unless he is a lawyer,
may not be permitted to represent himself as trustee *pro se, i.e.,* to litigate the
matter without counsel on behalf of the trust.[51]

Assume the trustee of the inn manages to locate a competent ironmonger,
who then properly repairs and re-installs the fire escape. For no good reason,
the trustee refuses to pay the competent ironmonger for his services. Whom/
what does the competent ironmonger name as defendant in a suit upon the
contract, the trustee or "the trust"? From the competent ironmonger's

---

[46] *See* 1 Restatement of Property at 3 (introductory note to Chapter 1). *See also* In re
Catherwood's Trust, 173 A.2d 86, 91 (1961) ("A gift of an equitable life estate in income or of a
remainder does constitute a grant of a vested property right of which the recipients cannot be
divested by legislative action.").

[47] *See generally* Bogert §§146 (Creditor), 146 (Spouse).

[48] 1 Scott & Ascher §2.3.3.

[49] *See* Galdjie v. Darwish, 113 Cal. App. 4th 1331, 1343, 7 Cal. Rptr. 3d 178, 187 (2003)
(confirming that at common law, the trustee was the legal owner of the underlying property).

[50] *See generally* 4 Scott on Trusts §280.2. *See also* Witzman v. Gross, 148 F.3d 988, 990 (1998)
(the general rule of trust law that a beneficiary cannot bring an action at law in a trust's stead
against a third party for torts or other wrongs extends to beneficiaries who attempt to sue a
trustee's attorneys for legal malpractice); Navarro Sav. Ass'n v. Lee, 446 U.S. 458 (1980) (for
purposes of determining federal diversity jurisdiction in an action brought by trustees against
third parties for breach of contract, the domiciles of the trustees, not those with the equitable
interests, is what is relevant, the trustees being the "real parties to the controversy").

[51] *See* C. E. Pope Equity Trust v. United States, 818 F.2d 696 (9th Cir. 1987) (citing the
language of the Judiciary Act of 1789, now found in 28 U.S.C. §1654, as indirect authority for the
proposition that a trustee who is neither a beneficiary nor a lawyer must retain a lawyer to represent
the trust in any federal court litigation).

perspective, the safer practice is to name the trustee,[52] although naming both nowadays is probably the safest.[53]

What if a fire escape fell on a passerby? If the inn were not the subject of a trust, the innkeeper-owner, whether or not under guardianship, could personally be liable in tort for any harm to the passerby caused by the innkeeper-owner's negligence.

If the inn were the subject of a trust, could the innkeeper-trustee be held personally liable for any harm to the third party caused by his negligence or the negligence of his agents? Under the common law, he could.[54] Moreover, whether or not he was entitled to indemnity, the liability could even exceed the value of the underlying trust property. At one time, merely his status as the holder of the legal title would subject him to liability that could exceed the value of the underlying trust property.[55] The current state of the law, however, is that the innkeeper-trustee can be held fully and personally liable only if he is "personally at fault."[56] To the extent there is personal fault, he would generally have no right to be indemnified from the entrusted property.[57] To the extent there is no personal fault, the risk of liability has generally shifted to the trust estate.[58] The matter of the trustee's external liability is discussed in greater detail in Section 7.3.3 of this handbook (Liability as Legal Owner in Tort to Nonbeneficiaries) and in Section 9.6 of this handbook (Trusts That Resemble Corporations or Agencies).

What if the trustee for full value sells the inn in violation of the terms of the trust to someone who has no notice of the trust (*i.e.*, to a BFP)? Under the common law, the sale is probably good with the result that the beneficiaries have no recourse against the BFP, just the trustee for the proceeds.[59]

When the trust terminates, must the trustee convey the trust property in whatever form to the remaindermen, or do the remaindermen take automatically? Under the common law, a conveyance would be required, with the possible exception of certain trusts involving real estate.[60] A conveyance, of course, would not be required if the remainder had been legal rather

---

[52] *See, e.g.*, Portico Mgmt. Grp., LLC v. Harrison, 202 Cal. App. 4th 464 (2011).

[53] *See generally* §8.15.77 of this handbook (the trust entity doctrine).

[54] *See generally* 4 Scott & Ascher §22.4; 4 Scott on Trusts §264.

[55] *See generally* 4 Scott & Ascher §26.4.5 (When Trust Estate Is Insufficient to Indemnify Trustee).

[56] 4 Scott & Ascher §22.4.

[57] 4 Scott & Ascher §22.4.

[58] 4 Scott & Ascher §22.4.

[59] *See generally* 4 Scott on Trusts §284. *See also* §§5.4.2 of this handbook (rights of the beneficiary as against BFPs and other transferees of the underlying trust property), 8.3.2 of this handbook (bona fide purchase for value of trust property, specifically what constitutes notice that a transfer is in breach of trust?), and 8.15.63 of this handbook (doctrine of bona fide purchase; the BFP). *See also* §8.3.6 of this handbook (negotiable instruments and the duty of third parties to inquire into the trustee's authority to transfer trust property). For a comparison of the BFP, a creature of equity, with the holder in due course, a creature of law, *see* §8.15.68 of this handbook (the holder in due course in the trust context).

[60] *See generally* 1A Scott on Trusts §88; §8.15.1 of this handbook (statute of uses).

than equitable. This is because title would have vested *ab initio* in the remaindermen.[61]

The trustee's ownership interest in the trust estate is subtle and complex and thus the rights, duties, and obligations of those who may come in contact with the trust estate are entangled.[62] As the trustee may be exposed to potential personal liability to third parties as an incident of the "ownership" interest in the trust estate, the potential trustee should seek the advice of counsel and purchase appropriate liability insurance before venturing into this strange world of bifurcated interests. With respect to a given situation, the trustee should also understand the extent to which these common law duties and obligations may be altered by statute, by decision, and by the terms of a particular governing instrument.[63] The Uniform Trust Code, for example, would afford the trustee who holds an interest as a general partner in a general partnership certain contract and tort liability protections.[64]

Finally, what about the agency? What if the guests own the inn and the innkeeper is operating the inn under a power of attorney? In that case, the innkeeper is their agent and he receives the citation on their behalf, as they possess both the legal estate and the equitable estate.[65] Were the innkeeper the trustee of the inn, his acts would be as principal with respect to the affairs of the inn. He would neither be an agent of the settlor nor an agent of the beneficiaries.[66]

§3.5.2 *Rights of the Trustee*

To the extent to which the trustee is entitled to indemnity, he has a security interest in the trust property. He will not be compelled to transfer the trust property to the beneficiary or to a transferee of the interest of the beneficiary or a successor trustee until he is paid or secured for the amount of expenses properly incurred by him in the administration of the trust.[67] . . .

The trustee need not pay over income without deducting the compensation to which he is entitled with respect to the income, and need not pay over principal without deducting the compensation to which he is entitled with respect to the principal. To this extent the trustee has a security interest in the trust property for his compensation.[68]

---

[61] *See generally* §8.27 of this handbook (comparing the legal life estate and the equitable life estate incident to a trust?).

[62] *See, e.g.,* Charles E. Rounds, Jr., *State Common Law Aspects of the Global Unwindings of the Madoff Ponzi Scheme and the Sub-Prime Mortgage Securitization Debacle,* 27 Wis. Int'l L.J. 99 (2009).

[63] *See, e.g.,* UTC §1010 (available at <http://www.uniformlaws.org/Act.aspx?title= Trust%20Code>) (Limitation on Personal Liability of Trustee).

[64] UTC §1011 (available on the Internet at http://www.uniformlaws.org/Act.aspx? title=Trust%20Code>).

[65] 1 Scott & Ascher §2.3.4.

[66] Lewin ¶1-17.

[67] Restatement (Second) of Trusts §244 cmt. c.

[68] Restatement (Second) of Trusts §242 cmt. e.

In the tangle of legal relationships that is the trust, the trustee as well as the beneficiary has certain rights. The trustee's rights are incident to holding the title (*e.g.*, the right of possession and alienation) and the office (*e.g.*, the right to reimbursement and reasonable compensation).

§3.5.2.1 Right at Law to Possession

[C]o-trustees bought a Mercedes-Benz with trust principal, took title in the name of one of them, and put the life beneficiary in possession. A court-appointed additional trustee insisted that the automobile be sold and the proceeds properly invested. The two original trustees took possession of the automobile and the life beneficiary sued to recover possession. It was held that, while the life beneficiary might be able to sue to surcharge the trustee for breach of trust, she was not entitled to possession of the automobile.[69]

In the absence of statute, decision, or the settlor's contrary intention, the trustee, as holder of the legal title, is entitled to the possession of the real property; thus the trustee may eject the beneficiary.[70] On the other hand, "the settlor may provide that the spouse may occupy the settlor's former residence rent free, in which event the spouse's occupancy would prevent the trustee from taking possession."[71] With the same qualifications, the trustee is entitled also to the possession of the personal property.

§3.5.2.2 Right at Law to Transfer Title

The trustee being as to the world the legal owner of the entrusted property may convey it to a third party. The third party then will stand at law entitled in place of the trustee.[72] Thus, a trustee may convey to a third party for fair market value an entrusted residence in furtherance of the trust's lawful purposes though a beneficiary has been occupying the residence.[73]

If, however, the terms of the trust purport to deprive the trustee of this default power to convey, any transferee with notice of the restriction takes the property subject to the trust, receiving no larger title than the trustee is

---

[69] 2A Scott on Trusts §170.17 n.2 (discussing Boalt v. Hanson, 412 So. 2d 880 (Fla. Ct. App. 1982)).

[70] *See generally* 2A Scott on Trusts §175. *But see generally* V. Woerner, Annot., *Right of appeal from order on application for removal of personal representative, guardian, or trustee*, 37 A.L.R.2d 751 (1954).

[71] UTC §809 cmt. (available at <http://www.uniformlaws.org/Act.aspx?title=Trust%20 Code>); *see also* Bogert §1 ("In rare cases the beneficiary may be allowed to enjoy the property directly.").

[72] *See generally* 4 Scott on Trusts §283.

[73] *See, e.g.*, Cavagnaro v. Sapone, 2014 WL 4808828 (Cal. Ct. App. Sept. 29, 2014) ("Although the trustors of the trust undoubtedly were concerned with the welfare of their daughter, a contingent remainder beneficiary of the trust, the evidence confirms that the sale is necessitated by current financial conditions and transgresses neither the terms nor purpose of the trust.").

authorized to convey.[74] In other words, the transferee is not a BFP.[75] Under these circumstances, the sale is voidable at the option of the beneficiary.[76] While it is preferable that the trustee sign a deed to real estate "as trustee" rather than individually, disclosing on the deed the trusteeship may not be a prerequisite to passing good title, as at least one court has held.[77]

Because of the trustee's right to transfer title, it is said that the trust is not a restraint on the alienability of property.[78] This is because "if the trustee makes a transfer under powers conferred by law or the terms of the trust, the transferee acquires the whole title, free of trust; if he makes a transfer in breach of trust to a bona fide purchaser, the transferee also acquires the whole title, free of trust; [e]ven a transfer in breach of trust to a donee, or to a purchaser with notice of the breach, carries the title, subject to the trust, which is all the trustee ever owned."[79]

For more on the concept of the good-faith purchaser for value or BFP, the reader is referred to Section 8.15.63 of this handbook.

§3.5.2.3 Right in Equity to Exoneration and Reimbursement, *i.e.*, Indemnity; Payment of Attorneys' Fees

If the trustee properly incurs a liability in the administration of the trust, he is entitled to indemnity out of the trust estate either by exoneration, that is using trust property in discharging the liability so that he will not be compelled to use his individual property in discharging it, or by way of reimbursement, that is if he has used his individual property in discharging the liability, by repaying himself out of the trust property.[80]

Exoneration and reimbursement. An agent generally incurs no liability for acting within the scope of the agency. It is the principal who is on the hook. By contrast, it is the trustee who acts as principal in connection with the administration of the trust. It is the trustee, not the beneficiary, who is

---

[74] *See generally* 4 Scott on Trusts §284.

[75] *See generally* 5 Scott & Ascher §29.1.1 (Bona Fide Purchaser); §§5.4.2 of this handbook (rights of the beneficiary as against BFPs and other transferees of the underlying trust property), 8.3.2 of this handbook (bona fide purchase for value of trust property, specifically what constitutes notice that a transfer is in breach of trust?), and 8.15.63 of this handbook (doctrine of bona fide purchase and the BFP). For a comparison of the BFP, a creature of equity, with the holder in due course, a creature of law, *see* §8.15.68 of this handbook (the holder in due course in the trust context).

[76] *See generally* 4 Scott on Trusts §291.

[77] Galdjie v. Darwish, 113 Cal. App. 4th 1331, 7 Cal. Rptr. 3d 178 (2003) (involving a conveyance of real estate by the trustee-beneficiaries of a revocable inter vivos trust).

[78] *See generally* Broadway Nat'l Bank v. Adams, 133 Mass. 170 (1882).

[79] W. F. Fratcher, Trust §95, in VI Intl. Encyclopedia of Comp. Law §108 at 89 (F. H. Lawson ed., 1973). *See also* §5.4.2 of this handbook (rights of the beneficiary as against transferees, including BFPS). *See also* 5 Scott & Ascher §29.1.1 (Bona Fide Purchaser).

[80] Restatement (Second) of Trusts §244 cmt. b.

personally liable to third parties in contract[81] and tort,[82] "whether or not he is acting in accordance with his powers and duties as trustee."[83] Again, a trustee is a principal. He is neither an agent nor, absent special facts, an employee of the trust.[84]

Inasmuch as there is a rigid restriction against personal participation by the trustee in any of the profits and gains resulting from the administration of the trust estate,[85] equity takes pains to hold the trustee harmless from personal liability for obligations properly incurred.[86] Thus, unless the terms of the trust provide otherwise,[87] a trustee is entitled to indemnity out of the trust estate, either by exoneration or reimbursement, for expenses properly incurred in the administration and management of the trust,[88] whether or not the trust contains a spendthrift provision.[89] In England, so too is an outgoing trustee, even after he has parted with the trust property,[90] as is the trustee of a voidable trust.[91] "A trustee has a first charge or lien upon the trust fund in respect of the liabilities, costs and expenses covered by his right of indemnity."[92] In some jurisdictions, this equitable right of indemnity has been codified by statute.[93] The trustee may even be entitled to interest on personal funds reasonably and appropriately advanced.[94] The trustee, of course, has no fiduciary duty to make advances out of his own pocket, absent special facts, but to the extent he chooses to do so, he is entitled to take "security for indemnification."[95] A trustee who has made good any loss occasioned by his breach of trust is entitled to be

---

[81] *See generally* §7.3.1 of this handbook (trustee's liability as legal owner in contract to nonbeneficiaries); Lewin ¶21-05 through ¶21-07 (England).

[82] *See generally* §7.3.3 of this handbook (trustee's liability as legal owner in tort to nonbeneficiaries); Lewin ¶21-08 (England).

[83] Lewin ¶21-04.

[84] *See generally* Loring v. United States, 80 F. Supp. 781 (D. Mass. 1948).

[85] *See generally* §6.1.3 of this handbook (the trustee's duty of loyalty).

[86] *See generally* 4 Scott & Ascher §221.1; Bogert §718. "Under the general law a trustee is in general not entitled to indemnity out of the trust property in respect of liabilities to third parties and costs and expenses incurred in consequence of unauthorised acts." Lewin ¶39-94 (England).

[87] 4 Scott & Ascher §22.1.4 (Terms of the Trust).

[88] Restatement (Third) of Trusts §38(2); Lewin ch. 21 (England); 3 Scott & Ascher §§18.1.2 (Power to Incur Expenses) (U.S.), 18.1.2.5 (Expenses of Management) (U.S.); 4 Scott & Ascher §22.1 (Expenses Properly Incurred).

[89] 4 Scott & Ascher §22.1.2 (Spendthrift Trusts).

[90] Lewin ¶14-50.

[91] Lewin ¶21-23. The purported trustee of a purported trust that is held void ab initio, however, may well not be entitled to indemnity out of the trust estate. Lewin ¶21-23.

[92] Lewin ¶21-26 (England); 4 Scott & Ascher §§22.1 (Expenses Properly Incurred) (U.S.), 22.1.1 (Lien for Indemnity) (U.S.).

[93] *See, e.g.,* §31(1) of the English Trustee Act 2000; §47(2) of the Cayman Islands Trust Law (2001 revision); §59(4) NSW Trustee Act 1924; Article 22(2) of the Trusts Jersey Law (1984) (as substituted by Trusts (Amendment) (Jersey) Law (1989)).

[94] 4 Scott & Ascher §22.1.

[95] 4 Scott & Ascher §22.1.1 (Lien for Indemnity).

indemnified for expenses reasonably incurred to the extent the trust estate is benefited thereby.[96] A beneficiary who seeks equity must do equity.[97]

A right of exoneration is a right in the trustee to pay creditors directly from the trust estate[98] all of the expenses "reasonably and appropriately"[99] incurred by him as its owner,[100] including taxes,[101] repair costs,[102] brokers' commissions,[103] expenses of running a trade or business on behalf of the trust,[104] premiums for insuring against liability in contract and tort to nonbeneficiaries,[105] and other legitimate expenses of prudently collecting, managing, preserving,[106] and protecting the trust property,[107] including those properly incurred in hiring agents,[108] traveling,[109] leasing,[110] investing,[111] borrowing,[112] and bringing, defending, and settling litigation, including attorneys' fees, and expenses of consulting counsel when there is reasonable cause.[113] The

---

[96] 4 Scott & Ascher §§22.1.3 (Trustee in Default), 22.2.1 (Benefit to Trust Estate).

[97] *See* §8.12 of this handbook (where the trust is recognized outside the United States) (containing a catalog of equity maxims).

[98] 4 Scott & Ascher §22.1 (defining exoneration as "the power to use trust funds to discharge obligations that have arisen out of trust administration").

[99] Restatement (Third) of Trusts §88 cmt. b.

[100] Restatement (Third) of Trusts §38 cmt. b; 4 Scott & Ascher §22.1.

[101] *See generally* §7.3.4.1 of this handbook (trustee's liability for taxes and shareholder assessments); 4 Scott & Ascher §22.1.

[102] Restatement (Third) of Trusts §88, cmt. b; 3 Scott & Ascher §18.1.2.2 (Repairs and Improvements); 4 Scott & Ascher §22.1 (Expenses Properly Incurred).

[103] 4 Scott & Ascher §22.1.

[104] Lewin ¶21-14 (England).

[105] Restatement (Third) of Trusts §88, cmt. b. *See generally* §§7.3.1 of this handbook (trustee's liability as legal owner in contract to nonbeneficiaries) and 7.3.3 of this handbook (trustee's liability as legal owner in tort to nonbeneficiaries); Lewin ¶21-17 (England); 3 Scott & Ascher §18.1.2.1 (U.S.).

[106] *See generally* 3 Scott & Ascher §18.1.2.1 (Preservation of the Trust Property).

[107] Restatement (Third) of Trusts §88 cmt. b.

[108] Restatement (Third) of Trusts §88 cmt. c; UTC §709 cmt. (available at <http://www.uniformlaws.org/Act.aspx?title=Trust%20Code>); 3 Scott & Ascher §18.1.2.3 (Employment of Agents) (noting, however, that unless the terms of the trust or a statute provides otherwise, the trustee ordinarily cannot properly at trust expense employ agents to perform services that the trustee is being compensated to perform, *e.g.*, keeping proper accounts or making the trust property productive, at least without an appropriate reduction of the trustee's own compensation). It goes without saying that a trustee may not retain an agent at trust expense to perform a nondelegable function, such as administering the dispositive provisions of a discretionary trust. 3 Scott & Ascher §18.1.2.3. *See also* 4 Scott & Ascher §22.1 (Expenses Properly Incurred).

[109] Lewin ¶21-13 (England).

[110] Restatement (Third) of Trusts §88 cmt. b.

[111] Restatement (Third) of Trusts §88 cmt. b.

[112] Restatement (Third) of Trusts §88 cmt. b. " . . . [I]f a trustee borrows funds from a third party for use in the administration of the trust, the interest on the loan is payable (or reimbursable) from the trust estate, provided the rate of interest is reasonable and borrowing serves an appropriate trust purpose and is otherwise consistent with the trustee's fiduciary duties." Restatement (Third) of Trusts §88 cmt. b.

[113] Restatement (Third) of Trusts §88 cmt. b; UTC §§709(a)(1), 1004 (available at <http://www.uniformlaws.org/Act.aspx?title=Trust%20Code>). *See generally* Bogert §718; 4 Scott &

expenditures must be in furtherance of the trust's purposes.[114] "Improvements may serve to make the property more productive,[115] or to make the premises safe and tenantable; therefore a trustee can properly incur improvement costs if and as the property's retention and improvement are prudent and suitable to the purposes of the trust."[116] This right of exoneration is coupled with a right of reimbursement for sums paid from the trustee's own pocket for expenses properly incurred.[117] The trustee, however, still needs to be "cost-conscious."[118] Unreasonable expenditures are not reimbursable.[119]

Premiums for internal fiduciary liability insurance are generally not chargeable to the trust estate. English default law is in accord,[120] although there is an exception for trustees of charitable trusts.[121]

What if the trustee without authority incurs an expense that confers a benefit on the trust estate? In that case, the trustee is ordinarily entitled to indemnity to the extent of the value of the benefit conferred.[122] The Restatement (Third) of Trusts is generally in accord.[123] Under the Uniform Trust Code, a trustee is entitled to be reimbursed out of the trust property, with interest as appropriate, expenses that were not properly incurred in the administration of the trust to the extent necessary to prevent unjust enrichment of the trust.[124] "Given this purpose, a court, on appropriate grounds, may delay or even deny

---

Ascher §22.1; 3 Scott on Trusts §188; Lewin ¶21-16 (England); Lee R. Russ, J.D., Annot., *Award of attorneys' fees out of trust estate in action by trustee against cotrustee*, 24 A.L.R.4th 624 (1983). *See also* F. M. English, Annot., *Right of coexecutor or cotrustee to retain independent legal counsel*, 66 A.L.R.2d 1169 (1959). *But see* Barber v. Barber, 915 P.2d 1204 (Alaska 1996) (trustee who brought complaint for instructions is a neutral party, not a "prevailing" party and therefore not entitled to legal fees); Malachowski v. Bank One, Indianapolis, 682 N.E.2d 530 (Ind. 1997) (though trustee prevailed, not awarded trustee fees because litigation not reasonably necessary). *See generally* §3.4.4.1 of this handbook (multiple trustees (cotrustees)) (discussing in part when a cotrustee is entitled to reimbursement from the trust estate for the costs of separate representation).

[114] (Third) of Trusts §88 cmt. b; 3 Scott & Ascher §18.1.2.4.

[115] 4 Scott & Ascher §22.2.2 (Separable Transactions).

[116] Restatement (Third) of Trusts §88 cmt. b; 3 Scott & Ascher §18.1.2.4. *See also* 3 Scott & Ascher §18.1.2.2 (Repairs and Improvements); 4 Scott & Ascher §22.1 (Expenses Properly Incurred).

[117] *See generally* Bogert §718; Hollaway v. Edwards, 68 Cal. App. 4th Supp. 94, 80 Cal. Rptr. 2d 166 (1998) (awarding trustee attorneys' fees incurred in defending a removal action brought by the cotrustee); Franzen v. Norwest Bank Colo., 955 P.2d 1018 (Colo. 1998) (holding that trustee was entitled to reimbursement of attorney's fees incurred in litigation initiated by beneficiary's agent seeking revocation of trust).

[118] 3 Scott & Ascher §18.1.2.6.

[119] 3 Scott & Ascher §18.1.2.6 (When Trustee Improperly Incurs Expense).

[120] Kemble v. Hicks [1999] P.L.R. 287 (England).

[121] Charities Act 1993 §73F (England).

[122] Restatement (Second) of Trusts §245 cmt. d. *See also* Lewin ¶21-25 (England); 3 Scott & Ascher §18.1.2.6 (When Trustee Improperly Incurs Expense) (U.S.); 4 Scott & Ascher §22.2.1 (Benefit to Trust Estate) (U.S.).

[123] Restatement (Third) of Trusts §88 cmt. a.

[124] UTC §709(a)(2) (available at <http://www.uniformlaws.org/Act.aspx?title=Trust%20Code>). *See generally* 4 Scott & Ascher §22.2.1 (Benefit to Trust Estate).

reimbursement for expenses which benefited the trust."[125] Also, if a trustee improperly incurs an expense the benefit of which the beneficiary can accept or reject, the trustee is not entitled to indemnity if the right of rejection is, in fact, exercised. Thus, if a trustee improperly purchases with his own funds an automobile for the trust, the trustee is not entitled to indemnity if the beneficiary declines to ratify the transaction. The trustee, however, may keep the automobile for himself.

If a trustee properly enters into a contract on behalf of the trust and thereby incurs personal liability, he is entitled to be indemnified from the trust estate.[126] "Although the trustee breaks a contract properly made by him in the administration of the trust and thereby incurs a liability for breach of contract, he is entitled to indemnity to the extent to which he thereby benefited the trust estate."[127] Also, "[w]here a tort to a third person results from the negligence of an agent or servant properly employed by the trustee in the administration of the trust, and the trustee is not personally at fault, although the trustee is liable to the third person, he is entitled to indemnity out of the trust estate."[128]

If the trustee in breach of trust satisfies from the trust estate a liability to a third person that was incurred in the course of administering the trust, the third person would not be obliged to make the trust estate whole if the third person were a BFP.[129] To qualify as a BFP, the third person would have to have given full value, taken legal title to the payment, and been reasonably unaware of the breach.[130] The beneficiary always has recourse against the wrongdoing trustee personally, whether or not the third person is a BFP:

---

[125] UTC §709 cmt. (available at <http://www.uniformlaws.org/Act.aspx?title=Trust%20Code>). "Appropriate grounds . . . [for delay or even denying reimbursement for expenses which benefited the trust] . . . include: (a) whether the trustee acted in bad faith in incurring the expense; (2) whether the trustee knew that the expense was inappropriate; (3) whether the trustee reasonably believed the expense was necessary for the preservation of the trust estate; (4) whether the expense has resulted in a benefit; and (5) whether indemnity can be allowed without defeating or impairing the purposes of the trust." UTC §709 cmt. (available at <http://www.uniformlaws.org/Act.aspx?title=Trust%20Code>).

[126] 4 Scott & Ascher §22.3 (Contractual Liability). *See generally* §7.3.1 of this handbook (trustee's contractual liability as the legal owner to nonbeneficiaries).

[127] Restatement (Second) of Trusts §246 cmt. c. "Thus, if the trustee in the proper exercise of a power makes a contract to sell trust property, and subsequently receives a better offer for the property and sells it, he is entitled to indemnity for his liability on the contract to the extent which the breach of contract resulted in his obtaining a higher price." Restatement (Second) of Trusts §246 cmt. c.

[128] Restatement (Second) of Trusts §247 cmt. b. *See generally* 4 Scott & Ascher §22.4 (Tort Liability). *See generally* §7.3.3 of this handbook (trustee's liability as legal owner in tort to nonbeneficiaries).

[129] *See generally* §5.4.2 of this handbook (rights of the beneficiary as against BFPs and other transferees of the underlying trust property), 8.3.2 of this handbook (bona fide purchase for value of trust property, specifically what constitutes notice that a transfer is in breach of trust?), and §8.15.63 of this handbook (doctrine of bona fide purchase; the BFP). *See also* §8.3.6 of this handbook (negotiable instruments and the duty of third parties to inquire into the trustee's authority). For a comparison of the BFP, a creature of equity, with the holder in due course, a creature of law, *see* §8.15.68 of this handbook (holders in due course in the trust context).

[130] 5 Scott & Ascher §29.2.7 (Debts Incurred During Trust Administration).

The Chancellors, when appealed to by the beneficiaries, felt that there was no reason in equity or conscience why a person who had acquired property in good faith and for value should be disturbed. They therefore kept their hands off. As between the two innocent parties, they let the loss that resulted from the breach of trust lie where it fell. They left the beneficiaries to seek redress against the wrongdoing trustee.[131]

Attorneys' fees. A trustee is entitled to exoneration or reimbursement from the trust estate for attorneys' fees, provided the services rendered are appropriate for handling by an attorney-at-law.[132] Legal fees incurred by a trustee in obtaining allowance of his accounts come to mind;[133] or in bringing a complaint for instructions or declaratory judgment;[134] or an action to collect or protect the trust property.[135] "A trustee is also entitled to indemnity for the reasonable expenses of obtaining advice of counsel as to trust administration, at least when the need for such advice arises out of circumstances that are not the trustee's fault."[136] One court has even ordered the beneficiaries of a terminated trust to return a portion of the final distribution so that the judicially removed trustee could mount a legal defense of his final accounts, accounts that were under attack by those very same beneficiaries.[137]

Functions that should not be delegated to counsel at trust expense. On the other hand, if the attorney-at-law is performing services that the trustee personally or through ministerial agents ought to be performing, such as collecting and keeping track of dividends, keeping the trust's records, or preparing accountings, then those legal costs are probably not reimbursable from the trust estate absent special facts.[138] The trustee will most likely have to pay those costs out of his own pocket.[139]

When the trustee is entitled to have counsel fees paid from the trust estate. What about nonroutine legal matters? Attorneys' fees reasonably incurred by the trustee in connection with the preservation, protection, administration, and

---

[131] 5 Scott & Ascher §29.1.1 (Bona Fide Purchaser).

[132] 4 Scott & Ascher §22.1.

[133] 4 Scott & Ascher §22.1.

[134] *See generally* 3 Scott & Ascher §16.8 (Application for Instructions); 4 Scott & Ascher §22.1 (Expenses Properly Incurred); Chapter 1 of this handbook (in part discussing the right of trustees and beneficiaries to seek instructions from the court); §8.42 of this handbook (the complaint for instructions versus the complaint for declaratory judgment). *See also* §8.13 of this handbook (when a beneficiary is entitled to have his or her legal fees paid from the trust estate).

[135] 4 Scott & Ascher §22.1 (Expenses Properly Incurred); Restatement (Third) of Trusts §88 cmt. d. "The right of indemnification applies even though the trustee is unsuccessful in the action, as long as the trustee's conduct was not imprudent or otherwise in violation of a fiduciary duty." Restatement (Third) of Trusts §88 cmt. d.

[136] 4 Scott & Ascher §22.1 (Expenses Properly Incurred).

[137] *See* Kasperbauer v. Fairfield, 170 Cal. App. 4th 785 (Cal. Ct. App. 2009).

[138] *See generally* Restatement (Third) of Trusts §88 cmt. c. *See, e.g.,* Mears v. Addonizio, 336 N.J. Super. 474, 765 A.2d 260 (App. Div. 2001) (providing that fees of attorney for trustee not payable from trust when the trustee was merely a nominal party in litigation). Attorneys' fees in bringing trustee's account before the court, however, would be allowable. *See, e.g.,* Mears v. Addonizio, 336 N.J. Super. 474, 765 A.2d 260 (App. Div. 2001).

[139] 4 Scott & Ascher §22.2 (Expenses Improperly Incurred).

distribution of the trust property are generally reimbursable from the trust estate, such as legal fees and costs incurred by a trustee in successfully defending allegations that the trustee had breached his trust.[140] Indenture trustees are no exception.[141] In Nebraska, the standard is "substantially successful"; the trustee's defense need not be "100 percent successful" in order for the trustee to be entitled to recover costs, including attorneys' fees.[142] "Ultimately, however, the issue of the trustee's entitlement to indemnification for litigation expenses lies in the sound discretion of the court."[143] As to the fees that the trustee's attorneys incur in litigation that is ongoing between the trustee and the beneficiaries, the trustee should seek permission from the court before deducting those fees from the trust estate.[144] This is because the litigation has placed the trustee's interests in conflict with those of the beneficiaries, thus requiring the trust to "report to the court for guidance."[145] In England, if the trustee has suspended income payments in the face of sufficient principal to cover any litigation costs that the court might eventually award the trustee, the court may order that the payments be resumed.[146]

The trustee's legal costs are not reimbursable from the trust estate when the trustee is personally at fault. All bets are off when the trustee is personally at fault.[147] The costs of mounting an unsuccessful defense to an allegation of breach of fiduciary duty are generally not reimbursable.[148] Certainly the obligation to pay any

---

[140] Restatement (Third) of Trusts §88 cmt. d; 3 Scott & Ascher §18.1.2.4 (Expenses of Judicial Proceedings); 4 Scott & Ascher §22.1 (Expenses Properly Incurred). *See* Regions Bank v. Lowrey, 101 So. 3d 210 (Ala. 2012) (confirming that a trustee may be reimbursed from the trust estate for expenses, including attorneys' fees, incurred by the trustee in defending a breach-of-trust action, provided the trustee had not been found to have committed a material breach of trust); Spencer v. Di Cola, 2014 WL 1775522 (Ill. App. Ct. May 1, 2014) (the appellate court not agreeing with the beneficiary that the defendant-trustee's successful defense of her position as trustee was inappropriately "self-serving," an office which, after all, had been authorized by the very terms of the trust, it affirmed the lower court's decision to award the defendant-trustee her legal defense costs and to allow her to satisfy those obligations with entrusted funds); National City Bank, N.E. v. Beyer, 2001 WL 1664079 (Ohio App.) (holding that a successful judicial defense against breach-of-trust allegations benefits the trust estate such that the trustee is entitled to reimbursement of his legal fees). *But see* Boatmen's Trust Co. of Ark. v. Buchbinder, 343 Ark. 1, 32 S.W.3d 466 (2000) (denying the trustee a right of indemnity from the trust estate for its attorneys' fees though it was the prevailing party in the breach-of-trust action).

[141] *See* Bogert §250, n. 44. *See generally* §9.31 of this handbook (corporate trusts; trusts to secure creditors; the Trust Indenture Act of 1939; Protecting bondholders).

[142] *See* In re Estate of Stuchlik, 289 Neb. 673 (2014).

[143] 4 Scott & Ascher §22.1.

[144] *See* J.P. Morgan Trust Co., N.A. v. Siegel, 965 So.2d 1193 (Fla. App. 4th Dist., 2007).

[145] J.P. Morgan Trust Co., N.A. v. Siegel, 965 So.2d 1193, 1195 (Fla. App. 4th Dist., 2007).

[146] Lewin ¶38-09.

[147] *See generally* 3 Scott & Ascher §18.1.2.4 (Expenses of Judicial Proceedings); 4 Scott & Ascher §22.2 (Expenses Improperly Incurred).

[148] Restatement (Third) of Trusts §88 cmt. d; 3 Scott & Ascher §18.1.2.4 (Expenses of Judicial Proceedings); 4 Scott & Ascher §§22.1 (Expenses Properly Incurred), 22.2 (Expenses Improperly Incurred). *See, e.g.*, Grate v. Grzetich, 373 Ill. App. 3d 228, 867 N.E.2d 577 (2007) (attorneys' fees incurred by a trustee in the unsuccessful defense of an action for conversion of trust assets brought by the guardian of the disabled beneficiary were not reimbursable from the trust estate as the fees had not been incurred in protecting the trust estate).

attorneys' fees that were incurred by a trustee in the unsuccessful defense of a breach of fiduciary duty action ought not to be directly or indirectly imposed on those to whom the duty ran.[149] Attorneys' fees incurred by the trustee in correcting a trustee error—such as misdelivery of the trust property—also are not reimbursable.[150] Accordingly, counsel would be well advised to personally bind the trustee in contract to pay his or her fees out of the trustee's own pocket to the extent those fees are held not to be an obligation of the trust estate.

The costs of a legal malpractice action against trust counsel are generally not reimbursable from the trust estate. Costs incurred by the trustee in bringing an action against trust counsel for rendering faulty legal advice that led to the trustee's breaching a fiduciary duty also would not be reimbursable from the trust estate. In principle, the trustee is personally obliged to make the beneficiaries whole for his breaches of fiduciary duty. Moreover, the beneficiaries are not obliged to fund a legal malpractice action the outcome of which could only inure to the benefit of the trustee. On the other hand, if the trustee is both impecunious and dilatory, the beneficiaries themselves, under principles of subrogation, may be entitled to initiate the malpractice action against counsel in order that they can be made whole.[151]

The trustee's legal defense costs are chargeable to the beneficiaries if it is found that the litigation was pursued in bad faith. In most states and under federal law, "when a baseless claim is maintained vexatiously, obdurately or in bad faith, an exception to the American Rule applies and allows the recovery of counsel fees against the opposing party."[152] When a beneficiary engages in frivolous litigation against the trustee, or against the trust relationship itself, the beneficiary's equitable interest under the trust may be charged with the attendant costs.[153] Thus, if a beneficiary engages in vexatious and burdensome litigation against the trustee and the other beneficiaries, the court may order that the attorneys' fees of all the defendants be charged against the plaintiff-beneficiary's equitable interest, to the extent the interest is identifiable, discrete, and severable.[154] To

---

[149] *See* Restatement (Third) of Trusts §88 cmt. d; UTC §709 cmt. (Reimbursement of Expenses) (available at <http://www.uniformlaws.org/Act.aspx?title=Trust%20Code>); 3 Scott & Ascher §18.1.2.4 (Expenses of Judicial Proceedings); 4 Scott & Ascher §§22.1 (Expenses Properly Incurred), 22.2 (Expenses Improperly Incurred); In re Estate of Stowell, 595 A.2d 1022 (Me. 1991) (denying reimbursement of attorneys' fees to trustee where litigation was result of his breach of fiduciary duties).

[150] 4 Scott & Ascher §22.2 (Expenses Improperly Incurred). *See, e.g.*, May v. Oklahoma Bank & Trust Co., 261 P.3d 1138 (Okla. 2011) (bank not entitled to legal fees it incurred in correcting its own negligence).

[151] *Cf.* §8.15.50 of this handbook (subrogation doctrine) (discussing the subrogation rights of third parties *against* the trust estate).

[152] Martin A. Heckscher, *Fees, Fees, Fees: A Blessing and a Bane, How to Charge, Collect and Defend Them*, 31 ACTEC L.J. 21, 30 (2005).

[153] *See* 3 Scott on Trusts §188.4 n.13 and accompanying text. *See generally* §8.13 of this handbook (in litigation pertaining to a trust, when is the beneficiary entitled to reimbursement from the trust estate for legal fees).

[154] *See, e.g.*, Larkin v. Wells Fargo Bank, N.A., No. A13-1839 (Minn. Ct. App. Oct. 6, 2014) (unpublished) (" [The plaintiff-beneficiary's] . . . continuing attempt to undermine the settlement

the extent the interest is not, the court may have the equitable power to impose on the plaintiff-beneficiary personal liability for the fees.[155]

When a trustee has prevailed in a suit for breach of trust brought vexatiously, obdurately, or in bad faith by a beneficiary, he may have a fiduciary duty to the other beneficiaries to bring an action against the beneficiary to compel the beneficiary to bear the burden of the trustees' attorneys' fees, rather than have the trust estate (and the other beneficiaries to the extent of their interest in the trust estate) bear that burden.[156] Circumstances may even warrant that the trustee also bring an action on behalf of the trust estate against the nuisance beneficiary's counsel.[157] As noted above, an advance by the trustee of money for the protection of the trust gives rise to a lien against trust property to secure reimbursement with reasonable interest.[158]

Whether expenses incurred by trust counsel in collecting his or legal fees are reimbursable from the trust estate. There is little law on the question of whether an attorney who has represented a trustee is entitled to be paid from the trust estate for time spent and costs incurred by the attorney in collecting or defending the attorney's reasonable legal fees.[159] If the attorney can demonstrate that his or her efforts to get paid have somehow benefited the trust estate, then a court should have no problem awarding "fees on fees" from the trust estate.[160] Absent a showing that the trust estate has received a benefit from the attorney's collection efforts, if the attorney has acted reasonably and in good faith in seeking to have his or her fees paid from the trust estate and the beneficiaries have acted unreasonably and in bad faith in opposing those efforts, then the equitable exception to the "fees-on-fees" or "fees-for-fees" prohibition should

---

was not beneficial, particularly after the settlement agreement was confirmed in binding arbitration, by the district court, and by this court on appeal, and his alternate proposed settlement agreement was nonsensical and included ad hominem attacks on other trust beneficiaries. The evidence supports the district court's finding that . . . [he] . . . engaged in vexatious and burdensome litigation."). It is interesting to note that the district court had ordered the plaintiff-beneficiary to pay the trustee's attorneys' fees "*either personally* or as a deduction from his share of the trust."

[155] *See generally* §5.6 of this handbook (in part discussing the potential personal liability of the litigious beneficiary).

[156] *See generally* 3 Scott & Ascher §18.1.2.4 (noting that "[i]f one beneficiary unsuccessfully tries, through litigation, to advance his or her own beneficial interest, the trustee may properly charge the resulting litigation expenses against the beneficiary's share").

[157] *See, e.g.,* Pederson Trust, 757 N.W.2d 740 (N.D. 2008) (nuisance beneficiary and his counsel jointly and severally liable for trustee's litigation costs).

[158] 4 Scott & Ascher §22.1.1 (Lien for Indemnity); UTC §709(b) (available at <http://www.uniformlaws.org/Act.aspx?title=Trust%20Code>). *Cf.* Nickerson v. Fiduciary Trust Co., 6 Mass. App. Ct. 317, 375 N.E.2d 357 (1978) (holding that probate court had not abused its discretion under Mass. Gen. Laws Ann. 215 §39A in awarding the trustee of an irrevocable trust the counsel fees it had incurred as a result of the settlor's unsuccessful action to invalidate or reform the trust).

[159] *See* Martin A. Heckscher, *Fees, Fees, Fees: A Blessing and a Bane, How to Charge, Collect and Defend Them*, 31 ACTEC L.J. 21, 32–36 (2005) (discussing the "fee on fees" issue in the context of attorneys representing fiduciaries of probate estates).

[160] In re Mary Ann O'Neill Revocable Trust, No. 319546 (Mich. Ct. App. May 19, 2015) (unpublished).

apply.[161] If the trustee has unreasonably or in bad faith been frustrating the attorney's efforts to get paid, it would seem that the trustee should be ordered to pay the "fees on fees" out of personal funds without recourse to the trust estate.

§3.5.2.4 Right in Equity to Compensation

Local custom is a factor to be considered in determining compensation. Other relevant factors are: the trustee's skill, experience and facilities, and the time devoted to trust duties; the amount and character of the trust property; the degree of difficulty, responsibility, and risk assumed in administering the trust, including in making discretionary distributions; the nature and costs of services rendered by others; and the quality of the trustee's performance.[162]

The English rule is that the trustee is not entitled to compensation unless the instrument expressly provides for it,[163] though there are now some statutory exceptions applicable to corporate and professional trustees.[164] In the United States and some parts of the British Commonwealth, however, a trustee is entitled in equity to reasonable compensation, even when the instrument is silent upon the subject,[165] "unless the terms of the trust provide otherwise or the trustee agrees to forgo compensation."[166] In some jurisdictions, a trustee's compensation is set by statute.[167] For a more detailed discussion of trustee compensation, see Section 8.4 of this handbook.

To the extent of his reasonable compensation, the trustee has a "security interest" in[168] or lien on[169] the trust property. "The trustee need not pay over income without deducting the compensation to which he is entitled with respect to the income, and need not pay over principal without deducting the compensation to which he is entitled with respect to the principal."[170] On the other hand, "[t]he trustee has no charge on the trust property to secure a beneficiary's indebtedness that is unconnected with the trust."[171] With respect to a debt that

---

[161] *See* In re Mary Ann O'Neill Revocable Trust, No. 319546 (Mich. Ct. App. May 19, 2015) (unpublished) (the fees-for-fees prohibition would not be applicable if the beneficiaries unjustifiably and in bad faith were to litigate in opposition to trust counsel's legitimate efforts to be compensated with entrusted funds).

[162] Restatement (Third) of Trusts §38 cmt. c(1). *See generally* §8.4 of this handbook (trustee compensation).

[163] *See generally* 4 Scott & Ascher §21.1; 3A Scott on Trusts §242.

[164] Lewin ¶20-132 through ¶20-158.

[165] *See generally* 4 Scott & Ascher §21.1; 3A Scott on Trusts §242. *See also* §8.4 of this handbook (trustee compensation).

[166] Restatement (Third) of Trusts §38(1).

[167] *See generally* Bogert §975; 4 Scott & Ascher §21.1.

[168] *See generally* Bogert §975.

[169] Restatement (Third) of Trusts §38 cmt. b.

[170] Restatement (Second) of Trusts §242 cmt. e; 4 Scott & Ascher §21.1.

[171] 4 Scott & Ascher §25.1 (Liability of Beneficiary to Trustee Individually).

the beneficiary owes to the trustee personally, the trustee is in no better position than the beneficiary's other general creditors.[172] That is not to say that under certain circumstances the beneficiary and the trustee could not enter into a binding agreement to secure a beneficiary's debt to the trustee with the beneficiary's equitable interest.[173] Due deference, however, would have to be given to the trustee's overarching duty of loyalty,[174] the equitable interest could not be spendthrifted,[175] and the beneficiary would have to be of full age and legal capacity.[176]

§3.5.2.5 Right in Equity to Rely on Trust Instrument

However, a trustee should also be able to administer a trust with some dispatch and without concern that a reasonable reliance on the terms of the trust instrument is misplaced.[177]

The Uniform Trust Code provides that a trustee who acts in reasonable reliance on the terms of the trust as expressed in the trust instrument is not liable to a beneficiary for a breach of trust to the extent the breach resulted from the reliance.[178] If a court may consider extrinsic evidence on the issue of a settlor's intent, then it is appropriate that the trustee be afforded this protection. Why? Because the court could, after the trustee has assumed office, determine that the "intended terms of the trust" are not the "expressed" terms of the trust.[179]

§3.5.2.6 Right in Equity to Seek Instructions from Court

Courts of equity, in the exercise of their jurisdiction over the administration of trusts, have long been willing to provide trustees instructions, upon request, as to their duties and powers.[180]

When the current rights, duties, and obligations of the trustee are uncertain due to problems with the governing instrument or the terms of the trust

---

[172] 4 Scott & Ascher §25.1 (Liability of Beneficiary to Trustee Individually).

[173] 4 Scott & Ascher §25.1 (Liability of Beneficiary to Trustee Individually).

[174] *See generally* §6.1.3.5 of this handbook (acquisition by trustee of equitable interest and the trustee's duty of loyalty to the beneficiary in nontrust matters generally).

[175] 4 Scott & Ascher §25.1 (Liability of Beneficiary to Trustee Individually).

[176] 4 Scott & Ascher §25.1 (Liability of Beneficiary to Trustee Individually).

[177] UTC §1006 cmt. (available at <http://www.uniformlaws.org/Act.aspx?title=Trust%20Code>).

[178] UTC §1006 (available at <http://www.uniformlaws.org/Act.aspx?title=Trust%20Code>).

[179] UTC §1006 cmt. (available at <http://www.uniformlaws.org/Act.aspx?title=Trust%20Code>).

[180] 3 Scott & Ascher §16.8.

generally, the trustee is entitled, at trust expense,[181] to initiate an action for instructions or declaratory judgment[182] in a court that has jurisdiction over the trust.[183] He is not obliged to rationalize conflicting provisions, resolve ambiguities, or supply missing terms on his own authority and at his own risk.[184] The trustee of a business trust is no exception.[185] Nor is the trustee of a charitable trust.[186] "Beneficiaries, too, are entitled to seek judicial instructions regarding trust administration."[187]

There must be reasonable doubt, however.[188] "Decisions of questions which may arise upon the happening of events in the future . . . [, however,] . . . must await those events."[189] Also, courts are generally not in the business of advising trustees on how to exercise their discretionary powers.[190] Subject to the trustee's (or beneficiary's) right of appeal and provided all necessary parties[191] have properly been made parties to the proceeding, instructions issued by the court are binding on trustees and beneficiaries alike, unless the instructions

---

[181] Restatement (Third) of Trusts §71 cmt. e; 3 Scott & Ascher §16.8.

[182] *See generally* §8.42 of this handbook (the complaint for instructions versus the complaint for declaratory judgment).

[183] *See* Restatement (Second) of Trusts §201 cmt. b (noting that if the trustee is in doubt as to the interpretation of the trust instrument, then he can protect himself by obtaining instructions from the court, the extent of his duties and powers being determined by the trust instrument and the rules of law which are applicable law, and not by his own interpretation of the instrument or his own belief as to the rules of law); UTC §201(c) (available at <http://www.uniformlaws.org/Act.aspx?title=Trust%20Code>) (Role of Court in Administration of Trust). For a catalog of other types of judicial proceedings involving trust administration that might be brought by a trustee or beneficiary, see UTC §112 cmt. (borrowing from California Probate Code §17200). In England, the courts exclusively have inter alia the power to vary the terms of trusts where they think fit (on the application of interested parties); the power to appoint trustees (when no other way of appointment can be used); the power to remove a trustee; the power to vary administrative provisions including investment powers; the power to determine the true construction of the terms of the trust; the power to enforce the terms of the trust; and the power to consider and award damages for breach of trust. Martyn Frost, Overview of Trusts in England and Wales, in Trusts in Prime Jurisdictions 19–20 (Alon Kaplan ed., 2000). *See generally* §9.4.4 of this handbook (whether the legislature may alter the terms of a charitable trust without violating the doctrine of separation of powers).

[184] *See generally* 3 Scott & Ascher §16.8 (noting that "[t]rustees have received instructions on a wide range of questions, including the extent of their powers and duties, the identity of the trust beneficiaries and the extent of their interests, the proper allocation and apportionment of receipts or expenditures between income and principal, and the identity of those entitled to the trust property upon the termination of the trust"); Thomas H. Belknap, Newhall's Settlement of Estates and Fiduciary Law in Massachusetts §2:15 (1994).

[185] *See, e.g.* Hauser v. Catlett, 197 Okla. 668, 173 P.2d 728 (1946) (a timely petition for instructions by the trustees of a business trust to resolve a trust termination issue).

[186] *See generally* 5 Scott & Ascher §37.3.12.

[187] 3 Scott & Ascher §16.8.

[188] Restatement (Third) of Trusts §71; 3 Scott & Ascher §16.8.

[189] Flye v. Jones, 283 Mass. 136, 138, 186 N.E. 64 (1933). *See also* In re Deed of Trust of McCargo, 652 A.2d 1330, 1337 (Pa. Super. 1994) (holding that an order of the lower court was improper because in part it purported to resolve a matter by declaratory judgment that was not based upon an event certain to occur); Restatement (Third) of Trusts §71 cmt. d.

[190] *See generally* 3 Scott & Ascher §16.8.

[191] *Cf.* §5.7 of this handbook (the necessary parties to a suit brought by a beneficiary).

were procured by fraud, duress, misrepresentation, concealment or, perhaps, as the result of manifest error.[192] "The court's determination of the questions involved marks them as res judicata."[193]

§3.5.3 The Powers of the Trustee in Equity to Manage the Trust Estate

A power differs from a duty. A duty imposes an obligation or a mandatory prohibition. A power, on the other hand, is a discretion, the exercise of which is not obligatory. The existence of a power, however created or granted, does not speak to the question of whether it is prudent under the circumstances to exercise the power.[194]

A trustee, being the absolute legal owner of the property, has under the default law at least all the powers over the property that a "legally competent and unmarried individual"[195] would have, subject however to the paramount equitable rights of the beneficiary.[196] The powers of the trustee of a charitable trust are similarly extensive.[197] Thus, in the case of either a private trust or a charitable one, a direction in the governing instrument to the trustee to employ a particular person as attorney is generally unenforceable.[198] A trustee will always have the inherent power to retain unconflicted counsel of his choice. On the other hand, the courts of equity will restrain the trustee from exercising any power inconsistent with the beneficiary's rights.[199] In other words, "all powers held as trustee, whether they are expressed or implied, are held in a fiduciary capacity and their exercise or nonexercise is subject to the fiduciary duties of trusteeship."[200] Moreover, "the comprehensive powers of a trustee under the default rule may be narrowed or qualified by statute or by the terms of the trust."[201]

Why a legally competent and unmarried individual rather than any absolute legal owner? The reason is that the default law generally places restrictions on what certain property owners, *e.g.*, corporations, persons under disability such as minors, and married persons, may do with their property. For

---

[192] Restatement (Third) of Trusts §71 cmt. b.

[193] 3 Scott & Ascher §16.8.

[194] UTC §815 cmt. (available at <http://www.uniformlaws.org/Act.aspx?title=Trust%20Code>). *See generally* 3 Scott & Ascher §16.1 (Duties and Powers of the Trustee) (suggesting that when say that the trustee has the power to do something, we mean that the trustee is under no duty to the beneficiaries not to do it).

[195] Restatement (Third) of Trusts §85(1)(a); 3 Scott & Ascher §18.1.

[196] *See generally* Bogert §146. The trustee may have additional powers granted by statute or the terms of the trust. *See* Restatement (Third) of Trusts §85(1)(b).

[197] 5 Scott & Ascher §37.3.2 (Extent of Powers of a Trustee of a Charitable Trust).

[198] 2 Scott on Trusts §126.3.

[199] *See* 3 Scott & Ascher §18.1; 3 Scott on Trusts §199.

[200] Restatement (Third) of Trusts §85 cmt. b(2); §86.

[201] Restatement (Third) of Trusts §85 cmt. c(1). *See generally* 4 Scott & Ascher §19.1.12 (Terms of the Trust).

example, while dower, tenancy-by-the-entirety ownership, marital support ob-ligations, and the like might place limitations on what a married person may do with his or her own property, a married person acting as trustee would not be subject to such limitations with respect to property that is the subject of a trust merely by virtue of the fact that legal title is in that person.[202]

There are two categories of trustee powers: Those that relate to the administration of the trust and those that relate to the disposition of income and principal.[203] The latter category is discussed in some detail in Section 3.5.3.2(a) of this handbook. Ordinarily these powers are discretionary.[204] Even when under the terms of the trust or applicable law a power is mandatory, the trustee generally has wide latitude in how that power is exercised.[205] A trustee vested with discretion is duty-bound to use his judgment.[206] "A trustee who does not use his or her judgment is not acting in the state of mind in which the settlor expected the trustee to act."[207] As a general rule, the court will not second-guess the trustee in the exercise of his discretion, unless there has been a clear abuse of that discretion.[208] Again, a trustee's discretion is never unlimited. It can never, for example, extend to subverting the interests of the beneficiaries in contravention of the trust's lawful terms.[209] In other words, a trustee's discretion no matter how broad the "band" is always subject to fiduciary constraints.[210] "No matter how broad the language of the trust instrument, the court will never permit the trustee to act dishonestly or in bad faith."[211] Moreover, unless the terms of the trust provide otherwise, a trustee in the exercise of his fiduciary powers will be expected to behave "reasonably."[212]

As noted, the trustee has only the powers—and all the powers—needed to carry out the terms of the trust and to protect the trust corpus.[213] When the two goals are in conflict or when a term of the trust or a provision of the applicable law is ambiguous, the trustee is entitled to petition the court for guidance.[214] Unless the terms of a trust provide otherwise, these powers of a trustee "pass to and are exercisable by substitute or successor trustees."[215] The reader is referred to Section 3.4.4.1 of this handbook for a discussion of the powers and duties of cotrustees.

---

[202] Restatement (Third) of Trusts §85 cmt. c.

[203] 3 Scott & Ascher §18.2.

[204] 3 Scott & Ascher §18.2.

[205] 3 Scott & Ascher §18.2.

[206] 3 Scott & Ascher §18.2.2 (When Trustee Fails to Use Judgment).

[207] 3 Scott & Ascher §18.2.2 (When Trustee Fails to Use Judgment).

[208] 3 Scott & Ascher §18.2.

[209] 3 Scott & Ascher §18.2. *See, however,* §6.2.12 of this handbook (trustee's duty not to comply with provisions that are unlawful or violate public policy).

[210] 3 Scott & Ascher §18.2.

[211] 3 Scott & Ascher §18.2.3 (When Trustee Acts Dishonestly).

[212] 3 Scott & Ascher §18.2.6 (Reasonableness of Trustee's Exercise of a Power).

[213] *See* Restatement (Third) of Trusts §186. *See generally* 3 Scott & Ascher §18.1.

[214] Restatement (Second) Trusts §259.

[215] Restatement (Third) of Trusts §85(2). *See generally* §3.4.4.3 of this handbook (successor trustees).

Ascertaining the limits of the trustee's equitable authority (in other words, the limits of the trustee's powers) is more an art than a science. The panoply of powers with respect to a given trust is drawn from long-established customs and practice, the common law, statute,[216] the terms of the trust itself,[217] and by implication from the general purposes of the trust.[218] In England, the trustee by statute "automatically has all the powers normally necessary or appropriate for efficient trust administration, even if the trust instrument is silent."[219]

The trustee's general powers incident to the office are numerous; to name just a few, they include: the power to sell,[220] lease,[221] sue and defend,[222] contract and incur expense,[223] and vote stock proxies.[224] In short, the trustee has all the powers needed to carry out the duties of a trustee.[225]

When it comes to trust powers, however, things are not always as they seem. Trustees should be cautious in exercising an express power that expands the common law authority of a trustee.[226] For example, one would be ill advised to rely on an expansive general power in the governing instrument "to do all things which the settlor could have done with his own property" or "to act unreasonably."[227] Courts are unlikely to interpret such language as a license to speculate or self-deal or otherwise engage in acts that are inconsistent with the concept of a trust.[228] To the extent they do, their inclination is to interpret such provisions strictly.[229] Moreover, language authorizing a trustee to deal with trust property as if he were its absolute owner ordinarily would not be construed as expanding the trustee's dispositive fiduciary powers, only his administrative ones. One court, however, has construed such language as authorizing the trustee of a certain charitable trust to make distributions to charities of his choosing, in addition to those specifically designated in the governing instrument.[230]

---

[216] Restatement (Third) of Trusts §85(1)(b). *See generally* 3 Scott & Ascher §§16.1 (Duties and Powers of the Trustee), 18.1 (The Extent of a Trustee's Powers).

[217] Restatement (Third) of Trusts §85(1)(b). *See also* 3 Scott & Ascher §18.1.1 (Conditional Powers) (noting that when the terms of the trust authorize the trustee to do a particular act only upon the happening of a particular event, the trustee ordinarily has no authority to do the act until the event actually happens, unless so empowered by the court); 4 Scott & Ascher §19.1.12 (Terms of the Trust).

[218] Restatement (Third) of Trusts §85 cmt. c.

[219] 3 Scott & Ascher §16.1. *See* Trustee Act, 1925, 15 Geo. V, c. 19, §69.

[220] *See* §3.5.3.1(a) of this handbook (trustee's power of sale).

[221] *See* §3.5.3.1(b) of this handbook (the trustee's power to lease trust property).

[222] *See* §3.5.3.1(c) of this handbook (the trustee's power to sue and defend).

[223] *See* §3.5.3.1(d) of this handbook (the trustee's power to bind the trust in contract).

[224] *See* §3.5.3.1(e) of this handbook (the trustee's power to vote proxies).

[225] *See generally* 3 Scott & Ascher §18.1.

[226] *See generally* 4 Scott & Ascher §19.1.12 (Terms of the Trust).

[227] *See generally* 3 Scott & Ascher §18.2.6 (Reasonableness of Trustee's Exercise of a Power).

[228] *See* Restatement (Second) of Trusts §186 cmt. f.

[229] *See generally* 4 Scott & Ascher §19.1.12 (Terms of the Trust).

[230] *See* Revocable Trust of Rice v. State of Ohio, 182 Ohio App.3d 605, 614, 914 N.E.2d 411, 418 (2009).

Even a tightly drafted specific power to retain a particular investment remains outstanding only as long as the investment furthers the general purposes and economic well-being of the trust.[231] If, for example, the investment is in an industry whose products are becoming obsolete and thus unmarketable, the trustee may have a duty to sell the investment notwithstanding the express retention authority.[232]

What if the investment is in a corporation that merges into another corporation?[233] "[I]f in any material respect there has been a change in the nature of . . . risk, security, or priority, the new property ought not to be held under the [retention] authorization clause . . . ; [i]f, considering the character of the business to be carried on by the new or revised corporation and the rights and liabilities of the shareholders, the new shares represent substantially the same type of investment, they may be retained under the settlor's authorization."[234]

The trustee who mechanically relies on powers expressly bestowed in the governing instrument does so at his peril. On the other hand, when the law is ambiguous as to whether the trustee has an implied power in a given situation, the trustee is entitled and advised to seek judicial guidance.

For a discussion of the trustee's implied right in equity to be indemnified from the trust estate for expenses reasonably incurred in the administration of the trust, the reader is referred to Section 3.5.2.3 of this handbook. Because the trustee as to the world is the owner of the trust property, he has the inherent power, both at law and in equity, to incur expenses.

§3.5.3.1 Some Specific Implied General Powers

The Uniform Trust Code is intended to grant trustees the broadest possible powers but to be exercised always in accordance with the duties of the trustee and any limitations stated in the terms of the trust. This broad authority is denoted by granting the trustee the powers of an unmarried competent owner of individually owned property, unlimited by restrictions that might be placed on it by marriage, disability, or cotenancy.[235]

Implied powers are granted to the trustee by operation of law, because without them it would be impossible to carry out the trustee's fiduciary responsibilities.[236] They need not be expressly granted in the terms of the trust.[237] The power to sell intangible personal property, lease, sue and defend, bind the trust

---

[231] *See* Restatement (Second) of Trusts §167 cmts. g, h; Restatement (Third) of Trusts §92, cmt. d [Restatement (Third) of Trusts: Prudent Investor Rule §229 cmt. d]; 4 Scott & Ascher §19.1.12 (Terms of the Trust).

[232] *See, e.g.,* Mueller v. Mueller, 28 Wis. 2d 26, 135 N.W.2d 854 (1965); Restatement (Third) of Trusts §92 cmt. d [Restatement (Third) of Trusts: Prudent Investor Rule §229 cmt. d]. *See generally* 4 Scott & Ascher §19.1.12 (Terms of the Trust).

[233] *See generally* Restatement (Second) of Trusts §231 cmt. f.

[234] Bogert §682.

[235] UTC §815 cmt. (available at <http://www.uniformlaws.org/Act.aspx?title=Trust%20Code>).

[236] *See generally* Bogert §551.

in contract, and vote proxies are a few of the more important powers that the trustee possesses incident to his office.[238] Thus, they are powers that the trustee possesses unless the settlor expressly or by implication denies them to the trustee.[239] Again, the list is by no means exclusive. Moreover, the Restatement (Third) of Trust's "comprehensive"[240] general articulation of the default authority that a trustee possesses over the trust property, namely, that of a "legally competent, unmarried individual,"[241] recognizes that any attempt to compile a "comprehensive" list of specific implied trustee powers applicable in every conceivable situation would be an act of futility and counterproductive.[242] It also evidences a "more expansive the better" policy:[243] The "breadth and simplicity" of the expansive approach to implied trustee powers "has the advantages (i) of facilitating fundamental efficiency in the use of family financial resources, with no course of action arbitrarily foreclosed, and (ii) of supplying both the *immediate* flexibility suitable to today's variety of trust purposes and circumstances and the adaptability *over time* to accommodate changing economic conditions and asset-management practices."[244]

The disadvantage of the expansive approach, of course, is that it can provide some cover for the unscrupulous. The authors of this handbook, however, are of the opinion that no trustee bent on making equitable mischief is going to be constrained or deterred by a miserly powers grant.[245] In any case, in earlier times, "[w]hen the purpose of the trust was not to manage wealth, but merely to ensure the safe passage of land through several generations,"[246] a trustee would have been kept on a much tighter leash, at least on paper:

> Protecting the beneficiary against . . . [trustee misbehavior] . . . has always been the central concern of trust law. In the early centuries of the trust, when trustees were mostly stakeholders of ancestral land, it was relatively easy to keep them in check,

---

[237] The phrase *terms of the trust* means the "settlor's intention 'with respect to the trust provisions' manifested 'in a manner that admits of its proof in judicial proceedings.'" Restatement (Third) of Trusts §85 cmt. b(1).

[238] *See generally* 3 Scott & Ascher §18.1.

[239] *See generally* 3 Scott & Ascher §16.2 (noting, however, that because "[n]ot all courts have fully accepted the notion that the trustee has such powers as are appropriate for effective trust administration," it is still common for a trust instrument to contain provisions expressly conferring on the trustee a wide variety of powers that he would or should have under the default law in any case).

[240] Restatement (Third) of Trusts §85 cmt. a.

[241] Restatement (Third) of Trusts §85(1).

[242] Restatement (Third) of Trusts §85 cmt. a.

[243] *See generally* 3 Scott & Ascher §18.1 (suggesting that there is "great wisdom" in the "expansive notion of trustees' powers").

[244] Restatement (Third) of Trusts §85 cmt. a.

[245] *See generally* 4 Scott & Ascher §19.1.12 (Terms of the Trust) (noting that if the terms of the trust narrow the field of permissible investments, the trustee who invests more broadly generally commits a breach of trust).

[246] 3 Scott & Ascher §18.1.

simply by disabling them from doing much with the trust property. Thus, trust default law deliberately supplied no trustee powers.[247]

(a)   The power to sell and buy; the power to invest.

Absent statutory authority[248] or authority in the governing instrument,[249] or a court order,[250] or beneficiary consent,[251] does the trustee have an implied power on behalf of the trust to sell the trust property to a third party for reasonable consideration? At early common law the answer was "no" when it came to land.[252] This was appropriate for a time when a family would derive its very identity from a specific parcel of land.[253] Justice Story summarized American law in his treatise of 1836: "[T]he trustee has no right (unless express power is given) to change the nature of the estate, as by converting land into money, or money into land."[254]

In the United States today courts will generally find a power of sale unless it appears from the language of the trust instrument, interpreted in light of the circumstances, that the settlor intended that the land should be retained by the trust.[255] Such a presumption is appropriate for a society that has come to look upon real estate as just one form of investment.[256] Moreover, unless there is an indication of a contrary intention in the terms of the trust, the trustee has had the implied or inherent authority to sell intangible personal property (*e.g.,*

---

[247] John H. Langbein, *Rise of the Management Trust,* Tr. & Est. 53–56 (Oct. 2004). "Early trust doctrine, especially as developed in England, severely limited the authority of trustees." Restatement (Third) of Trusts §85 cmt. a. "Over time, as equitable remedies and fiduciary standards have evolved and as the role of trusts has diversified, the powers allowed to trustees have gradually, rather steadily, expanded through judicial decisions and legislation and also through the drafting practices of experienced lawyers." Restatement (Third) of Trusts §85 cmt. a. *See generally* 3 Scott & Ascher §18.1 (The Extent of a Trustee's Powers).

[248] *See* 3 Scott & Ascher §18.1.4 n.9 (a list of citations to some American statutes that expressly confer on trustees broad powers of sale).

[249] *See generally* 3 Scott & Ascher §18.1.4.1 (The Terms of the Trust).

[250] *See generally* 3 Scott & Ascher §18.1.4.2 (Power of Court to Authorize Sale). *See, e.g.,* Matter of Pulitzer, 249 N.Y.S. 87 (Surr. Ct. 1931), *aff'd,* 260 N.Y.S. 975 (App. Div. 1932) (court authorizing sale of entrusted newspaper corporation though terms of trust had directed that the asset not be sold).

[251] *See generally* 3 Scott & Ascher §18.1.4.3 (Consent of Beneficiaries) (noting that regardless of whether the trustee has a power of sale, no beneficiary who has given informed consent to a sale can set it aside).

[252] *See generally* 3 Scott & Ascher §18.1.4; 3 Scott on Trusts §186.

[253] *See generally* 3 Scott on Trusts §190.

[254] John H. Langbein, *Rise of the Management Trust*, Tr. & Est. 54 (Oct. 2004) (citing to 2 Joseph Story, Commentaries on Equity Jurisprudence as Administered in England and America, 242 (1836)).

[255] *See generally* 3 Scott & Ascher §18.1.4; 3 Scott on Trusts §190; Bogert §741 (Statutes Regarding Court or Trustee's Sales).

[256] Types of property in estates in total taxable returns filed in 1998 were as follows: stocks, bonds, and mutual funds ($57.4 billion); real estate other than personal residences ($8.9 billion); personal residences ($6.3 billion). *Where the Money Is*, Wall St. J., Feb. 26, 2001, C13, col. 5. *See generally* 3 Scott & Ascher §18.1.4.1 (noting that land has no become a "commodity").

stocks and bonds) since the concept of a *Prudent Man Rule* took root.[257] "A trustee's powers in these matters include power to grant, for example, easements, rights to explore and remove natural resources, and options to lease or purchase."[258] A limitation on a trustee's power of sale might take the form of a direction to the trustee in the terms of the trust to allow the current beneficiary to occupy a particular dwelling comprising the trust estate or to distribute to the remaindermen shares of a particular closely held corporation once the trust terminates.[259] Express asset retention authority, however, is never a license to put the administration of the trust on automatic.[260]

With the express or implied duty to invest comes the power to buy and sell.[261] In many jurisdictions, the trustee is given by statute the power to sell personal property, unless the terms of the trust indicate a contrary intention.[262] The Restatement (Third) of Trusts provides that a trustee has an implied power of sale unless the terms of the trust indicate a contrary intent.[263]

A power of sale does not necessarily include the power to sell the trust property on credit.[264] Whether a sale on credit is allowed depends in large part on whether the receipt of notes in lieu of cash would put the trust at unnecessary risk.[265] If the buyer has a good credit rating, the sale may be proper, particularly if the sale is desirable and cannot otherwise be made.[266] A trustee would have the implied power to sell on credit, *i.e.*, in exchange for an unsecured promissory note, provided the promissory note is an appropriate trust investment.

While it may now be the default law that a power of sale brings with it a power in the trustee to grant an option,[267] caution nonetheless is advised.[268] Much will still depend upon whether granting the option

---

[257] *See generally* Restatement (Third) of Trusts at 3 (Prudent Investor Rule) (1992) (introduction to Topic 5); Harvard Coll. v. Amory, 26 Mass. (9 Pick.) 446 (1830). *See generally* 3 Scott & Ascher §18.1.4.1 (noting, however, that some courts may still find it "easier to find a power to sell personal property than a power to sell land").

[258] Restatement (Third) of Trusts §86 cmt. c.

[259] Restatement (Third) of Trusts §86 cmt. c.

[260] *See generally* §3.5.3.2(i) of this handbook (special investment powers).

[261] *See* Restatement (Third) of Trusts §190 cmts. b, d (Prudent Investor Rule) (1992).

[262] *See* 3 Scott on Trusts §190 n.10 and §190.4 n.10 for statutes governing the sale of trust property. *See also* Uniform Trustees' Powers Act §3(c)(7) (a trustee has power "to acquire or dispose of an asset, for cash or on credit, at public or private sale"); Bogert §743. Pursuant to §3(c)12 of the Uniform Trustees' Powers Act, a trustee would have the power to grant an option involving disposition of a trust asset.

[263] Restatement (Third) of Trusts §86 cmt. c; Restatement (Third) of Trusts §190 (Prudent Investor Rule) (1992).

[264] *See generally* 3 Scott on Trusts §190.7.

[265] *See generally* 3 Scott on Trusts §190.7.

[266] *See* Restatement (Third) of Trusts §190 cmt. j (Prudent Investor Rule) (1992).

[267] *See generally* 3 Scott & Ascher §18.1.4.6 (Power to Sell Options) (noting that at one time it was thought improper for a trustee to sell an option to purchase trust property as "the trustee should always be in a position to exercise discretion as to the amount of the purchase price and that it was therefore improper for a trustee to commit in advance by giving an option").

[268] *See* 3 Scott on Trusts §190.8.

is in the best interests of the trust, taking into account all the facts and circumstances.[269]

For a discussion of whether a power of sale includes a power to pledge or mortgage the trust estate, the reader is referred to Section 3.5.3.2(c) of this handbook.

A general power of sale or investment would allow the trustee to exchange trust property for property other than cash, provided the property received is a proper trust investment.[270] At one time, however, it was thought that an authorization to sell trust property connoted a sale for money only.[271] It is hard to come up with a better example of form trumping substance.

The state of the law as to whether a power of sale, in and of itself, will bring with it the power to incorporate the trust property appears to be in a state of flux.[272] Let us assume, for example, that a portion of the trust estate comprises an unincorporated business enterprise. The trustee may wish to exchange the assets of the enterprise for shares in an incorporated entity in order to insulate the other trust assets from the risks of the business.[273] Some commentators have suggested that court approval may be needed to effect such incorporation, absent express authority in the governing instrument.[274] The Restatement (Third) of Trusts is not in accord, finding a general authority to prudently incorporate already in the default law.[275]

Whatever the case, the trustee may not use the corporate form to escape the fiduciary duties of trust law.[276] The laws of England and the Isle of Man are generally in accord.[277] Trust law trumps corporate law.[278] By this we mean that one who as trustee controls a corporation holds its shares not for the benefit of the controlling shareholder but for the benefit of the trust beneficiaries.[279] The trust documentation establishes the bounds of the trustee's internal liability, *i.e.*,

---

[269] *See* 3 Scott on Trusts §190.8 n.3 and accompanying text.

[270] *See* Restatement (Third) of Trusts §190 cmt. m. *See also* 3 Scott on Trusts §190.9 n.2 and accompanying text. The trustee should be aware that, under certain circumstances, like-kind exchanges might offer income tax advantages for the trust. *See* I.R.C. §1031.

[271] *See generally* 3 Scott & Ascher §18.1.4.7 (Power to Exchange).

[272] *See generally* 3 Scott & Ascher §18.1.4.7 (Power to Exchange); 3 Scott on Trusts §190.9A; D. E. Ytreberg, Annot., *Trustee's power to exchange trust property for share of corporation organized to hold the property*, 20 A.L.R.3d 841 (1968).

[273] *See generally* 3 Scott & Ascher §18.1.4.7 (Power to Exchange); 3 Scott on Trusts §190.9A; D. E. Ytreberg, Annot., *Trustee's power to exchange trust property for share of corporation organized to hold the property*, 20 A.L.R.3d 841 (1968).

[274] *See generally* 3 Scott & Ascher §18.1.4.7 (Power to Exchange); 3 Scott on Trusts §190.9A; D. E. Ytreberg, Annot., *Trustee's power to exchange trust property for share of corporation organized to hold the property*, 20 A.L.R.3d 841 (1968).

[275] Restatement (Third) of Trusts §86 cmt. e.

[276] UTC §802 cmt. (available at <http://www.uniformlaws.org/Act.aspx?title =Trust%20Code>). *See generally* 3 Scott & Ascher §§18.1.4.7 (Power to Exchange), 18.1.8 (Powers With Respect to Shares of Stock).

[277] *See, e.g., In re Poyiadjis,* 2001-03 MLR 316 (Sept. 19, 2002) (Isle of Man High Court of Justice).

[278] 3 Scott & Ascher §18.1.8.

[279] Restatement (Third) of Trusts §86 cmt. e.

his liability to the beneficiaries. "Thus, for example, a trustee whose duty of impartiality would require the trustee to make current distributions for the support of current beneficiaries may not evade that duty by holding assets in corporate form and pleading the discretion of corporate directors to determine dividend policy."[280] Likewise, "[w]hen it is proper to form a charitable corporation to administer a charitable trust, the provisions of the corporate charter or certificate of incorporation must be in accordance with the terms of the trust."[281]

The corporate documentation and corporate law govern the trustee's external liability, *i.e.*, its liability to third parties in matters that pertain to the corporate entity, and, of course, govern what duties the trustee may have to minority shareholders, if any. The trustee of a controlling interest in a corporation who ignores or treats as a second-class citizen the trust documentation runs the risk of violating the fiduciary duties that are the subject of Chapter 6 of this handbook and incurring the liabilities that are the subject of Chapter 7.

It should be emphasized that a general express or implied power of sale does not contemplate sales to third parties for less than reasonable consideration.[282] Nor does it contemplate sales to the trustee himself. For the duties of a trustee in deciding whether and when to sell and in conducting a sale, the reader is referred to Bogert, Trusts and Trustees, Section 744.

(b)   The power to lease.

Associated with the trustee's duty to make the trust property productive is the power in the trustee to lease the real estate, or even the tangible personal property,[283] unless to do so would violate the express or implied intentions of the settlor.[284] The Restatement (Third) of Trusts is generally in accord.[285] "If a lease is improper, the beneficiaries can have it set aside, unless the lessee is a bona fide purchaser."[286]

---

[280] UTC §802 cmt. (available at <http://www.uniformlaws.org/Act.aspx?title= Trust%20Code>). *See, e.g.*, In re Koffend's Will, 218 Minn. 206, 219–220, 15 N.W.2d 590, 598 (1944).

[281] 5 Scott & Ascher §37.3.1.1 (Whether Trustee May Convey to or Form Charitable Corporation).

[282] *See* Restatement (Third) of Trusts §190 cmt. i.

[283] 3 Scott & Ascher §18.1.3.

[284] *See generally* Restatement (Second) of Trusts §189; 3 Scott & Ascher §18.1.3.

[285] Restatement (Third) of Trusts §86 cmt. c.

[286] 3 Scott & Ascher §18.1.3.1. *See also* §5.4.2 of this handbook (rights of the beneficiary as against BFPs and other transferees of the underlying trust property), §8.3.2 of this handbook (bona fide purchase for value of trust property, specifically what constitutes notice that a transfer is in breach of trust?), and §8.15.63 of this handbook (doctrine of bona fide purchase and the BFP). *Cf.* §8.3.6 of this handbook (negotiable instruments and the duty of third parties to inquire into the trustee's authority). For a comparison of the BFP, a creature of equity, with the holder in due course, a creature of law, *see* §8.15.68 of this handbook (the concept of the holder in due course in the trust context).

Because the remaindermen are entitled to the entire legal interest upon termination,[287] as well as full possession,[288] it was generally the case that a lease could not extend beyond the period of the trust,[289] unless the terms of the trust provided otherwise.[290] A lease that extended beyond the reasonably anticipated duration of the trust would not be binding on the remaindermen, but such a lease would be valid for the duration of the trust.[291] Thus, the trustee was cautioned to limit his lease to a reasonable or customary term. What *was* a "reasonable and customary duration" depended upon facts peculiar to each case. Thus, long-term leases had been approved when necessary to preserve the trust property,[292] even when forbidden by the terms of the trust.[293]

The Restatement (Third) of Trusts, however, suggests that a trustee *would* have default authority to lease real estate beyond the period of the trust, though it does acknowledge that "the duration of a lease may present special fiduciary concerns for the trustee to consider."[294] The transaction, for example, must make sense from an investment perspective.[295] It also must be done in a way that "respects" the remaindermen's equitable property rights.[296] Accordingly, a trustee contemplating leasing beyond the period of the trust may wish to give some advance notice at least to the presumptive remaindermen.[297]

If the trustee enters into a lease where the lessee undertakes to make improvements to the property in partial or total satisfaction of the lessee's rental obligation, *i.e.*, a building lease, the trustee should understand that such an arrangement could have the effect of shifting beneficial interests from the income beneficiary to the remaindermen.[298] Therefore, absent express or implied authority in the trust terms, the trustee should refrain from entering into such a lease, unless a way can be found to compensate the income account for the portion of the lessee's rental obligation that has taken the form of capital

---

[287] If the remainderman receive property that is subject to a lease, some sticks in the bundle of rights we call ownership would be lodged in the lessee, *e.g.*, the right to possession.

[288] *See generally* 3 Scott & Ascher §18.1.3.2.

[289] Restatement (Second) of Trusts §189 cmt. c; 3 Scott & Ascher §18.1.3.2.

[290] *See generally* 3 Scott & Ascher §18.1.3.3.

[291] Restatement (Second) of Trusts §189 cmt. c; 3 Scott & Ascher §18.1.3.2.

[292] *See, e.g.*, Myrick v. Moody Nat'l Bank, 336 S.W.3d 795 (Tex. App. 2011) (the trust property's highest and best use being to lease it out, the court authorized the trustee to extend the period of a lease beyond the trust's term, though the trustee had no express authority in the governing instrument to do so). *See generally* 3 Scott & Ascher §18.1.3.2; 3 Scott on Trusts §189.2.

[293] *See generally* 3 Scott & Ascher §18.1.3.3.

[294] Restatement (Third) of Trusts §86 cmt. c(1). *See generally* 3 Scott & Ascher §18.1.3.2.

[295] *See generally* §6.2.2.1 of this handbook (the *Harvard College* Prudent Man Rule and its progeny).

[296] Restatement (Third) of Trusts §86 cmt. c(1).

[297] *See generally* §6.1.5.1 of this handbook (the trustee's duty to provide information to the beneficiary).

[298] *See generally* 3 Scott & Ascher §18.1.3.4; 3 Scott on Trusts. §189.5.

improvements.[299] The Restatement (Third) of Trusts offers some general guidance to trustees contemplating such improvement-in-lieu-of-rent arrangements:

> It may be appropriate for a trustee to agree to reduced rental payments or a longer lease period, or both, in consideration of the lessee's agreement to make improvements that will belong to the trust when the lease expires, with no payment (or prescribed payment) to be made by the trust. The propriety of such an arrangement, however, depends on (i) whether it presents a productivity issue (see §79 on impartiality), and, if so, how that issue might be resolved (cf. §79, Comment i), and (ii) whether the additional "investment" in the property raises diversification or other issues of prudence under the principles of §90.[300]

(c)   The power to sue and defend.

The trustee has the duty of gathering and protecting the trust property,[301] hence the implied power to sue for it or for any damage to it; to defend suits against the trust; and to employ counsel and incur all necessary costs at the expense of the trust fund, whether successful or not in the litigation, unless the trustee has been imprudent.[302] These expenses are allowed not only in cases directly affecting the property but also where the trustee has acted reasonably and in good faith in attempting to protect the beneficiary (*e.g.*, where the trustee has attempted, though unsuccessfully, to have a guardian appointed for the beneficiary).

(d)   The power to bind the trust in contract.

If there is a fiduciary duty, the trustee has the power to enter into contracts, binding on the trust, for goods and services that are reasonably needed by him to carry out that duty.[303] This would include the costs of judicial proceedings and the expenses of managing, repairing, and improving the trust property.[304] The trustee has the inherent power to hire at trust expense agents such as attorneys and brokers, provided their services are needed for the proper

---

[299] *See generally* 3 Scott & Ascher §18.1.3.4 (noting also that a building lease that requires the trust to pay for improvements at the end of the lease term and/or grants the lessee some kind of option to purchase the improved land could be problematic, although such leases have often been permitted by the courts).

[300] Restatement (Third) of Trusts §86 cmt. c(1).

[301] *See* §6.2.1.1 of this handbook (duty to take active control of trust property) and §6.2.6 of this handbook (the trustee's duty to defend the trust against attack; the trustee's duty not to attack the trust).

[302] *See* Restatement (Second) of Trusts §188 cmt. b. *See generally* 3 Scott on Trusts §188.4.

[303] *See generally* 3 Scott on Trusts §188; Restatement (Second) of Trusts §271.

[304] *See generally* 3 Scott on Trusts §§188.4 (Judicial Proceedings), 188.2 (Repairs and Improvements).

administration of the trust.[305] The trustee, however, has no implied power to hire an agent for the purpose of performing services that the trustee personally ought to perform.[306] The trustee, for example, could not hire at trust expense an agent to decide who among a class of beneficiaries is entitled to discretionary distributions of principal.[307]

(e) The power to vote proxies.

One of the duties of the trustee is to actively manage and protect the trust estate.[308] Thus with respect to shares of stock the trustee has the power to exercise all of the ordinary rights of a stockholder, including the right to vote on corporate matters.[309] It is the duty of the trustee in voting shares of stock to act solely in the economic interest of the beneficiary in light of the manifested intentions of the settlor.[310] One has no power as trustee to indulge one's own social and political predilections with the stockholder franchise.[311] The lodestars must always be the economic well-being of the trust and the intentions of the settlor.[312]

If a minority interest in a corporation comprises a portion of the trust estate, the trustee probably has the implied power to vote the shares by proxy, provided the trustee is acquainted with the questions to be voted upon, has used due care in selecting the proxy, and has given suitable instructions with regard to the vote.[313] If the trust's interest in the corporation is a controlling one, the trustee has no power to give a general proxy.[314] The fiduciary responsibility of a trustee in voting a control block is heavier than where he holds only a small fraction of the shares.[315]

(f) The power to divide and combine trusts.

The Restatement (Third) of Trusts would have it the default law that a "trustee may divide a trust into two or more trusts or combine two or more trusts

---

[305] *See* 3 Scott on Trusts §188.3.

[306] *See* §6.1.4 of this handbook (the trustee's duty not to delegate critical functions).

[307] *See* §6.1.4 of this handbook (the trustee's duty not to delegate critical functions).

[308] *See* §6.2.1 of this handbook (trustee's duty to take active control of, segregate, earmark, and protect the trust property).

[309] *See generally* 3 Scott & Ascher §18.1.8; 3 Scott on Trusts §193.

[310] *See* 3 Scott & Ascher §18.1.8; 3 Scott on Trusts §193.1. *See also* UTC §802(g) (available at <http://www.uniformlaws.org/Act.aspx?title=Trust%20Code>).

[311] *See* §6.1.3 of this handbook (trustee's duty of loyalty to the beneficiaries or the trust's charitable purposes).

[312] 3 Scott & Ascher §18.1.8.

[313] *See* 3 Scott on Trusts §193.3. For a list of statutes providing that fiduciaries may vote by proxy, *see* 3 Scott on Trusts §193.3 nn.2–3.

[314] *See* 3 Scott on Trusts §193.3.

[315] UTC §802 cmt. (available at <http://www.uniformlaws.org/Act.aspx?title=Trust%20Code>).

into a single trust, if doing so does not adversely affect the rights of any beneficiary or the accomplishment of the trust purpose."[316] Absent implied authority to divide and combine, or absent express authority to do so in the terms of the trust, a trustee who wants such authority would have to obtain it from the court. There may be tax reasons why division is in the interest of the beneficiaries. The reader is referred to Section 3.5.3.2(m) of this handbook in this regard. Combining may promote administrative efficiency. The advantages of administering multiple trusts as a common fund, not to be confused with a common trust fund, are covered in Section 3.5.3.2(d) of this handbook.

(g) The power to incur and pay expenses.

The trustee has an implied power to pay from the trust estate reasonable expenses incurred in the course of administering the trust. The Restatement (Third) of Trusts is in accord.[317] "The trustee's right of indemnification entitles the trustee either to pay proper expenses directly from the trust estate (exoneration) or to obtain reimbursement from the trust when the trustee has personally paid those expenses."[318] For a discussion of what expenses are proper and reasonable, the reader is referred to Section 3.5.2.3 of this handbook.

(h) The power to disclaim or abandon property.

As a general rule, the trustee has a duty to protect the trust property, a topic that is covered in Section 6.2.1.3 of this handbook. On the other hand, it may be in the interest of the beneficiaries and in furtherance of the trust's purposes for the trustee to disclaim an item of property that would otherwise be held in trust, or to abandon an item of property that is already in the trust. When that is the case, the trustee would have an implied power to disclaim or abandon the item.[319]

(i) The power to appoint an ancillary trustee of property out-of-state.

Under Section 816(20) of the Uniform Trust Code, a trustee would have the default power to appoint an ancillary trustee for property situated out-of-state. The office of ancillary trustee is discussed in Section 9.32 of this handbook.

---

[316] Restatement (Third) of Trusts §68.

[317] Restatement (Third) of Trusts §88.

[318] Restatement (Third) of Trusts §88 cmt. a. *See generally* §3.5.2.3 of this handbook (right in equity to exoneration and reimbursement, *i.e.*, indemnity; payment of attorneys' fees).

[319] Restatement (Third) of Property (Wills and Other Donative Transfers) §86 cmt. f.

§3.5.3.2 Powers to Engage in Acts That Might Otherwise Be Breaches of Trust

[The specific powers granted to the trustee under the Uniform Trust Code] . . . are subsumed under the general authority granted in Section 815(a)(2) to exercise all powers over the trust property which an unmarried competent owner has over individually owned property, and any other powers appropriate to achieve the proper management, investment, and distribution of the trust property . . . . While the Committee drafting . . . [the] . . . Code discussed dropping the list of specific powers, it concluded that the demand of third parties to see language expressly authorizing specific transactions justified retention of a detailed list.[320]

Just as the aspirational law now would have no *per se* limitations on what a trustee may invest in,[321] so also it would have few if any *per se* limitations on the trustee's authority to carry out his fiduciary responsibilities.[322] For confirmation, one need only consult the Uniform Trustees' Powers Act and the applicable sections of the Uniform Trust Code.[323] Still, some acts have technically—perhaps *traditionally* is a better word—been considered *per se* breaches of trust, though it may have been in the interest of the trust and the proper execution of its purposes for the trustee to engage in such acts. Thus, since time immemorial, seasoned trust lawyers have proffered their fledglings, particularly those fledglings who see only bright lines, the following advice: "The main duty of a trustee is to commit judicious breaches of trust,"[324] or, perhaps, its variant: "A day should not go by without a benevolent breach of trust."[325]

Now, most trust instruments contain provisions that not only exculpate the trustee and others from all kinds of liability,[326] including some liabilities that no longer even exist,[327] but also bestow on the trustee powers that he might not

---

[320] UTC §816 cmt. (available at <http://www.uniformlaws.org/Act.aspx?title=Trust%20Code>).

[321] *See generally* §6.2.2.1 of this handbook (the *Harvard College* Prudent Man Rule and its progeny).

[322] *See* Restatement (Third) of Trusts §85 cmt. a (suggesting that the leading modern treatises in giving guidance to trustees, beneficiaries and courts accompany that guidance with "unfortunate statements about powers that are not ordinarily authorized by implication").

[323] UTC §§815, 816 (available at <http://www.uniformlaws.org/Act.aspx?title=Trust%20Code>). *See, e.g.,* Mass. Gen. Laws ch. 190B, §7-401 (a statutory list of powers that are granted to a trustee without court authorization or confirmation).

[324] Attributed by Lindley MR to Lord Justice Selwyn in argument in the case of Perrins v. Bellamy [1899] 1 Ch. 797 (England).

[325] Told in jest to the senior author shortly after his graduation from law school by his superior, Sanborn Vincent, Esq. (U.S.).

[326] *See generally* §7.2.6 of this handbook (exculpatory provisions that cover negligent breaches of trust).

[327] *See generally* §8.15.69 of this handbook (third-party liability for trustee's misapplication of payments to trustee; the purchaser's duty to monitor the trustee's application of the purchase price).

otherwise possess (or have possessed) under the common law.[328] Courts have tended to construe such provisions narrowly.[329] On the other hand, "the preferred construction" also is that a catalog of specific trustee powers in a trust instrument is not "exhaustive."[330] What follows is a discussion of some standard trustee powers clauses, which, with the exception of the power to make discretionary payments of income and principal, are generally considered "boilerplate."

(a)   **The power to use income for the beneficiary's benefit; to make discretionary payments of income and principal (the discretionary trust); principal invasion authority generally.**

The high court noted that sometimes the trustee's discretion is conditioned on a determination of the existence of certain facts such as the beneficiary is deserving or in need, whereas in other instances, the power is unconditional. In the present case, there were no conditions. Even in the absence of conditions, however, the trustee must not act capriciously, from careless good nature, or from the desire to relieve himself or herself of trouble, but only after consideration of all the circumstances.[331]

Beneficial applications of income. Most trust instruments bestow on the trustee the power to apply income for the benefit of the income beneficiary, as well as instruct the trustee how to administer the income account when the beneficiary is a minor or otherwise under an incapacity. However, if the instrument simply requires the trustee to pay the trust's income to the beneficiary, the traditional default law has been that payment must be made directly to the beneficiary at reasonable intervals, "normally monthly or quarter-annually,"[332] less expenses allocable to income.[333] The trustee would not have the power to choose the alternative of expenditures for the benefit of the

---

[328] Sample trustee powers language may be found in Bogert §§1281–1308; UTC §816 (available at <http://www.uniformlaws.org/Act.aspx?title=Trust%20Code>); and Uniform Trustees' Powers Act. In England, "[t]he current approach, in professionally drafted deeds, is to confer on trustees such wide powers of administration as are appropriate to the size and purpose of the trust." Martyn Frost, *Overview of Trusts in England and Wales,* in Trusts in Prime Jurisdictions 15 (2000). "This is especially true for investment powers, given the very narrow and prescriptive lists of permitted investments set out in the . . . [English] . . . Trustee Act 1961." Martyn Frost, *Overview of Trusts in England and Wales,* in Trusts in Prime Jurisdictions 15 (2000). *See generally* 3 Scott & Ascher §18.1 (noting that still to this day in the United States, "well-drafted trust instruments continue, almost uniformly, to contain extensive enumerations of trustees' powers").

[329] *See generally* §3.5.3.2(i) of this handbook (special investment powers). *Cf.* 3 Scott & Ascher §17.2.11 (noting that a court will generally construe narrowly a provision that authorizes a trustee to self-deal). "Even if the terms of the trust plainly authorize the trustee to deal with himself or herself, the trustee always must act fairly and in good faith." 3 Scott & Ascher §17.2.11.

[330] Restatement (Third) of Trusts §85 cmt. c(1); 3 Scott & Ascher §18.

[331] 5 Scott & Ascher §33.1.1 (referring to Boyden v. Stevens, 188 N.E. 741 (Mass. 1934)).

[332] Restatement (Third) of Trusts §49 cmt. c(1); 3 Scott & Ascher §17.14. *See generally* §5.4.1.3 of this handbook (beneficiary's right to income or possession).

beneficiary.[334] Thus, if the beneficiary is legally incapacitated, *e.g.*, by age or mental incompetency, a guardian would have to be appointed by the court to receive the income payments on behalf of the beneficiary—an expensive, time-consuming, and inconvenient process.[335]

Statutes have now been enacted in a number of jurisdictions allowing the trustee to make income payments for the benefit of an incapacitated beneficiary without the need for express authority in the terms of the trust.[336] The reader is particularly referred to the relevant sections of the Uniform Trustees' Powers Act[337] and the Uniform Trust Code.[338] The Restatement (Third) of Trusts, by generally endorsing this approach, would modify the default law: "Absent either express authorization or a contrary provision, it is implied from a direction to distribute income (or other amounts) that the trustee has authority to apply the funds for the beneficiary's benefit so long as no objection is raised by or on behalf of the beneficiary."[339]

The trustee has other options as well in the face of a beneficiary's inability for whatever reason to handle funds. If in good-faith doubt as to the beneficiary's "practical or legal capacity to handle funds," the trustee may segregate the funds in a separate account, "subject to the continuing right of withdrawal upon demand by or on behalf of the beneficiary."[340] The funds would be fully vested in the beneficiary.[341] Simply making distributions to a custodian under the applicable Uniform Transfers to Minors Act[342] (or to a custodial trustee under the Uniform Custodial Trustee Act)[343] may also be an option.

The discretionary trust. *First what the classic nondiscretionary trust looks like.* Perhaps the one trustee power that is clearly not buried somewhere in past or present default law is the power to make discretionary accumulations and/or distributions of income and principal.[344] Under a basic common law trust— *A* (the settlor) to *B* (the trustee) for C (the current beneficiary) for life, then to D (the remainder beneficiary)—C receives all net trust accounting income accrued to the date of death, and upon C's death, D receives the principal outright

---

[333] Restatement (Third) of Trusts §49 cmt. c(1). *See generally* 3 Scott & Ascher §17.14; 2A Scott on Trusts §182; §5.4.1.3 of this handbook (beneficiary's right to income or possession).

[334] *See generally* 2A Scott on Trusts §182; *but see* 3 Scott & Ascher §17.14.1 (suggesting that if the trustee applies a distribution for the "necessary support" of the incapacitated beneficiary, "the trustee is ordinarily not subject to surcharge, as otherwise the beneficiary would be unjustly enriched").

[335] 3 Scott & Ascher §17.14.1; 2A Scott on Trusts §182.1 n.1 and accompanying text.

[336] *See generally* 3 Scott & Ascher §17.14.1; 2A Scott on Trusts §182.1 n.1 and accompanying text.

[337] Uniform Trustees' Powers Act §3(c)(22).

[338] UTC §816(21) (available at <http://www.uniformlaws.org/Act.aspx?title=Trust%20Code>).

[339] Restatement (Third) of Trusts §49 cmt. c(2).

[340] Restatement (Third) of Trusts §49 cmt. c(2).

[341] Restatement (Third) of Trusts §49 cmt. c(2).

[342] *See generally* §3.5.3.2(l) of this handbook (the power to administer distributions to minors and other legally incapacitated persons).

[343] Uniform Custodial Trust Act §5.

[344] *See generally* 3 Scott & Ascher §18.2.

and free of trust.[345] The trustee has no power to invade principal for the benefit of the current beneficiary.[346] Because of the duty of impartiality, the trustee has no power to withhold income from *C* or take principal from D[347] and give it to C.[348] To do so would be a breach of trust.[349] Moreover, if there are multiple *C*s, the trustee has a common law duty to be impartial as among them.[350] Thus, each *C* would receive an equal portion of the income stream. A trustee has no authority to deviate from these precepts absent express authority in the terms of the trust.

The fiduciary dispositive power. It is now common practice for settlors to bestow on trustees the discretionary authority to favor the current beneficiary over the remainderman by invading principal, and vice versa by accumulating income; and to discriminate between and among members of a class of beneficiaries.[351] The trustee is said to possess a fiduciary dispositive power,[352] which is not to be confused with a personal nonfiduciary power of appointment.[353] "Once it is determined that the power in question is held in the role of trustee, words such as 'absolute' or 'sole and uncontrolled' or 'unlimited' are not interpreted literally."[354]

The classic discretionary trust grants the trustee broad generalized discretion in his fiduciary capacity to pay income and distribute principal to the beneficiary.[355] A grant of *sole, absolute, and uncontrolled discretion*, or words to that effect, is often referred to as language of "extended discretion."[356] A cousin of the discretionary trust is the *discretionary support trust*, in which the trustee's

---

[345] *See generally* 4 Scott & Ascher §20.1 (Impartiality Between Successive Beneficiaries).

[346] "In the absence of such authority the trustee has no power to invade principal for an income beneficiary." Restatement (Third) of Trusts §49 cmt. d.

[347] "In the absence of such authority the trustee has no power to invade principal for an income beneficiary." Restatement (Third) of Trusts §49 cmt. d.

[348] *See* §6.2.5 of this handbook (trustee's duty of impartiality). *See generally* 4 Scott & Ascher §20.1 (Impartiality Between Successive Beneficiaries) (confirming that "an income beneficiary has traditionally been entitled to the entire income, and nothing else").

[349] *See* §6.2.5 of this handbook (duty of impartiality).

[350] *See* §6.2.5 of this handbook (duty of impartiality).

[351] *See generally* 4 Scott & Ascher §20.1 (but noting that "despite the rise of the discretionary trust, there remain a great many beneficiaries whose only entitlement consists of an interest in income or an interest in principal").

[352] Lewin ¶20-119 (England).

[353] *See generally* §8.1 of this handbook (powers of appointment). *See also* 3 Scott and Ascher §13.2.3 (noting that if the terms of the trust require the trustee to pay to a beneficiary so much of the principal as the beneficiary may request, the trustee has no discretion to withhold any part of the principal if the beneficiary request it, the *beneficiary* essentially possessing a nonfiduciary general inter vivos power of appointment that trumps any fiduciary powers the trustee may possess).

[354] Restatement (Third) of Trusts §85 cmt. d. "It is contrary to sound policy, and a contradiction in terms, to permit the settlor to relieve a *trustee* of all accountability." Restatement (Third) of Trusts §85 cmt. d. *See generally* 3 Scott & Ascher §18.2 (Control of Discretionary Powers).

[355] *See* Bogert §228.

[356] Kevin D. Millard, *Rights of a Trust Beneficiary's Creditors under the Uniform Trust Code*, 34 ACTEC L.J. 58, 69 (2008).

discretion is limited by a standard such as health, maintenance, and support.[357] The Restatement (Third) of Trusts, unlike the Restatement (Second) of Trusts, does not attempt to draw a bright line between discretionary trusts and support trusts where distributions are subject to an exercise of trustee discretion.[358] The Uniform Trust Code is generally in accord with the Third Restatement, essentially deeming a support trust to be a discretionary trust with a support standard.[359] "Language of extended discretion may be used along with a standard, such as 'the trustee may distribute to the beneficiary as much of the net income and principal of the trust as the trustee determines advisable, in the trustee's *sole and absolute discretion*, for the beneficiary's health, education, maintenance, and support.' "[360] Sometimes a grant of discretion is coupled with language of direction, such as "my trustees *shall*, in their absolute discretion, distribute such amounts as are necessary for the beneficiary's support."[361] Still, the provision is discretionary, not mandatory, despite the presence of the imperative "shall."[362]

A permissible beneficiary of a discretionary trust also may be a beneficiary of mandatory distributions, that is to say a taker in default of exercise of the fiduciary power, if the terms of the trust so provide. The terms of the trust, however, also could call for the value of mandatory distributions to be reduced by the value of prior discretionary distributions, if any. Such a qualification is known as a hotchpot clause. Such clauses are the subject of Section 8.15.51 of this handbook.

A trustee's discretionary authority is not unlimited; at the very least it must be exercised in good faith and within its limits. In every U.S. jurisdiction, a trustee's exercise of discretionary authority, including absolute discretionary authority, is subject to judicial review.[363] "Notwithstanding the breadth of discretion granted to a trustee in the terms of the trust, including the use of such terms as 'absolute,' 'sole,' or 'uncontrolled,' the trustee shall exercise a discretionary power in good faith and in accordance with the terms and purposes of the trust

---

[357] In the context of creditor accessibility, the Uniform Trust Code has eliminated the distinction between discretionary and support trusts, unifying the rules for all trusts fitting within either of the former categories. UTC §504 cmt. (available at <http://www.uniformlaws.org/Act.aspx?title=Trust%20Code>). *See generally* 3 Scott & Ascher §15.3.

[358] Restatement (Third) of Trusts, Reporter's Notes on §60. *See generally* Kevin D. Millard, *Rights of a Trust Beneficiary's Creditors under the Uniform Trust Code*, 34 ACTEC L.J. 58 (2008).

[359] UTC §504 cmt. (citing (Third) of Trusts, Reporter's Notes on §60 cmt. a) (available at <http://www.uniformlaws.org/Act.aspx?title=Trust%20Code>). *See, e.g.*, Strojek v. Hardin County Bd. of Supervisors, 602 N.W.2d 566, 569 (Iowa Ct. App. 1999) (noting that while the definitional distinctions between support and discretionary trusts are limpid, provisions of particular trusts muddy these clear demarcations).

[360] Kevin D. Millard, *Rights of a Trust Beneficiary's Creditors under the Uniform Trust Code*, 34 ACTEC L.J. 58, 69 (2008).

[361] UTC §506 cmt (available at <http://www.uniformlaws.org/Act.aspx?title=Trust%20Code>).

[362] UTC §506 cmt (available at <http://www.uniformlaws.org/Act.aspx?title=Trust%20Code>).

[363] Ivan Taback & David Pratt, *When the Rubber Meets the Road: A Discussion Regarding a Trustee's Exercise of Discretion*, 49 Real Prop., Trust & Estate Law 491, 492 (2015).

and the interest of the beneficiaries."[364] The good-faith requirement is not surprising.[365] " . . . [G]ood faith is required even in arm's length business dealings when the parties are not in a fiduciary relationship . . . , and is referenced in at least 50 different provisions of the Uniform Commercial Code."[366] A trustee who exercises discretion in good faith does so fairly and honestly without fraud or collusion.[367] A trustee who exercises discretion in bad faith does so for fraudulent, selfish, or improper purposes.[368]

It is an open question, however, whether in the face a broad grant of discretionary authority the *reasonableness* of a trustee's actions also may be the subject of judicial second-guessing.[369] Some have even suggested that when there has been a generalized grant accompanied by language of extended discretion, the trustee is relieved of the default duty to act reasonably and in good faith.[370] What is left is essentially a duty not to act in bad faith.[371] If that is all that is left, do we really have a trust at all, at least of the Anglo-American

---

[364] UTC §814(a) (available at <http://www.uniformlaws.org/Act.aspx?title=Trust%20Code>) (codifying the common law principle that despite the breadth of discretion purportedly granted by the wording of a trust, no grant of discretion to a trustee, whether with respect to management or distribution, is ever absolute). *See generally* Frederick R. Franke, Jr., *Resisting the Contractarian Insurgency: The Uniform Trust Code, Fiduciary Duty, and Good Faith in Contract*, 36 ACTEC L.J. 517, 528 (2010) (noting that in practice the courts impose on trustees duties to act reasonably and in good faith even when their discretions are ostensibly absolute); Alan Newman, *Spendthrift and Discretionary Trusts: Alive and Well under the Uniform Trust Code*, 40 Real Prop. Prob. & Tr. J. 567, 612–614 (Fall 2005) (discussing the UTC's "in accordance with the terms and purposes of the trust and the interests of the beneficiaries" limitation on trustee discretion). *See, e.g.,* Griffin v. Griffin, 463 So. 2d 569, 574 (Fla. 1985) (confirming that a vesting of absolute discretion in a trustee does not relieve the trustee from the exercise of good faith or from being judicious in the administration of the trust). These equitable limitations on what a trustee may do in the exercise of his discretionary authority would not apply to powers that the trustee may exercise in a nonfiduciary capacity. UTC §814 cmt. (available at <http://www.uniformlaws.org/Act.aspx?title=Trust%20Code>).

[365] *See generally* Frederick R. Franke, Jr., *Resisting the Contractarian Insurgency: The Uniform Trust Code, Fiduciary Duty, and Good Faith in Contract*, 36 ACTEC L.J. 517 (2010).

[366] Alan Newman, *Spendthrift and Discretionary Trusts: Alive and Well under the Uniform Trust Code*, 40 Real Prop. Prob. & Tr. J. 567, 618, n.254 (Fall 2005). *See also* 5 Scott & Ascher §31.1.1; Frederick R. Franke, Jr., *Resisting the Contractarian Insurgency: The Uniform Trust Code, Fiduciary Duty, and Good Faith in Contract*, 36 ACTEC L.J. 517 (2010).

[367] Nelson v. First Nat'l Bank & Trust Co. of Williston, 543 F.3d 432, 435–436 (8th Cir. 2008).

[368] Nelson v. First Nat'l Bank & Trust Co. of Williston, 543 F.3d 432, 435–436 (8th Cir. 2008).

[369] *See generally* 3 Scott & Ascher §18.2.6 (Reasonableness of Trustee's Exercise of a Power); Frederick R. Franke, Jr., *Resisting the Contractarian Insurgency: The Uniform Trust Code, Fiduciary Duty, and Good Faith in Contract*, 36 ACTEC L.J. 517 (2010); Kevin D. Millard, *Rights of a Trust Beneficiary's Creditors under the Uniform Trust Code*, 34 ACTEC L.J. 58, 68–76 (2008); Alan Newman, *Spendthrift and Discretionary Trusts: Alive and Well under the Uniform Trust Code*, 40 Real Prop. Prob. & Tr. J. 567, 610–612 (Fall 2005); 5 Scott & Ascher §33.1.1 (fiduciary powers to terminate or modify).

[370] *See generally* Frederick R. Franke, Jr., *Resisting the Contractarian Insurgency: The Uniform Trust Code, Fiduciary Duty, and Good Faith in Contract*, 36 ACTEC L.J. 517 (2010); Kevin D. Millard, *Rights of a Trust Beneficiary's Creditors under the Uniform Trust Code*, 34 ACTEC L.J. 58, 68–76 (2008).

[371] *See generally* Frederick R. Franke, Jr., *Resisting the Contractarian Insurgency: The Uniform Trust Code, Fiduciary Duty, and Good Faith in Contract*, 36 ACTEC L.J. 517 (2010); Kevin D. Millard, *Rights of a Trust Beneficiary's Creditors under the Uniform Trust Code*, 34 ACTEC L.J. 58, 68–76 (2008).

equity-based variety that is the subject of this handbook?[372] In any case, the designated permissible current beneficiaries and presumptive remaindermen should still have standing to bring an action against the trustee for abuse of discretion.[373] Note that in England, this may be easier said than done; as a general rule, English "[t]rustees exercising a discretionary power are not bound to disclose their reasons, their role being a confidential one."[374] Even a personal *nonfiduciary* power of appointment whose exercise is limited by some standard, *e.g.*, a power in the beneficiary to demand principal from the trustee for the beneficiary's "support," generally must be exercised in good faith.[375]

For a state-by-state law survey (in chart format) of grounds for judicial interference in a trustee's exercise of discretionary authority, including the standard of care prevailing in each state to which a trustee in the exercise of that authority is held, see Taback and Pratt.[376]

May an exercise of trustee discretion lead to the trust's termination. Whether a fiduciary power in a trustee to invade principal encompasses the power to invade the principal down to zero and in so doing effect a termination of the trust will depend upon the terms of the trust.[377] It should be noted that the Uniform Trust Code negates any presumption that the presence of a spend-thrift clause evidences a material purpose that would bar the judicial termination or modification of a trust that has only one beneficiary.[378] The Restatement (Third) of Trusts is in accord.[379] There is much case law, however, that is not.[380] Under the Restatement, authority in the trustee to invade principal for the beneficiary's support, or otherwise for the beneficiary's benefit, does raise a

---

[372] *See generally* §6.1 of this handbook (general duties) (when a critical element of the trust relationship is lacking).

[373] *See generally* Frederick R. Franke, Jr., *Resisting the Contractarian Insurgency: The Uniform Trust Code, Fiduciary Duty, and Good Faith in Contract*, 36 ACTEC L.J. 517 (2010); Alan Newman, *Spendthrift and Discretionary Trusts: Alive and Well under the Uniform Trust Code*, 40 Real Prop. Prob. & Tr. J. 567, 604–609 (Fall 2005) (U.S.); Lewin ¶29-101 (England). *See also* Lewin ¶29-100 (England) (providing some examples of abuse of discretion). *But see* Regan v. Uebelhor, 690 N.E.2d 1222 (Ind. Ct. App. 1998) (holding that an Indiana virtual representation statute deprived granddaughter of standing to challenge actions of trustee that had been approved by mother and grandmother).

[374] Lewin ¶29-101 (England).

[375] *See generally* 3 Scott & Ascher §13.2.7; §8.1 of this handbook (powers of appointment); §8.15.26 of this handbook (fraud on a power doctrine).

[376] Ivan Taback & David Pratt, *When the Rubber Meets the Road: A Discussion Regarding a Trustee's Exercise of Discretion*, 49 Real Prop., Trust & Estate Law 491, 521–547 (2015).

[377] *See generally* 5 Scott & Ascher §33.1.1 (Termination or Modification by Trustee). *See, e.g.*, Boyden v. Stevens, 188 N.E. 741 (Mass. 1934); McKnight v. Bank of N.Y. & Trust Co., 173 N.E. 568 (N.Y. 1930).

[378] UTC §411(c) (available at <http://www.uniformlaws.org/Act.aspx?title=Trust%20Code>). *See generally* §8.15.7 of this handbook (the *Claflin* doctrine (material purpose doctrine)); 5 Scott & Ascher §34.1.2 (Spendthrift Trusts); 5 Scott & Ascher §34.1.4 (Support Trusts and Discretionary Trusts).

[379] Restatement (Third) of Trusts §65 cmt. e. *See generally* 5 Scott & Ascher §34.1.2 (Spendthrift Trusts). Likewise, a discretionary provision may or may not evidence a material purpose that would bar termination or modification. Restatement (Third) of Trusts §65 cmt. e.

[380] 5 Scott & Ascher §34.1.2 n.1.

strong material purpose presumption, but only a presumption.[381] The case law is less equivocal.[382] "In England, in contrast, the sole beneficiary of the trust can terminate the trust at any time, even if the trust is for the beneficiary's support or the trustee has discretion over distributions or when to terminate the trust."[383]

The exercise of a fiduciary dispositive power is nondelegable. A trustee with a fiduciary dispositive power may not delegate the exercise of that power to anyone, absent ultra-specific express authority in the terms of the trust to do so.[384] It is one of the few powers that remain to this day *per se* nondelegable.[385] Only the trustee may exercise the discretion. Thus, trust counsel may only advise. It falls to the trustee, and only the trustee, "to decide."[386] Also, the trustee may not bind himself in contract or otherwise to exercise a fiduciary dispositive power in a particular way in the future.[387] The trustee personally must exercise discretion at the time of each discretionary payment or distribution.[388] What applies to trustees in this regard would apply as well to trust protectors with fiduciary dispositive powers.[389] During World War I, Parliament created a limited statutory exception from the common law prohibition against a trustee's delegating the entire administration of a trust to others, particularly the exercise of fiduciary dispositive and administrative powers.[390] Available to trustees on active military duty, it allowed for the appointment of a "delegate" who would "attend meetings of the trustees in the place of an absent, delegating trustee and participate in the decisions of the trustees as one of their number."[391] Thus a "delegate" was more in the nature of a substitute trustee than an agent, an agent being one who acts at the direction of the principal.[392] "The English *Trustee Act* 1925, s 25, deriving from the War-time legislation, furnished

---

[381] Restatement (Third) of Trusts §65 cmt. e. *See generally* §8.15.7 of this handbook (the *Claflin* doctrine (material purpose doctrine)); 5 Scott & Ascher §34.1.4 (Support Trusts and Discretionary Trusts).

[382] 5 Scott & Ascher §34.1.4 n. 1.

[383] 5 Scott & Ascher §34.1.4. *See generally* §3.5.3.2(a) of this handbook (the discretionary trust, including the support invasion standard).

[384] *See generally* §6.1.4 of this handbook (trustee's duty to give personal attention, that is the duty not to delegate certain fiduciary functions).

[385] *See generally* §6.1.4 of this handbook (trustee's duty to give personal attention, that is the duty not to delegate certain fiduciary functions).

[386] *See* Scott v. The Nat'l Trust [1998] 2 All ER 705, 717 (England) ("It is however for advisors to advise and for trustees to decide: trustees may not (except insofar as they are authorized to do so) delegate the exercise of their discretions, even to experts.").

[387] *See generally* 5 Scott & Ascher §33.1.1.

[388] 5 Scott & Ascher §33.1.1.

[389] *See generally* §3.2.6 of this handbook (considerations in the selection of a trustee) (in part discussing the rights, duties, and obligations of a trust protector).

[390] Execution of Trusts (War Facilities) Acts 1914 and 1915 (England). *Cf.* British Columbia Trustee Act 1966 §14.

[391] W. A. Lee, *Purifying the dialect of equity*, 7 Tr. Q. Rev., Issue No.2, 12–13 (May 2009) [A STEP publication].

[392] W. A. Lee, *Purifying the dialect of equity*, 7 Tr. Q. Rev., Issue No.2, 12–13 (May 2009) [A STEP publication]. *See generally* §9.9.2 of this handbook (the agency relationship); Chapter 1 of this handbook (comparing the trust and agency relationships).

a more general power to trustees to delegate their *'trusts powers and discretions'* to others by way of a power of attorney during absence abroad."[393] Thus, when considering matters of fiduciary delegation, one needs to be attentive to the nomenclature.[394] A trustee may delegate certain functions to an agent.[395] An agent, however, is not a *delegate*, at least as that term is properly employed in the context of English trust law.

Trustee's failure to exercise discretion one way or the other does not cause trust to fail. The refusal of the trustee of a *noncharitable* trust to exercise discretionary dispositive authority generally does not warrant a judicial determination that the trust has failed and that a resulting trust should be imposed.[396] If a trust ought not to fail for want of a trustee, it certainly ought not to fail on account of a breach of trust, unless the terms of the trust so provide.[397] The breach is the failure to affirmatively act, that is to affirmatively carry out the terms of the trust. The trustee's duty to act is taken up in Section 6.1.2 of this handbook. In this case, the breach is not the failure to actually make discretionary distributions to the permissible beneficiaries but the failure to consider in good faith whether or not to do so.

In the event of a trustee's failure to exercise such a discretionary authority, the court may decline to compel the trustee to exercise the authority, appoint a special trustee solely for the purpose of exercising the authority, or exercise the authority itself.[398] The court also might order that the subject property be distributed in equal shares to the members of the beneficiary class.[399] When the class comprises "relatives" of a designated individual, there is precedent for the court ordering that the subject property be distributed in equal shares to those who would be the individual's heirs at law.[400] When the trustee of a testamentary trust refuses or neglects to select beneficiaries from an indefinite class, such as of the settlor's "friends," then a resulting trust may have to be imposed, it being "obviously impossible" for the court to divide the property among all of the class members.[401] The court, of course, always has the option of removing the trustee and appointing a suitable successor in furtherance of the trust's purposes and the interests of the beneficiaries.[402]

---

[393] W. A. Lee, *Purifying the dialect of equity*, 7 Tr. Q. Rev., Issue No.2, 12–13 (May 2009) [A STEP publication].

[394] *See* W. A. Lee, *Purifying the dialect of equity*, 7 Tr. Q. Rev., Issue No.2, 12–13 (May 2009) [A STEP publication] ("The error that has arisen in relation to the distinction between delegation and agency is that the two have become hopelessly confused and that that confusion has even reached the English *Trustee Act 2000* . . .").

[395] *See generally* §6.1.4 of this handbook (what functions a trustee may delegate to agents).

[396] *See generally* §4.1.1.1 of this handbook (the resulting trust).

[397] *Cf.* 6 Scott & Ascher §39.7.1 (No Reverter for Breach of Charitable Trust).

[398] *See generally* 6 Scott & Ascher §41.4.

[399] *See generally* 6 Scott & Ascher §41.4.

[400] *See generally* 6 Scott & Ascher §41.5 (Trust for Relatives). Heirs at law are those entitled to take under the laws of intestacy. *See generally* §5.2 of this handbook (class designations). *See also* 6 Scott & Ascher §41.10 (Trust for Several Valid Objects).

[401] 6 Scott & Ascher §41.6 (Testamentary Disposition for Members of Indefinite Class).

[402] *See generally* §7.2.3.6 of this handbook (removal).

The discretionary trust for an indefinite class of beneficiaries is covered in Section 9.29 of this handbook ("The Adapted Trust").[403] The discretionary trust for a specific noncharitable purpose is covered in Section 9.27 of this handbook ("The Purpose Trust").[404] Principles of agency law, more or less govern the inter vivos adapted trust, the trustee being a constructive agent of the settlor under such an arrangement.[405] The same can be said for the inter vivos purpose trust.[406] In the case of a testamentary adapted or purpose trust, however, even agency principles are inapplicable as the will speaks at death. Thus there is really no one with standing to seek its enforcement.[407]

When the trustee of a discretionary *charitable* trust with multiple charitable purposes fails altogether to exercise his discretionary dispositive authority, there are several possibilities: The court may remove the trustee and appoint a new one, or order application of the trust property *in equal shares* to the specified charitable purposes, unless such a resolution would violate the terms of the trust.[408] Equal allocation among the charitable purposes, for example, might not be what the settlor had in mind. Thus, "[i]f it is possible to ascertain the maximum amount necessary to accomplish one of the charitable purposes, the court will not require application of more than that amount, and will divide the balance among the other charitable purposes."[409] When the terms of the trust provide that "the power to allocate among charities is confined to the original trustee, and an equal division would be inconsistent with the settlor's intent, the court may frame a scheme for division of the property."[410]

A fiduciary dispositive power must be expressly granted. Unless a fiduciary dispositive power has been granted to the trustee by the terms of the trust, such a power would not be implied, even under modern default law.[411] When the terms of the trust do so provide, however, there is a default presumption that the discretionary power would pass to any successor trustees.[412]

The trustee's duty of impartiality. Is the trustee of a so-called discretionary trust[413] relieved of the common law duty of impartiality? Not really. "The duty

---

[403] *See also* 6 Scott & Ascher §41.6.

[404] *See also* 6 Scott & Ascher §41.8.

[405] *See generally* 6 Scott & Ascher §41.9.

[406] *See generally* 6 Scott & Ascher §41.9.

[407] *See generally* 6 Scott & Ascher §41.8.

[408] 6 Scott & Ascher §§39.3.4 (Power to Distribute Among Specified Charities), 39.3.5 (Power to Distribute Among Charitable and Other Valid Objects).

[409] 6 Scott & Ascher §39.3.4.

[410] 6 Scott & Ascher §§39.3.4, 41.10.

[411] 4 Scott & Ascher §20.1.

[412] Restatement (Third) of Trusts §85 cmt. d. *See generally* §3.4.4.3 of this handbook (successor trustees). On the other hand, a power of appointment conferred on a beneficiary is generally not transmissible. Restatement (Third) of Trusts §85 cmt. d. "A power of appointment is personal to the designated donee or donees, and is to be distinguished from a fiduciary power that runs with the office or is conferred upon a person as trustee." Restatement (Third) of Trusts §85 cmt. d. *See generally* §8.1 of this handbook (Powers of Appointment).

[413] A discretionary trust is a trust under which the trustee is granted discretion with respect to a beneficiary's rights to benefits. *See* Restatement (Third) of Trusts §50 cmt. a. A trustee, of course, may well have discretionary authority in other areas as well, such as in the selection of

to act impartially does not mean that the trustee must treat the beneficiaries equally . . . ; [r]ather, the trustee must treat the beneficiaries equitably in light of the purposes and terms of the trust."[414] Moreover, the trustee remains fully accountable even in the face of a broad grant of discretionary authority. "Even under the broadest grant of fiduciary discretion, a trustee must act honestly and in a state of mind contemplated by the settlor."[415] Again, a trustee's discretionary power with respect to trust benefits is a fiduciary power. It should not be confused with a nonfiduciary personal power of appointment.[416] A personal power of appointment "is not subject to fiduciary obligations and may be exercised arbitrarily within the scope of the power."[417]

Standards governing the exercise of a trustee's discretionary dispositive powers. Discretionary powers to sprinkle, spray, and accumulate income and to invade principal are governed by standards set forth in the terms of the trust.[418] A standard can be broadly drafted (*e.g.*, the power to invade principal for *C*'s "benefit") or narrowly drafted (*e.g.*, the power to invade principal to pay *C*'s "medical bills"). A typical standard found in many trusts permits payment for the "maintenance and support" of the beneficiary. A "support" standard falls somewhere between the underwriting of utility bills and the underwriting of a world cruise. Precisely *where* is not always easy to determine. Much depends on the beneficiary's station in life at the time the inter vivos trust was established,[419] or in the case of a testamentary trust, during the testator's lifetime;[420] the size of the trust estate; and the extent of the trustee's discretion.[421] The menu of standards available to the settlor is limited only by one's imagination. For a comparative analysis of the meanings of some frequently used standards, for example, "support or maintenance," "education," "health," "medical care," "comfort," "comfortable support," "support in reasonable comfort," "support and comfort," "generous support," "happiness," "benefit," "best interests,"

---

investments. Discretionary authority in the trustee to select investments alone, however, would not make the trust a discretionary trust.

[414] UTC §803 cmt. (available at <http://www.uniformlaws.org/Act.aspx?title=Trust%20Code>). In other words, "the trustee is under a duty to act with 'due regard' to the beneficiaries' respective interests." 4 Scott & Ascher §20.1.

[415] Restatement (Third) of Trusts §50, cmt. c. *See generally* §8.15.15 of this handbook (the ascertainable standard). *Cf.* §3.5.3.2(i) of this handbook (special investment powers).

[416] *See generally* §8.1 of this handbook (powers of appointment).

[417] Restatement (Third) of Trusts §50 cmt. a.

[418] Restatement (Third) of Trusts, §50 cmt. a. *See generally* 2 Scott on Trusts §§128.3, 128.7. *See also* Dobris, *New Forms of Private Trusts for the Twenty-First Century—Principal and Income*, 31 Real Prop. Prob. & Tr. J. 1 (Spring 1996).

[419] *See, e.g.*, In re Benjamin F. Haddad Trust, 2013 WL 4081031 (Mich. Ct. App. Aug. 13, 2013).

[420] *See generally* Halbach, *Problems of Discretion in Discretionary Trusts*, 61 Colum. L. Rev. 1425 (1961). *See also* I.R.C. §2041(b)(1)(A) (providing that a power holder's right to invade principal for his own "maintenance or support" is *not* treated as a general power for federal estate tax purposes); 2 Scott on Trusts §128.4 (suggesting that "support" encompasses support of a beneficiary's spouse and minor children).

[421] *See generally* 3 Scott & Ascher §13.2.4.

"welfare," "emergency," "severe hardship," and "disability," the reader is referred to the Restatement (Third) of Trusts.[422]

Letters of wishes. Some experienced practitioners have advocated that settlors prepare nonbinding confidential "letters of wishes" to assist their trustees in making discretionary decisions in given situations.[423] The authors have seen many of them over the years. To be sure, "[w]hen interpreting the provisions of a trust, 'the polestar in every trust is the settlor's intent and the intent must prevail.'"[424] Still, one needs to be cognizant of the risks of attaching an informal letter of wishes to a formal trust instrument. The letter itself can contain ambiguities, and is certain not to address all the situations that the trustee could encounter in the exercise of his discretionary authority. Or the contents of the letter could conflict with the contents of the trust instrument. To further muddy the waters, there is the ambiguous legal status of letters of wishes generally. Would a letter of wishes really be nonbinding if its contents constituted evidence of the trust's core purpose? Certainly it would be discoverable by the beneficiaries, warts and all, if it were.[425] So much for confidentiality. That being the case, what is to prevent a court in a given situation in the exercise of its equitable powers from deeming a letter of wishes either to be integrated into the trust instrument itself (assuming the letter was prepared at the time the trust was created), or an amendment to the trust to the extent that the trust was amendable at the time the letter of wishes was prepared?

On the other hand, a trustee generally need not disclose the process of deciding whether to exercise a particular discretionary power, such as the power to invade corpus.[426] This principle is ostensibly not for the benefit of the trustees but for the benefit of the beneficiaries. Thus, if a particular letter of wishes is intended merely to assist the trustee in making discretionary decisions and not to articulate a gloss on the settlor's intent, then perhaps the letter ought not to be discoverable by the beneficiaries. In England there are no bright lines. In one case involving a discretionary trust, the court was inclined to order disclosure of a letter of wishes to the beneficiaries only because the trustees were contemplating distributing the entirety of the trust corpus.[427] Otherwise there was a sense on the part of both the court and the trustees that the beneficiaries would be better served were the letter of wishes kept confidential.

---

[422] Restatement (Third) of Trusts §50 (comment on sub-section (2)). For a case in which the trial court had second-guessed discretionary distributions made by trustees who were limited by a hardship standard, *see* Griffin v. Griffin, 463 So. 2d 569 (Fla. 1985).

[423] *See, e.g.,* Alexander A. Bove, Jr. & Melissa Langa, *Distinguishing discretion in discretionary trusts,* 34 MLW 1203 (Jan. 23, 2006).

[424] In re Scheidmantel, 868 A.2d 464, 488 (2005) (citing In re Trust of Hirt, 832 A.2d 438, 448 (Pa. Super. 2003)).

[425] *See generally* §5.4.1.1 of this handbook (discussing the beneficiary's right to information and confidentiality).

[426] Re Londonderry's Settlement, [1965] Ch 918 CA (England).

[427] Breakspear v. Ackland All E.R. (D) 260 (19 February 2008); EWHC 220 (Ch.) (19 February 2008) (England).

In the face of all this uncertainty, there is really no substitute for the settlor of a discretionary trust gathering all its provisions within the four corners of a single formal instrument; for making sure that each provision is unambiguous and *sensibly comprehensive*; and, last but not least, for doing whatever it takes to find just the right trustee.[428] Whether there is any utility to adding a letter of wishes to the mix is an open question. Much may depend upon the particular facts and circumstances, as well as how skillfully and subtly the letter is drafted.[429] The case for adding a letter of wishes to the mix is made by Alexander A. Bove, Jr.[430]

When the beneficiary of a support trust gifts away a trust distribution. If a trustee makes a distribution to a beneficiary pursuant to a support invasion standard and the beneficiary turns around and gives away the distribution to a third person, the trustee may be in breach of trust.[431] This is because the distribution was not used for the beneficiary's support.[432] The fraud on a power doctrine may be implicated as well in that a nonobject of the trustee's discretionary power is being benefited. The doctrine of fraud on a power is covered in Section 8.15.26 of this handbook. On the other hand, "[w]hen the beneficiary of a support trust is married, the usual inference is that the beneficiary is entitled to enough to support not only the beneficiary, but also the beneficiary's spouse and minor children."[433] In fact, one court has broadly construed the term *support* to encompass discretionary distributions for the purpose of funding the private school educations of the beneficiary's children.[434] Another court has mused that authority in a trustee to invade principal to enable the widowed beneficiary to maintain the standard of living to which she had become accustomed when her husband was alive might encompass facilitating the making of gifts by the widow after his death via principal distributions to her, provided she had given similar gifts when *her husband* was alive and provided the types of gifts contemplated were "consistent with that standard of living."[435] A discretionary distribution to a beneficiary to enable the beneficiary to pay a

---

[428] *See generally* §5.2 of this handbook (particularly the introductory quote discussing the importance of good drafting); §3.2.6 of this handbook (considerations in the selection of a trustee).

[429] *See* the introductory quotation to §5.2 of this handbook (class designation: "children," "issue," "heirs," and "relatives" (some rules of construction)).

[430] *The Letter of Wishes: Can We Influence Discretion in Discretionary Trusts?* 35 ACTEC L.J. 38 (2009).

[431] *Cf.* McKnight v. Bank of N.Y. & Trust Co., 173 N.E. 568 (N.Y. 1930) (a trustee's invasion of principal other than pursuant to the support standard set forth in the terms of the trust tantamount to an unauthorized partial revocation).

[432] *See* Smith v. Deshaw, 78 A.2d 479, 116 Vt. 441 (1951). *But see* Finch v. Wachovia Bank & Trust Co., 577 S.E.2d 306 (N.C. 2003) (suggesting that full discretion in the trustee to invade principal to meet the beneficiary's "reasonable needs in her station of life" would include authority to invade principal to enable the beneficiary to make substantial gifts to her "church, charities and family members").

[433] 3 Scott & Ascher §13.2.4.

[434] *See* Estate of Stevens, 2005 WL 1211003 (S.C. Ct. App.).

[435] In re Van Dusen Marital Trust, 834 N.W.2d 514, n.1 (Minn. Ct. App. 2013).

debt the beneficiary's husband owes to the trustee, however, could well implicate the trustee's duty of loyalty.[436] At least one court has so held.[437] When a
beneficiary of a revocable trust is incompetent, the court may permit the trustee
to make gifts, either to other individuals or to charity, "if the beneficiary would
have made such gifts on his or her own."[438]

When HIPAA clashes with the law of trusts. As one can see, a number of these
standards will impose on the trustee an affirmative fiduciary duty to ascertain
and assess a beneficiary's health situation.[439] The challenge for the trustee is to
do so without running up against the Health Insurance Portability and Accountability Act (HIPAA) privacy rules. "The civil and criminal penalties authorized
under HIPAA offer no real incentive for a treating physician, hospital, or other
covered entity to assist a corporation, partnership, or trustee in obtaining
health information for purposes of evaluating an individual's disability, capacity, or medical condition."[440] Counsel who is called upon to assist a trustee in
getting around the HIPAA information roadblocks should find Jacqueline
Myles Crain's article[441] particularly helpful, both at the drafting stage and
thereafter.

The trustee-beneficiary of a discretionary trust. It may be the default rule that a
trustee-beneficiary may not participate in decisions regarding distributions of
principal to himself.[442] Presumably, the rule may be overridden by express
language in the governing instrument[443] or by an allocation in the terms of the
trust of decision-making responsibilities to an independent cotrustee who

---

[436] *See generally* §6.1.3 of this handbook (trustee's duty of loyalty to the beneficiary).

[437] Molyneux v. Fletcher, [1898] 1 Q.B. 648. *See generally* 3 Scott & Ascher §17.2.10 (Other
Situations Implicating the Duty of Loyalty).

[438] 3 Scott & Ascher §18.1.7.

[439] *See, e.g.,* Marsman v. Nasca, 30 Mass. App. 789, 573 N.E.2d 1025 (1991); Old Colony
Trust Co. v. Rodd, 356 Mass. 584, 254 N.E.2d 886 (1970). *See generally* Hayes & Wall, *Fiduciary
Discretion—Where Is the Better Part of Valor,* 132 Tr. & Est. 8 (1993) (discussing the practical
considerations of making and documenting discretionary distributions).

[440] Jacqueline Myles Crain, *HIPAA—A Shield for Health Information and a Snag for Estate
Planning and Corporate Documents,* 40 Real Prop. Prob. & Tr. J. 357, 360 (Summer 2005).

[441] *HIPAA—A Shield for Health Information and a Snag for Estate Planning and Corporate
Documents,* 40 Real Prop. Prob. & Tr. J. 357 (Summer 2005).

[442] *See generally* Bogert §129. *See, e.g.,* Dana v. Gring, 374 Mass. 109, 371 N.E.2d 755 (1977);
UTC §814(b)(2) (available at <http://www.uniformlaws.org/Act.aspx?title=Trust%20Code>)
(providing that a trustee may not exercise a power to make discretionary distributions to satisfy a
legal obligation of support that the trustee personally owes another person); Fla. Stat. Ann.
§737.402(4) (Florida). *But see* UTC §814(b)(1) (providing that a person other than a settlor who is
a beneficiary and trustee of a trust that confers on the trustee a power to make discretionary
distributions to or for the trustee's personal benefit may exercise the power only in accordance
with an ascertainable standard relating to the trustee's individual health, education, support, or
maintenance within the meaning of §2041(b)(1)(A) or 2514(c)(1) of the Internal Revenue Code).
A power that is subject to these exercise limitations may be exercised by a majority of the remaining
trustees whose exercise of the power is not so limited. UTC §814(c). These default exercise
limitations would not apply to non-QTIP marital deduction trusts, revocable trusts, and §2503(c)
minors trusts. UTC §814(d).

[443] *See, e.g.,* N.C. Gen. Stat. §32-34(b) (N.C.); Garfield v. United States, 47 A.F.T.R.2d
¶81-1583, 80-2 USTC ¶13,381 (D. Mass.).

directly or indirectly possesses no beneficial interest, contingent or otherwise, in the trust property, as well as holds no nonfiduciary powers of appointment over it. Absent special facts, though, it would have to be someone other than the beneficiary's personal attorney. The independence of the trusteeship of any agent-fiduciary of a beneficiary, for that matter, would likely be called into question. Within the scope of an agency, the agent's duty of loyalty to the principal is virtually absolute; the trustee, however, also is likely to have duties that run simultaneously to other beneficiaries, including the remaindermen. In New York, the override option had *at one time* been foreclosed by statute:

> Except in the case of a trust which is revocable by such person during lifetime, a power conferred upon a person in his or her capacity as trustee of an express trust to make discretionary distributions of either principal or income to himself or herself or to make discretionary allocations in his or her favor of receipts or expenses as between principal and income, cannot be exercised by him or her. If the power is conferred on two or more trustees, it may be executed by the trustees who are not so disqualified. If there is no trustee qualified to execute the power, its execution devolves on the supreme court or the surrogate's court, except that if the power is created by will, its execution devolves on the surrogate's court having jurisdiction of the estate of the donor of the power.[444]

There is generally nothing in the default law that would prevent the settlor of a discretionary trust from designating in its terms a trustee as one of the permissible beneficiaries, at least in principle. "The conflict . . . [however,] . . . between such a trustee's personal interest and that of the other trust beneficiaries is obvious."[445] And then there are the tax issues: "A trustee's discretionary power to make distributions in his or her own favor may cause the property subject to the power to be treated as the trustee's own, for purposes of the federal estate, gift, and income taxes."[446]

---

[444] Est. Powers & Trusts Law §10-10.1 (New York). The statute was amended in 2003 to permit express overrides:

> A power held by a person as trustee of an express trust to make a discretionary distribution of either principal or income to such person as a beneficiary, or to make discretionary allocations in such person's favor of receipts or expenses as between principal and income, cannot be exercised by such person unless (1) such person is the grantor of the trust and the trust is revocable by such person during such person's lifetime, or (2) the power is a power to provide for such person's health, education, maintenance or support within the meaning of §§2041 and 2514 of the Internal Revenue Code, or (3) *the trust instrument, by express reference to this section, provides otherwise.* If the power is conferred on two or more trustees, it may be exercised by the trustee or trustees who are not so disqualified. If there is no trustee qualified to exercise the power, its exercise devolves on the supreme court or the surrogate's court, except that if the power is created by will, its exercise devolves on the surrogate's court having jurisdiction of the estate of the donor of the power.Est. Powers & Trusts Law §10-10.1 (New York).

[445] 3 Scott & Ascher §18.2.5. *See also* §3.2.6 of this handbook (considerations in the selection of a trustee).

[446] *See generally* 3 Scott & Ascher §18.2.5. *See also* §8.9.3 of this handbook (tax-sensitive powers).

Tax-curative provisions in a discretionary trust. The Uniform Trust Code does not generally address the subject of tax curative provisions.[447] It does, however, put certain default law limitations on a beneficiary-trustee's exercise of discretion.[448] Why? Because "the unintended inclusion of the trust in the beneficiary-trustee's gross estate is a frequent enough occurrence that the drafters concluded that it is a topic that . . . [the] . . . Code should address."[449] Accordingly, the Uniform Trust Code provides that "a person other than a settlor who is a beneficiary and trustee of a trust that confers on the trustee a power to make discretionary distributions to or for the trustee's personal benefit may exercise the power only in accordance with an ascertainable standard relating to the trustee's individual health, education, support, or maintenance within the meaning of Section 2041(b)(1)(A) or 2514(c)(1) of the Internal Revenue Code . . . ."[450]

Courts will not second-guess a trustee's exercise of discretionary authority, unless there has been a clear abuse of discretion. In any case, courts will not second-guess the trustee's exercise of discretionary powers unless to prevent misinterpretation or abuse of discretion by the trustee, nor are they inclined to give advance rulings on the propriety of a contemplated exercise of a lawful discretionary power in the absence of a showing of bad faith or improper motive.[451] Similar deference is afforded trustees of charitable trusts.[452]

Of course, a trustee's failure to take some action can itself constitute an abuse of discretion warranting injunction, specific performance orders, removal, and other such equitable relief that can have the effect of stripping the

---

[447] UTC §814 cmt. (available at <http://www.uniformlaws.org/Act.aspx?title=Trust%20 Code>).

[448] UTC §814(b) (available at <http://www.uniformlaws.org/Act.aspx?title=Trust%20 Code>). So does Virginia. *See* Va. Code §§64.1–67.2.

[449] UTC §814 cmt (available at <http://www.uniformlaws.org/Act.aspx?title=Trust%20 Code>).

[450] UTC §814(b)(1). *See, e.g.,* Va. Code §§64.1–67.2 (Virginia). *See generally* 3 Scott & Ascher §18.2.5 (Trustee With Discretionary Power to Distribute to Self); §§8.9.3 of this handbook (tax-sensitive powers) and 8.15.15 of this handbook (the ascertainable standard).

[451] *See* Restatement (Third) of Trusts §50(1); In re Van Dusen Marital Trust, 834 N.W.2d 514, 524 (Minn. Ct. App. 2013) ("But a trustee may not exercise its discretion in a manner that defeats the grantor's intent or the trust's purpose."); Carter v. Carter, 965 N.E.2d 1146, 1153 (Ill. 2012) ("The exercise of discretion by the trustee is not subject to interference by the court absent proof of fraud, abuse of discretion or bad faith."). *See generally* 3 Scott & Ascher §18.2; 3 Scott on Trusts §187; Bogert §560; 5 Scott & Ascher §33.1.1. "The court will not ordinarily instruct trustees on how to exercise discretion . . . ." UTC §112 cmt. (available at <http://www.uniformlaws.org/ Act.aspx?title=Trust%20Code>). *See, e.g.,* Finch v. Wachovia Bank & Trust Co., N.A., 577 S.E.2d 306 (N.C. 2003) (the court having second-guessed the trustee's narrow interpretation of the scope of its invasion authority, declined to force the trustee to exercise that authority). *See also* Wright v. Blum, 114 N.E. 79 (Mass. 1916). This is not to say that if a trustee is committing or threatening to commit a breach of trust by abuse of discretion, the court would not or could not step in and compel the trustee prospectively to exercise his discretion in a particular way, particularly if the abuse or threatened abuse is occasioned by the trustee's dishonesty or bad faith. *See generally* 3 Scott & Ascher §18.2.1. Inaction as well as action can constitute an abuse of discretion. *See generally* 3 Scott & Ascher §18.2.1.

[452] *See generally* 5 Scott & Ascher §37.3.4.

trustee of his discretionary authority altogether.[453] English courts are similarly disinclined to second-guess trustees,[454] as is the Restatement (Third) of Trusts,[455] which explains abuse of discretion this way:

> An abuse of discretion may result from the exercise of discretionary authority in bad faith or from improper motive. Thus, a discretionary power is abused if a trustee acts dishonestly, such as when the trustee receives an improper inducement for exercising the power in question. Similarly, an abuse of discretion occurs when a trustee acts from an improper even though not dishonest motive, such as when the act is undertaken in good faith but for a purpose other than to further the purposes of the trust or, more specifically, the purposes for which the power was granted.[456]

Documenting the trustee's exercises of discretion. The trustee must be aware that the exercise of a discretionary power to pay income or distribute principal affects the property rights of the beneficiaries. Thus, executed discretionary decisions should be well documented: A trustee is well advised to keep accurate records of all requests, granted and denied. The Uniform Trust Code requires that a trustee send the permissible distributees of trust income and/or principal, at least annually and at the termination of the trust, a report of the trust property, liabilities, receipts, and disbursements, including the source and amount of the trustee's compensation, a listing of the trust assets, and, if feasible, their respective market values.[457]

Whether the trustee of a discretionary trust should take into account nontrust assets and benefits available to the beneficiary. The common law offers little useful guidance when it comes to whether the trustee shall take into account assets available to the beneficiary outside the trust (*e.g.*, a portfolio of securities) or take into account the beneficiary's collateral sources of support (*e.g.*, public benefits;[458] or a wealthy spouse; or the beneficiary's personal portfolio or earning power[459]). The issue most often arises when the standard is "maintenance" or "support." Suffice it to say, the cases are all over the lot.[460] The Restatement (Second) of Trusts took the position that in trusts for support the inference was that the trustee did not need to take into account other resources

---

[453] *See generally* 3 Scott & Ascher §18.2.1.

[454] Lewin ¶29-87 through ¶29-92 (England).

[455] Restatement (Third) of Trusts §87.

[456] Restatement (Third) of Trusts §87 cmt. c. *See generally* §8.15.26 of this handbook (fraud on a power doctrine).

[457] UTC §813(c) (available at <http://www.uniformlaws.org/Act.aspx?title=Trust%20Code>). *See generally* §6.1.5.2 of this handbook (trustee's duty to keep and render accounts).

[458] *See, e.g.*, Restatement (Third) of Trusts §50 cmt. e(4) (suggesting that "to the extent consistent with the terms and purposes of the trust, and allowable by applicable benefits statutes . . . , the presumption is that the trustee's discretion should be exercised in a manner that will avoid either disqualifying the beneficiary for other benefits or expending trust funds for purposes for which public funds would otherwise be available"). *See generally* §5.3.5 of this handbook (Medicaid eligibility and recoupment).

[459] *See generally* 3 Scott & Ascher §13.2.4.

[460] *See* 3 Scott & Ascher §13.2.4.

available to the beneficiary.[461] This position is followed by many, though not all, jurisdictions.[462] On the other hand, other resources of the beneficiary are to be considered when limitation language such as "when in need" and "if necessary" is employed.[463] At least one court has so held.[464]

The Restatement (Third) of Trusts has taken a position different from prior restatements, namely that if the trust's provisions do not address the question of whether the trustee is to take into account the beneficiary's other resources, particularly when the trustee's exercise of discretion is constrained by an objective standard of such support, the trustee is to consider the other resources but *has some discretion* in the matter.[465] A trustee of a discretionary trust in part for the education of the settlor's grandchildren has done just that.[466] Her reasoned failure to underwrite their education expenses with trust property was contested but found on appeal not to have been an abuse of discretion, the grandchildren having had multiple collateral sources of tuition support, including their own fully funded New York 529 College Savings accounts.

May a trustee exercise discretion to distribute income and/or invade principal for the "support" of a child in a way that relieves the child's parents of the burdens of their support obligation?[467] "The soundest and most substantial statutory and judicial authority supports the rule that the parents bear the primary obligation to support their child and that resort may be had to a child's own resources for his basic needs only if the parents are financially unable to fulfill the obligations themselves."[468] The Restatement (Third) of Trusts is generally in accord.[469] The rule is probably applicable as well to trusts that are funded by personal injury settlements.[470] "Ultimately . . . [however,] . . . a trustee's duty and authority with respect to other resources are matters of settlor intention, and it may be determined though interpretation that a particular

---

[461] *See* Restatement (Second) of Trusts §128(e). The Restatement (Third) of Trusts Tentative Draft No. 2, Mar. 10, 1999) in the comment on sub-section (2) of §50 at 308, suggests that if the governing instrument is silent on the matter, a trustee, in determining the distributions to be made to a beneficiary under an objective standard such as support, is "to consider the other resources but has some discretion in the matter."

[462] *See generally* 2 Scott on Trusts §128.4. (For a catalog of jurisdictions where the inference is that trustees do not have to consider collateral sources of support, *see* 2 Scott on Trusts §128.4 n.3.). *See also* 3 Scott & Ascher §13.2.4 (containing a similar catalog at n.6).

[463] *See* Harootian v. Douvadjian, 954 N.E.2d 560, 563–564 (Mass. App. Ct. 2011).

[464] Woodberry v. Bunker, 359 Mass. 239, 243 (1971). "However, it is not required, unless expressly stated by the testator, that the life beneficiary 'exhaust the whole of her individual estate before she is entitled to have any part of the principal.'" *Id.*

[465] Restatement (Third) of Trusts §50 cmt. e(2). *See generally* 3 Scott & Ascher §13.2.4 n.8 (containing citations to cases that have required the trustee to consider the beneficiary's other resources, the accompanying text however noting that "many of these cases seem to have found a manifestation of such an intention on the settlor's part").

[466] *See* Trusts for McDonald, 953 N.Y.S.2d 751 (2012).

[467] *See generally* 3 Scott & Ascher §13.2.4.

[468] Armstrong v. Armstrong, 544 P.2d 941, 943 (Cal. 1976).

[469] Restatement (Third) of Trusts §50 cmt. e(3).

[470] In the Matter of Allison Marmol, 640 N.Y.S.2d 969 (Sup. Ct. 1996). *See generally* §9.3 of this handbook (the self-settled "special needs"/"supplemental needs" trust).

settlor intended to provide for, or allow, the beneficiary's full support to come from the trust, and thus to assist and benefit the parent directly."[471] It should be noted that the Restatement (Third) of Trusts has created an opposite presumption with respect to a discretionary beneficiary who became such as a result of an adoption *after* the trust was created: The adopting parent's duty of support is *not* to be taken into account by the trustee when exercising discretion to make or not make distributions for the support of the adopted child.[472] The presumption is, of course, rebuttable.[473]

Again, a court asked to rule on an "other resource" issue will ground its ruling in the presumed intentions of the settlor as extracted from the particular discretionary language,[474] as will a court faced, say, with a support trust of residential real estate in which the beneficiary is no longer residing. "In the absence of evidence of a contrary intention, the usual inference is that the beneficiary remains entitled to support in any event."[475] The prudent prospective trustee of a support trust endeavors to have such issues resolved at the drafting stage.

The trustee's affirmative duty to ascertain the needs of the beneficiary. If the trust instrument grants the trustee the discretionary power to pay income or distribute principal to the beneficiary for the beneficiary's maintenance and support, the trustee will most likely be under an affirmative duty to determine if the beneficiary needs funds. Some recent cases are in accord,[476] as is the Restatement (Third) of Trusts.[477] Even when the fiduciary invasion power lacks limiting conditions, the trustee will still have an affirmative duty to apprise himself of all the relevant facts and circumstances.[478]

The trustee is not an agent of the beneficiary. On the other hand, if the trustee were to give the beneficiary free rein to withdraw at will trust principal, the trustee's duty not to delegate his discretionary authority would be implicated.[479] The trustee is a principal. He is not an agent of the beneficiary. Also, in bestowing on the beneficiary a constructive nonfiduciary general inter vivos power of appointment, the trustee violates his duty to carry out the terms of the trust.[480] This all assumes, of course, that the terms of the trust do not in fact grant the beneficiary such a power.

---

[471] Restatement (Third) of Trusts §50 cmt. e(3).

[472] Restatement (Third) of Trusts §50 cmt. e(3).

[473] Restatement (Third) of Trusts §50 cmt. e(3).

[474] *See generally* 2 Scott on Trusts §128.4.

[475] 3 Scott & Ascher §13.2.4.

[476] *See, e.g.,* Marsman v. Nasca, 30 Mass. App. 789, 573 N.E.2d 1025 (1991); Old Colony Trust Co. v. Rodd, 356 Mass. 584, 254 N.E.2d 886 (1970). *See generally* Hayes & Wall, *Fiduciary Discretion—Where Is the Better Part of Valor,* 132 Tr. & Est. 8 (1993) (discussing the practical considerations of making and documenting discretionary distributions).

[477] Restatement (Third) of Trusts §§50 cmt. e(1), 87, cmt. c.

[478] 5 Scott & Ascher §33.1.1. *See also* Boyden v. Stevens, 188 N.E. 741 (Mass. 1934).

[479] *See generally* 3 Scott & Ascher §17.3.2 (citing to Matter of Osborn, 299 N.Y.S. 593 (App. Div. 1937). *See also* McKnight v. Bank of N.Y. & Trust Co., 173 N.E. 568 (N.Y. 1930).

[480] *See generally* §6.1.2 of this handbook (the trustee's duty to carry out the terms of the trust).

The default authority of the trustee of a discretionary trust to pay the funeral bills of a permissible beneficiary. If authorized to pay income and/or principal to or for the benefit of a beneficiary, may the trustee pay the beneficiary's funeral bills with income accrued to the date of death? Absent express authority to do so, probably not. This is because the equitable property interest is now in someone other than the beneficiary's estate.[481] One learned commentator, however, disagrees, suggesting that the "usual inference is that the trustee's discretion as to the disposition of income accruing prior to the beneficiary's death does not end with the beneficiary's death, and that the trustee may in its discretion pay such income to the beneficiary's estate."[482] In the case of a support trust, the usual inference is that the trustee may pay the deceased beneficiary's funeral bills and postmortem debts with accrued income and/or principal, and may be required to do so, depending upon the terms of the trust.[483]

Inherent in a trustee's power to make discretionary distributions is the lesser power, in lieu thereof, to make loans. If an outright distribution would "fall . . . within the reasonable discretion of the trustee," so should a loan in lieu thereof.[484] As a practical matter, however, the trustee may not wish to get into the business of administering loans to beneficiaries. Moreover, what if the beneficiary defaults? Should the trustee seek to collect on behalf of the trust or should discretion be exercised and the original transaction treated as an outright distribution? Absent special circumstances, the trustee should keep things as clean and simple as possible. Note that a loan to a beneficiary is an investment and should be carried as such on the books of the trust. The loan, however, need not qualify as a prudent investment.[485]

Decanting: Discretionary fiduciary distributions of principal in further trust. Inherent in a trustee's unqualified power to make discretionary distributions of principal outright and free of trust to or for the benefit of a beneficiary is the lesser power to make a distribution of principal to another trustee upon a different trust to or for the benefit of that beneficiary.[486] The Restatement (Third) of Property is in accord.[487] Moving property from one trust to another

---

[481] *But see* 2 Scott on Trusts §128.4. The Restatement (Third) of Trusts §50 cmt. d(5) suggests that authority in the trustee to satisfy the postdeath obligations of a discretionary beneficiary is presumed "only to the extent that . . . [the] . . . probate estate, revocable trust, and other assets available for these purposes are insufficient or . . . the trustee, during the beneficiary's lifetime, either agreed to make payment or unreasonably delayed in responding to a claim by the beneficiary for which the terms of the trust would have required payment while the beneficiary was alive."

[482] 3 Scott & Ascher §13.2.3.

[483] 3 Scott & Ascher §13.2.4.

[484] Restatement (Third) of Trusts §50 cmt. d(6).

[485] Restatement (Third) of Trusts §90 [Restatement (Third) of Trusts: Prudent Investor Rule §227].

[486] Phipps v. Palm Beach Trust Co., 142 Fla. 782, 196 So. 299 (1940) (holding that the power vested in a trustee to create an estate in fee includes the power to create or appoint any estate less than a fee, unless the donor clearly indicates a contrary intent) (U.S.); Lewin ¶¶3-59, 3-67 (England). *See generally* Restatement (Second) of Property (Wills and Other Donative Transfers) §11.1; Restatement (Third) of Property (Wills and Other Donative Transfers) §19.14.

[487] Restatement (Third) of Property (Wills and Other Donative Transfers) §19.14, cmt. f.

in this way is referred to as decanting in some circles.[488] On the other hand, a decanting for the benefit of someone other than that beneficiary could implicate the fraud on a power doctrine, which is covered generally in Section 8.15.26 of this handbook. "While the tax treatment of F . . . [corporate] . . . reorganizations is well settled, with case law going back to the 1920s and statutes providing nonrecognition treatment, the tax treatment of decantings is surprisingly unsettled."[489]

In Massachusetts, the decanting authority of trustees is regulated by general principles of equity.[490] In New York, decanting distributions are regulated by statute.[491] It has been suggested that the legal premise underlying the statute is that a trustee with an absolute fiduciary power to invade principal is analogous to a donee of a nonfiduciary special/limited power of appointment who may exercise the power in further trust.[492] The analogy, however, would seem a false one as trustees are constrained by the fiduciary principle in the exercise of their powers; donees of nonfiduciary powers of appointment generally are not.[493] Thus, a power in a trustee to select his successor, by decanting or otherwise, is held in a fiduciary capacity. At minimum this translates into a fiduciary duty on the part of the trustee to exercise due diligence in the selection of an appropriate successor.

Decanting can be a way for *the trustee* of an irrevocable trust to modify its administrative provisions, accommodate a beneficiary-related change of circumstances, respond to changes in the tax laws, or correct errors or ambiguities in the governing trust instrument. The trustee, of course, would be subject to fiduciary constraints in the exercise of his discretionary decanting authority, and any such exercise would have to be done prudently. Thus, the failure of the trustee to give due advance consideration to the tax consequences, if any, of a discretionary trust-to-trust decanting would amount to a prima facie breach of his duty to administer the trust prudently.

A transfer of property to a trustee in breach of some fiduciary duty to the legal or equitable owner of the property is subject to rescission and restitution.[494] Thus, if an agent in breach of a fiduciary duty to the principal transfers the principal's property to a trustee, the trustee is "liable in restitution" to the

---

[488] Restatement (Third) of Property (Wills and Other Donative Transfers) §19.14, Reporter's Note.

[489] Jason Kleinman, *Trust Decanting: A Sale Without Gain Realization*, 49 Prop., Trust & Estate L. J. 453, 458 (2015).

[490] *See generally* Morse v. Kraft, 466 Mass. 92, 992 N.E.2d 1021 (2013).

[491] N.Y. Est. Powers & Trusts Law §10-6.6. Alaska, Arizona, Delaware, Florida, Illinois, Indiana, Kentucky, Missouri, Nevada, New Hampshire, North Carolina, Ohio, South Dakota, Tennessee, and Virginia also have decanting statutes.

[492] Matter of Estate of Mayer, 176 Misc. 2d 562, 672 N.Y.S.2d 998 (1998); Phipps v. Palm Beach Trust Co., 142 Fla. 782, 196 So. 299 (1940). *See generally* §8.1.2 of this handbook (exercising of powers of appointment in further trust).

[493] *See generally* §8.1.1 of this handbook (powers of appointment).

[494] *See* Restatement (Third) of Restitution and Unjust Enrichment §17 (lack of authority).

principal.[495] So also if a trustee in breach of trust decants to another trust with a different trustee and different beneficiaries, absent special facts. The trustee of the other trust and, indirectly, the beneficiaries of the other trust are "liable in restitution" to the beneficiaries of the inception trust "as necessary to avoid unjust enrichment."[496]

Ultimately, whether or not there is decanting authority in the trustee should simply hinge on the intent of the settlor of the trust as divined from its terms, as well as on the motives of the trustee. If, for example, decanting would thwart the wishes of the settlor, then such a distribution in further trust ought to be judicially voidable.[497] So also if decanting is merely an attempt on the part of the inception trustee to end-run the ancient proscription against delegating to agents the entire administration of the trust or to avoid having to monitor the activities of agents to whom fiduciary discretions have been properly delegated.[498] When it comes to the motives of a trustee, equity looks to substance rather than to form.[499] One cannot forget that the trust, first and foremost, is a principles-based creature of equity.[500] Thus, whether decanting is permissible should be determined on a case-by-case basis taking into account the terms of the particular trust and the motives of the particular trustee.[501] To promulgate some hard and fast rule either way by statute only serves to further stultify and barnicalize the law of trusts:

> The growing universe of state decanting rules has resulted in an increasingly complicated patchwork of state laws on the subject. In addition, many of the states that have passed decanting legislation have specifically sought to retain preexisting common law principles. Furthermore, state decanting statutes remain subject to varying judicial interpretation. One significant area of variation among states exists with regard to the distribution standards necessary to decant a trust.[502]

In any case, it is at least a settled and universal principle that decanting may not serve as a vehicle for subverting settlor intent, or at least that was the case. The material purpose doctrine (aka the Claflin Doctrine), which is covered

---

[495] *See* Restatement (Third) of Restitution and Unjust Enrichment §17 (lack of authority). *See generally* §3.4.1 of this handbook (whether an agent acting under a durable power of attorney can effectively transfer the principal's property in trust).

[496] *See* Restatement (Third) of Restitution and Unjust Enrichment §17 (lack of authority).

[497] *See, e.g.*, Ferri v. Powell-Ferri, 2013 WL 5289955 (Conn. Super. Ct. Aug. 23, 2013), 56 Conn. L. Rptr. 828 (2013) ("The decanting frustrates . . . [the settlor's intentions] . . . and, therefore, cannot stand.").

[498] *See generally* §6.1.4 of this handbook (delegation).

[499] *See generally* §8.12 of this handbook (equity's maxims).

[500] *See generally* Chapter 1 of this handbook (equity in the Anglo-American legal tradition).

[501] *See* Phipps v. Palm Beach Trust Co., 142 Fla. 782, 785, 196 So. 299, 301 (1940) (whether decanting is permissible turns on the facts of the particular case and the terms of the instrument creating the trust); Morse v. Kraft, 466 Mass. 92, 98, 992 N.E.2d 1021, 1026 (2013) ("We conclude that the terms of the 1982 Trust authorize the plaintiff to transfer property in the subtrusts to new subtrusts without the consent of the beneficiaries or a court.").

[502] Ivan Taback & David Pratt, *When the Rubber Meets the Road: A Discussion Regarding a Trustee's Exercise of Discretion*, 49 Real Prop., Trust & Estate L. 491, 515 (2015).

generally in Section 8.15.7 of this handbook and which has been the traditional doctrinal protector of settlor-intent, may have been neutralized in Washington State by an obscure piece of legislation known as the Trust and Estate Dispute Resolution Act (TEDRA).[503] Were it not for decanting one might be inclined to dismiss TEDRA as a doctrinal anomaly of minimal national relevance. We begin our explanation of what TEDRA does and why decanting makes TEDRA a matter of national relevance by recalling the current state of the material purpose doctrine. In recent years, reformers of trust law have been hard at work defanging the plain meaning rule, primarily by liberalizing the doctrines of reformation and deviation. The rule is discussed generally in Section 8.15.6 of this handbook, the doctrines generally in Section 8.15.22. That having been said, the reformers have generally been quick to caution that these liberalizations are intended to buttress settlor-intent, not subvert it. At minimum, lip service is being paid to settlor-intent. There is one notable exception: Professor Langbein's "intent-defeating" (his words) benefit-the-beneficiaries rule, which has been incorporated into the Uniform Trust Code. This is a topic that is taken up in Section 6.1.2 of this handbook. This radical intent-defeating policy reform embedded in the UTC has met with considerable push-back. Both the Massachusetts and the New Hampshire legislatures, for example, have said "no thanks." Even some denizens of the ivory tower have declined to fall in line.[504]

Now, while all this has been going on, in Washington State the material purpose doctrine may well have been effectively defanged by TEDRA.[505] The legislation in part provides that a trust may be reformed nonjudicially by agreement of the trustee and beneficiaries without regard to the trust's material purposes, at least that is what its drafters intended. The agreement is final and binding on all parties. Idaho is, so far at least, the only other TEDRA state. These developments, isolated though they may be, have national implications. Here is why: There have already been decantings from other states into trusts sited in Washington State to facilitate subversion of their material purposes. Assuming this practice takes on a head of steam, which is likely, the trust instrument scrivener should consider advising his or her settlor-client that the material purpose doctrine may well be TEDRA-vulnerable, unless effective countermeasures can be taken at the drafting stage to defang TEDRA, or forestall a decanting to a TEDRA state. In theory, a decanting from a non-TEDRA state to a TEDRA state in order to subvert a trust's material purposes would be subject to equitable reversal by the courts of the non-TEDRA state. As a practical matter, however, the pursuit by a beneficiary (presumably someone who had not been a party to the TEDRA agreement) of such an equitable multi-jurisdictional action would not be a realistic option, absent special facts, if only because of the numerous and substantial personal expenditures of time and treasure that likely would be required to maintain the action.

---

[503] Chap. 11.96A.220 RCW.

[504] *See generally* §6.1.2 of this handbook.

[505] Chap. 11.96A.220 RCW.

When there is a class of permissible beneficiaries some may have priority over others.
If there are competing requests, or needs, for discretionary distributions, it is up
to the trustee, not counsel to the trust,[506] not the courts, to determine the
proper allocation. In making discretionary payments among a group of beneficiaries, the trustee has reasonable latitude in favoring one beneficiary over the
other, or one generation of beneficiary over the other. In the absence of abuse,
the trustee's decisions are final.[507] The Restatement (Third) of Trusts has
identified "a few appropriate inferences and constructional preferences" as a
"starting point" when there is no clear guidance in the governing instrument:

- "Relationship to the settlor is relevant, leading in the most common
  situations to an inference that the beneficiary at the top of a line of
  descendants is favored over his or her own issue, with the settlor's
  spouse also so favored whether or not an ancestor of the others (*e.g.*,
  settlor's issue by prior marriage)";[508]
- "Among multiple lines of descent (*e.g.*, all of the settlor's issue) there is
  an inference of priorities *per stirpes*, that is, that (i) the various lines are
  entitled to similar, impartial (. . . but not necessarily equal) treatment,
  with disparities to be justified on a principled basis consistent with trust
  purposes, and that (ii) the inference of favored status with a descending
  line begins with the person(s) at the top (*e.g.*, the settlor's child or the
  children of a deceased child)";[509]
- "The preceding inference applies to the typical family trust for the
  support and education of minor or youthful beneficiaries following the
  death of one or both of their parents, with a preference for a common
  standard of living and similarity of opportunity to be balanced against
  usually modest funding and almost inevitably different beneficiary
  needs, capacities, and interests";[510] and
- "Because these various situations do not involve 'substantially separate
  and independent shares' for different lines of beneficiaries . . . , it is
  presumed that differences in benefits received by remainder beneficiaries or their ancestors during the trust period are not later to be taken
  into account in determining shares upon subsequent distribution, or in
  dividing the original trust for continuation thereafter in separate shares
  or trusts for separate lines of issue."[511]

The generation-skipping tax. Under no circumstances, however, should the
trustee make any discretionary distribution without a full understanding of the
generation-skipping tax consequences. In New York, by statute, a trustee with

---

[506] *Cf.* §8.32 of this handbook (whether the trustee can escape liability for making a mistake
of law if he acted in good faith on advice of counsel).

[507] *See* 2A Scott on Trusts §183.

[508] Restatement (Third) of Trusts §50 cmt. f.

[509] Restatement (Third) of Trusts §50 cmt. f.

[510] Restatement (Third) of Trusts §50 cmt. f.

[511] Restatement (Third) of Trusts §50 cmt. f.

"absolute" discretion to invade principal may use the invasion power to create a new trust for one or more of the permissible beneficiaries.[512] A purpose of the statute is to facilitate family-wide generation-skipping tax planning.[513]

Monies paid under a mistake of law. When a trustee transfers in breach of trust moneys to a good-faith purchaser for value (BFP), the moneys are not recoverable.[514] At common law, moneys paid under a mistake of law to an innocent non-BFP also were not recoverable.[515] Thus, when the insolvent trustee of an express trust pursuant to a mistake of law exercised his dispositive discretion in favor of an innocent non-BFP, the beneficiary was out of luck.[516] The injured beneficiary had no recourse against the transferee, although it is not entirely clear why the innocent transferee would not have held the property upon a resulting trust for the benefit of the rightful beneficiary, or, if not innocent, upon a constructive trust.[517] In any case, "[i]n one of the most significant changes of direction in private law in the twentieth century the . . . .[general] . . . rule was overturned in the House of Lords . . . by way of a lengthy deconstruction of the precedents and academic literature by Lord Goff of Chieveley."[518] In the trust context the rule is being nibbled away by particular exceptions.[519]

Note: For an exhaustive discussion of the current state of the case law on the subject of discretionary powers of trustees, the reader is referred to the Reporter's Notes on Section 50 of the Restatement (Third) of Trusts.

Principal invasion authority generally. As noted, the trustee generally has no authority to invade principal for the benefit of the current beneficiary, unless the terms of the trust so provide.[520] The current beneficiary is entitled to net trust accounting income only.[521] On the other hand, if the current beneficiary is entitled to an *annuity*, that is "a stated sum paid periodically," and the terms of the trust are silent as to the source of the payments, it seems the better view is that they are payable out of the funds of the trust without regard to distinction between income and principal,[522] although there are decisions out there to the contrary.[523]

---

[512] *See* Estate of Mayer, 176 Misc. 2d 562, 672 N.Y.S.2d 998 (Surr. Ct. 1998). *See also* §8.15.15 of this handbook (the ascertainable standard) (suggesting that it cannot be said that a trustee's discretion is ever unlimited).

[513] *See* Estate of Mayer, 176 Misc. 2d 562, 672 N.Y.S.2d 998 (Surr. Ct. 1998).

[514] *See generally* §8.15.63 of this handbook (doctrine of bona fide purchase; the BFP).

[515] *See generally* W.A. Lee, *Purifying the dialect of equity*, 7(2) Tr. Q. Rev.16–23 (May 2009) [A STEP publication].

[516] *See, e.g.*, Re Diplock [1948] Ch. 465 (England).

[517] *See generally* §3.3 of this handbook (the constructive trust) and §4.1.1.1 of this handbook (the resulting trust).

[518] W.A. Lee, *Purifying the dialect of equity*, 7(2) Tr. Q. Rev. .19 (May 2009) [A STEP publication] (referring to Kleinwort Benson v. Lincoln CC [1999] 2 AC 349 (England)).

[519] *See, e.g.*, Re Hastings-Bass [1975] Ch. 25; [1974] 2 WLR 904 (England).

[520] *See generally* 4 Scott & Ascher §20.1 (Impartiality Between Successive Beneficiaries).

[521] 4 Scott & Ascher §20.1.

[522] 3 Scott & Ascher §13.2.8.

[523] 3 Scott & Ascher §13.2.8, n.7.

At least when it comes to the default law, it seems all the more reasonable that a trustee ought to have inherent discretion to make *unitrust* distributions to the current beneficiary in whole or in part from the principal account.[524] Recall that a unitrust amount is "an amount equal to a fixed percentage of the value of the trust assets, redetermined annually."[525]

(b) The power to lease beyond the term of the trust.

Under certain circumstances, it may be in the economic interest of the trust for the trustee to enter into a lease that extends beyond the term of the trust.[526] If oil, gas, or valuable minerals are discovered under the surface of entrusted land, for example, the duty to preserve the trust property and make it productive may require that the trustee enter into a long-term extraction lease.[527] It is good practice, therefore, to provide express language in the governing instrument authorizing such leases.[528] Otherwise, there is the slight risk that the trustee would be held liable for failing to turn over to the remainderman possession of and the entire legal interest in the trust property.[529]

Because the remaindermen are entitled to the entire remainder interest upon termination, as well as full possession,[530] it was generally the case that a lease could not extend beyond the period of the trust,[531] unless the terms of the trust provided otherwise.[532] A lease that extended beyond the reasonably anticipated duration of the trust would not be binding on the remaindermen, but such a lease would be valid for the duration of the trust.[533] Thus, the trustee was cautioned to limit his lease to a reasonable or customary term. What *was* a "reasonable and customary duration" depended upon facts peculiar to each case. Thus, long-term leases had been approved when necessary to preserve the trust property,[534] even when forbidden by the terms of the trust.[535]

---

[524] 3 Scott & Ascher §13.2.8.

[525] 3 Scott & Ascher §13.2.8. *See also* §9.13 of this handbook (the unitrust).

[526] *See generally* 3 Scott on Trusts §189.2; L. S. Tellier, Annot., *Power of trustee and Court as regards term of lease of trust property*, 67 A.L.R.2d 978 (1959).

[527] *See generally* 3 Scott & Ascher §18.1.3.5. In the case of the discovery of oil, the trustee's duty to preserve could well be implicated were he to fail to enter into a long-term oil extraction lease, in that it is geologically possible for the entrusted oil to be physically drawn away from the entrusted parcel should the abutting landowners undertake their own drilling operations.

[528] *See generally* Bogert §790; 3 Scott & Ascher §18.1.3.3 (The Terms of the Trust).

[529] If the remainderman receives property that is subject to a lease, some sticks in the bundle of rights we call ownership would be lodged in a nonbeneficiary, namely, the lessee, such as the right, at least temporarily, to possess. *See generally* 4 Scott & Ascher §20.1 (Impartiality Between Successive Beneficiaries).

[530] *See generally* 3 Scott & Ascher §18.1.3.2.

[531] Restatement (Second) of Trusts §189 cmt. c; 3 Scott & Ascher §18.1.3.2.

[532] *See generally* 3 Scott & Ascher §18.1.3.3.

[533] Restatement (Second) of Trusts §189 cmt. c; 3 Scott & Ascher §18.1.3.2.

[534] *See generally* 3 Scott & Ascher §18.1.3.2; 3 Scott on Trusts §189.2.

[535] *See generally* 3 Scott & Ascher §18.1.3.3.

(c)   **The power to borrow on behalf of the trust or to pledge or mortgage the trust property.**

Whether the trustee has the power to borrow money on behalf of the trust and whether he or she has the right to pledge or mortgage the trust property as security for the loan are separate questions.[536] The trustee, for example, may well have a power to borrow money on the general credit of the trust for a particular trust purpose[537] but have no authority to pledge or mortgage the trust property.[538]

Because the trustee has a common law duty to exercise direct continuing control over the trust property, the trustee was considered to have had no inherent power to borrow on behalf of the trust absent express statutory authority or express authority in the terms of the trust.[539] It followed from this that the trustee had no implied general power to pledge or mortgage the trust property.[540] Nor would a general power of sale suffice.[541] The trustee also was considered not to have an inherent power to purchase property for the trust that was or would be subject to a mortgage.[542] However, under limited circumstances (*e.g.*, an emergency threatening the economic well-being of the trust), the powers to borrow and to encumber the trust property would be implied.[543]

The Restatement (Third) of Trusts, however, would reverse any default presumption that the trustee lacks the inherent power to grant a security interest in the trust property: "Unless prohibited by statute or the terms of the trust, a trustee has power to borrow for trust purposes and to pledge, mortgage, grant a deed of trust, or otherwise encumber the trust property."[544] Normally, however, a trustee will want to avoid encumbering any trust asset that has been specifically reserved by the terms of the trust for segregation and distribution.[545]

---

[536] *See* 2A Scott on Trusts §191.3.

[537] *See generally* 3 Scott & Ascher §18.1.5.2 (Power to Borrow Without Security).

[538] *See* 3 Scott & Ascher §18.1.5; 2A Scott on Trusts §191.3.

[539] *See* Restatement (Second) of Trusts §175. For a list of statutes enlarging the power of trustees to mortgage or pledge trust property, *see* 3 Scott & Ascher §18.1.5 n.4; 2A Scott on Trusts §191 n.17.

[540] *See generally* Bogert §752 (Express Grant of Power to Mortgage). *See, e.g.*, Tuttle v. First Nat'l Bank of Greenfield, 187 Mass. 533, 73 N.E. 560 (1905) (holding that because the trustee lacked authority to pledge trust assets, a third-party creditor who had made a loan to the trustee that was ostensibly secured by a pledge of part of the trust principal may not apply the trust property in its possession in payment of the debt even though the borrowed funds had been used for proper trust purposes, but instead must seek satisfaction by going against the trustee personally).

[541] *See generally* 3 Scott & Ascher §18.1.5.

[542] *See generally* 3 Scott & Ascher §18.1.5.1.

[543] Bogert §167; 3 Scott & Ascher §18.1.5.

[544] Restatement (Third) of Trusts §86 cmt. d.

[545] Restatement (Third) of Trusts §86 cmt. d; 3 Scott & Ascher §18.1.5. *See generally* §8.15.54 of this handbook (ademption by extinction in the trust context). *Cf.* UPC §2-606(b) (providing that if specifically devised property is mortgaged by a conservator or agent acting under a durable power of attorney for someone who is incapacitated, the specific devisee has a right to a general

Some courts have construed certain expressed powers of management as including the power to borrow.[546] What about the power to borrow for investment purposes? Is that implied in the direction "to invest and reinvest"? It was not thought so, as such a power was considered tantamount to a power to speculate.[547] Moreover, the mere power of sale was not thought to have carried with it a power to pledge or mortgage.[548] The Restatement (Third) of Trusts, however, is much more accommodating when it comes to leveraging for trust purposes:

> As increasingly recognized in legislation and drafting practices, and enabled by the comprehensive empowerment of trusts in §85, prudent borrowing may have advantages over liquidation of assets to raise funds for trust needs. This may be especially true in the case of relatively short-term requirements in situations involving martial-deduction trusts and revocable (or other estate-tax "grantor") trusts—postponing sale, for example, of a residence or appreciated assets. The power of trustees to borrow, however, with the exercise of fiduciary care and skill, may be of value in trust administration generally as a means of responding to shifting concerns or opportunities as a particular trust's circumstances change and as more general economic conditions, financial concepts or practices, and rules of taxation evolve over time.[549]

As to the related issue of whether a trustee may invest trust assets in leveraged derivatives, the reader is referred to Section 6.2.2.1 of this handbook. It should be noted that the recently revised *investment* sections of the Restatement of Trusts now grant the trustee an implied power to borrow, pledge, or otherwise encumber trust property for trust purposes, unless prohibited from so doing by statute or the terms of the trust.[550]

If a trustee may borrow on behalf of the trust, may the trustee lend his own funds to the trust? This question usually arises in the context of a corporate fiduciary that has general banking powers. While there is no absolute prohibition against the trustee's lending funds to the trust, if at all possible the practice should be avoided. Any loans that *are* made must be at competitive rates and terms. The issue of conflict of interest is always present whenever the trustee enters into transactions involving the trust estate for the trustee's own account.

---

pecuniary devise equal to the amount of the unpaid loan). *See generally* §8.15.55 of this handbook (antilapse in the trust context) and §8.15.56 of this handbook (the 120-hour survival requirement in the trust context). *See generally* Restatement (Third) of Property (Wills and Other Donative Transfers) §1.1 cmt f (abatement); UPC §3-902 (abatement).

[546] *See generally* 3 Scott on Trusts §191.3.

[547] *See* 3 Scott on Trusts §227.6.

[548] *See generally* 2A Scott on Trusts §191.

[549] Restatement (Third) of Trusts §86 cmt. d.

[550] *See* Restatement (Third) of Trusts §191 (Prudent Investor Rule) (provisional) (available at <http://www.uniformlaws.org/Act.aspx?title=Trust%20Code> as Article 9 of the UTC).

(d) Powers to invest in mutual funds and common trust funds; to administer common funds; and to combine trusts.

The commingled fund. In a jurisdiction where the investment of trust property in a mutual fund is considered a breach of the common law duty not to delegate investment discretion, the trustee will need express authority in the governing instrument.[551] To invest in a common trust fund, the trustee will need statutory authority or express authority in the trust instrument;[552] otherwise, the trustee runs afoul of the common law duty not to commingle the assets of the trust with the assets of other trusts.[553]

The common fund. Nowadays many trusts are designed to fracture into separate trust shares or sub-trusts upon the happening of a contingency, *e.g.*, when there is no child of the settlor that meets the two qualifications of being alive *and* under a specified age.[554] If the successor trusts are to be funded in kind, values are generally to be determined as of the time of allocation.[555] For a discussion of the myriad issues that can arise if the trustee unduly delays in dividing the trust, or fails to do so altogether, the reader is referred to Section 8.2.3 of this handbook.[556] In the case of a revocable inter vivos trust that divides into sub-trusts upon the settlor's death, the trustee may want to run it as an "administrative trust" once the settlor dies until such time as all the sub-trusts are actually funded. The administrative trust is discussed in Section 9.9.14 of this handbook.

It may be in the economic interest of all concerned, however, to keep the assets of the separate trusts together in a common fund. "Administrative economies promoted by combining trusts include a potential reduction in trustees' fees, particularly if the trustee charges a minimum fee per trust, the ability to file one trust income tax return instead of multiple returns, and the ability to invest a larger pool of capital more effectively."[557] Because of the

---

[551] *See* §6.1.4 of this handbook (trustee's duty not to delegate critical functions) and §6.1.3.4 of this handbook (indirect benefit accruing to the trustee) (many states by statute allow a trustee to invest in mutual funds). *See also* Fein, Securities Activities of Banks §11.05[B][c][E]. *See generally* Langbein & Posner, *Market Funds and Trust-Investment Law*, 1976 Am. B. Found. J. 1, 22 (1976); Shattuck, *The Legal Propriety of Investment by American Fiduciaries in the Shares of Boston-Type Open-End Investment Trusts*, 25 B.U. L. Rev. 1 (1945).

[552] *See* Restatement (Third) of Trusts §90 cmt. m [Restatement (Third) of Trusts §227 cmt. m]. *See generally* Bogert §677.

[553] *See* §6.2.1 of this handbook (trustee's duty to take active control of, segregate, earmark, and protect the trust property).

[554] *See generally* 5 Scott & Ascher §36.4.6 (When Property Is to Be Distributed to Several Trusts).

[555] *See generally* 5 Scott & Ascher §36.4.6 (When Property Is to be Distributed to Several Trusts); §8.2.3 of this handbook (trust termination and distribution issues).

[556] *See also* Restatement (Third) of Trusts §89, Reporter's Notes, cmt. g; John A. Hartog & George R. Dirkes, Assisting the Nonprofessional Trustee in Implementing the Administrative Trust (visited Sept. 2015) < http://www.hartogbaer.com/forms/USCArticle.pdf> (discussing the so-called stale trust). *See also* §9.9.14 of this handbook (the administrative trust).

[557] UTC §417 cmt. (available at <http://www.uniformlaws.org/Act.aspx?title=Trust%20Code>).

common law prohibition against commingling, the trustee may need express authority in the governing instrument to do so.[558] In any event, investing the property of several trusts as a single fund should not "require frustration of the settlor's intention to create separate trusts."[559]

Combining trusts. The Uniform Trust Code would authorize a trustee to combine two or more trusts into a single trust if the result would not impair the rights of any beneficiary or adversely affect achievement of the purposes of either trust, provided advance notice is given to the qualified beneficiaries.[560] Their consent, however, is not required.[561] Ohio has such a statute.[562] It has been suggested that a trustee may have a duty to combine trusts with identical terms if administrative economies can be achieved by so doing.[563] Combination may also be a solution to the small, *i.e.*, uneconomic, trust problem.[564] The trustee, however, must maintain records clearly indicating the respective interests.[565]

Thus, the trustee who lacks a sophisticated operational infrastructure should think twice before aggregating assets for investment purposes if the trustee has been given authority under one or more of the separate trusts to invade principal. This is because each time a distribution of principal is made out of the common fund to the beneficiary of one trust and not to the beneficiary of another, and each time the trustee makes unequal distributions out of the common fund to beneficiaries of different trusts, it becomes that much more difficult for the trustee to keep track of a separate trust's allocable share of principal and the income it generates. As a trustee's liability for misdelivery is virtually absolute, the benefits of aggregation need to be weighed against its risks, particularly the risk of improperly accounting for income and principal. A warning: The trustee's administration of the common fund is likely to be subject to particular scrutiny at the time the first separate trust terminates.

---

[558] *See generally* 2A Scott on Trusts §179.2. *But see* UTC §417 (available at <http://www.uniformlaws.org/Act.aspx?title=Trust%20Code>) (authorizing the trustee to combine trusts provided the combining "does not impair rights of any beneficiary or adversely affect achievement of the purposes of the trust").

[559] 2 Scott & Ascher §10.4.

[560] UTC §417 (available at <http://www.uniformlaws.org/Act.aspx?title=Trust%20Code>).

[561] UTC §417 cmt. (available at <http://www.uniformlaws.org/Act.aspx?title=Trust%20Code>).

[562] Ohio Rev. Code §13339.67.

[563] UTC §417 cmt. (available at <http://www.uniformlaws.org/Act.aspx?title=Trust%20Code>).

[564] UTC §417 cmt. (available at <http://www.uniformlaws.org/Act.aspx?title=Trust%20Code>). *See generally* §3.5.3.2(k) of this handbook (the trustee's power to terminate the trust).

[565] UTC §810(d) (available at <http://www.uniformlaws.org/Act.aspx?title=Trust%20Code>).

(e) **The power to hold the trust property in the name of a third party or in the trustee's own name without disclosing the fiduciary relationship.**

The trustee has a common law duty to earmark the trust property as the property of the trust.[566] On the other hand, the trustee may, for legitimate reasons, prefer not to disclose the fiduciary relationship. The process of security transfer, for example, is less complicated when securities are registered in the name of someone other than the trustee (there being no need to prove authority to brokers and transfer agents).[567] Any power in the trustee not to disclose the fiduciary relationship must be set forth expressly in the governing instrument or in a statute.[568]

When trust securities are registered in the name of a third party, the level of risk will vary depending on the type of intermediary. If, for example, trust securities are registered in the name of a partnership established under the auspices of a bank trust department (a nominee),[569] the securities are segregated from the general assets of the bank. In the event of the bank's insolvency, property subject to trust would promptly be transferred to another institution with little or no interruption in asset administration.[570]

When trust securities are registered in the name of a brokerage house (*street name*),[571] however, segregation will be less than absolute. The securities are not evidenced by identifiable certificates. Instead, they are held in a fungible bulk that is made up of the securities of all the broker-dealer's customers.[572] In the event of the broker-dealer's insolvency, special rules under the Bankruptcy Code and the Securities Investor Protection Act (SIPA) come into play.[573] These

---

[566] *See* 2A Scott on Trusts §179.3. *See* §6.2.1.2 of this handbook (the trustee's duty to segregate and earmark the trust property, that is to say the duty not to commingle); UTC §810(b) & (c) (available at <http://www.uniformlaws.org/Act.aspx?title=Trust%20Code>).

[567] *See generally* 3 Scott & Ascher §17.11.4.

[568] *See generally* Bogert §596; 3 Scott & Ascher §17.11.4.

[569] Bogert §596. *See generally* §6.2.1.2 of this handbook (the trustee's duty to segregate and earmark the trust property, that is to say the duty not to commingle); UTC §810 cmt. (available at <http://www.uniformlaws.org/Act.aspx?title=Trust%20Code>); 3 Scott & Ascher §17.11.4.

[570] *See* Mooney, *Beyond Negotiability: A New Model for Transfer and Pledge of Interests in Securities Controlled by Intermediaries*, 12 Cardozo L. Rev. 305, 361 n.200 (1990).

[571] "Street name" generally refers to a security intermediary's practice of holding a fungible bulk of securities in its own name or in that of its nominees, even though the securities may be beneficially owned by its customers. Mooney, *Beyond Negotiability: A New Model for Transfer and Pledge of Interests in Securities Controlled by Intermediaries*, 12 Cardozo L. Rev. 305, n.4 (1990). *See generally* 5 Scott on Trusts §521.6 n.9 and accompanying text; In re Bevill, Bresler & Schulman, Inc., 59 B.R. 353, 374 (1986); §6.2.1.2 of this handbook (the trustee's duty to segregate and earmark the trust property, that is to say the duty not to commingle).

[572] Mooney, *Beyond Negotiability: A New Model for Transfer and Pledge of Interests in Securities Controlled by Intermediaries*, 12 Cardozo L. Rev. 305, 331–342 (1990).

[573] Mooney, *Beyond Negotiability: A New Model for Transfer and Pledge of Interests in Securities Controlled by Intermediaries*, 12 Cardozo L. Rev. 305, 351–361 (1990). *See also* Don & Wang, *Stockbroker Liquidations under the Securities Investor Protection Act and Their Impact on Securities Transfers*, 12 Cardozo L. Rev. 509, 540–547 (1990); David A. Kessler, Note and Comment, *Investor Casualties in the War for Market Efficiency*, 9 Admin. L.J. Am. U. 1307 (1996).

rules could prevent the trustee from exercising immediate control over the trust property. They could also result in the trust taking a pro rata share of the fungible bulk, a share that could be less than what would be owed to it. Should there be a shortfall, recourse could then be had against the assets of the Securities Investor Protection Corporation (SIPIC). The settlor and the trustee will want to give careful consideration to whether SIPIC insurance adequately mitigates the risks of holding securities in street name with a broker-dealer.

The Uniform Trust Code provides that a trustee shall cause the trust property to be designated so that the interest of the trust, to the extent feasible, appears in records maintained by a party other than a trustee or beneficiary.[574] "While securities held in nominee form are not specifically registered in the name of the trustee, they are properly earmarked because the trustee's holdings are indicated in the records maintained by an independent party, such as in an account in a brokerage firm."[575]

> **(f) The power to compromise, arbitrate, and abandon claims, to include the power to disclaim or abandon property generally; the power to make gifts of trust property.**

A trustee has the duty to collect that which is owed the trust.[576] Take, for example, the trustee who holds legal title to contractual rights against a third party, such as rights against the corporate issuer of a bond or rights against an insurance company incident to an insurance policy. The third party, instead of making a payment to the trustee, who is the other party to the contract, takes it upon itself to makes a payment directly to a trust beneficiary who is not of full age and legal capacity. The trustee may have a fiduciary duty to seek to compel the third party to make the payment a second time, this time to the trustee.[577]

On the other hand, there is a duty not to squander trust assets in litigating claims that should be dealt with in some other way.[578] Thus, the trustee has the inherent common law power to compromise, arbitrate, and abandon claims to

---

[574] UTC §810(c) (available at <http://www.uniformlaws.org/Act.aspx?title=Trust%20Code>).

[575] UTC §810 cmt. (available at <http://www.uniformlaws.org/Act.aspx?title=Trust%20Code>).

[576] See 3 Scott & Ascher §18.1.6; Restatement (Second) of Trusts §177.

[577] The third-party obligor who makes a payment directly to the trust beneficiary instead of to the title-holding trustee, the other party to the contract, does so at his, her, or its peril, unless directed to do so by the trustee. 5 Scott & Ascher §32.1 (Discharge by Beneficiary of Claim Against Third Person). If the beneficiary is not of full age and legal capacity, the third party obligor runs the risk of having to pay twice. 5 Scott & Ascher §32.1 (Discharge by Beneficiary of Claim Against Third Person). There is a similar risk if following the direction were to constitute a knowing participation with the trustee in a breach of trust or if the trust were a spendthrift trust. 5 Scott & Ascher §32.1 (Discharge by Beneficiary of Claim Against Third Person).

[578] Restatement (Second) of Trusts §177 cmt. c; 3 Scott & Ascher §18.1.6; 3 Scott on Trusts §192. See UTC §805 (available at <http://www.uniformlaws.org/Act.aspx?title=Trust%20Code>) ("In administering a trust, the trustee may incur only costs that are reasonable in relation to the trust property, the purposes of the trust, and the skills of the trustee.").

the extent it is in the economic interest of the trust to do so.[579] Because of the tension between the two duties, the cautious trustee will seek judicial approval before compromising, arbitrating, or abandoning substantial claims, unless there is clear statutory authority to do so or the matter is expressly addressed in the governing instrument.[580] In furtherance of the trust's purposes, and provided it is in the beneficiaries' interest to do so, a trustee may abandon trust property or disclaim property that would otherwise become trust property.[581] "But such action may not be taken merely for the convenience, or to avoid or lessen the responsibilities, of the trustee."[582] For the trustee's power to disclaim a fiduciary power, the reader is referred to Section 3.5.3.4 of this handbook.

One commentator has suggested that a trustee may make a "gift" of trust property, provided the trust estate is somehow advantaged by the transfer.[583] A trustee, for example, might "donate" trust funds to a hotel company in order to "secure" the location of a hotel near entrusted land.[584] Certainly, such a transfer to a noncharity is problematic, unless it were actually a transfer for consideration incident to an enforceable contract between the trustee and the hotel company. The donative transfer of one of three parcels of entrusted land to a conservation charitable trust in order to protect and enhance the value of the other two seems less problematic, in that the Attorney General, at least in theory, is charged with enforcing the charitable trust.[585] Moreover, there is a compelling equitable argument that the land transfer is actually a defensive expenditure, analogous to insuring at trust expense an entrusted residence against fire and flood damage.[586] In any case, "[o]rdinarily, it is improper for a trustee to make a gift of trust property."[587]

(g)   The power to resolve questions.

What is income and what is principal? Absent authority in the governing instrument,[588] the trustee has no inherent power to deviate from generally accepted practices of fiduciary accounting when determining what is income and what is principal for purposes of crediting receipts or charging

---

[579] *See* Restatement (Third) of Trusts §86 cmt. f; Restatement (Second) of Trusts §177; 3 Scott & Ascher §18.1.6. *See also* C. C. Marvel, Annot., *Trustee's power to compromise and settle claims and actions by or against trust estate*, 35 A.L.R.2d 967 (1954).

[580] *See generally* 3 Scott & Ascher §18.1.6.

[581] Restatement (Third) of Trusts §86 cmt. f; 3 Scott & Ascher §18.1.7.

[582] Restatement (Third) of Trusts §86 cmt. f.

[583] 3 Scott & Ascher §18.1.7.

[584] 3 Scott & Ascher §18.1.7.

[585] *See generally* 3 Scott & Ascher §18.1.7. *See also* §9.4.2 of this handbook (standing to enforce charitable trusts).

[586] *See generally* §6.2.1.3 of this handbook (the trustee's duty to protect the trust property).

[587] 3 Scott & Ascher §18.1.7.

[588] *See generally* 4 Scott & Ascher §20.2.3 (noting that when a trustee is granted a discretionary power to allocate receipts and expenditures between income and principal, "the trustee's allocation is generally controlling, in the absence of an abuse of discretion").

disbursements.[589] Nor would most settlors want to bestow on the trustee such a power, for to do so would permit the trustee to shift beneficial interests arbitrarily between the income beneficiary and the remaindermen.[590] On the other hand, when the law provides no clear guidance on how to characterize a particular item, the trustee ought to have the power to decide such questions without resort to the courts.[591] Thus, the settlor should give the trustee the power in doubtful cases to determine which receipts are income and which are principal, and which expenses should be paid out of the income account and which out of the principal account.[592]

In one case, the trust instrument provided that the trustees were authorized and empowered to "determine the allocation of receipts and disbursements between principal and income, provided such allocation is not inconsistent with the beneficial enjoyment of trust property accorded to a life tenant under the general principles of the law of trusts." The current beneficiary was entitled to all the net trust accounting income. The trustees, who had authority to invade principal for the beneficiary's health, maintenance, and support, granted the beneficiary's request for a distribution of income before it had actually been earned. To do so, the trustees used assets from the principal account but treated the distribution as an advancement against future income receipts, rather than as an invasion of principal. Presumably, the principal account was reimbursed out of the income that was subsequently earned and received. The current beneficiary then went after the future income receipts, arguing that the trustees had actually exercised their principal invasion authority and that he was entitled to all the net trust accounting income. The trustees took the position that they were empowered to allocate to income the principal advancements in furtherance of their fiduciary duty to protect the interests of the remainder beneficiaries. The court agreed.[593]

In England, "[a] provision in a trust instrument that refers . . . [allocation and apportionment questions] . . . to the trustees and purports to make their determination conclusive and binding on the beneficiaries is void as repugnant to the interests conferred by the instrument and as an attempt to oust the jurisdiction of the court."[594] That is not to say that the terms of the trust may not

---

[589] *See* Restatement (Second) of Trusts §233 cmt. p.

[590] *See generally* 4 Scott & Ascher §20.1 (Impartiality Between Successive Beneficiaries). In Old Colony Trust Co. v. Silliman, 352 Mass. 6, 223 N.E.2d 504 (1967), the court held that broad discretion in the trustee to decide whether accretions are to be treated as income or principal did not empower trustee to shift the beneficial interests. It noted that "[a] fair reading of the whole of most trust instruments will reveal a 'judicially enforceable, external, and ascertainable standard' for the exercise of even broadly expressed fiduciary powers." Old Colony Trust Co. v. Silliman, 352 Mass. 6, 9, 223 N.E.2d 504, 506 (1967).

[591] *See generally* 4 Scott & Ascher §20.2.3.

[592] *See* R. P. Davis, Annot., *Construction of specific provision of will or trust instrument giving executor or trustee power to determine what is income or what is principal*, 27 A.L.R.2d 1323 (1953). *See generally* 3 Scott & Ascher §18.2.

[593] *See* Frazier v. Brechler, 28 Fla. L. Weekly D378, 839 So. 2d 761 (2003). *See generally* §5.4.1.3 of this handbook (right to income and possession) (discussing loans of trust principal to the income beneficiary).

[594] Lewin ¶25-01(England).

bestow on the trustees discretion to distribute income to the principal (capital) beneficiaries and principal (capital) to the income beneficiaries.

Instrument interpretation. If the terms of a trust authorize the trustee generally or "in situations of doubt or controversy" to render interpretations of the provisions of the trust instrument that are final and binding on all parties, may the court nonetheless overrule the trustee's interpretive decisions? The short answer is yes.[595] The settlor of a trust cannot deprive a court of equity of its inherent authority to construe the provisions of the trust's governing documentation.[596]

(h) The power to exclude the remainderman from the accounting process.

The trustee has a duty to render accounts at reasonable intervals not only to the income beneficiaries but also to the remaindermen.[597] The process of accounting to remaindermen can be expensive and time-consuming, particularly when interests are contingent or diffused.[598] Moreover, when remaindermen are unborn or unascertainable during a given accounting period, the involvement of a guardian ad litem may be required.[599] A trustee therefore welcomes an express power to exclude the remaindermen from the accounting process.[600] A word of caution: In some jurisdictions, the assent of the income beneficiary cannot bind the remaindermen no matter what the governing instrument may say, particularly when the assent relates to a shifting of beneficial interests.[601]

The Uniform Trust Code takes a compromise approach. Under the Uniform Trust Code, the trustee of an irrevocable trust periodically must furnish accountings or "reports" to the "qualified beneficiaries" who would include presumptive remaindermen twenty-five years of age or older.[602] The trustee cannot be relieved of this obligation by express language in the govern

---

[595] Restatement (Third) of Trusts §71 cmt. f.

[596] Taylor v. McClave, 128 N.J. Eq. 109, 14 A.2d 213 (1940). *See generally* 3 Scott & Ascher §18.2.

[597] *See* §6.1.5 of this handbook (the trustee's duty to account to the beneficiary).

[598] *See generally* Westfall, *Nonjudicial Settlement of Trustees' Accounts*, 71 Harv. L. Rev. 40, 49 n.34 and accompanying text (1957).

[599] Westfall, *Nonjudicial Settlement of Trustees' Accounts*, 71 Harv. L. Rev, 40, 49 n.34 and accompanying text (1957). *See also* Restatement (Second) of Trusts §214 cmt. a.

[600] For sample language, *see* Bogert §1295 n.11.

[601] *See, e.g.,* In re Crane, 34 N.Y.S.2d 9 (1942). *See generally* Westfall, *Nonjudicial Settlement of Trustees' Accounts*, 71 Harv. L. Rev. 40, n.187 and accompanying text (1957). *See also Matter of Omar*, N.Y.L.J. at 29 (col. 3) (Feb. 5, 1996) (Surry. Ct.) (invalidating provision relieving trustee of duty to account to remaindermen). *See generally* 4 Scott & Ascher §20.1 (Impartiality Between Successive Beneficiaries).

[602] *See* UTC §102(12) (available at <http://www.uniformlaws.org/Act.aspx?title=Trust%20Code>) (defining the term *qualified beneficiary*); UTC §105(b)(8) (providing that the trustee may not be relieved in the governing instrument of his duty to notify the qualified beneficiaries of an irrevocable trust who have attained 25 years of age of their right under §813 to request periodic trustee accountings or "reports").

ing instrument. The trustee, however, need not account to persons yet to be conceived. The intent here is to obviate the need for the appointment of a guardian ad litem in connection with the settlement of the trustee's accounts while at the same time ensuring a measure of trustee accountability when it comes to the remainder interests.

(i)   Special investment powers.

The trustee has a duty to invest the trust property prudently, balancing the obligation to preserve the principal for the remaindermen against the obligation to produce a reasonable rate of return for the income beneficiary.[603] Over the years, courts and legislatures have set down guidelines for trustees to follow in the carrying out of this duty.[604] A trustee who keeps within them will be protected regardless of how the portfolio actually performs.[605]

Many instruments, however, provide the trustee with powers to deviate from established guidelines, such as a power to speculate or to hold wasting assets or assets that present a high degree of risk.[606] Such provisions are for the most part interpreted "strictly" by the courts.[607] As a practical matter, the more general the fiduciary's power to veer from established investment practice, the more likely the power is illusory.[608] Short of that, a court might conclude "that the language of extended discretion and other evidence before it manifests a settlor intention to authorize the particular trustee to act with a lesser degree of *caution* (*e.g.*, to accept a greater degree of compensated risk), but not a lesser degree of *care*, than would otherwise be appropriate to the particular trust and its circumstances under the duty of prudence."[609]

If a settlor, for example, wants the family business retained in trust even though such an investment may amount to a speculation under the common law, the trustee will want an express power of retention that makes reference to

---

[603] *See* §6.2.2.1 of this handbook (the *Harvard College* Prudent Man Rule and its progeny); 4 Scott & Ascher §20.1 (Impartiality Between Successive Beneficiaries).

[604] *See* §6.2.2.1 of this handbook (the *Harvard College* Prudent Man Rule and its progeny); 4 Scott & Ascher §20.1 (Impartiality Between Successive Beneficiaries).

[605] *See* §6.2.2.1 of this handbook (the *Harvard College* Prudent Man Rule and its progeny); 4 Scott & Ascher §20.1 (Impartiality Between Successive Beneficiaries).

[606] *See generally* 4 Scott & Ascher §19.1.12. *See, however,* John H. Langbein, *Mandatory Rules in the Law of Trusts*, 98 Nw. U. L. Rev. 1105 (2004) (advancing the view "that in the future, the benefit-the-beneficiaries requirement will be especially consequential in the realm of trust-investment practice, where it will restrain the settler from imposing value-impairing investment directions").

[607] 4 Scott & Ascher §19.1.12.

[608] "A trust provision that authorizes investments to be made 'in the trustee's discretion,' or that confers on the trustee 'all of the powers of an owner' is not ordinarily to be construed as granting the trustee wider latitude than conferred by the Prudent Investor Rule." Restatement (Third) of Trusts §228 cmt. g (Prudent Investor Rule).

[609] Restatement (Third) of Trusts §87 cmt. d.

the business itself[610] as well as appropriate express powers to enable the trustee to run the business efficiently and cost-effectively.[611] "Any intention to abrogate a trustee's common law or statutory duty to diversify also should be clearly indicated in the terms of the trust."[612] Trust provisions fixing a standard of prudence lower than that otherwise required of trustees, however, are "strictly construed."[613]

Absent express authority to hold the settlor's business in trust, the trustee is under a duty to liquidate the business.[614] Certainly, a general authority to speculate is insufficient, because the trustee is at risk that some court would dismiss such language as "boilerplate" and then rule that the trustee's reliance upon it was unreasonable.[615] Even in the face of express retention language, the trustee will want to monitor the health of the subject investment.[616] This is because the trustee at some point may have an overriding duty incident to his general duty of care to seek authority from the court to liquidate should the investment subsequently becomes improper or inappropriate due to changed circumstances.[617]

It should be noted that one court has actually declined to hold a corporate trustee liable for self-dealing, in part *because of* its good faith reliance on boilerplate.[618] The trustee had invested trust assets in a life insurance contract. The contract had been purchased through the trustee's insurance affiliate. The affiliate's sizeable commission, $512,000, had been paid from trust assets. The trust instrument contained a general boilerplate provision authorizing the trustee "to deal with any trust hereunder without regard to conflicts of interest."[619] Here is the court's facts and circumstances rationale for blessing the actions of the trustee: "That Wachovia's insurance affiliate earned a substantial commission does not amount to bad faith; the trust instrument permitted this

---

[610] Restatement (Third) of Trusts §92 cmt. e [Restatement (Third) of Trusts: Prudent Investor Rule §229 cmt. e]. *See* M. L. Cross, Annot., *Construction and effect of instrument authorizing or directing trustee or executor to retain investments received under such instrument*, 47 A.L.R.2d 187 (1956).

[611] *See generally* 4 Scott & Ascher §§19.3.3 (Terms of the Trust), 19.3.4 (Duty to Wind up Testator's Business).

[612] Wood v. U.S. Bank, N.A., 828 N.E.2d 1072, 1078 (Ohio Ct. App. 1st Dist. 2005).

[613] Restatement (Third) of Trusts §77 cmt. d. *See generally* 4 Scott & Ascher §19.1.2 (Terms of the Trust).

[614] Restatement (Third) of Trusts §229 cmt. e (Prudent Investor Rule); 4 Scott & Ascher §19.3.4 (Duty to Wind up Testator's Business). *See* M. L. Cross, Annot., *Construction and effect of instrument authorizing or directing trustee or executor to retain investments received under such instrument*, 47 A.L.R.2d 187 (1956).

[615] Restatement (Third) of Trusts §228 cmt. g. For a discussion of the trustee's obligations as they relate to investments in life insurance contracts, *see* U.S. Trust, 1994 Life Insurance Trusts and Related Matters, Practical Drafting 3588 (1994). *See also* §9.2 of this handbook (the irrevocable life insurance trust). *See generally* 4 Scott & Ascher §19.1.12 (Terms of the Trust).

[616] *See generally* 4 Scott & Ascher §§19.2, 19.3.3.

[617] Restatement (Second) of Trusts §231. *See generally* 4 Scott & Ascher §§19.1.12 (Terms of the Trust), 19.3.4 (noting that if a trustee is in reasonable doubt as to whether he should carry on a business may apply to the court for instructions).

[618] *See* French v. Wachovia Bank, N.A., 722 F.3d 1079 (7th Cir. 2013).

[619] French v. Wachovia Bank, N.A., 722 F.3d 1079, 1086 (7th Cir. 2013).

kind of self-dealing, and the insurance exchange was a 'win-win' for both the trust and the bank."[620] The intersection of trust law and good faith doctrine is covered generally in Section 8.15.81 of this handbook.

(j) The power to loan money to the trust and charge a reasonable rate of interest.

As the trustee has no inherent power under the common law to transact with the trust property for his own account, it would seem he has no inherent power to loan his own money to the trust at interest. The cases suggest otherwise, however.[621] All things being equal, however, it is preferable that the trustee refrain from such activity in the absence of statutory or regulatory authority or authority in the governing instrument.[622]

(k) The power to terminate the trust for practical reasons; small trusts.

The trustee has no inherent power to terminate the trust before its purposes have been fulfilled.[623] The settlor may wish to provide such a power in the terms of the trust should the trust become impractical or uneconomical to administer.[624] Absent an express power of termination, for example, the trustee might feel obliged to seek judicial approval before terminating a trust that had become too small to cost-effectively manage.[625] The Restatement (Third) of Trusts provides as follows: "If the trust estate is or becomes so small that the interest of the beneficiaries, or the trust purposes, would be better served by terminating the trust, the court may so order . . . ."[626]

Many jurisdictions now have statutes authorizing the nonjudicial termination of small trusts.[627] The Uniform Trust Code has a default rule

---

[620] French v. Wachovia Bank, N.A., 722 F.3d 1079, 1088 (7th Cir. 2013).

[621] *See generally* Bogert §543(L).

[622] *See generally* Bogert §543(L). *But see* First Nat'l Bank of Boston v. Slade, 379 Mass. 243, 399 N.E.2d 1047 (1979) ("A rule of law would be too harsh and impractical which failed to recognize that a commercial bank and a business client may wish to maintain a relationship which involves the bank, in its various aspects, in the operations of the business and in the estate planning of one or more owners of that business.").

[623] *See generally* 4 Scott on Trusts §337.

[624] UTC §414 (available at <http://www.uniformlaws.org/Act.aspx?title=Trust%20Code>) provides for termination when the value of the trust property falls below $50,000.

[625] 5 Scott & Ascher §33.3 (When Continuing Trust Administration Becomes Uneconomic). *See also Procedures for Terminating Small Trusts: Report of the Committee on Formation, Administration and Distribution of Trusts*, 19 Real Prop. Prob. & Tr. J. 988 (1984). *See generally* 4 Scott & Ascher §20.1 (Impartiality Between Successive Beneficiaries).

[626] Restatement (Third) of Trusts §66 cmt. d. *See generally* 5 Scott & Ascher §33.3; §8.2.2.1 of this handbook (grounds for the mid-course termination of a trust).

[627] 5 Scott & Ascher §33.3 n. 5. *See also Procedures for Terminating Small Trusts: Report of the Committee on Formation, Administration and Distribution of Trusts*, 19 Real Prop. Prob. & Tr. J. 988 (1984). *See, e.g.*, Cal. Prob. Code §15408 (providing that when trust principal does not exceed

that authorizes the trustee of a trust consisting of trust property having a total value less than a specified amount to terminate the trust if the trustee concludes that the value of the trust property is insufficient to justify the cost of administration.[628]

It is important to keep in mind that for an express termination authorization to have any utility, the provision should direct where and how the property is to go once the trustee's power of termination has been exercised.[629] It is critical that the provision be drafted so as not to inadvertently generate adverse tax consequences, or to unintentionally render the settlor ineligible for Medicaid benefits. In one case involving an income-only irrevocable trust *for the benefit of the settlor* the mere existence of the trustee's boilerplate discretionary authority to terminate the trust for practical reasons and distribute the principal outright and free of trust "to the beneficiaries" rendered the principal "countable" for purposes of determining *the settlor's* eligibility for MassHealth Medicaid benefits.[630]

The Uniform Prudent Management of Institutional Funds Act (UPMIFA) would permit the trustees of a charitable trust or the directors of a charitable corporation to expend free of restriction "without an expensive trip to the court"[631] a gift that is too small to administer cost-effectively on a segregated basis, provided more than twenty years has elapsed since the gift was made.[632] The property must still be used for charitable purposes that are consistent with the donor's intent and the state attorney general must still be notified of what is being contemplated.[633] Under the official version of the model act, a fund of $25,000 or more in value would not qualify as "small."[634]

$20,000 in value, the trustee may terminate the trust without court involvement even if the trust has a spendthrift provision). In California, where the trust instrument does not provide a manner of distribution upon a §15408 termination and where the settlor's intent is not adequately expressed in the trust instrument, the trustee may distribute the trust property to the living beneficiaries on an "actuarial basis." Cal. Prob. Code §15410(d). In Massachusetts, Gen. Laws ch. 203, §25 provides that a court may order consolidation or termination and distribution if costs of administering the trust are uneconomical.

[628] UTC §414(a) (available at <http://www.uniformlaws.org/Act.aspx?title=Trust%20Code>).

[629] If, for example, the property of the trust upon an early termination is to pass to someone's issue, it should be made clear whether the issue take per stirpes, per capita, or in some other manner. *See generally* §5.2 of this handbook (class designations). *See Procedures for Terminating Small Trusts: Report of the Committee on Formation, Administration and Distribution of Trusts*, 19 Real Prop. Prob. & Tr. J. 988 (1984). *Cf.* UTC §414(c) (available at <http://www.uniformlaws.org/Act.aspx?title=Trust%20Code>) (providing that upon termination of an uneconomic trust the trustee shall distribute the trust property in a matter consistent with the purposes of the trust).

[630] *See* Doherty v. Director of the Office of Medicaid, 908 N.E. 390, 74 Mass. App. Ct. 439 (2009) [2009 WL 1664708]. *See generally* §5.3.5 of this handbook (Medicaid eligibility).

[631] Unif. Prudent Management Inst. Funds Act, Prefatory Note.

[632] Unif. Prudent Management Inst. Funds Act §6(d).

[633] Unif. Prudent Management Inst. Funds Act §6(d).

[634] Unif. Prudent Management Inst. Funds Act §6(d).

(l) The power to administer distributions to minors and other legally incapacitated persons.

Delivery of trust property into the hands of a legally incapacitated beneficiary is misdelivery for which there is absolute liability.[635] Thus, the cautious trustee, faced with having to make such a distribution, may well insist that a court-appointed guardian be in place to receive the property. Because of the general cost and inconvenience of the guardianship process, the prospective trustee will want to see a provision empowering the trustee to retain and administer the otherwise distributable property for the benefit of the incapacitated person. Typical language includes the power to deal with the beneficiary's relatives and others who have not been formally appointed to oversee his or her welfare. The prospective trustee should insist that any such provision address where the property is to go should the incapacitated person die prior to final distribution.

While it is far preferable that distributions to minors and other legally incapacitated persons be addressed by express language in the governing instrument, statutes have now been enacted in some jurisdictions allowing a trustee to make payments to or for the benefit of an incapacitated beneficiary without the need for express authority to do so in the terms of the trust.[636] The Restatement (Third) of Trusts, by generally endorsing this approach, would modify the default law: "Absent either express authorization or a contrary provision, it is implied from a direction to distribute income (or other amounts) that the trustee has authority to apply the funds for the beneficiary's benefit so long as no objection is raised by or on behalf of the beneficiary."[637] The trustee has other options as well in the face of a beneficiary's inability for whatever reason to handle funds. If in good-faith doubt as to the beneficiary's "practical or legal capacity to handle funds," the trustee may segregate the funds in a separate account, "subject to the continuing right of withdrawal upon demand by or on behalf of the beneficiary."[638] The funds would be fully vested in the beneficiary.[639] In addition, when appropriate, there is the option of making distributions to a custodian under the applicable Uniform Transfers to Minors Act.

---

[635] So, also, when a legally enforceable claim against a third person is held in trust for a minor and the third person pays the amount of the claim directly to the minor rather than the trustee, the third person can be compelled to pay the claim twice, unless the third person had been directed to make the payment by the trustee. 5 Scott & Ascher §32.1. The third party would still have had to pay twice had the third person been on notice that the issuing of the direction itself was a breach of trust on the part of the trustee. 5 Scott & Ascher §32.1. To follow the direction under such circumstances would have constituted participation with the trustee in a breach of trust. 5 Scott & Ascher §32.1. If the minor still has the payment at the time he or she attains majority or if the minor has used the payment for necessaries, then the third person might not have to pay twice after all. 5 Scott & Ascher §32.1. A trustee who fails to compel the third person to pay twice when the third person is obliged by law to do so has constructively misdelivered the trust property.

[636] 2A Scott on Trusts §182.1 n.1 and accompanying text.

[637] Restatement (Third) of Trusts §49 cmt. c(2).

[638] Restatement (Third) of Trusts §49 cmt. c(2).

[639] Restatement (Third) of Trusts §49 cmt. c(2).

For a general discussion of what a trustee needs to be concerned about when making a distribution of trust property to anyone, not just a minor, see Section 8.2.3 of this handbook.

(m)   The power to divide a trust.

The Uniform Trust Code would make it a default rule that a trustee may divide a trust into two or more separate trusts, provided the result does not impair the rights of any beneficiary or adversely affect achievement of the purposes of the trust.[640] Absent statutory division authority,[641] the trustee should have that authority in the governing instrument:

> Division of trusts is often beneficial and, in certain circumstances, almost routine. Division of trust is frequently undertaken due to a desire to obtain maximum advantage of exemptions available under the federal generation-skipping tax. While the terms of the trusts that result from such a division are identical, the division will permit differing investment objectives to be pursued and allow for discretionary distributions to be made from one trust and not the other. Given the substantial tax benefits often involved, a failure by the trustee to pursue a division might in certain cases be a breach of fiduciary duty. The opposite could also be true if the division is undertaken to increase fees or to fit within the small trust termination provision.[642]

If division would facilitate the conservation of the trust property for the beneficiaries, a trustee with neither statutory nor express or implied division authority in the governing instrument may, under certain circumstances, have a fiduciary duty to seek that authority from the court.[643]

Some states by statute, grant trustees some or all of the powers discussed in this section, unless a settlor by express language in the governing instrument provides otherwise.[644] Other states have on their statute books a selection of trustee powers, some or all of which may be incorporated by reference into a trust instrument.[645] See Section 551 of Bogert, Trusts and Trustees, for a full catalog of state trustee powers statutes of both the opt-out and opt-in variety. Section 816 of the Uniform Trust Code confers a number of special powers on the trustee. All the Section 816 powers are subject to alteration in the terms of

---

[640] UTC §417 (available at <http://www.uniformlaws.org/Act.aspx?title=Trust%20Code>).

[641] For a list of statutes authorizing the division of a trust, *see* Restatement (Third) of Property (Wills and Donative Transfers) §12.2 Statutory Note. *See also* UTC §417 cmt. (available at <http://www.uniformlaws.org/Act.aspx?title=Trust%20Code>) (listing cases in which division has been authorized by the courts in the absence of authorizing statute).

[642] UTC §417 cmt. (available at <http://www.uniformlaws.org/Act.aspx?title=Trust %20Code>). *See also* Suter & Repetti, *Trustee Authority to Divide Trusts*, 6 Prob. & Prop. 52 (Nov./Dec. 1992) (recommending that a trustee be given express division authority in the governing instrument).

[643] *See, e.g.,* Marquis v. Marquis, 437 Mass. 1010, 771 N.E.2d 133 (2002) (granting the trustee division authority in order to save federal generation-skipping transfer taxes).

[644] *See generally* Uniform Trustees' Powers Act, 7C U.L.A. 388 (2000).

[645] *See, e.g.,* Mass. Gen. Laws Ann. ch. 184B, §§1, 2 (Statutory optional fiduciary powers).

the trust. Many of the Section 816 powers are similar to the powers listed in Section 3 of the Uniform Trustees' Powers Act (1964).

For a discussion of the myriad issues that can arise if the trustee at the time of termination of a main trust is required by the terms of the trust to divide it into separate trust shares but unduly delays in doing so, or fails to do so altogether, the reader is referred to Section 8.2.3 of this handbook.[646]

(n)   The power to resign.

It is common practice for a settlor to bestow on the trustee by express language in the governing instrument the power to resign. If the terms of a trust make no provision for trustee resignation, the trustee will need either the unanimous consent of all beneficiaries or court authorization to resign.[647] If there are no cotrustees, a resignation by whatever method will only become effective upon acceptance of the trusteeship by a qualified successor.[648] Moreover, resignation in and of itself will not absolve a trustee from liability for prior breaches of trust.[649] Nor may the trustee resign for the purpose of escaping adverse circumstances occasioned by the breaches of his cotrustees, unless he has fully apprised the settlor, the beneficiaries, and/or the court as appropriate of all the relevant law and facts.[650]

Trustees of revocable trusts are subject to different rules when it comes to the power to resign. A trustee of a revocable trust may resign with the consent of the holder of the right of revocation; the consent of anyone else not being required.[651] "Even without the . . . [holder's] . . . consent, however, a trustee of a revocable trust may resign if the addition of property or a change in the trust terms significantly changes the trustee's responsibilities."[652]

(o)   The power to cooperate with others.

It is probably still a good idea to have express language in a governing trust instrument authorizing the trustee to deposit with a protective committee the securities of a financially distressed corporation that is an asset of the trust. Express authority to join in a representative suit affecting the trust property is

---

[646] *See also* Restatement (Third) of Trusts §89, Reporter's Notes, cmt. g.

[647] Restatement (Third) of Trusts §36.

[648] Restatement (Third) of Trusts §36 cmt. a. *See generally* §6.1.4 of this handbook (the trustee's duty not to delegate critical fiduciary functions).

[649] Restatement (Third) of Trusts §36 cmt. d.

[650] Restatement (Third) of Trusts §36 cmt. a.

[651] Restatement (Third) of Trusts §36 cmt. b. *See generally* §8.11 of this handbook (the duties of the trustee of a revocable inter vivos trust).

[652] Restatement (Third) of Trusts §36 cmt. b. *See generally* §8.11 of this handbook (the duties of the trustee of a revocable inter vivos trust).

probably also desirable. In the past, such acts raised delegation[653] and control[654] issues. Nowadays, however, the trustee's authority to perform them may well be implied. The Restatement (Third) of Trusts, for example, provides that a trustee may deposit the securities of a corporation in financial distress with a protective committee without violating the duty not to delegate, provided a reasonable individual owner would do the same.[655] It also provides that a trustee may participate with others in a representative suit involving the trust property, although by doing so the trustee surrenders control over the suit.[656]

(p)   **The power to hire agents and advisors at trust expense.**

As a general rule, "a trustee cannot properly incur expenses for another's performance of functions the trustee is compensated—and thus expected—to perform personally."[657] On the other hand, the trustee is empowered to retain agents and advisors at trust expense when it is appropriate to the sound administration of the trust. The Restatement (Third) of Trusts is in accord.[658] A gray area is when the trustee retains the services of an investment manager, advisor, or agent.[659] There is also the related matter of whether the trustee is entitled to full compensation, or whether the trustee's compensation should be offset by the investment advisory costs.[660] While there may be implied authority in the trustee to hire agents and advisors at trust expense when appropriate, it is probably in the interest of all parties that the settlor's expectations with respect to the hiring and compensation of investment managers be addressed square on and with appropriate specificity in the governing instrument. For the trustee's right to exoneration and reimbursement for reasonable attorneys' fees, the reader is referred to Section 3.5.2.3 of this handbook.

§3.5.3.3   The Power to Submit an Internal Trust Dispute to Arbitration; Mandatory Arbitration Clauses in Trust Instruments; Mediation

After careful consideration, we conclude that only the judicial system is equipped to handle incompetency hearings and the legal ramifications following a determination of . . . [a

---

[653] *See* §6.1.4 of this handbook (the trustee's duty not to delegate critical fiduciary functions).

[654] *See* §6.2.1.1 of this handbook (the trustee's duty to take active control of the trust property).

[655] Restatement (Third) of Trusts §80 cmt. i.

[656] Restatement (Third) of Trusts §80 cmt. i. *Cf.* §6.2.1.1 of this handbook (the trustee's duty to take active control of the trust property).

[657] Restatement (Third) of Trusts §88 cmt.

[658] Restatement (Third) of Trusts §88 cmt. c.

[659] *See generally* §6.1.4 of this handbook (the trustee's duty not to delegate critical fiduciary functions).

[660] *See generally* §6.2.1.3 of this handbook (the trustee's duty to protect the trust property) and §8.4 of this handbook (trustee compensation); Restatement (Third) of Trusts §88 cmt. c.

settlor's] . . . incompetency. As a matter of public policy, issues of incompetency cannot be submitted to arbitration.[661]

Not to be confused with an external contractual dispute between the trustee and a third party,[662] if a particular *internal* trust dispute is resolvable by agreement among all interested parties, including the trustee, then it follows that the parties are entitled to submit the dispute to nonjudicial binding arbitration.[663] But not all trust disputes are:

> In drawing attention to the benefits of mediation, it would be simplistic to suggest it is a cure-all for all trust and probate disputes. Some disputes will not be appropriate for mediation, in particular those that turn on technical construction of trust deeds or wills, cases in which injunctions are sought and claims involving allegations of fraud.[664]

So also some trust disputes, on public policy grounds, may not be arbitrated in a nonjudicial context—*e.g.*, a dispute over the validity of a testamentary trust or whether there has been a violation of the rule against perpetuities.[665] As a general matter, a trust term that purports to oust the court of its traditional equitable jurisdiction over trust matters has always been considered unenforceable, *e.g.*, one that purports to bestow on a member of the executive branch of a state's government the authority to make binding determinations as to whether the trustee is complying with the other trust terms.[666] Nor has it been considered possible to "oust" the court by an expansive grant of discretion to the trustee. "It is submitted . . . that, even as to matters thus firmly committed to the trustee's discretion, judicial review should remain available if the trustee acts in bad faith, contrary to the terms of the trust, or with an improper motive."[667]

In any case, assuming a particular trust dispute can be arbitrated nonjudicially, for the process to work, *i.e.*, for the arbitrator's decisions to be final and binding on all persons, each interested party will need to be represented by

---

[661] In re Trust of Fellman, 412 Pa. Super. 577, 586, 604 A.2d 263, 267 (1992) (involving a trustee who failed to honor the settlor's instrument of revocation though the trust was revocable by the settlor, the trustee being of the opinion that the settlor was incompetent). *See generally* §8.2.2.2 of this handbook (the revocable trust).

[662] *Cf.* In re Shalik, 2007 N.Y. Slip Op. 51942(U) (Sur. 2007) (2007 WL 2944758) (involving a probate estate, not a trust).

[663] *See generally* §8.44 of this handbook (mediation and arbitration have their limitations when it comes to trust disputes); R. Kabaker, J. Maier & F. Ware, *The Use of Arbitration in Wills and Trusts*, 17 ACTEC Notes 177 (1991).

[664] Jeremy Gordon, *More talk*, 15 The Journal, Issue 7 29 (July/Aug. 2007) 29 [A STEP publication]. *See generally* §8.44 of this handbook (mediation and arbitration have their limitations when it comes to trust disputes).

[665] R. Kabaker, J. Maier & F. Ware, *The Use of Arbitration in Wills and Trusts*, 17 ACTEC Notes 177 (1991).

[666] *See generally* 3 Scott & Ascher §18.2 (Executive Branch Encroachment on Court's Equitable Prerogatives). *Cf.* §9.4.4 of this handbook (legislative branch encroachment on court's equitable prerogatives).

[667] 3 Scott & Ascher §18.2 (Control of Discretionary Powers).

independent counsel, or to give an informed waiver of counsel, unless the trust is revocable, which is a whole other matter. As the typical noncommercial trust will have unborn and unascertained beneficiaries requiring the services of a guardian ad litem, it is hard to see how the court can be kept altogether out of the process.[668] If some of the current beneficiaries are minors, then the court almost certainly will have to be involved.[669] Thus, whether arbitration is an option worth pursuing when there are unborn and unascertained beneficiaries (or minor beneficiaries) will depend upon whether its attendant redundancies and inefficiencies are outweighed by its advantages.

Likewise, formal mediation can be both wasteful and futile when the unborn and unascertained are without representation, not to mention minors and others under some disability. It can also subject the trustee to personal liability for the attendant costs.[670] For more on how efforts to even formally *mediate* certain trust disputes can end up being counterproductive, the reader is referred to Section 8.44 of this handbook.

Still, there is little direct law on the subject of whether a settlor, by express language in the governing instrument, may compel the arbitration of those trust disputes that may be arbitrated.[671] Since the beginning of the country, such clauses have been utilized in testamentary instruments.[672] George Washington employed one in his will.[673] U.S. Supreme Court Chief Justice Marshall passed on such a clause in *Pray v. Belt*.[674]

Today, mandated will arbitration clauses are being enforced. "The sanctity with which courts respect a testator's last intents and wishes offers courts a solid foundation for enforcing testamentary arbitration clauses."[675] It has been suggested that there is no compelling reason to deny a *settlor's* intent comparable deference, particularly if the arbitration clause includes a "no-contest" or an "in terrorem" feature.[676] That may be the case, but the Court of Appeals of California is one court that remains unpersuaded.[677]

---

[668] *See generally* §8.14 of this handbook (when a guardian ad litem or special representative is needed and when virtual representation will suffice).

[669] *See* Mark S. Poker & Amy S. Kiiskila, *Prevention and Resolution of Trust and Estate Controversies*, 33 ACTEC L.J. 262, 266 (2008).

[670] *See generally* §8.44 of this handbook (mediation and arbitration have their limitations when it comes to trust disputes).

[671] *See generally* R. Kabaker, J. Maier & F. Ware, *The Use of Arbitration in Wills and Trusts*, 17 ACTEC Notes 177 (1991).

[672] *See generally* R. Kabaker, J. Maier & F. Ware, *The Use of Arbitration in Wills and Trusts*, 17 ACTEC Notes 177 (1991).

[673] 124 N.Y.L.J. 1558 (1950).

[674] 26 U.S. (1 Pet.) 670, 7 L. Ed. 309 (1828).

[675] R. Kabaker, J. Maier & F. Ware, *The Use of Arbitration in Wills and Trusts*, 17 ACTEC Notes 177, 179 (1991).

[676] *See generally* §5.5 of this handbook (voluntary or involuntary loss of the beneficiary's rights) (discussing in part "no-contest" or *in terrorem* trust clauses).

[677] *See* McArthur v. McArthur, 224 Cal. App. 4th 651 (2014) (" . . . [The Defendant] . . . contends that there is a national trend towards allowing arbitration in the trust context, and urges us to follow this 'trend.' These are arguments best addressed to the Legislature, not to this court. Moreover, '[e]ven the strong public policy in favor of arbitration does not extend to those who are

Some have cautioned that the right to compel arbitration is statutory and that the Uniform Arbitration Act, which has been adopted in a number of jurisdictions, makes no mention of trusts.[678] It provides that "[a] written agreement to submit any existing controversy to arbitration or a provision in a written contract to submit to arbitration any controversy thereafter arising between the parties is valid, enforceable and irrevocable, save upon such grounds as exist at law or in equity for the revocation of any contract."[679] The question then becomes whether a trust is a form of contract.[680] Some see them as two distinct legal relationships.[681] Others do not.[682] The better view is that a trust is *sui generis*,[683] and there is some case law to that effect.[684] It should be noted that Washington State has an arbitration statute that does make mention of trusts.[685] So has Missouri. Missouri's statute provides that "a provision in a trust instrument requiring the mediation or arbitration of disputes between or among the beneficiaries, a fiduciary, a person granted nonfiduciary powers under the trust instrument, or any combination of such persons is enforceable."[686] There is a critical exception, however: In the case of a dispute "relating to the validity of a trust," such a provision would not be enforceable "unless all interested persons with regard to the dispute consent to the mediation or arbitration of the dispute."[687]

The Supreme Court of Texas has ordered the enforcement of a trust arbitration clause over the objection of the settlor's two sons, whom the court

---

not parties to an arbitration agreement or have not authorized anyone to act for them in executing such an agreement.' [citations]" In any event, whatever the national trend might be , ... [the Defendant] . . . fails to demonstrate that any other jurisdiction would compel arbitration under the facts of this case, where the beneficiary has *not* either expressly or implicitly sought the benefits of a trust instrument containing the disputed arbitration provision.")

[678] *See, e.g.,* Alexis S. Hamdan & Ronald F. Kehoe, *Arbitration Clauses in Wills and Trusts: A Litigator's Perspective,* Mass. Lawyers Weekly, p. B4, col. 1, May 10, 1999 (27 M.L.W. 1984).

[679] Uniform Arbitration Act §1, 7. The language of §6(a) of the Uniform Arbitration Act (2000) is similar: "An agreement contained in a record to submit to arbitration any existing or subsequent controversy arising between the parties to the agreement is valid, enforceable, and irrevocable except upon a ground that exists at law or in equity for the revocation of a contract."

[680] *See, e.g.,* Schoneberger v. Oelze, 208 Ariz. 591, 96 P.3d 1078 (2005) (trusts being not "written contracts" subject to the provisions of an Arizona statute that enforced arbitration clauses in contracts, mandatory arbitration clauses in two inter vivos trusts were unenforceable as against the trusts' beneficiaries). *Schoneberger* may have been rendered moot by Ariz. Rev. Stat. Ann. § 14-10205.

[681] *See, e.g.,* Restatement (Second) of Trusts §§74 cmt. a, 197 cmt. b. *See also* 2A Scott on Trusts §169.

[682] *See generally* §8.22 of this handbook (whether we even need the trust when we have the corporation and the third party beneficiary contract).

[683] *See generally* §8.22 of this handbook (whether we even need the trust when we have the corporation and the third party beneficiary contract).

[684] *See, e.g.,* Schoneberger v. Oelze, 208 Ariz. 591, 595, 96 P.3d 1078, 1082 (2004) (a trust is not a contract).

[685] Wash. Rev. Code §11.96A.030(1).

[686] RSMO 456.2-205.1

[687] RSMO 456.2-205.2.

characterized as the trust's "sole beneficiaries."[688] The court based its ruling on two grounds: (1) Enforcement is in conformance with the intentions of the settlor, and (2) the applicability of the doctrine of direct benefits estoppel, a category of general equitable estoppel doctrine, satisfies the agreement requirement of the Texas Arbitration Act. The Act provides that a written agreement to arbitrate is enforceable if it provides for arbitration of either an existing controversy or one that arises between the parties after the date of the agreement. The court explains its application of a contract-based doctrine to a trust, a relationship that most serious scholars have concluded is not per se contract-based: " . . . [A] beneficiary who attempts to enforce rights that would not exist without the trust manifests her assent to the trust's arbitration clause. For example, a beneficiary who brings a claim for breach of fiduciary duty seeks to hold the trustee to her obligations under the instrument and thus has acquiesced to its provisions, including the arbitration clause. In such circumstances, it would be incongruent to allow a beneficiary to hold a trustee to the terms of the trust but not to hold the beneficiary to those same terms."[689] If, by implication, a trust arbitration clause would not be enforceable against someone incapable of granting such an assent, such as an unborn or unascertained equitable quasi remainderman, then the court, as a practical matter, may have neutered most Texas trust arbitration clauses, except those in commercial trust instruments.

Notwithstanding the paucity of law on the subject of the enforceability of trust arbitration clauses, settlors are employing them. For a collection of sample arbitration clauses, the reader is referred to an article by Bridget A. Logstrom.[690] The American Arbitration Association[691] offers the following as a model:

> In order to save the cost of court proceedings and promote the prompt and final resolution of any dispute regarding the interpretation of my trust or the administration of my trust, I direct that any such dispute shall be settled by arbitration administered by the American Arbitration Association under its Arbitration Rules for Wills and Trusts then in effect. Nevertheless the following matters shall not be arbitrable—questions regarding my competency, attempts to remove a fiduciary, or questions concerning the amount of bond of a fiduciary. In addition, arbitration may be waived by all *sui juris* parties in interest.
>
> The arbitrator shall be a practicing lawyer licensed to practice law in the state whose laws govern my trust. The arbitrator's decision shall not be appealable to any court, but shall be final and binding on any and all persons

---

[688] Hal Rachal, Jr. v. John W. Reitz, No. 11-0708 (Tex. May 3, 2013).

[689] *Rachal*, No. 11-0708, at 11. For a discussion of why the trust relationship per se is not contract-based, see §8.22 of this handbook.

[690] *Arbitration in Estate and Trust Disputes: Friend or Foe?* 30 ACTEC L.J. 266 (2005).

[691] 120 Broadway, New York, NY 10271. Phone: (212) 716-5800.

who have or may have an interest in my trust, including unborn or incapacitated persons, such as minors or incompetents. Judgment on the arbitrator's award may be entered in any court having jurisdiction thereof.[692]

For a discussion of the resolution of *external* disputes through arbitration and mediation, *i.e.*, disputes between the trustee and third parties such as those who owe the trust money or are owed money by the trust, the reader is referred to Section 3.5.3.2(f) of this handbook.

Again, for a general discussion of the limitations of mediation and arbitration when it comes to trust disputes, see Section 8.44 of this handbook.

§3.5.3.4   The Trustee's Power to Disclaim a Fiduciary Power

A beneficiary of full age and legal capacity may disclaim his or her equitable property interest under a trust. This matter is discussed in Section 5.5 of this handbook. When a trustee disclaims a legal or equitable interest that otherwise would have become trust property, then that interest does not become trust property.[693]

May a trustee, however, disclaim a *power* granted to the trustee by the terms of the governing instrument or by law? The answer is yes, provided the disclaimer is compatible with the fiduciary duties discussed in Chapter 6 of this handbook.[694] The Uniform Probate Code is in accord.[695] The Restatement (Third) of Trusts is generally in accord, as well.[696] "But such action may not be taken merely for the convenience, or to avoid or lessen the responsibilities, of the trustee . . . ."[697] Note that in England, discretionary fiduciary powers generally are not releasable.[698]

Let us assume that a trustee has a discretionary power to invade principal for the benefit of a class of permissible beneficiaries comprising the settlor's children. Under the terms of the trust, the settlor's widow receives all net trust accounting income. The settlor's children are the remaindermen. The trustee is a child of the settlor.[699] The trustee may disclaim the power to invade principal for his own benefit, *e.g.*, to avoid a tax liability,[700] without breaching his Chapter

---

[692] *See* American Arbitration Association pamphlet: Arbitration Rules for Wills and Trusts, effective October 1, 1995, at page 4. *See generally* Mary F. Radford, *An Introduction to the Uses of Mediation and Other Forms of Dispute Resolution* in Probate, Trust, and Guardianship Matters, 34 Real Prop. Prob. & Tr. J. 601 (No. 4) (Winter 2000).

[693] UPC §2-1108.

[694] UPC §2-1111 cmt. *See* 3 Scott & Ascher §18.1.7 n.7 (a listing of statutes authorizing fiduciaries to disclaim interests in property and powers).

[695] UPC §§2-1105(b), 2-1111.

[696] Restatement (Third) of Trusts §86 cmt. f.

[697] Restatement (Third) of Trusts §86 cmt. f.

[698] Lewin ¶29-83 (England).

[699] *See generally* §8.9.3 of this handbook (tax-sensitive powers).

[700] *See generally* §8.9.3 of this handbook (tax-sensitive powers).

6 fiduciary duties. This is because the disclaimer would adversely affect no other beneficiary. The disclaimer also would not have to bind successor trustees.[701]

On the other hand it is problematic whether the trustee could effectively disclaim his power to invade principal for the other children, even if the motive for disclaiming were to qualify the trust for QTIP status.[702] This is because the trustee would have a duty to treat all beneficiaries equitably in light of the purposes and terms of the trust.[703] He would need the consent of all the children for the disclaimer to be effective.[704] In this case, there are two possible exceptions to the consent requirement: (1) If there were authority, whether express or implied, vested in the trustee under the terms of the trust to disclaim the fiduciary power without the children's consent or (2) if engineering QTIP status were in fact in the interest of the children. If such a disclaimer would be in the interest of the children, then it would most likely be binding on successor trustees.[705] A disclaimer, in whole or in part, of the future exercise of a fiduciary power ought not to be barred merely because of the power's previous exercise.[706]

When having a trustee disclaim a fiduciary power is not an option, those who might benefit from such a disclaimer can always mount an effort to have the trust judicially reformed or modified.[707] Whether such an effort will be successful is another matter.

§3.5.3.5 A Trust Provision Granting the Trustee Express Authority to Redeem at Par Entrusted Flower Bonds Is Now Obsolete

Until the 1970s, it was considered a sine qua non that a trust instrument contain some version of the following boilerplate:

> If at the time of the death of the Settlor, the Trustee holds United States Treasury bonds redeemable at par for the payment of federal estate taxes (what we called in the trade "flower bonds"), then notwithstanding the provisions hereinbefore set forth or any provisions to the contrary contained in the Settlor's will, the Trustee shall in any event pay such portion of the federal estate taxes due by reason of the Settlor's death as is equal to the par value of said bonds.

---

[701] UPC §2-1111(c).

[702] *See* §8.9.1.3 of this handbook (the marital deduction) (discussing the QTIP trust).

[703] *See* §6.2.5 of this handbook (trustee's duty to treat the beneficiaries of impartially). *See also* Restatement (Third) of Trusts §86 cmt. f.

[704] *See, e.g.,* Cleaveland v. United States, 62 A.F.T.R.2d (RIA) 88-5992, 88-5994, 88-1 USTC ¶13,766 (C.D. Ill. 1988) (allowing a disclaimer as beneficiaries "received notice of the trustee's disclaimer and did not object").

[705] UPC §2-1111(c).

[706] UPC §2-1113(c).

[707] *See generally* §8.17 of this handbook (trust reformation to remedy mistakes); Restatement (Third) of Trusts §86 cmt. f; Restatement (Third) of Property (Wills and Donative Transfers) §§12.1 and 12.2.

A flower bond (also known as an estate tax anticipation bond) was a special type of United States Treasury bond that was redeemable in payment of federal estate taxes at its par value rather than at its market value, which tended to be less than its par value. If the bonds were entrusted, there had to have been an express redemption mandate similar to the above boilerplate in the trust instrument, or the redemption would not have been honored by the government. The Treasury ceased issuing flower bonds in 1971. The last of such bonds matured in 1998. Now that all live flower bonds have either been redeemed or matured, flower bond redemption authority in the boilerplate of trust instruments serves no practical purpose.

§3.5.4 Nature of Trustee's Liability

At common law, the trustee's liability was personal.[708] This is still the case when it comes to the trustee's internal dealings with the beneficiary.[709] Even in his external dealings on behalf of the trust with third parties it is still sometimes the case.[710]

The liability of one who contracts with a trustee generally runs to the trustee, and only indirectly to the beneficiaries.[711] One who commits a tort that harms the trust estate is primarily liable to the trustee, and only secondarily to the beneficiaries.[712] On the other hand, the liability of a third party who colludes with the trustee to commit a breach of trust runs in equity directly to the beneficiaries.[713]

§3.5.4.1 Personal Liability of Trustee (External and Internal)

Sir Leicester has no objection to an interminable Chancery suit. It is a slow, expensive, British, constitutional kind of thing.—Charles Dickens[714]

The trustee can take no benefit from ownership of the trust estate, nor deal with it for personal profit or for any purpose unconnected with the trust.[715] The

---

[708] *But see* Curtis, *The Transmogrification of The American Trust*, 31 Real Prop. Prob. & Tr. J. 251 (No. 2 1996) (suggesting that the trust is evolving into a "quasi-corporation" when it comes to the trustee's third-party liability).

[709] *See generally* §7.2 of this handbook (trustee's internal fiduciary liability to the beneficiaries).

[710] *See generally* §7.3 of this handbook (trustee's external liability as legal owner to nonbeneficiaries).

[711] *See generally* 5 Scott & Ascher §28.1.

[712] *See generally* 5 Scott & Ascher §28.2.

[713] *See generally* §7.2.9 of this handbook (personal liability of third parties, including the trustee's agents, to the beneficiary; investment managers; directors and officers of trust companies; lawyers; brokers).

[714] Bleak House, Chapter 2 (In Fashion).

[715] *See* §6.1.3 of this handbook (trustee's duty to be loyal to the trust).

trustee is nevertheless the "owner" of the property.[716] Thus, subject to certain exceptions (statutory and otherwise),[717] the general rule is that the trustee is personally liable as owner to nonbeneficiaries such as contract creditors, tort creditors, and the federal, state, and local governments in the same way and to the same extent as if the property were owned by the trustee individually.[718] Moreover, the trustee is personally liable in equity to the beneficiaries for breaches of fiduciary duty.[719]

§3.5.4.2 Insuring Against Trustee's Personal Liability

Chubb & Son, of Warren, N.J., has rejected a couple dozen companies' requests for coverage during recent months, said John Coonan, Chubb's vice president for world-wide fiduciary liability. He declined to identify specific companies, but said that if a company has a significant amount of employer stock . . . we may be inclined not to underwrite the risk. He defined significant as exceeding 10% total assets.[720]

As owner of the legal interest, the trustee is vulnerable on two fronts when it comes to personal liability. As the owner of the trust estate, the trustee is personally liable to nonbeneficiaries for negligent and intentional torts committed by him and his servants against nonbeneficiaries in the course of the administration of the trust estate.[721] As the fiduciary, the trustee is also personally liable to the beneficiaries for any negligent or intentional breaches of trust that cause injury to the trust itself.

As a practical matter, the individual trustee cannot obtain insurance that would cover the trustee's personal liability for intentional torts committed against nonbeneficiaries and for intentional breaches of trust.[722] Even if such insurance could be obtained, the premiums would have to be absorbed by the trustee personally as a cost of doing business—they may not be charged by the

---

[716] *See* §3.5.1 of this handbook (nature and extent of the trustee's estate).

[717] *See* §3.5.2.3 of this handbook (right in equity to exoneration and reimbursement, *i.e.*, indemnity; payment of attorneys' fees) and §7.3 of this handbook (trustee's liability as legal owner to nonbeneficiaries).

[718] *See* §7.3 of this handbook (trustee's liability as legal owner to nonbeneficiaries).

[719] *See* §7.2 of this handbook (trustee's liability as fiduciary to the beneficiary).

[720] Kathy Chen, *Insuring Trustees of Pension Plans Becomes Costlier*, Wall St. J., May 3, 2002, at C11.

[721] *See generally* §7.3 of this handbook (trustee's liability as legal owner to nonbeneficiaries). Note that in Louisiana, although a plaintiff generally may hold a trustee who makes a contract personally liable on the contract if its terms fail to exclude personal liability, the presence after where the trustee's signature appears on the contract of the word *trustee* or the words *as trustee* together with language identifying the trust shall be deemed prima facie evidence of the contracting parties' intention to exclude the trustee from personal liability. La. Rev. Stat. Ann. §9:2125(c).

[722] *See generally* R. Keeton & A. Widiss, Insurance Law, Guide to Fundamental Principles, Legal Doctrines, and Commercial Practices, Practitioner's Edition §5.4 (1988) (suggesting that it would be against public policy to be able to obtain insurance against one's intentional tortious acts).

trustee to the trust estate.[723] The insurance company that underwrites the
trustee's coverage for negligent acts against nonbeneficiaries essentially underwrites as well the costs of the trustee's defense against allegations that the acts
were intentional.

Internal liability. The individual trustee who is not also an attorney will
have a hard time finding inexpensive fiduciary liability insurance that will cover
the trustee's personal liability for negligent breaches of trust, particularly in the
carrying out of investment and property disbursement responsibilities.[724] Such
insurance falls outside the scope of coverage of most homeowner and umbrella
policies. It is generally underwritten on a per trust basis, with the insurance
company requiring the trustee, as part of the application process, to submit a
copy of the governing instrument. If the terms of the trust are amendable in any
manner that would change the potential liability of the trustee, a substantive
amendment will terminate coverage unless approved in advance by the insurance company. Premiums for internal fiduciary liability insurance are generally
not chargeable to the trust estate.[725] English law is in accord,[726] although there
is an exception for trustees of charitable trusts.[727] It has been reported, however,
that in England "a very inexpensive trustee liability insurance policy" is now
being marketed to lay trustees.[728] Moreover, in England trust instruments
executed in the late 1990s and thereafter tend to expressly grant to the trustee
the authority to charge fiduciary liability insurance premiums against the trust
estate as a trust expense.[729] Absent such authority, if the trustee's stockbroker or
investment advisor absorbs the cost of the trustee's fiduciary liability insurance
premiums in exchange for the trustee directing brokerage or advisory work his
or her way,[730] then the trustee's duty of undivided loyalty is implicated, a topic
we take up in Section 6.1.3.4 of this handbook.

On this side of the Atlantic, many insurance companies have a substantial
minimum premium for such fiduciary liability insurance. A negotiated annual
premium for $3 million of coverage, with a $50,000 deductible, could run as
high as $57,000. The trustee's counsel fees incurred in negotiating the contract
alone could exceed $10,000. The individual trustee of a private noncommercial
trust who seeks customized fiduciary liability insurance that would cover the
trustee's negligent breaches of trust probably should start with those companies
that write policies for fiduciaries of pension plans or directors and officers of

---

[723] *See generally* Bogert §599.

[724] Phone interviews with insurers offering professional liability products yielded no insurer
with a standard policy for the private trustee. Those insurers willing to consider underwriting
policies would negotiate the price and the coverage.

[725] *See generally* §3.5.2.3 of this handbook (right in equity to exoneration and reimbursement, *i.e.*, indemnity; payment of attorneys' fees).

[726] Kemble v. Hicks [1999] P.L.R. 287 (England).

[727] Charities Act 1993 §73F (England).

[728] Clive Barwell, *Can the trust pay?*, 17(1) STEP J.70 (Jan. 2009).

[729] Clive Barwell, *Can the trust pay?*, 17(1) STEP J. 70 (Jan. 2009).

[730] Clive Barwell, *Can the trust pay?*, 17(1) STEP J.71 (Jan. 2009) (apparently this is
happening in England).

corporations.[731] Again, premiums for such internal liability coverage generally may not be charged against the trust estate.

The attorney acting as trustee has an advantage over the layman when it comes to coverage for negligent breaches of trust. Standardized legal malpractice policies are available to the lawyer who acts as trustee of trusts in the ordinary course of his or her practice. However, the attorney should carefully read his or her particular policy to confirm that trustee services have not been excluded from the definition of *professional services*.[732] "For example, while an individual policy might cover the work of a lawyer acting 'as trustee,' that same policy could contain specific exclusions for claims arising out of an attorney acting in his or her capacity as a director or officer of a business entity."[733] Attorneys serving as trust protectors may have to negotiate coverage on a case-by-case basis, unless perhaps in cases or jurisdictions where a protectorship is essentially a cotrusteeship.[734]

The lawyer-trustee "of a trust holding a closely held business interest might find the business exclusion applied to deny coverage when the trustee by necessity is required to participate in active business management decisions and it is those actions which give rise to the claim."[735] All policies will contain coverage exclusion provisions for damages arising out of dishonest acts. A failure to disclose relevant information on a policy application (*e.g.*, the existence of potential liability for acts or omissions committed prior to the policy commencement date) could trigger the dishonesty exclusion.[736] Many policies will specifically exclude coverage for losses suffered by beneficiaries during the course of a lawyer's administration of an ERISA plan.[737] Legal malpractice policies also tend not to cover punitive damage awards and other awards in excess of actual damages. Most of these policies also exclude discrimination and environmental injury claims.

---

[731] A list of such companies is published by the International Risk Management Institute, 12222 Merit Drive, Suite 1450, Dallas, Texas 75251-2276, which can be reached at (972) 960-7693 or at <www.irmi.com>. The non-ERISA trustee may want to contact The Chubb Group of Insurance Companies, Warren, New Jersey 07059, <www.chubb.com> and ask about the *Wealth Managers Insurance Program From Chubb*.

[732] *See* Ronald E. Mallen, et al., Legal Malpractice: The Law Office Guide to Purchasing Legal Malpractice Insurance 11, §§1.53–1.55 (1998 ed.). *See generally* Andrew S. Hanen & Jett Hanna, *Legal Malpractice Insurance: Exclusions, Selected Coverage and Consumer Issues*, 33 S. Tex. L. Rev. 75, 93–96 (1992).

[733] ACTEC Practice Committee, Fiduciary Matters Subcommittee, *Guide for ACTEC Fellows Serving as Trustees*, 26 ACTEC Notes 313, 322 (2001).

[734] *See generally* §3.2.6 of this handbook (considerations in the selection of a trustee).

[735] *See generally* §3.2.6 of this handbook (considerations in the selection of a trustee).

[736] *See* Selko v. Home Ins. Co., 139 F.3d 146 (1998). *See also* Webster v. Powell, 98 N.C. App. 432, 391 S.E.2d 204 (1990) (suggesting informal fiduciary arrangements not requiring court approval may be excluded from scope of policy coverage). *But see* Continental Cas. Co. v. Burton, 795 F.2d 1187 (4th Cir. 1986) (noting that insurer seeking to apply coverage exclusion bears burden of demonstrating its applicability).

[737] *See* Edward J. Boyle et al., Insurance Coverage for Attorneys, Accountants, and Insurance Brokers Serving as ERISA Fiduciaries or Corporate Directors, in Professional Liability Insurance for Attorneys, Accountants, and Insurance Brokers 1986, at 481 (PLI Litig. & Admin. Practice Course Handbook Series No. 303, 1986).

There are standardized insurance products available to corporate trustees. This type of insurance is known in the trade as Bankers Professional Liability Insurance or BPL Insurance. BPL Insurance covers both the *internal* risk of breach of fiduciary duty and the *external* risk of liability to third parties with whom the trustee comes in contact in the course of administering a trust. The following are some of the more common trust activities that are covered by a typical BPL Insurance contract:[738]

- Administering trusts;
- Administering Individual Retirement Accounts and Keogh Plans;
- Acting as trustee in bankruptcy;
- Acting as an ERISA fiduciary;[739]
- Acting as tax planner and/or tax preparer to trusts, estates, and individuals;
- Acting as an investment or financial advisor; and
- Acting as an investment manager.

The corporate trustee is the named insured under a BPL Insurance policy. Also covered under the policy are the corporation's owners, partners, officers, stockholders, directors, and employees. Their estates are covered as well. BPL Insurance generally covers economic injury occasioned by negligent acts. It will not cover punitive, exemplary, and multiplied damages. Nor will it cover fines and penalties, such as fines resulting from unpaid tax liabilities.[740] Some policies have "recourse provisions." This means that if a covered individual such as a trust officer *willfully* injures a trust, *e.g.*, embezzles its funds, then the insurance company will not pay out under the policy if the corporate trustee can make itself whole in an action against the trust officer.

There are three types of exclusions found in BPL Insurance policies. They are exclusions for business risk; fraudulent, criminal, and dishonest acts; and exposures covered under other policies.

---

[738] Bankers Professional Liability Policy Supplemental Application (American International Specialty Lines Insurance Company) 89-182 (3/89).

[739] *See* ERISA §410 (29 U.S.C. §1110(a)); Edward J. Boyle et al., Insurance Coverage for Attorneys, Accountants, and Insurance Brokers Serving as ERISA, Fiduciaries or Corporate Directors, in Professional Liability Insurance for Attorneys, Accountants, and Insurance Brokers 1986, at 492 (PLI Litig. & Admin. Practice Course Handbook Series No. 303, 1986) (pointing out that ERISA permits a *plan* to purchase fiduciary liability insurance only if the policy allows insurer to seek recourse against breaching fiduciary; the insurer may waive this recourse right provided the *trustee* personally absorbs the cost of this additional coverage). *See* Kathy Chen, *Insuring Trustees of Pension Plans Becomes Costlier*, Wall St. J., May 3, 2002, at C11.

[740] *But see* Pens. Plan Guide (CCH) ¶23,931G, Board of Trustees of Int'l Bhd. of Elec. Workers' Local No. 141 Pension Fund v. Aetna Cas. & Sur. Co., 106 F.3d 389 (4th Cir. 1997) (unpublished table decision). In that case, the court held that an IRS settlement paid to maintain qualified status of plan was considered damages, rather than excluded fines and penalties under the insurance policy. The settlement was considered damages that the insured became obligated to pay, even though it represented fulfillment of what amounted to a tax liability. The court considered these damages compensatory tort damages, construing the ambiguous contract terms against the drafting insurer.

The trust officer who is employed by a corporate trustee seems particularly exposed when it comes to liability for breaches of trust. While the doctrine of *respondeat superior* will inevitably draw in the corporate trustee as a codefendant, it is the employment contract itself that determines whether the employer must defend and indemnify the trust officer or obtain insurance that will achieve the same result. If the terms are nonexistent or ambiguous in this regard, the trust officer would be well advised to consult with his or her insurance carrier. Again, little comfort will be found in the terms of personal homeowner and umbrella policies.

External liability. The trustee's liability for injury to nonbeneficiaries occasioned by acts of *ordinary negligence* (committed personally by the trustee or by his agents) is readily insurable, and in most cases its costs are chargeable to the trust estate.[741] For example, the cost of insuring an automobile that comprises a part of the trust estate is properly a trust expense.

§3.5.4.3 Fiduciary Bonds and Sureties (Internal Liability)

In most states, a *testamentary trustee* must execute a bond for the faithful performance of his duties.[742] (However, it is generally within the discretion of the court to require that the trustee of any type of trust give an appropriate bond.)[743] A fiduciary bond is a signed promise to be personally responsible for carrying out certain obligations. It neither increases nor decreases the trustee's general fiduciary responsibility, nor does it affect the trustee's liability. It is essentially a standardized enforcement mechanism. If a trustee who has given bond misdelivers or embezzles, for example, he is subject to suit "on the bond."

---

[741] *See generally* §3.5.2.3 of this handbook (right in equity to exoneration and reimbursement, *i.e.*, indemnity; payment of attorneys' fees).

[742] *See generally* Bogert §151; 76 Am. Jur. 2d *Trusts* §§427–440 (1992). *See also* §3.4.1 of this handbook (appointment). Note, however, that §7-304 of the UPC provides in part that "[a] trustee need not provide bond to secure performance of his duties unless required by the terms of the trust, reasonably requested by a beneficiary or found by the Court to be necessary to protect the interests of the beneficiaries who are not able to protect themselves and whose interests otherwise are not adequately represented." In 2008, Massachusetts adopted its own version of Section 7-304 that actually tracked the traditional default law, namely that "[i]n the case of a testamentary trust, a trustee shall furnish a bond for the performance of the trustee's fiduciary duties and a surety *shall be required* unless waived by the terms of the trust, or found by the court to be not necessary to protect the interests of the beneficiaries." Mass. Gen. Laws ch. 190B, §7-304. As far as distributions to a trustee from an estate are concerned, "if the trust instrument does not excuse the trustee from giving bond, the personal representative may petition the appropriate Court to require that the trustee post bond if he apprehends that distribution might jeopardize the interests of persons who are not able to protect themselves, and he may withhold distribution until the Court has acted." UPC §3-913(b). The citation to the Massachusetts version of this sub-section, which was enacted in 2008, is Mass. Gen. Laws ch. 190B, §3-913(a). The Massachusetts version reads slightly differently as well: "If *a* trust instrument does not excuse the trustee from giving bond, *before distributing to a* [sic] *trustee* a personal representative may petition the appropriate court to require that the trustee post bond *with sureties* if *the personal representative* apprehends that distribution might jeopardize the interests of persons who are not able to protect themselves, and *the personal representative* may withhold distribution until the *court* has acted."

[743] Bogert §151.

For a compilation of state statutes requiring certain trustees, including corporate trustees, to give bond, see Section 151 of Bogert, Trusts and Trustees.

In the case of a contemplated distribution from a probate estate to the trustee of a testamentary or inter vivos trust, the Uniform Probate Code provides that the personal representative in advance of making the distribution may petition the court to require that the trustee post bond if the personal representative "apprehends that distribution might jeopardize the interests of persons who are not able to protect themselves."[744] Distribution may be withheld until the court has acted.[745] The trust instrument may excuse the trustee from giving such a bond.[746]

It may be appropriate to have a surety on a trustee's bond.[747] A surety is either an individual or a company that agrees to be responsible (up to the dollar limits specified in the bond) in the event the beneficiary cannot be made whole in an action against the trustee. Surety fees are a proper trust expense generally charged to trust income. Usually corporate trustees, by statute, need not have sureties on their bonds.[748] Under the Uniform Trust Code, a regulated financial-service institution qualified to do business in a state need not give bond, even if required to do so by the terms of the trust.[749] "When a trustee-beneficiary commits a breach of trust that causes a loss to the trust estate, and the surety on the trustee's bond makes good the loss, the surety is entitled to be subrogated to the rights of the other beneficiaries to a charge on the trustee's interest."[750]

If the same person is both executor and testamentary trustee under a will, the surety on the trustee's bond would not be liable for the person's actions as executor.[751] In some jurisdictions, the surety is entitled to receive an accounting from the trustee.[752] The surety, however, does not have standing to petition for removal of the trustee.[753] Under the Uniform Trust Code, any liability of a resigning trustee or of any sureties on the trustee's bond for acts or omissions of the trustee is not discharged or affected by the trustee's resignation.[754]

In Section 6.1.3.6 of this handbook, we discuss the trustee's duty of impartiality in the context of transactions between trusts sharing the same trustee. Of course, the trustee's duty not to self- deal also would be implicated if a trustee of two separate trusts, say Trust X and Trust Y, were to misappropriate funds from one, say Trust X, and later make restitution with funds misappropriated from Trust Y. The trustee, of course, would be personally liable to

---

[744] UPC §3-913(b).

[745] UPC §3-913(b).

[746] UPC §3-913(b).

[747] *See generally* Bogert §864; 76 Am. Jur. 2d *Trusts* §§427–440 (1992).

[748] *See generally* Bogert §864; 76 Am. Jur. 2d *Trusts* §§427–440 (1992).

[749] UTC §702(c) (available at <http://www.uniformlaws.org/Act.aspx?title=Trust%20Code>).

[750] 4 Scott & Ascher §25.2.7. *Cf.* §8.15.50 of this handbook (subrogation doctrine in the trust context).

[751] 1 Scott & Ascher §2.3.2.2.

[752] Bogert §961.

[753] Bogert §522.

[754] UTC §705(c) (available at <http://www.uniformlaws.org/Act.aspx?title=Trust%20Code>).

make both trusts whole out of his own funds, if necessary, thus rendering any impartiality issues moot.[755] If the trustee, however, were judgment proof, Trust *X* would likely prevail over Trust *Y*, provided the Trust *X* beneficiaries were BFPs, as would likely be the case.[756] In other words, the funds would stay in Trust *X*. As we have noted elsewhere, the transfer of money in satisfaction of an antecedent debt can satisfy the BFP value requirement.[757] In this case, the antecedent debt would be the trustee's equitable obligation to make Trust *X* whole.[758] On the other hand, the beneficiaries of Trust *Y* would be entitled to recover from any surety on the bond of the trustee that might have been issued to the trustee in his capacity as trustee of Trust *X*.[759] "The beneficiaries of . . . [Trust *X*] . . . could have sued on the bond, and when they are paid with the funds of . . . [Trust *Y*] . . ., the beneficiaries of . . . [Trust *Y*] . . . are entitled to be subrogated to their rights on the bond."[760]

For the unrelated topic of corporate trusts established to secure bond investors, see Section 9.31 of this handbook (Corporate Trusts; Trusts to Secure Creditors; The Trust Indenture Act of 1939; Protecting Bondholders).

§3.6 External Inbound Liabilities of Third Parties to the Trustee and the Beneficiaries

It was once true that, in an action at law brought by the trustee against a third party, the beneficiaries were neither necessary nor proper parties. This was because, in an action at law, two or more persons could not join as plaintiffs, unless they had a joint interest because any judgment in their favor would be a judgment for them jointly. Obviously, the trustee and the beneficiaries do not have a joint interest. This difficulty, however, did not exist in the case of a suit in equity; nor does it exist after the merger of law and equity.[1]

External in-bound liability of third parties. As to the world, the trustee is the legal owner of the underlying trust property.[2] "As between the beneficiaries and the outside world, it is the trustee who represents both the trust and the beneficiaries."[3] As such he will have occasion to enter into contracts with third parties for goods and services that are necessary for the proper administration

---

[755] *See generally* §7.2.3 of this handbook (types of equitable relief for breaches of trust).

[756] *See generally* 5 Scott & Ascher §29.7 (Transfer in Restitution for Wrong).

[757] *See generally* §8.15.63 of this handbook (doctrine of bona fide purchase; the BFP).

[758] *Cf.* §2.3 of this handbook (wrongful defunding) ("A reasonable argument can be made that the absent trust property has merely been transformed into another type of property, namely the equitable personal obligation of the wrongdoer").

[759] 5 Scott & Ascher §29.7 (Transfer in Restitution for a Wrong). *See generally* §3.5.4.3 of this handbook (bonds and sureties).

[760] 5 Scott & Ascher §29.7.

§3.6 [1] 5 Scott & Ascher §28.1.2.

[2] *See generally* §3.5.1 of this handbook (nature and extent of the trustee's estate).

[3] 5 Scott & Ascher §28.2.

of the subject property, *e.g.*, hiring a contractor to re-shingle an entrusted apartment building.[4] The trustee also may hold in trust as an investment contractual rights against a third party.[5] In other words, bonds, insurance policies, and other such arrangements that impose enforceable obligations on third parties may constitute a part or all of the underlying trust property itself.[6] In such a situation, the third party who bypasses the trustee and pays the trust beneficiary directly risks having to pay twice.[7] The third party also would be ill-advised to set off a personal claim that the third party has against the beneficiary in lieu of making payments to the trustee, absent special facts.[8]

The trustee being the legal owner of the trust property, it is also possible for third parties to commit torts against the trustee with respect to the subject property.[9] A third party, for example, might without authority occupy the apartment building.[10] Finally, there is the situation where the trustee and the third party conspire to interfere with the beneficiary's equitable property rights.[11] In other words, the third party participates with the trustee in a breach of trust affecting the underlying trust property. The trustee might, for example, in violation of his duty of loyalty transfer the apartment building to someone in City Hall for less than adequate consideration in exchange for a building permit covering work on the trustee's personal residence.[12]

Nature of liability of third parties to the trustee. The right to bring an action in contract or tort against a third party to remedy harm done to the trust

---

[4] *See generally* 5 Scott & Ascher §28.1 (Actions by the Trustee). *Cf.* §7.3.1 of this handbook (trustee's external liability as legal owner in contract to nonbeneficiaries, *i.e.*, to third parties).

[5] *See generally* 5 Scott & Ascher §§28.1, 32.1 (Discharge by Beneficiary of Claim Against Third Person).

[6] *See generally* §9.9.1 of this handbook (life insurance and third party beneficiary contracts generally) and §9.9.4 of this handbook (bank accounts and other such debtor-creditor contractual arrangements are not trusts).

[7] The third party obligor who makes a payment directly to the trust beneficiary instead of to the title-holding trustee, the other party to the contract, does so at his, her, or its peril, unless directed to do so by the trustee. 5 Scott & Ascher §32.1 (Discharge by Beneficiary of Claim Against Third Person). If the beneficiary is not of full age and legal capacity, the third party obligor runs the risk of having to pay twice. 5 Scott & Ascher §32.1 (Discharge by Beneficiary of Claim Against Third Person). There is a similar risk if following the direction were to constitute a knowing participation with the trustee in a breach of trust, or if the trust were a spendthrift trust. 5 Scott & Ascher §32.1 (Discharge by Beneficiary of Claim Against Third Person). It would be risky as well for the third-party obligor to set off its own personal claim against the beneficiary in lieu of making payment to the trustee. *See* 5 Scott & Ascher §32.2 (Set-off of Claim of Third Person Against Beneficiary).

[8] 5 Scott & Ascher §32.2 (Set-off of Claim of Third Person Against Beneficiary).

[9] *See generally* 5 Scott & Ascher §28.1 (Actions by the Trustee). For a discussion of a trustee's outbound liability in tort, *see* §7.3.3 of his handbook (trustee's liability in tort to nonbeneficiaries, *i.e.*, to third parties).

[10] *See, e.g.*, 5 Scott & Ascher §28.1 ("Thus, if a third party disseises the trustee of land or wrongfully takes possession of the land, the trustee can maintain an action to recover possession").

[11] *See generally* 5 Scott & Ascher §28.2 (Actions by the Beneficiaries).

[12] *See also* §5.4.2 of this handbook (rights of the beneficiary as against transferees of the underlying property, including BFPs) and §6.1.3.4 of this handbook (indirect benefit accruing to the trustee [duty of loyalty]).

property is primarily in the trustee.[13] The Restatement (Third) of Trusts is generally in accord.[14] The principle applied even in the case of a feoffee to uses.[15] This right is incident to the trustee's duty to protect and preserve the trust property.[16] So also is the right to bring an action against the state for compensation should some or all of the trust property be taken by eminent domain, or against a third party who has been unjustly enriched at the expense of the trust estate.[17] If the trustee is induced by fraud, duress, undue influence, or mistake to enter into a contract with a third party to the detriment of the trust estate, the right to bring an action to reform or rescind the contract is in the trustee.[18] These rights of action pass by operation of law to the successor trustee.[19] "The policy that forbids assigning tort claims does not apply in the case of a successor trustee."[20] On the other hand, a claim brought by a trustee against a third party that was duly held by a court to be invalid may not be revived and re-litigated by the successor trustee, the matter being *res judicata*.[21] Likewise, if a trustee is barred by a statute of limitations from bringing an action *against a third party* on behalf of the trust estate, so will be his successor.[22] That does not mean, however, that the beneficiary might not have a claim in equity against the trustee, or, if the trustee is deceased, his personal representative, for the trustee's failure to take appropriate action against the third party within the period allowed by law, or even against a successor trustee or his personal representative for the successor's failure to compel the trustee to take appropriate action against the third party.[23]

A word about procedure: Again, the beneficiary would have the right in equity to bring an action *against the trustee* for failing to bring an action against a third party, provided it would have been a reasonable thing for the trustee to do so. "Judicial economy is probably best served if a wrongdoing trustee and the third-party participant in that wrongdoing are joined in one action, but this is not a prerequisite to recovery on behalf of the trust."[24] Still, the beneficiary could not bring an action directly against the third party,[25] except in the following situations:

---

[13] *See generally* 5 Scott & Ascher §28.1 (Actions by the Trustee).

[14] *See* Restatement (Third) of Trusts §107(1).

[15] *See* Chudleigh's Case, 1 Rep. 114 (1589-95). *See generally* §8.15.1 of this handbook (statute of uses).

[16] *See generally* §6.2.1.3 of this handbook (trustee's duty to protect and preserve trust property; to enforce claims; and to defend the trust in actions brought against the trust estate).

[17] *See generally* 5 Scott & Ascher §28.1 (Actions by the Trustee).

[18] 5 Scott & Ascher §28.1.

[19] 5 Scott & Ascher §28.1.3

[20] 5 Scott & Ascher §28.1.3.

[21] 5 Scott & Ascher §28.1.3.

[22] 5 Scott & Ascher §28.2.

[23] 5 Scott & Ascher §28.2.

[24] Restatement (Third) of Trusts §107 cmt. f.

[25] 5 Scott & Ascher §28.2 (Actions by the Beneficiaries).

— The trustee in breach of trust declines to bring an action against the third party[26]
— All trust purposes have been fulfilled and the trustee is a passive trustee[27]
— The trustee has properly assigned the cause of action to the beneficiary[28]
— The beneficiary is entitled immediately and unconditionally to any recovery against the third party[29]
— The third party has knowingly participated with the trustee in a breach of trust that somehow relates to the contract or the third party's tortious activity[30]

In an action in contract or tort *by the trustee* against the third party, the trustee proceeds as if he owned the underlying trust property outright and free of trust. This will usually entail an action at law against the third party. If however, the trustee could have sought equitable relief against the third party, *e.g.*, specific performance of a contract or specific reparation incident to a tort, then he may do so.[31]

Unless there is some dispute between the beneficiaries and the trustee (or among the beneficiaries) that is somehow relevant to the controversy or unless a "complete determination of the controversy" cannot somehow be had without the joinder of the beneficiaries,[32] the beneficiaries need not be made parties to actions brought by the trustee against third parties.[33] Thus, the trustee need not disclose to a third party the terms or even the very existence of the trust, or that he owns the subject property other than outright. The burden, however, would be on the plaintiff to prove that he rightfully holds *in some capacity* the legal title to, or some beneficial interest in, the subject property.[34] Thus, under certain circumstances, at least some portion of the governing trust instrument may have to be put into evidence by the plaintiff (*e.g.*, if the contract or tort action is being brought against the third party by a successor to the inception trustee).[35]

---

[26] 5 Scott & Ascher §28.2.1 (When the Trustee Fails to Sue). The Restatement (Third) of Trusts provides that the beneficiary may bring suit against a third party in the stead of the trustee if the trustee "is unable, unavailable, unsuitable, or improperly failing to protect the beneficiary's interest." *See* Restatement (Third) of Trusts §107(2)(b). The court will generally direct that the proceeds of any recovery be paid to the trustee, or if the trustee is unfit to receive them, to a successor trustee. *See generally* 5 Scott & Ascher §28.2.3.

[27] *See generally* 5 Scott & Ascher §28.2.

[28] *See generally* 5 Scott & Ascher §28.2.

[29] 5 Scott & Ascher §28.2 ("In such a case, the beneficiary can compel the trustee to assign the claim to the beneficiary, so that the beneficiary can enforce it directly"). *See also* Restatement (Third) of Trusts §107(2)(a).

[30] *See generally* 5 Scott & Ascher §28.1.

[31] 5 Scott & Ascher §28.1.

[32] 5 Scott & Ascher §28.1.2.

[33] *Cf.* §5.7 of this handbook (necessary parties to a suit brought by a beneficiary).

[34] *See* Moore v. Bowen, 73 Ga. App. 192, 35 S.E.2d 924 (1945).

[35] *See* Moore v. Bowen, 73 Ga. App. 192, 35 S.E.2d 924 (1945).

Even though the beneficiaries may possess the equitable interest, as the legal owner of the underlying property, the trustee, or a duly appointed successor, in the first instance takes title to the full recovery, absent special facts.[36] The Restatement (Third) of Trusts is generally in accord.[37] Moreover, the third party is generally not obliged to see to it that the trustee applies it for the benefit of the beneficiaries in a way that is consistent with the trustee's fiduciary obligations and the terms of the trust.[38]

If the trustee has a fiduciary duty to sue the third party but refuses to do so, then the beneficiaries may bring an action in equity to compel the trustee to do so.[39] The third party is then made a codefendant in the action, "thus avoiding multiple suits, one in equity by the beneficiaries against the trustee and another at law by the trustee against the third party."[40] Likewise, when a bond issuer defaults and the indenture trustee refuses to initiate a foreclosure action, the bondholders may do so, joining the trustee and issuer as defendants.[41] If a trustee cannot be made subject to the jurisdiction of the court, the beneficiaries may proceed against the third party without him.[42] Fewer than all beneficiaries may take appropriate action against a third party,[43] in which case the common fund doctrine may be applicable.[44] For more on the right and standing of trust beneficiaries to sue third parties, the reader is referred to Section 5.4.1.8 of this handbook.[45] For more on the necessary parties to a suit brought by the beneficiaries, see Section 5.7 of this handbook.

When the third party participates with the trustee in a breach of trust. When a third party participates with a trustee in a breach of trust, such as when the trustee transfers trust property to the third party in breach of trust and the third party knows or should know that the transfer is in breach of trust, the beneficiary may bring an equity action directly against the third party.[46] This is because "[t]he wrong is against the beneficiaries rather than the trustee, as the third party is interfering with the trust relationship."[47] That is not to say that the trustee—assuming the trustee is not time-barred—is foreclosed from bringing

---

[36] 5 Scott & Ascher §28.2.3.

[37] Restatement (Third) of Trusts §107 cmt. e ("A cause of action that may be brought on behalf of the trust is itself a trust asset, and any recovery ordinarily belongs to the trust estate, regardless of who prosecuted the action.").

[38] 5 Scott & Ascher §28.1.2. On the other hand, "[t]he situation is quite different when the suit against the third party is based on a transfer made by the trustee in breach of trust." 5 Scott & Ascher §28.1.2.

[39] *See generally* 5 Scott & Ascher §28.2 (Actions by the Beneficiaries).

[40] 5 Scott & Ascher §28.2.1.

[41] 5 Scott & Ascher §28.2.1. *See also* §9.31 of this handbook (corporate trusts; trusts to secure creditors; The Trust Indenture Act of 1939; protecting bondholders).

[42] 5 Scott & Ascher §28.2.2.

[43] 5 Scott & Ascher §28.2.4.

[44] *See generally* §8.15.13 of this handbook (common fund doctrine).

[45] *See also* §5.7 of this handbook (necessary parties to a suit brought by a beneficiary).

[46] *See generally* 5 Scott & Ascher §28.1.

[47] *See generally* 5 Scott & Ascher §28.1.

his own action against the third party.[48] A tip for the trust litigator: " . . . the fact that the trustee is barred by laches or the statute of limitations from maintaining a suit against the third party does not necessarily mean that the beneficiaries are also time barred."[49] On the other hand, the beneficiary of full age and legal capacity who unreasonably sleeps upon his or her rights after having personally acquired actual knowledge of a third party's knowing participation with the trustee in a breach of trust does risk bumping up against the laches defense.[50]

For more on the beneficiary's rights as against third-party transferees of the trust property, see Section 5.4.2 of this handbook and Section 8.3.6 of this handbook.[51] For more on the beneficiary's rights as against a third party who knowingly participates with the trustee in a breach of trust that does not entail a transfer of trust property to the third party, see Section 7.2.9 of this handbook.

For a discussion of the trustee's external outbound liability as legal owner to nonbeneficiaries, the reader is referred to Section 7.3 of this handbook, and its subsections.

The BFP has no duty to see to the proper application of the purchase price. As we have noted above and elsewhere, a third party who knowingly participates with a trustee in a breach of trust shares with the trustee liability for any loss caused by the breach.[52] Thus, if the trustee transfers trust property in breach of trust to a third-party purchaser who is aware of the breach, the third-party purchaser holds the trust property subject to the terms of the trust.[53] Otherwise, "such a purchaser is liable only if the trustee commits a breach of trust in making the transfer and the purchaser has notice that the trustee is doing so."[54] At common law, however, it was doctrine that even the innocent third-party purchaser had a continuing obligation running to the trust beneficiaries to see to it that the trustee properly applied the purchase price.[55] In the United States, such an innocent third party either by case law or statute has been

---

[48] *See generally* 5 Scott & Ascher §28.1.

[49] 5 Scott & Ascher §28.2. *See, however,* 5 Scott & Ascher §31.1.2 (noting that in the following situation if the trustee is time-barred from bring an action against a third party, the beneficiaries are likely to be as well: " . . . [W]hen the trustee does not intentionally commit a breach of trust in transferring the property and the transferee does not have actual knowledge that the transfer is in breach of trust but is chargeable with notice because he or she might have ascertained that the transfer was in breach of trust").

[50] *See generally* 5 Scott & Ascher §31.1.2. *See generally* §8.15.70 of this handbook (the laches doctrine).

[51] *See* §5.4.2 of this handbook (rights of the beneficiary as against transferees of the underlying property, including BFPs), and §8.3.6 of this handbook (negotiable instruments and the duty of third parties to inquire into the trustee's authority) (in part discussing the difference between a BFP and a holder in due course).

[52] *See* §7.2.9 of this handbook (personal liability of third parties to the beneficiary).

[53] *See* §5.4.2 of this handbook (rights of the beneficiary as against transferees of the underlying property).

[54] 5 Scott & Ascher §30.1 (Misapplication of Payments Made to Trustee).

[55] 5 Scott & Ascher §30.1.

relieved of such an obligation.[56] "In England, the old rule has been repudiated by statute."[57]

Liability of a third party who fails to honor a Uniform Trust Code Section 1013 certification. Again, the trustee of the typical trust will have numerous occasions to transact with third parties in furtherance of the trust's lawful purposes. This is appropriate as the trustee holds the legal title to the trust property and, thus, "as to the world" is its owner. A third party might be selling an asset to, or purchasing an entrusted asset from, the trustee. A third party might be loaning funds to the trustee in his or her fiduciary capacity or borrowing entrusted property from the trustee. A third party might be selling goods and services to the trustee or purchasing goods and services from the trustee, all in furtherance of the trust's lawful purposes. The trustee also may properly retain third-party agents in furtherance of the trust's lawful purposes, such as attorneys-at-law and investment managers.

Section 1013(h) of the Uniform Trust Code provides as follows: "A person . . . [other than a beneficiary] . . . making a demand for the trust instrument in addition to a certification of trust or excerpts is liable for damages if the court determines that the person did not act in good faith in demanding the instrument."

The information in a trustee's UTC Section 1013 certification is limited to the following bits of information:

- That the trust exists and its date of execution
- The identity of the settlors
- The powers of the trustee
- The revocability or irrevocability of the trust and the identity of any persons holding a power to revoke
- The authority of cotrustees to sign or otherwise authenticate and whether all or less than all are required in order to exercise the powers of the trustee
- The trust's taxpayer identification number
- The manner of taking title to trust property
- A statement that the trust has not been revoked, modified, or amended in any manner that would cause the representations contained in the certification to be incorrect

A UTC Section 1013 certification, however, "need not contain the dispositive terms of a trust." Unexplained are the nature of the "liability" and "damages" that are being contemplated by subsection (h). Nor is a definition of "good faith" even supplied in this context. Presumably, the third party is subject to some type of tort liability, but what duty of care is implicated by the "making of a demand for a trust instrument"? According to the section's official commentary, left to "other law" is the issue of "how damages for a bad faith refusal

---

[56] 5 Scott & Ascher §30.1, n.5 (case law) & n.7 (statutes).
[57] 5 Scott & Ascher §30.1 (referring to Trustee Act, 1925, 15 Geo. V., c. 19, §14).

are to be computed." Also unspecified is to whom this demanding "person" would be liable in the face of a judicial determination of liability.

A third party contemplating dealing with a trustee should be able contractually to defang UTC Section 1013(h), assuming it actually has fangs. Time will tell whether it does in the face of all this statutory vagueness.

May UTC Section 1013's general applicability be negated effectively *ab initio* by the trust's terms? In the face of subsection (g) of UTC Section 1013, some settlors may want to consider doing just that so as to better protect the equitable property rights of the beneficiaries of their trusts. Subsection (g) provides as follows: "A person who in good faith enters into a transaction in reliance upon a certification of trust may enforce the transaction *against the trust property* [emphasis supplied] as if the representations contained in the certification were correct." The problem is that the third party who is not furnished a copy of the trust instrument, only a cryptic trustee certification, will not be privy to the UTC Section 1013 negation provision and therefore may well not be bound by its terms.

Statutes of limitation and laches in contract and tort actions by the trustee and/or trust beneficiaries against third parties and in equitable actions by beneficiaries against third parties for participating with the trustee in breaches of trust. As the holder of the legal title to the underlying trust property, the trustee will have occasion to enter into contracts with third parties on behalf of the trust for goods and services. So also are such third parties (and others, as well) duty-bound not to commit torts against the trustee as holder of the legal title. Thus, if a third party breaches a contract with the trustee or commits a tort against the trustee to the detriment of the beneficiaries' equitable interests, the trustee may have a fiduciary duty to bring an action against the third party seeking such relief as will make the beneficiaries whole.[58] "We have also seen that a beneficiary cannot ordinarily maintain such an action, except when the trustee neglects or refuses to sue or is unavailable."[59] As a general rule, if the third party has not participated in some way with the trustee in a breach of trust, the third party will have the benefit of the statutes of limitations that are applicable to legal contract and tort actions generally, as though the trustee had owned the underlying property outright and free of trust.[60] "Indeed, in both England and the United States, it is well settled that when a third person wrongfully takes possession of land or chattels held in trust

---

[58] *See generally* §6.2.1.3 of this handbook (trustee's duty to protect and preserve the trust property).

[59] 5 Scott & Ascher §31.1.1 (Persons Acting Adversely to Trustee). "The theory underlying the beneficiary's right to sue is that the beneficiary can maintain a suit against the trustee to compel the trustee to sue the tortfeasor." 5 Scott & Ascher §31.1.1 (Persons Acting Adversely to Trustee). In an action against the trustee to compel the trustee to take action against the third party, "in order to avoid a multiplicity of suits," the tortfeasor should be joined as a codefendant. 5 Scott & Ascher §31.1.1 (Persons Acting Adversely to Trustee). *See generally* §5.4.1.8 of this handbook (right and standing of beneficiary to proceed in stead of trustee against those with whom the trustee has contracted, against tortfeasors, and against the trustee's agents, *i.e.*, against third parties).

[60] *See generally* 5 Scott & Ascher §31.1.1 "We have seen that the trustee can maintain such an action."

and remains in adverse possession for the period of the statute of limitations, neither the beneficiaries nor the trustee may maintain an action to recover the property or for damages."[61] If the trustee waits too long to bring suit, the beneficiaries will likely still have recourse against the trustee, unless they also have *sat on their hands* for too long, but only after their having received actual knowledge of the trustee's nonfeasance.[62]

On the other hand, if the third party's interactions with the trustee also constitute a knowing participation with the trustee in a breach of trust, then the trust beneficiaries themselves may well not be foreclosed from bringing suit against the third party, the allowable time for bringing an equitable action against the third party likely being governed by different rules, namely, the doctrine of laches as modified by any statute of limitations applicable to breaches of fiduciary duty.[63] To reiterate: What this all means is that the period in which the beneficiaries may bring an action against a third party does not begin to run against them until such time as the beneficiaries, their duly appointed guardians, or what have you, have received actual notice of the third party's participation in the breach of trust.[64] That is likely not to be good news for the third party. Again, just because the trustee is foreclosed by an applicable statute of limitations from bringing an action against a third party does not necessarily mean that the beneficiaries are as well.[65]

---

[61] 5 Scott & Ascher §31.1.1 (Persons Acting Adversely to Trustee).

[62] *See generally* §7.2.10 of this handbook (the laches doctrine as partially codified by a statute of limitations) and §8.15.70 of this handbook (laches doctrine generally).

[63] *See generally* 5 Scott & Ascher §31.1.1 (Persons Acting Adversely to Trustee); §7.1.3 of this handbook (defense of failure of beneficiary to take timely action against trustee) and §7.2.10 of this handbook (limitation of action by beneficiary against trustee (laches and statutes of limitation)) (discussing the laches doctrine and statutes of limitations that partially codify the doctrine). *See also* 5 Scott & Ascher §31.1.2 (Transferees of Trust Property).

[64] Note, however, that if the third party did not participate with the trustee in a breach of trust, then if the trustee is time-barred from bringing an action against the third party, the trust beneficiaries, including the unborn and unascertained remaindermen, are likely to be as well. This is because legal title is lodged in the trustee. In this regard, *see generally* §8.27 of this handbook (what is the difference between a legal life estate and an equitable life estate under a trust?) (noting that whether an interest is legal or equitable has practical consequences for its owner, such as in the context of establishing or preventing adverse possession by a third party).

[65] *See generally* 5 Scott & Ascher §31.1 (Rights of Beneficiaries When Trustee is Barred by Laches or Statute of Limitations).

CHAPTER 4

Interests Remaining with the Settlor

§4.1　Interests and Powers Remaining with the Settlor by Operation of Law

In the case of an irrevocable trust where the settlor has expressly reserved no beneficial interest and under which the settlor possesses no powers,[1] whether a vested equitable reversionary interest nonetheless attaches to the settlor by operation of law is a question of more than academic interest, particularly in the charitable context where property worth billions of dollars is currently held in trust. If some property rights remain back with the settlor at the time property is transferred in trust, then the settlor may have standing to compel the trustee to carry out the terms of the trust. Thus, for example, the trustee of a college endowment fund[2] could be accountable not only to the attorney general but also to benefactors.

Presently there is much authority to the effect that the settlor of such a trust retains no interest that would allow him or her to bring an action against the trustee for breach of trust,[3] such as the trustee's colluding with all the beneficiaries to subvert the trust's material purposes.[4] Nor does the settlor's executor, administrator, or personal representative retain such an interest.[5] "A trustee of a private trust is under a duty to follow the instructions of the settlor with regard to implementation of the terms of the trust, but only the beneficiary, not the settlor, may enforce this duty."[6]

However, some case law and commentary suggest that the settlor may not be entirely out of the picture *e.g.*, a spendthrift trust may not be terminated without the settlor's consent.[7]

---

§4.1 [1] In derogation of traditional trust law, §602(a) of the UTC provides that a trust is revocable by the settlor unless the terms of the trust provide otherwise. *See generally* Bogert §42; §8.2.2 of this handbook. It is traditional trust law that the express reservation of administrative powers, such as the power to direct investments or remove trustees, alone would afford the settlor standing to seek the trust's judicial enforcement. *See* Bogert §42.

[2] The Uniform Prudent Management of Institutional Funds Act (UPMIFA) §2(2), which covers charitable corporations as well as charitable trusts, defines an endowment fund as "an institutional fund or part thereof that, under the terms of a gift instrument, is not wholly expendable by the institution on a current basis." The term "does not include assets that an institution designates as an endowment fund for its own use."

[3] *See, e.g.,* 4 Scott & Ascher §24.4.1; 3 Scott on Trusts §200.1; Bogert §42; Russell v. Yale Univ., 54 Conn. App. 573, 737 A.2d 941 (Conn. App. 1999) (holding that *in the absence of an expressly reserved right to do so*, neither the settlor of a charitable trust nor the settlor's heir would have standing to bring an action against the trustee to enforce the terms of the trust).

[4] *See, e.g.,* 5 Scott & Ascher §34.6 (Conveyance by Trustee to or at the Direction of the Beneficiaries).

[5] 4 Scott & Ascher §24.4.1.

[6] Bogert §42.

[7] *See* 4 Scott & Ascher §24.4.1 n.2. *See, e.g.,* Carr v. Carr, 171 N.W. 785 (Iowa 1919) (holding that the donor of a trust has such interest therein as to entitle him to maintain a suit in equity to compel the carrying out of the terms thereof); 2A Scott on Trusts §151 ("It is held that even though the trust is a spendthrift trust, it can be terminated by the beneficiaries and the settlor if they all consent and are under no disability."); 4 Scott on Trusts §340 ("It is clear, therefore, that in New York the trust can be terminated with the consent of the settlor and all the beneficiaries, even

Moreover, some states have enacted legislation that directly addresses the issue.[8]

The Uniform Trust Code has gone a long way toward putting the settlor back in the picture. It provides, for example, that the settlor of a charitable trust, among others, may maintain a proceeding to enforce the trust.[9] The Uniform Prudent Management of Institutional Funds Act (UPMIFA), which covers charitable corporations as well as charitable trusts, does not entirely exclude the donor from the picture, although the fiduciary and the state attorney general are clearly the senior partners in the relationship.[10] Of course, in any state, the settlor with expressly retained interests or powers may bring an enforcement action against the trustee.[11]

---

though a beneficiary may have an interest in the income that cannot be assigned by him."); Bogert §1006 n.13 and accompanying text. *See generally* Gaubatz, *Grantor Enforcement of Trusts: Standing in One Private Law Setting,* 62 N.C. L. Rev. 905, 941 (1984); Note, *Right of a Settlor to Enforce a Private Trust,* 62 Harv. L. Rev. 1370 (1949); Rounds, *Social Investing, IOLTA and the Law of Trusts: The Settlor's Case Against the Political Use of Charitable and Client Funds,* 22 Loy. U. Chi. L.J. 163 (1990); Reid, Mureiko, & Mikeska, *Privilege and Confidentiality Issues When a Lawyer Represents a Fiduciary,* 30 Real Prop. Prob. & Tr. J. 542, 588 (1966); Langbein, *The Contractarian Basis of the Law of Trusts,* 105 Yale L.J. 625, 664 (1995); Bogert §871 (discussing when an action involving a trust may require notice to the settlor). *See* UTC §411 (available at <http://www.uniformlaws.org/Act. aspx?title=Trust%20Code>) ("A noncharitable irrevocable trust may be modified or terminated upon consent of the settlor and all beneficiaries even if the modification or termination is inconsistent with a material purpose of the trust"). *See also* UTC §706 (granting settlor standing to petition for removal of trustee); UTC §405(c) (granting settlor standing to maintain a proceeding to enforce a charitable trust); UTC §410b (granting the settlor standing to bring a *cy pres* petition). In Alaska, on petition of a settlor, a court may modify or terminate an irrevocable trust if all the beneficiaries consent and if continuation of the trust on the existing terms of the trust is not necessary to further a material purpose of the trust. Alaska Stat. §13.36.360. The presence of a spendthrift clause may constitute such a material purpose but is not presumed to do so. Alaska Stat. §13.36.360. *See generally* §8.2.2 of this handbook (when the trust may be modified or terminated) and §8.15.7 of this handbook (the *Claflin* doctrine). *But see* Mass. Gen. Laws ch. 214, §10B (providing that upon a petition commenced *after the death of the donor* for the application of *cy pres* to similar public charitable purposes of a gift for a public charitable purpose which has become impossible or impracticable of fulfillment, the court may exercise jurisdiction without requiring that the heirs or next of kin of the donor or others who would be entitled to take upon failure of any charitable gift be joined as parties).

[8] In 1990, California enacted legislation granting the settlor of an irrevocable living trust the right to petition to have the trustee removed for cause. Cal. Prob. Code §15642(a) (West 1991). California also provides for settlor involvement in the modification or termination of irrevocable trusts. Cal. Prob. Code §15404.

[9] UTC §405(c) (available at <http://www.uniformlaws.org/Act.aspx?title=Trust%20Code>). *Cf.* Uniform Management of Institutional Funds Act (UMIFA) §7 (providing that, "[w]ith the written consent of the donor, the governing board may release, in whole or in part, a restriction imposed by the applicable gift instrument on the use or investment of an institutional fund"). *But see* Carl J. Herzog Found., Inc. v. University of Bridgeport, 243 Conn. 1, 699 A.2d 995 (1997) (holding that §7 does not bestow standing on benefactor to enforce restriction).

[10] *See, e.g.,* Unif. Prudent Management Inst. Funds Act §6 (Release or Modification of Restrictions on Management, Investment, or Purpose).

[11] *See* Bogert §§42, 415.

China is another story. Under the trust code of the People's Republic of China, which was enacted on April 28, 2001, the settlor remains very much in the picture, even under the default law:[12]

> For Chinese scholars, the very notion of cutting off settlors from their own trusts is perverse. As Zhong Ruidong and Chen Xiangcong put it: "The trust relationship, after all, is established by the settlor." Moreover, the American approach misses another obvious point—the "constructive role" of settlors in enforcing their own trusts. Who better than settlors can determine whether the trust purposes, beneficiary rights, and trustee duties they themselves prescribed are "conscientiously fulfilled?" Yet, rather than promoting this beneficial, even indispensable, function of settlors, American trust law actually impedes it.[13]

§4.1.1 The Reversionary Interest

A reversion is never . . . created by deed or writing, but arises from construction of law; a remainder can never be limited, unless by either deed or devise. But both are equally transferable, when actually vested, being both estates in praesenti, though taking effect in futuro.[14]

If the settlor or the settlor's probate estate[15] is entitled by operation of law, *i.e.*, pursuant to the imposition of a resulting trust,[16] to a return of the trust property should the trust fail, the settlor possesses an equitable reversionary interest.[17] Such an interest is a property right. Moreover, this right is vested in the settlor from the trust's inception whether or not the trust ever does fail.[18] Reversionary interests are always vested. Thus the settlor of an ongoing express trust has a right *ab initio* to assign the equitable reversion to the trustee, to another beneficiary, or to a third party, who could even be the trustee of another express trust.[19] In other words, an equitable reversion incident to one express trust may be the *res* of another express trust. Whether the reversion ever

---

[12] Xintuo Fa [Trust Law] (promulgated by the Standing Comm. Nat'l People's Cong., Apr. 28, 2001, effective Oct. 1, 2001).

[13] Frances H. Foster, *American Trust Law in a Chinese Mirror*, 94 Minn. L. Rev. 602, 639 (2010). *See generally* §8.12 of this handbook (the idiosyncrasies of the Chinese Trust Law 2001).

[14] Blackstone's Commentaries, Book II, 175.

[15] *See generally* W. W. Allen, Annot., *Time of ascertainment of settlor's heirs and distributees who take on failure of trust*, 27 A.L.R.2d 691 (1953).

[16] *See* §4.1.1.1 of this handbook (defining and discussing the resulting trust).

[17] Thus, settlors or their successors "may attack the validity of the trust and seek recovery of the trust property if, for example, the rules regarding perpetuities or suspension of the power of alienation are violated by the terms of the trust." Bogert §42.

[18] Lewin ¶ 5-66 (England).

[19] *See, e.g.*, New England Trust Co. v. Sanger, 337 Mass. 342, 348–349, 149 N.E.2d 598, 602 (1958) (involving the effective funding of one express trust with the equitable reversion incident to another express trust). *See also* the introductory quotation at the beginning of this section, §4.1.1 of this handbook.

blossoms or transforms into the proceeds of an actual resulting trust of income or of principal, or of both, is another matter.[20]

In the United States, such reversionary interests are generally exempt from the Rule against Perpetuities.[21] In England, on the other hand, a reversion upon the happening of a condition subsequent now implicates the Rule.[22] The Rule also is implicated when the duration of an English charitable trust is subject to a contingency-based limitation, *e.g.*, as long as a certain state of affairs continues.[23] Thus, an equitable reversion upon the failure of an English charitable trust would be unenforceable if the interest were to become possessory beyond the period of the Rule.[24] *Cy pres* would then have to be applied.[25]

We should note here that in response to concerns "about the clogging of title and other administrative problems caused by remote default provisions upon failure of a charitable purpose,"[26] the Uniform Trust Code would sharply curtail the ability of a settlor to create a charitable trust whose property would revert to the settlor's personal representative, *i.e.*, the settlor's probate estate, upon the accomplishment of that purpose (or upon the impossibility of its fulfillment), even when the purpose is a limited one.[27] This is a topic we take up in Section 9.4.3 of this handbook as part of our coverage of the *cy pres* doctrine.

The Restatement (Third) of Property's failure to appreciate the intersection of resulting trust procedural doctrine and equitable future interest property doctrine comes through loud and clear when it purports to reform in one fell swoop the substantive law of future property interests:

> The reason for categorizing future interests as either reversions or remainders is that the legal profession, especially in describing future interests created in a trust, is accustomed to referring to a future interest retained by a transferor as a 'reversion' and a future interest created in a transferee as a "remainder." In addition, the Restatement Third of Trusts refers to a resulting trust as a "reversionary, equitable interest" . . . and the Restatement Third of Restitution and Unjust Enrichment variously refer to property as "reverting" or "reverting back" to the transferor or the transferor's estate or successors in interest in certain cases.[28]

Where to begin? First, a resulting trust is not a property interest. It is an equitable procedural device for moving title from the express trustee to the possessor of the equitable reversion, as we explain in Section 4.1.1.1 of this handbook. The resulting trust, itself, is not the reversion.

---

[20] *See generally* §4.1.1.1 of this handbook (resulting trusts of income and principal).

[21] 6 Scott & Ascher §39.7.2.

[22] *See generally* 6 Scott & Ascher §39.7.2

[23] 6 Scott & Ascher §39.7.3 (Limitations).

[24] *See generally* 6 Scott & Ascher §39.7.2

[25] *See generally* §9.4.3 of this handbook (the *cy pres* doctrine).

[26] UTC §413 cmt. (available at <http://www.uniformlaws.org/Act.aspx?title=Trust%20 Code>).

[27] UTC §413 (available at <http://www.uniformlaws.org/Act.aspx?title=Trust%20Code>). *See generally* 6 Scott & Ascher §39.5.2.

[28] Restatement (Third) of Property (Wills and Other Donative Transfers) §25.2, cmt. e.

Second, an equitable future interest is not created "in a trust." It is not the entrusted property title to which is in the trustee. An equitable future property interest is property that is created incident to the trust relationship itself. A share of a trusteed mutual fund is an equitable property interest.[29] Legal title to the fund itself is in the trustees.[30]

Third, the always-vested equitable reversion and the sometimes-vested equitable remainder are critically different property concepts, largely because of the former's inconvenient linkage with the resulting trust. In other words, far more is keeping the equitable reversion and the equitable remainder apart than just the collective stodginess of unenlightened trust lawyers.

Could it be that equitable future interests are not even intended to be covered in the Restatement (Third) of Property? It is hard to tell, but it would not be surprising if they were beyond its contemplated scope as coverage of equitable property interests years ago "dropped out" of the standard U.S. law school curriculum and soon thereafter "became unfamiliar to American lawyers, including law professors."[31] But if equitable future property interests are intended to be covered in the Restatement (Third), then its earnest obsession with simplification and with purging the law of future interests of its few remaining feudal vestiges may be doing more harm than good.[32] This is because the cleansing exercise perversely may be mucking up, and in the process profoundly obfuscating, critical and still-prevailing differences between the two foundational *property* regimes of the Anglo-American legal tradition, the legal and the equitable. Here is one such difference: In the case of a nonpossessory *legal* reversion, a piece of the full legal title to the subject property is in the holder of the reversion.[33] In the case of a nonpossessory equitable reversion, full legal title to the subject property is in the express trustee, who may pass good title to a BFP (good faith purchaser for value) in derogation of the equitable reversion.[34]

---

[29] *See generally* Charles E. Rounds, Jr. & Andreas Dehio, *Publicly-Traded Open End Mutual Funds in Common Law and Civil Law Jurisdictions: A Comparison of Legal Structures*, 3 N.Y.U J. L & Bus. 473, 476 (2007).

[30] *See generally* Charles E. Rounds, Jr. & Andreas Dehio, *Publicly-Traded Open End Mutual Funds in Common Law and Civil Law Jurisdictions: A Comparison of Legal Structures*, 3 N.Y.U J. L & Bus. 473 (2007).

[31] Restatement (Third) of Restitution and Unjust Enrichment §1, Reporter's Note e.

[32] Restatement (Third) of Property (Wills and Other Donative Transfers), ch. 25, Introductory Note: "The system of classification of present and future interests originated in feudal patterns of land holding and governmental finance that has been obsolete for centuries. This Restatement simplifies classification for its present purposes. The principal function of classification today is descriptive—a short-hand way of describing an interest that has specific characteristics."

[33] *See generally* Cornelius J. Moynihan, Introduction to the Law of Real Property 104 (2d ed. 1988) (the quantum theory of legal estates); §8.27 of this handbook (the legal versus the equitable estate).

[34] *See generally* §8.15.63 of this handbook (the BFP).

Here is another critical difference: A legal remainder must be supported by a prior estate, such as a legal life estate.[35] This is not true in the case of an equitable quasi-remainder.[36]

Let us assume that equitable reversions and remainders are, for whatever reason, simply not subjects of the Restatement (Third) of Property, at least not directly. In other words, on its face, Section 25.2, which compares and contrasts the reversion and the remainder, is only about legal interests. If one assumes that the adjective "legal" in the commentary to Section 25.2 means "as opposed to equitable," then the assertion that no *legal* consequences in property law flow from maintaining the reversion and remainder as separate future interest classifications would seem to confirm that their equitable counterparts, *particularly the property attributes of those counterparts*, are the domain of some other restatement, one that has yet to see the light of day. This is also supported by the absence of a trust fact pattern in any of the twelve illustrations in the Section 25.2 commentary. But as "Equity follows the law," equity's property regime is eventually bound to feel some ripple effects of all this slapdash "law" reform.[37]

Congress, for its purposes, has had no problem conflating the equitable reversion and equitable remainder. The term *reversionary interest* as employed in Section 2037(a)(2) of the Internal Revenue Code encompasses both equitable reversions[38] and equitable remainders expressly reserved by settlors.[39] Under Section 2037(a)(2), the value of property[40] transferred by a decedent during the decedent's lifetime is includible for federal estate tax computation purposes in the gross estate of the decedent, provided *both* of the following conditions are met:

- Possession or enjoyment of the property can be obtained only by surviving the decedent.[41]
- The decedent had a reversionary interest in the property, the value of which immediately before death exceeded 5 percent of the value of such property.[42]

---

[35] John Chipman Gray, The Rule Against Perpetuities §8 (4th ed. 1942) ("The particular estate and the remainders form an unbroken series. Each remainder is said to be supported by the preceding estates.").

[36] John Chipman Gray, The Rule Against Perpetuities §324 (4th ed. 1942) (Quasi Remainders).

[37] *See generally* §8.12 of this handbook (equity's maxims generally); Charles E. Rounds, Jr., *Proponents of Extracting Slavery Reparations from Private Interests Must Contend with Equity's Maxims*, 42 U. Tol. L. Rev. 673, 691–692 (2011) (explaining the jurisdictional underpinnings of the specific maxim "Equity follows the law").

[38] *See generally* §4.1.1.1 of this handbook (discussing in part the resulting trust).

[39] *See generally* §8.2.1.3 of this handbook (the vesting of interests under trusts), 8.30 of this handbook (the differences between a vested equitable remainder subject to divestment and a vested (transmissible) contingent equitable remainder), and §8.15.2 of this handbook (doctrine of worthier title).

[40] The value may have to be reduced by the value of one or more intervening interests. *See, e.g.,* Estate of Tarver v. Comm'r, 255 F.2d 913 (1958).

[41] I.R.C. §2037(a)(1).

[42] I.R.C. §2037(a)(2).

For purposes of Section 2037, the term *reversionary* interest in part includes a possibility that property transferred by the decedent "may return to him or his estate."[43] It is this language that picks up contingent remainders expressly reserved by settlors,[44] as well as reversions.

Finally, none of this should be confused with the situation where a settlor impresses a trust on a partial *legal* interest, such as on a *legal* term of years, but reserves the *legal* reversion. "If the subject matter of a trust was a partial interest in certain property (for example, . . . [a *legal*] . . . term of years), and consequently the settlor retained a . . . [*legal*] . . . reversion, the settlor may secure protection of the . . . [*legal*] . . . reversionary interest."[45]

§4.1.1.1 The Resulting Trust and the Equitable Reversionary Interest: A General Discussion

The default or last-resort character of the resulting trust is illustrated by its frequent avoidance through application of constructional rules, such as that providing for an acceleration of remainders . . . ; or even occasionally by finding gifts by implication.[46]

[A] contract, unlike a trust for a limited purpose, is not capable of occasioning a resulting trust.[47]

The rationale for the resulting trust. The governing instrument of a trust—if properly drawn—designates those who take title to the subject property once the trust terminates either intentionally or unintentionally. In the absence of such a designation, or if the anticipated takers are not then in existence, the beneficial interest does not usually accrue to the trustee, although there are some exceptions. To put it another way, if an express trust is fully performed without exhausting the trust estate or fails, the trustee may not walk away with the trust property,[48] unless there is properly admissible evidence that the settlor intended otherwise or the default law so provides.[49] This is because the settlor never intended to make a gift of the underlying property to the trustee personally.[50] The property reverts to the settlor, or passes to the settlor's probate estate if the settlor is deceased at the time the trust terminates. It is said the property passes "upon a resulting trust."

---

[43] I.R.C. §2037(b)(1).

[44] Estate of Allen v. United States, 558 F.2d 14 (Ct. Cl. 1977).

[45] Bogert §42.

[46] Restatement (Third) of Trusts, Reporter's Notes on §7 cmt. a. *See generally* §8.15.47 of this handbook (acceleration of vested and contingent equitable remainders).

[47] Lewin ¶ 8-52 (England).

[48] *See generally* 6 Scott & Ascher §§42.1.1 (When Trust Instrument Does Not Dispose of Entire Beneficial Interest), 41.1.1 (Ways in Which an Express Trust Can Fail).

[49] *See generally* 6 Scott & Ascher §41.2 (Rebutting the Resulting Trust).

[50] *See generally* Lewin ¶ 7-02 (England); 6 Scott & Ascher §40.1.1 (Distinguishing Resulting Trusts from Express Trusts) (U.S.).

A resulting trustee who wrongfully keeps the subject property for himself is unjustly enriched.[51] The procedural equitable remedy might well be his judicial conversion into a constructive trustee;[52] the substantive equitable remedy would likely be a specific enforcement or restitution order.[53]

Triggering events. A resulting trust is the equitable mechanism that gets the legal title of the balance of the trust estate from the trustee of an express trust back into the hands of the settlor or the settlor's probate estate[54] when the trust fails or has been fully performed.[55] In England, a resulting trust is imposed in the following situations:

- Trusts that fail at the outset for perpetuity, uncertainty, lapse, or some other reason;[56]
- Trusts to be declared in the future;[57]
- Events not provided for;[58]
- Surplus assets and surplus income;[59]
- Failure of marriage settlement;[60]
- Disclaimer, release or surrender by beneficiary;[61] and
- Trust declared as part of estate or fund.[62]

The United States differs only at the margins as to what events can trigger the imposition of a resulting trust. Here is one commentator's list:

- Failure to name a beneficiary;[63]
- Beneficiary nonexistent;[64]

---

[51] *See generally* §8.15.78 of this handbook (unjust enrichment). *See also* Restatement of Restitution §160 cmt. b (constructive trust and resulting trust).

[52] *See generally* §7.2.3.1.6 of this handbook (the constructive trust as a procedural equitable remedy).

[53] *See generally* §7.2.3.4 of this handbook (the specific enforcement order as a substantive equitable remedy) and §7.2.3.3 of this handbook (the restitution order as a substantive equitable remedy).

[54] Lewin ¶8-19 (England); 6 Scott & Ascher §40.1.1 (U.S.).

[55] Lewin ¶8-02.

[56] Lewin ¶8-04 (England). *See also* 6 Scott & Ascher §41.1.1 (U.S.).

[57] Lewin ¶8-05.

[58] Lewin ¶8-06 (England). *See also* 6 Scott & Ascher §§41.3–41.12.2 (U.S.).

[59] Lewin ¶8-07 (England). *See also* 6 Scott & Ascher §42.1.1 (U.S.). *See generally* §9.31 of this handbook (noting that with respect to property held in trust to secure the contractual rights of bondholders, any surplus reverts upon a resulting trust back to the issuer of the bonds). *See also* Bogert §250 (U.S.) (confirming that any entrusted surplus security held in a corporate trust would become the subject of a resulting trust, unless the governing trust indenture were to provide otherwise).

[60] Lewin ¶8-09 (England). *See generally* §9.30 of this handbook (the English marriage settlement).

[61] Lewin ¶8-11 (England). *See also* 6 Scott & Ascher §41.2.1 (U.S.).

[62] Lewin ¶8-12 (England).

[63] 6 Scott & Ascher §41.1.1 (U.S.).

[64] 6 Scott & Ascher §41.1.1 (U.S.).

- Beneficiary unascertainable;[65]
- Named beneficiary of testamentary trust predeceases testator causing a lapse;[66]
- Failure to designate beneficiary properly;[67]
- Beneficiary incapable of taking beneficial interest;[68]
- Indefiniteness of beneficiaries;[69]
- Indefiniteness of trust purposes;[70]
- Beneficiary renounces beneficial interest;[71]
- Disposition invalid for illegality;[72]
- Trust imposed on only a part of the trust res;[73]
- Trust imposed on all the res for a limited period only; and[74]
- Entire res not needed to accomplish the trust's purposes (surplus).[75]

Action of trustee generally not a triggering event. A breach of a trust generally does not cause its failure and the imposition of a resulting trust,[76] nor would the refusal of the trustee of a discretionary trust to consider in good faith whether or not to distribute income and/or principal.[77]

When a testamentary trust fails *ab initio*. If a *testamentary trust* fails at the outset, however, a resulting trust is not imposed, unless there has been a vesting of legal title to the subject property in the trustee.[78] The failed legacy or devise merely lapses.[79]

---

[65] 6 Scott & Ascher §41.1.1 (U.S.).

[66] 6 Scott & Ascher §41.1.1 (U.S.).

[67] 6 Scott & Ascher §41.1.1 (U.S.).

[68] 6 Scott & Ascher §41.1.1 (U.S.).

[69] 6 Scott & Ascher §41.1.1 (U.S.).

[70] 6 Scott & Ascher §41.1.1 (U.S.).

[71] 6 Scott & Ascher §41.1.1 (U.S.).

[72] 6 Scott & Ascher §41.1.1 (U.S.).

[73] 6 Scott & Ascher §42.1.1 (U.S.).

[74] 6 Scott & Ascher §42.1.1 (U.S.).

[75] 6 Scott & Ascher §42.1.2 (U.S.).

[76] If a trust ought not to fail for want of a trustee, it certainly ought not to fail on account of a breach of trust, unless the terms of the trust so provide. *See* 6 Scott & Ascher §39.7.1 (No Reverter for Breach of Charitable Trust).

[77] In the event of a trustee's failure to exercise such a discretionary authority, the court may decline to compel the trustee to exercise the authority, appoint a special trustee solely for the purpose of exercising the authority, or exercise the authority itself. The court also might order that the subject property be distributed in equal shares to the members of the class of permissible beneficiaries. *See generally* 6 Scott & Ascher §41.4 (Trust for Members of Definite Class); §3.5.3.2(a) of this handbook (the discretionary trust). In the face of a trustee's failure to exercise discretionary authority to apply income and/or principal for the benefit of the "relatives" of a designated individual, the court might order that the subject property be distributed to those who would be the individual's heirs at law. *See generally* 6 Scott & Ascher §41.5 (Trust for Relatives). Finally, the court may remove the trustee and appoint a suitable successor. *See generally* §7.2.3.6 of this handbook (removal).

[78] 6 Scott & Ascher §41.1.

[79] *See generally* §8.15.55 of this handbook (lapse and antilapse).

The partial failure of a trust. A trust's partial failure can trigger a resulting trust with respect to some but not all of the trust estate. There is the partial vertical failure and the partial horizontal failure.[80] An example of a partial vertical failure would be two sub-trusts, one of which lacks beneficiaries. The property in the failed sub-trust passes upon a resulting trust to the settlor or the settlor's probate estate, *together with the income that is thrown off by that property*.[81] The other sub-trust continues. An example of a partial horizontal failure would be a failed disposition of income but not of principal, or of principal but not of income.[82]

Some fact patterns. Here are three noncharitable trust fact patterns that do implicate the resulting trust. Only in the third would the subject property almost certainly return to the settlor or the settlor's probate estate upon a resulting trust.[83] In the first two, imposition of a resulting trust is just one of several possible outcomes.

Situation #1:
    A entrusts property to *B* for *C* in perpetuity. *C* subsequently dies.

Situation #2:
    A entrusts property to *B* for *C* for life, then to *D*. *C* disclaims at the outset, or renounces in mid-course, the equitable interest.

Situation #3:
    A entrusts property to *B* for *C* for life. *C* subsequently dies. There is no *D*.[84]

In Situation #1, there might well not be a reversion.[85] *C* arguably was the sole beneficiary, the one with the entire equitable interest other than the equitable right of reverter.[86] If that is the case, then upon *C*'s death, the trust property would become an asset of *C*'s probate estate.[87] The critical wording is

---

[80] 6 Scott & Ascher §41.1.2 (Partial Failure of Trust).

[81] 6 Scott & Ascher §41.1.2 (Partial Failure of Trust).

[82] 6 Scott & Ascher §41.1.2 (Partial Failure of Trust).

[83] *See generally* 6 Scott & Ascher §42.1.1 (When Trust Instrument Does Not Dispose of Entire Beneficial Interest).

[84] There could be any number of reasons why there is no remainderman, that is to say why there is no *D*. They range from a failure of the settlor to designate a remainderman in the terms of the trust to the creation of an equitable remainder that violates the rule against perpetuities. *See generally* 6 Scott & Ascher §41.1.1.

[85] *See generally* 6 Scott & Ascher §42.1.1 ("One must bear in mind, however, that although the terms of the trust provide for the payment of income to a designated beneficiary and fail to make any express provision with respect to the principal, the instrument may nevertheless be interpreted as giving the entire beneficial interest to the designated beneficiary, and not merely a life interest").

[86] Restatement (Third) of Trusts §49 cmt. c. *See generally* 3 Scott & Ascher §13.2.2.

[87] Restatement (Third) of Trusts §55.

in perpetuity.[88] Had *A* assigned the nonpossessory equitable reversionary interest to *C* and had *C* died intestate and without heirs at law, then the law is unsettled as to whether the subject property would escheat to the state or revert upon a resulting trust to the settlor (or to the settlor's probate estate), notwithstanding the assignment.[89]

In Situation #2, a resulting trust is not necessarily imposed upon the income stream until such time as *C* actually does die.[90] It all depends upon what the settlor would have wanted, or most likely would have wanted.[91] If *D*'s equitable remainder interest is indefeasibly vested, then there likely would be an immediate acceleration to *D*.[92] The topic of acceleration is further discussed in Section 8.15.47 of this handbook.[93] If acceleration is not an option, then the income stream is diverted to the presumptive remaindermen until such time as *C* actually does die; income is accumulated for eventual payment to the actual remaindermen; or a resulting trust is imposed upon the income stream until such time as *C* actually does die.[94] The troublesome wording in the terms of the trust that all parties, including the court, must contend with is *C for life*.

Situation #3 is a common resulting trust fact pattern. There almost certainly would be an equitable reversion upon the death of *C*.[95] If pursuant to the terms of an express trust the income interest is for the life of the beneficiary only[96] (or for a term of years) and there is no other disposition of the property upon the beneficiary's death (or expiration of the term of years), then the trust property returns free of trust to the settlor or the settlor's probate estate upon a resulting trust, which is the equitable equivalent of a legal reversion.[97] Thus it cannot be said that *C* was the sole beneficiary,[98] unless *C* also was the settlor, in which case there might well have been a state of merger *ab initio*.[99] In other words, there would never have been a trust in the first place.[100]

The procedural mechanics. Here are the mechanics of imposing a resulting trust. In response to the petition or complaint of someone with a property or fiduciary interest in the entrusted property, the court in the exercise of its equitable powers orders that the trustee hold the property "upon a

---

[88] A provision for the benefit of C only that contained no time limitation whatsoever might well bring about the same result, even in the absence of the words "in perpetuity" or their equivalent.

[89] *See generally* 6 Scott & Ascher §41.1.4 (When Settlor Disposes of Entire Beneficial Interest).

[90] 6 Scott & Ascher §42.1.2 (When There Is or Will Be a Surplus).

[91] 6 Scott & Ascher §41.2.1 (Acceleration).

[92] 6 Scott & Ascher §41.2.1 (Acceleration). *See also* §8.2.1.3 of this handbook (discussing the concept of vesting in the trust context).

[93] *See also* 6 Scott & Ascher §41.1.2.

[94] 6 Scott & Ascher §41.2.1 (Acceleration).

[95] *See generally* 3 Scott & Ascher §13.2.2.

[96] Restatement (Third) of Trusts §49 cmt. c.

[97] 5 Scott on Trusts §411. *See also* National Shawmut Bank v. Joy, 315 Mass. 457, 463, 53 N.E.2d 113, 119 (1944).

[98] 3 Scott & Ascher §13.2.2.

[99] *See generally* §8.7 of this handbook (merger).

[100] *See generally* §8.7 of this handbook (merger).

resulting trust" for the benefit of the settlor or the settlor's probate estate (or perhaps in the case of a valid assignment, for the benefit of the settlor's assignees); instructs the trustee as to who the rightful takers of the property are; and then orders that the legal title to the property be transferred to them. Once legal title duly leaves the trustee, the resulting trust terminates.[101] Because a resulting trust involves a fiduciary relationship between the trustee and the reversionary beneficiaries, the reversionary beneficiary who unreasonably delays in bringing an action against the trustee for breach of fiduciary duty must contend with the laches doctrine.[102] Laches is generally covered in Sections 7.2.10 of this handbook and 8.15.70 of this handbook.

The statute of frauds and the resulting trust. The resulting trust, as is also the case with the constructive trust, is exempt from the statute of frauds applicable to trusts, a topic we cover in Section 8.15.5 of this handbook.

The beneficiary of a resulting trust is the settlor. The beneficiary of a resulting trust is the settlor of the terminated express trust. If there are multiple settlors, each takes upon the imposition of a resulting trust a share of the trust estate that is proportional to his or her contribution.[103] In the case of the imposition of a resulting trust, if the settlor had died intestate without heirs at law, any personal property would pass upon a resulting trust to the Crown or the State as *bona vacantia*.[104] Otherwise, the property would follow the fortunes of the residue of the settlor's probate estate, or pass by the laws of intestate succession in the event that the trust's failure had resulted in the failure (lapse) of the will's residuary disposition as well.[105] An equitable reversion is fully vested and assignable *ab initio*.[106] Thus the settlor of an ongoing express trust could actually assign the equitable reversion to the trustee of another express trust.[107]

The settlor of a trust is not always the one designated as such in the documentation. An outstanding equitable reversionary interest is a beneficial interest in the trust property that remains back with the settlor. It is superior to the trustee's legal interest[108] and may become possessory by operation of law

---

[101] 6 Scott & Ascher §40.7 (Termination of Resulting Trust).

[102] 6 Scott & Ascher §40.6.

[103] *See generally* 6 Scott & Ascher §§41.1.5 (Trust Fails), 42.1.3. (Surplus), 42.3 (Surplus in the Case of a Charitable Trust).

[104] *See generally* §8.15.46 of this handbook (*bona vacantia* doctrine); 3 Scott & Ascher §14.10.3 (Death of Beneficiary without Heirs); 6 Scott & Ascher §41.1.3 (Resulting Trust When Testator Dies without Heirs).

[105] *See generally* §8.15.55 of this handbook (lapse and antilapse) and §8.26 of this handbook (will residue clauses).

[106] *See* §4.1.1 of this handbook (the reversionary interest), including the introductory quotation.

[107] *See, e.g.,* New England Trust Co. v. Sanger, 337 Mass. 342, 348–349, 149 N.E.2d 598, 602 (1958) (involving the effective funding of one express trust with the equitable reversion incident to another express trust).

[108] If, for example, those who take upon a resulting trust cannot be ascertained, absent a contrary statute or trust provision, the trust property will be held for the state. Restatement (Third) of Trusts §8 cmt. c(1). The trustee may not walk away with the property or divert it to other purposes. Restatement (Third) of Trusts §8 cmt. c(1).

through the mechanism of the resulting trust should the trust fail or become fully performed without the trust estate having been exhausted. By settlor we mean "the person who in reality provided the funds for the settlement, not necessarily the person who appears to be the settlor on the relevant documents."[109] Thus, if *A*, in exchange for fair consideration furnished by *B*, transfers certain property to *B* in trust for *C*, then *B* is both settlor and trustee.[110] Though the legal title came from *A*, equity considers the transferee to be the actual settlor, even when the documentation's terminology suggests otherwise.[111] "If the trust fails, the transferee can therefore keep the property, and no resulting trust arises."[112] The consideration, however, must have had a value that was more or less commensurate with the value of the entrusted property at the time of the exchange. In other words, the exchange cannot have been a sham, such as if the consideration had only been a nominal sum. The logic is the same when the owner of property transfers it for consideration provided *by a third person* upon a trust that fails, or whose purposes are subsequently accomplished without the trust estate being exhausted. In either case a resulting trust arises not in favor of the transferor but in favor of the person who provided the consideration.[113] A third person who provides consideration for the establishment of a declaration of trust also would be entitled to the trust property, not the one designated in the trust documentation as the declarant.[114]

Resulting trust versus *cy pres* **(charitable trusts).** In the case of a charitable trust, a court would be more amenable to enforcing a resulting trust in lieu of applying *cy pres* were the trust to fail at the outset than were it to fail in mid-course.[115] This is the case whether the purposes of an express trust cannot be accomplished[116] or have been fully accomplished without exhausting the trust estate.[117] For more on *cy pres* as an alternative to the imposition of a resulting trust, see Section 9.4.3 of this handbook.

Constraining the resulting trust in the charitable context. We should note here that in response to concerns "about the clogging of title and other administrative problems caused by remote default provisions upon failure of a charitable purpose,"[118] the Uniform Trust Code would sharply curtail the

---

[109] Lewin ¶ 8-18 (England). *See also* 6 Scott & Ascher §41.13 (U.S.).

[110] *See* 6 Scott & Ascher §41.13 (To Whom Trust Results).

[111] *See* 6 Scott & Ascher §41.14 (suggesting that under these circumstances *A* would simply be a vendor). *See also* 6 Scott & Ascher §42.4 (suggesting that when the transferor receives consideration for the transfer in trust, the transferor is merely a vendor and has no further interest in the property).

[112] 6 Scott & Ascher §41.14 (When Transferee Provides Consideration for Transfer in Trust).

[113] 6 Scott & Ascher §41.15 (Failure). The transferor is merely a "vendor." 6 Scott & Ascher §41.15 (Failure). *See also* 6 Scott & Ascher §42.5 (Surplus).

[114] 6 Scott & Ascher §§41.16 (Failure), 42.6 (Surplus).

[115] *See generally* 6 Scott & Ascher §41.3 (Failure of Charitable Trusts).

[116] *See generally* 6 Scott & Ascher §41.3 (Failure of Charitable Trusts).

[117] *See generally* 6 Scott & Ascher §42.3 (Surplus in the Case of a Charitable Trust).

[118] UTC §413 cmt (available at <http://www.uniformlaws.org/Act.aspx?title=Trust%20 Code>).

ability of a settlor to create *a charitable trust* whose property would revert to the settlor's personal representative, *i.e.*, the settlor's probate estate, upon the accomplishment of that purpose (or upon the impossibility of its fulfillment), even when the purpose is a limited one.[119] This is a topic we take up in Section 9.4.3 of this handbook as part of our coverage of the *cy pres* doctrine.

Dissolution of noncharitable unincorporated association. In the case of a trust established for the benefit of a noncharitable unincorporated association, the trustee may not walk away with the trust estate in the event the association dissolves.[120] Instead, depending upon what the association's purposes were and how the trust was funded, there should be:

- Retention of the subject property in trust for the benefit of the successor association, if there is one;[121]
- A division of the balance of the trust estate among the members who are on the rolls of the association at the time of dissolution, either in equal shares or in proportions that correspond to what was contributed by each to the trust fund;[122]
- An imposition of a resulting trust on the balance for the benefit of all contributors, each receiving an amount that is proportional to what he or she contributed to the trust fund;[123]
- Dedication of the subject property to an alternate purpose as provided by the terms of the trust;[124]
- Disposition of the subject property as provided by statute;[125] or
- A transfer of the balance to the state as *bona vacantia*.[126]

In the case of the dissolution of a business trust with transferable shares of beneficial interest, for example, those who own the shares at the time of dissolution are generally entitled to take pro rata legal interests in the underlying property.[127] When a country club dissolves, it is likely that any trust property held for the club will be distributed outright and free of trust to those who are on the club's membership rolls at the time of dissolution, *in equal shares*.[128] Had the trust been for the benefit of an association of workers should

---

[119] UTC §413 (available at <http://www.uniformlaws.org/Act.aspx?title=Trust%20Code>). *See generally* 6 Scott & Ascher §39.5.2.

[120] 6 Scott & Ascher §42.1.4.

[121] 6 Scott & Ascher §42.1.4.

[122] 6 Scott & Ascher §42.1.4.

[123] 6 Scott & Ascher §42.1.4.

[124] 6 Scott & Ascher §42.1.4.

[125] 6 Scott & Ascher §42.1.4.

[126] 6 Scott & Ascher §42.1.4.

[127] 6 Scott & Ascher §42.1.4. *See generally* §9.6 of this handbook (the business trust explained).

[128] 6 Scott & Ascher §42.1.4. "Former members have no claim to any part of the property because their interests ceased when their memberships ceased." 6 Scott & Ascher §42.1.4. "It is immaterial that some have paid dues for longer than others, because they have presumably received greater benefits." 6 Scott & Ascher §42.1.4.

they at some point go on strike, there is precedent for current members in the event of dissolution taking outright and free of trust the subject property, but *in proportion to what each had paid into the fund, i.e.,* not necessarily in equal shares.[129] Had the purpose of the trust merely been to provide financial assistance to workers who might from time to time fall on hard times, then, upon dissolution, a resulting trust might well be imposed on the balance of the trust estate for the benefit of all contributors, each taking in proportion to his or her contribution.[130] This result would be all the more likely if management has paid into the fund as well.[131] Take, however, a trust for the benefit of an unincorporated association whose purpose is to provide fixed annuities to the widows of its members from time to time. Should the association at some point become extinct, all members having died and all annuity obligations having been satisfied, then there is precedent for the balance of the trust estate passing to the state as *bona vacantia,* rather than upon a resulting trust to the contributors' personal representatives (probate estates).[132] The longer such an association has been in existence, the more attractive the *bona vacantia* option, at least from a practical standpoint.[133]

Restraints on alienation of reversionary interest are unenforceable. A spendthrift clause in a trust purporting to restrain alienation of the reversionary interest or to insulate it from the reach of the settlor's creditors is generally unenforceable.[134] This durable right of alienation accrues to the settlor's successors in interest as well.

Only an affirmative gift over can trump the equitable reversion. While the terms of a trust may provide that the equitable reversionary interest shall not accrue to the settlor's probate estate upon the death of the settlor should the trust fail or its purposes be fulfilled, such a provision would be unenforceable in the absence of an effective gift-over or an effective assignment of the reversion by the settlor.[135] In other words, there needs to be a remainderman available to take the legal title to the subject property from the trustee. "The settlor's heirs are excluded only if there is a provision, express or implied, that someone else is to have the property."[136] As Blackstone has noted:

> A reversion is never . . . created by deed or writing, but arises from construction of law; a remainder can never be limited, unless by either deed or devise. But both

---

[129] 6 Scott & Ascher §42.1.4.

[130] 6 Scott & Ascher §42.1.4.

[131] 6 Scott & Ascher §42.1.4.

[132] 6 Scott & Ascher §42.1.4. *See generally* §8.15.46 of this handbook (*bona vacantia* doctrine).

[133] 6 Scott & Ascher §42.1.4.

[134] 6 Scott & Ascher §40.4 (Transfer by Beneficiary). The settlor, however, could assign the equitable reversionary interest to the trustee of another spendthrift trust for the benefit of a third person. In that case, the spendthrift clause of the other trust might well be enforceable with respect to the assignment.

[135] 6 Scott & Ascher §41.2 (Rebutting the Resulting Trust).

[136] 6 Scott & Ascher §41.2 (Rebutting the Resulting Trust).

are equally transferable, when actually vested, being both estates *in praesenti*, though taking effect *in futuro*.[137]

The Rule against Perpetuities and the resulting trust. In the United States, reversionary interests are generally exempt from the Rule against Perpetuities as they are vested *ab initio*.[138] In England, on the other hand, a reversion upon the happening of a condition subsequent now implicates the Rule.[139] The Rule is also implicated when the duration of an English charitable trust is subject to a contingency-based limitation, *e.g.*, as long as a certain state of affairs continues.[140] Thus, an equitable reversion upon the failure of an English charitable trust would be unenforceable if the interest were to become possessory beyond the period of the Rule.[141] *Cy pres* would then have to be applied.[142]

Resulting trustee a fiduciary. From a trust's inception, the settlor possesses the possibility of reverter, which is a fully transferable nonpossessory vested equitable interest in the subject property.[143] The trustee is in a fiduciary relationship with the one who takes, or would take, upon imposition of a resulting trust, unless they are one and the same.[144] Just as one may not contract with oneself, so also one may not owe oneself a fiduciary duty.

Fiduciary duty of trustee to the settlor. The resulting trust represents the law's commitment to protecting the settlor's property rights. The concept of the trust begins with the settlor, exists to fulfill the settlor's wishes as reflected in the terms of the trust, and ultimately ends with the settlor or the settlor's probate estate to the extent that the terms of the trust cannot be fulfilled or are unknown.[145] "Every legal estate and interest not embraced in an express trust and not otherwise disposed of remains in the creator."[146] The trustee is the steward of someone else's property—in part the steward of the reversionary interest.[147] The scrupulous trustee understands this. On the other hand, "if the settlor is still alive and remains competent, he or she cannot ordinarily hold the trustee liable for distributing the trust property in accordance with the terms of the trust instrument, even if the trust is invalid."[148] It would be unfair for the

---

[137] Blackstone's Commentaries, Book II, 175.

[138] 6 Scott & Ascher §39.7.2.

[139] *See generally* 6 Scott & Ascher §39.7.2

[140] 6 Scott & Ascher §39.7.3 (Limitations).

[141] *See generally* 6 Scott & Ascher §39.7.2

[142] *See generally* §9.4.3 of this handbook (the *cy pres* doctrine).

[143] J. Gray, The Rule Against Perpetuities §§113, 603.9 (4th ed. 1942).

[144] 6 Scott & Ascher §40.6.

[145] *Cf.* §9.27 of this handbook (the purpose trust) and §9.29 of this handbook (the adapted trust).

[146] N.Y. Est. Powers & Tr. Law §7-1.7.

[147] *Cf.* §9.27 of this handbook (the purpose trust) and §9.29 of this handbook (the adapted trust).

[148] 4 Scott & Ascher §24.31.1 (Liability for Distributions Under Invalid, Amended, Revoked, or Ineffective Trust Instruments).

settlor to fault the trustee for endeavoring to carry out the settlor's own instructions.[149]

When the trustee may walk away with the property in lieu of the imposition of a resulting trust. When an express trust is fully performed and there is property still remaining in the trust estate, a resulting trust is imposed on the surplus.[150] Generally the trustee may not walk away with the property, unless the terms of the express trust provide otherwise.[151] "Whether the trust is inter vivos or testamentary, the traditional view is that extrinsic evidence of the settlor's declarations that the trustee is to be permitted to keep the property if the trust is fully accomplished without exhausting the trust estate is ordinarily inadmissible."[152]

At English common law, there were some quirky default exceptions to the general default rule that the beneficial interest in a trust may not accrue to the trustee. Here are two:

- If a person who held land free of trust died intestate and without heirs at law, the land escheated to his overlord.[153] "In the case of equitable interests, however, there was no tenure, and since the equitable interest was not held of any overlord, there was no escheat of the equitable interest."[154] The consequence of all of this was that the trustee actually could keep the land, the doctrine of *bona vacantia* applying only to personal property.[155] In 1884, Parliament closed this loophole.[156] It enacted a statute that provided that the beneficial interest in the land, rather than accruing to the trustee, passes to the Crown.[157]
- In the case of a trust for the benefit of one person, say *C*, whose duration was keyed to the life span of another, say *X*, *C* is said to have an "equitable estate *pur autre vie*."[158] At one time, if *C* were alive when the trust was created, assuming the underlying property were land, but died before *X*, and if the terms of the trust had not specified that the property was to be held for the benefit of "*C and his heirs*," then, after *C*'s death, "the trustee could simply hold the . . . [the property] . . . for the trustee's own benefit until the death of the measuring life,"[159] namely, *X*.

---

[149] 4 Scott & Ascher §24.31.1 (Liability for Distributions Under Invalid, Amended, Revoked, or Ineffective Trust Instruments).

[150] *See generally* 6 Scott & Ascher §42.2 (Rebutting the Resulting Trust).

[151] *See generally* 6 Scott & Ascher §42.2 (Rebutting the Resulting Trust).

[152] *See generally* 6 Scott & Ascher §42.2 (Rebutting the Resulting Trust).

[153] *See generally* 3 Scott & Ascher §14.10.3.

[154] Scott on Trusts §411.4 (1939 ed.).

[155] *See* §8.15.46 of this handbook (*bona vacantia*). *See also* 6 Scott & Ascher §41.1.5 (Multiple Donors).

[156] *See generally* 3 Scott & Ascher §14.10.3.

[157] *See* Intestates Estates Act, 1884, 47 & 48 Vict., c. 71, §4. *See also* 6 Scott & Ascher §41.1.3 (text in footnotes).

[158] *See generally* Restatement (Third) of Property (Wills and Other Donative Transfers) §24.5, cmt. c. (providing examples of estates *pur autre vie*).

[159] 3 Scott & Ascher §14.10.2.

Nowadays, the equitable interest would be held in the interim for the benefit of "those entitled to the . . . [probate] . . . estate . . . [of *C*] . . . , as determined under the law of intestate succession or by will,"[160] unless, of course, the terms of the trust had provided otherwise. Note that the law French term for the measuring life is *cestui que vie*.

The Restatement (Third) of Trusts has its own limited default exception to the imposition of a resulting trust upon the failure of an express trust, an exception that also could bring about a windfall for the trustee. If the express trust fails for illegality "and the policy against permitting unjust enrichment of a transferee is outweighed by the policy against giving relief to one who has entered into an illegal transaction,"[161] the trustee may keep the property free of trust.[162]

This is not new law. An example of such a situation would be the debtor who transfers property to an innocent trustee for the debtor's own benefit in an effort to defraud creditors. The court might well decide neither to enforce the terms of the express trust nor impose a resulting trust, leaving the trustee to walk away with the property.[163] So also if one establishes an inter vivos trust for one's own benefit in order to clothe *the trustee* with apparent ownership, causing those who may transact with the trustee in his individual capacity to be misled as to the trustee's personal creditworthiness.[164] The trustee may keep the property rather than return it.[165] He who comes into equity must come with clean hands.[166] Equity reluctantly would rather leave things as they are than afford "comfort and encouragement to wrongdoing."[167] The settlor's probate estate, or the assignee of the equitable nonpossessory reversionary for that matter, would generally be no better off.[168] Again, we are talking here about inter vivos trusts, not testamentary trusts.[169]

On the other hand, if the trustee has been more at fault than the settlor, then a resulting trust is imposed.[170] The parties are said not to be *in pari delicto*.[171] So also if the settlor demands the property back before the illegal

---

[160] 3 Scott & Ascher §14.10.2.

[161] Restatement (Third) of Trusts §8.

[162] Restatement (Third) of Trusts §8 cmt. i.

[163] *See generally* 6 Scott & Ascher §41.12.

[164] 6 Scott & Ascher §41.12.

[165] 6 Scott & Ascher §41.12.

[166] *See generally* §8.12 of this handbook (selected equity maxims).

[167] Haggerty v. Wilmington Trust Co., 194 A. 134, 137 (Del. Ch. 1937).

[168] 6 Scott & Ascher §41.12.6 (Transferees from Settlor). "Several cases, however, have reached the opposite result when the settlor had conveyed property in fraud of creditors on a secret trust to return the property to the settlor." 6 Scott & Ascher §41.12.6 (Transferees from Settlor). "In these cases, the courts allowed recovery after the settlor's death by the settlor's personal representatives, in whose hands the property would, of course, be subject to the claims of the settlor's defrauded creditors." 6 Scott & Ascher §41.12.6 (Transferees from Settlor).

[169] 6 Scott & Ascher §41.12.6 (Transferees from Settlor).

[170] 6 Scott & Ascher §41.12.1.

[171] 6 Scott & Ascher §§41.12.1, 41.12.3 (When Settlor and Trustee Are Not *In Pari Delicto*).

purpose is accomplished.[172] A settlor who is ignorant of the facts that make the trust illegal also may get the property back.[173] Finally, "[i]n the case of a *testamentary trust* for an illegal purpose, the trustee is never permitted to keep the property; a resulting trust always arises in favor of the testator's estate."[174]

Avoiding imposition of a resulting trust by power of appointment exercise. *Generally.* Assume the following poorly drafted testamentary trust: *A* (settlor/testator) to *B* (trustee) for *C* (equitable life beneficiary) for life. Unfortunately, no remainderman is designated. *C*, however, is granted a general testamentary power of appointment. If *C* were to effectively and fully exercise the power, no resulting trust of the trust corpus would be imposed in favor of *A*'s probate estate. This is clear. But what if *C*'s will makes no reference whatsoever to powers of appointment? The only dispositive term is a plain-vanilla residuary clause. And what if the trust were to continue for the benefit of certain other persons before failing for want of a remainderman to take the legal title from the trustee? And finally, what if *C* were to, say, exercise the testamentary power in a way that violates the rule against perpetuities? What then? We first consider whether a plain-vanilla will residue clause might serve, under certain circumstances, to effectively exercise a general testamentary power of appointment in favor of the residuary takers, thus obviating the need for the imposition of a resulting trust.

Plain-vanilla will residue clauses that exercise general testamentary powers of appointment. In Section 8.1.1 of this handbook, we note that there is some old law to the effect that a plain-vanilla will residue clause exercised all general testamentary powers of appointment that the testator had possessed over entrusted property. Of course, such a clause would not have exercised a power that by its terms could only have been exercised by an instrument making specific reference to the power.

At one time, Section 2-608 of the Uniform Probate Code provided that a general residuary clause in a will or a will making a general disposition of all of the testator's property did *not* exercise a power of appointment held by the testator, unless specific reference was made to the power or there was some other indication of intention to include the property subject to the power. In 1990, the negative rule was made subject to several exceptions. One is that if a

---

[172] 6 Scott & Ascher §41.12.2. For a resulting trust to be imposed on the property, the settlor must have a *locus poenitentiae*, which, according to the Oxford English Dictionary, is an "opportunity allowed by law to a person to recede from some engagement, so long as some particular step has not been taken." The literal translation of *locus* is place. In other words, if there is still time for the settlor to abort the illegal undertaking and the settlor does so, then the property may be recovered.

[173] 6 Scott & Ascher §41.12.4 (When Settlor Is Not Blameworthy). Violating the Rule against Perpetuities is not the type of illegal conduct that would prevent a settlor from recovering the entrusted property. 6 Scott & Ascher §41.12.4 (When Settlor Is Not Blameworthy). While it may be against public policy to enforce a provision that violates the Rule, it would not be against public policy to then enforce a resulting trust in favor of the settlor. 6 Scott & Ascher §41.12.4 (When Settlor Is Not Blameworthy). For a discussion of whether the settlor's right to recover from the trustee of an illegal trust depends upon whether it is necessary for the settlor to introduce evidence of the trust's illegality, *see* 6 Scott & Ascher §41.12.5.

[174] 6 Scott & Ascher §41.12.1.

power is a general one and there is no gift over in default of its exercise, a general residuary clause or general disposition in the will of the donee (holder) of the power will serve to exercise it.

The Restatement (Third) of Property (Wills and Other Donative Transfers), specifically Section 19.4, endorses with a vengeance the UPC's absence-of-taker-in-default exception, even upping the ante; and in so doing, sets a particularly nasty trap for the unwary trustee and estate planner. Here is the language: "A residuary clause in the donee's will or revocable trust does not manifest an intent to exercise any of the donee's power(s) [sic] of appointment, unless the power in question [sic] is a general power and the donor did not provide for takers in default *or the gift-in-default clause is ineffective.*"

And here is the trap: Assume the donee possessed a general testamentary power of appointment at the time of his death under his grandmother's trust. There is no express or blanket power-exercise clause in the donee's will, just a plain vanilla residue clause. What if the gift-in-default clause in the grandmother's trust is rendered "ineffective," say, twenty years after the donee's death but before the trust itself terminates? The comments, illustrations, and Reporter's Notes supporting the Restatement (Third)'s Section 19.4 only address the trust that terminates on its own terms *upon the death of the powerholder*. Distributing trustees beware. The trust property may well belong not to those who take by resulting trust, but to the lucky residuary takers under the will of the power-holder. Massachusetts has baked into its version of UPC 2-608 such a Restatement (Third)-type trap.

The doctrine of capture or the battle of the resulting trusts. If the donee (holder) of a general testamentary power of appointment exercises it by appointing the subject property to a trustee of a trust that fails *ab initio* or subsequently, a resulting trust is imposed.[175] The subject property, however, does not necessarily revert to the settlor of the original trust or to the settlor's probate estate.[176] Instead, a resulting trust might well be imposed in favor of the powerholder's probate estate under the so-called capture doctrine, a topic we take up in Section 8.15.12 of this handbook.

Expired general powers of appointment and the resulting trust. If the holder of a general inter vivos power of appointment dies without having effectively exercised the power, the power expires.[177] Likewise, if the holder of a general testamentary power of appointment fails to effectively exercise the power by will, the power expires at the holder's death. In either case, the gift-in-default clause in the granting instrument, if there is such a clause, controls the disposition of the unappointed property.[178] (So also if a power

---

[175] *See generally* 6 Scott & Ascher §41.17 (Trust Created by Exercise of General Power of Appointment); §8.1.1 of this handbook (powers of appointment).

[176] *See generally* 6 Scott & Ascher §41.17 (Trust Created by Exercise of General Power of Appointment).

[177] As we note in §8.1.1 of this handbook, a power of appointment is exercisable; it is never directly transferable.

[178] Restatement (Third) of Property (Wills and Other Donative Transfers) §19.22(a).

expires by inter vivos disclaimer or release.[179]) The time when a power expires "is almost invariably the death of the donee,"[180] although one could certainly fashion a grant of a general power that would be capable of expiring before its donee had, such as upon the exhaustion of an intervening equitable estate *pur autre vie*. The concept of the estate *pur autre vie* is discussed generally in Section 8.15.64 of this handbook.

The Restatement (Third) of Property speaks in terms of a general power "lapsing," an unfortunate innovation.[181] Its predecessors spoke in terms of a power "expiring,"[182] which is less ambiguous in that the term "lapse" can mean "to pass to another through neglect or omission."[183] As we note in Section 8.1.1 of this handbook, a power of appointment itself is never directly transmissible.

But what if the donor of an expired power had neglected to provide for takers-in-default in the granting instrument, or the instrument's gift-in-default clause was ineffective when the power expired? In that case, the unappointed property passes upon a resulting trust back to the donor if the donor is then living, or into the probate estate of the donor if the donor is not then living, but, again, not until all valid intervening equitable interests have themselves expired.[184] *In a radical departure from settled doctrine, the Restatement (Third) of Property provides that if the donee "merely failed to exercise the power," the unappointed property is captured by the donee or the donee's estate.*[185] A resulting trust, however, would still be imposed in the case of expiration by disclaimer or release,[186] or upon the expiration by any means of a power of revocation, amendment, or withdrawal.[187] In Section 8.15.12 of this handbook, we question the logic of treating a power of "revocation, amendment, or withdrawal" differently from other "types" of general inter vivos power of appointment, whether for capture purposes generally or for any other purpose. A resulting trust also would be imposed if the donee "expressly refrained from exercising the power."[188] Of course, this discussion is entirely academic if the donor is also the donee of the expired general power. The unappointed property would then end up in the probate estate of the donee in any case, whether by imposition of a resulting trust under traditional doctrine or by capture.

---

[179] Restatement (Third) of Property (Wills and Other Donative Transfers) §19.22(a).

[180] Restatement (First) of Property §367, cmt. d.

[181] *See* Restatement (Third) of Property (Wills and Other Donative Transfers) §19.22 (term lapse employed even in the section's title); §8.15.55 of this handbook (lapse and antilapse).

[182] *See, e.g.*, Restatement (First) of Property §367, cmt. d.

[183] The American Heritage Dictionary 1014 (3d ed. 1996).

[184] *See, e.g.*, Restatement (First) of Property §367(1).

[185] Restatement (Third) of Property (Wills and Other Donative Transfers) §19.22(b). For a discussion of traditional capture doctrine, *see* §8.15.12 of this handbook.

[186] Restatement (Third) of Property (Wills and Other Donative Transfers) §19.22(b).

[187] Restatement (Third) of Property (Wills and Other Donative Transfers) §19.22, cmt. f.

[188] Restatement (Third) of Property (Wills and Other Donative Transfers) §19.22(b).

The Restatement (Third) of Property exhibits a curious and tenacious aversion to invoking applicable resulting trust doctrine,[189] particularly in the sections devoted to unexercised or ineffectively exercised general powers of appointment. The result is an unhelpful dearth of context, particularly when it comes to following chains of title, as well as a fair amount of general incoherence. Take, for example, Section 19.22(b), which in part reads: "... but if the donee released the power or expressly refrained from exercising the power, the unappointed property passes under a reversionary interest to the donor or to the donor's transferees or successors in interest." The phrase "passes under a reversionary interest" is nonsensical in the trust context. What actually happens is that the legal title to the unappointed property passes from the trustee to the donor or his personal representative upon a resulting trust such that the equitable reversion, which had vested *ab initio*, becomes possessory. Nothing is passing from the trustee under, over, or in a reversionary interest.

We also quibble with the failure of all of the restatements to expressly confirm that in the face of an expired power of appointment, title to property unappointed does not leave the hands of the trustee until such time as all valid intervening equitable estates have themselves expired, unless the terms of the trust so provide. An intervening equitable estate typically would be an equitable life estate.[190]

Expired nongeneral powers of appointment and the resulting trust. If the donee of a *nonfiduciary*, nongeneral power of appointment allows the power to expire unexercised, the power-in-trust doctrine may be implicated, a topic we take up in Section 8.15.90 of this handbook. If it is, title to the appointive property is held *by the donor* of the power (or by the personal representative of the donor if the donor has predeceased the power's expiration) upon a constructive trust for the benefit of the permissible appointees, title to the appointive property having passed to the donor or his personal representative pursuant to the imposition of a resulting trust.

The purchase money resulting trust is actually an express trust. There is also something known as the purchase money resulting trust, which we cover in Section 3.3 of this handbook. The purchase money resulting trust is misnamed. It is actually a type of express trust.[191] The purchase money resulting trust does not arise automatically by operation of law.[192] Take a land transaction in which title to the land is transferred to someone other than the one who contributed the consideration, *i.e.*, the purchase price.[193] When there is intent on the part of the person who paid the consideration to make a gift of the land to the person who actually took the legal title to it, then no purchase money

---

[189] *See, e.g.*, Restatement (Third) of Property (Wills and Other Donative Transfers) §25.2 (although the title to the sections is *Reversion or Remainder*, the resulting trust is mentioned once, and only in passing).

[190] *See generally* §8.27 of this handbook (the equitable life estate).

[191] *See generally* 6 Scott & Ascher §40.1.1 (suggesting that the purchase money resulting trust is actually an express trust).

[192] *See, e.g.*, Ravi Vajpeyi v. Shuaib Yusaf, [2003] EWHC 2339 (Ch) (England) (presumption of resulting trust rebutted by evidence that a loan of the property in question was intended).

[193] *See generally* 6 Scott & Ascher §40.1.

resulting trust will arise in favor of the one who paid the consideration.[194] When such donative intent is lacking, however, the situation may call for the imposition of a purchase money resulting trust in favor of the one who paid the consideration. On the other hand, a resulting trust that is occasioned by the failure of an express trust or the accomplishment of its purposes arises automatically in favor of those who took vested reversionary interests at the express trust's inception. Again, reversionary interests are always vested.[195] The Ohio Supreme Court appears to have lost sight of this critical difference between the purchase money resulting trust and the other two types of resulting trust in a case involving an express trust that failed for want of an equitable remainder,[196] the court then further confusing matters by mischaracterizing the nonexistent equitable remainder as a nonexistent "residue."[197] It is high time that American law schools again make Trusts required, a topic we address in Section 8.25 of this handbook.

The constructive trust and resulting trust distinguished. The constructive trust is not a resulting trust, although the two are often confused.[198] "A constructive trust is imposed when a person holding title to property is subject to an equitable duty to convey it to another on the ground that the titleholder would be unjustly enriched if permitted to retain it."[199] We take up the constructive trust in Section 3.3 of this handbook. A constructive trust and not a resulting trust is imposed, for example, when *A* deeds land to *B* absolutely and *B* orally agrees at the time to hold the land for the benefit of *A* or a third person, though the deed makes no mention of this commitment.[200] In other words, *B*, the transferee, cannot hide behind the statute of frauds.[201] Similarly an absolute testamentary devise of land to *B* who has orally agreed to hold it for the benefit of *C* may warrant the imposition of a constructive trust for *C*'s benefit, notwithstanding the statute of wills.[202] On the other hand should an instrument of conveyance indicate a naked intention to impress a trust upon the subject property, then the imposition of a resulting trust may be appropriate, there being no indication on the face of the instrument of who the beneficiaries are and what the trust purposes might be.[203] This would essentially be a failed express trust. Had the conveyance been procured by fraud or had it been incident to the abuse of a fiduciary or confidential relationship, then there is precedent for imposing on the subject property a constructive trust for the

---

[194] Restatement (Third) of Trusts §9(1)(a).

[195] *See generally* §8.2.1.5 of this handbook.

[196] *See* Stevens v. Radey, 117 Ohio St. 3d 65, 881 N.E.2d 855 (2008).

[197] Stevens v. Radey, 117 Ohio St. 3d 65, 881 N.E.2d 855 (2008). *See* §8.15.2 of this handbook (remaindermen take "by purchase" from the trustee). See also introductory quote to §4.1.1 of this handbook (comparing a reversion with a remainder) and §8.26 of this handbook (will residue clauses).

[198] 6 Scott & Ascher §40.1.2 (Distinguishing Resulting Trusts from Constructive Trusts).

[199] 6 Scott & Ascher §40.1.2.

[200] 6 Scott & Ascher §40.1.7.

[201] 6 Scott & Ascher §40.1.7. *See generally* §8.15.5 of this handbook (statute of frauds).

[202] 6 Scott & Ascher §40.1.7.

[203] 6 Scott & Ascher §40.1.7.

benefit of the intended beneficiaries in lieu of imposing on it a resulting trust for the benefit of the transferor or the transferor's successors in interest.[204]

The resulting trust and express trust distinguished. The resulting trust differs from the express trust when it comes to burdens of proof in the litigation of trust matters. In the case of an express trust the burden is on the beneficiary who is alleging a breach of trust to prove that there had been an intention to impress a trust upon the subject property in the first place.[205] On the other hand, "[w]hen the circumstances are such as to give rise to a resulting trust, it is unnecessary for the person seeking to recover the property to prove that a trust was intended, since the inference that arises from the circumstances, until rebutted, suffices to justify recovery."[206]

The transfer of trust property to a BFP can cut off the reversionary interest. The transfer of a specific item of trust property *by the trustee* to a good-faith purchaser for value (bona fide purchaser, or BFP) cuts off any nonpossessory vested equitable reversionary interest which the settlor may possess in that property.[207] It also would cut off the rights of anyone who had succeeded to the interest by assignment, on account of the settlor's death, or otherwise. We cover the doctrine of bona fide purchase in Section 8.15.63 of this handbook.

The history of the resulting trust concept. The resulting trust is not a new concept. Not long after the chancellor began enforcing *uses* in fifteenth-century England, he was confronted with the issue of what was to happen to land that was enfeoffed by *A* to *B* and his heirs for the *use* of *C* for life when there was no mention of what was to be done with the beneficial interest once *C* died.[208] "The chancellor took the view that because there was nothing to indicate that *B* should have the use in himself, the inference was that *A* was entitled to it."[209] It was said that *B* held the property upon a resulting *use* for *A*, the transferor. In other words, the use "sprang back" or "resulted" to *A*.[210] Gratuitous land transfers also raised the presumption that the transferee held the property upon a resulting *use* for the transferor.[211] Finally even the purchase money resulting trust, a topic we take up in Section 3.3 of this handbook, can be traced back to what was essentially the purchase money resulting *use*.[212]

---

[204] 6 Scott & Ascher §40.1.7.

[205] *See generally* §8.24 of this handbook (burdens of proof in trust litigation).

[206] 6 Scott & Ascher §40.3.

[207] 6 Scott & Ascher §40.5 (Transfer by Trustee).

[208] *See generally* 6 Scott & Ascher §40.1 (When a Resulting Trust Arises); §8.15.1 of this handbook (statute of uses); Chapter 1 of this handbook (containing a list of all the Lord Chancellors since 1066).

[209] 6 Scott & Ascher §40.1.

[210] 6 Scott & Ascher §40.1 (When a Resulting Trust Arises).

[211] *See generally* 6 Scott & Ascher §§40.1 (When a Resulting Trust Arises), 40.2 (noting that "the old doctrine that a resulting use arose upon a gratuitous conveyance has nearly disappeared, although the old doctrine that a resulting use arose in favor of one who paid the purchase price for a conveyance to another still applies").

[212] *See generally* 6 Scott & Ascher §40.1.

The notional resulting trust. *Default law of antilapse.* The application of antilapse to certain equitable property interests under trusts is covered in Section 8.15.55 of this handbook, specifically the elaborate default antilapse regime that Section 2-707 of the Uniform Probate Code has concocted. A critical component of the regime is the notional resulting trust, which in this context is employed as a device for determining "substitute takers in cases of a beneficiary's failure to survive . . . [a] . . . distribution date."[213] These substitutes take the legal title from the trustee as remaindermen. No resulting trust is actually triggered.

The notional resulting trust as a trust instrument drafting tool. An experienced trust scrivener strives to avoid any possibility of the imposition of a resulting trust upon the trust's eventual termination. The judicial imposition of a resulting trust tends to be "cumbersome and costly," particularly if it involves "distributions to and through estates of deceased beneficiaries of future interest, who may have died long before the distribution date."[214] The notional resulting trust as a handy drafting tool for avoiding want-of-remaindermen trust failures is taken up in Section 5.2 of this handbook, specifically in conjunction with our discussion of the term "heirs."

§4.1.1.2 Charitable Trusts, Equitable Reversions, and Donor Intent

By expressly reserving a property interest such as a right of reverter, the donor of the gift or the settlor of the trust may bring himself and his heirs within the special interest exception to the general rule that beneficiaries of a charitable trust may not bring an action to enforce the trust, but rather are represented by the attorney general.[215]

Whether settlor of a charitable trust, *qua* settlor has standing to litigate trust matters: The general default law. Occasionally, the charitable purpose for which a settlor establishes a charitable trust will become impossible of fulfillment. This most often arises where the charity ceases to exist. In those cases, a *cy pres* petition may be brought by someone with the requisite standing[216] in order to determine if the settlor's charitable intent was sufficiently general such that the imposition of a resulting trust is unwarranted.[217] If general charitable intent is found, the court fashions a new purpose for the trust that approximates as nearly as possible the trust's original charitable purpose as set forth in its terms, this in order to carry out the settlor's general charitable

---

[213] UPC §2-707, cmt. (substitute gifts).

[214] UPC §2-707, cmt. (common-law background).

[215] Carl J. Herzog Found., Inc. v. University of Bridgeport, 243 Conn. 1, 9, 699 A.2d 995, 999 (1997). *See generally* §9.4.2 of this handbook (standing to enforce charitable trusts).

[216] *See generally* §9.4.2 of this handbook (standing to enforce charitable trusts).

[217] *See* §§8.15.5 of this handbook (statute of frauds) and 9.4.3 of this handbook (*cy pres*). *See* UTC §413(a) (available at <http://www.uniformlaws.org/Act.aspx?title=Trust%20Code>) (modifying the doctrine of *cy pres* by presuming that the settlor had a general charitable intent when a particular charitable purpose becomes impossible or impracticable to achieve).

intent. The doctrine of *cy pres* should not be confused with the doctrine of equitable deviation. The doctrine of equitable deviation, which is discussed in Section 8.15.20 of this handbook, "allows the court to authorize the breach of an administrative restriction on a charitable disposition."[218]

The settlor of a charitable trust who possesses a vested equitable reversionary property interest under it perforce should have the right to initiate/participate in litigation pertaining to the trust's administration. As a general rule, one who possesses property rights is granted standing to participate in litigation that could affect those rights. Under the default law, however, a settlor, *qua* settlor, possesses no reversionary interest under a trust with a general charitable purpose. Should such a trust become impossible of fulfillment, the court, instead of enforcing a resulting trust, will apply the doctrine of *cy pres*.[219]

Absent a statute to the contrary, the settlor of a trust with a limited charitable purpose does possess a vested reversionary interest, an interest that ripens into possession should the purpose become impossible of fulfillment.[220] Accordingly, the settlor of such a trust, *qua* settlor, ought to be made a party to any *cy pres* action brought by the trustee, the attorney general, or whomever.

The Uniform Trust Code. The Uniform Trust Code would afford the settlor, *qua* settlor, standing to bring a *cy pres* petition,[221] as well as maintain a proceeding to enforce the trust,[222] whether or not the charitable intent was a general one. "Responding to concerns about the clogging of title and other administrative problems caused by remote default provisions upon failure of a charitable purpose,"[223] the Uniform Trust Code, however, would sharply curtail the ability of a settlor to create a charitable trust whose property would revert to the settlor's personal representative, *i.e.*, the settlor's probate estate, upon the accomplishment of that purpose (or upon the impossibility of its fulfillment) even when the purpose is a limited one.[224] This is a topic we take up in Section 9.4.3 of this handbook.

The reversionary interest and the rule against perpetuities. In the United States, reversionary interests are generally exempt from the Rule against Perpetuities

---

[218] *See generally* Craig Kaufman, *Sympathy for the Devil's Advocate: Assisting the Attorney General When Charitable Matters Reach the Courtroom*, 40 Real Prop. Prob. & Tr. J. 705 (Winter 2006).

[219] *See generally* §4.1.1.1 of this handbook (defining the resulting trust) and §9.4.3 of this handbook (defining *cy pres*).

[220] J. Gray, The Rule Against Perpetuities §603.9 (4th ed. 1942); 4A Scott on Trusts §§399.3, 401.2–401.3. *But see* Mass. Gen. Laws ch. 214, §10B (providing that upon a petition commenced after the death of the donor for the application of *cy pres* to similar public charitable purposes of a gift for a public charitable purpose which has become impossible or impracticable of fulfillment, the court may exercise jurisdiction without requiring that the heirs or next of kin of the donor or others who would be entitled to take upon failure of any charitable gift be joined as parties).

[221] UTC §410(b) (available at <http://www.uniformlaws.org/Act.aspx?title=Trust%20 Code>).

[222] UTC §405(c) (available at <http://www.uniformlaws.org/Act.aspx?title=Trust%20 Code>).

[223] UTC §413 cmt. (available at <http://www.uniformlaws.org/Act.aspx?title=Trust%20 Code>).

[224] UTC §413 (available at <http://www.uniformlaws.org/Act.aspx?title=Trust%20Code>). *See generally* 6 Scott & Ascher §39.5.2.

as they are vested *ab initio*. In England, on the other hand, a reversion upon the happening of a condition subsequent now implicates the Rule.[225] The Rule also is implicated when the duration of an English charitable trust is subject to a contingency-based limitation, *e.g.*, as long as a certain state of affairs continues.[226] Thus, an equitable reversion upon the failure of an English charitable trust would be unenforceable if the interest were to become possessory beyond the period of the Rule.[227] *Cy pres* would then have to be applied.[228]

The Uniform Prudent Management of Institutional Funds Act (UPMIFA). The UPMIFA, which applies to charitable corporations as well as charitable trusts, makes provision for the release or modification of a restriction on the management, investment, or charitable purpose of an institutional fund with donor consent.[229] On the other hand, the UPMIFA does not require that the donor even be notified of an equitable deviation or *cy pres* proceeding.[230] Here is the rationale: "The trust law rules of equitable deviation and cy pres do not require donor notification and instead depend on the court and the attorney general to protect donor intent and the public's interest in charitable assets."[231] When in a given situation donor intent and the public interest cannot be reconciled, it would seem that the attorney general would have an ethical obligation to retain special outside counsel to advocate on behalf of donor intent.

Since time immemorial, effectively protecting a settlor's charitable intentions from future subversions has been a challenge. In any case, the default law of trusts/charitable corporations has traditionally never been particularly solicitous of the intentions of the charitable donor, particularly one who has deceased.[232] This is a subject we address in much greater detail in Sections 9.4.2, 9.4.3, and 9.8.1 of this handbook. As far back as the sixteenth century, upholding donor intent has been a concern, at least in some quarters. Sir Francis Moore, the drafter of the Statute of Charitable Uses (1601),[233] for example, had intentionally omitted entrusted religious benefactions from its preamble for reasons related to donor intent, . . .

> lest the gifts intended to be employed upon purposes grounded upon charity, might, in change of times (contrary to the minds of the givers) be confiscate into the King's treasury. For religion being variable, according to the pleasure of succeeding princes, that which at one time is held orthodox, may at another, be accounted superstitious, and then such lands are confiscate.[234]

---

[225] *See generally* 6 Scott & Ascher §39.7.2.

[226] 6 Scott & Ascher §39.7.3 (Limitations).

[227] *See generally* 6 Scott & Ascher §39.7.2.

[228] *See generally* §9.4.3 of this handbook (the *cy pres* doctrine).

[229] Unif. Prudent Management Inst. Funds Act §6(a).

[230] Unif. Prudent Management Inst. Funds Act §6 cmt.

[231] Unif. Prudent Management Inst. Funds Act §6 cmt.

[232] *See generally* Craig Kaufman, *Sympathy for the Devil's Advocate: Assisting the Attorney General When Charitable Matters Reach the Courtroom*, 40 Real Prop. Prob. & Tr. J. 705 (Winter 2006).

[233] *See generally* §8.15.4 of this handbook (charitable purpose doctrine (Statute of Elizabeth/charitable uses)) and §9.4.1 of this handbook (charitable purposes).

[234] Moore, *Readings upon the Statute of 43 Elizabeth*, in Duke, Law of Charitable Uses 131, 132 (1676).

Measures the *prospective* settlor can take to make it more difficult for the trustee to thwart donor intent once the charitable trust is established. For some high-profile charities, upholding donor intent has been something less than a sacred obligation.[235] A prospective charitable donor, however, should be able to structure the benefaction in a way that will at least cause the charity to think twice before it takes a future act in derogation of the donor's charitable intentions. In other words, there are some steps that a disgruntled donor perhaps could have taken *before* the gift was made. They include the following:

- Establish a charitable trust in a state whose courts have a good track record of respecting donor intent.[236]
- Establish a charitable trust in a state where the Office of the Attorney General has a good track record of both taking seriously its responsibility of overseeing public charities and respecting donor intent.[237]
- Avoid unrestricted gifts to charitable corporations.[238]
- Avoid making a charity the trustee of a restricted gift for the benefit of the charity.
- Avoid making a governmental entity the trustee of a charitable gift.[239]
- Put a sunset provision into the trust instrument, or provide that the trust estate shall be consumed within a reasonable period of time.
- Make sure that the purposes of the charitable trust are articulated with precision.[240]
- Appoint more than one trustee of the charitable trust.[241]
- Draft the charitable trust instrument in a way that bestows on the donor standing to seek enforcement of the trust in the courts,[242] such as a reserved right to receive and object to trustee accountings.[243]
- Draft the charitable trust instrument in a way that bestows standing on persons other than the donor to seek the trust's enforcement along with the attorney general.[244]
- Designate a trust protector in the charitable trust instrument.[245]

---

[235] *See, e.g.*, Doug White, Abusing Donor Intent: The Robertson Family's Epic Lawsuit against Princeton University (Saint Paul, Minn.: Paragon House, 2014).

[236] *See generally* §9.4.3 of this handbook (*cy près*).

[237] *See generally* §9.4.2 of this handbook (standing to enforce charitable trusts).

[238] *See generally* §9.8.1 of this handbook (the charitable corporation).

[239] *See generally* §9.8.21 of this handbook (the city, the state, or the United States as trustee).

[240] Ambiguity invites mischief-making by the attorney general and the courts. *See, e.g.*, Ebitz v. Pioneer Nat'l Bank, 372 Mass. 207, 361 N.E.2d 225 (1977).

[241] *See generally* §3.4.4.1 of this handbook (cotrustees) and §7.2.4 of this handbook (cofiduciary and predecessor liability and contribution in the trust context).

[242] *See* §4.2 of this handbook (expressly reserved beneficial interests and powers in the trust context).

[243] *See, e.g.*, Patton v. Sherwood, 152 Cal. App. 4th 339, 61 Cal. Rptr. 3d 289 (2007) (the court enforcing a reserved right to receive and object to the accountings of a trustee of a charitable remainder unitrust).

[244] *See* §3.2.6 of this handbook (considerations in the selection of a trustee).

[245] *See* §3.2.6 of this handbook (considerations in the selection of a trustee).

Note: Care should be taken to draft the "donor control" provisions of a charitable trust in a way that does not have adverse tax consequences. Also, a provision that calls for the donated property to pass on to noncharitable beneficiaries, *e.g.*, the settlor or the settlor's family members, upon the happening of certain contingencies could be problematic.[246] For more detail, the reader is referred to an article by Alan F. Rothschild, Jr.[247]

§4.1.2   *Settlor-Standing: Reversionary Interests, Expectation Interests, and Direct Grants of Standing*

The Restatement (Second) of Trusts. Let us assume for the sake of argument that a certain settlor reserves no power and no beneficial interest. Would the default law nonetheless afford the settlor standing to seek judicial redress for a breach of trust? It is generally assumed that neither the settlor nor the settlor's representatives can compel performance of the trust or redress a breach.[248] This assumption appears to take support from the Restatement (Second) of Trusts:

> Neither the settlor nor his heirs or personal representatives, as such, can maintain a suit against the trustee to enforce a trust or enjoin or obtain redress for a breach of trust. Where, however, the settlor retains an interest in the trust property, he can of course maintain a suit against the trustee to protect that interest. Thus, if the settlor is also a beneficiary of the trust, or if he has an interest by way of a resulting trust, or if he has reserved power to revoke the trust, he can maintain a suit against the trustee to protect his interest.[249]

Upon reflection, however, one realizes that while under this section the settlor of a trust with a general charitable purpose would lack standing to enforce the trust, perhaps the settlor of either a private trust or a charitable trust with limited purpose would not lack standing. The settlor of a private trust or a limited charitable purpose trust retains a vested reversionary equitable interest in the trust property that exists because of the possibility that the trust may fail at some future date for want of a purpose or beneficiary.[250] Upon the trust's failure, a resulting trust arises in favor of the settlor or the settlor's estate. Thus, the Restatement (Second) may support the proposition that the vested equitable reversionary equitable property interest—an interest that ripens into possession of title to the underlying trust property should the trust

---

[246] Such provisions are sometimes incorrectly referred to as "reversions." *See* §4.1.1 of this handbook (specifically the section's introductory italicized quotation).

[247] *The Dos and Don'ts of Donor Control*, 30 ACTEC L.J. 261 (2005).

[248] *See generally* 3 Scott on Trusts §200.1; Bogert §42.

[249] Restatement (Second) of Trusts §200 cmt. b.

[250] *See, e.g.*, Restatement (Third) of Trusts, ch. 9, Introductory Note (suggesting that one who takes a legally implied reversionary interest is actually a beneficiary). *But see* Estate of Leitner, 2004 WL 440202 (Cal. App.) (suggesting that a settlor of a charitable trust possesses no vested reversionary interest in the absence of an express reverter clause).

fail—provides a settlor with sufficient standing to seek enforcement of the trust's terms in the courts.[251]

The Restatement (Third) of Trusts. The Restatement (Third) of Trusts is also sending mixed signals as to whether the settlor of a noncharitable (private) trust, *qua* settlor, would have standing to seek its enforcement. The commentary to its Section 94 confirms that one "who holds a reversionary interest by operation of law" under a noncharitable (private) trust is a beneficiary of that trust. As we have already noted, under classic principles of property and trust law, the settlor of a noncharitable (private) trust retains by operation of law a nonpossessory vested equitable reversionary property interest.[252] If the trust eventually terminates in favor of designated equitable remaindermen, then the equitable reversionary property interest extinguishes before the settlor can ever come into possession of the legal title to the underlying property; if the trust fails in mid-course, then legal title to the underlying property becomes possessory via the imposition of a resulting trust.[253] Ergo, the settlor, *qua* settlor, is a beneficiary of the trust that he has established, and accordingly should have standing to seek the trust's enforcement in the courts. There is elsewhere, however, seemingly conflicting official Section 94 commentary that states: "Neither the settlor of a private trust nor the personal representative or successors in interest of the settlor can, *as such*, maintain a suit against the trustee to enjoin or redress a breach of trust or otherwise to enforce the trust, absent contrary legislation."[254] Perhaps this apparent conflict can be reconciled if, for the holder of an equitable reversionary property interest to qualify as a trust beneficiary, his interest in the underlying property has to have already ripened into a possessory right.

Adapted and purpose trusts. Of course, the settlor of an adapted trust, or the settlor's successors in interest, would have standing to bring an action against the trustee to prevent or redress a breach of trust.[255] A trust whose terms direct the trustee to distribute the trust property to those members of an

---

[251] There is ancient analogous English precedent, specifically in the context of outright transfers of fee simple interests, for granting transferors standing to enforce conditions. Prior to the Statute *Quia Emptores*, which was enacted by Parliament in 1290, a condition against alienation by the transferee of a fee simple interest in England would have been enforceable at the petition of the transferor. This is because "prior to that statute the feoffor or grantor of such an estate was entitled to the escheat on failure of heirs of the grantee, which was properly a possibility of reverter, and was treated as a reversion; so that the vendor did not, by the feoffment or conveyance, part with the entire estate; but this reversion, dependent on this contingency, remained in him and his heirs, which gave them an interest to insist upon the condition and take the benefit accruing to them upon the breach." Mandlebaum v. McDonell, 29 Mich. 78, 18 Am. Rep. 61 (1874).

[252] *See generally* §4.1.1.1 of this handbook (the equitable reversionary interest).

[253] *See generally* §4.1.1.1 of this handbook (the resulting trust).

[254] Restatement (Third) of Trusts §94 cmt. d(2).

[255] Restatement (Third) of Trusts §46 cmts. f, g (members of an indefinite class of beneficiaries); Restatement (Third) of Trusts §47 cmts. f, g (trust for noncharitable purposes).

indefinite class of beneficiaries whom the trustee shall select is an example of an adaptive trust.[256] So also is a purpose[257] or honorary[258] trust.

Charitable trusts. We should also note here that in response to concerns about the "clogging of title and other administrative problems caused by remote default provisions upon failure of a charitable purpose,"[259] the Uniform Trust Code would sharply curtail the ability of a settlor to create a charitable trust whose property would revert to the settlor's personal representative, *i.e.*, the settlor's probate estate, upon the accomplishment of that purpose (or upon the impossibility of its fulfillment), even when the purpose is a limited one.[260] This is a topic we take up in Section 9.4.3 of this handbook.[261] That having been said, both the Uniform Trust Code and the Restatement (Third) of Trusts, in a radical and, in our opinion, much-needed departure from traditional trust law doctrine, nonetheless would grant the settlor of a *charitable trust* broad default standing to seek its enforcement in the courts. The topic of settlor-standing in the charitable context is covered generally in Section 9.4.2 of this handbook.

Rule against Perpetuities. In the United States, reversionary interests are generally exempt from the Rule against Perpetuities as they are vested *ab initio*. In England, on the other hand, a reversion upon the happening of a condition subsequent now implicates the Rule.[262] The Rule also is implicated when the duration of an English charitable trust is subject to a contingency-based limitation, *e.g.*, as long as a certain state of affairs continues.[263] Thus, an equitable reversion upon the failure of an English charitable trust would be unenforceable if the interest were to become possessory beyond the period of the Rule.[264] *Cy pres* would then have to be applied.[265]

The settlor's expectation interest. In 1949, a Note in the Harvard Law Review questioned the now widely held assumption that the settlor lacks standing to seek enforcement of the trust and suggested that Professor Scott's positions were unsupported by judicial decision.[266] Thirty-five years later, Professor Gaubatz put forth in an article the thesis that in some situations a settlor of a trust should have standing to seek its enforcement because of the settlor's "expectation interest" in having the terms of the trust carried out.[267]

---

[256] *See* §9.29 of this handbook (the adapted trust).

[257] *See* §9.27 of this handbook (the purpose trust).

[258] *See* §9.27 of this handbook (the purpose trust). *See also* §9.9.5 of this handbook (honorary trusts including trusts for pets).

[259] UTC §413 cmt. (available at <http://www.uniformlaws.org/Act.aspx?title=Trust%20 Code>).

[260] UTC §413 (available at <http://www.uniformlaws.org/Act.aspx?title=Trust%20Code>). *See generally* 6 Scott & Ascher §39.5.2.

[261] Discussing the *cy pres* doctrine.

[262] *See generally* 6 Scott & Ascher §39.7.2.

[263] 6 Scott & Ascher §39.7.3 (Limitations).

[264] *See generally* 6 Scott & Ascher §39.7.2.

[265] *See generally* §9.4.3 of this handbook (the *cy pres* doctrine).

[266] *See* Note, *Right of a Settlor to Enforce a Private Trust*, 62 Harv. L. Rev. 1370 (1949).

[267] Gaubatz, *Grantor Enforcement of Trusts: Standing in One Private Law Setting*, 62 N.C.L. Rev. 905 (1984). Professor Gaubatz suggests that "the grantor's standing is analyzed better on the basis of whether he has an interest, economic or otherwise, in the performance of the trustee's duties.

Management of Institutional Funds. Even the Uniform Management of Institutional Funds Act (UMIFA) acknowledged that the donor of a gift to a charitable corporation ought not to be entirely out of the picture. Section 7 of UMIFA, for example, provided that, "[w]ith the written consent of the donor, the governing board may release, in whole or in part, a restriction imposed by the applicable gift instrument on the use or investment of an institutional fund."[268] UPMIFA, which superseded UMIFA in 2006, is at least as deferential to donor intent, if not more so:[269] "If the donor consents in a record, an institution may release or modify, in whole or in part, a restriction contained in a gift instrument on the management, investment, or purpose of an institutional fund."[270]

The public policy case for and against keeping the settlor in the picture. To be sure, enforceability and accountability are two features that distinguish the trust from the gift.[271] If a settlor has an expectation interest in having the terms of the trust carried out—and thus standing to seek judicial redress—this may add an extra measure of accountability to the trust relationship consistent with the imposition of fiduciary duties. It is that imposition, after all, which distinguishes a trust from a gift. Without some right of enforcement remaining back with the settlor, there is no practical way to prevent the trustee from colluding with beneficiaries to effect a breach of trust.[272]

In the context of charitable trusts, an element of "privatization" is called for, as attorneys general no longer have the resources to systematically police

---

If he possesses such an interest, and that interest is within the zone of interests sought to be protected by those duties, then the grantor can bring an action to enforce the trust. In a broad sense, if the grantor has an economic, *expectation* (emphasis added), or representational interest in the trust, such that he can be trusted to fully and fairly litigate the validity of the transactions that he challenges, and his interest was foreseeable at the time the trust was created, he can maintain an action." Gaubatz, *Grantor Enforcement of Trusts: Standing in One Private Law Setting*, 62 N.C.L. Rev. 905, 940–941 (1984). *See generally* Reid, Mureiko, & Mikeska, *Privilege and Confidentiality Issues When a Lawyer Represents a Fiduciary*, 30 Real Prop. Prob. & Tr. J. 541, 588 (1996); Langbein, *The Contractarian Basis of the Law of Trusts*, 105 Yale L.J. 625, 664 (1995). *But see* Sanders v. Citizens Nat'l Bank of Leesburg, 585 So. 2d 1064 (Fla. 1991) (court, having denied a settlor standing to enforce a trust that he had impressed upon his property, made an oblique reference to Professor Gaubatz's article).

[268] 7A U.L.A. (Part II) 475, 503 (1999). *But see* Carl J. Herzog Found., Inc. v. University of Bridgeport, 243 Conn. 1, 699 A.2d 995 (1997) (§7 does not bestow standing on benefactor to enforce restriction).

[269] The provisions of §4 of UPMIFA, which deal with appropriation for expenditure or accumulation of the endowment fund, for example, emphasize the importance of respecting the intent of the donor, as expressed in the gift instrument. *See generally* Unif. Prudent Management Inst. Funds Act §4 and the Comment thereto.

[270] Unif. Prudent Management Inst. Funds Act §6.

[271] *See generally* Restatement (Second) of Trusts §25 cmts. c, a. The settlor's standing, if any, to enforce a trust may have its roots in Anglo-Norman law. In the fourteenth century, if the *feoffee to uses* failed to perform his duties, the *feoffor* could seek enforcement in the Court of Common Pleas. Later, the *cestui que use* also gained a right to seek enforcement, but in the Court of Chancery. *See generally* W. F. Fratcher, 6 Intl. Encyclopedia of Comp. Law 14 (F. H. Lawson ed., 1973).

[272] *See, e.g.,* UTC §411(b) (available at <http://www.uniformlaws.org/Act.aspx?title= Trust%20Code>).

the administration of the nation's inventory of charitable trusts.[273] Moreover, in construing the terms of a trust, a court will attempt to divine the intent of the settlor as manifested at the time the interest was created.[274] Is there not then some irony when that settlor, himself, is denied standing to bring before the court issues relating to that intent?

One cannot deny the practical downside for the trustee if the settlor is to remain in the picture, particularly in situations where the trustee and settlor disagree as to how certain trust provisions should be interpreted and administered. And there will always be the situation where the settlor and beneficiaries are at loggerheads and the trustee is caught in the middle.

Under the Uniform Trust Code, the settlor is an interested person with respect to a judicial proceeding brought by beneficiaries to terminate or modify a trust.[275] The Code would also allow a settlor to request the court to remove a trustee.[276] "The right to petition for removal does not . . . [however] . . . give the settlor of an irrevocable trust . . . the right to an annual report or to receive other information concerning administration of the trust."[277]

The Uniform Trust Code would allow a noncharitable irrevocable trust to be modified or terminated upon consent of the settlor and all beneficiaries, even if the modification or termination is inconsistent with a material purpose of the trust.[278] The Restatement (Third) of Trusts is in accord.[279] The Code is silent, however, as to whether this right dies with the settlor.[280] Also, the settlor may commence a proceeding to approve or disapprove any proposed modification or termination.[281]

The Uniform Trust Code provides that the settlor of a charitable trust, among others, may maintain a proceeding to enforce the trust.[282] The settlor may also bring a *cy pres* petition.[283]

---

[273] *See generally* 4A Scott on Trusts §391. *See generally* §9.4.2 of this handbook (standing to enforce charitable trusts). *See* Estate of Leitner, 2004 WL 440202 (Cal. App.) (suggesting that because attorneys general "may not be in a position to become aware of . . . [the] . . . .wrongful conduct" of charitable trustees, settlors may provide an "investigative function" by "bringing to light conduct detrimental to a charitable trust so that remedial action may be taken").

[274] *See generally* Restatement (Second) of Trusts §164 cmt. b.

[275] UTC §410 cmt. (available at <http://www.uniformlaws.org/Act.aspx?title=Trust%20 Code>).

[276] UTC §706(a) (available at <http://www.uniformlaws.org/Act.aspx?title=Trust%20 Code>).

[277] UTC §706 cmt. (available at <http://www.uniformlaws.org/Act.aspx?title=Trust%20 Code>).

[278] UTC §411(a) (available at <http://www.uniformlaws.org/Act.aspx?title=Trust%20Code>).

[279] Restatement (Third) of Trusts §65.

[280] Section 65(2) of the Restatement (Third) of Trusts provides that if all beneficiaries consent but the settlor is deceased, the court could authorize termination or modification if it determines that the reasons for termination or modification outweigh the material purpose.

[281] UTC §410(b) (available at <http://www.uniformlaws.org/Act.aspx?title=Trust%20 Code>).

[282] UTC §405(c) (available at <http://www.uniformlaws.org/Act.aspx?title=Trust%20 Code>).

[283] UTC §410(b) (available at <http://www.uniformlaws.org/Act.aspx?title=Trust%20 Code>).

§4.1.3 Creditor Accessibility as a General Inter Vivos Power of Appointment

Thus the Massachusetts Court . . . [in Ware v. Gulda*] . . . held that creditors of the settlor-beneficiary could reach the trust assets despite the fact that under the terms of the trust instrument, distributions by the trustee to, or on behalf of, the settlor were completely within its discretion, and even though the interests of the remaindermen beneficiaries would be adversely affected by such action . . . The* Gulda *decision provided the basis for our holding in* Paolozzi v. Commissioner *. . . to the effect that a settlor-beneficiary of a discretionary trust had failed to relinquish dominion and control over such interest for gift tax purposes.*[284]

It is becoming a general rule that a settlor's creditors may reach the trust property to the extent the settlor reserves a beneficial interest.[285] For example, a trust for the benefit of the settlor—fully discretionary as to income and principal—will expose the entire property to creditor attack.[286] The law thus bestows on the settlor the ability to indirectly extract value from the trust by incurring debts and leaving it to the creditors to collect.[287] This right to direct trust property to creditors conforms to the Restatement of Property's definition of a general inter vivos power of appointment.[288] The possession of such a right may have estate and gift tax consequences[289] and may also bear on the settlor's eligibility for Medicaid and on the rights of the settlor's spouse to reach the trust property.[290] Does it also mean, however, that the settlor may terminate the trust other than by incurring debts? Probably not:

---

[284] Outwin v. Comm'r, 76 T.C.153, 164–165 (1981) (referring to Ware v. Gulda, 331 Mass. 68, 117 N.E.2d 137 (1954) and Paolozzi v. Comm'r, 23 T.C. 182 (1954)).

[285] *See* §5.3.3.1 of this handbook (when the settlor's creditors may reach any beneficial interest that have been reserved).

[286] *See* §5.3.3.1 of this handbook (when the settlor's creditors may reach any beneficial interest that have been reserved).

[287] *See* §5.3.3.1 of this handbook (when the settlor's creditors may reach any beneficial interest that have been reserved). *See, e.g.*, Johnson v. First Nat'l Bank of Jackson, 386 So. 2d 1112, 1115 (Miss. 1980) (deeming a self-settled irrevocable inter vivos trust to be "in effect revocable" because settlor could borrow money up to the value of the trust estate, donate that amount to the Church of Scientology, and then have the creditor levy on the trust estate in satisfaction of the debt). *See generally* §5.3.3.1 of this handbook (whether the settlor's creditors may gain access to beneficial interests that have been reserved).

[288] Restatement (Second) of Property §11.4 (Wills and Other Donative Transfers). *Cf.* 5 Scott & Ascher §34.3 (When Settlor Is Sole Beneficiary) ("When the settlor creates a trust of which the settlor is the sole beneficiary, the settlor can, at any time, terminate the trust, even if doing so would defeat a material trust purpose").

[289] *See* §5.3.3.1 of this handbook (reaching the settlor's reserved beneficial interest).

[290] *See* §5.3.4 of this handbook (rights of beneficiary's spouse and children to the underlying trust property or to the equitable interest) and §5.3.5 of this handbook (Medicaid eligibility and recoupment). The trustee will find helpful the chart entitled "Trusts Affected by the Omnibus Reconciliation Act of 1993" published in C. B. Kruse, Jr., *Third-Party and Self-Created Trusts* 19–22 (2d ed. 1998). An earlier version of the chart can be found in Kruse, *Self-Settled Trusts Following OBRA 1993*, 134 Tr. & Est. 66, 68 (Mar. 1995). *See also* Kruse, *OBRA '93 Disability Trusts—A Status Report*, 10 Prob. & Prop. 15 (No. 3) (1996).

Even if the spendthrift provisions in the trust under consideration are void as to the settlor-beneficiary, this does not mean that the trust is void or that the settlor-beneficiary can terminate the trust without the consent of the other beneficiaries. We think the spendthrift provisions as to the interest of the settlor-beneficiary are severable.[291]

On the other hand, were the settlor the sole beneficiary of the trust, the settlor at any time and notwithstanding the terms of the trust would be able to terminate it and receive back title to the subject property.[292] This would be the case even though the termination would defeat a material trust purpose.[293] There are two qualifications: The settlor must not be under some incapacity at the time of the termination and the terms of the trust must not require that the trustee give consent to the termination.[294]

In 1997, Alaska enacted a statute that may insulate reserved beneficial interests in certain irrevocable, "self-settled," independently trusteed, discretionary trusts (created after April 1, 1997) from the reach of the settlor's creditors.[295] If a settlor of one of these Alaska asset protection trusts has reserved no express right of revocation and if the statute is effective in insulating the reserved beneficial interest from creditor attack, then it could be said that for gift and estate tax purposes the settlor has reserved no general inter vivos power of appointment over the transferred property.[296] Accordingly, although the transfer might have gift tax consequences, down the road the property itself, along with any appreciation, could be out of the settlor's federal gross estate for estate tax purposes.[297] A number of other U.S. jurisdictions have followed Alaska's lead. For more on the domestic asset protection trust, the reader is referred to Section 5.3.3.1 (c) of this handbook.

§4.1.4   Reserved General Inter Vivos Power of Appointment Opens Door to Settlor's Postmortem Creditors

In Section 5.3.3.1(b.1) of this handbook, we confirm that the inter vivos creditors of the settlor of a revocable inter vivos trust will generally have access to the entrusted property while the settlor is alive. What about the settlor's postmortem creditors? They would have access as well. Although such a trust is nontestamentary and is therefore not subject to the Wills Act or to the usual

---

[291] Fewell v. Republic Nat'l Bank of Dallas, 513 S.W.2d 596, 598 (Tex. 1974).

[292] *See generally* 5 Scott & Ascher §34.3 (When Settlor Is Sole Beneficiary); §8.2.2.1 of this handbook (trust terminations by consent).

[293] *See generally* 5 Scott & Ascher §34.3. *See also* §8.15.7 of this handbook (the *Claflin* doctrine, also known as the material purpose doctrine).

[294] *See generally* 5 Scott & Ascher §34.3.

[295] *See generally* §5.3.3.1(c) of this handbook (domestic asset protection havens).

[296] *See* Paolozzi v. Comm'r, 23 T.C. 182, 186 (1954) (gift tax); Outwin v. Comm'r, 76 T.C. 153 n.5 (1981) (estate tax); Paxton v. Comm'r, 86 T.C. 785 (1986) (estate tax).

[297] *See* Paolozzi v. Comm'r, 23 T.C. 182, 186 (1954) (gift tax); Outwin v. Comm'r, 76 T.C. 153 n.5 (1981) (estate tax); Paxton v. Comm'r, 86 T.C. 785 (1986) (estate tax).

procedures of estate administration, property held in it is subject to the claims of the creditors of the deceased settlor's probate estate, provided the property would have been subject to the claims of the postmortem creditors had it been owned outright by the settlor at the time of his or her death, taking account of homestead and other exemptions.[298]

§4.2 Expressly Reserved Beneficial Interests and Powers

The evolution and clarification of judicial thought in this country on whether revocable trusts are testamentary is aptly illustrated in the leading cases in Massachusetts.[1]

A settlor may expressly reserve a beneficial interest in the income or the principal, or both, of the trust.[2] "If the settlor is the sole beneficiary of a trust and is not under an incapacity, he can compel termination of the trust, although the purposes of the trust have not been accomplished."[3]

The settlor may expressly reserve special and general powers of appointment.[4] If a power is exercisable by a will it is known as a testamentary power.[5] A power exercisable by a deed is known as an inter vivos power.[6] The settlor may reserve a power to amend or revoke the trust.[7] (The right to amend is tantamount to a general inter vivos power of appointment because such a power can be inserted into the instrument through the amendment process.[8]) It is now settled law that a reserved right of revocation neither invalidates the trust as an ineffective attempt at a testamentary disposition[9] nor makes it a constructive agency[10] that terminates upon the death of the putative settlor.[11]

---

[298] Restatement (Third) of Trusts § 25, cmt. e.

§4.2 [1] Restatement (Third) of Trusts, Reporter's Notes on Comment b to §25 (referring to McEvoy v. Boston Five Cents Sav. Bank, 201 Mass. 50, 87 N.E. 465 (1909); Jones v. Old Colony Trust Co., 251 Mass. 309, 146 N.E. 716 (1925); Roche v. Brickley, 254 Mass. 584, 150 N.E. 866 (1926); National Shawmut Bank v. Joy, 315 Mass. 457, 53 N.E.2d 113 (1944)).

[2] *See generally* Restatement (Second) of Trusts §114.

[3] Restatement (Second) of Trusts §339. *See generally* 6 Scott & Ascher §41.9. Upon the death of the settlor before the trust's termination, the subject property would have to pass either as a remainder or a reversion into the settlor's probate estate for the settlor to enjoy "sole beneficiary" status. This, of course, assumes that the settlor is the only designated income or permissible beneficiary.

[4] *See generally* National Shawmut Bank v. Joy, 315 Mass. 457, 53 N.E.2d 113 (1944); 4 Scott on Trusts §330.

[5] *See generally* §8.1 of this handbook (powers of appointment).

[6] *See generally* §8.1 of this handbook (powers of appointment).

[7] *See generally* 4 Scott on Trusts §§331, 331.1, 331.2; §§5.3.3.1 of this handbook (reaching settlor's reserved beneficial interest), 8.2.2.2 of this handbook (the revocable trust), and 8.11 of this handbook (the duties of the trustee of a revocable inter vivos trust).

[8] *See generally* §8.1 of this handbook (powers of appointment).

[9] *See* National Shawmut Bank v. Joy, 315 Mass. 457, 53 N.E.2d 113 (1944).

[10] *See* National Shawmut Bank v. Joy, 315 Mass. 457, 53 N.E.2d 113 (1944).

[11] Restatement (Third) of Trusts §25.

While a trust is revocable, "the trustee may follow a direction of the settlor that is contrary to the terms of the trust."[12] At the outset, the settlor may appoint himself trustee or cotrustee by declaration or reserve the right to do so thereafter.[13] These are the traditional ways the settlor may remain in the picture. Thus, the typical revocable inter vivos trust cannot serve as a vehicle for limiting tort liability in a noncommercial setting. If the owner of an automobile, for example, transfers legal title to it to the trustee of a nominee trust in exchange for fully vested transferable shares of beneficial/equitable interest, is the trustee or the owner of the shares, or neither, primarily liable in tort should there be an accident due to the beneficial/equitable owner's negligent operation of the vehicle? Or are they perhaps jointly liable? Or is only the trust estate at risk? It seems settled that the shareowner is the one primarily and personally exposed, absent special facts or a statute to the contrary.[14] Had title to the vehicle been transferred to the trustee of a garden-variety self-settled trust under which the transferor had reserved a general inter vivos power of appointment (such as a right to revoke the trust and get back title to the vehicle), it is suggested that the result would/should be the same.[15] The transferor would/should be the one exposed to primary and personal liability, absent special facts. Certainly for purposes of applying the rule against perpetuities, the holder of a general inter vivos power of appointment incident to a trust relationship is deemed to own the entrusted property outright and free of trust.[16] So also for taxation,[17] welfare-eligibility,[18] and creditor-accessibility purposes.[19] There is no discernible policy reason why this should not also be the case for tort liability purposes.

Nowadays settlors are resorting to more limited, subtler means of maintaining involvement with the trusts that they have created, such as by reserving rights to control investments, to remove trustees, or to receive accountings. These reservations are less burdensome for the settlor than the assumption of a cotrusteeship but not necessarily less burdensome for the trustee.

The practice of reserving the right to direct investments is a particularly worrisome development from the trustee's perspective because the law is not entirely clear whether the trustee has some fiduciary responsibility to monitor

---

[12] UTC §808(a) (available at <http://www.uniformlaws.org/Act.aspx?title=Trust%20Code>).

[13] *See generally* 2 Scott on Trusts §100.

[14] *See, e.g.*, Morrison v. Lennett, 415 Mass. 857, 616 N.E. 2d 92 (1993) ("In prior decisions, involving nominee provisions in trust instruments, the court has disregarded the trustees' record ownership of the property and liability has been imposed directly on the beneficiaries.").

[15] *See* Restatement (Third) of Property (Wills and Other Donative Transfers) § 17.4, cmt. f(1) ("A presently exercisable general power of appointment is an ownership-equivalent power."). *See also* Restatement (Third) of Trusts § 74.

[16] *See generally* §8.2.1.1 of this handbook.

[17] *See generally* §8.9.3 of this handbook.

[18] *See generally* §5.3.5 of this handbook.

[19] *See generally* §5.3.3.1 of this handbook.

and react to the settlor's investment activities.[20] Any ambiguity in the arrangement will pose a trap for the unwary trustee and an extraordinary burden for the cautious trustee. The trustee should not accept directed trust business unless these ambiguities can be resolved by express language in the governing instrument.

There is some authority to the effect that, in the case of an irrevocable trust, a nontrustee to whom investment discretion has been allocated will be held to a fiduciary standard in the exercise of that discretion.[21] It should be emphasized, however, that this will in no way diminish the general fiduciary duties of the trustee.

As to devices aimed at riding herd on the trustee—reserved rights of removal, consultation, and disclosure—the law has not settled on what constraints, if any, are placed on the holders of these rights. If they are fiduciaries, they are like cotrustees and presumably assume the burdens commensurate with that office, such as the risk of surcharge for unreasonable behavior. If they are *not* fiduciaries, then what are they? How does the law protect the trustee from assertions of these rights that are arbitrary, unreasonable, or imprudent—in short, that are not in the interest of the beneficiaries? The law is similarly unsettled when it comes to the allocation of trustee oversight responsibilities to third parties such as protectors,[22] although the Uniform Trust Code attempts to clear up some of this confusion.

The Code provides that if the terms of a trust confer upon a person other than the settlor of a revocable trust power to direct certain actions of the trustee, the trustee shall act in accordance with an exercise of the power unless the attempted exercise is manifestly contrary to the terms of the trust or the trustee knows the attempted exercise would constitute a serious breach of a fiduciary duty that the person holding the power owes to the beneficiaries of the trust.[23] What is that duty? A person, other than a beneficiary, who holds a power to direct, is presumptively a fiduciary who, as such, is required to act in good faith with regard to the purposes of the trust and the interests of the beneficiaries.[24] The Code further provides that the holder of a power to direct is liable for any

---

[20] *See generally* 2A Scott on Trusts §185; Restatement (Third) of Trusts §185 cmts. b–h (1992); Kemper, *Construction and Operation of Will or Trust Provision Appointing Advisors to Trustee or Executor,* 56 A.L.R.3d 1249 (1974). *See also* Cal. Prob. Code Ann. §16462 (1990) (providing that "a trustee of a revocable trust is not liable to a beneficiary for any act performed or permitted pursuant to written directions from the person holding the power to revoke, including a person to whom the power to direct the trustee is delegated."). *See generally* Hatamyar, *See No Evil? The Role of the Directed Trustee under ERISA,* 64 Tenn. L. Rev. 1, 38–41 (1996) (discussing the common law of directed trustees).

[21] *See* UTC §808(d) (available at <http://www.uniformlaws.org/Act.aspx?title=Trust%20Code>) (providing that the nonbeneficiary holder of a power to direct is presumptively a fiduciary).

[22] *See generally* §3.2.6 of this handbook (considerations in the selection of a trustee); UTC §808 cmt. (available at <http://www.uniformlaws.org/Act.aspx?title=Trust%20Code>).

[23] UTC §808(b) (available at <http://www.uniformlaws.org/Act.aspx?title=Trust%20Code>).

[24] UTC §808(d) (available at <http://www.uniformlaws.org/Act.aspx?title=Trust%20Code>).

loss that results from breach of a fiduciary duty.[25] On the other hand, "[a] trustee who administers a trust subject to a veto power occupies a position akin to that of a cotrustee and is responsible for taking appropriate action if the third party's refusal to consent would result in a serious breach of trust."[26]

§4.3   The Settlor-Brought Declaratory Judgment Action

It has been the general rule that the validity of a revocable inter vivos trust (or will) may not be determined in a declaratory judgment action during the lifetime of the settlor (or testator).[1] This is no longer the case in New Hampshire. In New Hampshire, by statute, a settlor during his or her life may commence a judicial proceeding to determine the validity of a trust, whether revocable or irrevocable, that he or she has created.[2]

---

[25] UTC §808(d) (available at <http://www.uniformlaws.org/Act.aspx?title=Trust%20 Code>).

[26] UTC §808 cmt. (available at <http://www.uniformlaws.org/Act.aspx?title=Trust%20 Code>).

§4.3 [1] *See* Ullman v. Garcia, 645 So. 2d 168 (Fla. 3d DCA 1994). Declaratory judgment actions are discussed generally in §8.42 of this handbook.

[2] *See* R.S.A. 564-B:4-406 (N.H.).

CHAPTER **5**

The Beneficiary

§5.1 Who/What May Be a Trust Beneficiary Generally; Who/What Are the Beneficiaries in a Given Situation

The term beneficiary includes not only beneficiaries who received their interests under the terms of the trust but also beneficiaries who received their interests by other means, including by assignment, exercise of a power of appointment, resulting trust upon the failure of an interest, gap in a disposition, operation of an antilapse statute upon the predecease of a named beneficiary, or upon termination of the trust.[1]

Human beings and corporations. A human being may be the beneficiary of a trust. An artificial legal entity, such as a corporation, may be as well.[2]

A trust may have one,[3] or more than one,[4] beneficiary. "If the terms of a trust require payment to one person of both the income for a period of time, and, thereafter, the principal, that person is the trust's sole beneficiary, unless there is a contingent gift to another or a resulting trust upon the designated person's failure to survive the stated period."[5] Generally for someone to qualify as the *sole beneficiary* of a trust, the underlying property must pass to that person's probate estate in the event of his or her death before final distribution.

A sole trustee may be one of several beneficiaries and a cotrustee may be a sole beneficiary.[6] A settlor may establish a trust for the settlor's own benefit.[7] "A person is a beneficiary of a trust if the settlor manifests an intention to give the person a beneficial interest...."[8]

A trust beneficiary's interest is an equitable property interest.[9] It can be a present interest or a future interest, and, whether vested or contingent, the interest is property.[10] Thus, entities capable of owning property, *i.e.*, with the

---

§5.1 [1] UTC §103 cmt. (available at <http://www.uniformlaws.org/Act.aspx?title=Trust%20Code>).

[2] Bogert §1.

[3] 2 Scott & Ascher §12.2.1.

[4] 2 Scott & Ascher §12.2.

[5] 3 Scott & Ascher §13.2.2.

[6] 2 Scott & Ascher §12.4; Bogert §1. *See generally* §8.7 of this handbook (merger).

[7] 2 Scott & Ascher §12.3.

[8] Restatement (Third) of Trusts §48.

[9] *See* Restatement of Property §6 cmt. a; Restatement (Second) of Trusts §2 cmt. f. *See generally* §3.5.1 of this handbook (nature and extent of the trustee's estate).

[10] *See* 2 Scott on Trusts §130 (The Property Subject to the Trust); 1 Restatement of Property at 3 (introduction to ch. 1) (the equitable interest); UPC §1-201(3) (providing that a beneficiary of a trust includes one who has any present or future interest, vested or contingent, under the trust); In re Catherwood's Trust, 173 A.2d 86, 91 (1961) ("A gift of an equitable life estate in income or of an estate in remainder does constitute a grant of a vested property right of which the recipients cannot be divested by legislative action."); Henry Hansmann and Ugo Mattei, *The Functions of Trust Law: A Comparative Legal and Economic Analysis*, 73 N.Y.U. L. Rev. 434, 469–473 (1998) (suggesting that a beneficiary's interest is property, at least to the extent of that beneficiary's interest under the trust); *see, e.g.*, Barber v. Barber, 837 P.2d 714 (Alaska 1992) (confirming that a contingent trust beneficiary has a constitutionally protected property interest). *See also* UTC §103(11) (available at

capacity to take and hold legal title to property,[11] are eligible to be trust beneficiaries; these are entities to whom enforceable personal rights with respect to tangible and intangible things may attach.[12] Such entities would include minors,[13] the insane,[14] certain corporations,[15] unincorporated associations,[16] noncitizens,[17] persons who are unborn[18] or unascertained,[19] the United States,[20] or a state[21] of the United States.

At common law, a child in gestation, *i.e.*, a child *en ventre sa mere*, who was born alive was deemed to have been alive at gestation.[22] Thus, "the common-law perpetuity period was comprised of three components: (1) a life in being (2) plus 21 years (3) plus a period of gestation when needed."[23] Although neither period of the Uniform Statutory Rule Against Perpetuities (USRAP) has a gestation extension,[24] the act makes no effort to interfere with whatever common law or statutory equitable property rights one born alive might possess by virtue of having been *in utero* at a given time.[25] In other words, someone *in utero*

<http://www.uniformlaws.org/Act.aspx?title=Trust%20Code>) ("'Property' means anything that may be the subject of ownership, whether real or personal, legal or equitable, or any interest therein.").

[11] Restatement (Third) of Trusts §43.

[12] *See generally* W. N. Hohfeld, Fundamental Legal Conceptions 23–124 (1923) (suggesting that property is a collection of rights, privileges, powers and immunities with respect to a thing rather than the thing itself); *see also* 1 Restatement of Property at 3 (introduction to ch. 1).

[13] *See* 2 Scott on Trusts §116; Restatement (Third) of Trusts §43 cmt. a (providing that a minor may be a trust beneficiary though he or she lacks the capacity to transfer property and enter into contracts).

[14] 2 Scott on Trusts §116.

[15] *See* 2 Scott on Trusts §117.1. *See also* 2 Scott & Ascher §12.5.1. *But see* Restatement (Third) of Trusts §43 cmt. c (providing that if, by statute, a corporation cannot take title to land, or to land of more than a certain value or for other than certain purposes, it cannot become the beneficiary of a trust of land, or of land of more than the designated value or for other than the designated purposes).

[16] Restatement (Third) of Trusts §43 cmt. d; 2 Scott & Ascher §12.6.

[17] Restatement (Third) of Trusts §43 cmt. b; 2 Scott & Ascher §12.5.2 (Aliens).

[18] 2 Scott & Ascher §12.1.1.

[19] Scott on Trusts §112.1. *See* Restatement (Third) of Trusts §44 cmt. c. In Louisiana, however, with the exception of the "class trust," a beneficiary must be in being and ascertainable on the date of the creation of the trust. La. Rev. Stat. Ann. §9:1803. An unborn child is deemed a person in being and ascertainable, if he is born alive. La. Rev. Stat. Ann. §9:18.03. In Louisiana, a "class trust" is enforceable even though some members of the class are not yet in being at the time of the creation of the trust, *provided at least one member of the class is then in being*. La. Rev. Stat. Ann. §9:1891(A). Under Louisiana law, a "class trust" is an inter vivos or testamentary trust in favor of a class consisting of some or all of the settlor's children, grandchildren, nieces, nephews, grandnieces, or grandnephews, or any combination thereof.

[20] Restatement (Third) of Trusts §43 cmt. a.

[21] Restatement (Third) of Trusts §43 cmt. a.

[22] UPC §2-901 cmt.

[23] UPC §2-901 cmt.

[24] *See* UPC §2-901. *See also* §8.2.1.7 of this handbook (the two USRAP periods).

[25] UPC §2-901 cmt.

may be a provisional trust beneficiary. "As to the legal status of conceived-after-death children, that question has not yet been resolved."[26]

One whose equitable interest under a trust has extinguished[27] or whose interest is an expectancy (not to be confused with a contingent equitable interest) is not a beneficiary and thus lacks the standing to maintain a suit against the trustee.[28] A beneficiary designation in the will of a living person is an example of an expectancy, assuming no contractual overlay. This is because the will does not speak until the testator's death. Until such time the will is said to be ambulatory.

As noted, a settlor or trustee of a trust may also be its beneficiary, provided the same person is not the sole trustee and sole beneficiary.[29] When the same person possesses the entire legal and the entire equitable interest, there is no trust. The interests are said to be merged. Under the doctrine of merger, a topic we take up in Section 8.7 of this handbook, that person owns the subject property outright and free of trust.

In the noncharitable context, the equitable interests of the unborn[30] and unascertained are represented by the guardian ad litem,[31] unless a living and identified beneficiary is allowed to represent their interests under the doctrine of virtual representation.[32]

Charities. In the charitable context, future unascertained recipients of charity are entitled to beneficiary status because the attorney general is charged with enforcing trusts established on their behalf.[33] Even a charitable

---

[26] UPC §2-901 cmt.

[27] *See, e.g.*, Matter of McDonough Living Trust, 2009 WL 2447481 (Minn. App. 2009) (denying standing to the personal representative of the probate estate of a deceased trust beneficiary whose interest under the trust terminated at death to petition for the removal of the trustee, the decedent's status as a trust beneficiary having terminated at death).

[28] 4 Scott & Ascher §24.19. For an example of what an expectancy interest would look like in the context of an inter vivos trust, consider Carolyn's interest in Moon v. Lesikar, 230 S.W.3d 800 (Tex. App. 2007) ("We conclude that because Mr. Lesikar was the settlor of the trust with the power to revoke the trust, the sole beneficiary of the trust while alive, and co-trustee of the trust, Carolyn . . . [, though designated in the terms of the trust as a successor beneficiary,] . . . has no standing to complain of Mr. Lesikar's . . . [inter vivos] . . . disposition of Family Trust assets, including the Airport Stock."). Under classic principles of trust and property law, Carolyn's equitable property interest, though ultra-contingent, would still be a property interest. The Texas court, by depriving her of standing to seek the trust's enforcement, effectively downgraded that interest to a mere expectancy.

[29] Restatement (Third) of Trusts §43 cmt. a.

[30] 2 Scott & Ascher §12.1.1.

[31] *See* Restatement (Second) of Trusts §214 cmt. a. *See generally* Begleiter, *The Guardian Ad Litem in Estate Proceedings*, 20 Willamette L. Rev. 643, 651–653 (1984). *See generally* §8.14 of this handbook (when a guardian ad litem or special representative is needed and when virtual representation will suffice).

[32] *See* §§8.15.34 of this handbook (virtual representation doctrine) and 8.14 of this handbook (when a guardian ad litem or special representative is needed and when virtual representation will suffice).

[33] *See* 4A Scott on Trusts §§364, 391. *See generally* §9.4.2 of this handbook (standing to enforce charitable trusts).

corporation yet to be formed may be the beneficiary of a trust.[34] As the beneficiaries are indefinite, the attorney general is charged with the duty of informing the court of any breach of duty by the trustee.[35] Under the Uniform Trust Code, the settlor and any person with a special interest in the charitable trust also may maintain an enforcement proceeding.[36] For purposes of the Uniform Probate Code, however, the beneficiary of a charitable trust is limited to anyone who has standing to seek its enforcement in the courts.[37]

Tombs and gravesites. The dead, who are without any status whatsoever under the common law, are entitled to beneficiary status, provided the legislature authorizes trusts for the perpetual care of gravesites and legal mechanisms for their enforcement.[38] Otherwise, a person who has already died before a trust is established cannot be a beneficiary.[39]

In the absence of statutory authority, the relatives[40] of the dead should have common law standing to enforce gravesite protection trusts during the period permitted by the rule against perpetuities.[41] Essentially, such trusts exist

---

[34] 2 Scott & Ascher §12.1.2 (noting that a trust for the benefit of a yet-to-be-organized noncharitable corporation might well violate the rule against perpetuities). *See generally* §8.2.1 of this handbook (rule against perpetuities).

[35] *See* §9.4.2 of this handbook (standing to enforce charitable trusts).

[36] UTC §405 cmt. (available at <http://www.uniformlaws.org/Act.aspx?title=Trust%20 Code>).

[37] UPC §1-201(3).

[38] *See, e.g.*, Bolton v. Stillwagon, 410 Pa. 618, 190 A.2d 105 (1963) (holding the trustees of a perpetual care trust personally liable for self-dealing with the trust property, a trust that was operating pursuant to statutory authority). *See generally* P. Jackson, The Law of Cadavers and of Burial and Burial Places (2d ed. 1950); G. Newhall, Settlement of Estates and Fiduciary Law in Massachusetts §10 (4th ed. 1958); 4A Scott on Trusts §374.9. *See generally* §9.9.5 of this handbook (honorary trusts), which discusses the extent to which the UTC and the UPC would recognize and provide for the enforcement of this type of honorary trust; 6 Scott & Ascher §39.7.5 (confirming that a trust for the perpetual maintenance of a grave or a tomb is noncharitable unless a statute provides otherwise, or unless, perhaps, the interred was a well-known public figure, such as a president or war-time general).

[39] 2 Scott & Ascher §12.1.3. *See generally* §§8.2.1 of this handbook (the rule against perpetuities) (discussing the concept of vesting) and 8.15.55 of this handbook (antilapse [the trust application]) (discussing antilapse principles applicable to trusts).

[40] *See, however,* §8.2.1.9 of this handbook (abolition of the rule against perpetuities) (suggesting how expansive the term *relatives* can be).

[41] *But see* 2 Scott on Trusts §124.2; Lucker v. Bayside Cemetery, 114 A.D.3d 162, 979 N.Y.S.2d 8 (2013). In New York, a trust for the perpetual care of a grave is by statute deemed a charitable trust. Thus, it is generally the New York Attorney General who is vested with the standing to seek enforcement of such trusts in the courts. "We hold that the *Lucker* plaintiffs and their class as they define it—indeed, whatever group categorization is used—are neither sufficiently 'sharply defined' nor sufficiently 'limited in number' to be eligible for standing to sue the cemetery as beneficiaries. To the contrary, aside from the use of the vague term 'near relatives,' plaintiffs can offer no rational limiting principle that would distinguish children from grandchildren—or, indeed, great-grandchildren—or from nieces or nephews or cousins and their children." Lucker v. Bayside Cemetery, 114 A.D.3d 162, 979 N.Y.S.2d 8, 14–15 (2013).

for the benefit of the relatives who themselves possess the common law right to visit, honor, and protect gravesites of their deceased relatives.[42]

One court has suggested that a "sort of trust" attaches to a burial plot, the trust being for the benefit of the "family" of the interred.[43] The Restatement (Third) of Trusts suggests that an honorary or adapted purpose trust that grants the trustee a "power to maintain a grave should be allowed for the lifetime of the decedent's spouse and children, or of other concerned individuals designated in the will . . . , all lives in being at the testator's death."[44]

At common law, a bequest for the purpose of maintaining an individual tomb or monument did not give rise to a charitable trust,[45] and thus violated the rule against perpetuities.[46] For Prof. John Chipman Gray, however, the vice was not "that the interests of the *cestui que trust* are too remote, but that there is no *cestui que trust* at all."[47]

Today, in most jurisdictions a trust for the perpetual care of someone's gravesite is by statute enforceable.[48] "Some of the statutes clearly treat such a trust as charitable for all purposes, some do not."[49] Presumably the state attorney general has some role to play in the supervision of a perpetual care trust that qualifies as charitable or quasi-charitable, along with the relatives of the interred.[50]

Holders of powers of appointment. Under the definition of property adopted by the Restatement of Property, the holder of a general inter vivos power of appointment would be a beneficiary because the holder would possess an enforceable equitable personal right relating to a tangible or intangible thing.[51] The Uniform Trust Code is in accord.[52] So also is the Restatement (Third) of Trusts.[53] In the pre-Restatement world, when personal rights and property rights were considered mutually exclusive, a powerholder had only a personal right.[54] The Uniform Probate Code considers the donee, appointee,

---

[42] *See generally* Rounds, *Protections Afforded to Massachusetts' Ancient Burial Grounds*, 73 Mass. L. Rev. 176 (1988).

[43] Sanford v. Vinal, 28 Mass. App. Ct. 476, 485–486, 552 N.E.2d 579, 584 (1990).

[44] Restatement (Third) of Trusts §47 cmt. d(2). *See generally* §§9.27 of this handbook (the purpose trust) and 9.29 of this handbook (the adapted trust).

[45] *See generally* 6 Scott & Ascher §§38.7.10, 39.7.5; In re Mary R. Latimer Trust, 2013 WL 4463388 (Del. Ch. Aug. 2, 2013).

[46] *See* John Chipman Gray, The Rule Against Perpetuities, Appendix H §898 (4th ed. 1942).

[47] John Chipman Gray, The Rule Against Perpetuities, Appendix H §898 (4th ed. 1942).

[48] 6 Scott & Ascher §38.7.10.

[49] 6 Scott & Ascher §38.7.10.

[50] *See generally* §9.4.2 of this handbook (standing to enforce charitable trusts).

[51] W. N. Hohfeld, Fundamental Legal Conceptions 23-124 (1923). *See generally* 1 Restatement of Property at 43 (introduction to ch. 1).

[52] UTC §103(2)(B) (available at <http://www.uniformlaws.org/Act.aspx?title=Trust%20Code>).

[53] Restatement (Third) of Trusts, ch. 9, Introductory Note.

[54] *See generally* National Shawmut Bank v. Joy, 315 Mass. 457, 472, 53 N.E.2d 113, 123 (1944) (suggesting that power of appointment is not property).

or taker in default of an exercise of a power of appointment to be a "beneficiary designated in a governing instrument."[55]

Beneficiary designations must be definite. Where there is no beneficiary, there is no trust.[56] In the case of private trusts (as opposed to charitable or public trusts), the beneficiary must be definite.[57] This does not mean that the beneficiary specifically must be named—a designation by description is sufficient,[58] *e.g.*, future issue or descendants.[59] The beneficiary is sufficiently definite, however, only if it is certain at the time when the trust takes effect that the beneficiary will be identified before the expiration of the period allowed by the Rule against Perpetuities.[60]

Class designations. It commonly is held that a trust for the benefit of the members of a class of persons is valid.[61] "When a trust is created for members of a class, suit to redress or enjoin a breach of trust can be maintained by any member of the class."[62] This would apply to declarations of trust as well.[63] Under the common law, however, a trust created for the benefit of an indefinite class of persons will fail, and a resulting trust will be imposed,[64] *e.g.*, a trust for all of *X*'s friends or for all of *X*'s relatives.[65] Note, however, that under the Uniform Trust Code, a trust may be created for a noncharitable purpose without a definite or definitely ascertainable beneficiary, or for a noncharitable but otherwise valid purpose to be selected by the trustee.[66] The trust, though,

---

[55] UPC §1-201(3).

[56] Restatement (Second) of Trusts §66. *See, however,* §9.9.5 of this handbook (honorary trusts).

[57] Restatement (Third) of Trusts §44; Restatement (Second) of Trusts §112; 2 Scott & Ascher §12.1.

[58] Restatement (Third) of Trusts §44 cmt. b; Restatement (Second) of Trusts §112 cmt. b. *See generally* §5.2 of this handbook (class designations such as children, issue, heirs, and, relatives).

[59] 2 Scott & Ascher §12.7. *See generally* §5.2 of this handbook (class designations such as children, issue, heirs, and relatives).

[60] 2 Scott & Ascher §12.7. *See generally* §8.2.1 of this handbook (rule against perpetuities) and UTC §402(b) (available at <http://www.uniformlaws.org/Act.aspx?title=Trust%20Code>).

[61] *See* Restatement (Second) of Trusts §120. *See generally* §5.2 of this handbook (class designations such as children, issue, heirs, and relatives).

[62] Restatement (Third) of Trusts §45 cmt. f. "The fact that a member of the class may ultimately take nothing does not prevent that beneficiary from maintaining suit; each of the beneficiaries of such a trust is in this position, for if none could sue the trustee might commit a breach of trust with impunity." Restatement (Third) of Trusts §45 cmt. f.

[63] Restatement (Third) of Trusts §45 cmt. g.

[64] *See* Restatement (Third) of Trusts §45; Restatement (Second) of Trusts §123. *See generally* 2 Scott on Trusts §123; National Shawmut Bank v. Joy, 315 Mass. 457, 463, 53 N.E.2d 113, 118 (1944).

[65] 2 Scott & Ascher §12.9 (noting, however, that a limited or special nonfiduciary power of appointment in someone that may be exercised in favor of *X*'s friends or relatives would not fail for indefiniteness). *See generally* §8.1 of this handbook (powers of appointment).

[66] UTC §409(1) (available at <http://www.uniformlaws.org/Act.aspx?title=Trust%20Code>). *See generally* §9.9.5 of this handbook (honorary trusts).

may not be enforced for more than twenty-one years.[67] The Restatement (Third) of Trusts is generally in accord.[68]

Animals and inanimate objects. Trusts for the benefit of animals or of inanimate objects have been sustained, even when not charitable.[69] These trusts, however, depend upon the honor of the trustee as there is no person who as beneficiary can apply to the court for enforcement.[70] If the named trustee does not carry out the trust, the property will be held upon a resulting trust.[71] The Restatement (Third) of Trusts would grant the person caring for a pet standing to enforce an "adapted trust" for the pet's benefit[72] and allow the trust to continue for the life of the pet.[73] The Uniform Trust Code is generally in accord.[74]

Standing to seek trust's enforcement. The beneficiary of a trust with even a "minute or remote" equitable interest has standing (*locus standi*) to seek its enforcement, to include having the trust property secured.[75] Nor is *locus standi* dependent upon the size of the equitable interest.[76] "It is different where- . . . [one] . . . has no existing equitable interest, vested or contingent, but only a mere possibility of a future interest—an expectancy or *spes successionis*."[77] Just as a person who might incidentally benefit from the performance of a contract cannot enforce the contract,[78] so also " . . . a person who merely benefits incidentally from the performance of the trust is not a beneficiary."[79] Thus, a trust to pay someone's tuition at a specified educational institution does not make the institution a trust beneficiary.[80] Nor usually would a direction to the trustee in the terms of the trust to employ a particular individual in the administration

---

[67] UTC §409(1) (available at <http://www.uniformlaws.org/Act.aspx?title=Trust%20Code>).

[68] Restatement (Third) of Trusts §§46 (Members of an Indefinite Class as Beneficiaries), 47 (Trusts for Noncharitable Purposes). *See generally* §9.29 of this handbook (the adapted trust) and §9.27 of this handbook (the purpose trust).

[69] *See generally* 2 Scott on Trusts §124. *See also* UTC §408 (available at <http://www.uniformlaws.org/Act.aspx?title=Trust%20Code>) (trust for care of animal); §9.9.5 of this handbook (honorary trusts).

[70] *See generally* Restatement (Second) of Trusts §124 cmt. d. *But see* UTC §408(b) (available at <http://www.uniformlaws.org/Act.aspx?title=Trust%20Code>) (authorizing enforcement of a trust for care of animal by a person appointed in the terms of the trust or, if no person is so appointed, by a person appointed by the court).

[71] *See generally* Restatement (Second) of Trusts §404. *But see* UTC §408(b) (available at <http://www.uniformlaws.org/Act.aspx?title=Trust%20Code>) (providing that a person having an interest in the welfare of the animal may request the court to appoint a person to enforce the trust or to remove a person appointed). *See, however,* §9.9.5 of this handbook regarding the enforceability of trusts for pets under the UTC and the UPC.

[72] Restatement (Third) of Trusts §47, cmt. f.

[73] Restatement (Third) of Trusts §47, cmt. d(2).

[74] *See* §9.9.5 of this handbook (honorary trusts).

[75] Lewin ¶38-11 (England); Farkas v. Williams, 125 N.E.2d 600 (Ill. 1955) (U.S.).

[76] Lewin ¶38-11 (England); Farkas v. Williams, 125 N.E.2d 600 (Ill. 1955) (U.S.).

[77] Lewin ¶38-11 (England).

[78] 2 Scott & Ascher §12.13; 4 Scott & Ascher §24.4.

[79] Restatement (Third) of Trusts §48.

[80] Restatement (Third) of Trusts §48 cmt. a, illus. 3.

of the trust bestow on that individual beneficiary status.[81] Likewise, that a
trustee is compensated from the trust estate for his services alone would not
make him a trust beneficiary.[82] Even though someone who benefits incidentally
from the performance of a trust may not enjoy the status of a beneficiary, that
person might still under certain circumstances have access to the trust estate as
a creditor of the trustee, provided there is recourse to the trust estate;[83] or as a
creditor of the beneficiary, provided the equitable interest is creditor
accessible.[84]

To summarize, any beneficiary of a trust would have standing to seek its
enforcement in the courts. The Restatement (Third) of Trusts, specifically the
official commentary to Section 94, is in accord:

> A suit to enforce a private trust ordinarily . . . may be maintained by any benefi-
> ciary whose rights are or may be adversely affected by the matter(s) at issue. The
> beneficiaries of a trust include any person who holds a beneficial interest, *present or*
> *future, vested or contingent.* . . . This includes a person who is eligible to receive a
> discretionary distribution . . . or who holds a reversionary interest by operation of
> law, as well as one who has succeeded to a beneficial interest by assignment,
> inheritance, or otherwise. The holder of a power of revocation or withdrawal . . . is
> a beneficiary; so is the donee of a special or general power of appointment, as is an
> expressed or implied . . . taker in default of appointment.[85]

The Restatement (Third), however, is sending mixed signals as to whether
the settlor of a trust, *qua* settlor, would have standing to seek its enforcement. As
noted above, the Section 94 commentary confirms that one "who holds a
reversionary interest by operation of law" under a noncharitable (private) trust
is a beneficiary of that trust. Under classic principles of property and trust law,
the settlor of a noncharitable (private) trust retains by operation of law a
nonpossessory vested equitable reversionary property interest.[86] If the trust
eventually terminates in favor of designated equitable remaindermen, then the
equitable reversionary property interest extinguishes before the settlor can ever
come into possession of the legal title to the underlying property; if the trust
fails in mid-course, then legal title to the underlying property becomes possessory via the imposition of a resulting trust.[87] Ergo the settlor, *qua* settlor, is a

---

[81] Restatement (Third) of Trusts §48 cmt. b; 2 Scott & Ascher §12.13.3 (noting, however, that
there is the rare case when a direction to employ someone is for the purpose of providing a benefit
to that person, in which case that person will enjoy the status of a beneficiary).

[82] Restatement (Third) of Trusts §48 cmt. c.

[83] *See generally* 2 Scott & Ascher §12.13.2 (Debts Arising During Administration); §7.3.2 of
this handbook (agreements with nonbeneficiaries to limit trustee's contractual liability) and §7.3.3
of this handbook (trustee's liability as legal owner in tort to nonbeneficiaries).

[84] *See generally* A.W. Gans, *Intervention in litigation by one claiming interest in fruits thereof as trust*
beneficiary, 2 A.L.R.2d 227; §5.3.3.3 of this handbook (discretionary provisions and other restraints
upon voluntary and involuntary transfers of the equitable interest including the spendthrift
clause).

[85] Restatement (Third) of Trusts §94 cmt. b (emphasis added).

[86] *See generally* §4.1.1.1 of this handbook (the equitable reversionary interest).

[87] *See generally* §4.1.1.1 of this handbook (the resulting trust).

beneficiary of the trust that he has established and accordingly would have standing to seek the trust's enforcement in the courts.

There is elsewhere, however, seemingly conflicting official Section 94 commentary, which states: "Neither the settlor of a private trust nor the personal representative or successors in interest of the settlor can, *as such*, maintain a suit against the trustee to enjoin or redress a breach of trust or otherwise to enforce the trust, absent contrary legislation."[88]

Perhaps this apparent conflict can be reconciled if, for the holder of an equitable reversionary property interest to qualify as a trust beneficiary, his interest in the underlying property has to have already ripened into a possessory right.

For a general discussion of whether the settlor of a trust, *qua* settlor, should have standing to seek the trust's enforcement in the courts, see Section 4.1.2 of this handbook.

Assignees of the equitable interest. Some equitable interests are not assignable, *e.g.*, a permissible beneficiary's contingent interest under a discretionary trust, but some are. A trustee on actual or constructive notice[89] of the valid assignment of an equitable interest under his trust, *e.g.*, the assignment by a beneficiary of his or her fully vested and assignable equitable remainder interest, owes "the same duties towards the assignee or disponee as he formerly owed to the beneficiary."[90] For all intents and purposes, the assignee or disponee is a beneficiary.[91]

§5.2 Class Designation: "Children," "Issue," "Heirs," and "Relatives" (Some Rules of Construction)

[I]n no branch of the law do mere words play a greater part. In drafting a will or trust involving future interests, no amount of clear thinking or appreciation of practical aspects of the problem will suffice, if the draughtsman does not know the significance which the courts attach to particular words or phrases.[1]

When, however, there is no evidence as to the settlor's intention, the court may be compelled to resort to a rule of construction. Such rules are supposed to reflect what most settlors would have intended, in the absence of further evidence. When the court construes the governing

---

[88] Restatement (Third) of Trusts §94 cmt. d(2).

[89] Lewin ¶ 26-47.

[90] Lewin ¶ 26-46.

[91] *See generally* 4 Scott & Ascher §24.4.3 (suggesting that "the transferee of a beneficiary's interest becomes, as a result of the transfer, a beneficiary and can maintain a suit against the trustee to enforce the trust or to enjoin or obtain redress for a breach of trust"); UPC §1-201(3) (deeming one who owns by assignment an equitable interest under a trust a beneficiary); A.W. Gans, *Intervention in litigation by one claiming interest in fruits thereof as trust beneficiary*, 2 A.L.R.2d 227.

§5.2 [1] Lewis M. Simes, Cases and Materials on the Law of Future Interests 1 (1951).

instrument, therefore, it simply loads the dice one way or the other, in the absence of further evidence.[2]

Class designations generally. When the settlor properly designates by name related beneficiaries such as children, there is little room for ambiguity as to who qualifies as a beneficiary.[3] What is lost, however, is the flexibility, adaptability, and economy of language that comes when the beneficiaries are designated not by name but by group or class membership,[4] which is permissible as long as it is done in a way that does not run afoul of an applicable Rule against Perpetuities.[5]

Suppose a trust provides that the trustee, upon the death of the settlor's spouse, shall distribute the corpus outright and free of trust to "the children then living of the settlor." It would bring in children born after the trust was executed and exclude children predeceasing the spouse.[6] Were the children specifically named, considerable additional language would be required to address such contingencies. "Class designations are valid as long as the membership of the class will finally be determined within the applicable perpetuities period."[7] For a discussion of when the default law deems a class to be "closed," the reader is referred to Section 8.15.52 of this handbook.[8]

If, due to sloppy drafting or otherwise, a settlor's intention as to the application of a particular class designation cannot be ascertained, the court will fall back on a rule of construction. Rules of construction, however, are themselves generally not all that easy to parse, many presuming a working knowledge of the arcane corners of the default substantive law of trusts.[9] And to make matters worse, these rules can vary from jurisdiction to jurisdiction, a topic we take up in Section 8.5 of this handbook:

---

[2] 7 Scott & Ascher §45.3.

[3] Shifting between specific designations and class designations in the same instrument, however, is not advised. When unavoidable, the drafting attorney needs to do this with care. In one case, a settlor established a testamentary trust for his son's named children. Upon termination, the property was to pass outright and free of trust to his son's "children." After the will had been executed, the son adopted a child. Was the adoptee entitled to a terminating distribution? Inferring the settlor's intent from a reading of the will as a whole, the court ruled that she was not. *See* Retseck v. Fowler State Bank, 782 N.E.2d 1022 (Ind. App. 2003). There would not have been this patent ambiguity with its attendant litigation had there been a proper definition of the term *children* somewhere in the will's boilerplate.

[4] Professor Leach advises against the use of class gifts: "Describe beneficiaries by name rather than by a class designation wherever that is possible; for this will eliminate many of the casualties of the 'fertile octogenarian' type." W. Barton Leach, *Perpetuities in a Nutshell,* 51 Harv. L. Rev. 638, 670 (1938). *See generally* §8.15.31 of this handbook (the fertile octogenarian principle).

[5] Restatement (Third) of Trusts §44 cmt. b; 2 Scott & Ascher §12.1.

[6] *See* Restatement (Third) of Trusts §45 cmt. a (providing that a class is not "indefinite" such that its members could not be the beneficiaries of a trust merely because the class consists of a changing or shifting group, the number of whose members may increase or decrease).

[7] UTC §402 cmt. (available at <http://www.uniformlaws.org/Act.aspx?title=Trust%20 Code>).

[8] Containing primarily a discussion of the so-called rule of convenience.

[9] In §8.25 of this handbook, we bemoan the fact that few American law schools these days even require instruction in the fundamentals of trust law, let alone in its nooks and crannies.

Thus, in some states, when there is a gift over to the settlor's or testator's heirs at law or next of kin, they are to be ascertained as of the time of the settlor's or testator's death, whereas in other states, they are to be ascertained as of the time when the interest vests in possession, in either case in the absence of a manifestation of a contrary intention. So also, the rules may vary, in the case of a gift over to a beneficiary's heirs or next of kin, as to whether they are to be determined by the intestacy provisions in force at the testator's domicil or at that of the beneficiary. The rules may also vary as to whether a beneficiary's spouse is to be included among the beneficiary's heirs or next of kin.[10]

When the permissible appointees under a nongeneral power of appointment are designated as a class. The Restatement (Third) of Property proposes that the "family definitions" in an instrument that grants a nongeneral power of appointment apply to the permissible appointees as well as to the takers in default, unless the terms of the grant manifest a contrary intent.[11] "For example, if the donor's document expressly excludes adopted children from the definition of 'children' or 'descendants,' the donee of a nongeneral power whose permissible appointees are the donee's descendants would not be permitted to appoint to the donee's adopted child."[12]

In the event a nongeneral power of appointment is allowed to expire unexercised, the power-in-trust or implied-gift-in-default doctrines may be implicated such that the permissible appointees take the appointive property nonetheless, a topic we take up in Section 8.15.90 of this handbook. For either doctrine to be implicated, however, the class of permissible appointees would have to be sufficiently defined and limited. If the permissible appointees are a class of someone's issue, descendants, or the like, all the restatements would have the appointive property pass to the members by representation rather than per capita in the event of nonexercise.[13]

Issue and descendants. Class designations in trust instruments need to be carefully drafted. Take, for example, the term *issue*, perhaps the most commonly used and most useful of the class designations. *Issue* includes not just children but the lineal descendants of all generations of the designated ancestor, *i.e.*, grandchildren, great grandchildren, and the like.[14] The public, however, is

---

[10] 7 Scott & Ascher §45.3.2. "Likewise, the rules may vary as to the circumstances under which the issue of a testator or of a beneficiary take per capita, per stirpes, or in some other way. The rules may vary as to whether a given disposition is vested or contingent. The rules may also vary as to the effect of a gift over if a beneficiary dies without issue. The rules may vary as to powers of appointment, as, for example, whether a special power is exclusive or nonexclusive; whether in the case of a special power of appointment there is an implied gift over to the objects of the power; and whether a will that does not mention a power of appointment can exercise it." 7 Scott & Ascher §45.3.2. Powers of appointment are taken up in §8.1 of this handbook.

[11] Restatement (Third) of Property (Wills and Other Donative Transfers) §19.14, cmt. b.

[12] Restatement (Third) of Property (Wills and Other Donative Transfers) §19.14, cmt. b.

[13] Restatement (First) of Property §367(4); Restatement (Second) of Property (Wills and Other Donative Transfers) §24.2, cmt. d; Restatement (Third) of Property (Wills and Other Donative Transfers) §19.23, cmt. a.

[14] UPC §1-201(25). *See generally* Fratcher, *Class Gifts to Heirs, Issue, and Like Groups*, 55 Alb. L. Rev. 1205 (1992).

inclined to see the term as encompassing only someone's children.[15] This confusion can lead to profound misunderstandings on the part of beneficiaries as to the nature of their equitable interests, and to breaches of trust on the part of their trustees. Again, issues are not just someone's children. To make matters worse, the terms *issue* and *descendants* are not necessarily synonymous. True, one's issue are also one's descendants,[16] but not all one's descendants are necessarily one's issue.[17]

The term *issue* or *descendants* ought not to stand alone in a trust instrument.[18] It needs to be accompanied by unambiguous qualifying language that explains who are to be included in the class and the size of each recipient's share, *i.e.*, whether a particular distribution is to be *per capita*,[19]

---

[15] The UPC defines "child" for its purposes as an "individual entitled to take as a child under . . . [the] . . . Code by intestate succession from the parent whose relationship is involved and excludes a person who is only a stepchild, a foster child, a grandchild, or any more remote descendant." UPC §1-201(5).

[16] UPC §1-201(9).

[17] At one time it was understood that there were two classes of descendants, lineal and collateral. *See* Best v. Stonehewer, 55 Eng. Rep. 557, 559 (1864), *aff'd*, House of Lords (1865). The transfer of an estate to whomever occasioned by the death of its holder was traditionally referred to as a "descent" of the estate. Best v. Stonehewer, 55 Eng. Rep. 557, 559 (1864), *aff'd*, House of Lords (1865). Accordingly a "descendant" need not have been an issue of the decedent. Best v. Stonehewer, 55 Eng. Rep. 557, 559 (1864), *aff'd*, House of Lords (1865). For a U.S. case in which the term "collateral descendant" was employed, *see* Estate of Pearson, 441 Pa. 172, 185, 275 A.2d 336, 341 (1971). Here is the UPC's "definition" of descendant: "'Descendant' of an individual means all of his [or her] descendants of all generations, with the relationship of parent and child at each generation being determined by the definition of child and parent contained in this Code." UPC §1-201(9). Article II of the Code, which covers intestacy, wills and donative transfers, now employs the designation descendant instead of the designation issue: "The word 'descendants' replaces the word 'issue' . . . throughout the revisions of Article II." UPC §2-103 cmt. "The term issue is a term of art having a biological connotation." UPC §2-103 cmt. "Now that inheritance rights, in certain cases, are extended to adopted children, the term *descendants* is a more appropriate term." UPC §2-103 cmt.

[18] *See, e.g.*, Mayhew's Estate, 307 Pa. 84, 160 A. 724 (1932) (the scrivener having "neither qualified, explained, nor modified by any context" the term *issue*, the court after reviewing the English and American cases on point construed "legal life estate to X, remainder to X's issue" to mean that the issue take per stirpes rather than per capita).

[19] "When property is distributed in a per capita fashion, each person takes, in his or her right, an equal portion of the property. . . . At common law, a devise to 'issue' or 'descendants' . . . [without qualifying language] . . . was presumed to have meant for those individuals to take equally, per capita." In re Lincoln-Alliance Bank & Trust Co., 2 Misc. 3d 1008(A), 2004 WL 750260 (N.Y. Sur.). To X's *then living issue per capita* would most likely mean that X's then living descendants of all generations would share *equally*. *See, e.g.*, First Ill. Bank v. Pritchard, 230 Ill. App. 3d 861, 595 N.E.2d 728 (1992). If, however, the word *issue* or the phrase *issue share and share alike* were employed, then a *per stirpital* distribution might be presumed. First Ill. Bank v. Pritchard, 230 Ill. App. 3d 861, 595 N.E.2d 728 (1992). The word *issue* in isolation might even be interpreted as calling for an *equally near, equally dear* allocation. *See, e.g.*, UPC §2-709(b). Even a phrase such as *equally to X's then living issue* might result in the issue taking *per stirpes*. *See, e.g.*, New England Trust Co. v. McAleer, 344 Mass. 107, 181 N.E.2d 569 (1962). In other words, *per capita* is likely to be construed as *equally* and *equally* is likely to be construed as something else, *e.g.*, *per stirpes*. A word of caution: Under the Restatement (Second) of Property (Wills and Other Donative Transfers) §28.5(1), a distribution to the "children of X" and the "issue of Y" with everyone sharing a common ancestor would result in the "children" and "issue" being deemed "the issue of the common

per stirpes,[20] *by right of representation*,[21] or *per-capita-at-each-generation*, the new "equally near, equally dear" concept that has been incorporated into the intestacy sections of the Uniform Probate Code and made applicable as well on a default basis to trust instruments that employ the term *by right of representation*.[22]

The following is a sample *per-capita-at-each-generation* trust provision that employs the term *per stirpes* to establish how much economic value is assigned to each generational level and who in each generational level is entitled to take:

> Upon the death of C [the life beneficiary] the trustee shall, for computation purposes only, allocate the balance of the trust estate as if it were to be distributed per stirpes to C's issue, with the stocks to be determined, however, at the generational level closest in degree to C that contains at least one then living person. Then, *at each generational level*, the trustee shall combine for computation purposes the shares allocated to that level, to the extent there has been any such allocation, and divide the total into as many equal shares as there are persons in

---

ancestor," *i.e.*, being lumped as a single class. Distribution then would be per stirpes with the stocks to be determined at the first generation below the common ancestor. *See* Restatement (Second) of Property (Wills and Other Donative Transfers) §28.2.

[20] To X's Issue *per stirpes* means by representation with the head of the respective stocks (stirps) being the children of X. *See* UPC §2-709(c). *See also* the graphic depiction in Figure 5-1.

[21] In the absence of language to the contrary in the governing instrument, most courts will look to an intestacy statute for guidance as to the legal meaning of the term *per stirpes*. *See* UPC §2-708. Until recently, the terms *by right of representation* and *per stirpes* were considered synonymous. Now their meanings may be diverging. The UPC provides that to X's issue *by right of representation* will result in an *equally near, equally dear* allocation while the term *per stirpes* would result in a traditional *per stirpes* allocation, with the stocks being determined at the generational level of X's children. UPC §2-709.

[22] *See* UPC §§2-106 (intestacy), 2-709(b) (trust instruments). To illustrate the concepts of *per capita* (equally), *per stirpes*, and *per-capita-at-each-generation* (equally near, equally dear), let us assume that a settlor provided that his trust shall terminate at his death and that the property shall then pass to his then living *issue, per stirpes*. Let us also assume that the settlor had three children (X, Y, and Z) and that during his lifetime, X predeceased the trust's termination, leaving one child who survived the termination; Y predeceased the trust's termination, leaving two children who survived the termination; and Z survived the termination as did her three children. Under the traditional application of *per stirpes*, X's child would take one third, Y's children would share one third, and Z would take one third. Z's children would take nothing. On the other hand, if the settlor had provided that his then living issue were to take *per capita* (equally), then Z and all the then living grandchildren would have taken equal shares. The hybrid concept, known as *per-capita-at-each-generation* (equally near, equally dear), was approved by the National Conference of Commissioners on Uniform State Laws and made a part of the Uniform Act on Intestacy, Wills and Donative Transfers. It has now been incorporated into the intestacy sections of the UPC, *see* §2-106, and made applicable to trust instruments on a default basis, *see* §2-709(b) when the term *by right of representation* is employed. It has been suggested that "[t]he per-capita-at-each-generation system is more responsive to the underlying premise of the original UPC system, in that it always provides equal shares to those equally related; the pre-1990 UPC achieved this objective in most but not *all cases*." UPC §2-106 cmt. To continue with our example, if the classic pre-1990 version of *per stirpes* is applicable, the child of X receives one-third; under the new *per-capita-at-each-generation* (equally near, equally dear) approach, the child of X would receive 2/9, because the children of deceased X and the children of deceased Y would share equally. Z, of course, would take to the exclusion of her children. UPC §2-106 cmt. *See generally* Restatement (Third) of Property (Wills and Other Donative Transfers) §2.3 cmt.

that level who would have partaken in the per stirpital distribution. Each such person shall then receive one such equal share outright and free of trust.

The Uniform Probate Code would say it more or less this way:

> Upon the death of C (the life beneficiary) the balance of the trust estate shall be divided into as many equal shares as there are (i) surviving descendants of C in the generation nearest to C which contains one or more surviving descendants of C (ii) and deceased descendants of C in the same generation who left surviving descendants of C, if any. Each surviving descendant in the nearest generation is allocated one share. The remaining shares, if any, are combined and then divided in the same manner among the surviving descendants of the deceased descendants as if the surviving descendants who were allocated a share [that is those who had received actual distributions] and their surviving descendants had predeceased C.[23]

For a graphic depiction of a classic per stirpital distribution see Figure 5-1.

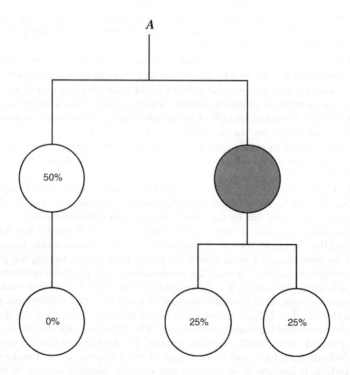

Figure 5-1. Percentage Allocation Illustration of Remainder to A's Issue Per Stirpes. The darkened circle represents a deceased child.

---

[23] UPC §2-709(b). *See also* Mass. Gen. Laws ch. 190B, §§2-106, 2-709.

The inherently and patently contradictory phrase *issue in equal shares by right of representation* should be avoided at all costs.[24] A trustee unable to avoid administering such a provision will need guidance from the court. Somehow, the concept of representation with its inherent potential for effecting unequal distributions among the members of a class of issue needs to be harmonized with the equality requirement, "or one of them must be rejected and given no effect."[25] It may well be that the phrase *in equal shares* refers to equality among the stocks ("stirpes"[26]), with the term *by right of representation* referring to the proportions that eligible issue within each stock ("stirps") take.[27] This interpretation makes particular sense when distribution to the issue of designated individuals is called for, rather than to the issue of a single individual, *e.g.*, the issue of the settlor.[28] A provision that couples two or more classes, for example, *equally to my children and the children of my deceased children*, also should be avoided.[29] It could mean that all take *per capita*.[30] Or it could mean that the children share equally 50 percent and the children of deceased children share equally 50 percent, or perhaps that all take *per stirpes*.[31] The phrase *to X and her children* is particularly unfortunate. One court confronted with such a phrase saw three possible interpretations, "namely (a) that . . . [X] . . . takes a fee simple absolute to the exclusion of her children, either on the theory that the words 'and to her children' are words of limitation, or that the word 'or' was intended for the word 'and' and that the gift to the children was substitutional; (b) that . . . [X] . . . takes a life estate with remainder on her death to her children, as similar devises or grants have been interpreted in other jurisdictions, notably Pennsylvania; and (c) that . . . [X] . . . and her two children are tenants in common, each having an undivided one-third interest in the property."[32] And there

[24] *See generally* U.S. Trust, *1992 New York Trusts and Estates Legislation: Meanings of Per Stirpes and In Equal Shares per Stirpes*, Practical Drafting 2939–2972 (1992).

[25] Bradlee v. Converse, 318 Mass. 117, 118, 60 N.E.2d 345, 346 (1945).

[26] *Stirps* is singular; *stirpes* is plural. *Stirps* is Latin for stem or stock. In legal parlance *stirps* means the branch of a family, *e.g.*, a child and his or her descendants. According to the Oxford English Dictionary, the adjectival form of *stirps* is stirpal, *e.g.*, a stirpal share.

[27] *See, e.g.*, In re Will of Lewis, 434 S.E.2d 472 (Ga. 1993).

[28] *See, e.g.*, Estate of Harrison, 456 Pa. Super. 114, 689 A.2d 939 (1997) (holding that equal shares meant equality among family groupings, with each family grouping being headed by a son of the settlor, not necessarily equality within each family grouping); Trust Estate of Dwight v. Keolanui, 80 Haw. 233, 909 P.2d 561 (1995) (the issue being of designated individuals and the designated individuals being the heads of their respective family groupings, the equality requirement applied among the family groupings but not necessarily within each family grouping); Bradlee v. Converse, 318 Mass. 117, 60 N.E.2d 345 (1945) (where provision is for the issue of designated individuals, the equality is among the stirpes, not necessarily within each stirps).

[29] *Cf.* Restatement of Property §303(2) (construing an outright gift to a person and his or her "family").

[30] Boston Safe Dep. & Trust Co. v. Doolan, 307 Mass. 233 (1940).

[31] *See generally* 96 C.J.S. Wills §708. *See also* Restatement (Second) of Property (Wills and Other Donative Transfers) §28.5(1).

[32] In re Parent's Will, 240 N.Y.S.2d 558 (1963) (holding that the mother and her children each took a one-third undivided interest as tenants in common).

is a fourth possible interpretation not mentioned by the court: that X takes 50 percent and her children share the other 50 percent.

Even without the reference to equal shares, a provision calling for distribution to someone's issue *by right of representation* or *per stirpes* may be ambiguous under certain circumstances, such as when the first generation of issue below that person dies before the time set for distribution. Let us take the following situation: The person has two children, A and B, both of whom have predeceased. A had one child (X) and B had two children (Y and Z). Do X, Y, and Z start the stocks ("stirpes") and share one-third each? Or do we begin at the level of A and B, giving X one-half and leaving Y and Z to share one-quarter each? The Restatement of Property Section 301, comment h, suggested that where the intent of the settlor was unclear, the stocks ("stirpes") began at the first generation where there was a living member at the time set for distribution. Thus, in our case, X, Y, and Z would have shared equally.[33] The Restatement (Second) of Property (Wills and Other Donative Transfers) Section 28.1(3), on the other hand, would start the stocks at the level of A and B.[34] Under the Uniform Probate Code if the term *per stirpes* is employed, the stocks (stirps) are determined at the level of A and B,[35] but not if the term *by right of representation* is employed.[36] Because the law is unsettled in this area, the prospective trustee will want the matter of "where to start the stocks" adequately addressed in the governing instrument.

Illegitimacy and adoption. A trust term that expressly limits a class of beneficial owners to "lawful issue" has traditionally signaled the intention to exclude illegitimate issue. "The great majority of courts that have examined the question have concluded that, when used in a testamentary instrument to modify words such as 'children,' 'issue,' or 'descendants,' the word 'lawful' must be read as representing the intent to limit a bequest to children of legally married parents."[37] At common law, a trust for the benefit of someone's children or issue was construed *prima facie* as excluding members of the class who were born or conceived out of wedlock, unless the context suggested otherwise.[38] In recent years, legislatures and courts, both here and in

---

[33] Restatement of Property §301 cmt. h. The comment to §2.3 of the Restatement (Third) of Property (Wills and Other Donative Transfers) refers to the situation in which X, Y, and Z share equally as *per-capita-with-representation* or *modified per stirpes*. One also sees the term *modern per stirpes*. The situation in which X would get one-half is referred to as *strict per stirpes* or *English per stirpes*.

[34] "Even though the possible takers under a gift to 'issue' include primarily descendants of every degree of relationship to the designated person, the conclusion is justified that the average donor does not intend that descendants in a lower degree of relationship to the designated person are to share equally with persons in a higher degree of relationship to the designated person." Restatement (Second) of Property (Wills and Other Donative Transfers) §28.2 cmt. a. *See also* Weller v. Sokol, 271 Md. 420, 318 A.2d 193 (1974). *See, e.g.*, Boston Safe Dep. & Trust Co. v. Goodwin, 59 Mass. App. Ct. 270, 795 N.E.2d 581 (2003).

[35] UPC §2-709(c).

[36] UPC §2-709(b).

[37] In re Estate of Wright, 147 Wash. App. 674, 196 P.3d 1075 (2008).

[38] Lewin ¶6-14 (England); Lowell v. Talcott, 86 Mass. App. Ct. 145, 148–149, 14 N.E.3d 332, 334–335 (2014) (the court noting, however, that "there also existed a corresponding 'strong

England,[39] have been redefining the term *issue* and other such group designations to include persons adopted and born out of wedlock.[40] The authors of the Uniform Probate Code have been at the forefront of this movement.[41] It is our view that such alterations in meaning should not apply retroactively to vested and contingent equitable property rights under irrevocable trusts, no matter how appealing on a personal level retroactivity may be.[42] Such alterations in meaning should apply only prospectively, unless the settlor has expressed a contrary intention.[43] Otherwise, this shifting of property interests from one group to another amounts to a governmental taking of property by redefinition, a topic we consider in Section 8.15.71 of this handbook. Be that as it may, the fact that should ultimately control whether an adoptee, or anyone else for that matter, is a trust beneficiary is what the settlor intended.[44] Granted, discerning such intent is sometimes easier said than done.

Heirs. *Heirs* is another term that often appears in trust instruments.[45] In the nontrust context it generally means those who *are* entitled to take under the laws of intestacy rather than by will. Under the intestacy provisions of the Uniform Probate Code, an individual in gestation at the time when the class of someone's "heirs" is determined is treated as living at that time if the individual lives 120 hours or more after birth. The Code also would include the surviving spouse and the state as someone's possible heirs.[46]

In the context of drafting trust instruments, however, the word heirs generally means those who *would* be entitled to take under some intestacy statute.[47] Thus, the word *heirs* accompanied by appropriate qualifying language can serve as a convenient formula for designating takers in default of named

---

legal presumption' that a child born in lawful wedlock was legitimate."). As to the child who is demonstrably born out of wedlock, *see, e.g.*, Powers v. Steele, 394 Mass. 306, 475 N.E.2d 395 (1985) (for purposes of construing the dispositive provisions of a particular inter vivos trust, the court deemed to be legitimate an out-of-wedlock-born "issue" who had been judicially legitimated post-birth).

[39] Lewin ¶6-14 (England).

[40] *See generally* Restatement (Second) of Property (Wills and Other Donative Transfers) §§25.2–25.5 *See also* In re Trusts of Harrington, 311 Minn. 403, 250 N.W.2d 163 (1977) (adoptees deemed issue of the body); In re Will of Hoffman, 53 A.D.2d 55, 385 N.Y.S.2d 49 (1976) (redefining the term *issue* to include illegitimates).

[41] *See* UPC §2-705.

[42] In England, for example, such modifying statutes generally have no "retrospective effect." Lewin ¶6-14.

[43] For an illustration of how an expression of settlor intent can trump the applicable default law, *see* Parker v. Parker, 131 S.W.3d 524 (Tex. 2004) (the settlor in one dispositive provision having expressly excluded adopteds as trust beneficiaries by employing the limitation "children born of her body" and in a nearby dispositive provision having not included such limiting language, the settlor demonstrated an intent to include adopteds as potential takers in the nearby provision).

[44] *See* Dennis v. Kline, 120 So. 3d 11, 20, 38 Fla. L. Weekly D1337 (Fla. Dist. Ct. App. 2013).

[45] The UPC narrowly defines *heirs* as those persons, including the surviving spouse, who are entitled under the statutes of intestate succession to the property of a decedent. UPC §1-201(21). *See also* §8.5 of this handbook (conflict of laws in the trust context).

[46] UPC §1-201(20) (defining "heirs").

[47] *See* National Shawmut Bank of Boston v. Joy, 315 Mass. 457, 462–467, 53 N.E.2d 113, 117–120 (1944) (construing a default clause to be in the subjunctive). *See generally* Casner,

beneficiaries. Such a provision-in-default is sometimes referred to as a disaster clause.[48]

It should be kept in mind, however, that the resulting trust is notional, not actual.[49] These takers in default, these notional "heirs," take the legal title directly from the trustee as mere remainderman. This is not about reversionary interests becoming possessory in someone's "heirs" incident to the imposition of an actual resulting trust. The actual resulting trust is the subject of Section 4.1.1.1 of this handbook.

The heirs designation in trust instruments, however, can carry with it all kinds of problems if it is used without proper qualification. To illustrate, assume that upon the death of a settlor's spouse the trustee shall pursuant to the terms of the trust distribute the trust property outright and free of trust to the settlor's heirs. Again, most courts will construe *heir* as someone who would take under some statute dealing with intestate succession.[50] But the statute of what jurisdiction? And is it the statute in effect at the creation of the trust, the death of the settlor, or the death of the spouse?[51] What if the statute treats real property differently from personal property? The same issues are present when a distribution is to be made to the "heirs" of someone other than the settlor.[52]

A prospective trustee should insist that the term *heirs* be accompanied with appropriate assumptions, exclusions, and qualifications to wring out such gaps and ambiguities.[53] In 1939, Professor Casner offered the following "basic form," which was intended to do just that in the context of devises under wills. Over the years since then, it has been revised and adapted to accommodate equitable interests under trusts:

Construction of Gifts to Heirs and the Like, 53 Harv. L. Rev. 207 (1939). *See also* §8.5 of this handbook (conflict of laws) and 8.15.2 of this handbook (doctrine of worthier title).

[48] One who possesses a contingent equitable interest by virtue of a disaster clause in a trust instrument generally qualifies as a beneficiary of the trust. *See* §5.1 of this handbook.

[49] The actual resulting trust is covered in §4.1.1.1 of this handbook.

[50] *See* Casner, *Construction of Gifts to Heirs and the Like*, 53 Harv. L. Rev. 207, 208–209 (1939): "When the devisees in a will are described as the 'heirs' . . . of a designated person, almost all courts agree that some statute dealing with the intestate succession of property is to be employed to ascertain the persons described, in the absence of additional language or circumstances which indicate a contrary intent on the part of the testator." *See also* Fratcher, *Class Gifts to Heirs, Issue and Like Groups*, 55 Alb. L. Rev. 1205 (1992); §8.5 of this handbook (conflict of laws in the trust context). *See, e.g.*, Ross v. Comm'r, 652 F.2d 1365, 1366 (1981) (suggesting that "estate" and "heirs at law" are not equivalent terms). *See generally* Restatement (Second) of Property (Wills and Other Donative Transfers) §§29.1–29.8.

[51] *See* W. E. Shipley, Annot., *Time as of which members of class described as grantor's or settlor's heirs, next of kin, relations, and the like to whom a future gift is made are to be ascertained*, 38 A.L.R.2d 327 (1954).

[52] *See generally* W. W. Allen, Annot., *Time of ascertaining persons to take, under deed or inter vivos trust, where designated as the heirs, next of kin, children, relations, etc. of the life tenant or remainderman*, 65 A.L.R.2d 1408 (1959). *See also* W. W. Allen, Annot., *Time of ascertaining persons to take where designated as the heirs, next of kin, descendants, etc. of one other than the testator, trustor, grantor, life tenant, or remainderman*, 60 A.L.R.2d 1394 (1958).

[53] *See generally* Casner, *Construction of Gifts to Heirs and the Like*, 53 Harv. L. Rev. 207 (1939). *See also* §8.5 of this handbook (conflict of laws in the trust context).

Legal Interests

then to those persons, and in such shares, as *would have taken* real property owned by me and situated in State *X* if I had died immediately after the termination of all prior interests in the land which is the subject of this devise, intestate and domiciled in State *X*, unless all prior interests expire by their terms before the will has taken effect, in which case, to those persons and in such shares as would have taken real property owned by me and situated in State *X* if I had died intestate and domiciled in State *X;* my intention is to include all persons who would take on such assumed intestacy whether they are related to me by blood or not, whether legitimate or illegitimate, and whether or not they have received any interest under this will.[54]

Here is a typical catch-all trust provision designed to avoid the imposition of a resulting trust[55] should there be, say, no issue of the settlor alive when the trust ultimately terminates, assuming it was contemplated that the settlor's then living issue would be the remaindermen:

Equitable interests under trusts

If there shall be a failure of disposition of any beneficial interest created under this trust, then the property comprising the beneficial interest which has failed of disposition shall be paid over and distributed, free of all trusts, to those persons to whom and in the proportions in which the same would have been distributed had the Settlor then died intestate and unmarried, domiciled in the State of *X* and owning such property absolutely.

A state legislature contemplating amending its intestacy statute, or replacing it altogether with a different one, should at least be aware of how the catch-all default clauses of irrevocable trusts could be affected by the legislation, particularly clauses of the type that incorporate by reference the dispositive scheme of some intestacy statute in the form that it is in *at the time of trust termination.* Section 2-103 of the model Uniform Probate Code, for example, "provides for inheritance by descendants of the decedent, parents and their descendants, and grandparents and collateral relatives descended from grandparents; . . . it eliminates more remote relatives tracing through great-grandparents."[56] If there are no takers, the intestate estate passes to the state.[57] Under Massachusetts' version of Section 2-103, there is essentially no cut-off. Intestate property passes to the next of kin, with degrees of kindred being computed according to the consanguinity table of the civil law, presumably subject to a parentelic preference to break a tie between kin of equal degree.[58]

---

[54] Casner, *Construction of Gifts to Heirs and the Like*, 53 Harv. L. Rev. 207, 249–250.

[55] *See generally* §4.1.1.1 of this handbook (the resulting trust).

[56] UPC §2-103, cmt.

[57] UPC §2-105.

[58] Mass. Gen. Laws Chap. 190B §2-103(4).

This was essentially what the law was before Massachusetts enacted its version of the UPC.[59] Had Massachusetts not rejected the UPC's intestacy cut-off, under certain facts and circumstances the assets of a terminated trust could well have ended up in the coffers of the Commonwealth rather than in the hands of some distant collateral relative. A prescient settlor might well have elected at the drafting stage to default to some charity, or even to the table of consanguinity, rather than to the Commonwealth.

If the trust instrument uses the term *heirs* without any qualifying language, or employs inappropriate qualifiers such as heirs *per stirpes* or heirs *in equal shares*, then prior to distribution the trustee should seek the advice of counsel. This will reduce the risk of misdelivery. Counsel may well advise the trustee to initiate an action for instructions and/or declaratory judgment to eliminate altogether the risk of this happening.[60]

The Uniform Probate Code would create a default presumption of the subjunctive when the term *heir* is employed in a trust instrument without qualification:

> If . . . a governing instrument calls for a present or future distribution to or creates a present or future interest in a designated individual's "heirs", "heirs at law", "next of kin", "relatives", or "family", or language of similar import, the property passes to those persons, including the state, and in such shares as *would succeed* to the designated individual's intestate estate under the intestate succession law of the designated individual's domicile if the designated individual died when the disposition is to take effect in possession or enjoyment. If the designated individual's surviving spouse is living but is remarried at the time the disposition is to take effect in possession or enjoyment, the surviving spouse is not an heir of the designated individual.[61]

Relatives. The term *relatives* probably should not be employed as a class description.[62] "If it is shown that, in using the word 'relatives,' the settlor intended to create a trust for all individuals who are related to the designated person, the intended class is not sufficiently ascertainable to sustain a trust, because a person has an indefinite number of close and remote relatives."[63] For illustrations of how a designated individual could have an astronomical number of ancestor-relatives or issue-relatives, not to mention collateral relatives, see Section 8.2.1.9 of this handbook. If the terms of the trust suggest that the word

---

[59] *See* Mass. Gen. Laws c. 190 §2.

[60] *See generally* §8.42 of this handbook (complaints for instructions and declaratory judgment).

[61] UPC §2-711.

[62] 2 Scott & Ascher §12.8.

[63] Restatement (Third) of Trusts §45 cmt. d. *Cf.* Lucker v. Bayside Cemetery, 114 A.D.3d 162, 970 N.Y.S.2d 8, 14–15 (2013) ("[N]ear relatives" of an interred did not have standing to seek judicial enforcement of a trust established for the perpetual care of the gravesite, the class not being "sufficiently sharply defined" and its likely members not being "sufficiently limited in number."). Note, however, that a "trust for the benefit of 'relatives' of the settlor or other designated person does not fail if the trustee has power to select who among the relatives shall take and in what proportions." Restatement (Third) of Trusts §45 cmt. d(1).

relatives is not intended to encompass all relatives of a designated individual, a court might be inclined to construe *relatives* more narrowly, *e.g.*, as a synonym for *heirs-at-law*, unless the terms of the trust clearly indicate a contrary intention.[64] It should be noted, however, that while a spouse of a designated individual will usually not be his or her close blood relative, the spouse could well be that person's heir-at-law under the applicable intestacy statute.

Who takes and in what proportions. The Restatement (Third) of Trusts provides a rule of thumb for determining the proportions that a class of beneficiaries will take in the absence of specific guidance in the governing instrument:

> If the settlor fails to specify the shares of class members or to provide for the manner in which they are to benefit, class members described as "children," "grandchildren," "brothers and sisters," or "nieces and nephews" are presumed to take equally. Those described as "issue," "descendants," "heirs," or "next of kin" of a person are presumed to take in the manner in which those class members would take the person's property as intestate successors under applicable law.[65]

Care must be taken in drafting a dispositive provision for multiple income beneficiaries. Take the following trust: *A* to *B*, net income to be paid to *C1* and *C2* with principal to be distributed outright and free of trust to the then living issue of *C1* and *C2* upon the death of the survivor of the two. If the terms of the trust are silent, what happens to *C1*'s portion of the income stream should he die survived by *C2*? Here are some possibilities:

- Whether or not *C1* and *C2* constitute a class, there is a "cross remainder," *i.e.*, *C2* gets the benefit of *C1*'s portion as well as his own.[66]
- *C1* has a life estate measured by the life of someone else, namely, *C2*, in other words, an estate *pur autre vie*,[67] with the result that *C1*'s portion of the income stream will now flow into the estate of *C1* as long as *C2* remains alive.[68]
- *C1*'s portion of the income stream accumulates for ultimate distribution to the remaindermen.[69]
- *C1*'s portion of the income stream flows upon a resulting trust back to *A* (the settlor) or his estate, *i.e.*, there is a reversion.[70]

---

[64] Restatement (Third) of Trusts §45 cmt. d.

[65] Restatement (Third) of Trusts §45 cmt. b.

[66] *See, e.g.*, Westervelt v. First Interstate Bank, 551 N.E.2d 1180 (Ind. Ct. App. 1990).

[67] For a history of the estate *pur autre vie, see* Cornelius J. Moynihan, Introduction to the Law of Real Property 45 (2d ed.). *See generally* 3 Scott & Ascher §14.10.2 (Estate *pur Autre Vie*); §8.15 of this handbook (discussing the "law French" phenomenon); Restatement (Third) of Property (Wills and Other Donative Transfers) §24.5, cmt. c. (providing examples of estates *pur autre vie*).

[68] Matter of Lopez, 64 Haw. 44, 636 P.2d 731 (1981) (though trust income was to be paid to a class of "children," each child took a life estate *pur autre vie*). *Cf.* Briggs v. Briggs, 950 S.W.2d 710 (Tenn. Ct. App. 1997) (involving a legal life estate *pur autre vie*).

[69] *See, e.g.*, Jorgensen v. Pioneer Trust Co., 198 Or. 579, 258 P.2d 140 (1953).

[70] *See, e.g.*, Union & New Haven Trust Co. v. Sellek, 128 Conn. 566, 24 A.2d 485 (1942).

According to the Restatement (Third) of Trusts, a fifth possibility should be the default law: "Where the terms of the trust make no express provision for the situation, the normal inference is that the settlor intended the income share to be paid to the issue (if any) of the deceased beneficiary in the typical case of this type in which the remainder is to pass to the descendants of the income beneficiaries upon the survivor's death."[71]

The survivorship condition precedent. Whether *survivorship* is a precondition of someone taking as a member of a class of remaindermen also should be resolved and addressed fully and unambiguously at the drafting stage.[72] In a jurisdiction that has enacted Section 2-707 of the Uniform Probate Code, this may be easier said than done.[73] For the reasons why this is so, the reader is referred to Section 8.15.55 of this handbook (antilapse [the trust application]). When it is not, there may have to be resort to the default law, *e.g.*, the doctrine of acceleration[74] or the rule of convenience.[75] To make things even more complicated, the default law may now have a statutory 120-hour survival requirement that is applicable to trusts.[76] It should not be left to the courts to wrestle with the applicable cases and the statutes.

Take, for example, the following testamentary trust: *A* to *B* for *C* for life then to the children of *C* in equal shares. If, at the death of *C*, there is a living child and living issue of a deceased child, it may well be that the living child receives 50 percent and the deceased child's estate receives 50 percent;[77] whereas, if one were to apply the same fact pattern to a slightly modified version of the trust, the results might be different. Let's replace children with issue: *A* to *B* for *C* for life then to the issue of *C*. In this case, the living child might receive 50 percent and the issue of the deceased child might receive 50 percent per stirpes.[78]

Care should be taken to address the contingency of survivorship in a way that does not make things worse. Let us take a testamentary trust that reads *A* to *B* for *C* for life and then to the surviving children of *A*; and let us assume that one child survives *C* and one does not. Both children, however, survived *A*. "When the future interest is in *surviving* or *living* persons, there may be ambiguity as to the time at which they must be living in order to take the gift; it may be the time

---

[71] Restatement (Third) of Trusts §49 cmt. c(3).

[72] *See generally* 3 Scott & Ascher §13.2.9 (Whether an Interest Is Conditional on Beneficiary's Survival).

[73] In 2008, Massachusetts enacted a somewhat less radical version of UPC §2-707. *See* Mass. Gen. Laws ch. 190B, §2-707 (b) (providing that "[if] an instrument is silent on the requirement of survivorship, a future interest under the terms of a trust is contingent on the beneficiary's surviving the distribution date").

[74] *See* §8.15.47 of this handbook (accelerating vested and contingent equitable remainders).

[75] *See generally* §8.15.52 of this handbook (class gifts and the rule of convenience); 2 Scott & Ascher §12.14.4.

[76] *See generally* §8.15.56 of this handbook (120-hour survival requirement [the trust application]).

[77] *See generally* Edward C. Halbach, Jr., *Future Interests: Express and Implied Conditions of Survival*, 49 Cal. L. Rev. 297, 308 (1961).

[78] *See generally* Edward C. Halbach, Jr., *Future Interests: Express and Implied Conditions of Survival*, 49 Cal. L. Rev. 297, 312–314 (1961).

of the testator's death, or it may be the time at which the preceding interest terminates."[79] It could well be that upon the death of C the living child receives 50 percent and the deceased child's estate receives the other 50 percent.[80] Actually, this result should be no surprise. Traditionally, the law has favored early vestings,[81] although there is now an effort to move the law in the other direction.[82] For more on this effort, the reader is referred to Section 8.15.55 of this handbook (antilapse [the trust application]).

In any case, it is always preferable if the trustee can with confidence extract from the plain language of the governing instrument answers to such questions as "Surviving whom?" or, if a person is to receive a distribution of trust property at a certain age, "What happens if he or she dies before attaining that age?"[83] In other words, "the question is whether the gift is subject to a condition, precedent or subsequent, of survival until the designated age, or whether the gift is absolute, subject only to postponement of enjoyment."[84] Or if the holder of the prior equitable estate, *e.g.*, the income or current beneficiary, dies after the person who is to receive the principal of the trust estate has attained the certain age, "Who gets the principal upon the death of the income beneficiary?"[85]

---

[79] 3 Scott & Ascher §13.2.9.

[80] *See, e.g.*, Parkhurst v. Jonsburg, 324 Mass. 66, 84 N.E.2d 538 (1949) (holding that the remainder interest of the settlor/testator's sister was conditioned upon her surviving the testator/settlor, not upon her surviving the expiration of the intervening equitable estate).

[81] *See* Jesse Dukeminier, *The Uniform Probate Code Upends the Law of Remainders*, 94 Mich. L. Rev. 148, 155 (1995). *See, e.g.*, Estate of Woodworth, 22 Cal. Rptr. 2d 676 (App. 1993) (a judicial application of traditional early-vesting doctrine).

[82] *See, e.g.*, UPC §2-707 (Survivorship with Respect to Future Interests Under Terms of Trust; Substitute Takers). *See generally* §8.15.55 of this handbook (antilapse in the trust context).

[83] If the word *at* means payable, the decedent's executor takes the distribution. *Cf.* Smith v. Morgan, 2004 WL 345303 (Mich. Ct. App.) (ruling an early vesting when a portion of the trust estate was payable to income beneficiary "upon attaining" a certain age). If the word *at* carries with it a survivorship condition, the provision fails because the condition has not been satisfied. *See, e.g.*, Roberts v. Squyres, 4 S.W.3d 485 (Tex. App. 1999) (finding no survivorship condition and imposing a resulting trust). *But see* Restatement of Property §258 (presuming a vested interest with no survivorship condition). *See generally* Clobberie's Case, 2 Vent. 342, 86 Eng. Rep. 476 (1677); §8.15.21 of this handbook (doctrine of Clobberie's Case versus the divide-and-pay-over-rule). *See, e.g.*, Parkhurst v. Jonsburg, 324 Mass. 66, 84 N.E.2d 538 (1949) (citing *Clobberie's Case* but finding it inapplicable because the language of the governing instrument had expressly created an interest that was subject to a condition subsequent of survivorship); 3 Scott & Ascher §13.2.9 (discussing the "divide-and-pay-over-rule," a rule that at least in part appears to conflict with the rule that was enunciated in the Clobberie's case,). *See generally* §8.30 of this handbook (the difference between a vested equitable remainder subject to divestment and a vested (transmissible) contingent equitable remainder). *See also* UPC §2-707 (establishing an "antilapse" type rule for future interests in trusts, whether revocable or irrevocable, whereby descendants of a beneficiary of a future interest who fails to survive the time when the future interest is to take effect in possession or enjoyment take in place of the deceased beneficiary's estate).

[84] 3 Scott & Ascher §13.2.9.

[85] *See, e.g.*, Lumbert v. Estate of Carter, 29 Fla. L. Weekly D509, 867 So. 2d 1175 (2004) (taking an early vesting approach in resolving a patent ambiguity in the governing instrument, the court construed the terms of the trust to provide that upon the death of the income beneficiary, a specified portion of the trust principal shall pass to the estate of the remainderman who had died 14 months after the income beneficiary but before the trustee could effect distribution, the

Again, in Section 8.15.55 of this handbook, we take up Uniform Probate Code Section 2-707, which would expand the concept of antilapse to include not only ambulatory testamentary dispositions but also to equitable future interests under trusts.

Adopting the intestacy statute's rules of construction; posthumous conception. With a few exceptions, the Uniform Probate Code on a default basis "invokes the rules of construction pertaining to intestate succession as rules of construction for interpreting terms of relationship in private instruments."[86] The rules of construction that govern the rights and status of children conceived posthumously come to mind.[87] The Uniform Trust Code provides that the rules of construction that apply to the interpretation of and disposition of property by will also apply as appropriate to the interpretation of the terms of a trust and the disposition of the trust property.[88]

Mistake. As to class designations that are the product of mistake, the reader is referred to Sections 8.15.22 of this handbook and 8.17 of this handbook. We take up the plain meaning rule and the parol evidence rule in Section 8.15.6 of this handbook.

Ambiguity. As a general rule, a latently ambiguous class designation, *i.e.*, a provision that is clear on its face but ambiguous in its application, may be resolved with the aid of extrinsic evidence.[89] Not so with a patent ambiguity, *i.e.*, an ambiguity that is apparent merely from a reading of the governing instrument.[90] "Not only may extrinsic evidence be used to clarify the meaning of a latent ambiguity, but it may be used to demonstrate that an ambiguity exists

---

remainderman having become entitled to a nonpossessory vested equitable interest in portions of the trust estate upon her attaining two of the three ages specified in the governing instrument, though the ages specified were attained during the lifetime of the income beneficiary and though there was a gift-over provision in the event the remainderman were to die before the "entire principal had been distributed to her in fee").

[86] UPC §2-705 cmt. *See also* Mass. Gen. Laws ch. 190B, §2-705.

[87] *See generally* Sheldon F. Kurtz & Lawrence W. Waggoner, *The UPC Addresses the Class-Gift and Intestacy Rights of Children of Assisted Reproduction Technologies*, 35 ACTEC L.J. 30 (2009); Susan N. Gary, *We Are Family: The Definition of Parent and Child for Succession Purposes*, 34 ACTEC L.J. 171 (2008); Kathryn Venturatos Lorio, *Conceiving the Inconceivable: Legal Recognition of the Posthumously Conceived Child*, 34 ACTEC L.J. 154 (2008).

[88] UTC §112 (available at <http://www.uniformlaws.org/Act.aspx?title=Trust%20Code>). "This section is patterned after Restatement (Third) of Trusts §25(2) and cmt. e (Tentative Draft No. 1, approved 1996), although this section, unlike the Restatement, also applies to irrevocable trusts." UTC §112 cmt.

[89] *See* Dennis v. Kline, 120 So. 3d 11, 38 Fla. L. Weekly D1337 (Fla. Dist. Ct. App. 2013). Ambiguity in application might take the form of two groups of persons meeting the class description or no group meeting the description. A provision for the benefit of the issue of "the Settlor's Uncle George" when there are two persons meeting the description of Uncle George, one on his mother's side and one on his father's, would be an example of the former type of latent ambiguity. A provision for the benefit of the issue of "the Settlor's Aunt Kate" when the settlor has only one aunt, but her name is Susan, would be an example of the latter type of latent ambiguity.

[90] *See* Trupp v. Naughton, No. 320843 (Mich. Ct. App. May 26, 2015) ("A patent ambiguity exists if an uncertainty concerning the meaning appears on the face of the instrument and arises from the use of defective, obscure, or insensible language.").

in the first place and to establish intent."[91] In the face of a "manifestly ambiguous document," however, at least one court has considered extrinsic evidence of settlor intent.[92] Sometimes, there is nothing a court can do:

> In conclusion, the Court "struggled manfully" to make sense of the trust deed; however, a sensible construction of its provisions was impossible. Although this is an extreme case (many of the critical provisions of the deed were a nonsense), the case does show that settlors and trustees need to err on the side of caution and, even with the smallest of changes to a deed, ensure their lawyers have dealt properly with the drafting. If you are not lawyers familiar with drafting trusts, it can be a false economy to draft without seeking professional assistance from trust lawyers qualified in the relevant jurisdiction.[93]

For more on when extrinsic evidence of settlor intent may be admissible, see Section 8.15.6 of this handbook.

§5.3 The Beneficiary's Property Interest

The beneficiary's equitable interest is an interest in property.[1] However, it is a type of interest that may, under certain circumstances, be inalienable or immune from attachment, or both. To the extent it is not, the beneficiary "can transfer his or her beneficial interest during life to the same extent as a similar legal interest."[2] That an equitable future interest is contingent alone does not preclude its transferability.[3] Unless the terms of the trust provide otherwise, a beneficiary may transfer his or her equitable interest without notice to or consent of the trustee.[4] Unless prevented by the terms of the trust, an equitable interest in a trust may be the subject of a gift[5] or a promise to transfer the interest in the future may be consideration for a contract.[6] "In some states a

---

[91] Trupp v. Naughton, No. 320843 (Mich. Ct. App. May 26, 2015).

[92] *See* In re Deed of Trust of McCargo, 652 A.2d 1330, 1335 (Pa. Super. 1994).

[93] Giles Corbin, *Watch Your Language*, Trusts & Estates L.J., No. 47, June 2003, at 22 (discussing Re The Double Happiness Trust, [2003] WTLR 367 (Royal Court of Jersey)). "The Court cited the case of Re Malabry Invs. Ltd., [1982] JJ 117, in which it was held that the validity of a trust depends upon there being certainty of subject matter, beneficial interests, and beneficiaries." Giles Corbin, Watch Your Language, Trusts & Estates L.J., No. 47, June 2003, at 22.

§5.3 [1] *See* In re Catherwood's Trust, 173 A.2d 86, 91 (1961). ("A gift of an equitable life estate in income or of an estate in remainder does constitute a grant of a vested property right of which the recipients cannot be divested by legislative action.").

[2] Restatement (Third) of Trusts §51. *But see* New York Est. Powers & Trusts Law §7-1.5(a) (prohibiting with certain exceptions an income beneficiary's transfer of the equitable income interest, unless the power to do so is a term of the trust).

[3] Restatement (Third) of Trusts §51 cmt. b.

[4] Restatement (Third) of Trusts §51 cmt. d.

[5] Restatement (Third) of Trusts §52(1).

[6] Restatement (Third) of Trusts §52(2).

writing is required for a transfer of the beneficiary's interest in a trust of land only; in some a writing is required for the transfer of a beneficial interest in any trust."[7]

Professor Maitland referred to the transmissibility and alienability of a beneficiary's equitable interest as attributes of its *internal* character.[8] This is unfortunate, as the term *internal* character can easily be misconstrued as referring to the nature of a beneficiary's interest, if any, in the trust's underlying property. In this handbook, the adjective *internal* is employed in quite a different context: We refer to a trustee's personal liability to the beneficiary as *internal*, to be distinguished from the trustee's external personal liability as owner of the underlying property to third parties.[9] In other words, the terms *internal* liability and *fiduciary* liability as employed in this handbook are in many cases synonymous, particularly when the duty of undivided loyalty is implicated. This is consistent with the Uniform Probate Code's taxonomy of trustee duties and obligations.[10]

A trust beneficiary's standing to seek enforcement of the trust in the courts, regardless of whether the beneficiary was a party to the trust's creation, or whether the trustee made any promises to the beneficiary, is what underpins the beneficiary's property interest.[11] "In this respect the law of trusts differs from the law of contracts where there have been some holdings that not all third party beneficiary contracts are enforceable."[12]

§5.3.1   Nature and Extent of Property Interest

Trusts have been creatures of English law since the 14th Century . . . At the beginning . . . , trusts were used for dividing estates in real estate, and facilitating the donor's testamentary plans in the face of the laws of primogeniture and other restrictions imposed by the Crown on transfers of land, which constituted most of the wealth of medieval society. Scholars suggest that the French Revolution ended similar efforts at dividing ownership in France, and ultimately throughout Europe and South America through the influence of the subsequent Napoleonic Code, because divided property rights came to be considered characteristic of feudalism.[13]

---

[7] Restatement (Third) of Trusts §53 cmt. a. *See generally* §8.15.5 of this handbook (statute of frauds).

[8] Maitland, Equity 112 (1936).

[9] *See generally* §7.1 of this handbook (trustee's liabilities generally).

[10] *See, e.g.,* UPC §7-201(a).

[11] Bogert §1; Scanlan v. Eisenberg, 669 F.3d 838 (7th Cir. 2012) (holding that even the beneficiary of a discretionary trust has standing to seek its enforcement in the courts, though beneficiary's equitable property interest is contingent).

[12] Bogert §1.

[13] Henry Christensen, III, *Foreign Trusts and Alternative Vehicles*, SH032 ALI-ABA 81, 83 (2002) (citing to Henry Hansmann & Ugo Mattei, *The Function of Trust Law: A Comparative Legal and Economic Analysis*, 73 N.Y.U. L. Rev. 434, 442 (1998)). *See generally* §8.12 of this handbook (where the trust is recognized outside the United States).

Is the beneficiary's equitable interest itself, as distinguished from any interest the beneficiary may have in the underlying property, an interest in property, or merely a personal claim against the trustee in the nature of an equitable chose in action? "When uses were first enforced in England by the chancellors of the fifteenth century, it is clear that they looked at the use primarily as a personal relationship between the feoffee and the cestui que use."[14] Today, it seems reasonably settled that a beneficiary has more than mere rights against the trustee,[15] although Professor Maitland disagreed.[16] The fact that we all are obligated not to collude with a trustee in breach of trust[17] supports the proposition that a beneficiary's equitable rights are, for all intents and purposes, rights in rem.[18] In other words, the beneficiary's equitable interest no matter how ephemeral is itself an interest in property.

In addition, the beneficiary as well possesses some type of proprietary interest in the underlying trust property that is either vested or contingent.[19] "The result is something unique: a form of double ownership . . . [in the underlying property], . . . with the trustee holding legal title, but the beneficiary having equitable ownership."[20] Certainly the doctrine of tracing,[21] together with the doctrine that a non-BFP takes the underlying property of a trust subject to its terms,[22] supports the proposition that the beneficiary has some kind of proprietary interest in the underlying property, along with the equitable

---

[14] Scott on Trusts §130. The phrase *cestui que trust* has evolved into a synonym for *beneficiary*. It is not known when this Norman-French phrase was introduced into our language, but it is believed to have been in the seventeenth century. For a discussion of such borrowings from the Norman French, *see* Sweet, 'Cestui Que Use': 'Cestui Que Trust,' 26 L.Q. Rev. 196 (1910). *See generally* §8.15 of this handbook (the doctrines ancient and modern) (discussing the "law French" phenomenon).

[15] *See generally* 3 Scott & Ascher §13.1; 2 Scott on Trusts §130.

[16] Maitland, Equity 107 (1936).

[17] *See generally* §7.2.9 of this handbook (personal liability of the trustee's agents and other third parties to the beneficiary).

[18] *See generally* 3 Scott & Ascher §13.1.

[19] *See generally* Bogert §183 (Beneficiary's Right in Personam or in Rem). *But see* Bogert §184 (Statutory Declarations as to the Nature of the Beneficiary's Interest); United States v. O'Shaughnessy, 517 N.W.2d 574, 577 (Minn. 1994) (holding that under Minnesota law, the beneficiary of a certain discretionary trust does not have "property" or any "right to property" in undistributed trust principal or income before the trustees have exercised their discretionary powers of distribution under the trust agreement).

[20] 1 Scott & Ascher §1.1 (noting, however, that Professors Ames and Maitland objected to the characterization of a trust beneficiary's interest as property in that legal title to the subject property is in the trustee).

[21] *See generally* §7.2.3.1 of this handbook (tracing and accounting for proceeds and profits in the trust context).

[22] *See generally* §8.15.63 of this handbook (doctrine of bona fide purchase; the BFP), §8.3.2 of this handbook (the bona fide purchase doctrine's notice requirement), and §5.4.2 of this handbook (rights of the beneficiary as against transferees of the underlying trust property). *See also* §8.3.6 of this handbook (negotiable instruments and the duty of third parties to inquire into the trustee's authority). For a comparison of the BFP, a creature of equity, with the holder in due course, a creature of law, *see* §8.15.68 of this handbook (holders in due course in the trust context).

interest.[23] That the beneficiary possesses at least an indirect interest in the underlying trust property via the beneficiary's equitable personal claim against the trustee is not in dispute.

Even in the case of a fully discretionary trust where one must strain to articulate a nexus between the beneficiary and the underlying property, the beneficiary still can enforce the trust against a non-BFP.[24] The outcome of a tax or other dispute, however, may hinge on the nature of and/or the intensity of a beneficiary's legal relationship with the underlying trust property.[25] For a discussion of the doctrine of equitable conversion as it may apply to a beneficiary's proprietary interest in entrusted real estate that the trustee is directed to liquidate, the reader is referred to Section 8.15.44 of this handbook.

The extent of the beneficiary's equitable interest—again, not to be confused with the beneficiary's interest in the underlying property—is usually governed by the terms of the trust. The settlor of the trust may create equitable interests that correspond to the comparable legal estates (e.g., the beneficiary may be given an equitable life estate or an equitable estate for years). With respect to transmissible vested equitable interests, if the trust principal is personal property, the beneficiary's interest is personal property, too, and follows personal property rules; if it is real estate, the beneficiary's interest is also regarded as realty.[26] "If, however, the trust property is real estate, but the beneficiary's interest is for a terms of years, the interest is personal property."[27] By statute, an equitable interest in an Illinois land trust is personal property as well.[28]

The equitable interest of the beneficiary may be a future interest, vested or contingent; it may rest solely in the discretion of the trustee; it may be limited to the occupation of the trust property. A trust under which the beneficiary gets the use or occupation of the underlying property but no entitlement to income or principal distributions has been referred to as a "personal trust."[29]

Co-owners of a beneficial interest ordinarily hold the interest jointly unless there is a statute to the contrary.[30] Of course, the terms of a governing

---

[23] 3 Scott & Ascher §13.1.

[24] Lewin ¶1-06. See generally §5.4.2 of this handbook (rights of the beneficiary as against transferees, including BFPs).

[25] See generally 3 Scott & Ascher §13.1.1, n.1 and accompanying text. See also United States v. O'Shaughnessy, 517 N.W.2d 574 (Minn. 1994) (involving an unsuccessful attempt by the IRS to reach a taxpayer's contingent equitable interest in a discretionary trust and/or the underlying property, this in order to satisfy an income tax deficiency); Cohen, Massachusetts Estate Tax Planning for Non-Massachusetts Residents Owning Real Estate in Massachusetts, 70 Mass. L. Rev. 124, 126 (1985) (tax); In re Grand Jury Subpoena, 973 F.2d 45 (1st Cir. 1992) (Fifth Amendment privilege not available to trustees of nominee trust).

[26] See generally Scott & Ascher §13.1.1.

[27] 3 Scott & Ascher §13.1.1 (citing to Restatement (Second) of Trusts §130(b) cmt. c, & illus. 6).

[28] 3 Scott & Ascher §13.1.1, n.3.

[29] 3 Scott & Ascher §13.2.6.

[30] In many states, such statutes have been enacted. See generally 2A Scott on Trusts §143. Many states' statutes impose a presumption of tenancy in common. See, e.g., N.Y. Est. Powers &

instrument may specify how the beneficial interest is to be held (jointly or as tenants in common) notwithstanding any common law or statutory presumption.[31]

Again, the issue of the beneficiary's relationship to the underlying property is separate from the issue of whether a particular equitable interest is vested or contingent. "[The equitable] . . . [i]nterests of beneficiaries of private express trusts run the gamut from valuable substantialities to evanescent hopes. Such a beneficiary may have any one of an almost infinite variety of the possible aggregates of rights, privileges, powers, and immunities."[32] Equitable interests in trusteed individual retirement accounts (IRAs) and realty or nominee trusts tend to crowd the substantial end of the rights spectrum,[33] and to the extent they are transferable may themselves constitute the underlying properties of other trusts.[34] One who unconditionally possesses the *entire* equitable interest in a parcel of real estate is even said to possess an equitable fee simple.[35] At the opposite extreme are the contingent equitable interests in charitable trusts.[36] At least from the perspective of any member of the public selected at random, such interests tend to be little more than evanescent hopes. A beneficiary's interest in a trust associated with a qualified employee benefit plan tends to move over time from the contingent end to the vested end of the rights spectrum.[37] "[A] . . . discretionary beneficiary, who is merely a member of a class to whom the trustees have a discretion to apply trust capital or income, . . . has a mere right to require the trustees to consider from time to time how to exercise their power."[38] The interest is contingent because it is subject to the condition precedent of the

---

Trusts Law §6-2.2 (Consol. 1979); Ill. Ann. Stat. ch. 76, §§1–1a, 2 (Smith-Hurd 1987); Cal. Civ. Code §683 (West 1982); Mass. Gen. Laws Ann. ch. 184, §7 (West 1987).

[31] *See, e.g.*, Anderson v. Bean, 220 Mass. 360, 107 N.E. 964 (1915).

[32] Farkas v. Williams, 5 Ill. 2d 417, 422–423, 125 N.E.2d 600, 603 (1955) (citing 4 Powell, The Law of Real Property, at 87).

[33] *See* §§9.5.2 of this handbook (the IRA trust) and 9.6 of this handbook (trusts that resemble corporations or agencies); Charles E. Rounds, Jr., *State Common Law Aspects of the Global Unwindings of the Madoff Ponzi Scheme and the Sub-Prime Mortgage Securitization Debacle*, 27 Wis. Int'l L.J. 99 (2009).

[34] *See generally* §2.1 of this handbook (the property requirement); Charles E. Rounds, Jr., *State Common Law Aspects of the Global Unwindings of the Madoff Ponzi Scheme and the Sub-Prime Mortgage Securitization Debacle*, 27 Wis. Int'l L.J. 99 (2009).

[35] *See generally* 3 Scott & Ascher §13.2.1 (noting also that words of inheritance such as "to *X* and his heirs" are no longer necessary to create an equitable fee simple). To possess the entire equitable interest is to be the sole beneficiary. "If the terms of a trust require payment to one person of both the income for a period of time, and, thereafter, the principal, that person is the trust's sole beneficiary, unless there is a contingent gift to another or a resulting trust upon the designated person's failure to survive the stated period." 3 Scott & Ascher §13.2.2. Generally for someone to qualify as the sole beneficiary of a trust, the underlying property must pass to that person's probate estate in the event of his or her death before final distribution.

[36] *See* §9.1 of this handbook (the grantor trust).

[37] I.R.C. §§401(a)(7), 411; ERISA §203 (ERISA vesting standards).

[38] Lewin ¶1-08 (England). *See generally* §3.5.3.2(a) of this handbook (the discretionary trust).

trustee exercising discretion. Nonetheless, the equitable interest is an interest in property; it is not merely a hope or expectancy.[39]

§5.3.2   Voluntary Transfers of the Equitable (Beneficial) Interest

Uses became assignable long before choses in action were. As Bacon wrote, "For the transferring of uses there is no case in law whereby an action is transferred, but the subpoena in case of use was always assignable."[40]

In the absence of restraint imposed by the terms of the trust or by statute,[41] the beneficiary's equitable estate may be transferred by the beneficiary as freely as might be done if it were a legal estate (beneficial interests after all being property interests).[42] The Restatement (Third) of Trusts is in accord.[43] In fact, it has been settled since the early seventeenth century that equitable property interests under active trusts are assignable, at least in principle.[44] "A beneficiary can make such a transfer whether the interest is a present or a future interest, vested or contingent."[45] By way of background, at early common law, a contingent legal remainder interest in land was generally not assignable during the remainderman's life and thus was not reachable by his creditors, a contingent interest not being considered property.[46] Today even such an interest as that would qualify as a property interest.

On the other hand, the beneficiary may not transfer the equitable interest if it is subject to the discretion of the trustee or if it is inseparable from that of

---

[39] *See* Kevin D. Millard, *Rights of a Trust Beneficiary's Creditors Under the Uniform Trust Code*, 34 ACTEC L.J. 58, 72 (2008) (the equitable interest of a beneficiary of a discretionary trust is more than a mere expectancy, it is an interest in property).

[40] 1 Scott & Ascher §1.1 (citing to Bacon, Reading upon the Statute of Uses 7, 16 (Rowe ed., 1804)).

[41] In New York, by statute, a trust is a spendthrift trust unless the governing instrument provides otherwise. N.Y. Est. Powers & Trusts Law §7-1.5(a). On the other hand, under §501 of the UTC (available at <http://www.uniformlaws.org/Act.aspx?title=Trust%20Code>), there is creditor accessibility unless the terms of the governing instrument provide otherwise. What we have here are opposite default rules. For a catalog of state statutes providing that a spendthrift clause is presumed even if not expressly included in the trust, *see* Jeffrey A. Schoenblum, 2000 Multistate Guide to Estate Planning 11-40 (2000); 3 Scott & Ascher §15.2.1, n.16.

[42] *See generally* Restatement of Property §5; Restatement of Property §3 (introduction to ch. 1); 3 Scott & Ascher §14.1; 2A Scott on Trusts §132; Restatement (Second) of Trusts §133; Brown v. Fletcher, 235 U.S. 589, 599 (1915); Charles E. Rounds, Jr., *State Common Law Aspects of the Global Unwindings of the Madoff Ponzi Scheme and the Sub-Prime Mortgage Securitization Debacle*, 27 Wis. Int'l L.J. 99 (2009).

[43] Restatement (Third) of Trusts §51.

[44] *See* Warmstrey v. Tanfield, 1 Ch. Rep. 29 (1628).

[45] 3 Scott & Ascher §14.1.

[46] Dukeminier, Krier, Alexander & Schill, Property 232 (6th. Ed) ("But oddly enough, when the question was whether the heirs of a dead remainderman inherited the remainder, the courts saw the remainder as an interest passing to them, if survivorship was not required by the instrument").

others.[47] *These are restraints imposed by the terms of the trust.*[48] Or a beneficial interest may be so personal in nature as to be unassignable (*e.g.*, support for the beneficiary's education).[49]

The reader is cautioned that whether a particular equitable interest is assignable is an issue separate and apart from whether the beneficiary holds a power of appointment over the underlying trust property.[50] An equitable interest is "assigned"; a power of appointment is "exercised."[51]

Unless it terminates with the beneficiary's death, the equitable or beneficial interest may pass by will[52] or by intestacy.[53] Otherwise it may be transferred inter vivos by deed.[54] Transfers may be in whole or in part, outright or by way of security, or in trust.[55] Requirements of capacity and present intention are identical at law and in equity,[56] to include when fraud, duress, undue influence, or mistake is grounds for the reformation or rescission of a particular transfer.[57] A transfer may be gratuitous or for consideration, and in either case irrevocable.[58] The transferee of a legal or equitable interest need not know of the transfer or assent to it, but both interests are of course disclaimable.[59] In the case of the transfer of an equitable interest, notice to and/or the consent of the trustee also is not required, unless the terms of the trust provide otherwise.[60] Having said that, a court might well take a beneficiary's failure to communicate to the trustee, the transferee, and appropriate third parties a present intention to transfer as evidence that such an intention was lacking.[61] Testamentary transfers of beneficial interests as well as legal interests require compliance with the statute of wills.[62]

That equitable interests can be assigned is one reason why it is risky for third parties to bypass the trustee. Assume, whether for investment purposes or

---

[47] *See generally* 2A Scott on Trusts §§132, 155, 161; E. Griswold, Spendthrift Trusts §§435–445 (2d ed. 1947) (discussing the separability of the beneficial interests).

[48] *See generally* 3 Scott & Ascher §14.1.

[49] *See generally* 2A Scott on Trusts §160.

[50] *See* §8.1 of this handbook (powers of appointment).

[51] *See generally* §8.1 of this handbook (powers of appointment).

[52] Restatement (Third) of Trusts §55(1); 3 Scott & Ascher §14.1.1.

[53] Restatement (Third) of Trusts §55(1); 3 Scott & Ascher §14.1.1.

[54] 3 Scott & Ascher §14.1.

[55] *See generally* 2A Scott on Trusts §132. *See also* Blair v. Comm'r, 300 U.S. 5, 13 (1937) (holding valid life beneficiary's assignment of portions of trust income).

[56] *See generally* Restatement (Third) of Trusts §51 cmt. c; Restatement (Second) of Trusts §133; 3 Scott & Ascher §14.2; 2A Scott on Trusts §§133–134 (Capacity, Intention); Chase Nat'l Bank of N.Y. v. Sayles, 11 F.2d 948, 955 (1st Cir. 1926) (a valid unrestricted assignment is irrevocable); Restatement (Second) of Trusts §134.

[57] 3 Scott & Ascher §14.8.

[58] 3 Scott & Ascher §14.4.

[59] *See generally* Restatement (Second) of Trusts §137; 3 Scott & Ascher §14.6; 2A Scott on Trusts §137; §5.5 of this handbook (voluntary or involuntary loss of the beneficiary's rights).

[60] *See* 3 Scott & Ascher §14.5 (noting, however, that a trustee who has no notice of the transfer incurs no liability for continuing to make payments to the original beneficiary).

[61] 3 Scott & Ascher §14.3.

[62] *See generally* Bogert §188; 2A Scott on Trusts §132.1.

otherwise, the trustee holds the legal title to contractual rights against a third party, such as rights against the issuer of a corporate bond or against an insurance company incident to one of its policies. In other words, assume that a bond or an insurance contract is a trust asset. If the third party makes a payment to the trust beneficiary rather than to the trustee, the other party to the contract, the third party does so at its peril: "When the beneficiary's interest is assignable and has been assigned, and the trust estate includes a claim against a third person, payment of the claim to the original beneficiary does not preclude the trustee from compelling the third person to pay again, even if, at the time of the initial payment, the third person has no notice of the assignment."[63] The trustee, the one to whom the obligation was due, never received the payment. Nor did the assignee receive it, the one with the current equitable property interest. If the third party has any recourse, it is against the assignor, the original or former beneficiary.

The statute of frauds may apply to the transfer of an equitable interest, particularly if the underlying property is realty.[64] Such a transfer may also require attention to the rules and regulations of the Securities and Exchange Commission.[65] On the other hand, some of the formalities required for the transfer of a legal interest may be dispensed with in the case of the transfer of the equitable interest. Thus, as a general rule, the transfer of a beneficial interest in a trust containing real estate need not be recorded in a registry of deeds.[66]

This then raises the question whether assignments of equitable or beneficial interests take priority in the order made or in the order in which notice is given to the trustee.[67] There is a division of authority on the issue,[68] although "in many states, on the ground that because the equities are otherwise equal, the prior prevails."[69] The Restatement (Third) of Trusts would resolve the issue this way: "Where the beneficiary of a trust makes successive transfers of an interest, the first transferee is entitled to the interest unless the subsequent transferee prevails under principles of estoppel."[70] The second transferee, however, would

---

[63] 5 Scott & Ascher §32.1 (Discharge by Beneficiary of Claim Against Third Person).

[64] 3 Scott & Ascher §14.7; Restatement (Third) of Trusts §53, cmt. a. *See generally* Bogert §190; Restatement (Second) of Trusts §138; §8.15.5 of this handbook (statute of frauds).

[65] *See* §7.3.3.3 of this handbook (registration and sale of securities) and §7.3.4.2(a) of this handbook (criminal and civil liability: securities laws); Charles E. Rounds, Jr., *State Common Law Aspects of the Global Unwindings of the Madoff Ponzi Scheme and the Sub-Prime Mortgage Securitization Debacle,* 27 Wis. Int'l L.J. 99 (2009).

[66] *See generally* Bogert §249.

[67] *See generally* 3 Scott & Ascher §14.9.

[68] *See generally* 2A Scott on Trusts §163; Bogert §195.

[69] 5 Scott & Ascher §29.1.2. We essentially have here a conflict between BFPs of the equitable interest. *See generally* §8.15.63 of this handbook (doctrine of bona fide purchase).

[70] Restatement (Third) of Trusts §54. "If the prior transferee of a beneficiary's interest induced the subsequent transferee to believe that no transfer had occurred, and the subsequent transferee in reliance thereon paid value without notice of the earlier transfer, the prior transferee is by estoppel postponed to the subsequent transferee." Restatement (Third) of Trusts §5 cmt. b. *See* §7.1.3 of this handbook (defense of failure of beneficiary to take timely action against trustee) for a definition of the term *estoppel.*

prevail if the first transfer were revocable or voidable;[71] or if the subsequent transferee were a bona fide purchaser (BFP), *i.e.*, if he or she without notice of the prior transfer, gave value for the underlying trust property and received the legal title thereto.

What if a trustee honors the beneficiary's assignment of an equitable interest in a spendthrift trust? Courts tend to absolve the trustee by treating the assignment as a revocable order to transfer accrued income or principal once it becomes possessory.[72] For this purpose, the trustee is essentially deemed an agent of the beneficiary. The relationship being an agency, it is revocable by the principal (in this case the beneficiary) up until the time accrued income or principal is transferred by the trustee outright and free of trust to the assignee.[73]

The transferee of an equitable or beneficial interest under a trust not only has standing to seek judicial enforcement of the trust but also standing to petition the court to compel the trustee to remedy any breaches of trust that may have occurred prior to the transfer.[74] On the other hand, it is questionable whether a purported transfer of just the breach-of-fiduciary-duty claim would be effective.[75]

§5.3.3 Rights of Beneficiary's Creditors and Others to the Equitable Interest and/or the Underlying Trust Property

The common law rule that appointive assets covered by an unexercised general power of appointment, created by a person other than the donee, cannot be reached by the donee's creditors results from adherence to the common law distinction between ownership and power. Until the donee exercises the power, he has not accepted control over the appointive assets that gives the donee the equivalent of ownership of them.[76]

Equity generally follows the law. In the case of involuntary transfers of the beneficiary's interest, the equitable estate is treated in many respects as if it were a legal estate;[77] except, perhaps, when it comes to

---

[71] Restatement (Third) of Trusts §54 cmt. c.

[72] *See* Restatement (Second) of Trusts §152 cmt. i; John P. Ludington, L.L.B, Annot., *Validity and construction of beneficiary's arrangement for payment to another, as they become due, of sums due under spendthrift trust*, 83 A.L.R.3d 1142 (1978).

[73] *See* Restatement (Second) of Trusts §152 cmt. i; John P. Ludington, L.L.B, Annot., *Validity and construction of beneficiary's arrangement for payment to another, as they become due, of sums due under spendthrift trust*, 83 A.L.R.3d 1142 (1978). *See also* UTC §502 cmt. (available at <http://www.uniformlaws.org/Act.aspx?title=Trust%20Code>) (citing to Restatement (Third) of Trusts §58 cmt. d (Tentative Draft No. 2, approved 1999) & Restatement (Second) of Trusts §152 cmt. i in support of the proposition that the beneficiary, not having made a binding transfer, can withdraw the beneficiary's direction but only as to future payments).

[74] 3 Scott & Ascher §14.1.2.

[75] 3 Scott & Ascher §14.1.2.

[76] Restatement (Second) of Property (Wills and Other Donative Transfers) §13.2 cmt. a.

[77] Bogert §193.

procedure.[78] Therefore, as a general rule, a beneficiary's creditors and spouse may reach that portion of the equitable interest or the underlying trust property itself over which the beneficiary possesses an affirmative right of consumption, such as in the case where there are no enforceable spendthrift restrictions.[79] The Restatement (Third) of Trusts is generally in accord,[80] as is the federal Bankruptcy Code (U.S.).[81]

Some exceptions. There are four important exceptions to this rule:

(1) *Powers of appointment.* At common law, a nonsettlor holder of a general power of appointment, whether testamentary[82] or inter vivos, could not be compelled by creditors or others to exercise it.[83] This is a remnant of the pre-Restatement of Property distinction between personal rights and property rights.[84] However, if the power is exercised, the property subject to the power may be fair game for the holder's creditors.[85] It should be noted that in some states, statutes permit the

[78] *See, e.g.,* Restatement (Third) of Trusts §56 cmt. e (providing that "except as modified by statute, a creditor can subject the beneficiary's interest to the satisfaction of a claim . . . after having attempted to satisfy the claim out of legal interests of the beneficiary, or when it appears that an attempt to do so would be unsuccessful or insufficiently productive"). *See also* 3 Scott & Ascher §14.11 (noting that "at common law, although a judgment creditor obtained, by virtue of the judgment, a lien on all of the lands of the judgment debtor, a judgment conferred no lien on the equitable interests of the judgment debtor, such as a beneficial interest in a trust," but noting, also, that "[i]n most states today, . . . a judgment lien extends, as well, to any equitable interests the debtor may have in land").

[79] *See generally* 2A Scott on Trusts §§147, 157. *See also* UTC §501 (available at <http://www.uniformlaws.org/Act.aspx?title=Trust%20Code>).

[80] Restatement (Third) of Trusts §56.

[81] *See generally* 3 Scott & Ascher §14.11.1 (noting that "[w]hen a trust beneficiary goes into bankruptcy, the beneficial interest vests in the trustee in bankruptcy, unless the terms of the trust or applicable law imposes a restraint on alienation of the interest").

[82] *See* Restatement (Third) of Trusts §56 cmt. b (noting that a general power to appoint only by will does not give the donee during his or her lifetime the equivalent of ownership of the appointive assets).

[83] *See, e.g.,* Gilman v. Bell, 99 Ill. 144 (1881); State St. Trust Co. v. Kissel, 302 Mass. 328, 333, 19 N.E.2d 25 (1939). *See generally* Ritchie et al., Decedent's Estates and Trusts 961–964 (8th ed. 1993).

[84] *See, e.g.,* Gilman v. Bell, 99 Ill. 144 (1881); State St. Trust Co. v. Kissel, 302 Mass. 328, 333, 19 N.E.2d 25 (1939). *See generally* Ritchie et al., Decedent's Estates and Trusts 961–964 (8th ed. 1993). *See also* National Shawmut Bank v. Joy, 315 Mass. 457, 472, 53 N.E.2d 113, 124 (1944); Jones v. Clifton, 101 U.S. 225, 231 (1879).

[85] *See, e.g.,* Gilman v. Bell, 99 Ill. 144 (1881); State St. Trust Co. v. Kissel, 302 Mass. 328, 333, 19 N.E.2d 25 (1939). *See generally* Ritchie et al., Decedent's Estates and Trusts 961–964 (8th ed. 1993). *See, e.g.,* Alaska Stat. §34.40.115 (Alaska). *See generally* Restatement (Second) of Property (Wills and Other Donative Transfers) §13.4 (providing that appointive assets covered by an exercised general power to appoint by will, created by a person other than the donee, can be subjected to the payment of claims against the donee's estate). "Appointive assets covered by an exercised general power to appoint by deed, created by a person other than a donee, can be subjected to the payment of the claims of creditors of the donee to whatever extent they could have been thus subjected, under the rules relating to fraudulent conveyances, if the appointive assets has been owned by the donee and transferred to the appointee." Restatement (Second) of Property (Wills and Other Donative Transfers) §13.5.

creditors of the holder of a non–self-settled general inter vivos power of appointment to reach the property, even if the power is unexercised.[86] The Restatement (Third) of Trusts takes this approach as well.[87] In fact, it would afford even *postmortem* creditors of the holder of the power access to the subject property to the extent the power had not been exercised during the holder's lifetime.[88] The Uniform Trust Code is generally in accord.[89] Property subject to a nongeneral, *i.e.*, limited/special, power of appointment, of course, can never be reached by the holder's creditors, whether or not the power is exercised, except to the extent required by rules of law relating to fraudulent conveyances.[90] Moreover, under the Uniform Trust Code, "a beneficiary may serve as trustee of a third-party created trust without being treated as the settlor of a revocable trust for creditors' rights purposes, if the beneficiary's power to distribute to himself or herself is limited by the requisite ascertainable standard."[91] In other words, a fiduciary general-type power that is limited by an ascertainable standard will not in and of itself expose the subject property to attack by the personal creditors of the trustee-beneficiary.

(2) *Employee benefit plans.* Even when employees have untrammeled access to their interests in trusts associated with qualified employee benefit plans, it does not necessarily mean that their creditors do as well. This is due to federal pension law.[92]

(3) *Indivisible equitable interests.* If the debtor-beneficiary holds the equitable interest jointly with another or as a tenant by the entirety, the

---

[86] Bogert §233; Restatement (Second) of Property (Wills and Other Donative Transfers) §13.2, Statutory Note to Section 13.2. *See also* UTC §505(b)(1) (available at <http://www.uniformlaws.org/Act.aspx?title=Trust%20Code>) (providing that for creditors' rights purposes, the holder of a presently exercisable power of withdrawal is treated in the same manner as the settlor of a revocable trust to the extent of the property subject to the power). *See generally* Restatement (Third) of Trusts §10, Reporter's Note to Comment g, re: Clause (e) (who is the nominal settlor of a trust and who is the actual settlor of a trust for purposes of taxation, creditor accessibility, and equitable distribution in the context of divorce hinges on the substance of the arrangement rather than its form).

[87] Restatement (Third) of Trusts §56 cmt. b.

[88] Restatement (Third) of Trusts §56 cmt. b.

[89] UTC §505(b)(1) (available at <http://www.uniformlaws.org/Act.aspx?title=Trust%20Code>).

[90] Restatement (Third) of Trusts §56 cmt. b; Restatement (Second) of Property (Wills and Other Donative Transfers) §13.1.

[91] Alan Newman, *Spendthrift and Discretionary Trusts: Alive and Well Under the Uniform Trust Code*, 40 Real Prop. Prob. & Tr. J. 568, 592–593 (Fall 2005) (referring to UTC §§103(10) & 103(2)). *See generally* §8.15.15 of this handbook (the ascertainable standard).

[92] *See* I.R.C. §401(a)(13) (1954) (trusts that are part of qualified plans must prohibit assignment or alienation of benefits); Patterson v. Shumate, 504 U.S. 753 (1992) (holding that assets held in a trust associated with a qualified plan may not be reached by the bankruptcy trustee though the trust would not qualify for spendthrift protection under state trust law). *But see* Marton, Gerson & Levine, *Qualified Plans May Not Be Protected in Bankruptcy*, 23 ACTEC Notes 75 (1997). *See generally* §5.3.3.3(d) of this handbook (trusteed employee benefit plans and IRAs).

creditors may not reach the equitable interest during the life of the cotenant.[93]

(4) *Corresponding legal interests that are exempt from creditors' claims.* "In all states, and under the federal Bankruptcy Act, certain kinds and amounts of property are exempt from creditors' claims within specified limits."[94] Generally, legal and equitable interests that correspond to one another are treated similarly in this regard.

Vulnerable equitable interests. An example of an equitable interest that is vulnerable to involuntary transfer would be an irrevocable, nondiscretionary, income-only trust created by *A* for the benefit of *C:* where, after the expiration of ten years, the property passes outright and free of trust to *D;* where *B* is the trustee; where *D* is ascertained at the time the property is transferred to *B;* and where there is no spendthrift provision. Under such a trust, the income stream itself would be reachable and attachable by *C*'s spouse and creditors during the ten-year period. If *C* were to die intestate during the ten-year period, the income stream would inure to the benefit of *C*'s heirs at law for the balance of the period, subject to any rights of the creditors and the spouse to the equitable interest. In addition, the present vested right to the future unrestricted enjoyment of the property would be reachable by *D*'s spouse and creditors during the ten-year period.[95] If *D* were to die intestate before ten years, the vested equitable remainder interest—that right of future enjoyment—would pass in accordance with the laws of distribution to *D*'s heirs at law, unless the underlying trust property were realty, in which case the equitable interest would pass to them by descent.[96] *D* could also designate by a will who is to succeed to *D*'s interest if death occurred during the ten-year period.

Were the debtor both the sole current beneficiary and the sole remainderman, *i.e.,* were the debtor the only beneficiary,[97] then the court would have the authority, if necessary, to order the trustee to sell the underlying property and pay the creditor what is due the creditor out of the proceeds, provided, of course, the equitable interest itself were free of enforceable spendthrift restrictions.[98] "In contrast, in the usual situation in which the debtor is not the sole beneficiary, the creditor of any one beneficiary cannot reach the . . . [underlying] . . . trust property, because doing so would interfere with the rights of the other beneficiaries."[99] In that case, only the debtor's equitable property interest, not the underlying property itself, would be creditor accessible, unless, perhaps, the trust were self-settled. In the non–self-settled context, at least, that

---

[93] *See generally* Bogert §230.

[94] Restatement (Third) of Trusts §56 cmt. d.

[95] *See generally* Restatement (Third) of Trusts §193.

[96] 2A Scott on Trusts §142.

[97] The debtor would still qualify as the "only beneficiary" if the debtor, say, alone possessed an equitable life estate, provided all the underlying trust property were to become part of the debtor's probate estate upon the life estate's expiration.

[98] The express restrictions of the non–self-settled spendthrift trust and the implied restrictions of the non–self-settled discretionary trust come to mind.

[99] 3 Scott & Ascher §14.11.2.

might translate into the creditor's right to receive periodic distributions of net trust accounting income or the right to receive trust principal outright and free of trust when the trust eventually terminates on its own terms. Whether it was the former or the latter would depend upon the type of equitable estate the debtor possessed.[100]

Homestead. While a trust beneficiary's vested equitable interest may be vulnerable to creditor attack, it also may be entitled to the same statutory protections as legal interests.[101] Homestead exemptions, for example, apply to equitable as well as legal interests.[102] Such exemptions are generally recognized by the bankruptcy code (U.S.), subject to certain limitations as to amount and availability.[103]

Non–self-settled discretionary trusts. An example of an equitable interest that traditionally has *not* been subject to involuntary transfer is a fully discretionary trust established by *A* for the benefit of *C* during *C*'s lifetime. Here *C* possesses no affirmative right to consume the income and principal: *C* gets whatever *B* chooses to release and no more, as do *C*'s spouse and creditors. Moreover, should *C* die intestate nothing would pass to *C*'s heirs at law, the interest having extinguished at *C*'s death. The Restatement (Third) of Trusts, however, has adopted a more creditor-friendly approach to a debtor's equitable interest under a non–self-settled discretionary trust.[104]

Reserved equitable interests under discretionary trusts. In many jurisdictions, the creditor of a settlor-beneficiary has now come to be fully in the driver's seat, even when it comes to *reserved* equitable interests under discretionary trusts. Where the settlor is also a beneficiary, *i.e.*, where *A* and *C* or *A* and *D* are the same, the equitable interest is vulnerable to attack by *A*'s spouse and creditors.[105] This is a manifestation of the public policy that a settlor-debtor may not eat his cake and have it too.[106] Alaska, Colorado, Delaware, Missouri, Nevada, New Hampshire, Oklahoma, Rhode Island, South Dakota, Tennessee, Utah, and Wyoming, however, have recently enacted legislation insulating

---

[100] 3 Scott & Ascher §14.11.2.

[101] Bogert §187.

[102] Bogert §187. *But see* Boyle v. Weiss, (461 Mass. 519, 962 N.E.2d. 169 2012) (holding that the owner of an equitable interest under a trust of a parcel of real estate and the dwelling upon it may not acquire an estate of homestead in the entrusted property though the equitable owner resides in the dwelling, legal title to the entrusted property being in the trustee and not the equitable owner); In re Bosonetto, 271 B.R. 403 (Bankr. M.D. Fla. 2001) (denying homestead exemption to a bankrupt because she held title to her home not in her individual capacity but as trustee of a revocable inter vivos trust for her benefit, finding that a trustee does not qualify as a "natural" person for purposes of the homestead eligibility provisions of the Florida constitution).

[103] 3 Scott & Ascher §14.11.4.

[104] Restatement (Third) of Trusts §60.

[105] Restatement (Third) of Trusts §56 cmt. b.

[106] *See generally* 2A Scott on Trusts §156; Restatement (Second) of Trusts §156; Ware v. Gulda, 331 Mass. 68, 117 N.E.2d 137 (1954) (holding the property of a fully discretionary trust to be reachable by the settlor-beneficiary's creditors). *See also* Vanderbilt Credit Corp. v. Chase Manhattan Bank, N.A., 100 A.D.2d 544, 546, 473 N.Y.S.2d 242, 245 (1984).

certain such self-settled discretionary trusts from creditor attack.[107] Whether these developments mark the start of a trend remains to be seen.

The charging order. The judicially granted *charging order* may be a fallback option for a debtor/beneficiary's creditor who is prevented from getting at the underlying assets of a spendthrift or discretionary trust.[108] A charging order would allow the creditor to at least snare any distributions that are actually made by the trustee before they reach the hands of the debtor/beneficiary.[109] As is generally the case when a creditor seeks to reach a trust beneficiary's interest, the court need not have personal jurisdiction over the beneficiary, just over the trustee, "at least when the court also has jurisdiction over the administration of the trust."[110] The charging order, however, is probably not a fallback option when it comes to Minnesota spendthrift trusts: "We therefore hold that a district court may not, before proceeds of a spendthrift trust are received by the beneficiary, determine what the beneficiary may or may not do with the proceeds."[111]

The Uniform Trust Code muddies the waters. Uniform Trust Code §501 provides as follows: "To the extent a beneficiary's interest is not subject to a spendthrift provision, the court may authorize a creditor or assignee of the beneficiary to reach the beneficiary's interest by attachment of present or future distributions to or for the benefit of the beneficiary or other means." It is not entirely clear what is meant by "reach the beneficiary's interest." Is it the beneficiary's equitable/beneficial interest under the trust? If so, as we have already discussed, equitable/beneficial interests themselves are generally per se attachable, unless subject to a spendthrift restraint, excessively contingent, or subject to statutory protections. Or is it the beneficiary's legal interest in distributed, or to-be-distributed, items of trust income and trust principal? If so, then perhaps UTC §501 is referring ultra-obliquely to the charging order. It may be that UTC §501 is conflating and muddling two very different processes: reaching a beneficiary's equitable interest under a trust and reaching a beneficiary's legal interest in trust distributions after legal title to them has left the trustee.

Introducing the next section. What follows is *not* a discussion of the charging order. What follows is a discussion of the circumstances under which

---

[107] Alaska Stat. §34.40.110(b)(2) (Michie 1997); Del. C. Ann. tit. 12, §§3570–3576, (1997); R.I. Stat. §§18-9.2-1 *et seq.*; Nev. Rev. Stat. §166.040.

[108] *See, e.g.,* Hamilton v. Drogo, 241 N.Y. 401, 150 N.E. 496 (1926). *See also* UTC §501 (available at <http://www.uniformlaws.org/Act.aspx?title=Trust%20Code>) (allowing for attachment under certain circumstances of "future distributions").

[109] The UTC would allow a creditor or assignee of a beneficiary of a spendthrift trust to reach a mandatory distribution of income or principal, provided the trustee has not made the distribution to the beneficiary within a reasonable time after the required distribution date. UTC §506 (available at <http://www.uniformlaws.org/Act.aspx?title=Trust%20Code>). "Following this reasonable period, payments mandated by the express terms of the trust are in effect being held by the trustee as agent for the beneficiary and should be treated as part of the beneficiary's personal assets." UTC §506 cmt.

[110] 3 Scott & Ascher §14.11.2.

[111] Fannie Mae v. Heather Apartments Ltd. P'ship, 799 N.W.2d 638, 642 (Min. Ct. App. 2012), *aff'd,* 811 N.W.2d 596 (Minn. 2012).

the creditor may reach the trust property *regardless of the terms of the trust and regardless of the actions or inactions of the trustee.*

§5.3.3.1   Reaching Settlor's Reserved Beneficial Interest

Note two essential components of the Restatement Rule. First, the rule grants to creditors greater rights than those retained by the settlor himself or herself: the settlor cannot compel trust distributions, but the settlor's creditors can. Second, the rule applies notwithstanding that allowing the settlor's creditors to reach the assets of the trust may defeat not just the settlor's interests, but also the interests of other beneficiaries. . . . The foregoing discussion suggests that in writing his treatise and drafting the Restatement, Professor Scott either misread the applicable precedent or simply focused on those aspects of the precedent that supported the position that he advocated, while ignoring those aspects that contradicted his position. More importantly, for several reasons, the discussion suggests that the Restatement rule stands on shaky theoretical ground.[112]

In the United States, for public policy reasons, a settlor[113] cannot place property in trust for the settlor's own benefit and keep it and/or the equitable interest beyond the reach of the settlor's[114] creditors.[115] (It has been likewise in England, at least as far back as the reign of Henry VII, and perhaps as far back as even the reign of Edward III.[116]) In other words, on public policy grounds, a spendthrift provision in a trust established for the settlor's own benefit is unenforceable, at least as against the settlor-beneficiary's creditors, *even if the conveyance in trust had not been fraudulent.*[117] In the United States, however, there

---

[112] Robert T. Danforth, *Rethinking the Law of Creditors' Rights in Trusts*, 53 Hastings L.J. 287, 294, 301 (2002).

[113] The beneficiary need not have made the actual transfer of the property to the trustee. A beneficiary who had paid consideration in return for which someone else made the transfer would be deemed the settlor with the result that the beneficiary's creditors would have access to the constructively retained interest. Restatement (Third) of Trusts §58 cmt. f. Also, "[a] life beneficiary of a spendthrift trust created by another who pays off encumbrances on the trust property becomes to that extent settlor of the trust." Restatement (Third) of Trusts §58 cmt. f.

[114] *See* Restatement (Third) of Trusts §58 cmt. e (confirming that the policy would not necessarily negate a spendthrift restraint with respect to the interests of persons other than the settlor).

[115] "Such interest will pass to the settlor's trustee in bankruptcy as 'a beneficial interest . . . in a trust that' is not subject to a restriction on transfer 'that is enforceable under applicable nonbankruptcy law' under the terms of Bankruptcy Code §541(c)(2)." Restatement (Third) of Trusts §58 cmt. e.

[116] 73 Hen. VII, c. 4 (1487); 50 Edw. III, c. 6 (1376). *See generally* Erwin N. Griswold, *Spendthrift Trusts Created in Whole of in Part for the Benefit of the Settlor*, 44 Harv. L. Rev. 203 (1930). *See also* 1 Scott & Ascher §1.1 (noting that "for six hundred years, people have resorted to trusts to evade creditors' claims, but, until very recently, it has always been recognized that permitting them to do so was contrary to sound policy"); 3 Scott & Ascher §15.4 (noting that these English statutes were also interpreted as "enabling the settlor's creditors to reach the settlor's beneficial interest by a proceeding at common law, without the expense of a creditor's suit in Chancery").

[117] *See* 3 Scott & Ascher §15.4. *See generally* The Fraudulent Conveyances Act 1571 (13 Eliz. 1, c5), otherwise known as the Statute of 13 Elizabeth (regulating fraudulent conveyances generally) [England].

are apparently no relevant cases dealing with whether a forfeiture provision in such a trust would violate public policy.[118] In England:

> . . . a provision requiring the forfeiture of a settlor's interest upon bankruptcy is invalid as a fraud on the bankruptcy law. But a provision for the forfeiture of the settlor's right to income upon voluntary alienation or if creditors attempt to reach it is valid.[119]

If the settlor retains the right during his or her lifetime[120] to revoke the trust, or retains an unrestricted right to amend it, the subject property will be reachable by the settlor's creditors, and later by the creditors of the settlor's estate, to the extent the property would be reachable were the settlor to own the property outright and free of trust.[121]

Of course, the reservation of a special/limited inter vivos power of appointment, in and of itself, will *not* subject the underlying trust property to the claims of the settlor's creditors, as the power may be exercised neither in favor of the settlor nor in favor of the settlor's creditors.[122] This is the case even though an exercise of the power could bring about the trust's termination.

It is not just the underlying property of revocable trusts that is creditor-vulnerable. A retained equitable or beneficial interest, such as a right to all net trust accounting income or a right to periodic unitrust distributions,[123] would be accessible to the settlor's creditors even if the settlor had not reserved a right to revoke or amend. Moreover, even if the trust contained a spendthrift provision and the trustee had full discretion and there were innocent remaindermen who could be harmed and the transfer was not procured by fraud,[124]

---

[118] *See* 3 Scott & Ascher §15.1.1. By forfeiture provision, we mean a provision that terminates the interest of a beneficiary "upon an attempt by the beneficiary to alienate the interest or an attempt by the beneficiary's creditors to reach it." 3 Scott & Ascher §15.1.1.

[119] 3 Scott & Ascher §15.1.1.

[120] *Cf.* Restatement (Third) of Trusts §58 cmt. e (providing that if the settlor reserves not only a right to receive the income of a trust for life but also a general power to appoint the remainder by will, neither the life interest nor the remainder subject to the right to appoint can be protected from the creditors of the settlor by a spendthrift restraint). "The settlor's creditors can reach the principal of the trust, provided there are no interests in others who can receive benefits during the settlor's lifetime." Restatement (Third) of Trusts §58 cmt. e.

[121] Restatement (Third) of Trusts §25 cmt. e; UTC §505(a)(1) (available at <http://www.uniformlaws.org/Act.aspx?title=Trust%20Code>); 3 Scott & Ascher §§14.11.3, 15.4.1.

[122] 3 Scott & Ascher §14.11.3. *See generally* §8.1 of this handbook (powers of appointment). Likewise, the reservation of a special/limited testamentary power of appointment, in and of itself, will not subject the underlying trust property to the claims of the settlor's creditors, as the power, by its terms, may not be exercised in favor of the settlor, the settlor's creditors, the settlor's probate estate, or the creditors of the settlor's probate estate.

[123] *See* 3 Scott & Ascher §15.4.

[124] *See generally* 3 Scott & Ascher §15.4.

the settlor's creditors would still be afforded access.[125] The Restatement (Third) of Trusts is in accord.[126]

The policy is reflected in Section 156(2) of the Restatement (Second) of Trusts,[127] which has been adopted by case law or statute in whole or in part by an ever-increasing number of jurisdictions: "[W]here a person creates for his own benefit a trust for support or a discretionary trust, his transferee or creditors can reach the maximum amount which the trustee under the terms of the trust could pay to him or apply for his benefit."[128] While unanimity across the jurisdictions on the rights of creditors to reach reserved beneficial interests has not been achieved, the law had been settling rapidly on the spirit, and in some cases even the language, of Section 156(2).[129] The Restatement (Third) of Trusts is generally in accord,[130] as is the Uniform Trust Code.[131]

Creditor accessibility can have gift and estate tax consequences as well. The settlor-beneficiary of a fully discretionary trust,[132] for example, may have failed to relinquish dominion and control over the trust property sufficient to have made a completed gift for gift tax purposes.[133] On the other hand, the "settlor's ability to secure the economic benefit of the trust assets by borrowing and relegating creditors to those assets for repayment may well trigger inclusion of the property in the settlor's gross estate under secs. 2036(a)(1) or 2038(a)(1)... [of the Internal Revenue Code]...."[134]

Under the Uniform Trust Code, if a trust has more than one settlor, the amount the creditor or assignee of a particular settlor may reach may not exceed the settlor's interest in the portion of the trust attributable to that settlor's contribution.[135] In one case, a husband and his wife owning property as tenants by the entireties transferred the property into an irrevocable self-settled spendthrift trust.[136] A judgment creditor of the husband tried unsuccessfully to reach the trust assets. The court reasoned that had the judgment been against the husband and wife jointly and severally, the creditor's claim would have been

---

[125] *See* Restatement (Second) of Trusts §156. *See, e.g.,* Spenlinhauer v. Spencer Press, Inc., 195 B.R. 543 (Bankr. D. Me. 1996), *aff'd,* 103 F.3d 106 (1st Cir. 1996). *See generally* Alan Newman, *Spendthrift and Discretionary Trusts: Alive and Well Under the Uniform Trust Code,* 40 Real Prop. Prob. & Tr. J. 567, 590 (Fall 2005).

[126] Restatement (Third) of Trusts §58 cmt. e.

[127] *See also* Ware v. Gulda, 331 Mass. 68, 117 N.E.2d 137 (1954).

[128] *See* Restatement (Second) of Trusts §156 appendix. *See also* UTC §505(a)(2) (available at <http://www.uniformlaws.org/Act.aspx?title=Trust%20Code>).

[129] *See* 2A Scott on Trusts §156 n.1.

[130] Restatement (Third) of Trusts §60 cmt. f.

[131] UTC §505(a)(2) (available at <http://www.uniformlaws.org/Act.aspx?title=Trust%20 Code>).

[132] That is a trust under which the trustee alone has full discretion to use income and/or principal to or for the benefit of the settlor.

[133] Outwin v. Comm'r, 76 T.C. 153, 164–165 (1981). *See generally* §4.1.3 of this handbook (creditor accessibility as a general inter vivos power of appointment).

[134] Outwin v. Comm'r, 76 T.C. 153, n.5 (1981).

[135] UTC §505(a)(2) (available at <http://www.uniformlaws.org/Act.aspx?title=Trust%20 Code>).

[136] Bolton Roofing Co. v. Hedrick, 701 S.W.2d 183 (Mo. Ct. App. 1985).

valid. The judgment, however, was against the husband only. Just as the creditor would have had no legal right to levy against the real estate before they conveyed it to the trustee, the legal title to the real estate having been held by them as tenants by the entireties, so it "stands to reason" that the creditor could not have access to it after the conveyance.

Recently, Alaska, Delaware, Hawaii, Missouri, Nevada, New Hampshire, Oklahoma, Rhode Island, South Dakota, Tennessee, Utah, Virginia, and Wyoming have seen fit by legislation to afford some creditor protection to certain "self-settled" discretionary trusts.[137] Whether this development marks the beginning of a trend remains to be seen.[138] These initiatives are discussed in greater detail in Section 5.3.3.1(c) of this handbook. In jurisdictions that are following the letter or spirit of Section 156(2), a transfer to an irrevocable trust by the settlor for the settlor's own benefit will not be a completed inter vivos transfer for federal gift tax or estate tax purposes.[139] This is true even if the settlor is only a discretionary beneficiary.[140]

Uniform Trust Code provides that a lapse, release, or waiver of a power of withdrawal, whether the power was reserved by or granted to the holder, will cause the holder to be treated as the settlor of the trust for creditor accessibility purposes only to the extent the value of the property affected by the lapse, release, or waiver exceeds the Crummey or "5 and 5" power.[141] For a discussion of the "5 and 5" power, see Section 9.18 of this handbook.

(a) The vulnerability of principal (reserved beneficial interest and powers). It is important to understand how radically Section 156(2), discussed immediately above, has altered the common law of property and trusts.[142] Let us assume that a settlor creates a trust for his or her own benefit, giving the trustee discretion over income and principal. Under Section 156(2), the principal is vulnerable to attack by the settlor's creditors even if: (1) the trustee never chooses to exercise this discretion; (2) the trustee is independent; (3) the remaindermen are unrelated third parties; and (4) the original transfer in trust

---

[137] Alaska Stat. §34.40.110(b)(2) (Michie 1997); Del. C. Ann. tit. 12 §§3570–3576 (1997); R.I. Gen. Laws §§18-9.2-1 *et seq.*; Nev. Rev. Stat. §166.040; Utah Code Ann. §25-6-14(4)(a).

[138] The drafters of the UTC have rejected the approach taken in states like Alaska and Delaware, both of which allow a settlor to retain a beneficial interest immune from creditor claims. UTC §505 cmt. (available at <http://www.uniformlaws.org/Act.aspx?title=Trust%20Code>).

[139] Paolozzi v. Comm'r, 23 T.C. 182, 186 (1954); Outwin v. Comm'r, 76 T.C. 153, 153 n.5 (1981); Paxton v. Comm'r, 86 T.C. 785 (1986). *See generally* §4.1.3 of this handbook (creditor accessibility as a general inter vivos power of appointment).

[140] Paolozzi v. Comm'r, 23 T.C. 182, 186 (1954); Outwin v. Comm'r, 76 T.C. 153, 153 n.5 (1981); Paxton v. Comm'r, 86 T.C. 785 (1986). *See generally* §4.1.3 of this handbook (creditor accessibility as a general inter vivos power of appointment).

[141] UTC §505(b)(2) (available at <http://www.uniformlaws.org/Act.aspx?title=Trust%20Code>). *See generally* Kevin D. Millard, *Rights of a Trust Beneficiary's Creditors under the Uniform Trust Code*, 34 ACTEC L.J. 58, 65–66 (2008).

[142] *See generally* 3 Scott & Ascher §15.4.3 (Discretionary Trust for the Settlor).

was *not* procured by fraud.[143] Vulnerability would be a given, of course, if the settlor were the sole beneficiary, *i.e.*, if the settlor were the only permissible beneficiary, with the underlying property to pass to the settlor's probate estate upon the settlor's death.[144]

What if the settlor reserves no beneficial interest, only a naked right of revocation? The state of the common law has been until relatively recently that an unexercised,[145] naked reserved right of revocation will not expose the principal, *i.e.*, the underlying trust property, to attack by the settlor's creditors.[146] It was reasonable to expect, however, that form would give way to substance sooner rather than later.[147] That process is well under way,[148] and probably was inevitable after *In re Totten*.[149] More and more, courts and legislatures are hard pressed to justify why, as a matter of public policy, the settlor's creditors should be thwarted by naked reserved rights of revocation under which settlors retain rights of consumption over the subject properties, rights that are the functional equivalent of ownership, but should not be thwarted by reserved beneficial interests in discretionary trusts where control is transferred to independent trustees. After all, a naked retained right of revocation enables a competent settlor to destroy the contingent equitable interests of all ostensible beneficiaries.[150] While in form the settlor may have only a personal right of disposition, in substance he is a beneficiary, in fact the primary beneficiary.[151] This is because the interests of the ostensible beneficiaries are subordinate to the settlor's right to get back the entrusted property.[152] It should be noted that

---

[143] The UTC does not address possible rights against a settlor who was insolvent at the time of the trust's creation or was rendered insolvent by the transfer of property to the trust, the subject instead being left to state fraudulent transfer law. UTC §505 cmt. (available at <http://www.uniformlaws.org/Act.aspx?title=Trust%20Code>). *See also* 3 Scott & Ascher §15.4.

[144] *See generally* 3 Scott & Ascher §15.4.3. *See also* §8.15.7 of this handbook (discussing the applicability of the *Claflin* doctrine even in the absence of spendthrift restraints).

[145] *See generally* 3 Scott & Ascher §14.11.3 (noting that "[t]here is authority for the proposition that if the donee of a general power exercises it, and if the donee's other assets are insufficient to pay the donee's debts, the donee's creditors can reach the appointed property, but . . . [that-] . . . there is also . . . [some] . . . authority to the contrary").

[146] *See* Restatement (Second) of Trusts §330 cmt. o; Jones v. Clifton, 101 U.S. 225, 230–231 (1879). For statutes providing otherwise, *see* 4 Scott on Trusts §330.12. *See also* UTC §505(a)(1) (available at <http://www.uniformlaws.org/Act.aspx?title=Trust%20Code>) (during the lifetime of the settlor, the property of a revocable trust is subject to the claims of the settlor's creditors).

[147] *See generally* Alan Newman, Spendthrift and Discretionary Trusts: Alive and Well Under the Uniform Trust Code, 40 Real Prop. Prob. & Tr. J. 567, 591–592 (Fall 2005).

[148] 3 Scott & Ascher §§14.11.3, 15.4.2.

[149] 179 N.Y. 112, 71 N.E. 748 (1904). *See generally* §9.8.5 of this handbook (the Totten or tentative trust).

[150] *See generally* 3 Scott & Ascher §§15.4.1, 15.4.2.

[151] *See generally* 3 Scott & Ascher §§15.4.1, 15.4.2.

[152] *See* UTC §505(a)(1) (available at <http://www.uniformlaws.org/Act.aspx?title=Trust%20Code>) (providing that the settlor's possession of a naked reserved right of revocation alone will subject the trust property to the claims of the settlor's creditors). *See also* UTC §603(a) (providing that while a trust is revocable and the settlor has capacity to revoke the trust, the rights of the beneficiaries are subject to the control of, and the duties of the trustee are owed exclusively to, the settlor).

the Uniform Trust Code would afford the creditors of the holder of a naked right of revocation access to the trust principal.[153] The Restatement (Third) of Trusts is in accord.[154] On the other hand, the reservation of a general testamentary power of appointment in and of itself will not subject the underlying trust property to the claims of the settlor's creditors during the settlor's lifetime.[155]

Is principal safe from attack by the settlor's creditors when the settlor creates an income-only spendthrift trust for the settlor's own benefit, notwithstanding the fact that the spendthrift clause cannot protect the income stream itself from the reach of the settlor's creditors?[156] Probably yes—at least for the foreseeable future.[157] There is a counterargument, however: The principal—the engine that generates the income—is employed for the benefit of the settlor. Thus, because the entire principal is dedicated to the benefit of the settlor, the spirit and letter of Section 156(2) dictate that the principal itself should be vulnerable to creditor attack.[158] While the engine argument is essentially the rationale in the estate tax context for the reserved life estate sections of the Internal Revenue Code,[159] it has so far proven of little utility to the settlor's creditors.[160] Note, however, that a self-settled income-only trust containing a reserved general power of appointment, be it inter vivos or testamentary, may well be creditor-vulnerable.[161]

(b)   The postmortem creditor of deceased settlor. It is self-evident that the legitimate postmortem creditors of the settlor of a testamentary trust will have access to that portion of the settlor's probate estate that is destined to fund the trust, *i.e.*, to the extent their lawful claims have not been or cannot be satisfied from other estate assets. Whether by statute or decision, the probate estate is generally where postmortem creditors are expected to look to first. Under certain circumstances, however, the postmortem creditors also may have access to the underlying property of a trust that the decedent had established during his or her lifetime. This is likely to be the case if the settlor has reserved a general inter vivos power of appointment, such as a right of revocation, or

---

[153] UTC §505(a)(1) (available at <http://www.uniformlaws.org/Act.aspx?title=Trust%20Code>).

[154] Restatement (Third) of Trusts §25 cmt. e.

[155] *See generally* 3 Scott & Ascher §15.4.1.

[156] *See generally* 3 Scott & Ascher §15.4.

[157] *See generally* 2A Scott on Trusts §156 n.2 and accompanying text.

[158] *See generally* Rounds, *The Vulnerability of Trust Assets to Attack by the Deceased Settlors Creditors, by the Commonwealth Should It Seek Reimbursement for Medicaid Payments, and by the Spouse,* 73 Mass. L. Rev. 67, 70 (1988).

[159] I.R.C. §2036(a)(1) (1978), *rev'g* May v. Heiner, 281 U.S. 238 (1930). *See also* Omnibus Budget Reconciliation Act of 1993 §13611 (1993) (making the principal of self-settled income-only trusts countable for Medicaid eligibility purposes).

[160] *See, e.g.,* Restatement (Third) of Trusts §58 cmt. e, illus. 8.

[161] Restatement (Third) of Trusts §58 cmt. e; Restatement (Second) of Trusts §156 cmt., illus. 1.c. *See, e.g.,* Phillips v. Moore, 286 Ga. 619, 690 S.E.2d 620 (2010) (holding that a reserved income interest under a trust, coupled with a reserved general *testamentary* power of appointment, will subject trust principal to the reach of the settlor's *inter vivos* creditors).

possibly even a general testamentary power of appointment. Finally, the proceeds of any insurance on the life of a settlor of a revocable inter vivos trust that are paid to the trustee also might be vulnerable to the claims of the settlor's postmortem creditors, unless there is a statute that provides otherwise.

(b.1) Reserved right of revocation or general inter vivos power of appointment. Although the "traditional thinking" was otherwise,[162] the current trend of the law favors allowing the settlor's postmortem creditors, as well as the surviving spouse, access to the principal of an inter vivos trust if the settlor reserved a personal power to consume[163] the underlying property *at the time of the settlor's death*.[164] By power to consume, we mean an express or constructive general inter vivos power of appointment. This should be contrasted with the lot of the inter vivos creditor where the focus traditionally was on the retention of a beneficial interest, rather than a power to consume.[165] Thus, we traditionally had such anomalies as the naked reserved right of revocation exposing trust assets to the reach of the settlor's postmortem creditors, but not the inter vivos ones;[166] or the property of a self-settled "irrevocable" discretionary trust being

---

[162] *See* 3 Scott & Ascher §14.11.3.

[163] *See generally* Uniform Nonprobate Transfers on Death Act §102(a) (defining a nonprobate transfer to include "a valid transfer effective at death by a transferor . . . to the extent that the transferor immediately before death had power, acting alone, to prevent the transfer by . . . withdrawal and instead to use the property for the benefit of the transferor or apply it to discharge claims against the transferor's probate estate." The Act provides that retention alone of a general testamentary power of appointment would not expose the subject property to attack by the settlor's postmortem creditors. Uniform Nonprobate Transfers on Death Act §102(a).

[164] Restatement (Third) of Trusts §25(2) cmt. e. *See, e.g.,* Estate of Nagel, 580 N.W.2d 810 (Iowa 1998); State St. Bank & Trust Co. v. Reiser, 7 Mass. App. Ct. 633, 389 N.E.2d 768 (1979) (creditor access because of power of consumption at time of debtor's death); Sullivan v. Burkin, 390 Mass. 864, 460 N.E.2d 572 (1984) (spousal access because of power of consumption during marriage). *See* Clifton B. Kruse, Jr. (compiler), *Summary of Case Law: Rights of Creditors Following Death of Settlor. Beneficiaries of Revocable Trusts,* 23 ACTEC Notes 155 (1997). *See also* UTC §505(a)(3) (available at <http://www.uniformlaws.org/Act.aspx?title=Trust%20Code>) (providing that "[a]fter the death of a settlor, and subject to the settlor's right to direct the source from which liabilities will be paid, the property of a trust that was revocable at the settlor's death is subject to claims of the settlor's creditors, costs of administration of the settlor's estate, the expenses of the settlor's funeral and disposal of remains, and statutory allowances to a surviving spouse and children to the extent the settlor's probate estate is inadequate to satisfy those claims, costs, expenses, and allowances"); Restatement (Second) of Property (Wills and Other Donative Transfers) §34.3 (rejecting the principle of Jones v. Clifton, 101 U.S. 225 (1879), that a trust settlor's reserved power to revoke is not an asset subject to creditors' claims and instead providing that a settlor's creditors may reach the assets of a revocable trust even when the trust transfer to the trustee was not fraudulent); UPC §6-102(b) (Revised 1998) (establishing liability of nonprobate transferees for creditor claims and statutory allowances). *See generally* Wellman & Brucken, *NCCUSL To Your Rescue: New UPC Sec. 6-102,* 26 ACTEC Notes 361 (2001).

[165] *See* 4 Scott on Trusts §330.12; Restatement (Second) of Trusts §330 cmt. o.

[166] *See* State St. Bank & Trust Co. v. Reiser, 7 Mass. App. Ct. 633, 638, 389 N.E.2d 768, 771 (1979) (in the postmortem context, a reserved general inter vivos power may be enough to expose trust property to creditor attack); Restatement (Second) of Trusts §330 cmt. o (in inter vivos context a naked reserved general inter vivos power may not be enough to expose property to creditor attack).

subject to the reach of the settlor's inter vivos creditors, but not the postmortem ones.[167] The law is now quickly evolving to the point where the settlor-beneficiary's inter vivos and postmortem creditors have coextensive access to the property of an inter vivos trust.[168] The Restatement (Third) of Property is fully there, in letter and in spirit.[169] Until this process is complete, however, such subtle divergences in the law will continue to complicate the already complicated life of the trustee.[170]

The Uniform Trust Code would provide that the property of a trust that was revocable at the settlor's death is subject to claims of the settlor's creditors, costs of administration of the settlor's estate, the expenses of the settlor's funeral and disposal of remains, and statutory allowances to a surviving spouse and children to the extent the settlor's probate estate is inadequate to satisfy those claims, costs, expenses, and allowances.[171] The Uniform Trust Code defines "revocable" as meaning "revocable" by the settlor "without the consent of the trustee or a person holding an adverse interest."[172] The settlor, of course, would retain the right to direct in his or her estate planning documents the source from which postmortem liabilities will be paid.[173] Florida already has such legislation on her books.[174]

On the other hand, the Uniform Probate Code (specifically Section 6-102) and the Uniform Nonprobate Transfers on Death Act (specifically Section 102) are somewhat less creditor-friendly. They provide by implication that if the settlor at the time of death possessed a right of revocation jointly *with a nonadverse party*, his or her postmortem creditors will not have access to the subject property. One learned but "puzzled" commentator explains how easily "Section 102" can be "manipulated to avoid creditors":

> To avoid the reach of Section 102, the trustor simply could require that to revoke the trust the nonadverse party must join the trustor in making the revocation. The

---

[167] *See generally* Elaine H. Gagliardi, *Remembering the Creditor at Death: Aligning Probate and Nonprobate Transfers*, 41 Real Prop. Prob. & Tr. J. 819, 858–859 (2007).

[168] *See generally* Elaine H. Gagliardi, *Remembering the Creditor at Death: Aligning Probate and Nonprobate Transfers*, 41 Real Prop. Prob. & Tr. J. 819 (2007).

[169] *See* Restatement (Third) of Property (Wills and Other Donative Transfers) §22.2, cmt. f.

[170] *See, e.g.*, UTC §505(a)(1) (available at <http://www.uniformlaws.org/Act.aspx?title= Trust%20Code>) (providing that during the lifetime of the settlor, the property of a revocable trust is subject to the claims of the settlor's creditors).

[171] UTC §505(a)(3) (available at <http://www.uniformlaws.org/Act.aspx?title=Trust%20 Code>).

[172] UTC §103(14) (available at <http://www.uniformlaws.org/Act.aspx?title=Trust%20 Code>).

[173] UTC §505(a)(3) (available at <http://www.uniformlaws.org/Act.aspx?title=Trust%20 Code>).

[174] Fla. Stat. §737.3054. *See also* In re Guardianship of Gneiser, 29 Fla. L. Weekly D1235, 873 So. 2d 573 (2004) (holding that although the trustee of a revocable trust whose settlor has died must by statute honor the request of the settlor's personal representative to have the claims of postmortem creditors satisfied from trust assets, the trustee may not honor such a request from the deceased settlor's guardian, nor may requests for payment that come directly from the creditors to the trustee be honored).

trust could then give the trustor the power to replace at will the joint powerholder with another powerholder of the trustor's own choosing. As a result, the trustor could remove and replace the joint powerholder until the trustor found one willing to agree with trustor that the trust should be revoked. Such a provision would be no more than a minor inconvenience in light of the greater benefit bestowed by the possibility of avoiding creditor claims following death.[175]

Because procedures for affording a decedent's postmortem creditors access to nonprobate assets, such as those in the hands of trustee transferees, are state specific, one is loath to generalize. With that caveat, it is probably safe to say that in most U.S. jurisdictions, the current state of the default procedural law is that the postmortem creditors of a decedent must (1) "pursue probate administration, even in the absence of probate assets, prior to pursuing the nonprobate transferee[s] directly" and (2) "pursue probate assets before pursuing nonprobate transferees."[176] This two-step process can pose a real problem for the postmortem creditor:

> At times, the creditor's search for a decedent's assets resembles a game of hide-the-ball, with the trustee distributing assets before being notified of any judgment on the creditor's claim, as was the case in Dobler v. Arluk Center Industrial Group. In that case, the trustee of decedent's revocable trust was able to evade creditors by transferring assets to beneficiaries prior to a judgment being issued in the probate court.[177]

(b.2)   Reserved general testamentary power of appointment. If a settlor establishes an inter vivos trust, reserving only a naked general testamentary power of appointment over the underlying trust property, then would the settlor's postmortem creditors have access to the property were the settlor to die not having exercised the power? The traditional answer was no. Only to the extent that the power was actually exercised by the terms of the settlor's will would the subject property become vulnerable to the claims of the settlor's

---

[175] Elaine H. Gagliardi, *Remembering the Creditor at Death: Aligning Probate and Nonprobate Transfers*, 41 Real Prop. Prob. & Tr. J. 819, 856 (2007). "The comments to Section 102 . . . [of the Uniform Nonprobate Transfers on Death Act] . . . indicate, however, that liability under Section 102 might attach regardless of whether the decedent holds the sole power to revoke 'if the trust is named as beneficiary of a nonprobate transfer, such as of securities registered in [transfer-on-death] form.'" Elaine H. Gagliardi, *Remembering the Creditor at Death: Aligning Probate and Nonprobate Transfers*, 41 Real Prop. Prob. & Tr. J. 819, 855–856 (2007) (citing to Uniform Nonprobate Transfers on Death Act §102 cmt. 7).

[176] Elaine H. Gagliardi, *Remembering the Creditor at Death: Aligning Probate and Nonprobate Transfers*, 41 Real Prop. Prob. & Tr. J. 819, 822–823 (2007). *See, e.g.*, State St. Bank & Trust Co. v. Reiser, 7 Mass. App. Ct. 633, 389 N.E.2d 768 (1979) (the court requiring an exhaustion of the probate estate before affording creditors access to the assets of a trust over which the decedent held a general inter vivos power of appointment at the time of death).

[177] Elaine H. Gagliardi, *Remembering the Creditor at Death: Aligning Probate and Nonprobate Transfers*, 41 Real Prop. Prob. & Tr. J. 819, 881 (2007) (citing to Dobler v. Arluk Med. Ctr. Indus. Group, 107 Cal. Rptr. 2d 478 (Ct. App. 2001), *aff'd*, 11 Cal. Rptr. 3d 194 (Ct. App. 2004)).

postmortem creditors.[178] Thus, if the deceased settlor by the terms of a valid will were to actually exercise the power over, say, 50 percent of the subject property, then the settlor's postmortem creditors would have access to that 50 percent, and only that 50 percent. What was left over from the 50 percent would then pass to the appointees. It should be borne in mind that the postmortem creditors would have had no need to turn to the assets of the inter vivos trust had there been sufficient assets in the settlor's probate estate to satisfy their claims in the first place. It should also be noted that the law may be trending in the direction of affording the settlor's postmortem creditors access to *all* property subject to the reserved general testamentary power of appointment, *whether or not there had been an actual exercise*.[179] The Restatement (Third) of Property (Wills and Other Donative Transfers) is already there.[180] Section 22.2 provides that "[p]roperty subject to a general power of appointment that was created by the donee is subject to the payment of the claims of the donee's creditors to the same extent that it would be subject to those claims if the property were owned by the donee."

The Restatement (Third), however, muddles its explanation of the mechanics of reaching entrusted appointive property. It suggests in an illustration supporting Section 22.2 that on the donor-donee's death, the claims against the donor-donee's estate "can be satisfied *out of the remainder* . . . to the same extent as if the Donor-Donee owned the remainder interest at Donor-Donee's death."[181] Because the *full legal title* to entrusted appointive property is in the trustee, it is the entire legal interest in the hands of the trustee *at the time of the donor-donee's death*, not just the equitable quasi-remainder, that is vulnerable to the claims of the donor-donee's postmortem creditors. That the underlying trust property itself is vulnerable to the claims of the donor-donee's creditors is buttressed by the wording of Section 22.2: It is the property that is "subject to a general power of appointment" that is vulnerable to external claims. There is nothing about going after the equitable property interests. Nor can there be a legal remainder in the traditional sense, full legal title to the entrusted appointive property, as we said before, being in the trustee.[182] The bottom line: The Restatement (Third) appears to have conflated and confused reaching entrusted property subject to an equitable power of appointment and attaching the equitable property interests that are thrown off incident to the trust relationship itself.

---

[178] *Cf.* State St. Trust Co. v. Kissel, 302 Mass. 328, 19 N.E.2d 25 (1939) (involving the actual exercise of a general testamentary power of appointment under a trust established by someone other than the deceased powerholder).

[179] *See generally* 3 Scott & Ascher §15.4.1.

[180] *See* Restatement (Third) of Property (Wills and Other Donative Transfers) §22.1, cmt. a.

[181] *See* Restatement (Third) of Property (Wills and Other Donative Transfers) §22.2, illus. 4.

[182] *See generally* §8.27 of this handbook (comparing and contrasting legal and equitable property interests).

(b.3) Life insurance proceeds. Life insurance proceeds paid to the insured's revocable inter vivos trust upon the death of the insured may, by statute, be beyond the reach of the settlor's postmortem creditors.[183] Prior to paying the settlor's postmortem creditors from life insurance proceeds payable to the trustee by reason of the settlor's death, the trustee should consult counsel.

(c) Domestic asset protection havens. For general discussion of the subject of conflict of laws in the trust context, particularly how public policy can influence which state's law shall govern a matter in dispute, the law of the litigation forum or some other law, the reader is referred to Section 8.5 of this handbook.[184] Here, however, we zero in on the self-settled trust with a spendthrift provision, particularly the trust whose property is sited and administered in a state that no longer has a public policy that would categorically prevent enforcement of the provision as against *the settlor's* creditors.[185] "All United States jurisdictions permit creditors to set aside fraudulent transfers."[186] A U.S. domestic asset protection (DAP) jurisdiction is a jurisdiction that seeks by legislation to protect the assets of a self-settled trust from attack by the settlor's *future* creditors, provided the establishment of the trust is not the result of a fraudulent conveyance and the provisions of the trust meet certain statutory requirements.[187]

In 1997, Alaska enacted a statute that may insulate certain self-settled discretionary trusts created after April 1, 1997, from the reach of the settlor's creditors.[188] The reserved contingent equitable interest may be unavailable to the settlor's creditors if (1) the trust is irrevocable,[189] (2) the trust is fully discretionary as to income and principal at its inception, (3) the trustee with the discretionary authority is someone other than the settlor, (4) the transfer in trust is not established to defraud preexisting creditors[190] and the settlor so swears in

---

[183] *See generally* 5 Scott on Trusts §508.4; Bogert §243. *Cf.* In re Estate of Clotworthy, 742 N.Y.S.2d 168 (App. Div. 2002) (involving a commercial structured settlement annuity).

[184] *See also* 7 Scott & Ascher §45.7.1.2 (Inter Vivos Trusts/Spendthrift Clauses/Conflict of Laws).

[185] *See also* 7 Scott & Ascher §45.7.1.2 (Inter Vivos Trusts/Spendthrift Clauses/Conflict of Laws).

[186] Richard W. Nenno, *Planning with Domestic Asset-Protection Trusts: Part I*, 40 Real Prop. Prob. & Tr. J. 263, 276–286 (Summer 2005). *See generally* Jeffrey A. Schoenblum, 1 Multistate and Multinational Estate Planning 1461 (1999) (The Onshore Alternative: Alaska and Delaware Asset Protection Trusts). *See also* John E. Sullivan III, *Gutting the Rule Against Self-Settled Trusts: How the New Delaware Trust Law Competes with Offshore Trusts*, 23 Del. J. Corp. L. 423 (1998); Gideon Rothschild, *Asset Protection Trusts*, in Trusts in Prime Jurisdictions 424 (Alon Kaplan ed., 2000).

[187] *See generally* 3 Scott & Ascher §15.4.3.

[188] Alaska Stat. §§34.40.010 to 34.40.130, 13.36.390, 34.40.110.

[189] Note that Alaska Stat. §13.36.360(b) provides that, unless there is an express provision to the contrary in the governing trust instrument, an irrevocable trust may not be modified or terminated under §13.36.360 while a settlor is also a discretionary beneficiary of the trust.

[190] *Cf.* Breitenstine v. Breitenstine, 2003 WY 16, 62 P.3d 587 (2003) (holding that an "intent to hinder or delay creditors," a phrase that has been excised from the Alaska statute, is enough to

an affidavit,[191] (5) at the time of transfer, the settlor is not in default by thirty or more days of making payment due under a child support judgment or order, and (6) the trust is sited in Alaska.[192] The Alaska statute rejects the public policy at the heart of Section 156(2) of the Restatement (Second) of Trusts, namely "that a settlor cannot place property in trust for his own benefit and keep it beyond the reach of creditors."[193]

Effective July 1, 1997, Delaware responded by enacting a similar but not identical statute.[194] In 1999, Rhode Island and Nevada did the same.[195] Utah has since joined the group,[196] as has South Dakota.[197] Oklahoma's DAP legislation, known as the Family Wealth Preservation Act, was enacted June 9, 2004, effective for trusts settled thereafter.[198] Oklahoma, however, has placed a cap on the amount that can be sheltered in a self-settled trust from attack by the settlor's creditors. Missouri's DAP legislation was signed into law July 9, 2004, as part of its Uniform Trust Code legislation.[199] It is effective for all trusts created on, before, or after January 1, 2005. In 2007, Tennessee and Wyoming followed suit.[200] On January 1, 2009, New Hampshire came on board.[201] Hawaii has done so as well, effective July 1, 2010.[202] As has Virginia, effective July 1, 2012;[203] Ohio, effective March 27, 2013;[204] and Mississippi, effective July 1, 2014.[205]

---

consider a conveyance fraudulent even if there is no actual fraud). *See generally* Henry J. Lischer, Jr., *Professional Responsibility Issues Associated with Asset Protection Trusts*, 39 Real Prop. Prob. & Tr. J. 561 (2004).

[191] Alaska Stat. §34.40.110(k). The affidavit requirement may afford some protection to the lawyer who drafts the trust.

[192] Alaska Stat. §34.40.110(k). The settlor, however, may serve as a cotrustee, may serve as an adviser, and/or may appoint a trust protector. *See* Alaska Stat. §§34.40.110(g), 34.40.110(i). An implied agreement, however, between the settlor and the trustee that attempts to grant or permit the retention of greater rights or authority than is stated in the trust instrument would be void as a matter of law. *See* Alaska Stat. §34.40.110(j).

[193] Ware v. Gulda, 331 Mass. 68, 117 N.E.2d 137 (1954).

[194] Del. Code Ann. 12, §§3570–3576. *See also* Douglas J. Blattmachr & Richard W. Hompesch II, Alaska v. Delaware: *Heavyweight Competition in New Trust Laws*, 12 Prob. & Prop. 32, 34–38 (Jan./Feb. 1998) (comparing Alaska and Delaware asset protection laws).

[195] R.I. Gen. Laws §§18-9.2-1 to 18-9.2-7; Nev. Rev. Stat. §§166.010 to 166.170.

[196] Utah Code Ann. §25-6-14.

[197] S.D. Codified Laws §§55-16-1 to 55-16-17.

[198] Okla. Stat. Ann. tit. 31, §§10 to 18.

[199] Mo. Rev. Stat. §456.5-505.

[200] Tenn. Code Ann. §35-16-101; Wyo. Stat. Ann. §§4-1-505, 4-10-510 to 4-10-523.

[201] N.H. Rev. Stat. Ann. §564-D: 1-18.

[202] Haw. Rev. Stat. §§554G-1 to 554G-12.

[203] Va. Code §§55-545.05, 55-545.03:2, 55-545.03:3. There must be a Virginia trustee who maintains custody within Virginia of some or all of the trust property, maintains records within Virginia, prepares within Virginia fiduciary income tax returns for the trust, or otherwise materially participates within Virginia in the administration of the trust.

[204] Ohio Rev. Code Ann. §§5816.01 to 5816.14.

[205] Mississippi Qualified Disposition in Trust Act, Miss. Code Ann. §§91-9-701 et seq. (effective July 1, 2014).

For an in-depth textual analysis of all this legislation, the reader is referred to Richard N. Nenno.[206] His article has a handy comparison in outline form of the provisions of the Alaska, Delaware, Nevada, Rhode Island, and Utah, statutes, as well as a Delaware asset protection trust form irrevocable trust agreement. The reader is also referred to David G. Shaftel.[207]

Colorado may or may not be a domestic asset protection jurisdiction.[208] On the books is a statute dating back to the time before Colorado was a state, which reads as follows: "All deeds of gift, all conveyances, and all transfers or assignments, verbal or written, of goods, chattels, or things in action, or real property, made in trust for the use of the person making the same shall be void as against the creditors existing of such person."[209] Some have suggested that because the statute only mentions "existing" creditors of the settlor, by implication a settlor's future creditors would not have access to the entrusted property. A number of experienced Colorado trusts and estates lawyers are not so sure. We know of no trial or appellate court decision that has yet addressed the issue.

Generally, existing creditors may attack a transfer by the later of four years from the transfer or one year from the time the transfer was or could reasonably have been discovered by the creditor.[210] Future creditors must make a claim within the four-year period. Nevada is the exception: Its periods are two and six months, respectively. Query: Might a trustee, under certain circumstances, have a duty to relocate the trust's principal place of administration to one of these DAP jurisdictions? The Uniform Trust Code provides that "[a] trustee is under a continuing duty to administer the trust at a place appropriate to its purposes, its administration, and the interests of the beneficiaries."[211]

One hope is that this asset protection legislation will save estate taxes. Here is how: The property of a fully discretionary "self-settled" irrevocable inter vivos trust has been subject to estate tax upon the death of the settlor-beneficiary *not* because the settlor died with a reserved contingent equitable interest[212] but because the property was reachable by the settlor's creditors such that Section

---

[206] *Planning with Domestic Asset-Protection Trusts: Part II*, 40 Real Prop. Prob. & Tr. J. 477 (Fall 2005).

[207] *Comparison of the Twelve Domestic Asset Protection Statutes* (updated through November 2008), 34 ACTEC L.J. 293 (2009).

[208] *See* Colo. Rev. Stat. §38-10-111; 3 Scott & Ascher §15.4.3 n.20 and accompanying text (observing that though the Colorado statute seems to be the exact opposite of an "asset protection" statute, it is open to interpretation that self-settled spendthrift limitations are effective as to posttransfer creditors). *See generally* David G. Shafter, *Comparison of the Twelve Domestic Asset Protection Statutes* (updated through November 2008), 34 ACTEC L.J. 293, 294 (2009) (accompanying the Colorado entry are some case and commentary citations).

[209] Colo. Rev. Stat. §38-10-111.

[210] *But see* Alaska Stat. §34.40.110(d) (narrowly defining a preexisting creditor as someone who demonstrates by a preponderance of the evidence that he or she asserted a specific claim against the settlor before the settlor transferred assets to the trust).

[211] UTC §108(b) (available at <http://www.uniformlaws.org/Act.aspx?title=Trust%20Code>).

[212] For a discussion of whether a self-settled fully discretionary trust might implicate I.R.C. §2036(a)(1) as a retained right to income or enjoyment, *see* David G. Shaftel, *Domestic Asset Protection Trusts: Key Issues and Answers*, 30 ACTEC L.J. 1024 (2004).

2038 of the Internal Revenue Code is implicated.[213] The legislation aims to eliminate what makes such arrangements tax-sensitive, namely, creditor accessibility.[214] The hope is that even if a gift tax should be owed at the time the trust is established, any subsequent appreciation in the value of the trust property would escape estate tax upon the settlor's death.[215] For a catalog of other possible uses of a DAP trust, the reader is referred to Richard W. Nenno.[216]

So far, "...there have been no significant court cases validating the benefits of...[domestic asset protection trusts]...in tough debtor-creditor situations."[217] Thus, with respect to an action brought by a creditor in a jurisdiction other than a DAP jurisdiction, it remains to be seen whether the court of the DAP jurisdiction will be bound by the full faith and credit clause[218] to enforce a judgment of the court of the other state that, for example, a particular transfer out of the other state into an asset protection trust established in the DAP jurisdiction constitutes a fraudulent conveyance under the laws of the other state.[219] The judgment would be against the settlor.[220]

---

[213] A general inter vivos power of appointment is the power to appoint to oneself *or* one's creditors. If the property of an irrevocable discretionary self-settled trust is reachable by the settlor's creditors, then the settlor has reserved a general inter vivos power of appointment exercisable by the incurring of debts. *See generally* §8.9.3 of this handbook (tax-sensitive powers).

[214] *See* Blattmachr, *Practice Alert: Alaska Trusts Offer New Estate Planning Opportunities*, 1997 RIA Estate and Financial Planners Alert, June 1997, at 3 (discussing how the Alaska asset protection legislation might enhance the attractiveness of Crummey Trusts; Life Insurance Trusts; Unified Credit and GST Exemption Trusts; GRATs, GRUTs, and GRITs; QPRTs; Charitable Lead Trusts; and Charitable Remainder Trusts and also discussing how non-U.S. persons might find an Alaska Trust advantageous). *See also* Douglas J. Blattmachr & Jonathan G. Blattmachr, A New Direction in Estate Planning: North to Alaska, Trusts & Estates, Sept. 1997, at 48 (suggesting that an Alaska asset protection trust can afford a settlor both protection from creditors and estate tax reduction).

[215] *See* Priv. Ltr. Rul. 9837007 (ruling that a transfer to an Alaska asset protection trust was a completed gift for tax purposes but not ruling on potential estate tax consequences of transfer).

[216] *Planning with Domestic Asset-Protection Trusts: Part I*, 40 Real Prop. Prob. & Tr. J. 263, 332–338 (Summer 2005).

[217] Jay D. Adkisson, *Five Concerns About Domestic Asset Protection Trusts*, Lawyers Weekly USA, T & E 2004, at H9. *See also* Richard W. Nenno, *Planning with Domestic Asset-Protection Trusts: Part I*, 40 Real Prop. Prob. & Tr. J. 263, 331 (Summer 2005) (confirming that "[n]o court has upheld the effectiveness of a DAPT").

[218] U.S. Const. Art. IV, §1.

[219] *See generally* Jeffrey A. Schoenblum, 1 Multistate and Multinational Estate Planning 1463 (1999) (Must Alaska and Delaware Recognize Other States' Judgments?); Karen Gebbia-Pinetti, *As Certain as Death and Taxes: Estate Planning, Asset-Protection Trusts, and Conflicting State Law*, A.L.I.-A.B.A. Course of Study Materials, Advanced Estate Planning Techniques, Feb. 19–21, 1998 (discussing conflict of laws issues raised by Alaska's and Delaware's asset protection legislation); Douglas J. Blattmachr & Richard W. Hompesch II, Alaska v. Delaware: *Heavyweight Competition in New Trust Laws*, 12 Prob. & Prop. 32, 34–38 (Jan./Feb. 1998) (discussing and comparing merits of Alaska's and Delaware's asset protection trust laws). *See also* John E. Sullivan III, *Gutting the Rule Against Self-Settled Trusts: How the New Delaware Trust Law Competes with Offshore Trusts*, 23 Del. J. Corp. L. 423 (1998).

[220] *See* Richard W. Nenno, *Planning with Domestic Asset-Protection Trusts: Part I*, 40 Real Prop. Prob. & Tr. J. 263, 293 (Summer 2005).

If the court is not so bound, then a creditor of the settlor would be left with having to bring an action in another state or federal court where there is jurisdiction either over the trustee or the trust assets,[221] bearing in mind that there is always the risk that the court of the other (forum) state would still defer to the laws of the DAP jurisdiction and/or that the court in the DAP jurisdiction would still not honor the other (forum) state's judgment.[222]

In the absence of jurisdiction over the trustee or the trust assets, the court of the other (forum) state might be tempted to invoke its contempt powers against the settlor if there were any indication that to do so would bring about a repatriation of the transferred assets.[223]

Should these issues play out in a federal bankruptcy court, the outcome is likely to hinge on whether the court recognizes the "applicable nonbankruptcy law" transfer restrictions of the DAP jurisdiction.[224] It should be noted that Congress amended the Bankruptcy Code in 2005 to allow a bankruptcy trustee to reach certain transfers to a DAP trust made by the debtor going back ten years from the filing of the bankruptcy petition.[225] One federal bankruptcy

---

[221] *See* Richard W. Nenno, *Planning with Domestic Asset-Protection Trusts: Part I*, 40 Real Prop. Prob. & Tr. J. 263, 294–299 (Summer 2005); David G. Shaftel, *Domestic Asset Protection Trusts: Key Issues and Answers*, 30 ACTEC L.J. 10, 13 (2004). *See generally* §8.40 of this handbook (judicial jurisdiction over the trustee). *Cf.* United States v. Bank of Nova Scotia, 740 F.2d 817 (11th Cir. 1984) (affirming order of civil contempt fine of $25,000 per day and total fine of $1.825 million against Miami branch of bank that refused to disclose to a federal grand jury the account records of its Bahamas branch).

[222] *See* Richard W. Nenno, *Planning with Domestic Asset-Protection Trusts: Part I*, 40 Real Prop. Prob. & Tr. J. 263, 292–319 (Summer 2005).

[223] *Cf., e.g.*, Federal Trade Comm'n v. Affordable Media, LLC, 179 F.3d 1228 (9th Cir. 1999) (the "Anderson Case") (affirming the judgment of the U.S. District Court for the District of Nevada holding a married couple in contempt of court for refusing to repatriate assets held in a Cook Islands trust). "Subsequent to the Andersons' appeal . . . , but prior to oral argument, the district court ordered the Andersons released from custody. . . . Because they remain in contempt, their appeal of the court's order finding them in contempt has not been rendered moot, even though they are no longer in custody." *Id.* n.3. In 2002, the FTC settled a $20 million suit against the trustee (AsiaCiti Trust Limited) for $1.2 million. *See also* Lawrence v. Goldberg, 279 F.3d 1294 (11th Cir. 2002); In re Lawrence, 238 B.R. 498 (Bankr. S.D. Fla. 1999) (a contempt of court incarceration case involving an offshore asset protection trust established in Mauritius).

[224] Under the Federal Bankruptcy Code, the bankruptcy estate does not include any beneficial interest of the debtor in a trust where the interest is subject to a restriction on alienation that is enforceable under "applicable nonbankruptcy law." 11 U.S.C.A. §541(c)(2). *See generally* Richard W. Nenno, Planning with Domestic Asset-Protection Trusts: Part I, 40 Real Prop. Prob. & Tr. J. 263, 292–319 (Summer 2005); §5.3.3.3(d) of this handbook (trusteed employee benefit plans and IRAs). *See also* Restatement, Second, Conflict of Laws §270 (1971) (suggesting that with respect to an inter vivos trust of movables, a court should look to the law of the state designated by the settlor in the governing instrument as the law that is to govern the validity of the trust).

[225] *See* 11 U.S.C. §548(e)1. *See, e.g.*, Waldron v. Huber (In re Huber), Adversary No. 12-04171, Bankruptcy No. 11-41013, Order Granting Trustee Partial Summary Judgment, Doc. 142, (Bankr. W.D. Wash. May 17, 2013).

court has voided the transfer of assets into an Alaska DAP trust with an Alaska choice-of-law provision, the trust having been established by a resident of Washington, a state that has a strong public policy against self-settled asset protection trusts. There were simply too few Alaska contacts: "In the instant case, it is undisputed that at the time the Trust was created, the settlor was not domiciled in Alaska, the assets were not located in Alaska, and the beneficiaries were not domiciled in Alaska. The only relation to Alaska was that it was the location in which the Trust was to be administered and the location of one of the trustees, AUSA."[226]

Finally, it does not necessarily follow that a creditor who is foreclosed from reaching into a DAP trust also would be foreclosed from obtaining a judicial charging order. Such an order would snare any distributions actually made by the trustee.[227]

In any case, let there be no misunderstanding: Domestic asset protection legislation is controversial. Some feel that placing one's assets in a DAP trust is fraught with risk.[228] Others are adamant that a state should not be enabling a debtor to eat his cake and have it too:

> Interestingly, the Uniform Trust Code flatly rejects the notion of an "asset protection trust." Likewise, the Third Restatement adheres unapologetically to the traditional rule. So also, the scholarly reaction to asset protection trusts has been almost universally negative . . . In any event, the concept of the asset protection trust has already generated an immense amount of commentary.[229]

Some non-U.S. jurisdictions also have rejected the creditor-friendly policy of Section 156(2) of the Restatement of Trusts. This has given rise to the so-called Offshore Asset Protection Trust discussed briefly in Section 9.10 of this handbook. For a discussion of how DAP trusts compare with offshore asset protection trusts, readers are referred to Jeffrey A. Schoenblum.[230]

(d) Qualified State Tuition Program (Alaska). In Alaska, property invested under the aegis of a Qualified State Tuition Program is exempt by statute from the claims of the creditors of the participant/settlor, *even though the participant/settlor may withdraw at will his or her allocable portion of the program's assets.* Creditor protection has been extended to the equitable interests of the contingent beneficiaries, *i.e.,* the students, as well. If such a "self-settled"

---

[226] Waldron v. Huber (In re Huber), Adversary No. 12-04171, Bankruptcy No. 11-41013, Order Granting Trustee Partial Summary Judgment, Doc. 142, (Bankr. W.D. Wash. May 17, 2013).

[227] *See, e.g.,* Hamilton v. Drogo, 241 N.Y. 401, 150 N.E. 496 (1926). *See also* UTC §501 (available at <http://www.uniformlaws.org/Act.aspx?title=Trust%20Code>) (allowing for attachment under certain circumstances of "future distributions").

[228] *See, e.g.,* Michael A. Passananti, *Domestic Asset Protection Trusts: The Risks and Roadblocks Which May Hinder Their Effectiveness,* 32 ACTEC L.J. 260, 271 (2006).

[229] 3 Scott & Ascher §15.4.3.

[230] 1 Multistate and Multinational Estate Planning 1467 (1999). *See also* Richard W. Nenno, *Planning with Domestic Asset-Protection Trusts: Part I,* 40 Real Prop. Prob. & Tr. J. 263, 338–348 (Summer 2005).

arrangement meets the requirements of Section 529 of the Internal Revenue Code, the taxation of income generated by the allocable portion is deferred until distribution. Participation may afford the participant/settlor and his or her beneficiaries certain gift, estate, and generation-skipping tax avoidance opportunities as well.

§5.3.3.2 Reaching the Equitable Interest of Beneficiary Who Is Not the Settlor

Except as modified by statute, the method by which a creditor can subject the beneficiary's interest to the satisfaction of his claim is by a proceeding in equity to reach and apply the beneficiary's interest, called a creditor's bill or a bill for equitable execution. Under this procedure the creditor cannot reach the beneficiary's interest until he has attempted without success to satisfy his claim out of the legal interests of the beneficiary, unless it appears that such an attempt would be unsuccessful. In some States this procedure is retained but is regulated by statute.[231]

Inter vivos. The trustee should understand that because the equitable interests of nonsettlor trust beneficiaries and remaindermen are property interests,[232] these interests might be subject to the claims of the beneficiaries' creditors.[233] If, however, the settlor has reserved beneficial interests or if the settlor has qualified the beneficiaries' equitable interests,[234] then the trust property may well not be available to the creditors of the nonsettlor beneficiaries.[235]

Let us look at a classic creditor-vulnerable trust that contains no such reservations or qualifications: *A* establishes an income-only trust for the benefit of *C* for *C*'s life. The income payments are mandatory.[236] The principal passes outright and free of trust to *D* at the death of *C*, *D* being a person ascertained at

---

[231] Restatement (Second) of Trusts §147 cmt. c. For a relatively recent case in which the creditor of a deceased settlor of a revocable trust was invited to file a complaint in equity to reach and apply the assets of the trust should the creditor be unable to obtain full satisfaction of the debt owed from the settlor's probate estate, *see* State St. Bank & Trust Co. v. Reiser, 7 Mass. App. Ct. 633, 389 N.E.2d 768 (1979). Today, many states have statutes authorizing a creditor to reach the interest of a beneficiary "by some form of legal execution, whether by levying directly upon the subject matter of the trust or by garnishing the trustee or by proceeding supplementary to execution." Restatement (Second) of Trusts §147 cmt. c. *See also* 3 Scott & Ascher §14.11 (confirming that at common law, "a trust beneficiary's creditors could not, by a proceeding at law, reach the beneficiary's interest, because it was *equitable*").

[232] *See generally* Alan Newman, *Spendthrift and Discretionary Trusts: Alive and Well Under the Uniform Trust Code*, 40 Real Prop. Prob. & Tr. J. 567, 585–586 (Fall 2005).

[233] *See* 3 Scott & Ascher §14.11; 2A Scott on Trusts §147.

[234] *See* §5.3.3.1 of this handbook (reaching settlor's reserved beneficial interest) and §5.3.3.3 of this handbook (discretionary provisions and other restraints upon voluntary and involuntary transfers of trust property, including the spendthrift trust).

[235] *See* Restatement (Second) of Trusts §§152, 155. *But see* Restatement (Second) of Trusts §157.

[236] *See* UTC §506(a) (defining mandatory in this context) (available at <http://www.uniformlaws.org/Act.aspx?title=Trust%20Code>).

the time of the trust's creation. *C* has a vested property interest in the stream of net income.[237] *C*'s creditors can seize the stream itself,[238] *i.e.,* they can seize the distribution rights themselves.[239] *D* has a vested nonpossessory property interest in the remainder. That interest is reachable by *D*'s creditors even before *C* dies, although it would not be possessory until *C* dies.[240] It should be emphasized that *all* equitable interests—contingent or otherwise—are *property* interests.[241] As such, they may not be taken by the state without just compensation.[242] Some equitable interests, however, such as those under the just-described trust, may be reached by the beneficiaries' creditors.

While an unqualified equitable interest in trust property may be vulnerable to the reach of the nonsettlor beneficiary's creditors, property subject to a general inter vivos power of appointment in a nonsettlor who possesses no other equitable interest traditionally has been creditor-vulnerable *only to the extent the power is actually exercised.*[243] The trustee should be aware of this subtle

---

[237] *See generally* Bogert §182 (section entitled "Vested and Contingent Interests").

[238] *See generally* Bogert §193.

[239] *See generally* Alan Newman, *Spendthrift and Discretionary Trusts: Alive and Well Under the Uniform Trust Code,* 40 Real Prop. Prob. & Tr. J. 567, 583 (Fall 2005).

[240] *See* 2A Scott on Trusts §147.2.

[241] *See* 2A Scott on Trusts §130.

[242] *See* Webb's Fabulous Pharmacies, Inc. v. Beckwith, 449 U.S. 155 (1980) (holding that for takings law purposes, interest follows principal); Sinibaldi, *The Taking Issue in California's Legal Services Trust Account Program,* 12 Hastings Const. L.Q. 463 (1985) (suggesting that IOLTA, the Interest on Lawyers' Trust Accounts program, implicates the Fifth Amendment takings clause). *See also* Washington Legal Found. v. Texas Equal Access to Justice Found., 94 F.3d 996 (1996) (holding that clients have a cognizable property interest in the interest earned on their deposits in IOLTA accounts), *aff'd on appeal,* Phillips v. Washington Legal Found., 118 S. Ct. 1925 (1998); *remanded* (for a determination as to whether such "property interest" had been taken in violation of the Fifth Amendment); Washington Legal Found. v. Texas Equal Access to Justice Found., 270 F.3d 180 (2001) (holding that Texas IOLTA program involves unconstitutional taking of property of clients); Schneider v. California Dept. of Corrections, 151 F.3d 1194 (1998) (holding that California statute requiring that interest earned on inmate funds placed in inmate trust accounts be diverted to an inmate welfare fund implicated the Fifth Amendment takings clause); Bockman v. Vail, 161 F.3d 11 (1998) (holding that inmate had a property interest in interest earned on deposits in a personal savings account that had been diverted to a prison welfare/betterment account). *See generally* In re Catherwood's Trust, 173 A.2d 86, 91 (1961) (holding that "[a] gift of an equitable life estate in income or of an estate in remainder does constitute a grant of a vested property right of which the recipients cannot be divested by legislative action"). *But see* Washington Legal Found. v. Massachusetts Bar Found., 993 F.2d 962 (1st Cir. 1993) (holding that interest earned on certain funds entrusted by a client to his attorney is not the client's property and accordingly "belongs to no one").

[243] *See generally* 3 Scott & Ascher §14.11.3 (but also citing to some contrary authority in note 3); Gilman v. Bell, 99 Ill. 144 (1881) (involving a general inter vivos power of appointment, the court noting that the doctrine had long been established in England that courts of equity will not aid creditors in cases where general inter vivos powers have not been exercised). *See also* Irwin Union Bank & Trust Co v. Long, 312 N.E.2d 908 (Ind. App. 1974). *Cf.* State St. Trust Co. v. Kissel, 302 Mass. 328, 19 N.E.2d 25 (1939) (holding the doctrine applicable to general testamentary powers of appointment as well). *But see* UTC §505(b)(1) (available at <http://www.uniformlaws.org/Act.aspx?title=Trust%20Code>) (providing that the creditors of holder of general inter vivos power of appointment *who is not the settlor* will have access to property subject to power even during periods when power is unexercised). The UTC does not address creditor issues

but substantive difference in vulnerability, a difference that has its origins in a vestigial distinction between property rights (*e.g.*, the equitable interest) and personal rights (*e.g.*, the power of appointment).[244]

In New York, however, and in an ever-growing number of other jurisdictions,[245] the creditors of the nonsettlor donee of an *unexercised* general inter vivos power of appointment will have access to the property subject to the power, even in cases where the donee is otherwise not a beneficiary.[246] The Uniform Trust Code[247] and the Restatement (Third) of Trusts[248] are generally in accord, as is the Restatement (Third) of Property.[249] And this is even in the face of a spendthrift clause,[250] the possession of an unlimited, presently exercisable general power of appointment nowadays more and more being considered the functional equivalent of outright ownership, whether or not the holder is the settlor.[251] The existence of a general inter vivos power of appointment whose exercise is governed by a standard, such as health, maintenance, or support, or that is held in a fiduciary capacity may well also have the effect of rendering unenforceable a spendthrift clause, at least to the extent that it is directed against the powerholder's creditors.[252]

Since *Crummey v. Commissioner*[253] was decided in 1968, the IRS has been making life difficult, but by no means impossible, for the settlors of Crummey trusts. The bone of contention is the Crummey trust's lapsing withdrawal-rights feature. To further complicate matters, there is the risk that this feature renders at least some of the underlying trust assets accessible to the powerholder's creditors, both pre- and post-lapse. The Crummey trust is discussed generally, and these specific tax-avoidance and creditor-access issues in particular, in §9.18 of this handbook.

It has been and continues to be settled law, however, that the possession of an unexercised general *testamentary* power of appointment, in and of itself, will not afford the creditors of the living donee (holder) access to the subject property.[254] Moreover, because a will "speaks only at death," it is self-evident that the donee would be foreclosed from actually exercising the power before death.

---

with respect to property subject to a special power of appointment or a testamentary general power of appointment. UTC §505 cmt. For creditor rights against such interests, *see* Restatement (Second) of Property (Wills and Other Donative Transfers) §§13.1–13.7.

[244] Gilman v. Bell, 99 Ill. 144 (1881); National Shawmut Bank v. Joy, 315 Mass. 457, 53 N.E.2d 113 (1944).

[245] *See* 3 Scott & Ascher §14.11.3 (listing some of the jurisdictions in note 7).

[246] N.Y. Est. Powers & Trusts Law §10-7.2.

[247] UTC §505(b)(1) (available at <http://www.uniformlaws.org/Act.aspx?title=Trust%20Code>).

[248] Restatement (Third) of Trusts §56 cmt. b.

[249] Restatement (Third) of Property (Wills and Other Donative Transfers) §22.3(a).

[250] *See* 3 Scott & Ascher §§14.11.3, 15.2.8.

[251] *See* 3 Scott & Ascher §15.2.8.

[252] *See* 3 Scott & Ascher §15.2.8.

[253] 397 F.2d 82 (9th Cir. 1968).

[254] Restatement (Third) of Trusts §56 cmt. b; 3 Scott & Ascher §15.2.8.

It is also self-evident that the possession of an inter vivos *special* (limited) power of appointment, in and of itself, will not subject the underlying trust property to the claims of the donee's (holder's) creditors.[255] Nor will the possession of a special (limited) testamentary power. This is because neither power may be exercised in favor of the donee or the donee's creditors, or the donee's probate estate or the creditors of the donee's probate estate for that matter.

Postmortem. As a general rule, if the equitable interest of a nonsettlor trust beneficiary terminates upon the beneficiary's death, neither the interest nor the subject property is reachable by the beneficiary's postmortem creditors, unless the terms of the trust provide otherwise. The funeral home is a possible exception.[256] Also, the creditors of a deceased beneficiary of a spendthrift trust may be entitled to reach any unpaid income attributable to the period prior to the beneficiary's death, notwithstanding the fact that the beneficiary's interest was inalienable.[257]

It has been settled law that the mere possession by a nonsettlor donee of an unexercised general *inter vivos* power of appointment at the time of the donee's death in and of itself will *not* subject the trust property to the claims of the donee's postmortem creditors. The Uniform Nonprobate Transfers on Death Act is in accord.[258] The Uniform Trust Code[259] and the Restatement (Third) of Trusts,[260] however, are not. Moreover, the Restatement (Third) of Trusts goes even further: It would afford the postmortem creditors of the nonsettlor donee of an unexercised general *testamentary* power of appointment access to the subject property.[261] So too would the Restatement (Third) of Property, to the extent that the donee's estate is insufficient to satisfy the claims of the creditors of the donee's estate.[262] Powers of appointment are covered generally in Section 8.1.1 of this handbook.

It has long been settled law that the actual exercise by a nonsettlor donee of a general testamentary power of appointment will subject the property affected by the exercise to the claims of the donee's postmortem creditors.[263] The Uniform Nonprobate Transfers on Death Act, however, appears not to be in accord.[264] The Restatement (Third) of Property provides that, "[t]o the extent that an appointee would have taken the appointed property as a taker in default

---

[255] 3 Scott & Ascher §§14.11.3, 15.2.8.

[256] *See generally* §3.5.3.2(a) of this handbook (in part discussing whether discretionary authority in a trustee to use income and/or principal to or for the benefit of a beneficiary would extend to the payment of the beneficiary's funeral bills). *See also* 2 Scott on Trusts §128.4; Restatement (Third) of Trusts §50 cmt. d(5).

[257] 3 Scott & Ascher §15.6.1 (Death of Beneficiary of Spendthrift Trust).

[258] *See* Uniform Nonprobate Transfers on Death Act §102 cmt. 3.

[259] UTC §501(b)(1) (available at <http://www.uniformlaws.org/Act.aspx?title=Trust%20Code>).

[260] Restatement (Third) of Trusts §56 cmt. b.

[261] Restatement (Third) of Trusts §56 cmt. b.

[262] Restatement (Third) of Property (Wills and Other Donative Transfers) §22.3(b).

[263] *See, e.g.*, State St. Trust Co. v. Kissel, 302 Mass. 328, 19 N.E.2d 25 (1939).

[264] Uniform Nonprobate Transfers on Death Act §102 cmt. 3.

of appointment had the appointment not been made, the appointee takes under the gift in default of appointment and not under appointment."[265] Here is why:

> Usually it makes no difference in legal consequences whether the appointee takes as appointee or as taker in default. The appointee takes the same amount in either capacity. The principal difference arises in jurisdictions that follow the rule that the estate creditors of the donee of a general testamentary power that was conferred on the donee by another have no claim on the appointive property unless the donee has exercised the power. Although . . . [the Restatement (Third) of Property] . . . does not follow that rule regarding creditor's rights . . . , some jurisdictions do.[266]

It goes without saying that the possession of a special (limited) testamentary power of appointment, in and of itself, will not subject the underlying trust property to the claims of the donee's creditors, *nor will its actual exercise.*[267] This is because the donee may not exercise the power in favor of the donee's probate estate or the creditors of the donee's probate estate. Recall that the donee of a power of appointment is the holder of the power, the one who has the right to exercise it, the donor of the power being the one who created the power in the first place.

§5.3.3.3 Discretionary Provisions, Forfeiture Provisions, and Other Restraints upon Voluntary and Involuntary Transfers, Including the Spendthrift Trust

New Mexico has developed little trust law over its approximately 395 years of political existence. Possibly because we have not been burdened by the weight of tradition in this area, New Mexico's attorneys and bankers did not object to . . . [Uniform Trust Code] . . . provisions that have often caused controversy in other states, such as beneficiary notice provisions and protections of spouses and children despite spendthrift clauses.[268]

The settlor may limit the circumstances under which income and principal will benefit the holder of an equitable interest.[269] Some limitations can so qualify the equitable interest that the beneficiary, as a practical matter, has a property right that is neither transferable nor attachable.[270] If, under applicable state law, the equitable interest is neither transferable by the beneficiary nor reachable by the beneficiary's creditors, then the equitable interest is

---

[265] Restatement (Third) of Property (Wills and Other Donative Transfers) §19.25.

[266] Restatement (Third) of Property (Wills and Other Donative Transfers) §19.25, cmt. d.

[267] *See generally* 3 Scott & Ascher §14.11.3; §8.1 of this handbook (powers of appointment).

[268] Fletcher Catron, Uniform Trust Code Notes (Summer 2003) at 5.

[269] Farkas v. Williams, 5 Ill. 2d 417, 422–423, 125 N.E.2d 600, 603 (1955) (citing 4 Powell, The Law of Real Property, at 87).

[270] *See, e.g.,* Brownell v. Leutz, 149 F. Supp. 98 (1957) (the interest of permissible beneficiary of a discretionary trust who was German alien was held not to be property interest susceptible of seizure during wartime by Alien Property Custodian).

unlikely to pass to the beneficiary's trustee in bankruptcy in the event of the beneficiary's bankruptcy.[271] Or take a transferable and/or creditor-accessible equitable interest in trust principal whose enjoyment is subject to some condition precedent such as the death of a third party before a certain date. Any transferees of the contingent equitable interest would still not be able to get at the underlying trust property itself until such time, if ever, that the condition precedent is actually fulfilled.[272]

The trustee should keep in mind—and this bears frequent repeating—that such limitations are not likely to thwart the settlor-beneficiary's creditors,[273] and that even in the face of such limitations, once income or principal is distributed from the trust to any beneficiary, whether or not the settler (*i.e.*, once title passes from the trustee to the beneficiary), the distributed property becomes alienable by the beneficiary and is reachable by the beneficiary's creditors.[274] Thus, it follows that the Uniform Trust Code would allow a creditor or assignee of a beneficiary of a spendthrift trust to reach a mandatory distribution of income or principal, provided the trustee has not made the distribution to the beneficiary within a reasonable time after the required distribution date.[275] The Restatement (Third) of Trusts is generally in accord.[276]

(a)   **The non–self-settled discretionary or discretionary support trust.** In the United States, and certainly in England,[277] the *discretionary trust* is perhaps the most effective means of keeping the nonsettlor beneficiary's creditors, including the beneficiary's trustee in bankruptcy,[278] away from the equitable interest.[279] This is because the beneficiary has no enforceable right to

---

[271] *See generally* 3 Scott & Ascher §15.2.2.

[272] *See generally* 3 Scott & Ascher §15.8.

[273] *See* §5.3.3.1 of this handbook (reaching settlor's reserved beneficial interest).

[274] *See* 3 Scott & Ascher §15.2.5 (noting, for example, that "when a beneficiary deposits a distribution in a bank account, creditors can access it").

[275] UTC §506 (available at <http://www.uniformlaws.org/Act.aspx?title=Trust%20Code>). "Following this reasonable period, payments mandated by the express terms of the trust are in effect being held by the trustee as agent for the beneficiary and should be treated as part of the beneficiary's personal assets." UTC §506 cmt.

[276] Restatement (Third) of Trusts §58 cmt. d(2). *See generally* 3 Scott & Ascher §15.2.5.

[277] Lewin ¶5-113.

[278] 11 U.S.C. §541(c)(2). *See generally* 3 Scott & Ascher §15.2.2 (Bankruptcy of Beneficiary).

[279] *See* Restatement (Second) of Trusts §155 cmt. b; United States v. O'Shaughnessy, 517 N.W.2d 574, 577 (Minn. 1994) ("Creditors, who stand in the shoes of the beneficiary, have no remedy against the trustee until the trustee distributes the property."); Pemberton v. Pemberton, 9 Mass. App. Ct. 9, 20, 411 N.E.2d 1305, 1308 (1980) (noting that "if even apart from the spendthrift clause a trustee is given the discretionary power to distribute income or principal to described beneficiaries [a] right of *any* beneficiary to receive *anything* is subject to the condition precedent of the trustee having first exercised his discretion" with the result that "the immunization of the trust assets from the reach of creditors of beneficiary is complete."); Morrison v. Doyle, 582 N.W.2d 237 (1998) (holding that assets subject to a discretionary trust are insulated from attack by the beneficiary's creditors *even though the beneficiary is also serving as the trustee*). *But see*

an identifiable portion of the income stream or to the principal.[280] Things may be slightly different in the case of a trust with only one beneficiary.[281] The Uniform Trust Code negates any presumption that the presence of a spend-thrift clause evidences a material purpose that would bar the judicial termination or modification of a trust that has only one beneficiary.[282] The Restatement (Third) of Trusts is in accord.[283] There is much case law, however, that is not.[284] Under the Restatement, authority in the trustee to invade principal for the beneficiary's support, or otherwise for the beneficiary's benefit, does raise a strong material purpose presumption, but only a presumption.[285] The case law is less equivocal.[286] "In England, in contrast, the sole beneficiary of the trust can terminate the trust at any time, even if the trust is for the beneficiary's support or the trustee has discretion over distributions or when to terminate the trust."[287]

The classic discretionary trust grants the trustee broad generalized discretion in his fiduciary capacity to pay income and distribute principal to the beneficiary.[288] A grant of *sole, absolute, and uncontrolled discretion*, or words to that effect, is often referred to as language of "extended discretion."[289] A cousin of the discretionary trust is the *discretionary support trust*, in which the trustee's discretion is limited by a standard such as health, maintenance, and support.[290]

UTC §504(c) (available at <http://www.uniformlaws.org/Act.aspx?title=Trust%20Code>) (providing that "[t]o the extent a trustee has not complied with a standard of distribution or has abused a discretion . . . a distribution may be ordered by the court to satisfy a judgment or court order against the beneficiary for support or maintenance of the beneficiary's child, spouse, or former spouse . . .").

[280] For a state-by-state compilation of cases and statutes that bear on the issue of whether or under what circumstances the creditors of the beneficiary of a discretionary trust may reach the assets of the trust, *see* Jeffrey A. Schoenblum, 2000 Multistate Guide to Estate Planning 11-66 (2000).

[281] *See generally* §8.15.7 of this handbook (the *Claflin* doctrine, also known as the material purpose doctrine).

[282] UTC §411(c) (available at <http://www.uniformlaws.org/Act.aspx?title=Trust%20 Code>). *See generally* §8.15.7 of this handbook (the *Claflin* doctrine (material purpose doctrine)); 5 Scott & Ascher §§34.1.2 (Spendthrift Trusts), 34.1.4 (Support Trusts and Discretionary Trusts).

[283] Restatement (Third) of Trusts §65 cmt. e. *See generally* 5 Scott & Ascher §34.1.2 (Spendthrift Trusts). Likewise, a discretionary provision may or may not evidence a material purpose that would bar termination or modification. Restatement (Third) of Trusts §65 cmt. e.

[284] 5 Scott & Ascher §34.1.2 n.1.

[285] Restatement (Third) of Trusts §65 cmt. e. *See generally* §8.15.7 of this handbook (the *Claflin* doctrine, also known as the material purpose doctrine); 5 Scott & Ascher §34.1.4 (Support Trusts and Discretionary Trusts); §3.5.3.2(a) of this handbook (the discretionary trust, including the support invasion standard).

[286] 5 Scott & Ascher §34.1.4 n.1.

[287] 5 Scott & Ascher §34.1.4. *See generally* §3.5.3.2(a) of this handbook (the discretionary trust, including the support invasion standard).

[288] *See* Bogert §228.

[289] Kevin D. Millard, *Rights of a Trust Beneficiary's Creditors under the Uniform Trust Code*, 34 ACTEC L.J. 58, 69 (2008).

[290] In the context of creditor accessibility, the UTC has eliminated the distinction between discretionary and support trusts, unifying the rules for all trusts fitting within either of the former

The Restatement (Third) of Trusts, unlike the Restatement (Second) of Trusts, does not attempt to draw a bright line between discretionary trusts and support trusts where distributions are subject to an exercise of trustee discretion.[291] The Uniform Trust Code is generally in accord with the Third Restatement, essentially deeming a support trust to be a discretionary trust with a support standard.[292] "Language of extended discretion may be used along with a standard, such as 'the trustee may distribute to the beneficiary as much of the net income and principal of the trust as the trustee determines advisable, in the trustee's *sole and absolute discretion*, for the beneficiary's health, education, maintenance, and support.' "[293] Sometimes a grant of discretion is coupled with language of direction, such as "my trustees *shall*, in their absolute discretion, distribute such amounts as are necessary for the beneficiary's support."[294] Still, the provision is discretionary, not mandatory, despite the presence of the imperative "shall."[295]

In England, one often encounters trusts that have both quasi-forfeiture and discretionary features. They are known as *protective trusts*. " . . . [A protective trust] . . . is a trust that is initially required to pay all of its income to one or more beneficiaries, until the occurrence of a disqualifying event, such as an attempted assignment, bankruptcy, or execution by creditors, whereupon the right to income ceases, and a discretionary trust for the benefit of the beneficiary, or the beneficiary and the beneficiary's family, arises automatically." No matter what the type of noncharitable discretionary trust, a member of the class of eligible beneficiaries, of course, would at least have standing to sue the trustee for abuse of discretion.[296]

Creditors. As a general rule, a creditor, not being a beneficiary, would lack such standing and thus could not force the trustee to make discretionary distributions.[297] The Uniform Trust Code is generally in

---

categories. UTC §504 cmt. (available at <http://www.uniformlaws.org/Act.aspx?title=Trust%20Code>). *See generally* 3 Scott & Ascher §15.3.

[291] Restatement (Third) of Trusts, Reporter's Notes on §60. *See generally* Kevin D. Millard, *Rights of a Trust Beneficiary's Creditors Under the Uniform Trust Code*, 34 ACTEC L.J. 58 (2008).

[292] UTC §504 cmt. (citing Restatement (Third) of Trusts, Reporter's Notes on §60 cmt. a) (available at <http://www.uniformlaws.org/Act.aspx?title=Trust%20Code>). *See, e.g.*, Strojek v. Hardin County Bd. of Supervisors, 602 N.W.2d 566, 569 (Iowa Ct. App. 1999) (noting that while the definitional distinctions between support and discretionary trusts are limpid, provisions of particular trusts muddy these clear demarcations).

[293] Kevin D. Millard, *Rights of a Trust Beneficiary's Creditors under the Uniform Trust Code*, 34 ACTEC L.J. 58, 69 (2008).

[294] UTC §506 cmt. (available at <http://www.uniformlaws.org/Act.aspx?title=Trust%20Code>).

[295] UTC §506 cmt. (available at <http://www.uniformlaws.org/Act.aspx?title=Trust%20Code>).

[296] *See* 3 Scott & Ascher §15.3; Restatement (Second) of Trusts §187 cmt. k. *See generally* Alan Newman, *Spendthrift and Discretionary Trusts: Alive and Well Under the Uniform Trust Code*, 40 Real Prop. Prob. & Tr. J. 567, 601–602 & 604–605 (Fall 2005).

[297] Restatement (Second) of Trusts §155 cmt. d. *See, e.g.*, In re Escher, 407 N.Y.S.2d 106 (Sur. Ct. Bronx Co. 1978), *aff'd*, 426 N.Y.S.2d 1008 (N.Y. App. Div. 1980), *aff'd*, 420 N.E.2d 91 (1981) (denying government-creditor of beneficiary access to trust property, the settlor's intent being to underwrite the costs of meeting the beneficiary's supplemental needs, not those health care costs

accord.[298] Moreover, "[u]nder the UTC, no creditor of a beneficiary (including the state) may compel discretionary distributions to satisfy claims based on the creditor's having provided support to the beneficiary."[299] Limited exceptions to this general rule may include support or discretionary trusts where the claimant is the beneficiary's spouse or child,[300] governmental entity,[301] or a supplier of necessaries,[302] in which case the creditor may seek a charging order attaching present or future distributions to or for the benefit of the beneficiary.[303] In one case, a creditor who had furnished necessary emergency medical services to the beneficiary of a support trust was allowed compensation from the trust estate.[304] Even in a case where creditors are granted standing, however, they generally can "fare no better than the beneficiary."[305]

When the debtor-beneficiary is not the settlor, the creditor will find it difficult if not impossible to reach property held in a discretionary support or fully discretionary trust because the trustee's fiduciary duty runs to the beneficiary, not to the creditor.[306] A creditor then is left with little recourse other than perhaps to attempt to obtain a judicial charging order that, if granted, might

---

that are routinely underwritten by the state). *See also* UTC §504(b) (available at <http://www.uniformlaws.org/Act.aspx?title=Trust%20Code>).

[298] UTC §504(b) (available at <http://www.uniformlaws.org/Act.aspx?title=Trust%20Code>). *See generally* Kevin D. Millard, *Rights of a Trust Beneficiary's Creditors under the Uniform Trust Code*, 34 ACTEC L.J. 58 (2008).

[299] *See generally* Alan Newman, *Spendthrift and Discretionary Trusts: Alive and Well Under the Uniform Trust Code*, 40 Real Prop. Prob. & Tr. J. 567, 588 (Fall 2005) (referring to UTC §504(b)).

[300] *See, e.g.*, Ventura County Dept. of Child Support Servs. v. Brown, 117 Cal. App. 4th 144, 11 Cal. Rptr. 3d 489 (2004) (holding, notwithstanding statutory authority to the contrary, that a court may compel the trustee of a non–self-settled trust to exercise the trustee's discretion under certain narrow circumstances, namely to satisfy an enforceable child support judgment against the discretionary beneficiary). *See generally* Dessin, *Feed a Trust and Starve a Child: The Effectiveness of Trust Protective Techniques Against Claims for Support and Alimony*, 10 Ga. St. U. L. Rev. 691 (1994); Restatement (Second) of Trusts §157.

[301] *See* 3 Scott & Ascher §15.5.4 (Claims for Taxes); Restatement (Second) of Trusts §157. *But see* Miller v. Department of Mental Health, 432 Mich. 426, 442 N.W.2d 617 (1989) (suggesting that Michigan may not seek reimbursement from discretionary trusts for public assistance rendered to nonsettlor beneficiaries but that support trusts may be vulnerable); Simpson v. Kansas Dept. of Soc. & Rehab. Servs., 906 P.2d 174 (Kan. Ct. App. 1995) (assets of an irrevocable discretionary trust for settlor's adult daughter not available to daughter for Medicaid eligibility purposes). *See generally* Silber, *The Effect of a Trust on the Eligibility or Liability of the Trust Beneficiary for Public Assistance*, 26 Real Prop. Prob. & Tr. J. 133 (1991). *But see also* United States v. O'Shaughnessy, 517 N.W.2d 574 (Minn. 1994); Texas Commerce Bank Nat'l Ass'n v. United States, 908 F. Supp. 453 (S.D. Tex. 1995) (each denying IRS access to a taxpayer-beneficiary's equitable interest in a discretionary trust).

[302] *See, e.g.*, Restatement (Second) of Trusts §157(b).

[303] *See, e.g.*, UTC §503 cmt. (available at <http://www.uniformlaws.org/Act.aspx?title=Trust%20Code>); 3 Scott & Ascher §15.5.4.

[304] Sherman v. Skuse, 59 N.E. 990 (N.Y. 1901). *See generally* 4 Scott & Ascher §26.5.2 (When Trust Estate Has Benefitted).

[305] 3 Scott & Ascher §15.3. *See generally* Kevin D. Millard, *Rights of a Trust Beneficiary's Creditors under the Uniform Trust Code*, 34 ACTEC L.J. 58 (2008).

[306] *See* 2A Scott on Trusts §154; Restatement (Second) of Trusts §170.

snare any discretionary distributions actually made to the beneficiary.[307] It would be difficult, however, to fashion an order broad enough to encompass payments made to third-party service providers for the benefit of the beneficiary.[308] In England it may be impossible.[309] A beneficiary's contingent equitable property interest[310] in a support or fully discretionary trust is generally not subject to execution sale.[311]

In the future, the discretionary trust may not be as impervious to creditor attack as has traditionally been the case. The reader's attention is called to the Restatement (Third) of Trusts Section 60 and the accompanying commentary. Section 60 provides as follows:

> Subject to the rules stated in §§58 and 59 (on spendthrift trusts), if the terms of a trust provide for a beneficiary to receive distributions in the trustee's discretion, a transferee or creditor of the beneficiary is entitled to receive or attach any distributions the trustee makes or is required to make in the exercise of that discretion after the trustee has knowledge of the transfer or attachment. The amounts a creditor can reach may be limited to provide for the beneficiary's needs (Comment c), or the amounts may be increased where the beneficiary either is the settlor (Comment f) or holds the discretionary power to determine his or her own distributions (Comment g).[312]

Comment g provides that if the nonsettlor beneficiary is the trustee of a discretionary trust with authority to determine his or her benefits, the beneficiary's creditors may reach from time to time the maximum amount the trustee-beneficiary can properly take. An ability of a nonsettlor beneficiary-trustee to run up debts and have them satisfied from the trust estate is likely to

---

[307] *See, e.g.*, Hamilton v. Drogo, 241 N.Y. 401, 150 N.E. 496 (1926). *See also* UTC §501 (available at <http://www.uniformlaws.org/Act.aspx?title=Trust%20Code>) (allowing under certain circumstances for attachment of "future distributions"). *See generally* Alan Newman, *Spendthrift and Discretionary Trusts: Alive and Well under the Uniform Trust Code*, 40 Real Prop. Prob. & Tr. J. 567, 584 (Fall 2005).

[308] *See generally* Alan Newman, *Spendthrift and Discretionary Trusts: Alive and Well under the Uniform Trust Code*, 40 Real Prop. Prob. & Tr. J. 567, 570–571 (Fall 2005).

[309] *See generally* 3 Scott & Ascher §15.3.1.

[310] *See generally* Alan Newman, *Spendthrift and Discretionary Trusts: Alive and Well Under the Uniform Trust Code*, 40 Real Prop. Prob. & Tr. J. 567, 602–603 (Fall 2005) (noting, however, that whether a beneficiary of a trust has a property interest in the trust's assets or merely a personal right against the trustee with respect to its administration is still the subject of debate).

[311] Restatement (Third) of Trusts §60 cmt. c. "If the interest of the beneficiary of a trust is so indefinite or contingent that it cannot be sold with fairness to both the creditors and the beneficiary, it cannot be reached by his creditors." Restatement (Second) of Trusts §162.

[312] *But see* Alaska Stat. §34.40.110(h) (providing that under Alaska law, a spendthrift provision is valid even though the beneficiary is named as the sole trustee of the trust). If the beneficiary is appointed as the sole trustee, Alaska law provides that trust distributions can only be made in accordance with an ascertainable standard that relates to the beneficiary's health, education, maintenance or support. Alaska Stat. §13.36.153. *See generally* §8.15.15 of this handbook (the ascertainable standard).

be construed by the taxing authorities as a constructive general inter vivos power of appointment.[313]

In 2004 the drafters of the Uniform Trust Code, out of concern that "adoption of the Restatement rule...[embedded in Comment g]...would unduly disrupt standard estate planning,"[314] added the following neutralizing language to Section 504 of the Code:

> If the trustee's or cotrustee's discretion to make distributions for the trustee's or cotrustee's own benefit is limited by an ascertainable standard, a creditor may not reach or compel distribution of the beneficial interest except to the extent the interest would be subject to the creditor's claim were the beneficiary not acting as trustee or cotrustee.[315]

Already, the Uniform Trust Code has created an exception for support claims of a child, spouse, or former spouse who has a judgment or order against a beneficiary, even a nonsettlor beneficiary, for support or maintenance:[316] To the extent a trustee has not complied with a standard of distribution or has abused a discretion, a distribution may be ordered by the court to satisfy a judgment or court order against the beneficiary for support or maintenance of the beneficiary's child, spouse, or former spouse.[317] The court shall direct the trustee to pay to the child, spouse, or former spouse such amount as is equitable under the circumstances but not more than the amount the trustee would have been required to distribute to or for the benefit of the beneficiary had the trustee complied with the standard or not abused the discretion.[318]

Assignees. In principle, is one's contingent equitable property interest under a non–self-settled discretionary or discretionary support trust assignable in the absence of a valid spendthrift clause? Our view is that both gratuitous and nongratuitous assignments of such interests are not. Some interests, particularly interests that are incident to certain fiduciary relationships, *e.g.*, the lawyer-client agency-contract relationship, are simply too personal in nature to

---

[313] *See generally* §8.1 of this handbook (powers of appointment). *Cf.* §4.1.3 of this handbook (creditor accessibility as a general inter vivos power of appointment) (discussing the constructive inter vivos power of appointment in the context of self-settled discretionary trusts).

[314] UTC §504 cmt (available at <http://www.uniformlaws.org/Act.aspx?title=Trust%20 Code>).

[315] UTC §504(e) (available at <http://www.uniformlaws.org/Act.aspx?title=Trust%20 Code>).

[316] UTC §504 cmt. (available at <http://www.uniformlaws.org/Act.aspx?title=Trust%20 Code>).

[317] UTC §504(c) (available at <http://www.uniformlaws.org/Act.aspx?title=Trust%20 Code>). *See generally* Alan Newman, *The Rights of Creditors of Beneficiaries under the Uniform Trust Code: An Examination of the Compromise*, 69 Tenn. L. Rev. 771, 832–843 (2002) (advocating a loosening of the UTC's "trustee has not complied with a standard of distribution or has abused a discretion" threshold requirement for affording children, spouses, and former spouses access to a nonsettlor beneficiary's interest in a discretionary trust).

[318] UTC §504 cmt. (available at <http://www.uniformlaws.org/Act.aspx?title=Trust%20 Code>).

be assignable. In the case of a purported gratuitous assignment of the contingent equitable interest under a non–self-settled discretionary or discretionary support trust, the purported assignee ought to be without recourse. The settlor intended John Jones to be a permissible beneficiary, not someone selected by John Jones.[319] It is the trustee who possesses the fiduciary power, not John Jones.[320]

In the case of a nongratuitous purported assignment, that is a purported assignment for consideration, the purported assignment is still invalid, but the purported assignee ought not necessarily to be without recourse. The purported assignee may be entitled to equitable relief incident to the contract breach. Such relief might take the form of a charging order capturing any distributions that are actually made by the trustee to or for the benefit of the permissible beneficiary. One should not, however, confuse the availability of equitable relief with assignment enforceability.

The reader is cautioned that the authors of the Restatement (Third) of Trusts and certain well-respected commentators have come to an opposite conclusion, namely, that "[r]egardless of the scope of the trustee's discretion, the beneficiary of a discretionary interest can... [in principle]... assign it...."[321] In any case, as a practical matter, "rather few ... assignees will actually be able to compel distributions under a discretionary trust."[322] Also working against the interests of the third-party assignee is the fact that the trustee's fiduciary duties run to the permissible beneficiary designated by the settlor in the terms of the trust, not to third-parties designated by the beneficiary through purported assignments.[323] Thus, the trustee risks liability, perhaps to the contingent remaindermen, for any discretionary distributions *to anyone* that happen to be captured by outstanding third-party charging orders. The fraud on a power doctrine also might be implicated.[324] An exception would be if such distributions were somehow authorized by the terms of the trust.

(b)   Forfeiture provisions in non–self-settled trusts. Another mechanism for thwarting a nonsettlor[325] beneficiary's creditors is a provision that terminates altogether the beneficiary's equitable interest upon the happening of some event, such as the beneficiary's entering a nursing home, assuming debtor status, or attempting an alienation of the equitable interest.[326] If the

---

[319] *See, e.g.*, Slattery v. Wason, 23 N.E. 843 (Mass. 1890).

[320] *See* §8.1 of this handbook (powers of appointment).

[321] *See* 3 Scott & Ascher §15.3, n. 7 and accompanying text (citing to Restatement (Third) of Trusts §60 & cmts. a, b.); 3 Scott & Ascher §15.3.2 (questioning the proposition that a support trust is necessarily also a spendthrift trust).

[322] 3 Scott & Ascher §15.3.1 *See also* 3 Scott & Ascher §15.3.2 (Support Trusts).

[323] *See, e.g.*, Slattery v. Wason, 23 N.E. 843 (Mass. 1890).

[324] *See generally* §8.15.26 of this handbook (the fraud on a power doctrine).

[325] *See* Restatement (Third) of Trusts §57 cmt. b (suggesting that if a forfeiture provision in a self-settled trust were enforceable, which is not likely to be the case, it would come "objectionably close to a pre-planned fraudulent conveyance that is to become effective on insolvency").

[326] *See generally* 2A Scott on Trusts §150.

beneficiary has no property interest, then there is nothing to alienate and nothing for the creditors to attach.[327] Often, but not always, the interest subject to forfeiture is a life interest in the trust's income stream.[328] Trust forfeiture provisions are generally enforced, even in those jurisdictions where trust spendthrift provisions generally are not.[329] By trust spendthrift provision, we mean a direct restraint on the alienability of the equitable interest.[330]

In lieu of total forfeiture, the trust might pursuant to its terms convert into a discretionary trust when or if a creditor of the beneficiary attempts to launch an attack on the equitable interest.[331] It is settled law, however, that a forfeiture provision is not effective to defeat a federal tax lien.[332] In England, a gift over on alienation or bankruptcy is generally enforceable.[333]

In U.S. jurisdictions, the reverse-forfeiture option can be an effective spendthrift restraint,[334] at least as effective as the forfeiture option.[335] By "reverse-forfeiture," we mean a provision in a trust that a beneficiary other than the settlor is not entitled to principal or other benefits from the trust until such time, if ever, that the beneficiary becomes financially solvent or receives a discharge in bankruptcy.[336] In England, on the other hand, a reverse-forfeiture provision is unlikely to be effective as a constructive spendthrift restraint, the English courts having held "that when a trustee is to pay a beneficiary income or principal when the beneficiary becomes solvent, the beneficiary has an interest that passes to assignees in bankruptcy."[337]

    (c) The non–self-settled spendthrift trust. *History of the spendthrift trust.* In England, trust spendthrift provisions have generally been unenforceable, at least since 1811.[338] In the United States this was generally also the case until 1875, when the U.S. Supreme Court handed down its spendthrift-friendly

---

[327] 3 Scott & Ascher §15.1.

[328] 3 Scott & Ascher §15.1.

[329] 3 Scott & Ascher §15.1.

[330] *See generally* §5.3.3.3(c) of this handbook (the non–self-settled spendthrift trust).

[331] Restatement (Third) of Trusts §57; 3 Scott & Ascher §15.1. *See, e.g.,* Nichols v. Eaton, 91 U.S. 716 (1875).

[332] United States v. Riggs Nat'l Bank, 636 F. Supp. 172 (D.D.C. 1986).

[333] Lewin ¶5-116. Note, however, that "[i]n England, a provision requiring the forfeiture of a *settlor's interest* upon bankruptcy is invalid as a fraud on the bankruptcy court." 3 Scott & Ascher §15.1.1.

[334] Restatement (Third) of Trusts §58 cmt. b(3).

[335] *See generally* 3 Scott & Ascher §15.7 (Solvency as Condition Precedent).

[336] Restatement (Third) of Trusts §57, cmt. d.

[337] *See generally* 3 Scott & Ascher §15.7 (Solvency as Condition Precedent).

[338] Lewin ¶5-109 (England); 3 Scott & Ascher §15.2.1 (the leading English case standing for the proposition that direct restraints on the alienability of equitable interests are unenforceable being *Brandon v. Robinson*, a case decided by Lord Eldon in 1811 [18 Ves. 429 (1811)]). Note, however, that while the English courts have generally never permitted restraints on the alienation of equitable interests, they have uniformly upheld restraints against the alienation of a married woman's equitable interest under a marriage settlement. Scott on Trusts §146.1 (1939 ed.). *See generally* §9.30 of this handbook (marriage settlements (England)).

decision in *Nichols v. Eaton*.[339] Once the Massachusetts Supreme Judicial Court had held—in *Broadway National Bank v. Adams* (1882)[340]—that a trust spendthrift provision was a permissible form of alienation restraint, there was little doubt that the spendthrift trust had gained an important strategic foothold on this side of the Atlantic, and that it was probably here to stay. Prof. John Chipman Gray was not amused:

> My modest task has been to show, that spendthrift trusts have no place in the system of the Common Law. But I am no prophet, and certainly do not mean to deny that they may be in entire harmony with the Social Code of the next century. Dirt is only matter out of place; and what is a blot on the escutcheon of the Common Law may be a jewel in the crown of the Social Republic.[341]

The spendthrift clause explained. A "spendthrift provision" is "a term of a trust which restrains both[342] voluntary[343] and involuntary . . . [irrevocable][344] . . . transfer[s] of a beneficiary's . . . [equitable or beneficial][345] . . . interest."[346] Again, it restrains alienation of the equitable or beneficial interest. Its purpose is not to tie up distributions of income and/or principal once in the hands of a beneficiary, nor could it do so.[347] Similarly a spendthrift clause in a trust purporting to restrain alienation of the outstanding nonpossessory vested equitable *reversionary interest* under that trust or to insulate that interest from the reach of the settlor's creditors would be unenforceable.[348] This durable right of alienation would accrue to the settlor's successors

---

[339] *See* Nichols v. Eaton, 91 U.S. 716, 727 (1875) ("Why a parent, or one who loves another, and wishes to use his own property in securing the object of his affection, as far as property can do it, from the ills of life, the vicissitudes of fortune, and even his own improvidence, or incapacity for self-protection, should not be permitted to do so, is not readily perceived."). Followed by Broadway Nat'l Bank v. Adams, 133 Mass. 170 (1882). *See also* 3 Scott & Ascher §15.2.1, n. 12 for a catalog of U.S. jurisdictions in which direct restraints on the alienability of equitable interests in non–self-settled trusts have been enforced by the courts in the absence of legislation addressing one way or another the enforceability issue. *But see* Restatement (Third) of Trusts §58 cmt. e (providing that a spendthrift restraint is not valid with respect to any interest retained by the settlor).

[340] 133 Mass. 170 (1882).

[341] John Chipman Gray, Restraints on the Alienation of Property x (2nd ed. 1895) (preface to the second edition).

[342] "For reasons of policy, a spendthrift restraint that seeks only to prevent creditors from reaching the beneficiary's interest, while allowing the beneficiary to transfer the interest, is invalid. . . ." Restatement (Third) of Trusts §58 cmt. b(2).

[343] "A spendthrift restraint prevents the transfer of a trust beneficiary's interest to another, whether the attempted assignment is by gift, sale, or exchange, or as security for a new or existing debt." Restatement (Third) of Trusts §58 cmt. c.

[344] Restatement (Third) of Trusts §58 cmt. d(1).

[345] Restatement (Third) of Trusts §58 cmt. d(1).

[346] UTC §103(15) (available at <http://www.uniformlaws.org/Act.aspx?title=Trust%20Code>). *See also* UTC §502(a).

[347] Restatement (Third) of Trusts §58 cmts. d. & d(2); 3 Scott & Ascher §15.2.5. *See, e.g.*, Alaska Stat. §34.40.110(c).

[348] 6 Scott & Ascher §40.4 (Transfer by Beneficiary). The settlor, however, could assign the equitable reversionary interest to the trustee of another spendthrift trust for the benefit of a third person. In that case, the spendthrift clause of the other trust might well be enforceable. An

in interest as well. Nor would a spendthrift provision in and of itself prevent a beneficiary's court-appointed guardian or agent acting under a durable power of attorney from compelling or taking distributions *on behalf of the beneficiary*.[349] Even in the face of a restriction on the right to alienate the *equitable interest*, the beneficiary of a spendthrift trust who has been granted a nonfiduciary power of appointment may effectively transfer the *underlying trust property* by an exercise of the power.

Rights of assignees of spendthrifted equitable interests. If the trustee of a spendthrift trust makes a distribution of a portion of the trust property to an assignee in the face of a valid spendthrift provision, the transfer is nonetheless effective[350] and the trustee is protected.[351] The beneficiary's assignment is treated as an agency, the trustee being the agent and the beneficiary the principal.[352] The terms of the constructive agency are that the trustee shall transfer to the purported assignee "whatever distributions the beneficiary is entitled to receive and has purported to assign."[353] The authorization, as with any agency, however, is revocable.[354] "Thus, a spendthrift restraint merely prevents the beneficiary from making an *irrevocable* transfer of his or her beneficial interest,"[355] that is of the equitable income stream itself. On the other hand, "[a] number of cases have held that an assignment is valid and presumably irrevocable as to income that is *already in the hands of the trustee at the time of the assignment*."[356]

Liability of third parties. Third parties, as well as the trustee, can incur liability for violating the terms of a valid spendthrift provision. Take, for example, the trustee who holds legal title to contractual rights against a third party, such as rights against the corporate issuer of a bond or rights against an insurance company incident to an insurance policy. The third party, instead of making a payment to the trustee, who is the other party to the contract, takes it upon itself to make a payment directly to the beneficiary. The trustee may have a fiduciary duty to seek to compel the third party to make the payment a second time, this time to the trustee.[357]

---

outstanding equitable reversionary interest would become possessory upon the imposition of a resulting trust, a topic we take up in §4.1.1.1 of this handbook.

[349] *See generally* 3 Scott & Ascher §15.6 (Disability of Beneficiary of Spendthrift Trust).

[350] Restatement (Third) of Trusts §58 cmt. d(1).

[351] Restatement (Third) of Trusts §58 cmt. d(1).

[352] Restatement (Third) of Trusts §58 cmt. d(1).

[353] Restatement (Third) of Trusts §58 cmt. d(1).

[354] "If the beneficiary of a spendthrift interest purports to transfer it to another for value but later revokes the assignment and the trustee's authority pursuant to it, the beneficiary is liable to that other person." Restatement (Third) of Trusts §58 cmt. d(1). "Although that person cannot reach the beneficiary's interest under the trust, satisfaction of the claim can be obtained from other property of the beneficiary or from trust funds after they have been distributed to the beneficiary." Restatement (Third) of Trusts §58 cmt. d(1). For a discussion of the "charging order" option, *see* §5.3.3 of this handbook.

[355] Restatement (Third) of Trusts §58 cmt. d(1).

[356] 3 Scott & Ascher §15.2.5, n.10 and accompanying text.

[357] The third-party obligor who makes a payment directly to the trust beneficiary instead of to the title-holding trustee, the other party to the contract, does so at his, her, or its peril, unless

Constructive receipt by the beneficiary of a spendthrift trust. When does a mandatory nondiscretionary distribution[358] "reach the hands" of the beneficiary? One court has held as early as when the trustee writes out the distribution check: Although the check for $862.95 representing "accrued income, ready for distribution" had not left the hands of the trustee, let alone been delivered to the beneficiary, the beneficiary's creditor was allowed to seize it. "[W]e think . . . [the beneficiary's right] . . . vested in his share of the income when the amount was ascertained, ready for distribution and the accounting made."[359] The Restatement (Third) of Trusts is generally in accord. It would deem distributable spendthrifted funds held by a trustee for an unreasonably long period of time to be constructively received by the beneficiary and therefore subject to attachment by his or her creditors.[360] The Uniform Trust Code similarly provides that the creditor of the beneficiary of a spendthrift trust can reach a mandatory distribution of income or principal that has not been made to the beneficiary "within a reasonable time after the designated distribution date."[361]

Discretionary payments to the creditors of the beneficiary. The trustee's fiduciary duties, of course, run to the beneficiary and not his or her creditors. Thus, when neither trustee retention nor distribution out is an attractive option from the beneficiary's perspective, the trustee of a spendthrift trust may want to consider a third option, namely, making distributions in the form of cash payments to certain creditors of the beneficiary, *e.g.*, credit card companies, automobile leasing companies, and the like, provided doing so is for the benefit of the beneficiary and provided the terms of the trust permit such indirect applications of trust funds. An indirect distribution out toward the outright purchase of

---

directed to do so by the trustee. 5 Scott & Ascher §32.1 (Discharge by Beneficiary of Claim Against Third Person). If the beneficiary is not of full age and legal capacity, the third party obligor runs the risk of having to pay twice. 5 Scott & Ascher §32.1 (Discharge by Beneficiary of Claim Against Third Person). There is a similar risk if following the direction were to constitute a knowing participation with the trustee in a breach of trust, or if the trust were a spendthrift trust. 5 Scott & Ascher §32.1 (Discharge by Beneficiary of Claim Against Third Person). In the case of a direct payment to the beneficiary in the face of a valid spendthrift provision, "[i]t would seem, . . . that the third person is entitled to maintain an action against the beneficiary personally to recover the amount paid to the beneficiary if the beneficiary was not under a legal incapacity at the time of the payment." 5 Scott & Ascher §32.1 (Discharge by Beneficiary of Claim Against Third Person). This claim for restitution would have to be satisfied from any property belonging to the beneficiary that is lawfully not in the trust.

[358] A mandatory distribution is "a distribution of income or principal which the trustee is required to make to a beneficiary under the terms of the trust, including a distribution upon termination of the trust." UTC §506(a) (available at <http://www.uniformlaws.org/Act.aspx?title=Trust%20Code>). "The term does not include a distribution subject to the exercise of the trustee's discretion even if (1) the discretion is expressed in the form of a standard of distribution, or (2) the terms of the trust authorizing a distribution couple language of discretion with language of direction." UTC §506(a).

[359] Knettle v. Knettle, 197 Wash. 225, 229, 84 P.2d 996, 998 (1938).

[360] Restatement (Third) of Trusts §58 cmt. d(2); UTC §506(b) (available at <http://www.uniformlaws.org/Act.aspx?title=Trust%20Code>). *See generally* 3 Scott & Ascher §15.2.5.

[361] UTC §506(b) (available at <http://www.uniformlaws.org/Act.aspx?title=Trust%20Code>).

an item of property, *e.g.*, an automobile, on the other hand, might well subject the item itself to creditor attachment. Carefully considered indirect applications of trust funds to certain creditors of and service providers to a beneficiary are likely to conform to the equitable spirit if not the letter of most trust spendthrift provisions.[362]

Drafting the spendthrift provision. "No specific form of words is necessary to impose a . . . [direct] . . . restraint on alienation."[363] The key is that the settlor intended to impose such a restraint. Some courts have even construed express voluntary restraints to include involuntary restraints, and vice versa.[364] Some have even enforced one-sided restraints that operate only against creditors.[365] "In their enactment of the UTC, Arizona, Kansas, Missouri, and North Dakota allow spendthrift provisions that restrain either the voluntary or involuntary transfer of the beneficiary's interest. The Ohio version of the UTC allows a trust to restrain involuntary transfers but to allow voluntary transfers with the consent of a trustee who is not the beneficiary."[366] Assuming, however, that a prospective settlor intends to create a spendthrift trust that is squarely in the mainstream, then he or she would be well advised to put in the governing instrument clear and unambiguous language to the effect "that the beneficiary may not assign, sell, mortgage, or otherwise dispose of the interest and that the interest is not liable for the beneficiary's debts."[367] To be valid under the model Uniform Trust Code, a spendthrift provision must restrain both voluntary and involuntary alienations of a beneficiary's equitable interest, except for the equitable reversion.[368]

Current and future equitable interests are generally protectable. By "interest" we mean not only the equitable right to benefit from a trust's income stream but also the equitable right to receive its principal in the future. At one time, however, a direct restraint on, say, a trust remainderman's right *during the lifetime of the income beneficiary* to alienate the equitable remainder interest was invalid.[369] This is generally no longer the case, with one possible exception; an exception, by the way, that should not be confused with the possession of a general testamentary power of appointment:[370]

---

[362] *See generally* Alan Newman, *Spendthrift and Discretionary Trusts: Alive and Well under the Uniform Trust Code*, 40 Real Prop. Prob. & Tr. J. 567, 570–571 (Fall 2005).

[363] 3 Scott & Ascher §15.2.4.

[364] *See generally* 3 Scott & Ascher §15.2.4.

[365] *See generally* 3 Scott & Ascher §15.2.3.

[366] Kevin D. Millard, *Rights of a Trust Beneficiary's Creditors under the Uniform Trust Code*, 34 ACTEC L.J. 58, 60 (2008) (citations omitted).

[367] 3 Scott & Ascher §15.2.4.

[368] UTC §502(a) (available at <http://www.uniformlaws.org/Act.aspx?title=Trust%20 Code>). *See generally* §4.1.1 of this handbook (the equitable reversion) and §4.1.1.1 of this handbook (the resulting trust).

[369] 3 Scott & Ascher §15.2.7. Apparently, the restraint seemed too much like a direct restraint on the alienability of a legal interest in land in fee simple or of an absolute legal interest in personality, both of which were, and today generally are, forbidden on public policy grounds.

[370] *See generally* §8.1 of this handbook (powers of appointment)

The rule is different, however, in the case of a restraint on the alienability of an interest of principal that is payable to the beneficiary's *estate*. Such a restraint *cannot* advantage the beneficiary. It would serve only to ensure that, at death, the beneficiary could dispose of the property free of the claims of creditors. Accordingly, such a restraint is not effective, and upon the beneficiary's death, creditors can reach the principal. In addition, it would seem that if the income is payable to a beneficiary for life and the principal is payable to the same beneficiary's estate, the beneficiary's creditors ought to be able, during the beneficiary's lifetime, to reach the interest in principal, even if a spendthrift provision denies them access to the income interest.[371]

Trustee of a spendthrift trust is still entitled to be indemnified from the trust estate. Notwithstanding the existence of a spendthrift clause, a trustee is entitled to indemnity out of the trust estate for expenses properly incurred by him in the administration of the trust.[372] Moreover, it would seem equally appropriate that the equitable interest of the beneficiary of a spendthrift trust should nonetheless be subject to a charge for losses caused by the beneficiary's wrongdoing.[373] "The relevant cases are, however, a mixed lot, including those dealing with pension plans subject to ERISA."[374] There is also a difference of opinion as to whether a trustee of a spendthrift trust who makes an advancement of trust property to a beneficiary is entitled to withhold future income to reimburse the trust.[375]

The public policy rationale for enforcing spendthrift provisions. The rationale for the court's enforcement of a spendthrift trust is that it is the prerogative of the settlor—the owner of the property—to determine what restrictions (if any) will be placed on the use of his property.[376] It is a privilege that comes with ownership.[377] After all, the settlor need not have created the trust in the first place but could have instead consumed the property or given it away outright and free of trust.[378] Other policy justifications for enforcing spendthrift clauses

---

[371] 3 Scott & Ascher §15.2.7. Some of this brings to mind the old Rule in Shelley's case, or at least its ghost, particularly when the terms of a trust are that principal is ultimately to be paid to the probate estate of the income beneficiary. *See generally* §8.15.3 of this handbook (Rule in Shelley's Case).

[372] Restatement (Second) of Trusts §244 cmt. d.

[373] 4 Scott & Ascher §25.2.3 (Beneficiary Who Deals Wrongfully with Trust Property). *See generally* §5.6 of this handbook (duties and liabilities of the beneficiary).

[374] 4 Scott & Ascher §25.2.3 n.7.

[375] *See generally* 4 Scott & Ascher §25.2.5.1 (Advances to Beneficiary of Spendthrift Trust).

[376] Nichols v. Eaton, 91 U.S. 716 (1875) (pro-spendthrift policy dicta); Broadway Nat'l Bank v. Adams, 133 Mass. 170 (1882) (actually upholding a direct restraint on the alienability of an equitable interest). For the public policy argument against enforcement of spendthrift trusts, *see* John Chipman Gray, Restraints on the Alienation of Property 262 (1883). *See also* Restatement (Third) of Trusts, Reporter's Notes on §58.

[377] Nichols v. Eaton, 91 U.S. 716 (1875) (pro-spendthrift policy dicta); Broadway Nat'l Bank v. Adams, 133 Mass. 170 (1882) (actually upholding a direct restraint on the alienability of an equitable interest).

[378] *See generally* 3 Scott & Ascher §15.2.1 (observing that "both those who have advocated and those who have opposed the validity of restraints on alienation have relied on the notion of individualism").

include the following: "[t]he public interest in protecting spendthrift individuals from personal pauperism, so that they do not become public burdens"[379] and "the responsibility of creditors to make themselves aware of their debtors' spendthrift trust protections."[380] The Restatement (Third) of Trusts accepts the spendthrift doctrine, except as it may apply to the settlor-beneficiary[381] and except as it may apply to a nonsettlor who has the equivalent of ownership in the trust property.[382] Ownership equivalence might take the form of possession of a general inter vivos power of appointment.[383]

Spendthrift protections afforded by New York default law. In New York, by statute, a non–self-settled trust is a quasi-spendthrift trust, absent language in the governing instrument to the contrary.[384] The statute appears to have left the door somewhat ajar when it comes to reaching certain otherwise exempt equitable interests that are not needed "for the reasonable requirements of the judgment debtor and his dependents,"[385] and perhaps in certain other situations as well.[386]

Special creditors of the beneficiary of a spendthrift trust may have access to the equitable interest, either by statute or case law. The express reference in many spendthrift clauses to creditors over the years has invited assaults on the very institution of the spendthrift trust.[387] In one dramatic case, the mother of a minor victim of sexual molestation unsuccessfully sought to reach in satisfaction of a default judgment the perpetrator's equitable interest in a non–self-settled spendthrift trust.[388] In another, the personal representative of a murder victim unsuccessfully attempted to reach the property of a spendthrift trust established for the benefit of the murderer by his mother in order to satisfy a tort judgment against the murderer.[389] While ordinary contract creditors may have only themselves to blame for failing to exercise due diligence when entering into

---

[379] Sligh v. First Nat'l Bank of Holmes County, 704 So. 2d 1020, 1027 (1997).

[380] Sligh v. First Nat'l Bank of Holmes County, 704 So. 2d 1020, 1027 (1997).

[381] Restatement (Third) of Trusts §58.

[382] Restatement (Third) of Trusts §58 cmt. b(1).

[383] A "presently exercisable general power of appointment" is a synonym for a "general inter vivos power of appointment." Restatement (Third) of Trusts §58 cmt. b(1).

[384] N.Y.C.P.L.R. 5205(c); N.Y. Est. Powers & Trusts Law §7-3.4. *See generally* 3 Scott & Ascher §15.2.1, n.23 and accompanying text; 2A Scott on Trusts §152.1 n.4 and accompanying text. Mich. Comp. L. §555.19 bars an assignment of the equitable interest if the trust property is land. *See also* Mont. Code §72-24-205. For a compilation of jurisdictions in which a spendthrift provision is presumed even if not addressed by express language in the governing instrument, *see* Jeffrey A. Schoenblum, 2000 Multistate Guide to Estate Planning 11-40 (2000).

[385] N.Y.C.P.L.R. 5205(d). *See generally* 3 Scott & Ascher §15.2.1, n.24 and accompanying text.

[386] *See generally* 3 Scott & Ascher §15.2.1 (observing that the New York statute does not always mean everything it "seems to say").

[387] *See* Bogert §222 (Arguments for and Against Spendthrift Trusts).

[388] Scheffel v. Krueger, 146 N.H. 669, 782 A.2d 410 (2001) (addressing the scope of New Hampshire's spendthrift statute (RSA 564:23)). *See generally* Douglas E. Zemel, *Underused Spendthrift Trusts Can be Bulletproof,* 2001 LWUSA 873 (in part discussing *Scheffel v. Krueger*).

[389] *See* Duvall v. McGee, 375 Md. 476, 826 A.2d 416 (2003).

transactions with beneficiaries of spendthrift trusts, this generally cannot be said for tort creditors[390] and other such "involuntary" creditors:

> This line of reasoning, however, is plainly insufficient to justify the exemption of a beneficiary's interest from the claims of those who have not voluntarily extended credit. It does not apply, for example, to tort creditors. Nor does it apply to governmental claims for taxes. It does not apply to the beneficiary's children when they claim support, and it may not apply to the claim of a beneficiary's spouse for support or alimony. Moreover, even a contract creditor who has furnished the beneficiary with necessaries stands in quite a different position from ordinary contract creditors.[391]

Some assaults on the clause have been partially or wholly successful, leading to noteworthy divergences across the jurisdictions.[392] A few states, such as North Carolina, will not enforce a spendthrift provision.[393] On the other hand, Minnesota has a long history of enforcing spendthrift trusts against all comers, including those seeking alimony and child support.[394] So does Massachusetts, with one possible divorce-related exception.[395] Arkansas, Kansas, and Maine have included no exceptions for certain creditors in their versions of the Uniform Trust Code.[396]

Mississippi's highest court has allowed attachment of a beneficiary's interest in a spendthrift trust by his intentional and gross negligence tort creditors, the court noting that "[a] man who is about to be knocked down by an automobile has no opportunity to investigate the credit of the driver of the automobile."[397] The Restatements would seem more or less in accord.[398] The Uniform Trust Code, however, does not appear to be.

Some states allow spendthrift provisions to protect the income stream only,[399] while others allow principal to be protected as well.[400] Some spendthrift

---

[390] *See generally* 3 Scott & Ascher §15.5.5 (Tort Claims).

[391] 3 Scott & Ascher §15.5.

[392] Bogert §222 n.59.

[393] Bogert §222 n.59. *See also* Annot., *Invalidity of Spendthrift Provision as Affecting Other Provisions of Trust*, 9 A.L.R.2d 1361 (1950).

[394] *See* In re Moulton's Estate, 233 Minn. 286, 46 N.W.2d 667 (1951).

[395] *See* Lauricella v. Lauricella, 409 Mass. 211, 565 N.E.2d 436 (1991) (nonsettlor beneficiary's interest in realty trust subject to equitable division in divorce proceeding notwithstanding spendthrift clause). *See generally* §5.3.4 of this handbook (rights of beneficiary's spouse and children to trust property or equitable interest).

[396] Kevin D. Millard, *Rights of a Trust Beneficiary's Creditors under the Uniform Trust Code*, 34 ACTEC L.J. 58, 61 (2008).

[397] *See* Sligh v. First Nat'l Bank of Holmes County, 704 So. 2d 1020 (Miss. 1997) (also providing a scholarly discussion of the pros and cons of creating a tort exception to the enforceability of spendthrift clauses). *Sligh* by legislation is no longer the law in Mississippi. *See* Miss. Code Ann. §91-9-503 (2003) (eliminating Mississippi's judicially created tort exception). *See also* Alaska Stat. §34.40.110(b) (amounting to a legislative rejection of the tort exception).

[398] *See* Restatement (Third) of Trusts §59 cmt. a; Restatement (Second) of Trusts §157 cmt. a.

[399] 2A Scott on Trusts §152.

[400] 2A Scott on Trusts §153.

jurisdictions draw a line when it comes to the beneficiary's spouse and children[401] or to a creditor who has supplied "necessaries,"[402] which has been held in some cases to include a government agency that has provided institutional care to the beneficiary.[403] As a general rule, governmental claims for unpaid taxes may be satisfied from the taxpayer's equitable interest in a spendthrift trust.[404] By statute, the equitable interests of enemy aliens in spendthrift trusts are generally subject to governmental seizure.[405] "As we have seen, ERISA, which preempts state law as to a great many retirement plans, requires that each plan prohibit the assignment or alienation of benefits but provides that benefits may be reached by a qualified domestic relations order for child support, alimony, and marital property rights."[406]

The Restatement (Third) of Trusts provides that the interest of a beneficiary in a valid spendthrift trust can be reached in satisfaction of an enforceable claim against the beneficiary for services or supplies provided for the protection of the beneficiary's interest in the trust,[407] e.g., services rendered by an attorney-at-law.[408] So does the Uniform Trust Code.[409]

In New York, that portion of the income stream of a spendthrift trust that is not needed to maintain the beneficiary in his station in life is accessible to the beneficiary's creditors.[410]

---

[401] *E.g.*, California, Kentucky, Louisiana, Missouri, New York, Oklahoma, Texas, Washington, and Wisconsin by legislation afford the spouse and dependents, under certain circumstances, access to a beneficiary's equitable interest in a spendthrift trust. *See* 3 Scott & Ascher §15.5.1 (Dependents of the Beneficiary); 2A Scott on Trusts §157.1 n.2. *See generally* Dessin, *Feed a Trust and Starve a Child: The Effectiveness of Trust Protective Techniques Against Claims for Support and Alimony*, 10 Ga. St. U. L. Rev. 691 (1994). *See also* UTC §503(b) (available at <http://www.uniformlaws.org/Act.aspx?title=Trust%20Code>) (providing that "[e]ven if a trust contains a spendthrift provision, a beneficiary's child, spouse, or former spouse who has a judgment or court order against the beneficiary for support or maintenance, or a judgment creditor who has provided services for the protection of a beneficiary's interest in the trust, may obtain from a court an order attaching present or future distributions to or for the benefit of the beneficiary."). The Restatement (Third) of Trusts is in accord. *See* Restatement (Third) of Trusts §59. *See* Marriage of Chapman, 297 Ill. App. 3d 611, 697 N.E.2d 365 (1998) (holding that the principal of a spendthrift trust was available to satisfy a child support judgment against the beneficiary because the beneficiary possessed a limited power to appoint the principal to a class of which his children were members).

[402] *See* 3 Scott & Ascher §15.5.2; 2A Scott on Trusts §§157.1, 157.2. Unlike Restatement (Third) of Trusts §59, and Restatement (Second) of Trusts §157(b) the UTC does not create an exception to the spendthrift restriction for nongovernmental creditors who have furnished necessary services or supplies to the beneficiary. UTC §503 cmt. (available at <http://www.uniformlaws.org/Act.aspx?title=Trust%20Code>).

[403] *See* 3 Scott & Ascher §15.5.4; 2A Scott on Trusts §§157.1, 157.2.

[404] *See generally* 3 Scott & Ascher §15.5.4.

[405] *See generally* 3 Scott & Ascher §15.5.4.

[406] *See* 3 Scott & Ascher §15.5.1 (referring to 29 U.S.C. §1056(d)(3)).

[407] Restatement (Third) of Trusts §59.

[408] *See generally* 3 Scott & Ascher §15.5.3.

[409] *See* UTC §503 cmt. (available at <http://www.uniformlaws.org/Act.aspx?title=Trust%20 Code>).

[410] N.Y. Est. Powers & Trusts Law §7-3.4 (1992).

A spendthrift provision will not prohibit the United States or a state from attaching the beneficial interest for taxes owed by the beneficiary.[411]

Assume the trustee of a spendthrift trust is among the beneficiaries of that trust. The trustee-beneficiary commits a breach of trust. Presumably the trust estate may be made whole out of the trustee-beneficiary's equitable interest, notwithstanding the presence of a spendthrift clause, assuming that interest is severable from the other equitable interests. At least one California court has so held.[412]

Bankruptcy of beneficiary. Unlike the settlor of a discretionary trust, the settlor of a spendthrift trust directly confronts the creditor by withholding from the trustee the authority to honor assignments and attachments of the equitable interests.[413] What the beneficiary cannot alienate, the creditor cannot attach.[414] If such restraints are valid under state law, they generally will be honored in the bankruptcy context.[415]

As a general rule, a beneficiary's equitable property interest in a trust with a spendthrift provision that is enforceable under state law is not reachable by the beneficiary's trustee in bankruptcy,[416] unless the trust is self-settled.[417] In one case, however, a bankruptcy trustee was afforded access to the assets of a spendthrift trust of which the bankrupt was a beneficiary. If the creditors of the beneficiary, notwithstanding the spendthrift clause and over the objections of the trustee, could have been reimbursed from the trust estate for "necessaries"

---

[411] *See* Restatement (Third) of Trusts §59 cmt. a(1); 2A Scott on Trusts §157.4; Bogert §224 (collecting the case law and relevant Internal Revenue Code provisions authorizing the satisfaction of federal tax claims from interests in spendthrift trusts). *See also* UTC §503(c) (available at <http://www.uniformlaws.org/Act.aspx?title=Trust%20Code>) (providing that a spendthrift provision is unenforceable against state and federal claims to the extent state or federal law so provides). *See, e.g.*, United States v. Riggs Nat'l Bank, 636 F. Supp. 172 (D.D.C. 1986); LaSalle Nat'l Bank v. United States, 636 F. Supp. 874 (N.D. Ill. 1986).

[412] *See* Chatard v. Oveross, 179 Cal. App. 4th 1098 (2009).

[413] *See* 2A Scott on Trusts §§151, 152 (Restraint on Alienation of Income), 153 (Restraint on Alienation of Principal, *i.e.*, Remainders); Bogert §222 n.59 (For the Current Status of Spendthrift Trusts in All States).

[414] Ritchie et al., Decedent's Estates and Trusts 630 (8th ed. 1993); 3 Scott & Ascher §15.2.3; 2A Scott on Trusts §152.3; UTC §502(a) (available at <http://www.uniformlaws.org/Act.aspx?title=Trust%20Code>) (providing that a spendthrift provision is valid only if it restrains *both* voluntary and involuntary transfers of the beneficial interest). *But see* Bank of New England v. Strandlund, 402 Mass. 707, 529 N.E.2d 394 (1988) (enforcing a one-sided restraint on involuntary alienation). On the subject of "one-sided restraints," *see generally* Restatement (Third) of Trusts, Reporter's Notes on §58; 3 Scott & Ascher §15.2.3 (Whether It Is Necessary to Restrain Both Voluntary and Involuntary Alienation) (containing at note 5 a catalog of jurisdictions in which one-sided restraints on the alienability of equitable interests, in this case restraints that operate against the creditor but not the beneficiary, are still enforced; and suggesting that while such one-sided restraints would seem contrary to public policy, one-sided restraints that operate only against the beneficiary would seem not to).

[415] Bankruptcy Code §541(c)(2). *See generally* 3 Scott & Ascher §15.2.2.

[416] *See, e.g.*, Kerr v. T.D. Bankworth, Slip Copy, 2008 WL 1827606 (Bankr. S.D. Tex.). *See generally* Kevin D. Millard, *Rights of a Trust Beneficiary's Creditors under the Uniform Trust Code*, 34 ACTEC L.J. 58, 75 (2008) ("The UTC should have no effect on the treatment of trusts in bankruptcy").

[417] 11 U.S.C. §541(c)(2). *See generally* 3 Scott & Ascher §15.2.2 (Bankruptcy of Beneficiary).

furnished the beneficiary, then the bankruptcy trustee can divert the reimbursements to the bankruptcy estate:

> [the bankrupt beneficiary] . . . incurred debts for numerous necessities such as doctors, ambulance services, telephone services, utilities and hospitals. . . . We modify the Court of Appeals decision by holding that the ability of the trustee in bankruptcy to reach a beneficiary's interest in a spendthrift trust is not dependent upon the exercising of the trustee's discretionary power. Section 70(c) of the Bankruptcy Act allows the trustee in bankruptcy, as a hypothetical lien creditor holding a judgment against the debtor on the date of the bankruptcy, to reach the spendthrift trust for debts incurred by . . . [the bankrupt beneficiary] . . . for necessities of life.[418]

English law has not been receptive to the spendthrift trust. As noted, English law, in contrast to U.S. law, has never recognized the spendthrift trust.[419] The English scrivener, however, is not without options when it comes to cordoning off the equitable interest. There is always the quasi-forfeiture provision; namely, in the event the beneficiary attempts to assign the equitable interest or becomes insolvent, the beneficiary loses the automatic right to receive income and instead becomes the permissible beneficiary of a discretionary trust.[420] Such a provision would be the functional equivalent of a direct restraint on the alienability of the equitable interest, but for the forfeiture of the beneficiary's autonomy. On this side of the Atlantic, a quasi-forfeiture provision in a U.S. trust was honored by none other than the Supreme Court in an 1875 federal bankruptcy case.[421]

Disclaimers, releases, and powers of appointment. Spendthrift restrictions on voluntary alienation generally do not cover proper disclaimers,[422] releases of powers of appointment, and exercises of powers of appointment.[423] One court has confirmed the validity of a permissible beneficiary's release of her equitable interest under a discretionary spendthrift trust.[424] The Uniform Trust Code negates any presumption that the presence of a spendthrift clause evidences a material purpose, which, under the *Claflin* (material purpose) doctrine, would bar the judicial termination or modification of a one-beneficiary trust.[425] The

---

[418] Erickson v. Bank of California, 97 Wash. 2d 246, 253–254, 643 P.2d 670, 674 (1982).

[419] Brandon v. Robinson, 34 Eng. Rep. 379 (ch. 1811). *See generally* Lewin ¶5-109 (England).

[420] 3 Scott & Ascher §15.1.

[421] Nichols v. Eaton, 91 U.S. 716 (1875).

[422] Restatement (Third) of Trusts §58 cmt. c; 3 Scott & Ascher §15.2.9.

[423] 3 Scott & Ascher §15.2.9, UTC §502 cmt. (available at <http://www.uniformlaws.org/Act.aspx?title=Trust%20Code>) (citing Restatement (Third) of Trusts §58 cmt. c (Tentative Draft No. 2, approved 1999)).

[424] *See* Guerriero v. Comm'r, 433 Mass. 628, 745 N.E.2d 324 (2001) (upholding the right of a beneficiary to release her equitable interest under a discretionary trust which also contained a spendthrift provision).

[425] UTC §411(c) (available at <http://www.uniformlaws.org/Act.aspx?title=Trust%20Code>). *See generally* 5 Scott & Ascher §34.1.2 (Spendthrift Trusts); §8.15.7 of this handbook (the *Claflin* doctrine, also known as the material purpose doctrine).

Restatement (Third) of Trusts is in accord.[426] There is much case law, however, that is not.[427] Merger may well extinguish any outstanding spendthrift restraints, a topic we cover in Section 8.7 of this handbook.[428]

The presently exercisable general inter vivos power of appointment. Involuntary alienation restraints are generally in abeyance as well in the face of an outstanding presently exercisable general inter vivos power of appointment. By that we mean that a trust spendthrift clause is not only ineffective as against the creditors of the powerholder insofar as the subject property is concerned[429] but also for all intents and purposes, redundant as against the creditors of the other beneficiaries, as long as the power is exercisable but unexercised. The very existence of such a power renders the equitable interests of the other beneficiaries so ephemeral, so expectancy-like, that *their* creditors have few practical options. Certainly they can do nothing that would interfere with the powerholder's functional equivalent of ownership.[430]

The Uniform Trust Code. The Uniform Trust Code provides that even if a trust contains a spendthrift provision, a beneficiary's child, spouse, or former spouse who has a judgment or court order against the beneficiary for support or maintenance, or a judgment creditor who has provided services for the protection of a beneficiary's interest in the trust, may obtain from a court an order attaching present or future distributions to or for the benefit of the beneficiary.[431] The Code, however, unlike the Restatements,[432] does not create an exception for tort claimants.[433] The court also may have discretionary authority incident to its general equitable powers to order that the legal fees of the child, spouse, or former spouse be paid from the trust estate.[434] "The third category of . . . [UTC] . . . exception creditor is the state or federal government, but only

---

[426] Restatement (Third) of Trusts §65 cmt. e. *See generally* 5 Scott & Ascher §34.1.2 (Spendthrift Trusts). Likewise, a discretionary provision may or may not evidence a material purpose that would bar termination or modification. Restatement (Third) of Trusts §65 cmt. e.

[427] 5 Scott & Ascher §34.1.2 n.1.

[428] *See* Restatement (Third) of Trusts §69 cmt. d; *but see* 5 Scott & Ascher §34.7 (Conveyance by Beneficiary to Trustee). *See also* 5 Scott & Ascher §34.5.1 (Acquisition of Legal Title by Beneficiary of Spendthrift Trust).

[429] *See generally* 3 Scott & Ascher §15.2.8.

[430] *See generally* §8.11 of this handbook (duties of the trustee of a revocable inter vivos trust).

[431] UTC §§503(b), 503(c) (available at <http://www.uniformlaws.org/Act.aspx?title=Trust%20Code>).

[432] Restatement (Third) of Trusts §59 cmt. a; Restatement (Second) of Trusts §157 cmt. a.

[433] UTC §503 cmt. (available at <http://www.uniformlaws.org/Act.aspx?title=Trust%20Code>). *See, however,* Alan Newman, *The Rights of Creditors of Beneficiaries under the Uniform Trust Code: An Examination of the Compromise,* 69 Tenn. L. Rev. 771, 825–830 (2002) (suggesting that at least when the beneficiary's tortious conduct is intentional, reckless, or grossly negligent, those injured by such conduct ought to be able to reach at least a part of trust assets available for distribution to or for the benefit of the beneficiary without regard to whether the trust instrument includes a spendthrift provision).

[434] UTC §1004 (available at <http://www.uniformlaws.org/Act.aspx?title=Trust%20Code>).

'to the extent a statute of this State or federal law so provides.'"[435] Under the Code, a provider of necessities to a beneficiary is not an exception creditor.[436] The Restatement of Trusts is not in accord in this regard.[437]

Section 503 of the model Uniform Trust Code is where the Code's categories of exception creditor are specified. It is a section that almost every enacting state has modified in some way. For more on these modifications the reader is referred to Kevin D. Millard.[438]

Alaska is an unusually strong spendthrift jurisdiction. The protection which an Alaska spendthrift clause provides against creditors is "extremely powerful because all creditors, of whatsoever nature and kind, are barred from attaching the trust assets before payment or delivery of the assets to the beneficiary."[439] In Alaska, there are no exceptions for spouses seeking support, ex-spouses seeking alimony, providers of necessaries, tort creditors, or children seeking support.[440]

Terminating the small spendthrift trust. In California, a spendthrift trust whose principal does not exceed $20,000 in value may be terminated by the trustee without court involvement.[441]

The spendthrift QTIP trust. A spendthrift clause will not jeopardize a trust's eligibility for QTIP status.[442] A spendthrift clause coupled with a forfeiture provision will.[443]

Nonenforceability of a contract to assign a spendthrifted equitable interest. If a beneficiary of a non–self-settled spendthrift trust enters into a contract to assign for consideration the equitable interest, or purports to make a present assignment of it for value, the contract is generally not *specifically enforceable.*[444] That does not mean, however, that the beneficiary could not be held personally liable to the other party, at least for restitution of amounts paid, and possibly also any damages occasioned by the contract breach. "Thus, the other party . . . [might be able to] . . . obtain a personal judgment against the beneficiary and obtain satisfaction out of any property available to creditors but . . . [could] . . . reach the beneficiary's interest in the trust only if and to the extent other

---

[435] Kevin D. Millard, *Rights of a Trust Beneficiary's Creditors under the Uniform Trust Code*, 34 ACTEC L.J. 58, 60 (2008) (referring to UTC §503(b)(3)).

[436] Kevin D. Millard, *Rights of a Trust Beneficiary's Creditors under the Uniform Trust Code*, 34 ACTEC L.J. 58, 61 (2008).

[437] Restatement (Second) of Trusts §157(b); Restatement (Third) of Trusts §59(b).

[438] *Rights of a Trust Beneficiary's Creditors under the Uniform Trust Code*, 34 ACTEC L.J. 58, 61–62 (2008).

[439] Stephen E. Greer, Esq., *Creditor Protection Vastly Improved with Enactment of 2003 Alaska Trust Bill*, available at <https://www.alaskabar.org/library/estate7-03_aktrustbill.pdf> (visited Sept. 2015).

[440] Alaska Stat. §34.40.110(h).

[441] Cal. Prob. Code §15408(c). *See generally* §3.5.3.2(k) of this handbook (the power to terminate the trust).

[442] Treas. Reg. §§20.2056(b)-5(f)(7) and 25.2523(e)-1(f)(7). *See generally* §8.9.1.3 of this handbook (the marital deduction) (discussing in part the QTIP trust).

[443] *See, e.g.,* Miller v. United States, 267 F. Supp. 326 (Fla. 1967). *See also* Technical Advice Memorandum 8248008.

[444] *See generally* 3 Scott & Ascher §15.2.6. (Contract to Assign Beneficiary's Interest).

creditors . . . [could] . . ."[445] We leave to the contracts treatises, however, the question of whether impossibility of performance should be a defense that is available to the beneficiary in these situations.

Why a spendthrift provision in a trust is not an impermissible alienation restraint. At this point, a comment on *alienation restraints* is in order. It is a cardinal principle of law that a restraint upon alienation of a legal fee simple, or of an absolute interest in personal property, is invalid.[446] Courts that enforce spendthrift provisions circumvent this rule by drawing a distinction between legal interests and equitable interests.[447] Because the spendthrift restraint goes to the equitable interest and not to the trustee's legal interest, the power of alienation under a spendthrift provision continues unimpaired.[448] And even when alienation of the legal interest is ostensibly restrained in perpetuity in the charitable context, such as when a specific parcel of real estate has been entrusted in perpetuity for a charitable purpose, the trustee may still irrevocably alienate the legal title to a BFP in contravention of the terms of the trust.[449] Thus, a provision in a "nonqualified" personal residence trust that limits the trustee's right to alienate the underlying property, *i.e.*, the residence, may be unenforceable under local law.[450] Note also that if one is designated the sole beneficiary and the sole trustee of a spendthrift trust, there is a merger[451] such that one holds legal title to the underlying property not only free of trust but also free of any enforceable spendthrift restrictions.[452] Recall that a proper trust spendthrift provision restrains alienation of the equitable interest only. In the case of merger, there is no equitable interest because there is no trust; there is only a

---

[445] 3 Scott & Ascher §15.2.6.

[446] *See generally* §8.15.40 of this handbook (the trust exception to the rule against direct restraints on one's ability to alienate one's property); 2A Scott on Trusts §152. *See also* 92 C.J.S. Vendor & Purchaser §311a.(2)(a) (noting that a covenant that absolutely prohibits a purchaser from selling or assigning his interest has been held to be an unlawful restriction on the power of alienation).

[447] *See* Broadway Nat'l Bank v. Adams, 133 Mass. 170 (1882).

[448] *See* Broadway Nat'l Bank v. Adams, 133 Mass. 170 (1882). *See also* 2A Scott on Trusts §152 n.8 (speculating on the politics behind the *Adams* case). New York, however, does not draw a distinction in the trust context between the legal interest and the equitable interest when it comes to the suspension of the power of alienation. There is a suspension of the alienability of the underlying trust property if the alienability of either interest is suspended. N.Y. Est. Powers & Trusts Law §9-1.1(a). Presumably, the New York statute that deems a trust to be a spendthrift trust, absent language in the governing instrument to the contrary, takes care of the common law alienability problem for trusts that do not violate the applicable Rule against Perpetuities. N.Y. Est. Powers & Trusts Law §7-1.5 (1998).

[449] *See generally* §8.15.63 of this handbook (doctrine of bona fide purchase).

[450] *See* Treas. Reg. §25.2702-5(b)(1) (providing that a trust shall not meet the requirements of a "nonqualified" personal residence trust if, during the original duration of the term interest, the residence may be sold or otherwise transferred by the trustee or may be used for a purpose other than as a personal residence of the term holder). *But see* Blattmachr & Slade, 836 T.M., Partial Interests—GRATs, GRUTs, QPRTs A-24 n.153 (1996) (suggesting that local law may make it impossible to comply with the anti-alienation requirements of Treas. Reg. §25.2702-5(b)(1)). *See generally* §9.15 of this handbook (the qualified personal residence or QPRT).

[451] *See generally* §8.15.36 of this handbook (merger).

[452] 3 Scott & Ascher §15.2.

legal interest that is pretending to be a trust. And a direct restraint on the alienation of a legal interest, say, a legal life estate, is generally invalid.[453]

(d) Trusteed employee benefit plans and IRAs. An employee benefit plan may well include an associated trust that serves as a receptacle for employer and employee contributions. Under federal law, contributions and the income generated by their investment are entitled to favorable tax treatment, provided the plan meets certain requirements (*i.e.*, is *tax-qualified*).[454] One such requirement is that the associated trust contain a spendthrift (anti-alienation) provision prohibiting the employee from alienating or assigning his beneficial interest and third parties from reaching it.[455]

An Employee Retirement Income Security Act (ERISA)-mandated anti-alienation provision may prevent a trustee in bankruptcy from reaching the debtor's interest in a tax-qualified plan, even though the associated trust would not have enjoyed spendthrift protection under state law.[456]

The trustee should be aware that no such federal spendthrift requirement applies to trusts associated with IRAs.[457] Thus, state statutes and the common law of trusts will determine whether property held by an IRA trustee is reachable by the taxpayer's creditors. In the federal bankruptcy context, however, IRA assets are now probably exempt from the bankruptcy estate.[458]

In Kansas, a taxpayer may designate an "individual" as the postmortem beneficiary of his IRA account and in so doing insulate the IRA funds from the

---

[453] 3 Scott & Ascher §15.2.1. *See generally* §8.27 of this handbook (the difference between a legal life estate and an equitable life estate incident to a trust).

[454] *See* I.R.C. §401(a) (2004) (listing numerous requirements that a plan must meet to receive tax-qualified status and favorable tax treatment). If a plan is tax-qualified under the Internal Revenue Code, the employer making the contributions to the plan may receive a tax deduction, and the employee may defer the payment of taxes on both the principal (contributions) held in trust on their behalf and the income generated therefrom until distribution is made to the employee. *See* I.R.C. §§404, 501(a), 402(a) (2004).

[455] *See* I.R.C. §401(a)(13)(A) (stating I.R.C. anti-alienation provision); ERISA §206(d)(1), 29 U.S.C.A. §1056(d)(1) (stating ERISA anti-alienation provision); *see also* Treas. Reg. §1.401(a)-13(b)(1) (1988) (providing that an ERISA-qualified anti-alienation provision is one that prohibits plan benefits from being "anticipated, assigned, . . . alienated or subject to attachment, garnishment, levy, execution or other legal or equitable process").

[456] *See* Patterson v. Shumate, 504 U.S. 753 (1992) (holding that an ERISA-qualified pension plan is excluded from bankruptcy estate under §541(c)(2) of the Bankruptcy Code (the Code), which precludes certain inalienable interests from becoming part of the debtor's bankruptcy estate, because ERISA constitutes "applicable nonbankruptcy law" for purposes of the Code); *see also* ERISA §206(d)(1), 29 U.S.C.A. §1056(d)(1). Section 541(a)(1) of the Code provides that the commencement of a bankruptcy case creates an estate consisting of "all legal or equitable interests of the debtor in property as of the commencement of the case." 11 U.S.C.A. §541(a)(1). The Code provides a narrow exception to this general rule, however, by excluding from the bankruptcy estate any beneficial interest of the debtor in a trust where the interest is subject to a restriction on alienation, which is enforceable under "applicable nonbankruptcy law." 11 U.S.C.A. §541(c)(2).

[457] *See* I.R.C. §408.

[458] *See* Rousey v. Jacoway, 125 S. Ct. 1561 (2005) (exempting IRA assets from the bankruptcy estate under 11 U.S.C. §522(d)(10)(E)). *See also* Bankruptcy Abuse Prevention and Consumer Protection Act of 2005 (amending the Bankruptcy Code to afford enhanced protection to IRA assets).

reach of the taxpayer's postmortem creditors.[459] In 2007, however, the Court of Appeals of Kansas ruled that Kansas's version of Uniform Trust Code Section 505(a)(3) eliminated this spendthrift protection in cases where IRA funds are payable postmortem not to "individuals" but to trustees of self-settled revocable inter-vivos trusts.[460] UTC Section 505(a)(3) provides that "[a]fter the death of a settlor . . . the property of a trust that was revocable at the settlor's death is subject to the claims of the settlor's creditors . . . to the extent the settlor's probate estate is inadequate to satisfy those claims. . . ."

The administration of employee benefit and IRA arrangements is a topic beyond the scope of this handbook. Trustees of property associated with tax-qualified employee benefit arrangements and IRAs, however, should at least understand the federal and state laws governing the rights of creditors to reach such property. And all trustees should be aware of how beneficiaries and their creditors may be affected by the movement of property from the shelter of tax-qualified employee benefit trusts and IRA trusts to other types of trusts.[461]

(e) **Personal trusts (non–self-settled).** A beneficiary's equitable interest under a non–self-settled trust may be so personal in nature as to evidence an intention on the part of the settlor that it be unassignable by the beneficiary and unreachable by the beneficiary's creditors.[462] One court, for example, has held that an equitable option granted to a beneficiary under the terms of a trust, namely, to purchase certain shares of stock comprising a portion of the underlying trust property, was too personal in nature to be assignable.[463] So also may one's equitable interest in a trust for one's education or one's funeral be unassignable, either voluntarily or involuntarily, or both.[464] Some courts have held that the equitable right to personally occupy a dwelling comprising the trust estate is unassignable.[465] At least one court, however, has held otherwise.[466]

(f) **Inseparable equitable interests.** "Another situation in which an intent to restrain alienation has been presumed is that in which there is a trust for a group of beneficiaries and the interests of the members of the group are

---

[459] See Kan. Stat. Ann. §60-2308(b).

[460] See Commerce Bank, N.A. v. Bolander, 154 P.3d 1184, 2007 WL 1041760 (Kan. Ct. App. 2007).

[461] See generally Natalie B. Choate, *Life and Death Planning for Retirement Benefits*, for a discussion of the tax consequences of moving property from tax-qualified employee benefit trusts to other types of trusts. Updates may be obtained by visiting <www.ataxplan.com>.

[462] See generally 3 Scott & Ascher §15.2.4.

[463] See Skelton v. Younghouse, [1942] A.C. 571, [1942] 1 All E.R. 650.

[464] See generally 3 Scott & Ascher §15.2.4.

[465] See 3 Scott & Ascher §15.2.4, n.13.

[466] See Matter of Enders, 13 N.Y.S.2d 766 (Surr. Ct. 1939).

inseparable."[467] A trust for the benefit of someone's "family," for example, may create equitable interests that are unassignable due to inseparability.[468]

§5.3.4 Rights of Beneficiary's Spouse and Children to Trust Property or Equitable Interest

Community property law in the United States is primarily of Spanish origin, although there remains some French influence in Louisiana. Community property law developed from Germanic tribal practices introduced in Spain following the fall of the Roman Empire. Early emigrants to the Spanish possessions in the New World carried with them elements of the Spanish legal system.[469]

The purpose of alimony is to meet one's continuing duty to support; while the purpose of property division is to unscramble the ownership of property, giving to each spouse what is equitably his.[470]

There are two marital property systems in the United States: the separate share system (common law) and the community property system (civil law).

Under a separate share system, whatever a spouse brings to the marriage, earns, and acquires in his or her own right during the marriage belongs to that spouse. The separate share system is of relatively recent origin. The regime that was in place before in the common law jurisdictions is discussed in Section 9.30 of this handbook.

Under a community property system, each spouse has an undivided one-half interest in property acquired during the marriage, other than property acquired by gift, devise, and descent.[471] Even separate property, however, can become community property "as the result of conversion, either through commingling or pursuant to spousal agreement, or as the result of the accumulation of income in a state in which the income derived from separate property during marriage is community property."[472]

---

[467] 3 Scott & Ascher §15.2.4.

[468] *See generally* 3 Scott & Ascher §15.2.4.

[469] Huston, Price & Treacy, 802 T.M., Community Property: General Considerations A-1. "In the United States, the Spanish system was retained in some of the territories acquired from Spain, Mexico, and France during the 1800s." Huston, Price & Treacy, 802 T.M., Community Property: General Considerations A-1. "Upon admission to statehood, several of the southwestern states adopted constitutional or statutory provisions continuing the community property system as practiced at that time." Huston, Price & Treacy, 802 T.M., Community Property: General Considerations A-1. "Other states, although having no substantial contact with Spanish culture or institutions, nevertheless adopted the community property system, due perhaps to their desire to attract women as settlers." Huston, Price & Treacy, 802 T.M., Community Property: General Considerations A-1.

[470] Rubin v. Rubin, 204 Conn. 224, 228, 527 A.2d 1184, 1186 (1987).

[471] *See generally* Jeffrey A. Schoenblum, 1 Multistate and Multinational Estate Planning 501–503 (1999). *See* Schoenblum, 1 Multistate Multinational Estate Planning at 559–588 for a discussion of the essential elements of community property. *See also* 1 Scott & Ascher §8.2.5; Bogert §26.

[472] 3 Scott & Ascher §14.10.6.

There are now nine community property states: Arizona, California, Idaho, Louisiana, Nevada, New Mexico, Texas, Washington, and Wisconsin, which has adopted the Uniform Marital Property Act.[473] The community property system also applies in the territory of Puerto Rico. The rest have systems that are more or less of the separate share variety.

For discussions of how migrating from a community property state to a common law state, or vice versa, could alter a married couple's collective and individual ownership rights, see Kenneth W. Kingma[474] and David W. Reinecke.[475]

It should be noted here that in Alaska a husband and wife, whether or not domiciled in Alaska, may convert their property (or some of it) into community property by transferring it to the trustee of a so-called Alaska Community Property Trust.[476] Each spouse will then own an undivided one-half interest in the community property.[477] At least one trustee must be an Alaska bank or trust company or an individual permanently residing in Alaska.[478] What are the possible favorable tax consequences of all of this? Upon the first death, the basis of the undivided one-half community property interest of the surviving spouse is stepped up along with the basis of the decedent's one-half interest.[479]

What are the amendment and revocation protocols for a revocable trust that is funded by both spouses at least in part with community property? The Uniform Trust Code provides that to the extent the trust consists of community property, the trust may be revoked by either spouse acting alone but may be amended only by joint action of both spouses.[480]

In a community property state, divorce will generally cause an equal partitioning of the community property between the parties.[481] Separate property, such as an equitable interest under a trust created before the marriage, is not likely to be reallocated. Death too is likely to result in an equal partitioning of community property. "Since each spouse owned half, the survivor is initially entitled to this amount and does not even confront statutory dower or elective

---

[473] Jeffrey A. Schoenblum, 1 Multistate and Multinational Estate Planning 502 n.10 (1999) and accompanying text.

[474] *Property Division at Divorce or Death for Married Couples Migrating between Common Law and Community Property States*, 35 ACTEC L.J. 74 (2009).

[475] *Community Property Issues for Non-Community Property Practitioners*, 28 ACTEC L.J. 224 (2002).

[476] Jeffrey A. Schoenblum, 1 Multistate and Multinational Estate Planning 1314–1316 (1999).

[477] Jeffrey A. Schoenblum, 1 Multistate and Multinational Estate Planning 1314–1316 (1999).

[478] Jeffrey A. Schoenblum, 1 Multistate and Multinational Estate Planning 1314–1316 (1999).

[479] Jeffrey A. Schoenblum, 1 Multistate and Multinational Estate Planning 1314–1316 (1999).

[480] UTC §602(b)(1) (available at <http://www.uniformlaws.org/Act.aspx?title=Trust%20 Code>).

[481] Jeffrey A. Schoenblum, 1 Multistate and Multinational Estate Planning 559–560 (1999) (noting some "equitable distribution" exceptions to the general rule that community property states require the equal division of community assets in the event of divorce).

share provisions, as does a surviving spouse in a common law property jurisdiction."[482] What follows is a brief discussion of how divorce or death in a non-community property jurisdiction can result in the reallocation of equitable interests under trusts.

§5.3.4.1   Spousal Rights in Common Law States

The trial court held that the remainder interest, though initially vested, no longer was vested by virtue of the mother's execution of a codicil to her will that would have defeated husband's interest. The Montana Supreme Court affirmed, but instead reasoned that husband's remainder could not be vested until the power holder's death. In the author's opinion, this logic is flawed and a consequence of attempting to reconcile the law of future interests with equitable property divisions. A more logical rationale is that, vested or not, some interest are simply to uncertain to constitute property.[483]

Divorce and separation. The purchase money resulting trust, a resulting trust/express trust hybrid, which is generally covered in Section 3.3 of this handbook, is one of several equitable devices that a court may deploy when reordering the economic interests of the parties to a divorce, particularly their interests in the marital home. Likewise, it may be used when unmarried cohabitants are going their separate ways.[484] The standard express trust is likely to figure prominently in divorce litigation when one spouse is the beneficiary of an express trust that has been established by a third party. The issue then is whether the other spouse may have access to the subject property, or failing that whether the beneficiary-spouse should be deemed to own the underlying property outright for purposes of allocating the contents of the marital estate between them.

The purchase money resulting trust. Assume a husband and wife had taken the legal title to the marital home jointly. Assume also that they had contributed disproportionately to the purchase price and that there is no written agreement as to the rights, duties, and obligations of the parties that complies with the statute of frauds.[485] In such case, the divorce court may impose a purchase money resulting trust on the property in favor of each in proportion to his or her contribution, unless there is evidence of a different understanding at the time of purchase.[486] This also would be the outcome if the legal title had been taken in the name of only one spouse.[487] The general rule is that in order to benefit from the imposition of a purchase money resulting trust, one must have

---

[482] Jeffrey A. Schoenblum, 1 Multistate and Multinational Estate Planning 502 (1999). *See generally* Huston, Price & Treacy, 802 T.M., Community Property: General Considerations.

[483] Marc A. Chorney, *Interests in Trusts as Property in Dissolution of Marriage: Identification and Valuation*, 40 Real Prop. Prob. & Tr. J. 1 (Spring 2005) (referring to In re Marriage of Beadle, 1998 MT 225, 968 P.2d 698 (1998)).

[484] *See generally* 6 Scott & Ascher §43.11.1 (Cohabitation without Marriage).

[485] *See generally* §8.15.5 of this handbook (Statute of Frauds).

[486] 6 Scott & Ascher §43.11 (Marital Home and Family Assets). *See also* §8.15.5 of this handbook (statute of frauds).

[487] 6 Scott & Ascher §43.11.

contributed to the purchase price *at the time of purchase*.[488] Marital home postpurchase mortgage payments and improvements may well be an exception, at least one commentator has so suggested.[489] A purchase money resulting trust may be imposed on personal property as well as real property.[490]

The imposition of a purchase money resulting trust is by no means the only equitable mechanism that courts employ in effecting an equitable division of the marital estate, nor is it likely the most utilized.[491] There also are the constructive trust and the equitable lien to prevent the unjust enrichment of one spouse at the expense of another.[492] Spousal agreements that are unenforceable at law may be enforceable in equity.[493] "Whatever the technical grounds, it would seem that, at bottom, the court is often simply enforcing a duty of fair dealing between spouses."[494] Unmarried cohabitants, of course, also may have contractual rights, duties, and obligations one to the other that are law-based.[495] Again, for a general discussion of the purchase money resulting trust, and the constructive trust, as well, the reader is referred to Section 3.3 of this handbook.

The express trust. If a trust is accessible to a beneficiary's creditors, it will be accessible to the beneficiary's spouse for the spouse's support, *i.e.*, alimony, and will be subject to property division in the event of divorce.[496] Under certain circumstances, the spouse will have access while the creditors will not.[497]

The spouse, for example, may be entitled to pierce a spendthrift trust for alimony and child support, even when the beneficiary is not the settlor.[498] Equitable interests of beneficiaries under such trusts have been subjected to division as marital property.[499] Some courts are viewing spouses and children as a class of claimant entitled to special deference.[500] The thought is that, as a matter of public policy, the beneficiary should not be permitted to enjoy the equitable interest while neglecting to support his dependents.[501] Some states

---

[488] 6 Scott & Ascher §43.11.

[489] 6 Scott & Ascher §43.11.

[490] *See generally* §3.3 of this handbook (purchase money resulting trusts).

[491] 6 Scott & Ascher §43.11.

[492] 6 Scott & Ascher §43.11. *See also* §3.3 of this handbook (the constructive trust).

[493] 6 Scott & Ascher §43.11.

[494] 6 Scott & Ascher §43.11.

[495] *See generally* 6 Scott & Ascher §43.11.1 (Cohabitation without Marriage).

[496] *See, e.g.*, Speed v. Speed, 263 Ga. 166, 430 S.E.2d 348 (1993). *See generally* Wofford, 515-2nd T.M., Divorce and Separation (focusing on the tax aspects of divorce and separation).

[497] Restatement (Third) of Trusts §59; 2A Scott on Trusts §157.1; Restatement (Second) of Trusts §157.

[498] Restatement (Second) of Trusts §157. *See generally* §5.3.3.3(c) of this handbook (the non–self-settled spendthrift trust).

[499] *See, e.g.*, Flaherty v. Flaherty, 138 N.H. 337, 638 A.2d 1254 (1994).

[500] *See* Wife v. Husband, Del. Ch., 286 A.2d 256 (1971); Bacardi v. White, 463 So. 2d 218 (Fla. 1985); Albertson v. Ryder, 85 Ohio App. 3d 765, 621 N.E.2d 480 (1993).

[501] *See* Carolyn L. Dessin, *Feed a Trust and Starve a Child: The Effectiveness of Trust Protective Techniques Against Claims for Support and Alimony*, 10 Ga. St. U. L. Rev. 691 (1994).

have enacted statutes allowing the spouse and children access to the beneficiary's interest in a spendthrift trust. The Restatement (Third) of Trusts, specifically Section 59, is in accord.

The Uniform Trust Code would allow a creditor or assignee of a beneficiary of a spendthrift trust to reach a mandatory distribution of income or principal, provided the trustee has not made the distribution to the beneficiary within a reasonable time after the required distribution date.[502] "Following this reasonable period, payments mandated by the express terms of the trust are in effect being held by the trustee as agent for the beneficiary and should be treated as part of the beneficiary's personal assets."[503] Likewise, "[t]he ex-spouse's remedy is to attach present or future distributions to or for the benefit of the beneficiary, provided the court may limit any award 'to such relief as is appropriate under the circumstances.' "[504]

As a general rule, the spouse of a beneficiary may *not* reach the beneficiary's contingent[505] equitable interest in a trust under which someone else possesses a general inter vivos power of appointment, *e.g.*, right of revocation,[506] or in a fully *discretionary trust* created by someone other than the beneficiary.[507] The Restatement (Third) of Trusts, however, would allow a beneficiary's spouse limited access to the beneficiary's contingent equitable

---

[502] UTC §506 (available at <http://www.uniformlaws.org/Act.aspx?title=Trust%20Code>).

[503] UTC §506 cmt. (available at <http://www.uniformlaws.org/Act.aspx?title=Trust%20 Code>).

[504] Alan Newman, *Spendthrift and Discretionary Trusts: Alive and Well under the Uniform Trust Code*, 40 Real Prop. Prob. & Tr. J. 567, 626 (Fall 2005) (referring to UTC §503(c).

[505] A contingent interest is an interest subject to a condition precedent such as nonrevocation, survivorship, or a trustee's exercise of discretion.

[506] *See, e.g.*, Dryfoos v. Dryfoos, 2000 WL 1196339 (July 28, 2000) (Conn. Super.); Rubin v. Rubin, 204 Conn. 224, 527 A.2d 1184 (1987).

[507] *See generally* Restatement (Second) of Trusts §155. *See also* Pemberton v. Pemberton, 9 Mass. App. Ct. 9, 411 N.E.2d 1305 (1980); In re Marriage of Jones, 812 P.2d 1152 (Colo. 1991); In re Marriage of Rosenblum, 602 P.2d 892 (Colo. Ct. App. 1979); §5.3.3.3(a) of this handbook (the non–self-settled discretionary trust). *See generally* Helen Brezinsky, *Trusts as Marital Property Still Safe/No Decisions Address Equitable Distribution*, N.Y.L.J., June 30, 1997, at 7, col. 1 (discussing New York's substantial body of matrimonial law with its ever-changing definition of marital property). *See also* M. L. Cross, Annot., *Trust income or assets as subject to claims against beneficiary for alimony, maintenance, or child support*, 91 A.L.R.2d 262 (1963). *But see* UTC §504(c) (available at <http://www.uniformlaws.org/Act.aspx?title=Trust%20Code>) (providing that to the extent a trustee has not complied with a standard of distribution or has abused a discretion, a distribution may be ordered by the court to satisfy a judgment or court order against the beneficiary for support or maintenance of the beneficiary's child, spouse, or former spouse). The court shall direct the trustee to pay to the child, spouse, or former spouse such amount as is equitable under the circumstances but not more than the amount the trustee would have been required to distribute to or for the benefit of the beneficiary had the trustee complied with the standard or not abused the discretion. UTC §504(c). *See, e.g.*, Mathews v. Mathews, 450 N.E.2d 278 (Ohio App. 1981) (ordering that trustee of a discretionary support trust satisfy out of income beneficiary's past due child support obligations); In re Will of John T. Sullivan, 12 N.W.2d 148 (Neb. 1943) (ordering trustee of a discretionary "support and maintenance" trust to support beneficiary's wife and child out of income and/or principal, the court however finding support of the wife and child to be in keeping with the intent of the settlor). *See also* Restatement (Third) of Trusts, Tent. Draft No. 2, §60 cmt. e (suggesting that a "creditor" seeking to enforce a support right or judgment against the

interest in a non–self-settled discretionary trust for purposes of enforcing a support right or judgment against the beneficiary.[508] The Uniform Trust Code is more or less in accord:

> If the trust provides for distributions to be at the trustee's discretion, the ex-spouse may compel distributions he or she can reach, but only if (1) he or she has a judgment or court order for support or maintenance and (2) in not making the distribution, the trustee has not complied with a standard of distribution or has abused a discretion. In that case, the UTC provides for the court to order the trustee to pay to the ex-spouse "such amount as is equitable under the circumstances but not more than the amount the trustee would have been required to distribute to or for the benefit of the beneficiary had the trustee complied with the standard or not abused the discretion."[509]

In some states, equitable interests under a *spendthrift* or *support* trust may *not* be reached by the spouse and children of the nonsettlor beneficiary.[510] The thinking is that if the settlor had wanted them in as beneficiaries, he would have named them as beneficiaries.[511] Of course, the trustee voluntarily might decide that it is in the interests *of the beneficiary* to make distributions to the spouse or children, subject, of course, to the terms of the governing instrument and the facts and circumstances prevailing.

Turning to the equitable division of marital assets in the context of divorce, depending upon the facts and circumstances, a beneficiary's equitable interest—perhaps the income stream, perhaps the principal's appreciation during the marriage, perhaps the whole thing—could itself be the subject of physical division or re-allocation; or in lieu of actual physical division, could be deemed an "economic circumstance" of the beneficiary for purposes of computing the value of the general marital estate. As a rule of thumb, the more contingent the equitable interest, the less likely will it be subject to actual physical division or re-allocation. That is not necessarily the case, however, when it comes to deeming an equitable interest an economic circumstance.

In a Colorado dissolution action, a spouse's contingent equitable interest in a trust that was revocable by his mother was deemed marital property for

---

trust beneficiary may be able to compel the trustee to make a distribution on the ground that a refusal to do so would constitute an abuse of discretion).

[508] Restatement (Third) of Trusts §60 cmt. e(1).

[509] Alan Newman, *Spendthrift and Discretionary Trusts: Alive and Well under the Uniform Trust Code*, 40 Real Prop. Prob. & Tr. J. 567, 626 (Fall 2005) (referring to UTC §§503(c) (1) & (2)).

[510] Comins v. Comins, 33 Mass. App. Ct. 28, 595 N.E.2d 804 (1992). *See also* Erickson v. Erickson, 197 Minn. 71, 266 N.W. 161 (Minn. 1936); In re Campbell's Trusts, 258 N.W.2d 856 (Minn. 1977). *But see* Lauricella v. Lauricella, 409 Mass. 211, 565 N.E.2d 436 (1991) (holding beneficiary's interest in realty trust subject to equitable division notwithstanding spendthrift clause).

[511] Comins v. Comins, 33 Mass. App. Ct. 28, 595 N.E.2d 804 (1992). *See also* Erickson v. Erickson, 197 Minn. 71, 266 N.W. 161 (Minn. 1936); In re Campbell's Trusts, 258 N.W.2d 856 (Minn. 1977). *But see* Lauricella v. Lauricella, 409 Mass. 211, 565 N.E.2d 436 (1991) (holding beneficiary's interest in realty trust subject to equitable division notwithstanding spendthrift clause).

valuation purposes.[512] A Massachusetts divorce court has deemed a current beneficiary's contingent equitable interest in a non–self-settled discretionary trust, to be a marital asset belonging to the beneficiary for purposes of determining how the other items of marital property are to be allocated between the parties, *i.e.*, for valuation purposes.[513] Another Massachusetts court has assigned a value of $128,000 to a remainderman's interest in a discretionary trust, even though the current beneficiary was alive and eligible to receive distributions.[514] Colorado has a similar case.[515] A third Massachusetts court has awarded the wife alimony, after the husband received a contingent equitable interest in a non–self-settled discretionary trust to be shared with other permissible beneficiaries, the husband's shared contingent equitable interest being deemed to be a "substantial inheritance" for asset valuation purposes.[516] Some divorce courts in England also have been treating the trust as a financial resource:

> Although it is possible to attack the integrity of a trust, cases . . . [in England] . . . where a successful attack can be mounted will be rare. A more common way for a trust to be affected by divorce proceedings is for the claimant to seek financial settlement from the other party to the marriage which treats trust assets, or income from such assets (even where the assets are held on discretionary trusts), as a financial resource of that party. This justifies the making of an order against that party which is higher than would otherwise be made. In extreme cases, the financial order made is one with which the party cannot comply without financial

---

[512] *See* Marriage of Gorman, 36 P.3d 211 (2001) (mischaracterizing a contingent equitable interest as a vested interest subject to divestment upon the happening of a condition subsequent). *Gorman* was subsequently reversed by statute (C.R.S. §14-10-113 (7)(b)). It provides that expectancies such as one's contingent equitable interest in a living person's revocable trust may not be considered as an economic circumstance in a divorce proceeding. *See generally* National Shawmut Bank v. Joy, 315 Mass. 457, 53 N.E.2d 113 (1944) (confirming that one's possession of a right of revocation as a matter of property law renders all other equitable interests contingent). *See generally* §8.30 of this handbook (the difference between a vested equitable remainder subject to divestment and a vested (transmissible) contingent equitable remainder).

[513] *See* Comins v. Comins, 33 Mass. App. Ct. 28, 595 N.E.2d 804 (1992). *But see* Child v. Child, 58 Mass. App. Ct. 76, 84 n.4, 787 N.E.2d 1121, 1126 n.4 (2003) (a divorce case in which the appellate court speculated that had the husband raised at the trial level the issue of the valuation of his equitable interest under two non–self-settled discretionary trusts, the principal might have been entered on the husband's side of the ledger at a discounted value, the husband seeming to lack a "present, enforceable, equitable right to use the trust property for his own benefit").

[514] *See* Chilkot v. Chilkot, 607 A.2d 883 (Vt. 1992). *See also* Davidson v. Davidson, 474 N.E.2d 1137 (Mass. App. Ct. 1985) (a remainder valuation case where the current discretionary beneficiary died after the divorce decree but before the conclusion of litigation to modify property division and support orders). *But see* Williams v. Massa, 728 N.E.2d 932 (Mass. 2000) (finding the contingent equitable remainder interest in a discretionary trust to be a "mere expectancy" and therefore not susceptible of valuation).

[515] In re Marriage of Balanson, 25 P.3d 28 (Colo. 2001), *appeal after remand*, 2004 Colo. App. LEXIS 1716 (Colo. Ct. App. Sept. 23, 2004). For an in-depth discussion of Balanson, *see* Marc A. Chorney, *Interests in Trusts as Property in Dissolution of Marriage: Identification and Valuation*, 40 Real Prop. Prob. & Tr. J. 1 (Spring 2005).

[516] Dwight v. Dwight, 52 Mass. App. Ct. 739 (2001).

assistance from the trustees—this indirectly applies pressure (or "judicious en-couragement," as one leading case states) on the trustees to release funds to that beneficiary.[517]

In a child support dispute incident to an Illinois divorce action, the ex-wife sought to discover information relating to two trusts established by her husband in the offshore jurisdiction of Jersey. She and her disabled daughter were beneficiaries among others, including the ex-husband himself. The ex-wife, however, also asserted that the trusts were shams. While sympathetic to her plight, the Jersey Royal Court rejected the ex-wife's discovery requests, at least for the time being:

> Accordingly, we wish to make it clear that, in the event of the mother dropping the allegation of invalidity—so that the Illinois proceedings return to a straightfor-ward dispute over child maintenance—this Court would be likely to view sympa-thetically any application by the mother and/or S for disclosure of the trust accounts (containing sufficient details to show the contribution and value of the trust assets and giving details of any distributions made to the settlor over the years).[518]

Some courts have avoided the problems inherent in valuing equitable interests under discretionary trusts by providing that at least a portion of any future distributions made by the trustee be physically allocated to the nonben-eficiary spouse. One court has issued an order to the trustee allocating 20 percent of any future distributions actually made to the wife (in her capacity as beneficiary of a discretionary trust) to her husband.[519] This is known as a "when, as, and if received" or "if and when received" or "if, as, and when received" order.[520] It is a form of charging order.[521] In Florida, it is referred to as a writ of garnishment.[522] Courts in other states also have issued such orders in the divorce context.[523]

---

[517] James Ferguson & Anne Exton, *Trusts under Attack*, Trusts and Estates L.J., No. 43 (Jan./Feb. 2003), at 22.

[518] Nearco Trust Co. (Jersey) Ltd. v. AM, [2003] JRC 002A. *See generally* §6.2.6 of this handbook (the trustee's duty to defend the trust and certainly not to attack it).

[519] Leavitt v. Leavitt, Commonwealth of Massachusetts, The Trial Court, Probate and Family Court Dept., Essex Division, Docket No. 95D-1951-DVI (1995) (order upheld in S.L. v. R.L., 55 Mass. App. Ct. 880, 774 N.E.2d 1179 (2002)). *See also* van Oosting v. van Oosting, 521 N.W.2d 93, 98 (N.D. 1994) (holding that "[o]n remand the appropriate method of distribution, therefore, would be the award to Shirley of a percentage of future payments that would have otherwise gone to Bruce").

[520] Williams v. Massa, 431 Mass. 619, 628, 728 N.E.2d 932, 941 (2000).

[521] Hamilton v. Drogo, 241 N.Y. 401, 150 N.E. 496 (1926) (ordering attachment of future discretionary distributions, if any, after "allotment" by the trustee but before delivery is effected to the beneficiary). *See generally* §5.3.3 of this handbook (rights of beneficiary's creditors and others to trust property).

[522] *See, e.g.*, Berlinger v. Casselberry, 2013 WL 62212023 (Fla. Dist. Ct. App. Nov. 27, 2013).

[523] *See, e.g.*, van Oosting v. van Oosting, 521 N.W.2d 93 (N.D. 1994) (snaring any distribu-tions to the current beneficiary); Flaherty v. Flaherty, 638 A.2d 1254 (N.H. 1994) (snaring any remainder distributions). In Zuger v. Zuger, 563 N.W.2d 804 (N.D. 1997), the North Dakota court

Some divorce courts, however, have declined to include contingent interests in the calculation of the value of marital estates for equitable distribution purposes. One court, for example, did not include the value of a spouse's equitable contingent remainder in computing the marital estate.[524] It also declined to issue a charging order.[525] The appellate court affirmed the decision, noting that "[n]either the present assignment of a percentage of a contingent interest's value, nor a future award on an 'if and when' basis, avoids administrative hardships inherent in the valuation of expectant interests or in the requirement of continued court supervision."[526] Another divorce court took a spouse's vested equitable remainder off the table for marital estate computation purposes. Why? Because the equitable interest was subject to the condition subsequent of his mother not exercising her limited testamentary power of appointment. This decision also was affirmed on appeal.[527]

One court has endeavored to clear up some confusion as to what equitable property interests are vested and what are contingent under long-standing principles of property and trust law.[528] An interest subject to the condition precedent of the trustee's exercise of discretion, for example, is contingent.[529] So is an interest subject to the condition precedent of survivorship.[530] "However, even when a party's remainder interest in a trust cannot strictly be characterized as vested, it still may be included, in appropriate instances, within the marital estate."[531] One's contingent equitable interest in a discretionary trust is still technically an interest in property, *i.e.,* something more than a mere expectancy or hope.[532]

Presumably a court should give serious consideration to discounting a spouse's nonpossessory equitable interest to its present value. For some interesting and helpful musings on how a court might go about valuing future equitable interests in the divorce context, the reader is referred to Marc A.

---

again took the charging order route, although its grasp of the fundamentals of property and trust law seems less than firm: Zuger v. Zuger, 563 N.W.2d 804, 806 (N.D. 1997). As to why, *see generally* §8.30 of this handbook (the difference between a vested equitable remainder subject to divestment and a vested (transmissible) contingent equitable remainder).

[524] Williams v. Massa, 431 Mass. 619, 628, 728 N.E.2d 932, 941 (2000).

[525] Williams v. Massa, 431 Mass. 619, 628, 728 N.E.2d 932, 941 (2000).

[526] Williams v. Massa, 431 Mass. 619, 628, 728 N.E.2d 932, 941 (2000).

[527] Marriage of Beadle, 1998 Mont. 225, 968 P.2d 698 (1998). *Cf.* S.L. v. R.L., 55 Mass. App. Ct. 880, 774 N.E.2d 1179 (2002) (a spouse's contingent equitable remainder interest in a trust established by her father was taken off the table for marital estate computation purposes not because of her mother's general inter vivos power of appointment over the trust property but because of her mother's testamentary power of appointment over the trust property, although the nonexercise of both powers was a condition precedent to the spouse receiving an interest under the trust as was the condition precedent that she survive her mother).

[528] D.L. v. G.L., 61 Mass. App. Ct. 488, 811 N.E.2d 1013 (2004).

[529] D.L. v. G.L., 61 Mass. App. Ct. 488, 811 N.E.2d 1013 (2004).

[530] D.L. v. G.L., 61 Mass. App. Ct. 488, 811 N.E.2d 1013 (2004).

[531] D.L. v. G.L., 61 Mass. App. Ct. 488, 811 N.E.2d 1013 (2004).

[532] *See generally* Kevin D. Millard, *Rights of a Trust Beneficiary's Creditors under the Uniform Trust Code,* 34 ACTEC L.J. 58, 72 (explaining the difference between an expectancy and a contingent equitable property interest in the context of divorce litigation).

Chorney.[533] In some situations, a court may want to piggy-back on the Internal Revenue Code's actuarial valuation tables in order to avoid getting bogged down in the actual facts and circumstances of a given situation, *e.g.*, "the health of beneficiaries, the specific assets held in trust, the past performance of trust investments, the projections for future performance, the prior trust distributions, the identity of the trustees, and a number of other subjective factors."[534] IRC Section 7520 "is a present value calculation that applies mortality and interest rate factors mandated by the Code."[535] Unfortunately, these tables are not particularly helpful when it comes to valuing equitable interests that are subject to possible diversion to third parties due to the exercise of fiduciary or nonfiduciary powers of appointment, or the happening of other such difficult-to-quantify contingencies.

For purposes of ascertaining the economic circumstances of parties to a divorce, the estate plans of third parties may be discoverable, *e.g.*, the revocable inter vivos trust of a spouse's living parent. In Massachusetts, "expectancy" discovery would generally be limited to obtaining an affidavit from the parent as to his or her net worth, rounded to the nearest $550,000; a general description of the current estate plan; and the date the estate plan was last revised.[536] Still, one cannot help but wonder whether the U.S. Constitution would impose additional limitations on how far a state incident to a divorce action could intrude upon the privacy expectations of innocent third parties.

For more on the laws of property division in the context of divorce, the reader is referred to John Gregory, Janet Richards, and Sheryl Wolf.[537]

Whatever the degree of the trust's vulnerability, it always should be kept in mind that the trustee's primary allegiance is to the beneficiary, not to the nonbeneficiary spouse or ex-spouse. Thus, when there is marital discord, the trustee must suppress any personal feelings as to who may be "at fault" and vigorously defend—within reason and to the extent the law allows—the beneficiary's equitable property interest. As the English say, "[t]rustees have the custody of the property: they do not keep the conscience of their beneficiary."[538] A trustee may even have a fiduciary duty to challenge, at trust expense, a charging order that interferes with the trustee's ability to carry out the settlor's intentions.[539] "Although the process and division may reflect the concept of marriage as a shared enterprise or partnership, this process and division likely

---

[533] *Interests in Trusts as Property in Dissolution of Marriage: Identification and Valuation*, 40 Real Prop. Prob. & Tr. J. 1, 30–35 (Spring 2005).

[534] Marc A. Chorney, *Interests in Trusts as Property in Dissolution of Marriage: Identification and Valuation*, 40 Real Prop. Prob. & Tr. J. 1, 31 (Spring 2005).

[535] Marc A. Chorney, *Interests in Trusts as Property in Dissolution of Marriage: Identification and Valuation*, 40 Real Prop. Prob. & Tr. J. 1, 31 (Spring 2005).

[536] *See generally* Gerald L. Nissenbaum & Wendy J. Overbaugh, *What you need to know about Vaughn affidavits*, 35 MLW 575 (Oct. 30, 2006) [Massachusetts Lawyers Weekly].

[537] Property Division in Divorce Proceedings: A Fifty State Guide (Aspen Publishers Inc. 2004).

[538] Lewin ¶ 20-161 (England).

[539] *See* Hodel v. Irving, 481 U.S. 704, 715 (1987) (noting that the right to pass on property is a property right subject to Fifth Amendment protection).

will be counter to the intent of the trust's settlor and perhaps will require the participation of the family members of a beneficiary in the proceedings."[540] The trustee's duty to defend the trust and its dispositive terms is taken up in Section 6.2.6 of this handbook.

. . .

Divorce, dissolution, or annulment of a marriage can sometimes trigger by operation of law the partial revocation of a trust.[541] The Uniform Probate Code, for example, provides that with respect to a trust under which the settlor has reserved a right of revocation, any provisions in favor of the settlor's spouse are revoked upon their divorce or marriage annulment.[542] This includes any provisions designating the ex-spouse as a fiduciary.[543] The Restatement (Third) of Property is generally in accord.[544] Under the Code, however, the property passes as if the settlor's ex-spouse had disclaimed the beneficial interest.[545] Under the Restatement, the property passes as if the settlor's ex-spouse had predeceased the settlor.[546] Under the Code, divorce extinguishes not only the equitable interests of the ex-spouse but also those of the ex-spouse's relatives,[547] except those relatives who remain related to the settlor by blood, adoption, or affinity postdivorce.[548]

Postmortem. *The nonsettlor beneficiary.* Upon the death of the nonsettlor beneficiary, his or her surviving spouse will not have access to the trust property unless the terms of the governing instrument expressly provide so, unless the deceased beneficiary's equitable interest does not terminate at death,[549] or unless the trust distributes to the deceased beneficiary's estate.[550]

Reserved rights of revocation and spousal election. In an ever-increasing number of jurisdictions, however, the spouse through the spousal election statute,

---

[540] Marc A. Chorney, *Interests in Trusts as Property in Dissolution of Marriage: Identification and Valuation*, 40 Real Prop. Prob. & Tr. J. 1, 3 (Spring 2005).

[541] *See generally* 5 Scott & Ascher §35.1.6.

[542] UPC §2-804(b)(1). *See, e.g.*, Mass. Gen. Laws ch. 190B, §2-804 (partial revocation of certain trusts by divorce).

[543] UPC §2-804(b)(1). *See, e.g.*, Mass. Gen. Laws ch. 190B, §2-804 (partial revocation of certain trusts by divorce).

[544] Restatement (Third) of Property (Wills and Other Donative Transfers) §4.1(b) cmt. p.

[545] UPC §2-804(d).

[546] Restatement (Third) of Property (Wills and Other Donative Transfers) §4.1 cmt. o.

[547] UPC §2-804(b).

[548] UPC §2-804(a)(5).

[549] Restatement (Third) of Trusts §55(2).

[550] *See* 2A Scott on Trusts §§144, 145, 146A. *See, e.g.*, Bongaards v. Millen, 440 Mass. 10, 793 N.E. 2d 335 (2003) (the court in denying a surviving spouse access to a trust that was established for the benefit of the deceased spouse by a third party criticized the augmented estate concept embodied in Restatement (Third) of Property (Wills and Other Donative Transfers) §9.1(c) as being vague, unsupported, contradictory, and poorly reasoned). "[W]hile this court often considers the various Restatements of the Law as prestigious sources of potentially persuasive authority, we have never taken the position that this court should abdicate to the views of the American Law Institute as set forth in its various Restatements." *See, e.g.*, Bongaards v. Millen, 440 Mass. 10, 793 N.E. 2d 335 (2003). *See also* Restatement (Third) of Property (Wills and Other Donative Transfers) §23.1, Reporter's Notes (responding to the *Bongaards* rebuke).

the successor to common-law dower and curtesy,[551] may be afforded postmortem access to the trust if it was created by the deceased spouse *and* if the deceased spouse had reserved the power to revoke or amend the trust or a general inter vivos power of appointment.[552] The Uniform Probate Code is in accord,[553] as is the Restatement (Third) of Property[554] and the Restatement (Third) of Trusts.[555] The Uniform Probate Code, however, would go farther in that it would expose to spousal election other types of self-settled trusts, as well as non–self-settled trusts established by the deceased spouse for the benefit of third parties during marriage and within two years of death.[556] In 2008, Massachusetts enacted a number of sections of the Uniform Probate Code. Not included were those sections of the Code that deal with spousal election.[557]

---

[551] *See* UPC §2-112, cmt. *See also* §9.30 of this handbook (marriage settlements (England)).

[552] 1 Scott & Ascher §8.2.5; Bogert §233 (Surviving Spouse's Marital Rights). *See, e.g.,* Sullivan v. Burkin, 390 Mass. 864, 460 N.E.2d 572 (1984) (holding prospective, however); Staples v. King, 433 A.2d 407 (Me. 1981); Knell v. Price, 569 A.2d 636 (Md. 1990); Sieh v. Sieh, 713 N.W.2d 194 (Iowa 2006). *But see* Friedberg v. Sunbank/Miami, N.A., 648 So. 2d 204 (Fla. Dist. Ct. App. 1994) (denying surviving spouse access to assets of revocable inter vivos trust when seeking elective share). *See generally* Charles E. Rounds, Jr., *The Common Law Is Not Just about Contracts: How Legal Education Has Been Short-Changing Feminism*, 43 U. Rich L. Rev. 1185 (2009 (in part discussing *Sullivan v. Burkin*).

[553] UPC §2-205, cmt. (Example 3); UPC §6-102(b) (added to the Code in 1998 and replacing §6-107 of the original Code and its 1989 sequel, §6-215).

[554] Restatement (Third) of Property (Wills and Other Donative Transfers) §9.1(c) and cmt. j. thereto.

[555] Restatement (Third) of Trusts §25 and cmt. d thereto.

[556] UPC §2-205. The authors of the UPC have evolved a fiendishly complicated spousal election regime reminiscent of ERISA and the Internal Revenue Code, complete with a vesting-schedule analog, which is intended to "bring elective-share law into line with the contemporary view of marriage as an economic partnership." UPC, Art. II, Part 2, General Comment. "The original elective-share fraction of one-third of the decedent's estate," they suggest, "plainly does not implement a partnership principle." UPC, Art. II, Part 2, General Comment. They note that "the economic partnership theory of marriage is already implemented under the equitable-distribution system applied in both the common-law and community-property states when a marriage ends in divorce." UPC, Art. II, Part 2, General Comment. "The marital-property portion of the augmented estate is computed by . . . applying the percentages set forth in a graduated schedule that increases annually with the length of the marriage (each "marital-portion percentage" being double the percentage previously set forth in the "elective-share percentage" schedule)." UPC, Art. II, Part 2, General Comment. Included in the UPC augmented estate is "property over which the decedent alone, immediately before death, held a presently exercisable general power of appointment." UPC §2-205(1)(A). *See also* §8.1 of this handbook (powers of appointment). Property held in income-only self-settled trusts would seem to be captured by Section 2-205 as well. *See* UPC §2-205(2)(A). Section 2-214 purports to afford liability protection to the trustee who makes a distribution in accordance with the terms of the trust prior to receiving written notice of a surviving spouse's intention to make an election against the trust property. We call the reader's attention to §8.25 of this handbook in which we express our concern that few American law schools now require Agency, Trusts and Equity. Though UPC §2-205 and its supporting sections attempt through codification to touch all bases, to address all contingencies, they nevertheless presume more than just a passing understanding of the core common law legal relationships of agency and trusts, the latter being a creature of equity. They also presume a basic understanding of how those two fiduciary relationships intersect and blend with the laws of contract and property.

[557] *See* Chapter 521 of the Acts of 2008 (Massachusetts).

Florida has modified its spousal election share statute in part to capture property held in the deceased spouse's self-settled revocable trust,[558] although one Florida court has declined to apply the statute retroactively.[559] A surviving spouse who had knowingly waived his or her rights to the trust property, however, would not be afforded access.[560]

Conflict of laws and the spousal election. Take a revocable inter vivos trust of movables. The settlor's domicile, State *X*, has an expansive postmortem spousal election statute that would capture the entrusted property. The election statute of another state, State *Y*, would not. Could the settlor effectively insulate the entrusted property from the reach of State *X*'s statute by establishing the trust in State *Y* and designating in the terms of the trust that the law of State *Y* shall govern the trust's validity? On public policy grounds such countermeasures would likely be ineffective. The Restatement (Second) of Conflict of laws is in accord.[561] The topic of conflict of laws in the trust context is covered generally in Section 8.5 of this handbook.

The illusory trust doctrine. And then there is the illusory trust doctrine, which Massachusetts, by the way, has rejected.[562] In Illinois, whether a surviving spouse will have access to the property held in the deceased spouse's revocable trust appears to hinge on whether there was an intent to defraud on the part of the deceased spouse. "As interpreted by Illinois courts, intent to defraud has become a strange combination of intent and control and has resulted in a body of law almost unique in its lack of protection for the surviving spouse."[563] The illusory trust doctrine is taken up in Section 8.15.41 of this handbook.

When the deceased donee of an unexercised general inter vivos power of appointment was not the settlor. In New York, on the other hand, the surviving spouse now has postmortem access to the trust property whether the deceased spouse died possessed of a reserved inter vivos power of appointment (right to revoke) or died possessed of a general inter vivos power that had been given to him or her by a third party.[564] The Restatement (Third) of Property is fully in accord in both situations.[565] If access is foreclosed due to the fact that the trust's place of administration is in another state, the New York court may well allow the surviving spouse to elect *against the deceased spouse's probate estate* an amount computed as if the assets of the trust were a part of the local probate estate.[566]

Unexercised general testamentary powers of appointment. Property subject to an unexercised general testamentary power of appointment has traditionally not been deemed to have been *owned* at death by the deceased donee for purposes of sorting out the surviving spouse's elective-share rights. The Restatement

---

[558] Fla. Stat. §732.207.

[559] Estate of Heid v. Heid, 863 So. 2d 1259 (Fla. 2004).

[560] *See, e.g.,* Briggs v. Wyoming Nat'l Bank of Casper, 836 P.2d 263 (Wyo. 1992).

[561] Restatement (Second) of Conflict of Laws §270, cmt. e.

[562] *See* Sullivan v. Burkin, 390 Mass. 864, 869 n.4, 460 N.E.2d 572, 572 n.4 (1984).

[563] Helene S. Shapo, *The Widow's Mite Gets Smaller: Deficiencies in Illinois Elective Share Law,* 24 S. Ill. U. L.J. 95, 98 (1999).

[564] N.Y. Est. Powers & Trusts Law §5-1.1-A(b)(1)(h) (1998).

[565] *See* Restatement (Third) of Property (Wills and Other Donative Transfers) §23.1, cmt. d.

[566] *See generally* 7 Scott & Ascher §45.4.2.4. *See also* §8.5 of this handbook (conflict of laws).

(Third) of Property would make an exception for the surviving spouse of a deceased settlor-donee.[567] Here is the rationale: "The reservation of a general testamentary power over property once owned by the donee allows the donee to maintain control of the death-time disposition of that property."[568]

§5.3.4.2 Rights of Children

I'll strip you of your commission; I'll lodge a five-and-threepence in the hands of trustees, and you shall live on the interest.—I'll disown you, I'll disinherit you, I'll unget you! And damn me! If ever I call you Jack again!— Sir Anthony in Richard Brinsley Sheridan's play *The Rivals*.[569]

The omitted-child statute. An omitted-child statute in a common law jurisdiction is designed to prevent unintentional disinheritance *by will* of the members of a designated class of individuals. At minimum, the class will comprise the children of the testator. In Section 8.15.89 of this handbook, we consider how the revocable inter vivos trust can be employed as an instrument of pretermission; specifically, technical pretermission by pour-over devise and substantive pretermission by predeath funding.

Piercing the spendthrift trust on behalf of a child of the beneficiary. Section 503 of the Uniform Trust Code provides that even if a trust contains a spendthrift provision, a beneficiary's child who has a judgment or court order against the beneficiary for support or maintenance may obtain from a court an order attaching present or future distributions to or for the benefit of the beneficiary.[570] There is nothing new here:

The . . . [Uniform Trust Code's] . . . exception . . . for judgments or orders to support a beneficiary's child . . . is in accord with . . . numerous state statutes.[571] It is also consistent with federal bankruptcy law, which exempts such support orders from discharge. The effect of this exception is to permit the claimant for unpaid support to attach present or future distributions . . . [from a spendthrift trust] . . . that would otherwise be made to the beneficiary. Distributions subject to attachment include distributions required by the express terms of the trust, such as mandatory payment of income, and distributions the trustee has otherwise decided to make, such as through the exercise of discretion.[572]

---

[567] *See* Restatement (Third) of Property (Wills and Other Donative Transfers) §23.1(2).

[568] *See* Restatement (Third) of Property (Wills and Other Donative Transfers) §23.1, cmt. b.

[569] Brander Mathews, Sheridan's Comedies 117 (1885).

[570] UTC §503(b) (available at <http://www.uniformlaws.org/Act.aspx?title=Trust%20 Code>).

[571] The exception also is in accord with Restatement (Third) of Trusts §59(a) (Tentative Draft No. 2, approved 1999); Restatement (Second) of Trusts §157(a).

[572] UTC §503 cmt. (available at <http://www.uniformlaws.org/Act.aspx?title=Trust %20Code>). *See also* Restatement (Third) of Trusts §59(a) (providing that the interest of a beneficiary in a valid spendthrift trust can be reached in satisfaction of an enforceable claim against the beneficiary for support of a child).

Piercing the discretionary trust on behalf of a child of the beneficiary. Section 504 of the Uniform Trust Code, which deals with access to equitable interests under discretionary trusts, authorizes a child with a support claim against a beneficiary of a discretionary trust to compel a distribution to the child to the extent the trustee has abused a discretion or failed to comply with a standard of distribution. The court, however, may not compel the trustee to pay out to the child more than the amount the trustee would have been required to distribute to or for the benefit of the beneficiary had the trustee complied with the standard or had not abused the discretion.[573]

In California, a state that has not adopted the Code, "a court may overcome a trustee's discretion . . . when there is an enforceable child support judgment that the trustee refuses to satisfy."[574]

The germ of a common law postmortem support obligation. There is a Massachusetts Supreme Judicial Court decision that possibly contains the germ of a common law postmortem child support obligation. Time will tell. The probate court had ordered the father of his illegitimate child to pay child support "until further order of the court." It was the father's intention that neither his will nor his revocable inter vivos trust contain any provisions for the benefit of the child. At the time of the father's death, he was current on his child support payments. The Supreme Judicial Court, in an action initiated by a guardian ad litem appointed to represent any interests the child might have in her father's estate, held that the father's child support obligation survived his death and that it could be satisfied from the assets of the revocable, now irrevocable, inter vivos trust.[575] The court invoked no statutory authority for the action it took relative to the trust.

§5.3.5 Medicaid Eligibility (Means Testing) and Recoupment

Given the general ineffectiveness of spendthrift language to insulate a settlor's own beneficial interest from the claims of creditors, one would surely expect that the general rule would be that the retention of a beneficial interest in trust would, notwithstanding spendthrift language or other limitations on the trustee's discretion to spend on behalf of the settlor, disqualify the settlor from . . . [governmental benefits or programs, such as Medicaid, that are means tested] . . . Indeed, this is generally the case.[576]

---

[573] UTC §504(c)(2) (available at <http://www.uniformlaws.org/Act.aspx?title=Trust%20 Code>).

[574] Ventura County Dep't of Child Support Servs. v. Brown, 117 Cal. App. 4th 144, 11 Cal. Rptr. 3d 489 (2004) (involving efforts by Ventura County and the mother of minor children to seek satisfaction of judgments against father for child support arrearages and ongoing support from father's interest in trust of father's deceased mother).

[575] L.W.K. v. E.R.C., 432 Mass. 438, 735 N.E.2d 359 (Mass. 2000).

[576] 3 Scott & Ascher §15.4.3.

Medicaid not to be confused with Medicare,[577] is a medical assistance welfare program established under the federal Social Security Act, administered by the states, and supported by federal and state tax revenues.[578] To be eligible for Medicaid benefits, such as coverage for nursing home costs, an applicant must be needy.[579] Since Medicaid's inception, creative lawyers have been employing the self-settled trust as a vehicle for rendering their clients "needy" in form, though not necessarily in substance, and thus, with any luck, eligible for Medicaid. Legislatures and welfare bureaucracies have responded with statutes and regulations designed to thwart these efforts.[580] One ought not to be able to eat one's cake and have it too.

Among the property transfers that must be disclosed on a Medicaid application form are all transfers of property—both outright and in trust—that the applicant has made for less than adequate consideration during the prior sixty months.[581] If there have been any such transfers, the applicant will be disqualified from receiving Medicaid for a length of time that is calculated in part with reference to the aggregate value of the property that was transferred during the look-back period. A transfer to the applicant's disabled child or to an applicant's child who is under 21, on the other hand, is unlikely to affect eligibility. And, of course, for Medicaid eligibility purposes, an inter vivos transfer to an applicant's spouse is not a "spend-down" event. It is tantamount to a transfer to oneself.

While the trust has from the beginning been a high-profile tool in the Medicaid planner's kit, the plight of the poor trustees has garnered little attention. They are often left to administer poorly drawn instruments long after the settlors have died and memories faded as to why such arrangements were made in the first place. The prospective trustee of a trust designed to render the settlor eligible for Medicaid should pay particular attention to the provisions that kick in *after* the settlor has died. In addition, whether the trust is long or short term, the prospective trustee should be particularly wary of taking on a trust that contains a single illiquid asset, such as a residence. How are the expenses of maintaining the residence, including property taxes, and the trustees' fees to be paid?[582]

---

[577] 42 U.S.C. §§1395-97 *et seq.*; 42 C.F.R. pt. 401–498 *et seq.* (Medicare).

[578] *See* 42 U.S.C. §§1396 *et seq. See also* Dobris, *Medicaid Asset Planning by the Elderly: A Policy View of Expectations, Entitlement and Inheritance*, 24 Real Prop. Prob. & Tr. J. 1, 10 (1989).

[579] *See* 42 U.S.C. §§1396 *et seq. See also* Dobris, *Medicaid Asset Planning by the Elderly: A Policy View of Expectations, Entitlement and Inheritance*, 24 Real Prop. Prob. & Tr. J. 1, 10 (1989).

[580] *See, e.g.,* 42 U.S.C. §1396p (deeming property in certain self-settled trusts to be countable for Medicaid eligibility purposes); 42 U.S.C. §1320a-7b(a) (criminalizing certain transfers made for purposes of achieving Medicaid eligibility). *See generally* Ahern v. Thomas, 248 Conn. 708 (1999) (discussing in part congressional efforts to tighten up Medicaid eligibility).

[581] 42 U.S.C. §1396p(c)(1)(B)(i).

[582] *See, e.g.,* Cavagnaro v. Sapone, 2014 WL 4808828 (Cal. Ct. App. Sept. 29, 2014) (trustee of a subtrust ordered to liquidate entrusted residence due to the fact that the subtrust's expenses were approximately $3,000 per month, while the income generated by the entrusted property was only in the range of $1,800).

While Medicaid planning issues are well beyond the scope of this handbook, several trust-related points are worth making here.

Medicaid planning has two parts: *eligibility*,[583] *i.e.*, means testing,[584] and *recoupment*.[585] A self-settled trust, for example, that contains the settlor's residence may not jeopardize the settlor's eligibility for Medicaid assistance,[586] but the residence may be subject to postmortem recoupment by the state.[587] The two should not be confused.[588]

Eligibility. When the settlor of a trust is also its beneficiary, with some exceptions the subject property will be deemed owned outright by the settlor for purposes of determining the settlor's eligibility for Medicaid.[589] In the case of a *self-settled revocable inter vivos trust*, the settlor-beneficiary is deemed to own outright and free of trust the subject property for Medicaid eligibility determination purposes. Moreover, any transfers of trust property to third parties by the trustee during the lifetime of the settlor-beneficiary are deemed to have been made by the settlor-beneficiary, and thus are subject to the sixty-month look-back period.[590]

Even self-settled *irrevocable and fully discretionary* inter vivos trusts are problematic. The principal of a trust under which the settlor-beneficiary may receive principal distributions only in the discretion of the independent trustee, for example, would still be deemed owned by the settlor-beneficiary, thus rendering the principal countable for Medicaid eligibility determination

---

[583] 3 Scott & Ascher §15.3.

[584] *See generally* 3 Scott & Ascher §15.4.3.

[585] *See* 42 U.S.C. §1396p(b) (mandating postmortem "estate" recovery of three kinds of inter vivos Medicaid payments). Express authority in the trustee of an irrevocable, self-settled inter vivos trust to pay the settlor's "indebtedness" from corpus during the settlor's lifetime would enable the Medicaid authorities to recover postmortem from corpus the Medicaid benefit payments that had been paid to the settlor. *See, e.g.,* Estate of Melby, 841 N.W.2d 867 (Iowa 2014). It is suggested that the corpus also would be so vulnerable postmortem had the corpus by operation of law been reachable inter vivos by the settlor's creditors. For a general example of creditor accessibility by operation of law, see Ware v. Gulda, 331 Mass. 68, 117 N.E.2d 137 (1954).

[586] *See* 42 U.S.C. §1382b(a)(1) (excluding home when assessing Medicaid eligibility). *See* Dobris, *Medicaid Asset Planning by the Elderly: A Policy View of Expectations, Entitlement and Inheritance*, 24 Real Prop. Prob. & Tr. J. 1, 15 (1989).

[587] *See* 42 U.S.C. §§1396p(a)–(b) (providing for recovery against augmented estate of Medicaid recipient). *See also* Dobris, *Medicaid Asset Planning by the Elderly: A Policy View of Expectations, Entitlement and Inheritance*, 24 Real Prop. Prob. & Tr. J. 1, 17 (1989).

[588] *See generally* Bradley E. S. Fogel, *Scylla and Charybdis Attack: Using Trusts for Medicaid Planning and Non-Medicaid Asset Protection*, 35 ACTEC L.J. 45 (2009).

[589] For purposes of determining Medicaid eligibility, a trust established by a beneficiary's guardian or conservator with the beneficiary's property is deemed to be established by the beneficiary. Strand v. Rasmussen, 2002 WL 1558529 (Iowa Sup. Ct. 2002). Contrary interpretation would create an absurd result by permitting guardians and others acting on behalf of an individual to do what the law prevents the actual individual from doing himself or herself. Strand v. Rasmussen, 2002 WL 1558529 (Iowa Sup. Ct. 2002).

[590] 42 U.S.C. §1396p(d)(3)(A).

purposes.[591] Such a trust at one time was inappropriately referred to as a "Medicaid qualifying trust."[592]

A self-settled trust with a *forfeiture provision* is likely to prove ineffective in rendering the settlor Medicaid eligibile.[593] And whether or not a self-settled trust contains a forfeiture provision, there is no value discount, even though the applicant's equitable interest is subject to a condition precedent of the exercise of trustee discretion.[594] As to the ongoing rights of the applicant's general creditors to reach the underlying assets of such self-settled discretionary trusts, the reader is referred to Section 5.3.3.1(a) of this handbook.

A *naked reserved right in the settlor to borrow* from trust principal also could render the subject property countable for purposes of determining the settlor's Medicaid eligibility.[595] The right is naked in that the designated beneficiary in the terms of the trust is someone other than the settlor.

The principal of a *self-settled income-only trust*, however, may well be noncountable for purposes of determining Medicaid eligibility,[596] as well as inaccessible to the settlor's creditors.[597] But upon the death of the settlor, the retention of the equitable life estate may have estate tax, as well as income tax cost basis, consequences that are unrelated to Medicaid.

Definitely noncountable—though fully creditor accessible[598]—is the principal of a *"(d)(4)(A)" or "payback" trust* established by the court or some third party for the benefit of a permanently disabled Medicaid applicant who was under the age of 65, even though the trust was funded *with the applicant's own*

---

[591] *See* 42 U.S.C. §1396p(d)(3)(B)(i) (deeming property in certain self-settled trusts countable for Medicaid eligibility purposes). *See generally* §9.3 of this handbook (the self-settled "special needs"/"supplemental needs" trust). *Cf.* Guerriero v. Comm'r of the Div. of Med. Assistance, 433 Mass. 628, 745 N.E.2d 324 (2001) (holding that the settlor's release as beneficiary of her equitable interest under a discretionary trust successfully rendered the trust principal noncountable for Medicaid eligibility purposes); Lebow v. Comm'r of the Div. of Med. Assistance, 433 Mass. 171, 740 N.E.2d 978, *passim* (2001) (deeming the assets of a trust under which the settlor possesses no beneficial interest but under which the trustee possesses an amendment power to be available to settlor for purposes of determining the settlor's Medicaid eligibility, *i.e.*, deeming the trust to be what has been misnamed a "Medicaid qualifying trust").

[592] *See* 42 U.S.C. §1396a(k) (repealed).

[593] *See, e.g.*, Cohen v. Comm'r of the Div. of Med. Assistance, 423 Mass. 399, 668 N.E.2d 769 (1996). *See generally* §5.3.3.3(b) of this handbook (forfeiture provisions).

[594] Cohen v. Comm'r of the Div. of Med. Assistance, 423 Mass. 399, 668 N.E.2d 769 (1996).

[595] *See, e.g.*, Edholm v. Minnesota Dep't of Human Servs., 2013 WL 2926468 (Minn. Ct. App. July 17, 2013).

[596] *See, e.g.*, Ahern v. Thomas, 248 Conn. 708 (1999) (pre-OBRA '93 trusts). *See* Harry S. Margolis, 2 Elder Law Forms Manual 12.1–12.2 (1999): The passage of the Omnibus Budget Reconciliation Act of 1993 (OBRA '93) (Pub. L. No. 103-66) (codified at 42 U.S.C. §1396p(d)) on August 10, 1993, greatly confused Medicaid trust law. Since then, the Health Care Financing Administration (HCFA) has taken significant steps to clarify confusing language in the federal law.... Through HFCA Transmittal 64 along with correspondence to various elder law practitioners, HFCA has answered some questions raised by OBRA '93. For instance, HFCA seems to read OBRA '93 to permit income-only trusts.

[597] *See generally* §5.3.3.1(a) of this handbook (the self-settled income-only trust and whether principal is accessible to the settlor's creditors).

[598] *See generally* §5.3.3.1(a) of this handbook (creditor access to the settlor-beneficiary's retained equitable interest).

funds and thus was constructively self-settled.[599] Such trusts, and the pooled disability trust as well, are discussed in Section 9.3 of this handbook.

If a Medicaid applicant were to transfer property to the trustee of an irrevocable inter vivos trust, fully discretionary or otherwise, *for the benefit of a third party other than the applicant's spouse*, the property would be rendered noncountable for Medicaid eligibility purposes, the applicant having retained no beneficial interest in the property. The gift in trust, however, would trigger the Medicaid sixty-month look-back period in that the transfer would have been for less than fair market value.[600]

Finally, an anomaly in the self-settled area: For eligibility purposes, an *inter vivos* trust established by the applicant's spouse for the benefit of the applicant is deemed a self-settled trust established by the applicant for the applicant's benefit. A *testamentary* fully discretionary trust established by a deceased spouse for the benefit of the applicant, however, is not.[601] Here, the spousal unity principle does not apply. For purposes of determining Medicaid eligibility, a testamentary trust is treated as if it were created by a third party for the benefit of the applicant.[602] At least one court, however, would deem the applicant a constructive settlor as to that portion of the trust property that would have passed to the applicant had the applicant exercised his or her statutory spousal election rights.[603]

On the other hand, *when neither the Medicaid applicant nor his or her spouse is the settlor of a trust for the benefit of the applicant*, the rule of thumb is that the trust property is countable for Medicaid eligibility purposes only to the extent the property is accessible to the beneficiary-applicant's general creditors.[604] Thus, a fully discretionary trust[605] created by a third party for the applicant's benefit should not render the applicant ineligible for Medicaid.[606] If the terms of the trust grant the trustee discretion to pay income and/or principal to or for the

---

[599] *See* 42 U.S.C. §1396p(d)(4)(A). See also the quoted passage that introduces §9.3 of this handbook (the constructive settlor may not handle the mechanics of establishing the trust).

[600] 42 U.S.C. §1396p(d)(3)(B)(ii).

[601] 42 U.S.C. §1396p(d)(2)(A) (2002). *See, e.g.*, Pohlman v. Nebraska Dep't of Health & Human Servs., 271 Neb. 272, 710 N.W.2d 639 (2006). *But see* Miller v. Kansas Dep't of Soc. & Rehab. Servs., 275 Kan. 349, 350, 64 P.3d 395, 397 (2003) (holding that a widow was the constructive cosettlor of a discretionary testamentary trust established for her benefit by her deceased husband and that she was therefore ineligible for Medicaid; she in lieu of electing to take a statutory share of her husband's probate estate accepted her beneficial interest under the testamentary trust). *See* §5.3.4 of this handbook (rights of beneficiary's spouse and children to the underlying trust property, or at least to the beneficiary's equitable interest).

[602] 42 U.S.C. §1396p(d)(2)(A).

[603] *See* Miller v. State Dep't of Soc. & Rehab. Servs., 274 Kan. 349, 359–361, 64 P.3d 395, 402–404 (2003).

[604] *See* Canter v. Comm'r of Pub. Welfare, 423 Mass. 425 (1996); Dobris, *Medicaid Asset Planning by the Elderly: A Policy View of Expectations, Entitlement and Inheritance*, 24 Real Prop. Prob. & Tr. J. 1 (1989). *See also* 45 Code Fed. Reg. §233.20(a)(3)(ii)(D) (1998). *See generally* §5.3.3.3 of this handbook (creditor accessibility).

[605] *See generally* §3.5.3.2(a) of this handbook (the fully discretionary trust).

[606] *See generally* Bradley E. S. Fogel, *Scylla and Charybdis Attack: Using Trusts for Medicaid Planning and Non-Medicaid Asset Protection*, 35 ACTEC L.J. 45 (2009); §5.3.3.3(a) of this handbook (creditor accessibility and the discretionary trust).

applicant's support, then it is a matter of interpretation as to whether the assets of the trust will render the applicant ineligible for Medicaid.[607] When it comes to taking into account for Medicaid eligibility determination purposes entrusted assets, the law is inclined to ignore contingent equitable interests that have been bestowed on the applicant *by third parties*; that cannot be said, however, for contingent equitable interests that have been retained by the applicant.[608]

Recoupment. As to *postmortem recoupment* for lifetime Medicaid payments, the state essentially has the status of a creditor of the deceased Medicaid recipient.[609] Accordingly, if the recipient had been the settlor and/or beneficiary of a trust during his or her lifetime, the trustee would have a duty to the successor beneficiaries to afford the Medicaid authorities only such access to the trust property as the law requires.

The ElderLaw Report. The trustee wishing to keep abreast of trust-related developments in the Medicaid area would do well to subscribe to *The ElderLaw Report*.[610]

§5.4   Rights of the Beneficiary

A right is a legally enforceable claim against another, that the other shall do a given act or shall not do a given act.— Restatement of Property Section 1.

The beneficiary has, by virtue of the equitable interest in the trust property, rights against the trustee. The trustee must perform certain duties or be held accountable to the wronged beneficiary.

§5.4.1   Certain Incidental Rights of the Beneficiary Against the Trustee

The beneficiary's equitable interest is an interest in property, a property right being a bundle of personal rights associated with something of value.[1] It

---

[607] *See, e.g.*, Eckes v. Richland County Soc. Servs., 621 N.W.2d 851 (2001); Kryzsko v. Ramsey County Soc. Servs., 2000 N.D. 43, 607 N.W.2d 237 (2000); Simpson v. Kansas Dep't of Soc. & Rehab. Servs., 906 P.2d 174 (Kan. Ct. App. 1995). *See generally* §3.5.3.2(a) of this handbook (the support standard for principal invasion); §5.3.3.3(a) of this handbook (creditor access to the assets of a support trust).

[608] *See generally* Bradley E. S. Fogel, *Scylla and Charybdis Attack: Using Trusts for Medicaid Planning and Non-Medicaid Asset Protection*, 35 ACTEC L.J. 45 (2009); Dobris, *Medicaid Asset Planning by the Elderly: A Policy View of Expectations, Entitlement and Inheritance*, 24 Real Prop. Prob. & Tr. J. 1 (1989).

[609] *See* 42 U.S.C. §1396p(a)–(b) (providing for recovery against estate of Medicaid recipient).

[610] Published eleven times a year by Wolters Kluwer.

§5.4   [1] *See* Restatement of Property §§1–5, 6 cmt. a; 2 Scott on Trusts §130.

could be said that the various rights of the beneficiary are subsumed in the general right that fiduciary duties be carried out; however, to the trustee operating on the front lines, such a general description does not offer much practical guidance. Accordingly, this section addresses some of the more important specific rights incidental to that general right.

§5.4.1.1 Right to Information and Confidentiality

[N]o beneficiary (and least of all a discretionary beneficiary) has any entitlement as of right to disclosure of anything which can plausibly be described as a trust document. Especially when there are issues as to personal or commercial confidentiality, the court may have to balance the competing interests of different beneficiaries, the trustees themselves, and third parties.[2]

The trustee's duty to account to the beneficiary. A trustee has a duty to account to the beneficiary.[3] As a practical matter this duty translates into a right in the beneficiary to all information needed to protect the beneficiary's equitable interest.[4] Moreover, this right is not limited to "qualified" or "fairly representative" beneficiaries.[5] The beneficiary has a right to full information about the concerns of the trust at all reasonable times[6] and may examine the trust instrument,[7] the trust property,[8] accounts, vouchers,[9] and usually the opinions of counsel consulted by the trustee in respect to trust affairs.[10] The

---

[2] Judicial Committee of the Privy Council. Vadim Schmidt v. Rosewood Trust Ltd., [2003] UKPC 26 (¶67) (involving an Isle of Man trust).

[3] *See* §6.1.5 of this handbook (trustee's duty to account to the beneficiaries).

[4] UTC §813(a) (available at <http://www.uniformlaws.org/Act.aspx?title=Trust%20Code>) (Duty to Inform and Report). *See also* Restatement (Second) of Trusts §173 cmt. c (suggesting that "[a]lthough the terms of the trust may regulate the amount of information which the trustee must give and the frequency with which it must given, the beneficiary is always entitled to such information as is reasonably necessary to enable him to enforce his rights under the trust or to prevent or redress a breach of trust"); Healy v. Axelrod Constr. Co. Pension Plan & Trust, 787 F. Supp. 838, 844 (N.D. Ill. 1992) (holding that an ERISA fiduciary has a duty to disclose and inform a beneficiary of material facts which affect the interests of the beneficiary and of the fiduciary's knowledge of prejudicial acts by an employer such as failing to contribute to a pension fund); §6.1.5.1 of this handbook (the trustee's duty to provide necessary information to the beneficiaries). *See generally* Reid, Mureiko, & Mikeska, *Privilege and Confidentiality Issues When a Lawyer Represents a Fiduciary*, 30 Real Prop. Prob. & Tr. J. 541 (1996).

[5] Restatement (Third) of Trusts §82 cmt. e.

[6] Restatement (Third) of Trusts §82 cmt. e; Bogert §§961, 861.

[7] Lewin ¶23-07 (England).

[8] Lewin ¶23-04 (England).

[9] Lewin ¶23-04 (England).

[10] *See, e.g.*, Fletcher v. Fletcher, 253 Va. 30, 480 S.E.2d 488 (Va. 1997) (affording beneficiary access to copies of trust instrument and schedule of assets); Taylor v. Nations-Bank Corp., 481 S.E.2d 358 (N.C. App. 1997) (affording beneficiaries access to instruments of trusts that were currently operative but denying them access to documentation which pertained to trusts that the settlor had revoked before his death); Gump v. Wells Fargo Bank, Nat'l Ass'n, 237 Cal. Rptr. 311, 335 (1987) (concluding that when an attorney counsels a trustee to aid him in his duties as administrator of a trust, the trust beneficiaries are ordinarily to be treated as clients of the attorney

Restatement (Third) of Trusts is generally in accord.[11] The trustee has a duty to furnish this information "with reasonable promptness" to the beneficiary and/or the beneficiary's accountant and attorney.[12] "A beneficiary who shows that the trust fund is in danger can obtain, not only an interim injunction, but also an interim order directing a party to provide information about the location of trust property, or property claimed to be trust property, or property into which trust property can be traced."[13]

Right of assignees of equitable interests to information. The general right to information applies as well to an assignee of the beneficial interest.[14] "On petition by the trustee or a beneficiary, however, a court may limit the frequency or extent of such inquiries by one or more of the beneficiaries, weighing the remoteness or substantiality of their interest in the trust against the burdens, intrusiveness, and privacy considerations that may be involved."[15]

Information pertaining to the trustee's interactions with regulators and counsel. That having been said, the beneficiary may not discover the work product of a bank examining agency, *e.g.*, the Comptroller of the Currency, unless the agency waives its bank examination privilege.[16] Also, in England, it has been held that one's right not to answer questions or give information that would incriminate oneself extends to trustees in civil accounting actions brought by beneficiaries.[17] For a discussion of possible limitations on a beneficiary's right to gain access to the trustee's communications with trust counsel, the reader is referred to Section 8.8 of this handbook.

Rights of remaindermen to information. The most important thing that the trustee must keep in mind is that the income beneficiary does not possess this right to information alone: The remaindermen, including in some cases those with contingent interests,[18] also share this right. Unless limited by the

---

and the "joint clients" exception to the attorney-client privilege established by Evidence Code §962 (California) applies). *See generally* 2A Scott on Trusts §173 n.5 and accompanying text; Lewin ¶23-08 (England); §8.8 of this handbook (whom does counsel represent?); Revised Reg. 9 (available on the Internet at <www.gpoaccess.gov/cfr/index.html>) (providing that a national bank administering a collective investment fund shall provide the fund's financial report to beneficiaries of participating trusts entitled to periodic accountings. 12 C.F.R. §9.18(b)(6)(iv) (1997)). Note, however, that the examination reports of bank examination agencies have a "qualified" privilege. *See, e.g.*, Leslie Fay Cos., Inc. Securities Litigation, 152 F.R.D. 42, 44 (S.D.N.Y. 1993); In re Subpoena Served upon Comptroller of Currency, 967 F.2d 630, 633 (D.C. Cir. 1992); First E. Corp. v. Mainwaring, 21 F.3d 465 (D.C. Cir. 1994).

[11] Restatement (Third) of Trusts §82, cmt.

[12] Restatement (Third) of Trusts §82(2).

[13] Lewin ¶38-09. *See generally* §7.2.3.1.5 of this handbook (the preliminary or temporary injunction to preserve trust property) and §7.2.3.1.3 of this handbook (tracing (following property into its product)).

[14] Lewin ¶23-11A (England).

[15] Restatement (Third) of Trusts §82 cmt. e.

[16] Frankford Trust Co. v. Advest, Inc., 1995 WL 491300, at *2 (E.D. Pa.).

[17] Lewin ¶23-14 (England).

[18] UTC §813(a) (available at <http://www.uniformlaws.org/Act.aspx?title=Trust%20Code>) (providing that unless reasonable under the circumstances, a trustee shall promptly respond to a beneficiary's request for information related to the administration of the trust). *See* 2A Scott on Trusts §§172, 173. *But see* Bogert §961 n.23 and accompanying text.

terms of the trust,[19] a trustee must not succumb to the pressure of a beneficiary to withhold information about the trust from other beneficiaries. This situation usually occurs when the current beneficiary is a member of a generation older than the remainder interests and does not want the existence of the trust disclosed. Typically, the current beneficiary is a parent of the beneficiaries who will take the remainder. To be sure, the settlor by express language may limit the rights of the remaindermen to information, but there is a limit to what a court will tolerate when it comes to limiting a beneficiary's right to protect the equitable interest.[20] A trustee who may operate in secret is essentially unaccountable—a condition that is inimical to the concept of the trust.

The qualified beneficiary concept. Under the Uniform Trust Code, any person who has a present or future interest in an irrevocable trust, whether vested or contingent, and any holder of a power of appointment over the trust property is entitled upon request to the trustee's accountings or "reports," as well as any other information reasonably related to the trust's administration.[21] This right may not be waived by the settlor.[22] The Uniform Trust Code further provides that the trustee has an affirmative duty to notify the "qualified beneficiaries" of an irrevocable trust who are 25 years of age or older of the existence of the trust and of their right to request accountings or "reports" and other information related to the administration of the trust.[23] The trustee may not be relieved of this duty by express language in the governing instrument.[24] A "qualified beneficiary" is either a current beneficiary or a presumptive remainderman.[25]

---

[19] *See* Restatement (Second) of Trusts §173 (providing that beneficiaries may examine trust instrument unless its terms provide otherwise). *See, e.g.*, Taylor v. Nationsbank, 481 S.E.2d 358 (N.C. App. 1997), *review granted, then withdrawn*, 493 S.E.2d 57 (1997); Fletcher v. Fletcher, 480 S.E.2d 488 (Va. 1997) (both affording beneficiaries full access to trust instruments).

[20] *Cf.* UTC §105(b)(9) (available at <http://www.uniformlaws.org/Act.aspx?title=Trust%20Code>) (providing that the settlor may not waive the trustee's duty to respond to the request of a beneficiary of an irrevocable trust for trustee's accountings and "reports" and other information reasonably related to the administration of the trust). *Cf. also* UTC §105(b)(8) (providing that the settlor may not waive the trustee's duty to notify the current beneficiaries and the presumptive remaindermen of an irrevocable trust who are 25 years of age or older of the existence of the trust and of their right to request trustee's accountings and "reports" and other information reasonably related to the administration of the trust).

[21] UTC §105(b)(9) (available at <http://www.uniformlaws.org/Act.aspx?title=Trust%20Code>).

[22] UTC §105(b)(9) (available at <http://www.uniformlaws.org/Act.aspx?title=Trust%20Code>).

[23] UTC §105(b)(8) (available at <http://www.uniformlaws.org/Act.aspx?title=Trust%20Code>).

[24] UTC §105(b)(8) (available at <http://www.uniformlaws.org/Act.aspx?title=Trust%20Code>).

[25] UTC §103(12) (available at <http://www.uniformlaws.org/Act.aspx?title=Trust%20Code>).

Under the Uniform Trust Code, in a critical matter such as when equitable property rights, whether vested or contingent, are at stake, notice to the qualified beneficiaries would *not* relieve the trustee of the duty to give adequate notice *to the nonqualified beneficiaries*, either by giving actual notice to them or by giving notice to a duly appointed guardian ad litem charged with representing their interests. The virtual representation exception to the rule applies only if there is no conflict of interest between the qualified and nonqualified beneficiaries. In most cases, however, there will be such a conflict. Here is the Code's commentary on the limitations of the qualified beneficiary concept:

> Due to the difficulty of identifying beneficiaries whose interests are remote and contingent, and because such beneficiaries are not likely to have much interest in the *day-to-day affairs of the trust*, the Uniform Trust Code uses the concept of "qualified beneficiary" . . . to limit the class of beneficiaries to whom certain notices must be given or consents received.[26]

Examples given are trustee resignations, successor trustee appointments, combining trusts, and the like. In other words, notice to the qualified beneficiaries is sufficient only in quasi-ministerial undertakings that generally do not affect one way or another equitable property rights, absent special facts. A trustee who fails to parse the due process limitations of the qualified beneficiary concept does so at his peril. In the words of Justice J.D. Heydon of the High Court of Australia, "the silent waters of equity run deep—often too deep for legislation to obstruct."[27]

Waiver by the settlor via the trust terms of the trustee's duty to keep the beneficiaries informed. Section 105 of the Uniform Trust Code imposes some mandatory duties on the trustee. Two of them "have been extremely controversial and have failed to gain traction in UTC-adopting jurisdictions." Here are the two Section 105 mandatory duties:

- [8]the duty under Section 813(b)(2) and (3) to notify qualified beneficiaries of an irrevocable trust who have attained 25 years of age of the existence of the trust, of the identity of the trustee, and of their right to request trustee's reports.
- [9] the duty under Section 813(a) to respond to the request of a [qualified] beneficiary of an irrevocable trust for trustee's reports and other information reasonably related to the administration of the trust.

As of 2013, only Nebraska, New Mexico, and Florida "have actually and substantially adopted the duty to notify found in section 105(b) (8)."[28] There is less to this mini-revolt, however, than meets the eye. "Waiver by a settlor of the

---

[26] UTC §103, cmt. (available at <http://www.uniformlaws.org/Act.aspx?title=Trust%20 Code>).

[27] The Hon. Justice J.D. Heydon, A.C., *Does statutory reform stultify trust law analysis?*, 6 Tr. Q. Rev., Issue 3, at 28 (2008) [a STEP publication].

[28] John Spencer Treu, *The Mandatory Disclosure Provisions of the Uniform Trust Code: Still Boldly Going Where No Jurisdiction Will Follow*, 82 Miss. L.J. 597, 611 (2013).

trustee's duty to keep the beneficiaries informed of the trust's administration does not otherwise affect the trustee's duties. The trustee remains accountable to the beneficiaries for the trustee's actions."[29] All beneficiaries are owed this general duty, not just the qualified beneficiaries. True, the Code imposes on the trustee a duty to involve the qualified beneficiaries in the "day-to-day affairs of the trust" to a limited degree, such as by keeping them informed of trustee resignations and the like. This is an additional burden imposed on the trustee by the Code. In no way does this imposition, however, derogate from, or otherwise erode, the trustee's critical general duty—a duty that trustees have had since time immemorial—to account to all the beneficiaries, qualified and nonqualified alike, for his or her actions. It remains the case that the beneficiary is entitled to whatever information the beneficiary must have in order to effectively defend and protect his or her equitable property rights, whether those rights be vested or contingent, except, perhaps, (1) while the trust is revocable or (2) if the five-year period of the UTC's Section 1005(c) statute of ultimate repose has run.

Sensitive personal information. On the other hand the beneficiary's right to information, under certain circumstances, may conflict with another beneficiary's right to confidentiality, the latter right being an incident of the trustee's duty of loyalty.[30] The conflict arises not in the context of the trustee's duty to refrain from making unnecessary disclosures of the affairs of the trust to third parties, which is virtually absolute; it arises in the context of balancing the interests of multiple classes of beneficiaries. Is someone with a remote contingent remainder interest, for example, entitled to all the information that the trustee was privy to when a discretionary distribution to a permissible life beneficiary was made? That information might include medical information or intimate details of the beneficiary's marital situation. The answer is "of course not." On the other hand, an abuse of the trustee's discretion could improperly eliminate the remainderman's property interest altogether.[31]

There are no easy answers. The trustee must exercise good judgment in distinguishing the fishing expedition from legitimate efforts to protect one's property. "Appropriate disclosure can usually be provided in general terms that allow reasonable protection for confidential, private, or sensitive information."[32] While the contingent remaindermen ought not to be furnished with all

---

[29] UTC §105, cmt. (available at <http://www.uniformlaws.org/Act.aspx?title=Trust%20 Code>).

[30] *See* §6.2.3 of this handbook (duty of confidentiality); Restatement (Third) of Trusts §78 cmt. i. Reid, Mureiko, & Mikeska, *Privilege and Confidentiality Issues When a Lawyer Represents a Fiduciary*, 30 Real Prop. Prob. & Tr. J. 541, 590 (1996) ("Like an umpire who must call a runner either safe or out, the trustee must make decisions that almost always could be considered adverse to some beneficiary's interest."). For a case illustrating the tension between the trustee's duty to disclose and the beneficiary's right to confidentiality, *see* Fletcher v. Fletcher, 480 S.E.2d 488 (Va. 1997) (the fact that plaintiff was beneficiary of one of three trust shares not grounds for denying him access to entire trust document and its schedule of assets).

[31] *See* Bogert §961 n.4 and accompanying text; 2A Scott on Trusts §173 n.3 and accompanying text.

[32] Restatement (Third) of Trusts §50 cmt. e(1).

the details of the discretionary distribution, they at least are entitled to know that discretion has been exercised; they certainly are entitled to a copy of the governing instrument. When the trustee is unable to reconcile a beneficiary's "need to know" with the "privacy concerns" of the cobeneficiary, then the trustee may have to give some thought to asking the court to fashion some response to the beneficiary's information request that balances the competing considerations of interest protection and confidentiality.[33] Involving the courts, however, should not be undertaken lightly. Besides the attendant time and expense, the very purpose of the endeavor could be compromised by the attendant publicity.

Whether the trustee may disclose to the beneficiary only selected excerpts from the trust instrument. The practice of furnishing certain classes of beneficiaries with excerpts only of a governing instrument is a questionable one,[34] even in the face of express, unambiguous authority to do so in the governing instrument.[35] This Restatement (Third) of Trusts is generally in accord:

> Because one's enforcement of his or her rights as a trust beneficiary normally requires an awareness of the terms of the trust, a beneficiary is ordinarily entitled to obtain a copy of the trust. Sometimes, a request for the needed terms of the trust can be satisfied by copies of relevant provisions or a suitably redacted copy of the trust instrument. In situations involving or likely to involve litigation, however, selected or edited terms of the trust will be unsatisfactory. Accordingly, the easiest and most helpful response to a beneficiary's request (and ordinarily *required* if demanded) is for the trustee simply to send a copy of the instrument when the request is made.[36]

The trust term that purports to partially negate the trustee's duty to inform. Under the Uniform Trust Code, the settlor may negate the trustee's duty to provide a beneficiary upon request with a copy of the trust instrument and the requirement that the trustee provide annual reports to the "qualified beneficiaries."[37] On the other hand, "[t]he furnishing of a copy of the entire trust instrument and preparation of annual reports may be required in a

---

[33] Restatement (Third) of Trusts §82, cmt. f. *See generally* §8.42 of this handbook (the difference between a complaint (petition) for instructions and a complaint (petition) for declaratory judgment).

[34] *See, e.g.*, UTC §813(b)(1) (available at <http://www.uniformlaws.org/Act.aspx?title=Trust%20Code>) (providing that upon request of a beneficiary, the trustee shall promptly provide the beneficiary with a copy of the trust instrument); Taylor v. Nationsbank Corp., 125 N.C. App. 515, 520; 481 S.E.2d 358, 362 (1997) (holding that beneficiaries are entitled to review the entire trust instrument, not just the clauses that grant them their equitable interests).

[35] "Even limitations of these types, however, cannot properly prevent beneficiaries, even underage beneficiaries (or their duly appointed representatives), from requesting and receiving information currently necessary for the protection of their interests. . . ." Restatement (Third) of Trusts §82 cmt. e.

[36] Restatement (Third) of Trusts §82 cmt. e.

[37] UTC §105 cmt. (available at <http://www.uniformlaws.org/Act.aspx?title=Trust%20Code>).

particular case . . . if such information is requested by a beneficiary and is reasonably related to the trust's administration."[38]

Upon death of settlor of revocable trust. Upon the death of the settlor of a revocable trust, the trustee upon request may be obliged to furnish those succeeding to the equitable interests with a copy of the instrument.[39] In one jurisdiction, by statute, this obligation extends upon request to the "heirs" of the deceased settlor.[40]

§5.4.1.2 Right to Prompt and Efficient Administration

Upon acceptance of a trusteeship, the trustee shall administer the trust in good faith.[41] The beneficiary's equitable interest is an interest in property. Thus, to the extent the trustee is dilatory or inefficient in the administration of his trust, he interferes with that property interest and is in breach of trust.[42] Where, for example, a trustee is directed to pay the trust's income to a beneficiary for life or a designated period, in the absence of other direction the beneficiary is entitled to have the net income of the trust property paid to him or her at reasonable intervals, normally monthly or quarter-annually, but at least annually.[43] The beneficiary has a right to expect that his or her checks will arrive on time, that tax returns will be filled out properly and filed when due, that investment decisions will be made and executed in a timely fashion, and that accountings will be submitted at regular intervals.

§5.4.1.3 Right to Income or Possession

The Court of Chancery had an ancient jurisdiction to authorise the application of income and, in more limited circumstances, capital, for the maintenance of a minor even if this was not authorised by the terms of the trust.[44]

---

[38] UTC §105 cmt. (available at <http://www.uniformlaws.org/Act.aspx?title=Trust%20 Code>).

[39] *Cf.* UTC §813(b)(3) (available at <http://www.uniformlaws.org/Act.aspx?title=Trust%20 Code>) (requiring the trustee of a revocable trust within sixty days after acquiring knowledge of the settlor's death to notify the qualified beneficiaries, usually the current beneficiaries and the presumptive remaindermen, of the trust's existence, of the identity of the settlor or settlors, of the right to request a copy of the trust instrument, and of the right to a trustee's report).

[40] Cal. Prob. Code §16061.5 (1999).

[41] UTC §801 (available at <http://www.uniformlaws.org/Act.aspx?title=Trust%20Code>).

[42] *See* Bogert §541 n.60 and accompanying text (the requirement of diligence applies to the uncompensated as well as the compensated trustee). *See also* §8.33 of this handbook (whether the level of an uncompensated trustee's duty of care is less than that of a compensated trustee).

[43] Restatement (Third) of Trusts §49 cmt. c(1).

[44] CD (a minor) v. O, [2004] EWHC Ch 1036 (High Court of Justice (Chancery Division)) (England).

Nowadays, it is default law that the current beneficiary of a trust is entitled to the net trust-accounting income.[45] It is also default law that a trust is income only, *i.e.*, the current beneficiary is not entitled to principal, unless the governing instrument indicates that the settlor intended otherwise.[46] Thus, a trust for the "benefit" of *C*, remainder to D^{47} is normally income only absent additional language suggesting the contrary.[48] Without such additional language, the trustee would have no power to invade principal for the income beneficiary.[49] On the other hand, when the purpose of a trust is to "support" the current beneficiary, there may be an implied authority in the trustee to invade principal, at least some courts have so held.[50]

Income generally need not be paid out as soon as it has been received by the trustee.[51] Keep in mind that the dividends, interest, and rents that are generated by the underlying trust property are paid in the first instance to the trustee, *i.e.*, the trustee has the legal title to the income account as well as to the principal account. The trustee in turn deducts as appropriate trust expenses chargeable to income, and then transfers title to what is left over in the income account to the current beneficiaries. "The trustee, . . . [however] . . . , can properly withhold enough of the gross income to meet not only present but also anticipated expenses that are properly chargeable to income."[52] While it is customary to pay out income quarterly, sometimes monthly, the terms of the trust may provide for pay-outs that are more frequent or less frequent, as well as for pay-outs that are more irregular, or even for no income pay-outs at all.[53] If the trust requires a mandatory distribution of all net income to the beneficiary, the trustee must do so at regular intervals, normally monthly or quarter-annually.[54] The beneficiary has no right to the possession of the trust property unless there is clear indication that the settlor intended otherwise,[55] such as in the case of a personal trust under which the beneficiary is entitled to occupy an entrusted residence.[56]

---

[45] For the mechanics of distributing income to or for the benefit of a beneficiary under an incapacity, *e.g.*, minority, *see* §3.5.3.2(a) of this handbook.

[46] Bogert §812 n.72 and accompanying text; 4 Scott & Ascher §20.1. *See also* §3.5.3.2(a) of this handbook regarding application rather than direct payment of income.

[47] Were there no gift over to another, that is were there no "D," then the current beneficiary's right to principal might be inferred. 3 Scott & Ascher §13.2.7.

[48] 3 Scott & Ascher §13.2.7.

[49] Restatement (Third) of Trusts §49 cmt. d.; 4 Scott & Ascher §20.1 (Impartiality Between Successive Beneficiaries); 3 Scott & Ascher §17.14 (Duty to Keep and Render Accounts).

[50] 3 Scott & Ascher §13.2.7.

[51] *See generally* 3 Scott & Ascher §17.14.

[52] 3 Scott & Ascher §17.14 (noting that "[i]n order to equalize the income from year to year, the trustee may estimate in advance probable expenditures, such as for repairs, and create a reserve to meet them").

[53] *See generally* 3 Scott & Ascher §17.14.

[54] Restatement (Third) of Trusts §49 cmt. c(1).

[55] Bogert §181 n.14 and accompanying text.

[56] 3 Scott & Ascher §13.2.6.

If the beneficiary is entitled to an annuity[57] or unitrust[58] amount *payable only out of income*,[59] and there is a deficiency, it is a question of interpretation of what happens then.[60] With any luck, the matter is addressed completely and unambiguously in the governing instrument.[61] If not, unfortunately there is no satisfactory default law and no generally applicable body of rules of construction governing how to handle the situation,[62] the principal presumably being off limits.[63] The deficiency in one year might be made up from any excess income earned in subsequent years.[64] Or when there is excess trust-accounting income in one year, it might be set aside as a rainy-day fund to make up for any deficiencies in future years.[65]

Ordinarily the right to possession of real estate and chattels belongs to the trustee,[66] but if the settlor intended that the beneficiary have the use of the property in specie, the beneficiary will be entitled to possession.[67]

Presumably, the trustee's general authority to determine allocation of receipts and disbursements between principal and income would encompass a loan of principal to the income beneficiary secured against future income receipts.[68] The trustee, however, should not make an *unsecured* loan of principal to the beneficiary of an income-only trust in the absence of express or implied authority to do so in the governing instrument. If the beneficiary defaults on the unsecured loan, the trustee would have participated in an unauthorized invasion of principal.

Any loan that the trustee does make to the beneficiary should be somehow *secured*. There should be written loan documentation that adequately spells out the rights, duties, and obligations of the parties. To further protect the remaindermen's interest, the trustee may want to take out insurance on the beneficiary's life. The loan is a fixed-income trust investment and should be carried as such on the trustee's schedule of assets.

All this having been said, even a secured loan of principal to the beneficiary of an income-only trust is likely to be a bad idea. The trustee needs a compelling reason for putting the economic interests of the remaindermen at

---

[57] Under a trust annuity provision, the beneficiary is to receive periodically a stated sum.

[58] Under a unitrust provision, the beneficiary is to receive periodically "a sum determined by some mathematical formula, such as a stated percentage of the trust's estate value determined annually." Restatement (Third) of Trusts §49 cmt. e.

[59] *Cf.* §6.2.4.7 of this handbook (the noncharitable unitrust, also known as the noncharitable total return trust).

[60] Restatement (Third) of Trusts §49 cmt. e.

[61] *See generally* 3 Scott & Ascher §13.2.8.

[62] Restatement (Third) of Trusts §49 cmt. e.

[63] *See, however,* §8.17 of this handbook (trust reformation and modification).

[64] Restatement (Third) of Trusts §49 cmt. e.

[65] Restatement (Third) of Trusts §49 cmt. e.

[66] Bogert §181 n.14 and accompanying text.

[67] Bogert §181 n.14 and accompanying text.

[68] *See, e.g.,* Frazier v. Brechler, 28 Fla. L. Weekly D378, 839 So. 2d 761 (2003). *See* §3.5.3.2(g) of this handbook (the trustee's power to resolve questions as to what is income and what is principal).

risk in this way. From the remaindermen's perspective, it is unlikely that such a high maintenance asset can be justified on investment grounds alone. If it cannot, it must fall to someone other than the remaindermen to absorb the initial and ongoing costs of the loan.[69] Again, all this assumes that the terms of the income-only trust do not address the matter of principal loans. If the settlor intends that such loans be made, then the trustee must take his cue from the governing instrument when it comes to such matters.

As mentioned, there is a presumption that a *trust* is income only, that the trustee may make no principal invasions for the current beneficiaries, unless the governing instrument clearly indicates that the settlor intended otherwise.[70] When it comes to the *charitable corporation*,[71] however, there is an opposite presumption. An unrestricted gift to a charitable corporation carries with it the presumption that principal as well as income may be devoted to its charitable purpose.[72]

§5.4.1.4 Right to Enjoin Abuse of Discretion

By express language in the governing instrument, the settlor may provide—in lieu of the common law right to the income from or the use of the trust property—that the beneficiary shall have a right to income or principal or both, in the discretion of the trustee.[73] Usually the settlor provides some standard to guide the trustee in the exercise of discretion ("support" and "education" being some common examples).[74] While the general rule is that a court will not second-guess the trustee's exercise of discretion, a beneficiary does have the right to seek judicial relief should the trustee abuse that discretion.[75]

§5.4.1.5 Right to Remedies for Breaches of Trust

The beneficiary has standing to seek judicial enforcement of the terms of the trust and to have the trust made whole for any loss occasioned by the trustee's breach of trust.[76] This is true whether the beneficiary's interest is vested or contingent; or whether the beneficiary is a life beneficiary or a remainderman; or whether the beneficiary is one of several beneficiaries.[77] Under the Uniform Trust Code, a beneficiary would have standing to seek the

---

[69] *See generally* §6.2.4.4 of this handbook (what expenses are allocated entirely to trust income, entirely to trust principal, and apportioned between income and principal).

[70] *See generally* 4 Scott & Ascher §20.1 (Impartiality Between Successive Beneficiaries).

[71] *See generally* §9.8.1 of this handbook (the charitable corporation).

[72] *See generally* §9.8.1 of this handbook (the charitable corporation).

[73] *See* §3.5.3.2(a) of this handbook (the trustee's power to make discretionary payments of income and principal (the discretionary trust)).

[74] Bogert §§182 (Support or Education), 229 (Support).

[75] 52 Scott on Trusts §128.3.

[76] Bogert §871.

[77] 4 Scott & Ascher §24.19 (Several Beneficiaries).

trustee's removal.[78] The judicial remedies available to the beneficiary, including trustee removal, are covered in Section 7.2.3 of this handbook.[79] Of course, a beneficiary whose interest has extinguished or whose interest is a mere expectancy (not to be confused with a contingent equitable interest) may not maintain a suit against the trustee.[80]

It should be emphasized that under the UTC, any beneficiary, not just the qualified beneficiary, would have standing to request the court to remove a trustee.[81] Any beneficiary also may commence a proceeding to approve or disapprove modification of the trust's terms, even a proceeding that leads to a termination altogether of the trust relationship itself.[82] Not so in Kansas. Under the version of the Code that Kansas has enacted, a nonqualified beneficiary is apparently foreclosed from defending his or her equitable property rights, at least via a trustee-removal or trust-reformation proceeding.[83] "As such, contingent beneficiaries cannot request removal of a trustee or seek modification of a trust."[84] It remains to be seen whether the settlor of a Kansas trust could effectively, via its terms, grant a nonqualified beneficiary standing to commence any proceeding in defense of the beneficiary's equitable property rights, even a trustee-removal or term-reformation proceeding.

§5.4.1.6 Rights to Appoint, Remove, Direct, and Advise Trustee in the Absence of Fault

While a trust is revocable, the trustee may follow a direction of the settlor that is contrary to the terms of the trust.[85]

The trustee is not an agent of the beneficiary. Thus the beneficiary has no inherent common law right to appoint or remove the trustee, nor to direct the trustee or even have the beneficiary's advice considered by the trustee.[86] The beneficiary can bring an action to remove the trustee, but there must be grounds for removal,[87] and the ultimate decision rests with the court.

---

[78] UTC §706(a) (available at <http://www.uniformlaws.org/Act.aspx?title=Trust%20Code>).

[79] *See* §7.2.3 of this handbook (types of equitable relief for breaches of trust). *See also* Bogert §§861–871.

[80] 4 Scott & Ascher §24.19 (Several Beneficiaries).

[81] UTC §706(a) (available at <http://www.uniformlaws.org/Act.aspx?title=Trust%20Code>).

[82] UTC §410(b) (available at <http://www.uniformlaws.org/Act.aspx?title=Trust%20Code>).

[83] *See generally* Kastner v. Intrust Bank, 569 Fed. Appx. 593 (2014).

[84] Kastner v. Intrust Bank, 569 Fed. Appx. 593, 598 (2014).

[85] UTC §808(a) (available at <http://www.uniformlaws.org/Act.aspx?title=Trust%20Code>).

[86] *See* 2 Scott on Trusts §§107.3, 185.

[87] UTC §706(a) (available at <http://www.uniformlaws.org/Act.aspx?title=Trust%20Code>) (granting a beneficiary among others standing to petition the court to remove a trustee). *See generally* Bogert §527 (Grounds for Removal); §7.2.3.6 of this handbook (trustee removal). *See*

The settlor, however, may bestow on the beneficiary by express language in the governing instrument any one or more of these rights as against the trustee. These rights may be exercised even when the trustee is not at fault, if such is the wish of the settlor. The prospective trustee should be aware of all such common law derogations that may lurk in a governing instrument. The existence of certain ones—such as the right to give investment directions—may bear on how the trustee's services should be priced or on the advisability of even taking on the trusteeship at all.[88] Directed trustees have not always been certain of their oversight responsibilities.[89]

The Uniform Trust Code endeavors to correct the situation: If the terms of a trust confer upon a person other than the settlor of a revocable trust power to direct certain actions of the trustee, the trustee shall act in accordance with an exercise of the power unless the attempted exercise is manifestly contrary to the terms of the trust or the trustee knows the attempted exercise would constitute a serious breach of a fiduciary duty that the person holding the power owes to the beneficiaries of the trust.[90] A trustee who is subject to a veto power would have heightened oversight responsibilities. "A trustee who administers a trust subject to a veto power occupies a position akin to that of a cotrustee and is responsible for taking appropriate action if the third party's refusal to consent would result in a serious breach of trust."[91]

The Uniform Trust Code provides that a vacancy in a trusteeship required to be filled shall be filled by a person designated in the terms of the trust to act as successor trustee.[92] When there is no such designation, the vacancy shall be filled by a person appointed by unanimous agreement of the qualified beneficiaries.[93] If all else fails, the vacancy shall be filled by a person appointed by the

---

also UTC §706 (providing that a court has the discretion to remove a trustee not only for serious breaches of trust but also for lack of cooperation among cotrustees; for "persistent failure of the trustee to administer the trust effectively;" because of a "substantial change of circumstances"; or in response to a removal request by all of the qualified beneficiaries).

[88] Bogert §122.

[89] *See* §6.1.4 of this handbook (duty to give personal attention (not to delegate)). *See also* UTC §808(b) (available at <http://www.uniformlaws.org/Act.aspx?title=Trust%20Code>) (providing that if the terms of a trust confer upon a person other than the settlor of a revocable trust power to direct certain actions of the trustee, the trustee shall act in accordance with an exercise of the power unless the attempted exercise is manifestly contrary to the terms of the trust or the trustee knows the attempted exercise would constitute a serious breach of a fiduciary duty that the person holding the power owes to the beneficiaries of the trust).

[90] UTC §808(b) (available at <http://www.uniformlaws.org/Act.aspx?title=Trust%20Code>).

[91] UTC §808 cmt. (available at <http://www.uniformlaws.org/Act.aspx?title=Trust%20Code>).

[92] UTC §704(c)(1) (available at <http://www.uniformlaws.org/Act.aspx?title=Trust%20Code>).

[93] UTC §704(c)(2) (available at <http://www.uniformlaws.org/Act.aspx?title=Trust%20Code>). Qualified beneficiaries are essentially the current beneficiaries and the presumptive remaindermen. UTC §103(12) (defining the term *qualified beneficiary*).

court.[94] Of course, the court always possesses equitable powers to appoint an additional trustee or special fiduciary "whenever the court considers the appointment necessary for the administration of the trust."[95]

It goes without saying that a beneficiary who holds a power of appointment has constructive authority to remove the trustee. A living beneficiary who possesses a right of revocation or other form of general inter vivos power of appointment unilaterally may remove the trustee.[96] So also may the beneficiary who possesses a general testamentary power of appointment, but not during the beneficiary's lifetime. This is because a will speaks at death.[97] Inherent in a general power of appointment, *e.g.*, the right to appoint property outright and free of trust to oneself or one's estate, is the lesser right to remove the trustee. A beneficiary may effectively terminate a trustee's tenure through the exercise of a limited/special power of appointment as well, either by an appointment of the property to another trustee in further trust if such an appointment is permitted by case law, statute, or the governing instrument, or by an appointment outright and free of trust to a third-party permissible appointee.

§5.4.1.7 Right to Conveyance

The remainderman has a right to conveyance of the trust property within a reasonable time after the trust has terminated, assuming title has not already vested in the remainderman by operation of law.[98]

Are there any circumstances under which a remainderman is entitled to a conveyance before the end of a trust's natural life? Assume the following transfer in trust: *A* to *B* for *C* for ten years, remainder to *C;* the trust is inter vivos; no other person has a beneficial interest; and *C* is of full age and legal capacity. Does *C* have a right to the property outright and free of trust before the expiration of the ten-year period? The American Rule is that if the trust has a purpose (*e.g.*, if it is a spendthrift or discretionary trust), *C* would have no such right.[99] (The English Rule is to the contrary.[100]) If the trust has no purpose, or its purpose had been accomplished, *C* would have a right to conveyance before the period's expiration.[101]

---

[94] UTC §704(c)(3) (available at <http://www.uniformlaws.org/Act.aspx?title=Trust%20Code>).

[95] UTC §704(d) (available at <http://www.uniformlaws.org/Act.aspx?title=Trust%20Code>).

[96] UTC §603(d) (available at <http://www.uniformlaws.org/Act.aspx?title=Trust%20Code>).

[97] UTC §602 cmt. (available at <http://www.uniformlaws.org/Act.aspx?title=Trust%20Code>).

[98] Restatement (Second) of Trusts §345 cmt. e. *See generally* §3.5.1 of this handbook (nature and extent of the trustee's estate) and §8.15.1 of this handbook (statute of uses).

[99] *See* Claflin v. Claflin, 149 Mass. 19, 20 N.E. 454 (1889); Restatement (Second) of Trusts §337. *See generally* §8.15.7 of this handbook (the *Claflin* doctrine (material purpose doctrine)).

[100] Restatement (Second) of Trusts §337, reporter's notes.

[101] Restatement (Second) of Trusts §337, reporter's notes.

As a practical matter, *C* may be able to persuade the trustee to convey in the face of an unfulfilled trust purpose. However, some have suggested that the settlor ought to have a cause of action against the trustee for interfering with the settlor's expectation interest in having the terms of the trust carried out.[102] In any case, while *C* may succeed in obtaining the property, there is no enforceable right to a premature conveyance in the face of an unfulfilled purpose as would be the case under the more liberal English Rule.[103] Therefore, if the aid of the court is sought in accelerating *C*'s remainder interest, it will not be given.[104]

In any event, nothing less than the whole of an absolute estate will entitle the beneficiary to a conveyance, even under the English Rule.[105] Therefore, if there are contingent or unascertained interests, there can be no agreement to convey, and a beneficiary who has a life estate, with power of disposition by a will, has not such an absolute estate as entitles him to a conveyance. Thus, the settlor can prevent the beneficiary's call for a conveyance even under the English Rule by the simple expedient of making a small provision for some person unascertained.[106]

Under a traditional "net income only to *C* for life, remainder to *D*"-type of trust, may the trustee make a loan of *trust principal* to the remainderman (*D*) before the trust has terminated even if the interest rate is reasonable? Probably not, unless there is express authority to do so in the governing instrument or all parties who have, or could have, income and remainder interests (or their personal representatives) give informed consent. The effect of such a loan is to constructively delegate to the remainderman aspects of the trust's administration.[107] Moreover, by making such loans the trustee is asking for trouble. If the remainderman is slow to make the interest payments or pay back the principal, the equitable interests of the income beneficiaries (*C*) are compromised. If the remainderman defaults, the trust is prematurely terminated to the detriment of the income beneficiaries and in contravention of the intentions of the settlor. If something should go wrong, it is guaranteed that the income beneficiaries will call the trustee to account for having made the loan. Why could the remainderman not obtain a bank loan? In the absence of consent by all parties or express authority in the governing instrument, the prudent trustee usually will want authority of the court before making pretermination loans of trust assets to remaindermen.

May the trustee, without express authority in the governing instrument, make a pretermination loan *of his own funds* to the remainderman and secure the

---

[102] *See* §4.1.2 of this handbook (the settlor's reversionary or expectation property interest). *But see* Bogert §1006 n.13 and accompanying text (premature terminations upheld when the trustee and beneficiary joined in a transfer of trust property outright and free of trust back to the settlor). *See also* Bogert §1008 (implying that settlor has standing to litigate issues of premature termination).

[103] Bogert, Trusts and Trustees §1008.

[104] *See* Bogert §1008.

[105] *See* Bogert §1007 n.7 and accompanying text.

[106] *See* Bogert §1007 n.9 and accompanying text.

[107] *See generally* §6.1.4 of this handbook (the trustee's duty not to delegate critical fiduciary functions).

loan with trust assets? If the trust is a spendthrift trust, the answer is no.[108] If the remainderman's equitable interest is nonvested, the value of the security is problematic. If the trust is not a spendthrift trust and the remainderman equitable interest is vested, then the concerns relating to constructive premature termination expressed in the prior paragraph would still apply to a loan of the trustee's own funds that is secured by trust assets. And one cannot forget that there are loyalty issues attendant when such loans are secured by trust assets.[109] There is probably no impediment, however, to a trustee making a loan at interest to the remaindermen of his own funds, either unsecured or secured by nontrust assets, provided the transaction is fair and untainted by undue influence.[110]

§5.4.1.8 Right and Standing of Beneficiary to Proceed in Stead of Trustee Against Those with Whom the Trustee Has Contracted, Against Tortfeasors, and Against the Trustee's Agents, *i.e.*, Against Third Parties

In the old law of uses, it was held that where the feoffee to uses was disseised by a third person the cestui que use could not maintain a suit in equity against the third person even though he had notice of the use.[111]

In the present situation, it is clear from the complaint the beneficiary could prove facts showing she had standing to bring suit against the third parties for the improper distribution of stock. She could show, at the very least, the trustee improperly neglected to bring action against the appellees when he waited over ten years after the improper transfer and still did not bring suit.[112]

Standing and procedure. The trustee is the one primarily responsible for seeing to it that harm done to the trust by a third party such as an investment advisor is remedied.[113] This is an affirmative common law duty. If the trustee fails to take suitable action, then the beneficiary may step into the shoes of the

[108] 4 Scott & Ascher §25.1 (Liability of Beneficiary to Trustee Individually).

[109] *See generally* §6.1.3.5 of this handbook (acquisition by trustee of the equitable Interest, as well as the trustee's general duty of loyalty to the beneficiary in nontrust matters); 4 Scott & Ascher §25.1 (Liability of Beneficiary to Trustee Individually).

[110] *See generally* §6.1.4 of this handbook (trustee's duty not to delegate critical fiduciary functions) and §8.32 of this handbook (whether the trustee can escape liability for making a mistake of law if he acted in good faith on advice of counsel).

[111] 4 Scott on Trusts §282 (citing to Chudleigh's Case, 1 Rep. 114, 139b (1589–1595). *See generally* §8.15.1 of this handbook (statute of uses).

[112] Anderson v. Dean Witter Reynolds, Inc., 841 P.2d 742, 745 (Utah 1992) (citing with approval Restatement (Second) of Trusts §282, which in part provides that if a trustee improperly refuses or neglects to bring an action against a third person, the beneficiary can maintain a suit in equity against the third person).

[113] *See generally* 5 Scott & Ascher §28.1.

trustee and deal directly with the third party.[114] This could include bringing an equitable derivative suit on behalf of the trust against the third party if all else fails.[115] To memorialize the trustee's inaction, the beneficiary will want to make a formal written demand upon the trustee before taking matters into his or her own hands. The court may award the beneficiary litigation costs if the litigation is deemed beneficial to the trust.[116] Any common law causes of action would be based on one or more of the following: breach of contract (contract); tortious conduct (tort); and breach of fiduciary duty (agency).[117] Analogous derivative doctrine prevails in the wills context: "Although court-appointed fiduciary managers in probate proceedings have broad statutory authority to bring all actions necessary to collect assets, preserve and protect the estate, . . . nothing in that body of law expressly prohibits a court from granting a beneficiary leave to bring an action on behalf of the estate when there are special circumstances that take the case out of the general rule."[118]

The Restatement (Third) of Trusts provides that a trust beneficiary may maintain a proceeding related to the trust or its property against a third party only if the beneficiary is in possession, or entitled to immediate distribution, of the trust property involved; *or* if the trustee is "unable, unavailable, unsuitable or improperly failing to protect the beneficiary's interest."[119] There is an admonition that accompanies the authorization: "It bears repeating that the trustee, and not a beneficiary, is ordinarily the only proper person to bring (and to decide whether to bring) an action on behalf of the trust against a third party."[120]

The Uniform Probate Code would grant the beneficiary standing to petition the court directly, *i.e.*, without having first made a demand upon the trustee, to "review the propriety of employment of any person by a trustee including any attorney, auditor, investment advisor or other specialized agent or assistant, and the reasonableness of the compensation of any person so employed. . . ."[121]

In the case of a trusteed mutual fund, before an investor-beneficiary may bring a derivative suit on behalf of the fund against, say, the third-party fund sponsor, it is likely that the investor-beneficiary must first make a formal

---

[114] 4 Scott on Trusts §§282, 282.1; Restatement (Second) of Trusts §§281–282; 5 Scott & Ascher §28.2.1.

[115] *See* UTC §1004 cmt. (available at <http://www.uniformlaws.org/Act.aspx?title=Trust%20Code>); Lewin ¶43-05 (England); 5 Scott & Ascher §28.2.1 (U.S.).

[116] 3 Scott on Trusts §188.4; UTC §1004 cmt. (available at <http://www.uniformlaws.org/Act.aspx?title=Trust%20Code>).

[117] *See generally* 5 Scott & Ascher §28.2.1 (When the Trustee Fails to Sue).

[118] Estate of Bleeker v. Arvest Trust Co., 2007 OK 68, 168 P.3d 774 (2007).

[119] Restatement (Third) of Trusts §107(2).

[120] Restatement (Third) of Trusts §107 cmt. c(2).

[121] UPC §7-205. "Any person who has received excessive compensation from a trust may be ordered to make appropriate refunds." UPC §7-205.

demand upon the trustees to take suitable action.[122] This is an example of the statutory law of corporations encroaching back upon the law of trusts. "Likewise, when property is conveyed by deed of trust to . . . [an indenture trustee] . . . to secure an issue of bonds, and the trustee, upon default, refuses to bring a proceeding for foreclosure, one or more of the bondholders can maintain a suit for foreclosure, joining the trustee and obligor as defendants."[123]

For more on the inbound external liabilities of third parties to the trustee or the beneficiary, or both, see Section 3.6 of this handbook.

Contract and tort. For a successful breach of contract action to lie against the third party, the beneficiary would have to prove that the trustee had entered into a contract for goods or services with the third party on behalf of the trust, that the third party had breached the contract, and that the beneficiary's equitable interest had been harmed as a result thereof.

For a successful tort action to lie, the beneficiary would have to prove that the third party had committed some tort that had adversely affected in some way the beneficiary's equitable interests, *e.g.*, trespassing on trust land.[124] Should the beneficiary successfully prove the third party's knowing participation in a breach of trust, many of the remedies that are available as against the trustee would be available as well as against the third party (in fact, their liability would be joint and several).[125] "Thus, if the trustee directs an agent to sell trust property, which the agent knows the trustee is not authorized to sell, and he does sell it, he is liable for participation in the breach of trust."[126] If the agent takes title to the property, he becomes an involuntary trustee, technically a constructive trustee, of the property.[127]

Agency. If a third party is acting as an agent of the trustee for purposes of assisting the trustee in carrying out his fiduciary responsibilities, there are three possibilities, assuming the third party has *not* been knowingly facilitating and participating in any breaches of trust by the trustee: The third party could have fiduciary duties that ran to the trustee alone, to the beneficiary alone, or to both.[128]

---

[122] ING Principal Protection Funds Derivative Litigation, 369 F. Supp. 2d 163, 170–171 (2005) (suggesting that the prederivative litigation universal demand requirement is applicable to business trusts such as trusteed mutual funds, as well as to corporations).

[123] 5 Scott & Ascher §28.2.1. *See generally* §9.31 of this handbook (corporate trusts; trusts to secure creditors; the trust indenture act of 1939; protecting bondholders).

[124] Scott on Trusts §§280.2, 280.3.

[125] Bogert §868. *See also* 5 Scott & Ascher §28.2.

[126] Restatement (Second) of Trusts §326 cmt. a.

[127] Scott on Trusts §288; 5 Scott & Ascher §28.2. *See generally* §3.3 of this handbook (involuntary trustees) (discussing the constructive trust).

[128] With respect to the trustee's legal counsel, *see* Chinello v. Nixon, Hargrave, Devans & Doyle, 788 N.Y.S.2d 750 (2005) (confirming that in New York, absent fraud, collusion, malicious acts, or other special circumstances, counsel to the trustee is not liable to third parties not in privity, *e.g.*, the beneficiaries of the trust, for harm caused by counsel's professional negligence).

If the agent has fiduciary duties that ran to the beneficiary alone, an unlikely if not illogical scenario, the beneficiary would have standing to bring an action against the third party for any breach of fiduciary duty to the beneficiary.

If the agent has fiduciary duties that ran to the trustee alone, the beneficiary would have no standing to go against the agent. Some courts, for example, have held that trust counsel is such an agent.[129] Other courts have granted beneficiaries standing, holding that trust counsel has some duties that run to the beneficiary as well as to the trustee.[130]

If the agent has fiduciary duties that run to both the trustee and the beneficiary, presumably each would have standing to sue the agent. What if a trust officer, an agent of his or her corporate employer, knowingly causes the employer to commit a breach of trust? Would the beneficiary, as well as the trustee-employer, have standing to sue the trust officer and could the trust officer be found personally liable? The answer is likely to be yes on both counts.[131] "The question is of great importance to the beneficiaries if the bank is insolvent."[132] The Uniform Prudent Investor Act provides that an agent in performing a delegated function owes a duty *to the trust* to exercise reasonable care to comply with the terms of the delegation.[133] One can reasonably assume that one consequence of an agent having duties that run *to the trust* is that the trustee and the beneficiary each would have standing to sue the agent.

§5.4.1.9   Right and Standing of Beneficiary to Petition Court for Instructions or Declaratory Judgment

The law affords the beneficiary a means of heading off or mitigating harm to the trust occasioned by trustee mistake,[134] *e.g.*, the misdelivery of trust property. When there is reasonable doubt as to the powers and duties of the trustee, the beneficiary may petition the court for instructions and/or a declaratory judgment.[135] Trustees, of course, also have authority to bring such petitions.[136] For a discussion of the differences between a complaint for instructions and a complaint for declaratory judgment, see Section 8.42 of this handbook.

---

[129] *See generally* §8.8 of this handbook (whom trust counsel represents); 4 Scott on Trusts §326.4.

[130] *See generally* §8.8 of this handbook (whom trust counsel represents); 4 Scott on Trusts §326.4.

[131] *See generally* §7.2.9 of this handbook (personal liability of the trustee's agents and other third parties to the beneficiary); 4 Scott on Trusts §326.3.

[132] Scott on Trusts §326.3 at 303.

[133] Uniform Prudent Investor Act §9(b).

[134] Restatement (Third) of Trusts §71 cmt. a.

[135] Restatement (Third) of Trusts §71; 3 Scott & Ascher §16.8.

[136] *See* Chapter 1 of this handbook.

§5.4.2 Rights of the Beneficiary as Against Transferees of the Underlying Property, Including BFPs

A person other than a beneficiary who in good faith . . . and for value deals with a trustee without knowledge that the trustee is exceeding or improperly exercising the trustee's powers is protected from liability as if the trustee properly exercised the power.[137]

The principles that apply to the choice of remedies against a trustee who has committed a breach of trust apply as well in the case of a person to whom the trustee has transferred property in breach of trust, when the transferee had notice of the breach.[138]

A trustee, being the holder of legal title to the trust property, has the inherent power to transfer the title to a BFP,[139] "and thereby cut off the beneficiaries' interests in the trust property, *even if, in so doing, the trustee also commits a breach of trust.*"[140] The trustee holds the legal title for the benefit of the beneficiary; each person who receives the legal title from the trustee in breach of trust also holds the property in trust, unless the transferee has a special and valid equitable claim of his own.[141] The law has concluded that the transferee has such an equitable claim when title is acquired in a wholly innocent manner in exchange for full value,[142] in other words, when the transferee is a BFP. Whenever a person acquires the title under these circumstances, the equity court declines to interfere.[143] This is the doctrine of bona fide purchase, a subject that is covered generally in Section 8.15.63 of this handbook. It is substantially a rule of inaction:[144]

Undoubtedly, the reason why the chancellors refused to give relief to a cestuis que use against a bona fide purchaser derived from considerations of conscience. Equity refused to give a remedy unless there was an affirmative reason in point of justice for giving it. The cestui que use and the bona fide purchaser were equally innocent, and the chancellor refused to interpose.[145]

---

[137] UTC §1012(a) (available at <http://www.uniformlaws.org/Act.aspx?title=Trust%20Code>).

[138] 5 Scott & Ascher §29.1.8.7.

[139] *See generally* §8.15.63 of this handbook (doctrine of bona fide purchase).

[140] 3 Scott & Ascher §18.1. There should be no misunderstanding. The sales proceeds belong to the trust, not to the trustee personally. The property that was transferred out of the trust was merely replaced by different property of equal value. *See also* 5 Scott & Ascher §29.1.1.

[141] *See* 4 Scott on Trusts §288; 5 Scott & Ascher §29.1.1.

[142] *See* 4 Scott on Trusts §284; 5 Scott & Ascher §29.1.1.

[143] *See* 4 Scott on Trusts §284; 5 Scott & Ascher §29.1.1.

[144] *See* 4 Scott on Trusts §284; 5 Scott & Ascher §29.1.1.

[145] 3 Scott & Ascher §13.1. *See also* 5 Scott & Ascher §29.1.1. *See generally* §8.12 of this handbook (containing a catalog of equity maxims, including "Where there is equal equity, the law shall prevail"); Chapter 1 of this handbook (containing the names of all the Lord Chancellors from 1066 to the present). The "use" is discussed in §8.15.1 of this handbook.

Thus, if the trustee transfers trust property in breach of trust to a BFP, the purchaser acquires the title free of trust.[146] Moreover, nowadays a BFP would have no duty to the trust beneficiaries to see to it that the trustee properly applies the purchase price.[147] The trust beneficiaries, of course, would still have recourse against the trustee personally for what the BFP paid for the entrusted property. In many jurisdictions the rule has been codified.[148] For the transferee to be protected, each of the rule's three conditions must be satisfied: actual acquisition of title,[149] the payment of value,[150] and a lack of notice.[151] For a comparison of the holder in due course, a creature of law, with the BFP, a creature of equity, the reader is referred to Sections 8.15.68 of this handbook and 8.3.6 of this handbook.

A transferee with actual or constructive knowledge of the trust also qualifies as a BFP if the transferee pays value and takes title in good-faith

---

[146] 4 Scott on Trusts §284. *See also* 5 Scott & Ascher §29.1.1. *See generally* §8.21 of this handbook (duty of third parties to investigate whether trustee has power to act or is properly exercising the power) and §8.15.63 of this handbook (doctrine of bona fide purchase). Were the trustee or a prior transferee-with-notice to reacquire the subject property from a BFP, then the property would be held subject to the trust. If the trustee reacquired the property as trustee of a new trust with different beneficiaries, however, then the remedy of specific reparation might well not be an option. *See generally* 5 Scott & Ascher §29.6.5 (Retransfer by a Bona Fide Purchaser on a New Trust). *See generally* §7.2.3.9 of this handbook (the equitable relief of specific reparation). Also, were the trustee to reacquire the trust property by fraud from a BFP, he would hold the subject property as a constructive trustee for the benefit of the BFP, the equitable rights of the beneficiaries of the originating trust having been cut off back when the BFP took title to the subject property. *See* 5 Scott & Ascher §29.6.5. For a detailed discussion of how the law deals with the clash of equities that can occur when "one person wrongfully transfers to a bona fide purchaser property that belongs to another person and thereafter wrongfully reacquires the property or acquires other property from the purchaser and with the property so acquired makes restitution to the original victim," *see* 5 Scott & Ascher §29.7 (Transfer in Restitution for a Wrong).

[147] *See generally* §8.15.69 of this handbook (third party liability for trustee's misapplication of payments to trustee).

[148] *See* 4 Scott on Trusts §288 n.7 (Listing the State BFP Statutes).

[149] *See generally* 5 Scott & Ascher §29.4 (Transfer of Title to Trust Property). Title also will be deemed to have passed to a purchaser when only the accomplishment of third party ministerial acts stands in the way of a consummation of the transfer of title. Assume, for example, that a trustee in breach of trust delivers stock certificates to a good faith purchaser for value and there is a delay in reflecting the transfer on the books of the issuing corporation. The transferee would be a BFP, even if the transferee were to receive notice of the breach before the transfer had actually been formalized. *See* 5 Scott & Ascher §29.4.3 (Notice Before Transfer but After Trustee Has Completed Breach of Trust).

[150] The BFP value requirement is covered in §8.15.63 of this handbook (doctrine of bona fide purchase; the BFP).

[151] *See generally* §8.3.2 of this handbook (the doctrine of bona fide purchase and its notice requirement); 5 Scott & Ascher §29.1.5 (Transferee with Notice); 4 Scott on Trusts §288 n.6 (containing a collection of cases involving transferees who were deemed to have taken with notice). *See also* Bogert §§891 (Notice), 894 (Facts Putting on Inquiry), 885 (Title), 887 (Value). For a discussion of the bona fide purchase value and passage-of-title requirements, *see* §8.15.63 of this handbook (doctrine of bona fide purchase; the BFP).

reliance on representations within the four corners of the trust instrument that the trustee has the power to convey.[152]

If the trustee wrongfully contracts to sell the trust property to an innocent purchaser, the beneficiary's right remains unclouded if the purchaser then learns of the trust relationship before the passage of title,[153] unless the beneficiary by word or conduct induced the purchaser to pay value.[154] "A court will not compel a trustee to complete a breach of trust."[155]

For more on the bona fide purchase lack-of-notice requirement, the reader is referred to Section 8.3.2 of this handbook. For a discussion the lack-of-notice requirement when the subject property is a negotiable instrument, the reader is referred to Section 8.3.6 of this handbook.[156]

One who in breach of trust is transferred trust property by *gift* must disgorge it, even when one is ignorant of the trust's existence.[157] Otherwise, the donee would be unjustly enriched.[158] A "donee" of entrusted property who pays value after receiving notice that the transfer was in breach of trust is still not a BFP.[159] "A transferee of trust property who is not a bona fide purchaser before receiving notice cannot become a bona fide purchaser after receiving notice."[160]

The innocent donee who has restored the property to the trust is under no further duty.[161] So too is the donee who subsequently learns that the transfer was in breach of trust.[162] The donee who has sold it need only restore the proceeds.[163] Should the donee, while still ignorant of the trust, in turn give it away to someone else, then the donee (now a donor) is not liable.[164] "The principle of public policy that requires a trustee or a transferee with notice from

---

[152] Bogert §897 (Duty to Inquire Resulting From Terms of Documents). *See generally* §8.21 of this handbook (duty of third parties to investigate whether trustee has power to act or is properly exercising the power). The UTC would authorize the trustee to furnish third parties a certification of trust in lieu of the trust instrument. UTC §1013 (available at <http://www.uniformlaws.org/Act.aspx?title=Trust%20Code>). *See generally* §9.6 of this handbook (trusts that resemble corporations or agencies) (discussing in part the "autonomous" power of the trustee of a nominee trust to transfer the underlying property).

[153] *See* 5 Scott & Ascher §§29.4.1 (Contract to Transfer Trust Property), 29.4.2 (Transfer After Notice); Restatement (Second) of Trusts §§310, 311.

[154] Complicit beneficiaries would be "estopped" or barred under equitable principles from successfully "setting up their equitable interest as against the purchaser." *See* 5 Scott & Ascher §29.5 (Estoppel of Beneficiaries). *See also* 5 Scott & Ascher §§29.5.1 (Rights of Creditors When Beneficiaries Are Estopped), 29.5.2 (Rights of Equitable Claimants When Beneficiaries Are Estopped), 29.5.3 (Rights of Transferee When Beneficiaries Consent to Transfer).

[155] 5 Scott & Ascher §29.1.2. *See generally* §8.15.63 of this handbook (doctrine of bona fide purchase).

[156] *See also* §8.15.68 of this handbook (the holder in due course in the trust context).

[157] 5 Scott & Ascher §§29.1.6 (Donee), 29.1.9 (Extent of Liability of Donee); Restatement (Second) of Trusts §289.

[158] 5 Scott & Ascher §29.1.9 (Extent of Liability of Donee)

[159] 5 Scott & Ascher §29.3.4 (Payment of Value After Notice).

[160] 5 Scott & Ascher §29.3.4.

[161] *See* 4 Scott on Trusts §292; 5 Scott & Ascher §29.1.9 (Extent of Liability of Donee).

[162] 5 Scott & Ascher §29.1.8.2.

[163] 5 Scott & Ascher §29.1.9 (Extent of Liability of Donee)

[164] 4 Scott on Trusts §292.1; 5 Scott & Ascher §29.1.9.1 (Extent of Liability of Donee).

a trustee who incurs a loss to make good the loss and to surrender any profit does not apply to an innocent donee."[165] If an innocent donee sells the property to a BFP and then reacquires the property from a BFP, "the donee is under no greater liability, except that if the donee elects to keep the proceeds, the beneficiaries can compel the donee either to pay the value of the property at the time the donee originally held it or to surrender the property itself."[166]

If, on the other hand, the innocent donee sells or gives away the property after acquiring knowledge of the trust, liability attaches.[167] The innocent donee who has consumed the trust property may be liable if these expenditures qualify as "ordinary";[168] if they are "extraordinary," and if the donee has changed position detrimentally in reasonable reliance upon the transfer, then the donee may not be liable.[169]

If trust property is used in breach of trust to improve property belonging to a third party who was on notice of the breach, the third party is "liable for the value of the trust property used to improve his or her property, increased or decreased to reflect the results of a prudent course of investment, and the beneficiaries are entitled to an equitable lien on the property for this amount."[170] The third party, however, is not a constructive trustee of his own property.[171] Nor is the innocent "donee" of trust property transferred in breach of trust: " . . . [T]he beneficiaries are not entitled to enforce a constructive trust of the property benefited, since the property is not the product of the trust funds, but the owner would be unjustly enriched if not required to pay for the benefit conferred."[172] Thus, "[i]f the amount spent improving the property exceeds the amount of the benefit conferred, the beneficiaries are not entitled to a lien for the full amount expended, but only to the extent of the benefit conferred."[173]

A third party who borrows trust funds knowing the loan to be a breach of trust holds the funds as a constructive trustee.[174] A third party who actually pays for and receives title and possession of an item of trust property knowing that the transfer is in violation of the beneficiary's prior rights also holds the item in

---

[165] 5 Scott & Ascher §29.1.9 (Extent of Liability of Donee)

[166] 5 Scott & Ascher §29.6.4 (Retransfer by Bona Fide Purchaser to Donee).

[167] 4 Scott on Trusts §292.3; 5 Scott & Ascher §29.1.9.3 (Extent of Liability of Donee).

[168] Restatement (Second) of Trusts §292 cmt. j; 5 Scott & Ascher §29.1.9.2 (Extent of Liability of Donee).

[169] Restatement (Second) of Trusts §292 cmt. j; 5 Scott & Ascher §29.1.9.2 (Extent of Liability of Donee).

[170] 5 Scott & Ascher §29.1.8.9 (When Trust Funds Are Used to Improve Property of Another).

[171] 5 Scott & Ascher §29.1.8.9.

[172] 5 Scott & Ascher §29.1.9.5 (When Trust Funds Are Used to Improve Property of Another).

[173] 5 Scott & Ascher §29.1.9.5 (When Trust Funds Are Used to Improve Property of Another).

[174] 5 Scott & Ascher §29.1.8.1.

constructive trust for the beneficiary,[175] unless the beneficiary elects to affirm the transaction.[176] So too is the case if the third party ought to have known of the outstanding beneficial interest.[177] The third party, however, is entitled to be reimbursed from the trust estate for what was paid for the item, provided that the trustee has not misappropriated the payment.[178] In other words, the payment must have been added to the trust estate and held for the benefit of the beneficiary, as provided by the trust's terms.[179]

The third party also may be entitled to reimbursement for any reasonable or necessary expenditures that the third party made in order to maintain or improve the item prior to its return to the trust estate, provided the third party had had no actual knowledge that there had been a breach of trust when the expenditures were made, and thus was not an "officious intermeddler."[180] On the other hand, even the officious intermeddler may be entitled to reimbursement for expenditures made in satisfaction of any obligations that run with the property, *e.g.*, real estate taxes.[181]

What if the trustee in breach of trust transfers trust funds to a third party incident to an illegal transaction, *e.g.*, to satisfy a personal illegal gambling debt? Can the third party ever be a BFP? Yes. If the third party pays full value, is unaware of the trust, and is unaware "of the circumstances that make the transaction illegal."[182] Otherwise, the third party takes the property subject to the trust.[183] An innocent transferee who has paid no value would be liable at least to the extent that there has been unjust enrichment at the expense of the trust estate.[184] A third party who takes with actual or constructive notice of the

---

[175] 5 Scott & Ascher §29.1.8.1 (Restitution of Trust Property); 5 Scott on Trusts §462.4; 5 Scott & Ascher §28.2. *See generally* §8.15.63 of this handbook (doctrine of bona fide purchase). "The transferee is also chargeable as constructive trustee of any income received from the property, and, if the transferee has had the use of the property, the transferee is chargeable with the value of such use." 5 Scott & Ascher §29.1.8.1.

[176] 5 Scott & Ascher §29.1.8.8 (Election by Beneficiaries to Affirm). If the value of the subject property has declined since it was transferred in breach of trust by the trustee to the third party, then the beneficiaries will be sorely tempted to affirm the transaction, absent special facts.

[177] Bogert §894.

[178] Had the third party been a BFP or had the sale not been in breach of trust, the third party could keep the item whether or not the proceeds of the sale had been misappropriated by the trustee. *See* 5 Scott & Ascher §29.1.8.5.

[179] 5 Scott & Ascher §29.1.8.5.

[180] 5 Scott & Ascher §29.1.8.6 ("But if the transferee makes expenditures for repairs or improvements, the transferee is entitled to credit for only the amount by which the estate has benefited, even if the transferee has spent more. . . . The basis for the credit is to avoid unjust enrichment of the beneficiaries"). However, when it comes to innocent "donees," *see* 5 Scott & Ascher §29.1.9.4 ("The donee has a lien on the property for the amount so expended, even though the property was not benefited to the same extent") See generally §8.15.35 of this handbook (trustees *de son tort*; *de facto* trustees and officious intermeddlers).

[181] 5 Scott & Ascher §29.1.8.6. *See, e.g.*, Hawley v. Tesch, 88 Wis. 213, 59 N.W. 670, 677 (1894).

[182] 5 Scott & Ascher §29.1.7 (Transferee in an Illegal Transaction).

[183] 5 Scott & Ascher §29.1.7 (Transferee in an Illegal Transaction).

[184] 5 Scott & Ascher §29.1.10 (Extent of Liability of Transferee in an Illegal Transaction).

illegality also would be liable for any profits that are subsequently generated from the exploitation of funds that rightfully belong to the trust.[185]

In lieu of a restoration of the item to the trust estate, *i.e.*, the equitable relief of specific restitution, equity may, depending upon the facts and circumstances, permit the beneficiary to elect to have the third party transfer to the trust estate cash or other property equivalent in value to what the item was worth at the time the third party wrongfully received it.[186] In any case, if the third party has disposed of the item such that tracing is not an option, the third party is personally liable to the beneficiary for its value,[187] or, if the item was sold, for the actual sale proceeds, should the beneficiary so elect.[188] Until the matter is resolved, the beneficiaries are entitled to an equitable lien on the item, or on the sales proceeds.[189] In ancient Rome, things would have been quite different had the property been held by a *fiduciarius*. A *fiducia* was similar to an Anglo-American common law trust in that the fiduciarius took title to property for the benefit of someone else. Moreover, creditors of the fiduciarius could not get at the property. There is an important difference, however, between the fiducia concept and the trust concept: If a fiduciarius transferred the property to a non-BFP, the beneficiary was essentially a general creditor whose only recourse was to go against the fiduciarius personally.[190] He could not go against the transferee of the property.

And then there is the purchase with trust funds of a specific item from a third party in breach of trust. If the third party is not a BFP, then the third party holds the purchase money subject to the trust. If the proceeds have left the hands of the third party and cannot be traced, the beneficiaries are entitled to seek a judgment against the third party for the amount of the proceeds, "but they are not entitled to priority over the seller's other creditors."[191]

What about a transfer of title to trust property that is occasioned by the trustee's death to one or more of the following: the trustee's personal representative, heirs-at-law, legatees, devisees, or surviving spouse? It is now settled law that none would qualify as a BFP.[192] Unless the transfer was pursuant to the

[185] 5 Scott & Ascher §29.1.10 (Extent of Liability of Transferee in an Illegal Transaction).

[186] 5 Scott & Ascher §§29.1.8.2 (Recovery of Value of Trust Property), 29.1.8.7 (Choice of Remedies) (noting that "[w]hen the beneficiary or one of the beneficiaries is under an incapacity, or when there are several beneficiaries and they do not all agree on a remedy, the court will choose the remedy that best effectuates the trust purposes").

[187] 5 Scott & Ascher §29.1.8.2 (Recovery of Value of Trust Property). "It would seem that the beneficiaries should, at their option, be able to charge the transferee with the value of the property at the time when the transferee disposed of it, increased or decreased to reflect the results of a prudent course of investment, or with the value of the property at the time of the decree, together with any income received." 5 Scott & Ascher §29.1.8.2.

[188] 5 Scott & Ascher §29.1.8.3. "The transferee is thus accountable for any profit." 5 Scott & Ascher §29.1.8.3.

[189] 5 Scott & Ascher §29.1.8.4 (Lien on Property or Its Proceeds).

[190] Jeffrey A. Schoenblum, 1 Multistate and Multinational Estate Planning 1252 (1999).

[191] 5 Scott & Ascher §29.1.8.1.

[192] *See generally* 5 Scott & Ascher §29.1.6.1 (Devolution on Death of Trustee). *See also* §3.4.3 of this handbook (death of trustee).

terms of the trust, the postmortem transferee or transferees would hold the property subject to those terms.[193] One or more of the following: the trustee,[194] his cotrustee, his successor,[195] and the beneficiaries (including the remaindermen) would have standing in the first instance to bring an equitable recovery action against a non-BFP to whom trust property has been transferred in breach of trust.[196] The beneficiary's right of action against the transferee is a direct one,[197] except, perhaps, when there is an innocent cotrustee[198] or successor trustee[199] in the picture. The doctrine of laches, as tweaked by a statute of limitations applicable to breaches of fiduciary duty,[200] will generally govern when such an action must be brought.[201]

The beneficiary's direct right to go against a non-BFP is not to be confused with the derivative right of a beneficiary to sue a third party who has breached a contract with the trustee or has committed a tort against the trustee to the detriment of the trust estate.[202] Still, the trustee—as the legal titleholder, if for no other reason—ought to be made a party so that all aspects of the controversy may be resolved without resort to a separate judicial proceeding,[203] unless the trustee cannot be made subject to the court's jurisdiction.[204] In a recovery action brought by the beneficiaries against a transferee, the trustee in any case would be a necessary party because the transfer would have been incident to a breach of trust.[205] The transferee, on the other hand, would not necessarily need to be made a party if the only relief that is being sought is against the trustee personally, *e.g.*, to recover for the trust estate amounts paid to the trustee by the third-party transferee.[206] A beneficiary who seeks relief from the trustee and the transferee in separate actions, of course, would not be entitled to a

---

[193] *See generally* §3.3 of this handbook (involuntary trustees).

[194] *See generally* 5 Scott & Ascher §29.1.11.2 (Suit by Trustee) (citing to Wetmore v. Porter, 92 N.Y. 76, 85 (1883) ("We see no reason why a trustee who has been guilty even of an intentional fault is not entitled to his *locus penitentiae* and an opportunity to repair the wrong which he may have committed.").

[195] 5 Scott & Ascher §29.1.11.4 (Suit by Successor Trustee).

[196] 5 Scott & Ascher §29.1.11 (Who Can Maintain Action) ("The beneficiary, however, can maintain an action at law when the property transferred is money or tangible personal property and the beneficiary is entitled to an immediate and unconditional payment or transfer thereof from the trustee").

[197] *See generally* 5 Scott & Ascher §29.1.11.1 (Suit by Beneficiary).

[198] 5 Scott & Ascher §29.1.11.3.

[199] 5 Scott & Ascher §29.1.11.4.

[200] *See generally* §8.15.70 of this handbook (laches doctrine)

[201] *See generally* §3.6 of this handbook (just because the trustee is time-barred does not necessarily mean that the beneficiaries are as well).

[202] *See generally* §3.5.4.4 of this handbook (external inbound liabilities of third parties in contract and tort).

[203] 5 Scott & Ascher §29.1.11.1 (Suit by Beneficiary).

[204] 5 Scott & Ascher §29.1.12.

[205] 5 Scott & Ascher §29.1.12. *See also* §5.7 of this handbook (the necessary parties to a suit brought by a beneficiary).

[206] 5 Scott & Ascher §29.1.12.

"double satisfaction."[207] The liability would have to be equitably apportioned between the defendants.[208]

For why innocent personal creditors of a trustee are generally not BFPs, the reader is referred to Sections 8.3.1 of this handbook and 8.15.63 of this handbook.[209] Suffice it to say that the unauthorized use of trust property to satisfy (cancel) an antecedent (preexisting) personal debt owed by the trustee to a third party has traditionally been problematic not because of the bona fide purchase doctrine's lack-of-notice requirement but because of its payment-of-value requirement.[210]

§5.4.3 Beneficiary's Right to Legal Fees from Trust Estate or from Trustee Personally

In litigation involving a good-faith difference of opinion among the parties to a trust as to the meaning of a material trust term, the beneficiaries may be entitled to reimbursement for their legal fees *from the trust estate*. This matter is covered in Section 8.13 of this handbook.[211] In litigation against a trustee for breach of trust, the beneficiary, if successful, may be entitled to have the beneficiary's legal fees made a personal obligation of the trustee.[212]

§5.4.4 Beneficiary's Right to Terminate the Trust

This protective measure, securing the rights of cestuis que trustent to grant or withhold consent . . . [to the revocation or amendment of a trust] . . . , was the aftermath of legislative indulgence of settlors of trusts, who, having foundered in the 1907 economic depression, sought to fuel a financial comeback by access to assets they had locked into trusts in balmier times. . . .[213]

---

[207] 5 Scott & Ascher §29.1.12.1 (Effect of Judgment).

[208] 5 Scott & Ascher §29.1.12.1 (Effect of Judgment).

[209] *See also* 5 Scott & Ascher §29.3.7 (Satisfaction of Antecedent Debt as Value) ("If a trustee in breach of trust transfers trust property in satisfaction of a debt or other obligation owed by the trustee to the transferee, the weight of authority is to the effect that, subject to various exceptions, the transferee takes the property subject to the trust").

[210] While the satisfaction of an antecedent debt may serve as consideration for a legally enforceable contract, it has traditionally not been considered the kind of value contemplated by the equitable bona fide purchase doctrine. *See generally* 5 Scott & Ascher §29.3 (Value).

[211] Bogert §871. *See also* §8.15.13 of this handbook (the common fund doctrine).

[212] Bogert §871.

[213] Estate of Cord, 58 N.Y.2d 539, n.5, 449 N.E.2d 402, n.5, 462 N.Y.S.2d 622, n.5 (1983) (referring to Est. Powers & Trust Law §7-1.9 (New York), under which formal consent of all parties "beneficially interested" in a trust is a prerequisite to its revocation or amendment).

Termination. A beneficiary may terminate a trust without court permission if there is express authority to do so in the governing instrument.[214] A beneficiary who holds a power of appointment may terminate the trust by exercising that power. Someone else who holds a power may do so as well at the beneficiary's request. Again, no court involvement would be required. A beneficiary may terminate an irrevocable inter vivos trust without going to court if the beneficiary obtains the consent of the trustee and all the other beneficiaries, including all the remaindermen.[215] In some cases, the settlor's consent would be required as well.[216] The court would have to get involved if a beneficiary who possesses no express right of termination or general power of appointment were to seek termination of a testamentary trust or termination of any trust that is in part or in whole for the benefit of unrepresented[217] minors, incompetents, persons unborn, or persons unascertained.[218] Only the court may appoint a guardian ad litem.[219] Even if the beneficiary were the only one with the equitable interest, a court in the United States probably would not order termination if the trust still had a valid material purpose.[220] Under what circumstances would the court even get involved, if there were only one beneficiary and that beneficiary had the entire equitable interest, if the trust were testamentary, or if the trustee had declined to accede to the beneficiary's request?

---

[214] For a discussion of the termination rights of a settlor of a revocable trust, *see* §8.2.2.2 of this handbook.

[215] *See, e.g.,* Estate of Cord, 58 N.Y.2d 539, 449 N.E.2d 402, 462 N.Y.S.2d 622 (1983). *See generally* §8.2.2.1 of this handbook (mid-course modification, termination, or rescission of an irrevocable trust).

[216] *See generally* §4.1.2 of this handbook (the settlor's reversionary or expectation interest).

[217] *See generally* UTC Art. 3 (available at <http://www.uniformlaws.org/Act.aspx?title=Trust%20Code>) (dealing with representation of beneficiaries, *e.g.*, personal representatives, trustees, guardians, and conservators, and what is known as virtual representation).

[218] *See, e.g.,* Nitsche v. St. Clair State Bank, 46 S.W.3d 682 (Mo. App. 2001) (declining to approve the termination of a trust without the consent of the unborn and unascertained contingent remainder interests or their disinterested representatives). *See generally* §8.14 of this handbook (when a guardian ad litem (or special representative) is needed: virtual representation issues) and §8.11 of this handbook (what are the duties of the trustee of a revocable inter vivos trust?) (noting that the holder of a right of revocation or general inter vivos power of appointment may terminate a trust and in so doing extinguish the contingent interests of the other beneficiaries including the unborn and unascertained remaindermen). The holder of a general testamentary power of appointment could, under certain circumstances, consent to the termination of an irrevocable trust notwithstanding the interests of the unborn and unascertained remaindermen. *See generally* UTC §302 (available at <http://www.uniformlaws.org/Act.aspx?title=Trust%20Code>) (providing that to the extent there is no conflict of interest between the holder of a general testamentary power of appointment and the persons represented with respect to the particular question or dispute, the holder may represent and bind persons whose interests, as permissible appointees, takers in default, or otherwise, are subject to the power).

[219] *Cf.* UTC §305 (available at <http://www.uniformlaws.org/Act.aspx?title=Trust%20Code>) (substituting the term representative for the term guardian ad litem in part to signal that a representative may consider general benefit accruing to the living members of the family of the otherwise unrepresented beneficiary).

[220] *See generally* §8.15.7 of this handbook (the *Claflin* doctrine (material purpose doctrine)).

To summarize: In the United States, a beneficiary may not effect termination of a trust absent one or more of the following: express termination language; a power of appointment in the beneficiary or someone else; consent of the trustee, the beneficiaries, and perhaps the settlor; accomplishment of the trust's material purpose; or some insurmountable obstacle that makes it impossible for a trustee to carry out the settlor's intentions.[221]

Destination of trust property upon termination. Whether the trust property passes to the beneficiary upon termination will depend upon how the trust was terminated and/or its terms. If the governing instrument so provides, the trust property will pass to the beneficiary upon termination. The beneficiary with a general power of appointment may appoint the property to himself, or to his estate if the power is testamentary.[222] If the beneficiary effects a termination by exercising a limited/special power of appointment, the beneficiary may not direct the property to himself.[223] If a third party terminates the trust through the exercise of a general power of appointment, the property may be appointed outright and free of trust to the beneficiary. Only if the beneficiary is a permissible appointee could the third-party exercise a limited/special power in favor of the beneficiary.

If the trust terminates because all beneficiaries have consented, there are a number of possibilities. The property could revert back to the settlor or his estate upon a resulting trust, be distributed among the current beneficiaries, or pass by acceleration to the remaindermen. Presumably, the beneficiary would be a member of one of those classes. If the beneficiary had the entire equitable interest and it was fully vested, and if the trust were to terminate for lack of a material purpose, the property would pass only to the beneficiary.[224]

§5.5   Involuntary or Voluntary Loss of the Beneficiary's Rights

The mere fact that the beneficiary knows that the trustee is committing a breach of trust and fails to make any objection is not sufficient to preclude him from holding the trustee liable for breach of trust.[1]

Acquisition of beneficial interests by the trustee. The trustee, being a fiduciary, has an affirmative equitable duty to act solely in the interest of the

---

[221] Restatement (Second) of Trusts §335 (Accomplishment of Purposes Becoming Impossible or Illegal).

[222] *See generally* §8.1 of this handbook (powers of appointment).

[223] *See generally* §8.1 of this handbook (powers of appointment).

[224] *See generally* §8.15.7 of this handbook (the *Claflin* doctrine (material purpose doctrine)).

§5.5 [1] Stowers v. Norwest Bank Indiana, N.A., 624 N.E.2d 485, 488 (1993)—(reversing the trial court's grant of summary judgment in favor of the trustee and citing to Scott, *The Law of Trusts* §216 at 1733 (3d ed. 1967), for the proposition that a beneficiary's failure to object in and of itself cannot give rise to the defenses of waiver and estoppel).

beneficiaries. Thus, a former or present trustee may not acquire the property of the trust by adverse possession.[2] In theory, however, the trustee may acquire the property with the informed consent of all beneficiaries.[3] Likewise, their informed[4] consent, ratification, or release may be sufficient to discharge the trustee from breaches of trust.[5] "The mere fact, however, that the beneficiary does not object to a deviation from the terms of the trust is not consent to such deviation."[6] The beneficiary owes no fiduciary duties to the trustee. A binding consent to a breach of trust requires some "affirmative act" by the beneficiary.[7]

It is clear, however, that such discharge is not binding if given in reliance upon fraudulent representation or under circumstances of concealment of material facts by the trustee.[8] It equally is well settled that the beneficiary must be of full age and legal capacity or else the beneficiary's consent is not binding.[9] In acts involving the shifting of beneficial interests, the assent of one beneficiary will not bind the others,[10] nor is the assent of the income beneficiaries binding on the remaindermen.[11] Thus, it is impossible for a trustee to obtain release by private agreement when there are beneficiaries who are unborn, unascertained, or under some legal disability.[12] (Such would certainly be the case for most cemetery trustees and trustees of charitable trusts.[13]) On the other hand, the assent of the beneficiary who holds a general inter vivos power of appointment

---

[2] 5 Scott on Trusts §495. *See also* §6.1.3 of this handbook (trustee's duty of loyalty to the beneficiaries).

[3] 5 Scott on Trusts §496.

[4] The consent of the beneficiary, however, would not preclude the beneficiary from holding the trustee liable for a breach of trust if the beneficiary when consent was given did not know of his rights and of the material facts which the trustee knew or should have known and which the trustee did not reasonably believe that the beneficiary knew. Restatement (Second) of Trusts §216(2)(b).

[5] 5 Scott on Trusts §216. *See generally* W. W. Allen, Annot., *Beneficiary's consent to, acquiescence in, or ratification of trustee's improper allocation or distribution of assets*, 29 A.L.R.2d 1034 (1953). A beneficiary cannot give an informed consent, ratification, or release without all the material facts. What facts are material? All the facts that the beneficiary needs to protect his or her equitable interests. As the trustee, not the beneficiary, is the fiduciary, it is the affirmative duty of the trustee to apprise the beneficiary of those facts. In most cases the vehicle for transmitting those facts will be the trustee's accounting or trustee's report as that term is defined in the Uniform Trust Account. UTC §813 (available at <http://www.uniformlaws.org/Act.aspx?title=Trust%20Code>). *See generally* §6.1.5.2 of this handbook (trustee's duty to keep and render accounts) and §5.4.1.1 of this handbook (the beneficiary's right to information and confidentiality). *See generally* UTC §802 cmt. (noting that no breach of the duty of loyalty occurs if the beneficiary ratified the transaction either prior to or subsequent to its occurrence).

[6] Restatement (Second) of Trusts §216 cmt. a.

[7] UTC §1009 cmt. (available at <http://www.uniformlaws.org/Act.aspx?title=Trust%20Code>); Restatement (Third) of Trusts §97 cmt. b.

[8] 5 Scott on Trusts §216; Restatement (Second) of Trusts §216(2)(b); UTC §1009(2) (available at <http://www.uniformlaws.org/Act.aspx?title=Trust%20Code>).

[9] 5 Scott on Trusts §216.3.

[10] 5 Scott on Trusts §216.2. *See also* In re Crane, 34 N.Y.S.2d 9 (1942).

[11] 13 Scott on Trusts §216.2; Restatement (Second) of Trusts §216 cmt. g.

[12] *See* Bogert §1007 n.9 and accompanying text.

[13] Rounds, *Protections Afforded to Massachusetts' Ancient Burial Grounds*, 73 Mass. L. Rev. 176 (1988).

or reserved right of revocation may well be binding on all other beneficiaries, including the unborn and unascertained.[14]

Laches and statutes of limitations (breach of trust actions). Delay on the part of the beneficiary in compelling a trustee to redress negligent breaches of trust apparent from a scrutiny of the trustee's accounts may constitute laches sufficient to release the trustee from such liabilities.[15] A cause of action against a trustee for breaches of the duty of loyalty, however, is not barred by laches until a reasonable time after *all* beneficiaries become aware of the breach and fail to take appropriate action.[16] What constitutes laches depends upon the circumstances of each case, but the mere lapse of time alone will not bar the beneficiary where the position of others has not been changed.[17] Circumstances indicating an intention to abandon one's equitable remedies, along with a lapse of time, will be sufficient to bar a recovery.[18] A beneficiary with a contingent remainder interest may interfere to protect the estate during the life tenancy but is not guilty of laches or acquiescence until the estate comes into the beneficiary's possession. Even the contingent remaindermen are well advised to take action immediately upon receiving notice of a breach, whether or not prior interests have terminated.[19]

Some states have enacted statutes of limitations for actions against trustees. In Georgia, for example, the applicable statute of limitations for a breach of trust claim is six years from the date the beneficiary discovered, or reasonably should have discovered, the subject of the claim.[20]

The Uniform Trust Code establishes two limitation periods in which a beneficiary may bring a claim against the trustee: a one-year period for the beneficiary who has received notice of a potential claim for breach of trust[21] and a five-year period for the beneficiary who has not.[22] A beneficiary may not

---

[14] *See* 3 Scott on Trusts §216.2; UPC §1-108 (acts by holder of general power). *See generally* §8.11 of this handbook (duties of trustee of a revocable inter vivos trust).

[15] *See* 3 Scott on Trusts §219. *See also* Bogert §964; UTC §802 cmt. (available at <http://www.uniformlaws.org/Act.aspx?title=Trust%20Code>) (confirming that no breach of the duty of loyalty occurs with respect to a particular transaction if the beneficiary failed to commence a judicial proceeding within the time allowed).

[16] *See* Lawson v. Haynes, 170 F.2d 741 (10th Cir. 1948); Bogert §543(U). *See also* §6.1.3.5 of this handbook (acquisition by trustee of the equitable interest and the trustee's duty of loyalty to the beneficiary generally in nontrust matters).

[17] *See* Bogert §§948, 949.

[18] Bogert §949 n.36 and accompanying text.

[19] *See* Bogert §949 n.66 and accompanying text; 3 Scott on Trusts §219.4. *See, e.g.,* Mayer v. M. S. Bailey & Son, Bankers, 347 S.C. 353, 555 S.E.2d 406 (2001) (holding that UPC §7-307 short statute of limitations commenced to run as to the remaindermen before the death of the life tenant when they received the trustee's final account).

[20] *See, e.g.,* Snuggs v. Snuggs, 571 S.E.2d 800 (Ga. 2002).

[21] UTC §1005(a) (available at <http://www.uniformlaws.org/Act.aspx?title=Trust%20Code>). *Cf.* Mayer v. M. S. Bailey & Son, 347 S.C. 353, 555 S.E.2d 406 (2001) (holding that UPC §7-307 short statute of limitations commenced to run as to the remaindermen before the death of the life tenant when they received the trustee's final accounting).

[22] UTC §1005(c) (available at <http://www.uniformlaws.org/Act.aspx?title=Trust%20Code>).

commence a proceeding against a trustee for breach of trust more than one year after the date the beneficiary or a representative of the beneficiary was sent a report that adequately disclosed the existence of a potential claim for breach of trust and informed the beneficiary of the time allowed for commencing a proceeding.[23] Otherwise, a judicial proceeding by the beneficiary against a trustee for breach of trust must be commenced within five years after the first to occur of (1) the removal, resignation, or death of the trustee; (2) the termination of the beneficiary's interest in the trust; or (3) the termination of the trust.[24]

The one-year statute of limitations does not begin to run against a beneficiary who has waived the furnishing of a report.[25] If the trustee wishes to foreclose possible claims immediately, he should endeavor to obtain consent to the report from the beneficiaries and/or their representatives.[26]

Missing beneficiaries. What does the trustee do when a beneficiary cannot be found? He looks for a state statute such as one that applies to abandoned property.[27] In some states, by statute, the trustee, after a specified period of time, may bring an action to have the equitable interest pass to those who would be entitled to it if the beneficiary had died.[28] Under the Uniform Probate Code, a beneficiary who has been missing without a trace and for no apparent reason for a continuous period of five years is *presumed* dead, providing there has been a diligent good faith inquiry into the circumstances surrounding the beneficiary's absence that has turned up nothing definitive.[29]

Proof of beneficiary's death. In the case of the death of a beneficiary, "[m]any states have statutes that require the courts to receive, as evidence of death, a finding of presumed death by an official of the United States authorized to make such findings."[30] Under the Uniform Probate Code, a certified or authenticated copy of a death certificate purportedly issued by an official or agency of the place where the death purportedly occurred is prima facie evidence of the identity of the decedent and the fact of his or her death.[31] It also

---

[23] UTC §1005(a) (available at <http://www.uniformlaws.org/Act.aspx?title=Trust%20Code>). "A report adequately discloses the existence of a potential claim for breach of trust if it provides sufficient information so that the beneficiary or representative knows of the potential claim or should have inquired into its existence." UTC §1005(b).

[24] UTC §1005(c) (available at <http://www.uniformlaws.org/Act.aspx?title=Trust%20Code>). "If a trusteeship terminates by reason of death, a claim against the trustee's estate for breach of fiduciary duty would, like other claims against the trustee's estate, be barred by a probate creditor's claim statute even though the statutory period prescribed by this section has not yet expired." UTC §1005 cmt.

[25] UTC §1005 cmt. (available at <http://www.uniformlaws.org/Act.aspx?title=Trust%20Code>).

[26] UTC §1005 cmt. (available at <http://www.uniformlaws.org/Act.aspx?title=Trust%20Code>).

[27] 3 Scott & Ascher §14.10.4 n.3; 2A Scott on Trusts §142.3 n.3.

[28] 3 Scott & Ascher §14.10.4 n.1; 2A Scott on Trusts §142.3 n.1.

[29] UPC §1-107(5). "His [or her] death is presumed to have occurred at the end of the period unless there is sufficient evidence for determining that death occurred earlier." UPC §1-107(5).

[30] 3 Scott and Ascher §14.10.4 (containing a catalog of such statutes at note 2).

[31] UPC §1-107(2).

is prima facie evidence of the place, date, and time of death.[32] A certified or authenticated copy of any record or report of a governmental agency, domestic or foreign, that an individual has died is prima facie evidence of that fact, as well as of any circumstances surrounding the event that are disclosed by the record or report.[33] Otherwise, the fact of death must be established by clear and convincing evidence, which may include circumstantial evidence.[34] An undisputed entry on one of the aforementioned official documents of a time of death that is 120 hours or more after the time when another person was purported to have died establishes clear and convincing that there has been compliance with the Code's 120-hour survivorship requirement, no matter how the other person's time of death was determined.[35]

Homicide [Trust beneficiaries murdering settlors or one another]. The Restatement of Property provides that a remainder beneficiary whose interest is contingent upon surviving the current beneficiary forfeits the equitable interest if he or she murders the current beneficiary.[36] The principle has been codified in at least one state's "Slayer's Act."[37] The beneficiary who murders the holder of a right of revocation also forfeits the equitable interest.[38] The Uniform Probate Code is in accord. It provides that the felonious and intentional killing of the settlor of a revocable trust, whether or not the killing results in a criminal conviction, extinguishes any provisions in the trust for the benefit of the killer, any powers of appointment granted to the killer, and any present or future role fiduciary role the killer might have in the administration of the trust.[39] Likewise for any testamentary trust created under the victim's will.[40] The killer is deemed to have disclaimed all beneficial interests and powers, and, in the case of any fiduciary roles, to have predeceased the settlor.[41] Although the equitable principle that a wrongdoer may not profit by his or her own wrong, namely *Nullus commodum capere potest de injuria sua propia*, is borrowed from the civil law,[42] a court of equity, such as the probate court, is perfectly competent to adjudicate whether a killer may be allowed to succeed to the property of his or her victim.[43]

Divorce. Divorce, dissolution, or annulment of a marriage can sometimes trigger by operation of law the partial revocation of a trust.[44] The Uniform

---

[32] UPC §1-107(2).

[33] UPC §1-107(3).

[34] UPC §1-107(4).

[35] UPC §1-107(6). *See generally* §8.15.56 of this handbook (120-hour survival requirement in the trust context).

[36] Restatement (Third) of Property (Wills and Other Donative Transfers) §8.4 cmt. n, illus. 9.

[37] *See* In re Trust Estate of Jamison, 431 Pa. Super. 486, 636 A.2d 1190 (1994).

[38] Restatement (Third) of Property (Wills and Other Donative Transfers) cmt. k, illus. 2.

[39] UPC §2-803(c)(1). *See, e.g.*, Mass. Gen. Laws ch. 190B, §2-803.

[40] UPC §2-803(c)(1).

[41] UPC §2-803(e). *See generally* §8.15.55 of this handbook (lapse and antilapse).

[42] UPC §2-803 cmt.

[43] UPC §2-803 cmt.

[44] *See generally* 5 Scott & Ascher §35.1.6.

Probate Code, for example, provides that with respect to a trust under which the settlor has reserved a right of revocation, any provisions in favor of the settlor's spouse are revoked upon their divorce or marriage annulment.[45] This includes any provisions designating the ex-spouse as a fiduciary.[46] The Restatement (Third) of Property is generally in accord.[47] Under the Code, however, the property passes as if the settlor's ex-spouse had disclaimed the beneficial interest.[48] Under the Restatement, the property passes as if the settlor's ex-spouse had predeceased the settlor.[49] Under the Code, divorce extinguishes not only the equitable interests of the ex-spouse but also those of the ex-spouse's relatives,[50] except those relatives who remain related to the settlor by blood, adoption, or affinity postdivorce.[51]

Beneficiary's consent to a breach of trust. A trustee is not liable to a beneficiary for breach of trust if the beneficiary, while having capacity, consented to the conduct constituting the breach, released the trustee from liability for the breach, or ratified the transaction constituting the breach.[52] As we discuss in greater detail in §7.1.2 of this handbook, the trustee, however, will not be off the hook if the purported consent, release, or ratification of the beneficiary was induced by improper conduct of the trustee;[53] or if, at the time of the purported consent, release, or ratification, the beneficiary did not actually understand his or her legal rights and the material facts relating to the breach.[54] "Where a beneficiary has requested or consented to what essentially amounts to mismanagement by a fiduciary, equitable rather than contractual principles must govern."[55] The burden will be on the trustee to demonstrate

---

[45] UPC §2-804(b)(1). *See, e.g.*, Mass. Gen. Laws ch. 190B, §2-804 (partial revocation of certain trusts by divorce).

[46] UPC §2-804(b)(1). *See, e.g.*, Mass. Gen. Laws ch. 190B, §2-804 (partial revocation of certain trusts by divorce).

[47] Restatement (Third) of Property (Wills and Other Donative Transfers) §4.1(b) cmt. p.

[48] UPC §2-804(d).

[49] Restatement (Third) of Property (Wills and Other Donative Transfers) §4.1 cmt. o.

[50] UPC §2-804(b).

[51] UPC §2-804(a)(5).

[52] UTC §1009 (available on the Internet at <http://www.uniformlaws.org/Act.aspx?title=Trust%20Code>). *See also* UTC §1009 cmt. (available at <http://www.uniformlaws.org/Act.aspx?title=Trust%20Code>) (advising that more than a mere failure to object is necessary to effect a consent, release, or ratification); 4 Scott & Ascher §24.21 (Consent of Beneficiary) ("Likewise, one must distinguish a beneficiary's consent from a beneficiary's failure to object"); §7.1.2 of this handbook; §7.1.4 of this handbook (trustee's defense that beneficiary consented to or ratified breach of trust); Restatement of Restitution §191.

[53] UTC §1009(1) (available at <http://www.uniformlaws.org/Act.aspx?title=Trust%20Code>); 4 Scott & Ascher §24.21 (Consent of Beneficiary); Restatement of Restitution §191 cmt. d.

[54] UTC §1009(2) (available at <http://www.uniformlaws.org/Act.aspx?title=Trust%20Code>); Restatement of Restitution §191 cmt. b & c.

[55] Estate of Saxton, 274 A.D.2d 110, 119, 712 N.Y.S.2d 225, 231 (2000).

that the beneficiary had actual and full knowledge and understanding of his or her legal rights.[56] In other words, the consent must be a fully informed one.[57]

A trustee who enters into a self-dealing transaction with a beneficiary will have the burden of proving that the beneficiary has given his or her informed consent.[58] Undue influence is presumed.[59] "If the beneficiary's approval involves a self-dealing transaction, the approval is binding only if the transaction was fair and reasonable."[60] In addition, the beneficiary's approval must be with "full knowledge of all relevant facts and complete awareness of the resultant divided loyalty and its possible consequences."[61] For more on informed consent to fiduciary self-dealing, the reader is referred to Sections 7.1.1, 6.1.3.3, and 7.2.7 of this handbook, particularly Section 7.1.1 of this handbook.

Beneficiary's disclaimer, renunciation, or release of equitable interest or nonfiduciary power. A disclaimer is "the refusal to accept an interest in or power over property."[62] It is not a transfer, assignment, or release of the property.[63] A trust beneficiary at common law,[64] or by statute,[65] may disclaim his or her equitable interest, provided the beneficiary has not accepted it,[66] has not

---

[56] Estate of Saxton, 274 A.D.2d 110, 119, 712 N.Y.S.2d 225, 231 (2000). *See also* 4 Scott & Ascher §24.21 (Consent of Beneficiary); Restatement of Restitution §191 cmt. a (burden of proof).

[57] *See generally* 4 Scott & Ascher §24.21 (Consent of Beneficiary). *See also* §7.1.2 of this handbook (defenses to allegations that the trustee breached the duty of loyalty) and §7.2.7 of this handbook (beneficiary consent to or ratification of a breach of trust). *Cf.* §6.1.3.3 of this handbook (discussing appointment of scrivener as trustee).

[58] *See generally* §7.1.2 of this handbook (defenses to allegations that trustee breached the duty of loyalty) and §8.24 of this handbook (the burden of proof in an action for breach of trust brought by the beneficiary against the trustee).

[59] *See generally* §8.24 of this handbook (the burden of proof in an action for breach of trust brought by the beneficiary against the trustee).

[60] UTC §1009 cmt. (available at <http://www.uniformlaws.org/Act.aspx?title=Trust %20Code>). *See also* 4 Scott & Ascher §24.21 (Consent of Beneficiary); §7.1.2 of this handbook (informed consent); Restatement of Restitution §191 cmt. e (self-dealing transaction must be fair and reasonable).

[61] Cohen v. First Camden Nat'l Bank & Trust Co., 51 N.J. 11, 18–19, 237 A.2d 257, 261 (1967). *See also* §7.1.2 of this handbook (defenses of allegations that the trustee breached the duty of loyalty) (discussing in part the concept of informed consent); Restatement of Restitution §191(2)(b).

[62] UPC §2-1102(3). *See, e.g.,* Mass. Gen. Laws ch. 190B, §2-801 (Massachusetts disclaimer statute, which was formerly Mass. Gen. Laws ch. 191A).

[63] UPC §2-1105(f).

[64] *See generally* UPC §2-1104 (providing that the Code does not limit any right of a person to make a common law disclaimer); UPC §2-1113 cmt. (noting that under the common law an effective disclaimer had to be made only within a "reasonable" time).

[65] *See, e.g.,* UPC §2-1105 (power to disclaim). *See generally* Richard V. Wellman, *Disclaimer Talk*, 27 ACTEC L.J. 243 (2001) (reporting on the NCCUSL discussions that took place during preparation of revisions to its uniform acts on disclaimers, including §2-801 of the UPC, particularly as to the appropriate rule for directing where disclaimed gifts go when the donor made no provision for their disposition).

[66] 1 Scott on Trusts §36.1; UPC, Part 11, General Comment ("Because a disclaimer is a refusal to accept, the only bar to a disclaimer should be acceptance of the offer."). *See, e.g.,* Whitney v. Faulkner, 502 Utah Adv. Rep. 43, 95 P.3d 270 (2004) (although the applicable disclaimer statute

waived the right to disclaim,[67] and has not already assigned the interest.[68] Powers of appointment may be disclaimed as well.[69] The Restatement (Third) of Trusts is in accord.[70] So also is the Uniform Probate Code.[71] In old New York, it was the custom of the Dutch to disclaim an estate by laying a key on the coffin.[72] Needless to say, a writing will generally suffice today.[73]

Having accepted the equitable interest under a trust, the beneficiary would still have the option of releasing or renouncing it,[74] or electing not to continue to receive its benefits.[75] Even one's contingent equitable interest under a fully discretionary trust may be renounced.[76] "Disclaimers are to be distinguished from releases or elections which involve either the surrender of a property interest already accepted or the choice of one interest rather than another."[77] Powers of appointment are generally releasable, a topic we take up in Section 8.1.1 of this handbook.

Under the Uniform Probate Code acceptance is now the only bar to disclaiming equitable interests and powers under trusts.[78] There is no longer a time limit.[79] On the other hand, for estate, gift, and generation-skipping tax avoidance purposes, a disclaimer must comply with Section 2518 of the Internal Revenue Code.[80] It must be made not later than the date that is nine months after the later of the day on which the transfer creating the interest in the disclaiming beneficiary is made, or the day on which he or she attains age 21.[81] The problem here is that under state law, the nonaccepting recipient of a vested (transmissible) contingent remainder or a vested remainder subject to divestment, has a reasonable time, nine months, or no time limitation after the interest becomes indefeasibly vested to disclaim, *i.e.* when the condition

---

authorized partial disclaimers, a debtor-beneficiary's general disclaimer of all his interest in a terminating trust was ineffective as to his undistributed interest in the trust, he already having received and accepted certain items of tangible personal property that had comprised a portion of the trust estate).

[67] UPC §2-1113(a).

[68] UPC §2-1113(b)(2).

[69] Restatement (Third) of Trusts §51 cmt. f(1); UPC §2-1105(a). *See generally* §8.1.1 of this handbook (disclaiming and releasing powers of appointment).

[70] Restatement (Third) of Trusts §51 cmt. f.

[71] UPC §2-1105(a).

[72] Chester, Courts and Lawyers of New York (1925).

[73] *See, e.g.*, UPC §2-1105(c) (providing for written disclaimers).

[74] *See, e.g.*, Guerriero v. Comm'r, 433 Mass. 628, 745 N.E.2d 324 (2001) (involving the release of a contingent equitable interest under a discretionary trust).

[75] 1 Scott & Ascher §5.6.1.

[76] *See, e.g.*, In re Estate of Gilbert, 592 N.Y.S.2d 224 (Sup. Ct. N.Y. Cnty. 1992).

[77] Roche & Carlson, *The Dynamic Disclaimer*, 14 New Eng. L. Rev. 401 (1979).

[78] UPC §2-1113 cmt.

[79] UPC §2-1113 cmt.

[80] *See* Wenig, 848 T.M., Disclaimers; Connelly, *Constructing Qualified Disclaimers*, 11 Prob. & Prop. 47 (Jul./Aug. 1997). A disclaimer that meets the requirements of the transfer tax provisions of the Internal Revenue Code (I.R.C. §2518) will be deemed to have met the requirements for an effective disclaimer under the UPC. *See* UPC §2-1114 (tax qualified disclaimer).

[81] Roche & Carlson, *The Dynamic Disclaimer*, 14 New Eng. L. Rev. 401, 416–441 (1979).

precedent is fulfilled or the condition subsequent extinguishes unfulfilled, as the case may be.[82] For tax purposes, however, the recipient must disclaim within nine months after the interest is created, *i.e.*, when there is still a possibility that the condition precedent may not be fulfilled or that the condition subsequent will.[83] Generally, the equitable interest will then pass as if the beneficiary had predeceased the time of transfer.[84] "The traditional judicial approach . . . [had-] . . . presume[d] . . . acceleration absent contrary intent."[85]

In any case, for the disclaimer to be valid for tax avoidance purposes, the disclaimant must be without authority to direct where the property goes next. Also, it goes without saying that the property must pass to someone other than the disclaimant. Accordingly, if the alternate taker would be the trustee of a trust under which the disclaimant would have an equitable interest or power of appointment, then the prospective disclaimant will want to consult his or her tax advisor before proceeding. Depending on the terms of the recipient trust, it may be necessary for the disclaimant to disclaim his or her interest under that trust as well. Qualified disclaimers also can be employed to prune trusts that do not qualify for the marital deduction into trusts that do.[86]

The presence of a spendthrift clause ought not to be an impediment to disclaiming for the reason that a disclaimer is a refusal to accept ownership of an interest, not a transfer of an interest already owned.[87] Nor should the beneficiary's insolvency or bankruptcy be an impediment.[88] The U.S. Supreme Court, however, has held that a disclaimer does not defeat federal tax liens.[89]

One court has reformed the disclaimer of an equitable interest under a trust: "We determine that a disclaimer may be reformed in circumstances like those presented here, where there is decisive evidence of the . . . [disclaimant's] . . . intent to minimize tax consequences and where that intent was clearly frustrated."[90] In this case, the disclaimant had been unaware

---

[82] *See, e.g.*, UPC §2-1105 (no time limit). *See generally* §8.30 of this handbook (the difference between a vested equitable remainder subject to divestment and a vested (transmissible) contingent equitable remainder).

[83] I.R.C. §2518(b)(2). *See generally* UPC, Part II, General Comment (noting that the absence of any mention of time limits in the UPC disclaimer sections is intended to send a clear signal to the practitioner that the requirements for a tax qualified disclaimer are set by "different law").

[84] UPC §2-1106.

[85] Patricia G. Roberts, *The Acceleration of Remainders: Manipulating the Identity of the Remaindermen*, 42 S.C. L. Rev. 295, 297 (1991).

[86] *See, e.g.*, Lassiter v. Comm'r, T.C. Memo. 2000-324.

[87] *See* UTC §502 cmt. (available at <http://www.uniformlaws.org/Act.aspx?title=Trust%20Code>); UPC §2-1105(a).

[88] 1 Scott & Ascher §5.6.1.

[89] Drye v. United States, 1999 WL 1100445 (U.S.) (Dec. 7, 1999). The law is unsettled as to whether *Drye* applies in the bankruptcy context. *See, e.g.*, Nistler v. Nistler, 259 B.R. 723 (Bankr. D. Or. 2001) (holding that a disclaimer cannot be a transfer of an interest in a decedent's estate and therefore cannot be a fraudulent transfer under bankruptcy law). The *Nistler* court did not find compelling the reasoning in In re Kloubec, 247 B.R. 246 (Bankr. N.D. Iowa 2000), that *Drye* is applicable in the bankruptcy context. 54 Kaufman v. Richmond, 442 Mass. 1010, 811 N.E.2d 987 (2004).

[90] Kaufman v. Richmond, 442 Mass. 1010, 811 N.E.2d 987 (2004).

of the adverse federal generation-skipping transfer tax consequences of her disclaimer at the time it was made.

In the absence of restraint imposed by the trust instrument or by statute, the beneficiary's equitable estate may be transferred by the beneficiary as freely as might be done if it were a legal estate. A beneficial interest in a trust after all is itself property. The voluntary assignment of equitable interests is covered elsewhere in this handbook.[91]

The subject of the disclaimer by a trustee of one or more of his fiduciary powers is taken up in Section 3.5.3.4 of this handbook.

No-contest or *in terrorem* provisions. A "no-contest" or "*in terrorem*" clause in a trust instrument provides for the forfeiture or reduction of the interest of a beneficiary who "contests" the arrangement.[92] An "anti-contest" clause would be such a clause. The hope is that the beneficiaries will be deterred from engaging in costly litigation against the trustee, and one another, and in generally subjecting the settlor's personal affairs to unwanted publicity. "Such clauses promote the public policies of honoring the intent of the donor and discouraging litigation by persons whose expectations are frustrated by the donative scheme of the instrument."[93] Some courts have enforced such clauses.[94] (One court would even go so far as to enforce a provision forfeiting the equitable interest of a trust beneficiary who urges or voluntarily aids someone else to contest.[95]) Other courts, however, citing public policy considerations, do not enforce *in terrorem*/no-contest clauses.[96] In recognition of the fact that "the validity of no-contest clauses is not universally accepted, nor is (where these clauses are valid) the probable-cause exception," such clauses are generally construed narrowly.[97]

In England, a no-contest clause is probably enforceable, provided it is coupled with an express gift over.[98] Overreaching is always a concern. The *in*

---

[91] *See* §5.3.2 of this handbook (voluntary transfers).

[92] *See generally* Annot., *Validity and enforceability of provisions of will or trust instrument for forfeiture or reduction of share of contesting beneficiary*, 23 A.L.R.4th 369 (1983).

[93] Donkin v. Donkin, 314 P.3d 780, 787 (Cal. 2013) ("In tension with these public policy interests are the policy interests of avoiding forfeitures and promoting full access of the courts to all relevant information concerning the validity and effect of a will, trust, or other instrument.").

[94] *See generally* Annot., *Validity and enforceability of provisions of will or trust instrument for forfeiture or reduction of share of contesting beneficiary*, 23 A.L.R.4th 369 (1983). *See also* Restatement (Third) of Property (Wills and Other Donative Transfers) §8.5 (Tentative Draft No. 3, Apr. 4, 2001) (providing that a provision in a donative document purporting to rescind a donative transfer to, or a fiduciary appointment of, any person who institutes a proceeding challenging the validity of all or part of the document is enforceable unless probable cause existed for instituting the proceeding).

[95] *See* Estate of Stewart, 230 Ariz. 480, 286 P.3d 1089, 1094 (2012) (The court, however, would not enforce a provision forfeiting the interests of a trust beneficiary who is subpoenaed to testify in a court proceeding or to provide documentary evidence or when sworn to provide truthful testimony in court.).

[96] *See generally* Annot., *Validity and enforceability of provisions of will or trust instrument for forfeiture or reduction of share of contesting beneficiary*, 23 A.L.R.4th 369 (1983).

[97] Restatement (Third) of Trusts §96 cmt. e.

[98] Lewin ¶ 5-10 (England).

terrorem clause contained in the 1046 will of the widow Wolgith for the benefit of King Edward the Confessor and others, for example, is the type of clause that one who is concerned about enforceability should probably avoid:

> "[A]nd, he who would ignore my will, which I have executed with the witness of God, may he be denied this earth's joy and may the Almighty Lord who created and shaped all beings shut him out of the gathering of all the holy ones on Doomsday; and, may he be taken to Satan, the devil, and to all his be damned companions, to the pit of Hell, and there suffer, with the enemies of God, without ceasing, and never bother my heirs."[99]

In the case of the trust, there are really three categories of "contest." One can contest the circumstances surrounding a trust's creation,[100] its purposes, or *how* it is being administered, or any combination thereof. Assuming that the settlor intended to impress a trust upon the property, not to make a gift to the "trustee," then it would seem inconsistent with the concept of the trust for a court to apply a "no contest" clause to the third category, *e.g.*, good-faith actions brought by beneficiaries to construe the terms of governing instruments or to remedy breaches of trust.[101] Accountability, after all, is the glue that holds the institution of the trust together.[102] Under the Uniform Trust Code, a "contest" is "an action to invalidate all or part of the terms of the trust or of property transfers to the trustee."[103] Thus, a beneficiary who in good faith brings a

---

[99] Malcolm A. Moore, *The Joseph Trachtman Lecture—The Origin of Our Species: Trust and Estate Lawyers and How They Grew*, 32 ACTEC L.J., 159, 160 (2006).

[100] *See, e.g.*, Ackerman v. Genevieve Ackerman Family Trust, 908 A.2d 1200 (D.C. App. 2006) (no-contest clause enforced after beneficiary brought an unsuccessful action to exclude a certain residence from the trust estate, though both the beneficiary *and the settlor* had testified that the settlor had never intended that the residence be the subject of a trust). *Cf.* Claudia G. Catalano, *What constitutes contest or attempt to defeat will within provision thereof forfeiting share of contesting beneficiary*, 3 A.L.R. 5th 590 §11 (noting that an appeal of an order admitting or denying a will to probate could itself constitute the type of contest contemplated by the will's no-contest clause).

[101] *See* Restatement (Third) of Property (Wills and Other Donative Transfers) §8.5 cmt. a (suggesting that a clause that purports to prohibit beneficiaries from enforcing fiduciary duties owed to the beneficiaries by the trustee is unenforceable). *See, e.g.*, Callaway v. Willard, 739 S.E.2d 533 (Ga. App. 2013) ("Further, our Supreme Court has held that, as a matter of public policy, *in terrorem* clauses may not be construed so as to immunize a fiduciary from the law that imposes certain duties upon and otherwise governs the actions of such fiduciaries."); Conte v. Conte, 56 S.W.3d 830 (Tex. App. 2001) (an action to remove trustee not being an effort to vary the settlor's intent, *in terrorem* clause not triggered when beneficiary commenced action to remove cotrustee); Boles v. Lanham, 865 N.Y.S.2d 360 (App. Div. 2008) (trust "incontestability" clause held not to have been triggered against a beneficiary when the beneficiary brought suit against the trustee for breach of fiduciary duty, the trustee having acted in bad faith in failing to make income and principal distributions to the beneficiary). *But see* Estate of Pittman, 63 Cal. App. 4th 290, 73 Cal. Rptr. 2d 622 (1998) (holding that beneficiaries' attempt to use legal proceedings to obtain a determination/clarification as to the legal character of property in a joint trust, *i.e.*, whether it was community or separate property, constituted a "contest" within meaning of broadly worded *in terrorem* clause).

[102] *See generally* §6.1.5 of this handbook (duty to account to the beneficiary).

[103] UTC §604 cmt. (available at <http://www.uniformlaws.org/Act.aspx?title=Trust%20 Code>).

complaint for instructions merely to clarify the terms of the trust probably has little to worry about. On the other hand, the beneficiary should think twice before appealing whatever decision the trial court ultimately hands down, particularly if the appeal could result in a diminution of the size or scope of someone's equitable interest under the trust.[104] One court has held that merely a complaint to convert a trust into a unitrust would trigger a forfeiture under the trust's no-contest clause.[105]

Also, *the trustee* should think twice before challenging a judicial ruling that a no-contest clause has been violated by some but not all beneficiaries. In a New Hampshire case involving a trustee who had attempted to do just that, the court concluded that the trustee lacked the requisite standing to pursue the appeal.[106] The court mused that the trustee might have been in violation of the duty of loyalty, specifically the derivative duty of impartiality, in appealing the clause's enforcement.[107] Invoking the exception to the American rule, a topic we take up in Section 8.15.13 of the handbook, the court upheld the ruling of the trial court that the trustee must personally bear the burden of the legal fees of the innocent beneficiaries who had mounted a defense to the ill-fated contest.[108] The trustee's removal from office was also upheld.[109] The equitable relief of trustee removal is taken up in Section 7.2.3.6 of this handbook.

Some states have statutes that enable a prospective contestant to seek an advance determination from the court as to whether a contemplated action would trigger a forfeiture of his or her equitable interest under the trust's no contest clause, assuming the trust has one.[110] In the absence of such a statute, a court might be persuaded to render an advance determination in the context of a complaint for declaratory judgment.[111]

---

[104] *Cf.* Claudia G. Catalano, *What constitutes contest or attempt to defeat will within provision thereof forfeiting share of contesting beneficiary*, 3 A.L.R.5th 590 §11 (Appeal of order admitting or denying will to probate).

[105] McKenzie v. Vanderpool, 151 Cal. App. 4th 1442, 61 Cal. Rptr. 3d 129 (2d Dist. 2007). *See generally* §6.2.2.4 of this handbook (the noncharitable unitrust and the investment considerations).

[106] *See* Shelton v. Tamposi, 164 N.H. 490, 499, 62 A.3d 741, 749 (2013).

[107] *See Shelton*, 164 N.H. 490, 500, 62 A.3d 741, 750. *See generally* §6.2.5 of this handbook (the trustee's duty of impartiality).

[108] *See Shelton*, 164 N.H. 490, 503, 62 A.3d 741, 752.

[109] *See Shelton*, 164 N.H. 490, 505, 62 A.3d 741, 754.

[110] California at one time by statute had made it possible for a trust beneficiary with impunity to indirectly challenge a no-contest clause in the governing instrument via a safe harbor declaratory relief proceeding. *See* Donkin v. Donkin, 314 P.3d 780, 787–789 (Cal. 2013).

[111] *See generally* §8.42 of this handbook for a discussion of the difference between a complaint (petition) for instructions and a complaint (petition) for declaratory judgment. For an example of a declaratory judgment action that did not lead to forfeiture, see In re Miller Osborne Perry Trust, 299 Mich. App. 525, 831 N.W.2d 251 (2013) (the plaintiff-trust beneficiary's seeking a determination via a naked action for declaratory judgment as to whether he would have probable cause to contest an amendment to the governing trust instrument altering the trust's dispositive provisions and adding a no-contest clause held not to constitute the type of contest the particular clause was meant to deter, this though the court had found that probable cause to contest would have been lacking).

Under the Restatement (Third) of Property, a no-contest clause is enforceable unless there was probable cause for instituting the proceeding.[112] "Probable cause exists when, at the time of instituting the proceeding, there was evidence that would lead a reasonable person, properly informed and advised, to conclude that there was a substantial likelihood that the challenge would be successful."[113] The Restatement (Second) of Property had a similar definition of probable cause.[114] Under the Restatement (Third) of Trusts, a no-contest clause is not *per se* unenforceable. It would, however, be unenforceable "to the extent that...[enforcing it]...would interfere with the enforcement or proper administration of the trust."[115] The Restatement (Third) obliquely endorses the probable-cause enforceability exception.[116] Alaska, by statute, has no such probable cause exception.[117]

What about a provision in a QTIP trust that subjects the surviving spouse's interest under the trust to the condition that he or she elect within six months of the settlor's death not to contest the trust. Would the presence of such a limited preacceptance no-contest clause jeopardize the QTIP election and the estate tax marital deduction?[118] Probably, it would not be. In the eyes of the IRS, that type of no-contest provision merely creates "alternatives" for the spouse; it does not create a "power to appoint" to persons other than the surviving spouse during the surviving spouse's lifetime, a power that would be fatal for marital deduction eligibility purposes.[119]

A trust no-contest provision, by statute, is generally unenforceable in Florida.[120] On the other hand, a trust provision granting the settlor's surviving spouse trust-beneficiary status, provided he or she refrains from exercising his or her spousal election rights, would be enforceable in Florida.[121] "...[A]n optional alternative to a statutory minimum benefit...is unlike a no contest clause due to the different purposes behind the legal right that the beneficiary must forfeit under each type of clause."[122]

---

[112] Restatement (Third) of Property (Wills and Other Donative Transfers) §8.5. *See, e.g.,* Russell v. Wachovia Bank, N.A., 370 S.C. 5, 633 S.E.2d 722 (S.C. 2006) (the court holding a trust no-contest clause enforceable against certain beneficiaries when there had been no probable cause for them to contest the trust's validity, it being self-evident that the settlor had not been the subject of undue influence). *Cf.* UPC §3-905 (providing that a will no-contest clause is unenforceable if probable cause exists for instituting proceedings).

[113] Restatement (Third) of Property (Wills and Other Donative Transfers) §8.5 cmt. c.

[114] *See* Hamel v. Hamel, 299 P.3d 278, 289–290 (2013) (parsing Restatement (Second) of Property (Wills and Other Donative Transfers) §9.1, cmt. j).

[115] Restatement (Third) of Trusts §96(2).

[116] Restatement (Third) of Trusts §96 cmt. e.

[117] Alaska Stat. §13.36.330 (2008).

[118] *See generally* §8.9.1.3 of this handbook (the marital deduction).

[119] Priv. Ltr. Rul. 9244020.

[120] Dinkins v. Dinkins, 120 So. 3d 601, 603 (Fla. 2013).

[121] Dinkins v. Dinkins, 120 So. 3d 601 (Fla. 2013).

[122] "The purpose of statutory minimum benefits is generally to ensure that surviving family members are provided for and do not become dependent on the public treasury, regardless of the decedent's intent... This purpose is not thwarted by providing an optional alternative devise

Assume a trust beneficiary's litigation counsel has negligently commenced a contest in the face of a fully enforceable *in terrorem* clause. Can he or she get the horse back into the barn by withdrawing the suit? Or is it too late? It is probably too late. The California court explains:

> Respondent contends, applying the familiar rule of strict construction where forfeiture is involved, that "contest" here means a legal opposition, pressed home to a decision, and that nothing short of this fulfills the terms of the condition subsequent. But having regard, as we must, to the controlling consideration of the purpose of the testator, can this be true? If so, then the testator contemplated permission to any disaffected heir, devisee, or legatee to use all of the machinery of the law to overthrow his wishes; to urge upon the court any of the "technical rules" which it may be thought were trespassed upon; to drag into publicity matters of the testator's private life; to assail his sanity—all to thwart "the testator's manifest purpose." And, after having done all this, if before a judicial determination has been actually rendered he has been able to force a compromise through the fears of the other beneficiaries under the will, or, failing this, has reached the conclusion that his efforts for the destruction of the instrument will prove abortive, he may dismiss his petition, receive the benefit of the testator's bounty, and be heard to declare, "I have not contested." This cannot be.[123]

The Restatement (Third) of Property (Wills and Other Donative Transfers) would seem in accord with the thinking of the California court: "In the absence of specific language to the contrary, the clause should be construed to be violated regardless of whether the action is subsequently withdrawn immediately after its institution, prior to a hearing, at the trial, or at any time thereafter."[124] Efforts short of filing an action that are aimed solely at procuring time to gather the facts, however, ought not to spring the *in terrorem* trap.[125]

Assume the terms of a revocable inter vivos trust include an *in terrorem* provision; for whatever reason, a companion *in terrorem* provision is lacking in the settlor's pour-over will.[126] Could the trust's *in terrorem* clause be triggered by a will contest, the theory being that the will and will substitute (the revocable inter vivos trust) are parts of a single estate plan?[127] Probably not, and it should be no surprise that at least two courts have so held.[128] Because equity does not favor forfeitures, courts are inclined to construe *in terrorem* clauses narrowly.[129]

The mere presence of an enforceable *in terrorem* clause in a trust ought not to negate a beneficiary's standing to invoke the jurisdiction of the court,

---

[sic], because the beneficiary is free to reject it for any reason, including that it is less valuable than the statutory benefit." Dinkins v. Dinkins, 120 So. 3d 601, 603 (Fla. 2013).

[123] In re Hite's Estate, 101 P. 443, 445 (1909).

[124] Restatement (Third) of Property (Wills and Other Donative Transfers) §8.5 cmt. d.

[125] Restatement (Third) of Property (Wills and Other Donative Transfers) §8.5 cmt. d.

[126] *See generally* §2.1.1 of this handbook (testamentary pour-overs to inter vivos trusts).

[127] *See generally* Chapter 1 of this handbook (unifying the law of probate and nonprobate transfers).

[128] *See* Savage v. Oliszczak, 77 Mass. App. Ct. 145, 928 N.E.2d 995 (2010); Keener v. Keener, 278 Va. 435, 682 S.E.2d 545 (2009).

[129] Bogert §181.

provided that the beneficiary's allegations of injury, causation, and "redressabil-ity" are sufficiently particularized. At least one court has so held.[130] While the presence of an enforceable *in terrorem* clause in a trust may ultimately turn out to be an effective defense to an action brought by a beneficiary to, say, reform the trust, the mere existence of such a clause cannot deprive the beneficiary of standing to bring the action in the first place.[131] Otherwise such clauses would be self-executing.

§5.6   Duties and Liabilities of the Beneficiary

The trustee is bound to know what his duty is, and can not throw upon the cestui que trustent the obligation of telling him what such duty is. Mere knowledge and noninterference by the cestui que trust before his interest has come into possession do not always bind him as acquiescing in the breach of trust.[1]

External liability. Except perhaps in certain cases where the beneficiary controls the trustee, the beneficiary will not be held liable as the constructive owner of the *underlying trust property*.[2] In other words, absent special facts, a beneficiary is not personally liable to a third party for an obligation incurred by the trustee in the administration of the trust.[3] Thus, in matters involving the trust estate and third parties, the beneficiary is liable neither in contract[4] nor in tort;[5] nor criminally for a nuisance on the trust property,[6] nor for a trustee's unlawful acts of discrimination,[7] nor as a stockholder.[8]

Ownership of the equitable interest generally does not bring with it liabilities. With the possible exception of those trusts under which the beneficiary for all intents and purposes controls the trustee (*e.g.*, the revocable inter vivos trust, the realty trust, or the nominee trust), the beneficiary also incurs no liabilities arising inherently out of *ownership of the equitable or beneficial interest*, except when it comes to taxation.[9]

---

[130] Sonntag v. Ward, 253 P.3d 1120, 1121 (Utah. Ct. App. 2011).

[131] Sonntag v. Ward, 253 P.3d 1120, 1121 (Utah. Ct. App. 2011).

§5.6 [1] White v. Sherman, 168 Ill. 589, 606, 48 N.E. 128, 132 (1897).

[2] *See* 3 Scott on Trusts §§274, 274.1.

[3] Restatement (Third) of Trusts §103.

[4] *See* 3 Scott on Trusts §275.

[5] *See* 3 Scott on Trusts §276.

[6] *See* 3 Scott on Trusts §265.3.

[7] *See* Bogert §731.

[8] *See* 3A Scott on Trusts §265.2.

[9] 4 Scott & Ascher §22.6 (Indemnity from Beneficiaries); 3A Scott on Trusts §274. *See generally* §7.3.3 of this handbook (trustee's liability as legal owner in tort to nonbeneficiaries) and §9.6 of this handbook (trusts that resemble corporations or agencies).

Internal liability. The Restatement (Third) of Trusts, specifically Section 104, lists four general areas in which the beneficiary's actions may lead to an assumption of internal liability, that is to say liability "to the trust":

1. A loan or advance to the beneficiary from the trust
2. The beneficiary's debt to the settlor that has been placed in the trust, unless the settlor manifested a contrary intention
3. The trust suffered a loss resulting from a breach of trust in which the beneficiary participated
4. Liability imposed by other law, such as the law of contract, tort, or unjust enrichment

To the extent the beneficiary's equitable interest under the trust can be untangled and separated out from the interests of the other beneficiaries, then "the trust" is entitled to a charge on the interest to secure payment of the beneficiary's liability.[10] That the interest is subject to a spendthrift restraint would not be a defense.[11] In the case of the unwarrantedly litigious beneficiary, "the trust," under certain circumstances, may be entitled to satisfaction from the beneficiary's personal funds. This is a topic that is taken up at the end of this section.

The trustee is not an agent of the beneficiary.[12] The trustee's duty not to delegate the administration of the trust could well be implicated if the trustee without authority were to behave as if he were the beneficiary's agent.[13] In the absence of agreement, the beneficiary is not personally bound to indemnify the trustee for trust administration expenses.[14] The beneficiary may voluntarily undertake to make himself or herself liable to the trustee, *e.g.*, by furnishing funds to enable the trustee to improve the trust estate or by litigating in order to collect insurance proceeds.[15] In England, on the other hand, the beneficiary in some cases may be personally bound to indemnify the trustee to the extent there are insufficient assets in the trust estate to do so.[16]

The beneficiary of a trust is not an agent of the trustee. The beneficiary *qua* beneficiary is not an agent of the trustee. The trustee owes the beneficiary duties, not the other way around. Thus, it is a "well-established principle that a trustee cannot simply delegate his own duty to provide information to his

---

[10] Restatement (Third) of Trusts §104(2).

[11] Restatement (Third) of Trusts §104 cmt. h.

[12] *See, e.g.*, Buck v. Haas, 180 La. 188, 156 So. 217 (1934). *But see* UTC §108(e) (available at <http://www.uniformlaws.org/Act.aspx?title=Trust%20Code>) (providing that a trustee may not transfer a trust's principal place of administration over the objections of a qualified beneficiary without court approval).

[13] *See generally* 3 Scott & Ascher §17.3.2 (citing to Matter of Osborn, 299 N.Y.S. 593 (App. Div. 1937); Matter of JPMorgan Chase Bank, N.A. (Roby) 2014 N.Y. Slip Op. 07799 (Nov. 14, 2014) (confirming that it is default law that a trustee of an irrevocable trust may not delegate away his investment authority to the beneficiary).

[14] *See* Bogert §718; 4 Scott & Ascher §22.6.

[15] Restatement (Second) of Trusts §278.

[16] *See generally* 4 Scott & Ascher §22.6 (Indemnity from Beneficiaries).

beneficiary or force the beneficiary to find avenues for information he is rightfully owed."[17] The trustee's fiduciary duty to keep the beneficiaries reasonably informed is taken up generally in Section 6.1.5.1 of this handbook.

Beneficiary generally must return overpayments. Both in England and the United States, the beneficiary would generally be liable to indemnify the trustee for liability occasioned by overpayment or misdelivery of the trust property *to the beneficiary.*[18] Otherwise, the beneficiary would be unjustly enriched.[19] If a beneficiary wrongfully deals with trust property, any loss can be made up from the beneficiary's interest;[20] in the case of overpayment, as noted above, the beneficiary may be personally liable.[21] "One who seeks equity must do equity."[22] Where an innocent overpayment has been made, there may be a change of position by the beneficiary, however, that makes it inequitable to compel repayment.[23] See generally the Restatement (Third) of Restitution and Unjust Enrichment for a general discussion of position change as a defense to restitution.[24] A trustee makes distribution at his peril: An overpayment that is not repaid by the beneficiary is a personal obligation of the trustee.[25] "A beneficiary of a trust that is determined to have been invalid is liable to return any distribution received."[26]

Beneficiary may not knowingly participate in a breach of trust. A beneficiary is liable to the same extent as any other person for participation or collusion in a

---

[17] Janowiak v. Tiesi, 932 N.E.2d 569 (Ill. 2010) (the court noting that there is "no authority for the bold assertion that a trust beneficiary has a duty to . . . ferret out information for himself ").

[18] 4 Scott & Ascher §22.6.1 (When Trust Estate Has Already Been Conveyed).

[19] Restatement of Restitution §163 ("Where the owner of property transfers it as a result of mistake of such a character that he is entitled to restitution, the transferee holds the property upon a constructive trust for him"); Restatement (Third) of Restitution and Unjust Enrichment §17 (fiduciary misdeliveries).

[20] Restatement (Second) of Trusts §253; 4 Scott & Ascher §25.2 (Liability of Beneficiary to Trust Estate).

[21] Restatement (Second) of Trusts §254; Restatement of Restitution §163 (1937) (U.S.); 4 Scott & Ascher §§22.6.1 (U.S.) (When Trust Estate Has Already Been Conveyed), 25.2 (Liability of Beneficiary to Trust Estate) (U.S.), 25.2.4 (Beneficiary Who Receives Overpayment) (U.S.); Lewin ¶42-04 through ¶42-10 (England) (discussing a trustee's common law right of recovery and equitable right of recoupment).

[22] *See generally* 4 Scott & Ascher §25.2 (Liability of Beneficiary to Trust Estate); §8.12 of this handbook (containing a list of equity maxims); Snell's Equity ¶5-09.

[23] 4 Scott & Ascher §25.2.4.1 (Change of Position); Restatement (Second) of Trusts §254; Restatement of Restitution §178 (Change of Position). *But see* First Union Nat'l Bank v. Mcgill, 684 So. 2d 845 (Fla. Ct. App. 1996) (trustee's improper allocation of capital gains to the income account shall be made up by a remedial allocation to principal of future income payments, rather than by surcharging the trustee).

[24] Restatement (Third) of Restitution and Unjust Enrichment §65.

[25] *See generally* 4 Scott & Ascher §§24.31 (Liability for Incorrect Distributions), 25.2.4.2 (Rights of Trustee and Other Beneficiaries).

[26] UTC §604(c) (available at <http://www.uniformlaws.org/Act.aspx?title=Trust%20 Code>). *See also* 4 Scott & Ascher §25.2 (Liability of Beneficiary to Trust Estate).

breach of trust.[27] "Although there is not the same fiduciary relationship between trust beneficiaries as there is between them and the trustee, there is enough of a fiduciary element in their relationship to make it inequitable for one to seek to obtain an advantage over another."[28] The English cases are in accord.[29] If beneficiary X persuades the trustee improperly to lend or distribute to him trust property, X may be liable to beneficiaries Y and Z.[30] X's own interest in the trust estate may be subjected to an equitable lien in their favor.[31] The beneficiary would be ill advised to instruct the trustee in matters concerning management of the trust estate.[32]

The trustee takes directions from the beneficiary at his peril, unless the terms of the trust provide otherwise. The trustee would be equally ill advised to blindly follow the beneficiary's instructions.[33] The trustee is in no way excused from liability merely because some of the beneficiaries insisted upon an improper action—except perhaps as to a claim presented by those who did the insisting.[34] Moreover, as noted, the interfering beneficiaries may be held to have colluded in the breach of trust.[35]

Beneficiary's liability is generally limited. The beneficiary may not be forced to contribute personal funds in order to prevent the trust property from being taken by foreclosure.[36] Nor is the trustee "entitled to a charge on the beneficiary's interest in the trust to secure a liability of the beneficiary to the trustee not connected with the administration of the trust, unless the beneficiary contracts to give him such a charge."[37] Neither is a third party who owes a contractual obligation to the trustee, *e.g.*, the issuer of a bond or an insurance policy that is an asset of the trust, generally entitled, in lieu of making payments to the

---

[27] Bogert §256; 4 Scott & Ascher §§25.2 (Liability of Beneficiary to Trust Estate), 25.2.6 (Beneficiary Who Consents to or Participates in Breach of Trust), 25.2.6.3 (Participation by Beneficiary in Breach of Trust). *See generally* §5.4.1.8 of this handbook (right and standing of beneficiary to proceed in stead of trustee against those with whom the trustee has contracted, against tortfeasors, and against his agents, *i.e.*, against third parties).

[28] 4 Scott & Ascher §25.3 (Beneficiary's Duty to Other Beneficiaries).

[29] Lewin ¶40-06 (England).

[30] Bogert §256; 4 Scott & Ascher §§25.2 (Liability of Beneficiary to Trust Estate), 25.2.4.2 (Rights of Trustee and Other Beneficiaries).

[31] Bogert §256; 4 Scott & Ascher §§25.2 (Liability of Beneficiary to Trust Estate), 25.2.3 (Beneficiary Who Deals Wrongfully with Trust Property).

[32] Bogert §216; 4 Scott & Ascher §25.2 (Liability of Beneficiary to Trust Estate).

[33] Bogert §256(2) (One Beneficiary's Consent to a Breach of Trust Will Not Relieve Trustee from Liability to the Other Beneficiaries); 1 Scott on Trusts §8 (Trustee Not an Agent of the Beneficiary). *See also* Restatement (Third) of Trusts §80 cmt. b (noting that the trustee can properly take into account information or suggestions furnished by a beneficiary but then "must exercise independent, prudent, and impartial fiduciary judgment on the matters involved").

[34] Restatement (Second) of Trusts §216 cmt. g.

[35] Restatement (Second) of Trusts §256; 4 Scott & Ascher §25.2 (Liability of Beneficiary to Trust Estate).

[36] *See* 2A Scott on Trusts §176.

[37] Restatement (Second) of Trusts §250; 4 Scott & Ascher §25.1 (Liability of Beneficiary to Trustee Individually).

trustee, to set off a personal claim that the third party has against the beneficiary.[38]

Beneficiary may voluntarily assume trust liabilities. A trust beneficiary, of course, may voluntarily enter into an enforceable contract to pay money or property into the trust (or back into the trust in the case of a loan or advancement),[39] in which case the beneficiary's interest is subject to a charge for the amount of the obligation.[40] In spite of the public policy implications, even a beneficiary's agreement to indemnify the trustee against losses occasioned by a breach of trust *that the beneficiary had asked the trustee to commit* may be enforceable.[41]

The litigious beneficiary. In litigation pertaining to a trust, the court has discretion to order the trustee to reimburse the beneficiary from the trust estate for the beneficiary's reasonable legal fees and other litigation costs.[42] The litigation, however, must be indispensable to the proper administration of the trust or confer a benefit on the beneficiary class.[43] If the trustee is found to be personally at fault, the trustee may then be required to reimburse the trust estate out of his own funds for what was paid out to the beneficiary.[44] If a trustee has prevailed in a suit for breach of trust, he is entitled to be indemnified from the trust estate for his litigation costs.[45]

If a beneficiary engages in frivolous litigation against the trustee, or against the trust relationship itself, the beneficiary's equitable interest under the trust may be charged with the attendant costs.[46] Thus, if a beneficiary engages in vexatious and burdensome litigation against the trustee and the other beneficiaries, the court may order that the attorneys' fees of all the defendants be charged against the plaintiff-beneficiary's equitable interest to the extent the interest is identifiable, discrete, and severable.[47]

---

[38] 5 Scott & Ascher §32.2 (Set-Off of Claim of Third Person Against Beneficiary).

[39] *See generally* 4 Scott & Ascher §25.2.5 (Beneficiary Who Receives Advance or Loan of Trust Funds). *But see* 4 Scott & Ascher §25.2.5.1 (Advances to Beneficiary of Spendthrift Trust).

[40] 4 Scott & Ascher §25.2.2 (Beneficiary's Contractual Obligations to Trust).

[41] 4 Scott & Ascher §25.2.6.2 (When Consenting Beneficiary Agrees to Indemnify Trustee).

[42] *See generally* §8.13 of this handbook (when the beneficiary may be entitled to be reimbursed from the trust estate for his or her legal fees).

[43] *See generally* §8.13 of this handbook (when the beneficiary may be entitled to be reimbursed from the trust estate for his or her legal fees).

[44] *See generally* §7.2.3.7 of this handbook (assessment of attorneys' fees and other costs against the trustee personally).

[45] *See generally* §3.5.2.3 of this handbook (the trustee's right to exoneration and reimbursement).

[46] *See* 3 Scott on Trusts §188.4 n.13 and accompanying text. *See generally* §8.13 of this handbook (in litigation pertaining to a trust, when is the beneficiary entitled to reimbursement from the trust estate for legal fees).

[47] *See, e.g.,* Larkin v. Wells Fargo Bank, N.A., No. A13-1839 (Minn. Ct. App. Oct. 6, 2014) (unpublished) (". . . [The plaintiff-beneficiary's] . . . continuing attempt to undermine the settlement was not beneficial, particularly after the settlement agreement was confirmed in binding arbitration, by the district court, and by this court on appeal, and his alternate proposed settlement agreement was nonsensical and included ad hominem attacks on other trust beneficiaries. The evidence supports the district court's finding that . . . [he] . . . engaged in vexatious and

When a beneficiary litigates vexatiously, obdurately, or in bad faith, the trustee may have a fiduciary duty to the other beneficiaries to bring an action against the beneficiary to compel the beneficiary to reimburse the trust estate for the trustee's attorneys' fees and other litigation costs.[48] Circumstances even may warrant that an action be brought on behalf of the trust against the nuisance beneficiary's counsel as well.[49] In Missouri, the litigious nonprevailing beneficiary need not have engaged in intentional misconduct or litigated in bad faith to end up personally on the hook for the trustee's attorney's fees, at least to the extent of his distributive share.[50] In Wisconsin, the court in the exercise of its general equitable powers may specifically order the beneficiary to pay the trustee's attorney's fees from nontrust assets.[51]

Another arrow in the court's quiver is the litigation injunction. Where a vexatious trust beneficiary engages in a manifest abuse of the judicial process, the court may enjoin him from pursuing future litigation involving the trust without leave of the court.[52] "Stated most simply, a court considering the propriety of a litigation injunction must first consider whether the vexatious litigant 'is likely to continue to abuse the judicial process and harass other parties,' and from such a determination, assess whether an injunction is appropriate."[53]

An exception to the fees-on-fees/fees-for-fees prohibition. If the beneficiaries of a trust unreasonably or in bad faith force trust counsel to litigate to collect the fees to which he or she is lawfully entitled, then trust counsel's personal collection-litigation costs may well be reimbursable from the trust estate. This is the equitable exception to the "fees-on-fees" or "fees-for-fees" prohibition, a topic that is taken up in §3.5.2.3 of this handbook.

---

burdensome litigation."). It is interesting to note that the district court had ordered the plaintiff-beneficiary to pay the trustee's attorneys' fees *"either personally* or as a deduction from his share of the trust.") [italics added.]

[48] *See generally* §3.5.2.3 of this handbook (tagging the nuisance beneficiary with all litigation costs).

[49] *See, e.g.,* Pederson Trust, 757 N.W.2d 740 (N.D., 2008) (beneficiary and his counsel held joint and severally liable for the trustee's attorneys' fees).

[50] O'Riley v. U.S. Bank, N.A., 412 S.W.3d 400, 418–420 (W.D. Mo. 2013).

[51] *See, e.g.,* French v. Wachovia Bank, N.S., 722 F.3d 1079 (7th Cir. 2013) (the court having held that the corporate trustee was not liable for its act of indirect self-dealing, in part because of its good faith reliance on the boilerplate provisions of the trust instrument, ordered the beneficiaries to pay the trustee's attorney's fees out of personal funds).

[52] Kates v. Pressley, 2013 WL 495415 (E.D.N.Y. Feb. 7, 2013) (chronicling the deployment of litigation injunctions against one particularly vexatious trust beneficiary in a federal court, a New York state court, and a Florida state court).

[53] Kates v. Pressley, 2013 WL 495415 (E.D.N.Y. Feb. 7, 2013).

§5.7   The Necessary Parties to a Suit Brought by a Beneficiary

And it is a general rule in equity . . . that all persons materially interested, either legally or beneficially, in the subject-matter of a suit, are to be made parties to it, either as plaintiffs or as defendants, however numerous they may be, so that there may be a complete decree, which shall bind them all.[1]

In an action brought by the beneficiary to construe the terms of the trust or for breach of fiduciary duty, one or more of the following are necessary party defendants: the trustee, the cotrustee, the trustee's executor, the successor trustee, beneficiaries with vested interests,[2] beneficiaries with contingent interests,[3] remaindermen with vested interests,[4] remaindermen with contingent interests,[5] the state's attorney general, the settlor, the settlor's executor, and third parties who in some way may have caused some harm to the beneficiary's equitable interest.[6] "Ordinarily, a trust beneficiary may not bring a class suit on behalf of himself or herself and all other beneficiaries to enforce the trust or to recover damages for breach of trust."[7] Such suits are not unknown, however.[8] Moreover, an investor class action would seem the preferred vehicle for maintaining a breach of fiduciary duty suit *against the trustees or director-trustees* of a mutual fund.[9]

At minimum, whoever currently has title to the trust property is a necessary party. If the fiduciary's only interest in the litigation is that of stakeholder, *e.g.*, a complaint for instructions to construe the meaning of an ambiguous term, then he should be sued in his representative capacity.[10] On the other hand, if the suit is for some breach of his duty to the beneficiary, then he should be sued individually as well.[11]

Likewise, the capacity in which the other fiduciaries are sued will depend on whether they are stakeholders or are themselves alleged to have breached some duty to the beneficiary.[12] Those beneficiaries and remaindermen whose

---

§5.7 [1] Old Colony Trust Co. v. Wood, 321 Mass. 519, 525, 74 N.E.2d 141, 145 (1947).

[2] *See generally* 4 Scott & Ascher §24.19 (Several Beneficiaries).

[3] *See generally* 4 Scott & Ascher §24.19 (Several Beneficiaries).

[4] *See generally* 4 Scott & Ascher §24.19 (Several Beneficiaries).

[5] *See generally Beneficiaries as necessary parties to action relating to trust or its property,* 9 A.L.R.2d 10; 4 Scott & Ascher §24.19 (Several Beneficiaries).

[6] *See generally* Bogert §871.

[7] 4 Scott & Ascher §24.19 (Several Beneficiaries).

[8] 4 Scott & Ascher §24.19 n.15.

[9] *See generally* Charles E. Rounds, Jr. & Andreas Dehio, *Publicly-Traded Open End Mutual Funds in Common Law and Civil Law Jurisdictions: A Comparison of Legal Structures,* 3 N.Y.U.J.L. & Bus. 473 (2007).

[10] *See generally* Bogert §871.

[11] *See generally* Bogert §871.

[12] *See generally* Bogert §871. *See also* §7.2.4 of this handbook (cofiduciary and predecessor liability and contribution in the trust context).

equitable interests could be affected by the litigation are necessary parties.[13] This might include the unborn; the unascertained; minors and other legally incompetent individuals; and those whose equitable interests are contingent.[14] The state attorney general is a necessary party if the trust in whole or in part has a charitable purpose.[15] Under certain circumstances, the settlor or his executor may be a necessary party.[16] So too might be a third party who in some way has harmed or is harming the beneficiary's equitable interest, *e.g.*, a trespasser on trust real estate.[17]

For a discussion of who may qualify as interested parties in a suit brought by a trustee against third parties, see Section 3.5.4.4 of this handbook. In a breach of contract or tort action brought by a trustee against a third party for harming the trust estate, for example, absent special facts the beneficiaries need not be made parties to the action. For a discussion of who may qualify as interested parties in a suit occasioned by a transfer of trust property in breach of trust to a third party, see Section 5.4.2 of this handbook.

---

[13] *See generally* Bogert §871.

[14] *See generally* Bogert §871. *See also* §8.14 of this handbook (whether a guardian ad litem or special representative is needed); 4 Scott & Ascher §24.19.

[15] *See generally* §9.4.2 of this handbook (standing to enforce charitable trusts).

[16] *See generally* §4.1 of this handbook (interests and powers remaining with the settlor by operation of law). *See also* UTC §410 cmt. (suggesting that the settlor is an interested person with respect to a judicial proceeding brought by the beneficiaries to terminate or modify a noncharitable irrevocable trust) (available at <http://www.uniformlaws.org/Act.aspx?title=Trust%20Code>).

[17] *See generally* §5.4.1.8 of this handbook (right and standing of beneficiary to proceed in stead of trustee against third parties, such as those with whom the trustee has contracted, tortfeasors, and the trustee's agents).

CHAPTER *6*

The Trustee's Duties

§6.1 General Duties

The trust concept straddles the law of property and the law of personal obligations and allows circumvention of the English privity of contract doctrine that prevents third parties from enforcing a contract for their benefit made by others. . . . As emphasized by Millet LJ in Armitage v. Nurse[1] there is an irreducible core of obligations owed by the trustees to the beneficiaries and enforceable by them which is fundamental to the concept of a trust. If the beneficiaries have no rights of enforcement against the trustees there are no trusts.[2]

When property is transferred from one person to another, the transferee's legal status with respect to the property will depend in large part on the transferor's intent.[3] If the intent is to make an outright gift or bequest, then the transferor imposes no duties on the transferee with respect to the property.[4]

---

§6.1 [1] [1998] Ch. 241, 253.

[2] David Hayton, *The Uses of Trusts in the Commercial Context*, in Trusts in Prime Jurisdictions 431 (Alon Kaplan ed., 2000).

[3] *See, e.g.,* Jimenez v. Lee, 547 P.2d 126 (Or. 1976) ("There was nothing about either of the gifts which would suggest that the beneficial ownership of the subject matter of the gift was to vest in defendant to use as he pleased. . . .").

[4] McNeil v. McNeil, 798 A.2d 503 (Del. 2002); Wood v. Honeyman, 178 Or. 484, 559–561, 169 P.2d 131, 163–164 (1946). *See generally* 3 Scott & Ascher §§17.4 (Duty to Keep and Render Accounts), 18.2.3 (When Trustee Acts Dishonestly); Frederick R. Franke, Jr., *Resisting the Contractarian Insurgency: The Uniform Trust Code, Fiduciary Duty, and Good Faith in Contract*, 36 ACTEC L.J. 517, 530 (2010).

That means that a resulting trust cannot be imposed upon the property once the unrestricted donative transfer has been completed.[5]

The trustee's five fundamental duties. If the intent is to create an agency, contract, bailment, or trust, then the transferor imposes certain enforceable duties on the transferee with respect to the transferred property.[6] "Unless a testator or other transferor manifests an intention to impose enforceable duties on the transferee, the intention to create a trust is lacking and no trust is created."[7] A trust relationship, whether private or charitable,[8] brings with it five fundamental duties:

(1) The duty to be generally prudent (to include the duty to segregate the property);
(2) The duty to act and to carry out the terms of the trust;[9]
(3) The duty to be loyal to the beneficiaries and/or the trust's charitable purposes (which would include the duty to act honestly and in good faith);[10]
(4) The duty to give personal attention to the affairs of the trust; and
(5) The duty to account to the beneficiary.[11]

---

[5] 6 Scott & Ascher §41.7. *See generally* §4.1.1.1 of this handbook (the resulting trust).

[6] Jacob v. Davis, 128 Md. App. 433, 450–451, 738 A.2d 904, 912–913 (1999).

[7] Restatement (Third) of Trusts §13 cmt. d. No trust is created if the transferor intends merely to impose a moral obligation on the transferor. "It is no longer the case, as it once appeared to be in England, that the wish of a testator, like that of a sovereign, is to be taken as a command." Restatement (Third) of Trusts §13 cmt. d.

[8] *See generally* 5 Scott & Ascher §37.3.1 (The Duties of the Trustee of a Charitable Trust).

[9] "Simply stated, a trustee's duty is to obey the directions of the trust. However in the performance of that a trustee must have regard to additional duties, in particular: (a) to act with care; (b) to act impartially with respect to beneficiaries; (c) to invest the trust funds and manage them prudently; (d) to act jointly and unanimously with cotrustees, unless the governing deed permits otherwise; (e) to inform (not advise) the beneficiaries; and (f) to keep and supply accounts and other information." Martyn Frost, *Overview of Trusts in England and Wales*, in Trusts in Prime Jurisdictions 13 (Alon Kaplan ed., 2000).

[10] *See generally* §6.1.3 of this handbook (the trustee's duty of loyalty); Frederick R. Franke, Jr., *Resisting the Contractarian Insurgency: The Uniform Trust Code, Fiduciary Duty, and Good Faith in Contract*, 36 ACTEC L.J. 517 (2010) (the trustee's duty of good faith).

[11] A term in a trust that the trustee shall not be accountable to anyone for his actions is unenforceable. Bogert §542. *See, e.g.*, Matter of Kornrich, 854 N.Y.S.2d 293 (Surr. Ct. 2008). *See generally* §7.2.6 of this handbook (discussing types of exculpatory clauses that may be enforceable and thus protective of the trustee). "Waiver by a settlor of the trustee's duty to keep the beneficiaries informed of the trust's administration does not otherwise affect the trustee's duties." UTC §105 cmt. (available at <http://www.uniformlaws.org/Act.aspx?title=Trust%20Code>). "The trustee remains accountable to the beneficiaries for the trustee's actions." UTC §105 cmt. *See also* Scanlan v. Eisenberg, 669 F.3d 838, 846–847 (7th Cir. 2012) (confirming that a trustee of a discretionary trust as a matter of public policy must be accountable to the beneficiaries, or the trustee would be insulated from suits for breach of trust); T.P. Gallanis, *The Trustee's Duty to Inform*, 85 N.C.L. Rev. 1595, 1621 (2007) ("The trustee has a mandatory duty to inform the beneficiaries because only they have both the financial incentive and legal authority to fulfill the monitoring and enforcement functions."); John H. Langbein, *Mandatory Rules in the Law of Trusts*, 98 Nw. U. L. Rev. 1105, 1126 (2004) (suggesting that "like a term purporting to abrogate all fiduciary duties, or a term authorizing the trustee to act in bad faith, a term that prevents the beneficiary from

If any one of these duties is totally lacking, there is a good chance that the transferee's legal status with respect to the property is something other than that of a trustee.[12] But if his status is that of a trustee, then his duty to act in good faith and in accordance with the purposes of the trust may not be waived by the settlor.[13] The fundamental requirement that a trust and its terms be for the benefit of its beneficiaries also is not waivable,[14] nor as a matter of public policy[15] is the trustee's duty to account.[16] In other words, "a settlor may not so negate the responsibilities of a trustee that the trustee would no longer be acting in a fiduciary capacity."[17] On the other hand, "[i]f a transaction is called a trust but leaves the settlor with too much control and the so-called trustee without any real power or duty, it may be held to be a mere agency."[18]

The power of appointment exception. There is an exception: If the settlor were to reserve or grant to the trustee *in the trustee's individual capacity*, whether the trustee be the settlor himself or a third party, a general inter vivos power of appointment (otherwise known as a presently exercisable general power of appointment), then the trustee would be immunized from surcharge for all acts committed while in possession of the power.[19] This would be the case even if the acts otherwise would constitute a breach of one or more of the fiduciary duties that are the subject of this chapter.[20] In other words, a breach-of-trust action brought by the other beneficiaries against the trustee (or

---

obtaining the information needed to enforce the trust entails the risk of making the trust unenforceable and hence illusory"). On the other hand, a provision purporting to relieve the transferee of the need to account "may indicate an intention on the part of the . . . [transferor] . . . to make an outright gift, rather than to create a trust." 3 Scott & Ascher §17.4. "No matter how broad the language of the trust instrument, the court will never permit the trustee to act dishonestly or in bad faith." 3 Scott & Ascher §18.2.3.

[12] "A [testator] who attempts to create a trust without accountability in the trustee is contradicting himself." Jacob v. Davis, 128 Md. App. 433, 450, 738 A.2d 904, 913 (1999) (holding remainderman of testamentary trust was entitled to accounting during lifetime of income beneficiary notwithstanding language in will to contrary and citing to Bogert §973). *See also* 3 Scott & Ascher §17.4.

[13] UTC §105(b)(2) (available at <http://www.uniformlaws.org/Act.aspx?title=Trust%20 Code>). *See generally* Frederick R. Franke, Jr., *Resisting the Contractarian Insurgency: The Uniform Trust Code, Fiduciary Duty, and Good Faith in Contract*, 36 ACTEC L.J. 517 (2010).

[14] UTC §105(b)(3) (available at <http://www.uniformlaws.org/Act.aspx?title=Trust%20 Code>).

[15] 1 Scott & Ascher §9.3.14.

[16] *See, e.g.,* Hollenback v. Hanna, 802 S.W.2d 412, 414 (Tex. App. San Antonio 1991) (holding a provision relieving a trustee of the duty to account to be against public policy and therefore void); In re Kassover, 124 Misc. 2d 630, 476 N.Y.S.2d 763 (Surr. Ct. 1984) (holding void as against public policy a trust term that would relieve the settlor-trustee of an irrevocable trust of the duty to account to anyone but himself); Restatement (Third) of Trusts §83 cmt. d (suggesting that a trust term providing that the trustee shall have no accountability should be interpreted as having the same effect as an exculpatory clause and thus as being subject to the same limitations). *See generally* §7.2.6 of this handbook (when the terms of a trust provide for trustee exculpation).

[17] UTC §105 cmt. (available at <http://www.uniformlaws.org/Act.aspx?title=Trust%20 Code>).

[18] Bogert §15.

[19] Restatement (Third) of Trusts §74 cmt. a(1). *See generally* 3 Scott & Ascher §17.4.

[20] *See generally* 3 Scott & Ascher §17.4.

by a successor trustee against a predecessor trustee) for acts committed, while
the fiduciary held in a nonfiduciary capacity a general inter vivos power of
appointment, would be an act of futility.[21]

Let there be no misunderstanding, however; possession of such a power by
the trustee in no way invalidates the trust itself.[22] What it does do is relieve the
trustee of fiduciary duties that he would otherwise have.

**The equitable fiduciary standard is more intense than the legal good-
faith standard.** The parties to a mere contract owe each other nonwaivable legal
duties of good faith and fair dealing.[23] A trustee of a trust, on the other hand,
owes the beneficiaries not only a nonwaivable equitable duty of good faith but
also a nonwaivable equitable duty of undivided loyalty.[24] The parties to a
contract generally have no duty to act solely for the benefit of one another.
While a trust, a creature of equity, can arise incident to a legal contract, such as
to function as a bargained-for vehicle for securing a contracting party's obligation to make certain payments, the trust itself is not a contract.[25] It has evolved
to the point where it is *sui generis*.[26]

A trustee may not limit his duties unilaterally. As a general rule, a trustee
may not limit his duties unilaterally, absent express authority in the governing
instrument.[27] There are some exceptions. Under Illinois law, for example, a
trustee may disclaim or release fiduciary powers and presumably avoid the duties
associated with those powers, *e.g.*, the authority to invade principal.[28] Under the
Prudent Investor Rule, investment discretion may be prudently delegated by the
trustee to agents.[29] In New York, a trustee with unlimited discretion to invade
principal for a beneficiary may impress a different trust upon the trust property,
provided the new trust is for the benefit of the beneficiary.[30]

Breach of trust defined. The Restatement (Third) of Trusts defines a
breach of trust as "a failure by the trustee to comply with any duty that the
trustee owes, as trustee, to the beneficiaries, or to further the charitable
purposes, of the trust."[31]

---

[21] *See generally* 3 Scott & Ascher §17.4.

[22] *See generally* §8.7 of this handbook (merger).

[23] Frederick R. Franke, Jr., *Resisting the Contractarian Insurgency: The Uniform Trust Code,
Fiduciary Duty, and Good Faith in Contract*, 36 ACTEC L.J. 517, 533 (2010).

[24] Frederick R. Franke, Jr., *Resisting the Contractarian Insurgency: The Uniform Trust Code,
Fiduciary Duty, and Good Faith in Contract*, 36 ACTEC L.J. 517, 519 (2010).

[25] *See generally* Frederick R. Franke, Jr., *Resisting the Contractarian Insurgency: The Uniform
Trust Code, Fiduciary Duty, and Good Faith in Contract*, 36 ACTEC L.J. 517 (2010).

[26] *See generally* Frederick R. Franke, Jr., *Resisting the Contractarian Insurgency: The Uniform
Trust Code, Fiduciary Duty, and Good Faith in Contract*, 36 ACTEC L.J. 517 (2010); §8.22 of this
handbook (the *sui generis* nature of the trust relationship).

[27] *See generally* 3 Scott & Ascher §16.1 (noting, also, that today, trustees often have duties not
because the terms of the trust so provide, but simply because there is a trust relationship).

[28] 755 Ill. Comp. Stat. 5/2-7 (for testamentary transfers); 760 Ill. Comp. Stat. 20/25 (for
nontestamentary transfers); 765 Ill. Comp. Stat. 325 (permitting the release of fiduciary powers).

[29] *See* §6.1.4 of this handbook (trustee's duty not to delegate critical fiduciary functions).

[30] N.Y. Est. Powers & Trusts Law §10-6.6 (New York). *See* §3.5.3.2(a) of this handbook (the
discretionary trust).

[31] Restatement (Third) of Trusts §93.

A breach of trust is not necessarily a breach of fiduciary duty. Some duties that a trustee owes the beneficiary are fiduciary duties. Some are not. The duty of loyalty is a fiduciary duty. It is a standard of conduct. The trustee's duty of prudence is a standard of care that is judged on the basis of conduct not consequences. Nonfiduciaries also are held to standards of care, sometimes to standards that are higher than those to which trustees are held, surgeons and airline pilots, for example. In other words, a breach of trust is not necessarily a breach of fiduciary duty.[32] The Restatement (Third) of Trusts is *not* in accord. It deems all breaches of trust to be breaches of fiduciary duty: "A breach of trust is a violation by a trustee of a fiduciary duty—that is, of any duty the trustee owes, *as trustee*—to the trust beneficiaries or to further the trust's charitable purpose(s)."[33]

The trustee's obligation to the beneficiary is equitable, except in rare instances. Be that as it may, the duties that the trustee owes the beneficiary are generally equitable.[34] In rare instances, however, a trustee's obligation to a beneficiary is treated as legal such that it is enforceable in a legal action.[35] "First, where the controversy over the meaning and administration of the trust is so one-sided that the trustee is clearly bound to pay the beneficiary a certain sum of money or turn over definite property, so that the extent of the trustee's liability can be ascertained without a long and complicated accounting, a court of law will sometimes undertake to fix the amount due and enforce the obligation of the judgment. . . . Second, a court of law also can give a judgment against a trustee for a definite amount that the trustee has separated from the trust property and promised to pay to the beneficiary."[36]

§6.1.1 Duty to Be Generally Prudent

A trustee shall administer the trust as a prudent person would, by considering the purposes, terms, distributional requirements, and other circumstances of the trust. In satisfying this standard, the trustee shall exercise reasonable care, skill, and caution.[37]

The directors of an ordinary business corporation often have been called trustees and their relation to the corporation is at least fiduciary. They are bound to act with absolute fidelity and must place their duties to the corporation above every other financial or business

---

[32] *Cf.* Charles E. Rounds, Jr., *Lawyer Codes are Just About Licensure, the Lawyer's Relationship with the State: Recalling the Common Law Agency, Contract, Tort, and Property Principles that Regulate the Lawyer-Client Fiduciary Relationship*, 60 Baylor L. Rev. 771 (2008) (noting that while an act of legal malpractice may be a legal tort, it is not necessarily an equitable breach of the lawyer's fiduciary duty to his or her client).

[33] Restatement (Third) of Trusts §93 cmt. b.

[34] Bogert §1.

[35] Bogert §1.

[36] Bogert §1, n.28.

[37] UTC §804 (available at <http://www.uniformlaws.org/Act.aspx?title=Trust%20Code>).

obligation. They must act, also, with reasonable intelligence, although they cannot be held
responsible for mere errors of judgment or want of prudence.[38]

It is said that the "[t]wo grand principles underlie much of the Anglo-
American law of trusts: the trustee's duties of loyalty and of prudence."[39] Each
is not all that susceptible to being precisely defined, however. As for the duty of
loyalty in the trust context:

> . . . the most that can honestly be said about the duty of loyalty is that it is the result
> of the courts' efforts at *regulating* the actions of trustees in situations in which their
> own interests conflict with those of the beneficiaries, to increase the likelihood, in
> the first instance, that the trustee will choose to advance the beneficiaries' best
> interests and, when the trustee fails to do so, to allow the beneficiaries an unusually
> generous selection of remedies.[40]

The general concept of prudence is even less susceptible to being defined
precisely. The Right Honorable Edmund Burke explains: "Prudence is not only
the first in rank of the virtues political and moral, but she is the director, the
regulator, the standard of them all. Metaphysics cannot live without definition;
but prudence is cautious how she defines."[41]

In the narrower trust context, the duty of prudence requires that the
trustee exercise "reasonable care, skill, and caution"[42] in the administration of
the trust generally, not just in investment matters.[43] "It is not sufficient that a
trustee uses such diligence as the trustee ordinarily employs in the trustee's own
affairs."[44] The standard is intended as an objective one, that of the prudent
person.[45] While the terms of the trust may dispense with the trustee's duty to be
prudent in specific situations, a "vice" mutual fund comes to mind, the trustee
is still saddled with a general duty of prudence.[46]

The duty of loyalty is a fiduciary duty. The duty of prudence in and of itself
is not. A fiduciary is generally saddled with a duty of care, though one need not

---

[38] Spiegel v. Beacon Participations, 297 Mass. 398, 410–411, 8 N.E.2d 895, 904 (1937)
(enunciating the Massachusetts business judgment rule).

[39] John H. Langbein & Bruce A. Wolk, Pension and Employee Benefit Law 678 (2000).

[40] 3 Scott & Ascher §17.2.

[41] 1 The Works of the Right Hon. Edmund Burke 498 (1834).

[42] Restatement (Third) of Trusts §77(2).

[43] A distinction should be drawn here between this overarching duty to act reasonably and
competently in all matters of trust administration and the so-called *prudent man rule* that provides
the trustee with a standard of conduct for the investment of trust assets. *See* §6.2.2.1 of this
handbook (the *Harvard College* prudent man rule and its progeny). UTC §804 (available at
<http://www.uniformlaws.org/Act.aspx?title=Trust%20Code>) provides that a trustee "shall ad-
minister the trust as a prudent person would, by considering the purposes, terms, distributional
requirements, and other circumstances of the trust." In satisfying this standard, "the trustee shall
exercise reasonable care, skill, and caution." In other words, there is a duty of "prudent administration."

[44] 3 Scott & Ascher §17.6 (Duty to Exercise Reasonable Care and Skill).

[45] *See generally* 3 Scott & Ascher §17.6 (Duty to Exercise Reasonable Care and Skill).

[46] *See generally* 3 Scott & Ascher §17.6.

be a fiduciary to owe someone a duty of care.[47] On the other hand, if the trustee's imprudent act is incident to a breach of the trustee's duty of loyalty, then the trustee's imprudence would constitute a breach of fiduciary duty.[48]

This standard of prudence is judged on the basis of conduct, not performance.[49] A trustee's action or inaction will not be judged in hindsight.[50] It will, however, be judged in light of the "purposes, terms, and other circumstances of the trust."[51] Thus if the trustee deposits or keeps trust cash in a bank that he knows or should know is in a precarious financial condition, then he could be liable to the beneficiaries for any losses to the trust that are occasioned by the bank's failure. The failure of the bank *per se*, however, would not give rise to liability.[52] As to entrusted bank deposits generally, there is no reason that the trustee should allow FDIC insurance limits to be exceeded.[53] In this regard, the reader is referred to the FDIC Guide to Calculating Deposit Insurance Coverage for Revocable and Irrevocable Trusts.[54]

The trustee in the administration of the trust at least must have and employ the skills of an individual of ordinary intelligence; and, to the extent he lacks the requisite technical skills in a given area, *e.g.*, law or investing, the trustee has a duty prudently to obtain competent guidance and assistance to make up for the deficiency.[55] "A trustee who does the best it can . . . [still commit] . . . a breach of trust if the trustee's best is not good enough."[56] Again, the standard for assessing whether one possesses or possessed the skills necessary to assume a trusteeship is an objective one.[57] "The duty to act with caution does not, of course, mean the avoidance of all risk, but refers to a degree of caution that is reasonably appropriate or suitable to the particular trust, its

---

[47] *See generally* Charles E. Rounds, Jr., *Lawyer Codes Are Just About Licensure, the Lawyer's Relationship with the State: Recalling the Common Law Agency, Contract, Tort, Trust, and Property Principles the Regulate the Lawyer-Client Fiduciary Relationship*, 60 Baylor L. Rev. 771 (2008).

[48] *Cf.* Ray Ryden Anderson & Walter W. Steele, Jr., *Fiduciary Duty, Tort and Contract: A Primer on the Legal Malpractice Puzzle*, 47 SMU L. Rev. 235, 250 (1994). *See, e.g.*, Holmes v. Drucker, 411 S.E.2d 728 (Ga. Ct. App. 1991) (involving a lawyer who negligently failed to file a lawsuit in a timely matter, a tortuous act, and then lied to the client about the negligence in breach of his fiduciary duty to the client).

[49] Restatement (Third) of Trusts §77 cmt. a (matters relating to the administration of the trust generally); Harvard Coll. v. Amory, 26 Mass. (9 Pick.) 446, 461 (1830) (investment matters); Restatement (Third) of Trusts §90 [Restatement (Third) of Trusts: Prudent Investor Rule §227]; 3 Scott & Ascher §17.6; 3 Scott on Trusts §§204, 227. *See also* Restatement (Third) of Trusts §204 (provisional—1992) (nonliability for loss in absence of breach of trust).

[50] Restatement (Third) of Trusts §77 cmt. a.

[51] Restatement (Third) of Trusts §77(1).

[52] *See generally* 3 Scott & Ascher §17.12.1 (Negligent Selection [Bank Deposits]).

[53] *See* 73 Fed. Reg. 56706-01 (Sept. 30, 2008).

[54] *See* <http://www.fdic.gov/regulations/laws/federal/2008/08sep26rule.html>.

[55] Restatement (Third) of Trusts §77 cmt. b. *See generally* §6.1.4 of this handbook (trustee's duty not to delegate critical fiduciary functions).

[56] 4 Scott & Ascher §24.5.

[57] Restatement (Third) of Trusts §77 cmt. b; 3 Scott & Ascher §17.6.

purposes and circumstances, the beneficiaries' interests, and the trustee's plan for administering the trust and achieving its objectives."[58]

As a general rule, the amateur trustee must exercise "such care and skill as a man of ordinary prudence would exercise in dealing with his own property."[59] On the other hand, one who holds oneself out as a professional with special skills is under a duty to employ those skills.[60] Thus the trustee's administration had better be as advertised.[61] The Uniform Probate Code would hold any trustee, amateur or professional, at least to the standard of a prudent man who deals with the property of another.[62] For quite some time now, the law has been trending in the direction of holding the corporate trustee to a higher standard of care than the standard to which an individual nonprofessional trustee is generally held,[63] a topic that is covered in more detail in Section 6.1.4 of this handbook.

The trustee's general duty of prudence ought not to be confused with an expansive discretionary power or specific direction in the trust's terms to act "unreasonably" in a given situation.[64] Generally the courts will not second-guess the trustee in the exercise of such a power or the carrying out of such a direction, provided the trustee has acted "in good faith, in accordance with the terms of the trust, and not capriciously."[65]

§6.1.2 Duty to Act; Duty to Carry Out the Terms of the Trust and the Settlor's Intentions Generally as Reflected in the Terms

Upon acceptance of a trusteeship, the trustee shall administer the trust in good faith, in accordance with its terms and purposes and the interests of the beneficiaries. . . . [66]

---

[58] Restatement (Third) of Trusts §77 cmt. b; 3 Scott & Ascher §17.6.

[59] Restatement (Second) of Trusts §174 cmt. a; 2A Scott on Trusts §174; Harvard Coll. v. Amory, 26 Mass. (9 Pick.) 446, 461 (1830). *But see* UPC §7-302 (1998) (holding trustee to standard of "a prudent man" dealing with the property of another).

[60] Restatement (Third) of Trusts §77 cmt. a; UTC §801 (available at <http://www.uniformlaws.org/Act.aspx?title=Trust%20Code>); 3 Scott & Ascher §17.6; 2A Scott on Trusts §174.1; UPC §7-302.

[61] *See generally* 3 Scott & Ascher §17.6.

[62] UPC §7-302.

[63] *See generally* 3 Scott & Ascher §17.6.

[64] *See generally* 3 Scott & Ascher §18.2.6 (Reasonableness of Trustee's Exercise of a Power).

[65] 3 Scott & Ascher §18.2.6.

[66] UTC §801 (available at <http://www.uniformlaws.org/Act.aspx?title=Trust%20Code>). "Upon acceptance of the trust by the trustee, he is under a duty to the beneficiary to administer the trust." Restatement (Second) of Trusts §169. If the trustee has not accepted, he can disclaim and is under no liability; but once having accepted he is under a duty to administer the trust as long as he continues to be trustee. Restatement (Second) of Trusts §169 cmt. a. "Even though by the terms of the trust the trustee is to receive no compensation, he is under a duty if he has accepted the trust to administer it." Restatement (Second) of Trusts §169 cmt. b. *See generally* §3.4.2 of this handbook (accepting or disclaiming a trusteeship).

*Having impulsively . . . revealed the prime but private purpose of the Pequod's voyage, Ahab . . . had indirectly laid himself open to the unanswerable charge of usurpation; and with perfect impunity, both moral and legal, his crew if so disposed, and to that end competent, could refuse all further obedience to him, and even violently wrest from him the command—*Herman Melville[67]

While one has no duty to accept the office of trustee, a person who has done so has an affirmative duty to act. While one has no duty to accept the office of trustee,[68] a person who has done so has an affirmative duty[69] to act, *i.e.,* to administer the trust diligently.[70] In England, it is said that upon acceptance of the office, a trustee must not "sleep upon it."[71] An agent, even an agent designated as such under a durable power of attorney, generally has no duty to act.[72] The agent is merely "authorized" to act. This is a core difference between the two fundamental legal relationships.

The settlor's lawful intentions still should be paramount. Unless applicable law provides otherwise,[73] the trustee has an overarching duty to carry out the intentions of the settlor as they have been manifested in the terms of the trust[74] or interpreted by a court.[75] A settlor via the terms of the trust traditionally has even been able to dilute, though not neutralize altogether, the duties of prudence and loyalty that the trustee owes the beneficiaries.[76] The wishes of the beneficiaries are subordinate, or should be subordinate, to those of the settlor.[77]

---

[67] Moby-Dick Ch. 46.

[68] *See generally* §3.4.2 of this handbook (acceptance and disclaimer).

[69] Restatement (Third) of Trusts §76 cmt. b.

[70] Restatement (Third) of Trusts §76(1). *See generally* 3 Scott & Ascher §17.1.

[71] Lewin ¶12-47.

[72] *See generally* §9.9.2 of this handbook (agency arrangements).

[73] Restatement (Third) of Trusts §76(1).

[74] Restatement (Second) of Trusts §164 cmt. a; 2A Scott on Trusts §§164, 164.1. *But see* 2A Scott on Trusts §§165–168 (deviation from terms of trust permitted in cases of impossibility, illegality, or a change in circumstances). *See generally* §8.17 of this handbook (trust reformation to remedy mistakes; trust modification; tax objectives). Unless the settlor has reserved a power to modify or revoke the trust, however, subsequent oral expressions of the settlor are not admissible to vary the terms of the trust. 2A Scott on Trusts §164.1. *See generally* §8.15.6 of this handbook (parol evidence rule). *See also* Bogert §683 (Duty to Use Reasonable Care in Following Settlor's Directions [with regard to trust investments]).

[75] Restatement (Second) of Trusts §8; 1 Scott on Trusts §8.

[76] *See, e.g.,* Bartlett v. Dumaine, 128 N.H. 497, 507–508 (1986) (trust settlor may choose to apply more liberal and forgiving "business judgment rule" to trustee's investments in lieu of "prudent conservator" rule then prevailing under New Hampshire common law); In re Frolich's Estate, 112 N.H. 320, 327 (1972) (" . . . a person's right to dispose of property by . . . trust in such manner and by such means as he sees fit includes the right to increase or decrease those burdens which are ordinarily imposed upon fiduciaries . . . , including the duty of loyalty").

[77] *See, e.g.,* Church of the Little Flower v. U.S. Bank, 979 N.E.2d 106 (Ill. App. Ct. 2012) (holding that the trial court's granting of an equitable deviation petition to terminate a split-interest trust upon a finding that the substantial fees that the trustee had been collecting from the trust estate had been interfering with the trust's charitable purposes was unwarranted in light of the trust's particular terms); American Nat'l Bank of Cheyenne v. Miller, 899 P.2d 1337 (Wyo. 1995) (trustee had a duty and standing to oppose termination of trust even though termination was requested and consented to by all current beneficiaries and remaindermen if the termination

One practitioner-scholar, however, is suggesting that, via the Uniform Trust Code and other such partial codifications, settlor intent is being sacrificed on the altar of flexibility. He writes: "During the past couple of decades . . . the term 'irrevocable,' as used in estate planning, has taken on a new, counter-intuitive meaning. In the 21st century, a trust that's said to be irrevocable is, in truth, often nothing of the sort."[78]

In any case, while legally the trustee is neither an agent of the settlor nor an agent of the beneficiary,[79] it can do no harm for a trustee to consider himself a steward of the trust's purposes as they have been expressed by the settlor in the terms of the trust.[80] The Uniform Prudent Management of Institutional Funds Act (UPMIFA) is generally in accord.[81] In fact, it has been billed as an "improvement" over its predecessor, the Uniform Management of Institutional Funds Act (UMIFA), when it comes to protecting donor intent.[82]

Trustee may not alter trust terms by contract or disclaimer. The trustee has no authority to enter into a contract that would have the effect of altering the terms of the trust,[83] absent the consent of *all* the beneficiaries (and perhaps the settlor) or a court order (*e.g.*, a *cy pres* action).[84] Nor should the trustee be allowed to alter the terms of a trust by selectively disclaiming fiduciary powers.[85]

Trustee's duty to honor spendthrift restraints. The conscientious trustee of a spendthrift trust is attentive to the wishes of the settlor, as they are reflected in the terms of the trust, even when no one is looking over his shoulder. Let us assume that notwithstanding its anti-alienation provisions, the beneficiary intends to assign the beneficial interest. Moreover, it may be in the beneficiary's interest

---

would frustrate a material purpose of the trust). The clearly expressed intention of the settlor should be "zealously guarded." American Nat'l Bank of Cheyenne v. Miller, 899 P.2d 1337, 1339 (Wyo. 1995).

[78] Charles A. Redd, *Flexibility vs. Certainty—Has the Pendulum Swung Too Far?*, Trts. & Estates (Feb. 23, 2015).

[79] "It sometimes happens that the intended terms of the trust differ from the apparent meaning of the trust instrument." UTC §1006 cmt. (available at <http://www.uniformlaws.org/Act.aspx?title=Trust%20Code>). "This can occur because the court, in determining the terms of the trust, is allowed . . . [under the UTC] . . . to consider evidence extrinsic to the trust instrument." UTC §1006 cmt. *See generally* §3.5.2.5 of this handbook (discussing trustee's right to rely on the terms of the trust as expressed in the trust instrument).

[80] *But see* Alan Newman, *The Intention of the Settlor: Under the Uniform Trust Code: Whose Property Is It, Anyway?*, 38 Akron L. Rev. 649 (2005).

[81] Unif. Prudent Management Inst. Funds Act §4, Prefatory Note.

[82] Unif. Prudent Management Inst. Funds Act, Prefatory Note.

[83] The terms of a trust include not just what lies within the four corners of the governing trust instrument but also the "entire manifestation of the settlor's intention, whether in words or by conduct, as apparent from all of the circumstances at the creation of the trust, insofar as such evidence is admissible." 1 Scott & Ascher §2.2.4. "As to any matter expressly addressed in the governing instrument, the terms of the governing instrument ordinarily are the terms of the trust," unless the relevant provision is ambiguous. 1 Scott & Ascher §2.2.4. *See generally* §8.15.6 of this handbook (parol evidence rule).

[84] *See generally* Bogert §713. The *cy pres* doctrine is discussed in §9.4.3 of this handbook.

[85] *Cf.* UPC §2-1105 cmt. ("As a policy matter, the creator of a trust or other arrangement creating a fiduciary relationship should be able to prevent a fiduciary accepting office under the arrangement from altering the parameters of the relationship").

to do so. The trustee's first and foremost duty, however, is to the intentions of the settlor.[86] The assignment must not be honored;[87] the trustee is not an agent of the beneficiary. If the trustee honors the assignment, the settlor ought to have recourse. Would not the trustee's obligation to carry out the settlor's intentions be an illusory one if only the beneficiary could seek its enforcement? Certainly the beneficiary will not be raising any objections in the situation just described. As for the settlor, the matter of what rights, if any, are lodged with the settlor is covered in Chapter 4.

Trustee's affirmative duty to ascertain the purposes of the trust. In administering the trust, the trustee has a duty to ascertain his duties and obligations, the beneficiaries, and the purposes of the trust.[88] He is then under a duty "to comply with the terms of the trust and applicable law in distributing or applying income and principal to or for the benefit of the beneficiaries."[89] English law is in accord.[90] Thus, under traditional principles of trust law, a trustee is absolutely liable for misdelivery,[91] *i.e.*, there is liability even in the absence of fault.[92] So also is the trustee who honors a powerholder's direct appointment of the trust property to a nonobject of the power.[93] The transferee who was unjustly enriched by the misdelivery, however, would be obliged to indemnify the trustee, or otherwise make restitution.[94] UPMIFA expressly charges the fiduciary with considering the charitable purposes of the institutional fund and making a reasonable effort to verify facts relevant to its management and investment.[95]

---

[86] *Cf.* Estate of Somers, 277 Kan. 761, 89 P.3d 898, 907 (2004) (a case in which a corporate trustee opposed partial termination by modification of a split-interest charitable trust "because of its duty to carry out the terms of the instrument and the wishes of the settlor," the court noting cynically, however, that the trustee "stood to lose management fees should the Trust be terminated or reduced in corpus").

[87] *See, e.g.*, Restatement (Second) of Trusts §164. *But see* §5.3.2 of this handbook (discussing in part how courts tend to react when such assignments are honored).

[88] Restatement (Third) of Trusts §76(2).

[89] 3 Scott & Ascher §17.14 (Duty to Distribute or Apply Income and Principal in Accordance with Terms of Trust). *See also* §3.5.3.2(a) of this handbook (the discretionary trust)) and §5.4.1.3 of this handbook (beneficiary's right to income or possession).

[90] Lewin ¶ 12-49 (England).

[91] Lewin ¶ 26-02 through ¶ 26-04 (England); 4 Scott & Ascher §24.5 (U.S.). "The trustee is liable although he makes the payment or conveyance under a reasonable mistake of law or fact." Restatement (Second) of Trusts §226 cmt. b. *See generally* §8.32 of this handbook (whether the trustee can escape liability for making a mistake of law if he acted in good faith on advice of counsel).

[92] 4 Scott & Ascher §24.5 (Liability without Actual Fault). *See also* Restatement (Third) of Restitution and Unjust Enrichment §17 (fiduciary misdeliveries).

[93] Restatement (Third) of Property (Wills and Other Donative Transfers) §19.17(a). Powers of appointment are covered generally in §8.1.1 of this handbook. The fraud on a special power doctrine is taken up in §8.15.26 of this handbook.

[94] Restatement of Restitution §163 ("Where the owner of property transfers it as a result of mistake of such a character that he is entitled to restitution, the transferee holds the property upon a constructive trust for him."). *See generally* §7.2.3.1.6 of this handbook (the constructive trust as a procedural equitable remedy).

[95] Unif. Prudent Management Inst. Funds Act, §3.

Trustee's affirmative duty to ascertain the proper beneficiaries of the trust. This duty to read the governing instrument and get the facts is all part and parcel of the trustee's general duty to carry out the terms of the trust.[96] "If he is in doubt as to the proper person to whom a payment or conveyance should be made, he can apply to the court for instructions and will be protected by the order of the court against claims of all persons who were made parties to the proceeding."[97] The trustee, however, is entitled to bring an action on his own behalf against the transferee to recover the misdelivered property.[98]

Trustee's good-faith failure to ascertain external facts. The Uniform Trust Code, however, would relieve the trustee from liability for a good faith failure to "ascertain external facts, often of a personal nature, that might affect administration or distribution of the trust" in ways that thwart the intentions of the settlor.[99] It provides that if the happening of an event, including marriage, divorce, performance of educational requirements, or death, affects the administration or distribution of a trust, a trustee who has exercised reasonable care to ascertain the happening of the event is not liable for a loss resulting from the trustee's lack of knowledge.[100] The Restatement (Third) of Trusts is generally in accord.[101]

Capricious purposes. It should be noted that the settlor's latitude when it comes to defining the purposes of the trust is not unlimited.[102] "[T]he principle that a trust have a purpose which is for the benefit of its beneficiaries precludes unreasonable restrictions on the use of trust property."[103] Likewise, "[a]n owner's freedom to be capricious about the use of the owner's own property ends when the property is impressed with a trust for the benefit of others."[104]

A trust term that purports to oust the court of its traditional equitable jurisdiction over trust matters. Nor is a trust term that purports to oust the court of its traditional equitable jurisdiction over trust matters enforceable, *e.g.*, one that purports to bestow on a member of the executive branch of a state's government the authority to make binding determinations as to whether the trustee is complying with the other trust terms.[105] Nor can the court be "ousted" by an expansive grant of discretion to the trustee. "It is submitted . . . that, even as to matters thus firmly committed to the trustee's discretion,

---

[96] Restatement (Third) of Trusts §76 cmt. f.

[97] Restatement (Second) of Trusts §226 cmt. b. *See also* Restatement (Third) of Trusts §76 cmt. f; 4 Scott & Ascher §24.31 (Liability for Incorrect Distributions).

[98] Restatement (Third) of Trusts §76 cmt. f. *See also* Old Colony Trust Co. v. Wood, 321 Mass. 519, 526, 74 N.E.2d 141, 145–146 (1947).

[99] UTC §1007 cmt. (available at <http://www.uniformlaws.org/Act.aspx?title=Trust%20Code>).

[100] UTC §1007 (available at <http://www.uniformlaws.org/Act.aspx?title=Trust%20 Code>). *See also* 4 Scott & Ascher §24.31 (Liability for Incorrect Distributions).

[101] Restatement (Third) of Trusts §76 cmt. f.

[102] UTC §412 cmt. (available at <http://www.uniformlaws.org/Act.aspx?title=Trust%20Code>).

[103] UTC §412 cmt. (available at <http://www.uniformlaws.org/Act.aspx?title=Trust%20Code>).

[104] UTC §412 cmt. (available at <http://www.uniformlaws.org/Act.aspx?title=Trust%20Code>).

[105] *See generally* 3 Scott & Ascher §18.2 (Executive Branch Encroachment on Court's Equitable Prerogatives). *Cf.* §9.4.4 of this handbook (legislative branch encroachment on court's equitable prerogatives).

judicial review should remain available if the trustee acts in bad faith, contrary to the terms of the trust, or with an improper motive."[106]

Trust terms that are unlawful or violate public policy. While the trustee has a duty to carry out the terms of the trust, he has a countervailing duty to the beneficiaries "*not* to comply with a provision of the trust that the trustee knows or should know is invalid because the provision is unlawful or contrary to public policy."[107] This duty not to comply is covered in Section 6.2.12 of this handbook. The trustee also may not attempt to comply with a provision if compliance would be impossible or incur unreasonable expense. This other duty not to comply is addressed in Section 6.2.13 of this handbook.

Whether the UTC benefit-the-beneficiaries rule erodes the principle that settlor intent is paramount. Section 404 of the Uniform Trust Code codifies what facially are plain vanilla principles of trust law: "A trust may be created only to the extent its purposes are lawful, not contrary to public policy, and possible to achieve. A trust and its terms must be for the benefit of the beneficiaries." Yale Law School Professor John H. Langbein, however, "believes," and, one senses, fervently hopes, that in the future the Code's "benefit-the-beneficiaries" rule "will interact with the growing understanding of sound fiduciary investing practices to restrain the settlor's power to direct a course of investment imparting risk and return objectives contrary to the interests of the beneficiaries."[108] In other words, there is actually an "intent-defeating" aspect to the Uniform Trust Code provision.[109] "Under Professor Langbein's formulation of the benefit-the-beneficiaries rule, the 'benefit' of a trust provision is determined by reference to objective notions of prudence and efficiency rather than the settlors' subjective intent."[110]

The courts, however, have been delivering a resounding "no thanks" to Professor Langbein's formulation.[111] So have the legislatures.[112] And so have

---

[106] 3 Scott & Ascher §18.2 (Control of Discretionary Powers).

[107] Restatement (Third) of Trusts §72.

[108] John H. Langbein, *Mandatory Rules in the Law of Trusts*, 98 Nw. U. L. Rev. 1105, 1111(2004).

[109] John H. Langbein, *Mandatory Rules in the Law of Trusts*, 98 Nw. U. L. Rev. 1105 (2004).

[110] Jeffrey A. Cooper, *Empty Promises: Settlor's Intent, the Uniform Trust Code, and the Future of Trust Investment law*, 88 Boston Univ. L. Rev. 1165, 1168–1169 (2008).

[111] *See, e.g.*, Carter v. Carter, 965 N.E.2d 1146 (Ill. 2012); Ladysmith Rescue Squad, Inc. v. Newlin, 694 S.E.2d 604 (Va. 2010) ("We conclude that the UTC has not altered the fundamental principles that in construing, enforcing and administering wills and trusts, the testator's or settlor's intent prevails over the desires of the beneficiaries, and that intent is to be ascertained by the language the testator or settlor used in creating the will or trust."); Parker v. Shullman, 983 So. 2d 643 (Fla. App. 4th Dist. 2008); In re Trust Created by Charlotte P. Hyde, 845 N.Y.S.2d 833 (2007); *cf.* Church of the Little Flower v. U.S. Bank, 979 N.E.2d 106 (Ill. App. Ct. 2012) (holding that the trial court's granting of an equitable deviation petition to terminate a split-interest trust upon a finding that the trustee's continuing to deduct from the trust estate its substantial but lawful fees would not be in furtherance of the interests of the beneficiaries was unwarranted in light of the trust's particular terms).

[112] *See, e.g.*, Ohio Rev. Code Ann. §5804.04; Ga. Code Ann. §53-12-341(2); N.H. Rev. Stat. Ann. §564-B:1-112/1-105(b)(3)/4-404 (generally providing that a trustee is not liable to a beneficiary to the extent that the trustee acted in reasonable reliance on the provisions of the trust or court order or determined not to diversify the investments of a trust in good faith in reliance on

the legal academics. Quinnipiac University School of Law School Professor Jeffrey A. Cooper, for one, has weighed in on the side of the settlor.[113] Professor Cooper outlines numerous reasons, some practical, some grounded in public policy, why any court would be ill-advised to put an "intent-defeating" gloss on the Code's "benefit-the-beneficiaries" rule. The first victim of the gloss would be the Uniform Trust Code itself: "The approach would render the UTC a fundamentally incomprehensible piece of trust legislation, requiring a reader seeking to understand the UTC's meaning to look to the pages of law reviews rather than the UTC's own text."[114] In his *Dead Hand Investing: The Enforceability of Trust Investment Directives*, Professor Cooper articulates his global policy objection to the rule, namely that it "can be read to materially alter key principles of traditional trust law, creating significant complexities of statutory interpretation and precipitating a host of undesirable, likely unintended, consequences."[115] His many reasons for coming to this conclusion are fleshed out in the article.

The UTC's mandatory rules also appear to be muddling certain aspects of our conflict of laws jurisprudence that are trust-focused, a subject covered generally in Section 8.5 of this handbook. For some reason, the Uniform Trust Code does not codify the settlor's general, though not limitless, common law right to designate which state's laws shall govern the resolution of questions bearing on the trust's validity.[116] University of Texas Professor Mark L. Ascher speculates on what that reason could be:

> One senses in all this the icy hand of section 105 of the UTC, which lists those issues as to which the UTC purports to be mandatory law, i.e., those issues as to which the settlor may not, by the terms of the trust, effectively provide otherwise. Among the issues listed in section 105 are "the requirements for creating a trust." Thus, it may be that the unwillingness of section 403 to allow the settlor, by the terms of the trust, to designate the law that is to apply in determining whether the trust has been "validly created" is simply a consequence of an almost entirely cosmetic effort at buttressing section 105.[117]

---

the express terms of the trust). *See also* Joseph F. McDonald, III, *Open Architecture Trust Designs under New Hampshire Law Provide Flexibility and Opportunities*, N.H. B.J. (Autumn 2008), at 38 ("A beneficiary seeking to surcharge a trustee for relying on an authority to retain under a governing instrument or court order have a formidable evidentiary burden: they now must show that the trustee acted in bad faith in following a direction or authorization not to diversify."). Massachusetts registered its "no thanks" by leaving out of its version of UTC §404 the following sentence: "A trust and its terms must be for the benefit of its beneficiaries." *See* M.G.L.A. 203E §404. So did Iowa by opting not to include any mandatory rules in its trust code.

[113] *Empty Promises: Settlor's Intent, the Uniform Trust Code, and the Future of Trust Investment law*, 88 B.U. L. Rev. 1165 (2008).

[114] Jeffrey A. Cooper, *Empty Promises: Settlor's Intent, the Uniform Trust Code, and the Future of Trust Investment law*, 88 B.U. L. Rev. 1165, 1179 (2008).

[115] Jeffrey A. Cooper, *Dead Hand Investing: The Enforceability of Trust Investment Directives*, 37 ACTEC L.J. 365, 405 (Winter 2011).

[116] *See generally* 7 Scott & Ascher §45.4.2.1.

[117] 7 Scott & Ascher §45.4.2.1.

§6.1.3 Trustee's Duty of Loyalty to the Beneficiaries or to the Trust's Charitable Purposes

A trustee is held to something stricter than the morals of the marketplace. Not honesty alone, but the punctilio of an honor the most sensitive, is then the standard of behavior. As to this there has developed a tradition that is unbending and inveterate. Uncompromising rigidity has been the attitude of courts of equity when petitioned to undermine the rule of undivided loyalty by the disintegrating erosion of particular exceptions.[118]

The principle. As noted earlier, "[t]wo grand principles underlie much of the Anglo-American law of trusts: the trustee's duties of *loyalty* and of *prudence*."[119] As to the duty of loyalty, the more "fundamental" of the two,[120] a trustee is under a duty to act solely in the interest of the beneficiaries as to matters that directly and indirectly involve the trust property.[121] In the case of a charitable trust, the trustee must administer the trust "solely in the interests of effectuating the trust's charitable purposes."[122] The members of the board or council of a civil law foundation, on the other hand, owe their primary

---

[118] Meinhard v. Salmon, 249 N.Y. 458, 464, 164 N.E. 545, 546 (1928) (Cardozo, C.J.). *But see* Restatement (Third) of Trusts §78 cmt. b (suggesting that the Cardozo quote now fails "to capture either the experience or the true policy of American trust law"). *See also* Pegram v. Herdrich, 120 S. Ct. 2143 (2000) (discussing the meaning of the word *fiduciary* as that term is employed in ERISA, distinguishing the duties of a common law trustee from that of an HMO physician, and citing to the passage of *Meinhard v. Salmon* that accompanies this footnote). One commentator finds the Cardozo passage's "rhetorical excess" not only a bit much but also not an entirely accurate summary of the state of the law: "In addition, the courts have often loaded the dice rhetorically, stating proudly that a trustee's duty not to engage in transactions that involve self-dealing or that involve or might create conflicts of interest is 'strict' or 'absolute'"). 3 Scott & Ascher §17.2. Still, with loyalty jurisprudence now riddled with "particular exceptions" and with U.S. law schools, for the most part, no longer requiring that their students take courses in the agency and trust relationships, the two core fiduciary relationships from which all others derive, it would be unfortunate if the rhetorical excesses and now unfashionable earnestness of the Cardozo passage were to detract and distract one from an appreciation of the fact that democratic capitalism functions best not only when contracts are generally enforced but also when fiduciaries (or their civil law counterparts) can generally expect to be held accountable for their actions. *See generally* Charles E. Rounds, Jr., *The Case for a Return to Mandatory Instruction in the Fiduciary Aspects of Agency and Trusts in the American Law School*, 18 Regent U. L. Rev. 251 (2005–2006).

[119] John A. Langbein & Bruce A. Wolk, Pension and Employee Benefit Law 678 (2000).

[120] 3 Scott & Ascher §17.2.

[121] UTC §802(a) (available at <http://www.uniformlaws.org/Act.aspx?title=Trust%20 Code>). *See* Restatement (Third) of Trusts §78(1); 3 Scott & Ascher §17.2; 2A Scott on Trusts §170. The Employee Retirement Income Security Act (ERISA), 29 U.S.C. §§1104(a)1, 404 (1974) codifies this duty for fiduciaries of employees' pension plans; Revised Reg. 9 (effective Jan. 29, 1997 and available at <www.gpoaccess.gov/cfr/index.html> provides that a national bank exercising fiduciary powers shall adopt and follow written policies and procedures that address, where appropriate, the bank's methods for preventing self-dealing and conflicts of interest. *See* 12 C.F.R. §9.5(c).

[122] UTC §802 cmt. (available at <http://www.uniformlaws.org/Act.aspx?title=Trust%20 Code>). *See also* Restatement (Third) of Trusts §78(1). *See generally* §9.4 of this handbook (The Charitable Trust).

allegiance to the entity itself, even when there are noncharitable beneficiaries.[123]

A trustee is always a fiduciary with a general duty of loyalty, even the interested trustee whose duties are, for all intents and purposes, ministerial.[124] "Even if the terms of the trust plainly authorize the trustee to deal with himself or herself, the trustee always must act fairly and in good faith."[125] Even the indenture trustee whose duties are little more than custodial owes the bondholder-beneficiaries its undivided loyalty.[126] This general duty of loyalty runs to the beneficiary.[127] Thus, neither a cotrustee nor a successor trustee can authorize or ratify a trustee's breach of the general duty of loyalty.

Reconciling the trustee's duty of loyalty to the beneficiary and his duty to carry out the settlor's intentions. As to how the trustee's duty of undivided loyalty to the beneficiaries is reconciled with the trustee's overarching duty to carry out the settlor's intentions as manifested in the terms of the trust, the reader is referred to Section 6.1.2 of this handbook and Jeffrey A. Cooper.[128]

A brief history of the loyalty principle. The "foundation" of Anglo-American loyalty jurisprudence is the holding in *Keech v. Sandford*, a 1726 English case in which the court admonished a trustee of a lease for renewing it in his own name.[129] From it has evolved the general profit rule, which is this: "If a trustee . . . without authority makes a profit directly or indirectly from the use of the property subject to the trust . . . , or in the course of the fiduciary relationship and by reason of his fiduciary position, then he is not permitted to retain the profit."[130] It must accrue one way or the other to the trust estate. Otherwise the trustee would be unjustly enriched, a topic we take up in Section 8.15.78 of this handbook. The Restatement (Third) of Restitution and Unjust

---

[123] *See generally* §8.12.1 of this handbook (the civil law foundation).

[124] *See generally* 3 Scott & Ascher §17.2; Charles E. Rounds, Jr., *Lawyer Codes Are Just About Licensure, the Lawyer's Relationship with the State: Recalling the Common Law Agency, Contract, Tort, Trust, and Property Principles the Regulate the Lawyer-Client Fiduciary Relationship*, 60 Baylor L. Rev. 771 (2008).

[125] 3 Scott & Ascher §§17.2.11 (The Terms of the Trust), 18.2.3 (When Trustee Acts Dishonestly).

[126] E.F. Hutton Southwest Properties II, Ltd. v. Union Planters Nat'l Bank, 953 F.2d 963, 969 (1992). *See generally* §9.31 of this handbook (corporate trusts; trusts to secure creditors; the Trust Indenture Act of 1939; protecting bondholders).

[127] *See generally* 3 Scott & Ascher §17.2 (Duty of Loyalty).

[128] *Empty Promises: Settlor's Intent, The Uniform Trust Code, and the Future of Trust Investment Law*, 88 B.U. L. Rev. 1165 (2008).

[129] (1726) 2 Eq. Cas. Abr. 741, Sel. Cas. Ch. 61, 25 Eng. Rep. 223 (1726); Lewin ¶¶20-02 to 20–27. *See also* Restatement (Third) of Trusts §78 cmt. e (confirming that "a trustee must not acquire, for the trustee's personal account, a lease or encumbrance held by another on trust property") and the Reporter's Notes thereto; 3 Scott & Ascher §17.2.7 (Purchase of Adverse Interest from Third Person). *Cf.* Meinhard v. Salmon, 164 N.E. 545 (N.Y. 1928) (holding an agent fiduciary, in this case a "joint adventurer," liable for renewing a lease for his own benefit behind the back of his coadventurer). Had the coadventurer declined to participate in the lease renewal after having been given a fair opportunity to do so, the plaintiff likely would not have prevailed. *See, e.g.*, Ebberts v. McLean, 98 S.W.2d 352 (Tex. 1937).

[130] Lewin ¶20-26 (England).

Enrichment is fully in accord.[131] In England, the profit, whether in cash or in kind, is held upon a constructive trust for the benefit of the beneficiaries.[132] So also on this side of the Atlantic.[133]

The loyalty principle is embedded in the trust relationship itself. The duty of undivided loyalty springs from the trust relationship rather than from any provision of the trust instrument.[134] It is the bedrock of the trust relationship.[135] "Reasons behind the establishment of the loyalty rule by equity are that it is generally, if not always, humanly impossible for the same person to act fairly in two capacities and on behalf of two interests in the same transaction."[136] A trustee, like an agent with discretionary authority, is a fiduciary;[137] but unlike the principal in an agency relationship, the trust beneficiary, at least under the default law, cannot fire or vote out his or her fiduciaries.[138] Moreover, under the terms of the typical noncommercial trust, it would not be possible for the beneficiary to cut his or her losses by selling or otherwise disposing of the beneficial or equitable interest.[139]

Voidable transactions. "A transaction affected by a conflict between the trustee's fiduciary and personal interests is voidable by a beneficiary who is affected by the transaction."[140] The following transactions are likely voidable,

---

[131] Restatement (Third) of Restitution and Unjust Enrichment §3 (wrongful gain).

[132] Lewin ¶ 20-28. *See* §3.3 of this handbook (discussing generally the constructive trust); §7.2.3.1.6 of this handbook (the constructive trust as a procedural equitable remedy).

[133] Restatement of Restitution §190. *See also* §3.3 of this handbook (discussing generally the constructive trust); §7.2.3.1.6 of this handbook (the constructive trust as a procedural equitable remedy).

[134] *See generally* 3 Scott & Ascher §17.2.

[135] *See* Restatement (Third) of Trusts §78 cmt. c(2) (noting that even if the terms of the trust authorize the trustee to act in a way that would otherwise constitute a breach of the duty of loyalty, the express authorization . . . would not completely dispense with the trustee's underlying fiduciary obligations to act in the interest of the beneficiaries and to exercise prudence in administering the trust"); 3 Scott & Ascher §17.2 (noting that the duty of loyalty is the trustee's "most fundamental duty" and that "it arises not from any provision in the terms of the trust but simply on account of the relationship that is inherent in every trust").

[136] Bogert §543. "Consciously or unconsciously he will favor one side as against the other, where there is or may be a conflict of interest." Bogert §543. *See also* 3 Scott & Ascher §17.2.14.6 (noting that "[a]s long as banks have both trust departments and commercial banking departments, questions of divided loyalty, sometimes quite difficult, will continue to arise").

[137] For a discussion of the meaning of the word *fiduciary* and for a comparison of the two principle fiduciary relationships, *i.e.*, the agency and the trust, *see* Chapter 1 of this handbook.

[138] Restatement (Third) of Trusts §78 cmt. b.

[139] Restatement (Third) of Trusts §78 cmt. b.

[140] UTC §802 cmt. (available at <http://www.uniformlaws.org/Act.aspx?title=Trust%20 Code>).

unless authorized by the terms of the trust, by a court order,[141] by legislation or regulation, or by the informed consent of all beneficiaries:[142]

- Trustee selling trust property and keeping the proceeds for himself;[143]
- Trustee buying at trustee's own sale, even if the sale is a public one and the trustee is the highest bidder;[144]
- Trustee leasing trust property to self;[145]
- Trustee buying at sale forced by third person;[146]
- Trustee buying for self-encumbrances (outstanding claims against, or interests in, trust property);[147]

---

[141] *See generally* 3 Scott & Ascher §17.2.12 (Court Approval) (noting that the "key" to whether a court would authorize a trustee to enter into a transaction that would implicate the duty of loyalty is whether the transaction would be in the best interest of the beneficiaries).

[142] *See generally* 3 Scott & Ascher §17.2 (confirming that "self-interested trustee transactions may well be proper when they have been authorized by the terms of the trust, a court order, or the consent of the beneficiaries").

[143] *See* Restatement of Restitution §198 ("Where a fiduciary in violation of his duty to the beneficiary disposes of property entrusted to him as fiduciary, he holds any property received in exchange upon a constructive trust for the beneficiary"); §3.3 of this handbook (discussing generally the constructive trust); §7.2.3.1.6 of this handbook (the constructive trust as a procedural equitable remedy).

[144] *See generally* Bogert §543(A); Restatement (Third) of Trusts §78 cmt. b (suggesting that "otherwise the possibility of purchase by the trustee would create a temptation for the exercise of less than the trustee's best efforts and business judgment on behalf of the trust to determine whether sale is appropriate and to obtain the most favorable price and terms from others for the trust property"); Restatement of Restitution §192, cmt. b (purchase by fiduciary individually of property entrusted to him as fiduciary/private or public sale).

[145] Bogert §543(B); Lewin ¶20-62 (England). *See also* Lewin ¶20-65 (providing that if trust property is subject to a lease that is assignable only with consent of the trustee-lessor, the self-dealing rule is violated if the trustee-lessor consents to the assignment of the lease by the tenant to one of the trustees).

[146] Bogert §543(C); 3 Scott & Ascher §17.2.1.

[147] Bogert §543(D); Restatement of Restitution §196 ("Where a fiduciary in violation of his duty to the beneficiary purchases or retains an encumbrance upon property entrusted to him as fiduciary, he holds the encumbrance upon a constructive trust for the beneficiary"); Restatement of Restitution §196, cmt. b ("The rule is not based upon the existence of harm to the beneficiary in the particular case. The purpose of the rule is to prevent a conflict of opposing interests in the minds of fiduciaries, whose duty is to act solely for the benefit of their beneficiaries"); §3.3 of this handbook (discussing generally the constructive trust); §7.2.3.1.6 of this handbook (the constructive trust as a procedural equitable remedy); 3 Scott & Ascher §17.2.7 (Purchase of Encumbrance) (noting that though a trustee may purchase from a third party for the trustee's own account an encumbrance on the trust property, the trustee may not profit thereby). Also, if a trustee is entrusted with property for the benefit of a class of creditors, the trustee may purchase the claim of one of the creditor-beneficiaries without the informed consent of the others, but any profit accruing to the trustee as a result of the purchase must be held for the benefit of the others. The trustee is entitled only to the purchase price, plus interest. 3 Scott & Ascher §17.2.7. The seller of the encumbrance, on the other hand, may be without recourse if the sale price was fair and the seller had full knowledge of the applicable facts and law. 3 Scott & Ascher §17.2.7.

- Trustee purchasing substantial interests in a business association both for the trust estate and for the trustee personally at the same time;[148]
- Trustee purchasing in his fiduciary capacity (from a third party) a substantial interest in a business association in which the trustee already holds an interest in a personal capacity;[149]
- Trustee purchasing in his individual capacity (from a third party) a substantial interest in a business association in which the trustee already holds an interest in a fiduciary capacity;[150]
- Trustee selling own property to the trust;[151]
- Corporate trustee buying earmarked pool of investments for trusts;[152]
- Corporate trustee buying or holding its own stock for a trust;[153]
- Trustee of one trust selling to itself as trustee of another trust;[154]
- Trustee of lease taking renewal or buying reversion for self;[155]
- Trustee lending funds to himself, herself, or itself;[156]
- Corporate trustee depositing funds with its own banking department;[157]
- Trustee lending own funds to trust;[158]

---

[148] Restatement (Third) of Trusts §78 cmt. e (noting that such a transaction could give rise to a temptation on the part of the trustee to consider his own advantage rather than solely the interests of the trust beneficiaries, *e.g.*, "in the exercise of voting rights, in later decisions to sell or retain the interest held either in the trust or by the trustee personally, and in situations in which the trustee might consider making further equity or debt investment in the enterprise"); 3 Scott & Ascher §17.2.9 (Competition with the Trust).

[149] Restatement (Third) of Trusts §78 cmt. e; 3 Scott & Ascher §17.2.9 (Competition with the Trust).

[150] Restatement (Third) of Trusts §78 cmt. e; 3 Scott & Ascher §17.2.9 (Competition with the Trust).

[151] Bogert §543(E) (U.S.); Lewin ¶20-63 (England). *See generally* 3 Scott & Ascher §17.2.2 (Purchase of Trustee's Own Property by Trust); Restatement of Restitution §193 ("Where a fiduciary who has power to purchase property for the beneficiary purchases property from himself individually in violation of his duty to the beneficiary, he holds the purchase money upon a constructive trust for the beneficiary"); §3.3 of this handbook (a general discussion of the constructive trust); §7.2.3.1.6 of this handbook (the constructive trust as a procedural equitable remedy).

[152] Bogert §543(F).

[153] Bogert §543(G).

[154] Bogert §543(H); Lewin ¶20-76 (England).

[155] Bogert §543(I) (U.S.); Lewin ¶2-02 through ¶20-25 (England). *See also* Restatement (Third) of Trusts §78 cmt. e; 3 Scott & Ascher §17.2.7 (Purchase of Adverse Interest from Third Person); Restatement of Restitution §195 ("A person holding as fiduciary a leasehold interest who in violation of his duty to the beneficiary obtains a renewal of the lease for himself holds the new lease upon a constructive trust for the beneficiary"); §3.3 of this handbook (a general discussion of the constructive trust); §7.2.3.1.6 of this handbook (the constructive trust as a procedural equitable remedy).

[156] Bogert §543(J); Lewin ¶20-64 (England); 3 Scott & Ascher §17.2.4 (When Trustee Borrows Trust Funds) (U.S.).

[157] Bogert §543(K); 3 Scott & Ascher §17.2.14.6.

[158] Bogert §543(L); Lewin ¶20-64 (England); 3 Scott & Ascher §17.2.6 (Loan by Trustee to the Trust) (U.S.).

- Trustee employing self to do specialized work for the trust;[159]
- Trustee of corporate stock voting for election of himself, herself, or itself as director or officer of corporation;[160]
- Trustee of a business enterprise engages in competing business for personal profit;[161]
- Trustee accepting a gift from one with whom the trustee conducts trust business;[162]
- Trustee securing incidental benefit such as bonuses and commissions for self from third parties incidental to the administration of the trust estate;[163]
- Trustee with a duty to buy for the trust purchases for himself;[164]
- Trustee acting for the trust and also for a third party who deals with the trust;[165]
- Trustee exploiting confidential information for personal benefit;[166]
- Indirect disloyalty: dealings with relatives, affiliated corporations, and similar persons.[167]

The no-further-inquiry rule. Under classic principles of trust law, the fact that the trustee engaged in an unauthorized act of self-dealing was all that the beneficiary needed to prove in an action to void the transaction. As no further

---

[159] Bogert §543(M).

[160] Bogert §543(N); Lewin ¶ 20-37 (England). *But see* Restatement (Third) of Trusts §78 cmt. d(1) (providing that although technically a form of self-dealing results, there is no breach of trust if the trustee's position is procured to serve the interests of the trust and its beneficiaries, provided the salary is not greater than what is warranted by the services the trustee performs for the enterprise on behalf of the trust and its beneficiaries). *See also* 3 Scott & Ascher §17.2.8.

[161] Bogert §543(O); Restatement of Restitution §199 ("Where a fiduciary acquires property by competing with the beneficiary in violation of his duty to the beneficiary, he holds the property upon a constructive trust for the beneficiary"); §3.3 of this handbook (a general discussion of the constructive trust); §7.2.3.1.6 of this handbook (the constructive trust as a procedural equitable remedy); *see also* Restatement (Third) of Trusts §78 cmt. e; 3 Scott & Ascher §17.2.9.

[162] Bogert §543(P).

[163] Bogert §543(Q); 3 Scott & Ascher §§17.2.3 (Use of Trust Property for Trustee's Own Benefit),17.2.8 (Bonus, Commission, or Other Compensation); Restatement of Restitution §197 ("Where a fiduciary in violation of his duty to the beneficiary receives or retains a bonus or commission or other profit, he holds what he receives upon a constructive trust for the beneficiary"); §3.3 of this handbook (a general discussion of the constructive trust); §7.2.3.1.6 of this handbook (the constructive trust as a procedural equitable remedy).

[164] Bogert §543(R); 3 Scott & Ascher §§17.2.7,17.2.9; Restatement of Restitution §194 ("A fiduciary who purchases from a third person for himself individually property which it is his duty to purchase for the beneficiary holds it upon a constructive trust for the beneficiary"); §3.3 of this handbook (a general discussion of the constructive trust); §7.2.3.1.6 of this handbook (the constructive trust as a procedural equitable remedy).

[165] Bogert §543(S); Lewin ¶ 20-75 (England); 3 Scott & Ascher §17.2.1.3 (U.S.).

[166] Restatement of Restitution §200 ("Where a fiduciary in violation of his duty to the beneficiary acquires property through the use of confidential information, he holds the property so acquired upon a constructive trust for the beneficiary"): §3.3 of this handbook (a general discussion of the constructive trust); §7.2.3.1.6 of this handbook (the constructive trust as a procedural equitable remedy).

[167] Bogert §543(T); Lewin ¶ 20-72 through ¶ 20-74 (England).

proof was required, this came to be known as the "no further inquiry rule."[168] Whether the trustee acts in good faith[169] or pays a fair consideration[170] or erects a Chinese wall between its commercial and fiduciary departments[171] is immaterial.[172] The rule was marbled through the English common law[173] and is consistent with traditional civil law (continental) fiduciary principles.[174] It is a rule that the Restatement (Third) of Trusts for "prophylactic reasons"[175] has given its unqualified endorsement and ratification.[176] It recognizes, however, that there are some long-standing exceptions to the rule that, for reasons of practicality, efficiency, and beneficiary interest, should be allowed to stand, *e.g.*, when the terms of the trust[177] or rulings of the court authorize a transaction that involves conflicting fiduciary and personal interests.[178] One learned commentator has articulated the rule's general policy underpinnings: In its wish to guard the highly valuable fiduciary relationships against improper administration, equity deems it better to forbid disloyalty and strike down all disloyal acts,

---

[168] *See* Girod v. Girod, 45 U.S. 503, 553 (1846). *See generally* 3 Scott & Ascher §17.2.

[169] *See* In re Gleeson's Will, 124 N.E.2d 624 (Ill. App. 1955) ("The good faith and honesty of the . . . [trustee] . . . can avail . . . [him] . . . nothing so far as justification of the course he chose to take in dealing with trust proper is concerned.").

[170] *See* In re Gleeson's Will, 124 N.E.2d 624 (Ill. App. 1955) (" . . . [T]he fact that the trust sustained no loss on account of his dealings therewith . . . can avail . . . [the trustee] . . . nothing so far as justification of the course he chose to take in dealing with trust proper is concerned.").

[171] Lewin ¶ 20-61 (England); 3 Scott & Ascher §17.2.14.6 (noting that Chinese walls have generally proven "not very effective").

[172] *See* Girod v. Girod, 45 U.S. 503, 553 (1846).

[173] *See generally* Lewin ¶ 20-60.

[174] Girod v. Girod, 45 U.S. 503, 552–562. *See generally* §8.12.1 of this handbook (civil law alternatives to the trust).

[175] Restatement (Third) of Trusts §78 cmt. b. "In such situations, for reasons peculiar to typical trust relationships, the policy of the trust law is to prefer (as a matter of default law) to remove altogether the occasions of temptation rather than to monitor fiduciary behavior and attempt to uncover and punish abuses when a trustee has actually succumbed to temptation." Restatement (Third) of Trusts §78 cmt. b. "The inherent subjectivity and impracticability of second guessing a trustee's application of business judgment or exercise of fiduciary discretion are aggravated by the opportunities and relative ease of concealing misconduct—or at least by the absence of timely information and the likely disappearance of relevant evidence—that results from the trustee's day-to-day, usually long-term, management of the trust property and control over the trust records." Restatement (Third) of Trusts §78 cmt. b. "Viewed from the beneficiaries' perspective, especially that of remainder beneficiaries, efforts to prevent or detect actual improprieties can be expected to be inefficient if not ineffective." Restatement (Third) of Trusts §78 cmt. b. "Such efforts are likely to be wastefully expensive and to suffer from time lag and inadequacies of information, from a lack of relevant experience and understanding, and perhaps from want of resources to monitor trustee behavior and ultimately to litigate and expose actual instances of fiduciary misconduct." Restatement (Third) of Trusts §78 cmt. b. *But see* John H. Langbein, *Questioning the Trust Law Duty of Loyalty: Sole Interest or Best Interest?*, 114 Yale L.J. 929 (2005) (suggesting that profound historical changes over the past two centuries have rendered the no further inquiry rule obsolete). For the counterargument, *see* Leslie, *In Defense of the No Further Inquiry Rule: A Response to Professor John Langbein*, 47 Wm. & Mary L. Rev. 541 (2005).

[176] Restatement (Third) of Trusts §78 cmt. b.

[177] *See generally* 3 Scott & Ascher §17.2.11.

[178] Restatement (Third) of Trusts §78 cmt. c. *See generally* §7.1.2 of this handbook (defenses to allegations that the trustee breached the duty of loyalty); 3 Scott & Ascher §§17.2, 17.2.12.

rather than to attempt to justify...[the trustee's]...representation of two interests.[179]

For some time now, John H. Langbein, an influential trust academic who has had little real-world law practice experience, has been advocating a generalized defanging of the no-further-inquiry rule.[180] The ivory tower, however, is not the real world, as another trust academic has reminded us:

> Under the influence of law and economics theory, prominent scholars and reformers are rapidly dismantling the traditional legal and moral constraints on trustees. Trusts are becoming mere "contracts," and trust law nothing more than "default rules." "Efficiency" is triumphing over morality. In the law and economics universe of foresighted settlors, loyal trustees, informed beneficiaries, and sophisticated family and commercial creditors, trusting trustees may make sense. In the real world, however, it does not. A trust system that exalts trustee autonomy over accountability can and increasingly does impose significant human costs on all affected by trusts.[181]

Whether charitable and noncharitable fiduciaries are held to different loyalty standards. It has been suggested that different standards of loyalty apply to directors of charitable corporations and trustees of charitable trusts.[182] In the former case, it is a "best interest" standard; in the latter, it is the "sole interest" standard that we have been discussing in this section of the handbook.[183] It is also being put forth in some quarters that these standards are "merging," and perhaps this is a good thing.[184] If it is in fact the case that the "sole interest" rule is under some kind of attack, then there really needs to be more public discussion about what such a "merger" would look like, and whether it really would be a good thing, as well as what the likely ramifications for the institution of the trust itself would be should such a merger actually be effected. With the fiduciary relationship being marginalized both in the academy[185] and in the marketplace,[186] now may not be the time to replace the no-further-inquiry rule, riddled with exceptions though it may now be, with some kind of facts-and-circumstances test. Certainly, human nature being what

---

[179] Bogert §543; Leslie, *In Defense of the No Further Inquiry Rule: A Response to Professor John Langbein*, 47 Wm. & Mary L. Rev. 541 (2005). *But see* John H. Langbein, *Questioning the Trust Law Duty of Loyalty: Sole Interest or Best Interest?*, 114 Yale L.J. 929 (2005) (suggesting that profound historical changes over the past two centuries have rendered the no further inquiry rule obsolete).

[180] For the case against a defanging of the no-further-inquiry rule, see Melanie B. Leslie, *In Defense of the No Further Inquiry Rule: A Response to Professor Langbein*, 47 Wm. & Mary L. Rev. 541, 550–567 (2005).

[181] Frances H. Foster, *American Trust Law in a Chinese Mirror*, 94 Minn. L. Rev. 602, 651 (2010). *See also* Frederick R. Franke, Jr., *Resisting the Contractarian Insurgency: The Uniform Trust Code, Fiduciary Duty, and Good Faith in Contract*, 36 ACTEC L.J. 517 (2010).

[182] Unif. Prudent Management Inst. Funds Act §3 cmt.

[183] Unif. Prudent Management Inst. Funds Act §3 cmt.

[184] Unif. Prudent Management Inst. Funds Act §3 cmt.

[185] *See generally* Charles E. Rounds, Jr., *The Case for a Return to Mandatory Instruction in the Fiduciary Aspects of Agency and Trusts in the American Law School, Together With a Model Fiduciary Relations Course Syllabus*, 18 Regent U. L. Rev. 251 (2005–2006).

[186] *See generally* §8.10 of this handbook (particularly the introductory quote).

it is, a general facts-and-circumstances approach to divided loyalties is easier for the ignorant and the negligent and the mischief makers to game, and for their lawyers to manipulate, than is a general bright-line no-further-inquiry approach:

We have alluded to the fact that some courts have applied the "sole interest" rule mechanically,[187] while others have not. In one case, a trustee sold trust property to his wife and his father at fair market value. The court found the trustee's transaction with his wife voidable on public policy grounds[188] but not the one with his father:

> In Bogert on Trusts & Trustees, Vol. 3, §484, at page 1520, the author says: "If the trustee sells to his own wife, the courts have tended to treat the transaction as subject to avoidance. The common law identity of husband and wife, the fact that a benefit to the wife would generally inure to the advantage of the husband, and the difficulty of uncovering collusion between them, all argue in favor of treating the sale to the trustee's wife as equivalent in legal effect to a sale to himself. The same doctrine should control if a woman who is trustee sells to her husband."[189]

The court applied a facts-and-circumstances test in failing to void the sales to the trustee's father:

> But no legal presumption of self-dealing or bad faith arises simply because the sale of trust property was made by the trustee to his father. In this case the trustee introduced substantial evidence of the care exercised in determining the true value of the securities sold and the manner in which the sales were made. The objectors failed to produce any evidence that there was a breach of the duty by the trustee in making such sales other than that the purchaser was the father of said trustee and therefore such sale must be sustained.[190]

Avoiding liability before and after the fact. Because a trustee must not allow personal interests to compete with the interests of the beneficiaries arising under the trust,[191] the trustee who has an interest adverse to the trust that he intends to assert must resign from the trust,[192] unless all the beneficiaries give their informed consent to his retention of the office.[193] The acquisition of a conflicting interest even may be grounds for removal.[194] Likewise, the trustee of

---

[187] *See, e.g.,* In re Kline, 142 N.J. Eq. 20, 59 A.2d 14 (1948); Slay v. Burnett Trust, 143 Tex. 621, 642–643, 187 S.W.2d 377, 389 (1945).

[188] *See generally* 3 Scott & Ascher §17.2.1.3 (Sale to Third Person for Trustee's Benefit).

[189] In re Minch's Will, 71 N.E.2d 144, 146 (Ohio 1946).

[190] In re Minch's Will, 71 N.E.2d 144, 147 (Ohio 1946).

[191] *See* Restatement (Second) of Trusts §170 cmt. p; 2A Scott on Trusts §170.23. *See, e.g.,* Johnson v. Witkowski, 30 Mass. App. Ct. 697, 573 N.E.2d 513 (1991) (use of trust property to effect cancellation of a trustee's personal guarantee can constitute a breach of the duty of loyalty).

[192] *See* 2A Scott on Trusts §170.23.

[193] *See* Restatement (Second) of Trusts §216 cmt. g; 3 Scott on Trusts §§216, 216.2; 3 Scott & Ascher §17.2.1 (citing to Fox v. Mackreth, Bros. C.C. 400 (1788), a venerable English informed consent case).

[194] Restatement (Third) of Trusts §37 cmt. e; 3 Scott & Ascher §17.2.9.

a business may not enter into a competing business for personal benefit[195] or purchase an investment that, as the facts suggest, the trustee was expected to purchase for the trust.[196] "While normally associated with corporations and with their directors and officers, what is usually referred to as the corporate opportunity doctrine also applies to . . . [trustees]. . . ."[197] English law seems to be in accord.[198] So also an indenture trustee of a corporate trust may not compete with the beneficiary-bondholders in matters relating to the administration and disposition of the entrusted security.[199]

A trustee may not assert a claim of adverse possession against the trust estate. It is also the case that a trustee of land may not assert a claim of adverse possession against the trust.[200] A trustee of two trusts may sell property from one trust to the other only if neither trust is disadvantaged.[201]

Voting trusts. In voting shares of stock or otherwise exercising powers of control over enterprises, the trustee shall act in the best interests of the beneficiaries.[202] The trustee shall elect or appoint directors or other managers who will manage the corporation or enterprise in the best interest of the beneficiaries.[203] The trustee may use the voting power to procure a position as director, officer or manager of the enterprise, provided the position is procured to serve the interests of the trusts and its beneficiaries.[204] In other words, "[t]he

---

[195] Restatement (Third) of Trusts §78 cmt. e; 3 Scott & Ascher §17.2.9 (Competition with the Trust); Restatement of Restitution §199 (competition by fiduciary); Lewin ¶ 20-40 (England)

[196] *See* Restatement (Third) of Trusts §78 cmt. e; 3 Scott & Ascher §§17.2.7 (Purchase of Adverse Interest from Third Person), 17.2.9 (Competition with the Trust); 2A Scott on Trusts §170.23; 3 Scott on Trusts §206; Restatement of Restitution §194 (purchase by fiduciary of property that he should purchase for the beneficiary). *See also* UTC §802(e) (available at <http://www.uniformlaws.org/Act.aspx?title=Trust%20Code>). *See, e.g.,* Wootten v. Wootten, 151 F.2d 147 (1945) (a trustee who held title to a block of stock of a corporation in his individual capacity, title to a block of stock in the corporation as trustee, and who while trustee acquired from a third party for his own account enough additional stock to give him a majority interest in the corporation could be in breach of the duty of loyalty to the trust beneficiaries depending upon the facts and circumstances).

[197] UTC §802 cmt. (available at <http://www.uniformlaws.org/Act.aspx?title=Trust%20 Code>). *See also* Restatement (Third) of Trusts §78 cmt. e; 3 Scott & Ascher §§17.2.7 (Purchase of Adverse Interest from Third Person), 17.2.9 (Competition with the Trust).

[198] Lewin ¶ 20-41 through ¶ 20-43.

[199] *See generally* §9.31 of this handbook (corporate trusts; trusts to secure creditors; the Trust Indenture Act of 1939; protecting bondholders).

[200] Railroad Co. v. Durant, 95 U.S. 576 (1877); Smith v. Dean, 240 S.W.2d 789 (Tex. Civ. Ct. App. 1951). *See generally* Lewin ¶ 20-160 (England).

[201] *See* Restatement (Third) of Trusts §78 cmt. c(7); 2A Scott on Trusts §170.16.

[202] UTC §802(g) (available at <http://www.uniformlaws.org/Act.aspx?title=Trust%20 Code>); 3 Scott & Ascher §§18.1.8 (Powers with Respect to Shares of Stock), 18.1.8.1 (Duty of Trustee in Voting Shares), 18.1.8.2 (When Trustee Has Controlling Interest).

[203] UTC §802(g) (available at <http://www.uniformlaws.org/Act.aspx?title=Trust%20 Code>); 3 Scott & Ascher §§18.1.8 (Powers with Respect to Shares of Stock), 18.1.8.1 (Duty of Trustee in Voting Shares), 18.1.8.2 (When Trustee Has Controlling Interest).

[204] Restatement (Third) of Trusts §78 cmt. (d)1. An appropriate compensation arrangement for the trustee's services to the corporation or other enterprise held in the trust would be for the trustee to turn over to the trust any compensation the trustee receives from the corporation or other enterprise, with "the reasonable compensation (or special compensation) as trustee to

trustee may not use the corporate form to escape the fiduciary duties of trust law."[205] Thus, if a trustee were to engineer his appointment to an official position with the enterprise for the purpose of supplementing his compensation as trustee, then he could well be compelled to turn over the corporate salary to the trust.[206] He might even be forced to step down from the trusteeship itself.[207] The laws of England and the Isle of Man are generally in accord.[208] J.P. Morgan on general principles never thought much of the idea of a voting trustee of an entrusted corporation serving on the company's board of directors: "I cannot agree that (consistently with a proper interpretation of the Trust) the Voting Trustees can or should vote themselves in as Directors. How can they fairly judge of the wisdom or policy of the management if they are in advance committed to its action by the presence of its members or some of them in the Board of Directors?"[209]

Trust law generally trumps corporate law. Take an individual trustee who also happens to be a director of a corporation. Some shares of the corporation are in the trust. If the director negligently or intentionally harms the corporation and in so doing causes the entrusted shares to depreciate in value, he or she has a fiduciary duty *to the trust beneficiaries* to make the trust whole.[210] Of course, if the trustee reimburses the corporation out of his personal assets, "there is no impairment in the value of the shares and, thus, no liability to the trust beneficiaries."[211]

The duty of loyalty, however, does not make the trustee an agent of the beneficiary. A trustee, for example, is ordinarily "not required to vote shares held in trust in accordance with the instructions of the beneficiaries."[212] Nor may the trustee yield to a demand by the beneficiaries to commit a breach of

---

include the value of the special services rendered in the trustee's role with the corporation or other enterprise"). Restatement (Third) of Trusts §78 cmt. (d)1. *See generally* 3 Scott & Ascher §18.1.8.2 (When Trustee Has Controlling Interest).

[205] UTC §802(g) (available at <http://www.uniformlaws.org/Act.aspx?title=Trust%20 Code>). "Thus, for example, a trustee whose duty of impartiality would require the trustee to make current distributions for the support of current beneficiaries may not evade that duty by holding assets in corporate form and pleading the discretion of corporate directors to determine dividend policy." UTC §802(g). "Rather, the trustee must vote for corporate directors who will follow a dividend policy consistent with the trustee's trust-law duty of impartiality." UTC §802(g). *See, e.g.,* Koffend's Will v. First Nat'l Bank of Minneapolis, 218 Minn. 206, 219–220, 15 N.W.2d 590, 598 (1944) (confirming that when a corporation is used as an agency to effectuate a settlor's intention, the law of trusts trumps the law of corporations).

[206] *See generally* 3 Scott & Ascher §17.2.8 (Bonus, Commission, or Other compensation).

[207] *See generally* 3 Scott & Ascher §17.2.8 (Bonus, Commission, or Other Compensation).

[208] *See, e.g., Re Poyiadjis* 2001-03 MLR 316, Sept. 19, 2002 (Isle of Man High Court of Justice).

[209] Jean Strouse, Morgan 253 (Random House 1999). "Late in 1887 . . . [Morgan] . . . vetoed a suggestion that Reading trustee J. Lowber Welsh be elected to the . . . [railroad's] . . . board of directors." Strouse, Morgan 253 (Random House 1999).

[210] 3 Scott & Ascher §18.1.8.

[211] 3 Scott & Ascher §18.1.8.

[212] 3 Scott & Ascher §18.1.8.1.

trust, for that would be putting the interests of the trustee before the interests of the trust.[213]

The duty of loyalty is not a passive one. The duty of loyalty requires affirmative action by the trustee, who must do all that can honestly be done for the furtherance of the interests of the trust.[214] The trustee cannot consent to a judgment invalidating the trust nor pay a creditor who has a claim that cannot be enforced by suit. All demands must be pressed, even to the extent of bringing suit, unless it is evident that it is useless to do so. The trustee must not unreasonably fail to appeal adverse decisions.[215] The trustee must defend the trust. If a successful action is brought by a third party against the trust, the trustee is under a duty to the beneficiary to appeal to a higher court if it is reasonable to do so.[216]

When the trustee may have a fiduciary duty to resign the trusteeship. A trustee is under a continuing duty to administer the trust at a place appropriate to the purposes of the trust and to its sound, efficient management.[217] Section 7-305 of the Uniform Probate Code provides that "[i]f the principal place of administration becomes inappropriate for any reason, the Court may enter an order furthering efficient administration and the interests of the beneficiaries, including, if appropriate, release of registration, removal of the trustee and appointment of a trustee in another state."[218] The trustee who puts fiduciary compensation considerations ahead of the interests of the beneficiaries in having the trust administered at a place and by a trustee that are more appropriate to the purposes of the trust and to its sound, efficient management runs the risk of incurring liability for violating the duty of loyalty. This would certainly be the case in those jurisdictions that have enacted the section.[219]

The compensation exception to the duty of loyalty. A trustee is entitled to take a reasonable fee from the trust estate for all fiduciary services.[220] This is an inherent conflict,[221] but it is nonetheless permitted since it would be

---

[213] In Estate of Carmean, L.A. Super. Ct. Civ. P374331 (1984) (unpublished), the court held that the duty of loyalty was breached when a trust officer imprudently diverted income from the maintenance of the trust property to the beneficiaries in order to keep them quiet, that is, in order to "rid herself of the burden of handling requests and listening to hard luck stories."

[214] *See* Restatement (Second) of Trusts §2 cmt. b, §170.

[215] *See* Restatement (Second) of Trusts §177 cmt. d.

[216] *See* Restatement (Second) of Trusts §178 cmt. a; 2A Scott on Trusts §178.

[217] UPC §7-305.

[218] UPC §7-305. *See also* Mass. Gen. Laws ch. 190B, §7-305.

[219] *See, e.g.*, Mass. Gen. Laws ch. 190B, §7-305.

[220] *See* §3.5.2.4 of this handbook (right in equity to compensation) and §8.4 of this handbook (the trustee's compensation).

[221] *See* Restatement (Third) of Trusts §78 cmt. c(4) (noting that "[t]he strict prohibitions against transactions by trustees involving conflicts between their fiduciary duties and personal interests do not apply to the trustee's taking of reasonable compensation for services rendered as trustee"); Lewin ¶20-132 (England); 3 Scott & Ascher §17.2 (U.S.) ("noting that though '[p]aying oneself for one's own services is blatant self–dealing, . . . [it is] . . . clear, at least in . . . [the U.S.] . . . , that trustees are normally entitled to compensate themselves for their services as trustee' ").

unreasonable to expect trustees to serve without compensation.[222] The Restatement (Third) of Trusts is in accord.[223] (While it remains the default law of England that the office of trustee is gratuitous, the terms of a trust or the beneficiaries may authorize trustee compensation; in addition, recent legislation has carved out exceptions in the default law for corporate and professional trustees.)[224]

If trustees starting tomorrow were no longer allowed to take a reasonable fee for their services, the institution of the trust probably would not long survive, human nature and the laws of economics being what they are. This practical exception to a fiduciary's duty of loyalty, however, may have a cost to the equitable interests beyond that of the compensation itself, as at least one investment professional[225] has so opined in the mutual fund context:[226]

> ... [T]he evidence showed me that the mutual-fund industry has completely failed to provide reasonable active-management returns to individuals.... The crux of the failure is with the for-profit management of funds for individuals. Mutual-fund managers have a fiduciary responsibility to investors. Obviously if they are operating in a for-profit mode, they have a profit motive. When you put the profit motive up against fiduciary responsibility, that fiduciary responsibility loses and profits win.... If you limit assets under management,... [for example]..., you have a much better chance of beating the market. But asset gathering improves profits.[227]

In the United States, "[t]he trustee need not pay over income without deducting the compensation to which he is entitled with respect to the income, and need not pay over principal without deducting the compensation to which he is entitled."[228] It is said that the trustee has a "security interest"[229] in the trust property for his reasonable compensation. A trustee may enter into an agreement between the trustee and a beneficiary relating to the appointment or compensation of the trustee, provided the transaction is fair to the beneficiaries.[230] If the trustee overcharges the trust in violation of an agreement that fixed his compensation, he may be in breach of the duty of loyalty.[231]

---

[222] UTC §802(h)(2) (available at <http://www.uniformlaws.org/Act.aspx?title=Trust%20 Code>).

[223] Restatement (Third) of Trusts §78 cmt. c(4).

[224] *See* 3A Scott on Trusts §242; Lewin ¶ 20-132 through ¶ 20-158 (England).

[225] David F. Swenson, who has been overseeing Yale's $19 billion endowment fund.

[226] *See generally* §8.10 of this handbook (fiduciary principles applicable to the mutual fund).

[227] Tom Lauricella, *Yale Manager Blasts Industry,* Wall St. J., Sept. 6, 2005, R1, col. 1 (an interview with David Swenson in which he advises individuals to choose index funds and ETFs over active managers).

[228] Restatement (Second) of Trusts §242 cmt. e.

[229] Restatement (Second) of Trusts §242 cmt. e.

[230] UTC §802(h)(1) (available at <http://www.uniformlaws.org/Act.aspx?title=Trust%20 Code>).

[231] *See, e.g.,* Nickel v. Bank of Am. Nat'l Trust & Sav. Ass'n, 290 F.3d 1134 (2002) (referring to Prof. John Langbein's testimony suggesting that it is "an open-and-shut breach of the trustee's duty of loyalty" when a bank overcharges its trust accounts).

The trustee is entitled to be reimbursed from the trust estate for expenses reasonably incurred. The trustee is also entitled to reimbursement for reasonable expenses[232] and, to the extent to which the trustee is entitled to indemnity, he has a security interest in the trust property.[233] The general rule, however, is that, apart from the right to reasonable compensation and to be indemnified for reasonable expenses, a trustee may not receive direct or indirect economic benefit from the trust estate[234] unless authorized to do so by the settlor of a revocable trust, by the nonsettlor holder of a general inter vivos power of appointment, by the terms of the trust instrument,[235] by the court,[236] by statute, or by all of the beneficiaries including the remaindermen after full and fair disclosure.[237] As a practical matter, the trustee bent on transacting with the trust estate "for his own account" seldom will find the last option (beneficiary informed consent in a nonjudicial setting) a viable one. Most trusts will have some beneficiaries who are unborn, unascertained, or under legal disabilities such as minority or mental incapacity, thereby making the informed consent of all the beneficiaries unobtainable.

Some exceptions to the duty of loyalty that are rooted in custom and practice. Other exceptions to the duty of loyalty having their roots in custom and practice as well as case law include the following transactions, if fair to the beneficiaries:

- A transaction between a trust and another trust, decedent's estate, or conservatorship of which the trustee is a fiduciary or in which a beneficiary has an interest;[238]
- A deposit of trust money in a regulated financial service institution operated by the trustee;[239] and

---

[232] *See* §3.5.2.3 of this handbook (trustee's right in equity to exoneration and reimbursement from the trust estate).

[233] Restatement (Second) of Trusts §244 cmt. c.

[234] *See generally* 3 Scott & Ascher §17.2.8.

[235] *See generally* J.D. Perovich & J.D. Annot, *Validity and Construction of Trust Provision Authorizing Trustee to Purchase Trust Property*, 39 A.L.R.3d 836 (1971).

[236] *See generally* 3 Scott & Ascher §17.2.12 (Court Approval).

[237] *See* Restatement (Third) of Trusts §78 cmt. c(3); 2A Scott on Trusts §170.

[238] UTC §802(h)(3) (available at <http://www.uniformlaws.org/Act.aspx?title=Trust%20Code>); Restatement (Third) of Trusts §78 cmt. c(7); 3 Scott & Ascher §17.2.

[239] UTC §802(h)(4) (available at <http://www.uniformlaws.org/Act.aspx?title=Trust%20Code>); Restatement (Third) of Trusts §78 cmt. c(6); 3 Scott & Ascher §§17.2 (Duty of Loyalty), 17.2.14.1 (Deposit by Corporate Trustee in its Own Banking Department), 17.2.14.6 (noting, however, that there is always "the temptation to leave the funds on deposit for longer than necessary"). *See also* Comptroller of the Currency Regulation 9 at 12 C.F.R. §9.10(b) (providing that a national bank may deposit funds of a fiduciary account that are awaiting investment or distribution in the commercial, savings, or another department of the bank, unless prohibited by applicable law).

- An advance by the trustee of his own money at a reasonable rate of interest for the protection of the trust.[240]

The trustee who breaches the duty of loyalty becomes essentially an insurer of the subject property. As noted, so rigorous is the duty of loyalty that an unauthorized act of self-dealing will be regarded as constructively fraudulent and, at the option of the beneficiary, will be set aside.[241] The trustee is not given an opportunity to justify his action; an untrammeled choice of affirmance or rejection rests with the beneficiary.[242] If the beneficiary elects to affirm the transaction, the trustee must account for all profit;[243] if the beneficiary disaffirms, the trustee must make good all losses:[244]

> If a breach of trust has turned out well, as when gains have resulted from the breach, the beneficiaries will ordinarily choose to hold the trustee accountable for the gains. If the breach of trust has gone badly, the beneficiaries will ordinarily choose to surcharge the trustee for both losses incurred and gains forgone.[245]

Thus, if a trustee, motivated by divided loyalties, imprudently acquires or retains on behalf of the trust a particular investment, the trustee will be held liable for any resulting loss suffered by the trust whether or not the investment is a sound fiduciary investment. Moreover, the trustee—at the election of the beneficiaries—may be liable even for the difference between the highest unrealized value of the investment and its realized value.[246]

It is obvious that the trustee should scrupulously avoid the assumption of so serious a risk; no intelligent person desires to become an insurer against loss under such circumstances. The trustee's invariable rule should be to avoid dealing with the trust property in this way.

Trustee may not exploit confidential information for personal purposes. This rule sounds almost unreasonably harsh, but it is required because of the demonstrated fallibility of humanity. There are no exceptions, although there are limits. Thus if the trustee honestly sells the trust property to a third person and *there is no scheme to repurchase*, the trustee is not conclusively forbidden from acquiring it in his individual capacity later on.[247] So also after

---

[240] UTC §802(h)(5) (available at <http://www.uniformlaws.org/Act.aspx?title=Trust%20 Code>); Restatement (Third) of Trusts §78 cmt. c(6); 3 Scott & Ascher §17.2. *See generally* §6.1.3.1 of this handbook (trustee benefiting as borrower and lender; bank deposits on commercial side of trustee bank).

[241] *See* Restatement (Second) of Trusts §206 cmt. b; 3 Scott on Trusts §§206, 208.4; 3 Scott & Ascher §17.2.1.1.

[242] *See* 2A Scott on Trusts §170.2.

[243] *See generally* 3 Scott & Ascher §17.2.1.1.

[244] *See* Restatement (Second) of Trusts §206 cmt. b; 2A Scott on Trusts §170.2; 3 Scott on Trusts §206; 3 Scott & Ascher §17.2.1.1.

[245] 4 Scott & Ascher §24.9.

[246] *See* the following sections of this handbook: §7.1 (trustee's liabilities generally), §7.2.3.1 (tracing and accounting for proceeds and profits), and §7.2.3.2 (damages).

[247] *See* Restatement (Third) of Trusts §78 cmt. d; 2A Scott on Trusts §170.6; 3 Scott & Ascher §§17.2.1.3, 17.2.1.5.

the trustee has stepped down.[248] A trustee, including a former trustee, however, may not use knowledge acquired in the course of administering the trust to gain a personal advantage at the expense of the beneficiaries.[249] "[C]onflict-of-interest problems might be ameliorated by the appointment of an additional trustee, or by the appointment of a trustee *ad litem* to handle a specific, conflict-sensitive transaction."[250]

When the trustee acquires the equitable interest itself. When a beneficiary transfers the equitable interest itself—not the underlying property—to the trustee, the burden is on the trustee to demonstrate that his actions were fair and reasonable under the circumstances.[251] Resignation or removal does not relieve the trustee of the duty of undivided loyalty. Unless a cotrustee remains in office or the court otherwise orders, and until the trust property is delivered to a successor trustee or other person entitled to it, a trustee who has resigned or been removed has the duties of a trustee and the powers necessary to protect the trust property.[252] "A trustee who has resigned or been removed shall proceed expeditiously to deliver the trust property within the trustee's possession to the cotrustee, successor trustee, or other person entitled to it."[253]

The trustee's duty of loyalty survives the due assumption of trusteeship by his successor. Again, the trustee's fiduciary duties to the beneficiaries (or to the trust's charitable purposes, as the case may be) continue although there has been a proper transfer of legal title to a qualified successor trustee. The transferor-trustee, for example, remains burdened with the duty of undivided loyalty, to include the incidental sub-duties of not depriving the beneficiaries of critical information and maintaining confidences.[254] In the face of such residual

---

[248] *See* Restatement (Second) of Trusts §170 cmt. g. But if the trustee steps down for the purpose of purchasing the trust property, then the sale can be set aside at the election of the beneficiary. 3 Scott & Ascher §17.2.1.5 (When Purchaser Is No Longer Trustee); 2A Scott on Trusts §170.8.

[249] *See generally* 3 Scott & Ascher §17.2.1.5.

[250] Restatement (Third) of Trusts §37 cmt. g.

[251] *See* 3 Scott & Ascher §17.2.1 (Sale of Trust Property to Trustee Individually) (noting that the burden of proof is on the trustee who self-deals to show that he has not taken advantage of the fiduciary relationship); Restatement of Restitution §191 cmt. e (self-dealing transaction must be fair and reasonable); Restatement of Restitution §191 cmt. a (burden of proof is upon the self-dealing fiduciary to demonstrate that transaction was fair and reasonable). *See generally* §8.24 of this handbook (who has the burden of proof in an action for breach of trust brought by the beneficiary against the trustee).

[252] UTC §707(a) (available at <http://www.uniformlaws.org/Act.aspx?title=Trust%20 Code>). *See also* §3.4.3 of this handbook (death of trustee, resignation of trustee, or, disqualification trustee due to physical or mental ill health) and §7.2.3.6 of this handbook (trustee removal).

[253] UTC §707(b) (available at <http://www.uniformlaws.org/Act.aspx?title=Trust%20 Code>). *See also* §3.4.3 of this handbook (death of trustee, resignation of trustee, or disqualification trustee due to physical or mental ill health) and §7.2.3.6 of this handbook (trustee removal).

[254] *See, e.g.,* Janowiak v. Tiesi, 932 N.E.2d 569 (Ill. 2010) (holding that a trustee's duty of undivided loyalty, including the sub-duty to disclose to the trust beneficiaries critical/material information acquired in the course of the fiduciary relationship, survives the trusteeship). Not only is a former trustee-fiduciary saddled with such residual fiduciary duties, so also is the former agent-fiduciary. The attorney-at-law in the post-termination-of-the-representation period particularly comes to mind in this regard.

trust-related burdens, divestiture of bare legal title, in and of itself, ought not also divest the transferor-trustee of standing to litigate matters pertaining to the trust's proper administration.[255] The trustee's duty of confidentiality is taken up generally in Section 6.2.3 of this handbook.

Restitution of consequential gains occasioned by trustee self-dealing. A breach of trust that has a self-dealing component to it can subject the trustee to liability for consequential gains, if any. If no self-dealing is involved, then the trustee may well incur no such liability. Equitable relief and the loyalty factor are taken up in Section 7.2.3.1.3 of this handbook.

§6.1.3.1 Trustee Benefiting as Borrower and Lender; Bank Deposits on Commercial Side of Trustee Bank

Borrowing for personal purposes. Nothing good can come of a trustee's borrowing from the trust estate no matter how competitive the interest rate may be and no matter how complete the paper trail, with perhaps the limited exception of the short-term deposit of funds awaiting distribution on the commercial side of the trustee bank.[256] The thief when caught asserts it is only a loan. "A trustee who uses trust funds in the trustee's own business is chargeable with principal and interest or with a pro rata share of the business' profits, at the option of the beneficiaries."[257] In the case of a loan of trust funds to a cotrustee, a family member of the trustee, or to the trustee's lawyer, the beneficiaries may have recourse against both the trustee and the borrower.[258] A bank deposit, of

---

[255] *But see* Old Nat'l Bancorp v. Hanover College, 15 N.E.3d 574 (Ind. Sup. Ct. 2014) (the court apparently oblivious of the maxim that equity exalts substance over form, which maxim is discussed in §8.12 of this handbook).

[256] *See generally* 3 Scott & Ascher §17.2.14.6 (noting that there is always "the temptation to leave the funds on deposit for longer than necessary"); Comptroller of the Currency Regulation 9, Fiduciary Funds Awaiting Investment or Distribution, 12 C.F.R. §9.10(b) (self-deposits) (1997) (available at <www.gpoaccess.gov/cfr/index.html>). The Employee Retirement Income Security Act (ERISA) permits the fiduciary ("a bank or similar financial institution supervised by the United States or a State") under an employee's pension plan to invest all or part of the plan's assets in deposits with itself that bear a reasonable rate of interest if either a provision of the plan expressly authorizes it to do so or the plan covers only employees of the fiduciary. ERISA §408, 29 U.S.C. §1108(b)(4) (1974). Most banks now have the operational capability of "sweeping" uninvested trust cash into short-term investments on a daily basis, thus reducing substantially the occasions when it would be appropriate for a bank trustee to deposit trust funds in noninterest-bearing accounts. *See, e.g.,* Upp v. Mellon Bank, N.A., 799 F. Supp. 540 (E.D. Pa. 1992), *rev'd*, 994 F.2d 1039 (1993). Revised Reg. 9 (effective Jan. 29, 1997 and available at <www.gpoaccess.gov/cfr/index.html>) provides that a national bank exercising fiduciary powers shall adopt and follow written policies and procedures that address, where appropriate, the bank's investment of funds held as fiduciary, including short-term investments and the treatment of fiduciary funds awaiting investment and distribution. *See* 12 C.F.R. §9.5(e) (1997) (available at <www.gpoaccess.gov/cfr/index.html>). *See generally* Melanie L. Fein, Securities Activities of Banks, §11.06(A) (1997) (textual material on brokerage, 12b-1, and sweep fees and nn.283, 284–285).

[257] 3 Scott & Ascher §17.2.4.

[258] *See generally* 3 Scott & Ascher §17.2.4; §5.4.2 of this handbook (rights of the beneficiary as against BFPs and other transferees of the trust property).

course, is a loan.[259] An individual trustee, however, ordinarily may park trust cash in a bank of which he is a shareholder or officer, that is in the absence of special facts suggesting that by so doing the trustee would be in breach of his duties of loyalty and prudence *to the trust beneficiaries*.[260] The larger the amounts relative to the size of the bank, the more problematic the practice. Also, because of the trustee's special relationship with the bank, it is a given that he knows or should know at all times the bank's financial condition. Thus, in the event of the bank's insolvency, the trustee will have a tough time rebutting allegations that it was at least imprudent for him to park trust cash in that bank of all banks.[261]

Even when borrowing is duly authorized, it will always bring with it the appearance of impropriety, the trustee being on both sides of the transaction.[262] Was the authority fairly obtained? Why didn't the trustee go to the marketplace? Who represented the trust in the transaction? Will the trust be thought of first if the trustee's personal financial situation begins to sour? Who will represent the trust in the event of default? What happens if the trustee goes bankrupt?

Moreover, from the perspective of the trustee, when a portion of the trust assets is invested in a personal obligation, the trustee ventures outside the safe harbor of the Prudent Man Rule (which is a rule of conduct, not performance) to become an insurer of the value of the portion.[263]

The Uniform Trust Code recognizes and broadens a long-standing exception to the borrowing prohibition by authorizing a deposit of trust money in a regulated financial service institution operated by the trustee, provided the transaction is fair to the beneficiaries.[264] Restatement (Third) of Trusts is generally in accord.[265] The corporate trustee, however, needs to be extra vigilant when exercising its limited statutory authority to deposit entrusted funds "on the commercial side" or with an affiliate as such authority in no way

---

[259] *See generally* §9.9.4 of this handbook (noting that a bank account is a contract, the bank being the debtor and the depositor being the creditor).

[260] *See generally* 3 Scott & Ascher §17.2.5.

[261] *See generally* 3 Scott & Ascher §17.12.1 (Negligent Selection [Bank Deposits]).

[262] The case of John Zaccaro, husband of former vice-presidential candidate Geraldine Ferraro, and his handling of the estate of an elderly woman in New York illustrates the pitfalls of fiduciaries' borrowing from their estates and trusts. Mr. Zaccaro had borrowed from the estate $175,000, which he paid back with interest. Nonetheless, he was removed as conservator of the woman's estate. The judge in the case, New York Supreme Court Justice Edwin Kassof, wrote, "Thus it is generally accepted that the fiduciary is not permitted to use estate funds for his own benefit or for investments in his own business. There is no necessity for finding malicious intent, deliberate wrongdoing or criminal conduct. The mere appearance of impropriety must be assiduously avoided. This standard has been applied with uncompromising rigidity by the courts." Wash. Post, Aug. 31, 1984, §1, at A1.

[263] *See* §6.1.1 of this handbook (the trustee's duty to be generally prudent) and §6.2.1 of this handbook (the trustee's duty to take active control of, segregate, earmark, and protect the trust property).

[264] UTC §802(h)(4) (available at <http://www.uniformlaws.org/Act.aspx?title=Trust%20 Code>). *See also* 3 Scott & Ascher §17.2.14.1 (Deposit by Corporate Trustee in Its Own Banking Department).

[265] Restatement (Third) of Trusts §78 cmt. c(6). In England, the two-party rule of English contract law is often circumvented by express language in a governing trust instrument authorizing a bank trustee to deposit trust money in an account at the bank. *See generally* Lewin ¶ 20-58.

abrogates the trustee's general duty of loyalty.[266] The "temptation to leave the funds on deposit for longer than necessary" must be resisted.[267] One court has offered these words of caution:

> A trustee bank which exercises its statutory right to hold trust funds in its commercial department accepts, however, the increased responsibilities which the circumstances impose. The permission of the statute to deposit in the commercial department funds awaiting distribution or investment does not remove the factors which support the arguments advanced for the contrary rule. These include that there may be "a temptation to leave money on deposit for an unnecessarily long time, since the bank is making a profit by lending the money at a greater rate of interest than it pays on the account, if indeed any interest at all is paid on such accounts." . . . If, in the afterlook, the time of withholding of funds from investment appears too long, questions of the trustee's motive will inevitably press themselves forward. . . .[268]

The *no-further-inquiry rule*[269] should continue to apply to unauthorized trustee borrowings for personal purposes,[270] and the courts should resist the temptation to recognize "fairness" and "benign intentions" as legitimate defenses to such activity. To do otherwise is to tempt the honest and afford avenues of escape to the dishonest. The law should be absolutely unambiguous in this regard and ignorance of it should never be a judicially recognized excuse.

Lending personal funds. On the other hand, there is some social utility in allowing the trustee to lend his, her, or its personal funds *to* the trust if there is sensitivity to the loyalty considerations attendant even when funds flow from

---

[266] *See generally* 3 Scott & Ascher §17.2.14.1 (noting that undue delay on the part of a corporate trustee in investing trust cash temporarily parked on its commercial side might well constitute a breach of the corporate trustee's duty of loyalty *to the trust beneficiaries*). The duty of loyalty would certainly be implicated if the corporate trustee were in a precarious financial condition. 3 Scott & Ascher §17.2.14.1. Moreover, the directors and principal officers of the corporate trustee could well be called upon personally to make *the beneficiaries* whole in the event of the corporate trustee's insolvency. 3 Scott & Ascher §17.2.14.1. *See generally* §7.2.9 of this handbook (in part discussing the personal liability of directors and officers of trust companies).

[267] 3 Scott & Ascher §17.2.14.6. *Cf.* 3 Scott & Ascher §17.12.3 (Leaving Funds on Deposit for an Unreasonable Time) (noting that apart from the loyalty issues, it would likely be imprudent *from an investment perspective* to leave large sums on deposit in an account that bears little or no interest for a long period of time, even if the deposit is in an institution that has no other affiliation with the trustee).

[268] New England Trust Co. v. Triggs, 334 Mass. 324, 334–335, 135 N.E.2d 541, 548 (1956).

[269] *See* Estate of Rothko, 43 N.Y.2d 305, 372 N.E.2d 291 (1977), *aff'g* 56 A.D.2d 499, 392 N.Y.S.2d 870 (1977), *aff'g* 84 Misc. 2d 870, 379 N.Y.S.2d 923 (1975). *See generally* 3 Scott on Trusts §206. *See also* Stegemeier v. Magness, 728 A.2d 557, 562 (Del. Sup. 1999) (noting that the absolute prohibition under common law against self-dealing by a trustee has been modified in the corporate setting to offer a safe harbor for the directors of a corporation if the transaction is approved by a majority of disinterested directors). *See generally* §9.8.1 of this handbook (in part comparing a charitable trust with a charitable corporation); UTC §802 cmt. (available at <http://www.uniformlaws.org/Act.aspx?title=Trust%20Code>).

[270] Restatement (Third) of Trusts §78 cmt. c(6).

the trustee to the trust.[271] For that reason, the Restatement (Third) of Trusts does not have a blanket prohibition against such activity.[272] The interest rate, however, must be reasonable.[273] The borrowing also must be "necessary for proper needs of administration because (and for as long as) funds for this purpose are not reasonably available from other sources on equally favorable or better terms."[274] In some states, trustees have statutory authority under certain circumstances to make loans to their trusts.[275]

A strict definition of self-dealing would encompass trustee lending in that the trustee receives from the trust estate not only trustee fee compensation but also interest income.[276] Moreover, if for some reason the creditworthiness of the trust erodes, does the duty of loyalty require some forbearance on the part of the lending trustee? The outcome of a particular case is likely to depend on its own set of facts and circumstances.[277] It is recommended, however, that unless the trust instrument specifically permits the trustee to lend funds to the trust, the trustee should refrain from engaging in such activity.[278] (Under the Uniform Trust Code, an advance by the trustee of money for the protection of the trust gives rise to a lien against trust property to secure reimbursement with reasonable interest.)[279] Even when the trust terms specifically permit the trustee to lend funds to the trust, the terms of the loan must be competitive.

The duty of loyalty is also implicated when the trustee of a trust loans its own funds to a corporation some of whose shares are in the trust. "In voting these trust shares there may be a temptation to consider the bank's own interests, and not merely those of the trust beneficiaries," particularly when there are merger or takeover proposals on the table.[280]

With respect to a trustee's loan to a corporation that is owned and controlled by the trust, the law is somewhat ambiguous as to whether the trustee may protect its position to the detriment of the corporation and of course the

---

[271] UTC §802(h)(5) (available at <http://www.uniformlaws.org/Act.aspx?title=Trust%20 Code>).

[272] Restatement (Third) of Trusts §78 cmt. c(6).

[273] Restatement (Third) of Trusts §78 cmt. c(6). *See generally* 3 Scott & Ascher §17.2.6 (noting, however, that the trustee would not be entitled to interest if the advance was unnecessary due to the fact that the trust already had sufficient uninvested cash).

[274] Restatement (Third) of Trusts §78 cmt. c(6).

[275] *See* 3 Scott & Ascher §17.2.6 n.5.

[276] *But see* First Nat'l Bank of Boston v. Slade, 379 Mass. 243, 399 N.E.2d 1047 (1979); Bullivant v. First Nat'l Bank of Boston, 246 Mass. 324, 141 N.E. 41 (1923). *See generally* 3 Scott & Ascher §17.2.6; 2A Scott on Trusts §170.20; Bogert §543(L).

[277] *See generally* First Nat'l Bank of Boston v. Slade, 379 Mass. 243, 399 N.E.2d 1047 (1979); Bullivant v. First Nat'l Bank of Boston, 246 Mass. 324, 141 N.E.41 (1923); Bogert §543(L); 2A Scott on Trusts §§170.20, 170.23A, 170.24.

[278] *See* §3.5.3.2(c) of this handbook (the trustee's power to borrow on behalf of the trust or to pledge or mortgage the trust property).

[279] UTC §709(b) (available at <http://www.uniformlaws.org/Act.aspx?title=Trust%20 Code>). *See generally* 3 Scott & Ascher §17.2.6.

[280] 3 Scott & Ascher §17.2.14.6.

trust.[281] What if the lending trustee calls the loan, driving the corporation into bankruptcy and the trust into oblivion?[282] In this context, may the commercial side and the trust side of a bank be treated as separate entities? As the bank has only one management pyramid and one set of shareholders, the answer has to be no.[283] Thus, while such activity is not per se a breach of trust,[284] it is recommended that trustees refrain from loaning to corporations that are owned and controlled by their trusts. As a practical matter, the attorney for the trust will find it a difficult task leading the lending trustee through a gauntlet of federal insider trading compliance requirements on one side and state-imposed fiduciary obligations on the other.[285]

§6.1.3.2 Corporate Trustee Invests in Its Own Stock

[N]ormal assurances concerning proper fiduciary behaviour would be undermined (especially regarding the trustee's future conduct) if a bank were allowed to purchase its own shares for a trust it is administering, even though the shares were purchased from third persons at market price and would be a prudent investment for the trust.[286]

When trustees lend to themselves without authority they breach the duty of loyalty.[287] Are things any different if a corporate trustee invests trust assets in itself, *i.e.*, in its own stock?[288] In each case, the trustee is contracting with itself.[289] Certainly the duty of loyalty is implicated when a corporation in its capacity as trustee purchases directly from itself stock in itself.[290] These self-ownership situations, however, usually come about inadvertently and innocently when the stock pours over by will into a trust of which the corporation also happens to be trustee, or as an incident to the corporation merging with another entity. Nothing good can come of such entanglements.

---

[281] *See generally* First Nat'l Bank of Boston v. Slade, 379 Mass. 243, 399 N.E.2d 1047 (1979); Bullivant v. First Nat'l Bank of Boston, 246 Mass. 324, 141 N.E. 41 (1923); 2A Scott on Trusts §170.20; Bogert §543(L).

[282] *See generally* First Nat'l Bank of Boston v. Slade, 379 Mass. 243, 399 N.E.2d 1047 (1979); Bullivant v. First Nat'l Bank of Boston, 246 Mass. 324, 141 N.E. 41 (1923); 2A Scott on Trusts §170.20; Bogert §543(L).

[283] 2A Scott on Trusts §170.18.

[284] *See generally* 3 Scott & Ascher §17.2.10.

[285] *See generally* 3 Scott & Ascher §17.2.14.6 (suggesting that these colliding duties can put the corporate trustee in a "dilemma").

[286] Restatement (Third) of Trusts §78 cmt. b.

[287] *See generally* §6.1.3.1 of this handbook (when the trustee benefits as a borrower or lender of the trust property).

[288] *See generally* 3 Scott & Ascher §17.2.14.5.

[289] *See generally* §9.9.4 of this handbook (a debt is a contract) and §9.9.7 of this handbook (shareholders in a corporation are in a contractual relationship with the corporation).

[290] 3 Scott & Ascher §17.2.14.5.

If the corporate entity is publicly traded, the entity as trustee may not exploit nonpublic inside information on behalf of its trusts.[291] Independent judgment in the voting of the shares is virtually impossible.[292] If the financial condition of the corporation becomes precarious, its trust department may be tempted to hold on to its own stock for any number of business considerations unrelated to the welfare of its trusts, such as supporting the stock's price in order to maintain the confidence of trust or commercial customers.[293] In either case, such nonfeasance constitutes a continuing act of self-dealing arising out of the entity's divided loyalties.[294]

By regulation, national banks may not purchase their own shares—or shares in their affiliates—for their trusts.[295] There are a number of state statutes that proscribe such activity as well.[296] "The mere fact that the trustee has broad discretionary powers in making investments does not mean that the trustee has the authority to invest trust funds in its own shares."[297] Even when self-ownership is expressly authorized by the terms of a trust, a court order, a statute, or beneficiary consent,[298] the corporate trustee will always owe the trust beneficiaries a general duty of loyalty and prudence. Moreover, it is not always that easy to divine the limits of a particular authorization, *e.g.*, whether it would cover stock dividends (and/or rights to subscribe) or the merger of the corporate trustee with another entity.[299]

---

[291] *See generally* §7.3.3.3 of this handbook (registration and sale of entrusted securities) and §7.3.4.2(a) of this handbook (securities laws). *See also* 3 Scott & Ascher §17.2.14.6.

[292] *See, e.g.*, Ledbetter v. First State Bank & Trust Co., 85 F.3d 1537 (11th Cir. 1996). *See generally* Report, *Voting by Corporate Trustee of Its Own Stock Held in Trust*, 3 Real Prop. Prob. & Tr. J. 517 (1968); Barclay, *Voting Bank's Own Stock Held in Trust* (pts. 1–2), 106 Tr. & Est. 70, 678 (1967). In some jurisdictions, the right of a corporate fiduciary to vote its own shares is addressed by statute. *See* 3 Scott & Ascher §17.2.14.5, n.4.

[293] *See generally* 3 Scott & Ascher §17.2.14.5; 2A Scott on Trusts §170.15.

[294] In 3 Scott & Ascher §17.2.14.5, however, it is suggested that it is self-evident that a corporate trustee is guilty of no self-dealing when it purchases its own shares from a third party for one of its trusts, or when it retains its own shares in one of its trusts. All we have is a conflict of interest. But is that really all we have? It is not hard to conjure up a set of facts and circumstances where *the fiduciary's very purpose* in purchasing or retaining its stock is to self-deal. In the former case it might be to buttress the stock's market price; in the latter, it might be to control how entrusted shares are voted. It would seem that only when *the settlor's clear purpose*, as manifested by the terms of the trust, is that the trust contain an investment in the corporate trustee can it be said that the corporate trustee in holding its own stock has a conflict of interest, but is not engaged in self-dealing, at least absent special facts or subsequent self-dealing behavior.

[295] Comptroller of the Currency Reg. §9.12(a), 12 C.F.R. §9.12(a).

[296] 3 Scott & Ascher §17.2.14.5 n.8.

[297] 3 Scott & Ascher §17.2.14.5.

[298] *See generally* 3 Scott & Ascher §17.2.14.5 (noting that the informed consents of some trust beneficiaries to the corporate trustee investing the assets of the trust in itself will generally not bind the nonconsenting beneficiaries). There is an exception: The informed consent of the holder of a general inter vivos power of appointment, *e.g.*, a reserved right of revocation, would generally bind all other equitable interests, including those who have not given consent. 3 Scott & Ascher §17.2.14.5.

[299] *See generally* 3 Scott & Ascher §17.2.14.5.

Any intentional misrepresentation by the corporate trustee to the beneficiary of the facts and law that relate to the self-dealing could constitute fraud. A negligent misrepresentation could constitute constructive fraud,[300] a topic that is covered in Section 8.15.59 of this handbook. Moreover, any misrepresentations made by the corporate trustee's agents, *e.g.*, trust counsel, would likely be imputed to the corporate trustee.[301]

A beneficiary cannot consent to or ratify retention of trustee stock in the trust portfolio, unless the beneficiary actually understands the applicable law, particularly his or her legal rights.[302] And even in the face of a duly obtained authorization to self-deal, the trustee is saddled with the overarching obligation to be prudent, fair, and reasonable.[303] Thus, express language in the governing instrument authorizing the trustee to retain its own stock as an "inception asset"[304] cannot relieve the trustee of its duty to monitor the investment.[305]

Such entanglements never should be initiated by the trustee and, when they inadvertently develop, should be ended as soon as it is prudent to do so.[306] The Restatement (Third) of Trusts is generally in accord.[307] Prudent disengagement, however, is the key.[308] One court has surcharged a corporate successor trustee for mechanically liquidating a large position in its own parent company without first having conducted an assessment of the trust's particular purposes and circumstances, to include the current income needs and life expectancy of the life beneficiary.[309]

If stock in the corporate trustee is part of the holdings of a revocable trust and the settlor wants the trustee to retain it in the trust, the trustee at a minimum should require a letter from the settlor directing retention of the stock and holding the trustee harmless from the consequences of so doing.[310] Such an authorization, though, would not relieve the corporate trustee of the

---

[300] *See, e.g.*, In re Gillies' Will, 98 N.Y.S.2d 853 (1950).

[301] *See, e.g.*, In re Gillies' Will, 98 N.Y.S.2d 853 (1950).

[302] *See, e.g.*, In re Gillies' Will, 98 N.Y.S.2d 853, 857–858 (1950). *See generally* Restatement of Restitution §191 (informed consent to fiduciary self-dealing); §7.1.2 (informed consent to trustee self-dealing).

[303] Restatement of Restitution §191 cmt. e.

[304] Restatement (Third) of Trusts §78 cmt. e(2).

[305] *See* Restatement (Third) of Trusts §78 cmt. e(2); Restatement (Second) of Trusts §231 cmts. a, b (1959); Mueller v. Mueller, 28 Wis. 2d 26, 135 N.W.2d 854 (1965).

[306] *See generally* American Bar Association, A Fiduciary's Guide to Federal Securities Laws 46 (1994).

[307] Restatement (Third) of Trusts §78 cmt. e(2) (noting, however, that it would "normally be permissible for a relatively modest portion of the trustee's stock to be held indirectly through an appropriate holding of shares in a mutual fund or other pooled investment vehicle").

[308] *See generally* 3 Scott & Ascher §17.2.14.5 (noting that a trustee under a duty to sell its own shares, it is not subject to surcharge unless it fails to sell within a reasonable time). "If the trustee holds a considerable block of such shares, if there is no ready market for them, or if they cannot be sold except at a discount, the trustee may be justified in failing to sell them for quite a while." 3 Scott & Ascher §17.2.14.5.

[309] *See* In re Scheidmantel, 868 A.2d 464 (Pa. Super. 2005).

[310] Restatement (Third) of Trusts §74 cmt. b.

general duty of loyalty and prudence, nor, absent special facts, should it be construed as granting the corporate trustee a license to self-deal.

§6.1.3.3   Trustee Benefiting as Buyer and Seller

When a trust company buys for its ward's estate securities from its banking adjunct or affiliate, with the same identity of interest between the two shown to exist in the instant case, it comes within the following well-established rule of law: Where a trustee buys with trusts funds property which the trustee owns or is materially interested in, or sells trust property to himself, or to one whom the trustee is materially interested in, such a transaction is voidable at the option of the cestui.[311]

Generally. Any act that appears to be in the interest of the trustee instead of the trust estate may constitute a breach of trust for which the remedies are as complete as the equity court can make them.[312] The trustee cannot make any profit out of the use of the trust property or gain any advantage, direct or indirect, by its purchase or sale.[313] This trustee is accountable even for an economic benefit that falls into his lap innocently, that is not as the result of some breach of trust.[314] Otherwise, the trustee would be unjustly enriched.[315] "The situation of a trustee gives him an opportunity of knowing the value of the property, and, as he acquires that knowledge at the expense of the beneficiary, he is bound to apply it for the beneficiary's benefit."[316]

Sales and purchases for trustee's own account. The trustee—whether an individual or an institution—must not sell trust property to himself personally,[317] sell his own property to the trust,[318] sell property under circumstances

---

[311] Baxter v. Union Indus. Trust & Sav. Bank, 273 Mich. 642, 645–647, 263 N.W. 762, 763 (1935).

[312] *See generally* §7.2.3 of this handbook (types of equitable relief for breaches of trust).

[313] Restatement of Restitution §§190–200 (acquisition of property by a fiduciary) (U.S.); Lewin ¶ 20-26 through ¶ 20-54 (England).

[314] 4 Scott & Ascher §24.7 (Accountability for Profits in the Absence of a Breach of Trust).

[315] *See generally* §8.15.78 of this handbook (unjust enrichment).

[316] Lewin ¶ 20-60.

[317] *See* Restatement (Third) of Trusts §77 cmt. b; 3 Scott & Ascher §17.2.1; Restatement of Restitution §192 ("Where a fiduciary who has power to sell property of the beneficiary sells it to himself individually in violation of his duty to the beneficiary, he holds the property upon a constructive trust for the beneficiary") (U.S.); Lewin ¶ 20-60 (England). *See generally* §3.3 of this handbook (a general discussion of the constructive trust); §7.2.3.1.6 of this handbook (the constructive trust as a procedural equitable remedy). *Cf.* Restatement of Restitution §196 ("Where a fiduciary in violation of his duty to the beneficiary purchases or retains an encumbrance upon property entrusted to him as fiduciary, he holds the encumbrance upon a constructive trust for the beneficiary"). "The rule is not based upon the existence of harm to the beneficiary in the particular case. The purpose of the rule is to prevent a conflict of opposing interests in the minds of fiduciaries, whose duty it is to act solely for the benefit of their beneficiaries." Restatement of Restitution §196, cmt. a.

[318] *See* Restatement (Third) of Trusts §77 cmt. d; 3 Scott & Ascher §17.2.2 (Purchase of Trustee's Own Property by Trust); Restatement of Restitution §193 ("Where a fiduciary who has power to purchase property for the beneficiary purchases property from himself individually in violation of his duty to the beneficiary, he holds the purchase money upon a constructive trust for

where his personal interest might affect his judgment,[319] renew the trust lease in his own name,[320] buy property for himself that he ought to have bought for the trust,[321] or be guided by the interests of any third person including other trusts.[322] "Nor can this salutary rule be evaded by circuity of conveyances"[323] or other "subterfuges."[324] Nor is it a defense that the trustee acquired trust property for himself at a public auction.[325] Moreover, "[i]t is now generally the case, in both the United States and England, that a court may set aside a trustee's purchase of trust assets for his or her own account if the beneficiaries have not . . . [given their informed consent] . . . , *even of the trustee has acted in good faith and paid a fair price.*"[326]

If the trustee with his own funds purchases from a third party a share of stock for $10 *with the intention of selling it to the trust* for $15, and does so, then the trustee is personally accountable to "the trust" for his profit on the transaction, namely $5.[327] In the alternative, the beneficiaries could compel the trustee to

---

the beneficiary"). *See generally* §3.3 of this handbook (a general discussion of the constructive trust); §7.2.3.1.6 of this handbook (the constructive trust as a procedural equitable remedy).

[319] Restatement (Third) of Trusts §77 cmt. d; 3 Scott & Ascher §17.2.1.4 (When Trustee Has Personal Interest in Purchase).

[320] *See generally* 2A Scott on Trusts §170.23; Restatement of Restitution §195 ("A person holding as fiduciary a leasehold interest who in violation of his duty to the beneficiary obtains a renewal of the lease for himself holds the new lease upon a constructive trust for the beneficiary"). *See generally* §3.3 of this handbook (a general discussion of the constructive trust); §7.2.3.1.6 of this handbook (the constructive trust as a procedural equitable remedy).

[321] *See* Restatement (Third) of Trusts §78 cmt. c(5); Bogert §483; Restatement of Restitution §194 ("A fiduciary who purchases from a third person for himself individually property which it is his duty to purchase for the beneficiary holds it upon a constructive trust for the beneficiary"). *See also* §3.3 of this handbook (the constructive trust generally); §7.2.3.1.6 of this handbook (the constructive trust as a procedural equitable remedy).

[322] Restatement (Third) of Trusts §78 cmt. e, c(7).

[323] Arnold v. Brown, 41 Mass. (24 Pick.) 89, 97 (1832). *See generally* 3 Scott & Ascher §17.2.1.3.

[324] Bogert §543; 3 Scott & Ascher §17.2.1.3.

[325] Restatement of Restitution §192, cmt. b (private or public sale) (U.S.); Whichcote v. Lawrence, Ves. Jr. 740 (1798) (England); Campbell v. Walker, 5 Ves. 678 (1800), 13 Ves. 601 (1807) (England). *See generally* 3 Scott & Ascher §§17.2.1, 17.2.1.2 (U.S.). One commentator has suggested that perhaps the self-dealing trustee should be cut some slack if the trust property is acquired by the trustee at an auction that is sponsored and administered by an independent third party, perhaps a mortgagee of the trust property, provided the trustee could not have prevented the forced sale and has no direct or indirect role in determining the purchase price. *See* 3 Scott & Ascher §17.2.1.2. Presumably, a "softening" of the no further inquiry rule from a conclusive to a rebuttable presumption of impropriety in such situations is the type of "particular exception" that Justice Cardozo would have looked at with a jaundiced eye. For those whose views of human nature range from the pessimistic to the cynical, his slippery slope argument is likely to be a compelling one. The trustee can always seek court approval to put in a bid. *See generally* 3 Scott & Ascher §17.2.12 (Court Approval).

[326] 3 Scott & Ascher §17.2.1; Restatement of Restitution §191 (effect of consent of beneficiary to the fiduciary's self-dealing); §7.1.2 of this handbook (beneficiary's informed consent to the trustee's self-dealing).

[327] *See generally* 3 Scott & Ascher §17.2.2 (Purchase of Trustee's Own Property by Trust); §7.2.3.2 of this handbook (in part discussing damage calculation options that may be available to the beneficiaries when the trustee has breached the duty of loyalty).

take back the purchase price, with interest.[328] The trustee, however, would be entitled to get the stock back, together with any dividends that had been thrown off while the stock was in "the trust."[329] On the other hand, "if the trustee did not purchase the property for the purpose of reselling it to the trust, and sells it to the trust for no more than its value at the time of the sale, the trustee is ordinarily not accountable for any profit, as the trust made no profit *on the transaction*."[330]

With mortgage participations, it is generally the other way around. Take a corporate trustee who makes a series of loans to third parties with its own funds. The loans are secured by mortgages. The trustee then puts these mortgages together in a bundle and sells interests or participations in the bundle to certain trusts of which it is a trustee, making no profit on the transactions. In this case, the better view is that the practice does not implicate the trustee's duty of loyalty, provided the purpose of the exercise *from the very beginning* was to get the participations into the trusts.[331] In other words, the trustee advances its own funds merely as an accommodation to the beneficiaries. Whether it is prudent to have the participations in the trusts in the first place is another matter. The assumption here is that it is.

If a trustee may not transact directly with the trust estate, so too the trustee may not do so through straw men,[332] relatives,[333] dummies, specially organized corporations, and affiliated or subsidiary corporations.[334] "If the trustee's

---

[328] *See generally* 3 Scott & Ascher §17.2.2 (Purchase of Trustee's Own Property by Trust); §7.2.3.2 of this handbook (in part discussing damage calculation options that may be available to the beneficiaries when the trustee has breached the duty of loyalty).

[329] *See generally* 3 Scott & Ascher §17.2.2 (Purchase of Trustee's Own Property by Trust); §7.2.3.2 of this handbook (in part discussing damage calculation options that may be available to the beneficiaries when the trustee has breached the duty of loyalty).

[330] 3 Scott & Ascher §17.2.2 (Purchase of Trustee's Own Property by Trust). *See also* §7.2.3.2 of this handbook (in part discussing damage calculation options that may be available to the beneficiaries when the trustee has breached the duty of loyalty).

[331] *See generally* 3 Scott & Ascher §17.2.14.2 (Mortgage Participations).

[332] Smith v. SunTrust Bank, 325 Ga. App. 531, 754 S.E.2d 117 (2014) ("Accordingly, we conclude that the Trustees' use of a straw man created a jury issue on the question of fraudulent concealment."); Hayes v. Hall, 188 Mass. 510, 74 N.E. 935 (1905) (involving an auction sale of trust property to the trustee's wife through a third-party conduit). Louis Brandeis used himself as a straw in certain transactions involving The Warren Trust. *See* §8.38 of this handbook (the Warren Trust (a.k.a. the Mills Trust)). The *Hayes* ruling was based upon a report that Brandeis's law partner, Edward F. McClennen, had submitted as a court-appointed special master. *See generally* Richard W. Painter, *Contracting Around Conflicts in a Family Representation: Louis Brandeis and the Warren Trust*, 8 U. Chi. L. Sch. Roundtable 353, 365–366 (2001) (suggesting that Brandeis's use of himself as a straw or conduit in the lease transaction between The Warren Trust and the Firm rendered the lease "clearly vulnerable to legal challenge"). *See generally* 3 Scott & Ascher §17.2.1.3 (Sale to Third Person for Trustee's Benefit).

[333] *See generally* 3 Scott & Ascher §17.2.1.3 (Sale to Third Person for Trustee's Benefit).

[334] Bogert §543; 3 Scott & Ascher §17.2.1.4 (When Trustee Has Personal Interest in Purchase).

attorney purchases trust property, the sale is generally voidable."[335] So also is a sale to an employee or other such agent of the trustee.[336]

In England, the trustee's use of a nominee to acquire an interest in the trust property would violate the so-called genuine transaction rule.[337] The secret use of a straw could also constitute a breach of the trustee's duty of full disclosure.[338] "Courts . . . [however] . . . have recognized that a sale by a trustee with a personal interest is not voidable, if there is a before-the-fact approval by the grantor, the court, or the beneficiaries."[339]

In England, the rule that it takes two to make a contract, that one cannot enter into an enforceable contract with oneself, the so-called two party rule,[340] may well make it difficult mechanically for the trustee to, say, purchase a trust asset,[341] absent express authority to do so in the terms of the trust or the interposition of a nominee.[342] This is because the trustee would be on both sides of the transaction, on one side in his individual capacity and on the other in his fiduciary capacity. "In the United States, however, identity of parties may not prevent a contract being made if the capacities are different."[343]

To be sure, the terms of the trust may authorize the trustee to purchase trust property, but the trustee must still act fairly, reasonably, and in good faith.[344] Thus the beneficiaries could have the sale set aside if the price were not a fair one.[345] On the other hand, if the terms of the trust were that the trustee could acquire the property at less than its fair market value, then the trustee would also have the status of a beneficiary, which would be a whole other matter.

A court could also authorize the trustee to purchase trust property. "The key, of course, is whether allowing the transaction to occur is in the best interest of the beneficiaries."[346] Chancellor Kent said it best in an 1816 decision:

---

[335] 3 Scott & Ascher §17.2.1.3.

[336] 3 Scott & Ascher §17.2.1.3.

[337] Lewin ¶20-59 (noting that the two-party rule of English contract law, which is discussed later in this section, is easily circumvented because it has no application to a sale to a nominee). *See generally* §8.15.49 of this handbook (the genuine transaction rule).

[338] *See* §5.4.1.1 of this handbook (the beneficiary's right to information and confidentiality) and §6.1.5.1 of this handbook (the trustee's duty to provide necessary information to the beneficiaries).

[339] Stegemeier v. Magness, 728 A.2d 557, 563 (Del. Super. 1999).

[340] *See generally* §8.15.48 of this handbook (the two-party rule).

[341] Lewin ¶20-56 (England).

[342] Lewin ¶20-58.

[343] Lewin ¶20-56, n.43 (citing to Restatement (2d) Contracts, §9 cmt. (b)).

[344] *See generally* 3 Scott & Ascher §17.2.11. *Cf.* Restatement of Restitution §191 cmt. e ("A transaction between the fiduciary and the beneficiary in which the fiduciary is dealing on his own account in regard to a matter within the scope of the relation can be set aside if the transaction is not fair and reasonable. Thus, if a trustee purchases for himself trust property with the consent of the beneficiary, the beneficiary can set aside the sale if the price paid by the trustee was not in fact an adequate price, even though at the time of the sale the parties believed that it was adequate.").

[345] Restatement of Restitution §191 cmt. e.

[346] 3 Scott & Ascher §17.2.12.

The only way for a trustee to purchase safely, if he is willing to give as much as anyone else, is by filing a bill, and saying, so much is bid, and I will bid more, and the court will then examine into the case, and judge whether it be advisable to let the trustee bid.[347]

Trustee as counsel, broker, or consultant. A gray area has developed in the law, namely, the selling by the trustee of legal, brokerage, and consulting services to the trust.[348] Again, as with the sale of goods, such transactions fall within the strict definition of *self-dealing* in that economic benefit is accruing to the trustee from the trust estate over and above the trustee fees.[349] In England the practice is forbidden,[350] but in most American jurisdictions it is not.[351] In 1988, for example, the Boston law firms, in the aggregate, had assets under fiduciary management in the range of $3 billion to $4 billion.[352]

In those jurisdictions where trust counsel represents the trustee and not the trust,[353] the American Bar Association (ABA) sees no conflict of interest in cases where the lawyer-trustee or his firm is furnishing legal services to the fiduciary, provided the compensation is reasonable.[354] Its formal opinion in this regard, however, relates to licensure only, *i.e.*, the lawyer-trustee's regulatory relationship with the state. It cannot and should not be construed as eroding or limiting a lawyer-trustee's liability to his client for breach of the common law or equitable duty of undivided loyalty.

The Restatement (Third) of Trusts would allow compensated self-employment, provided the special services rendered by the trustee "are necessary or appropriate to prudent administration of the trust."[355] After all, if the trustee possesses special skills and facilities that would be useful in the administration of the trust, why should they not be utilized in furtherance of the trust's purposes?[356] The trustee, however, would have a duty to disclose to the beneficiaries the special services performed and the compensation received for those services.[357] (Note that under the Restatement (Third) of Trusts, it would still be

---

[347] Davoue v. Fanning, 2 Johns. Ch. 252, 261 (N.Y.1816). *See also* Master of the Rolls in Campbell v. Walker, 5 Ves. 678, 681 (1800), 13 Ves. 601 (1807) (England).

[348] *See* Restatement (Third) of Trusts §78 cmt. d; Restatement (Second) of Trusts §242 cmt. d; 2A Scott on Trusts §170.22; 3A Scott on Trusts §242.2.

[349] *See generally* 3 Scott & Ascher §17.2.8 (Bonus, Commission, or Other Compensation).

[350] *See* Robinson v. Pett, 3 P. Wms. 249 (1734). *See generally* Bogert §975.

[351] *See* Martin A. Heckscher, *Fees, Fees, Fees: A Blessing and a Bane, How to Charge, Collect and Defend Them*, 31 ACTEC L.J. 21, 36–42 (2005); Restatement (Second) of Trusts §242 cmts. d, k; 3A Scott on Trusts §242.2; Bogert §975. *Cf.* L.S. Tellier, Annot., *Right of Executor or Administrator to Extra Compensation for Legal Services Rendered by Him*, 65 A.L.R.2d 809 (1959).

[352] William D. Haught, *Attorneys Take Fiduciary Roles*, 127 Tr. & Est. 10 (Feb. 1988).

[353] *See* §8.8 of this handbook (whom trust counsel represents).

[354] ABA Formal Op. 02-426.

[355] Restatement (Third) of Trusts §78 cmt. c(5).

[356] It is reasonable to expect "that the trustee's familiarity with the purposes and affairs of the trust will result in efficiency and cost advantages to the trust." Restatement (Third) of Trusts §78 cmt. c(5). *See generally* §6.2.7 of this handbook (duty to use special skills or expertise).

[357] Restatement (Third) of Trusts §78 cmt. c(5). *See also* 3 Scott & Ascher §17.2.8.

a breach of trust for the trustee to hire close relatives, *e.g.*, his spouse, son, or daughter, to provide legal services to the trust.)[358]

It is, nonetheless, troubling when a trustee hires himself as trust counsel.[359] The trustee is on both sides of the service contract, so the arrangement on its face is the product of divided loyalties.[360] At the very least such transactions put great stress on the trustee's independent judgment.[361] Thus, to avoid even the appearance of impropriety, the trustee should not charge for routine, legal, or consulting tasks[362] and should turn over to the trust any routine brokerage commissions that are generated as a consequence of these transactions with the trust estate.[363] Extraordinary legal, consulting, and brokerage services should be purchased by the trust at arm's length from independent third parties.[364]

When the trustee is also the service vendor, accountability is reduced: The trust is deprived of the benefit of independent advice, and the beneficiaries are deprived of the benefit of the checks and balances inherent in arm's-length contractual relationships.[365] When the trustee, for example, acts also as attorney, it must fall to the court or to the beneficiaries to monitor the quality of the legal work, the commitment to the expeditious resolution of the legal matter,

---

[358] Restatement (Third) of Trusts §78 cmt. e(1) (noting that the hiring of a close relative as trust counsel "would create a temptation for the trustee to consider the interests of others rather than to act solely in the interests of the beneficiaries").

[359] "[T]he risks inherent in sacrificing independence and objectivity of judgment in deciding these matters must be justifiable in terms of the expected benefits to the trust through greater efficiency and reduced time and expense in allowing the trustee to render the services." Restatement (Third) of Trusts §78 cmt. c(5).

[360] *See* Bogert §543(m).

[361] *See, e.g.*, In re Matter of Klarner, 2003 WL 22723228.

[362] The author acknowledges that there is a divergence of opinion over whether the trustee who renders legal services to his or her trust is entitled to additional compensation. In recent years, bills have been filed in both the California and New York legislatures aimed at what is perceived by the sponsors to be "double dipping." *See* Pollock, *State Legislators Move to Curb Double Dipping by Estate Lawyers*, Wall St. J., June 23, 1993, at B5, col. 1. The American Bar Association, however, has opposed any legislative initiatives to limit or regulate the practice of lawyer-trustees' taking double compensation. *See* Ronald C. Link, *Developments Regarding the Professional Responsibility of the Estate Administration Lawyer: The Effect of the Model Rules of Professional Conduct*, 26 Real Prop. Prob. & Tr. J. 1 (1991); Bogert §975.

[363] *See* Restatement (Third) of Trusts §78 cmt. d(1); Restatement (Second) of Trusts §206 cmt. k (1959); 3 Scott & Ascher §17.2.8; 2A Scott on Trusts §170.22.

[364] *See, e.g.*, Estate of Haviside v. Sheehan, 102 Cal. App. 3d 365, 368, 162 Cal. Rptr. 393, 395 (1980) (suggesting that it is contrary to public policy to allow a trustee to be paid for legal services he or she renders to the trust estate, that the attorney-trustee must hire a third party or perform such services without compensation). *See generally* Brown, *The Punctilio of an Honor the Most Sensitive*, 131 Tr. & Est. 24 (1992). *See also* First Nat'l Bank of Boston v. Brink, 372 Mass. 257, 268, 361 N.E.2d 406, 412 (1977) (Liacos, J., concurring in part and dissenting in part) (commenting on the perceived or actual conflicts of interest that can arise when an attorney and fiduciary are one and the same).

[365] *See* §3.2.2 of this handbook (the lawyer) and §3.2.3 of this handbook (the stockbroker). *See also* Blake v. Pegram, 109 Mass. 541, 553 (1872) (suggesting that charges to the trust of legal fees by the lawyer/trustee are "open to serious question, because of the liability to abuse, or, at least, to the suspicion of abuse," this because the lawyer/trustee "is his own client").

and the reasonableness of the legal fees.[366] Because court oversight is inefficient and beneficiary oversight often illusory, neither alternative is particularly satisfactory.

The Uniform Trust Code "does not take a specific position on whether dual fees may be charged when a trustee hires its own law firm to represent the trust."[367] The Restatement (Third) of Trusts, as noted, sort of does:

> A trustee who renders special services in the administration of the trust, for example as an attorney or real estate agent, may be awarded compensation for such services when it is advantageous to the trust that the trustee rather than another perform those services.[368]

Appointment of scrivener[369] as trustee. It is one thing when the trustee hires himself as trust counsel after the trust has been established. It is quite another when the settlor's estate planning lawyer drafts a trust instrument under which the lawyer is designated as the trustee. Ethical red flags are certainly raised when the scrivener writes himself or herself in as trustee or cotrustee.[370] The attorney-client relationship is an agency relationship.[371] The client is the principal; the lawyer is the agent. There are two types of agencies: ministerial and fiduciary. Most attorney-client relationships are of the latter variety. As such, the lawyer generally has a duty to act solely in the interest of the client as to matters that fall within the scope of the agency.[372] To the extent the lawyer receives a gift from the client or enters into a self-dealing transaction with the client, there is a presumption that the lawyer has exerted undue influence on the client. The burden is on the lawyer to prove that the client has given his or her informed consent to the conflict of interest and that the lawyer's conduct has been fair to

---

[366] *See, e.g.,* In re Testamentary Trust of Flynn, Slip Copy, 2005 WL 1846520 (Ohio App. 2 Dist.), 2005-Ohio-4028 (in affirming the lower court's decision to reduce for excessiveness the attorney-trustee's compensation, the appellate court resolved its doubts against the attorney-trustee observing that it should be the responsibility of the attorney-trustee, not the Court or the trial court, to sort out what services she had been performing as a trustee and what services as attorney).

[367] UTC §708 cmt. (available at <http://www.uniformlaws.org/Act.aspx?title=Trust%20 Code>).

[368] Restatement (Third) of Trusts §38 cmt. d.

[369] For a brief history of the Worshipful Company of Scriveners of London, visit <http:// www.scriveners.org.uk/history.htm>.

[370] *See, e.g.,* Paula A. Monopoli, *Drafting Attorneys as Fiduciaries: Fashioning an Optimal Ethical Rule for Conflicts of Interest,* 66 U. Pitt. L. Rev. 411 (2004); Paula A. Monopoli, *Fiduciary Duty: New Ethical Paradigm for Lawyer/Fiduciaries,* 67 Mo. L. Rev. 309 (2002).

[371] *See generally* Charles E. Rounds, Jr., *Lawyer Codes Are Just About Licensure, the Lawyer's Relationship with the State: Recalling the Common Law Agency, Contract, Tort, Trust, and Property Principles the Regulate the Lawyer-Client Fiduciary Relationship,* 60 Baylor L. Rev. 771 (2008).

[372] *See generally* Charles E. Rounds, Jr., *Lawyer Codes Are Just About Licensure, the Lawyer's Relationship with the State: Recalling the Common Law Agency, Contract, Tort, Trust, and Property Principles the Regulate the Lawyer-Client Fiduciary Relationship,* 60 Baylor L. Rev. 771 (2008).

the client.[373] As noted in the first chapter of this handbook, the lawyer-client agency relationship, absent special facts, is not also a confidential one. Nor need it be for the burden of proving the absence of undue influence to fall on the lawyer in the first instance. New York law, however, would appear not to be in accord when it comes to who has the burden of proof in such situations.[374]

According to a Formal Ethics Opinion of the ABA, the scrivener's acceptance of the trusteeship constitutes neither the acceptance of a gift from the client-settlor nor the lawyer entering into a business transaction with his or her client-settlor.[375] If it were a business transaction, Rule 1.8 of the ABA's Model Rules of Professional Conduct (MRPC) would be implicated: The client-settlor's "signed, informed consent to the essential terms of the arrangement after receiving the lawyer's written advice to seek independent legal advice" would be required.[376] If the offer and acceptance of a compensated trusteeship is neither a gift nor a business transaction, what is it? The Opinion is silent on that issue. If it involves a contract, then the ABA Opinion, not to mention the American College of Trust and Estate Counsel's (ACTEC's) objective informed consent standard discussed below, conflicts with both the letter and the spirit of the Restatement (Second) of Contracts.[377] In any case, the reader should be cautioned that the Opinion relates to licensure, *i.e.*, the lawyer's regulatory relationship with the state.[378] It does not and should not be construed as in any way eroding a lawyer's civil liability to his client for a breach of the duty of loyalty under fundamental common law principles of agency law.[379]

As noted, the ABA's MRPC are designed "to provide a structure for regulating conduct through disciplinary agencies," not to serve as a basis for civil liability.[380] That being the case, it seems only equitable that the Rules also not serve as a basis for exempting a scrivener-trustee from fiduciary duties that

---

[373] Restatement of Restitution §191 cmt. e (self-dealing transaction must be fair and reasonable); Restatement of Restitution §191 cmt. a (burden on the fiduciary to prove that self-dealing transaction was fair and reasonable).

[374] *See* In re Construction & Reformation of Matthews Trust No. 1, 878 N.Y.S.2d 8 (App. Div. 2009) (citing as authority dicta in Matter of Weinstock, 40 N.Y.2d 1, 7, 386 N.Y.S.2d 1, 351 N.E.2d 647 (1976)).

[375] ABA Formal Op. 02-426.

[376] ABA Formal Op. 02-426 at n.7.

[377] Restatement (Second) of Contracts §173(b) (providing in part that if a fiduciary makes a contract with his beneficiary relating to matters within the scope of the fiduciary relation, the contract is voidable by the beneficiary, unless all parties beneficially interested manifest assent with full understanding of their legal rights and of all relevant facts that the fiduciary knows or should know).

[378] *See generally* Charles E. Rounds, Jr., *Lawyer Codes Are Just About Licensure, the Lawyer's Relationship with the State: Recalling the Common Law Agency, Contract, Tort, Trust, and Property Principles the Regulate the Lawyer-Client Fiduciary Relationship*, 60 Baylor L. Rev. 771 (2008).

[379] *See generally* Charles E. Rounds, Jr., *Lawyer Codes Are Just About Licensure, the Lawyer's Relationship with the State: Recalling the Common Law Agency, Contract, Tort, Trust, and Property Principles the Regulate the Lawyer-Client Fiduciary Relationship*, 60 Baylor L. Rev. 771 (2008).

[380] ABA Model Rules of Professional Conduct, Preamble. *See generally* Charles E. Rounds, Jr., *Lawyer Codes Are Just About Licensure, the Lawyer's Relationship with the State: Recalling the Common Law Agency, Contract, Tort, Trust, and Property Principles the Regulate the Lawyer-Client Fiduciary Relationship*, 60 Baylor L. Rev. 771 (2008).

he might otherwise have under fundamental principles of agency and trust law. Beneficiaries, their counsel, and courts should take note. What is sauce for the goose ought also to be sauce for the gander.

Take, for example, what constitutes "informed consent" to the scrivener acting as trustee, a situation that is typically fraught with information asymmetry. For civil liability purposes, the laws of agency and trusts require, and have always required, that a scrivener-trustee may not avail himself of the informed consent defense, unless the client, when the consent was given, was of full age and legal capacity, free of undue influence, and *actually understood* the applicable facts and law,[381] to include the inherent conflicts of interest.[382] In other words, the client needs to subjectively understand the situation, warts and all.[383] Whether a particular consent was sufficiently informed to take the scrivener-trustee off the common law hook will depend upon the particular facts and circumstances. Thus beneficiaries and courts should take with a grain of salt ACTEC's position, as reflected in its Commentaries on the Model Rules, namely that for purposes of regulatory compliance there is informed consent even if the client is merely provided with certain unprocessed information sanitized of any references to inherent conflicts of interest:

> For the purposes of this Commentary, a client is properly informed if the client is provided with information regarding the role and duties of the fiduciary, the ability of a lay person to serve as fiduciary with legal and other professional assistance, and the comparative costs of appointing the lawyer or another person or institution as fiduciary. The client should also be informed of any significant lawyer-client relationship that exists between the lawyer or the lawyer's firm and a corporate fiduciary under consideration for appointment.[384]

This is essentially a partial consumer disclosure that is similar in approach to what is generally required by statute in certain transactions between contracting parties who are not in a fiduciary relationship, *e.g.*, the disclosure that a seller of a share of stock must make to a prospective buyer, a commercial lender of funds to a prospective borrower, or a commercial borrower to a prospective

---

[381] *Cf.* 3 Scott & Ascher §17.2.4 (noting that "[a] beneficiary's consent or acquiescence may bar the beneficiary from holding the trustee liable for improper lending of trust funds, but only if the beneficiary had full knowledge of the facts and his or her legal rights"); Matter of Audrey Carlson Revocable Trust, 873 N.Y.S.2d 669 (App. Div. 2009) (in the agency context, a self-dealing transaction entered into by the agent is voidable without the "clearest showing" that the principal actually intended that the agent engage in such activity).

[382] *See generally* §7.1.2 of this handbook (defenses to allegations that the trustee breached the duty of loyalty); Restatement of Restitution §191 (effect of consent of beneficiary).

[383] *Cf., e.g.,* Pascale, Sr. v. Pascale, 113 N.J. 20, 37–38, 549 A.2d 782, 791 (1988) (suggesting that when economic benefit passes between parties to a confidential relationship, there is a presumption of undue influence if the party in whom the confidence has been placed is a recipient of that benefit, unless there is clear and convincing evidence that the party who placed the confidence actually understood the inherent conflicts). *See generally* §7.1.2 of this handbook (defenses to allegations that the trustee breached the duty of loyalty).

[384] ACTEC Commentaries on the Model Rules of Professional Conduct 95 (4th ed. 2006) (ACTEC Commentary on MRPC 1.7).

lender.[385] There is generally no obligation on the part of the lender, for example, to ascertain whether the borrower actually understands what is being disclosed. As a general rule, a creditor-debtor relationship is not a fiduciary one.[386] Real estate agents, on the other hand, are generally required by law at least to address the issue of inherent conflicts of interest in their disclosure materials.[387] The irony with the ACTEC position on informed consent to a scrivener serving as trustee is that any lawyer retained *as independent counsel* to advise a client on whether or not to give consent would be expected *even by the regulatory authorities* to proactively assist that client in connecting the dots. As an agent-fiduciary hired to scrutinize the behavior of another fiduciary, independent counsel would be expected to do more than merely "provide information" to the client. Luckily, as one learned commentator has noted, "intimations that probate practice has a law unto itself come only from probate practitioners themselves."[388]

A scrivener's intentional misrepresentation of the applicable law or facts for the purpose of procuring from his or her client a compensated trusteeship, of course, may constitute common law fraud.[389] Negligent misrepresentations may constitute common law constructive fraud, a topic that is covered in Section 8.15.59 of this handbook.

---

[385] *See, e.g.*, Wells v. Stone City Bank, 691 N.E.2d 1246 (Ind. Ct. App. 1998) (while the relationship between a bank (the debtor) and a checking account holder (the creditor) is contractual rather than fiduciary, the bank nonetheless has a duty to act fairly and in good faith).

[386] *See generally* §9.9.4 of this handbook (bank accounts and other such debtor-creditor contractual arrangements are not trusts).

[387] There are statutes on the books in various states allowing a single real estate operation through employees it designates to service both the buyer and the seller in a real estate deal. One-stop shopping is efficient and is what the consumer wants. These statutes generally provide that the signing by the parties of a disclosure form that outlines the inherent conflicts of interest will give rise to a "conclusive presumption" of informed consent. One learned commentator has advocated something similar for scrivener-trustees. She suggests that furnishing clients at the instrument drafting stage with an "off the rack" disclosure form "is the most efficient and predictable way to make sure that full disclosure and informed consent has been obtained, given the nature of the conflict of interest and the transactional information asymmetry." *See* Paula A. Monopoli, *Drafting Attorneys as Fiduciaries: Fashioning an Optimal Ethical Rule for Conflicts of Interest*, 66 U. Pitt. L. Rev. 411, 444 (2005). Unfortunately, if the client must actually understand the nature of the "conflict of interest" and the "transactional information asymmetry," then "off the rack" disclosure materials alone can do more harm than good in that "equity looks to the intent rather than to the form." *See generally* §8.12 of this handbook (containing a catalog of equity maxims). Fiduciary relationships are not contracts. *See* Scott FitzGibbon, *Fiduciary Relationships Are Not Contracts*, 82 Marq. L. Rev. 303 (1999). Thus, it is suggested that a compelling case has yet to be made for sacrificing subjective informed consent on the altar of efficiency, particularly when it comes to agent-fiduciaries entering into self-dealing transactions with their principals and trustees with their beneficiaries.

[388] Geoffrey C. Hazard, Jr., *Conflict of Interest in Estate Planning for Husband and Wife*, 20 The Probate Lawyer 1 (1994) (delivered as The Joseph Trachtman Lecture at the 1994 Annual Meeting of the American College of Trust and Estate Counsel).

[389] *See generally* Charles E. Rounds, Jr., *Lawyer Codes Are Just About Licensure, the Lawyer's Relationship with the State: Recalling the Common Law Agency, Contract, Tort, Trust, and Property Principles the Regulate the Lawyer-Client Fiduciary Relationship*, 60 Baylor L. Rev. 771 (2008).

For a comprehensive discussion of the conflicts of interest considerations that are present whenever a lawyer drafts for a client a trust instrument that designates the lawyer as trustee, the reader is referred to Joseph W. deFuria, Jr.[390] For a discussion of what constitutes informed consent to a lawyer-trustee entering into self-dealing transactions with the trust estate generally, see Section 7.1.1 of this handbook.

Enforceability of exculpatory clauses. The enforceability of exculpatory clauses inserted by scrivener-trustees is discussed in Section 7.2.6 of this handbook. The insertion of a provision purporting to relieve the scrivener-trustee of any duty to account to the beneficiary would not only be a breach of fiduciary duty under agency principles[391] but also strongly suggest a violation of professional ethics.[392] Because such a provision would be unenforceable on public policy grounds,[393] its insertion also would constitute a legal tort, namely, the commission of an act of malpractice in the rendering of legal services.[394]

Brokerage activities of a bank trustee. On November 12, 1999, President Clinton signed into law the Gramm-Leach-Bliley Financial Modernization Bill Act,[395] which implements fundamental changes in how the U.S. financial services industry is regulated. The Act provides for "functional" regulation of bank securities activities.

Section 201 of the Act provides in part that a bank shall not be required to register as a broker under the federal securities laws because it effects transactions in a "trustee capacity," or because it effects transactions in a "fiduciary capacity" in its trust department or other departments that are regularly examined by bank examiners for compliance with fiduciary principles and standards. For the exemption to apply, the bank must be chiefly compensated for such transactions, consistent with fiduciary principles and standards, on the basis of an administration or annual fee (payable on a monthly, quarterly, or other basis), a percentage of assets under management, or a flat or capped per order processing fee equal to not more than the cost incurred by the bank in connection with executing securities transactions for trustee and fiduciary customers, or any combination of such fees.[396] An additional requirement is that the bank may not publicly solicit brokerage business. It may, however, advertise in its trust promotional literature that it effects transactions in

---

[390] *A Matter of Ethics Ignored: The Attorney-Draftsman as Testamentary Fiduciary*, 36 U. Kan. L. Rev. 275 (1988).

[391] *See generally* Charles E. Rounds, Jr., *Lawyer Codes Are Just About Licensure, the Lawyer's Relationship with the State: Recalling the Common Law Agency, Contract, Tort, Trust, and Property Principles the Regulate the Lawyer-Client Fiduciary Relationship*, 60 Baylor L. Rev. 771 (2008) (agency principles).

[392] *See, e.g.,* In re Kornich, 854 N.Y.S.2d 293, 296 (2008) (professional ethics).

[393] *See, e.g.,* In re Kornich, 854 N.Y.S.2d 293, 296 (2008) (public policy).

[394] *See generally* Charles E. Rounds, Jr., *Lawyer Codes Are Just About Licensure, the Lawyer's Relationship with the State: Recalling the Common Law Agency, Contract, Tort, Trust, and Property Principles the Regulate the Lawyer-Client Fiduciary Relationship*, 60 Baylor L. Rev. 771 (2008).

[395] 113 Stat. 1338, 1384–1390.

[396] *See generally* 3 Scott & Ascher §17.2.8 (Bonus, Commission, or Other Compensation).

securities on behalf of its trust accounts.[397] Section 202 of the Act provides that a bank shall not be a dealer within the meaning of the federal securities laws because it buys or sells securities for investment purposes for accounts for which the bank acts as a trustee or fiduciary.[398]

Multidisciplinary professional practices. In the world of agency, the duty of undivided loyalty is under attack on two fronts: by the real estate brokers and by the lawyers. Legislation is being pushed through in a number of states that would enable a single real estate agency to serve both the seller and the buyer in a transaction.[399] The concept is known as dual agency.

As for the lawyers, the ABA House of Delegates has voted not to accept recommendations contained in a report of its Commission on Multidisciplinary Practice. The vote was taken July 11, 2000. The report had recommended allowing lawyers to share fees with, or even be supervised by, nonlawyers such as accountants, stockbrokers, and insurance salesmen. These affiliations are known as MDPs. An MDP was defined in the Report as "a partnership, professional corporation, or other association or entity that includes lawyers and nonlawyers and has as one, but not all, of its purposes the delivery of legal services to a client(s) [sic] other than the MDP itself or that holds itself out to the public as providing non-legal, as well as legal, services." "The proposals would . . . [have ended] . . . the legal profession's 30-year self-imposed business isolation from other disciplines."[400] It is expected that MDP proponents will continue to press their case in the years to come.

These pressures on the duty of undivided loyalty in the agency context cannot help but put yet more pressure on the trustee's duty of undivided loyalty. It can be expected, for example, that MDPs, should they ever be authorized, would push for legal authority to include trust services as part of their product inventory, to the extent such authority does not exist already. As to the mechanics of bringing trusteeships into the MDP fold, common law trustees presumably would join MDP affiliations or MDP entities themselves would take title to property as common law trustees. Of course, MDPs would want to supplement their take of trustee fees with revenues generated from servicing in-house the legal, accounting, and brokerage needs of their trusts. The MDP concept is not new. In *Jothann v. Irving Trust Co.*, a 1934 New York case involving the drafting of a trustee exculpation provision by a lawyer who was acting on behalf of the trustee, the court, invoking fundamental principles of trust and agency law, struck the provision:

> Notwithstanding the forms that were followed, it must in all candor be said that the plaintiff actually received no independent legal advice in connection with the

---

[397] 15 U.S.C.A. §78c.

[398] 15 U.S.C.A. §78c.

[399] *See generally* Vickie J. Brady, *The Brokerage Relations Addition to the Illinois Real Estate Act: The Case of the Legalized Conflict of Interest,* 22 S. Ill. U. L.J. 725 (1998); Sherry A. Mariea & Timothy T. Sigmund, *Real Estate Agents Bid Farewell to Common Law,* 54 J. Mo. B. 96 (1998); Valerie M. Sieverling, *The Changing Face of the Real Estate Professional: Keeping Pace,* 63 Mo. L. Rev. 581 (1998).

[400] John Gibeaut, *Share the Wealth: ABA Panel Proposes Fee-Splitting with Other Professions,* ABA J., July 1999, at 14, col. 1.

preparation or execution of the trust agreement in controversy. She did not have the benefit of independent counsel, devoted solely to her interests, in explaining the significance and the legal and practical effects of the instrument she signed. She was entitled to actual, rather than absentee, counsel and advice. Holden, an employee of the defendant, was in effect acting in a dual capacity, attempting to serve two principals with conflicting interests.[401]

In the years to come, we will chronicle the extent to which courts and legislatures alter the trustee's duty of undivided loyalty to accommodate the MDP concept.

§6.1.3.4 Indirect Benefit Accruing to the Trustee

When it's good, it's very, very good. When it's bad, it's better. So runs the slogan of the Vice Fund, a new investment group that will begin buying stocks next week, with portfolios in alcohol, tobacco, gun makers and casinos. Fund manager Dan Aherns told Investor's Business Daily: There's nothing wrong with [socially conscious] investing if it helps you sleep at night. But he believes investing should be about making money, not salving one's conscience.[402]

Mutual funds that call themselves socially responsible have had striking growth in assets over the last decade, fueled in part by the perception that they can more than hold their own with the rest of the fund industry. A new study, however, calls that idea into doubt.[403]

Generally. *The principles.* A trustee commits a breach of trust if he uses the trust property for his own purposes without authority in the terms of the trust,[404] statutory authority, the informed consent of all the beneficiaries,[405] or a court order.[406] "Thus, where a trust is created of an estate that, as not infrequently happens in England, has valuable sporting privileges, the trustee cannot properly enjoy the privilege of shooting game on the estate, but where it is practicable to do so should lease the privilege for the benefit of the trust estate."[407] Nor may a South Carolina trustee take a spin in a Corvette that happens to comprise a portion of the trust estate, unless the spin is in furtherance of the trust's purposes.[408] A trustee who is authorized to reside on trust property is nonetheless chargeable with the occupancy's fair rental value, unless the terms of the trust provide otherwise.[409] Otherwise the trustee would be unjustly enriched.[410] If the trustee

---

[401] 270 N.Y.S. 721, 726 (1934).

[402] Naomi Schaefer, *Accountable to God*, Wall St. J., Aug. 30, 2002, at W21.

[403] Mark Hurlbert, *Good for Your Conscience, If Not for Your Wallet*, N.Y. Times, July 20, 2003, at p. 6 BU.

[404] *See generally* 3 Scott & Ascher §17.2.11.

[405] *See generally* 3 Scott & Ascher §17.2.3 (Use of Trust Property for Trustee's Own Benefit).

[406] *See generally* 3 Scott & Ascher §17.2.12 (Court Approval).

[407] 2A Scott on Trusts §170.17. *See also* 3 Scott & Ascher §17.2.3.

[408] *See, e.g.*, Yates v. Yates, 292 S.C. 49, 354 S.E.2d 800 (S.C. Ct. App. 1987).

[409] *See generally* 3 Scott & Ascher §17.2.3.

without authority leases the trust property to himself, then "the beneficiaries can ordinarily set the lease aside or charge the trustee with the fair rental value or with the profits, if any, that the trustee derives."[411]

Using the trust estate to dispense patronage. Vast wealth is concentrated in the hands of the nation's relatively small corps of trustees.[412] With wealth comes patronage and with patronage comes the opportunity and the temptation to benefit indirectly from its dispensation.[413] The opportunities are virtually unlimited and the benefits to be gained subtle and often difficult to detect.[414] Nevertheless, the conscientious and ethical trustee resists the temptation to benefit personally from the economic power that comes with the right to control the property of others.

Benefiting the trustee's friends and family. Trustees should think twice before selling or loaning trust property to—or purchasing goods and services with trust property from—their spouses,[415] close relatives,[416] business

---

[410] *See generally* §8.15.78 of this handbook (unjust enrichment).

[411] 3 Scott & Ascher §17.2.3.

[412] Today, a relatively small number of institutional fiduciaries collectively have the power to control most of the nation's large companies. "This phenomenon has been labeled 'fiduciary capitalism.'" *See* John H. Langbein & Bruce A. Wolk, Pension and Employee Benefit Law 803 (2000) (citing James P. Hawley & Andrew T. Williams, *The Emergence of Fiduciary Capitalism*, 5 Corporate Governance 206 (1997)). Such a high concentration of economic power carries with it a danger that these fiduciaries could either become inappropriately engaged or disengaged in matters that relate to the exercise of that power. Some fear that this small cadre of trustees and agents might someday improperly exploit this power to control the economy in ways that are not in the interests of beneficial owners. Others fear that these fiduciaries will refrain altogether from monitoring the myriad enterprises over which they have voting control. *See generally* Chapter 1 of this handbook.

[413] *See generally* 3 Scott & Ascher §17.2.14.6 (offering as an example the temptation of a bank trustee to promote good commercial relations with a corporate customer by investing trust assets in the customer's stock or debt). The bank might similarly be tempted at some point not to sell the stock or debt, though it would be prudent and in the best interests of the trust beneficiaries to do so. 3 Scott & Ascher §17.2.14.6.

[414] A mutual fund trustee, for example, who for his own personal and/or professional reasons allows a wealthy and powerful fund investor to "market time" to the detriment of the other investors would be breaching his common law duty of undivided loyalty to the other investors. *See* Securities & Exch. Comm'n v. Treadway, 354 F. Supp. 2d 311, 314 (2005). *See generally* 3 Scott & Ascher §17.2.14.6 (noting that "when a corporate fiduciary has both a trust department and a commercial banking department, conflicts of interest are inevitable, and they are often subtle").

[415] *See, e.g.*, Hartman v. Hartle, 95 N.J. Eq. 123, 122 A. 615 (1923) (noting that "it is settled law . . . that a trustee cannot purchase from himself at his own sale, and that his wife is subject to the same disability, unless leave so to do has been previously obtained under an order of the court"). *See also* UTC §802(c)(1) (available at <http://www.uniformlaws.org/Act.aspx?title=Trust%20 Code>); 3 Scott & Ascher §17.2.1.3 (Sale to Third Person for Trustee's Benefit).

[416] UTC §802(c)(2) (available at <http://www.uniformlaws.org/Act.aspx?title=Trust%20 Code>) (presuming a conflict of interest when trustee enters into transactions involving the investment or management of the trust property with his descendants, siblings, parents, or their spouses). *See also* Restatement (Third) of Trusts §78 cmt. e (prohibiting fiduciary transactions with trustee's spouse, parents, descendants and their spouses, and other individuals who are natural objects of the trustee's bounty); 3 Scott & Ascher §17.2.1.3 (Sale to Third Person for Trustee's Benefit).

associates[417] and enterprises in which the trustee has an interest,[418] entities who have an interest in the trustee,[419] attorneys,[420] as well as persons in a position to offer indirect considerations.[421] A transaction with an entity such as a partnership or a corporation—even a charitable corporation—of which the trustee is a principal officer also may implicate the duty of loyalty, and could well expose the entity itself to liability for participating in a breach of trust.[422] Because of the trustee's significant involvement in the entity's governance, the entity will find it difficult, though not necessarily impossible, to make the case that it was a bona fide purchaser (BFP).[423]

The Restatement (Third) of Trusts would prohibit altogether fiduciary transactions with the trustee's close family members.[424] This would include, for example, the hiring of the trustee's spouse, son, or daughter to provide legal services to the trust.[425] The general prohibition, however, would not apply to dealings with family members who are trust beneficiaries, provided the dealings are in keeping with the letter and spirit of the terms of the trust.[426]

As it is improper for an individual trustee to enter into a fiduciary transaction with a close family member who is not a beneficiary, so also is it improper for a corporate trustee to enter into a fiduciary transaction with one of its officers or directors. "Although not involving self-dealing (as would occur in the case of affiliates . . .), these transactions involve individuals closely

---

[417] See generally 3 Scott & Ascher §17.2.1.3 (Sale to Third Person for Trustee's Benefit). See, however, Restatement (Third) of Trusts §78 cmt. e (providing that neither a strict prohibition nor a presumption of divided loyalty applies to transactions with a business acquaintance of the trustee, unless there are "expectations of reciprocity" that are disadvantageous to the trust).

[418] See, e.g., InterFirst Bank Dallas, N.A. v. Risser, 739 S.W.2d 882 (Tex. Ct. App. 1987) (trustee bank assessed punitive damages and actual damages and was removed for selling trust assets to a commercial customer). See also UTC §802(c)(4) (available at <http://www.uniformlaws.org/Act.aspx?title=Trust%20Code>) (presuming a conflict of interest when the trustee enters into a transaction involving the investment or management of the trust property with "a corporation or other person or enterprise in which the trustee, or a person that owns a significant interest in the trustee, has an interest that might affect the trustee's best judgment"); 3 Scott & Ascher §17.2.1.3 (Sale to Third Person for Trustee's Benefit). But see UTC §802f (allowing a trustee to invest trust assets in its proprietary mutual fund provided the trustee discloses at least annually to the beneficiaries entitled to accountings the rate and method by which the additional compensation was determined).

[419] UTC §802(c)(4) (available at <http://www.uniformlaws.org/Act.aspx?title=Trust%20Code>).

[420] Restatement (Third) of Trusts §78 cmt. e (noting that "[a]ny fiduciary transaction with a personal agent or personal attorney of the trustee is presumed to be affected by a conflict between the fiduciary and personal interests of the trustee"); 3 Scott & Ascher §17.2.1.3 (confirming that if the trustee's attorney purchases trust property, the sale is generally voidable).

[421] See generally 3 Scott & Ascher §17.2.14.6.

[422] See generally 3 Scott & Ascher §17.2.1.4.

[423] See generally §5.4.2 of this handbook (rights of the beneficiary as against BFPs and other transferees of the trust property).

[424] Restatement (Third) of Trusts §78 cmt. e(1).

[425] Restatement (Third) of Trusts §78 cmt. e(1).

[426] Restatement (Third) of Trusts §78 cmt. e.

associated with a corporate trustee in a manner comparable to family members of an individual trustee)."[427]

Kickbacks and nonpecuniary benefits from service providers. Trustees should not accept benefits of a pecuniary or nonpecuniary nature from a provider of services to the trust.[428] Bonuses and commissions received from third parties, *e.g.*, from a buyer or insurer of trust property, should be turned over to the trust,[429] as should bribes.[430] In England, the no-further-inquiry rule applies to bribes and secret commissions received by the trustee.[431]

Premiums for internal fiduciary liability insurance are generally not chargeable to the trust estate.[432] English law is in accord,[433] although there is an exception for trustees of charitable trusts.[434] In England, trust instruments executed in the late 1990s and thereafter tend to expressly grant to the trustee the authority to charge fiduciary liability insurance premiums against the trust estate as a trust expense.[435] Absent such authority, if the trustee's stockbroker or investment advisor absorbs the cost of the trustee's fiduciary liability insurance premiums in exchange for the trustee directing brokerage or advisory work his or her way,[436] then the trustee's duty of undivided loyalty is implicated.

Windfalls belong to the trust, not to the trustee. Thus, a trustee who incurs litigation costs in successfully defending a breach-of-fiduciary-duty claim may not be reimbursed from the trust estate for those costs if those costs were actually paid by the trustee's insurance carrier, not the trustee.[437] Otherwise the

---

[427] Restatement (Third) of Trusts §78 cmt. e.

[428] Restatement of Restitution §197 (bonus or commission received by fiduciary). *See, e.g.,* In re Estate of Rothko, 43 N.Y.2d 305, 372 N.E.2d 291 (1977), *aff'g* 56 A.D.2d 499, 392 N.Y.S.2d 870 (1977), *aff'g* 84 Misc. 2d 830, 379 N.Y.S.2d 923 (1975) (a case in which independent judgment was called into question because of professional advantages and financial opportunities that accrued to coexecutors from the sale of estate assets); Brown, *The Punctilio of an Honor the Most Sensitive*, 131 Tr. & Est. 24 (1992) (referring to a case, ultimately settled, involving an executor who selectively revealed information regarding real property in the estate in order to give an advantage to a friend participating in the subsequent auction of that piece of property).

[429] Restatement (Third) of Trusts §78 cmt. d(1) (noting also that even informal prearrangements for future considerations are covered by the proscription); 3 Scott & Ascher §17.2.8 (Bonus, Commission, or Other Compensation); Restatement of Restitution §190 ("Where a fiduciary in violation of his duty to the beneficiary receives or retains a bonus or commission or other profit, he holds what he receives upon a constructive trust for the beneficiary"). *See also* §3.3 of this handbook (a general discussion of the constructive trust); §7.2.3.1.6 of this handbook (the constructive trust as a procedural equitable remedy).

[430] *See generally* 3 Scott & Ascher §17.2.8.

[431] Lewin ¶ 20-33 (England). *See generally* §6.1.3 of this handbook (in part discussing the no-further-inquiry rule) and §8.15.30 of this handbook (no-further-inquiry rule).

[432] *See generally* §3.5.2.3 of this handbook.

[433] Kemble v. Hicks [1999] P.L.R. 287 (England).

[434] Charities Act 1993 s. 73F (England).

[435] Clive Barwell, *Can the trust pay?*, 17(1) STEP J. 70 (Jan. 2009).

[436] Clive Barwell, *Can the trust pay?*, 17(1) STEP J. 71 (Jan. 2009) (apparently this is happening in England).

[437] *See, e.g.*, Foulston Siefkin LLP v. Wells Fargo Bank of Tex. N.A., 465 F.3d 211 (5th Cir. 2006) (trustee incurred attorneys' fees of approximately $1.5 million). *See generally* §3.5.2.3 of this handbook (trustee's equitable right to exoneration and reimbursement from the trust estate).

trustee would be unjustly enriched.[438] This assumes that the trustee plans to pocket the reimbursement, *i.e.*, that the insurance company has no subrogation rights in equity or otherwise to be reimbursed from the trust estate.[439]

Allowing the trustee to accept compensation from third parties is bad policy. Like Caesar's wife, the trustee must be above suspicion. When the trustee yields to these temptations, it is not long before rationalizing takes over and the interests of the beneficiaries are compromised. The Restatement (Third) of Trusts has endorsed the policy that underlies the traditional proscription against a trustee taking outside compensation for acts performed as trustee: "If a trustee were allowed to keep any form of compensation from a third person for acts performed in the administration of the trust, a temptation would exist that would deprive the beneficiaries of the circumstantial assurance of independent and objective fiduciary judgment that the trust law seeks to provide."[440]

Social investing. The practice of *social investing* (*socially responsible investing* or *SRI* to its proponents) illustrates how seductive this economic power can be.[441] Corralling a workable definition of social investing is not all that easy. One social investor, for example, purports to define it this way: "Social investing is about investing in solutions in education, economic development, health, climate change and poverty alleviation."[442] That is only not a definition but also descriptive of an investment strategy that one unmotivated by social investment considerations might pursue.

Social investing has been defined by Professor Langbein and Judge Posner as the "pursuit of an investment strategy that tempers the conventional objective of maximizing the investor's financial interests by seeking to promote nonfinancial social goals as well."[443] In the latter part of the twentieth century, considerable social investing energy was focused on pressuring the trustees of charitable and pension funds to disinvest in companies that were doing business in apartheid South Africa. A similar campaign is currently under way targeting companies that do business in the Sudan and Iran.[444]

"A trustee ordinarily violates the duty of loyalty by using trust property to benefit anyone other than the beneficiaries, or to accomplish any objective

---

[438] *See generally* §8.15.78 of this handbook (unjust enrichment).

[439] *See generally* §8.15.50 of this handbook (the subrogation doctrine in the trust context).

[440] Restatement (Third) of Trusts §78 cmt. d(1).

[441] *See generally* 4 Scott & Ascher §19.1.13 (Moral Considerations in Investing).

[442] Geoff Burnand, *Social value of money*, 16(30) STEP J. 21 (Mar. 2008) (Mr. Burnand is Chief Executive at Investing for Good).

[443] Langbein & Posner, *Social Investing and the Law of Trusts*, 79 Mich. L. Rev. 72, 73 (1980). *See, e.g.*, Andrew Ross Sorkin, *Court Ties Up Hershey Deal, For Time Being*, N.Y. Times, Sept. 5, 2002, at C1, col. 5 (reporting the Pennsylvania attorney general's opposition to the efforts of the trustees of The Hershey Trust to diversify a portfolio that is heavily concentrated in the stock of Hershey Foods Corporation and his intention to "propose legislation that would change laws that govern charitable trusts so that trustees could consider the interests of a community before selling a controlling stake in a for-profit company"). *See generally* §8.35 of this handbook (the Hershey Trust).

[444] *See* Jane Spencer, Sudan-Divestment Laws Draw Attacks From Fund Managers, Business Groups, Wall St. J., May 3, 2006, at p. C1.

other than a trust purpose."[445] A trustee who *without express authority in the governing instrument*[446] voluntarily undertakes to practice social investing uses the trust estate, *i.e.*, other people's property,[447] to promote the trustee's own political and social goals—a clear case of indirect self-dealing.[448] The trustee who yields to third-party pressure to practice social investing is acting on divided loyalties;[449] the trustee who seeks the acclaim of particular constituencies, or at least the cessation of their criticisms,[450] may be subordinating the interests of the trust to the interests of the trustee,[451] particularly when under-diversification or sub-par investment performance, or both, is the likely or

---

[445] 3 Scott & Ascher §17.2.3.

[446] *See generally* 3 Scott & Ascher §17.2.11 (Terms of the Trust).

[447] "During his lengthy career as a self-appointed 'consumer advocate,' . . . [Ralph Nader-] . . . has lectured others about the evils of monopolists, corporate polluters, and weapons makers." James M. Sheehan, The Free Market, May 2002, at 6. "Among his recent . . . [personal] . . . holdings: router monopolist Cisco Systems, fossil-fuel giant Occidental Petroleum, and missile manufacturer Raytheon." James M. Sheehan, The Free Market, May 2002, at 6.

[448] *See* Rounds, *Social Investing, IOLTA, and the Law of Trusts: The Settlor's Case Against the Political Use of Charitable and Client Funds*, 22 Loy. U. Chi. L.J. 163, 170–172 nn.27, 31 (1990).

[449] *See, e.g.*, Sarah Ellison, *Sale of Hershey Foods Runs Into Opposition*, Wall St. J., Aug. 26, 2002, at A3, col. 1 (reporting that the Pennsylvania attorney general who at one time called for diversification of The Hershey Trust investment portfolio has since reversed his position: "While the recent opposition by Mr. Fisher is viewed by many as political posturing, it could complicate the sale . . . [of the trust's 77 percent stake in Hershey Foods Corp.] . . . by scaring off bidders and giving some board members of the trust, already being criticized from local officials and employees, the cover they need to scrap the sale, say takeover experts.").

[450] *See, e.g.*, Sarah Ellison, *Hershey Foods' Controlling Trust Says It Has No Intentions to Sell*, Wall St. J., Sept. 27, 2002, B5, col. 1 (reporting that the trustees of The Hershey Trust, by "pulling Hershey Foods from the auction block at the eleventh hour despite receiving a $12.5 billion offer from Wm. Wrigley Jr. Co.," were attempting to "appease" local residents and other constituencies who had been strenuously and publicly criticizing the portfolio diversification initiatives of the trustees and calling for the trustees to resign). *See generally* §8.35 of this handbook (the Hershey Trust).

[451] Langbein & Posner, *Social Investing and the Law of Trusts*, 79 Mich. L. Rev. 72, 96–104 (1980). "We conclude that the duty of loyalty . . . forbid[s] social investing in its current form." Langbein & Posner, *Social Investing and the Law of Trusts*, 79 Mich. L. Rev. 72, 76 (1980). *See also* Restatement (Second) of Trusts §170 cmt. q (providing that "[t]he trustee is under a duty to the beneficiary in administering the trust not to be guided by the interest of any third person"); comment to §5 of Uniform Prudent Investor Act (available at <http://www.uniformlaws.org/Act.aspx?title=Trust%20Code> as Article 9 of the UTC) (suggesting that "[n]o form of so-called 'social investing' is consistent with the duty of loyalty if the investment activity entails sacrificing the interests of trust beneficiaries."). *Cf.* Cryan v. Crocker Nat'l Bank, No. 721368 (Cal. Sup. Ct., Mar. 10, 1981) (surcharging bank trustee for selling trust property to a charity on whose board a trust committee member was serving). It should be noted, however, that the Report of the Massachusetts Prudent Investor Act Committee, which forms a part of the legislative history of Mass. Gen. L. ch. 203C (the Massachusetts Prudent Investor Act), by implication, endorses the practice of social investing: "Social investing using screens of socially responsible criteria to select a universe of investments from which to select a portfolio that the trustee *believes*" "[emphasis added] will accomplish the objectives of the trust [is] allowed." Whether Massachusetts courts will apply the Report's subjective "belief" standard to trustees who practice social investing remains to be seen. *See also* 29 C.F.R. §2509.94-1 (1995). Section 2509.94-1, the U.S. Labor Department's Interpretive Bulletin relating to ERISA, states that §§403 and 404 of ERISA do not prevent trustees of private employee benefit trusts who comply with ERISA prudence requirements from

actual consequence. In any case, regardless of the consequences, unauthorized social investing implicates the fraud on a power doctrine.[452] In this case the power is a discretionary administrative power.[453] The court, for example, will "interpose" if a trustee takes a bribe for making an investment.[454] The considerations that flow to the trustee and/or third parties for social investing need not be so crass, however, for the doctrine to be implicated.[455]

Nor are benign motives a defense.[456] "Even if the trustee does not act in bad faith, the court will interfere if the trustee acts with an improper motive." Thus the trustees of a miners' pension fund who have adopted a policy of not investing in any form of energy that competes with coal are on shaky legal ground:

> In considering what investments to make, trustees must put aside their own personal views and interests. Trustees may have strongly held social or political views. They may be firmly opposed to any investment in South Africa or other countries, or they may object to any form of investment in companies concerned with alcohol, tobacco, armaments or many other things. In the conduct of their own affairs, of course, they are free to abstain from making any such investments. Yet, under a trust, if investments of this type would be more beneficial to the beneficiaries than other investments, the trustees must not refrain from making the investments by reason of the views they hold.[457]

This is a critical excerpt from the decision of the English judge (Megarry VC) in *Cowan v. Scargill* (1985).[458] Since 1985, proponents of social investing have been endeavoring to make the difficult case that the "Megarry Judgment"

---

investing in Economically Targeted Investments (ETIs). Section 2509.94-1 defines ETI's as investments "selected for the economic benefits they create apart from their investment return to the employee benefit plan." 29 C.F.R. §2509.94-1 (1995). "Secretary of Labor Robert Reich interpreted IB-1 to mean that 'a pension trustee, given two investment choices of equal risk and return, may pick an investment based on social goals.'" John H. Langbein & Bruce A. Wolk, Pension and Employee Benefit Law 845 (2000) (citing 63 Tax Notes 1745 (1994)). For a brief discussion of the concept of "costless social investing" in the ERISA context, *see* John H. Langbein & Bruce A. Wolk, Pension and Employee Benefit Law at 844–845. On May 9, 1995, U.S. Representative Jim Saxton (R-N.J.) introduced a bill that would effectively rescind the Interpretive Bulletin. *See* H.R. 1594, 104th Cong., 1st Sess. (1995). For an analogous controversy in the corporate area, *see* Medical Comm. for Human Rights v. SEC, 432 F.2d 659, 681 (D.C. Cir. 1970), wherein the court noted "that there is a clear and compelling distinction between management's legitimate need for freedom to apply its expertise in matters of day-to-day business judgment, and management's patently illegitimate claim of power to treat modern corporations with their vast resources as personal satrapies implementing personal political or moral predilections." *But see* 404 U.S. 403 (vacating the lower court decision as moot because after certiorari was granted to the U.S. Supreme Court, the corporation acquiesced to the stockholder's request and included anti-napalm proposal in its 1971 proxy statement).

[452] *See generally* §8.15.26 of this handbook (the fraud on a power doctrine).
[453] *See generally* §3.5.3 of this handbook (discussing discretionary administrative powers).
[454] 3 Scott & Ascher §18.2.3.
[455] *See generally* §8.15.26 of this handbook (the fraud on a power doctrine).
[456] *See generally* §8.15.26 of this handbook (the fraud on a power doctrine).
[457] Cowan v. Scargill, [1985] 1 Ch. 270, [1984] 2 All E. R. 750 (England).
[458] [1985] Ch 270.

in no way closed the door on social investing by fiduciaries. "Commentators supporting social investing tend to concede the overriding force of the duty of loyalty" arguing instead "that particular schemes of social investing may not result in below-market returns."[459] They advocate a "facts and circumstances" or "no harm no foul" test. In other words, to the extent actual investment performance is unaffected by the trustee's social investing activities, the fiduciary duty of undivided loyalty that is owed *to the trust beneficiaries* or *to the trust's specific charitable purposes* is not implicated. In fact, the manager of one mutual fund has consistently outperformed the market by adhering to the Shariah code of the Islamic faith in the selection of the fund's underlying assets. In any case, the fund trustees' fiduciary's duty of loyalty would not be implicated as the fund's goals and purposes are fully disclosed to prospective investors:

> The limits to investing are many: most financial firms that earn interest, such as banks and brokerages, as well as tobacco and alcohol companies and any venture engaged in adult entertainment. Companies that have a lot of debt are frowned upon—yet so are those that have piled up too much interest-bearing cash.[460]

It should be noted here that social investing is sometimes confused with mere efforts at enhancing shareholder value. A trustee, for example, who attempts to influence by proxy voting the internal governance of a company would not be engaging in social investing, provided the investment is prudent and the goal of the voting is a narrow one, namely the enhancement of shareholder value in furtherance of the specified purposes of the trust.[461] In fact, the trustee may have an affirmative duty to exert his influence in this way.

It appears that under the Restatement (Third) of Trusts (and the Uniform Prudent Investor Act), social investing has no place in the default law of trusts.[462] If social investing has a place, as Professor Scott suggested it had,[463] then it is incumbent upon the courts and the legislatures to create objective standards, *i.e.*, to define this exception to the trustee's duty of undivided loyalty

---

[459] UTC §5 cmt. (available at <http://www.uniformlaws.org/Act.aspx?title=Trust%20 Code>).

[460] Karen Richardson, *Extra Work: Investing by Rules of Islamic Faith*, Wall. St. J., July 19, 2006, at pg. C3. *See generally* 4 Scott & Ascher §19.1.13 (Moral Considerations in Investing) (confirming that the policy of both the Restatement (Third) of Trusts and the Uniform Prudent Investor Act is that "[o]nly to the extent permitted by the terms of the trust or the consent of the beneficiaries may the trustees of private trusts properly take social considerations into account in making investment decisions").

[461] *See* Uniform Prudent Investor Act §5 cmt (suggesting that "[n]o form of so-called 'social investing' is consistent with the duty of loyalty if the investment activity entails sacrificing the interest of trust beneficiaries—for example, by accepting below-market returns—in favor of the persons supposedly benefited by pursuing the particular social cause"). *But see* 3 Scott on Trusts §227.17 (suggesting that a trustee is "entitled to consider the welfare of the community, and refrain from allowing the use of the funds in a manner detrimental to the community" even if it were not so that "a corporation that has a proper sense of social obligation is more likely to be successful in the long run than those that are bent on obtaining the maximum amount of profits").

[462] Restatement (Third) of Trusts §78 cmt. f. *See also* Restatement (Third) of Trusts: Prudent Investor Rule §227 cmt. c.

[463] 3 Scott on Trusts §227.17.

in a way that establishes reasonable limits on a trustee's right to promote with the trust estate his own personal, political, and social goals, or the personal, political, and social goals of third parties,[464] something Professor Scott did not do particularly well. The only guidance he offered us was that the trustees who have a "concern in the social behavior of the corporations in whose securities they invest" could decline to invest in companies "whose activities or some of them are contrary to fundamental and generally accepted ethical principles."[465] Identifying someone's "favorite cause" is one thing.[466] Identifying "fundamental and generally accepted ethical principles," however, is quite another.[467] The problem is that what is "ethics" to one man is often mere "politics" to another.[468]

In 2002, for example, in response to calls for Harvard to divest itself of stock in companies that do business with or in Israel, Harvard University President Lawrence Summers "criticized . . . [such calls for] . . . divestment as an unwarranted attempt to 'single out' Israel as an odious abuser of human rights," condemning "the divestment movement and other extreme anti-Israel efforts as anti-Semitic in effect, if not in intent."[469]

On February 8, 2015, The University of California Student Association, which purports to represent all 240,000 students enrolled in the UC system's 10 campuses, passed (9-1-5) a disinvestment resolution which, in part, purports to proscribe fiduciary investing by UC in U.S. debt, such as U.S. treasuries. Here is the wording:

> THEREFORE BE IT FURTHER RESOLVED, That the Board of Directors of the University of California Student Association determines if it is found that UC funds are being invested in any of the aforementioned governments [Brazil, Egypt, Indonesia, Israel, Russia, Turkey, Sri Lanka, Mexico, and the United States], the University of California Student Association calls upon the University

---

[464] *See, e.g.,* Jenna Russel, *Some on Harvard, MIT faculties urge divestment in Israel,* Boston Globe, May 6, 2002, at B3, col. 1 (reporting that about seventy-five faculty members at the two institutions have signed an online petition asking the schools to divest from companies doing business in Israel until its forces withdraw from occupied territories). "[Paul Nemirovsky, a doctoral student at MIT] . . . wrote a response pointing out that other nations responsible for 'infinitely larger' civilian casualties haven't been similarly condemned. . . ." Jenna Russel, *Some on Harvard, MIT faculties urge divestment in Israel,* Boston Globe, May 6, 2002, at B3, col. 1. With the abolition of South Africa's system of apartheid, social investors have been focusing much of their attention on companies that make tobacco products. As of June 2000, approximately 14.5 percent of all U.S. charitable foundations were employing some sort of social or political investment screen. "A growing number of funds have been set up to invest in a socially responsible manner." Chart, *Different Definitions of Responsibility,* N.Y. Times, Feb. 11, 2001, at NE 26, col. 3. "But there are many different ideas about what this means." Chart, *Different Definitions of Responsibility,* N.Y. Times, Feb. 11, 2001, at NE 26, col. 3.

[465] 3 Scott on Trusts §227.17.

[466] 4 Scott & Ascher §19.1.13.

[467] 4 Scott & Ascher §19.1.13.

[468] *See generally* Pension Fund Politics: The Dangers of Socially Responsible Investing, American Enterprise Institute (John Entine ed., 2005).

[469] Jon Berkon, *Levin Must Speak Out Against Divestment,* 34 Yale Herald, No. 12 (Nov. 21, 2002).

of California to divest all stocks and securities of such governments, at such time and in such manner as fund trustee[sic] may determine, and maintain divestment from said governments, in accordance with the fund trustees' fiduciary duty, until they meet the University of California endorsed Principles of Responsible Investment.

Note that in the resolution there is reference to some fiduciary duty of the fund trustees. There is, however, no accompanying commentary shedding light on the nature of the duty that is being contemplated by the students, nor on to whom (or to what) that duty runs. In any case, the resolution probably should have been expanded to include personal disclaimers by the students of any federal funds to which they, themselves, might otherwise be entitled, now and in the future. If it is socially irresponsible to purchase a U.S. debt instrument with other people's money, surely it is even more so to personally partake, whether directly or indirectly, in the proceeds from its sale.

Swarthmore, too, has been pressured to socially invest its charitable assets. In 2013 Danielle Charette wrote in The Wall Street Journal: "The latest upheaval has centered on the school's radical environmentalist club, Montana Justice, which has led a multiyear campaign calling on the college to divest its $1.5 billion endowment—one of the highest endowments-per-student in the nation—of fossil fuel companies."[470]

Cambridge University (England) in 2015 established a working group to devise rules to "ensure" that a significant portion of the investments made by the managers of its endowment is socially responsible.[471] The group included three students.[472]

Are fiduciaries constrained only by their subjective social and political predilections in deciding whether to yield to third-party pressure to make political statements with endowments? Is SRI so subjective as to be, for all intent and purposes, "what you make of it"[473] or "whatever the loudest person in the room says it is,"[474] as some have suggested? If it is, should it be? If not, and assuming social investing by fiduciaries such as trustees is to be tolerated, if not encouraged, there need to be objective criteria to guide them in the selection of those companies and countries that are fair game for targeting and those that are not. Otherwise, we run the risk of trusteeships, particularly charitable and

---

[470] Danielle Charette, *My Top-Notch Illiberal Arts Education,* Wall St. J., May 16, 2013, at A13.

[471] *See* Juliet Samuel, *Cantabrigian Investing Hopes to Get an Ethical Edge,* Wall St. J., May 19, 2015, at C1, col. 4.

[472] Putting aside the question of whether the social investment of entrusted charitable funds can ever be regulated objectively by rules objectively arrived at, one wonders why the powers-that-be of any charitable educational institution would ever delegate to students *qua* students the task of endeavoring to come up with such rules. Students come and go. Moreover, even most university professors will lack the requisite qualifications to competently perform such a task.

[473] Joel C. Dobris, *SRI-Shibboleth or Canard,* 42 Real Prop. Prob. & Tr. J. 755, 756 (No.4-2008) (the opinion of the article's author).

[474] Joel C. Dobris, *SRI-Shibboleth or Canard,* 42 Real Prop. Prob. & Tr. J. 755, 756, n.4. (No.4-2008) (the opinion of a friend of the article's author).

pension trusteeships, becoming political footballs.[475] Take the overwhelming vote (431–462) of the General Assembly of the Presbyterian Church (USA) calling for a divestment campaign targeted at corporations doing business in Israel:

> The church is not calling for divestment of its $7 billion portfolio from China, despite China's denial of the most basic political and religious rights and its particularly harsh treatment of followers of Falun Gong. It is not condemning Russia, even though Russia's policies in Chechnya are by any human-rights standard atrocious. It is not even calling for economic sanctions against Syria or Iran, whose human-rights records for their own people are egregious and whose Jewish citizens are denied the basic civil rights and liberties afforded to all Israelis, including its Arab citizens, some of whom even serve in the Knesset.[476]

In any case, knowledgeable commentators remind us that promoting a particular social or political goal by social investing is one thing, achieving it by social investing is quite another:

> According to Doug Henwood, editor of *Left Business Observer* and a well-known socialist critic of the stock market, there is simply no way to invest responsibly. . . . Social responsibility, he warns, is an exercise of futility in a capitalist system. . . . Oddly, I find myself in agreement with these leftist thinkers. They are right: their ambitions are not achievable in the stock market. Capitalism is too complex to serve a narrow political ideology.[477]

Let there be no misunderstanding: Congress—and probably the state legislatures, as well—can always make it a crime for private fiduciaries to invest in certain companies. Criminal proscriptions will almost always trump the fiduciary principles that are the subject of this handbook, provided the proscriptions are the product of statutes that are both duly enacted and constitutional. IOLTA's quasi-criminal proscriptions are problematic on both counts.

IOLTA. In 1978, Florida's lawyer-trustees received by judicial fiat a limited exemption from the duty of undivided loyalty that each had owed his or

---

[475] At a conference on social investing, one panelist, a proponent of social investing, publicly suggested to the author that the investment decisions of trustees of charitable and pension funds as a matter of public policy ought to be subject to political influence.

[476] Jay Lefkowitz, *Singled Out*, Wall St. J., July 30, 2004, at W13, col. 1. *See also* Jim Roberts, *Turn Left at the Presbyterian Church*, Wall St. J., June 15, 2006, at A14 (suggesting that a large majority of the members of the Presbyterian Church are of the opinion that the church needs to abandon divestment as a hostile action against Israel in favor of "investment" in Israel and Palestinian groups that are working as "bridge-builders for peace").

[477] James M. Sheehan, The Free Market, May 2002, at 6. *See also* Elizabeth Benton, *Yale's New Political Activism: Middle and Center*, 34 Yale Herald, No. 7 (Oct. 18, 2002) (reporting that in response to calls for Yale to divest itself of countries doing business in Israel, its president made the following observation: "The University has investments in many public companies that do business in America—I'd bet that if you looked at the 1,000 biggest companies in America, 900 do business in Israel . . . [T]o divest of holdings in Israel, one would have to divest in a great portion of the American economy").

her clients when Florida's highest court adopted the first Interest on Lawyers Trust Accounts (IOLTA) program.[478] Soon, the *judiciaries* of a number of states[479] also began authorizing or compelling lawyer-trustees to apply the income earned on client commingled trust accounts to charitable and professional organizations. For IOLTA administration purposes, what would otherwise have been an equitable duty on the part of the lawyer to obtain from the client an informed consent to the diversion was generally suspended, also by judicial fiat. In the First Circuit, the IOLTA diversion withstood challenges on First, Fifth, and Fourteenth Amendment grounds.[480] The U.S. Court of Appeals for the Fifth Circuit, however, held that IOLTA income is the property of the client.

On appeal, the U.S. Supreme Court affirmed, holding that, "for purposes of the Takings Clause of the Fifth Amendment," gross IOLTA income is the property of the client.[481] This was in line with long-standing principles of Anglo-American property and trust law.[482]

The Ninth Circuit en banc then held that a government appropriation of IOLTA interest for public purposes did not constitute a taking without just compensation in violation of the Fifth Amendment.[483] A decision of the U.S. Court of Appeals for the Fifth Circuit, however, held that it did.[484] The U.S. Supreme Court granted certiorari June 10, 2002, to hear an appeal of the Ninth Circuit decision. Oral arguments were heard December 9, 2002.

In 2003, the U.S. Supreme Court ruled that though gross IOLTA income constitutes the property of clients and though the gross income has been taken

---

[478] *See generally* Comment, *IOLTA—Overcoming Its Current Obstacles*, 18 Stetson L. Rev. 415 (1989). *See also* §9.7.2 of this handbook (IOLTA trusts). *See generally* Charles E. Rounds, Jr., *Lawyer Codes Are Just About Licensure, the Lawyer's Relationship with the State: Recalling the Common Law Agency, Contract, Tort, Trust and Property Principles that Regulate the Lawyer-Client Relationship*, 60 Baylor L. Rev. 771 (2008).

[479] *See* A.B.A. IOLTA Clearinghouse, IOLTA Profiles, 7 IOLTA Update 1, 4–7 (1991). It should be noted, however, that there is legislative involvement in the Maryland, New York, Ohio, and Pennsylvania IOLTA programs. The IOLTA Update was a valuable resource for statistics relating to the various state programs.

[480] *See, e.g.*, Washington Legal Found. v. Massachusetts Bar Found., 993 F.2d 962 (1st Cir. 1993) (holding in part that an IOLTA account is not a "formal" trust and that the "interest earned on IOLTA accounts belongs to no one"). *But see* Ritchie et al., Decedents' Estates and Trusts 1318 (8th ed. 1993) ("Funds received by a lawyer on behalf of a client are held in trust for the client."); Sinibaldi, *The Taking Issue in California's Legal Services Trust Account Program*, 12 Hastings Const. L.Q. 463 (1985) ("the laudable purpose of California's [IOLTA] program should not sustain it against a Takings Clause challenge").

[481] *See* Phillips v. Washington Legal Found., 118 S. Ct. 1925, 141 L. Ed. 2d 174 (1998). *See also* Schneider v. California Dep't of Corr., 151 F.3d 1194 (1998); Bockman v. Vail, 161 F.3d 11 (1998) (each citing *Phillips* and holding that interest on personal funds of an incarcerated prisoner belongs to the prisoner).

[482] Lewin ¶ 23-23 (noting that the House of Lords has held that a sole life tenant of shares in a company is the equitable owner of dividends as soon as they are received by the trustees, even though they are entitled to deduct expenses before transmitting them to the beneficiary).

[483] Washington Legal Found. v. Legal Found. of Wash., 271 F.3d 835 (9th Cir. 2001).

[484] Washington Legal Found. v. Texas Equal Access to Justice Found., 2001 WL 1222105 (5th Cir.).

from them by the state, there is no compensation due them.[485] This is because under a properly administered program, principal sums that could generate net income for a client may not be deposited in an IOLTA account.[486] Would the lawyer-trustee still have a common law duty incident to the duty of loyalty to inform the client in advance that the client's property, *i.e.*, the equitable interest, is being taken by the state under the auspices of an IOLTA program?[487] "Despite their widespread acceptance, these programs have always been controversial, in large part because they appear to deprive clients of the interest on their funds."[488] In other words, third parties to the lawyer-client trust relationship are unjustly enriched.[489] Moreover, "[t]here seem no longer to be any practical impediments to making trust funds productive, even on a temporary basis, while retaining a very high level of liquidity, whether by bank deposits or investment in money-market funds or other short-term funds."[490]

Notwithstanding the decision of the U.S. Supreme Court upholding the constitutionality of IOLTA, the lawyer-trustee will continue to have an obligation to properly account for each client's allocable share of IOLTA principal.[491] Accordingly, the lawyer-trustee who does not have an in-house trust accounting infrastructure that is up to the task of properly administering IOLTA principal may want to employ the standard retail "sub-accounting"/"sweep" product of a reputable financial services institution. Not only would such a product facilitate keeping track of a client's allocable share of principal, it would also facilitate the generation of appropriate trust accountings. The lawyer-trustee may well find that the costs of administering IOLTA principal in-house, particularly secretarial and other labor costs, approximate or exceed the costs in fees and charges of farming the work out to a financial services institution.

Inside the corporate trustee. The corporate trustee (*e.g.*, a bank or a trust company) is a collection of human beings performing myriad tasks in furtherance of myriad corporate purposes. Thus, there is ample opportunity for the corporation and the individual directors and officers to directly and indirectly self-deal.[492] The breaches can be subtle.[493] They are often hidden in a thicket of complicated financial transactions and thus difficult to sort out, let alone prevent and detect by those not privy to the inner workings of the institution.[494]

---

[485] Brown v. Legal Found. of Wash., 123 S. Ct. 1406 (2003).

[486] *See* Schneider v. California Dep't of Corr., 345 F.3d 716 (9th Cir. 2003) (remanding for a determination of whether an individual prison inmate was unconstitutionally deprived of any net interest earned on funds held in his state prison inmate trust account).

[487] *See* §6.1.5.1 of this handbook (the trustee's duty to furnish the beneficiaries with critical information).

[488] 1 Scott & Ascher §2.3.8.1.

[489] *See generally* §8.15.78 of this handbook (unjust enrichment).

[490] 3 Scott & Ascher §17.13.

[491] *See* §6.1.5.2 of this handbook (the trustee's duty to keep and render accounts).

[492] *See generally* 3 Scott & Ascher §17.2.14 (Corporate Trustees).

[493] *See generally* 3 Scott & Ascher §17.2.14.6.

[494] *See* Brown, *The Punctilio of an Honor the Most Sensitive*, 131 Tr. & Est. 24–25 (1992). "If an intended act is even faintly suggestive of impropriety, don't do it." Brown, *The Punctilio of an Honor the Most Sensitive*, 131 Tr. & Est. 24, 26 (1992). *See also* Revised Reg. 9 (12. C.F.R. §9.12)

As a general rule, neither the corporate trustee nor its directors and officers[495] should directly or indirectly enter into self-dealing transactions that involve the trust property.[496] Unless authorized by the terms of the trust[497] or by statute,[498] the corporate trustee should not direct trust business to its in-house real estate sales operation; its securities[499] and banking departments;[500] subsidiary corporations and affiliates in which it has a controlling interest;[501] or its proprietary mutual funds.[502] "So also, in the absence of authorization, a purchase by a

---

(Self-dealing and conflicts of interest) (available at <www.gpoaccess.gov/cfr/index.html>). Section 9.12(b), for example, provides that "[a] national bank may not lend, sell, or otherwise transfer assets of a fiduciary account for which a national bank has investment discretion to the bank or any of its directors, officers, or employees, or to affiliates of the bank or any of their directors, officers, or employees, or to individuals or organizations with whom there exists an interest that might affect the exercise of the best judgment of the bank. . . ."

[495] *See generally* 3 Scott & Ascher §17.2.14.

[496] The duty of loyalty extends to employees and agents of the trustee. The focus is on the functions performed, not just on the entity holding legal title. *See* Bogert §543 n.21 and accompanying text. *See, e.g.,* In re Bond & Mortgage Guar. Co., 303 N.Y. 423, 103 N.E.2d 721 (1952) (holding that counsel to the trustee also may not self-deal). *See also* 3 Scott & Ascher §17.2.14.

[497] *See generally* 3 Scott & Ascher §§17.2.11 (The Terms of the Trust), 17.2.14 (Corporate Trustees).

[498] *See generally* 3 Scott & Ascher §17.2.14 (Corporate Trustees).

[499] *See generally* 3 Scott & Ascher §§17.2.8 (Bonus, Commission, or Other Compensation), 17.2.14 (Corporate Trustees) (noting that when a bank or trust company underwrites securities, "it has usually agreed with the other underwriters not to sell at less than the public offering price"). There also is the danger that the bank or trust company will "make its trusts a dumping ground for unsold securities"). 3 Scott & Ascher §§17.2.8 (Bonus, Commission, or Other Compensation), 17.2.14 (Corporate Trustees).

[500] Restatement (Third) of Trusts §78 cmt. d (noting that self-dealing is involved because the various departments are not "separate persons"); 3 Scott & Ascher §17.2.4 (noting that because trust officers owe fiduciary duties not only to the shareholders of the bank or trust company that employees them but also to the beneficiaries of the trusts that they are managing, the temptation to favor the shareholders "is likely to be far more insidious than the temptation of an individual trustee to favor himself or herself "). *See also* 3 Scott & Ascher §17.2.14.6 (General Observations on Conflicts of Interest on the Part of Corporate Trustees).

[501] Restatement (Third) of Trusts §78 cmt. d (noting that transactions with subsidiaries and affiliates controlled by the trustee, or in which the trustee has a substantial interest, could tempt a trustee to consider its own financial advantage in the transaction rather than the interests of the beneficiaries); 3 Scott & Ascher §17.2.14.

[502] At the very least, a trust company should set high ethical standards for its employees. Brown, *The Punctilio of an Honor the Most Sensitive,* 131 Tr. & Est. 24, 31 (1992). *See* Comptroller of the Currency Trust Interpretation No. 273 (Sept. 25, 1992) (concerning trust department purchase of securities through affiliated discount brokerage companies). 12 C.F.R. §9.5(a) & (c) (available at <www.gpoaccess.gov/cfr/index.html>) provides that a national bank exercising fiduciary powers shall adopt and follow written policies and procedures that address, where appropriate, the bank's brokerage placement practices and methods for preventing self-dealing and conflicts of interest. *See generally* 3 Scott & Ascher §17.2.14.4 (Proprietary Mutual Funds); §9.7.1 of this handbook (the common trust fund and the proprietary mutual fund) (discussing in part conversions by banks of their common trust funds into mutual funds). A number of states, by statute, authorize a bank, under certain circumstances, to invest trust assets in mutual funds to which the bank acts as investment advisor.. *See also* UTC §802(f) (available at <http://www.uniformlaws.org/Act.aspx?title=Trust%20Code>) (providing that an investment by a trustee

corporate trustee of securities from an apparently unrelated company may be improper if the companies have directors and officers in common and enjoy a close business relationship."[503]

A proprietary mutual fund is a mutual fund for which the trustee, or its affiliate,[504] provides investment advice and operational support for a fee. Under the Uniform Trust Code, the no-further-inquiry rule would not apply to a trustee whose trusts contain shares in its own proprietary mutual funds, provided the trustee annually discloses to beneficiaries the rate and method by which the additional compensation is determined.[505] The Restatement (Third) of Trusts, however, contains a warning for corporate trustees: Despite the permissive language of a statute authorizing a corporate trustee to invest trust assets in its proprietary mutual funds, the corporate trustee is still saddled with a duty to be prudent in the carrying out of its investment responsibilities:

> [T]he trustee cannot properly confine its investments to the proprietary-mutual fund offerings if this would impair the trustee's ability to manage both uncompensated and compensated risk through proper diversification and through asset allocation appropriate to the particular trust; and the trustee must be sufficiently aware of overall costs associated with other mutual-fund alternatives to enable the trustee to fulfill its important responsibility to be cost conscious in managing the trust's investment program and more generally.[506]

When the corporate trustee receives "soft dollars"[507] from its security trading activities or "financial incentives" for doing business on behalf of

---

in securities of an investment company or investment trust to which the trustee, or its affiliate, provides services in a capacity other than as trustee is not presumed to be affected by a conflict between personal and fiduciary interests if the investment complies with the prudent investor rule). "The trustee may be compensated by the investment company or investment trust for providing those services out of fees charged to the trust if the trustee at least annually notifies-... [the current beneficiaries and presumptive remaindermen]... of the rate and method by which the compensation was determined." UTC §802(f). *See generally* 3 Scott & Ascher §17.2.14 (Corporate Trustees).

[503] 3 Scott & Ascher §17.2.14.

[504] UTC §802 cmt. (available at <http://www.uniformlaws.org/Act.aspx?title=Trust%20Code>) (suggesting that an affiliate of the trustee would include a corporation or other person or enterprise in which the trustee, or a person that owns a significant interest in the trustee, has an interest that might affect the trustee's best judgment).

[505] UTC §802 cmt. (available at <http://www.uniformlaws.org/Act.aspx?title=Trust%20Code>). *See generally* §9.7.1 of this handbook (the common trust fund and the proprietary mutual fund).

[506] Restatement (Third) of Trusts §78 cmt. c(8).

[507] Soft dollar purchases occur when "a national bank chooses to purchase products or services and pay for them with brokerage commissions arising from securities transactions for trust accounts...." Comptroller of the Currency Regulation TBC-17 Banking Issuance 267 (1990). For an in-depth discussion of the fiduciary issues that are raised when brokers and *agents with investment discretion* (investment managers) enter into soft dollar compensation arrangements, *see* Joseph A. Franco, *Rethinking Brokerage Rebate Arrangements: The Case for Collective Cash Pass-Through Arrangements,* 1 Vill. J. L. & Inv. Mgmt. 143, 154 (1999).

fiduciary accounts with third-party vendors,[508] issues of indirect self-dealing, as well as of unjust enrichment generally, present themselves.[509] A trustee who enters into a "soft dollar" arrangement with a broker uses the trust's property (in the form of brokerage commissions) to obtain "rebates" that may be used to purchase investment research useful to some or all of the other accounts managed by the trustee, including the trustee's other trusts.[510] The practice was not an issue for fiduciaries until 1975, when the current negotiated rate system replaced a fixed rate system. With the unbundling of brokerage and research products, it was thought that trustees who entered into "soft dollar" full-commission arrangements might be breaching their duty of loyalty.[511] Should they not be purchasing investment research products with their own funds? After all, a trustee may not use trust funds to pay for services that the trustee ought personally to perform. The practice of fiduciaries entering into soft dollar transactions has its critics, both here and abroad:

> In Britain, two reports on fund management written in the past couple of years, by Ron Sandler and Paul Myers respectively, pinpointed various problems. For instance, "softing" arrangements, common in many rich countries, involve a fund manager paying commission to stockbrokers out of the investor's pot of money—over and above the percentage fee for fund management. In return for these commissions, fund managers get newswire services, access to people who analyze stocks—and, from time to time, tempting invitations. Mr. Myers said that softing ought to stop.[512]

In 1975, the U.S. Congress squarely addressed the issue when it added Section 28(e) to the Exchange Act.[513] Section 28(e), *which preempts state trust law insofar as applicable*, provides a "safe harbor" for those trustees with investment discretion.[514] Thus, when such a trustee enters into a "soft dollar" full-commission transaction with a broker on behalf of his trust, the trustee will not be in breach of his common law duty of loyalty, provided he has determined "in good faith that [the] commission [is] reasonable in relation to the value of the brokerage and research services . . . viewed in terms of either that particular

[508] Brown, *The Punctilio of an Honor the Most Sensitive*, 131 Tr. & Est. 24, 27 (1992).

[509] *See generally* 3 Scott & Ascher §17.2.8 (Bonus, Commission, or Other Compensation); Restatement of Restitution §197 ("Where a fiduciary in violation of his duty to the beneficiary receives or retains a bonus or commission or other profit, he holds what he receives upon a constructive trust for the beneficiary"); §8.15.78 of this handbook (unjust enrichment); §3.3 of this handbook (the constructive trust generally); §7.2.3.1.6 of this handbook (the constructive trust as a procedural equitable remedy).

[510] *See generally* American Bar Association, A Fiduciary's Guide to Federal Securities Laws 192 (1994).

[511] *See generally* 3 Scott & Ascher §17.2.8 (Bonus, Commission, or Other Compensation).

[512] *Other People's Money*, Economist, July 5, 2003, at 4.

[513] *See generally* American Bar Association, A Fiduciary's Guide to Federal Securities Laws 192 (1994).

[514] *See* Foley & Lardner, SEC staff no-action letter (pub. avail. Jan. 3, 1977).

transaction or his overall responsibilities with respect to the accounts as to which he exercises investment discretion."[515]

On the other hand, the Uniform Trust Code provides that a trustee is accountable to an affected beneficiary for any profit made by the trustee arising from the administration of the trust, even absent a breach of trust.[516] "A typical example of a profit is receipt by the trustee of a commission or bonus from a third party for actions relating to the trust's administration."[517] While the trustee may not be in breach of trust when he enters into soft dollar arrangements with third parties, he may have a fiduciary duty to see to it that the economic benefit of those soft dollars accrues to the trust and not to the trustee personally.[518] Otherwise the trustee is unjustly enriched.[519]

In investment matters, the trust officer, as an employee of the trustee, has a common law duty of loyalty to the trust. This duty coexists with (and occasionally is superseded by) the trading proscriptions of the Securities Exchange Act of 1934.[520] The nature and scope of these proscriptions[521] have been poorly explained by securities lawyers to the fiduciary community, with the result that trust officers have been frightened into an obsessive concern with avoiding the act's criminal sanctions. In fact, this obsession has led to allegations of breaches of the common law duty of loyalty.[522]

---

[515] American Bar Association, A Fiduciary's Guide to Federal Securities Laws at 194 (1994).

[516] UTC §1003(a) (available at <http://www.uniformlaws.org/Act.aspx?title=Trust%20 Code>).

[517] UTC §1003 cmt. (available at <http://www.uniformlaws.org/Act.aspx?title=Trust%20 Code>). *See also* Restatement of Restitution §197.

[518] UTC §1003 cmt. (available at <http://www.uniformlaws.org/Act.aspx?title=Trust%20 Code>). *See generally* 3 Scott & Ascher §17.2.8 (Bonus, Commission, or Other Compensation); Restatement of Restitution §197 ("Where a fiduciary in violation of his duty to the beneficiary receives or retains a bonus or commission or other profit, he holds what he receives upon a constructive trust for the beneficiary"); §8.15.78 of this handbook (unjust enrichment); §3.3 of this handbook (the constructive trust generally); §7.2.3.1.6 of this handbook (the constructive trust as a procedural equitable remedy).

[519] *See generally* §8.15.78 of this handbook (unjust enrichment).

[520] *See* §7.3.4.2(a) of this handbook (securities laws). Revised Reg. 9 (available at <www.gpoaccess.gov/cfr/index.html>) provides that, "unless authorized by applicable law, a national bank may not invest funds of a fiduciary account for which a national bank has investment discretion in the stock or obligations of, or in assets acquired from: the bank or any of its directors, officers, or employees; affiliates of the bank or any of their directors, officers, or employees; or individuals or organizations with whom there exists an interest that might affect the exercise of the best judgment of the bank." 12 C.F.R. §9.12(a)(1) (1997).

[521] *See* §7.3.3.3 of this handbook (registration and sale of securities). *See generally* American Bar Association, A Fiduciary's Guide to Federal Securities Laws 228, 229 (1994).

[522] In a suit against the FDIC by the beneficiaries of a testamentary trust containing a large concentration of stock in the insolvent parent corporation of the bank cotrustee, it was alleged that the bank breached its fiduciary duty by failing to evaluate, manage, or analyze the stock during a period when the stock went from a high of $6,030,726 in June 1986 to a low of $260,605 in August 1990. The Bank in its answer had suggested that the Bank lawfully "could not" have evaluated, managed, or analyzed the stock and accordingly had not done so. The case was settled before trial. *See* Godfrey v. FDIC, Civil No. 90-0290-B-C (D. Me. 1990).

The "34 Act," for example, does not abrogate the trust officer's common law duty to exploit public information (even public information derived from colleagues on the commercial side) in furtherance of the interests of the trust.[523] The failure to utilize such information out of an irrational fear of criminal sanction is in itself a breach of the duty of loyalty.

On the other hand, the trust officer may not exploit any inside information relating to the trust itself directly or indirectly for personal benefit.[524] The general rule is that as much relevant information as is legally permissible should flow to the trust and as little as possible should flow out of the trust.[525] Confidential information, as with light in a black hole, stays in the trust officer's file. The trust officer conducting an auction of trust property, for example, violates the duty of loyalty by disclosing nonpublic information relating to asset value to certain bidders with whom the officer has a direct or indirect relationship and not to the others.[526]

Moreover, as with the trust company itself, the trust officer should refrain from directly or indirectly transacting with the trust property.[527] This will usually take the form of contracting on behalf of the trust for goods and services

---

[523] *See* Comptroller of the Currency Regulation, 12 C.F.R. §9.7(d) (1963). This has been superseded by a full revision, effective January 29, 1997. Revised 12 C.F.R. Part 9, available at <www.gpoaccess.gov/cfr/index.html>, provides that a national bank exercising fiduciary powers shall adopt and follow written policies and procedures that in part should address methods for ensuring that fiduciary officers and employees not use material inside information in connection with any decision or recommendation to purchase or sell any security:

> The Chinese Wall provision [embodied in 12 C.F.R. §9.7(d)] has been misinterpreted at times as an absolute barrier. The doctrine does not require the total separation of trust and commercial functions within the bank. Neither does it prohibit the integration of joint marketing and servicing of fiduciary and commercial department customers. The original and continuing intent of the Chinese Wall was to prevent the passage of material inside information between a bank's fiduciary and commercial departments in violation of securities laws and regulations.

Comptroller's Handbook for Fiduciary Activities, Fiduciary Activities—Conflicts of Interest, 71, 72 (Sept. 1990). *See generally* Melanie L. Fein, Securities Activities of Banks, §§7.03[D], 7.03[C]; Allan Horwich, *Bank Fiduciaries with Material Inside Information: Responsibilities and Risks*, 113 Banking L.J. 4 (1996) (discussing the prohibited use of nonpublic information with respect to ERISA Fiduciaries); Michael P. Malloy, *Can 10b-5 for the Banks? The Effect of an Antifraud Rule on the Regulation of Banks*, 61 Fordham L. Rev. 507, 527 (1993) (focusing in on the repercussions of Texas Gulf Sulphur and the alleged tipping between the commercial and trust departments of a large New York bank); Condus v. Howard Sav. Bank, 781 F. Supp. 1052 (D.N.J. 1992) (upholding state tort actions for negligent misrepresentation claims to remedy injury from reliance on inside information given by bank officers).

[524] *See* Restatement of Restitution §200 ("Where a fiduciary in violation of his duty to the beneficiary acquires property through the use of confidential information, he holds the property so acquired upon a constructive trust for the beneficiary"). *See also* §3.3 of this handbook (the constructive trust generally); §7.2.3.1.6 of this handbook (the constructive trust as a procedural equitable remedy).

[525] *See* §6.2.3 of this handbook (the trustee's duty of confidentiality).

[526] *See* Brown, *The Punctilio of an Honor the Most Sensitive*, 131 Tr. & Est. 24–25 (1992).

[527] *See* Bogert §543 n.21; 4 Scott on Trusts §326.3.

with persons in a position to directly or indirectly further the personal interests of the trust officer.[528]

§6.1.3.5 Acquisition by Trustee of Equitable Interest; Duty of Loyalty to the Beneficiary in Nontrust Matters

However, a purchase by a trustee from his beneficiary . . . [of the equitable interest] . . . is at all times a transaction of great nicety, and one which the courts will watch with the utmost jealousy, and will be set aside if the consideration was insufficient.[529]

A transaction between a trustee and a beneficiary that does not concern trust property but that occurs during the existence of the trust or while the trustee retains significant influence over the beneficiary and from which the trustee obtains an advantage is voidable by the beneficiary unless the trustee establishes that the transaction was fair to the beneficiary.[530]

Acquisition by trustee of equitable interest. *At the time of entrustment.* Assume two parties are in a principal-agency relationship. The principal owns Blackacre outright and free of trust. The terms of the agency are set forth in an expansive durable power of attorney instrument. Without informing the principal and without express authority to do so in the terms of the agency, the agent transfers legal title to Blackacre to himself as trustee for the benefit of the principal, with the property to pass outright and free of trust to the agent upon the principal's death. The principal, upon learning of the purported entrustment, demands the return of Blackacre free of trust. The agent refuses and in so doing triggers a common law termination of the agency. Will the former principal prevail in the equity court in getting Blackacre back? Most likely yes: "Such self-dealing by an agent, in the absence . . . of distinct authority from the principal expressly granted in the empowering instrument, has been continuously and uniformly denounced as one of the most profound breaches of fiduciary duty, irrespective of the agent's good faith and however indirect or circuitous the accomplishment of the benefit to the agent."[531] The former principal's procedural equitable remedy is a judicial decree that the former agent is now a constructive trustee of Blackacre.[532] The substantive equitable remedy is a judicial order that the constructive trustee transfer legal title to Blackacre back to the former principal.[533]

Post entrustment. While the no-further-inquiry rule[534] may not apply to a purchase by the trustee of a beneficiary's equitable interest,[535] the burden is on

---

[528] *See generally* 3 Scott & Ascher §17.2.8.

[529] Lewin ¶20-127 (England).

[530] UTC §802(d) (available at <http://www.uniformlaws.org/Act.aspx?title=Trust%20Code>).

[531] Gagnon v. Coombs, 39 Mass. App. Ct. 144, 654 N.E.2d 54 (1995).

[532] *See generally* §7.2.3.1.6 of this handbook (the constructive trust).

[533] *See generally* §7.2.3.4 of this handbook (the specific performance remedy).

[534] *See generally* §6.1.3 of this handbook (duty to be loyal to the trust) and §8.15.30 of this handbook (the no-further-inquiry rule).

[535] Lewin ¶20-126 (England).

the trustee to demonstrate that "he has taken no advantage of his position and has made full disclosure to the beneficiary, and that the transaction is fair and honest."[536] In England, this is known as the fair dealing rule.[537] Thus, when the trustee purchases a beneficiary's equitable interest, "the selling beneficiary cannot thereafter set the sale aside, assuming that he or she had full knowledge and the sale was for an adequate price and was in all other respects proper."[538]

The burden would certainly be on the trustee, a fiduciary, to demonstrate that a gratuitous transfer of the equitable interest to the trustee by the beneficiary was on the up and up.[539] The equitable interest would have to be transferable; the beneficiary would have to be of full age and legal capacity and fully understand the applicable law and facts; and there could not be any undue influence on the part of the trustee.[540]

As to whether a transfer of the equitable interest to the trustee would extinguish the trust by merger, the reader is referred to Section 8.7 of this handbook.

Nontrust matters. As we have seen, a trustee is under a duty to act solely in the interest of the beneficiaries as to matters that directly and indirectly relate to the trust property.[541] The trustee, however, may have occasion to deal with a beneficiary in matters unrelated to the trust property or the equitable interest, such as selling the beneficiary life insurance or providing the beneficiary with brokerage or legal services.[542] Such activity is permissible, but the trustee must be scrupulously fair.[543] The Restatement (Third) of Trusts is generally in accord.[544] While such dealings may not be forbidden per se, they carry with them the presumption, albeit rebuttable, of undue influence.[545]

---

[536] Lewin ¶ 20-126 (England). *See also* 3 Scott & Ascher §17.5 (Duty to Furnish Information); 5 Scott & Ascher §34.7 (Conveyance by Beneficiary to Trustee).

[537] Lewin ¶ 20-126.

[538] 3 Scott & Ascher §17.2.7.

[539] *See generally* §7.1.2 of this handbook (defenses to allegations that the trustee breached the duty of loyalty); §8.24 of this handbook (who has the burden of proof in an action for breach of trust brought by the beneficiary against the trustee); Restatement of Restitution §191, cmt. e (a fiduciary self-dealing transaction, though properly consented to by the beneficiary, still must be fair and reasonable); Restatement of Restitution §191, cmt. a (the burden of proof is upon the fiduciary).

[540] *See generally* 5 Scott & Ascher §34.7 (Conveyance by Beneficiary to Trustee) (noting that a spendthrift restraint could call into question the effectiveness of the transfer itself); Restatement of Restitution §191 (effect of consent of beneficiary); §7.1.2 of this handbook (for the transfer to be effective, the beneficiary must be privy to all the applicable facts and law, including the loyalty considerations); Restatement (Third) of Trusts §69 cmt. d (an effective transfer to the trustee would extinguish any outstanding spendthrift restraints).

[541] *See* §6.1.3 of this handbook (trustee's duty of loyalty to the beneficiaries or to the trust's charitable purposes).

[542] *See generally* 3 Scott & Ascher §17.5 (Duty to Furnish Information).

[543] *See* Restatement (Third) of Trusts §78(3); Bogert §544. *See also* discussion of the Multidisciplinary Practice (MDP) in §6.1.3.3 of this handbook (trustee benefiting as buyer or seller of trust property).

[544] Restatement (Third) of Trusts §78 cmt. g.

[545] *See* Bogert §544.

A transaction between a trustee and a beneficiary is particularly vulnerable to attack if the parties were in a confidential relation at the time of the transaction and the trustee abused that relationship.[546] "A confidential relation exists between two persons when one has gained the confidence of the other and purports to act or advise with the other's interest in mind."[547] Although the trustee-beneficiary relationship is a fiduciary relationship, it is not necessarily one of confidence.[548] Whether it also is a confidential relationship will depend upon the facts and circumstances. "A confidential relationship is not presumed to exist, however, with regard to beneficiaries whose interests in the trust are remote and whose interactions with the trustee as fiduciary are insignificant."[549]

When the relationship also is one of confidence, the trustee's duty to the beneficiary is one of full disclosure. Note that the Restatement (Third) of Trusts would require communication to the beneficiary of all material facts the trustee knows or should know in connection with the particular matter, whether or not the fiduciary relationship is coupled with a classic confidential relationship.

Let us assume, for example, that a trustee wishes to purchase for his own use the beneficiary's personal residence. The parties because of special facts and circumstances are in a confidential relation. The trustee while on vacation quite by chance learns from a third party that a proposed change in the zoning law is likely to increase the property's market value. The beneficiary is unaware of the proposed zoning change and its possible significance. The trustee does not inform the beneficiary of the proposed zoning change. Instead, the trustee induces the beneficiary not to seek independent advice and proceeds to exploit the beneficiary's ignorance for the trustee's own advantage. The trustee by so doing has abused the confidential relationship. The consequence is that the beneficiary may elect to have the sale of the residence set aside.[550] Had a confidential relationship been lacking, then the sale could not be set aside.

---

[546] Restatement (Second) of Trusts §2 cmt. b. illus. 1; Chapter 1 of this handbook (discussing in part those relationships that are confidential but not fiduciary); Restatement (Second) of Trusts §2 & cmt. b; Bogert §§544 nn.15–23 and accompanying text, 482 (Abuse of Confidential Relationship); Restatement of Restitution §200 ("Where a fiduciary in violation of his duty to the beneficiary acquires property through the use of confidential information, he holds the property so acquired upon a constructive trust for the beneficiary"); §3.3 of this handbook (the constructive trust generally); §7.2.3.1.6 of this handbook (the constructive trust as a procedural equitable remedy); Restatement (Third) of Trusts (Reporter's Notes on §2) (discussing efforts on the part of courts and commentators to define the nature and scope of various confidential relationships); UTC §802(d) & cmt. (available at <http://www.uniformlaws.org/Act.aspx?title=Trust%20 Code>) (creating a presumption that certain transactions between a trustee and beneficiary outside of trust are an abuse by the trustee of a confidential relationship with the beneficiary).

[547] Restatement (Second) of Trusts §2 cmt. b.

[548] Restatement (Second) of Trusts §2 cmt. b. *But see* Restatement (Third) of Trusts §78 cmt. a (referring to a "broader" confidential relationship that the trustee ordinarily has with respect to the trust beneficiaries during the existence of the trust).

[549] Restatement (Third) of Trusts §78 cmt. g.

[550] Restatement (Second) of Trusts §2 cmt. b, illus. 1.

Reminder: Even in the absence of a confidential relationship, the trustee who intends to exploit confidential information *gained in the course of administering the trust* will need the beneficiary's informed consent to do so.[551]

The Uniform Trust Code would allow a trustee to implement a contract that the trustee had entered into before he contemplated becoming trustee.[552] Preexisting claims could also be pursued.[553] The Restatement (Third) of Trusts is generally in accord.[554] While such transactions may proceed without automatically being voidable by the beneficiary, they are "not necessarily free from scrutiny."[555] Moreover, a failure on the part of the trustee to disclose to the beneficiaries at the time of appointment any conflict of interest that is incident to a preappointment agreement or transaction could be grounds for removing the trustee.[556]

To recap, the trustee may not through abuse of confidence gain a direct or indirect advantage in outside transactions with beneficiaries.[557] Unlike dealing with a stranger, the trustee may not take advantage of his peculiar knowledge or

---

[551] Restatement of Restitution §200 (using confidential information); §7.1.2 of this handbook (a beneficiary may give informed consent to trustee self-dealing). A trustee who intends to exploit confidential information in a transaction between the trustee and the beneficiary and the lawyer who intends to exploit confidential information in a transaction between the lawyer and the lawyer's client both are treading on thin ice. Rule 1.8 of the American Bar Association's Model Rules of Professional Conduct (MRPC) sets forth the conditions that must be satisfied before a lawyer may transact with his or her client. While Rule 1.8 was not written with trustees in mind, a trustee who intends to transact with a beneficiary could do worse than look to Rule 1.8 for guidance as to how to be "scrupulously fair." Rule 1.8(a) provides that a lawyer shall not enter into a business transaction with a client, or knowingly acquire an ownership, possessory, security or other pecuniary interest adverse to a client, unless the following conditions are met:

(1) The transaction and terms on which the lawyer acquires the interest are fair and reasonable to the client and are fully disclosed and transmitted in writing in a manner that can be reasonably understood by the client;

(2) The client is advised in writing of the desirability of seeking and is given a reasonable opportunity to seek the advice of independent legal counsel on the transaction; and

(3) The client gives informed consent, in a writing signed by the client, to the essential terms of the transaction and the lawyer's role in the transaction, including whether the lawyer is representing the client in the transaction.

Rule 1.8(b) provides that a lawyer "shall not use information relating to representation of a client to the disadvantage of the client unless the client gives informed consent." MRPC1.0 (e) defines informed consent as "the agreement by a person to a proposed course of conduct after the lawyer has communicated adequate information and explanation about the material risk of and reasonably available alternatives to the proposed course of conduct."

[552] UTC §802(b)(5) (available at <http://www.uniformlaws.org/Act.aspx?title=Trust%20 Code>).

[553] UTC §802(b)(5) (available at <http://www.uniformlaws.org/Act.aspx?title=Trust%20 Code>).

[554] Restatement (Third) of Trusts §78 cmt. h.

[555] UTC §802 cmt. (available at <http://www.uniformlaws.org/Act.aspx?title=Trust%20 Code>).

[556] Restatement (Third) of Trusts §78 cmt. h. *See generally* §7.2.3.6 of this handbook (trustee removal).

[557] *See* Bogert §544; Restatement of Restitution §200 (acquisition of property by a fiduciary).

position, either for personal gain or for the profit of some of the beneficiaries to the exclusion of others.[558] This prohibition against the exploitation of information acquired in the course of administering the trust, whether for personal gain or in violation of the duty of impartiality,[559] applies to former trustees as well as to trustees currently in office.[560]

The best course is for the trustee to avoid commercial and financial dealings with the beneficiaries altogether; if such activity must be pursued, it should be done only after they have obtained competent independent advice on those matters that directly and indirectly relate to the activity.[561] The trustee always has the burden of showing that the beneficiaries were fully informed and thoroughly understood the matter and that no advantage of position or influence was taken.[562]

It goes without saying that the trustee should never solicit gifts or other favors from beneficiaries. At the very least such solicitations would have the appearance of extortion. Nor should the trustee accept unsolicited gifts or favors from the beneficiaries, for to do so cannot help but cloud independent judgment—particularly should the wishes of the settlor as manifested in the governing instrument and the wishes of the beneficiaries come in conflict. Matters are worsened if unsolicited gifts or favors from fewer than all beneficiaries are accepted, because then the trustee's ability to be impartial is called into question.[563] The trustee's duty of impartiality in matters relating to the beneficiaries is an incident of the general duty of loyalty, so it goes without saying that the trustee ought not to act as an agent (e.g., as attorney-at-law) for a beneficiary whose interests are in conflict with the interests of the other trust beneficiaries, whether or not the conflicting interests are trust-related.[564]

The ABA House of Delegates has voted not to accept recommendations contained in a report of its Commission on Multidisciplinary Practice.[565] The vote was taken July 11, 2000. The report had recommended allowing lawyers to share fees, or even be supervised by, nonlawyers such as accountants, stockbrokers, and insurance salesman. Should the concept ever become a reality, more likely than not many MDPs would want to include trust services in their product inventories. Either MDP entities would take title as common law trustees to the

---

[558] Bogert §544.

[559] See generally §6.2.5 of this handbook (trustee's duty of impartiality).

[560] Restatement (Third) of Trusts §78 cmt. h.

[561] See Bogert §544.

[562] Bogert §544; Restatement of Restitution §191 cmt. e (self-dealing transaction must be fair and reasonable); Restatement of Restitution §191 cmt. a (the burden is upon the fiduciary to prove informed consent and that the self-dealing transaction was fair and reasonable; 3 Scott & Ascher §17.2.10 (Other Situations Implicating the Duty of Loyalty); §7.2.3 of this handbook (types of equitable relief for breaches of trust).

[563] See Restatement (Third) of Trusts §79.); 2A Scott on Trusts §183; §6.2.5 of this handbook (trustee's duty of impartiality).

[564] See Restatement (Third) of Trusts §79.); 2A Scott on Trusts §183; §6.2.5 of this handbook (trustee's duty of impartiality). See generally §8.8 of this handbook (whom trust counsel represents).

[565] See generally §6.1.3.3 of this handbook (trustee benefiting as buyer and seller).

property of their clients or common law trustees would join MDP affiliations. Whatever the mechanics, a beneficiary could well end up purchasing legal, accounting, brokerage, or investment advisory services from an MDP that is somehow involved in the administration of his or her trust. Such transactions, even those that do not do involve trust property, would carry with them, *as a matter of trust law*, a rebuttable presumption of undue influence on the part of the MDP.

§6.1.3.6 Breaches of Duty of Loyalty Not Involving Self-Dealing

Most cases involve conflicts of duty rather than conflicts of interest. In other words, the professional owes duties to two clients with conflicting interests.[566]

In every case, a breach of the duty of loyalty involves some conflict of interest. In most cases, as we have seen, the conflict is between the interests of the trustee and the interests of the beneficiary. In other words, the breach will have a self-dealing component to it. A trustee, however, can breach the duty of loyalty without engaging in acts of self-dealing.[567]

When the trustee favors one trust over another. Here is an example of how: John Jones is trustee of Trust 1 and Trust 2. Part of each trust's investment portfolio is 50 shares of *X* Corporation. Jones knows that *X* has become an imprudent investment and must be sold. To sell all 100 shares at one time, however, would be imprudent because of market conditions. Jones sells Trust 1's 50 shares. *X* goes bankrupt before Trust 2's shares can be sold. We have here a possible breach of the duty of loyalty. In this case, however, it involves not an act of self-dealing but a breach of the "duty of impartiality as to the several trusts."[568] Jones should have sold 25 shares from each trust,[569] *i.e.*, there should have been a pro rata partial liquidation.[570]

Here is another example of a trustee favoring one trust over another in breach of the duty of undivided loyalty. Trust 1 is a charitable trust. Trust 2 is a noncharitable trust for the benefit of someone's issue. The trustee, in violation of the terms of Trust 2, decants stock valued at $1 million into Trust 1. The charitable purposes of Trust 1 have been unjustly enriched by the trustee's disloyalty to the beneficiaries of Trust 2.[571] What is the procedural equitable judicial remedy? The trustee holds the stock as a constructive trustee for the

---

[566] David Halpern, *Conflicts of Interest*, 2(1) Trust Q. 28 (2004). *See, e.g.*, In re Estate of Klarner, 2003 WL 22723228 (Colo. Ct. App.) (involving trusts with conflicting interests).

[567] Lewin ¶ 20-01 (England).

[568] *See generally* 2A Scott on Trusts §170.16. *See also* §6.2.5 of this handbook (trustee's duty of impartiality, particularly the trustee's duty of loyalty to all beneficiaries *within the same trust*).

[569] 2A Scott on Trusts §170.16.

[570] 3 Scott & Ascher §17.2.15 (Duty of Trustee Under Separate Trusts).

[571] *See, e.g.* Reinhardt Univ. v. Castleberry, 318 Ga. App. 416, 734 S.E.2d 117 (2012).

benefit of the beneficiaries of Trust 2.[572] What is the central substantive equitable judicial remedy? It is restitution.[573] A specific performance order to pour the stock back into Trust 2 is issued against the trustee. There may be incidental substantive equitable judicial remedies to which the beneficiaries of Trust 2 are entitled, as well, such as denial of trustee compensation and an assessment of legal fees against the trustee personally.[574]

Trust-to-trust transactions where the trusts share the same trustee. Another loyalty pitfall not involving self-dealing is when the trustee of one trust sells to himself as trustee of another trust.[575] The trustee must take care that the transaction is fair to both trusts.[576] The Restatement (Third) of Trusts is fairly accommodating when it comes to such trust-to-trust transactions:

> The duty of loyalty does not preclude trustees in their fiduciary capacity from dealing with other trusts or with decedents' or conservatorship estates, including trusts and estates of which the trustee is a fiduciary. Any such sale, exchange, loan, or other transaction, however, must be consistent with the purposes of each fiduciary relationship and for a consideration that is fair to the beneficiaries of the relationships. Even the fair-consideration requirement does not necessarily apply if the arrangement is appropriate to the terms or beneficial interests of those relationships and to the applicable requirements of impartiality.[577]

The English default law is probably not as accommodating as the Restatement (Third) of Trusts when it comes to sales between trusts sharing a common trustee, although there is now some doubt as to whether the no-further-inquiry rule in all its severity should be applied.[578] This doubt, in large part, is being fostered by the American courts, which for some time have been applying a fairness test to such trust-to-trust transactions.[579]

Of course, the trustee's duty not to self-deal also would be implicated if a trustee of two separate trusts, say Trust X and Trust Y, were to misappropriate funds from one, say Trust X, and later make restitution with funds misappropriated from Trust Y. The trustee, of course, would be personally liable to make both trusts whole out of his own funds, if necessary, thus rendering any impartiality and other loyalty-related issues moot.[580] If the trustee, however, were judgment proof, Trust X would likely prevail over Trust Y, provided the Trust X beneficiaries were BFPs, as would likely be the case.[581] In other words,

---

[572] *See, e.g.* Reinhardt Univ. v. Castleberry, 318 Ga. App. 416, 734 S.E.2d 117 (2012). *See generally* §7.2.3.1.6 of this handbook (the constructive trust).

[573] *See generally* §7.2.3.3 of this handbook (restitution).

[574] *See generally* §7.2.3.7 of this handbook (denial of trustee's compensation and assessment of attorneys' fees against the trust personally).

[575] Bogert §543(H).

[576] UTC §802(h)(3) (available at <http://www.uniformlaws.org/Act.aspx?title=Trust%20Code>). *See generally* 3 Scott & Ascher §17.2.15; 2A Scott on Trusts §170.16.

[577] Restatement (Third) of Trusts §78 cmt. c(7).

[578] Lewin ¶20-76 (England).

[579] Lewin ¶20-76.

[580] *See generally* §7.2.3 of this handbook (types of equitable relief for breaches of trust).

[581] *See generally* 5 Scott & Ascher §29.7 (Transfer in Restitution for Wrong).

the funds would stay in Trust *X* and not return to Trust *Y*. As we have noted elsewhere, the transfer of money in satisfaction of an antecedent debt can satisfy the BFP value requirement.[582] In this case, the antecedent debt would be the trustee's equitable obligation to make Trust *X* whole.[583] On the other hand, the beneficiaries of Trust *Y* would be entitled to recover from any surety on the bond of the trustee that might have been issued to the trustee in his capacity as trustee of Trust *X*.[584] "The beneficiaries of . . . [Trust *X*] . . . could have sued on the bond, and when they are paid with the funds of . . . [Trust *Y*] . . . , the beneficiaries of . . . [Trust *Y*] . . . are entitled to be subrogated to their rights on the bond."[585]

When the trustee unnecessarily puts the interests of creditors ahead of the beneficiary's. A third example of a loyalty breach that does not involve self-dealing is when the trustee places the interests of creditors ahead of the interests of the beneficiary when the law does not require it. In one case, a trustee of a revocable trust successfully thwarted the postmortem creditors of the deceased settlor by making distribution to the trust beneficiaries prior to the creditor's claim having been reduced to a judgment.[586] Had the trustee not pursued this course of action, he could well have been in breach of his duty *to the beneficiaries* of undivided loyalty.

When the trustee is the agent of an independent third party in a transaction involving the trust. A fourth example of a loyalty breach that does not necessarily involve self-dealing is when the trustee purchases the trust property for the benefit of an independent third party.[587] Of course, if the trustee is to receive compensation from the third party for his agency services or is somehow indirectly benefited by the transaction, then the trustee would be self-dealing.

Mistake-based reformation actions brought by trustees. A fifth example of a loyalty breach that does not necessarily involve self-dealing is when the trustee seeks to reorder the equitable interests by bringing a mistake-based reformation action.[588] Legal title to the property of a trust being in the trustee, it is likely that the trustee would have standing to bring such an action.[589] Whether under equitable principles the trustee should do so is another matter. If the trustee is seeking to bring about a reordering of the equitable property interests at the expense of one or more of the beneficiaries designated within

---

[582] *See generally* §8.15.63 of this handbook (doctrine of bona fide purchase; the BFP).

[583] *Cf.* §2.3 of this handbook (wrongful defunding of the trust: "A reasonable argument can be made that the absent trust property has merely been transformed into another type of property, namely the equitable personal obligation of the wrongdoer").

[584] 5 Scott & Ascher §29.7 (Transfer in Restitution for a Wrong). *See generally* §3.5.4.3 of this handbook (bonds and sureties).

[585] 5 Scott & Ascher §29.7.

[586] *See* Dobler v. Arluk Med. Ctr. Indus. Group, 107 Cal. Rptr. 2d 478 (Ct. App. 2001), *aff'd*, 11 Cal. Rptr. 3d 194 (Ct. App. 2004).

[587] *See generally* 3 Scott & Ascher §17.2.1.3.

[588] *See generally* §8.15.22 of this handbook (reformation actions).

[589] *See, e.g.*, Reid v. Temple Judea & Hebrew Union Coll. Jewish Inst. of Religion, 994 So. 2d 1146 (Fla. App. 2008).

the four corners of the governing instrument, then his initiating the reformation action, and certainly his appealing of any lower court decision not to reform, would be difficult to square with his fiduciary duties of loyalty and impartiality, not to mention his duty to defend the trust, a topic we take up in Section 6.2.6 of this handbook.[590] Even as a nominal defendant in a mistake-based reformation action brought by someone else, the trustee should be wary of taking a position that is adverse to any designated beneficiary.

§6.1.3.7 Defenses to Allegations That the Trustee Breached the Duty of Loyalty

The trust law sole interest rule is Bleak House law, born of the despair that Lord Chancellor Eldon voiced in 1803 that however honest the circumstances of a particular transaction, no Court is equal to the examination and ascertainment of the truth in much the greater number of cases.[591]

A transaction involving investment or management of trust property entered into by the trustee for the trustee's own personal account which is affected by a conflict between the trustee's fiduciary and personal interests is voidable by a beneficiary, unless the trustee has the authority to enter into the transaction.[592] Defenses to allegations of divided loyalty include the following: (1) the transaction was authorized by the terms of the trust;[593] (2) the transaction was approved by the court;[594] (3) the beneficiary did not commence a judicial proceeding within the time allowed by law;[595] (4) the beneficiary consented to the trustee's conduct, ratified the transaction, or released the trustee;[596] (5) or the transaction involves a contract entered into or claim acquired by the trustee before the person became the trustee.[597] The topic of defenses to a disloyalty allegation is addressed in more detail in Section 7.1.1 of this handbook.

---

[590] *See* §6.2.5 of this handbook (the trustee's duty of impartiality).

[591] John H. Langbein, *Questioning the Trust Law Duty of Loyalty: Sole Interest or Best Interest?*, 114 Yale L. J. 929, 947 (2005) (citing to *Ex parte* James, 8 Ves. June. 337, 345, 32 Eng. Rep. 385, 388 (Ch. 1803)).

[592] UTC §802(b) (available at <http://www.uniformlaws.org/Act.aspx?title=Trust%20 Code>).

[593] *See generally* 3 Scott & Ascher §17.2.11.

[594] Lewin ¶20-92 (England); 3 Scott & Ascher §17.2.12 (U.S.).

[595] Lewin ¶20-106 through ¶20-112 (England).

[596] Restatement of Restitution §191 (effect of consent of beneficiary) (U.S.); Lewin ¶20-91 (England).

[597] Lewin ¶20-91 (England). *See also* Restatement (Third) of Trusts §78 cmt. c.

§6.1.4 Duty to Give Personal Attention (Not to Delegate)

The fiduciary powers of trustees were classically personal and non-delegable.[598]

A downward adjustment of fees may be appropriate if a trustee has delegated significant duties to agents, such as the delegation of investment authority to outside managers.[599]

Trustee may not delegate entire trust administration. It has long been the case in the United States that a trustee, even in the absence of express authority in the governing trust instrument or statutory authority, may "properly employ professional agents, such as attorneys, bankers, or brokers, and entrust them with money, securities, or other property of the trust, where under the circumstances a prudent man would employ such agents and entrust them with such property."[600] The authority is inherent and equitable.

Because the trustee's relationship with the trust beneficiaries is a personal[601] one, however, the entire administration of the trust may not be delegated,[602] unless prudently and on a temporary basis to enable the trustee to take reasonable vacations (including overseas travel), to deal with health issues, to serve in the military,[603] and the like.[604] "The fact that a trustee leaves the country and expects to remain abroad indefinitely does not, in the absence of proper authorization, justify delegating to another the power to administer the trust."[605] If the trustee could avoid responsibility by delegating fundamental duties to a third party, the settlor's intention in selecting a particular trustee would be thwarted.[606] On the other hand, as we shall see, the trustee has a fiduciary obligation to seek whatever assistance necessary to execute the efficient and competent administration of the trust.[607]

---

[598] Joshua Getzler, *Legislative Incursions Into Modern Trusts Doctrine in England: The Trustee Act 2000 and the Contracts (Rights of Third Parties) Act 1999*, 2 Global Jurist Topics, Issue 1, Art. 2 (2002).

[599] UTC §708 cmt. (available at <http://www.uniformlaws.org/Act.aspx?title=Trust%20Code>).

[600] 11 Scott on Trusts §171.2 (Fratcher ed.) (citing to, among numerous other cases, Vigdor v. Nelson, 322 Mass. 670, 79 N.E.2d 288 (1948)).

[601] Restatement (Third) of Trusts §80 cmt. d.

[602] *See* Restatement (Third) of Trusts §80; 3 Scott & Ascher §17.3.1; 2A Scott on Trusts §171. *See generally* §7.2.4 of this handbook (cofiduciary and predecessor liability and contribution in the trust context).

[603] *See* 2 Scott & Ascher §11.9 (noting that both in England and the United States, statutes have been enacted to facilitate delegation of fiduciary duties and/or fiduciary succession when a trustee goes off to war).

[604] Restatement (Third) of Trusts §80 cmt. c.

[605] 3 Scott & Ascher §17.3.1 If the trustee expects to be abroad indefinitely, he may well have a duty to resign the trusteeship in favor of a qualified successor. This may, but not necessarily, require judicial authorization.

[606] UTC §703(e) (available at <http://www.uniformlaws.org/Act.aspx?title=Trust%20Code>).

[607] *See* Restatement (Third) of Trusts §§80 cmt. d(1) (delegation generally), 227 cmt. j (prudent investor rule); 3 Scott & Ascher §17.3; 2A Scott on Trusts §§171.2, 227.1.

During World War I, Parliament created a limited statutory exception from the common law prohibition against a trustee's delegating the entire administration of a trust to others.[608] Available to trustees on active military duty, it allowed for the appointment of a "delegate" who would "attend meetings of the trustees in the place of an absent, delegating trustee and participate in the decisions of the trustees as one of their number."[609] Thus a "delegate" was more in the nature of a substitute trustee than an agent, an agent being one who acts at the direction of the principal.[610] "The English *Trustee Act* 1925, s 25, deriving from the War-time legislation, furnished a more general power to trustees to delegate their '*trusts powers and discretions*' to others by way of a power of attorney during absence abroad."[611] Thus, when considering matters of fiduciary delegation, one needs to be attentive to the nomenclature.[612] A trustee may delegate certain functions to an agent. An agent, however, is not a *delegate*, at least as that term is properly employed in the context of English trust law.

Specific nondelegable functions. As a general rule, the trustee may not delegate to an agent[613] the responsibility to coordinate the trust's administration and to supervise other agents.[614] "Thus, when an agent does an act that, if done by the trustee, would have constituted a breach of trust, the trustee is liable if the trustee directed, permitted, approved, acquiesced in, or concealed the doing of the act, or if the trustee fails to take reasonable steps to compel the agent to redress the wrong."[615] Even if the terms of the trust have expressly bestowed on the trustee expansive authority to delegate ministerial and non-ministerial functions, this would still be the case.

Moreover, some specific functions are nondelegable no matter how intense the supervision,[616] such as discretion as to how income and principal may

---

[608] Execution of Trusts (War Facilities) Acts 1914 and 1915 (England). *Cf.* British Columbia Trustee Act 1966, s. 14.

[609] W. A. Lee, *Purifying the dialect of equity*, 7(2) Tr. Q. Rev 12–13 (May 2009) [A STEP publication].

[610] W. A. Lee, *Purifying the dialect of equity*, 7(2) Tr. Q. Rev. 12–13 (May 2009) [A STEP publication]. *See generally* §9.9.2 of this handbook (the agency relationship); Chapter 1 of this handbook (comparing the trust and agency relationships).

[611] W. A. Lee, *Purifying the dialect of equity*, 7(2) Tr. Q. Rev. 12–13 (May 2009) [A STEP publication].

[612] *See* W. A. Lee, *Purifying the dialect of equity*, 7(2) Tr. Q. Rev. 12–13 (May 2009) [A STEP publication] ("The error that has arisen in relation to the distinction between delegation and agency is that the two have become hopelessly confused and that that confusion has even reached the English *Trustee Act 2000* . . .").

[613] The Restatement (Third) of Trusts defines an agent in the delegation context as "a person (other than a cotrustee) to whom a trustee delegates the performance of specified fiduciary duties or functions and grants authority to exercise corresponding powers of trusteeship." *See generally* 4 Scott & Ascher §24.30 (Liability for Acts of Agents).

[614] *See* Restatement (Third) of Trusts §80 cmt. d(2); 4 Scott & Ascher §24.30; 2A Scott on Trusts §171.1.

[615] 4 Scott & Ascher §24.30.

[616] *See* Restatement (Third) of Trusts §80 cmt. f(3); 2A Scott on Trusts §171.1; Bogert §555.

be used in furtherance of the purposes of the trust.[617] Thus, the trustee of a discretionary trust with a support standard who gives the beneficiary free rein to make principal withdrawals is not only breaching his duty to carry out the terms of the trust[618] but also the duty not to delegate.[619] "A trustee who does not use his or her judgment is not acting in the state of mind in which the settlor expected the trustee to act."[620]

Consequences of trustee's improper delegation. The consequences of improper delegation to agents are severe: (1) The trustee becomes personally liable for the errors and omissions of the agents[621] and (2) the trustee may not be reimbursed from the trust estate for the costs of employing them.[622] The delegation of fiduciary duties, however, should not be confused with the hiring of consultants and advisors.[623]

Specific trustee functions that are delegable. On the other hand, asset custody, record keeping, and other such ministerial tasks generally may be delegated to others.[624] An agent may be allowed to collect dividends and rents, keep the books, and act for the trustee where a "prudent man of business" would employ an agent.[625] Thus, the trustee employs a stock brokerage to purchase stocks and pays for the same through it.[626] In such cases, the trustee will not be held liable for the default of an agent, unless due care in selecting that agent was not exercised.[627] Likewise, a trustee who has employed a reputable conveyancer is not responsible for a flaw in the title that the conveyancer overlooked.[628]

If, however, a loss occurs through the careless failure of the trustee to see that the agent uses due diligence, it really is the trustee's own negligence that triggers liability.[629] If, for example, "one assumes that it would be proper in the case of a given trust for the trustee to delegate to a broker the duty of selling trust securities, delivering the negotiable instruments to him for that purpose, and permitting him to receive the purchase price, this privilege is qualified by

---

[617] Restatement (Third) of Trusts §80 cmt. f(3); 3 Scott & Ascher §17.3.2; 2A Scott on Trusts §171.2.

[618] *See generally* §6.1.2 of this handbook (trustee's duty to carry out the terms of the trust).

[619] *See generally* 3 Scott & Ascher §17.3.2.

[620] 3 Scott & Ascher §18.2.2 (When Trustee Fails to Use Judgment).

[621] *See* Restatement (Second) of Trusts §225(2)(b) (1959); 4 Scott & Ascher §24.30; 2A Scott on Trusts §171.1; 3 Scott on Trusts §225.1.

[622] *See generally* 3 Scott & Ascher §18.1.2.3 (Employment of Agents); 4 Scott & Ascher §24.30 (Liability for Acts of Agents).

[623] Restatement (Third) of Trusts §80 cmt. a.

[624] *See* Restatement (Third) of Trusts §80 cmt. e; 2A Scott on Trusts §171.2; Bogert §555.

[625] *See* Restatement (Third) of Trusts §80 cmt. e; 2A Scott on Trusts §171.2; Bogert §555.

[626] *See* 2A Scott on Trusts §171.2.

[627] It would be unreasonable to require the trustee to be a guarantor of the conduct of the agent where the delegation was proper and the trustee has otherwise acted prudently. *See* Restatement (Second) of Trusts §225(2)(c); 2A Scott on Trusts §171.2; 3 Scott on Trusts §225.1; Bogert §557. On the other hand, a beneficiary may have a cause of action against a corporate trustee who negligently retains and supervises an incompetent trust office. Levinson v. Citizens Nat'l Bank of Evansville, 644 N.E.2d 1264, 1269–1270 (Ind. Ct. App. 1994).

[628] *See generally* 4 Scott & Ascher §24.30 (Liability for Acts of Agents).

[629] *See generally* 4 Scott & Ascher §24.30 (Liability for Acts of Agents).

duties on the part of the trustee to determine whether the broker to whom he contemplates giving this power is experienced and of good reputation, to direct the broker as to terms of sale and methods of managing the transaction, if such would be the normal procedure for sellers of securities, to promptly review the results of the delegation, and to learn whether the broker has made the sale, how much he obtained, and what he did with the proceeds."[630]

Proxy voting. The trustee may vote stock by proxy at shareholder meetings, unless the block of stock represents a controlling interest or there are other than routine matters on the table.[631] Many states have statutes to that effect.[632] As to controlling interests or nonroutine matters, delegation by means of a general proxy is inappropriate.[633] On the other hand, when the number of shares held by the trust is not substantial relative to shares outstanding, the trustee ordinarily would not be justified in attending in person shareholders' meetings, at least at trust expense.[634]

Protective committees and class actions. Nowadays, a trustee may deposit the securities of a corporation in financial distress with a protective committee without violating the duty not to delegate, provided a reasonable individual owner would have done the same.[635] Likewise, the trustee may participate with others in a representative suit or class action involving the trust property, although by doing so the trustee surrenders control over the suit.[636]

When trustee liable for acts of his agents. The Restatement (Second) of Trusts[637] provides that the trustee is liable to the beneficiary for the act of an agent[638] only if:

---

[630] Bogert §557.

[631] *See* Restatement (Second) of Trusts §193 cmt. b; 3 Scott & Ascher §18.1.8.3; 3 Scott on Trusts §193.3. *See also* 3 Scott & Ascher §18.1.8.3 n.1 and Bogert §556 nn.97–98 for lists of state statutes authorizing trustees to vote stock by proxy. In its Interpretive Bulletin 94-2, the U.S. Department of Labor suggests that ERISA plan fiduciaries have a duty to vote proxies where proxy voting decisions will affect the value of an investment. *See* Department of Labor Interpretive Bulletin 94-2, 29 C.F.R. 2509.

[632] 3 Scott & Ascher §18.1.8.3 n.1; 3 Scott on Trusts §193.3.

[633] 3 Scott & Ascher §18.1.8.3.

[634] 3 Scott & Ascher §18.1.8.3. *See generally* §6.2.1.3 of this handbook (incurring unnecessary expenses is not protecting the trust property).

[635] Restatement (Third) of Trusts §80 cmt. i; 3 Scott & Ascher §§17.3.3 (Power to Cooperate with Others), 18.1.8.4 (Deposit of Shares with Protective Committee).

[636] Restatement (Third) of Trusts §80 cmt. i; 3 Scott & Ascher §§17.3.3 (Power to Cooperate with Others), 18.1.8.4 (Deposit of Shares with Protective Committee).*Cf.* §6.2.1.1 of this handbook (trustee's duty to take active control of trust property).

[637] Restatement (Second) of Trusts §225.

[638] "A corporate trustee is liable to the beneficiary for the neglect or default of its officers or its own employees within the course of the employment." Restatement (Second) of Trusts §225 cmt. b. "They are not agents employed in the administration of the trust within the meaning of the rule stated in this Section, which includes only such agents as are employed in connection with the administration of the trust and whose compensation can properly be paid out of the trust property." Restatement (Second) of Trusts §225 cmt. b.

(1) The act would have constituted a breach of trust if done by the trustee; and

(2) The trustee did one or more of the following:

- Directed or permitted the act of the agent;
- Delegated to the agent the performance of acts that he was under a duty not to delegate;
- Did not use reasonable care in the selection or retention of the agent;
- Did not exercise proper supervision over the conduct of the agent;
- Approved or acquiesced in or concealed the act of the agent; and
- Neglected to take proper steps to compel the agent to redress the wrong.[639]

Trustee delegating investment functions to agents. In the gray area is the matter of asset selection.[640] In the past, investment discretion was considered a nondelegable function.[641] The principle was best illustrated by the sale of real estate or personal property: The trustee could not delegate the essential matters of the sale (*i.e.*, the determination of the price and terms and the central question whether the sale had best be made).[642] Now the trustee, on occasion, even may have a duty to do so, *e.g.*, "in the case of a trust that conducts a business or other activities the administration of which involves numerous transactions."[643]

Similarly, the trustee could not give a general power of attorney to make sales or purchases of trust securities, but having reached a decision to sell certain trust securities he ordinarily would deliver a special power of transfer, thus employing an agent to perform a purely ministerial act.[644]

The modern trend is to permit the trustee to delegate some investment discretion to investment advisors and others, provided there is adequate supervision by the trustee.[645] This allows the trustee to retain an investment advisor

---

[639] *See generally* 4 Scott & Ascher §24.30 (Liability for Acts of Agents).

[640] *See generally* 3 Scott & Ascher §17.3.2 (Delegation of Authority to Do Particular Acts).

[641] *See* Restatement (Second) of Trusts §171 cmt. h; 2A Scott on Trusts §171.2; 3 Scott on Trusts §227.9A.

[642] *See* Restatement (Second) of Trusts §171 cmt. g; 2A Scott on Trusts §171.2; Bogert §556. *See generally Trustee's Power to Employ Broker or Agent to Sell or Lease Estate Property*, 47 A.L.R.2d 1379 (1995).

[643] Restatement (Third) of Trusts §80 cmt. f(2) (noting that in "situations of this type the trustee may not only be permitted but virtually compelled by considerations of time, efficiency, or even competence, and thus effectiveness of administration, to delegate to properly selected agents the power to hire employees of a trust business, to fix prices or the terms of contracts, and to carry out sales, purchases, and other transactions").

[644] *See* Restatement (Second) of Trusts §171 cmt. g; 2A Scott on Trusts §171.2; Bogert §556. *See generally Trustee's Power to Employ Broker or Agent to Sell or Lease Estate Property,* 47 A.L.R.2d 1379 (1995).

[645] *See* Restatement (Third) of Trusts §80 cmt. f; UTC §807 (available at <http://www.uniformlaws.org/Act.aspx?title=Trust%20 Code>); 3 Scott & Ascher §17.3.2 (Delegation of Authority to Do Particular Acts); 4 Scott & Ascher

and to pay for the advisor's services from the trust. The theory of the early common law that the trustee—and certainly the experienced professional or corporate trustee[646]—needed no assistance in investment matters has been discarded.[647] In the world of the mutual fund, such common law delegation proscriptions seem never to have been taken seriously. Since at least the 1920s, mutual fund trustees and mutual fund director-trustees have been delegating investment discretion to agents.[648] To be sure, in the typical situation, the practice is expressly contemplated in the governing documentation.[649]

This relaxation of the prohibition against delegation in the investment context is embodied in Section 80 of the Restatement (Third) of Trusts, which recognizes that some "fiduciary authority" may with adequate supervision be delegated.[650] "The trustee," however, "personally must at least define the trust's investment objectives."[651] The trustee must also make the decisions that establish the trust's investment strategies and programs, at least to the extent of approving plans developed by agents and advisors.[652] Section 80 thus gives trustees the flexibility to carry out their investment duties and does away with the general prohibition against trustees' delegating investment discretion.[653] As long as trustees are prudent in selecting their advisors, participate in setting trust investment objectives, and routinely monitor the advisors' performance, they should not be liable for delegating to advisors.[654]

---

§24.30 (Liability for Acts of Agents). *See also* John H. Langbein, *The Uniform Prudent Investor Act and the Future of Trust Investing,* 81 Iowa L. Rev. 641, 650 (1996) (casting a positive light on the relaxation of the trustee's duty not to delegate: "The last of the great reforms of the Uniform Prudent Investor Act is to put the final nails in the coffin of the much criticized former rule that forbade trustees to delegate investment and management functions."). *But see* Jerome J. Curtis, Jr., *The Transmogrification of the American Trust,* 31 Real Prop. Prob. & Tr. J. 251 (No. 2 1996) (suggesting that this relaxation of the trustee's duty not to delegate "has diminished the protections afforded trust assets and has fundamentally changed the relationship between the trustee, beneficiary, and other parties").

[646] Restatement (Third) of Trusts §80 cmt. f(1).

[647] Restatement (Third) of Trusts §80 cmt. f(1).

[648] *See generally* Charles E. Rounds, Jr. & Andreas Dehio, *Publicly-Traded Open End Mutual Funds in Common Law and Civil Law Jurisdictions: A Comparison of Legal Structures,* 3 N.Y.U.J.L. & Bus. 473 (2007).

[649] *See generally* Charles E. Rounds, Jr. & Andreas Dehio, *Publicly-Traded Open End Mutual Funds in Common Law and Civil Law Jurisdictions: A Comparison of Legal Structures,* 3 N.Y.U.J.L. & Bus. 473 (2007).

[650] Restatement (Third) of Trusts §80 cmt. e. *See also* 4 Scott & Ascher §24.30 (Liability for Acts of Agents).

[651] Restatement (Third) of Trusts §80 cmt. f(1). *See also* 4 Scott & Ascher §24.30 (Liability for Acts of Agents).

[652] Restatement (Third) of Trusts §80 cmt. f(1).

[653] Restatement (Third) of Trusts §80 cmt. f(1).

[654] Uniform Prudent Investor Act §9 (providing that if a trustee exercises reasonable care, skills and caution in selecting an agent, he will not be liable to the beneficiaries or to the trust for the decisions or actions of the agent to whom the function was delegated). This partial relaxation of the duty not to delegate is embodied in the Uniform Prudent Investor Act, promulgated in 1994 by the National Conference of Commissioners on Uniform State Laws. The Uniform Prudent Investor Act is also available at <http://www.uniformlaws.org/Act.aspx?title=Trust%20Code> as Article 9 of the UTC. *See also* 4 Scott & Ascher §24.30 (Liability for Acts of Agents).

In language that tracks the spirit if not the letter of the Prudent Investor Rule, the Uniform Trust Code grants a trustee general authority to delegate "duties and powers that a prudent trustee of comparable skills could properly delegate under the circumstances."[655] The Restatement (Third) of Trusts is in accord,[656] as is the Uniform Prudent Management of Institutional Funds Act (UPMIFA).[657] The trustee, of course, has a continuing duty to supervise and monitor the agent's performance and compliance with the terms of the delegation,[658] which ordinarily should not include an exculpatory provision covering the agent's conduct.[659]

In other words, whether there has been prudent delegation of a particular duty is dependent on the facts and circumstances of the particular trust relationship.[660] "For example, delegating some administrative and reporting duties might be prudent for a family trustee but unnecessary for a corporate trustee."[661]

When the trustee's agent acts improperly. A trustee who exercises reasonable care, skill, and caution in delegating his duties is not liable to the beneficiaries or the trust for an improper action of the agent to whom the performance of a particular function was delegated.[662] That liability has been shifted by the Uniform Trust Code and Uniform Prudent Investor Act onto the shoulders of the agent: "In performing a delegated function, an agent owes a duty to the trust to exercise reasonable care to comply with the terms of the delegation."[663] As between the trustee and the beneficiary, the beneficiary now would bear the loss.[664] The beneficiary must look to the agent for satisfaction.[665]

Prof. Stewart E. Sterk, in a law review article, explains the politics behind the liability-shift, a shift which he emphatically does not endorse: " . . . [B]ecause modern portfolio theory requires a financial sophistication that many trustees—especially family members—do not possess, both the Restatement (Third) and the UPIA reversed the traditional rule that prohibited trustees from delegating investment functions," and then complemented this reversal with

---

[655] UTC §807 (available at <http://www.uniformlaws.org/Act.aspx?title=Trust%20 Code>).

[656] Restatement (Third) of Trusts §80 cmt. e.

[657] Unif. Prudent Management Inst. Funds Act §5.

[658] Restatement (Third) of Trusts §80 cmt. d(2).

[659] Restatement (Third) of Trusts §80 cmt. d(2).

[660] UTC §807 cmt. (available at <http://www.uniformlaws.org/Act.aspx?title=Trust%20 Code>).

[661] UTC §807 cmt. (available at <http://www.uniformlaws.org/Act.aspx?title=Trust%20 Code>).

[662] UTC §807(c) (available at <http://www.uniformlaws.org/Act.aspx?title=Trust%20 Code>); 4 Scott & Ascher §24.30 (Liability for Acts of Agents).

[663] Uniform Prudent Investor Act §9(b). *See also* Restatement (Third) of Trusts §80 cmt. g (noting that in "accepting the delegation of a trust function from a trustee, an agent assumes a fiduciary role with fiduciary responsibilities").

[664] UTC §807(c) cmt. (available at <http://www.uniformlaws.org/Act.aspx?title=Trust%20 Code>).

[665] *See generally* 3 Scott & Ascher §17.3.2.

the aforementioned liability-shift.[666] First, there has been no such equitable blanket prohibition against delegation since well before the UPIA was even on the drawing board.[667] Second, no one has proffered a serious explanation as to why it makes good public policy to shift the burden of loss in the case of a delegation gone awry from the shoulders of the innocent fiduciary, who did the delegating, onto the shoulders of the innocent nonfiduciary-beneficiary, who did not do the delegating.

Trustee and his agents share fiduciary liability. The movement to do away with the common law principle that a trustee may not delegate away discretionary duties related to the administration of the trust estate has many adherents.[668] A comment in the Restatement (Third) of Trusts, for example, suggests that beneficiaries have nothing to fear from these developments: "The combined responsibilities of trustee and agent in a delegation situation supply the reasonable assurance trust law requires that the trust relationship and the interests of the beneficiaries will be protected."[669] Others are not so sure. One learned commentator has written:

> The first of the so-called reforms permits trustees to delegate even the most sensitive duties without liability to trust beneficiaries. The trustees are liable only when their delegatees engage in conduct that would have constituted a breach of trust if committed by the trustee. In the past, trustees were the insurers of the conduct of those to whom nonministerial duties were delegated. To the extent that nonministerial duties may be delegated with impunity, beneficiaries have lost a valuable guarantee that their interests will be protected. If all duties are delegable, trustees will be tempted to follow the advice to "Delegate as much as possible." Certainly, trust beneficiaries gain when their trustees seek expert opinions, but there is little justification for permitting trustees to transfer their nonministerial duties to others without taking responsibility for the consequences of the delegation. Liberalizing the common-law prohibitions on delegation cuts at the heart of the traditional role of the trustee, leaving trustees who delegate with only one duty: to exercise care in selecting and, perhaps, supervising their delegatees. While the law may have been too quick in the past to dictate that a particular function could not be delegated, the remedy does not lie with a blanket approval of all delegations.[670]

---

[666] *See* Stewart E. Sterk, *Rethinking Trust Law Reform: How Prudent is Modern Prudent Investor Doctrine?*, 95 Cornell L. Rev. 851, 863 (2010).

[667] *See* Scott on Trusts §171.2.

[668] *See generally* 3 Scott & Ascher §17.3.2.

[669] Restatement (Third) of Trusts §80 cmt. g.

[670] Jerome J. Curtis, Jr., *The Transmogrification of the American Trust*, 31 Real Prop. Prob. & Tr. J. 251, 309–310 (No. 2 1996) (taking the "Delegate as much as possible" quotation from Charles M. Bennett, *When The Fiduciary's Agent Errs—Who Pays The Bill—Fiduciary, Agent, or Beneficiary?*, 28 Real Prop. Prob. & Tr. J. 429, 481 (1993)).

Trustees investing in mutual funds. It is now settled law that a trustee may prudently invest in a mutual fund without breaching the duty not to delegate.[671]

Incorporating the trust estate. But what about the practice of incorporating the trust estate itself? The argument has been advanced that if the trust estate is incorporated, the trustees are thereafter freed from the inherent limitations of the trust and even from their liability for the continued administration. A trust, however, is a personal confidence. Thus, the better view is that the corporation will act simply as an agency to carry out the trust[672] and that the trustees are in no way liberated from their fiduciary responsibilities.[673] The Uniform Trust Code is in accord.[674] A trustee who holds the working control of the stock is accountable as a fiduciary for the administration of corporate affairs absent express language in the governing instrument to the contrary.[675] Corporate transactions will be treated as though they were the trustee's.[676]

The trustee may have a duty to seek the advice of consultants and advisors. An advisor is not necessarily an agent of the advisee. As stated above, the trustee has an affirmative fiduciary obligation—and therefore the implied authority—to seek out the advice of experts if it is prudent to do so. If the specialized services of lawyers, accountants, genealogists, private investigators, and the like are necessary for the proper administration of the trust,[677] then the trustee has a duty to consult them at trust expense on behalf of the trust.[678] As noted, the Restatement (Third) of Trusts draws a distinction between delegation and the hiring of consultants and advisors.[679] So do the English.[680]

While a trustee's consulting advisors may be part of acting prudently and exercising care, the failure to follow their advice is not *per se* a breach of trust, at

---

[671] Restatement (Third) of Trusts §90 cmt. m [Restatement (Third) of Trusts: Prudent Investor Rule §227 cmt. m]; 4 Scott & Ascher §19.1.10; 3 Scott on Trusts §227.9A; Bogert §673; Langbein & Posner, *Market Funds and Trust-Investment Law,* 1976 Am. B. Found. Res. J. 1, 22 (1976).

[672] *See generally* 3 Scott on Trusts §190.9A.

[673] 3 Scott on Trusts §190.9A. *See also* 3 Scott on Trusts §225; UTC §802 cmt. (available at <http://www.uniformlaws.org/Act.aspx?title=Trust%20Code>).

[674] UTC §802 cmt. (available at <http://www.uniformlaws.org/Act.aspx?title=Trust%20 Code>).

[675] *See generally* 3 Scott & Ascher §17.3.1 (Delegation of Entire Administration).

[676] UTC §802 cmt. (available at <http://www.uniformlaws.org/Act.aspx?title=Trust%20 Code>). *See also* 2A Scott on Trusts §§171.1, 171.4; Annot., *Trustee's Power to Exchange Trust Property for Share of Corporation Organized to Hold the Property,* 20 A.L.R.3d 841 (1968); Uniform Trustees' Power Act §3(c)(3) (providing that a trustee has the power "to continue or participate in the operation of any business or other enterprise, and to effect incorporation, dissolution, or other change in the form of the organization of the business or enterprise").

[677] *See, e.g.,* C.E. Pope Equity Trust v. United States, 818 F.2d 696 (9th Cir. 1987) (citing the language of the Judiciary Act of 1789, now found in 28 U.S.C. §1654, as indirect authority for the proposition that a trustee who is neither a beneficiary nor a lawyer must retain a lawyer to represent the trust in any federal court litigation).

[678] Restatement (Third) of Trusts §77 cmt. b; UTC §709 cmt. (available at <http://www.uniformlaws.org/Act.aspx?title=Trust%20Code>). *See generally* Restatement (Third) of Trusts §80 cmt. b; 2A Scott on Trusts §171.2.

[679] Restatement (Third) of Trusts §80 cmt. a.

[680] Lewin ¶ 29-42 (England).

least one court has so held. The court explains its rationale: "In contrast, were we to require a trustee to follow investment advice it receives, we would in effect mandate delegation of a trustee's duties. We decline to require a trustee to abdicate this fundamental function of a trustee to make investment decisions merely because the trustee seeks advice on acting prudently."[681]

Amateur trustees. The "amateur" trustee should guard against the natural inclination to delegate the entire administration of the trust to "experts" such as lawyers,[682] investment advisors, brokers, financial planners, and institutions acting as agents for fiduciaries.[683] That even goes for the business-savvy mutual fund trustee or mutual fund director trustee.[684] There is more to trust administration than a series of legal tasks; than making investment decisions; than security custody and record keeping. On the other hand, "[a] trustee's discretionary authority in matters of delegation may be abused by imprudent failure to delegate as well as by making an imprudent decision to delegate."[685] Conscientious and reasonable "amateurs" make excellent trustees, provided they actively coordinate and supervise.[686]

When a trustee delegates fiduciary functions to a cotrustee. A trustee should guard against delegating the entire administration not only to "experts" and others but also to the cotrustee.[687] Cotrustees hold the trust property in joint tenancy;[688] accordingly there is authority that one of them alone may demand and receive interests, rents, dividends, and other sums of money due

---

[681] The Woodward School for Girls, Inc. v. City of Quincy, trustee, SJC-11390, 2013 WL 8923423 (Mass. July 23, 2014).

[682] *See, e.g.,* Anton v. Anton, 815 So. 2d 768 (Fla. Ct. App. 2002) (finding the lay-trustee liable for the defalcations of the lawyer-trustee).

[683] *See* Restatement (Third) of Trusts §227 cmt. j (Prudent Investor Rule). *See, e.g.,* Shriners Hosps. for Crippled Children v. Gardiner, 152 Ariz. 527, 733 P.2d 1110 (1987) (holding that express authority to employ and compensate attorneys, accountants, agents and brokers merely a recognition of the trustee's obligation to obtain expert advice, not a license to remove himself from the role as trustee).

[684] *See generally* Charles E. Rounds, Jr. & Andreas Dehio, *Publicly-Traded Open End Mutual Funds in Common Law and Civil Law Jurisdictions: A Comparison of Legal Structures,* 3 N.Y.U.J.L. & Bus. 473 (2007).

[685] Restatement (Third) of Trusts §80 cmt. d(1).

[686] Restatement (Third) of Trusts §90 cmt. d [Restatement (Third) of Trusts: Prudent Investor Rule §227 cmt. d]; 4 Scott & Ascher §24.30 (Liability for Acts of Agents). *See generally* Charles E. Rounds, Jr. & Andreas Dehio, *Publicly-Traded Open End Mutual Funds in Common Law and Civil Law Jurisdictions: A Comparison of Legal Structures,* 3 N.Y.U.J.L. & Bus. 473 (2007).

See generally J.R. Kemper, L.L.B., Annot., *Construction and Operation of Will or Trust Provision Appointing Advisors to Trustee or Executor,* 56 A.L.R.3d 1249 (1974). The trustee's duty to use care and skill, two of the basic standards of trusteeship, "are neither excessively demanding nor monolithic, neither precluding conscientious service by friends or family members nor permitting casual, inattentive behavior by trustees who are able to meet a standard of competence and conduct higher than the ordinary." Restatement (Third) of Trusts §77 cmt. b.

[687] *See* Restatement (Third) of Trusts §81 cmt. c(1); 3 Scott & Ascher §17.16 (Duty with Respect to Co-Trustees); 4 Scott & Ascher §24.29 (Liability for Co-Trustee's Breach of Trust); 2A Scott on Trusts §184; Bogert §555.

[688] *See* Bogert §§145, 554.

the trust.[689] It has been stated to be the rule, in the absence of any knowledge of unfitness, that the "other" trustees may permit one of their number to exercise the trust powers and will not be liable if the designee abuses them.[690] It also has been said that in cases where the trust duties cannot conveniently be exercised by joint action, the trustees may make a reasonable apportionment of them and that an individual trustee will not, under these circumstances, be liable for the loss of funds caused by the neglect of the other.[691] Although the rule forbidding delegation has thus been relaxed, there are distinct limitations. In fact it is very dangerous for one cotrustee to fall into the habit of leaving the trust business to another.[692] "A trustee who remains inactive is guilty of a breach of trust."[693]

It is the duty of all trustees, unless excused by the instrument,[694] to participate in the trust administration.[695] May one cotrustee allow the other cotrustee to make and execute investment decisions without prior consultation or approval? Typically, this issue arises when a trust has a professional cotrustee and a nonprofessional cotrustee. In the context of a nonprofessional delegating to a professional cotrustee, the answer is probably yes. The Prudent Investor Rule would now seem to permit this delegation, but this may not be the rule in all jurisdictions.[696]

The question that is difficult, in practice, is the extent to which one of several cotrustees may be subject to surcharge as a result of allowing one or more of the others to assume custody and control of part or all of the trust property. These cases ordinarily do not involve an active participation in a wrongful act. Nevertheless the ensuing loss may well have been "made possible" by the "neglect" of the inactive trustee.[697] It is improper for a trustee to allow a cotrustee to act generally as the trustee's agent[698] and to do alone what ought to have been done jointly (*e.g.*, allowing the cotrustee, without express authority under the terms of the trust,[699] to invest the trust funds without consultation or

---

[689] "[I]f the performance of an act may be properly delegated by the trustee he may give such power to a cotrustee as well as to any other qualified person." Bogert §555. *See also* Bogert §554; Restatement (Second) of Trusts §194 cmt. b; 3 Scott on Trusts §194.

[690] *See* Restatement (Second) of Trusts §224; 3 Scott on Trusts §224.

[691] *See* Bogert §589.

[692] *See, e.g.,* Anton v. Anton, 815 So. 2d 768 (Fla. Ct. App. 2002) (finding a passive cotrustee liable for the economic loss to the trust occasioned by the active trustee's absconding with trust property).

[693] 3 Scott & Ascher §17.16. *See also* 4 Scott & Ascher §24.29 (Liability for Co-Trustee's Breach of Trust); Charles E. Rounds, Jr. & Andreas Dehio, *Publicly-Traded Open End Mutual Funds in Common Law and Civil Law Jurisdictions: A Comparison of Legal Structures*, 3 N.Y.U.J.L. & Bus. 473 (2007).

[694] *See* Restatement (Third) of Trusts §81 cmt. b; 2A Scott on Trusts §§184, 185.

[695] *See* Restatement (Third) of Trusts §81 cmt. c; 4 Scott & Ascher §24.29; 2A Scott on Trusts §184; Bogert §584.

[696] *See* Restatement (Third) of Trusts §80 cmt. f(1).

[697] *See* Restatement (Second) of Trusts §224(2)(d); 4 Scott & Ascher §24.29; 3 Scott on Trusts §224.3.

[698] *See* Restatement (Second) of Trusts §224(2)(b); 3 Scott on Trusts §224.2.

[699] *See* Restatement (Third) of Trusts §80 cmt. h.

supervision[700] or by standing by and allowing the cotrustee to commit a breach of trust).[701] "Often the fees of cotrustees will be in the aggregate higher than the fees for a single trustee because of the duty of each trustee to participate in administration and not delegate to a co-trustee duties that the settlor expected the co-trustees to perform jointly."[702]

When one cotrustee commits a breach of trust. If one trustee commits a breach of trust, the cotrustee is liable if redress is not sought.[703] Under the Uniform Trust Code, however, the cotrustee's responsibility to take preventive and/or remedial action is limited only to serious breaches of trust.[704] Otherwise, a dissenting trustee who participates in a nonserious breach of trust at the direction of the majority of the trustees is not liable for the breach, provided the dissenter notifies any cotrustee of the dissent at or before the time of the breach.[705]

As may be expected, it is doubly dangerous for one trustee to allow a cotrustee to have exclusive management of the trust estate after the latter has proved unreliable.[706] Thus in one case the trust instrument provided that each trustee was to be held liable for his own defaults only (a fairly common clause). The active management of the estate was entrusted to a person who had been the testator's financial advisor. This person collected and embezzled $30,000, which the inactive trustee discovered. The inactive trustee nevertheless allowed the cotrustee to continue to manage the estate, and the latter then embezzled additional monies from the trust estate. The inactive trustee was not held liable for the first embezzlement but was surcharged with the amount of the second.[707] Had the financial advisor been a mere alternate trustee, the court might not have been so deferential.[708]

When one cotrustee handles trust operations. A delegation issue is raised by the practice, now commonly followed by corporate cotrustees, of retaining exclusive possession of the trust property and of issuing checks and making distributions without signature of the remaining trustees. It is probable that the

---

[700] *See* Restatement (Third) of Trusts §81 cmt. c; 3 Scott on Trusts §224.3.

[701] *See* Restatement (Second) of Trusts §224(2)(d); 4 Scott & Ascher §24.29; 3 Scott on Trusts §224.3.

[702] UTC §708 cmt. (available at <http://www.uniformlaws.org/Act.aspx?title=Trust%20 Code>).

[703] *See* Restatement (Second) of Trusts §224(2)(e); 4 Scott & Ascher §24.29 (Liability for Co-Trustee's Breach of Trust); 3 Scott & Ascher §17.16 (Duty with Respect to Co-Trustees); 3 Scott on Trusts §224.5. *See generally* Lee R. Russ, J.D., Annot., *Award of Attorney's Fees Out of Trust Estate in Action by Trustee Against Co-Trustee*, 24 A.L.R.4th 624 (1981). *See also* §3.4.4.1 of this handbook (cotrustees) and §7.2.4 of this handbook (cofiduciary and predecessor liability and contribution in the trust context).

[704] UTC §703(g) (available at <http://www.uniformlaws.org/Act.aspx?title=Trust%20 Code>).

[705] UTC §703(h) (available at <http://www.uniformlaws.org/Act.aspx?title=Trust%20 Code>).

[706] 4 Scott & Ascher §24.29 (Liability for Co-Trustee's Breach of Trust).

[707] In re Mallon's Estate, 43 Misc. 569, 89 N.Y. Supp. 554 (1904), *aff'd sub nom.*, In re Howard, 110 App. Div. 61, 97 N.Y. Supp. 23 (1905), *aff'd*, 185 N.Y. 539, 77 N.E. 1189 (1906).

[708] *See, e.g.*, Shriners Hosps. v. Gardiner, 152 Ariz. 527, 733 P.2d 1110, 1113 (1987).

courts will approve this practice under most circumstances.[709] Yet the principle remains unshaken that the trustee will be liable if the trust property is unjustifiably left in the exclusive control of the cotrustee and is lost.[710] The representations of the cotrustee as to the status of the property may not be relied upon; personal investigation is required.[711] It is not clear whether trustees may delegate access to a safe deposit box to one of their number. Professor Scott cites several state statutes that indicate approval.[712] Good practice suggests access by more than one person, as by one trustee and a deputy or agent of another.[713]

Allocating fiduciary functions among the cotrustees. Occasionally trustees adopt a program of divided custody and responsibility short of delegation.[714] Thus a trustee who is particularly skilled in real estate matters is given charge of that part of the trust portfolio or one who lives near a fraction of the trust property is expected to manage that fraction. It is, of course, possible to make these arrangements and yet to avoid criticism, if all of the trustees keep themselves informed of the facts and problems as they arise and participate in all decisions of significance.[715] The habit is not a salutary one in the absence of express permission.

Professional trustees now held to a higher fiduciary standard than amateur trustees. For some time, a principle has been developing in law that the professional or corporate fiduciary is held to a standard higher than that of an amateur.[716] This concept of a higher standard for professional trustees has matured to the point where it is now a part of the Restatement:

> On the other hand, it follows from the requirement of care as well as sound policy that, if the trustee possesses a degree of skill greater than that of an individual of ordinary intelligence, the trustee is liable for a loss that results from failure to make reasonably diligent use of that skill. So also, if a trustee, such as a corporate or professional fiduciary, procured appointment as trustee by expressly or impliedly representing that it possessed greater skill than that of an individual of ordinary intelligence, or if the trustee has or represents that it has special facilities for

---

[709] See Restatement (Second) of Trusts §194 cmt. b; 3 Scott on Trusts §194; Bogert §555.

[710] See Restatement (Second) of Trusts §224(2)(d); 3 Scott on Trusts §224.3.

[711] See Restatement (Third) of Trusts §227 cmt. j (Prudent Investor Rule); 4 Scott & Ascher §24.29 (Liability for Co-Trustee's Breach of Trust).

[712] 3 Scott on Trusts §224.2.

[713] See generally 3 Scott & Ascher §17.3.2 (suggesting that "it is ordinarily improper for a trustee to give another person access to a safe-deposit box containing trust securities").

[714] Restatement (Third) of Trusts §81 cmt. c.

[715] Restatement (Third) of Trusts §81 cmt. c. See generally 4 Scott & Ascher §24.29 (Liability for Co-Trustee's Breach of Trust).

[716] See New Eng. Trust Co. v. Paine, 317 Mass. 542, 59 N.E.2d 263, 269 (1945) ("The law does not look with special favor upon attempts to impair the breadth and strength of the safeguards that experience has erected for the protection of those whose property has been confided to the good faith and sound judgment of trustees. And certainly this general attitude should not be softened first for the benefit of trust companies and professional trustees who hold themselves out as fully conversant with the duties of trustees and fully competent to perform them."). See generally James L. Rigelhaupt, Jr., J.D., Annot., *Standard of Care Required of Trustee Representing Itself to Have Expert Knowledge or Skill*, 91 A.L.R.3d 904 (1980).

investment management, the trustee is liable for a loss that results from failure to make reasonably diligent use of that skill or of those special facilities.[717]

The professional should take heed. The amateur, however, would be well advised not to let down his guard. The greater expertise of the professional trustee is only one factor a court would be expected to consider in determining degrees of comparative fault. Had the amateur, for example, been the active trustee or had the amateur fraudulently induced the professional trustee to commit the breach, the court would be expected to assign at least a portion of the liability to the amateur.[718]

It is permissible for the terms of the trust to break out certain fiduciary responsibilities and allocate them exclusively to a cotrustee or an agent, *e.g.*, the duty to make investments:[719]

> For example, the terms of the trust may commit investment powers to a corporate trustee and discretionary powers of distribution to an individual co-trustee, or vice versa. So also, the terms of the trust may provide for the administration of one part of the trust assets by one trustee and the administration of the rest by another. So also, as is common in England, the terms of the trust may commit title to and custody of the trust property to a corporate trustee, while committing all of the powers of administration to managing trustees.[720]

A trustee's duty to monitor the activities of his cotrustees. Express allocations of fiduciary responsibilities, however, can raise troubling issues. If, for example, the governing instrument allocates investment discretion to one trustee, to what extent does the "other" trustee have a fiduciary obligation to monitor the activities of the investing trustee?[721]

The California courts were asked to consider this perplexing issue in *Kirkbride v. First Western Bank*.[722] In *Kirkbride* a corporate trustee was held liable for the speculative investments of a cotrustee, even in the face of explicit

---

[717] Restatement (Third) of Trusts §90 cmt. d [Restatement (Third) of Trusts: Prudent Investor Rule §227 cmt. d]. *See also* Bogert §612; James L. Rigelhaupt, Jr., J.D., Annot., *Standard of Care Required of Trustee Representing Itself to Have Expert Knowledge or Skill*, 91 A.L.R.3d 904 (1980); UTC §806 (available at <http://www.uniformlaws.org/Act.aspx?title=Trust%20Code>) (Trustee's Skills); UPC §7-302 (providing that if the trustee has special skills or is named trustee on the basis of representations of special skills or expertise, that trustee is under a duty to use those skills); §6.2.7 of this handbook (trustee's duty to employ special skills or expertise).

[718] UTC §1002 cmt. (available at <http://www.uniformlaws.org/Act.aspx?title=Trust%20 Code>).

[719] Restatement (Third) of Trusts §80 cmt. h.

[720] 3 Scott & Ascher §18.3.

[721] *See generally* Hatamyar, *See No Evil? The Role of the Directed Trustee Under ERISA*, 64 Tenn. L. Rev. 1, 38–41 (1996) (discussing the common law of directed trustees); 4 Scott & Ascher §24.29 (Liability for Co-Trustee's Breach of Trust); Restatement (Second) of Trusts §185 (addressing a trustee's oversight responsibility when the settlor allocates an element of control to a nontrustee); Charles E. Rounds, Jr. & Andreas Dehio, *Publicly-Traded Open End Mutual Funds in Common Law and Civil Law Jurisdictions: A Comparison of Legal Structures*, 3 N.Y.U.J.L. & Bus. 473 (2007).

[722] Civ. No. 58254, Super. Ct. No. 101232 (Cal. App. 2d 1981) (unpublished).

allocations of investment responsibilities to the cotrustee.[723] Moreover, the speculations with trust assets were made when the trust was revocable by the settlor who at all relevant times was of full age and legal capacity and fully informed. Ordinarily, "[t]he courts have no place in trying to save persons, such as . . . [a] *competent settlor of a revocable trust*, from what may or may not be her own imprudence with her own assets."[724]

To be sure the California legislature responded to *Kirkbride* by amending the California Probate Code to provide trustees some limited prospective relief from the holding.[725] It now provides that "a trustee of a revocable trust is not liable to a beneficiary for any act performed or permitted pursuant to written directions from the person holding the power to revoke, including a person to whom the power to direct the trustee is delegated."[726] The Uniform Trust Code employs similar language.[727]

Nevertheless, the message of the California courts and legislature is clear: In the face of express allocation of investment responsibilities to one trustee the "other" trustee needs to be careful not to drop his guard when it comes to coordination and supervision. This is critical, particularly for trustees of trusts that are irrevocable. The noninvesting cotrustee needs to stay engaged, even in the face of language in the governing instrument exculpating the noninvesting trustee from liability for the investing trustee's imprudent investments.[728]

Take, for example, a trust whose terms call for a growth investment strategy and whose terms allocate sole investment responsibility to a cotrustee. If the designated investing cotrustee, instead, were to pursue an income-at-the-expense-of-growth investment strategy, the other cotrustee would have a residual fiduciary duty to get the investing cotrustee to change course and pursue a growth strategy. If the investing trustee is uncooperative, then the matter may have to be brought before the court.[729] While the exculpatory language may have relieved the noninvesting trustee of stock-picking responsibilities, it would not have relieved the noninvesting trustee of the duty to make sure that whatever investment strategy the investing trustee is pursuing is in keeping with, and furthers the purposes of, the trust; and it certainly would not relieve

---

[723] Civ. No. 58254, Super. Ct. No. 101232 (Cal. App. 2d 1981) (unpublished).

[724] In re Revocable Trust of Fellman, 412 Pa. Super. 577, 581, 604 A.2d 263, 265 (1992) (quoting from Florida Nat'l Bank v. Genova, 460 So. 2d 895, 898 (Fla. 1984) with emphasis by the court). *See also* McGinley v. Bank of Am., N.A., 109 P.3d 1146 (Kan. 2005) (where trustee of a revocable trustee was held harmless for retaining Enron stock in accordance with the written directions of the settlor).

[725] Cal. Prob. Code §16462 (West 1991). *See generally* §8.11 of this handbook (the duties of the trustee of a revocable inter vivos trust).

[726] Cal. Prob. Code §16462 (West 1991).

[727] UTC §808(a) (available at <http://www.uniformlaws.org/Act.aspx?title=Trust%20 Code>).

[728] *But see* Restatement (Third) of Trusts §81 cmt. b (suggesting that the settlor's limiting of a trustee's functions or allocation of functions among the trustees usually, either explicitly or as a matter of interpretation, has the effect of relieving the trustee(s) to whom a function is not allocated of any affirmative duty to remain informed or to participate in deliberations about matters within that function).

[729] *Cf.* 3 Scott & Ascher §18.3 (When Powers are Exercisable by Several Trustees).

him of the duty to take remedial action in the face of actual knowledge, however acquired, of a breach of fiduciary duty by the investing trustee, whether or not the breach relates to the investment function.[730]

If a prospective "other" trustee practically or politically[731] would be unable to supervise the active trustee and appropriately respond to a breach of trust by the active trustee, including if necessary bringing the breach to the attention of the court, or if it is likely that the prospective "other" trustee could not be adequately compensated for the extra effort and liability attendant with such divisions of responsibility, then the prospective "other" trustee should give serious consideration to declining the business.[732]

Residual responsibilities of the trustee who is subject to third-party direction and veto. It is the default rule that even trustees subject to third-party direction have oversight responsibilities. It is true that if the terms of a trust confer upon a person other than the settlor of a revocable trust power to direct certain actions of the trustee, the trustee "shall act in accordance with an exercise of the power."[733] The trustee, however, may not do so if the attempted exercise is manifestly contrary to the terms of the trust or the trustee knows the attempted exercise would constitute a serious breach of a fiduciary duty that the person holding the power owes to the beneficiaries of the trust.[734] In other words, even when it comes to directed trusts, the trustee must remain engaged.[735] The New Hampshire legislature has addressed the issue of a directed trustee's residual duties square on by providing that a directed trustee shall have no duty to review the actions of an exclusive *powerholder*.[736] It would insulate the directed trustee from liability for losses occasioned by following, pursuant to the terms of the trust, the *powerholder*'s directions, or for the actions and inactions of the *powerholder* generally.[737] Whether a directed trustee who knowingly assists a powerholder in breaching the *powerholder*'s fiduciary duties could escape liability altogether remains to be seen. For more on the effects of a power to direct or control the trustee, the reader is referred to Section 3.2.6 of this handbook.[738]

Trustees subject to third-party veto definitely have oversight responsibilities. "A trustee who administers a trust subject to a veto power occupies a position akin to that of a cotrustee and is responsible for taking appropriate

---

[730] Restatement (Third) of Trusts §81 cmt. b.

[731] *See, e.g.,* Anton v. Anton, 815 So. 2d 768 (Fla. Ct. App. 2002) (involving cotrustees who were brothers).

[732] *See generally* §3.4.4.1 of this handbook (cotrustees) and §7.2.4 of this handbook (cofiduciary and predecessor liability and contribution in the trust context).

[733] UTC §808(b) (available at <http://www.uniformlaws.org/Act.aspx?title=Trust%20 Code>).

[734] UTC §808(b) (available at <http://www.uniformlaws.org/Act.aspx?title=Trust%20 Code>).

[735] *See, e.g.,* Tittle v. Enron, 284 F. Supp. 2d 511, 591 (2003) (noting that even in the case of an Employee Stock Ownership Plan (ESOP), there is some duty on the part of a directed trustee to keep apprised of the company's financial condition to the extent that the trustee can determine whether the stock is an appropriate, *i.e.*, prudent investment).

[736] N.H. Rev. Stat. Ann. §564-B: 12-1204.

[737] N.H. Rev. Stat. Ann. §564-B: 12-1205.

[738] *See also* 3 Scott & Ascher §16.7.

action if the third party's refusal to consent would result in a serious breach of trust."[739]

Internal agents (employees) of the corporate trustee. It is self-evident that a corporate trustee generally may delegate the administration of its trusts to its employees and other agents. This delegation authority, however, is not absolute:

> Some acts in the administration of a trust are of such importance that it may be improper for a corporate trustee to entrust them to mere employees. Instead, the board of directors, or a responsible committee or officer, should be in charge of these sorts of decisions. As to national banks, the Comptroller of the Currency has promulgated relevant regulations.[740]

The Uniform Trust Code provides that a corporate trustee has notice or knowledge of a fact involving a trust only from the time the information was received by an employee having responsibility to act for the trust or would have been brought to the employee's attention if the corporate trustee had exercised reasonable diligence.[741] A corporate trustee exercises reasonable diligence if it maintains reasonable routines for communicating significant information to the employee having responsibility to act for the trust and there is reasonable compliance with the routines.[742] By exercising "reasonable diligence," could a corporate trustee avoid liability for breaches of trust committed not only by its external agents but also by its internal agents, *e.g.*, its trust officers?

Abandoning the trust by resignation or otherwise, the ultimate act of delegation. *Abandonment by resignation.* This discussion of delegation would be incomplete without reference to the ultimate delegation breach: the resignation of the trustee without a qualified successor in place, even when the governing instrument purports to grant the trustee such authority.[743] In England, a trustee who declines to commit a breach of trust but resigns in favor of someone less scrupulous who is prepared to and does commit it may well be liable anyway for the breach, provided the office was vacated in order to clear the way for the successor to commit the breach.[744]

" . . . [A] trustee's resignation becomes effective only upon the acceptance of the trusteeship by a new trustee."[745] Once having accepted a trust, the trustee

---

[739] UTC §808 cmt. (available at <http://www.uniformlaws.org/Act.aspx?title=Trust%20 Code>).

[740] 3 Scott & Ascher §17.3.4 (referring to Comptroller of the Currency Reg. §9.4, 12 C.F.R. §9.4).

[741] UTC §104(b) (available at <http://www.uniformlaws.org/Act.aspx?title=Trust%20 Code>).

[742] UTC §104(b) (available at <http://www.uniformlaws.org/Act.aspx?title=Trust%20 Code>).

[743] *See* Bogert §511; 2A Scott on Trusts §171.1. *See also* §3.4.3 of this handbook (death of trustee, resignation of trustee, or disqualification of trustee because of physical or mental ill health).

[744] Lewin ¶ 14-43 (England).

[745] Restatement (Third) of Trusts §36 cmt. a.

is under a duty to administer the trust as long as he continues to be trustee.[746] A resignation provision is never a license to abandon a trust once accepted.[747] "[U]ntil the trust property is delivered to a successor trustee or other person entitled to it, a trustee who has resigned or been removed has the duties of a trustee and the powers necessary to protect the trust property."[748] The Restatement (Third) of Trusts is generally in accord.[749]

Accordingly, a resigning trustee is well advised to obtain a signed acceptance from the successor trustee before relinquishing dominion and control of the trust property. Many trust instruments provide for trustee succession. In that case, the signed acceptance should be obtained from the designated successor, provided the successor is of full age and legal capacity. If the designated successor is not of full age and legal capacity or if the governing instrument lacks a trustee succession provision, then the resigning trustee will have to wait until the court appoints a successor. In the interim, the resigning trustee must remain fully engaged in the affairs of the trust until ordered by the court to do otherwise. Not to remain fully engaged could constitute a constructive abandonment of the trust subjecting the trustee to personal liability for any harm to the trust estate or the interests of the beneficiaries occasioned by the abandonment.

To the extent the resigning trustee has a role to play in the selection of his or her successor, then the resigning trustee must exercise due diligence in the selection of the successor. In other words, resigning trustee must see to it that the successor is qualified because of a residual fiduciary obligation to do so. Otherwise, if the resigning trustee is on actual notice that his or her designated successor is unqualified, then there is a residual fiduciary duty to do something about it, such as to bring the matter to the attention of the court. An extreme example is the outgoing trustee who is on actual notice that the designated successor intends to run off with the trust property.

Abandonment by delegation. A trustee may prudently delegate to agents discrete, delegable fiduciary functions. What the trustee may not do is then proceed to delegate to an agent the task of monitoring the activities of those agents. That would constitute a constructive abandonment of the trust. A trustee, for example, might hire a contractor to construct with trust funds an apartment building on entrusted real estate. While it falls to the contractor to monitor the activities of his sub-agents, it falls to the trustee to prudently monitor the activities of the contractor. That is a nondelegable function. The trustee may wish to retain the services of an architect to assist the trustee in carrying out his monitoring responsibilities. But the architect is not an agent of the trustee, the architect not having been granted discretionary authority over

---

[746] Restatement (Second) of Trusts §169 cmt. a.

[747] UTC §707 cmt. (available at <http://www.uniformlaws.org/Act.aspx?title=Trust%20Code>).

[748] UTC §707(a) (available at <http://www.uniformlaws.org/Act.aspx?title=Trust%20Code>).

[749] Restatement (Third) of Trusts §80 cmt. c.

the contractor. The architect is merely a consultant/advisor. In matters pertaining to the trustee's general oversight responsibilities, the buck stops with the trustee.

§6.1.5 Duty to Account to the Beneficiary

If the settlor attempts to eliminate any accounting duty of the trustee, by providing that it shall not be necessary for his trustee to account to anyone at any time, it would seem that the clause should be invalid and the duty of the trustee unaffected. . . . Provisions of this sort in deeds and wills would seem against public policy and void. . . . [750]

The trustee assumes enforceable obligations. In the absence of enforceability, there is no trust; rather there is a gift from the purported settlor to the trustee.[751] Thus the trustee's general duty to account to someone other than himself[752] is an indispensable one.[753] "Even under the broadest grant of fiduciary discretion, a trustee must act honestly and in a state of mind contemplated by the settlor."[754] When it comes to specifics, however, "to account" has many meanings. It can relate to

- The duty of the trustee to keep internal financial records respecting the trust property;
- The duty of the trustee to report to the beneficiary about the trust property;
- The duty of the trustee to report to the court for purposes of obtaining a final and binding approval of the trustee's actions;

---

[750] Hollenback v. Hanna, 802 S.W.2d 412, 414 (Tex. Ct. App. San Antonio 1991).

[751] 3 Scott & Ascher §17.4; 2A Scott on Trusts §172. *See, e.g.,* Siefert v. Leonhardt, 975 S.W.2d 489, 492 (Mo. Ct. App. E.D. 1998) (suggesting that affording future beneficiaries standing to bring an accounting action against the trustee even when their interests are contingent is premised on the strong public policy consideration of ensuring that someone has the power to enforce the trustee's fiduciary duties). *See generally* Bogert §961. *See* Briggs v. Crowley, 352 Mass. 194, 224 N.E.2d 417 (1967) (finding from a reading of the trust instrument as a whole that the settlor intended to impose a trust and not to make a gift, notwithstanding that there was a provision in the instrument that the trustee shall not be called upon to account to anyone except the "donor").

[752] *See, e.g.,* Trust of Malasky, 290 A.D.2d 631, 736 N.Y.S.2d 151 (2002) (holding that although an inter vivos trust may limit the right of beneficiaries to compel an accounting, any attempt to completely excuse the obligation of a trustee to account is void as against public policy). A "circumstance in which the settlor who is the trustee and accountable only to himself is the equivalent of a provision in which the trustee is accountable to no one." Trust of Malasky, 290 A.D.2d 631, 736 N.Y.S.2d 151 (2002).

[753] "The essential ingredient of trusteeship is the duty to account which affords the beneficiaries a correlative right to have the court enforce the trustees' fundamental obligation to account." D.J. Hayton, *The Irreducible Core Content of Trusteeship,* 5 JTCP 3, 5 (1996).

[754] Restatement (Third) of Trusts §50 cmt. c.

- The obligation of the trustee to remit to the trust estate profits that the trustee has made from the trust in the absence of a breach of trust; or
- The equitable remedy afforded to a beneficiary in an action against the trustee "which arises from equity's power of discovery, and which commonly entails the use of a master or referee to examine and offset financial records and prepare consolidated accounts."[755]

The duty to account runs *to the beneficiary*. While the trustee also may have an obligation to keep cotrustees fully informed[756] and to render a proper final accounting to a successor trustee,[757] a particular trustee's duty to account *to the beneficiary* means just that: *to the beneficiary*.[758] It does not mean to other fiduciaries, other than perhaps to a guardian ad litem or a beneficiary's court-appointed guardian. Thus, a statute of limitations for bringing an action against a trustee for breach of fiduciary duty will not begin to run until there has been a proper accounting *to the beneficiary*.[759] In the event the beneficiary is under a disability or unborn or unascertained, this is likely to entail court involvement. A trustee who refuses to account, at minimum, is subject to removal.[760]

§6.1.5.1   Duty to Provide Information

A particularly appropriate circumstance justifying removal of the trustee is a serious breach of the trustee's duty to keep the beneficiaries reasonably informed of the administration of the trust or to comply with a beneficiary's request for information. . . . Failure to comply with this duty may make it impossible for the beneficiaries to protect their interests. . . . It may also mask more serious violations by the trustee.[761]

Together these Sections . . . [of the Restatement (Third) of Trusts] . . . foster a reasonable degree of openness and transparency suitable to the underlying principles that, under modern default law, trustees have comprehensive authority subject to their fiduciary

---

[755] John H. Langbein, *Mandatory Rules in the Law of Trusts*, 98 Nw. U. L. Rev. 1105 n.107 (2004).

[756] *See generally* §3.4.4.1 of this handbook (cotrustees).

[757] *See generally* §3.4.4.3 of this handbook (successor trustees).

[758] The board or council of a civil law foundation, on the other hand, would not necessarily have a duty to account to its noncharitable beneficiaries, a topic we take up in §8.12.1 of this handbook.

[759] *See generally* §§7.1.1–7.1.8 of this handbook (discussing what defenses to allegations of breach of fiduciary duty may be available to the trustee).

[760] 3 Scott & Ascher §17.4.

[761] UTC §706 cmt. (available at <http://www.uniformlaws.org/Act.aspx?title=Trust%20Code>). *See, e.g.,* Wood v. Honeyman, 178 Or. 484, 561, 169 P.2d 131, 164 (1946) (the court observing that a provision in the terms of a trust relieving a trustee of the duty to furnish the beneficiary on an ongoing basis with whatever information the beneficiary would need to protect the equitable interest would render equity "impotent" and is therefore unenforceable; otherwise, should the settlor's confidence in the trustee prove mistaken, the provision could be "virtually a license to the trustee to convert the fund to his own use and thereby terminate the trust").

responsibilities and that a trust is to be administered for its beneficiaries and to be enforceable by them.[762]

The historical context and utilitarian rationale. The trustee's duty to inform the beneficiaries about the trust and its administration is of ancient origin. In the 1818 Chancery case of *Walker v. Symonds*, Lord Chancellor Eldon stated: "It is the duty of trustees to afford to their [beneficiaries] accurate information of the disposition of the trust-fund; all the information of which they are, or ought to be, in possession..."[763] In 2007, one commentator articulated the utilitarian rationale for imposing on trustees such a duty: "The trustee has a mandatory duty to inform the beneficiaries because only they have both the financial incentive and legal authority to fulfill the monitoring and enforcement functions."[764]

Information to which the beneficiary is entitled. An incident of the trustee's general duty to account is the specific affirmative duty to furnish the beneficiary with all the information that the beneficiary needs to protect his, her, or its equitable property rights.[765] Or, to put it another way, a beneficiary is entitled to all the information "that is reasonably necessary to the prevention or redress of a breach of trust or otherwise to the enforcement of the beneficiary's rights under the trust."[766] A trustee who breaches this duty to inform may be compelled by the court to do so incident to an equitable action to account, an action that is typically brought by the beneficiary.[767] Even a beneficiary whose equitable interest is contingent on the trustee's exercise of discretion would have standing to bring such an action.[768] Having said that, certain opinions of counsel, a special category of "information" that is covered in Section 8.8 of this handbook, may not be discoverable. "When the trust is in favor of successive beneficiaries, a beneficiary who has a future interest, as well as a beneficiary who is presently entitled to receive income, is ordinarily entitled to this information,

---

[762] Restatement (Third) of Trusts §82 cmt. a.

[763] (1818) 3 Swanst. 1,59, 36 Eng. Rep. 751, 772 (Ch.).

[764] T.P. Gallanis, *The Trustee's Duty to Inform*, 85 N.C.L. Rev. 1595, 1621 (2007).

[765] UTC §813(a) (available at <http://www.uniformlaws.org/Act.aspx?title=Trust%20 Code>) (Duty to Inform and Report). *See also* Bogert §961; Restatement (Third) of Trusts §82(1)(c); Restatement (Second) of Trusts §173; 3 Scott & Ascher §17.5; 2A Scott on Trust §173. *See* §5.4.1.1 of this handbook (the beneficiary's right to information and confidentiality) and §8.8 of this handbook (whom trust counsel represents). For a comparison of the trustee's common law duty to provide information with the ERISA fiduciary's statutory duty to disclose, *see* John H. Langbein & Bruce A Wolk, Pension and Employee Benefit Law 697–701 (2000) (suggesting that the courts have become "more insistent about developing disclosure standards under ERISA than in the common law of trusts" because "disclosure duties in ERISA plan settings demarcate the tension between the employer's two roles, that is, between the employer's so-called 'business' or 'settlor' functions and the ERISA fiduciary functions").

[766] In re Matter of the Kipnis Section 3 Trust, 2014 WL 2515207 (Ariz. Ct. App. June 13, 2014).

[767] Bogert §970 (Parties and Procedures on Accounting).

[768] Bogert §970 (Parties and Procedures on Accounting).

whether the interest is vested or contingent. . . ."[769] Recent English case law is generally in accord.[770] Secrecy and accountability are incompatible.[771] Again, this is an affirmative duty, not a passive one.[772] That the beneficiary did not ask for the information is no excuse. The Restatement (Third) of Trusts is generally in accord,[773] as is the Uniform Probate Code.[774]

The UTC's qualified beneficiary concept. Under the Uniform Trust Code, any person who has a present or future interest in an irrevocable trust, whether vested or contingent, and any holder of a power of appointment over the trust property is entitled upon request to the trustee's accountings or "reports," as well as any other information reasonably related to the trust's administration.[775] This right may not be waived by the settlor.[776] The Uniform Trust Code further provides that the trustee has an affirmative duty to notify the "qualified beneficiaries" of an irrevocable trust who are 25 years of age or older of the existence of the trust and of their right to request accountings or "reports" and other information related to the administration of the trust.[777] The trustee may not be relieved of this duty by express language in the governing instrument.[778] A "qualified beneficiary" is either a current beneficiary or a presumptive remainderman.[779]

Under the Uniform Trust Code, in a critical matter such as when equitable property rights, whether vested or contingent, are at stake, notice to the qualified beneficiaries would not relieve the trustee of the duty to give adequate notice to *the nonqualified beneficiaries*, either by giving actual notice to them or by giving notice to a duly appointed guardian ad litem charged with representing their interests. (The Restatement (Third) of Trusts confirms that even nonqualified beneficiaries have enforceable property rights.)[780] The virtual representation exception to the notice requirement applies only if there is no conflict of

---

[769] 3 Scott & Ascher §17.5. Note, however, that if beneficiary *X* has a "right of revocation, a general power of appointment, or an unrestricted right of withdrawal" and beneficiary *Y* does not, then while *X* is of full age and legal capacity, the trustee generally has no duty to keep *Y* informed.

[770] *See, e.g.,* Schmidt v. Rosewood Trust Ltd. [2003] WTLR 565 (Privy Council).

[771] *See generally* Kevin D. Millard, *The Trustee's Duty to Inform and Report Under the Uniform Trust Code,* 40 Real Prop. Prob. & Tr. J. 373 (Summer 2005).

[772] *See, e.g.,* McNeill v. Bennett, 798 A.2d 503, 510 (Del. 2002). *See generally* 3 Scott & Ascher §17.5.

[773] Restatement (Third) of Trusts §§82, 82(1)(c), & 83.

[774] UPC §7-303.

[775] UTC §105(b)(9) (available at <http://www.uniformlaws.org/Act.aspx?title=Trust%20 Code>).

[776] UTC §105(b)(9) (available at <http://www.uniformlaws.org/Act.aspx?title=Trust%20 Code>).

[777] UTC §105(b)(8) (available at <http://www.uniformlaws.org/Act.aspx?title=Trust%20 Code>).

[778] UTC §105(b)(8) (available at <http://www.uniformlaws.org/Act.aspx?title=Trust%20 Code>).

[779] UTC §103(12) (available at <http://www.uniformlaws.org/Act.aspx?title=Trust%20 Code>).

[780] *See* Restatement (Third) of Trusts §94 cmt. b ("A suit to enforce a private trust ordinarily . . . may be maintained by any beneficiary whose rights are or may be adversely affected

interest between the qualified and nonqualified beneficiaries. In most cases, however, there will be such a conflict.

Here is the Code's commentary on the limitations of the qualified beneficiary concept: "Due to the difficulty of identifying beneficiaries whose interests are remote and contingent, and because such beneficiaries are not likely to have much interest in the *day-to-day affairs of the trust*, the Uniform Trust Code uses the concept of 'qualified beneficiary'... to limit the class of beneficiaries to whom certain notices must be given or consents received."[781] Examples given are trustee resignations, successor trustee appointments, combining trusts, and the like. In other words, notice to the qualified beneficiaries is only sufficient in quasi-ministerial undertakings that generally do not affect one way or another equitable property rights, absent special facts. A trustee who fails to parse the due process limitations of the qualified beneficiary concept does so at his peril. In the words of Justice J.D. Heydon of the High Court of Australia, "the silent waters of equity run deep—often too deep for legislation to obstruct."[782]

Waiver by the settlor via the trust terms of the trustee's duty to keep the beneficiaries informed. Section 105 of the Uniform Trust Code imposes some mandatory duties on the trustee. Two of them "have been extremely controversial and have failed to gain traction in UTC-adopting jurisdictions." Here are the two mandatory duties:

- [8] the duty under Section 813(b)(2) and (3) to notify qualified beneficiaries of an irrevocable trust who have attained 25 years of age of the existence of the trust, of the identity of the trustee, and of their right to request trustee's reports.
- [9] the duty under Section 813(a) to respond to the request of a [qualified] beneficiary of an irrevocable trust for trustee's reports and other information reasonably related to the administration of the trust.

As of 2013, only Nebraska, New Mexico, and Florida "have actually and substantially adopted the duty to notify found in section 105(b)(8)."[783] There is less to this mini-revolt, however, than meets the eye. "Waiver by a settlor of the trustee's duty to keep the beneficiaries informed of the trust's administration does not otherwise affect the trustee's duties. The trustee remains accountable to the beneficiaries for the trustee's actions."[784] All beneficiaries are owed this

---

by the matter(s) at issue. The beneficiaries of a trust include any person who holds a beneficial interest, present or future, vested or contingent.").

[781] UTC §103, cmt. (available at <http://www.uniformlaws.org/Act.aspx?title=Trust%20Code>) (emphasis added).

[782] The Hon. Justice J.D. Heydon, A.C., *Does statutory reform stultify trust law analysis?*, 6 Tr. Q. Rev., 3, 28 (2008) (a STEP publication).

[783] John Spencer Treu, *The Mandatory Disclosure Provisions of the Uniform Trust Code: Still Boldly Going Where No Jurisdiction Will Follow*, 82 Miss. L.J. 597, 611 (2013). The author refers to Ohio as a "partially-mandatory disclosure jurisdiction." *See also* Zimmerman v. Zirpolo Trust, 2012 WL 346657 (Ohio App. 5 Dist.).

[784] UTC §105, cmt. (available at <http://www.uniformlaws.org/Act.aspx?title=Trust%20Code>).

general duty, not just the qualified beneficiaries. True, the Code imposes on the trustee a duty to involve the qualified beneficiaries in the "day-to-day affairs of the trust" to a limited degree, such as by keeping them informed of trustee resignations and the like. This is an additional burden imposed on the trustee by the Code. In no way does this imposition, however, derogate from, or otherwise erode, the critical general duty—a duty that trustees have had since time immemorial—to account to all the beneficiaries, qualified and nonqualified alike, for his or her actions. It remains the case that the beneficiary is entitled to whatever information the beneficiary must have in order to effectively defend and protect his or her equitable property rights, whether those rights be vested or contingent, except, perhaps, (1) while the trust is revocable or (2) if the five-year period of the UTC's Section 1005(c) statute of ultimate repose has run. And, except for the statute of repose, the statute limiting actions for breaches of trust will not begin to run against the beneficiary until such time as that information has been received and comprehended by the beneficiary.[785]

The information surrogate. In several states, the terms of a trust may authorize the trustee to account to a "surrogate" of the beneficiary in lieu of accounting to the beneficiary.[786] The trustee is said to be a "quiet trustee." The surrogate is designated in the trust's terms and would seem to meet the definition of a trust protector.[787] If one assumes that the protector/information surrogate is a fiduciary, which is likely to be the case, then the tangle of possible intersecting fiduciary relationships and duties could get mind-boggling. The protector/information surrogate, for example, might well owe a fiduciary duty to a minor beneficiary to report to the minor's guardian about the activities of the protector's cofiduciary, namely the quiet trustee. In turn, the guardian might well owe a fiduciary duty to the minor to apprise himself of all the critical information he can get his hands on relative to the minor's equitable property rights under the quiet trust. In other words, the guardian might well owe the minor a duty to monitor the relevant activities of both the protector/information surrogate and the quiet trustee.

Once the minor beneficiary attains the age of majority, it could get even more interesting. Presumably, both the guardian and the protector/information surrogate would then owe the beneficiary a fiduciary duty to convey in good faith to the beneficiary all the critical information that they had acquired while the beneficiary was a minor regarding the terms of the quiet trust and the activities of the quiet trustee. What information would be critical? Whatever information the beneficiary would need to protect and defend his equitable property rights under the quiet trust. Moreover, if the quiet trustee upon being confronted by the beneficiary intentionally deceives the beneficiary as to the existence and/or terms of the trust, then the quiet trustee risks incurring liability for committing acts of fraud against the beneficiary.

---

[785] *See generally* §7.1.3 of this handbook (defense of failure of beneficiary to take timely action against trustee).

[786] *See, e.g.,* D.C. Code Ann. §19-1301.05(c)(3).

[787] *See generally* §3.2.6 of this handbook (discussing the office of trust protector).

Prof. Alan Newman has written a law review article that, in part, flags some "additional questions" that are raised by a quiet trusteeship that has a protector/information surrogate feature to it, such as whether there is a tolling of the applicable statute of limitations for breaches of fiduciary duty until such time as the beneficiary is put on actual or constructive notice of the relevant facts and law.[788] Under the Restatement (Third) of Trusts, one has a sense that notice only to the protector/information surrogate would not start the applicable breach of trust statute of limitations running against the clueless beneficiary. It provides that "[b]y the terms of a trust, the settlor may reserve or confer upon others the power to enforce the trust. The holder of such a power has standing, on behalf of the beneficiaries, to bring suit against the trustee, although the power does not prevent a beneficiary from acting on his or her own behalf."[789]

Now, if the protector/information surrogate, by statute, case law, or trust term, is truly not a fiduciary, then it is hard to see how a quiet trust can be a true trust, a trust being a fiduciary relationship with respect to property. It cannot be said that the quiet trustee owes any fiduciary duties to the protector/information surrogate, the protector/information surrogate not being a beneficiary. Certainly the protector/information surrogate owes the quiet trustee no fiduciary duties. No fiduciary duties, no trust, at least not of the kind that is the subject of this handbook.

Some beneficiaries may now be more equal than others, but only as to things ministerial. As noted, the Uniform Trust Code and the Restatement (Third) of Trusts would limit those who must be kept informed *on an ongoing basis* to those entitled or eligible to receive distributions of income and principal and to those who *would be entitled* to take upon the termination of the current interest or the trust itself, whether their interests are contingent or vested.[790] This class is referred to in the Uniform Trust Code as "qualified beneficiaries"[791] and in the Restatement as "fairly representative" beneficiaries.[792] On occasion, this ongoing duty to inform may run to a holder of a general testamentary or nongeneral power of appointment, a power to veto or direct acts of the trustee, or a power to modify the trust.[793] Absent special facts, this ongoing duty would not run to representatives of unborn and unascertained contingent interests.[794] The trustee, however, may "for some matters and some

---

[788] *See* Alan Newman, *The Intention of the Settlor Under the Uniform Trust Code: Whose Property Is It, Anyway?*, 38 Akron L. Rev. 649, 680–681 (2005).

[789] Restatement (Third) of Trusts §94 cmt. d(1).

[790] *See, e.g.,* Barber v. Barber, 837 P.2d 714 (Alaska 1992) (a contingent trust beneficiary having a constitutionally protected property interest, the beneficiary was entitled to notice of a contemplated sale of real estate comprising the trust estate).

[791] *See* UTC §103(12) (available at <http://www.uniformlaws.org/Act.aspx?title=Trust%20 Code>) (defining "qualified" beneficiary).

[792] *See* Restatement (Third) of Trusts §82 cmt. a(1) (defining "fairly representative" beneficiary).

[793] Restatement (Third) of Trusts §82 cmt. a(1).

[794] *See, however,* Restatement (Third) of Trusts §83 cmt. b (suggesting that it is "essential to the enforceability of a meaningful duty of impartiality" that the trustee's duty to "report on request" extend when appropriate in light of a particular set of facts and circumstances to

trustee concerns" provide information to additional beneficiaries, if the trustee "wishes or deems appropriate to the circumstances."[795] In the case of a charitable trust, the duty to be kept informed would run to the appropriate attorney general, and to identifiable charities, if any, with equitable interests under the trust.[796]

Sensitive personal information. At any given time, though, it may be appropriate for the trustee to furnish certain types of information to some beneficiaries and not to others, *e.g.*, information on the health condition of a particular beneficiary. This should not implicate the duty of impartiality,[797] provided "the trustee's selection—or exclusion—of those to be informed or consulted is fair, reasonable, and impartial in light of the context and reasons for the communication."[798] For a discussion of the dilemma a trustee can face when one beneficiary's right to information conflicts with another's right to confidentiality, see Section 5.4.1.1 of this handbook. Absent special facts, however, "[w]hen a trustee prepares and provides a report in response to a request by a beneficiary, the trustee might wish to follow a simple, routine practice of also sending a copy to other beneficiaries, particularly to fairly representative beneficiaries and perhaps to others as well."[799]

The revocable trust exception. There is another exception to the trustee's duty to provide information, namely if the trust is revocable by the settlor alone and the settlor has the capacity to revoke it.[800] During the period when he does, the trustee may not disclose any information pertaining to the trust to the other beneficiaries, if any, *i.e.*, to those who possess equitable contingent remainder interests.[801] The trustee's duty to inform under these circumstances runs to the

---

beneficiaries who are not "fairly representative," presumably even on occasion to appropriate representatives of the unborn and unascertained). *See generally* §8.14 of this handbook (guardian ad litem and virtual representation issues).

[795] Restatement (Third) of Trusts §82 cmt. a(1). Take, for example, a trust for the benefit of a widow for her lifetime. Upon her death, the subject property passes outright and free of trust to her then living issue. The widow, her terminally ill daughter, the daughter's husband and guardian, and the daughter's two adult children are all alive. Under the circumstances, namely, that in all likelihood the daughter will predecease her widowed mother, the trustee may want to provide appropriate information regarding the trust to the two adult children (the widow's grandchildren) on an ongoing basis, although neither meets the technical definition of a "fairly representative" beneficiary. The trustee may want to do this if only to smoke out and informally address any misconceptions they may have about how the trust is being administered, or should be administered, in anticipation of sooner rather than later having to put before them his final accounts.

[796] Restatement (Third) of Trusts §82 cmt. a. *See generally* §9.4.2 of this handbook (standing to enforce charitable trusts).

[797] *See generally* §6.2.5 of this handbook (the trustee's duty of impartiality in his dealing with the beneficiaries).

[798] Restatement (Third) of Trusts §79 cmt. d.

[799] Restatement (Third) of Trusts §83 cmt. b.

[800] Restatement (Third) of Trusts §82 cmt. a; 3 Scott & Ascher §17.5. *See generally* Frances H. Foster, *Privacy and the Elusive Quest for Uniformity in the Law of Trusts*, 38 Ariz. St. L.J. 713 (2006).

[801] UTC §603 (available at <http://www.uniformlaws.org/Act.aspx?title=Trust%20 Code>) (providing that while a trust is revocable and the settlor has capacity to revoke the trust,

settlor and to the settlor alone.[802] It is likely that the Uniform Probate Code is in accord.[803] Otherwise, the trustee should respond to a reasonable request for information as soon as possible after the request is received.[804]

The trustee's duty to inform upon creation of an irrevocable trust or upon a revocable trust becoming irrevocable. As noted above, the Uniform Trust Code provides that upon the creation of an irrevocable trust or upon a revocable trust becoming irrevocable, whether by death of the settlor or otherwise, the trustee has an affirmative duty immediately to notify the beneficiaries of the existence of the trust, of the identity of the settlor or settlors, of the right to request a copy of the trust instrument,[805] and of the right to the accountings or "reports" of the trustee.[806] After accepting a trusteeship, the trustee should notify the beneficiaries of the acceptance and of the trustee's name, address, and telephone number.[807] Under the Uniform Trust Code, notice to current beneficiaries and to the presumptive remaindermen, *i.e.*, the "qualified beneficiaries," would satisfy these notice requirements.[808]

The Restatement (Third) of Trusts catalogs the "initial information" that the trustee should furnish the "fairly representative" beneficiaries of a trust that is irrevocable, or has just become so:[809]

---

rights of the beneficiaries are subject to the control of, and the duties of the trustee are owed exclusively to, the settlor). *See also* §8.11 of this handbook (the duties of a trustee of a revocable inter vivos trust).

[802] Restatement (Third) of Trusts §74 cmt. e.

[803] *See* UPC §§1-403(2)(A), 7-303(a).

[804] *See generally* Bogert §961. *See also* UTC §813(a) (available at <http://www.uniformlaws.org/Act.aspx?title=Trust%20Code>) (providing that unless unreasonable under the circumstances, a trustee shall promptly respond to a beneficiary's request for information related to the administration of the trust). A trustee upon request shall promptly furnish to the beneficiary a copy of the trust instrument. UTC §813(b)(1) (available at <http://www.uniformlaws.org/Act.aspx?title=Trust%20Code>).

[805] *See generally* 3 Scott & Ascher §17.5; UPC §7-303(b), however, would only require that the trustee upon reasonable request provide the beneficiary with a copy of the terms of the trust that describe or affect his interest and with relevant information about assets of the trust and the particulars relating to the administration.

[806] The UTC §813(b)(3) (available at <http://www.uniformlaws.org/Act.aspx?title=Trust%20Code>) provides that this shall be done within sixty days after the date the trustee acquires knowledge of the creation of an irrevocable trust or within sixty days after the date the trustee acquires knowledge that a formerly revocable trust has become irrevocable, whether by the death of the settlor or otherwise. UPC provides that within thirty days after his acceptance of the trust, the trustee shall inform in writing the current beneficiaries and if possible one or more persons who under §1-403 may represent beneficiaries with future interests, of the Court in which the trust is registered and of his name and address. UPC §7-303(a).

[807] UTC §813(b)(2) (available at <http://www.uniformlaws.org/Act.aspx?title=Trust%20Code>) provides that this shall be done within sixty days after the trusteeship is accepted. *See generally* Bogert §961. *See also* §3.4.2 of this handbook (acceptance or disclaimer of the trusteeship); §3.4.4.3 of this handbook (successor trustees); and §8.2.4 of this handbook (a trust termination checklist).

[808] *See* UTC §103(12) (available at <http://www.uniformlaws.org/Act.aspx?title=Trust%20Code>) (defining the term *qualified beneficiary*); UTC §813(b) (describing the events that trigger an affirmative duty on the part of the trustee to supply qualified beneficiaries with information).

[809] Restatement (Third) of Trusts §82 cmt. b.

- "The existence, source, and name (or descriptive reference) of the trust;[810]
- The extent and (present or future, discretionary or conditional, etc.) nature of their interests;[811]
- The name(s) of the trustee(s), contact and compensation information, and perhaps the roles of the cotrustees;[812] and
- The beneficiaries' right to further information, including the usual right to request information concerning the terms of the trust or a copy of the trust instrument."[813]

A beneficiary might not qualify as "fairly representative" at the time when an irrevocable trust is funded or when a revocable trust becomes irrevocable. Should the beneficiary, however, later achieve "fairly representative" status, perhaps because of the death of a "higher" remainder beneficiary, the trustee would have a duty to furnish the beneficiary with the initial information described immediately above.[814] "If a beneficiary becomes currently entitled to distributions (such as by obtaining a specified age or because of another's death), or becomes eligible to receive or request discretionary distributions, or if a beneficiary ceases to be entitled or eligible to receive distributions, the trustee should appropriately inform the beneficiary."[815]

There are limits on a settlor's ability to limit the trustee's duty to keep the beneficiaries informed. Under the Uniform Trust Code, the settlor by the terms of the trust may not relieve the trustee of the duty to inform "qualified beneficiaries" 25 years of age or older of the existence of the trust, to provide them upon request with such accountings or "reports" as the trustee may have prepared, and to respond to their request for other information reasonably related to the trust's administration.[816] The settlor, however, by the terms of the trust may relieve the trustee of the duty to provide a beneficiary upon request with a copy of the trust instrument and the requirement that the trustee provide annual reports to the "qualified beneficiaries,"[817] a radical divergence from

---

[810] Restatement (Third) of Trusts §82 cmt. b.

[811] Restatement (Third) of Trusts §82 cmt. b.

[812] Restatement (Third) of Trusts §82 cmt. b.

[813] Restatement (Third) of Trusts §82 cmt. b. "It is appropriate, and will ordinarily be simplest, for the trustee to provide a copy of the trust instrument to fairly representative beneficiaries as a part of the initial information at the outset of administration." Restatement (Third) of Trusts §82 cmt. b.

[814] Restatement (Third) of Trusts §82 cmt. c.

[815] Restatement (Third) of Trusts §82 cmt. c.

[816] *See* UTC §105(b)(8) (available at <http://www.uniformlaws.org/Act.aspx?title=Trust%20Code>).

[817] *See* UTC §105 cmt. (available at <http://www.uniformlaws.org/Act.aspx?title=Trust%20Code>). *See also* Taylor v. Nationsbank Corp., 481 S.E.2d 358 (N.C. App. 1997). *But see* Fletcher v. Fletcher, 253 Va. 30, 480 S.E.2d 488 (1997) (although the settlor may have orally asked the trustee not to disclose to the beneficiaries the details of the trust, the court held that a beneficiary may inspect the entire trust document, not just redacted portions).

traditional trust principles that unsurprisingly is not without its detractors.[818] "The furnishing of a copy of the entire trust instrument and preparation of annual reports may be required in a particular case, however, if such information is requested by a beneficiary and is reasonably related to the trust's administration."[819] Certainly, as we have already discussed, the "provisions of the UTC [Uniform Trust Code] that codify the trustee's duty to inform and report are among the most controversial portions of the UTC and, as a result, have become the least uniform among jurisdictions that have enacted the UTC."[820]

At the other end of the spectrum, the Uniform Probate Code (UPC) encountered resistance when it came to limiting a trust beneficiary's access to the entire trust document. Section 7-303(b) of the UPC provided that "[u]pon reasonable request the Trustee shall provide the beneficiary with a copy of the terms of the trust which describe or affect his interest...." In 2010, Section 7-303(b) was purged from the model UPC. The Restatement (Third) of Trust falls generally in line with the Uniform Trust Code in permitting a settlor in the terms of the trust to limit the trustee's duty to inform beneficiaries under the age of 25,[821] suggesting, however, that "a court that is troubled about such specificity and arbitrariness as a matter of common-law principle might consider a more flexible approach to reconciling" the "policy favoring a settlors' freedom of disposition" with "the policies of facilitating enforcement and limiting dead-hand control."[822]

While the Restatement (Third) of Trusts would tolerate some alteration in the amount of information a trustee must give to the beneficiaries initially and on an ongoing basis, as well as some alteration in the "circumstances and frequency with which, and persons to whom, it must be given," it cautions that a beneficiary is "always entitled ... to request such information ... as is reasonably necessary to enable the beneficiary to prevent or redress a breach of trust and otherwise to enforce his or her rights under the trust," except, of course, when the trust is self-settled and revocable, the settlor is alive and not legally incapacitated, and the beneficiary is not the settlor.[823] Moreover, it is not just the "qualified" or "fairly representative" beneficiary who is entitled to information.[824] As to the trustee's duty to furnish information to a beneficiary who is

---

[818] *See, e.g.*, Frances H. Foster, *Privacy and the Elusive Quest for Uniformity in the Law of Trusts*, 38 Ariz. St. L.J. 713 (2006).

[819] UTC §105 cmt. (available at <http://www.uniformlaws.org/Act.aspx?title=Trust%20 Code>).

[820] Kevin D. Millard, *The Trustee's Duty to Inform and Report Under the Uniform Trust Code*, 40 Real Prop. Prob. & Tr. J. 373, 400 (Summer 2005). *See also* Frances H. Foster, *Privacy and the Elusive Quest for Uniformity in the Law of Trusts*, 38 Ariz. St. L.J. 713 (2006).

[821] Restatement (Third) of Trusts §82 cmt. e.

[822] Restatement (Third) of Trusts §82 cmt. e, Reporter's Notes thereto. *See generally* Frances H. Foster, *Privacy and the Elusive Quest for Uniformity in the Law of Trusts*, 38 Ariz. St. L.J. 713 (2006).

[823] Restatement (Third) of Trusts §82 cmt. a(2). *See generally* 3 Scott & Ascher §17.5; Frances H. Foster, *Privacy and the Elusive Quest for Uniformity in the Law of Trusts*, 38 Ariz. St. L.J. 713 (2006).

[824] Jacob v. Davis, 128 Md. App. 433, 738 A.2d 904 (1999).

under a legal disability,[825] the trustee may furnish the requisite information to the beneficiary's legal or natural guardian, conservator, agent under a durable power of attorney, or such "one or more trust beneficiaries whose concerns can be expected reasonably to coincide with those of the disabled beneficiary."[826]

The Uniform Probate Code's trust registration requirement. When it comes to the trustee's duty to inform and account to the beneficiaries, the model Uniform Probate Code was sort of the black sheep, in large part due to its trust registration requirement. Section 7-303(a) provided that "[w]ithin 30 days after his acceptance of the trust, the trustee shall inform in writing the current beneficiaries and if possible one or more persons who . . . may represent beneficiaries with future interests, of the Court in which the trust is registered and of his name and address." Section 7-303(b) required the trustee "upon request" to furnish the beneficiary with a copy of the "terms of the trust which describe or affect his interest." This obligation on the part of trustees to register their trusts was the centerpiece of the Uniform Probate Code's system of trust-related codifications and thus indispensable to the system's internal coherence and logic. Again, the portions of the model UPC dealing with trust administration, housed mainly in its Article VII, were purged in 2010.

When the trustee may have a duty to give beneficiaries advance notice of an important or significant event. The trustee may have a duty to give advance notice to the beneficiaries of important or significant events affecting the trust property, such as a change in the method or rate of the trustee's compensation or an important transaction involving an asset that is difficult to value or to replace, *e.g.*, real estate or a closely held business interest.[827] Under the Uniform Trust Code, the trustee would have a duty to notify the current beneficiaries and the presumptive remaindermen of a proposed transfer of a trust's principal place of administration not less than sixty days before initiating the transfer.[828] A self-dealing transaction that involves the underlying trust property also would warrant the giving of advance notice. To the extent readily available, remainder beneficiaries, whether ascertained or presumptive, are

[825] Restatement (Third) of Trust §82 cmt. a(1).

[826] Restatement (Third) of Trust §82 cmt. a(1). If, for example, two children, with more or less identical equitable interests under a trust are entitled to be furnished information about the trust on an ongoing basis, but one is a minor, ordinarily the trustee's duty to furnish information to the minor is satisfied if he furnishes only the adult child with the requisite information. If, however, the interests of the two children are in potential conflict, *e.g.*, if the two are permissible beneficiaries under a discretionary trust, *see* §3.5.3.2(a) of this handbook, then keeping just the adult beneficiary informed will not satisfy the trustee's duty to keep the minor informed.

[827] *See* UTC §813(a), (b)(4) & cmt. (available at <http://www.uniformlaws.org/Act.aspx?title=Trust%20Code>) (suggesting that notice to qualified beneficiaries would satisfy the advance notice requirement); Restatement (Third) of Trusts §82(1)(c); 3 Scott & Ascher §17.5. *See also* Allard v. Pacific Nat'l Bank, 663 P.2d 104 (Wash. 1983) (surcharging trustee for failing to give beneficiaries advance notice of proposed sale of a parcel of real estate that was sole asset of trust); In re Green Charitable Trusts, 172 Mich. App. 298, 431 N.W.2d 492 (1988) (affirming trial court finding that trustee was in breach of trust for failing to inform beneficiaries of a contemplated transaction involving the trust estate).

[828] UTC §108(d) (available at <http://www.uniformlaws.org/Act.aspx?title=Trust%20Code>).

shut out of the process, the trustee could be in breach of the duty of impartiality.[829] A trustee's duty under the default law to give advance notice to a beneficiary of a contemplated action, however, does not in and of itself afford the beneficiary a nonjudicial power to veto the contemplated action.[830] A general power in the beneficiary to veto contemplated actions of the trustee would conflict with a core principle of the default law of trusts, namely, that the trustee is not an agent of the beneficiary.[831] The source of any veto powers must be the terms of the trust.[832] The Restatement (Third) of Trusts lists some situations which could give rise to a requirement on the part of a trustee to give advance notice to qualified or fairly representative beneficiaries of a contemplated action:

- "significant changes in trustee circumstances, including changes in the identities, number, or roles of trustees or in methods of determining trustee compensation;
- decisions regarding delegation of important fiduciary responsibilities or significant changes in arrangements for delegation;
- important adjustments being considered in investment or other management strategies;
- significant actions under consideration involving hard-to-value assets or special sensitivity to beneficiaries (such as liquidating or selling shares of a closely held business or a sale or long-term lease of a major real estate holding);
- plans being made for distribution on termination or partial termination (or perhaps subdivision) of the trust; and
- other transactions or developments of which beneficiaries should be made aware and thereby allowed an opportunity to offer suggestions, comments, or information, or to request reports or accountings. . . ."[833]

This duty to inform in advance has its limitations, particularly if the trustee is engaged in sensitive contract negotiations with third parties on behalf of the trust:

Confidential information may take more than one form. Trustees negotiating a contract may obtain confidential information of the other party. To allow a beneficiary to see that information might be a breach of contract: a beneficiary having the information might wish to intervene concerning the conduct of negotiations, thereby compromising the trustees' autonomy. Trustees who own shares may receive confidential information in that capacity. If they breach

---

[829] Restatement (Third) of Trusts §79 cmt. d. *See generally* §6.2.5 of this handbook (trustee's duty of impartiality in his dealings with the beneficiaries); 4 Scott & Ascher §20.1 (Impartiality Between Successive Beneficiaries).

[830] Restatement (Third) of Trusts §82 cmt. d.

[831] *See generally* §5.6 of this handbook (duties and liabilities of the beneficiary).

[832] *See generally* §3.2.6 of this handbook (considerations in the selection of a trustee) and §4.2 of this handbook (expressly reserved beneficial interests and powers).

[833] Restatement (Third) of Trusts §82 cmt. d.

confidentiality the value of the shares might be diminished: *Neagle v. Remington* [2002] 3 NZLR 827 at 32(e) per Patterson J.[834]

The trustee's duty to render accounts to the court and to the beneficiaries. Apart from the duty to provide advance notice of important or significant events, "[t]he trustee . . . owes his beneficiary a duty to render at suitable intervals, upon resignation or removal, and upon termination of the trust, a formal and detailed account of his receipts, disbursements, and property on hand, from which the beneficiary can learn whether the trustee has performed his trust and what the current status of the trust is."[835] This we refer to as the duty to keep and render accounts, a topic that is covered next in Section 6.1.5.2 of this handbook.

Self-dealing transactions. The trustee's duty to inform also may be implicated when the trustee transacts with a beneficiary, a topic that is covered in Section 6.1.3.5 of this handbook (acquisition by trustee of equitable interest; duty of loyalty to the beneficiary in nontrust matters).

The quiet or silent trust. Is a quiet or silent trust illusory? The question is intentionally ambiguous. Is the question whether the trust itself is illusory, or just its quietness? A quiet or silent trust has been defined as "an irrevocable trust that, by its terms, directs the trustee not to inform the beneficiaries of the existence of the trust, its terms and the details of the administration of the trust."[836] South Dakota, for example, would seem to authorize such trusts by statute. See S.D. Codified Laws §55-2-13, which provides that "[t]he settlor, trust advisor, or trust protector, may, by the terms of the governing instrument, or in writing delivered to the trustee, expand, restrict, eliminate, or otherwise modify the rights of beneficiaries to information relating to the trust." It seems there are two possibilities.

The first is that S.D. Codified Law §55-2-13 means what it says, in which case a quiet or silent trust is something other than the legal/equitable relationship that is the subject of this handbook. Perhaps it is just a constructive principal/agency relationship, the "settlor" being the principal and the "trustee" being the agent. Or perhaps it is just a fancy completed common law gift to the "trustee."

The second is that a quiet or silent trust is a true trust. If that is the case, then how, as a practical matter, is the trustee to hide the existence of the trust from the beneficiary and comply with applicable tax laws?[837] Assuming that that is possible, then how is the trustee to handle a request for information from the curious beneficiary about the terms of the trust should the beneficiary somehow otherwise get wind of its existence? If the trustee lies to the beneficiary, or intentionally obfuscates, is he not committing an act of actual, or constructive,

---

[834] W. A. Lee, *Purifying the dialect of equity*, 7(2) Tr. Q. Rev. 14 (May 2009) [a STEP publication]. *See generally* §3.5.1 of this handbook (the trustee is a principal, not someone's agent).

[835] Bogert §963.

[836] Joyce Crivellari, *Trust & Estate Insights*, May 2013 (A UBS Private Wealth Management Newsletter).

[837] *See generally* Alan Newman, *The Intention of the Settlor Under the Uniform Trust Code: Whose Property Is It, Anyway?*, 38 Akron L. Rev. 659, 679 (2005) (taxation and the quiet/silent trust).

fraud against the beneficiary, such that any applicable statute of ultimate repose is tolled?[838] Finally, the trustee's duty to account is a two-edged sword. Yes, it is burdensome for the trustee. But rendering accounts to the beneficiary is also the tried-and-true vehicle for limiting the trustee's liability.

The quiet or silent trust is not to be confused with the secret (or semi-secret) trust, which is the subject of Section 9.9.6 of this handbook.

Countervailing considerations. It may not always be in the best interests of a beneficiary, or of his or her cobeneficiaries, for the trustee to disclose to the beneficiary confidential legal advice which counsel has rendered to the trustee. It could even be "prejudicial to the ability of the trustees to discharge their obligations under the trust."[839] This is a topic we take up in Section 8.8 of this handbook in our discussion of trust counsel and the attorney-client privilege.

§6.1.5.2 Duty to Keep and Render Accounts

Upon reasonable request, a beneficiary is entitled to a statement of the accounts of the trust annually and on termination of the trust or change of the trustee.[840]

The Uniform Trust Code employs the term report instead of accounting in order to negate any inference that the report must be prepared in any particular format or with a high degree of formality.[841]

An incident of the trustee's general duty to account and the trustee's particular duty to provide information is the trustee's duty to keep written accounts that show the nature, amount, and administration of the trust property.[842] All doubts are resolved against the trustee who does not keep accurate accounts.[843] Implicit in the trustee's duty to inform and report is the duty to keep adequate records of the administration of the trust.[844] The trustee further

---

[838] *See generally* §7.1.3 of this handbook (the UTC's statute of ultimate repose).

[839] David Hayton, Paul Mathews, & Charles Mitchell, *Underhilll and Hayton, Law Relating to Trusts and Trustees* §60.58 (17th ed. 2006).

[840] UPC §7-303(c). *See also* Restatement (Third) of Trusts §83 (providing that a trustee has a duty at reasonable intervals upon request to provide beneficiaries with reports or accountings).

[841] UTC §813 cmt. (available at <http://www.uniformlaws.org/Act.aspx?title=Trust%20 Code>) (suggesting that the reporting requirement might even be satisfied by providing the beneficiaries with copies of the trust's income tax returns and monthly brokerage account statements if the information on those returns and statements is complete and sufficiently clear).

[842] *See* Restatement (Second) of Trusts §172; 3 Scott & Ascher §17.4; 2A Scott on Trusts §172; Bogert §962; Lewin ¶ 23-05 (England). For a comprehensive list of local statutes regulating the duty of a trustee to account in court for the administration of a trust, *see* Bogert §§965–968. *See also* 2A Scott on Trusts §172 n.10 and accompanying text.

[843] *See* Restatement (Second) of Trusts §1 72 cmt. b; 3 Scott & Ascher §17.4; 2A Scott on Trusts §172; Bogert §962. *See, e.g.,* Markus v. Markus, 119 N.E.2d 415, 418 (1954) (noting that because the burden is upon a trustee to show that he acted with reasonable skill and judgment, to include accounting for all the trust property which came into his possession, the failure to do so will require the trustee to "stand the loss").

[844] UTC §810(a) (available at <http://www.uniformlaws.org/Act.aspx?title=Trust%20 Code>).

has a duty at reasonable intervals on request to provide beneficiaries with such reports or accountings as will enable them to protect their equitable interests.[845] The court has exclusive jurisdiction of proceedings initiated by interested parties to review and settle the accounts of a trustee.[846]

A total negation of the duty to account is unenforceable. A trust provision that states that the trustee does not have to account to anyone will not be enforced.[847] The courts consider such a provision as being against public policy, so it is without effect.[848] The English cases are generally in accord,[849] as is the Restatement (Third) of Trusts:

> Occasionally the terms of a trust provide that the trustee shall have no accountability for his or her conduct in the administration of the trust. Assuming that the settler intended to create a trust relationship, however, this does not preclude the beneficiaries from holding the trustee liable for a breach of trust or otherwise accountable for the trust property and its administration. A trust provision of this type may be interpreted as having the same effect as an exculpatory clause, and thus as being subject to the same limitation.[850]

Formatting the accounting. As to the mechanics of putting together a trustee accounting, first things first: It is critical that the file contain a complete and accurate inventory of the items that were in the trust at the time it was created, with their inception values and tax costs readily apparent. The inventory is the key to the code. Second, the trustee from inception to termination should reflect trust accounting income and trust accounting principal on separate schedules. Income and principal should never be blended, except when income has been duly added to principal. On the other hand, within the four corners of the principal account itself, it may be appropriate for practical reasons to ascribe an average or "blended" inception value to the shares of a particular company that have been brought into the trust's portfolio over time in increments, unless in a given situation the beneficiaries would somehow be materially disadvantaged by such an accounting shortcut.[851]

Jurisdictions will vary as to the necessary form of an account,[852] but in every trust account there should be a clear showing of the following: income

---

[845] Restatement (Third) of Trusts §83; 3 Scott & Ascher §17.4.

[846] UPC §7-201(a).

[847] *See* 3 Scott & Ascher §17.4; 2A Scott on Trusts §172 n.16 and accompanying text.

[848] *See* Trust of Malasky, 290 A.D.2d 631, 632, 736 N.Y.S.2d 151, 153 (2002) (holding that although an inter vivos trust may limit the right of beneficiaries to compel an accounting, any attempt to completely excuse the obligation of a trustee to account is void as against public policy).

[849] Lewin ¶ 23-14 (England).

[850] Restatement (Third) of Trusts §83 cmt. d. *See generally* §7.2.6 of this handbook (when the terms of the trust provide for trustee exculpation).

[851] Matter of Hunter, 27 Misc. 3d 1205(A) (Surr. Ct. Westchester County 2010)

[852] "The UTC employs the term 'report' instead of 'accounting' in order to negate any inference that the report must be prepared in any particular format or with a high degree of formality." UTC §813 cmt. (available at <http://www.uniformlaws.org/Act.aspx?title=Trust%20 Code>). "The reporting requirement might even be satisfied by providing the beneficiaries with copies of the trust's income tax returns and monthly brokerage account statements if the

received, income paid, balance of income, additions to principal, deductions from principal, principal on hand, and changes in investments.[853] The account will ordinarily be presented with debtor and creditor sides. By that we mean that the trustee is "charged" or "debited" with whatever property enters the trust and "credited" with whatever property that properly leaves the trust. And with any luck, at termination there will be nothing but zeros.

Thus, a traditional trust accounting would have a Schedule A (principal items on hand at the beginning of the accounting period that were "charged" to the trustee); Schedule B (principal distributions that were made during the accounting period that were "credited" to the trustee); Schedule C (balance of principal items on hand at the end of the accounting period that are "charged" to the trustee); Schedule D (income items on hand at the beginning of the accounting period that were "charged" to the trustee); Schedule E (income items paid out during the accounting period that were "credited" to the trustee); and Schedule F (balance of income items on hand at the end of the accounting period that are "charged" to the trustee). Thus, "Schedules B, E, and C together should equal the total of Schedules A and D."[854]

Now, for all this to work, "THE INVENTORY VALUES FOR ORIGINAL ITEMS AND THE COST OF AFTER-ACQUIRED ITEMS SERVE AS THE BASIS IN ALL FUTURE ACCOUNTS FOR DETERMINING THE PROFIT AND LOSS ON THE SALES OF SECURITIES."[855] If market values are used, the accounts will be not only out of balance but also nonsensical. Once one realizes that for trust accounting purposes, the value of an entrusted item is fixed as of the time the trustee takes the legal title to it, or is deemed to have taken the legal title to it, the logic of the trust accounting process becomes apparent. Of course, market values should also be reflected somewhere on the accounting, as the trustee has a general affirmative duty to furnish the beneficiary with critical information, a topic that we covered in the prior section of this handbook. But if there is to be an orderly keeping track of receipts and expenditures over time, the value of each entrusted item needs to be fixed for trust accounting purposes as of the time the trustee takes, or is deemed to have taken, the legal title to it.

The acquisition value of each asset, as well as its market value at the beginning and end of the accounting period, should be readily ascertainable from a casual scrutiny of the account by anyone of average intelligence who is unfamiliar with the practices and terminology of trust administration.[856] For trust accounting purposes, the acquisition value of a life insurance contract (policy) is generally its net cash surrender value (plus any unexpired premium)

---

information on those returns and statements is complete and sufficiently clear." UTC §813 cmt. "The key factor is not the format chosen but whether the report provides the beneficiaries with the information necessary to protect their interests." UTC §813 cmt.

[853] *See generally* 3 Scott & Ascher §17.4.

[854] Thomas H. Belknap, Newhall's Settlement of Estates and Fiduciary Law in Massachusetts §29:2 (5th ed. 1997) (form of accounts).

[855] Thomas H. Belknap, Newhall's Settlement of Estates and Fiduciary Law in Massachusetts §29:2 (5th ed. 1997) (form of accounts).

[856] Restatement (Third) of Trusts §83 cmt. b and the Reporter's Notes thereto.

as of the time the trustee acquired, or was deemed to have acquired, the contract. Going forward, absent special facts, the contract's market values for trust accounting purposes are its net cash surrender value (plus any unexpired premium) as of the beginning and end of each accounting period.[857] This all assumes that any mid-administration sale of the contract on the open market (life settlement) by the trustee—to the extent such a sale would even be legally permissible and a practical option—would not command a price that is greater than its net cash surrender value. For a model trustee's accounting, the reader is referred to Bogert.[858] A trustee also should not deny a beneficiary's request for any additional information which the beneficiary would reasonably need to monitor and protect the equitable interest.[859]

Testamentary trusts. Some states require the testamentary trustee to file an inventory with the court soon after appointment,[860] and then to file accounts regularly with the court thereafter throughout the life of the trust. It should be noted here that the Uniform Probate Code would relieve the testamentary trustee of this account filing obligation, "substituting clear remedies and statutory duties to inform beneficiaries."[861] In any case, the trustee of a testamentary trust should take care to ensure that the inventory is accurate. The balance of personal and real property set forth on the inventory will be the beginning balances of a testamentary trustee's first account. Also, the values of the property on the inventory establish the trustee's financial responsibility for those assets. Even in the case of the inter vivos trust where there is usually no court involvement, the inventory is indispensable from every standpoint. It is the starting point for all subsequent accounts.

To reiterate, on failure to keep adequate accounts, all doubts are resolved against the trustee, and the trustee may be denied compensation.[862] The beneficiary may demand an accounting.[863] Compelling an accounting is within the jurisdiction of a court of equity.[864]

Judicial settlement of trustees' accounts. The trustee as a matter of right is entitled periodically to a discharge of liability by means of the judicial

---

[857] Special circumstances may call for a different valuation method, *e.g.*, the ratable charge method, the interest-adjusted ratable charge method, the deferred-premium asset method, the accrual basis (policy reserve) method, or the economic benefit method.

[858] Bogert §970, n.59. *See also* Robert Whitman, Fiduciary Accounting Guide (2nd ed. 1998).

[859] Restatement (Third) of Trusts §83 cmt. b.

[860] *See* Bogert §597.

[861] UPC, Part 4, Powers of Trustees, Comment; UPC §7-201(b).

[862] *See* Restatement (Second) of Trusts §243; 3 Scott & Ascher §17.4; 2A Scott on Trusts §172; 3A Scott on Trusts §243; Bogert §962.

[863] *See* Restatement (Second) of Trusts §172 cmt. c; 3 Scott & Ascher §17.4; 2A Scott on Trusts §172; Bogert §963. Some beneficiaries, however, are more equal than others when it comes to the right to information. In the case of a revocable inter vivos trust under which the settlor has reserved a right of revocation, for example, the trustee may not provide reports or accountings or other information concerning the terms or administration of the trust to other beneficiaries while the settlor is alive and has capacity, unless authorized to do so by the settlor, the terms of the trust, or statute. Restatement (Third) of Trusts §74 cmt. e.

[864] *See* 3 Scott & Ascher §17.4; 2A Scott on Trusts §172; Bogert §963.

settlement of accounts (allowance of accounts).[865] The trustee is discharged of any liability for transactions covered by the account.[866] A judicial settlement of a trust account entails the filing of the account in a court that has jurisdiction over the trust, properly notifying by service or otherwise those who may have an interest in the trust, and requesting the court to render an approval or allowance of the account that is binding on all persons who are interested, or may become interested, in the trust once the applicable appeal period has run. "If, therefore, on a trustee's accounting, the court determines that the trustee is not subject to surcharge and that the beneficiaries' have had proper notice and an opportunity to be heard, the court's judgment complies with the requirements of due process and is entitled to full faith and credit throughout the country."[867] For a discussion of the practice in some quarters of trustees encouraging beneficiaries to give the trustees releases and indemnities in consideration of the trustees not seeking judicial approval/allowance/settlement of their accounts, the reader is referred to Section 8.2.3 of this handbook.

A careful examination of local statute and case law should be made to determine the extent to which the judicial allowance of the trustee's account acts as a discharge from further obligation for the transaction covered thereby,[868] i.e., the extent to which allowance affords the trustee a defense of *res judicata*.[869] "In some states, a decree approving an intermediate account is final and conclusive as to all matters disclosed therein, but in others the beneficiaries are permitted on the final accounting to reopen matters already disclosed in prior accountings."[870] Commonly the statutes require notification of the interested parties, either by personal service, mailing, or publication.[871] The procedure followed in most states provides for the appointment of a guardian ad litem to represent persons unborn or unascertained and often to represent persons under some legal disability.[872] For more on the role of the guardian ad litem, to

---

[865] *See* Bogert §970; 4 Scott & Ascher §§23.1 (The Settlement of Accounts), 24.25 (Judicial Discharge).

[866] *See* Bogert §974; 4 Scott & Ascher §§23.1 (The Settlement of Accounts), 24.25 (Judicial Discharge).

[867] 4 Scott & Ascher §24.25 (Judicial Discharge).

[868] *See generally* 4 Scott & Ascher §23.1.

[869] *See generally* 4 Scott & Ascher §23.1.

[870] 4 Scott & Ascher §23.1. *Cf.* Matter of JP Morgan Chase Bank, N.A. (Strong), 2013 WL 6182548 (N.Y. Sur.) ("The burden of proof is on the Trustee to show clearly that the issue of the proper calculation of the tax-basis of the stock in Trust I was litigated and determined by the Supreme Court in the intermediate account proceeding. . . . The trustee has not met its burden[,] . . . and as such the Objectants cannot be estopped from making the argument in this . . . [final judicial settlement] . . . proceeding.").

[871] *See* Restatement (Second) of Trusts §220 cmt. d; 3 Scott on Trusts §220; Bogert §974. *See, e.g.,* UPC §1-108 (providing that for purposes of granting approval of a trustee's account, the holder of a presently exercisable general power of appointment, including one in the form of a power of amendment or revocation, is deemed to act for those who possess contingent equitable interests).

[872] *See generally* 4 Scott & Ascher §23.1.

include a discussion of the doctrine of virtual representation,[873] the reader is referred to Section 8.14 of this handbook.

It is critical that the trustee obtain a written legal opinion advising the trustee who are entitled to receive notice of an accounting, *i.e.*, who generically are entitled. The opinion should be retained in the trustee's permanent file. Commonly, one or more of the following will be on the list of those so entitled: current beneficiaries, remaindermen with vested interests, presumptive remaindermen, the guardian ad litem, and the court.[874] "As a general matter, the fact that a beneficiary has only a future interest, and that it is contingent, does not preclude the beneficiary from compelling an accounting."[875] In the case of a trust with charitable interests, the state attorney general may also be entitled to some accounting-related information.

It is default law, however, that only the settlor of a revocable inter vivos trust is entitled to an accounting while the settlor is alive and has legal capacity.[876] It would be a breach of a trustee's fiduciary duty to the settlor for the trustee to furnish the other beneficiaries[877] with an accounting, unless authorized to do so by the settlor, the terms of the trust, or statute.[878] On the other hand, during the period of a settlor's incapacity, "the other beneficiaries are ordinarily entitled to exercise, on their own behalf, the usual rights of trust beneficiaries, and the trustee is ordinarily under a duty to provide them with accountings and other information concerning the trust and its administration."[879]

The opinion also should advise the trustee what information satisfies the notice requirement. When in doubt, the trustee should furnish each person and entity entitled to notice with a copy of the entire accounting. It also is critical that the trustee take reasonable steps to confirm all external facts referenced expressly or by implication in the accounting. The trustee would be well advised, for example, to have in his files copies of birth certificates, adoption decrees, diplomas, marriage certificates, death certificates, and any other such documentation that would evidence that the trustee has been reasonably diligent ascertaining who is and who is not entitled to share in the equitable interest.

Finally, it is advisable that the trustee have in his files evidence that whoever was entitled to notice actually received it. Section 7-307 of the Uniform Probate Code, for example, provides that a beneficiary who has *personally* received a trustee's final account would have only three years from its receipt to

---

[873] *See* UPC §1-403(2)(iii) (providing that unless otherwise represented, a minor or an incapacitated, unborn, or unascertained beneficiary is bound by an order to the extent the beneficiary's interest is adequately represented by another party having a substantially identical interest in the proceeding).

[874] *See generally* 4 Scott & Ascher §20.1 (Impartiality Between Successive Beneficiaries).

[875] 3 Scott & Ascher §17.4.

[876] Restatement (Third) of Trusts §74 cmt. e.

[877] The interests of the other beneficiaries are contingent, the condition precedent being that the settlor not exercise his or her right of revocation.

[878] Restatement (Third) of Trusts §74 cmt. e.

[879] Restatement (Third) of Trusts §74 cmt. e.

assert any claims against the trustee. This would be the case even if the trustee had failed to disclose critical information on the account.[880] When personal service is not required by statute or court order, the trustee should employ a delivery service that employs tracking numbers. The trustee is advised to print out and place in his files hard-copy evidence that appropriate accounting documentation arrived at its intended destination and was duly accepted. Generating all this paperwork is well worth the cost. An action brought against the trustee years in the future for failure to properly account would be a far more costly proposition; and were the trustee to be found liable, the attendant costs would not be reimbursable from the trust estate.[881]

A reminder: Except in those jurisdictions that have enacted Section 7-307 of the Uniform Probate Code,[882] no amount of paperwork can protect a trustee who has prepared and disseminated an accounting that has material inaccuracies and/or omissions.[883] This would apply as well to the nonjudicial accounting or report,[884] a subject covered below. The trustee is a fiduciary, not an adversary:

> Because the beneficiary may rely upon the disclosures in the trustee's account and the petition for its allowance, a proceeding for the allowance of the account does not impose upon the beneficiary as an ordinary adversary the burden of making his own inquiry to ascertain the truth of the trustee's disclosures. The beneficiary may accept them as true. In this respect the rule is different from what it is in ordinary litigation, where the parties are not only adversary, but where there is no fiduciary relationship.[885]

The final decree allowing a trustee's account can be reopened only under circumstances that would allow the reopening of an ordinary decree of the equity or probate court (*e.g.*, to correct fraud).[886] Finality in the settlement of accounts furthers the public interest that there be honest people willing to serve

---

[880] *See, e.g.*, Mass. Gen. Laws ch. 190B, §7-307.

[881] *See generally* 3 Scott & Ascher §17.4 (noting that "[a]ny expenses and costs that arise as a result of the trustee's failure to keep proper accounts are chargeable against the trustee personally, rather than against the trust estate").

[882] *See* Unif. Prob. Code §7-307 which provides as follows: "In any event and *notwithstanding lack of full disclosure* a trustee who has issued a final account or statement received by the beneficiary and has informed the beneficiary of the location and availability of records for his examination is protected after 3 years."

[883] Restatement (Third) of Trusts §83 cmt. c. *See, e.g.*, In re Anger's Will, 225 Minn. 229, 330 N.W.2d 694 (1948) (decree allowing trustees' annual accounts not res judicata (final) as to acts of self-dealing on the part of the trustees, the trustees having failed to disclose fully, frankly, and without reservation in the documentation facts relevant to the self-dealing).

[884] Restatement (Third) of Trusts §83 cmt. c.

[885] In re Anger's Will, 225 Minn. 229, 330 N.W.2d 694 (1948).

[886] *See* Restatement (Second) of Trusts §220 cmt. a; 3 Scott on Trusts §220; Bogert §974. For a case involving the reopening of allowed accounts for "constructive fraud," *see* National Acad. of Sci. v. Cambridge Trust Co., 370 Mass. 303, 346 N.E.2d 879 (1976), which involved a trustee's good faith representation on its accountings that a widow had not remarried and thus was entitled to income payments when in fact she had remarried and under the governing instrument was not so entitled. The court found that the trustee had made "no reasonable efforts to ascertain the true state of the facts it [had] misrepresented in the accounts."

as trustees. Thus, a decree allowing an account ordinarily cannot be questioned in a collateral proceeding in law or in equity.[887] Of course, for a decree to be final, the court must have jurisdiction to make the decree, and the machinery for giving notice must satisfy due process.[888] Thus, if an executor of an estate or trustee of a terminating trust is accounting to himself as the sole successor fiduciary, notice needs to be given to the equitable interests.[889]

For a discussion of fraud or constructive fraud as a basis for the reopening of a previously allowed trustee account, the reader is referred to Section 8.15.59 of this handbook.[890] On the other hand, the Uniform Trust Code would relieve the trustee from liability for a good-faith failure to "ascertain external facts, often of a personal nature, that might affect administration or distribution of the trust" in ways that thwart the intentions of the settlor.[891] It provides that if the happening of an event, including marriage, divorce, performance of educational requirements, or death, affects the administration or distribution of a trust, a trustee who has exercised reasonable care to ascertain the happening of the event is not liable for a loss resulting from the trustee's lack of knowledge.[892]

The nonjudicial settlement of trustees' accounts. The trustee of a testamentary trust will likely be unable to obtain a final and binding settlement (approval) of his accounts without court involvement. The general procedural requirements for getting the court involved will likely be found in a state statute.[893] The specifics are usually laid out in a body of court rules. Inter vivos trust instruments, on the other hand, often expressly provide for periodic accountings in a nonjudicial setting.[894]

When the beneficiary withholds approval in a nonjudicial setting. The typical inter vivos accounting provision provides that the trustee shall be discharged of further liability upon assent of certain adult beneficiaries.[895] Sometimes there is a clause expressly providing for release upon the beneficiary's failure to object within a certain period, usually within sixty days of receipt.[896] Under the default

---

[887] *See* 3 Scott on Trusts §220.

[888] *See* Restatement (Second) of Trusts §220 cmt. c; 3 Scott on Trusts §220. *See, e.g.,* Shirk v. Walker, 298 Mass. 251, 10 N.E.2d 192, 198–199 (1937) (vacating the portion of the trial court decision that relates to the trust's principal account because the remainder interests had not been made a party to the litigation); Mullane v. Central Hanover Bank & Trust Co., 339 U.S. 306 (1950).

[889] *See, e.g.,* In re Hunter, 6 App. Div. 3d 117, 775 N.Y.S.2d 42 (2004).

[890] *See generally* 4 Scott & Ascher §24.31 (Liability for Incorrect Distributions).

[891] UTC §1007 cmt. (available at <http://www.uniformlaws.org/Act.aspx?title=Trust%20 Code>). *See generally* 4 Scott & Ascher §24.31 (Liability for Incorrect Distributions); §8.15.59 of this handbook (constructive fraud).

[892] UTC §1007 (available at <http://www.uniformlaws.org/Act.aspx?title=Trust%20 Code>). *See generally* 4 Scott & Ascher §24.31 (Liability for Incorrect Distributions).

[893] *See* 3 Scott & Ascher §17.4 n.13 for citations to a number of such state statutes.

[894] *See generally* Westfall, *Nonjudicial Settlement of Trustees' Accounts,* 71 Harv. L. Rev. 40 (1957); 3 Scott & Ascher §17.4; 2A Scott on Trusts §172.

[895] *See generally* Westfall, *Nonjudicial Settlement of Trustees' Accounts,* 71 Harv. L. Rev. 40, 60–63 (1957); 3 Scott & Ascher §17.4; 2A Scott on Trusts §172.

[896] *See generally* Westfall, *Nonjudicial Settlement of Trustees' Accounts,* 71 Harv. L. Rev. 40 (1957); 3 Scott & Ascher §17.4; 2A Scott on Trusts §172. *Cf.* UTC §1009 cmt. (available at <http://

common law, as well as general principles of equity, the failure of a beneficiary to object within such a short period of time would unlikely result in a foreclosing of the trustee's liability for a breach of trust, even for a breach that was unambiguously disclosed in the accounting. As a general rule, the beneficiary's informed consent to a breach of trust must be manifested by some affirmative act.

> Consent or ratification ordinarily requires more than mere failure of the beneficiary to object to conduct that the beneficiary was aware would or did constitute a breach of trust (but cf. . . . [laches doctrine] . . .); the consent or ratification is normally expressly communicated to the trustee, orally or by delivery of a writing, although the consent or ratification may be implied by the beneficiary's conduct in some circumstances.[897]

The doctrine of laches is taken up in Section 7.1.3 of this handbook. In Section 5.5 of this handbook we remind the reader that a trust beneficiary, *qua* beneficiary, generally owes the trustee no duties, fiduciary or otherwise.[898]

In jurisdictions that have enacted Section 7-307 of the Uniform Probate Code, it is default statute-law that "any claim against a trustee for breach of trust is barred as to any beneficiary who has received a final account or other statement fully disclosing the matter and showing termination of the trust relationship between the trustee and the beneficiary unless a proceeding to assert the claim is commenced within [6 months] after receipt of the final account or statement."[899] Article VII of the model Uniform Probate Code was superseded by the model Uniform Trust Code and withdrawn in 2010 following widespread enactment of assorted versions of the Uniform Trust Code.

Whether the assent of a beneficiary can bind the nonassenting cobeneficiaries. It is settled law that the assent of the holder of a right of revocation who is of full age and legal capacity may bind all contingent equitable interests.[900] It is unsettled, however, whether, in a nonjudicial setting, the assent of present beneficiaries of an irrevocable trust can bind future beneficiaries, remaindermen, and others including minors, the unborn, and the unascertained.[901] In this regard, the law is particularly uncertain when it comes to the nonjudicial settlement of an

---

www.uniformlaws.org/Act.aspx?title=Trust%20Code>) (suggesting that as a matter of default law, a beneficiary's failure to object is not sufficient to relieve a trustee of liability for breach of trust); 4 Scott & Ascher §24.21 (Consent of Beneficiary) ("The fact that a beneficiary knows the trustee is committing a breach of trust and fails to object is insufficient to preclude the beneficiary from holding the trustee accountable for the breach of trust").

[897] Restatement (Third) of Trusts §97 cmt. b.

[898] *See also* the introductory quotation to §5.5 of this handbook.

[899] *See,* Mass. Gen. Laws ch. 190B, §7-307.

[900] *See generally* §8.11 of this handbook (what are the duties of the trustee of a revocable inter vivos trust?); 3 Scott & Ascher §17.4. *See, e.g., Trust of Malasky,* 290 A.D.2d 631, 632, 736 N.Y.S.2d 151, 153 (2002) (deeming remaindermen to have "no pecuniary interest" in trust during period when settlor possessed right of revocation).

[901] *See, e.g.,* Jacob. V. Davis, 128 Md. App. 433, 738 A.2d 904 (1999) (suggesting that such an assent should be nonbinding). *See generally* 3 Scott & Ascher §17.4.

account that reflects a shifting of beneficial interests.[902] This is because such a shifting may implicate the following principle:

> If the trustee commits a breach of trust... with the consent of one of the beneficiaries, and the breach results in a benefit to the consenting beneficiary and a loss to the trust estate or one or more other beneficiaries, the trustee is entitled to impound the share of the consenting beneficiary, to make good the loss suffered by the trust estate or the other beneficiaries, at least to the extent of the benefit received by the consenting beneficiary.[903]

Thus the Restatement (Third) of Trusts provides that a "designated person's approval... is subject to court review for abuse, with particular attention to neglect or to the possible effects of a conflict of interests between that person and a beneficiary" and that "this review is available to a beneficiary regardless of a trust provision to the contrary, such as one purporting to make the trustee's discharge final or conclusive upon the designated person's approval."[904]

In a landmark case out of New York, the court held that the assent to an account of the trustee of an inter vivos trust by the income beneficiary could not bind the remaindermen:

> If the settlor intended by paragraph Twelfth to deprive the vested remaindermen of their right to question the acts of the trustees, then the validity of that paragraph—as regards the remaindermen—is, to say the least, doubtful. The effect of such deprivation would prevent the vested remaindermen from protecting their interests for the duration of the life estate. Even if the trust were not being performed, they would be without redress. Denial of "the equitable right to enforce the trust" is "inconsistent with its necessary and essential qualities as such." This puts the creator of the trust "in the attitude of deliberately nullifying his own evident purpose." That he meant to create an effective trust is beyond all question; and a construction which makes him destroy in the very effort to create, should not prevail if there be any other rational interpretation.[905]

In any case, a provision purporting to relieve the trustee of the obligation to account to future beneficiaries is unlikely to deprive a future beneficiary of

---

[902] *See, e.g.*, Trust of Malasky, 290 A.D.2d 631, 736 N.Y.S.2d 151 (2002) (holding that when a cotrustee or trustee is the sole income beneficiary, a trust provision that limits the trustees' accounting responsibilities to the income beneficiaries is violative of public policy). *See generally* 4 Scott & Ascher §20.1 (Impartiality Between Successive Beneficiaries).

[903] 4 Scott & Ascher §25.2.6.1 (When Consenting Beneficiary Profits from Breach of Trust).

[904] Restatement (Third) of Trusts §83 cmt. d (providing also that even a settlor-accountee may employ the accounting in derogation of the rights of the beneficiaries). *See also* In re Cassover, 124 Misc. 2d 630, 46 N.Y.S.2d 763 (Surr. Ct. 1984) (the court disregarding on public policy grounds a provision in an irrevocable trust that the settlor-trustee shall be accountable only to himself).

[905] In re Crane, 34 N.Y.S.2d 9 (1942) (citing Van Cott v. Prentice et al., 104 N.Y. 45, 52, 10 N.E. 257, 260). *See also* 3 Scott & Ascher §17.4 (discussing *In re Crane*).

standing to bring an accounting action against the trustee.[906] It is likely that standing would be granted even if the future beneficiary's equitable interest were contingent.[907] The Restatement (Third) of Trusts is generally in accord.[908] Given this uncertainty, the trustee needs to understand in advance of taking a particular action whether binding approval of that action can be obtained nonjudicially through the accounting process. Accordingly, the trustee would be well advised to have in his files a written legal opinion that addresses the types of actions that may not be covered by the settlement provisions of the particular trust's accounting clause, *e.g.*, deducting an income expense from principal, invading principal for the benefit of a current beneficiary, or pursuing an income-at-the-expense-of-growth investment strategy.[909]

Having taken an action that is appropriate but which falls outside the nonjudicial settlement provisions of the accounting clause, the trustee will need to make a cost-benefit analysis. The trustee could have the accounting that covers the period in which the action was taken approved by the court.[910] From the perspective of the beneficiary, however, the privacy and efficiencies attendant with a nonjudicial settlement are preferable to the publicity, time, and expense attendant with a judicial proceeding.[911] Moreover, a frivolous trip to the probate court itself could constitute a breach of the duty of loyalty.

The Uniform Trust Code offers a partial compromise. It would have the trustee periodically account to so-called qualified beneficiaries.[912] For purposes of the Act, a qualified beneficiary is a beneficiary who, on the date the beneficiary's qualification is determined: (A) is a distributee or permissible distributee of trust income or principal; (B) *would be* a distributee or permissible distributee of trust income or principal if the interests of the distributees in . . . (A) . . . [above] . . . terminated on that date; or (C) *would be* a distributee or permissible distributee of trust income or principal if the trust were to terminate on that date.[913] In other words, the trustee would have to render routine periodic written accountings to the presumptive remaindermen as well as to the current beneficiaries. A word of caution is in order here: There is less to the UTC's qualified-beneficiary concept than meets the eye. As we note in Section 6.1.5.1 of this handbook, "[u]nder the Uniform Trust Code, in a critical matter such as when equitable property rights, whether vested or contingent, are at stake, notice to the qualified beneficiaries would not relieve the trustee of the

---

[906] *See, e.g.*, Trust of Malasky, 290 A.D.2d 631, 736 N.Y.S.2d 151 (2002) (holding that when a cotrustee or trustee is the sole income beneficiary, a trust provision that limits the trustees' accounting responsibilities to the income beneficiaries is violative of public policy); Briggs v. Crowley, 224 N.E.2d 417, 421 (1967).

[907] *See, e.g.*, Siefert v. Leonhardt, 975 S.W.2d 489 (Mo. Ct. App. 1998).

[908] Restatement (Third) of Trusts §83 cmt. d.

[909] *See generally* 4 Scott & Ascher §20.1 (Impartiality Between Successive Beneficiaries).

[910] *See generally* 4 Scott & Ascher §24.31 (Liability for Incorrect Distributions).

[911] *See generally* Bogert §973 (Settlor's Control Over Duty to Account).

[912] UTC §813(c) (available at <http://www.uniformlaws.org/Act.aspx?title=Trust%20 Code>).

[913] UTC §103(12) (available at <http://www.uniformlaws.org/Act.aspx?title=Trust%20 Code>).

duty to give adequate notice to the nonqualified beneficiaries, either by giving actual notice to them or by giving notice to a duly-appointed guardian ad litem charged with representing their interests."

Laches and statutes of limitation. A beneficiary's claim against the trustee may be barred by principles arising in equity under the common law of trusts, *e.g.*, estoppel and laches.[914] The Uniform Trust Code establishes two limitation periods: a one-year period for the beneficiary who has received notice of a potential claim for breach of trust[915] and a five-year period for the beneficiary who has not.[916] A beneficiary may not commence a proceeding against a trustee for breach of trust more than one year after the date the beneficiary or a representative of the beneficiary was sent a report that adequately disclosed the existence of a potential claim for breach of trust and informed the beneficiary of the time allowed for commencing a proceeding.[917] Otherwise, a judicial proceeding by a beneficiary against a trustee for breach of trust must be commenced within five years after the first to occur of (1) the removal, resignation, or death of the trustee; (2) the termination of the beneficiary's interests in the trust; or (3) the termination of the trust.[918] Thus, under the Uniform Trust Code it is conceivable that a trustee could achieve finality without ever having rendered an accounting to the beneficiaries.[919] This is a radical departure from long-standing common law fiduciary principles.

Note, however, that the Uniform Trust Code one-year statute of limitations does not begin to run against a beneficiary who has waived the furnishing of a report.[920] If the trustee wishes to foreclose possible claims immediately, he should endeavor to obtain a consent to the report from the beneficiaries and/or their representatives.[921]

In Florida, an action against a trustee for breach of trust must be brought by a beneficiary within six months after the beneficiary receives from the trustee two items, an accounting (or other report) that "adequately discloses the matter" and a so-called limitation notice.[922] The six-month period begins to run once both items, which may be contained in a single document, have been received. The accounting or report adequately discloses a matter if it provides

---

[914] UTC §1005 cmt. (available at <http://www.uniformlaws.org/Act.aspx?title=Trust%20 Code>). *See generally* §7.1.3 of this handbook (discussing the equitable doctrines of laches and estoppel).

[915] UTC §1005(a) (available at <http://www.uniformlaws.org/Act.aspx?title=Trust%20 Code>).

[916] UTC §1005(c) (available at <http://www.uniformlaws.org/Act.aspx?title=Trust%20 Code>).

[917] UTC §1005(a) (available at <http://www.uniformlaws.org/Act.aspx?title=Trust%20 Code>).

[918] UTC §1005(c) (available at <http://www.uniformlaws.org/Act.aspx?title=Trust%20 Code>).

[919] *See generally* 4 Scott & Ascher §23.1.

[920] UTC §1005 cmt. (available at <http://www.uniformlaws.org/Act.aspx?title=Trust%20 Code>).

[921] UTC §1005 cmt. (available at <http://www.uniformlaws.org/Act.aspx?title=Trust%20 Code>).

[922] Fla. Stat. §737.307.

sufficient information so that a beneficiary knows of a claim or reasonably should have inquired into the existence of a claim with respect to that matter.[923] The following communication would satisfy the limitation notice requirement:

> An action for breach of trust based on matters disclosed in a trust accounting or other written report of the trustee may be subject to a 6-month statute of limitations from the receipt of the trust accounting or other written report. If you have questions, please consult your attorney.[924]

Under the Uniform Trust Code, if a cotrustee remains in office, a trustee who has resigned or been removed need not submit a final accounting or trustee's report.[925]

Tax filings. The trustee's duty to periodically render accountings to the beneficiaries should not be confused with the trustee's tax filing obligations.[926] For example, "[t]he determination of whether a trust is terminated for tax purposes generally depends upon whether the property held in trust has been distributed to the persons entitled to succeed to the property upon termination of the trust rather than upon the technicality of whether the trustee has rendered a final accounting."[927] While in general, a taxpayer's taxable year is the annual accounting period that it uses to keep its books, which may be a calendar year or a fiscal year, all trusts, other than charitable and tax-exempt trusts, must adopt or change to a calendar taxable year.[928] In the case of domestic trusts, returns are due on or before the fifteenth day of the fourth month following the close of the taxable year.[929] Foreign trusts are generally not required to file before the fifteenth day of the sixth month following the close of the taxable year.[930]

Liability of the trustee who fails to account. The trustee who fails to properly account to the beneficiary may be held personally liable for any harm to the beneficiary's equitable interests that is directly or indirectly attributable to that failure. This is a topic that is taken up in Section 8.24 of this handbook.

Burdens of proof. In the case of a failure on the part of the trustee to properly account, all doubts are resolved against the trustee and in the beneficiary's favor. This is a topic that is taken up in Section 8.24 of this handbook.

---

[923] Fla. Stat. §737.307(2).

[924] Fla. Stat. §737.307(3)(b).

[925] UTC §707 cmt. (available at <http://www.uniformlaws.org/Act.aspx?title=Trust%20 Code>).

[926] *See generally* Chapter 10 of this handbook (the income taxation of trusts).

[927] Polito, 574 T.M., Accounting Periods A-46 (1997).

[928] Polito, 574 T.M., Accounting Periods A-2, A-21 (1997).

[929] Polito, 574 T.M., Accounting Periods A-40 (1997).

[930] Polito, 574 T.M., Accounting Periods A-40 (1997).

§6.2   Specific Duties Incident to General Duties

The trustee has myriad duties that are offshoots of the general duties to be prudent, to carry out the terms of the trust, to be loyal to the trust, to give personal attention, and to account.[1] Some particular duties are offshoots of other particular duties. The duty to follow the Prudent Man Rule, for example, is not only an offshoot of the general duty to be prudent but also of the specific duty to protect the trust property, the specific duty to make the trust property productive, and the specific duty to balance the interests of income beneficiaries and remaindermen.

§6.2.1   Duty to Take Active Control of, Segregate, Earmark, Preserve, and Protect Trust Property

The trustee is under a duty to use proper care to prevent theft of the subject matter of the trust and to prevent damage from the unlawful acts of third persons. . . . When it is possible to take steps necessary to preserve the trust property, it is his duty to take such steps.[2]

The trustee's duty to identify, take active control of, segregate, earmark, and protect the trust property is implicit in all the trustee's general duties. If the trust is to do its job, the trust property must be kept safe.

§6.2.1.1   Duty to Identify and Take Active Control of Trust Property

In Ex parte Ogle, a debtor assigned his property to the defendant, a trustee for his creditors. Among the trust property was a quantity of wine and spirits that the trustee permitted to remain in the possession of the debtor, who drank most of it. The court held that the trustee was liable to the creditors.[3]

It is axiomatic that a new trustee should forthwith ascertain what property is, or is to be, the subject of the trust.[4] Having identified and located the property, the trustee must take reasonable steps to take control of it,[5] or face the prospect of liability for any loss incurred due to delay or inaction, *e.g.*, any loss occasioned by the failure to cash a check before the settlor-drawer stops payment or dies.[6] Or in the case of a testamentary trust, "[i]f the trustee does not

---

§6.2   [1] *See* §6.1 of this handbook (the trustee's general duties).

[2] 2A Scott on Trusts §176.

[3] 3 Scott & Ascher §17.7 (referring to *Ex parte* Ogle, L.R. 8 Ch. App. 711 (1873) (England)).

[4] Lewin ¶ 12-50 (England).

[5] *See generally* Restatement (Second) of Trusts §175. *See also* UTC §809 (available at <http://www.uniformlaws.org/Act.aspx?title=Trust%20Code>); 3 Scott & Ascher §17.7.

[6] 1 Scott & Ascher §10.11.3.

within a reasonable time take such steps as are prudent . . . [to take control] . . . , and the executor absconds with the trust property, the trustee may be liable for the loss."[7] The English cases are in accord.[8] Disclaiming is generally not an option, except in the rarest of cases when taking a particular item of property into the trust would run counter to the beneficiaries' interests or the trust's purposes.[9]

This duty to collect[10] encompasses redressing breaches of trust by predecessor fiduciaries,[11] such as executors of pour-over wills[12] and predecessor trustees,[13] and may even entail the trustee's suing an executor personally for the amounts the executor overpaid in inheritance taxes.[14] The trustee is deemed to know about a predecessor's breach if he has actual knowledge of it; has received a notice or notification of it; or from all the facts and circumstances known to the trustee, has reason to know it.[15]

The trustee of an irrevocable trust has an affirmative duty to take reasonable steps to locate all life insurance contracts of which the trustee is a vested third-party beneficiary. MIB Solutions, Inc. has a well-regarded policy locator service.[16] The duty to take control of trust property, an aspect of the trustee's duty of prudent administration, would include bringing suit against an insurance company that refuses to pay what is due the trust under an insurance contract. The trustee, however, has no obligation personally to fund remedial litigation[17] or litigation to collect insurance proceeds unless indemnified by the trust beneficiaries, although there may be an affirmative duty to solicit their voluntary indemnity.[18]

Accordingly, if the trust estate is inadequate to fund the litigation, the trustee should send to the beneficiaries a formal written request for indemnification.[19] If the request is denied, the trustee should so inform the court having jurisdiction over the trust and seek its guidance. If some beneficiaries agree to assume the litigation costs and others do not, those beneficiaries who do are

---

[7] 3 Scott & Ascher §17.7.

[8] Lewin ¶ 34-02 through ¶ 34-22 (England).

[9] Restatement (Third) of Trusts §86 cmt. f.

[10] Restatement (Third) of Trusts §76(b).

[11] *See* Restatement (Second) of Trusts §223(2)(a); 2A Scott on Trusts §177; Bogert §583. *See, e.g.*, Peterson v. McMahon, 99 P.3d 594 (2004) (an action for breach of fiduciary duty brought by a successor trustee against a predecessor trustee).

[12] *See, e.g.*, Pepper v. Zions First Nat'l Bank, N.A., 801 P.2d 144 (Utah 1990). *See generally* 3 Scott & Ascher §17.7.

[13] *See generally* 4 Scott & Ascher §22.6.1.

[14] *See, e.g.*, In re First Nat'l Bank of Mansfield, 37 Ohio St. 2d 60, 307 N.E.2d 23, 24 (1974) (involving a nonrefundable overpayment by the executor of state inheritance taxes).

[15] *See generally* UTC §812 (available at <http://www.uniformlaws.org/Act.aspx?title=Trust%20Code>) (collecting trust property); UTC §104 (knowledge).

[16] Visit <http://www.policylocator.com/estate/>.

[17] Lewin ¶ 21-50 (England); 4 Scott & Ascher §22.1.1 (U.S.). *See also* 4 Scott & Ascher §22.6.1 (When Trust Estate Has Already Been Conveyed).

[18] Restatement (Third) of Trusts §76 cmt. d. *See generally* Bogert §582; 3 Scott & Ascher §17.8; 2A Scott on Trusts §175.

[19] *See generally* 4 Scott & Ascher §22.6.1

entitled to reimbursement from the trust estate in the event the litigation is successful. Litigation costs should be equitably apportioned.

The trustee takes control of the trust property by re-registration, through agents, or by acquiring physical possession, as appropriate.[20] For example, it is now a standard practice of mutual funds to evidence ownership by means of the computer-generated account statement rather than a paper certificate. Re-registration would therefore be enough. On the other hand, with respect to closely held corporations where paper certificates remain the standard means of evidencing ownership, physical possession would be required as well.[21] Much will depend on the terms of the trust. "For example, the settlor may provide that the spouse may occupy the settlor's former residence rent-free, in which event the spouse's occupancy would prevent the trustee from taking possession."[22]

The failure to re-register securities can have unfortunate practical consequences, particularly when it comes to declarations of trust. A declaration of trust is a trust in which the same person is both settlor and trustee. If securities held in a declaration of trust are not re-registered in a way that discloses that they are the subject of a trust, then upon the death of the settlor, the settlor's personal representative and the designated successor trustee each may have a fiduciary duty to attempt to prevent the other from taking title to and control of the securities.

While the absence of a paper trail clearly evidencing to third parties, *e.g.*, transfer agents *and/or beneficiaries*, the settlor's intent to impress a trust upon the securities does not necessarily mean that the requisite intent was lacking, it doesn't help the successor trustee's case.[23] So that there can be no doubt as to who should take title to and control of the securities upon the settlor's death, the settlor-trustee should have them re-registered in a way that discloses that they are the subject of a trust. As title to trust property is in the trustee, the securities should be re-registered in the name of the trustee, *e.g.*, "John Jones, Trustee of the XYZ Trust." They should not be re-registered merely in the name of the trust.

When the trust estate includes contractual rights that were created in a noncommercial setting, such as an unsecured personal IOU of someone to whom the settlor has loaned money, formal registration with a third party may not be a practical option. At the time when the IOU became an asset of the trust estate, therefore, the trustee had a duty to inform the obligor (the one who owes the money) of the existence of the trust and to make arrangements for receiving on behalf of the trust payments of income and principal.[24] If a parcel of land was subject to a lease at the time it was transferred to the trustee, the trustee had a

---

[20] *See generally* Bogert §583; 2A Scott on Trusts §175. *See also* UTC §809 cmt. (available at <http://www.uniformlaws.org/Act.aspx?title=Trust%20Code>).

[21] *See generally* Bogert §583; 2A Scott on Trusts §175.

[22] UTC §809 cmt. (available at <http://www.uniformlaws.org/Act.aspx?title=Trust%20 Code>).

[23] Restatement (Third) of Trusts §14 cmt. c.

[24] Restatement (Third) of Trusts §76 cmt. d.

duty to inform the lessee of the existence of the trust and to direct the lessee to pay the rent to the trustee.[25]

§6.2.1.2   Duty to Segregate and Earmark Trust Property (Duty Not to Commingle)

The animals were known also by their earmarks, the specific notch an owner had carved in their ears. The earmarks always resembled something else: a swallow's tail, a half-moon, a penny. For example, on February 29, 1659, Walter listed his horse in the Animal Book, a bay gelding . . . For a marking, Walter chose a short horizontal line curving into a vertical cut that lopped off the bottom third of the ear—Sarah Messer, Red House ("being a most accurate account of New England's oldest continuously lived-in house").[26]

The terms of a trust may permit trust property to be mingled or jointly held with the trustee's own property . . . This, however, does not relieve the trustee of the duty to earmark if and as feasible; thus, the duty recognizes that, for example, in the matter of earmarking property that a trustee holds both personally and in trust, a herd of cattle on the family farm presents a more difficult problem than does the farm itself—Restatement (Third) of Trusts.[27]

Introduction. It is the duty of the trustee to earmark the trust property and to keep it separate from the trustee's own property and from other property not subject to the trust (including funds of different trusts).[28] Unless authorized by statute, decision, or the governing instrument, the trustee should not commingle. "This rule is designed to protect the trustee from temptation, from the hazard of loss, and of being a possible defaulter, as well as to protect the trust fund . . . [itself]. . . ."[29] Here is just one of an infinite number of examples of what can go wrong where there has been a failure to earmark on the part of a trustee: " . . . [I]f a third person lends money to the trustee personally; and, subsequently, the trustee lends trust funds to the same person, who has no notice that the borrowed funds are trust funds, the third person can set off the two claims."[30] The corporate trustee whose internal division of labor makes it prone to incidents of institutional memory loss should take particular heed, particularly when the situation is exacerbated by a high rate of personnel turnover.

---

[25] Restatement (Third) of Trusts §76 cmt. d.

[26] Sarah Messer, Red House 48 (2004).

[27] Restatement (Third) of Trusts §84 cmt. e.

[28] UTC §810(b) (available at <http://www.uniformlaws.org/Act.aspx?title=Trust%20Code>). *See generally* Restatement (Third) of Trusts §84; Restatement (Second) of Trusts §179; 3 Scott & Ascher §§17.11.1 (Duty Not to Mingle Trust Property with Trustee's Own Property), 17.11.2 (Duty Not to Mingle Funds of Separate Trusts); 2A Scott on Trusts §179.3; Bogert §596. *See also* §8.15.11 of this handbook (rule in Clayton's case) (addressing who is entitled to what when withdrawals are made from an account containing funds that have been wrongfully commingled); 12 C.F.R. §9.13(b) (1997) (Revised Reg. 9) (available at <www.gpoaccess.gov/cfr/index.html>) (providing that a national bank shall keep the assets of fiduciary accounts separate from the assets of the bank); §8.18 of this handbook (Regulation 9 revised).

[29] In re Hodges' Estate, 66 Vt. 70, 28 A. 663, 664 (1894).

[30] 5 Scott & Ascher §30.3 (Set-Off of Claim of Third Person Against Trustee). *See generally* §8.15.63 of this handbook (doctrine of bona fide purchase; the BFP).

Breaches of trust attributable to the internal management structures of corporate trustees are fast becoming the bread and butter of trust litigators.[31]

Dematerialization and the trustee's duty to earmark. The law of trusts has had little choice but to adapt to the dematerialization phenomenon, *i.e.,* to the reality that electronic record-keeping is causing paper certificates to go the way of carbon copies.[32] If the Depository Trust & Clearing Corporation (DTCC) has its way, the SEC sooner rather than later will effectively outlaw altogether the issuance of paper certificates by companies subject to its regulation.[33] How the law can keep alive the spirit of the traditional proscription against fiduciary commingling and still adapt to dematerialization's operational realities is an implicit theme of this section.

Commingling trustee's personal assets with trust assets. The Restatement (Third) of Trusts endorses a strict application of the rule against commingling trust property with the trustee's own as incident to the trustee's duty of loyalty, specifically the trustee's duty not to create potentially conflicting interests.[34] "Particular concern exists when commingling (or lack of identification) might make misconduct or abuses difficult to detect."[35]

Commingling the trust funds with funds belonging to the individual trustee generally is held to be a breach of trust.[36] Many states have statutes covering such activity, which is a *criminal act* in some states.[37] "An exception is recognized, however, when a commingling results from . . . the settlor's creation of a trust to hold an undivided interest in property in which an undivided interest also is given or already belongs to the trustee personally, or is given or already held by the trustee as property of another trust in which the trustee in

---

[31] *See generally* §6.2.11 of this handbook (duty of institutional trustee to have an effective organizational structure).

[32] *See* Richard R. Stanley, *Global Custody Operations of Banks,* 114 Banking L.J. 418, 423 (1997) (noting that modern trend is to use the electronic medium instead of paper certificates). The process of using electronic data entry in lieu of paper certificates is known as "dematerialization." *See* Richard R. Stanley, *Global Custody Operations of Banks,* 114 Banking L.J. 418, 423 (1997). *See also* Group of 30, Clearance and Settlement Systems in the World's Securities Markets (1988) (recommending a worldwide move to "dematerialize" securities); Peers, *Paperless Wall Street,* Wall St. J., June 7, 1994, at C1.

[33] *See* Matt Jarzemsky, *End Looming for Paper Certificates,* Wall St. J., Mar. 13, 2013, at C3.

[34] Restatement (Third) of Trusts §84 cmt. b. *See also* Restatement (Second) of Trusts §179 cmt. b (trustee's duty not to mingle trust funds with his own).

[35] Restatement (Third) of Trusts §84 cmt. b. The Restatement (Third) of Trusts looks askance at the "no harm no foul" approach to a trustee's failure to earmark which was taken by the court in Miller v. Pender, 93 N.H. 1, 34 A.2d 663 (1943) (the court failing to assign liability in an absence of a demonstrated causal connection between the loss suffered by the trust and the trustee's failure to earmark), the Restatement "recognizing the mismatch between relatively sophisticated trustees in control of records and the time lag suffered by often unsophisticated beneficiaries, a matter of concern when some investments succeed while others fail and it becomes necessary to determine who owns what." Restatement (Third) of Trusts §84, Reporter's Notes to Comments b and c.

[36] *See generally* Restatement (Third) of Trusts §84 cmt. b; Restatement (Second) of Trusts §§179 cmt. d, 205 cmt. f; Bogert §§596, 707; 3 Scott & Ascher §17.11.1.

[37] *See* 3 Scott & Ascher §17.11.1 n.4 and 2A Scott on Trusts §179.1 n.5 for citations to state statutes criminalizing the commingling of trust funds.

beneficially interested."[38] Even when commingling is not a *per se* breach of trust, the trustee who commingles nevertheless invites full personal responsibility if anything goes wrong as a result,[39] such as the trust property falling into the hands of a BFP,[40] the trustee's personal creditors,[41] or the trustee's executor. In Section 7.2.3.2 of this handbook, we consider whether a trustee's failure to earmark, in and of itself, will warrant an assessment of equitable damages against the trustee personally.

Incremental additions to a trust fund. Additions to a trust fund, whether by the settlor or others, ought to be permissible as not the type of commingling contemplated by the prohibition.[42] Management of additions as separate trusts seems unnecessary and in most cases not in the economic interest of the beneficiaries. However, there may be a tax consideration or a creditor-protection consideration that warrants having additions to a trust segregated. And there is the rare case where the transferor actually intended to create a new trust with the addition.[43] When there is, the trustee should obtain a written opinion of counsel explaining why the additions should be administered as separate trusts notwithstanding the administrative costs. The legal opinion should then be affixed to the governing instrument.

Earmarking. The trustee should deposit trust funds only in a properly identified trust account.[44] "Thus, it is improper for a trustee to deposit money of the trust in the trustee's personal account in a bank, even if the trustee maintains records continuously and carefully showing the trust's interest in the account."[45] If the deposit is made in the individual name of the trustee, however, the trustee will be treated as a guarantor of the solvency of the bank even though due care was used in the choice of the bank and the funds were not

---

[38] Restatement (Third) of Trusts §84 cmt. b.

[39] *See, e.g.,* Kirby v. Frank, 132 N.J. Eq. 378, 28 A.2d 267 (1942) (a trustee is held strictly accountable when he commingles trust funds with those of his own, and any doubt will be resolved against him). *But see* Miller v. Pender, 98 N.H. 1, 34 A.2d 663 (1943) (the court requiring a demonstrated causal connection between the loss to the trust and the trustee's failure to earmark).

[40] *See generally* §5.4.2 of this handbook (rights of the beneficiary as against BFPs and other transferees, of the trust property); 3 Scott & Ascher §17.11.3.

[41] *See generally* 3 Scott & Ascher §17.11.1.

[42] *See* 3 Scott & Ascher §17.11.2 (Duty Not to Mingle Funds of Separate Trusts); 2A Scott on Trusts §179.2; Smith v. Shanahan, 314 Mass. 329, 335, 50 N.E.2d 397, 400 (1943) ("The futility of having two or more parallel trusts in the hands of the same trustee to accomplish the same objects in the same way is plainly apparent").

[43] *See generally* 3 Scott & Ascher §17.11.2.

[44] UTC §810(c) (available at <http://www.uniformlaws.org/Act.aspx?title=Trust%20 Code>) (providing that a trustee shall cause the trust property to be designated so that the interest of the trust, to the extent feasible, appears in records maintained by a party other than a trustee or beneficiary). *See generally* Bogert §598; Restatement (Second) of Trusts §180; ACTEC Practice Committee, Fiduciary Matters Subcommittee, *Guide for ACTEC Fellows Serving as Trustees*, 26 ACTEC Notes 313, 317 (advising that the trustee should maintain a separate bank checking account for each trust, to be the trust's repository of receipts, such as dividends and the proceeds of security sales, and as the source for funds drawn by the trustee in checks remitted to the beneficiaries and for the purchase of new investments).

[45] Restatement (Third) of Trusts §84 cmt. b. *See also* Restatement (Second) of Trusts §179 cmt. b. *See generally* 3 Scott & Ascher §17.12.2 (Deposit in Personal Account).

in any way misused.[46] One learned commentator, however, has suggested that the rule is perhaps a bit too hard and fast and may not even reflect the current state of the law:

> This, however, seems completely unfair; the loss was entirely due to the bank's failure and had nothing to do with the commingling. Fortunately, the more recent authority suggests that, when the trustee improperly mingles trust property with the trustee's own, the trustee is not liable for losses that are not the result of the commingling, particularly when the trustee has been essentially honest.[47]

In any case, upon accepting a trusteeship, the trustee should open a checking account in the individual name of the trustee, but with the express qualification that it is as trustee of the particular trust. Going forward, the trustee should then run trust cash through that account, not through his personal account. The designation and qualification of the trust account should be along the lines of the following: "John Jones, Trustee of the ABC Trust."[48] It would not be advisable, appropriate, or customary for the account to be opened in the name of "the trust." Remember, title to the trust property is in the trustee. Under classic principles of trust law, the trust is not a legal entity as is corporation. The Restatement (Third) of Trusts is generally in accord.[49]

"It is arguable that a trustee ought not to invest in bonds or other securities that are payable to bearer, because they are not, and cannot be, properly earmarked."[50] Having said that, all negotiable securities, and even partially negotiable securities such as registered coupon bonds, should be deposited in a safe deposit vault.[51] If that is inconvenient, they should be kept in a separate strongbox and properly identified as trust property. Trust securities ought not

---

[46] *See generally* 2A Scott on Trusts §180.2; Bogert §§596, 598. *But see* 3 Scott & Ascher §17.11.1.

[47] 3 Scott & Ascher §17.11.1. *See also* 3 Scott & Ascher §17.12.2 ("Thus, as in these other sorts of . . . [earmark] . . . cases, we believe that absolute liability is inappropriate"). It should be noted here that the author of this handbook does not share the commentator's view that absolute liability is inappropriate in cases where entrusted cash is deposited in the personal bank accounts of trustees. It is suggested that replacing absolute liability with some kind of good-faith facts-and-circumstances test is not in the public interest, or in the long-term interest of the institution of the trust, particularly considering how easy and cost-effective sub-accounting has become operationally. There is now a wide variety of commercial sub-accounting programs, both off-the-shelf and offered by financial services institutions, from which the amateur as well as the professional trustee may choose.

[48] *See* Restatement (Second) of Trusts §179 cmt. d ("It should be taken in the name of the trustee as 'trustee under the will of' the settlor, or 'as trustee under a certain deed of trust' or 'as trustee for' certain beneficiaries").

[49] Restatement (Third) of Trusts §84 cmt. d. *See also* Restatement (Second) of Trusts §179 cmt. d.

[50] 3 Scott & Ascher §17.11.3; *but see* Restatement (Second) of Trusts §179 cmt. d ("If a bond is otherwise a proper trust investment, however, the mere fact that it is payable to bearer does not render it an improper trust investment, unless the terms of the trust prohibit holding securities payable to bearer; but the trustee should keep records showing that the bond is held by him as trustee").

[51] *See generally* Bogert §598.

be kept in the trustee's personal safe deposit box even if they are in a separate envelope. The particular danger to be avoided here is the commingling of assets of the trust estate with the trustee's own property.[52] Segregation and earmarking facilitate identification of trust property should a trustee die in office, deter a trustee from using funds for personal benefit,[53] and facilitate an equitable enforcement action by beneficiaries or creditors against a trustee who is uncooperative, disloyal, or insolvent.[54] When neither earmarking nor vault storage is feasible, as would be the case with certain items of tangible personal property, *e.g.*, furniture, "the trustee must maintain records clearly reflecting that the property belongs to the trust."[55] It goes without saying that the trustee must keep trust furniture and other such items physically separate from property belonging to the trustee personally. "As to all of these kinds of property, earmarking in the conventional sense is either impossible or impracticable."[56] Thus good record keeping is critical,[57] if only because any doubts will be resolved against the trustee.[58]

Commingling the assets of multiple trusts established under one instrument or different instruments. The Uniform Prudent Management of Institutional Funds Act (UPMIFA) expressly authorizes an institution to pool two or more institutional funds for purposes of management and investment.[59] Ordinarily, however, the default duty of a trustee is not to mingle property held upon one trust with property held upon another trust, whether the two or more trusts are created by the same or different settlors.[60] More often than not, a single trust instrument will provide for the creation of more than one trust.[61]

The common fund. A single discretionary trust, for example, might be established at the outset under the terms of the instrument, and there might then be a provision for the trust to divide into separate trust shares at some future time, perhaps when no child of the settlor is both alive and under the age of 21. It is likely that the terms of the trust would then authorize the trustee to manage the properties of the various separate trust shares as a common

---

[52] *See* Bogert §596 (providing the following reasons for the duty to earmark: (1) to facilitate identification of trust property were the trustee to die in office; (2) to deter a trustee from using trust funds for personal benefit; (3) to facilitate an equitable enforcement action by beneficiaries or creditors against a trustee who is uncooperative, disloyal, or insolvent). *See also* UTC §810(a) (available at <http://www.uniformlaws.org/Act.aspx?title=Trust%20Code>) (providing that a trustee shall keep trust property separate from the trustee's own property).

[53] *See* 3 Scott & Ascher §17.11.3 (a failure to earmark could tempt the trustee "to contend that the investments that prove profitable are the trustee's own, while those that prove unprofitable are the trust's").

[54] *See generally* Bogert §596.

[55] Restatement (Third) of Trusts §84 cmt. d(2). *See generally* 3 Scott & Ascher §17.11.3.

[56] 3 Scott & Ascher §17.11.3.

[57] *See generally* 3 Scott & Ascher §17.11.3.

[58] *See generally* §6.2.9 of this handbook (trustee's duty to keep precise, complete and accurate records).

[59] The Unif. Prudent Management of Inst. Funds Act §3(d).

[60] Restatement (Third) of Trusts §84 cmt. c. *See generally* 3 Scott & Ascher §17.11.2 (Duty Not to Mingle Funds of Separate Trusts).

[61] *See generally* 3 Scott & Ascher §17.11.2.

fund[62]—not to be confused of course with a common trust fund[63]—in order to reduce the administrative costs of running separate trusts. The Uniform Trust Code would make it default law that a trustee may invest as a whole the property of two or more separate trusts, provided the trustee maintains records clearly indicating the respective interests.[64] The Restatement (Third) of Trusts is generally in accord.[65] It is already default law that a corporate trustee may deposit cash held in its various trusts in a single bank account in its own name as trustee, provided there is adequate sub-accounting.[66] For more on the common fund concept, the reader is referred to 3.5.3.2(d) of this handbook.

The practical downside, however, to the common fund is this: The effectiveness of the trustee's defense against an allegation of breach of trust may depend upon the faithful and productive management of each of the individual trust shares. Thus managing separate trusts as a common fund might cause a problem involving only one trust to spread throughout the instrument's entire system of trusts.[67]

The common trust fund. Over the years, it has become apparent that it is in the economic interest of trustees and beneficiaries alike to permit some commingling.[68] Legislatures and courts from time to time have responded by relaxing somewhat the general prohibition against commingling.[69] The practice of corporate trustees investing in mortgage participations predates the Great Depression.[70] A post-Depression example of this relaxation is the *common trust fund*, a bank-sponsored mutual fund-like investment vehicle available only to the bank's fiduciary accounts.[71] The now ubiquitous proprietary mutual fund is a relative newcomer.[72]

The common trust fund was a response to a general concern that a small trust estate offers little possibility of diversification or of yield and would be better off commingled with other trust estates similarly situated.[73] The concept of the

---

[62] *See generally* 3 Scott & Ascher §17.11.2; 2A Scott on Trusts §179.2; Maxwell, Comment, *Statutory Procedures for the Combination or Division of Trusts,* 21 Real Prop. Prob. & Tr. J. 561 (1986).

[63] *See generally* Bogert §677; 3 Scott on Trusts §227.9; §9.7.1 of this handbook (the common trust fund and the proprietary mutual fund).

[64] UTC §810(d) (available at <http://www.uniformlaws.org/Act.aspx?title=Trust%20 Code>). *See generally* 3 Scott & Ascher §17.11.2.

[65] Restatement (Third) of Trusts §84 cmt. c. *See generally* 3 Scott & Ascher §17.11.2.

[66] *See generally* 3 Scott & Ascher §17.11.2.

[67] A problem in a common trust fund can also spill over to its participating trusts. *See* First Ala. Bank of Montgomery, NA. v. Martin, 425 So. 2d 415 (Ala. 1982) (involving a class action against a bank trustee for making imprudent investments in two common trust funds whose participation units were held in 1,250 individual trusts).

[68] *See generally* Bogert §677; Restatement (Second) of Trusts §179 cmt. e.

[69] *See generally* Bogert §677.

[70] *See generally* 3 Scott & Ascher §17.11.3; 4 Scott & Ascher §19.1.9.

[71] *See generally* Bogert §677; 4 Scott & Ascher §19.1.9; Restatement (Second) of Trusts §227 cmt. k (common trust funds).

[72] *See generally* 3 Scott & Ascher §17.11.2; 4 Scott & Ascher §19.1.10. *See generally* §9.7.1 of this handbook (the common trust fund and the proprietary mutual fund).

[73] *See generally* Bogert §677; Restatement (Second) of Trusts §227 cmt. k (common trust funds).

common trust fund was floated in the early part of the twentieth century.[74] As time went on, many states were prepared through legislation to exempt the arrangement from the common law prohibition against commingling.[75] Aside from the segregation issue, however, there was the issue of whether a common trust fund would be deemed an association for federal income tax purposes.[76] Beginning in 1936 the tax roadblock was removed: The Federal Revenue Act of 1936 (now Section 584 of the 1986 Code) allows a pass-through of the income tax liability to the participating trusts.[77] Until relatively recently, thousands of common trust funds were administered by hundreds of banks across the country.[78] Today, however, the proprietary mutual fund would appear to be on the road to becoming the preferred commingled investment vehicle for corporate fiduciaries.[79]

The Internal Revenue Code defines a common trust fund as a fund maintained by a bank exclusively for the collective investment and reinvestment of monies contributed thereto by the bank in its capacity as a trustee, executor, administrator, or guardian and in conformity with federal rules and regulations.[80] The Comptroller of the Currency regulates national banks in the exercise of their trust powers.[81] This includes the administration of their common trust funds.[82] The compilation of the regulations applicable to the fiduciary activities of national banks is known in the trade as "Regulation 9" or simply "Reg. 9."[83] As no common trust fund gains the Section 584 income tax advantage unless it conforms to the requirements of federal law, common trust funds administered by state banks, as a practical matter, must also comply with Reg. 9's provisions with respect to common trust funds.[84]

The common trust fund itself is a trust with its own governing instrument.[85] Its trustee is a bank, and can only be a bank.[86] When the bank's own trust accounts—its fiduciary customers if you will—invest or participate in the common trust fund, funds from a number of trusts come together.[87] The

---

[74] *See* Bogert §677.

[75] Bogert §677; Restatement (Second) of Trusts §227 cmt. k (common trust funds).

[76] *See* Brooklyn Trust Co. v. Comm'r, 80 F.2d 865 (2d Cir. 1936), *cert. denied*, 298 U.S. 659 (1936) (holding that a common trust fund was essentially conducting an investment business for profit, and thus, is "taxable as an association").

[77] *See generally* Bogert §261.

[78] *See* Bogert §677 n.34.

[79] *See generally* §9.7.1 of this handbook (the common trust fund and the proprietary mutual fund).

[80] *See* 3 Scott on Trusts §227.9.

[81] *See* Revised Reg. 9 (12 C.F.R. Part 9) (effective Jan. 29, 1997) (available at <www.gpoaccess.gov/cfr/index.html>).

[82] *See* Bogert §§677, 270.25.

[83] *See generally* Bogert §134; 2 Scott on Trusts §96.5.

[84] *See generally* Bogert §677.

[85] *See* 12 C.F.R. §9.18(b)(1) (Revised Reg. 9) (effective Jan. 29, 1997) (available at <www.gpoaccess.gov/cfr/index.html>).

[86] *See* Bogert §677; Restatement (Second) of Trusts §227 cmt. k (common trust funds).

[87] Restatement (Second) of Trusts §227 cmt. k (common trust funds).

resulting commingling would place the bank, as trustee of the various participating trusts, in breach of its duty to segregate were it not entitled to the statutory common trust fund exemption.[88]

Taking title in the name of a third person. The duty to earmark is implicated not only when the trustee takes title to trust property in his own name without disclosing the existence of the trust, but also when he takes title in the name of a third person, "regardless of whether there is disclosure of the existence of the trust."[89] Over the years, the cost somewhat the common law duty to earmark.[90] The practice of holding certificates in bulk with book entry,[91] in special purpose depository institutions,[92] in the name of nominees,[93] and in street name has been the result.[94] "Many states have statutes that permit a trustee to deposit with a federal reserve bank securities guaranteed by the United States."[95] With the exception of bank deposits and street name registration, the traditional proscription against the commingling of trust property with the personal assets of the trustee or the nominee remains largely intact.[96] "What is important in the matter of earmarking is that, to the extent feasible, the property is shown to be property of the trust in records maintained by and within the control of a party other than the trustee or beneficiary,"[97] and that the property not be commingled with the third party's own assets.

The trustee, however, should exercise due diligence before placing trust property in "street name" with a broker.[98] Due diligence would entail an

---

[88] Restatement (Second) of Trusts §227 cmt. k (common trust funds).

[89] 3 Scott & Ascher §17.11.4.

[90] *See* Bogert §596. *See also* Restatement (Second) of Trusts §179 cmt. e (taking title in the name of a third person).

[91] *See generally* 3 Scott & Ascher §17.11.4.

[92] *See generally* 3 Scott & Ascher §17.11.4.

[93] *See also* UTC §810 cmt. (available at <http://www.uniformlaws.org/Act.aspx?title=Trust %20Code>) (suggesting that "[w]hile securities held in nominee form are not specifically registered in the name of the trustee, they are properly earmarked because the trustee's holdings are indicated in the records maintained by an independent party, such as in an account at a brokerage firm"). The Restatement (Third) of Trusts is generally in accord. *See* Restatement (Third) of Trusts §84 cmt. d(1). For a list of citations to state statutes regarding fiduciary registration of securities in the name of a nominee, *see* 3 Scott & Ascher §17.11.4. n.7. *See also* Restatement (Second) of Trusts §325 cmt. e (use of nominees).

[94] *See generally* 1 Whitney, Trust Department Administration and Operations §3.01[11] (1995). *See also* §3.5.3.2(e) of this handbook (the power to hold the trust property in the name of a third party or in the trustee's own name without disclosing the fiduciary relationship); ACTEC Practice Committee, Fiduciary Matters Subcommittee, 26 ACTEC Notes, 313, 317 (2001).

[95] 3 Scott & Ascher §17.11.4.

[96] *See* UTC §810(b) (available at <http://www.uniformlaws.org/Act.aspx?title=Trust%20 Code>) (providing that a trustee shall keep trust property separate from the trustee's own property).

[97] Restatement (Third) of Trusts §84 cmt. d.

[98] *See generally* In re Bevill, Bresler & Schulman, Inc., 59 B.R. 353, 374 (1986) ("Customers . . . who [leave] securities with a broker in street name or in negotiable form do not retain full property ownership of the securities in the event a SIPA liquidation proceeding is initiated against the broker. These customers are treated as preferred creditors entitled to receive a ratable share of

investigation of the broker's capitalization, as well as experience and track record rendering stock custody and transfer services.[99]

Mutual funds. When a trustee invests trust assets in mutual fund participations, he is commingling the assets of the trust with the assets of other investors in the mutual fund. While technically a breach of the duty not to commingle, this practice is acceptable, provided the trustee in so doing is not in breach of other fiduciary duties, *e.g.*, the duty of loyalty, the duty to give personal attention, the duty not to incur unreasonable costs, and the duty to prudently invest.

The "informal" pooled trust accounts of attorneys, collecting agents, auctioneers, and stockbrokers. The subject of the judicially mandated commingling of funds of law clients is addressed in Section 9.7.2 of this handbook (IOLTA trusts).[100] "Custom or the character of a trust" may also make it proper for a collection agent, auctioneer, and stockbroker to mingle the property of one trust with property of another trust in a single fiduciary account, provided meticulous records are kept of the pro rata equitable interests.[101] "In some situations of this type it may be unclear whether there is a trust or some other relationship, but in any event the amount on the deposit is not to be diminished by withdrawals or disbursements, or otherwise below the aggregate amount to which the clients or customers are entitled."[102]

---

customer property (plus an appropriate SIPIC allowance)."). *See generally* Mooney, *Beyond Negotiability: A New Model for Transfer and Pledge of Interests in Securities Controlled by Intermediaries,* 12 Cardozo L. Rev. 305 n.4 ("Street Name" generally refers to the practice of securities intermediaries' holding fungible bulks of securities in their own names, or that of their nominees, even though the securities may be beneficially owned by their customers); Don & Wang, *Stockbroker Liquidations Under the Securities Investor Protection Act and Their Impact on Securities Transfers,* 12 Cardozo L. Rev. 509 (1990); Kessler, *Investor Casualties in the War for Market Efficiency,* 9 Admin. L.J. Am. U. 1307 (1996); §3.5.3.2(e) of this handbook (the trustee's power to hold the trust property in the name of a third party or in the trustee's own name without disclosing the fiduciary relationship); ACTEC Practice Committee, Fiduciary Matters Subcommittee, *Guide for ACTEC Fellows Serving as Trustees,* 26 ACTEC Notes 313, 317 (2001) (suggesting that notwithstanding SIPIC insurance, the "general creditor consequence" can be "problematic" with brokerage firms that are smaller or not well capitalized and citing to "*Brokers' Legal Woes Can Strand Investors,*" Wall St. J., May 24, 2000, at C1).

[99] This may be easier said than done. After the recent collapse of MJK Clearing, Inc., SIPIC commissioned a study by Fitch Risk Management. One conclusion of the study was that current federal reporting regulations are not adequate to enable regulators, let alone customers, to assess the risks of doing business with a particular securities firm. *See* John R. Emshwiller, *A Trading Firm's Failure Lands Deutsche Bank in Court,* Wall St. J., May 2, 2003, at C1, col. 2.

[100] *See also* Restatement (Second) of Trusts §179 cmt. f ("In the case of informal trusts where the trustee holds the funds of numerous beneficiaries it may be proper to mingle the funds of all the beneficiaries. Thus, ordinarily an attorney, a collecting agent or auctioneer can properly deposit in a single trust account the funds of all his clients provided he keeps an accurate record of the contributions of the separate trusts").

[101] Restatement (Third) of Trusts §84 cmt. e. *See also* Restatement (Second) of Trusts §179 cmt. f.

[102] Restatement (Third) of Trusts §84 cmt. e. *See also* Restatement (Second) of Trusts §179 cmt. f.

§6.2.1.3 Duty to Protect and Preserve Trust Property; Duty to Enforce Claims; Duty to Defend Actions

To protect the beneficiary against excessive costs, the trustee should also be alert to adjusting compensation for functions that the trustee has delegated to others.[103]

If mutual fund firms ran gas stations, the fees would be posted in tiny letters on the bathroom ceiling.[104]

Introduction. Except for the rare case where abandonment of an item of trust property serves the interest of the beneficiaries and is in furtherance of the trust's purposes,[105] the trustee is under a duty to take all reasonable steps to protect[106] and preserve/conserve the trust property.[107] Indenture trustees are no exception.[108] The reasonable costs of doing so are a legitimate trust expense.[109] This duty is not delegable.[110] A necessary part of this general duty encompasses vigilant protection of the trust property against deterioration or loss.[111] The trustee could be liable, for example, if he permitted stock subscription rights to expire[112] or an entrusted life insurance contract to lapse due to premium nonpayment.[113] Tax penalties or obligations unreasonably incurred, *e.g.*, as a result of the trustee's negligence, are a personal expense of the trustee.[114] In order to avoid the underpayment or overpayment of capital

---

[103] UTC §805 cmt. (available at <http://www.uniformlaws.org/Act.aspx?title=Trust%20 Code>).

[104] Charles Stein, *Only Scandal in High Fees Is Ignorance*, Boston Globe, Dec. 14, 2003, at p. G5.

[105] *See* Restatement (Third) of Trusts §86 cmt. f.

[106] Restatement (Third) of Trusts §76(2)(b). *See, e.g.*, S. Leinberg & A. Gibbons, *Performing Due Diligence With Respect to Life Insurance Trusts Is Crucial*, 30 Estate Planning 748 (2003) (discussing the trustee's duty of due diligence when the trust is funded with contractual rights incident to a life insurance or annuity contract).

[107] *See* Bogert §582; 3 Scott and Ascher §§17.8, 18.1.2.1; 2A Scott on Trusts §176; Lewin ¶ 34-23 through ¶ 34-29 (England). *See also* UTC §809 (available at <http://www.uniformlaws.org/ Act.aspx?title=Trust%20Code>).

[108] Bogert §250, n.45. *See generally* §9.31 of this handbook (corporate trusts; trusts to secure creditors; the Trust Indenture Act of 1939; protecting bondholders).

[109] *See generally* §3.5.2.3 of this handbook (trustee's equitable right to exoneration and reimbursement from the trust estate); 3 Scott & Ascher §18.1.2.1 (Preservation of the Trust Property).

[110] *See generally* 2A Scott on Trusts §171.

[111] *See* Restatement (Second) of Trusts §176 cmts. b, c; 3 Scott & Ascher §17.8. *See also* United States v. White Mt. Apache Tribe, 537 U.S. 465, 475–476 (2003).

[112] *See* 3 Scott & Ascher §17.8; 2A Scott on Trusts §176 n.28 and accompanying text.

[113] *See, e.g.*, Rafert v. Meyer, 859 N.W.2d 332 (Neb. 2015). That having been said, it is generally the case that the trustee would have no duty to pay the premium with his personal funds.

[114] *See generally* 3 Scott & Ascher §18.1.2.6 (When Trustee Improperly Incurs Expense). *Cf.* McCormick v. Cox, 118 So. 3d 980, 38 Fla. L. Weekly D1723 (Fla. Dist. Ct. App. 2013) (the appellate court upholding a finding of the trial court that the trustee's negligent failure to correct the undervaluation of the trust's sole asset, a golf course, via an amended estate tax return

gains taxes, it is critical that the trustee keep proper track of the tax basis/cost of each item of trust property, a topic we take up in Section 11.1 of this handbook.

Unwarranted administrative costs. Administrative costs should be reasonable in relation to the trust property, the purposes of the trust, and the skills of the trustee.[115] "If a trustee incurs a greater expense that is reasonable, the trustee cannot charge the trust estate with the excess."[116] The costs of the trustee's unwarranted litigiousness, for example, are not reimbursable.[117] Creditors' claims should not be satisfied from trust assets unnecessarily.[118] Public policy dictates that the terms of a trust may go only so far in "relaxing" this general duty to preserve the trust property.[119] On the other hand, a trustee is not an insurer:

> A trustee has a duty to use reasonable care and skill to preserve the trust property. The applicable standard is that of a person of ordinary prudence. If the trust property is lost or destroyed or declines in value, the trustee is not subject to surcharge unless the trustee has failed to exercise reasonable care and skill.[120]

Below-market sales. A sale by a trustee of trust property to a third party for less than its market value[121] is not protecting the trust

---

necessitated a 1031 like-kind exchange transaction, at an additional cost to the trust of $2,146,812.00, so as to avoid "an immediate and adverse capital gain tax to the . . . trust and beneficiaries").

[115] UTC §805 (available at <http://www.uniformlaws.org/Act.aspx?title=Trust%20Code>). *Cf.* The Uniform Prudent Management of Institutional Funds Act §3(c)(1) (UPMIFA) (imposing on an institution a duty to incur only costs that are appropriate and reasonable).

[116] 3 Scott & Ascher §18.1.2.6 (When Trustee Improperly Incurs Expense). *See, e.g.,* McCormick v. Cox, 118 So. 3d 980, 982, 38 Fla. L. Weekly D1723 (Fla. Dist. Ct. App. 2013) (upholding a finding of the trial court that legal fees paid by the trustee to trust counsel's law firm were "substantially unreasonable and unsupported by the evidence"). The court also found that counsel having participated in the trustee's breach of trust must share the trustee's liability. *See generally* §7.2.9 of this handbook (trust counsel liability).

[117] *See generally* 3 Scott & Ascher §18.1.2.6 (When Trustee Improperly Incurs Expense).

[118] *See, e.g.,* Dobler v. Arluk Med. Ctr. Indus. Group, 107 Cal. Rptr. 2d 478 (Ct. App. 2001), *aff'd,* 11 Cal. Rptr. 3d 194 (Ct. App. 2004) (in which a trustee of a revocable trust successfully avoided having to satisfy from trust assets the claims of the postmortem creditors of the deceased settlor by transferring assets to the trust beneficiaries before the claims were reduced to judgment). *See generally* 3 Scott & Ascher §17.10 (Duty to Defend Actions).

[119] 3 Scott & Ascher §17.8.

[120] 3 Scott & Ascher §17.8.

[121] Market value is "the most probable price which property should bring in a competitive and open market under all conditions requisite for a fair sale, the buyer and seller each acting prudently and knowledgeably, and assuming the price is not affected by undue stimulus." Glossary of the Uniform Standards of Professional Appraisal Practice (2000 ed.). "Implicit in this definition is the consummation of a sale as of a specified date and the passing of title from seller to buyer under certain conditions whereby: (1) buyer and seller are typically motivated; (2) both parties are well informed or well advised, and acting in what they consider their best interests [or in the case of a trustee, the best interests of the beneficiaries]; (3) a reasonable time is allowed for exposure in the open market; (4) payment is made in terms of cash in United States dollars or in terms of financial arrangements comparable thereto; and (5) the price represents the normal consideration for the property sold unaffected by special or creative financing or sales concessions granted by

property.[122] "Conceivably, a sale at the prevailing market price might be improper if, owing to economic conditions or the conditions of the market in question, prices are depressed."[123]

Unless it is imprudent to do so under the circumstances, or the trust terms provide otherwise, a parcel of trust real estate should be listed for sale on the open market[124] with independent brokers, *i.e.*, brokers who are free of conflicts of interest, and only after the trustee has obtained at least one current appraisal by an independent competent appraiser[125] who has employed one or more of the following standard valuation methods as appropriate: Sales Comparison,[126] Cost,[127] and Income Capitalization.[128] Receiving a secured promissory note in lieu of cash is generally permissible, provided the note standing on its own two feet would be a suitable investment for the particular trust.[129] "In some circumstances, however, it may be proper for a trustee to accept from the buyer a note or other asset of a type or in an amount that the trustee would not otherwise acquire for the trust portfolio when it is prudent under the circumstance to do so, considering any special advantages of the sale opportunity along with the tax as well as investment aspects of the transaction."[130]

Relocating the trust's situs. If the location of the trust's principal place of administration puts the trust property at unreasonable risk, the trustee may have a duty to transfer the trusteeship to someone who is in a position to

---

anyone associated with the sale." Glossary of the Uniform Standards of Professional Appraisal Practice (2000 ed.). Treas. Reg. §25.2512-1 has a similar definition of fair market value for federal gift tax purposes:

> "... The value of ... [gifted] ... property is the price at which such property would change hands between a willing buyer and a willing seller, neither being under any compulsion to buy or to sell, and both having reasonable knowledge of relevant facts. The value of a particular item of property is not the price that a forced sale of the property would produce. Nor is the fair market value of an item of property the sale price in a market other than that in which such item is most commonly sold to the public, taking into account the location of the item wherever appropriate. ..."

[122] 3 Scott & Ascher §18.1.4.4 (confirming that a trustee who sells trust property at an unreasonably low price is liable for the loss).

[123] 4 Scott & Ascher §24.11.4 (When Trustee Has Power of Sale).

[124] On the trustee's duty to "test the market," *see* Rippey v. Denver United States Nat'l Bank, 273 F. Supp. 718 (D. Colo. 1967).

[125] *See, e.g.*, Lincoln Nat'l Bank & Trust Co. v. Shriners Hosps. for Crippled Children, 588 N.E.2d 597 (Ind. Ct. App. 1992); Allard v. Pacific Nat'l Bank, 99 Wash. 2d 394, 405, 663 P.2d 104, 111 (1983); Belcher v. Birmingham Trust Nat'l Bank, 348 F. Supp. 61, 158 (Ala. 1968).

[126] Comparative analysis of the subject with other similar properties that have recently sold and for which the sales price and terms are known.

[127] Land value added to the estimated reproduction cost new of the improvements less depreciation from all causes.

[128] Analysis of income and expenses and conversion of the net incomes stream(s) into an estimate of value.

[129] Restatement (Third) of Trusts §86 cmt. c(2). *See generally* §6.2.2.1 of this hand book (the *Harvard College* prudent man rule and its progeny).

[130] Restatement (Third) of Trusts §86 cmt. c(2). *See also* 3 Scott & Ascher §18.1.4.5 (Power to Sell on Credit).

administer the trust at a place appropriate to its sound, efficient management.[131] When it comes to taxation, divorce, and creditor access, some jurisdictions are more favorable to the interests of trust beneficiaries than others. New York, for example, imposes a tax on undistributed dividends and capital gains. Delaware, on the other hand, does not. Alaska, unlike many jurisdictions, will enforce the spendthrift provisions of certain self-settled trusts. The general subject of conflict of laws is taken up in Section 8.5 of this handbook; the general subject of judicial jurisdiction in Section 8.40 of this handbook.

A trustee may have a duty to move the situs of the trust if to do so would substantially further the interests of the beneficiaries, would not be in contravention of the terms of the trust, and would be both possible and practical.[132] If such a move were only possible were the trustee to relinquish the trusteeship, then so be it.[133] "[C]hanges in the place of administration, location of beneficiaries, or other developments causing serious geographic inconvenience to the beneficiaries or to the administration of the trust" may even be grounds for removal.[134]

Section 7-101 of the Uniform Probate Code would require a trustee to register the trust in an appropriate court at the trust's principal place of administration. This registration requirement is in part designed to facilitate administratively the appropriate relocation of a trust's principal place of administration by keeping court involvement in the process to a minimum.[135] In 2008, Massachusetts adopted a gutted version of Section 7-101 that imposed on trustees no such obligation to register with the court.[136]

On the other hand, changing trust situs might not be in the best interests of the beneficiaries, all things considered. The state in which the trust was established, for example, might attempt to continue to tax the income of the trust even after all the trustees and all the beneficiaries had moved elsewhere.[137] A trustee who is contemplating making a significant change in the place of administration of an inter vivos trust should so inform the beneficiaries and solicit their comments.[138] While they ordinarily would not have a power to veto the move, they should be given the opportunity in advance of the move to petition the court for instructions should they object to what is being contemplated.[139] A change of situs of a testamentary trust generally requires court

---

[131] UPC §7-305.

[132] Restatement (Third) of Trusts §76 cmt. b(2).

[133] Restatement (Third) of Trusts §76 cmt. b(2). *See also* UPC §7-305; Mass. Gen. Laws ch. 190B, §7-305.

[134] Restatement (Third) of Trusts §76 cmt. b(2); UPC §7-305 (providing also that "[v]iews of adult beneficiaries shall be given weight in determining the suitability of the trustee and the place of administration").

[135] UPC, Part 1, Trust Registration, General Comment.

[136] Mass. Gen. Laws ch. 190B, §7-101.

[137] *See generally* Bernard E. Jacob, *An Extended Presence, Interstate Style: First Note on a Theme from* Saenz, 30 Hofstra L. Rev. 1133 (2002) (considering claims of constitutional protection that ought to be erected against literal application of the "Founder-State Trust" concept).

[138] Restatement (Third) of Trusts §76 cmt. b(2).

[139] Restatement (Third) of Trusts §76 cmt. b(2).

approval, and in Massachusetts also the consent of all living beneficiaries.[140] Now that Massachusetts has adopted Section 7-305 of the Uniform Probate Code, however, beneficiary consent may no longer be a requirement: It provides that the views of adult beneficiaries shall be "given weight" in determining who would be a suitable successor trustee, as well as the trust's next principal place of administration.[141] It needs to be kept in mind that any trust terms that address where the trust is to be administered and/or trustee succession should still control, unless compliance would be contrary to the "efficient administration or the purposes of the trust."[142]

Investing imprudently. It is implicit in the so-called Prudent Man Rule in all its manifestations, including the Restatement's recently adopted *Prudent Investor Rule*, that the trustee, in investing the trust estate, must strive to protect trust principal from the ravages of inflation.[143]

Transaction costs should be kept to a minimum.[144] The trustee intending to purchase mutual fund shares through a broker, for example, must do so prudently. Whether A shares, B shares, or C shares are taken into the trust can make a difference to the trust's bottom line depending upon the given facts and circumstances, *e.g.*, the expected duration of the investment. With A shares, there is an initial sales commission and an annual 12b-1 fee in the range of 0.25 percent, which is over and above the fund's other annual expenses. With B shares, there is an annual 12b-1 fee of 1 percent and a back-end (exit) commission that declines the longer the shares are held. Eventually the B shares will convert into A shares, which have a lower 12b-1 fee structure. With C shares, there is an annual 12b-1 fee of 1 percent, but no upfront or back-end commission charges. "In the vast majority of cases, the B shares are never the most advantageous of the share classes."[145] For a brief discussion of 12b-1 fees, see Section 8.10 of this handbook.

---

[140] Mass. Gen. Laws Ann. 206, §29.

[141] UPC §7-305; Mass. Gen. Laws ch. 190B, §7-305.

[142] UPC §7-305; Mass. Gen. Laws ch. 190B, §7-305.

[143] *See* Restatement (Third) of Trusts §90 cmt. e [Restatement (Third) of Trusts: Prudent Investor Rule §227 cmt. e].

[144] *See, e.g., Municipal Bonds: Tax Free Income vs. Trustee Obligation to Avoid Unwarranted Costs*, 33 ACTEC L.J. 195 (2008). While monitoring transaction costs is relatively easy when the trust assets are individually invested, it is another matter when the assets are mutual fund participations. Still, the trustee still has a duty to scrutinize a mutual fund's cost structure, even if it is an index fund. *See generally* Luther J. Avery & Patrick J. Collins, *Managing Investment Expenses: Trustee Duty to Avoid Unreasonable or Inappropriate Costs*, 25 ACTEC Notes 123 (1999) (covering the following topics: The Unsophisticated Fiduciary and the Decision to Obtain Investment Expertise; Hiring a Professional Trustee; Seeking Asset Management Advice from a Broker; Costs of Investment Management Strategies; Range of Expenses for Managed Investment Funds; Commissions and Fees; Whether Expensive Investment Programs Produce Superior Returns; Market Impact and Liquidity Costs; and Taxes, Inflation and Turnover). *See also* Tom Lauricella, *This Is News? Fund Fees Are Too High, Study Says*, Wall St. J., Aug. 27, 2001, at C1, col. 5; Danny Hakim, *Index Fund Fees Are Not Created Equal*, N.Y. Times, Jan. 14, 2001, at BU8, col. 2.

[145] Jonathan Clements, *Why B Shares Deserve to Get an F: These Broker-Sold Funds Are a Bad Deal*, Wall St. J., July 2, 2003, at D1 (quoting Edward O'Neal, a finance professor at Wake Forest University in Winston-Salem, N.C.).

Tax liabilities should be prudently incurred if they must be incurred. The trustee must be aware that almost anything he does can have positive or negative tax consequences for the trust.[146] The trustee's duty to keep track of the tax basis/cost of the trust property is discussed in Section 11.1 of this handbook.

Costs of unreasonably delegating tasks to agents. The duty not to incur unreasonable costs also applies when a trustee decides whether and how to delegate tasks to agents, including investment managers and attorneys.[147] "In deciding whether and how to delegate, the trustee must be alert to balancing projected benefits against the likely costs."[148] The trustee, for example, will want to ascertain to what extent, if at all, fees paid to investment advisors are a deductible expense for income tax purposes.[149] Even though a trustee has properly employed an attorney, only that portion of the legal fee that is reasonable under all of the circumstances is a legitimate trust expense.[150] Any excess would be a personal obligation of the trustee.[151]

Insuring the trust property. The trustee should insure the trust property to the extent it is reasonable to do so against losses occasioned by theft, fire, severe weather, injury to third parties, and the like, and may do so at trust expense.[152] Again, the entrusted property must be reasonably insured. Thus, when a particular risk of loss is slight and the cost to the trust estate of insuring against that risk excessive, the trustee, absent special facts, may elect not to insure against the risk and may well be duty-bound not to do so. Should the remote risk later materialize, the trust estate, not the trustee personally, bears the burden of the loss.[153] As to entrusted bank deposits, the reader is referred to the FDIC Guide to Calculating Deposit Insurance Coverage for Revocable and Irrevocable trusts.[154]

Looking after entrusted real estate. Trust real estate should be routinely inspected, at least annually or more often as circumstances warrant, and

---

[146] See, e.g., Jonathan G. Blattmacher, Put In Trust, D-1, D-4 (1999) (suggesting that the rent-free use of property owned by a trust by its beneficiary does not result in imputed income to either the trust or the beneficiary). See generally Mark L. Ascher, The Fiduciary Duty to Minimize Taxes, 20 Real Prop. Prob. & Tr. J. 663 (1985).

[147] UTC §805 cmt. (available at <http://www.uniformlaws.org/Act.aspx?title=Trust%20Code>); Restatement (Third) of Trusts §88 cmt. c.

[148] UTC §805 cmt. (available at <http://www.uniformlaws.org/Act.aspx?title=Trust%20Code>).

[149] See, e.g., Mellon Bank, N.A. v. United States, 47 Fed. Cl. 186 (Fed. Cl. 2000) (holding that income tax deduction for fees paid by trustee to outside investment advisors subject to two percent floor).

[150] 3 Scott & Ascher §18.1.2.6 (When Trustee Improperly Incurs Expense).

[151] 3 Scott & Ascher §18.1.2.6 (When Trustee Improperly Incurs Expense).

[152] See Bogert §599; 3 Scott & Ascher §17.8 (noting that a trustee who has used reasonable care in the selection of an insurer will not be liable for a loss caused by the insurer's failure).

[153] See, e.g., Regions Bank v. Lowrey, 101 So. 3d 210 (Ala. 2012) (trustee's failure to have insured an extensive tract of entrusted timberland against the hurricane damage that had befallen the tract held not a breach of trust).

[154] <http://www.fdic.gov/regulations/laws/federal/2008/08sep26rule.html>. See also <http://www.bankrate.com/btm/news/sav/20030820a1.asp> (The CDARS Program).

appraised at least every three years. Property taxes should be paid in a timely fashion to avoid a tax sale.[155] If the trust property is subject to a mortgage, the trustee must take reasonable steps to prevent a loss of the property due to foreclosure. A trustee may properly use trust funds to keep entrusted buildings and equipment in good repair.[156]

Looking after entrusted insurance contracts. While it is true that a trustee generally has no duty to use personal funds to keep entrusted insurance contracts in force, he is nonetheless duty-bound to take reasonable steps to see to it that the premiums are either paid with entrusted funds or by someone else, such as a willing beneficiary of the trust. The typical trust instrument will contain exonerating boilerplate similar to the following:

> The Trustee shall be under no obligation to pay the premiums which may become due and payable under the provisions of such policy of insurance, or to make certain that such premiums are paid by the Settlor or others, or to notify any persons of the non-payment of such premiums, and the Trustee shall be under no responsibility or liability of any kind in the event such premiums are not paid as required.

One thing is for sure: No matter how expansive and detailed the purported exoneration, if the trustee is on actual or constructive notice that an entrusted policy is about to lapse due to unintentional premium nonpayment, he is duty-bound to take reasonable steps to prevent the lapse, short of reaching into his own pocket.

> Perhaps the most fundamental aspect of acting for the benefit of the beneficiaries is protecting the trust property.... [Such exonerating language]...cannot be relied upon to abrogate...[the Trustee's]...duty to act in good faith and in accordance with the terms and purposes of the trust and the interests of the beneficiaries.[157]

If the risk to the trust estate is attributable to the trustee's own negligence, say the trustee had undertaken to furnish the insurance company with an address to which notifications should be sent and the address had been wrong, then he could well be financially on the hook for any consequential economic harm to the trust estate.[158]

The trustee should not compete with the trust. "While normally associated with corporations and with their directors and officers, what is usually referred to as the corporate opportunity doctrine also applies to...[trustees]...."[159] Accordingly, a beneficiary may void a transaction

---

[155] *See* Bogert §602; 3 Scott & Ascher §17.8; 2A Scott on Trusts §176.

[156] 3 Scott & Ascher §17.8 (noting that if the trustee's failure to keep a premises in good condition causes it to be "untenantable," the trustee may be liable for the loss of rentals).

[157] Rafert v. Meyer, 859 N.W.2d 332 (Neb. 2015).

[158] *See, e.g.*, Rafert v. Meyer, 859 N.W.2d 332 (Neb. 2015).

[159] UTC §802 cmt. (available at <http://www.uniformlaws.org/Act.aspx?title=Trust%20Code>).

entered into by the trustee that involved an opportunity belonging to the trust, *e.g.*, the trustee's entering into a business in direct competition with a business owned by the trust or purchasing an investment for himself that the facts suggest should have been purchased for the trust.[160]

A trustee wishing to exploit an opportunity belonging to the trust or otherwise compete with the trust, of course, may do so notwithstanding the aforementioned proscriptions if the terms of the trust authorize it. Absent express authority in the governing instrument or some enabling statute, the trustee could attempt to obtain the informed consent of all beneficiaries, both current beneficiaries and remaindermen, or a court order. Either option, however, can be expensive if not problematic when there are unborn or unascertained beneficiaries in the picture. However the trustee attempts to get around the default law, the trustee has an internal overarching duty to act in good faith. This would include fully disclosing to the beneficiaries all information, both of a factual and legal nature, they would need to protect their equitable interests.

Legitimate claims against predecessor fiduciaries and cotrustees. A legitimate claim against a predecessor trustee or the settlor's estate (or personal representative) should be pursued on behalf of the trust.[161] A trustee who has reason to suspect that a cotrustee is depleting or about to deplete the trust property must take reasonable steps to prevent him from doing so.[162]

Claims by and against third parties. A trustee shall take reasonable steps to enforce claims of the trust against third parties and, as we shall see, to defend claims against the trust by third parties.[163] (One court has even found that a trustee had a duty to enforce a claim against a contingent remainderman that predated the trust).[164] Accordingly, the trustee has full power to sue on behalf of the trust estate and to defend suits that put the trust estate at risk.[165]

One court has authorized a trustee to assign away *for adequate consideration* a trust claim against a third party.[166] The assignee was better equipped to prosecute the claim, the trust being cash-starved and no lawyer being found willing to take the matter on a contingent fee basis. The court found 55 percent of any recovery to be adequate consideration. This contractual right to a percentage of the recovery replaced the claim as a trust asset.

---

[160] UTC §802 cmt. (available at <http://www.uniformlaws.org/Act.aspx?title=Trust%20 Code>).

[161] *See* 3 Scott & Ascher §17.9; 2A Scott on Trusts. §177; Bogert §§592, 594.

[162] *See* Restatement (Third) of Trusts §81 cmt. d.

[163] UTC §811 (available at <http://www.uniformlaws.org/Act.aspx?title=Trust%20 Code>); Restatement (Third) of Trusts §76 cmt. d. *See also* 3 Scott & Ascher §§17.9 (Duty to Enforce Claims), 17.10 (Duty to Defend Actions); 2A Scott on Trusts §178; Bogert §581. *Cf.* §6.2.6 of this handbook (trustee's duty to defend the trust against attack, and certainly not to attack the trust).

[164] *See, e.g.*, New Haven Sav. Bank v. LaPlace, 66 Conn. App. 1, 783 A.2d 1174 (2002) (noting that the defendant failed to cite any law holding that a trustee must forbear foreclosing a mortgage on a note held by the trust because the maker of the note is a contingent remainderman).

[165] *See* Bogert §§594, 869; §6.2.6 of this handbook (trustee's duty to defend the trust against attack, and certainly not to attack the trust).

[166] *See* Dunmore v. Dunmore, 2012 WL 267725 (Cal. App. 3d Dist.).

The trustee's duty to prudently litigate. Again, the trustee of a trust that is strapped for cash has no obligation to use his personal funds to underwrite remedial litigation[167] or litigation to collect insurance proceeds or other assets due the trust, unless the beneficiaries are willing to foot the bill with their own funds, although there may be an affirmative duty to solicit their voluntary indemnity.[168] "A trustee who can obtain the necessary funds by a sale or a mortgage of trust property may be under a duty to do so,"[169] provided it is reasonably likely that the costs of selling or encumbering the trust property is worth the benefits that could reasonably be expected to be obtained from the litigation. In any case, a trustee who is contemplating serious litigation at trust expense would be well advised to seek a second legal opinion before proceeding.[170] He may even have a fiduciary duty to do so. Perhaps taking security for the claim in lieu of litigating it is a better option.[171] Or possibly putting the collection process on temporary hold would be a better way to go, provided there is a chance that doing so would increase the chances of a satisfactory resolution of the matter.[172] Likewise, a trustee has no duty to employ personal funds to fend off claims *against the trust estate*, unless the claims have been occasioned by some breach of trust.

As a general rule, all demands must be pressed, even to the extent of bringing suit,[173] or else the trustee will be liable for any loss caused by unjustified forbearance.[174] Take, for example, the trustee who holds legal title to contractual rights against a third party, such as rights against the corporate issuer of a bond or rights against an insurance company incident to an insurance policy. The third party, instead of making a payment to the trustee, who is the other party to the contract, takes it upon itself to makes a payment directly to a trust beneficiary who is not of full age and legal capacity. The

---

[167] Lewin ¶ 21-50 (England).

[168] Restatement (Third) of Trusts §76 cmt. d. *See generally* Bogert §582; 3 Scott & Ascher §17.8; 2A Scott on Trusts §175.

[169] 3 Scott & Ascher §17.8.

[170] *See also* §8.25 of this handbook (noting that trustees can no longer assume that every lawyer has been exposed in an academic setting, or anywhere for that matter, to the fundamentals of agency and trust law).

[171] *See generally* 3 Scott & Ascher §17.9 (noting that "it may be reasonable for the trustee to take security for the claim, even if doing so would not otherwise be part of a prudent investment strategy for the trust").

[172] *See generally* 3 Scott & Ascher §17.9.

[173] *See* 3 Scott & Ascher §17.9; 2A Scott on Trusts §177; UTC §812 (available at <http://www.uniformlaws.org/Act.aspx?title=Trust%20 Code>). *See, e.g.*, PriceWaterhouseCoopers, LLP v. Bassett, 666 S.E.2d 721 (Ga. Ct. App. 2008) (trustees of interests in a now bankrupt business enterprise successfully brought suit against its corporate accountants for negligently misrepresenting the financial condition of the enterprise, a misrepresentation that had induced the trustees to acquire the interests for various family trusts).

[174] *See* 3 Scott & Ascher §17.9; 2A Scott on Trusts §177; UTC §812 (available at <http://www.uniformlaws.org/Act.aspx?title=Trust%20Code>).

trustee may have a fiduciary duty to seek to compel the third party to make the payment a second time, this time to the trustee.[175]

A trustee who is unsuccessful at the trial level in pressing a claim may have a duty to appeal the decision to a higher court, provided it would be reasonable and in the interests of the beneficiaries to do so.[176] "The trustee is not excused from enforcing a claim merely because the settlor would not have pressed it or because of generous feelings for the obligor."[177] On the other hand, it may be in the economic interest of the beneficiaries, and therefore prudent and reasonable, to forbear or to compromise a claim or submit it to arbitration.[178] Because of the attendant expense to the trust, the patently futile prosecution of a claim itself can constitute a breach of the specific duty to protect the trust property.[179] State statutes authorize a trustee to compromise, usually with court approval.[180]

Imprudently compromising claims by and against the trust estate. In the absence of express authority in the governing instrument to do so, the trustee inclined to compromise a claim should check for an applicable statute. If one is found, its provisions should be followed. In the absence of such a statute, the trustee has two options: to obtain the consent of the current beneficiaries and remaindermen, if feasible, or to seek court approval. Note: If the claim is *de minimis*, taking such precautions would not be commensurate with the trustee's potential liability and thus could constitute a breach of the trustee's duty of loyalty, and ironically his duty not to waste the trust property.

Ordinarily, the trustee has a duty to defend third-party actions that might result in a loss to the trust estate, and to appeal adverse decisions to the extent it is reasonable and in the interest of the beneficiaries to do so.[181] "It might also be reasonable to settle an action or suffer a default rather than to defend an

---

[175] The third-party obligor who makes a payment directly to the trust beneficiary instead of to the title-holding trustee, the other party to the contract, does so at his, her, or its peril, unless directed to do so by the trustee. 5 Scott & Ascher §32.1 (Discharge by Beneficiary of Claim Against Third Person). If the beneficiary is not of full age and legal capacity, the third party obligor runs the risk of having to pay twice. 5 Scott & Ascher §32.1 (Discharge by Beneficiary of Claim Against Third Person). There is a similar risk if following the direction were to constitute a knowing participation with the trustee in a breach of trust or if the trust were a spendthrift trust. 5 Scott & Ascher §32.1 (Discharge by Beneficiary of Claim Against Third Person).

[176] *See generally* 3 Scott & Ascher §17.9 (noting that the trustee generally has "wide discretion" whether or not to appeal and risks being second-guessed only when there has been an abuse of that discretion).

[177] 3 Scott & Ascher §17.9 (noting that "[t]he trustee may not be generous, at the beneficiaries' expense").

[178] *See* Restatement (Third) of Trusts §76 cmt. d; Restatement (Second) of Trusts §192; 3 Scott & Ascher §17.9.

[179] *See* Restatement (Second) of Trusts §192 cmt. c; 3 Scott on Trusts §192; §6.2.6 of this handbook (the trustee's duty to defend the trust against attack, and certainly not to mount an attack against the trust).

[180] *See* 3 Scott on Trusts §192.

[181] *See generally* 3 Scott & Ascher §17.10.

action."[182] Consuming trust property in a patently futile defense of a claim against the trust estate can itself constitute a breach of trust.

Administering provisions that are unlawful or violate public policy. Likewise, notwithstanding the duty to carry out the terms of his trust,[183] there is a countervailing duty on the part of the trustee, a duty that runs to the beneficiaries, not to carry out provisions that are unlawful or violate public policy.[184] The trustee also has a duty not to attempt to comply with a provision if compliance would be impossible or incur unreasonable expense.[185]

§6.2.1.4   Operations: Asset Custody and Transfer

Institutional custody programs for use by lawyers and other trustees have been developed by stock brokerage firms and bank trust departments. A lawyer or law firm having even a modest volume of trusteeships may choose a custody program to serve literally as the trustee's back office.[186]

"In earlier times, equities commonly were held and transferred in certificate form, and bonds commonly had coupons for manual clippings as interest came due."[187] The trustee would keep the certificates in designated safe deposit boxes. He would "maintain a separate bank checking account for each trust, to be the trust's repository of receipts, such as dividends and the proceeds of security sales, and as the source for funds drawn by the trustee in checks remitted to the beneficiaries and for the purchase of new investments."[188] It fell to the trustee or his clerical staff to "account for the transactions, keeping income items separate from principal, on the books of the trust."[189]

In most cases today, a U.S. trustee will hold shares in U.S. corporations in either of two ways: He will be registered as the legal owner on the books of the corporation or he will hold the shares in the form of a computerized book entry, directly (or indirectly through a bank or a broker) at The Depository Trust and

---

[182] UTC §811 cmt. (available at <http://www.uniformlaws.org/Act.aspx?title=Trust%20Code>). *See generally* 3 Scott & Ascher §17.10.

[183] *See* §6.1.2 of this handbook (the trustee's duty to affirmatively carry out the terms of the trust).

[184] Restatement (Third) of Trusts §72. *See generally* §6.2.12 of this handbook (the trustee's duty not to comply with provisions that are unlawful or violate public policy).

[185] Restatement (Third) of Trusts §73. *See generally* §6.2.13 of this handbook (the trustee's duty not to attempt to comply with a trust provision if compliance would be impossible or incur unreasonable expense).

[186] ACTEC Practice Committee, Fiduciary Matters Subcommittee, *Guide for ACTEC Fellows Serving as Trustees*, 26 ACTEC Notes, 313, 317 (2001).

[187] ACTEC Practice Committee, Fiduciary Matters Subcommittee, *Guide for ACTEC Fellows Serving as Trustees*, 26 ACTEC Notes, 313, 317 (2001).

[188] ACTEC Practice Committee, Fiduciary Matters Subcommittee, *Guide for ACTEC Fellows Serving as Trustees*, 26 ACTEC Notes, 313, 317 (2001).

[189] ACTEC Practice Committee, Fiduciary Matters Subcommittee, *Guide for ACTEC Fellows Serving as Trustees*, 26 ACTEC Notes, 313, 317 (2001).

Clearing Corporation (DTCC).[190] (The shareholder books of the U.S. corporation itself will be maintained by a bank transfer agent, by an independent agent, or in-house.)

DTCC came into existence in 1999.[191] It is a holding company that combines the functions of the former Depository Trust Company (DTC) and the National Securities Clearing Corporation (NSCC). Between them, these two firms provide the primary infrastructure for the clearance, settlement, and custody of the vast majority of equity, corporate debt, and municipal bond transactions in the United States. The DTC subsidiary, for instance, provides for the custody and safekeeping of traded securities, proxy distribution services, principal and income distribution, corporate action processing, withholding tax services, collateral loan services, and delivery and payment services, sets and enforces settlement risk controls, and provides clearing and settlement links.

DTCC, a member of the Federal Reserve System, is a limited-purpose trust company organized under the banking laws of New York. It is owned by members of the financial industry, principally its participating broker-dealers and banks. DTCC is registered with the SEC as a clearing agency pursuant to Section 17A of the Securities Exchange Act of 1934 and is subject to regulation by the SEC and the New York State Department of Banking. It is also a clearing agency within the meaning of Article 8 of the Uniform Commercial Code (UCC). Section 8-320 of the UCC authorizes and governs the computerized book-entry method of holding securities.

DTCC is governed by a board of directors that is elected annually under a system of cumulative voting. Today, through its nominee Cede & Co. (a contraction of "central depository"), DTCC holds approximately $20 trillion worth of debt and equity securities for most of the nation's banks and brokers; $75 trillion worth of assets pass through its system annually in connection with transactions that call for book-entry delivery. Physical possession of certificated securities is either with DTCC itself or with transfer agents participating in a Fast Automated Securities Transfer (FAST) program. DTCC has no investment authority. Nor does it have an equitable or beneficial interest in the securities that are registered in the name of Cede & Co. Proxy authority flows through the depositing entities to those who would have the voting rights were the shares in question not with DTCC.

An individual trustee can indirectly participate in DTCC by entering into an asset custody and transfer agency agreement[192] with a bank or broker that either participates directly in DTCC or offers asset custody and transfer services through an entity that does. The practice is known as "piggy-backing." In most

---

[190] *See generally* <www.dtcc.org> (visited Oct. 1, 1999).

[191] *See* Self-Regulatory Organizations; The Depository Trust Company; Order Granting Accelerated Approval of a Proposed Rule Change Relating to Arrangements to Integrate the Depository Trust Company and the National Securities Clearing Corp., Release No. 34-41786, 70 S.E.C. Docket 948, File No. SR-DTC-99-17, 1999 WL 651555 (S.E.C.) (Aug. 24, 1999). For the companion NSCC release, *see* 1999 WL 681506 (S.E.C.).

[192] *See generally* §6.2.4.8 of this handbook (the operational aspects of keeping track of trust income and trust principal).

cases, those with the equitable or beneficial interest in the security, in this case the trust beneficiaries, would be unknown to DTCC.

The law of trusts has had little choice but to adapt to the dematerialization phenomenon, *i.e.,* to the reality that electronic record-keeping is causing paper certificates to go the way of carbon copies.[193] If DTCC has its way, the SEC sooner rather than later will effectively outlaw altogether the issuance of paper certificates by companies subject to its regulation.[194] How the law can keep alive the spirit of the traditional proscription against fiduciary commingling and still adapt to dematerialization's operational realities is an implicit theme of Section 6.2.1.2 of this handbook.

A U.S. investor may hold foreign securities in the form of an American Depositary Receipt (ADR). An ADR represents an ownership interest in securities (on a share-for-share or share-for-fractional-share basis) that have been deposited with a depositary, typically a U.S. bank or trust company. Custody of the underlying security is in an overseas branch of the depositary bank or with its agent. The ADR itself is a negotiable certificate issued by the depositary and is a security subject to U.S. securities laws. It is tradable on the U.S. exchanges, NASDAQ, and OTC in the same manner as the securities of domestic issuers. An ADR is easier to price and trade than the underlying foreign security, because prices are denominated in U.S. currency and the trading (including clearance and settlement) takes place in the United States where transactions are processed efficiently and with a high degree of reliability. Also, the process of paying out dividends to a U.S. investor would be easier than would be the case were title to the underlying security in the investor.[195]

The process of security "dematerialization" is well along in England as well. For a discussion of how English trustees are adapting, the reader is referred to ¶ 34-40 through ¶ 34-53 of Lewin on Trusts.

The trustee should maintain personal custody of deeds and other indicia of real estate ownership. "There may be advantages in maintaining a nominee sub-trust or partnership to hold the legal title to the real estate."[196] However title is held, "the trustee should exercise ownership control by arranging for regular inspection and monitoring of the land and improvements and their condition."[197]

---

[193] *See* Richard R. Stanley, *Global Custody Operations of Banks,* 114 Banking L.J. 418, 423 (1997) (noting that modern trend is to use the electronic medium instead of paper certificates). The process of using electronic data entry in lieu of paper certificates is known as "dematerialization." *See* Richard R. Stanley, *Global Custody Operations of Banks,* 114 Banking L.J. 418, 423 (1997). *See also* Group of 30, Clearance and Settlement Systems in the World's Securities Markets (1988) (recommending a worldwide move to "dematerialize" securities); Peers, *Paperless Wall Street,* Wall St. J., June 7, 1994, at C1.

[194] *See* Matt Jarzemsky, *End Looming for Paper Certificates,* Wall St. J., Mar. 13, 2013, at C3.

[195] *See generally* American Depositary Receipts, Securities Act Release No. 6894 (May 30, 1991).

[196] ACTEC Practice Committee, Fiduciary Matters Subcommittee, *Guide for ACTEC Fellows Serving as Trustees,* 26 ACTEC Notes 313, 318 (2001).

[197] ACTEC Practice Committee, Fiduciary Matters Subcommittee, *Guide for ACTEC Fellows Serving as Trustees,* 26 ACTEC Notes, 313, 318 (2001).

§6.2.2 Duty to Prudently Make Trust Property Productive

A trustee is not an insurer.[198]

Trustees did not always have a default duty to make the trust property productive. At the close of the Middle Ages, land was the subject of most trusts and trustees were little more than passive titleholders.[199] "Centuries later, as the tie between land and wealth was swept away by the Industrial Revolution, the trustee became a more active steward."[200] Today, rather than land, a typical trust is likely to contain intangible personal property such as equities, bonds, insurance contracts, and bank accounts, which are essentially contract rights against the issuers, as well as equitable interests in other trusts such as mutual funds. Complex financial instruments cry out for active fiduciary management. "As the jurist Roscoe Pound observed in an arresting epigram, 'Wealth in a commercial age is made up largely of promises.'"[201] Again, active management is critical, particularly as the discretionary fiduciary power to invest in "securities," which is now a default power, is generally not construed to mean that the trustee is foreclosed from investing in unsecured obligations.[202]

The duty to make the trust property productive. Today, a trustee has a specific duty to make the trust property productive,[203] *i.e.*, "to provide returns or other benefits from the trust property,"[204] unless the circumstances suggest otherwise, or the terms of the trust provide otherwise.[205] In fact, a trustee risks personal liability for unreasonably failing to invest the trust property.[206] Thus, parking large amounts of trust cash for an extended period of time in a bank account that bears little or no interest is likely to be a breach of trust,[207] as would ordinarily allowing a beneficiary to park a vehicle rent free on entrusted land or the failure to lease out an entrusted vehicle.[208] The trustee who invests trust funds in a parcel of commercial real estate that is unproductive of net trust accounting income risks having to compensate the current beneficiaries out of

---

[198] UTC §1003 cmt. (available at <http://www.uniformlaws.org/Act.aspx?title=Trust%20 Code>).

[199] *See generally* §8.15.1 of this handbook (statute of uses).

[200] Donald D. Kozusko, *Be Positive About Trusts*, UTC Notes (Summer 2003), at p. 7.

[201] John H. Langbein, *Rise of the Management Trust*, Tr. & Est. 53 (2004) (citing Roscoe Pound, An Introduction to the Philosophy of Law, 236 (1922)).

[202] 4 Scott & Ascher §19.1.12.

[203] Lewin ¶ 35-01 (England); 3 Scott & Ascher §17.13 (U.S.); 4 Scott & Ascher §19.1 (The Trustee's Investment Duties—In General) (U.S.).

[204] Restatement (Third) of Trusts §76(2)(c).

[205] Restatement (Third) of Trusts §76(2)(c); Restatement (Third) of Trusts §90 cmt. a [Restatement (Third) of Trusts: Prudent Investor Rule §227 cmt. a]. *See generally* Bogert §611; §3.5.3.1(a) of this handbook (noting that the trustee's duty to invest and the trustee's power are incident to the trustee's overarching duty to make the trust property productive).

[206] *See generally* 4 Scott & Ascher §24.15 (Liability for Breach of Trust by Failing to Invest); §7.2.3.2 of this handbook (damages as an equitable remedy for a breach of trust).

[207] *See generally* 3 Scott & Ascher §17.12.3 (Leaving Funds on Deposit for an Unreasonable Time).

[208] *See generally* 3 Scott & Ascher §17.13 (Duty to Make the Trust Property Productive).

his own pocket for the income that they would have received had the entrusted funds been productively and prudently invested.[209] Again, to the extent the terms of the trust contemplate such nonincome-generating arrangements, the duty to make the trust property productive is not implicated.[210] "The fiduciary duty of a trustee to maintain capital and generate income, with concomitant investment powers, was established by the late seventeenth century."[211] This specific duty flows from the general duties to be prudent and carry out the intentions of the settlor.[212]

For a trust portfolio to qualify as "productive," must trust accounting income be generated, or will mere principal appreciation suffice? It depends. One court having parsed the language of the governing instrument held the former.[213] What about an income-only perpetual trust? Need the trustee invest for capital appreciation? Yes, at least one appellate court, parsing and then applying its state's version of the Prudent Investor Rule, has so held.[214]

The duty to invest. Inherent in the duty to make the trust property productive is the duty to invest[215] the trust property and to do so prudently.[216] The Prudent Man Rule in its original manifestation,[217] and as it has evolved in the various jurisdictions by statute and decision,[218] is intended as a safe harbor for the trustee faced with the stark reality that there is no such thing as a risk-free investment:

> Keeping the money under the bed is not risk-free; you are subject both to inflation and burglars (though not necessarily in that order). Even if money at the bank ought probably to remove the burglar risk, it will not remove the inflation risk.[219]

The prudence safe harbor. The safe harbor is this: A trustee is held to a standard of care in the carrying out of his investment responsibilities that is

---

[209] *See, e.g.,* Miller v. Bank of Am., N.A. 326 P.3d 20 (N.M. 2013).

[210] *See generally* Trent S. Kiziah, *The Trustee's Duty to Diversify: An Examination of the Developing Case Law,* 36 ACTEC L.J. 357 (2010).

[211] Joshua Getzler, *Legislative Incursions Into Modern Trusts Doctrine in England: The Trustee Act 2000 and the Contracts (Rights of Third Parties) Act 1999,* 2(1) Global Jurist Topics, Art. 2 (2002).

[212] Restatement (Third) of Trusts §90 cmt. i [Restatement (Third) of Trusts: Prudent Investor Rule §227 cmt. i].

[213] *See* In re Van Dusen Marital Trust, 834 N.W.2d 514, 525 (Minn. App. 2013).

[214] *See* The Woodward School for Girls, Inc. v. City of Quincy, trustee, SJC-11390, 2013 WL 8923423 (Mass. July 23, 2014) ("On remand, an assessment of what a prudent investor would have done requires expert testimony on the minimum level of growth equities that would have been prudent for an income-only fund, with consideration of the potential shifts over the lengthy period at issue.").

[215] Lewin ¶ 35-01 (England); 4 Scott & Ascher §19.1 (U.S.).

[216] Restatement (Third) of Trusts §90 cmt. a [Restatement (Third) of Trusts: Prudent Investor Rule. §227 cmt. a]; Bogert §702.

[217] Harvard Coll. v. Amory, 26 Mass. (9 Pick.) 446, 461 (1830).

[218] *See generally* 3 Scott on Trusts §227.13.

[219] Geoffrey Shindler, *Should We Be Devoted Followers of Investment Fashion?,* Tr. & Est. L.J. 3 (Oct. 2003).

judged on the basis of the trustee's *conduct, not investment performance.*[220] Prudence is evaluated at the time of the investment, and on an ongoing basis without the benefit of hindsight.[221] The Uniform Prudent Management of Institutional Funds Act (UPMIFA), applicable to both charitable trusts and charitable corporations, is fully in accord with this principle.[222] A prospective trustee need not be concerned that he is being asked to be a guarantor of the inception value of the trust property.[223] The Restatement (Third) of Trusts is in accord.[224] "For the most part, the same principles that govern the investment practices of the trustees of private trusts also govern the investment practices of the trustees of charitable trusts."[225]

For a discussion of the special productivity issues associated with tenants' security deposits and escrow funds in the hands of mortgagees, the reader is referred to Section 9.9.4 of this handbook.

§6.2.2.1 The *Harvard College* Prudent Man Rule and Its Progeny

Absent a breach of trust, a trustee is not liable to a beneficiary for a loss or depreciation in the value of trust property or for not having made a profit.[226]

The *Harvard College* Prudent Man Rule. In the extraordinarily influential 1830 case of *Harvard College v. Amory,*[227] the Supreme Judicial Court of Massachusetts set forth the following safe harbor rule:

All that can be required of a trustee to invest is that he shall conduct himself faithfully and exercise a sound discretion. He is to observe how men of prudence, discretion, and intelligence manage their own affairs, not in regard to speculation,

---

[220] 4 Scott & Ascher §19.1.2. *See, e.g.,* Uniform Prudent Investor Act §8 (available at <http://www.uniformlaws.org/Act.aspx?title=Trust%20Code>) (providing that compliance with the prudent investor rule is determined in light of the facts and circumstances existing at the time of a trustee's decision or action and not by hindsight). *See also* Restatement (Third) of Trusts §90 cmt. b [Restatement (Third) of Trusts: Prudent Investor Rule §227 cmt. b]. Note that at one time the pocket part for reporting cases involving the Prudent Investor Rule could be found in the back of Appendix Volume 5 of the Restatement of the Law (Second), Trusts (1987). Note also that the Uniform Prudent Investor Act is available at <http://www.uniformlaws.org/Act.aspx?title=Trust%20Code> as Article 9 of the UTC. *See also* Bogert §612 n.23 and accompanying text. *But see* UTC §706 cmt. (suggesting that the court may remove a trustee for consistently poor investment performance as compared with the performance of trustees of comparable trusts).

[221] 4 Scott & Ascher §19.1.2. *See, e.g.,* Metzler v. Graham, 112 F.3d 207, 209 (5th Cir. 1997) (an ERISA case); Stuart Cochran Irrevocable Trust v. Keybank, 901 N.E.2d 1128 (Ind. Ct. App. 2009) (investing in insurance contracts).

[222] Unif. Prudent Management Inst. Funds Act §7 (reviewing compliance).

[223] 4 Scott & Ascher §24.8 (Nonliability for Loss in the Absence of a Breach of Trust).

[224] Restatement (Third) of Trusts §99 cmt. b.

[225] 5 Scott & Ascher §37.3.8.

[226] UTC §1003(b) (available at <http://www.uniformlaws.org/Act.aspx?title=Trust%20Code>).

[227] 26 Mass. (9 Pick.) 446 (1830).

but in regard to the permanent disposition of their funds, considering the probable income as well as the probable safety of the capital to be invested.[228]

This is a "default" rule in that it applies absent an expression of a contrary intention in the governing instrument[229] or preemption by some other body of law.[230] Essentially, the trustee is to prudently balance the considerations of risk and reward, to strike as well a reasonable balance between the extreme of the nonincome-producing speculation[231] that subverts the interests of the income beneficiary and the extreme of the wasting asset that subverts the interests of the remainderman.[232] A middle ground that allows for a reasonable flow of income while preserving principal is the goal.[233] While English trustees could not invest in privately issued securities, *i.e.*, securities not issued or backed by the government, the Court in *Harvard College v. Amory* went out of its way to assure Massachusetts trustees that they were under no such constraints.[234] It was not until much later, 1859 in fact, that England began allowing her trustees to invest in the private sector.[235]

In selecting investments, the trustee must exercise reasonable care,[236] skill,[237] and caution.[238] What is a reasonable investment strategy for principal preservation today? Probably a strategy that strives to maintain the purchasing power of the principal.[239] For a trust of short duration, the purchasing power

---

[228] Harvard Coll. v. Amory, 26 Mass. (9 Pick.) 446, 461 (1830). *See generally* 4 Scott & Ascher §19.1.2 (Trust Investments in the United States).

[229] 4 Scott & Ascher §19.1.2 (noting that in the case of trusts that are not governed by ERISA, "[i]f the terms of a trust enlarge or restrict the scope of the trustee's investment responsibilities-, . . . the terms of the trust ordinarily control"). *See, e.g.*, Howard v. Howard, 211 Or. App. 557, 156 P.3d 89 (2007) (the court parsing the language of the trust instrument to ascertain whether the settlor intended that the trustee take into account the current beneficiary's personal assets in fashioning an investment policy for the trust).

[230] "In ordinary private trust law, the settlor may use the trust instrument to override most of the otherwise applicable rules . . . [, t]hat is to say, almost all trust law is default law, rules of law that apply only when the instrument does not direct something contrary." John H. Langbein & Bruce A. Wolk, Pension and Employee Benefit Law 682 (2000). "To the extent that ERISA forbids the plan sponsor and others to depart from 'the provisions of [ERISA],' it transforms default law into mandatory law." John H. Langbein & Bruce A. Wolk, Pension and Employee Benefit Law 682 (2000).

[231] For musings on the meaning of the word *speculation, see* Joel C. Dobris, *Speculations on the Idea of Speculation in Trust Investing: An Essay,* 39 Real Prop. Prob. & Tr. J. 439 (2004).

[232] *See generally* 4 Scott & Ascher §20.1 (Impartiality Between Successive Beneficiaries).

[233] *See generally* 4 Scott & Ascher §20.1 (Impartiality Between Successive Beneficiaries).

[234] 4 Scott & Ascher §19.1.2 (Trust Investments in the United States).

[235] Law of Property (Amendment) Act. 1859, 22 & 23 Vict., c. 35, §32.

[236] *See generally* 4 Scott & Ascher §19.1.3 (Requirement of Care).

[237] *See generally* 4 Scott & Ascher §19.1.4 (Requirement of Skill).

[238] *See generally* 4 Scott & Ascher §19.1.5 (Requirement of Caution).

[239] *See* 4 Scott & Ascher §19.1.5 n.4 and accompanying text; Trent S. Kiziah, *The Trustee's Duty to Diversify: An Examination of the Developing Case Law,* 36 ACTEC L.J. 357, 359 (2010). *See, e.g.,* Estate of Cooper v. Cooper, 81 Wash. App. 79, 87–88, 913 P.2d 393, 397–398 (1996) (trustee faulted for growing the principal between 1978 and 1987 at an average rate of 2.15 percent per year while the yearly rate of inflation averaged 6 percent over the same period); Restatement (Third) of Trusts: Prudent Investor Rule §232 cmt. c. One commentator, however, has suggested

can be eroded by a temporary decline in the stock or bond markets.[240] For a trust of long duration, inflation is likely to be the greater threat to the principal's purchasing power.[241] The longer the duration of a trust, all things being equal, the more consideration the trustee needs to give to investing in equities.[242] Whether a trustee has a fiduciary duty to the remainder beneficiaries to strive to keep up with inflation, however, will ultimately depend upon the terms of the trust.[243] One court has determined that when there is a duty to distribute all net income to the life beneficiary, there is a duty to preserve and protect the corpus of the trust, but not to "increase" it.[244]

Down through the years, many jurisdictions, either judicially or legislatively, have adopted some form of the rule. Some have adopted the rule almost verbatim;[245] others have tinkered with its language.[246]

In 1900, however, the "legal list" was the norm:

> In fact, by 1900, seventy years after *Amory*, most states still followed the New York "legal list" rule, and only a distinct minority had embraced the Massachusetts prudent man rule. During the 1930s and 1940s, it became increasingly difficult for trustees to find legal investments to purchase. More importantly, because at the time the dividend yield from common stocks substantially exceeded the rate of return then available from fixed income investments found on state law legal lists, many states began adopting the prudent man standard as a means to allow trustees to capture for the current beneficiary the higher yields then available from safe equity investments. As a result, by the late 1940s, the Massachusetts rule had become the majority rule.[247]

---

that under the *Harvard College* prudent man rule, a trustee was only expected to strive to maintain the nominal value of the principal, not the real inflation-adjusted value as would be the case under the prudent investor rule. *See* C. Boone Schwartzel, *Is the Prudent Investor Rule Good for Texas?*, 54 Baylor L. Rev. 701 (2002). *See* Sarlin v. Sarlin, 430 S.E.2d 530, 532 (S.C. Ct. App. 1993) (trustee faulted for investing almost exclusively for growth); In re Trust Created by Martin, 266 Neb. 353, 664 N.W.2d 923 (2003) (holding that trustee who invested preponderance of the trust assets in fixed-income investments did not breach its fiduciary duty to the remaindermen).

[240] *See generally* 4 Scott & Ascher §19.1.7 (suggesting that a trust's portfolio should probably become more liquid as its termination date approaches, particularly if the trustee has no authority to distribute in kind).

[241] *See* In re Trusteeship under Agreement with Mayo, 105 N.W.2d 900 (Minn. 1960). *See generally* 4 Scott & Ascher §19.1.5 (Requirement of Caution) (suggesting that in an inflationary economy, purchasing power typically "decays" when a portfolio is invested in an "overly cautious" way).

[242] For more on the trustee's duty of impartiality, *see* §6.2.5 of this handbook.

[243] *See generally* 4 Scott & Ascher §19.1.7 (Selection of Investments).

[244] SunTrust Bank v. Merritt, et al., 612 S.E.2d 818 (Ga. Ct. App. 2005). *See generally* Trent S. Kiziah, *The Trustee's Duty to Diversify: An Examination of the Developing Case Law*, 36 ACTEC L.J. 357 (2010).

[245] *See generally* 3 Scott on Trusts §227.5; Restatement (Third) of Trusts (Prudent Investor Rule) topic 5 (Investment of Trust Funds) introduction 3 (1992); Bogert §§612–613.

[246] *See, e.g.*, Bogert §§612 n.17 cmt., 613 n.14.

[247] C. Boone Schwartzel, *Is the Prudent Investor Rule Good for Texas?*, 54 Baylor L. Rev. 701, 710–711 (2002). *See generally* 4 Scott & Ascher §19.1.2.

For many states the problem with the "legal list" approach to fiduciary investing was its perceived inflexibility.[248] There have been some hold-outs, however. "Virginia . . . [, for example] . . . is one of the very few states, if not the only, that affords a fiduciary, whether individual or corporate, absolute immunity from claims . . . [of imprudent investing of] . . . trust assets, provided the fiduciary invests in the assets specified by statute."[249]

The *Harvard College* Prudent Man Rule has shown itself remarkably adaptable to changing economic environments.[250] In 1974 Congress included a modified version of the rule in the Employee Retirement Income Security Act (the *Federal Prudent Man Rule*).[251]

It should be noted here, however, that while most states had by 1981 adopted some version of the Prudent Man Rule for trust investments,[252] a number of states have retained the statutory "legal list" for personal representatives (executors and administrators), guardians, and conservators.[253] "In addition, all state investment statutes made certain federal, state and local bonds or other obligations 'legal investments' for trustees and other fiduciaries."[254] The investment statutes of all states, the District of Columbia, and the United Kingdom are reproduced in Sections 615–666 of Bogert, Trusts and Trustees.

The prudent investor rule. As the twentieth century was drawing to a close, some academics and investment professionals had become persuaded that "much of the apparent and initially intended generality and adaptability of the *Harvard College* prudent man rule [had been] lost as it [had been] elaborated in the courts and applied case by case."[255] In some jurisdictions, certain investment practices, as a practical matter, had come to be off-limits to even the most careful, skillful, and cautious of trustees (*e.g.*, engaging in futures and option trading and venture capital programs), at least that was the conventional

---

[248] *See* 3 Scott on Trusts §227.13 (New York is a good example); today only two states have legal lists limited to debt securities. Ala. Const. art. IV, §74 (1901, amended 1939); Ala. Code §19-3-120-128 (1994); Ky. Rev. Stat. Ann. §§386.020 and 386.800(3) (Michie/Bobbs-Merrill 1994). *See also* First Ala. Bank v. Martin, 425 So. 2d 415, 427 (Ala. 1982) (beneficiary consent not a defense to trustee investing off the legal list).

[249] J. H. Scott v. United States, 186 F. Supp. 2d 664, 667 (2002) (citing to Va. Code Ann. §§26-40, 26-40.01 (Michie 1992)).

[250] *See* Bergquist, *The Prudent Man Rule in Massachusetts Today,* 122 Tr. & Est. 44 (Dec. 1983).

[251] *See* 29 C.F.R. §2550.404a-1 (1974); Bogert §612 n.20; Restatement (Third) of Trusts (Prudent Investor Rule) §227 Reporter's Note 66–67 (1992).

[252] *See generally* 4 Scott & Ascher §19.1.2.

[253] Bogert §613.

[254] Bogert §613.

[255] *See* Restatement (Third) of Trusts (Prudent Investor Rule) topic 5 (Investment of Trust Funds) introduction 3 (1992). *See generally* 4 Scott & Ascher §19.1.2.

wisdom in some circles.[256] As interpreted, the Rule had become "in the eyes of many quite obstreperous."[257]

Moreover, the need for a clear distinction between trust accounting income and principal implicit in the *Harvard College* Prudent Man Rule arguably had become somewhat blunted by three developments: (1) the eclipse of the income-only[258] trust by the discretionary trust, particularly of the type that has principal invasion provisions;[259] (2) the practice of gauging investment performance not only by the income that is produced but also by how much the principal has appreciated (the *total return* concept);[260] and (3) the economic reality[261] that many good companies had not been issuing, or had never issued, dividends.[262] One learned commentator has elaborated on the shrinking-dividend phenomenon:

---

[256] Restatement (Third) of Trusts §90 cmt. f. [Restatement (Third) of Trusts: Prudent Investor Rule. §227 cmt. f]. *See generally* 4 Scott & Ascher §19.1.6 (Kinds of Investments); Gordon, *The Puzzling Persistence of the Constrained Prudent Man Rule*, 62 N.Y.U. L. Rev. 52 (1987) (arguing that a constrained conception of the prudent man rule deters trustees from making many favorable investments such as start-up enterprises, short sales, options, and futures).

[257] 4 Scott & Ascher §19.1.2.

[258] By "income only," we mean the governing instrument mandates distribution of all net trust accounting income to the current beneficiary and makes no provision for the invasion of principal. *See generally* 4 Scott & Ascher §20.1 (Impartiality Between Successive Beneficiaries) (noting that "an income beneficiary has traditionally been entitled to the entire income and nothing else").

[259] Under a typical discretionary trust, the trustee, among other things, has a discretionary power to invade principal to or for the benefit of the current beneficiary. *See generally* 4 Scott & Ascher §20.1 (Impartiality Between Successive Beneficiaries) (noting, however, that "despite the rise of the discretionary trust, there remain a great many beneficiaries whose only entitlement consists of an interest in income or an interest in principal").

[260] *See* Restatement (Third) of Trusts §90 cmt. i [Restatement (Third) of Trusts: Prudent Investor Rule §227 cmt. i.]; §6.2.4.6 of this handbook (noting that a portfolio's total return is the sum of income, *e.g.*, dividends, interest, and the like, and realized and unrealized capital gains); 4 Scott & Ascher §20.1 (Impartiality Between Successive Beneficiaries); Trent S. Kiziah, *The Trustee's Duty to Diversify: An Examination of the Developing Case Law*, 36 ACTEC L.J. 357 n.11 (2010) ("For all purposes of this outline, the phrase 'modern portfolio theory' is meant to encompass Markowitz's portfolio theory, the capital asset pricing model, the efficient market theory and other similar modern theories of investing"). *See generally* Robert B. Wolf, *Total Return Trusts—A Decade of Progress, But Are We There Yet?* (Parts 3 & 4 of 4), 32 ACTEC L.J. 101 (2006); Robert B. Wolf, *Total Return Trusts: Can Your Clients Afford Anything Less?*, 24 ACTEC Notes 45 (1998); Jerold I. Horn, *Prudent Investor Rule, Modern Portfolio Theory, and Private Trusts: Drafting and Administration Including the Give-Me-Five Unitrust*, 33 Real Prop. Prob. & Tr. J. 1 (No. 1 Spring 1998); Robert B. Wolf, *Defeating the Duty to Disappoint Equally—The Total Return Trust*, 32 Real Prop. Prob. & Tr. J. 45 (1997); Dobris, *New Forms of Private Trusts for the Twenty-First Century*, 31 Real Prop. Prob. & Tr. J. 1 (Spring 1996).

[261] *But see* Jonathan Clements, *FedEx Delivers: Its Small New Dividend Gives Hope That More Firms Will Follow*, Wall St. J., June 5, 2002, at D1.

[262] *See* Kenneth N. Gilpin, *The Dividend Check Isn't in the Mail*, N.Y. Times, Feb. 4, 2001, at BU10, col. 2; Karen Hube, *More Dividends Go the Way of the Dinosaur*, Wall St. J., Feb. 24, 2000, at R6; Jeremy J. Siegel, *The Dividend Deficit*, Wall St. J., Feb. 12, 2002, at A20, col. 4 (blaming in part the U.S. tax laws for the dramatic decline in the dividend yield and thus the "concrete evidence" of real earnings: "Since realized capital gains are now taxed at a maximum 20% (half the top rate on dividends), shareholders prefer that companies use earnings to lift the price of their shares rather than pay taxes on dividends.").

[T]he dividend yield, and thus the concrete evidence of real earnings, has declined dramatically in recent years. In the 19th century and first half of the 20th century the average dividend yield on stocks was 5.8%. It was not until 1958 that the dividend yield on stocks fell below the interest rate on long-term government bonds and even through the 1980s the dividend yield averaged 4.3%. But during the great bull market of the 1990s, dividends fell out of favor. The dividend yield sunk to 1.2% at the market peak in March 2000 and has subsequently risen to only 1.6%.[263]

Committed to the proposition that investment prudence ought not to be judged on the basis of each individual security in isolation,[264] but on the basis of the portfolio as a whole, these law reformers set about crafting model legislation that would codify this portfolio-as-a-whole bias.[265] It was also felt that the hard-and-fast default rule that a trustee shall not speculate needed to be moderated somewhat.[266] In 1992, the American Law Institute promulgated the culmination of these reform efforts, the so-called *Prudent Investor Rule*:

> **§227 *General Standard of Prudent Investment* [Now Restatement (Third) of Trusts §90]**
>
> *The trustee is under a duty to the beneficiaries to invest and manage the funds of the trust as a prudent investor would, in light of the purposes, terms, distribution requirements, and other circumstances of the trust.*
>
> *(a) This standard requires the exercise of reasonable care, skill, and caution, and it is to be applied to investments not in isolation but in the context of the trust portfolio and as a part of an overall investment strategy, which should incorporate risk and return objectives reasonably suitable to the trust.*
>
> *(b) In making and implementing investment decisions, the trustee has a duty to diversify the investments of the trust unless, under the circumstances, it is prudent not to do so.*[267]

---

[263] Jeremy J. Siegel, *The Dividend Deficit*, Wall St. J., Feb. 12, 2002, at A20, col. 4.

[264] *See generally* 4 Scott & Ascher §19.1.2 (noting that the "requirement of caution gave rise to an interpretation of the prudent person rule itself that allowed beneficiaries to contest the prudence of a trustee's investments on an asset-by-asset basis").

[265] *See generally* 4 Scott & Ascher §19.1.2. *See, e.g.*, 12 C.F.R. §9.18(a) n.1 (1997) (Revised Reg. 9) (available at <www.gpoaccess.gov/cfr/index.html>) (providing that in determining whether investing fiduciary assets in a collective investment fund is proper, the bank may consider the fund as a whole and, for example, shall not be prohibited from making that investment because any particular asset is nonincome producing).

[266] *See generally* 4 Scott & Ascher §19.1.2.

[267] Restatement (Third) of Trusts §90 [Restatement (Third) of Trusts: Prudent Investor Rule §227]. The Uniform Prudent Investor Act is available at <http://www.uniformlaws.org/ Act.aspx?title=Trust%20Code> as Article 9 of the UTC. *See generally* Martin D. Begleiter, *Does the Prudent Investor Need the Uniform Prudent Investor Act—An Empirical Study of Investment Practices*, 51 Me. L. Rev. 27 (1999). *See generally* 4 Scott & Ascher §19.1.2.

The Uniform Prudent Investor Act incorporates these revised standards for prudent trust investment promulgated by the American Law Institute in its Restatement (Third) of Trusts.[268] The Uniform Prudent Management of Institutional Funds Act (UPMIFA) has taken the principles of the Uniform Prudent Investor Act and modified them to fit the "special needs" of charitable trusts and charitable corporations.[269]

As of 2011, the Uniform Prudent Investor Act had been enacted by 41 states and the District of Columbia. Only Colorado had done so, however, without any changes.

Are the Prudent Investor Rule (PIR) and modern portfolio theory (MPT) joined at the hip? As we shall see later in this section, there seems to be a general perception among its detractors that that is the case, that modern portfolio theory is in fact a gloss on the Rule.[270] Was that intended by the American Law Institute? This is hard to tell as the commentary in the Restatement (Third) of Trusts is ambiguous. There is much general commentary to the effect that "specific investments *or techniques* are not per se prudent or imprudent."[271] And then there is other more-specific commentary suggesting a modern portfolio theory bias, such as the following: "These criticisms of the prudent man rule are supported by a large and growing body of literature that is in turn supported by empirical research, well documented and essentially compelling. Much but not all of the criticism is found in writings that have collectively and loosely come to be called modern portfolio theory."[272] For what it is worth, the Supreme Judicial Court of Massachusetts (the court that authored the venerable and now-discarded Harvard College Prudent Man Rule) takes it as a given that the PIR and MPT are a package, at least the version of the PIR that was enacted in Massachusetts.[273]

If the PIR and MPT actually are a package, then trustees and jurists alike need to be mindful of the growing disenchantment of investment professionals with MPT, a phenomenon we address later in this section.[274] The PIR may already be on the road to becoming obsolete.

For an explanation of MPT that is written "by a layperson for laypersons," the reader is referred to Paul G. Haskell, *The Prudent Person Rule for Trustee Investment and Modern Portfolio Theory*.[275] For a succinct explanation of the case

---

[268] The full text of the Act is reprinted in Bogert §613. It is also available at <http://www.uniformlaws.org/Act.aspx?title=Trust%20Code> (UTC, Art. 9).

[269] Unif. Prudent Management of Inst. Funds Act, Prefatory Note.

[270] *See, e.g.,* Stewart E. Sterk, *Rethinking Trust Law Reform: How Prudent is Modern Prudent Investor Doctrine?*, 95 Cornell L. Rev. 851 (2010).

[271] *See* Restatement (Third) of Trusts §90 [Restatement (Third) of Trusts: Prudent Investor Rule §227 cmt. f] (emphasis added).

[272] *See* Restatement (Third) of Trusts §90 [Restatement (Third) of Trusts: Prudent Investor Rule §227 Introduction].

[273] *See* The Woodward School for Girls, Inc. v. City of Quincy, trustee, SJC-11390, 2013 WL 8923423, n.17 (Mass. July 23, 2014).

[274] *See, e.g.,* Stewart E. Sterk, *Rethinking Trust Law Reform: How Prudent is Modern Prudent Investor Doctrine?*, 95 Cornell L. Rev. 851 (2010).

[275] 69 N.C. L. Rev. 87 (1990).

against MPT, see Brown Brothers Harriman & Co.'s investment manifesto *What We Believe, BBH's Principles of Investing*. Here is the gist of its message: "So we find that the fundamental assumption of Modern Portfolio Theory is imperfect at best, and one that we do not share."

One has a sense that the PIR may be suffering death by a thousand tweaks, tweaks that are being administered by statute, commentary, and court decision. Trent S. Kiziah's *Remaining Heterogeneity in Trust Investment Law after Twenty-Five Years of Reform* chronicles state by state the legislative tweaking.[276] As for skeptical commentary, Brown Brothers Harriman & Co. anti-MPT investment manifesto is just the tip of the iceberg. Toward the end of this section we flag some commentary that presumes to attack the Prudent Investor Rule head on.

And as for tweaking by court decision, *Carter v. Carter* (2012) out of the Appellate Court of Illinois, which one commentator has characterized as "eviscerating" the Illinois Prudent Investor Rule, is as good an example as any.[277] The case involved a trustee/current beneficiary who invested 100 percent of the trust portfolio in municipal bonds. At minimum it would be fair to say that the PIR has suffered some significant judicial marginalization in the State of Illinois as a result of the *Carter* case. Here is an excerpt from the decision: "...we find that the trial court did not err in finding that...[the Plaintiff]...failed to establish a cause of action under the prudent investor rule where there is no evidence that...[the trustee's]...decision to invest in municipal bonds was arbitrary or unreasonable."[278] The words of Justice J.D. Heydon of the High Court of Australia come to mind: "...[Still, over the long term,]...the silent waters of equity run deep—often too deep for legislation to obstruct."[279]

For more on the delegation aspects of the Uniform Prudent Investor Act, the reader is referred to Section 6.1.4 of this handbook.

The trustee's duty to monitor investments. On this side of the Atlantic, a trustee has a continuing duty to monitor trust investments and remove imprudent ones. This continuing duty exists separate and apart from the trustee's duty to exercise prudence in selecting investments at the outset.[280] So also on the other side of the Atlantic: "The England and Wales *Trustee Act 2000* states in s4(2): 'A trustee must from time to time review the investments of the trust.' This reiterates the common-law position set out by Leggatt LJ in *Nestle v National*

---

[276] 37 ACTEC L.J. 317 (Fall 2011).

[277] Carter v. Carter, 965 N.E.2d 1146 (2012).

[278] Carter v. Carter, 965 N.E.2d 1146, 1158 (2012).

[279] The Hon. Justice J.D. Heydon, A.C., *Does statutory reform stultify trusts law analysis?*, 6 Tr. Q. Rev. 3, 28 (2008) [a STEP publication].

[280] *See* Bogert §§684 & 685; 4A Scott & Ascher §19.3.1; Uniform Prudent Investor Act §2, cmt.; Restatement (Third) of Trusts §90, cmt. b; In re Stark's Estate, 15 N.Y.S. 729, 731 (Surr. Ct. 1891) (a trustee must "exercise[e] a reasonable degree of diligence in looking after the security after the investment has been made"); Johns v. Herbert, 2 App. D.C. 485, 499 (1894) (trustee liable for failure to discharge his "duty to watch the investment with reasonable care and diligence").

Westminster Bank Plc,[281] which confirmed that periodic reviews of investments should be undertaken."[282]

In the face of such a "continuing duty," a statute of limitations that purports to set up a time defense to actions against trustees for imprudent investing is likely to be a paper tiger as a practical matter, absent special facts.[283] Statutes of limitations in the fiduciary context are discussed generally in §7.1.3 of this handbook.

A gain may not offset a loss occasioned by a breach. It is traditional default law that a trustee is not entitled to offset a loss occasioned by a breach of trust with a gain that has *not* been occasioned by a breach of trust.[284] Thus, before the PIR came on the scene, the trustee in some jurisdictions may have risked *per se* liability if he invested, say, 5 percent of the portfolio in gold ingots and another 5 percent in a gold mine, the former, taken in isolation, being a classic speculation and the latter, taken in isolation, being a classic wasting asset. But if the appropriateness of an investment is assessed in the context of the trust portfolio as a whole, then no investment is *per se* prudent or imprudent. The particular circumstances of the trust, the reasonableness of the trustee's choice of an overall investment strategy, and the extent to which the investment complements that strategy are all factors that the court must take into account in determining whether the trustee was imprudent in investing in the gold ingots or the gold mine, as the case may be.[285] Clearly it will take some time to harmonize the Prudent Investor Rule with the rule that a trustee may not offset a breach with a gain.[286] The process began a decade before the advent of the Prudent Man Rule with *Matter of Bank of New York,*[287] which one learned commentator has characterized as a "transitional case":[288]

> The record of any individual investment is not to be viewed exclusively, of course, as though it were in its own water-tight compartment; since to some extent individual investment decisions may properly be affected by considerations of the performance of the fund as an entity, as in the instance, for example, of individual security decisions based in part on considerations of diversification of the fund or of capital transactions to achieve sound tax planning for the fund as a whole.[289]

---

[281] [1992] EWCA (Civ) 12.

[282] Tom Glanville, *Time for your check-up*, 23/Issue 4 STEP J. 69 (May 2015).

[283] *Cf.* Tibble v. Edison Int'l, 575 U.S. ___ (2015), U.S. Sup. Ct., No. 13-550 (May 18, 2015) (an ERISA case in which the court piggybacked on the common law of trusts).

[284] 4 Scott & Ascher §24.18 (Balancing Losses Against Gains). *See, e.g.,* JP Morgan Chase Bank, N.A. (Strong), 2013 WL 6182548 (N.Y. Sur.) (holding that a loss occasioned by a single imprudent investment made by the trustee may not be offset for damages-computation purposes by an overall gain (net gain) in the value of the trust's portfolio).

[285] *Cf.* In re Hyde, 44 A.D.3d 1195, 845 N.Y.S.2d 833 (2007) (that the trust's portfolio "heavily concentrated" in the stock of a closely held family corporation not *per se* imprudent).

[286] 4 Scott & Ascher §24.18 (Balancing Losses Against Gains).

[287] 323 N.E.2d 700 (N.Y. 1974).

[288] 4 Scott & Ascher §24.18 (Balancing Losses Against Gains).

[289] Matter of Bank of N.Y., 323 N.E.2d 700, 703 (N.Y. 1974).

Asset allocation. What is the optimal asset mix for a trust?[290] That is a subject beyond the scope of this handbook and far better covered by others.[291] The traditional trust portfolio consists of a mix of equities (common stock) and indebtedness (*e.g.*, bonds, debentures, promissory notes, and money market instruments).[292] At one time, the prevailing practice was to weight the mix in favor of fixed income securities; today, the prevailing practice is to weight the mix in favor of equities.[293] Whether the prevailing practice is a prudent one is another matter. One commentator and fiduciary litigator has his doubts: "The standard 60/40 allocation between equities and bonds may no longer work, disrupted by the periodic crashes in the equity markets that have crippled returns, and the low return of bonds, which no longer provide either the assured high income or the downside protection of earlier decades."[294] Suffice it to say that in the case of a widespread market decline, the trustee *as a matter of law* would not be immune from liability for any losses that are occasioned by misallocation merely because those losses happen to "correlate" with the market's decline.[295] "Coincide" is, perhaps, the better word in this context.

While investing in fixed-income securities presumably generates a predictable stream of income, they can lose some of their real value in periods of inflation and/or escalating interest rates.[296] Equities, on the other hand, tend to keep pace with inflation but can lose their value in periods when the market is

---

[290] *See generally* 4 Scott & Ascher §19.1.6 (Kinds of Investments) (noting that "at one time in England, and at various times and in various places in the United States, there were restrictions on the types of investments that were considered proper for a trustee").

[291] Restatement (Third) of Trusts §90 cmt. k [Restatement (Third) of Trusts: Prudent Investor Rule §227 cmt. k]; 4 Scott & Ascher §19.1.7 (Selection of Investments).

[292] Restatement (Third) of Trusts §90 cmts. k, l, & m [Restatement (Third) of Trusts: Prudent Investor Rule §227 cmts. k, l, & m].

[293] Restatement (Third) of Trusts §90 cmts. k, l, & m [Restatement (Third) of Trusts: Prudent Investor Rule §227 cmts. k, l, & m]. *See generally* 4 Scott & Ascher §19.2.

[294] Dominic J. Campisi, *Fiduciary Liability*, 136 ABA Trust & Investments, July–August 2010, at 12 [American Bankers Association].

[295] *See* Greenberg v. JP Morgan Chase Bank, N.A., 2014 N.Y. Slip Op. 31122(U) (Apr. 25, 2014).

[296] A bond is a fixed-income security that is subject to market value fluctuation over its life. It is referred to as a "fixed-income" security because the *amount* of interest it generates is set. To illustrate how a bond's value can fluctuate, let us take a U.S. Treasury thirty-year bond that was issued and sold in 1993. The initial investor/lender purchased it for $1,000. The bond is generating interest at an annual rate of 6.25 percent ($62.50). At the expiration of the thirty-year period, the terms provide that the then-holder will receive $1,000. In 1994, only a year or so into the life of the bond, the interest rate of newly issued bonds went up to 8.1 percent. Our investor/lender, for whatever reason, sold the bond. He only got $782 for it, 22 percent less than he paid for it. Why was this? Because the potential buyers in 1994 would naturally settle for no less than an 8.1 percent return on their investments (the prevailing rate). With the bond's stream of interest being "fixed," the only play was in the market price of the bond itself. Accordingly, for the bond's return to get up to 8.1 percent, the price of the bond had to go down to $782. The point again: The market value of fixed-income investments can fluctuate from the time of issue to the time of maturity. A debenture is essentially an unsecured bond. *See generally* §9.31 of this handbook (corporate trusts; trusts to secure creditors; the Trust Indenture Act of 1939; protecting bondholders).

down.[297] "Do what you will, the capital is at hazard."[298] Even inflation-indexed U.S. Treasury bonds "can post nasty short-term losses" should interest rates rise.[299] Thus the prudent trustee not only calls for a reasonable balance between equities and fixed income securities but also diversification among economic sectors, geographical areas,[300] and maturity dates,[301] of course taking into account in the formulation of investment objectives the settlor's intentions.[302] If the trustee's only breach of trust is negligently investing too large a portion of the trust estate in a single investment or type of investment, the trustee is liable "for such loss as results from investment of the excess over what would have been a proper investment."[303]

---

[297] Restatement (Third) of Trusts §90 [Restatement (Third) of Trusts: Prudent Investor Rule §227].

[298] Harvard Coll. v. Amory, 26 Mass. (9 Pick.) 446, 461 (1830). *See generally* Trent S. Kiziah, *The Trustee's Duty to Diversify: An Examination of the Developing Case Law*, 36 ACTEC L.J. 357, 359 (2010) ("A fundamental tenet of MPT is the premise that all investments, including U.S. Treasuries, may become worthless or more commonly, may not perform in the manner anticipated, a concept referred to as 'risk.' Every investment faces internal and external factors which give rise to risk, known as 'firm risk.'").

[299] *See* Jonathan Clements, *One of the World's 'Safest' Investments Still Carries the Risk of Painful Losses*, Wall St. J., Aug. 27, 2003, at D1. *Cf.* GIW Indus. v. Trevor, Stewart, Burton & Jacobsen, Inc., 895 F.2d 729 (11th Cir. 1990) (investing in mortgage notes with a long history of repayment nonetheless exposes ERISA plan assets to risks of holding fixed-return obligations in a period of volatile interest rates, default not being only risk addressed by ERISA §404(a)(1)(C)). *See also* John H. Langbein, *Mandatory Rules in the Law of Trusts*, 98 Nw. U. L. Rev. 1105, 1113 (2004) (advising that "[e]ven a blue chip can suffer catastrophic and wholly unpredictable losses—as happened, for example, to the share of the Union Carbide Company in the wake of the 1984 Bhopal disaster or to Texaco, then independent and one of the major international oil companies, when a fluke lawsuit forced it into bankruptcy in 1987").

[300] *See generally* Frederic J. Bendremer, *Modern Portfolio Theory and International Investments Under the Uniform Prudent Investor Act*, 35 Real Prop. Prob. & Tr. J. 791 (2001) (examining Modern Portfolio Theory as a basis for diversification and the role of international investments within fiduciary portfolios). *See also* 4 Scott & Ascher §19.1.11 (confirming that "numerous cases have held that a trustee does not commit a breach of trust merely by investing in property the situs of which lies outside the state . . . [in which the trust was created and administered] . . . ," although there are some older cases that hold otherwise).

[301] *See, e.g.,* GIW Indus. v. Trevor, Stewart, Burton & Jacobsen, Inc., 895 F.2d 729 (11th Cir. 1990) (investment of 70 percent of ERISA plan assets in government bonds with a single maturity date and 15 percent in zero coupon bonds with a different maturity date exposes plan assets to unacceptable risk in that the trustee might need to liquidate a portion or all of the portfolio when the bond market is down).

[302] *See* Restatement (Third) of Trusts §90 cmts. e–h [Restatement (Third) of Trusts: Prudent Investor Rule §227 cmts. e–h]; 4 Scott & Ascher §19.2 (The Duty to Diversify); In re Dickinson, 152 Mass. 184, 25 N.E. 99 (1890). *But see* In re Adriance's Estate, 145 Misc. 345, 260 N.Y.S. 173 (Surr. Ct. 1932) ("It is entirely true that many financial authorities advocate wide diversity of investment. It is equally true that others as strenuously affirm the contrary, and agree with the familiar admonition of the late Andrew Carnegie: 'Put all your eggs in one basket and watch the basket.' "). It should be noted that in 1995 New York adopted a version of §227 [now Restatement (Third) of Trusts §90], including its diversification requirements. N.Y. Est. Powers & Trusts Law §11-2.3 (1995). *See generally* Estate of Cooper, 913 P.2d 393 (Wash. Ct. App. 1996) (trustee surcharge for imprudent asset balance).

[303] 4 Scott & Ascher §19.2.1 (Extent of Liability). *See generally* §7.2.3.2 of this handbook (damages as an equitable relief for the trustee failing to properly invest the trust property).

The insurance contract as an investment. The terms of the trust may require that the trust's principal investment be a *life insurance contract* on the settlor's life.[304] Still, "[a] survey of the literature following the 1992 publication of Restatement Third reveals several articles suggesting that life insurance is a 'fiduciary' asset that requires the trustee to devote a level of care, skill, and caution comparable to other traditional investments (*e.g.*, stocks and bonds)."[305] Upon the death of the insured, whether the trustee should elect to leave the proceeds with the insurance company or take a lump sum will generally depend upon whether leaving the proceeds with the company would be a prudent investment under the given circumstances.[306]

A trustee who purchases with trust principal a commercial *annuity contract* on the life of the current beneficiary is investing in what amounts to a speculative wasting asset. On its face, at least, it would appear that the remaindermen are being disadvantaged, particularly if the annuity payments are to be paid to the current beneficiary.[307] Also, "[a]t one time, such a purchase might have been deemed improper, as an unsecured loan to the life insurance company."[308] While today purchasing with principal an annuity contract is not *per se* imprudent,[309] in most actual situations it probably is. Of course, if the trustee is authorized to invade principal, such an investment may be less problematic.[310] Still, a trustee who contemplates making such an investment should document in advance why he considers it a prudent thing to do under the circumstances, as well as why his duty of loyalty to the remaindermen[311] and his duty to give personal attention to the affairs of the trust[312] are not implicated. Certainly the trustee would be ill-advised to rely on the advice and counsel of the insurance broker as to what his fiduciary duties are with respect to the purchase and administration of the annuity contract.[313] That function is best left to independent legal counsel.[314]

---

[304] *See generally* 4 Scott & Ascher §§19.2 (The Duty to Diversity), 19.1.8 (Questions Relating to Life Insurance); §9.2 of this handbook (the irrevocable life insurance trust).

[305] Kathryn A. Ballsun, Patrick J. Collins, & Dieter Jurkat, *Standards of Prudence and Management of the Insurance Portfolio*, 32 ACTEC L.J. 66, 67 (2006). *See, e.g.*, Stuart Cochran Irrevocable Trust v. Keybank, 901 N.E.2d 1128 (Ind. Ct. App. 2009). *See also* Kathryn A. Ballsun, Patrick J. Collins, & Dieter Jurkat, *Evidencing Care, Skill and Caution in The Management of ILITs (Part 3 of 4)*, 32 ACTEC L.J. 145 (2006); Kathryn A. Ballsun, Patrick J. Collins, & Dieter Jurkat, *ILIT Asset Management: The Written Investment Policy Statement (Part 4 of 4)*, 32 ACTEC L.J. 229 (2006).

[306] *See generally* 4 Scott & Ascher §§19.1.8 (Questions Relating to Life Insurance), 19.2 (The Duty to Diversify).

[307] *See generally* 4 Scott & Ascher §19.1.8.

[308] 4 Scott & Ascher §19.1.8.

[309] 4 Scott & Ascher §19.1.8.

[310] 4 Scott & Ascher §19.1.8. For a discussion of trustee powers to invade principal and discretionary trusts in general, the reader is referred to §3.5.3.2(a) of this handbook.

[311] *See generally* §6.2.5 of this handbook (trustee's duty of impartiality).

[312] *See generally* §6.1.4 of this handbook (trustee's duty not to delegate critical fiduciary functions).

[313] *Cf.* §8.32 of this handbook (whether the trustee can escape liability for making a mistake of law if he acted in good faith on advice of counsel).

[314] *See generally* §8.8 of this handbook (whom trust counsel represents).

For a discussion of whether a particular annuity payment belongs entirely in the income account or entirely in the principal account, or whether it is to be somehow apportioned between the two accounts, the reader is referred to Section 6.2.4.3 of this handbook.

Diversification. The law as to what constitutes prudent diversification is not settled.[315] Empirical studies examining the number of stocks needed to diversify diversifiable risk are all over the lot: "Several empirical studies have shown that as few as ten to fifteen securities can significantly reduce compensated risk. Other studies showed that twenty stocks are necessary for optimal diversification. One recent study has concluded that 120 stocks are now required in order to reach an optimal level of diversification."[316] Rodney Sullivan, editor of Financial Analysts Journal, puts the number at 40.[317] And then there is Pudd'nhead Wilson's Calendar:

> Behold, the fool saith, "Put not all thine eggs in the one basket"—which is but a manner of saying, "Scatter your money and your attention"; but the wise man saith, "Put all your eggs in the one basket and –WATCH THAT BASKET."[318]

Section 3 of the Uniform Prudent Investor Act requires that "[a] trustee shall diversify the investments of the trust unless the trustee reasonably determines that, because of special circumstances, the purposes of the trust are better served without diversifying."[319] This has sparked a debate between the "indexers" and the "stock pickers."

An index fund is a type of mutual fund or unit investment trust "whose investment objective typically is to achieve approximately the same return as a particular market index, such as the S & P 500 Composite Stock Price Index, the Russell 2000 Index or the Wilshire 5000 Total Market Index. An index fund will attempt to achieve its investment objective primarily by investing in securities (stocks and bonds) of companies that are included in a selected index."[320] It is said that the fund is "passively" invested.

Passive investing in the commercial context is nothing new. The Massachusetts Investors Trust (MIT), said to be the first open-end mutual fund to be established in the United States (March 1924), started out being passively

---

[315] *See generally* 4 Scott & Ascher §19.2 (How Much Diversification Is Enough?); 76 Am. Jur. 2d, *Trusts* §542. In the ERISA context, there is no "empirical formula" used to determine whether a portfolio is adequately diversified. *See* Meyer v. Berkshire Life Ins. Co., 250 F. Supp. 2d 544 (2003); Olsen v. Hegarty, 180 F. Supp. 2d 552 (2001).

[316] Trent S. Kiziah, *The Trustee's Duty to Diversify: An Examination of the Developing Case Law*, 36 ACTEC L.J. 357, 362–363 (2010).

[317] Jason Zweig, *Simple Index Funds May Be Complicating the Markets*, Wall St. J., Feb. 18–19, 2012, at B1.

[318] Mark Twain, Pudd'nhead Wilson and Those Extraordinary Twins 79 (Norton Critical Edition, 2d ed. 2005).

[319] Available at <http://www.uniformlaws.org/Act.aspx?title=Trust%20Code> as Article 9 of the UTC. 29 U.S.C. §1104(a)(1)(C) is the ERISA section that "guards against undiversified investment schemes that subject ERISA plans to undue risk of loss." Olsen v. Hegarty, 180 F. Supp. 2d 552 (2001).

[320] *See* <https://www.sec.gov/answers/indexf.htm> (an SEC on-line publication).

invested. A 1925 MIT promotional brochure explained: "The Trust, by complete diversification, both geographically and industrially, has eliminated the human element of prediction by adopting the mechanical Law of Averages as successfully demonstrated by insurance companies. The Trust's holdings of over 120 representative stocks cover about sixty different industries."[321]

Present-day indexers accept the proposition that over time, the market cannot be beaten.[322] They find the efficient markets theory compelling, namely that "the trading by investors in a free and competitive market drives security prices to their true 'fundamental' values,"[323] that "large-scale arbitrage in capital markets is an optimal mechanism for dissemination of information to investors and hence an optimal method of capital allocation in the aggregate economy."[324] Accordingly, "[t]he market can better assess what a stock or a bond is worth than any individual stock trader."[325] An anti-indexer put it this way:

> Perhaps the most compelling evidence in favor of market efficiency is the inability of even the shrewdest investors to consistently beat the market. It isn't just that individual investors trail the passive benchmarks, such as the Standard & Poor's 500, by 2% to 3% a year. Nearly all mutual and pension funds also fail to beat the market on a consistent basis. Even the savviest investors—George Soros, Warren Buffett, Julian Robertson—occasionally stumble.[326]

Indexers also accept the proposition that industry risk and firm risk, for all intents and purposes, are absent in a portfolio of "hundreds of issues."[327] Accordingly, the indexers assert that only by passively investing in index funds can most trustees efficiently and cost-effectively construct portfolios that are

---

[321] According to Michael R. Yogg, "MIT eliminated the human element in favor of the mechanical law of averages because, in fact, it had no research department for the first eight years of its operation." Michael R. Yogg, *Passion for Reality: The Extraordinary Life of the Investing Pioneer Paul Cabot* 39 (Columbia University Press 2014).

[322] *See generally* Jonathan R. Macey, An Introduction to Modern Financial Theory 75 (The American College of Trust and Estate Counsel Foundation 2d ed. 1998) (suggesting that those who would "ignore the learning of modern corporate financial theory and continue to try to beat the market by selecting 'winners' on the basis of fundamental values" do so at their peril). *See also* Langbein & Posner, *Market Funds and Trust-Investment Law*, 1977 Am. B. Found. Res. J., 1, n.3 (1977).

[323] Andrei Shleifer, *Are Markets Efficient? No, Arbitrage Is Inherently Risky*, Wall St. J., Dec. 28, 2000, at A10, col. 3 (defining arbitrage as betting against security mispricing, *i.e.*, that prices will converge to true values).

[324] Joshua Getzler, *Legislative Incursions into Modern Trusts Doctrine in England: The Trustee Act 2000 and the Contracts (Rights of Third Parties) Act 1999*, 2(1) Global Jurist Topics, Art. 2 (2002).

[325] Andrei Shleifer, *Are Markets Efficient? No, Arbitrage Is Inherently Risky*, Wall St. J., Dec. 28, 2000, at A10, col. 3.

[326] Andrei Shleifer, *Are Markets Efficient? No, Arbitrage Is Inherently Risky*, Wall St. J., Dec. 28, 2000, at A10, col. 3.

[327] John H. Langbein, *The Uniform Prudent Investor Act and the Future of Trust Investing*, 81 Iowa L. Rev. 641, 649 (1996). *See generally* 4 Scott & Ascher §19.2.

broad-based enough to satisfy the diversification requirements of Section 3 of the Act.[328]

The stock-pickers counter by asserting that active stock selection based on valuation "fundamentals" is the way to go.[329] Winners can be selected that beat the market, particularly when it is down.[330] Moreover, markets are not efficient. In fact, "deviations from efficiency can be large and persistent, especially with no catalysts to bring markets back to efficiency."[331]

As markets are inefficient, active investment management will pay off in the long run.[332] Because not all stocks in an index will have good fundamentals, a trustee who pursues a passive investment strategy by gathering into a portfolio "hundreds of issues" may well be imprudently overdiversifying that portfolio:

> The portfolio theory was introjected by Posner and Langbein into United States trusts law in the 1970's; they used the theory purely as a micro-economic argument for maximizing return to trust funds. It was not long until linkages were made between the efficacy of portfolio investment and the wider justifications of stock market activity provided by the efficient market hypothesis: portfolio investment enriches the individual investor and at the same time improves the liquidity and

---

[328] John H. Langbein, *The Uniform Prudent Investor Act and the Future of Trust Investing*, 81 Iowa L. Rev. 641, 658 (1996). An index or market fund is designed to hold a basket of securities that approximates the diversification of some index of market performance such as the Standard and Poor's 500 Composite Index. *See generally* Langbein & Posner, *Market Funds and Trust-Investment Law (pts. 1–2)*, 1976 Am. B. Found. Res. J., 1 (1977); 1977 Am. B. Found. Res. J., 1 (1977). *But see* Luther J. Avery & Patrick J. Collins, *Managing Investment Expenses: Trustee Duty to Avoid Unreasonable or Inappropriate Costs*, 25 ACTEC Notes 123, 128 (1999) (suggesting that "[I]ndex funds are, *on average*, less expensive . . . [than their actively managed counterparts] . . . but there is no guarantee that a particular index fund is less expensive than an actively managed counterpart"); Tom Lauricella, *This Is News? Fund Fees Are Too High, Study Says*, Wall St. J., Aug. 27, 2001, at C1, col. 5; Aaron Lucchetti, *Index Funds Aren't Always Tax Efficient*, Wall St. J., July 28, 2000, C1 (noting that rapid run-ups in stock prices and other factors in recent years have meant more-frequent changes to the makeup of indexes, causing more trading and more taxable distributions for investors holding index funds outside tax-sheltered accounts). *See also* Burton G. Malkiel, *Investors Shouldn't Fear Spiders*, Wall St. J., May 30, 2000, at A26 (comparing the open-end index mutual fund with the exchange-traded index fund (ETF) and noting that the latter may offer some advantages over the former when it comes to transaction costs, taxable capital gains realization, and pricing). *See generally* Mutual Funds, Quarterly Review, Wall St. J., Apr. 9, 2001, at R1.

[329] *See, e.g.*, E.S. Browning & Greg Ip, *Back to Basics, After Tech Bubble Bursts, Value Investing Suddenly Makes Sense Again*, Wall St. J., Nov. 27, 2000, at C1, col. 3.

[330] *See generally* Harvey E. Bines, *Modern Portfolio Theory and Investment Management Law: Refinement of Legal Doctrine*, 76 Colum. L. Rev. 721 (1976). *See also* Jonathan R. Macey, An Introduction to Modern Financial Theory 75 (The American College of Trust and Estate Counsel Foundation 2d ed. 1998) (suggesting that "[e]mpirical studies have shown that a small amount of diversification goes a long way"); Joanne Legomsky, *Active Managers Await the Verdict*, N.Y. Times, Apr. 8, 2001, at BU 30, col. 1 (noting that "falling stock prices, which offer precious little consolation to anyone but short-sellers, have at least given actively managed mutual funds a chance to prove something they have claimed: that in bear markets, they are better equipped to outperform their passively managed index-fund cousins").

[331] Burton G. Malkiel, *Are Markets Efficient? Yes, Even if They Make Errors*, Wall St. J., Dec. 28, 2000, at A10, col. 5.

[332] Burton G. Malkiel, *Are Markets Efficient? Yes, Even if They Make Errors*, Wall St. J., Dec. 28, 2000, at A10, col. 5.

efficiency of the entire market, truly the work of a beneficent and invisible hand. However, both justificatory theories are today subject to sustained theoretical and empirical assault by leading economists.[333]

"Efficient-market theorists believe that the stock market acts like a massive computer, with investors acting like microcircuits that quickly marshal all the information at hand and crunching out share prices that represent a rational view of each stock's fundamental value."[334] The efficient market hypothesis,[335] which was "thought up by a French mathematician a century ago and rediscovered by American finance professors in the 1960s,"[336] arguably works only when many investors, believing that the market is actually inefficient, "busy themselves looking for trends, analyzing balance sheets and trading feverishly."[337] Were all investors to become converts to the Hypothesis, the market would then become inefficient. Why? Because they would "lazily put their money in unmanaged index funds, and the market . . . [would] . . . cease to incorporate new information. . . ."[338]

Some who reject the efficient market hypothesis opt for indexing anyway. The markets are so "loony" that one is compelled to invest as if they were efficient:

> According to Kahneman's "prospect theory," most of us find losses roughly twice as painful as we find gains pleasurable. This radical precept subverts much of the "utility theory," the longstanding economic doctrine that says we weigh gain and loss rationally. When combined with the reality that some market winners display the same recklessness as some victorious gamblers—a phenomenon that Richard Thaler, an economist at the University of Chicago, calls "the house-money effect"—the market is often revealed to be downright loony. Indeed, the findings of "behavioral finance" in recent years have increasingly challenged the fundamental rationality assumed by defenders of "efficient markets," those who believe Eugene Fama's famous dictum that prices "fully reflect available information."[339]

And then there is the "black swan" phenomenon. "Critics of investment theory highlight the limitations of standard statistical models, which are

---

[333] Joshua Getzler, *Legislative Incursions into Modern Trusts Doctrine in England: The Trustee Act 2000 and the Contracts (Rights of Third Parties) Act 1999*, 2(1) Global Jurist Topics, Art. 2 (2002).

[334] Justin Lahart, *Blue Screen (Ahead of the Tape)*, Wall St. J., Oct. 5, 2005, C1, col. 1.

[335] For a discussion of the "efficient frontier" in the context of modern portfolio theory and the prudent man rule, *see* Edward A. Moses, J. Clay Singleton, & Stewart A. Marshall, III, *Modern Portfolio Theory and the Prudent Investor Act*, 30 ACTEC L.J. 166 (2004).

[336] Jim Holt, *He Figured the Odds, and They Still Beat Him*, Wall St. J., July 16, 2003, at D8, WL-WSJ 3974156 (reviewing A Mathematician Plays the Stock Market, by John Allen Paulos).

[337] Jim Holt, *He Figured the Odds, and They Still Beat Him*, Wall St. J., July 16, 2003, at D8, WL-WSJ 3974156 (reviewing A Mathematician Plays the Stock Market, by John Allen Paulos).

[338] Jim Holt, *He Figured the Odds, and They Still Beat Him*, Wall St. J., July 16, 2003, at D8, WL-WSJ 3974156 (reviewing A Mathematician Plays the Stock Market, by John Allen Paulos).

[339] Dirk Olin, *Crash Course: Prospect Theory*, N.Y. Times Mag., June 6, 2003, at p. 33.

generally poor at capturing the effect of improbable and unpredictable market crises, which can have an enormous impact on markets."[340]

The index fund. Whatever the case, the fact is that all stock indexes are not the same.[341] Among other things, they will not share the same risk characteristics. Nor are trust purposes all the same. Accordingly, a mechanical or passive approach to index selection would seem ill advised.[342] Certainly, the trustee should eschew "[a] slavish devotion to indexing ... by which money is thrown blindly and in great force at pieces of corporate paper that have been gathered together by the 500s."[343] A trustee, for example, might consider implementing a long-term buy and hold investment strategy using two index funds, one that tracks the Standard & Poor's 500 Composite Index and the other that tracks the Nasdaq-100 Index:[344]

- *Standard & Poor's 500 Composite Index.* The S&P 500 is composed of 500 of the largest companies that trade on the New York Stock Exchange and the NASDAQ. The 500 stocks are grouped into business segments: 400 industrials, 40 financial companies, 40 utilities, and 20 transportations. The S&P 500 more accurately reflects the overall market activity than the Dow because it includes a greater number of stocks. The S&P 500's values are weighted. The price of each stock in the index is multiplied by the number of outstanding stocks and is then divided by the total number of shares included in the index. The weighting of stocks allows the larger companies to have a greater influence on performance than the smaller companies. Starting January 1, 2005, the weighting will reflect available float market capitalization. "That just means it will be based on the value of a company's shares that are available to be traded, and no longer will include shares held by family interests and others."[345]
- *Nasdaq-100 Index.* The Nasdaq-100 Index is composed of the largest nonfinancial U.S. and non-U.S. companies listed on the National Market tier of the Nasdaq Stock Market. It was launched in 1985 with a

---

[340] Mathew Clark, *Investment risk*, 17(1) STEP J 65 (Jan. 2009).

[341] *See generally* Gretchen Morgenson, *Why an Index Isn't a Mirror of the Market*, N.Y. Times, Apr. 9, 2000, at BU 17 (noting that that an S&P 500 stock index fund is not an investment in the broadly diversified overall market and that the investment performance of some funds that track the S&P 500 stock index has been inferior to the performance of the index itself).

[342] *See generally* Jonathan R. Macey, An Introduction to Modern Financial Theory 75, 92 (The American College of Trust and Estate Counsel Foundation 2nd ed. 1998) (suggesting that "even in light of ECMH [The Efficient Capital Markets Hypothesis], there is a demand for financial experts who can assemble well-diversified portfolios because different portfolios will have different risk characteristics"); Patrick Collins, *Fiduciary Duty to Monitor and Review Passively Managed Mutual Funds*, J. Investing (Fall 1999).

[343] Jeffrey Bronchick, *We Need Better Stock Analysis, Not More Info*, Wall St. J., Aug. 6, 2002, at A20, WL-WSJ 3402731.

[344] *See generally* Aaron Lucchetti, *Investors Find Nasdaq Funds Are Elusive*, Wall St. J., Mar. 20, 2000, at C23 (noting that the Nasdaq 100 over the years has beaten the composite).

[345] Gregory Zuckerman, *Float-Weighted S&P 500 Likely to Pressure Some Stocks*, Wall St. J., Sept. 10, 2004, at C1, col. 2.

value set at 250. The Nasdaq-100 is a "modified capitalization-weighted index," *i.e.*, it is designed to prevent a few large companies from dominating the index. The Nasdaq-100 list is revised each December.

The broader "benchmark" indexes include the Wilshire 5000 Equity Index and the NASDAQ Composite Index. *The Wilshire 5000 Equity Index* is the broadest measure of the market. It is a weighted index that is based on the dollar value of more than 7,000 common stocks traded on the NYSE and AMEX.[346] It also has a selection of OTC stocks. The 5,000 in the title is the number of companies that made up the index at its inception. The *NASDAQ Composite Index* is composed of all stocks of companies, domestic and foreign, that trade on the NASDAQ. The index reflects the percentage change in the market value of these stocks traded since February 5, 1971. The current index is determined by the ratio change in the market value from the base period to the current period multiplied by 100. Stocks from six different sub-indexes representing different business segments make up the composite index.

The *Dow Jones Industrial Average* tracks the performance on the New York Stock Exchange on a given day of the stock of thirty major U.S. companies. The thirty blue chips represent a cross-section of U.S. industry. The Dow began in 1896 with twelve companies. Over time, the number has increased. Also, companies have come and gone as American industry has evolved. Dow Jones & Company selects which companies are to be added to the index and which are to be deleted according to undisclosed criteria. Each stock in the DJIA is unweighted. At the end of each day, each company's closing share price is totaled and divided by a number that has been adjusted over time to accommodate splits, spin-offs, and substitutions. The result is the day's "average" (originally, the divisor was 12). This means that each dollar in price carries equal weight regardless of the capitalization or the size of the company. The system allows for companies with higher stock prices to have a greater influence on the average, unlike the S&P 500 and the Wilshire 5000 Equity Index, which employ weighting. Although the number of stocks in the Dow is less than in other indexes, the concept is that each particular stock represents a sector of the economy and thus serves as a reliable measure of the market as a whole.

The *Russell 2000 Index*, created in 1978 by Frank Russell Company in Tacoma, Washington, is a small-capitalization stock index. The index is weighted by capitalization. Once a year, the company reconstitutes the index.[347]

The *Russell 3000 Index* contains the 3,000 largest U.S. stocks, which represent about 98 percent of the investable U.S. equity market. The CREF Stock Account variable annuity uses two benchmarks: The Russell 3000 index for about 80 percent of its portfolio (domestic) and the *MSCI Europe, Australia,*

---

[346] The Vanguard Total Stock Market Index Fund seeks to replicate the Wilshire 5000. Another "total market fund" is the TIAA-CREF Equity Index Fund, which tracks the Russell 3000. Schwab's Total Stock Market Index Fund also tracks the total market.

[347] *See* Tom Lauricella & Ken Brown, *What Constitutes a Russell 2000 Stock Is No Small Matter,* Wall St. J., May 31, 2001, at C1, col. 3 (discussing the mechanics of the annual reconstitution of the index).

Far East (EAFE)+Canada Index for about 20 percent of the portfolio (international).[348] For brief descriptions of *non-U.S. stock indexes*, the reader is referred to the Wall Street Journal.

What is an "underdiversified" portfolio? Perhaps a portfolio that has not diversified out industry and firm risk.[349] One thing is certain: In the years to come, more than one court will be called upon to consider how far below the diversification level of the average index fund is too far.[350]

Sentimentality and other emotions. Sentimentality, public pressure, or inertia can lead to portfolios that are self-evidently underdiversified.[351] So can favoring a professional or social relationship at the expense of the fiduciary relationship, a practice that also would implicate the trustee's duty of loyalty.[352]

Inception assets. The trustee should be particularly wary of retaining property in the form received from the settlor[353] or a prior fiduciary, unless prudent to do so or unless there is authority to do so in the terms of the trust.[354]

---

[348] "By combining two broadly diversified benchmarks and applying an approach that keeps us close to that composite benchmark, we ensure that investors get a very broadly diversified fund to meet their equity allocation." Scott Biddle, director of Equity Portfolio Analytics at TIAA-CREF, in 7 Investment Forum No. 1 (Mar. 2003) at p. 3. "Although this portfolio mix probably won't stand out during the short term, such an approach has a track record of providing competitive long-term returns while keeping the volatility of the returns lower than equity funds that are more specialized." Scott Biddle, director of Equity Portfolio Analytics at TIAA-CREF, in 7 Investment Forum No. 1 (Mar. 2003) at p. 3.

[349] *See, e.g.,* §8.35 of this handbook (the Hershey Trust) (discussing a trust portfolio that has a 50 percent concentration in the stock of one company).

[350] *See* Jonathan R. Macey, An Introduction to Modern Financial Theory 75 (The American College of Trust and Estate Counsel Foundation 2d ed. 1998) (noting that "[t]he availability of index funds which permit investors to diversify away all of the firm-specific risk associated with owning stock strongly suggests that investment managers who cause their clients to bear firm-specific risk are in violation of their fiduciary duties").

[351] *See generally* 4 Scott & Ascher §§19.3.2 (Inception Assets), 19.4, 19.4.1 (Investments That Subsequently Become Inappropriate); Matter of JPMorgan Chase Bank, N.A. (Strong), 2013 WL 6182548 (N.Y. Sur.) (corporate trustee's unjustified inertia in liquidating imprudently concentrated holdings of Kodak stock resulted in it being surcharged); §8.35 of this handbook (the Hershey Trust) (examining a trust established in 1909 by chocolate industrialist Milton S. Hershey and his wife that now contains 31 percent of the outstanding common shares of Hershey Foods Corporation and roughly 76 percent of its voting stock, an ownership interest which in the aggregate has a market value in the range of $10 billion).

[352] *See, e.g.,* Attorney Grievance Comm'n v. Sachse, 693 A.2d 806 (Md. 1997) (involving a lawyer serving as a trustee who invested the entire trust corpus in an enterprise that a woman with whom he had a preexisting professional and social relationship had been running out of her basement). *See generally* 3 Scott & Ascher §17.2.10 (Other Situations Implicating the Duty of Loyalty).

[353] *See, e.g.,* Estate of Saxton, 274 A.D.2d 110, 712 N.Y.S.2d 225 (2000) (trustee surcharged for failing to diversify portfolio that since the trust's inception was comprised only of IBM stock). *See generally* Trent S. Kiziah, *The Trustee's Duty to Diversify: An Examination of the Developing Case Law,* 36 ACTEC L.J. 357, 374–376 (2010) ("Unless the trust specifically references the grantor's special relationship to a publicly held stock, trustees should be extremely cautious about retaining a concentration in a publicly held company on the special relationship exception to the duty to diversify.").

[354] *See generally* 4 Scott & Ascher §§19.3, 19.3.1, 19.3.2, 19.3.3; Trent S. Kiziah, *The Trustee's Duty to Diversify: An Examination of the Developing Case Law,* 36 ACTEC L.J. 357, 372–376 (2010)

"Retaining investments is in effect making them."[355] The closely held business;[356] the stock that has been in the family for generations, particularly stock that has been integral to the family's financial success;[357] and unproductive real estate are common traps for the unwary trustee.[358] For a thorough discussion of the history, evolution, and current state of inception-asset investment doctrine in the trust context, see Kiziah, Singleton, and Marshall.[359]

Express or implied authority to be underdiversified. That is not to say that a trust cannot have as its very purpose the retention and administration of a single asset, *e.g.*, keeping the farm or ranch in the family for future generations, in which case fiduciary prudence may well be expected to play second fiddle to sentimentality.[360] One court has even surcharged a corporate successor trustee for mechanically embarking on a diversification program, a program that in part entailed the liquidation of a large block of stock in its own parent company, without first having conducted an assessment of the trust's particular purposes and circumstances, to include the current income needs and life expectancy of the life beneficiary.[361] Another court, in a case involving the corporate trustee of a family trust whose sole asset since inception was 20,000 acres of timberland that had sustained severe hurricane damage, found that the trustee's failure to diversify prior to the hurricane was neither imprudent nor in bad faith in light of the trust's implied purposes and "other circumstances."[362]

Of course, when it comes to operating any corporation or other business entity out of a trust, there is no substitute for a provision in the trust instrument that unambiguously bestows authority on the trustee to retain the particular enterprise, if that is what is desired.[363] It is also critical that the trustee be able to readily ascertain *from the trust instrument* whether the Prudent Investor Rule or the business judgment rule is to govern the administration of the enterprise, as

---

(when a business has a special relationship to the purposes of the trust). *See, e.g.*, In re Estate of Rowe, 712 N.Y.S.2d 662 (2000) (affirming surcharge and removal of trustee for failure to diversify 30,000 shares of IBM bequeathed to a charitable lead annuity trust).

[355] Dickerson v. Camden Trust Co., 140 N.J. Eq. 34, 42, 53 A.2d 225, 231 (1947). *See generally* 4 Scott & Ascher §19.3.2; John Jeffrey Pankauski & Robert E. Conner, *Looking for the Exits: A Fiduciary's Sell Strategy Under the Prudent Investor Act*, 20(6) Prob. & Prop. 40 (Nov./Dec. 2006). *But see* In re HSBC Bank USA, N.A., 947 N.Y.S.2d 292, 300 (N.Y. App. Div. 2012) ("Moreover, it is well established 'that retention of securities received from the creator of the trust may be found to be prudent even when purchase of same might not'. . . .").

[356] *See generally* 4 Scott & Ascher §19.3.4.

[357] *See generally* 4 Scott & Ascher §19.3.

[358] *See generally* 3 Scott on Trusts §230.

[359] Trent S. Kiziah, J. Clay Singleton & Stewart A. Marshall, III, *The Persistent Preference for Inception Assets*, 40 ACTEC L.J. 151 (2014).

[360] *See generally* 4 Scott & Ascher §19.3.3; Trent S. Kiziah, *The Trustee's Duty to Diversify: An Examination of the Developing Case Law*, 36 ACTEC L.J. 357, 371–372 (2010) (family farms and branches).
    See, e.g., In re Trust Created by Inman, 693 N.W.2d 514, 521 (Neb. 2005).

[361] *See* In re Scheidmantel, 868 A.2d 464 (Pa. Super. 2005). *See generally* §6.1.3.2 of this handbook (trustee invests in its own stock).

[362] Regions Bank v. Lowrey, 101 So. 3d 210 (Ala. 2012).

[363] *See generally* 4 Scott & Ascher §§19.1.12, 19.3.3 (Terms of the Trust).

well as the circumstances under which it may be sold or the otherwise disposed of.[364] The trustee should also be instructed how to handle stock dividends, stock splits, subscription rights, and corporate mergers.[365]

No investment is *per se* imprudent. What specific investments are then improper for trustees? The drafters of the Prudent Investor Rule would say that it depends on the facts and circumstances of the particular trust[366]—*no* investment is considered *per se* imprudent or prudent.[367] In some quarters and at some times and in certain situations in the past, one or more of the following investments may have been deemed *per se* imprudent: enterprises lacking in seasoned performance as to safety and yield;[368] junior mortgages;[369] wasting assets (*e.g.*, leaseholds, royalties, patents, oil wells, natural gas wells, timberlands, and coal mines);[370] most family businesses;[371] commodities;[372] and other speculations of one sort or another.[373] It goes without saying that under any default rule, investment in an enterprise in which the trustee has a personal interest is off limits.[374] In any case, it should be emphasized that these proscriptions were generally default proscriptions.[375] They applied in a given situation absent an expression of a contrary intention in the governing instrument or preemption by some other body of law (*e.g.*, ERISA).[376]

Derivatives and leverage. Under the Prudent Investor Rule, so-called derivatives, *e.g.*, option contracts,[377] would not be *per se* off limits to trustees.[378]

---

[364] *See generally* 4 Scott & Ascher §19.1.12 (Terms of the Trust). As to some default law when the intentions of the settlor are not all that easy to discern, see Rollins v. Rollins, 294 Ga. 711 (2014) (Where a trust properly holds only a minority interest in family entities, "it is generally best to allow the trustees to act in the interest of all the shareholders and to require that they be held to a corporate level fiduciary standard when acting as directors.").

[365] 4 Scott & Ascher §19.4.2 (Changes in Trust Investments).

[366] *See* Restatement (Third) of Trusts §90 cmt. k [Restatement (Third) of Trusts: Prudent Investor Rule §227 cmt. k].

[367] *See* Restatement (Third) of Trusts (Prudent Investor Rule) §227 cmt. k. *See generally* 4 Scott & Ascher §19.1.7 (Selection of Investments).

[368] *See generally* Bogert §§612, 679; 4 Scott & Ascher §19.1.6 (Kinds of Investments). *But see* Restatement (Third) of Trusts §90 cmt. l [Restatement (Third) of Trusts: Prudent Investor Rule §227 cmt. l].

[369] *See* Bogert §674; 4 Scott & Ascher §19.1.6 (Kinds of Investments). *But see* Restatement (Third) of Trusts §90 cmt. n [Restatement (Third) of Trusts: Prudent Investor Rule §227 cmt. n].

[370] *See* Bogert §827.

[371] Bogert §§571–577; 4 Scott & Ascher §19.1.6 (Kinds of Investments).

[372] *See, e.g.*, Hadleigh D. Hyde Trust v. Gridley, 458 N.W.2d 802 (1990).

[373] *See* Bogert §612.

[374] Bogert §543.

[375] *See generally* 4 Scott & Ascher §19.1.12 (Terms of the Trust).

[376] *See* Lurie & Clews v. Fenchel, Elman & Burger, No. 95C 6525, 1997 WL 566393 (N.D. Ill.) (Illinois court held that a trustee did not breach his fiduciary duty by holding many income-oriented securities because his primary duty, according to the governing instrument, was to the income beneficiary who was suffering from a serious illness and required expensive treatment).

[377] *See generally* Michael D. Cohn, *Using Options as a Tool to Protect Assets, Increase Investment Income, and Improve Risk Reward Ratios*, 31 ACTEC L.J. 74 (2005).

[378] "A derivative is a financial product the value of which is determined by reference to the value and characteristics of another financial product." Anthony P. Marshall, *The Taxation of*

Under certain circumstances, for example, a portfolio of low basis stock held in the revocable trust of an elderly woman, a trustee may have a duty to invest in derivatives to reduce the risks inherent in a portfolio that is both underdiversified and otherwise undiversifiable.[379]

The trustee, however, would be well advised to have a compelling reason, backed up by a well-documented record of diligence, before venturing into the realm of leveraged derivatives.[380] "Any use of leverage carries with it the multiplication of risk which can render the investment extremely risky. . . . Especially close monitoring of highly leveraged investment strategies is necessary, and even then there may be substantial losses."[381] Trustees are being advised to be particularly wary of leveraged hedge funds:

> Sometimes, investors use large losses to justify leaping into programs that offer the potential for quick recovery through the use of leverage, short selling, and other "high-tech" strategies. Although hedge funds may be appropriate complements

---

Derivative Solutions to Wealth Building Problems, 27 ACTEC L.J. 143 (2001) (containing a handy "derivative glossary" of the following terms: option, equity option, index option, strike price, put, call, long and short positions, in-the-money, intrinsic value, time value, European-style and American-style options, notional principal amount, constructive sales, and Section 1256 contracts). A derivative also has been defined as a financial instrument "whose value derives from some other, more fundamental asset." Roberta Romano, *A Thumbnail Sketch of Derivative Securities and Their Regulation,* 55 Md. L. Rev. 1, 2 (1996) (containing also an in-depth explanation of the more common derivatives, specifically forward contracts, futures contracts, options, swaps, mortgage-based derivatives, and structured notes). *See also* Andrea S. Kramer & Anne K. Hilker, *Understanding Financial Products Used to Diversify Investment Risk,* American College of Trust and Estate Counsel, Summer 2000 Meeting, Session III. The Unif. Principal & Income Act (1997) §414 (available at <http://www.uniformlaws.org/Act.aspx?title=Trust%20Code>), defines a derivative as "a contract or financial instrument or a combination of contracts and financial instruments which gives a trust the right or obligation to participate in some or all changes in the price of a tangible or intangible asset or group of assets, or changes in a rate, an index of prices or rates, or other market indicator for an asset or a group of assets." Professor Langbein writes: "There are, however, risk-reducing uses of derivatives. . . . The . . . [Uniform Prudent Investor Act's] . . . abrogation of categoric restrictions on types of investments allows trustees to use derivatives in such cases." John H. Langbein, *The Uniform Prudent Investor Act and the Future of Trust Investing,* 81 Iowa L. Rev. 641, 661 (1996).

[379] Randall H. Borkus, *A Trust Fiduciary's Duty to Implement Capital Preservation Strategies Using Financial Derivative Techniques,* 36 Real Prop. Prob. & Tr. J., 127 (Spring 2001) (exploring plausible hedging strategies using financial derivatives or derivative-like products to maximize portfolio wealth and concluding that trust fiduciary duties require implementing and understanding modern hedging techniques); George Crawford, *A Fiduciary Duty to Use Derivatives?,* 1 Stan. J.L. Bus. & Fin. 307 (1995). *See also* Levy v. Bessemer Trust Co., 1997 U.S. Dist. LEXIS 11056 (S.D.N.Y.); Comm. Fut. L. Rep. (CCH) ¶27,249 (suggesting that investment agent may have had a duty to use hedge strategies such as private sales to an investment house, deep-in-the-money calls, cash settled collars, and out-of-the-money calls to insure principal's heavy and illiquid concentration in Corning, Inc., stock against possible market decline). *See, e.g.,* Joanne Legomsky, *Covered Calls Can Erase Some Risk,* N.Y. Times, June 3, 2001, at 8, col. 1 (defining a call option as the right, for a fee, to buy a certain number of shares at a specified strike price for a set time). "[A] . . . call option is 'covered' because you own the shares on which it is based, as opposed to the riskier 'naked' option, in which you do not own any of the shares." Joanne Legomsky, *Covered Calls Can Erase Some Risk,* N.Y. Times, June 3, 2001, at 8, col. 1.

[380] *See generally* 4 Scott & Ascher §19.1.6 (Kinds of Investments).

[381] Crawford, *A Fiduciary Duty to Use Derivatives?,* 1 Stan. J.L. Bus. & Fin. 307 (1995).

to the portfolios of large institutional investors that command significant resources and leverage with the financial services community (i.e., investors such as Harvard and Yale endowments or CalPERS), hedge funds may be unsuitable for more modest pensions, trusts and endowments.[382]

A simple rule of thumb for trustees when it comes to derivatives: insurance, yes; gambling, no.[383] For a discussion of various derivative products, as well as an explanation of the income and estate tax consequences of their use, see Anthony P. Marhall.[384]

The prudent investor rule has its proponents. One learned commentator has suggested that the Prudent Investor Rule is "more an attempt to restore flexibility" than an attempt to change the "foundation statement."[385] In the eyes of some, the Prudent Man Rule was drifting off course in that it was tending to:

- Focus upon the propriety of each asset in isolation rather than as an integral part of a portfolio;[386]
- Focus upon preservation of nominal value of principal rather than upon maintenance of purchasing power;[387]
- Prohibit certain investments entirely;[388]
- Provide a "safe harbor" for certain investments;[389]
- Deter the fiduciary from delegating management;[390] and
- Deter the fiduciary from acquiring new types of investment products.[391]

---

[382] Patrick J. Collins, *Hedge Funds: A Critical Examination*, 28 ACTEC Notes 36, 44 (2002) (explaining that "hedge fund" is now an umbrella term; that although, originally, hedge funds were used to hedge the systematic risk of equity markets (market-neutral funds), they now encompass a wide variety of investment styles and objectives including investments in private equity, leveraged buyouts, distressed securities, third-world debt, and event-driven arbitrage (merger and acquisition funds)).

[383] *See* Hadleigh D. Hyde Trust v. Gridley, 458 N.W.2d 801, 805 (1990) (concluding that the Prudent Man Rule does not authorize trust investments in commodities but noting that some limited commodity transactions for the purpose of hedging a trust's farming operation may be permissible).

[384] *The Taxation of Derivative Solutions to Wealth Building Problems*, 27 ACTEC Notes 143 (2001).

[385] Jerold I. Horn, *Flexible Trusts and Estates for Uncertain Times*, SH092 ALI-ABA 775, 825 (2003).

[386] Jerold I. Horn, *Flexible Trusts and Estates for Uncertain Times*, SH092 ALI-ABA 775, 825 (2003).

[387] Jerold I. Horn, *Flexible Trusts and Estates for Uncertain Times*, SH092 ALI-ABA 775, 825 (2003).

[388] Jerold I. Horn, *Flexible Trusts and Estates for Uncertain Times*, SH092 ALI-ABA 775, 826 (2003).

[389] Jerold I. Horn, *Flexible Trusts and Estates for Uncertain Times*, SH092 ALI-ABA 775, 826 (2003).

[390] Jerold I. Horn, *Flexible Trusts and Estates for Uncertain Times*, SH092 ALI-ABA 775, 826 (2003).

[391] Jerold I. Horn, *Flexible Trusts and Estates for Uncertain Times*, SH092 ALI-ABA 775, 826 (2003).

The Prudent Investor Rule is merely a tweak, a mid-course correction, say its proponents; it is not a shrine to Modern Portfolio Theory.[392]

The prudent investor rule also has its detractors. The prudent investor movement, however, is not without its detractors in the investment community. One skeptic has written:

> Alas, as every practitioner knows, there is no such thing as a permanent investment truth. As circumstances change, so do ideas. Similarly with the law: It has "never stood for long in the path of progress," as eminent jurists have written. Thus, it would come as no surprise that Wall Street and the trust-and-estates bar are today making their intellectual peace not only with the new investment ideas, but also with resurgent, one-way markets. Out is hyper-caution: in is sensible risk-taking (it being understood by every modern that risk and reward are opposite sides of the same coin). Out is the fetish of safety: in are diversification and total return. The great issue as always, however, is timing. Does this sea change in fiduciary law constitute unalloyed progress? Has the world arrived at a better and higher understanding of investment theory? Or is it giving in to the spirit of an age that dresses down on Fridays and puts its fiduciary money (or some of it) on the horse of momentum? Our conclusion: there is more capitulation than meets the eye.[393]

In 1987, one law academic had endeavored to make the case that the "unconstrained" Harvard College Prudent Man Rule was not broke.[394].More recently, others have suggested that while the judicial constraints that may have infected the old rule in some quarters were unfortunate,[395] the legislative cure has been worse than the disease.[396] For 175 years, the old rule had accommodated evolving notions of prudent investing. It had brought us through a civil war, a world war, a great depression, another world war, and the Cold War. Why should it now choke on the total return concept and the current thinking on diversification?[397] The Prudent Investor Rule *is*, they say, a shrine to modern

---

[392] *But cf.* Meyer v. Berkshire Life Ins. Co., 250 F. Supp. 2d 544, 566 (2003) (suggesting that in the pension investment context, the failure on the part of the investing fiduciary to adhere to principles of Modern Portfolio Theory may be evidence of a breach of the duty to invest prudently).

[393] 13 Grant's Interest Rate Observer, No. 21, Nov. 10, 1995, at 3, col. 3. *But see* Ken Brown, *Momentum Trades Offer Success, as Well as Bumps*, Wall St. J., Aug. 6, 2001, at C1, col. 3 (defining momentum investing as "You buy stocks that are going up—regardless of price—and sell when they turn down" and noting that "the momentum crowd has been blamed in recent years for piling into hot stocks and pushing them up to unreasonable levels, then rushing out at the whiff of bad news, heightening market volatility").

[394] *See* Jeffrey N. Gordon, *The Puzzling Persistence of the Constrained Prudent Man Rule*, 62 N.Y.U. L. Rev. 52 (1987).

[395] *See, e.g.*, Paul G. Haskell, *The Prudent Person Rule for Trustee Investment and Modern Portfolio Theory*, 69 N.C. L. Rev. 87 (1990) (suggesting that the traditional prudent person rule needs some retuning, but that for family trusts it remains essentially a sound rule).

[396] *See, e.g.*, C. Boone Schwartzel, *Is the Prudent Investor Rule Good for Texas?*, 54 Baylor L. Rev. 701 (2002).

[397] *See* Jeffrey N. Gordon, *The Puzzling Persistence of the Constrained Prudent Man Rule*, 62 N.Y.U. L. Rev. 52 (1987) ("Professor Gordon concludes by arguing that, contrary to courts' fears,

portfolio theory,[398] which one commentator has referred to as the product of "a quiet conspiracy of pension-fund consultants and the Nobel Prize committee to dominate otherwise reasonably intelligent discourse in regard to the management of large pools of assets."[399] Is it not unwise to build a standard of prudence around a single investment philosophy? Sooner or later, the old rule will be back they say, or hope.

One commentator is even suggesting that, "with Alan Greenspan recanting his belief in the ability of the market to manage risk," the "reign" of modern portfolio theory may have already reached an "inflection point," that "[t]he results of the 2000-2003 crash and the more recent great recession call into question many of the assumptions on which fiduciary investment models have been built."[400] Events, for example have called into question the critical assumption that self-interest moderates risk: " . . . [T]rust in the self-interest of corporations and their officers and boards to take no unnecessary risks was compromised when events showed that huge financial institutions relied on black boxes supervised by the most highly compensated employees outside of American athletics, using the salaries as a measure of their competence."[401]

And even if one assumes that the old rule has been roughed up a bit by the occasional state appellate court,[402] why the wholesale destabilization of the law of trusts? The old rule was two sentences. The Massachusetts Prudent Investor Act, on the other hand, is somewhere around twenty-one sentences, plus fourteen pages of explanatory legislative history that is inconsistent in part with the text and commentary that make up the Restatement (Third) of Trust Prudent Investor Rule and the Uniform Prudent Investor Act's Rule. Moreover, it is not only in Massachusetts, the birthplace of the old common law rule, where this has happened. Many of the other adopting states also have tinkered with, and in some cases substantially altered, the text of the model statute.[403] In fact, of the 41 states (and the District of Columbia) that have enacted the Uniform Prudent Investor Act as of 2011, only Colorado has done so without modification. Trent S. Kiziah has catalogued the tinkerings and substantial alterations in his *Remaining Heterogeneity in Trust Investment Law after Twenty-Five Years of Reform*, which concludes with a plea for each state to give serious consideration

---

the only significant clash between portfolio theory and trust doctrine arises in the allocation of returns between life beneficiaries and remaindermen, and he analyses ways of resolving the conflict.").

[398] *See, e.g.,* Stewart E. Sterk, *Rethinking Trust law Reform: How Prudent is Modern Prudent Investor Doctrine?*, 95 Cornell L. Rev. 851 (2010).

[399] Jeffrey Bronchick, *We Need Better Stock Analysis, Not More Info,* Wall St. J., Aug. 6, 2002, at A20, WL-WSJ 3402731.

[400] Dominic J. Campisi, *Fiduciary Liability,* 136 ABA Trust & Investments, July–August 2010, at 12 [American Bankers Association].

[401] Dominic J. Campisi, *Fiduciary Liability,* 136 ABA Trust & Investments, July–August 2010, at 13 [American Bankers Association].

[402] *See generally* Paul G. Haskell, *The Prudent Person Rule for Trustee Investment and Modern Portfolio Theory,* 69 N.C. L. Rev. 87, 100–109 (2003).

[403] Trent S. Kiziah, *The Trustee's Duty to Diversify: An Examination of the Developing Case Law,* 36 ACTEC L.J. 357 n.1 (2010) (for an excellent discussion of how state specific modifications of the UPIA bear on the duty to diversify, *see* Practical Drafting, 7026–7058 (Oct. 2002)).

to legislating away its deviations from the model Act.[404] One take-away from the article is that nationally trust investment law is in a state of total disarray:

> Trustees operating in multiple jurisdictions should bear in mind that a super-majority of the states that have enacted UPIA have modified it to a certain degree. Many of the modifications are editorial, but many are significant. . . . Rather than making broad statements concerning investment law, legal counsel should focus on the particulars of the trust and the peculiarities of each state's UPIA.[405]

Perhaps the time has come to declare the Uniform Prudent Investor Act a failed experiment. Perhaps the time has come to give serious thought to an across-the-board total repeal that would return trust investment law to the relative homogeneity, stability, simplicity, flexibility, and adaptability of the status quo ante, which was a regime of trust investment law that was principles-based rather than statute-based, subject to the occasional legal-list-type exception. There is some conceptual logic to returning to the status quo ante. The institution of the trust being a creature of equity is itself principles-based, not statute-based. In the meantime, it is a virtual certainty that the disparate decisions that are coming down and will be coming down from the various state courts in the years ahead will be exacerbating further this lack of statutory uniformity when it comes to the Prudent Investor Rule. In other words, things are only going to get more chaotic in the trust-investment-law space.

The Prudent Investor Rule now rules, at least on paper. Whether a carbuncle on the common law has been lanced or a jewel hacked from its crown, one thing is certain: The investment theories that are perceived to underpin the Prudent Investor Rule have all but carried the day, at least for now.[406] *Even in the hold-out states*, litigators on the prowl will find underdiversified,[407] underperforming portfolios tempting targets of opportunity.[408] A court is unlikely to buck all the diversification legislative history, scholarship, and publicity that inevitably will come in at trial.[409] On the other hand, as noted above, an increasing number of academics and practitioners have taken to criticizing

---

[404] Trent S. Kiziah, *Remaining Heterogeneity in Trust Investment Law After Twenty-Five Years of Reform*, 37 ACTEC L.J. 317 (Fall 2011).

[405] Trent S. Kiziah, *Remaining Heterogeneity in Trust Investment Law After Twenty-Five Years of Reform*, 37 ACTEC L.J. 317, 361 (Fall 2011).

[406] *See* Edward A. Moses, J. Clay Singleton, & Stewart A. Marshall III, *Measuring the Effectiveness of a Trust Portfolio's Diversification*, 35 ACTEC L.J. 303, 309 (2009) ("MPT is now an integral part of trust law").

[407] *See, e.g.,* Jonathan Clements, *Why 15 Stocks Just Aren't Enough*, Wall St. J., Mar. 13, 2001, at C1, col. 3.

[408] *See* Collins, Savage, & Stampfli, *Financial Consequences of Distribution Elections From Total Return Trusts*, 35 Real Prop. Prob. & Tr. J., 243, 258–259 (Summer 2000) (concluding from the statistical evidence that "trustees who eschew broad diversification in hopes of capturing superior investment returns from a narrow range of investments may have a heavy burden of proof if poor future performance prompts trust beneficiaries to file fiduciary surcharge actions"). For practical advice on how to prove a trustee's failure to diversify in breach of trust litigation, *see* William L. Velton, *Trustee's Failure to Diversify Investments*, 14 Am. Jur. *Proof of Facts* 2d 253 (as of Aug. 2003).

[409] *See, e.g.,* Edward A. Moses, J. Clay Singleton, & Stewart A. Marshall III, *Measuring the Effectiveness of a Trust Portfolio's Diversification*, 35 ACTEC L.J. 303, 309 (2009) ("The diversification

modern portfolio theory and its tenets of diversification "as not being grounded in reality."[410] So we shall have to see.

Rebalancing the portfolio. Once the trust property is well invested, the investments should not be changed without good reason. The trustee should strive to assess market panics or dramatic inflations in market values with professional detachment.[411] It is not the duty of the trustee to follow the ticker as might a speculator.[412] No investment should be liquidated before tax and transaction costs are estimated and duly considered.[413] Above all, the trustee in carrying out his investment responsibilities should resist blindly accepting each new "paradigm" that comes along. A healthy dose of skepticism always is in order:

> While we have witnessed many "new paradigms" over the years, none have persisted. The "concept" stocks of the Go-Go years in the 1960s came, and went. So did the "Nifty-Fifty" era that soon followed. The "January Effect" of small-cap superiority came, and went. Option-income funds and "Government Plus" funds came, and went. High-tech stocks and "new economy" funds came as well, and the survivors remain far below their peaks. Intelligent investors should approach with extreme caution any claim that a "new paradigm" is here to stay. That's not the way financial markets work.[414]

The trust's portfolio should be prudently rebalanced when it is appropriate to do so.[415] If a trust security has acquired a speculative value much above its true value as an investment, it is obviously time to reduce the trust's position in

---

measure described in this article allows fiduciaries to defend the employment of less than strictly optimal portfolios and provides an additional strategy to assist in exercising their business judgment").

[410] Dominic J. Campisi, *Fiduciary Liability*, 136 ABA Trust & Investments, July–August 2010, at 14 [American Bankers Association] (offering as an example Didier Sornette, "Why Stock Markets Crash" at 38 (Princeton, 2003)).

[411] *See generally* 4 Scott & Ascher §19.4 (Investments That Subsequently Become Inappropriate).

[412] *See generally* 4 Scott & Ascher §19.4 (Investments That Subsequently Become Inappropriate).

[413] *See generally* 4 Scott & Ascher §§19.2, 19.3.1, 19.4 (Taxes); Trent S. Kiziah, *The Trustee's Duty to Diversify: An Examination of the Developing Case Law*, 36 ACTEC L.J. 357, 367-370 (2010) (tax considerations). *See* In re Janes, 90 N.Y.2d 41, 681 N.E.2d 332, 659 N.Y.S.2d 165 (1997) (in which the New York Supreme Court applied New York's prudent person rule, the predecessor of New York's prudent investor rule adopted Jan. 1, 1995, to hold that a trustee who failed to divest the trust estate of substantial holdings in a growth stock in the face of a seven-year decline in the value of the stock breached his fiduciary duty). *See also* UTC §805 (available at <http://www.uniformlaws.org/Act.aspx?title=Trust%20Code>) (providing that in administering a trust, the trustee may incur costs that are reasonable in relation to the trust property, the purposes of the trust, and the skills of the trustee). *See generally* Luther J. Avery & Patrick J. Collins, *Managing Investment Expenses: Trustee Duty to Avoid Unreasonable or Inappropriate Costs*, 25 ACTEC Notes 123 (1999).

[414] John C. Bogle & Burton G. Malkiel, *Turns on a Paradigm*, Wall St. J., June 27, 2006, at A14.

[415] 4 Scott & Ascher §19.4.1; Trent S. Kiziah, *The Trustee's Duty to Diversify: An Examination of the Developing Case Law*, 36 ACTEC L.J. 357, 362 (2010) ("The duty to diversify requires a concentration be sold even if analysts are predicting that the concentration will outperform similar

that investment, if not sell out altogether.[416] And yet a mere increase in market value is not enough, for the doctrine "can readily be pressed so far as to sanction a practice of trading and trafficking in trust securities, which would be attended with dangerous results to the trust fund."[417]

The written investment policy statement. As noted above, the safe harbor rules that govern whether trustees have been prudent in carrying out their investing responsibilities are rules of conduct. A trustee is not a contract-insurer of the inception value of the trust portfolio, nor is he a contract-guarantor of any particular level of investment performance. Nowadays, a trustee, particularly a trustee of a charitable trust, is expected to have prepared, or carefully overseen the preparation of a written investment policy statement that articulates an investment strategy that is both prudent and appropriate for the particular trust.[418] Such a statement can be a double-edged sword. While it can serve as documentary evidence of thoughtful stewardship, it also can serve as evidence of maladministration, particularly if the trustee has negligently failed to adhere to its guidelines, or negligently failed to keep the guidelines appropriately updated as circumstances change.[419] Here is a suggested Table of Contents for an investment policy statement:

_____Investment Policy Statement for *X* Trust

_____*Table of Contents*

- *Statement of Investment Objectives*
- *Investment Policy and Guidelines*
  - *Time Horizon*
  - *Risk Tolerance*
  - *Liquidity Requirements*
  - *Diversification*
  - *Asset allocation*
  - *Rebalancing frequency*

---

assets. Diversification does not focus on future anticipated performance; rather, diversification focuses on the fact that the trustee has too many eggs in one basket.").

[416] *See* 4 Scott & Ascher §19.4.1; 3 Scott on Trusts §231.

[417] New England Trust Co. v. Eaton, 140 Mass. 532, 537, 4 N.E. 69, 72 (1886).

[418] *See, e.g.,* Matter of JP Morgan Chase Bank N.A. (Strong), 2013 WL 6182548 (N.Y. Sur. 2013) (the court finding that the trustee had failed "to undertake an adequate analysis of the Trusts by creating an investment plan"); Matter of Hunter, 100 A.D.3d 996, 998, 955 N.Y.S.2d 163 (2012) (the court finding the failure of the corporate trustee of a charitable remainder trust to formulate a specific investment plan that included diversification evidence that the trustee's investment conduct had been imprudent).

[419] *See, e.g.,* Matter of JP Morgan Chase Bank N.A. (Strong), 2013 WL 6182548 (N.Y. Sur. 2013) ("The evidence demonstrates that the Trustee did not meet its own internal guidelines, and when the sporadic and cursory internal reviews of the Trust holdings did occur, the Trustee did not act upon its own recommendations"); Matter of Hunter, 100 A.D.3d 996, 998, 955 N.Y.S.2d 163 (2012) (the court finding the failure of the corporate trustee of a charitable remainder trust to follow its own internal investment policies evidence that the trustee's investment conduct had been imprudent).

§6.2.2.2 The Prudent Investor's Code of Conduct

*Seated on the transom was what seemed to me a most uncommon and surprising figure. It turned out to be Captain Bildad, who along with Captain Peleg was one of the owners of the vessel; the other shares, as is sometimes the case in these ports, being held by a crowd of old annuitants; widows, fatherless children, and chancery wards; each owning about the value of a timber head, or a foot of plank, or a nail or two in the ship. People in Nantucket invest their money in whaling vessels, the same way that you do yours in approved state stocks bringing in good interest.—*Ishmael[420]

The *Harvard College* Prudent Man Rule and its progeny are rules of conduct, not performance. While the prudence of the trustee's conduct will be judged in light of the facts and circumstances applicable in a given situation,[421] there are some long-accepted indicia of prudent conduct. At minimum the trustee should always:

(1) Decide whether to accept a trust only after making an exhaustive examination of the trust portfolio and only after a thorough audit of the accountings of the prior fiduciary is completed;[422]

(2) Require, before taking on a trusteeship, that a predecessor fiduciary remedy any breaches of fiduciary duty and cleanse the portfolio of improper investments, absent compelling reasons to do otherwise;[423]

(3) Upon accepting a trusteeship, immediately ascertain what property comprises the trust estate,[424] take control of the

---

[420] Herman Melville, Moby-Dick, Ch. 16 (The Ship).

[421] Bogert §706.

[422] Restatement (Third) of Trusts §76 cmt. d. *See, e.g.,* Dickerson v. Camden Trust Co., 140 N.J. Eq. 34, 53 A.2d 225 (1947) (suggesting that a trustee could be exposed to liability for accepting unauthorized investments from a predecessor fiduciary). *See generally* Bogert §684. Note, also, that Revised Reg. 9 (available at <www.gpoaccess.gov/cfr/index.html>) provides that, before accepting a fiduciary account, a national bank shall review the prospective account to determine whether it can properly administer the account. 12 C.F.R. §9.6(a) (1997). UTC §701(c)(2) (available at <http://www.uniformlaws.org/Act.aspx?title=Trust%20Code>) authorizes a nominated trustee to investigate trust property to determine potential liability for violation of environmental law or other law without accepting the trusteeship. *See generally* §6.2.1.1 of this handbook (trustee's duty to take active control of trust property). *Cf.* UTC §812 (requiring the trustee to take reasonable steps to compel a former trustee or other person to deliver trust property to the trustee and to redress a breach of trust known to the trustee to have been committed by a former trustee); UTC §705(c) (providing that any liability of a resigning trustee or of any sureties on the trustee's bond for acts or omissions of the trustee is not discharged or affected by the trustee's resignation); 4 Scott & Ascher §§24.4.2 (Co-Trustees and Successor Trustees), 24.28 (Liability of Successor Trustee), 24.28.1 (When Successor Trustee Permits Continuation of Breach), 24.28.2 (When Successor Trustee Fails to Compel Predecessor to Deliver Trust Property), 24.28.3 (When Successor Trustee Fails to Compel Predecessor to Redress Breach of Trust).

[423] *See generally* 4 Scott & Ascher §24.28.3 (When Successor Trustee Fails to Compel Predecessor to Redress Breach of Trust); Restatement (Second) of Trusts §223; 4 Scott & Ascher Ch. 19 (The Investment of Trust Funds); §6.2.1.1 of this handbook (trustee's duty to take active control of trust property).

[424] Restatement (Third) of Trusts §76 cmt. d.

property,[425] and set about cleansing the portfolio of improper investments;[426]

(4) Understand the intentions of the settlor as they are expressed in the
governing instrument and invest accordingly;[427]

(5) Consider drafting an Investment Policy Statement;[428]

(6) Investigate each investment,[429] personally monitor the portfolio on
a regular basis, and respond to changed circumstances in a timely
fashion to the extent a response is deemed appropriate;[430]

(7) On an ongoing basis, "engage in a thoughtful process and make
considered decisions" about whether or not to adjust between principal and income or convert to a unitrust, assuming the trustee

---

[425] Restatement (Third) of Trusts §76 cmt. d. *See, e.g.,* In re First Nat'l Bank of Mansfield, 37
Ohio St. 2d 60, 307 N.E.2d 23 (1974) (holding a testamentary trustee personally liable for the value
of a nonrefundable state inheritance tax overpayment by the executor). *See generally* §6.2.1.1 of this
handbook (trustee's duty to take active control of trust property). *See also* UTC §812 (available at
<http://www.uniformlaws.org/Act.aspx?title=Trust%20Code>) (providing that the trustee shall
take reasonable steps to compel a former trustee or other person to deliver trust property to the
trustee and to redress a breach of trust known to the trustee to have been committed by a former
trustee). Note: "[T]he beneficiaries may relieve the trustee from potential liability for failing to
pursue a claim against a predecessor trustee or other person holding trust property." UTC §812
cmt. "The obligation to pursue a successor trustee can also be addressed in the terms of the trust."
UTC §812 cmt. Note, however, that a trustee in rare instances may have a duty to disclaim an item of
property that would otherwise be held in trust when doing would serve the beneficiaries' interests
and further the trust's purposes. *See* Restatement (Third) of Trusts §86 cmt. f.

[426] Bogert §583. For a discussion of the personal liability of a trustee who imprudently or
improperly fails to sell trust property, *see generally* 4 Scott & Ascher §24.12 (Liability for Breach of
Trust by Failing to Sell Trust Property); §7.2.3.2 of this handbook (damages as an equitable relief
for breaches of trust). *See also* Revised Reg. 9, which is applicable to national banks. 12 C.F.R.
§9.6(b) (1997) (Initial Post-acceptance Review) (available at <www.gpoaccess.gov/cfr/
index.html>). *See generally* Report, *Duties and Responsibilities of a Successor Trustee*, 10 Real Prop.
Prob. & Tr. J. 310 (1975). A trustee shall take reasonable steps to compel a former trustee or other
person to deliver trust property to the trustee and to redress a breach of trust known to the trustee
to have been committed by a former trustee. UTC §812 (available at <http://www.uniformlaws.org/
Act.aspx?title=Trust%20Code>) (collecting trust property). A breach of trust is known to the
trustee if he has actual knowledge of it; has received a notice or notification of it; or from all the
facts and circumstances known to him, has reason to know it. UTC §104 (knowledge). *See also* 4
Scott & Ascher Ch. 19 (The Investment of Trust Funds).

[427] Bogert §683. In order to carry out the intentions of the settlor, "[t]he trustee must know
who the beneficiaries are and their ages, locations, sources of support apart from the trust
(including, for instance, entitlement to social, medical and public benefits), and other circumstances relevant to their entitlement as beneficiaries." ACTEC Practice Committee, Fiduciary
Matters Subcommittee, *Guide for ACTEC Fellows Serving as Trustees*, 26 ACTEC Notes 313, 322
(2001). "The trustee must regularly review and confirm the current accuracy and completeness of
all such information." ACTEC Practice Committee, Fiduciary Matters Subcommittee, *Guide for
ACTEC Fellows Serving as Trustees*, 26 ACTEC Notes 313, 322 (2001).

[428] *See generally* §6.2.2.1 of this handbook (how the Investment Policy Statement can be a
double-edged sword).

[429] *See, e.g.,* Kathryn A. Ballsun, Patrick J. Collins, & Dieter Jurkat, *Evidencing Care, Skill and
Caution in The Management of ILITs (Part 3 of 4)*, 32 ACTEC L.J. 145 (2006).

[430] Bogert §612. *See also* Uniform Prudent Investor Act §2(c) (available at <http://
www.uniformlaws.org/Act.aspx?title=Trust%20Code> as Article 9 of the UTC) (listing "circumstances" that a trustee shall consider in investing and managing trust assets).

possesses such a fiduciary power either under the default law or the terms of the trust.[431]

(8) Obtain expert investment advice as appropriate;[432]

(9) Maintain prudent diversification at all times, unless it is clearly the intention of the settlor that this not be done;[433]

(10) Maintain an adequate cushion of liquidity so that the cash needs of the trust may be accommodated in an orderly fashion;[434]

(11) Understand that no capital is risk-free and that even insured bank accounts and fixed-income government issues are "at hazard" in that their value erodes with inflation, and act upon that understanding;[435]

(12) Invest for the long term unless there is a legitimate reason not to do so;[436]

(13) Keep all trust property invested at all times unless there is a legitimate reason not to do so;[437]

---

[431] *See* Margaret E. W. Sager, *Litigation and the Total Return Trust*, 35 ACTEC L.J. 206, 214–215 (2009) (addressing what the trustee's "process" in considering the total return statutes should be and whether a prudent process can insulate the trustee from liability in the face of poor investment performance). *See generally* §6.2.2.4 of this handbook (the noncharitable total return trust).

[432] *See generally* Bogert §§555, 556, 701; Restatement (Third) of Trusts §80 cmt. b.

[433] *See* 4 Scott & Ascher §§19.2, 19.3.2, 19.4.1; 3 Scott on Trusts §228; Restatement (Third) of Trusts §90 [Restatement (Third) of Trusts: Prudent Investor Rule) §227]. *See generally* P. G. Guthrie, Annot., *Duty of Trustee to Diversify Investments, and Liability for Failure to Do So*, 24 A.L.R.3d 730 (1969). *See, e.g.,* In re Maxwell, 306 N.J. Super. 563, 704 A.2d 49 (1997) (allowing prayer for punitive damages and recoupment of fees where trustee allegedly failed to diversify and actively concealed a substantial decrease in the value of the trust assets); In re Estate of Janes, 630 N.Y.S.2d 472 (Surr. Ct. 1995) (trustee surcharged $6 million for failure to diversify). Note: In re Estate of Janes, 223 A.D.2d 20, 643 N.Y.S.2d 972 (1996), *aff'd,* 659 N.Y.S.2d 165, 681 N.E.2d 332 (1997) (damage amount modified on appeal to $4,065,029). *See also* Estate of Maxedon, 946 P.2d 104 (Kan. App. 1997) (suggesting a common law duty to diversify absent language in governing instrument to contrary); Malachowski v. Bank One, Indianapolis, 667 N.E.2d 780 (Ind. App. 1996) (rebuffing plaintiff's claim that the trustee diversified only to further its own interests).

[434] *See generally* Bogert §612. If a particular hedge fund allows investors only one or two opportunities each year to cash out, then for extended periods of time its participations are illiquid. Limited partnership interests are often even more illiquid. The trustee who has committed trust assets to an illiquid hedge fund or limited partnership that has done poorly may be called upon in some court proceeding to explain why something more marketable would not have served the trust just as well. *See also* 3 Scott & Ascher §17.12.4 (Restrictions on Withdrawals [Bank Deposits]).

[435] *See* Bogert §612 n.90. *See also* Restatement (Third) of Trusts §90 cmt. e [Restatement (Third) of Trusts: Prudent Investor Rule §227 cmt. e]; 4 Scott & Ascher §19.2.

[436] *See generally* Bogert §612.

[437] *See generally* Bogert §611; 3 Scott & Ascher §17.13 (Duty to Make the Trust Property Productive). Revised Reg. 9 (available at <www.gpoaccess.gov/cfr/index.html>) provides that with respect to a fiduciary account for which a national bank has investment discretion or discretion over distributions, the bank may not allow funds awaiting investment or distribution to remain uninvested and undistributed any longer than is reasonable for the proper management of the account and consistent with applicable law. 12 C.F.R. §9.10(a) (1997).

(14) Keep meticulous permanent records of all investment research, deliberations, and decisions;[438]

(15) Assess the tax consequences of contemplated investment changes;[439]

(16) Assess the transaction costs of contemplated investment changes;[440] and

(17) Obtain, keep current, and periodically review basic personal and financial information on each beneficiary.[441]

Adherence to this code of conduct does not mean that the trustee will be immune from suit for improper investing, but it will help to show that the trustee's conduct was prudent:

> A prudent process may protect a trustee from liability. How the trustee "got there" is probably more important than where the trust ends up. As one commentator has noted: "[T]here is little protection in arguing historical averages, . . . protection for the fiduciary rests in pretty old-fashioned efforts: good personal relationships, communication and consultation, sign-offs and accountings." In addition, as ACTEC Fellow Dom Campisi has observed, "[b]ad results from a carefully structured portfolio may not constitute a breach of trust; bad results from a poor economic plan will doubtless lead to surcharge."[442]

---

[438] UTC §810(a) (available at <http://www.uniformlaws.org/Act.aspx?title=Trust%20 Code>). *See generally* Bogert §962. *See also* Revised Reg. 9 (available at <www.gpoaccess.gov/cfr/ index.html>) setting forth the record-keeping responsibilities of national banks in the conduct of their fiduciary activities. 12 C.F.R. §9.8 (1997).

[439] *See generally* 4 Scott & Ascher §§19.2, 19.3.1, 19.4 (Taxes); Luther J. Avery & Patrick J. Collins, *Managing Investment Expenses: Trustee Duty to Avoid Unreasonable or Inappropriate Costs,* 25 ACTEC Notes 123, 133 (1999) (Taxes, Inflation and Turnover).

[440] *See* Uniform Prudent Investor Act §7 (providing that "[i]n investing and managing trust assets, a trustee may only incur costs that are appropriate and reasonable in relation to the assets, the purposes of the trust, and the skills of the trustee"). Section 7 is also available at <http:// www.uniformlaws.org/Act.aspx?title=Trust%20Code> as a part of Article 9 of the UTC. *See generally* Luther J. Avery & Patrick J. Collins, *Managing Investment Expenses: Trustee Duty to Avoid Unreasonable or Inappropriate Costs,* 25 ACTEC Notes 123 (1999); Pamela D. Perdue, *Satisfying ERISA's Fiduciary Duty Requirements with Respect to Plan Costs,* 25 J. Pension Planning & Compliance 1 (Spring 1999); Tom Lauricella, *This Is News? Fund Fees Are Too High, Study Says,* Wall St. J., Aug. 27, 2001, at C1, col. 5; Danny Hakim, *Index Fund Fees Are Not Created Equal,* N.Y. Times, Jan. 14, 2001, at BU8, col. 2. *See also* UTC §805 (providing that in administering a trust, the trustee may incur only costs that are reasonable in relation to the trust property, the purposes of the trust, and the skills of the trustee).

[441] ACTEC Practice Committee, *Fiduciary Matters Subcommittee,* 26 ACTEC Notes 313, 322 (2001).

[442] Margaret E. W. Sager, *Litigation and the Total Return Trust,* 35 ACTEC L.J. 206, 214 (2009) (referring to Deborah S. Gordon, *Living With The Total Return Litigation Threat,* SH002 ALI-ABA 253 (2002) and Dominic J. Campisi, *Fiduciary Litigation: Case Law,* FFIEC July 2, 2003).

§6.2.2.3 The Prudent Investor and the Charitable Corporation

It has been suggested that there is no compelling reason to maintain the trust's traditional line of demarcation between income and principal when it comes to tax-exempt funds managed by charitable corporations, except when private beneficiaries are involved.[443] Assuming that to be the case, then it follows that a charity's day-to-day cash requirements ought not to influence one way or another the implementation of a reasonable growth investment strategy. Accordingly, Section 2 of the Uniform Management of Institutional Funds Act (UMIFA),[444] which has been enacted in a number of jurisdictions since it came on the scene in 1994, allowed for some tapping of principal appreciation:

> The governing board may appropriate for expenditure for the uses and purposes for which an endowment fund is established so much of the net appreciation, realized and unrealized, in the fair value of the assets of an endowment fund over the historic dollar value of the fund as is prudent under the standard established by Section 6. This Section does not limit the authority of the governing board to expend funds as permitted under other law, the terms of the applicable gift instrument, or the charter of the institution.[445]

In 2006, the Uniform Prudent Management of Institutional Funds Act (UPMIFA) replaced UMIFA as the model statute regulating fiduciaries charged with investing the endowment funds of charitable trusts and charitable corporations.[446] The new act does away with the historic dollar value concept.[447] In the words of the National Conference of Commissioners on Uniform State Law, "instead of using historic dollar value as a limitation, UPMIFA applies a more carefully articulated prudence standard to the process of making decisions about expenditures from an endowment fund."[448] The new act gives a welcome nod to the principle that donor intent is generally paramount, and otherwise uniformly applies the principles of the Uniform Prudent Investor Act to the endowments of charitable trusts and charitable corporations alike.[449] Its prudence standard "is consistent with the business judgment standard under corporate law, *as applied to charitable corporations.*"[450]

---

[443] *See generally* 4 Scott & Ascher §20.1 (Impartiality Between Successive Beneficiaries); 5 Scott & Ascher §37.3.8 (Investments in the Charitable Context).

[444] *See generally* 5 Scott & Ascher §37.3.8.

[445] *See generally* 5 Scott & Ascher §37.3.8.

[446] *See generally* 5 Scott & Ascher §37.3.8.

[447] Unif. Prudent Management Inst. Funds Act §4 cmt. *See generally* 5 Scott & Ascher §37.3.8.

[448] Unif. Prudent Management Inst. Funds Act §4 cmt. *See generally* 5 Scott & Ascher §37.3.8.

[449] Unif. Prudent Management Inst. Funds Act, Prefatory Note. *See generally* 5 Scott & Ascher §37.3.8.

[450] Unif. Prudent Management Inst. Funds Act §3 cmt. *See generally* 5 Scott & Ascher §37.3.8.

§6.2.2.4   The Noncharitable Unitrust (Total Return Trust): Investment Considerations

Macroeconomics narrowly beats out Modern Portfolio Theory as the most destructive invention of the 20th century.[451]

The noncharitable unitrust concept. There is a school of thought that even in the noncharitable context,[452] the rigid demarcation between income and principal is counterproductive when it comes to trust investments.[453] The trustee is caught in the middle between the life beneficiaries who are clamoring for more income and the remaindermen who are clamoring for more growth.[454] Under these conditions, a total return investment strategy aimed at growth rather than income is difficult.[455] "The significant decline in interest rates and an unprecedented decline in dividend yields produces an impossible task for the trustee today to satisfy both the income beneficiary and the remainder-men."[456] The problem is further exacerbated by the fact that a number of good companies have not been paying dividends.[457] Moreover, when it comes to investment performance, the trustee is unfairly compared with those investors who are not shackled by a traditional trust's income requirements.[458]

For some, the noncharitable "unitrust" is the way to go.[459] Instead of the traditional "all net income to *C*, remainder to *D*" design, a typical "unitrust" governing instrument will provide that all trust accounting net income shall be added to principal and the life beneficiary in a given year shall then receive a

---

[451] John Rutledge, *Follow the Money*, Am. Spectator, Jan./Feb. 2002, at 18.

[452] "Most of our recent learning and practices on the use and drafting of unitrusts and annuity interests, however, arise from the 1969 enactment of the split-interest (specifically the charitable lead and remainder-interest) rules of Internal Revenue Code §2055(e)(2)(A) and (B)." Restatement (Third) of Trusts, Reporter's Notes on §49. *See generally* §9.4.5 of this handbook (tax-oriented trusts that mix charitable and noncharitable interests (split-interest trusts)).

[453] *See generally* 4 Scott & Ascher §20.1 (Impartiality Between Successive Beneficiaries); 4 Scott & Ascher §§20.6.10 (Effect of Rules Relating to Principal and Income on Investments by Trustee), 20.11 (Total Return Unitrusts).

[454] *See generally* 4 Scott & Ascher §§20.1 (Impartiality Between Successive Beneficiaries), 20.11 (Total Return Unitrusts).

[455] *See generally* 4 Scott & Ascher §§20.6.10 (Effect of Rules Relating to Principal and Income on Investments by Trustee), 20.11 (Total Return Unitrusts).

[456] Robert B. Wolf, *Total Return Trusts: Can Your Clients Afford Anything Less?*, 24 ACTEC Notes 45 (1998). *See also* Robert B. Wolf, *Total Return Trusts—A Decade of Progress, But Are We There Yet?* (Parts 3 & 4 of 4), 32 ACTEC L.J. 101 (2006). *See generally* 4 Scott & Ascher §20.6.10 (Effect of Rules Relating to Principal and Income on Investments by Trustee).

[457] Karen Hube, *More Dividends Go the Way of the Dinosaur*, Wall St. J., Feb. 24, 2000, at R6. *But see* Karen Talley, *Dividend Payouts May Cushion Small Caps' Fall*, Wall St. J., June 3, 2002, at C8 (noting that 630 stocks on the Russell 2000 small-cap index pay dividends, "belying the perception that these companies prefer to pour capital into operations because they are generally young and in a growth mode").

[458] *See generally* 4 Scott & Ascher §20.6.10.

[459] *See* Patrick J. Collins and Josh Stampfli, *Promises and Pitfalls of Total Return Trusts*, 27 ACTEC L.J. 205 (2001). *See generally* 4 Scott & Ascher §20.1 (Impartiality Between Successive Beneficiaries).

fixed percentage, typically 5 percent,[460] of the net market value of the trust estate valued at the end of the prior year. There are many variations on the theme.[461] For example, one learned commentator, an admitted unitrust skeptic, advises no more than 3 percent.[462] The point is that now both constituencies, the life beneficiaries and the remaindermen, at least will be badgering the trustee for the same thing: growth.[463]

For a collection of sample unitrust clauses, the reader is referred to Jerold I. Horn, Esq.[464]

Express authority in the trustee to invade principal should obviate the need to convert. Granted, a traditional trust under which the current beneficiary is entitled only to net trust accounting income poses a particular challenge for the trustee who wishes to pursue a total return investment strategy: The more he invests for growth, the more the duty of impartiality is implicated.[465] On the other hand, the trustee of a trust with fiduciary and/or nonfiduciary powers of appointment, *e.g.* the trustee of a discretionary trust, is not necessarily faced with such a conundrum, at least not to the same degree.[466] Actually, any express fiduciary authority to invade principal for the benefit of the current beneficiary should go a long way toward reducing the urgency of maintaining for trust accounting purposes a strict demarcation between income and principal.[467] Moreover, a trust under which the trustee has full discretion to distribute or withhold income and to invade or not invade principal may be administered as a unitrust, even in the absence of express unitrust provisions, provided that doing so does not conflict with the settlor's intentions. No reformation by a court would be required. The discretionary trust may even be preferable to the

---

[460] *See generally* Edward A. Moses, J. Clay Singleton, & Stewart Andrew Marshall, III, *The Appropriate Withdrawal Rate: Comparing a Total Return Trust to a Principal and Income Trust*, 31 ACTEC L.J. 118 (2005). For an exhaustive and sophisticated discussion of how much a trust can pay out and still keep up with inflation, see Robert B. Wolf, *Total Return Trusts—A Decade of Progress, But Are We There Yet?* (Parts 3 & 4 of 4), 32 ACTEC L.J. 101 (2006); Robert B. Wolf, *Total Return Trusts—Can Your Clients Afford Anything Less?*, 33 Real Prop. Prob. & Tr. J. 131 (No. 1, Spring 1998).

[461] *See* Robert B. Wolf, *Total Return Trusts—A Decade of Progress, But Are We There Yet?* (Parts 3 & 4 of 4), 32 ACTEC L.J. 101 (2006); Robert B. Wolf, *Defeating the Duty to Disappoint Equally the Total Return Trust*, 23 ACTEC Notes 46 (1997).

[462] Joel C. Dobris, *Why Five? The Strange, Magnetic, and Mesmerizing Affect of the Five Percent Unitrust and Spending Rate on Settlors, Their Advisers, and Retirees*, 41 Real Prop. Prob. & Tr. J. 39 (Spring 2005).

[463] *But see* Collins, Savage & Stampfli, *Financial Consequences of Distribution Elections from Total Return Trusts*, 35 Real Prop. Prob. & Tr. J. 243, 249 (Summer 2000) (suggesting that grantor selection and trustee implementation of irrevocable distribution formulae may create a level of antagonism between beneficiary classes equal to that found in the more traditional net income trusts).

[464] *Prudent Investor Rule, Modern Portfolio Theory, and Private Trusts: Drafting and Administration Including the "Give-Me-Five" Unitrust*, 33 Real Prop. Prob. & Tr. J. 1 (No. 1, Spring 1998).

[465] 4 Scott & Ascher §20.11.

[466] 4 Scott & Ascher §20.11.

[467] 4 Scott & Ascher §20.11.

unitrust in that it "allows investment for total return . . . [yet] . . . does not tie the trustee to an annual payout that may not be sustainable in a particular year."[468]

Taxation. "Traditional fiduciary income tax rules are tied to traditional state law concepts of income and principal and do not afford trustees much latitude in treating capital gains as part of the trust income distributable to the income beneficiary."[469] On February 15, 2001, the IRS issued proposed regulations that in part would permit a reasonable allocation of capital gains tax treatment to unitrust distributions.[470] "The Proposed Regulations offer[ed] far greater latitude and increased flexibility for trustees in the tax treatment of distributions to income beneficiaries of noncharitable trusts than the existing Treasury regulations."[471] The IRS issued final regulations on December 30, 2003.[472] "For the most part, the final regulations are not substantially different from the proposed regulations. . . ."[473]

Unitrust-conversion and adjustment-power statutes. Almost every state now has a statute that either authorizes a trustee to convert a traditional trust, *i.e.*, one that calls for the periodic distribution of trust accounting income, into a unitrust,[474] or a statute that authorizes a trustee under certain circumstance to reallocate or adjust returns between income and principal.[475] In some states, trustees have been given the power to do both.[476] Pennsylvania has a typical "ordering" rule for satisfying its 4 percent statutory unitrust rate: The trustee shall satisfy the 4 percent distribution amount first from ordinary income, then from short-term capital gains, then from long-term capital gains, and finally from principal.[477] A judicial reformation of an irrevocable traditional trust into a unitrust does raise some constitutional red flags, a topic we take up in Section 8.15.71 of this handbook. Presumably that is why New York's unitrust conversion statute has settlor intent high on its nonexclusive list of "relevant factors"

---

[468] Joel C. Dobris, *Why Five? The Strange, Magnetic, and Mesmerizing Affect of the Five Percent Unitrust and Spending Rate on Settlors, Their Advisers, and Retirees*, 40 Real Prop. Prob. & Tr. J. 39, n.10 (Spring 2005).

[469] George L. Cushing, *Income Tax Treatment of Total Return Trusts*, ACTEC Course Outline of Total Return Trusts B-1-GLC (Feb. 21, 2001).

[470] Prop. Treas. Reg. §1.643(b)-1 (Feb. 15, 2001).

[471] George L. Cushing, *Income Tax Treatment of Total Return Trusts*, ACTEC Course Outline of Total Return Trusts B-21-GLC (Feb. 21, 2001).

[472] Treas. Reg. §1.643(b)-1.

[473] Barbara A. Sloan, *§643 Regulations: Use of Non-Charitable Unitrusts and Other Issues Raised under the Final Regulations*, 30 ACTEC L.J. 23 (2004).

[474] 4 Scott & Ascher §20.11 n.9 (a listing of state conversion statutes).

[475] Robert B. Wolf, *Total Return Trusts—A Decade of Progress, But Are We There Yet?* (Parts 1 & 2 of 4), 32 ACTEC L.J. 5, 13 (2006); Robert B. Wolf, *Total Return Trusts—A Decade of Progress, But Are We There Yet?* (Parts 3 & 4 of 4), 32 ACTEC L.J. 101 (2006). *See generally* 4 Scott & Ascher §20.2 n.9 (a listing of state statutes bestowing on trustees a discretionary power to adjust); §6.2.4.3 of this handbook (what trust receipts are apportioned between the income and the principal accounts).

[476] Robert B. Wolf, *Total Return Trusts—A Decade of Progress, But Are We There Yet?* (Parts 1 & 2 of 4), 32 ACTEC L.J. 5, 13 (2006); Robert B. Wolf, *Total Return Trusts—A Decade of Progress, But Are We There Yet?* (Parts 3 & 4 of 4), 32 ACTEC L.J. 101 (2006).

[477] Robert B. Wolf, *Total Return Trusts—A Decade of Progress, But Are We There Yet?* (Parts 1 & 2 of 4), 32 ACTEC L.J. 5, 14 (2006); Robert B. Wolf, *Total Return Trusts—A Decade of Progress, But Are We There Yet?* (Parts 3 & 4 of 4), 32 ACTEC L.J. 101 (2006).

that courts are encouraged to consider when deciding whether or not to grant conversion applications.[478] And should a trustee's unitrust election implicate the trustee's duty of loyalty, such as when the trustee happens also to be a remainderman, the election is "scrutinized" by the courts "with special care."[479]

The 1997 version of the Uniform Principal and Income Act grants the trustee a general discretionary power to make adjustments from principal to income to avoid any unfairness to the income beneficiary, a topic that is covered in Section 6.2.4.3 of this handbook.

The Restatement (Third) of Trusts, specifically Section 111, provides that a trustee, under certain circumstances, would have an affirmative duty to exercise a statutory unitrust election. This is a topic that is taken up in Section 6.2.4 of this handbook.

The trustee's duty to inform. The trustee with a default discretionary power to convert or adjust may well have a fiduciary duty to so inform all beneficiary classes, sooner rather than later, and certainly before any relevant decisions are made with respect to any exercise or nonexercise. As we note in Section 6.1.5.1 of this handbook, a trustee has a specific duty to furnish the beneficiary with all the information that the beneficiary needs to protect his, her, or its equitable interest. That the trustee holds a power to re-order the equitable property interests is a critical piece of information that each beneficiary should have. For a discussion of other duties that a trustee may owe the beneficiaries incident to his exercise or nonexercise of the default fiduciary power to convert or adjust, as well as the equitable remedies that may be available to the beneficiaries in the event the trustee breaches one or more of these duties, the reader is referred to Margaret E. W. Sager.[480] Her article also contains a discussion of what duties the lawyers for the various parties to a trust relationship may owe their respective clients and others in the face of an exercise or nonexercise of such a power. The defenses that may be available to the trustee in a surcharge action or to trust counsel in a malpractice action arising out of the exercise or nonexercise of the power to convert or adjust also are touched upon.[481]

Beware of the *in terrorem* clause. A *beneficiary* seeking to have a trust converted into a unitrust would be well advised to first read carefully the governing instrument. One court at least has held that merely a complaint to convert a trust into a unitrust would trigger a forfeiture under the trust's no-contest clause.[482] For more on no-contest and *in terrorem* clauses, the reader is referred to Section 5.5 of this handbook.

---

[478] *See, e.g.*, In re Moore, 41 Misc. 3d 687, 971 N.Y.S.2d 419 (2013).

[479] In re Heller, 849 N.E.2d 262 (N.Y. 2006).

[480] Margaret E. W. Sager, *Litigation and the Total Return Trust*, 35 ACTEC L.J. 206 (2009). For a general discussion of equitable remedies for breaches of trust, the reader is referred to §7.2.3 of this handbook.

[481] Margaret E. W. Sager, *Litigation and the Total Return Trust*, 35 ACTEC L.J. 206, 219–220 (2009).

[482] McKenzie v. Vanderpool, 151 Cal. App. 4th 1442, 61 Cal. Rptr. 3d 129 (Cal. App. 2 Dis., 2007).

The case against the unitrust concept. Not everyone endorses the unitrust concept. One learned commentator has written:

> We believe that unitrusts are a bad idea. Those who establish unitrusts today are exposing their trusts' beneficiaries to risks that neither may understand and neither may want. We are not predicting that the stock market will drop 50% in the next few years, as it did following the last great market highs in the late 1960s and early 1970s. Nor are we opposed to trustees distributing something other than accounting interest and dividend income. Our concern is simply that market values are not the best foundation for trust distributions. Using unitrusts, particularly today in what surely is an artificially high stock market, is likely to have unanticipated and adverse consequences. The most significant consequence is counterintuitive: While unitrusts would seem to encourage greater equity exposure, in practice they will discourage it. . . . For long-lived taxable trusts seeking even-handed treatment for income and remainder beneficiaries, the best distribution rule remains "real interest from bonds plus dividends from stocks." Unitrusts are not a good solution.[483]

The power to divide a trust. The Uniform Trust Code would authorize a trustee to divide a trust even if the trusts that result are dissimilar.[484] This could, under certain circumstances, offer a way out for the trustee confronted with conflicts among the beneficiaries and between the beneficiaries and the trustee over the trustee's investment objectives.[485] "[However,] . . . the more the terms of the divided trusts diverge from the original plan, the less likely it is that the settlor's purposes would be achieved and that the division could be approved."[486]

The nonstatutory equitable conversion. Assume there is no unitrust-conversion statute on the books. Nor is there a statute vesting trustees with a power to adjust. Principal-invasion authority is lacking in the terms of the trust. Might the court nonetheless have the inherent equitable authority in a given situation to order a conversion? Yes. Should it exercise that authority? It probably should, provided the answers to the following three questions are "No," "No," and "Yes":

1. Would an equitable conversion compromise the equitable property rights, whether vested or contingent, of a class of trust beneficiaries, or of any beneficiary, for that matter?
2. Would an equitable conversion thwart a material purpose of the trust?

---

[483] James P. Garland, *The Problems With Unitrusts*, I The Journal of Private Portfolio Management No. 4 (Spring 1999). *See also* Reni Gertner, *More States Allowing Unitrusts*, 2002 LWUSA 353 (May 27, 2002) (listing some of the disadvantages of the noncharitable unitrust); Alvin J. Golden, *Total Return Unitrusts: Is This a Solution in Search of a Problem?*, 28 ACTEC L.J. 121 (2002).

[484] UTC §417 cmt. (available at <http://www.uniformlaws.org/Act.aspx?title=Trust%20Code>).

[485] UTC §417 cmt. (available at <http://www.uniformlaws.org/Act.aspx?title=Trust%20Code>).

[486] UTC §417 cmt. (available at <http://www.uniformlaws.org/Act.aspx?title=Trust%20Code>).

3. Would an equitable conversion be beneficial to all current and noncurrent beneficiaries of the trust?

§6.2.3   Duty of Confidentiality

Moreover, since a fiduciary relationship exists even before the trust instrument is finally executed, if a settlor has imparted confidential information to the trustee, the fiduciary relationship will forbid its disclosure to anybody else. Indeed, it is wholly offensive to Equity's standards of integrity that the trustee could take personal advantage of the settlor's confidence.[487]

The current trustee. *Intentional breaches*. A corollary of the trustee's general duty of loyalty is the specific duty to keep all the affairs of the trust confidential.[488] The trustee's duty to act solely in the interest of the beneficiaries means that third parties are told only what the law requires the trustee to divulge, *e.g.*, information mandated by regulatory, supervisory, and taxing authorities,[489] or what furthers the interests of all the beneficiaries, *e.g.*, information needed by executors of pour-over wills and trustees of related trusts.[490] "Even in providing information to or on behalf of beneficiaries, however, the trustee has a duty to act with sensitivity and, insofar as practical, with due regard for considerations of relevancy and sound administration, and for the personal concerns and privacy of the trust beneficiaries." Breach of confidence was one of three traditional bases for equity jurisdiction, the others being fraud and accident. The law of trusts, the law of agency, and the law governing lawyers are separate offshoots of the branch of equity that remedied breaches of confidence.[491] Unauthorized disclosure to third parties, at minimum, is grounds for removal.[492]

Negligent breaches. A breach of confidence need not necessarily implicate the trustee's duty of loyalty. The trustee who maintains in digital form confidential information pertaining to the terms of the trust, its settlor, its beneficiaries, and/or the subject property assumes a duty to keep that information secure.[493] Thus, the trustee could be held personally liable for the consequences of negligently failing to protect such information from the predations of

---

[487] Paul-Jean Le Cannu, Trusts and Money Laundering in English Law: The Duties of Confidentiality and Disclosure of Trustees and the Obligations Arising Out of Sections 93a, 93b and 93d of the Criminal Justice Act 1988, 2 Global Jurist Topics No. 2, Article 4 (2002).

[488] *See* Restatement (Second) of Trusts §170 cmt. s. *See also* §5.4.1.1 of this handbook (the trust beneficiary's right to information and confidentiality) and §8.8 of this handbook (whom trust counsel represents).

[489] Restatement (Third) of Trusts §78 cmt. i.

[490] *See* Restatement (Third) of Trusts §78 cmt. i; Restatement (Second) of Trusts §170. *See also* 2A Scott on Trusts §170.

[491] *See generally* Chapter 1 of this handbook.

[492] *See* Bogert §527. *See generally* §7.2.3.6 of this handbook (trustee removal).

[493] *See generally* Huw Thomas, *Defend your data*, Dec. 2014/Jan. 2015 STEP J. 55 (how trustees should approach information security).

cybercriminals. The trustee's costs of prudently insuring against the quantifi-
able costs of cybercrimes, both avoidable but for the trustee's ordinary negli-
gcnce and unavoidable, ought to be reimbursable from the trust estate.[494]

Co-liability of third parties. What about the liability of the third party who
receives the confidential information? If the third party exploits the information in ways that are injurious to the trust, or if the third party and the trustee are
somehow connected such that the trustee is in conflict of interest, then the third
party may well share liability with the trustee, provided the third party knew of
the trust's existence.[495] In England, a third party may incur liability if he, she, or
it exploits confidential information pertaining to the trust in order to "dishonestly assist" the trustee in misapplying the trust property, or to induce him to do
so.[496] If the misapplication was for the third party's benefit, then the third party
might well be held accountable as a constructive trustee of the misapplied
property.[497] For a detailed discussion of third-party fiduciary liability of the
trustee's agents, see Section 7.2.9 of this handbook.

Keeping critical information from beneficiaries themselves. As to whether a
trustee may keep information pertaining to the affairs of the trust secret not
only from third parties but also from the beneficiaries themselves, see Section
5.4.1.1 of this handbook (right to information and confidentiality).

The former trustee. The trustee's fiduciary duties to the beneficiaries (or
to the trust's charitable purposes, as the case may be) will not cease even upon
the proper transfer of legal title to a qualified successor trustee. The transferor-
trustee, for example, remains burdened with the duty of undivided loyalty, to
include the incidental sub-duty of confidentiality.[498] In the face of such residual
trust-related burdens, divestiture of bare legal title, in and of itself, will not also
divest the transferor-trustee of standing to litigate matters pertaining to the
trust's proper administration.[499]

§6.2.4 Duty to Separate Income from Principal and the Right to Income

*Because the interests of income beneficiaries and remainder beneficiaries . . . are in many
ways quite antagonistic, the trustee has a fundamental duty to administer the trust so as to
preserve a fair balance between them. Capturing exactly what this means in any particular
case, however, may be difficult, for it is clear that the duty of impartiality does not require that
the trustee treat each beneficiary exactly the same. Just as apples and oranges are inherently*

---

[494] *See generally* §3.5.2.3 of this handbook (expenses reimbursable from the trust estate).

[495] *See generally* Lewin ¶ 20-49 through ¶ 20-50 (England).

[496] Lewin ¶ 20-49 through ¶ 20-50 (England).

[497] Lewin ¶ 20-49 (England).

[498] Not only is a former trustee-fiduciary saddled with such residual fiduciary duties, so also
is the former agent-fiduciary. The attorney-at-law in the post-termination-of-the-representation
period particularly comes to mind in this regard.

[499] *But see* Old Nat'l Bancorp v. Hanover College, 15 N.E.3d 574 (Ind. Sup. Ct. 2014) (the
court apparently oblivious of maxim that equity exalts substance over form that is discussed in
§8.12 of this handbook).

different, and require different treatment, so also, successive beneficiaries are inherently different and require different treatment.[500]

Unless a contrary intention is expressed in the governing instrument,[501] one class of beneficiaries will get the net income or use of as the trust property and another will ultimately get the principal (or as the English say the "capital") free of trust.[502] As a matter of law, unless the settlor intended otherwise, a current beneficiary is entitled to the net income as it accrues.[503] It must be distributed periodically at reasonable intervals.[504] Thus, one offshoot of the trustee's general duty to impartially carry out the terms of the trust will likely be the specific affirmative duty to separately account for income and principal.[505] The Restatement (Third) of Trusts is generally in accord, although it suggests that the trustee of a "purely" discretionary trust, a "pure" annuity trust, or a "pure" unitrust would not be equitably burdened with such a duty to separately account.[506] In the case of the purely discretionary trust, the trustee would need to have the discretionary fiduciary power to distribute principal, as well as income. Absent such principal-invasion authority, the trustee would still be saddled with the duty to separately account. The Restatement coins a term for traditional net trust-accounting income. It is "§110 income."[507]

Assume the trustee of a discretionary trust that is less than "purely" discretionary commingles trust accounting income and principal for administrative purposes without express authority in the governing instrument to do so. There may be some risk that some court somewhere might order the trustee to unscramble the egg. The risk, however, is a remote one. Equity concerns itself (or should concern itself) with the substance of a matter, not the technicalities. As a practical matter, there are no income beneficiaries and principal beneficiaries when the trustee has discretion to distribute either income or principal in mid-course. There are only current beneficiaries and remainder beneficiaries. Moreover, if periodically adding accumulated income to principal would further both the trust's material purposes and the interests of all classes of

---

[500] 4 Scott & Ascher §20.1.

[501] *See generally* 4 Scott & Ascher §20.2.3

[502] *See generally* 4 Scott & Ascher §20.1 (Impartiality Between Successive Beneficiaries); 3A Scott on Trusts §232.

[503] 4 Scott & Ascher §20.1. Note, however, that a life beneficiary is entitled to income in the form of corporate distributions to stockholders once the distribution becomes payable to shareholders of record on a designated date after the creation of the beneficial interest. *See generally* Restatement (Second) of Trusts §236. Income in the form of periodic payments such as interest and rents, however, is treated as accruing from day to day. *See generally* Restatement (Second) of Trusts §235 cmt. a. *See also* Revised Unif. Principal & Income Act §4.

[504] Although the trustee is not obligated to distribute income upon receipt, it is reasonable, where the trust does not specify the frequency of income payments, to distribute income semiannually or quarterly. *See generally* 2A Scott on Trusts §182; Bogert §814. It might in fact be reasonable in certain instances for the trustee to withhold income to build up a reserve for payment of future expenditures. 2A Scott on Trusts §182; Bogert §814.

[505] *See generally* 4 Scott & Ascher §20.1; 2A Scott on Trusts §183. *See also* Bogert §816.

[506] Restatement (Third) of Trusts §109 cmt. b.

[507] *See, e.g.,* Restatement (Third) of Trusts §109 cmt. a.

beneficiary, then the trustee may well have a default equitable *duty* to do just that. If adding income to principal would have no impact one way or the other on the trust's material purposes and the equitable interests, then it would seem that the trustee ought to have the *right* to do so without risk of sanction.

When a trust truly has income beneficiaries, the trustee's duty to separately account for income and principal is a critical duty. The determination where to credit a receipt or debit an expense directly affects the property interests of the income beneficiary and the remainderman: A receipt credited to income will benefit the income beneficiary whereas a receipt credited to principal will benefit the remainderman. Similarly, a decision where to charge an expense directly affects the beneficiary's property interests. Failure to properly credit a receipt or charge an expense is a breach of trust. Occasionally, how the trustee should handle a particular type of receipt or expense is expressly addressed in the terms of the trust.[508] More often, the terms of the trust grant the trustee a discretionary power to determine in doubtful cases which receipts are income and which are principal, and which expenses should be paid out of the income account and which out the principal account, a topic that is covered in Section 3.5.3.2(g) of this handbook.

A trustee is also under a duty to act impartially.[509] Thus, the trustee must be careful to distinguish between principal and income with regard both to receipts and expenditures so that neither the current beneficiary nor the remainderman will be deprived of what is due to each.[510]

The trustee must decide what qualifies as income and what qualifies as principal for trust accounting purposes. For guidance, the trustee should look to the law that governs the administration of the trust.[511] Most jurisdictions now have comprehensive statutory rules that, unless the terms of a trust provide otherwise, determine allocation and apportionment issues.[512] Most likely these rules have been borrowed from the Uniform Principal and Income Act (1997).[513] Still, "no statute, no matter how well drafted and carefully thought through, can answer every conceivable question."[514] Thus, the trustee will still need the common law and the generally accepted practices and lore of the

---

[508] *See generally* 4 Scott & Ascher §20.2.3 (Terms of the Trust).

[509] 3 Scott & Ascher §17.15 (Duty of Impartiality); 4 Scott & Ascher §20.1 (Impartiality Between Successive Beneficiaries).

[510] *See generally* 4 Scott & Ascher §20.1 (Impartiality Between Successive Beneficiaries).

[511] When the terms of the trust provide neither for the allocation of receipts and expenses nor for the applicable law, a conflict of laws question may arise. *See* 5A Scott on Trusts §586. The trustee or court may resolve such questions by ascertaining the intention of the settlor. Otherwise, matters of administration might be resolved through application of the law of the place of administration, and matters of construction might be resolved through application of the law of the settlor's domicile. 5A Scott on Trusts §586. See generally Jeffrey A. Schoenblum, 1 Multistate and Multinational Estate Planning §§17.02, 17.03 (2000).

[512] For a catalog of state legislation applicable to the allocation of income and principal and the apportionment of expenses, *see* Bogert §816 nn.64–66.

[513] 4 Scott & Ascher §20.2.

[514] 4 Scott & Ascher §20.2.

jurisdiction to catch what falls between the legislative cracks.[515] The law of principal and income has always been a minefield that even the experienced trustee—or particularly the experienced trustee—ventures into with some trepidation:

> The law of principal and income, which we are about to take up, seeks to allocate each and every receipt that comes into a trustee's hands, and each and every expense that a trustee pays, between principal and income. It is both an intricate and a rigid body of law, and close examination almost inevitably conveys the impression that much of it is more than usually arbitrary.[516]

Of course, if the terms of the trust direct where a receipt is to be credited or where an expense is to be debited, then the trust term controls.[517] Even when the state of the settlor's domicile has one set of rules for the allocation of receipts and expenses between income and principal and the state where the trust is being administered has another, there is no conflict of laws problem if the terms of the trust address the situation, "because such matters, not involving questions of validity, are almost entirely within the settlor's control."[518] A trustee who fails to honor the settlor's intentions in this regard would be in breach of trust, absent special circumstances or prior court approval.[519]

Above all the trustee must understand that the rules governing what is income for tax purposes are separate from the rules governing what is allocated to income for trust accounting purposes.[520] A receipt of income in respect of a decedent (IRD), for example, may be income for tax purposes but principal for trust accounting purposes.[521] And of course, *when in doubt, the prudent trustee allocates receipts to principal and expenses to income.*[522]

Until recently, in most states a trustee would have been subject to some version of the 1931 Uniform Principal and Income Act or the 1962 Revised Uniform Principal and Income Act. The reader should be aware, however, that in 1997, the National Conference of Commissioners on Uniform State Laws

---

[515] *See generally* Bogert §816 n.67 and accompanying text.

[516] 4 Scott & Ascher §20.1.

[517] *See generally* 4 Scott & Ascher §§20.2.3, 20.6.9; 7 Scott & Ascher §45.3.10; 2A Scott on Trusts §164.

[518] 7 Scott & Ascher §45.3.10. *See generally* §8.5 of this handbook (conflict of laws).

[519] *See generally* §6.1.2 of this handbook (the trustee's duty to carry out the terms of the trust).

[520] *See* Bogert §816. The trustee should note that the economic theories that form the basis for principles of accounting for tax purposes and of accounting for trust purposes differ substantially. *See* Bogert §816 n.63 and accompanying text.

[521] Receipt of income in respect of a decedent (*IRD receipt*) is income received to which a decedent had rights prior to death but which was not payable or collected until after death. *See generally* M. C. Ferguson et al., Federal Income Taxation of Estates, Trusts, and Beneficiaries Chapter 3 (3d ed. 2000). Once the receipt is paid, it must be included in the gross income of the estate or trust of the decedent for the taxable year when received. I.R.C. §691(a)(1) (1992). For trust accounting purposes, however, the receipt is treated as principal. *See* Revised Unif. Principal & Income Act §4(b)(1) ("receipts due but not paid at the date of death of the testator are principal") (available at <http://www.uniformlaws.org/Act.aspx?title=Trust%20Code>).

[522] *See generally* Bogert §810 (Readjustments).

approved a new version of the model statute.[523] The 1997 version would allow trustees who are authorized and inclined to pursue total return investment strategies to make appropriate reallocations or adjustments between the income and principal accounts in furtherance of these strategies.[524] Trust accounting rules relating to a number of asset categories, including S-corporation stock, partnership interests, derivatives, and timber, have been amended, clarified, or expanded.[525] The 1997 revision has now been enacted in almost all the States:[526]

> There was at one time doubt about the constitutionality of applying a principal and income statute to a trust or an estate that pre-dated the statute. Now, however, it seems clear that retroactive application of principal and income legislation is constitutionally possible.[527]

The Restatement (Third) of Trusts, specifically Section 111, would impose an *affirmative* duty on the trustee to exercise a statutory adjustment power (or statutory unitrust election) if such an exercise would enable the trustee to better carry out his duty of impartiality to the various classes of beneficiary, assuming under the particular trust there are various classes and he has such a duty of impartiality. Absent such statutory authority, the Restatement provides that the trustee nonetheless would have what amounts to a common law/equitable duty to equitably adjust the income and principal accounts as appropriate. Section 111 has no counterpart in the Restatement (Second) of Trusts. Here is the official rationale for breaking all this new doctrinal ground:

> It is normally advantageous to beneficiaries collectively and therefore prudent for the trustee to seek a total return that is optimal in light of the trust's purposes and circumstances, especially the risk tolerance of the trust and its beneficiaries. But a significant aspect of the duty of impartiality in many trusts is the requirement . . . of suitable income productivity. The ideal way of reconciling these potentially conflicting responsibilities . . . is to invest for optimal total return and, if necessary, to adjust principal and income . . . or to make a unitrust election . . . in order to achieve an appropriate level of income productivity.[528]

In other words, this is all about fashioning a trust accounting regime that can comfortably accommodate the prudent investor rule: "The 'prudent investor rule' *encourages* trustees to invest for optimal total return (i.e., to make a reasonable effort to invest the highest total return that is suitable to the trust's purposes and the circumstances of the trust and its beneficiaries, especially risk

---

[523] Unif. Principal & Income Act (1997) (available at <http://www.uniformlaws.org/Act.aspx?title=Trust%20Code>).

[524] *See generally* 4 Scott & Ascher §20.2.

[525] The full text with commentary of the Unif. Principal & Income Act (1997) is available at <http://www.uniformlaws.org/Act.aspx?title=Trust%20Code>.

[526] *See* 4 Scott & Ascher §20.2 n.9.

[527] 4 Scott & Ascher §20.2. *See also* 4 Scott & Ascher §20.6.2.

[528] Restatement (Third) of Trusts §111 cmt. a.

tolerance)."[529] Time will tell whether a regime of trust accounting that is so profoundly total-return focused is capable of comfortably adapting to the ongoing and inexorable evolution in trust-investment doctrine.[530]

For a discussion of the English rules governing the allocation and apportionment of capital (principal) and income receipts, the reader is referred to chapter 25 of Lewin on Trusts. Also addressed in the chapter are the rules pertaining to the allocation and apportionment of trust expenses.

§6.2.4.1 What Receipts Are Entirely Allocated to Income for Trust Accounting Purposes?

Income includes any return on capital that does not impair it, but not returns that represent an accretion to capital.[531]

The ordinary current receipts of a trust are income.[532] They should be credited to the income account and distributed, after making provision for ordinary expenses, to the beneficiary who is entitled to receive income.[533] This includes routine rents; ordinary[534] and extraordinary[535] cash dividends, including dividends on preferred stock;[536] items of current interest;[537] accrued increment on bonds or other obligations issued at discount;[538] shares in a corporation other than the distributing corporation;[539] and a pro rata share of the income earned during administration of the settlor's estate.[540] As to extraordinary cash dividends, the majority rule is that they belong to income, although some jurisdictions have held that they are apportionable between

---

[529] Restatement (Third) of Trusts, Ch. 23, Introductory Note (accounting for principal and income) (emphasis added).

[530] *See generally* §6.2.2.1 of this handbook (whether the prudent investor rule is already passing into obsolescence).

[531] 4 Scott & Ascher §20.2.1

[532] *See generally* 4 Scott & Ascher §20.2.1.

[533] Ordinary current receipts will generally include the earnings, profits, and products that result from use or investment of the trust corpus. *See* 3A Scott on Trusts §233.1. Ordinary receipts that indicate merely a change in the form of the corpus, however, are not to be credited to the income account but are retained as principal. 3A Scott on Trusts §233.1. *See also* Bogert §816. The Revised Unif. Principal & Income Act provides rules for the allocation of most receipts. Revised Unif. Principal & Income Act §3. For a catalog of states where the Act has been adopted, *see* Bogert §816 nn.64, 65.

[534] *See generally* 4 Scott & Ascher §20.6.1 (Ordinary Cash Dividends).

[535] *See generally* 4 Scott & Ascher §20.6.2 (Extraordinary Distributions Including Stock Dividends).

[536] 4 Scott & Ascher §20.6.4 (Dividends on Preferred Stock).

[537] *See* 3A Scott on Trusts §233.1.

[538] 3A Scott on Trusts §233.1. *See also* Revised Unif. Principal & Income Act §7.

[539] A dividend in the form of shares in a corporation other than the distributing corporation is generally allocable as income unless the dividend is declared out of capital. 3A Scott on Trusts §236.5. *See, e.g.,* Mass. Gen. Laws ch. 203, §21A.

[540] *See* 3A Scott on Trusts §234.4.

income and principal.[541] For a discussion of the Massachusetts rule governing the allocation of extraordinary dividends, the reader is referred to Section 8.15.14 of this handbook.

§6.2.4.2   What Receipts Are Entirely Allocated to Principal for Trust Accounting Purposes?

On the other hand, profits on the sale or exchange of any part of the principal are ordinarily principal.[542]

Proceeds from the sale by the trustee of trust principal are considered principal; thus, realized capital gains, although income for tax purposes, are considered items of principal for trust accounting purposes.[543] So also are most distributions of stock, including ordinary and extraordinary stock dividends;[544] regular or small stock dividends; subscription rights;[545] distributions resulting from corporate reorganizations, spin-offs, etc.; and dividends in liquidation.[546] In California, money received by the trustee in partial liquidation of an entity is allocated to principal if the total amount of money received *by the trustee* (not the amount of the entire distribution by the entity) is greater than 20 percent of the entity's gross assets, as shown by the entity's year-end financial statements immediately preceding the initial receipt.[547]

Additional shares resulting from stock splits are of course items of principal, as are capital gain distributions from mutual funds.[548] Actually, under the

---

[541] 4 Scott & Ascher §20.6.2; 3A Scott on Trusts. §236.4.

[542] 4 Scott & Ascher §20.2.1.

[543] Bogert §§822–823; 4 Scott & Ascher §10.2.1. *See generally* §10.2 of this handbook (capital gains income for tax purposes) and §11.1 of this handbook (tax basis/cost of trust property).

[544] *See generally* 4 Scott & Ascher §20.6.2 (Extraordinary Distributions Including Stock Dividends); §8.15.14 of this handbook (the Massachusetts rule of allocation).

[545] *See generally* 4 Scott & Ascher §20.6.5 (Subscription Rights).

[546] *See generally* 4 Scott & Ascher §20.6.2. For a discussion of the rules of allocation for ordinary and extraordinary stock dividends, including a discussion of why the "Massachusetts rule of allocation" now governs in most jurisdictions and why the "Pennsylvania rule of apportionment" has fallen out of favor, *see* 4 Scott & Ascher §20.6.2; 3A Scott on Trusts §§236.3–236.8. For a discussion of the constitutional implications of making adoption of the Massachusetts rule applicable to preexisting trusts, *see* 4 Scott & Ascher §20.6.2. For a discussion of the treatment of rights to subscribe to shares of stock and the treatment of dividends in liquidation, *see* 4 Scott & Ascher §20.6.2; 3A Scott on Trusts. §§236.9–236.10. *See* John P. Ludington, Annot., *Modern Status of Rules Governing Allocation of Stock Dividends or Splits Between Principal and Income*, 81 A.L.R.3d 876 (1977). *See also* §8.15.14 of this handbook (the Massachusetts rule of allocation).

[547] Estate of Thomas, 124 Cal. App. 4th 711, 21 Cal. Rptr. 3d 741 (2004) (involving distributions of the undistributed income of a subchapter S corporation to a qualified subchapter S trust).

[548] *See generally* 4 Scott & Ascher §20.6.6 (Distributions from Mutual Funds). *See, e.g.*, Tait v. Peck, 346 Mass. 521, 194 N.E.2d 707 (1963) (holding that capital gains distributions from mutual funds are principal). *See generally* Annot., *Allocation Between Income and Principal of Capital Gains Dividend of Mutual Fund or Investment Trust or Corporation*, 98 A.L.R.2d 511 (1964).

1997 revision of the Uniform Principal and Income Act, "all corporate distributions in 'property other than money' are principal."[549]

If the trust estate is taken by eminent domain, the compensation therefor is a principal item.[550] When entrusted property is destroyed by fire or other casualty, any insurance proceeds are also principal.[551]

§6.2.4.3 What Receipts Are Apportioned Between the Income and Principal Accounts?

As we have seen, after Congress changed the tax rules relating to depletion, there was no reason to continue with the $27\frac{1}{2}$ percentage. But the switch from $27\frac{1}{2}$ to 90, as the percentage of most receipts from mineral interests allocable to principal . . . [called for by the 1997 revision of the Uniform Principal and Income Act . . .], is nothing short of staggering.[552]

The concept of apportionment. At common law, interest earned generally accrued daily to the one who was entitled to it, say, for life. Take the income-only nondiscretionary trust for the benefit of C for life. Upon the death of C, C's probate estate was entitled to undistributed net trust investment interest accrued to the date of C's death, but not to what was left over, if any. Some other trust beneficiary was entitled to that. In other words, the accumulated and undistributed interest income at the time of C's death had to be "apportioned" by B, the trustee. On the other hand, rents would accrue on rent days and ordinary dividends on record dates. Thus, if C died just before a rent day or a record date, his probate estate was out of luck as to the particular income receipt, unless the terms of the trust provided otherwise. The rent or the dividend, as the case may be, went somewhere else, perhaps to C2, or perhaps into the trust's principal account for ultimate distribution to D. There was no apportionment of the rent payment or the dividend payment between or among the various equitable property interests extant incident to the trust relationship. Then, in 1931, default apportionment doctrine suddenly got complicated and volatile:

> Modern statutes (including the 1931 and 1962 versions of the Uniform Principal and Income Act) liberalized these common-law rules, directing that certain periodic payments (including both interest and rent, but not dividends) be apportioned between successive owners on the basis of a day-to-day accrual. Reversing this development, the most recent and widely-adopted version of the Uniform Principal and . . . [Income] . . . Act (the 1997 Act) restricts apportionment of trust income even more narrowly than does the common law. The 1997 Uniform Act determines entitlement to any periodic payment (including interest) by its date of receipt, disregarding any prior date of accrual or due date.[553]

---

[549] 4 Scott & Ascher §20.6.3 (referring to Unif. Principal & Income Act §401(c)(1) (1997)).

[550] 4 Scott & Ascher §20.2.1.

[551] 4 Scott & Ascher §20.2.1.

[552] 4 Scott & Ascher §20.7.3.

[553] Restatement (Third) of Restitution and Unjust Enrichment §47 cmt. f.

The Restatement (Third) of Restitution and Unjust Enrichment, specifically in the commentary to §47, suggests that trust receipt apportionment doctrine is little more than a specific application of general unjust enrichment doctrine: "Allocation and apportionment between competing claims of ownership . . . reflect the same principles of unjust enrichment that underlie the rule of the present section, even though the claimant does not literally seek 'restitution' unless the defendant has been paid money to which the claimant was entitled inter se."[554] Here is §47 verbatim: "If a third person makes a payment to the defendant in respect of an asset belonging to the claimant, the claimant is entitled to restitution from the defendant as necessary to prevent unjust enrichment."

Wasting or overproductive property. The money received by way of "yield" from a wasting investment presents a peculiar problem.[555] Such a yield involves a continuing dissipation of principal to the economic detriment of the remainderman.[556] In order to be impartial, therefore, the trustee should set aside some part of the yield to protect the remainderman from this gradual loss,[557] unless the interests of the remainderman can better be protected in some other way[558] or the terms of the trust call for the income beneficiary to be favored.[559] "Wasting or overproductive property consists of property interests that terminate or tend to depreciate over the course of time."[560] Examples of wasting or overproductive investments are "leaseholds; royalties, whether from books or inventions or from leases of mineral or timber lands; patent rights; interests in things the substance of which is consumed, such as mines, oil and gas wells, quarries, and timber lands; and interests in things that are subject to obsolescence, are consumed in the using, or are worn out by use, such as buildings, furniture, machinery, and equipment."[561]

The apportionment of wasting assets is purely a matter of calculation. It may be done by fixing the value of the property at the time of creation of the trust and paying the life tenant from time to time that part of the yield which would equal the usual rate of return in trust investments.[562] It also may be done by apportioning the proceeds of sale when the property is sold.[563] The decisions in cases involving mining operations, quarries, and oil wells are numerous and

---

[554] Restatement (Third) of Restitution and Unjust Enrichment §47 cmt. c.

[555] A *wasting asset* is one whose value will depreciate or be destroyed in time, thus favoring the life beneficiary at the expense of the remainderman who is left with an asset of little or no value. *See generally* 3A Scott on Trusts §239; Bogert §827; Revised Unif. Principal & Income Act §§9–11.

[556] *See* 4 Scott & Ascher §20.7; 3A Scott on Trusts §239; Restatement (Third) of Trusts §239.

[557] 4 Scott & Ascher §20.7; 3A Scott on Trusts §239; Restatement (Third) of Trusts §239. The Revised Unif. Principal & Income Act sets specific guidelines for apportioning receipts from wasting assets such as minerals and other natural resources, timber, royalties, patents, and so forth. *See* Revised Unif. Principal & Income Act §§9–11; Restatement (Third) of Trusts §239.

[558] 4 Scott & Ascher §20.7.

[559] 4 Scott & Ascher §20.7.1 (Terms of the Trust).

[560] 4 Scott & Ascher §20.7.

[561] 4 Scott & Ascher §20.7. *See generally* 3A Scott on Trusts §239.

[562] *See* 3A Scott on Trusts. §239 n.4, §241.4.

[563] *See* 3A Scott on Trusts. §239 n.4, §241.4.

diverse in their holdings.[564] Obviously if the instrument shows that the life beneficiary is to enjoy all benefits of wasting property, neither amortization of receipts nor apportionment of proceeds is necessary.[565]

The practice of amortizing bond premiums traditionally worked this way: When a trustee purchases a bond (or other fixed-income obligation) for the principal account at a premium, *i.e.*, at a price in excess of its value at maturity, the trustee deducts over time from the income stream such sums as are necessary to reimburse the principal account for the premium.[566] This is done particularly if the trustee expects to hold the bond to maturity, as its market value at the time of purchase will inevitably decline over time to face value.[567] Moreover, it is likely that the purchase price exceeds the face value because the bond's interest rate is a particularly generous one. Thus, absent some adjustments over time, the income account is advantaged over time at the expense of the principal account. The bond would be characterized on a trust accounting report or statement as an "amortized investment."

The concept of apportioning accretions, on the other hand, works this way: Where a trustee purchases a bond (or other fixed-income obligation) bearing no stated interest that is redeemable at a future time for an amount in excess of its purchase price, the accretion belongs to the income account. In this case, the bond would be characterized as an "accreted investment."

Under the common law, the trustee had a duty to the remainderman to amortize bond premiums.[568] Thus, the purchase of a bond at a price in excess of its face amount called for the allocation of some of the bond income, as it was received, to the principal account.[569] "*[A]ll three versions of the . . . [Uniform Principal and Income Act] . . . have eliminated any duty on the part of a trustee to amortize bond premiums.*"[570] It should be noted that, for purposes of tax accounting, premiums on purchases on tax-exempt bonds must be amortized.[571]

The 1997 revision of the Uniform Principal and Income Act calls for an allocation of 90 percent of most receipts from mineral interests to principal.[572] This is a radical departure from past practice. Under the prior version of the Act, 27½ percent was allocated to principal.[573] In the case of timber harvesting on entrusted land, the proceeds attributable to "annual growth" is apportioned to income, and the balance to principal.[574]

---

[564] For a general discussion of the wide range of holdings among the jurisdictions in this area, *see* 3A Scott on Trusts §239.3.

[565] *See generally* 4 Scott & Ascher §20.7.1; 3A Scott on Trusts. §239.1.

[566] 4 Scott & Ascher §20.7.2 (Bonds Purchased at Premium).

[567] 4 Scott & Ascher §20.7.2.

[568] 4 Scott & Ascher §20.7.2; 3A Scott on Trusts. §239.2.

[569] 4 Scott & Ascher §20.7.2 (Bonds Purchased at Premium).

[570] 4 Scott & Ascher §20.7.2.

[571] For the federal tax treatment of premiums paid in purchasing tax-exempt bonds, *see* I.R.C. §171 (1992).

[572] 4 Scott & Ascher §20.7.3 (referring to Unif. Principal & Income Act §411(a)(1) (1997)).

[573] 4 Scott & Ascher §20.7.3 (referring to Unif. Principal & Income Act §9(a)(3) (1962)).

[574] 4 Scott & Ascher §20.7.4 (referring to Unif. Principal & Income Act §412 (1997)).

Sometimes, the trust property includes equipment and/or a building that generates income. Should a trustee apportion some of this income over time to principal to establish a depreciation reserve? Such items "tend, over time, to decline in value, not only due to physical deterioration but also as they become less well-suited to their original purposes."[575] Under the 1997 revision of the Uniform Principal and Income Act, the trustee has a discretionary power to set aside a depreciation reserve.[576] It will depend upon the particular facts and circumstances whether he has a fiduciary duty to do so.

The 1997 revision of the Uniform Principal and Income Act defines a "liquidating asset" as "an asset whose value will diminish or terminate because the asset is expected to produce receipts for a period of limited duration."[577] Examples of liquidating assets are leaseholds, patents, copyrights, and royalty rights. Ten percent of a liquidating asset receipt is allocated to income, and the balance to principal.[578]

The 1997 revision provides that the portion of a deferred compensation or annuity payment that has been characterized *by the payor* as (or in lieu of) interest or a dividend is income.[579] The balance is principal.[580] A payment of the entire account balance is principal, as is that portion of a payment that is attributable to the exercise by the trustee of a right of withdrawal.[581] "If no part of a payment is characterized as interest, a dividend, or an equivalent payment, and all or part of the payment is 'required to be made,' the trustee is to allocate to income 10 percent of the part that is required to be made during the accounting period, and the balance to principal."[582]

Because the revision's allocation and apportionment rules for deferred compensation, annuities, and similar payments are so arcane, the trustee is advised not to rely on a paraphrase of what they are. Rather, the trustee faced with administering such a payment is advised to download a copy of Section 409 of the 1997 revision of the Uniform Principal and Income Act from the web and endeavor to parse the actual text.[583] After doing so, if the trustee is in reasonable doubt as to whether the receipt is entirely income or entirely principal, or whether it is to be apportioned somehow between the two accounts, trust counsel should be asked to characterize the receipt in a written opinion, which then should be placed in the trust's permanent file.

---

[575] 4 Scott & Ascher §20.7.5.

[576] 4 Scott & Ascher §20.7.5 (referring to Unif. Principal & Income Act §503(b) (1997)).

[577] Unif. Principal & Income Act §410(a) (1997).

[578] Unif. Principal & Income Act §410(b) (1997).

[579] Unif. Principal & Income Act §409(b) (1997).

[580] Unif. Principal & Income Act §409(b) (1997).

[581] Unif. Principal & Income Act §409(c) (1997).

[582] 4 Scott & Ascher §20.7.6 (Liquidating Assets) (referring to Unif. Principal & Income Act §409(c) (1997)).

[583] The full text is available at <http://www.uniformlaws.org/Act.aspx?title=Trust%20Code>.

Unproductive or underproductive property. On the other hand, unproductive property can work a hardship on the income beneficiary.[584] Thus, upon the sale of such property, an appropriate portion of the proceeds traditionally was required to be allocated to the income account,[585] unless the terms of the trust suggested that the settlor intended otherwise.[586] Likewise, the proceeds from the settlement of a note long in default were required to be appropriately apportioned between both accounts.[587] When the proceeds were brought into the hands of the trustee, a calculation was made which attempted to award to the life tenant the income that would have been received if the unproductive property actually had produced at a current rate of return.[588] In the case of unproductive property, an income allocation was appropriate even when a particular investment has resulted in a capital loss.[589]

Unless the terms of the trust provided otherwise,[590] a trustee traditionally was under a duty to the income beneficiary to sell unproductive property within a reasonable time.[591] The rules expressed herein also applied to underproductive property.[592] Thus if property that produced income substantially less than the current rate of return on trust investments was held, the trustee, absent a

---

[584] Restatement (Third) of Trusts §240 (provisional); 4 Scott & Ascher §20.6.7 (Undistributed Earnings).

[585] 4 Scott & Ascher §20.8 (Unproductive or Underproductive Property).

[586] *See generally* 4 Scott & Ascher §20.8.1 (Terms of the Trust). Section 241 (provisional) of the Restatement (Third) of Trusts provides a methodology for apportioning the net proceeds from the sale of unproductive property between income and principal. The portion of the proceeds allocable to principal we will call the principal amount. The principal amount is that which when added to what that amount would earn in interest at the current rate of return on trust investments for the period the unproductive asset was in the trust equals the net proceeds. The net proceeds minus the principal amount is then what is allocated to income. For an algebraic depiction of the methodology, *see* Jesse Dukeminier & Stanley M. Johanson, Wills, Trusts, and Estates 937 (2000). On the other hand, the income account receives no portion of proceeds from the sale of unproductive property that the trustee, in the governing instrument, is directed or specifically authorized to retain. *See* Restatement (Third) of Trusts §241. *See also* Bogert §824; 4 Scott & Ascher §20.6.7 (noting that under the 1997 version of the Uniform Principal and Income Act, upon the sale of stock in a company that has distributed none of its earnings, the trustee would have the discretionary power to make an adjustment from principal to income in order to avoid any unfairness to the income beneficiary); Restatement (Second) of Trusts §241(2). *Cf.* Revised Unif. Principal & Income Act §12 (income should be determined as if principal had been invested to yield 4 percent per annum).

[587] A default in interest payment on a bond may be an example of a productive asset that becomes nonproductive. *See generally* 3A Scott on Trusts §§240.3, 241.3–241.3A; 4 Scott & Ascher §20.9.1 (Mortgages in Default).

[588] *See generally* 4 Scott & Ascher §20.9 (discussing the mathematics of determining what portion of the proceeds from the delayed sale of unproductive property should be allocable to income).

[589] Restatement (Third) of Trusts §241 cmt. b.

[590] 4 Scott & Ascher §20.8.1 (Terms of the Trust).

[591] 4 Scott & Ascher §20.6.7; 3A Scott on Trusts §240; Restatement (Third) of Trusts §240 (provisional).

[592] *See* 4 Scott & Ascher §20.9; 3A Scott on Trusts §240; Restatement (Third) of Trusts §240 cmt. b (provisional).

contrary intention, was required to make an appropriate apportionment when the property was sold.[593]

The 1997 Uniform Principal and Income Act modifies the asset-by-asset approach of its predecessor acts when it comes to allocating to income a portion of the proceeds from the delayed sale of an unproductive or underproductive asset.[594] The 1997 Act allocates proceeds from the sale or other disposition of an asset to principal "without regard to the amount of income the asset produces during any accounting period."[595] In other words, it abolishes the apportionment rule in favor of bestowing on the trustee a discretionary power to make equitable adjustments between the income and principal accounts.[596] Now, in determining the trustee's duty to make an item of property productive of income, it is the performance of the portfolio as a whole and the trustee's practice of making principal distributions to the income beneficiary that are the primary considerations.[597] While trustees will continue to have under the Prudent Investor Rule a duty to diversify trust investments, a trustee with an equitable power of adjustment[598] should no longer feel obliged to dispose of a particular unproductive or underproductive stock position "just to plump up the income stream."[599]

The 1997 version of the Uniform Principal and Income Act has made two important departures from past practices. Under the 1997 version, the trustee who controls and runs an entrusted business now has broad discretion in allocating the profits between income and principal,[600] subject, of course, to his overarching duty to act solely in the interests *of the trust beneficiaries*.[601] The second departure relates to "non-interest-bearing securities, such as U.S. savings bonds, that are payable or redeemable under a fixed schedule of appreciation."[602] The 1997 version, unless the maturity of the security is less than one year, allocates all such increment in value to principal.[603] On the other hand,

---

[593] The trustee, when allocating proceeds from the sale of underproductive property, must modify the general rule for allocating proceeds from the sale of unproductive property to account for the small income received as well as for the associated carrying charges of the underproductive asset. *See* 4 Scott & Ascher §20.9; 3A Scott on Trusts §241.1.

[594] 4 Scott & Ascher §20.9.

[595] *See* Unif. Principal & Income Act (1997) §413(b) (available at <http://www.uniformlaws.org/Act.aspx?title=Trust%20Code>).

[596] 4 Scott & Ascher §20.9.

[597] Unif. Principal & Income Act (1997) §413(b) cmt., paragraph 2.

[598] *See generally* 4 Scott & Ascher §20.10 (Equitable Adjustments).

[599] 4 Scott & Ascher §20.8.

[600] *See generally* 4 Scott & Ascher §20.2.1 (Receipts).

[601] *See generally* §3.5.3.1(a) of this handbook (noting that the trustee of an entrusted business owes an overarching duty to the trust beneficiaries, though the trustee himself is the shareholder of record). The fiduciary duties that the trustee may simultaneously owe to the minority corporate shareholders, if any, is beyond the scope of this handbook. Whether there is a satisfactory harmonization of these potentially conflicting sets of fiduciary duties may well depend upon the quality of coordination between trust and corporate counsel. *See generally* §8.25 of this handbook (which American law schools still require Trusts).

[602] 4 Scott & Ascher §20.2.1 (Receipts).

[603] *See generally* 4 Scott & Ascher §20.2.1.

"[t]he 1997 Uniform Act continues the general rule that gain realized upon the maturity or other disposition of discount bonds is principal ..."[604]

§6.2.4.4   What Expenses Are Allocated Entirely to Income, Entirely to Principal, and Apportioned Between Income and Principal?

Expenses that are connected with the everyday administration of the trust property are chargeable entirely to income.[605] Examples include ordinary repairs to real estate, annual real property taxes, insurance premiums, premiums on the trustee's bond, and legal expenses incurred in collecting income.[606] Income taxes attributable to trust accounting income are charged to income.[607]

Expenses incurred primarily for the protection and preservation of the principal are chargeable entirely to principal.[608] This includes legal expenses that relate to the interpretation of the trust, the appointment or removal of the trustee, and litigation;[609] alterations and additions to real estate;[610] expenses for preparation of property for rental or sale; income taxes on capital gains;[611] brokers' commissions;[612] the costs of a guardian ad litem appointed to represent remainder interests; that portion of a mortgage payment that amortizes a debt the trust owes;[613] and the expenses of making final distribution.[614] "If a trustee borrows money from income to make an expenditure which should have been borne by principal, he should repay the sum at the earliest opportunity, even if he is obliged to get court consent to a mortgage on the trust property to raise the amount."[615] On the other hand, an incremental equitable apportionment of income to principal may be appropriate to fund certain capital improvements.[616]

---

[604] 4 Scott & Ascher §20.8.2 (Discount Bonds).

[605] 4 Scott & Ascher §20.2.2.

[606] The Revised Unif. Principal & Income Act provides that "ordinary expenses" are chargeable against income. Revised Unif. Principal & Income Act §13(a). *See generally* 4 Scott & Ascher §20.2.2; 3A Scott on Trusts §233.2; Bogert §802.

[607] Revised Unif. Principal & Income Act §13(a)(6); 4 Scott & Ascher §20.2.2.

[608] 4 Scott & Ascher §20.2.2.

[609] 4 Scott & Ascher §20.2.2.

[610] 4 Scott & Ascher §20.2.2.

[611] 4 Scott & Ascher §20.2.2 ("Such gains may well be income for federal tax purposes, but, since they are in fact accretions of principal, it would be unfair to pay the tax out of income").

[612] 4 Scott & Ascher §20.2.2.

[613] 4 Scott & Ascher §20.2.2.

[614] Revised Unif. Principal & Income Act. §13(c). *See generally* 4 Scott & Ascher §20.2.2; 3A Scott on Trusts §233.3.

[615] Bogert §810. *See, e.g.,* In re Peoples' Nat'l Bank & Trust Co. of White Plains, 90 N.Y.S.2d 384 (1949) (providing that when the principal is illiquid, the income beneficiaries may be granted a lien on the principal for any income disbursements that were made to cover principal expenses).

[616] 4 Scott & Ascher §20.2.2.

Some expenses are chargeable in part to income and in part to principal, such as regular trustee's fees and costs of periodic accountings that pertain both to the income and the remainder interests.[617] Under both the 1962 and the 1997 versions of the Uniform Principal and Income Act, no matter how trustee compensation is *computed*, *e.g.*, solely as a percentage of income or solely as a percentage of principal, it is default law that the *burden* is shared equally between the income and the principal accounts.[618] "Chargeable... [entirely]... to principal... [, however,]... are fees for acceptance, distribution, or termination of the trust, and fees charged on disbursements made to prepare property for sale."[619]

The trust may include property that does not produce any current income. Where should the expenses of the unproductive property be charged? The answer to this difficult question depends on the terms of the trust. Generally, the current as well as extraordinary expenses of unproductive property are payable from principal unless the terms of the trust provide otherwise.[620]

It should be noted that some jurisdictions require a trustee to adjust the income and principal amounts when certain tax elections upset the equilibrium between the competing equitable interests.[621] Let us take a residuary testamentary trust, for example. Administration expenses paid from the principal of the probate estate are elected to be taken as an income tax deduction, rather than as an estate tax deduction. This reduces the taxable income of, but not the income actually paid to, the life beneficiary.[622] Some jurisdictions require that some income be transferred to the principal account so that the trust remainderman is compensated for not benefiting from an estate tax deduction (and so

---

[617] Revised Unif. Principal & Income Act §13(a)(3). Ordinary practice is to pay the trustee a commission on income earned that is chargeable against income. *See* 4 Scott & Ascher §20.2.2; 3A Scott on Trusts §233.3. The trustee is also ordinarily paid a commission, either upon acceptance of the trust or upon the distribution of principal, which is chargeable against principal. 4 Scott & Ascher §20.2.2; 3A Scott on Trusts §233.3. To determine how any other service is to be charged, the nature of the service must be considered. 4 Scott & Ascher §20.2.2; 3A Scott on Trusts §233.3. *See also* Bogert §§806, 975. *Cf.* Revised Unif. Principal & Income Act §13(a)(5) (providing that one-half of the trustee's regular compensation, whether based on a percentage of principal or income, and all expenses reasonably incurred for current management of principal and application of income, are chargeable against income).

[618] 4 Scott & Ascher §20.2.2.

[619] UTC §708 cmt. (available at <http://www.uniformlaws.org/Act.aspx?title=Trust%20 Code>). *See also* 4 Scott & Ascher §20.2.2 (Expenses).

[620] Where the trustee by terms of the trust is directed to sell unproductive property, and the property is not immediately sold, the ordinary expenses of carrying the property should generally be charged to principal. *See* 3A Scott on Trusts §233.4. *See also* Restatement (Second) of Trusts §233 cmt. m. However, if the terms of the trust direct the trustee to retain unproductive property, it is assumed that the settlor intended carrying costs to be paid out of income. 3A Scott on Trusts §233.4.

[621] *See generally* 4 Scott & Ascher §20.10.1 (Equitable Adjustments Relating to Taxes). *See, e.g.*, Matter of Warms' Estate, 140 N.Y.S.2d 169 (Surr. Ct. 1955) (the "Warms' adjustment").

[622] *See generally* 4 Scott & Ascher §20.10.1 (Equitable Adjustments Relating to Taxes).

that the income beneficiary is not given a free ride).[623] This is known as the "*Warms* adjustment."[624]

And then there is the situation where a trust owns an interest in a pass-through entity, such as a partnership or S corporation. "Because the trust's taxes and amounts distributed to a beneficiary are interrelated, the trust may be required to apply . . . [an algebraic] . . . formula to determine the correct amount payable to a beneficiary."[625] In the comment to Section 505 of the Uniform Principal and Income Act (1997) such a formula is supplied.

§6.2.4.5 When Does a Beneficiary's Entitlement to Income Begin and What Happens to Accrued but Undistributed Income When the Trust's Term Expires or the Beneficiary Dies?[626]

Many QTIP trusts provide for the payment of stub income to the spouse's estate. Stub income is the income earned during the period immediately following the last distribution of income and ending at the spouse's death. Under Regulations sections 20.2056(b)-7(d)(4) and 25.2523(f)-1(c)(1)(ii), distribution of such income is not required to qualify for QTIP treatment. To enhance the asset protection aspects of the trust, it should contain a provision directing its stub income to be distributed to the successor beneficiaries or successor trusts.[627]

The initial income beneficiary of an inter vivos trust is entitled to income earned on the trust property from the date the trust is deemed to have been created.[628] In the case of a testamentary trust of the residue of a probate estate, it is generally from the testator's death, rather than from when the subject property is actually segregated from the probate estate.[629] In the case of an inter vivos trust that receives a pour-over distribution of the residue, net income accrues to the trust beneficiary from the date of the testator's death, even though there will be some time thereafter before the trustee actually receives the property.[630] In other words, income generated postmortem by the residuary property retains its character as accounting income when is passes to the

---

[623] *See generally* M. L. Ferguson et al., Federal Income Taxation of Estates, Trusts and Beneficiaries §3.06[D] (2000). *See also* In re Estate of Holloway, 323 N.Y.S.2d 534 (Surr. Ct. 1971), *modified,* 327 N.Y.S.2d 865 (Surr. Ct. 1972) (when a trust accounting principal distribution from an estate to a trust carries out distributable net income (DNI), *i.e.,* is taxable as income, then the income account must reimburse the principal account for the tax benefit) (the "Holloway Adjustment"). *See generally* Boyle, *Equitable Adjustments and GST Taxes,* 6 Prob. Prac. Rep. 1 (Nov. 1994); Bogert §807 n.17 and accompanying text.

[624] *See generally* 4 Scott & Ascher §20.10.1 (Equitable Adjustments Relating to Taxes).

[625] Unif. Principal & Income Act (1997) §505 cmt.

[626] For a general discussion of such questions, *see* Bogert §818.

[627] Jonathan E. Gopman, *Optimizing Asset Protection with QTIPs,* 15(6) Prob. Prac. Rep. 2 (June 2003). *See generally* §8.9.1.3 of this handbook (the marital deduction).

[628] *See* 4 Scott & Ascher §20.3; 3A Scott on Trusts §234.

[629] *See generally* 4 Scott & Ascher §20.3.

[630] 4 Scott & Ascher §20.3.3; 3A Scott on Trusts §234. *See, e.g.,* Old Colony Trust Co. v. Smith, 266 Mass. 500, 165 N.E. 657 (1929). *See generally* §9.9.14 of this handbook (administering the trust while assets are being marshaled).

trustee. This would include income that had been generated by assets destined to be entrusted that had to be liquidated during the probate process to pay bequests, debts, and expenses.[631] "If the subject matter of the trust is a fractional share of the residuary estate, the trustee is entitled to receive a corresponding fraction of the estate's income, which remains income for trust accounting purposes."[632] These, of course, are all default rules. The terms of a trust may specify its own rules as to when trust income begins.[633] For a discussion of why a trustee generally needs to know something about will residue clauses, the reader is referred to Section 8.26 of this handbook.

A specific devise of property or a specific legacy of property to a trustee carries with it the income earned on the property.[634] In some cases the settlor will create a trust by a general pecuniary legacy, *i.e.*, a cash bequest. When the executor distributes the pecuniary legacy to the trustee, the general rule has been that the trustee is entitled to a proportionate share of the income earned by the estate during its administration, possibly without taking into account the residue's diminishing value occasioned by the payment of debts, taxes, and expenses.[635]

As noted, the initial income beneficiary's right to income is deemed to commence at the time the trust is deemed to arise. Sometimes, all this "deeming" can be a trap for the unwary. Take a corporate cash distribution where the shareholder of record date was before the trust was deemed to have been created but where the distribution found its way into the hands of the trustee, the successor shareholder, after the trust was deemed to have been created. The distribution is generally trust accounting principal, not income:

> The general rule is that a corporate distribution belongs to those who are shareholders on the shareholder of record date, and not to those who are shareholders when the distribution actually becomes payable. The thinking is that declaring a distribution separates it from the corporation's other assets and creates a debt to those who are shareholders on the shareholder of record date, even though payment occurs later.[636]

When estate property is transferred to a trustee by the settlor's executor, the trustee has a duty to review the executor's account to determine that the

---

[631] *See generally* 4 Scott & Ascher §20.3.4. For a catalog of states where income earned by the assets of the estate used to pay debts, taxes, and administrative expenses is payable to the life beneficiary, *see* 4 Scott & Ascher §20.3.4 n.1; 3A Scott on Trusts §234.4 n.1. *See generally* Revised Unif. Principal & Income Act §5; D. E. Buckner, Annot., *Allocation, as Between Income and Principal, of Income Property Used in Paying Legacies, Debts and Expenses,* 2 A.L.R.3d 1061 (1965).

[632] 4 Scott & Ascher §20.3.5 (Bequest of Share of Residuary Estate).

[633] 4 Scott & Ascher §20.3.3.

[634] *See* 4 Scott & Ascher §20.3.1; 3A Scott on Trusts §234.1; *see, e.g.,* Mass. Gen. Laws ch. 197, §26.

[635] *See* 4 Scott & Ascher §30.3.2; 3A Scott on Trusts §§234.2, 234.4. *But see* Unif. Principal & Income Act §202(b)(1) (1997) (available at <http://www.uniformlaws.org/Act.aspx?title=Trust%20Code>).

[636] 4 Scott & Ascher §20.6.8 (Allocating Distributions at Beginning or End of Income Interest).

trust has received its share of income.[637] Periodic rental, interest, and annuity payments that continue after the testator's death accrue on a daily basis.[638] Thus periodic payments accruing to the testator before his or her death are items of trust principal, and payments accruing afterward are items of trust income.[639] "In all other cases, any receipt from an income producing asset is income even though the receipt was earned or accrued in whole or in part before the date when the asset became subject to the trust."[640] The 1997 version of the Uniform Principal and Income Act endeavors to take some of the labor out of the administration of income accruals:

> In contrast, the 1997 Uniform Act largely eliminates day-to-day apportionment, except as to receipts and disbursements that are not periodic or have no due date. Instead, receipts and disbursements that are due prior to the testator's death or before an income interest begins are allocable entirely to principal. Periodic receipts and disbursements that are due thereafter and would otherwise be allocable to income are, in fact, allocable entirely to income.[641]

On termination of an income interest under a trust that is up and running, the income beneficiary or his or her estate traditionally received net trust accounting income that was then due or already in the hands of the trustee but yet to be distributed, as well as income that had accrued to the date of termination but was payable after termination.[642]

Under the 1997 version of the Uniform Principal and Income Act, however, *unless the terms of the trust provide otherwise*,[643] the beneficiary or his or her estate is not entitled to income that was due but had yet to find its way into the hands of the trustee at the time of termination.[644] In addition, there is no longer an accrual to date of termination of payable income.[645] Finally, "[i]f the beneficiary of the terminating interest has an 'unqualified power to revoke more than five percent of the trust immediately before the income interest ends,' the 1997 Act provides that income already received by the trustee with respect to the portion of the trust that the beneficiary could have revoked is instead treated as principal."[646] Thus, it is critical that the terms of the trust expressly direct where undistributed and accrued income is to go at all times and under all circumstances.[647] For a general discussion of what happens to income when

---

[637] *See generally* 2A Scott on Trusts §177; Bogert §817 n.11; §§6.2.1.1 of this handbook (the trustee's duty to identify and take active control of trust property) and 6.2.2.2 of this handbook (the prudent investor's code of conduct).

[638] Revised Unif. Principal & Income Act §4(b)(2).

[639] Revised Unif. Principal & Income Act §4(b)(2).

[640] Revised Unif. Principal & Income Act §4(c).

[641] 4 Scott & Ascher §20.4.

[642] 4 Scott & Ascher §20.5 (Apportionment When Income Interest Ends).

[643] 4 Scott & Ascher §20.5.

[644] 4 Scott & Ascher §20.5.

[645] 4 Scott & Ascher §20.5.

[646] 4 Scott & Ascher §20.5 (referring to Unif. Principal & Income Act §303(b) (1997)).

[647] *See generally* 4 Scott & Ascher §20.5.

there is no current beneficiary, the reader is referred to Section 8.41 of this handbook.

Upon the death between distribution dates of the beneficiary of an annuity trust or unitrust, should the probate estate receive a pro rata share of what was to be the next scheduled payment? Professor Scott suggested that it should. "An annuitant naturally incurs day-to-day expenses in reliance on the annuity payments."[648] The 1997 version of the Uniform Principal and Income Act is not in accord, suggesting that as between the remaindermen and the takers of the probate estate, the typical settlor would favor the former.[649] Again, all this is subject to the terms of the trust addressing such issues square on.

When an accrual determination is called for, these have been the traditional rules: If the day fixed by a corporation for determining which stockholders of record are entitled to a dividend—that is the day the dividend is "declared"—comes before the termination date of the income interest, the dividend goes to the beneficiary or the beneficiary's estate, even though the dividend is not mailed out until after the termination date.[650] Ordinary dividends, as a general rule, are not apportioned.[651] Unpaid rents, interest, and annuities accrue on a daily basis to the beneficiary up to the date of termination.[652] If the beneficiary's death triggers the termination, then accrued income will be paid to the beneficiary's estate.[653] Under the Uniform Principal and Income Act (1997), "... [a]n income interest ends on the day before an income beneficiary dies...."[654] Note, however, that "[o]rdinarily, the estate of the beneficiary of a support trust is not entitled to income that accrued prior to the beneficiary's death."[655] Nor is the estate of the permissible beneficiary of a discretionary trust.[656]

Again, these income accrual rules apply unless the settlor expressed a contrary intention in the governing instrument.[657] As most modern trust instruments will address the matter of undistributed and accrued income, the trustee is likely to find the answers to most accrual questions simply by reading the governing instrument.

---

[648] 4 Scott & Ascher §20.5.1.

[649] 4 Scott & Ascher §20.5.1 (referring to Unif. Principal & Income Act §303 cmt. (1997)).

[650] 4 Scott & Ascher §20.6.1; Revised Unif. Principal & Income Act. §4(e).

[651] 4 Scott & Ascher §20.6.1.

[652] Revised Unif. Principal & Income Act. §4(d).

[653] Restatement (Second) of Trusts §235A.

[654] Unif. Principal & Income Act (1997) §301(d).

[655] 3 Scott & Ascher §13.2.4. See generally §3.5.3.2(a) of this handbook for a discussion of the characteristics of a support trust.

[656] 4 Scott & Ascher §20.5.

[657] *See generally* 4 Scott & Ascher §20.4; 3A Scott on Trusts §234.

§6.2.4.6 Rethinking Traditional Principles of Income/Principal Allocation and Apportionment (Investment Considerations)

At this point, it remains unclear how successful the power of adjustment will be in freeing the trustee's investment decisions from the icy grip of traditional principal and income law—Mark L. Ascher[658]

Although much of the discussion of the power to adjust focuses on the re-allocation of principal (capital gains) to income, which is a nod to the bull market available during much of the early life of the power to adjust, the power to adjust can also work the other way—S. Alan Medlin[659]

The Drafting Committee of the National Conference of Commissioners on Uniform State Laws has redrafted the Revised Uniform Principal and Income Act—1962 (the "1962 Act").[660] At its 1997 annual meeting, the Conference approved the redraft and recommended it for enactment in all of the states. The new act, known as the Uniform Principal and Income Act (1997), attempts to achieve some coordination with the Uniform Prudent Investor Act[661] by making certain accommodations to "total return" or "growth" investment strategies:[662]

> The fiduciary who exploits the investment flexibility of modern portfolio theory to optimize total return (consistent with an appropriate level of risk and the applicable time horizons), but who allocates the receipts among the beneficiaries in accordance with the traditional principal and income rules, is therefore likely to violate the duty of impartiality, by favoring one beneficiary over another. One of the primary goals of the 1997 version of the Uniform Principal and Income Act was to address this conundrum.[663]

A portfolio's total return is the sum of income (*e.g.*, dividends, interest, and the like) and realized and unrealized capital gains.[664] For an excellent discussion of portfolio theory, the efficient markets hypothesis, option theory, and the

---

[658] 4 Scott & Ascher §20.6.10.

[659] S. Alan Medlin, *The Uniform Principal and Income Act's Power to Adjust*, 18(6) Prob. Prac. Rep. 4 (June 2006).

[660] *See generally* 4 Scott & Ascher §20.6.10; Schaengold, *New Uniform Principal and Income Act in Progress*, 133 Tr. & Est. 42 (1994).

[661] Uniform Prudent Investor Act (available at <http://www.uniformlaws.org/Act.aspx?title=Trust%20Code> as Article 9 of the UTC).

[662] 4 Scott & Ascher §§20.6.10 (Effect of Rules Relating to Principal and Income on Investments by Trustee), 20.10.2 (Equitable Adjustments Relating to Investments).

[663] 4 Scott & Ascher §20.10.2. *See generally* §6.2.5 of this handbook (duty of impartiality).

[664] *See generally* Anderson, *Use of Trusts in Estate Planning: Drafting Tips, Tax Consequences and Ethical Considerations—The Prudent Investor Trustee: Trust Design and Drafting Techniques in an Era of Prudent Investor Rule and Uniform Principal and Income Act*, 49 PLI N.Y. 291 (May 1999); Joel C. Dobris, *New Forms of Private Trusts for the Twenty-First Century—Principal and Income*, 31 Real Prop. Prob. & Tr. J. 1 (Spring 1996); Jonathan R. Macey, An Introduction to Modern Financial Theory (The American College of Trust and Estate Counsel Foundation 2d ed. 1998).

other scholarship that has helped to fashion these "growth" strategies, the reader is referred to Jonathan R. Macey.[665]

Specifically, the 1997 Act allows for some adjustment between income and principal accounts to compensate income beneficiaries for shifts in beneficial interest occasioned by the pursuit of such growth strategies.[666] It should be noted, however, that these are default rules: Settlors may insist in their instruments that trustees cleave to traditional principles of income allocation. Again, the full text of the Uniform Principal and Income Act (1997) is available at <http://www.uniformlaws.org/Act.aspx?title=Trust%20Code>.

§6.2.4.7   The Noncharitable Unitrust (Total Return Trust): Applying Income to Principal

Patti Spencer, a Lancaster, Pa., estate planner who has written about total return unitrusts, said that some professional trustees aren't equipped to handle the computations necessary to set up and manage them.[667]

It is not only in the charitable context that one sees the erosion of traditional principles of income segregation and allocation.[668] In order to accommodate the current economic reality that many good companies at least until recently have not been issuing dividends[669] and to facilitate "total return" and growth investment strategies,[670] practitioners are beginning to draft noncharitable "unitrust" instruments.[671]

A typical "unitrust" calls for a trustee to apply all net trust accounting income to principal.[672] The trustee then distributes to the life beneficiaries in a given year a fixed percentage (typically 5 percent)[673] of the net market of the

---

[665] An Introduction to Modern Financial Theory (The American College of Trust and Estate Counsel Foundation 2d ed. 1998).

[666] *See generally* Restatement (Third) of Trusts §79 cmt. I; 4 Scott & Ascher §20.6.10.

[667] Reni Gertner, *More States Allowing New Unitrusts*, 2002 LWUSA 353, 383 (May 27, 2002).

[668] *See generally* Robert B. Wolf, *Total Return Trusts—A Decade of Progress, But Are We There Yet? (Parts 1 & 2 of 4)*, 32 ACTEC L.J. 5 (2006); Robert B. Wolf, *Total Return Trusts—A Decade of Progress, But Are We There Yet? (Parts 3 & 4 of 4)*, 32 ACTEC L.J. 101 (2006).

[669] *See generally* 4 Scott & Ascher §20.6.10; Karen Hube, *More Dividends Go the Way of the Dinosaur*, Wall St. J., Feb. 24, 2000, at R6.

[670] *See generally* §6.2.2.1 of this handbook (the *Harvard College* prudent man rule and its progeny).

[671] *See* Anderson, *Use of Trusts in Estate Planning: Drafting Tips, Tax Consequences and Ethical Considerations—The Prudent Investor Trustee: Trust Design and Drafting Techniques in an Era of Prudent Investor Rule and Uniform Principal and Income Act*, 49 PLI N.Y. 291 (May 1999). *See generally* §6.2.2.4 of this handbook (the noncharitable unitrust or noncharitable total return trust and the investment considerations).

[672] *See generally* §9.13 of this handbook (the unitrust).

[673] For an exhaustive and sophisticated discussion of how much a trust can pay out and still keep up with inflation, *see* Robert B. Wolf, *Total Return Trusts—Can Your Clients Afford Anything Less?*, 33(1) Real Prop. Prob. & Tr. J. 131 (Spring 1998). *See also* Robert B. Wolf, *Total Return Trusts—A Decade of Progress, But Are We There Yet? (Parts 3 & 4 of 4)*, 32 ACTEC L.J. 101 (2006).

trust estate valued at the end of the prior year.[674] There are many variations on the theme.[675] For a collection of sample unitrust clauses, the reader is referred to Jerold I. Horn, Esq.[676]

Generally the terms of the trust specify whether unitrust amounts are to come in whole or in part from net trust accounting income, in whole or in part from the principal account, or whether the settlor has left it to the trustee to make the call. Absent such guidance, the better view is that the trustee has default authority to make the unitrust distributions from the general funds of the trust without regard to distinction between income and principal.[677]

It should be noted, however, that a trust under which the trustee has full discretion to distribute or withhold income and to invade or not invade principal may be administered as a unitrust, even in the absence of express unitrust provisions, provided doing so does not conflict with the settlor's intention. No reformation by a court would be required. Legislatures are also stepping in to give trustees the "power to adjust":

In order to remove the obstacle presented by the (old) definition of the word "income" and allow for "total return" investing, approximately 38 states have now adopted a version of the Uniform Principal and Income Act ("UPIA"). This act in one variation encourages a trustee to invest for "total return" (read emphasize equities in lieu of fixed income) and, without a court order, allows trustees to "recast" principal items as "income" so as to increase the payout to an income beneficiary up to a given level.[678]

For more on noncharitable unitrusts including the case against them, the reader is referred to Section 6.2.2.4 of this handbook (the noncharitable unitrust (total return trust): investment considerations).

The Restatement (Third) of Trusts, specifically Section 111, provides that under certain circumstances a trustee would have an affirmative duty to exercise a statutory unitrust election. This is a topic that is taken up in Section 6.2.4 of this handbook.

---

[674] *See* Anderson, *Use of Trusts in Estate Planning: Drafting Tips, Tax Consequences and Ethical Considerations—The Prudent Investor Trustee: Trust Design and Drafting Techniques in an Era of Prudent Investor Rule and Uniform Principal and Income Act*, 49 PLI N.Y. 291 (May 1999). *See also* Ward, *Use of Trusts in Estate Planning: Drafting Tips, Tax Consequences and Ethical Considerations—Fiduciary Income Tax*, 49 PLI N.Y. 237 (May 1999).

[675] *See* Robert B. Wolf, *Total Return Trusts—A Decade of Progress, But Are We There Yet? (Parts 3 & 4 of 4)*, 32 ACTEC L.J. 101 (2006); Robert B. Wolf, *Defeating the Duty to Disappoint Equally—the Total Return Trust*, 23 ACTEC Notes 46 (1997). *But see* Joel C. Dobris, *Why Do Trustee Investors Often Prefer Dividends?*, 32(2) Real Prop. Prob. & Tr. J. 255 (Summer 1997).

[676] *Prudent Investor Rule, Modern Portfolio Theory, and Private Trusts: Drafting and Administration Including the "Give-Me-Five" Unitrust*, 33(1) Real Prop. Prob. & Tr. J. 1 (Spring 1998).

[677] 3 Scott & Ascher §13.2.8.

[678] Michael J. Zdeb, *Trustees Lose an Excuse: Modern Investment Theory Comes to the Aid of Beneficiaries*, Fiduciary Fun 5 (Winter 2002). *See generally* §6.2.4.6 of this handbook (rethinking traditional principles of income allocation in the trust context).

§6.2.4.8 Operations: Keeping Track of Income and Principal

The individual trustee. What are the options for the individual trustee who wishes to keep track of in-house income and principal? He can manually enter each receipt and disbursement into a ledger. Or he can use a personal computer that runs on trust accounting software that is either tailor-made or off-the-shelf.[679]

A description of each asset and its cost basis is entered into the computer. Each disbursement, distribution, and deposit also is manually entered into the system, as are the relevant data appearing on the monthly statements issued by the banks and brokerage houses that have actual custody of the assets, such as dividends and interest, current market price, splits, mergers, and corporate name changes. From time to time, the trustee reconciles the computer's bottom line with the bottom lines of the various statements generated externally.

Usually, each receipt and disbursement is entered with an expense code to facilitate data collection for tax return preparation. The accounting module and the tax preparation module, each of which generally may be purchased separately, should be appropriately linked or integrated so as to facilitate not only the preparation of periodic trust accounting statements in probate format but also tax forms.

While these PC software programs are an improvement over the ledger book, they still are high-maintenance. Someone still must manually type in the raw data. To alleviate somewhat the trustee's data entry burden, several off-the-shelf software packages allow for interface with whatever facility has custody of the assets. Transaction information is formatted so that it may be downloaded from the facility's system directly to the trustee's system. To maintain valuations that are close to current, it is now possible to directly link such programs via modem to security pricing services.

A custody agreement with a bank is another option. The bank receives the interest and dividends, generates disbursement checks, prices the investments, and does the accounting. Compensation is based on a percentage of the market value of the trust. The bank also may assess fees for transactions. It is important to note here that in this scenario, the bank is only providing back office services; it is not serving as a cotrustee. The bank provides all of the reports for the beneficiaries and, for an extra fee, will produce probate accountings.

Larger nonbank trust operations. When a trust operation becomes too large to operate off a personal computer, then it is common practice for the custody and accounting function to be handled by a bank or by a service provider with whom the bank has contracted. Deposit and disbursement checks are run between the trustee and the bank by courier several times a day. Some banks allow the trustee to enter check requests directly into the trust accounting system via a computer terminal in the trustee's office. To accommodate beneficiaries who come in on short notice, the trustee and bank can set up a "zero

---

[679] Daniel B. Evans, Wills, Trusts, and Technology: An Estate and Trust Lawyer's Guide to Automation (2d ed.) published jointly by the Real Property, Probate and Trust Law and Law Practice Management Sections of the American Bar Association.

balance" checking account, which allows the trustee to generate checks in-house. The trustee notifies the bank by phone to cover checks drawn on the zero balance account.

The bank typically provides the trustee with PC software that enables the trustee to obtain current information on the trust and to generate customized reports. In addition, the bank will provide information the trustee will need to prepare the fiduciary tax returns. For an extra fee, some banks will prepare the actual returns.

§6.2.5 Duty of Impartiality

The sole interest rule undertakes to prevent conflicts; the duty of impartiality regulates trustee/beneficiary conflicts when the trust terms create a conflict that abridges the sole interest rule.[680]

The duty to act impartially does not mean that the trustee must treat the beneficiaries equally. Rather, the trustee must treat the beneficiaries equitably in light of the purposes and terms of the trust.[681]

Within a trust. A difficult aspect of the trustee's general duty of loyalty is the specific duty to treat all beneficiaries, charitable[682] and otherwise, impartially,[683] *i.e.*, not to favor one beneficiary over another, unless authorized to do so by the governing instrument.[684] And even when so authorized the trustee's discretionary acts favoring one beneficiary over another must be in furtherance of the intentions of the settlor, not in furtherance of the trustee's own biases and predilections.[685] "Nor is it permissible for a trustee to ignore the interests of some beneficiaries merely as a result of oversight or neglect, or because a particular beneficiary has more access to the trustee or is more aggressive, or simply because the trustee is unaware of the duty"[686] of impartiality.[687] It is not

---

[680] John H. Langbein, *Questioning the Trust Law Duty of Loyalty: Sole Interest or Best Interest?*, 114 Yale L.J. 929, 939 (2005).

[681] UTC §803 cmt. (available at <http://www.uniformlaws.org/Act.aspx?title=Trust%20Code>). In other words, "the trustee is under a duty to act with 'due regard' to the beneficiaries' respective interests." 4 Scott & Ascher §20.1.

[682] Restatement (Third) of Trusts §79(2) and cmt. h thereto.

[683] Restatement (Third) of Trusts §79; 3 Scott & Ascher §17.15.

[684] 3 Scott & Ascher §17.15; 2A Scott on Trusts §183; Restatement (Third) of Trusts §79 cmt. c. *See generally* §6.1.3.6 of this handbook (breaches of duty of loyalty that do not involve self-dealing on part of trustee).

[685] Restatement (Third) of Trusts §79 cmt. b; Revised Unif. Principal & Income Act §4(e). *See generally* 3 Scott & Ascher §17.15 (noting that "[i]f the trustee does have discretion to favor one beneficiary over another, the court will not control the exercise of this discretion, except to prevent an abuse of discretion").

[686] Restatement (Third) of Trusts §79 cmt. b.

[687] *See generally* 3 Scott & Ascher §17.15.

just the squeaky wheel that may need the oil.[688] An indenture trustee of a corporate trust, for example, would owe each bondholder a duty of impartially should the issuer default, particularly when it comes to parceling out the liquidated security.[689] The duty of impartiality also may be implicated when a trustee furnishes material information about the affairs of the trust to some members of a beneficiary class but not to others.[690] The trustee runs the risk of breaching the duty of impartiality in conflicts between and among beneficiaries as well. Neutrality is generally the order of the day.[691] Moreover, in a dispute between two parties claiming to be beneficiaries, a trustee may not advocate for either side or assume the validity of either side's position.[692]

Mistake-based reformation actions. The duty of impartiality is implicated when the trustee seeks to reorder the equitable interests by bringing a mistake-based reformation action.[693] Legal title to the property of a trust being in the trustee, it is likely that the trustee would have standing to bring such an action.[694] Whether under equitable principles the trustee should do so is another matter. If the trustee is seeking to bring about a reordering of the equitable property interests at the expense of one or more of the beneficiaries designated within the four corners of the governing instrument, then his initiating the reformation action, and certainly his appealing of any lower court decision not to reform, would be difficult to square with his fiduciary duties of loyalty and impartiality, not to mention his duty to defend the trust, a topic we take up in Section 6.2.6 of this handbook.[695] Even as a nominal defendant in a mistake-based reformation action brought by someone else, the trustee should be wary of taking a position that is adverse to any designated beneficiary.

The current beneficiaries and the remaindermen have inherently competing interests. The trustee runs a major risk of breaching the duty of impartiality in the context of the competing interests of income beneficiaries and remaindermen.[696] "If there are several beneficiaries, whether concurrent or successive, the

---

[688] *See generally* 3 Scott & Ascher §17.15 (discussing the "procedural aspects" of the trustee's duty of loyalty).

[689] *See generally* §9.31 of this handbook (corporate trusts; trusts to secure creditors; the Trust Indenture Act of 1939; protecting bondholders).

[690] *See, e.g.,* McNeil v. Benet, 792 A.2d 190 (Del. Ch. 2001), *aff'd in part, rev'd in part,* McNeil v. McNeil, 798 A.2d 503 (Del. 2002) (involving the selective furnishing of material information to members of a class of current beneficiaries). *See generally* 3 Scott & Ascher §17.15.

[691] Restatement (Third) of Trusts §79 cmt. c. "Even in the role of a neutral 'stakeholder,' however, the trustee may have a duty to provide relevant information of which the trustee has knowledge and to make reasonable efforts to assure that all interested beneficiaries are (or have an opportunity to be) adequately represented." Restatement (Third) of Trusts §79 cmt. c.

[692] In re Doris Duke Trust, 702 A.2d 1008, 1023–1024 (N.J. Super. Ch. 1995).

[693] *See generally* §8.15.22 of this handbook (reformation actions).

[694] *See, e.g.,* Reid v. Temple Judea & Hebrew Union Coll. Jewish Inst. of Religion, 994 So. 2d 1146 (Fla. Ct. App. 2008).

[695] *See* §6.1.3.6 of this handbook (breaches of duty of loyalty not involving self-dealing).

[696] 4 Scott & Ascher §20.1 (Impartiality Between Successive Beneficiaries); 3 Scott & Ascher §17.15 (Duty of Impartiality); 3A Scott on Trusts §232; Restatement (Third) of Trusts §232 cmt. b. *See also* Morse v. Stanley, 732 F.2d 1139, 1145 (2d Cir. 1984) (an ERISA case involving a trustee's duty to impartially balance the interests of present claimants and future claimants).

consent of one of them to a deviation from the terms of the trust does not preclude the other beneficiaries from holding the trustee liable for breach of trust so far as their interests are affected."[697] Unless the terms of the trust provide otherwise,[698] the trustee has a duty to make the trust property reasonably productive of trust-accounting income.[699] Thus, it is the default law that the trustee has a duty to separate income from principal and then to distribute the net income to the income beneficiary and eventually to turn over the principal free of trust to the remaindermen.[700] This is implied by the trustee's general duty to carry out the terms of the trust. The general duty of loyalty, however, requires that the trustee balance the interests of the income beneficiaries and the remaindermen—in other words, *the trustee must be impartial when dealing with those with conflicting equitable interests*.[701] "Just as apples and oranges are inherently different, and require different treatment, so also, successive beneficiaries are inherently different and require different treatment."[702] Treating impartially interests that are conflicting but different is easier said than done: For example, which should absorb the expense of the insurance premium, the income account, or the principal account?[703] The applicable default law is addressed in Section 6.2.4 of this handbook.

Allocation of receipts and disbursements between the income and principal accounts. In fulfilling the duty to act impartially in the allocation of receipts and disbursements between income and principal, the trustee should consider in appropriate cases reallocation of income to the principal account and vice versa, if allowable under local law.[704] Under the Restatement (Third) of Trusts, the trustee would be allowed to make appropriate accounting adjustments to comply with the duty of impartiality even absent permissive legislation.[705]

During a period of high inflation, for example,[706] a trustee might wish to invest in bonds that yield a high rate of interest.[707] Although it may be prudent from an investment perspective to do so, the trustee worries that over time an erosion of the purchasing power of the trust accounting principal will result.[708]

---

[697] Restatement (Second) of Trusts §216 cmt. g.

[698] Restatement (Third) of Trusts §79 cmt. g(2).

[699] Restatement (Third) of Trusts §79 cmt. e.

[700] *See* §6.2.4 of this handbook (trustee's duty to separate income from principal and the beneficiary's right to income); 4 Scott & Ascher §20.1 (Impartiality Between Successive Beneficiaries).

[701] 4 Scott & Ascher §20.1 (Impartiality Between Successive Beneficiaries); 2A Scott on Trusts §183; Restatement (Third) of Trusts §79 cmt. b.

[702] 4 Scott & Ascher §20.1.

[703] *See* §6.2.4.4 of this handbook (expenses allocated entirely to trust income, entirely to trust principal, and apportioned between trust income and trust principal?).

[704] *See generally* §6.2.4.6 of this handbook (rethinking traditional principles of income allocation in the trust context).

[705] Restatement (Third) of Trusts §79 cmt. i.

[706] UTC §803 cmt. (available at <http://www.uniformlaws.org/Act.aspx?title=Trust%20 Code>). "For an example of such authority, *see* Unif. Principal & Income Act §104 (1997)." UTC §803 cmt.

[707] *See generally* 4 Scott & Ascher §20.1 (Impartiality Between Successive Beneficiaries).

[708] *See generally* 4 Scott & Ascher §20.1 (Impartiality Between Successive Beneficiaries).

Armed with the authority to transfer a portion of the income account to the principal account, the trustee could invest in the bonds without advantaging the current beneficiaries at the expense of the remaindermen.

Reallocation authority also would be helpful in cases in which a particular investment could advantage the remaindermen at the expense of the current beneficiaries. Take, for example, a trust that contains a large parcel of undeveloped real estate. Net accounting income is being used to pay property taxes. If the trustee had reallocation authority, he could transfer a portion of principal cash to the income account to compensate for the tax payments.

How investment decisions can implicate a trustee's duty of impartiality. The difficulty in balancing competing equitable interests manifests itself most dramatically, however, in matters of *investment*[709] and of *disclosure of information*. With respect to investments, the trustee of a trust that requires periodic disbursement of all net trust accounting income and makes no provision for invasion of principal, *i.e.*, an income-only trust, has traditionally walked a tightrope.[710] Investing for maximum income may sacrifice growth, to the displeasure of the remainderman;[711] investing for maximum growth may cause the income beneficiary to complain.[712] This is an inevitable outgrowth of the traditional distinction between income and principal, a trust accounting concept that takes no account of the investment concept of *total return*.[713] Additional authority in the trustee to invade principal does not eliminate the inherent tension or "economic competition" between the equitable estates, although it does mitigate it somewhat.[714]

---

[709] Restatement (Third) of Trusts §79 cmt. f; 4 Scott & Ascher §20.1.

[710] *See generally* 4 Scott & Ascher §20.1 (Impartiality Between Successive Beneficiaries); Edward J. Beckwith, *Is It Possible to Provide a Fair Return to Both Current and Future Trust Beneficiaries?,* SC 60 ALI-ABA 31 (1998).

[711] *See generally* 4 Scott & Ascher §20.1 (Impartiality Between Successive Beneficiaries). *See* Dennis v. Rhode Island Hosp. Trust Nat'l Bank, 744 F.2d 893, 897 (1st Cir. 1984) (in holding the trustee liable to the remaindermen, the court said: "[T]here is evidence that the trustee did little more than routinely agree to the requests of the trust income beneficiaries that it manage the trust corpus to produce the largest possible income."). *See also* In re Mulligan, 1 N.Z.L.R. 481 (1998) (a cofiduciary liability case involving a corporate trustee that pursued to the economic detriment of the remaindermen a high income low growth investment strategy at the insistence of the individual cotrustee who was also the income beneficiary).

[712] *See generally* 4 Scott & Ascher §20.1 (Impartiality Between Successive Beneficiaries). In In re Francis M. Johnson Trust, 211 Neb. 750, 320 N.W.2d 466, 469 (1982), the trustees held onto stock in a corporation that paid no dividends and upon dissolution of the corporation allocated a part of the gain to income. A minor beneficiary challenged the allocation. Although the court held the allocation to be a proper exercise of discretion, it did say: "Trustees may not, however, sacrifice income for the purpose of increasing the value of the principal of the trust."

[713] *See* Restatement (Third) of Trusts §90 cmt. e [Restatement (Third) of Trusts: Prudent Investor Rule §227 cmt. e]; 4 Scott & Ascher §20.1. *See, however,* §6.2.4.6 of this handbook (rethinking traditional principles of income allocation in the trust context), §6.2.2.4 of this handbook (the noncharitable unitrust or noncharitable total return trust and the investment considerations), and §6.2.4.7 of this handbook (the noncharitable unitrust or noncharitable total return trust: applying income to principal).

[714] Restatement (Third) of Trusts §79 cmts. f, g(2).

The *Harvard College* Prudent Man Rule[715] and the Prudent Investor Rule acknowledge the income/principal conflict and attempt to balance the competing interests. In practice, this probably means the pursuit of an investment strategy geared to generating a reasonable stream of net trust accounting income for the current beneficiaries while maintaining the principal's purchasing power[716] for the remaindermen.[717] For a trust of short duration, the purchasing power can be eroded by a temporary decline in the stock or bond markets. For a trust of long duration, inflation is likely to be the greater threat to the principal's purchasing power.[718] The longer the duration of a trust, all things being equal, the more consideration the trustee needs to give to investing in equities. "It is important to note that the protection or growth of the purchasing power of principal tends as well to preserve or enhance the purchasing power of the income flow over the duration of the income interest."[719]

The Prudent Man Rule was first enunciated at a time when the psychological wall between the income beneficiary and the remainderman was higher than it is today.[720] Then, income-only trusts and use-only trusts involving land were the rule.[721] Now, settlors tend to bestow on their trustees considerable discretionary authority, particularly the authority to invade principal for the benefit of the life beneficiaries and to accumulate income for the benefit of the remaindermen.[722] The result is that it is more difficult for the trustee of a discretionary trust to breach the duty of impartiality in carrying out his investment responsibilities than it is for the trustee of a traditional income-only trust.[723] The same goes for the trustee of an annuity or unitrust.[724] In any case,

---

[715] Harvard Coll. v. Amory, 26 Mass. (9 Pick.) 446, 461 (1830). *See also* 3 Scott on Trusts §227.

[716] Restatement (Third) of Trusts §79 cmt. g.

[717] Restatement (Third) of Trusts: Prudent Investor Rule §232 cmt. c (provisional). *But see* Tovrea v. Nolan, 875 P.2d 144, 149 (Ariz. 1993) (suggesting that the interests of the remaindermen are subordinate to the interests of the income beneficiary and in support thereof citing to Restatement (Second) of Trusts §232 cmt. b, since superseded by the Restatement (Third) of Trusts: Prudent Investor Rule §232 cmt. c (provisional)).

[718] *See, e.g.,* Estate of Cooper v. Cooper, 81 Wash. App. 79, 87–88, 913 P.2d 393, 397–398 (1996) (faulting a trustee for pursuing an investment strategy that failed to keep up with inflation).

[719] Restatement (Third) of Trusts §79 cmt. g. *But see* Howard v. Howard, 156 P.3d 89 (Or. App. 2007) (the court and the parties to the litigation taking as a given that investing to preserve or enhance the purchasing power of the principal and investing to preserve or enhance the purchasing power of the income flow are mutually exclusive investment strategies).

[720] *See generally* 4 Scott & Ascher §20.1.

[721] Bogert §§5–8; 4 Scott & Ascher §20.1.

[722] *See generally* Restatement (Third) of Trusts §90 cmt. i [Restatement (Third) of Trusts: Prudent Investor Rule §227 cmt. i]; 4 Scott & Ascher §20.1.

[723] Restatement (Third) of Trusts §79 cmt. f; 3 Scott & Ascher §17.15 (noting that "[i]f the trustee does have discretion to favor one beneficiary over another, the court will not control the exercise of this discretion, except to prevent an abuse of discretion"); 4 Scott & Ascher §20.1 (noting, however, that "despite the rise of the discretionary trust, there remain a great many beneficiaries whose only entitlement consists of an interest in income or an interest in principal"); 2A Scott on Trusts §155.

[724] Restatement (Third) of Trusts §79 cmt. f (noting, however, that the trustee of an annuity or unitrust still must be sensitive to impartiality issues in investing, *e.g.,* "issues about possible emphasis on tax-exempt earnings or about trade-offs between the high total-return objectives of

it remains the rule that a trustee has a duty to treat the current beneficiaries and remaindermen impartially to the extent their interests clash.[725]

Information disclosure and the trustee's duty of impartiality. When it comes to the disclosure of information, the conflicting interests of the current beneficiaries and the remaindermen can put the trustee between a rock and a hard place. As we have seen, an incident of the trustee's general duty to account is the specific duty of disclosure,[726] while at the same time an incident of the trustee's general duty of loyalty is the specific duty of confidentiality.[727] What is a trustee to do if disclosures to the remaindermen would violate the confidences of the current beneficiary? Suppose the current beneficiary's alcoholism were the basis for a proper exercise of the trustee's discretion to invade principal. Should the current beneficiary's medical history be disclosed to the remaindermen? In theory the answer lies in another specific duty: the duty to balance the interests of the life beneficiary and the remainderman. Thus the way out of this impasse is for the trustee to provide the remaindermen with only so much information about the current beneficiary as they would need to enable them to protect their equitable interests. In this case it would be the information they would need to ascertain whether the trustee had committed an abuse of discretion.[728] What this would actually mean in practice is harder to say. This is all easier said than done. The remaindermen are certainly not entitled to the medical file, but they should not be stonewalled either. And there is an added complication: a trustee generally need not disclose the process of deciding whether to exercise a particular discretionary power, a topic we take up in Section 3.5.3.2(a) of this handbook in our discussion of letters of wishes.

Competing interests within a class of trust beneficiary. The duty of impartiality applies not only to successive equitable interests but also to concurrent ones,[729] *i.e.*, to the "simultaneous" beneficiaries.[730] The members of a class of current beneficiaries—whether income beneficiaries or discretionary beneficiaries, or both—are likely to have significantly differing needs and tax positions, while the members of a class of remaindermen are likely to have significantly different objectives and risk tolerances.[731] "In other words, the duty of impartiality is also relevant to a trustee's treatment of several beneficiaries, each of whom has the same or a similar interest in the trust."[732]

The trustee of more than one trust. In Section 6.1.3.6 of this handbook, we discuss the trustee's duty of impartiality in the context of transactions

---

some beneficiaries and the low-risk tolerance of others"); 4 Scott & Ascher §20.1. *See generally* §6.2.2.4 of this handbook (the noncharitable unitrust (total return trust): investment considerations).

[725] *See generally* 4 Scott & Ascher §20.1 (Impartiality Between Successive Beneficiaries).

[726] *See* §6.1.5 of this handbook (trustee's duty to account to the beneficiary).

[727] *See* §6.2.3 of this handbook (trustee's duty of confidentiality).

[728] *See generally* Bogert §961; 3 Scott & Ascher §17.15; 2A Scott on Trusts §173; §8.8 of this handbook (whom trust counsel represents).

[729] Restatement (Third) of Trusts §79 cmt. a; 3 Scott & Ascher §17.15.

[730] 3 Scott & Ascher §17.15.

[731] Restatement (Third) of Trusts §79 cmt. a; 3 Scott & Ascher §17.15.

[732] 3 Scott & Ascher §17.15.

between trusts sharing the same trustee. Of course, the trustee's duty not to self-deal also would be implicated if a trustee of two separate trusts, say Trust X and Trust Y, were to misappropriate funds from one, say Trust X, and later make restitution with funds misappropriated from Trust Y. The trustee, of course, would be personally liable to make both trusts whole out of his own funds, if necessary, thus rendering any impartiality issues moot.[733] If the trustee, however, were judgment proof, Trust X would likely prevail over Trust Y, provided the Trust X beneficiaries were BFPs, as would likely be the case.[734] In other words, the funds would stay in Trust X. As we have noted elsewhere, the transfer of money in satisfaction of an antecedent debt can satisfy the BFP value requirement.[735] In this case, the antecedent debt would be the trustee's equitable obligation to make Trust X whole.[736] On the other hand, the beneficiaries of Trust Y would be entitled to recover from any surety on the bond of the trustee that might have been issued to the trustee in his capacity as trustee of Trust X.[737] "The beneficiaries of... [Trust X]... could have sued on the bond, and when they are paid with the funds of... [Trust Y]..., the beneficiaries of... [Trust Y]... are entitled to be subrogated to their rights on the bond."[738]

§6.2.6 Duty to Defend the Trust Against Attack; Duty Not to Attack the Trust; Indirect Attacks (Construction Proceedings)

The trustee's duty to defend the trust. The trustee has a duty to defend the trust.[739] The trust may be attacked by those who have an economic interest in bringing about its cancellation or termination.[740] It may be attacked by those who oppose its purposes.[741] To fail to mount a vigorous defense is to thwart the intentions of the settlor and may be grounds for the trustee's removal. Moreover, the trustee would be liable to the beneficiaries for any injury occasioned by an unwarranted capitulation.[742]

However, if it is clear to a reasonable person who has sought and obtained independent, competent legal advice that an attack is warranted or that resistance would be futile, then a defense should not be mounted.[743] This

---

[733] *See generally* §7.2.3 of this handbook (types of equitable relief for breaches of trust).

[734] *See generally* 5 Scott & Ascher §29.7 (Transfer in Restitution for Wrong).

[735] *See generally* §8.15.63 of this handbook (doctrine of bona fide purchase in trust context).

[736] *Cf.* §2.3 of this handbook (wrongful defunding of trust by trustee) ("A reasonable argument can be made that the absent trust property has merely been transformed into another type of property, namely the equitable personal obligation of the wrongdoer").

[737] 5 Scott & Ascher §29.7 (Transfer in Restitution for a Wrong). *See generally* §3.5.4.3 of this handbook (bonds and sureties in the trust context).

[738] 5 Scott & Ascher §29.7.

[739] *See generally* Bogert §581. *See also* 2A Scott on Trusts §178.

[740] *See generally* Bogert §581. *See also* 2A Scott on Trusts §178.

[741] *See generally* Bogert §581. *See also* 2A Scott on Trusts §178.

[742] *See generally* Bogert §581. *See also* 2A Scott on Trusts §178.

[743] *See generally* Bogert §581. *See also* 2A Scott on Trusts §178.

exception would not apply when there is reasonable uncertainty as to the facts or the law.[744]

The trustee must do what is necessary within the bounds of law and reason to defend the trust and thus may retain counsel for that purpose and is entitled to have the costs of such representation absorbed by the trust.[745] All reasonable appeals should be taken.[746] The trustee who is unprepared to go the distance should seek to have the trusteeship transferred to someone who is. He probably should not have accepted the trust in the first place.

In the case of an action for instructions or declaratory judgment to clarify the terms of a trust and/or sort out the rights of its beneficiaries,[747] it would seem that the trustee may assume a neutral posture,[748] once he has assured himself that all parties, including the unborn and unascertained, are properly represented.[749] On the other hand, if the action is actually a vehicle for attacking the trust itself, *e.g.*, if there are allegations that the trust was the product of fraud, duress, or undue influence, then the trustee is duty bound to advocate for the trust's validity,[750] unless to do so would be self-evidently futile and/or unreasonable. Likewise, if the judgments that are ultimately issued by the trial court amount to a "total or partial destruction of the trust," then the trustee may have a fiduciary duty to appeal to a higher court if to do so would be reasonable and in the interests of the beneficiaries.[751] Unless an appeal would be self-evidently unreasonable and/or futile, then its costs may be borne by the trust.[752]

Divorce proceedings. The trustee is not relieved of the duty to defend the trust and its dispositive terms just because the beneficiary happens to be getting divorced. The trustee's primary allegiance is to the beneficiary, not to the nonbeneficiary spouse or ex-spouse, unless the express terms of the trust provide otherwise. Thus, when there is marital discord, the trustee must suppress any personal feelings as to who may be at fault and vigorously defend—within reason and to the extent the law allows—the beneficiary's equitable property interest. As the English say, "[t]rustees have the custody of

---

[744] *See generally* Bogert §581. *See also* 2A Scott on Trusts §178.

[745] *See generally* Bogert §581. *See also* 2A Scott on Trusts §178. *See generally* 3 Scott & Ascher §18.1.2.4 (noting also that the trustee can properly "pay out of the trust estate the expenses of resisting an attempt by the beneficiaries to terminate the trust prematurely").

[746] Bogert §581; 2A Scott on Trusts §178. *See* P.H. Vartanian, Annot., *Right of Trustee of Express Trust to Appeal from Order or Decree Not Affecting His Own Personal Interest*, 6 A.L.R.2d 147 (1949).

[747] *See generally* §8.42 of this handbook (complaints for instructions versus complaints for declaratory judgment).

[748] *See generally* §6.2.5 of this handbook (trustee's duty of impartiality); 3 Scott & Ascher §17.10. *Cf.* 3 Scott & Ascher §18.1.2.4 (noting that "if the trustee is reasonably in doubt about the terms of the trust or the scope of the trustee's duties or powers, the trustee can properly incur the expense of a judicial proceeding to construe the terms of the trust or for instructions").

[749] *See generally* §6.2.5 of this handbook (trustee's duty of impartiality); 3 Scott & Ascher §17.10.

[750] *See generally* 3 Scott & Ascher §17.10.

[751] 3 Scott & Ascher §17.10.

[752] *See generally* 3 Scott & Ascher §17.10.

the property: they do not keep the conscience of their beneficiary."[753] A trustee may even have a fiduciary duty to challenge, at trust expense, a charging order against discretionary distributions that interferes with the trustee's ability to carry out the settlor's intentions. "Although the process and division may reflect the concept of marriage as a shared enterprise or partnership, this process and division likely will be counter to the intent of the trust's settlor and perhaps will require the participation of the family members of a beneficiary in the proceedings."[754] Reaching equitable interests in the context of divorce proceedings is taken up in Section 5.3.4.1 of this handbook.

The trustee's duty not to attack the trust. The trustee being a fiduciary, he may not mount an attack against his own trust.[755] It has been said that the trustee, having accepted the trust, is "estopped" from then setting up its invalidity.[756] At minimum, such acts of betrayal are grounds for removal. This would include attacks on only some of the equitable interests. Take the mistake-based reformation suit.[757] Legal title to the property of a trust being in the trustee, it is likely that the trustee would have standing to bring such an action.[758] Whether under equitable principles the trustee should do so is another matter. If the trustee is seeking to bring about a reordering of the equitable property interests at the expense of one or more of the beneficiaries designated within the four corners of the governing instrument, then his initiating the reformation action, and certainly his appealing of any lower court decision not to reform, would be difficult to square with his fiduciary duties of loyalty and impartiality, not to mention his duty to defend the trust.[759] Even as a nominal defendant in a mistake-based reformation action brought by someone else, the trustee should be wary of taking a position that amounts to a constructive attack on the equitable interests of any designated beneficiary.

The Uniform Trust Code. The Uniform Trust Code neglects to "state" in its Article 8 the trustee's critical common law duty to defend his or her trust. But the Code also neglects to expressly negate the duty. Thus, the duty remains very much alive and well in the jurisdictions that have enacted the Code. "The Uniform Trust Code is supplemented by the common law of trusts and

---

[753] Lewin ¶ 20-161 (England).

[754] Marc A. Chorney, *Interests in Trusts as Property in Dissolution of Marriage: Identification and Valuation*, 40 Real Prop. Prob. & Tr. J. 1, 3 (Spring 2005).

[755] *See generally* Bogert §581; 2A Scott on Trusts §178 ("Clearly, the trustee owes a duty to the beneficiaries not to destroy the trust"); P.H. Vartanian, Annot., *Right of Trustee of Express Trust to Appeal from Order or Decree Not Affecting His Own Personal Interest*, 6 A.L.R.2d 147 (1949).

[756] *See generally* Bogert §581; 2A Scott on Trusts §178 ("Clearly, the trustee owes a duty to the beneficiaries not to destroy the trust"); P.H. Vartanian, Annot., *Right of Trustee of Express Trust to Appeal from Order or Decree Not Affecting His Own Personal Interest*, 6 A.L.R.2d 147 (1949).

[757] *See generally* §8.15.22 of this handbook (reformation actions).

[758] *See, e.g.*, Reid v. Temple Judea & Hebrew Union Coll. Jewish Inst. of Religion, 994 So. 2d 1146 (Fla. Ct. App. 2008).

[759] *See* §6.1.3.6 of this handbook (breaches of the trustee's duty of loyalty that do not involve self-dealing) and §6.2.5 of this handbook (the trustee's duty of impartiality).

principles of equity."[760] Actually, vice versa is more precise. In any case, the application of the doctrine of substantive equitable deviation, a topic we take up generally in Section 8.15.20 of this handbook, and the application of the doctrine of substantive equitable reformation, a topic we take up generally in Section 8.15.22 of this handbook, are constrained and tempered by the trustee's duty to defend. The Code's failure to expressly "state" the trustee's duty to defend is a trap for the unwary trust professional who labors under the misconception that in any given situation all applicable trust law lurks only within the Code's four corners. What applies to the trustee's duty to defend the trust applies also to his or her duty not to attack it.

§6.2.7   Duty to Use Special Skills or Expertise

It follows from the requirement of care, as well as from sound policy, that if the trustee actually possesses a degree of skill greater than that of an individual of ordinary intelligence . . . , the trustee has a duty to make use of that skill, and is ordinarily liable for a loss that results from failure to do so.[761]

The Uniform Trust Code provides that a trustee who has special skills or expertise has a duty to use those special skills or expertise.[762] The Restatement (Third) of Trusts is generally in accord,[763] as is the Uniform Probate Code[764] and UPMIFA.[765] One who represents himself as possessing special skills or expertise and is named as trustee in reliance upon those representations shall be held to the standard of one who in fact possesses those special skills and expertise.[766] That is why the professional trustee would be well advised to have all marketing brochures and other promotional materials carefully reviewed before they are disseminated to the public to make sure that he, she, or it is able and prepared to perform as advertised. It is a certainty that should a disgruntled beneficiary file suit against the trustee for breach of some fiduciary duty, those materials will be discovered and made part of the litigation record.

§6.2.8   Duty to Administer Promptly and Efficiently

To the extent the trustee is dilatory or inefficient in the administration of his trust, he is in breach of trust in that he is interfering with the beneficiary's

---

[760] UTC, General Comment to Article 1 (available at <http://www.uniformlaws.org/Act.aspx?title=Trust%20Code>).

[761] Restatement (Third) of Trusts §77 cmt. e.

[762] UTC §806 (available at <http://www.uniformlaws.org/Act.aspx?title=Trust%20Code>).

[763] Restatement (Third) of Trusts §77(3).

[764] See UPC §7-302.

[765] Unif. Prudent Management Inst. Funds Act §3(e)(6).

[766] UTC §806 (available at <http://www.uniformlaws.org/Act.aspx?title=Trust%20Code>).

property rights, the equitable interest itself being an interest in property. "Where . . . [, for example,] . . . a trustee is directed to pay the trust's income to a beneficiary for life or a designated period, in the absence of other direction the trustee is under a duty to pay the beneficiary the net income of the trust property at reasonable intervals, normally monthly or quarter-annually, but at least annually. . . ."[767] The trustee has a duty to see to it that checks arrive on time,[768] tax returns are filled out properly and filed when due,[769] that investment decisions are made and executed in a timely fashion,[770] and that accountings[771] are submitted at regular intervals.[772]

§6.2.9 Duty to Keep Precise, Complete, and Accurate Records

Obscurity visits responsibility upon the trustee.[773]

An incident of the trustee's duty to be generally prudent[774] and to account (or report)[775] to beneficiaries is the trustee's duty to keep adequate records of the administration of the trust.[776] "The performance of these record-keeping responsibilities is also essential to a trustee's duty to collect and safeguard the trust property and to the beneficiaries' right to enforce the trustee's duty to act with prudence, loyalty and impartiality, as well as to the trustee's duty regarding reasonable and appropriate costs of administration."[777] By adequate we mean precise, complete, and accurate.[778] The Restatement (Third) of Trusts is generally in accord calling for the maintenance of books and records that are clear, complete, and accurate.[779] The information, however, need not be arranged in

---

[767] Restatement (Third) of Trusts §49 cmt. c(1).

[768] *See generally* §6.1.2 of this handbook (trustee's duty to affirmatively carry out the terms of the trust).

[769] *See generally* §7.3.4.1 of this handbook (liability for taxes and shareholder assessments in the trust context).

[770] *See generally* §6.2.2 of this handbook (trustee's duty to make trust property productive).

[771] *See generally* §6.1.5.2 (trustee's duty to keep and render accounts).

[772] UTC §801 (available at <http://www.uniformlaws.org/Act.aspx?title=Trust%20Code>); Bogert §541 n.60 and accompanying text (the requirement of diligence applies to the uncompensated as well as compensated trustee); §8.33 of this handbook (whether the level of an uncompensated trustee's duty of care is lower than that of a compensated trustee).

[773] Berlage v. Boyd, 206 Md. 521, 532, 112 A.2d 461, 466 (1955).

[774] *See* §6.1.1 of this handbook (trustee's duty to be generally prudent).

[775] *See* §6.1.5 of this handbook (trustee's duty to account to the beneficiary).

[776] UTC §810(a) cmt. (available at <http://www.uniformlaws.org/Act.aspx?title=Trust%20Code>). *See generally* Bogert §962; Scott on Trusts §172; Restatement (Second) of Trusts §172.

[777] Restatement (Third) of Trusts §83 cmt. a.

[778] Jimenez v. Lee, 547 P.2d 126 (Or. 1976); Berlage v. Boyd, 206 Md. 521, 532, 112 A.2d 461, 466 (1955); Wood v. Honeyman, 178 Or. 484, 555–556, 169 P.2d 131, 162 (1946).

[779] Restatement (Third) of Trusts §83.

any special format.[780] On the other hand, any expenses occasioned by the inadequacy of the trustee's records, *e.g.*, the expenses of hiring a CPA, should be borne personally by the trustee.[781] It is critically important that the trustee keep a proper record of the tax basis/cost of each item of trust property. We explain why in Section 11.1 of this handbook.

In litigating a corporate trustee's conduct in a given situation, whether it kept proper records could well have a bearing on whether it maintained an effective organizational structure, which in turn could have a bearing on whether it had exercised reasonable care and skill under the circumstances.[782] A national bank is required to retain the records for a period of three years from the later of the termination of the trust or the termination of any litigation relating to the trust.[783] But because allowed accounts generally may be re-opened upon a showing of fraud or manifest error,[784] the trustee is well advised to retain indefinitely materials that evidence the trustee's due diligence and prudence.[785]

The Prudent Man Rule and Prudent Investor Rule are rules of conduct, not performance.[786] Accordingly, the trustee is well advised to keep meticulous permanent records of all investment research, deliberations, and decisions.[787] At minimum, the trustee needs to create and place in a permanent file a writing that sets forth the circumstances and rationale behind a particular investment decision. In addition, any collateral materials that demonstrate due diligence and prudence on the part of the trustee in making the decision, *e.g.*, investment committee minutes, recommendations of investment experts, legal memoranda, correspondence, and the paper trail from the persons or persons who made the investment decision to the person or persons who implemented the investment decision, should be retained.

There are practical reasons why one might want to retain indefinitely the entire trust file.[788] Long after a trust has terminated, the trustee can expect tax

---

[780] Wylie v. Bushnell, 277 Ill. 484, 115 N.E. 618, 622 (1917). *See also* Restatement (Third) of Trusts §83 cmt. a.

[781] Miller v. Pender, 93 N.H. 1, 34 A.2d 663 (1943).

[782] *See generally* 3 Scott & Ascher §17.7 (Duty to Exercise Reasonable Care and Skill); §6.2.11 of this handbook (the institutional trustee's duty to have an effective organizational structure).

[783] 12 C.F.R. §9.8 (1997) (Reg. 9) (available at <www.gpoaccess.gov/cfr/index.html>).

[784] For a case involving the reopening of allowed accounts for "constructive fraud," *see* National Acad. of Sci. v. Cambridge Trust Co., 370 Mass. 303, 346 N.E.2d 879 (1976). This case involved a trustee's good faith representation on its accountings that a widow had not remarried and thus was entitled to income payments when in fact she had remarried and under the terms of the governing instrument was not so entitled. The court found that the trustee had made "no reasonable efforts to ascertain the true state of the facts it . . . [had] . . . misrepresented in the accounts." *See generally* 4 Scott & Ascher §24.31 (Liability for Incorrect Distributions).

[785] *See generally* 4 Scott & Ascher §24.31 (Liability for Incorrect Distributions).

[786] *See* §6.2.2.2 of this handbook (the prudent investor's code of conduct).

[787] *See* §6.2.2.2 of this handbook (the prudent investor's code of conduct). *See generally* 3 Scott & Ascher §17.6 (Duty to Exercise Reasonable Care and Skill).

[788] Lewin ¶26-67 through ¶26-68 (England).

basis/cost,[789] genealogical, and land title inquiries, as well as inquiries from trustees administering related trusts. Even when an ex-trustee has no legal duty to respond to such requests, the ex-trustee may wish to in order to maintain good public relations, or out of simple courtesy. As reconstructing the file of a trust long terminated can be both time-consuming and expensive, it may be worth the cost of storage to keep the entire file extant indefinitely.

When there is a failure to keep adequate records, all doubts are resolved against the trustee.[790] The Restatement (Third) of Trusts is generally in accord:

> A trustee who fails to keep proper records is liable for any loss or expense resulting from that failure. A trustee's failure to maintain necessary books and records may also cause a court in reviewing a judicial accounting to resolve doubts against the trustee. These failures by trustees may furnish grounds for reducing or denying compensation, or even for removal, or for charging the trustee with the costs of corrective procedures or of having to conduct otherwise unnecessary accounting proceedings in court.[791]

§6.2.10 Duty to Petition Court for Modification of or Deviation from Terms of Trust When Appropriate

This duty . . . [to invoke the doctrine of equitable deviation] . . . is not generally extended to distributive provisions . . . because of concern that to do so might create unfair risks and burdens for trustees and also might, in some situations, present impartiality problems.[792]

The court may modify an administrative or distributive provision of a trust if, because of circumstances that were not anticipated by the settlor, the modification or deviation would further the purposes of the trust. This is known as the equitable deviation doctrine.[793] The Restatement (Third) of Trusts would impose an affirmative duty on the trustee to initiate a modification or deviation action when circumstances warrant invocation of the doctrine.[794] The duty is generally limited to the trust's administrative provisions. The circumstances must have the potential to cause substantial harm to the trust or its beneficiaries. The duty arises only if the trustee knows about the circumstances or should have known about them. If the trustee is actually aware that a purpose of the settler would be jeopardized by adhering to existing provisions governing

---

[789] *See generally* §11.1 of this handbook (tax basis/cost of trust property).

[790] *See generally* §8.24 of this handbook (who has the burden of proof in an action for breach of trust brought by the beneficiary against the trustee); *see, e.g.*, Matter of JP Morgan Chase Bank N.A. (Strong), 2013 WL 6182548 (N.Y. Sur. 2013) ("Case law has repeatedly held that if a fiduciary 'fails to maintain adequate records of its conduct and transactions, all doubts and presumptions are resolved adversely against it.'").

[791] Restatement (Third) of Trusts §83 cmt. a(1). *See generally* §7.2.3 of this handbook (types of equitable relief for breaches of trust).

[792] Restatement (Third) of Trusts, Reporter's Notes on §66(2) and cmt. c thereto.

[793] *See generally* §8.15.20 of this handbook (doctrine of equitable deviation).

[794] Restatement (Third) of Trusts §66(2).

distribution, "the trustee would have a duty to petition the court for instructions or for appropriate deviation or modification."[795]

For a discussion of some of the extraordinary circumstances under which a court may order the early termination of a noncharitable irrevocable inter vivos trust, or the reformation or modification of its dispositive terms, the reader is referred to Section 8.2.2.1 of this handbook. The doctrine of equitable deviation is covered more fully in Section 8.15.20 of this handbook. In Section 8.15.22 of this handbook, we examine the doctrines of reformation, modification, and rectification. Finally, in Section 8.17 of this handbook we wrestle with mistake-based trust reformation or modification actions that are tax-driven, *i.e.*, actions that are brought to achieve tax efficiencies.

As a general rule, a trustee should refrain from taking sides in judicial proceedings that could bring about a shifting of the equitable or beneficial interests.[796] In any proceeding that involves the reformation, modification, or outright elimination of a dispositive provision it is critical that each interested party be represented by independent counsel, or a guardian ad litem to the extent appropriate.[797] For a discussion of who would be a necessary party and thus entitled to such representation, the reader is referred to Section 5.7 of this handbook.

§6.2.11 Duty (of Institutional Trustee) to Have an Effective Organizational Structure

Some acts in the administration of a trust are of such importance that it may be improper for a corporate trustee to entrust them to mere employees. Instead, the board of directors, or a responsible committee or officer, should be in charge of these sorts of decisions. As to national banks, the Comptroller of the Currency has promulgated relevant regulations.[798]

The public trust company. Because the obligations of an institutional trustee are at least as onerous as those of an individual trustee,[799] a dysfunctional or ineffective internal organization is not a defense to an allegation of breach of fiduciary duty.[800] To the contrary, it might be evidence of negligence, or even reckless conduct.[801] The failure of the directors of the institutional trustee to put in place and maintain an effective organizational structure would

---

[795] Restatement (Third) of Trusts §66(2) cmt. e. *See generally* §8.42 of this handbook (discussing the differences between a petition (complaint) for instructions and a complaint (petition) for declaratory relief).

[796] *See generally* §6.2.5 of this handbook (the trustee's duty of impartiality).

[797] *See generally* §8.14 of this handbook (when a guardian ad litem (or special representative) is needed, including a discussion of virtual representation issues).

[798] 3 Scott & Ascher §17.3.4 (Delegation by Corporate Trustees) (referring to Comptroller of the Currency Reg. §9.4, 12 C.F.R. §9.4).

[799] *See generally* §6.1.4 (discussing in part the principle that the professional or corporate trustee is held to a higher fiduciary standard than is an amateur trustee).

[800] *See generally* 3 Scott & Ascher §17.6.

[801] *See generally* 3 Scott & Ascher §17.6.

constitute a breach of the institution's duty to administer the trust prudently.[802] It may even constitute an improper delegation of their fiduciary duties, *i.e.*, of those of their duties that run *to the trust beneficiaries*.[803] Personal liability as well could attach to the directors themselves.[804] Proper record keeping is critical.[805] Indenture trustees particularly should take note in this regard.[806] The following are indicia of an effective fiduciary organization:

- "The organizational structure...[is]...designed to promote an orderly flow of the daily work and...[is]...sufficiently flexible to accommodate peak work loads without sacrificing efficiency or accuracy."[807]
- "Fiduciary committees...[are]...so structured as to constitute flexible, workable entities. Functions...[are]...clearly defined and effectively executed."[808]
- "...[T]he...plan of organization...include[s]...procedures for personnel recruitment, training, evaluation and salary administration."[809]
- "Staff...[is]...sufficient to handle the volume of work. Lines of authority, duties and responsibilities...[are]...clearly defined and effectively communicated to all personnel to promote efficiency, productivity and the orderly execution of the...[institution's]...functions."[810]
- "The organization plan...facilitate[s]...the implementation of an adequate program of internal controls and a system of checks and balances designed to ensure proper administration of

---

[802] *See generally* 3 Scott & Ascher §17.6; §6.1.1 (Trustee's Duty to Be Generally Prudent).

[803] *See generally* 3 Scott & Ascher §17.3.4 (Delegation by Corporate Trustees).

[804] *See generally* §7.2.9 of this handbook (personal liability of third parties including the trustee's agents).

[805] *See generally* 3 Scott & Ascher §17.6 (noting that it is "crucial" that a corporate trustee "keep detailed records of all aspects of the administration of each of its trusts, including, for example, the minutes of the proceedings of its investment committee"); §6.2.9 of this handbook (noting that all doubts are resolved against the trustee who fails to keep precise, complete and accurate records) and §8.24 of this handbook (noting that all doubts are resolved against the trustee who fails to properly account). *See, e.g.*, Matter of JP Morgan Chase Bank N.A. (Strong), 2013 WL 6182548 (N.Y. Sur. 2013) ("The...[corporate trustee]...cannot argue that its own inability to preserve its own records (or those of its predecessors) for three Trusts of such high value forecloses the ability of the Objectants to challenge how those Trusts were administered.").

[806] *See generally* §9.31 of this handbook (corporate trusts; trusts to secure creditors; the Trust Indenture Act of 1939; protecting bondholders).

[807] Comptroller's Handbook for Fiduciary Activities, Management Appraisal, Organizational Structure (Sept. 1990).

[808] Comptroller's Handbook for Fiduciary Activities, Management Appraisal, Organizational Structure (Sept. 1990).

[809] Comptroller's Handbook for Fiduciary Activities, Management Appraisal, Organizational Structure (Sept. 1990).

[810] Comptroller's Handbook for Fiduciary Activities, Management Appraisal, Organizational Structure (Sept. 1990).

the . . . [institution's] . . . fiduciary business. Such controls . . . include a procedure for management review of actions taken by all personnel."[811]

- "The organization plan . . . include[s] . . . procedures for effective communication among all levels of management. Procedures . . . facilitate the dissemination of information necessary to:

  — Inform all supervisory personnel of senior management's policies and directives,

  — Apprise senior management of its subordinates' activities in implementing such policies and directives, and

  — Effect the orderly execution of administrative details."[812]

- "Authority to make discretionary decisions and the matters in which independent judgment may be exercised . . . [are] . . . defined expressly and communicated to supervisory personnel. Sufficient flexibility . . . [is] . . . allowed to permit expedient action where it would be essential to the best interests of . . . [the beneficiary]. . . ."[813]

The private trust company. In Section 8.6 of this handbook we discuss the private trust company (a.k.a. family trust company or exempt trust company). State-chartered private trust companies, while generally less regulated and more intimate than their public counterparts, should still have organizational structures with clear lines of authority and built-in systems of checks and balances for monitoring the activities of company personnel who have access to entrusted assets.[814] There should be in place a written plan, approved and administered by the board of directors, for a truly independent and fully competent regular auditing of *fiduciary activity*.[815] "A private trust company should also have a due diligence process for not only selecting third party service providers and advisors, but also for monitoring their performance."[816] Trust counsel should be competent, independent, proactive, and kept fully informed. He or she should have primary responsibility for the safekeeping, interpretation, and proper implementation of the terms of all governing trust instruments and associated documentation.

---

[811] Comptroller's Handbook for Fiduciary Activities, Management Appraisal, Organizational Structure (Sept. 1990).

[812] Comptroller's Handbook for Fiduciary Activities, Management Appraisal, Organizational Structure (Sept. 1990). *See also* 3 Scott & Ascher §17.6 ("Thus, when beneficiaries seek to surcharge a corporate trustee, it is important, in proving that it acted prudently, for the trustee to be able to show that it gave careful consideration to the decision at hand, in accordance with its own, internal procedures").

[813] Comptroller's Handbook for Fiduciary Activities, Management Appraisal, Organizational Structure (Sept. 1990).

[814] *See generally* Alan V. Ytterberg & James P. Weller, *Managing Family Wealth Through A Private Trust Company*, 36 ACTEC L.J. 623, 636–639 (2010).

[815] *See generally* Alan V. Ytterberg & James P. Weller, *Managing Family Wealth Through A Private Trust Company*, 36 ACTEC L.J. 623, 638–639 (2010).

[816] *See generally* Alan V. Ytterberg & James P. Weller, *Managing Family Wealth Through A Private Trust Company*, 36 ACTEC L.J. 623, 639 (2010).

The unincorporated family trust office. It is critical that an unincorporated family office of individuals and/or entities providing agency services to a constellation of family trustees have an effective organizational structure. In the absence of the corporate template to channel the lines of fiduciary authority and to allocate fiduciary responsibilities, it will fall to trust counsel to perform those channeling and allocation functions, to be the fiduciary traffic cop, as it were. A newly minted lawyer is simply not going to have the requisite experience to handle the legal, operational, and political complexities of the job, particularly as the legal titles to the constellation's assets will not be concentrated in one entity. In order to minimize the risk of a catastrophic blindsiding down the road, the prudent prospective "office" trust counsel will want to make the granting of such channeling and allocation authority a condition of his or her employment.

The multi-participant trust. A multi-participant trust is a single trust that is administered by a constellation of fiduciaries and quasi-fiduciaries in addition to the title-holding trustee, such as protectors, removers, appointers, and the like. The functions of the traditional "plenipotent" trustee are sliced, diced, and the pieces parceled out; a process we discuss in some detail in Section 3.2.6 of this handbook. The ACTEC article *Achieve the Promise—and Limit the Risk—of Multi-Participant Trusts* is all about making sure that critical fiduciary functions do not fall between the cracks along the way.[817] The authors lay out twelve requirements for a well-functioning multi-participant trust. Here is what they have to say about the Uniform Trust Code in this regard: "The UTC in the form recommended by the Uniform Law Commissioners not only fails to successfully address these twelve items, its recommended provisions may block effectively addressing some of them in the trust instrument."[818]

§6.2.12 Duty Not to Comply with Provisions That Are Unlawful or Violate Public Policy

In determining whether a trustee should have known that a provision was unlawful or contrary to public policy, or should have investigated the provision's validity, among the relevant factors for a court to consider are the particular trustee's experience, familiarity with trust law and practice, and representations concerning competence to serve as trustee.[819]

The trustee's duty to carry out the terms of the trust is covered in Section 6.1.2 of this handbook. "A trustee . . . [however] . . . has a duty not to comply with a provision of the trust that the trustee knows or should know is invalid because

---

[817] John P.C. Duncan & Anita M. Sarafa, *Achieve the Promise—and Limit the Risk—of Multi-Participant Trusts*, 36 ACTEC L.J. 769 (Spring 2012).

[818] John P.C. Duncan & Anita M. Sarafa, *Achieve the Promise—and Limit the Risk—of Multi-Participant Trusts*, 36 ACTEC L.J. 769, 798 (Spring 2012).

[819] Restatement (Third) of Trusts §72 cmt. c.

the provision is unlawful or contrary to public policy."[820] It is obvious that the trustee has a duty not to commit a crime or a serious tort even if instructed to do so by the terms of the trust. It is also obvious that a trustee may not comply with a provision that instructs the trustee to, say, erect a building that violates local zoning laws or will constitute a public nuisance.[821] This duty on the part of the trustee not to engage in "illegal" activity, however, also encompasses activity that merely violates public policy,[822] an "unruly horse" that is not all that easy to corral.[823] While it may not violate public policy for a parent to disinherit a child who chooses to marry, for example, a trust provision that cuts off the child's equitable interest if the child marries at all very well might.[824] For a discussion of some incentive provisions that are likely to violate public policy, see Section 9.24 of this handbook.[825] A provision that runs afoul of the applicable rules against perpetuities[826] or the applicable rule against accumulations[827] also would violate public policy. These are all public policy-based proscriptions that, ostensibly, at least, are of some interest to the community. The focus, in other words, is to some extent external to the trust relationship itself.

On the other hand, whether or not a trustee has a duty to carry out "value-impairing investment instructions," *e.g.*, a provision that directs the trustee to invest the entire trust corpus in shares of a single large publicly traded company, is really more a question of what makes sound general trust law.[828] In other words, to the extent there is a "public-policy" component, it is internally focused on the trust relationship itself. In this case, it is the extent to which the economic interests of the beneficiary should be allowed to trump the settlor's intentions.[829] Thus, when it comes to a petition for equitable deviation, the test is not what is in the "best interests" of the beneficiaries; rather, the petitioners must establish that the settlor's presumed intent is incapable of fulfillment.[830]

And then there are trust terms that are in the interest of neither the community at large nor the beneficiaries. An instruction to use trust assets to erect buildings in the financial and business district of a large city that are no more than three stories high, for example, would likely fall into that category.[831]

---

[820] Restatement (Third) of Trusts §72. *Cf.* §8.15.39 of this handbook (noting that the rule against capricious purposes and the rule that a trust purpose may not violate public policy are easily conflated).

[821] *See generally* 3 Scott & Ascher §16.3 (Illegality).

[822] *See generally* 3 Scott & Ascher §16.3 (Illegality).

[823] *See* Richardson v. Mellish, 2 Bing. 229, 252 (1824) (an English case).

[824] *See generally* §9.24 of this handbook (the incentive trust).

[825] *See also* 3 Scott & Ascher §16.3.

[826] *See* §8.2.1 of this handbook (the rule against perpetuities).

[827] *See* §8.15.8 of this handbook (the rule against accumulations).

[828] *See, e.g.,* In re J.P. Morgan Chase Bank, N.A., 19 Misc. 3d 337, 852 N.Y.S.2d 718 (2008) (the court enforcing a provision in a trust restricting the trustee from selling 18 Broadway and 562 Park Avenue).

[829] *See generally* 3 Scott & Ascher §16.3 (Illegality).

[830] *See, e.g.,* In re J.P. Morgan Chase Bank, N.A., 19 Misc.3d 337, 342, 852 N.Y.S.2d 718, 722 (2008). *See generally* §8.15.20 of this handbook (the doctrine of equitable deviation).

[831] *See generally* 3 Scott & Ascher §16.3 (discussing Colonial Trust Co. v. Brown, 135 A. 555 (Conn. 1926)).

Whether a provision violates public policy is determined at the time of performance, not at the time of the trust's creation.[832] "A trustee 'should know' what the trustee would have learned through the exercise of reasonable care."[833] When there is reasonable doubt, the trustee at trust expense may and should petition the court for instructions.[834]

There is more than a technical difference between the absence of a duty to comply with a particular trust term on grounds of "illegality" and a fiduciary duty not to comply. Clearly a trustee has no duty to comply with an instruction to commit a crime or serious tort, or to violate some recognized public policy. To the extent engaging in any of these activities would constitute a breach of trust, the trustee also has an affirmative fiduciary duty *not* to comply. While the trustee may have a duty to the community at large not to erect a public nuisance with trust assets, even if instructed to do so by the terms of the trust, he also has a fiduciary duty not to do so, a duty that runs to the beneficiaries.[835] Thus, if the trustee were subsequently ordered by the municipality to tear the offending structure down, the trustee personally must bear the burden of the attendant costs, as well as otherwise making the trust estate whole.[836]

§6.2.13 Duty Not to Attempt to Comply with a Trust Provision If Compliance Would Be Impossible or Incur Unreasonable Expense

I do not think it is legitimate for any . . . [settlor] . . . to invoke our law of trusts . . . and at the same time attempt to prohibit these trustees from exercising the most characteristic function which falls to be discharged by every trustee,—the preservation of the trust estate.[837]

The trustee's duty to carry out the terms of the trust is covered in Section 6.1.2 of this handbook. "A trustee . . . [, however,] . . . has a duty not to attempt to comply with a trust provision directing the trustee to do an act if the trustee knows or should know (a) that compliance is impossible, or (b) that the expense of attempting to comply is unreasonable."[838] This is in keeping with the trustee's duty to protect the trust property, a topic that is covered in Section of this handbook. The trustee must "reasonably believe" that performance of the terms of the trust is impossible.[839] That means that the trustee must exercise "due diligence in ascertaining whether it is possible to comply with the terms of

---

[832] *See generally* 3 Scott & Ascher §16.3.

[833] Restatement (Third) of Trusts §72 cmt. c. *See generally* §6.1.1 of this handbook (the trustee's duty to be generally prudent).

[834] *See generally* 3 Scott & Ascher §16.3 (Illegality); §8.42 of this handbook (the complaint (petition) for instructions versus the complaint (petition) for declaratory judgment).

[835] *See generally* 3 Scott & Ascher §16.3.

[836] *See generally* 3 Scott & Ascher §16.3.

[837] Thompson's Trs. v. Davidson, [1947] S.C. (Scotland) 654, 658.

[838] Restatement (Third) of Trusts §73.

[839] 3 Scott & Ascher §16.2.

the trust before the trustee is justified in abandoning the attempt."[840] For a discussion of some of the extraordinary circumstances that may warrant the early termination of an irrevocable trust, the reader is referred to Section 8.2.2.1 of this handbook.

When in doubt as to whether it would be possible or cost-effective to carry out a particular provision, the trustee may petition the court for instructions.[841] "If it appears to the court that compliance with a trust provision is not possible, or that it would be wasteful to attempt to comply, and if the impossibility or impracticability is a result of unanticipated circumstances, not only may the court direct or authorize the trustee to deviate from the provision, but it may modify the terms of the trust."[842] The doctrine of equitable deviation is addressed in Section 8.15.20 of this handbook. We cover the doctrines of reformation, modification, and rectification in Section 8.15.22 of this handbook. Reformation and modification of trusts to achieve tax efficiencies are considered in Section 8.17 of this handbook.

If complying with the terms of the trust is impossible due to the trustee's breach of trust, then the trustee, of course, may well be personally liable for the consequences.[843]

§6.2.14   Duty of Reasonable Cooperation with Cotrustee(s)

A trustee has a duty to cooperate with his cotrustee or cotrustees, unless it would be unreasonable to do so.[844] This duty is incident to the duty to prudently participate in the administration of the trust.[845] On the other hand, a trustee would be liable for cooperating with a cotrustee in a breach of trust.[846] Such unreasonable cooperation could take the form of:

- Participating in the breach;
- Acquiescing in the breach;
- Concealing the breach;
- Improperly delegating the administration of the trust to the breaching cotrustee;[847]
- Enabling the cotrustee to commit the breach by "failing to exercise reasonable care, including by failing to make reasonable effort to enjoin or otherwise prevent the breach";[848] and
- Neglecting to take reasonable steps to obtain redress for the breach.

---

[840] 3 Scott & Ascher §16.2.

[841] See generally 3 Scott & Ascher §16.2. See also §8.42 of this handbook (the complaint (petition) for instructions versus the complaint (petition) for declaratory judgment).

[842] Restatement (Third) of Trusts §73 cmt. c.

[843] See generally 3 Scott & Ascher §16.2.

[844] Restatement (Third) of Trusts §81 cmt. c.

[845] Restatement (Third) of Trusts §81 cmt. c.

[846] Restatement (Third) of Trusts §81 cmt. e.

[847] See §6.1.4 of this handbook (trustee's duty not to delegate critical fiduciary functions).

[848] Restatement (Third) of Trusts §81 cmt. e.

For more on the topic of when it would be unreasonable for a trustee to cooperate with his cotrustee, the reader is referred to Sections 3.4.4.1 of this handbook (multiple trustees (cotrustees)); 6.1.4 of this handbook (duty to give personal attention (not to delegate)); and 7.2.4 of this handbook (cofiduciary and predecessor liability and contribution).

§6.2.15 *Duty to Administer Trust at an Appropriate Place*

A trustee is under a continuing duty "to administer the trust at a place appropriate to the purposes of the trust and to its sound, efficient management."[849] As we note in Section 6.2.1.3 of this handbook, this duty can implicate the trustee's duty to protect and preserve trust property. It also can implicate the trustee's duty of loyalty, as we note in Section 6.1.3 of this handbook. "If it is an inter vivos trust and the trustee has not become subject to the jurisdiction of any particular court to which the trustee is thereafter accountable, it is not ordinarily necessary to apply to a court for permission to move the trust assets to another state and to administer the trust there, unless the terms of the trust, express or implied, are to the contrary."[850] For the relocation of a testamentary trust to be final and binding on all parties, however, such an application for permission will likely be necessary, absent special facts. The Restatement (Second) of Conflict of Laws is in accord.[851] Judicial relinquishment of jurisdiction over the administration of a trust is taken up generally in Section 8.40 of this handbook. What law governs the trust's administration postrelocation is discussed in Section 8.5 of this handbook. Both the Uniform Trust Code and the Uniform Probate Code would involve the beneficiaries in the process of considering and effecting a relocation of the trust's principal place of administration.[852] If a trust's principal place of administration becomes inappropriate for any reason, the court may remove the trustee if such drastic action is necessary to make a relocation happen.[853] We discuss the equitable relief of trustee removal in Section 7.2.3.6 of this handbook.

§6.3   Governmental Reporting Obligations

The trustee must be attentive to federal and state governmental reporting obligations. In addition to those obligations arising under the tax and securities

---

[849] UPC §7-305. *See also* Mass. Gen. Laws ch. 190B, §7-305; UTC §108(b) (available at <http://www.uniformlaws.org/Act.aspx?title=Trust%20Code>); 7 Scott & Ascher §45.5.3.1.

[850] 7 Scott & Ascher §45.5.3.

[851] Restatement (Second) of Conflict of Laws §271, cmt. g.

[852] UTC §108 (d) & (e) (available at <http://www.uniformlaws.org/Act.aspx?title=Trust%20 Code>); UPC §7-305. *See generally* 7 Scott & Ascher §45.5.3.1.

[853] UPC §7-305. *See also* Mass. Gen. Laws ch. 190B, §7-305; 7 Scott & Ascher §45.5.3.1.

laws, the trustee of a pension trust may be required to file periodic reports with the Department of Labor; the trustee of a charitable trust with the state attorney general; the corporate trustee with the Comptroller of the Currency or state banking commissioner; and so forth. Do not forget property tax filings with City Hall and of course abatement notices. The list of governmental reports and filings is long and will vary from jurisdiction to jurisdiction. A caution is therefore in order: This handbook presents only a few of the more common reports and filings.

§6.3.1   *Tax Filings*

(a) **Domestic trusts.** After a trust becomes irrevocable it is likely to be treated as a separate taxable entity for federal and state tax purposes.[1] If the trust does not already have an Employer Identification Number at that time, one must be applied for on Form SS-4.[2] For any year in which the trust has taxable income or gross income exceeding $600, or if beneficiary is a nonresident alien, the trustee must file a federal fiduciary income tax return, Form 1041, on or before April 15 of the following year.[3] Beneficiaries are notified of taxable and nontaxable distributions on the form's Schedule K-1. While the K-1 must be in the hands of the beneficiaries by April 15, it is good practice for the trustee to send it sooner in order that the beneficiaries may prepare their own tax returns in a timely fashion. Also, the trustee must make quarterly estimated tax payments, which are due April 15, June 15, September 15, and January 15.[4]

The trust's federal income tax must be carefully estimated, since the trustee who substantially and negligently overpays may be personally liable for interest on the overpayment, while the consequences of substantially and negligently underpaying taxes include personal liability for any penalties that may be assessed as a result of the underpayment. Even negligent failures to file can lead to awards of punitive damages against the trustee if complemented by evidence from which another element of aggravation can be inferred.[5] Further, many states impose a tax on the trust's taxable income. This may impose certain

---

§6.3 [1] In matters involving the income taxation of trusts, the trustee is referred to Chapters 10 and 11 of this handbook, as well as to Ferguson, Freeland & Ascher, Federal Income Taxation of Estates, Trusts, and Beneficiaries (2000). For a compilation of the income tax rates for trusts in the various states as of 3/1/00, *see* Jeffrey A. Schoenblum, 2000 Multistate Guide to Estate Planning 9-1 (2000). As to each state's own unique matrix of statutory rules governing what contacts justify the taxation by the state of a particular trust's income, *see* Jeffrey A. Schoenblum, 2000 Multistate Guide to Estate Planning 9-1 (2000). *See also* Jeffrey A. Schoenblum, 2 Multistate and Multinational Estate Planning 427–493 (2000) (Multi-jurisdictional Income Tax Considerations for Trusts and Estates); Gutierrez, *Oops! The State Income Taxation of Multi-Jurisdictional Trusts*, 25 U. Miami Est. Plan. Inst. Ch. 12 (1991). *See generally* §8.34 of this handbook (when an employer identification number (EIN) is not required).

[2] *See* 26 C.F.R. §301.6109-1 (1992).

[3] *See* Bogert §265.

[4] Bogert §265.

[5] *See* Smith v. Underwood, 487 S.E.2d 807, 818 (N.C. Ct. App. 1997).

state tax reporting and payment obligations on the trustee. The matter of the income taxation of trusts is covered in greater depth in Chapter 10 of this handbook. Chapter 11 of this handbook is devoted entirely to the subject of determining the income tax basis/cost of entrusted property.

The generation-skipping tax on certain transfers is a relatively new tax that places additional tax-reporting burdens on trustees.[6] A federal GST tax payment obligation may arise upon one or more of the following events: (1) a trust's creation, (2) a trust's termination, and (3) a distribution of principal or income from a trust.[7] If either the trust itself or the recipient of the property interest enjoys an exemption, a federal GST tax may *not* be due.[8] The tax is generally separate from and independent of the federal estate, gift, and income tax. Under certain circumstances, the trustee may be obliged to file a GST tax return[9] as well as pay the tax due. For some GSTs, the trustee files an informational return and provides the recipient with data that the recipient will need to prepare the GST tax return and pay the tax. In matters related to the GST tax the prudent trustee communicates and coordinates with the settlor's executor and the trust beneficiaries as appropriate and raises any cash needed to pay the tax in an orderly and timely fashion.

The trustee of an individual retirement account (IRA) or Simplified Employee Plan IRA (SEP-IRA) is required to make yearly reports to the IRS and to the taxpayer on the status of the account.[10] Employee benefit plan trustees must report distributions to participants on Form 1099-R.[11]

(b) Foreign trusts.

Clearly there are a number of factors to consider, but naming a private trust company in the U.S. as successor trustee of a foreign trust can be a key step toward domesticating the trust to eliminate this ... [IRS Form 3520] ... reporting requirement.[12]

---

[6] I.R.C. §2601. *See generally* Berteau, Gregoria, & Seitl, 822 T.M. 2d, Estate and Gift Tax Returns and Audits; Stephens et al., Federal Estate and Gift Taxation ¶ 12.03[1] (8th ed. 2002).

[7] Stephens et al., Federal Estate and Gift Taxation ¶ 13.02 (8th ed. 2002).

[8] Stephens et al., Federal Estate and Gift Taxation ¶ 15.02 (8th ed. 2002).

[9] Stephens et al., Federal Estate and Gift Taxation ¶ 18.02 (8th ed. 2002). For information on when and under what circumstances such returns must be filed, as well as other matters related to the federal generation-skipping-transfer tax, the trustee is referred to Stephens et al., Federal Estate and Gift Taxation (8th ed. 2002). *See generally* Jon J. Gallo, *Estate Planning and the Generation-Skipping Tax,* 33 Real Prop. Prob. & Tr. J. 457 (1998).

[10] *See* Treas. Reg. §§1.408-5, 1.408-9.

[11] A complete list of federal tax forms (as well as the forms themselves) may be found in *IRS Forms,* published by BNA Tax Management, 1250 23rd Street, N.W., Washington, D.C. 20037-1166 (1-800-223-7270).

[12] Alan V. Ytterberg & James P. Weller, *Managing Family Wealth Through a Private Trust Company,* 36 ACTEC L.J. 623, 630-631 (2010).

"The trustee[13] of a foreign trust must file . . . [with the IRS] . . . three returns and statements if the trust has U.S. income."[14] They are Form 56 (notice Concerning Fiduciary Relationship), Form 1040R (Nonresident Alien Income Tax Return), and Forms 8288 and 8288-A (involving transfers by the trustee of interests in U.S. real property). A U.S. person who creates a foreign trust or transfers property directly or indirectly to the trustee of a foreign trust must report on Form 3520 to the IRS, within ninety days, written notice of the amount of money or other property transferred, the identity of the recipient trust, its trustees, and its beneficiaries.[15]

The Small Business Job Protection Act provides tests to determine if a trust is foreign or domestic.[16] The death of a U.S. citizen who possessed a beneficial interest under a foreign trust is also a reportable event provided that the trust is included in the decedent's gross estate.[17] In addition, a reportable event includes the creation of any foreign trust by a U.S. person, the transfer of any money or property (directly or indirectly) to a foreign trust by a U.S. person,

---

[13] *See generally* McCaffrey, Harrison, & Kirschner, *U.S. Taxation of Foreign Trusts, Trusts with Non-U.S. Grantors and Their U.S. Beneficiaries*, 26 ACTEC Notes 159 (2000).

[14] Zaritsky, 854-2nd T.M., U.S. Taxation of Foreign Estates, Trusts, and Beneficiaries A-87-A-97 (also providing details as to when, where, and how these returns must be filed to include copies of the forms themselves in the Appendix). *See generally* McCaffrey, Harrison, & Kirschner, *U.S. Taxation of Foreign Trusts, Trusts with Non-U.S. Grantors and Their U.S. Beneficiaries,* SJ027 ALI-ABA 137 (2003).

[15] I.R.C. §6048(a)(1), (a)(2)(A), (B), further interpreted by Notice 97-34, 1997-2, I.R.B. 22. Parts of this have been repealed by Notice 2003-75. The reporting regime for Canadian RRSPs & RRIFs have been simplified. The penalty for failure to report the transfer to a foreign trust is 35 percent of the gross value of the transfer. *See* I.R.C. §6677(a)(2). Additional penalties may be levied as well for chronic failure to report. *See also* IRS Forms 3520, 3520A.

[16] Pub. L. No. 104-188, 110 Stat. 1755, 104 H.R. 3448. There are two tests courts apply to determine whether the trust is foreign or domestic. *See* Frederick Tansill, *Offshore Asset Protection Trusts: Emphasizing Non-Tax Issues,* SB45 ALI-ABA 389, 400–404 (1998). The first is the court test. Tansill, *Offshore Asset Protection Trusts: Emphasizing Non-Tax Issues,* SB45 ALI-ABA 389, 401 (1998). A trust will meet the court test if the trust is registered by a U.S. fiduciary in a U.S. court under a state statute that has provisions substantially similar to Article VII, Trust Administration, of the UPC if, in the case of a testamentary trust, all fiduciaries of the trust have been qualified as trustees of the trust by a court within the U.S. or, in the case of an inter vivos trust, the fiduciaries and/or beneficiaries take steps with a court within the U.S. that cause the administration of the trust to be subject to the primary supervision of the court. Tansill, *Offshore Asset Protection Trusts: Emphasizing Non-Tax Issues,* SB45 ALI-ABA 389, 402 (1998). The second test is the control test. Tansill, *Offshore Asset Protection Trusts: Emphasizing Non-Tax Issues,* SB45 ALI-ABA 389, 403 (1998). The control test is met only if all substantial decisions are made by U.S. fiduciaries. Tansill, *Offshore Asset Protection Trusts: Emphasizing Non-Tax Issues,* SB45 ALI-ABA 389, 403 (1998). Substantial decisions of the trust include, but are not limited to, whether and when to distribute income or corpus; the amount of any distributions; the selection of a beneficiary; the power to make investment decisions; whether a receipt is allocable to income or principal; whether to terminate the trust; whether to compromise, arbitrate, or abandon claims of the trust; whether to sue on behalf of the trust or defend suits against the trust; and whether to remove, add, or replace a trustee. Tansill, *Offshore Asset Protection Trusts: Emphasizing Non-Tax Issues,* SB45 ALI-ABA 389, 403 (1998). If both of these tests are met, the trust will be treated as a U.S. trust but if only one test is met it will be treated as a foreign trust. Tansill, *Offshore Asset Protection Trusts: Emphasizing Non-Tax Issues,* SB45 ALI-ABA 389, 401 (1998).

[17] I.R.C. §6048(a)(3)(A)(iii).

including transfer by reason of death, and the death of a citizen or resident of the United States if the decedent was treated as the owner of any portion of a foreign trust under the rules of subpart E of Part I of subchapter J or Chapter 1 or if any portion of a foreign trust was included in the gross estate of the decedent, as previously mentioned.[18]

A U.S. person treated as the owner of a foreign trust under the Foreign Grantor Trust Rules[19] must ensure that the trustee (or trust) files an annual report on Form 3520A with the IRS providing full accounting of trust activities, information on each U.S. person who (a) is treated as the owner of any portion of the trust, or (b) receives directly or indirectly any distribution from the trust.[20] The trustee must attach a "Foreign Grantor Trust Information Statement" to Form 3520A and send a copy of the same to each U.S. beneficiary or owner of the trust. The Foreign Grantor Trust Information must include certain background information, including the trust's employer identification number; a trust balance sheet; an annual income statement; an owner statement that includes a statement of net trust income attributable to the owner; and a beneficiary statement, which includes a statement for each U.S. beneficiary receiving a trust distribution.[21] A U.S. person annually must report to the IRS all distributions made to him or her from foreign trusts.[22] The beneficiary of a foreign trust must disclose distributions from the trust on Schedule B of his or

---

[18] I.R.C. §6048(a)(3)(A)(i)–(iii).

[19] I.R.C. §679. *See generally* §9.1 of this handbook (the grantor trust).

[20] I.R.C. §6048(b)(1)(A), (B). *See also* Frederick Tansill, *Offshore Asset Protection Trusts: Emphasizing Non-Tax Issues,* SB45 ALI-ABA 389, 410–412 (1998). The penalty for failing to file the annual report on the foreign trust is 5 percent of the value of the portion of the trust assets as owned by the U.S. person. *See* I.R.C. §6677(b), (c). Additional penalties may be levied as well for chronic failure to report. *See* I.R.C. §6677(a)(2). Each taxpayer subject to tax under I.R.C. §679 with respect to a foreign trust having one or more U.S. beneficiaries must file Form 3520-A, Annual Return of Foreign Trust with U.S. Beneficiaries, together with any additional schedules or other information required by the form or the instructions to the form. 26 C.F.R. 404.6048-1. If the taxpayer's spouse is also subject to tax under I.R.C. §679 with respect to the same foreign trust for the same taxable year, and if both taxpayer and spouse file a joint return of income tax for that year, a single Form 3520A may be filed jointly with respect to such trust for the year. 26 C.F.R. 404.6048-1. A U.S. person who directly or indirectly transfers property to a foreign trust shall be treated as the owner for his taxable year of the portion of such trust attributable to such property if for such a year there is a U.S. beneficiary of any portion of such trust. I.R.C. §679. *See also* I.R.C. §679 for exceptions to treating the U.S. transferor as the owner, special rules applicable to a foreign grantor who later becomes a U.S. person, and outbound trust migrations.

[21] *See* Frederick Tansill, *Offshore Asset Protection Trusts: Emphasizing Non-Tax Issues,* SB45 ALI-ABA 389, 411–412 (1998).

[22] I.R.C. §6048(c)(1). The penalty for failure to report a distribution is 35 percent of the gross amount. I.R.C. §6677(a)(2). Additional penalties may be levied as well for chronic failure to report. *See also* IRS Forms 3520, 3520A. *See generally* Carlyn S. McCaffrey, Ellen K. Harrison & Elyse G. Kirschner, *U.S. Taxation of Foreign Trusts, Trusts with Non-U.S. Grantors and Their U.S. Beneficiaries,* SJ027 ALI-ABA 137 (2003).

her Form 1040.[23] United States persons must report to the IRS on Form 4789 cash transfers of $10,000 or more pursuant to Section 6039F.[24]

In addition, the Small Business Protection Act provides that a trustee must appoint a U.S. agent to accept service of process with respect to taxes or else the Treasury Secretary may determine the tax consequences under the grantor trust rules.[25] For a more in-depth treatment of the subject of the taxation by the United States of certain foreign trusts and the reporting obligations of their settlors, trustees, and beneficiaries, the reader is referred to Howard M. Zaritsky and Jeffrey A. Schoenblum.[26]

§6.3.2 SEC Filings

When the trust acquires voting rights or a power of disposition over more than 5 percent of a class of registered securities, the trustee *may* have to report the event to the Securities and Exchange Commission, the issuer, and each exchange on which the security is traded.[27] The same may be necessary when the trust acquires voting rights or a power of disposition over more than 10 percent of a class of registered securities.[28] If the trustee proposes to sell restricted securities or control securities, the trustee or the trust itself could be deemed a statutory underwriter. "If so, the sale must be made pursuant to an effective registration statement or the . . . [trustee] . . . must determine that some exemption from registration other than Section 4(1) . . . [of the Securities Act] . . . is available."[29] More often than not, registration can be avoided if the sale meets the requirements of SEC Rule 144. "A family office pooled investment vehicle may fall within the definition of an investment company, and, if it does, it will be subject to registration with the SEC unless an exemption from registration is available or the SEC issues an order that declares that the investment vehicle is not an investment company."[30] As to whether the trustee, himself, needs to register with the Commission as an investment advisor, see Section 8.15.10 of this handbook.

---

[23] I.R.C. §6048(c). *See also* I.R.C. §6677(a).

[24] *See* I.R.C. §6039F. In addition, the U.S. person is subject to a penalty equal to 5 percent of the amount of the gift for each month the failure continues, not to exceed 25 percent of the amount. I.R.C. §6039F.

[25] *See* I.R.C. §6048(b)(2)(B). *See generally* §9.1 of this handbook (the grantor trust).

[26] Howard M. Zaritsky, 854-2nd T.M., U.S. Taxation of Foreign Estates, Trusts and Beneficiaries, and Howard M. Zaritsky, 911-2nd T.M., U.S. Taxation of Foreign Estates, Trusts and Beneficiaries (each containing forms and worksheets in the Appendix); Jeffrey A. Schoenblum, 2 Multistate and Multinational Estate Planning 456–493 (2000).

[27] 17 C.F.R. §240.13d-1 (2004). *See generally* American Bar Association, A Fiduciary's Guide to Federal Securities Laws 61–62 (1994).

[28] *See generally* American Bar Association, A Fiduciary's Guide to Federal Securities Laws (1994). Some states may require their own filings. If a SEC report has been triggered, local law should be consulted.

[29] American Bar Association, A Fiduciary's Guide to Federal Securities Laws 8 (1994). *See generally* §7.3.4.2 of this handbook (criminal and civil liability under the securities laws).

[30] Audrey C. Talley, *Family Offices: Securities and Commodities Law Issues*, 34 ACTEC L.J. 284, 287–288 (2009).

§6.3.3   Bank Regulatory Filings

Each national bank that exercises fiduciary powers must periodically submit reports to myriad governmental agencies, including the Comptroller of the Currency. The Treasury Department, the Commerce Department, as well as the Office of Management and Budget, FDIC, and the Federal Reserve Board require certain fiduciaries to make periodic general reports of their activities.[31]

A bank that fails to file such regulatory documentation when required to do so may be subject to federal prosecution. Moreover, it may not be reimbursed from trust assets for any penalties and fees incurred as a result of such failure to file.

§6.3.4   Uniform Probate Code §7-101 Registration with the Court [now withdrawn/repealed]

Section 7-101 of the Uniform Probate Code [now withdrawn/repealed] would have imposed on a trustee the duty to register the trust in an appropriate court located at the trust's principal place of administration. This duty to register applied not only to trustees of testamentary trusts but also to trustees of inter vivos trusts.[32] No exception was made for trust declarations or oral trusts.[33] A provision in the terms of the trust purporting to relieve the trustee of this registration obligation would have been ineffective.[34] The registration, which would have taken the form of a "statement" of acknowledgement of trusteeship, would, among other things, have disclosed the trustee's name and address.[35] "The statement shall identify the trust: (1) in the case of a testamentary trust, by the name of the testator and the date and place of domiciliary probate; (2) in the case of a written inter vivos trust, by the name of each settlor and the original trustee and the date of the trust instrument; or (3) in the case of an oral trust, by information identifying the settlor or other source of funds and describing the time and manner of the trust's creation and the terms of the trust, including the subject matter, beneficiaries and time of performance."[36] Any trustee who failed to so register would have risked removal, denial of compensation, and/or surcharge.[37]

---

[31] For a list of these reports, *see* Victor P. Whitney, 2 Trust Dept. Admin. & Operations §15.20 (Updated on Lexis 2004).

[32] UPC §7-102 [withdrawn/repealed].

[33] UPC §7-102 [withdrawn/repealed].

[34] UPC §7-104 [withdrawn/repealed].

[35] UPC §7-102 [withdrawn/repealed].

[36] UPC §7-102 [withdrawn/repealed].

[37] UPC §7-104 [withdrawn/repealed]; *cf.* §7.2.3 of this handbook (types of relief (equitable remedies)).

CHAPTER **7**

Liabilities Incident to the Trust Relationship

§7.1 Trustee's Liabilities Generally (Breaches of Trust; Beneficiary's Standing to Seek Judicial Relief; Defenses; Equitable Excuses; Remedies)

Definitions. A breach of trust is a violation by the trustee of any duty that as trustee he owes to the beneficiary.[1] The trustee's internal liabilities are sanctions imposed on the trustee by the court in the exercise of its equitable powers as a consequence of the trustee's breaching at least one internal duty that the trustee owes to beneficiaries and/or the trust's purposes. A trustee who commences to engage in activity that could constitute a breach of trust is exposing himself to the possibility of liability. Whether a trustee's "liability" is realized or potential depends upon the context in which the word is employed. A trustee's liability to third parties in his capacity as the holder of the legal title to the entrusted property is an external liability.

The trustee who breaches no internal duty exposes himself to no internal liability.[2] The Restatement (Third) of Trusts is in accord.[3] That having been said, "[w]hen the administration of a trust produces a profit, whether there has or has not been a breach of trust, the trustee is accountable for the profit, including any income, realized gains, and unrealized appreciation in the value of the trust property," notwithstanding the fact that legal title to the entrusted property is in the trustee.[4] "This accountability reflects the fundamental principle that value generated by the trust estate and trust activities belongs to the trust, not to the trustee personally, and is to be held or applied for trust purposes."[5]

Breaches of trust. The trustee is liable to the beneficiary for injury caused by negligent and intentional breaches of trust. There are some internal breaches of trust, however, for which the trustee may be held absolutely liable even when acting in good faith. The trustee, for example, has traditionally been absolutely liable for injury to the beneficiary's equitable interest occasioned by misdelivery,[6] or by the trustee's misconstruing the nature and extent of the

---

§7.1 [1] Restatement (Second) of Trusts §201. *See generally* Chapter 6 of this handbook (the trustee's duties).

[2] 3 Scott & Ascher §16.1 The statement is not entirely accurate. It is conceivable that the trustee could incur external liability, that is, liability to third parties, without breaching any duty to the beneficiaries.

[3] Restatement (Third) of Trusts §99.

[4] Restatement (Third) of Trusts §99 cmt. c.

[5] Restatement (Third) of Trusts §99 cmt. c.

[6] *See generally* 4 Scott & Ascher §24.31 (Liability for Incorrect Distributions). *See, e.g.,* Stowers v. Norwest Bank Ind., N.A., 624 N.E.2d 485 (Ind. Ct. App. 1993) (holding trustee liable for distributing trust property *per capita* rather than *per stirpes* as required by the governing instrument, notwithstanding beneficiary's failure to object to the erroneous distribution when it was proposed). *See generally* Restatement (Second) of Trusts §226 cmts. a, b; Annot., *Payment or distribution under invalid instruction as breach of trust*, 6 A.L.R. 4th 1196 (1981). Note, however, that the Uniform Trust Code would not impose absolute liability on the trustee for misdelivery. *See*

trustee's powers.[7] One who has been unjustly enriched by the misdelivery, however, would be obliged to indemnify the trustee, or otherwise make restitution.[8]

There are also some breaches for which the trustee may be held liable even in the absence of a causal connection between the injury and the breach,[9] such as the failure to segregate and earmark[10] and engaging in unauthorized acts of self-dealing,[11] although the trend of the law is to relieve trustees of some of this internal absolute liability.[12] As a general rule, the trustee is not liable to the

---

UTC §1007 (available at <http://www.uniformlaws.org/Act.aspx?title=Trust%20Code>) (providing that if the happening of an event, including marriage, divorce, performance of educational requirements, or death, affects the administration or distribution of a trust, a trustee who has exercised reasonable care to ascertain the happening of the event is not liable for a loss resulting from the trustee's lack of knowledge).

[7] *See* 4 Scott & Ascher §24.31 (Liability for Incorrect Distributions); Restatement (Second) of Trusts §201 cmt. b; R. D. Hursh, Annot., *Trustee's liability for payments of trust funds to one whose interest has terminated*, 48 A.L.R.2d 1252 (1956).

[8] Restatement of Restitution §163 ("Where the owner of property transfers it as a result of a mistake of such a character that he is entitled to restitution, the transferee holds the property upon a constructive trust for him"); Restatement (Third) of Restitution and Unjust Enrichment §17 (fiduciary misdeliveries). *See generally* §7.2.3.1.6 of this handbook (the constructive trust as a procedural equitable remedy).

[9] *See generally* 3 Scott on Trusts §205.1.

[10] *See* Restatement (Third) of Trusts: Prudent Investor Rule §205 cmt. f. *See, e.g.*, In re Hodges' Estate, 28 A. 663 (1894) (holding a trustee who had made a loan partly of trust money and partly of his own in exchange for a note made payable to the trustee individually liable for any loss of interest on the trust money, whatever may have been the reason or motive that prompted the transaction). The earmarking requirement "is designed to protect the trustee from temptation, from the hazard of loss, and of being a possible defaulter, as well as to protect the trust fund." In re Hodges' Estate, 28 A. 663, 664 (1894). *See also* Kirby v. Frank, 132 N.J. Eq. 378, 28 A.2d 267 (1942) (sustaining a master's report fixing indebtedness of a cemetery superintendent to cemetery where it was unclear what were personal transactions and what were cemetery transactions). "Where a trustee co-mingles funds of a *cestui que trust* with those of his own, the court will hold such trustee to a strict accountability and any doubt will be resolved against the trustee." Kirby v. Frank, 132 N.J. Eq. 378, 28 A.2d 267 (1942). If the trustee deposits in a bank trust funds in his, her, or its name without disclosing the fiduciary capacity, the trustee will be treated as a guarantor of the solvency of the bank, even though due care was used in the choice of the bank and the funds were not in any way misused. *See generally* 2A Scott on Trusts §180.2; Bogert §§596, 598.

[11] *See, e.g.*, Mosser v. Darrow, 341 U.S. 267 (1951) (reorganization trustee held personally liable for permitting key employees to profit from trading in securities of the debtors' subsidiaries, whether or not the trust was harmed or the trustee benefited thereby); Slay v. Burnett Trust, 143 Tex. 621, 187 S.W.2d 377 (1945) (holding that in an action by a successor trustee against a predecessor trustee for "secret profits" from the trust estate, recovery may be had on behalf of the beneficiary whether or not the trustee acted in good faith and whether or not the trust was harmed thereby, the profits having resulted from a loan of trust funds to buy units in an oil syndicate in receivership); In re Kline, 59 A.2d 14 (N.J. 1948) (confirming that the rule that a trustee may not self-deal in matters pertaining to the trust "operates irrespectively of the good faith or bad faith of such dealing").

[12] *See, e.g.*, Griffin v. Griffin, 463 So. 2d 569 (Fla. Ct. App. 1985) (there being abundant evidence on the record to support the trial court's finding that the trustees' monthly payments to non-income beneficiaries were made in good faith and without malice, the trustees held not personally liable for these disbursements). *See also* UTC §1007 (available at <http://www.uniformlaws. org/Act.aspx?title=Trust%20Code>) (mitigating misdelivery exposure by providing that if the

beneficiary if the trust sustains economic injury (*e.g.*, investment losses or poor investment performance), unless there has been a breach of trust.[13] Thus, if the trust property is stolen through no fault of the trustee, the trustee is not liable.[14]

Generally, mistakes as to the law and in the interpretation of the terms of the trust are no excuse.[15] "A trustee commits a breach of trust not only where he violates a duty in bad faith, or intentionally although in good faith, or negligently, but also where he violates a duty because of a mistake as to the extent of his duties and powers."[16] When in doubt as to the terms of the trust, the trustee can always protect himself by obtaining instructions from the court.[17]

Under the common law, the trustee, as holder of the legal title to the trust property, is liable in contract and in tort to third parties (nonbeneficiaries) as if the trustee were the absolute owner of the property,[18] although under certain circumstances indemnification and reimbursement from the trust estate for such third-party liability may be possible.[19] This we refer to as the trustee's external liability.[20]

Standing to seek judicial relief for a breach of trust. Standing is the right or capacity to initiate a suit. All beneficiaries have standing to bring a petition to

---

happening of an event, including marriage, divorce, performance of educational requirements, or death, affects the administration or distribution of a trust, a trustee who has exercised reasonable care to ascertain the happening of an event is not liable for a loss resulting from the trustee's lack of knowledge); Restatement (Second) of Trusts §179 cmt. d (providing that a trustee is not liable for the failure to earmark where the loss is unconnected with the failure to earmark, "except in a situation where as a matter of policy an absolute liability is imposed upon the trustee in order to deter him from committing such a breach of trust").

[13] 4 Scott & Ascher §24.8. *But see* UTC §706 cmt. (available at <http://www.uniformlaws.org/Act.aspx?title=Trust%20Code>) (suggesting that a persistent failure to administer the trust effectively might include a long-term pattern of mediocre performance, such as consistently poor investment results when compared to comparable trusts).

[14] 4 Scott & Ascher §24.8 (Nonliability for Loss in the Absence of a Breach of Trust).

[15] Restatement (Second) of Trusts §201 cmt. b. *See generally* 4 Scott & Ascher §24.31 (Liability for Incorrect Distributions). On the other hand, "[w]hen the question whether the trustee has committed a breach of trust depends not upon the extent of his powers and duties, but upon whether he has acted with proper care or caution, the mere fact that he has made a mistake of fact or law in the exercise of his powers or performance of his duties does not render him liable for breach of trust . . . [in the absence of negligence on his part]. . . ." Restatement (Second) of Trusts §201 cmt. c. "Thus, if the trustee is authorized to invest funds in such securities as a prudent man would purchase, he is not liable if he invests in bonds which on the facts known to him are the sort in which prudent men would invest, although, owing to facts which he did not know and was not negligent in not knowing, the bonds were not in fact properly secured." Restatement (Second) of Trusts §201 cmt. c.

[16] Restatement (Second) of Trusts §201 cmt. b; 4 Scott & Ascher §24.5 (What Constitutes a Breach of Trust).

[17] *See, e.g.,* 4 Scott & Ascher §24.31 (Liability for Incorrect Distributions).

[18] *See generally* Bogert §§712 (Contractual Liability), 731 (Tort Liability); Restatement (Second) of Trusts §261; 3A Scott on Trusts §261. *See generally* §3.5.1 of this handbook (nature and extent of the trustee's estate).

[19] *See* §3.5.2.3 of this handbook (trustee's equitable right to exoneration and reimbursement from the trust estate).

[20] *See generally* §7.3 of this handbook (trustee's liability as legal owner to nonbeneficiaries).

the court to remedy a trustee's breach of fiduciary duty,[21] provided there is no one of full age and legal capacity who possesses a right of revocation or power of withdrawal.[22] While a trust is revocable and the settlor has capacity to revoke the trust, however, the rights of the beneficiaries are subject to the control of, and the duties of the trustee are owed exclusively to, the settlor.[23] Then it is only the settlor who has standing to bring such a petition. Also, anyone with a power of withdrawal who is of full age and legal capacity is deemed a settlor for standing purposes, at least to the extent of the property subject to the power.[24] Otherwise, anyone who has a present or future beneficial interest in a trust, whether vested or contingent,[25] would have standing to bring the petition. This would include the following in addition to those who take their interests pursuant to the terms of the trust:

- Assignees of the equitable interest;[26]
- Appointees pursuant to exercise of powers of appointment;[27]
- Takers upon the imposition of a resulting trust;[28]
- Creditors of the beneficiary who have enforceable claims against the equitable interest; and
- Takers pursuant to the terms of an antilapse statute.[29]

The Uniform Trust Code broadens the common law concept of trust beneficiary for standing purposes to include someone other than the trustee who holds a power of appointment over the trust property, even a nongeneral testamentary power of appointment.[30] "Holders of powers are included on the assumption that their interests are significant enough that they should be afforded the rights of beneficiaries."[31] Again, during those periods when

---

[21] UTC §1001 cmt. (available at <http://www.uniformlaws.org/Act.aspx?title=Trust%20Code>).

[22] *See generally* Lewin ¶ 38-11 (*locus standi* to be a claimant to secure the trust property).

[23] UTC §603(a) (available at <http://www.uniformlaws.org/Act.aspx?title=Trust%20Code>).

[24] UTC §603(c (available at <http://www.uniformlaws.org/Act.aspx?title=Trust%20Code>)

[25] UTC §103(2) (available at <http://www.uniformlaws.org/Act.aspx?title=Trust%20Code>).

[26] UTC §103 cmt. (available at <http://www.uniformlaws.org/Act.aspx?title=Trust%20Code>).

[27] UTC §103 cmt. (available at <http://www.uniformlaws.org/Act.aspx?title=Trust%20Code>). Takers in default of exercise of a power of appointment take pursuant to the terms of the trust.

[28] UTC §103 cmt. (available at <http://www.uniformlaws.org/Act.aspx?title=Trust%20Code>). *See generally* §4.1.1.1 of this handbook (defining the resulting trust).

[29] UTC §103 cmt. (available at <http://www.uniformlaws.org/Act.aspx?title=Trust%20Code>).

[30] UTC §103 cmt. (available at <http://www.uniformlaws.org/Act.aspx?title=Trust%20Code>).

[31] UTC§103 cmt. (available at <http://www.uniformlaws.org/Act.aspx?title=Trust%20Code>).

someone of full age and legal capacity possesses a right of revocation or right of withdrawal, only one person has standing to bring a petition to remedy the trustee's breach of fiduciary duty: the one who possesses that right. All other powers of appointment are deemed nonexistent for standing purposes.

A trustee has standing to bring a petition to remedy a cotrustee's breach of trust.[32] A successor trustee would have standing to sue a predecessor for breach of trust.[33] Likewise, a trustee designated to receive a portion of someone's probate estate would have standing to sue the personal representative for any breach of fiduciary duty that compromised the pour-over.[34]

For a discussion of the standing of the settlor of a noncharitable trust who has reserved no power or beneficial interest to bring an action against the trustee for breach of fiduciary duty, see Section 4.1.2 of this handbook. For a discussion of the standing of the settlor of a charitable trust, see Section 4.1.1.2.

The attorney general of the state that has jurisdiction over a particular charitable trust has standing to maintain a proceeding to seek its enforcement.[35] This has been the tradition both in England and the United States.[36] Blackstone discusses the source of the attorney general's power:

> The king, as parens patriae, has the general superintendence of all charities; which he exercises by the keeper of his conscience, the chancellor. And therefore, whenever it is necessary, the attorney general, at the relation of some informant, (who is usually called the relator) files ex officio an information in the court of chancery to have the charity properly established.[37]

Parens patriae, literally parent of the country, refers traditionally to the role of the state as sovereign and guardian of persons under legal disability, such as juveniles or the insane.[38] It is a concept of standing utilized to protect those

---

[32] UTC §1001 cmt. (available at <http://www.uniformlaws.org/Act.aspx?title=Trust%20Code>). *See* Restatement (Second) of Trusts §224; Lee R. Russ, J.D., Annot., *Award of attorneys' fees out of trust estate in action by trustee against cotrustee*, 24 A.L.R.4th 624 (1983); F. M. English, Annot., *Right of coexecutor or trustee to retain independent legal counsel*, 66 A.L.R.2d 1169 (1959); UTC §703(g)(1) & (2) (available at <http://www.uniformlaws.org/Act.aspx?title=Trust%20Code>) (providing that each trustee shall exercise reasonable care to prevent a cotrustee from committing a serious breach of trust and to compel a cotrustee to redress a serious breach of trust).

[33] UTC §1001 cmt. (available at <http://www.uniformlaws.org/Act.aspx?title=Trust%20Code>).

[34] *See, e.g.,* In re First Nat'l Bank of Mansfield, 37 Ohio St. 2d 60, 307 N.E.2d 23 (1974) (holding a testamentary trustee personally liable for the value of a nonrefundable state inheritance tax overpayment by the personal representative).

[35] Restatement (Second) of Trusts §391. "In some States the local district or country attorney can maintain such a suit." Restatement (Second) of Trusts §391 cmt. "Such a duty may be maintained either with or without a relator." Restatement (Second) of Trusts §391 cmt. "When a suit is brought by the Attorney General on the relation of a third person, the relator is liable for the costs which would otherwise have to be paid by the State." Restatement (Second) of Trusts §391 cmt. A relator is a beneficially interested person on whose behalf the sovereign or a state brings an action.

[36] *See generally* Jackson v. Phillips, 96 Mass. (14 Allen) 539, 579 (1867).

[37] 3 Blackstone, Commentaries 427.

[38] Black's Law Dictionary 1114 (6th ed. 1990).

quasi-sovereign interests such as health, comfort, and welfare of the people, interstate water rights, and the like.[39] Although some courts in the United States do not subscribe to the doctrine of *parens patriae* as being the source of an attorney general's authority in relation to charitable trusts,[40] most do.[41]

The Uniform Trust Code affords the attorney general the status of a beneficiary for such purposes as receiving notice of a transfer of the trust's principal place of administration, notice of a trust division or combination, notice of a trustee's resignation, and notice of a trustee's annual report or accounting.[42]

Charitable organizations expressly mandated to receive distributions under the terms of a trust have standing to seek enforcement of the trust.[43] According to Professor Scott, individuals having a special interest in the performance of a charitable trust can maintain a suit for its enforcement.[44] They, however, must show that their interest is not merely derived from their status as members of the general public. Thus, the incumbent of an endowed chair at a medical research facility would have standing to seek enforcement of the endowment trust.[45] Rights of enforcement also would accrue to a minister entitled to income distributions from a clergy support trust.[46]

The subject of who has standing to enforce charitable trusts is also addressed in Section 9.4.2 of this handbook.

7.1.1 Defenses to Breach-of-Trust Claims

Depending upon the particular facts and circumstances, legal and equitable defenses may be available to a trustee who has been sued for a breach of his trust.

7.1.2 Defenses to Allegations That the Trustee Breached the Duty of Loyalty; Informed Consent, Release, Ratification, and Affirmance

Clearly, the position of the Bank as trustee of, and at the same time creditor secured by, the trust assets gave rise to a conflict of interest incompatible with its duty of undivided loyalty to

---

[39] Black's Law Dictionary 1114 (6th ed. 1990).

[40] *See, e.g.,* Powers v. First Nat'l Bank of Corsicana, 138 Tex. 604, 161 S.W.2d 273 (1942).

[41] *See, e.g.,* State v. Taylor, 58 Wash. 2d 252, 362 P.2d 247 (1961); Late Corp. of the Church of Jesus Christ of Latter-Day Saints v. United States, 136 U.S. 1 (1890); Wallace v. Graff, 104 F. Supp. 925 (D.C. 1952); In re Quinn's Estate, 156 Cal. App. 2d 684, 320 P.2d 219 (1958); In re Katz's Estate, 40 N.J. Super. 103, 122 A.2d 185 (1956).

[42] UTC §110(c) (available at <http://www.uniformlaws.org/Act.aspx?title=Trust%20 Code>).

[43] UTC §110(b) (available at <http://www.uniformlaws.org/Act.aspx?title=Trust%20 Code>). *See also* Restatement (Second) of Trusts §391 cmt.

[44] 4A Scott on Trusts §391. *See also* Restatement (Second) of Trusts §391.

[45] 4A Scott on Trusts §391.

[46] 4A Scott on Trusts §391. *See also* Restatement (Second) of Trusts §391 cmt. c.

its trust. . . . This liability may be avoided only if it can be shown that . . . [the settlor-beneficiary] . . . consented to the transaction with full knowledge of all relevant facts and complete awareness of the resultant divided loyalty and its possible consequences.[47]

Breaches of the duty of loyalty. A trustee owes a duty of undivided loyalty to the beneficiaries. Thus, a sale, encumbrance, or other transaction involving the investment of the trust property entered into by the trustee for the trustee's own personal account, or which is otherwise affected by a conflict between his fiduciary and personal interests, is generally voidable[48] by those who possess the equitable interests.[49] The burden is on the trustee to prove the beneficiary's informed consent.[50]

The trustee's defenses. The fairness of the transaction is generally not a defense.[51] One or more of the following defenses, however, may be available to the trustee, depending upon the facts and circumstances of the transaction:

- The transaction is authorized by the terms of the trust.[52]
- The transaction was approved by the court.[53]

---

[47] Cohen v. First Camden Nat'l Bank & Trust Co., 51 N.J. 11, 18–19, 237 A.2d 257, 261 (1967).

[48] Equity is more flexible and "less severe" when an affiliate of the trustee transacts with the trust estate than when the trustee, himself, does so. A transaction involving the investment or management of the property of the trust is only presumed to be affected by a conflict between personal and fiduciary interests if it is entered into by the trustee with his spouse, descendants, siblings, parents, agents, or attorneys. *See* UTC §802(c) (available at <http://www.uniformlaws.org/Act.aspx?title=Trust%20Code>). The presumption is also raised if the transaction is with a corporation or other person or enterprise in which the trustee, or a person that owns a significant interest in the trustee, has an interest that might affect the trustee's best judgment. *See* UTC §802(c)(4). A transaction with the spouse of a descendant, sibling, or parent of the fiduciary will raise the presumption as well. *See* UTC §802(c)(2). The trustee has the burden of proving that the trustee's duty of loyalty has not been breached by his allowing his affiliates to transact with the trust estate, or that the beneficiaries have given their informed consent to the transactions, assuming they would otherwise constitute a breach of *the trustee's* duty of loyalty. *See* Restatement of Restitution §191. cmt. a.

[49] UTC §802(b) (available at <http://www.uniformlaws.org/Act.aspx?title=Trust%20 Code>).

[50] Restatement of Restitution §191, cmt. a; Restatement (Third) of Trusts §97 cmt. e.

[51] This is referred to as the "no further inquiry rule." *See generally* UTC §802 cmt. (available on at <http://www.uniformlaws.org/Act.aspx?title=Trust%20Code>); §6.1.3 of this handbook (trustee's duty of loyalty to the beneficiaries or to the trust's charitable purposes), §8.15.30 of this handbook (the no-further-inquiry rule), and §8.24 of this handbook (who has the burden of proof in an action for breach of trust brought by the beneficiary against the trustee).

[52] *See* UTC §802(b)(1) (available at <http://www.uniformlaws.org/Act.aspx?title=Trust%20 Code>); Restatement (Third) of Trusts §78, cmt. c(2); 3 Scott & Ascher §17.2.11 (noting that "[e]ven if the terms of the trust plainly authorize the trustee to deal with himself or herself, the trustee always must act fairly and in good faith"); Lewin ¶ 20-51 (England).

[53] *See* UTC §802(b)(2) (available at <http://www.uniformlaws.org/Act.aspx?title=Trust%20 Code>); Lewin ¶ 20-53 (England); 3 Scott & Ascher §17.2.12 (U.S.). *See also* Restatement (Third) of Trusts §78, cmt. c(1) (suggesting that "[i]n many situations involving a conflict of a trustee's fiduciary duties and personal interests, especially in significant matters involving complexity and business judgment, the interests of sound administration may be better served if the court were to appoint a trustee ad litem . . . to reach a decision on the matter in question and then, if

- An action is not brought against the trustee within the time allowed.[54]
- Those with the equitable interests gave informed consent to the trustee's action.[55]
- Those with the equitable interests ratified the transaction.[56]
- Those with the equitable interests released the trustee from liability.[57]
- The transaction involves a contract entered into or claim acquired by the trustee before the person became or contemplated becoming a trustee.[58]

---

appropriate, to arrange the terms of the transaction and its implementation"); 3 Scott & Ascher §17.2.12 (or the court might appoint another trustee, "who has no conflict of interest, to deal with a particular asset or proposed transaction").

[54] *See* §7.1.3 of this handbook (defense of failure of beneficiary to take timely action against trustee) and §8.15.70 of this handbook (laches doctrine generally); UTCe §802(b)(3) (available at <http://www.uniformlaws.org/Act.aspx?title=Trust%20Code>). "Claims may be barred by principles such as estoppel and laches arising in equity under the common law of trusts." UTC §1005 cmt. *See generally* §5.5 of this handbook (voluntary or involuntary loss of the beneficiary's rights). The UTC creates two limitation periods for actions by beneficiaries against trustees, a one-year period and a five-year period. A beneficiary may not commence a proceeding against a trustee for breach of trust more than one year after the date the beneficiary or representative of the beneficiary was sent a report that adequately disclosed the existence of a potential claim for breach of trust and informed the beneficiary of the time allowed for commencing a proceeding. *See* UTC §1005(a). Otherwise, a judicial proceeding by a beneficiary against a trustee for breach of trust must be commenced within five years after the first to occur of the removal, resignation, or death of the trustee; the termination of the beneficiary's interest in the trust; or the termination of the trust. *See* UTC §1005(c). *See also* Lewin ¶ 20-54 (England).

[55] *See* UTC §802(b)(4) (available at <http://www.uniformlaws.org/Act.aspx?title=Trust%20 Code>); Restatement (Third) of Trusts §78 cmt. c(3) and §97; Restatement of Restitution §191; §5.5 of this handbook (voluntary or involuntary loss of the beneficiary's rights); 3 Scott & Ascher §17.2.1 (citing to Fox v. Mackreth, Bro. C.C. 400 (1788), a venerable English informed consent case); 4 Scott & Ascher §24.21 (Consent of Beneficiary). For a discussion of the authority of holders of certain types of powers of appointment to consent to breaches of trust, *see* §8.14 of this handbook (guardian ad litem and virtual representation issues); Lewin ¶ 20-52 (England).

[56] *See* UTC §802(b)(4) (available at <http://www.uniformlaws.org/Act.aspx?title=Trust%20 Code>); Restatement (Third) of Trusts §78 cmt. c(3); §5.5 of this handbook (voluntary or involuntary loss of the beneficiary's rights); 3 Scott & Ascher §17.2.1 (citing to Fox v. Mackreth, Bro. C.C. 400 (1788), a venerable English informed consent case); 4 Scott & Ascher §24.21 (Consent of Beneficiary). For a discussion of the authority of holders of certain types of powers of appointment to consent to breaches of trust, *see* §8.14 of this handbook (guardian ad litem and virtual representation issues); Lewin ¶ 20-52 (England).

[57] *See* UTC §802(b)(4) (available at <http://www.uniformlaws.org/Act.aspx?title=Trust%20 Code>); Restatement (Third) of Trusts §78 cmt. c(3); §5.5 of this handbook (voluntary or involuntary loss of the beneficiary's rights); 3 Scott & Ascher §17.2.1 (citing to Fox v. Mackreth, Bro. C.C. 400 (1788), a venerable English informed consent case); 4 Scott & Ascher §24.21 (Consent of Beneficiary). For a discussion of the authority of holders of certain types of powers of appointment to consent to breaches of trust, *see* §8.14 of this handbook (guardian ad litem and virtual representation issues); Lewin ¶ 20-52 (England).

[58] *See* UTC §802(b)(5) (available at <http://www.uniformlaws.org/Act.aspx?title=Trust%20 Code>). "In implementing the contract or pursuing the claim, the trustee must still complete the transaction in a way that avoids conflict between the trustee's fiduciary and personal interests." UTC §802 cmt. "Because avoiding such a conflict will frequently be difficult, the trustee should consider petitioning the court to appoint a special fiduciary . . . to work out the details and complete the transaction." Uniform Trust Code §802 cmt.

The particular defenses of informed consent, release, ratification, and affirmance. A beneficiary's consent to a breach of trust, such as unauthorized acts of self-dealing, may be given before or at the time of the trustee's act or omission.[59] A release, ratification, or affirmance occurs when a beneficiary "subsequently, with knowledge of the breach, affirms a trustee's improper conduct or agrees to discharge the trustee from liability."[60] In this section, as well as in Section 7.1.3, the term *consent* is employed broadly to encompass both beneficiary-consent to a breach of trust given before the breach has occurred and beneficiary-consent to a breach of trust given after the breach has occurred, the latter technically bring a release, ratification, or affirmance.

As noted above, a trustee may enter into a self-dealing transaction involving the trust property if the beneficiary has given informed consent.[61] The beneficiary, of course, must be of full age and legal capacity,[62] and there must be an absence of undue influence on the part of the trustee.[63] Even "over-persuasion" may be problematic.[64] For the consent to be informed, however, the beneficiary must "know"[65] or have "complete awareness"[66] of the material facts[67] and critical law,[68] to include the "possible consequences"[69] of the trustee's divided loyalties. In other words, there must be "full knowledge."[70] As

---

[59] *See* Restatement (Third) of Trusts §97 cmt. b.

[60] Restatement (Third) of Trusts §97 cmt. b.

[61] Restatement (Third) of Trusts §97 cmt. b; Restatement of Restitution §191. *See, e.g.,* In re Gillies' Will, 98 N.Y.S.2d 853 (1950) (involving the effectiveness of a beneficiary's waiver and release when a portion of the trust estate constituted stock in the corporate cotrustee).

[62] *See generally* 4 Scott & Ascher §24.21.3 (When Consent Is Effective); Restatement of Restitution §191, cmt. b.

[63] 5 Scott & Ascher §34.7 (Conveyance by Beneficiary to Trustee); Restatement of Restitution §191, cmt. d; Restatement (Third) of Trusts §97(c).

[64] Restatement of Restitution §191, cmt. d. ("Thus, the transaction can be set aside where the fiduciary over-persuades the beneficiary, even though he is not guilty of fraud, duress, or of conduct which would justify setting aside the transaction for undue influence if he were not a fiduciary").

[65] UTC §1009(2), (available at <http://www.uniformlaws.org/Act.aspx?title=Trust%20Code>); Restatement (Second) of Trusts §216(2)(b); Restatement of Restitution §191(2)(b).

[66] Cohen v. First Camden Nat'l Bank & Trust Co., 51 N.J. 11, 18, 237 A.2d 257, 261 (1967).

[67] 4 Scott & Ascher §24.21 (Consent of Beneficiary); Restatement of Restitution §191(2)(b) (beneficiary must know the material facts which the fiduciary knew or should have known).

[68] *See* 4 Scott & Ascher §24.21 (Consent of Beneficiary) (full knowledge of "legal rights" required); 3 Scott & Ascher §17.2.4 (noting that "[a] beneficiary's consent or acquiescence may bar the beneficiary from holding the trustee liable for improper lending of trust funds, but only if the beneficiary had full knowledge of the facts and his or her legal rights"); Restatement of Restitution §191, cmt. c ("If he knows or should know that the beneficiary is not aware of his rights, the fiduciary should inform him of his rights").

[69] Cohen v. First Camden Nat'l Bank & Trust Co., 51 N.J. 11, 18, 237 A.2d 257, 261 (1967).

[70] 4 Scott & Ascher §24.21 (Consent of Beneficiary); 3 Scott & Ascher §17.2.4 (When Trustee Borrows Trust Funds); 5 Scott & Ascher §34.7 (When Trustee Acquires the Equitable Interest from the Beneficiary); Restatement of Restitution §191(2)(b) (for a beneficiary's consent to be sufficiently informed, the beneficiary must "know his rights and the material facts which the fiduciary knew or should have known").

equitable rather than contractual principles must govern,[71] the test is a subjective one.[72] It is not enough that the trustee furnished the beneficiary with the requisite information.[73] The particular beneficiary in fact had to have understood the implications of the trustee's actions as well.[74] That having been said, the Restatement (Third) of Trusts provides that if the trustee reasonably believes that the beneficiary subjectively understands the relevant facts and applicable law, then the breaching trustee may well be off the hook. Here is the wording verbatim: "If . . . the trustee is led by the beneficiary reasonably to believe that the beneficiary is *aware of the relevant information and rights,* and the trustee acts in reliance on that belief, the beneficiary cannot hold the trustee liable even though the beneficiary was in fact insufficiently informed."[75]

As a general rule, the beneficiary's informed consent must be manifested by some affirmative act.

> Consent or ratification ordinarily requires more than mere failure of the beneficiary to object to conduct that the beneficiary was aware would or did constitute a breach of trust (but cf. . . . [laches doctrine] . . .); the consent or ratification is normally expressly communicated to the trustee, orally or by delivery of a writing, although the consent or ratification may be implied by the beneficiary's conduct in some circumstances.[76]

The doctrine of laches is taken up in Section 7.1.3 of this handbook. In Section 5.5 of this handbook we remind the reader that a trust beneficiary, *qua* beneficiary, generally owes the trustee no duties, fiduciary or otherwise.[77]

Burden of proof and constructive fraud. The burden is on the trustee to demonstrate that the beneficiary had actual and full knowledge of his or her legal rights.[78] Moreover, misrepresentations of the material facts and critical law by the trustee or his agents to the beneficiary could constitute constructive fraud.[79]

Informed consent of beneficiary's surrogate can bind the beneficiary. A beneficiary's duly appointed and duly authorized personal fiduciary (such as a guardian,

---

[71] Estate of Saxton, 712 N.Y.S.2d 225, 231, 274 A.D.2d 110, 119 (2000).

[72] Restatement of Restitution §191, cmt. b ("Thus, if a trustee purchases for himself trust property with the consent of the beneficiary who has just come of age, or is an aged person who has lost his capacity for exercising judgment, or a person wholly unfamiliar with business affairs, the transaction may be set aside").

[73] 4 Scott & Ascher §24.21 (Consent of Beneficiary); Restatement of Restitution §191(2)(b) (beneficiary must subjectively "know" his rights and the material facts).

[74] Restatement (Second) of Trusts §216 cmt. k.

[75] Restatement (Third) of Trusts §97 cmt. e (emphasis added).

[76] Restatement (Third) of Trusts §96 cmt. b.

[77] *See also* the introductory quotation to §5.5 of this handbook.

[78] Estate of Saxton, 712 N.Y.S.2d 225, 231, 274 A.D.2d 110, 119 (2000). *See generally* 4 Scott & Ascher §24.21 (Consent of Beneficiary); Restatement of Restitution §191, cmt. a (the burden is upon the trustee to prove that the beneficiary has given his or her informed consent to the self-dealing transaction); §8.24 of this handbook (who has the burden of proof in an action for breach of trust brought by the beneficiary against the trustee).

[79] *See generally* §8.15.59 of this handbook (constructive fraud in the trust context).

a conservator, or an agent acting under a power of attorney) may consent to the trustee's breach of trust in the stead of the beneficiary and in so doing bind the beneficiary. The personal fiduciary (himself, herself, or itself), however, must have had a subjective understanding of the relevant facts and applicable law pertaining to the breach for the proxy consent to be effective in taking the breaching trustee off the hook.[80]

As a general rule, the informed consent of a beneficiary to a breach of trust does not bind a nonconsenting cobeneficiary.[81] That having been said, the doctrine of virtual representation provides that under certain limited circumstances, a cobeneficiary may consent to a breach of trust and, in so doing, bind another cobeneficiary, though the consenting cobeneficiary is not acting in a fiduciary capacity, provided the consent is sufficiently informed and the interests of the cobeneficiaries are not in conflict.[82] The doctrine of virtual representation is taken up in Section 8.14 of this handbook. And, of course, the informed consent of the holder of a nonfiduciary general inter vivos power to appoint entrusted property, whether reserved or granted, binds all other beneficiaries under the trust, such a power being the equivalent of full ownership of the property.[83] This is the case even though legal title to the entrusted property is in the trustee.

The ACTEC exception. It is the position of the American College of Trust and Estate Counsel (ACTEC), however, that lawyer-trustees who enter into self-dealing transactions with their trusts are entitled to the benefit of an objective standard of informed consent: If the rules require a lawyer to obtain a client's informed consent, confirmed in writing, the lawyer should at the outset provide the client with information *sufficient to allow the client to understand the matter.*[84] This would constitute the type of "particular exception"[85] to the duty of undivided loyalty of an agent[86]

---

[80] Restatement (Third) of Trusts §97 cmt. d.

[81] *See* Restatement (Third) of Trusts §97 cmt. c(1).

[82] Restatement (Third) of Trusts §97 cmt. d.

[83] *See* Restatement (Third) of Trusts §97 cmt. c(2). *See also* §8.11 of this handbook (the rights and powers of the holder of a general inter vivos power of appointment).

[84] ACTEC Commentaries on the Model Rules of Professional Conduct 13 (4th ed. 2006) (ACTEC Commentary on MRPC 1.0). *But see* Restatement (Second) of Agency §393 cmt. a (subjective standard); Restatement of Restitution §191 (subjective standard); Webster v. Kelly, 175 N.E. 69, 71–72 (Mass. 1931) (subjective standard); Cleary v. Cleary, 692 N.E.2d 955 (Mass. 1988) (subjective standard); Model Rules of Professional Conduct, Rule 1.7, Official Comment (subjective standard). *Cf.* Pascale, Sr. v. Pascale, 113 N.J. 20, 37–38, 549 A.2d 782, 791 (1988) (subjective standard [in the context of a lawyer's simultaneously representing parties whose interests are in conflict]); In re Gillies' Will, 98 N.Y.S.2d 853, 858 (1950) (subjective standard [when a corporate trustee retains its own stock in the trust, the effectiveness of a beneficiary's waiver and release is conditioned in part on the beneficiary's actually understanding the applicable law]). *See also* 3 Scott & Ascher §17.2.4 (noting that a beneficiary's consent or acquiescence may bar the beneficiary from holding the trustee liable for improper lending of trust funds, but only if the beneficiary actually had full knowledge of the facts and his or her legal rights).

[85] Meinhard v. Salmon, 249 N.Y. 458, 464, 164 N.E. 545, 546 (1928) (Cardozo, C.J.).

[86] *See* Estate of Kramer, 2003 WL 22889500 (Pa. Com. Pl.), 23 Fiduc. Rep. 2d 245 (2003) (rejecting an objective standard of informed consent to a lawyer-trustee's drafting an exculpatory clause into the trust instrument, the scrivener being an agent-fiduciary of the settlor). *But see*

or trustee[87] that so concerned Justice Cardozo.[88] The reader should be aware, however, that ACTEC's objective standard of informed consent to such fiduciary self-dealing would relate to licensure regulation only, *i.e.*, the lawyer-trustee's relationship with the state.[89] It ought not to degrade the lawyer-trustee's internal equitable fiduciary relationship *with the trust beneficiary*.[90]

For purposes of any trustee's internal civil liability for engaging in self-dealing transactions with the trust estate, the test of whether the beneficiary has given informed consent remains a subjective one, *i.e.*, whether the particular beneficiary in fact understood in a general way (1) the material facts of and critical law that related to the proposed self-dealing transaction, (2) the effect, if any, that the transaction would likely have on the beneficiary's equitable property rights under the trust, and (3) that the beneficiary was free to abort the transaction by withholding consent.[91] The test of whether a beneficiary's ratification of a completed self-dealing transaction was sufficiently informed would be similarly subjective.

An "actual understanding" standard attempts to compensate for the information asymmetries that are inherent in the trustee-beneficiary fiduciary

---

Restatement of Restitution §191, cmt. c ("The beneficiary may in the case of some fiduciary relations, such as that of principal and agent, waive his right to have a full disclosure; thus, if the principal manifests that he knows all material facts or is willing to deal without knowing them, the agent is not under a duty to disclose them, and a transaction between the principal and agent will not be set aside because of the failure of the agent to disclose the facts").

[87] Restatement of Restitution §191, cmt. c.

[88] Meinhard v. Salmon, 249 N.Y. 458, 464, 164 N.E. 545, 546 (1928) (Cardozo, C.J.).

[89] *See generally* Charles E. Rounds, Jr., *Lawyer Codes Are Just About Licensure, the Lawyer's Relationship with the State: Recalling the Common Law Agency, Contract, Tort, Trust, and Property Principles the Regulate the Lawyer-Client Fiduciary Relationship*, 60 Baylor L. Rev. 771 (2008).

[90] *See generally* 4 Scott & Ascher §24.21 (Consent of Beneficiary); Charles E. Rounds, Jr., *Lawyer Codes Are Just About Licensure, the Lawyer's Relationship with the State: Recalling the Common Law Agency, Contract, Tort, Trust, and Property Principles the Regulate the Lawyer-Client Fiduciary Relationship*, 60 Baylor L. Rev. 771 (2008).

[91] Restatement (Second) of Agency §393 cmt. a (subjective standard); Restatement of Restitution §191, cmt. c (subjective standard); Webster v. Kelly, 175 N.E. 69, 71–72 (Mass. 1931) (subjective standard); Cleary v. Cleary, 692 N.E.2d 955 (Mass. 1988) (subjective standard); Model Rules of Professional Conduct, Rule 1.7, Official Comment (subjective standard). *Cf.* Pascale, Sr. v. Pascale, 113 N.J. 20, 37–38, 549 A.2d 782, 791 (1988) (subjective standard [in the context of a lawyer's simultaneously representing parties whose interests are in conflict]); In re Gillies' Will, 98 N.Y.S.2d 853, 858 (1950) (subjective standard [when a corporate trustee retains its own stock in the trust, the effectiveness of a beneficiary's waiver and release is conditioned in part on the beneficiary's actually understanding the applicable law]). *Cf.* 3 Scott & Ascher §18.1.4.3 (noting that regardless of whether the trustee has a power of sale, "no beneficiary who has consented to a sale can set it aside or hold the trustee liable for a breach of trust in making it, if the beneficiary was adult and competent and had knowledge of all relevant facts and of the beneficiary's legal rights and the trustee did not improperly induce consent"). If a trustee needs the subjective informed consent of a beneficiary to sell entrusted property to third parties in contravention of the terms of the trust, it seems logical that the trustee also would need the subjective informed consent of the beneficiary to engage in unauthorized self-dealing transactions that involve the trust estate.

relationship. The Restatement of Contracts is in accord,[92] as are the Restatement of Restitution[93] and the Restatement (Third) of Trusts, which would require that the consenting beneficiary have an actual "awareness" of the relevant facts and applicable law.[94] It is the price a trustee should pay for wanting to eat his cake and have it too, for eschewing the resignation option. In some cases, the physical, mental, or emotional state of the beneficiary, or perhaps the beneficiary's dearth of life experiences, will make it impossible for the beneficiary to give a consent that is sufficiently informed,[95] unless, of course, he or she is represented by fully informed independent counsel. The elderly woman with no business experience[96] and the "unsophisticated country lad, incapable of properly transacting his own business,"[97] come to mind.[98]

Fraud, duress, undue influence, or fiduciary abuse by the trustee. The trustee who by fraud, duress, undue influence, or "fiduciary abuse" induces a beneficiary to consent to a breach of trust remains liable for the breach.[99] "Fiduciary abuse may result if the trustee brings unwarranted pressure to bear on the beneficiary, for example, by threatening to withhold a distribution to which the beneficiary is entitled unless the beneficiary executes a release."[100]

The self-dealing transaction still must be fair and reasonable. Informed consent to a self-dealing transaction that is neither fair nor reasonable would still be problematic. If, for example, "a trustee purchases for himself trust property with the consent of the beneficiary, the beneficiary can set aside the sale if the price paid by the trustee was not in fact an adequate price, even though at the time of the sale the parties believed that it was adequate."[101] The Restatement (Third) of Trusts is in accord.[102]

---

[92] Restatement (Second) of Contracts §173(b) (providing that when a fiduciary makes a contract with his beneficiary relating to matters within the scope of the fiduciary relation, the contract is voidable unless all parties beneficially interested manifest assent with full understanding of their legal rights and of all relevant facts that the fiduciary knows or should know).

[93] Restatement of Restitution §191(2)(b) (a beneficiary cannot give informed consent to a self-dealing transaction without knowing his or her rights and the material facts).

[94] Restatement (Third) of Trusts §97(b).

[95] *See generally* 4 Scott & Ascher §24.21.3 (When Consent Is Ineffective); Restatement of Restitution §191, cmt. b.

[96] *See, e.g.,* Ball v. Hopkins, 167 N.E. 338 (Mass. 1929). *See generally* Restatement of Restitution §191, cmt. b.

[97] *See, e.g.,* Boehmer v. Silvertone, 186 P. 26 (Or. 1920). *See generally* Restatement of Restitution §191, cmt. b. ("Thus, if a trustee purchases for himself trust property with the consent of the beneficiary who has just come of age, or who is an aged person who has lost his capacity for exercising judgment, or a person wholly unfamiliar with business affairs, the transaction may be set aside").

[98] *See generally* 4 Scott & Ascher §24.21.3 ("Thus, a trustee relies, at the trustee's own risk, on the consent of a beneficiary who, although technically not under any legal incapacity, is especially vulnerable").

[99] Restatement (Third) of Trusts §97 cmt. f.

[100] Restatement (Third) of Trusts §97 cmt. f. Liability releases in the context of the nonjudicial settlement of trust accounts are discussed generally in §8.2.3 of this handbook.

[101] Restatement of Restitution §191, cmt. e.

[102] Restatement (Third) of Trusts §97 cmt. f.

English law. English informed consent doctrine and informed doctrine prevailing on this side of the Atlantic are generally in accord, at least in the trust context.[103]

Cross-references. For a discussion of the related issue of what constitutes informed consent to a lawyer serving as trustee of a trust when he or she has drafted the governing instrument, the so-called scrivener trustee problem, the reader is referred to Section 6.1.3.3 of this handbook.

§7.1.3 Defense of Failure of Beneficiary to Take Timely Action Against Trustee

At one end of the spectrum, the doctrine of laches applies where the claimant's delay in bringing proceedings makes it impossible for a fair trial of the action to take place, e.g., because of the loss or destruction of evidence. In that context, the defence of laches has much in common with the principle of procedure, which enables the court to strike out stale claims for want of prosecution. At the other end of the spectrum, the doctrine of laches applies where the claimant's delay induces the defendant to act on the basis that the claim will not be asserted or pursued. In that context, laches overlaps considerably with the doctrines of affirmation, acquiescence and estoppel.... [104]

"Claims may be barred by principles such as estoppel and laches arising in equity under the common law of trusts."[105] These two principles are easily confused. Moreover, the defense of laches is sometimes confused with the defense of acquiescence and the defense of acquiescence with the defense of estoppel.

Acquiescence. The defense of acquiescence, which rests upon the doctrine of election, is available to a trustee if a beneficiary, fully apprised of all the relevant facts and law, of full age and legal capacity, and under no undue influence, "stands by" and in so doing induces the trustee to believe that the beneficiary has assented to a breach of trust. The beneficiary, for example, would be well advised not to hold back to see whether an imprudent investment appreciates or depreciates in value. He or she should promptly either affirm the actions of the trustee or call the trustee to account.

Estoppel. A beneficiary cannot hold the trustee liable for a breach of trust if the beneficiary consents to the breach.[106] For the beneficiary to be "estopped" from holding the trustee liable, however, the beneficiary must have been fully apprised of the relevant facts and law and the trustee cannot have improperly induced the beneficiary to give consent. If, for example, the trustee transfers trust property to a third person in violation of the terms of the trust with the

---

[103] Lewin ¶ 20-128 (England).

[104] Tom Leech, *What Is Laches?*, Tr. & Est. L.J. (Dec. 2002) at i (pull-out).

[105] UTC §1005 cmt. (available at <http://www.uniformlaws.org/Act.aspx?title=Trust%20 Code>). *See generally* §5.5 of this handbook (voluntary or involuntary loss of the beneficiary's rights).

[106] *See generally* §5.5 of this handbook (voluntary or involuntary loss of the beneficiary's rights).

informed consent of the beneficiary, the beneficiary is precluded from holding the trustee liable, and also from retrieving the property from the third person. This is the case even when the third person is not a good-faith purchaser for value, *i.e.*, a bona fide purchaser (BFP).[107]

Laches and statutes of limitations that partially codify the laches doctrine. *While the trustee is in office.* For the beneficiary to be prevented by "laches" from holding the trustee liable for a breach of trust, the beneficiary must have so delayed in bringing an action against the trustee that it would be inequitable to permit the beneficiary to hold the trustee liable.[108] As a matter of public policy, suits should be brought with reasonable promptness.[109] With the passage of time, it becomes difficult to ascertain the truth.[110] The enforcement of a constructive trust also may be barred by laches.[111] Laches generally will not bar a beneficiary while under a legal incapacity, such as minority or incompetence, or bar the holder of an outstanding contingent equitable remainder interest until the intervening interest has expired.[112]

A cause of action against a trustee for breaches of the duty of loyalty (or any type of breach for that matter) would not be barred by laches until a reasonable time after all beneficiaries, both current beneficiaries and remaindermen, had become fully aware of the breach and its legal implications[113] and failed to take appropriate action.[114] The Restatement (Third) of Trusts is generally in

---

[107] *See, e.g.*, Mathews v. Thompson, 186 Mass. 14, 71 N.E. 93 (1904) (consent to transfer as gift to third person); Preble v. Greenleaf, 180 Mass. 79, 61 N.E. 808 (1901) (consent to transfer in payment of personal debt of trustee). *See generally* §5.4.2 of this handbook (rights of the beneficiary as against BFPs and other transferees of the underlying trust property), §8.3.2 of this handbook (the doctrine of bona fide purchase and its notice requirement), and §8.15.63 of this handbook (doctrine of bona fide purchase). *See also* §8.3.6 of this handbook (negotiable instruments and the duty of third parties to inquire into the trustee's authority). For a comparison of the BFP, a creature of equity, with the holder in due course, a creature of law, *see* §8.15.68 of this handbook (holders in due course in the trust context).

[108] 4 Scott & Ascher §24.24.1 (Laches); Restatement (Third) of Trusts §98 cmt. b(2) (delay prejudicial to trustee); §8.15.70 of this handbook (laches doctrine generally).

[109] 4 Scott & Ascher §24.24.1 (Laches).

[110] *See* Restatement (Third) of Trusts §98 cmt. b; §8.15.70 of this handbook (laches doctrine generally).

[111] *See generally* 3 Scott & Ascher §17.2.7; §3.3 of this handbook (involuntary trustees) (in part discussing the remedial constructive trust).

[112] *See* 4 Scott & Ascher §24.24.1; Restatement (Third) of Trusts §98 cmt. b(1); §8.15.70 of this handbook (laches doctrine generally).

[113] *See generally* §8.15.70 of this handbook (laches doctrine generally). *Cf.* 3 Scott & Ascher §17.2.4 (noting that a beneficiary's consent or acquiescence may bar the beneficiary from holding the trustee liable for improper lending of trust funds, but only if the beneficiary had full knowledge of the facts and his or her legal rights). Note, however, that if laches or the applicable statute of limitation forecloses the trustee from filing suit against a third party for harming the trust estate, so too are the remaindermen, including the unborn and unascertained, likely to be foreclosed. *See generally* §8.27 of this handbook (the difference between a legal life estate and an equitable life estate incident to a trust).

[114] *See, e.g.*, Lawson v. Haynes, 170 F.2d 741 (10th Cir. 1948). *See generally* Bogert §542(U); §5.5 of this handbook (voluntary or involuntary loss of the beneficiary's rights). For a discussion of the current state of the doctrine of laches in England, the reader is referred to Tom Leech, *What Is Laches?*, Tr. & Est. L.J. (Dec. 2002) at i (pull-out).

accord.[115] In one state, a remainderman has a reasonable time after his interest vests *in possession* to bring suit against the trustee for a breach of trust.[116] This would be the case even if he had become aware of the breach prior to the time of such vesting.[117]

To start the running of an applicable statute of limitations, it would generally require a subjective awareness *on the part of the beneficiary* of the relevant facts and law.[118] Statutes of limitations applicable to actions by beneficiaries against trustees for breaches of trust should be looked upon as little more than partial codifications of equity's laches doctrine.[119]

The trustee's duty to monitor investments. A trustee has a continuing duty to monitor trust investments and remove imprudent ones. This continuing duty exists separate and apart from the trustee's duty to exercise prudence in selecting investments at the outset.[120] In the face of such a "continuing duty," a statute of limitations that purports to set up a time defense to actions against trustees for imprudent investing is likely to be a paper tiger as a practical matter, absent special facts.[121] Fiduciary investing is discussed generally in Section 6.2.2.1 of this handbook.

Repudiating the trust. In the case of a breach of trust, it is a principle of equity that the laches period, or the applicable statute of limitations period, as the case may be, does not commence to run against the beneficiary until the trustee "openly" makes the beneficiary aware that he is "repudiating" his fiduciary duty not to be in breach of trust.[122] Thus, when one hears that the trustee has "repudiated" his trust, it is likely that he is openly in breach of one or more of his trustee duties, not that he has denied the very existence of, or

---

[115] Restatement (Third) of Trusts §98 cmt. b(1).

[116] Eldridge v. Eldridge, 398 S.C. 113, 728 S.E.2d 24 (2012).

[117] Eldridge v. Eldridge, 398 S.C. 113, 728 S.E.2d 24 (2012).

[118] *See generally* 4 Scott & Ascher §24.24.2 (Statutes of Limitations). *See, e.g.*, Beck v. Mueller, 848 N.W.2d 903 (Wis. Ct. App. 2014) (statute of limitations began to run against trust beneficiaries upon their failure to receive incremental distributions over time as expressly and unambiguously required by terms of governing trust instrument, terms which they had been well aware of, or should have been well aware of, at the various times the distributions should have been made); Koob v. Koob, A14-0506 (Minn. Ct. App., filed Nov. 24, 2014) (though the appellant informally on numerous occasions within the period of the applicable statute of limitations expressed his concerns orally and in writing to the trustees that he should have received a distribution of a certain percentage of the trust estate, he failed to bring a formal action against them within the period prescribed by the statute, and, thus, when he did get around to bringing the action, it was time-barred).

[119] *See generally* 3 Scott & Ascher §17.2.1.1; Restatement (Third) of Restitution and Unjust Enrichment §70, cmt. f (discovery rule); §8.15.70 of this handbook (laches doctrine).

[120] *See* Bogert §§684 & 685; 4A Scott & Ascher §19.3.1; Uniform Prudent Investor Act §2, cmt.; Restatement (Third) of Trusts §90, cmt. b; In re Stark's Estate, 15 N.Y.S. 729, 731 (Surr. Ct. 1891) (a trustee must "exercise[e] a reasonable degree of diligence in looking after the security after the investment has been made"); Johns v. Herbert, 2 App. D. C. 485, 499 (1894) (trustee liable for failure to discharge his "duty to watch the investment with reasonable care and diligence").

[121] *Cf.* Tibble v. Edison Int'l, No. 13-550, 575 U.S. ___ (May 18, 2015) (an ERISA case in which the court piggybacked on the common law of trusts).

[122] Matter of Barabash, 31 N.Y.2d 76, 286 N.E.2d 268 (1972).

abandoned altogether, the trust.[123] By way of example, an unequivocal failure to render a proper accounting in a timely fashion to the beneficiary upon request may well constitute an act of "repudiation" sufficient to trigger an applicable statute of limitations running against the beneficiary. So, too, might the rendering of an accounting to the beneficiary, say, via the beneficiary's counsel, that reveals on its face a breach of trust.[124] If, on the other hand, the trustee in bad faith or otherwise is stringing the beneficiary along when it comes to furnishing information to which the beneficiary is entitled, then the trustee has yet to openly repudiate the trust.[125]

A beneficiary might be foreclosed by laches or an applicable statute of limitations from extracting damages from the trustee personally for a particular breach of trust.[126] That having been said, the beneficiary generally would not otherwise be foreclosed from seeking the trust's enforcement in the courts.[127] If, however, the alleged trustee has repudiated the very existence of the trust, and the beneficiary with knowledge or reason to know of the wholesale repudiation fails to bring suit within a reasonable time or a time prescribed by statute, the beneficiary may well be barred from seeking the trust's enforcement.[128]

The court and the state attorney general are not bound by laches doctrine when it comes to charitable trusts. The state attorney general under the so-called public rights principle is not bound by the doctrine of laches when it comes to the enforcement of charitable trusts.[129] The court is not so bound, as well. "The mere fact that the trustees of a charitable trust have long applied the trust property to purposes other than those designated by the settlor does not preclude the court from directing that the trust be administered according to its terms."[130]

The Uniform Trust Code. In the case of an irrevocable trust, the Uniform Trust Code creates two limitation periods for actions by beneficiaries against trustees, a one-year period and a five-year period. "A beneficiary may not commence a proceeding against a trustee for breach of fiduciary duty more than one year after the date the beneficiary or representative of the beneficiary was sent a report or accounting that adequately disclosed the existence of a potential claim for breach of trust and informed the beneficiary of the time allowed

---

[123] *See, e.g.,* 5 Scott, Trusts [3d ed.], §409, p. 3226 ("A fiduciary is not entitled to rely upon the laches of his beneficiary as a defense, unless he repudiates the . . . [trust] . . . relation to the knowledge of the beneficiary.").

[124] *See, e.g.,* Matter of JP Morgan Chase Bank N.A. (Strong), 2013 WL 6182548 (N.Y. Sur. 2013).

[125] *See, e.g.,* Matter of JP Morgan Chase Bank N.A. (Strong), 2013 WL 6182548 (N.Y. Sur. 2013).

[126] Restatement (Third) of Trusts §98 cmt. a(1).

[127] Restatement (Third) of Trusts §98 cmt. a(1).

[128] Restatement (Third) of Trusts §98 cmt. a(1).

[129] Restatement (Third) of Trusts §98 cmt. a(2).

[130] 5 Scott & Ascher §37.3.10.

for commencing the proceeding."[131] The five-year period is taken up at the end of this section.

In the case of a revocable trust, the Uniform Trust Code, specifically §604(a), provides that "a person may commence a judicial proceeding to contest the *validity* of a trust that was revocable at the settlor's death within the earlier of: (1) [three] years after the settlor's death; or (2) [120] days after the trustee sent the person a copy of the trust instrument and a notice informing the person of the trust's existence, of the trustee's name and address, and of the time allowed for commencing a proceeding."[132] One court has held that an action to establish that a revocable trust had terminated as a matter of law by merger constituted a challenge to the trust's *validity*, thus subjecting the action to the time limitations of Missouri's version of UTC §604(a).[133]

Once a trustee leaves office. It has been a core principle of trust law that "[t]he resignation of the trustee, although in accordance with the terms of the trust, will not relieve the trustee from liability for breaches of trust committed by him."[134] Thus a trustee's departure from office does not relieve him of the duty to properly account *to the beneficiaries*. A former trustee who has failed to properly account for his actions while in office will have the same equitable and legal defenses to a beneficiary's breach of trust allegations that the former trustee would have were he still in office. In one former-trustee liability case, however, the New York court, for reasons of practicality, held that New York's six-year statute of limitations for breach-of-trust actions began to run against a beneficiary from the time the successor trustee was "put in place," *because the beneficiary knew of the trustee's resignation and never demanded an accounting, the beneficiary at all relevant times having been of full age and legal capacity.*[135]

The highest Massachusetts court took a radical and unprecedented departure from traditional trust law principles when it held that a statute of limitations had begun to run *against the beneficiaries* of a trust whose former trustees had never properly accounted to them when the *successor trustee* knew or should have known of the predecessors' breaches.[136] At the time the successor was deemed to know of the predecessor's breach, one beneficiary was a minor and the other was missing. No guardian ad litem had ever been duly and formally appointed by the court to represent their interests.[137] It appears that the court

---

[131] UTC §1005(a) (available at <http://www.uniformlaws.org/Act.aspx?title=Trust%20 Code>).

[132] UTC §604(a) (available at <http://www.uniformlaws.org/Act.aspx?title=Trust%20 Code>).

[133] *See* Morris v. Trust Co. of the Ozarks, 423 S.W.3d 918 (Mo. App. 2014). Merger is discussed generally in §8.7 and §8.15.36 of this handbook).

[134] 2 Scott on Trusts §106.2.

[135] Tydings v. Greenfield, Stein & Senior, LLP, 11 N.Y.3d 195, 897 N.E.2d 1044, 868 N.Y.S.2d 563 (N.Y. 2008). *See generally* §6.1.5 of this handbook (the trustee's affirmative duty to furnish the beneficiary with critical information).

[136] O'Connor v. Redstone, 452 Mass. 537, 896 N.E.2d 595 (2008). *See generally* Heidi A. Seely, Knowledge of Successor Trustee Sufficient to Commence Statute of Limitations—*O'Connor v. Redstone*, XLIII Suffolk Univ. L. Rev. 519 (2010).

[137] *See generally* §8.14 of this handbook (when there is a need for a guardian ad litem).

had confused and conflated the limitation rules applicable to external *legal* actions by third-party tort and contract claimants against trustees with the rules applicable to internal breach of fiduciary *equitable* actions by beneficiaries against their trustees.[138]

The principle that a successor trustee owes a duty to the beneficiaries to compel the predecessor to account has traditionally meant that upon acceptance of the successor trusteeship the successor merely joins the predecessor on the fiduciary hook.[139] Succession generally has not also started a process of phasing out the predecessor's liability *to the beneficiaries*, come what may.[140] Having said that, Judge Cardozo saw it otherwise, although, we suggest, he had conveniently ignored the fact that lawyers and trustees upon leaving office are not relieved of all their fiduciary duties, this in accordance with long-standing common law agency and trust principles.[141] Here is Judge Cardozo: "While an express trust subsists and has not been openly renounced, the Statute of Limitations does not run in favor of the trustee. But after the trust relation is at an end, the trustee has yielded the estate to a successor the rule is different. The running of the statute then begins, and only actual or intentional fraud will be effective to suspend it."[142] Maybe the trust relation ends upon a yielding of the trust estate, but surely elements of the fiduciary relation continue, such as the duty to provide the beneficiaries with critical information and the duty of confidentiality.[143] Just as a breach of trust is not always the breach of a fiduciary duty to the beneficiaries,[144] so also a breach of fiduciary duty to the beneficiaries is not always a breach of trust.

Still, until these issues of residual predecessor-trustee liability sort themselves out a bit more in the courts and the legislatures, the trustee would be well advised to look upon the Uniform Trust Code (UTC) statutes of limitation as little more than partial codifications of laches doctrine.[145] They are by no means self-contained. Particularly in cases of unauthorized acts of trustee self-dealing, "other law" will generally determine which trustee "misdeeds" will cause them to toll,[146] as well as the level of "understanding" a beneficiary must have before

---

[138] *See generally* §7.3 of this handbook (trustee's external liability to third parties in contract and tort) and §8.25 of this handbook (few American law schools still require instruction in Agency, Trusts and Equity).

[139] *See generally* §7.2.4 of this handbook (successor trustee liability).

[140] *See generally* §7.2.4 of this handbook (predecessor trustee fiduciary liability).

[141] *See generally* Charles E. Rounds, Jr., *Lawyer Codes Are Just About Licensure, the Lawyer's Relationship with the State: Recalling the Common Law Agency, Contract, Tort, Trust, and Property Principles that Regulate the Lawyer-Client Fiduciary Relationship*, 60 Baylor L. Rev. 771 (2008) (certain fiduciary duties are owed by the lawyer to the client even after representation has terminated).

[142] Spallholz v. Sheldon, 216 N.Y. 205, 209, 110 N.E. 431 (1915).

[143] *See generally* §6.1.5.1 of this handbook (the trustee's duty to provide information) and §6.2.3 of this handbook (the trustee's duty of confidentiality).

[144] *See generally* §6.1.1 of this handbook (while the trustee's duty of loyalty is a fiduciary duty, his duty of prudence really is not).

[145] *See* §8.15.70 of this handbook (laches doctrine generally).

[146] *See* UTC §1005 cmt. (available at <http://www.uniformlaws.org/Act.aspx?title=Trust%20Code>).

the statutory periods will begin to run.[147] The level, by the way, is likely to be high, namely, a full subjective understanding of the facts and law applicable to the self-dealing.[148] That is either traditional laches, or laches by analogy.[149]

The Uniform Trust Code's statute of ultimate repose. The Uniform Trust Code, too, opts for practicality over principle when it comes to predecessor-trustee liability. Under the Code, specifically Section 1005(c), a judicial proceeding by a beneficiary against a trustee for breach of trust must be commenced within five years after the first to occur of the removal, resignation, or death[150] of the trustee; the termination of the beneficiary's interest in the trust; or the termination of the trust. The five-year limitation period, which is intended to provide some ultimate repose for actions against a trustee,[151] may or may not cover fraudulent acts on the part of the trustee, the drafters of the Uniform Trust Code having preferred "to leave that question to . . . [laws that deal with fraudulent acts generally]. . . ."[152] If Section 1005(c) is subject to a fraud exception, then possibly it would be subject to a constructive fraud exception as well. Constructive fraud is taken up generally in Section 8.15.60 of this handbook. The trust reformation action, a topic that is taken up in Section 8.15.22 of this handbook, also would not be subject to the Code's ultimate repose provisions, it not being an action against the trustee for a breach of his trust.

Section 1005(c) provides that under certain circumstances a trust beneficiary has only five years to bring a breach-of-trust action against the trustee *even should the beneficiary lack actual or constructive notice of the breach.* Assume four years have run since a breach of trust has occurred. The trustee and the beneficiary remain totally in the dark as to the fact and nature of the breach. One more year and the trustee is off the hook. Trust counsel, on the other hand, becomes aware of the breach. Here is a situation in which counsel may have to respond to two potentially conflicting duties: (1) to represent the trustee in his official capacity, and (2) to protect the trustee personally. If counsel informs the trustee of the breach and the trustee takes no action to remedy it, the trustee's fraudulent inaction may toll the running of the statute. On the other hand, if counsel keeps quiet, the five-year period will expire and the trustee is personally off the hook. Still, the trustee will have breached virtually the entire panoply of fiduciary duties that had been owed to the beneficiary, duties that are the subject of

---

[147] *See generally* §7.1.2 of this handbook (defenses to allegations that the trustee breached the duty of loyalty).

[148] *See generally* §7.1.2 of this handbook (defenses to allegations that the trustee breached the duty of loyalty).

[149] *See* §8.15.70 of this handbook (laches doctrine generally).

[150] "If a trusteeship terminates by reason of death, a claim against the trustee's estate for breach of fiduciary duty would, like other claims against the trustee's estate, be barred by a probate creditor's claim statute even though . . . [the five-year statutory period] . . . had not yet expired." UTC §1005 cmt. (available at <http://www.uniformlaws.org/Act.aspx?title=Trust%20 Code>).

[151] UTC §1005 cmt. (available at <http://www.uniformlaws.org/Act.aspx?title=Trust%20 Code>).

[152] UTC §1005 cmt. (available at <http://www.uniformlaws.org/Act.aspx?title=Trust%20 Code>).

Chapter 6 of this handbook. What is an innocent trust counsel to do in such a situation?

One court has proffered the following advice: When a trustee is faced with a personal-fiduciary conflict, "the trustee can mitigate or avoid the problem by retaining and paying out of his own funds separate counsel for legal advice that is personal in nature."[153] But how exactly is trust counsel to get the trustee to retain at his own expense separate personal counsel without causing a fraud-based tolling of the running of the statute and/or without trust counsel, himself, ending up constructively participating in the breach of trust? Perhaps the only way out of the cul-de-sac is the *deus ex machina* of a repeal of Section 1005(c). Under default laches doctrine, trust counsel would no longer be conflicted in that the trustee would be personally benefited by a full disclosure of the breach to the beneficiary. This is because full disclosure would trigger a start of the running of any statute of limitations that might be applicable to such a breach of fiduciary duty or, in the absence of such a statute, a start of the running of the "reasonable" laches period that a fully informed trust beneficiary would have to bring suit against the trustee for a breach of trust.

One commentator on ethical lawyering is floating a general proposal that might at least eliminate our Section 1005(c) fraud-disclosure conundrum, though in a given situation the fall-out from the cure would most likely be worse than the disease. He proposes that each state "adopt a rule" along the lines of the following: "A lawyer, to the extent the lawyer reasonably believes necessary, may reveal information relating to the representation of a client to inform a tribunal or a beneficiary about any material breach of fiduciary responsibility when the client is serving as a fiduciary such as a guardian, personal representative, trustee, or receiver."[154]

Does the running of the UTC Section 1005(c) statute of ultimate repose shut the door once and for all on all claims against the trustee arising out of his maladministration of the trust? Maybe not: Let us assume that the trustee innocently or negligently makes off with the trust property in violation of the terms of the trust. The beneficiary neither knew nor should have known of the trustee's personal enrichment at trust expense. Five years elapse such that the beneficiary under Section 1005(c) is foreclosed from bringing a *breach of trust* action against the trustee. In this particular situation, however, the beneficiary may well have another arrow in his quiver, namely, an equitable action against the trustee not for his breach of trust but for the equitable wrong of his unjust enrichment. The equitable action of restitution for unjust enrichment is taken up generally in Section 7.2.3.3 of this handbook. The equitable wrong of unjust enrichment itself is taken up generally in Section 8.15.78 of this handbook. Presumably, the trustee was not only unjustly enriched by the trust property but

[153] *See* Stewart v. Kono, 2012 WL 4427096 (Cal. App. 2 Dist.).
[154] Kennedy Lee, *Representing the Fiduciary: To Whom Does The Attorney Owe Duties?*, 37 ACTEC L.J. 469, 492 (Winter 2011).

also by any compensation he took for "services" performed during the period of maladministration.[155]

The Georgia Trust Code lacks a comparable ultimate repose feature. Taking a page from traditional laches doctrine it provides that "[i]f the beneficiary has not received a report which adequately discloses the existence of a claim against the trustee for a breach of trust, such claim shall be barred as to that beneficiary unless a proceeding to assert such claim is commenced within six years after the beneficiary discovered, or reasonably should have discovered, the subject of such claim."[156] Thus, the trustee's fraudulent concealment will toll the limitation period.[157]

§7.1.4 Defense of Consent, Release, Ratification, or Affirmance by the Beneficiary (to Breaches of Trust Generally)

A trustee who commits a breach of trust without the beneficiaries' prior consent may nevertheless avoid liability if the beneficiaries subsequently discharge the trustee by contract, accord and satisfaction, or release. The applicable principle is the same as that which governs the discharge of contractual liability, except that, since the relationship is fiduciary, the limitations that apply to beneficiaries' consent apply here, as well.[158]

A trustee is not liable to the beneficiary for a breach of trust if the beneficiary consented to the conduct constituting the breach;[159] released the trustee from liability for the breach;[160] or ratified or affirmed[161] the transaction constituting the breach.[162] Ratification or affirmance is an option if the trustee's questionable transaction can be undone or set aside.[163] "This principle rests on the doctrine of election of remedies."[164]

---

[155] *See generally* Charles E. Rounds, Jr., *Chinks in the Armor: Three Exceptions to the Uniform Trust Code's 5-Year Ultimate Repose Provision Suggest that a Trustee May Not Be Home Free from Liability*, Trusts & Estates (Nov. 19, 2013), available at <http://wealthmanagement.com/estate-planning/chinks-armor>.

[156] O.C.G.A. §53-12-307(a).

[157] *See, e.g.*, Smith v. SunTrust Bank, 325 Ga. App. 531, 754 S.E.2d 117 (2014).

[158] 4 Scott & Ascher §25.2.6 (Beneficiary Who Consents to or Participates in Breach of Trust); 4 Scott & Ascher §24.22 (Discharge of Liability by Release or Contract).

[159] Lewin ¶ 39-60 (England).

[160] *See generally* 4 Scott & Ascher §24.22 (Discharge of Liability by Release or Contract).

[161] Lewin ¶ 39-71 (England); 4 Scott & Ascher §24.23 (U.S.).

[162] UTC §1009 (available at <http://www.uniformlaws.org/Act.aspx?title=Trust%20Code>. *See generally* §7.2.7 of this handbook (beneficiary consent, release, or ratification). *See, e.g.*, Buchbinder v. Bank of Am., N.A., 342 Ark. 632, 640–641, 30 S.W.3d 707, 712–713 (2000) (holding that beneficiary's knowing consent, manifested by his acquiescence and actual demand for payments he later challenged, precluded a subsequent action against the trustee to enforce the trust's terms).

[163] 4 Scott & Ascher §24.23 (Discharge of Liability by Ratification or Subsequent Affirmance).

[164] 4 Scott & Ascher §24.23.

A beneficiary's consent to a breach of trust may be given before or at the time of the trustee's act or omission.[165] "A 'ratification' or 'release' occurs when a beneficiary subsequently, with knowledge of the breach, affirms a trustee's improper conduct or agrees to discharge the trustee from liability for the conduct."[166]

The trustee, however, is not relieved of liability if the consent, release, ratification, or affirmance was induced by improper conduct of the trustee.[167] Nor is the trustee off the hook if, at the time of the consent, release, ratification, or affirmance, the beneficiary did not fully understand his or her legal and equitable rights or the material facts, at least insofar as they relate to the breach.[168] In other words, the consent, release, ratification, or affirmance must be informed.[169]

For a discussion of the doctrine of informed consent, release, ratification, and affirmance in the specific context of breaches of the trustee's duty of loyalty, the reader is referred to Section 7.1.2 of this handbook. For a discussion of the authority of holders of certain types of powers of appointment to consent to breaches of trust and so bind appointees and takers in default, see Section §8.14 of this handbook.[170]

§7.1.5 Defense That the Governing Instrument Contains Exculpatory Language

A provision in a trust instrument relieving the trustee of liability for ordinary negligence is generally enforceable.[171] Such a provision, however, is not enforceable to the extent that it was inserted as the result of an abuse by the trustee of a fiduciary or confidential relationship to the settlor.[172] The Uniform Trust Code presumes that "[a]n exculpatory term drafted or caused to be drafted by the trustee is invalid as an abuse of a fiduciary or confidential relationship unless the trustee proves that the exculpatory term is fair under the

---

[165] Restatement (Third) of Trusts §97 cmt. b.

[166] Restatement (Third) of Trusts §97 cmt. b.

[167] Restatement (Third) of Trusts §97 cmt. f.

[168] UTC §1009 (available at <http://www.uniformlaws.org/Act.aspx?title=Trust%20 Code>). *See generally* 4 Scott & Ascher §24.22 (Discharge of Liability by Release or Contract). *See, e.g.*, Nalley v. Langdale, 319 Ga. App. 354, 366, 734 S.E.2d 908, 918 (2012) (the court confirming that even though an act of a trustee is unauthorized and constitutes a breach of trust, it may be acquiesced in, confirmed, or ratified by a beneficiary with "full knowledge of all facts and of his or her legal rights" such that the beneficiary is estopped from repudiating the breach and attempting to hold the trustee liable for it.)

[169] *See, e.g.*, Miller v. Bank of Am., N.A., 326 P.3d 20, 26 (N.M. 2013) ("Without a fully informed consent or ratification from Beneficiaries, the Bank's imprudent conduct that resulted from rashly investing the entirety of the Trusts' assets in unproductive and declining Building reflected a failure to exercise to reasonable care, special skills, or expertise required of a trustee.").

[170] *See also* UPC §1-108 (acts of holder of general power).

[171] *See* §7.2.6 of this handbook (express trustee exculpation).

[172] UTC §1008(a)(2) (available at <http://www.uniformlaws.org/Act.aspx?title=Trust%20 Code>).

circumstances and that its existence and contents were adequately communicated to the settlor."[173]

As a matter of public policy, an exculpatory provision may not relieve a trustee of liability for a breach of fiduciary duty committed in bad faith or with reckless indifference to the purposes of the trust or the interests of the beneficiaries.[174] In England, a trustee who commits a breach of trust in reliance upon an exculpatory or indemnity clause risks losing its protections.[175] For more on trustee exculpation, see Section 7.2.6 of this handbook.

§7.1.6 Defense That Trustee Lacked Knowledge of Some Event

The common law imposed absolute liability against a trustee for misdelivery regardless of the trustee's level of care.[176] Courts in recent years, however, have been reluctant to impose liability on a trustee who has acted reasonably and in good faith.

In one case, the trustee of a testamentary trust misdelivered income to a former beneficiary. The trust had provided that net income shall be distributed to the settlor's wife "during her lifetime so long as she remained unmarried." In the event of her remarriage, the trust property was to be held for the benefit of a charity. After the trust was established, the wife remarried but failed to so inform the trustee. In fact she went to great lengths to hide her marital status from the bank. As a result, the trustee paid to her the net trust income until the time of her death. Among other acts of concealment, she would endorse trust checks by signing her name as it was when she was married to the settlor. Once she had remarried, all net income pursuant to the terms of the trust should have inured to the benefit of the charity. The trustee discovered its error after her death. The court held that the trustee had engaged in "constructive fraud" in that it had failed to take reasonable steps to ascertain the true state of the facts that it had been misrepresenting in its periodic accountings:

> This rule is not a strict liability standard, nor does it make a trustee an insurer against active fraud of all parties dealing with the trust. Entries in the accounts honestly made, after reasonable efforts to determine the truth or falsity of the representations therein have failed through no fault of the trustee, will not be deemed fraudulent or provide grounds for reopening properly allowed accounts. However, in the instant case, the probate judge found that the bank, through twenty-two years covered by the disputed accounts, exerted "no effort at all . . . to

---

[173] UTC §1008(b) (available at <http://www.uniformlaws.org/Act.aspx?title=Trust%20 Code>).

[174] UTC §1008(a)(1) (available at <http://www.uniformlaws.org/Act.aspx?title=Trust%20 Code>).

[175] Lewin ¶ 39-81 (England).

[176] UTC §1007, cmt. (available at <http://www.uniformlaws.org/Act.aspx?title=Trust%20 Code>).

ascertain if . . . [the wife] . . . had remarried even to the extent of annually requesting a statement or certificate from her to that effect" and that "in administering
the trust acted primarily in a ministerial manner and in disregard of its duties as
a trustee to protect the terms of the trust."[177]

The Uniform Trust Code mitigates somewhat the harshness of the misdelivery liability rule in order to "encourage trustees to administer trusts expeditiously and without undue concern about liability for failure to ascertain
external facts, often of a personal nature, that might affect administration or
distribution of the trust."[178] It provides that "[I]f the happening of an event,
including marriage, divorce, performance of educational requirements, or
death, affects the administration or distribution of a trust, a trustee who has
exercised reasonable care to ascertain the happening of the event is not liable
for a loss resulting from the trustee's lack of knowledge."[179] This provision is
based on Washington Revised Code Section 11.98.100. Oklahoma and Texas
have similar statutes.[180]

§7.1.7 Defense That Trustee Relied on Trust Instrument

The terms of a trust and the terms of its instrument may not necessarily be
the same.[181] Under the Uniform Trust Code, for example, a court may consider
evidence extrinsic to the trust instrument in ascertaining the settlor's intent.[182]
A court also may add and delete language from the instrument upon clear and
convincing evidence that both the settlor's intent and the terms of the trust were
affected by a mistake of fact or law, whether in expression or inducement.[183] A
trustee who acts in reasonable reliance on the terms of the trust as expressed in
the trust instrument is not liable to a beneficiary for a breach of fiduciary duty
to the extent the breach resulted from the reliance.[184]

---

[177] National Acad. of Sci. v. Cambridge Trust Co., 370 Mass. 303, 309, 436 N.E.2d 879, 884
(1976).

[178] UTC §1007 cmt. (available at <http://www.uniformlaws.org/Act.aspx?title=Trust%20
Code>).

[179] UTC §1007 (available at <http://www.uniformlaws.org/Act.aspx?title=Trust%20
Code>).

[180] *See* 3 Scott on Trusts §226 n.7.

[181] UTC §1006 cmt. (available at <http://www.uniformlaws.org/Act.aspx?title=Trust%20
Code>).

[182] UTC §103(17) (available at <http://www.uniformlaws.org/Act.aspx?title=Trust%20
Code>).

[183] UTC §415 (available at <http://www.uniformlaws.org/Act.aspx?title=Trust%20
Code>).

[184] UTC§1006 (available at <http://www.uniformlaws.org/Act.aspx?title=Trust%20
Code>).

§7.1.8 *The Equitable Excuse (for a Breach of Trust)*

The general rule has been that a trustee who breaches his trust is not absolved of liability merely because he did so in good faith. As we explain in Section 8.15.81 of this handbook, under the Uniform Trust Code the good faith of the trustee may well now be an effective defense, at least in some situations. The Restatement (Third) of Trusts would seem to be more or less in accord with the Code in this regard. The Restatement (Third), specifically the commentary to Section 95, talks in terms of the equitable excuse: "If, however, the court concludes that, in the circumstances, it would be unfair or unduly harsh to require the trustee to pay, or pay in full, the liability which would normally result from a breach of trust, the court has equitable authority to excuse the trustee in whole or in part for having to pay the liability."[185] It proffers some examples of trustee behavior that might warrant a particular breach of trust being equitably excused:

- Good faith reliance on overruled precedent
- Good faith observance of "typical fiduciary practice"
- Good faith selection and monitoring of agents[186]
- Good faith purchase of trust property out of apparent necessity "to further interests of beneficiaries"[187]
- Good faith reliance on advice of counsel[188]
- Good faith/"sincere" effort to ascertain applicable facts and law
- Good faith ignorance of the complaint/petition for instructions option[189]

§7.2   Trustee's Internal Liability as Fiduciary to the Beneficiary

But to say that a man is a fiduciary only begins analysis; it gives direction to further in inquiry. To whom is he a fiduciary? What obligations does he owe as a fiduciary? In what respect has he failed to discharge those obligations? And what are the consequences of his deviation from duty?[1]

---

[185] Restatement (Third) of Trusts §95 cmt. d.

[186] *See generally* §6.1.4 of this handbook (delegation).

[187] *See generally* §6.1.3.3 of this handbook (trustee benefiting as buyer).

[188] *See generally* §8.32 of this handbook (reliance on advice of counsel as a defense to a breach of trust allegation).

[189] *See generally* §8.42 of this handbook (the complaint for instructions and the complaint for declaratory judgment).

§7.2 [1] S.E.C. v. Chenery, 318 U.S. 80, 85–86 (1943).

By 1464, it was acknowledged that a *cestui qui use* could bring an action in the court of chancery against the *feofee* to uses for the latter's breaching of his duties.[2] Today, the trustee, the successor to the *feofee* to uses, is accountable in equity to the beneficiary, the successor to the *cestui qui use*, for his breaches of trust.[3] The duties of the trustee, fiduciary, and otherwise, are enumerated and discussed in Chapter 6 of this handbook. Much difficulty can be avoided if the trustee takes the time to learn each of his many duties. Specificity is the key. A general uninformed concern about breaches of trust is unlikely to keep the trustee out of trouble. On the other hand, the beneficiary who puts forth without more the general allegation that there has been a breach of trust should be called upon to elaborate:[4] What specific duties allegedly have been breached? How did these breaches allegedly occur? Which breaches allegedly were intentional and which were negligent? And why are there are no credible defenses available to the trustee in light of the particular facts and circumstances?

"The Court has exclusive jurisdiction of proceedings initiated by interested parties concerning the internal affairs of trusts."[5] The equitable remedies available to the beneficiary are not available to a stranger to the trust. They are available, however, to anyone having a right to represent the interest of the beneficiary, including an assignee or a creditor with a lien.[6] Even persons to whom income or principal is payable at the discretion of the trustee would have standing to bring the matter of the trustee's abuse of discretion before the court.[7] If the trustee refuses to sue or defend on behalf of the trust estate, the beneficiary may proceed against the trustee and the third party as codefendants, but the trustee must be shown to be in default.[8]

In the litigation context, the consequences of a breach of fiduciary duty are likely to be different from the consequences of a breach of a nonfiduciary duty, *e.g.*, failing to carry out one's obligations under a sales contract. In the case of a breach of fiduciary duty, there are likely to be more remedy options available to the party to whom the duty is owed,[9] burdens of proof are likely to fall more heavily on the fiduciary,[10] and periods in which actions must be brought will tend to run from the time when actual notice of the breach is received by the

---

[2] *See* Anonymous. Y.B. 4 Edw. IV, fol. 8, pl. 9 (1464). *See also* Weakly v. Rogers, 5 East 138, note (a).

[3] 4 Scott & Ascher §24.1.

[4] *See, e.g.,* Hartlove v. Maryland Sch. for the Blind, 111 Md. App. 310, 681 A.2d 584 (1996) (after wrestling with the question of whether "breach of fiduciary duty" in the estate context can constitute an independent and viable cause of action, the court held that it can).

[5] UPC §7-201(a).

[6] *See* Bogert §970 (Creditor of Beneficiary or of Trust Itself Has Standing to Demand an Accounting); 3 Scott on Trusts §200.

[7] *See* Bogert §871 n.10 and accompanying text. *See generally* 2 Scott on Trusts §128.3.

[8] *See* Bogert §869 n.35 and accompanying text.

[9] *See generally* §7.2.3 of this handbook (types of equitable relief for breaches of trust).

[10] *See generally* §8.24 of this handbook (who has the burden of proof in an action for breach of trust brought by the beneficiary against the trustee).

party to whom the duty is owed.[11] This is generally the case whether the fiduciary relationship is incident to a trust or to an agency.

§7.2.1 Intentional Breaches

In the world of trusts, an intentional breach is usually two or more breaches: a breach of the duty of loyalty coupled with other breaches. For example, when a trustee without authority borrows from the trust estate at no interest, both the duty of loyalty *and* the duty to make the trust property productive have been breached, as well as the duty to segregate and earmark. The breach of the duty of loyalty never travels alone, and it always constitutes a breach of fiduciary duty.[12] Moreover, the element of self-dealing tends to make the associated breach a continuing one. Thus the self-dealing menu of damage theories may be more extensive than the negligence menu.[13] The assessment of appreciation damages against a trustee who has self-dealt comes to mind.[14] The Restatement (Third) of Restitution and Unjust Enrichment is in accord in part for public policy reasons: "Restitution requires a full disgorgement of profit by a conscious wrongdoer, not just because of the moral judgment implicit in the rule of this section, ... [namely, that a person is not permitted to profit by his wrong,] ... but because any lesser liability would provide an inadequate incentive to lawful behavior."[15]

§7.2.2 Negligent Breaches

Like the intentional breach, the negligent breach is actually two or more breaches: a breach of the duty to be generally prudent in conducting the affairs of the trust coupled with some other breach. Let us assume, for example, that the trustee negligently makes an unauthorized distribution of principal to an income beneficiary. Here the trustee has breached both the duty to be prudent and the duty to carry out the terms of the trust. A negligent breach of trust, however, does not necessarily rise to the level of a breach of fiduciary duty.[16]

---

[11] *See generally* §7.2.10 of this handbook (laches and statutes of limitation in the trust context).

[12] *See generally* William A. Gregory, *The Fiduciary Duty of Care: A Perversion of Words*, 38 Akron L. Rev. 181 (2005).

[13] *See* 4 Scott & Ascher §24.10; 3 Scott on Trusts §205.1.

[14] *See generally* 4 Scott & Ascher §24.10 (Liability for Breach of Duty of Loyalty).

[15] Restatement (Third) of Restitution and Unjust Enrichment §3, cmt. c.

[16] *See generally* William A. Gregory, *The Fiduciary Duty of Care: A Perversion of Words*, 38 Akron L. Rev. 181 (2005).

§7.2.3   Types of Relief (Equitable Remedies for Breaches of Trust)

The Australian courts have held that fiduciary obligations are the proscriptive counterpart of the prescriptive duties at common law. In other words they create restrictions rather than positive duties. In my view the same analysis holds good in English law.[17]

To remedy a breach of trust that has occurred or may occur, the court may . . . void an act of the trustee, impose a lien or a constructive trust on trust property, or trace trust property wrongfully disposed of and recover the property or its proceeds.[18]

Trust beneficiary traditionally was not entitled to legal relief. The types of relief available to a trust beneficiary for breaches of fiduciary duty have traditionally been exclusively equitable.[19] Thus, *the beneficiary* was traditionally foreclosed from bringing a legal action against the trustee, such as an action of trespass, trover, detinue, replevin, or case.[20] Nor could *the beneficiary* bring a legal action in tort or contract against the trustee for an internal breach of fiduciary duty.[21]

Equitable remedies for breaches of trust. It is said that the "plastic remedies of the chancery" were "moulded to the needs of justice."[22] If the trustee committed an intentional breach or fell below the required standard of care, it was equity that sought to place the beneficiary at least in the position that he, she, or it would have been in had there not been a breach of trust.[23] "Nor did equity courts insist upon a showing of detrimental reliance in cases where they ordered 'surcharge.' Rather, they simply ordered a trust or beneficiary made whole following a trustee's breach of trust."[24] Little has changed, at least in principle.[25] The equitable liabilities that may be imposed upon today's defaulting trustee, *i.e.*, the tools the court has at its disposal for making the beneficiary whole,[26]

---

[17] David Halpern, *Conflicts of Interest*, 2(1) Tr. Q. Rev. 28 (2004). "Kelley v. Cooper ([1993] A.C. 205) at first sight might be thought to suggest that there can in some cases be a positive fiduciary duty of disclosure, but the better analysis is that the mere failure to disclose is not of itself a breach of fiduciary duty in a case of potential conflicts of interest. . . . It only becomes so where the failure is intentionally disloyal. . . ." 2(1) Tr. Q. Rev. 28 (2004) at n.6.

[18] UTC §1001(b)(9) (available at <http://www.uniformlaws.org/Act.aspx?title=Trust%20 Code>).

[19] *See* Hunter v. United States, 30 U.S. 173, 188 (1831) ("It is the peculiar province of equity, to compel the execution of trusts."); CIGNA Corp. v. Amara, 131 S. Ct. 1866, 1879 (2011).

[20] 4 Scott & Ascher §24.1.1 (Action at Law in Tort).

[21] 4 Scott & Ascher §§24.1.1 (Action at Law in Tort), 24.1.2 (Action at Law for Breach of Contract).

[22] Foreman v. Foreman, 167 N.E. 428, 429 (N.Y. 1929).

[23] *See* CIGNA Corp. v. Amara, 131 S. Ct. 1866, 1881 (2011).

[24] *See* CIGNA Corp. v. Amara, 131 S. Ct. 1866, 1881 (2011).

[25] *See generally* Restatement (Third) of Trusts §95 ("With limited exceptions, the remedies of trust beneficiaries are equitable in character and enforceable against trustees in a court exercising equity powers.").

[26] 4 Scott & Ascher §24.3 (The Beneficiary's Equitable Remedies).

have changed little over the centuries.[27] The court in the exercise of its inherent equitable powers[28] may grant the beneficiary a single remedy or mix for him a cocktail of remedies should a single remedy afford less than full relief.[29] It may grant one or more of the following *substantive* equitable remedies in order to make the beneficiaries whole:

- Compel the trustee to redress a breach of fiduciary duty by paying money, restoring property (restitution and reparation), or other means.[30]
- Void an act of the trustee.[31]
- Permanently enjoin the trustee from committing a breach of fiduciary duty (injunction).[32]

---

[27] *See* CIGNA Corp. v. Amara, 131 S. Ct. 1866 (2011) (an ERISA case).

[28] It should be noted that the court also has inherent equitable powers to excuse when appropriate good faith breaches of trust. *See generally* 4 Scott & Ascher §24.9.2 (Power of Court to Excuse Breach of Trust).

[29] *See, e.g.*, Miller v. Bank of Am., N.A., 326 P.3d 20, 30 (N.M. 2013) (holding that in light of the particular facts and circumstances of this case, which involves the mismanagement of an item of entrusted real estate, "[t]he award of prejudgment interest and the inflation adjustment are not duplicative.")

[30] UTC §1001(b)(3) (available at <http://www.uniformlaws.org/Act.aspx?title=Trust%20 Code>); 4 Scott & Ascher §24.3.3 (Damages). *See, e.g.*, Estate of Wilde, 708 A.2d 273 (Me. 1978) (having found the trustee liable for imprudently investing the trust estate, the court adopted the following formula for calculating damages: the value of the trust as if it had been managed by a prudent professional trustee in Portland, Maine, less the value of the assets actually delivered to the trustee, rejecting a more mechanical method based upon the value of the trust as if it been invested in an S & P index fund); Matter of Will of Janes, 643 N.Y.S.2d 972 (App. Div. 1996) (rejecting a hypothetical market value appreciation measure of damages in the case of a trustee's negligent retention of Kodak stock in favor of the following measure: the value of the 12,087 shares of Kodak stock on August 9, 1973, the date on which they should have been sold, minus the value of the shares when they were ultimately sold or transferred, minus any income attributable to the stock retained, plus interest at the legal rate compounded from August 9, 1973); First Ala. Bank v. Spragins, 515 So. 2d 962 (Ala. 1987) (using as a benchmark for the measure of damages the S & P 500 Index). Restoration of the Trust Property (Specific Reparation). *See generally* 4 Scott & Ascher §24.11.3. *See, e.g.*, Staley v. Kreinbihl, 152 Ohio St. 315, 89 N.E.2d 593 (1949) (holding that where a beneficiary has traced trust property into hands of the deceased trustee, the income on the property is subject to the short statute of limitations for claims against decedent while an action to recover property itself is not).

[31] UTC §1001(b)(9) (available at <http://www.uniformlaws.org/Act.aspx?title=Trust%20 Code>). *See, e.g.*, Estate of Rothko, 43 N.Y.2d 305, 372 N.E.2d 291 (1977) (the court in part voiding and setting aside a contract made by the coexecutors of an estate with a corporation, this because a coexecutor had a personal interest in the corporation and because the contract favored the coexecutor at the expense of the estate).

[32] UTC §1001(b)(2) (available at <http://www.uniformlaws.org/Act.aspx?title=Trust%20 Code>); 4 Scott & Ascher §24.3.2 (Injunction). *See, e.g.*, In re Gould's Will, 234 N.Y.S.2d 825 (1962) (enjoining trustee at request of beneficiary from performing on a contract to sell stock comprising the trust estate when disposing of the stock would be imprudent); Ohio Oil Co. v. Daughetee, 88 N.E. 818 (1909) (enjoining trustee at request of beneficiary from entering into an oil and gas lease in that to do so would impair the interest of the remainderman; McHenry v. Jewett, 90 N.Y. 58 (1882) (enjoining trustee at request of beneficiary from voting stock in a particular way).

- Compel the trustee to perform a specific duty (specific enforcement).[33]
- Suspend the trustee.[34]
- Remove the trustee.[35]
- Reduce or deny compensation to the trustee.[36]
- Appoint a special fiduciary or receiver to take possession of and administer the trust property.[37]
- Order any other appropriate substantive relief.[38]

To assist it in fashioning an appropriate mix of *substantive* equitable remedies for a particular breach of trust, the court has at its disposal a variety of *procedural* equitable remedies. They include the following:

---

[33] UTC §1001(b)(1) (available at <http://www.uniformlaws.org/Act.aspx?title=Trust%20 Code>); 4 Scott & Ascher §24.3.1 (Specific Enforcement of Trust). *See, e.g.*, In re Koffend's Will, 218 Minn. 206, 15 N.W.2d 590 (1944) (holding that the court may direct the trustee to vote for directors of a corporation comprising the trust estate who would vote dividends for the benefit of the trust beneficiary); Nash v. Sutton, 117 N.C. 231, 23 S.E. 178 (1895) (holding that trustees may be compelled by the court to convey real estate to a successor); Merkel v. Long, 368 Mich. 1, 117 N.W.2d 130 (1962) (in a matter involving the settlement of a controversy as to the effect of provisions of will creating trust, the court may order the trustees to sign the agreement reached by the parties unless they resign).

[34] UTC §1001(b)(6) (available at <http://www.uniformlaws.org/Act.aspx?title=Trust%20 Code>).

[35] UTC §1001(b)(7) (available at <http://www.uniformlaws.org/Act.aspx?title=Trust%20 Code>). *See, e.g.*, Steele v. Kelley, 710 N.E.2d 973, 994 (Mass. App. Ct. 1999) (noting that the fundamental question in trustee removal cases is not the wishes of the beneficiaries, but rather whether the circumstances are such that the degree of the trustee's discretion makes it detrimental to the trust for the trustee to continue in office); Shear v. Gabovitch, 685 N.E.2d 1168, 1194 (Mass. App. Ct. 1997) (ordering removal of trustee who possessed "almost plenary discretion over all distributions to a beneficiary" because he could not "be expected to exercise his power with desirable perspective and detachment when his motives and integrity" were constantly being "impugned by the beneficiary," the parties having been "mired for years in a draining legal equivalent of total war"). *See, however*, Symmons v. O'Keefe, 419 Mass. 288, 644 N.E.2d 631 (1995) (the mere fact that there is friction or hostility between the trustee and beneficiaries would not necessarily be a sufficient ground for removal, the reason being that beneficiaries desiring a trustee's removal would have an incentive to quarrel with the trustee).

[36] UTC §1001(b)(8) (available at <http://www.uniformlaws.org/Act.aspx?title=Trust%20 Code>). *See, e.g.*, Matter of Estate of Gump, 2 Cal. Rptr. 2d 269 (1991) (holding that trial court had not abused its discretion in denying trustee compensation and costs that related to the negligent administration of a lease of trust real estate).

[37] UTC §1001(b)(5) (available at <http://www.uniformlaws.org/Act.aspx?title=Trust%20 Code>) (making explicit the court's authority to appoint a special fiduciary, also sometimes referred to as a receiver); 4 Scott & Ascher §24.3.4 (Appointment of Receiver). *See also* Restatement (Second) of Trusts §199(d) (providing that a beneficiary of a trust can maintain a suit to appoint a receiver to take possession of the trust property and administer the trust). *See, e.g.*, Boyce v. Wendt, 305 Mich. 254, 9 N.W.2d 531 (1943) (holding that where trustees have failed to keep records, have mingled the trust funds with their own, and are insolvent, the court may appoint a receiver to conserve the property); Smith v. Fleetwood Bldg. Corp., 120 Fla. 481, 163 So. 293 (1935) (where trustee is seeking to enforce a lien on the trusts property for advances made by him and in so doing asserting an interest adverse to the trust, he may be removed and replaced by a receiver).

[38] UTC §1001(b)(10) (available at <http://www.uniformlaws.org/Act.aspx?title=Trust%20 Code>).

- Order the trustee to account.[39]
- Follow the trust property wrongfully disposed of *in specie.*
- Trace the trust property wrongfully disposed of and recover the property or its proceeds (following the property into its product).[40]
- Issue temporary injunctions.
- Impose an equitable lien or constructive trust on property that belongs to the trust.[41]

The procedural versus the substantive equitable remedy. Equitable accounting; following; tracing (following property into its product); the imposition of an equitable lien; and the imposition of a constructive trust are not equitable remedies in the sense that a permanent injunction or a decree for specific performance or a restitution order is an equitable remedy. They are just "part of the process of establishing the substantive rights of the parties."[42] The court, for example, having held that the beneficiary has a right to follow a particular item of property and that the transferee of that property has the duties of a constructive trustee with respect to it (in other words, the court having adjudicated the rights, duties, and obligations of the parties to the dispute) it can now fashion whatever substantive remedies are appropriate to make the beneficiary whole.[43] Perhaps it will issue a restitution order coupled with a permanent injunction. Still, the imposition of a constructive trust on identifiable property is a remedy in the sense that it freezes the status quo, *i.e.,* it prevents the transferee from consuming or alienating the subject property to

---

[39] UTC §1001(b)(4) (available at <http://www.uniformlaws.org/Act.aspx?title=Trust%20 Code>). *See, e.g.,* Corsi v. Corsi, 302 Ill. App. 3d 519, 706 N.E.2d 956 (1998) (holding that the plaintiffs' allegations of breach of trust and inadequacy of accountings are sufficient to support a motion to compel an accounting); Estate of P.K.L. v. J.K.S., 189 Ariz. 487, 943 P.2d 847 (1997) (stating that a trust income beneficiary has a right to require the trustee to produce a copy of the trust terms describing or affecting the beneficiary's interest, relevant information about the trust assets, and the annual statement of the accounts of the trust). *See, however,* Johnson v. Kotyck, 90 Cal. Rptr. 2d 99, 76 Cal. App. 4th 83 (1999) (holding contingent beneficiaries of a revocable inter vivos trust not entitled to an accounting though the settlor's conservator had come into possession of the revocation power).

[40] UTC §1001(b)(9) (available at <http://www.uniformlaws.org/Act.aspx?title=Trust%20 Code>); 4 Scott & Ascher §24.6 (Following Trust Property into Its Product). *See, e.g.,* Bowling v. Bowling, 252 N.C. 527, 114 S.E.2d 228 (1960) (providing that though the beneficiary acquiesced in the trustee taking control of the trust property and investing it in a nonlegal investment for his own benefit, the trust fund may be traced into such investment).

[41] UTC §1001(b)(9) (available at <http://www.uniformlaws.org/Act.aspx?title=Trust%20 Code>). *See, e.g.,* Nile v. Nile, 432 Mass. 390, 734 N.E.2d 1153 (2000) (upholding the imposition of a constructive trust on the assets of the decedent's revocable inter vivos trust in order to secure the decedent's obligations under a postdivorce settlement agreement between the decedent and his former wife); Lackey v. Lackey, 691 So. 2d 990 (Miss. 1997) (trust beneficiary entitled to have constructive trust imposed on proceeds of life insurance policy purchased with property embezzled from trust).

[42] Snell's Equity 314–315 (31st ed. 2005).

[43] *See* Head v. Head, 323 P.3d 505, 510 (Or. Ct. App. 2014) ("As a general rule, a court in equity has broad discretion in crafting relief, and the parties in equity are not necessarily limited to the relief that they seek in their complaint.").

third parties, and so we are treating it as a *procedural* remedy for purposes of this handbook. The least remedy-like of the procedural remedies is the equitable accounting, which is essentially little more than litigation discovery "in aid of a purely equitable right."[44]

Allow us one final illustration of our simple taxonomy of equitable remedies. Take the imposition of a constructive trust to facilitate restitution for unjust enrichment.[45] Unjust enrichment is the wrong, restitution is the substantive remedy; and the imposition of a constructive trust is the procedural remedy.[46] It is unfortunate that Equity is no longer required in most American law schools, and now offered at all in only a few, a topic we address in Section 8.25 of this handbook.

Choice of equitable remedies. When a trust has multiple classes of beneficiary, *e.g.*, equitable life interests and equitable remainder interests, not all classes are likely to be equally advantaged by the equitable relief that the court fashions. If *all* beneficiaries cannot agree on what the court should do, "the court ordinarily elects the remedy that in its opinion is the most advantageous to the beneficiaries as a whole."[47]

When there is a right to a jury trial. In an action at law, the parties may be entitled to a jury trial. That is generally not the case with equitable actions,[48] although there have been some trust-related exceptions.[49] An action brought by a beneficiary against a trustee for breach of trust is historically an equitable action, and, therefore, one in which there is no right to a jury trial.[50] If the trustee, however, is under a duty to pay money immediately and unconditionally to a beneficiary, the payment may be enforced against the trustee in an action at law.[51] In that case, the parties may have a right to a jury trial. "These situations are unlike a suit in equity to compel a trustee to restore misappropriated money, or a misappropriated chattel, that is to remain an asset of the trust."[52] Otherwise, a damage award against a trustee is likely to be an equitable remedy, and in any case the availability of a legal remedy ought not to "oust the

---

[44] Snell's Equity ¶ 18-04 (31st ed. 2005).

[45] *See generally* §8.15.78 of this handbook (unjust enrichment).

[46] *See* Nelson v. Nelson, 288 Kan. 570, 205 P.3d 715 (2009) ("The [defendants] correctly assert that a constructive trust is an equitable remedy; and a request to impose such a trust is not a cause of action that will stand independent of some wrongdoing."). For a general discussion of the constructive trust, see §3.3 of this handbook.

[47] 4 Scott & Ascher §24.19.1 (Choice of Remedies).

[48] 4 Scott & Ascher §24.1.2; Restatement (Third) of Trusts §95 cmt. a.

[49] *See, e.g.*, 4 Scott & Ascher §24.1.2 n.11.

[50] Carstens v. Central Nat'l Bank Co. of Des Moines, 461 N.W.2d 331 (Iowa 1990); Brown v. United Mo. Bank, N.A., 78 F.3d 382 (8th Cir. 1996); Magill v. Dutchess Bank & Trust Co., 150 A.D.2d 531, 541 N.Y.S.2d 437 (1989).

[51] Restatement (Second) of Trusts §198(1); 4 Scott & Ascher §§24.2 (The Beneficiary's Legal Remedies), 24.2.1 (When Money Is Due to Beneficiary) (noting also that "if the trustee has misappropriated trust funds due to a beneficiary, the trustee is liable in an action at law"); Restatement (Third) of Trusts §95 cmt. a ("[T]raditional principles allow a beneficiary to proceed against a trustee at law to enforce a right to a chattel or money if the trustee has violated an immediate, unconditional duty to transfer the chattel or pay the money to the beneficiary.").

[52] Restatement (Third) of Trusts §95 cmt. a.

jurisdiction of the court in equity to compel delivery of the money."[53] Occasionally, actions at law have been maintained by beneficiaries to compel trustees to disgorge items of tangible personal property,[54] although it would seem that such a remedy is actually an equitable one.[55]

Under the Uniform Probate Code, in any proceeding involving a trust where the parties have no right under the Constitution, by statute, or otherwise to a jury trial, "the Court in its discretion may call a jury to decide any issue of fact, *in which case the verdict is advisory only.*"[56] The court may do so notwithstanding the fact that the parties have waived any rights they may have to a jury trial.[57]

§7.2.3.1 Equity's Procedural Remedies of Accounting, Following *in Specie*, Tracing (Following Property into Its Product), Equitable Lien, Injunction and Constructive Trust

§7.2.3.1.1 Equitable Accounting

In probate court, nothing speaks more eloquently or provides more insight into factual and legal issues than an accounting.[58]

An equitable accounting is not only a form of litigation discovery but also a critical procedural equitable remedy, critical in that it lays the informational groundwork for all the other equitable remedies, both procedural and substantive. "Save in exceptional cases, the right to an account is dependent upon the existence of a fiduciary relationship," such as the relationship of trustee and beneficiary or agent and principal.[59] Because one's beneficial interest in a trust is an equitable right, it is in equity that one petitions for an accounting of the trustee's actions.[60] Who is entitled to an equitable accounting in the trust context? As we discuss more generally in Section 6.1.5.1 of this handbook, all the beneficiaries of a trust would have standing. This would include the remaindermen, as well as those whose equitable interests are contingent. For a more detailed and general discussion of who would qualify as the beneficiary of a particular trust, the reader is referred to Section 5.1 of this handbook.

---

[53] Wilkinson v. Stitt, 56 N.E. 830, 831 (Mass. 1900). *See generally* 4 Scott & Ascher §24.2.3 (Whether Legal Remedy Is Exclusive).

[54] *See, e.g.,* 4 Scott & Ascher §24.2.2 n.1.

[55] 4 Scott & Ascher §24.2.2. *See generally* §7.2.3.9 of this handbook (the equitable relief of specific reparation).

[56] UPC §1-306(b).

[57] UPC §1-306(b).

[58] Opening sentence of decision in Christie v. Kimball, 202 Cal. App. 4th 1407, 136 Cal. Rptr. 3d 516 (2012).

[59] Snell's Equity ¶ 18-04 (31st ed. 2005).

[60] Snell's Equity ¶ 18-04 (31st ed. 2005).

An incident of the trustee's general duty to account is the specific affirmative duty to furnish the beneficiaries with all the information that the beneficiaries need to enable them to protect their equitable interests under the trust.[61] That is the type of information that the typical decree or order for an equitable accounting is designed to uncover.

As a practical matter, a court with jurisdiction over the trustee of a trust, or its property, is entitled to any and all information pertaining to the trust that it can get its hands on.[62] Accordingly, its powers to extract information that is relevant to the affairs of the trust are expansive. One procedural vehicle for exercising these powers is the decree for an equitable accounting.[63] At least one court has even exercised this power *sua sponte* (on its own motion).[64]

In *Bleak House*, Dickens caricatured the consequences of the failure of a fiduciary to obey a judicial order for general accounting: "A sallow prisoner has come up, in custody, for the half-dozenth time, to make a personal application 'to purge himself of his contempt'; which, being a solitary surviving executor who has fallen into a state of conglomeration about accounts of which it is not pretended that he had ever any knowledge, he is not at all likely ever to do.... In the meantime his prospects in life are ended."[65]

§7.2.3.1.2   Following *in Specie*

Following property *in specie* (in kind) is essentially a rule of evidence that allows a claimant to identify misapplied property.[66] It is the process of "identifying the same property as it is transferred from one person to another."[67] On the other hand, tracing (following property into its product), a topic we take up in Section 7.2.3.1.3 of this handbook, is the process of "identifying a new asset as the substitute for an original asset which was misappropriated from the claimant."[68] The Restatement (Third) of Restitution and Unjust Enrichment's explanation of why following and tracing are not synonymous is helpful: "If the property in question may still be identified in its original form—whether in the recipient's hands or those of the subsequent transferee—there is no need to 'trace' anything, because the claimant obtains restitution of (or from) the original asset."[69]

---

[61] *See generally* §6.1.5.1 of this handbook (the trustee's duty to provide information to the beneficiary).

[62] *See generally* §8.40 of this handbook (jurisdiction over the trustee).

[63] *See, e.g.*, Jimenez v. Lee, 547 P.2d 126 (Or. 1976) ("This is a suit brought by plaintiff against her father to compel him to account for assets which she alleges were held by defendant as trustee for her.").

[64] *See* Christie v. Kimball, 202 Cal. App. 4th 1407, 136 Cal. Rptr. 3d 516 (2012) ("We conclude the probate court's general power to supervise administration of trusts permits it to order a trustee's accounting on its own motion.").

[65] Charles Dickens, *Bleak House*, Ch. 1 (In Chancery).

[66] Snell's Equity ¶ 28-32.

[67] Snell's Equity ¶ 28-32.

[68] Snell's Equity ¶ 28-32.

[69] Restatement (Third) of Restitution and Unjust Enrichment §58, cmt. c.

For purposes of this handbook, we are classifying following *in specie* as a procedural equitable remedy, rather than a substantive equitable remedy.[70] The assessment of damages and the issuing of a restitution order are examples of substantive equitable remedies.[71] A procedural equitable remedy supports a substantive equitable remedy. The procedural equitable remedy of following property *in specie*, for example, is tailor-made to support the substantive equitable remedy of restitution for the wrong of unjust enrichment, a topic we take up in Section 8.15.78 of this handbook.

If a trustee wrongfully transfers entrusted property to a third person who is not a good faith purchaser for value (BFP),[72] the beneficiary may choose the more advantageous procedural equitable remedy.[73] "He may either follow the original asset and enforce his equitable title to the original asset, or trace into the substituted asset in the hands of the trustee and enforce a proprietary remedy against it."[74] The former option we refer to in this handbook as following *in specie*; the latter as following property into its product (tracing).[75] Had the entrusted asset passed *in specie* into the hands of a BFP, then following *in specie* would not be an option.[76]

§7.2.3.1.3 Tracing (Following Property into Its Product)

Where a person wrongfully disposes of property of another knowing that the disposition is wrongful and acquires in exchange other property, the other is entitled at his option to enforce either (a) a constructive trust of the property so acquired, or (2) an equitable lien upon it to secure his claim for reimbursement from the wrongdoer.[77]

Tracing (following property into its product) in the trust context is about going after any *proceeds* from the wrongful disposition of entrusted property.[78] Following *in specie* is about going after the entrusted property itself. Though tracing was thought at one time to be a substantive equitable remedy, the better and current view is that it is a procedure for establishing the chain of evidence

---

[70] *See generally* §7.2.3 of this handbook (the procedural equitable remedy and the substantive equitable remedy compared).

[71] *See* §7.2.3.2 of this handbook (damages); §7.2.3.3 of this handbook (restitution).

[72] *See generally* §8.15.63 of this handbook (the BFP).

[73] Snell's Equity ¶ 28-36.

[74] Snell's Equity ¶ 28-36.

[75] *See generally* §7.2.3.1.3 of this handbook (following property into its product (tracing)).

[76] *See* Restatement (Third) of Restitution and Unjust Enrichment §17, illus. 4 (a non-BFP fact pattern). *See, e.g.,* Hartman v. Hartle, 122 A. 615 (N.J. Ch. 1923) (following real estate *in specie* not an option, the property now being "owned" by BFPs).

[77] Restatement of Restitution §202.

[78] *See, e.g.,* Lackey v. Lackey, 691 So.2d 990 (Miss. 1997) (a constructive trust for the benefit of the beneficiary of a certain express trust may be imposed on the proceeds of a certain life insurance policy that are attributable to policy premiums that had been paid from funds embezzled from the express trust, the policy proceeds now being in the hands of presumably innocent third parties).

from res to res.[79] Thus, for purposes of this handbook, we are referring to tracing (following property into its product) as a procedural equitable remedy, as opposed to a substantive equitable remedy. An example of a substantive equitable remedy would be the assessment of damages or a specific reparation order.[80]

The procedural equitable remedy of tracing (following property into its product) is not available to the beneficiary unless the economic value is physically traceable into the hands of the trustee and extant.[81] "Thus, if a trustee sells trust property and dissipates the proceeds, the beneficiary of the trust is not entitled to priority over other claimants of the trustee. The claimant must prove not only that the wrongdoer once had property legally or equitably belonging to him, but that he still holds the property or property which is in whole or in part its product."[82] Commingling the property "in one indistinguishable mass" does not necessarily preclude tracing; a total dissipation of the product, however, would.[83] A total dissipation would render the beneficiary a mere general creditor of the trustee personally.[84]

Thus, one of the possible advantages of being able to trace (follow into the product) is that "the equitable owner (the restitution claimant) recovers in priority to general creditors, . . . [though] . . . only to the extent that the creditors would otherwise be unjustly enriched at the owner's expense."[85] But what's sauce for the goose is sauce for the gander. The beneficiary (the trust) also may not be unjustly enriched.[86] Thus, when traced property has been put to profitable use, the Restatement (Third) of Restitution and Unjust Enrichment would not allow the beneficiary (the trust) to obtain a recovery in excess of what had been lost if to do so would be at the expense of the trustee's personal creditors, or at the expense of his innocent surviving dependents.[87]

It is fundamental that the trust property and any income earned on it be kept within the trustee's control.[88] This obligation extends not only to the property in its original form but to any new form into which it has been changed

---

[79] W. A. Lee, *Purifying the dialect of equity*, 7(2) Tr. Q. Rev. 20–21 (May 2009) [a STEP publication].

[80] *See generally* §7.2.3.2 of this handbook (equitable damages); §7.2.3.3 of this handbook (specific reparation).

[81] *See, e.g.,* Jimenez v. Lee, 547 P.2d 126 (Or. 1976) ("The money from the savings bond and savings account are clearly traceable into the bank stock.").

[82] Restatement of Restitution §215, cmt. a.

[83] Restatement of Restitution §215, cmt. a.

[84] Restatement of Restitution §215, cmt. a. *See, e.g.,* Jimenez v. Lee, 547 P.2d 126 (Or. 1976) ("Whether or not the assets of plaintiff's trust are traceable into a product, defendant is personally liable for that amount which would have accrued to plaintiff had there been no breach of trust.").

[85] Restatement (Third) of Restitution and Unjust Enrichment §58, cmt. b.

[86] *See, e.g.,* Jimenez v. Lee, 547 P.2d 126 (Or. 1976) ("Defendant [self-dealing trustee] is, of course, entitled to deduct the amount which he expended out of the trust estate for plaintiff's [beneficiary's] educational needs.").

[87] Restatement (Third) of Restitution and Unjust Enrichment §61.

[88] *See generally* 2A Scott on Trusts §175. *See also* §6.2.1.2 of this handbook (trustee's duty to segregate and earmark trust property).

or converted.[89] This is what tracing (following property into its product) is about. "What is traced is not the physical asset itself but the value inherent in it."[90] Again, tracing is not a substantive remedy. Rather, it is a mechanism or "process by which a claimant demonstrates what has happened to his property, identifies its proceeds and the persons who have handled or received them, and justifies his claim that the proceeds can probably be regarded as representing his property."[91] If the trustee, in breach of trust, allows specific trust property to pass for full value to a purchaser who is innocently unaware of the beneficiary's equitable interest in the property, i.e., to a BFP,[92] then the purchaser is entitled to keep the specific property.[93] The trustee, however, would be accountable to the beneficiary for the proceeds.[94] For more on the concept of the good faith purchaser for value (BFP), the reader is referred to Section 8.15.63 of this handbook. If the transferee is not a BFP, then the beneficiary is entitled to follow the asset *in specie* and have the asset itself brought back into the trust, assuming that that is physically possible,[95] or to trace and recoup its economic value if not, i.e., to follow the property into its product.

It is said that tracing (following property into its product) is concerned with the same person but different assets, while following *in specie* is concerned with the same asset but different persons.[96] Recovery through following or tracing (following property into its product) is usually effected judicially by the imposition of a constructive trust upon the asset or the proceeds as the case may be,[97] a topic we take up in Section 3.3 of this handbook. Again, the constructive trust also is not a substantive equitable remedy. Rather it is a procedural equitable remedy, that is to say an equitable device or mechanism for freezing and securing the followed or traced property so that the court may issue

---

[89] 4 Scott & Ascher §24.6 (Following Trust Property into Its Product).

[90] Lewin ¶41-05 (England). *See also* 4 Scott & Ascher §24.11.2 (Accountability for Proceeds).

[91] Foskett v. McKeown [2001] 1 AC 102, 128D; [2002] 2 WLR 1299.

[92] *See* Lewin ¶41-102 through ¶41-127 (England) (discussing the good-faith purchaser for value, *i.e.*, the BFP). As to the United States, *see* §5.4.2 of this handbook (rights of the beneficiary as against BFPs and other transferees of the underlying trust property), §8.3.2 of this handbook (the doctrine of bona fide purchase and its breach of trust notice requirement), and §8.15.63 of this handbook (doctrine of bona fide purchase in the trust context). *See also* §8.3.6 of this handbook (negotiable instruments and the duty of third parties to inquire into the trustee's authority). For a comparison of the BFP, a creature of equity, with the holder in due course, a creature of law, *see* §8.15.68 of this handbook (holders in due course in the trust context).

[93] *See, e.g.*, Stegemeier v. Magness, 728 A.2d 557 (Del. 1999). *See generally* Restatement (Second) of Trusts §284 §8.3.2 of this handbook (purchasers for value of trust property); Restatement of Restitution, Chap. 13, Introductory Note (1937) (the BFP).

[94] Lewin ¶41-05 (England); 4 Scott & Ascher §24.11.2 (Accountability for Proceeds) (U.S.); Restatement of Restitution §198 ("Where a fiduciary in violation of his duty to the beneficiary disposes of property entrusted to him as fiduciary, he holds any property received in exchange upon a constructive trust for the beneficiary") (U.S.).

[95] *See generally* Bogert §§866, 921, 922; 4 Scott & Ascher §24.11.2 (Accountability for Proceeds). *See also* §7.2.3.9 of this handbook (the equitable relief of specific reparation) and §8.3.2 of this handbook (purchasers for value of trust property).

[96] Lewin ¶41-05.

[97] 4 Scott & Ascher §24.6.

equitable specific performance/enforcement orders with respect to it.[98] It is the specific performance/enforcement order that is the substantive equitable remedy.[99]

The value to the beneficiary of being able to trace (follow the trust property into its product) is twofold: Any increase in its value since the wrongful disposition accrues to the beneficiary, and the beneficiary with respect to the property obtains priority over the trustee's general creditors.[100] Otherwise, the claim against the trustee for breach of trust could well be that of a general creditor.[101] Again, even if the plaintiff is successful in asserting a trust relationship, the property must still be identified with reasonable precision for a tracing order to issue.[102]

The self-dealing factor. Assume *B* is trustee of $5000 for the benefit of *C*. In breach of trust *B* purchases for himself Blackacre with the money. Immediately thereafter the market value of Blackacre doubles. *C* can charge *B* as constructive trustee of Blackacre for the benefit of *C*, or can hold *B* personally liable for $5000 and enforce an equitable lien upon Blackacre.[103] On the other hand, if *B* in good faith misdelivers $5000 to *X* who then purchases with the funds Blackacre for himself, *X* is unjustly enriched, but only to the tune of $5000 plus interest. In other words, there is no tracing. The critical difference between the two fact patterns is that in the first the trustee was engaged in fiduciary self-dealing, whereas in the second he had not been personally aggrandized by his breach of trust.[104] Had *X* received the $5000 as trustee of another trust, the result would have been the same.[105] No tracing, no restitution of consequential gains, only the restitution of $5000 plus interest. "...[R]estitution for an inadvertent breach of trust will not impose a liability for consequential gains if the result would be to strip one innocent beneficiary of a gain and confer it as a windfall on another."[106] Where there is equal equity, the law shall prevail.[107]

Third party's knowing participation in a breach of trust. A third party to a trust relationship who knowingly participates in a breach of trust incurs fiduciary-like liabilities. This is a topic we take up in Section 7.2.9 of this handbook. Thus, to the extent trust property is wrongfully separated from the trust estate and traceable to the noninnocent third party, the BFP defense is

---

[98] *See generally* §7.2.3.1.6 (the constructive trust).

[99] *See generally* §7.2.3.4 of this handbook (specific performance).

[100] 4 Scott & Ascher §§24.11.2 (Accountability for Proceeds), 24.6 (Following Trust Property into Its Product); Restatement (Second) of Trusts §202.

[101] 4 Scott & Ascher §§24.11.2 (Accountability for Proceeds), 24.6 (Following Trust Property into Its Product); Restatement (Second) of Trusts §202; Restatement of Restitution §215, cmt. a. *But see* §7.4 of this handbook (noting that claims for money damages against a trustee for fraud, embezzlement, defalcation, or other such acts of willful and malicious injury to a trust are not dischargeable in bankruptcy).

[102] *See* Bogert §921; Restatement of Restitution §215, cmt. a.

[103] Restatement of Restitution §202, illus. 1.

[104] *See generally* Restatement (Third) of Restitution and Unjust Enrichment §43.

[105] *See generally* Restatement (Third) of Restitution and Unjust Enrichment §43, illus. 35.

[106] Restatement (Third) of Restitution and Unjust Enrichment §53, cmt. d.

[107] *See generally* §8.12 of this handbook (equity's maxims).

unavailable to the third party. Here is an illustration taken verbatim from the Restatement (Third) of Restitution and Unjust Enrichment:

> Title to Owner's restaurant is held by Trustee for owner. Acting without authority, Trustee sells the restaurant to Purchaser, who acquires the property with notice of the breach of trust. The restaurant, now insured for the benefit of the Purchaser, is destroyed by fire. Purchaser's rights under the policy, and any insurance proceeds that may eventually be payable, are the traceable product of Owner's interest in the property. They are held by Purchaser in constructive trust for Owner.[108]

Tracing funds into a common account or commingled fund. If by ordinary accounting methods the beneficiary can show that trust cash has been deposited to the personal account of the trustee, a lien may be placed upon all the funds in the account.[109] If the trustee is insolvent, the "trust" is entitled to priority over the trustee's general creditors when it comes to satisfying its claim from funds in the account.[110] To the extent that assets in the account and traceable property that has left the account are insufficient to satisfy the claim, the trust becomes a personal general creditor of the trustee for the balance owed.[111]

It should be noted, however, that in the past if there had been incremental withdrawals from an account in which trust funds and the personal funds of the trustee had been commingled, a court might well have felt the need to make a determination as to whose money it was, the trustee's or the trust's. The determination, which was based on certain traditional presumptions and fictions, could well have had varying economic consequences for the parties, *i.e.*, the trust beneficiaries and the trustee's personal creditors, particularly if the balance in the account was less than the claim and the money that had been withdrawn had subsequently been dissipated, or if the money that was withdrawn had been invested in an asset that had appreciated and what remained in the account had been dissipated. Many courts, both here and in England,[112] felt constrained to apply one or more of the following presumptions, a process that Professor Scott felt has unnecessarily muddied the waters:

- The trustee was presumed to have withdrawn his own money first.
- The one, be it the trustee or the "trust," whose funds had first entered the account was deemed the owner of the funds that had first exited the account.
- The trustee was presumed to have acted honestly, and pursued a withdrawal program that was most advantageous to the trust.

---

[108] Restatement (Third) of Restitution and Unjust Enrichment §58, illus. 13.
[109] *See generally* Bogert §924; Restatement of Restitution §211, cmt. a.
[110] Restatement of Restitution §209, cmt. a.
[111] Restatement of Restitution §215, cmt. a.
[112] For a discussion of the English bank account tracing cases, *see* Mark Pawlowski, *Tracing into Assets*, Tr. & Est. L.J., No. 40 (Oct. 2002), at 4.

The Restatement of Restitution (1937) would limit tracing in such circumstances to the proportion that the trust's money bore to the total of the commingled fund at the time of the wrongful withdrawal by the trustee.[113] "In part, at least, the impetus of the proportionality rule . . . was a concern that the claimant might otherwise obtain a fortuitous windfall recovery at the expense of the recipient's general creditors."[114]

The approach of the Restatement (Third) of Restitution and Unjust Enrichment to such withdrawals has more of an equitable flavor to it than either the traditional approach or the approach of the 1937 Restatement. Disadvantageous or untraceable withdrawals are attributed to the wrongdoing trustee's personal funds, to the extent the available balance permits.[115] Conversely, any withdrawal that yields a traceable product may be attributable to the trustee's personal funds to the extent the beneficiaries so elect and the available balance permits.[116] This dual presumption in favor of the trust beneficiaries is "counterbalanced" by an "equally significant" presumption in favor of the trustee (and, by extension, in favor of the trustee's personal creditors). Here it is: A contribution by the trustee to the common fund postwithdrawal is not put toward making the trust estate whole, unless it can be shown that the trustee affirmatively intended otherwise.[117]

Warning: The much-criticized Rule in Clayton's Case, covered in Section 8.15.11 of this handbook, is inapplicable to commingling of trust funds with the trustee's personal funds. The Rule in Clayton's Case, which takes a "first in, first out" approach, applies when the trustee has commingled the funds of two or more trusts in a single account. In any case, the Restatement of Restitution is not in accord with Clayton: "Where a person wrongfully mingles money of two or more persons and subsequently wrongfully withdraws and dissipates a part of the money, the claimants are entitled to share the balance proportionately. . . . It is immaterial in what order the deposits were made. . . ."[118] In other words, the equality is equity maxim informs tracing doctrine in cases where the assets of multiple trusts are wrongly commingled in a single fund.[119]

All profits gained by verifiable use of the trust fund belong to the trust estate and not to the trustee. This is true whether the profits have been gained rightfully or wrongfully. "The principle is that, in the management of a trust, the trustee may lose but cannot gain."[120] Otherwise, the trustee would be unjustly enriched. The subject of unjust enrichment is taken up in Section 8.15.78 of this handbook.

---

[113] Restatement of Restitution §§210-211 (1937).

[114] Restatement (Third) of Restitution and Unjust Enrichment §59, cmt. d.

[115] Restatement (Third) of Restitution and Unjust Enrichment §59, cmt. d.

[116] Restatement (Third) of Restitution and Unjust Enrichment §59, cmt. d.

[117] Restatement (Third) of Restitution and Unjust Enrichment §59, cmt. d.

[118] Restatement of Restitution §213, cmt. c.

[119] *See, e.g.,* Matter of Michigan Boiler & Eng'g Co., 171 B.R. 565 (Bankr. E.D. Mich. 1993). The equity maxims are covered generally in §8.12 of this handbook.

[120] Baker v. Disbrow, 18 Hun 29, 30 (1879), *aff'd mem.* 79 N.Y. 631 (1880). *See generally* 4 Scott & Ascher §24.9 (Liability in the Case of a Breach of Trust).

§7.2.3.1.4   Equitable Lien

The imposition of a constructive trust, a subject that is covered in Section 7.2.3.1.6 of this handbook, is a procedural equitable remedy that is tailor-made to support the substantive equitable remedy of restitution for the wrong of unjust enrichment.[121] Sometimes, however, the facts are such that the judicial imposition of a constructive trust is not an option, such as where the trustee wrongfully uses entrusted property to improve property that the trustee has rightfully acquired with his personal funds.[122] In that case, the beneficiaries are entitled to the imposition of an equitable lien on the trustee's improved property, but not to the imposition of a constructive trust on it.[123]

The equitable lien is an asset-based procedural equitable remedy for unjust enrichment. So is the constructive trust and subrogation.[124] "All three remedies allow the claimant to assert rights in specific property as an alternative (or a supplement) to a money judgment against the defendant in personam."[125] In the case of the equitable lien, however, its function is to secure the defendant's equitable obligation to make a money payment.[126] There still, however, needs to be some nexus between the specific asset that one wishes to equitably encumber and the unjust enrichment event.[127] As an equitable lien has the "ordinary characteristics of a lien for security," the one who has been unjustly enriched may bring about its discharge by paying the claimant the amount of the underlying liability.[128] In other words, the wrongdoer has a right of redemption.

An equitable lien secures a fixed amount; a constructive trust corrals identifiable property that can fluctuate in value. Thus, the constructive trust is the "natural choice for a case in which a wrongdoer has acquired an asset that has appreciated in value, while equitable lien will be more favorable if the value of the asset has declined."[129]

Had the trustee wrongfully swapped entrusted property for other property, which he then wrongfully kept for himself, then the court could impose either a constructive trust or an equitable lien on the other property, a fact pattern we consider in Section 7.2.3.1.3 of this handbook.[130] If the wrongfully acquired property has fallen in value, then the equitable lien is the beneficiary's better procedural remedy; if it has risen in value, then the constructive trust

---

[121] *See also* §7.2.3.3 of this handbook (restitution); §8.15.78 of this handbook (unjust enrichment).

[122] Restatement of Restitution §206 (Improvements upon Wrongdoer's Property).

[123] Restatement of Restitution §206, cmt. b.

[124] Subrogation is covered in §7.2.3.1.7 of this handbook.

[125] Restatement (Third) of Restitution and Unjust Enrichment §56, cmt. a.

[126] Restatement (Third) of Restitution and Unjust Enrichment §56, cmt. a.

[127] Restatement (Third) of Restitution and Unjust Enrichment §56, cmt. a.

[128] Restatement (Third) of Restitution and Unjust Enrichment §56, cmt. c.

[129] Restatement (Third) of Restitution and Unjust Enrichment §56, cmt. b.

[130] *See also* Restatement of Restitution §202, illus. (U.S.); Snell's Equity ¶ 28-36 (England). *See, e.g.,* Jimenez v. Lee, 547 P.2d 126 (Or. 1976).

is.[131] If the wrongfully acquired property becomes less valuable than the wrongfully alienated entrusted property, the trustee is still personally liable for the full value of the wrongfully alienated entrusted property, the equitable lien being merely security for the beneficiary's equitable claim against the trustee.[132] English law is in accord:

> Against an asset in the hands of the trustee, the claimant has an election between two proprietary remedies. He may enforce an equitable lien against it for the value of the original asset which was applied to acquire it. The lien is for this fixed amount, and does not change in value even if the substituted asset rises or falls in value. Alternatively, he may claim the entire beneficial ownership of the substituted asset under a constructive trust. The value of this proprietary security will vary in accordance with fluctuations in the value of the substituted asset. The claimant has an unrestricted election between whichever of the remedies is more advantageous to him.[133]

If the property subject to an equitable lien is encumbered or transferred, the fate of the lien will depend upon the particular facts and circumstances. "The equitable claimant is entitled to priority over the creditors of the owner of the property, since the creditors are not bona fide purchasers . . . [for value (BFPs)] . . ."[134] On the other hand, an equitable lien could be cut off if title to the subject property were to pass to a legitimate BFP,[135] or if it were disposed of in such a way as to be rendered untraceable.[136] Still, "[w]here property is subject to an equitable lien and the owner of the property disposes of it and acquires other property in exchange, he holds the property so acquired subject to the lien. . . . So also, where the property which is subject to the lien is mingled with other property in one indistinguishable mass, the lien can be enforced against the mingled mass."[137]

There is little difference between the equitable lien and the equitable charge, except in the way that each can come about. The equitable lien is a judicially imposed procedural equitable remedy, whereas the equitable charge is the product of an initially private and voluntary reordering of the rights, duties, and obligations of the parties. An equitable lien "arises by operation of equity from the relationship between the parties rather than by any act of theirs."[138] The equitable charge is taken up in Section 9.9.10 of this handbook.

---

[131] Restatement of Restitution §161, cmt. a; Snell's Equity ¶ 28-36 (England).

[132] Restatement of Restitution §202, cmt. d. (U.S.); Snell's Equity ¶ 28-36 (England).

[133] Snell's Equity ¶ 28-36.

[134] Restatement of Restitution §161, cmt. c. *See generally* §8.15.63 of this handbook (the doctrine of bona fide purchase; the BFP).

[135] Restatement of Restitution §161, cmt. d.

[136] Restatement of Restitution §161, cmt. e.

[137] Restatement of Restitution §161, cmt. e.

[138] Snell's Equity ¶ 34-07.

§7.2.3.1.5 Preliminary or Temporary Injunction to Preserve Trust Property (the Procedural Equitable Remedy)

A preliminary/temporary injunction to preserve trust property—the English employ the term interim injunction—is a procedural equitable remedy.[139] Its purpose is to maintain the *status quo* pending a final determination of the substantive rights of the parties.[140] "A court of equity has never hesitated to use the strongest powers to protect and preserve a trust fund in interlocutory proceedings on the basis that, if the trust fund disappears by the time the action comes to trial, equity will have been invoked in vain."[141]

If the property to be frozen is not in the hands of the trustee, it at least must be susceptible of being followed *in specie* or traced (followed into its product).[142] Otherwise the issuance of a preliminary or temporary injunction to preserve trust property is not an option. The subject of following trust property *in specie* is covered in §7.2.3.1.2 of this handbook; the subject of following trust property into its product (tracing) is covered in §7.2.3.1.3 of this handbook.

If trust property is in the hands of a third party, a preliminary or temporary injunction against the third party would be justified if there were a possibility that that trust property could pass into the hands of a good faith purchaser for value (BFP).[143] The BFP is discussed in §8.15.63 of this handbook. Enjoining further alienation of the trust property to anyone pending a final determination of the substantive rights, duties and obligations of the parties is usually advisable. The more parties that have to be brought into the litigation the more inconvenience and expense for all concerned.[144]

In §5.4.1.1 of this handbook, we consider the beneficiary's general right to be kept informed about the affairs of the trust. "A beneficiary who shows that the trust fund is in danger can obtain, not only an interim injunction, but also an interim order directing a party to provide information about the location of trust property, or property claimed to be trust property, or property into which trust property can be traced."[145] As to who qualifies as a beneficiary a trust for standing purposes (*locus standi*), the reader is referred to §5.1 of this handbook.[146]

---

[139] Lewin ¶ 38-09.
[140] Lewin ¶ 38-09.
[141] Lewin ¶ 38-09.
[142] Lewin ¶ 38-09.
[143] Lewin ¶ 38-10.
[144] Lewin ¶ 38-10.
[145] Lewin ¶ 38-09.
[146] As to who would have standing under English law, see Lewin ¶ 38-11 (*locus standi* to be a claimant to secure the trust property).

§7.2.3.1.6   Constructive Trust

Constructive trust doctrine. A general discussion of constructive trust doctrine is contained in Section 3.3 of this handbook, which the reader is advised to consult before proceeding further. A constructive trust is an express trust which doubles as a procedural equitable remedy, that is to say its purpose is to support the substantive equitable remedy of restitution for unjust enrichment.[147] The Restatement of Restitution (1937) is not in accord, suggesting that a constructive trust is something other than a true trust.[148] For the same reason, neither is the Restatement (Third) of Restitution and Unjust Enrichment in accord.[149]

The substantive equitable remedy of restitution is covered in Section 7.2.3.3 of this handbook. The wrong of unjust enrichment is taken up in Section 8.15.78 of this handbook. "Where a person holding title to property is subject to an equitable duty to convey it to another on the ground that he would be unjustly enriched if he were permitted to retain it, a constructive trust arises."[150] As we discuss in greater detail in Section 6.1.3 of this handbook, there are many ways that a trustee can unjustly enrich himself from the trust property in breach of the duty of loyalty such that the judicial imposition of a constructive trust is warranted.[151] Here are a few:

- Purchase by trustee for his own account of property entrusted to him as fiduciary;[152]
- Sale of trustee's individual property to himself as fiduciary;[153]
- Purchase by trustee of property that he should purchase for the beneficiary;[154]
- Renewal of lease by trustee for his personal benefit;[155]
- Purchase by trustee for his own account of an encumbrance upon property held by him as fiduciary;[156]
- Bonus or commission received by trustee;[157]

---

[147] *See generally* Charles E. Rounds, Jr., *Relief for IP Rights Infringement Is Primarily Equitable: How American Legal Education Is Short-Changing the 21st Century Corporate Litigator*, 26 Santa Clara Computer & High Tech L.J. 313 (2010).

[148] Restatement of Restitution §160, cmt. a.

[149] *See* Restatement (Third) of Restitution and Unjust Enrichment §55, cmt. b.

[150] Restatement of Restitution §160.

[151] *See generally* Restatement of Restitution §190.

[152] Restatement of Restitution §192.

[153] Restatement of Restitution §193.

[154] Restatement of Restitution §194.

[155] Restatement of Restitution §195 (providing that a person holding as trustee a leasehold interest who in violation of his duty to the beneficiary obtains a renewal of the lease for himself holds the new lease upon a constructive trust for the beneficiary).

[156] Restatement of Restitution §196.

[157] Restatement of Restitution §197 (providing that where a trustee in violation of his duty to the beneficiary receives or retains a bonus or commission or other profit, he holds what he receives upon a constructive trust for the beneficiary).

- Sale of entrusted property in breach of trust;[158]
- Competition by trustee;[159] and
- Exploiting confidential information for personal purposes.[160]

A constructive trust can also be judicially imposed as a procedural equitable remedy on property wrongfully in the hands of a third party to a trust relationship. "Where a fiduciary in violation of his duty to the beneficiary transfers property or causes property to be transferred to a third person, the third person, if he gave no value or if he had notice of the violation of duty, holds the property upon a constructive trust for the beneficiary."[161] If the third party were a good faith purchaser for value (BFP) of the entrusted property, there would no unjust enrichment and thus there could be no imposition of a constructive trust on the property that had been transferred out. The rights of a BFP are considered in Section 8.15.63 of this handbook. If circumstances warrant, however, a constructive trust could be judicially imposed on the proceeds from the sale of entrusted property to a BFP.[162]

Creditors of the constructive trustee. It is said that "[t]he preference that the constructive trust claimant acquires over general creditors of the defendant is usually the object of the . . . [procedural] . . . remedy."[163] The restitution claimant will generally prevail over a judgment creditor, "though not over a secured creditor who qualifies as a bona fide purchaser of the assets in question."[164] Otherwise the judgment creditor would be unjustly enriched. "The practical advantages of asset-based restitution are particularly apparent when the claimant obtains restoration of appreciated property without the need to prove its value."[165]

The claimant's property must be identifiable and titled in the one who is unjustly enriched. The procedural equitable remedy of constructive trust is only available, however, if the specific property at issue is identifiable, that is capable of either being followed *in specie* or followed (traced) into its product,[166] and if the property has not found its way into the hands of a good faith

---

[158] Restatement of Restitution §198 (providing that where a trustee in violation of his duty to the beneficiary disposes of property entrusted to him as fiduciary, he holds any property received in exchange upon a constructive trust for the beneficiary).

[159] Restatement of Restitution §199 (providing that where a trustee acquires property by competing with the beneficiary, *i.e.*, with the "trust," in violation of his duty to the beneficiary, he holds the property upon a constructive trust for the beneficiary).

[160] Restatement of Restitution §200 (providing that where a trustee in violation of his duty to the beneficiary acquires property through the use of confidential information, he holds the property so acquired upon a constructive trust for the beneficiary).

[161] Restatement of Restitution §201(1).

[162] Restatement of Restitution §198, cmt. a.

[163] Restatement (Third) of Restitution and Unjust Enrichment §55, cmt. a. *See also* cmt. d.

[164] Restatement (Third) of Restitution and Unjust Enrichment §55, cmt. d.

[165] Restatement (Third) of Restitution and Unjust Enrichment §55, cmt. i.

[166] *See generally* §7.2.3.1.2 of this handbook (following *in specie*); §7.2.3.1.3 of this handbook (following property into its product or tracing); Restatement (Third) of Restitution and Unjust Enrichment §55, cmt. g.

purchaser for value (BFP).[167] The one who is unjustly enriched needs to have the legal title to the identifiable property, not just the possession of the property. Otherwise, the claimant will have to resort to some other remedy.[168] Thus, the constructive trust coupled with an equitable restitution order would not be a suitable judicial vehicle for recovering stolen property *in specie* directly from its thief, the thief having possession of but not legal title to the property. All is not necessarily lost, however. The mere fact that title never left the claimant ought not to prevent the claimant from recovering the property *in specie* from the thief via an action at law for replevin.[169]

The constructive trustee will generally be called upon to render an equitable accounting. The procedural equitable remedy of constructive trust may be coupled with the procedural equitable two-pronged remedy of a judicial specific performance order to the constructive trustee to account to the claimant for net profits accruing to the constructive trustee incident to the constructive trustee's unjustifiable use of the identified property over time, "in the same manner as a trustee's accounting under an express trust, for the purpose of determining . . . net liability in restitution."[170]

Joint ownership in constructive trust. What about joint ownership in constructive trust? Say an express trustee purchases identifiable property for personal purposes for $20,000. It turns out that $10,000 of the purchase price was obtained in breach of trust from the trust estate. The value of the property doubles. The express trustee is a constructive trustee of 50 percent of the property for the benefit of the beneficiaries of the express trust. The express trust is the equitable owner of the property acquired in the proportion that its asset contribution bears to the total amount invested.[171] Thus, the current market value of the express trust's share of the property is $20,000.[172] "A case in which the claimant's funds supply a portion of the purchase price must be distinguished from one in which the claimant's funds are used to enhance the value of the property the defendant owns."[173] In the latter case, the claimant's remedy is likely to be an equitable lien, a topic we take up in Section 7.2.3.1.4 of this handbook.

The constructive trust versus the resulting trust. Sometimes it is not all that clear whether the constructive trust or the resulting trust is the appropriate procedural equitable remedy for innocent unjust enrichment. Sometimes it may not matter. Assume the owner of an identifiable item of property transfers it by mistake to *B* in trust. Assume that the legal title to the property metaphorically just falls into *B*'s lap. No express trust beneficiaries are designated or ascertainable. The transferor then dies. Finally, assume that *B* would be unjustly

---

[167] *See generally* Restatement (Third) of Restitution and Unjust Enrichment §55, cmt. m; §8.15.63 of this handbook (the BFP).

[168] Restatement (Third) of Restitution and Unjust Enrichment §55, cmt. f.

[169] Restatement (Third) of Restitution and Unjust Enrichment §55, cmt. f.

[170] Restatement (Third) of Restitution and Unjust Enrichment §55, cmt. l. *See, e.g.*, Jimenez v. Lee, 547 P.2d 126 (Or. 1976).

[171] Restatement (Third) of Restitution and Unjust Enrichment §55, cmt. n.

[172] Restatement (Third) of Restitution and Unjust Enrichment §55, illus. 32.

[173] Restatement (Third) of Restitution and Unjust Enrichment §55, cmt. n.

enriched were he to retain title to the property. In other words, title to the item should somehow find its way into the hands of the executor of the transferor's probate estate. But what procedural vehicles are available to the court for bringing about such a result? The resulting trust might be one, a topic we take up generally in Section 4.1.1.1 of this handbook. *B* is judicially determined to hold the item upon a resulting trust for the benefit of the executor.[174] The constructive trust is another. The transfer of legal title having been the product of a unilateral mistake on the part of the transferor, that is to say there having been no intention on the part of the transferor to make a gift of the item to *B*, the court declares *B* a constructive trustee of the item for the benefit of the executor. "Liability in restitution is often independent of fault."[175] In either case, the court follows up with an equitable specific performance order compelling *B* to transfer title to the executor.

§7.2.3.1.7 Subrogation

Where a trustee has been unjustly enriched at the expense of the beneficiaries, there are certain situations where an equitable subrogation order is the appropriate procedural equitable remedy rather than the imposition of a constructive trust[176] or equitable lien.[177] One situation is where the trustee wrongfully uses trust funds to release a mortgage on his personal property. This is a topic we take up in Section 8.15.50 of this handbook. In Section 9.9.23 of this handbook we explain generally what equitable subrogation is and why the remedy itself does not put the parties in some kind of trust relationship. In a nutshell, subrogation "is a doctrine under which one person is entitled to stand in the shoes of another in respect of certain legal or equitable rights."[178]

§7.2.3.2 Damages (a Substantive Remedy)

The reference to paying money . . . [in the Uniform Trust Code] . . . includes liability that might be characterized as damages, restitution, or surcharge.[179]

Cases awarding money damages for consequential injury, either to the trust or to the beneficiary, exist in profusion in trust remedy law. Accordingly, money damages were and are as much an equitable remedy as a legal remedy. Justice Scalia was correct to say that [m]oney damages are . . . the classic form of legal relief, but flatly wrong to assert that money damages

---

[174] *See, e.g.,* Stephenson v. Spiegle, 429 N.J. Super. 378, 58 A.3d 1228 (2013) (endorsing the resulting trust option).

[175] Restatement (Third) of Restitution and Unjust Enrichment §1, cmt. f.

[176] *See generally* §7.2.3.1.6 of this handbook (the constructive trust).

[177] *See generally* §7.2.3.1.4 of this handbook (the equitable lien).

[178] Harold Greville Hanbury & Ronald Harling Maudsley, Modern Equity 574 (10th ed. 1976).

[179] UTC §1001 cmt. (available at <http://www.uniformlaws.org/Act.aspx?title=Trust%20Code>).

are not equally characteristic of equity when it enforces equity-based causes of action such as those arising from breach of trust.[180]

A general Introduction to equitable damages. The wronged beneficiary is not necessarily limited to the remedy of tracing and recovery.[181] If tracing is impossible or impractical, equitable damages from the trustee's personal assets may be an option.[182] Damages in equity, especially for breach of trust, are sometimes called surcharge.[183] Trust beneficiaries, however, need to be fairly certain that they have a good case before bringing their trustee to court as "a trustee can ordinarily pay out of the trust estate litigation expenses incurred in a successful attempt to prevent the beneficiaries from subjecting the trustee to surcharge."[184] Also, a beneficiary's claim against the trustee for damages for breach of trust does not in itself entitle the beneficiary to priority over the trustee's other claimants.[185] In other words, when it comes to a claim against the trustee for damages, the beneficiary generally is in no better position than a general creditor of the trustee, unless the trustee also possesses an equitable interest under the trust.[186] "If the trustee is also a beneficiary, the other beneficiaries are entitled to a charge upon the trustee's beneficial interest to secure their claims for breach of trust."[187] Still, under certain circumstances, a damages election on balance will be worth the risks. Under Kansas' version of the Uniform Trust Code, for example, a trustee who embezzles or knowingly converts to the trustee's own use trust property would be liable for double the property's value.[188]

Ordinarily the trust estate is augmented by the money judgment. The court, however, would have the equitable authority to order that the surcharged

---

[180] John H. Langbein, *What ERISA Means by Equitable: The Supreme Court's Trail of Error in* Russell, Mertens, *and* Great-West, 103 Colum. L. Rev. 1317, 1337 (2003) (citing to Mertens v. Hewitt Assocs., 508 U.S. 248, 255 (1993)). *See generally* 4 Scott & Ascher §24.9.

[181] Restatement (Second) of Trusts §202(2).

[182] Note, however, that if the trustee also happens to be a beneficiary, then "the other beneficiaries can compel the trustee-beneficiary to make good the breach of trust out of his or her beneficial interest." 4 Scott & Ascher §25.2.7 (Impounding Trustee-Beneficiary's Share). *But see* 4 Scott & Ascher §25.2.7.1 (Trustee-Beneficiary of Spendthrift Trust).

[183] *See* Restatement (Third) of Trusts §95 cmt. b (surcharge liability for breach of trust); CIGNA Corp. v. Amara, 131 S. Ct. 1866, 1880 (2011) ("Indeed, prior to the merger of law and equity this kind of monetary remedy against a trustee, sometimes called a 'surcharge,' was 'exclusively equitable.'"); John H. Langbein, *What ERISA Means by Equitable: The Supreme Court's Trail of Error in* Russell, Mertens, *and* Great-West, 103 Colum. L. Rev. 1317, 1352-1353 (2003) ("The concept . . . [of a surcharge] . . . , evoking the days when English lawyers still spoke law French, is that the Chancellor grants monetary relief by a charge on (sur) the account filed by the breaching trustee."). The law French phenomenon is explained in §8.15 of this handbook (doctrines ancient and modern).

[184] 3 Scott & Ascher §18.1.2.4.

[185] Restatement (Second) of Trusts §202(2).

[186] 4 Scott & Ascher §24.6; Restatement (Second) of Trusts §202(2).

[187] 4 Scott & Ascher §24.6.

[188] Kan. Stat. Ann. §58a-1002(a)(3). *See also* McCabe v. Duran, 180 P.3d 1098 (Kan. Ct. App. 2008) (the court declining to retroactively apply the double-damages provision of Kansas's version of the UTC).

amount be paid directly to the beneficiary should the particular facts and circumstances warrant bypassing the trustee.[189]

Damage computation methodologies. As a general rule, damages would be computed on the basis of any loss occasioned by a breach of trust, to include the value of any subsequent earnings and gains that would have accrued to the trust were it not for the breach and to include interest thereon if appropriate.[190] To restore the real value of the trust principal, an upward inflation adjustment may be warranted.[191] In other words, a trustee who commits a breach of trust is liable to the beneficiary for the greater of the following amounts:

- What is required to restore the value of the trust or estate property and distributions to what they would have been, had the breach not occurred.[192]

---

[189] Restatement (Third) of Trusts §100 cmt. a(2).

[190] *See generally* Bogert §862; 4 Scott & Ascher §§24.9 (Liability in the Case of a Breach of Trust), 24.17 (Effect of General Increase or Decrease in Market Values). For when compound interest, as opposed to simple interest, is appropriate, *see* Bogert §863; Restatement (Second) of Trusts §207(2) (1959) (providing that where the trustee is chargeable with interest, he is chargeable with simple and not compound interest, unless he has received compound interest, or he has received a profit which cannot be ascertained but is presumably at least equal to compound interest, or it was his duty to accumulate the income). Prior to 1987, long-standing California law permitted a court to award compound interest in some cases of breach of fiduciary duty. *See* Nickel v. Bank of Am. Nat'l Trust & Sav. Ass'n, 290 F.3d 1134, 1137 (9th Cir. 2002). In 1987, the California legislature eliminated compounding as an option. Nickel v. Bank of Am. Nat'l Trust & Sav. Ass'n, 290 F.3d at 1139. For a case in which compound interest was assessed, *see, e.g.,* Matter of Will of Janes, 643 N.Y.S.2d 972, 982 (App. Div. 1996) (rejecting a hypothetical market value appreciation measure of damages in the case of a fiduciary's negligent retention of Kodak stock in favor of the following measure: the value of the 12,087 shares of Kodak stock on August 9, 1973, the date on which they should have been sold, minus the value of the shares when they were ultimately sold or transferred, minus any income attributable to the stock retained, plus interest at the legal rate, compounded from August 9, 1973). For a case in which the court did employ a hypothetical market value appreciation measure of damages, *see* First Ala. Bank v. Spragins, 515 So. 2d 962 (Ala. 1987) (using as a benchmark the S & P 500 Index). *But see* Estate of Wilde, 708 A.2d 273 (Me. 1998) (adopting the following method of damage calculation: the value of the trust as if it has been managed by a prudent professional trustee in Portland, Maine, less the value of the assets actually delivered to the trustee and rejecting a more mechanical method based upon the value of the trust had it been invested in an S & P index fund less the value of assets actually delivered). *See generally* Restatement (Third) of Trusts §211(2) [provisional and now superseded by §100] (providing that, in a case where the trustee fails to acquire property constituting a proper investment, the beneficiaries may "charge the trustee with the amount of the funds the trustee failed properly to invest, adjusted for the amount of the total return, positive or negative, that would have accrued to the trust estate had the funds been invested in a timely fashion, this return to be based on a total return experience for suitable investments of generally comparable trusts"). *See also* UTC §1002 (available at <http://www.uniformlaws.org/Act.aspx?title=Trust%20Code>) (Damages Against Trustee for Breach of Trust); Stephen C. Fulton, *Interest on Money Damages for Periods Before and After Judgment: A Guide for the Massachusetts Practitioner,* 85 Mass. L. Rev. 146 (No. 4, Spring 2001) (including a discussion of interest on money damages for periods before and after entry of judgment in the United States courts).

[191] *See, e.g.,* Miller v. Bank of Am., N.A. 326 P.3d 20, 29-30 (N.M. 2013).

[192] *See, e.g.,* 4 Scott & Ascher §24.17 (Effect of General Increase or Decrease in Market Values).

• The profit the trustee made by reason of the breach.[193]

Here is the general damage computation methodology of the Restatement (Second) of Trusts:

§205 Liability in Case of Breach of Trust

If the trustee commits a breach of trust, he is chargeable with

(a) *any loss or depreciation in value of the trust estate resulting from the breach of trust; or*

(b) *any profit made by him through the breach of trust; or*

(c) *any profit which would have accrued to the trust estate if there had been no breach of trust*

In 1990, Section 205 was tentatively revised, pending its being put in final form, renumbered, and integrated into the Restatement (Third) of Trusts:

§205 Trustee's Liability in Case of Breach of Trust [tentative revision]

A trustee who commits a breach of trust is

(a) *accountable for any profit accruing to the trust through the breach of trust; or*

(b) *chargeable with the amount required to restore the values of the trust estate and trust distributions to what they would have been if the trust has been properly administered.*

In addition, the trustee is subject to such liability as necessary to prevent the trustee from benefitting personally from the breach of trust.

In 2012, Section 205 [tentative revision] of the Restatement (Third) of Trusts was put in final form, renumbered as Section 100, adopted, and promulgated:

§100 Liability of Trustee for Breach of Trust

A trustee who commits a breach of trust is chargeable with

(a) *the amount required to restore the values of the trust estate and trust distributions to what they would have been if the portion of the trust affected by the breach had been properly administered; or*

(b) *the amount of any benefit to the trustee personally as a result of the breach.*

---

[193] UTC §1002 (available at <http://www.uniformlaws.org/Act.aspx?title=Trust%20 Code>). *See also* Restatement (Third) of Trusts §205 [provisional and now superseded by §100]; 4 Scott & Ascher §24.9. *See, e.g.*, Nickel v. Bank of Am. Nat'l Trust & Sav. Ass'n, 290 F.3d 1134 (9th Cir. 2002) (holding that the appropriate remedy for a corporate trustee's overcharging its trust accounts is to allot to those accounts a proportionate share of the bank's profits during the years of misappropriation).

Section 100, on its face, would appear to present the beneficiary with an illogical and inequitable election: Have the beneficiary (or trust) made whole or compel the trustee to make restitution for his unjust enrichment. In other words, it appears that Section 100 would make these equitable remedies mutually exclusive. Traditionally, the beneficiary (or trust) would be entitled to both remedies, provided there is no inequitable double-dipping. Thus, the trustee who loans his personal funds at interest to himself as trustee and then invests those funds in an entrusted business, which he then proceeds in breach of trust to mismanage, would have been liable both for the diminution of the value of the trust estate that had been occasioned by the breach and his having been unjustly enriched by the interest payments, with a possible equitable offset for the unpaid balance of the loan. Otherwise, there is a built-in incentive for the trustee to self-deal. Section 205 (the tentative draft) created no such incentive. See its last sentence in this regard.

If a trustee is liable for a loss occasioned by a breach of trust, the amount of the liability is not reduced by profits accruing to the trust as a result of other actions of the trustee that do not involve a breach of trust.[194] The amount of the liability also may not be reduced by profits that accrue as a result of another and distinct breach of fiduciary duty.[195] On the other hand, if the trustee makes a profit and also incurs a loss through breaches that are not separate and distinct, the beneficiary is entitled to the amount of the profit less the amount of the loss,[196] or if there has been a net loss the amount of the loss less the amount of the profit.[197]

Factors to be considered in determining whether breaches of trust are distinct include whether the breaches are the result of a single policy, judgment, or set of interrelated decisions; the amount of time elapsing between the

---

[194] Restatement (Second) of Trusts §213 cmt. b; Restatement (Third) of Trusts §213 cmt. c [provisional and now superseded by §101 cmt. a]. *See generally* 4 Scott & Ascher §24.18 (Balancing Losses Against Gains). *See, e.g.,* Grate v. Grzetich, 373 Ill. App. 3d 228, 867 N.E.2d 577 (2007) (sterling investment performance not a mitigating circumstance that warranted allowing the trustee to deduct from the trust estate attorneys' fees incurred in an unsuccessful defense of an action against the trustee for conversion of a portion of the trust property, nor, of course, did it warrant retention of the funds that the trustee had converted).

[195] Restatement (Third) of Trusts §213 [provisional and now superseded by §101 cmt. a & cmt. c]. Factors to be considered in determining whether breaches of fiduciary duty are distinct include whether the breaches are the result of a single policy, judgment, or set of interrelated decisions; the amount of time elapsing between the breaches of duty; whether between breaches the fiduciary has become aware of the earlier breach; and whether there was self-dealing involved. Restatement (Third) of Trusts §213 cmt. f [provisional and now superseded by §101 cmt. c].

[196] Restatement (Second) of Trusts §213; Restatement (Third) of Trusts §213 cmt. e [provisional and now superseded by §101 cmt. a & cmt. b]. If, however, the profits and losses from the breaches of fiduciary duty affect different beneficial interests differently in a way that would have inequitable consequences if gains were to be offset against losses, then netting may not be appropriate though the breaches are the result of a single policy, judgment, or set of interrelated decisions. Restatement (Third) of Trusts §213 cmt. f [provisional and now superseded by §101 cmt. b & cmt. c].

[197] Restatement (Third) of Trusts §213 cmt. e [provisional and now superseded by §101 cmt. b & cmt. c].

breaches;[198] whether between breaches the trustee had become aware of the earlier breach; and whether there was self-dealing involved.[199]

Liability for interest. Absent an applicable statutory provision to the contrary, a trustee who exploits trust funds for his own personal purposes in breach of his trust may be liable for prejudgment interest. This liability is rooted in unjust enrichment doctrine. "To the extent the . . . [trustee's] . . . supplemental enrichment derives from the use of money, the corresponding liability in restitution constitutes 'prejudgment interest.'"[200] If the cause of action is based on the trustee's unjust enrichment and if the substantive remedy being sought is equitable restitution, then "the question of 'prejudgment interest' becomes merely one aspect of the overall calculation of the . . . [trustee's] . . . enrichment from the transaction in question."[201] Thus, if the trustee misapplies trust funds in a self-dealing transaction, he is liable for interest on the funds from the date of their misapplication. This would be the case even if the trustee's breach of trust had not been intentional.[202]

In Massachusetts, an award of prejudgment interest (*i.e.*, an award of interest "on the measure of damages from the last date on which the damage was sustained") need not be preconditioned on a finding that the trustee had been unjustly enriched by his breach of trust. The Commonwealth's highest court explains: "Making the beneficiary whole, particularly where the breach stems from imprudent investment decisions having an impact on the growth of the trust's assets, may require awarding interest beginning from the time of the breach, such that the trust's assets resemble what they would have but for the breach."[203]

Here is how the Restatement (Second) of Trusts handles the calculation of interest damages: "Where the trustee commits a breach of trust and thereby incurs a liability for a certain amount of money with interest thereon, he is chargeable with interest at the legal rate or such other rate as the court in its sound discretion may determine, but in any event he is chargeable with interest actually received by him or which he should have received."[204] The trustee is chargeable with simple interest, not compound interest, unless he has received compound interest or "he has received a profit which cannot be ascertained but is presumably at least equal to compound interest" or the trustee had a duty to accumulate income.[205] If, for example, the trustee used trust funds in his own business, charging him with compound interest may be appropriate "on the

---

[198] *See generally* 4 Scott & Ascher §24.9.

[199] Restatement (Third) of Trusts §213 cmt. f [provisional and now superseded by §101 cmt. c].

[200] Restatement (Third) of Restitution and Unjust Enrichment §53 cmt. e.

[201] Restatement (Third) of Restitution and Unjust Enrichment §53 cmt. e.

[202] Restatement (Third) of Restitution and Unjust Enrichment §53 illus. 13.

[203] The Woodward School for Girls, Inc. v. City of Quincy, trustee, SJC-11390, 2013 WL 8923423 (Mass. July 23, 2014).

[204] Restatement (Second) of Trusts §207(1).

[205] Restatement (Second) of Trusts §207(2). *See generally* 4 Scott & Ascher §24.9.3 (Liability for Interest).

ground that he probably received a return from the trust fund so used at least equal to compound interest."[206]

Today, it would seem that interest keyed to the usual rate of return on trust investments and compounded may be more in keeping with the spirit of the Prudent Investor Rule than simple interest computed at some fixed legal rate.[207] In light of the widespread adoption of the Uniform Prudent Investor Act, the traditional methodology for computing equitable damages is undergoing a thorough review. How does one come up with an appropriate return rate for damage computation purposes that conforms to the spirit of the prudent investor rule? One might base it on the "total return experience (positive or negative) for other investments of the trust in question, or possibly that of portfolios of other trusts having comparable objectives and circumstances."[208] The use of some benchmark index or combination of indexes[209] may be appropriate if a trustee with general investment authority imprudently invests the assets of the trust.[210] The total return approach may not always be the right one, particularly when a breach is recent.[211] In such cases, it may be appropriate just to charge the trustee with simple interest at the fixed legal rate.[212] The rate may be based on the income yields of investments of generally comparable entities.[213]

Appreciation damages. Take the case of trustee *with a general authority to sell* who proceeds to sell trust property to a BFP in a self-dealing transaction. The law has been somewhat unsettled as to whether money damages are limited to the proceeds, plus any profit made *by the trustee* at the time of the sale; or may include as well the value of the unrecoverable property's appreciation as of the time of the decree.[214] The current state of the law appears to be that it is as of

---

[206] Restatement (Second) of Trusts §207 cmt. d; Lewin ¶ 39-34 (England).

[207] 4 Scott & Ascher §24.9.3 (Liability for Interest).

[208] Restatement (Third) of Trusts §205 cmt. a [provisional and subject to re-numbering]. *See generally* 4 Scott & Ascher §24.9.

[209] *See* §6.2.2.1 of this handbook (the *Harvard College* prudent man rule and its progeny).

[210] Restatement (Third) of Trusts, Reporter's Notes on §§205 and 208–211 [provisional and now superseded by §100]. *See generally* 4 Scott & Ascher §§24.17 (Effect of General Increase or Decrease in Market Values), 24.9.3 (Liability for Interest). *But see* Edward A. Moses, J. Clay Singleton, & Stewart Andrew Marshall, III, *Computing Market Adjusted Damages in Fiduciary Surcharge Cases Using Modern Portfolio Theory*, 31 ACTEC L.J. 60, 62 (2005) (advocating the use of a market-adjusted damage model portfolio rather than a single index as a benchmark for measuring damages and offering a methodology for creating such a model portfolio).

[211] 4 Scott & Ascher §24.9.

[212] 4 Scott & Ascher §§24.9 (Liability in the Case of a Breach of Trust), 24.9.3 (Liability for Interest).

[213] Restatement (Third) of Trusts §211 cmt. f [provisional and now superseded by §100]; 4 Scott & Ascher §24.9.3 (Liability for Interest).

[214] *See generally* Note, *Trustee Liability for Breach of the Duty of Loyalty*, 49 Fordham L. Rev. 1012 (1981). Section 1002 of the UTC (available at <http://www.uniformlaws.org/Act.aspx?title=Trust%20Code>) would appear to allow for the awarding of appreciation damages. *Cf.* 4 Scott & Ascher §24.9 (suggesting that when there is authority to sell, the trustee who sells to a third party for less than full value "is not . . . liable for any subsequent increase in the value of the property sold, because the trust did not forgo that particular gain *as a result of a breach of trust*").

the time of the decree.[215] If the sale is to a non-BFP, *e.g.*, the trustee himself, the beneficiaries may elect to set aside the sale and recover the property. If the property has subsequently appreciated in value, this is most likely what they will do. If a trustee has *no authority to sell*, the beneficiary, of course, is entitled to appreciation damages fixed at the time of the decree.[216]

If a trustee with no duty to retain a particular entrusted asset sells it for a price that is below market, an assessment of appreciation damages is unwarranted, provided the trustee is found not to have engaged in fraudulent conduct. At least one New York court has so held: Appreciation damages are only appropriate where a trustee fraudulently sells property he or she was duty-bound to retain, "the theory being that the beneficiaries are entitled to be placed in the same position they would have been in had the breach not consisted of a sale of property that should have been retained."[217] Under the Restatement (Third) of Trusts an assessment of appreciation damages would have been warranted had the trustee sold the property to himself or otherwise self-dealt, whether or not the trustee had committed the breach of trust in good faith.[218]

In a Uniform Trust Code jurisdiction, the beneficiary may hold the trustee liable for the amount necessary to compensate fully for a loss occasioned by a breach of trust. This would include any "lost income, capital gain, or appreciation that would have resulted from proper administration."[219]

In New York, which has not enacted the Uniform Trust Code (or some version of it), appreciation damages may be calculated in a given situation by the market index damages calculation method, provided the breach of trust that damaged the beneficiary's equitable interest had a self-dealing flavor to it. One New York court explains:

> The market index damages calculation method that the Objectants advocate for in this case compares the actual portfolio against an alternative hypothetical portfolio that was managed properly during the same time period. See, Matter of Rothko, 43 N.Y.2d 305 (1977) [a case that involved a probate estate, not a trust, and a collection of oil paintings, not a portfolio of securities]. This method attempts to turn back the clock and calculate the outcome of the trust management that allegedly should have occurred. However, the Rothko case upon which this calculation method is based concerned fiduciaries [executors] that sold assets that they should have retained, as opposed to retaining assets that they should have sold. . . . Additionally, the fiduciaries in Rothko engaged in a long pattern of flagrant self-dealing. . . . The Objectants argue that the Trustee's behavior goes

---

[215] 4 Scott & Ascher §24.10 (Liability for Breach of Duty of Loyalty).

[216] Restatement (Second) of Trusts §208 (1959); 4 Scott & Ascher §§24.9, 24.10.

[217] *See* Estate of Sonnelitter, 983 N.Y.S.2d 149, 152 (2014).

[218] Restatement (Third) of Trusts §100 cmt. c. This is an application of the "no further inquiry" principle, which is discussed in §6.1.3 of this handbook and in §78, cmt. d of the Restatement (Third) of Trusts.

[219] UTC §1002 cmt. (available at <http://www.uniformlaws.org/Act.aspx?title=Trust%20 Code>). *See generally* 4 Scott & Ascher §24.17 (Effect of General Increase or Decrease in Market Values); 4 Scott & Ascher §24.9 (Liability in the Case of a Breach of Trust).

beyond mere negligence, arising to a level of misconduct and self-dealing allowing this method of damages calculation.[220]

The review and revision of the Restatement (Second) of Trust's sections on damages, which had been ongoing since 1990, is now complete. The Restatement (Second) of Trusts addresses the trustee's liability for damages in Sections 197 through 213. As of 2010, there were 92 sections of the Restatement (Third) of Trusts that had come off the assembly line. While there was tangential coverage of damages in those sections, we awaited the final approval of the sections of the Restatement (Third) of Trusts that directly dealt with damages. In the meantime, Sections 197 through 213 of the Restatement (Second) of Trusts were *tentatively* revised and included in a separate part of the 1992 Prudent Investor Rule single blue-covered volume, which was approved May 18, 1990. Once the revisions to the damage-related sections of the Restatement (Second) of Trusts were approved, they would have to be renumbered to fit in with the section number sequencing of the Restatement (Third) of Trusts, which is radically different from the sequencing of the Restatement (Second) of Trusts. Finally, on May 18, 2011, Sections 93 through 111 of the Restatement (Third) of Trusts were adopted and promulgated by The American Law Institute. Sections 100 through 102 generally deal with the calculation of damages incident to a breach of trust.

Wrongful acquisition, retention, and disposition of specific property/ damages. We now consider the liability of a trustee for a loss resulting from selling specific trust property which it is his duty to retain, or failing to sell specific trust property which it is his duty to sell, or purchasing specific property which it is his duty not to purchase, or failing to purchase specific property when there is a duty to do so.

Selling specific property when there is a duty to retain it. If the trustee has no authority to sell a specific item of property but does so, he is liable for the market value of the property as of the time of the decree, not at the time of commencement of the suit,[221] plus the value of the income that would have accrued to the trust if the property had been retained.[222] If the proceeds of the sale have been paid into the trust, the trustee will be credited with the amount so paid and any income that has been earned thereon.[223] If the proceeds have

---

[220] Matter of JP Morgan Chase Bank N.A. (Strong), 2013 WL 6182548 (N.Y. Sur. 2013).

[221] *See generally* 4 Scott & Ascher §24.11.1 (Value at Time of Suit); Restatement (Second) of Trusts §208(1)(b); Restatement (Third) of Trusts §208 [provisional and now superseded by §100].

[222] Restatement (Second) of Trusts §208(1)(b); Restatement (Third) of Trusts §208 [provisional and now superseded by §100]; Lewin ¶ 39-27 (England); 4 Scott & Ascher §§24.9 (Liability in the Case of a Breach of Trust) (U.S.), 24.11 (Liability for Breach of Trust by Selling Trust Property) (U.S.). *See also* Bogert §862, n.44 and accompanying text.

[223] Restatement (Second) of Trusts §208 cmt. c; Restatement (Third) of Trusts §208 cmt. c [provisional and now superseded by §100]; 4 Scott & Ascher §24.11.1.

been invested, the trustee is entitled to an offset for any appreciation.[224] Of course, the beneficiaries may elect instead to affirm the sale.[225]

Failure to sell a specific asset when there is a duty to sell. If the trustee fails to sell a specific asset which he has a duty to sell and the property depreciates in value, the trustee is personally liable for the value of the proceeds that the trust would have received had the property been properly sold.[226] In addition, the beneficiary can charge the trustee with interest on the amount,[227] or possibly in the alternative with an appropriate additional amount to compensate for loss of return on those proceeds.[228] The depreciated property itself will then belong to the fiduciary.[229]

In one case involving a probate estate, the will directed the executors to convert into cash all property except that specifically bequeathed.[230] The executors delayed the sale of an interest in a closely held corporation beyond six months from their appointment. The executors were surcharged "in an amount equal to the difference between the amount which would have been realized if each stock had been sold at the lowest price reached during the 6-month period following their appointment and the price at which the stock was eventually sold."[231]

Absent such special facts, however, one should expect only rough justice when it comes to a judicial determination of *when* a specific trust asset should have been sold. One court explains:

> [T]he Trustee does raise an important issue, and one that plagues cases in which a violation of the Prudent Investor Rule is alleged. There is no way to turn back the clock, and expert testimony at trial will always be colored by hindsight. This is of particular concern in this case, when the date of prudent divestiture, whatever it might be, is so many years before trial. There is no bright line rule, or controlling statute or regulation. "[N]o fixed standard exists for the time in which divestiture of an imprudently held investment must occur."[232]

Purchasing with trust funds specific property when no duty to do so. If the trustee in breach of trust purchases with trust funds specific property from a

---

[224] *See, e.g.*, In re Scheidmantel, 868 A.2d 464, 494 (Pa. Super. 2005).

[225] Restatement (Second) of Trusts §208(1)(a); Restatement (Third) of Trusts §208 [provisional and now superseded by §100].

[226] Restatement (Second) of Trusts §209(1); Restatement (Third) of Trusts §209(1) [provisional and now superseded by §100].

[227] Restatement (Second) of Trusts §209(1).

[228] Restatement (Third) of Trusts §209(1) [provisional and subject to re-numbering]; Lewin ¶ 39-29 (England); 4 Scott & Ascher §§24.9 (U.S.) (Liability in the Case of a Breach of Trust), 24.12 (Liability for Breach of Trust by Failing to Sell Trust Property) (U.S.).

[229] Restatement (Second) of Trusts §209 cmt. b; Restatement (Third) of Trusts §209 cmt. b [provisional and now superseded by §100]; 4 Scott & Ascher §24.12 (Liability for Breach of Trust by Failing to Sell Trust Property).

[230] In re Estate of Campbell, 190 Neb. 456, 209 N.W.2d 165 (1973).

[231] In re Estate of Campbell, 190 Neb. 456, 209 N.W.2d 165 (1973).

[232] Matter of JP Morgan Chase Bank, N.A. (Strong), 2013 WL 6182548 (N.Y. Sur. 2013) (quotation from Matter of Saxton, 274 A.D.2d 110, 120 (N.Y. App. Div. 2000)).

third party, the beneficiary can elect either to affirm[233] or reject the purchase.[234] If rejection is elected, the Restatement (Second) of Trusts provides that the trustee must augment the trust estate out of his own pocket an amount equal to the purchase price, plus interest thereon.[235] Having done so, the trustee is entitled to remove from the trust estate and take ownership of the specific property that should not have been purchased.[236] An alternative to the purchase-price-plus-interest approach to damages computation is "to charge the trustee with the amount of trust funds expended in the purchase plus or minus the amount of a reasonably appropriate positive or negative total return thereon."[237]

Failing to purchase specific property. If the trustee in breach of trust fails to purchase specific property, "the beneficiary can charge him with its value at the time of the decree together with the income which would have accrued thereon if he had purchased it."[238] If reasonable and possible under the circumstances, the trustee in the alternative might be required to purchase the specific property and hold it in trust, "paying therefor out of the trust property only so much as he would have had to pay if he had properly purchased it, and charge him with the income which would have accrued thereon if he had properly purchased it."[239] This is not to say that the beneficiaries may not affirm the trustee's inaction.[240]

If the specific property has depreciated in value so that its value at the time of the decree, together with the income it would have produced, would not exceed the amount of the funds initially available for purchase, plus any income (or adjusted for the positive or negative return) actually received from the improper investment thereof, the trustee is under no liability to the beneficiaries for failing to make the purchase.[241]

Failure to make proper investment/damages. If the trustee has a duty to purchase *specific* property and fails to do so, the beneficiaries may charge the trustee with the value of the specified property at the time of the decree, plus the

---

[233] Restatement (Third) of Trusts §210(1)(b) [provisional and now superseded by §100]. If the improperly purchased property has already been sold, the fiduciary must account for the proceeds and for the return that is traceable to the property. Restatement (Third) of Trusts §210(1)(b).

[234] Restatement (Second) of Trusts §210 cmt. b; Restatement (Third) of Trusts §210(1)(b) [provisional and now superseded by §100].

[235] Restatement (Second) of Trusts §210(1)(a).

[236] Restatement (Second) of Trusts §210 cmt. b; Restatement (Third) of Trusts §210(2) [provisional and now superseded by §100].

[237] Restatement (Third) of Trusts §210(1)(a) [provisional and now superseded by §100]. *See, however,* Gillespie v. Seattle-First Nat'l Bank, 70 Wash. App. 150, 855 P.2d 680 (1993) (holding trustee liable for amount expended in making the purchase, plus compound interest).

[238] Restatement (Second) of Trusts §211. *See also* Restatement (Third) of Trusts §211(2) [provisional and now superseded by §100].

[239] Restatement (Second) of Trusts §211. *See also* Restatement (Third) of Trusts §211 cmt. g [provisional and now superseded by §100].

[240] Restatement (Third) of Trusts §211(1) [provisional and now superseded by §100]. *See generally* §7.1.4 of this handbook (trustee's defense of beneficiary affirmance).

[241] Restatement (Third) of Trusts §211 cmt. d [provisional and now superseded by §100].

income that the property would have produced had it been purchased within a reasonable time.[242] Income amounts for which the trustee is charged are compounded.[243] Except for the compounding, the Restatement (Second) of Trusts is more or less in accord.[244] A failure on the part of the trustee to invest or prudently invest when there is a *general duty to invest* is another matter.

The failure to invest at all. Nowadays, a trustee has a default *duty* to make the trust property productive, that is to say a duty to invest the assets of the trust.[245] As a corollary, a trustee will generally have a default *power* to invest.[246] The general default power to invest perforce brings with it the default sub-power to sell the trust property,[247] as well as the default sub-power to purchase property for the trust with the proceeds.[248]

The Restatement (Second) of Trusts provides that if the trustee "can properly invest in any securities which are proper trust investments and he neglects to make any investment, he is chargeable with the amount of income which normally would accrue from proper trust investments" but "is not chargeable...with a loss of the profit which might have resulted from the investment of the trust funds because of a general rise of values in the security market."[249]

The final version of the Restatement (Third) of Trusts is unlikely to be in accord. It is likely to provide that if the trustee possesses a general duty to invest prudently and fails to do so,[250] the trustee may be charged with the amount of the funds the trustee failed properly to invest, adjusted for the amount of the total return, positive or negative, that would have accrued to the trust had the funds been invested in a timely fashion.[251] The return would be based on a total

---

[242] Restatement (Third) of Trusts §211(2) [provisional and now superseded by §100]. If the trustee has the duty to purchase one or more of several designated securities and neglects to invest in any of them, it is in the discretion of the court to calculate the damages based on either the least profitable of the designated securities or on their average profitability. Restatement (Third) of Trusts §211 cmt. e [provisional and now superseded by §100]. *See also* Restatement (Third) of Trusts §211 cmt. g [provisional and now superseded by §100]; 4 Scott & Ascher §§24.9 (Liability in the Case of a Breach of Trust), 24.14 (Liability for Breach of Trust by Failing to Purchase Specific Property).

[243] Restatement (Third) of Trusts §211(2) [provisional and now superseded by §100].

[244] Restatement (Second) of Trusts §211. *See also* Restatement (Second) of Trusts §207 (simple interest).

[245] *See generally* §6.2.2 of this handbook (trustee's duty to make trust property productive).

[246] *See generally* §3.5.3.1(a) of this handbook (the trustee's powers to sell and buy).

[247] *See generally* 4 Scott & Ascher §24.11.4 (When Trustee Has Power of Sale); §3.5.3.1(a) of this handbook.

[248] *See generally* 4 Scott & Ascher §24.14 (Liability for Breach of Trust by Failing to Purchase Specific Property), 24.13 (Liability for Breach of Trust by Purchasing Property) (noting, however, that a trustee may commit a breach of trust by making an improper investment); §3.5.3.1(a) of this handbook.

[249] Restatement (Second) of Trusts §211 cmt. f.

[250] *See* 4 Scott & Ascher §24.15 (Liability for Breach of Trust by Failing to Invest Property).

[251] Restatement (Third) of Trusts §211 (U.S.) [provisional and subject to re-numbering]; Lewin ¶39-26 (England). *See generally* 4 Scott & Ascher §24.17 (Effect of General Increase or Decrease in Market Values); 4 Scott & Ascher §19.2.1 (Extent of Liability); 4 Scott & Ascher §24.9

return experience for suitable investments of generally comparable trusts.[252] The measure of damages would also take account of a compounding of that return.[253] The liability of the trustee is reduced by the value at the time of the decree of any investments the trustee actually made and by the amount of any income produced by the improper investments.[254] Income amounts for which the trustee is credited are compounded.[255]

If the trustee has a duty to invest a specified amount of money in certain designated securities and in breach of that duty fails to do so, he may be compelled to purchase the securities if it is reasonable under the circumstances then to do.[256] If the securities have appreciated in value since the time when they should have been purchased, then the trustee is personally liable for the value of the appreciation.[257] The trustee is also chargeable with the amount of income, compounded, that would have accrued had the specified securities been purchased within a reasonable period of time.[258] Except for the compounding, the Restatement (Second) of Trusts is more or less in accord.[259] "A similar rule applies if it is the duty of the trustee to purchase a specified number of the designated securities and in breach of trust the trustee neglects to do so."[260]

(Liability in the Case of a Breach of Trust); 4 Scott & Ascher §24.11.4 (When Trustee Has Power of Sale); 4 Scott & Ascher §24.15 (Liability for Breach of Trust by Failing to Invest).

[252] Restatement (Third) of Trusts §211(2) [provisional and now superseded by §100]; 4 Scott & Ascher §24.17 (Effect of General Increase or Decrease in Market Values); 4 Scott & Ascher §24.15 (Liability for Breach of Trust by Failing to Invest).

[253] Restatement (Third) of Trusts §211 cmt. f [provisional and now superseded by §100]. If the period during which the fiduciary has failed to make investments is not significantly prolonged, at least if the fiduciary is not guilty of bad faith or other serious misconduct, it would ordinarily be an appropriate exercise of equitable discretion to measure the performance of proper fiduciary investments only by applying a suitable rate of interest, based on the income yields of investments of generally comparable entities. Restatement (Third) of Trusts §211 cmt. f [provisional and now superseded by §100].

[254] Restatement (Third) of Trusts §211(2) [provisional and now superseded by §100].

[255] Restatement (Third) of Trusts §211(2) [provisional and now superseded by §100].

[256] Restatement (Second) of Trusts §211 cmt. g; Restatement (Third) of Trusts §211 cmt. g [provisional and now superseded by §100]. Lewin ¶39-25 (England); 4 Scott & Ascher §24.14 (Liability for Breach of Trust by Failing to Purchase Specific Property) (U.S.); 4 Scott & Ascher §24.9 (Liability in the Case of a Breach of Trust) (U.S.).

[257] Restatement (Second) of Trusts §211cmt. g; Restatement (Third) of Trusts §211 cmt. g [provisional and now superseded by §100]; 4 Scott & Ascher §24.14. If the designated securities have depreciated in value, the trustee may still have some personal liability if the value of the assets traceable to the designated funds are inadequate to purchase the requisite number of shares. Restatement (Third) of Trusts §211 cmt. g [provisional and now superseded by §100]. *See generally* Bogert §862, n.43 and accompanying text; 4 Scott & Ascher §24.9.

[258] Restatement (Third) of Trusts §211 cmt. g [provisional and now superseded by §100]. *See also* Restatement (Third) of Trusts §211(2) [provisional and now superseded by §100] (compounding).

[259] Restatement (Second) of Trusts §211 cmt. g; Restatement (Second) of Trusts §207(2) (simple interest only).

[260] Restatement (Third) of Trusts §211 cmt. g [provisional and now superseded by §100].

The trustee is entitled to be credited with the income, if any, actually received in the meantime on the funds that should have been so invested.[261] Income amounts for which the trustee is credited are compounded.[262] Except possibly for the compounding, the Restatement (Second) of Trusts is more or less in accord.[263]

Depreciation or sub-par appreciation occasioned by the failure to invest prudently. When there is depreciation or sub-par appreciation[264] occasioned by the failure to invest prudently, the trustee is liable for any income, capital gain, and appreciation that would have accrued had the trust been properly administered;[265] likewise if the trustee imprudently fails altogether to make part or all of the trust property productive.[266] "Thus the recovery for an improper investment by a trustee would ordinarily be the difference between (1) the value of the investment and its income and other product at the time of surcharge and (2) the amount of the funds expended in making the investment, increased (or decreased) by the amount of the total return (or negative total return) that would have accrued to the trust and its beneficiaries if the funds had been properly invested."[267]

So also if the trustee in breach of trust accepts too low a price in an otherwise proper sale of trust property, "the trustee's liability would be the amount by which the sale price was inadequate and a compound return on the amount to the date of surcharge."[268] It should be noted that "[I]f the breach of trust consists only in selling it for too little, he is not chargeable with the amount of any subsequent increase in value of the property . . . as he would be if he were not authorized to sell the property."[269] In England, a sale or lease "at an undervalue" constitutes a "wilful default." In this context, willful default means wrongful omission rather than conscious wrongdoing.[270]

---

[261] Restatement (Second) of Trusts §211 cmt. g; Restatement (Third) of Trusts §211 cmt. g [provisional and now superseded by §100].

[262] Restatement (Third) of Trusts §211(2) [provisional and now superseded by §100].

[263] Restatement (Second) of Trusts §211 cmt. g.

[264] *See generally* Restatement (Third) of Trusts Reporter's Notes on §§205 and 208–211 [provisional and now superseded by §100]; 4 Scott & Ascher §24.17 (Effect of General Increase or Decrease in Market Values).

[265] UTC §1002 cmt. (available at <http://www.uniformlaws.org/Act.aspx?title=Trust%20 Code>); 4 Scott & Ascher §§24.9 (Liability in the Case of a Breach of Trust), 24.12 (Liability for Breach of Trust by Failing to Sell Trust Property), 24.17 (Effect of General Increase or Decrease in Market Values); Restatement (Third) of Trusts §210 [provisional and now superseded by §100].

[266] 4 Scott & Ascher §24.15 (Liability for Breach of Trust by Failing to Invest); Restatement (Third) of Trusts §211(2) [provisional and now superseded by §100].

[267] Restatement (Third) of Trusts §205 cmt. a [provisional and subject to re-numbering]. *See generally* 4 Scott & Ascher §§24.9 (Liability in the Case of a Breach of Trust), 24.9.1 (When Loss Would Have Occurred in Absence of Breach of Trust), 24.17 (Effect of General Increase or Decrease in Market Values).

[268] Restatement (Third) of Trusts §205 cmt. a [provisional and now superseded by §100].

[269] Restatement (Second) of Trusts §205 cmt. d. *See generally* 4 Scott & Ascher §§24.9 (Liability in the Case of a Breach of Trust), 24.11.4 (When Trustee Has Power of Sale). *See, e.g.*, Hopkins v. Loeber, 332 Ill. App. 140, 74 N.E.2d 39 (1947).

[270] Lewin ¶39-21 (England).

If the trustee is authorized to purchase property for the trust but overpays, the trustee is chargeable with the amount paid in excess of its value.[271] He is not, however, chargeable with a subsequent depreciation in value, absent a depreciation occasioned by a breach of fiduciary duty.[272]

In one case, a bank trustee was held to have been in breach of trust for pursuing an investment strategy that failed to properly balance the interests of the income beneficiaries and remaindermen.[273] In this case, the trustee had made no effort to grow the corpus for the benefit of the remainderman. The court measured the sub-par appreciation for damage computation purposes against how the corpus would have appreciated had the bank utilized its own common equity trust fund. The court declined to measure the lost appreciation against "objective market criteria."[274] In another case, however, a trustee was held liable for sub-par appreciation occasioned by the improper retention of an investment.[275] For damage computation purposes, the benchmark used to measure the value of the foregone appreciation was the Standard and Poor's 500 index. In yet another case, a trustee was held liable for lost appreciation occasioned by the failure to invest a portion of the portfolio in equities, most of the investments having been in tax-exempts.[276] The proper measure of damages was the difference between the actual value of the portfolio and what its value would have been had 40 percent of the portfolio been made up of an appropriate mix of equities.

What if a trust has no remaindermen? Should total return considerations still inform how equitable damages are calculated? The Supreme Judicial Court of Massachusetts (SJC), in a case involving what was essentially an income-only perpetual charitable trust, a trust that had been invested almost exclusively for income generation, criticized the trustee, as had the trial judge, for failing to pursue an investment strategy that had an appropriate capital-appreciation component to it as required by the Massachusetts Prudent Investor Act. The SJC, however, disagreed with the trial judge as to what specific strategy would have been appropriate and, in particular, how the foregone capital appreciation should be calculated for damages computation purposes.[277] The SJC referred to the foregone portfolio appreciation as "unrealized gains." The usual understanding of the term "unrealized gains" is actual paper gains that have yet to be locked in by a cash sale, which was not what the case was about. The Restatement (Second) of Trusts is generally not in accord with the total return approach to damages computation. It provides that "where a trustee makes an improper investment, although he is liable for any loss which results, he is not liable in

[271] Restatement (Second) of Trusts §205 cmt. e. *See generally* 4 Scott & Ascher §24.9.
[272] Restatement (Second) of Trusts §205 cmt. e.
[273] Noggle v. Bank of Am., 70 Cal. App. 4th 853 (1999).
[274] Noggle v. Bank of Am., 70 Cal. App. 4th 853, 862 (1999).
[275] First Ala. Bank v. Spragins, 515 So. 2d 962 (Ala. 1987).
[276] Baker Boyer Nat'l Bank v. Garver, 43 Wash. App. 673, 719 P.2d 583 (1986).
[277] *See* The Woodward School for Girls, Inc. v. City of Quincy, trustee, SJC-11390, 2013 WL 8923423 (Mass. July 23, 2014).

addition for any profit which might have been made if he had made a proper investment."[278]

Trustee acquires or exploits trust property in breach of duty of loyalty/ damages. If the trustee self-deals in breach of his duty of loyalty, he is chargeable with any loss or depreciation in value of the property of the trust that results from the breach.[279] On the other hand, the trustee would be chargeable with any profit he makes from the transaction, or any profit that would have accrued to the trust had there not been a breach.[280]

Acquisition of an entire trust asset. A trustee who acquires the trust property is unjustly enriched, unless there is some legal or equitable basis for the acquisition.[281] "If the trustee in breach of trust sells trust property to himself individually, and the price paid by him was less than the value of the property at the time when the trustee purchased it, the beneficiary can compel him to pay the difference; or, at his option, the beneficiary can set aside the sale and compel the trustee to reconvey the property and account for any income which he has received therefrom, in which case the trustee will be entitled to receive from the trust estate the amount which he paid for the property and income thereon actually received by the trust estate, if any; or he can compel the trustee to offer the property for sale and if it is sold for more than the amount which the trustee paid for it, compel him to account for the excess."[282] If the property is subsequently sold to someone who is unaware of the trust and pays full value, *i.e.*, a BFP,[283] the trustee is accountable for the profit he makes on the sale.[284] To be more precise, if the property has been sold to a BFP, the beneficiaries are entitled to the difference between the sales price and the appreciated value of the property *at the time of the decree*,[285] not at the time the suit is commenced.[286] Bottom line: The self-dealing trustee may not benefit from any appreciation in

---

[278] Restatement (Second) of Trusts §211 cmt. f.

[279] *See generally* 4 Scott & Ascher §24.13 (Liability for Breach of Trust by Purchasing Property).

[280] Restatement (Second) of Trusts §206 cmt. a. *See generally* Bogert §543 (Measure of Damages); 4 Scott & Ascher §24.9 (Liability in the Case of a Breach of Trust).

[281] Restatement of the Law of Restitution §190.

[282] Restatement (Second) of Trusts §206 cmt. b; 3 Scott & Ascher §17.2.1.1 (Remedies); 4 Scott & Ascher §24.9 (Liability in the Case of a Breach of Trust).

[283] *See generally* §5.4.2 of this handbook (rights of the beneficiary as against BFPs and other transferees of the underlying trust property), §8.3.2 of this handbook (the doctrine of bona fide purchase and its breach of trust notice requirement), and §8.15.63 of this handbook (doctrine of bona fide purchase in the trust context). *See also* §8.3.6 of this handbook (negotiable instruments and the duty of third parties to inquire into the trustee's authority). For a comparison of the BFP, a creature of equity, with the holder in due course, a creature of law, *see* §8.15.68 of this handbook (holders in due course in the trust context).

[284] Restatement (Second) of Trusts §206 cmt. b.

[285] 4 Scott & Ascher §24.10 (Liability for Breach of Duty of Loyalty); Restatement (Second) of Trusts §208, cmt. d (Value at time of decree).

[286] 4 Scott & Ascher §24.11.1 (Value at Time of Suit).

the value of the property from the time of sale to the time of the decree.[287] One way or another, any appreciation must inure to the benefit of the beneficiaries. On the other hand, if the property has depreciated in value since the sale, that is the trustee's problem.[288]

Acquisition of an interest in a trust asset. Let us assume that the trustee purchases for himself an interest in a trust asset in breach of his duty of undivided loyalty. The beneficiaries seek to have him charged as constructive trustee of the interest so purchased and ordered to remit to the trust any profits related to the self-dealing.[289] If, for example, the trustee purchases a $5,000 mortgage on the property of the trust for $3,000, at foreclosure he may only pocket up to $3,000 from the proceeds of the sale plus any interest thereon.[290] Or if a lease is an asset of the trust, the trustee cannot renew the lease for himself and then sell it to a third party at a profit. If he does so, the profit belongs to the trust estate.[291]

Trustee purchases property for himself which he should have purchased for the trust. If the trustee purchases property for himself that he had a duty to purchase for the trust, the trustee can be charged as a constructive trustee of the property and be compelled to account for any profit he makes as a result of the purchase.[292] He is, however, entitled to be reimbursed from the trust for what he paid for the property.

In one case, the defendant held title to two blocks of stock in a corporation. One block he held as trustee of a trust for the benefit of the widow and children of his deceased brother. The other block he owned in his individual capacity. The defendant then purchased for his own account from a third party enough shares of the stock to give him a majority interest. The plaintiffs sought to establish a constructive trust of those shares. The court denied the defendant's motion to dismiss and remanded the case for a determination as to whether the trustee had acted in good faith and in the exercise of a wise discretion in acquiring for himself the majority interest:

> A trustee must not compete with his beneficiary in the acquisition of property. The principle is not limited to cases where the fiduciary acquires property entrusted to him, nor to cases where the fiduciary competes with the beneficiary in the

---

[287] UTC §1002(a)(1) (available at <http://www.uniformlaws.org/Act.aspx?title=Trust%20 Code>); 4 Scott & Ascher §24.10 (Liability for Breach of Duty of Loyalty). *See also* Restatement (Second) of Trusts §205 cmt. i (Failure to make a profit); Restatement (Second) of Trusts §208 cmt. d. (Value at time of decree).

[288] 4 Scott & Ascher §24.10 (Liability for Breach of Duty of Loyalty); Restatement (Second) of Trusts §208 cmt. c (Value at time of sale).

[289] Restatement (Second) of Trusts §206 cmt. h. *Cf.* Pomeroy v. Bushong, 317 Pa. 459, 177 A. 10 (1935) (executor's purchase of estate asset voidable by beneficiaries whether or not executor had acted in good faith in making the purchase); Hartman v. Hartle, 95 N.J. Eq. 123, 122 A. 615 (1923) (where executor's wife purchased an estate asset without leave of court and resold it to a BFP so that the asset could not be recovered, the executor was accountable for the profit the wife made on the sale to the BFP).

[290] Restatement (Second) of Trusts §206 cmt. h, illus. 5.

[291] Restatement (Second) of Trusts §206 cmt. h.

[292] Restatement (Second) of Trusts §206 cmt. i.

purchase of property which the trustee has undertaken to purchase for the beneficiary.[293]

Trustee uses property of trust for own purposes. If the trustee in breach of his fiduciary duty uses the property of the trust for his own purposes and makes a profit thereby, he is accountable for the profit so made.[294] Thus, if he uses trust money in his own business, he is chargeable with the profit.[295] In England, he will hold the profit upon a constructive trust for the benefit of the trust estate.[296] Or if he lends trust property to himself at one rate of interest and relends it to a third party at a higher rate of interest, the trust is entitled to the spread.[297]

In one case, a testatrix, who died in 1938, devised 50 percent of a four-family dwelling outright and free of trust to her daughter and 50 percent to her daughter as trustee for the benefit of the testatrix's granddaughter until she arrived at the age of 27 years. Upon obtaining that age, the granddaughter's 50 percent share was to go outright and free of trust to the granddaughter. The trustee had lived in a portion of the dwelling before and after her mother's death. After her mother's death, the trustee had charged herself and other relatives' rents that were below market. The court found that there were conflicts of interest between the trustee and the beneficiary and that the trustee in breach of trust had been "resolving" those conflicts in her own favor:

> The argument is made that the trustee carried on, in the management of the property, as did the settlor (her mother) during her lifetime. Whatever the settlor did in dealing with her property, no one has a right to question, particularly where most of the tenants were her children. One has a right to deal with the property as he may desire. A trustee, however, cannot seek shelter from improvident or overly generous conduct toward herself and other tenants, some of whom are relatives of the settlor because that was the way the settlor dealt with those in possession of her property during her lifetime. A trustee is charged with the absolute necessity of protecting the trust estate with the utmost fidelity in the interest of the beneficiary. In this case that means collecting a reasonable rent under the economic conditions of today and not to continue rents or a slight variation of them as charged in the depths of the depression.[298]

---

[293] Wootten v. Wootten, 151 F.2d 147, 150 (1945).

[294] Restatement (Second) of Trusts §206 cmt. j; 4 Scott & Ascher §24.7. *See, e.g.,* Nickel v. Bank of Am. Nat'l Trust & Sav. Ass'n, 290 F.3d 1134 (2002) (holding that the appropriate remedy when a bank trustee overcharges its trust accounts is to allot to those accounts a proportionate share of the bank's profits during the years of misappropriation).

[295] Restatement (Second) of Trusts §206 cmt. j; 4 Scott & Ascher §24.7.

[296] Lewin ¶ 20-32. "But if the trustee's personal use of the trust property results in both a profit to the trustee and a loss in respect of the beneficiaries being deprived of the use of the property, the beneficiaries cannot recover both the profit and the loss." Lewin ¶ 20-32.

[297] Restatement (Second) of Trusts §206 cmt. j; 4 Scott & Ascher §24.7.

[298] Estate of Fiorelli, 74 Ohio Law Abs. 38, 134 N.E.2d 576, 580 (1956).

Unless the terms of the trust provide otherwise, a trustee of a large country estate "cannot properly enjoy the privilege of shooting game on the estate."[299] The privilege should be leased out for the benefit of the trust estate.[300]

Bonus, commission, or other compensation. The trustee in the course of carrying out his property administration responsibilities may not accept for himself a bonus, commission, or other compensation from a third party.[301] Anything of that nature that does come his way must be turned over to the trust or estate.[302] A lawyer for the trustee would have the same obligation.[303]

Trustee sells own property to trust (using trust as a dumping ground). If a trustee in breach of trust sells his own property to the trust, the beneficiaries have several options.[304] If the price was more than the value of the property, the beneficiaries can compel him to repay the difference or, at their option, set aside the sale and compel the trustee to repay the amount of the purchase price with interest thereon.[305] With the latter option, the trustee is allowed to take back the property and any income that was earned thereon.[306] "If the trustee sells his individual property to himself as trustee and the property subsequently depreciates in value, the trustee is chargeable with the amount of the depreciation even though he sold the property at a fair market value and even though had he purchased it from a third person it would have been a proper trust investment."[307]

In one case, the trustee purchased some bonds in his own name and then sold them to himself as trustee of a trust. The appellate court confirmed the finding and recommendation of the special master that the trustee should replace the bonds with cash:

> In making this investment the defendant violated various rules by which equity seeks to secure funds from mismanagement and waste. One of these rules is that the trustee who invests such funds in his own name becomes personally responsible. This is only a corollary of the rule that if he deals with the estate on his own account it must be at his own risk. Were he permitted to do otherwise it would place before him the constant temptation to make the trust fund a dumping ground for his own unsatisfactory ventures.[308]

---

[299] 2A Scott on Trusts §170.17.

[300] Webb v. Earl of Shaftesbury, 7 Ves. 480 (1802); Hutchinson v. Morritt, 3 Y. & C. Ex. 547 (1839).

[301] Restatement (Second) of Trusts §170 cmt. o.

[302] Restatement (Second) of Trusts §206 cmt. k. *See generally* 4 Scott & Ascher §24.7.

[303] *See, e.g.,* In re Clarke's Estate, 12 N.Y.2d 183, 188 N.E.2d 128, 237 N.Y.S.2d 694 (1962) (an attorney for fiduciary who received a kickback of $800 from a real estate broker was ordered to add back that amount to the fiduciary estate).

[304] *See generally* 4 Scott & Ascher §24.10 (Liability for Breach of Duty of Loyalty); Restatement (Second) of Trusts §206 cmt. c.

[305] Restatement (Second) of Trusts §206 cmt. c. *See generally* 4 Scott & Ascher §§24.9 (Liability in the Case of a Breach of Trust), 24.10 (Liability for Breach of Duty of Loyalty). *See also* 2A Scott on Trusts §170.2.

[306] Restatement (Second) of Trusts §206 cmt. c.

[307] Restatement (Second) of Trusts §206 cmt. d.

[308] Cornet v. Cornet, 269 Mo. 298, 190 S.W. 333 (1916).

What if the trustee purchases property from a third person for the purpose of reselling it to himself as trustee, does sell it to himself as trustee, and makes a profit thereby? He is chargeable with the excess of the amount that he received from the trust over the amount he paid for it, unless the property has depreciated in value.[309] If at the time of resale the property has depreciated in value, the trustee is chargeable with the difference between the value of the property at resale and what the trust paid for it.[310] Note, however, that if the trustee acquired the property for a purpose other than reselling it to himself as trustee and the property appreciates in value prior to the resale, the trustee is only chargeable with the "excess, if any, of the amount which he received from the trust over the value of the property at the time when he sold it to himself as trustee."[311]

Trustee competes with trust. A trustee may not enter into a substantial competition with the equitable interests of the trust.[312] If he does, he is chargeable with any resulting loss and is accountable for any profit he personally makes conducting the competing enterprise.[313] Assume an oil well is an asset of a trust. The trustee may not start up his own drilling operation on a contiguous parcel of real estate and in so doing draw oil away from the reach of the well. If he does, the trustee can be compelled to hold the contiguous parcel and any profit that he makes running the competing enterprise upon a constructive trust for the trust.[314] The trustee, however, would be entitled to reimbursement for out-of-pocket expenditures.

In one case, a testator's liquor business became an asset of his probate estate upon his death.[315] Toward the end of his life, as his health had begun to fail, he had entrusted to his son the running of the business. Once the testator had died, the son, instead of running the business for the benefit of the probate estate, claimed the business as his own. The son, being both trustee and agent-employee of the enterprise, was ordered by the court to account for all the property of the probate estate that was in his possession and to put the probate estate in the same condition that it would have been in had he not repudiated his fiduciary relationships as trustee and employee and wrongfully assumed the position of owner.

Multiple breaches of trust (Damages for violations of more than one duty with respect to the same portion of the trust property). Both in the United States and in England,[316] a trustee may not reduce his liability for a

---

[309] Restatement (Second) of Trusts §206 cmt. e.

[310] Restatement (Second) of Trusts §206 cmt. f.

[311] Restatement (Second) of Trusts §206. cmt. g.

[312] Restatement (Second) of Trusts §170 cmt. p.

[313] Restatement (Second of Trusts §206 cmt. l.

[314] Restatement (Second) of Trusts §206 cmt. l, illus. 12.

[315] *See* Jubinville v. Jubinville, 313 Mass. 103, 46 N.E.2d 533 (1943). *See also* Sauvage v. Gallaway, 329 Ill. App. 38, 66 N.E.2d 740 (1946), 331 Ill. App. 309, 72 N.E.2d 133 (1947) (trustee could be enjoined from carrying on an advertising business that would compete with an asset of the trust estate).

[316] Lewin ¶ 39-17 (England).

breach of trust with a gain from a separate and distinct breach of trust.[317] This is known as the anti-netting rule.[318] If, however, a trustee makes a profit and also suffers a loss through the *same* breach of trust, the beneficiaries are entitled only to the amount of the profit less the amount of the loss or they may charge the trustee with the loss reduced by the amount of the profit.[319]

If a trustee commits multiple breaches of trust in the course of administering the same portion of the trust property, is the beneficiary entitled to multiple damage awards? The answer is generally no, absent a statutory provision to the contrary. On the other hand, "[i]f a trustee violates two or more . . . investment duties . . . , he should be liable for all the damages which the beneficiary can prove were caused by each breach, and the beneficiary should not be required to make an election between suing the trustee for one breach or another."[320]

Damages for wrongful sale of specific property and wrongful purchase with the proceeds thereof. If the trustee sells a specific asset which the terms of the trust had directed be retained[321] and uses the proceeds to purchase other property,[322] his liability for damages would hinge on the subsequent fortunes of the two assets. If the sold asset appreciates in value, he is liable for its value.[323] The value is pegged at the time of the decree. He is also entitled to offset the phantom asset's value by the value of the improperly purchased asset. If the value of the unauthorized asset appreciates, the trustee is accountable for the gain.[324] If both assets appreciate, those possessing equitable interests in the trust may elect the more profitable.[325] If the unauthorized asset depreciates in value, the trustee is chargeable with the loss.[326] He may, however, offset the loss by any depreciation in the value of the sold asset.

In one case, a corporate trustee wrongfully sold a fixed-income asset and wrongfully invested the proceeds in another fixed-income asset, namely, its own "matured passbook accounts." The court awarded the beneficiaries interest on the entrusted monies at the legal rate of 6 percent per annum, compounded annually, less the amounts which were actually paid out by the trustee. The court

---

[317] *See* Restatement (Second) of Trusts §213 (balances losses and gains); Restatement (Third) of Trusts §213 (balancing losses against profits) [provisional and now superseded by §101].

[318] *See generally* §8.15.33 of this handbook (the anti-netting rule for multiple breaches of trust); Restatement (Second) of Trusts §213 (balancing losses and gains); Restatement (Third) of Trusts §213 (balancing losses against profits) [provisional and now superseded by §101].

[319] *See generally* §8.15.33 of this handbook (the anti-netting rule for multiple breaches of trust); Lewin ¶ 39-17 (England); Restatement (Second) of Trusts §213 (balancing losses and gains); Restatement (Third) of Trusts §213 (balancing losses against profits) [provisional and now superseded by §101] (U.S.).

[320] Bogert §707.

[321] *See generally* 4 Scott & Ascher §24.11 (Liability for Breach of Trust by Selling Trust Property).

[322] *See generally* 4 Scott & Ascher §24.13 (Liability for Breach of Trust by Purchasing Property).

[323] Restatement (Second) of Trusts §212 cmt. b.

[324] Restatement (Second) of Trusts §212 cmt. b.

[325] Restatement (Second) of Trusts §212 cmt. b.

[326] Restatement (Second) of Trusts §212 cmt. b.

declined to compel the trustee to account for any profits in excess of the legal rate:

> Upon consideration of the circumstances of this case, . . . including the difficulty and expense involved in an attempt to arrive at an accurate accounting of the profits earned from the use of these funds, we believe that a final judgment and decree should be entered upon the remanding of this case, to include an award of interest, to be computed as previously stated, but without provision for a further accounting.[327]

Damages for wrongful purchase and wrongful failure to purchase specific property as directed. If the trustee in breach of trust purchases with trust funds what he should not have purchased[328] and fails to purchase what was directed to be purchased by the terms of the trust,[329] his liability for damages would depend on the subsequent fortunes of the two assets. If the specific asset that should have been purchased appreciates in value, the trustee is accountable for the value of the asset at the time of the decree.[330] If the property that was purchased appreciates in value, he is accountable for the gain.[331] If both assets appreciate, the beneficiaries may elect the more profitable.[332] If the property which was wrongfully purchased depreciates in value, the trustee is chargeable with the loss.[333] The trustee may, however, offset the loss by any depreciation in the value of the asset that he had wrongfully neglected to purchase.

When the trustee is not directed to purchase a specific item of property but breaches a general duty to invest prudently, the court, in coming up with a damage figure, must wrestle with the question of what exactly it was that the trustee wrongfully failed to purchase. In one case, a corporate trustee, pursuant to the terms of the governing instrument and in accordance with the general default law, had a general duty to purchase investments that prudently balanced the interests of the income beneficiaries and the remaindermen. Instead, the trustee invested the trust estate entirely in fixed-income securities in order to maximize current income. There had been no growth in the principal. The appellate court addressed the failure-to-purchase issue this way:

> The remaindermen also contend the trial court miscalculated their damages by using a formula based on its findings that the "most accurate rate of appreciation for the determination of . . . damages . . . would be the rate of appreciation experience[d] by the common equity funds utilized by the [B]ank." The way the remaindermen see it, they are "entitled to appreciation damages based upon objective market criteria." They are mistaken. It is undisputed that whatever

---

[327] Stephan v. Equitable Sav. & Loan Ass'n, 268 Or. 544, 522 P.2d 478 (1974).

[328] *See generally* 4 Scott & Ascher §24.13 (Liability for Breach of Trust by Purchasing Property).

[329] *See generally* 4 Scott & Ascher §24.14 (Liability for Breach of Trust by Failing to Purchase Specific Property).

[330] Restatement (Second) of Trusts §212 cmt. c.

[331] Restatement (Second) of Trusts §212 cmt. c.

[332] Restatement (Second) of Trusts §212 cmt. c.

[333] Restatement (Second) of Trusts §212 cmt. c.

portion of the trust estates that should have been invested in assets that would have benefited the remaindermen over their parents would have been invested in the Bank's common equity fund. It follows that it was appropriate for the probate court to approve the referee's calculation of damages based on the amount the trusts actually would have earned. . . .[334]

Damages for wrongful failure to sell specific property and wrongful failure to purchase other specific property. If the trustee fails to sell specific property which the terms of the trust directed be sold[335] and fails to purchase with the proceeds other specific property which the terms of the trust directed be purchased,[336] his liability for damages would depend on the subsequent fortunes of the two assets. If the asset that he should have purchased appreciates in value, the trustee is accountable for the value of the asset at the time of the decree.[337] If the improperly retained asset appreciates in value, he is accountable for the gain.[338] If both assets appreciate, the beneficiaries may elect the more profitable.[339] If the improperly retained asset depreciates in value, the trustee is chargeable with the loss.[340] He may, however, offset the loss by any depreciation in the value of the asset he should have purchased but did not.

And then there is the analogous failure to prudently disinvest and reinvest. In one case, a trustee was found in breach of trust for failing promptly to dispose of bonds that had come into default. The trial court's computation of the trustee's damage liability was based on the interest stipulated in the bonds that were in default. The appellate court rejected that approach:

It is clear to us that in surcharging the trustee's account, the amount should be measured by the return that the trustee could have made had he promptly disposed of the bonds and reinvested in safe and lawful securities. It is not to be concluded without proof that such securities would produce the same income as the bonds in question. We think that this issue was not tried and that the interests of justice require a return of the record for further evidence upon this point.[341]

---

[334] Noggle v. Bank of Am., 70 Cal. App. 4th 853, 862 (1999). In First Alabama Bank of Montgomery v. Martin, 425 So. 2d 415 (Ala. 1982), a case involving imprudent investments within the bank's equity and bond common trust funds, the court determined that the benchmark for measuring loss of principal for damage computation purposes should be one-year Treasury bills. As to the income that the common trust funds would have earned without the transactions complained of, the court ordered the bank to calculate the accounts as if it had fully performed the duties as the plaintiffs claimed it should have performed, and to recalculate the account as if it had promptly invested all the additional income at specified one-year Treasury bill rates ranging from 4.61 percent to 12.23 percent and averaging 7.5 percent. Compounding was appropriate because the trustee had breached its duty to reinvest income. See 3 Scott on Trust §207.2.

[335] See generally 4 Scott & Ascher §24.12 (Liability for Breach of Trust by Failing to Sell Trust Property).

[336] See generally 4 Scott & Ascher §24.14 (Liability for Breach of Trust by Failing to Purchase Specific Property).

[337] Restatement (Second) of Trusts §212 cmt. d.

[338] Restatement (Second) of Trusts §212 cmt. d.

[339] Restatement (Second) of Trusts §212 cmt. d.

[340] Restatement (Second) of Trusts §212 cmt. d.

[341] In re North's Will, 294 N.W. 15, 17 (1940).

Damages in absence of causal connection between breach of trust and loss. As a general rule, if the trustee commits a breach of trust and for reasons unrelated to the breach the trust suffers an economic loss, the trustee generally is not chargeable with the amount of the loss if it would have occurred in the absence of a breach of trust.[342] A trustee, for example, who fails to prudently diversify should be liable only for that portion of a portfolio's investment losses that are attributable to the breach.[343] Let us assume that a trust holds a block of shares in a certain company. The trustee sells the block and realizes $1,000 in losses. If the block had comprised 20 percent of the portfolio when prudence dictated that it should have comprised no more than 10 percent, then the trustee's personal liability should be capped at $500. There are several exceptions to this causal connection liability principle:

Self-dealing by trustee. A trustee who sells his own property to the trust is liable for any depreciation in the value of the property.[344] "[I]t is immaterial that the trustee could properly have purchased similar property from a third person and that in such a case he would not have been liable for the loss."[345] The policy behind the no-further-inquiry rule is to deter fiduciaries from engaging in acts of self-dealing.[346]

In one case, a bank sold certain bonds that it owned outright or through an affiliate to itself as trustee of a living trust. The life beneficiary and the remaindermen objected.[347] Although the bonds were subsequently sold at loss, the trustee most likely would not have been in breach of trust had it purchased them for the trust from a third party. The core of the objection was that the trustee had breached its duty of loyalty. The original cost of the bonds was $54,597.95. They were ultimately sold for $43,428.69, resulting in a loss to the trust of $11,169.26. The trial court sustained the contention of the objectors and surcharged the trustee's account with such loss, together with interest amounting to $8,735.12, aggregating a total sum of $19,904.38. The order of the trial court was affirmed on appeal.

---

[342] *See generally* 4 Scott & Ascher §24.9.1 (When Loss Would Have Occurred in Absence of Breach of Trust); Restatement (Second) of Trusts §205 cmt. f.

[343] 4 Scott & Ascher §24.9.1 (When Losses Would Have Occurred in Absence of Breach of Trust); Restatement (Second) of Trusts §205 cmt. f.

[344] Restatement (Second) of Trusts §205 cmt. f. *See generally* Bogert §543(E) (Trustee Selling His Own Property to the Trust); 4 Scott & Ascher §24.9.

[345] Restatement (Second) of Trusts §205 cmt. f. *See generally* 2A Scott on Trusts §170.2.

[346] Restatement (Second) of Trusts §205 cmt. f. *See generally* §7.1 of this hand book and §8.15.30 of this handbook (discussing the no-further-inquiry rule). *See also* 4 Scott & Ascher §24.9.1 (When Loss Would Have Occurred in Absence of Breach of Trust).

[347] In re Anneke's Trust v. First & Am. Nat'l Bank, 229 Minn. 60, 38 N.W.2d 177 (1949). Note: If authorized by statute, a corporate trustee may purchase mutual fund participations or other securities from its affiliate, provided the transaction is prudent, fair to the beneficiaries, and not forbidden by the terms of the trust. *See* Supervisory Letter (SR 99-7, Mar. 26, 1999) (Federal Reserve Board, Division of Banking Supervision) (raising concerns that banks that invest their fiduciary funds in their proprietary mutual funds may be subject to suit for breach of the common law duty of undivided loyalty if they are not careful, notwithstanding general statutory authority to do so).

Failure of trustee to earmark. When a trustee, in breach of his fiduciary duty, fails to earmark an investment,[348] he is not necessarily liable for a loss resulting from his making what is otherwise a prudent investment.[349] Much will depend on the circumstances surrounding the failure to earmark.[350] In some cases, absolute liability will attach in order to discourage fiduciaries from engaging in certain activities. If, for example, the failure is such that it could facilitate his claiming personal ownership were the asset to appreciate and disclaiming personal ownership were it to depreciate, then liability might well attach regardless of the absence of a causal connection between the failure to earmark and the loss and regardless of the trustee's actual motivations.[351] On the other hand, if the particular failure to earmark cannot in and of itself elevate the investment's exposure to risk, then liability may well not attach.[352]

As a general rule, the trustee who deposits funds in a bank account without designating the account as a trust account is personally liable for any loss occasioned by the insolvency of the bank. The rule applies even when no personal funds of the trustee are in the account. Courts are not inflexible, however, in applying the rule.[353] In one case, a trustee deposited the funds of a trust un-earmarked in his firm's account. The account also contained un-earmarked funds from other trusts. After the trustee died but before the bank failed, the trustee's personal representative properly earmarked the funds. The court declined to impose liability on the trustee's estate:

> Our conclusion, therefore, is that the mingling of the trust funds . . . by the trustee was an irregularity which beyond question would have made his estate liable, had the deposits to the credit of these trusts remained commingled down to the time of the failure of the . . . [bank]. . . . As, however, this irregularity had been fully cured by deposits made by the administrator of the deceased trustee under proper trust designations at the time of the failure of the . . . [bank] . . . , we are of the opinion that no liability attaches to the estate of the trustee by reason of the former manner in which the deposits were carried.[354]

---

[348] *See generally* §6.2.1.2 of this handbook (trustee's duty to segregate and earmark trust property); Restatement (Second) of Trusts §179 cmt. d (duty to earmark trust property); Restatement (Second) of Trusts §205 cmt. f (earmarking/damages).

[349] Restatement (Second) of Trusts §205 cmt. f.

[350] *See generally* §6.2.1.2 of this handbook (trustee's duty not to commingle trust property); Restatement (Second) of Trusts §179 cmt. d (duty to earmark trust property); Restatement (Second) of Trusts §205 cmt. f (earmarking/damages).

[351] Restatement (Second) of Trusts §179 cmt. d (duty to earmark trust property); Restatement (Second) of Trusts §205 cmt. f; 4 Scott & Ascher §24.9.1. (When Loss Would Have Occurred in Absence of Breach of Trust).

[352] Restatement (Second) of Trusts §179 cmt. d (duty to earmark trust property); Restatement (Second) of Trusts §205 cmt. f. *See generally* 4 Scott & Ascher §24.8 (Nonliability for Loss in the Absence of a Breach of Trust).

[353] *See generally* §6.2.1.2 of this handbook (trustee's duty to segregate and earmark the trust property); 4 Scott & Ascher §24.9.1 (When Loss Would Have Occurred in Absence of Breach of Trust).

[354] Carey v. Safe Deposit & Trust Co. of Baltimore, 178 A. 242, 246 (Md. 1935).

In another case, one Daniel Yturria purchased a certificate of deposit with trust funds. The bank issued the certificate to "D. Yturria, Trustee." The beneficiary, however, was not designated. At the time the deposit was made, the bank was a solvent, reputable institution. Thereafter, it went into receivership. The court declined to impose liability on the trustee:

> By procuring from that bank its certificate for the amount deposited, made payable to "D. Yturria, Trustee," that bank was put on notice that the fund represented by that certificate was not the individual property of the depositor, but was a fund held by him in a trust relation, though the name of the cestui que trust was not stated or disclosed; and that fund could not be applied, by the depository bank or another, on the individual indebtedness of the depositor.[355]

Damages in absence of breach of trust. The trustee's duty of loyalty, including the no further inquiry rule, is generally covered in Section 6.1.3 of this handbook. A trustee must turn over to the trust any profit made by the trustee in the course of administering the trust, unless the terms of the trust provide otherwise.[356] The principle applies even when the profit has not been occasioned by some breach of fiduciary duty.[357] A typical example of a profit that may not accrue to the trustee is a commission or bonus from a third party for a transaction involving the trust property.[358]

Whether a personal benefit accruing to the trustee constitutes a windfall or legitimate compensation or "profits earned outside of trust administration"[359] depends upon the facts and circumstances. In one case, a bank took a mortgage on certain store and apartment buildings and allocated participations to trust estates under its administration. It also undertook the task of acting as rental agent for the mortgagor and received from him a commission of 5 percent on rents collected. This commission was over and above its standard charges for fiduciary services. The court, however, held that the commission need not be remitted to the trust estate:

> Such an arrangement, far from amounting to a secret profit received by the trustee at the expense of the trust estates, was for their benefit and enabled the trustee at

---

[355] Anguera v. Yturria, 80 F.2d 57, 58 (1935).

[356] 4 Scott & Ascher §24.7 (Accountability for Profits in the Absence of a Breach of Trust); Restatement (Second) of Trusts §203 cmt. a (accountability for profits in the absence of a breach of trust).

[357] UTC §1003(a) (available at <http://www.uniformlaws.org/Act.aspx?title=Trust%20Code>); 4 Scott & Ascher §24.7 (Accountability for Profits in the Absence of a Breach of Trust); Restatement (Second) of Trusts §203 cmt. a (accountability for profits in the absence of a breach of trust).

[358] UTC §1003 cmt. (available at <http://www.uniformlaws.org/Act.aspx?title=Trust%20Code>); 4 Scott & Ascher §24.7 (Accountability for Profits in the Absence of a Breach of Trust); Restatement (Second) of Trusts §203 cmt. a (accountability for profits in the absence of a breach of trust).

[359] 4 Scott & Ascher §24.7 (Accountability for Profits in the Absence of a Breach of Trust); Restatement (Second) of Trusts §203 cmt. b (trustee accountable for profit made through the use of trust property); Restatement (Second) of Trusts §203 cmt. e (trustee not accountable for profit unconnected with administration of trust).

all times to see that the property was efficiently managed to advantage of all. The compensation received by the trustee as rental agent for the owner was not money which the participating trust interests would otherwise be entitled to. They would have belonged to the owner, or would have been paid to some other rental agent as fair compensation for services rendered. It was not shown that the rental commissions were in any sense a profit; on the contrary, they were just charges for services performed . . . [by the trustee] . . . in its required administration of the trust, and their receipt does not offend the admitted rule against a trustee's obtaining a bonus or commission from dealings with specific trust property. . . .[360]

Punitive or exemplary damages. The courts of equity had no power to award punitive damages.[361] "Equity suffers not Advantage to be taken of a Penalty or Forfeiture, where Compensation can be made."[362] It therefore followed that an award of damages for breach of fiduciary duty could not have a punitive element to it, the office of trustee itself being a creature of equity.[363] Thus there is an absence of any mention of punitive damages in the body of the Restatement (Third) of Trusts.[364] Courts, in any case, have always considered it within their equitable powers to reduce or deny compensation—and reimbursement for expenses—to trustees who are held to be in breach of trust.[365] Still, some courts have begun to assess punitive damages against professional trustees and these assessments are being upheld, particularly in cases where the breach of fiduciary duty involves fraud or malice.[366] Without an award of actual

---

[360] In re Harton's Estate, 331 Pa. 507, 515–516, 1 A.2d 292, 296 (1938). *See generally* Scott on Trusts §170.22.

[361] "Traditionally, remedies for breach of trust at law were limited to suits to enforce unconditional obligations to pay money or deliver chattels." UTC §1001 cmt. (available at <http://www.uniformlaws.org/Act.aspx?title=Trust%20Code>). "Otherwise, remedies for breach of trust were exclusively equitable, and as such, punitive damages were not available and findings of fact were made by the judge and not the jury." UTC §1001 cmt.

[362] Richard Francis, Maxims of Equity 44 (London, Bernard Lintot 1728) (maxim no. 12).

[363] *See generally* 22 Am. Jur. 2d *Equity* §738 (1990).

[364] *But see* Restatement (Third) of Trusts §100, cmt. d ("In the egregious case, however, punitive damages are permissible under the laws of many jurisdictions. This is especially so if the trustee has acted maliciously, in bad faith, or in a fraudulent, particularly reckless, or self-serving manner."). *See also* UTC §1001 cmt. (available at <http://www.uniformlaws.org/Act.aspx?title= Trust%20Code>) (noting that the UTC does not preclude the awarding of punitive damages for breaches of fiduciary duty).

[365] *See* Bogert §861 n.60 and accompanying text. *See also* Restatement (Third) of Trusts: Prudent Investor Rule §205 cmt. a (1992). *Cf.* Estate of Gould, 547 S.W.2d 863 (Mo. Ct. App. 1977) (an attorney's conduct as executor being improper and his conduct as attorney wrong, he was properly removed from those positions and denied all compensation). For a discussion of the difference between punitive damages and appreciation damages, *see* Estate of Rothko, 379 N.Y.S.2d 923, 84 Misc. 2d 830 (1975).

[366] *See* Bogert §862 n.34 and accompanying text; 4 Scott & Ascher §24.9 n.36 and accompanying text; 3 Scott on Trusts §205 n.1 and accompanying text; Campisi et al., *Emerging Damages Claims and the Right to Jury Trials in Fiduciary Litigation*, 27 Real Prop. Prob. & Tr. J. 541, 542–553 (1992) (containing a review of availability of punitive damages and appreciation damages in fiduciary litigation in the various states). *See, e.g.*, Smith v. Underwood, 487 S.E.2d 807 (N.C. Ct. App. 1997) (allowing punitive damages where a plaintiff has proven at least nominal damages and where an element of aggravation, such as fraud, causes the injury); Shoemaker v. Estate of

damages, however, there can be no award of punitive damages, at least that is the case in Missouri.[367] And certainly stonewalling the court is not a good idea:

> Moreover we agree with the district court that the size of the punitive damages award is not out of proportion to the actual damages sustained. Evidence in the record revealed that Mercantile is part of a twenty-one-bank holding company. Mercantile, standing alone, claims assets in excess of $48 million. Clearly a substantial sting would be required to deter this financial institution from profiting in the future by ignoring—and thereby impairing—the rights of trust beneficiaries such as Virginia Haberstick. . . . The complete and utter failure of the bank to offer an explanation for its inaction bespeaks an ulterior motive. One can only assume from this record that more remunerative trusts occupied the trust officers' time.[368]

One court has upheld an award of exemplary damages against a predecessor trustee in an action for breach of fiduciary duty brought by the successor.[369] It did so, however, by misconstruing the nature of the action as legal rather than equitable. As the dissent pointed out: "While the nature of the available remedies may be a strong indicator of the legal or equitable nature of an action, . . . the fact that a plaintiff seeks a money judgment has by no means been considered decisive that the action is one at law."[370]

The Uniform Trust Code would not preclude the awarding of punitive damages for breaches of fiduciary duty.[371] In fact, under Kansas's version of the Uniform Trust Code, a trustee who embezzles or knowingly converts to the trustee's own use trust property would be liable for double the property's value.[372]

Freeman, 967 P.2d 871 (Okla. 1998) (holding that evidence supports an award of punitive damages where trustee has failed to transfer farm to remaindermen as required by terms of the trust); InterFirst Bank of Dallas, N.A. v. Risser, 739 S.W.2d 882 (Tex. Ct. App. Texarkana 1987) (assessing $10 million in punitive damages against trustee bank that sold trust property to a debtor of the bank). *But see* Kann v. Kann, 690 A.2d 509, 520 (Md. 1997) (holding "allegations of breach of fiduciary duty, in and of themselves, do not give rise to an omnibus or generic cause of action at law. . . . [H]ere . . . the claim is exclusively equitable and not triable of right before a jury. . . . [P]unitive damages are not at all available in equity".).

[367] *See* O'Riley v. U.S. Bank, N.A., 412 S.W.3d 400, 418 (2013).

[368] Hamilton v. Mercantile Bank of Cedar Rapids, 621 N.W.2d 401 (Iowa 2001) (assessing punitive damages against a successor trustee for making "absolutely no effort" to ascertain condition of degraded trust real estate upon and after it assumed the trusteeship).

[369] Peterson v. McMahon, 99 P.3d 594 (Colo. 2004).

[370] Peterson v. McMahon, 99 P.3d 594, 600 (Colo. 2004).

[371] UTC §1001 cmt. (available at <http://www.uniformlaws.org/Act.aspx?title=Trust%20Code>).

[372] Kan. Stat. Ann. §58a-1002(a)(3). *See also* McCabe v. Duran, 180 P.3d 1098 (Kan. Ct. App. 2008) (the court declining to retroactively apply the double-damages provision of Kansas's version of the UTC).

§7.2.3.3 Restitution and Specific Reparation/Restitution, a.k.a. Restitution *in Specie* as Substantive Remedies

Restitution is the law of nonconsensual and nonbargained benefits in the same way that torts is the law of nonconsensual and nonlicensed harms.—Restatement Third, Restitution and Unjust Enrichment.[373]

The Treaty of Versailles (1919) formally asserted Germany's war guilt and ordered it to pay reparations to the Allies . . . A reparations commission fixed sums in money; some payments were to be in kind (i.e., coal, steel, ships).—The Columbia Encyclopedia.[374]

General restitution. Restitution is the primary remedy for the wrong of unjust enrichment.[375] Unjust enrichment is covered in Section 8.15.78 of this handbook. "A person obtains restitution when he is restored to the position he formerly occupied either by the return of something which he formerly had or by the receipt of its equivalent in money."[376] In Section 7.2.3.1 of this handbook, we cover the procedural mechanics for effecting a restitution for unjust enrichment in the context of a breach of trust, such as the imposition of a constructive trust. The topic of the constructive trust is generally covered in Section 3.3 of this handbook. "With few exceptions, a claimant entitled to a disgorgement remedy in restitution might instead recover compensation for the injury caused by the defendant's tort or other breach of duty. Restitution becomes significant when it affords remedial or procedural advantages by comparison with an action for damages."[377] Damages as an equitable relief for breach of trust is covered in Section 7.2.3.2 of this handbook.

The equitable remedy of restitution for unjustified enrichment is concerned with "the receipt of benefits that yield a measurable increase in the recipient's wealth."[378] The wealth-shifting, however, is not of the type that is incident to an enforceable contract.[379]

At one time restitution was limited to the return of a specific item of property.[380] In other words, it was a synonym for specific reparation. "In modern legal usage, its meaning has frequently been extended to include not only the restoration or giving back of something to its rightful owner and

---

[373] Restatement (Third) of Restitution and Unjust Enrichment §1, cmt. d.

[374] The Columbia Encyclopedia 2304 (5th ed. 1993).

[375] Restatement of Restitution §1.

[376] Restatement of Restitution §1, cmt. a; *see also* Restatement (Third) of Restitution and Unjust Enrichment §1, cmt. a.

[377] Restatement (Third) of Restitution and Unjust Enrichment §3, cmt. b.

[378] Restatement (Third) of Restitution and Unjust Enrichment §1, cmt. d.

[379] "There are remedies for breach of contract that have frequently been called 'restitution' and have sometimes been explained in terms of unjust enrichment. . . . [The Restatement (Third) of Restitution and Unjust Enrichment, however] . . . describes them as a part of contract law, not restitution, and it rejects the supposed connection with principle of unjust enrichment." Restatement (Third) of Restitution and Unjust Enrichment §1, cmt. e.

[380] Anne M. Payne and Monique Leahy, Restitution and Implied Contracts, 66 Am. Jur. 2d Restitution and Implied Contracts §1; *see also* Restatement (Third) of Restitution and Unjust Enrichment §1, cmt. c (restitution and restoration).

returning to the status quo, but also compensation, reimbursement, indemnification, or reparation for benefits derived from, or for loss or injury caused to, another."[381] Thus, under the right circumstances, restitution would be available to remediate an unauthorized distribution of fungible trust monies.[382]

The Restatement (Third) of Restitution and Unjust Enrichment provides that one who is unjustly enriched is "liable in restitution," an unfortunate definitional innovation in that it implies that the one who is unjustifiably enriched must be at fault, which is not necessarily the case.[383] "There are prominent instances of unjust enrichment in which a negligent claimant recovers from a blameless defendant."[384] The negligent misdelivery of trust property to an innocent non-BFP comes to mind. The topic of BFPs is taken up in Section 8.15.63 of this handbook.

Restitution in specie or in kind (specific reparation/specific/asset-based restitution). When a trustee wrongfully acquires from the trust estate by sale or otherwise an item of tangible personal property, a parcel of real estate, or a nonfungible item of intangible personal property, the beneficiaries may compel the trustee to put the specific property, or its in-kind equivalent, back in the trust.[385] The same applies when a trustee in violation of his duty to the beneficiary transfers specific property or causes property to be transferred to a third person.[386] The third person holds the property *in specie* upon a constructive trust for the beneficiaries.[387] This type of equitable relief is known as specific reparation, or restitution *in specie* or in kind.[388] The Restatement (Third) of Restitution and Unjust Enrichment refers to such remedies as "asset-based" or "property-based." Specific reparation is not necessarily an exclusive remedy.[389] It may be an ingredient in a cocktail of equitable remedies that the court in a given situation mixes in order to make the beneficiaries whole.[390] This in-kind relief is expansive enough to capture like properties:

> If the trustee owns similar property of his or her own, the court may compel the trustee to hold the trustee's own property subject to the trust. Or the court may compel the trustee to procure similar property for the trust if it is readily available in the market.[391]

---

[381] Anne M. Payne and Monique Leahy, Restitution and Implied Contracts, 66 Am. Jur. 2d Restitution and Implied Contracts §1.

[382] *See* Restatement (Third) of Restitution and Unjust Enrichment §17, illus. 18.

[383] Restatement (Third) of Restitution and Unjust Enrichment §1 ("A person who is unjustly enriched at the expense of another is subject to liability in restitution.")

[384] Restatement (Third) of Restitution and Unjust Enrichment §1, cmt. f.

[385] 4 Scott & Ascher §24.11.3 (Specific Reparation); Restatement of Restitution §190.

[386] Restatement of Restitution §201(1).

[387] Restatement of Restitution §201(1).

[388] Restatement of Restitution §4, cmt. d.

[389] Restatement of Restitution §4 (Remedies).

[390] Restatement of Restitution §4 (Remedies); Restatement of Restitution 640.

[391] 4 Scott & Ascher §24.11.3 (Specific Reparation).

Not only the trustee's improper acquisition of trust property can warrant a decree for specific reparation, but also the trustee's improper failure to purchase specific property for the trust. " ... [I]f the trustee has improperly failed to purchase specific property, the court may order specific reparation, and compel the trustee to purchase the property, if it is reasonable to do so, to pay out of the trust fund only so much as the property would have cost at the time the trustee should have purchased it, and to pay any deficit out of the trustee's own pocket."[392] The term "specific restitution" as employed in the Restatement (Third) of Restitution and Unjust Enrichment is only a partial synonym for the term specific reparation:

> References to "specific restitution" are themselves ambiguous. Sometimes the expression is used to describe a remedy that restores the identical asset that the claimant has lost, while at other times it describes a remedy that gives substitute rights in specific property as opposed to money judgment. This Restatement attempts to minimize confusion on this score by avoiding the term "specific restitution," except when the claimant recovers the very thing that was lost.[393]

The potential advantages of seeking an asset-based remedy. Under certain circumstances, a trust beneficiary may be better off seeking an asset-based equitable remedy for a breach of trust than seeking an assessment against the trustee personally for equitable damages. Again, it all depends on the particular set of facts and circumstances. Here are some *possible* advantages in opting for an asset-based equitable remedy:

- Avoidance of valuation litigation
- Capture of postbreach appreciation
- Preference over trustee's creditors
- Accommodation of emotional attachment to a specific asset
- End-running the Uniform Trust Code's statute of ultimate repose (§1005(c)).[394]

Of course an asset-based remedy for unjust enrichment would not be available if the particular asset in question is no longer identifiable. The process of identifying the particular asset is called "following," a topic we take up in Section 7.2.3.1.2 of this handbook. The Restatement (Third) of Restitution and

---

[392] 4 Scott & Ascher §24.14 (Liability for Breach of Trust by Failing to Purchase Specific Property). *See generally* §7.2.3.2 of this handbook (assessing damages for a breach of trust).

[393] Restatement (Third) of Restitution and Unjust Enrichment §1, cmt. e. "The broader set of remedies that is sometimes and more loosely called 'specific restitution' (or what English writers call 'proprietary restitution') appears in this Restatement under the heading 'Restitution Via Rights in Identifiable Property.'" Restatement (Third) of Restitution and Unjust Enrichment §1, cmt. e.

[394] *See generally* §7.1.3 of this handbook (the UTC's five-year statute of ultimate repose forecloses breach-of-trust actions, not necessarily actions for restitution to remedy unjust enrichment).

Unjust Enrichment describes the process as tracing,[395] which conflicts with the nomenclature of this handbook. *Tracing*, as the term is employed in this handbook, is the process of tracking property into its product, a topic we take up in Section 7.2.3.1.3 of this handbook.

§7.2.3.4   Specific Performance/Enforcement and Permanent Injunction as Substantive Remedies

A typical characteristic of equity is that it operates by means of prohibitions and orders directed to the parties (equitable remedies). This is often expressed with the phrase equity acts in personam. . . . In this way equity created, for instance, the possibility to demand specific performance; according to common law, the owner could by means of writ of detinue demand the delivering of unlawfully retained personal property, but the defendant could by his own choice pay compensation.[396]

The court may issue a decree of specific performance/enforcement[397] or a permanent injunction,[398] as well as assess damages, a topic we take up in §7.2.3.2 of this handbook; order restitution, a topic we take up in §7.2.3.3 of this handbook; reduce or deny the trustee's compensation, a topic we take up in §7.2.3.7 of this handbook; appoint a receiver, a topic we take up in §7.2.3.8 of this handbook; and/or remove the trustee, a topic we take up in §7.2.3.6 of this handbook.[399] These are all substantive equitable remedies. The beneficiaries' rights are fundamentally equitable; their remedies are correspondingly broad: "Since both the beneficiaries' rights and the trustee's duties are equitable, the situation differs from that in which the plaintiff seeks specific performance of a contract or specific redress for a tort. Ordinarily, equity does not specifically enforce a contract or grant specific redress for a tort when damages are inadequate. A trust beneficiary, however, is entitled to specific enforcement of the trust even if the subject matter is not unique."[400]

Permanent injunction. A trustee may be permanently enjoined from committing in the future a particular breach of trust.[401] "Trustees have been restrained from distributing an estate inconsistently with the terms of the

---

[395] *See* Restatement (Third) of Restitution and Unjust Enrichment, Chap. 7, Topic 2, Introductory Note.

[396] Michael Bogdan, Comparative Law 111 (1994).

[397] *See generally* 4 Scott & Ascher §24.3.1 (Specific Enforcement of Trust).

[398] *See generally* Lewin ¶ 38-09 through ¶ 38-13 (England) (including a discussion of interim injunctions to preserve trust property); 4 Scott & Ascher §24.3.2 (Injunction) (U.S.).

[399] *See generally* Bogert §861. *See, e.g.*, Koffend's Will v. First Nat'l Bank of Minneapolis, 218 Minn. 206, 220, 14 N.W.2d 590, 598 (1944) (confirming that a court has the power to direct a trustee of a corporation to select corporate directors who will run the corporation as the settlor intended notwithstanding the default law of corporations). "A court of equity may specifically direct a trustee to exercise a power which was given him where such action is necessary to give a cestui a remedy." Koffend's Will v. First Nat'l Bank of Minneapolis, 218 Minn. 206, 220, 14 N.W.2d 590, 598 (1944).

[400] 4 Scott & Ascher §24.3.1 (Specific Enforcement of Trust).

[401] 4 Scott & Ascher §24.3.2.

instrument; and from electing as minister to a Presbyterian chapel a person not licensed as a preacher in the Church of Scotland; or from selling under depreciatory conditions of sale; or from selling for a price below that offered firmly by a prospective purchaser; or selling as tenant for life inconsistently with the tenant for life's position as trustee; or selling land held on trust for sale without appointing a second trustee and without consulting the beneficiary."[402]

Specific performance/enforcement. The institution of the trust owes its very existence to the equitable remedy of specific performance/enforcement. One of Equity's maxims was and is that Equity will not suffer a wrong to be without a remedy, the maxim referring to rights which are suitable for judicial enforcement, but are not enforceable at common law owing to some technical defect.[403] It was on that maxim that the Court of Chancery based its interference to enforce uses and trusts, a topic we consider in more detail in Chapter 1 of this handbook.[404] "Where A conveyed land to B to hold to the use of, or on trust for, C, and B claimed to keep the benefit of the land for himself, C had no remedy at law. Yet such an abuse of confidence was most distinctly wrong, and a wrong capable of easy redress in a court of justice."[405]

Today, when it comes to specific breaches of trust, Equity will impel a court that has taken jurisdiction to retain jurisdiction until the entire matter is "cleaned up" once and for all. If a trustee of a discretionary trust, for example, has abused his discretion with respect to trust benefits, the court may "direct the trustee to make or refrain from making certain payments; issue instructions to clarify the standards or guidelines applicable to the exercise of the power; or rescind the trustee's payment decisions, usually directing the trustee to recover amounts improperly distributed and holding the trustee liable for failure or inability to do so."[406]

§7.2.3.5 Statutory Penalties

The trustee must monitor not only developments in the common law of trusts but also developments in the judicial construction of certain criminal and civil statutes. The racketeering and consumer protection statutes should be of particular concern because of their generous treble-damage provisions. Such provisions provide the trial bar with an economic incentive to take on the smaller breach-of-fiduciary-duty cases.

---

[402] Harold Greville Hanbury & Ronald Harling Maudsley, Modern Equity 106 (10th ed. 1976).

[403] Snell's Equity ¶ 5-02.

[404] *See generally* Snell's Equity ¶ 5-03. *See also* §8.15.1 of this handbook (statute of uses).

[405] Snell's Equity ¶ 5-03.

[406] Restatement (Third) of Trusts §50, cmt. b; Restatement (Third) of Trusts §87, cmt. b. *See generally* §3.5.3.2(a) of this handbook (the power to make discretionary applications of income and principal); 3 Scott & Ascher §8.2.1 (Methods of [Judicial] Control).

(a) Consumer protection. In suits by beneficiaries against professional trustees,[407] it is now common practice to allege violations of the consumer protection statutes, which in some jurisdictions can bring treble-damage recoveries to successful consumer-beneficiaries.[408] The defendant professional trustee should take such allegations particularly seriously when they are made by a settlor of a funded revocable trust.[409] This is because the professional trustee of such a trust is likely to have, or have had, a contractual relationship with the settlor and because the professional trustee advertises fiduciary services to the public. Private "intra-enterprise" conflicts, however, are another matter. The Massachusetts consumer protection statute, for example, has been held not to apply to internal disputes between beneficiaries and trustees over the administration of trusts.[410] On the other hand, the same statute has been held applicable to egregious breaches of fiduciary duty on the part of a trustee who had sold his services as a financial manager and self-styled independent trustee to members of the public in the ordinary course of business.[411] Some of the plaintiffs were nonsettlor beneficiaries of trusts that the defendant had been administering.

Apart from matters of litigation, there are innumerable consumer-oriented laws and regulations governing transactions between the trustee and the settlor and the trustee and the beneficiary. At the point when a trust is established, for example, the trustee may be required to make certain disclosures to the settlor such as the trustee's prevailing fee structure.

(b) RICO. In suits by beneficiaries against trustees for breaches of fiduciary duty, it is now not unusual to see a count alleging that the trustee engaged in a pattern of racketeering activity in violation of Title IX of the Organized Crime Control Act of 1970 (the "RICO Statute").[412] A successful civil RICO action against a trustee could result in the beneficiary's being awarded treble damages.[413] In addition to the federal RICO statute, over twenty states now have "little RICO" statutes.[414]

(c) Failure to file a UPC §7-101 registration with court. Section 7-101 of the Uniform Probate Code would require the trustee of a testamentary or inter

---

[407] *See* §7.3.3.1 of this handbook (consumer protection in the trust context); 17 Am. Jur. 2d *Consumer Protection* §§280–305 (1990).

[408] *See generally* Sovern, *Deceptive Trade Practices*, 52 Ohio St. L.J. 437, 448 n.66 and accompanying text (1991).

[409] *Cf.* Grand Pac. Fin. Corp. v. Brauer, 57 Mass. App. Ct. 407, 783 N.E.2d 849 (2003) (an attorney-agent found liable under the Massachusetts consumer protection statute for self-dealing with escrowed funds).

[410] Steele v. Kelley, 46 Mass. App. Ct. 712, 710 N.E.2d 973 (1999).

[411] Quinton v. Gavin, 64 Mass. App. Ct. 792, 835 N.E.2d 1124 (2005).

[412] "Racketeer-Influenced and Corrupt Organizations," 18 U.S.C. §§1961–1968 (1988). *See generally* D. Abrams, The Law of Civil RICO (1991).

[413] 18 U.S.C. §1964. *See generally* 31A Am. Jur. 2d *Extortion, Blackmail* §227 (1989).

[414] *See generally* 31A Am. Jur. 2d *Extortion, Blackmail* §§241–259.

vivos trust, even the trustee of a trust declaration or oral trust, to register the trust in an appropriate court at the trust's principal place of administration. A trustee who failed to do so would risk being surcharged by the court.[415] In 2008, Massachusetts adopted a gutted version of Section ¶ 7-101 that imposed no such registration obligation on trustees.[416]

§7.2.3.6 Removal

The court will remove a trustee if it is in the interest of the trust to do so.[417]

In one case, a trustee pertinaciously insisted on being continued in office, though his co-trustees were unwilling to act with him, and Lord Nottingham said that he liked not that a man should be ambitious of a trust when he could get nothing but trouble by it, and without any reflection on the conduct of the trustee, declared that he should meddle no further in the trust.[418]

The trial court has the discretionary authority to remove a trustee for cause.[419] This includes the trustee of a charitable trust.[420] As a general rule, however, for there to be cause, there needs to be some evidence that the trustee's continuation in office would be detrimental to the trust.[421] English law is in accord.[422] In any removal proceedings, the trustee is entitled to the usual due process protections including notice and an opportunity to be heard.[423] Moreover, the costs incurred by the trustee in defending an unsuccessful removal proceeding are ordinarily chargeable to the trust estate,[424] and sometimes even to the plaintiffs themselves. In the case of a testamentary trust, the court in which the trustee has qualified as trustee may remove the trustee and appoint another, even if the trustee has left the state and relocated the trust

---

[415] UPC §¶ 7-104.

[416] Mass. Gen. Laws ch. 190B, §¶ 7-101.

[417] *See* Restatement (Second) of Trusts §107 cmt. a. *See also* 2 Scott on Trusts §107. *See generally* E. Le Fevre, Annot., *Removal of trustee of voting trust*, 34 A.L.R.2d 1136 (1954).

[418] Lewin ¶ 13-54 (referring to Uvedale v. Ettrick (1682) 2 Ch. Cas. 130 at 131).

[419] 2 Scott & Ascher §11.10; 4 Scott & Ascher §24.3.5. *See also* Trustee Act 1925, s 41 (England) (expressly granting the court the power to remove trustees). "It is interesting to note that the Commonwealth jurisdictions have followed the English Court in adopting an inherent jurisdiction to remove a trustee: *see Miller v. Cameron* (1936) 54 CLR 572 in Australia, *Hunter v. Hunter* [1938] NZLR 520 in New Zealand, *MacLaren v. Grant* (1894) 23 SCR 310 in Canada and *Parujan v. Atlantic Western Trustees Limited* [2003] JLR N[11] in Jersey." Ruth Hughes, *The removal of a trustee*, 7(2) Tr. Q. Rev. 27 n.2 (May 2009) [a STEP publication].

[420] *See generally* 5 Scott & Ascher §37.3.6 (Removing the Trustee of a Charitable Trust).

[421] 2 Scott & Ascher §11.10; 4 Scott & Ascher §24.3.5.

[422] *See* Letterstedt v. Broers, (1884) 9 App Cas 371, 386 (England).

[423] 2 Scott & Ascher §11.10; 4 Scott & Ascher §24.3.5.

[424] *See generally* 3 Scott & Ascher §18.1.2.4.

property.[425] Absent special facts, the removal judgment is enforceable in all the other states.[426]

Removal may be ordered because of hostility between the trustee and a beneficiary,[427] but only in rare cases.[428] "[R]emoval ... [, for example,] ... might be justified if a communications breakdown is caused by the trustee or appears to be incurable."[429] On the other hand, relief has been denied if the trustee's duties are essentially ministerial or if the proper administration of the trust is not jeopardized by the hostility,[430] or if the beneficiary "is merely a remainder beneficiary" and there is "no necessity of communication and personal contact between the trustee and the remainderman."[431] Without more, hostility or friction between the trustee and the beneficiaries is seldom grounds for removal.[432] The English cases are generally in accord.[433] "This is because if hostility were a substantive ground alone any dissatisfied beneficiary could create a disagreement and the Court would then be forced to investigate the source of the hostility to see if it was genuine."[434] A trustee's hostility toward a trust's lawful charitable purposes, however, would, and should, warrant removal.[435]

The court has removed trustees, or said that it would do so, for the following reasons: insanity, habitual drunkenness, criminality involving moral

---

[425] 7 Scott & Ascher §45.2.2.5. *See generally* §8.40 of this handbook (jurisdiction over the affairs of a trust).

[426] 7 Scott & Ascher §45.2.2.5.

[427] *See, e.g.*, Maydwell v. Maydwell, 135 Tenn. 1, 185 S.W. 712 (1916).

[428] 1 Scott & Ascher §11.10.

[429] UTC §706 cmt. (available at <http://www.uniformlaws.org/Act.aspx?title=Trust%20Code>).

[430] *See* Bogert §527. *See, e.g.*, Shear v. Gabovitch, 685 N.E.2d 1168, 1194 (Mass. App. Ct. 1997) (ordering removal of trustee who possessed almost plenary discretion over all distributions to a beneficiary because he could not be expected to exercise his power with desirable perspective and detachment when his motives and integrity were constantly being impugned by the beneficiary, the parties having been mired for years in a draining legal equivalent of total war); Steele v. Kelley, 710 N.E.2d 973, 994 (Mass. App. Ct. 1999) (noting that the fundamental question in trustee removal cases is not the wishes of the beneficiaries, but rather whether circumstances such as the degree of the trustee's discretion make it detrimental to the trust for the trustee to continue in office); Symmons v. O'Keeffe, 419 Mass. 288, 644 N.E.2d 631(1995) (the mere fact that there is friction or hostility between the trustee and beneficiaries is not necessarily a sufficient ground for removal, because otherwise the beneficiaries would be quarreling with the trustee with the intent of forcing his removal).

[431] Krug v. Krug, 838 S.W.2d 197, 202 (Tenn. 1992).

[432] UTC §706 cmt. (available at <http://www.uniformlaws.org/Act.aspx?title=Trust%20Code>); Restatement (Third) of Trusts §37 cmt. e(1).

[433] Lewin ¶ 13-47. For a selection of grounds for removal culled from the English cases, see Lewin ¶ 13-51.

[434] Ruth Hughes, *The removal of a trustee*, 7(2) Tr. Q. Rev. 28 (May 2009) [a STEP publication]. (citing to Forster v. Davies (1861) 4 De G F & J 133) (England)). As to the United States, *see* Symmons v. O'Keeffe, 419 Mass. 288, 644 N.E.2d 631 (1995) (the mere fact that there is friction or hostility between the trustee and beneficiaries is not necessarily a sufficient ground for removal, because otherwise the beneficiaries would be quarreling with the trustee with the intent of forcing his removal).

[435] *See generally* 5 Scott & Ascher §37.3.6.

turpitude, failure to obey trust-related court orders, thwarting the purposes of the trust to include abuses of discretion,[436] chronic inactivity, unauthorized commingling, failure to account,[437] a personal interest adverse to the trust, the taking of excessive and unauthorized compensation, favoring the interests of some beneficiaries over the interests of others in violation of the duty of impartiality,[438] and embezzlement, as well as a myriad of other serious and material breaches of trust too numerous to mention here.[439] Most jurisdictions have statutes covering one or more of the above cases.[440] Many states now have statutes revoking the nomination of a former spouse of the settlor.[441] The Restatement (Third) of Trusts suggests that a trustee's failure to maintain necessary books and records may be grounds for removal.[442] The trustee's personal bankruptcy does not necessarily warrant removal, but may do so.[443] The court is entitled to take into account the trustee's past maladministration of a comparable trust, trustee removal being an equitable relief.[444]

In voting shares of stock or otherwise exercising powers of control over enterprises, the trustee shall act in the best interests of the beneficiaries.[445] The trustee shall elect or appoint directors or other managers who will manage the corporation or enterprise in the best interest of the beneficiaries.[446] The trustee may use the voting power to procure a position as director, officer or manager of the enterprise, provided the position is procured to serve the interests of the trusts and its beneficiaries.[447] In other words, "[t]he trustee may not use the

---

[436] 3 Scott & Ascher §18.2.1.

[437] *See* Restatement (Third) of Trusts §37, cmt. e (suggesting that repeated or flagrant failure or delay in providing proper information or accountings to beneficiaries may be grounds for removal); 3 Scott & Ascher §17.4.

[438] *See, e.g.,* Shelton v. Tamposi, 164 N.H. 490, 62 A.3d 741 (2013). The trustee's duty of impartiality is taken up in §6.2.5 of this handbook.

[439] *See* Bogert §527; 2 Scott on Trusts §107; Restatement (Third) of Trusts §37 cmt. e.

[440] *See generally* Bogert §527 nn.7, 8; 2 Scott on Trusts §107 n.22; *see, e.g.,* Cal. Prob. Code §15642 (West 1994) (court may remove trustee for, among other things, excessive compensation, failure to act, and insolvency); Mass. Gen. Laws Ann. ch. 203, §12 (West 1990) (providing that a trustee may be removed if such removal is for the interests of the beneficiaries of the trust or if the trustee has become incapacitated by reason of mental illness).

[441] 2 Scott & Ascher §11.10.

[442] Restatement (Third) of Trusts §83 cmt. a(1). *See generally* §6.2.9 of this handbook (trustee's duty to keep precise, complete, and accurate records). *Cf.* 3 Scott & Ascher §17.4 (noting also that a trustee's refusal to account is grounds for removal).

[443] 1 Scott & Ascher §11.10 (noting that failure of a corporate trustee would certainly justify its removal).

[444] *See* Quincy Trust Co. v. Taylor, 317 Mass. 195, 57 N.E.2d 573 (1944).

[445] UTC §802(g) (available at <http://www.uniformlaws.org/Act.aspx?title=Trust%20Code>).

[446] UTC §802(g) (available at <http://www.uniformlaws.org/Act.aspx?title=Trust%20Code>).

[447] Restatement (Third) of Trusts §78 cmt. (d)1. An appropriate compensation arrangement for the trustee's services to the corporation or other enterprise held in the trust would be for the trustee to turn over to the trust any compensation the trustee receives from the corporation or other enterprise, with "the reasonable compensation (or special compensation) as trustee to

corporate form to escape the fiduciary duties of trust law."[448] Thus, if a trustee were to engineer his appointment to an official position with the enterprise for the purpose of supplementing his compensation as trustee, then he could well be compelled to turn over the corporate salary to the trust.[449] The court might even be justified in removing him as trustee.[450] The laws of England and the Isle of Man are generally in accord.[451]

The court has declined to remove trustees for the following causes: irregularity in the way a trustee was appointed, personal insolvency, nonresidency, good-faith error in judgment, and isolated acts of negligence.[452] "Not every breach of trust warrants removal of the trustee . . . , but serious or repeated misconduct, even unconnected with the trust itself, may justify removal."[453] Where the same person serves as both executor and testamentary trustee under a will, removal from the executorship will not necessarily warrant removal from the trusteeship.[454]

The Uniform Trust Code provides that the court may remove a trustee if the trustee has committed a serious breach of trust; if there has been lack of cooperation among cotrustees that substantially impairs administration of the trust; or if, because of unfitness, unwillingness, or persistent failure of the trustee to administer the trust effectively, the court determines that removal of the trustee best serves the interests of the beneficiaries.[455] "A 'persistent failure to administer the trust effectively' might include a long-term pattern of mediocre performance, such as consistently poor investment results when compared

---

include the value of the special services rendered in the trustee's role with the corporation or other enterprise"). Restatement (Third) of Trusts §78 cmt. (d)1.

[448] UTC §802(g) (available at <http://www.uniformlaws.org/Act.aspx?title=Trust%20 Code>). "Thus, for example, a trustee whose duty of impartiality would require the trustee to make current distributions for the support of current beneficiaries may not evade that duty by holding assets in corporate form and pleading the discretion of corporate directors to determine dividend policy." UTC §802(g). "Rather, the trustee must vote for corporate directors who will follow a dividend policy consistent with the trustee's trust-law duty of impartiality." UTC §802(g). *See, e.g.,* Koffend's Will v. First Nat'l Bank of Minneapolis, 218 Minn. 206, 219–220, 15 N.W.2d 590, 598 (1944) (confirming that when a corporation is used as an agency to effectuate a settlor's intention, the law of trusts trumps the law of corporations).

[449] *See generally* 3 Scott & Ascher §17.2.8 (Bonus, Commission, or Other Compensation).

[450] *See generally* 3 Scott & Ascher §17.2.8 (Bonus, Commission, or Other Compensation).

[451] *See, e.g.,* Re Poyiadjis, 2001-03 MLR 316, Sept. 19, 2002 (Isle of Man High Court of Justice).

[452] *See, e.g.,* Unfunded Insurance Trust Agreement of Capaldi, 870 A.2d 493 (Del. 2005) (confirming that in Delaware the Vice Chancellor may only remove a trustee who fails to perform his duties through more than mere negligence). *See generally* Bogert §527; Lewin ¶ 13-53 (England).

[453] Restatement (Third) of Trusts §37 cmt. e.

[454] 1 Scott & Ascher §2.3.2.1.

[455] UTC §707(b) (available at <http://www.uniformlaws.org/Act.aspx?title=Trust%20 Code>).

to comparable trusts."[456] A "substantial change of circumstances" might also justify removal.[457]

Under the Uniform Trust Code, the court is authorized to grant a request by all the qualified beneficiaries, *i.e.*, the current beneficiaries and the presumptive remaindermen, that the trustee be removed, provided the designation of the trustee was not a material purpose of the trust, removal best serves the interests of all of the beneficiaries, and a suitable cotrustee or successor is available.[458] Under the Code, a "substantial change of circumstances" would suffice in lieu of a request by the qualified beneficiaries, provided all three conditions are satisfied. In one Code state, Pennsylvania, "a family's movement over time from northwestern Pennsylvania to the Tidewater region of Virginia, coupled with the fact that the original trustee institution ha[d] gone through approximately six corporate mergers leading to entirely different bank officers involved in administering the trusts, represent[ed] a change of circumstances substantial enough" to warrant a judicial no-fault removal of the incumbent corporate trustee.[459]

Connecticut has similar no-fault legislation. It authorizes a court having jurisdiction to remove a trustee even in the absence of a "blamable act," *i.e.*, even without cause, provided all beneficiaries request the removal, a material purpose of the trust would not be compromised by the removal, and a suitable cofiduciary or successor fiduciary is available to step in.[460]

So too the Uniform Probate Code provides for removal in the absence of trustee culpability, though not without cause. Section 7-305, for example, provides that "[i]f the principal place of administration becomes inappropriate for any reason, the Court may enter any order furthering efficient administration and the interests of the beneficiaries, including, if appropriate, . . . removal of the trustee and appointment of a trustee in another state."[461]

By the terms of the trust, a power to remove the trustee may be lodged in one or more individuals.[462] In England, a power of removal is a "fiduciary power," which "must be exercised for the benefit of the beneficiaries, not for the

---

[456] UTC §706 cmt. (available at <http://www.uniformlaws.org/Act.aspx?title=Trust%20 Code>). *See also* Restatement (Third) of Trusts §37 cmt. e (suggesting that "gross or continued inadequacies in matters of investment" may be grounds for removal).

[457] UTC §706(b) (available at <http://www.uniformlaws.org/Act.aspx?title=Trust%20 Code>). *See, e.g.*, The Vincent J. Fumo Irrevocable Children's Trust for the Benefit of Allison Fumo (Appeal of Vincent J. Fumo), 2014 PA Super 235, No. 2459 EDA 2013 (Oct. 17, 2014) (" . . . [W]e hold that the Orphan's Court acted within its discretion by ordering Repici's removal and substituting DiBona as trustee . . . due to a 'substantial change in circumstances' in the management of Daughter's trust.")

[458] UTC §706(b) (available at <http://www.uniformlaws.org/Act.aspx?title=Trust%20 Code>).

[459] In re McKinney, 67 A.3d 824, 2013 Pa. Super. Ct. 123 (2013).

[460] *See* In re Fleet Nat'l Bank's Appeal from Probate, 267 Conn. 229, 837 A.2d 785 (2004) (involving the other-than-for-cause provision in Connecticut's fiduciary removal statute, specifically Conn. Gen. Stat. Ann. §45a-242(a)(4)).

[461] *See also* Mass. Gen. Laws ch. 190B, §7-305.

[462] *See generally* 5 Scott & Ascher §37.3.6 (The Charitable Trust).

benefit of the person upon whom the power is conferred."[463] In the United States, a removal power is generally not a fiduciary power, unless the terms of the trust provide otherwise.[464]

A power granted to a beneficiary or some other person to terminate the trust has been said to involve a power to remove the trustee.[465] If all beneficiaries acting in concert have the inherent power to terminate the trust, they can effect a removal of the trustee by terminating the trust and creating another trust with a different trustee.[466] The trustee of an irrevocable trust should be aware that the retained power in a settlor (or the power in a beneficiary) to remove and replace the trustee may, under certain circumstances, subject the trust property to estate taxes upon the powerholder's death.[467]

Under the Uniform Trust Code, the settlor, a cotrustee, or a beneficiary may request the court to remove a trustee, or a trustee may be removed by the court on its own initiative.[468] Pending a final decision on a request to remove a trustee, or in lieu of or in addition to removing a trustee, the court may order such appropriate relief as may be necessary to protect the trust property or the interests of the beneficiaries to include the appointment of a special fiduciary,[469] or trustee *ad litem* as per the Restatement (Third) of Trusts.[470]

Unless a cotrustee remains in office or the court otherwise orders, a trustee who has been removed retains the duties of a trustee and the powers necessary to protect the trust property until such time as the trust property is delivered to a successor trustee or other person entitled to it.[471] "A trustee who has . . . been removed shall proceed expeditiously to deliver the trust property within the trustee's possession to the cotrustee, successor trustee, or other person entitled

---

[463] Lewin ¶ 13-41 (England).

[464] 2 Scott & Ascher §11.10.2 (The Private Trust); 5 Scott & Ascher §37.3.6 (The Charitable Trust).

[465] *See* 2 Scott on Trusts §107.3. *See also* Restatement (Second) of Trusts §107 cmt. i.

[466] 2 Scott & Ascher §11.11 (noting that a trust with a material purpose generally may not be terminated in this way). *See generally* §8.15.7 of this handbook (the *Claflin* or material purpose doctrine).

[467] *See generally* Estate of Wall v. Comm'r, 101 T.C. 300 (1993) (holding that the settlor's reserved power to remove and replace corporate trustees would not generate adverse estate tax consequences upon the death of the settlor); Rev. Rul. 95-58, 1995-2 C.B. 191 (suggesting that a reserved power to remove and replace trustees will not bring adverse estate tax consequences upon death of settlor provided the power does not extend to appointing an individual or corporate successor trustee that is related or subordinate to the settlor within the meaning of §672(c) of the Internal Revenue Code). *See generally* §8.9.3 of this handbook (tax-sensitive powers) and §8.15.15 of this handbook (the ascertainable standard).

[468] UTC §706(a) (available at <http://www.uniformlaws.org/Act.aspx?title=Trust%20 Code>).

[469] UTC §706(c) & cmt. (available at <http://www.uniformlaws.org/Act.aspx?title=Trust %20Code>). *See also* 2 Scott & Ascher §11.10.

[470] Restatement (Third) of Trusts §78, Reporter's Notes.

[471] UTC §707(a) (available at <http://www.uniformlaws.org/Act.aspx?title=Trust%20 Code>).

to it."[472] In England, a trustee who is being "compulsorily retired" normally may have his accounts settled before parting with trust assets, "or alternatively have security to cover the costs of any dispute which may arise in relation to accounts whether by reason of an alleged breach of trust or otherwise."[473] He, however, cannot demand a release as a *quid pro quo*.[474]

Section 7-101 of the Uniform Probate Code would require the trustee of a testamentary or inter vivos trust, even the trustee of a trust declaration or oral trust, to register the trust in an appropriate court at the trust's principal place of administration. A trustee who failed to do so would risk removal by the court.[475] In 2008, Massachusetts adopted a gutted version of Section 7-101 that imposed no such registration obligation on trustees.[476]

§7.2.3.7 Reduction or Denial of Compensation and/or Assessment of Attorneys' Fees and Other Costs Against the Trustee Personally

There are cases denying compensation when a trustee has repudiated the trust, misappropriated trust property, mingled trust property with the trustee's own, failed to keep accounts, been guilty of gross negligence, or committed other serious breaches of trust.[477]

While a trustee may be entitled to attorney fees incurred in the protection and preservation of the estate, he is not entitled to charge the trust estate with fees for defending his own maladministration against the [justifiable] complaint of the beneficiaries.[478]

The compensation and attorneys' fees of the trustee. To remedy a breach of trust that has occurred or may occur, the court may reduce or deny compensation to the trustee.[479] "In deciding whether to reduce or deny a trustee compensation, the court may wish to consider (1) whether the trustee acted in good faith; (2) whether the breach of trust was intentional; (3) the nature of the breach and the extent of the loss; (4) whether the trustee has restored the loss; and (5) the value of the trustee's services to the trust."[480] If the trustee is found to be at fault, he also will not be entitled to reimbursement from the trust estate

---

[472] UTC §707(b) (available at <http://www.uniformlaws.org/Act.aspx?title=Trust%20Code>).

[473] Lewin ¶ 13-29 (England).

[474] Lewin ¶ 13-29 (England).

[475] UPC §7-104.

[476] Mass. Gen. Laws ch. 190B, §7-101.

[477] 4 Scott & Ascher §21.2 (Effect of Breach of Trust on Compensation).

[478] Citizens & S. Nat'l Bank v. Haskins, 254 Ga. 131, 143, 327 S.E.2d 192, 203 (1985).

[479] 4 Scott & Ascher §21.2 (Effect of Breach of Trust on Compensation); UTC §1001(b)(8) (available at <http://www.uniformlaws.org/Act.aspx?title=Trust%20Code>). In one case, the court denied the trustee interest on the fees that were ultimately determined to be due the trustee, the trustee having been found to be in breach of trust. Citizens & S. Nat'l Bank v. Haskins, 254 Ga. 131, 143, 327 S.E.2d 192, 203 (1985).

[480] UTC §1001 cmt. (available at <http://www.uniformlaws.org/Act.aspx?title=Trust%20Code>). *See also* 4 Scott & Ascher §21.2.

for his own attorneys' fees and expenses.[481] The Restatement (Third) of Trusts suggests that a trustee's failure to maintain necessary books and records could be grounds for reducing or denying compensation.[482] Certain abuses of discretion also may warrant a denial or reduction of the trustee's compensation.[483] "When the court reduces or denies compensation, it does so not to impose a penalty for committing a breach of trust but because the trustee has not properly performed the services for which compensation is given."[484] Section 7-101 of the Uniform Probate Code would require the trustee of a testamentary or inter vivos trust, even the trustee of a trust declaration or oral trust, to register the trust in an appropriate court at the trust's principal place of administration. A trustee who failed to do so would risk denial of compensation.[485] In 2008, Massachusetts adopted a gutted version of Section 7-101 that imposed no such registration obligation on trustees.[486]

In one case, the corporate trustee was held in breach of its fiduciary duties in its management of the principal income-generating asset of a trust during two accounting periods and accordingly was denied a portion of its compensation and out-of-pocket expenses.[487] The asset was "a 60.41 percent interest in real property at 250 Post Street leased to the venerable San Francisco business firm known as Gump's retail store."

The trustee was found during the two accounting periods to have (1) failed vigorously to monitor and enforce the rent provisions of the lease; (2) failed to demand the lessee's compliance with the terms of the lease, including certification of rent statements; (3) failed to require the lessee to maintain records and accounts in accordance with generally accepted accounting principles (as required by the lease), which are necessary to ensure accurate computation of rents; (4) failed to monitor properly the sales records of the lessee; and (5) failed to obtain necessary assistance despite its knowledge that it was not competent to monitor the accuracy of the rental statements or record keeping. Furthermore, the corporate trustee breached its duty of loyalty by threatening objecting beneficiaries that it would charge the substantial expense of an audit to their income shares. This attempt to pressure the beneficiaries into dropping their contests and withdrawing their objections constituted a "knowing" or intentional breach of trust.

The court denied the trustee compensation for services *connected with the leased property* during the two accounting periods. It also denied the trustee reimbursement for attorneys' fees and costs incurred *in connection with the administration of the leased property* during the two accounting periods.[488]

---

[481] *See generally* 3 Scott & Ascher §18.1.2.4.

[482] Restatement (Third) of Trusts §83, cmt. a(1).

[483] *See* 3 Scott & Ascher §18.2.1 n.9 and accompanying text.

[484] 4 Scott & Ascher §21.2.

[485] UPC §7-104.

[486] Mass. Gen. Laws ch. 190B, §7-101.

[487] Estate of Gump, 1 Cal. App. 4th 582, 2 Cal. Rptr. 2d 269 (1992).

[488] *See generally* 3 Scott & Ascher §18.1.2.4. *Cf.* Friedman v. Hazen, 328 Mass. 233, 102 N.E.2d 777 (1952) (where executor's antagonism to sole beneficiary had resulted in expensive

The court, however, ruled that the trustee was entitled to ordinary trustee's fees and ordinary attorneys' fees for services *unconnected* with the administration of the leased property or the related litigation.

Again, if the trustee is found to be at fault, he will not be entitled to reimbursement from the trust estate for his *own* attorneys' fees and expenses.[489]

The beneficiary's attorneys' fees. In an action by a beneficiary against the trustee, a court in its discretion may hold the trustee personally liable for the beneficiary's attorneys' fees and other costs, provided the trustee is personally at fault.[490] The Restatement (Third) of Trusts is in accord.[491] This is an exception to the American rule that each party bears his own attorneys' fees in the absence of a statutory or contractual exception.[492] Successful actions by beneficiaries against trustees for unjustified refusal to distribute trust principal, for imprudent investing, for failing to render clear and accurate accountings, for commingling, and for not obtaining the best possible price for a trust asset have resulted in the assessment of attorneys' fees and costs against trustees personally.[493]

---

proceedings not of benefit to estate, it was error to make an allowance against the estate for attorneys' fees for defending executor in removal proceeding).

[489] Bogert §871 n.50; 3 Scott & Ascher §18.1.2.4. *See also* §7.2.8 of this handbook (trustee's liability though the beneficiary has suffered no economic harm). *See generally* UTC §708 cmt. (available at <http://www.uniformlaws.org/Act.aspx?title=Trust%20Code>).

[490] *See generally* Bogert §871; 3 Scott & Ascher §18.1.2.4. *See, e.g.*, Davis v. Davis, 889 N.E.2d 374, 388 (Ind. Ct. App. 2008) (" . . . [W]e reverse the trial court's attorney fee award in the amount of $4,000.00 and remand this issue to the trial court to determine what attorney fees were reasonably incurred by . . . [the beneficiary] . . . in securing from the Trust a proper and timely accounting, in uncovering the need for the Trustee to repay loans made to him from Trust funds, and in ensuring that the Trust received the appropriate interest on money loaned from the Trust. We order the Trust to pay . . . [the beneficiary] . . . such reasonable attorney fees as the court shall determine, and order the Trustee to reimburse the Trust for such sums"); Citizens & S. Nat'l Bank v. Haskins, 254 Ga. 131, 327 S.E.2d 192 (1985) (providing that a trustee who has acted in bad faith, has been stubbornly litigious, or has caused the beneficiary unnecessary trouble and expense may be liable for the plaintiff's attorneys' fees in an equity action against the trustee).

[491] *See* Restatement (Third) of Trusts §100, cmt. b(2).

[492] *See* Trusteeship of Trust of Williams, 631 N.W.2d 398 (Minn. Ct. App. 2001) (defining the American rule and declining to introduce the trust exception into Minnesota's jurisprudence).

[493] Trusteeship of Trust of Williams, 631 N.W.2d 398 (Minn. Ct. App. 2001) at n.53. *See also* UTC §1004 (available at <http://www.uniformlaws.org/Act.aspx?title=Trust%20Code>). *See, e.g.*, Wolf v. Calla, 288 F. Supp. 891 (E.D. Pa. 1968) (trustee having breached his trust by refusing to distribute to the beneficiary the trust corpus, court may order trustee to pay beneficiary's counsel fees out of the trustee's personal funds, the aged and blind beneficiary having been unjustifiably deprived of his interest in the trust for nine years); Estate of Bonin, 457 A.2d 1123 (Me. 1983) (personal representative who failed to deposit proceeds from the sale of real estate and other funds into an interest-bearing bank account ordered to pay out of his own pocket the actual attorneys' fees of beneficiary); Heller v. First Nat'l Bank of Denver, N.A., 657 P.2d 992 (Colo. 1982) (court may order trustee to pay out of its own pocket a portion of the fee of the beneficiary's accountant and a portion of the fee of the beneficiary's attorney, the trustee having been found to have breached its duty to provide the beneficiary with clear and accurate trust accountings); Donahue v. Watson, 413 N.E.2d 974 (Ind. 1980) (evidence of the trustee's improper commingling of trust funds, as well as other breaches of fiduciary duty, was sufficient to support an attorney fee award of $10,000 against former trustee and in favor of trust beneficiaries); Wills of Jacobs v. Weinstein, 91 N.C. App. 138, 370 S.E.2d 860 (1988) (the trustee having been removed for breaching his duty of loyalty to

In one case, the coexecutor of an estate that contained a number of shares of a closely held corporation was ordered to pay out of his personal funds the attorneys' fees of certain beneficiaries who had brought an action against him for breach of certain of his fiduciary duties.[494] The remaining shares had been held by the coexecutor and his family members in their individual capacities, and in another estate of which he was a fiduciary. The residue of the testatrix's estate was to pass into a trust for the benefit of the testatrix's grandchildren and a charity. The coexecutor sold the shares of the corporation that were held in the estate back to the corporation. At the shareholders' meeting that approved the purchase, the coexecutor voted all the outstanding shares of the corporation either in his individual capacity or in some representative capacity. Four days later he purchased for his own account the shares held in the other estate. At that point, the coexecutor effectively owned all the outstanding shares of the corporation.

The sale price per share was $1,800, although the coexecutor had shortly before the sale engaged a professional appraiser. The appraiser determined the sale value to be in excess of $2,400 per share for majority interest shares and $2,000 per share for minority interest shares. The net worth of the company was appraised at $4,040.84 per share. Soon after the coexecutor had effectively acquired all shares in the corporation himself, he liquidated the corporation at a per-share value substantially above what he had paid for the shares.

For these acts of self-dealing, the court declared the coexecutor a constructive trustee of the liquidation proceeds for the benefit of the beneficiaries of both estates. As one of a number of equitable remedies fashioned by the court, the coexecutor was ordered to pay out of his own pocket the fees and costs of those plaintiff attorneys who were at the center of the litigation.

In another case against a trustee, this time a class action for imprudent investment of the assets of 1,250 individual trusts, the plaintiffs won a judgment of $5,753,747. Their attorneys were awarded a fee of one-third of that amount, or $1,795,200:

> In the present case, there was evidence before the court from which it could conclude that the bank concealed the existence of its own written investment standards, violated its own written minimum standards of safety,

---

the beneficiary, the court's order that the trustee pay out of his own pocket the beneficiary's litigation costs, including witness fees and attorneys' fees, was a proper assessment of damages).

[494] Parker v. Rogerson, 76 Misc. 2d 705, 350 N.Y.S.2d 950 (1973). *See also* Feinberg v. Adolph K. Feinberg Hotel Trust, 922 S.W.2d 21 (Mo. 1996) (adopting a rule that permits courts to assess attorney fees against trustees who engage in self-dealing and in so doing creating a limited exception to the American rule that litigants must bear the expense of their own attorneys' fees); Murphy v. Murphy, 1997 Me. 103, 694 A.2d 932 (1997) (trustee having borrowed $11,000 from his child's trust fund for his personal use, the court had authority to order trustee to pay out of his own pocket $10,000 of the child's attorneys' fees); Allard v. Pacific Nat'l Bank, 99 Wash. 2d 394, 663 P.2d 104 (1983) (the trustee having breached its fiduciary duties in the administration and disposition of real estate held in trust, the court had authority to order trustee to pay out of own pocket the plaintiff's attorneys' fees).

attempted to conceal the holding of REIT's under the heading of insurance, and attempted to conceal the fact that it had sold Associated Coca-Cola stock at a loss in January 1975 by lumping the sale of this stock with the sale of 1,000 shares of a parent company Coca-Cola stock.[495]

The attorneys then sought to have that amount paid from the trustee's personal funds rather than from the award. The court ordered the trustee to pay out of its own pocket $1 million:

> In assessing the fee against the defaulting bank, as opposed to the fund, one factor that we have considered has been the quality of the actions of the bank. Although the bank's actions were considerably below the standards required of a paid fiduciary, yet they fall far short of actions which would justify a fee award of 33% of the recovery, or even 20% or 25% of the recovery, which is more in line with most of the stockholders, securities, and civil rights cases that we have reviewed.[496]

In yet another case, a corporate trustee who had been found liable for imprudent investing was ordered to pay out of its own pocket the legal bills of the beneficiaries and individual trustees because of the unnecessary trouble and expense its stubbornly litigious defense had caused them.[497]

A trustee should think twice before challenging a judicial ruling that a no-contest clause has been violated by some but not all of the beneficiaries.[498] In a New Hampshire case involving a trustee who had attempted to do just that, the court concluded that the trustee lacked the requisite standing to pursue the appeal.[499] The court mused that the trustee might have been in violation of the duty of loyalty, specifically the derivative duty of impartiality, in appealing the clause's enforcement.[500] Invoking the exception to the American rule, a topic we take up generally in Section 8.15.13 of the handbook, the court upheld the ruling of the trial court that the trustee must personally bear the burden of the legal fees of the innocent beneficiaries who had mounted a defense to the ill-fated contest.[501] The trustee's removal from office was also upheld.[502] The equitable relief of trustee removal is taken up generally in Section 7.2.3.6 of this handbook.

When there may be beneficiary liability. Under certain circumstances a beneficiary may be ordered to pay out of personal funds the fees of *the trustee's*

---

[495] Reynolds v. First Ala. Bank of Montgomery, N.A., 471 So. 2d 1238, 1243 (Ala. 1985).

[496] Reynolds v. First Ala. Bank of Montgomery, N.A., 471 So. 2d 1238, 1245 (Ala. 1985).

[497] Citizens & S. Nat'l Bank v. Haskins, 327 S.E.2d 192 (Ga. 1985).

[498] Trust no-contest/*in terrorem* provisions are covered generally in §5.5 of this handbook.

[499] *See* Shelton v. Tamposi, 164 N.H. 490, 499, 62 A.3d 741, 749 (2013).

[500] *See* Shelton v. Tamposi, 164 N.H. 490, 500, 62 A.3d 741, 750 (2013). *See generally* §6.2.5 of this handbook (the trustee's duty of impartiality).

[501] *See* Shelton v. Tamposi, 164 N.H. 490, 503, 62 A.3d 741, 752 (2013).

[502] *See* Shelton v. Tamposi, 164 N.H. 490, 505, 62 A.3d 741, 754 (2013).

attorneys, a topic we take up in Section 5.6 of this handbook.[503] In one case, a nuisance beneficiary and his counsel were held jointly and severally liable for the trustee's litigation defense costs.[504]

§7.2.3.8   Appointment of Receiver, Special Fiduciary, or Trustee ad Litem

A receiver is certainly a fiduciary. But a receiver is not a trustee in the strict sense for a receiver does not have title to the property under administration.[505]

Receiver or special fiduciary. To remedy a breach of trust that has occurred or may occur, the court may appoint a receiver, which the Uniform Trust Code refers to as a special fiduciary, to take possession of the trust property and administer the trust.[506] The Code provides that "[t]he authority of the court to appoint a special fiduciary is not limited to actions alleging breach of trust but is available whenever the court, exercising its equitable jurisdiction, concludes that an appointment would promote administration of the trust."[507] The differences between a trustee and a receiver are taken up in Section 9.9.17 of this handbook. "Ordinarily, the court simply removes a trustee who is not properly administering the trust. While removal proceedings are pending, however, the court may appoint a receiver."[508]

In England, judicial trustees rather than receivers are generally sought for ordinary trusts.[509] A judicial trustee, a creature of The Judicial Trustees Act of 1896, is appointed by and under the control of the court.[510]

Trustee ad litem. One California court, invoking its general equitable powers over trusts, appointed a "trustee ad litem" to perform certain functions with respect to some but not all of the assets of a trust. The effect of the appointment was to remove from the incumbent trustee the power to conduct certain lawsuits. "Since the interests of the third party plaintiffs and the trustee are similar and inimical to those of the beneficiaries who seek to preserve the trust assets, there is sufficient showing that . . . [the trustee's] . . . personal

---

[503] *See also* §3.5.2.3 of this handbook.

[504] *See* Pederson Trust, 757 N.W.2d 740 (N.D. 2008).

[505] 1 Scott & Ascher §2.3.12. *See also* Bogert §14 (receivership).

[506] UTC §1001(b)(5) (available at <http://www.uniformlaws.org/Act.aspx?title=Trust%20 Code>); 4 Scott & Ascher §24.3.4 (Appointment of Receiver); Bogert §14 (receivership).

[507] UTC §1001 cmt. (available at <http://www.uniformlaws.org/Act.aspx?title=Trust%20 Code>).

[508] 4 Scott & Ascher §24.3.4; *see also* Lewin ¶ 38-23 (England) ("Receivers are seldom sought for ordinary trusts nowadays, a judicial trustee being generally preferred, or in less serious cases, the appointment of a new trustee under section 41 of the Trustee Act of 1925"); Snell's Equity ¶ 17-21 (England) ("But the modern practice in appropriate cases is to apply for the appointment of a judicial trustee . . . rather than a receiver").

[509] Lewin ¶ 38-24.

[510] Lewin ¶ 19-01 (England).

interests conflict with the interests of those beneficiaries seeking only to preserve the assets of the trust."[511]

The Restatement (Third) of Trusts formally recognizes the office of trustee ad litem. In appropriate circumstances, for example, a trustee ad litem may be appointed to consider and, if appropriate, to maintain a proceeding in the stead of the incumbent trustee against a third party on behalf of the trust and its beneficiaries.[512]

> The appointment of a trustee ad litem is particularly useful in circumstances in which it may be unnecessary or premature, or the need for action too urgent, to remove and replace the trustee, even temporarily with respect to other aspects of administration, and in which the court finds it to be in the best interests of the beneficiaries and appropriate to the trust purposes to assure independent and disinterested decisions regarding the prosecution of the proceeding in question.[513]

In the case of a trustee of a charitable trust who ceases to serve as trustee after having breached his trust, his cotrustee or his successor in office would have standing to sue him for the breach. "Similarly, if a sole trustee who committed a breach of trust nevertheless continues to serve as trustee, a trustee ad litem . . . may be appointed . . . [by the court] . . . to sue for redress."[514]

§7.2.4   Cofiduciary Liability and Contribution; Predecessor and Successor Trustee Liability

Joint and several liability also is imposed on a nonparticipating cotrustee who . . . failed to exercise reasonable care (1) to prevent a cotrustee from committing a serious breach of trust, or (2) to compel a cotrustee to redress a serious breach of trust.[515]

One of the best ways for a successor trustee to get off on the right foot . . . is to require the prior trustee to account, or to review the prior trustee's accounts.[516]

Cotrustee liability. The trustee will be liable for an improper delegation of a duty, a topic discussed in Section 6.1.4 of this handbook;[517] on the other hand, it has been well settled since the 1633 English case of *Townley v. Sherborne*[518] that

---

[511] Getty v. Getty, 205 Cal. App. 3d 134, 141 (1988).

[512] Restatement (Third) of Trusts §107(3).

[513] Restatement (Third) of Trusts §107 cmt. d.

[514] Restatement (Third) of Trusts §94 cmt. f.

[515] UTC §1002 cmt. (available at <http://www.uniformlaws.org/Act.aspx?title=Trust%20 Code>).

[516] 4 Scott & Ascher §24.28.

[517] *See* Restatement (Third) of Trusts: Prudent Investor Rule §171 (provisional). *See generally* §6.1.4 of this handbook (trustee's duty not to delegate critical fiduciary functions); 4 Scott & Ascher §24.29 (Improper Delegation to Co-Trustee).

[518] (1633) Bridg. 35; 2 W & T.L.C. (9th ed.) 577.

a trustee is not responsible for a cotrustee's breach of trust,[519] unless the trustee participated in, approved, acquiesced in, or concealed the breach, or failed to take what steps were necessary to compel the cotrustee to redress the breach.[520] Thus, a trustee has the requisite standing to bring a breach-of-trust action against his cotrustee. This would include the trustee of a charitable trust.[521]

In one case, Mary Jane, an inexperienced investor, was appointed trustee of a trust with charitable and noncharitable interests. An individual was the current beneficiary. Charles was designated the first alternate trustee and Robert the second alternate trustee. Mary Jane placed the trust assets with Dean Witter Reynolds, a brokerage house. Charles, an investment counselor and stockbroker, made all investment decisions concerning the trust assets. The accountings, as well as certain admissions, established that Charles was functioning as a "surrogate trustee." At some point, Charles embezzled $317,234.36 from the trust. Mary Jane having become an invalid and Charles having been determined to be untrustworthy, Robert succeeded to the trusteeship. Robert was Mary Jane's guardian-conservator. The court remanded the case for a determination as to whether Mary Jane would be personally liable for Charles's embezzlement, *i.e.*, whether she improperly delegated the entire trust administration to Charles and then failed to bring a timely action against Charles to recover what was embezzled. If, after remand, it turns out that Mary Jane was in breach of trust, Robert would have to be removed as trustee as he would then be faced with an irreconcilable conflict of interest:

> If, after remand, the trial court determines that Mary Jane is personally liable for the diversion of funds, Robert must be removed as trustee. A trustee is liable to a beneficiary if he fails to "redress a breach of trust committed by the predecessor [trustee.]" Restatement (Second) of Trusts §223(2). Robert would, therefore, have a duty to enforce the surcharge against his aunt and ward, Mary Jane. The conflict between personal responsibilities and trust obligations is obvious and great. Estate of Rothko, 43 N.Y.2d 305, 319, 401 N.Y.S.2d 449, 454, 372 N.E.2d 291, 296 (1977) (while a trustee is administering the trust he must refrain from placing himself in position where his personal interest does or may conflict with interest of beneficiaries). Another trustee, without such conflicts, would have to be appointed.[522]

---

[519] Lewin ¶ 39-52 (England).

[520] *See* Restatement (Third) of Trusts §81(2); Restatement (Second) of Trusts §224; 4 Scott & Ascher §24.29 (U.S.); Lewin ¶ 39-57 (England); Lee R. Russ, J.D., Annot., *Award of attorneys' fees out of trust estate in action by trustee against cotrustee*, 24 A.L.R.4th 624 (1983). *See also* F. M. English, Annot., *Right of coexecutor or trustee to retain independent legal counsel*, 66 A.L.R.2d 1169 (1959). *See generally* §6.1.4 of this handbook (trustee's duty not to delegate critical fiduciary functions). *See also* UTC §703(g)(1) & (2) (available at <http://www.uniformlaws.org/Act.aspx?title=Trust%20 Code>) (providing that each trustee shall exercise reasonable care to prevent a cotrustee from committing a serious breach of trust and to compel a cotrustee to redress a serious breach of trust).

[521] *See* Restatement (Third) of Trusts §94 cmt. f.

[522] Shriners Hosp. for Crippled Children v. Gardiner, 152 Ariz. 527, 531, 733 P.2d 1110, 1114 (1987). *Cf.* Estate of Chrisman, 746 S.W.2d 131 (Mo. 1988) (personal representative held jointly and severally liable with her co-personal representative for the mismanagement of the estate by improperly retaining investments, where the representative had considerable business acumen and was aware of the financial condition of estate assets on a day-to-day basis).

Under the Uniform Trust Code, the nonbreaching trustee's responsibility to take preventive and/or remedial action against the cotrustee is limited only to serious breaches of trust.[523] Otherwise, a dissenting trustee who participates in a nonserious breach of trust at the direction of the majority of the trustees is not liable for the breach, provided the dissenter notifies any cotrustee of the dissent at or before the time of the breach.[524]

The Restatement (Third) of Trusts, however, draws no distinction between serious and nonserious breaches when it comes to a trustee's duty to take remedial action against a breaching cofiduciary.[525] According to the Restatement, there is a duty to obtain redress whether or not the breach is serious, unless to do so would be unreasonable.[526] On the other hand, the Restatement provides that "[a] trustee who opposed an action taken upon decision by a majority of the trustees and who made that opposition known to a co-trustee but thereafter reasonably joined in the action in order to avoid obstructing its execution, is not liable for the action *unless the dissenting trustee was aware that the action was a breach of trust.*"[527]

In any case, when some form of preventive or remedial action is called for, resignation may not be enough:

> [A] trustee may not exercise a power of resignation or otherwise resign for the purpose of facilitating a breach of trust by the remaining cotrustee(s) or of escaping adverse circumstances without disclosing the breach or circumstances to the beneficiaries, settlor, or court, as the case may be . . . [,] all trustee powers . . . [being] . . . subject to a duty of good-faith exercise. . . .[528]

When cotrustee 1 is uncertain as to whether cotrustee 2 is reliable, cotrustee 1 should request from cotrustee 2 all the information that cotrustee 1 would need to make that determination. Cotrustee 2 would have a correlative duty of full disclosure. If the requested information is not forthcoming, *e.g.*, cotrustee 2 unreasonably refuses to hand over vouchers that would support certain expenses that cotrustee 2 has paid from the trust estate, then cotrustee 1 would be well advised to retain independent counsel to assist with the investigation. If counsel is unable to extract the information, then the matter of cotrustee 2's reliability will have to be put before the court. Regardless of the outcome of the litigation, cotrustee 2 clearly has breached the duty to keep

---

[523] Shriners Hosp. for Crippled Children v. Gardiner, 152 Ariz. 527, 531, 733 P.2d 1110, 1114 (1987). *Cf.* Estate of Chrisman, 746 S.W.2d 131 (Mo. 1988) (personal representative held jointly and severally liable with her co-personal representative for the mismanagement of the estate by improperly retaining investments, where the representative had considerable business acumen and was aware of the financial condition of estate assets on a day-to-day basis).

[524] UTC §703(h) (available at <http://www.uniformlaws.org/Act.aspx?title=Trust%20 Code>).

[525] Restatement (Third) of Trusts §81 cmt. b. *See generally* 4 Scott & Ascher §24.29 (Liability for Co-Trustee's Breach of Trust).

[526] Restatement (Third) of Trusts §81 cmt. b.

[527] Restatement (Third) of Trusts §81 cmt. e.

[528] Restatement (Third) of Trusts §36 cmt. a.

cotrustee 1 fully informed. Accordingly, the court at minimum can be expected to hold cotrustee 2 personally liable for cotrustee 1's reasonable attorneys' fees.

"If several trustees unite in a breach of trust, they are jointly and severally liable and the entire claim of the beneficiary may be satisfied from the property of one trustee."[529] A trustee who has made good a loss occasioned by a breach of trust is entitled to contribution from those cotrustees participating in the wrong,[530] but in this day and age, a professional trustee may well find it difficult to persuade a court to order a participating "amateur" cotrustee to make contribution.[531] Difficult, but not impossible.[532]

The Uniform Trust Code (as does the Restatement of Trusts[533]) provides that if more than one trustee is liable to the beneficiaries for a breach of trust, a trustee is entitled to contribution from the other trustee or trustees.[534] A trustee, however, is not entitled to contribution if the trustee was substantially more at fault than another trustee or if the trustee committed the breach of trust in bad faith or with reckless indifference to the purposes of the trust or the interests of the beneficiaries.[535] A trustee who received a benefit from the breach of trust is not entitled to contribution from another trustee to the extent of the benefit received.[536] The subject of liability for attorneys' fees and costs occasioned by disputes between and among cotrustees is addressed in Section 3.4.4.1 of this handbook.

What if contribution cannot be obtained from an insolvent cotrustee? "To the extent that contribution cannot be obtained from an insolvent trustee, the other trustees with contribution rights and obligations share the insolvent

---

[529] Bogert §862 n.25 and accompanying text. *See also* 4 Scott & Ascher §24.29 (liability for cotrustee's breach of trust); Restatement (Third) of Trusts §102(1) ("Except as otherwise provided in this Section, if two or more trustees are liable for a breach of trust, they are jointly and severally liable, with contribution rights and obligations between or among them reflecting their respective degrees of fault.").

[530] Bogert §862 n.29 and accompanying text.

[531] *See generally* Restatement (Third) of Trusts §90 cmt. d [Restatement (Third) of Trusts: Prudent Investor Rule §227 cmt. d].

[532] *See, e.g.,* In re Knox, 96 A.D.3d 1652, 946 N.Y.S.2d 817 (2012).

[533] Restatement (Third) of Trusts §102; Restatement (Second) of Trusts §258.

[534] UTC §1002(b) (available at <http://www.uniformlaws.org/Act.aspx?title=Trust%20 Code>).

[535] UTC §1002(b) (available at <http://www.uniformlaws.org/Act.aspx?title=Trust%20 Code>); Restatement (Third) of Trusts §102(2) ("A trustee who committed a breach in bad faith is not entitled to contribution unless the trustee or trustees from whom contribution is sought also acted in bad faith."). Among the factors to consider when assessing the liability, if any, of the less active trustee: "(1) Did the trustee fraudulently induce the other trustee to join in the breach? (2) Did the trustee commit the breach intentionally while the other trustee was at most negligent? (3) Did the trustee, because of greater experience or expertise, control the actions of the other trustee? (4) Did the trustee alone commit the breach with liability imposed on the other trustee only because of an improper delegation or failure to properly monitor the actions of the cotrustee?" UTC §1002(b).

[536] UTC §1002(b) cmt. (available at <http://www.uniformlaws.org/Act.aspx?title=Trust%20 Code>); Restatement (Third) of Trusts §102(3).

trustee's liability, equally if they are substantially equally at fault or proportionately if not."[537]

Successor trustee liability. It long has been stated as the general rule that the successor trustee is in no way liable for the acts of the predecessor.[538] This statement undoubtedly is correct, but there is an equally well-settled rule that the successor trustee has a positive duty, upon taking over the trust estate, to see that the predecessor has properly accounted for the whole of it.[539] Thus, a trustee has the requisite standing to bring a breach-of-trust action against his predecessor. This would include the trustee of a charitable trust.[540]

Indeed, failure to prosecute any claim that may exist against the predecessor may constitute a breach of trust on the part of the successor.[541] Moreover, with the array of criminal statutes on the books covering everything from money laundering to hazardous waste, the successor trustee now more than ever cannot afford to dispense with an examination into the doings of his predecessor in office and into the condition of the trust property, particularly if it is real property. Due diligence is the order of the day.

At minimum, the successor should require an accounting if one has not been formally made.[542] Copies of the fiduciary income tax returns for the previous three years should be scrutinized. All real estate should be inspected.[543] If the property is coming from the settlor's estate the successor should also obtain copies of federal and state estate tax returns. This matter is of growing practical importance especially as so many inter vivos trusts are conducted without formal accountings.[544] The person proposed as successor trustee should insist, whenever it is reasonably possible, that accounts of the

---

[537] Restatement (Third) of Trusts §102, cmt. c.

[538] *See* Restatement (Second) of Trusts §223.

[539] In re Will of Crabtree, 449 Mass. 128, 138, 865 N.E.2d 1119, 1129 (2007) (citing the Handbook as authority). *See generally* Bogert §583 (Duty of Trustee to Take Possession); UTC §812 (available at <http://www.uniformlaws.org/Act.aspx?title=Trust%20Code>) (requiring the trustee to take reasonable steps to compel a former trustee or other person to deliver trust property to the trustee and to redress a breach of trust known to the trustee to have been committed by a former trustee); UTC §705(c) (providing that any liability of a resigning trustee or of any sureties on the trustee's bond for acts or omissions of the trustee is not discharged or affected by the trustee's resignation); 4 Scott & Ascher §§24.4.2 (Co-Trustees and Successor Trustees), 24.28 (Liability of Successor Trustee), 24.28.1 (When Successor Trustee Permits Continuation of Breach), 24.28.2 (When Successor Trustee Fails to Compel Predecessor to Deliver Trust Property), 24.28.3 (When Successor Trustee Fails to Compel Predecessor to Redress Breach of Trust).

[540] *See* Restatement (Third) of Trusts §94 cmt. f.

[541] *See* 4 Scott & Ascher §24.28.3 (When Successor Trustee Fails to Compel Predecessor to Redress Breach of Trust); Restatement (Second) of Trusts §223 cmt. d; §6.2.1.1 of this handbook (trustee's duty to identify and take active control of trust property).

[542] *See generally* 4 Scott & Ascher §24.28 (Liability of Successor Trustee); §6.2.2.2 of this handbook (the prudent investor's code of conduct).

[543] *See, e.g.,* Hamilton v. Mercantile Bank of Cedar Rapids, 621 N.W.2d 401 (Iowa 2001) (assessing damages, including punitive damages, against a successor trustee for failing to inspect degraded real estate upon and after assuming the trusteeship and for failing to take appropriate steps to protect and preserve the trust property).

[544] *See generally* §6.1.5.2 of this handbook (trustee's duty to keep and render accounts).

predecessor be made up and allowed or the assents obtained as provided in the trust instrument. Furthermore, it is often possible (and always desirable) to require that unsuitable holdings in the trust portfolio be removed before the succession is completed, or at least marked for very early removal after the succession.

It is of little importance to a successor trustee whether the theoretical basis for surcharge is the predecessor's malfeasance or the successor's nonfeasance in prosecuting the trust's just claims against the predecessor.[545] Moreover, the bringing of a suit against a predecessor may have unpleasant collateral social and financial consequences for the successor, particularly if the predecessor is a relative, friend, business associate, or customer of the successor. The prudent person makes certain, before succeeding to the trust office, that all things are in order and does not rely on any express language in the governing instrument purporting to relieve a successor of the duty to investigate the acts of the predecessor.[546]

As to the liability of a trustee for following the improper directions of a holder of an express power to direct the trustee when the holder is a fiduciary but not a trustee, the reader is referred to Section 3.2.6 of this handbook.

Predecessor trustee liability. It has been a core principle of trust law that "[t]he resignation of the trustee, although in accordance with the terms of the trust, will not relieve the trustee from liability for breaches of trust committed by him."[547] Thus a trustee's departure from office does not relieve him of the duty to properly account *to the beneficiaries*. A former trustee who has failed properly to account for his actions while in office will have the same equitable and legal defenses to a beneficiary's breach of trust allegations that the former trustee would have were he still in office, such as laches and any associated statute of limitations that partially codifies the laches doctrine. The defense of failure of the beneficiary to take timely against the trustee is taken up in Section 7.1.2 of this handbook.

In one predecessor-trustee liability case, however, the New York court, for reasons of practicality, held that New York's six-year statute of limitations for

---

[545] Bogert §583 (Duty of Trustee to Take Possession); UTC §812 (available at <http://www.uniformlaws.org/Act.aspx?title=Trust%20Code>) (requiring the trustee to take reasonable steps to compel a former trustee or other person to deliver trust property to the trustee and to redress a breach of trust known to the trustee to have been committed by a former trustee); UTC §705(c) (requiring the trustee to take reasonable steps to compel a former trustee or other person to deliver trust property to the trustee and to redress a breach of trust known to the trustee to have been committed by a former trustee); UTC §705(c) (providing that any liability of a resigning trustee or of any sureties on the trustee's bond for acts of omissions of the trustee is not discharged or affected by the trustee's resignation); 4 Scott & Ascher §§24.4.2 (Co-Trustees and Successor Trustees), 24.28 (Liability of Successor Trustee), 24.28.1 (When Successor Trustee Permits Continuation of Breach), 24.28.2 (When Successor Trustee Fails to Compel Predecessor to Deliver Trust Property), 24.28.3 (When Successor Trustee Fails to Compel Predecessor to Redress Breach of Trust).

[546] *See generally* 4 Scott & Ascher §24.28 (Liability of Successor Trustee) (noting that "[o]ne of the best ways for a successor trustee to get off on the right foot . . . is to require the prior trustee to account, or to review the prior trustee's records").

[547] 2 Scott on Trusts §106.2.

breach-of-trust actions began to run against a beneficiary from the time the successor trustee was "put in place," *because the beneficiary knew of the trustee's resignation and never demanded an accounting, the beneficiary at all relevant times having been of full age and legal capacity.*[548]

The highest Massachusetts court took a radical and unprecedented departure from traditional trust law principles when it held that a statute of limitations had begun to run *against the beneficiaries* of a trust whose former trustees had never properly accounted to them when the *successor trustee* knew or should have known of the predecessors' alleged breaches.[549] At the time the successor was deemed to know of the predecessor's alleged breaches, one beneficiary was a minor and the other was missing. No guardian ad litem ever was duly and formally appointed by the court to represent their interests.[550] It appears that the court had confused and conflated the limitation rules applicable to external *legal* actions by third-party tort and contract claimants against trustees with the rules applicable to internal breach of fiduciary *equitable* actions by beneficiaries against their trustees.[551]

The principle that a successor trustee owes a duty to the beneficiaries to compel the predecessor to account has traditionally meant that upon acceptance of the successor trusteeship the successor merely joins the predecessor on the fiduciary hook, albeit a different type of act. Succession generally has not also started a process of phasing out the predecessor's liability *to the beneficiaries,* come what may. Having said that, Judge Cardozo saw it otherwise, although, we suggest, he had conveniently ignored the fact that lawyers and trustees upon leaving office are not relieved of all their fiduciary duties, this in accordance with long-standing common law agency and trust principles.[552] Here is Judge Cardozo: "While an express trust subsists and has not been openly renounced, the Statute of Limitations does not run in favor of the trustee. But after the trust relation is at an end, the trustee has yielded the estate to a successor the rule is different. The running of the statute then begins, and only actual or intentional fraud will be effective to suspend it."[553] Maybe the trust relation ends upon a yielding of the trust estate, but surely elements of the fiduciary relation continue, such as the duty to provide the beneficiaries with critical information and

---

[548] Tydings v. Greenfield, Stein & Senior, LLP, 11 N.Y.3d 195, 897 N.E.2d 1044, 868 N.Y.S.2d 563 (N.Y. 2008). *See generally* §6.1.5 of this handbook (the trustee's affirmative duty to furnish the beneficiary with critical information).

[549] O'Connor v. Redstone, 452 Mass. 537, 896 N.E.2d 595 (2008).

[550] *See generally* §8.14 of this handbook (when there is a need for a guardian ad litem).

[551] *See generally* §7.3 of this handbook (trustee's external liability to third parties in contract and tort), §7.1.3 of this handbook (the laches doctrine), and §8.25 of this handbook (few American law schools still require instruction in Agency, Trusts and Equity).

[552] *See generally* Charles E. Rounds, Jr., *Lawyer Codes Are Just About Licensure, the Lawyer's Relationship with the State: Recalling the Common Law Agency, Contract, Tort, Trust, and Property Principles that Regulate the Lawyer-Client Fiduciary Relationship*, 60 Baylor L. Rev. 771 (2008) (certain fiduciary duties are owed by the lawyer to the client even after representation has terminated).

[553] Spallholz v. Sheldon, 216 N.Y. 205, 209, 110 N.E. 431 (1915).

the duty of confidentiality.[554] Just as a breach of trust is not always the breach of a fiduciary duty to the beneficiaries,[555] so also a breach of fiduciary duty to the beneficiaries is not always a breach of trust.

The Uniform Trust Code, too, opts for practicality over principle when it comes to predecessor-trustee liability. Under the Code, a judicial proceeding by a beneficiary against a trustee for breach of fiduciary duty must be commenced within five years after the first to occur of the removal, resignation, or death[556] of the trustee; the termination of the beneficiary's interest in the trust; or the termination of the trust. The five-year limitation period, which is intended to provide some ultimate repose for actions against a trustee,[557] may or may not cover fraudulent acts on the part of the trustee, the drafters of the Uniform Trust Code having preferred "to leave that question to . . . [laws that deal with fraudulent acts generally]. . . ."[558]

Still, until these issues of residual predecessor-trustee liability sort themselves out a bit more in the courts and the legislatures, the trustee would be well-advised to look upon the UTC statutes of limitation as little more than partial codifications of laches doctrine.[559] They are by no means self-contained. Particularly in cases of unauthorized acts of trustee self-dealing, "other law" will generally determine what trustee "misdeeds" will cause them to toll,[560] as well as the level of "understanding" a beneficiary must have before they will begin to run.[561] The level, by the way, is likely to be high, namely a full subjective understanding of the facts and law applicable to the self-dealing.[562] That is either traditional laches, or laches by analogy.[563]

---

[554] *See generally* §6.1.5.1 of this handbook (the trustee's duty to provide information); §6.2.3 of this handbook (the trustee's duty of confidentiality).

[555] *See generally* §6.1.1 of this handbook (while the trustee's duty of loyalty is a fiduciary duty, his duty of prudence really is not).

[556] "If a trusteeship terminates by reason of death, a claim against the trustee's estate for breach of fiduciary duty would, like other claims against the trustee's estate, be barred by a probate creditor's claim statute even though . . . [the five-year statutory period] . . . had not yet expired." UTC §1005 cmt. (available at <http://www.uniformlaws.org/Act.aspx?title=Trust%20Code>).

[557] UTC §1005 cmt. (available at <http://www.uniformlaws.org/Act.aspx?title=Trust%20Code>).

[558] UTC §1005 cmt. (available at <http://www.uniformlaws.org/Act.aspx?title=Trust%20Code>).

[559] *See* §8.15.70 of this handbook (laches doctrine generally).

[560] *See* UTC §1005, cmt. (available at <http://www.uniformlaws.org/Act.aspx?title=Trust%20Code>).

[561] *See generally* §7.1.2 of this handbook (defenses to allegations that the trustee breached the duty of loyalty).

[562] *See generally* §7.1.2 of this handbook (defenses to allegations that the trustee breached the duty of loyalty).

[563] *See* §8.15.70 of this handbook (laches doctrine generally).

§7.2.5   Insurance and Indemnification for Liability Arising Out of a Breach of Fiduciary Duty to the Beneficiary

Unless the trustee is an attorney[564] or a bank, inexpensive fiduciary liability insurance will be exceedingly difficult, if not impossible, to obtain for coverage for breaches of fiduciary duty; if it *is* obtained, the premium costs must be borne personally by the trustee and not by the trust estate, unless the terms of the trust provide otherwise.[565] Moreover, it goes without saying that a trustee may not be indemnified from the trust estate for an adverse judgment arising out of a breach of fiduciary duty.

It has been reported, however, that in England "a very inexpensive trustee liability insurance policy" is now being marketed to lay trustees.[566] Moreover, in England trust instruments executed in the late 1990s and thereafter tend to expressly grant to the trustee the authority to charge fiduciary liability insurance premiums against the trust estate as a trust expense.[567] Absent such authority, if the trustee's stockbroker or investment advisor absorbs the cost of the trustee's fiduciary liability insurance premiums in exchange for the trustee directing brokerage or advisory work his or her way,[568] then the trustee's duty of undivided loyalty is implicated, a topic we take up in Section 6.1.3.4 of this handbook.

Prospective insurers are more receptive to full-time professional individual trustees who have investment experience and who are backed up by well-constructed operational infrastructures than they are to amateurs.[569]

For more on insuring the trustee against internal fiduciary liability, the reader is referred to Section 3.5.4.2 of this handbook.

---

[564] *See generally* ACTEC Practice Committee, Fiduciary Matters Subcommittee, *Guide for ACTEC Fellows Serving as Trustees*, 26 ACTEC Notes 313, 321 (2001) (addressing in part professional liability insurance and bonding and warning that while an individual policy might cover the work of a lawyer acting "as trustee," that same policy could contain specific exclusions for claims arising out of an attorney acting in his or her capacity as a director or officer of a business entity). "As a practical matter, a lawyer acting as trustee of a trust holding a closely-held business interest might find the business exclusion applied to deny coverage when the trustee by necessity is required to participate in active business management decisions and it is those actions which give rise to the claim." ACTEC Practice Committee, Fiduciary Matters Subcommittee, *Guide for ACTEC Fellows Serving as Trustees*, 26 ACTEC Notes 313, 322 (2001).

[565] *See* §3.5.4.2 of this handbook (insuring against personal liability). *See also* Bogert §599 (Insuring Against Personal Liability).

[566] Clive Barwell, *Can the trust pay?*, 17(1) STEP J. 70 (Jan. 2009).

[567] Clive Barwell, *Can the trust pay?*, 17(1) STEP J. 70 (Jan. 2009).

[568] Clive Barwell, *Can the trust pay?*, 17(1) STEP J. 71 (Jan. 2009) (apparently this is happening in England).

[569] For more on fiduciary liability insurance, *see* §3.5.4.2 of this handbook (insuring the trustee against personal liability).

§7.2.6　Exculpatory (also Exemption or Indemnity) Provisions Covering Breaches of Trust; Trustee Exoneration Provisions

We note initially that courts have long distinguished between negligence-type claims and mistakes for mere errors of judgment. . . . Moreover, this distinction has existed since before the trust instrument at issue here was created. Thus, we can reasonably assume that the trust creator was aware of these distinctions and could have exculpated a trustee for negligent acts had he wished to do so. Because our task is to find the intent of the trust's creator, and trust instruments are to be strictly construed, we conclude that while the exculpatory clause protects a trustee from liability for mistakes or errors of judgment, it does not do so for negligent acts.[570]

The trustee's acts of ordinary negligence. Many trust instruments contain exculpatory provisions that purport to limit the trustee's liabilities to the beneficiary. Sometimes they are enforceable; sometimes they are not.[571] In Massachusetts and North Carolina they generally are.[572] In New York such provisions in *testamentary trusts* are void as against public policy.[573] Not in the case of New York inter vivos trusts, however. In fact, the term of an inter vivos trust purporting to relieve the trustee of liability for breaches of trust occasioned by the good faith reliance on the advice of counsel has been found not to violate New York public policy.[574] Under the federal Trust Indenture Act of 1939, a provision purporting to exculpate an indenture trustee from liability for ordinary negligence is unenforceable as against the bondholders.[575] The Restatement (Third) of Trusts is more tolerant of fiduciary exculpation, although its tolerance is not unlimited:

A provision in the terms of a trust that relieves a trustee of liability for breach of trust, and that was not included in the instrument as a result of the trustee's abuse

---

[570] Trusteeship of Williams, 591 N.W.2d 743, 747–748 (Minn. 1999).

[571] In Bogert §1295, there is the following example of an exculpatory provision: No Trustee, acting hereunder, shall be held responsible for the defaults of any cotrustee or for any loss sustained by the trust estate through any error of judgment made in good faith, but he shall be liable only for his own willful misconduct or breach of good faith.

[572] *See* J.P. Morgan Chase, N.A. v. Loutit, 2013 WL 497329 (N.Y. Sup.).

[573] N.Y. Est. Powers & Trusts Law §11-1.7 (providing that any attempted exoneration of a testamentary trustee from liability for failure to exercise reasonable care, diligence, and prudence is against public policy and void). A New York court, however, has honored an immunity for a testamentary trustee's "errors of judgment." *See* In re White, 31 N.Y.2d 681, 337 N.Y.S.2d 258 (1972). N.Y. Est. Powers & Trusts Law §11-1.7 does not apply to trustees of inter vivos trusts. *See* Carey v. Cunningham, 595 N.Y.S.2d 185 (1st Dep't 1993); Kolentus v. Avco Corp., 798 F.2d 949 (7th Cir. 1986). *See generally* Whitman, *Exoneration Clauses in Wills and Trust Instruments*, 4 Hofstra Prop. L.J. 123 (1992); Bogert §542; 4 Scott & Ascher §24.27.3; 3 Scott on Trusts §222; Restatement (Second) of Trusts §222; 7 Scott & Ascher §45.6.6 (conflict of laws and fiduciary exculpation).

[574] *See* In re HSBC Bank USA, N.A., 947 N.Y.S.2d 292 (N.Y. App. Div. 2012). *See generally* §8.32 of this handbook (the trustee's good faith reliance on advice of counsel as a defense to a breach of trust claim).

[575] 15 U.S.C.A. §77ooo. *See generally* §9.31 of this handbook (corporate trusts; trusts to secure creditors; the Trust Indenture Act of 1939; protecting bondholders).

of a fiduciary or confidential relationship, is enforceable except to the extent that it purports to relieve the trustee (a) of liability for a breach of trust committed in bad faith or with indifference to the fiduciary duties of the trustee, the terms or purposes of the trust, or the interests of the beneficiaries, or (b) of accountability for profits derived from a breach of trust.[576]

For a discussion of what might constitute good faith conduct on the part of a trustee, see generally Section 8.15.81 of this handbook.

In those jurisdictions where trust exculpatory clauses are enforceable, including England,[577] courts will go only so far in giving them force and effect.[578] As a general rule, anything beyond exculpation for ordinary negligence is of doubtful validity.[579] "No matter how broad the provision, the trustee is liable for committing a breach of trust in bad faith or with reckless indifference to the interests of the beneficiaries."[580] Moreover, a valid exculpatory clause will not necessarily deter a court in a given situation from denying the trustee compensation.[581] By federal statute, a mutual fund trustee may not be relieved of liability for acts that are occasioned by "willful misfeasance, bad faith, gross negligence or reckless disregard of the duties of his office."[582] ERISA essentially does away with fiduciary exculpation altogether.[583] In Texas, however, an exculpatory clause may relieve a trustee of liability for acts of self-dealing.[584] The exceptions are a corporate trustee loaning trust money to itself, buying trust property from itself, or selling trust property to itself.

An exculpatory clause that purports to limit a trustee's liability for a particular type of breach of trust ought not to be confused with a clause that grants the trustee a discretionary power to engage in an act that might otherwise be a breach of trust.[585] This is easier said than done, however, when an exculpatory clause is narrowly drawn, such as a clause that purports to exculpate the trustee from liability for retaining the family business. Whether the trustee

---

[576] Restatement (Third) of Trusts §96(1). The "good faith" standard of conduct in the trust context is discussed in §8.15.81 of this handbook.

[577] Lewin ¶ 39-82 (England).

[578] Lewin ¶ 39-82 (England).

[579] Lewin ¶ 39-82 (England). *See generally* 4 Scott & Ascher §§24.27 (U.S.), 24.27.3 (Extent to Which Exculpatory Provisions Are Against Public Policy).

[580] 4 Scott & Ascher §24.27.3 (Extent to Which Exculpatory Provisions Are Against Public Policy).

[581] *See generally* 4 Scott & Ascher §24.27.1. *See also* §7.2.3.7 of this handbook (reduction or denial of compensation).

[582] 15 U.S.C.A. §80a-17(h) (Investment Company Act of 1940).

[583] *See* 4 Scott & Ascher §24.27.3 (referring to ERISA §410(a), 29 U.S.C. §1110(a)).

[584] Texas Commerce Bank v. Grizzle, 46 Tex. Sup. Ct. J. 318, 96 S.W.3d 240 (2002).

[585] *See generally* 4 Scott & Ascher §24.27.1 (Distinction Between Exculpatory Provisions and Provisions That Enlarge Trustee's Powers); 7 Scott & Ascher §45.6.6 (fiduciary exculpation versus enlarging the trustee's powers/conflict of laws); §3.5.3.2 of this handbook (the trustee's express authority to engage in acts that might ordinarily be considered breaches of trust).

is entitled to compensation may well hinge on whether it is actually a discretionary power.[586]

Exculpatory clauses tend to be strictly construed by the courts.[587] In one case, a provision exculpating a trustee for ordinary negligence was held not to cover a breach of the duty to keep the beneficiaries informed and a breach of the duty to treat them impartially. "The duties to furnish information and to act impartially are not subspecies of the duty of care, but separate duties."[588] In another case, the court would not allow a trustee who had committed a breach of trust to compensate himself from the trust estate, even though the trustee, because of an exculpatory clause, had been relieved of liability for losses that had been occasioned by the breach.[589]

A trustee may not hide behind an exculpatory provision that has been improperly inserted.[590] An issue of the improper insertion of an exculpatory provision is likely to come up when the drafting attorney, or his law partner,[591] is also the named trustee.[592] When the attorney-trustee drafts into the instrument a provision limiting liability, there is at best an appearance of impropriety and conflict of interest.[593] After all, he has a duty to represent the interests of the settlor, his client—not his own interests.[594] In situations where the drafting attorney is the named trustee, the best practice is for the attorney to insist that the settlor seek competent, independent legal advice on the matter of trustee exculpation.[595] The benefit to the settlor is self-evident; the benefit to the trustee is that the exculpation is less vulnerable to attack than it would be otherwise. The next best practice is for the attorney to fully disclose to the settlor the existence and import of such a provision.[596] In no event should the drafting attorney casually dismiss as mere boilerplate an exculpatory provision—neither

---

[586] *See generally* 4 Scott & Ascher §24.27.1 (Distinction Between Exculpatory Provisions and Provisions That Enlarge Trustee's Powers).

[587] Lewin ¶ 39-90 (England); 4 Scott & Ascher §24.27.2 (U.S.). *But see* Texas Commerce Bank v. Grizzle, 46 Tex. Sup. Ct. J. 318, 96 S.W.3d 240 (2002) (liberally construing an exculpatory clause in a trust and holding that the clause relieved the trustee of liability for losses to the trust caused by a liquidation of trust assets incident to a merger of the bank with another bank).

[588] McNeil v. McNeil, 798 A.2d 503, 509 (Del. 2002).

[589] Warren v. Pazolt, 89 N.E. 381 (Mass. 1909). *See also* In re Chamberlain, 156 A. 42 (N.J. Prerog. Ct. 1931); Restatement (Second) of Trusts §243 cmt. g.

[590] *See generally* 4 Scott & Ascher §24.27; Young, *Exculpatory Clauses*, 13 Prob. L.J. 63 (1995).

[591] *See, e.g.*, Estate of Kramer, 2003 WL 22889500 (Pa. Com. Pl.), 23 Fiduc. Rep. 2d 245 (2003) (ruling that law partner stands in the shoes of the scrivener).

[592] *See generally* 4 Scott & Ascher §24.27.4; Restatement (Second) of Trusts §222 cmt. d.

[593] *See generally* 4 Scott & Ascher §24.27.4 (Exculpatory Provision Improperly Inserted).

[594] *See generally* 4 Scott & Ascher §24.27.4 (Exculpatory Provision Improperly Inserted).

[595] Restatement (Second) of Trusts §222 cmt. d. *See also* UTC §1008 cmt. (available at <http://www.uniformlaws.org/Act.aspx?title=Trust%20Code>) (suggesting that if the settlor was represented by independent counsel, the settlor's attorney is considered the drafter of the instrument even if the attorney used the trustee's form).

[596] *See* Marsman v. Nasca, 30 Mass. App. 789, 573 N.E.2d 1025 (1991), *review denied*, 411 Mass. 1102, 579 N.E.2d 1361 (1991) (exculpatory clause upheld in face of unrefuted testimony that the settlor asked the attorney-trustee to insert the clause). *But see* UTC §1008(b) (available at <http://www.uniformlaws.org/Act.aspx?title=Trust%20Code>) (disapproving of the *Marsman* case and providing that an exculpatory provision drafted by or on behalf of the trustee is presumed

in practice nor in response to client inquiries.[597] That practice is unacceptable.[598]

By the time the trust instrument is executed, the relationship between a prospective corporate trustee and a prospective settlor may well have developed into a confidential one.[599] "When a corporate officer drafts the trust instrument, even in a state in which this is permissible, there is such a relationship between the parties, even prior to the creation of the trust, that inclusion of a provision relieving the trustee of liability for breach of trust is ineffective unless the settlor fully understood the nature of the provision and freely agreed to it."[600]

In England, clauses that exonerate or indemnify trustees for negligent breaches of trust are recognized.[601] "The Trust Law Committee, a privately-funded body working for reform of trust law, . . . [however] . . . has started a consultation exercise on reforming this area of the law to bar such clauses from general use by professional trustees."[602]

While there are important similarities between the charitable trust and the charitable corporation,[603] fiduciary exculpation is one area where there is a fundamental difference. *Settlors* of charitable trusts generally control the insertion of exculpatory provisions into trust instruments, not the trustees. When it comes to charitable corporations, however, it is the *directors*—the fiduciaries themselves—who generally have authority, by statute,[604] to determine whether there is fiduciary exculpation.

As to boilerplate exculpatory-type provisions that would relieve an innocent third-party purchaser of trust property of the now nonexistent duty to see to it that the trustee properly applies the purchase price, see Section 8.15.69 of this handbook.

The trustee who relies on the terms of the trust. The Uniform Prudent Investor Act provides as follows: "The prudent investor rule, a default rule, may be expanded, restricted, eliminated, or otherwise altered by the provisions of a trust. A trustee is not liable to a beneficiary to the extent that the trustee acted

---

to have been inserted as a result of an abuse of a fiduciary or confidential relationship). *See generally* 4 Scott & Ascher §24.27.4 (Exculpatory Provision Improperly Inserted).

[597] *See* Jothann v. Irving Trust Co., 151 Misc. 107, 270 N.Y.S. 721 (1934), *aff'd*, 243 A.D. 691, 277 N.Y.S. 955 (1935) (striking exculpatory provision, which had been drafted by attorney acting as agent for the trustee). *See generally* Rutanen v. Ballard, 424 Mass. 723, 678 N.E.2d 133 (1997) (excerpting §7.2.6 of this handbook (exculpatory (also exemption or indemnity) provisions covering breaches of fiduciary duty to the beneficiary).

[598] *See generally* 4 Scott & Ascher §24.27.4 (Exculpatory Provision Improperly Inserted).

[599] *See generally* 4 Scott & Ascher §24.27.4 (Exculpatory Provision Improperly Inserted). *See also* Chapter 1 of this handbook (in part defining a confidential relationship).

[600] 4 Scott & Ascher §24.27.4 (Exculpatory Provision Improperly Inserted).

[601] Armitage v. Nurse, [1997] 2 ALL ER 705.

[602] Martyn Frost, *Overview of Trusts in England and Wales*, in Trusts in Prime Jurisdictions 13, 22 (Alon Kaplan ed., 2000).

[603] *See* §9.8.1 of this handbook (the charitable corporation).

[604] *See* Revised Model Nonprofit Corporation Act Subchapter E cmt. 1 (1987). *See also* Moody, *State Statutes Governing Directors of Charitable Corporations*, 18 U.S.F. L. Rev. 749, 782–783 (1984) (tabulating state indemnification provisions applicable to nonprofit corporations).

in reasonable reliance on the provisions of the trust."[605] The Uniform Trust Code is in accord.[606] A warning: The reliance must be reasonable. Take, for example, the entrusted insurance contract. The typical trust instrument will contain exonerating boilerplate similar to the following: "The Trustee shall be under no obligation to pay the premiums which may become due and payable under the provisions of such policy of insurance, or to make certain that such premiums are paid by the Settlor or others, or to notify any persons of the non-payment of such premiums, and the Trustee shall be under no responsibility or liability of any kind in the event such premiums are not paid as required." One thing is for sure: No matter how expansive and detailed the purported exoneration, if the trustee is on actual or constructive notice that an entrusted policy is about to lapse due to unintentional premium nonpayment, he is duty-bound to take reasonable steps to prevent the lapse, short of reaching into his own pocket. "Perhaps the most fundamental aspect of acting for the benefit of the beneficiaries is protecting the trust property . . . [Such exonerating language] . . . cannot be relied upon to abrogate . . . [the Trustee's] . . . duty to act in good faith and in accordance with the terms and purposes of the trust and the interests of the beneficiaries."[607] If the risk to the trust estate is attributable to the trustee's own negligence, say, the trustee had undertaken to furnish the insurance company with an address to which notifications should be sent and the address had been wrong, then he could well be financially on the hook for any consequential economic harm to the trust estate.[608]

A boilerplate clause purporting to exonerate the trustee for breaches of trust occasioned by the good-faith reliance on the opinions of counsel can be a two-edged sword. This is because the trustee who pursues an advice-of-counsel defense risks partially waiving the attorney-client privilege. Such partial waivers are taken up in Section 8.8 of this handbook.

§7.2.7 Beneficiary Consent, Release, or Ratification

Where a beneficiary has requested or consented to what essentially amounts to mismanagement by a fiduciary, equitable rather than contractual principles must govern. . . . Hence, petitioner, as the fiduciary, must demonstrate, if the IDA is to be enforced as a contract, that the beneficiaries had the intent to form a contract and so formed it with actual and full knowledge of all legal rights.[609]

The beneficiary's informed consent, ratification, or release is sufficient to discharge the trustee from liability to the beneficiary for a breach of trust, a

---

[605] Uniform Prudent Investor Act §1(b).
[606] *See generally* §3.5.2.5 of this handbook.
[607] Rafert v. Meyer, 859 N.W.2d 332 (Neb. 2015).
[608] *See, e.g.*, Rafert v. Meyer, 859 N.W.2d 332 (Neb. 2015).
[609] Estate of Saxton, 712 N.Y.S.2d 225, 231, 274 A.D.2d 110, 119 (2000).

topic that is addressed more fully in Section 7.1.2 of this handbook.[610] This applies even in the case of spendthrift trusts.[611] The burden, however, will be on the trustee to demonstrate that the beneficiary had actual and full knowledge and understanding of all legal rights.[612] As we note in Section 7.1.2 of this handbook, the test is a subjective one, both in the United States and in England.[613] Under the Uniform Trust Code, a purported consent, release, or ratification is ineffective to the extent it was induced by improper conduct of the trustee[614] or to the extent the beneficiary did not know at the time of the purported consent, release, or ratification of the beneficiary's rights or of the material facts relating to the breach.[615] "If the beneficiary's approval involves a self-dealing transaction, the approval is binding only if the transaction was fair and reasonable"[616] in the context of the particular facts and circumstances.[617] The Restatement of Restitution is in accord.[618] Again, for more on informed consent in the trustee self-dealing context, see Section 7.1.2 of this handbook.

---

[610] *See* 3 Scott & Ascher §17.2.1 (citing to the following venerable informed consent loyalty cases: Morse v. Royal, 12 Ves. 355, 373 (1806) (England); Davoue v. Fanning, 2 Johns. Ch. 252 (N.Y. Ch. 1816); Michoud v. Girod, 45 U.S. (4 How.) 503 (1846); Restatement (Second) of Trusts §§216–218. In some states, the beneficiary's right to release the trustee from liability is covered by statute. *See, e.g.,* N.C. Stat. §36A-79 (West 1999); N.M. Stat. Ann. 1978, §46-2-15 (West 1999). *See also* UTC §1009 (available at <http://www.uniformlaws.org/Act.aspx?title=Trust%20 Code>) (Beneficiary's Consent, Release, or Ratification); UTC §111(d)(6) (Nonjudicial Settlement Agreements).

[611] *See generally* 4 Scott & Ascher §24.21.1 (Consent by Beneficiary of Spendthrift Trust).

[612] Estate of Saxton, 712 N.Y.S.2d 225, 231, 274 A.D.2d 110, 119 (2000). *See generally* 4 Scott & Ascher §24.21 (Consent of Beneficiary); 3 Scott & Ascher §17.2.4 (noting that "[a] beneficiary's consent or acquiescence may bar the beneficiary from holding the trustee liable for improper lending of trust funds, but only if the beneficiary had full knowledge of the facts and his or her legal rights"); Restatement of Restitution §191, cmt. a (burden of proof); §8.24 of this handbook (who has the burden of proof in an action for breach of trust brought by the beneficiary against the trustee).

[613] *See generally* Lewin ¶ 20-128 (England) (suggesting that the beneficiary must actually understand the conflicts inherent in a trustee entering into a self-dealing transaction with his beneficiary); §7.1.2 of this handbook (defenses to allegations that the trustee breached the duty of loyalty) (U.S.); Restatement of Restitution §191 (U.S.).

[614] UTC §1009(1) (available at <http://www.uniformlaws.org/Act.aspx?title=Trust%20 Code>) (Beneficiary's Consent, Release, or Ratification); UTC §817(c)(1) (Distribution Upon Termination). *See also* Restatement of Restitution §191, cmt. d (improper conduct by trustee).

[615] UTC §1009(2) (available at <http://www.uniformlaws.org/Act.aspx?title=Trust%20 Code>) (Beneficiary's Consent, Release, or Ratification); UTC §817(c)(2) (Distribution Upon Termination). *See also* Restatement of Restitution §191, cmts. b & c. *See, e.g.,* Janowiak v. Tiesi, 932 N.E.2d 569 (Ill. 2010) (to be effective, a release must be informed).

[616] UTC §1009 cmt. (available at <http://www.uniformlaws.org/Act.aspx?title=Trust%20 Code>). *See also* Restatement of Restitution §191, cmt. e (self-dealing transaction must be fair and reasonable).

[617] *See generally* 4 Scott & Ascher §24.21.3 ("Thus, a trustee relies, at the trustee's own risk, on the consent of a beneficiary who, though technically not under any legal incapacity, is especially vulnerable"). In order for a beneficiary's consent to or ratification of a trustee's act of self-dealing to be binding, the beneficiary must subjectively, that is actually, understand the applicable facts and the law.

[618] Restatement of Restitution §191, cmt. e.

The trustee must understand that each of the following qualifies as a *beneficiary:* those with remainder interests as well as those with income interests; those with contingent interests as well as those whose interests have vested.[619] Thus, the informed consent of only the current beneficiaries to what otherwise might constitute a breach of trust may not be sufficient to bind the remaindermen.[620] While it is true that the informed consent of one of several beneficiaries, even beneficiaries of the same class, is generally binding only on the consenter, there is one notable exception: The informed consent of the holder (donee) of a *general inter vivos power of appointment,* such as a reserved right of revocation, will generally bind all other beneficiaries.[621] There is even some law to the effect that the informed consent of the holder (donee) of a *general testamentary power of appointment* binds at least the appointees and takers in default.[622] For a more detailed discussion of the extent to which the informed consent of the holder (donee) of a general testamentary power of appointment binds the trust's other beneficiaries, the reader is referred to Section 8.14 of this handbook.

For more on the topic of the limitation of a trustee's liability to the beneficiary through the beneficiary's own actions or inactions, to include more on informed consent, see Section 5.5 of this handbook.

§7.2.8 Liability Without Economic Injury to the Beneficiary

A trustee is liable for intentional breaches of trust, whether or not the breach caused economic injury to the trust. This is particularly the case when it comes to breaches of the duty of loyalty. Lack of economic injury is no more a defense to a trustee's breach of the duty of loyalty than is the failure to steal a defense to the crime of breaking and entering. While money damages may not be an available remedy in the absence of economic harm, there is always injunction, removal, and assessment of costs—and possibly even criminal sanction.[623] Under the Uniform Trust Code, a trustee is accountable to an affected beneficiary for any profit made by the trustee arising from the administration of the trust, even absent a breach of trust.[624] "A typical example of a profit is receipt by the trustee of a commission or bonus from a third party for actions relating to the trust's administration."[625]

---

[619] *See generally* 3 Scott on Trusts §216.2 (U.S.); Lewin ¶38-11 (England).

[620] *See generally* 4 Scott & Ascher §§24.21.2, 24.19 (Several Beneficiaries).

[621] *See generally* 4 Scott & Ascher §24.21.2 (Several Beneficiaries).

[622] *See generally* 4 Scott & Ascher §24.21.2 (Several Beneficiaries).

[623] *But see* Bogert §861 n.57 and accompanying text. *See generally* §7.2.3.7 of this handbook (the equitable relief of reduction or denial of compensation and/or assessment of attorneys' fees and other costs against the trustee personally).

[624] UTC §1003(a) (available at <http://www.uniformlaws.org/Act.aspx?title=Trust%20Code>).

[625] UTC §1003 cmt. (available at <http://www.uniformlaws.org/Act.aspx?title=Trust%20Code>).

Negligent breaches also can bring liability without economic injury. One court, for example, has held a trustee liable for the legal costs that a beneficiary incurred in getting the trustee to properly account.[626] The Restatement (Third) of Trusts is generally in accord.[627]

The beneficiary's costs of getting a trustee to prudently invest the trust property also should be absorbed by the trustee personally. Let us take, for example, the trustee who negligently concentrates the trust estate in only one stock. Last year the stock's performance was well below the market average; this year its performance is, and continues to be, well above the market average. The beneficiary, concerned that the portfolio is at an unacceptable level of risk, retains counsel who finally manages either by litigation or negotiation to get the trustee to diversify. While ultimately the trust suffered no resulting economic injury, the trustee nonetheless was in breach of the duty to diversify. Thus, while money damages may be inappropriate, it would be appropriate for the trustee personally to bear the burden of all legal fees and associated costs incurred by the beneficiary and others in getting the trustee to prudently diversify.[628] Had the trustee sold when the stock was down, there would have been realized losses that could have formed the basis for an assessment of damages.[629] There is some irony here. Had the stock been sold in a down market in a conscientious—albeit belated—effort to carry out the duty to diversify, the trustee's liability could well be keyed to those losses.[630]

§7.2.9   Personal Liability of Third Parties, Including the Trustee's Agents, to the Beneficiary; Investment Managers; Directors and Officers of Trust Companies; Lawyers; Brokers

A third party may not knowingly participate in a breach of trust. The trust beneficiary has an equitable property right that is enforceable against "every person in the world" because "every person in the world" is obligated not to collude with the trustee in a breach of trust.[631] That includes trust counsel, brokers, and other such agents of the trustee.[632] "A third person who, although not a transferee of trust property, has notice that the trustee is committing a

---

[626] James v. Newington & ors, [2004] JRC 059 (Jersey Royal Court (Samedi Division)).

[627] Restatement (Third) of Trusts §83 cmt. a(1) and §100, cmt. b(2).

[628] *See generally* §8.13 of this handbook (in litigation pertaining to a trust, when the beneficiary is entitled to reimbursement from the trust estate for legal fees).

[629] *See* Restatement (Third) of Trusts: Prudent Investor Rule §205.

[630] In one case, a bank trustee was held liable for the failure to diversify even though "the value of the trust principal increased and 'substantial income' was earned throughout the bank's tenure as trustee." First Ala. Bank of Huntsville, N.A. v. Spragins, 515 So. 2d 962 (Ala. 1987). Liability was based on the difference between the actual increase and the increase that might have been achieved with a diversified portfolio. *See also* Restatement (Third) of Trusts §§209–211.

[631] 3 Scott & Ascher §13.1.

[632] As to the complicit broker, *see* Restatement (Third) of Restitution and Unjust Enrichment §17, illus. 12 (a securities broker having received trust funds in payment for securities that he knew

breach of trust and participates therein is liable to the beneficiary for any loss caused by the breach of trust."[633] As to the liabilities, if any, of third-party transferees of trust property, the reader is referred to Section 8.15.63 of this handbook.[634]

A trustee's nonministerial agents generally owe fiduciary duties to the beneficiaries. An agent-fiduciary of a trustee who is knowingly involved in matters relating to the administration of a trust generally has fiduciary duties that run also to the beneficiaries.[635] A broker retained by the trustee to find a buyer for a parcel of entrusted real estate, for example, may well have fiduciary duties that run to the beneficiaries as well as the trustee. The more discretionary the broker's authority, the more likely the broker is a fiduciary. As we discuss in Section 8.8 of this handbook, there may be a trust counsel exception in some jurisdictions. In some jurisdictions, trust counsel's fiduciary duties may run exclusively to the trustee. Still, as noted above, any lawyer who knowingly assists the trustee in committing a breach of trust may be held liable to the beneficiaries for the consequences.[636] Under common law agency principles, for the lawyer's partner to be liable to the trust beneficiaries, however, the partner would have to have, at minimum, actual knowledge of the conspiracy.[637]

The Uniform Prudent Investor Act expressly provides that "[i]n performing a delegated function, an agent owes a duty to the trust to exercise care to comply with the terms of the delegation."[638] In England, however, there appears to be more deference to those who negligently assist trustees in breaching their trusts, the torts of conspiracy and unlawful interference having yet to intrude upon its law of trusts.[639]

By federal statute, one who advises the trustees of a mutual fund on investment matters is expressly deemed to have a fiduciary duty to the investors, *i.e.*, the trust beneficiaries, not to take compensation that is unreasonable.[640] Moreover, the advisor may not be exculpated from liability to the investors for acts of "willful misfeasance, bad faith, or gross negligence, in the performance of his duties, or by reason of his reckless disregard of his duties and obligations,"

---

had been purchased in violation of the terms of the trust, the successor trustee has a claim against the broker to rescind the sale and recover the original purchase price).

[633] Restatement (Second) of Trusts §326; 4 Scott on Trusts §326; 5 Scott & Ascher §§28.2, 30.6.5. One Missouri court, however, seems to have assumed that civil conspiracy doctrine, not general principles of equity, governs the liability of an agent of a trustee who knowingly participates in the trustee's breaches of trust. *See* Brock v. McClure, 404 S.W.3d 416 (Mo. App. 2013). Apparently, the law in Missouri has become unsettled as to whether civil conspiracy liability can attach to a conspirator who is not personally benefited by the conspiracy. *See Brock*, 404 S.W.3d 416 n.3. Civil conspiracy is a tort.

[634] *See also* §8.15.69 of this handbook (third party liability for trustee's misapplication of payments to trustee).

[635] Lattuca v. Robsham, 2004 WL 1636979 (Mass). *See also* Restatement (Second) of Trusts §326, cmt. a.

[636] *See generally* 4 Scott on Trusts §326.4; 5 Scott & Ascher §28.2.

[637] Babb v. Bynum & Murphrey, PLLC, 643 S.E.2d 55 (N.C. Ct. App. 2007).

[638] Uniform Prudent Investor Act §9(b).

[639] Lewin ¶ 40-48 through ¶ 40–49 (England).

[640] 15 U.S.C.A. §80a-35(b) (Investment Company Act of 1940).

contractual and other-wise, under the investment management agency agreement.[641]

Whether the directors of a trust company owe fiduciary duties to trust beneficiaries. A corporation that holds property in trust has fiduciary duties that run to the trust beneficiaries.[642] In the United States, so too do the directors and officers of the corporation.[643] "[R]ecognition of a duty of a director to those for whom a corporation holds funds in trust may be viewed as another application of the general rule that a director's duty is that of an ordinary prudent person under the circumstances."[644] A corporate officer would have a similar duty.[645] Thus, a director or officer of a trust company may be held liable to the trust beneficiaries for directly harming their equitable interests, either negligently or intentionally, in violation of his or her fiduciary duties to them, or for participating with the corporation in a breach of trust.[646] "It is no defense that a director or officer did not personally profit from the breach of trust or that the conduct was not dishonest."[647] For liability to attach, however, the director or officer must be personally at fault.[648] Just because the trust company is liable does not necessarily mean that its directors and officers are as well.[649] Even a director who is passive or disengaged may be personally liable to the beneficiaries for the breaches of his codirectors.[650] The same goes for the officers.[651]

Here is another rationale for allowing the trust beneficiaries to seek redress from a trust company's directors and officers, one that is not based on a duty that runs directly from the directors and officers to the beneficiaries: "Such directors and officers are personally liable to the corporation, and its claim against them is a corporate asset, which the beneficiaries can reach, as creditors of the corporation."[652] One commentator has suggested that under this theory of liability, the claims of the trust beneficiaries ought to have priority over the claims of the corporation's general creditors.[653]

---

[641] 15 U.S.C.A. §80a-17(i) (Investment Company Act of 1940).

[642] Francis v. United Jersey Bank, 87 N.J. 15, 432 A.2d 814 (1981).

[643] *See generally* 3 Scott & Ascher §17.2.14.1 (the directors of an insolvent trust company may be held personally liable to the trust beneficiaries for trust cash that had been parked on its commercial side, at least to the extent that the cash cannot be traced and recovered for the trusts); 5 Scott & Ascher §30.6.3 (Directors and Officers of Corporate Trustee).

[644] Francis v. United Jersey Bank, 87 N.J. 15, 432 A.2d 814 (1981). *See also* 5 Scott & Ascher §30.6.3 ("A director or officer is under a duty to the beneficiaries to use reasonable care in the exercise of his or her powers and the performance of his or her duties as director or officer").

[645] 5 Scott & Ascher §30.6.3

[646] 5 Scott & Ascher §30.6.3.

[647] 5 Scott & Ascher §30.6.3.

[648] 5 Scott & Ascher §30.6.3.

[649] 5 Scott & Ascher §30.6.3.

[650] Francis v. United Jersey Bank, 87 N.J. 15, 432 A.2d 814 (1981). *See generally* 5 Scott & Ascher §30.6.3 ("It would seem, however, that the mere fact that the director or officer is guilty of inaction rather than of intentionally wrongful or negligent action should not negate personal liability").

[651] 5 Scott & Ascher §30.6.3.

[652] 5 Scott & Ascher §30.6.3.

[653] 5 Scott & Ascher §30.6.3.

In England, the director of a trust company owes no fiduciary duties or duties of care to the beneficiaries of the trusts of which the trust company is a trustee, unless he or she has dishonestly assisted the trust company in a breach of trust.[654] Moreover, English case law does not support the proposition that a trust company's claim against an honest but negligent director constitutes a corporate asset that is reachable in a "dog leg" action by trust beneficiaries.[655] "The validity or invalidity of the dog-leg claim, of course, is of only theoretical interest where the corporate trustee has assets adequate to meet a claim for breach of trust or where it has insurance."[656] A "dog leg" action is analogous to a derivative suit in the corporate context, or in the trust context for that matter.[657]

Personal liability of trust officers and other agents of the corporate trustee. A corporate trustee would be liable to the beneficiary for neglect or default of an internal agent, *i.e.*, an officer or employee, provided that the agent had been acting within the course of the employment.[658] This would be the case whether or not the corporate trustee, itself, had engaged in any breach of trust in connection with the matter.[659] The corporate trustee, for example, would be on the hook even if it had acted prudently in hiring and overseeing the activities of the internal agent.

On the other hand, if the activities of an external agent, *i.e.*, independent contractor, had been the cause of the problem, whether or not there was liability to the beneficiary *on the part of the corporate trustee* would in part depend upon the prudence or lack thereof of the corporate trustee in selecting and retaining the external agent.[660] As a general rule, a natural person has knowledge of a fact if the person has actual knowledge of it; has received a notice or notification of it; or from all the facts and circumstances known to the person at the time in question, has reason to know it.[661] On the other hand, a corporate trustee would have notice or knowledge of a fact only when the information is received by an employee having responsibility to act for the trust, or would have been brought to the employee's attention had the corporate trustee exercised reasonable diligence.[662] In other words, notice to a corporate trustee is not necessarily

---

[654] HR v. JAPT, [1997] O.P.L.R. 123 [England].

[655] Gregson v. H.A.E. Trustees Ltd., [2008] EWHC 1006 (ch), [2008] All E.R. (D) 105 (May).

[656] Nicholas Le Poidevin, *Corporate trustees: The limits of responsibility*, 6(4) Tr. Q. Rev. 7 [a STEP publication].

[657] *See generally* §5.4.1.8 of this handbook (right and standing of beneficiary to proceed in stead of trustee against those with whom the trustee has contracted, against tortfeasors, and against the trustee's agents *i.e.*, against third parties).

[658] Restatement (Second) of Trusts §225 cmt. b.

[659] Restatement (Second) of Trusts §225 cmt. b.

[660] Restatement (Second) of Trusts §225(2)(c).

[661] UTC §104(a) (available at <http://www.uniformlaws.org/Act.aspx?title=Trust%20Code>).

[662] UTC §104(a) cmt. (available at <http://www.uniformlaws.org/Act.aspx?title=Trust%20Code>).

achieved by giving notice to a branch office.[663] Nor does it necessarily acquire knowledge at the moment a notice arrives in the mailroom.[664] A corporate trustee exercises reasonable diligence if it maintains reasonable routines for communicating significant information to the employee having responsibility to act for the trust and there is reasonable compliance with the routines.[665] In any case, that a corporate trustee is found not liable to the beneficiaries for the malfeasance or nonfeasance of an external agent does not mean that the agent must be so found as well.

There are also instances where internal agents such as trust officers have been sued personally, along with their corporate employers, for breaches of fiduciary duty, notwithstanding the fact that the corporate employer was the named trustee.[666] True, the trust company may be held liable for the acts of the trust officer under the doctrine of *respondeat superior*.[667] It does not follow from this, however, that the trust officer is then relieved of liability.[668] A trust officer is at some personal financial risk if the trust company does not carry employee liability insurance; the trust company is financially weak, bankrupt,[669] or otherwise unable or unwilling to indemnify the trust officer; or the trust officer's homeowner's policy does not cover acts performed in the course of employment. Certainly the trust beneficiaries would be tempted to mount an effort to have the officer of the insolvent trust company saddled with liabilities that run to them directly. Why? Because the beneficiaries would merely be general creditors of the insolvent trust company, at least to the extent the trust property itself could not be traced into the bankruptcy estate.[670] Thus, it would be particularly unwise for a trust officer to park trust cash on the commercial

---

[663] UTC §104(a) cmt. (available at <http://www.uniformlaws.org/Act.aspx?title=Trust%20Code>).

[664] UTC §104(a) cmt. (available at <http://www.uniformlaws.org/Act.aspx?title=Trust%20Code>).

[665] UTC §104(b) (available at <http://www.uniformlaws.org/Act.aspx?title=Trust%20Code>).

[666] *See generally* 5 Scott & Ascher §30.6.3, n. 1; 4 Scott on Trusts §326.3.

[667] *See generally* §6.1.4 of this handbook (the trustee's duty not to delegate critical fiduciary functions). *See also* §7.3.3 of this handbook (trustee's liability as legal owner in tort to nonbeneficiaries) and §8.32 of this handbook (whether the trustee may escape liability for making a mistake of law if he acted in good faith on advice of counsel). The UTC provides that a corporate trustee that conducts activities through employees has notice or knowledge of a fact involving a trust only from the time the information was received by an employee having responsibility to act for the trust, or would have been brought to the employee's attention if the corporate trustee had exercised reasonable diligence. UTC §104(b) (available at <http://www.uniformlaws.org/Act.aspx?title=Trust%20Code>). A corporate trustee exercises reasonable diligence if it maintains reasonable routines for communicating significant information to the employee having responsibility to act for the trust and there is reasonable compliance with the routines. UTC §104(b). Would a corporate trustee's exercise of "reasonable diligence" insulate it from vicarious liability for the actions of the employees?

[668] *See* Bogert §901 n.10 and accompanying text; 4 Scott on Trusts §326.3; 5 Scott & Ascher §30.6.3 (noting that the claim of a corporation against its directors or officers for causing it to incur fiduciary liability is a corporate asset).

[669] *See generally* 4 Scott on Trusts §326.3.

[670] 5 Scott & Ascher §30.6.3 (Directors and Officers of Corporate Trustee).

side if the trust company's insolvency is a real possibility. Actual insolvency could well expose the trust officer to personal liability *to the beneficiaries* for any of the cash that could not be traced and recovered for the trusts, at least to the extent the trust officer knew or should have known about the entity's precarious financial situation.[671]

Whether trust counsel has a fiduciary duty to the trust beneficiaries. As discussed in Section 8.8 of this handbook, the cases are all over the lot on the question of whether trust counsel represents the trustees, the beneficiaries, or both classes together. It is settled law, however, that in matters unrelated to the rendering of legal advice, a lawyer for a trustee has the same duty of undivided loyalty to the beneficiaries as does the trustee.[672] In one case, for example, a lawyer who was representing trustees in the sale of trust real estate secretly arranged with the brokers to take a portion of any commissions they might earn on the transaction. While the trustees were not found culpable, and although the trust ultimately was not harmed by the lawyer's machinations, the court nonetheless reduced the lawyer's compensation and ordered him to turn over the kickback to the trust estate.[673]

When trust counsel knowingly participates in a breach of trust. It goes without saying that trust counsel may not knowingly participate with the trustee in an act that would constitute a breach of trust, such as the sale of a parcel of trust real estate to counsel for less than fair market value in violation of the terms of the trust.[674] A trustee who pays counsel out of entrusted funds legal fees that are demonstrably excessive is wasting trust assets.[675] It is self-evident that counsel is a knowing participant in that breach.[676] Suffice it to say, a trust counsel who knowingly participates in any act that might reasonably be considered by a court to be a breach of trust is asking for trouble.[677]

On the other hand, trust counsel generally would not be liable to the trust beneficiaries for participating in a breach of trust if all that counsel did was render naked legal advice to the trustee as to the law applicable to an act of the trustee that was in a breach of trust, or to an act that if undertaken by the trustee would be in breach of trust.[678] That is not to say that counsel could not incur liability to the trustee, and possibly to the beneficiaries, as well, for negligently

---

[671] *See generally* 3 Scott & Ascher §17.2.14.1.

[672] *See* Clarke's Estate, 12 N.Y.2d 183, 187, 188 N.E.2d 128, 130, 237 N.Y.S.2d 694, 697 (1962).

[673] Clarke's Estate, 12 N.Y.2d 183, 187, 188 N.E.2d 128, 130, 237 N.Y.S.2d 694, 697 (1962). *See also* In re Bond & Mortgage Guar. Co. (In re Half Moon Hotel), 303 N.Y. 423, 103 N.E.2d 721 (1952) (attorneys for trustee held liable for breach of the duty of undivided loyalty to the trust beneficiaries when they purchased at arm's length through third-party brokers interests in the underlying property, though there was no evidence of actual fraud, bad faith, or "manipulation of the trust dealings" by the attorneys).

[674] 5 Scott & Ascher §30.6.4 (Attorneys and Other Agents).

[675] *See generally* §6.2.1.3 of this handbook (the trustee's duty not to waste the trust property).

[676] *See, e.g.*, McCormick v. Cox, 118 So. 3d 980, 982, 38 Fla. L. Weekly D1723 (Fla. Dist. Ct. App. 2013) (upholding a finding of the trial court that the legal fees paid to trust counsel were "substantially unreasonable and unsupported by the evidence").

[677] 5 Scott & Ascher §30.6.4.

[678] 5 Scott & Ascher §30.6.4.

rendering faulty legal advice.[679] But that would be for the commission of a tort, a legal proscription, not for the participation in a breach of trust, which is an equitable proscription.[680]

The third party who pays directly to the beneficiary a debt owed the trust. A third party who bypasses the trustee does so at his, her, or its peril. Take, for example, the trustee who holds legal title to contractual rights against a third party, such as rights against the corporate issuer of a bond or rights against an insurance company incident to one of its insurance policies.[681] In other words, a bond or an insurance contract is a trust asset. The third party, instead of making a payment to the trustee, who is the other party to the contract, takes it upon itself to make a payment directly to the trust beneficiary, who is not of full age and legal capacity. The trustee may have a fiduciary duty to seek to compel the third party to make the payment a second time, this time to the trustee.[682]

A third party definitely risks having to pay twice if it makes a payment to the beneficiary designated in the governing instrument in the face of a valid assignment of the equitable interest, even when the "original" beneficiary is of full age and legal capacity and even if the third party had no notice, actual or constructive, of the assignment.[683] The trustee to whom the obligation ran and to whom the payment should have been made did not receive it.[684] Nor did the assignee, the current possessor of the equitable property interest, receive the payment.[685] If the third party has any recourse, it is against the original or former beneficiary.

Liability of third-party purchasers of trust property to the beneficiaries. As we have noted throughout this handbook, a third party who knowingly participates with a trustee in a breach of trust shares with the trustee liability for any losses occasioned by the breach. If the trustee transfers trust property in breach of trust to a third-party purchaser who is aware of the breach, the third-party purchaser holds the trust property subject to the terms of the

---

[679] *See generally* §8.8 of this handbook (whom trust counsel represents).

[680] *See generally* §8.8 of this handbook (whom trust counsel represents).

[681] *See generally* §9.9.4 of this handbook (bank accounts and other such debtor-creditor contractual arrangements are not trusts) and §9.9.1 of this handbook (life insurance and other such third-party beneficiary contracts are not trusts).

[682] The third-party obligor who makes a payment directly to the trust beneficiary instead of to the title-holding trustee, the other party to the contract, does so at his, her, or its peril, unless directed to do so by the trustee. 5 Scott & Ascher §32.1 (Discharge by Beneficiary of Claim Against Third Person). If the beneficiary is not of full age and legal capacity, the third-party obligor runs the risk of having to pay twice. 5 Scott & Ascher §32.1 (Discharge by Beneficiary of Claim Against Third Person). There is a similar risk if following the direction were to constitute a knowing participation with the trustee in a breach of trust, or if the trust were a spendthrift trust. 5 Scott & Ascher §32.1 (Discharge by Beneficiary of Claim Against Third Person).

[683] 5 Scott & Ascher §32.1 (Discharge by Beneficiary of Claim Against Third Person). *See generally* §5.3.2 of this handbook (voluntary transfers of the equitable (beneficial) interest under a trust).

[684] 5 Scott & Ascher §32.1.

[685] 5 Scott & Ascher §32.1.

trust.[686] Otherwise, "such a purchaser is liable only if the trustee commits a breach of trust in making the transfer and the purchaser has notice that the trustee is doing so."[687] At common law, however, it was doctrine that even the innocent third-party purchaser had a continuing obligation running to the trust beneficiaries to see to it that the trustee properly applied the purchase price.[688] In the United States, such an innocent third party either by case law or by statute has been relieved of such an obligation.[689] "In England, the old rule has been repudiated by statute."[690]

    Liability of a third party who fails to honor a Uniform Trust Code Section 1013 certification. The trustee of the typical trust will have numerous occasions to transact with third parties in furtherance of the trust's lawful purposes. This is appropriate as the trustee holds the legal title to the trust property, and, thus, "as to the world" is its owner. A third party might be selling an asset to, or purchasing an entrusted asset from, the trustee. A third party might be loaning funds to the trustee in his fiduciary capacity or borrowing entrusted property from the trustee. A third party might be selling goods and services to the trustee or purchasing goods and services from the trustee, all in furtherance of the trust's lawful purposes. The trustee also may properly retain third-party agents in furtherance of the trust's lawful purposes, such as attorneys-at-law and investment managers.

    Section 1013(h) of the Uniform Trust Code provides as follows: "A person . . . [other than a beneficiary] . . . making a demand for the trust instrument in addition to a certification of trust or excerpts is liable for damages if the court determines that the person did not act in good faith in demanding the instrument."

    The information in a trustee's Uniform Trust Code §1013 certification is limited to the following bits of information:

- That the trust exists and its date of execution
- The identity of the settlors
- The powers of the trustee
- The revocability or irrevocability of the trust and the identity of any persons holding a power to revoke
- The authority of cotrustees to sign or otherwise authenticate and whether all or less than all are required in order to exercise the powers of the trustee
- The trust's taxpayer identification number
- The manner of taking title to trust property

---

[686] *See generally* §5.4.2 of this handbook (rights of the beneficiary as against transferees of the underlying trust property).

[687] 5 Scott & Ascher §30.1 (Misapplication of Payments Made to Trustee).

[688] 5 Scott & Ascher §30.1. *See also* §8.15.69 of this handbook (third party liability for trustee's misapplication of payments to the trustee).

[689] 5 Scott & Ascher §30.1, n.5 (Case Law) & n.7 (Statute).

[690] 5 Scott & Ascher §30.1 (referring to Trustee Act, 1925, 15 Geo. V., c. 19, §14 (England)).

- A statement that the trust has not been revoked, modified, or amended in any manner that would cause the representations contained in the certification to be incorrect.

A Uniform Trust Code §1013 certification, however, "need not contain the dispositive terms of a trust." Unexplained are the nature of the "liability" and "damages" that are being contemplated by subsection (h). Nor is a definition of "good faith" even supplied in this context. Presumably, the third party is subject to some type of tort liability, but what duty of care is implicated by the "making of a demand for a trust instrument"? According to the section's official commentary, left to "other law" is the issue of "how damages for a bad faith refusal are to be computed." Also unspecified is to whom this demanding "person" would be liable in the face of a judicial determination of liability.

A third party contemplating dealing with a trustee should be able contractually to defang Uniform Trust Code §1013(h), assuming it actually has fangs. Time will tell whether it actually does in the face of all this statutory vagueness.

May Uniform Trust Code §1013's general applicability be negated effectively *ab initio* by the trust's terms? In the face of subsection (g) of Uniform Trust Code §1013, some settlors may want to consider doing just that so as to better protect the equitable property rights of the beneficiaries of their trusts. Subsection (g) provides as follows: "A person who in good faith enters into a transaction in reliance upon a certification of trust may enforce the transaction *against the trust property* [emphasis supplied] as if the representations contained in the certification were correct." The problem is that the third party who is not furnished a copy of the trust instrument, only a cryptic trustee certification, will not be privy to the Uniform Trust Code §1013 negation provision and therefore may well not be bound by its terms.

Related sections. As to whether a trustee may shift liability for breaches of fiduciary duty on to the shoulders of his agents, see Section 3.2.6 of this handbook (Considerations in the Selection of a Trustee). As to the beneficiary's right to proceed in the stead of the trustee directly against the trustee's agents, the reader is referred to Section 5.4.1.8 of this handbook (Right (of Beneficiary) to Proceed in Stead of Trustee against Those with Whom the Trustee Has Contracted, against Tortfeasors, and against His Agents, *i.e.*, against Third Parties). As to the duties, if any, that a trustee's counsel may have to the beneficiaries, the reader is referred to Section 8.8 of this handbook (Whom Does Counsel Represent?). So too *a beneficiary* who consents to a breach of trust and/or participates in a breach of trust may incur liability to the other beneficiaries for so doing, a topic that is covered in Section 5.6 of this handbook.[691] For a discussion of the inbound external liabilities of third parties generally to the trustee or the beneficiary, or both, see Section 3.6 of this handbook.

---

[691] *See also* 4 Scott & Ascher §95.2.6.3 (Participation by Beneficiary in Breach of Trust).

§7.2.10   *Limitation of Action by Beneficiary Against Trustee (Laches and Statutes of Limitation)*

The expressions "the Statutes of Limitation" or the "Statute of Limitations" or simply "the Statute" are often used to denote collectively the series of statutes, commencing with the Limitation Act 1623, which dealt with the limitation of actions. The present statutes are the Limitation Act 1980 (which repealed and replaced the former statutes) and the Latent Damage Act 1986 (which amended the Act of 1980)—Snell's Equity.[692]

Whether a relationship is one of debtor-creditor or trustee-beneficiary can matter greatly in the litigation context.[693] A collection action at law against a contract debtor, for example, might be barred by a statute of limitations that would not be applicable to actions by beneficiaries against their trustees.[694]

Equitable defenses. A beneficiary's claim against the trustee, however, might still be barred by principles arising in equity under the common law of trusts, *e.g.*, estoppel and laches.[695] Or, perhaps it would not. For the beneficiary to be prevented by "laches" from holding the trustee liable for a breach of trust, the beneficiary must have so delayed in bringing an action against the trustee that it would be inequitable to permit the beneficiary to hold the trustee liable.[696] As a matter of public policy, suits should be brought with reasonable promptness.[697] With the passage of time, it becomes difficult to ascertain the truth.[698] A cause of action against a trustee for breaches of the duty of loyalty (or any other type of breach for that matter) would not be barred by laches until a reasonable time after all beneficiaries, both current beneficiaries and remaindermen, had become aware of the breach and failed to take appropriate action.[699] Those who would take upon imposition of a resulting trust would similarly not be barred.[700]

The state attorney general is not bound by the doctrine of laches when it comes to the enforcement of charitable trusts.[701] Neither is the court. "The mere fact that the trustees of a charitable trust have long applied the trust property to purposes other than those designated by the settlor does not

---

[692] Snell's Equity ¶ 5-16, n. 52 (England).

[693] *See generally* §9.9.4 of this handbook (bank accounts and other such debtor-creditor contractual arrangements are not trusts).

[694] 1 Scott & Ascher §2.3.8.2.

[695] UTC §1005 cmt. (available at <http://www.uniformlaws.org/Act.aspx?title=Trust%20 Code>). *See also* §5.5 of this handbook (voluntary or involuntary loss of the beneficiary's rights).

[696] *See generally* Restatement (Third) of Trusts §98 cmt. b; §8.15.70 of this handbook (laches doctrine generally).

[697] Restatement (Third) of Trusts §98 cmt. b.

[698] Restatement (Third) of Trusts §98 cmt. b.

[699] *See, e.g.*, Lawson v. Haynes, 170 F.2d 741 (10th Cir. 1948). *See generally* Bogert §542(U); Restatement (Third) of Trusts §98 cmt. b(1); §5.5 of this handbook (voluntary or involuntary loss of the beneficiary's equitable rights); §7.1.2 of this handbook (defenses to allegations that the trustee breached the duty of loyalty); §7.1.2 of this handbook (defense of failure to take timely action against trustee); §8.15.70 of this handbook (the laches doctrine in the trust context).

[700] *See generally* 6 Scott & Ascher §40.6.

[701] *See* Restatement (Third) of Trusts §98 cmt. a(2) (immunity of attorneys general).

preclude the court from directing that the trust be administered according to its terms."[702]

The Uniform Trust Code. The Uniform Trust Code establishes two limitation periods: a one-year period for the beneficiary who has received notice of a potential claim for breach of trust[703] and a five-year period for the beneficiary who has not.[704] A beneficiary may not commence a proceeding against a trustee for breach of trust more than one year after the date the beneficiary or a representative of the beneficiary was sent a report that adequately disclosed the existence of a potential claim for breach of trust and informed the beneficiary of the time allowed for commencing a proceeding.[705]

Otherwise, a judicial proceeding by a beneficiary against a trustee for breach of trust must be commenced within five years after the first to occur of (1) the removal, resignation, or death of the trustee; (2) the termination of the beneficiary's interest in the trust; or (3) the termination of the trust.[706]

Uniform Trust Code §1005(c)'s five-year repose provisions are a radical departure from the Anglo-American legal tradition. It bars actions against a trustee by beneficiaries, even in cases where the trustee has failed to disclose critical information to the beneficiaries. In other words, it stands the ancient doctrine of laches on its head. The equitable remedies catalogued and discussed in Section 7.2.3 of this handbook are what give the fiduciary principle, as applied in the trust context, teeth. UTC §1005(c) would work a substantial defanging of that principle. That a legislature would intentionally enact into law an incentive not to engage in proper fiduciary conduct would seem ill-advised, and certainly unfair to trust counsel, a topic we ruminate on in Section 7.1.2 of this handbook.

Legislative revival of time-barred claims constitutionally questionable. Assume a two-year statute of limitations for breach of trust claims has just run against the beneficiaries of an irrevocable trust. Today, however, the legislature has repealed the statute and enacted a successor statute with a four-year time period. Are the beneficiaries of the trust foreclosed from availing themselves of the new four-year time period in a breach of trust action against the trustee? In other words, have their claims been legislatively revived? Probably they have not

---

[702] 5 Scott & Ascher §37.3.10.

[703] UTC §1005(a) (available at <http://www.uniformlaws.org/Act.aspx?title=Trust%20 Code>).

[704] UTC §1005(c) (available at <http://www.uniformlaws.org/Act.aspx?title=Trust%20 Code>).

[705] "A report adequately discloses the existence of a potential claim for breach of trust if it provides sufficient information so that the beneficiary or representative knows of the potential claim or should have inquired into its existence." UTC §1005(b) (available at <http:// www.uniformlaws.org/Act.aspx?title=Trust%20Code>).

[706] UTC §1005(c) (available at <http://www.uniformlaws.org/Act.aspx?title=Trust%20 Code>). "If a trusteeship terminates by reason of death, a claim against the trustee's estate for breach of fiduciary duty would, like other claims against the trustee's estate, be barred by a probate creditor's claim statute even though the statutory period prescribed by this section has not yet expired." UTC §1005 cmt.

been.[707] The Uniform Trust Code would seem to be in accord. It provides that "[i]f a right is acquired, extinguished, or barred upon the expiration of a prescribed period that has commenced to run under any other statute before [the effective date of the [Code]], that statute continues to apply to the right even if it has been repealed or superseded."[708]

California. California has a three-year statute of limitations for an action by a beneficiary against a trustee for breach of trust.[709] It runs from the time the beneficiary receives a writing that adequately discloses the claim.[710]

Statutes of limitations as partial codifications of laches doctrine. Insofar as they apply to internal breaches of fiduciary duty by trustees, such statutes of limitations are really little more than partial codifications of laches doctrine.[711] Particularly in cases of unauthorized acts of trustee self-dealing, "other law" will generally determine what trustee "misdeeds" will cause them to toll,[712] as well as the level of "understanding" a beneficiary must have before they will begin to run. When fiduciary self-dealing is involved, these statutes are unlikely to begin to run against the beneficiary until the beneficiary acquires a full subjective understanding of the applicable facts and law.[713] In other words, principles of laches will still generally apply, whether actually or by analogy.[714]

Fraudulent activity. The Uniform Probate Code provides that if a trustee's fraudulent activity is used to avoid or circumvent its provisions, any beneficiary harmed thereby must commence an action for relief against the trustee within two years after the discovery of the fraud, "but no proceeding may be brought against one not a perpetrator of the fraud later than five years after the time of commission of the fraud."[715] Should trust property pass to a BFP (good-faith purchaser for value) incident to the trustee's fraudulent activity, however, the BFP will be allowed to keep the property.[716] The beneficiary then will have to look elsewhere for restitution.[717]

Former trustees. For a general discussion of time barring breach of trust actions against *former trustees*, the reader is referred to Section 7.1.2 of this handbook.

---

[707] *See, e.g.,* Newcomer v. National City Bank, 19 N.E.3d 492, 500 (Ohio 2014).

[708] UTC §1106(b) (available at <http://www.uniformlaws.org/Act.aspx?title=Trust%20 Code>).

[709] *See* Noggle v. Bank of Am., 70 Cal. App. 4th 853 (1999).

[710] Noggle v. Bank of Am., 70 Cal. App. 4th 853 (1999).

[711] *See* §8.15.70 of this handbook (laches doctrine generally).

[712] *See* UTC §1005 cmt. (available at <http://www.uniformlaws.org/Act.aspx?title=Trust %20Code>).

[713] *See generally* §7.1.2 of this handbook (defenses to allegations that the trustee breached the duty of loyalty).

[714] *See* §8.15.70 of this handbook (laches doctrine in the trust context).

[715] UPC §1-106 (effect of fraud and evasion). *See also* §8.15.63 of this handbook (the BFP).

[716] *See generally* §8.15.63 of this handbook (doctrine of bona fide purchase; the BFP).

[717] UPC §1-106 (effect of fraud and evasion).

§7.2.11 Liability of a Trustee Who Honors a Fraudulent Exercise of a Power of Appointment

The fraud on a special power doctrine is covered generally in Section 8.15.26 of this handbook. A trustee who transfers trust property to a permissible appointee for the benefit of an impermissible appointee such that the fraud on a special power doctrine is implicated incurs no liability as a consequence, unless the trustee knew or should have known of the *donee's* (powerholder's) fraud.[718] If the trustee knew or had reason to know of the donee's fraud, then the transfer would constitute a breach of trust.[719] In the case of such a breach of trust, the person entitled to the appointive assets may seek recovery from the trustee personally, as well as from the impermissible appointee who has been unjustly enriched.[720] Otherwise, the trustee would still have an obligation upon learning of the fraud "to notify the persons entitled to the appointive assets of their rights and to initiate action against the mistaken payee to recover the wrongfully dispensed assets."[721] When there is reasonable doubt as to whether there actually has been a fraud perpetrated on the special power, the trustee should petition the court for instructions and/or a declaratory judgment.[722] Powers of appointment are covered generally in Section 8.1.1 of this handbook.

§7.3 Trustee's External Liability as Legal Owner to Nonbeneficiaries (Third Parties)

Insofar as the internal administration of the trust was concerned, the beneficiaries were regarded as the owners of the trust property, but insofar as the external administration was concerned, the trustee was regarded as the property's sole owner.[1]

The traditional default law. It has been seen that the trustee, so far as concerns the outside world, is the owner of the trust property and that the duty to account to the beneficiary is primarily an internal matter.[2] It follows that in dealing with strangers the trustee is the responsible party, even though the trustee has no beneficial interest in the trust property.[3] It is traditional default

---

[718] Restatement (Third) of Property (Wills and Other Donative Transfers) §19.17(b).

[719] Restatement (Third) of Property (Wills and Other Donative Transfers) §19.17, cmt. b.

[720] Restatement (Third) of Property (Wills and Other Donative Transfers) §19.17, cmt. b; §8.15.78 of this handbook (unjust enrichment).

[721] Restatement (Third) of Property (Wills and Other Donative Transfers) §19.17, cmt. b.

[722] Restatement (Third) of Property (Wills and Other Donative Transfers) §19.17, cmt. b; §8.42 of this handbook (actions for instructions and/or declaratory judgment).

§7.3 [1] 4 Scott & Ascher §26.1.

[2] *See* §3.5.1 of this handbook (nature and extent of the trustee's estate); Portico Mgmt. Grp., LLC v. Harrison, 202 Cal. App. 4th 464 (2011) (the "trust" itself is not a person but simply a collection of assets and liabilities).

[3] *See generally* 4 Scott & Ascher §26.1 (The Trustee's Liability—In General).

law that trustees of both private and charitable trusts are personally liable on the contracts that they enter into with third parties on behalf of their trusts.[4]

Uniform Probate Code §7-306(a), now withdrawn. The Uniform Probate Code, however, would have taken the trustee off the hook with respect to a contract properly entered into in his fiduciary capacity in the course of administration of the trust estate, unless the trustee had failed "to reveal his representative capacity and identify the trust estate in the contract."[5]

Restatement (Third) of Trusts. The Restatement (Third) of Trusts, specifically Section 105, provides that "[a] third party may assert a claim against a trust for a liability incurred in trust administration by proceeding against the trustee *in the trustee's representative capacity*, whether or not the trustee is personally liable."[6] The particular liability may arise from a trustee's ownership or control of the trust property; from contracts made by the trustee; from torts committed by the trustee; or from torts committed by the trustee's agents, such as the trustee's employees.[7] Section 105 does not immunize the trustee from being sued personally, as well, or instead.[8] Suing the trustee in his representative capacity is how a third party procedurally should go about asserting a claim against "the trust" or, to be more precise, against the trust estate.[9] Under classic principles of trust law, a trust is not a juristic person.

Uniform Trust Code. Here is how the Uniform Trust Code would regulate the trustee's personal liability to third parties:

- Except as otherwise provided in the contract, a trustee is not personally liable on a contract properly entered into in the trustee's fiduciary capacity in the course of administering the trust if the trustee in the contract disclosed the fiduciary capacity.[10]
- A trustee is personally liable for torts committed in the course of administering a trust, or for obligations arising from ownership or control of trust property, including liability for violation of environment law, only if the trustee is personally at fault.[11]
- A claim based on a contract entered into by a trustee in the trustee's fiduciary capacity, on an obligation arising from ownership or control of trust property, or on a tort committed in the course of administering a trust, may be asserted in a judicial proceeding against the trustee in the

---

[4] *See generally* 5 Scott & Ascher §37.3.14.

[5] UPC §7-306(a) [revoked/withdrawn in 2010].

[6] Restatement (Third) of Trusts §105 (emphasis added).

[7] Restatement (Third) of Trusts §105, cmt. b.

[8] Restatement (Third) of Trusts §105, cmt. c.

[9] Restatement (Third) of Trusts §105, cmt. c.

[10] UTC §1010(a) (available at <http://www.uniformlaws.org/Act.aspx?title=Trust%20 Code>).

[11] UTC §1010(b) (available at <http://www.uniformlaws.org/Act.aspx?title=Trust%20 Code>).

trustee's fiduciary capacity, whether or not the trustee is personally liable for the claim.[12]

Uniform Statutory Trust Entity Act. In Section 9.6 of this handbook, we consider the common law external liabilities of trustees (and the beneficiaries in some cases) of trusts that resemble corporations or agencies. For the most part, these trusts are employed as instruments of commerce. In the case of a statutory trust created under the Uniform Statutory Trust Entity Act, legal liability in contract and/or tort *to third parties* is expressly limited to the trust assets.[13] "A beneficial owner, trustee, agent of the trust, or agent of the trustee is not personally liable, directly or indirectly, by way of contribution or otherwise, for a debt, obligation, or other liability of the trust or series thereof solely by reason of being or acting as a trustee, beneficial owner, agent of the trust, or agent of the trustee."[14] This would be the case even if the beneficiaries had the legal and equitable power and authority to control the trustee.[15] (That is not to say that the trustee of a statutory trust could not be held personally liable in equity to the trust "entity," and thus indirectly to the beneficiaries, for a breach of trust.)[16]

Uniform Voidable Transactions Act (formerly Uniform Fraudulent Transfer Act). The now-superseded Uniform Fraudulent Transfer Act (UFTA) expressly captured the deemed fraudulent transfer of the assets of a trust from the trustee to the trust beneficiary or a third party.[17] Thus, certain transfers made or obligations incurred the effect of which was to hinder, delay, or defraud, actually or constructively, creditors "of the trust" were subject to full or partial equitable avoidance, as appropriate. The Uniform Voidable Transactions Act (UVTA), on the other hand, expressly references neither the trustee nor the trust in its extensive definitional list of covered persons/entities.[18] Does the omission constitute an exclusion-by-implication of entrusted-property transfers from the Act's coverage? It is our understanding from conversations with several members of the UVTA drafting committee that the committee had assumed that such transfers would be covered by the Act.

Trustee still not an agent of "the trust." It remains ill-advised to regard the trustee as an agent of "the trust" or to assume that the trust estate or beneficiary will be primarily liable; for the most part the trustee has full and primary liability,[19] unless perhaps when the terms of the trust provide that external claims against the trustee shall be enforced directly against the trust

---

[12] UTC §1010(c) (available at <http://www.uniformlaws.org/Act.aspx?title=Trust%20 Code>).

[13] Uniform Statutory Trust Entity Act §304(a).

[14] Uniform Statutory Trust Entity Act §304(a).

[15] Uniform Statutory Trust Entity Act §304, cmt.

[16] Uniform Statutory Trust Entity Act §304, cmt. ("However, nothing in this section limits the personal liability of a trustee to the statutory trust for breach of duty under Section 505.")

[17] *See* UFTA §1(9) (including the "trust" in its list of individuals and entities qualifying as a person for purposes of the UFTA).

[18] *See* UVTA §1(10) [defining "organization] & §1(11) [defining "person"].

[19] *See generally* Restatement (Second) of Trusts §261; §3.5 of this handbook (trustee's relationship to the trust estate). In recent years, in matters of delegation and third-party claims,

estate.[20] The beneficiary ordinarily has no liability to third parties, except in the case where the trustee has been stripped of substantial control over management of the trust property and the law of the jurisdiction finds the essence of the relationship to be that of principal-agent.[21]

Trustee's right of reimbursement and exoneration. Because the trustee must bear this burden of full personal responsibility and because all gains must accrue to the trust estate, the trustee who has acted properly is given certain rights against the trust estate. These rights are equitable in nature and include the right of reimbursement and exoneration.[22] In cases where the creditor, whether in contract or in tort, finds difficulty in collecting directly from the trustee, may the trust estate be reached instead? Or should the creditor be limited, by subrogation, to whatever rights of indemnity the trustee may have? These and other such questions are considered below. However, it should be noted:

> Where a liability to third persons is imposed upon a person, not as a result of a contract made by him or a tort committed by him but because he is the holder of the title to the trust property, a trustee as holder of the title to the trust property is subject to personal liability, but only to the extent to which the trust estate is sufficient to indemnify him.[23]

Entrusted partnership interests. Under the common law, a trustee assumes unlimited personal liability if he invests trust assets in a partnership as a general partner.[24] This means that the trustee's personal liability could run to beneficiaries and nonbeneficiaries alike *as to matters involving the partnership*. It also means that to the extent the enforceable claims of nonbeneficiaries cannot be satisfied from the trust estate the trustee would be personally liable. That is why the Comptroller of the Currency may well object to a bank trustee's investing in general partnerships, unless its liability is effectively limited by the governing instrument or by state law.[25] The Uniform Trust Code would afford a trustee who holds an interest as a general partner certain contract liability and

---

the trust has begun to take on some corporate-like aspects. *See generally* Curtis, *The Transmogrification of the American Trust*, 31 Real Prop. Prob. & Tr. J. 251 (1996).

[20] *See generally* 4 Scott & Ascher §26.5.3 (When Terms of Trust Provide for Liability of Trust Estate) (the claims, however, have to be trust-related).

[21] *See* Bogert, §§247E–247F (discussing the liability of beneficiaries of certain business trusts); §9.6 of this handbook (trusts that resemble corporations or agencies).

[22] *See* Restatement (Second) of Trusts §244; §3.5.2.3 of this handbook (trustee's equitable right to exoneration or reimbursement from the trust estate).

[23] Restatement (Second) of Trusts §265.

[24] *See generally* Bogert, §679.

[25] Bogert, §679. *See also* UTC §1011(b) (available at <http://www.uniformlaws.org/Act.aspx?title=Trust%20Code>) (relieving a trustee who holds an interest as a general partner from personal liability for torts committed by the partnership or for obligations arising from ownership or control of the interest unless the trustee is personally at fault).

tort liability protections, provided he does so in a fiduciary capacity.[26] Note that if the trustee of a revocable trust holds an interest as a general partner, the settlor is personally liable for contracts and other obligations of the partnership as if the settlor were the general partner.[27]

Cross references. For a discussion of the external *inbound* liability of third parties in contract and tort to the trustee or the beneficiaries, or both, with respect to the trust estate, see Section 3.5.4.4 of this handbook. Questions of liability as between a trustee and the trust estate might be determined in the context of a proceeding for an accounting (see Section 7.2.3.1.1 of this handbook), a trustee surcharge proceeding (see Section 7.2.3.2 of this handbook), or a proceeding to seek or oppose trustee indemnification (see Section 7.2.3.7 of this handbook).[28] In Section 3.5.2.3 of this handbook, we cover the trustee's substantive rights of indemnification.

§7.3.1 Trustee's External Liability as Legal Owner in Contract to Nonbeneficiaries (Third Parties)

"Contracting with a trust fund" is, of course, an elementary legal blunder, since it is trite law that any contract is and has to be with the trustees in their personal capacity. But to the business and lay community this is an incomprehensible and hugely unrealistic pedantry. The supplier of expensive software to a charity, the broker executing million pound stock purchases for a pension fund, both look solely to the credit of the fund in question. The credit of the individuals comprising the trustee board is a matter of irrelevance, and indifference—Keith Wallace, Esq., Reed Smith LLP, London.[29]

Except as otherwise provided in the contract, a trustee is not personally liable on a contract properly entered into in the trustee's fiduciary capacity in the course of administering the trust if the trustee in the contract disclosed the fiduciary capacity—Uniform Trust Code (U.S.).[30]

At common law. At common law, when the trustee entered into a contract with a nonbeneficiary, *i.e.*, a third party, even though he did so rightfully and on behalf of the trust estate, it nevertheless was the trustee's contract and not that of the trust estate.[31] Thus, a suit at law upon the contract would be against the

---

[26] UTC §1011 (available at <http://www.uniformlaws.org/Act.aspx?title=Trust%20 Code>).

[27] UTC §1011(d) (available at <http://www.uniformlaws.org/Act.aspx?title=Trust%20 Code>).

[28] UPC §7-306(d). *See, e.g.*, Mass. Gen. Laws ch. 190B, §7-306(d).

[29] Keith Wallace, *Recourse revisited—what are the risks for trustees' counterparties?* 8 Trust Quarterly Review, Issue 1, 2010, at 5 [a STEP publication].

[30] UTC §1010(a) (available at <http://www.uniformlaws.org/Act.aspx?title=Trust%20 Code>).

[31] Bogert §712; 4 Scott & Ascher §26.2; 5 Scott & Ascher §28.1.

trustee personally; a judgment for damages issued against the trustee individually;[32] execution upon such a judgment could not issue against the trust assets.[33]
Trust assets could be reached upon execution only through subrogation[34] to
whatever equitable rights of exoneration[35] or indemnity the trustee might have
had against the trust estate.[36] This would be in a separate action in equity.[37] An
actual right of exoneration or indemnification is a personal asset of the
trustee.[38] If the trustee had acted in breach of trust or outside the scope of a
proper trust administration, exoneration or indemnity might not have been in
the cards.[39] The third party would then have had no subrogation rights against
the trust estate.[40] As we elaborate in the next paragraph, in many jurisdictions,
either by statute or on different theories of law, the trust assets now may be
reached directly,[41] unless the contract was outside the scope of proper administration.[42] In at least one jurisdiction, by statute, a contract action by a third
party against a trustee or the trust estate must be brought within two years after
the right of action accrues, instead of within the normal six-year limitation
period.[43]

As noted, the contract creditor's access to the trust estate for damages
traditionally was measured strictly by the extent of the trustee's equitable

---

[32] Bogert §712; 4 Scott & Ascher §26.2; 5 Scott & Ascher §28.1.

[33] Bogert §712; 4 Scott & Ascher §26.2; 5 Scott & Ascher §28.1.

[34] Subrogation is the legal doctrine of substituting one creditor for another. Thus, if the
trustee is a creditor of the trust by virtue of his right to be indemnified for a third-party contractual
liability, the third-party creditor under the doctrine may take the place of the trustee and seek
satisfaction directly from the trust estate up to the limit of the trustee's right of indemnity. Lewin
¶ 21-31 through ¶ 21-36 (England). *See generally* §3.5.2.3 of this handbook (trustee's equitable
right to exoneration or reimbursement from the trust estate) and §8.15.50 of this handbook (the
subrogation doctrine in the trust context).

[35] *See generally* 4 Scott & Ascher §26.5.1 (When Trustee Is Entitled to Exoneration).

[36] Bogert §716; 4 Scott & Ascher §26.2; §3.5.2.3 of this handbook (trustee's equitable right
to exoneration or reimbursement from the trust estate).

[37] *See generally* 4 Scott & Ascher §26.5 (The Power of a Creditor to Reach the Trust Property).

[38] 4 Scott & Ascher §26.5.1 (When Trustee Is Entitled to Exoneration).

[39] *See generally* §3.5.2.3 of this handbook (trustee's equitable right to exoneration or
reimbursement from the trust estate); 4 Scott & Ascher §26.5.1.1 (When Trustee Is Not Entitled to
Exoneration).

[40] *See* §8.15.50 of this handbook (subrogation rights); Keith Wallace, *Recourse revisited—what
are the risks for trustees' counterparties?* 8 Trust Quarterly Review, Issue 1, 2010, at 5 [a STEP
publication] ("The case neatly illustrates the principle that the third party's subrogation to the
trustee's own right of recourse to the fund is limited to what right of recourse the trustee possesses,
referring to the case of *Re Pumfrey, Worcester City & County Banking v. Blick*, 22 Ch 255 (1882)
[England]").

[41] *See generally* 4 Scott & Ascher §26.5 (The Power of a Creditor to Reach the Trust Property).

[42] Bogert §712; 4 Scott & Ascher §26.2. *See* Curtis, *The Transmogrification of the American Trust*,
31 Real Prop. Prob. & Tr. J. 251 (1996) (suggesting that the trend to allow direct actions against
trustees in their representative capacities diminishes "the protections afforded trust assets and has
fundamentally changed the relationship between the trustee, beneficiary, and other parties").

[43] Mass. Gen. L. Ann. ch. 260, §11 (West 1992). Note: two-year limitation period has been
held inapplicable to businesses conducted in trust form, *e.g.*, realty trusts. Hull v. Tong, 14 Mass.
App. Ct. 710, 713 (1982).

authority to act.[44] It followed that a creditor who intended to contract with the trustee was well advised to ascertain that the trustee had the authority to enter into the transaction on behalf of the trust. In the absence of such authority, the creditor could only look to the trustee's personal assets. Thus, the prudent prospective creditor called for the trust instrument and examined its provisions. Even when the trustee lacked the equitable authority to enter into a particular contract on behalf of the trust, however, the creditor could at least look to the trust estate to the extent the trust benefited from the transaction.[45] And a trustee, of course, could be compelled to specifically perform a contract that had not been made in breach of trust.[46]

The restatements. The Restatement (Second) of Trusts, which came along in 1959, advocated a less dogmatic, less procedure-driven general approach to third-party access that was grounded in general equitable principles.[47] The Restatement (Third) of Trusts has followed suit. It provides that a trustee is personally liable on a contract entered into in the course of trust administration only if, in so doing, the trustee committed a breach of trust, the trustee's representative capacity was undisclosed and unknown to the third party, *or the contract so provides.*[48] Today, the default law has evolved to the point where much of the risk is now on the trust estate rather than the creditor, *assuming the trustee's fiduciary capacity was properly disclosed when the contract was struck*[49] and assuming that the contract itself was not outside the scope of a proper trust administration:[50]

> It is when the trustee not only is insolvent but also has acted unreasonably or unfaithfully in entering into a contract that the new rules change the ultimate outcome. In such a case, the third party can now reach the trust estate directly, notwithstanding the trustee's insolvency, leaving the trust estate with no effective recourse against the insolvent trustee.[51]

The Uniform Trust Code. For how the Uniform Trust Code would regulate the trustee's personal liability to third parties, see §7.3 of this handbook.

---

[44] *See* 4 Scott & Ascher §26.2; 3A Scott on Trusts §268.2.

[45] *See* 4 Scott & Ascher §26.5.2 (When Trust Estate Has Been Benefited) ("Such relief derives from the general principle that one should not be unjustly enriched at the expense of another"); 4 Scott & Ascher §26.2 (Contractual Liability); 3A Scott on Trusts. §269.1.

[46] *See generally* 4 Scott & Ascher §26.6.1.

[47] Restatement (Second) of Trusts §271A. *See generally* 4 Scott & Ascher §26.5.5 (When Equity Requires).

[48] Restatement (Third) of Trusts §106. "[I]f the trustee's representative capacity is undisclosed and unknown to the third party, the trustee is personally liable on the contract though entitled to indemnification from the trust estate if the contract is otherwise proper." Restatement (Third) of Trusts §106 cmt. b(1). The trustee's right to exoneration and indemnification is taken up in §3.5.2.3 of this handbook.

[49] *See generally* 4 Scott & Ascher §26.2.1 (Terms of the Trust).

[50] 4 Scott & Ascher §26.2.2.

[51] 4 Scott & Ascher §26.2.

Uniform Voidable Transactions Act, formerly Uniform Fraudulent Transfer Act. As to whether the Uniform Voidable Transactions Act captures transfers of entrusted property, see §7.3 of this handbook.

The trustee's residual liabilities. Even today, however, a solvent trustee who properly enters into a contract with a third party assumes some personal risk. "Though the trustee has acted properly in making the contract, if the trustee, by breach of trust, has so diminished the trust estate that the other party is unable to obtain full satisfaction from the trust estate, the trustee is personally liable . . . [on the contract to the third party] . . . for the deficiency."[52] Internally, the trustee is in breach of his equitable fiduciary duties to the beneficiaries; externally, he has committed what amounts to a legal tort against the creditor.[53]

Uniform Statutory Trust Entity Act. In Section 9.6 of this handbook, we consider the common law external liabilities of trustees (and the beneficiaries in some cases) of trusts that resemble corporations or agencies. For the most part, these trusts are employed as instruments of commerce. In the case of a statutory trust created under the Uniform Statutory Trust Entity Act, legal liability in contract *to third parties* is expressly limited to the trust assets.[54] "A beneficial owner, trustee, agent of the trust, or agent of the trustee is not personally liable, directly or indirectly, by way of contribution or otherwise, for a debt, obligation, or other liability of the trust or series thereof solely by reason of being or acting as a trustee, beneficial owner, agent of the trust, or agent of the trustee."[55] This would be the case even if the beneficiaries had the legal and equitable power and authority to control the trustee.[56] (That is not to say that the trustee of a statutory trust could not be held personally liable in equity to the trust "entity," and thus indirectly to the beneficiaries, for a breach of trust.)[57]

Cross references. For a discussion of the *inbound* contractual liabilities of third parties to the trustee or the beneficiary, or both, see Section 3.5.4.4 of this handbook.

§7.3.2 Agreements of Trustee with Nonbeneficiaries (Third Parties) to Limit External Contractual Liability

Except as otherwise provided in the contract, a trustee is not personally liable on a contract properly entered into in the trustee's fiduciary capacity in the course of administering the trust if the trustee in the contract disclosed the fiduciary capacity.[58]

---

[52] 4 Scott & Ascher §26.2.3 (Personal Liability of Trustee to Creditor When Trustee Is Liable to Trust Estate).

[53] 4 Scott & Ascher §26.2.3 (Personal Liability of Trustee to Creditor When Trustee Is Liable to Trust Estate).

[54] Uniform Statutory Trust Entity Act §304(a).

[55] Uniform Statutory Trust Entity Act §304(a).

[56] Uniform Statutory Trust Entity Act §304, cmt.

[57] Uniform Statutory Trust Entity Act §304, cmt. ("However, nothing in this section limits the personal liability of a trustee to the statutory trust for breach of duty under Section 505.")

[58] UTC §1010(a) (available at <http://www.uniformlaws.org/Act.aspx?title=Trust%20Code>). "However, unlike the UPC [§7-306(a), now withdrawn], which requires that the contract

The trustee may contractually limit personal liability in matters involving nonbeneficiaries,[59] or have it limited to the extent of the trust estate.[60] As to a problem asset, the trustee may even be able to limit the exposure of the trust estate to the asset itself by moving the asset into a limited liability company (LLC).[61]

Thus a trustee may contract in such a way as to preclude personal liability by adding after his signature the qualification "as trustee, but not individually."[62] (With respect to negotiable instruments, a duly authorized trustee is not personally liable if he simply signs "as trustee," provided the instrument identifies the trust.)[63] Trust instruments sometimes are recorded and often contain clauses exempting the trustee from personal liability;[64] in such cases a reference to the trust in the contract may suffice to do away with the trustee's liability.[65] Any creditor who is on actual notice of the existence of such a clause should be taken to have excused the trustee[66] It will not do, however, in the present state of the law, for a trustee to rely upon a provision in the instrument of which the creditor has no notice.[67]

The Uniform Trust Code provides that a claim based on a contract entered into by a trustee in the trustee's fiduciary capacity may be asserted in a judicial

---

both disclose the representative capacity and identify the trust, subsection (a) protects a trustee who reveals the fiduciary capacity either by indicating a signature as trustee or by simply referring to the trust." UTC §1010 cmt. (noting also that subsection (a) in no way excuses any liability the trustee may have for breach of trust). Again, UPC §7-306(a) was withdrawn in 2010.

[59] 4 Scott & Ascher §26.2.1; 3A Scott on Trusts. §263.

[60] *See generally* Bogert §714; 4 Scott & Ascher §§26.5.4 (When Contract Binds Trust Estate), 26.2.1 (Terms of Trust); Lewin ¶21-48 (England). *But see* Restatement (Second) of Trusts §263 cmt. a (words "as trustee" or "as trustee for" without more until relatively recently might not have been enough to limit the trustee's contractual personal liability). *See, e.g.*, Sylvia v. Johnson, 44 Mass. App. Ct. 483, 691 N.E.2d 608 (1998) (holding beneficiaries were not personally liable on contract with third party even though beneficiaries were also trustees and controlled the trust because third party had knowledge of nonrecourse clause in trust). *See generally* §9.6 of this handbook (trusts that resemble corporations or agencies).

[61] *See generally* Suzanne L. Shier, Using LLCs to Manage Risk in the Administration of Personal Trust Special Assets, Passthrough Entities 20 (Jan.–Feb. 2000). *See also* §8.22 of this handbook (why we need the trust when we have the corporation and the third party beneficiary contract).

[62] 4 Scott & Ascher §26.2.1; Restatement (Second) of Trusts §263 cmt. a. *See* Uniform Commercial Code §3-403. *But see* Apahouser Lock & Sec. Corp. v. Carvelli, 26 Mass. App. Ct. 385, 528 N.E.2d 133 (1988) (holding trustees of a nominee trust personally liable on a purchase order on which they had disclosed their fiduciary capacities because they owned and controlled the property of the trust estate). *See generally* §9.6 of this handbook (discussing in part the nominee trust). *See also* §5.6 of this handbook (duties and liabilities of the beneficiary).

[63] *See* Uniform Commercial Code §3-403. *But see* 3A Scott on Trusts §263.1 n.2 and accompanying text.

[64] *See generally* Bogert §714. *Cf.* UTC §1010(a) (available at <http://www.uniformlaws.org/Act.aspx?title=Trust%20Code>) (Limitation on Personal Liability of Trustee).

[65] *See generally* Bogert §714. *Cf.* UTC §1010(a) (available at <http://www.uniformlaws.org/Act.aspx?title=Trust%20Code>) (Limitation on Personal Liability of Trustee).

[66] *See generally* Bogert §714. *Cf.* UTC §1010(a) (available at <http://www.uniformlaws.org/Act.aspx?title=Trust%20Code>) (Limitation on Personal Liability of Trustee).

[67] *See generally* 3A Scott on Trusts §263.2.

proceeding against the trustee in the trustee's fiduciary capacity, whether or not the trustee is personally liable for the claim.[68]

§7.3.3   Trustee's External Liability as Legal Owner in Tort to Nonbeneficiaries (Third Parties)

A trustee is personally liable for torts committed in the course of administering a trust, or for obligations arising from ownership or control of trust property, including liability for violation of environmental law, only if the trustee is personally at fault.[69]

Even if the trustee is not at fault in committing a tort, the trustee may nevertheless be precluded from indemnity if the trustee committed the tort while acting outside the scope of proper trust administration.[70]

At common law. At common law, the trustee was as responsible for the torts which he committed in the course of administering the trust estate as he would have been for those committed in the course of administering his own affairs.[71] Thus, the trustee was personally liable to nonbeneficiaries for any injury to them occasioned by a failure to keep the trust property in proper repair.[72] Moreover, under the doctrine of *respondeat superior*,[73] if servants were employed on behalf of the trust, the trustee's personal liability for their torts was determined exactly as though they were employed for the trustee's own affairs.[74] For a discussion of how the Uniform Prudent Investor Act under certain circumstances would shift personal liability from the trustee to the trustee's agents, the reader is referred to Section 6.1.4 of this handbook. This liability was personal to the trustee; execution therefore ran against the trustee irrespective of whether he had a right to indemnity from the trust fund.[75] On the other hand, successor trustees did and do not succeed to this liability[76] nor was or is a

---

[68] UTC §1010(c) (available at <http://www.uniformlaws.org/Act.aspx?title=Trust%20 Code>).

[69] UTC §1010(b) (available at <http://www.uniformlaws.org/Act.aspx?title=Trust%20 Code>). "[Subsection (b)] . . . is contrary to Restatement (Second) of Trusts §264, which imposes liability on a trustee regardless of fault, including liability for acts of agents under respondeat superior." UTC §1010 cmt. *See generally* §7.3.4.2(b) of this handbook (environmental protection).

[70] 4 Scott & Ascher §22.4.

[71] *See* 4 Scott & Ascher §§22.4, 26.3; Restatement (Second) of Trusts §264.

[72] *See* 4 Scott & Ascher §§22.4, 26.3; 3A Scott on Trusts §264. *See generally* §3.5.1 of this handbook (nature and extent of the trustee's estate).

[73] *See* Restatement of Agency 2d §§212–267; 4 Scott & Ascher §26.3 (Tort Liability).

[74] *See* 4 Scott & Ascher §§22.4 (Tort Liability), 24.30 (Liability for Acts of Agents), 26.3 (Tort Liability); Restatement (Second) of Trusts §264 cmt. b.

[75] *See generally* 4 Scott & Ascher §§22.4 (Tort Liability), 24.30 (Liability for Acts of Agents); 3A Scott on Trusts §264.

[76] *See generally* Bogert §731 n.19 and accompanying text.

trustee in bankruptcy necessarily liable for the torts of his agents.[77] A successor trustee, however, can be enjoined from using trust property in such a way as to constitute a tort to a third person, even when the particular problem began with the predecessor trustee.[78]

The right of the tort creditor to reach the trust estate had been a matter of great confusion in the cases. The principal difficulty lay in the fact that the trustee's right of exoneration or indemnity had not been clear.[79] It was reasonably settled that if the trustee was not personally at fault *and* was not negligent in the selection of his agents, he had a right to exonerate or indemnify himself from the trust estate,[80] and the tort creditor had the right in a separate action in equity to levy against the trustee's right of exoneration or indemnity.[81] If a tort had been committed while the trustee was acting beyond the scope of his duties, however, trust assets could not be reached[82] and judgment would be against the trustee personally.[83]

At common law, a third-party tort action had to be commenced against the trustee personally.[84] Any recovery was satisfied from the trustee's personal assets.[85] The trustee was then entitled *in a separate action in equity*[86] to seek indemnification from the trust estate.[87] In that action the beneficiaries would have had standing to oppose the trustee's request for indemnification if the trustee, for example, had acted beyond the scope of his authority.[88] If there were not enough in the trust estate to make the trustee whole, the trustee would have had no recourse. He would have been obliged personally to bear the loss.

At common law, if the trustee had insufficient assets to satisfy his personal obligation to the third party, the third party *in a separate action in equity*[89] would have been obliged to levy on any right of exoneration or indemnification the trustee might have had.[90] As noted above, any actual right of exoneration or

---

[77] *See generally* 3A Scott on Trusts §264. *But see* Bogart, *Liability of Directors of Chapter 11 Debtors in Possession: Don't Look Back—Something May Be Gaining on You*, 68 Am. Bankr. L.J. 155, 208–212 (1994).

[78] *See generally* 4 Scott & Ascher §26.6.2 (Injunction Against Torts).

[79] *See generally* Curtis, *The Transmogrification of the American Trust*, 31 Real Prop. Prob. & Tr. J. 251, 276–294 (1996); 4 Scott & Ascher §26.3 (Tort Liability).

[80] *See generally* 4 Scott & Ascher §§24.30 (Liability for Acts of Agents), 26.3 (Tort Liability).

[81] *See generally* 4 Scott & Ascher §§22.4, 26.3, 26.5.1; 3A Scott on Trusts §264. *But see* Bogart, *Liability of Directors of Chapter 11 Debtors in Possession: Don't Look Back—Something May Be Gaining on You*, 68 Am. Bankr. L.J. 155, 208–212 (1994).

[82] 4 Scott & Ascher §26.5.1.1 (When Trustee Is Not Entitled to Exoneration).

[83] 4 Scott & Ascher §22.4; 3A Scott on Trusts §271A.2.

[84] 4 Scott & Ascher §26.3 (Tort Liability).

[85] 4 Scott & Ascher §26.3 (Tort Liability).

[86] *See generally* 4 Scott & Ascher §26.5 (The Power of a Creditor to Reach the Trust Property).

[87] 4 Scott & Ascher §26.3 (Tort Liability).

[88] 4 Scott & Ascher §26.5.1.1 (When Trustee Is Not Entitled to Exoneration).

[89] *See generally* 4 Scott & Ascher §26.5 (The Power of a Creditor to Reach the Trust Property).

[90] *See generally* 4 Scott & Ascher §26.5.1 (When Trustee Is Entitled to Exoneration).

indemnification is a personal asset of the trustee.[91] In that equitable action, the beneficiaries, however, could have blocked the third party's efforts to reach the trust estate if the trustee otherwise would not have been entitled to exoneration or indemnification.[92] The Restatement (Second) of Trusts, which came along in 1959, advocated a less dogmatic, less procedure-driven general approach to third-party access; an approach that was grounded in general equitable principles.[93] It provided that "[a] person to whom the trustee has incurred a liability in the course of the administration of the trust may be permitted to obtain satisfaction of this claim out of the trust estate if it is equitable to permit him to do so. . . ."[94] The Restatement (Third) of Trusts has followed suit. It provides that a trustee is personally liable for a tort committed in the course of trust administration, or for an obligation arising from the trustee's ownership of or control of trust property, *only if the trustee is personally at fault.*[95] "Thus, a trustee is not personally liable for a tort committed by the trustee's agent or employee where there is no personal fault on the part of the trustee."[96] If the trustee is not personally at fault, then it is the trust estate, and only the trust estate, that can be on the hook.[97]

The Uniform Trust Code. The Uniform Trust Code, which was finalized in 2005, provides that a claim based on an obligation arising from ownership or control of trust property, or on a tort committed in the course of administering a trust, may be asserted in a judicial proceeding against the trustee in the trustee's fiduciary capacity, whether or not the trustee is personally liable for the claim.[98] In other words, the tort victim in the first instance may go directly against the trust estate.[99]

The Uniform Probate Code. Warning: The sections of the model Uniform Probate Code referenced in this paragraph and the next were withdrawn in 2010. In jurisdictions that have adopted Section 7-306(b) of the Uniform Probate Code, the trustee would be liable to nonbeneficiaries in tort "only if he is personally at fault."[100] As a procedural matter, Section 7-306(c) permits claims to be asserted against the trust estate by proceeding against the trustee in

---

[91] *See generally* 4 Scott & Ascher §26.5.1 (When Trustee Is Entitled to Exoneration).

[92] *See generally* 4 Scott & Ascher §§26.5.1 (When Trustee Is Entitled to Exoneration), 26.5.1.1 (When Trustee Is Not Entitled to Exoneration).

[93] Restatement (Second) of Trusts §271A. *See generally* 4 Scott & Ascher §26.5.5 (When Equity Requires).

[94] Restatement (Second) of Trusts §271A cmt. a.

[95] Restatement (Third) of Trusts §106 (adopted and promulgated May 18, 2011).

[96] Restatement (Third) of Trusts §106 cmt. b(2).

[97] *See* Restatement (Third) of Trusts §105 cmt. b.

[98] *See* UTC §1010(c) (available at <http://www.uniformlaws.org/Act.aspx?title=Trust%20 Code>). *See generally* 4 Scott & Ascher §26.3 (Tort Liability).

[99] *See generally* 4 Scott & Ascher §§26.3 (Tort Liability), 26.5.1 (When Trustee Is Entitled to Exoneration).

[100] *See generally* James S. Sligar, *Executor and Trustee Liability to a Third Party*, 132 Tr. & Est. 30 (Apr. 1993); Bogert §732; 4 Scott & Ascher §§22.4 (Tort Liability), 24.30 (Liability for Acts of Agents), 26.3 (Tort Liability). *See, e.g.*, Mass. Gen. Laws ch. 203, §14A.

his fiduciary capacity, whether or not the trustee is personally liable therefor.[101] The sections are intended to offer some protection to the trustee. As noted above, under the common law, a trustee though not personally at fault could be held liable for the torts of his agents.[102] He would then have a right of indemnity against the trust estate.[103] If there were not enough in the trust estate to make the trustee whole, however, he would be out of luck. The trustee is cautioned, however, that this trend of deeming for certain purposes trusts to be entities can be a double-edged sword, particularly when it comes to asserting the attorney-client privilege, a topic that is covered in Section 8.8 of this handbook.[104]

The trustee also is warned that the protections afforded trustees by Section 7-306(b) go only so far. The careful tort claimant, for example, can be expected not only to sue the trustee in his representative capacity but also to sue the trustee in his individual capacity. There need only be an allegation of "personal fault." Moreover, it is unlikely that a judgment for the nonbeneficiary plaintiff will contain no finding whatsoever of "personal fault" on the part of the trustee. Even when the wrongful acts were committed by the trustee's agents, there is the matter of their negligent selection and supervision.[105] And there is the matter of divided loyalty: When a trustee asserts the absence of "personal fault," he is calling for imposition of the economic burden of the tort on the trust estate and indirectly on the beneficiaries whose interests he is charged with protecting.[106] Because of this conflict, it is important that the beneficiaries be represented in the litigation by separate independent counsel. And again, "[e]ven if the trustee is not at fault in committing a tort, the trustee may nevertheless be precluded from indemnity if the trustee committed the tort while acting outside the scope of proper trust administration."[107] In Massachusetts, Section 7-306(a) liability protection is not available to trustees of business trusts created to develop real

---

[101] *See generally* 4 Scott & Ascher §26.3 (Tort Liability). *See e.g.*, Mass. Gen. Laws ch. 190B, §7-306(c).

[102] 4 Scott & Ascher §26.3 (Tort Liability).

[103] 4 Scott & Ascher §26.3 (Tort Liability).

[104] Again, it long has been a general principle of law and equity that the trust relationship is not a juristic entity. *See, e.g.*, Jimenez v. Corr, 764 S.E.2d 115 (Va. 2014) ("In contrast, an inter vivos trust is inseparable from the parties related to it, and the trust does not have a separate legal status.").

[105] Bogert §731; 4 Scott & Ascher §24.30 (Liability for Acts of Agents). *See generally* §6.1.4 of this handbook (discussing in part how the Uniform Prudent Investor Act allows a trustee under certain circumstances to insulate himself from the consequences of the decisions or actions of his agents).

[106] 4 Scott & Ascher §§22.4 (Tort Liability), 24.30 (Liability for Acts of Agents). In some cases, a trustee may even be entitled to be indemnified from the trust estate for liability to a third party occasioned by an intentional tort, provided the trustee's tortious conduct has bestowed some benefit on the trust estate. 4 Scott & Ascher §§22.4 (Tort Liability), 24.30 (Liability for Acts of Agents).

[107] 4 Scott & Ascher §22.4 (Tort Liability).

estate;[108] so also in Florida.[109] It should be noted that M.G.L.A. 190B §7-306 (Massachusetts) was repealed, effective July 8, 2012.[110]

Warning: Article VII of the *model* Uniform Probate Code addressed selected issues of trust administration, including trust registration, the jurisdiction of courts concerning trusts, and the duties and liabilities of trustees. Article VII of the *model* UPC was superseded by the Uniform Trust Code, approved in 2000, and was withdrawn in 2010 following the widespread enactment of the UTC.

The risk of the trustee's insolvency is shifting against the beneficiary. The risk of the trustee's insolvency is shifting inexorably from the tort victim to the trust estate in situations where the trustee is at fault.[111] "In such ... [situations] ..., the tort victim can now reach the trust estate directly, notwithstanding the trustee's insolvency, leaving the trust with no effective recourse against the insolvent trustee."[112] This is one more reason why the trustee should insure himself both as an individual and as trustee against nonbeneficiary claims in tort arising from the ownership or operation of the trust estate.[113] The expense of such insurance is a proper charge against the trust estate.[114]

Cross references. A number of federal and state statutes have been enacted into law that are designed to protect consumers and redress acts of discrimination against certain classes of individuals. The trustee who deals with nonbeneficiaries on behalf of the trust estate may be bound by the requirements of these statutes and personally subject to their sanctions. See generally Section 7.3.3.1 of this handbook (consumer protection) and Section 7.3.3.2 of this handbook (civil rights). For a discussion of the inbound liabilities of third parties in tort to the trustee or the beneficiary, or both, see Section 3.6 of this handbook.

§7.3.3.1 Consumer Protection

A substantial majority of the states have enacted, in one form or another, statutes designed to protect consumers from unfair or deceptive trade practices.[115] Most if not all of these consumer protection statutes will cover trustees who render goods and services to the public on behalf of their trusts.[116]

---

[108] First E. Bank, N.A. v. Jones, 413 Mass. 654, 602 N.E.2d 211 (1992).

[109] *See* Taylor v. Richmond's New Approach Assoc., Inc., 351 So. 2d 1094 (Fla. 1977).

[110] M.G.L.A. Chap.190B is where Massachusetts' version of the UPC, which contains a multitude of deviations from the model Code, may be found.

[111] *See generally* 4 Scott & Ascher §26.3 (Tort Liability).

[112] 4 Scott & Ascher §26.3 (Tort Liability).

[113] *See generally* 4 Scott & Ascher §26.3 (Tort Liability).

[114] Bogert §803; §3.5.2.3 of this handbook (trustee's equitable right to exoneration and reimbursement from the trust estate).

[115] *See generally* 17 Am. Jur. 2d *Consumer Protection* §280 (1990). *See also* Dunbar, Comment, *Consumer Protection: The Practical Effectiveness of State Deceptive Trade Practices Legislation*, 59 Tul. L. Rev. 427, Tab. III at 441–448 (1984) (listing and analyzing consumer protection statutes by state).

[116] *See generally* 17 Am. Jur. 2d *Consumer Protection* §285 (1990). *See, e.g.*, Vogt v. Seattle First Nat'l Bank, 117 Wash. 2d 541, 817 P.2d 1364 (1991). *Cf.* Baker Boyer Nat'l Bank v. Garver, 43

If an unincorporated automobile dealership, for example, were operated out of a trust, the trustee might be held personally liable to customers for statements by employees of the trust that the automobiles are of a particular quality when they are not, that repairs may be needed when they are not, or that there is a specific price advantage when there is not.[117]

Under some state statutes, consumers have a private right of action,[118] while under others the attorney general must bring the action on behalf of the consumers.[119] In some states both options are available.[120] Private relief usually takes the form of rescission, restitution, and consequential damages.[121] In a number of jurisdictions, customers are entitled to treble damages and the recovery of attorneys' fees.[122] If the dealership was incorporated, legal liability for damages under the statute might run in the first instance to the corporate enterprise. The trust beneficiaries, however, would have a right in equity to compel the trustee personally to make good any loss to the trust occasioned by the assessment of damages against the dealership, provided the loss could be tied to a breach of trust. In Massachusetts, however, they would not have a consumer protection cause of action.[123]

Not all consumer protection statutes cast the broad "unfair and deceptive" net. Some target specific activities such as odometer tampering, pyramid schemes, and telephone sales solicitations.[124]

§7.3.3.2 Discrimination Based on Race, Color, Religion, Sex, Age, or Disability

As a general rule, the trustee may not discriminate on the basis of race, color, religion, sex, age, or disability in transactions with nonbeneficiaries on behalf of the trust.[125] This includes discrimination not only in the sale of goods and services to the public but also in matters relating to the hiring and employment of the trust's servants.[126] There are numerous exceptions and

---

Wash. App. 673, 719 P.2d 583 (1986) (holding that trustee not liable under Consumer Protection Act because trustee's acts did not extend to a widespread pattern of deceptive practices and were unlikely to be repeated).

[117] *See* 17 Am. Jur. 2d *Consumer Protection* §297 (1990).

[118] 17 Am. Jur. 2d *Consumer Protection* §302.

[119] 17 Am. Jur. 2d *Consumer Protection* §300.

[120] 17 Am. Jur. 2d *Consumer Protection* §301.

[121] *See generally* J. Sovern, *Deceptive Trade Practices*, 52 Ohio St. L.J. 437 (1991).

[122] J. Sovem, *Deceptive Trade Practices*, 52 Ohio St. L.J. 437 n.66 (1991). Multiplying a damage award is not limited to consumer protection actions. Under Kansas' version of the UTC, for example, a trustee who embezzles or knowingly converts to the trustee's own use trust property would be liable for double the property's value. *See* Kan. Stat. Ann. §58a-1002(a)(3). *See also* McCabe v. Duran, 180 P.3d 1098 (Kan. Ct. App. 2008) (the court declining to retroactively apply the double-damages provision of Kansas' version of the UTC).

[123] Steele v. Kelley, 46 Mass. App. Ct. 712, 710 N.E.2d 973 (1999).

[124] *See generally* 17 Am. Jur. 2d *Consumer Protection* §299 (1990).

[125] *See generally* 14 C.J.S. *Civil Rights* §§43-101 (1991).

[126] 14 C.J.S. *Civil Rights* §§143-217.

exemptions, which are beyond the scope of this handbook. Persons subject to unlawful discrimination may recover compensatory damages from the trustee, and in some cases punitive damages.[127] The trustee's liability to nonbeneficiaries for intentional acts of discrimination is not indemnifiable from the trust estate.[128] If liability runs to a corporation held in the trust, the trustee may be compelled in equity to reimburse the trust estate for any resulting economic loss to the extent the loss is attributable to a breach of trust.

§7.3.3.3   Registration and Sale of Securities

Fiduciary obligations of directors ought not to be made so onerous that men of experience and ability will be deterred from accepting such office, wrote Chief Justice Arthur Prentice Rugg. Law in its sanctions is not coexistence with morality. It cannot undertake to put all parties to every contract on an equality as to knowledge, experience, skill and shrewdness. For nearly the next 30 years, insider-trading cases generally followed Goodwin v. Agassiz. In 1934, Congress passed the Securities Exchange Act, under whose anti-fraud provisions insider-trading prosecutions are now brought.[129]

The trustee may not engage in the sale of securities held in the trust—or of securities representing beneficial interests in the trust itself—unless the securities are registered under the federal Securities Act of 1933 or unless the sale falls under one or more of a number of statutory exemptions.[130] The determination of whether a particular interest constitutes a security and, if it does, whether it needs to be registered requires the specialized expertise of a securities lawyer.[131] It certainly is not a job for the layman. The trustee who sells securities representing interests held by the trust, or beneficial interests in the trust itself, in violation of the registration requirements of federal law could be held personally liable to purchasers for their investment losses.[132] There are state registration requirements as well; known collectively as Blue Sky Laws, they carry their own private rights of action.[133]

---

[127] 14 C.J.S. *Civil Rights* §§222–475.

[128] *See generally* Bogert §734.

[129] Rick Wartzman, *A 1920s Insider Trade Was Ruled by Court to Be Merely a Perk*, Wall St. J., July 3, 2002, at B1 (discussing Goodwin v. Agassiz, 283 Mass. 358, 186 N.E. 659 (1933)). *See generally* Henry G. Manne, *The Case for Insider Trading*, Wall St. J., Mar. 17, 2003, at A14 (suggesting that insider-trading proscriptions lack social utility and economic sense).

[130] *See generally* American Bar Association, A Fiduciary's Guide to Federal Securities Laws 5–59 (1994). A bank administering a collective investment fund may not issue any certificate or other document representing a direct or indirect interest in the fund, except to provide a withdrawing account with an interest in a segregated investment. 12 C.F.R. §9.18(b)(11) (1997) (available at <www.gpoaccess.gov/cfr/index.html>).

[131] *See generally* Harvey Bines & Steve Thel, *Investment Management Arrangements and the Federal Securities Laws*, 58 Ohio St. L.J. 459 (1997).

[132] *See generally* American Bar Association, A Fiduciary's Guide to Federal Securities Laws (1994).

[133] *See generally* Bogert §247R.

Most states have modeled their blue sky laws after the Uniform Securities Act.[134] The Act imposes registration requirements on securities, broker-dealers, sales representatives, and investment advisors. These requirements tend to track federal law. Many state blue sky regimes, small and private, offer exemptions similar to federal Regulation D.[135] The Uniform Securities Act provides copious antifraud provisions that carry criminal and civil penalties.

The National Securities Market Improvement Act of 1996 has preempted some blue sky laws.[136] Notably, certain "federally covered securities" no longer need be registered with the states. The filing of a notice may be sufficient.[137] Also, investment advisor supervision is now shared between the SEC and the states.[138]

Even as to the states that have adopted the Uniform Securities Act, blue sky case laws, regulations, and practices can differ from state to state.[139]

The trustee also could incur personal civil liability to nonbeneficiaries for the unlawful insider trading of securities held in the trust estate.[140] This is the case even when the trustee acts solely in the interests of the beneficiaries, that is, when the trustee in no way profits personally. *Insider trading* is trading in the securities markets while in possession of nonpublic information that would be important to a reasonable investor in making a decision to buy or sell a security. Section 10(b) of the Securities Exchange Act of 1934 and Rule 10(b)(5) provide the legal framework for private rights of action in the insider-trading context:

> In 1934 Congress refused an early draft of the Securities and Exchange Act that contained a provision outlawing insider trading, perhaps because it would have covered members of Congress. But in 1961 the SEC, not to be denied, invented a new theory to force insiders either to "disclose or abstain from trading." In 1968 this unorthodox bit of lawmaking received judicial sanction, and subsequently Congress itself recognized *fait accompli* in what the SEC had ordained.[141]

The trustee must make the trust whole for any losses to it occasioned by running afoul of the securities laws; and of course the trustee, not the trust, must

---

[134] The Uniform Securities Act of 1985, with 1988 amendments, has been adopted by nine states. The Uniform Securities Act of 1956 (as amended in 1958) has been adopted in 35 states. *See generally* Blue Sky Law Reporter (CCH); Fein, Securities Activities of Banks §2.03[B][2].

[135] *See also* John C. Williams, J. D., Annot., *What constitutes public or private offering within meaning of state securities regulation*, 84 A.L.R.3d 1009 (Supp. 1998).

[136] Pub. L. No. 104-290 (1996).

[137] Blue Sky Law Reporter (CCH).

[138] Harold S. Bloomenthal et al., Securities Law Series, Securities Law Hand Book (2002 ed).

[139] Gary M. Brown et al., Nuts and Bolts of Securities Law, at 25 (1998).

[140] *See generally* 14 C.J.S. *Civil Rights* §§43–101 (1991). *See also* M.P. Malloy, *Can 10b-5 for the Banks? The Effect of an Antifraud Rule on the Regulation of Banks*, 61 Fordham L. Rev. S23 (1993); Allan Horwich, *Bank Fiduciaries with Material Inside Information, Responsibilities and Risks*, 113 Banking L.J. 4 (1996).

[141] Henry G. Manne, *The Case for Insider Trading*, Wall St. J., Mar. 17, 2003, at A14.

bear the burden of attorneys' fees and other litigation costs that are a conse-quence of the illegal activities.[142]

§7.3.4 External Liability as Titleholder Arising Other Than in Contract or Tort; Unauthorized Practice of Law by Trustee; Tax Liabilities Occasioned by Trustee's Death; Trustee's External Liability to Third Parties Who Possess Some Interest in the Underlying Trust Property

Where the liability arises out of the ownership of the trust property the third person is entitled not only to reach the trust estate through the trustee's right of indemnity, but also to reach the trust estate directly in an action brought against the trustee as such. He can reach the trust estate even though the trustee by reason of some breach of trust is indebted to the trust estate and is thereby precluded from asserting a right to indemnity. In such a case the third person is entitled not only to reach the trust estate but to reach the claim against the trustee for breach of trust.[143]

The trustee as holder of the legal title has certain duties and obligations that run to third parties, including the city, the state, and the United States.[144] It is in the areas of taxation, securities regulation, and environmental protection discussed below that most of the title-holder-per se-liability landmines have been strewn. But there are *per se* liability landmines strewn elsewhere as well: a shareholder call or assessment,[145] an unruly entrusted dog or other animal; a covenant to pay rent with respect to an entrusted leasehold; or a dangerous fence on a entrusted premises come to mind.[146]

As a general rule, "[w]here a liability to third persons is imposed upon a person, not as a result of a contract made by him or a tort committed by him but because he is the holder of the title to property, a trustee as holder of the title to the trust property is subject to personal liability, but only to the extent to which the trust estate is sufficient to indemnify him."[147] This was not always the case.[148] On the other hand, the trustee is not entitled to indemnity if the behavior that generated the external liability constitutes an internal breach of trust, *e.g.*, if the trustee negligently and unnecessarily failed to pay a tax

---

[142] *See* Bogert §801 n.15 and accompanying text.
[143] Restatement (Second) of Trusts §265 cmt. d.
[144] 4 Scott & Ascher §26.4 (Liability as Owner of Trust Property).
[145] *See generally* 4 Scott & Ascher §26.4.2; §7.3.4.1 of this handbook.
[146] *See generally* 4 Scott & Ascher §26.4.4.
[147] Restatement (Second) of Trusts §265. *See generally* 4 Scott & Ascher §§22.5 (Liability as Title Holder), 26.4 (Liability as Owner of Trust Property). In England, on the other hand, the beneficiary in some cases may be personally bound to indemnify the trustee to the extent there are insufficient assets in the trust estate to do so. 4 Scott & Ascher §22.6 (Indemnity from Beneficiaries).
[148] *See generally* 4 Scott & Ascher §26.4.5 (When Trust Estate Is Insufficient to Indemnify Trustee).

obligation of the trust such that a penalty is assessed. The penalty then is the trustee's personal obligation for which he is not entitled to be indemnified from the trust estate.[149]

§7.3.4.1   Liability for Taxes; Liability for Shareholder Calls and Assessments

When a tax is owed on account of ownership of property, it is usually the case that the applicable statute imposes a duty on someone to pay the tax.[150] (The other alternative is for the taxing statute to bestow on some governmental agency the authority to impose a lien on the subject property, and to sell the property in the event the tax is not paid.)[151] In the case of a trust in which the beneficiary controls the trustee, *e.g.*, a nominee trust,[152] the obligation to pay the tax may well fall on the beneficiary.[153] Generally, however, it is the trustee who has the obligation, an obligation that is coupled with an equitable right of exoneration or indemnity from the trust estate.[154]

It was once the case that the trustee of entrusted stock was personally liable for any calls or assessments with respect to that stock.[155] As with tax obligations, this was an obligation that was coupled with an equitable right of exoneration or indemnity from the trust estate.[156] "In any event, there is now widespread statutory authority for the proposition that a trustee is ordinarily liable for calls and assessments in a representative capacity only, and not personally."[157]

Property taxes. In the absence of statute, the trustee as legal owner would be personally liable for any taxes owed on tangible, intangible,[158] and real property held in the trust.[159] In most cases, however, the trustee, as legal owner, is relieved by statute of personal liability either through the imposition of such liability on the beneficiary or on the property itself.[160] Consequently, as a practical matter, most property tax obligations are now directly imposed by statute on the trust estate.[161] Even if the trustee could not resort to a statute

---

[149] *See generally* 4 Scott & Ascher §22.5 (Liability as Title Holder).

[150] *See generally* 4 Scott & Ascher §26.4.1 (Taxes).

[151] *See generally* 4 Scott & Ascher §26.4.1 (Taxes).

[152] *See generally* §9.6 of this handbook (trusts that resemble corporations or agencies).

[153] *See generally* 4 Scott & Ascher §26.4.1 (Taxes).

[154] *See generally* §3.5.2.3 of this handbook (right in equity to exoneration and reimbursement, i.e., indemnity); *See generally* 4 Scott & Ascher §26.4.1 (Taxes).

[155] *See generally* 4 Scott & Ascher §26.4.2 (Assessments on Shareholders).

[156] *See generally* §3.5.2.3 of this handbook (trustee's equitable right to exoneration or reimbursement from the trust estate); 4 Scott & Ascher §26.4.2 (Assessments on Shareholders).

[157] 4 Scott & Ascher §26.4.2 n.5.

[158] *See generally* Property tax: business situs of intangibles held in trust in state other than beneficiary's domicile, 59 A.L.R.3d 837; 4 Scott & Ascher §26.4.1 (Taxes).

[159] *See generally* 3A Scott on Trusts §265.

[160] 3A Scott on Trusts §265.1; 4 Scott & Ascher §26.4.1 n.4.

[161] 3A Scott on Trusts §265.1; 4 Scott & Ascher §26.4.1

relieving him of personal liability for property taxes, he would have an equitable right to reimbursement from the trust estate.[162]

Federal income taxes.[163] Unless we have a grantor trust,[164] "[t]he trust's . . . income tax return (Form 1041) is filed and the tax paid by the . . . [trustee] . . . , but the taxpayer primarily liable for the tax is the . . . trust."[165] The trustee, however, may have secondary liability for any tax obligations that remain unsatisfied due to the unlawful disposition of trust assets.[166]

The trustee also may be responsible for making timely estimated tax payments. The failure to do so may cause the trustee to be internally liable to the beneficiaries for any injury to the trust occasioned thereby. The income taxation of business trusts is covered in Section 10.7 of this handbook.

Estate taxation. "Although the Code does not specifically impose personal liability upon the executor with respect to the estate tax, §2002 does provide that the executor shall pay the estate taxes."[167] What if no personal representative has been appointed? What if all the settlor's property, for example, has been transferred inter vivos to the trustee of a revocable trust so that there is no probate estate? In that case, the Internal Revenue Code places the responsibility for preparing and filing the federal estate tax return on the trustee.[168] The Internal Revenue Code also imposes secondary personal liability on the trustee for the estate tax:

> If the estate tax imposed by chapter 11 is not paid when due, then the spouse, transferee, trustee (except the trustee of an employees' trust which meets the requirements of section 401(a)), surviving tenant, person in possession of the property by reason of the exercise, nonexercise, or release of a power of appointment, or beneficiary, who receives, or has on the date of the decedent's death, property included in the gross estate under sections 2034 or 2042, inclusive, to the

---

[162] *See generally* Bogert §807; Restatement (Second) of Trusts §265 cmt. b; §3.5.2.3 of this handbook (trustee's equitable right to exoneration or reimbursement from the trust estate).

[163] *See generally* Chapter 10 of this handbook (the income taxation of trusts).

[164] *See generally* Zaritsky, 858 T.M., Grantor Trusts: Sections 671–679. *See also* §9.1 of this handbook (the grantor trust).

[165] *See generally* Jeffrey G. Sherman, *All You Really Need to Know About Sub-chapter J You Learned from this Article*, 63 Mo. L. Rev. 1, 7 (1998). *See also* J. R. Kemper, Annot., *Liability of executor, administrator, trustee, or his counsel, for interest, penalty, or extra taxes assessed against estate because of tax law violations*, 47 A.L.R.3d 507 (1973) (collecting cases in which courts have considered whether to hold the trustee personally liable for taxes assessed against the trust).

[166] *See generally* Norman M. Lane & Howard M. Zaritsky, Federal Income Taxation of Estates and Trusts ¶ 16.04[10] (3rd ed. 2000); Zaritsky, 854-2nd T.M., U.S. Taxation of Foreign Estates, Trusts and Beneficiaries A-133. *See, e.g.*, Want v. Comm'r, 280 F.2d 777 (2d Cir. 1960) (addressing requirement of knowledge of tax obligation). For a discussion of the various income tax elections a trustee may be called upon to make, *see* 855 T.M., Estate and Trust Administration—Tax Planning. The many civil penalties that may be imposed for various tax offenses are covered in 634 T.M., Civil Tax Penalties. For a discussion of the liability of a foreign fiduciary for U.S. income taxes, *see* 854 T.M., U.S. Taxation of Foreign Estates, Trusts and Beneficiaries.

[167] Blum, 219 T.M., Estate Tax Payments and Liabilities A-45.

[168] I.R.C. §2203. *See generally* §8.16 of this handbook (the trustee of revocable trust as "inadvertent executor").

extent of the value, at the time of the decedent's death, of such property, shall be personally liable for such tax.[169]

A trustee may be called upon to make various estate tax elections.[170] If the trustee's breach of a fiduciary duty causes a nonrecoverable overpayment of estate taxes or the assessment of penalties and interest to be assessed against the trust, the trustee may be held personally liable to the beneficiaries for his failing to protect the trust property. In making tax elections, the trustee should be attentive to his duty of impartiality.[171]

Generation-skipping taxes. The trustee is responsible for filing the generation-skipping tax return and seeing to it that the tax is paid from trust assets in the following situations: taxable terminations and direct skips from trusts.[172] The personal representative is responsible for a "direct skip at death" filing and seeing to it that the tax obligation is satisfied from estate assets.[173] Recipients are responsible for "taxable distribution" filings.[174]

Shareholder calls and assessments. The shareholder of a corporation may have paid less to the corporation for a share of its stock than the stock's par value.[175] This could subject the shareholder to a personal obligation to pay into the corporation the difference.[176] A direction to pay the difference is known as a "call."[177] Also, should the corporation fail, the shareholder could be "assessed" an amount equal to the stock's par value.[178] "Where by statute the registered owners of shares of stock are subject to liability for an assessment, if shares are registered in the name of a person as trustee, he is liable only to the extent to which the trust estate is sufficient to indemnify him."[179] The trustee would likely be personally liable, however, if the shares were registered in his individual name without disclosing the fact that he is a trustee.[180]

§7.3.4.2 Criminal and Civil Liability

It has always been the case that the trustee may be held criminally liable for misappropriation of the trust funds.[181] In recent years, however, we have seen a

---

[169] I.R.C. §6324.

[170] For a discussion of the various estate tax elections a trustee may be called upon to make, *see* 822 T.M., Estate and Gift Tax Returns and Audits, and Frayda L. Bruton, *Post Mortem Trust Administration Checklist*, 25 ACTEC Notes 331 (2000).

[171] *See generally* §6.2.5 of this handbook (trustee's duty of impartiality to the beneficiaries).

[172] 850 T.M., Generation-Skipping Tax.

[173] 850 T.M., Generation-Skipping Tax.

[174] 850 T.M., Generation-Skipping Tax.

[175] 4 Scott & Ascher §26.4.2.

[176] 4 Scott & Ascher §26.4.2.

[177] 4 Scott & Ascher §26.4.2.

[178] 4 Scott & Ascher §26.4.2.

[179] Restatement (Second) of Trusts §265 cmt. c; 4 Scott & Ascher §26.4.2 n.5.

[180] Restatement (Second) of Trusts §265 cmt. c; 4 Scott & Ascher §26.4.2.

[181] *See generally* 2A Scott on Trusts §179.1 (Intentional Misappropriation Constitutes the Crime of Embezzlement).

proliferation of statutes designed to regulate the advertising and sale of products and services to the public. These statutes have broadened substantially the trustee's opportunity to incur criminal liability in the course of administering a trust. Civil liability traps for the unwary trustee are being set as a result of the ongoing movement to codify large swathes of the law of trusts. In this regard we particularly have in mind the Uniform Probate Code's trust registration requirement.

(a) **Securities laws.** The trustee as holder of the title to the trust portfolio has ample opportunity to run afoul of the criminal laws pertaining to the issuance, acquisition, and transfer of securities. Accordingly, the trustee should have near at hand a copy of A Fiduciary's Guide to Federal Securities Laws.[182]

1. *Insider Trading (SEC).* The trustee may be held criminally liable for insider trading in violation of the federal securities laws even in those cases where the trustee does not profit personally.[183] Conviction can result in substantial fines being levied against the trustee—and this would include the corporate trustee and its officers, directors, and supervisory personnel. In addition, conviction can bring long jail terms. The key, however, is that the information must be nonpublic. The trustee may—and has a duty to—use public information in furtherance of the interests of the trust.

2. *Securities Registration.* The trustee who transfers unregistered or restricted securities held in the trust in violation of the securities laws may be criminally liable.[184] Moreover a transferable share of beneficial interest in the trust itself may be a "security" subject to regulation.[185] If the trustee proposes to sell restricted securities or control securities, the trustee or the trust itself could be deemed a statutory underwriter. "If so, the sale must be made pursuant to an effective registration statement or the ... [trustee] ... must determine that some exemption from registration other than section 4(1) ... [of the Securities Act] ... is

---

[182] *See generally* Audrey C. Talley, *Family Offices: Securities and Commodities Law Issues,* 34 ACTEC L.J. 284 (2009); American Bar Association, A Fiduciary's Guide to Federal Securities Laws (1994) (hereinafter "the Guide"); Melanie L. Fein, Securities Activities of Banks §11 (2d Supp. 1998).

[183] *See generally* Audrey C. Talley, Family Offices: Securities and Commodities Law Issues, 34 ACTEC L.J. 284 (2009); American Bar Association, A Fiduciary's Guide to Federal Securities Laws (1994) (hereinafter "the Guide"); Melanie L. Fein, Securities Activities of Banks §11 (2d Supp. 1998).

[184] *See generally* Audrey C. Talley, Family Offices: Securities and Commodities Law Issues, 34 ACTEC L.J. 284 (2009); American Bar Association, A Fiduciary's Guide to Federal Securities Laws (1994) (hereinafter "the Guide"); Melanie L. Fein, Securities Activities of Banks §11 (2d Supp. 1998).

[185] *See* Bogert §247R (Registration of Beneficial Interests Under State Securities Laws).

available."[186] More often than not, registration can be avoided if the sale meets the requirements of SEC Rule 144.

3. *Ownership Disclosure.* When a trust acquires more than 5 percent of a class of registered securities, the trustee may be required to file certain disclosure forms with the Securities and Exchange Commission and with the Exchanges.[187] Determining who is and what securities are subject to these disclosure obligations is a complicated matter. It is a topic that falls beyond the scope of this handbook and beyond the ken of most trust attorneys as well. However, because the cost of noncompliance could be criminal sanctions, the trustee should consult a qualified securities lawyer if there is reason to believe that a holding is approaching (or has exceeded) the 5 percent point.

4. *40 Act Registration.* The Investment Advisers Act of 1940 may require the trustee, himself, to register with the Securities and Exchange Commission, file annual reports with the Commission, and conduct his business in certain specified ways. This matter is covered in Section 8.15.10 of this handbook.

5. *33 Act Limited Offering Exemption for Trusts: Regulation D [Rule 501(a)(7)].* When is a trustee qualified under the federal securities laws to purchase on behalf of his trust securities exempt from the registration requirements of section 5 of the Securities Act of 1933? Answer: When he is the trustee of a trust "with total assets in excess of $5,000,000, not formed for the specific purpose of acquiring the securities offered, whose purchase is directed by a sophisticated person as described in §230.506(b)(2)(ii)."

(b) Environmental protection. As holder of the title to the trust property, the trustee is likely to face criminal sanctions if he intentionally or negligently, in the course of his administration, violates environmental statutes.[188] In addition to a number of major federal environmental statutes on the books, each state as well has its own set of environmental laws, as does England.[189]

While most environmental statutes require intent or negligence on the part of the trustee, under the federal Comprehensive Environmental Response, Compensation, and Liability Act (CERCLA), as initially enacted,[190] an innocent trustee's liability as the "owner" for the clean-up of hazardous waste on or within

---

[186] American Bar Association, A Fiduciary's Guide to Federal Securities Laws 8 (1994). *See also* Audrey C. Talley, *Family Offices: Securities and Commodities Law Issues*, 34 ACTEC L.J. 284 (2009). *See generally* §6.3.2 of this handbook (SEC filings).

[187] *See generally* American Bar Association, A Fiduciary's Guide to Federal Securities Laws (1994).

[188] 4 Scott & Ascher §26.4.3 (Environmental Cleanup Costs). *See, e.g.,* California v. Campbell, 138 F.3d 772, 782 (9th Cir. 1998).

[189] 4 Scott & Ascher §26.4.3 n.4 (U.S.); Lewin ¶21-10 (England).

[190] 42 U.S.C. §9601 et seq. (1983). *See generally* 4 Scott & Ascher §26.4.3 (Environmental Cleanup Costs).

the trust property may not have been limited by the trust's ability to indemnify the trustee *except when the property [was] contaminated at the time of acquisition and the trustee [undertook] promptly to correct the situation or when the trustee [had] no control over the use of the trust property*—at least one federal district court had so held.[191] In other words, the trustee under certain circumstances may well have been held strictly (and personally) liable as titleholder for the full clean-up costs even if those costs *exceeded* the value of the trust estate.

In September 1996, CERCLA was amended to relieve a trustee of personal liability for the release or threatened release of a hazardous substance merely because the trustee held the legal title.[192] The amendment shifted the risk of CERCLA liability from the trustee personally to the trust estate itself, except for environmental injury resulting from the trustee's intentional or negligent acts.[193] The amendment is effective for any claim against a trustee that had not been finally adjudicated as of September 30, 1996.

Because the amendment does nothing to alleviate the trust estate itself from the economic risk of CERCLA remedies and because the trustee would still be personally liable for negligent and intentional violations of CERCLA, it will still behoove the prudent prospective trustee to commission an exhaustive and comprehensive environmental inspection of land comprising the trust estate before deciding whether to accept its trusteeship.

A trustee of clean real estate will not want to infect a trust with contaminated real estate, nor will a trustee of contaminated real estate want to accept additions of clean real estate. Liability might well attach to a trustee who negligently failed to disclaim the clean property, or otherwise insulate it from having to contribute to the costs of bringing the contaminated property into conformance with environmental laws. Finally, the amendment does nothing to change environmental laws that may be on the books in the state in which the land is located.[194] The Uniform Trust Code, however, purports to do just that.

To encourage trustees to accept and administer trusts containing real property, the Uniform Trust Code contains several provisions designed to limit a trustee's exposure under state law to possible liability for violation of environmental law.[195] The Uniform Trust Code would enable a nominated trustee to

---

[191] *See* City of Phoenix, Ariz. v. Garbage Servs. Co., 827 F. Supp. 600 (D. Ariz. 1993). *See generally* Graham & Lindquist, *The Application of CERCLA and Other Strict Liability Environmental Statutes to Fiduciary Relationships—Putting City of Phoenix in Context*, 29 Real Prop. Prob. & Tr. J. 1 (1994). *See generally* 4 Scott & Ascher §26.4.3 (Environmental Cleanup Costs).

[192] 42 U.S.C. §9607(n). *See generally* 4 Scott & Ascher §26.4.3 (Environmental Cleanup Costs).

[193] 42 U.S.C. §9607(n)(2) and (3). *See generally* 4 Scott & Ascher §26.4.3 (Environmental Cleanup Costs).

[194] *See generally* 4 Scott & Ascher §26.4.3 (Environmental Cleanup Costs).

[195] UTC §103 cmt. (available at <http://www.uniformlaws.org/Act.aspx?title=Trust%20Code>). *See generally* 4 Scott & Ascher §26.4.3 (Environmental Cleanup Costs).

investigate trust property to determine potential liability for violation of environmental law or other law without accepting the trusteeship.[196] The prospective trustee, however, needs to do so in a way that does not constitute a constructive acceptance of the trust. At minimum, the current trustee and/or the current beneficiaries should be informed in writing that a preacceptance investigation is to be undertaken, not a postacceptance exercise of fiduciary powers or performance of fiduciary duties.

A trustee also is granted comprehensive and detailed powers to deal with property involving environmental risks.[197] Finally, the trustee is immunized under state law from personal liability for violation of environmental law arising from the ownership and control of trust property.[198]

Under the Uniform Probate Code, a trustee would be personally liable for obligations arising from ownership or control of property of the trust estate only if he is "personally at fault."[199]

(c) **Unauthorized practice of law by trustee; civil liability of trustee for rendering faulty legal advice.** The nonlawyer trustee, whether a corporation or an individual, should leave the drafting of the trust instrument to the settlor's lawyer.[200] To be sure, practicing law without a license is a crime in some jurisdictions.[201] At the very least the trustee risks losing the right to be compensated for his services *as trustee*.[202] But what is perhaps of greater practical concern is that the nonlawyer trustee (be it an individual or an institution like a bank) will be held to the standard of a competent trust lawyer in any *civil* action brought for negligent drafting.[203] Unlike the licensed attorney, however, the nonlawyer trustee will have no legal malpractice insurance to fall back on.

When the settlor is not represented by an attorney, the trustee may have a "duty of vigilance" to advise the settlor to retain one for purposes of determining whether the governing instrument or prospective instrument accurately

---

[196] UTC §701(c)(2) (available at <http://www.uniformlaws.org/Act.aspx?title=Trust%20 Code>).

[197] UTC §816(13) (available at <http://www.uniformlaws.org/Act.aspx?title=Trust%20 Code>). *See generally* 4 Scott & Ascher §26.4.3 (Environmental Cleanup Costs).

[198] UTC §1010(b) (available at <http://www.uniformlaws.org/Act.aspx?title=Trust%20 Code>). *See generally* 4 Scott & Ascher §26.4.3 (Environmental Cleanup Costs).

[199] UPC §7-306(b). *See generally* 4 Scott & Ascher §26.4.3 (Environmental Cleanup Costs).

[200] *See generally* Bogert §136 nn.7–10 and accompanying text.

[201] *See* Powell, *The Problem of the Parachuting Practitioner*, 1992 U. Ill. L. Rev. 105, 123–124 nn.97–98 and accompanying text (listing state unauthorized practice of law statutes with respective enforcement systems). *See, e.g.*, Akron Bar Ass'n v. Miller, 684 N.E.2d 288 (Ohio 1997); Trumbull County Bar Ass'n v. Hanna, 684 N.E.2d 329 (Ohio 1997) (enjoining the marketing of standardized living trust documentation).

[202] *Cf.* Franklin v. Chavis, 371 S.C. 527, 640 S.E.2d 873 (S.C. 2007) (nonlawyer scrivener of will that designated scrivener as personal representative not entitled to be compensated for his services *as personal representative*).

[203] Harper, James & Gray, 3 The Law of Torts §16.6 (1986).

reflects the settlor's intent and is legally effective.[204] One court has criticized the corporate trustee of a revocable trust for failing to "warn" the settlor that the trust document's "easily identifiable impediments or pitfalls" would lead to a frustration of her expressed donative intent and that a properly drawn amendment would be needed to rectify the situation.[205]

Even when there is counsel in the picture, the nonlawyer trustee who renders faulty legal or quasi-legal advice to the settlor runs the risk of committing "professional malpractice." One court has held a corporate trustee of an irrevocable trust with defective Crummey provisions liable in tort for negligently advising the settlor to continue making Crummey contributions to the trust.[206] The settlor at the time the trust instrument was drafted and thereafter was represented by independent counsel, who also happened to have been the scrivener. Before rendering the advice, the trustee had become aware of the defects and had been in communication with the settlor's counsel about them. Damages were apportioned: The corporate trustee was found 60 percent liable, while counsel was found 40 percent liable.

And then there is the matter of fiduciary exculpation. By the time the trust instrument is executed, the relationship between a prospective corporate trustee and a prospective settlor may well have developed into a confidential one.[207] "When a corporate officer drafts the trust instrument, even in a state in which this is permissible, there is such a relationship between the parties, even prior to the creation of the trust, that inclusion of a provision relieving the trustee of liability for breach of trust is ineffective unless the settlor fully understood the nature of the provision and freely agreed to it."[208]

(d) Failure to file a UPC §7-101 registration with court. Section 7-101 of the Uniform Probate Code would require the trustee of a testamentary or inter vivos trust, even the trustee of a trust declaration or oral trust, to register the trust in an appropriate court at the trust's principal place of administration. A trustee who failed to do so would risk being surcharged by the court.[209] In 2008, Massachusetts adopted a gutted version of Section 7-101 that imposed no such registration obligation on trustees.[210]

---

[204] *See* Wisconsin Acad. of Sci., Arts and Letters v. First Wis. Nat'l Bank of Madison, 142 Wis. 2d 750, 419 N.W.2d 301 (1987).

[205] *See* Wisconsin Acad. of Sci., Arts and Letters v. First Wis. Nat'l Bank of Madison, 142 Wis. 2d 750, 419 N.W.2d 301 (1987).

[206] *See* Hatleberg v. Norwest Bank Wis., 283 Wis. 2d 234, 700 N.W.2d 15 (2005).

[207] *See generally* 4 Scott & Ascher §24.27.4 (Exculpatory Provision Improperly Inserted). *See also* Chapter 1 of this handbook (in which a confidential relationship is defined).

[208] 4 Scott & Ascher §24.27.4 (Exculpatory Provision Improperly Inserted).

[209] UPC §7-104.

[210] Mass. Gen. Laws ch. 190B, §7-101.

§7.3.4.3   When Death of a Trustee Who Possessed No Beneficial Interest in the Trust Will Subject the Trust Property to Federal Estate Tax Liability

The personal obligations to private third parties of a trustee *who possesses no beneficial interest* in the trust property may not be satisfied out of that property even though title was in the trustee.[211] Neither his spouse nor his creditors may reach the trust property.[212] Generally, the trust property is unaffected by his death as well: In the absence of language in the governing instrument addressing the matter of trustee succession, the court will appoint his successor.[213] With an important exception, the death of a trustee who possessed no beneficial interest in the trust property also will not subject the trust property to federal estate transfer tax liability. The exception: the death of a trustee *who possessed no beneficial interest* in the trust can trigger federal estate tax liability if:

- The trustee was the settlor;[214]
- The trustee *in his fiduciary capacity*, either alone or with any other person,[215] possessed at death[216] the power to change enjoyment of the beneficial interest by altering, amending, revoking, or terminating the trust *in favor of someone other than the trustee*;[217] and
- The power was not limited by an ascertainable standard.[218]

This exception comes about because of Section 2038(a) of the Internal Revenue Code. Take the discretionary trust. Even if a settlor-trustee has untrammeled discretion to apply income and/or invade principal for the benefit of a class *limited to persons other than himself or his creditors*, at his death the then value

---

[211] *See generally* §8.3.1 of this handbook (the trustee's personal creditors and the trustee's spouse).

[212] *See generally* §8.3.1 of this handbook (the trustee's personal creditors and the trustee's spouse).

[213] *See generally* §3.4.4.3 of this handbook ("It is an equitable maxim that a trust shall not fail for want of a trustee.").

[214] *See* I.R.C. §2038(a).

[215] *See generally* Helvering v. City Bank Farmers Trust Co., 296 U.S. 85 (1935) (holding that any other person includes adverse parties, *e.g.*, beneficiaries).

[216] There also would be includibility under I.R.C. §2038(a) if the settlor-trustee's power to alter, amend, revoke, or terminate is relinquished during the three-year period ending on the date of his death. This three-year rule is expressly addressed in I.R.C. §2038(a).

[217] If the settlor-trustee had reserved the right to make discretionary distributions to himself, his lifetime creditors likely would have had access to the trust property. *See generally* §5.3.3.1 of this handbook (reaching settlor's reserved beneficial interest). This lifetime creditor accessibility would have caused the trust property to be subject to the federal estate tax at the settlor's death under I.R.C. §2041(a)(2), which deals with general powers of appointment in the federal estate tax context. *See generally* §4.1.3 of this handbook (creditor accessibility as a general inter vivos power of appointment). *See also* Round v. Comm'r, 332 F.2d 590 (1st Cir. Mass. 1964) (holding that though a decedent was unable because of a legal or factual constraint to exercise the power, trust property was still subject to the estate tax).

[218] *See generally* Jennings v. Smith, 161 F.2d 74 (2d Cir. 1947).

of the trust property must still be reflected on the trustee's own "personal" federal estate tax return. This is because the transfer tax liability triggered by his death results from the power he possessed predeath to change the enjoyment of the beneficial interest in the property that he predeath had made subject to a trust. There is inclusion even in the case where the trustee had no biological and economic relationship with the permissible beneficiaries and even though the power is exercisable only in his fiduciary capacity.

On the other hand, if the trustee's exercise of discretion had been limited by an ascertainable standard, there would be no such inclusion. While the law is somewhat fuzzy on what does or does not constitute an ascertainable standard, "health," "maintenance," "support," and "education" are generally considered well within the "ascertainable" category.[219]

Note also that if Section 2038(a) of the Code is implicated because the trustee's discretion is not limited by an ascertainable standard, distributions of income and/or principal to permissible beneficiaries may be deemed gifts *from the settlor-trustee* for federal gift tax purposes.[220]

§7.3.4.4   Trustee's External Liability to Third Party Who Possesses Some Interest in the Underlying Trust Property

A third party who possesses some interest in the underlying trust property may not maintain a suit to enforce the trust.[221] Being a co-owner does not in and of itself make one a beneficiary.[222] A third-party co-owner may, however, bring suit against the trustee to protect the co-owner's property interest.[223] If, for example, a majority interest in a closely held corporation constitutes a trust asset, the minority corporate shareholder may maintain a suit against the trustee for a breach of the trustee's fiduciary duty as majority shareholder *to the minority shareholder*. A third person who possesses an interest in the subject property that is superior or adverse to that of the trust's may maintain an action against the trustee to protect the interest.[224] "In such a case it is generally not necessary to make the trust beneficiaries parties defendant, as the trustee represents them."[225]

---

[219] Analogizing to the standards expressly set forth in I.R.C. §2041(b)(1), which deal with what constitutes a general power of appointment for federal estate tax purposes. *See* Jennings v. Smith, 161 F.2d 74 (2d Cir. 1947).

[220] Treas. Reg. §25.2511-2(f).

[221] 4 Scott & Ascher §24.4 (Persons Other Than the Beneficiaries).

[222] 4 Scott & Ascher §24.4 (Persons Other Than the Beneficiaries).

[223] 4 Scott & Ascher §§24.4 (Persons Other Than the Beneficiaries), 26.7 (Protection of Third Party's Interest in Trust Property).

[224] 4 Scott & Ascher §26.7 (Protection of Third Party's Interest in Trust Property).

[225] 4 Scott & Ascher §26.7 (Protection of Third Party's Interest in Trust Property).

§7.4 Discharge in Bankruptcy of Trustee's Personal Debt to Trust Owed as a Result of a Breach of Trust

Of course, the personal creditors of the trustee cannot reach the trust property, because the trustee, as trustee, has no beneficial interest in either the trust or the trust property.[1]

Because the assets of a trust are supposed to be segregated from the personal assets of the trustee, the personal bankruptcy of the trustee should be a nonevent insofar as the equitable interests of the beneficiaries are concerned.[2] "Although a bona fide purchaser for some purposes, the trustee in bankruptcy holds trust property subject to the trust."[3] Moreover, any claims *for money damages* for fraud, embezzlement, defalcation,[4] or other such acts of willful and malicious injury to a formal express trust by the trustee are not dischargeable, as per Section 523(a)(4) of the Federal Bankruptcy Code.[5] Surcharges occasioned by the trustee's ordinary negligence generally are.[6]

In 2013, the U.S. Supreme Court clarified the scope of the term *defalcation* as it is employed in Section 523(a)(4): "We hold that it includes a culpable state of mind requirement akin to that which accompanies application of the other terms in the same statutory phrase. We describe the state of mind as one involving knowledge of, or gross recklessness in respect to, the improper nature of the relevant fiduciary behavior."[7]

With respect to *the trust property* itself, if it can be traced, the trustee in bankruptcy (not to be confused with the bankrupt trustee) will hold the property subject to the trust.[8] The beneficiary then will have priority over the general creditors with respect to that property.[9] An exception is land, subject to an oral trust that is unenforceable because of the statute of frauds.[10] Title to the land passes from the bankrupt trustee to the trustee in bankruptcy, even if the

---

§7.4 [1] 3 Scott & Ascher §14.11. For a discussion of ways to limit the trustee in bankruptcy's access to the equitable interest in the event of the *beneficiary's* bankruptcy, the reader is referred to §5.3.3.3 of this handbook, as well as its sub-sections.

[2] *See generally* 4 Scott & Ascher §24.26.

[3] 4 Scott & Ascher §24.26. *See also* 5 Scott & Ascher §29.3.10 (Trustee in Bankruptcy). *See generally* §8.3.1 of this handbook (the trustee's personal creditors and the trustee's spouse) and §8.15.63 of this handbook (doctrine of bona fide purchase; the BFP).

[4] *See* In re Baylis, 313 F.3d 9 (2002); 4 Scott & Ascher §24.26 (wrestling with the meaning of "defalcation" in the context of bankruptcy law).

[5] 4 Scott & Ascher §24.26; 3 Scott on Trusts §221. "An individual cannot obtain a bankruptcy discharge from a debt for fraud or defalcation while acting in a fiduciary capacity, embezzlement, or larceny." 11 U.S.C. §523(a)(4).

[6] 4 Scott & Ascher §24.26.

[7] Bullock v. BankChampaign, N.A., 2013 WL 1942393 (U.S.).

[8] 4 Scott & Ascher §24.26; 3 Scott on Trusts. §221.1 (U.S.); Lewin ¶ 22-50 (England).

[9] 4 Scott & Ascher §24.26; 3 Scott on Trusts §221.1.

[10] *See generally* §8.15.5 of this handbook (statute of frauds).

latter has notice of the oral trust and becomes available to the general creditors.[11] Likewise with most properties that are the subject of implied trusts, constructive trusts, agencies, and the like.[12]

To summarize: A trustee in bankruptcy of another trustee's personal estate is generally not a good-faith purchaser for value (BFP) of the property which the other trustee had been holding in trust.[13] That property the trustee in bankruptcy holds "subject to the trust or other equity."[14] On the other hand, "although the beneficiary retains his or her equitable interest in the trust property, some claims for damages against a trustee or one who has assisted or participated in a breach of trust may be discharged in bankruptcy."[15]

---

[11] 1 Scott & Ascher §6.14. *See, e.g.,* 4 Scott & Ascher §24.26 n.16.

[12] *See* 4 Scott & Ascher §24.26 n.16.

[13] 5 Scott & Ascher §29.3.10 (Trustee in Bankruptcy). *See generally* §8.3.1 of this handbook (the trustee's personal creditors and the trustee's spouse) and §8.15.63 of this handbook (doctrine of bona fide purchase in the trust context).

[14] 5 Scott & Ascher §29.3.10 (Trustee in Bankruptcy).

[15] 5 Scott & Ascher §29.3.10 (Trustee in Bankruptcy).

CHAPTER *8*

Miscellaneous Topics of General Interest to the Trustee

§8.1 Powers of Appointment

Because of their incredible flexibility, powers of appointment are important in the drafting of trusts. Indeed, the late Professor Leach described powers of appointment as the most efficient dispositive device that the ingenuity of Anglo-American lawyers has ever worked out.[1]

Professor W. Barton Leach (1900–1971) was an able steward of the power of appointment doctrine. The same cannot be said for his successors. We explain in Old Doctrine Misunderstood, New Doctrine Misconceived: Deconstructing the Newly-Minted Restatement (Third) of Property's Power of Appointment Sections.[2] Section 8.1.1 of this handbook, immediately following, is a general primer on the current state of the power of appointment doctrine.

§8.1.1 Power of Appointment Doctrine

A trustee's discretionary power with respect to trust benefits is to be distinguished from a power of appointment. The latter is not subject to fiduciary obligations and may be exercised arbitrarily within the scope of the power.[3]

History. In England up until the second half of the seventeenth century, certain interests in land could not be devised, *i.e.*, transferred by will. The power of appointment was invented by creative lawyers to circumvent such proscriptions. An owner could "achieve the practical equivalent of a devise by granting the property in the owner's lifetime upon uses to be appointed by the owner's will."[4] Thus, "[t]he exercise of the power was effective, although a devise would have been void."[5]

---

§8.1 [1] Ira Mark Bloom, *How Federal Transfer Taxes Affect the Development of Property Law*, 58 Clev. St. L. Rev. 661 (2000) (citing to W. Barton Leach, *Powers of Appointment*, 24 A.B.A. J. 807, 807 (1938)). "In the history of English law powers of appointment were primarily the outgrowth of efforts to circumvent the rule, existing prior to 1540, that many of the most important types of interests in land could not be devised." Restatement (Second) of Property: (Wills and Other Donative Transfers), Division II, Part V, Introductory Note. "Despite this rule it became possible for an owner to achieve the practical equivalent of a devise by granting the property in the owner's lifetime upon uses to be appointed by the owner's will." Restatement (Second) of Property (Wills and Other Donative Transfers), Division II, Part V, Introductory Note.

[2] Charles E. Rounds, Jr., *Old Doctrine Misunderstood, New Doctrine Misconceived: Deconstructing the Newly-Minted Restatement (Third) of Property's Power of Appointment Sections*, 26 Quinnipiac Prob. L.J. 240 (2013).

[3] Restatement (Third) of Trusts §50 cmt. a. *See generally* §8.15.26 of this handbook (fraud on a power doctrine).

[4] Restatement (Third) of Property (Wills and Other Donative Transfers), Scope of Division VI. *See generally* §8.15.1 of this handbook (Statute of Uses).

[5] Restatement (Third) of Property (Wills and Other Donative Transfers), Scope of Division VI.

In the 1930s, the modern law of powers of appointment on this side of the Atlantic was still in its infancy.[6] It is now fully developed, in large part thanks to the "pioneering work" of Prof. W. Barton Leach, who died in 1971.[7]

Creating powers of appointment. In explaining how a power of appointment is created, the Uniform Powers of Appointment Act muddles trust declaration doctrine. An equitable nonfiduciary power of appointment is granted via the terms of a trust. A trust may arise either by a transfer of property from the settlor to the trustee or by the settlor's declaration. As to the latter method, an enforceable trust can arise if the owner of an interest in property, say X, declares himself trustee of the property for the benefit of another. This is known as a declaration of trust. It has long been the general rule that there need not be a conveyance of legal title from the settlor to himself as trustee for such a trust to arise. Predeclaration the legal title was in X. Postdeclaration the legal title is still in X. In each case, as to the world X is the legal owner of the subject property.[8]

In the Comment to Section 201 of the Uniform Powers of Appointment Act there is the assertion that a declaration of trust "necessarily entails a transfer of legal title from the owner-as-owner to the owner-as-trustee. . . ." No authority is supplied for this general proposition, because there is none.

What we may have here is a botched attempt to clean up one of the doctrinal messes of the Restatement (Third) of Property (Wills and Other Donative Trusts), which makes a blanket assertion that a power of appointment arises incident to a transfer of property.[9] Not so in the case of equitable powers of appointment incident to declarations of trust. It appears that the commentary to the Uniform Powers of Appointment Act is attempting to come to the rescue of the Restatement (Third) by asserting, without any authority whatsoever and in the face of a massive amount of authority to the contrary, that a declaration of trust that grants an equitable power-of-appointment arises incident to a transfer of legal title from the settlor to the settlor as trustee. That a legal power of appointment can only arise incident to a property transfer may be the source of all this confusion.[10]

---

[6] A. James Casner, *In Memoriam: W. Barton Leach*, 85 Harv. L. Rev. 717 (1972).

[7] A. James Casner, *In Memoriam: W. Barton Leach*, 85 Harv. L. Rev. 717 (1972).

[8] *See generally* Restatement (Second) of Trusts §17 cmt. a (1957) (stating that "[i]f the owner of property declares himself trustee of the property, a trust may be created without a transfer of title to the property"); I Scott & Fratcher §17.1 (4th ed. 1987) (transferring the property to a trustee is not necessary to create a trust by declaration, since the settlor already holds legal title); Bogert & Bogert §141 (2d ed. Rev. 1979) (stating that when a trust is created by declaration, a property interest does not truly transfer to the trustee because the settlor already owned the property); §3.4.1 of this handbook. *See, e.g.*, Taliaferro v. Taliaferro, 921 P.2d 803 (Kan. 1996).

[9] *See generally* Charles E. Rounds, Jr., *Old Doctrine Misunderstood, New Doctrine Misconceived: Deconstructing the Newly-Minted Restatement (Third) of Property's Power of Appointment Sections*, 26 Quinnipiac Prob. L.J. 240, 246 (2013).

[10] *See, e.g.*, Doan v. Vestry of Parish of Ascension of Carroll Cnty., 103 Md. 662, 64 A. 313 (1906). The court, having found no intention to impress a trust on the subject property, considered whether a *legal* fee simple in X and a naked *legal* collateral power of appointment in Y may be allowed to coexist. Its conclusion: "It is . . . a naked collateral power repugnant to the fee devised . . . and for that reason void."

A personal power of disposition. A power of appointment is a personal power of disposition.[11] It is a power given by the donor to someone—usually a beneficiary, sometimes a third party—to short-circuit, alter, or extend the terms of the trust.[12] That someone is known as the donee. In other words, a power of appointment is a power "that enables the donee of the power to designate recipients of beneficial ownership interests in or powers of appointment over the appointive property."[13] A power of appointment that is conferred on a donee who is unborn arises on the donee's birth.[14] On the other hand, "[a] power cannot be conferred on an individual who is deceased at the time of the disposition purporting to create the power."[15]

Doctrine of independent legal significance not applicable. To the extent an exercise of an inter vivos power of appointment created under the terms of a power-grantor's will is enforceable, it is not on account of the doctrine of independent legal significance. Rather, the exercise would be enforceable "on the theory that the exercise relates back and becomes part of the . . . [power-grantor's] . . . will, even if the writing exercising the power is not executed in accordance with the statutory formalities for wills."[16] We take up the doctrine of independent legal significance in Section 8.15.9 of this handbook.

The Restatement (Third) of Property further muddles the definition of a power of appointment. Under the Restatement (Second) of Property (Wills and Other Donative Transfers), a power of amendment, revocation, or termination among other powers qualified as a power of appointment.[17] The newly minted Restatement (Third) of Property (Wills and Other Donative Transfers) deletes a power of termination from the list.[18] Here is the reason given in the Reporter's Notes for the deletion: A power of termination "merely enables the donee of the power to convert ownership interests into possessory interests, but does not enable the donee to shift ownership interests from one beneficiary to another."[19] We are not so sure.

---

[11] Restatement (Second) of Property (Wills and Other Donative Transfers) §11.1. *See also* UTC §103 cmt. (available at <http://www.uniformlaws.org/Act.aspx?title=Trust%20 Code>) (defining a power of appointment as authority to designate the recipients of beneficial interests in property).

[12] Restatement (Third) of Property (Wills and Other Donative Transfers) §17.1 cmt. c. In the case of a power to designate the recipient of a remainder interest, for example, the power is also a power to divest the interest of the beneficiaries who would take the remainder interest were the power not exercised, which would typically be the interest of the takers in default of appointment. *Id.*

[13] Restatement (Third) of Property (Wills and Other Donative Transfers) §17.1 (power of appointment defined).

[14] Restatement (Third) of Property (Wills and Other Donative Transfers) §17.2 cmt. d.

[15] Restatement (Third) of Property (Wills and Other Donative Transfers) §17.2 cmt. e.

[16] Restatement (Third) of Property (Wills and Other Donative Transfers) §3.7 cmt. e.

[17] *See* Restatement (Second) of Property (Wills and Other Donative Transfers) §11.1 cmt. c.

[18] Restatement (Third) of Property (Wills and Other Donative Transfers) §17.1 cmt. e.

[19] Restatement (Third) of Property (Wills and Other Donative Transfers) §17.1, Reporter's Note to comment e. *See generally* Charles E. Rounds, Jr., *Old Doctrine Misunderstood, New Doctrine Misconceived: Deconstructing the Newly-Minted Restatement (Third) of Property's Power of Appointment Sections*, 26 Quinnipiac Prob. L.J. 240, 250 (2013).

Let's apply this to the classic trust formula: *A* to *B*, for *C* for life, then to *D*. *X* is granted an equitable power to terminate *D*'s interest. *D*'s equitable interest vests *ab initio*, subject to being divested upon *X*'s exercise of the termination power. In the event of exercise, a resulting trust would be triggered, and *A*'s vested equitable reversionary interest would become posessory.[20] But does *X* not then also possess a power to shift an "ownership" interest between *D* and *A*? This seems different from the mere power to terminate *C*'s interest and, in so doing, open the way for *D*'s interest to become possessory by acceleration. No wonder the Restatement (First) of Property and the Restatement (Second) of Property had deemed a power of termination to be a power of appointment, as does Section 2041 of the Internal Revenue Code. For tax purposes, a retained power to terminate would be taxable, whether exercise triggers an equitable acceleration or an equitable reversion.[21] In The Uniform Powers of Appointment Act there is no mention of powers of termination, neither in the text nor in the accompanying commentary.

The appointive property. The appointive property is the property or property interest that is subject to a power of appointment.[22] In the trust context, title to the subject property is in a trustee. The trustee takes title to the appointive property either by transfer or by declaration.[23]

A management power is not a power of appointment. A power over the management of trust property, sometimes called an administrative power, is not a power of appointment.[24] Neither is a power to designate or remove the trustee.[25]

Agencies are not powers of appointment. A power of attorney creates an agency relationship, not a power of appointment.[26] In other words, "[a] power of appointment does not create an agency relationship between the donor and the donee of the power."[27]

Powers appendant (or appurtenant). Whether an appendant (or appurtenant) power of appointment would have any validity is taken up in Section 8.15.85 of this handbook.

Fiduciary and nonfiduciary powers. A power of appointment, as it is generally understood in the nontax context, is not a discretionary power *in* a trustee to invade principal for the benefit of the beneficiary or to select remaindermen.[28] For purposes of this handbook, with the exception of Section

---

[20] *See generally* §4.1.1 of this handbook (the equitable reversionary interest).

[21] *See* Lober v. United States, 346 U.S. 335, 336–337 (1953).

[22] Restatement (Third) of Property (Wills and Other Donative Transfers) §17.2(g).

[23] *See generally* Charles E. Rounds, Jr., *Old Doctrine Misunderstood, New Doctrine Misconceived: Deconstructing the Newly-Minted Restatement (Third) of Property's Power of Appointment Sections*, 26 Quinnipiac Prob. L.J. 240, 246 (2013).

[24] Restatement (Third) of Property (Wills and Other Donative Transfers) §17.1 cmt. h.

[25] Restatement (Third) of Property (Wills and Other Donative Transfers) §17.1 cmt. i.

[26] *See generally* §9.9.2 of this handbook (powers of attorney).

[27] Restatement (Third) of Property (Wills and Other Donative Transfers) §17.1 cmt. j.

[28] *But see* Restatement (Second) of Property (Wills and Other Donative Transfers) §11.1 cmt. d. Under UTC §402(c) cmt. (available at <http://www.uniformlaws.org/Act.aspx?title=Trust%20 Code>) a power in a trustee to select a beneficiary from an indefinite class is valid, even if the class from whom the selection may be made cannot be ascertained. "Such a provision would fail under

(tax-sensitive powers), a power of appointment is not a power *in the trustee;* it is a power *to give directions to* the trustee.

A power held by a trustee in his fiduciary capacity, sometimes referred to as a power in trust,[29] a fiduciary power,[30] a power annexed to the office,[31] a power coupled with an interest,[32] or a fiduciary distributive power[33] is taken up in Section 3.5.3.2(a) of this handbook, which covers the power to make discretionary payments of income and principal under a discretionary trust.[34] The Restatement (Third) of Property generally defers to the Restatement (Third) of Trusts for the law governing such nongeneral fiduciary powers.[35]

It should be noted that the Uniform Trust Code contemplates that a power of appointment may be held in either a fiduciary[36] or nonfiduciary capacity, as does the Restatement of Property.[37] The Code's definition of "beneficiary," however, excludes powers held by a trustee, though not powers held by others in a fiduciary capacity.[38] The Restatement (Third) of Trusts has carved out altogether a trustee's discretionary power with respect to trust benefits from the definition of a power of appointment.[39] A trustee's power to disclaim a fiduciary power is covered in Section 4.5.3.4 of this handbook.[40]

As a general rule, a holder of a personal power of appointment, even if it happens to be the trustee, does not hold the power in a fiduciary capacity; has no duty to exercise it; and may disclaim it, release it, or allow it to lapse.[41] Such

---

traditional doctrine; it is an imperative power with no designated beneficiary capable of enforcement." UTC §402(c) cmt. If the trustee does not exercise the power within a reasonable time, the power fails and the property will pass to the settlor or his estate by resulting trust. UTC §402(c) cmt. *See also* Restatement (Third) of Property §46(2) (providing for the establishment of an "adapted trust" in the event a trustee is directed to distribute trust property to those members of an indefinite class of beneficiaries whom he shall select). *See generally* §9.29 of this handbook (the adapted trust).

[29] *But see* Restatement (Second) of Property (Wills and Other Donative Transfers) §11.1 cmt. a (providing that the power-holder may hold the power in a fiduciary or nonfiduciary capacity).

[30] Lewin ¶ 29-07 (England).

[31] Lewin ¶ 29-18 (England).

[32] Lewin ¶ 29-18 (England).

[33] Restatement (Third) of Property (Wills and Other Donative Transfers) §17.1 cmt. *g.*

[34] *See also* Lewin ¶ 29-09 (England).

[35] Restatement (Third) of Property (Wills and Other Donative Transfers) §17.1 cmt. *g.*

[36] *See generally* 1 Scott on Trusts §27 (1939) (discussing the academic debate between Professors Gray and Ames over whether powers can be held in trust).

[37] UTC §103 cmt. (available at <http://www.uniformlaws.org/Act.aspx?title=Trust%20 Code>); Restatement (Second) of Property (Wills and Other Donative Transfers) §11.1 cmt. a; Restatement (Third) of Property (Wills and Other Donative Transfers) §17.1 cmt. g.

[38] UTC §103 cmt. (available at <http://www.uniformlaws.org/Act.aspx?title=Trust%20 Code>). *See also* Restatement (Second) of Property (Wills and Other Donative Transfers) §11.1 cmt. a.

[39] Restatement (Third) of Trusts §50 cmt. a.

[40] *See also* UPC §2-1105(b) (the power to disclaim a fiduciary power); UPC §2-1111 (the consequences of disclaiming a fiduciary power).

[41] Restatement (Third) of Trusts §46 cmt. c.

discretionary nonfiduciary powers may be exercised arbitrarily, provided that the exercise is within the scope of the power.[42]

Nonfiduciary powers of appointment are either general or nongeneral/special/limited. A power of appointment is general "to the extent that the power is exercisable in favor of the donee, the donee's estate, or the creditors of either, regardless of whether the power is also exercisable in favor of others."[43] All other nonfiduciary powers of appointment are nongeneral.[44] A nongeneral power is sometimes referred to as a special or limited power of appointment.[45]

A power in the trustee to toggle a testamentary power of appointment or a nongeneral inter vivos power of appointment. The settlor of a trust may empower the trustee, or a trust protector, to convert a donee's equitable general testamentary power into an equitable nongeneral testamentary power, or to convert a donee's equitable nongeneral testamentary power into an equitable general testamentary power prior to the donee's death. The donee's power is either general or nongeneral depending on the scope of the donee's power at any particular time.[46] Because a living donee of an equitable testamentary power of appointment, whether general or nongeneral, does not enjoy the functional equivalent of an ownership interest in the subject property, a power in a trustee to upgrade and downgrade a nonfiduciary testamentary power does little more than give rise to a plain vanilla *discretionary trust.*

The same can be said for a power in the trustee to upgrade a nongeneral inter vivos power of appointment. Such an upgrade would be the functional equivalent of a discretionary distribution outright and free of trust of the subject property to the donee.

A power in a trustee to toggle down an inter vivos power of appointment. The Restatement (Third) of Property (Wills and Other Donative Transfers), however, would seem to contemplate the enforceability of downgrades of equitable

---

[42] Restatement (Third) of Property (Wills and Other Donative Transfers) §17.1 cmt. g.

[43] Restatement (Third) of Property (Wills and Other Donative Transfers) §17.3(a).

[44] Restatement (Third) of Property (Wills and Other Donative Transfers) §17.3(b).

[45] The Restatement of Property §320 had defined a special power as one that could be exercised only in favor of persons, not including the donee or his estate, who constitute a group "not unreasonably large." Expansively drawn powers, such as the power to appoint to anyone in the world except the powerholder, were thought of as general/special hybrids. Such powers were adjudged so rare that "it would not be useful to state the rules applicable to them in situations where the distinction between general and special powers is significant." *Id.,* cmt. a. By the time the Restatement Second was promulgated in 1983, however, such powers had become fairly common, as the tax laws were treating them as nontaxable. In the late 1930s, law professors had been engaged in heated debates between and among themselves over whether the holders of unexercised powers of appointment should be taxed for federal estate and gift tax purposes as if the holders had owned outright the appointive property. For a brief but colorful account of these debates, *see* the introductory quotation to §8.9.3.1 of this handbook.

[46] Restatement (Third) of Property (Wills and Other Donative Transfers) §17.3 cmt. d, illus. 4.

general inter vivos powers of appointment as well.[47] Because the donee of an equitable nonfiduciary general inter vivos power of appointment enjoys the functional equivalent of a legal fee simple in the subject property, it is disappointing that neither the commentary nor the reporter's note addresses the public policy and practical aspects of bestowing on a trustee such a discretionary equitable defeasement power, particularly as such an encumbrance in the legal context would likely be void as an impermissible alienation restraint. As the authority in a trustee to downgrade a nonfiduciary general inter vivos power of appointment would certainly itself be held in a fiduciary capacity, it is also disappointing that the Restatement (Third) of Property neglects to offer practical guidance to the trustee as to how such a defeasement power should be administered. At the very least, the prudent trustee would want to sort out the fiduciary, tax, and fraudulent conveyance implications, if any, of exercising such a downgrade before deciding whether or not to actually "toggle" down. And in the event there is a toggling down against the wishes of the powerholder, the trustee may wish to retain the services of a personal bodyguard.

When joinder of an adverse party is required for an effective power exercise. No matter how inclusive the class of objects/permissible appointees, a power of appointment exercisable only with the joinder of an adverse party is a special or limited power.[48] Who would qualify as an adverse party in this context is taken up in Section 8.15.83 of this handbook.

Classifying nonfiduciary powers of appointment as inter vivos or testamentary. A nonfiduciary power of appointment that is not exercisable by will is an inter vivos power. A power exercisable "by deed," for example, is an inter vivos power.[49] A power is testamentary if it is exercisable only by the donee's will.[50]

Classifying nonfiduciary powers as presently exercisable, postponed/deferred or testamentary. A *presently exercisable power of appointment* is immediately exercisable inter vivos, that is to say during the lifetime of the donee/holder of the power.[51] An inter vivos *postponed power* (sometimes referred to as a *deferred power*) is not exercisable until the occurrence of a specified event.[52] A postponed power becomes presently exercisable once the specified event occurs.[53] A power is *testamentary* if it is exercisable only by the donee's will.[54]

A power exercisable by deed or will. A power of appointment that is exercisable either inter vivos or by will is in substance two powers: an inter vivos

---

[47] *See* Restatement (Third) of Property (Wills and Other Donative Transfers) §17.3 cmt. d. *See generally* Charles E. Rounds, Jr., *Old Doctrine Misunderstood, New Doctrine Misconceived: Deconstructing the Newly-Minted Restatement (Third) of Property's Power of Appointment Sections*, 26 Quinnipiac Prob. L.J. 240, 280 (2013).

[48] *See* Restatement (Third) of Property (Wills and Other Donative Transfers) §17.3 cmt. e.

[49] *See* Restatement (Third) of Property (Wills and Other Donative Transfers) §17.4 cmt. e.

[50] *See* Restatement (Third) of Property (Wills and Other Donative Transfers) §17.4 cmt. c.

[51] *See* Restatement (Third) of Property (Wills and Other Donative Transfers) §17.4 cmt. a.

[52] *See* Restatement (Third) of Property (Wills and Other Donative Transfers) §17.4 cmt. d.

[53] *See* Restatement (Third) of Property (Wills and Other Donative Transfers) §17.4 cmt. d.

[54] *See* Restatement (Third) of Property (Wills and Other Donative Transfers) §17.4 cmt. c.

power and a testamentary power. Confusing syntax with substance, the Restatement (Third) of Property conflates the two distinct powers and then labels the conflation a presently exercisable power, which the testamentary component of the conflation is not.[55]

Classifying powers of appointment as "collateral," "in gross," or appendant/appurtenant. Whether there is utility in continuing to classify nonfiduciary powers of appointment as either *collateral* or *in gross* is taken up in Section 8.15.84 of this handbook. The *appendant/appurtenant power of appointment* is taken up in Section 8.15.85 of this handbook.

The parties. The *donor* of a power of appointment determines the nature and scope of the power and how it may be exercised by the powerholder.[56] In brief, the donor is the person who created or reserved the power.[57] In the case of a power of appointment created under the terms of a trust, the donor of the power would be the trust's settlor; unless the power of appointment had been created as a result of the exercise of a preexisting power of appointment in further trust, in which case the donor of the new power would be the donee of the preexisting power. Thus, "[b]efore creating the power, the donor was either the owner of the appointive property or the donee of a power of appointment with respect to the appointive property."[58]

The powerholder is referred to as the *donee* of the power.[59] "The 'donee' is the person on whom the power was conferred or in whom the power was reserved."[60] Thus, in the case of a reserved power, the donor and the donee are one and the same.[61]

Although some powers may be exercised postmortem, that is to say after the death of the donee, a power of appointment may not be created in someone who is already deceased.[62]

A power of appointment created under the will of the donor of the power comes into existence at the date of the testator's/donor's death, which is when the will speaks, not when the will is executed (signed and witnessed).[63] On the other hand, a power of appointment created under the terms of a revocable inter vivos trust comes into existence when the trust is funded, which could

---

[55] *See* Restatement (Third) of Property (Wills and Other Donative Transfers) §17.4 cmt. a. *See generally* Charles E. Rounds, Jr., *Old Doctrine Misunderstood, New Doctrine Misconceived: Deconstructing the Newly-Minted Restatement (Third) of Property's Power of Appointment Sections*, 26 Quinnipiac Prob. L.J. 240, 265–266 (2013).

[56] Restatement (Second) of Property (Wills and Other Donative Transfers) §11.2(1).

[57] Restatement (Third) of Property (Wills and Other Donative Transfers) §17.2(a).

[58] Restatement (Third) of Property (Wills and Other Donative Transfers) §17.2(a).

[59] Restatement (Second) of Property (Wills and Other Donative Transfers) §11.2(2).

[60] Restatement (Third) of Property (Wills and Other Donative Transfers) §17.2(b).

[61] Restatement (Third) of Property (Wills and Other Donative Transfers) §17.2(b) (noting that the holder of a reserved power is sometimes referred to as the donor-donee of the power).

[62] Restatement (Third) of Property (Wills and Other Donative Transfers) §19.11.

[63] Restatement (Third) of Property (Wills and Other Donative Transfers) §19.11 cmt. b.

be well before the death of the settlor/donor.[64] A revocable inter vivos trust may be a will substitute, but it is most certainly not a will.

While the terms of a will may not effectively grant a power of appointment to someone who predeceases the testator, it may be possible for the will's scrivener to exploit as a fall-back the doctrine of incorporation by reference or the doctrine of independent legal significance to bring about the practical equivalent of such a grant. The doctrine of incorporation by reference is taken up in Section 8.15.17 of this handbook and the doctrine of independent legal significance in Section 8.15.9 of this handbook. In either case, the will would be borrowing the language of an extrinsic document that had been prepared by the predeceasing power-grantee for purposes of designating who gets what under the power-grantor's will.[65] A power of appointment may be effectively conferred on a donee who is incapacitated, whether on account of the donee's mental condition or minority.[66] "A power of appointment that was previously conferred on a donee who then had capacity is not invalidated if the donee subsequently becomes incapacitated, nor does subsequent incapacity invalidate an exercise of the power that was executed when the donee had capacity."[67]

The *objects or permissible appointees* are the persons to whom an appointment can be made.[68] In other words, "[t]he 'permissible appointees' are the persons to whom an appointment is authorized."[69] A court must be capable of determining from a power's authorizing language who would have the status of a permissible appointee and who would not should it be called upon to make such a determination.[70] If the description of the class is so vague or so indefinite that such a determination is not possible, then the power is unenforceable.[71] A permissible appointee does not have a transferable property interest.[72] "Were it otherwise, a permissible appointee could transform an impermissible appointee into a permissible appointee, exceeding the intended scope of the power and thereby violating the donor's intention."[73]

The death of the last survivor of all possible permissible appointees of an equitable nonfiduciary nongeneral power of appointment prior to its exercise triggers a termination of the power.[74] Had all of them predeceased the entrustment that was to give rise to the power, then the power would never have come

[64] *See* National Shawmut Bank v. Joy, 315 Mass. 457, 53 N.E.2d 113 (1944) (a reserved right of revocation does not make a revocable inter vivos trust a will). *See also* Restatement (Third) of Property (Wills and Other Donative Transfers) §19.11 cmt. c.

[65] *See generally* Restatement (Third) of Property (Wills and Other Donative Transfers) §19.11 cmt. d(1) & cmt. d(2).

[66] Restatement (Third) of Property (Wills and Other Donative Transfers) §19.8 cmt. b.

[67] Restatement (Third) of Property (Wills and Other Donative Transfers) §19.8 cmt. b.

[68] Restatement (Second) of Property (Wills and Other Donative Transfers) §11.2(3).

[69] Restatement (Third) of Property (Wills and Other Donative Transfers) §17.2(c).

[70] Restatement (Third) of Property (Wills and Other Donative Transfers) §18.1 cmt. i.

[71] Restatement (Third) of Property (Wills and Other Donative Transfers) §18.1 cmt. i.

[72] Restatement (Third) of Property (Wills and Other Donative Transfers) §17.2 cmt. f.

[73] Restatement (Third) of Property (Wills and Other Donative Transfers) §17.2 cmt. f.

[74] Restatement (Third) of Property (Wills and Other Donative Transfers) §18.1 cmt. h.

into existence in the first place.[75] This having been said, in the future, the prepower-exercise death of all permissible appointees expressly specified in a power grant may not necessarily extinguish the power.[76] Take, for instance, the radical departure from the settled law proposed by the Restatement (Third) of Property (Wills and Other Donative Transfers), specifically its Section 19.12(c).[77] It would afford the donee of an equitable nongeneral power of appointment default authority to exercise the power directly in favor of a descendant of a predeceasing permissible appointee, *even though the descendant himself was not a permissible appointee under the express terms of the power grant.*[78] The predeceasing appointee apparently need not even be a relative protected by some antilapse statute: "If an antilapse statute can substitute the descendants of a deceased appointee, the donee of the power should be allowed to make a direct appointment to one or more descendants of a deceased permissible appointee."[79] Why not just let the trust instrument speak for itself? Paper logic seems to be trumping common sense in this particular corner of the Restatement (Third) of Property. It should be noted that the Restatement proposes that even when an antilapse statute fails to expressly address an appointment to a deceased appointee, its "purpose and policy" should still apply to such an appointment *as if the appointed property were owned by either the donor or the donee.*[80] For the policy debate over whether antilapse should be applied in the trust context in the first place, the reader is referred to Section 8.15.55 of this handbook.

The *appointees* are the persons to whom an appointment has actually been made.[81] "An appointment cannot be validly made to an impermissible appointee of the power."[82]

And then there are the *takers in default of a power's exercise*. A "taker in default of appointment" is a person who takes part or all of the appointive property to the extent that the power has not been effectively exercised.[83] Having said that, the Uniform Probate Code would apply its antilapse provisions to exercised testamentary powers of appointment such that if a designated appointee fails to survive the testator, *i.e.*, fails to survive the one who exercised the power, the subject property would then pass to the appointee's descendants rather than to the takers in default, unless the language that created the power

---

[75] Restatement (Third) of Property (Wills and Other Donative Transfers) §18.1 cmt. h.

[76] *See generally* Charles E. Rounds, Jr., *Old Doctrine Misunderstood, New Doctrine Misconceived: Deconstructing the Newly-Minted Restatement (Third) of Property's Power of Appointment Sections*, 26 Quinnipiac Prob. L.J. 240, 278–279 (2013).

[77] California has had such a statute since 1982. *See* Cal. Prob. Code §674 (Death of permissible appointee before exercise of special power).

[78] The deceased permissible appointee, however, would have to have survived the execution of the instrument that created the power.

[79] Restatement (Third) of Property (Wills and Other Donative Transfers) §19.12 cmt. f.

[80] Restatement (Third) of Property (Wills and Other Donative Transfers) §19.12(b).

[81] Restatement (Second) of Property (Wills and Other Donative Transfers) §11.2(4); Restatement (Third) of Property (Wills and Other Donative Transfers) §17.2(e).

[82] Restatement (Third) of Property (Wills and Other Donative Transfers) §17.2 cmt. g.

[83] Restatement (Third) of Property (Wills and Other Donative Transfers) §17.2(f).

had expressly ruled out such a substitution.[84] While a power of appointment is *per se* nontransferable, the interest of the taker in default is not *per se* nontransferable.[85]

The Restatement (Third) of Property endorses the following intent-based default assumption: "If the donee of a power of appointment makes a valid partial appointment to a taker in default, the taker in default-appointee also takes his or her share of any unappointed property as taker in default...."[86] The donor of a power of appointment may expressly provide in the terms of the grant that, to the extent the donee makes an appointment to a taker in default, the appointee must elect either to take by appointment or to take in default thereof.[87] The donor though might provide that in the case of an actual partial appointment to a taker in default, the appointee may elect to take in default as well, provided the appointee's share of the fund to be divided up among all the takers in default is determined by hotchpot calculation.[88] As the English say, the appointed property notionally needs to be "brought into hotchpot."[89] The hotchpot concept generally is taken up in Section 8.15.51 of this handbook.

An *impermissible appointee* of a power of appointment would be anyone who is not a permissible appointee.[90] An appointment, or a contract to appoint, to an impermissible appointee might well constitute a fraud on the power, a topic we take up in Section 8.15.26 of this handbook. The doctrine of infectious invalidity might well be implicated should the donee of a power of appointment exercise it in favor of both permissible and impermissible appointees in a common disposition, a topic we take up in Section 8.15.72 of this handbook.

The appointive property. As noted, the appointive property is the property or property interest that is subject to a power of appointment.[91] In the trust context, title to the appointive property is lodged in the trustee, at least until the power is exercised. The Restatement (Third) of Property would appear to muddle this fairly straightforward concept when it comes to equitable remainders under trusts.[92] It does so by proffering without any explanation the following illustration:

> Donor died, leaving a will that devised property in trust, directing the trustee to pay the net income to Donee for life, then to distribute the trust principal to such

[84] UPC §2-603. *See also* Restatement (Third) of Property (Wills and Other Donative Transfers) §19.12; §8.15.55 of this handbook (lapse and antilapse).

[85] Restatement (Third) of Property (Wills and Other Donative Transfers) §17.2 cmt. h.

[86] Restatement (Third) of Property (Wills and Other Donative Transfers) §19.24.

[87] Restatement (Third) of Property (Wills and Other Donative Transfers) §19.24 cmt. b.

[88] Restatement (Third) of Property (Wills and Other Donative Transfers) §19.24 cmt. b.

[89] Lewin ¶ 28-02. *See also* §8.15.51 of this handbook (hotchpot).

[90] Restatement (Third) of Property (Wills and Other Donative Transfers) §17.2(d).

[91] Restatement (Third) of Property (Wills and Other Donative Transfers) §17.2(g).

[92] *See generally* Charles E. Rounds, Jr., *Old Doctrine Misunderstood, New Doctrine Misconceived: Deconstructing the Newly-Minted Restatement (Third) of Property's Power of Appointment Sections*, 26 Quinnipiac Prob. L.J. 240, 246–249 (2013).

persons as Donee shall appoint. Donee has a power of appointment over the remainder interest in the trust.[93]

The problem, however, is that, as Prof. John Chipman Gray pointed out more than 100 years ago, there is, strictly speaking, no such thing as a remainder incident to a trust relationship.[94] This is because legal title to the subject property is in the trustee. Unlike a legal future interest, no equitable future interest requires a previous estate to support it.[95] In other words, the packets of equitable property interests thrown off by a trust relationship may be independent and discrete. The interests may even be separated by time gaps, legal title to the subject property safely being in the trustee. For that reason Gray was wont to refer to equitable remainders as quasi remainders.[96]

In the case of a power of appointment incident to a clutch of legal interests the mechanics are very different.[97] Take a legal life estate in realty and its associated remainder. Those interests are the product of the fee having been "cut across" into successive interests.[98] "But they are all parts of the same fee...."[99] Thus, in the case of the exercise of a "legal" power of appointment that is exercisable during the lifetime of the legal life tenant, the legal title to the fee comes to the appointee directly from both the legal life tenant and the legal remainderman.

The above illustration from the Restatement, therefore, would be more precise if its second sentence had read either that the Donee has a power of appointment over the property to which the trustee has the legal title, or that the Donee has a power to designate equitable quasi remaindermen. But upon the death of the Donee there is in existence, strictly speaking, no property interest comparable to a legal remainder that could be the subject of an appointment. In this particular fact pattern, upon termination of the equitable life estate, there is only the equitable reversion, which is in the settlor or his successors in interest, and the entrusted property itself, legal title to which is in the trustee.[100]

The comment in which the illustration is nestled has the following sentence, which is unsupported by any commentary in the Reporter's Note: "The appointive property is the remainder interest."[101] If the suggestion is that the equitable quasi remainder is the appointive property, then the sentence would

---

[93] Restatement (Third) of Property (Wills and Other Donative Transfers) §17.1 cmt. d, illus. 1.

[94] John Chipman Gray, The Rule Against Perpetuities §324 (1942) (quasi remainders).

[95] John Chipman Gray, The Rule Against Perpetuities §324 (1942) (quasi remainders). *See generally* §8.30 of this handbook (the fiction of the equitable remainder).

[96] John Chipman Gray, The Rule Against Perpetuities §324 (1942) (quasi remainders).

[97] The legal property interest and the equitable property interest are compared in §8.27 of this handbook.

[98] Oliver Wendell Holmes, Jr., The Common Law 352 (59th prtg. 1923).

[99] Oliver Wendell Holmes, Jr., The Common Law 352 (59th prtg. 1923).

[100] *See generally* §4.1.1 of this handbook (the equitable reversion); §3.5.1 of this handbook (the trustee's legal estate).

[101] Restatement (Third) of Property (Wills and Other Donative Transfers) §17.1 cmt. d.

seem nonsensical. If the suggestion is that the entire trust corpus, title to which is in the trustee, shall be deemed a remainder under these special circumstances, then there is probably some logic to it. Here is one Restatement comment that is desperately in need of some attention in the Reporter's Note.

Inapplicability of spendthrift restraints. As we shall see, a power of appointment, whether general or limited, would allow the holder either indirectly or directly to divert the subject property to another. "If the donee of a power to direct a trustee to distribute income or principal to another is the income beneficiary of the trust, the donee's power is effective despite any spendthrift restraint on the donee's income or remainder interest."[102] Spendthrift restraints are covered in Section 5.3.3.3(c) of this handbook.

The general inter vivos power of appointment. A general inter vivos power over trust principal would give the powerholder, *i.e.*, the donee, the right while alive to direct the trustee to turn over the principal at least to the holder or the holder's creditors.[103] That right is the functional equivalent of ownership of the underlying trust property.[104] This would be the case even if the powerholder were also the trustee.[105] "Also, by implication, a power of revocation or withdrawal of principal . . . is a power to direct a trustee to distribute principal to another, because such a power permits the donee not only to withdraw principal for himself or herself but also to direct the trustee to distribute principal to another."[106]

The power of revocation, amendment, or withdrawal. A power of revocation, amendment, or withdrawal, whether reserved or bestowed on someone other than the settlor, meets the definition of a general inter vivos power of appointment.[107] By "power of revocation," we mean the power to revoke a trust and assume legal title to, and acquire a full beneficial in, the entrusted property. Such ownership-equivalent powers are held by the powerholder "individually and not in a fiduciary capacity," even if the power holder also serves as trustee.[108]

When a donee may consent to a breach of trust. The holder of a general inter vivos power of appointment over principal, if of full age and legal capacity, may consent to a breach of trust and in so doing bind the other beneficiaries,

---

[102] Restatement (Third) of Property (Wills and Other Donative Transfers) §17.1 cmt. f.

[103] *See* Restatement (Second) of Property (Wills and Other Donative Transfers) §11.4; Lewin ¶ 29-12 (England) (defining general and limited powers under English law).

[104] Restatement (Third) of Trusts §74 cmt. a. *See generally* 6 Scott & Ascher §41.17; Restatement (Third) of Property (Wills and Other Donative Transfers) §17.4 cmt. f(1) (suggesting that a presently exercisable general power of appointment is an ownership-equivalent power).

[105] *See* Fulp v. Gilliland, 972 N.E.2d 955 (Ind. Ct. App. 2012).

[106] Restatement (Third) of Property (Wills and Other Donative Transfers) §19.3(a) & §17.1 cmt. f.

[107] UTC §505 cmt. (available at <http://www.uniformlaws.org/Act.aspx?title=Trust%20 Code>); UPC §1-108; Restatement (Third) of Property (Wills and Other Donative Transfers) §17.1 cmt. e.

[108] Restatement (Third) of Trusts §74 cmt. a.

including the takers in default.[109] A general inter vivos power of appointment, however, may be limited by the provisions of the trust to the withdrawal of income only.[110] In other words, the appointive property is only the income stream itself.

The general (as opposed to nongeneral) presumption. Ordinarily, the terms of a general inter vivos power of appointment will expressly authorize the holder to appoint the appointive property to the holder or the holder's creditors. Absent such express authorization, the Restatement (Third) of Property suggests that language creating an inter vivos power of appointment should be construed as creating a general power unless the language "expressly prohibits" exercise in favor of the donee and the donee's creditors. Presumably an express designation of a limited class of permissible appointees that does not include the donee and the donee's creditors would constitute such an express prohibition.[111]

Partial revocations. The Restatement (Third) of Property proposes that any express limitation on the right to partially revoke (or withdraw), or on the number of partial revocations (or withdrawals) that may be executed, is unenforceable.[112]

Constructively transferring a nonfiduciary general inter vivos power of appointment. Inherent in the right to revoke (withdraw) is the right to directly grant a right of revocation (withdrawal) over the entrusted property to another, such as by the exercise of the power in further trust.[113] The Restatement falsely analogizes such a constructive transfer to a delegation of the power of revocation.[114] Rather, such a constructive transfer is analogous to an irrevocable transfer by assignment of the entrusted property itself.[115]

A power to appoint only to the donee's creditors. The Restatement (Third) of Property (Wills and Other Donative Transfers) proposes that a power to appoint only to the donee's creditors permits only such an appointment, *even though the power is general.*[116] The Restatement (Second) of Property adopted a similar posture.[117] In neither Restatement, however, is, nor was, any light shed on the

---

[109] UPC §1-108 (acts of holder of general inter vivos power); §8.14 of this handbook (representing the beneficiary); §7.1.4 of this handbook (consenting to a breach of trust); §8.11 of this handbook (duties of trustee of a revocable trust).

[110] Restatement (Third) of Property (Wills and Other Donative Transfers) §17.1 cmt. e.

[111] Restatement (Third) of Property (Wills and Other Donative Transfers) §17.3 cmt. a. *See particularly* illus. 2.

[112] Restatement (Third) of Property (Wills and Other Donative Transfers) §19.13 cmt. c.; Restatement (Second) of Property (Wills and Other Donative Transfers) §19.1 cmt. d.

[113] Restatement (Third) of Property (Wills and Other Donative Transfers) §19.13 cmt. f.; Restatement (Second) of Property (Wills and Other Donative Transfers) §19.2.

[114] Restatement (Third) of Property (Wills and Other Donative Transfers) §19.13 cmt. g; Restatement (Second) of Property (Wills and Other Donative Transfers) §19.2, cmt. b.

[115] *See* Marx v. Rice, 3 N.J. Super. 581, 585–586, 67 A.2d 918, 920–921 (1949) (in the case of a general inter vivos power of appointment the analogy is to property, whereas in the case of a nongeneral inter vivos power, the analogy is to agency). *See generally* Charles E. Rounds, Jr., *Old Doctrine Misunderstood, New Doctrine Misconceived: Deconstructing the Newly-Minted Restatement (Third) of Property's Power of Appointment Sections*, 26 Quinnipiac Prob. L.J. 240, 256 (2013).

[116] Restatement (Third) of Property (Wills and Other Donative Transfers) §19.13(b).

[117] Restatement (Second) of Property (Wills and Other Donative Transfers) §19.1 cmt. b.

policy behind the proposition, in the Reporter's Notes, or anywhere else for that matter. The proposition just hangs there. Presumably the donee could fairly easily circumvent the creditor-only limitation simply by contracting with third parties for goods and services using a credit card.[118]

The general testamentary power of appointment. While a presently exercisable general power of appointment is a right in the powerholder *currently* to appoint the underlying trust property directly to the powerholder,[119] a general testamentary power would give the powerholder a right *only by will* to direct the trustee to turn over the trust property at least to the powerholder's estate, or to the estate's creditors.[120] Remember, a will speaks at death, not at the time of its execution.[121]

Assume the terms of a power specify that the donee may appoint the subject property by will to his estate. No other permissible appointee is mentioned in the terms of the power. The donee may nonetheless appoint the property by will directly to anyone to whom the donee could have devised the property had the donee owned the subject property outright and free of trust.[122] On the other hand, the donee of a general testamentary power grant that expressly limits the universe of permissible appointees to the creditors of the donee's estate is restricted to appointing only to those creditors, at least that is the view of the Restatement of Property.[123]

Must the will be probated, however, to effectively exercise the testamentary power? Perhaps not. At least one court has held that there was an effective exercise of a general testamentary power of appointment, though the will was

---

[118] *See generally* Charles E. Rounds, Jr., *Old Doctrine Misunderstood, New Doctrine Misconceived: Deconstructing the Newly-Minted Restatement (Third) of Property's Power of Appointment Sections*, 26 Quinnipiac Prob. L.J. 240, 280 (2013).

[119] *See* Restatement (Third) of Trusts §74 cmt. a.

[120] Restatement (Second) of Property (Wills and Other Donative Transfers) §11.4. For a discussion of the authority of the holder of a testamentary power of appointment to consent to a breach of trust and in so doing bind the appointees and takers in default, *see* §8.14 of this handbook (when is a guardian ad litem needed?). In a few states, a general residuary clause in a will is presumed to exercise a *general* testamentary power of appointment, unless the settlor (the donor of the power) indicated a contrary intention in the instrument that created the power. *See generally* Ritchie et al., Decedents' Estates and Trusts 929 (8th ed. 1993); §8.15.12 of this handbook (doctrine of capture).

[121] UPC §2-603 cmt. The time of a will's execution is the time when the last witness to sign has affixed his or her signature to the paper.

[122] Restatement (Third) of Property (Wills and Other Donative Transfers) §19.13(a); Restatement (Second) of Property (Wills and Other Donative Transfers) §19.1.

[123] Restatement (Third) of Property (Wills and Other Donative Transfers) §19.13(b); Restatement (Second) of Property (Wills and Other Donative Transfers) §19.1 cmt. b. In neither version, however, is (or was) any light shed on the policy behind the proposition, in the Reporter's Notes, or anywhere else for that matter. The proposition just hangs there. As the *primary* subjective motive behind the typical creditor-focused general testamentary power grant surely is to benefit the donee's legatees and devisees by indirection, not to bestow some gratuitous benefit on the estate's creditors, it is hard to see how, absent special facts, a deviation from the express terms of such a grant would rise to the level of an actual fraud on the *general* power, particularly in light of the maxim: Equity looks to the intent rather than to the form. Equity maxims are catalogued and discussed in §8.12 of this handbook. The fraud on a *special* power doctrine is taken up in §8.15.26 of this handbook.

not probated and though the period of time after the testator's death in which the will could have been probated had lapsed.[124] The "written document" was sufficient.[125] A more systematic discussion of the *mechanics* of exercising a power of appointment, including by unprobated will, may be found further on in this section.

Tax sensitivity. For federal estate tax purposes, "[p]roperty over which a decedent holds a general power of appointment is included in the gross estate of the donee unless it was a general power created on or before October 21, 1942 and is not exercised (or was partially released or otherwise converted to a nongeneral power before November 1, 1951)."[126] The prospective donor of a general power is well advised to make express mention in the granting language of whichever of the "dreaded four"[127] object categories is appropriate: the donee himself or herself, the donee's creditors, the donee's estate, or the creditors of the donee's estate. This will avoid confusion down the road as to whether the donor intended to grant a general or nongeneral power. The default law, however, is that the "scope of the donee's authority as to appointees and the time and manner of appointment is unlimited except as to the extent the donor effectively manifests an intent to impose limits."[128] Accordingly, one court has construed the power to appoint by will "to such person or persons as she may designate" as a general power, though none of the "dreaded four" objects was expressly mentioned in the granting language.[129]

Cross-reference. For the intersection of power of appointment doctrine and the federal income tax regime, see Section 8.9.3 of this handbook.

The nongeneral (special/limited) power of appointment. On the other hand, the holder of a nongeneral power of appointment, sometimes referred to as a special, limited, or specific power of appointment, may appoint only to members of a specified class of permissible appointees.[130] The class, however, may not comprise the donee, creditors of the donee, the donee's probate estate, and the creditors of the donee's probate estate. If the class comprises even one of the aforementioned, the power is a general one.

In the case of a member of a class of permissible appointees of a non-general power who predeceases the appointment, the Restatement (Third) of Property proposes that the specified class be expanded under default law to encompass the member's descendants even though the express terms of the

---

[124] *See* Lumbard v. Farmers State Bank, 812 N.E.2d 196 (2004).

[125] *See generally* Charles E. Rounds, Jr., *Old Doctrine Misunderstood, New Doctrine Misconceived: Deconstructing the Newly-Minted Restatement (Third) of Property's Power of Appointment Sections*, 26 Quinnipiac Prob. L.J. 240, 284–285 (2013) (the exercise by unprobated will trap).

[126] Blattmachr, Kamin & Bergman, *Estate Planning's Most Powerful Tool: Powers of Appointment Refreshed, Redefined, and Reexamined*, 47 Real Prop., Trust & Est. L J. 529, 543 (2013).

[127] *See generally* §5.3.3 of this handbook (rights of beneficiary's creditors and others to trust property); §8.9.3 of this handbook (tax-sensitive powers).

[128] Restatement (Second) of Property (Wills and Other Donative Transfers) §12.2.

[129] *See* Dickinson v. Wilmington Trust Co., 734 A.2d 605 (1999).

[130] Restatement (Second) of Property (Wills and Other Donative Transfers) §11.4 cmt. b; Restatement (Third) of Property (Wills and Other Donative Transfers) §17.3 cmt. b.

power grant make no mention of them.[131] For more on this radical proposition, the reader is referred to Section 8.15.26 of this handbook.[132]

Whether the nongeneral power is inter vivos or testamentary, these permissible appointees are the objects of the power. "The donor may define the permissible appointees of a nongeneral power by exclusion, by inclusion, or by a combination of the two."[133] The class of permissible appointees or objects of a limited power may be expansively defined as everyone in the world except the powerholder, his creditors, his estate, and the creditors of his estate.[134] This is defining by exclusion. Or the class of permissible appointees may be defined narrowly by inclusion. The class, for example, might be limited to someone's issue, children, or descendants.[135] Class designations are taken up generally in Section 5.2 of this handbook.

It is said that "[w]hen the donee can appoint only among the members of a class of which the donee is not a member, there is no sense in which the donee is the owner of the property."[136] In England a jointly held power and a power to appoint with the consent of another person are *per se* limited powers.[137] Again, that the holder of a limited power of appointment over income and/or principal is also a beneficiary of the trust will in no way limit the holder's right of exercise, even should the terms of the trust contain a spendthrift provision.[138]

Fraudulent exercise of nongeneral powers. A trustee called upon to distribute trust property to someone pursuant to the exercise of a power of appointment has a fiduciary duty to the takers in default to ascertain whether the procedures and formalities called for by the power were followed.[139] Thus, a contract to exercise a nongeneral power that is not presently exercisable is unenforceable, absent special circumstances.[140] When there is reasonable doubt as to who is entitled to the appointive property, particularly if the power is testamentary, the trustee may want to seek instructions from the court in order to avoid the risk of misdelivery.[141] In Section 8.15.79 of this handbook we discuss the doctrine of allocation (marshalling), which may empower the court

---

[131] Restatement (Third) of Property (Wills and Other Donative Transfers) §19.12(c).

[132] *See also* Charles E. Rounds, Jr., *Old Doctrine Misunderstood, New Doctrine Misconceived: Deconstructing the Newly-Minted Restatement (Third) of Property's Power of Appointment Sections*, 26 Quinnipiac Prob. L.J. 240, 275–279 (2013) (antilapse run amok).

[133] Restatement (Third) of Property (Wills and Other Donative Transfers) §19.15 cmt. d.

[134] Restatement (Third) of Property (Wills and Other Donative Transfers) §17.3(b) (U.S.); Lewin ¶5-67 (England).

[135] Restatement (Second) of Property (Wills and Other Donative Transfers) §11.4 cmt. b (U.S.); Restatement (Third) of Property (Wills and Other Donative Transfers) §17.2 cmt. f (U.S.).

[136] 6 Scott & Ascher §41.18.

[137] Lewin ¶5-67.

[138] Restatement (Third) of Property (Wills and Other Donative Transfers) §17.1 cmt. f.

[139] Lewin ¶26-52.

[140] *See* Restatement (Third) of Property (Wills and Other Donative Transfers) §21.2 cmt. a (" . . . [T]he donor of a power not presently exercisable has manifested an intent that the selection of the appointees and the determination of the interests they are to receive is to be made in the light of the circumstances that exist on the date that the power becomes exercisable. Were a contract to appoint to be enforceable, the donor's intent would be defeated.").

[141] Lewin ¶26-52.

to effect an equitable allocation of assets in the event there has been an innocent ineffective exercise of a limited/special testamentary power of appointment in favor of a nonobject. The subject of fraudulent exercises of limited powers is addressed in Section 8.15.26 of this handbook.

Exclusive (exclusionary) and nonexclusive (nonexclusionary) limited powers. The holder (donee) of an *exclusive/exclusionary* limited power may exercise the power in favor of fewer than all of the members of the permissible class of appointees (objects).[142] If the power were *nonexclusive/nonexclusionary*, for the exercise to be valid, it would have to be in favor of all members of the class. No one could be left out.[143] The permissible appointees, however, would have to have been sufficiently defined and limited by the terms of the power.[144]

The exclusivity presumption. The Restatement (Third) of Property would presume exclusivity: "In determining whether a power is exclusionary or nonexclusionary, the power is exclusionary unless the terms of the power expressly provide that an appointment must benefit each permissible appointee or one or more designated permissible appointees."[145]

The illusory appointments doctrine. Should the donee/holder of a nonexclusionary/nonexclusive power of appointment exercise the power in a way that effectively excludes one or more of the permissible appointees from a share of the appointive property, then the illusory appointments doctrine could be implicated, a topic we take up in Section 8.15.86 of this handbook.

Hotchpot clauses. A permissible appointee of an exclusionary nongeneral power of appointment also may be a taker in default of its exercise should the terms of the trust so provide. As a qualification, however, the terms of the trust might call for the value of mandatory principal distributions to the taker in default to be reduced by the value of prior principal discretionary distributions to the taker in default incident to any exercises of the power. The power could be of the fiduciary or nonfiduciary variety. In the case of the former, the powerholder is likely to be the trustee of a discretionary trust.[146] Such a set-off provision is known as a hotchpot clause and is the subject of Section 8.15.51 of this handbook.[147] In any case, "[s]uch a clause does not make the power nonexclusionary, because the terms do not prevent the donee from making an appointment that excludes a permissible appointee."[148]

---

[142] Restatement (Third) of Property (Wills and Other Donative Transfers) §17.5.

[143] *See, e.g.,* Hargrove v. Rich, 278 Ga. 561, 604 S.E.2d 475 (2004) (a limited power to appoint to a class of "nieces and nephews" is a nonexclusive power and thus could not be exercised in favor of only one niece to the exclusion of other members of the class, the court holding that the conjunctive "and" denotes nonexclusivity).

[144] Restatement (Third) of Property (Wills and Other Donative Transfers) §17.5 cmt. b & cmt. h.

[145] Restatement (Third) of Property (Wills and Other Donative Transfers) §17.5.

[146] *See generally* §3.5.3.2(a) of this handbook (the discretionary trust).

[147] *See also* Charles E. Rounds, Jr., *Old Doctrine Misunderstood, New Doctrine Misconceived: Deconstructing the Newly-Minted Restatement (Third) of Property's Power of Appointment Sections,* 26 Quinnipiac Prob. L.J. 240, 261 (2013) (the hotchpot calculation n the trust context).

[148] Restatement (Third) of Property (Wills and Other Donative Transfers) §17.5 cmt. k.

The Restatement (Third) of Property endorses the following intent-based default assumption: "If the donee of a power of appointment makes a valid partial appointment to a taker in default, the taker in default-appointee also takes his or her share of any unappointed property as taker in default. . . ."[149] As noted, the donor of a power of appointment may expressly provide in the terms of the grant that, to the extent the donee makes an appointment to a taker in default, the appointee must elect either to take by appointment or to take in default thereof.[150] The donor, though, might provide that in the case of an actual partial appointment to a taker in default, the appointee may elect to take in default as well, provided that the appointee's share of the fund to be divided up among all the takers in default is determined by hotchpot calculation.[151] As the English say, the appointed property notionally needs to be "brought into hotchpot."[152]

Nonexclusionary general powers. There are some musings in the Restatement (Third) of Property to the effect that even general powers of appointment can be nonexclusionary.[153] The examples proffered in support of the proposition, however, actually are not supportive.[154] For an explanation of why they are not supportive, see Rounds, *Old Doctrine Misunderstood, New Doctrine Misconceived: Deconstructing the Newly-Minted Restatement (Third) of Property's Power of Appointment Sections.*[155]

A power of appointment is exercised; neither the power itself nor the appointive property is transferred. The holder of a power "exercises" the power; he or she does not "transfer" it or the appointive property. Professor Lewis M. Simes said it best: "Perhaps the most significant aspect of the operation of powers of appointment is involved in the doctrine that the exercise of the power is an event and not a conveyance. . . ."[156] In the case of entrusted property, title moves from the trustee to the appointee in and on the event of exercise. Thus, "[i]f the donee dies without exercising the power, the power lapses (expires). The power does not pass through the donee's estate to the

---

[149] Restatement (Third) of Property (Wills and Other Donative Transfers) §19.24.

[150] Restatement (Third) of Property (Wills and Other Donative Transfers) §19.24 cmt. b.

[151] Restatement (Third) of Property (Wills and Other Donative Transfers) §19.24 cmt. b.

[152] Lewin ¶ 28-02. *See also* §8.15.51 of this handbook (hotchpot).

[153] Restatement (Third) of Property (Wills and Other Donative Transfers) §17.5 cmt. b. *See generally*, Charles E. Rounds, Jr., *Old Doctrine Misunderstood, New Doctrine Misconceived: Deconstructing the Newly-Minted Restatement (Third) of Property's Power of Appointment Sections*, 26 Quinnipiac Prob. L.J. 240, 274–275 (2013).

[154] *See* Restatement (Third) of Property (Wills and Other Donative Transfers) §17.5 cmt. g. *See generally*, Charles E. Rounds, Jr., *Old Doctrine Misunderstood, New Doctrine Misconceived: Deconstructing the Newly-Minted Restatement (Third) of Property's Power of Appointment Sections*, 26 Quinnipiac Prob. L.J. 240, 274–275 (2013).

[155] Charles E. Rounds, Jr., *Old Doctrine Misunderstood, New Doctrine Misconceived: Deconstructing the Newly-Minted Restatement (Third) of Property's Power of Appointment Sections*, 26 Quinnipiac Prob. L.J. 240, 274–275 (2013).

[156] Lewis M. Simes, Cases and Materials on the Law of Future Interests 208 (2d ed. 1951). *But see* Restatement (Third) of Property (Wills and Other Donative Transfers) §19.7 cmt. a ("A donee of a power of appointment who exercises the power is like any other transferor of property in regard to authority to revoke or amend the transfer.").

donee's successors in interest."[157] English tradition is in accord: "In general, a person to whom a discretion has been given, whether personally or by virtue of his being in a fiduciary relationship, may not delegate his discretion to others. *Delegatus non potest delegare.*"[158]

Appointment to a trustee as a constructive transfer of the power. A holder of a nonfiduciary power of appointment, however, may be able to effect the functional equivalent of its transfer, provided that the holder is entitled to exercise the power in further trust, which nowadays is likely to be the case.[159]

A general power to appoint to the holder or the holder's estate encompasses a right in the holder to exercise the power in further trust without restriction as to the terms of the further entrustment. Thus, the terms of the further entrustment may grant general powers of appointment (and nongeneral powers, as well) to anyone in the universe.[160] For more on the exercise of powers in further trust, the reader is referred to Section 8.1.2 of this handbook.[161] Whether the exercise of a general power fails at the outset or at a later time, the doctrine of capture may be implicated, a topic that is taken up in Section 8.15.12 of this handbook.

As noted, inherent in an equitable nonfiduciary power to revoke a trust and take ownership of the subject property is the power to constructively transfer the power irrevocably via an exercise of the power in further trust.[162] The Restatement (Third) of Property (Wills and Other Donative Transfers) falsely analogizes such a constructive transfer to a delegation of the power of revocation.[163] Such a constructive transfer is better analogized to an irrevocable

---

[157] Restatement (Third) of Property (Wills and Other Donative Transfers) §17.1 cmt. b.

[158] Hansbury and Maudsley, Modern Equity 145–146 (10th ed. 1976). *See, however,* the Restatement (Third) of Property (Wills and Other Donative Transfers) §19.13 cmt. g, which suggests that "[a]n appointment that creates a power of appointment in another in effect delegates to the other the right to complete the exercise of the donee's power." In the case of the exercise of a general inter vivos power, at least, it would seem the better analogy is to that of an irrevocable assignment of a vested property interest in the subject property. The Restatement (First) of Property (194) [§359 cmt. a.] is in accord: "When the donee of a special power appoints by creating a general power in an object of the original power this is effective, not as a delegation of the power, but because it is an appointment of a valuable interest approximating ownership to the object himself." *See generally* W. Barton Leach, *Perpetuities in a Nutshell*, 51. Harv. L. Rev. 638, 653 (1938) (A general inter vivos power of appointment "is the equivalent of ownership since it enables the donee of the power to become the owner at any time by appointing to himself.").

[159] *See* Restatement (Third) of Property (Wills and Other Donative Transfers) §17.1 cmt. b.

[160] Restatement (Third) of Property (Wills and Other Donative Transfers) §19.13 cmt. f.

[161] If the donee (holder) of a general testamentary power of appointment exercises it by appointing the subject property to a trustee of a trust that fails *ab initio* or subsequently, a resulting trust is imposed. *See generally* §4.1.1.1 of this handbook (the resulting trust). The subject property, however, does not necessarily revert to the settlor of the original trust, or to the settlor's probate estate. Instead, a resulting trust might well be imposed in favor of the powerholder's probate estate under the so-called capture doctrine, a topic we take up in Section 8.15.12 of this handbook.

[162] Restatement (Third) of Property (Wills and Other Donative Transfers) §19.3 cmt. f; Restatement (Second) of Property (Wills and Other Donative Transfers) §19.2.

[163] Restatement (Third) of Property (Wills and Other Donative Transfers) §19.13 cmt. g.

transfer by assignment of the entrusted property itself.[164] "A presently exercisable general power of appointment is an ownership-equivalent power."[165] An agency, on the other hand, is revocable at the will of either party to it. Moreover, a discretionary agency imposes fiduciary duties on the agent. The constructive transferee of a general inter vivos power of appointment owes no fiduciary duties to the constructive transferor, absent special facts.

In the case of an equitable nongeneral power that may be exercised in further trust, the holder of the power may grant a *general inter vivos power of appointment* to a permissible appointee of the nongeneral power.[166] The Restatement (Third) of Property would go further and allow the holder to grant a general testamentary power of appointment to a permissible appointee of the nongeneral power. Here is the rationale: "If the general power created in the second donee is a testamentary power, the second donee does not have, in substance, the equivalent of ownership, but the second donee is close to having the equivalent of ownership, especially in a case in which the second donee is given an interest in the appointive assets."[167]

In the case of an equitable nongeneral power that may be exercised in further trust (Special Power #1), any grant of *another nongeneral power of appointment* incident to the exercise in further trust (Special Power #2) must be for the benefit of the permissible appointees of Special Power #1.[168] Under the Restatement (First) of Property, only a permissible appointee of Special Power #1 could be a grantee of Special Power #2.[169] Under the Restatement (Third) of Property (Wills and Other Donative Transfers), specifically Section 19.14, however, an impermissible appointee of Special Power #1 may be a grantee, as well.[170]

The impermissible appointee however, holds Special Power #2 in "confidence" for the benefit of the permissible appointees of Special Power #1.[171] Unexplained in the commentary and Reporter's Notes to Section 19.14 is whether the impermissible appointee assumes any fiduciary duties incident to his stewardship of Special Power #2. Here is the only guidance proffered; guidance that is fraught with ambiguity: "Because the donor has imposed confidence in the donee to select which permissible appointees to benefit by an

---

[164] *See* Marx v. Rice, 67 A.2d 918, 920–921 (N.J. Super. Ct., Ch. Div. 1949) (In the case of a general inter vivos power of appointment, such as a right of revocation, the donee of the power is the constructive owner of the subject property, not just some kind of quasi agent of the donor of the power).

[165] Restatement (Third) of Property (Wills and Other Donative Transfers) §17.4 cmt. f(1).

[166] Restatement (Third) of Property (Wills and Other Donative Transfers) §19.14 cmt. g(1).

[167] Restatement (Third) of Property (Wills and Other Donative Transfers) §19.14 cmt. g(1). *See also* Restatement (First) of Property §359 (2) cmt. a (1940).

[168] Restatement (Third) of Property (Wills and Other Donative Transfers) §19.14.

[169] Restatement (First) of Property §359(2) ("The donee of a special power can effectively exercise it by creating in an object an interest for life and a special power to appoint among persons all of whom are objects of the original power, unless the donor manifests a contrary intent.").

[170] Restatement (Third) of Property (Wills and Other Donative Transfers) §19.14 cmt. g(4).

[171] *See generally*, Charles E. Rounds, Jr., *Old Doctrine Misunderstood, New Doctrine Misconceived: Deconstructing the Newly-Minted Restatement (Third) of Property's Power of Appointment Sections*, 26 Quinnipiac Prob. L.J. 240, 269–271 (2013).

appointment, the donee is authorized to grant the selection power to any other person."[172]

By definition, the original donee of an equitable nonfiduciary nongeneral power is unconstrained by the fiduciary principle. The status of the donee's surrogate, however, is another matter. Loaded words like "confidence" and "benefit" suggest that the donee's surrogate may well be holding Special Power #2 itself in trust for the benefit of the Special Power #1's permissible appointees. If what we have here is essentially the conversion of an equitable nonfiduciary power into some kind of a fiduciary one, then there is nothing in the Restatement (Third) of Property about how the fiduciary duties of the surrogate are to be coordinated with those of the express trustee in whom the legal title to the trust property resides, or even what the scope of those duties might be. Perhaps some useful coordination analogies may be found elsewhere, such as in trust protector doctrine, which is rapidly moving out of the development state. The office of trust protector is covered generally in Section 3.2.6 of this handbook.

Adapted trusts are sui generis. Upon the disclaimer by the trustee of an adapted trust of an unexercised power to select those among an indefinite class of beneficiaries who are to receive the trust property, the power could pass to the successor trustee.[173] The settlor, however, must have designated, or provided a means for designating, a successor trustee, or intended that the power not be personal to the original trustee.[174]

Donee's authority to revoke or amend exercise. Take a trust that contains the following terms: A (settlor) to B (trustee) for C1 (first income beneficiary) for life, then to C2 for life (second income beneficiary), and upon the death of C2, legal title to the entrusted property passes outright and free of trust from B to D (the remainderman). C2 is also granted a nongeneral inter vivos power of appointment over the trust property, *subject to C1's equitable life estate.* C2 exercises the power by deed in favor of X while C1 is still alive. Can C2 undo the exercise prior to C2's death, legal title to the appointive property still being in the trustee? Or is the exercise irrevocable?

Here is the traditional black-letter law: "The donee of a power of appointment lacks the authority to revoke or amend an exercise of the power, except to the extent that the donee reserved a power of revocation or amendment when exercising the power, and the terms of the power do not prohibit the reservation."[175] The rule of irrevocability of appointments has its origins in the 1717 English case of *Hele v. Bond.*[176] "When an appointment presently and unreservedly transfers appointive property to an object, the rule of irrevocability derived

---

[172] Restatement (Third) of Property (Wills and Other Donative Transfers) §19.14 cmt. g(4).
[173] Restatement (Third) of Trusts §46 cmt. d(3).
[174] Restatement (Third) of Trusts §46 cmt. d(3).
[175] Restatement (Third) of Property (Wills and Other Donative Transfers) §19.7.
[176] Hele v. Bond, [1717] Prec. Ch. 474, 24 Eng. Rep. 213. *See also* Saunders v. Evans, [1861] 8 H.L. Cas. 721, 11 Eng. Rep. 611; Shirley v. Fisher, [1882] 43 Ch. Div. 290.

from *Hele v. Bond*... is recognized by American authorities without exception."[177] Now comes the Restatement (Third) of Property and unsettles the doctrine.

In that a will speaks at death, an exercise of a testamentary power of appointment cannot be undone. The Restatement (Second) of Property confirms that if *C2*'s power were testamentary, then there could be no exercise until *C2* dies, which is when the terms of *C2*'s will speak. Any exercise of a testamentary power of appointment perforce is irrevocable, because the power itself is not exercisable until the powerholder's death.[178] The Restatement (Third) of Property seems to be in accord, although it is hard to tell for sure. There may be some text missing. Here is what there is: "Because a will does not become effective as a dispositive instrument until the testator dies..., a testamentary exercise of a power—whether the power is testamentary or presently exercisable—may be revoked or amended by the donee to the same extent as any other provision of the donee's will."[179] A testamentary exercise of a presently exercisable power of appointment may be revoked?[180] Again, once a testamentary power is exercised by will it is too late to revoke the exercise, because the testator is dead and thus unavailable to execute the revocation. Nor can the testator's agent exercise the revocation as an agency terminates upon the principal's death. Also, some preliminary background commentary on exercises by will of presently exercisable powers would have been helpful. The revocability of such exercises is difficult enough to grasp.

Power exercisable by donee's last unrevoked deed. The Restatement (Third) of Property alludes to a "power that is exercisable by the donee's last unrevoked instrument."[181] No context or example is supplied. It is self-evident that a testamentary power of appointment can only be exercised by the donee's last unrevoked will. But what about an inter vivos power of appointment that is exercisable by the donee's last unrevoked exercise by deed? How would that work in practice? The Reporter's Notes are of no help.

Take the inter vivos power of appointment. Its terms provide that (1) the interests of the appointees can only become possessory upon the expiration of a prior equitable interest, such as the *C1* equitable life estate in the *A-B-C1-C2* entrustment described immediately above, and (2) the power is exercisable by the donee's last unrevoked deed. In this context, the donee's "last unrevoked instrument" would be the last unrevoked deed of inter vivos exercise that was executed before the termination of the preceding equitable life estate. This presumption is buttressed by the comprehensive and scholarly Reporter's Notes to the now-superseded Section 15.2 of the Restatement (Second) of Property (Donative Transfers). But we are still left with the question of whether

---

[177] Restatement (Second) of Property (Wills and Other Donative Transfers) §15.2, Reporter's Notes.

[178] Restatement (Second) of Property (Wills and Other Donative Transfers) §15.2 cmt. c.

[179] Restatement (Third) of Property (Wills and Other Donative Transfers) §19.7 cmt. c.

[180] The language of the Restatement (Second) of Property (Wills and Other Donative Transfers) is less muddled. It speaks in terms of revoking inter vivos the "terms" of a testamentary power exercise rather than revoking the testamentary exercise itself. *See* §15.2 cmt. b.

[181] Restatement (Third) of Property (Wills and Other Donative Transfers) §19.7 cmt. b.

C2's exercise by deed was revocable in the first place. Presumably that would hinge on whether there has been an express reservation of such a right. The Restatement (Third) of Property, for example, would deem an exercise "by revocable trust" to be an "exercise by deed," a convoluted fiction that should have been fleshed out with some thoughtful commentary.

Power revocation by power exercise. In the case of a power exercisable either by deed or by will, which is actually two powers, the last unrevoked inter vivos exercise by deed of exercise trumps any testamentary exercise,[182] with the effective date of the inter vivos exercise presumably being *retroactive to the date the deed was executed*. Thus, we have a nasty trap for the unwary trustee saddled with absolute liability for misdelivering the property of his terminating trust: "If a power is exercisable by deed or by will, the provisions in the will in regard to the exercise of the power may be nullified by an inter vivos appointment by the donee that may cause what in effect is an ademption or a satisfaction of the provisions exercising the power in the will."[183]

The mechanics of exercising a power of appointment. Most if not all powers of appointment specify that any exercise be by written instrument. The authors have never seen a power of appointment that expressly provides for its oral exercise, although a settlor's telephone request for funds from the trustee of his revocable inter vivos trust would actually be tantamount to such an exercise. The terms of a particular power might specify that the instrument of exercise shall be a will. Or it might specify that it shall be a deed. In any case, the *will* and the *deed* have been the two main categories of exercise vehicles. A will that has been duly admitted to probate has generally more than sufficed.[184] So also has a deed "that would be formally sufficient under applicable law to be legally operative in the donee's lifetime to transfer an interest to the appointee if the donee owned the appointive assets."[185] And if the mode of exercise is not expressly specified? "A power in which the document of exercise is not specified (as in 'to such as the donee shall appoint') is exercisable by deed or will."[186] A

---

[182] Restatement (Third) of Property (Wills and Other Donative Transfers) §19.7 cmt. c ("If the power is presently exercisable, an irrevocable inter vivos appointment may defeat a testamentary exercise.").

[183] Restatement (Second) of Property (Wills and Other Donative Transfers) §15.2 cmt. b. *See generally* §8.15.54 of this handbook (ademption in the trust context).

[184] The level of capacity a donee of a power of appointment would need to have possessed in order to effectively exercise it by will is the same level of capacity that the donee would need to have possessed in order to effectively transfer by will property which the donee had owned outright and free of trust. *See* Restatement (Third) of Property (Wills and Other Donative Transfers) §19.8(a) (capacity of donee of a power of appointment to exercise the power by will); Chapter 1 of this handbook (capacity to transfer one's property generally by will).

[185] Restatement (Third) of Property (Wills and Other Donative Transfers) §19.9 cmt. d. The level of capacity a donee of a power of appointment would need to possess in order to effectively exercise the power by deed is the same level that the donee would need to possess in order to effectively transfer by deed of gift property which the donee owns outright and free of trust. *See* Restatement (Third) of Property (Wills and Other Donative Transfers) §19.8(a) (capacity of donee of power of appointment to exercise the power of appointment by deed); Chapter 1 of this handbook (capacity generally to transfer one's property by deed of gift).

[186] Restatement (Third) of Property (Wills and Other Donative Transfers) §19.9 cmt. g.

power exercisable by deed or will is in substance two powers.[187] The Restatement (Third) of Property would drop two additional types of exercise vehicle into the mix: the unprobated but duly executed will and the revocable inter vivos trust.[188]

The unprobated but duly executed will as a power-exercise vehicle. The Restatement (Third) of Property would have a power of appointment that is exercisable "by will" exercisable by an unprobated instrument that is "formally" sufficient to be admitted to probate under applicable law.[189] On the other hand, if the instrument ends up actually being submitted to probate and probate is denied, then the exercise is retroactively ineffective.[190] What is left unexplained is how prudent trustees are to practically and cost-effectively smoke out enforceable exercises of testamentary powers of appointment by unprobated wills. Recall the general rule that a trustee is absolutely liable for misdelivering the trust property.[191]

Going forward, scriveners should give serious consideration to drafting testamentary powers of appointment that are expressly exercisable only by wills that have actually been probated. With respect to testamentary powers that have already been granted, there are things that trustees can do to insulate themselves from personal liability for misdelivery in the absence of such an express limitation. In the face of reasonable doubt as to whether or not in a given situation a testamentary power may have been exercised via nonprobated will, for example, the trustee is entitled at trust expense to seek guidance from the court, such as by filing a complaint for instructions and/or declaratory judgment.[192]

Power exercise via a revocable inter vivos trust instrument. The Restatement (Third) of Property would have an equitable power of appointment that is exercisable "by will" exercisable "in a revocable-trust document, as long as the revocable trust remained revocable at the donee's death."[193] The reason? Because "a revocable trust operates in substance as a will."[194] The problem with such one-dimensional thinking is that a self-settled revocable inter vivos trust is still not a true testamentary instrument; and it is certainly much more than just a will substitute. It can also function, for example, as a static inter vivos property-management vehicle for competent and incompetent settlors alike, a function that wills can never perform for their testators, the will being merely a property transfer vehicle that speaks only at death. But things get even more

---

[187] *But see* Restatement (Third) of Property (Wills and Other Donative Transfers) §19.9 cmt. e (a nonsensical conflation of two powers of appointment, one exercisable by deed and the other by will, into a single "presently exercisable" power of appointment).

[188] Restatement (Third) of Property (Wills and Other Donative Transfers) §19.9 cmt. b.

[189] Restatement (Third) of Property (Wills and Other Donative Transfers) §19.9 cmt. b.

[190] Restatement (Third) of Property (Wills and Other Donative Transfers) §19.9 cmt. b.

[191] *See generally* §6.1.2 of this handbook (liability of trustees for misdelivery of trust property).

[192] *See generally* §8.42 of this handbook (the complaint for instructions and the complaint for declaratory judgment).

[193] Restatement (Third) of Property (Wills and Other Donative Transfers) §19.9 cmt. b.

[194] Restatement (Third) of Property (Wills and Other Donative Transfers) §19.9 cmt. b.

muddled and convoluted . . . and ungrammatical. Apparently, "[t]he exercise of a power of appointment by [sic] a revocable trust would be an exercise 'by deed.'"[195]

How would one who had been granted, say, an equitable nongeneral power of appointment exercisable "by will" actually go about exercising it "by revocable trust"? What would such an exercise look like? Presumably the power-grantee-settlor via the terms of this revocable trust would direct the trustee of the revocable trust upon the grantee's death to, in turn, direct the trustee of the original trust—the trust containing the power grant—to distribute the subject property to one or more of the permissible appointees.

Guidance is lacking as to whether a trustee of a revocable trust may be granted fiduciary discretion to exercise or not exercise the power to appoint by will upon the death of the settlor of the revocable trust, that is to say, upon the death of the grantee of the power. If a trustee were granted such fiduciary discretion, how long would the trustee have to make up his mind following the death of the power grantee? And finally, what is the Restatement (Third) of Property's purpose in deeming an exercise by revocable trust to be an exercise by deed? And who would be the deemed grantor of the deed, the settlor or the trustee of the revocable trust that has the power-exercise provision?

The grantor of a power to appoint "by will" may effectively prohibit exercise "by revocable trust" in the express terms of the power grant. The grantor who wishes to authorize exercise "by revocable trust" would be well advised to specify with detailed precision, in the terms of the power grant, the process that must be followed to effect such an exercise, step by step.[196]

When the exercise is the product of someone's wrongdoing. It is self-evident that in order for an attempted exercise of a power of appointment to be effective, the exercise must not be the product of fraud, duress, or undue influence perpetrated against the donee by one who would be unjustly enriched by the exercise. The Restatement (Third) of Property, however, garbles the transmission. It asserts that the "donee must be free from . . . wrongdoing."[197] The power's

---

[195] Restatement (Third) of Property (Wills and Other Donative Transfers) §19.9 cmt. d.

[196] It is critical that the scrivener know whether the grantor of the testamentary power contemplated that the trustee of the exercising trust be a ministerial agent of the grantee of the power, or whether the grantor of the power contemplated something more intensive, such as that the trustee of the exercising trust being vested via the terms of the exercising trust with fiduciary discretion to exercise or not exercise the power. If the trustee of the exercising trust may be vested with fiduciary discretion via the terms of the exercising trust to exercise the power, then the scrivener of the exercising trust needs to know the limits of the discretion and to whom the fiduciary duties are to be owed. In any case, as the trustee possesses the legal title to the property that is the subject of the exercising trust, a trust that was once revocable, it would seem that it is the trustee of the exercising trust who needs to be the mechanical centerpiece of any exercise "by revocable trust," the grantee-settlor perforce being dead. While the exercising trust may be a will substitute, it is not a will. Rather, it is an ongoing fiduciary relationship with respect to property to which the trustee has the legal title. That being the case, a "testamentary" power-exercise by the trustee of an exercising trust would bear some resemblance to an exercise "by deed" in that the trustee would be alive at the time the instrument of exercise speaks. The Restatement (Third), however, fails to connect the dots, so this is only a surmise.

[197] Restatement (Third) of Property (Wills and Other Donative Transfers) §19.8(b).

exercise cannot be the result of wrongdoing perpetrated by others *against the donee*. Wrongdoing *by donees*, which is a whole other matter, implicates the unrelated fraud on a special power doctrine, a topic we take up in Section 8.15.26 of this handbook.

The effectiveness of a purported inter vivos exercise of a general power of appointment by the donee's guardian or agent under a durable power of attorney. This is a topic that is covered in Section 8.2.2.2 of this handbook.

The blanket-exercise clause. A blanket instrument of exercise exercises, or attempts to exercise, all powers of appointment possessed by the one who has executed the instrument. The form blanket-exercise language proffered by the Restatement (Third) of Property refers to "any power of appointment I may have,"[198] which is unfortunate, the amorphous "any" being defined as "one, some, every, or all without specification."[199] Replacing the word "any" with the word "each," together with a few minor wording adjustments, should do the trick. Though syntactically singular, "each" unambiguously conveys the intention that *all* possessed powers be exercised.

A provision in a will that expressly or by implication purports to exercise all testamentary powers of appointment generally captures powers created after the will was executed, that is to say after the will was duly signed and witnessed. "A will speaks as of the date it becomes legally operative, which is the date the testator dies. It disposes of after-acquired property, and by analogy after-acquired powers should be similarly treated."[200] Section 17.6 of the now-superseded Restatement (Second) of Property (Donative Transfers) sets forth the traditional black-letter law applicable to such blanket exercises: "A manifestation of intent in the donee's will to exercise powers includes powers acquired after the execution of the donee's will, unless the exercise of the after-acquired powers is specifically excluded." Note that Section 17.6 addressed only appointments by will; an appointment by deed, unlike a will, generally being effective and final at the time the deed of exercise is executed and delivered.

The successor to Section 17.6, namely Section 19.6 of the Restatement (Third) of Property (Wills and Other Donative Transfers), is much broader in scope, so much so, in fact, that it appears that more has been bitten off than is chewable. Not only are blanket exercises by will covered, but apparently also blanket exercises by testamentary trust, revocable trust, and irrevocable inter vivos trust, as well. No illustrations, however, are supplied that would enlighten one as to what an exercise "by trust" would actually look like in practice. Presumably, the internal exercise clause would have to be triggered by some event, such as someone's death. The illustrations address only exercises by will. The cryptic Reporter's Notes are similarly silent. Here is the Restatement (Third) of Property's problematic comment, specifically comment b to Section 19.6: "The donee's exercising document is any document that the donee

---

[198] Restatement (Third) of Property (Wills and Other Donative Transfers) §19.2 cmt. d.

[199] The American Heritage Dictionary of the English Language 83 (3d ed. 1996).

[200] Restatement (Second) of Property (Wills and Other Donative Transfers) §17.6 cmt. a. *See generally* §8.15.9 of this handbook (doctrine of independent legal significance).

executes that contains an exercise clause. Thus, the donee's exercising document could be the donee's will, a testamentary trust, a revocable or irrevocable
inter vivos trust, or any other document that contains an exercise clause."[201]
That is it. Even one illustration would have been nice.

When a general testamentary power of appointment is exercised by a
catch-all provision in the will of the donee (holder) of the power, a catch-all
provision being one that not only disposes of the property the donee owned but
also exercises all unspecified powers of appointment that the donee may have
possessed, we may have a "blending" of the appointive assets with the property
that was owned by the donee.[202] In the case of a blending, the blended property
is allocated ratably to the various interests, including claims of creditors, taxes,
and expenses of administration.

Under the Uniform Probate Code, a blanket-exercise clause in the will of
the donee (holder) of a testamentary power of appointment, whether the power
is general or nongeneral, will effect its exercise.[203] "If a governing instrument
creating a power of appointment expressly requires that the power be exercised
by a reference, an express reference, or a specific reference, to the power or its
source, it is presumed that the donor's intention, in requiring that the donee
exercise the power by making reference to the particular power or to the
creating instrument, was to prevent an inadvertent exercise of the power."[204]
Thus, if there is clear and convincing extrinsic evidence that the purpose of a
blanket-exercise clause, at least in part, was to exercise a particular power that
has a specific-reference requirement associated with it, then the blanket-
exercise clause might well serve to exercise the power, unless the presumption as
to the limited purpose of the requirement, namely, just to avoid inadvertent
exercise, is overcome.[205]

The specific exercise clause. A testamentary instrument of specific exercise
might look like this: "I hereby exercise the power of appointment conferred
upon me by [my mother's will] as follows: I appoint [fill in details of appoint-
ment]."[206] Note that the mother's will is not referred to by date "because the
donee's mother might subsequently revoke her will and replace it with another."[207] It has been suggested that the specific-reference requirement actually
owes its current ubiquity to a pre-1942 provision of the Internal Revenue Code:

---

[201] The preoccupation of the Restatement (Third) of Property with unifying the law of wills
and will substitutes is ubiquitous. *See, for example,* Section 19.6's second illustration, which deals
with the situation where the same person is both the donor and the donee of a power of
appointment: "Since a revocable inter vivos trust is in practical effect a substitute for a will, it is not
likely that Donee intended that the [blanket exercise] provisions of his existing will should in effect
nullify the provisions of the gift-in-default clause in Donee's subsequently executed revocable
trust."

[202] Restatement (Second) of Property (Wills and Other Donative Transfers) §22.1; 6 Scott &
Ascher §41.17.

[203] UPC §2-608 cmt.

[204] UPC §2-704.

[205] UPC §2-704 cmt. *See generally* §8.24 of this handbook (burdens of proof).

[206] Restatement (Third) of Property (Wills and Other Donative Transfers) §19.2 cmt. c.

[207] Restatement (Third) of Property (Wills and Other Donative Transfers) §19.2, Reporter's
Note.

"Specific-reference clauses were a pre-1942 invention to prevent an inadvertent exercise of a general power.... The federal estate-tax law then provided that the value of property subject to a general power was included in the donee's gross estate *only if the general power was exercised.*"[208] For general powers created after October 1, 1942, the mere possession of an unexercised power can have adverse estate tax consequences.[209] A technical violation of the terms of a specific-exercise clause will not necessarily render the exercise ineffective, a topic that is taken up in Section 8.15.88 of this handbook.[210]

The blending clause. A blending clause "purports to blend the appointive property with the donee's own property in a common disposition."[211] The vehicle of disposition is typically the will residue clause:

> The exercise portion of a blending clause can take the form of a specific exercise or, more commonly, a blanket exercise. For example, a clause providing "All the rest, residue, and remainder of my estate, including the property over which I have a power of appointment under my mother's will, I give, devise, and bequeath as follows" is a blending clause with a specific reference. A clause providing "All the rest, residue, and remainder of my estate, including any property over which I have a power of appointment, I give, devise, and bequeath as follows" is a blending clause with a blanket exercise.[212]

Partial exercise. Unless the terms of the power provide otherwise, a partial exercise of a general inter vivos power of appointment, perhaps over income alone[213] or over a certain percentage of the principal, is usually permissible and would not extinguish the power over the unaffected property. Moreover, merely amending the trust by means of an exercise of the general inter vivos power would not extinguish the power as to both the affected and unaffected property, unless a purpose of the amendment was to renounce or otherwise do away with the power in whole or in part. In other words, absent special facts and circumstances, the exercise of a general inter vivos power of appointment need not be a one-shot deal.

A power over a portion of the trust property. A partial exercise of a power of appointment is not to be confused with a power of appointment that is granted only over a portion of the trust property. If only a portion of the trust estate is subject to a general inter vivos power of appointment, then the holder is the constructive owner of only that portion, as long as he or she is of full age

---

[208] Restatement (Third) of Property (Wills and Other Donative Transfers) §19.10 cmt. d.

[209] *See* I.R.C. §2041.

[210] *But see* Estate of Christiansen v. Stevens, 127 So. 3d 675, 678 (Fla. 2013) ("The donor of a power, inasmuch as he is disposing of his own property, may prescribe whatever ceremonies he pleases for its execution; and although these may be perfectly arbitrary, yet, being required by the creator of the power, they can be satisfied only by a strictly literal and precise performance of them.").

[211] Restatement (Third) of Property (Wills and Other Donative Transfers) §19.2 cmt. e.

[212] Restatement (Third) of Property (Wills and Other Donative Transfers) §19.2 cmt. e.

[213] As to what an exercise of a power of appointment over income alone would look like, *see* Loring v. Marshall, 396 Mass. 166, 484 N.E.2d 1315 (1985) (involving the partial exercise of a limited/special testamentary power of appointment).

and legal capacity.[214] This would include the power to subvert the interests of the other beneficiaries as to that portion.[215] It also would include the power to segregate the portion subject to the power from the rest of the trust estate and impress a different trust upon that portion, provided, however, that the donee's exercise of authority over the portion "does not intrude upon the administration of, or the rights of others in, the other share or shares of the trust."[216]

Exercise before power created. A power of appointment cannot be effectively exercised before the power itself comes into existence or before a condition precedent to the power's exercise has been satisfied.[217] A testamentary power of appointment, however, may be exercised by a will that is executed, *i.e.*, signed and witnessed, before the power is created but takes effect after the power is created.[218] Why? Because a will speaks at death.[219]

Some powers of appointment are exercisable by dispositive instruments that make no specific or general mention whatsoever of powers of appointment. Some powers of appointment are exercisable by dispositive instruments that make neither specific nor general mention of powers of appointment. There is, for example, some old law to the effect that a plain-vanilla will residue clause exercised all general testamentary powers of appointment that the testator had possessed over entrusted property. Of course, such a clause would not have exercised a power that by its terms could only have been exercised by an instrument making specific reference to the power. In the case of any type of power, whether inter vivos or testamentary, and whether general or nongeneral, there is always a risk that an instrument that is merely intended to transfer the powerholder's unentrusted property will unintentionally effect an exercise of the power in favor of the transferees of that property. We start, however, with the naked disposition by will or deed of a specified item of entrusted property by someone other than the trustee.

Appointive assets specifically identified in a dispositive instrument of donee that contains no mention of powers of appointment. A power of appointment is properly exercised by an instrument that makes some reference to the power, or at least to powers of appointment in general. In the case of a "carelessly drawn" instrument of exercise that makes no such reference,[220] all is not necessarily lost: "A disposition by the donee of property over which the donee has a power of appointment

---

[214] Restatement (Third) of Trusts §74 cmt. h.

[215] Restatement (Third) of Trusts §74 cmt. h.

[216] Restatement (Third) of Trusts §74 cmt. h.

[217] Restatement (Second) of Property (Wills and Other Donative Transfers) §18.4. "The second Restatement differs from the first, however, in adding the rule that a power cannot be exercised before a condition precedent to its exercise has been satisfied." Restatement (Second) of Property (Wills and Other Donative Transfers), Reporter's Note to §18.4.

[218] Restatement (Second) of Property (Wills and Other Donative Transfers) §17.6.

[219] Restatement (Second) of Property (Wills and Other Donative Transfers) §17.6 cmt. a. "[A will] . . . disposes of after-acquired owned property, and by analogy after-acquired powers should be similarly treated." Restatement (Second) of Property (Wills and Other Donative Transfers) §17.6 cmt. a. *See generally* 1 Scott & Ascher §7.1.4.

[220] Restatement (Second) of Property (Wills and Other Donative Transfers) §17.4 cmt. b ("In situations where the rule of this section applies, the deed or will in question has been carelessly drawn.").

manifests an intent to exercise the donee's power over the property."[221] Here is the underlying policy: "When the donee purports to dispose of property covered by a power, even though the donee does not refer to the power, it is a fair inference that the donee's dominant purpose is to cause the designated beneficiary to receive the property. The method by which this result is obtained is secondary."[222] Of course, such a naked disposition in favor of impermissible objects of the power would not be effective in exercising the power.

Exercise of general testamentary powers of appointment by plain-vanilla will residue clauses. In a few states, the most notable being New York,[223] a general residuary clause in a will that makes no specific reference to powers of appointment (such as "all the rest, residue, and remainder of my estate, I devise to . . .") is presumed nevertheless to exercise a *general* testamentary power of appointment, unless the settlor (the donor of the power) has indicated a contrary intention in the instrument that created the power.[224] In those few states, exercise could be effected as well by a catch-all provision disposing of all of the testator's estate.[225] Such a presumption or "rule of construction" at one time prevailed in Massachusetts.[226] In most states, however, there is now no such presumption.[227] In New York, a residuary clause might even exercise a *limited* testamentary power, provided the legatees and devisees are permissible takers, *i.e.*, permissible objects of the power.[228] "When a general power to appoint by will is exercised by the residuary clause in the donee's will, the appointive property is blended with the donee's owned property that is disposed of by the residuary clause."[229]

At one time, Section 2-608 of the Uniform Probate Code (UPC) provided that a general residuary clause in a will or a will making a general disposition of all of the testator's property did *not* exercise a power of appointment held by the testator, unless specific reference was made to the power or there was some other indication of intention to include the property subject to the power.[230] In 1990 the negative rule was made subject to several exceptions. One exception is that if a power is a general one and there is no gift over in default of its exercise, a general residuary clause or general disposition in the will of the donee of the

---

[221] Restatement (Third) of Property (Wills and Other Donative Transfers) §19.3.

[222] Restatement (Second) of Property (Wills and Other Donative Transfers) §17.4 cmt. a.

[223] *See* N.Y. Est. Powers & Trusts Law §10-6.1(a)(4) (1999).

[224] *See generally* Susan F. French, *Exercise of Powers of Appointment: Should Intent to Exercise Be Inferred from a General Disposition of Property?*, 1979 Duke L.J. 747. *See also* §§8.15.12 of this handbook (doctrine of capture) and 8.26 of this handbook (why trustees need to know about will residue clauses).

[225] *See* Restatement (Third) of Property (Wills and Other Donative Transfers) §19.4 cmt. a ("A disposition of all of the testator's property (such as 'All of my estate, I devise to . . . ') is the equivalent of a residuary clause.").

[226] *See* Beals v. State St. Bank & Trust Co., 326 N.E.2d 896 (Mass. 1975); Restatement (Third) of Property (Wills and Other Donative Transfers) §19.10 cmt. d.

[227] *See, e.g.*, UPC §2-608.

[228] *See generally* Susan F. French, *Exercise of Powers of Appointment: Should Intent to Exercise Be Inferred from a General Disposition of Property?*, 1979 Duke L.J. 768.

[229] Restatement (Second) of Property (Wills and Other Donative Transfers) §22.1 cmt. d.

[230] UPC §2-608 cmt.

power will serve to exercise it.[231] The Restatement (Second) of Property (Wills and Other Donative Transfers) Section 17.3 was generally in accord with UPC Section 2-608, although it had no absence-of-taker-in-default exception: "If the donee by deed or will manifests an intention to dispose of all of the donee's property, this of itself does not manifest an intention to exercise any power possessed by the donee." Note that Section 17.3 also contemplated exercises by deed.

The successor to Section 17.3, namely Section 19.4 of the Restatement (Third) of Property (Wills and Other Donative Transfers), leaves something to be desired in the grammar department. It also endorses with a vengeance the Uniform Probate Code's absence-of-taker-in-default exception, and ups the ante; in so doing, it sets a particularly nasty trap for the unwary trustee and estate planner. Here is the language: "A residuary clause in the donee's will or revocable trust does not manifest an intent to exercise any of the donee's power(s) [sic] of appointment, unless the power in question [sic] is a general power and the donor did not provide for takers in default *or the gift-in-default clause is ineffective.*"[232]

Here is the trap: Assume the donee possessed an equitable general testamentary power of appointment at the time of his death under his grandmother's trust. There is no express or blanket power-exercise clause in the donee's will, just a plain-vanilla residue clause. What if the gift-in-default clause in the grandmother's trust is rendered "ineffective," say, not until 20 years after the donee's death.?[233] All equitable quasi remainderman end up predeceasing the equitable income beneficiaries. The comments, illustrations, and Reporter's Notes supporting the Restatement (Third)'s Section 19.4 only address the trust that terminates on its own terms *upon the death of the powerholder*. The trustee of a terminated trust that, for whatever reason, has no remainderman to take needs to be careful. The trust property could actually now belong not to those who take incident to the imposition of a resulting trust, but to the lucky plain vanilla residuary takers under the will of some long-dead donee of an equitable general testamentary power of appointment. The terms of the power grant are buried in some strange place within the governing instrument. The donee, himself, is buried who knows where. Massachusetts has baked into its version of UPC 2-608 such a Restatement (Third)-type trap. The resulting trust is covered generally in Section 4.1.1.1 of this handbook

The property rights of the holder of an equitable reversion under a trust that fails for want of a remainderman has traditionally vested *ab initio*, a topic we

---

[231] UPC §2-608 cmt.

[232] If "any" is shorthand for "any one," then the option of selecting "power" in its singular form renders the sentence nonsensical.

[233] Assume, for example, that someone other than the donee of the general testamentary possesses an equitable life estate under the trust and that the trust is to terminate upon the death of the life beneficiary in favor of the settlor's (donor's) issue then living. Twenty years after the donee has died but before the death of the life beneficiary, the last survivor of the settlor's (donor's) issue dies rendering the gift-in-default clause "ineffective." Does this event now clear the way for the residuary takers under the donee's will (and the executors of those takers who have died in the interim) to take the legal title from the trustee once the trust terminates?

take up in Section 4.1.1 of this handbook. The Restatement (Third)'s Section 19.4 would render such a reversion subject to divestment upon the exercise of a general testamentary power by plain-vanilla will residue provision.[234] This is not the only layer of complexity of recent vintage that has been introduced into resulting trust jurisprudence. The other is the expansion of the application of antilapse principles to equitable interests under trusts, a topic that is taken up in Section 8.15.55 of this handbook. The resulting trust is covered generally in Section 4.1.1.1 of this handbook.

That the Uniform Probate Code is synchronized neither with the Restatement (Second) of Property nor with the Restatement (Third) of Property contributes to the general chaos in this once relatively orderly corner of the law of powers of appointment. Perhaps the law reformers should go back to their drawing boards and start over. Or, better still, they should stand aside and allow the law of powers of appointment to evolve organically and incrementally over time by old-fashioned trial and error.

Nonresiduary property dispositions that in retrospect served to exercise powers of appointment. The Restatement (Second) of Property (Wills and Other Donative Transfers) generally tracked the black-letter law: "If the donee's deed or will, read with reference to the property the donee owned and other circumstances existing at the time of the execution of the donee's deed or will, indicates that the donee understood that he was disposing of property covered by a power, the donee thereby manifests an intent to exercise the power."[235] So as not to open wide the litigation floodgates, the Restatement (Second) of Property emphasized that the only circumstances that were material were those that existed at the time the language of alleged appointment was formulated: "Later changes in circumstances have no importance except so far as they were foreseeable and therefore constituted elements in the situation then existing."[236] Donee intent is an important public policy consideration, but so is transactional finality.

The Restatement (Third) of Property (Wills and Other Donative Transfers), specifically its Section 19.5, would inject all kinds of uncertainty and instability into this once quiet corner of the law of powers of appointments. A powerholder's intent to exercise is manifested in a "disposition," a term that is not defined. Presumably not just inter vivos deeds of exercise and testamentary appointments are contemplated, but other types of property dispositions as well. Neither the illustrations nor the Reporter's Notes that accompany the section, however, shed any light on what such dispositions might look like.[237] Might the term "disposition," for example, capture inter vivos assignments of property to the trustees of revocable and irrevocable inter vivos trusts? Now there is a trap for the unwary trust practitioner, as we explain at the end of this segment.

---

[234] *Cf.* §8.30 of this handbook (vested remainders that are subject to divestment).

[235] Restatement (Second) of Property (Wills and Other Donative Transfers) § 17.5.

[236] Restatement (Second) of Property (Wills and Other Donative Transfers) § 17.5 cmt. a.

[237] *See, however,* Restatement (Third) of Property (Wills and Other Donative Transfers) §19.3, illus. 2 (the granting of a 50-year lease on real estate a partial exercise of a general inter vivos power of appointment over the real estate).

But it gets worse. The Restatement (Third) ventures into territory which the Restatement (Second) had declared off-limits: Namely, the taking into account of future unanticipated changed circumstances in determining the intentions of the powerholder at the time he executes the instrument of exercise. Postexecution events apparently "can sometimes be relevant in determining the donee's intention,"[238] an insight the logic of which had escaped the more practical drafters of the Restatement (Second) of Property. "Post-execution evidence of intention may properly be considered in resolving an ambiguity, if it sheds light on the donee's intention at the time of execution or on what the donee's intention would probably then have been had the ambiguity been recognized *or had the subsequent event been anticipated*."[239] It will take decades for the courts to untangle the hairs of that fur ball, should they elect to apply its wisdoms and insights to actual cases and controversies. The term "ambiguity," for example, is defined elsewhere as "an uncertainty in meaning that is revealed by the text or by extrinsic evidence other than direct evidence of intention contradicting the plain meaning of the text."[240] We take direct evidence of intention contradicting the plain meaning of the text to refer primarily to direct evidence of scrivener error.[241] Presumably, an ambiguity in the context of a possible exercise of a power of appointment has something to do with confusion as to the powerholder's intentions vis-à-vis the power, whether the confusion is language-based (a patent ambiguity in the instrument of exercise) or fact-based (a latent ambiguity revealed by extrinsic evidence).[242]

One can imagine a nightmare scenario where the settlor of a revocable inter vivos trust dies years after it had been funded with all of his property. There are certain unforeseeable events subsequent to the execution of the inter vivos funding assignment that eroded the value of the trust corpus prior to his death. Perhaps his granddaughter became afflicted with a life-threatening disease. Someone postmortem now raises the question of whether the inter vivos "disposition" by assignment had actually exercised at the time a certain general inter vivos power of appointment that the settlor had possessed under his grandfather's trust? Or does the subject property now belong to the takers in default under the grandfather's trust?

Not to worry say the nonpracticing academics: "As with any other evidence bearing on the donee's intention, the probative force of post-execution evidence of intention is for the trier of fact to evaluate."[243]

For estate planners practicing in the trenches who may not be convinced or who, in any case, would prefer not to have their work products scrutinized

---

[238] Restatement (Third) of Property (Wills and Other Donative Transfers) §19.5 cmt. a.

[239] Restatement (Third) of Property (Wills and Other Donative Transfers) §19.5 cmt. a.

[240] Restatement (Third) of Property (Wills and Other Donative Transfers) §11.1.

[241] *See* Restatement (Third) of Property (Wills and Other Donative Transfers) §11.1 cmt. c.

[242] *See* Restatement (Third) of Property (Wills and Other Donative Transfers) §11.1 cmt. b & cmt. c. The traditional rule of construction has been that extrinsic evidence is not allowed in to resolve patent ambiguities, only latent ambiguities. *But see* Restatement (Third) of Property (Wills and Other Donative Transfers) §11.1 cmt. a ("Although it is customary to distinguish between latent and patent ambiguities, no legal consequences attach to the distinction.").

[243] Restatement (Third) of Property (Wills and Other Donative Transfers) §19.5 cmt. a.

retrospectively by "triers of facts" if at all possible, there is this advice: Never draft a power of appointment that is exercisable other than by a deed or a will that makes specific reference to the particular power. The Restatement (Third), in a welcome flush of common sense, is unambiguously supportive: "Even if the donee's disposition would otherwise be deemed to manifest an intent to exercise a power, the intended exercise is not effective if the donor has imposed the requirement (which is common) that the power can only be effectively exercised by language that makes specific reference to the power."[244]

Powers of appointment can travel in disguise. "Any words or phrases are sufficient to create a power of appointment if they establish that the transferor so intended."[245] In other words, a power of appointment is not always labeled as such in the governing instrument. It sometimes travels in disguise. For example, a general inter vivos power might take the form of a reserved right of revocation, a beneficiary's right to have his debts satisfied from the trust estate, or simply an unrestricted right in someone to demand principal.[246] A nongeneral inter vivos power of appointment might take the form of a right of disposition: "Donee shall have the right to dispose of the remainder interest among her children as she pleases."[247] Replace the words "dispose of" with the word "devise" and the power would be testamentary.[248] Precatory words are words of entreaty, request, desire, wish, or recommendation, rather than command. As to whether in a given situation such words might nonetheless indicate an intention to create a power of appointment, whether of the fiduciary or nonfiduciary variety, the reader is referred to Section 8.15.58 of this handbook.

Ineffective appointment to impermissible appointee. In the case of an equitable nongeneral power of appointment, an attempted appointment to an impermissible appointee is ineffective to pass legal title to the trust principal from the trustee to the impermissible appointee. The Restatement (Third) of Property appears to address such ineffective appointments only in the nontrust context: "An attempted appointment of a *beneficial* interest to an impermissible appointee fails. The impermissible appointee receives no better *title* than the impermissible appointee would receive in any other case in which a nonowner purports to transfer property to another."[249] A power of appointment over a legal remainder comes to mind. This statement is problematic in the trust context, however, as legal title to entrusted property is in the trustee, while title to the equitable/beneficial interest is in the beneficiary. Generally it is the legal interest in the trustee that is the subject of any attendant power of appointment. While it is possible to possess a power that limits the donee to appointing an equitable/beneficial interest in trust principal, such as a stream of income, the

---

[244] Restatement (Third) of Property (Wills and Other Donative Transfers) §19.5 cmt. d.

[245] Restatement (Third) of Property (Wills and Other Donative Transfers) §18.1 cmt. b.

[246] Restatement (Second) of Property (Wills and Other Donative Transfers) §12.1 cmt. a & Reporter's Note to §12.1.

[247] Restatement (Third) of Property (Wills and Other Donative Transfers) §18.1 cmt. b, illus. 1.

[248] Restatement (Third) of Property (Wills and Other Donative Transfers) §18.1 cmt. b, illus. 2.

[249] Restatement (Third) of Property (Wills and Other Donative Transfers) §19.15 cmt. g.

usual power grant is more expansive, encompassing principal as well as income. Moreover, in the case of a failed exercise in further trust, not only does the appointment of the equitable/beneficial interest fail but also the appointment of the legal title in the property that is the subject of the trust. The Restatement (Second) of Property did a better job of sorting out and keeping straight the shifting legal and equitable relationships incident to an ineffective exercise of an equitable power of appointment.[250]

When a provision-in-default-of-exercise is lacking. *The general testamentary power.* A prospective trustee should make sure there are provisions in default of exercise. Let us take as an example the following trust: *A* to *B* for *C* for life, with *C* possessing a general testamentary power of appointment. What happens if *C* were to die, say, intestate? The instrument being silent, it is likely that the death of *C* would trigger a resulting trust in favor of *A* or *A*'s estate.[251]

The nongeneral power. Were *C* to possess instead a nongeneral power, there is a split of authority as to whether a resulting trust is triggered or whether the property passes in equal shares to the permissible appointees, provided that the class is sufficiently defined and limited.[252] In England, the permissible appointees may be in luck as well.[253]

Traditional doctrines. A court inclined to favor in a given situation the permissible appointees over the holders of the equitable reversion traditionally has had to resort to either the power-in-trust rationale (or its variant, the mandatory-power-in trust rationale) or the implied-gift-in-default rationale. The latter is what the Restatements have been pushing.[254] All three doctrines are explained in Section 8.15.90 of this handbook.

The Restatements. In a break with tradition, the Restatement (Third) of Property would have antilapse principles apply in situations where, in the absence of a taker-in-default provision in the granting instrument, a permissible appointee has predeceased an unexercised nongeneral power's expiration.[255] Lapse and antilapse in the trust context are covered generally in Section 8.15.55 of this handbook. In another break with tradition, if the permissible appointees are a class of someone's issue, descendants, or the like, all the

---

[250] *See, e.g.*, Restatement (Second) of Property (Wills and Other Donative Transfers) §20.1 cmt. e (an exercise in further trust in part entails the appointment of an equitable (beneficial) interest in the appointive property).

[251] Restatement (Second) of Property (Wills and Other Donative Transfers) §24.1.

[252] *See generally* 1 Scott on Trusts §27. *See, e.g.*, Restatement (Second) of Property (Wills and Other Donative Transfers) §24.2 (presuming an implied gift in default of appointment to the objects of the limited power in the absence of a manifestation by the donor of the power of a contrary intention). It should be noted that if the objects of the limited power could be from more than one generation, *e.g.*, "issue," then distribution would be *per stirpes*. Restatement (Second) of Property (Wills and Other Donative Transfers) §24.2 cmt. d.

[253] Lewin ¶29-03 through ¶29-05.

[254] *See* Restatement (First) of Property §367 cmt. b; Restatement (Second) of Property (Wills and Other Donative Transfers) §24.2, cmt. a; Restatement (Third) of Property (Wills and Other Donative Transfers) §19.23(b).

[255] Restatement (Third) of Property (Wills and Other Donative Transfers) §19.23(b).

Restatements would have the appointive property pass to the members by representation rather than per capita in the event of nonexercise.[256]

All this having been said, "[i]f the donor manifests an intent that the defined and limited class of permissible appointees are to receive the appointive property only by appointment, the donor's manifestation of intent eliminates any implied gift in default to the permissible appointees."[257] In that case, title to the appointive property passes upon a resulting trust from the trustee to the donor of the power, or the donor's personal representative if the donor is deceased at the time of the power's expiration.[258] The Restatement (Third) suggests that the appointive property "passes under a reversionary interest," which is nonsensical.[259] The nonpossessory equitable reversion vested *ab initio*.[260] The resulting trust, which the Restatement (Third) makes no mention of in this context, is merely the equitable procedural device employed by the court to effect a flowering of the equitable reversion into a possessory *legal* interest in the subject property.[261]

A practice tip. In any case, the settlor's counsel should have supplied the trust with terms that would become operative in the event *C* fails in whole or in part effectively to exercise the power.[262]

When the taker-in-default disclaims. "A disclaimer of an interest in property by a ... taker in default of an exercise of a power of appointment takes effect as of the time the instrument creating the power becomes irrevocable."[263]

The expired general power of appointment: The Restatement (Third) of Property muddles the interplay of lapse, resulting trust, and capture doctrine. If the holder of a general inter vivos power of appointment dies without having effectively exercised the power, the power expires.[264] Likewise, if the holder of a general testamentary power of appointment fails to effectively exercise the power by will, the power expires at the holder's death. In either case, the gift-in-default clause in the granting instrument, if there is such a clause, controls the disposition of the unappointed property.[265] (So also if a

---

[256] Restatement (First) of Property §367(4); Restatement (Second) of Property (Wills and Other Donative Transfers) §24.2 cmt. d; Restatement (Third) of Property (Wills and Other Donative Transfers) §19.23 cmt. a. *See generally* §5.2 of this handbook (class designations).

[257] Restatement (Third) of Property (Wills and Other Donative Transfers) §19.23 cmt. a.

[258] Restatement (Second) of Property (Wills and Other Donative Transfers) §24.2(2). *See generally* §4.1.1.1 of this handbook (the resulting trust).

[259] Restatement (Third) of Property (Wills and Other Donative Transfers) §19.23(c).

[260] *See generally* §4.1.1 of this handbook (the vested reversionary interest).

[261] *See generally* §4.1.1.1 of this handbook (the vested reversionary interest). If the subject property itself were an equitable interest, such as a share of a trusteed mutual fund, then the donor of the expired power (or his personal representative) would take full ownership of the equitable interest upon imposition of the resulting trust.

[262] *See* Bogert §1064 for a sample provision in default of the exercise of a power of appointment (art. fourth, §3).

[263] UPC §2-1110(b).

[264] As we note in Section 8.1.1 of this handbook, a power of appointment is exercisable; it is never directly transferable.

[265] Restatement (Third) of Property (Wills and Other Donative Transfers) §19.22(a).

power expires by inter vivos disclaimer or release.[266]) The time when a power expires "is almost invariably the death of the donee,"[267] although one could certainly fashion a grant of a general power that would be capable of expiring before its donee had, such as upon the exhaustion of an intervening equitable estate *pur autre vie*. The concept of the estate *pur autre vie* is discussed generally in Section 8.15.64 of this handbook.

The Restatement (Third) of Property speaks in terms of a general power "lapsing," an unfortunate innovation.[268] Its predecessors spoke in terms of a power "expiring,"[269] which is less ambiguous in that the term "lapse" can mean "to pass to another through neglect or omission."[270] See above for an explanation of why a power of appointment itself is never directly transmissible.

But what if the donor of an expired power had neglected in the granting instrument to provide for takers-in-default, or the instrument's gift-in-default clause was ineffective when the power expired? In that case, the unappointed property passes upon a resulting trust back to the donor if the donor is then living, or into the probate estate of the donor if the donor is not then living, but, again, not until all valid intervening equitable interests have themselves expired.[271] Resulting trusts are covered generally in Section 4.1.1.1 of this handbook. *In a radical departure from settled doctrine, the Restatement (Third) of Property provides that if the donee "merely failed to exercise the power" the unappointed property is captured by the donee or the donee's estate.*[272] There is no resulting trust. There is no antilapse.[273]

A resulting trust, however, would still be imposed in the case of expiration by disclaimer or release,[274] or upon the expiration by any means of a power of revocation, amendment, or withdrawal.[275] Again, as we did in more detail in our discussion of ineffective exercises of general powers in Section 8.15.12 of this handbook, we question the logic of treating a power of "revocation, amendment, or withdrawal" differently from other "types" of general inter vivos power of appointment, whether for capture purposes generally or for any other purpose. A resulting trust also would be imposed if the donee "expressly refrained from exercising the power."[276] Of course, this discussion is entirely academic if the donor is also the donee of the expired general power. The unappointed property would then end up in the probate estate of the donee in

---

[266] Restatement (Third) of Property (Wills and Other Donative Transfers) §19.22(a).

[267] Restatement (First) of Property §367 cmt. d.

[268] *See* Restatement (Third) of Property (Wills and Other Donative Transfers) §19.22 (term lapse employed even in the section's title).

[269] *See, e.g.,* Restatement (First) of Property §367 cmt. d.

[270] The American Heritage Dictionary 1014 (3d ed. 1996).

[271] *See, e.g.,* Restatement (First) of Property §367(1).

[272] Restatement (Third) of Property (Wills and Other Donative Transfers) §19.22(b).

[273] For a general discussion of antilapse doctrine, *see* §8.15.55 of this handbook.

[274] Restatement (Third) of Property (Wills and Other Donative Transfers) §19.22(b).

[275] Restatement (Third) of Property (Wills and Other Donative Transfers) §19.22 cmt. f.

[276] Restatement (Third) of Property (Wills and Other Donative Transfers) §19.22(b).

any case, whether by imposition of a resulting trust under traditional doctrine or by quasi-capture.[277]

The Restatement (Third) of Property's tenacious aversion to acknowledging applicable resulting trust doctrine comes through loud and clear in the sections devoted to unexercised or ineffectively exercised powers of appointment.[278] The result is an unhelpful dearth of context, particularly when it comes to following chains of title. Take, for example, Section 19.22(b), which reads in part: "... but if the donee released the power or expressly refrained from exercising the power, the unappointed property passes under a reversionary interest to the donor or to the donor's transferees or successors in interest." The phrase "passes under a reversionary interest" is inappropriate in the trust context. What actually happens is that the legal title to the unappointed property passes from the express trustee, now a resulting trustee, back to the settlor-donor or his personal representative upon a resulting trust such that the equitable reversion, which had vested *ab initio*, flowers into possession.[279] Nothing is passing from the express trustee under, over, or in a reversionary interest.

We also quibble with the failure of all of the Restatements to expressly confirm that in the face of an expired power of appointment, title to property unappointed does not leave the hands of the trustee until such time as all valid intervening equitable estates have themselves expired, unless the terms of the trust so provide. An intervening equitable estate typically would be an equitable life estate.[280]

Creditor access. *Reserved general inter vivos powers.* When a settlor bestows on himself a *general* inter vivos power to appoint the trust property (*e.g.*, a reserved right of revocation), his creditors may have access to the property whether or not the power is ever exercised.[281] This is consistent with the long-standing public policy that one may not place property beyond the reach

---

[277] The traditional capture doctrine is discussed generally in Section 8.15.12 of this handbook.

[278] *See, e.g.*, Restatement (Third) of Property (Wills and Other Donative Transfers) §25.2 (although the title to the sections is *Reversion or Remainder*, the resulting trust is mentioned once, and only in passing).

[279] John Chipman Gray, The Rule Against Perpetuities §113 (4th ed. 1942) ("All reversions are vested interests. From their nature they are always ready to take effect in possession whenever and however the preceding estates determine."). In the case of an equitable reversion that has become possessory, legal title to the entrusted property somehow still needs to get from the trustee to the holder of the equitable reversion. That is where the resulting trust comes in. It is essentially a procedural equitable device for divesting the express trustee of a failed trust of the legal title to the subject property. *See generally* §4.1.1.1 of this handbook (the resulting trust as an equitable title-transfer mechanism).

[280] *See generally* §8.27 of this handbook (the equitable life estate).

[281] 2A Scott on Trusts §156. *See also* §5.3.3.1 of this handbook (reaching settlor's reserved beneficial interest); UTC §505(a)(1) (available at <http://www.uniformlaws.org/Act.aspx?title= Trust%20Code>) (providing that during the settlor's lifetime, the property of a revocable trust is subject to claims of the settlor's creditors). *But see* 4 Scott §330.12 (suggesting that property subject to an unexercised naked reserved right of revocation may not be reachable by the settlor's creditors). For more on the naked reserved right of revocation, *see* §5.3.3.1(a) of this handbook.

of one's creditors and still retain the right to enjoy it.[282] It is the settlor's *right* of exercise that makes the property vulnerable, not the fact of exercise. The right of exercise is treated as equivalent to an ownership interest in the property subject to the power. The Restatement (Third) of Property is in accord.[283] For more on creditor accessibility in the context of reserved general inter vivos powers of appointment, such as reserved rights of revocation, the reader is referred to Section 5.3.3.1(b.1). of this handbook.

When the donee of a general inter vivos power is not the settlor. On the other hand, if the holder of the general inter vivos power is not the settlor, the property traditionally has been creditor-accessible only to the extent that the holder in fact exercises the power.[284] This restriction on access may not apply to the trustee in bankruptcy.[285] This restriction also no longer may apply generally, as we explain in Section 5.3.3.2 of this handbook.

General testamentary powers. The access of the donee's creditors to property subject to a reserved general testamentary power of appointment is taken up in Section 5.3.3.1(b.2) of this handbook. As to creditors of the nonsettlor donee of such a power of appointment, see Section 5.3.3.2 of this handbook.

Nongeneral powers. With respect to a *limited/special/nongeneral* power to appoint trust property, the holder is treated as though an agent of the settlor; thus the holder's creditors would have no access to the property whether the power is ever exercised.[286] There is an important exception: "If the gift in default of appointment is to the donee's estate, the donee's power, though in form a nongeneral power, is in substance a general power to appoint by will, and the rights of the donee's creditors are governed . . . [accordingly]. . . ."[287]

In the case of the bankruptcy of a donee of a nongeneral power of appointment, the appointive property is excluded from the federal bankruptcy estate under Section 541(b)(1) of Bankruptcy Code of 1978, absent special facts.[288] This is because the power may not be exercised in favor of the donee-debtor.

When the nondonee of an unexercised power of appointment may effect its negation. *The donor*. The donor of an equitable power of appointment may expressly reserve the right to amend the terms of the power or revoke the power altogether.[289] The donor also may reserve such a power indirectly. Take, for instance, a revocable inter vivos trust. Pursuant to its terms, following the death of the settlor (the one with the reserved right of revocation), various takers in default are to become holders of various types of powers of appointment over various portions of the trust property. Now, it is self-evident that the donee of a

---

[282] *See generally* 2A Scott on Trusts §156.

[283] Restatement (Third) of Property(Wills and Other Donative Transfers) §22.2.

[284] *See generally* 2A Scott on Trusts §147.3.

[285] 2A Scott on Trusts §147.3.

[286] *See* 2A Scott on Trusts §147.3; 3 Scott & Ascher §14.11.3; Restatement (Second) of Property (Wills and Other Donative Transfers) §13.1; Restatement (Third) of Property (Wills and Other Donative Transfers) §22.1 (2010).

[287] Restatement (Third) of Property (Wills and Other Donative Transfers) §22.1 cmt. c.

[288] Bankruptcy Code of 1978 (11 U.S.C. §541(b)(1)).

[289] Restatement (Third) of Property (Wills and Other Donative Transfers) §18.2.

power of appointment can effect its extinguishment by exercising the power completely such that the subject/appointive property is no longer a trust asset.[290] But is it also possible for the *donor* of a yet-to-be-exercised power of appointment over trust property indirectly to undo the power grant, to effectively call back the power? The answer is yes, provided the *donor* has reserved to himself or herself a power of appointment over the very same property. That seems to be the gist of Section 18.2 of the Restatement (Third) of Property (Wills and Other Donative Transfers), although it is hard to tell. Here is the text: "The donor of a power of appointment lacks the authority to revoke or amend the power, except to the extent the donor reserved a power of revocation or amendment when creating the power."

In the trust context, the usual understanding of a power of revocation is a power to revoke the trust itself. The usual understanding of a power of amendment is a power to alter the trust's terms. In each case, however, the power meets the definition of a general inter vivos power of appointment, which, if superior, *encompasses a power to negate other powers*. But a superior reserved limited or testamentary power can also, under certain circumstances, effect the negation by its exercise of other powers. Bottom line: the qualification *except to the extent that the donor reserved a power of revocation or amendment when creating the power* should, by implication, encompass the reservation to the *donor* of any kind of superior power the exercise of which could have the effect of negating or altering the terms of other unexercised powers granted by the donor. The Restatement (Third)'s Section 18.2 still needs a lot of work.

The holder of another power of power of appointment. Who besides the donor and donee of a particular unexercised power of appointment might be in a position to negate it? The nondonor holder of another power of appointment the exercise of which could effect a negation of the particular unexercised power. Thus, the nondonor holder of a presently exercisable general inter vivos power of appointment over certain entrusted property can proceed to negate a testamentary power of appointment over the same property, provided the testamentary power is in the hands of someone who is still alive. Recall that prior to the death of its donee, a testamentary power of appointment perforce is unexercised, a will speaking only at death.

Disclaimer of a nonfiduciary power of appointment by the intended donee. A nonfiduciary power of appointment is generally disclaimable by the intended donee of the power, provided the power has not been accepted.[291] The Restatement (Third) of Property is generally in accord.[292] Under the Uniform Probate Code, the following rules apply in the event a power is disclaimed:

---

[290] *See* Restatement (Third) of Property (Wills and Other Donative Transfers) §18.2 cmt. d (releasing powers).

[291] *See* UPC §2-1105(a). *See generally* §5.5 of this handbook (disclaiming equitable property interests and powers under trusts).

[292] Restatement (Third) of Property (Wills and Other Donative Transfers) §20.4.

1. "If the holder has not exercised the power, the disclaimer takes effect as of the time the instrument creating the power becomes irrevocable
2. If the holder has excrcised the power and the disclaimer is of a power other than a presently exercisable general power of appointment, the disclaimer takes effect immediately after the last exercise of the power
3. The instrument creating the power is construed as if the power expired when the disclaimer became effective"[293]

Item 2 is nonsensical on its face. How can one disclaim an already-exercised power? Perhaps "last exercise" means "last *partial* exercise"? By process of elimination it would seem that the subject of Item 2 is only the inter vivos (presently exercisable) nongeneral power of appointment. The general inter vivos power of appointment is expressly excluded. As a will speaks at death, it is impossible for the donee of a testamentary power of appointment, whether of the general or nongeneral variety, to exercise it in any way before death. Thus Item 2 must be referring only to the partially exercised inter vivos (presently exercisable) nongeneral power of appointment. Still, how can one disclaim such a power if it has already been exercised, either fully or partially? In the latter case, hasn't the power itself been constructively accepted at the time of first exercise, if not earlier?

The key to unlocking this mystery is hidden in the Uniform Disclaimer of Property Interests Act (1999), specifically Section 13(d), which reads as follows: "A disclaimer, in whole or part, of the *future exercise* of a power not held in a fiduciary capacity is not barred by its previous exercise unless the power is exercisable in favor of the disclaimant." Disclaiming a future exercise? It would seem that what we have here is actually just a garden-variety release of the power itself, not some kind of disclaimer. "A disclaimer prevents acquisition *of the power*, and consequently the donee who has accepted *the power* can no longer disclaim."[294] We now take up the topic of releasing powers of appointment by their donees.

Release of a power of appointment by its donee. *The general inter vivos power.* The Restatement (Third) of Property provides that the donee of an accepted general inter vivos power of appointment may irrevocably release the power in whole or in part, unless the donor of the power has effectively manifested an intent that it not be releasable.[295] The Restatement (Second) does as well.[296] Why the holder of a general inter vivos power of appointment, which is tantamount to an absolute ownership interest in the subject property, may be prevented from getting rid of it other than by exercising it into oblivion is not explained.[297] The Restatement (First) of Property provided, quite sensibly, that such a power is releasable even if the donor had expressly provided in

---

[293] UPC §2-1109.

[294] Restatement (Third) of Property (Wills and Other Donative Transfers) §20.4 cmt. b.

[295] Restatement (Third) of Property (Wills and Other Donative Transfers) §20.1.

[296] Restatement (Second) of Property (Wills and Other Donative Transfers) §14.1.

[297] Restatement (Third) of Property (Wills and Other Donative Transfers) §20.1 cmt. d.

the power grant to the contrary.[298] The analogy of a nonreleasable general inter vivos power of appointment to a spendthrifted equitable interest under a trust, floated in the Restatement (Second), is a false one.[299] It should be to an impermissible *legal* alienation restraint, a topic we take up in Section 8.15.40 of this handbook, and which the law has traditionally disfavored in principle.

The general testamentary power of appointment. The analogy of a general testamentary power of appointment to a property interest in the holder is also valid.[300] Thus, a general testamentary power of appointment is generally releasable,[301] and should be so even in the face of an express spendthrift restraint.[302]

The nongeneral power of appointment. A nongeneral power is generally releasable,[303] although the rationale cannot be based on quasi-property principles.[304] In the case where the permissible appointees and the takers in default are one and the same, the rationale seems to be no harm/no foul.[305] In the case when they aren't, it has been suggested that "the fact that the objects of the power are not takers in default of an exercise indicates they are not of primary concern to the donor."[306]

In the case of the inter vivos release of a nongeneral testamentary power of appointment, however, the effect could be to alter the express terms of the trust. If, for example, a taker in default had a vested interest subject to divestment upon the exercise of a certain nongeneral testamentary power, upon release of the power the interest would become indefeasibly vested in the taker-in-default *during the donee's lifetime*, an event not provided for in the terms of the trust.[307] The release also would "close the door prematurely on the objects of the power in a manner not contemplated by the donor."[308] The vested interest subject to divestment is taken up in Section 8.30 of this handbook.

The mechanics of releasing a nonfiduciary power of appointment. Delivering a written declaration of release is the preferred way for a donee of a releasable *nonfiduciary* power of appointment incident to a trust relationship to release the power, but to whom? The answer cannot be found by looking to the Restatement (Third) of Property (Wills and Other Donative Transfers) for guidance.

The donee should deliver the writing to those who could be adversely affected by an appointment, such as the takers in default, *and to the trustee*. In the case of an equitable nongeneral power of appointment whose class of permissible appointees is limited and defined, it would seem that they should receive

---

[298] *See* Restatement (First) of Property §334 cmt. b.

[299] See Restatement (Second) of Property (Wills and Other Donative Transfers) §14.1 cmt. a.

[300] *See* Hodel v. Irving, 481 U.S. 704, 715 (1987) (the right to pass property postmortem is a property right subject to Fifth Amendment protections).

[301] See Restatement (Third) of Property (Wills and Other Donative Transfers) §20.1 cmt. a.

[302] *See* Restatement (First) of Property §334 cmt. b.

[303] Restatement (Third) of Property (Wills and Other Donative Transfers) §20.2.

[304] Restatement (Second) of Property (Wills and Other Donative Transfers) §14.2.

[305] Restatement (Third) of Property (Wills and Other Donative Transfers) §20.2 cmt. a.

[306] Restatement (Second) of Property (Wills and Other Donative Transfers) §14.2 cmt. a.

[307] Restatement (Second) of Property (Wills and Other Donative Transfers) §14.2 cmt. a.

[308] Restatement (Second) of Property (Wills and Other Donative Transfers) §14.2 cmt. a.

some kind of notice of the release as well, they being not only quasi contingent trust beneficiaries[309] but also the ones who, after all, would be adversely affected by the release itself. But from whom should they receive the notice? Presumably from the trustee, the trustee being the fiduciary in the equation, although the Restatement fails even to flag the issue.

The Restatement, specifically Section 20.3, catalogs various methods of releasing releasable powers of appointment, none of which seems particularly appropriate when there is a trustee in the picture. In fact there is not a single illustration with a release fact pattern that involves an equitable power of appointment, which is yet more evidence that what coverage there is of equitable powers in the Restatement was an afterthought, and a last-minute one at that.

Taxation. The release of some powers, however, can have tax consequences.[310] Note also that the Uniform Trust Code would provide that upon the lapse, release, or waiver of a general inter vivos power of appointment, the holder would be treated as the settlor of the trust for creditor accessibility purposes to the extent the value of the property affected by the lapse, release, or waiver exceeds the greater of the Crummey or "5 and 5" power.[311]

The fiduciary discretionary power. A trustee's discretionary power to apply income and/or principal to a class of permissible takers, *i.e.*, a power in trust, however, more likely than not would not be of the variety that is releasable (or disclaimable) *by the powerholder trustee*.[312] Why? Because if the power is released (or disclaimed), the equitable interests would no longer be subject to the condition precedent of the trustee's from time to time exercising his discretion, a condition precedent that the settlor presumably put in place for a reason.[313] There are no bright lines, however, as reasonable people can disagree as to what the settlor's intent actually was.[314]

Lapse of general inter vivos power of appointment other than by the death of the holder. Since *Crummey v. Commissioner* was decided in 1968, the IRS has been making life difficult, but by no means impossible, for the settlors of Crummey Trusts.[315] While the Crummey Trust continues to be an effective tax avoidance vehicle, the very feature that makes it effective potentially exposes

---

[309] *See generally* UTC §103(3)(A) (available at <http://www.uniformlaws.org/Act.aspx?title=Trust%20Code>) (deeming a permissible appointee to be a trust beneficiary).

[310] As to the tax consequences of releasing general powers, *see* Restatement (Second) of Property (Wills and Other Donative Transfers) §14.2 at 129 (Reporter's Tax Note to §14.1). As to the tax consequences of releasing limited powers, *see* Restatement (Second) of Property (Wills and Other Donative Transfers) §14.2 at 140 (Reporter's Tax Note to §14.2).

[311] UTC §505(b)(2) (available at <http://www.uniformlaws.org/Act.aspx?title=Trust%20Code>). *See also* §9.18 of this handbook (the Crummey trust) (discussing in part the "5 and 5" limitation).

[312] *See generally* §3.5.3.4 of this handbook (trustee's power to disclaim a fiduciary power); UPC §2-1111 (disclaimer of power held in fiduciary capacity).

[313] *See generally* §6.1.2 of this handbook (trustee's duty to carry out terms of the trust).

[314] *See* §6.1.2 of this handbook (trustee's duty to carry out the terms of the trust); Restatement (Second) of Property (Wills and Other Donative Transfers) §14.5 cmt. c, illus. 1 & 2; UPC §2-1105 cmt.; §3.5.3.4 of this handbook (disclaiming fiduciary powers); John J. Roche & Christopher T. Carlson, *The Dynamic Disclaimer*, 14 New Eng. L. Rev. 399, 419 (1979).

[315] 397 F.2d 82 (9th Cir. 1968).

the underlying property to the reach of the creditors of the holders of the withdrawal rights, namely, the short-term Crummey withdrawal rights themselves. Crummey Trusts are discussed generally, and these specific tax-avoidance and creditor-access issues in particular, in §9.18 of this handbook.

Disclaimer by appointee or taker in default of exercise of power of appointment. An actual appointee of a power of appointment may disclaim the subject property.[316] So too may the takers in default of the power's exercise.[317]

Failed exercise in further trust: the capture doctrine. If the donee or holder of a general testamentary power of appointment exercises it by appointing the subject property to a trustee of a trust that fails *ab initio* or subsequently, a resulting trust is imposed.[318] The subject property, however, does not necessarily revert to the settlor of the original trust, or to the settlor's probate estate.[319] Instead, a resulting trust might well be imposed in favor of the powerholder's probate estate under the so-called *capture doctrine*, a topic we take up in Sections 8.1.2 of this handbook and 8.15.12 of this handbook.

The chain of legal title to, versus the transmission of the economic interest in, the appointive property. Here is the chain of legal title to entrusted property that is subject to an exercised power of appointment: *The settlor/donor of the power—trustee—appointee*. If the power is nongeneral/limited/special, however, the appointee in substance takes the economic interest directly from the settlor/donor of the power, not from the trustee.[320] In the case of a general inter vivos power of appointment, the appointee in substance takes the economic interest from the donee/holder of the power.[321] In the case of a general testamentary power, for some purposes, *e.g.*, rule against perpetuities analysis, the economic interest is deemed to pass directly from the settlor/donor of the power to the appointee.[322] For other purposes, *e.g.*, estate taxation, the appointee is deemed to take the economic interest from the donee/holder of the power.[323] Deeming the economic interest in appointive property to pass directly from the settlor/donor of the power to the appointee is called in some quarters the relation-back theory.[324] Again, in all cases, the appointee takes the legal title to the appointive property from the trustee.

Conflict of laws and powers of appointment. In Section 8.5 of this handbook, we consider which state's law shall govern the validity of an inter vivos trust of movables should not all the parties and not all the entrusted assets

---

[316] UPC §2-1110(a). *See generally* §5.5 of this handbook (disclaimers by beneficiaries).

[317] UPC §2-1110(b). *See generally* §5.5 of this handbook (disclaimers by beneficiaries).

[318] *See generally* 6 Scott & Ascher §41.17 (Trust Created by Exercise of General Power of Appointment); §4.1.1.1 of this handbook (the resulting trust) and §8.1.2 of this handbook (exercise of powers of appointment in further trust).

[319] *See generally* 6 Scott & Ascher §41.17 (Trust Created by Exercise of General Power of Appointment).

[320] Restatement (Third) of Property (Wills and Other Donative Transfers) §17.4 cmt. f(2).

[321] Restatement (Third) of Property (Wills and Other Donative Transfers) §17.4 cmt. f(1).

[322] *See generally* §8.2.1.8 of this handbook (perpetuities and powers of appointment).

[323] *See generally* §8.9.3 of this handbook (the tax-sensitivity of the general testamentary power of appointment).

[324] Restatement (Third) of Property (Wills and Other Donative Transfers) §17.4 cmt. f.

be located together in one state. As a general rule, the law that governs the validity of such a trust would likewise govern the validity of any powers of appointment created pursuant to its terms.[325] "Thus, the law which determines the validity of the trust determines whether a power of appointment is invalid as in violation of the rule against perpetuities on the ground that it is a special power or testamentary power which might be exercised at a time beyond the permissible period."[326] The intersection of power of appointment doctrine and remoteness (perpetuities) doctrine is covered generally in Section 8.2.1.8 of this handbook.

§8.1.2   Exercise of Powers of Appointment in Further Trust

The donee of a presently exercisable general . . . [inter vivos] . . . power to appoint or power to withdraw trust property has the equivalent of the ownership of that property.[327]

General powers. If the governing instrument is silent on the issue, may the holder of a *general* power of appointment exercise it in further trust (*e.g.*, instead of appointing the property outright and free of trust to *X*, appoint it to a trustee for the benefit of *X*)? The answer is yes.[328] This is inherent in the holder's overarching right to appoint to anyone, including himself,[329] or if the power is testamentary, including his probate estate. Even if the holder of a general power were not entitled to appoint in further trust, the same result could still be achieved in two steps: by first appointing to himself (or his estate if the power is testamentary) and then by impressing a trust upon the property for the benefit of *X*. The Restatement (Third) of Property goes so far as to propose that any term in a general power grant that purports to restrict the donee's right to appoint in further trust is ineffective.[330] Whether the exercise of a general power fails at the outset or at a later time, the doctrine of capture may be implicated, a topic that is taken up in Section 8.15.12 of this handbook.

Nongeneral powers. Authority, however, is split on whether, absent express authority in the governing instrument,[331] the holder of a *limited/special* power may exercise it in further trust.[332] If the holder may appoint to members of a class comprised of *X*, *Y*, and *Z*, some courts would hold an exercise in further trust to be impermissible, because title would pass to the trustee who would be someone other than a designated member of the class.[333] In the

---

[325] *See* Restatement (Second) of Conflict of Laws §270 cmt. f.

[326] Restatement (Second) of Conflict of Laws §270 cmt. f.

[327] Restatement (Third) of Trusts §74 cmt. g.

[328] *See generally* 1 Scott on Trusts §§17.2, 21; 1 Scott & Ascher §3.1.2; Bogert §43; Restatement (Third) of Property (Wills and Other Donative Transfers) §19.13(a).

[329] Restatement (Third) of Trusts §74 cmt. g.

[330] Restatement (Third) of Property (Wills and Other Donative Transfers) §19.13 cmt. d.

[331] 1 Scott & Ascher §3.1.2.

[332] *See generally* 1 Scott & Ascher §17.2; Bogert §43.

[333] *See* 1 Scott & Ascher §17.2 n.5 and accompanying text. *Cf.* Jimenez v. Corr, 764 S.E.2d 115 (Va. Sup. Ct. 2014) (In a case involving the interpretation of a corporate shareholders'

opinion of one learned commentator, however, the scales have now tipped in favor of a default presumption that such exercises are permissible.[334]

Thus, other courts would enforce the exercise in further trust of a limited power in the absence of express language in the granting instrument prohibiting such an exercise.[335] The Restatement (Third) of Property is fully supportive.[336] The class of trust beneficiaries, however, would have to be limited to X, Y, and/or Z, i.e., to the specified objects of the power.[337] In one case, the holder of a limited testamentary power granted in a provision of her husband's inter vivos trust, attempted to exercise it in further trust by giving X, Y, and Z equitable life estates, but remainder interests to others, i.e., to nonobjects. The court enforced the life estate provisions but severed and struck the remainder provisions.[338] Upon the termination of the life interests, the subject property would have to pass in accordance with the default provisions of the husband's inter vivos trust.[339]

The matter of appointments in further trust should be addressed in the governing instrument. When it is not, the trustee should next check for an applicable statute before turning to the cases.[340] As to how an exercise of a limited power of appointment in further trust could violate the Rule against Perpetuities, the reader is referred to Section 8.2.1.8 of this handbook. If the exercise of a nongeneral power of appointment in further trust creates another nongeneral power of appointment, it has been suggested that the *donee* of the new power need not necessarily be a permissible appointee under the old. This is a topic we take up in Section 8.1.1 of this handbook.

Whether the exercise of a power in further trust creates a new trust. If a *general* power of appointment is exercised in further trust, is a new trust created or are the terms of the original trust merely altered or extended? Most general powers are drafted broadly enough so that either result is permissible.[341] Unfortunately, the question is not susceptible of any easy answer.[342]

In the case of the exercise of a general inter vivos power, a new trust is probably created, the donee of such a power having the equivalent of outright

---

agreement, the court held that the non-immediate-family-member trustees of a revocable inter vivos trust for the benefit of certain immediate family members of a signatory to the agreement are legally/equitably autonomous, that is to say they may not be deemed mere alter egos of the family members).

[334] 1 Scott & Ascher §3.1.2. *See also* Bogert, Trusts and Trustees §43 (in accord).

[335] *See, e.g.*, Vetrick v. Keating, 2004 WL 1254356 (Fla. Ct. App.).

[336] Restatement (Third) of Property (Wills and Other Donative Transfers) §19.14 cmt. e.

[337] Vetrick v. Keating, 2004 WL 1254356 (Fla. Ct. App.). *See generally* 1 Scott & Ascher §3.1.2; Restatement (Third) of Property (Wills and Other Donative Transfers) §19.15 cmt. e.

[338] Vetrick v. Keating, 2004 WL 1254356 (Fla. Ct. App.) (finding authority in Restatement (Second) of Property §23.1 cmts. a, d).

[339] *See generally* 1 Scott & Ascher §3.1.2.

[340] *See* 1 Scott on Trusts §17.2 n.7 and accompanying text. *See, e.g.*, Mass. Gen. Laws ch. 190B, §2-608(b) (presuming that limited powers may be exercised in further trust).

[341] Lewin ¶ 3-57.

[342] *See generally* Scott on Trusts §17.2.

ownership of the underlying property.[343] If the power included a right to terminate, which is likely the case, then it is hard to see how the donee is not the constructive settlor of the new trust.[344] When the power was exercised in further trust, the trustee of the old trust essentially also became an agent of the donee for purposes of transferring the subject property to the trustee of the new trust.[345] Thus, should the new trust fail at some point or its purposes be accomplished without the trust estate having been exhausted,[346] the property would revert upon a resulting trust to the donee or the donee's probate estate.[347] "The result is the same as if the beneficiary had terminated the old trust, received a conveyance of the trust property from the original trustee, and then transferred the property to the new trustee."[348]

In the case of a general testamentary power, however, it may depend upon how the power is exercised. If, for example, a general testamentary power is exercised without specific reference to the power so that the trust property is "blended" with the assets of the powerholder's probate estate, we could well have a two-trust situation.[349] Ultimately it's a question of the intention of the donee of the power.[350] Recall that "[a] blending clause purports to blend the appointive property with the donee's property in a common disposition." The subject of blending will come up again in our discussion of the doctrine of selective allocation (marshalling), specifically at Section 8.15.79 of this handbook, and in our discussion of the capture doctrine, specifically at Section 8.15.12 of this handbook.

While it is the default law that the exercise of a *limited* power in further trust does not give rise to a second trust, the terms of the trust that grant the *limited* power may authorize an exercise that creates a second settlement,[351] in which case the donor of the power will be deemed the settlor of the new trust.[352] Thus, whether after the exercise of such a power we are then left with the original trust constructively amended or a separate new trust that either coexists with the original or supersedes it will depend upon the terms of its exercise.[353] Whether we have one or two trusts also may depend upon who wants to know. Let us assume, for example, that *A* transfers property inter vivos to *B* in trust for *C*, who is given a *general* testamentary power of appointment. *C* exercises the power by providing in his or her will that *B* shall continue to hold the property in trust for the benefit of *X*. In this case *C* has expressed the intention that no new trust be created and that the terms of the original trust are merely to be extended. On

---

[343] *See, e.g.*, 1 Scott & Ascher §3.1.2 (confirming that the donee of the general inter vivos power would be the settlor of the new trust). *See also* 6 Scott & Ascher §41.19.

[344] 6 Scott & Ascher §41.19.

[345] 6 Scott & Ascher §41.19.

[346] *See generally* 6 Scott & Ascher §41.19 (Failure); 6 Scott & Ascher §42.9 (Surplus).

[347] 6 Scott & Ascher §41.19. *See generally* §4.1.1.1 of this handbook (the resulting trust).

[348] 6 Scott & Ascher §41.19.

[349] Restatement (Second) of Property (Wills and Other Donative Transfers) §22.1.

[350] Lewin ¶3-57.

[351] Lewin ¶¶3-58, 3-63, 3-64, 3-65, 3-66.

[352] 1 Scott & Ascher §3.1.2.

[353] Lewin ¶3-62.

the other hand, the creditors of *C* might demand that *B* turn the trust property over to *C*'s estate so that it may be available to satisfy their claims.[354] Once the claims are satisfied, a new trust presumably would arise for the benefit of *X*. Moreover, the court having jurisdiction over *C*'s estate might assert that this new trust is now a testamentary trust requiring its continuing supervision.

Regardless of the form of the arrangement, *i.e.*, whether there is a continuing trust or the termination of one and the starting up of another, when it comes to substantive rights there are two trusts. The donee who exercises the general power for all intents and purposes is the settlor of a new trust to which his or her creditors, spouse, the taxing authorities—perhaps even the welfare department—all may have access.[355] Even for purposes of the Rule against Perpetuities, the holder of a general inter vivos power is deemed to have a vested interest in the property subject to the power.[356]

The form of the arrangement seems to be up to the settlor. If the settlor expresses an intention that the *limited/special/nongeneral* powerholder may appoint new trustees upon an exercise in further trust, then such an appointment will be honored.[357] One learned commentator, however, suggests that absent language in the governing instrument to the contrary, inherent in the right to exercise a limited power in further trust, express or otherwise, is the right to appoint new trustees, although there are older cases to the contrary.[358] There is generally no requirement that the new trustees be members of the class of permissible appointees.[359]

Whether the exercise of a testamentary power in further trust converts an inter vivos trust into a court trust. Could the exercise of a *general* testamentary power of appointment have the effect of converting an inter vivos trust into a testamentary trust requiring subsequent periodic accountings to the court?[360] The attendant publicity and expense would make this an unfortunate result. Moreover, it would fly in the face of the very concept of the power of appointment—a power of disposition, a power to direct. The holder who exercises the general testamentary power in further trust is either directing that the property stay with the current trustee or directing one trustee to transfer title to another. In neither case is it expected that the estate of the powerholder will take unto itself more of an interest in the property (or that the court will

---

[354] Restatement (Second) of Property (Wills and Other Donative Transfers) §22.1.

[355] *See generally* 2A Scott on Trusts §147.3. *See also* UTC §401(3) (available at <http://www.uniformlaws.org/Act.aspx?title=Trust%20Code>) (providing that a trust may be created by the exercise of a power of appointment in favor of a trustee). *Cf.* Restatement (Third) of Trusts §10, Reporter's Note to Comment g, re: Clause (e) (discussing who may be deemed a settlor for purposes of taxation, creditor accessibility, and equitable division in the context of divorce).

[356] Leach, *Perpetuities in a Nutshell*, 51 Harv. L. Rev. 638, 654 (1938).

[357] *See* Lovejoy v. Bucknam, 299 Mass. 446, 13 N.E.2d 23 (1938).

[358] 1 Scott & Ascher §3.1.2.

[359] 1 Scott & Ascher §3.1.2.

[360] *See generally* Restatement (Second) of Property (Wills and Other Donative Transfers) §§11.1 cmt. b, 13.4 cmt. b.

acquire more supervision over the new arrangement) than is reasonably necessary to accommodate the interests of those having a claim against the estate.[361]

With respect to the exercise of a *limited* testamentary power of appointment in further trust, there should be no excuse whatsoever for a court's converting an inter vivos trust into a testamentary trust. The deceased holder is for all intents and purposes no more than an agent of the settlor, the holder's estate having no ownership interest, constructive or otherwise, in the property subject to the power. On the other hand, the exercise in further trust of a general testamentary power created under a *testamentary* trust as a practical matter might bring about a transfer of jurisdiction over the testamentary trust to the court supervising the administration of the powerholder's estate. This, however, is as much a conflict-of-laws issue as it is an issue rooted in the nature of the power of appointment itself.

The failed exercise in further trust. If the holder of a *general* power of appointment attempts to exercise the power in further trust and the "new" trust fails at the outset, or later fails or is fully performed without the trust estate having been exhausted,[362] the property may well pass as a resulting trust to the powerholder or the powerholder's probate estate under the doctrine of capture, a topic we take up in Section 8.15.12 of this handbook.[363] It does *not* pass back to the settlor of the "original" trust, or to the settlor's probate estate, unless the "original" trust instrument provides for a different disposition or unless the powerholder provided otherwise.[364] It is said that the property has been *captured* by the powerholder or the powerholder's probate estate.[365] The Restatement (Third) of Property would make certain alterations in traditional capture doctrine, a topic that is covered in some detail in Section 8.15.12 of this handbook.

If the holder of a *limited* power of appointment attempts to exercise the power in further trust and the "new" trust fails at the outset, or later fails or is fully performed without the trust estate having been exhausted,[366] there is no capture.[367] There are instead three possibilities, depending on the terms of the original trust or the law of the applicable jurisdiction: the property passes (1) to the takers in default,[368] (2) in equal shares to the class of permissible appointees,[369] or (3) back to the settlor of the "original" trust or his or her probate

---

[361] *See generally* Restatement (Second) of Property (Wills and Other Donative Transfers) §§11.1 cmt. b, 13.4 cmt. b. *See also* In re Estate of Wylie, 342 So. 2d 996 (Fla. Dist. Ct. App. 1977); Aurora Nat'l Bank v. Old Second Nat'l Bank, 59 Ill. App. 3d 384, 375 N.E.2d 544 (1978).

[362] *See generally* 6 Scott & Ascher §§41.17 (Failure), 42.7 (Surplus).

[363] *See generally* 6 Scott & Ascher §41.17 (Trust Created by Exercise of General Power of Appointment). *See also* §4.1.1.1 of this handbook (the resulting trust).

[364] 5 Scott on Trusts §426; 6 Scott & Ascher §41.17.

[365] *See generally* §8.15.12 of this handbook (the capture doctrine).

[366] *See generally* 6 Scott & Ascher §41.17 (Failure); 6 Scott & Ascher §42.8 (Surplus).

[367] *See generally* 6 Scott & Ascher §§41.17 (Trust Created by Exercise of General Power of Appointment), 41.18 (Trust Created by Exercise of Special Power of Appointment).

[368] *See generally* 6 Scott & Ascher §41.18 (Gift Overs in Default of Effective Exercise).

[369] *See generally* 6 Scott & Ascher §41.18 (Trust Created by Exercise of Special Power of Appointment). *See* Loring v. Marshall, 396 Mass. 166, 484 N.E.2d 1315 (1985) (citing with

estate.[370] In no event can the trustee keep the property.[371] "If the donee of a special power of appointment by deed or by will makes an appointment by deed that is ineffective, there is nothing, of course, to preclude the donee from making another appointment, either by deed or by will."[372]

The donee's capacity to exercise in further trust. The Restatement (Third) of Trusts speaks to the capacity of the holder, *i.e.*, the donee, of a power to exercise it in further trust: "The donee of a power of appointment has the capacity to make an effective appointment in trust if the donee has capacity to make an effective transfer of owned property of like type to the trustee of a trust that is similar in testamentary, revocable, or irrevocable character."[373] Thus, the holder/donee of a testamentary power of appointment must have testamentary capacity to exercise it in further trust. The testamentary standard of capacity also would apply to a holder/donee who wished to establish a revocable trust by means of the exercise of a general inter vivos power of appointment. An exercise of a general inter vivos power of appointment in further trust giving rise to an irrevocable trust requires either a donative or contractual standard of capacity on the part of the holder/donee of the power.[374]

Cross-reference. For a discussion of how an exercise in further trust could violate the Rule against Perpetuities, the reader is referred to Section 8.2.1.8 of this handbook.

§8.2 Termination of the Trust and Final Distribution

Generally, the terms of a trust determine when it terminates.[1] When the terms of a trust are silent, termination will occur when its purposes have been fulfilled.[2] The Restatement (Third) of Trusts defines termination date as the "time at which it becomes the duty of the trustee to wind up administration of the trust."[3] The law places a limit on how long a noncharitable trust may

---

approval Tentative Draft No. 7, 1984, of Restatement (Second) of Property (Wills and Other Donative Transfers) §24.2, which provides that in the absence of takers in default of the exercise of a limited power of appointment and in the absence of an expression of contrary intention in the instrument creating the power, property that is not appointed passes to the objects of the power).

[370] 5 Scott on Trusts §427; 6 Scott & Ascher §41.18. *See generally* §4.1.1.1 of this handbook (the resulting trust).

[371] 6 Scott & Ascher §41.18. For a discussion of the few situations in which a trustee with impunity may walk away with the trust property, see §4.1.1.1 of this handbook.

[372] 6 Scott & Ascher §41.18.

[373] Restatement (Third) of Trusts §11 cmt. d. *See generally* Chapter 1 of this handbook (discussing in part the capacity one needs to establish a trust other than through the exercise of a power of appointment).

[374] *See* the capacity discussion in Chapter 1 of this handbook.

§8.2 [1] Restatement (Third) of Trusts §61; 5 Scott & Ascher §33.1.

[2] Restatement (Third) of Trusts §61; 5 Scott & Ascher §33.1.

[3] Restatement (Third) of Trusts §89 cmt. a.

continue before termination. This constraint has come to be known as the *Rule against Perpetuities* (hereinafter "the Rule"). As long as the Rule is not violated, the settlor is entitled to set forth in the governing instrument when and under what circumstances the trust shall terminate. If the settlor fails to do so, the trust shall terminate when its purposes are fulfilled.[4] If the terms of the governing instrument are silent on what then happens to the trust property, the property shall pass back to the settlor or the settlor's estate upon a resulting trust. As to the related *Rule against Accumulations*, see Section 8.15.8 of this handbook.

The wind-up period is the period after the termination date and before "trust administration ends by complete distribution of the trust estate."[5] During the wind-up period, the trustee has a duty to preserve the trust estate. This means keeping any real property and tangible personal property insured and in repair.[6] Decisions as to whether and how to invest should be made in consultation with the distributees.[7] The trustee's lot is not any easy one. There are competing considerations that must be balanced. On the one hand, a trustee is generally expected to keep the trust estate preserved and reasonably productive during the wind-up period.[8] Reducing the entire portfolio to cash, therefore, probably is not an option. On the other hand, the trustee is generally expected to distribute out property that is unencumbered, readily marketable, and more or less intact.[9] That probably rules out remaining fully invested. Prevailing market conditions and the trust's tax picture are likely to constrain somewhat the trustee's maneuverability, thus further complicating matters. For a detailed discussion of selected distribution issues, the reader is referred to Section 8.2.3 of this handbook.

§8.2.1   *The Rule Against Perpetuities*

No interest is good unless it must vest, if at all, not later than 21 years after some life in being at the creation of the interest.[10]

---

[4] 5 Scott & Ascher §33.1.

[5] Restatement (Third) of Trusts §89 cmt. b.

[6] Restatement (Third) of Trusts §89 cmt. d.

[7] Restatement (Third) of Trusts §89 cmt. d.

[8] Restatement (Third) of Trusts §89 cmt. d.

[9] Restatement (Third) of Trusts §89 cmt. d.

[10] John Chipman Gray, The Rule Against Perpetuities §201 (4th ed. 1942). *See* Duke of Norfolk's Case, 3 Ch. Cas. 1, 22 Eng. Rep. 931 (Ch. 1682) (setting in motion a process that culminated in Gray's classic articulation of the Rule against Perpetuities). The Rule is said to have three purposes: (1) to provide "an adjustment or balance between the desire of the current owner of property to prolong indefinitely into the future his control over the devolution and use thereof and the desire of the person who will in the future become the owner of the affected land or other thing to be free from the dead hand," (2) to "contribute . . . to the increased use of the wealth of society," and (3) to "aid . . . current owners in responding to exigencies with their property." Restatement (Second) of Property (Wills and Other Donative Transfers) 8–9.

The history of perpetuities (remoteness) regulation. Professor John Chipman Gray asserted that the Anglo-American rule against perpetuities was not of feudal origin, that "it has its support in the practical needs of modern times."[11] That may be true, but the concept of a rule against perpetuities goes back to Roman times, if not earlier. In the third century A.D., there are indications that a *fideicommissum*[12] could not burden property beyond persons in being and the next (unborn) generation.[13] In the sixth century A.D., in a case involving a will,[14] the Roman emperor Justinian decreed that in that case and in all future cases the *fideicommissum* could not burden property beyond the fourth generation.[15] By 1472, English courts were not looking favorably on efforts to burden property in perpetuity.[16] In 1682, certain key elements of the modern common law Rule against Perpetuities were first articulated in the Duke of Norfolk's Case.[17] It is said that an impetus for the subsequent development of this judge-made rule was the exemption of legal executory interests from the application of yet another judge-made rule, namely, the destructibility of contingent remainders rule,[18] a topic we cover in some detail in Section 8.15.65 of this handbook. "The Rule against Perpetuities, as part of the Common Law, has been carried to all the English colonies where the principles of that Law prevail."[19] It was not until the 1960s, however, that the "life in being plus

---

[11] John Chipman Gray, The Rule Against Perpetuities §203 (4th ed. 1942).

[12] *See* §8.12.1 of this handbook (civil law alternatives to the trust).

[13] R. W. Lee, The Elements of Roman Law 246 (1956).

[14] Novel 159.

[15] *See* John Chipman Gray, The Rule Against Perpetuities, Appendix D (4th ed. 1942) (Roman law's *fideicommissum*). "'Fideicommissary substitutions,' as they were called, were sufficiently popular among the French nobility for the . . . [four-generation] . . . period to be reduced by legislation in 1650 to two generations, and one of the early acts of the reformers of the French Revolution was to forbid such substitutions altogether." Barry Nichols, An Introduction to Roman Law 269 (1962). *See generally* §8.12.1 of this handbook (the *fideicommissum*). In Malta in 1784, the Code of Rohan provided that no primogenitura could be instituted so as to extend beyond the fourth degree or "grado." Before that time, one's property could descend in perpetuity in accordance with rules laid down in one's will. *See* George Cessar Desain v. James Cessar Desain Viani, [1948] A.C. 18 P.C. (on appeal from the Court of Appeal, Malta).

[16] Taltarum's Case, Y.B. 12 Edw. IV, pl. 25 (1472). *See generally* George H. Haskins, *Extending the Grasp of the Dead Hand: Reflections on the Origins of the Rule Against Perpetuities*, 126 U. Pa. L. Rev. 19, 29 n.34 and accompanying text (discussing the historical significance of Taltarum's Case). *See, however*, Ritchie, Alford, & Effland, Decedents' Estates and Trusts 1082 (6th ed. 1982) (suggesting that the decision in D'Arundel's Case (1225) that the present holder of the fee could defeat the claim of his heirs by conveyance was the first of a series of judicial efforts to make land freely alienable by the present holder).

[17] 3 Ch. Cas. 1, 22 Eng. Rep. 931 (Ch. 1682). *See generally* Tye J. Klooster, *Are the Justifications for the Rule against Perpetuities Still Persuasive? A Survey of the Modern Policy Arguments Cast for and against Retention of the Rule against Perpetuities*, 30 ACTEC L.J. 95 (2004) (in part discussing the Duke of Norfolk's Case and its progeny).

[18] *See generally* Dukeminier, Krier, Alexander & Schill, Property 242 (6th ed. 2006).

[19] John Chipman Gray, The Rule Against Perpetuities §200 (4th ed. 1942). "Considering the unformed condition of the doctrine of remoteness at the time when the American Colonies were planted, it would have been quite possible for it to have developed there in a different shape from that which it assumed in England. But as a matter of fact the rule seems, in the absence of statute, to be always adopted throughout the United States in its modern English form." *Id.*

twenty-one" rule came to New York. Before then New York had a "two-life" rule.[20] It would be fair to say that in the United States the Rule is now in "free fall," a number of state legislatures having made it inapplicable to noncharitable trusts that meet certain statutory specifications.[21] This movement to "abolish" the Rule as it applies to certain contingent equitable property interests we take up in Section 8.2.1.9 of this handbook. Though a trust analog, the modern civil law foundation, even one with noncharitable beneficiaries, generally need not be limited in its duration.[22] An exception is the Austrian *privatstiftung* (foundation), whose maximum term is 100 years, although duration may be extended for another 100 years maximum each time foundation property vests. Extension is effected by resolution of the "ultimate beneficiaries," that is to say by resolution of those in whom the foundation property from time to time vests.

The Rule explained. The Rule against Perpetuities (*no interest is good unless it must vest, if at all, not later than twenty-one years after some life in being at the creation of the interest*) in its equitable application[23] places a limit on how long certain types of trusts may continue and is applicable even if a trustee has a power of sale.[24] During the life of a trust (*i.e.*, during the period when the trustee has legal title to the property), ascertained and unascertained beneficiaries and remaindermen have equitable interests in the trust property.[25] If during that time there is a condition that must be fulfilled before an equitable interest becomes possessory, if, for example, the terms of the trust provide that the youngest descendant of the settlor who is alive at the death of the current beneficiary shall take outright the trust's terminating distribution,[26] that equitable interest, in this case that equitable remainder interest, is said to be a *contingent* one, at least while the current beneficiary is alive.[27] (The condition of

---

[20] It has been the practice among some New York scriveners to designate in a trust instrument for the client interested in a New York trust that continues out as long as possible into the future ten or so of the scrivener's law partners and associates, and the children of the law partners and associates, as nonbeneficiary lives in being.

[21] 1 Scott & Ascher §9.3.9.

[22] *See generally* §8.12.1 of this handbook (the civil law foundation).

[23] For purposes of this section, an equitable interest is a property interest that arises incident to a trust relationship. *See generally* John Chipman Gray, The Rule Against Perpetuities §200.1 (4th ed. 1942) (noting that "[t]he practical importance of tracing the history of the Rule against Perpetuities lies in the proof it affords that the Rule is not confined, as has been sometimes contended, to interests arising under the Statutes of Uses and Wills, but that it was developed by cases on executory devises of chattels, which were common-law interests, *and that it should govern all kinds of future contingent interests*.") Thus, "[a]ll future equitable interests, not vested, are subject to the Rule against Perpetuities." *Id.* at §323. It follows that vested equitable interests, either of realty or personalty, are *not* subject to the Rule. *Id.* at §322 (4th ed. 1942).

[24] 1 Scott & Ascher §9.3.9; John Chipman Gray, The Rule Against Perpetuities §§202.1 & 487 (4th ed. 1942).

[25] *See generally* Bogert §181.

[26] *See generally* 3 Scott & Ascher §13.2.9 (Whether an Interest is Conditional on Beneficiary's Survival).

[27] *Cf.* John Chipman Gray, The Rule Against Perpetuities §101 (4th ed. 1942) (noting that as to legal interests in real estate "[a] remainder is contingent if, in order for it to come into possession, the fulfillment of some condition precedent other than the determination of the

survivorship is perhaps the most common such condition precedent the trustee is likely to encounter today.[28]) Note that the survivorship condition precedent is not that the current beneficiary dies but that someone else outlives the current beneficiary. Note also that in our example, survivorship is not necessarily the only condition precedent. Another is conception. Obviously to be eligible to receive the terminating distribution, one also must at least be *in utero* at the time the current beneficiary dies.[29] Thus, in our example, we actually have two conditions precedent: existence and survivorship. We take up the topic of gestation in more detail later on in this section. To summarize, "[t]he distinction . . . [between vested and contingent interests] . . . is of great importance as concerns the Rule against Perpetuities, for a true vested interest is never obnoxious to the Rule, while a contingent interest not only may be, but often is."[30]

In the context of trusts, the Rule governs how long equitable contingent *nonfiduciary* interests may remain outstanding before they must extinguish or be converted into vested interests (interests that are held by someone unconditionally).[31] Thus the Rule generally does not apply to fiduciary asset administration powers; nor will it invalidate a power in the trustee to dispose of a portion or all of the underlying trust property for full consideration; nor will it prevent payment to the trustee of reasonable compensation; nor will it invalidate a trustee's discretionary power to make pretermination distributions of vested interests; nor will it prevent a trust from continuing after the period of the Rule, provided all contingent equitable interests have vested within the period of the Rule; nor will it apply to a power to appoint a fiduciary.[32]

Probabilities are immaterial. Under the Rule's classic application, if a contingent event could possibly happen too remotely, there would be a violation *ab initio* as to the interest that is conditioned upon that event.[33] There is no better illustration of the immateriality of probabilities when it comes to the Rule's application than the case of the unborn widow, which is the topic of Section 8.15.32 of this handbook.[34]

---

preceding freehold estates is necessary"). *See also* §8.15.65 of this handbook (the trust exemption to the destructibility of contingent remainders rule).

[28] *See generally* §8.15.56 of this handbook (120-hour survival requirement applicable to trusts); 3 Scott & Ascher §13.2.9.

[29] *See generally* UPC §2-901 cmt. (gestation).

[30] John Chipman Gray, The Rule Against Perpetuities §99 (4th ed. 1942).

[31] *See generally* Bogert §181.

[32] *See* UPC §2-904 (2) (The Uniform Statutory Rule Against Perpetuities (USRAP) does not apply to "a fiduciary's power relating to the administration or management of assets, including the power of a fiduciary to sell, lease, or mortgage property, and the power of a fiduciary to determine principal and income"); UPC §2-904(3) (rule not applicable to power to appoint a fiduciary); UPC §2-904 (4) (rule not applicable to pretermination distributions of vested interests); Scott & Ascher §9.3.9 (suggesting that when it is permissible for a trust to continue longer than the period of the Rule, *e.g.*, when all interests have vested within the period of the Rule, the trustee may exercise his administrative powers, *e.g.*, his powers to sell, mortgage, and lease, until termination without violating the Rule).

[33] John Chipman Gray, The Rule Against Perpetuities §§214 & 268 (4th ed. 1942).

[34] John Chipman Gray, The Rule Against Perpetuities §214 (4th ed. 1942).

The public policy that the Rule aims to promote. Professor John Chipman Gray was adamant that the rule against perpetuities was not aimed at limiting restraints upon alienation but at restraining the creation of indestructible future contingent estates.[35] A legal future interest does not render a present future interest inalienable.[36] In the case of a trust, the trustee is vested with the legal title to the entrusted property. That being the case, he will generally have the inherent power to sell it.[37] Moreover, many equitable interests, be they present or future, will themselves be freely alienable.[38] In Gray's view, "[i]t would have been better had it been called the Rule against Remoteness."[39] The rule against perpetuities (remoteness) and the rules disallowing restraints on alienation do share a common policy purpose, however, namely, to "forward the circulation of property."[40] In other words, the rule against perpetuities has always been about marketability, not alienability,[41] about mitigating the commercial impediments that are the inevitable consequence of the judicial enforcement of future rights in property.[42] At least that was Gray's considered opinion. It was also his considered opinion that the Rule struck an appropriate balance between allowing each generation "the power of providing for those who come immediately after it in the way it thinks best" and enabling one to "make the most" of one's property.[43]

Other learned commentators have their own views as to the Rule's true policy objectives:

> Most discussion of the anti-dead-hand policy has centered on the rule against perpetuities and has emphasized the need to promote alienability of land. Simes rightly pointed out that this rationale does not explain why the rule should apply to trusts in which the trustee has the power of sale. Lewis M. Simes, Public Policy and the Dead Hand 40 (1955). Simes's alternative justification, "strik[ing] a fair balance between the desires of members of the present [and] succeeding generations," *Id.* at 58, is a slogan, not an explanation. . . .[44]

---

[35] John Chipman Gray, The Rule Against Perpetuities §2 (4th ed. 1942).

[36] John Chipman Gray, The Rule Against Perpetuities §2 (4th ed. 1942).

[37] John Chipman Gray, The Rule Against Perpetuities §§414.1 & 269 (4th ed. 1942).

[38] John Chipman Gray, The Rule Against Perpetuities §§119.1 & 269 (4th ed. 1942).

[39] John Chipman Gray, The Rule Against Perpetuities §2 (4th ed. 1942).

[40] John Chipman Gray, The Rule Against Perpetuities §2.1 (4th ed. 1942).

[41] John Chipman Gray, The Rule Against Perpetuities §2 (4th ed. 1942). *See also* §268 ("If there is a gift over of an estate on a remote contingency, the market value of the interest of the present owner will be greatly reduced, while the executory gift will sell for very little, or, in other words, the value of the present interest *plus* the value of the executory gift will fall far short of what would be the value of the property if there were no executory interest. Further, if the owner of the present interest wishes to convey an absolute fee, the holder of the executory gift can extort from him a price which exceeds what it ought to be, if based on the chance of his succeeding to the property.").

[42] John Chipman Gray, The Rule Against Perpetuities §268 (4th ed. 1942).

[43] John Chipman Gray, The Rule Against Perpetuities §268 (4th ed. 1942).

[44] John H. Langbein, *Mandatory Rules in the Law of Trusts*, 98 Nw. U. L. Rev. 1105 n.33 (2004).

The Court of Appeals of North Carolina in 2010 tried its hand at divining the public policy behind the Rule.[45] It found that the Rule's purpose was in fact to limit alienation restraints, that its purpose was *not* to limit how long the vesting of remote interests, equitable or otherwise, could be postponed. "The common law rule against perpetuities developed to prevent shifting future interests from effecting an unreasonable restraint on alienation. The rule attempts to prevent the creation of a fixed succession of future interests that will cause ownership of property to shift perpetually among devisees who have no power to alienate the property."[46] Thus, abolishing the Rule insofar as it applies to contingent equitable interests under trusts would not run counter to prevailing public policy, at least with respect to trusts whose trustees possess the power to sell or otherwise alienate. And every trust may well fall into that category, regardless of its terms. This is because a trustee, being the holder of the legal title, has the inherent power to convey trust property to a good faith purchaser for value (BFP), regardless of whether the conveyance would be in breach of trust. The concept of the BFP is taken up in Section 8.15.63 of this handbook.

Related sections in this handbook. For a discussion of when the condition precedent of survivorship is presumed and when it is not when the governing instrument is silent on the subject, as well as of the law's preference for early vesting in such cases, the reader is referred to Section 5.2 of this handbook. The section also contains examples of contingent equitable interests. For a discussion of when contingent interests are transmissible and when they are not, the reader is referred to Section 8.30 of this handbook. For a discussion of the application of antilapse concepts in the trust context, see Section 8.15.55 of this handbook. For a discussion of the Uniform Probate Code's 120-hour survival requirement applicable to trusts, see Section 8.15.56 of this handbook. For a discussion of the "all-or-nothing" rule applicable to class gifts and its exceptions, see Section 8.15.73 of this handbook; of the fertile octogenarian principle, see Section 8.15.31 of this handbook; of the doctrine of infectious invalidity, see Section 8.15.72 of this handbook; and of the unborn widow principle, see Section 8.15.32 of this handbook.

The concept of vesting. A vested equitable remainder under a trust is a future property interest that is subject to no condition precedent other than the termination of "the preceding equitable estate."[47] An equitable remainder interest that is subject to a condition precedent other than "the termination of the preceding equitable estate" is a contingent property interest. Survivorship is a common condition precedent in the world of trusts. A current equitable property interest, in this context "a preceding equitable estate," also can be either vested or contingent. A current equitable property interest in the income stream of a trust which interest is subject to the condition precedent of the

---

[45] Brown Bros. Harriman Trust Co. v. Benson, 688 S.E.2d 752 (N.C. App. 2010).

[46] Brown Bros. Harriman Trust Co. v. Benson, 688 S.E.2d 752, 755 (N.C. App. 2010).

[47] *See generally* John Chipman Gray, The Rule Against Perpetuities, Appendix M, §970 (4th ed. 1942).

trustee's exercise of discretion to distribute the income to the current beneficiary rather than apply it to principal comes to mind.[48]

The Rule is against the remoteness of vesting in interest,[49] not remoteness of *vesting in possession*.[50] To illustrate the difference between the two, let us assume *A* transfers property to *B* in trust for Mr. Jones for life, remainder to Mrs. Jones, *who is alive* and currently lives in a common law jurisdiction.

From the time the trust is created, Mrs. Jones's equitable remainder interest is *vested*, though not possessory.[51] This is because at the time the trust is created, she is ascertained and during the life of Mr. Jones there is no event that will extinguish her interest. At the death of Mr. Jones, the underlying trust property passes outright and free of trust either to Mrs. Jones or to her probate estate,[52] *unless perhaps there is an applicable antilapse statute*.[53] In other words, Mrs. Jones then gets possession of the property, be she dead[54] or alive.

Had Mrs. Jones had been dead at the time Mr. Jones transferred title to the property to *B* (the trustee), no equitable future property interest could have passed to her or her personal representative (probate estate). One cannot make a gift to one lacking juridical personality, such as a dead person. The Restatement (Third) of Property's articulation of the principle is garbled, at least in the case of the irrevocable transfer in trust. Here it is: "A beneficiary of a present or a future interest who is deceased when the donative document takes effect as a

---

[48] *See, e.g.*, Newcomer v. National City Bank, 19 N.E.3d 492, 511–515 (Ohio 2014).

[49] Lewin ¶ 5-22.

[50] Bogert §213; John Chipman Gray, The Rule Against Perpetuities, Appendix M, §972 (4th ed. 1942).

[51] *See generally* John Chipman Gray, The Rule Against Perpetuities §102 (4th ed. 1942). A *legal* future interest requires a previous estate to support it. *See generally* §8.27 of this handbook. Because no *equitable* future interest incident to a trust relationship requires a previous supporting estate, legal title being in the trustee, there is technically no such thing as an equitable remainder. Thus, Professor John Chipman Gray, exhibiting his characteristic scholarly precision, has labeled the equitable equivalent of a legal remainder a quasi remainder. *See generally* John Chipman Gray, The Rule Against Perpetuities §324 (4th ed. 1942).

[52] *But see* UPC §2-707 (providing that property would pass to the "descendents" of Mrs. Jones). *See generally* Halbach & Waggoner, *The UPC's New Survivorship and Antilapse Provisions*, 55 Alb. L. Rev. 1091, 1131–1133 (1992); Dukeminier, *The Uniform Probate Code Upends the Law of Remainders*, 94 Mich. L. Rev. 148, 149–150, 166 (1995). In a case where property is distributable by a trustee to a closed probate estate, a court can avoid the inconvenience and expense of having the estate reopened by ordering the trustee to make distribution directly to those who are entitled to the estate. *See, e.g.*, Cooling v. Security Trust Co., 29 Del. Ch. 286, 76 A.2d 1, 5 (1950).

[53] *See, e.g.*, UPC §2-707(b) ("A future interest under the terms of a trust is contingent on the beneficiary's surviving the distribution date."). The UPC's trust antilapse regime, however, is merely a rule of construction. *See* UPC §2-701. Thus, in trusts like "income to . . . [C] . . . for life, remainder in corpus to . . . [D] . . . whether or not . . . [D]. . . . survives . . . [C] . . . ," or "income to . . . [C] . . . for life, remainder in corpus to . . . [D] . . . or [D's] . . . estate," this section would not apply and, "should . . . [D] . . . predecease . . . [C] . . . , . . . [D's] . . . future interest would pass through . . . [D's] . . . estate to . . . [D's] . . . successors in interest, who would be entitled to possession or enjoyment at . . . [C's] . . . death." UPC §2-707 cmt. *See generally* §8.15.55 of this handbook (antilapse [the trust application]).

[54] Had she died intestate without heirs at law and had the trust been comprised of personal property, then the doctrine of *bona vacantia* might be applicable, in which case the property would pass to the Crown or the state. *See* §8.15.46 of this handbook (*bona vacantia* doctrine).

dispositive instrument takes no interest."[55] Take Mrs. Jones. She being alive at the time her husband created the trust relationship is a beneficiary of that relationship, not of the equitable remainder that is incident to it. As to the equitable remainder itself, which is a property interest, she is its actual owner. Had she been dead at the time of the transfer, Mrs. Jones could neither be a beneficiary of the trust relationship nor the recipient of an ownership interest in an equitable remainder incident to that relationship. The Restatement (Third) appears to have confused beneficiary status with beneficial ownership, and then conflated the two.

Section 2-707 of the Uniform Probate Code. An early-vesting presumption has been a critical component of traditional perpetuities doctrine.[56] Perhaps no longer. The Uniform Probate Code, specifically Section 2-707, provides that a future interest under the terms of a trust is contingent on the beneficiary surviving the distribution date. That presumption is coupled with a complicated antilapse feature, which is discussed in Section 8.15.55 of this handbook. Thus, should Mrs. Jones predecease Mr. Jones, her probate estate would be out of luck. The Restatement (Third) of Property (Wills and Other Donative Transfers) shies away from endorsing some kind of equitable presumption comparable to the UPC's statutory one. The traditional "rule of construction is the rule best suited within the confines of the common-law tradition to approximate the likely preference of the transferor, and is supported by the constructional preference for the construction that does not disinherit a line of descent."[57] The Restatement (Third), however, does call upon the state legislatures to enact UPC Section 2-707, suggesting that it "provide[s] a more direct and efficient means of protecting equality among different lines of descent" than having the trust property augment the probate estate of a beneficiary who predeceases the distribution date, as did Mrs. Jones.[58]

Likely preferences? Protecting equality among different lines of descent? One learned commentator was struck by the fact that Section 2-707 had made it to promulgation unsupported by any credible "empirical evidence indicating that most trust settlors want a remainderman to lose the remainder if he does not survive the life tenant, substituting his descendants for him if he leaves descendants."[59] In other words, the drafters appear to have been "proceeding purely on their own speculation."[60] The same might be said for the authors of the Restatement (Third) of Property.

---

[55] Restatement (Third) of Property (Wills and Other Donative Transfers) §26.1.

[56] For an application of the traditional early-vesting principle, see Estate of Woodworth, 22 Cal. Rptr. 2d 676 (App. 1993).

[57] Restatement (Third) of Property (Wills and Other Donative Transfers) §26.3 cmt. c.

[58] Restatement (Third) of Property (Wills and Other Donative Transfers) §26.3 cmt. h. *But see* Mark L. Ascher, *The 1990 Uniform Probate Code: Older and Better, Or More Like the Internal Revenue Code?*, 77 Minn. L. Rev. 639, 640 (1993) ("To be blunt, the 1990 version . . . [of the UPC] . . . is also quite pretentious.").

[59] Jesse Dukeminier, *The Uniform Probate Code Upends the Law of Remainders*, 94 Mich. L. Rev. 148, 149–150 (1995).

[60] Jesse Dukeminier, *The Uniform Probate Code Upends the Law of Remainders*, 94 Mich. L. Rev. 148, 149–150 (1995).

Vested equitable interests subject to divestment. If Mrs. Jones's interest were vested subject to divestment upon the happening of a condition subsequent (*e.g.*, if her interest passes to X in the event, say, that E marries F),[61] then X's contingent interest is said to be executory, provided E and F are alive at the time the underlying property is transferred in trust.[62] X's contingent equitable executory interest is subject to the traditional Rule against Perpetuities.[63] Mrs. Jones's equitable remainder interest vested *ab initio* and therefore cannot be obnoxious to the Rule.[64] As we shall see, however, neither interest in our particular hypothetical would have a Rule problem in any case, both spouses being lives in being.[65]

The Restatement (Third) of Property further complicates matters by pretzeling the traditional vested equitable future interest that is subject to a condition subsequent into an interest that is subject to a condition precedent.[66] "A condition subsequent is a condition that is expressed as a condition that, if satisfied on or before the distribution date, extinguishes the possibility that the future interest will take effect in possession or enjoyment."[67] This intentional conflation is unfortunate as the transmissibility of the vested remainder subject to divestment is easier to grasp conceptually than the transmissibility of the contingent remainder, a topic we take up generally in Section 8.30 of this handbook. Moreover, while all such vested remainders are transmissible, the same cannot be said for all versions of the contingent remainder.[68]

Vested income interests. Note, also, that if Mr. Jones had been entitled to an income interest for a fixed period, say ten years, rather than for life, then in the event of his death before the end of the fixed period, the trust's income stream would have flowed into his probate estate for the balance of the period, unless the terms of the trust had provided otherwise.[69] If the terms of the trust had provided that Mrs. Jones's vested equitable remainder interest would become possessory only upon the expiration of the ten-year period, then the underlying trust property could have ultimately ended up in her probate estate as well in the event she also had died in the interim. This is, of course, all classic default law.[70] The terms of the trust could easily have provided for "gifts over" to others in the event of the premature death of the current beneficiary and in the event

---

[61] *See generally* §8.30 of this handbook (the difference between a vested equitable remainder subject to divestment and a vested (transmissible) contingent equitable remainder).

[62] *See generally* Cornelius J. Moynihan, Introduction to the Law of Real Property 191 (2d ed. 1988); §8.15.80 of this handbook (springing and shifting equitable executory interests).

[63] *See, e.g.*, Warner v. Whitman, 353 Mass. 468, 233 N.E.2d 14 (Mass. 1968) (involving a collection of executory equitable interests in the income stream of a trust).

[64] *See* John Chipman Gray, The Rule Against Perpetuities §102 (4th ed. 1942).

[65] *See, however,* Warner v. Whitman, 353 Mass. 468, 233 N.E.2d 14 (Mass. 1968) (offering an example of how shifting executory equitable interests in the income stream of a trust could violate the Rule against Perpetuities as traditionally applied).

[66] Restatement (Third) of Property (Wills and Other Donative Transfers) §26.2 cmt. c ("This Restatement declines to perpetuate a difference in classification between a condition precedent and a condition subsequent.").

[67] Restatement (Third) of Property (Wills and Other Donative Transfers) §26.2 cmt. b.

[68] *See generally* §8.30 of this handbook.

[69] *See generally* 3 Scott & Ascher §14.10.1.

[70] *See, however,* §8.15.55 of this handbook (antilapse [*the trust application*]).

of the death before possession of the remainderman. The "gifts over" would be examples of equitable interests that are contingent.

Nonpossessory vested interests. On the other hand, were *A* to make a simple unconditional gift of the property outright and free of trust directly to Mrs. Jones, bypassing the trustee altogether, Mrs. Jones's interest at the time of transfer would be both *vested* and *possessory*. For purposes of the Rule, however, vesting only is what matters. Under either of the above Jones scenarios, by the way, the current equitable income interest fully vested in Mr. Jones *ab initio*. Under neither is survivorship the type of condition precedent that would have made *his* interest contingent at the time the underlying property was transferred in trust, or thereafter.[71]

Members of unincorporated associations. Or take a trust for the individual members of an unincorporated association. If the class of beneficiaries is fixed at the time the trust is created, the trust is enforceable. If the trust is for the benefit of the individual members of the association as it is constituted from time to time, "their interests would not comply with the vesting requirements of the traditional rule against perpetuities,"[72] the condition precedent of membership being a fatal flaw.[73]

The perpetual trust with a gift over to a noncharity. An irrevocable trust for a charitable purpose with a gift over to a named individual should the trust at some point in the future fail would not violate the Rule even if the failure could occur long after the individual had died, provided the individual was in existence at the time of the trust's creation.[74] Even if the failure might happen more than twenty-one years after the death of the last life-in-being, the gift over to the individual or the personal representative of the individual's probate estate would be valid because the individual took *ab initio* a vested (transmissible) contingent equitable remainder interest.[75] Recall that the Rule is about interests that could vest *remotely*.[76] The oxymoronic concept of the vested (transmissible) contingent equitable remainder is taken up in Section 8.30 of this handbook.

Conclusion. An exhaustive study of the Rule is beyond the scope of this book; moreover, it would duplicate the efforts of others.[77] Rather, the trustee should use the guidelines that follow to assist in developing a methodology for ruling out Rule problems and for framing appropriate questions for counsel when such problems are encountered. Ideally, the trustee will be able to confront the Rule efficiently and cost-effectively, with courage and with confidence.

---

[71] *See, e.g.,* Hochberg v. Proctor, 441 Mass. 403, 414–415, 805 N.E.2d 979, 989 (2004).

[72] Restatement (Third) of Trusts §43 cmt. e(1).

[73] *See* John Chipman Gray, The Rule Against Perpetuities, Appendix H, §§896, 896.1, & 896.2 (4th ed. 1942).

[74] *See generally* John Chipman Gray, The Rule Against Perpetuities, Appendix M (4th ed. 1942).

[75] *See* 6 Scott & Ascher §39.7.6 (Gift Over from Charity to Non-Charity); John Chipman Gray, The Rule Against Perpetuities, Appendix M (4th ed. 1942).

[76] *See, e.g.,* Hochberg v. Proctor, 441 Mass. 403, 805 N.E.2d 979 (2004).

[77] *See* Bogert §213 nn.1, 2 and accompanying text.

Charitable interests are not entirely exempt from the Rule's application. It should first be made clear that charitable trusts generally are *not* exempt from the Rule.[78] If property, however, will become the subject of a charitable trust in all events within the period of the Rule, *i.e.*, if an equitable interest under a trust will become available in all events for one or more charitable purposes within the period of the Rule, then such a trust may last forever.[79] Shifting of the equitable interests between and among charitable purposes would then be permissible in perpetuity.[80] In the words of Prof. Gray: "But although a charitable trust is to begin at a remote period, yet if it is preceded by another charitable trust, it has been held not to be void, even if there be a change of trustee."[81] The Uniform Probate Code is in accord.[82]

A gift over from a noncharity to a charity certainly would not pose a Rule problem if the charity's remainder interest had vested *ab initio*.[83] When a gift over from an individual to a charity fails, there is generally a resulting trust if the intervening noncharitable equitable interest had been subject to a limitation.[84] Had the noncharitable interest had been subject to a condition subsequent, the individual might well have been allowed to keep the property free of trust.[85]

Even without an intervening noncharitable equitable interest, the Rule against Perpetuities is not implicated when a charity takes a vested equitable interest *ab initio* though application is postponed until certain things happen, such as fundraising activities are undertaken.[86] Presumably if insufficient funds are raised, the court will apply *cy pres*.[87] On the other hand if vesting of the equitable charitable interest is made contingent upon the raising of sufficient funds, the Rule would be violated and a resulting trust may well be imposed by the court.[88] The matter of accumulating the net income of a charitable trust for

---

[78] *See generally* 5 Scott & Ascher §37.4.1; John Chipman Gray, The Rule Against Perpetuities §591 (4th ed. 1942).

[79] *See generally* 4A Scott on Trusts §365; 5 Scott & Ascher §37.4.1; 6 Scott & Ascher §39.7.7; John Chipman Gray, The Rule Against Perpetuities §589 (4th ed. 1942).

[80] John Chipman Gray, The Rule Against Perpetuities §§328 & 597 (4th ed. 1942). *See generally* 5 Scott & Ascher §37.4.1; 6 Scott & Ascher §39.5.2 ("It is immaterial that the gift over to the other charity may occur beyond the period of the rule against perpetuities, because the rule does not apply to a gift over from one charity to another"); 6 Scott & Ascher §39.7.5 (noting, however, that if the express condition that could bring about a charity-to-charity shift involves an event that is unrelated to a charitable purpose, such as the failure of the first charity also to see to it that the settlor's issue are taken care of, the condition itself might well be invalid as tending to create a perpetuity).

[81] John Chipman Gray, The Rule Against Perpetuities §328 (4th ed. 1942).

[82] UPC §2-904(5).

[83] *See generally* 6 Scott & Ascher §39.7.7.

[84] *See generally* 6 Scott & Ascher §39.7.7 (Gift Over from Non-Charity to Charity); John Chipman Gray, The Rule Against Perpetuities §414 (4th ed. 1942) ("When, by reason of an equitable interest being too remote, there is a legal interest vested in trustees, without any corresponding equitable interest, there is a resulting trust to the heir or next of kin."). *C.f.* §8.41 of this handbook (what is to be done with net income when there is no current beneficiary).

[85] *See generally* 6 Scott & Ascher §39.7.7 (Gift Over from Non-Charity to Charity).

[86] *See generally* 6 Scott & Ascher §39.7.8 (Gift to Charity without Intermediate Disposition).

[87] *See generally* §9.4.3 of this handbook (*cy pres*).

[88] *See generally* 6 Scott & Ascher §39.7.8 (Gift to Charity without Intermediate Disposition).

more than twenty-one years following the death of the last life in being is taken up in Section 8.15.8 of this handbook.

In the United States there likely would be no Rule violation should the trust property *revert* to the settlor or his or her probate estate upon a resulting trust in the event that at some point there is no charity to shift the equitable interest to, reversionary interests being always vested.[89] In England, on the other hand, a reversion upon the happening of a condition subsequent now implicates the Rule.[90] The Rule also is implicated when the duration of an English charitable trust is subject to a contingency-based limitation, such as so long as a certain state of affairs continues.[91] Thus, an equitable reversion upon the failure of an English charitable trust would be unenforceable were the interest to become possessory beyond the period of the Rule.[92] *Cy pres* would then have to be applied. Still, as we have been emphasizing, even in the United States one cannot say that the Rule is never applicable to charitable trusts.[93] What follows is an example of a charitable trust that has no Rule problem and one of a charitable trust that does:

To illustrate first a *nonviolation* in the charitable context, let us take a scholarship trust fund for gifted and needy U.S. citizens. Each U.S. citizen, born and unborn, has a contingent equitable interest in the trust.[94] The interests are contingent because certain conditions precedent—prior conditions as it were—must be satisfied before the citizen may receive a scholarship distribution from the trust. The conditions are that the citizen must be alive, gifted, needy, a scholar, a U.S. citizen, duly selected, and so forth. The beneficial interests are equitable and not legal because legal title to the property is in the trustee. As a matter of public policy the use of the trust property for such a charitable purpose perpetually may be subject to such conditions.[95] Not so, however, with noncharitable trusts.

To illustrate a *violation* of the Rule in the charitable context, let us take the following trust: A to B for the benefit of the issue[96] of C for a period of 100 years; and upon the expiration of the 100-year period, the trust property shall pass outright and free of trust to the then-living issue of C, by right of representation; but if there are no issues of C then living, then to the United Way. In this case, the contingent interest in the United Way could vest beyond the period of the Rule and is, therefore, bad, even though the United Way is a charity.[97]

---

[89] *See generally* 6 Scott & Ascher §§39.7.2, 39.7.3; John Chipman Gray, The Rule Against Perpetuities §603.9 (4th ed. 1942).

[90] *See generally* 6 Scott & Ascher §§39.7.2 (Conditions Subsequent), 39.7.3 (Limitations).

[91] 6 Scott & Ascher §39.7.3 (Limitations).

[92] *See generally* 6 Scott & Ascher §§39.7.2 (Conditions Subsequent), 39.7.3 (Limitations).

[93] Bogert §341; 1 Scott & Ascher §9.3.9.

[94] *But see* John Chipman Gray, The Rule Against Perpetuities §590 (4th ed. 1942) (suggesting that ordinarily no one has any equitable property rights incident to a charitable trust).

[95] *See generally* Bogert §351.

[96] *See generally* §5.2 of this handbook (class designation: "children," "issue," "heirs," and "relatives" (some rules of construction)).

[97] *See* John Chipman Gray, The Rule Against Perpetuities §594 (4th ed. 1942).

The charitable corporation. A restricted gift to a charitable corporation is subject to the same perpetuities limitations and exemptions as a transfer to the trustee of a charitable trust.[98]

The STAR trust [Cayman Islands]. In Section 9.8.10 of this handbook we take up the Cayman Islands STAR trust, which has some of the attributes of the benevolent trust[99] and some of the purpose trust.[100] Though the STAR trust needs to have a charitable purpose or equitable owners, it is exempt from the Rule against Perpetuities.

Honorary trusts. Under the Uniform Trust Code, a trust may be created for a noncharitable purpose without a definite or definitely ascertainable beneficiary, or for a noncharitable but otherwise valid purpose to be selected by the trustee.[101] But the trust may not be enforced for more than twenty-one years.[102]

The measuring life concept. Under the common law, a contingent interest in a noncharitable trust with ascertainable beneficiaries must extinguish by vesting or otherwise within the period allowed by the Rule. That period is twenty-one years after the death of certain people, expressly designated or inferred, who are alive at the time the contingent interest is created.[103] These people are known as *measuring lives* or *lives in being*.[104] That a settlor could, for example, provide that the trust shall terminate, say, twenty years after the death of the last survivor of the members of an expansive class of designated living individuals without violating the Rule, such as of all the living descendants of some European monarch.[105] "The language of all the cases is, that property may be so limited as to make it unalienable during any number of lives, not exceeding that to which testimony can be applied, to determine when the survivor of them drops."[106]

If at the time the interest is created one could conjure up a possible *fact or circumstance*—a worst-case scenario as it were—that would cause a condition precedent to remain outstanding beyond the period of the Rule, there may be a common law Rule problem that the trustee will have to confront.[107] At the very least, the trustee will have some analytical work to do as it is more than likely there are provisions in the governing trust instrument or somewhere in a state

---

[98] St. Joseph's Hosp. v. Bennett, 281 N.Y. 115, 22 N.E.2d 305 (1939).

[99] *See* §9.4.1 of this handbook (in part discussing the benevolent trust).

[100] *See* §9.27 of this handbook (the purpose trust).

[101] UTC §409 (available at <http://www.uniformlaws.org/Act.aspx?title=Trust%20 Code>). *See generally* §9.9.5 of this handbook (honorary trusts).

[102] *See generally* §9.9.5 of this handbook (honorary trusts).

[103] *See generally* John Chipman Gray, The Rule Against Perpetuities §216 (4th ed. 1942).

[104] *See generally* Dukeminier, Perpetuities: *The Measuring Lives*, 85 Colum. L. Rev. 1648 (1985); Becker, *A Methodology for Solving Perpetuities Problems Under the Common Law Rule: A Step by Step Process That Carefully Identifies All Testing Lives in Being*, 67 Wash. U. L.Q. 949 (1989).

[105] John Chipman Gray, The Rule Against Perpetuities §217 (4th ed. 1942).

[106] John Chipman Gray, The Rule Against Perpetuities §217 (4th ed. 1942) (Per Lord Eldon, C., 11 Ves. 146).

[107] Lewin ¶5-21 (England).

statute that will have some bearing on whether the trustee actually has a perpetuities problem with the trust.

The term of twenty-one years is in gross. It is said that the Rule's twenty-one-year term is in gross, *i.e.*, the term is fixed.[108] At one time, it had been thought that the period following the death of the last life in being might need to be keyed to the period remaining of an actual person's minority, which could be less than twenty-one years.[109] In other words, should a designated taker die while still a minor, the interest needed to immediately vest. In 1832, the House of Lords settled the matter: " . . . [T]he term of twenty-one years need have no reference to the minority of a devisee, nor, indeed, to any minority at all."[110] The reader should bear in mind that it was not until late into the twentieth century that the age of majority was generally reduced from 21 to 18. In any case, either of the following two dispositions will not violate the Rule, whether the age of majority is 21 or 18:

- "Bequest 'to all descendants of mine who shall be born within 21 years after my death.' "[111]
- "Bequest to a trustee 'to pay the income to A for life and then to pay the principal to such children of A as reach the age of 21.' "[112]

Gestation. At common law, a child in gestation, *i.e.*, a child *en ventre sa mere*, who was born alive was deemed to have been alive at gestation.[113] Thus, "the common-law perpetuity period was comprised of three components: (1) a life in being (2) plus 21 years (3) plus . . . period[s] of gestation when needed."[114] A devise in trust to such of the testator's grandchildren as shall reach the age of 21, for example, would not have run afoul of the Rule, even had the testator's only child been conceived minutes before his death.[115] The child would still have been deemed a life in being.[116] Professor Gray put it this way: "It is submitted that the true doctrine is that in applying the Rule against Perpetuities a child *en ventre sa mere* will be considered as born."[117]

Although neither period of the Uniform Statutory Rule Against Perpetuities (USRAP) has a gestation extension,[118] the act makes no effort to interfere with whatever common law or statutory equitable property rights one born alive might possess by virtue of having been *in utero* at a given time.[119] "As to the legal

---

[108] *See* W. Barton Leach, *Perpetuities in a Nutshell*, 51 Harv. L. Rev. 638, 641 (1938).

[109] *See generally* John Chipman Gray, The Rule Against Perpetuities §183 (4th ed. 1942).

[110] John Chipman Gray, The Rule Against Perpetuities §185 (4th ed. 1942).

[111] W. Barton Leach, *Perpetuities in a Nutshell*, 51 Harv. L. Rev. 638, 641 (1938).

[112] W. Barton Leach, *Perpetuities in a Nutshell*, 51 Harv. L. Rev. 638, 641 (1938).

[113] UPC §2-901 cmt.

[114] UPC §2-901 cmt. *See also* John Chipman Gray, The Rule Against Perpetuities §§221 & 222 (4th ed. 1942) (confirming that multiple periods of gestations are allowed).

[115] John Chipman Gray, The Rule Against Perpetuities §220 (4th ed. 1942).

[116] John Chipman Gray, The Rule Against Perpetuities §220 (4th ed. 1942).

[117] John Chipman Gray, The Rule Against Perpetuities §222 (4th ed. 1942).

[118] *See* UPC §2-901. *See also* §8.2.1.7 of this handbook (the two USRAP periods).

[119] UPC §2-901 cmt.

status of conceived-after-death children, that question has not yet been resolved."[120]

The methodology for determining Rule violations. How does one go about determining whether a particular contingent equitable interest violates the Rule in its classical form? First, determine when the contingent interests were created. Second, determine who the lives in being are. Third, determine who under the terms of the trust are to take vested interests. And, finally, calculate whether such a vesting, under a worst-case scenario, could occur more than twenty-one years after the time when the last survivor of the lives in being dies. In the words of Prof. John Chipman Gray, ". . . [E]very provision in a will or settlement is to be construed as if the Rule did not exist, and then to the provision so construed the Rule is to be remorselessly applied."[121]

To illustrate the process and to expose uninitiated readers to the complexity and subtlety of the Rule's application, throughout this section the following hypothetical trust will be subjected to the four-step analysis:

> A settlor transfers property inter vivos to a trustee. The settlor reserves an inter vivos right to the net income as well as a right of revocation. Upon the death of the settlor the trust converts to an irrevocable discretionary trust. The provisions of the discretionary trust are that the trustee may apply income and invade principal for one or more of the settlor's grandchildren, whenever born, who are alive when a particular discretionary distribution from the trust is made. At the point in time after the death of the settlor when no grandchild of the settlor is both alive and under the age of 30 years,[122] the trust shall be held for the benefit of the youngest then-living great-grandchild of the settlor. That great-grandchild, if there is one, shall have a right to all the net income in all events as well as a general inter vivos power to appoint the trust property. Any property remaining in the trust at the death of that great-grandchild shall be paid to the executor of the great-grandchild's estate.

A time line of the trust would look like this:

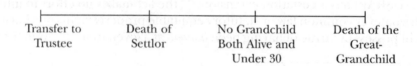

| Transfer to Trustee | Death of Settlor | No Grandchild Both Alive and Under 30 | Death of the Great-Grandchild |

§8.2.1.1   The Creation of the Interest

It is self-evident that because a will speaks at death, a contingent equitable interest under a testamentary trust cannot be created before the testator dies.[123] The rule that the question of remoteness is to be determined from the time of

---

[120] UPC §2-901 cmt.

[121] John Chipman Gray, The Rule Against Perpetuities §629 (4th ed. 1942).

[122] *See, e.g.,* Estate of Kreuzer, 674 N.Y.S.2d 505 (App. Div. 1998) (involving a common law violation where the age requirement was 35).

[123] *See generally* John Chipman Gray, The Rule Against Perpetuities §231 (4th ed. 1942).

the testator's death, and not from the date of the testator's will, has long been settled.[124] Thus, the testator can never be the life in being at the time of the creation of the testamentary trust.

With respect to any trust, whether testamentary or inter vivos, insofar as the Rule is concerned, contingent interests do not exist while a trust is revocable, *i.e.*, while there is an outstanding unexercised general inter vivos power to appoint the trust property.[125] Thus, contingent interests are deemed created at the time when a trust becomes irrevocable[126]—a time that will not always coincide with when property is transferred to the trustee. On the other hand, " . . . interests in property later added to . . . [an irrevocable] . . . trust are not 'created' until the addition occurs, or until a beneficiary designation becomes irrevocable when insurance or pension proceeds are made payable to . . . [the] . . . trustee."[127]

In our hypothetical trust, the equitable contingent interests of the grandchildren and great-grandchildren, born and unborn, are created at the death of the settlor when the reserved right of revocation (assuming it is never exercised) extinguishes. At that time certain of the settlor's issue receive equitable interests that are contingent upon survivorship and the trustee's exercise of discretion.[128] During the lifetime of the settlor of our hypothetical trust, the settlor alone, as holder of the power, is deemed to hold unconditionally all the equitable interests and is deemed to possess a vested interest in the property.[129] Or, to put it another way, while someone possesses a general inter vivos power of appointment or right to revoke, the contingent equitable interests of the successor beneficiaries to include the remaindermen are deemed for Rule analysis purposes not to exist. Therefore, as the Rule is concerned with when vesting must occur, there cannot be a Rule violation until after the extinguishment, by the settlor's death or otherwise, of the power.

§8.2.1.2   Validating Life or Worst-Case Life in Being

New Hampshire has played an important role in judicial modernization of the rule. First, Edgerly v. Barker[130] . . . [in 1891] . . . presaged the cy pres or reformation movement in this

---

[124] John Chipman Gray, The Rule Against Perpetuities §231 (4th ed. 1942).

[125] *See* Leach, *Perpetuities in a Nutshell*, 51 Harv. L. Rev. 638, 654 (1938). *See, e.g.*, Ohio Rev. Code §2131.08(B) (providing that contingent interests are deemed created for purposes of starting the period of the Rule against Perpetuities upon the death of the settlor of a revocable trust, or upon release of the right of revocation, unless the settlor has opted out of the Rule's application under §2131.09).

[126] 1 Scott & Ascher §9.3.9.

[127] Restatement (Third) of Trusts §29 cmt. g(1).

[128] *See* Restatement (Third) of Trusts §29 cmt. h (confirming that discretionary interests may not be subject to a condition precedent of the trustee's exercise of discretion beyond the perpetuities period); W. Barton Leach, *Perpetuities in a Nutshell*, 51 Harv. L. Rev. 638, 652 (1938) (suggesting that a discretionary trust created to last during unborn lives is in essence a power of appointment in the trustee and thus void if it can be exercised too remotely).

[129] *See* UPC §1-403 cmt. (confirming that a general inter vivos power is one that enables the powerholder to draw absolute ownership to himself).

[130] 66 N.H. 434, 31 Atl. 900 (1891).

context; and that movement was, energized in 1962 by Carter v. Berry[131] *...; and also by Estate of Foster*[132]*. ... Second, wait-and-see was advocated and relied on by the New Hampshire Supreme Court, although there was an alternative basis for the result that could have been employed, in Merchants National Bank v. Curtis*[133] *..., which stated that [w]hen a decision is made at a time when the events have happened, the court should not be compelled to consider only what might have been and completely ignore what was.*[134]

In order to come up with a hypothetical worst-case scenario to see whether there is a violation of the Rule in a given fact pattern, we need to identify the validating life[135] or worst-case life in being. It is unfortunate, but a mastery of the many nuances of worst-case life-in-being identification takes good intuition and much practice.[136] By way of illustration, the worst-case life in being in our hypothetical trust is the last survivor of the children of the settlor who were alive at the death of the settlor, assuming the reserved right of revocation—which is tantamount to a general power of appointment—is never exercised. Children *en ventre sa mere*[137] at that time would also qualify as lives in being.[138] (As to children *en ventre sa frigidaire*, the reader is referred to Professor W. Barton Leach's somewhat tongue-in-cheek 1962 article.[139])

Why must some child of the settlor be the life in being? Because, taking the period of gestation into account and ignoring, for purposes of the Rule, recent developments in the science of postmortem reproduction,[140] the child cannot come into existence after the settlor's death, which is when the reserved right of revocation is extinguished and when the contingent interests are created. A child cannot be conceived from the grave. (Likewise, an entrusted testamentary gift "to such of the testator's grandchildren as attain 21 is valid because the testator's children, though not expressly mentioned, are relevant lives in being."[141])

Why is that child the worst-case life in being? Because that child, after the death of all other lives in being (namely, the settlor and the settlor's issue living

---

[131] 243 Miss. 321, 140 So. 2d 843 (1962), 95 A.L.R.2d 791 (noted in 76 Harv. L. Rev. 1308, 61 Mich. L. Rev. 609, and 23 Ohio St. L.J. 545).

[132] 190 Kan. 498, 376 P.2d 784 (1962), 98 A.L.R.2d 795 (noted in 24 Ohio St. L.J. 651 and 12 Kan. L. Rev. 460).

[133] 98 N.H. 225, 97 A.2d 207 (1953).

[134] Restatement (Third) of Trusts §29, Reporter's Notes. *See also* Estate of Chun Quan Yee Hop, 469 P.2d 183 (Haw. 1970) (avoiding a rule violation by applying the doctrine of equitable approximation also known as the *cy pres* doctrine).

[135] Jesse Dukeminier & James E. Krier, Property 292 (4 ed. 1988).

[136] W. Barton Leach, *Perpetuities in a Nutshell*, 51 Harv. L. Rev. 638, 641–642 (1938).

[137] *En ventre sa mere* means conceived but not born. *See* §8.15 of this handbook for a general discussion of the law French phenomenon.

[138] Lewin ¶ 5-45.

[139] *Perpetuities in the Atomic Age: The Sperm Bank and the Fertile Decedent*, 48 A.B.A. J. 942 (1962).

[140] *See generally* Les A. McCrimmon, *Gametes, Embryos and the Life in Being: The Impact of Reproductive Technology on the Rule Against Perpetuities*, 34 Real Prop. Prob. & Tr. J. 697 (2000).

[141] Lewin ¶ 5-24 (England).

at the time of the settlor's death) could then produce nonlives-in-being grand-children of the settlor whose equitable interests during the discretionary phase of the trust are contingent and whose ages will govern the time when the remainder interests will ultimately vest in a great-grandchild.

What is the worst case? The worst case is that the only child of the settlor dies immediately after conceiving a grandchild of the settlor, the conception having taken place *after* the settlor's death. At that point all lives in being at the death of the settlor are dead and vesting now must occur before the expiration of twenty-one years. Had another life in being been in existence at that time (*e.g.*, another child of the settlor), then the day of reckoning could have been postponed. For a discussion of the common law "all-or-nothing" rule applicable to class gifts and its two exceptions, see Section 8.15.73 of this handbook.

Professor Leach, with characteristic clarity and economy of language, went to the heart of the problem in *Perpetuities in a Nutshell*, when he wrote that the lives in being "need not be mentioned in the instrument, need not be holders of previous estates, and need not be connected in any way with the property or the persons designated to take it."[142] In our hypothetical trust, the children of the settlor are neither mentioned nor holders of previous estates; yet they are lives in being for purposes of the Rule, assuming that at the death of the settlor there is at least one child of his then living and at least one grandchild of his then alive and under the age of 30. The trustee wishing to learn the art of life in being identification would do well to begin by studying the representative measuring life illustrations in Part III of Professor Leach's article.[143]

§8.2.1.3 The Vesting of Interests Under Trusts

A great deal of difficulty has beset courts and lawyers in interpreting this generally accepted terminology of contingent remainders and vested remainders subject to be divested or vested defeasible remainders. A long step has been taken in Restatement of the Law of Property, Section 157, in reducing this confusion. The term, contingent remainder, has been abandoned in the Restatement in favor of the term, remainder subject to a condition precedent. Such change makes less likely confusion between an interest subject to a condition precedent and a vested defeasible interest subject to a condition subsequent.[144]

A reversion, whether legal or equitable, and a vested remainder, whether legal or equitable, are not subject to the Rule.[145] Other types of future interests

---

[142] W. Barton Leach, *Perpetuities in a Nutshell*, 51 Harv. L. Rev. 641.

[143] *Perpetuities in a Nutshell*, 51 Harv. L. Rev. 641, 641–642.

[144] First Nat'l Bank v. Tenney, 165 Ohio St. 513, 516, 138 N.E.2d 15, 17–18 (1956). *See generally* §8.30 of this handbook (the difference between a vested equitable remainder subject to divestment and a vested (transmissible) contingent equitable remainder).

[145] John Chipman Gray, The Rule Against Perpetuities §205 (4th ed. 1942) (noting, however, in §205.2 that "[w]hen a remainder is given to a class, and such remainder is vested in certain members of the class, subject to open and let in other members, born afterwards or afterward fulfilling a condition, the shares in such remainder or interest may be obnoxious to the Rule against Perpetuities, because their number and therefore their size may not be determinable until too remote a period").

are not vested and therefore generally are subject to the Rule.[146] "In modern law when we speak of a remainder as being 'vested' we mean that it has certain definite characteristics, namely, that the remainderman is a presently identifiable person and that the remainder is not subject to a condition precedent."[147] A trust remainderman's interest is vested, for example, if the interest is not subject to the condition precedent that he or she survive the current beneficiary.[148] When an ascertained person is entitled, whether dead or alive, to an ascertained portion of the trust property, chances are the equitable interest in that portion is vested.[149]

What the trustee may find difficult to grasp about the vesting aspect of the Rule is that an interest may vest in someone for purposes of the Rule; yet the person may not get the use of the interest before death.[150] It is the person's probate estate that will ultimately get the use of the property,[151] unless an antilapse statute[152] is applicable or the interest that has vested is an equitable life estate.[153] (As to how the Rule applies to a direction to the trustee to accumulate income once vesting has occurred, see Section 8.15.8 of this handbook.) The trustee cannot begin to understand the Rule without having solved the vesting riddle.[154]

---

[146] John Chipman Gray, The Rule Against Perpetuities §205 (4th ed. 1942).

[147] Cornelius J. Moynihan, Introduction to the Law of Real Property 121 (2d ed. 1988).

[148] See J. C. Gray, The Rule Against Perpetuities §§101–103 (4th ed. 1942); *but see generally* §8.15.55 of this handbook (antilapse [the trust application]).

[149] *See, e.g.*, In re Darrell V. Wright Trust Agreement, No. 319832 (Mich. Ct. App. Mar. 17, 2015) (unpublished) (Although the trustee has discretion as to the *manner and timing* of disbursement, the beneficiary's equitable interest, in this particular case, at least, is nonetheless indefeasibly vested in the beneficiary as any balance of the dedicated trust corpus passes upon the beneficiary's death to the beneficiary's executor.). A word of caution: If it is up to the trustee whether or not the beneficiary, dead or alive, ever receives a disbursement, the condition precedent of the trustee exercising discretion renders the permissible beneficiary's equitable interest contingent.

[150] J. C. Gray, The Rule Against Perpetuities. §102 (4th ed. 1942).

[151] Note, however, that if the person dies intestate without heirs at law and the trust is comprised of personal property, then the doctrine of *bona vacantia* may be applicable, in which case the equitable interest would pass to the Crown or the State. See §8.15.46 (*bona vacantia* doctrine).

[152] *See generally* §8.15.55 of this handbook (antilapse [the trust application]).

[153] *See* Hochberg v. Proctor, 441 Mass. 403, 414–415, 805 N.E.2d 979, 989 (2004) (noting that if the vested equitable remainder is a life estate, the remainderman will enjoy the possession only if he survives the termination of the preceding life estate). The death of the remainderman, however, is not a condition precedent that would make the interest contingent; rather it is merely a limitation on the character of the remainderman's property interest. Hochberg v. Proctor, 441 Mass. 403, 414–415, 805 N.E.2d 979, 989 (2004).

[154] The trustee may wish to consult chapter 3 of Thomas F. Bergin and Paul G. Haskell's Preface to Estates in Land and Future Interests (2d ed. 1984), which has a useful section on the "concept of vestedness." *See also* Thomas F. Bergin & Paul G. Haskell, Preface to Estates in Land and Future Interests 66–73 (2d ed. 1984); J. C. Gray, The Rule Against Perpetuities §§99–118 (4th ed. 1942). *See generally* §5.2 of this handbook (class designation: "children," "issue," "heirs," and "relatives" (some rules of construction)) (discussing in part the law's preference for when a survivorship condition is satisfied and its preference for when an interest vests) and §8.30 of this handbook (the difference between a vested equitable remainder subject to divestment and a vested (transmissible) contingent equitable remainder).

In our hypothetical trust, the words *then living* make the interests of conceived and unconceived great-grandchildren contingent in part on their being born before and not dying before the trust terminates. (For a discussion of the Uniform Probate Code's 120-hour survival requirement, see Section 8.15.56 of this handbook.) These contingencies—or conditions precedent—will remain outstanding during that phase of the trust's life after the death of the settlor when there exists a grandchild of the settlor who is both alive and under the age of 30 years.

The instrument provides that at the point in time after the settlor's death when no grandchild of the settlor is both alive and under the age of 30, someone is then either going to hold a vested remainder interest or a vested reversionary interest under a resulting trust. The remainder interests will then be vested for two reasons, of which either one is sufficient vesting for purposes of the Rule: (1) the subsequent death of the great-grandchild, if any, who met the implicit conditions of birth, survivorship, and age will not extinguish his or her interest, because in that event the trust property would merely find its way into the great-grandchild's probate estate; (2) the qualifying great-grandchild will be the holder of an inter vivos power of appointment which, for purposes of the Rule, is tantamount to the great-grandchild possessing a vested interest in the trust property which is the subject of the power. If there is no great-grandchild around to take when there is no grandchild both alive and under the age of 30, the property will pass to the settlor's probate estate upon a resulting trust, the reversionary interest having been vested in the settlor and the settlor's estate during the entire life of the trust.[155]

§8.2.1.4 A Possible Vesting Beyond the Period of the Common Law Rule

My intent, however, is not to decide whether or not repeal is the proper alternative to the common law RAP. Nor is my goal to teach the intricacies of the Rule; I leave that to the dying number of law school professors who actually teach the Rule.[156]

Applying the Rule to our hypothetical trust, we assume the settlor and all the settlor's descendants who were alive at the settlor's death have died, except for one child of the settlor. After the death of the settlor, that child produces a grandchild of the settlor. The child then dies when the grandchild is a day old. Now all lives in being are dead and we have a day-old non-life-in-being grandchild of the settlor. If we can conjure up only one scenario whereby there could be a vesting in someone later than a day after the grandchild's 21st birthday, we have a common law Rule violation. We can. Here is one such scenario: At the age of 25, the grandchild receives a discretionary distribution of

---

[155] *See* John Chipman Gray, The Rule Against Perpetuities §327.1 (4th ed. 1942).

[156] Tye J. Klooster, *Are the Justifications for the Rule against Perpetuities Still Persuasive? A Survey of the Modern Policy Arguments Cast for and against Retention of the Rule against Perpetuities*, 30 ACTEC L.J. 95, 96 (2004).

income or principal from the trust.[157] Here is another: The grandchild has a 30th birthday at which point the property vests in a non-life-in-being great-grandchild of the settlor. In both cases, property would vest in non-lives in being more than twenty-one years after the death of the life in being child of the settlor.

§8.2.1.5   Consequences of a Violation of the Common Law Rule

If an equitable contingent interest fails, it does not mean necessarily that the entire trust fails.[158] The tainted interests are constructively stricken from the instrument and the trustee will continue to administer any remaining equitable interests that may be in compliance with the Rule, unless the doctrine of infectious invalidity is applicable, a topic we take up in Section 8.15.72 of this handbook or the "all-or-nothing" rule is applicable, a topic we take up in Section 8.15.73 of this handbook.

In our hypothetical trust, for example, the provisions for the benefit of the settlor are valid because he had reserved to himself a right of revocation in the nature of a general inter vivos power of appointment that, for purposes of the Rule, is tantamount to retaining a vested interest in the trust property. If the instrument had provided that the settlor's children were to have beneficial interests in the discretionary trust, the trustee could continue to administer their interests as they would be lives in being. Unfortunately the instrument did not so provide. Therefore, effective immediately upon the death of the settlor—which is when the interests are created under our hypothetical trust—the contingent equitable interests of the settlor's grandchildren during the discretionary phase of the trust are deemed *nonexistent* because of the possibility of a discretionary distribution of income or principal to a non-life-in-being grandchild more than twenty-one years after the death of the last life in being child of the settlor. Under the common law, the interests of those grandchildren who happen to be alive when the settlor dies might also fail.[159] This is a variation on the infamous "all or nothing" rule, a topic we take up in more detail in Section 8.15.73 of this handbook.[160] As vesting in a "then-living" grandchild may occur beyond the permissible period of the Rule, the entire remainder provision fails as well.

---

[157] *See* W. Barton Leach, *Perpetuities in a Nutshell*, 51 Harv. L. Rev. 638, 652 (1938) (noting that a discretionary trust is in essence a power of appointment and that a discretionary power is void if it can be exercised too remotely). *See generally* 1 Scott & Ascher §9.3.9 (noting that a trust is invalid to the extent that the interests of its beneficiaries are subject to the exercise of discretion by the trustee beyond the period of the rule); §8.1 of this handbook (powers of appointment); Lewin ¶ 5-70 (England).

[158] *But see* W. Barton Leach, *Perpetuities in a Nutshell*, 51 Harv. L. Rev. 638, 1336 (1938) (if equitable contingent interest is an "integral part of the dispositive scheme," then entire trust may indeed fail).

[159] W. Barton Leach, *Perpetuities in a Nutshell*, 51 Harv. L. Rev. 638, 649 (1938) (suggesting that no satisfactory rationalization of this application of the Rule has ever been advanced).

[160] 1 Scott & Ascher §9.3.9.

What are the consequences of these failures? The consequences are that upon the death of the settlor the trust stops—drops off into thin air as it were. By operation of law there are no more terms governing the disposition of income and principal. Thus, the life of the trust has come to an end. The trustee, however, may not consume the property.[161] Rather the trustee, now holding the property upon a resulting trust,[162] must transfer title to the executor or administrator of the settlor's probate estate. The trust property will then follow the fortunes of the settlor's probate estate, passing either in accordance with the terms of the settlor's will or under the laws of intestacy.[163] Remember, reversionary interests are always vested.[164] Had the children of the settlor, along with the grandchildren, been permissible beneficiaries during the discretionary phase of the trust, the life of the trust would have continued (for the benefit of the children only, however) until the death of the last life-in-being child of the settlor; then the trust would fail. Our hypothetical trust instrument, however, contained no such provision for the benefit of the settlor's children.

§8.2.1.6 The Perpetuities Saving Clause

Courts are urged to consider reforming . . . [pre-existing] . . . dispositions . . . [that violate the common law rule against perpetuities] . . . by judicially inserting a perpetuity saving clause, because a perpetuity saving clause would probably have been used at the drafting stage of the disposition had it been drafted competently.[165]

Today, a trust instrument is likely to contain a so-called perpetuities saving clause that triggers the termination of the trust at a time certain, unless the trust in the ordinary course of things terminates at an earlier time.[166] This time certain provision is designed to trigger a vesting within the period of the common law Rule no matter what.[167] Most such clauses operate by providing for a termination in all events twenty-one years after the death of the last survivor of specified lives-of-being when the trust became irrevocable, at which point the property is distributed outright and free of trust to remaindermen specified in the saving clause.[168]

---

[161] *See* Restatement (Second) of Trusts §345 cmt. i.

[162] *See generally* Bogert §468.

[163] Bogert §468.

[164] Lewin ¶ 5-66 (England).

[165] UPC §2-905 cmt. (Uniform Statutory Rule Against Perpetuities). *See generally* §8.15.22 of this handbook (reformation) and §8.15.71 of this handbook (retroactive application of new law governing trusts).

[166] For a sample saving clause, *see* Bogert §1046(VIII(k)) (provision entitled "Maximum Duration of Trusts"). *See also* David M. Becker, Perpetuities and Estate Planning 133–184 (1993) (Saving Clauses and Their Impact on Planning).

[167] Bogert §1046(VIII(k)). *See also* David M. Becker, Perpetuities and Estate Planning 133–184 (1993).

[168] Bogert §1046(VIII(k)). *See also* David M. Becker, Perpetuities and Estate Planning 133–184 (1993).

If such a provision were in the governing instrument of our hypothetical trust—perhaps providing for termination twenty-one years after the death of the last survivor of all issue of the settlor alive at the death of the settlor—there is no way that a non-life in being might receive a discretionary distribution or a vested remainder interest more than twenty-one years after the death of the last survivor of all lives in being.

The lesson here is: *Check for a saving clause*. The trustee should be faulted—if not held liable—for allowing a perpetuities panic to build before someone discovers that there is a valid governing saving clause, particularly if the trust is charged for any legal and administrative expenses attributable to the nonfeasance.

§8.2.1.7   Perpetuities Legislation

The perpetuity period under Isle of Man law is 150 years, recently extended from 80 years by the Trustee Act 2001. All trusts formed after 1 January 2001 may have a 150-year perpetuity period.[169]

Prof. John Chipman Gray was of the view that the rule against perpetuities should be remorselessly applied:

The Rule against Perpetuities is not a rule of construction, put a peremptory command of law. It is not, like a rule of construction, a test, more or less artificial to determine intention. Its object is to defeat intention. Therefore every provision in a will or settlement is to be construed as if the Rule did not exist, and then to the provision so construed the Rule is to be remorselessly applied.[170]

Since World War II there have been waves of legislative initiatives on this side of the Atlantic designed to corral and mitigate the harshness of the Rule.[171] So also on the other side of the Atlantic.[172] It was Professor Leach who more than anyone else was responsible for setting things in motion when, in 1952, he published several law review articles calling for legislative modification of the Rule.[173] He suggested that the Rule be applied on the basis of events that

---

[169] Paul Dougherty, *Focus: Trust Law in the Isle of Man*, 11(2) STEP J. 12 (May 2003).

[170] John Chipman Gray, The Rule Against Perpetuities §629 (4th ed. 1942).

[171] For a catalog of pre-World War II perpetuities statutes, both in England and in the United States, *see* John Chipman Gray, The Rule Against Perpetuities, Appendix C (4th ed. 1942). Prior to the War, seven U.S. states had anti-perpetuities provisions in their constitutions. *Id*. at §730.

[172] *See* Futter v. Comm'r, [2013] UKSC 26 (paragraph 15) (England) ("The rule against perpetuities has lost its terrors since the Perpetuities and Accumulations Act 1964 (which was almost completely non-retrospective) gradually came to apply to more and more trusts, followed by the Perpetuities and Accumulations Act 2009.").

[173] W. Barton Leach, *Perpetuities: Staying the Slaughter of the Innocents*, 68 L.Q. Rev. 35 (1952); W. Barton Leach, *Perpetuities in Perspective: Ending the Rule's Reign of Terror*, 65 Harv. L. Rev. 721 (1952). *See also* Restatement (Third) of Trusts §29, Reporter's Notes (confirming that Prof. Leach was the founder of the movement in this country to reform the Rule).

actually happen[174] and that offending provisions be reformed to approximate as near as possible the settlor's intent.

Whether the ensuing legislation has had or will have any social utility is a matter beyond the scope of this book. What is clear, however, is that these initiatives have added additional complexities to the Rule.[175] Take for example the USRAP.[176] It essentially grafts on to the common law Rule a ninety-year wait-and-see provision[177] and provides for judicial reformation in lieu of the imposition of a resulting trust.[178] Thus, even in a USRAP jurisdiction the trustee may not ignore the common law Rule.[179] That having been said, USRAP's wait-and-see and reformation features, for all intents and purposes, do away with the common law doctrine of infectious invalidity, a topic we take up in Section 8.15.72 of this handbook. Severability and reformation is now the order of the day. The same can be said for the common law "all-or-nothing" rule, which is discussed in Section 8.15.73 of this handbook.

In our hypothetical trust, for example, the USRAP would allow discretionary distributions to the settlor's grandchildren for a ninety-year period beginning with the settlor's death. The interest of a great-grandchild would be good if it were to vest within that period. There is another lesson here for a trustee faced with a common law Rule violation: If a review of the governing instrument does not turn up a saving clause, do not forget to check for an applicable statute.[180] England has had a wait-and-see statute since 1964.[181]

Under the model Uniform Probate Code's antilapse default provisions applicable to trusts certain equitable future interests that had traditionally been construed as vested would become subject to the condition precedent of survivorship, this in the absence of an overt expression on the part of the settlor

---

[174] *See, e.g.*, Merchants Nat'l Bank v. Curtis, 98 N.H. 225, 97 A.2d 207 (1953) (advocating and applying a wait-and-see approach).

[175] *See, e.g.*, White v. Fleet Bank of Maine, 1999 Me. 148, 739 A.2d 373 (1999) (holding Maine's wait-and-see statute inapplicable to the Rule Against Accumulations). *See generally* §8.15.8 of this handbook (Rule Against Accumulations).

[176] Uniform Statutory Rule Against Perpetuities (USRAP) has been incorporated into Part 9 of the UPC. *See, e.g.*, Mass. Gen. Laws ch. 190B, §2-901 (Mass. USRAP). Florida has adopted a 360-year USRAP period. Fla. Stat. Ann. §689.225(2)(f).

[177] It should be noted, however, that the common law did have a limited but long-standing "wait and see" exception to the general principle that the Rule is violated if there *could* be a vesting beyond the period of the Rule regardless of the actual facts and circumstances. The exception related to alternate contingent interests where at least one could not vest too remotely. "The rule has most often been applied where there is a perpetuities limitation to the issue of a living person and a valid limitation to take effect on that person's death without issue." Lewin ¶ 5-64. "In such a case, if the person in question dies without issue, the latter limitation is allowed to take effect." Lewin ¶ 5-64.

[178] UPC §2-903 (URAP reformations). *But see* In re Estate of Keenan, 519 N.W.2d 373 (Iowa 1994).

[179] UPC §2-901(a). *See generally* David M. Becker, *If You Think You No Longer Need to Know Anything About the Rule Against Perpetuities, Then Read This!*, 74 Wash. U. L.Q. 713 (1996).

[180] *See, e.g.*, Estate of Kreuzer, 674 N.Y.S.2d 505 (App. Div. 1998) (involving application of a New York statute allowing reformation in cases where the Rule has been violated because of an age requirement that is higher than 21).

[181] Lewin ¶ 5-21 (England).

of an intent that the interest be vested.[182] This could, for example, cause the contingent equitable interests of some takers in default of survivorship to violate the Rule against Perpetuities, at least in jurisdictions where the rule is still enforced.[183] What had once been safely vested would no longer be.[184] "To prevent an injustice from resulting because of this, the Uniform Statutory Rule Against Perpetuities, which has a wait-and-see element, is incorporated into the Code as part 9."[185]

As codification in a common law environment generally fosters more complexity and ambiguity in the law, not less,[186] it is only a matter of time before the trial lawyers are called in. A good example of how codification can fuel litigation is the New York legislature's well-intentioned but misguided tweaking back in 1828 of the rule against perpetuities.[187] Prof. John Chipman Gray explains:

> Before the year 1828, the forty or fifty volumes of the New York Reports disclose but one case involving a question of remoteness. In that year the reviewers (clever men they were, too) undertook to remodel the Rule against Perpetuities, and what a mess they made of it! Between four and five hundred cases [as of 1886] have come before the New York Courts under the statute as to remoteness,—an impressive warning on the danger of meddling with the subject.[188]

For a discussion of statutes that have abolished altogether the Rule against Perpetuities in the trust context, see Section 8.2.1.9 of this handbook.

§8.2.1.8   Perpetuities and Powers of Appointment

Validity of power itself. John Chipman Gray in the third edition of his treatise on the rule against perpetuities asserted that a power of appointment itself cannot be too remote. Rather, it is "the estate or interest appointed by it"[189] that can be. Thus, "[w]hen we say that a power is too remote, we mean that each and every estate or interest appointed under it is on a contingency which may happen at such a time that the estate appointed will be too remote."[190] The critical condition precedent that gives rise to the contingency is that the power

---

[182] *See generally* UPC §2-707; §8.15.55 of this handbook (lapse and antilapse); §8.2.1.3 of this handbook (vested and contingent equitable interests).

[183] *See generally* §§8.2.1 of this handbook (the Rule against Perpetuities), 8.2.1.9 of this handbook (abolishing the Rule against Perpetuities).

[184] *See generally* §8.2.1 of this handbook (the vesting concept).

[185] UPC §2-707 cmt.

[186] *See generally* Frances H. Foster, *Privacy and the Elusive Quest for Uniformity in the Law of Trusts*, 38 Ariz. St. L.J. 713 (2007). *See also* Bogert §7 ("In some states, the law governing trusts is not collected in a single title of the state code and finding all of the provisions that are relevant to trusts can be quite difficult.")

[187] *See generally* §8.2.1 of this handbook (the rule against perpetuities).

[188] John Chipman Gray, The Rule Against Perpetuities, Appendix G, §871 (4th ed. 1942).

[189] John Chipman Gray, The Rule Against Perpetuities §474.1 (4th ed. 1942).

[190] John Chipman Gray, The Rule Against Perpetuities §474.1 (4th ed. 1942).

be exercised.[191] There is a Rule problem in a given situation if an exercise of the power is possible more than twenty-one years after the death of the last life in being.[192]

In the fourth edition, his son, Roland Gray, sought to qualify his father's assertion that it is improper to speak of powers themselves as being too remote under the Rule, particularly if one accepts the proposition, as the son did, that a power of appointment, even an immediately exercisable general inter vivos power of appointment, is a contingent future interest. It is contingent because the ongoing preceding estate, which is less marketable by virtue of the outstanding power, is not cut short until the power is actually exercised:

> It is true that in the case of a general power presently exercisable, the holder of the power is treated for some purposes as if he were the present owner of the property over which the power is exercisable. But he is not so treated for all purposes; and the courts regularly point out that although his interest is treated as equivalent to ownership in some respects, he is not the owner. It is therefore not only natural, but permissible, to speak of a power as being itself invalid under the Rule. And this is a common usage.[193]

Under the USRAP, a general testamentary power of appoint is invalid unless it is certain to extinguish or be exercised within one of the statute's two allowable perpetuity periods.[194] The same goes for limited/special powers of appointment, whether inter vivos or testamentary, the so-called nongeneral powers.[195]

The initial holder of a general inter vivos power of appointment that is *presently exercisable*, such as the settlor of a revocable trust, is deemed to possess a vested interest in the subject property *ab initio*.[196] Thus the initial creation of such a power cannot violate the Rule against Perpetuities.[197] How that power is ultimately exercised is another matter.[198] Certain exercises in further trust, for example, could well trigger a rule violation, a topic we take up next.[199]

Validity of an exercise of the power in further trust. Let us assume the following *testamentary* trust: A to B (the trustee) for C for life. Under the governing instrument, C is granted a power to appoint the property in further

---

[191] John Chipman Gray, The Rule Against Perpetuities §474.1 (4th ed. 1942).

[192] John Chipman Gray, The Rule Against Perpetuities §474.1 (4th ed. 1942).

[193] John Chipman Gray, The Rule Against Perpetuities §474.2 (4th ed. 1942).

[194] UPC §2-901(c). *See generally* §8.2.1.7 of this handbook (USRAP); §8.1.1 of this handbook (the four categories of power of appointment)

[195] UPC §2-901(c). *See generally* §8.1.1 of this handbook (the four categories of power of appointment).

[196] John Chipman Gray, The Rule Against Perpetuities §524.1 (4th ed. 1942) (revocable trusts).

[197] *See* John Chipman Gray, The Rule Against Perpetuities §§477 & 524.1 (4th ed. 1942); UPC §2-901(b) (implications for the Rule against Perpetuities when the exercise of a general inter vivos power of appointment is subject to a condition precedent).

[198] *See generally* John Chipman Gray, The Rule Against Perpetuities §510 (4th ed. 1942) (only actual appointment considered).

[199] *See generally* UPC §2-902 cmt.

trust. *C* appoints the property in further trust for the benefit of *X*, an ascertained individual. The governing instrument further provides that *when X dies, B* shall distribute the trust property outright and free of trust to the *then*-living issue of *A*. Does the creation of the contingent equitable interests in the issue of *A* pursuant to *C*'s exercise of the power of appointment violate the classic common law Rule? The answer will depend upon what type of power *C* possessed. It may also depend upon when *X* was conceived.[200]

General inter vivos power of appointment. If *C* possessed a presently exercisable general inter vivos power of appointment, the lives in being are determined for Rule analysis purposes at the time the power is *exercised*,[201] or at the death of *C* in default of exercise.[202] The Uniform Probate Code is in accord,[203] as is the Restatement (Third) of Property.[204] Thus, there can be no violation under this fact pattern: Even if *X* were not conceived when *A* died, *X* was conceived when *C* exercised the power.[205] Accordingly, the issue of *A* take a vested interest immediately upon the death of *X* who is a life in being for Rule analysis purposes. There is no need even to count to 21.

Limited powers and general testamentary powers. If *C* possessed a limited/ special/nongeneral inter vivos power, a limited/special/nongeneral testamentary power, or a general testamentary power, *X* would have to have been alive *when A died* in order to qualify as a life in being for Rule analysis purposes.[206] In other words, *X* would have to have been alive at the time the power was *created*, a will speaking at death and this being a testamentary trust.[207] Again, the Uniform Probate Code is in accord,[208] as were Prof. John Chipman Gray[209] and Prof. Leach.[210] The Restatement (Third) of Property is in accord as

---

[200] *See generally* UPC §2-901 cmt. (gestation).

[201] John Chipman Gray, The Rule Against Perpetuities §524 (4th ed. 1942); Restatement of Property §391 (Exercise of a General Power Which Is, or Becomes, Presently Exercisable by Deed). *See generally* W. Barton Leach, *Perpetuities in a Nutshell*, 51 Harv. L. Rev. 638, 654 (1938); §8.2.1.1 of this handbook (the creation of the interest).

[202] John Chipman Gray, The Rule Against Perpetuities §524.1 (4th ed. 1942).

[203] *See* UPC §2-902 cmt.

[204] *See* Restatement (Third) of Property (Wills and Other Donative Transfers) §27.1, cmt. j(1).

[205] *See generally* John Chipman Gray, The Rule Against Perpetuities, Appendix L, §950 (4th ed. 1942).

[206] Restatement of Property §392 (Exercise of a General Testamentary Power or of a Special Power). *See generally* W. Barton Leach, *Perpetuities in a Nutshell*, 51 Harv. L. Rev. 638, 653–654 (1938). *See, e.g.,* Minot v. Paine, 230 Mass. 514, 523, 120 N.E. 167 (1918) (involving a power to appoint by will in further trust); Marx v. Rice, 3 N.J. Super. 581, 67 A.2d 918 (1949) (involving the exercise of a general testamentary power of appointment in further trust).

[207] John Chipman Gray, The Rule Against Perpetuities §514 (4th ed. 1942) ("If this were not the case, estates for life, with powers of appointment by will might be created; the tenants for life might appoint for life, with powers to the appointees to appoint by will; these appointees might, in their turn, appoint in like manner, and so an indefinite series of life estates could be created."). *See also* §§525 (special powers) and 526 (general powers to appoint by will).

[208] *See* UPC §2-902 cmt.

[209] *See* John Chipman Gray, The Rule Against Perpetuities, Appendix L, §950 (4th ed. 1942).

[210] *See* W. Barton Leach, *Perpetuities in a Nutshell*, 51 Harv. L. Rev. 638, 653–654 (1938).

well.[211] This gathering up of actual lives-in-being is a gloss on the traditional "relation-back" doctrine under which "the appointed interests or powers are created when the power was created, not when it was exercised, if the exercised power was a nongeneral power or a general testamentary power."[212] (The Restatement (Third) of Property professes not to "rely" upon the relation-back doctrine "for resolving the full array of questions that arise under power-of-appointment law" because the "theory" is "not uniformly applied and does not predict the outcome in any particular case."[213])

What if *X* had not been alive when the power was created? If he had not been, *C* would have been the only eligible life in being for Rule analysis purposes. This would have caused the contingent equitable interests in *A*'s issue to be invalid. Why? Because *X* could have lived well beyond twenty-one years after the death of *C*, our only available life in being. If it had been a general testamentary power of appointment that had been exercised in further trust, then there might still be hope if the doctrine of selective allocation (marshalling) is applicable. This is a topic we take up in Section 8.15.79 of this handbook.

Had *X* been alive at *A*'s death when the power was created, the contingent equitable interests in *A*'s issue would be valid because both *C* and *X* would be lives in being for Rule analysis purposes. This right to draw in for Rule analysis purposes more lives in being, provided they were conceived at the time the limited or general testamentary power was created, is what commentators mean when they talk about "taking into account facts and circumstances existing at the time of appointment," "taking a second look at the time of appointment," or, as the English say, calculating "with an eye to all events that have happened before the power is exercised."[214]

In the event of an ineffective exercise of a general testamentary power of appointment in further trust, for reason of remoteness or otherwise, the doctrine of capture may be implicated, a topic we take up in Section 8.15.12 of this handbook.

"In the case of a testamentary power over personalty, where the domicil of the donee of the power differs from that of the donor, the validity of the limitations of the appointment is governed, in general, by the law of the donor's domicil. Accordingly, questions of remoteness are governed by the law of the domicil of the donor of the power."[215] For a general discussion of conflict of laws in the trust context, the reader is referred to Section 8.5 of this handbook.

The Delaware Tax Trap. In 1933, Delaware enacted a statute which provided that for Rule analysis purposes, a person would qualify as a life in being if he were alive at the time a limited power *was exercised*.[216] Professor Leach noted that this development had two consequences: "(1) Property . . . [could] . . . thus

---

[211] *See* Restatement (Third) of Property (Wills and Other Donative Transfers) §27.1, cmt. j(3).

[212] UPC §2-902, cmt.

[213] Restatement (Third) of Property (Wills and Other Donative Transfers) §17.4, cmt. f.

[214] Lewin ¶ 5-71 (England).

[215] John Chipman Gray, The Rule Against Perpetuities §540.2 (4th ed. 1942).

[216] Del. Laws 1933, c. 198.

be tied up in a family *forever*—a result which . . . [had] . . . not been possible in Anglo-American law since Taltarum's Case, Y.B. 12 Edw. IV, pl. 25 (1472), emasculated the Statute De Donis; (2) No federal estate tax . . . [was] . . . payable after such tax has been paid in the estate of A."[217] In the 1950s, Congress responded by enacting Section 2041(a)(3) of the Internal Revenue Code, which made the creation of a power of appointment through the exercise of a limited power of appointment a taxable event (estate tax) if the exercise of the second power could postpone vesting (or suspend the power of alienation) for a period that was not anchored *to the time when the first power was created.*[218] This Code section, colloquially referred to by estate planners as the Delaware Tax Trap, is the subject of Section 8.15.18 of this handbook. As property snared in the trap receives a basis step-up for income tax purposes, the trap can also serve as a tax-avoidance vehicle.[219]

§8.2.1.9   Abolition of the Rule Against Perpetuities

This is a lawyer's law, made by lawyers for the use of lawyers, completely incomprehensible to the public. If it is working badly, it is the job of lawyers to change it.[220]

One might even venture the observation that, for better or for worse, the rule against perpetuities is currently in free fall.[221]

At least thirty-three states now would exempt contingent equitable interests under certain trusts from the application of the traditional rule against perpetuities or, in some cases, from any perpetuities restrictions whatsoever.[222] They are Alabama (360 years); Alaska; Arizona (500 years); Colorado (1,000 years); Delaware (entrusted personal property); District of Columbia; Florida (360 years); Hawaii; Idaho; Illinois; Kentucky; Maine; Maryland; Michigan (except real estate limited to greater of life-in-being plus 21 years, or 90 years); Mississippi (360 years for personalty, 110 years for realty); Missouri; Nebraska; Nevada (365 years); New Hampshire; New Jersey; North Carolina; North Dakota; Ohio (excluding trusts created by the exercise of a nongeneral power of appointment); Oklahoma[223]; Pennsylvania; Rhode Island; South Dakota; Tennessee (360 years); Utah (1,000 years); Virginia; Washington (150 years);

---

[217] W. Barton Leach, *Perpetuities in a Nutshell*, 51 Harv. L. Rev. 638, 653, n.37 (1938).

[218] I.R.C. §2041(a)(3). As to the corresponding gift tax section, *see* I.R.C. §2514(d).

[219] *See generally* Chapter 11 of this handbook (Tax Basis/Cost of Trust Property).

[220] W. Barton Leach, *Perpetuities in Perspective: Ending the Rule's Reign of Terror*, 65 Harv. L. Rev. 721, 728 (1952).

[221] 1 Scott & Ascher §9.3.9.

[222] Presumably, if the trustee has a power of sale, it cannot be said that abolition of the rule against perpetuities as it applies to spendthrift trusts amounts to a disabling restraint on the alienability of property. *See generally* §5.3.3.3(c) of this handbook (the non–self-settled spendthrift trust); Restatement (Second) of Property (Wills and Other Donative Transfers) ch. 4 (Validity of Restraints on Alienation).

[223] *See* Pipkin v. Pipkin, 370 P.2d 826 (Okla. 1962) (holding that the Oklahoma RAP limits only how long the trustee's power of alienation may be suspended).

Wisconsin; and Wyoming (1,000 years). Some are "opt-out" states. In some, the Rule will continue to apply to trusts of real property.[224] Nevada has a finite period as the Rule's total abolition would violate the Nevada constitution.[225]

A competition among the states seems to be under way, in part to attract the trust business of those wishing to leverage the $1 million + federal generation-skipping transfer tax exemption, particularly through the use of life insurance products.[226] Bear in mind that a trust under which the trustee does *not* have a power of sale will likely still be subject to the Rule in those jurisdictions that are said to have "abolished" the Rule. Pennsylvania may be an exception. The practicality and utility of a private perpetual dynastic trust with a relentlessly expanding class of beneficiaries (*e.g.*, the "issue" of the settlor) remains to be seen, however:

> Historians say that 26 of the 102 people who crossed the Atlantic on the Mayflower in 1620 and later celebrated the first Thanksgiving had children who had children who had children. Today, approximately 12 generations later, the Mayflower passengers may well have 25 million descendants. "It could be one out of every 10 people on the street," says Cay Lanham, the governor general of the General Society of Mayflower Descendants.[227]

While we perhaps can only estimate the size of the class of currently living Mayflower descendants, Blackstone teaches us that the size of the *ancestor* class of a single currently living Mayflower descendant can be calculated with mathematical certainty:

> The doctrine of lineal consanguinity is sufficiently plain and obvious; but it is at the first view astonishing to consider the number of lineal ancestors which every man has, within no great number of degrees: and so many different bloods is a man said to contain in his veins, as hath lineal ancestors. Of these he hath two in the first ascending degree, his own parents; he hath four in the second, the parents of his father and the parents of his mother; he hath eight in the third, the parents of his two grandfathers and two grandmothers; and, by the same rule of progression, he hath an hundred and twenty-eight in the seventh; a thousand and

---

[224] Wyoming allows a trust to be governed by a 1,000 year perpetuities period, provided certain conditions specified in W.S. 34-1-139(b) are satisfied. Under W.S. 34-1-139(c), however, the common law rule against perpetuities would still govern the entrustment of real property (the "realty exception"). Not a problem. W.S. 34-1-139(b) provides that for its purposes real property shall not include an interest in a corporation, LLC, partnership, or business trust. Thus, in Wyoming one may effectively get around its realty exception by transferring real estate to the trustee of a realty trust and then transferring the shares of beneficial interest to the trustee of a separate trust governed by the 1,000 year perpetuities period. As the shares of beneficial interest are intangible personal property, the realty exception will not apply to their entrustment.

[225] *See* Nev. Const. art. XV §4-4 ("No perpetuities shall be allowed except for eleemosynary purposes").

[226] *See generally* 1 Scott & Ascher §9.3.9 (noting that the "resulting legislative spectacle seems mostly to represent interstate (and sometimes even international) competition, stoked by the banks, for repute as hospitable jurisdictions in which to create so-called 'dynasty trusts' "); Dukeminier, *Dynasty Trusts: Sheltering Descendants from Transfer Taxes*, 23 Est. Plan. 417 (1996).

[227] Wall St. J., Nov. 25, 1987, at 1, col. 4.

twenty four in the tenth; and at the twentieth degree, or the distance of twenty generations, every man hath a million ancestors, as common arithmetic will demonstrate.[228]

It is said that the average settlor of a dynastic trust can expect to have 450 direct descendants 150 years after the trust is established.[229] While the settlor's genetic affinity with each of his natural children is 50 percent, his genetic affinity with a direct descendant six generations removed is no more than 1.6 percent.[230]

If the Rule against Perpetuities is on its last legs, as some have suggested, we are likely to see an ever greater willingness on the part of the courts to order the equitable modification or termination of noncharitable irrevocable trusts due to such "traditional notions" as mistake, changed circumstances, and impossibility.[231] The law of trusts was already "loosening up" in this regard,[232] as we note in Sections 8.2.2.1 of this handbook, 8.15.22 of this handbook, and 8.17 of this handbook, which address from one perspective or another when the dispositive terms of irrevocable noncharitable trusts may be altered in mid-course, or the trusts themselves terminated altogether. As time goes by, it is inevitable that some dynasty trusts[233] will become just plain "irksome."[234] It is also inevitable that the courts will find creative ways to effect their "dispatch."[235] As noted, the courts already have a number of arrows in their quiver in this regard. Also, there is always the trustee's duty not to attempt to comply with a trust provision if compliance would be impossible or incur unreasonable expense, a topic we cover in Section 6.2.13 of this handbook.[236]

§8.2.1.10 The Dynasty Trust

The Rule Against Perpetuities is under siege in the United States. . . . What is sparking the perpetuities repeal movement? Is it the recognition that this ancient property rule no longer serves any social policy? No. The rule is being repealed so that wealthy individuals will be able to create perpetual dynasty trusts to exploit the generation-skipping transfer (GST) tax system.[237]

---

[228] William Blackstone, 2 Commentaries on the Laws of England 203 (1979).
[229] Laura Saunders, *Dynasty Trusts Under Attack*, Wall St. J., Mar. 5–6, 2011, at B9.
[230] Laura Saunders, *Dynasty Trusts Under Attack*, Wall St. J., Mar. 5–6, 2011, at B9.
[231] 5 Scott & Ascher §33.6 (Loosening the Standards for Termination and Modification).
[232] 5 Scott & Ascher §33.6 (Loosening the Standards for Termination and Modification).
[233] *See generally* §8.2.1.10 of this handbook (the dynasty trust).
[234] 5 Scott & Ascher §33.6 (Loosening the Standards for Termination and Modification).
[235] 5 Scott & Ascher §33.6 (Loosening the Standards for Termination and Modification).
[236] *See also* §6.2.10 of this handbook (trustee's duty to petition court for modification of or deviation from terms of trust when appropriate).
[237] Ira Mark Bloom, *The GST Tax Tail Is Killing the Rule Against Perpetuities*, 87 Tax Notes 569 (2000). *See generally* Jesse Dukeminier, *Dynasty Trusts: Sheltering Descendants from Transfer Taxes*, 23 Est. Plan. 417 (1996).

At heart, the Rule is about land, and we are no longer land-minded in the areas of wealth or trusts. We only care about land when an issue of land use is before the court. Today, wealth lies in securities. And we cannot become very excited about whether or not some shares get tied up forever. The corporate assets likely will reach their highest and best use even if owned by the trustee of a perpetual trust. Additionally, to the extent land fails to reach its highest development use, a meaningful segment of the population is delighted.[238]

But who is likely to derive the most benefit from the existence of Dynasty Trusts? Upon close inspection, it seems clear that in reality, corporate fiduciaries . . . are likely to reap the major benefits from a Dynasty Trust, rather than the descendants of the settlor. That may explain why the banks lobbied so hard to try to get states to adopt the legislation that made Dynasty Trusts possible.[239]

In formal remarks[240] to the Fellows of the American College of Trust and Estate Counsel (ACTEC) at their fall 1999 meeting in Boston, Thomas P. Sweeney, Esq.[241] and Malcolm A. Moore, Esq.[242] catalogued the pitfalls of perpetual private (noncharitable) trusts, *i.e.*, dynasty trusts,[243] both for the settlor and for his or her counsel:

(1) Inability to know the direction that the applicable tax laws will evolve, (2) Inability to know the characters and personalities of future beneficiaries, (3) Difficulty in coming up with appropriate generically designated individuals to serve as trustees of trusts that, at least in theory, can last forever, (4) Inability to know what a corporate fiduciary's course of corporate evolution will look like, (5) Inability to know the direction that applicable state property and trust laws will evolve, (6) Difficulty of settling upon satisfactory provisions in default of issue, and (7) The virtual inevitability of future conflicts involving beneficiaries, trustees and advisors.

Because the dynasty trust presents, in their words, a "dizzying array" of potential problems and risks for all concerned, the commentators urged the

---

[238] Joel C. Dobris, *The Death of the Rule Against Perpetuities, or the RAP Has No Friends—An Essay*, 35 Real Prop. Prob. & Tr. J. 601, 635 (Fall 2000).

[239] Lucy A. Marsh, *The Demise of Dynasty Trusts: Returning the Wealth to the Family*, 5 Est. Plan. & Community Prop. L.J. 23, 24 (2012).

[240] Perpetual Trusts: Dynasty or Disaster? Will Beneficiaries Be Happy Campers or Plaintiffs? (Oct. 15, 1999).

[241] Richards, Layton & Finger, 920 N. King St., Wilmington, DE 19801.

[242] Davis Wright Tremaine, LLP, Suite 2200, 1201 Third Ave., Seattle, WA 98101-3045.

[243] A dynasty trust might work like this: At its inception, trust shares are allocated to the issue of the settlor as if distribution were to be outright and free of trust *per stirpes*. See §5.2 of this handbook (class designation: "children," "issue," "heirs," and "relatives" (some rules of construction)). Each issue allocated a trust share is designated the sole beneficiary of that share. Upon the issue's death, his or her trust share further divides per stirpes into trust shares to be held for the benefit of that person's then living issue eligible to take per stirpes. In theory, this process of dividing and subdividing into "trustlets" on a per stirpital basis continues ad infinitum down through the generations, unless aborted by a failure of issue, the trustee's exercise of discretion to invade principal, the exercise of powers of appointment, a change in the law, a court decree, or an act of God.

Fellows to draft for "flexibility." It was recommended that consideration be given to:

    a. Creating separate shares rather than "one pot" trusts;

    b. Inserting appropriate tax clauses;

    c. Inserting trustee removal, resignation, and replacement provisions;

    d. Segregating administration, distribution, and investment functions;

    e. Granting trustees administrative amendment authority in order to accommodate future changes in the tax laws;

    f. Inserting "portability" provisions;

    g. Granting issue limited powers of appointment;

    h. Granting trustees the power to sever and merge trusts;

    i. Granting trustees the power to terminate;

    j. Inserting discretionary income distribution and principal invasion provisions[244] that are appropriate for trusts of long duration; and

    k. Inserting perpetuities savings clauses.[245]

The default law is also going to have to adapt, as not all dynasty trusts will have "flexible" terms. Such noncharitable trusts, "which can endure indefinitely, or for absurdly long periods of time, will inevitably overstay their welcome."[246] Thus, we are likely to see an ever greater willingness on the part of the courts to order equitable reformations, modifications, and terminations due to such "traditional notions" as mistake, changed circumstances, and impossibility.[247] The law of trusts was already "loosening up" in this regard,[248] as we note in Sections 8.2.2.1 of this handbook, 8.15.22 of this handbook, and 8.17 of this handbook, which address from one perspective or another when the dispositive terms of irrevocable noncharitable trusts may be altered in midcourse, or the trusts themselves terminated altogether. As time goes by, some dynasty trusts will become just plain "irksome"[249] It is also inevitable that the courts will find creative ways to effect their "dispatch."[250] As we have noted, the courts already have a number of arrows in their quiver in this regard. And there is always the trustee's duty not to attempt to comply with a trust provision if compliance would be impossible or incur unreasonable expense, a topic we cover in Section 6.2.13 of this handbook.[251]

---

[244] *See* §3.5.3.2(a) of this handbook (the power to make discretionary payments of income and principal (the discretionary trust)).

[245] *See* §8.2.1.6 of this handbook (the perpetuities savings clause).

[246] 5 Scott & Ascher §33.6 (Loosening the Standards for Termination and Modification).

[247] 5 Scott & Ascher §33.6 (Loosening the Standards for Termination and Modification).

[248] 5 Scott & Ascher §33.6 (Loosening the Standards for Termination and Modification).

[249] 5 Scott & Ascher §33.6 (Loosening the Standards for Termination and Modification).

[250] 5 Scott & Ascher §33.6 (Loosening the Standards for Termination and Modification).

[251] *See also* §6.2.10 of this handbook (trustee's duty to petition court for modification of or deviation from terms of trust when appropriate).

§8.2.1.11 Professor Leach's Perpetuities in a Nutshell

In 1938, Professor Leach's *Perpetuities in a Nutshell* came out in the Harvard Law Review.[252] In 1972, his colleague and friend, Prof. A. James Casner, wrote this about it in *In Memoriam: W. Barton Leach*:

> Even before Bart dug in deeply on powers of appointment, he had begun writing about the Rule Against Perpetuities. The culmination of this work was his classic piece *Perpetuities in a Nutshell* . . . "If this paper fails of its purpose it has, at least, eminent company. Lord Thurlow undertook to put the Rule in Shelley's Case in a nutshell. 'But,' said Lord Macnaghten, 'it is one thing to put a case like Shelley's in a nutshell, and another thing to keep it there.' "[253] But Bart's paper did not fail of its purpose.[254]

What Prof. Leach had essentially done was boil Prof. John Chipman Gray's monumental treatise on the Rule Against Perpetuities[255] down to its essence, a monumental task in itself. As noted, however, putting, or attempting to put, big things physically or metaphorically into little nutshells is not a twentieth-century phenomenon. It has a long history. In ancient times, it was said that the *Iliad* was copied in so small a hand that the entire work could rest comfortably in a walnut shell.[256] Peter Bales, a clerk in England's court of chancery around 1590, was said to have written a bible so small that it was stored in a walnut shell "of English growth."[257] As to the metaphorical, the narrator in Joseph Conrad's *Heart of Darkness* observes that "[t]he yarns of seamen have a direct simplicity, the whole meaning of which lies within the shell of a cracked nut."[258]

In 1938, it could be said that thanks to Prof. Leach the common law Rule Against Perpetuities had finally after so many centuries been wrestled into its own nutshell. After the war, however, the waves of legislative initiatives designed to mitigate the harshness of the Rule[259] have had an unintended consequence, namely an exacerbation of the complexity of the Rule's application. It is ironic that Prof. Leach is also the godfather of these initiatives.[260] Now an effort is under way to do away with the Rule altogether.[261] Soon there may be nothing to put in a nutshell. Time will tell whether it perhaps would have been better to

---

[252] W. Barton Leach, *Perpetuities in a Nutshell*, 51 Harv. L. Rev. 638 (1938).

[253] W. Barton Leach, *Perpetuities in a Nutshell*, 51 Harv. L. Rev. 638 (1938) (quoting Van Grutten v. Foxwell, [1897] A.C. 658, 671).

[254] A. James Casner, *In Memoriam: W. Barton Leach*, 85 Harv. L. Rev. 717 (1972).

[255] John Chipman Gray, The Rule Against Perpetuities (4th ed. 1942).

[256] Pliny (vii, 21) (citing to Cicero (Apud Gellium, ix, 421)).

[257] Harleian mss. (530). For the Lord Chancellor in office at the time, *see* Chapter 1 of this handbook.

[258] The Portable Conrad 493 (Zabel ed.) 1947.

[259] *See generally* §8.2.1.7 of this handbook (perpetuities legislation).

[260] A. James Casner, *In Memoriam: W. Barton Leach*, 85 Harv. L. Rev. 717 n.11 (1972).

[261] *See generally* §8.2.1.9 of this handbook (abolition of the Rule Against Perpetuities).

leave the Rule alone, and nestled safely in the nutshell that Prof. Leach put it in back in 1938 before he went off to war.[262]

§8.2.2   When the Trust May Be Modified or Terminated in Mid-Course: A Brief Preliminary Overview

On the other hand, in cases of more complicated trusts involving retained interests in settlors, a presumption of revocability is justified by the risk of confusion and doubts about a settlor's understanding, uncertainties that are aggravated by the patently deficient performance of counsel in failing expressly to deal with the obviously important matter of revocability.[263]

A trust, once established, ordinarily cannot be terminated or its terms modified in mid-course, except as provided by its terms, *e.g.*, pursuant to a reserved power to revoke, a reserved power to amend, a nonfiduciary power of appointment, a power to demand principal, or a fiduciary power in the trustee to invade principal.[264] The list is by no means an exhaustive one. In Section 8.2.2.2 of this handbook, we cover express and implied powers of termination and modification in some detail.

But here are some excerpts: A trustee vested with the power to modify or terminate is presumed to hold it in a fiduciary capacity.[265] When a beneficiary holds such a power, the presumption is the opposite.[266] Particularly when it comes to reserved powers, "the same principles apply to the modification of a trust as apply to the revocation of a trust."[267] Inherent in the unrestricted right to modify or amend a trust is the right to revoke it.[268] "A power to revoke the trust includes the power to modify the terms of the trust. . . ."[269] In an increasing number of states, a trust is deemed revocable by the settlor, unless there is

---

[262] A. James Casner, *In Memoriam: W. Barton Leach*, 85 Harv. L. Rev. 717 (1972) (in part discussing Prof. Leach's military career).

[263] Restatement (Third) of Trusts §63 cmt. c(1).

[264] *See generally* Restatement (Third) of Trusts §61; 4 Scott on Trusts §330.1; 5 Scott & Ascher §33.1.2. *See, e.g.*, Phelps v. State St. Trust Co., 330 Mass. 511, 512, 115 N.E.2d 382 (1953) (the settlor having reserved the right to amend or revoke by an instrument in writing acknowledged and delivered to the trustee, any instrument purporting to amend the trust that had not been acknowledged by the settlor before a public officer authorized by law to take acknowledgments of other writings was ineffective). *But see* Johnson v. First Nat'l Bank of Jackson, Miss., 386 So. 2d 1112 (1980) (allowing the settlor of an ostensibly irrevocable inter vivos trust that contained a spendthrift provision to directly revoke the trust as she could have done so indirectly in any case by incurring debts). *See* §8.15.2 of this handbook (doctrine of worthier title) (discussing how in some jurisdictions an ostensibly irrevocable trust could be revocable if the settlor's executor, *i.e.*, the settlor's probate estate, takes the remainder interest).

[265] 5 Scott & Ascher §33.1.1 (Termination or Modification by Trustee).

[266] 5 Scott & Ascher §33.1.2 (Termination or Modification by Beneficiary).

[267] 5 Scott & Ascher §35.2 (Modification by Settlor).

[268] Restatement (Third) of Trusts §63 cmt. g; 5 Scott & Ascher §35.2.2 (Whether Power to Modify Includes Power to Revoke).

[269] 5 Scott & Ascher §35.2.2 (Whether Power to Modify Includes Power to Revoke). *See also Power to revoke trust as including power to amend*, 62 A.L.R.2d 1412; 5 Scott & Ascher §35.2.1 (Whether Power to Revoke Includes Power to Modify).

express language in the governing instrument to the contrary.[270] The impetus for the trend is the fact that the Uniform Trust Code prospectively would reverse the presumption of nonrevocability.[271] The Restatement (Third) of Trusts and the Uniform Trust Code are not entirely in sync in this regard.[272] The Restatement (Third) of Trusts would admit extrinsic evidence on whether a trust is revocable if its written terms do not adequately address the issue.[273] If a settlor retains no beneficial interest other than by resulting trust, there is a rebuttable presumption that the trust is irrevocable.[274] On the other hand, if the settlor retains some beneficial interest[275] in addition to what might be due him or her pursuant to the imposition of a resulting trust,[276] there is a rebuttable presumption that the trust is revocable and amendable.[277] If a settlor has reserved a right to revoke the trust, an exercise of that right need not be an all or nothing proposition, unless the terms of the trust provide otherwise.[278] The default law is that the settlor may make partial revocations[279] over time.[280] Again, express and implied powers of modification and termination are covered in much greater detail in Section 8.2.2.2 of this handbook.[281]

Under exceptional circumstances, however, a court may order that an ostensibly irrevocable trust be revoked, rescinded, voided, or terminated in mid-course, or its terms altered, amended, reformed, modified, or rectified.[282] These exceptional circumstances we cover in Section 8.2.2.1 of this handbook. We note that the termination of a trust also may be achieved if all the equitable and all the legal interests have been merged in one person,[283] if its purposes

---

[270] California, Montana, and Texas are among these states. *See* 4 Scott on Trusts §330.1 n.6 and accompanying text. The UTC §602(a) (available at <http://www.uniformlaws.org/Act .aspx?title=Trust%20Code>) also presumes revocability unless the terms of the trust provide otherwise. *See generally* §8.2.2.2 of this handbook.

[271] UTC §602(a) (available at <http://www.uniformlaws.org/Act.aspx?title=Trust%20 Code>). *See generally* §8.2.2.2 of this handbook.

[272] *See* Restatement (Third) of Trusts §63(1). *See generally* §8.2.2.2 of this handbook; 5 Scott & Ascher §35.1 (Revocation by Settlor).

[273] *See generally* 5 Scott & Ascher §35.1 (Revocation by Settlor).

[274] Restatement (Third) of Trusts §63 cmt. c. *See generally* §8.2.2.2 of this handbook.

[275] A reserved power of appointment would qualify as beneficial interest for purposes of the presumption of revocability.

[276] *See generally* §4.1.1.1 of this handbook (defining the resulting trust).

[277] Restatement (Third) of Trusts §63 cmt. c.

[278] *See generally* 5 Scott & Ascher §35.1.6 (Partial Revocation).

[279] Restatement (Third) of Trusts §63 cmt. e; 5 Scott & Ascher §35.1.6 (Partial Revocation). *See generally* §8.2.2.2 of this handbook.

[280] Restatement (Third) of Trusts §63 cmt. f; 5 Scott & Ascher §35.1.6 (Partial Revocation).

[281] *See also* 5 Scott & Ascher, Ch. 35 (Termination and Modification Pursuant to Settlor's Power to Revoke or Modify).

[282] *See, e.g.*, Generaux v. Dobyns, 205 Or. App. 183, 134 P.3d 983 (2006) (material unilateral mistake warranting rescission).

[283] *See generally* §8.2.2.1 of this handbook (trust terminations in mid-course); 5 Scott & Ascher §34.5 (Merger); 4 Scott on Trusts §330.1 (Merger); §§8.7 of this handbook (merger) and 8.15.36 of this handbook (merger).

are impossible of fulfillment, or if its purposes have been fully accomplished.[284] Some states have enacted statutes providing for the termination of small trusts.[285] In the United States, the coalescing of all *beneficial* interests in one person who is not the trustee ordinarily will not trigger a termination of the trust, unless the material purposes of the trust have been accomplished.[286] A trust may be cancelled/voided/rescinded because, at the time the trust was "created," the "settlor" (1) was under a legal incapacity; (2) was induced to establish the trust because of someone's fraud, duress, or undue influence; or (3) the arrangement was the product of the "settlor's" mistaken understanding of the applicable law or facts.[287] Actually, annulling rather than terminating better describes the consequences of cancelling, voiding, and rescinding. The Restatement (Third) of Trusts provides that a gratuitous transfer in trust may be "rescinded" if occasioned by fraud, duress, undue influence, or mistake.[288] In New Hampshire, a *settlor* during his or her life may commence a judicial proceeding to determine the validity of a trust, whether revocable or irrevocable, that he or she created.[289]

For a discussion of when a trust may be modified or reformed to remedy faulty tax planning and other such mistakes, the reader is referred to Section 8.17 of this handbook. A court may order termination of a trust if its purposes have become unlawful or contrary to public policy.[290] The Uniform Trust Code would allow the court to terminate a trust if, because of circumstances not anticipated by the settlor, termination would further the purposes of the trust.[291] It also makes provision for the mid-course termination of uneconomic trusts, or the mid-course modification of their terms.[292] Again, we cover all of this in much greater detail in Section 8.2.2.1 of this handbook.

---

[284] *See generally* §8.2.2.1 of this handbook; 4 Scott on Trusts §335; §8.15.7 of this handbook (the *Claflin* doctrine (material purpose doctrine)).

[285] *See generally* §8.2.2.1 of this handbook; Committee on Formation, *Administration, and Distribution of Trusts, Procedures for Terminating Small Trusts*, 19 Real Prop. Prob. & Tr. J. 988 (1984). *See, e.g.,* UTC §413 (available at <http://www.uniformlaws.org/Act.aspx?title=Trust%20 Code>) (authorizing a trustee to terminate a trust whose property has a value of less than $50,000 upon notice to qualified beneficiaries).

[286] *See generally* §8.2.2.1 of this handbook; 5 Scott & Ascher §34.1 (Consent of Beneficiaries); 4 Scott on Trusts §337.1; §8.15.7 of this handbook (the *Claflin* doctrine (material purpose doctrine)).

[287] *See generally* §8.2.2.1 of this handbook; 4 Scott on Trusts §§333.1 (Fraud), 333.3 (Undue Influence), 333.4 (Mistake). *See also* Rebidas v. Murasko, 677 A.2d 331 (Pa. Super. Ct. 1996) (suggesting an abuse of confidential relationship on part of lawyer/cotrustee).

[288] Restatement (Third) of Trusts §62 cmt. a. *See, e.g.,* Generaux v. Dobyns, 205 Or. App. 183, 134 P.3d 983 (2006) (material unilateral mistake warranting rescission).

[289] *See* RSA 564-B:4-406.

[290] UTC §410(a) (available at <http://www.uniformlaws.org/Act.aspx?title=Trust%20 Code>). *See generally* 8.2.2.1 of this handbook.

[291] UTC §412(a) (available at <http://www.uniformlaws.org/Act.aspx?title=Trust%20 Code>). *See generally* §8.2.2.1 of this handbook. *See also* §8.15.20 of this handbook (doctrine of [equitable] deviation).

[292] UTC §415 (available at <http://www.uniformlaws.org/Act.aspx?title=Trust%20 Code>). *See generally* §8.2.2.1 of this handbook.

§8.2.2.1 Exceptional Circumstances Warranting Mid-Course Modification, Reformation, or Rectification of the Terms of an Irrevocable Trust, or the Mid-Course Voidance, Rescission, Revocation, or Termination of the Trust Relationship Itself

The . . . [Uniform Trust Code] . . . contains a number of provisions that make it easier to modify or terminate a trust.[293] These provisions are controversial because they give beneficiaries more power and because a court's power to modify or terminate cannot be overridden by the trust language. We tried to nudge the law along a little bit, says . . . [David] . . . English.[294]

Generally. The behavior of the nonbeneficiary settlor of an irrevocable trust after the trust has been created cannot cause the trust to become revocable.[295] As discussed in the previous section, whether or not a trust is revocable depends either on its terms or on the default law, not on someone's behavior. Thus, just because the trustee in breach of his fiduciary duty has allowed the nonbeneficiary settlor to loot the trust or promiscuously borrow from the trust does not make the trust revocable.[296]

Except in the exceptional circumstances hereinafter listed, neither the trustee nor the beneficiaries nor third parties nor the court may terminate a trust or change its terms, unless the power to do so is granted in the terms of the trust.[297] If the trustee[298] or a third party,[299] such as a trust protector,[300] holds such a power, he is presumed to hold it in a fiduciary capacity.[301] Ultimately, it is a matter of interpretation whether the beneficiary holds such a power in a fiduciary capacity.[302] If not, it may be in the nature of a personal power of appointment.[303]

---

[293] "Where no consideration is involved in the creation of a trust, it can be rescinded . . . upon the same grounds, such as fraud, duress, undue influence, or mistake, as those upon which a gratuitous transfer of property not in trust can be rescinded or reformed." Restatement (Third) of Trusts §62 cmt. a.

[294] Sylvia Hsieh, *Trusts Will Be Overhauled by New Uniform National Rules*, Lawyers Weekly USA, May 14, 2001, at 1. *See* UTC §105(b)(4) (available at <http://www.uniformlaws.org/Act.aspx?title=Trust%20Code>) (providing that the power of the court to modify or terminate a trust may not be overridden by the terms of the trust).

[295] *See, e.g.*, Laycock v. Hammer, 141 Cal. App. 4th 25, 44 Cal. Rptr. 3d 921 (4th Dist.2006).

[296] Laycock v. Hammer, 141 Cal. App. 4th 25, 44 Cal. Rptr. 3d 921 (4th Dist. 2006).

[297] Restatement (Third) of Trusts §64(1).

[298] Restatement (Third) of Trusts §64 cmt. b.

[299] Restatement (Third) of Trusts §64(2); 5 Scott & Ascher §33.1.3 (Termination or Modification by Third Person).

[300] *See generally* §3.2.6 of this handbook (considerations in the selection of a trustee) (in part discussing the office of trust protector).

[301] *See generally* 5 Scott & Ascher §33.1.1.

[302] Restatement (Third) of Trusts §64 cmt. c.; 5 Scott & Ascher §33.1.2 (Termination or Modification by Beneficiary).

[303] Restatement (Third) of Trusts §64 cmt. c. *See generally* §8.1.1 of this handbook (powers of appointment).

Here is[304] the list of exceptional circumstances when mid-course judicial voidance, rescission, revocation, or termination of a trust, notwithstanding its terms, may be appropriate, or when the court may decree a mid-course modification, amending, reformation, or rectification of the terms themselves:

- The purported trust property was not owned by the settlor (voidance);[305]
- The purported trust property was not transferable (voidance);[306]
- Uncertainty (voidance);[307]
- The trust is a noncharitable purpose trust (voidance);[308]
- The transfer of the purported trust property was in fraud of creditors (voidance);[309]
- The trust is a sham (voidance);[310]
- Trust instrument is a testamentary document that violates the statute of wills (voidance);[311]
- Consent of all the equitable interests (revocation);
- Absence of trust purpose (revocation);[312]
- Accomplishment of trust purposes becomes impossible (modification or revocation);[313]
- Accomplishment of trust purposes becomes illegal (modification or revocation);[314]
- Continuing administration uneconomic (termination);[315]
- Taxation avoidance (modification or revocation);[316]
- Mistake (reformation, modification, rectification, rescission, or termination);[317]

---

[304] Restatement (Third) of Trusts §64 cmt. c; 5 Scott & Ascher §§33.1.1 (Termination or Modification by Trustee), 33.1.2 (Termination or Modification by Beneficiary). "Moreover, even if the beneficiary holds the power in a nonfiduciary capacity, there may be situations in which he or she has 'a duty not to exercise it in a manner that is unnecessarily harmful or unfair to other beneficiaries'" 5 Scott & Ascher §§33.1.1 (Termination or Modification by Trustee), 33.1.2 (Termination or Modification by Beneficiary) (quoting Restatement (Third) of Trusts §64 cmt. c).

[305] Lewin ¶ 12–30 (England).

[306] *See generally* Chapter 2 of this handbook (the property requirement).

[307] Lewin ¶ 12–30 (England).

[308] Lewin ¶ 12–30 (England). *See generally* §9.27 of this handbook (the purpose trust).

[309] Lewin ¶ 12–30 (England).

[310] Lewin ¶ 12–30 (England).

[311] Lewin ¶ 12–30 (England). *See generally* §8.15.9 of this handbook (doctrine of [facts or acts of] independent legal significance).

[312] *See generally* §8.15.7 of this handbook (the *Claflin* doctrine (material purpose doctrine)).

[313] *See generally* 5 Scott & Ascher §33.2.

[314] *See generally* 5 Scott & Ascher §33.2.

[315] *See generally* 5 Scott & Ascher §33.3.

[316] *See generally* 5 Scott & Ascher §33.5.

[317] *See generally* §8.15.22 of this handbook (doctrines of reformation and rectification).

- Unanticipated change of circumstances (reformation, modification, or revocation);[318]
- Fraud (voidance);[319]
- Undue Influence (voidance);[320]
- Duress (voidance);[321]
- Lack of mental capacity (voidance);[322]
- Combining of two like trusts, thus terminating one or both (termination); and[323]
- Merger (voidance or termination).[324]

Termination and modification by consent. An irrevocable trust may be able to be terminated in mid-course notwithstanding its terms, provided all beneficiaries, including the remaindermen,[325] are in a position to and do give their informed consents thereto.[326] In the United States, however, even though all the beneficiaries including the remaindermen are in existence and of full age and legal capacity, they may not collude with the trustee to terminate an inter vivos trust if its material purposes have yet to be accomplished,[327] at least in principle.[328] "Professor Scott wrote that the most common application of the principle that the beneficiaries cannot compel termination or modification of a trust if continuance in accordance with its current terms is necessary to carry out a material purpose was in the case of a spendthrift trust."[329] There is much case law that is in accord.[330]

---

[318] *See generally* 5 Scott & Ascher §33.4 (Termination or Modification on Account of Unanticipated Circumstances); §8.15.20 of this handbook (doctrine of [equitable] deviation).

[319] 1 Scott & Ascher §4.6.1; 4 Scott on Trusts §333.1.

[320] 1 Scott & Ascher §4.6.2; 4 Scott on Trusts §333.3.

[321] 1 Scott & Ascher §4.6.2; 4 Scott on Trusts §333.3.

[322] 1 Scott & Ascher §3.2; 4 Scott on Trusts §333.2.

[323] *See generally* §3.5.3.2(d) of this handbook (the power to invest in mutual funds and common trust funds; to administer common funds; and to combining trusts).

[324] *See generally* §§8.7 of this handbook (merger) and 8.15.36 of this handbook (merger); 5 Scott & Ascher §34.5 (Merger).

[325] *See* 5 Scott & Ascher §§34.1.1 (Successive Beneficiaries), 34.4 (When Some of the Beneficiaries Do Not or Cannot Give Binding Consent).

[326] 5 Scott & Ascher §34.1 (Consent of Beneficiaries).

[327] *See generally* 5 Scott & Ascher §§34.1 (Consent of Beneficiaries), 34.1.1 (Successive Beneficiaries); §8.15.7 of this handbook (the *Claflin* doctrine (material purpose doctrine)). *See also* UTC §411(b) (available at <http://www.uniformlaws.org/Act.aspx?title=Trust%20 Code>) (providing that a noncharitable irrevocable trust may be terminated upon consent of all the beneficiaries if the court concludes that continuance of the trust is not necessary to achieve any material purpose of the trust); *but see* UTC §411(a) (providing that a noncharitable irrevocable trust may be modified or terminated upon consent of the settlor and all beneficiaries even if the modification or termination is inconsistent with a material purpose of the trust).

[328] *See generally* 5 Scott & Ascher §34.1 (Consent of Beneficiaries). A few jurisdictions now have statutes making it somewhat easier to get around the material purpose limitation. *See* 5 Scott & Ascher §34.1 n.14.

[329] 5 Scott & Ascher §34.1.2.

[330] *See* 5 Scott & Ascher §34.1.2 n.1.

Would the settlor or the settlor's estate have any standing to object if the trust nonetheless were terminated? One could well imagine, for example, a situation whereby the spendthrift adult children of a settlor collude with the trustee to break the provisions of an income-only spendthrift trust that was established for their benefit by the parent.[331] Certainly the prevailing view today is that the complicitous beneficiaries have forfeited their right to hold the trustee accountable for the breach.[332] Some commentators have argued, however, that the settlor, as a matter of public policy, ought to have standing to compel the trustee faithfully to carry out the terms of his trust.[333] Others, most notably Prof. Scott, would seem to disagree.[334]

On the other hand,[335] under the Uniform Trust Code, a noncharitable irrevocable trust may be modified or terminated upon consent of the settlor and all beneficiaries, even if the modification or termination is inconsistent with a material purpose of the trust.[336] This merely reflects what has come to be the state of the case law:[337]

> Thus, when the trust is for the benefit of successive beneficiaries, and one of the settlor's purposes in creating the trust was to deprive the income beneficiary of the management of the property, so that the beneficiaries alone cannot compel termination, the trust can be terminated if the settlor consents. Similarly, when the trust is for the benefit of a sole beneficiary who is not to receive the principal prior to attaining a certain age, the beneficiary can compel the trustee to turn over the trust property earlier, if the settlor consents. Likewise, if the settlor consents, the beneficiaries may be able to compel termination of the trust, though, under its terms, the interests of the beneficiaries are inalienable.[338]

---

[331] *See* 2A Scott on Trusts §151 ("It is held that even though the trust is a spendthrift trust, it can be terminated by the beneficiaries and the settlor if they all consent and are under no disability.").

[332] *See generally* 5 Scott & Ascher §34.6.1 (Spendthrift Trusts).

[333] *See, e.g.,* 5 Scott & Ascher §37.3.10 (granting settlors standing to enforce their charitable trusts would be a "step in the right direction" and "a small price to pay for . . . [their] . . . generosity"). *See* §4.1 of this handbook (interests and powers remaining with the settlor by operation of law). UTC §411(a) (available at <http://www.uniformlaws.org/Act.aspx?title=Trust%20Code>) provides that a noncharitable irrevocable trust may be modified or terminated upon consent of the settlor and all beneficiaries, even if the modification or termination is inconsistent with a material purpose of the trust.

[334] *See* §4.1 of this handbook (interests and powers remaining with the settlor by operation of law). *See also* 5 Scott & Ascher §34.6 (Conveyance by Trustee to or at the Direction of the Beneficiaries) (suggesting that the settlor would be without recourse in the face of such collusion between the trustee and all of the beneficiaries).

[335] UTC§410(b) (available at <http://www.uniformlaws.org/Act.aspx?title=Trust%20Code>).

[336] UTC §411(a) (available at <http://www.uniformlaws.org/Act.aspx?title=Trust%20Code>). *See generally* 5 Scott & Ascher §34.1.3 (Postponement of Enjoyment). No restrictions are imposed on consent by the settlor's conservator or guardian, other than prohibiting such action if the settlor is represented by an agent. *See* UTC §411 cmt.

[337] 5 Scott & Ascher §34.2 n.4.

[338] 5 Scott & Ascher §34.2.

After the settlor's death, however, the settlor's personal representative or heirs may not step into the shoes of the settlor and, along with all the beneficiaries, effect a termination of the trust, at least to the extent that that it continues to have a material purpose.[339] This is because "the settlor's ability to consent to the termination of the trust is personal to the settlor."[340]

The Uniform Trust Code provides that the settlor may commence a proceeding to approve or disapprove a proposed modification or termination of a noncharitable trust.[341] The Uniform Trust Code also grants the settlor of a charitable trust standing to bring a *cy pres* petition.[342]

In the rare case where the settlor of a trust is also its only beneficiary, the settlor will have an unrestricted right at any time to terminate the trust and regain title to the subject property, notwithstanding the absence of an express right of revocation and in contravention of the terms of the trust generally.[343] There are two qualifications: The settlor must be competent at the time of the termination and the terms of the trust must not require that the trustee give consent.[344] Even if the trustee were to withhold consent to the termination, however, the trust would still be constructively revocable, at least in many jurisdictions. This is because the underlying trust property would be subject to the claims of the settlor's creditors.[345] We discuss the concept of the constructively revocable self-settled trust in Section 4.1.3 of this handbook.

Merely tracking what has been the case law, primarily *Claflin* and its progeny, the Uniform Trust Code expressly provides that a noncharitable irrevocable trust may be *terminated* upon consent of all of the beneficiaries if the court concludes that continuance of the trust is not necessary to achieve any material purpose of the trust.[346] The court may do this even over the objections of the settlor and without the consent of the trustee. There is nothing new here.[347] The Code further provides that a noncharitable irrevocable trust may be modified upon consent of all of the beneficiaries if the court concludes that modification is not inconsistent with a material purpose of the trust.[348] Again, the Restatement (Third) of Trusts is generally in accord.[349]

---

[339] 5 Scott & Ascher §34.2 (Consent of Beneficiaries and Settlor).

[340] 5 Scott & Ascher §34.2.

[341] UTC §410(b) (available at <http://www.uniformlaws.org/Act.aspx?title=Trust%20 Code>).

[342] UTC §410(b) (available at <http://www.uniformlaws.org/Act.aspx?title=Trust%20 Code>).

[343] *See generally* 5 Scott & Ascher §34.3 (When Settlor Is Sole Beneficiary).

[344] 5 Scott & Ascher §34.3. The trustee, however, may not withhold consent if to do so would be an abuse of discretion. 5 Scott & Ascher §34.3.

[345] *See generally* §5.3.3.1 of this handbook (creditor access to settlor's reserved beneficial interest); *but see* §5.3.3.1(c) of this handbook (the domestic asset protection jurisdictions).

[346] UTC §411(b) (available at <http://www.uniformlaws.org/Act.aspx?title=Trust%20 Code>).

[347] *See generally* 5 Scott & Ascher §34.1 (Consent of Beneficiaries).

[348] UTC §411(b) (available at <http://www.uniformlaws.org/Act.aspx?title=Trust%20 Code>).

[349] Restatement (Third) of Trusts §65.

Under the Code, a spendthrift restraint in the terms of a trust is not presumed to constitute a material purpose,[350] a nonpresumption that "has proven exceedingly controversial and has now been made 'optional.' "[351] Nevertheless, the Restatement (Third) of Trusts is generally in accord with the Code as to the nonpresumption.[352]

It is fairly well settled that a discretionary or support provision in a trust will generally infuse it with a material purpose.[353] So would a provision that postpones a beneficiary's access to the underlying property for a terms of year, or until the beneficiary attains a certain age.[354] A single-beneficiary trust to manage the underlying property while the beneficiary is under a legal, physical, or mental incapacity also would have a material purpose.[355] In this case, the trust would be terminable in favor of the beneficiary upon the beneficiary's attaining or regaining capacity, absent special additional facts.[356] The material purpose doctrine allows for severability, *i.e.*, for partial terminations in the event that only a portion of the underlying property is needed to carry out the trust's material purpose or purposes.[357] For more on the material purpose or *Claflin* doctrine, the reader is referred to Section 8.15.7 of this handbook.

The Code also provides that a noncharitable irrevocable trust may be *modified* upon consent of all the beneficiaries over the objections of the settlor and without the concurrence of the trustee if the court concludes that modification is not inconsistent with a material purpose of the trust.[358] One court, by authorizing a cash-out of the charitable remainder interests with the consent of the noncharitable interests, has effected a partial termination by modification of a split-interest trust, ruling that to do so would not compromise any material purpose of the trust.[359]

Section 65 of the Restatement (Third) of Trusts is generally in accord with the Code with respect to the circumstances under which a trust may be terminated or modified over the objections of the settlor and without the concurrence of the trustee. Comment a to Section 65 suggests that the "settlor's

[350] UTC §411(c) (available at <http://www.uniformlaws.org/Act.aspx?title=Trust%20Code>).

[351] 5 Scott & Ascher §34.1.2 (Spendthrift Trusts).

[352] Restatement (Third) of Trusts §65 cmt. e. *See generally* 5 Scott & Ascher §34.1.2.

[353] 5 Scott & Ascher §34.1.4 (Support Trusts and Discretionary Trusts).

[354] 5 Scott & Ascher §34.1.3 (Postponement of Enjoyment).

[355] *See generally* 5 Scott & Ascher §34.1.5 (When Beneficiary Is Under Disability That Subsequently Ceases).

[356] 5 Scott & Ascher §34.1.5.

[357] 5 Scott & Ascher §34.1.7 (Partial Termination).

[358] UTC §411(b) (available at <http://www.uniformlaws.org/Act.aspx?title=Trust%20Code>).

[359] Estate of Somers, 277 Kan. 761, 89 P.3d 898 (2004). *See also* University of Me. Found. v. Fleet Bank, 817 A.2d 871 (Me. 2003) (granting a partial distribution of the trust's surplus corpus to the remainder beneficiary, a charity, and requiring the trustee to retain sufficient assets to meet the trust's obligations to the life beneficiaries).

testimony would be relevant in a material-purpose inquiry." Also, the trustee would have standing to object to a proposed modification or termination.[360]

It is self-evident that anyone contemplating setting in motion proceedings to modify or terminate an irrevocable trust notwithstanding its terms will have an easier time of it if he or she obtains the consent of all beneficiaries, including potential ones[361] and those who lack capacity, not just the life beneficiaries.[362] In most cases, even in California where by statute the presumption of fertility is rebuttable,[363] this will be easier said than done:

> This requirement of unanimous consent also includes, for example, beneficiaries who are relatively unlikely ever to receive distributions, those whose interests arise by operation of law (*i.e.*, reversionary, or "resulting trust," interests), and persons who hold powers of appointment under the trust, as well as those who would take in default of the exercise of any but a presently exercisable general power. . . . Also included among those whose consent is required are successors in interest of prior beneficiaries, and the potential unborn (including after-adopted) or unascertainable beneficiaries so often provided for by class description, as in a seemingly simple trust designed to pay income to *A* for life and then to distribute the principal to *A*'s descendants who are living at her death.[364]

On the other hand, a beneficiary whose equitable interests will be unaffected or "unprejudiced" whatever the outcome of the proceeding might well not be a necessary party, such as in the case of a petition or complaint to terminate a segregated trust share that is being administered exclusively for the benefit of other beneficiaries.[365] A beneficiary with a contingent equitable interest that is certain never to vest might not be as well.[366] Or take a trust that is to terminate in favor of the issue of a designated individual who has no children and can never acquire any, either biologically or by adoption. There is probably no need for the never-to-exist class to be represented by a guardian ad litem in a proceeding to terminate the trust.[367] "If there are lingering doubts as

---

[360] *See, e.g.*, UTC §410 (available at <http://www.uniformlaws.org/Act.aspx?title=Trust%20 Code>).

[361] *See generally* §8.14 of this handbook (when is a guardian ad litem (or special representative) needed?) (covering also the doctrine of virtual representation); 5 Scott & Ascher §34.4 (When Some of the Beneficiaries Do Not or Cannot Give Binding Consent).

[362] *See generally* 5 Scott & Ascher §§34.1.1 (Successive Beneficiaries), 34.4 (When Some of the Beneficiaries Do Not or Cannot Give Binding Consent).

[363] Cal. Prob. Code §15406. *See generally* 5 Scott & Ascher §34.4.1 (noting that persons incapable of producing biological children are not necessarily incapable of acquiring children by adoption).

[364] Restatement (Third) of Trusts §65 cmt. b. *See also* 5 Scott & Ascher §34.4 (When Some of the Beneficiaries Do Not or Cannot Give Binding Consent).

[365] *See generally* 5 Scott & Ascher §§34.4 (When the Interests of the Nonconsenting Beneficiaries Are Not Affected), 34.4.2 (Partial Termination).

[366] *See generally* 5 Scott & Ascher §34.4.1 (Contingent Interests That Are Certain Never to Vest).

[367] 5 Scott & Ascher §34.4.1.

to the possibility of additional children, the court can require that security be given to restore the property upon a child's subsequent birth or adoption."[368]

In the case of a *testamentary* trust with a material purpose, the beneficiaries should not be allowed to effect its termination (or to effect a "stripping" from their equitable interests of the restrictions imposed by the testator, such as spendthrift restrictions) through a manufactured judicial proceeding to compromise the will.[369] Even in the case of litigation that is bona fide, the court should only approve a compromise that, to the extent possible, both protects the beneficiaries' interests and maintains the lawful restrictions imposed by the settlor-testator.[370] The settlor-testator being dead, it falls to the court to see to it that the lawful purposes of the trust are carried out, at least insofar as they can be divined from the will's four corners.

Recall that in Section 5.1 of this handbook, we noted that a trust beneficiary would include the holder of a general inter vivos power of appointment. Under the Uniform Trust Code, "withdrawal of the trust property is not an event terminating a trust."[371] The concept is that "[t]he trust remains in existence although the trustee has no duties to perform unless and until property is later contributed to the trust."[372] This assertion would seem a bit overinclusive. The exercise of a reserved right of revocation or a general inter vivos power of appointment over all the property of a trust in favor of the trustee of a different trust, for example, would be a terminating event, at least it should be, particularly if that were the intention of the powerholder.[373]

As a general rule, an irrevocable properly created charitable trust with a material purpose cannot be terminated by the settlor, with or without the consent of the trustee.[374] Nor can it be modified by the settlor, absent a reserved right to do so.[375] The power under the *cy pres* doctrine to alter the charitable purposes of a trust is with the court, not the settlor.[376] The Uniform Prudent Management of Institutional funds Act does, however, provide for some donor involvement when a court is deliberating whether "to release or modify a restriction on the management, investment, or purpose of an institutional fund."[377] The prospective settlor of an irrevocable charitable trust, however, needs to be careful: Once the ship sets sail, it will not be all that easy *for the settlor*

---

[368] 5 Scott & Ascher §34.4.1.

[369] 5 Scott & Ascher §34.1.6 (Compromise Agreement).

[370] 5 Scott & Ascher §34.1.6 (Compromise Agreement).

[371] UTC§410 cmt. (available at <http://www.uniformlaws.org/Act.aspx?title=Trust%20 Code>).

[372] UTC §410 cmt. (available at <http://www.uniformlaws.org/Act.aspx?title=Trust%20 Code>). *Compare* §2.2.1 of this handbook (the pour-over statute) (discussing how the Uniform Testamentary Additions to Trusts Act has done away with the need to token fund when there is an associated pour-over will).

[373] *See* 5 Scott & Ascher §35.1 (noting that "[a] settlor who has an unrestricted right to withdraw principal ordinarily has the power to revoke the trust").

[374] *See generally* 5 Scott & Ascher §37.4.2.1.

[375] *See generally* 5 Scott & Ascher §37.4.2.2.

[376] *See generally* 5 Scott & Ascher §37.4.2.2. *See generally* §9.4.3 of this handbook (*cy pres*).

[377] *See generally* 5 Scott & Ascher §37.4.2.2.

to alter its set course, let alone call it back. "The settlor's control over the property ceases immediately upon the creation of the trust, unless the terms of the trust or applicable law provides the settlor with such a power."[378] On the other hand, in Section 4.1.1.2 of this handbook we suggest some things that a prospective settlor can do at the drafting stage to increase the chances that the ship will actually be allowed to stay on the course that the settlor has set for it. For whether a state's legislature may modify of the terms of a charitable trust, the reader is referred to Section 9.4.4 of this handbook.

Absence of trust purpose (revocation). In England, if the entire equitable interest of a trust has vested in the beneficiary, the beneficiary may compel termination of the trust, notwithstanding its terms. In the United States, the beneficiary also may do so, provided, however, that the trust has no material purpose. The material purpose doctrine, sometimes referred to as the *Claflin* doctrine, is covered in Section 8.15.7 of this handbook.

Merger (voidance or termination). In Sections 8.7 of this handbook and 8.15.36 of this handbook we consider how the merger of all legal and equitable interests in one person can render a trust void *ab initio* or trigger its mid-course termination.[379]

When trust purposes become impossible to carry out or illegal (modification or revocation). In Section 6.2.13 of this handbook, we note that the trustee has a duty not to attempt to comply with a trust provision that directs the trustee to do the impossible. If the impossibility of carrying a trust's provision or provisions is so profound that that there is no sufficient reason for the trust to continue, then the court will find that the entire trust has terminated.[380] Absent special facts, the death or incapacity of the trustee is not the type of event that will trigger a trust termination, at least for reasons of administrative impossibility, as a trust shall not fail for want of a trustee.[381] As a last resort, the court will appoint a suitable successor. The total destruction of the trust property through no fault of anyone will obviously trigger a termination.[382] So too would a change in the form of the trust property that renders irrelevant the purposes of the trust, *e.g.*, a trust established for the sole purpose of administering a closely held business which is then sold for cash.[383] In the case of an impossibility trust termination other than one that is occasioned by the total destruction of the underlying property, any property remaining passes as directed by the terms of the trust. If the terms are silent as to what happens next, then the property reverts to the settlor or the settlor's estate upon a resulting trust.[384]

---

[378] 5 Scott & Ascher §37.4.2.2.

[379] *See also* 5 Scott & Ascher §34.5 (Merger).

[380] *See generally* 5 Scott & Ascher §33.2 (When Accomplishment of Trust Purposes Is Impossible or Illegal).

[381] *See generally* 5 Scott & Ascher §33.2 (When Accomplishment of Trust Purposes Is Impossible or Illegal). *See also* quotation introducing §3.4.1 of this handbook (appointment).

[382] 5 Scott & Ascher §33.2.

[383] 5 Scott & Ascher §33.2.

[384] 5 Scott & Ascher §33.2. *See generally* §4.1.1.1 of this handbook (in part defining the resulting trust).

In Section 6.2.12 of this handbook, we note that the trustee has a duty not to comply with a provision that is unlawful or violates public policy. In Section of this handbook, we cover incentive trusts whose purposes are either illegal or violate public policy. If the core purposes of a trust are so infected with illegality that it would be impossible for the trustee to carry out its terms, or that in carrying out its terms the trustee would subject himself to civil or criminal sanction, then the court will find that the trust itself has terminated.[385] In the case of a charitable trust, impossibility or illegality will not necessarily trigger a termination, at least not in all cases. *Cy pres* modification may be an option. Applications of the *cy pres* doctrine are covered in Sections 8.15.28 of this handbook and 9.4.3 of this handbook.

Continuing administration uneconomic (termination). It has long been the default law that the court may terminate a trust due to the happening of an event unanticipated by the settlor, provided the continued existence of the trust "would defeat or substantially impair the accomplishment of the trust purpose."[386] A gradual or precipitous decline in the market value of the trust's underlying assets through no fault of anyone might be just such an event,[387] particularly if there will be little left over for the beneficiaries after the trustee deducts from the trust estate the reasonable and customary fees to which he is entitled.[388] Nowadays, a trustee both in the governing instrument and by statute is likely to be granted the power to terminate the trust in mid-course should its continuation become "uneconomic," a topic we cover in Section 3.5.3.2(k) of this handbook.

Under the Uniform Trust Code, the trustee of a trust consisting of trust property having a total value less than a specified value may terminate the trust if the trustee concludes that the value of the trust property is insufficient to justify the cost of administration.[389] This is a default rule.[390] The court may modify or terminate a trust if it determines that the value of the trust property is insufficient to justify the cost of administration.[391] This is not a default rule, *i.e.*, the court may order a termination even if the settlor has forbidden it.[392] That such terminations are either trustee-initiated or court-ordered is the

---

[385] *See generally* 5 Scott & Ascher §33.2.

[386] 5 Scott & Ascher §33.3.

[387] 5 Scott & Ascher §33.3.

[388] *See generally* §8.4 of this handbook (the trustee's compensation).

[389] UTC §414(a) (available at <http://www.uniformlaws.org/Act.aspx?title=Trust%20 Code>) (noncharitable trusts); Estate of Somers, 277 Kan. 761, 89 P.3d 898 (2004) (charitable trusts).

[390] UTC §414 cmt. (available at <http://www.uniformlaws.org/Act.aspx?title=Trust%20 Code>) (noncharitable trusts); Estate of Somers, 277 Kan. 761, 89 P.3d 898 (2004) (charitable trusts).

[391] UTC §414(b) (available at <http://www.uniformlaws.org/Act.aspx?title=Trust%20 Code>).

[392] UTC §414 cmt. (available at <http://www.uniformlaws.org/Act.aspx?title=Trust%20 Code>).

Code's rationale for why the presence of a spendthrift provision would not be an impediment.[393]

Unilateral mistake as grounds for reformation, modification, rectification, rescission, or termination. A court will, as appropriate, reform, modify, or rectify the terms of a trust, or even order its termination altogether, upon clear and convincing evidence that a material mistake has caused the terms not to reflect the settlor's intent, or that but for the mistake the settlor would have used different terms.[394] So also a settlor may, "based on the equitable ground of mistake, seek judicial rescission of an irrevocable trust."[395]

Cross referencing. See generally Sections 8.15.20 of this handbook (deviation); 8.15.22 of this handbook (reformation, modification, and rectification); and 8.17 of this handbook (tax-focused reformation and modification).

Failure of consideration. A trust relationship can arise incident to a contract. "If a trust was created for consideration and the consideration fails, the settlor may rescind and retake the trust property."[396]

Taxation avoidance (reformation, modification, rescission, or termination). In the interest of achieving "tax efficiency" in the administration of trusts, "the courts have seemed especially ready, perhaps sometimes overly so, to rectify 'mistakes,'" as long as equitable property interests are not materially rearranged in the process.[397] As one learned commentator has noted, "the only real losers in such litigation are the tax collector and, hence, the tax-paying public, neither of which, typically, is before the court."[398] For more on terminating trusts or modifying their terms in order to save taxes, the reader is referred to Section 8.17 of this handbook.

Unanticipated change of circumstances (modification or termination). It has long been settled law that a court may terminate a trust or modify its dispositive provisions in response to an unanticipated change of circumstances that "would defeat or substantially impair the accomplishment of the trust purposes,"[399] a topic we cover in Section 8.15.22 of this handbook. In recent years, the bar has been lowered somewhat: "In particular, it is no longer necessary . . . to prove that either the trust or the beneficiaries would suffer dire consequences in the absence of judicial intervention."[400] Still, the wishes of the settlor as they are reflected in the terms of the trust will generally trump those of the beneficiaries to the extent there is a divergence.[401] Also, "it is appropriate

---

[393] UTC §414 cmt. (available at <http://www.uniformlaws.org/Act.aspx?title=Trust%20 Code>).

[394] *See generally* Bogert §42.

[395] Generaux v. Dobyns, 205 Or. App. 183, 134 P.3d 983 (2006).

[396] Bogert §42.

[397] 5 Scott & Ascher §33.5.

[398] 5 Scott & Ascher §33.5 n.5 (noting, however, that the U.S. Supreme Court in the *Bosch* decision "has imposed substantial limitations on the effectiveness, for federal tax purposes, of state court decrees reforming trust instruments"). *See generally* §8.15.27 of this handbook (the *Bosch* decision).

[399] 5 Scott & Ascher §33.4.

[400] 5 Scott & Ascher §33.4.

[401] 5 Scott & Ascher §33.4.

that courts act with particular caution in considering a modification or deviation that can be expected to diminish the interest(s) of one or more of the beneficiaries in favor of more or more others."[402]

Fraud (voidance). If one was induced by fraud to impress a trust upon one's property, one may petition the court to have the trust declared void and the petition will likely be granted.[403] Whether the trustee, the beneficiary, or a third person was unjustly enriched by the fraud is irrelevant.[404] This has been the law since time immemorial, or at least since 1816:

> In *Gordon v. Gordon*, a deed of settlement of property within a family was entered into by the eldest son in the belief that he was illegitimate, though a younger son knew of a secret marriage of his parents by virtue of which the eldest son was legitimate. Lord Eldon held that a duty of candour recognized in equity had been breached so that the settlement should be set aside.[405]

Undue influence and duress (voidance). That the settlor was induced by the undue influence of the trustee, the beneficiary, or a third person to create a trust also can be grounds in equity for its judicial voidance.[406] Otherwise, the wrongdoer would be unjustly enriched.[407]

Mere persuasion is not enough, however.[408] The settlor has to have had his or her free will supplanted by that of the influencer,[409] or, at least, so unfairly manipulated "that it would be inequitable not to permit the settlor to set it aside."[410] On the other hand, "[t]he settlor will get no relief if he has knowingly . . . [and freely] . . . acquiesced in the settlement."[411] In this day and age of enormous pressure on the elderly and the handicapped to divest themselves of their property, the trustee should exercise due diligence before accepting an irrevocable inter vivos trust. He should assure himself that he is neither buying a lawsuit nor expected to violate that trust. There are two categories of undue influence.

---

[402] Restatement (Third) of Trusts §66 cmt. b. *Cf.* §6.2.5 of this handbook (the trustee's duty of impartiality).

[403] 1 Scott & Ascher §4.6.1; 4 Scott on Trusts §333.1; Bogert §42; UTC §406 (available at <http://www.uniformlaws.org/Act.aspx?title=Trust%20Code>).

[404] 1 Scott & Ascher §4.6.1; 4 Scott on Trusts §333.1; UTC §406. *See generally* §8.15.78 of this handbook (unjust enrichment).

[405] Harold Greville Hanbury & Ronald Harling Maudsley, Modern Equity 627 (10th ed. 1976) (the *Gordon v. Gordon* citation being: (1816) 3 Swan. 400). In the Introduction to this handbook, we note that in England, the term *settlement* is sometimes employed as a synonym for *inter vivos* trust. Marriage settlements are covered in §9.30 of this handbook.

[406] 1 Scott & Ascher §4.6.2; 4 Scott on Trusts §333.3; Bogert §42.

[407] *See generally* §8.15.78 of this handbook (unjust enrichment).

[408] 1 Scott & Ascher §4.6.2; 4 Scott on Trusts §333.3.

[409] *See generally* Underhill & Hayton, Law Relating to Trusts and Trustees 347–348 (17th ed. 2007) (the settlor's conduct must be an expression of his or her free will).

[410] 1 Scott & Ascher §4.6.2.

[411] Underhill & Hayton, Law Relating to Trusts and Trustees 352 (17th ed. 2007).

The first category comprises "overt acts of improper pressure or coercion such as unlawful threats."[412] The coercion can be physical, psychological, or economic.[413] There seems to be little practical difference between overt or direct undue influence and duress.[414] In any case, we are happy to report that "[p]hysical violence or the threat of it rarely figures in the procuring of a trust."[415]

The second category of undue influence involves the taking of an unfair advantage of a fiduciary or confidential relationship by the dominant or ascendant party to it.[416] In the context of influencing someone to create a trust, a presumption of undue influence is raised if the influencer is in a fiduciary relationship with the settlor and somehow benefits directly or indirectly from the entrustment.[417] The influencer might be an agent of the settlor (perhaps the settlor's lawyer) or a trustee of another and preexisting trust under which the settlor possesses an equitable or beneficial interest.[418] A presumption of undue influence also would be raised if the advantaged influencer occupied a dominant or ascendant position of confidence vis-à-vis the settlor, *e.g.*, if their relationship were one of parent and child, doctor and patient, teacher and student, or priest and penitent.[419] Just as it can be said that direct or overt undue influence is a species of duress, so also it can be said that the taking of unfair advantage of a fiduciary or confidential relationship is a "species of fraud."[420]

Lack of mental capacity (voidance). Lack of mental capacity to impress a trust on one's property is grounds for a judicial determination that the purported trust was void *ab initio*. If one has the mental capacity to make a will, one has the mental capacity to create a testamentary trust or a revocable inter vivos trust,[421] or to exercise a testamentary power of appointment in further trust.[422] "While the courts have differed as to the precise test for mental capacity, they are agreed that a testator is mentally deficient for the purpose of making a will if the testator lacks the ability to understand the general nature of the testamentary act, to know the nature and extent of the testator's property and the

---

[412] Snell's Equity ¶ 8-12.

[413] Snell's Equity ¶ 8-12.

[414] Snell's Equity ¶ 8-12.

[415] L.A. Sheridan, The Law of Trusts 130 (12th ed. 1993) (suggesting ominously, however, that other forms of duress in the procuring of trusts "abound").

[416] Snell's Equity ¶ 8-12.

[417] Snell's Equity ¶ 8-12.

[418] Underhill & Hayton, Law Relating to Trusts and Trustees 347–348 (17th ed. 2007); Snell's Equity ¶ 8-12.

[419] Underhill & Hayton, Law Relating to Trusts and Trustees 347–348 (17th ed. 2007); Snell's Equity ¶ 8-12. *See generally* Chapter 1 of this handbook (in part distinguishing the confidential relationship from the fiduciary relationship).

[420] In re Reddaway's Estate, 214 Or. 410, 419–420, 329 P.2d 886 (1958).

[421] UTC §601 (available at <http://www.uniformlaws.org/Act.aspx?title=Trust%20 Code>). *See, e.g.*, Bonady v. Bonady-Napier, 2005 WL 91252 (Cal. App. 2005); 1 Scott & Ascher §3.2. The subject of grounds for contesting inter vivos trusts is touched on in the footnote accompanying §8.2.4(2) of this handbook (trust termination checklist).

[422] 1 Scott & Ascher §3.2.

natural objects of his or her bounty, and to interrelate these factors."[423] The settlor of a trust possesses the mental capacity to exercise any reserved right of revocation if and when he or she possesses the mental capacity to make a will.[424] The capacity standard for present irrevocable inter vivos transfers in trust (and for the exercise of inter vivos powers of appointment in further trust[425]) is either the higher contractual standard or the higher donative transfer standard.[426] The Restatement (Third) of Trusts is generally in accord.[427]

Wrongful interference with donative transfer. One who is wrongfully deprived of a beneficial interest under a trust before it is even established may have two arrows in his or her quiver: a legal action in tort for damages against the wrongdoer and an equitable action for restitution against those who, whether innocently or not, have been unjustly enriched by the wrongful acts. "Assuming that such a tort is recognized under local law, and that the measurable loss to the claimant is the same as the resulting gain to the recipient, the choice between an action for damages and for restitution . . . may make no practical difference."[428]

As to the equitable arrow, take the situation where the father of four adult children initially intends to impress an express trust upon his property for their benefit. Each child is to be allocated an equal share of the beneficial interest. By fraudulent representations, the father is persuaded by two of the four children to exclude a third child from the trust. The fourth child is totally in the dark as to the unsavory machinations of her two siblings. If the wronged child can prove that, but for the wrongful interference of his two sibling, he would have been included as a trust beneficiary on equal terms with the others, then the trustee of the express trust can be declared by the court a constructive trustee of an appropriate portion of the trust estate for the benefit of the wronged child. *Under unjust enrichment principles*, the shares of all three siblings are partially tapped pro rata to fund the constructive trust, which is the court's equitable

---

[423] Ritchie, Alford, Effland & Dobris, Cases and Materials on Decedents' Estates and Trusts 399 (1993). *See also* Restatement (Third) of Property (Wills and Other Donative Transfers) §8.1(b) (Tentative Draft No. 3, Apr. 4, 2001) (providing that "[t]o have mental capacity to make or revoke a revocable will substitute the donor must be capable of knowing and understanding in a general way the nature and extent of his or her property, the natural objects of his or her bounty, and the disposition that he or she is making of that property, and must also be capable of relating these elements to one another and forming an orderly desire regarding the disposition of the property").

[424] Restatement (Third) of Property (Wills and Other Donative Transfers) §8.1(b) (Tentative Draft No. 3, Apr. 4, 2001).

[425] 1 Scott & Ascher §3.2.

[426] *See* Restatement (Third) of Property (Wills and Other Donative Transfers) §8.1, Reporter's Note 3 (Tentative Draft No. 3, Apr. 4, 2001) (suggesting a contractual standard). A person lacks capacity to contract if by reason of mental illness or defect he is unable to understand in a reasonable manner the nature and consequences of the transaction. Restatement (Second) of Contracts §15. *See, however*, 1 Scott & Ascher §3.2 (Endorsing A Gift Standard). *See also* UTC §402 cmt. (available at <http://www.uniformlaws.org/Act.aspx?title=Trust%20Code>) (suggesting that to create an irrevocable trust, the settlor must have capacity during lifetime to transfer the property free of trust). *See also* UTC §601 cmt.

[427] Restatement (Third) of Trusts §11.

[428] Restatement (Third) of Restitution and Unjust Enrichment §46 cmt. a.

vehicle for making the wronged beneficiary whole. Because the innocent sibling is not a good faith purchaser for value (BFP), her share may not be spared.[429] "Restitution defendants who are innocent recipients . . . [, however,] . . . are entitled to the standard affirmative defenses, the most significant in this context being change of position. . . ."[430]

The combining of two or more like trusts, thus terminating one or both. The Uniform Trust Code would authorize a trustee to combine two or more trusts into a single trust if the result would not impair the rights of any beneficiary or adversely affect achievement of the purposes of the trusts.[431] Sometimes the governing instruments themselves will contain such an authorization, or even a mandate to combine upon the happening of some event.[432] In any case, it is likely to be more cost-effective to run one larger trust than two smaller ones. The professional trustee, for example, typically charges on a sliding scale that is keyed to the market value of the underlying assets of the trust.[433] Many trustees also charge a minimum annual fee.[434] For more on the extinguishment of a trust by its merger with another trust, the reader is referred to Section 3.5.3.2(d) of this handbook.

Cross references to other sections of this handbook that contain material that touches directly or indirectly on the voidance, rescission, reformation, modification, rectification, and termination of trusts. For a discussion of when a noncharitable trust may be reformed or terminated to remedy faulty tax planning, the reader is referred to Section 8.17 of this handbook. Section 8.15.20 of this handbook is devoted to the doctrine of equitable deviation. In Section 8.15.22 of this handbook we cover the doctrines of reformation, modification and rectification. As to when a charitable trust may be reformed in a *cy pres* action, the reader is referred to Section 9.4.3 of this handbook. In Section 8.15.2 of this handbook we consider how the doctrine of worthier title might cause certain ostensibly irrevocable trusts to be actually revocable. In Sections 8.7 of this handbook and 8.15.36 of this handbook we consider how merger could void a trust *ab initio* or trigger its mid-course termination. In Section 8.15.7 of this handbook, we delve into when a beneficiary who possesses the entire equitable interest under a trust may effect its termination consistent with the *Claflin* or material purpose doctrines.[435] In Section 5.7 of this handbook we discuss who would be the necessary parties in an action to reform or terminate an irrevocable trust. We have considered in this section how a declaration of trust or a conveyance in trust may be rescinded or set aside if its creation was induced by fraud, duress, or undue influence, or if the settlor was mentally incapacitated at the time of the trust's creation.

---

[429] Restatement (Third) of Restitution and Unjust Enrichment §46, illus. 10. *See generally* §8.15.63 of this handbook (the BFP).

[430] Restatement (Third) of Restitution and Unjust Enrichment §46 cmt. h.

[431] UTC §417 (available at <http://www.uniformlaws.org/Act.aspx?title=Trust%20Code>).

[432] *See generally* §3.5.3.2(d) of this handbook (a trustee the power to combine trusts).

[433] *See generally* §8.4 of this handbook (the trustee's compensation).

[434] *See generally* §8.4 of this handbook (the trustee's compensation).

[435] *See also* 5 Scott & Ascher §34.1 (Consent of Beneficiaries).

§8.2.2.2   Trusts Revocable and Amendable by Settlors, Beneficiaries, and Other Nonfiduciaries; Trusts Revocable and Amendable by Trustees and Other Fiduciaries

When the terms of the trust authorize the trustee to terminate the trust, the trustee may be guilty of an abuse of discretion in terminating the trust as well as in refusing to do so.[436]

For purposes of this section, a trust is revocable if someone possesses an inter vivos power of appointment over the trust property.[437] It is now settled law that the reservation in the settlor of a right of revocation will not in and of itself prevent a trust from coming into existence and functioning as a will substitute, notwithstanding the considerable control that is lodged in someone other than the trustee.[438] This includes even self-settled declarations of trust.[439] At one time, however, there was concern that such an arrangement might not be a trust but be a constructive agency and/or a failed attempt at a testamentary disposition.[440]

Some relevant power of appointment doctrine. A nonfiduciary power to revoke a trust and assume legal title to the entrusted property would include the power to cause the title to pass directly from the trustee to others, including to other trustees upon different trusts.[441] Such a power meets the definition of a general inter vivos power of appointment.[442] The Restatement (Third) of Property proposes that any express limitation on the power to partially revoke, or on the number of partial revocations that may be executed, is unenforceable.[443] Inherent in the power to revoke is the power to directly grant a power of revocation over the entrusted property to another, such as by the exercise of the power in further trust.[444] The Restatement incorrectly analogizes such a grant to an agency-type delegation of the power of revocation.[445] Rather, such a grant

---

[436] *See generally* Berall, Campfield, & Zaritsky, 468-2d T.M., Revocable Inter Vivos Trusts (describing the creation and use of revocable inter vivos trusts for asset management and estate planning).

[437] *But see* UTC §103(13) (available at <http://www.uniformlaws.org/Act.aspx?title=Trust%20Code>) (narrowly defining "revocable," as applied to a trust, to mean revocable by the settlor without the consent of the trustee or a person holding an adverse interest).

[438] 1 Scott & Ascher §5.7.

[439] 1 Scott & Ascher §8.2.6.

[440] 1 Scott & Ascher §§5.7, 8.2.1 (Will Substitute), 8.2.2 (Agency Substitute).

[441] Restatement (Third) of Property (Wills and Other Donative Transfers) §19.13(a).

[442] *See generally* §8.1.1 of this handbook (powers of appointment).

[443] Restatement (Third) of Property (Wills and Other Donative Transfers) §19.13 cmt. c; Restatement (Second) of Property (Wills and Other Donative Transfers) §19.1 cmt. d.

[444] Restatement (Third) of Property (Wills and Other Donative Transfers) §19.13 cmt. f; Restatement (Second) of Property (Wills and Other Donative Transfers) §19.2.

[445] Restatement (Third) of Property (Wills and Other Donative Transfers) §19.13 cmt. g; Restatement (Second) of Property (Wills and Other Donative Transfers) §19.2 cmt. b.

is more analogous to an irrevocable assignment of vested property rights in the entrusted property.[446]

Powers of appointment are covered generally in Section 8.1.1 of this handbook. The Restatement (Third) of Property floats by implication the novel proposition that a power of revocation, amendment, or withdrawal should be treated as a distinct species of general inter vivos power of appointment for purposes of avoiding application of the doctrine of capture in the face of an ineffective power exercise.[447] We challenge the logic of the proposition in Section 8.15.12 of this handbook.

The settlor. *The traditional default presumption was that a trust was irrevocable.*[448] Still, the settlor of a trust could expressly reserve an inter vivos right to revoke the trust, either in one shot or incrementally through partial revocations.[449] " . . . [I]n most states, the fact that the settlor has retained a testamentary power of appointment is not sufficient to allow the settlor to revoke the trust without the consent of all of the beneficiaries."[450]

In the absence of an expressly reserved power to revoke a trust or reform its terms, a court may be willing to grant the settlor such a power, provided there is clear and convincing evidence that the absence of such a power was occasioned by scrivener error, or by the settlor's mistaken understanding of the applicable facts or law at the time the trust was created.[451] In Section 8.2.2.1 of this handbook, we cover mistake-based trust terminations generally, including reformation actions.

The UTC creates a presumption of revocability. Under the Uniform Trust Code, however, a trust, whether private or charitable,[452] is presumed revocable by the settlor unless the terms of the trust expressly provide that the trust is irrevocable.[453] The Restatement (Third) of Trusts and the Uniform Trust Code are not entirely in sync in this regard.[454] The Restatement (Third) of Trusts would admit extrinsic evidence on whether a trust is revocable if its written terms do not adequately address the issue. If a settlor retains no beneficial interest other than by resulting trust, there is a rebuttable presumption that the trust is

---

[446] *See* Marx v. Rice, 3 N.J. Super. 581, 585–586, 67 A.2d 918, 920–921 (1949) (in the case of a general inter vivos power of appointment the analogy is to property, whereas in the case of a nongeneral inter vivos power, the analogy is to agency).

[447] *See* Restatement (Third) of Property (Wills and Other Donative Transfers) §19.21 cmt. f.

[448] 5 Scott & Ascher §35.1 (Revocation by Settlor).

[449] *See* 5 Scott & Ascher §35.1; 4 Scott on Trusts §330; Bogert §993. *See also* 5 Scott & Ascher §35.1.6 (Partial Revocation) (". . . . [A] settlor who has the power to revoke ordinarily may exercise it by withdrawing part of the trust property at one time and another part or all of the remaining trust property at one or more subsequent times").

[450] *See generally* 5 Scott & Ascher §34.4; §8.2.2.1 of this handbook (trust terminations by consent).

[451] 5 Scott & Ascher §35.3 (Power of Revocation or Modification Omitted by Mistake).

[452] 5 Scott & Ascher §37.4.2 (Revocation and Modification of Charitable Trusts).

[453] UTC §602(a) (available at <http://www.uniformlaws.org/Act.aspx?title=Trust%20 Code>). *See generally* 5 Scott & Ascher §35.1.

[454] *See* Restatement (Third) of Trusts §63(1); 5 Scott & Ascher §35.1 (observing that the Restatement (Third) of Trusts "in some sense splits the difference between the traditional view and the merging view" as embodied in the provisions of the UTC).

irrevocable.[455] On the other hand, if the settlor retains some beneficial interest[456] in addition to what might be due him or her pursuant to the imposition of a resulting trust,[457] there is a rebuttable presumption that the trust is revocable and amendable.[458] Under the Restatement (Third) of Trusts, a so-called adapted trust is revocable until the earlier of the settlor's death and the exercise by the trustee of his power to select among those of an indefinite class of beneficiaries who shall take the trust property.[459]

Evidence of the filing of a gift tax return might overcome the presumption of revocability. It has been suggested, however, that the failure to file a gift tax return ought not to overcome the presumption of irrevocability.[460] This is "because failure to file even a required gift-tax return is too common to be revealing of the settlor's intention or understanding of the trust."[461]

Whether a trust nowadays can ever be truly irrevocable. One practitioner-scholar is suggesting that, via the Uniform Trust Code and other such partial codifications, settlor-intent is being sacrificed on the altar of flexibility. He writes: "During the past couple of decades . . . the term 'irrevocable,' as used in estate planning, has taken on a new, counter-intuitive meaning. In the 21st century, a trust that's said to be irrevocable is, in truth, often nothing of the sort."[462]

The UTC's default revocation methodologies. In the pre-UTC days, unless the terms of a revocable inter vivos trust provided otherwise, the trust could not have been revoked by the settlor's will. A will speaks at the time of the testator's death, an event that happens also to render the trust irrevocable.[463] Section 602(c) of the UTC has turned this settled doctrine on its head and generally muddied the waters in the process. In its original manifestation, Section 602(c) provided as follows:

> The settlor may revoke or amend a revocable trust: (1) by substantial compliance with a method provided in the terms of the trust; or (2) if the terms of the trust do not provide a method or the method provided in the terms is not expressly made exclusive, by: (A) executing a later will or codicil that expressly refers to the trust or specifically devises property that would otherwise have passed according to the terms of the trust; or (B) any other method manifesting clear and convincing evidence of the settlor's intent.

---

[455] Restatement (Third) of Trusts §63 cmt. c.

[456] A reserved power of appointment would qualify as beneficial interest for purposes of the presumption of revocability.

[457] *See generally* §4.1.1.1 of this handbook (The Noncharitable Trust; Resulting Trust Defined) (in part defining the resulting trust).

[458] Restatement (Third) of Trusts §63 cmt. c.

[459] Restatement (Third) of Trusts §46 cmt. f. *See generally* §9.29 of this handbook (The Adapted Trust).

[460] Restatement (Third) of Trusts §63 cmt. c(1).

[461] Restatement (Third) of Trusts §63 cmt. c(1).

[462] Charles A. Redd, *Flexibility vs. Certainty—Has the Pendulum Swung Too Far?*, Trusts & Estates (Feb. 23, 2015).

[463] *See, e.g.*, Brown v. International Trust Co., 130 Colo. 543, 278 P.2d 581, 583 (Colo. 1954) (en banc).

By amendment to the UTC in 2001, the word "executing" was deleted "to avoid an implication that the trust is revoked immediately upon execution of the will or codicil and not at the testator's death." Quaere: What about the jurisdictions that allow a will with a trust-revocation provision to be effectively executed (signed by the witnesses) after the settlor has died, as per Section 2-502 of the Uniform Probate Code?[464]

Now comes *In re Schlicht*,[465] a 2014 trust-revocation case, which further muddies the waters. New Mexico has enacted the modified version of Section 602(c) of the UTC. The trust at issue expressly provided that the settlor may revoke the trust "by a duly executed instrument to that effect, signed by the [settlor] and delivered to the Trustee." The will had an express partial trust-revocation provision. The court held that the revocation-by-will was effective, notwithstanding the express language of the trust, which the court deemed to be nonexclusive. Here is the court's rationale: "[T]he will executed during the settlor's lifetime constituted substantial compliance with a method provided in the terms of the trust." It should be noted that Massachusetts has declined to enact the substantial compliance and revocation-by-will features of UTC §602(c). It has, however, adopted the vaguely worded "any other method of revocation" feature.

Acknowledging the uncertainty that is inherent in Section 602(c), the UTC has thrown a bone to the trustee community. Section 602(g) provides that "[a] trustee who does not know that a trust has been revoked or amended is not liable to the settlor or settlor's successors in interest for distributions made and other actions taken on the assumption that the trust has not been amended or revoked." What if the trustee should have known? It is suggested that the prospective settlor of a revocable inter vivos trust would be well-advised to give UTC §602(c) the widest possible berth by expressly providing in the terms of the trust an unambiguously exclusive method of revoking it, and by requiring that compliance be literal.

A general assignment to a trustee for the benefit of creditors. In England and Canada, the default presumption is that a *general assignment* to a trustee for the benefit of creditors is revocable by the debtor up until the time when the terms of the assignment are accepted by at least one of the creditors.[466] In the United States, there is a default presumption of irrevocability in the absence of an applicable statute.[467] Of course, if the debtor's intention is that the assignee be just an agent of the debtor, then title to the subject property never leaves the debtor,[468] although there are some exceptions to this general rule, which we cover in Section 9.9.2 of this handbook. "When a debtor delivers money or other property to a third person with instructions to pay a *particular creditor*, the relationship that arises may be a contract for the benefit of the creditor, an

---

[464] In Massachusetts, there is no express statutory requirement that the postmortem will execution must take place within a reasonable period of time post mortem.

[465] 329 P.3d 733 (N.M. Ct. App. 2014).

[466] 5 Scott & Ascher §35.1.8.

[467] 5 Scott & Ascher §35.1.8.

[468] 5 Scott & Ascher §35.1.8. *See generally* §9.9.2 of this handbook (agency arrangements).

agency for the debtor, or a trust," depending generally on the collective intention of the parties.[469] Thus, before assessing whether a "trust" for the benefit of a particular creditor is revocable, one would be well-advised to first make sure that the property that was delivered actually is the subject of a trust.[470]

Inherent in the reserved right to revoke is the right to amend. Inherent in the right to revoke a trust is the lesser right to amend it;[471] inherent in the right to amend is the right to insert by amendment into the trust instrument a revocation provision.[472] Thus, the law that is applicable to reserved powers of revocation is generally applicable as well to reserved powers of modification.[473] A settlor who has expressly or by implication reserved only the power to substitute beneficiaries may still be able to effect a termination of the trust by "indirection," namely, by substituting himself or herself in as the sole beneficiary.[474] Recall that in Section 8.2.2.1 of this handbook, we note that when the settlor is the sole beneficiary and under no legal disability, the settlor may revoke the trust and take back the subject property.

Mechanics of exercising a reserved right of revocation or amendment. How does a settlor with the right to revoke or amend exercise that right? When the instrument is silent on the mechanics of revocation or amendment, methods should be employed that manifest clear and convincing evidence of the settlor's present intent.[475] Often the methods of revoking and amending a trust are prescribed in its governing instrument.[476] It is generally some variation of the following: "by an instrument, in writing, delivered to the trustee." When the revocation procedure is specified, it should be followed to the letter,[477] though

---

[469] 5 Scott & Ascher §35.1.9.

[470] 4 Scott & Ascher §35.1.9. *See generally* §8.25 of this handbook (few American law schools still require Agency, Trusts, and Equity).

[471] Restatement (Third) of Trusts §63 cmt. g; *see generally* Bogert §1001 (The Exercise of a Power of Revocation or Termination); UTC §602 cmt. (available at <http://www.uniformlaws.org/Act.aspx?title=Trust%20Code>) (suggesting that a power of revocation includes the power to amend); 5 Scott & Ascher §35.2.1 (Whether Power to Revoke Include Power to Modify).

[472] Restatement (Third) of Trusts §63 cmt. g; UTC §602 cmt. (available at <http://www.uniformlaws.org/Act.aspx?title=Trust%20Code>) (suggesting that an unrestricted power to amend may also include the power to revoke a trust); 5 Scott & Ascher §35.2.2 (Whether Power to Modify Includes Power to Revoke).

[473] *See generally* 5 Scott & Ascher §35.2 (Modification by Settlor).

[474] *See generally* §3.5.2.2 of this handbook (whether power to modify includes power to revoke).

[475] UTC §602(c)(2)(B) (available at <http://www.uniformlaws.org/Act.aspx?title=Trust%20Code>); Restatement (Third) of Trusts §63 cmt. h. *See generally* 5 Scott & Ascher §35.1.1 (When No Method of Revocation Is Specified).

[476] *See generally* 5 Scott & Ascher §35.1.2 (When Method of Revocation Is Specified).

[477] Restatement (Third) of Trusts §63 cmt. i. *See, e.g.*, Salem United Methodist Church v. Bottorff, 138 S.W.3d 788 (2004) (while a physical act such as a tearing might serve to revoke a will if the act were coupled with a present intent to revoke, the deceased settlor's revocable trust had not been revoked during the settlor's lifetime by the settlor's act of tearing out the distributive provisions from the governing instrument, the governing instrument having provided for a specific method of revocation that did not involve the act of tearing); Austin v. City of Alexandria, 574 S.E.2d 289 (Va. 2003) (holding that a settlor having failed to follow revocation procedures set

the law may be trending in the direction of substantial compliance.[478] Both the Uniform Trust Code and the Restatement (Third) of Trusts have come down on the side of substantial compliance.[479] Some courts are even declining to enforce a provision seen in many trust instruments, namely, that for an amendment to be effective, the trustee must consent to it.[480] Concern has been expressed that such a requirement is tantamount to a "veto power" in the trustee, a power that could be wielded in ways that might frustrate the legitimate intentions of competent settlors.[481] Also, if the method of revocation specified in the terms of the trust was intended to be a method—but not the only method—of effecting a revocation, then "the settlor may revoke by any method that sufficiently manifests the intent to do so."[482]

On the other hand, when it comes not to the procedure for revoking but the *circumstances* under which revocation by the settlor is permissible, *e.g.*, only as necessary for the settlor's support[483] or only with the consent of the other beneficiaries,[484] then there must be literal compliance.[485] If the settlor may revoke the trust only with the consent of the trustee, then the consent power

---

forth in a deed of real estate to the trustee of his revocable trust, the real estate was still in the trust at the time of the settlor's death notwithstanding the settlor's efforts during his lifetime to transfer the real estate to the trustee of another trust); Reid v. McCoy, 46 P.3d 188 (Okla. Ct. App. 2002) (finding support in Restatement (Second) of Trusts §220 cmt. j, the court held that where the terms of a revocable and amendable inter vivos trust called for delivery of instrument of amendment to the trustee, an instrument of amendment delivered to the trustee after the death of the settlor was ineffective, the trust having been rendered irrevocable by the settlor's death); One Valley Bank, N.A. v. Hunt, 205 W. Va. 112, 516 S.E.2d 516 (1999) (holding that a reserved power to modify or revoke during the settlor's lifetime cannot be exercised by the settlor's will); Phelps v. State St. Trust Co., 330 Mass. 511, 512, 115 N.E.2d 382 (1953) (the settlor having reserved the right to amend or revoke by an instrument in writing acknowledged and delivered to the trustee, any instrument that purported to amend the trust that had not been acknowledged by the settlor before a public officer authorized by law to take acknowledgments of other writings held ineffective). *But see* UTC §602(c)(1) (available at <http://www.uniformlaws.org/Act.aspx?title=Trust%20Code>) (allowing for substantial compliance with execution formalities prescribed in the governing instrument).

[478] *See generally* 5 Scott & Ascher §35.1.2; §8.15.53 of this handbook (the harmless-error rule [the trust application]).

[479] UTC §602(c)(1) (available at <http://www.uniformlaws.org/Act.aspx?title=Trust%20Code>); Restatement (Third) of Trusts §63 cmt. i.

[480] *See, e.g.,* Godley v. Valley View State Bank, 277 Kan. 736, 89 P.3d 595 (2004); Huscher v. Wells Fargo Bank, 18 Cal. Rptr. 3d 27 (2004).

[481] It should be kept in mind that the purpose of the consent requirement is first and foremost to protect the trustee. Presumably there is always the option of resignation if the terms of the trust have metamorphosed in ways that the trustee finds objectionable. The problem is that even in the face of express resignation authority, a trustee is not relieved of his fiduciary responsibilities until such time as a qualified successor is in place. *See* §6.1.4 of this handbook (duty to give personal attention (not to delegate)).

[482] 5 Scott & Ascher §35.1.2.

[483] *See generally* 5 Scott & Ascher 35.1.3 n.24 and accompanying text.

[484] *See generally* 5 Scott & Ascher §35.1.3 (When Power to Revoke Is Subject to Consent of Beneficiaries) (noting that a beneficiary generally may withhold consent for no reason at all, that is a beneficiary's consent power is generally not a fiduciary power).

[485] 5 Scott & Ascher §35.1.2.

would likely be a fiduciary one.[486] It would then depend on the terms of the trust whether the trustee's fiduciary duty incident to holding the power to grant or withhold consent runs to the settlor or to the beneficiaries, or to both, and whether the power is discretionary or ministerial.[487] " . . . [I]f the terms of the trust neither expressly nor by implication limit the power of the trustee to consent to revocation, it would seem that the giving or withholding of consent ordinarily should be effective, as long as the trustee does not act dishonestly or form an improper motive."[488]

The Uniform Trust Code, in derogation of the common law,[489] provides that a revocable trust even may be revoked by a later will or codicil that expressly refers to the trust, or specifically devises property that would otherwise have passed according to the terms of the trust.[490] It is "understandable" that this provision of the Code "has proven controversial, and a number of states have rejected it."[491]

The effective time of revocation. Absent special facts or a specific trust provision to the contrary, a trust is deemed revoked as of the time the trustee receives the notice of revocation, not at the time the trustee relinquishes physical control of the subject property.[492] The revocation may even be effective as of the time notice is dropped in the mail, a consequence that would have a bearing on the rights, duties, and obligations of the parties should the settlor die before the notice is physically received by the trustee.[493] When it comes to trust revocations, there is much to be said for delivery by fax or email, followed by the mailing of a hard-copy back-up, particularly for the settlor who is in ill health.[494] A fax or email precisely sets the time of revocation, creates an evidentiary record, and eliminates any hiatus between the signing of the

---

[486] 5 Scott & Ascher §35.1.4.

[487] 5 Scott & Ascher §35.1.4.

[488] 5 Scott & Ascher §35.1.4.

[489] *See generally* 5 Scott & Ascher §35.1.2 (noting that "the vast majority of the cases have held that a settlor who has reserved the right to revoke a trust *during his or her lifetime* has not also reserved the power to revoke the trust by will"). *See, e.g.,* Last Will and Testament of Tamplin, 48 P.3d 471 (Alaska 2002) (holding that settlor's will ineffective to revoke her trust).

[490] UTC §602(c)(2)(A) (available at <http://www.uniformlaws.org/Act.aspx?title=Trust%20 Code>). "A revocation in a will ordinarily becomes effective only upon probate of the will following the testator's death." UTC §602 cmt. Under the UTC, a residuary clause in a will disposing of the settlor's estate in a way that conflicts with the trust's dispositive provisions alone would be insufficient to revoke the trust. For a testamentary revocation to be effective, there would need to be some reference to the trust. UTC §602 cmt. *See also* UTC §602(c) (each providing for the revocation of a revocable trust by a later will). *See generally* §8.26 of this handbook (why trustees need to know about will residue clauses).

[491] 5 Scott & Ascher §35.1.2 n.19 and accompanying text.

[492] 5 Scott & Ascher §35.1.2.

[493] 5 Scott & Ascher §35.1.2.

[494] *See, e.g.,* Estate of Noell v. Norwest Bank, 960 P.2d 499 (Wyo. 1998) (delivery of letter of revocation by fax).

instrument of revocation by the settlor and its receipt by the trustee.[495] Litigation thrives on ambiguous situations and language. As to language, "I hereby revoke" is obviously preferable to "I hereby intend to revoke," which could be construed as words of futurity.

The Code provides that a trustee who does not know that a trust has been revoked is not liable to the settlor or the settlor's successors in interest for distributions made and other actions taken on the assumption that the trust had not been revoked.[496] The Restatement (Third) of Trusts is generally in accord,[497] as is the Restatement (Third) of Property.[498]

The settlor grants a power of attorney and in so doing amends the terms of his amendable/revocable inter vivos trust. Whether an agent acting under a durable power of attorney may impress a trust on the principal's property for the benefit of the principal is taken up in Section 3.4.1 of this handbook. Whether the agent could effectively amend/revoke a trust that had already been settled by the principal, assuming a right to amend/revoke had been reserved, is taken up immediately below. But first, is it possible for the power of attorney instrument itself to double as an amendment to the trust? One court has so held.[499]

Whether an agent of the settlor may exercise a reserved right to amend or revoke.. A legally incapacitated settlor cannot exercise a reserved right of amendment or revocation.[500] May, however, the settlor's agent, acting under a durable power of attorney,[501] exercise it? In theory, yes, provided three conditions are met: (1) the applicable durable power of attorney statute authorizes such an agency, (2) the durable power of attorney under which the agent purports to act is either sufficiently broad or sufficiently precise to cover the purported act of amendment or revocation,[502] and (3) the governing trust instrument itself contains a provision that authorizes amendment or revocation by proxy.[503] Under the

---

[495] *See, e.g.,* Estate of Noell v. Norwest Bank, 960 P.2d 499 (Wyo. 1998) (delivery of letter of revocation by fax).

[496] UTC §602(g) (available at <http://www.uniformlaws.org/Act.aspx?title=Trust%20 Code>).

[497] Restatement (Third) of Trusts §63 cmt. h.

[498] Restatement (Third) of Property (Wills and Other Donative Transfers) §7.2 cmt. e.

[499] In Strange v. Towns, No. A14A0983, 2015 WL 895236 (Ga. Ct. App. Mar. 4, 2015), the court held that the settlor of an inter vivos trust that was subject to a reserved right to amend/ revoke had effectively amended the trust's terms in granting a particular durable power of attorney to her son. The facts of the case were unusual and somewhat murky.

[500] *See generally* 5 Scott & Ascher §35.1; 4 Scott on Trusts §330 n.7 and accompanying text. *But see* Florida Nat'l Bank of Palm Beach v. Geneva, 460 So. 2d 895 (Fla. 1985).

[501] UPC §5-501. *See also* §9.9.2 of this handbook (agency arrangements) (discussing the differences between a trust and an agency).

[502] *Cf.* Perosi v. LiGreci, 918 N.Y.S.2d 294 (Sup. Ct. 2011) (though the settlor of an "irrevocable" trust possessed the statutory right to revoke or amend the trust with the consent of all of the beneficiaries, his agent could not have exercised that right on the settlor's behalf as there was no provision in the governing power of attorney instrument expressly granting the agent the authority to exercise that statutory right).

[503] *See, e.g.,* Matter of Goetz, 793 N.Y.S.2d 318 (Surr. Ct. 2005); Muller v. Bank of Am., 12 P.3d 899 (Kan. Ct. App. 2000); In re Guardianship of Lee, 1999 Okla. Civ. App. 50, 982 P.2d 539 (1999) (each holding that the holder of general durable power of attorney of settlor could not amend or revoke settlor's revocable trust as the right to amend or revoke was reserved to the settlor

Restatement (Third) of Trusts, only conditions (1) and (2) or (1) and (3) need be satisfied.[504] The trustee honors at his peril a revocation executed by an agent, unless all three conditions have been met. So also in the case of an amendment by proxy.[505] This is, of course, subject to there being a case or statute on point suggesting otherwise.[506]

There are now statutes on the books in some jurisdictions subjecting to liability one who, without reasonable cause, fails to honor the instructions of an agent acting under a durable power of attorney. The trustee's lot is not an easy one. But it gets worse: The Restatement (Third) of Property (Wills and Other Donative Transfers) would arm the agent-fiduciary with a default "assumption" of authority to exercise a nonfiduciary general inter vivos power of appointment, such as a reserved right of revocation, but then impose *on the trustee* a duty to make a preliminary investigation of certain facts before honoring such an exercise. The trustee would have such a duty even if the trustee were to lack actual or constructive notice of any wrongdoing on the part of the third-party agent-fiduciary. Here is the actual wording:

> Unless the donor has manifested a contrary intent, it is assumed that the donor intends that the . . . agent under the authority of a durable power of attorney of the incapacitated donee of a presently exercisable general power is to be permitted to exercise the power for the benefit of the donee to the same extent the . . . agent could make an effective transfer of similar owned property for the benefit of the donee.[507]

To paraphrase, the trustee, before honoring such an exercise, would not only need to assure himself of the agent-fiduciary's general authority, but also that the purported proxy power-exercise is sufficiently for the benefit of the donee of the power and that the agent-fiduciary would have the specific authority to make an effective transfer of "similar owned property" for the benefit of the

---

personally, neither the trust nor the power of attorney having expressly authorized amendment or revocation by agents of the settlor). *See also* Kline v. Utah Dep't of Health, 776 P.2d 57 (Utah 1989); Cal. Prob. Code §15401(c) (Deering 1999) (providing that authority to revoke a trust by proxy must be in both instruments: the trust and the power of attorney). In Colorado, by statute, an agent of the settlor may revoke a trust under which the settlor has reserved a right of revocation, provided specific reference is made to the trust in the agency agreement. Colo. Rev. Stat. §15-14-608(2) (1998). Is not a written power of attorney making express reference to an amendable trust for all intents and purposes also a trust amendment? *Cf.* UTC §602(e) (available at <http://www.uniformlaws.org/Act.aspx?title=Trust%20 Code>) (providing that a settlor's powers with respect to revocation, amendment, or distribution of trust property may be exercised by an agent under a power of attorney only to the extent expressly authorized by the terms of the trust or the power); UTC §411(a) (providing that a settlor's power to consent to the termination of a noncharitable irrevocable trust may be exercised by an agent under a power of attorney only to the extent expressly authorized by the power of attorney or the terms of the trust).

[504] Restatement (Third) of Trusts §63 cmt. l.

[505] *See, e.g.,* Gurfinkel v. Josi, 972 So. 2d 927 (Fla. App. 3 Dist. 2007).

[506] *See, e.g.,* 5 Scott & Ascher §35.1 n.20 (catalog of citations to cases and statutes that pertaining to the revoking of trusts by proxy).

[507] Restatement (Third) of Property (Wills and Other Donative Transfers) §19.8 cmt. d.

donee. The concept of "similar owned property" presumably refers to property owned outright *by the principal*, although the Reporter's Notes are silent on the subject, as they are on the subject of how directly the donee needs to be benefited for the proxy exercise to be effective. This is all default law. Presumably the scrivener of a power-of-appointment grant is free to specify in the terms of the grant that the trustee may reasonably rely on the affidavit of the agent of the donee as to the agent's authority to exercise the power on behalf of the donee, and that the trustee shall be held harmless if he does so to the detriment of the donee.

Whether the settlor's guardian or conservator may exercise, or have a duty to exercise, a reserved right of revocation. Close attention to matters of authority is warranted as well if the trustee is in receipt of an instrument of revocation submitted by the settlor's conservator or guardian,[508] a right of revocation generally being considered a personal right.[509] A guardian or conservator of the settlor of a revocable trust may not exercise the settlor's right of revocation unless granted such authority in a statute and in the governing instrument.[510] Not all jurisdictions are in accord.[511] In Ohio, the guardian may exercise the ward's right of revocation with court approval.[512] In Connecticut, the conservator's inventory shall include the value of the ward's interest in all property in which the ward has an "equitable present interest."[513] "Increasingly, there is authority relating to whether the guardian of a settlor who is under an incapacity . . . may exercise the settlor's power to revoke a trust."[514]

As between the trustee and those expressly authorized to exercise the settlor's power to revoke or amend, *e.g.*, the settlor's conservator, guardian, or agent acting under a durable power of attorney, the Restatement (Third) of Trusts offers some general guidance as to who should be responsible for what: "In short, conservatorship action (or action by an agent who is expressly authorized to exercise the settlor's power to revoke or amend) may be appropriate to substitute for the judgment an incapacitated *settlor* can no longer exercise when need appears—for example, to compensate for short-comings in the planning of the trust or to make necessary or desirable gifts from the trust; but conservatorship or agency action exercising a settlor's power would normally not be appropriate to substitute for (*i.e.*, to interfere with) the judgments the *trustee* was expected and adequately empowered to make."[515]

Suppose the governing trust instrument contains a revocation provision that *excludes* revocation by proxy. Would such a qualified revocation provision effectively foreclose revocation by the settlor's conservator or guardian? Why

---

[508] *See, e.g.*, In re Bo, 365 N.W.2d 847 (N.D. 1985).

[509] Restatement (Third) of Trusts §74, Reporter's Notes (Comments *a*(2) and *e*).

[510] Bogert §1000.

[511] *See, e.g.*, In re Rudwick, 2002 WL 31730757 (Va. Cir. Ct.) (the settlor's court-appointed conservator allowed to exercise the settlor's reserved right of revocation though the governing instrument made no provision for revocation by proxy).

[512] *See* Friedrich v. BancOhio Nat'l Bank, 14 Ohio App. 3d 247, 470 N.E.2d 467 (1984).

[513] Conn. Stat. §45a-655(a).

[514] *See* 5 Scott & Ascher §35.1 n.20 (Catalog of Statutes and Cases).

[515] Restatement (Third) of Trusts §74 cmt. a(2).

not?[516] Presumably, it is the intention of the settlor that during periods of incapacity the trust be irrevocable and that the revocation provision be suspended so that there is no basis of authority on which the conservator or guardian can act.[517] To the extent the conservator or guardian is foreclosed from terminating an irrevocable trust created before incapacity, so too should it be foreclosed from terminating a trust where the power of revocation is suspended.

If a settlor's guardian or conservator has either a general or default fiduciary duty to attempt to obtain a court order transferring the ward's entrusted property into the guardianship or conservatorship estate, a duty that is incident to the duty to take control of all the ward's property, including the equitable interests, then things can get expensive. Under the Uniform Trust Code, the settlor's conservator or guardian could exercise a settlor's power of revocation upon approval of the court supervising the conservatorship.[518] However, "[b]ecause a settlor often creates a revocable trust for the very purpose of avoiding conservatorship, this power should be exercised by the court reluctantly."[519] Thus, the court should only override an express restriction if it concludes that the action furthers the interests of justice.[520] The Restatement (Third) of Trusts provides that "unless the trust terms provide otherwise, the settlor's power to revoke or amend a revocable trust may be exercised by a conservator, guardian, or other legal representative if and to the extent authorized by the appropriate court."[521]

---

[516] *See, e.g.,* Smith v. Department of Health, 895 So. 2d 735, 39, 368 (La. Ct. App. 2005) (suggesting that the rule at common law is that a guardian of an incompetent person does not have a power to revoke a trust created by the ward while he or she was competent under which the ward had reserved a right of revocation, even when there is no express prohibition against revocation by the guardian, the right to revoke being nontransferable and personal to the settlor).

[517] "Where the settlor reserves a power to revoke the trust under certain circumstances, he can revoke it only under those circumstances." 4 Scott on Trusts §330.8. *See, e.g.,* In re Guardianship of Lee, 1999 Okla. Civ. App. 50, 982 P.2d 539 (1999) (denying settlor's guardian access to assets of revocable trust, the settlor having expressly reserved only to herself the right to revoke and having made no mention of revocation by proxy). *But see* Johnson v. Kotyck, 76 Cal. App. 4th 83, 90 Cal. Rptr. 2d 99 (1999) (trust instrument being silent on the issue of conservator access to trust assets, the conservator of settlor of revocable trust allowed to revoke trust instead of settlor); UTC §602(f) (available at <http://www.uniformlaws.org/Act.aspx?title=Trust%20Code>) (apparently providing that conservator or guardian of incapacitated settlor of revocable trust may with court approval revoke trust in stead of settlor). *Cf.* UTC §411(a) (providing that a settlor's power to consent to the termination of a noncharitable irrevocable trust may be exercised by the settlor's conservator with the approval of the court supervising the conservatorship if an agent is not so authorized, or by the settlor's guardian with the approval of the court supervising the guardianship if an agent is not so authorized and a conservator has not been appointed).

[518] UTC §602(f) (available at <http://www.uniformlaws.org/Act.aspx?title=Trust%20Code>).

[519] UTC §602 cmt. (available at <http://www.uniformlaws.org/Act.aspx?title=Trust%20Code>).

[520] UTC §602 cmt. (available at <http://www.uniformlaws.org/Act.aspx?title=Trust%20Code>).

[521] Restatement (Third) of Trusts §63 cmt. l.

The Restatement (Third) of Property (Wills and Other Donative Transfers) would arm the legal representative of a donee of a nonfiduciary general inter vivos power of appointment, such as a reserved right of revocation, with a default "assumption" of authority to exercise the power by proxy, but then impose *on the trustee* a duty to make a preliminary investigation of certain facts before honoring such an exercise. The trustee would have such a duty even if the trustee were to lack actual or constructive notice of any wrongdoing on the part of the legal representative.

Here is the actual wording:

> Unless the donor has manifested a contrary intent, it is assumed that the donor intends that the legal representative . . . of the incapacitated donee of a presently exercisable general power is to be permitted to exercise the power for the benefit of the donee to the same extent the legal representative . . . could make an effective transfer of similar owned property for the benefit of the donee.[522]

To paraphrase, the trustee before honoring such an exercise would not only need to assure himself of the legal representative's general authority, but also that the purported proxy power-exercise is sufficiently for the benefit of the donee of the power and that the legal representative would have the specific authority to make an effective transfer of "similar owned property" for the benefit of the donee. So also if the trustee is in receipt of an instrument of proxy exercise submitted by the legal representative of a minor donee.[523]

The concept of "similar owned property" presumably refers to property owned outright *by the donee*, although the Reporter's Notes are silent on the subject, as they are on the subject of how directly the donee needs to be benefited for the proxy exercise to be effective. The judicial complaint for instructions or declaratory judgment is tailor-made for protecting the trustee in the face of such factual and legal uncertainties, a topic we take up in Section 8.42 of this handbook.[524]

Revocation occasioned by undue influence. In Florida, a competent settlor of a revocable trust, though subject to undue influence, apparently may effectively revoke the trust:

> The courts have no place in trying to save persons such as Mrs. Genova, the otherwise competent settlor of a revocable trust, from what may or may not be her own imprudence with her assets. When she created this trust, she provided a means to save herself from her own incompetence, and the courts can and should zealously protect her from her own mental in-capacity. However, when she created

---

[522] Restatement (Third) of Property (Wills and Other Donative Transfers) §19.8 cmt. d.

[523] Restatement (Third) of Property (Wills and Other Donative Transfers) §19.8 cmt. e. "A purported inter vivos exercise of a presently exercisable power by a minor is subject to ratification or disaffirmance by the minor when the minor becomes of age, as with a purported transfer by the minor of owned property." *Id.* An effective proxy exercise would negate these rights of ratification and disaffirmance.

[524] *See* Restatement (Third) of Property (Wills and Other Donative Transfers) §19.8 cmt. f ("A court may have jurisdiction apart from the donative document to authorize a legal representative to exercise the incapacitated donee's power.").

this trust, she also reserved the absolute right to revoke if she were not incompetent. In order for this to remain a desirable feature of the trust instrument, the right to revoke should be absolute.[525]

We leave to the reader to contemplate the public policy implications of the *Genova* holding, which is probably an aberration. The dissent suggested that the settlor's act was "not the exercise of *her* right to revoke, but rather was the will of another foisted on her."[526]

A revocable trust with multiple settlors. What if a revocable trust is created or funded by more than one settlor?[527] To the extent the trust consists of community property, the trust may be revoked by either spouse acting alone but may be amended only by joint action of both spouses.[528] To the extent the trust consists of property other than community property, each settlor may revoke or amend the trust with regard to the portion of the trust property attributable to that settlor's contribution.[529] Upon the revocation or amendment of the trust by less than all of the settlors, the trustee must notify the other settlors of the revocation or amendment.[530] In the case of a revocable trust created by a husband and wife in a common law jurisdiction, there is some default law to the effect that upon the death of the first spouse to die, the survivor's power of revocation over even *the survivor's* allocable portion of the trust estate dies as well.[531]

When revocation is subject to third-party consent. If a settlor may revoke the trust only with the consent of a third party, the third party may not act in bad faith or from an improper motive in granting or withholding consent.[532] If the trustee holds the power of consent, it is likely that he holds it in a fiduciary capacity.[533]

When the holder of a reserved right to revoke a trust dies: quasi-probating the will substitute. A trust under which the settlor has reserved a right of revocation is a type of will substitute. Thus, it is not surprising that the trend of the default law is in the direction of treating, at least for certain purposes, the settlor as if he or she were a testator/testatrix and the subject property as if it were probate property once the settlor dies, this even though title to the trust property does

---

[525] Florida Nat'l Bank of Palm Beach Cnty. v. Genova, 460 So. 2d 895, 898 (Fla. Sup. Ct. 1984).

[526] Florida Nat'l Bank of Palm Beach Cnty. v. Genova, 460 So. 2d 895, 898 (1984).

[527] *See, e.g.,* §9.25 of this handbook (the joint trust).

[528] Restatement (Third) of Trusts §63 cmt. k; UTC §602(b)(1) (available at <http://www.uniformlaws.org/Act.aspx?title=Trust%20Code>).

[529] 5 Scott & Ascher §35.1.10 (Trust with Multiple Settlors); Restatement (Third) of Trusts §63 cmt. k.; UTC §602(b)(2) (available at <http://www.uniformlaws.org/Act.aspx?title=Trust%20 Code>). The Code, however, does not address how a trustee calculates a settlor's pro rata contribution of interests held jointly or as tenancies by the entirety.

[530] UTC §602(b)(3) (available at <http://www.uniformlaws.org/Act.aspx?title=Trust%20 Code>).

[531] 5 Scott & Ascher §35.1.10 (Trust with Multiple Settlors). *See also* §9.25 of this handbook (the joint trust).

[532] Restatement (Third) of Trusts §63 cmt. j.

[533] Restatement (Third) of Trusts §63 cmt. j.

not transfer to the deceased settlor's executor/executrix, administrator/administratrix, or personal representative, as the case may be. These purposes include the following:

- Satisfaction of claims against the probate estate, to include certain statutory allowances;[534]
- Application of the 120-hour requirement;[535]
- Application of the harmless-error rule;[536]
- Revocation or amendment by a subsequent will;[537]
- Revocation by marriage;[538]
- Ademption by extinction;[539]
- Antilapse;[540]
- Invalidity due to incapacity or wrongdoing;[541]
- Application of construction, reformation, and modification doctrines generally;[542]
- Application of rules of construction governing class gifts specifically;[543] and

---

[534] Restatement (Third) of Property (Wills and Other Donative Transfers) §7.2 cmt. b. *See generally* §§5.3.3.1(b) of this handbook (the postmortem creditor), 5.3.4.1 of this handbook (spousal rights in common law states) and 8.9.1 of this handbook (the federal estate tax).

[535] Restatement (Third) of Property (Wills and Other Donative Transfers) §7.2 cmt. c: "The original Uniform Probate Code [§2-601] introduced a rule of construction that devisees must survive the decedent by 120 hours or more, but the terms of the statute applied only to transfers by will . . . The Revised Uniform Simultaneous Death Act and the Revised Uniform Probate Code expanded the 120-hour requirement of survival to all donative documents (wills and inter vivos donative documents, including will substitutes) that require the donee to survive the donor." *See generally* §8.15.56 of this handbook (120-hour survival requirement [the trust application]).

[536] Restatement (Third) of Property (Wills and Other Donative Transfers) §7.2 cmt. d. The harmless-error rule applicable to wills is as follows: "A harmless error in executing a will may be excused if the proponent establishes by clear and convincing evidence that the decedent adopted the document as his or her will." Restatement (Third) of Property (Wills and Other Donative Transfers) §3.3. *See generally* §8.15.53 of this handbook (harmless-error rule [the trust application]).

[537] Restatement (Third) of Property (Wills and Other Donative Transfers) §7.2 cmt. e. *See also* the text of §8.2.2.2 of this handbook (the revocable trust).

[538] Restatement (Third) of Property (Wills and Other Donative Transfers) §7.2 cmt. f. *See generally* §5.3.4.1 of this handbook (spousal rights in common law states) (rights of spouses of trust beneficiaries [divorce and separation]); UPC §2-804 (revocation of non probate transfers by divorce); *see also* Restatement (Third) of Property (Wills and Other Donative Transfers) §4.1 cmt. p (application to will substitutes).

[539] Restatement (Third) of Property (Wills and Other Donative Transfers) §7.2 cmt. f. *See generally* §8.15.54 of this handbook (ademption by extinction [the trust application]).

[540] Restatement (Third) of Property (Wills and Other Donative Transfers) §7.2 cmt. f. *See also* §8.11 of this handbook (what are the duties of the trustee of a revocable inter vivos trust?) (in part discussing the concept of antilapse in the trust context). *See generally* §8.15.55 of this handbook (antilapse [the trust application]).

[541] Restatement (Third) of Property (Wills and Other Donative Transfers) §7.2 cmt. g.

[542] Restatement (Third) of Property (Wills and Other Donative Transfers) §7.2 cmt. h.

[543] Restatement (Third) of Property (Wills and Other Donative Transfers) §7.2 cmt. i. *See generally* §5.2 of this handbook (class designation: "children," "issue," "heirs," and "relatives" (some rules of construction)).

- Application of social restrictions on freedom of disposition.[544]

For a thorough discussion of the applicability of certain rules governing testamentary dispositions to self-settled revocable trusts, the reader is referred to Section 7.2 of the Restatement (Third) of Property (Wills and Donative Transfers), particularly the accompanying commentary and Reporter's Notes. "These rules . . . [also] . . . inform the federal common law of will substitutes under the Employee Retirement Income Security Act (ERISA). . . ."[545]

Termination or modification by beneficiary; nonsettlor holder (donee) of a presently exercisable inter vivos power of appointment. The terms of a trust may bestow on its beneficiaries a power to terminate it or modify its terms.[546] The presumption is that the power is held in a nonfiduciary capacity.[547] There is an opposite presumption when the power is in the trustee.[548]

With the possible exception of creditor access to the subject property,[549] the default law treats the nonsettlor holder of a general inter vivos power of appointment (or its equivalent, *e.g.*, a right to demand principal) pretty much as it does a trust under which the settlor has reserved a right of revocation.[550] Like the settlor, the holder has the equivalent of an ownership interest in the portion[551] or all of the property that is the subject of the power. Like the settlor, the holder has the power to extinguish the rights of the other beneficiaries.[552] While the holder is of full age and has mental capacity, the exercise of such a power also will trump any coexisting discretionary authority in the trustee to make distributions to the holder, or anyone else for that matter.[553]

There are some differences, however. The trustee, for example, has a duty to apprise the other beneficiaries of the existence and nature of the power in the nonsettlor and to furnish them with accountings and reports until such time as the holder instructs otherwise.[554] The holder, of course, needs to be legally competent to issue such an instruction. In the event of the donee's incapacity, the other beneficiaries' right to trust accountings and reports revives.[555]

If the general inter vivos power, on the other hand, is only exercisable with the consent of the trustee, another beneficiary, or a third party not beneficially

---

[544] Restatement (Third) of Property (Wills and Other Donative Transfers) §7.2 cmt. j.

[545] Restatement (Third) of Property (Wills and Other Donative Transfers) §7.2 cmt. k.

[546] 5 Scott & Ascher §33.1.2 (Termination or Modification by Beneficiary).

[547] 5 Scott & Ascher §33.1.2 (Termination or Modification by Beneficiary).

[548] 5 Scott & Ascher §33.1.1 (Termination or Modification by Trustee).

[549] *See* §5.3.3 of this handbook (rights of beneficiary's creditors and others to trust property) (discussing in part powers of appointment and creditor accessibility).

[550] Restatement (Third) of Trusts §74 cmt. g.

[551] Restatement (Third) of Trusts §74 cmt. h.

[552] Restatement (Third) of Trusts §74 cmt. g.

[553] *See, e.g.*, Fleck-Rubin v. Fleck, 2006 WL 1300609 (Fla. Ct. App. 2006).

[554] Restatement (Third) of Trusts §74 cmt. g. "This is because the donee, unlike the settlor of a revocable trust, is not the source of the beneficiaries' rights, and the beneficiaries are entitled to know of the donee's actions and to know of and verify the donee's authority over the trust." Restatement (Third) of Trusts §74 cmt. g.

[555] Restatement (Third) of Trusts §74 cmt. g.

interested, then the interests of the other beneficiaries are less easily subverted by the holder.[556] This is because the holder's power then would not be the equivalent of ownership. A single-holder general inter vivos power of appointment subject to another's consent is not to be confused with a jointly held general inter vivos power of appointment (or power of withdrawal), which can only be exercised by all holders acting in concert. The joint power is a property equivalent that belongs to the holders collectively. It would enable them, acting in concert, to issue binding instructions to the trustee, to include instructions that if carried out could have the effect of subverting the interests of the other beneficiaries.[557]

Whether a third person holds in a fiduciary rather than personal capacity an express power to terminate or modify the trust will ultimately depend on the terms of the trust.[558] If, in the event of its exercise, the subject property passes or must pass to someone other than the third person, then the status of the third person may well be that of a fiduciary,[559] and quite possibly that of a trust protector.[560] If, on the other hand, the third person may exercise the power in his or her own favor, then chances are we have a nonfiduciary general inter vivos power of appointment.[561] The holder of a personal nonfiduciary limited/special inter vivos power of appointment over the entire corpus of a trust generally may revoke the trust by exercising the power, and do so without regard to fiduciary considerations.[562] There is an important caveat: The terminating exercise cannot be a fraud on the power.[563]

Termination by trustee or protector. The terms of a trust may bestow on the trustee a discretionary power to invade principal to or for the benefit of the beneficiary or beneficiaries. A trust with such a provision is known as a discretionary trust, a topic we cover in Section 3.5.3.2(a) of this handbook. Unless the terms provide otherwise, the power is held in a fiduciary capacity and must be exercised accordingly.[564] So also with an express discretionary power in the trustee to terminate the trust and revest the underlying property in the settlor.[565] Whether the trustee may "invade the principal down to zero" and in

---

[556] Restatement (Third) of Trusts §74 cmt. g(1).

[557] Restatement (Third) of Trusts §74 cmt. g.

[558] *See generally* 5 Scott & Ascher §33.1.3 (Termination or Modification by Third Person).

[559] *See generally* 5 Scott & Ascher §33.1.3 (Termination or Modification by Third Person).

[560] *See generally* §3.2.6 of this handbook (in part discussing the rights, duties, and obligations of a trust protector). *See also* 5 Scott & Ascher §33.1.3, n.1.

[561] *See generally* §8.1.1 of this handbook (powers of appointment).

[562] *See generally* §8.1.1 of this handbook (powers of appointment); *but see* 5 Scott & Ascher §33.1.2 (suggesting that even if a beneficiary holds a nonfiduciary power, there may be situations in which there is a duty not to exercise it in a manner that is "unnecessarily harmful or unfair to other beneficiaries" and finding support for the proposition in Restatement (Third) of Trusts §64 cmt. c).

[563] *See generally* §8.15.26 of this handbook (fraud on a power doctrine).

[564] *See generally* 5 Scott & Ascher 33.1.1 (Termination or Modification by Trustee); §3.5.3.2(a) of this handbook (the discretionary trust).

[565] 5 Scott & Ascher §33.1.1.

so doing effect its termination will depend upon the terms of the trust.[566] Thus, if the trustee has been given a personal nonfiduciary inter vivos power of appointment,[567] then the trustee may effect the trust's termination through the exercise of the power unencumbered by fiduciary constraints, provided the exercise would not constitute some kind of a fraud on the power.[568] Whether a trust protector with a direct or indirect discretionary power to terminate a trust is subject to trustee-like fiduciary constraints is discussed in Section 3.2.6 of this handbook.

The Restatement (Third) of Property would inject some quasi-capture doctrine into the law applicable to expired general powers of appointment. If the holder of a general inter vivos power of appointment dies without having effectively exercised the power, the power expires.[569] Likewise, if the holder of a general testamentary power of appointment fails to effectively exercise the power by will, the power expires at the holder's death. In either case, the gift-in-default clause in the granting instrument, if there is such a clause, controls the disposition of the unappointed property.[570] (So also if a power expires by inter vivos disclaimer or release.[571]) The time when a power expires "is almost invariably the death of the donee,"[572] although one could certainly fashion a grant of a general power that would be capable of expiring before its donee had, such as upon the exhaustion of an intervening equitable estate *pur autre vie*. The concept of the estate *pur autre vie* is discussed generally in Section 8.15.64 of this handbook.

The Restatement (Third) of Property speaks in terms of a general power "lapsing," an unfortunate innovation.[573] Its predecessors spoke in terms of a power "expiring,"[574] which is less ambiguous in that the term lapse can mean "to pass to another through neglect or omission."[575] As we note in Section 8.1.1 of this handbook, a power of appointment itself is never directly transmissible.

But what if the donor of an expired power had neglected in the granting instrument to provide for takers-in-default, or the instrument's gift-in-default clause was ineffective when the power expired? In that case the unappointed property passes upon a resulting trust back to the donor if the donor is then living, or into the probate estate of the donor if the donor is not then living, but,

---

[566] 5 Scott & Ascher §33.1.1.

[567] *See generally* §8.1 of this handbook (powers of appointment).

[568] *See generally* §8.15.26 of this handbook (fraud on a power doctrine).

[569] As we note in Section 8.1.1 of this handbook, a power of appointment is exercisable; it is never directly transferable.

[570] Restatement (Third) of Property (Wills and Other Donative Transfers) §19.22(a).

[571] Restatement (Third) of Property (Wills and Other Donative Transfers) §19.22(a).

[572] Restatement (First) of Property §367 cmt. d.

[573] *See* Restatement (Third) of Property (Wills and Other Donative Transfers) §19.22 (term lapse employed even in the section's title).

[574] *See, e.g.,* Restatement (First) of Property §367 cmt. d.

[575] The American Heritage Dictionary 1014 (3d ed. 1996).

again, not until all valid intervening equitable interests have themselves expired.[576] Resulting trusts are covered generally in Section 4.1.1.1 of this handbook. *In a radical departure from settled doctrine, the Restatement (Third) of Property provides that if the donee "merely failed to exercise the power" the unappointed property is captured by the donee or the donee's estate.*[577] A resulting trust, however, would still be imposed in the case of expiration by disclaimer or release,[578] or upon the expiration by any means of a power of revocation, amendment, or withdrawal.[579] Again, as we did in more detail in our discussion of ineffective exercises of general powers in Section 8.15.12 of this handbook, we question the logic of treating a power of "revocation, amendment, or withdrawal" differently from other "types" of general inter vivos power of appointment, whether for capture purposes generally or for any other purpose. A resulting trust also would be imposed if the donee "expressly refrained from exercising the power."[580] Of course, this discussion is entirely academic if the donor is also the donee of the expired general power. The unappointed property would then end up in the probate estate of the donee in any case, whether by imposition of a resulting trust under traditional doctrine or by quasi-capture.

The Restatement (Third) of Property exhibits a curious and tenacious aversion to invoking applicable resulting trust doctrine,[581] particularly in the sections devoted to unexercised or ineffectively exercised general powers of appointment. The result is an unhelpful dearth of context, particularly when it comes to following chains of title, as well as a fair amount of general incoherence. Take, for example, Section 19.22(b), which in part reads: " . . . but if the donee released the power or expressly refrained from exercising the power, the unappointed property passes under a reversionary interest to the donor or to the donor's transferees or successors in interest." The phrase "passes under a reversionary interest" is nonsensical in the trust context. What actually happens is that the legal title to the unappointed property passes from the trustee to the donor or his personal representative upon a resulting trust such that the equitable reversion, which had vested *ab initio*, becomes possessory. Nothing is passing from the trustee under, over, or in a reversionary interest.

We also quibble with the failure of all of the Restatements to expressly confirm that in the face of an expired power of appointment, title to property unappointed does not leave the hands of the trustee until such time as all valid intervening equitable estates have themselves expired, unless the terms of the trust so provide. An intervening equitable estate typically would be an equitable life estate.[582]

---

[576] *See, e.g.*, Restatement (First) of Property §367(1).

[577] Restatement (Third) of Property (Wills and Other Donative Transfers) §19.22(b).

[578] Restatement (Third) of Property (Wills and Other Donative Transfers) §19.22(b).

[579] Restatement (Third) of Property (Wills and Other Donative Transfers) §19.22 cmt. f.

[580] Restatement (Third) of Property (Wills and Other Donative Transfers) §19.22(b).

[581] *See, e.g.*, Restatement (Third) of Property (Wills and Other Donative Transfers) §25.2 (although the title to the sections is *Reversion or Remainder*, the resulting trust is mentioned once, and only in passing).

[582] *See generally* §8.27 of this handbook (the equitable life estate).

§8.2.3   *Termination and Distribution Issues*

Upon the occurrence of an event terminating or partially terminating a trust, the trustee shall proceed expeditiously to distribute the trust property to the persons entitled to it, subject to the right of the trustee to retain a reasonable reserve for the payment of debts, expenses, and taxes.[583]

Termination and distribution. *A trustee of a terminated trust has continuing fiduciary responsibilities.* The trustee's responsibilities include "applying or distributing trust income and principal during the administration of the trust and upon its termination."[584] The job of the trustee is not finished on the date the trust terminates,[585] nor is necessarily the court's.[586] It is not until the trustee is done "winding up" the trust's administration, to include making distribution "in a manner consistent with the purposes of the trust and the interests of the beneficiaries," is the trustee relieved of fiduciary duties.[587] Upon termination, for example, the trustee may have to delay distribution until such time as the legitimate expenses of the trust have been paid,[588] or until certain tax or asset liquidity issues have been resolved.[589] "Although the termination date has arrived, the trustee cannot be compelled to transfer the trust property to the appropriate beneficiaries until the trustee is paid or adequately secured for any compensation to which the trustee is entitled, as well as for any expenses properly incurred."[590] The subject of the posttermination "administrative trust" is covered in Section 9.9.14 of this handbook.

The terminated self-settled trust. In the case of a self-settled revocable trust that terminates upon the death of the settlor, the trustee will need to assure himself that the trust was not amended, or even revoked, during the settlor's lifetime.[591] "Or the trust assets may be subject, under applicable law, to payment

---

[583] UTC §817(b) (available at <http://www.uniformlaws.org/Act.aspx?title=Trust%20 Code>).

[584] Restatement (Third) of Trusts §76(2)(d). *See generally* 5 Scott & Ascher §36.2 (Duty of Trustee to Transfer Title or Possession on Termination of Trust).

[585] Termination date means "the time at which it becomes the duty of the trustee to wind up administration of the trust." Restatement (Third) of Trusts §89 cmt. a. "This time ordinarily arrives at the expiration of the period for which the trust was created, not at the time when distribution is actually accomplished." Restatement (Third) of Trusts §89 cmt. a. *See generally* 5 Scott & Ascher §36.1 (Powers and Duties of Trustee on Termination of Trust).

[586] Up until final distribution—and sometimes thereafter—"the court retains jurisdiction, when called upon, to settle accounts and to resolve issues regarding trust management and distribution." Restatement (Third) of Trusts §89 cmt. b.

[587] Restatement (Third) of Trusts §89. *See generally* 5 Scott & Ascher §§36.1 (Powers and Duties of Trustee on Termination of Trust), and 36.2.1 (Delay in Making Conveyance).

[588] Lewin ¶ 24-02 (England); 5 Scott & Ascher §36.2.1 (Delay in Making Conveyance) (U.S.).

[589] *See generally* Restatement (Third) of Trusts, §89 cmt. b; 5 Scott & Ascher §36.2.1 (Delay in Making Conveyance).The importance of ascertaining and communicating the tax basis/cost of an in-kind trust distribution is covered in §§11.1 and 11.4 of this handbook.

[590] 5 Scott & Ascher §36.2.2 (Trustee's Lien). *See generally* §3.5.2.3 of this handbook (trustee's right in equity to exoneration and reimbursement).

[591] 4 Scott & Ascher §24.31.1 (Liability for Distributions Under Invalid, Amended, Revoked, or Ineffective Instruments).

of a spouse's elective share, family allowances, the expenses of administering the settlor's estate, or the claims of the settlor's creditors."[592] A trustee who does not come to grips with these "complications" runs the risk of misdelivery, particularly if he knew or should have known about them.[593] Even inter vivos distributions to an incompetent settlor can become problematic postmortem.[594] Having said that, one who has been unjustly enriched by a misdelivery is obliged to indemnify the trustee, or otherwise make restitution.[595]

Until a trust asset is distributed, title to the asset is likely to remain in the trustee. As a general rule, legal title to the underlying trust property of a trust that has terminated will remain lodged in the trustee until the trustee formally conveys it out to the remaindermen. "Even if it is technically unnecessary for the trustee to convey legal title to the appropriate beneficiaries, because title is already vested in them, the court may compel the trustee to execute a deed of conveyance, simply to ensure marketable title." Thus, even if at the time of a trust's termination legal title passes by operation of law in accordance with the statute of uses, a topic we cover in Section 8.15.1 of this handbook, a formal conveyance of title is probably a good idea, if only because formal instruction in the statute of uses, in the words of Professor Moynihan "perhaps the most important single statute in the long history of the land law,"[596] has not been a high priority in the law schools for quite some time now.[597] Also, in Section 2.1 of this handbook we note that in the rare case when the remaindermen have shared the legal title with the trustee, a formal conveyance of the underlying property upon termination of the trust might theoretically not be necessary.[598] For practical reasons, however, it would probably be advisable.

A vacancy in the office of trustee during the wind-up period. A trustee also retains all necessary fiduciary powers up until the wind-up process is completed.[599] The Restatement (Third) of Trusts is in accord.[600] In the event that for whatever

---

[592] 4 Scott & Ascher §24.31.1 (Liability for Distributions Under Invalid, Amended, Revoked, or Ineffective Instruments).

[593] 4 Scott & Ascher §24.31.1 (Liability for Distributions Under Invalid, Amended, Revoked, or Ineffective Instruments).

[594] 4 Scott & Ascher §24.31.1 (Liability for Distributions Under Invalid, Amended, Revoked, or Ineffective Instruments).

[595] Restatement of Restitution §163 ("Where the owner of property transfers it as a result of mistake of such a character that he is entitled to restitution, the transferee holds the property upon a constructive trust for him"). *See generally* §7.2.3.1.6 of this handbook (the constructive trust as a procedural equitable remedy); §8.15.78 of this handbook (unjust enrichment).

[596] Cornelius J. Moynihan, Introduction to the Law of Real Property 24 (2d ed.).

[597] *See generally* §8.25 of this handbook (few American law schools still require Agency, Trusts, and Equity).

[598] *See also* 5 Scott & Ascher §36.2 (Duty of Trustee to Transfer Title or Possession on Termination of Trust).

[599] "The period for winding up the trust is the period after the termination date and before trust administration ends by complete distribution of the trust estate." Restatement (Third) of Trusts §89 cmt. b. *See generally* 5 Scott & Ascher §36.1 (Powers and Duties of Trustee on Termination of Trust).

[600] Restatement (Third) of Trusts §89.

reason a vacancy occurs in the office of trustee during the wind-up period, a successor will be appointed either pursuant to the terms of the trust or by the court.[601]

A trustee's general wind-up responsibilities. The trustee's wind-up responsibilities include the following:

- Determining and satisfying trust obligations, including those to taxing authorities;[602]
- Ascertaining the proper distributees and their shares, and planning and making distribution accordingly;[603] and
- Preparing and submitting an accounting or report to the court or the beneficiaries.[604]

Misdelivery. The trustee who distributes the wrong amount or pays it to the wrong person must bear the loss.[605] "If the trustee conveys trust property to a person who is not entitled to it, the trustee is liable to the beneficiary even though he reasonably believes that the person to whom he conveys the property is the beneficiary or that the conveyance was authorized or directed by the beneficiary."[606] Thus, in one case a trustee was held personally liable for making a terminating distribution per capita to the settlor's children and grandchildren when the distribution should have been made *per stirpes* only to the children.[607] The trustee, of course, was entitled to bring an action against the grandchildren

---

[601] Restatement (Third) of Trusts §89 cmt. b.

[602] Restatement (Third) of Trusts §89 cmt. c. The importance of ascertaining and communicating the tax basis/cost of an in-kind trust distribution is covered in §§11.1 and 11.4 of this handbook.

[603] Restatement (Third) of Trusts §89 cmt. c. *See generally* 4 Scott & Ascher §24.31 (Liability for Incorrect Distributions); 5 Scott & Ascher §§36.2.1 (Delay in Making Conveyance), 36.2.3 (To Whom Trustee Should Convey). One who has been unjustly enriched by a misdelivery is obliged to indemnify the trustee, or otherwise make restitution. Restatement of Restitution §163 ("Where the owner of property transfers it as a result of mistake of such a character that he is entitled to restitution, the transferee holds the property upon a constructive trust for him"). *See generally* §7.2.3.1.6 of this handbook (the constructive trust as a procedural equitable remedy). The importance of ascertaining and communicating the tax basis/cost of an in-kind trust distribution is covered in §§11.1 and 11.4 of this handbook.

[604] Restatement (Third) of Trusts §89 cmt. c. The importance of ascertaining and communicating the tax basis/cost of an in-kind trust distribution is covered in §§11.1 and 11.4 of this handbook.

[605] Restatement (Second) of Trusts §§226, 345 cmt. j (1959). *See generally* 4 Scott & Ascher §24.31 (Liability for Incorrect Distributions); 5 Scott & Ascher §36.2.3 (To Whom Trustee Should Convey).

[606] Restatement (Second) of Trusts §345 cmt. j. *See also* Restatement (Second) of Trusts §226 (addressing the trustee's liability for payments or conveyances made to persons other than the beneficiary); 4 Scott & Ascher §24.31 (Liability for Incorrect Distributions); 5 Scott & Ascher §36.2.3 (To Whom Trustee Should Convey).

[607] Stowers v. Norwest Bank Ind., N.A., 624 N.E.2d 485 (Ind. 1993). For a discussion of the meaning of the terms *per capita* and *per stirpes, see* §5.2 of this handbook (class designations and rules of construction: "children," "issue," "heirs," and "relatives").

to attempt to recover the property that had been misdelivered.[608] One who has been unjustly enriched by a misdelivery is obliged to indemnify the trustee, or otherwise make restitution.[609]

In another case, the trustee was fraudulently induced to make distributions to the wife of the beneficiary.[610] In this case, the trustee managed to dodge the bullet, because the wife, before absconding with the funds, had deposited them in a joint account in her name and that of the beneficiary.

Administering a trust provision that on its face may be invalid is particularly risky.[611] The topic of how a trustee should construe certain trust-related dispositive terms and phrases is covered in Section 5.2 of this handbook. If the trustee reads it carefully, he should be in a position to spot and avoid the more common misdelivery traps, such as the one mentioned above. And as we have noted throughout this handbook, the trustee is entitled to seek instructions from the court at "trust" expense when there is reasonable doubt as to the meaning of a trust term, or as to the very validity of the trust itself.[612]

When a terminated trust is treated as a quasi-probate estate. To further complicate the lot of the trustee of a trust that is terminating, some states by statute are now subjecting certain trust distributions to rules that traditionally have been applied only to legacies and devises under wills. In this regard, the reader is referred to Sections 8.15.54 of this handbook (ademption by extinction [the trust application]); 8.15.55 of this handbook (antilapse [the trust application]); and 8.15.56 of this handbook (the 120-hour requirement of survival [the trust application]). These statutory rules are loaded with arcane exceptions. Accordingly, the trustee of a trust that is terminating would be well advised to ascertain before commencing distribution whether or not any of these rules may be applicable.[613] When in reasonable doubt, the trustee should consider seeking the advice of counsel.[614] The failure to recognize the applicability of an antilapse rule can easily result in misdelivery for which the trustee could personally be liable.[615] For a discussion of hotchpot, the equitable device for calculating any offsets for prior distributions and advancements, the reader is referred to Section 8.15.51 of this handbook.

---

[608] *See also* Old Colony Trust v. Wood, 321 Mass. 519, 526, 74 N.E.2d 141, 145–146 (1947) (acknowledging that a trustee has standing to bring an action on his own behalf to recover misdelivered property).

[609] Restatement of Restitution §163 ("Where the owner of property transfers it as a result of mistake of such a character that he is entitled to restitution, the transferee holds the property upon a constructive trust for him"). *See generally* §7.2.3.1.6 of this handbook (the constructive trust as a procedural equitable remedy); §8.15.78 of this handbook (unjust enrichment).

[610] *See* DeRouen v. Bryan, 2012 WL 4872738 (Tex. App. Austin)).

[611] 4 Scott & Ascher §24.31.1 (Liability for Distributions Under Invalid, Amended, Revoked, or Ineffective Instruments).

[612] 4 Scott & Ascher §24.31.1 (Liability for Distributions Under Invalid, Amended, Revoked, or Ineffective Instruments); 5 Scott & Ascher §36.2.3 (To Whom Should Trustee Convey).

[613] *See generally* 4 Scott & Ascher §24.31 (Liability for Incorrect Distributions).

[614] 5 Scott & Ascher §36.2.1 (Delay in Making Conveyance).

[615] *See generally* 4 Scott & Ascher §24.31 (Liability for Incorrect Distributions).

It is virtually always the case that at least one person somewhere will have equitable remainder or reversionary property rights in the assets of a terminated trust. It needs to be kept in mind that at least one person or institution (or if worse comes to worse, the state[616]) will have an equitable property right in the underlying property of a trust upon its termination, although who that person or institution is may not be all that easy to discern in a given situation.[617] Nevertheless, it is to that person or institution that the outgoing trustee's fiduciary duties will run.[618] This is the case even during the period when there is uncertainty as to who actually is or are entitled to take.[619] If it turns out, for example, that, for whatever reason, there are no designated remaindermen, then the property is likely to pass upon a resulting trust back to the settlor, or to the settlor's probate estate should the settlor be deceased at the time the trust terminates, that is at the time the trust "fails."[620] In such a situation, the trustee's fiduciary duties from the time of termination to final distribution would run primarily to the settlor, or to those with an economic interest in the settlor's probate estate, as the case may be.[621]

When in reasonable doubt as to the rightful owner of the equitable interests, the trustee of a terminated trust may and should seek the guidance of the court. Again, there is a simple solution when the trustee and his counsel are in doubt as to the proper person to whom a conveyance should be made, or as to the shares to which the beneficiaries are entitled: "He can apply to the court for instructions and will be protected by the order of the court against claims of all persons who were made parties to the proceeding."[622] The cases that surcharge the trustee for making erroneous distributions are peculiarly distressing.[623] It has been held that if the trustee pays the wrong person even under advice of counsel,[624] the trustee will be obliged to refund the amount with interest.[625] Particular care must be taken when a power of attorney or order for payment or assignment is presented. It is as dangerous to pay over to one whose interest has terminated as to pay over on an invalid assignment.[626] The fact that the trustee has been

---

[616] *See, e.g.,* §8.15.46 of this handbook (*bona vacantia* doctrine).

[617] 5 Scott & Ascher §36.2.3 (To Whom Trustee Should Convey).

[618] 5 Scott & Ascher §36.2.3 (To Whom Trustee Should Convey).

[619] 5 Scott & Ascher §36.2.3 (To Whom Trustee Should Convey).

[620] 5 Scott & Ascher §36.2.3 (To Whom Trustee Should Convey). *See generally* §4.1.1.1 of this handbook (defining the resulting trust).

[621] 5 Scott & Ascher §36.2.3 (To Whom Trustee Should Convey). *See generally* §4.1.1.1 of this handbook (reversionary property rights, whether legal or equitable, are vested *ab initio*)

[622] Restatement (Second) of Trusts §345 cmt. j. *See generally* 5 Scott & Ascher §§36.2.1 (Delay in Making Conveyance), 36.2.3 (To Whom Trustee Should Convey); 4 Scott & Ascher §24.31 (Liability for Incorrect Distributions).

[623] *See generally* 4 Scott & Ascher §24.31 (Liability for Incorrect Distributions).

[624] *See generally* §8.32 of this handbook (whether the trustee can escape liability for making a mistake of law if he acted in good faith on advice of counsel).

[625] *See generally* 4 Scott & Ascher §24.31 (Liability for Incorrect Distributions); 5 Scott & Ascher §36.2.3 (To Whom Trustee Should Convey).

[626] *See generally* 4 Scott & Ascher §24.31 (Liability for Incorrect Distributions).

diligent or has taken advice will not be of any help when it comes to misdelivery.[627] The trustee's only protection for misdelivery is if it were done under a court order obtained without fraud and with proper notice having been given to all interested parties.[628] Again, one who has been unjustly enriched by a misdelivery will be obliged to indemnify the trustee, or otherwise make restitution,[629] unless there has been a change of position.[630]

Distributing to adoptees. The trustee should develop protocols for handling claims of beneficiary status due to adoption.[631] Before making a distribution to anyone, the trustee at minimum should have on file a written legal opinion that the claimant is in fact a lawful adoptee, that the terms of the trust and the applicable law entitle the adoptee to beneficiary status, and that the adoptee has not waived the equitable interest in consideration of the adoption. If the adoption took place in one jurisdiction but the laws of another jurisdiction govern how the trust is interpreted and administered, a lawyer from each jurisdiction may have to be retained.

Distributing to persons under legal disability. A distribution to a beneficiary who is under legal disability is fraught with danger for the trustee,[632] and for third persons as well.[633] The trustee, for example, ought not to pay a minor's share to the minor or the minor's natural parent without express authority to do so in the governing instrument, lest the trustee be required to pay again when the minor comes of age. Payment should be made only to the minor's formally appointed guardian (which may of course be the child's natural parent) or to

---

[627] *See generally* 4 Scott & Ascher §24.31 (Liability for Incorrect Distributions).

[628] *See generally* 5 Scott & Ascher §36.2.3 (To Whom Trustee Should Convey); 4 Scott & Ascher §24.31 (Liability for Incorrect Distributions); §§6.1.5.2 of this handbook (duty to keep and render accounts) and 7.1 of this handbook (trustee's liabilities generally).

[629] Restatement of Restitution §163 ("Where the owner of property transfers it as a result of mistake of such a character that he is entitled to restitution, the transferee holds the property upon a constructive trust for him"). *See generally* §7.2.3.1.6 of this handbook (the constructive trust as a procedural equitable remedy); §8.15.78 of this handbook (unjust enrichment).

[630] Restatement of Restitution §178 (change of position).

[631] *See, e.g.*, Old Colony Trust Co. v. Wood, 321 Mass. 519, 74 N.E.2d 141 (1947) (involving a trustee who was personally liable to the intended remaindermen for misdelivering principal to an adoptee).

[632] *See generally* §3.5.3.2 (l) of this handbook (the power to administer distributions to minors and other legally incapacitated persons).

[633] When, for example, a legally enforceable claim against a third person is held in trust for a minor and the third person pays the amount of the claim directly to the minor rather than to the trustee, the third person can be compelled to pay the claim twice, unless the third person had been directed to make the payment by the trustee. 5 Scott & Ascher §32.1. The third party would still have had to pay twice had the third person been on notice that the issuing of the direction itself was a breach of trust on the part of the trustee. 5 Scott & Ascher §32.1. To follow the direction under such circumstances would have constituted participation with the trustee in a breach of trust. 5 Scott & Ascher §32.1. If the minor still has the payment at the time he or she attains majority or if the minor has used the payment for necessaries, then the third person might not have to pay twice after all. 5 Scott & Ascher §32.1. A trustee who fails to compel the third person to pay twice when the third person is obliged by law to do so has constructively misdelivered the trust property.

someone informally appointed pursuant to the terms of a statute enacted to facilitate the distribution of trust property to minors.[634]

For the farseeing trustee, the doctrine of equitable deviation can be a godsend. Here is a real-life example: In lieu of the eventual outright distribution of the assets of an ongoing trust to the victim of schizophrenia affective disorder and bipolar disorder, which was the mode of terminating distribution called for by the trust's terms, the court, invoking the doctrine of equitable deviation, let it be known that it would uphold a diversion of the distribution to the trustee of a third-party special needs trust established down the road for the benefit of the victim.[635] Circumstances had changed.[636] The deceased settlors had been unaware of their granddaughter's disability and would not have wanted trust assets squandered to no avail, or unnecessarily diverted into the coffers of the state.[637] Had the trust already terminated, an equitable deviation might well not have been an option, the property having already vested in the victim. Then the fate of the distribution would probably have to be sorted out in the context of a guardianship proceeding. The doctrine of equitable deviation is covered generally in Section 8.15.20 of this handbook. Third-party special needs trusts are covered in Section 9.3 of this handbook.

Retaining a minor's share in further trust. A well-drafted trust instrument will make provision for retaining, at the option of the trustee, the minor's share in trust until the minor reaches the age of majority.[638] Such a provision, however, is not helpful when small amounts are involved. Accordingly, the instrument also should contain a provision authorizing distribution of a minor's share to a relative or friend of the minor for the benefit of the minor. One practitioner includes in his boilerplate optional authority in the trustee to transfer a minor's share to a qualified tuition program under Section 529 of the Internal Revenue Code for the benefit of the minor.

While it is far preferable that distributions to minors and other legally incapacitated persons be addressed by express language in the governing instrument, statutes have now been enacted in some jurisdictions allowing a trustee to make payments to or for the benefit of an incapacitated beneficiary without the need for express authority to do so in the terms of the trust.[639] The Restatement (Third) of Trusts, by generally endorsing this approach, would modify the default law: "Absent either express authorization or a contrary provision, it is implied from a direction to distribute income (or other amounts) that the trustee has authority to apply the funds for the beneficiary's benefit so long as no objection is raised by or on behalf of the beneficiary."[640] The trustee has other options as well in the face of a beneficiary's inability for whatever

[634] *See, e.g.*, Uniform Transfers to Minors Act, 8B U.L.A. 497 (1993).
[635] In re Riddell, 138 Wash. App. 485, 157 P.3d 888 (2007).
[636] In re Riddell, 138 Wash. App. 485, 157 P.3d 888 (2007).
[637] In re Riddell, 138 Wash. App. 485, 157 P.3d 888 (2007).
[638] *See generally* §3.5.3.2(l) of this handbook (the power to administer distributions to minors and other legally incapacitated persons).
[639] 2A Scott on Trusts §182.1 n.1 and accompanying text.
[640] Restatement (Third) of Trusts §49 cmt. c(2).

reason to handle funds. If in good-faith doubt as to the beneficiary's "practical or legal capacity to handle funds," the trustee may segregate the funds in a separate account, "subject to the continuing right of withdrawal upon demand by or on behalf of the beneficiary."[641] The funds would be fully vested in the beneficiary.[642] And when appropriate, there is the option of making distributions to a custodian under the applicable Uniform Transfers to Minors Act.

A good-faith failure on the part of the trustee to ascertain external facts. The Uniform Trust Code, however, would relieve the trustee of liability for a good-faith "failure to ascertain external facts, often of a personal nature, that might affect administration or distribution of the trust."[643] It provides that if the happening of an event, including marriage, divorce, performance of educational requirements, or death, affects the administration or distribution of a trust, a trustee who has exercised reasonable care to ascertain the happening of the event is not liable for a loss resulting from the trustee's lack of knowledge.[644] The trustee still would be required to make a "genuine investigation."[645] The trustee who makes distribution on the basis of information gleaned merely through "hearsay" does so at his peril.[646] In any case, one who is unjustly enriched by a misdelivery is obliged to make appropriate restitution.[647]

Receipts and releases. The trustee who by fraud, duress, undue influence, or "fiduciary abuse" induces a beneficiary to consent to a breach of trust remains liable for the breach.[648] "Fiduciary abuse may result if the trustee brings unwarranted pressure to bear on the beneficiary, for example, by threatening to withhold a distribution to which the beneficiary is entitled unless the beneficiary executes a release."[649]

In New York, it is common practice when there is no ambiguity as to who is to get what for the beneficiary to give the trustee a release and indemnity as consideration for the trustee's not seeking judicial approval/settlement of his accounts. Otherwise, the trustee is entitled to hold back a reasonable portion of the trust property pending judicial approval/settlement as a source for the payment of reasonable legal fees and other expenses incurred in connection

---

[641] Restatement (Third) of Trusts §49 cmt. c(2).

[642] Restatement (Third) of Trusts §49 cmt. c(2).

[643] UTC§1007 cmt. (available at <http://www.uniformlaws.org/Act.aspx?title=Trust%20 Code>). *See generally* 4 Scott & Ascher §24.31 (Liability for Incorrect Distributions).

[644] UTC§1007 (available at <http://www.uniformlaws.org/Act.aspx?title=Trust%20 Code>). *See generally* 4 Scott & Ascher §24.31 (Liability for Incorrect Distributions).

[645] Welch v. Flory, 294 Mass. 138, 143, 200 N.E. 900, 902 (1936) (applying trust principles to the failure of an administrator to locate heir-at-law of intestate).

[646] *See generally* 4 Scott & Ascher §24.31 (Liability for Incorrect Distributions).

[647] Restatement of Restitution §163 ("Where the owner of property transfers it as a result of mistake of such a character that he is entitled to restitution, the transferee holds the property upon a constructive trust for him"). *See generally* §7.2.3.1.6 of this handbook (the constructive trust as a procedural equitable remedy); §8.15.78 of this handbook (unjust enrichment).

[648] Restatement (Third) of Trusts §97 cmt. f.

[649] Restatement (Third) of Trusts §97 cmt. f.

with getting the court involved.[650] One Florida court has held that it would not be "prudent" for a trustee to make distribution without the consent of the beneficiaries to its final accounts, or approval of the accounts by the court. "Otherwise, one of the Beneficiaries could object to the accounting after the distribution of the Trust, resulting in litigation over assets that have already been distributed."[651] In England, it is common practice for a trustee to seek a release under seal prior to making final distribution, although the trustee in general would have no right to insist upon one.[652] Thus, the trustee's duty of loyalty would be implicated if the trustee (or trust counsel, for that matter) threatened or was otherwise abusive to a beneficiary who declined to grant a release.[653]

It is traditional equity doctrine that a nonjudicial release of trustee liability is "inapplicable to unknown claims."[654] The Uniform Trust Code is generally in accord. Under the UTC, a release by a beneficiary from liability for breach of trust is invalid to the extent it was induced by improper conduct of the trustee.[655] Thus, it would be ineffective to the extent the beneficiary, at the time of the release, did not know of the beneficiary's rights or of the material facts relating to the breach.[656] Moreover, a trustee's intentional failure to fully apprise the beneficiary of the applicable facts and law could constitute fraud, while the negligent failure to do so might constitute constructive fraud.[657] By accepting a distribution, the beneficiary submits personally to the jurisdiction of the courts of the state where the trust has its principal place of administration.[658]

Trustee compensation. "The trustee need not pay over income without deducting the compensation to which he is entitled with respect to the income, and need not pay over principal without deducting the compensation to which he is entitled with respect to the principal."[659] To the extent of his reasonable

---

[650] *See* Matter of JPMorgan Chase Bank N.A. (trust for the benefit of Mary Gill Roby, et al.), 2014 N.Y. Slip Op. 07799 (Nov. 14, 2014) ("Finally, objectants cite no legal authority prohibiting . . . [the trustee] . . . from delaying distribution of trust assets pending judicial settlement in order to pay for legal fees and other expenses.")

[651] Merrill Lynch Trust Co. v. Alzheimer's Lifeliners Assoc., 832 So. 2d 948, 954 (Fla. 2002). *See generally* 4 Scott & Ascher §24.31 (Liability for Incorrect Distributions).

[652] Lewin ¶ 26-63 (England).

[653] *See generally* 3 Scott & Ascher §17.2.10. *See, e.g.*, Ingram v. Lewis, 37 F.2d 259, 263 (10th Cir. 1930) ("It is legal duress for a trustee to refuse to turn over property to his beneficiary rightfully entitled thereto, except upon condition of signing a release").

[654] *See* Janowiak v. Tiesi, 932 N.E.2d 569 (Ill. 2010).

[655] UTC §817(c)(1) (available at <http://www.uniformlaws.org/Act.aspx?title=Trust%20 Code>). *See, e.g.*, Ingram v. Lewis, 37 F.2d 259 (1930).

[656] UTC §817(c)(2) (available at <http://www.uniformlaws.org/Act.aspx?title=Trust%20 Code>).

[657] *See generally* §8.15.59 of this handbook (constructive fraud).

[658] UTC §202(b) (available at <http://www.uniformlaws.org/Act.aspx?title=Trust%20 Code>).

[659] Restatement (Second) of Trusts §242 cmt. e. *Cf.* Restatement (Third) of Trusts §49 cmt. c(1) (providing that "despite a duty to distribute all income periodically, the trustee may properly

compensation, the trustee has a "security interest"[660] in the trust property. Termination fees are controversial and the subject of much litigation.[661] "Factors relevant to whether . . . [a termination fee] . . . is appropriate include the actual work performed; whether a termination fee was authorized in the terms of the trust; whether the fee schedule specified the circumstances in which a termination fee would be charged; whether the trustee's overall fees for administering the trust from the date of the trust's creation, including the termination fee, were reasonable; and the general practice in the community regarding termination fees."[662]

Expenses to include tax obligations. "Although a trust instrument directs termination of the trust and the distribution of the principal to the beneficiaries . . . , the trustee cannot make complete distribution until provision has been made for all the expenses, claims and taxes the trust may be obligated to pay, and certainly not before these amounts have been fully ascertained."[663] Prior to making distributions the trustee should make certain that all taxes due with respect to the property have been paid, including income, estate, and generation-skipping transfer taxes. The trustee who distributes property needed to satisfy a tax obligation may be personally liable for all or a portion of the tax.[664] The key to an orderly and satisfactory settlement of the trust's tax obligations is timely coordination with the settlor's executor, the beneficiary, or the beneficiary's executor, as appropriate. The Uniform Probate Code would authorize a trustee concerned about being saddled with an estate tax liability to do one or more of the following:

- Defer a distribution until the trustee is satisfied that adequate provision for payment of the estate tax has been made.
- Withhold from a distributee an amount equal to the amount of estate tax apportioned to an interest of the distributee.
- As a condition to a distribution, require the distributee to provide a bond or other security for the portion of the estate tax apportioned to the distributee.[665]

The importance of ascertaining and communicating the tax basis/cost of an in-kind trust distribution is covered in Sections 11.1 and 11.4 of this handbook.

---

withhold a reasonable amount of income receipts to meet present or anticipated expenses that are properly payable to the income beneficiary").

[660] Restatement (Second) of Trusts §242 cmt. e.

[661] UTC §708 cmt. (available at <http://www.uniformlaws.org/Act.aspx?title=Trust%20Code>).

[662] UTC §708 cmt. (available at <http://www.uniformlaws.org/Act.aspx?title=Trust%20Code>).

[663] First Union Nat'l Bank v. Jones, 768 So. 2d 1213, 1215 (Fla. Dist. Ct. App. 2000).

[664] *See generally* Bogert §265 (Income Tax); Stephens et al., Federal Estate and Gift Taxation ¶ 8.02 (estate tax), ¶ 12.03 (generation-skipping tax) (7th ed. 1997). *See also* §8.16 of this handbook (the trustee of revocable trust as "inadvertent executor").

[665] UPC §3-9A-108 (securing payment of estate tax from property in possession of fiduciary).

Methods of distribution. Upon termination of the trust, it is the trustee's duty to distribute the trust principal to the remainder beneficiaries. The trust instrument will often contain specific provisions directing the method of distribution.[666] If there are none, the method of distribution intended by the settlor may be inferred from the general language of the instrument. Generally, the remainder beneficiaries may determine the method, as long as all are in agreement as to what it should be. Even if the trustee is directed by the terms of the trust to use a particular method of distribution, the remainder beneficiaries acting in concert may require that a different method be employed.[667] The Restatement (Third) of Trusts is generally in accord.[668]

The Uniform Trust Code provides that upon termination or partial termination of a trust, the trustee may send to the beneficiaries a proposal for distribution.[669] The right of any beneficiary to object to the proposed distribution terminates if the beneficiary does not notify the trustee of an objection within thirty days after the proposal is sent.[670] For the beneficiary's right of objection to be foreclosed, however, the proposal must inform the beneficiary of the right to object and of the time allowed for objection.[671] The Restatement (Third) of Trusts, however, offers these well-chosen words of caution: "Especially if the plan...[for distribution]...is complicated, the trustee should consider obtaining the informed consent of the beneficiaries when it is practical to do so, although the trustee must also consider the possibility that adverse tax consequences may follow from relying on beneficiary consent—rather than on independent fiduciary judgment in the matter, informed by careful consultation."[672]

Absent specific provisions, general guiding language, or agreement among the remainder beneficiaries, the proper mode of distribution, *i.e.*, in what form the property is to exit the trust, depends upon all the facts and circumstances. The traditional default law was that land went out in kind and personal property as cash.[673] Nowadays, the law is more nuanced when it comes to what form a terminating trust distribution should take.[674] "Absent guidance in the terms of the trust, it would appear that the mode or modes of distribution

---

[666] *See generally* 5 Scott & Ascher §36.4.1 (Specific Provisions in Trust Instrument).

[667] *See* 5 Scott & Ascher §36.4.1; 4 Scott on Trusts §347.1; Restatement (Second) of Trusts §346.

[668] Restatement (Third) of Trusts §89 cmt. e(3).

[669] UTC §817(a) (available at <http://www.uniformlaws.org/Act.aspx?title=Trust%20 Code>).

[670] UTC §817(a) (available at <http://www.uniformlaws.org/Act.aspx?title=Trust%20 Code>).

[671] UTC §817(a) (available at <http://www.uniformlaws.org/Act.aspx?title=Trust%20 Code>).

[672] Restatement (Third) of Trusts §89 cmt. e(2).

[673] *See generally* 5 Scott & Ascher §36.4.4 (Personal Property).

[674] *See generally* 5 Scott & Ascher §36.4.4 (Personal Property).

are to be determined by the trustee, based not only on what is in the beneficiaries' interest but also on what is fair and reasonable."[675] In a number of states there are now statutes that would afford the trustee default authority to distribute in cash or in kind, partly in cash and partly in kind.[676] Even in the absence of statutory authority, a court, "by virtue of its general jurisdiction over the administration of trusts," would have inherent equitable powers to order distribution in cash or in kind, partly in cash and partly in kind, in furtherance of the trust's material purposes and the interests of its beneficiaries.[677]

Where a single beneficiary is entitled to the trust property, the trustee would be expected to distribute the property in kind.[678] "If under the terms of the trust there is no equitable conversion, but the trustee sells . . . land . . . [constituting some or all of the trust estate] . . . , the proceeds pass as the land would have."[679] That having been said, a single beneficiary generally may countermand an express provision in the terms of the trust that distribution of the underlying property shall be in kind.[680] So too the beneficiary may countermand an express direction that the trustee reduce the underlying property to cash prior to distributing it out.[681] When there are multiple beneficiaries all of whom are of full age and legal capacity and in accord, then they as well may elect whether the property comes out in cash or in kind, partly in cash and partly in kind, notwithstanding the terms of the trust.[682]

Generally a provision in the terms of the trust directing the trustee to make a distribution outright and free of trust in the form of an annuity contract on the life of a beneficiary and on no other may be countermanded by the beneficiary.[683] The distribution then would be made in cash or in kind, partly in cash and partly in kind, as the beneficiary shall elect.[684] "Thus the American courts often seem to have understood that it would be useless to require the trustee to purchase the annuity, as the annuitant could immediately sell it and obtain substantially the same amount as the purchase price."[685] In some states, however, beneficiaries do not have this right of election, either by case law or by statute.[686]

---

[675] 5 Scott & Ascher §36.4.2 (listing some "factors" which the trustee may find relevant in fashioning a mode of distribution).

[676] 5 Scott & Ascher §36.4 n.1.

[677] 5 Scott & Ascher §36.4.2 (No Specific Provision in Trust Instrument).

[678] *See* Restatement (Third) of Trusts §89 cmt. e(1); Restatement (Second) of Trusts §345 cmt. d.

[679] 3 Scott & Ascher §13.1.1. *See generally* §8.15.44 of this handbook (the doctrine of equitable conversion).

[680] *See generally* 5 Scott & Ascher §36.3 (Direction to Convert).

[681] *See generally* 5 Scott & Ascher §36.3 (Direction to Convert).

[682] *See generally* 5 Scott & Ascher §36.3 (Direction to Convert).

[683] *See generally* 5 Scott & Ascher §36.3 (Direction to Convert).

[684] *See generally* 5 Scott & Ascher §36.3 (Direction to Convert).

[685] 5 Scott & Ascher §36.3.

[686] 5 Scott & Ascher §36.3 n.7.

Unless the terms of the trust provide otherwise, express provisions for distribution of stated or formula-determined pecuniary amounts may be satisfied in kind, as well as in cash, or even partly in cash and partly in kind. Property that is distributed in kind to satisfy a pecuniary provision is valued at its fair market value at the time of actual distribution. The Restatement (Third) of Trusts is in accord.[687]

Where there are several remainder beneficiaries, three methods of distribution are possible: (1) transferring the trust property in kind to the remainder beneficiaries as tenants in common, (2) dividing the trust property into equal shares and distributing the trust property in kind to each remainder beneficiary, or (3) selling the trust property and dividing the proceeds among the remainder beneficiaries.[688] If appropriate, distribution might be made partly in cash and partly in kind.[689] The proper method of distribution depends upon what is reasonable under all the circumstances.[690] The trustee should consider the nature of the assets, the number of remainder beneficiaries, market conditions, tax implications, and so forth.[691] When making a distribution, be it in cash or in kind, the trustee is under a duty to the remainder beneficiaries to act impartially.[692] The Restatement (Third) of Trusts gets down to some helpful administrative and operational specifics:

> Unless otherwise required by trust provision, or by fiduciary duties in other aspects of the windup process, considerations of prudence and impartiality will often cause trustees to prefer—so far as practical—to distribute trust property in kind on a pro rata basis, that is, by transferring real property (and possibly other nonfungibles) to the remainder beneficiaries as tenants in common and by dividing and distributing fungibles among the beneficiaries so that each receives his or her proportionate share of each of the fungible asset holdings. To the extent this form of distribution would be undesirable, however, particularly because of impracticality (e.g., numerous tenants in common) or other disadvantages it may have for some or all of the distributees, distribution can properly be facilitated by some combination of liquidation and non-pro rata division of some of the trust estate. Furthermore, if required to meet trust obligations or to make distribution, the trustee may borrow funds on a prudent basis from a third party; or, if authorized by the terms of the trust or approved by the affected beneficiaries, the trustee may even facilitate distribution through borrowing/lending on fair terms

---

[687] *See* Restatement (Third) of Trusts §89 cmt. e(3) (noting that the pecuniary amount does not function as a fractional share of the trust estate).

[688] Restatement (Second) of Trusts §347 cmt. a.

[689] Restatement (Third) of Trusts §89 cmt. e(2).

[690] Restatement (Third) of Trusts §89 cmt. e(2); Restatement (Second) of Trusts §347 cmt. c.

[691] Restatement (Third) of Trusts §89 cmt. e(2). *See also* Boston Safe Deposit & Trust Co. v. Boone, 21 Mass. App. Ct. 637, 489 N.E.2d 209 (1986). *See generally* 5 Scott & Ascher §§36.4.2 (listing some "factors" which the trustee may find relevant in fashioning a mode of distribution), 36.4.3 (noting that "when the subject matter of a trust consists of land, it is easier to infer that the settlor intended that, upon termination, the land would go to the beneficiaries in kind than when the subject matter is personal property").

[692] Restatement (Third) of Trusts §89 cmt. e(2). *See generally* 5 Scott & Ascher §36.4.1 ("[W]hen either fairness or the best interests of the beneficiaries require, the court may authorize or direct distribution by a mode different than that specified in the terms of the trust").

between or among distributable shares, and by including promissory note(s) in the distributive share(s) as appropriate.[693]

If at the termination of a trust each remainderman is to receive free of shared ownership a selection of tangible and intangible items of trust property equal in value to that of a specified fractional share or percentage of the net trust estate, or if at termination a fixed pecuniary amount is to be satisfied in kind, then the trustee needs to be certain that each item's assigned value is defensible. It is not uncommon for the terms of a trust to specify that the trustee's determination as to the value of an item shall be final and binding on all the beneficiaries.[694] This is all well and good. "Values thereby fixed are not, however, binding if the trustees are guilty of an abuse of discretion, as when they fail to exercise their judgment or act arbitrarily."[695]

These valuation considerations would apply as well to in-kind distributions incident to certain partial terminations, such as when the older child of the settlor is to receive outright and free of trust upon the child's attaining the age of 30 a selection of items of trust property which, taken together, equal 50 percent of the value of the trust estate, all valuations being as of the time of actual distribution.[696] Any postdistribution appreciation in the value of what was distributed, or postdistribution diminution in the value of what was left behind, will not impose on the distributee any duty "to make restitution to the trust on the ground that he or she has been overpaid."[697] The amount to which the distributee is entitled is fixed as of the time of distribution.[698] This applies even if what was distributed subsequently depreciates in value or what was left behind subsequently appreciates in value.[699] In either case, the distributee would not be entitled to anything more from the trust estate, at least in the way of a make-up distribution.[700] The importance of ascertaining and communicating the tax basis/cost of an in-kind trust distribution is covered in Sections 11.1 and 11.4 of this handbook.

Mid-course terminations. The Uniform Trust Code makes provision for termination of an irrevocable noncharitable trust if the settlor and all the beneficiaries give their consent.[701] A noncharitable irrevocable trust may be terminated upon consent of all of the beneficiaries if the court concludes that continuance of the trust is not necessary to achieve any material purpose of the

---

[693] Restatement (Third) of Trusts §89 cmt. e(2).

[694] *See generally* 5 Scott & Ascher §36.4.4 (noting in footnote 11 that such a provision may violate New York public policy when it comes to testamentary trusts).

[695] 5 Scott & Ascher §36.4.4.

[696] 5 Scott & Ascher §36.4.5 (Termination of Trust in Part).

[697] 5 Scott & Ascher §36.4.5.

[698] 5 Scott & Ascher §36.4.5.

[699] 5 Scott & Ascher §36.4.5.

[700] 5 Scott & Ascher §36.4.5.

[701] UTC §411(a) (available at <http://www.uniformlaws.org/Act.aspx?title=Trust%20Code>). *See generally* §8.2.2.1 of this handbook (mid-course trust terminations).

trust.[702] If not all the beneficiaries consent, the termination still may be approved by the court if the court is satisfied that the interests of a beneficiary who does not consent will be adequately protected.[703] "Once termination has been approved, how the trust property is to be distributed is solely for the beneficiaries to decide."[704] The settlor does not control the subsequent distribution of the trust property.[705]

The Code would allow the court to fashion an appropriate order protecting the interests of the nonconsenting beneficiaries while at the same time permitting the remainder of the trust property to be distributed without restriction.[706] "The order of protection for the nonconsenting beneficiaries might include partial continuation of the trust, the purchase of an annuity, or the valuation and cashout of the interest."[707]

When distribution is delayed. If, for whatever reason, the trustee of a terminated trust delays unduly in effecting distribution to the remaindermen, each remainderman, as a practical matter, should be treated as the outright owner of an appropriate portion of the underlying property. Equity looks on that as done which ought to be done.[708] In earlier times, title might well have already vested in the remaindermen.[709] If distribution is delayed due to litigation, the "better practice may be to interplead the funds during the pendency of the litigation."[710] That way the trustee can place the burden of resolving the troubling question of whether to liquidate or stay in the market squarely on the shoulders of those who have, or who may have, the vested equitable property rights in the

---

[702] UTC §411(b) (available at <http://www.uniformlaws.org/Act.aspx?title=Trust%20 Code>). *See generally* §8.2.2.1 of this handbook (mid-course trust terminations).

[703] UTC §411(e) (available at <http://www.uniformlaws.org/Act.aspx?title=Trust%20 Code>). *See generally* §8.2.2.1 of this handbook (mid-course trust terminations).

[704] UTC §411 cmt. (available at <http://www.uniformlaws.org/Act.aspx?title=Trust%20 Code>). *See generally* §8.2.2.1 of this handbook (mid-course trust terminations).

[705] UTC §411 cmt. (available at <http://www.uniformlaws.org/Act.aspx?title=Trust%20 Code>). *See generally* §8.2.2.1 of this handbook (mid-course trust terminations).

[706] UTC §411 cmt. (available at <http://www.uniformlaws.org/Act.aspx?title=Trust%20 Code>). *See generally* §8.2.2.1 of this handbook (mid-course trust terminations).

[707] UTC §411 cmt. (available at <http://www.uniformlaws.org/Act.aspx?title=Trust%20 Code>). *See generally* §8.2.2.1 of this handbook (mid-course trust terminations).

[708] *See generally* §8.12 of this handbook (containing a general discussion of equity maxims).

[709] *See generally* §§2.1 of this handbook (noting that at common law, in a situation where the remaindermen shared the legal title with the trustee, there need not be a conveyance to them upon the trust's termination) and 8.15.1 of this handbook (noting that at common law in a situation where the statute of uses was applicable, a conveyance to the designated remaindermen would not have been necessary for title to pass to pass to them).

[710] Heinitsh v. Wachovia Bank, 665 S.E.2d 541, 545 (N.C. Ct. App. 2008).

subject property.[711] They will have only themselves to blame if it is determined with the benefit of hindsight that things should have been done differently.[712]

Termination and division. It is not always the case that the property of a trust distributes out at termination. The terms of the trust could well provide that the trust is to be fractured or divided into separate sub-trusts whose terms and beneficiaries are often different from those of the mother trust, with title to the underlying property remaining in the trustee.[713] See generally Section 8.9 of this handbook (why more than one trust: the estate and generation-skipping tax). For the investment-related implications of dividing a trust, see Section 3.5.3.2(d) of this handbook (discussing the common investment fund). The trustee may want to administer the one-pot trust as an "administrative trust" until such time as all the sub-trusts are funded, a topic we cover in Section 9.9.14 of this handbook.

If funding of the successor sub-trusts is to be in kind, values for funding purposes generally must be as of the time of allocation.[714] A valuation that is as of an inappropriate time or an appraisal that is poorly done might well have the effect of improperly reordering the equitable property rights of the beneficiaries of the various trusts, such as in the situation where pursuant to the terms of the governing trust instrument one successor trust is to be funded with a fixed sum, while the other successor trusts are to share equally in what remains of the trust estate.[715] If the aggregate value of the items allocated in kind to the "pecuniary" trust is greater than what it should be, either due to the poor quality of the appraisals or the fact that valuations were not as of the time of distribution, then the beneficiaries of the trusts that are receiving what is left over would be advantaged at the expense of the beneficiaries of the "pecuniary" trust.[716] The importance of ascertaining and communicating the tax basis/cost of an in-kind trust distribution is covered in Sections 11.1 and 11.4 of this handbook.

If the trustee unduly delays or fails altogether to effect division as required by the terms of the trust, over time "serious and difficult controversies can be expected to arise."[717] There is interference with the property rights of those

---

[711] Heinitsh v. Wachovia Bank, 665 S.E.2d 541 (N.C. Ct. App. 2008) (holding the trustee harmless for retaining disputed funds in a "low-risk" money market account while awaiting resolution of litigation concerning the classification of the funds as either trust accounting income or principal).

[712] Nelson v. First Nat'l Bank & Trust Co. of Williston, 543 F.3d 432 (8th Cir. 2008) (whether a trustee should be held liable for not liquidating a block of stock during the two weeks following the settlor's death).

[713] *See generally* 5 Scott & Ascher §36.4.6 (When Property Is to Be Distributed to Several Trusts).

[714] 5 Scott & Ascher §36.4.6.

[715] *See generally* 5 Scott & Ascher §36.4.6 (When Property Is to Be Distributed to Several Trusts).

[716] *See generally* 5 Scott & Ascher §36.4.6 (When Property Is to Be Distributed to Several Trusts). *See also* §6.2.5 of this handbook (trustee's duty of impartiality).

[717] Restatement (Third) of Trusts §89, Reporter's Notes, Comment *g (Aside: Failure to subdivide trust)*. *See also* John A. Hartog & George R. Dirkes, Assisting the Nonprofessional Trustee in Implementing the Administrative Trust (visited Aug. 13, 2008) <http://www.jahartog.com/materials-1.html> (discussing the so-called stale trust).

with equitable interests under the phantom separate trusts. Some who are reporting income to the taxing authorities probably should not be, while others who are not probably should be. Inevitably a beneficiary of a phantom separate trust will die further exacerbating the problem.

Take a revocable declaration of trust whose cotrustees are a husband and a wife unschooled in estate planning matters. The couple places their property, including their residence, in the trust. Upon the first death, the trust for tax and other reasons is supposed to split pursuant to its terms into separate trust shares. That, however, does not occur. The surviving spouse, who also is the surviving cotrustee, continues out of ignorance to deal with the underlying property as if nothing had happened. Years later someone somehow learns of the nonfeasance, most likely someone from among the following cast of characters:

- A beneficiary of one of the phantom separate trusts;
- The accountant of a beneficiary of one of the phantom separate trusts;
- A creditor of a beneficiary of one of the phantom separate trusts;
- The guardian or conservator for a beneficiary of one of the phantom separate trust;
- The executor, administrator, or personal representative of a beneficiary of one of the phantom separate trusts;
- The surviving spouse's accountant;
- Prospective lenders to the surviving spouse;
- A creditor of the surviving spouse;
- The surviving spouse's guardian or conservator;
- The surviving spouse's executor, administrator, or personal representative;
- The lawyer for the prospective buyer of some trust real estate;
- An IRS agent in the course of auditing an estate and/or income tax return;
- A state tax agent in the course of auditing an estate and/or income tax return;
- The successor trustee; and
- Counsel to the successor trustee.

Some will have fiduciary incentives to see to it that things are put right, *e.g.*, the successor trustee.[718] Others will be motivated by self interest, *e.g.*, the beneficiaries of the phantom separate trusts. However a failure to divide comes to light, the more time that has passed before its discovery, the greater the legal and administrative headaches for the fiduciary charged with putting things right. The Restatement (Third) of Trust, invoking the maxim "Equity looks on that as done which ought to be done,"[719] suggests that going forward, "[t]he

---

[718] *See generally* §7.2.4 of this handbook (cofiduciary and predecessor liability and contribution).

[719] *See generally* §8.12 of this handbook (where the trust is recognized outside the United States) (containing a catalog of equity maxims).

separate trusts should be deemed to have been established at some (necessarily estimated) time when division *should have* occurred (possibly allowing interest until the deemed 'funding' of a pecuniary formula), with the 'trusts' thereafter holding undivided (fractional) interests in all assets of the trust estate that was then subject to division."[720] Issues of personal liability arising out of the fiduciary nonfeasance may have to be addressed at some point as well.

§8.2.4   Trust Termination Checklist

The fiduciary of a trust (or estate) may elect under §663(b) to treat any amount that is properly paid or credited to a beneficiary within the first 65 days following the close of the taxable year as an amount properly paid or distributed on the last day of such taxable year . . .[721] *This . . . [is known as the] . . . 65-day rule. . . . The election, of course, has an impact on the distribution deduction of the trust and the amounts reportable as income by the beneficiaries.*[722]

Winding up the affairs of a trust that has terminated can be a difficult and time-consuming process. Who qualify as remaindermen is not always clear;[723] tax filings can get complicated; valuing and splitting the portfolio can be tricky. The importance of ascertaining and communicating the tax basis/cost of an in-kind trust distribution is covered in Sections 11.1 and 11.4 of this handbook. And then there are the remaindermen who have been waiting in the wings for years. Now that the life beneficiary has died, they want their property.[724] The trustee does not want the process to drag on, for there is always the danger that a remainderman will die during the process.[725] That can only further complicate and delay things. Moreover, "a trustee who unduly delays in winding up the trust may be liable for depreciation in the value of the trust property and for interest."[726]

The following is a trust termination checklist designed to help the trustee get through this difficult period as quickly as possible, bearing in mind that there is absolute liability for misdelivery.[727] Upon the event that triggers the

---

[720] Restatement (Third) of Trusts §89, Reporter's Notes, Comment *g* (*Aside: Failure to subdivided trust*). *See, e.g.,* Penny v. Wilson, 123 Cal. App. 4 596, 20 Cal. Rptr. 3d 212 (2004).

[721] For a much more detailed checklist, *see* Frayda L. Bruton, *Post Mortem Trust Administration Checklist,* 25 ACTEC Notes 331 (2000). *See generally* §§8.16 of this handbook (the trustee of revocable trust as "inadvertent executor") and 9.9.14 of this handbook (the administrative trust).

[722] John R. Price, Price on Contemporary Estate Planning §10.4.16 (2d ed. 2000). *See generally* §10.3 of this handbook (deductions (fiduciary income tax)).

[723] UTC §112 (available at <http://www.uniformlaws.org/Act.aspx?title=Trust%20 Code>) (providing that rules of construction that apply to the interpretation of and disposition of property by will also apply as appropriate to the interpretation of the terms of a trust and the disposition of the trust property). *See also* §5.2 of this handbook (class designations such as "children," "issue," "heirs," and "relatives" (some rules of construction)).

[724] *See generally* 5 Scott & Ascher §36.2.1 (Delay in Making Conveyance).

[725] *See generally* 5 Scott & Ascher §36.2.1 (Delay in Making Conveyance).

[726] 5 Scott & Ascher §36.2.1.

[727] *See generally* §8.2.3 of this handbook (avoiding misdelivery liability).

termination, for example, the death of the life beneficiary,[728] the trustee should:

Legal

1. Notify counsel for the trust, as well as the tax accountant (or tax officer) and the broker, if any, that the trust has terminated;
2. If the trust was revocable, confirm that it was properly executed and valid;[729]

---

[728] Events triggering trust terminations include the following: someone's death; a nondeath occurrence such as marriage of a beneficiary, loss of charitable standing with the IRS, or vacancy of entrusted real estate; passage of time; and revocation. Upon accepting a trusteeship, the prudent trustee establishes and maintains adequate internal controls to enable the trustee to promptly identify and appropriately respond to an event that will trigger the particular trust's termination.

[729] *See generally* 4 Scott & Ascher §24.31.1 (Liability for Distributions Under Invalid, Amended, Revoked, or Ineffective Instruments). The grounds for contesting an inter vivos trust are lack of due execution; mental incapacity; undue influence; mistake; fraud; and/or tortious interference of someone other than the settlor in connection with the creation of the trust. *See generally* Chapter 1 of this handbook and §3.4.1 of this handbook (appointment). "The capacity required to create, amend, revoke, or add property to a revocable trust . . . is the same as that required to make a will." UTC §601 (available at <http://www.uniformlaws.org/Act.aspx?title=Trust%20Code>). "To create an irrevocable trust, the settlor must have the capacity that would be needed to transfer the property free of trust." UTC §601. "There are no execution requirements under . . . [the Uniform Trust Code] . . . for a trust not created by will." UTC §507 cmt. *See also* Restatement (Third) of Property (Wills and Other Donative Transfers) §8.1 (Tentative Draft No. 3, Apr. 4, 2001) (providing that to have the mental capacity to make or revoke a revocable inter vivos trust, the settlor must be capable of knowing and understanding in a general way the nature and extent of his or her property, the natural objects of his or her bounty, and the disposition that he or she is making of that property, and must also be capable of relating these elements to one another and forming an orderly desire regarding the disposition of the property). *See generally* Nunan, *Trustee Liability: The Ghost of Distributions Past*, 9 Prob. & Real Prop. 8 (Nov./Dec. 1995). *See also* Jay M. Zitter, J.D., *Liability of Trustee for Payments or Conveyances Under a Trust Subsequently Held to Be Invalid*, 77 A.L.R. 4th 1177 (1990). *See* Davison v. Feuerherd, 391 So. 2d 799 (Fla. Ct. App. 1980) (upholding a complaint alleging tortious prevention of an amendment to a trust). *See generally* Restatement (Second) of Torts §774B (recognizing tortious interference with an expectancy as a valid cause of action). *See, e.g.*, Martin v. Martin, 687 So. 2d 903, 907 (Fla. Ct. App. 1997) (upholding tortious interference with expectancy claim against beneficiaries of inter vivos trust as amended); Wickert v. Burggraf, 214 Wis. 2d 426, 570 N.W.2d 889 (1997) (holding that the will and trust of elderly women the product of intentional interference with an expected inheritance). The UTC would not permit a person to commence a judicial proceeding to contest the validity of a trust that was revocable at the settlor's death later than the earlier of the following dates: (1) the expiration of three years after the settlor's death and (2) the expiration of 120 days after the trustee sends the person a copy of the trust instrument and a notice informing the person of the trust's existence, of the trustee's name and address, and of the time allowed for commencing a proceeding. UTC §604(a). "The trustee . . . [, however,] . . . may distribute the trust property in accordance with the terms of the trust until and unless the trustee receives notice of a pending proceeding contesting the validity of the trust, or until notified by a potential contestant of a possible contest, followed by its filing within 60 days." UTC §604(b) & cmt. *But see* Estate of Pew, 440 Pa. Super. 195, 655 A.2d 521 (1994) (suggesting that in Pennsylvania the revocable trust might have to be "probated" to trigger certain short probate-related statutes of limitations relating to creditors claims and those seeking to challenge the validity of the trust).

3. Ascertain who is entitled to undistributed income that has accrued to the time of termination;
4. Obtain for the file a written legal opinion (and, if necessary, a judicial determination) that specifies who the remaindermen are;[730]
5. Check for QTIP elections, GST elections, disclaimers, and assignments that may have been made in the past with respect to the trust;
6. Prepare and have approved (or judicially allowed, if necessary) accountings for the period beginning immediately after the period covered by the last approved account and ending at the time of termination;
7. If the trust contains real estate, ascertain whether some action must be taken pursuant to some environmental statute or regulation;

Tax

1. Early on, estimate the federal tax consequences for the trust estate *and for the remaindermen* of termination distributions (transfer tax) and posttermination sales (income tax);[731]
2. Early on, estimate the state tax consequences for the trust estate *and for the remaindermen* of termination distributions (transfer tax) and posttermination sales (income tax);
3. Early on, understand the tax consequences, if any, of making distributions in one year rather than another;
4. Early on, ascertain whether prior tax returns will have to be amended;

---

[730] *See generally* 4 Scott & Ascher §24.31 (Liability for Incorrect Distributions); §8.15.54 of this handbook (Ademption by Extinction [the trust application]); §8.15.55 of this handbook (Antilapse [the trust application]); §8.15.56 of this handbook (120-Hour Survival Requirement [the trust application]). UPC §2-707 has established an "anti-lapse-type" default rule for future interests in trusts, whether revocable or irrevocable, whereby descendants of a beneficiary of a future interest who fails to survive the time when the future interest is to take effect in possession or enjoyment take in place of the deceased beneficiary's estate, absent a contrary intention in the governing instrument. *But see* First Nat'l Bank v. Tenney, 165 Ohio St. 513, 138 N.E.2d 15 (1956); Randall v. Bank of Am., 48 Cal. App. 2d 249, 119 P.2d 754 (1941) (though trust revocable, property passes to estate of remainderman who predeceased settlor absent a contrary expression of intent in the governing instrument). *See generally* §5.2 of this handbook (class designation: "children," "issue," "heirs," and "relatives" (some rules of construction)). Particular care also should be taken in cases where a person asserts that he or she has the status of a remainderman by reason of adoption. The trustee should obtain from counsel a written opinion that an adoptee qualifies as a remainderman under the terms of the governing trust instrument, that the adoption was valid, and that the adoption was not conditioned on the adoptee's waiving his or her rights under the trust. In no case should a trustee anoint someone as a remainderman on the basis of hearsay evidence alone.

[731] Stock valuations as of a particular date may be obtained by subscribing to an online valuation service. *See, e.g.*, Evaluation Services, Inc.; Estate Valuations & Pricing Systems, Inc.; and Wallace Historical Pricing. CUSIP (Committee on Uniform Security Identification Procedures) numbers may be obtained from AP's Markets Web Ticker website or from Cornell University's Johnson Graduate School of Management website. The importance of ascertaining and communicating the tax basis/cost of an in-kind trust distribution is covered in Sections 11.1 and 11.4 of this handbook.

5. Early on, ascertain whether there is a need to file for tax rebates;

6. Meet regularly and often with the tax accountant (or tax officer) to make sure that no tax balls are being dropped;

Operations

1. Locate and gather in one easily accessible location all past accountings, tax returns, brokerage statements, portfolio valuations, and legal opinions that pertain to the trust and keep the file current going forward;[732]

2. Early on, get the current full names, current full addresses, current telephone and fax numbers, current email addresses, and the social security numbers of the remaindermen (or the tax ID numbers of personal representatives of any deceased remaindermen), and double-check the information for accuracy;[733]

3. Early on, obtain complete and accurate written transfer instructions from each remainderman;

4. Early on, obtain complete tax cost information on the trust assets and put that information in a format that the remaindermen and their tax advisers can understand;[734]

5. Prepare an estimate of the termination costs that must be borne by the trust, such as accrued trustee fees, distribution fees, court filing fees, attorneys' fees, tax return preparation fees, brokerage commissions, interest on pecuniary distributions,[735] and taxes;

6. Early on, prepare a game plan for raising cash, dividing the portfolio, and dealing with fractional shares, odd lots, and illiquid items;

7. Establish an appropriate reserve for meeting estimated termination costs, a reserve that has a little extra in it to accommodate the unforeseen;[736]

8. Keep income carefully segregated from principal and make sure each termination expense is charged to the appropriate account;

9. If a broker has custody of the portfolio, make sure he or she has the operational capability to separately account for income and principal;

---

[732] The importance of ascertaining and communicating the tax basis/cost of an in-kind trust distribution is covered in §§11.1 and 11.4 of this handbook.

[733] *See generally* 4 Scott & Ascher §24.31 (Liability for Incorrect Distributions). One of the reasons why the social security numbers of the remaindermen should be collected relates to any fiduciary income tax returns that the trustee may be required to prepare and file. The numbers will be needed for the Schedule K-1s.

[734] The importance of ascertaining and communicating the tax basis/cost of an in-kind trust distribution is covered in §§11.1 and 11.4 of this handbook.

[735] *See, e.g.,* Mass. Gen. Laws ch. 197, §20 (Rate and Payment of Interest on Pecuniary Legacies or Pecuniary Distributions Under Trust Instrument).

[736] UTC §817(b) (available at <http://www.uniformlaws.org/Act.aspx?title=Trust%20 Code>).

Public Relations

1. Early on, furnish the remaindermen with a proposal for distribution and a provisional timetable for distributions outlining how and when partial and final distributions are expected to be made and thereafter, at reasonable intervals, keep them informed as to how things are going;[737]
2. Early on, furnish the remaindermen with tax cost information;[738]
3. Early on, if appropriate, warn the remaindermen that *they* may be responsible for paying certain tax obligations *of the trust* and advise them to so notify their tax advisors;
4. Early on, consult with the remaindermen on posttermination investment strategy;
5. Unless inappropriate for some reason, circulate to the remaindermen drafts of accountings for their review and comment and suggest to them that they may want to furnish the trustee with releases and refunding agreements in lieu of the trustee's seeking at trust expense judicial approval of his accounts;[739]
6. Once an appropriate reserve has been established, immediately begin the process of making partial distributions and paying bills, unless there is a good reason not to do so (*e.g.*, ongoing litigation);[740]
7. Do not procrastinate in tying up the final loose ends: As soon as possible, get the final accounts prepared and approved (or judicially allowed, if appropriate); and

---

[737] *See* UTC §817(a) (available at <http://www.uniformlaws.org/Act.aspx?title=Trust%20 Code>) (providing that upon termination or partial termination of a trust, the trustee may send to the beneficiaries a proposal for distribution). "The right of any beneficiary to object to the proposed distribution terminates if the beneficiary does not notify the trustee of an objection within 30 days after the proposal was sent but only if the proposal informed the beneficiary of the right to object and of the time allowed for objection." UTC §817(a). *See generally* 5 Scott & Ascher §36.2.1 (Partial Terminating Distributions).

[738] The importance of ascertaining and communicating the tax basis/cost of an in-kind trust distribution is covered in §§11.1 and 11.4 of this handbook.

[739] *See* UTC §817(c) (available at <http://www.uniformlaws.org/Act.aspx?title=Trust%20 Code>) (providing that a release by a beneficiary of a trustee from liability for breach of trust is invalid to the extent it was induced by improper conduct of the trustee). A release also would be invalid to the extent the beneficiary, at the time of the release, did not know of the beneficiary's rights or of the material facts relating to the breach. UTC §817(c). The importance of ascertaining and communicating the tax basis/cost of an in-kind trust distribution is covered in §§11.1 and 11.4 of this handbook.

[740] *See* UTC §817(c) (available at <http://www.uniformlaws.org/Act.aspx?title=Trust%20 Code>) (providing that a release by a beneficiary of a trustee from liability for breach of trust is invalid to the extent it was induced by improper conduct of the trustee). A release also would be invalid to the extent the beneficiary, at the time of the release, did not know of the beneficiary's rights or of the material facts relating to the breach. UTC §817(c).

8. If a remaindermen with a vested beneficial interest in the trust has died before final distribution, ascertain whether you are that remainderman's inadvertent executor.[741]

§8.3   The Transfer of Trust Property

Purchase without notice is a cast-iron defence to the beneficiary's proprietary claim to a trust asset. . . .[1]

When the trustee transfers trust property to a bona fide purchaser, title passes free of trust.[2] Such a transfer forecloses the beneficiary's rights against the transferee, though not necessarily against the trustee,[3] as it cannot be said that the transferee has been unjustly enriched.[4] Any rights the beneficiary may have against nonbeneficiary takers of the trust property, including those who fail to qualify as bona fide purchasers, are covered elsewhere in this handbook.[5] Recall, however, that a transferee only secures the protection and status afforded a bona fide purchaser if title to the property is obtained for value and without notice.[6] The concept of the good faith purchaser for value or BFP is generally discussed in Section 8.15.63 of this handbook.[7]

---

[741] *See generally* §8.16 of this handbook (the trustee of revocable trust as "Inadvertent Executor").

§8.3 [1] Lewin ¶41-04 (England). *See also* 5 Scott & Ascher §29.1.1 (U.S.) (in accord). *See generally* §§5.4.2 of this handbook (rights of the beneficiary as against transferees of the underlying property, including BFPs), 8.3.2 of this handbook (bona fide purchase for value of trust property: what constitutes notice that transfer in breach of trust?), and 8.15.63 of this handbook (doctrine of bona fide purchase; the BFP). *See also* §8.3.6 of this handbook (negotiable instruments and the duty of third parties to inquire into the trustee's authority). For a comparison of the BFP, a creature of equity, with the holder in due course, a creature of law, *see* §8.15.68 of this handbook (holder in due course (the trust application)).

[2] Restatement (Second) of Trusts §284. *See generally* 4 Scott on Trusts §284.

[3] Lewin ¶41-04 (England).

[4] Restatement of Restitution §172; §8.15.78 of this handbook (unjust enrichment).

[5] *See* §5.4.2 of this handbook (rights of the beneficiary as against transferees, including BFPs).

[6] Restatement of Restitution §172.

[7] *See also* §§5.4.2 of this handbook (rights of the beneficiary as against transferees of the underlying property, including BFPs); 8.3.2 of this handbook (bona fide purchase for value of trust property: what constitutes notice that transfer in breach of trust?); Restatement of Restitution §172 (the defense of bona fide purchase). *Cf.* §8.3.6 of this handbook (negotiable instruments and the duty of third parties to inquire into the trustee's authority). For a comparison of the BFP, a creature of equity, with the holder in due course, a creature of law, *see* §8.15.68 of this handbook (holder in due course (trust application)).

§8.3.1 The Trustee's Personal Creditors and the Trustee's Spouse

Although a beneficial interest in a trust may generally be reached by creditors of the beneficiary . . . , the trustee's personal creditors or trustee in bankruptcy may not reach either the trust property or the trustee's nonbeneficial interest therein.[8]

In the early law of uses, it was held that, on the death of a trustee, the trustee's surviving spouse was entitled to dower or curtesy, free of the use. Thus it was stated as late as 1656, that the tenant in dower, and by curtesie, should not be seised to uses in being, for all these wanted privity of estate. . . . Today, . . . it is clear that the trustee's surviving spouse has no interest in the trust property, whether by dower, curtesy, or otherwise.[9]

As a general rule, an attachment of the trust property in a judicial proceeding by the trustee's personal creditors is subject to the rights of the beneficiaries.[10] In other words, the personal creditors of a nonbeneficiary trustee who resort to the courts are not BFPs[11] and thus may not acquire a beneficial interest in the trust property.[12] "A creditor who seizes a debtor's property under judicial process is not entitled to assume that the debtor holds the property free of equities."[13] Thus, it cannot be said that a trust is a form of contract:

> The main difficulty in the obligational view of trusts is that it does not explain the effect of the trust in relation to the rights of creditors—the "insolvency effect". This (the priority which the beneficiaries have over the trustee's creditors) is surely the central fact of the trust which any theory must recognize and explain. If the trust is in its essence a contract, it will not defeat the rights of the owner's . . . [, *i.e.*, the trustee's] . . . other creditors.[14]

---

[8] Restatement (Third) of Trusts §42 cmt. c. *See generally* §9.11 of this handbook (the bankruptcy trustee).

[9] 5 Scott & Ascher §29.1.6.1 (Devolution on Death of Trustee) (citing to Compleat Attorney 310 (1656).

[10] *See, e.g.,* 4 Scott & Ascher §§25.2.7.2 (Trustee-Beneficiary's Creditors), 25.2.7.3 (Transfer of Trustee-Beneficiary's Interest); 5 Scott & Ascher §29.3.11 (Creditors of Trustee). Note, however, that "[w]ith respect to trusts of land and other equitable interests in land, recording statutes may affect the question of whether the equitable interests of the beneficiaries or other claimants are entitled to priority over the rights of the trustee's creditors." 5 Scott & Ascher §29.3.11 (Creditors of Trustee).

[11] "The policy in favor of encouraging sales and security transactions does not apply." 5 Scott & Ascher §29.3.11 (Creditors of Trustee). *See generally* §8.15.63 of this handbook (doctrine of bona fide purchase; the BFP).

[12] Restatement (Third) of Trusts §42 cmt. c; Restatement (Second) of Trusts §308. *See generally* 4 Scott on Trusts §308. *See also* UTC §507 (available at <http://www.uniformlaws.org/Act.aspx?title=Trust%20Code>). *See, e.g.,* Universal Bonding Ins. Co. v. Gittens & Sprinkle Enters., 960 F.2d 366 (3d Cir. 1992).

[13] 5 Scott & Ascher §29.3.11 (Creditors of Trustee).

[14] George L. Gretton, *Trusts Without Equity*, 49 Int'l & Comp. L.Q. 599, 602–603 (July 2000).

In any case, if a trustee in breach of trust voluntarily or involuntarily transfers trust property to a third person, the third person may only retain the property if the third person is a bona fide purchaser for value or BFP.[15] In order to qualify as a BFP, the third person has to have taken title, given value, and had no actual or constructive notice of the breach.[16] With some exceptions, see Section 8.15.63 of this handbook, the satisfaction (cancellation) of an antecedent (preexisting) debt which the transferor owes the transferee will not satisfy the BFP value requirement.[17] The creditor-transferee thus not being a BFP, the property must be returned to the trust estate. Likewise, an assignment of trust property for the benefit of the trustee's personal creditors is ineffective.[18] "When a debtor makes an assignment for the benefit of creditors, the assignee is not a purchaser for value."[19] Neither is the trustee in bankruptcy of another trustee's personal estate.[20]

Because a trustee holds the legal title to the trust estate and as to the world is its owner, it is easy to see how the trust estate could end up in the hands of the trustee's personal creditors, albeit wrongfully, if the trustee were not careful.[21] The trustee would then have a fiduciary duty to get it back.[22] If the cause of the diversion were a failure on the part of the trustee to adequately segregate and earmark,[23] then the trustee might have to personally shoulder the burden of the retrieval costs.[24]

Certain attachments of real estate, however, may be exempted by statute from the general rule that trust property is off limits to the trustee's personal creditors.[25] Many states, for example, now have statutes subordinating the interest of the beneficiary to that of the trustee's personal creditor when the attached real estate is held in an unrecorded trust.[26] Thus, it is of critical importance for the trustee of an inter vivos trust containing real estate to record the governing instrument; timely recording effectively deprives the personal creditor of the trustee of any access to the trust's real estate.[27] Under most such statutes, the attaching creditor who has no notice of an unrecorded trust of real

---

[15] *See generally* §8.15.63 of this handbook (doctrine of bona fide purchase; the BFP).

[16] *See generally* §8.15.63 of this handbook (doctrine of bona fide purchase; the BFP).

[17] *See generally* §8.15.63 of this handbook (doctrine of bona fide purchase; the BFP).

[18] *See generally* 5 Scott & Ascher §29.3.9.

[19] 5 Scott & Ascher §29.3.9.

[20] *See generally* 5 Scott & Ascher §29.3.10 (Trustee in Bankruptcy).

[21] *See generally* §3.5.1 of this handbook (nature and extent of the trustee's estate).

[22] *See generally* §6.2.1 of this handbook (duty to take active control of, segregate, earmark, preserve and protect trust property).

[23] *See generally* §6.2.1.2 of this handbook (duty to segregate and earmark trust property (not to commingle)).

[24] *See generally* §3.5.2.3 of this handbook (right in equity to exoneration and reimbursement, *i.e.*, indemnity; payment of attorneys' fees).

[25] *See generally* 5 Scott & Ascher §29.3.11 (Creditors of Trustee).

[26] *See* 5 Scott & Ascher §29.3.11 (Creditors of Trustee); Restatement (Second) of Trusts §308 cmt. b. *See generally* §8.3.2 of this handbook (bona fide purchaser for value of trust property: what constitutes notice that a transfer is in breach of trust).

[27] *See generally* §8.3.2 of this handbook (bona fide purchaser for value of trust property: what constitutes notice that a transfer is in breach of trust).

estate will prevail over the beneficiary even though the creditor receives notice before taking the property on execution.[28] The statutes that give this unusual right do not ordinarily apply to personal property.[29]

As a general rule, the trustee's spouse will have no present or future rights to the trust property.[30] This holds true, both in the divorce context and upon the death of the trustee.[31] In neither case would the spouse qualify as a BFP.[32]

§8.3.2 Bona Fide Purchaser for Value of Trust Property: What Constitutes Notice That a Transfer Is in Breach of Trust?

But doubtless in the back of the minds of the equity judges, considerations of economic expediency also played a role. If the doctrines derived from conscience had not been commercially expedient, they would not have survived. The doctrine of bona fide purchase survives today precisely because it is commercially expedient.[33]

As we cover the doctrine of bona fide purchase in the trust context in some detail in Section 8.15.63 of this handbook, suffice it to say here that equity generally will not reverse a transfer of title to trust property to a bona fide purchaser for value (BFP),[34] even one made in breach of trust. For a transferee of title to trust property to qualify as a BFP, the transferee must have paid value for the property and have had no notice, actual or constructive, of the breach of trust.[35] Notice to a straw or other agent of the transferee would, of course, constitute notice to the transferee-principal.[36] Likewise, a transferee with notice of the breach could not achieve BFP status simply by having someone with no notice of the breach take the legal title to the subject property as trustee for the transferee's benefit.[37]

---

[28] *See generally* 5 Scott & Ascher §29.3.11; 4 Scott on Trusts §308.2.

[29] *See generally* Bogert §884; 3 Scott & Ascher §13.1. *See also* 5 Scott & Ascher §29.3.11.

[30] *See generally* Bogert §146.

[31] Bogert §146.

[32] *See generally* 5 Scott & Ascher §29.1.6.1 (Devolution on Death of Trustee); §8.15.63 of this handbook (doctrine of bona fide purchase).

[33] Scott & Ascher §13.1.

[34] *See generally* 5 Scott & Ascher §29.1.1.

[35] *See generally* 5 Scott & Ascher §§29.1 (General Principles), 29.1.5 (Transferee with Notice), 29.2 (Notice to Transferee of Trust Property) (suggesting that the term *constructive* is not a "happy" one: "It would be more accurate to say that a person has notice of a breach of trust where he or she has actual knowledge of the breach or knowledge of such facts that the person ought to inquire into whether the trustee is committing a breach of trust.").

[36] 5 Scott & Ascher §29.2.8 (Notice to Transferee's Agent).

[37] 5 Scott & Ascher §29.2.9 (Purchase in Trustee's Name). Assume the transferee-trustee innocently initiated the purchase but his beneficiary was aware of the breach. In that case, the transferor-trustee would have to disgorge the purchase price before getting the subject property back. 5 Scott & Ascher §29.2.9 (Purchase in Trustee's Name). An innocent transferee for value who takes title in the name of a trustee who has notice of the transferor-trustee's breach would still be

In the case of entrusted real estate, a prospective purchaser is on notice that the property is held in trust if the trust instrument is a matter of record.[38] The purchaser must then determine whether the trustee has the power of sale.[39] If the trustee has that power, the transferee will take clear title even though the trustee thereafter misappropriates the proceeds.[40] In England and in many American jurisdictions the purchaser expressly is exempted by statute from monitoring the application of the purchase price.[41]

In the case of unrecorded trust instruments, whether of real estate or personal property, or both, the first matter to be determined is whether the purchaser had notice of a trust's existence.[42] There being no instrument of public record this question becomes one of fact.[43] In the case of *real estate*, for example, the purchaser may be put on notice of the trust as a result of the explicit use of the word *trustee* in a previous deed,[44] material information communicated to the purchaser orally, or the existence of some peculiar circumstance, such as occupation of the property by a person who claims to have a beneficial interest in it.[45]

When there is no apparent evidence of the existence of a trust other than a recorded deed of real estate to the grantee "as trustee," then the prospective purchaser for value must investigate whether or not the subject property is actually entrusted, unless relieved of this duty of inquiry by statute.[46] If a reasonable and good-faith inquiry turns up nothing, then the purchaser will likely take the title as a BFP, with all the attendant protections.[47] "When a deed of land runs to the grantee personally but recites that the conveyance is in consideration of a payment by the grantee as trustee, a subsequent grantee is chargeable with notice that the land is held in trust."[48]

In the case of *securities*, the word *trustee* appearing upon the face of the certificate is sufficient to put the purchaser on notice of the trust's existence.[49]

---

a BFP. 5 Scott & Ascher §29.2.9 (Purchase in Trustee's Name). On the other hand, if a trustee-with-notice initiates a purchase for value from a wrongdoing trustee, neither the trustee-with-notice nor his beneficiary is a BFP. 5 Scott & Ascher §29.2.9 (Purchase in Trustee's Name).

[38] *See generally* 5 Scott & Ascher §29.2.1 (Notice Under Recording Statutes). *See also* 5 Scott & Ascher §29.2.3

[39] *See* §3.5.3 of this handbook (the powers of the trustee in equity to manage the trust estate).

[40] *See generally* 4 Scott on Trusts §321.

[41] 4 Scott on Trusts §321; 5 Scott & Ascher §30.1 (Misapplication of Payments Made to Trustee). *See also* §8.21 of this handbook (duty of third parties to investigate whether trustee is properly exercising power).

[42] *See generally* 5 Scott & Ascher §29.2.3 (Notice of Existence of Trust).

[43] *See generally* 5 Scott & Ascher §29.2.3 (Notice of Existence of Trust).

[44] *See generally* 4 Scott on Trusts §297.3; 5 Scott & Ascher §29.2.3.

[45] *See generally* 4 Scott on Trusts §297.3.

[46] 5 Scott & Ascher §29.2.3 (Notice of Existence of Trust).

[47] 5 Scott & Ascher §29.2.3 (Notice of Existence of Trust).

[48] 5 Scott & Ascher §29.2.3.

[49] *See generally* 5 Scott & Ascher §29.2.3; 4 Scott on Trusts §297.3. However, under the Uniform Commercial Code, the issuer or its transfer agent registering a security for transfer is not bound to inquire into the trustee's power. U.C.C. §8-404. *See also* Uniform Act for Simplification

In any case, the prospective purchaser of entrusted property of whatever sort who has constructive or actual notice of the entrustment may need to determine whether the trustee has the requisite authority to enter into the transaction,[50] unless relieved of such obligation by statute or otherwise.[51] Thus, if there is a trust instrument, prudence may dictate that, at minimum, a copy be obtained and its terms scrutinized.[52] For a general discussion of when such further inquiry is and is not warranted, the reader is again referred to Section 8.21 of this handbook.

A personal creditor of the trustee who in a judicial proceeding obtains an attachment of trust property in satisfaction of the debt would not take title as a bona fide purchaser, even if the creditor were unaware of the trust.[53] A judgment creditor takes subject to preexisting equities.[54] Having said that, "[w]ith respect to trusts of land and other equitable interests in land, recording statutes may affect the question of whether the equitable interests of the beneficiaries or other equitable claimants are entitled to priority over the rights of the trustee's creditors."[55] Also, one who purchases for value and in good faith trust property at a judicial sale of the trustee's personal assets may well be a BFP, a trustee having title to the property and the power to convey it.[56] On the other hand, there is some authority to the effect that if the judgment creditor is the purchaser, then the judgment creditor is not a BFP, "either because he or she is not a purchaser for value or because he or she is said to have 'constructive' notice of any equities."[57]

For more on why the satisfaction (cancellation) of an antecedent (preexisting) debt generally will not satisfy the BFP value requirement, see Section 8.15.63 of this handbook. For a general discussion of the rights of the trustee and trust beneficiaries as against transferees of the underlying property, see Section 5.4.2 of this handbook. As to the duty of third parties to investigate whether a trustee has power to act or is properly exercising the power, the reader is referred to Sections 8.21 of this handbook and 8.15.69 of this handbook. As to what constitutes third-party notice of a breach of trust when the

---

of Fiduciary Security Transfers §2. *See also* §8.21 of this handbook (duty of third parties to investigate whether trustee has power to act or is properly exercising the powers).

[50] Restatement (Second) of Trusts §297 cmts. d, k–n.

[51] 5 Scott & Ascher §29.2.4 (Notice of Terms of Trust).

[52] 5 Scott & Ascher §29.2.5 (Notice of Deviation from Terms of Trust) (in the absence of actual knowledge that the transaction would be in breach of trust, the prospective purchaser may rely on the language within the four corners of the governing instrument).

[53] UTC §507 cmt. (available at <http://www.uniformlaws.org/Act.aspx?title=Trust%20 Code>); 5 Scott & Ascher §29.3.11 (Creditors of Trustee). Property in which the trustee holds legal title as trustee is not part of the trustee's bankruptcy estate. 11 U.S.C. §541(d).

[54] 5 Scott & Ascher §29.3.11 (Creditors of Trustee).

[55] 5 Scott & Ascher §29.3.11 (Creditors of Trustee).

[56] 5 Scott & Ascher §29.3.12 (Purchaser at Judicial Sale) ("It is often said that a purchaser at an execution sale purchases at his or her peril . . . This is undoubtedly true to a certain extent, because if the judgment debtor does not have title, the purchaser cannot acquire title").

[57] 5 Scott & Ascher §29.3.12.

subject property is a negotiable instrument, see Section 8.3.6 of this handbook.[58] "Even at common law, . . . the duty of inquiry of a depository of trust funds differed substantially from that of a purchaser, mortgagee, or pledgee of trust property."[59] For more on a bank's duty of inquiry when it comes to deposits and withdrawals of trust funds, see Section 8.3.4 of this handbook. For a discussion of the differences between the BFP, a creature of equity, and the holder in due course, a creature of law, the reader is referred to Section 8.15.68 of this handbook.

§8.3.3   Pledgees of Trust Property and the Bona Fide Purchase Doctrine

So[60] also, when securities are held in trust but there is nothing on the face of the securities to indicate that they are held in trust, a purchaser or pledgee takes them free of the trust if the purchaser has no actual knowledge of the existence of the trust and no reason to believe that the securities are held in trust.[61]

Let us assume that the trustee pledges trust property to secure the trustee's own personal obligation. What are the rights of the pledgee as against the beneficiary? The pledgee is in a critical position: He may be a bona fide purchaser and fully protected in his security rights or, if the circumstances are against him, he may be at the extreme opposite pole, in the position of colluding in a breach of trust with full responsibility to the beneficiary as a constructive trustee.[62] Thus, a person who in good faith lends money to the trust and accepts a pledge of trust property will be fully protected despite a subsequent misappropriation of the proceeds of the loan.[63] However, if the lender accepts a pledge of known trust property to secure what the lender knows to be the trustee's personal indebtedness, the lender colludes in a breach of the trustee's duty of loyalty.[64] It should be noted that a pledgee of stock would be put upon inquiry by the presence of the word *trustee* on the face of the certificate.[65]

---

[58] *See also* §8.15.68 of this handbook (holder in due course (trust application)).

[59] 5 Scott & Ascher §30.4 (Depositories of Trust Funds). *See also* §§8.3.2 (bona fide purchaser for value of trust property: what constitutes notice that transfer in breach of trust?), 8.3.3 of this handbook (pledgees of trust property and the bona fide purchase doctrine), and 8.15.63 of this handbook (doctrine of bona fide purchase; the BFP).

[60] Restatement (Second) of Trusts §297 cmts. d, k–n.

[61] 5 Scott & Ascher §29.2.3.

[62] *See generally* §8.15.63 of this handbook (doctrine of bona fide purchase); 5 Scott & Ascher §29.1.1 (Bona Fide Purchaser).

[63] Restatement (Second) of Trusts §284 cmt. g.

[64] *See generally* §7.2.9 of this handbook (personal liability of third parties to the beneficiary).

[65] *See generally* 4 Scott on Trusts §297.3.

§8.3.4 Banks Receiving Deposits from Trustees and the Duty to Inquire into the Trustee's Authority

Even at common law, . . . the duty of inquiry of a depository of trust funds differed substantially from that of a purchaser, mortgagee, or pledgee of trust property.[66]

A bank generally is not bound to see that the trustee properly administers the trust's bank account even when it has notice that the money belongs to the trust.[67] It would be impossible to conduct business under any other rule. Therefore, in cases where the trustee, apparently acting in the ordinary course of business, draws funds from the trust account and deposits them in his own account, or in situations where the trustee deposits a trust check in his own account, the bank is not in any way liable.[68] There needs to be actual notice of a misappropriation,[69] nor at common law would there have been a presumption of misappropriation.[70] "Such a trustee may merely be taking reasonable compensation for serving as trustee, reimbursing himself or herself for reasonable expenses incurred on behalf of the trust, or taking a distribution of either income or principal to which the trustee is entitled as beneficiary." The Uniform Fiduciaries Act is generally in accord as to the lack of a presumption of misappropriation.[71] The Uniform Commercial Code, however, appears not to be.[72] The Restatement (Third) of Restitution and Unjust Enrichment would appear in solidarity with the U.C.C. in this regard.[73] Among the jurisdictions that have enacted both statutes, only a handful has endeavored to reconcile the conflicting presumptions.[74]

If the bank is on actual notice that a deposit of funds by a trustee into a trust checking or savings account with the bank is in breach of trust, then the bank risks liability for participating in the breach, even when there has been proper earmarking.[75] The bank, for example, could be chargeable as a constructive trustee of the funds were it on notice that under some federal, state, or

---

[66] 5 Scott & Ascher §30.4 (Depositories of Trust Funds). *See also* §§8.3.2 (bona fide purchaser for value of trust property: what constitutes notice that transfer in breach of trust?), 8.3.3 of this handbook (pledgees of trust property and the bona fide purchase doctrine), and 8.15.63 of this handbook (doctrine of bona fide purchase; the BFP).

[67] *See generally* 4 Scott on Trusts §324; Restatement (Second) of Trusts §324.

[68] *See generally* 4 Scott on Trusts §324.3.

[69] Bogert, Trusts and Trustees §21.

[70] 5 Scott & Ascher §30.4.2 (Deposit in Personal Account). *See generally* §§3.5.2.4 of this handbook (trustee's right in equity to compensation), 3.5.2.3 of this handbook (trustee's right in equity to exoneration and reimbursement), and 3.2.5 of this handbook (trustee as beneficiary).

[71] Unif. Fiduciaries Act §9.

[72] U.C.C. §§3-307(b)(2)(iii), 3-307 cmt. 3, 3-307(b)(4)(iii). *See generally* 5 Scott & Ascher §30.4.2 (Deposit in Personal Account).

[73] *See* Restatement (Third) of Restitution and Unjust Enrichment §69, illus. 13.

[74] 5 Scott & Ascher §30.4.2, n.11.

[75] *See generally* 5 Scott & Ascher §30.4.1 (Deposit in Trust Account); Bogert §21 (Deposit of Trust Funds). *See also* §6.2.1.2 of this handbook (trustee's duty to earmark trust property).

local regulation it was not a proper depository for them.[76] Note, also, that though "the bank at the time of the deposit did not have notice that the depositor was committing a breach of trust in making the deposit, if it receives such notice before the funds are withdrawn, it may be liable for permitting the withdrawal."[77] The lot of the trustee is not an easy one.[78]

If the trustee, in breach of trust, attempts to satisfy his personal obligation to the bank with trust funds on deposit in a checking or savings account with the bank[79] and the bank is on notice of the breach, then the bank must recredit the trust account.[80] Although at law the bank may have given value in releasing the trustee's personal debt to it, its notice of the trustee's breach of trust coupled with the antecedence of the personal debt[81] in equity would disqualify the bank as a BFP of the release of the debt that it owes to the trust, the debt taking the form of the account and the release taking the form of a debiting of that account.[82] By thus "setting one debt against the other" without the consent of the trust beneficiaries, it is said that such a transaction "in equity cannot stand."[83] The Restatement (Third) of Restitution and Unjust Enrichment is in accord.[84]

At common law, when a trustee gave a release in breach of trust and the obligor was not in a position of a bona fide purchaser, either because the obligor gave no value or because the obligor had notice that the trustee was committing a breach of trust in giving the release, the release was effective as a legal discharge but it would be set aside by a court of equity. After the merger of law and equity, the obligor is not permitted to avail himself or herself of the release even in an action at law.[85]

Today, whether and when a bank may debit a checking or savings account in satisfaction of a debt that the depositor owes to the bank is largely governed by statute.[86] As a general rule, if a trustee in breach of trust pays a personal debt

---

[76] 5 Scott & Ascher §30.4.1; Bogert §21. *See also* §§3.3 of this handbook (the constructive trustee) and 7.2.3.1 of this handbook (tracing and accounting for proceeds and profits).

[77] 5 Scott & Ascher §30.4.1 (Deposit in Trust Account).

[78] *See generally* 5 Scott & Ascher §30.4.3 (Permitting Withdrawals) (a bank permitting a trustee to withdraw funds after the bank has been put on actual notice that the withdrawal would be in breach of trust risks liability for participating in a breach of trust). *See generally* §3.5.4.1 of this handbook (in part discussing third-party participation in a breach of trust).

[79] *See generally* §9.9.4 of this handbook (bank accounts and other such debtor-creditor contractual arrangements are not trusts).

[80] *See generally* 4 Scott on Trusts §324.4; 5 Scott & Ascher §30.2 (Release of Claim Against Third Person by Trustee).

[81] *See generally* 5 Scott & Ascher §29.3.7 (Satisfaction of Antecedent Debt as Value).

[82] 5 Scott & Ascher §30.2. *See generally* §8.15.63 of this handbook (doctrine of bona fide purchase; the BFP).

[83] Pannell v. Hurley, 2 Coll. 241, 245 (1845) (England). The opinion was rendered by Vice-Chancellor Knight Bruce.

[84] Restatement (Third) of Restitution and Unjust Enrichment §17, illus. 14 ("Bank's affirmative defense as a bona fide payee (§67) is foreclosed by its notice of the breach of trust.").

[85] 5 Scott & Ascher §30.2.

[86] *See generally* 5 Scott & Ascher §30.4.4 (Application of Deposit to Depositor's Individual Indebtedness to Bank).

that the trustee owes the bank with a personal check drawn on the trustee's personal account with the bank, the bank may accept the check in payment of the personal indebtedness, unless the bank has actual knowledge of the breach.[87] On the other hand, if the check is drawn in breach of trust on an account that is designated as a trust account, then the bank is deemed to have notice of the breach.[88] In addition, under the Uniform Commercial Code, if the trustee's personal account in breach of trust contains entrusted funds, the bank would risk liability for participating in the breach.[89] The Uniform Fiduciaries Act is not in accord in this regard.[90] Note, also, that what generally applies to a bank in the context of taking a fiduciary's check would also apply to the bank in the context of a unilateral set-off against the fiduciary's personal indebtedness to the bank.[91]

Section 104(b) of the Uniform Trust Code addresses when a corporate trustee would have notice or knowledge of a fact involving its trust: "...[O]nly from the time the information was received by an employee having responsibility to act for the trust, or would have been brought to the employee's attention if the organization had exercised reasonable diligence." The corporate trustee is deemed to exercise reasonable diligence "if it maintains reasonable routines for communicating significant information to the employee having responsibility to act for the trust and there is reasonable compliance with the routines."[92] Notice to a branch office generally would not suffice.[93] "Nor does the organization necessarily acquire knowledge at the moment the notice arrives in the organization's mailroom."[94] While Section 104(b) does not appear to squarely address what would constitute notice to a corporate depository of entrusted funds of critical matters involving the trust, such as a material breach of trust, presumably the notice standard to which a corporate depository is held is no higher than the notice standard to which a corporate trustee, a fiduciary *ab initio*, is held.

§8.3.5 The Duty of an Issuing Corporation and Its Stock Transfer Agent to Inquire into the Trustee's Authority

In the absence of statutory guidance, the weight of authority in the United States was that, whenever the securities were registered in the name of the trustee as such, the corporation was

---

[87] 5 Scott & Ascher §30.4.4.

[88] 5 Scott & Ascher §30.4.4.

[89] U.C.C. §3-307(b)(2)(iii), (4)(iii). *See generally* 5 Scott & Ascher §30.4.4.

[90] Unif. Fiduciaries Act §9.

[91] 5 Scott & Ascher §30.4.4.

[92] "Reasonable diligence does not require an employee of the organization to communicate information unless the communication is part of the individual's regular duties or the individual knows a matter involving the trust would be materially affected by the information." UTC §104(b).

[93] UTC §104 cmt. (available at <http://www.uniformlaws.org/Act.aspx?title=Trust%20Code>).

[94] UTC §104 cmt. (available at <http://www.uniformlaws.org/Act.aspx?title=Trust%20Code>).

on notice of the trust's existence and therefore under an obligation to inquire whether the trustee was authorized to make the transfer, and was liable for participation in the breach of trust if such inquiry would have indicated that, in making the transfer, the trustee was committing a breach of trust. In stark contrast, the courts in England had long held that a corporation whose securities were held by a trustee was not liable for registering a transfer without inquiring into the trustee's authority to make the transfer, even if the transfer was, in fact, in breach of trust.[95]

The stock transfer agent, who is asked to effect transfer of a trust's shares in a corporation, and the corporation itself, are placed in an unpleasant position whenever the trustee is engaged in a wrongful assignment or sale of the shares. The underlying rule is that any person who knowingly assists in the wrongful disposition of the trust property is fully responsible.[96] "This was true whether the securities were registered in the name of the trustee individually or as trustee."[97] This means that, in the absence of a statute, whenever the corporation or its transfer agent knows of the existence of a trust it must ascertain whether the trustee has the power of sale.[98] As the duty to ascertain the trustee's authority is placed upon the corporation, it or its agent would be justified in declining to make transfer unless the trustee supplies the certificates for inspection or produces other evidence showing a right to make the transfer.

Prodded in large part by the "unfortunate decision"[99] in the 1943 landmark case of *King v. Richardson*,[100] in which the trustees of some shares in a chemical company were held liable for selling the shares in contravention of the terms of the trust and in which the company itself was held liable for participating in the breach by reregistering the shares, most states have now adopted statutes relieving corporations and their transfer agents of the duty to investigate a trustee's authority to transfer securities absent actual knowledge of the lack thereof.[101] They have generally done so either by enacting some version of the Uniform Act for Simplification of Fiduciary Security Transfers or some version of Article 8 of the Uniform Commercial Code, or both.[102]

For a more general discussion of the duty of third parties to investigate whether a trustee has the authority to take a particular action, the reader is referred to Section 8.21 of this handbook.

---

[95] 5 Scott & Ascher §30.5.

[96] *See generally* Bogert §901; 5 Scott & Ascher §30.5 (Registration of Transfer of Securities Held by Trustee); §8.21 of this handbook (duty of third parties to investigate whether trustee has power to act or is properly exercising the power).

[97] 5 Scott & Ascher §30.5.

[98] *See generally* Bogert §905.

[99] 5 Scott & Ascher §17.11.4 (noting that the ensuing flurry of legislation in the various states authorizing the nominee registration of entrusted securities was another response to the *King v. Richardson* decision).

[100] 136 F.2d 849 (4th Cir.), *cert. denied*, 320 U.S. 777 (1943).

[101] *See generally* Bogert §905; 5 Scott & Ascher §30.5 (Registration of Transfer of Securities Held by Trustee).

[102] *See* Unif. Act for Simplification of Fiduciary Security Transfers §3; U.C.C. §§8-804, 8-404, 8-403. *See generally* 5 Scott & Ascher §30.5, nn.11–19.

§8.3.6 Negotiable Instruments and the Duty of Third Parties to Inquire into the Trustee's Authority

The general principle that when a trustee in breach of trust transfers property to one who has notice of the breach of trust the transferee takes subject to the trust applied, as well, at common law, in the case of negotiable instruments. Given the widespread enactment of the Uniform Commercial Code, however, what constitutes notice of a breach of trust in the case of the transfer of a negotiable instrument is now almost entirely statutory.[103]

A negotiable instrument is a special type of contract, namely, "a written promise, or order, to pay to the order of a named payee, or to bearer, a specified sum of money" that on its face is unilateral and unconditional.[104] An individual promissory note in bearer form and a check made payable to "cash" are examples of negotiable instruments.[105] An assignment is a transfer of one's rights under a contract to a third party; a negotiation is a transfer of one's rights under a negotiable instrument.[106] Generally the assignee of contract rights takes only the rights that the assignor possessed, unless the assignee is a BFP.[107] The transferee of rights under a negotiable instrument takes only the rights that the transferor possessed, unless the transferee is a holder in due course.[108] Thus if *X* transfers to *Y* a check made out to cash in the amount of $50 in exchange for *Y*'s promise to mow *X*'s lawn, and *Y* does not mow the lawn, then *X* is entitled to get the check back from *Y*. But if *Y* in the interim has negotiated the check to a holder in due course, the holder in due course may keep the check and enforce its terms against *X*.[109] Any recourse *X* may have is against *Y* alone.[110]

A holder in due course[111] is like a BFP in the following respects:

- Each has to have paid value.[112]
- Each has to have had lack of notice that the transfer might be in derogation of the legal or equitable property rights of others.[113]

---

[103] 5 Scott & Ascher §29.2.6.

[104] Arthur Linton Corbin, Corbin on Contracts §863 (1952).

[105] U.C.C. §3-102 cmt.

[106] Arthur Linton Corbin, Corbin on Contracts §863 (1952) ("In so far as the rules applicable to negotiable instruments differ from those applicable to the assignment of other contract rights, they are due to the commercial advantages accruing from the use of a readily transferable credit instrument").

[107] *See generally* §8.15.63 of this handbook (doctrine of bona fide purchase; the BFP).

[108] U.C.C. §3-302 (Holder in Due Course); Bogert §883 (The Rule of Negotiability).

[109] U.C.C. §3-302 cmt.

[110] U.C.C. §3-302 cmt.

[111] *See generally* §8.15.68 of this handbook (holder in due course (trust application)).

[112] *See generally* §8.15.63 of this handbook (doctrine of bona fide purchase; the BFP); U.C.C. §3-302 (Holder in Due Course).

[113] *See generally* §8.15.63 of this handbook (doctrine of bona fide purchase; the BFP); U.C.C. §3-302 (Holder in Due Course). *See also* U.C.C. §3-307 (Notice of Breach of Fiduciary Duty).

There are some critical differences, however:

- The BFP is an equitable concept while the holder in due course is a legal one that is now generally codified, at least in the United States.[114] See Article 3 of the Uniform Commercial Code, versions of which have been enacted into law in most if not all the states.
- Cancellation of an antecedent debt can satisfy the holder-in-due-course value requirement but not the BFP value requirement.[115]
- In a case where trust property is transferred for value to a third party in breach of trust and the third party is to pay the funds *to the trustee personally*, it is unlikely that the third party would qualify as a BFP,[116] whereas if the property were a negotiable instrument, a third party who pays value and who has no actual knowledge of the breach would likely qualify as a holder in due course.[117]

If a trustee in breach-of-trust transfers an entrusted negotiable instrument to a third party for value who has actual notice of the breach, the third party is not a holder in due course.[118] Moreover, under Section 3-307 of the Uniform Commercial Code, the party has notice of a possible breach of trust if the third party has actual knowledge that the transferor is a fiduciary[119] and that (1) the payment is in satisfaction of the trustee's personal obligation; (2) the payment is otherwise to be applied for the trustee's personal benefit; or (3) the payment is not to be deposited into an account of the trust.[120] No such inference is raised, however, if the payment is made to the trustee personally.[121] The Uniform Fiduciaries Act is generally in accord.[122]

For a general discussion of whether a third party who transacts with the trustee has a duty to ascertain the trustee's authority in equity to enter into the transaction and to ascertain whether the authority is being properly exercised, the reader is referred to Section 8.21 of this handbook.

§8.3.7 The Duty of Stockbrokers to Inquire into the Trustee's Authority to Transact

Securities brokers who have assisted a fiduciary or a trustee in speculating with trust funds and deceiving the beneficiaries of an investment trust as to the financial stability of the trust

---

[114] *See* Dearman v. Trimmier, 26 S.C. 506, 2 S.E. 501, 504 (1887).

[115] 5 Scott & Ascher §29.3.7 (Satisfaction of Antecedent Debt as Value). *See, e.g.*, Dearman v. Trimmier, 26 S.C. 506, 2 S.E. 501, 504 (1887).

[116] *See generally* §8.15.63 of this handbook (doctrine of bona fide purchase; the BFP).

[117] U.C.C. §3-307 (Notice of Breach of Fiduciary Duty).

[118] U.C.C. §3-307 (Notice of Breach of Fiduciary Duty).

[119] *See generally* 5 Scott & Ascher §29.2.6 (Negotiable Instruments).

[120] *See generally* 5 Scott & Ascher §29.2.6 (Negotiable Instruments).

[121] U.C.C. §3-307 (Notice of Breach of Fiduciary Duty).

[122] Unif. Fiduciaries Act §§4 & 6.

are directly liable to the beneficiaries themselves both for breach of the brokers' fiduciary duties, and for aiding and abetting the trustee's breach in order to further the brokers' own economic interests—City of Atascadero v. Merrill Lynch, Pierce, Fenner & Smith, Inc.[123]

A stockbroker who knowingly participates with a trustee in a breach of trust may be liable to the beneficiaries, along with the trustee, for any attendant harm to their equitable interests.[124] At common law, a stockbroker would risk liability even if the stockbroker were on notice that a contemplated stock acquisition or disposition might constitute a breach of trust.[125] On the other hand, "[t]he mere fact that the account was in a customer's name, as trustee, did not impose on the broker a duty to examine the trust instrument to determine whether the trustee was authorized to purchase or sell the securities."[126] Under the Uniform Act for Simplification of Fiduciary Security Transfers, the stockbroker has somewhat less of a burden: For the stockbroker to incur liability, there has to be "actual knowledge" that the transaction would be in breach of trust.[127] Under Article 8 of the Uniform Commercial Code, the stockbroker's burden is further reduced: There has to be actual "collusion" with the trustee in a breach of trust:[128]

Knowledge that the action of the customer is wrongful is a necessary but not sufficient condition of the collusion test. The aspect of the role of securities intermediaries and brokers that Article 8 deals with is the clerical or ministerial role of implementing and recording the securities transactions that their customers conduct. Faithful performance of this role consists of following the instructions of the customer. It is not the role of the record keeper to police whether the transactions recorded are appropriate, so mere awareness that the customer may be acting wrongfully does not itself constitute collusion. That, of course, does not insulate an intermediary or broker from responsibility in egregious cases where its action goes beyond the ordinary standards of the business of implementing and recording transactions, and reaches a level of affirmative misconduct in assisting the customer in the commission of a wrong.[129]

For a more general discussion of the duty of third parties to investigate whether a trustee has the authority to engage in a particular activity, the reader is referred to Section 8.21 of this handbook.

---

[123] 80 Cal. Rptr. 2d 329 (Ct. App. 1998).

[124] 5 Scott & Ascher §30.6.2 (Brokers).

[125] 5 Scott & Ascher §30.6.2.

[126] 5 Scott & Ascher §30.6.2.

[127] Unif. Act for Simplification of Fiduciary Securities Transfers §7(a).

[128] U.C.C. §8-115.

[129] U.C.C. §8-115 cmt. 5.

§8.3.8   The Trust Safe Deposit Box: The Duty of the Lessor to Ascertain One's Equitable Authority to Gain Access

A bank, trust company, or safe deposit company (the "lessor") is generally the custodian, not the trustee, of the items of property in the safe deposit boxes that it rents out to the public. Title to each item remains in its owner. The laws of bailment, a nonfiduciary legal relationship, are applicable, absent special facts.[130] In the case of a safe deposit box that has been rented to a trustee and his agent, the question may arise whether the lessor risks liability for participating with the trustee in a breach of trust if it affords the agent access to the box and the agent thereafter absconds with its contents. What if putting the agent's name on the access card in the first place was a breach of trust on the part of the trustee? Perhaps doing so violated the express terms of the trust. "It would seem . . . that the . . . [lessor] . . . is not bound to inquire whether the trustee is committing a breach of trust in permitting an agent access to the safe-deposit box and that, unless the . . . [lessor] . . . knows or has reason to believe that the trustee is committing a breach of trust, the . . . [lessor] . . . should not be liable."[131]

When cotrustees grant to one of their number authority to access the trust safe deposit box alone, their collective fiduciary duty not to imprudently delegate the trust's administration may be implicated, a topic that is touched upon in Section 6.1.4 of this handbook.

§8.4   The Trustee's Compensation

Even though by the terms of the trust the trustee is to receive no compensation, he is under a duty if he has accepted the trust to administer it.[1]

"Sanders, the late-18th-century English treatise writer, explained: '[C]ourts of equity look upon trusts as honorary, and as a burden upon the honor and conscience of the [trustee], and not undertaken upon mercenary motives.' "[2] Subject to a contrary provision in the governing instrument,[3] the general rule now in the United States is that the trustee is entitled to reasonable

---

[130] *See generally* Chapter 1 of this handbook (in part outlining the differences between the trust and the bailment).

[131] 5 Scott & Ascher §30.6.5.

§8.4 [1] Restatement (Second) of Trusts §169 cmt. b.

[2] John H. Langbein, *Rise of the Management Trust*, Tr. & Est. 53 (Oct. 2004) (citing to Francis W. Sanders, An Essay on the Nature and Laws of Uses and Trusts, Including a Treatise on Conveyances at Common Law 256 (London, 1791).

[3] *See generally* Bogert §976 (Control of Compensation by Settlor or Beneficiary).

compensation.[4] Even the trustee of a charitable trust is so entitled, unless the terms of the trust provide otherwise.[5]

In some states, such as New York, the trustee's fees are set by statute,[6] and in others, such as Massachusetts, it is a matter of custom and practice.[7] "The trustee need not pay over income without deducting the compensation to which he is entitled with respect to the income, and need not pay over principal without deducting the compensation to which he is entitled with respect to the principal."[8] To the extent of his earned reasonable compensation, the trustee has a "security interest"[9] in or lien on[10] the trust property. On the other hand, a trustee or his probate estate going forward is not entitled to fiduciary compensation once the trustee for whatever reason ceases to serve as trustee.[11]

"The fact that a trustee is entitled to compensation for serving in that capacity . . . , however, does not make the trustee a beneficiary of the trust."[12] Thus, "if all of the beneficiaries wish to terminate a trust, it will not be continued merely to enable the trustee to earn additional compensation."[13] The terms of the trust, however, may bestow on the trustee beneficiary status.[14] Unless the terms of the trust provide otherwise, the presumption is that the equitable interest of a trustee-beneficiary is in addition to his regular compensation, not in lieu of compensation or the compensation itself.[15] Also, the presumption is that serving as trustee is not a condition of the trustee-beneficiary's enjoying the equitable interest.[16] Ultimately it is a question of interpretation of the settlor's intent.[17]

---

[4] *See generally* 4 Scott & Ascher §21.1; 3A Scott on Trusts §242; Restatement (Second) of Trusts §242; Restatement (Third) of Trusts §38 (1); Revised Reg. 9, 12 C.F.R. §9.15(a) (1997) (available at <www.gpoaccess.gov/cfr/index.html>) (providing that if the amount of a national bank's compensation for acting in a fiduciary capacity is not set or governed by applicable law, the bank may charge a reasonable fee for its service); UTC §708(a) (available at <http://www.uniformlaws.org/Act.aspx?title=Trust%20Code>) (providing that if the terms of a trust do not specify the trustee's compensation, a trustee is entitled to compensation that is reasonable under the circumstances).

[5] *See generally* 5 Scott & Ascher §37.3.9 (noting, however, that "in the case of charitable corporations, the members of the board of trustees ordinarily serve without compensation").

[6] *See* Bogert §§806, 975; 4 Scott & Ascher §21.1 notes 8, 13 (citations to numerous state trustee compensation statutes).

[7] Restatement (Second) of Trusts §242 cmt. b.

[8] Restatement (Second) of Trusts §242 cmt. e. *See also* 4 Scott & Ascher §21.1 (The Trustee's Compensation—in General); 5 Scott & Ascher §36.2.2 (Trustee's Lien).

[9] Restatement (Second) of Trusts §242 cmt. e.

[10] Restatement (Third) of Trusts §38 cmt. b.

[11] *See generally* 4 Scott and Ascher §21.1.10 (When Trustee Fails to Complete Administration).

[12] Restatement (Third) of Trusts §48 cmt. c.

[13] 5 Scott & Ascher §24.1. *See generally* §8.15.7 of this handbook (the *Claflin* doctrine (material purpose doctrine)).

[14] *See generally* 4 Scott & Ascher §21.1.3 (Terms of the Trust).

[15] Restatement (Third) of Trusts §38 cmt. e.

[16] Restatement (Third) of Trusts §38 cmt. e.

[17] Restatement (Third) of Trusts §38 cmt. e.

The prevailing practice in this country and in England is to calculate the trustee's compensation on the basis of a fixed percentage of income and/or principal,[18] *i.e.,* of the net principal. "Thus, with respect to land that is subject to a mortgage, the trustee's fee is ordinarily computed on the value of the trust's equity, not on the land's total value."[19] In Florida, however, the fixed-percentage approach to trustee compensation may be suspect.[20]

When the trustee is also counsel to the trust, however, the practice of charging on a time basis for the legal work and on a percentage basis for the fiduciary responsibility can give the appearance that the trust is being double-billed.[21] In this situation, it is probably better both for the attorney-trustee and the beneficiary if all compensation is time based,[22] provided the attorney-trustee segregates his trustee fees from his attorneys' fees in his time records and fee applications.[23] There is a general sense that the attorney-trustee's hourly rate for trust administration services ought to be materially lower than his hourly rate for performing trust counsel services, absent special facts. In one case the attorney-trustee had charged the trust estate the same hourly rate, $185–$195, for performing both types of services.[24] The court accepted the rate of $185–$195 for his legal work but reduced to $100 the rate he was allowed to charge for his trust administration work.[25]

In any case, as one may not contract with oneself, any agreement that the trustee makes with himself to furnish compensated legal services to the trust is unenforceable.[26] "In other words, a trustee who renders extra services can recover only so much as the court deems reasonable compensation under all the

---

[18] *See* 4 Scott & Ascher §21.1; Bogert §§806, 975; Restatement (Second) of Trusts §242 cmt. b; Lewin ¶ 19-58 (England). *But see* In re Estate of Sonovick, 373 Pa. Super. 396, 541 A.2d 374 (1988) (suggesting that compensation should be based on actual services rendered and not upon some arbitrary formula). In England, trust corporations sometimes charge fees on a time spent basis. Lewin ¶ 19-58.

[19] 4 Scott & Ascher §21.1.

[20] *Cf.* In re Platt's Estate, 586 So. 2d 328 (Fla. 1991) (compensating the personal representative).

[21] *See* UTC §708 cmt. (available at <http://www.uniformlaws.org/Act.aspx?title=Trust%20 Code>) (not taking a specific position on whether dual fees may be charged but noting that the trend is to authorize dual compensation as long as the overall fees are reasonable).

[22] *See, e.g.,* Grimes v. Perkins Sch. for the Blind, 22 Mass. App. Ct. 439, 494 N.E.2d 406 (1986) (suggesting that percentages are rules of thumb, useful as a guide, but not to be mechanically applied without consideration of the services actually performed). *See generally* §§3.2.2 of this handbook (the lawyer [as trustee]) and 6.1.3.3 of this handbook (trustee benefiting as buyer and seller); B. Glenn, Annot., *Right to double compensation where same person (Natural or Corporate) Acts as Executor and Trustee,* 85 A.L.R.2d 537 (1962).

[23] *See* In re Testamentary Trust of Flynn, Slip Copy, 2005 WL 1846520 (Ohio App. 2d Dist.), 2005-Ohio-4028 (in affirming the judgment of the lower court reducing the compensation of an attorney-trustee of a small trust, the court found compelling that a sizable amount of the work for which the attorney-trustee billed attorneys' fees fell within the scope of tasks that would typically be performed by a trustee and that her hourly attorney-fee rate was substantially higher than what a trustee should charge for administering a small trust).

[24] *See* Barron Revocable Trust v. Barron, 2013 WL 275913 (Mich. App.).

[25] *See* Barron Revocable Trust v. Barron, 2013 WL 275913 (Mich. App.).

[26] 4 Scott & Ascher §21.1.2.

circumstances."[27] The Uniform Trust Code requires that the trustee notify the qualified beneficiaries, usually the current beneficiaries and presumptive remaindermen, in advance of any change in the method or rate of the trustee's compensation.[28]

With respect to a given trust, beneficiaries, cotrustees, and other such interested persons would have standing to bring an action challenging "the reasonableness of the compensation determined by the trustee for his own services."[29] A trustee who has received excessive compensation from a trust may be ordered to make "appropriate refunds."[30] The reasonableness of a trustee's compensation is typically raised in the context of a proceeding for the allowance of the trustee's accounts,[31] though there is no impediment to a beneficiary reasonably and in good faith bringing the matter of fiduciary compensation before the court at any other time and in any other context, including in a proceeding for the sole purpose of adjudicating trustee compensation issues.

When the rule is that a trustee is entitled to reasonable compensation, what is "reasonable" depends upon the facts and circumstances.[32] Courts consider "the amount and difficulty of the services rendered by the trustee, the risks run by the trustee, and the responsibilities imposed upon him, and his skill and success in administering the trust."[33] The California Rules of Court advise that in determining or approving compensation of a trustee, the court may consider, among other factors, the following:

- "The gross income of the ... [trust] ... estate
- The success or failure of the trustee's administration
- Any unusual skill, expertise, or experience brought to the trustee's work
- The fidelity or disloyalty shown by the trustee
- The amount of risk and responsibility assumed by the trustee
- The time spent in the performance of the trustee's duties
- The custom in the community where the court is located regarding compensation authorized by settlors, compensation allowed by the court, or charges of corporate trustees for trusts or similar size and complexity

---

[27] 4 Scott & Ascher §21.1.2.

[28] UTC §813(b)(4) (available at <http://www.uniformlaws.org/Act.aspx?title=Trust%20 Code>).

[29] UPC §7-205. *See, e.g.*, Mass. Gen. Laws ch. 190B, §7-205.

[30] UPC §7-205. *See, e.g.*, Mass. Gen. Laws ch. 190B, §7-205.

[31] *See generally* §6.1.5.2 of this handbook (the trustee's duty to render accounts).

[32] *See generally* 4 Scott & Ascher §21.1.

[33] 4 Scott & Ascher §21.1; 3A Scott on Trusts §242 at 277. *See* Restatement (Second) of Trusts §242 cmt. b (listing factors that courts are to consider in determining amount of reasonable trustee compensation). *See also* UTC §708 cmt. (available at <http://www.uniformlaws. org/Act.aspx?title=Trust%20Code>) (noting that relevant factors in determining ... [reasonable] ... compensation ... include the custom of the community; the trustee's skill, experience, and facilities; the time devoted to trust duties; the amount and character of the trust property; the degree of difficulty, responsibility, and risk assumed in administering the trust, including in making discretionary distributions; the nature and costs of services rendered by others; and the quality of the trustee's performance).

- Whether the work performed was routine, or required more than ordinary skill or judgment"[34]

When the trustee properly delegates to agents particular tasks, the cost of doing so is generally a legitimate trust expense.[35] "A downward adjustment of fees may be appropriate . . . , [however] . . . , if a trustee has delegated significant duties to agents, such as the delegation of investment authority to outside managers,"[36] assuming, of course, that the trustee is being compensated for doing what the agents are doing.[37]

A downward adjustment certainly is appropriate if the trustee invests in a mutual fund whose fees, expenses, and other internal charges are unreasonably high.[38] It may be appropriate even if the fees are reasonable. "Mutual fund shares held in the trust are . . . subject to inherent management compensation (normally in the range of one percent of asset value), which suggests the need for a proportionate discount from the trustee's regular fee schedule, as to those shares."[39] On the other hand, "if the trustee improperly delegates, not only may the trustee incur liability for doing so, but the trustee may not be allowed reimbursement for the expense of employing the agent."[40]

The use by a corporate trustee of its proprietary mutual funds for a trust's investment program "must not result in the trustee receiving more than the reasonable overall compensation appropriate to its services to the trust, taking account of the trustee's mutual-fund duties and compensation."[41] The same approach should be taken when the trustee serves as director, officer, or manager of an enterprise in which the trust owns a controlling interest.[42] The Restatement (Third) of Trusts suggests that compensation received by the trustee from the enterprise should be handled this way: The trustee should

---

[34] UTC §813(b)(4) (available at <http://www.uniformlaws.org/Act.aspx?title=Trust%20 Code>).

[35] See generally 3 Scott & Ascher §18.1.2.3.

[36] UTC §708 cmt. (available at <http://www.uniformlaws.org/Act.aspx?title=Trust%20 Code>). The deductibility of investment advisory fees may have a bearing on whether or not a downward adjustment of trustee fees is in order. See also Restatement (Third) of Trusts §88 cmt. c; 3 Scott & Ascher §18.1.2.3 (Employment of Agents). See, e.g., Mellon Bank, N.A. v. United States, 47 Fed. Cl. 186 (Ct. Fed. Cl. 2000) (holding income tax deduction for fees paid by trustee to outside investment advisers subject to two percent floor). "On the other hand, a trustee with special skills, such as those of a real estate agent, may be entitled to extra compensation for performing services that would ordinarily be delegated." UTC §708 cmt.

[37] See generally 3 Scott & Ascher §18.1.2.3.

[38] See, e.g., Danny Hakim, Index Fund Fees Are Not Created Equal, N.Y. Times, Jan. 14, 2001, at BU8, col. 2 (noting that "[a]mong the seven equity mutual funds that it offers through its ONE Fund subsidiary, Ohio National has a Standard & Poor's 500 index mutual fund that is more than 10 times as expensive as some of its competitors, even though all such index funds track the same benchmark").

[39] ACTEC Practice Committee, Fiduciary Matters Subcommittee, Guide for ACTEC Fellows Serving as Trustees, 26 ACTEC Notes 313, 324 (2001).

[40] 3 Scott & Ascher §18.1.2.3.

[41] Restatement (Third) of Trusts §78 cmt. c(8).

[42] See generally 4 Scott & Ascher §21.1.1

"account to the trust for all of the compensation, with the reasonable compensation (or special compensation) as trustee to include the value of the special services rendered in the trustee's role with the corporation or other enterprise."[43] When the trustee's compensation is keyed to income, "it would obviously be unfair to the beneficiaries to allow the trustee percentage commissions based on gross receipts."[44] They should be based on the net income of the business.[45] "In states in which executors and trustees are entitled to such compensation as the court deems reasonable, a person who acts as both executor and trustee is entitled to such compensation as is reasonable in view of all of the duties informed."[46]

In voting shares of stock or otherwise exercising powers of control over enterprises, the trustee shall act in the best interests of the beneficiaries.[47] He must elect or appoint directors or other managers who will manage the corporation or enterprise in the best interest of the beneficiaries.[48] The trustee may use the voting power to procure a position as director, officer or manager of the enterprise, provided the position is procured to serve the interests of the trusts and its beneficiaries.[49] In other words, "[t]he trustee may not use the corporate form to escape the fiduciary duties of trust law."[50] Thus, if a trustee were to engineer his appointment to an official position with the enterprise for the purpose of supplementing his compensation as trustee, then he could well be compelled to turn over the corporate salary to the trust.[51] He might even be forced to step down from the trusteeship itself.[52] The laws of England and the Isle of Man are generally in accord.[53]

---

[43] Restatement (Third) of Trusts §78 cmt. d(1).

[44] 4 Scott and Ascher §21.1.1.

[45] *See generally* 4 Scott and Ascher §21.1.1.

[46] 4 Scott & Ascher §21.1.8 (Double Commissions).

[47] UTC §802(g) (available at <http://www.uniformlaws.org/Act.aspx?title=Trust%20 Code>).

[48] UTC §802(g) (available at <http://www.uniformlaws.org/Act.aspx?title=Trust%20 Code>).

[49] Restatement (Third) of Trusts §78 cmt. (d)1. An appropriate compensation arrangement for the trustee's services to the corporation or other enterprise held in the trust would be for the trustee to turn over to the trust any compensation the trustee receives from the corporation or other enterprise, with "the reasonable compensation (or special compensation) as trustee to include the value of the special services rendered in the trustee's role with the corporation or other enterprise"). Restatement (Third) of Trusts §78 cmt. (d)1.

[50] UTC §802(g) (available at <http://www.uniformlaws.org/Act.aspx?title=Trust%20 Code>). "Thus, for example, a trustee whose duty of impartiality would require the trustee to make current distributions for the support of current beneficiaries may not evade that duty by holding assets in corporate form and pleading the discretion of corporate directors to determine dividend policy." UTC §802(g). "Rather, the trustee must vote for corporate directors who will follow a dividend policy consistent with the trustee's trust-law duty of impartiality." UTC 802(g). *See, e.g.,* Koffend's Will v. First Nat'l Bank of Minneapolis, 218 Minn. 206, 219–220, 15 N.W.2d 590, 598 (1944) (confirming that when a corporation is used as an agency to effectuate a settlor's intention, the law of trusts trumps the law of corporations).

[51] *See generally* 3 Scott & Ascher §17.2.8 (Bonus, Commission, or Other Compensation).

[52] *See generally* 3 Scott & Ascher §17.2.8 (Bonus, Commission, or Other Compensation).

[53] *See, e.g., Re Poyiadjis* 2001-03 MLR 316, Sept. 19, 2002 (Isle of Man High Court of Justice).

If, by the terms of the trust instrument or by prior agreement with the settlor, the amount of compensation has been fixed, the trustee is generally entitled to that amount.[54] This applies all the more in the context of the trusteed mutual fund, the trustees of a mutual fund generally being in a contractual as well as trust relationship with the fund's investors.[55] If the trustee charges more than that amount without leave of court, he may be in breach of the duty of loyalty.[56] The trustee's compensation, of course, may be enlarged or diminished by agreement between the trustee and the beneficiaries.[57] A beneficiary who is not a party to the agreement, however, would not be bound by the agreement,[58] nor would the agreement be enforceable if the consenting beneficiaries were not apprised of and did not understand the applicable law and facts.[59]

Under the Uniform Trust Code, the court in the exercise of its equitable powers may order that the trustee receive more compensation than the governing instrument prescribes, provided the responsibilities and liabilities of the trustee turn out to be substantially greater than what was contemplated when the trust was created, or if the prescribed compensation is unreasonably low.[60] On the other hand, the court may order that compensation be less than what is set forth in the governing instrument when circumstances warrant.[61] The Restatement (Third) of Trusts provides that "[i]f the amount of compensation

[54] *See* 4 Scott & Ascher §§21.1.3 (Terms of the Trust), 21.1.5 (Agreement with Settlor); 3A Scott on Trusts §242.6; Restatement (Second) of Trusts §242 cmts. f, h; Restatement (Third) of Trusts §38. *See, e.g.,* Nickel v. Bank of Am. Nat'l Trust & Sav. Ass'n, 290 F.3d 1134 (2002) (addressing the appropriate method of damage computation when a bank trustee, whose compensation was set by contract and could only be increased by consent or by order of court, nine times between 1975 and 1990 raised its fees without consent or court order); Rutanen v. Ballard, 424 Mass. 723, 678 N.E.2d 133 (1997) (holding that trustee was entitled only to $50 per week based on her agreement entered into with settlor). "Where the trustee...agrees to a fixed payment with the settlor of the trust, he is bound by that agreement and is not entitled to a judicial determination of what is fair and reasonable." Rutanen v. Ballard, 424 Mass. 723, 735, 678 N.E.2d 133, 142 (1997). *See also* UTC §708 cmt. (available at <http://www.uniformlaws.org/Act.aspx?title=Trust%20Code>) (advising that compensation provisions should be drafted with care in order to avoid such questions as whether a provision in the terms of the trust setting the amount of the trustee's compensation is binding on a successor trustee, whether a dispositive provision for the trustee in the terms of the trust is in addition to or in lieu of the trustee's regular compensation, and whether a dispositive provision for the trustee is conditional on the person performing services as trustee).

[55] *See* Kleinman v. Saminsky, 41 Del. Ch. 572, 578, 200 A.2d 572, 576 (1964).

[56] *See, e.g.,* Nickel v. Bank of Am. Nat'l Trust & Sav. Ass'n, 290 F.3d 1134 (2002) (referring to the testimony of Prof. John Langbein that charging in excess of a fixed amount without leave of court is "an open-and-shut breach of the trustee's duty of loyalty").

[57] Restatement (Third) of Trusts §38 cmt. f; 4 Scott & Ascher §21.1.6.

[58] Restatement (Third) of Trusts §38 cmt. f.

[59] *See generally* 4 Scott & Ascher §21.1.6 (Agreement with Beneficiaries); §7.1.2 of this handbook (defenses to allegations that the trustee breached the duty of loyalty).

[60] UTC §708(b) (available at <http://www.uniformlaws.org/Act.aspx?title=Trust%20Code>). *See also* Restatement (Third) of Trusts §38 cmt. e.

[61] UTC §708(b) (available at <http://www.uniformlaws.org/Act.aspx?title=Trust%20Code>).

provided by the terms of the trust is or becomes unreasonably high or unreasonably low, the court may allow a smaller or larger compensation, or may allow the trustee to resign."[62]

A trustee may expressly or impliedly waive his right to compensation.[63] As a general rule, however, the level of a trustee's duty of care is the same whether or not he takes a fee.[64] Where the trustee commits a breach of trust, the court, in its discretion, may reduce or deny compensation.[65]

As to the tax consequences of the waiver of a right to fiduciary compensation, one learned commentator has written as follows:

> The crucial test of whether . . . [a trustee] . . . may waive his right to receive statutory commissions without thereby incurring any income or gift tax liability is whether the waiver involved will at least primarily constitute evidence of an intent to render a gratuitous service. If the timing, purpose, and effect of the waiver make it serve any other important objective, it may then be proper to conclude that the . . . [trustee] . . . has thereby enjoyed a realization of income by means of controlling the disposition thereof, and at the same time, has also effected a taxable gift by means of any resulting transfer to a third party of his contingent beneficial interest in a part of the assets under his fiduciary control. Rev. Rul. 66-167, 1966-1 C.B. 20.[66]

When there are cotrustees, some jurisdictions hold that compensation for all should not exceed an amount that would be charged if there were only one.[67] Others permit total compensation to reasonably exceed the amount a single trustee would charge, provided the trust benefits from the special skills and expertise that each cotrustee brings to the table.[68] "Often the fees of cotrustees will be in the aggregate higher than the fees for a single trustee because of the duty of each trustee to participate in administration and not delegate to a

---

[62] Restatement (Third) of Trusts §38 cmt. e. *See also Limiting effect of provision in contract, will, or trust instrument fixing trustee's or executor's fees*, 19 A.L.R.3d 520.

[63] 4 Scott & Ascher §21.1.7; 3A Scott on Trusts §242.8; Restatement (Second) of Trusts §242 cmt. j; Restatement (Third) of Trusts §38 cmt. g. *See also* UTC §708 cmt. (available at <http://www.uniformlaws.org/Act.aspx?title=Trust%20 Code>) (advising that a trustee should waive compensation prior to rendering significant services if concerned about possible gift and income taxation of the compensation accrued prior to the waiver and citing Rev. Rul. 66-167, 1966-1 C.B. 20).

[64] *See generally* §8.33 of this handbook (is the level of an uncompensated trustee's duty of care less than that of a compensated trustee?).

[65] 4 Scott & Ascher §21.2; Restatement (Second) of Trusts §243. *See also* Lowery v. Evonuk, 95 Or. App. 98, 767 P.2d 489 (1989) (holding that trustee was not entitled to compensation after point in time when breach was committed).

[66] John R. Price, Price on Contemporary Estate Planning §12.8 (2d ed. 2000). *See also* Bogert §980.

[67] 4 Scott & Ascher §21.1.9; 3A Scott on Trusts §242.10.

[68] 4 Scott & Ascher §21.1.9; 3A Scott on Trusts §242.10. *See also* Restatement (Third) of Trusts §38 cmt. i.

cotrustee duties the settlor expected the trustees to perform jointly."[69] In some states, cotrustee fees are set by statute.[70] Occasionally, a trust instrument will fix the trustee's fee at a certain percentage or amount.[71]

Table 8-1 is an analysis of the standard graduated fee schedules of professional trustees in Boston, Chicago, Los Angeles, Miami, and New York. "Published fee schedules are subject to the same standard of reasonableness under the Uniform Trust Code as are other methods for computing fees."[72] A review of this representative sampling should assist the trustee in formulating a fee schedule that conforms to industry standards.

Table 8-1.
Standard Charge Schedules of Professional Trustees[73]

Principal	Boston (Private)	Boston (Corporate)	Chicago (Corporate)	Los Angeles (Corporate)	Miami (Corporate)	New York (Corporate)	
First $1 million	0.744	1.129	0.913	1.150	1.133	1.129	0-1
Next $2 million	0.369	0.911	0.813	0.967	0.900	1.030	1-3
Next $2 million	0.300	0.675	0.609	0.683	0.800	0.710	3-5
Next $5 million	0.275	0.615	0.488	0.550	0.600	0.566	5-10
Above $10 million	0.275	0.515	0.400	0.450	0.516	0.490	>10

---

[69] UTC §708 cmt. (available at <http://www.uniformlaws.org/Act.aspx?title=Trust%20 Code>). "The trust may benefit . . . from the enhanced quality of decision-making resulting from the collective deliberations of the trustee." UTC §708 cmt.

[70] 3A Scott on Trusts §242.10.

[71] *See* J. P. Ludington, Annot., *Limiting effect of provision in contract, will, or trust instrument fixing trustee's or executor's fees*, 19 A.L.R.3d 520 (1968). *See also* Bogert §976 (Control of Compensation by Settlor or Beneficiary).

[72] UTC §708 cmt. (available at <http://www.uniformlaws.org/Act.aspx?title=Trust%20 Code>).

[73] Heirs, Inc., maintains an exclusive collection of bank trust department standard charge schedules. Contact: Heirs® Inc., P.O. Box 292, Villanova, PA 19085; tel. (610) 525-4442; fax: (610) 527-6260; email: standcedar@comcast.net; website: <www.heirs.net>.

The figures in Table 8-1 are percentages of principal. Many trustees charge a minimum annual fee ranging from $1,500 to $7,500. One bank is charging a minimum annual fee of $50,000. Some trustee compensation schedules are calculated not only on a percentage of the value of principal but also on a percentage of the value of income earned.[74] Income charges, as with principal charges, are typically set on a sliding scale.[75] The range of income charges is 1 percent at the low end and 7 percent at the high end. In addition to annual charges, some trustees charge for principal distributions during the term of a trust and upon its termination.[76] The range for principal distributions is 0.5 percent of principal at the low end and 2 percent at the high end. In England, "[a] trust corporation will normally charge an acceptance fee upon its appointment as trustee, an annual administration fee while it acts as trustee, and a withdrawal fee upon its retirement as trustee or upon distribution of the trust fund."[77]

Standard charge schedules for professional trustees in the United States are anything but standard when it comes to format. Here are a few that were in force and effect in 2007:

---

[74] *See generally* Bogert §975.

[75] The English actually refer to these as "scale fees." *See* Lewin ¶ 19-58.

[76] From 1945 to 1965, it was customary in California for scriveners to draft into trust instruments a one percent termination fee provision. At one time, many Florida banks charged a 1 percent termination fee. Most no longer do. *See* UTC §708 cmt. (available at <http://www.uniformlaws.org/Act.aspx?title=Trust%20Code>) (noting that factors relevant to whether a termination fee is appropriate include the actual work performed; whether a termination fee was authorized in the terms of the trust; whether the fee schedule specified the circumstances in which a termination fee would be charged; whether the trustee's overall fees for administering the trust from the date of the trust's creation, including the termination fee, were reasonable; and the general practice in the community regarding termination fees). "Because significantly less work is normally involved, termination fees are less appropriate upon transfer to a successor trustee than upon termination of the trust." UTC §708 cmt.

[77] Lewin ¶ 19-58 (England).

Example 1		Example 3	
1.10% of first	$ 500,000	0.80% of first	$ 500,000
1.00% of next	$ 1,500,000	0.70% of next	$ 500,000
0.75% of next	$ 3,000,000	0.60% of next	$ 500,000
0.50% of next	$ 5,000,000	0.50% of next	$ 500,000
0.40% of next	$ 5,000,000	0.35% of next	$ 1,000,000
0.30% of balance over	$15,000,000	0.30% of next	$ 2,000,000
		0.25% of next	$10,000,000
		0.20% of balance over	$15,000,000

Example 2	
0.55% of first	$ 1,000,000
0.20% of balance	

Example 4	
1.25% of first	$2.000,000
0.75% of next	$3,000,000
0.50% of balance	

Example 5	
1.25% of first	$2,000,000
0.50% of balance	

Under the Uniform Trust Code, the trustee of a trust consisting of trust property having a total value less than a specified amount may terminate the trust if the trustee concludes that the value of the trust property is insufficient to justify the cost of administration.[78] This is a default rule.[79] Also, the court may modify or terminate a trust or remove the trustee and appoint a different trustee if it determines that the value of the trust property is insufficient to justify the cost of administration.[80] This is not a default rule.[81]

It is advisable for a trustee to deduct his compensation on a regular basis. Otherwise, he may be deemed to have waived it if enough time goes by, particularly if the chronic failure to deduct compensation causes the beneficiary

---

[78] UTC §414(a) (available at <http://www.uniformlaws.org/Act.aspx?title=Trust%20 Code>).

[79] UTC §414 cmt. (available at <http://www.uniformlaws.org/Act.aspx?title=Trust%20 Code>).

[80] UTC §414(b) (available at <http://www.uniformlaws.org/Act.aspx?title=Trust%20 Code>).

[81] UTC §414 cmt. (available at <http://www.uniformlaws.org/Act.aspx?title=Trust%20 Code>).

innocently and reasonably to change his or her position.[82] "It has been pointed out that where trustees paid over income for many years without deducting their commissions, to allow them to deduct these commissions out of income thereafter accruing would be to give to the beneficiary years of plenty followed by a period when her income would be entirely withheld"[83]

As a trustee would have a duty to give advance notice to the beneficiaries of a change in the method or rate of the trustee's compensation,[84] the trustee would have a duty to give advance notice to the beneficiaries of the trustee's intention to deduct from the trust estate accrued compensation that the trustee had not been deducting on a regular basis. This is an incident of the trustee's duty to furnish the beneficiaries with all the information they need to protect their equitable interests.[85]

"Under Sections 501-502 of the Uniform Principal and Income Act (1997), one-half of a trustee's regular compensation is charged to income and the other half to principal . . . ; [c]hargeable to principal are fees for acceptance, distribution, or termination of the trust, and fees charged on disbursements made to prepare property for sale."[86] The Act is available on the Internet at <http://www.uniformlaws.org/Act.aspx?title=Trust%20Code>. Actually, under both the 1962 and the 1967 versions of the Uniform Principal and Income Act, no matter how trustee compensation is *computed*, *e.g.*, solely as a percentage of income or solely as a percentage of principal, it is default law that the *burden* is shared equally between the income and the principal accounts.[87]

For special service above and beyond the call of duty, the trustee may be entitled to extra compensation, but the matter is not without some controversy.[88] A trustee certainly would not be entitled to deduct a special fee from the

---

[82] *See generally* 4 Scott & Ascher §21.1.7; 3A Scott on Trusts §242.8 (Waiver of Compensation); Restatement (Third) of Trusts §38 cmt. *g* (as well as Reporter's Notes thereon); Restatement (Second) of Trusts §242 cmt. *j*; Lyons ex rel. Lawing v. Holder, 38 Kan. App. 2d 131, 139, 163 P.3d 343, 349 (2007) ("Lyons argued to the district court and now argues on appeal, however, that the trustee's failure to assert his contractual [sic] right of compensation for nearly 12 years should be considered waiver by inference. Although we decline to ascertain the weight of such evidence, we conclude that Holder's standing mute on his right to compensation for 12 years under these circumstances was some evidence of waiver. Moreover, although the record on appeal is not entirely clear on this, Holder's failure to address fees upon each accounting submitted to the beneficiary may also be considered a reasonable inference that waiver was intended." [The reader should note that the court mischaracterized the trustee's right to compensation as contractual. As is pointed out in §3.5.2.4 of this handbook, a trustee's right to compensation is equitable, not contractual.]).

[83] 3A Scott on Trusts §242.8.

[84] UTC §813(b)(4) (available at <http://www.uniformlaws.org/Act.aspx?title=Trust%20Code>).

[85] *See generally* §§5.4.1.1 of this handbook (right to information and confidentiality) (discussing the beneficiary's right to information) and 6.1.5.1 of this handbook (duty to provide information).

[86] UTC §708 cmt. (available at <http://www.uniformlaws.org/Act.aspx?title=Trust%20Code>).

[87] 4 Scott & Ascher §20.2.2.

[88] *See generally* 4 Scott & Ascher §21.1; 3A Scott on Trusts §242.2; Restatement (Second) of Trusts §242 cmt. d; Restatement (Third) of Trusts §38 cmt. d. Suffice it to say, a trustee may not

trust estate for the time and trouble he took to correct his own negligent or intentional errors.[89]

In recent years, corporate fiduciaries have been the subject of class action suits for their compensation practices.[90] Revised Regulation 9 (available at <www.gpoaccess.gov/cfr/index.html>) provides that a bank administering a collective investment fund may charge a reasonable fund management fee only if (1) the fee is permitted under applicable law and (2) the "amount of the fee does not exceed an amount commensurate with the value of legitimate services of tangible benefit to the participating fiduciary accounts that would not have been provided to the accounts were they not invested in the fund."[91] "A bank administering a collective investment fund may charge reasonable expenses incurred in operating the collective investment fund, to the extent not prohibited by applicable law in the state in which the bank maintains the fund."[92] The bank, however, must absorb the expenses of establishing or reorganizing a collective investment fund.[93]

Under the Uniform Trust Code, an investment by a trustee in securities of an investment company or investment trust to which the trustee, or its affiliate, provides services in a capacity other than as trustee is not presumed to be affected by a conflict between fiduciary interests if the investment complies with the Prudent Investor Rule.[94] "The trustee may be compensated by the investment company or investment trust for providing those services out of fees charged to the trust if the trustee at least annually notifies... [the current beneficiaries and presumptive remaindermen]... of the rate and method by which the compensation was determined."[95]

On November 12, 1999, President Clinton signed into law the Gramm-Leach-Bliley Financial Modernization Bill Act,[96] which implements fundamental changes in how the U.S. financial services industry is regulated. The Act provides for "functional" regulation of bank securities activities. Section 201 of the Act provides in part that a bank shall not be required to register as a broker under the federal securities laws because it effects transactions in a "trustee capacity," or because it effects transactions in a "fiduciary capacity" in its trust

---

enter into an enforceable contract with himself for extra compensation for extra services. For authority to take extra compensation, the trustee must look to the governing instrument, statute, or the court.

[89] See, e.g., May v. Oklahoma Bank & Trust Co., 261 P.3d 1138, 1143 (2011).

[90] See, e.g., Upp v. Mellon Bank, N.A., 799 F. Supp. 540 (E.D. Pa. 1992), rev'd, 994 F.2d 1039 (1993). See also UTC §708 cmt. (available at <http://www.uniformlaws.org/Act.aspx?title=Trust%20Code>) (noting that courts have generally upheld published fee schedules but this is not automatic).

[91] See 12 C.F.R. §9.18(b)(9)(ii) (1997).

[92] See 12 C.F.R. §9.18(b)(10) (1997).

[93] 12 C.F.R. §9.18(b)(10) (1997).

[94] UTC §802(f) (available at <http://www.uniformlaws.org/Act.aspx?title=Trust%20Code>).

[95] UTC §802(f) (available at <http://www.uniformlaws.org/Act.aspx?title=Trust%20Code>).

[96] 113 Stat. 1338, 1384-1390.

department or other departments that are regularly examined by bank examiners for compliance with fiduciary principles and standards.

For the exemption to apply, the bank must be chiefly compensated for such transactions, consistent with fiduciary principles and standards, on the basis of an administration or annual fee (payable on a monthly, quarterly, or other basis), a percentage of assets under management, or a flat or capped per-order processing fee equal to not more than the cost incurred by the bank in connection with executing securities transactions for trustee and fiduciary customers, or any combination of such fees. An additional requirement is that the bank may not publicly solicit brokerage business. It may, however, advertise in its trust promotional literature that it effects transactions in securities on behalf of its trust accounts.[97] Section 202 of the Act provides that a bank shall not be a dealer within the meaning of the federal securities laws because it buys or sells securities for investment purposes for accounts for which the bank acts as a trustee or fiduciary.[98]

§8.5 Conflict of Laws

A trustee is under a continuing duty to administer the trust at a place appropriate to the purposes of the trust and to its sound, efficient management.[1]

Introduction. In Section 8.40 of this handbook, we consider the rules that apply when two or more states have concurrent jurisdiction over the affairs of a trust. In this section, we consider whose laws are to be applied by the court that ultimately exercises jurisdiction, those of the forum state or those of some other state. When a trust instrument was prepared and executed in one state and the trust itself is being administered in another and its validity, or, perhaps, the meaning of a provision, is being litigated in a third, what is the court to do if the relevant laws of the various states are in conflict? Which state's law is to be applied? Much depends upon the issue. Laws may be contradictory when it comes to the validity of the trust itself;[2] the construction of its terms;[3] rules of

---

[97] 15 U.S.C.A. §78c.

[98] 15 U.S.C.A. §78c.

§8.5 [1] UPC §7-305.

[2] *See generally* Jeffrey A. Schoenblum, Multistate and Multinational Estate Planning §17.01 (1999). "A trust not created by will is validly created if its creation complies with the law of the jurisdiction in which the trust instrument was executed, or the law of the jurisdiction in which, at the time of creation: (1) the settlor was domiciled, had a place of abode, or was a national; (2) a trustee was domiciled or had a place of business; or (3) any trust property was located." UTC §403 (available on the Internet at <http://www.uniformlaws.org/Act.aspx?title=Trust%20Code>). "This section is comparable to Section 2-506 of the Uniform Probate Code, which validates wills executed in compliance with the law of a variety of places in which the testator had a significant contact." UTC§403 cmt. (available at <http://www.uniformlaws.org/Act.aspx?title=Trust%20 Code>). "Unlike the UPC, however, this section is not limited to execution of the instrument but

administration;[4] the validity of the exercise of a power of appointment;[5] or the rights, duties, and obligations of fiduciaries, beneficiaries, creditors, and others who may come in contact with the trust.[6] One state may recognize spendthrift trusts, while the other may not;[7] one may have adopted the Uniform Statutory Rule Against Perpetuities, while the other may not have done so;[8] in one state, a word such as *heirs* or *issue* might encompass illegitimates, while in the other state it might not.[9] States will have differing approaches to compensation, apportionment, revocability, disposition in default, and investing. Such inconveniences are the inevitable consequence of a federal system of government, inconveniences that are only exacerbated, as we shall see, by the multiplicity of parties to the trust relationship.

In this section, the term "immovable" is employed. Only land is an immovable.[10] By that we mean the land itself.[11] If an item of property is not land, it is a "movable."[12] An interest in an immovable can either be real property, *e.g.*, a freehold, or personal property, *e.g.*, a leasehold.[13] An immovable that has been *equitably converted* is also personal property.[14] So too is the mortgagee's interest in a mortgage.[15]

---

applies to the entire process of a trust's creation, including compliance with the requirements that there be trust property." UTC§403 cmt. "In addition, unlike the UPC, this section validates a trust valid under the law of the domicile or place of business of the designated trustee, or if valid under the law of the place where any of the trust property is located." UTC§403 cmt.

[3] Jeffrey A. Schoenblum, Multistate and Multinational Estate Planning §17.02 (1999).

[4] Jeffrey A. Schoenblum, Multistate and Multinational Estate Planning §§17.03–17.04 (1999).

[5] *See generally* Sloan v. Segal, 2008 WL 81513 (the Delaware court asserting jurisdiction and applying Delaware law in a matter involving the purported exercise of a limited testamentary power of appointment over property in a Delaware-based trust, the will, however, having been executed under questionable circumstances in Florida by a Florida domiciliary).

[6] Jeffrey A. Schoenblum, Multistate and Multinational Estate Planning §17.05 (1999).

[7] *See* §5.3.3.3(c) of this handbook (the non–self-settled spendthrift trust); Jeffrey A. Schoenblum, Multistate and Multinational Estate Planning §17.07 (1999); 5A Scott on Trusts §§625–628, 660. *See* Restatement (Second) of Conflict of Laws §273 (Restraints on Alienation of Beneficiaries' Interests).

[8] *See* §8.2.1.7 of this handbook (perpetuities legislation) (discussing the Uniform Statutory Rule Against Perpetuities (USRAP)).

[9] *See* §5.2 of this handbook (class designation: "children," "issue," "heirs," and "relatives" (some rules of construction)).

[10] 7 Scott & Ascher §46.5.

[11] *See generally* 7 Scott & Ascher §46.5.

[12] 7 Scott & Ascher §46.5.

[13] 7 Scott & Ascher §46.5 (the leasehold/conflict of laws). When it comes to the testamentary disposition of a leasehold, the validity of the will's execution or whether the testator had testamentary capacity or whether there are any restrictions on such a disposition to charity or the applicability of a spousal election statute is generally determined by the law of the situs of the land, as to the disposition of the leasehold. 7 Scott & Ascher §46.5.2. "In the United States, it would seem that if the leasehold is to be retained in trust, the courts of the situs would apply their local law, just as they do in the case of a freehold interest." 7 Scott & Ascher §46.5.2.

[14] *See generally* §8.15.44 of this handbook (equitable conversion). As to equitable conversion in a multi-jurisdictional context, *see* 7 Scott & Ascher §46.5.1.1 (Equitable Conversion—Validity of the Will/Conflict of Laws); 7 Scott & Ascher §46.5.1.2 Equitable Conversion—Validity of Trust

"Local law" means "the law which the courts of a jurisdiction apply in adjudicating legal questions that have no relation to another jurisdiction."[16]

The bulk of this section of the handbook deals with the trust of movables that has contacts in more than one state. Whose law is applicable in a given situation? The law of the state in which the trust is being administered (the "place of administration"), or of the state in which the underlying trust property is located (the "situs"), or of the state in which the settlor was domiciled when the trust was created (the "settlor's domicile"), or of the state in which the beneficiaries are domiciled (the "beneficiaries' domicile"), or of the state in which the trustee is domiciled (the "trustee's domicile"), or of the state in which the court handling the matter is located (the "forum")?

In the case of an entrusted parcel of land, as we shall see, it is the law of the situs of the land that generally governs most questions.[17] But it is not quite that simple. One commentator proffers a methodology for sorting out what law is applicable when it comes to a trust of land that has contacts in more than one state:

- "The law of the situs determines whether an interest in the land is personal property or real property.

Provisions/Conflict of Laws). The law of the situs of land governs whether there has been an equitable conversion. 7 Scott & Ascher §46.5.1. It also governs the effect of the equitable conversion. 7 Scott & Ascher §46.5.1. " . . . [I]f a court other than the court of the situs makes a determination as to the disposition of the land, or its proceeds, the courts of the situs are not bound to give the decree full faith and credit." 7 Scott & Ascher §46.5.1. When a will directs that a parcel of land be sold, the validity of the will's execution or whether the testator had testamentary capacity or whether there are any restrictions on such a devise being made to charity or the applicability of a spousal election statute is determined by the law of the situs of the land, as to the administration and disposition of that land. 7 Scott & Ascher §46.5.1.1. If the equitable conversion occurred predeath, however, then "the law of the testator's domicile may well govern." 7 Scott & Ascher §46.5.1.1. "The local law of the situs determines questions about whether an equitable conversion has occurred, and its effect. But the courts of the situs may decide to apply the conflicts law of the situs, rather than its local law. And if the courts of the situs would apply the law of the testator's domicil, and not the local law of the situs, other courts will do the same." 7 Scott & Ascher §46.5.1.1. "When the owner of land devises or conveys it in trust, subject to a direction that the land is to be sold and that a trust of the proceeds is to be administered in the state of the situs, the courts have held that the local law of the situs determines the validity of the trust, even when the testator or settlor was domiciled elsewhere." 7 Scott & Ascher §46.5.1.2 (Equitable Conversion—Validity of Trust Provisions/Conflict of laws). If the equitable conversion occurred predeath, then "the courts of the situs might well apply the law of the . . . [testator's] . . . domicil in order to uphold the trust, just as they do in the case of movables." 7 Scott & Ascher §46.5.1.2.

[15] In England, "the courts say that the mortgage gives the mortgagee an interest in an immovable, and that interests in immovables are governed by the local law of the situs, even if under the law of the situs such interests are personal property." 7 Scott & Ascher §46.5.3. In most of the United States, though the mortgagee has only a security interest in the land, title remaining in the mortgagor, the situs of the land and its courts control the fate of the security interest. 7 Scott & Ascher §46.5.3. That is not to say that a court of the situs of a mortgaged parcel of land might not apply the law of some other state in a given situation that involves the mortgage, such as the death intestate of the mortgagee. 7 Scott & Ascher §46.5.3.

[16] 7 Scott & Ascher §46.5 (citing to N.Y. Est. Powers & Trusts Law §3-5.1(a)(7)).

[17] 7 Scott & Ascher §46.5.

- If the law of the situs determines that the interest is personal property, it then determines whether it will apply, as to the disposition of the interest, its own local law or that which it applies to other kinds of personal property.
- Whether it will apply its own local law or that of another state will depend on the issue raised and the policies involved.
- In the United States . . . courts have frequently held that if the interest is personal property under the law of the situs, the applicable law in many situations is not the local law of the situs but instead that which applies to other personal property."[18]

Validity questions (conflict of laws). In Chapter 1 of this handbook, we consider some situations that might cause a trust to be invalid *ab initio*, or to become so in mid-course. They range from the absence of legal capacity to impress a trust upon one's property to the wholesale violation of the rule against perpetuities. In the case of a trust with multi-jurisdictional contacts, a trust might be valid under the laws of one state but not so under the laws of another. How does one go about sorting out whose laws are applicable? Much is likely to hinge on whether the trust is testamentary or inter vivos, and whether or not the subject property is land (immovables). A trust that contains a single parcel of real estate is governed by the laws of the state in which the parcel is located.[19] Unfortunately, if the trust contains real estate located in more than one state, or both real estate and movables, no similarly simple rule covers such variations on the theme.[20] A trust containing only personal property (movables) is governed by the laws of the state in which the trust is being administered.[21] There are many exceptions to this rule, which we shall go into later. For example, what if a testamentary trust is being administered in a state other than the state where the will was probated? Under those circumstances, the laws of the state of probate might govern.[22] Moreover, what is the state of administration? Where the trustee resides? Where the movables are located? Which movables? These issues we will now delve into in some detail.

Validity of testamentary trust of movables (conflict of laws). In adjudicating the validity of a testamentary trust of movables that has multi-jurisdictional contacts, a court must first determine whether the will itself is valid. If it is not, then the testamentary trust purported to be established under it is a nullity.[23] Just

---

[18] 7 Scott & Ascher §46.5.

[19] *See generally* Jeffrey A. Schoenblum, Multistate and Multinational Estate Planning §§17.01.1, 17.01.3, 17.02.1, 17.03.1 (1999); 5A Scott on Trusts §§648, 649, 652, 659; Restatement (Second) Conflict of Laws §§277–278.

[20] *See generally* 5A Scott on Trusts §§643–663.

[21] *See generally* Jeffrey A. Schoenblum, Multistate and Multinational Estate Planning §§17.01.2, 17.01.4-5, 17.02.2, 17.03.2-3 (1999); 5A Scott on Trusts §§574, 592, 605–607.

[22] *See generally* Jeffrey A. Schoenblum, Multistate and Multinational Estate Planning §17.01.2 (1982); 5A Scott on Trusts §592.

[23] 7 Scott & Ascher §45.4.1.

because the will is valid, however, does not mean that the trust must be as well.[24] The status of the trust calls for a separate analysis.

Validity of will itself. First we consider the validity of the will itself. In the case of a will that purports to dispose of movables situated in a state other than the state where the testator died domiciled, the court where the movables are situated will ordinarily apply the law of the last domicile in sorting out whether or not the will is a valid one.[25] This applies to questions of testamentary capacity, as well as compliance with execution formalities.[26] If compliance with the last domicile's will execution formalities is lacking, all is not lost, however. It may suffice if the mode of execution complied with the law of the state where the testator was domiciled *at the time of execution*; or the law of the state where the will's execution actually took place; or even the law of the forum, that is to say the law of the state where the movables happen to be physically located at the time of death and whose court is now considering the matter.[27] It will depend upon the language of the applicable statute in force in the state *where the testator died domiciled*.[28]

In a case where the will due to improper execution is invalid no matter what under the laws of the state of last domicile but is valid under the laws of the forum, that is to say valid under the laws of the state where the movables happen to be situated at the time of death, the question is whether the court may probate *those movables* or whether it must order them removed to the state of last domicile for disposition in accordance with its intestacy laws. It is likely to be the latter, with New York being a notable exception.[29] In any case, if the state *where the movables are physically located* has a statute that addresses the invalid-foreign-will problem, its provisions will govern.[30]

Questions pertaining to the validity of a purported will revocation are ordinarily determined by the laws of the state in which the testator died domiciled.[31] In Oklahoma, however, a revocation also would be effective if it complied with the laws of the state in which the purported revocation took place, or of the state in which the decedent was domiciled when it took place.[32]

The doctrine of incorporation by reference is covered in Section 8.15.17 of this handbook; the doctrine of independent legal significance in Section 8.15.9 of this handbook. The focus is on the practical applications of these doctrines,

---

[24] 7 Scott & Ascher §45.4.1.

[25] 7 Scott & Ascher §45.4.1.1.

[26] Note, however, that when it comes to adjudicating testamentary capacity, some states have limited statutory exceptions to this general rule. Under New York law, for example, a testator who dies domiciled elsewhere owning personal property situated in New York may provide in the will that New York law shall govern the will's intrinsic validity for purposes of disposing of the New York property. *See* N.Y. Est. Powers & Trusts Law §3-5.1(h).

[27] 7 Scott & Ascher §45.4.1.1.

[28] 7 Scott & Ascher §45.4.1.1.

[29] *See generally* 7 Scott & Ascher §45.4.1.1. As to applicable New York law, see N.Y. Est. Powers & Trusts Law §3-5.1(c).

[30] *See* 7 Scott & Ascher §45.4.1.1.

[31] *See generally* 7 Scott & Ascher §45.4.1.1.

[32] Okla. Stat. Ann. tit. 84, §§71 to 73.

particularly those applications that exploit the intersection of wills law and trust law. We consider the pour-over will in Section 2.2.1 of this handbook, a practical application that had originally been validated under the doctrine of independent legal significance. Just as no testamentary trust can arise under a will that is invalid, so also each of these practical applications presumes a valid will.[33]

As we note in Section 2.1.2 of this handbook, the subject property of a testamentary trust, at least initially, is some portion or all of the testator's/settlor's net probate estate. By "net probate estate" we mean that portion of the probate estate that is not needed to satisfy statutory obligations, such as the testator's/settlor's just debts and taxes. In common law jurisdictions, there is another statutory obligation that is subject to election by and for the benefit of the testator's/settlor's surviving spouse. The subject of statutory spousal election rights is taken up in Section 5.3.4.1 of this handbook. In any case, when the testator/settlor dies domiciled in a state other than the state where some or all of his or her personal property is situated, there may be a question as to which state's spousal election statute is applicable with respect to that property. Ordinarily, it is that of the state in which the testator/settlor died domiciled.[34] "On the other hand, when it was the testator who changed his or her domicil shortly prior to death, leaving the surviving spouse in what was previously the marital domicil, the courts have occasionally applied the law of the testator's former domicil."[35] Also, when a testator/settlor dies domiciled in one state having specified in the will that the law of another state with a different spousal election statute shall govern the will's validity and effect, the surviving spouse may well be entitled to elect the more generous share.[36]

In Section 9.8.1 of this handbook, we consider ancient and now largely superannuated restrictions on the ability of testators to devise land to charitable corporations and on the authority of the charitable corporations themselves even to take and hold land. If there are in force any similar restrictions on a testator's ability to bequeath movables for charitable purposes, at best a remote possibility, there may be a conflict-of-laws issue if the movables at death are situated out-of-state. Are the relevant laws of the state where the testator died domiciled applicable, or those of the state where the movables are situated? It is likely to be the former.[37] Moreover, "[i]f, as is considerably more likely, there is no such restriction in the state of the testator's domicil at death, the disposition is valid, notwithstanding the fact that there is such a restriction in the state in which the testator's movables are situated."[38] On the other hand, if the intended legatee is an out-of-state charitable corporation that may be subject to

---

[33] See generally 7 Scott & Ascher §45.4.1.1.

[34] See 7 Scott & Ascher §45.4.1.1 (noting that the state where the testator/settlor was last domiciled is the one that is ordinarily "most concerned" with the protection of the surviving spouse).

[35] 7 Scott & Ascher §45.4.1.1.

[36] See 7 Scott & Ascher §45.4.4.1.

[37] Restatement (Second) of Conflict of Laws §269 cmts. c, h.

[38] 7 Scott & Ascher §45.4.1.1.

restrictions on its authority to take and hold personal property, the effectiveness of those restrictions are determined by the laws of the state of incorporation.[39]

Validity of the testamentary trust where the will is valid. That a will is valid does not necessarily mean that the testamentary trust to be created under it is as well. The validity of the provisions of a testamentary trust of movables, as is the case with the validity of the will itself, is ordinarily determined by the laws of the testator's/settlor's domicile at death.[40] There are two exceptions. The first exception is when the testator/settlor provides in the will that the laws of another state shall govern.[41] If the other state has a "substantial connection" with the trust[42] and if the choice-of-law designation does not somehow subvert a public policy of the state in which the testator/settlor died domiciled,[43] the designation ordinarily will be honored by the courts of the domicile state.[44]

The second exception is when the administration *of the trust* is fixed expressly or by inference in another state. In that case, it is ordinarily the laws of the state where the trust is to be administered that govern its validity, and the validity of its terms, "unless the trust or a provision thereof is not only invalid under the law of the testator's domicil but also contrary to one of its strong public policies."[45] Having said that, if a certain testamentary trust of movables, whether charitable or noncharitable, would be valid under the laws of one state but not under the laws of the other, the court ordinarily will apply the law that supports a finding of validity.[46]

This would be the case, for example, if the rule against perpetuities or accumulations would be violated under the laws of the administration state, the situs state and/or the forum state but not under the laws of the domicile state, or vice versa, the public policy that these rules are designed to implement being

---

[39] 7 Scott & Ascher §§45.4.1.1 & 45.4.1.4.

[40] 7 Scott & Ascher §45.4.1.2.

[41] *See generally* 7 Scott & Ascher §45.4.1.3.

[42] "Such a designation is ordinarily effective if the designated state has a substantial connection with the trust, as when it is the testator's domicil, the place of trust administration, the trustee's domicil or place of business, or the place where the property is situated at the testator's death." 7 Scott & Ascher §45.4.1.3.

[43] A trust may violate the public policy of the state of the testator's/settlor's domicile at death if its provisions would tend to encourage immorality, divorce/ separation, or neglect of parental duties. A provision tending to restrain marriage, religious freedom, or the performance of public duties might also be violative of the state's public policy. These public policy considerations we take up in §9.24 of this handbook. In the conflict of laws context, a "strong" public policy needs to be implicated. "Thus, the trust will ordinarily be upheld if it is valid under the rule against perpetuities of the place of administration, notwithstanding the fact that it would be invalid under the law of the testator's domicil." 7 Scott & Ascher §45.4.1.4. So also with the rule against accumulations, a topic we take up in §8.15.8 of this handbook. 7 Scott & Ascher §45.4.1.4. *See generally* 7 Scott & Ascher §45.4.1.8 (Public Policy of the Testator's Domicil).

[44] *See generally* 7 Scott & Ascher §45.4.1.3; 7 Scott & Ascher §45.4.1.8.

[45] 7 Scott & Ascher §45.4.1.4; 7 Scott & Ascher §45.4.1.8.

[46] 7 Scott & Ascher §45.4.1.5. *See also* 7 Scott & Ascher §45.4.1.6 (Validity of a Charitable Trust). If a charitable testamentary trust would be valid under the laws of the state in which the testator/settlor died domiciled but not under the laws of the state fixed in the will as the place of administration, then the court in the domicile state may well appoint a local trustee to administer the trust. 7 Scott & Ascher §45.4.1.6. A trust ought not to fail merely for want of a trustee.

not so "strong" as to tip the judicial scales in favor of a choice-of-law selection that would defeat some or all of the equitable property interests.[47] That some states, most notably Delaware and Alaska, have come to allow perpetual non-charitable trusts has prompted one learned commentator to make this observation: "It is perhaps timely, therefore, to ask whether a court in a state in which the rule against perpetuities still prevails might not today be somewhat less willing to set aside its own state's policy, and to apply instead the rule of some other state, in order to enforce a perpetual or other exceedingly long-lived private trust."[48] Perpetuities we take up in Section 8.2.1 of this handbook and accumulations in Section 8.15.8 of this handbook.

When neither exception is applicable, what is the default law if the testator/settlor was domiciled in one state at the time the will was executed but domiciled in another at death as to matters related to the *validity* of a testamentary trust of movables created under it? Which state's laws are applicable? " . . . [T]he law of the testator's domicil at death remains central in determining the substantive validity of the will and its provisions."[49] Thus, even if the trust would have been valid under the laws of the state in which the testator/settlor was domiciled at the time of the will's execution, its validity is governed by the laws of the state in which the testator/settlor died domiciled.[50] On the other hand, as to issues related to whether the will was properly executed and how the testamentary trust's terms should be construed, the applicable law is ordinarily that of the state in which the testator/settlor was domiciled at the time the will was executed.[51]

In Section 8.12.1 of this handbook, we take up the subject of civil law trust analogs, it not being possible to impress a trust upon property in a number of civil law jurisdictions.[52] A testator who dies domiciled in a civil law jurisdiction such as France or Germany, however, should be able to impress a testamentary trust on movables that are situated and to be administered in a common law jurisdiction such as New York or Massachusetts.[53] On the other hand, a testator who dies domiciled in a common law state is generally precluded from fixing the administration of a testamentary trust in a civil law jurisdiction that has not introduced into its jurisprudence by statute or otherwise the Anglo-American trust.[54]

The doctrine of *cy pres* is covered in Section 9.4.3 of this handbook.[55] If it is impossible *at the outset* to carry out the charitable purposes of a testamentary trust of movables, the court will ordinarily look to the law of the testator's/

[47] 7 Scott & Ascher §45.4.1.5; 7 Scott & Ascher §45.4.1.8.

[48] 7 Scott & Ascher §45.4.1.5. *See also* 7 Scott & Ascher §45.4.1.8. *See generally* §8.2.1.9 of this handbook (abolition of the rule against perpetuities).

[49] 7 Scott & Ascher §45.4.1.9 (Change of Domicil After Execution of the Will).

[50] *See generally* 7 Scott & Ascher §45.4.1.9.

[51] *See generally* 7 Scott & Ascher §45.4.1.9.

[52] *See also* 7 Scott & Ascher §45.4.1.5.

[53] 7 Scott & Ascher §45.4.1.5.

[54] *See generally* §8.12.2 of this handbook (The Hague Convention on the Law Applicable to Trusts and on Their Recognition).

[55] *See also* §8.15.28 of this handbook.

settlor's last domicile in determining whether *cy pres* should be applied in lieu of the imposition of a resulting trust.[56] Should those charitable purposes only *subsequently* become impossible of fulfillment, it is the version of the *cy pres* doctrine prevailing in the state of administration that ordinarily governs.[57]

The law is unsettled as to the rights, duties, and obligations of the parties to a "trust" that has a noncharitable purpose and lacks ascertainable beneficiaries. The validity of such arrangements is considered in Section 9.27 of this handbook under the heading "The Purpose Trust" and in Section 9.29 of this handbook under the heading "The Adapted Trust." If a testator/settlor of a purpose or adapted testamentary trust of movables dies domiciled in one state having fixed the place of trust administration in another state, which state's laws govern the nature and validity of the equitable relationship, as well as the rights, duties, and obligations, if any, of the parties to that relationship? "It would seem that the disposition should be valid if it would be valid in either state," unless its purpose violates a strong public policy of the domicile state or would be considered capricious under its laws.[58]

Validity of inter vivos trusts of movables (conflict of laws). It is likely the case that unless the terms of an inter vivos trust of movables provide otherwise, it is the law of the place of administration that governs the trust's validity.[59] That is not to say that in a given instance, a court might not apply the law of the settlor's domicile or the law of the place of execution of the trust instrument or the law of the domicile of one or more beneficiaries or the law of the forum state or the law of the situs of the property.[60] Each alternative, however, has its drawbacks. The place where an inter vivos trust instrument is executed is often fortuitous, as is the location of the litigation forum.[61] Any trust nowadays is likely to have multiple beneficiaries scattered about the country.[62] Nor are all movables likely to be situated in the same state.[63] And certainly when it comes to sorting out a choice-of-law question, the inter vivos settlor's chance domicile at funding lacks the gravitational pull that his or her last domicile would have had the trust been testamentary, the last domicile being where the will itself would have been probated.[64] One learned commentator offers the following practice tip:

> . . . [I]f it is important that the law of the place of administration apply in determining the validity of the trust, the settlor may be well advised, prior to creating the trust, to deliver the trust property to the trustee, at the place of administration. Nor is this the only way to increase the likelihood that the law of the place of administration will apply. The settlor may also be well advised to execute the trust instrument at the place of administration; to include, in the

---

[56] 7 Scott & Ascher §45.4.1.6.

[57] 7 Scott & Ascher §45.4.1.6.

[58] 7 Scott & Ascher §45.4.1.7; 7 Scott & Ascher §45.4.1.8.

[59] *See generally* 7 Scott & Ascher §45.4.2.

[60] *See generally* 7 Scott & Ascher §45.4.2.

[61] 7 Scott & Ascher §45.4.2.

[62] 7 Scott & Ascher §45.4.2.

[63] 7 Scott & Ascher §45.4.2.

[64] 7 Scott & Ascher §45.4.2.

terms of the trust, a provision expressly designating as applicable the law of the place of administration; and, if feasible, to select trustees who are domiciled or have a place of business in the place of administration.[65]

Validity of an inter vivos trust—law designated by the settlor. Assume a settlor creates an inter vivos trust of movables under circumstances that would ordinarily call for the laws of one state, the default state, to be applied in resolving issues of its validity but designates expressly in the terms of the trust or by implication that the laws of some other state shall be applicable in such situations.[66] In deference to settlor intent, the court will ordinarily apply the designated law, unless to do so would violate a strong public policy of the default state, or unless the state whose laws have been designated has no substantial connection with the trust.[67] In the case of a revocable self-settled inter vivos trust of movables, for example, a court might well defer on public policy grounds to the law of the settlor's domicile in matters pertaining to the reach of that state's spousal election statute, though the settlor had specified in the terms of the trust that the law of some other state shall govern the trust's validity generally.[68] It should be noted that while the substantial connection requirement applies to validity questions, it ordinarily does not apply to construction questions.[69] For some reason, the Uniform Trust Code does not codify the settlor's general, though not limitless, common law right to designate which state's laws shall govern the resolution of trust validity questions.[70] One learned commentator speculates on what the reason could be:

> One senses in all this the icy hand of section 105 of the UTC, which lists those issues as to which the UTC purports to be mandatory law, i.e., those issues as to which the settlor may not, by the terms of the trust, effectively provide otherwise. Among the issues listed in section 105 are "the requirements for creating a trust." Thus, it may be that the unwillingness of section 403 to allow the settlor, by the terms of the trust, to designate the law that is to apply in determining whether the trust has been "validly created" is simply a consequence of an almost entirely cosmetic effort at buttressing section 105.[71]

---

[65] 7 Scott & Ascher §45.4.2, n.5.

[66] " . . . [T]he courts have held that when the settlor has failed by express provision to designate as applicable the law of any particular state, but has fixed the place of administration, the law of the place of administration may be applied to validate the trust." 7 Scott & Ascher §45.4.2.1. This is an example of what we mean by designating by implication.

[67] *See generally* 7 Scott & Ascher §45.4.2.1.

[68] *See* Restatement (Second) of Conflict of Laws §270 cmt. e. The topic of postmortem spousal rights to the entrusted property of decedents is covered generally in §5.3.4.1 of this handbook.

[69] 7 Scott & Ascher §45.4.2.1.

[70] *See generally* 7 Scott & Ascher §45.4.2.1.

[71] 7 Scott & Ascher §45.4.2.1.

The Uniform Trust Code has another validity-related mandatory rule, namely the benefit-of-the-beneficiaries rule.[72] It too is generating some robust scholarly debate, a debate that we cover in Section 6.1.2 of this handbook.

Validity of an inter vivos trust—no designation of applicable law. As a general rule, an inter vivos trust of movables is valid if it would be valid in the state fixed by the settlor as the place of administration.[73] "In the case of charitable trusts, the courts have been even more ready than in the case of private trusts to uphold the trust if it was valid at the place of administration, although it would not have been valid under either the law of the settlor's domicil or that of the place where it was created."[74] Naming as trustee an individual domiciled in a particular state, or a trust company having a place of business there, is a way of "fixing" a trust's place of administration.[75] When the place of administration has not been fixed, it is the law of the state having the most significant contacts with the particular trust.[76] "Such contacts may include the trustee's domicil, the settlor's domicil at the time of the creation of the trust, the place where the trust assets were located at the time of the creation of the trust, the place where the trust instrument was executed, and the domicil of one or more of the beneficiaries."[77] The Uniform Trust Code would seem to be generally in accord.[78]

The Uniform Trust Code, however, has a special section that sets out which states' laws may be applicable in determining whether a particular inter vivos trust has been "validly created." Possibilities are the law of the jurisdiction in which the trust instrument was executed or the law of the jurisdiction in which, at the time of the creation, the settlor was domiciled, had a place of abode, or was a national; a trustee was domiciled or had a place of business; or any trust property was located.[79] In a state that has not enacted the UTC, an inter vivos trust of movables is valid if its execution complies with the formal requirements, if any, of the place of administration, even if there has not been compliance with the formal requirements of the settlor's domicile.[80] "The common law is less clear when the trust is executed in compliance with the formal requirements of the settlor's domicil, but not with those of the situs of the property."[81] In the case of questions related to one's capacity to create an inter vivos trust of movables, it is the opposite: "It is not entirely clear whether a settlor who lacks capacity to create a trust under the law of the settlor's domicil can create an inter vivos trust

---

[72] UTC §105(b)(3) (available at <http://www.uniformlaws.org/Act.aspx?title=Trust%20Code>).

[73] 7 Scott & Ascher §45.4.2.2.

[74] 7 Scott & Ascher §45.4.2.3.

[75] 7 Scott & Ascher §45.4.2.2.

[76] 7 Scott & Ascher §45.4.2.2.

[77] 7 Scott & Ascher §45.4.2.2.

[78] 7 Scott & Ascher §45.4.2.2.

[79] UTC §403 (available at <http://www.uniformlaws.org/Act.aspx?title=Trust%20Code>).

[80] 7 Scott & Ascher §45.4.2.5 (Formalities in Creating an Inter Vivos Trust).

[81] 7 Scott & Ascher §45.4.2.5

by conveying movables in another state, in which the settlor has capacity."[82] Under the UTC, it would appear that that is possible.[83]

In a case where a purported inter vivos trust of movables has a significant relationship with several states but would be found to be valid only under the law of one of them, the court will be inclined to apply the law that would support a validity finding, absent strong countervailing public policy considerations.[84] Presumably the settlor did not intend to impress an invalid trust upon his or her property.[85] On the other hand, the court will be disinclined to apply the supportive law if the very creation of the trust were to violate some strong public policy of the settlor's domicile, such as a policy of affording certain economic protections to the spouses of settlors or of not enforcing spendthrift clauses in self-settled trusts or of limiting the permissible duration of private trusts.[86]

Avoiding a violation of a particular version of the rule against perpetuities, however, has traditionally not implicated a state's strong public policy, whether it be the state where the inter vivos trust of movables is to be administered or the state where the settlor was domiciled when the trust was created, although there is some law to the contrary.[87] Having said that, now that some states have actually or effectively *abolished altogether* the rule against perpetuities, how a court resolves the question of whether it should apply foreign perpetuities law such that an otherwise unenforceable private perpetual inter vivos trust of movables would become enforceable would have public policy implications that could reasonably be characterized as "strong."[88] Dueling versions of the Rule is one thing; abolishing the Rule altogether in some states but not in others is quite another.

In Section 8.15.8 of this handbook we take up the rule against accumulations. " . . . [T]here is authority for the proposition that a provision in an inter vivos trust for the accumulation of income is valid if it is valid under the law of the state of the settlor's domicil, or that of the state in which the property was situated at the time of the creation of the trust, or perhaps that of the state in which the trust instrument was executed, although it would not be valid under

---

[82] 7 Scott & Ascher §45.4.2.6 (The Settlor's Capacity to Create an Inter Vivos Trust). The level of capacity that one must have to impress a trust upon one's property is considered in Chap. 1 of this handbook.

[83] *See* UTC §403 & cmt. (available at <http://www.uniformlaws.org/Act.aspx?title=Trust%20 Code>) ("Unlike [UPC §2-506], §403 is not limited to execution of the instrument but applies to the entire process of a trust's creation . . .").

[84] 7 Scott & Ascher §45.4.2.3.

[85] 7 Scott & Ascher §45.4.2.3.

[86] *See generally* 7 Scott & Ascher §45.4.2.4 (Public Policy of the Settlor's Domicil). The general topic of spousal rights in the trust context is taken up in §5.3.4 of this handbook, the general topic of self-settled spendthrift trusts in §5.3.3.1 of this handbook, and the general topic of perpetual private trusts in §8.2.1.9 of this handbook.

[87] 7 Scott & Ascher §45.4.2.3. For a general discussion of the rule against perpetuities, *see* §8.2.1 of this handbook.

[88] *See* 7 Scott & Ascher §45.4.2.3 (Law Upholding an Inter Vivos Trust); §8.2.1.9 of this handbook (abolition of the rule against perpetuities).

the law of the place of administration."[89] On the other hand, if the accumulation provision is enforceable under the law of the place of administration, that should end the matter.[90]

In many civil law jurisdictions, most notably France and Germany, it is neither possible to impress an Anglo-American-type trust upon property nor is such an equity-based arrangement even recognized, topics we take up in Section 8.12 of this handbook.[91] A citizen of France or Germany, however, would not be foreclosed from relocating his or her movables to this country and impressing a valid inter vivos trust upon them here, at least not under generic trust law principles.[92]

Entrusted Land
(trust validity/conflict of laws)

As a general rule, the validity of an *outright* devise of land is governed by the law of the situs of that land.[93] The law of the situs, for example, would govern whether the will's execution complied with formal requirements and whether there was testamentary capacity.[94] Spousal elective share rights to a devise are governed by the law of the situs; so too are any civil law forced share rights afforded the testator's children.[95] Such will-trumping statutory rights are covered generally in Section 5.3.4 of this handbook, and in its sub-sections. The law of the situs also regulates the rights, if any, of pretermitted (omitted) children to devised land.[96] One would also look to the law of the situs for any restrictions on one's right to devise land for charitable purposes, a topic we cover generally in Section 8.15.4 of this handbook.[97]

The validity of a *testamentary trust* of land is governed by the law of the situs, particularly when its terms call for the land to be retained by the trustee.[98] The situation is different, however, when a testator devises to a trustee land that is situated in the state where the will is being probated and directs the trustee to sell the land and remit the proceeds to another state for administration as trust property. In that case, the trust is valid if it is valid at the place of administration, although it would have been invalid at the situs of the land, at least when there is no violation of a strong policy of the situs of the land.[99] The trust also would be valid if the land were sited out-of-state and the place of trust administration were the testator's/settlor's last domicile.[100] Such directions to sell entrusted real property may implicate the doctrine of equitable conversion, a topic we take up

---

[89] 7 Scott & Ascher §45.4.2.3.

[90] 7 Scott & Ascher §45.4.2.3.

[91] *See also* 7 Scott & Ascher §45.4.2.3.

[92] 7 Scott & Ascher §45.4.2.3.

[93] 7 Scott & Ascher §46.4.1.1 (Validity of the Will/Conflict of Laws/Land).

[94] 7 Scott & Ascher §46.4.1.1.

[95] 7 Scott & Ascher §46.4.1.1.

[96] 7 Scott & Ascher §46.4.1.1.

[97] 7 Scott & Ascher §46.4.1.1.

[98] 7 Scott & Ascher §46.4.1.2.

[99] 7 Scott & Ascher §46.4.1.2.

[100] 7 Scott & Ascher §46.4.1.2.

in Section 8.15.44 of this handbook. Note also that the land could be deemed personal property under certain circumstances, such as if it were a leasehold interest or serving as security for a debt.[101]

The validity or partial validity of *an inter vivos trust* of land is generally governed by the law of the situs of the land, unless there is a direction to sell the land and remit the proceeds to another state for administration there.[102] It is the law of the situs of the land that determines whether its owner has the capacity to impress a trust upon it.[103] In Section 8.11 of this handbook, we allude to the fact that at one time, though generally no longer, the revocable inter vivos trust was considered by some to be invalid for failing to comply with the statute of wills. To the extent there is any lingering doubt as to the enforceability of a revocable inter vivos trust, "it would seem that when the subject matter of the trust is land, the validity of the trust should depend upon the local law of the situs of the land."[104]

In Section 8.15.5 of this handbook, we discuss generally the statute of frauds as it applies to entrusted land. The creation of an inter vivos trust being a disposition of the beneficial interest in the subject property rather than a contract, "courts have generally held that whether a trust of land can be validly created without a writing depends upon the local law of the situs of the land, as does whether a memorandum suffices to comply with the statute of frauds."[105] If an oral trust of land fails under the statute of frauds, the transferee either holds the land outright and free of trust, or, in order to avoid unjust enrichment, as a constructive trustee for the benefit of the transferor.[106] The law of the situs will generally govern which it is to be.[107]

The purchase money resulting trust is discussed generally in Section 3.3 of this handbook. Whether a resulting trust of a parcel of land arises when someone other than the transferee of the land pays its purchase price "is determined by the local law of the state of the situs of the land."[108]

In Section 4.1.1.1 of this handbook, we consider the type of resulting trust that can arise when an express trust fails, or when there is property left over after an express trust has been fully performed. In the case of a trust of land, the courts of the state of the situs of the land have the last word on whether the trustee holds the property upon a resulting trust, or takes it outright and free of trust.[109] "In the case of a . . . [testamentary] . . . trust of land, the ultimate control is in the state of the situs, but in some situations its courts may apply the law of

---

[101] *See generally* 7 Scott & Ascher §46.4.1.2.

[102] 7 Scott & Ascher §46.4.2.

[103] 7 Scott & Ascher §46.4.2.

[104] 7 Scott & Ascher §46.4.2.

[105] 7 Scott & Ascher §46.4.2.

[106] 7 Scott & Ascher §46.4.2. *See generally* §3.3 of this handbook (the constructive trust).

[107] 7 Scott & Ascher §46.4.2.

[108] 7 Scott & Ascher §46.4.2. *See also* 7 Scott & Ascher §46.8.

[109] 7 Scott & Ascher §46.8.

the testator's domicil. In any event, the purpose is, as far as possible, to ascertain the state whose rules of construction the settlor would have preferred."[110]

In Section 3.4.2 of this handbook, we consider whether an inter vivos trust can arise without delivery of the subject property to the prospective trustee. "There is some authority to the effect that if the conveyance is ineffective for want of delivery the trust does not arise, but that if it fails merely because no trustee is named in the instrument of conveyance or the trustee is incapable of taking title to the property, the trust nevertheless arises."[111] There is some contra authority as well.[112] In any case, if the property is land, the law of the situs generally governs.[113]

Construing trust's dispositive provisions (conflict of laws). The settlor's lawful intentions govern the interpretation of the terms of a trust. "If, however, it is impossible to ascertain from the evidence the settlor's intention with respect to the matter at hand, the court may be forced to resort to a rule of construction."[114] Rules of construction relating to the disposition of trust property are covered generally in Section 5.2 of this handbook. We first consider what happens when a particular nonadministrative rule of construction varies materially from jurisdiction to jurisdiction.

Law designated by settlor or testator. As a general rule, the meaning and legal effect of the terms of a trust are determined by the laws of the jurisdiction *selected in the governing instrument,*[115] unless the selection of that jurisdiction's law is contrary to a strong public policy of the jurisdiction having the most significant relationship to the matter at issue.[116] The Uniform Probate Code is in accord.[117] So is the Uniform Trust Code.[118] "Since the court's purpose is to carry out the

---

[110] 7 Scott & Ascher §46.8.

[111] 7 Scott & Ascher §46.4.2.

[112] 7 Scott & Ascher §46.4.2.

[113] 7 Scott & Ascher §46.4.2.

[114] 7 Scott & Ascher §45.3. The question of a settlor's intention is one of fact, not law. 7 Scott & Ascher §45.3. The "ordinary meaning of the words used, the context in which they appear, and the circumstances under which the instrument was drafted" all can be factual evidence of how a particular trust provision should be interpreted. 7 Scott & Ascher §45.3. The court may consider where the settlor was domiciled at the time the instrument was executed and at the time it became effective. 7 Scott & Ascher §45.3. Whether the instrument was drafted by a layman or by experienced counsel may have relevance as to what the settlor's intentions were. 7 Scott & Ascher §45.3. The court may consider "whether the settlor used the language of his or her domicil, that of the place where the instrument was executed, or that of the place in which the trust was to be administered." 7 Scott & Ascher §45.3.

[115] *See* 7 Scott & Ascher §45.3.1. *See, e.g.,* Sloan v. Segal, 2008 WL 81513.

[116] UTC §107 (available at <http://www.uniformlaws.org/Act.aspx?title=Trust%20 Code>). *See generally* 7 Scott & Ascher §45.4.1.8 (public policy of the state in which the testator/ settlor of a testamentary trust of movables died domiciled); §8.39 of this handbook (settlor's choice of law as to meaning and effect of terms of trust).

[117] *See* UPC §2-703 (choice of law as to meaning and effect of governing instrument).

[118] UTC §107 (available at <http://www.uniformlaws.org/Act.aspx?title=Trust%20Code>). "Among the states that have enacted the UTC, however, there have been a significant number of departures from the official language." *See* 7 Scott & Ascher §45.3.1 n.8.

settlor's or testator's intention, it is immaterial whether the designated state has any connection with the creation or administration of the trust."[119]

Courts are somewhat less deferential to settlor intent when it comes to choosing what laws shall govern determinations relating to the *validity* of either the trust itself or its terms.[120] Having said that, the laws of the designated state are generally applied for purposes of determining whether an inter vivos trust of movables is revocable by the settlor, unless the terms of the trust have expressly addressed the matter.[121] A Totten trust is "ordinarily upheld if it is valid under either the law of the depositor's domicil or that of the state where the bank is located."[122] The subject of Totten trusts is covered in Section 9.8.5 of this handbook,

If a settlor provides that the laws of a particular state are to govern the construction of its terms, then the court will honor the provision as to movables, except when the designated state has no substantial relation to the trust or when to do so would violate the public policy of the state in which the trust is being administered.[123] A court having jurisdiction over a trust's administration, for example, would not enforce a spendthrift clause in a state that looks with disfavor on spendthrift trusts, even if the settlor's choice of law were that of some other state more favorably disposed toward such trusts.[124]

In the international context, the Hague Convention on the law applicable to trusts, a topic we take up in Section 8.12.2 of this handbook, also allows the settlor to designate the governing law and, absent a designation, would apply the law of the place having the closest connection to the trust.[125] "The Convention . . . lists particular public policies for which the forum may decide to override the choice of law that would otherwise apply."[126]

No designation of applicable law. Generally speaking, factors to consider in determining what law governs a particular trust matter include the place of the trust's creation, the location of the trust property, the domicile of the settlor, and the domicile of the trustee.[127] A rule of thumb is that the law of the trust's

---

[119] 7 Scott & Ascher §45.3.1.

[120] *See* 7 Scott & Ascher §45.3.1.

[121] 7 Scott & Ascher §45.3.5.2.

[122] 7 Scott & Ascher §45.3.5.2.

[123] *See generally* Jeffrey A. Schoenblum, Multistate and Multinational Estate Planning §17.01.6 (1999); *see also* Restatement (Second) Conflict of Laws §§267, 271, 272, 279. *See generally* Restatement (Second) Conflict of Laws §270.

[124] *See generally* Jeffrey A. Schoenblum, Multistate and Multinational Estate Planning §17.07 (1999).

[125] UTC §107 cmt. (available at <http://www.uniformlaws.org/Act.aspx?title=Trust%20Code>).

[126] UTC §107 cmt. (available at <http://www.uniformlaws.org/Act.aspx?title=Trust%20Code>). "These policies are protection of minors and incapable parties, personal and proprietary effects of marriage, succession rights, transfer of title and security interests in property, protection of creditors in matters of insolvency, and, more generally, protection of third parties acting in good faith." UTC §107 cmt.

[127] UTC §107 cmt. (available at <http://www.uniformlaws.org/Act.aspx?title=Trust%20Code>). *But see* 7 Scott & Ascher §45.3.5 ("As to matters not pertaining to trust administration, the settlor's domicil is certainly of less importance in the case of an inter vivos trust than in the case of

principal place of administration will govern administrative matters and the law of the place having the most significant relationship to the trust's creation will govern how one is to construe the dispositive provisions.[128]

Having said that, when it comes to construing the dispositive terms of an *inter vivos trust* of movables the settlor's domicile lacks the significance that it would have had it been testamentary.[129] In the case of a Totten Trust, for example, it is the state where the bank is organized and does business rather than the state of the depositor's domicile.[130] In the absence of a controlling designation in the terms of an inter vivos trust of movables,[131] the laws of the jurisdiction having the most significant relationship to the matter at issue ordinarily apply.[132] When it comes to identifying the beneficiaries, that is likely to be the laws of the state in which the trust is principally being administered rather than the laws of the settlor's domicile, unless, of course, the terms of the trust suggest otherwise.[133] On the other hand, in the case of cotrustees domiciled in different states or a trustee who is likely to be peripatetic such that it cannot be said that the place of administration has been "fixed" in any particular place, "the law of the settlor's domicil may well apply, in the absence of other significant contacts."[134] In the case of multiple settlors domiciled in different states, the court may have to "resort to other contacts" to determine the applicable law.[135] It might, for example, apply the laws of the state in which the trustee who has custody of the trust property is domiciled.[136]

---

a testamentary trust. . . . Accordingly, it has been held that in identifying the beneficiaries of an inter vivos trust, the applicable law is that of the state of administration, notwithstanding the fact that the settlor was domiciled elsewhere").

[128] UTC §107 cmt. (available at <http://www.uniformlaws.org/Act.aspx?title=Trust%20 Code>). Without precluding other means for establishing a sufficient connection with the designated jurisdiction, terms of a trust designating the principal place of administration are valid if a trustee's principal place of business is located in (or a trustee is a resident of) the designated jurisdiction, or all or part of the administration occurs in the designated jurisdiction. UTC §108. *See* UTC §108 cmt. (noting that a concept akin to principal place of administration is used by the Office of the Comptroller of the Currency, namely that reserves that national banks are required to deposit with state authorities is based on the location of the office where trust assets are primarily administered). *See* 12 C.F.R. §9.14(b) (Reg. 9) (available at <www.gpoaccess.gov/cfr/index.html>).

[129] 7 Scott & Ascher §45.3.5.

[130] 7 Scott & Ascher §45.3.5.2. *See generally* §9.8.5 of this handbook (the Totten trust).

[131] *See generally* 7 Scott & Ascher §45.3.5 (when the settlor of an inter vivos trust has designated that law that is to be applied).

[132] *See* UTC §107(2) (available at <http://www.uniformlaws.org/Act.aspx?title=Trust%20 Code>); 7 Scott & Ascher §45.3.5. *See, e.g.,* Seizer v. Sessions, 132 Wis. 2d 642, 940 P.2d 261 (1997).

[133] 7 Scott & Ascher §45.3.5. In §8.41 of this handbook, we take up the question of what is to be done with net income when there is no current beneficiary. "In the case of an inter vivos trust, as to which the settlor's domicil is often less important than in the case of a testamentary trust, the court may apply the law of the place of administration." 7 Scott & Ascher §45.3.7 (Income Not Specifically Disposed Of). Under §107(2) of the UTC, it is the law of the jurisdiction having the most significant relationship to the matter at issue.

[134] 7 Scott & Ascher §45.3.5.

[135] 7 Scott & Ascher §45.3.5.

[136] 7 Scott & Ascher §45.3.5.

If the terms of an inter vivos trust of movables fix the place of administration in a state other than the state where the settlor is or was domiciled, such as by the appointment of an out-of-state trust company, but fail to address whether the trust is revocable by the settlor, one ordinarily looks to the laws of the administration state to fill in the gap.[137] If the place of administration has not been fixed by the terms of the trust, its revocability is determined "by those contacts that for this purpose are most significant."[138] Under the Uniform Trust Code it would be the laws of the jurisdiction having the most significant "relationship" to the matter at issue.[139] So also when determining which jurisdiction's default law applies when there is a question as to how a trustee should allocate or apportion a particular receipt (or expense) between the income and principal accounts,[140] a topic that is covered generally in Section 6.2.4 of this handbook. We consider the general topic of revocability in Section 8.2.2.2 of this handbook.

Tax apportionment rules also can differ from state to state.[141] Thus, if the settlor of a funded revocable trust dies domiciled in a state other than the one in which the trust is being administered, which jurisdiction's default tax apportionment rules are applicable? There is not a lot of helpful law out there.[142] One learned commentator proffers the following intent-focused advice:

> Proper resolution of cases of this sort, however, is not to be achieved by mechanically applying either the law of the situs of the nonprobate assets or that of the decedent's domicil, but instead by trying to ascertain what the decedent, in view of all the circumstances, would probably have preferred. In this inquiry, any number of factors may prove relevant. As we have seen, the fact that the tax attributable to nonprobate assets is very large in comparison with the fund out of which it might under the law of one of the relevant states be payable seems almost undeniably relevant in determining what the decedent actually or presumably intended. This is especially so when it appears that the decedent did not realize how large the taxes were, or that the nonprobate assets would be part of the gross estate.[143]

Now we turn to the *testamentary trust*. "When it is necessary to apply a rule of construction in determining who are the beneficiaries of a testamentary trust of movables, and the testator has not designated the applicable law, the courts ordinarily apply the rule of the state of the testator's domicil, even when trust administration has been fixed elsewhere."[144] Ordinarily it is the state where the

---

[137] 7 Scott & Ascher §45.3.5.2

[138] 7 Scott & Ascher §45.3.5.2.

[139] UTC §107(2) (available at <http://www.uniformlaws.org/Act.aspx?title=Trust%20Code>).

[140] *See generally* 7 Scott & Ascher §45.3.10 (Allocation of Receipts and Expenses to Income or Principal/Conflict of Laws).

[141] *See generally* 7 Scott & Ascher §45.3.11 (Allocation of Estate Taxes/Conflict of Laws); §8.5 of this handbook (conflict of laws).

[142] *See* 7 Scott & Ascher §45.3.11.

[143] 7 Scott & Ascher §45.3.11.

[144] 7 Scott & Ascher §45.3.2. In §5.1 of this handbook, we take up the question of whether one who may only incidentally benefit from the performance of a trust, such as the creditor of a

testator was domiciled when the will was executed, not the state where he or she died domiciled, assuming they were not one and the same.[145] The model Uniform Trust Code would seem to be in accord.[146] If execution took place in a state other than the state where the testator was domiciled at the time of execution, the version of the rule of construction prevailing in the state of execution is the one that is likely to be applied.[147]

In Section 6.2.4 of this handbook, we consider the trustee's duty to separate income from principal, to include the associated duty to properly allocate receipts and expenses between the two accounts. Should a question arise as to how this should be done in a given situation, which is more a construction problem than an administrative one, the terms of the trust often provide the requisite guidance.[148] When such guidance is lacking, however, the trustee must search for an applicable default rule of construction.[149] In the case of a testamentary trust of movables whose settlor was last domiciled in a state other than the state where the trust is being administered, the trustee also may have to wrestle with the question of which state's default law governs.[150] Having said that, we should note that in cases involving testamentary trusts of movables,

---

designated beneficiary, would have standing to seek judicial enforcement of the trust. In the case of a testamentary trust of movables, the question is ordinarily determined by the laws of the state of the testator's/settlor's domicile. *See* 7 Scott & Ascher §45.3.6 (incidental beneficiaries/conflict of laws). Under the §107(2) of the UTC, it is the law of the jurisdiction having the most significant relationship to the matter at issue. In §8.41 of this handbook, we take up the question of what is to be done with net income when there is no current beneficiary. In the case of a testamentary trust of movables, the laws of the testator's/settlor's domicile are ordinarily determinative. *See* 7 Scott & Ascher §45.3.7 (Income Not Specifically Disposed Of). In §4.1.1.1 of this handbook, we discuss what happens when income is payable to a certain beneficiary but there is no provision for the ultimate distribution of the trust principal. Does the beneficiary take the principal as well? Or is there eventually a resulting trust of the principal? In the case of a testamentary trust of movables, again, the rules of construction followed in the state of the settlor's/testator's domicile ordinarily apply, unless the terms of the trust suggest otherwise. *See* 7 Scott & Ascher §45.3.8 (Principal Not Specifically Disposed Of). Under §107(2) of the UTC, it would be the rules of construction of the jurisdiction having the most significant relationship to the matter at issue. In §6.2.4.5 of this handbook, we take up the question of what is to be done with undistributed income upon the death of a life income beneficiary. Does income accrued to the date of death become a part of the beneficiary's probate estate; or is it distributed to the successor income beneficiary, if any; or does it become a part of the principal? In the case of a testamentary trust of movables, the applicable law is that of the settlor's/testator's domicile, unless the terms of the trust provide otherwise. *See* 7 Scott & Ascher §45.3.9 (Disposition of Income on Death of Life Beneficiary). Under §107(2) of the UTC, it is the law of the jurisdiction having the most significant relationship to the matter at issue.

[145] 7 Scott & Ascher §45.3.2.

[146] UTC §107 cmt. (available at <http://www.uniformlaws.org/Act.aspx?title=Trust%20 Code>). *See, however*, 7 Scott & Ascher §45.3.2 n.29 ("A number of states that have enacted the UTC, however, have enacted different rules for the situation in which the settlor has failed to designate the applicable law.").

[147] 7 Scott & Ascher §45.3.2.

[148] *See generally* §3.5.3.2(g) of this handbook (authorizing the trustee to resolve income/ principal allocation and apportionment questions); 7 Scott & Ascher §45.3.10 (confirming that in determining the allocation of receipts between income and principal, the courts have treated the question not as one of administration but as one of construction).

[149] *See generally* 7 Scott & Ascher §45.3.10.

[150] *See generally* 7 Scott & Ascher §45.3.10.

the courts, in determining the allocation of receipts between income and principal, ordinarily apply the law of the testator's domicile, rather than that of the place of administration.[151]

***

Entrusted Land
(rules of construction/dispositive provisions/conflict of laws)

Before we consider the problem of conflicting rules of construction in the multi-jurisdictional setting when land is involved, some context. In the days when the rule in Shelley's Case, the doctrine of worthier title, and other such fixed policy-based glosses on the law of real property were not mere rules of construction, the law of the situs of the entrusted land governed their applicability.[152] Now these rules and doctrines have largely morphed into rules of construction. Also, when it is a question of the interpretation of the language of a trust provision, that is of ascertaining what the settlor had in mind, rather than how a particular provision should be construed when the settlor's intentions are not readily discernable, "the court, in ascertaining the testator's intention, is likely to consider the ordinary usage at the testator's domicil, particularly at the time of the execution of the will, or at the place where the testator executed the will."[153] Whether we have a testamentary or inter vivos trust, and whether the subject of the trust is movables or immovables, "[i]n ascertaining the settlor's intent, the court should consider all of the circumstances bearing on that intent, including the usage at the settlor's domicil."[154] A rule of construction, on the other hand, is what the court applies when "[i]t is impossible to ascertain from the evidence the settlor's intention with respect to the issue at hand."[155] When it comes to parsing the provisions of a trust of land, the relevant rules of construction that prevail in the situs state could, for example, be different from those that prevail in the forum state. Whose rules, then, are applicable? First, the courts of the state of the situs of the entrusted land have the last word.[156] Second, all courts will generally honor any provision in the governing instrument calling for the trust's terms to be construed in accordance with the laws of a particular state.[157]

<hr>

[151] *See* 7 Scott & Ascher §45.3.10. "In considering a will, however, one should keep in mind that, although the applicable rules of construction ordinarily are those of the testator's domicil at death, if the testator was domiciled in another state at the time of execution of the will, the rules of construction of that state may well apply." 7 Scott & Ascher §45.3.10.

[152] 7 Scott & Ascher §46.3. *See generally* §8.15.3 of this handbook (Rule in Shelley's Case); §8.15.2 of this handbook (doctrine of worthier title).

[153] 7 Scott & Ascher §46.3.

[154] 7 Scott & Ascher §46.3.

[155] 7 Scott & Ascher §46.3. "In construing an instrument, the court applies a rule that is supposed to be in accord with what most settlors would have intended, in the absence of further evidence as to their actual intent." 7 Scott & Ascher §46.3. "A rule of construction merely loads the dice, one way or the other, in the absence of further evidence." 7 Scott & Ascher §46.3.

[156] 7 Scott & Ascher §46.3.

[157] 7 Scott & Ascher §46.3.

In the absence of such a provision and when the settlor's dispositive intentions are not otherwise discernable, the courts are "divided" on the question of whether the applicable law is that of the situs of a testamentary trust of land or that of the testator's domicil at execution, at least as to matters that relate to the very nature of the equitable interest and who might be entitled to it.[158] In the case of an inter vivos trust of land, however, the applicable law generally is that of the situs.[159]

Trust administration questions (conflict of laws). As to matters relating to the general administrative powers and duties of a trustee of an inter vivos or testamentary trust of movables,[160] particularly investment responsibilities,[161] compensation,[162] right to indemnity for expenses incurred in trust administration, and liabilities for breaches of trust,[163] the relevant provisions of the governing instrument are ordinarily construed in accordance with the laws of the state that the settlor expressly or by implication fixed as the place of administration, unless the terms of the trust provide otherwise.[164] These are construction matters that relate to the trust's administration, as opposed to the disposition of its property. In both categories of construction matter, however, when it comes to the Totten trust, a topic we take up in Section 9.8.5 of this handbook, "[i]t would seem that the applicable law should be that of the state where the bank is organized and does business, rather than the state of the settlor's domicil."[165]

In any case, the general rule is that the law of a trust's principal place of administration ordinarily governs its administration, a rule that is subject to a number of exceptions, which are discussed next.[166] Thus, an authorized mid-course relocation of a trust's principal place of administration to another might well cause a different law to govern the administration going forward, unless the

---

[158] 7 Scott & Ascher §46.3. "Apart from the testator's supposed familiarity with the law of his or her domicil, application of the rules of construction of the testator's domicil is desirable, in that it applies a single law not only to the testator's movables, but also to the testator's land, wherever situated." 7 Scott & Ascher §46.3. Otherwise, one could conjure up a fact pattern involving a trust of multiple parcels of land that are scattered about the country where applying the law of the situs to a beneficiary status question could result in each parcel having its own unique cohort of beneficiaries. 7 Scott & Ascher §46.3.

[159] 7 Scott & Ascher §46.3

[160] *See generally* 7 Scott & Ascher §45.6.3 (Powers and Duties of the Trustee/Conflict of Laws); §3.5.3 of this handbook (powers of the trustee); Chapter 6 of this handbook (duties of the trustee).

[161] *See generally* 7 Scott & Ascher §45.6.2 (Investment of Trust Funds/Conflict of Laws); §6.2.2.1 of this handbook (investing trust assets).

[162] *See generally* 7 Scott & Ascher §45.6.1 of this handbook (Compensation of the Trustee/Conflict of laws); §8.4 of this handbook (trustee compensation).

[163] *See generally* 7 Scott & Ascher §45.6.4 (Liabilities of the Trustee/Conflict of Laws); Chapter 7 of this handbook (the trustee's liabilities).

[164] 7 Scott & Ascher §45.3.2. *See generally* §6.2.2 of this handbook (the trustee's investment responsibilities); §8.4 of this handbook (trustee compensation); §3.5.2.3 of this handbook (trustee's right to indemnity); §7.2 of this handbook (liabilities of trustee for breaches of trust).

[165] 7 Scott & Ascher §45.3.5.2. A Totten trust, on the other hand, is upheld if it is valid either under the laws of the depositor's domicile or those of the state where the bank is located. 7 Scott & Ascher §45.3.5.2.

[166] 7 Scott & Ascher §45.5.3.2 (Whether to Permit a Change in the Applicable Law).

terms of the trust provide otherwise.[167] On the other hand, at least under the common law, the mere fact that the trustee has moved out of state ought not to warrant a change in the law applicable to the trust's administration.[168] Nor should a change in the place of administration alone render a valid trust invalid as a matter of law, even if the relocation has been authorized by the terms of the trust.[169] "When the court authorizes a change in the place of trust administration for reasons of convenience, as when there has been a change in the domicil of one or more of the beneficiaries or trustees, it is not clear whether trust administration is thereafter governed by the law of the new state."[170] The case law is mixed.[171]

Administration of testamentary trusts of movables generally (conflict of laws). With some exceptions, most notably those relating to the alienability of the equitable interests and fiduciary exculpation, the testator/settlor of a testamentary trust of movables may designate expressly or by implication the law of a state other than the state of last domicile as the law that shall govern its administration.[172] It may even be the law of a state that has no connection with the trust.[173] "Alternatively, the testator can designate the law of different states to govern different matters of trust administration."[174] The Uniform Trust Code is in accord,[175] as is the Restatement (Second) of Conflict of Laws.[176]

We turn now to the situation where the testator/settlor of a testamentary trust of movables makes no express designation in the will as to the law that shall govern the trust's administration.[177] Ordinarily, the law of the testator's/settlor's domicile at death governs the trust's administration,[178] unless the place of

---

[167] 7 Scott & Ascher §45.5.3.2 (Whether to Permit a Change in the Applicable Law). *See generally* §6.2.15 of this handbook (the trustee's duty to administer trust in an appropriate place); §8.40 of this handbook (judicial jurisdiction over the trustee, the beneficiaries, and the trust property).

[168] 7 Scott & Ascher §45.5.3.2.

[169] 7 Scott & Ascher §45.5.3.2.

[170] 7 Scott & Ascher §45.5.3.2.

[171] 7 Scott & Ascher §45.5.3.2.

[172] *See generally* 7 Scott & Ascher §45.5.1.1 (Administration of a Testamentary Trust—Law Designated by the Testator). "The designation of the state whose law is to govern the administration of the trust may be implied from the language of the will or from other circumstances indicating that the testator intended that the law of a particular state would govern trust administration." 7 Scott & Ascher §45.5.1.1.

[173] 7 Scott & Ascher §45.5.1.1.

[174] 7 Scott & Ascher §45.5.1.1.

[175] *See* UTC §107 (available at <http://www.uniformlaws.org/Act.aspx?title=Trust%20Code>).

[176] Restatement (Second) of Conflict of Laws §271 cmt. c.

[177] *See generally* Restatement (Second) of Conflict of Laws §271 (administration of trust of movables created by will).

[178] *Cf.* 7 Scott & Ascher §45.5.1.3 ("If, by the terms of the will, the property is left to a trustee in the testator's domicil, charged with a duty to invest the property or its proceeds and pay the income to trustees in another state, for administration there for charitable purposes, the administration of the trust, insofar as it is situated in the testator's domicil, is governed by the law of the testator's domicil . . . [, but having said that,] . . . 'the administration and disposition of the income received by the trustee in the other state . . . may well be governed by the law of the other state'").

administration has been fixed elsewhere, such as by a provision in the will naming an out-of-state trust company as the trustee, in which case the law of the state in which the trust company is organized and does business shall govern.[179]

If, instead, the named trustee of the testamentary trust were a nonresident individual rather than a corporation, then there would be a similar inference that the testator/settlor intended that the law of the trustee's domicile shall govern the trust's administration, provided the will expressly or by implication called for the trust to be administered there.[180] When a testamentary trust of movables has out-of-state cotrustees one of whom is actively engaged in the business of serving as a trustee, be the cotrustee a corporation or an individual, there is an inference that the testator/settlor intended the trust's administration to take place in and be governed by the law of the state in which the corporation or individual does business.[181] When the testator/settlor has not manifested in the will an intention that the trust be administered in another state, the law of the testator's/settlor's domicile ordinarily governs the trust's administration.[182] This is particularly the case when the designated trustee is an amateur.[183]

The Uniform Trust Code would seem *not* to be in accord. According to the official commentary, "[u]sually, the law of the trust's principal place of administration will govern administrative matters..."[184] This has always been the general rule when it comes to a charitable testamentary trust of movables which is to be administered in a state other than the testator's/settlor's last domicile, particularly if the trust is to be for the benefit of a community that is located within the state of administration.[185] So also the *cy pres* law of the place of administration is likely to apply should the purposes of the charitable testamentary trust become illegal, impossible, impracticable or wasteful in mid-course.[186] On the other hand, if it becomes impossible at the outset to carry out a trust's designated charitable purpose, the availability of *cy pres* may well be determined by the law of the testator's/settlor's domicile at death.[187] The general topic of *cy pres* is taken up in Section 9.4.3 of this handbook.

Under the UTC, it is not clear whether a testator/settlor could constructively select which state's law shall govern a trust's administration merely by designating in the terms of the trust its place of administration, particularly if no part of the administration is actually to occur there and the trustee is not domiciled or doing business there.[188] Here is one commentator's articulation of the cause of the confusion: "When the testator designates a jurisdiction as the

---

[179] 7 Scott & Ascher §45.5.1.2.

[180] 7 Scott & Ascher §45.5.1.2.

[181] 7 Scott & Ascher §45.5.1.2.

[182] 7 Scott & Ascher §45.5.1.2.

[183] 7 Scott & Ascher §45.5.1.2.

[184] UTC §107 cmt. (available at <http://www.uniformlaws.org/Act.aspx?title=Trust%20 Code>). *See generally* 7 Scott & Ascher §45.5.1.2.

[185] 7 Scott & Ascher §45.5.1.3 (Administration of a Charitable Trust/Conflict of Laws).

[186] 7 Scott & Ascher §45.5.1.3.

[187] 7 Scott & Ascher §45.5.1.3.

[188] UTC §§107(2) & 108(a) (available at <http://www.uniformlaws.org/Act.aspx?title= Trust%20Code>).

place of administration, whether the law of the designated jurisdiction will actually control the administration of the trust seems to depend, at least in part, under ... [UTC] ... sections 107(2) and 108(a), on whether that jurisdiction is also a jurisdiction in which a trustee resides or has a principal place of business, or in which at least a part of the administration of the trust occurs."[189]

It is important to keep in mind what we have been considering here, namely which state's law shall govern the administration of a *testamentary trust* of movables.[190] Impressing a testamentary trust on a portion or all of one's probate estate is quite different from a *testamentary pour over* into an inter vivos trust, a topic which is covered generally in Section 2.1.1 of this handbook. The law of the testator's last domicile will govern the validity of the will's pour-over provision while the law which was governing the administration of the recipient inter vivos trust before the pour-over will continue to do so even after it, absent special facts.[191]

Administration of inter vivos trust of movables generally (conflict of laws). The settlor of an inter vivos trust of movables may effectively provide expressly or by implication via its terms that the law of a particular state law shall always govern those aspects of the trust's administration that are within the settlor's power to regulate, such as trustee compensation and investment policy.[192] The Uniform Trust Code is generally in accord,[193] as is the Restatement (Second) of Conflict of Laws.[194] Just about any law may be chosen.[195] It need be neither the law of the settlor's domicile nor that of the trust's place of administration.[196] Moreover, the terms of the trust may provide that the law of one state shall govern some aspects of the trust's administration while the law of another state shall govern other aspects.[197] The settlor will not have such a free hand when it comes to an administrative matter that implicates a strong public policy of the state whose court is exercising jurisdiction over the trust's administration, such as the state's policy on spendthrift restraints or fiduciary exculpation.[198] The court is likely to be that of a state that has a substantial connection with the trust's administration.[199]

---

[189] 7 Scott & Ascher §45.5.1.2.

[190] *See generally* §2.1.2 of this handbook (the testamentary trust).

[191] 7 Scott & Ascher §45.5.1.4 (Pour-Over Wills/Conflict of Laws).

[192] 7 Scott & Ascher §45.5.2.1 (Administration of an Inter Vivos Trust—Law Designated by the Settlor). Thus, when a settlor does not intend his choice of governing law to be *permanent* and the trust instrument includes a power to appoint a successor trustee, at least one court has held that the law governing the administration of the trust may be changed. *See* In re Peierls Family *Inter Vivos* Trusts, 77 A.3d 249 (Del. 2013).

[193] UTC §107 (available at <http://www.uniformlaws.org/Act.aspx?title=Trust%20Code>).

[194] *See* Restatement (Second) of Conflict of Laws §272 (1971).

[195] 7 Scott & Ascher §45.5.2.1.

[196] 7 Scott & Ascher §45.5.2.1.

[197] 7 Scott & Ascher §45.5.2.1.

[198] 7 Scott & Ascher §45.5.2.1.

[199] 7 Scott & Ascher §45.5.2.1.

When the terms of an inter vivos trust of movables are silent as to the law that shall govern its administration, it is usually the law of the state that has the most significant relationship with the trust's administration, such as the state in which the administration has been fixed, if it has been.[200] Appointing a trust company as the trustee is one way to "fix" the trust's administration in the state where the company has its offices.[201] "Of course, a settlor who wishes to make doubly sure that the law of the place of administration will govern trust administration may wish to execute the trust instrument there, and to deliver the property to the trustee there, either before or at the creation of the trust."[202] If the trustee is not a corporation but an individual, there is a somewhat weaker inference that the trust's administration has been fixed in and is to be governed by the laws of the state of the trustee's domicile.[203]

If the terms of an inter vivos trust of movables neither expressly nor by implication fix its administration in a particular state, then the law of the state that has the most significant relationship with the administration governs the administration.[204] The Uniform Trust Code is in accord.[205] "It is in cases of this sort that the court is compelled to consider all of the contacts with the various states and to attempt to evaluate them:

> ... [T]he court will consider such contacts as the settlor's domicil at the time of the creation of the trust, the situs of the trust property at that time, the place of execution of the trust instrument, the purposes the settlor is seeking to accomplish with trust, the settlor's connection with states other than that of his or her domicil, and any other factors that seem to the court helpful in determining what the settlor intended or would or might have intended if he or she had considered what law should apply."[206]

As we have noted above in our discussion of the testamentary trust of movables, it is not clear whether under the UTC the settlor of a trust could constructively select which state's law shall govern a trust's administration merely by designating in the terms of the trust its place of administration, particularly if no part of the administration is actually to occur there and the trustee is not domiciled or doing business there.[207] We repeat here one commentator's articulation of the cause of the confusion: "When the testator designates a jurisdiction as the place of administration, whether the law of the designated jurisdiction will actually control the administration of the trust seems to depend, at least in part, under ... [UTC] ... sections 107(2) and

---

[200] 7 Scott & Ascher §45.5.2.2.

[201] 7 Scott & Ascher §45.5.2.2.

[202] 7 Scott & Ascher §45.5.2.2.

[203] 7 Scott & Ascher §45.5.2.2.

[204] 7 Scott & Ascher §45.5.2.2.

[205] UTC §107(2) (available at <http://www.uniformlaws.org/Act.aspx?title=Trust%20 Code>).

[206] 7 Scott & Ascher §45.5.2.2.

[207] UTC §§107(2) & 108(a) (available at <http://www.uniformlaws.org/Act.aspx?title= Trust%20Code>).

108(a), on whether that jurisdiction is also a jurisdiction in which a trustee resides or has a principal place of business, or in which at least a part of the administration of the trust occurs."[208]

Trust termination issues specifically (conflict of laws). In Section 8.2.2 of this handbook we consider the circumstances under which the beneficiaries of a trust may compel its termination in mid-course. The jurisdictions are not in accord as to what those circumstances are. The right to terminate a trust of movables ordinarily is governed by the law of the place of administration, unless the settlor has designated the law of another state as controlling.[209] So also "[w]hen . . . [a testator/settlor] . . . dies domiciled in one state and by will creates a trust to be administered in another state and provides that the beneficiaries are not entitled to terminate the trust, and under the law of one of the states the provision is effective but under the law of the other it is not, the court may apply the law that effectuates the . . . [testator's/settlor's] . . . intent."[210] Thus, it stands to reason that if a testamentary trust of movables is irrevocable under the law of the testator's/settlor's last domicile and if its place of administration has been fixed there by the terms of the will, then the fact that the trust would be terminable by a beneficiary under the law of *the beneficiary's domicile* will not make it so.[211]

Entrusted Land
(rules of construction/administrative provisions/conflict of laws)

When it comes to parsing the administrative provisions of a trust of land, the relevant rules of construction that prevail in the situs state can differ from those that prevail in the forum state. As we have already noted, the courts of the state of the situs of the entrusted land have the last word.[212] Second, all courts will generally honor any provision in the governing instrument calling for the trust's terms to be construed in accordance with the laws of a particular state.[213] In the absence of such a provision and when the settlor's intentions are not otherwise discernable, the rules of construction prevailing in the situs state generally apply to administrative matters, specifically those that relate to the trustee's compensation, powers, duties, and liabilities,[214] except when there has been an equitable conversion.[215] "When the terms of the trust direct or authorize the trustee to sell the land and remit the proceeds to another state for administration there, the courts of the place of administration will, after the sale and remittance, exercise jurisdiction over the administration of the trust. Likewise, after the sale and remittance, the law applicable to the administration

---

[208] 7 Scott & Ascher §45.5.1.2.

[209] 7 Scott & Ascher §45.6.5 (Termination of the Trust).

[210] 7 Scott & Ascher §45.6.5.

[211] 7 Scott & Ascher §45.6.5.

[212] *See generally* 7 Scott & Ascher §46.3.

[213] 7 Scott & Ascher §46.3.

[214] 7 Scott & Ascher §46.3; 7 Scott & Ascher §46.6.

[215] 7 Scott & Ascher §46.6. *See generally* §8.15.44 of this handbook (equitable conversion).

of the trust of the proceeds is ordinarily that of the state in which the trust is to be administered."[216]

As to land that is the subject of a testamentary trust, there is little authority as to whether the law of the testator's/settlor's domicile or that of the situs applies to questions arising out of the trustee's duty to properly allocate receipts and expenses between income and principal, a topic we cover generally in Section 6.2.4 of this handbook.[217]

The intersection of public policy and trust administration (conflict of laws). We have just come off a discussion of whose law should govern those aspects of a trust's administration that the settlor may generally regulate via the terms of the trust. "Certain matters of administration, however, may not be controlled by the terms of the trust."[218] Whose law governs these matters in a given situation we take up next.

Fiduciary exculpation (conflict of laws). In Section 7.2.6 of this handbook we discuss the effectiveness of a trust provision that would relieve the trustee of liability for breaching a duty that the trustee owes to the beneficiaries. We suggest that when it comes to a testamentary trust of movables, the law of the testator's/settlor's domicile at death should govern the construction of an exculpatory provision, while the public policy of the place of administration should dictate its enforceability. The enforceability of an exculpatory clause in an inter vivos trust of movables also should hinge on the applicable public policy in the state in which the trust is being administered. We can offer no law, however, that would directly support or call into question these suggestions.[219]

Fiduciary self-dealing (conflict of laws). In Section 6.1.3 of this handbook we discuss the trustee's duty not to self-deal with the trust property. In Section 7.1 of this handbook we outline the equitable defenses that may be available to a trustee who has engaged in self-dealing. "It appears that the law of the place of administration ordinarily determines whether a trustee is liable for self-dealing."[220] Having said that, one commentator has questioned whether the testator/settlor of a testamentary trust who dies domiciled in a state with a restrictive policy on fiduciary self-dealing should be able to fix the trust's administration in a state with a more permissive policy and in so doing avoid the consequences of the more restrictive public policy.[221] Certainly a mere designation in the will, without more, that the more permissive law shall control would be problematic.[222]

Consequences of third-party participation in a breach of trust (conflict of laws). In Section 7.2.9 of this handbook we examine generally how a third party who has knowingly participated with a trustee in a breach of trust could incur liability to

---

[216] 7 Scott & Ascher §46.6.

[217] 7 Scott & Ascher §46.3.

[218] 7 Scott & Ascher §45.6.6 (Matters of Administration that Cannot Be Controlled by the Terms of the Trust).

[219] *See generally* 7 Scott & Ascher §45.6.6.

[220] 7 Scott & Ascher §45.6.6.

[221] 7 Scott & Ascher §45.6.6.

[222] 7 Scott & Ascher §45.6.6.

the beneficiaries for any harm to them that is attributable to the participation. In Section 8.3.4 of this handbook, we focus on the question of whether a third-party bank depository of trust funds is bound to inquire into the trustee's authority to withdraw those funds. Whatever the case, when a trustee in breach of trust withdraws trust funds from a bank that has actual notice of the breach, the bank's liability is determined by the law of the place where the bank does business, not the law of the place where the trust is being administered.[223]

In Section 8.3.5 of this handbook we consider whether third-party corporation some of whose shares are the subject of a trust, as well as its stock transfer agent, owe any duty to the beneficiaries to ascertain the trustee's equitable authority to transfer the stock. Whatever the case, the applicable law is likely to be that of the state in which the corporation or transfer agent is organized, not the law of the trust's principal place of administration, unless the locations coincide.[224]

In Section 8.3.7 of this handbook we consider whether a stockbroker prior to getting operationally involved with a trustee in a transaction involving the purchase or sale on behalf of the trust of a block of securities would have a duty to the beneficiaries to make sure that the trustee had the equitable authority to do what was being contemplated.[225] Under the Uniform Act of Simplification of Fiduciary Security Transfers, the law that governs is the law of the state in which the broker committed the act or omission in question, not the law of the state in which the trust is being administered, unless the locations coincide.[226] Under the Uniform Commercial Code, the "local" law of the broker's "jurisdiction" governs.[227]

Charitable immunity issues (conflict of laws). The charitable immunity doctrine is covered in Section 8.15.38 of this handbook. It is now probably no longer good law most everywhere that though a charitable corporation lacks immunity from tort liability under the laws of its state of organization, it would still enjoy liability immunity for torts committed in and covered by the charitable immunity doctrine of another state.[228] "It seems clear enough that, when there is no immunity in the state in which the charitable corporation is incorporated, in which it conducts its principal activities, in which plaintiff resides, and in which plaintiff enters into some relationship with the corporation, the corporation should not be relieved of liability merely because the injury takes place in a state allowing immunity."[229]

---

[223] *See* 7 Scott & Ascher §45.6.6.1 (Participation in a Breach of Trust/Conflict of Laws) (citing to Uniform Commercial Code §4-102(b)).

[224] 7 Scott & Ascher §45.6.6.1 (citing to Unif. Act for Simplification of Fiduciary Security Transfers §8(a); U.C.C. §8-110(a), (b), (d) & (e)).

[225] *See generally* 7 Scott & Ascher §45.6.6.1.

[226] Unif. Act for Simplification of Fiduciary Security Transfers §8(b).

[227] U.C.C. §8-110(b) & (e).

[228] 7 Scott & Ascher §45.6.6.2.

[229] 7 Scott & Ascher §45.6.6.2. "If the purpose of the immunity rule is to preserve the corporation's assets, it would seem that there should be no immunity if the state of incorporation has no such policy." 7 Scott & Ascher §45.6.6.2.

The Restatement (Second) of Conflict of Laws provides that the law applicable to a particular charitable immunity conflict of laws issue is that of the jurisdiction that has "the most significant relationship to the occurrence and the parties."[230] Thus, if the charitable corporation's principal place of business also happens to be the plaintiff's domicile, the law of that jurisdiction would most likely govern.[231]

Nature of beneficiary's property interest (conflict of laws). It is not entirely settled whether a trust beneficiary possesses a direct proprietary interest *in the underlying trust property itself* or merely an indirect interest in the property incident to the beneficiary's equitable personal claim against the trustee, which itself is a property right. This is a question we consider in Section 5.3.1 of this handbook,[232] and which was considered by the House of Lords when it applied New York law in a high-profile trans-Atlantic tax case.[233] In a given matter involving a trust of movables that calls for a definitive answer to the question, a court would likely do as the House of Lords did and apply the law of the state in which the trust had been created, provided it was also the state in which the trust was being administered.[234] In the case of an entrusted parcel of land, it would apply the law of the land's situs.[235]

Enforceability of trust spendthrift provisions (conflict of laws). In Section 5.3.3.1 of this handbook, we consider whether the creditor of one who has reserved an equitable interest under a self-settled inter vivos spendthrift trust may reach that interest in satisfaction of the debt. In Section 5.3.3.3 of this handbook we consider the plight of the creditor of a nonsettlor beneficiary of either a testamentary or an inter vivos trust that has a spendthrift provision. Restrictions on voluntary assignments of the equitable interest also are discussed. All things being equal, the law of the situs of the trust will ordinarily govern.[236] "The law of the forum merely because it is the law of the forum, should not apply. It should also generally be immaterial where the beneficiary is domiciled, where the creditor or assignee is domiciled, and where the debt was incurred or the assignment was made."[237]

In the case of a *testamentary spendthrift trust of movables*, the enforceability of any spendthrift provisions is ordinarily governed by the law of the place that the testator/settlor expressly or by implication fixed as the trust's place of administration, at least under the common law.[238] In the absence of such a "fixing," it is likely to be the law of the testator's/settlor's domicile at death.[239] So too when it

---

[230] Restatement (Second) of Conflict of Laws §§145(1), 168.

[231] *See* Restatement (Second) of Conflict of Laws §§145 cmt. d; 168 cmt. b (1971).

[232] *See also* 7 Scott & Ascher §45.6.6.3 (The Nature of the Beneficiary's Interest/Conflict of Laws).

[233] Archer-Shee v. Garland, [1931] A.C. 212.

[234] 7 Scott & Ascher §45.6.6.3.

[235] 7 Scott & Ascher §45.6.6.3.

[236] 7 Scott & Ascher §45.7.3.

[237] 7 Scott & Ascher §45.7.3.

[238] 7 Scott & Ascher §45.7.1.1.

[239] 7 Scott & Ascher §45.7.1.1.

comes to questions regarding the assignability of the equitable interest.[240] The Restatement (Second) of Conflict of Laws seems generally in accord.[241]

If the beneficiary is not subject to the court's jurisdiction, "the court can entertain the proceeding as a proceeding *quasi in rem* to reach the beneficiary's interest in the trust estate, and to apply it to the creditor's claim against the beneficiary."[242] If the situs of the trust is in one state and the litigation forum is in another, the law of the situs would still govern even if the court were to have personal jurisdiction over the trustee.[243] "A spendthrift provision would be of little value if it could be ignored in any jurisdiction that happened to acquire jurisdiction over the trustee."[244] The same principle would apply if the court of a state other than the state of administration were to acquire by happenstance jurisdiction over an entrusted item of personal property, such as a block of a corporation's stock.[245]

So too the enforceability of a spendthrift term in an *inter vivos trust of movables* is likely to be governed by the law of the place of the trust's administration, and otherwise by the law of the state with the most significant relationship to the trust administration,[246] except, perhaps, in cases where the beneficiary-debtor is also the settlor:

> As we have seen, ... there are now, in a few states, statutes that permit, under various circumstances, the settlor of a trust to subject even the settlor's own beneficial interest to various levels of spendthrift protection.[247] Without question, these statutes are a remarkable departure from traditional trust law. It would hardly be surprising, therefore, if a court of the settlor's domicil, in considering the right of one or more of the settlor's creditors to reach the settlor's own, retained beneficial interest, were to conclude that it was contrary to a strong public policy of the forum to enforce a self-settled spendthrift provision, even if, under the law of the place of administration, such a provision were enforceable.[248]

---

[240] 7 Scott & Ascher §45.7.2 (Assignees of a Beneficiary's Interest/Conflict of Laws).

[241] Restatement (Second) of Conflict of Laws §273 (providing that "[w]hether the interest of a beneficiary of a trust of movables is assignable by him and can be reached by his creditors is determined ... in the case of a testamentary trust ... by the local law of the testator's domicil at death, unless the testator has manifested an intention that the trust is to be administered in another state, in which case it is governed by the local law of that state ...").

[242] 7 Scott & Ascher §45.7.1.1. *See also* §8.40 of this handbook (discussing the concept of *quasi in rem* jurisdiction).

[243] 7 Scott & Ascher §45.7.1.1.

[244] 7 Scott & Ascher §45.7.1.1.

[245] 7 Scott & Ascher §45.7.1.1.

[246] *See generally* Restatement (Second) of Conflict of Laws §273 (providing that "[w]hether the interest of a beneficiary of a trust of movables is assignable by him and can be reached by his creditors is determined ... in the case of an inter vivos ... by the local law of the state, if any, in which the settlor has manifested an intention that the trust is to be administered, and otherwise by the local law of the state to which the administration of the trust is most substantially related").

[247] *See generally* 7 Scott & Ascher §45.7.1.2.

[248] 7 Scott & Ascher §45.7.1.2. *See generally* §5.3.3.1 of this handbook (reaching settlor's reserved beneficial interest). *Cf.* In re Huber v. Huber, 493 B.R. 798 (2013) [U.S. Bankruptcy Court, W.D. Washington, at Tacoma] (relying heavily on the Restatement (Second) of Conflict of Laws §270, which addresses the validity of trusts of movables created inter vivos, but not on §273,

For more on the enforceability of the spendthrift provisions of a self-settled domestic asset protection trust in a multi-jurisdictional setting, the reader is referred to Section 5.3.3.1(c) of this handbook.[249]

The law that governs involuntary assignments of the equitable interest under an inter vivos trust of movables in a multi-jurisdictional setting will generally govern voluntary assignments as well.[250] Thus, "[i]f the settlor has not fixed a place of administration, the assignability of the beneficiary's interest depends on the law of the state that has the most significant relationship to the trust."[251]

The Uniform Trust Code would seem to be in accord with the common law when it comes to a *testamentary or inter vivos spendthrift trust of movables*, namely that the law of the place of trust administration ordinarily governs whether a beneficiary's interest would be vulnerable to the reach of his or her creditors,[252] or voluntarily assignable.[253] Still the Code is not a model of clarity in this regard. One commentator explains:

> Section 105 of the Uniform Trust Code designates as mandatory law "the effect of a spendthrift provision and the rights of certain creditors and assignees to reach a trust as provided in [Article] 5." At a minimum, therefore, it would seem that, as to these matters, any *direct* designation of applicable law by the testator would be ineffective. On the other hand, the UTC gives the ... [testator/settlor] ... far-reaching, though not unlimited, authority to designate the trust's "principal place of administration." Though the matter is far from clear, it is earnestly to be hoped that under the UTC, properly construed, the law applicable to the rights of ... [creditors or assignees] ... of a beneficiary of ... [a testamentary/inter vivos] ... spendthrift trust ... [of movables] ... is ordinarily that of the trust's principal place of administration.[254]

As a general rule, federal tax law trumps state spendthrift law. "Federal law gives the government a lien on all of a taxpayer's property, for unpaid income taxes, and the cases have all but unanimously held that the lien applies even to beneficial interests under spendthrift trusts."[255] We hasten to add, however, that only the equitable property interest of the delinquent taxpayer is vulnerable,

---

which addresses restraints on alienation of trust beneficiaries' interests, a U.S. bankruptcy court applies the law of the state in which the debtor-settlor and his creditors reside (Washington) rather than the debtor-friendly law of the state in which the trust, a self-settled spendthrift trust, was created (Alaska), with the result that the way is opened for the entrusted property to be brought into the federal bankruptcy estate).

[249] *See also* 7 Scott & Ascher §45.7.1.2.

[250] 7 Scott & Ascher §45.7.2.

[251] 7 Scott & Ascher §45.7.2.

[252] 7 Scott & Ascher §45.7.1.1.

[253] 7 Scott & Ascher §45.7.2.

[254] 7 Scott & Ascher §45.7.1.1 (referring to UTC §§105(b)(5) and 108(a) in that order and elaborating extensively in footnote 34). *See also* 7 Scott & Ascher §45.7.1.2 (Inter Vivos Trust/ Spendthrift Provisions/Conflict of Laws); 7 Scott & Ascher §45.7.2 (Assignees of a Beneficiary's Interest/Conflict of Laws).

[255] 7 Scott & Ascher §45.7.1.4 (Tax Claims of the United States/Conflict of Laws). As to the federal tax lien, see I.R.C. §6321.

that is to say the federal tax lien is subject to the equitable interests of innocent third parties. Thus, if the taxpayer is a remainderman, the lien may not capture the intervening equitable life estates, absent special facts. The United States may reach the taxpayer's equitable interest by bringing a proceeding at the situs of the trust, which would be *quasi in rem* if the taxpayer-beneficiary were not personally subject to the court's jurisdiction.[256]

When it comes to the federal Bankruptcy Code, however, there is some deference given to state spendthrift law. In Sections 5.3.3.1(c) and 5.3.3.3(c) of this handbook, we consider the vulnerability of the equitable interest of a trust beneficiary who has filed for personal bankruptcy.[257] Under federal bankruptcy law, title to the equitable as well as the legal property interests of a bankrupt passes to the trustee in bankruptcy.[258] There are exceptions, one of which is that "[a] restriction on the transfer of a beneficial interest of the debtor in a trust that is enforceable under applicable nonbankruptcy law is enforceable."[259] The question then becomes whether the law of the bankrupt's domicile or the law of some other state, such as the law of the situs of the trust, is applicable. As a rule of thumb, it is the law of the state in which the trust is being administered that governs the enforceability of any transfer restraints that may be lurking in its terms.[260]

In the case of a *trust of immovables*, the right of a beneficiary to assign the beneficial interest, as well as the rights of creditors to reach it, are ordinarily governed by the law of the situs of the land, unless there has been an equitable conversion.[261] "When the trustee is directed to sell land and remit the proceeds to, and administer a trust of the proceeds in, a state other than that of the situs, the alienability of a beneficiary's interest, and the rights of creditors to reach it, are determined, ordinarily at least, by the law of the state in which the trust of the proceeds is to be administered."

Construing class designations when beneficiaries are domiciled out of state (conflict of laws). We have touched briefly on the problems that arise when the settlor was domiciled in one state and the trust is administered in another. But more likely it is the beneficiary—not the settlor—who was domiciled in a state other than the administration state. This situation can bring with it its own set of conflict-of-law issues (*e.g.*, when the settlor provides for distribution upon the death of a beneficiary to the beneficiary's "issue").[262]

Issue. The word *issue* can mean one thing in the settlor's domicile and quite another thing in the beneficiary's. In the settlor's state it may include illegitimates; in the beneficiary's it may not. Which meaning applies? The better view

---

[256] 7 Scott & Ascher §45.7.1.4. *See also* §8.40 of this handbook (containing a general discussion of the concept of *quasi in rem* jurisdiction).

[257] *See also* 7 Scott & Ascher §45.7.1.3 (Bankruptcy of a Beneficiary/Conflict of Laws).

[258] 11 U.S.C. §541(a)(1).

[259] 11 U.S.C. §541(c)(2).

[260] *See generally* 7 Scott & Ascher §45.7.1.3.

[261] 7 Scott & Ascher §46.7. *See generally* §8.15.44 of this handbook (equitable conversion).

[262] *See* §5.2 of this handbook (class designation: "children," "issue," "heirs," and "relatives" (some rules of construction)).

seems to be the state where the instrument was prepared and signed, particularly if it was the settlor's domicile, unless the settlor had expressed a contrary intention in the governing instrument.[263] To some extent, it is a rule of administrative convenience: While a trust may have many beneficiaries in many different states, there is usually only one settlor. Moreover, it is reasonable to expect that the settlor and the drafting attorney were relying on the prevailing meaning of the word in the state of preparation and execution, particularly if it was the state of the settlor's domicile. Otherwise, the meaning of the word is held hostage to the migratory habits of the beneficiaries. "While transfer of the principal place of administration will normally change the governing law with respect to administrative matters, a transfer does not normally alter the controlling law with respect to . . . construction of its dispositive terms."[264]

Heirs of the beneficiary. Suppose a settlor of a trust of movables provides that upon the death of the beneficiary, the trust property passes outright and free of trust to the beneficiary's heirs. If the term *heirs* refers to intestate takers, as it generally does, which intestacy law is being referred to, that of the beneficiary's domicile or that of the settlor's? Does *heirs* cover only those persons, if any, who *actually* inherited the beneficiary's property under the laws of intestacy or those persons who *would have* inherited the property, assuming the beneficiary had died intestate?[265] If the latter, it is said that the would-be heirs take title "by purchase" from the trustee.[266] If the former, then the laws of the beneficiary's domicile would of course govern.

If the term heirs imports the subjunctive, as is likely to be the case nowadays,[267] the intestacy laws *of the settlor's domicile* are ordinarily used to determine who *would have been* the beneficiary's heirs-at-law.[268] In the case of a testamentary trust of movables, if the life beneficiary dies domiciled in a state other than the state in which the settlor (testator) had died domiciled, "the courts have generally held that in the absence of evidence indicating that the testator had a different intention, the beneficiary's 'heirs' are those who would have been the beneficiary's heirs if the beneficiary had died domiciled in the state in which the testator died domiciled."[269] This same default principle applies as well to inter vivos trusts: it is the intestacy statute of the settlor's domicile, not the intestacy statute of the deceased trust beneficiary's domicile, that is borrowed for purposes of determining who the beneficiary's would-be heirs at law are, that is to say who are the ones who take the underlying trust

---

[263] *See generally* 5A Scott on Trusts §578.

[264] UTC §108 cmt. (available at <http://www.uniformlaws.org/Act.aspx?title=Trust%20Code>).

[265] *See generally* National Shawmut Bank v. Joy, 315 Mass. 457, 462–467, 53 N.E.2d 113, 117–120 (1944).

[266] *See generally* §8.15.2 of this handbook; National Shawmut Bank v. Joy, 315 Mass. 457, 53 N.E.2d 113 (1944) (taking by purchase rather than by descent).

[267] *See generally* §5.2 of this handbook (legal and equitable class gift provisions that employ the subjunctive).

[268] 5A Scott on Trusts §578.

[269] 7 Scott & Ascher §45.3.4.

property outright and free of trust by purchase from the trustee upon the beneficiary's death.[270] The Uniform Trust Code would seem to be in accord.[271]

What if the state of last domicile and the state of execution are different? As between the state where the settlor (testator) died domiciled and the state where he or she was domiciled when the will was executed, the would-be heirs-at-law of the beneficiary of the testamentary trust may well be determined in accordance with the rules of construction applicable in the state of execution.[272] "Although ordinarily a will is construed in accordance with the law of the state in which the testator dies domiciled, the fact that the testator executed the will while domiciled in another state may indicate that the testator probably intended that the rules of construction of that other state would apply."[273]

Then the question becomes which version of the applicable intestacy statute is to be consulted? The one in force when the instrument trust was executed? The one in force at the time of the trust beneficiary's death? The jurisdictions are not in accord.[274] In New York, for example, it is the intestacy laws in force at the time of the settlor's death, while in Massachusetts it is the intestacy laws in force at the time of the beneficiary's death.[275] In either case, it is generally still the intestacy laws *of the settlor's domicile* that is consulted for purposes of determining who would have been the deceased life beneficiary's heirs-at-law, that is absent language in the governing instrument to the contrary, or, perhaps, if execution of the instrument had taken place in another state.[276]

Heirs of the settlor. An inter vivos trust under which the settlor has reserved a right to the income for life and under which the subject property is to pass outright and free of trust to the settlor's "heirs" upon the settlor's death could implicate the doctrine of worthier title, a topic we take up in Section 8.15.2 of this handbook. Under the doctrine in its classic form, it was a rule of law that such an arrangement created an equitable reversion in the settlor, not a remainder in the settlor's heirs.[277] That being the case, the trust was constructively revocable, the settlor being the only one with an equitable interest.[278] It followed that the underlying property was subject to the claims of the settlor's creditors, as well as transferable by the settlor both inter vivos and postmortem.[279]

---

[270] 7 Scott & Ascher §45.3.4.

[271] UTC §107 cmt. (available at <http://www.uniformlaws.org/Act.aspx?title=Trust%20 Code>) ("Usually, the law of the trust's principal place of administration will govern administrative matters and the law of the place having the most significant relationship to the trust's creation will govern the dispositive provisions"). *See generally* 7 Scott & Ascher §45.3.5.

[272] 7 Scott & Ascher §45.3.4.

[273] 7 Scott & Ascher §45.3.4.

[274] 7 Scott & Ascher §45.3.4.

[275] 7 Scott & Ascher §45.3.4 (*Matter of Lefferts*, 112 N.Y.S.2d 874 (Surr. Ct.), *aff'd* 117 N.Y.S.2d 652 (App. Div. 1952) (New York); Lincoln v. Perry, 21 N.E. 671 (Mass. 1889) (Massachusetts)).

[276] *See* 7 Scott & Ascher §45.3.4.

[277] *See* 7 Scott & Ascher §45.3.5.1 (Inter Vivos Trust for the Settlor and the Settlor's Heirs).

[278] *See* 7 Scott & Ascher §45.3.5.1.

[279] *See* 7 Scott & Ascher §45.3.5.1.

In jurisdictions that have not abolished the doctrine, and many have, it has morphed into little more than a rule of construction.[280] In practical terms, the rule of construction is this: If "the owner of property transfers it inter vivos, in trust, to pay the income to the settlor for life and on the settlor's death to convey the property to the settlor's heirs," the settlor is deemed to hold a reversionary interest, unless the settlor has manifested an intention that upon the trust's termination the subject property passes outright and free of trust to those persons who would have been the settlor's heirs-at-law had he or she then died intestate.[281] Those persons then are remaindermen who take title directly from the trustee by "purchase," rather than by "descent."[282] Equitable remainder dispositions to would-be heirs-at-law are covered in greater detail in Section 5.2 of this handbook.

Now if the settlor is domiciled in one state and the trust is to be, or is being, administered in another, the question of whether the settlor has created a reversion or a remainder in his would-be heirs-at-law is ordinarily determined by the laws of the place of administration, not of the settlor's domicile, absent language in the governing instrument to the contrary.[283] Under the Uniform Trust Code it is "the law of the jurisdiction having the most significant relationship to the matter at issue."[284]

A prospective trustee should think long and hard before accepting a trust that employs without appropriate elaboration the term *heirs*.[285] And should there be a need to resort to a rule of construction, it would be nice if the terms of the trust were to make which state's rules are to be applied.

Powers of appointment (conflict of laws). Powers of appointment are covered generally in Section 8.1.1 of this handbook. As one court has opined, "[t]here are strong, logical reasons for turning to the law of the donee's domicil at the time of death to determine whether a donee's will has exercised a testamentary power of appointment over movables."[286] (The grantor of a power of appointment is referred to as the donor of the power; the holder of the power is referred to as the donee of the power.) That having been said, "[m]ost courts in this country which have considered the question, however, ... [have interpreted] ... the donee's will under the law governing the administration of the trust, which is usually the law of the donor's domicil."[287] The restatements are definitely not in accord: "The law of the donee's domicile governs whether the

---

[280] *See* 7 Scott & Ascher §45.3.5.1.

[281] 7 Scott & Ascher §45.3.5.1.

[282] *See generally* §8.15.2 of this handbook (taking by purchase rather than by descent).

[283] *See generally* 7 Scott & Ascher §45.3.5.1.

[284] UTC §107(2) (available at <http://www.uniformlaws.org/Act.aspx?title=Trust%20Code>).

[285] M. Reutlinger, Wills, Trusts, and Estates: Essential Terms and Concepts 99–100 (1993); 5A Scott on Trusts §578. *See generally* §5.2 of this handbook (class designation: "children," "issue," "heirs," and "relatives" (some rules of construction)).

[286] *See* Beals v. State St. Bank & Trust Co., 326 N.E.2d 896 (Mass. 1975).

[287] *See* Beals v. State St. Bank & Trust Co., 326 N.E.2d 896 (Mass. 1975).

donee has effectively exercised a power of appointment, unless the instrument creating the power expresses a different intention."[288]

Jurisdiction. The Uniform Trust Code provides that with respect to their interests in a trust, the beneficiaries of a trust having its principal place of administration in a particular state are subject to the jurisdiction of the courts of the state regarding any matter involving the trust.[289] "It . . . seems reasonable to require beneficiaries to go to the seat of the trust when litigation has been instituted there concerning a trust in which they claim beneficial interests, much as the rights of shareholders of a corporation can be determined at a corporate seat."[290] For a general discussion of *in personam* jurisdiction over the trustee and/or the beneficiaries, as well as a discussion of *in rem* jurisdiction over the trust property, the reader is referred to Section 8.40 of this handbook.

Drafting tip. The prospective trustee should make sure that as many potential conflict-of-laws issues as possible are preempted in the governing instrument and should be particularly wary of "boilerplate" language, especially if it causes unfamiliar laws to apply to the trust's administration and to the construction of its terms. The prospective trustee should know the rules of the game before the game starts.[291]

Foreign trust companies. The topic of foreign trust companies and foreign charitable corporations serving as testamentary trustees is taken up in Section 8.6 of this handbook.

§8.6 Qualifying the Non-Human Being to Serve as a Trustee: Corporations Domestic and Foreign; Partnerships

Over the years, however, corporations gradually acquired the power to administer trusts. Indeed, in 1743, Lord Hardwicke stated that nothing was clearer than that corporations might be trustees.[1]

As we explain in Section 3.1 of this handbook, since time immemorial it has been a general principle of the common law as enhanced by equity that a human being may serve as a trustee of another's property. There are limited obvious exceptions, such as in the case of an infant. Idaho is the only state known to the authors of this handbook that by statute or otherwise has turned

---

[288] Restatement (Third) of Property (Wills and Other Donative Transfers) §19.1 cmt. e (citing Restatement (Second) of Conflict of Laws §275 cmt. c).

[289] UTC §202(b) (available at <http://www.uniformlaws.org/Act.aspx?title=Trust%20 Code>).

[290] UTC §202(b) cmt. (available at <http://www.uniformlaws.org/Act.aspx?title=Trust%20 Code>) (citing Comment to UPC §7-103).

[291] *See generally* Rosepink, *Representing Clients With Ties to Multiple States or Counties*, 22 ACTEC Notes 78 (1996).

§8.6 [1] 2 Scott & Ascher §11.1.6 (citing to Attorney-Gen. v. Landerfeld, 9 Mod. 286 (1743)).

this general principle on its head. In Idaho, only in exceptional situations may a human being act as a trustee for another's benefit, such as for the benefit of "relatives" or incident to "an existing attorney-client relationship or certified public accountant-client relationship."[2]

Conflating judicial qualification and regulatory qualification. In this section, unless a statute provides otherwise or the context suggests otherwise, a corporation "qualifies" as the trustee of a particular trust by an act of the judiciary, namely, by the court formally confirming the trustee's appointment. Judicial qualification is not to be confused with, say, a state banking commissioner authorizing or qualifying a corporation to engage generally in the business of serving as trustee. In the trust context, the concepts of judicial qualification and regulatory qualification are easily confused and conflated.

Corporations serving as trustees. At early common law, a corporation could not be seised to a use.[3] Today, it is settled law both in England and the United States that "[t]o the extent, by statute or otherwise, a partnership, unincorporated association, limited-liability company, or other entity can, as such, take and hold property beneficially, it can take, hold, and administer property in trust."[4] In most jurisdictions, however, a bank needs governmental authority to engage in the business of acting as trustee.[5] The requirement is statutory, there being no common law impediment *per se* to a corporation's engaging in such activity as long as it possesses the general authority to hold *property*.[6] It is self-evident that a corporation that takes title to property as trustee owes fiduciary duties to the beneficiaries, or, in the case of a charitable trust, owes fiduciary duties to the community as a whole. Thus, a corporate trustee can be in breach of trust and incur liability as a consequence. In fact, there are even cases "that have imposed liability on directors or officers of corporations that held property in trust and committed breaches of trust, though the corporations were not in the business of administering trusts."[7]

In Massachusetts not only may a plain-vanilla business corporation be in the business of serving as trustee of inter vivos and testamentary trusts if its articles of organization so provide, but if it is not a bank, the state banking commissioner has no authority to regulate its fiduciary activities.[8] "There is no rational legislative objective in treating corporate fiduciaries differently from individuals or other business organizations performing the same function."[9] To qualify as a "bank," the entity would also have to be in the business of taking

---

[2] Idaho Code Ann. §26-3205 (2000).

[3] 2 Scott & Ascher §11.1.6 (noting that there were various explanations including that the corporation was a dead body; that equity, *i.e.*, the chancellors, could not compel performance of a trust by a corporation; and that it was *ultra vires* for a corporation to serve as trustee).

[4] Restatement (Third) of Trusts §33 cmt. f; 1 Scott & Ascher §11.1.6.

[5] *See generally* 2 Scott on Trusts §§96.3, 96.5; Bogert, Trusts and Trustees §131.

[6] *See generally* 2 Scott on Trusts §96.

[7] *See* 5 Scott & Ascher §30.6.3, n.2.

[8] First Fiduciary Corp. v. Office of Comm'r of Banks, 43 Mass. App. Ct. 457, 684 N.E.2d 1 (1997).

[9] First Fiduciary Corp. v. Office of Comm'r of Banks, 43 Mass. App. Ct. 457, 463, 684 N.E.2d 1, 5 (1997).

deposits and making loans.[10] An entity that takes deposits is a contract debtor; an entity that makes loan is a contract creditor. As a general rule, the debtor-creditor contractual relationship, in and of itself, is not a fiduciary relationship.[11]

Qualifying foreign trust companies. In the case of a corporate trustee that has been incorporated in one state but is maintaining a particular trust's principal place of administration in another state, Section 7-105 of the Uniform Probate Code (repealed/withdrawn in 2010) had provided that the corporate trustee must qualify in the state of administration as a foreign corporation doing business in that state. On the other hand, if a corporation is administering a particular trust in the corporation's home state, it may receive on behalf of the trust a distribution incident to a foreign probate without the need to qualify as a trustee in the foreign jurisdiction.[12] Trustee qualification is generally not a concern, and generally never has been a concern, when a settlor domiciled in one state transfers *inter vivos* a portion or all of his or her property to a corporate trustee headquartered in another state, that is to a "foreign trust company."[13] On the other hand, when the settlor of a *testamentary* trust dies domiciled in one state and the designated trustee is a foreign trust company, the entity's qualification to serve locally as testamentary trustee traditionally has been regulated by local statute.[14] Some statutes are reciprocity-focused, that is to say "trust companies of another state are permitted to qualify as testamentary trustees if, but only if, the state's own trust companies are permitted to qualify in the other state."[15] If a state has a statute that authorizes foreign trust companies to serve as trustees of the testamentary trusts of its deceased domiciliaries, the authority is likely to be conditioned on the foreign trust company filing an instrument appointing some local public officer to receive service of process on behalf of the foreign trust company in actions that relate to its local fiduciary activities.[16] Such a filing "qualifies" the foreign trust company to serve as a testamentary trustee incident to a local probate. "The fact that a foreign trust company qualifies in a state as trustee under a will does not mean that it is engaging in business in the state," or that it may do so.[17] In a few states, foreign trust companies are precluded altogether by statute from serving as trustees of trusts locally established.[18] Such statutes likely do not violate the privileges and immunities clause of the U.S. Constitution in that for purposes of the clause's application, a corporation is not a citizen of the United States.[19]

---

[10] First Fiduciary Corp. v. Office of Comm'r of Banks, 43 Mass. App. Ct. 457, 684 N.E.2d 1 (1997).

[11] *See generally* §9.9.4 of this handbook (bank accounts and other such debtor-creditor contractual arrangements are not trusts).

[12] *See also* 7 Scott & Ascher §45.2.1.1 (Foreign Trust Companies).

[13] *See* 7 Scott & Ascher §45.2.1.1.

[14] *See* 7 Scott & Ascher §45.2.1.1, n.1.

[15] 7 Scott & Ascher §45.2.1.1.

[16] 7 Scott & Ascher §45.2.1.1.

[17] 7 Scott & Ascher §45.2.1.1.

[18] 7 Scott & Ascher §45.2.1.1.

[19] 7 Scott & Ascher §45.2.1.1.

A foreign trust company generally must satisfy local statutory qualification requirements when the subject of the testamentary trust is locally situated land.[20] However, when the subject of the testamentary trust is intangible personal property that ultimately will be administered in the foreign jurisdiction, such as a portfolio of publicly traded stocks and bonds, one learned commentator has questioned on public policy grounds any justification for requiring that the foreign trust company be locally qualified that is grounded in protectionism.[21] Trusts are created for the benefit of the beneficiaries, not for the benefit of the local trust companies.[22] And if continuing court supervision of a testamentary trust is deemed warranted, the local court in the exercise of its inherent equitable powers should simply condition the appointment of a foreign trust company on some appropriate court in the foreign jurisdiction agreeing to supervise on an ongoing basis the trust's administration, bearing in mind that there is a general trend in this country to legislatively replace continuing judicial supervision of trusts with judicial "intervention on demand."[23] In any case, there are some states that still require any foreign trust company that is designated as the trustee of a testamentary trust incident to a local probate to qualify locally, even when land is not involved.[24]

It seems one may draft around New York's fiduciary qualification reciprocity statute: "It has been held that under this statute a foreign trust company need not qualify as testamentary trustee in New York if the testator has manifested an intention that the trust be administered in the state in which the company is organized and does business."[25] One practical effect of avoiding the statute's application is to eventually remove the subject property from the jurisdiction of the New York courts.[26] Some states will similarly defer to settlor intent; others will not.[27] On the other hand, if the terms of a will were to condition a foreign trust company's appointment as testamentary trustee on its qualifying as such in New York, then it is likely that the condition would be enforced by the New York court.[28]

Qualifying foreign charitable corporations. There is some confusion as to whether an inter vivos or testamentary transfer of property to a charitable corporation subjects the property to a true trust, a topic we take up in Section 9.8.1 of this handbook. One Massachusetts court has described the arrangement as a quasi trust.[29] In California, a charitable corporation formed in

---

[20] 7 Scott & Ascher §45.2.1.1.

[21] See 7 Scott & Ascher §45.2.1.1.

[22] 7 Scott & Ascher §45.2.1.1.

[23] 7 Scott & Ascher §45.2.1.1 (noting that UTC §201(b) provides that even a testamentary trust is not subject to continuing judicial supervision, unless ordered by the court).

[24] See 7 Scott & Ascher §45.2.1.1.

[25] 7 Scott & Ascher §45.2.1.1.

[26] See 7 Scott & Ascher §45.2.1.1 (Foreign Trust Companies); §8.40 of this handbook (judicial jurisdiction over trustee and beneficiary).

[27] See 7 Scott & Ascher §45.2.1.1.

[28] See 7 Scott & Ascher §45.2.1.1.

[29] See American Institute of Architects v. Attorney General, 332 Mass. 619, 624, 127 N.E.2d 161, 164 (1955).

California has statutory authority to serve as a trustee.[30] In any case, "[i]t has been held that even though a bequest to a foreign charitable corporation is to be applied to a specific charitable purpose, the corporation is entitled to the legacy without qualifying in a court of the testator's domicil."[31] Local qualification may be required, however, if the property is for the benefit of persons in the state of the testator's domicil.[32] Qualification might entail the execution by the foreign charitable corporation of a power of attorney appointing an in-state official to accept service of process in proceedings relating to the administration of the local charitable trust, quasi trust, or whatever.[33]

National banks. By statute, the Comptroller of the Currency is vested with the authority to grant a federal trust charter to national banks.[34] A corporation with federal trust powers will carry the official designation of a national bank, whether or not it is authorized to engage in commercial banking activities as well.[35]

Federal savings banks. The Office of Thrift Supervision (OTS) is charged with the supervision of federal savings associations.[36] The regulation governing fiduciary activities of federal savings bank (FSBs) is 12 C.F.R. 550, which is promulgated under Section 5(n) of the Home Owners' Loan Act (HOLA).[37] Part 550 was designed to closely parallel 12 U.S.C. 92a, which authorizes the Comptroller of the Currency to grant fiduciary powers to national banks. Thus, OTS regulations closely parallel Regulation 9. A federal savings bank may have fewer limits on its ability to market and render fiduciary services nationwide if it possesses trust powers and is owned by a unitary thrift holding company and if the holding company was in existence May 4, 1999 (or had an application pending as of that date).[38]

State trust charters. The authority to grant a state trust charter, more often than not, is vested by statute in a state's banking commissioner.[39] Corporations with state trust charters often carry the designation *trust company*. A granting authority, whether federal or state, usually is charged by statute with the responsibility of regulating how the grantee corporation then carries out its trust charter.

A number of states have adopted the Conference of State Bank Supervisors' model Statutory Options for Multistate Trust Activities. It is referred to as the Multistate Trust Institutions Act. According to its author, the Act has

---

[30] Cal. Prob. Code §15604.

[31] 7 Scott & Ascher §45.2.1.3.

[32] 7 Scott & Ascher §45.2.1.3.

[33] 7 Scott & Ascher §45.2.1.3.

[34] 12 U.S.C. §92a(a) (1989).

[35] *See* 12 C.F.R. §5.22(a)(2) (1992).

[36] 12 U.S.C. §1463(a) ("Home Owners' Loan Act" or HOLA).

[37] 12 U.S.C. §1463(a) (HOLA).

[38] Gramm-Leach-Bliley Act §401 (grandfathering preexisting unitary thrift holding companies from the Act's restrictions on offering trust products on a nationwide basis, said restrictions in part having been aimed at keeping Wal-Mart from chartering a thrift or from conducting Wal-Mart brand banking operations in its stores).

[39] *See generally* Bogert §§135, 136.

dramatically reduced the cost of forming and operating private trust companies. According to its author, "new private trust company charters crafted in . . . [states that have adopted the Act] . . . are characterized by:

- Modest capital and other charter requirements;
- Flexibility to charter in one state while maintaining a full-service office in another;
- Risk-appropriate levels of regulatory supervision and support for fiduciary policies tailored to the clientele of a private trust company;
- Substantial protection for family and company private; and
- Reasonable staffing, space and activities requirements for both chartered state and family offices."[40]

Whether a particular group of organizers should seek a federal or state trust charter is well beyond the scope of this handbook.[41] It will depend upon many things, including which statutory and regulatory scheme best accommodates the group's business objectives and expectations.[42] Chartering authorities, for example, will differ as to capital and surplus requirements.[43] It should be noted, however, that no federal trust charter may be issued to a national bank operating in a state whose capital and surplus requirements for banks are *below* levels set for trust institutions chartered by that state.[44]

Private trust companies (a/k/a family trust companies and exempt trust companies). A private trust company is generally authorized to act as a trustee by state character.[45] It, however, may not solicit business from the general public.[46] "A private trust company can only provide trust and fiduciary services to a limited class of family members and, in some cases, charities and family employees. Many states define this class by reference to a specified degree of

---

[40] John P. C. Duncan, *The Private Trust Company: It Has Come of Age*, 142 Tr. & Est. 49 (Issue 8/Aug. 2003).

[41] For a discussion of choice of chartering authority, *see* Symons & White, Banking Law 63–69 (3d ed. 1991).

[42] *See* Symons & White, Banking Law at 72–75 for a discussion of the factors which the Office of the Comptroller of the Currency considers in deciding whether to grant a federal charter. Anyone interested in acquiring a national charter may obtain the Comptroller's Manual for Corporate Activities, a three-volume guidebook containing the policies, procedures, and forms used in the application process. The manual may be ordered by writing to the Comptroller of the Currency at the following address: Comptroller of the Currency, P.O. Box 70004, Chicago, IL 60673-0004. A $90 fee, payable to the Comptroller of the Currency, should accompany the written request. For a listing of state statutes relating to the chartering of bank and trust companies, see M. P. Malloy, The Corporate Law of Banks; appendix, chart 2.1 (State Bank Charters: Requirements) and chart 2.2 (Availability of Trust Powers: State Requirements) (1988).

[43] *See generally* John P. D. Duncan, *Forming A Private Trust Company: Elements and Process*, 136 Tr. & Est. 36 (Aug. 1997).

[44] 12 U.S.C. §92a(i) (1989).

[45] *See generally* Alan V. Ytterberg & James P. Weller, *Managing Family Wealth Through a Private Trust Company*, 36 ACTEC L.J. 623 (2010).

[46] *See generally* Alan V. Ytterberg & James P. Weller, *Managing Family Wealth Through a Private Trust Company*, 36 ACTEC L.J. 623, 624 (2010).

kinship to a certain relative designated in the charter application."[47] A private trust company will tailor its services to the particular financial goals and aspirations of the family group.

Some states do not require that a private trust company be chartered.[48] A nonchartered, unregulated private trust company, however, may be subject to SEC registration under the Investment Advisers Act of 1940 and limited in its ability to engage in interstate activities.[49] In Nevada, a family trust company can elect to be regulated, but regulated "litely," by the Nevada Financial Institutions Division so as to avoid having to register with the SEC.

The state that has a nuanced trust company regulatory regime and exempts its trusts from income taxation will have a leg up when it comes to attracting trust company start-ups. New Hampshire and South Dakota come to mind in this regard.

Private trust companies, while generally less regulated and more intimate than their public counterparts, should still have organizational structures with clear lines of authority and built-in systems of checks and balances for monitoring the activities of company personnel who have access to entrusted assets.[50] There should be in place a written plan, approved and administered by the board of directors, for a truly independent and fully competent regular auditing of *fiduciary activity*.[51] "A private trust company should also have a due diligence process for not only selecting third party service providers and advisors, but also for monitoring their performance."[52] Trust counsel should be competent, independent, proactive, and kept fully informed. He or she should have primary responsibility for the safekeeping, interpretation, and proper implementation of the terms of all governing trust instruments and associated documentation.

Trust Indenture Act of 1939. For a discussion of the requirement under the federal Trust Indenture Act of 1939 that at least one indenture trustee of a corporate trust established to secure the contractual rights of a class of bondholders be a bank or trust company, see Section 9.31 of this handbook. The reader is cautioned not to confuse a "corporate trust" of assets segregated to secure a bond issue with a trust that merely happens to have as a trustee a corporation.

Regulation of corporate trustees began with the Magna Carta. As we noted at the beginning of this section, a corporation that can take and hold

---

[47] *See generally* Alan V. Ytterberg & James P. Weller, *Managing Family Wealth Through a Private Trust Company*, 36 ACTEC L.J. 623, 624 (2010).

[48] *See generally* Alan V. Ytterberg & James P. Weller, *Managing Family Wealth Through a Private Trust Company*, 36 ACTEC L.J. 623, 629 (2010).

[49] *See generally* Alan V. Ytterberg & James P. Weller, *Managing Family Wealth Through a Private Trust Company*, 36 ACTEC L.J. 623, 629 (2010).

[50] *See generally* Alan V. Ytterberg & James P. Weller, *Managing Family Wealth Through a Private Trust Company*, 36 ACTEC L.J. 623, 636–639 (2010).

[51] *See generally* Alan V. Ytterberg & James P. Weller, *Managing Family Wealth Through a Private Trust Company*, 36 ACTEC L.J. 623, 638–639 (2010).

[52] *See generally* Alan V. Ytterberg & James P. Weller, *Managing Family Wealth Through a Private Trust Company*, 36 ACTEC L.J. 623, 639 (2010).

property in its own right can generally take and hold property in trust. It was not always the case, however, that a corporation could take and hold land. Early on, Parliament took to placing certain restrictions on the ability of a corporation, which in most cases would be the church, to take and hold land, this so as not to "deprive the overlord, including the king as lord paramount, of the benefits accruing from human tenants, who would live, marry, have children, and die" and so as not "to undermine the defense of the realm, which was based on the relationship between land-lord and tenant."[53] The process of imposing such restrictions began with the signing of the Magna Carta.[54] In 1960, they were removed once and for all by an act of Parliament.[55]

§8.7 Merger

Because one cannot be under an obligation to oneself, the same individual cannot be settlor, trustee, and sole beneficiary, and the trust parties can never be fewer than two.[1]

[E]ven[2] where the legal and equitable titles are both vested in the same person, equity will under certain conditions refuse to recognize a merger which might exist in law, as where such result would be contrary to the intention of the trustor and would destroy a valid trust.[3]

The doctrine of merger is occasionally a trap for the unwary; more often it is invoked in situations where it is inapplicable.[4] Thus, the trustee needs to

---

[53] *See generally* 5 Scott & Ascher §37.2.6.1.

[54] *See generally* 5 Scott & Ascher §37.2.6.1.

[55] *See generally* 5 Scott & Ascher §37.2.6.1.

§8.7 [1] Bogert §1.

[2] For a discussion of the concept of merger in Roman law, *see* §8.15.36 of this handbook.

[3] 90 C.J.S. §283 (citing to Dennis v. Omaha Nat'l Bank, 153 Neb. 865, 46 N.W.2d 606 (1951); Mesce v. Gradone, 1 N.J. 159, 62 A.2d 394 (1948); Quinn v. Pullman Trust & Sav. Bank, 98 Ill. App. 2d 402, 240 N.E.2d 791 (1st Dist. 1968); In re Haskell's Trust, 59 Misc. 2d 797, 300 N.Y.S.2d 711 (Sup. 1969)). *See also* Tretola v. Tretola, 2004 WL 1586999 (Mass. App. Ct.) (footnote 10 and accompanying text).

[4] As a general rule, a trust may be created solely for the benefit of the settlor, provided the settlor is not also the sole trustee. See UTC §402 cmt. (available at <http://www.uniformlaws.org/Act.aspx?title=Trust%20Code>), specifically the commentary on §402(a)(5). The Bogert treatise, however, appears to have fallen into the false merger trap by suggesting that one of the three "requirements" for the establishment of a valid private trust is "an expression of intent that property be held, at least in part, for the benefit of one other than the settlor." *See* Bogert §1, in which UTC §402(a)(3) is cited as authority for the proposition. It does not appear, however, that §402(a)(3) even addresses the settlor-as-sole-beneficiary question. Some courts also have inappropriately invoked the doctrine of merger, such as to invalidate self-declarations of trust in which the settlor is the sole current beneficiary but other persons are designated as beneficiaries of the remainder. *See* UTC §402 cmt. Presumably a so-called adapted trust would not fall prey to this particular misapplication of the merger doctrine as an adapted trust may not arise by declaration. *See* Restatement (Third) of Trusts, Reporter's Notes on §46, specifically on cmt. f thereto. The adapted trust is generally discussed in §9.29 of this handbook.

understand the concept if only to recognize when the doctrine is not a concern.[5]

Merger occurs when one person possesses the entire legal interest and the entire beneficial interest in property.[6] In such a case, there is no trust;[7] the person simply owns the property outright and free of trust, all interests having "merged" in that person.[8] Thus, the creditors, the spouse, and the taxing authorities might well have greater access to the property than would be the case were the property the subject of a viable trust.[9] If merger has occurred, at death the property passes in accordance with the terms of the person's will or by intestate succession, not in accordance with the terms of the instrument governing the purported trust.[10] Obviously, if those who are mentioned in the trust instrument are different from those mentioned in the will, merger will benefit the latter. Merger may have consequences as well in the welfare eligibility and recoupment area.

Merger would trigger a termination of a valid trust, for example, if a beneficiary with the entire equitable interest transfers that interest to the trustee, provided there is no cotrustee.[11] The equitable interest, however, would have to be transferable; the beneficiary would have to be of full age and legal capacity and fully understand the applicable law and facts; and there could not be any undue influence on the part of the trustee.[12] Assuming the trustee managed to get over these hurdles, the trustee would then have the full ownership interest with rights of personal consumption, even if all the trust purposes had not been accomplished.[13] Under the Restatement (Third) of Trusts, this would be the case even if there had been a spendthrift restraint in place.[14] The property is said to be "at home," the equitable interest having been

---

[5] *See, e.g.,* Hansen v. Bothe, 10 So. 3d 213 (Fla. App. 2009) (reversing the Circuit Court's finding that a trust had terminated by merger, the Circuit Court having failed to appreciate the fact that the continued existence of remainder beneficiaries under the trust meant that the legal and beneficial interests thereunder were not "completely coextensive," which they would have to be for a termination by merger to occur).

[6] *See generally* Restatement (Third) of Trusts §69; 5 Scott & Ascher §34.5; 2 Scott on Trusts §99; Restatement (Second) of Trusts §99; Bogert §§129, 1003.

[7] 2 Scott on Trusts §99. *See also* UTC §402(a)(5) (available at <http://www.uniformlaws.org/Act.aspx?title=Trust%20Code>).

[8] Bogert §129; 5 Scott & Ascher §34.5. *See generally* Larry D. Scheafer, Annot., *Trusts: merger of legal and equitable estates where sole trustees are sole beneficiaries,* 7 A.L.R.4th 621 (1996).

[9] *See generally* 2 Scott on Trusts §99.

[10] 2 Scott on Trusts §99.

[11] Restatement (Second) of Trusts §343 cmt. a; 5 Scott & Ascher §§34.7 (Conveyance by Beneficiary to Trustee), 34.5.2 (When Sole Beneficiary Does Not Become Sole Trustee). *See generally* 5 Scott & Ascher §34.5 (Merger).

[12] *See generally* 5 Scott & Ascher §34.7 (Conveyance by Beneficiary to Trustee) (a spendthrift restraint could render ineffective the transfer itself); Restatement (Third) of Trusts §69 cmt. d (an effective merger will extinguish spendthrift restraints). *See generally* §§6.1.3.5 of this handbook (acquisition by trustee of equitable interest: the loyalty issues) and 7.1 (the beneficiary's informed consent to a trustee's act of self-dealing).

[13] *See generally* 5 Scott & Ascher §34.7 (Conveyance by Beneficiary to Trustee).

[14] Restatement (Third) of Trusts §69 cmt. d.

"swallowed up" in the full ownership.[15] Of course, merger could be avoided if the trustee were to resign in a timely fashion, or to execute a timely disclaimer of the equitable interest.[16]

Going the other way, there would be a merger in the beneficiary of a single-beneficiary trust if the legal title were to pass from the trustee to the beneficiary and to no other,[17] whether or not this was done at the instigation of the beneficiary and whether or not the purposes of the trust had been fulfilled.[18] Under the Restatement (Third) of Trusts, any spendthrift protections would extinguish.[19] Thus, if that is not the desired result, the beneficiary should either disclaim the trusteeship or see to it that there is a cotrustee in place.[20] The Restatement (Second) of Trusts took the position that "when the sole beneficiary of a spendthrift trust, without his or her consent, became the sole trustee, he or she should be able to procure the appointment of a new trustee and have the trust reconstituted as a spendthrift trust."[21] One learned commentator finds the position of the Third Restatement plainly "more consonant with the surrounding doctrine").[22]

A state of merger also could exist *ab initio*. If, for example, *X* purports to declare himself trustee of certain property for a period of ten years after which the property is to pass outright and free of trust to *X*, there is no trust. All interests, both legal and equitable, remain merged in *X*.[23] A trust was never created.[24]

But more often than not there is no merger. Let us assume a trust, *A* to *B* for *C* for life, then to *D*. If the same person is the sole trustee and the sole income beneficiary, and if upon death the property passes to the person's executor or administrator—in other words to the estate—then there is a merger.[25] In other words, if *B*, *C*, and *D* are the same person, there is no trust—in fact there never was one. *A* simply made a gift to the person that was outright and free of trust. Nowadays one seldom runs across trust instruments where the one who possesses the equitable life estate also possesses the equitable remainder interest (*i.e.*, where the trust property ultimately passes into the probate estate of the life tenant), with the possible exception of nominee or

---

[15] Lewin ¶ 1-09 (England). *See also* 5 Scott & Ascher §34.5 (U.S.) ("The equitable interest is said to merge into the legal title").

[16] Restatement (Third) of Trusts §69 cmt. d. *See generally* §5.5 of this handbook (voluntary or involuntary loss of the beneficiary's rights) (in part discussing the subject of disclaimers of equitable interests under trusts).

[17] 5 Scott & Ascher §34.5 (Merger).

[18] 5 Scott & Ascher §34.6 (Conveyance by Trustee to or at the Direction of the Beneficiaries).

[19] Restatement (Third) of Trusts §69 cmt. d. *See generally* 5 Scott & Ascher §34.5.1 (Acquisition of Legal Title by Beneficiary of Spendthrift Trust).

[20] Restatement (Third) of Trusts §69 cmt. d; 5 Scott & Ascher §34.5.1.

[21] 5 Scott & Ascher §34.5.1 (referring to Restatement (Second) of Trusts §341(2) cmt. c & illus. 4, 7).

[22] 5 Scott & Ascher §34.5.1.

[23] *See* Odom v. Morgan, 99 S.E. 195 (1919).

[24] Restatement (Third) of Trusts §69 cmt. e.

[25] UTC §402 cmt. (available at <http://www.uniformlaws.org/Act.aspx?title=Trust%20 Code>).

realty trusts.[26] The property usually passes directly by purchase to someone's relatives.[27]

Where the group of trustees and the group of beneficiaries are identical, the fact that the trustees hold the legal title jointly with right of survivorship and the beneficiaries hold the equitable interest as tenants in common ought to prevent the destruction of the trust through merger.[28] One learned commentator is of the view that on policy grounds alone, namely, the policy of effectuating settlor intent whenever possible, there should be no merger in such cases.[29]

As one can see, not much need be done to prevent a merger of interests. The simple introduction of a cotrustee into the formula should avoid such a result.[30] Or if upon the death of *C* the property passes to the then-living issue of *C* rather than to *C*'s estate there is no merger.[31] " . . . [A] . . . trust is created even though the only interests of other beneficiaries are contingent, subject to revocation, or otherwise uncertain."[32] In this day and age, one has to work hard to back into a merger.

The trustee should always keep in mind that, as we have alluded to above, a right to revoke or the possession of a general inter vivos power of appointment is not what triggers a merger.[33] Thus, if *A*, *B*, and *C* are the same but *D* is the *issue* of *B/C* living at the termination of the trust, there is no merger even in the face of a reserved right of revocation or general inter vivos power of appointment in *B/C*.[34] It is when *D* is the estate of *B/C* and *B/C* are the same person that merger comes about. The existence of a reserved right of revocation or general inter vivos power of appointment does not affect the situation one way or the other.[35]

With the revocable living trust now the core of most estate plans, it is important that the trustee separate issues relating to merger from issues relating to powers of revocation and general inter vivos powers of appointment.

---

[26] *See* §9.6 of this handbook (trusts that resemble corporations or agencies) (discussing the nominee trust).

[27] *See generally* National Shawmut Bank v. Joy, 315 Mass. 457, 462–467, 53 N.E.2d 113, 117–120 (1944).

[28] *See generally* 2 Scott on Trusts §99.5; First Ala. Bank of Tuscaloosa, N.A. v. Webb, 373 So. 2d 631 (Ala. 1979).

[29] 2 Scott & Ascher §11.2.5.

[30] Restatement (Third) of Trusts §69 cmt. c. *See, e.g.*, First Ala. Bank of Tuscaloosa, N.A. v. Webb, 373 So. 2d 631 (Ala. 1979); Smith v. Francis, 221 Ga. 260, 144 S.E.2d 439 (1965).

[31] *See generally* 2 Scott on Trusts §99.3. *See also* Fratcher, *Trustor as Sole Trustee and Only Ascertainable Beneficiary*, 47 Mich. L. Rev. 907, 934 (1949).

[32] Restatement (Third) of Trusts §69 cmt. e.

[33] *See* National Shawmut Bank v. Joy, 315 Mass. 457, 469–478, 53 N.E.2d 113, 124–126 (1944).

[34] *See* Harrison, *Structuring Trusts to Permit the Donor to Act as Trustee*, 22(6) Est. Planning 331 (Nov./Dec. 1995).

[35] *See* Restatement (Third) of Property (Wills and Other Donative Transfers) §7.1 cmt. b (Tentative Draft No. 3, Apr. 4, 2001) (providing that "the fact that the interest of the remainder beneficiary is subject to the settlor's power to revoke or amend the trust . . . does not transform the inter vivos trust into a will").

These powers are technically personal rights of disposition, not interests in property.[36]

There is no merger even in a case where title to the entire beneficial interest in a nominee trust[37] is held by the trustee of some other trust and the same person is the sole trustee of each trust, unless that same person also possesses the entire beneficial interest in the other trust.

As suggested in the introductory quotation, the coalescing of all property interests, both legal and equitable, in one person may not effect a merger in every case. Nor would the chance merger of the legal interest away from the trustee necessarily mean that in equity the trust itself extinguishes.[38] It may be that the one in whom the legal interest merges holds the legal interest as constructive trustee for the benefit of the trust beneficiaries, unless that person is a BFP.[39] As constructive trustee, he or she would then have a duty to transfer title to the subject property to an appropriate successor trustee, presumably one appointed by the court.[40]

The merger concept is not new. It was woven into the fabric of Roman law, as we have noted in Section 8.15.36 of this handbook.

§8.8   Whom Does Counsel Represent?

The drafters of . . . [the Uniform Trust] . . . Code decided to leave open for further consideration by the courts the extent to which a trustee may claim attorney-client privilege against a beneficiary seeking discovery of attorney-client communications between the trustee and the trustee's attorney. The courts are split because of the important values that are in tension on this question.[1]—Uniform Trust Code

---

[36] *See* National Shawmut Bank v. Joy, 315 Mass. 457, 474, 53 N.E.2d 113, 124 (1944). *See also* In re Armstrong, 17 Q.B.D. 521, 531 (1886).

[37] *See generally* §9.6 of this handbook (trusts that resemble corporations or agencies) (discussing the nominee trust).

[38] *See generally* 5 Scott & Ascher §33.2.

[39] *See generally* 5 Scott & Ascher §33.2. *See generally* §8.15.63 of this handbook (doctrine of bona fide purchase and the BFP).

[40] *See generally* 5 Scott & Ascher §33.2. *See generally* §3.3 of this handbook (the remedial constructive trust).

§8.8   [1] UTC §813 cmt. (available at <http://www.uniformlaws.org/Act.aspx?title=Trust%20 Code>). On the one hand, the attorney-client privilege "recognizes that sound legal advice or advocacy serves public ends and that such advice or advocacy depends upon the lawyer's being fully informed by the client." UTC §813 cmt. (citing Upjohn Co. v. United States, 449 U.S. 383 (1981)). On the other hand, the UTC "requires that a trustee keep the qualified beneficiaries reasonably informed about the administration of the trust and of the material facts necessary for them to protect their interests, which could include facts that the trustee has revealed only to the trustee's attorney." UTC §813 cmt.

When the roles and objectives of legal consultation are unclear, the question of who has paid for the legal services, or who ultimately will be required to pay those expenses, although potentially relevant, involves other and complicated considerations so that this matter is not determinative in resolving issues of privilege.[2]—Restatement (Third) of Trusts

At the drafting stage. *The privity of contract sticking point.* As a general rule, the lawyer who drafts a trust instrument represents the settlor and only the settlor. Thus, under classic common law principles, the lawyer cannot be held liable to third parties, such as the beneficiaries or the intended beneficiaries, for professional negligence in preparing the trust document itself, absent special facts.[3] Such third parties are not in privity of contract with the lawyer, *i.e.*, they are not parties to a lawyer-client agency relationship.[4] The lawyer and the settlor, however, are.[5] The lawyer-agent's duties run solely to the client-principal.[6] The so-called privity barrier in estate planning malpractice cases has been under attack for some time, at least since *Lucas v. Hamm* was decided in California in 1961.[7] In Pennsylvania, for example, the intended beneficiary of a trust may not necessarily be foreclosed from also qualifying as the intended third-party beneficiary of an *enforceable* contract between the deceased settlor and the settlor's estate planning lawyer, whether or not the governing instrument makes mention of the intended beneficiary.[8]

The attorney-client privilege. Counsel's direct inter vivos communications with the settlor regarding estate planning matters, *as well as communications with other true agents of the settlor*, generally are protected postmortem by the attorney-client privilege.[9] Thus, counsel's inter vivos discussions with the trustee of the settlor's revocable inter vivos trust regarding how the settlor's various estate planning instruments might be fine-tuned, or better effectuate the settlor's

---

[2] Restatement (Third) of Trusts §82 cmt. f.

[3] *See, e.g.*, Fredrikson v. Fredrikson, 817 N.Y.S.2d 320 (App. Div. 2006).

[4] *See, e.g.*, Peleg v. Spitz, 2007 WL 4200611 (Ohio App. 8th Dist.) (in part defining the concept of privity).

[5] *See generally* Charles E. Rounds, Jr., *Lawyer Codes Are Just About Licensure, the Lawyer's Relationship with the State: Recalling the Common Law Agency, Contract, Tort, Trust, and Property Principles the Regulate the Lawyer-Client Fiduciary Relationship*, 60 Baylor L. Rev. 771 (2008).

[6] *See generally* Charles E. Rounds, Jr., *Lawyer Codes Are Just About Licensure, the Lawyer's Relationship with the State: Recalling the Common Law Agency, Contract, Tort, Trust, and Property Principles the Regulate the Lawyer-Client Fiduciary Relationship*, 60 Baylor L. Rev. 771 (2008).

[7] *See, e.g.*, Fabian v. Lindsay. 410 S.C. 475, 765 S.E.2d 132 (2014) ("We find . . . [the *Lucas v. Hamm*] . . . reasoning sound and adopt it here."); Lucas v. Hamm, 56 Cal. 2d 583, 15 Cal. Rptr 821, 364 P.2d 685 (1961).

[8] *See* Agnew v. Ross, No. 2195 EDA 2014 (Pa. Super. Ct. Feb. 2, 2015).

[9] *See, e.g.*, Adler v. Greenfield, 990 N.E.2d 1219 (Ill. App. Ct. 2013).

intentions, may well be privileged,[10] unless the testamentary exception to the attorney-client privilege is applicable.[11]

Cross-reference. For more on the privity defense in the trust drafting context, the reader is referred to Section 8.15.61 of this handbook.

The funding Achilles' heel. That is not to say that trust beneficiaries litigating in a jurisdiction that has a privity barrier will never have any arrows in their quivers. If, for example, the drafting attorney had also prepared the funding documentation, then he or she might be liable to the beneficiaries for any harm to the trust that was funding related. Faulty advice rendered to the trustee of an irrevocable life insurance trust with respect to the purchase of a life insurance contract and the negligent preparation of a deed of real estate into the trust come to mind.[12] The trustee, of course, might be liable as well.[13]

Statutes of limitations for estate planning malpractice. In any case, the trust scrivener whose professional duties to the settlor-client actually do cease at the time of document execution may expect that the applicable statute of limitations for lawyer malpractice will then begin to run against the settlor-client. At least one court has so held.[14] Whether a trust scrivener owes continuing postexecution duties will hinge on the particular facts and circumstances of the representation.[15] Note also that if the scrivener breached a *fiduciary* duty to the settlor-client in the course of preparing the documentation, such as the duty of undivided loyalty, then the applicable statute of limitations, at least under classic agency principles, ought not to run against the settlor-client until such time as the settlor-client acquires an actual subjective understanding of the material facts of the breach, as well as a general appreciation of why as a matter of law there has been a breach.

---

[10] *See, e.g.,* Adler v. Greenfield, 990 N.E.2d 1219 (Ill. App. Ct. 2013).

[11] *See, e.g.,* Zook v. Pesce, 438 Md. 232, 91 A.3d 1114 (2014) (the court not finding the exception applicable "in this case" but reaffirming "that in a dispute between putative heirs or devisees under a will or trust, the attorney-client privilege does not bar admission of testimony and evidence regarding communication between the decedent and any attorneys involved in the creation of the instrument, provided that evidence or testimony tends to help clarify the donative intent of the decedent").

[12] *See generally* §§5.4.1.8 of this handbook (right and standing of beneficiary to proceed in stead of trustee against those with whom the trustee has contracted, against tortfeasors, and against the trustee's agents, *i.e.,* against third parties) and 7.2.9 of this handbook (personal liability of third parties, including the trustee's agents, to the beneficiary; investment managers; directors and officers of trust companies; lawyers; brokers).

[13] *See generally* §8.32 of this handbook (can the trustee escape liability for making a mistake of law if he acted in good faith on advice of counsel).

[14] *See* Babb v. Hoskins, 733 S.E.2d 881 (N.C. App. 2012).

[15] *See, e.g.,* G. William Carlson, as Trustee of Bernice G. Carlson Charitable Uni-Trust No. 1, et al. v. Houk, A14-0633 (Minn. Ct. App., Filed Nov. 17, 2014) (alleged negligent providing of estate-planning and charitable-giving legal advice and drafting of two trust instruments),

Scrivener liability in tort to settlor's probate estate likely to be a hard sell. Assume the scrivener negligently prepares an estate plan for a client. A revocable inter vivos trust is a component of that estate plan. Due to scrivener's substandard estate planning, upon the death of the settlor-client, more estate taxes are owed than would have been owed had the estate plan conformed to the standards of the estate planning profession. May the personal representative of the deceased settlor-client maintain a legal malpractice tort action against the scrivener for substandard estate planning? Probably not. At least one Kansas court has so held. "We answer this question 'no' because the cause of action arose after the decedent's death which means it does not qualify as a survival claim under K.S.A 60-1801."[16]

After the trust has been created. *Whether trust counsel owes duties to the beneficiaries as well as the trustee.* The question of whether counsel represents the trustee, the beneficiaries, or both, is a difficult one[17] and depends to some extent on the facts and circumstances. The issues are subtle.[18] When the trust is revocable and the settler is of full age and legal capacity, counsel represents the settlor and only the settler. Otherwise, if counsel is advising the *office of trustee* as it were, the trustee is the primary client.[19] Some courts have ruled, however, that counsel has certain "restrictive" duties that run to the beneficiary as well.[20]

---

[16] Jeanes v. Bank of Am., N.A., 295 P.3d 1045, 1046 (2013).

[17] Existing case law is confused, incomplete, and insufficient. *See* Dominic J. Campisi, *The Search for the Deep Pocket—Is It Yours?*, 25 ACTEC Notes 246 (1999) (noting that the law regarding the role and liability of counsel for the fiduciary is in a state of perpetual flux because of the balancing tests used to determine the status, standards, and liabilities involved in such representation); Pennell, *Representations Involving Fiduciary Entities: Who Is the Client?*, 62 Fordham L. Rev. 1319, 1321–1326 (1994); ACTEC Commentaries on Model Rules of Professional Conduct (ACTEC Foundation) (3d ed. June 1999): Reporter's Note, Reporter's Note (2d ed.), Reporter's Note (3d ed.) (hereinafter "ACTEC Commentaries")). *See generally* Reid, Mureiko, & Mikeska, *Privilege and Confidentiality Issues When a Lawyer Represents a Fiduciary*, 30 Real Prop. Prob. & Tr. J. 541 (1996); Johns, *Fickett's Thicket: The Lawyer's Expanding Fiduciary and Ethical Boundaries When Serving Older Americans of Moderate Wealth*, 32 Wake Forest L. Rev. 445 (1997). *See also* §5.4.1.1 of this handbook (right to information and confidentiality) (discussing the beneficiary's right to information).

[18] *See generally* Frank, *The Legal Ethics of Louis D. Brandeis*, 17 Stan. L. Rev. 683, 694 (1965) (the Warren matter). *See generally* §8.38 of this handbook (the Warren trust (a.k.a. the Mills trust)).

[19] *See* Gadsden, *Ethical Guidelines for the Fiduciary's Lawyer*, 134 Tr. & Est. 8, 10 (Mar. 1995); Ross, *Particularized Guidance for the Estate and Trust Lawyer*, 133 Tr. & Est. 10, 14 (July 1994).

[20] *See* Gadsden, *Ethical Guidelines for the Fiduciary's Lawyer*, 134 Tr. & Est. 8, 10 (Mar. 1995) (stating duties are restrictive in nature). *But see* Roberts v. Fearey, 162 Or. App. 546, 986 P.2d 690 (1999) (where no allegation that attorney knowingly aided or assisted the trustee in the commission of a breach of fiduciary duty, attorney's duty of care ran only to trustee); Spinner v. Nutt, 417 Mass. 549, 631 N.E.2d 542 (1994) (holding no duty of reasonable care imposed with respect to beneficiaries if it would conflict with duty owed to fiduciary-client); 2A Scott on Trusts §173. *Cf.* Witzman v. Gross, 148 F.3d 988, 990 (1998) (holding that the general rule of trust law that a

Counsel, for example, may not exploit, to the detriment of either party, confidential information acquired in the course of his or her representation.[21] Nor may counsel withhold from the beneficiary information to which the beneficiary is entitled.[22] The Restatement (Third) of Trusts, for example, takes the position that "legal consultations and advice obtained in the trustee's fiduciary capacity concerning decisions or actions to be taken in the course of administering the trust . . . are subject to the general principle entitling a beneficiary to information that is reasonably necessary to the prevention or redress of a breach of trust or otherwise to the enforcement of the beneficiary's rights under the trust."[23] Because counsel has an obligation to advise the trustee on the nature of the trustee's fiduciary responsibilities and how best to carry them out, as well as a right to be paid from the trust, it is said that the beneficiary enjoys the status of a "derivative" or "secondary" client.[24] (It is even suggested that counsel would have an affirmative duty to disclose to the beneficiary any serious wrongdoing on the part of the trustee, e.g., embezzlement). Commentators have referred to this as the *entity* approach.[25]

Other courts, however, have held that the trustee is the only client,[26] suggesting that to say that the *trust* is the real client is inconsistent with the law of trusts.[27] At least one jurisdiction has confirmed this by statute:

Unless expressly provided otherwise in a written employment agreement, the creation of an attorney-client relationship between a lawyer and a person serving as fiduciary shall not impose upon the lawyer any duties or obligations to other persons interested in the estate, trust estate, or other fiduciary property, even though fiduciary funds may be used to compensate the lawyer for legal services rendered by the fiduciary. This section is intended to be declaratory of the

---

beneficiary cannot bring an action at law in a trust's stead against a third party for torts or other wrongs extends to beneficiaries who attempt to sue a trustee's attorneys for legal malpractice).

[21] *See* Gadsden, *Ethical Guidelines for the Fiduciary's Lawyer*, 134 Tr. & Est. 8, 16 (Mar. 1995) (confidentiality requirements).

[22] *See* Gadsden, *Ethical Guidelines for the Fiduciary's Lawyer*, 134 Tr. & Est. 8, 16 (Mar. 1995) (confidentiality requirements).

[23] Restatement (Third) of Trusts §82 cmt. f. *See generally* 3 Scott & Ascher §17.5.

[24] *See* Hazard & Hodes, The Law of Lawyering, A Handbook on the Model Rules of Professional Conduct §1.3:108 (2d ed. 1994).

[25] *See, e.g.*, J. Pennell, *Representation Involving Fiduciary Entities: Who Is the Client?*, 62 Fordham L. Rev. 1319 (1994); Restatement (Third) of Trusts §82 cmt. f, Reporter's Notes thereto.

[26] *See* Sullivan v. Dorsa, 128 Cal. App. 4th 947, 964, 27 Cal. Rptr. 3d 547, 560 (2005) (noting that, in general, an attorney engaged by a trustee does not thereby become an attorney for the trust's beneficiaries).

[27] *See, e.g.*, Huie v. DeShazo, 39 Tex. Supp. Ct. J. 288, 922 S.W.2d 920 (1996) (holding that the attorney-client privilege protects communications between a trustee and his or her attorney relating to trust administration from discovery by a trust beneficiary, only the trustee, not the beneficiary, being the client of the trustee's attorney); Spinner v. Nutt, 417 Mass. 549, 631 N.E.2d 542 (1994) (holding trustee owed no duty of reasonable care to beneficiaries if it would conflict with duty owed to fiduciary-client). *See generally* §3.5 of this handbook (trustee's relationship to the trust estate) (suggesting that a trust, unlike a corporation, is not a legal entity).

common law and governs relationships in existence between lawyers and persons serving as fiduciaries as well as such relationships hereafter created.[28]

Representing cotrustees. A lawyer may represent cotrustees in their fiduciary capacity.[29] The lawyer, however, should make it clear that each cotrustee is entitled to all information that flows between the lawyer and the other cotrustee or cotrustees. Accordingly, it is difficult to see how one lawyer can practically or ethically represent cotrustees, in either their representative or individual capacities, who are in conflict with one another.

Representing trustees of different trusts. The lawyer who simultaneously represents the trustee of Trust *X* and the trustee of Trust *Y* is asking for trouble if the trusts themselves are in conflict. This could happen if, for example, Trust *X* is a QTIP trust and Trust *Y* is a revocable trust established by the beneficiary of the QTIP trust. Let us assume the beneficiary has died. If Trust *X*'s class of remaindermen does not perfectly intersect with Trust *Y*'s class of remaindermen and if the tax apportionment provision of Trust *Y* is vague or ambiguous, the trustee of the QTIP trust may have a fiduciary duty to take the position that Trust *Y* should bear the burden of the federal estate tax liability attributable to the inclusion of the QTIP assets in the federal gross estate of the decedent. The trustee of the revocable trust may have a fiduciary duty to take the position that the default law applies, namely that the QTIP assets must bear the burden of their allocable share of the estate taxes. The situation would be exacerbated if the lawyer also were the trustee of one of the trusts, as was the case in *In re Estate of Klarner*:

> The Law Firm is also a trustee of the QTIP Trust and owes a fiduciary duty to Albert's daughters. Simultaneously, the Law Firm is a trustee of Marian's [revocable] Trust and represents the cotrustees, Marian's sons, in this litigation. Therefore, the Law Firm owes fiduciary duties to its clients, Marian's sons, while also owing fiduciary duties to Albert's daughters. The Law Firm is in the precarious position of advocating in this litigation an advantageous position for its clients, Marian's sons, that, if successful, would operate to the detriment of the beneficiaries to whom it owes a duty of loyalty.[30]

The trustee's personal defense counsel. If counsel has been retained by the trustee as his *personal lawyer* to advise him on matters such as how to defend an action for breach of trust, counsel would have no duties to the beneficiary.[31] The

---

[28] S.C. Code §62-1-109.

[29] ACTEC Commentary on MRPC 1.2.

[30] In re Estate of Klarner, 2003 WL 22723228 (Colo. App. 2003).

[31] *See, e.g.,* First Nat'l Bank of Fla. v. Whitener, 715 So. 2d 979, 982 (Fla. 1998) (holding that trustee was the "true client," the trustee having retained counsel after it realized "there were problems, including a perceived conflict of interest" and after the beneficiary had retained counsel). *See also* Wingfield, *Fiduciary Attorney-Client Communications: An Illusory Privilege?*, 8 Prob. & Prop. 60, 62 (1994) (protected communications); §3.5.2.3 of this handbook (right in equity to exoneration and reimbursement, *i.e.*, indemnity; payment of attorneys' fees). *See generally* 3 Scott & Ascher §17.5.

Restatement (Third) of Trusts is generally in accord.[32] The important thing to remember when it comes to legal representation is that the parties at all times must understand who represents whom. Or perhaps more important, who does *not* represent whom.[33] If it is reasonable for a beneficiary to assume that counsel is representing the beneficiary's interests when counsel is not, then, at minimum, counsel has a duty to communicate to the beneficiary that the beneficiary is in fact unrepresented.[34]

The way around all of this is for counsel, at the time he or she is hired by the trustee, to communicate directly with the beneficiaries regarding the nature of the representation. Certainly when storm clouds are gathering on the horizon—when trouble is brewing between the trustee and the beneficiary or between the beneficiary and other beneficiaries—counsel and the trustee have an affirmative duty to advise the beneficiary in a timely fashion that the beneficiary ought to retain his or her own independent counsel. The prudent trustee sees to it that this advice is rendered in writing and that there is a record of its having been received.

The relevancy of who pays trust counsel. Ordinarily the trustee's counsel fees are deductible from the trust estate, unless they relate to matters in which the trustee is personally at fault, *e.g.*, unauthorized acts of self-dealing. On the other hand, even in cases when the trustee is not personally at fault, " . . . [I]f the trustee employs an attorney for the trustee's own benefit and not for that of the trust, the trustee is personally liable for the attorney's fees and is not entitled to reimbursement from the trust estate."[35] Thus, absent special facts, fees incurred by a trustee in obtaining a legal opinion as to whether he would be entitled to charge the trust estate a commission for his brokerage services that is over and above his regular fiduciary compensation ordinarily would not be reimbursable, particularly if the trust would not have been disadvantaged had the brokerage business been directed to a third party. They certainly would not be reimbursable if the trust would have been advantaged had the business been directed elsewhere.

The attorney-client privilege. Whom trust counsel does and does not represent implicates the attorney-client privilege, which has the following elements: "Where legal advice of any kind is sought (2) from a professional legal advisor in his capacity as such, (3) the communications relating to that purpose, (4) made in confidence (5) by the client, (6) are at his instance permanently protected (7)

---

[32] Restatement (Third) of Trusts §82 cmt. f.

[33] *See, e.g.*, Chinello v. Nixon, Hargrave, Devans & Doyle, 788 N.Y.S.2d 750 (2005) (beneficiary who had at one time been represented by the law firm representing the trustee unsuccessfully sued the firm for legal malpractice and breach of fiduciary duty based on the beneficiary's execution of a waiver of citation and consent to accounting). *See generally* Reid, Mureiko, & Mikeska, *Privilege and Confidentiality Issues When a Lawyer Represents a Fiduciary*, 30 Real Prop. Prob. & Tr. J. 541, 556 (1996).

[34] *See* Gadsden, *Ethical Guidelines for the Fiduciary's Lawyer*, 134 Tr. & Est. 8, 17 (Mar. 1995) (citing Butler v. State Bar, 42 Cal. 3d 323, 721 P.2d 585 (1986)).

[35] 3 Scott & Ascher §18.1.2.4.

from disclosure by himself or by the legal advisor . . ."[36] Voluntary disclosure by the privilege-holder, in this case the trustee, to a third party constitutes a waiver of the privilege. The privilege-holding trustee's pursuit of an advice-of-counsel defense in a breach-of-trust action could constitute a partial waiver of the privilege.[37]

Whether the trustee may assert the attorney-client privilege against the beneficiary. In a suit by the beneficiary against the trustee, is the trustee entitled to assert the attorney-client privilege *against the beneficiary, or is there a fiduciary exception to the privilege?*[38] As to communications with trust counsel uttered *after* the onset of hostilities, the trustee may effectively assert the privilege.[39] As to communications uttered *before* the onset of hostilities, he may well not be able to.[40] One Arizona court has drawn a line between legal advice that the trustee seeks in his fiduciary capacity and legal advice that he seeks in his individual or corporate capacity.[41] The former is discoverable by the beneficiary under the fiduciary exception to the attorney-client privilege. The latter is not. Thus, legal advice on "matters of trust administration" is discoverable by the beneficiary, while legal advice sought by the trustee "for purposes of . . . [the trustee's] . . . self-protection" is not.[42]

One South Carolina court in denying a trustee the right to assert the attorney-client privilege against his beneficiary found persuasive the fact that counsel fees had been paid from the trust estate.[43] The Restatement (Third) of Trusts, on the other hand, downplays the significance of "who pays,"[44] as did the Arizona court.[45]

---

[36] United States v. Evans, 113 F.3d 1457, 1461 (7th Cir. 1997) (citing 8 John Henry Wigmore, Evidence in Trials at Common Law §2292 (John T. McNaughton ed., 1961)).

[37] *See* Mennen v. Wilmington Trust Co., Master's Report, C.A. No. 8432-ML (Del. Ch. Sept. 18, 2013) ("The waiver is 'partial' in the sense that it does not open to discovery all communications between the client and its attorney, but only those communications that relate to the subject matter of the disclosed communications.").

[38] *See generally* 3 Scott & Ascher §17.5 (Duty to Furnish Information).

[39] *See generally* 3 Scott & Ascher §17.5 (Duty to Furnish Information). *See, e.g.*, First Union Nat'l Bank of Fla. v. Whitener, 715 So. 2d 979, 982 (1998) (the court finding no fraud that would abrogate the trustee's right to assert the attorney-client privilege). *See generally* Gibbs & Hanson, *The Fiduciary Exception to a Trustee's Attorney/Client Privilege*, 21 ACTEC Notes 236 (1995).

[40] Gibbs & Hanson, *The Fiduciary Exception to a Trustee's Attorney/Client Privilege*, 21 ACTEC Notes 239; Lewin ¶23-08 (England). In New York, a trustee may invoke the attorney/client privilege only for "good cause." *See* Hoopes v. Carota, 142 A.D.2d 906, 531 N.Y.S.2d 407 (App. Div. 1988), *aff'd*, 74 N.Y.2d 716, 543 N.E.2d 73, 544 N.Y.S.2d 808 (1989). *But see* Huie, individually and as executor and trustee, v. the Honorable Nikki DeShazo, Judge, 922 S.W.2d 920 (Tex. 1996) (suggesting there is no "fiduciary exception" to the attorney/client privilege); Wells Fargo, N.A. v. Superior Court, 990 P.2d 591 (Cal. 2000) (denying beneficiary access even to attorney-trustee communications that involved routine trust administration matters).

[41] *See* In re The Kipnis Section 3.4 Trust, 2014 WL 2515207 (Ariz. App. Div. 1 2014).

[42] In re The Kipnis Section 3.4 Trust, 2014 WL 2515207 (Ariz. App. Div. 1 2014).

[43] Floyd v. Floyd, 365 S.C. 56, 87–88, 615 S.E.2d 465, 482 (2005).

[44] Restatement (Third) of Trusts §82 cmt. f, Reporter's Notes thereto. *See also* 3 Scott & Ascher §17.5.

[45] In re The Kipnis Section 3.4 Trust, 2014 WL 2515207 (Ariz. App. Div. 1 2014).

In any case, the prudent trustee should assume that any preconfrontation communications with counsel are discoverable and act accordingly.[46] And if it is any consolation to the trustee, the attorney-client privilege has its limitations. One court has issued the following general warning: "The attorney-client privilege does not permit a trustee to withhold 'material facts' from a beneficiary simply because the trustee has communicated those facts to the attorney."[47] Another court, after having ruled that certain documents in the trustee's file were covered by the privilege, cautioned against employing the privilege as a litigation tactic: "Nonetheless, the trustee may not use the privilege as a shield, and then, at trial, surprise the movants by using any of the requested documents as a sword."[48] Still another court has provided a useful hypothetical to explain how a no-exception approach to the attorney-client privilege arguably squares with the trustee's fiduciary duty to disclose material facts to the beneficiary:

Assume that a trustee who has misappropriated money from a trust confidentially reveals this fact to his or her attorney for the purpose of obtaining legal advice. The trustee, when asked at trial whether he or she misappropriated the money, cannot claim the attorney-client privilege. The act of misappropriation is a material fact of which the trustee has knowledge independently of the communication. The trustee must therefore disclose the fact (assuming no other privilege applied), even though the trustee confidentially conveyed the fact to the attorney. However, because the attorney's only knowledge of the misappropriation is through the confidential communication, the attorney cannot be called on to reveal this information.[49]

As noted above, the drafters of the Uniform Trust Code decided to leave open for further consideration by the courts the extent to which a trustee may claim attorney-client privilege against a beneficiary seeking discovery of attorney-client communications between the trustee and the trustee's lawyer, the courts now being profoundly split on the question of whom trust counsel represents.[50]

Asserting the privilege against the inquisitive successor trustee. In a suit by a successor trustee against a predecessor trustee, is the predecessor entitled to assert

---

[46] Gibbs & Hanson, *The Fiduciary Exception to a Trustee's Attorney/Client Privilege*, 21 ACTEC Notes, 236, 240 (1995) ("Assuming the inchoate existence of some fiduciary exception rule in your jurisdiction, the question for the attorney is: how do my fiduciary clients and I conduct our communications *prior* to the time a beneficiary asserts a claim . . . ? Alertly, carefully, and clearly is the certain answer."). *See generally* Desmarais, *The Fiduciary, His Counsel and the Attorney-Client Privilege*, 136 Tr. & Est. 29 (No. 6, May 1997).

[47] In re The Kipnis Section 3.4 Trust, 2014 WL 2515207 (Ariz. App. Div. 1 2014).

[48] Matter of Will of Poster, 884 N.Y.S.2d 838, 842 (Sur. 2009).

[49] Huie v. DeShazo, 39 Tex. Sup. Ct. J. 288, 922 S.W.2d 920, 923 (1996). *See generally* §§5.4.1.1 of this handbook (discussing the beneficiary's right to information) and 6.1.5.1 of this handbook (duty to provide information) (discussing duty of trustee to provide information to the beneficiary).

[50] UTC §813 cmt. (available at <http://www.uniformlaws.org/Act.aspx?title=Trust%20Code>).

the attorney-client privilege against the successor? Courts have held that when the office of trustee passes from one person to another, the power to assert the attorney-client privilege passes as well.[51] This would include the power to assert the privilege with respect to confidential communications between a predecessor trustee and an attorney on matters of trust administration. Bottom line: The predecessor may not assert the privilege as against the successor. The predecessor, however, would still retain the right to claim the attorney-client privilege as to communications between the predecessor and his, her or its personal attorney.[52]

Asserting the attorney-client privilege against those not party to the trust relationship. Assume the following: (1) counsel renders confidential tax advice to the trustee, which the trustee voluntarily passes on to the beneficiary; (2) the IRS seeks to discover that advice; and (3) the trustee asserts the attorney-client privilege against the IRS. Has the trustee waived the privilege by so informing the beneficiary of that advice? If there is a fiduciary exception to the attorney-client privilege, then the privilege presumably has not been waived, the trustee and the beneficiary being essentially coclients. Now if trust counsel represents the trustee and only the trustee, then the privilege may have been waived *by the trustee* when he communicated the confidential tax advice to the beneficiary, who would essentially have been a third party to the attorney-client relationship. The waiver might even apply to all the other beneficiaries, as well. "In view of the unsettled state of the law in the US regarding the existence of, and basis for, the fiduciary exception to the attorney-client privilege, trustees should carefully consider the potential waiver implications of disclosing privileged legal advice to beneficiaries. Moreover, in appropriate circumstances, trustees may wish to obtain Court directions before disclosing confidential legal advice."[53]

In Section 6.1.5.1 of this handbook, we discuss the trustee's duty to provide information to the beneficiaries of the trust. There is, however, a countervailing duty not to furnish beneficiaries with information if doing so would "not be in the best interests of the beneficiaries as a whole, but ... [would]...be prejudicial to the ability of the trustees to discharge their obligations under the trust."[54]

The perverse incentives inherent in Section 1005(c) of the Uniform Trust Code. The Uniform Trust Code, specifically Section 1005(c), provides that under certain circumstances a trust beneficiary has only five years to bring a breach-of-trust action against the trustee even should the beneficiary lack actual or constructive notice of the breach. Assume four years have run since a breach of trust has occurred. The trustee and the beneficiary remain totally in the dark as to the fact and nature of the breach. One more year and the trustee is off the hook. Trust counsel, on the other hand, becomes aware of the breach. Here is a

---

[51] *See, e.g.,* In re Estate of Fedor and Catherine M. Fedor Revocable Trust, 356 N.J. Super. 218, 811 A.2d 970 (2001).

[52] *See, e.g.,* In re The Kipnis Section 3.4 Trust, 2014 WL 2515207 (Ariz. App. Div. 1 2014).

[53] Basil Zirinis, Marina Bezrukova, Richard Corn, & James Gadwood, *Unintended Consequences*, 8(4) Tr. Q. Rev. 15 (2010) [a STEP publication].

[54] David Hayton, Paul Mathews, & Charles Mitchell, *Underhilll and Hayton, Law Relating to Trusts and Trustees* §60.58 (17th ed. 2006).

situation in which counsel may have to respond to two potentially conflicting duties: (1) to represent the trustee in his official capacity and (2) to protect the trustee personally. If he informs the trustee of the breach and the trustee takes no action to remedy it, the trustee's fraudulent inaction may toll the running of the statute. On the other hand, if counsel keeps quiet, the five-year period will expire and the trustee will be personally off the hook. Still the trustee will have breached virtually the entire panoply of fiduciary duties that had been owed to the beneficiary, duties that are the subject of Chapter 6 of this handbook.

What is an innocent trust counsel to do in such a situation? One court has proffered the following advice: When a trustee is faced with a personal-fiduciary conflict, "the trustee can mitigate or avoid the problem by retaining and paying out of his own funds separate counsel for legal advice that is personal in nature."[55] But how exactly is trust counsel to get the trustee to retain at his own expense separate personal counsel without causing a fraud-based tolling of the running of the statute and/or without trust counsel, himself, ending up constructively participating in the breach of trust? Might the only way out of the cul-de-sac be the *deus ex machina* of a repeal of Section 1005(c)? Under default laches doctrine trust counsel would no longer be conflicted in that the trustee would be personally benefited by a full disclosure of the breach to the beneficiary. This is because full disclosure would trigger a start of the running of any statute of limitations that might be applicable to such a breach of fiduciary duty, or, in the absence of such a statute, a start of the running of the "reasonable" laches period that a fully informed trust beneficiary would have to bring suit against the trustee for a breach of trust.

One commentator on ethical lawyering is floating a general proposal that might at least eliminate our Section 1005(c) fraud-disclosure conundrum, although in a given situation the fall-out from the cure would likely be nastier than the disease. He proposes that each state "adopt a rule" along the lines of the following: "A lawyer, to the extent the lawyer reasonably believes necessary, may reveal information relating to the representation of a client to inform a tribunal or a beneficiary about any material breach of fiduciary responsibility when the client is serving as a fiduciary such as a guardian, personal representative, trustee, or receiver."[56]

This UTC Section 1005(c) statute of ultimate repose is covered generally in Section 7.1.3 of this handbook and in Section 7.2.10 of this handbook.

---

[55] Stewart v. Kono, 2012 WL 4427096 (Cal. App. 2 Dist. 2012).

[56] Kennedy Lee, *Representing the Fiduciary: To Whom Does the Attorney Owe Duties?*, 37 ACTEC L.J. 469, 492 (Winter 2011).

§8.9 Why More Than One Trust: The Estate and Generation-Skipping Tax

Because this handbook focuses on the rights, duties, and obligations of the parties *after* the trust is established, a thorough treatment of the tax considerations that go into the *initial design* of a trust is beyond its scope. On the other hand, the trustee should have some inkling of why a trust looks the way it does. Why, for instance, did the same settlor create more than one trust for the same beneficiary? Or why did the trustee divide one trust into two identical ones?[1] There is also the rare occasion when it falls to the trustee to act as "inadvertent executor" (for tax purposes) of the settlor's estate.[2]

Because the majority of trusts are established to minimize estate and generation-skipping taxes, that is where the authors focus and limit the discussion. In Section 9.1 of this handbook, however, there are brief discussions of a few of the more exotic estate tax minimization vehicles, namely the GRIT (grantor retained interest trust), the GRAT (grantor retained annuity trust), and the GRUT (grantor retained unitrust).[3] Also, there are brief discussions of the QPRT (qualified personal residence trust) in Section 9.15 of this handbook, the CRUT (charitable remainder unitrust) in Section 9.4.5.1(a) of this handbook, the CRAT (charitable remainder annuity trust) in Section 9.4.5.1(b) of this handbook, the charitable lead trust in Section 9.4.5.2 of this handbook, and the Crummey trust in Section 9.18 of this handbook.

---

§8.9 [1] *See generally* §3.5.3.2(m) of this handbook (the trustee's power to divide a trust). *See also* UTC §417 cmt. (available at <http://www.uniformlaws.org/Act.aspx?title=Trust%20 Code>) (noting that division is frequently undertaken due to a desire to obtain maximum advantage of exemptions available under the federal generation-skipping tax). For a discussion of the myriad issues that can arise if the trustee unduly delays or fails altogether to effect a required division into separate trust shares, *see* §8.2.3 of this handbook (termination and distribution issues). *See also* Restatement (Third) of Trusts §89, Reporter's Notes, Comment *g* (Aside: Failure to subdivide trust).

[2] *See generally* §8.16 of this handbook (the trustee of revocable trust as "inadvertent executor").

[3] "The grantor retained annuity trust (GRAT) or grantor retained unitrust (GRUT) is often used to transfer large assets at a substantially reduced gift tax cost." Howard M. Zaritsky, *A GRAT (Or GRUT) Checklist*, 12(8) Prob. Prac. 1 (Aug. 2000). "A GRAT or GRUT . . . is an irrevocable gift of a remainder interest in a trust, in which the grantor (or an applicable family member) reserves for a term of years either a fixed annuity or a fixed percentage of the annual value of the trust fund (a unitrust amount)." Zaritsky, *A GRAT (Or GRUT) Checklist*, 12(8) Prob. Prac. 1 (Aug. 2000). For a checklist that can be used in planning and drafting a GRAT or a GRUT, *see* Zaritsky, *A GRAT (Or GRUT) Checklist*, 12(8) Prob. Prac. 1 (Aug. 2000). at 1–5.

§8.9.1 The Federal Estate Tax

Rules specifying the government's share of an estate has been a feature of western law for many centuries as it has been in other parts of the world.[4] By way of illustration, while the first clause of the Magna Carta of 1215 focuses on the spiritual side of life by proclaiming the freedom of the English church, the second through seventh clauses pertains to the material side of life—the taxation of inheritances.[5]

The federal estate tax is a tax on certain property transfers occasioned by the death of a beneficial owner.[6] (An inheritance tax is a tax "on the receipt of wealth, burdening the beneficiary of the transferred property rather than the decedent's estate."[7]) If appointed, the owner's executor has the obligation to file the federal estate tax return and pay any tax due from the property that the decedent beneficially owned. If there is no probate estate, anyone in possession of the property, such as a trustee, files the return. The trustee as an "inadvertent executor" is discussed in Section 8.16 of this handbook. The federal estate tax is due no later than nine months from the decedent's death; though an executor may obtain an automatic additional six months extension by filing IRS Form 4768. The party responsible for filing the return may also have an obligation to

---

[4] For an exhaustive survey of state gift, estate, inheritance, and generation-skipping transfers tax statutes, *see* Jeffrey A. Schoenblum, 2 Multistate and Multinational Estate Planning 755–961 (Appendix C) (1999). "In virtually all states, death taxes, whether of the estate or inheritance variety, . . . [were] . . . designed simply to soak up the credit provided by I.R.C. §2011." Schoenblum, 2 Multistate and Multinational Estate Planning at 755. This is known as a "sponge" or "pick-up" tax. *See generally* Schoenblum, 2 Multistate and Multinational Estate Planning at 8–11 (discussing the interplay of state death taxation and federal estate taxation including the statutory evolution of the sponge or pick-up tax). The Economic Growth and Tax Relief Reconciliation Act of 2001 (EGTRRA) has "changed the landscape" by gradually eliminating "federal estate taxes between 2001 and 2010 and their return in 2011." Jeffrey A. Cooper, John R. Ivimey & Donna D. Vincenti, *State Estate Taxes After EGTRRA: A Long Day's Journey Into Night*, 17 Quinnipiac Prob. L.J. 317 (2004). "EGTRRA also provides for the elimination of the state death tax credit over a period of 4 years, with the credit being reduced by 25% for estates of decedents dying in 2002, by 50% for decedents dying in 2003, and by 75% for decedents dying in 2004." Jeffrey A. Cooper, John R. Ivimey & Donna D. Vincenti, *State Estate Taxes After EGTRRA: A Long Day's Journey Into Night*, 17 Quinnipiac Prob. L.J. 317 (2004). "For the years 2005 and beyond, the credit is fully repealed and replaced with a deduction against the federal estate tax for state taxes paid." Jeffrey A. Cooper, John R. Ivimey & Donna D. Vincenti, *State Estate Taxes After EGTRRA: A Long Day's Journey Into Night*, 17 Quinnipiac Prob. L.J. 317(2004). In response to this "decoupling" of the state tax systems from the federal, state legislatures are establishing tax systems that are independent of the federal system. For country-by-country summaries of death and gift tax statutes, *see* Jeffrey A. Schoenblum, 2 Multistate and Multinational Estate Planning 1073–1147 (Appendix I) (1999).

[5] Margo Thorning, *The U.S. Tax Code in the 21st Century: Does the Estate Tax Fit?*, Special Report, American Council for Capital Formation (Mar. 2004).

[6] I.R.C. §2001(a). *See also* Treas. Reg. §20.2033-1(a). In 1862, a tax on intergenerational transfers was instituted to finance the Civil War. It was repealed in 1870. The estate tax was reinstituted in 1898 to finance the Spanish-American War. That tax was repealed in 1902. The current federal estate tax system was instituted in 1916. Since then, it has been subject to numerous legislative modifications. *See generally* Tom Herman, *A Change in Death & Taxes*, Wall St. J., Feb. 26, 2001, at C1, C13 (discussing the long history of estate taxes in the U.S.).

[7] Jeffrey A. Schoenblum, 2 Multistate and Multinational Estate Planning 6 (1999).

file a state estate tax return.[8] Not all states have an estate tax. Massachusetts does; Colorado does not. A state estate tax payment is currently a deduction, not a credit, on the federal estate tax return.

A discussion of what property interests generate an estate tax—*i.e.*, what property interests may comprise the federal gross estate—could fill volumes.[9] Briefly, the federal gross estate includes the value, at the time of the decedent's death, or in the case of a missing person, at the time he or she is declared dead,[10] of all his or her property, real or personal, tangible or intangible, wherever situated.[11] This would include the interests described in Code Sections 2033 through 2046. For settlors and trustees, however, key Code Sections are 2036, 2037, 2038, and 2034, in part because they can bring the value of previously transferred property into the federal gross estate for computation purposes.[12] Thus, certain powers of appointment and reversionary interests must be assigned dollar values.[13] Securities should be valued at the mean between the high and low price as of the date of death, which is the valuation method the IRS would employ in an audit.

The value of the net taxable estate is the value of the federal gross estate less certain deductions, such as the marital deduction, the charitable deduction, funeral expenses, and administration expenses, including trustee fees. There is an alternate valuation election on the federal estate tax return.[14] If it is made, all assets are then valued on the return as of six months after the date of death. This election is only available if it reduces the total value of the federal gross estate and estate tax liability. It cannot be made merely to effect an increase in the tax cost of the assets for capital gains income tax computation purposes when the assets are ultimately sold. In other words, the election would not be available merely to maximize the basis step-up that was occasioned by the property owner's death.

Suffice it to say that in the context of trusts, property subject to the federal estate tax is likely to include the property of a deceased settlor that was held in a revocable inter vivos trust or that became the subject of a trust upon the settlor's death.[15] (At one time, the IRS was even requiring the date of death

---

[8] *See* Charles D. Fox, IV and Adam M. Damerow, *The ACTEC State Death Tax Chart—Still Going Strong After Seven Years*, 35 ACTEC L.J. 53 (2009).

[9] *See generally* I.R.C. §§2031–2046; 34A Am. Jur. 2d, *Federal Taxation* ¶143,001 et seq.; Stephens et al., Federal Estate and Gift Taxation ¶¶4.01–4.18 (gross estate) (8th ed. 2002). *See also* Streng, 800 T.M., Estate Planning A-8 (discussing property includible in Gross Estate).

[10] An executor may elect to use an "alternate valuation date" of six months after the date of death, provided the values of the gross estate and the estate tax itself would be lower than what they would be were date of death valuations used. I.R.C. §2032. *See generally* Acker, 855 T.M., Estate and Trust Administration—Tax Planning A-7, A-8, A-9, & A-10 (discussing the §2032 alternate valuation date election).

[11] I.R.C. §2031.

[12] I.R.C. §2031.

[13] I.R.C. §2031.

[14] I.R.C. §2032.

[15] *See* I.R.C. §§2036–2038 (discussing taxability of transfers with retained life estates, transfers taking effect at death, and revocable transfers); Stephens et al., Federal Estate and Gift Taxation ¶¶4.08–4.10 (8th ed. 2006).

value of property that a decedent had gifted out of a revocable inter vivos trust in the three-year period before his or her death to be included in the value of the federal gross estate.[16]) A general understanding of what the tax is about and how it may have influenced the architecture of a particular trust, however, requires some familiarity with the following: (1) the unified credit, (2) the estate tax tables, and (3) the marital deduction.

A frequently updated catalog of state death tax statutes (U.S.), including a current status report on pending state death tax legislation, may be obtained from Charles D. Fox, IV, Esq., McGuireWoods LLP, Court Square Building, 310 Fourth St., N.E., Ste. 300, Charlottesville, VA 22902-1288;[17] tel. 434-977-2597.[18]

§8.9.1.1 The Unified Credit[19]

Under the Internal Revenue Code (the "Code"), the net taxable estate of approximately $675,000 or less for someone dying in 2001 generated no federal estate tax.[20] The number $675,000 is called the "credit equivalent" or "applicable exclusion amount" (or nowadays the "basic exclusion amount") because the Code allowed for 2001 decedents a total "credit" of $220,550 against a person's *aggregate* transfer tax liabilities, *i.e.*, gift tax (lifetime) and estate tax (postdeath).[21] In 2001, this translated into $675,000 worth of property.[22]

For example, assuming no lifetime taxable transfers, the computation of a $220,550 estate tax would have meant no federal estate tax due on the 2001 postmortem otherwise taxable transfer of $675,000. Again, the $675,000 figure was essentially the 2001 economic value of the "unified credit" or "applicable exclusion amount." It was an upper limit on the value of property that could

---

[16] *See* I.R.C. §2035(a) (Certain Gifts Within Three Years of Death Includible in Gross Estate). *But see* A.O.D. 1995-006 (providing that the three-year rule would not be applied by the IRS to donative transfers from a trust under which the deceased settlor had reserved rights of withdrawal).

[17] *See* Charles D. Fox, IV & Adam M. Damerow, *The ACTEC State Death Tax Chart—Still Going Strong After Seven Years*, 35 ACTEC L.J. 53 (2009).

[18] https://www.mcguirewoods.com/Offices/Charlottesville.aspx#professionals (accessed Sept. 19, 2013).

[19] *See generally* Kessler, 844 T.M., Estate Tax Credits and Computations A-1 through A-7 (discussing the §2010 unified credit against the estate tax).

[20] *See* I.R.C. §2010; Stephens et al., Federal Estate and Gift Taxation at ¶ 3.02 (8th ed. 2006) (assuming, in addition, decedent died after 1976 and there are no adjusted taxable gifts).

[21] *See* I.R.C. §2010(a). If the decedent made inter vivos gifts between September 8, 1976 and December 31, 1976, the unified credit is reduced by 20 percent of the portion of the $30,000 gift tax exclusion applicable to gifts made by the decedent during that time. I.R.C. §2010(b).

[22] *See* Stephens et al., Federal Estate and Gift Taxation at ¶ 3.01 (8th ed. 2002). A tax credit operates to reduce the tax directly on a dollar-for-dollar basis. Stephens et al., Federal Estate and Gift Taxation at ¶ 3.01. For 2000, the estate tax on the first $675,000 of taxable estate is $220,550. I.R.C. §2001(c).

pass tax-free in 2001 to someone other than the spouse or a charity.[23] The term *unified* is employed because it applies to both lifetime and postdeath transfers.[24] Thus, anyone who was responsible for preparing and filing a 706 estate tax return for someone who had died in 2001 would have needed to investigate whether the decedent had filed any gift tax returns, because the amount of the applicable exclusion amount that is available postmortem in part depends upon how much of it was "used up" inter vivos.

Portability. The Tax Relief Unemployment Insurance Reauthorization and Job Creation Act (the "2010 Tax Act") provided that if someone died survived by a spouse, the executor of the decedent's estate could elect to transfer any unused portion of the decedent's basic exclusion amount (exemption) to the surviving spouse. That portion augmented the surviving spouse's own unused basic exclusion amount (exemption).

The American Taxpayer Relief Act of 2012 (ATRA-2012) made the portability feature of the tax code permanent.

The applicable exclusion amount has been increasing in yearly increments (Table 8-2). Table 8-2 records the yearly increases in the credit equivalent/applicable exclusion amount/basic exclusion amount that have occurred or are scheduled, beginning with 2001.

Table 8-2. Unified Gift and Estate Tax Credit

In the case of estates of decedents dying, and gifts made, during:	Credit Equivalent/ Applicable Exclusion Amount/ Basic Exclusion Amount
2001	$675,000
2002/2003	$1,000,000
2004 and 2005	$1,500,000
2006, 2007, and 2008	$2,000,000
2009	$3,500,000
2010 [superseded]	No Federal Estate Tax [superseded]
2011 [superseded]	$1,000,000 [superseded]

---

[23] *See* I.R.C. §2010; Stephens et al., Federal Estate and Gift Taxation at ¶ 3.02 (8th ed. 2006) (assuming, in addition, decedent died after 1976 and there are no adjusted taxable gifts).

[24] *See* I.R.C. §2010 (unified transfer tax). Effective for decedents dying after 1976 and gifts made after 1976, the estate and gift tax rates are combined in a single rate schedule. I.R.C. §2010.

On June 7, 2001, the President signed into law the Economic Growth and Tax Relief Act of 2001,[25] which put in place the schedule of accelerated increases in the credit equivalent/applicable exclusion amount, followed by a return to the 2002 amount, that are depicted in Table 8-2.

On December 17, 2010, the 2010 Tax Act was signed into law. It retroactively created an estate tax option (in lieu of carry-over basis) for 2010 decedents and set the credit equivalent/applicable exclusion amount/basic exclusion amount for 2010, 2011, and 2012 at $5, million. In 2013 and beyond, the $5 million amount then drops back to $1 million, the credit equivalent/applicable exclusion amount in effect in 2002. See Table 8-2. The 2010 Tax Act requires that Table 8-2 be modified as follows:

2010 Tax Act Modifications to Table 8-2:

2010 [Estate tax may be elected in lieu of carry-over basis]	$5,000,000
2011	$5,000,000
2012	$5,000,000
2013 and beyond	$1,000,000 [superseded]

> **The American Taxpayer Relief Act of 2012 (AFTRA-2012) made permanent the $5 million per decedent applicable exclusion amount (indexed for inflation) for deaths in 2013 and beyond.**

The gift tax. At one time, the gift tax and the estate tax were fully unified in that they shared a single exemption and were subject to the same rates. In 2002, the available gift tax exemption was capped at $1 million through 2010, the year the estate tax was scheduled for temporary exile. Through 2009, however, the estate and gift tax regimes remained "unified" in the sense that a draw-down of the $1 million was also a draw-down of the overall credit equivalent/applicable exclusion amount. Under the 2010 Tax Act, the two regimes again became fully unified, which means that both regimes shared the same $5 million exemption for 2011 and 2012.

> **The American Taxpayer Relief Act of 2012 (AFTRA-2012) made permanent the $5 million per decedent unified exemption (indexed for inflation) for deaths in 2013 and beyond.**

---

[25] Pub. L. No. 107-16, 107th Cong., 1st Sess. (2001).

§8.9.1.2   The Estate Tax Rates

The federal estate tax rates[26] had been steeply graduated. The highest estate tax rate, however, began dropping in increments: 2002—50 percent, 2003—49 percent, 2004—48 percent, 2005—47 percent, 2006—46 percent, 2007—45 percent, 2008—45 percent, and 2009—45 percent. The 2010 Tax Act set for 2010, 2011, and 2012 a flat 35 percent tax rate above the basic exclusion amount for all states above $500,000.

The American Taxpayer Relief Act of 2012 (AFTRA-2012) increased the top estate and gift tax rate (and the only GST tax rate) to 40% for deaths in 2013 and beyond

---

IT IS IMPORTANT 'TO KEEP IN MIND THAT THE ESTATE TAX REGIME (UNLIKE THE GIFT TAX REGIME[27]) IS "TAX INCLUSIVE." THIS MEANS THAT THE AMOUNT OF THE ESTATE TAX TO BE PAID IS INCLUDED IN THE COMPUTATION OF THE "TAXABLE ESTATE." THUS IT IS SAID THAT THE ESTATE TAX IS, IN PART, A "TAX ON A TAX."[28]

§8.9.1.3   The Marital Deduction[29]

Foreshadowing the spousal deduction in the U.S. tax code, the seventh clause of the Magna Carta specifies that: after her husband's death, a widow shall have her marriage portion and her inheritance at once and without hindrance; nor shall she pay anything for her dower, her marriage portion, or her inheritance which she and her husband held on the day of her husband's death. . . .[30]

Finally, the . . . [settlor] . . . may choose to approximate the effect of a . . . [marital deduction-] . . . formula clause by making a pecuniary nonmarital deduction (or credit shelter) gift of an amount equal to the credit equivalent and leaving the balance of his or her estate to the surviving spouse. While this approach may not yield the optimum tax result, it is simple and easy to understand.[31]

---

[26] I.R.C. §2001(c). For a comparison of the U.S. estate tax rate structure with the estate tax rate structures of other countries, *see* Geoff Winestock, *Other Nations' Levies Make U.S. Look Bad—and Good*, N.Y. Times, Feb. 26, 2001, at C13, col. 5.

[27] Note, however, that "[t]he amount of gift tax paid by the decedent (or the decedent's estate) on any gift made by the decedent (or the decedent's spouse) within three years of death is included in a decedent's gross estate, regardless of whether the gift with respect to which the gift tax was paid is includible in the gross estate under §2035." Streng, 800 T.M., Estate Planning A-67 (referring to I.R.C. §2035(c)).

[28] *See generally*, Kunes, *More Blessed to Give Than to Devise* 10 Prob. & Prop. 20 (Sept./Oct. 1996).

[29] *See generally*, Pennell, 843 T.M., Estate Tax Marital Deduction.

[30] Margo Thorning, *The U.S. Tax Code in the 21st Century: Does the Estate Tax Fit?*, Special Report, American Council for Capital Formation (Mar. 2004).

[31] John R. Price, Price on Contemporary Estate Planning §5.32 (2d ed. 2000).

The value of property passing to the settlor's surviving spouse is not considered part of the taxable estate.[32] It is "deducted" from the gross estate. For property to be eligible for the marital deduction, it either must pass outright to the surviving spouse or must be transferred to a trust in such a way as to bring about its functional equivalent.[33] For example, a transfer to a trust of which the spouse is a mandatory income beneficiary and under which the spouse is given a general power of appointment qualifies for the marital deduction. The concept here is that the estate of the surviving spouse will pay for the favorable tax treatment afforded the estate of the first to die. For special rules that are applicable if the surviving spouse is not a U.S. citizen, see Section 9.14 of this handbook (the qualified domestic trust (QDOT)).

The transfer to a surviving spouse of a fully vested equitable remainder interest under a trust also would qualify for the marital deduction. Thus, the predeceasing spouse could provide by testamentary trust or revocable inter vivos trust that upon his or her death, child X shall receive an equitable life estate and the surviving spouse shall receive a fully vested equitable remainder. Needless to say, this is not a utilization of the marital deduction that one encounters often. It is usually the other way around, the surviving spouse receiving at least an equitable life estate and the children receiving equitable remainders, albeit ones that are usually ultra-contingent.

There is one major exception to the requirement that the surviving spouse must be given the functional equivalent of full control over the disposition of the property—either inter vivos or postmortem—in order for the transfer to qualify for the marital deduction: When the surviving spouse is given a qualified terminable interest in the decedent's property.[34] This is what the so-called QTIP trust is all about.[35] Generally, a terminable interest that passes to a surviving spouse will not qualify for the marital deduction, unless it has been coupled with a general inter vivos power of appointment. A terminable interest is an interest that passes to a person other than the surviving spouse upon the lapse of time or the occurrence of an event.[36] An equitable life estate would be a terminable interest.

Property that is entrusted by a predeceasing spouse is eligible for QTIP treatment if (1) *during the lifetime of the surviving spouse*, the surviving spouse has the right to all the net trust accounting income in all events,[37] (2) only the surviving spouse, if anyone, would have a right to the principal while he or she

---

[32] I.R.C. §2056(a).

[33] *See* Stephens et al., Federal Estate and Gift Taxation at ¶5.06[2] (8th ed. 2006).

[34] *See* Stephens et al., Federal Estate and Gift Taxation at ¶5.06[8] (discussing terminable interests qualifying for marital deduction).

[35] Stephens et al., Federal Estate and Gift Taxation at ¶5.06[8]. *See generally* Sebastian V. Grassi, Jr., *Estate Planning with QTIP Trusts after the 2001 Tax Act*, 30 ACTEC L.J. 111 (2004).

[36] Treas. Reg. §20.2056(b)-1(b).

[37] *See, however*, Treas. Reg. §§20.2056(b)-7(d)(4) and 25.2523(f)-1(c)(1)(ii) (providing that for a trust to qualify for QTIP status, stub income need not be paid into the spouse beneficiary's probate estate upon his or her death but may be added to principal or paid to successor beneficiaries). Stub income is income accrued between the date of the last distribution to the spouse beneficiary and the date of the spouse beneficiary's death.

is alive,[38] and (3) the surviving spouse is authorized to direct the trustee to convert unproductive property into income-producing property.[39] If these major conditions are satisfied, *upon the death of the surviving spouse*, the property may pass to a person or persons who the deceased settlor had designated (often the children by a first marriage).

If the trust is QTIP-eligible, generally it is the settlor's executor who elects to have a portion or all of the property in the QTIP trust treated as marital deduction property under Code Section 2056(b)(7).[40] The piper, of course, must then be paid. Upon the death of the surviving spouse, the *balance* remaining in the QTIP-elected[41] trust must be included in the estate of the surviving spouse for tax purposes.[42] The estate, however, may recover from the QTIP trust amounts necessary to pay the estate tax attributable to the inclusion of the value of the QTIP's assets in the computation of the total estate tax liability, unless the will or the revocable trust of the now deceased surviving spouse specifically provides that the liability attributable to the QTIP assets is to be satisfied from some other source, such as from the now deceased surviving spouse's probate estate or from the assets of his or her revocable trust.[43] For more on the apportionment of estate taxes upon the death of a QTIP trust income beneficiary, the reader is referred to Section 8.20 of this handbook.

Assume that a husband dies survived by his wife. How much of his property goes into the marital deduction trust, *e.g.*, a QTIP trust, and how much into the credit shelter trust? All things being equal, enough goes into the marital deduction trust so that there is no federal estate tax due, but not so much so as

---

[38] Treas. Reg. §20.2056(b)-1(b).

[39] Treas. Reg. §20.2056(b)-5(f)(5) (also providing that the trustee could resolve the unproductive asset problem by tapping other trusts' assets to make up for any deficiencies in trust accounting income). *See generally* §6.2.2.4 of this handbook (the noncharitable unitrust (total return trust): investment considerations).

[40] *See* Stephens et al., Federal Estate and Gift Taxation at ¶ 5.06[8][d][iii] (8th ed. 2002). *See generally* §8.16 of this handbook (the trustee of revocable trust as "inadvertent executor"). The election is made on Schedule M of the settlor's federal estate tax Form 706. "Under the terms of a *Clayton*-style QTIP trust, if a personal representative fails to make a QTIP election over all or a portion of the trust property, then that property (or portion thereof) will be disposed of in an alternative disposition that typically would not qualify for a marital deduction such as to a wholly discretionary trust for the benefit of a spouse and other beneficiaries." Jonathan E. Gopman, *Optimizing Asset Protection with QTIPs*, 15(6) Prob. Prac. Rep. 4 (June 2003). *See* Estate of Clayton v. Comm'r, 976 F.2d 1486 (1992). *See generally* §3.5.3.4 of this handbook (the trustee's power to disclaim a fiduciary power). *Cf.* Spencer v. Comm'r, 43 F.3d 226 (1995) (property "appointed" by decedent's executrix to a QTIP trust before QTIP election was made was QTIP property qualifying for the marital deduction).

[41] *See generally* Berteau, Gregoria & Seitl, 822 T.M., Estate and Gift Tax Returns and Audits A-49 (discussing GST exemption allocations and reverse QTIP elections).

[42] *See* Stephens et al., Federal Estate and Gift Taxation ¶ ¶ 4.01–4.18 (gross estate) (8th ed. 2006).

[43] *Cf., e.g.*, In re Estate of Klarner, 98 P.3d 892 (Colo. Ct. App. 2003) (holding that in Colorado, to be effective, a waiver of a statutory right to recover *state* estate taxes attributable to QTIP property need not make express reference to the QTIP liability). Overruled on appeal. *See* In re Estate of Klarner, 113 P.3d 150 (Colo. 2005).

to cause his unified credit to be underutilized.[44] If his unified credit is underutilized, more estate taxes may have to be paid upon her death than would otherwise have to be paid had his unified credit been fully utilized.

How is the amount that is to fund the marital deduction trust generally determined? A formula is set forth in the estate planning documentation, *e.g.*, in the revocable inter vivos trust instrument or in the will if the trusts are to be testamentary. Funding formulas are of two general types, pecuniary and fractional.

A pecuniary amount formula instructs the fiduciary to place a specific amount in the marital deduction trust. A fractional formula instructs the fiduciary to fund the marital deduction trust with a fractional interest in a pool of assets on a "pro rata" or "pick and choose basis."[45]

A pecuniary funding may be satisfied by cash. It also may be satisfied with noncash assets, *i.e.*, "in kind." If the fiduciary sells assets in order to fund the marital or QTIP with cash, then there may be capital gains consequences.

If the pecuniary funding is accomplished by an "in kind" allocation of property, then how and when may the property be valued and what property may be selected? One method is to value the assets as of the date of distribution. This is known as the "true worth" method. There is also the estate tax value method. If estate tax values are used, then there are no capital gains income tax consequences because the tax cost basis of an asset is set at its estate tax value. The fiduciary, however, could have a "64-19 problem":

> [the non-recognition of a gain or loss] . . . tempted fiduciaries to allocate assets that had declined in value to the marital share and assets that had increased in value to the other beneficiaries. Such an allocation was made in order to minimize the amount of property includible in the estate of the surviving spouse. . . . The IRS responded by issuing Revenue Procedure 64-19, 1964 C.B. 682. . . . [I]t provides . . . [in part] . . . that . . . the fiduciary "must distribute assets, including cash, fairly representative of appreciation or depreciation in the value of all property thus available for distribution in satisfaction of such pecuniary bequest or transfer."[46]

And then there is the "minimum value method" under which "assets distributed in kind . . . [to satisfy a pecuniary allocation] . . . have an aggregate fair market value on the date or dates of distribution no lower than the amount of the pecuniary marital deduction gift."[47]

The prospective trustee should carefully scrutinize the marital deduction formula clause in the proposed governing instrument. He should take a good hard look at the asset valuation and funding instructions. All contingencies

---

[44] When the credit shelter is underutilized, the marital deduction trust is said to be "overfunded."

[45] A gain or loss for capital gains income tax purposes is not recognized when a fractional share allocation is made. Treas. Reg. §§1.661(a)-2(f), 1.1014-4(a)(3).

[46] John R. Price, Price on Contemporary Estate Planning §5.37.3 (2d ed. 2000).

[47] Price, Price on Contemporary Estate Planning at §5.37.4.

should be addressed. There should be no gaps and/or ambiguities. When in doubt, the prospective trustee should run the instrument past counsel.

For a discussion of the pros and cons of selecting one marital deduction funding formula over another, as well as a selection of sample pecuniary and fractional formula clauses, the reader is referred to Price.[48] Professor Price's treatise also covers the income tax aspects of a formula fractional gift.[49] The reader also is referred to Sebastian V. Grassi, Jr.[50]

What does all this mean when it comes to the trustee? It means that a trustee may find himself administering several trusts created by the same settlor for the same person. For example, the governing instrument may call for a "bypass" trust to administer the credit equivalent property and a QTIP trust to handle the rest, with the surviving spouse being the primary beneficiary of both.[51] Why more than one trust? Because the settlor wants to keep the property in the credit equivalent "bypass" trust from being taxed again upon the death of the surviving spouse. If the surviving spouse has some property of his or her own, then those steeply graduated estate tax rates may well make the several-trust strategy an economically viable one.

Moreover, once the trusts are up and running, the trustee with an invasion right may want to draw down the principal of the QTIP trust before tapping the principal of the "bypass" trust and to invest the "bypass" trust more for growth and the QTIP more for income. Both strategies are designed to minimize the aggregate amount of estate tax liability resulting from the deaths of the settlor and his or her spouse.

§8.9.2. *The Generation-Skipping Transfer Tax*

The establishment of a trust which would skip generations, often available under foreign trust structures, is not available in Israel. Therefore, . . . [in Israel,] . . . there is a need for probate proceedings in order to achieve the settlor's goal of creating a trust that will exist for a number of generations.—Alon Kaplan, Tel Aviv, Israel, September 2005[52]

---

[48] Price, Price on Contemporary Estate Planning at §§5.10–5.40.

[49] Price, Price on Contemporary Estate Planning at §5.39.

[50] *A Practical Guide to Drafting Marital Deduction Trusts*, ALI-ABA 2004.

[51] For starters, the trustee needs to be attentive to which asset is allocated to which trust. Let us assume that a "pecuniary formula" marital deduction trust could be funded with assets that are valued as of the date of the decedent's death. If that were the case, the executor or trustee would have a tax avoidance incentive to allocate those assets that had declined in value to the marital deduction trust and those assets that had appreciated in value to the credit shelter or family trust. Why? All things being equal, less economic value would then be subject to the estate tax upon the death of the surviving spouse. Unfortunately, under Rev. Proc. 64-19, such cherry picking would disqualify the marital deduction. There are three exceptions: (1) If the marital deduction trust were allocated a fractional share of all assets, (2) if the marital deduction trust were allocated items that fairly represented those assets that had increased in value and those assets that had decreased in value, or (3) if all allocations were made at date of death values.

[52] *See generally* Harrington & Acker, 850 T.M., Generation-Skipping Tax.

The generation-skipping transfer tax. The U.S. federal generation-skipping transfer (GST) tax is imposed on transfers that skip the generation immediately below the transferor.[53] In the context of trusts, a GST event could be triggered when a settlor creates a trust for his or her grandchildren, when the trustee makes a distribution of income or principal to the grandchildren, or when the trust terminates in favor of them.[54] The GST tax rate had been 55 percent.[55] From 2002 through 2010, the GST tax rate descended in increments from 50 percent to 35 percent. The 2010 Tax Act had set the GST tax rate at 35 percent for 2011 and 2012.

> **The American Taxpayer Relief Act of 2012 (ATRA-2012) increased the GST tax rate to 40%.**

In 2003, the Code allowed each transferor a $1,120,000 GST exemption, which could be "spent" by the transferor during life to exempt lifetime GSTs or "saved" until death to exempt testamentary GSTs.[56] From year 2004 through year 2010, the GST exemption incrementally moved up in tandem with the estate tax exemption equivalent.[57] The 2010 Tax Act had set the GST exemption for 2011 and 2012 at $5 million, with no portability.

> **The American Taxpayer Relief Act of 2012 (ATRA-2012) made permanent the $5 million GST exemption (indexed for inflation after 2010).**

The interaction of the estate and generation-skipping tax regimes. It should be kept in mind that an estate (or gift) tax *and* a GST tax can be assessed simultaneously against a single transfer. Let us take a year 2001 $4 million direct skip to a grandchild by a decedent who has previously exhausted his unified credit and GST exemption. Assuming a 55 percent estate tax rate and a 55 percent GST tax with respect to the transfer, can there be anything left? Yes, there can. This is because the GST percentage is applied against the $4 million *net of the estate tax*. Moreover, the GST tax on direct skips is "tax exclusive." Thus, the total transfer tax bill on the gross $4 million is in round numbers $2,838,710 or 70.97 percent.[58] The net amount ultimately received by the grandchild is $1,161,290.[59]

---

[53] I.R.C. §§2601, 2611. *See generally* Bogert, Trusts and Trustees §284.

[54] *See generally* Stephens et al., Federal Estate and Gift Taxation ¶¶13.01–13.03 (8th ed. 2002).

[55] *See* I.R.C. §2641(b) (GST tax rate equals the maximum federal estate tax rate).

[56] I.R.C. §2631. *See generally* Stephens et al., Federal Estate and Gift Taxation at ¶¶15.01–15.03 (8th ed. 2002) (generation-skipping transfer exemption).

[57] I.R.C. §2631(c), as amended by the Economic Growth and Tax Relief Reconciliation Act of 2001.

[58] Harrington & Acker, 850 T.M., Generation-Skipping Tax A-58 (1996).

[59] Harrington & Acker, 850 T.M., Generation-Skipping Tax A-58 (1996).

Tax considerations in the administration of a constellation of related trusts. With the GST exemption in mind, a settlor might well provide for the creation of several trusts upon the settlor's death, with one to be fully exempt from the GST tax. It alone would be allocated the entire available GST exemption. In other words, it would have a zero inclusion ratio.[60] Thus, along with the "bypass" trust and the QTIP trust, the trustee would be administering a third trust: a GST "exempt" trust. Still, all three trusts would have been created by the same settlor, and their dispositive terms typically would be similar, if not identical.

The trustee in this situation will need to take a system-wide approach when it comes to formulating investment strategies and making principal distributions. Generation-skipping principal distributions should probably be made from an exempt trust. When principal distributions to the surviving spouse are in order, the trustee probably should draw down the nonexempt QTIP trust before looking elsewhere. The trustee should probably first exhaust the nonexempt "bypass" trust if principal distributions to the children are in order. In formulating these strategies, the trustee needs to at least understand the tax strategies that gave rise to the system of trusts that he finds himself administering.[61] Certainly, the trustee does not want to generate tax liabilities inadvertently.[62]

§8.9.3   *Tax-Sensitive Powers*

If the settlor impresses a trust upon property and reserves to himself or bestows on his spouse an income[63] interest that is either vested or subject to the trustee's exercise of discretion, the income generated by the trust property is taxable to the settlor; and upon the settlor's death, provided the settlor reserved a vested interest in the income, the then value of the principal is taken into account in the computation of the estate tax.[64]

If the settlor, the beneficiary, or a third party possessed at the time of death a *general inter vivos or testamentary power of appointment*, the trust property may be included in that person's federal gross estate for tax purposes even if the power was not exercised.[65] There also may be adverse estate tax consequences if a settlor-trustee or a beneficiary-trustee possessed at the time of *death a power not*

---

[60] *See generally* Jonathan G. Blattmachr & Diana S. C. Zeydal, *Adventures in Allocating GST Exemption in Different Scenarios*, 35 Est. Plan. 3 (Apr. 2008).

[61] *See, e.g.,* UTC §814(b) (available at <http://www.uniformlaws.org/Act.aspx?title=Trust%20Code>) (rewriting the terms of a trust that might otherwise result in adverse estate and gift tax consequences to a beneficiary-trustee).

[62] *See generally* Mark L. Ascher, *The Fiduciary Duty to Minimize Taxes*, 20 Real Prop. Prob. & Tr. J. 663 (1985).

[63] The grantor of a trust is treated as its owner and taxed on its income if the trust income is distributed actually or constructively to the grantor's spouse. I.R.C. §§671–677.

[64] I.R.C. §§677 (income tax), I.R.C. §2036(a) (estate tax). For more on the income tax consequences, the reader is referred to Zaritsky, 858-2d T.M., Grantor Trusts: Sections 671–679.

[65] I.R.C. §§2041(a)(2), 2041(b)(1).

limited by an ascertainable standard to determine who would enjoy the equitable interest.[66] These powers are generally disclaimable.[67]

A settlor's retained power, in a nonfiduciary capacity, to remove items of property from the trust and replace them with other items, a so-called power of substitution, in and of itself will not generally cause the trust corpus to be included in the settlor's taxable estate under Sections 2036 and 2038 of the Code, provided the trustee has a fiduciary duty to ensure that (1) the property acquired and substituted is in fact of equivalent value and (2) the substitution power cannot be exercised to shift benefits among the trust beneficiaries.[68]

Similar rules apply in the income tax context where the settlor has reserved the power to control disposition of trust property, revoke, or amend the trust.[69] A power to revoke the trust, a form of general inter vivos power of appointment, also will cause capital gains realized on the sale of trust assets to be taxable to the powerholder.[70] On the other hand, the power to dispose of property via one's will, a general testamentary power of appointment, will not subject the powerholder to *income* tax liability, although as noted above there could be estate tax consequences.[71] If the holder of a tax-sensitive power renounces it or allows it to lapse, a gift tax may be due.[72]

In the next section we have a checklist of questions designed to assist the domestic trustee in identifying *tax-sensitive powers*. If the answer to any question is "yes," the settlor (or his or her estate) or the holder of the power (or his or her estate) *may be subject to a tax liability*. Further investigation is then in order. The trustee should understand that in the tax area, powers of appointment are not always clearly labeled as such. For example, the express reservation of the right to "demand" principal is a tax-sensitive power of appointment even though the term "power of appointment" is not employed. For a more in-depth treatment of the subject of tax-sensitive powers, the reader is referred to Akers and Holt.[73]

It should be noted that the Uniform Trust Code does not generally address the subject of tax-curative provisions.[74] It does, however, put certain

---

[66] I.R.C. §§2036, 2038, 2041. In New York, by legislation, a trustee may not make discretionary distributions of either principal or income to himself as beneficiary, with the following exceptions: The governing instrument provides otherwise; the trust is revocable and the trustee is the settlor; or the discretionary authority is constrained by an ascertainable standard. N.Y. Est. Powers & Trusts Law §§10–10.1. *See generally* 3 Scott & Ascher §18.2.5 (Trustee with Discretionary Power to Distribute to Self). *See* Treas. Reg. §25.2514-1(c) (ascertainable standards that negate the characterization of a trustee power as a personal general power for tax purposes; discretionary distributions to satisfy trustee's own legal obligations).

[67] *See generally* §5.5 of this handbook (disclaiming equitable interests under trusts). *See also* Treas. Reg. §25.2518-2(e).

[68] Treas. Reg. §2008-22.

[69] I.R.C. §674 (retained control over beneficial interests—income tax).

[70] I.R.C. §§671, 676.

[71] I.R.C. §§674(b)(3) (income tax), §2041(a)(2) (estate tax).

[72] *See, e.g.,* Treas. Reg. §25.2511-2(f); I.R.C. §2041(b)(2).

[73] Steve R. Akers & Eric S. Holt, *Structuring Trustee Powers to Avoid a Tax Catastrophe*, Denver Estate Planning Council, Sept. 18, 2008 (Bessemer Trust Company, N.A.).

[74] UTC §814 cmt. (available at <http://www.uniformlaws.org/Act.aspx?title=Trust%20 Code>).

default law limitations on a beneficiary-trustee's exercise of discretion.[75] Why? Because "the unintended inclusion of the trust in the beneficiary-trustee's gross estate is a frequent enough occurrence that the drafters concluded that it is a topic that . . . [the] . . . Code should address."[76] Accordingly, the Uniform Trust Code provides that "a person other than a settlor who is a beneficiary and trustee of a trust that confers on the trustee power to make discretionary distributions to or for the trustee's personal benefit may exercise the power only in accordance with an ascertainable standard relating to the trustee's individual health, education, support, or maintenance within the meaning of Section 2041(b)(1)(A) or 2514(c)(1) of the Internal Revenue Code. . . ."[77]

In the future, the discretionary trust may not be as impervious to creditor attack as has traditionally been the case.[78] The reader's attention is called to the Restatement (Third) of Trusts Section 60 and the accompanying commentary. Section 60 provides as follows:

> Subject to the rules stated in §§58 and 59 (on spendthrift trusts), if the terms of a trust provide for a beneficiary to receive distributions in the trustee's discretion, a transferee or creditor of the beneficiary is entitled to receive or attach any distributions the trustee makes or is required to make in the exercise of that discretion after the trustee has knowledge of the transfer or attachment. The amounts a creditor can reach may be limited to provide for the beneficiary's needs (Comment c), or the amounts may be increased where the beneficiary either is the settlor (Comment f) or holds the discretionary power to determine his or her own distributions (Comment g).[79]

Comment g provides that if the nonsettlor beneficiary is the trustee of a discretionary trust with authority to determine his or her benefits, the beneficiary's creditors may reach from time to time the maximum amount the trustee-beneficiary can properly take. An ability of a nonsettlor beneficiary-trustee to run up debts and have them satisfied from the trust estate is likely to

---

[75] UTC §814(b) (available at <http://www.uniformlaws.org/Act.aspx?title=Trust%20Code>). So does Virginia. *See* Va. Code §§64.1–67.2.

[76] UTC§814 cmt. (available at <http://www.uniformlaws.org/Act.aspx?title=Trust%20Code>).

[77] UTC §814(b) (available at <http://www.uniformlaws.org/Act.aspx?title=Trust%20Code>). *See generally* 3 Scott & Ascher §18.2.5 (Trustee with Discretionary Power to Distribute to Self).

[78] *See generally* §5.3.3.3(a) of this handbook (the non–self-settled discretionary trust and creditor access).

[79] *But see* Alaska Stat. §34.40.110(h) (providing that under Alaska law, a spendthrift provision is valid even though the beneficiary is named as the sole trustee of the trust). If the beneficiary is appointed as the sole trustee, Alaska law provides that trust distributions can only be made in accordance with an ascertainable standard that relates to the beneficiary's health, education, maintenance or support. Alaska Stat. §13.36.153. *See generally* §8.15.15 of this handbook (the ascertainable standard).

be construed by the taxing authorities as a constructive general inter vivos power of appointment.[80]

In 2004 the drafters of the Uniform Trust Code, out of concern that "adoption of the Restatement rule...[embedded in Comment g]...would unduly disrupt standard estate planning,"[81] added the following neutralizing language to Section 504 of the Trust Code:

> If the trustee's or cotrustee's discretion to make distributions for the trustee's or cotrustee's own benefit is limited by an ascertainable standard, a creditor may not reach or compel distribution of the beneficial interest except to the extent the interest would be subject to the creditor's claim were the beneficiary not acting as trustee or cotrustee.[82]

As an aside, the Uniform *Probate* Code would establish an analogous matrix of "sensitive" powers that could expose the value of any subject property to inclusion in some UPC "augmented estate" for spousal election purposes. For more on the subject of spousal-election-sensitive powers, the reader is referred to the Comment to Section 2-205 of the Uniform Probate Code. For a discussion of spousal election generally, see Section 5.3.4.1 of this handbook.

Whether or not a power is exercisable with the joinder of an adverse party may well have tax implications. Who would qualify as an adverse party in this context is taken up in Section 8.15.83 of this handbook.

§8.9.3.1   A Checklist for Settlors

It was during this period of intense work in the field of powers of appointment that the famous verbal exchange took place between Bart Leach and Erwin Griswold. Griswold published an article entitled Powers of Appointment and the Federal Estate Tax in 1939.[83] *The thrust of this article was that the donee of a power of appointment, whether general or, with some suggested modifications, special, should be taxed for federal estate and gift tax purposes as though he owned the appointive assets, whether the power was exercised or not. Bart filed a dissent,*[84] *pointing out the great utility of powers of appointment in providing flexible family plans and abhorring the development of the tax laws in a way that would drive family plans into fixed and rigid molds. He observed that those who tinker with powers had better be lawyers rather than ribbon clerks.*[85] *In a reply,*[86] *Griswold responded that [t]he elimination*

---

[80] *See generally* §8.1 of this handbook (powers of appointment). *Cf.* §4.1.3 of this handbook (discussing the constructive inter vivos power of appointment in the context of self-settled discretionary trusts).

[81] UTC §504 cmt. (available at <http://www.uniformlaws.org/Act.aspx?title=Trust%20 Code>).

[82] UTC §504(e) (available at <http://www.uniformlaws.org/Act.aspx?title=Trust%20 Code>).

[83] Griswold, *Powers of Appointment and the Federal Estate Tax*, 52 Harv. L. Rev. 929 (1939).

[84] Leach, *Powers of Appointment and the Federal Estate Tax—A Dissent*, 52 Harv. L. Rev. 961 (1939).

[85] Leach, *Powers of Appointment and the Federal Estate Tax—A Dissent*, 52 Harv. L. Rev. 961, 961 (1939).

[86] Griswold, *In Reply*, 52 Harv. L. Rev. 967 (1939).

of discrimination and loopholes from our tax laws does not necessarily come from . . . the viewpoint of a ribbon clerk.[87]—In Memoriam: W Barton Leach.[88]

The Estate Tax

At the time of the settlor's death[89] . . .

(1) Did the settlor have the power to revoke the trust and get back the trust property?

(2) Did the settlor, alone or with another person, have the power to direct the property to the settlor's creditors or to someone whom the settlor had an obligation to support?

(3) Did the settlor have the power to direct the property by will to the settlor's estate?

(4) Did the settlor have the power to direct the property by will to the creditors of the settlor's estate?

(5) Did the settlor's creditors have access to income or principal?

(6) Did the settlor *as trustee* have *unlimited* discretion to apply income and/or invade principal for the benefit of *persons other than the settlor*?[90]

(7) Did the settlor as trustee of a trust of which the settlor was not a beneficiary have unlimited discretion to pay or accumulate income?[91]

(8) Did the settlor have the power to amend the trust?[92]

(9) Did the settlor possess in a nonfiduciary capacity a limited (special) inter vivos power of appointment?[93]

(10) Did the settlor reserve a power to remove the trustee and appoint a successor trustee who is related or subordinate to the settlor within the meaning of Code Section 672(c)?[94]

(11) Did the settlor have the right, alone or in conjunction with any person, to designate the persons who shall possess or enjoy the trust property or the income therefrom?[95]

---

[87] Griswold, *In Reply*, 52 Harv. L. Rev. 967 (1939).

[88] A. James Casner, *In Memoriam: W. Barton Leach*, 85 Harv. L. Rev. 717 (1972).

[89] Note an exception: the value of the following transfers, releases, and exercises that occur within three years of death are included in the value of the federal gross estate for estate tax computation purposes: (1) transfers of life insurance by the insured, (2) releases or exercises of general powers of appointment, and (3) releases of certain powers over retained property interests. *See* I.R.C. §2035(a).

[90] *See generally* Louis S. Harrison, *Structuring Trusts to Permit the Donor to Act as Trustee*, 22(6) Est. Planning 331 (Nov./Dec. 1995). *See also* §7.3.4.3 of this handbook (when death of a trustee who possessed no beneficial interest in the trust will subject the trust property to federal estate tax liability).

[91] I.R.C. §2036.

[92] I.R.C. §2038.

[93] I.R.C. §2036.

[94] *See* Rev. Rul. 95-58, 1995-2 C.B 191. *See generally* §3.2.6 of this handbook (considerations in the selection of a trustee) (in discussing the office of trust protector).

[95] I.R.C. §2036(a)(2). Thus, a reserved limited testamentary power of appointment could generate adverse estate tax consequences upon the death of the settlor. *See* Priv. Ltr. Rul.

(12) Did the trustee have an obligation under the terms of the trust to discharge legal obligations of the settlor with trust property?[96]

The Income Tax

During the settlor's lifetime . . .[97]

(1) Can the settlor or the settlor's spouse get at the trust property by revocation, amendment, or otherwise?

(2) Does the settlor or the settlor's spouse, *as trustee*, have *sole and unlimited discretion* to apply income and/or invade principal for the benefit of a class of *persons other than the settlor?*

(3) Does the settlor or the settlor's spouse possess in a nonfiduciary capacity a limited (special) inter vivos power of appointment?

(4) Does the settlor, the settlor's spouse, or a nonadverse party possess in a nonfiduciary capacity even a limited right to reacquire or acquire the trust property by substituting assets of equivalent value?[98]

(5) Does a trustee having no beneficial interest in the trust have the discretion without the consent of an adverse party to pay income directly to the settlor or the settlor's spouse?[99]

(6) Does the settlor or the settlor's spouse have the power to direct the trustee to invest in an entity that he or she controls?

(7) Does the settlor or the settlor's spouse have voting control over a trust investment?

(8) Has the settlor retained a reversionary interest?

(9) May the trustee use trust income to pay premiums on policies of insurance on the life of the settlor or the settlor's spouse?[100]

200502014 (Jan. 14, 2005). The power in a settlor to change the charitable remainder beneficiary of a charitable remainder trust when someone other than the settlor (or perhaps the settlor's spouse) is the income beneficiary could be a tax-sensitive power. *See* Rev. Rul. 76-8, 1976-1 CB 179. So also could be a retained power in the settlor of a charitable lead trust to designate or alter the charitable beneficiaries. *See* Priv. Ltr. Rul. 200328030 (CLT). *See generally* §8.15.9 of this handbook (doctrine of [facts or acts of] independent legal significance) (suggesting that the settlor's ability to alter the terms of an irrevocable trust by conceiving or adopting a child would not rise to the level of a tax-sensitive power).

[96] Rev. Rul. 2004-64 (addressing the potential adverse estate tax consequences upon the death of the settlor of an intentionally defective grantor trust if the trustee is obligated to satisfy with the trust property the income tax liability of the settlor).

[97] *See generally* Zaritsky, 858-2d T.M., Grantor Trusts: Sections 671–679. *See also* §9.1 of this handbook (the grantor trust).

[98] Priv. Ltr. Rul. 200434012 (Aug. 20, 2004). Who would qualify as an adverse party in this context is taken up in Section 8.15.83 of this handbook.

[99] Who would qualify as an adverse party in this context is taken up in Section 8.15.83 of this handbook.

[100] I.R.C. §677(a)(3). Note, however, that the trustee's power to use trust income to pay premiums on policies of insurance on the life of the grantor would not be tax-sensitive if the proceeds are irrevocably payable for a charitable purpose.

(10) Do the terms of the governing instrument provide that income and/or principal shall or may be paid to the settlor or the settlor's spouse?[101]

(11) Can the settlor's creditors gain access to the trust income or principal?

(12) May the settlor borrow the income and/or principal without adequate interest or security?

§8.9.3.2 A Checklist for Nonsettlors

The Estate Tax

At the time of the nonsettlor's death . . .

(1) Could the nonsettlor have terminated the trust and gained unrestricted access to the trust property?

(2) Could the nonsettlor have directed the trust property to the nonsettlor's creditors?[102]

(3) Could the nonsettlor have directed the property by will to the nonsettlor's estate?

(4) Could the nonsettlor have directed the property by will to the creditors of the nonsettlor's estate?

(5) Did the nonsettlor, *as trustee*, have sole discretion, *unlimited by an ascertainable standard such as health, education, support, or maintenance*, to invade principal for the nonsettlor's benefit?[103]

---

[101] *See* I.R.C. §677. If, for example, a settlor were to establish a lifetime QTIP trust for the benefit of his or her spouse, the trust would be deemed a grantor trust as to the trust accounting income. *See generally* §8.9.1.3 of this handbook (the marital deduction) (noting that one of the conditions for a trust having QTIP status is that all net trust accounting income must be paid to the spouse and only the spouse). Were the trustee to have authority to invade principal for the benefit of the spouse, the QTIP also would be deemed a grantor trust for capital gains income tax purposes.

[102] *See, e.g.*, Restatement (Third) of Trusts §60 cmt. g, which provides that when a nonsettlor is a trustee-beneficiary of a discretionary trust with authority to determine his or her benefits, his or her creditors may reach from time to time the maximum amount the trustee-beneficiary can properly take.

[103] *See generally* 3 Scott & Ascher §18.2.5 (Trustee with Discretionary Power to Distribute to Self). *But see* UTC §814(b)(1) (available at <http://www.uniformlaws.org/Act.aspx?title=Trust%20Code>) (providing that a person other than a settlor who is a beneficiary and trustee of a trust that confers on the trustee a power to make discretionary distributions to or for the trustee's personal benefit may exercise the power only in accordance with an ascertainable standard relating to the trustee's individual health, education, support, or maintenance within the meaning of §2041(b)(1)(A) or 2514(c)(1) of the Internal Revenue Code). *See generally* §8.15.15 of this handbook (the ascertainable standard).

Miscellaneous Topics of General Interest to the Trustee **§8.10**

(6) Did the nonsettlor, as trustee, have sole discretion, *whether or not limited by an ascertainable standard*, to invade principal for the benefit of someone to whom the trustee owed a legal obligation of support?[104]

The Income Tax[105]

During the nonsettlor's lifetime . . .

(1) Does the nonsettlor as trustee-beneficiary have unlimited access to trust corpus or income?
(2) Does the nonsettlor possess the power to amend or revoke the trust?
(3) Does the nonsettlor possess a general inter vivos power of appointment?
(4) Has the nonsettlor released a general inter vivos power of appointment?
(5) Has the nonsettlor sole trustee made an actual distribution of trust income to discharge a legal obligation of the trustee?
(6) Does the nonsettlor sole trustee possess the power to use the trust property to discharge his nonsupport legal obligations?
(7) Does the beneficiary possess the power to use trust property to discharge his or her nonsupport legal obligations?

§8.10 Fiduciary Principles Applicable to the Mutual Fund

Basic fiduciary duty too often has been forgotten in the high-voltage, high-velocity financial environment that has emerged in recent decades . . . the notion of financial trusteeship is frequently lost in the shuffle.[1]

---

[104] *See* Treas. Reg. §20.2041-1(c)(1) (providing that the ascertainable exception applies only to distributions for the benefit of the decedent, not to distributions to those to whom the decedent owes a legal obligation of support). *But see* UTC §814(b)(2) (available at <http://www.uniformlaws.org/Act.aspx?title=Trust%20Code>) (providing that a trustee may not exercise a power to make discretionary distributions to satisfy a legal obligation of support that the trustee personally owes another person). *See generally* 3 Scott & Ascher §18.2.5 (Trustee with Discretionary Power to Distribute to Self) (suggesting that "thoughtful drafters . . . generally prohibit the exercise of discretionary fiduciary powers in satisfaction of any legal obligation of the trustee"); §8.15.15 of this handbook (the ascertainable standard).

[105] *See generally* Zaritsky, 858-2d T.M., Grantor Trusts: Sections 671–679; Jonathan G. Blattmachr, Mitchell M. Gans, Alvina H. Lo, A Beneficiary as Trust Owner: Decoding Section 678, 35 ACTEC Journal 106 (2009) (examining "whether a non-grantor holding a power to distribute trust property to himself or herself, subject to an 'ascertainable standard, is properly treated as the trust's owner for income tax purposes and the extent to which a non-grantor who held an unrestricted power of withdrawal that has lapsed may continue to be treated, for income tax purposes, as the owner of the portion of the trust with respect to which the power lapsed").

§8.10 [1] John C. Bogle, *How Mutual Funds Lost Their Way*, Wall St. J., June 20, 2000 (citing Henry Kaufman, On Money and Markets). *But see* Aaron Lucchetti, *A Mutual-Fund Giant Is Stalking*

In the words of a former SEC chairman, [n]o issuer of securities is subject to more detailed regulation than a mutual fund. Unfortunately, as we shall see, decades of SEC-commissioned studies, rule-making, and jawboning have led to a system that, for the most part, works beautifully for those who sell funds to the public, or sell services to funds, but much less admirably for the industry's investors.[2]

A U.S. or U.K. mutual fund—even a mutual fund packaged as a corporation—is a trusteed portfolio of securities.[3] Legal title is either in an individual (or individuals) as trustee or in a corporation. The investors—those who purchase shares or participations in the fund—are both settlors and the owners of fully vested (equitable) property interests. Employing the formula set out in Section 3.5.3.2(a) of this handbook, one could say that each investor is simultaneously *A, C,* and *D* as to the investor's allocable share of the fund. The relationship between the trustee or trustee-director of a U.S. or U.K. mutual fund and the investor is a fiduciary one, both under common law principles and by statute.[4]

There usually is an investment manager/advisor in the picture who provides portfolio selection and administrative services to the title-holding fiduciary,[5] although there is no common law or statutory impediment to the titleholder of the underlying assets of a mutual fund performing investment management functions in-house.[6] The investment manager/advisor is an *agent*

Excessive Pay, Wall St. J., June 12, 2002, at C1 (reporting that Fidelity mutual fund trustees may withhold votes for corporate directors who overpay their senior executives).

[2] John P. Freeman & Stewart L. Brown, *Mutual Fund Advisory Fees: The Cost of Conflicts of Interest*, 26 J. Corp. L. 609, 613 (2001).

[3] *See generally* Charles E. Rounds, Jr. & Andreas Dehio, *Publicly-Traded Open End Mutual Funds in Common Law and Civil Law Jurisdictions: A Comparison of Legal Structures*, 3 N.Y.U.J.L & Bus. 473 (2007) (noting, however, that a statutory U.K.-REIT, is not a trust); Bogert §248; Anderson, *Rights and Obligations in the Mutual Fund: A Source of Law*, 20 Vand. L. Rev. 1120 (1967); American Bar Association, A Fiduciary's Guide to Federal Securities Laws 254 (1994).

[4] *See* Kleinman v. Saminsky, 41 Del. Ch. 572, 578, 200 A.2d 572, 576 (1964). *See generally* Charles E. Rounds, Jr. & Andreas Dehio, *Publicly-Traded Open End Mutual Funds in Common Law and Civil Law Jurisdictions: A Comparison of Legal Structures*, 3 N.Y.U.J.L & Bus. 473 (2007).

[5] *See generally* Richard A. Booth, *Who Should Recover What for Late Trading and Market Timing?*, 1 J. Bus. & Tech. L. 101, 102–103 (2006) (confirming that it is industry practice for trustees of a mutual fund (or for the investment company in the case of an incorporated mutual fund) to contract with a separate entity, the so-called investment adviser, to manage fund assets).

[6] *See* Kleinman v. Saminsky, 41 Del. Ch. 572, 578, 200 A.2d 572, 576 (1964). Actually, the common law traditionally looked favorably on the nondelegation of fiduciary functions such as investment management. *See generally* Charles E. Rounds, Jr. & Andreas Dehio, *Publicly-Traded Open End Mutual Funds in Common Law and Civil Law Jurisdictions: A Comparison of Legal Structures*, 3 N.Y.U.J.L. & Bus. 473 (2007); §6.1.4 of this handbook (discussing the trustee's duty to give personal attention to the affairs of the trust).

of *B*, the title-holding fiduciary.[7] The manager/advisor also will have a compensation contract with the title-holding fiduciary.[8] "The largest portion of a fund's expense ratio is generally the fund advisor's compensation, which is used to cover its operating costs and earned profits for its owners."[9] *The manager/advisor more often than not is also the creator, sponsor, and promoter of the mutual fund, i.e., the owner of the product.*[10] "For example, Boston's Fidelity Investments, the nation's largest fund firm, has a unit called Fidelity Management & Research Co., which manages most of its portfolios, even though Fidelity's fund board, which oversees all its funds, has the authority to go anywhere to find an investment manager."[11] A third party, usually a bank, serves as custodian of the fund assets.[12]

The British equivalent of the mutual fund is the unit trust.[13] "More than any other financial product, these vehicles have brought shareholder capitalism to the masses."[14] On the Continent, however, mutual funds are generally not trusteed.[15] That being the case, readers interested in learning something about how mutual funds actually are legally structured in civil law jurisdictions, particularly Germany and Luxembourg, are referred to the law review article by Rounds and Dehio.[16]

---

[7] While the investment advisor is an agent of *B*, the fiduciary, in the real world the investment advisor may well be the creator, sponsor, administrator, and promoter of the mutual fund. *See generally* Charles E. Rounds, Jr. & Andreas Dehio, *Publicly-Traded Open End Mutual Funds in Common Law and Civil Law Jurisdictions: A Comparison of Legal Structures*, 3 N.Y.U.J.L. & Bus. 473 (2007). *See, e.g.*, Krantz v. Fidelity Mgmt. & Research Co. (FMR), 98 F. Supp. 2d 150 (2000) (granting in part defendants' motion to dismiss because allegations in plaintiff's complaint did not rebut statutory presumption of noncontrol by investment advisor (FMR) over the fund trustees).

[8] *See generally* Charles E. Rounds, Jr. & Andreas Dehio, *Publicly-Traded Open End Mutual Funds in Common Law and Civil Law Jurisdictions: A Comparison of Legal Structures*, 3 N.Y.U.J.L. & Bus. 473 (2007).

[9] GAO/GGD-00-126 Mutual Fund Fees, at 5.

[10] *See generally* Charles E. Rounds, Jr. & Andreas Dehio, *Publicly-Traded Open End Mutual Funds in Common Law and Civil Law Jurisdictions: A Comparison of Legal Structures*, 3 N.Y.U.J.L & Bus. 473 (2007).

[11] John Shipman, *So Who Owns Your Mutual Fund?*, Wall St. J., May 5, 2003, at R1.

[12] *Cf.* Charles E. Rounds, Jr. & Andreas Dehio, *Publicly-Traded Open End Mutual Funds in Common Law and Civil Law Jurisdictions: A Comparison of Legal Structures*, 3 N.Y.U.J.L. & Bus. 473 (2007) (in part discussing the quasi-fiduciary role of the *Depotbank* or *dépositaire* in civil law jurisdictions).

[13] *See generally* Charles E. Rounds, Jr. & Andreas Dehio, *Publicly-Traded Open End Mutual Funds in Common Law and Civil Law Jurisdictions: A Comparison of Legal Structures*, 3 N.Y.U.J.L. & Bus. 473 (2007).

[14] The Law of Averages, 368 Economist No. 8331, July 5, 2003, at 6.

[15] *See generally* Charles E. Rounds, Jr. & Andreas Dehio, *Publicly-Traded Open End Mutual Funds in Common Law and Civil Law Jurisdictions: A Comparison of Legal Structures*, 3 N.Y.U.J.L. & Bus. 473 (2007).

[16] *See generally* Charles E. Rounds, Jr. & Andreas Dehio, *Publicly-Traded Open End Mutual Funds in Common Law and Civil Law Jurisdictions: A Comparison of Legal Structures*, 3 N.Y.U.J.L. & Bus. 473 (2007).

In the United States, there is much federal regulation of mutual funds.[17] "The Investment Company Act and Investment Advisers Act, both passed in 1940, provide overriding organizational form and rules regulating the business of mass-produced and offered trust services."[18] The rights, duties, and obligations of the parties, however, are first and foremost grounded in the common law principles of fiduciary law that are the subject of this handbook.[19] Were it not for federal preemption, for example, the taking of so-called 12b-1 fees by the fund advisor or sponsor probably would violate default common law loyalty principles:[20] Included as part of the operating expenses that are directly deducted from some funds are fees that go to compensate sales professionals and others for selling the fund's shares as well as for advertising and promoting them. These fees, known as "12b-1 fees," are named after Securities and Exchange Commission (SEC) rules authorizing mutual funds to pay for marketing and distribution expenses directly from fund assets. Any 12b-1 fees included in a fund's total expense ratio are limited to a maximum of 1 percent per year.[21]

For more information on the fiduciary aspects of mutual fund structuring and administration, the reader is referred to Sections 9.6, 9.7.1, and 9.7.5 of this handbook.

---

[17] *See generally* Charles E. Rounds, Jr. & Andreas Dehio, *Publicly-Traded Open End Mutual Funds in Common Law and Civil Law Jurisdictions: A Comparison of Legal Structures*, 3 N.Y.U.J.L. & Bus. 473 (2007).

[18] Tamar Frankel, *The Delaware Business Trust Act Failure as the New Corporate Law*, 23 Cardozo L. Rev. 325, n.28 (2001) (suggesting that the death of business trusts (investment companies) in the beginning of the 1930s and the death of the investment management industry ended in federal legislation).

[19] *See generally* Charles E. Rounds, Jr. & Andreas Dehio, *Publicly-Traded Open End Mutual Funds in Common Law and Civil Law Jurisdictions: A Comparison of Legal Structures*, 3 N.Y.U.J.L. & Bus. 473 (2007). "The structure of most mutual funds embodies a potential conflict of interest between the fund shareholders and the adviser." GAO/GGD-00-126 Mutual Fund Fees, at 14. "This conflict arises because the fees the fund charges the shareholders represents revenue to the adviser." GAO/GGD-00-126 Mutual Fund Fees, at 14. *See also* §6.1.3.3 of this handbook (trustee benefiting as buyer and seller).

[20] *See* §6.1.3 of this handbook (duty to be loyal to the trust). *See also* Aaron Lucchetti, *Fund Fees Get SEC Scrutiny: Intended as Temporary Measure, 12b-1 Payments Have Become An Important Revenue Source*, Wall St. J., May 28, 2002, at C1, col. 5; Jonathan Clements, *How to Make Money in Mutual Funds: Start Your Own*, Wall St. J., Feb. 5, 2002, at C1, col. 3 (the "unseemliness" of 12b-1 fees).

[21] GAO/GGD-00-126 Mutual Fund Fees. It also is unlikely that the common law would look favorably on the practice of having a mutual fund share auditors with its investment adviser. Why? Because the auditor, in violation of common law agency principles relating to conflicts of interest, would be an agent of parties on opposites sides of a supposedly arm's length employment contract.

§8.11 What Are the Duties of the Trustee of a Revocable Inter Vivos Trust?

Neither the First nor the Second Restatement of Trusts . . . have been as clear as one might have hoped in articulating the effect of a power of revocation on trust administration. One might speculate that one of the reasons for this deficiency was the need to paper over the dirty little secret that, in terms of trust theory, a revocable trust has always had but a tenuous claim to being a real trust.[1]

A revocable inter vivos trust is a true trust. For purposes of this section of the handbook, the term "powerholder" is shorthand for holder of a *general inter vivos power of appointment/revocation*, whether or not the holder is also the settlor of the trust. In the United States, it is now settled law that a revocable inter vivos trust legally is a trust, not an agency.[2] This is the case even when the trust arises by declaration.[3] Nor is it merely an invalid will that has been formatted to look like a trust.[4] It is a real trust. That means that the legal title to the subject property actually is in the trustee. Under classic principles of property and trust law, the "other" beneficiaries, as well as the principal beneficiary, *i.e.*, the powerholder, have equitable property interests.[5] The equitable property interests of the "others," though, are hypercontingent.[6]

But a revocable inter vivos trust has agency attributes. In the United States, however, it also is now virtually settled law that the trustee is the constructive agent of the powerholder, be the powerholder the settlor or someone else,[7] provided and as long as the powerholder is of full age and legal capacity.[8] No fiduciary duties are owed by the trustee to the other

---

§8.11 [1] 3 Scott & Ascher §16.5 (citing to the text in footnote 3). *See also*, Frances H. Foster, *Privacy and the Elusive Quest for Uniformity in the Law of Trusts*, 38 Ariz. St. L.J. 713 (2006).

[2] National Shawmut Bank v. Joy, 315 Mass. 457, 53 N.E.2d 113 (1944); Estate of West v. West, 331 Utah Adv. Rep. 11, 948 P.2d 351, 351 n.1 (1997) (noting that while revocable trusts may be a "legal fiction," they are "well entrenched in the law, useful, and accepted"). *See also* 3 Scott & Ascher §16.5 (suggesting that "revocable trusts are here to stay, it seems"). *See generally* §9.9.2 of this handbook (discussing the differences between a trust and an agency).

[3] *See, e.g.*, Farkas v. Williams, 125 N.E.2d 600 (Ill. 1955) (the court holding that though it has a "testamentary look" to it, the particular written revocable inter vivos declaration at issue is a true trust).

[4] *See generally* 3 Scott & Ascher §16.5 (noting that as late as the middle of the twentieth century, "there remained serious questions whether, in certain circumstances, a revocable trust was not invalid, under the statute of wills, as a 'testamentary transfer'"); Farkas v. Williams, 125 N.E.2d 600 (Ill. 1955).

[5] *See generally* 3 Scott & Ascher §16.5 (noting that "one of the primary theoretical steps" in validating the revocable trust was the proposition that persons other than the holder of the power of revocation have property "interests").

[6] National Shawmut Bank v. Joy, 315 Mass. 457, 53 N.E.2d 113 (1944).

[7] *See generally* 3 Scott & Ascher §16.6 (Effect of Presently Exercisable General Power of Appointment or Right of Withdrawal).

[8] UTC §603(a) (available at <http://www.uniformlaws.org/Act.aspx?title=Trust%20Code>) provides that while a trust is revocable and the settlor has capacity to revoke the trust, rights of the beneficiaries are subject to the control of, and the duties of the trustee are owed exclusively to, the

beneficiaries under such circumstances.[9] They are owed only to the powerholder.[10]

That power of revocation then is the functional equivalent of full owner-ship,[11] unless the power is held only in a fiduciary capacity, which is unlikely.[12] A transfer of property to the trustee of a revocable inter vivos trust, therefore, is constructively a transfer directly to the holder of the right of revocation.[13] It is no wonder, then, that more and more courts are deeming the "other" equitable interests, i.e., the interests of those other than the powerholder, not to be interests in property at all, just expectancies.[14] Accordingly, while the power-holder is of full age and legal capacity, the trustee is constructively subject to the laws of agency.[15] When the powerholder ceases to have the requisite mental capacity, the constructive agency terminates.[16] Until such time, the trustee will generally have no duty to communicate with the "other" beneficiaries, and most likely will have a fiduciary duty to the powerholder not to.[17] Until such time, the powerholder may remove, replace, or add trustees without grounds and gener-ally without court involvement.[18] The powerholder's informed consent to the trustee's accountings, or even to a breach of trust on the part of the trustee, will generally bind the other beneficiaries, including the takers in default.[19]

When two or more persons simultaneously hold a general inter vivos power of appointment. The prudent trustee will think long and hard before serving under a trust that has two or more persons simultaneously holding rights of revocation (or general inter vivos powers).[20] Such a situation brings with it property and tax problems too intricate to be covered by a handbook of

---

settlor. See generally 2 Scott on Trusts §216.2; Canter v. Comm'r, 423 Mass. 425, 668 N.E.2d 783 (1996). Retention of control is not without consequences for the settlor: If the trustee of a revocable trust holds an interest as a general partner, the settlor is personally liable for contracts and other obligations of the partnership as if the settlor were a general partner. UTC §1011(d).

[9] See, e.g., Fulp v. Gilliland, 998 N.E.2d 204 (Ind. 2013) (the court musing that to hold that a trustee of a revocable trust also owes duties to the remainder beneficiaries "would create conflicting rights and duties for trustees and essentially render revocable trusts irrevocable").

[10] See Fulp v. Gilliland, 998 N.E.2d 204 (Ind. 2013).

[11] See generally 3 Scott & Ascher §16.5 (Effect of Power of Revocation).

[12] See generally 3 Scott & Ascher §16.5.

[13] See Brown v. Miller, 2 So. 3d 321 (Fla. Ct. App. 2009).

[14] Canter v. Commissioner of Pub. Welfare, 423 Mass. 425, 429–431, 668 N.E.2d 783, 786–787 (1996). See also Restatement (Third) of Trusts §40, Reporter's Notes on §40.

[15] 1 Scott & Ascher §2.3.4 (noting that when a single person is both agent of, and trustee for, another, it is ordinarily the agency relationship that predominates, with the principles of agency, rather than those of trusts, applying).

[16] Restatement (Third) of Trusts §74 cmt. a(2).

[17] See generally 3 Scott & Ascher §16.5. See also Frances H. Foster, Privacy and the Elusive Quest for Uniformity in the Law of Trusts, 38 Ariz. St. L.J. 713 (2006). See, however, Turney P. Berry, David M. English, & Dana G. Fitzsimons, Longmeyer Exposes (or Creates) Uncertainty About the Duty to Inform Remainder Beneficiaries of a Revocable Trust, 35 ACTEC Journal 125 (2009) (referring to J. P. Morgan Chase Bank, N.A. v. Longmeyer, 275 S.W.3d 697 (Ky. 2009)).

[18] 3 Scott & Ascher §16.5.

[19] See generally 3 Scott & Ascher §16.5; UPC §1-108 (acts by holder of general inter vivos power of appointment); §7.1.4 of this handbook (consenting to or ratifying a breach of trust).

[20] See, however, §9.25 of this handbook (the joint trust).

this scope and size.[21] The Uniform Trust Code, however, does provide that if a revocable trust has more than one settlor, the duties of the trustee are owed to all of the settlors having capacity to revoke the trust.[22]

When the powerholder relies on the trustee's discretion. If the power-holder in practice defers to the trustee's discretion in matters pertaining to the administration and investment of the trust property, then the trustee ought to be held to the standards of loyalty and care of an agent-fiduciary.[23] As to entrusted bank deposits, for example, the trustee should see to it that FDIC insurance limits are not exceeded. In this regard, the reader is referred to the FDIC Guide to Calculating Deposit Insurance Coverage for Revocable and Irrevocable trusts.

Even when the trustee is authorized by the settlor to deviate from the terms of the trust or to contravene standard principles of trust law, the trustee in exercising this type of empowerment must do so prudently and in good faith.[24]

When the trustee is permitted to perform ministerial functions only. On the other hand, if the powerholder expects the trustee to perform only minis-terial functions, then the trustee ought to be held to a less rigorous standard.[25] Nevertheless, he remains a fiduciary. "Thus, if the settlor of a revocable trust simply directs the trustee to sell certain real property held in the trust, the trustee must, for example, act with prudence in arranging the price and other terms of the sale."[26] One consequence of this constructive agency is that the settlor of a revocable inter vivos trust (or the holder of an inter vivos power of appointment such as a right of withdrawal)[27] calls the shots.[28] The settlor (or

---

[21] UTC §602 cmt. (available at <http://www.uniformlaws.org/Act.aspx?title=Trust%20Code>) (suggesting that no important reason exists for the creation of a joint trust in a noncommunity property state).

[22] UTC §603(c) (available at <http://www.uniformlaws.org/Act.aspx?title=Trust%20Code>).

[23] *See, e.g.*, Wisconsin Acad. of Sci., Arts & Letters v. First Wis. Nat'l Bank of Madison, 142 Wis. 2d 750, 419 N.W.2d 301 (1987) (finding that a corporate trustee of a revocable trust had a duty of vigilance to advise settlor that the trust instrument as drafted would not serve to carry out her donative intent); Cohen v. First Camden Nat'l Bank & Trust (Matter of McCoy), 51 N.J. 11, 18, 237 A.2d 257, 261 (1967) (a trustee of a revocable trust may not enter into a self-dealing transaction with the trust, in this case by accepting a collateral assignment from the settlor-beneficiary of trust assets, unless the settlor-beneficiary consented to the transaction with full knowledge of all relevant facts and complete awareness of the resultant divided loyalty and its possible conse-quences). *See generally* Chapter 1 of this handbook (discussing the agent as fiduciary).

[24] *See, e.g.*, Namik v. Wachovia Bank of Ga., 612 S.E.2d 270 (Ga. 2005) (holding the trustee liable for the adverse estate tax consequences occasioned by its breach of the duty to exercise judgment and due care, namely, by failing to follow the directions of the settlor, a nonresident alien, to invest the trust property in U.S. government issues).

[25] *See, e.g.*, McGinley v. Bank of Am., N.A., 109 P.3d 1146 (Kan. 2005) (where trustee was held harmless for retaining Enron stock in accordance with the written directions of the settlor).

[26] Restatement (Third) of Trusts §74 cmt. b.

[27] UTC §603(d) (available at <http://www.uniformlaws.org/Act.aspx?title=Trust%20Code>).

[28] *See, e.g.*, McGinley v. Bank of Am., 109 P.3d 1146 (Kan. Sup. Ct. 2005) (though 77 percent of portfolio of revocable inter vivos trust had at one time been comprised of Enron stock, the

nonsettlor powerholder), for example, may give a binding consent to a trustee account that has the effect of ratifying a breach of trust, provided the consent is informed.[29] As noted, he or she may remove, replace, or add trustees, though there is no express authority to do so.[30] He or she even may override the express terms of the governing instrument[31] to include subverting the interests of the contingent beneficiaries, *i.e.*, the takers in default of the power's exercise.[32] After all, inherent in the right to revoke the trust is the lesser right to modify its terms.[33]

Exculpation of the directed trustee. Nowadays, the trustee is expected to take directions from a competent settlor who has retained a right to revoke[34] (or from the third party who holds a general inter vivos power of appointment);[35] and the trustee, in most cases,[36] will be held harmless for so doing.[37] The responsibility, however, falls on the shoulders of the trustee to ascertain the powerholder's capacity. "In the absence of reason for the trustee to believe that the settlor or donee lacks the requisite capacity, . . . [however,] . . . the trustee is entitled to proceed on the assumption that the settlor or donee possesses that capacity."[38]

Generally it is the powerholder who is entitled to be notified when the trustee intends to take an important action, such as resign. The Uniform Trust Code provides as follows: "In the case of a revocable trust, because the rights of the qualified beneficiaries are subject to the settlor's control, resignation of the trustee is accomplished by giving notice to the settlor instead of the beneficiaries."[39] Other situations in which the holder of the right of revocation

---

trustee was held not liable for losses occasioned by the Enron stock's subsequent substantial loss of value, the trustee having been directed by the settlor to retain the Enron stock). *See generally* 3 Scott & Ascher §16.5 (Effect of Power of Revocation).

[29] Restatement (Third) of Trusts §74 cmt. d. *See generally* §7.1.2 of this handbook (defenses to allegations that the trustee breached the duty of loyalty) (containing a discussion of the concept of informed consent).

[30] Restatement (Third) of Trusts §74 cmt. e.

[31] Restatement (Third) of Trusts §74.

[32] *See, e.g.*, Restatement (Third) of Trusts §74(1)(b) (suggesting that the rights of the beneficiaries of a revocable trust are exercisable by and subject to the control of the settlor).

[33] Restatement (Third) of Trusts §74 cmt. d.

[34] *See generally* 3 Scott & Ascher §16.5 (Effect of Power of Revocation).

[35] UTC §603(a) (available at <http://www.uniformlaws.org/Act.aspx?title=Trust%20Code>); Restatement (Third) of Trusts §74 (suggesting that the trustee of a revocable trust has a duty to comply with a direction of the settlor even though the direction is contrary to the terms of the trust or the trustee's normal duties, if the direction is communicated to the trustee in writing in a manner by which the settlor could properly amend or revoke the trust). The trustee has a similar duty to honor the directions of the donee of a presently exercisable general power of appointment or power of withdrawal, provided the donee has capacity to act. *See* Restatement (Third) of Trusts §74(2).

[36] *See generally* §6.1.4 of this handbook (duty to give personal attention (not to delegate)).

[37] Restatement (Third) of Trusts §74(1)(a)(ii).

[38] Restatement (Third) of Trusts §74a(2).

[39] UTC §707 cmt. (available at <http://www.uniformlaws.org/Act.aspx?title=Trust%20Code>). *See also* Restatement (Third) of Trusts §36 cmt. b.

stands in the shoes of others are gathered together in Section 1-108 of the Uniform Probate Code:

> For the purpose of granting consent or approval with regard to the acts or accounts of a personal representative or trustee, including relief from liability or penalty for failure to post bond, to register a trust, or to perform other duties, and for purposes of consenting to modification or termination of a trust or to deviation from its terms, the sole holder or all co-holders of a presently exercisable general power of appointment, including one in the form of a power of amendment or revocation, are deemed to act for beneficiaries to the extent their interests (as objects, takers in default, or otherwise) are subject to the power.

Incapacitation of powerholder. Once the powerholder becomes incapacitated, the trustee's fiduciary duties and liabilities ratchet up, particularly with respect to distributions.[40] An outright distribution to an incapacitated powerholder could well constitute misdelivery[41] for which the trustee could be held personally liable even after the powerholder's death.[42]

Once a settlor becomes incapacitated, the trustee is obligated to accommodate the equitable interests of the other beneficiaries as well as the powerholder's,[43] such as by providing them with relevant information about the trust, unless the incapacity is expected to be short term.[44] The prudent trustee, therefore, will endeavor to mitigate the risk of having to cross swords[45] with the other beneficiaries while the powerholder is still alive (or after the settlor's death[46]) by having a questionable direction of the powerholder put into the format of a written amendment[47] (or written partial exercise of the general

---

[40] 4 Scott & Ascher §24.31.1 (Liability for Distributions Under Invalid, Amended, Revoked, or Ineffective Instruments).

[41] *See generally* 4 Scott & Ascher §24.31 (Liability for Incorrect Distributions).

[42] 4 Scott & Ascher §24.31.1 (Liability for Distributions Under Invalid, Amended, Revoked, or Ineffective Instruments).

[43] UTC §603(b) (available at <http://www.uniformlaws.org/Act.aspx?title=Trust%20 Code>); Restatement (Third) of Trusts §74 cmt. a(2).

[44] Restatement (Third) of Trusts §74, Reporter's Notes (Comments a(2) and (e)). *See also* Frances H. Foster, *Privacy and the Elusive Quest for Uniformity in the Law of Trusts*, 38 Ariz. St. L.J. 713 (2006).

[45] "As a practical matter, . . . in the event of a surcharge action the trustee . . . [runs] . . . a risk in relying on unwritten evidence to support a defense based on settlor direction or authorization." Restatement (Third) of Trusts §74 cmt. c.

[46] *See, e.g.*, Siegal v. Novak, 920 So. 2d 89 (Fla. 2006) (the court granting standing to successor beneficiaries after the settlor's death to challenge distributions made before the settlor's death by the corporate trustee of a self-settled revocable inter vivos trust). *But see* In re Trust of Malasky, 290 App. Div. 2d 631, 736 N.Y.S. 2d 151 (2002) (successor beneficiaries denied standing to object to a postdeath accounting of a revocable trust, an accounting that covered a period when the settlor-trustee was alive, had capacity, and possessed a personal right of revocation). *Siegel* perhaps can be distinguished from *Malasky* in that in *Siegal* the settlor had not been serving as a trustee.

[47] UTC §808 cmt. (available at <http://www.uniformlaws.org/Act.aspx?title=Trust%20 Code>).

power[48]). If the trustee determines that a particular direction needs to be in writing, he has a fiduciary duty promptly to so notify the powerholder.[49] For a writing to constitute an enduring amendment, *i.e.*, an amendment that survives the death or incapacity of the powerholder, its terms may not be unlawful or violate public policy.[50]

For a discussion of whether the powerholder's court-appointed guardian, court-appointed conservator, and/or the holder of the powerholder's durable power of attorney would have revocation, amendment, or withdrawal authority, the reader is referred to Section 8.2.2.2 of this handbook (the revocable trust). When such authority exists, it is exercised in a fiduciary capacity.[51]

Death of powerholder. *Notice to qualified beneficiaries upon settlor's death of existence of trust and other such critical details.* The Uniform Trust Code[52] provides that within sixty days after the trustee acquires knowledge of the death of the settlor of a revocable trust, the trustee shall inform the qualified beneficiaries of the trust's existence, of the identity of the settlor or settlors, of the right to request a copy of the trust instrument, and of the right to trustee reports or accountings.[53]

Applying antilapse principles to the revocable trust. Section 2-707 of the Uniform Probate Code establishes an antilapse-type rule for revocable trusts. *In the absence of a contrary intention in the governing instrument,* upon the death of the settlor, the then-living issue of the designated successor beneficiary who has failed to survive the settlor shall take by right of representation what the beneficiary would have taken had he or she survived the settlor. This is in lieu of the imposition of a resulting trust or distribution to the beneficiary's estate.[54]

The revocable inter vivos trust as will substitute. A trust under which the settlor has reserved a right of revocation is a type of will substitute.[55] Thus, it is not surprising that the trend of the default law is in the direction of treating, at least for certain purposes, the settlor as if he or she were a testator/testatrix and the

---

[48] *Cf.* Restatement (Third) of Trusts §74(1)(a)(i) (providing that if the settlor of a revocable trust issues to the trustee a direction that is contrary to the terms of the trust or the trustee's normal fiduciary duties, the trustee has a duty to follow it, provided the direction is communicated in a manner by which the settlor could properly amend or revoke the trust).

[49] Restatement (Third) of Trusts §74 cmt. c.

[50] Restatement (Third) of Trusts §74 cmt. i. *See generally* §9.24 of this handbook (the incentive trust (and the public policy considerations); marriage restraints).

[51] Restatement (Third) of Trusts §74 cmt. a(2).

[52] UTC §813(b)(3) (available at <http://www.uniformlaws.org/Act.aspx?title=Trust%20 Code>).

[53] Upon the death of the settlor of a revocable inter vivos trust, the trustee will want to ascertain the applicable statute of limitations governing creditor claims, as well as actions by those seeking to defeat the trust. *See, e.g.,* Estate of Pew, 440 Pa. Super. 195, 248, 655 A.2d 521, 548 (1994). *See generally* Frances H. Foster, *Privacy and the Elusive Quest for Uniformity in the Law of Trusts,* 38 Ariz. St. L.J. 713 (2006).

[54] For a case where distribution was to the estate of the beneficiary of a revocable trust who had predeceased the settlor, *see* First Nat'l Bank v. Tenney, 165 Ohio St. 513, 138 N.E.2d 15 (1956). *See also,* Randall v. Bank of Am., 48 Cal. App. 2d 249, 119 P.2d 754 (1941).

[55] *See generally* Frances H. Foster, *Privacy and the Elusive Quest for Uniformity in the Law of Trusts,* 38 Ariz. St. L.J. 713 (2006).

subject property as if it were probate property once the settlor dies, this even though title to the trust property does not transfer to the deceased settlor's executor/executrix, administrator/administratrix, or personal representative, as the case may be.[56] These purposes include the following:

- Satisfaction of claims against the probate estate, to include certain statutory allowances;[57]
- Application of the 120-hour requirement;[58]
- Application of the harmless-error rule;[59]
- Revocation or amendment by a subsequent will;[60]
- Revocation by marriage;[61]
- Ademption by extinction;[62]
- Antilapse;[63]
- Invalidity due to incapacity or wrongdoing;[64]
- Application of construction, reformation, and modification doctrines generally;[65]

---

[56] *See generally* Frances H. Foster, *Privacy and the Elusive Quest for Uniformity in the Law of Trusts*, 38 Ariz. St. L.J. 713 (2006).

[57] Restatement (Third) of Property (Wills and Other Donative Transfers) §7.2 cmt. b. *See generally* §§5.3.3.1(b) of this handbook (the postmortem creditor), 5.3.4.1 of this handbook (spousal rights in common law states), 8.9.3 of this handbook (tax-sensitive powers).

[58] Restatement (Third) of Property (Wills and Other Donative Transfers) §7.2 cmt. c. "The original Uniform Probate Code introduced a rule of construction that devisees must survive the decedent by 120 hours or more, but the terms of the statute applied only to transfers by will. *See* Original UPC §2-601." Restatement (Third) of Property (Wills and Other Donative Transfers) §7.2 cmt. c. "The Revised Uniform Simultaneous Death Act and the Revised Uniform Probate Code expanded the 120-hour requirement of survival to all donative documents (wills and inter vivos donative documents, including will substitutes) that require the donee to survive the donor." Restatement (Third) of Property (Wills and Other Donative Transfers) §7.2 cmt. c. *See generally* §8.15.56 of this handbook (120-hour survival requirement [the trust application]).

[59] Restatement (Third) of Property (Wills and Other Donative Transfers) §7.2 cmt. d. The harmless-error rule applicable to wills is as follows: "A harmless error in executing a will may be excused if the proponent establishes by clear and convincing evidence that the decedent adopted the document as his or her will." Restatement (Third) of Property (Wills and Other Donative Transfers) §3.3. *See generally* §8.15.53 of this handbook (harmless-error rule [the trust application]).

[60] Restatement (Third) of Property (Wills and Other Donative Transfers) §7.2 cmt. e. *See also* §8.2.2.2 of this handbook (the revocable trust).

[61] Restatement (Third) of Property (Wills and Other Donative Transfers) §7.2 cmt. f. *See generally* §5.3.4.1 of this handbook (spousal rights in common law states rights of spouses of trust beneficiaries [divorce and separation]); UPC §2-804 (revocation of non probate transfers by divorce); *see also* Restatement (Third) of Property (Wills and Other Donative Transfers) §4.1 cmt. p (application to will substitutes).

[62] Restatement (Third) of Property (Wills and Other Donative Transfers) §7.2 cmt. f. *See generally* §8.15.54 of this handbook (ademption by extinction [the trust application]).

[63] Restatement (Third) of Property (Wills and Other Donative Transfers) §7.2 cmt. f. *See generally* §8.15.55 of this handbook (antilapse [the trust application]).

[64] Restatement (Third) of Property (Wills and Other Donative Transfers) §7.2 cmt. g.

[65] Restatement (Third) of Property (Wills and Other Donative Transfers) §7.2 cmt. h.

- Application of rules of construction governing class gifts specifically;[66] and
- Application of social restrictions on freedom of disposition.[67]

For a discussion of the applicability of certain rules governing testamentary dispositions to self-settled revocable trusts, the reader is referred to Section 7.2 of the Restatement (Third) of Property (Wills and Other Donative Transfers), particularly the accompanying commentary and Reporter's Notes.[68] "These rules . . . [also] . . . inform the federal common law of will substitutes under the Employee Retirement Income Security Act (ERISA). . . ."[69]

Mortmain principles applied to the will substitute. To the extent any statutory restrictions on one's ability to devise to a charity still remain in place, a topic we touch on in Section 8.15.4 of this handbook, on policy grounds they should probably apply as well to dispositions by will substitute, particularly the revocable inter vivos trust.[70] In England, the Georgian Statute of Mortmain, which was enacted by Parliament in 1736, lumped testamentary dispositions and revocable inter vivos dispositions together in imposing restrictions on one's ability to make dispositions for charitable purposes.[71]

Liability of trustee of revocable trust for breaches of trust committed before the powerholder died. Upon the death of the powerholder, either his or her personal representative or the successor trust beneficiaries would have standing to bring an action against the trustee for any breaches of duty that the trustee owed *to the powerholder* during the powerholder's lifetime.[72] The successor beneficiaries, however, would have standing to bring an action against the trustee only to the extent their equitable property interests were adversely affected by the trustee's maladministration.[73] That having been said, in Iowa, the trustee of a self-settled revocable trust has no duty to account to the successor beneficiaries for the period when the deceased settlor was of full age and legal capacity, thus rendering such a right of action illusory, at least as a practical matter.[74]

---

[66] Restatement (Third) of Property (Wills and Other Donative Transfers) §7.2 cmt. i. *See generally* §5.2 of this handbook (class designation: "children," "issue," "heirs," and "relatives" (some rules of construction)).

[67] Restatement (Third) of Property (Wills and Other Donative Transfers) §7.2 cmt. j.

[68] *See also* Frances H. Foster, *Privacy and the Elusive Quest for Uniformity in the Law of Trusts*, 38 Ariz. St. L.J. 713 (2006).

[69] Restatement (Third) of Property (Wills and Other Donative Transfers) §7.2 cmt. k.

[70] *See generally* 5 Scott & Ascher §37.2.6.6 (The Revocable Inter Vivos Charitable Trust).

[71] *See* Stat. 9 Geo. II, c. 36 (1736).

[72] *See, e.g.*, Estate of William A. Giraldin v. Christine Giraldin, 55 Cal. 4th 1058, 290 P.3d 199 (2012).

[73] *See, e.g.*, Estate of William A. Giraldin v. Christine Giraldin, 55 Cal. 4th 1058, 290 P.3d 199 (2012).

[74] *See* In re Trust # T-1 of Mary Faye Trimble, 826 N.W.2d 474 (Iowa 2013).

Some non-U.S. trust jurisdictions may not recognize the revocable trust. In closing, a note of caution: Not all jurisdictions have been receptive to the concept of a "revocable" inter vivos trust:

> For example, trusts with assets and objects totally under the control of the settlor until death or incapacity may well be held invalid in the common-law jurisdictions of England, New Zealand, Australia, and Canada (omitting Quebec, as a civil law province). . . . Courts in those countries, like early cases in this country . . . may conclude that no trust can come into existence until such extensive settlor control is removed, characterizing the arrangement as "testamentary" or as an agency rather than a trust relationship.[75]

§8.12   Where the Trust Is Recognized Outside the United States

The exemption of the trust property from the personal obligations of the trustee is the most significant feature of Anglo-American trust law by comparison with the devices available in civil law countries.[1]

Liechtenstein has recognized and enforced trusts as a matter of internal, domestic law, since 1928. As in any civil law country, this is based on statute. However, the Liechtenstein trust is based upon the Massachusetts business trust, not the general trust law of Massachusetts, but the business trust.[2]

The trust is an English cultural institution that may have Germanic roots. It was once thought that the trust had its origins in Roman law.[3] The currently accepted theory is that uses and trusts have their roots in ancient German law.[4] Modern Germany, however, does not recognize the trust.[5] It was

---

[75] Restatement (Third) of Trusts §74, Reporter's Notes. *See generally* §9.9.2 of this handbook (discussing the differences between a trust and an agency).

§8.12 [1] UTC §507 cmt. (available at <http://www.uniformlaws.org/Act.aspx?title=Trust%20Code>).

[2] Henry Christensen, III, *Foreign Trusts and Alternative Vehicles*, SH032 ALI-ABA 82, 97 (2002). *See generally* §9.6 of this handbook (trusts that resemble corporations or agencies) (discussing the nominee trust).

[3] 1 Scott on Trusts §1.9.

[4] 1 Scott on Trusts §1.9. *See generally* §8.37 of this handbook (the origin of the English trust). *See also* Oliver W. Holmes, *Law in Science and Science in Law*, 12 Harv. L. Rev. 443 (1899) (arguing that the trust is based on the Salic Salmannus). *Cf.* Frederick W. Maitland, *The Origin of Uses*, 8 Harv. L. Rev. 127 (1894) (arguing that both Roman and German elements contributed to the emergence of the use). *But see generally* Avisheh Avini, *The Origins of the Modern English Trust Revisited*, 70 Tul. L. Rev. 1139 (1996) (suggesting that the Islamic "waqf" is the precursor of the modern trust, the "waqf" having been introduced into England in the thirteenth century by the Franciscan friars returning from the crusades). *See generally* Jeffrey A. Schoenblum, 1 Multistate and Multinational Estate Planning §18.05 (1999) (The *Waqf*—An Islamic Law Alternative).

[5] Bogert §9.

in England that the use or trust evolved into the relationship that is the subject of this handbook.[6] This, in part, was because the English had separate courts of law and equity.[7]

The non-U.S. common law jurisdictions. Today, England, Northern Ireland, Wales, Australia,[8] Canada,[9] India,[10] and "a number of former British territories in the Caribbean"[11] cultivate the type of trust that is the subject of this handbook.[12] It should be noted, however, that each jurisdiction has its own body of trust law that on the margins is unique. Nor does one of these common law jurisdictions have a body of trust law that is identical to that of a U.S. state.[13] In England, New Zealand, Australia, and Canada (omitting Quebec, as a civil law province), for example, "trusts with assets and objects totally under the control of the settlor until death or incapacity may well be held invalid."[14] In the United States, on the other hand, the use of revocable inter vivos trusts as substitutes for both wills and conservatorships is widespread.[15] In the United States, spendthrift provisions generally are enforced by the courts.[16] In England they are not.[17] (For a discussion of other special aspects of English trust law, the reader is referred to Professor Schoenblum's Multistate and Multinational Estate Planning.[18])

Common law versus civil law. Jurisdictions in Europe and the Americas tend to fall into two general categories: common law and civil code.[19] France is now a civil code jurisdiction. England is and was a common law jurisdiction.

The trust is a creature of equity, an invention of the English court of chancery. By the fifteenth century, the English court system had evolved into two subsystems: the courts of the common law and the chancery courts. Equity,

---

[6] *See generally* §8.15.1 of this handbook (statute of uses).

[7] 1 Scott on Trusts §1.9.

[8] *See generally* Terry Johansson, *Trusts in Australia*, in Trusts in Prime Jurisdictions 157 (Alon Kaplan ed., 2000).

[9] *See generally* Martin J. Rochwerg & Michelle T. Cass, *Taxation of Trusts in Canada*, in Trusts in Prime Jurisdictions 221 (Alon Kaplan ed., 2000).

[10] *See generally* Revinder Nath, *Trusts in India*, in Trusts in Prime Jurisdictions 303 (Alon Kaplan ed., 2000).

[11] *See generally* Peter D. Maynard, *Trusts in the Bahamas*, in Trusts in Prime Jurisdictions 187 (Alon Kaplan ed., 2000); Christopher J. McKenzie, *Trust Law in the British Virgin Islands*, in Trusts in Prime Jurisdictions 207 (Alon Kaplan ed., 2000); Anthony Travers & Justin Appleyard, *Trusts in the Cayman Islands*, in Trusts in Prime Jurisdictions 239 (Alon Kaplan ed., 2000); St. John A. Robilliard, *Trusts in Guernsey*, in Trusts in Prime Jurisdictions 283 (Alon Kaplan ed., 2000).

[12] Bogert §9. *See generally* §9.10 of this handbook (the offshore asset protection trust).

[13] *See generally* Jeffrey A. Schoenblum, 2 Multistate and Multinational Estate Planning §18.18 (1999) (Special Aspects of English Trust Law).

[14] Restatement (Third) of Trusts §74, Reporter's Notes.

[15] *See* §8.11 of this handbook (what are the duties of the trustee of a revocable inter vivos trust?).

[16] *See generally* §5.3.3.3(c) of this handbook (the non–self-settled spendthrift trust).

[17] *See generally* Jeffrey A. Schoenblum, 1 Multistate and Multinational Estate Planning §17.07 (1999) (Spendthrift Trusts).

[18] Jeffrey A. Schoenblum, 2 Multistate and Multinational Estate Planning §18.18 (1999).

[19] *See generally* Michael Bogdan, Comparative Law (1994).

an invention of the chancery courts, affords remedies that are generally unavailable at law, such as the injunction and specific performance order. The trust is an institution that essentially evolved from an equitable remedy which has some of the attributes of the modern-day remedy of restitution for unjust enrichment.[20] Equity is also an application of maxims that were formulated in decisions of England's chancery courts. These maxims are as relevant today as they were when separate courts of law and equity were the norm.[21] They include the following:

- Equity will not suffer a wrong to be without a remedy.[22]
- Equity follows the law.[23]
- Where there is equal equity, the law shall prevail.[24]
- Where the equities are equal, the first in time shall prevail: *qui prior est tempore, potior est jure*.[25]
- He who seeks equity must do equity.[26]
- He who comes into equity must come with clean hands.[27]

---

[20] *See generally* Restatement of Restitution (1937).

[21] *See generally* Charles E. Rounds, Jr., *Proponents of Extracting Slavery Reparations from Private Interests Must Contend with Equity's Maxims*, 42 U. Tol. L. Rev. 673 (2011).

[22] Snell's Equity ¶ 5-02 through ¶ 5-04.

[23] Snell's Equity ¶ 5-05 through ¶ 5-07.

[24] The maxim's application is best exemplified by equity's forbearance when it comes to bona fide purchasers for value or BFPs, a topic that is covered in §5.4.2, 8.3.2 and §8.15.63 of this handbook:

> Undoubtedly, the reason why the chancellors refused to give relief to a cestui que use against a bona fide purchaser derived from considerations of conscience. Equity refused to give a remedy unless there was an affirmative reason in point of justice for giving it. The cestui que use and the bona fide purchaser were equally innocent, and the chancellor refused to interpose. 3 Scott & Ascher §13.1.

[25] Snell's Equity ¶ 5-08. Assume a trust beneficiary transfers for full value his equitable interest to *X*, a transferee in good faith, and then later purports to transfer for full value the same equitable interest to *Y*, who is also wholly innocent. *X* will generally prevail in equity, the transfer to him being the prior one. *See* §8.15.63 of this handbook (doctrine of bona fide purchase).

[26] Snell's Equity ¶ 5-09 through ¶ 5.14. For an example of the application of the maxim "He who seeks equity must do equity," *see* §3.3 of this handbook (involuntary trustees), specifically the discussion of remedial constructive trusts. For other trust-related applications of the maxim, *see* 4 Scott & Ascher §§22.1.3 (Trustee in Default) (noting that "there is no reason why a trustee who has properly incurred an expense and made good any loss that has resulted from a breach of trust should not be entitled to indemnity"), 25.2 (Liability of Beneficiary to Trust Estate) (noting that "[t]he interest of a beneficiary who is under a liability to pay money into the trust is subject to a charge for the amount of the liability," that is "a person entitled to participate in a fund and also bound to contribute to the same fund cannot receive the benefit without discharging the obligation").

[27] Snell's Equity ¶ 5-15. *See, e.g.*, The Vincent J. Fumo Irrevocable Children's Trust for the Benefit of Allison Fumo (Appeal of Vincent J. Fumo), 2014 PA Super. 235, No. 2459 EDA 2013 (Oct. 17, 2014). Note, however, that a trustee's own misconduct ordinarily does not prevent the trustee from maintaining a suit against a cotrustee to remedy a breach of trust. This is because the purpose of the suit is not to benefit the trustee but to benefit the beneficiaries. *See generally* 4 Scott & Ascher §24.4.2. On the other hands, the clean hands doctrine may well mean that a trustee who

- Delay defeats equities.[28]
- Equality is equity.[29]
- Equity looks to the intent (substance) rather than to the form.[30]
- Equity looks on that as done which ought to be done.[31]

---

commits a breach of trust in bad faith is entitled neither to contribution nor indemnity from his cotrustees. *See generally* 4 Scott & Ascher §24.32.3; Restatement (Third) of Trusts §102(2). *Cf.* Restatement (Third) of Restitution and Unjust Enrichment §63 (Equitable Disqualification (Unclean Hands)) ("Recovery in restitution to which an innocent claimant would be entitled may be limited or denied because of the claimant's inequitable conduct in the transaction that is the source of the asserted liability."). On the other hand, "[i]f a trustee from whom contribution is sought *also* acted in bad faith, contribution is required. . . . A bad-faith trustee may not hide behind another's unclean hands." Restatement (Third) of Trusts §102 cmt. d.

[28] Or equity aids the vigilant and not the indolent: *vigilantibus, non dormientibus, jura subveniunt.* Snell's Equity ¶5-16 through ¶5-19. *See* §§3.6 of this handbook (in part discussing statutes of limitation and laches in contract and tort actions by the trustee and/or trust beneficiaries against third parties and in equitable actions by beneficiaries against third parties for participating with the trustee in breaches of trust), 7.1.3 of this handbook (trustee's defense that beneficiary failed to take timely action against trustee), 7.2.10 of this handbook (limitation of actions by beneficiary against trustee: (laches and statutes of limitation)), and 8.15.70 of this handbook (laches doctrine generally).

[29] Snell's Equity ¶5-20 through ¶5-23. In England, when a court is compelled to take over the work of the trustee of a discretionary trust because of the trustee's nonexecution, the court will be inclined to invoke the equality is equity maxim and effect an equal division. Lewin on Trusts ¶29-96. In the U.S., the spirit of the maxim often manifests itself in the context of the apportionment of tax obligations (1) between and among classes of takers under a will, (2) between and among classes of trust beneficiaries, (3) between a trust and a probate estate, and (4) between a trust and other trusts. *See generally* §§8.15.62 (doctrine of equitable apportionment) and 8.20 of this handbook (tax apportionment within and without trust). The "equality is equity" maxim also informs tracing doctrine, particularly in cases where the assets of multiple trusts are wrongly commingled in a single fund. *See, e.g.,* Matter of Mich. Boiler & Eng'g Co., 171 B.R. 565 (Bankr. E.D. Mich. 1993).

[30] Snell's Equity ¶5-24. *See, e.g.,* The Vincent J. Fumo Irrevocable Children's Trust for the Benefit of Allison Fumo (Appeal of Vincent J. Fumo), 2014 PA Super. 235, No. 2459 EDA 2013 (Oct. 17, 2014). "Since paragraph 14 expressly proscribes Father from appointing himself as succesor trustee, this provision implicitly prohibits the appointment of Father's alter egos to this position." As employed by the Pennsylvania court in this trust case, the term *alter ego* is essentially a synonym for agent. The rule that equity will aid the defective exercise of a power of appointment, a specific application of the general maxim that equity looks to substance (intent) rather than to form, is taken up in §8.15.88 of this handbook. In Inglis v. Casselberry, 137 So. 3d 389 (Fla. Dist. Ct. App. 2013), the court, invoking the maxim that equity will not countenance an argument that elevates form over substance, ruled that the trustee had voluntarily submitted to the court's jurisdiction by participating in the litigation, such as by moving the court to grant requests materially beneficial to himself and the trust beneficiaries.

[31] Snell's Equity ¶5-25. For the maxim's application in the context of delayed trust terminations and distributions, *see* §8.2.3 of this handbook (termination and distribution issues). The doctrine of equitable conversion has been offered as another of the maxim's applications, a topic that is discussed in §§8.15.44 of this handbook (equitable conversion doctrine) and 9.9.11 of this handbook (a contract to convey land is not a trust). *See, however,* 3 Scott & Ascher 13.1.1 (suggesting that the maxim "equity regards as done that which ought to be done" is a "fictitious" explanation of the equitable conversion doctrine). In the trust context, the equitable conversion of land that the trustees have been directed to sell is an application of the maxim "Equity sees as done that which ought to be done." The word "ought" is employed not in the moral sense but in the legal/equitable sense. The rights to the land having already been re-ordered by the terms of the

- Equity imputes an intention to fulfill an obligation.[32]
- Equity acts *in personam*.[33]
- Equity will not aid a volunteer.[34]
- Equity will not suffer a trust to fail for want of a trustee.[35]
- Equity suffers not advantage to be taken of a penalty or forfeiture, where compensation can be made.[36]

"Just as the thirteen original states adopted substantially the entire common law of England, so they took over with little change the English system of equity jurisprudence, a portion of which was the subject of trusts."[37] In some jurisdictions, however, it took some time before trusts were judicially enforced. It was not until 1877, for example, that "equity won full recognition as a complementary part of the judicial system of Massachusetts."[38]

While it is said that equity affords relief when there is no common law remedy, equity is still very much a creature of case law. It is far from a "code" as that term is understood in France, Germany, Italy, and the other civil law jurisdictions. One learned commentator has articulated the case against codification:

> The main argument against codification is immobility. . . . A code corresponds to the state of legal developments at a given moment and it aims to fix that state so that it will not be changed. . . . The settled text can, at the very most, be the object of interpretation. . . . The fixing of the law by codification causes internal contradictions and intolerable tensions within a society. Every codification therefore poses a dilemma: if the code is not modified, it loses all touch with reality, falls out of date and impedes social development; yet if the components of the code are constantly modified to adapt to new situations, the whole loses its logical unity and increasingly exhibits divergences and even contradictions. These dangers are real,

---

trust, equity sees to it that "the land will devolve as personalty irrespective of the precise time at which the sale takes place, thus preventing the devolution of beneficial interests from being altered by failure or delay on the part of the trustees in executing this duty to sell." Hanbury & Maudsley, Modern Equity 277 (10th ed. 1976). A direction to purchase also might implicate equitable conversion doctrine.

[32] Snell's Equity ¶ 5-26.

[33] Snell's Equity ¶ 5-27 through ¶ 5-28. A judgment in an action at law creates rights in the plaintiff, whereas a decree in equity imposes duties on the defendant. *See generally* 1 Scott on Trusts §1.

[34] Though a court of equity generally will not enforce a gratuitous promise to create a trust, it will enforce a present gratuitous declaration of, or transfer in, trust. 1 Scott & Ascher §3.3.2.

[35] 2 Scott & Ascher §11.4. *See, however,* 2 Scott & Ascher §11.4.1 (noting that the maxim is inapplicable if the settlor intends for the trust to continue only so long as the designated trustee continues as trustee).

[36] Richard Francis, Maxims of Equity 44 (London, Bernard Lintot 1728) (maxim no. 12). This maxim is cited in support of the proposition that a court may not assess punitive damages against a trustee in an equitable action for breach of trust. *See generally* §7.2.3.2 of this handbook (punitive or exemplary damages). A legal action in contract or tort brought by a third party against the trustee would be another matter.

[37] Bogert §6.

[38] Edwin H. Woodruff, *Chancery in Massachusetts*, 5 The L.Q. Rev. 370, 383 (Oct. 1889).

for experience shows that the compilation of a new code is a difficult enterprise that rarely meets with success.[39]

Introducing the trust by statute into non-common law jurisdictions. In some civil law jurisdictions, such as Louisiana, Puerto Rico,[40] Panama,[41] Liechtenstein,[42] Quebec,[43] Mexico,[44] South Africa, Israel,[45] Venezuela,[46] and Monaco, the law of trusts has been introduced by statute.[47] That happened in Louisiana in 1964,[48] although Louisiana's first trust statute was enacted in 1920.[49]

In other civil law jurisdictions, most notably France and Germany,[50] the concept of the trust has generally made little headway.[51] "Under Danish law, the trust concept and its division between legal and equitable interests are completely unknown."[52]

The EU (European Union) has yet to officially define a trust.[53] "Misleadingly, Russian civil law has a concept of 'trusted management' (doveritelnoe upravlenie), which is often (erroneously) translated into English as 'trust', however, the Russian concept of trusted management and the Anglo-Saxon

---

[39] R. C. van Caenegem, An Historical Introduction to Private Law 14 (D. E. L. Johnston trans., Cambridge University Press 1992) (1998). *See also* David Wessel, *The Legal DNA of Economics*, Wall St. J., Sept. 6, 2001, at 1 (suggesting that "rule-laden civil-law countries aren't well adapted to cope with change").

[40] Bogert §9.

[41] Bogert §9.

[42] *See generally* Guido Meier, *The Trust in the Liechtenstein Law on Persons and Companies*, in Trusts in Prime Jurisdictions 349 (Alon Kaplan ed., 2000).

[43] On January 1, 2014, a new *Civil Code* became effective in the Czech Republic. It makes provision for a partial trust analog known as "Administration of Third Parties' Assets." The legislation is modeled somewhat after the "trust" sections of the *Civil Code of Quebec*, specifically Sections 1260–1370.

[44] Bogert §9.

[45] *See generally* Alon Kaplan, *Trusts in Israel*, in Trusts in Prime Jurisdictions 317 (Alon Kaplan ed., 2000).

[46] Bogert §9.

[47] *See generally* Jeffrey A. Schoenblum, 1 Multistate and Multinational Estate Planning 1280–1314 (1999).

[48] Bogert §9.

[49] *See generally* John Chipman Gray, The Rule Against Perpetuities, Appendix D, §§771 & 772 (4th ed. 1942) (Louisiana trust legislation).

[50] *See generally* Hein Kotz, *The Hague Convention on the Law Applicable to Trusts and Their Recognition*, in Trusts in Prime Jurisdictions 3, 12 (Alon Kaplan ed., 2000) (advising that the German government does not intend, in the foreseeable future, to commence ratification proceedings for The Hague Convention); Bogert §9.("The French code contains an exclusive list of recognized rights and property interests that generally prevents recognition of separate property interests in a trustee and beneficiary. . . . In Germany the concept of the trust is unknown, and German courts often treat the common law trust as a mere contractual relationship."

[51] Jeffrey A. Schoenblum, 1 Multistate and Multinational Estate Planning 1245–1247 (1999).

[52] Bogert §9.

[53] Henry Christensen, III, *Foreign Trusts and Alternative Vehicles*, SH032 ALI-ABA 81, 92 (2002).

common law trusts are based on different principles, have different natures and different characteristics and are used for different practical purposes."[54]

As noted above, Latin America has seen some trust legislation.[55] "In Latin America...[,however,]...with relatively few exceptions, the trust has been used solely for business purposes."[56]

Japan is a code jurisdiction that has a trust statute on its books, which is largely ignored.[57] "There is a trust law which attempts to codify the law of trusts but for lack of use and lack of tradition and most importantly, the lack of any tax benefits from the use of a trust, it largely lies fallow. However, it does provide some support when U.S. trusts have assets or beneficiaries in Japan."[58]

The Chinese Trust Law 2001 (PRC) appears to have created a trust-contract hybrid. Assets are segregated from the personal assets of the trustee, as is the case with a trusteeship. On the other hand, "...the settlor after trust creation remains very much in the picture, with considerable authority, and the more secondary position of the trustee suggests a contract between settlor and trustee—sometimes for the benefit of the settlor, sometimes for the settlor and trustee, and sometimes for a third party beneficiary."[59] For a behind-the scenes look at how China's legal scholars went about tweaking the trust, a quintessential common law institution, so that it could be retrofitted into a legal system that was not only socialist and civil law–based but also culturally alien in the extreme, the reader is referred to Frances H. Foster, American Trust Law in a Chinese Mirror.[60] "According to Chinese drafters and scholars, the initial impetus for the legislation was the urgent need to promote China's accession to the World Trade Organization and to address China's troubled financial sector by adopting 'an important pillar of the modern financing industry in developed countries,' the trust."[61]

As far as the United States is concerned, the Uniform Trust Code, although comprehensive in scope, is not intended to codify all aspects of the law of trusts. The National Conference of Commissioners on Uniform State Laws fully contemplated that the Uniform Trust Code, which is available on the Internet at <http://www.uniformlaws.org/Act.aspx?title=Trust%20Code>, would be supplemented by the common law of trusts and principles of equity.

---

[54] Olga Boltenko, *Trusts for Russians*, 17(5) STEP J. 43 (May 2009).

[55] Bogert §9.

[56] Bogert §9; *see generally* §9.6 of this handbook (the business trust).

[57] Bogert §9.

[58] Griffith Way, Planning the Estates of Americans Residing in Japan n. 26 [ABA Sections of Int'l Law and Real Prop., Prob., & Trust Law, *Current Legal Aspects of International Estate Planning* (Robert A. Hendrickson & William K. Stevens eds., 1982)].

[59] Donovan Waters, *Cross-Border Trusts and the Conflict of Laws (Part 1)*, 3(2) Trust Q. Rev. 7 (2005).

[60] Frances H. Foster, *American Trust Law in a Chinese Mirror*, 94 Minn. L. Rev. 602 (2010).

[61] Frances H. Foster, *American Trust Law in a Chinese Mirror*, 94 Minn. L. Rev. 602, 627–628 (2010).

§8.12.1   Civil Law Alternatives to the Trust

Dutch civil law, in keeping with many continental European legal systems, is based on Roman law as codified during the Napoleonic period. The trust form, as it is known under common law jurisdictions, does not therefore appear in the Dutch legal system. That is not to say that there is no similar institution or arrangement with which a foreign trust might be compared. Examples include the Roman law concept of usufruct, custodianship (bewind), foundations (stichting) and capital funds (doelvermogen).[62]

Sixteen months after Mr. Herrhausen's murder, the Red Army Faction claimed its last victim, killing Detlev Karsten Rohwedder, the head of the Treuhandanstalt, the powerful trust that controlled most state-owned assets in the former East Germany and was overseeing their privatization.[63]

There is really nothing comparable to the common law trust in civil law jurisprudence. "In surveying the varied civil law alternatives, it becomes clear that no one device serves all the purposes a single trust is capable of achieving."[64] That is not to say, however, that "in terms of any particular objective sought, there will undoubtedly be some technique of the civil law capable of securing the desired objective."[65]

For a discussion of how civil law trust analogs, which one commentator refers to as "trust-like devices,"[66] might be cobbled together to accomplish a particular task now routinely performed by the common law trust, the reader is referred to Pierre Lepaulle.[67] For a discussion of how civil law trust analogs are employed on the Continent in the mutual fund context, the reader is referred to Charles Rounds and Andreas Dehio.[68]

Fiducia; Fiducie. The concept of the *fiducia* can be traced to Roman law.[69] Its modern counterpart is the French *prete nom* and the German or Swiss *treuhand*.[70] Like a common law trust, the *fiducia* involves a transfer of property

---

[62] Barry Larking & Jan A. Dekker, *Use of Trust-Held Dutch Companies for International Tax Planning*, in Trusts in Prime Jurisdictions 293 (Alon Kaplan ed., 2000). Prof. Fratcher catalogs 26 diverse purposes for which trusts are commonly used. W. F. Fratcher, *Trust §101*, in Intl. Encyclopedia of Comp. Law, Vol. VI, ch. 11, p. 84 (F. H. Lawson ed., 1973). "The Roman law of the sixth century codifications and the codes presently in force on the continent of Europe contain no single legal device capable of achieving all of the 26 purposes. . . ." Fratcher, *Trust §101*, in Intl. Encyclopedia of Comp. Law, Vol. VI, ch. 11, p. 84 (F. H. Lawson ed., 1973).

[63] David Crawford, *The Murder of a CEO*, Wall St. J, Sep. 15, 2007, at pg. A5.

[64] Jeffrey A. Schoenblum, 1 Multistate and Multinational Estate Planning 1247 (1999).

[65] Schoenblum, 1 Multistate and Multinational Estate Planning 1247 at 1247–1248.

[66] *See* Bogert §9 ("In many civil law countries various statutory arrangements exist for the holding and disposition of property which can achieve at least some of the purposes or effects of a trust. These arrangements are sometimes called 'trust-like devices.'").

[67] *Civil Law Substitutes for Trusts*, 36 Yale L.J. 1126 (1927).

[68] *Publicly-Traded Open End Mutual Funds in Common Law and Civil Law Jurisdictions: A Comparison of Legal Structures*, 3 N.Y.U.J.L. & Bus. 473 (2007).

[69] *See* Bogert §9.

[70] *See generally* Jeffrey A. Schoenblum, 1 Multistate and Multinational Estate Planning 1252–1253 (1999). *See also* Harold Parize, *Utilisation of Foreign Trust Structures in Luxembourg*, in Trusts in Prime Jurisdictions 375 n.3 and accompanying text (Alon Kaplan ed., 2000) (discussing Luxembourg's *fiducie*).

to someone (the *fiduciarius*) who must administer it for the benefit of another. Unlike a trustee, however, the *fiduciarius* has both the legal and the equitable interest. The consequence? Creditors of the *fiduciarius* can get at the property and the beneficiary has no equitable property right. The beneficiary has only a personal claim against the *fiduciarius* in the event of an unauthorized transfer of the property to a third person. However, in several jurisdictions a level of protection has been introduced by, for example, applying agency principles to the transferee.[71] In February 2007, the French *Fiducie* came into being by an act of the French parliament.[72] The French *Fiducie* appears to resemble the Roman special patrimony.[73] As we shall see, however, whether a special patrimony is a trust, a quasi-trust, or merely an arrangement that can do some of the things that a trust can do is the subject of a scholarly debate that is ongoing. Luxembourg's *Fiducie* is a statutory partial trust-analog that is contract-based.

Usufruct. The *usufruct* is a Roman invention that involves "an analytical division of ownership"[74] into "three rights: *usus, fructus, abusus, i.e.,* the right to use the res . . . , the right to gather its fruits and products which can be taken without endangering its substance . . . , [and] . . . the right to dispose of the substance by partition, destruction, sale, or gift."[75] While the *usufructuary*, the one who possesses the *usus* and *fructus*, may resemble a trustee in that he is charged with some management responsibilities, he is not a trustee.[76] This is because the *usufructuary*[77] also must possess the beneficial interest.[78] The laws governing usufruct in Louisiana are incorporated in Louisiana Civil Code, Articles 535–629.

Fideicommissum. The *fideicommissum* is a gift to one person for life (the institute) and then to another (the substitute) upon the death of the institute, provided the substitute is alive at the death of the institute.[79] The substitute is like a trust remainderman in that he or she may be unborn and unascertained at the time of the transfer to the institute.[80] Unlike a trust remainderman, however, the substitute cannot take a vested transmissible interest at the time of the transfer to the institute. The *fideicommissum* itself is unlike a trust in that the institute has management responsibilities as well as the beneficial interest.[81] Moreover, it generally cannot be created by inter vivos transfer.[82]

---

[71] Henry Beckwith, *The Trust—Your Flexible Friend*, 45 Tr. & Est. L.J., iii (Apr. 2003) (pull-out).

[72] Act 2007-211.

[73] In French the arrangement is described as a *patrimoine d'affectation*.

[74] Jeffrey A. Schoenblum, 1 Multistate and Multinational Estate Planning 1255–1257 (1999).

[75] Pierre Lepaulle, *Civil Law Substitutes for Trusts*, 36 Yale L.J. 1126, 1140 (1927).

[76] *See generally* Bogert §9.

[77] In Italy today, the *usufruttario*.

[78] *See generally* Jeffrey A. Schoenblum, 1 Multistate and Multinational Estate Planning 1255–1257 (1999).

[79] Schoenblum, 1 Multistate and Multinational Estate Planning at 1258–1260.

[80] Schoenblum, 1 Multistate and Multinational Estate Planning at 1258–1260.

[81] Schoenblum, 1 Multistate and Multinational Estate Planning at 1258–1260.

[82] Schoenblum, 1 Multistate and Multinational Estate Planning at 1258–1260.

Today, the *fideicommissum* exists in Italy, France, and Spain, and in those Latin American countries, *e.g.*, Chile, whose jurisprudence is of Spanish origin. "In Colombia, since 1873 the Civil Code has provided for the 'propriedad fiduciaria,' an entity similar to the fideicomisum."[83] A Colombian bank, by statute, may act as a testamentary trustee.[84]

Emphyteusis. "While there are diverse ways of characterizing this interest, it is essentially an arrangement whereby the settlor grants a leasehold for a period of time, occasionally as long as 99 years, and also appoints what amounts to a . . . [trust] . . . remainderman."[85] There are two key differences, however, between the *emphyteusis* and the common law trust: The one who holds the leasehold (the *emphyteuticary*), unlike a trust beneficiary, is charged with preserving and improving the subject property; and the designated taker, unlike a trust remainderman, must be in existence at the time the *emphyteusis* was created.[86] (If the designated taker dies before the leasehold expires, however, he or she may transmit the remainder interests to persons unborn and ascertained at the time the *emphyteusis* was created.[87]) Another difference is that personal property may not be the subject of an *emphyteusis* but may be the subject of a trust.[88]

"Emphyteusis has two lines of ancestry, one Roman, one Greek. . . . The Greek States would make grants under the name Emphyteusis, a Greek word meaning 'grafting' or 'planting.'"[89] In the early Roman empire, municipal authorities would grant leases of agricultural land in perpetuity or for extended periods of time, subject to the payment of rent or vectigal.[90] The land was termed *ager vectigalis*.

Other civil law trust analogues, each with its own set of limitations, include the civil law guardianship; the curatorship; the donation or legacy with a charge or under a condition; third-party beneficiary contract; deposit; and mandate.[91]

Treuhand. The *treuhand*, recognized in Germany, Austria, and Switzerland, is a creature of case law and has many of the limitations of a third-party beneficiary contract.[92] "By the treuhand, or mandat, the settlor (treugeber) transfers property to the fiduciary (treuhänder), and gives him instructions on

---

[83] Henry Christensen, III, *Foreign Trusts and Alternative Vehicles*, SH032 ALI-ABA 81, 96 (2002).

[84] Colombian Civil Code, Law 45 of 1990, Law 35 of 1993.

[85] Jeffrey A. Schoenblum, 1 Multistate and Multinational Estate Planning 1257–1258 (1999).

[86] Jeffrey A. Schoenblum, 1 Multistate and Multinational Estate Planning 1257–1258 (1999).

[87] Jeffrey A. Schoenblum, 1 Multistate and Multinational Estate Planning 1257–1258 (1999).

[88] Jeffrey A. Schoenblum, 1 Multistate and Multinational Estate Planning 1257–1258 (1999).

[89] R. W. Lee, The Elements of Roman Law 173 (4th ed. 1956).

[90] R. W. Lee, The Elements of Roman Law 173 (4th ed. 1956).

[91] *See generally* Jeffrey A. Schoenblum, 1 Multistate and Multinational Estate Planning §18.03 (1999).

[92] *See generally* §8.22 of this handbook (why do we need the trust when we have the corporation and the third party beneficiary contract?).

its management and for whose benefit he holds the property."[93] A *treuhand* is not enforceable by the person for whom it has been established. Being a contract, it can only govern inter vivos relationships, and thus generally cannot be employed as an estate planning vehicle.[94] Finally, in the event of the fiduciary's insolvency, the *treuhand* assets become subject to the claims of his creditors, unless there is a statute that provides otherwise.[95] For how the *treuhand* is employed on the Continent in the mutual fund context, the reader is referred to Charles Rounds and Andreas Dehio.[96]

Civil law foundation. The private civil law foundation, unlike the trust, is a creature of statute.[97] Also, unlike the trust, the civil law foundation is a separate juristic entity or legal person.[98] It resembles a corporation, only without shareholders, in that the entity itself owns the managed assets.[99] A noncharitable civil law foundation may have individual beneficiaries, although it is a principle of foundation law that the members of the foundation's board or council owe their primary allegiance to the entity itself rather than to the beneficiaries.[100] This is a critical difference between the civil law noncharitable foundation and the noncharitable trust.[101] A discretionary permissible beneficiary of a civil law foundation has no enforceable legal or quasi-equitable property rights in foundation assets,[102] which can pose a problem for the beneficiary's creditors;[103] nor would the beneficiary have a default right to scrutinize the foundation's books or otherwise demand an accounting from the foundation's board or council,[104] which could pose a problem for the beneficiary himself.

---

[93] Henry Christensen, III, *Foreign Trusts and Alternative Vehicles*, SH032 ALI-ABA 81, 95 (2002).

[94] *See generally* §8.22 of this handbook (why we need the trust when we have the corporation and the third party beneficiary contract).

[95] *Cf.* §8.3.1 of this handbook (trustee's personal creditors and the trustee's spouse).

[96] *Publicly-Traded Open End Mutual Funds in Common Law and Civil Law Jurisdictions: A Comparison of Legal Structures*, 3 N.Y.U. J. L. & Bus. 473 (2007).

[97] Unlike a statutory civil law noncharitable foundation, a trust may change its situs without having to be dissolved and reconstituted, the trustee being the legal "owner" of the subject property.

[98] The trust is a legal relationship between the trustee and the beneficiaries rather than an entity.

[99] *See generally* James Quarmby, *The rise of alternative vehicles in private wealth planning*, Offshore Investment Issue 241, at 15 (Nov. 2013) [a STEP publication] ("Foundations are interesting vehicles because they have a legal personality, like a company, but have neither share capital nor any shareholders.").

[100] A civil law private noncharitable foundation also may exist to carry out a noncharitable purpose, such as the furtherance of a family business.

[101] *See generally* §6.1.3 of this handbook (the trustee's duty of loyalty to the beneficiaries).

[102] *See generally* §5.3.1 of this handbook (the trust beneficiary's property interest).

[103] *See generally* §5.3.3.3 of this handbook (the creditors of a trust beneficiary).

[104] *See generally* §6.1.5 of this handbook (the trustee's duty to account to the beneficiary) and §5.4.1.1 of this handbook (the trust beneficiary's right to information).

Another critical difference between the noncharitable civil law foundation and the common law trust is that the duties of the members of the foundation's board or council, who do not hold legal title to the foundation's assets, are contractual in nature, rather than fiducial. Their duties are set forth in the foundation's bylaws or regulations. A noncharitable civil law foundation may have a perpetual duration.[105] In the United States, there is no such thing as a noncharitable foundation, or a charitable foundation for that matter. Under the U.S. tax laws, a "charitable foundation" is either a charitable trust or a charitable corporation, each being a creature of state law.[106] A trustee of a common law trust, however, would likely have the *legal authority* to establish with trust assets a noncharitable foundation in a civil law jurisdiction.[107] Whether under equitable principles the trustee would be violating the terms of that particular trust in so doing is a separate issue.

In Switzerland, a *stiftung*, a type of civil law foundation, may be established for a charitable purpose.[108] "A family foundation, or Familienstiftung, may be created under a separate statute, art. 335 SCC, to pay costs of education, succor and other assistance of the donor's family."[109] In Liechtenstein, however, the purpose of a *stiftung* may be either personal or charitable. Variants of stiftungs also exist in Germany and Austria.[110] An Austrian *privatstiftung* is not limited to nonprofit purposes. In Italy, a civil law foundation is known as a *fondazione;* in the Netherlands, as a *stichting*.[111]

The French *fondation* is created via a deed. The grantor or grantors irrevocably settle assets for the achievement of a not-for-profit-purpose of general interest. The *fondation* owns the subject property absolutely. A related arrangement is the *fonds de dotation*, which roughly corresponds to an endowment fund. Both entities must be registered. The creation of a *fondation* requires government approval. In France, a *fondation* for the purpose of benefiting one's family is void as a matter of public policy.

The Fuggerei in Augsburg, Germany is said to be the oldest social settlement in existence in the world. Administration of the Fuggerei Foundation (*Stiftung*) and eight other foundations is carried out by the Fürstlich und Gräflich Fuggersche Stiftungs-Administration, which manages the estates

---

[105] *See generally* §8.2.1 of this handbook (the Rule against Perpetuities).

[106] *See generally* §§9.4 of this handbook (the charitable trust) and 9.8.1 of this handbook (the charitable corporation).

[107] *Cf.* §3.5.3.1(a) of this handbook (incorporating the trust estate).

[108] Articles 80 to 89 of the Swiss Civil Code.

[109] Henry Christensen, III, *Foreign Trusts and Alternative Vehicles*, SH032 ALI-ABA 81, 94 (2002) ("Family foundations cannot be created for general management of assets and payment of income to a family.").

[110] Henry Christensen, III, *Foreign Trusts and Alternative Vehicles*, SH032 ALI-ABA 81, 94 (2002).

[111] "Managers of former Russian oil giant Yukos Oil Co. were able to shield billions of dollars in cash and international assets of Yukos from the Russian government by using two Dutch stichtings. The foundations, which continue to hold those assets on behalf of Yukos shareholders, have played a central role in a decade-long legal battle between Yukos and the Russian Government." Shayndi Raice & Margot Patrick, *The Obscure Power of a Dutch "Stichting,"* Wall St. J., Apr. 23, 2015, at B6, col. 5.

owned by the foundation. A portion of the income from these forestry and real property interests is dedicated to maintaining the Fuggerei. Tourism has become an additional source of financial support. The Fuggerei was established in 1521 by Jakob Fugger the Rich[112] as a residential settlement for Augsburg citizens in need. The annual (net) rent for an apartment in the Fuggerei still is the nominal value of the Rhenish Guilder, in the range of 0.88 Euro, together with prayers three times a day for the founder and his family. About 150 people live at present in the 140 apartments in 67 houses.[113] Master Mason Franz Mozart, the great-grandfather of the composer W. A. Mozart, resided in the Fuggerei. The Fuggerei is a town within a city with its own church, town walls, and three entrance gates. The headquarters of the Stiftungs-Administration is in the Fuggerei.

Anstalt. A Liechtenstein *anstalt* has no shareholders but it does have beneficiaries; and it may, unlike a *stiftung*, conduct business. The settlor of an *anstalt* retains "founder's rights" to vary its terms. "Indeed, because of the founder's rights... [the anstalt]... share[s] many characteristics with... [the] ...revocable trust, and American lawyers using anstalts as part of an off-shore structure need to be careful of the possible estate tax consequences of doing so."[114]

It seems that the "courts of civil law countries... [are making]... every effort to uphold a trust, as long as its assets do not include realty located in the civil law country, and perhaps subject to claims of heirs under forced heirship."[115] For a discussion of the possible civil law origins of the English trust, see Section 8.37 of this handbook.

Now, not all scholars buy into the notion that the trust is incompatible with civil law tradition. According to one, the *special patrimony*, a civil law construct, is a trust. An ordinary patrimony is the totality of one's assets, the general rule being "[e]veryone has a patrimony, no one has more than one."[116] A special patrimony, *e.g.*, a *dos* or *peculium* in the Roman law, however, is an exception to

---

[112] Jakob Fugger II (the Rich) (1459 to 1525) was a Renaissance merchant and banker with extensive mining interests. Popes; the emperors Maximilian I, Karl V and Ferdinand I of Habsburg; the kings of Germany, Spain and Portugal, England and Hungary; as well as the Medici family of Florence transacted with the Fugger Company. The Fugger Company's trading operations reached out as far as India, South America and Africa. The zenith of the Fugger commercial empire was reached in 1546 under the administration of Anton Fugger, Jakob's nephew and successor. It was Jakob who helped secure the installation of Charles V as its emperor of the Holy Roman Empire by bribing the electors.

[113] While those benefiting from Jakob Fugger's charitable foundation are obliged to pay nominal rents, those benefiting from Benjamin Franklin's charitable trust were obliged to pay nominal interest on loans made to them from the trust. *See generally* §8.31 of this handbook (Boston's Franklin trust).

[114] Henry Christensen, III, *Foreign Trusts and Alternative Vehicles*, SH032 ALI-ABA 81, 95 (2002). *See generally* §9.10 of this handbook (the offshore asset protection trust); §8.9.3 of this handbook (tax-sensitive powers).

[115] Henry Christensen, III, *Foreign Trusts and Alternative Vehicles*, SH032 ALI-ABA 81, 100 (2002).

[116] George L. Gretton, *Trusts Without Equity*, 49 Intl. & Comp. L.Q. 599, 609 (2000).

this general rule.[117] " . . . [T]he assets of the special patrimony are segregated from the general patrimony, and to some extent the civilian tradition has likewise accepted segregation of liabilities also."[118] In other words, creditors may only seek satisfaction from the special patrimony. Thus, Gretton questions why the common law lawyer and the civil law lawyer should have difficulty understanding one another:

> One frequently meets continental lawyers who fret and puzzle about the trust, to whom the trust is an *Arcanum*, to be understood only in terms of the mysteries of equity, those who have swallowed whole that remarkable statement in the preamble to the Hague Convention on the Recognition of Trusts about the trust being a "unique legal institution" which "was developed in courts of equity in common law jurisdictions," those who accept at face value the assertion that the right of the beneficiary is a right *in rem*. Yet the civilian tradition actually has and has always had the appropriate concepts.[119]

Hungary's contract-based trust analog. On February 11, 2013, the Hungarian Parliament enacted the New Hungarian Civil Code, which has a contract-based trust-analog feature.[120] The details of this special type of contract may be found in the Code's Sixth Book, which is devoted to the law of obligations. Though contract-based, a Hungarian trust analog can be impressed on property by declaration or testamentary transfer, as well as by inter vivos transfer. Title to the subject property is in the obligor, who is a quasi fiduciary. The third-party obligees, the ones with the beneficial interest, have a reinforced *in personam* right in the subject property, which has some of the characteristics of a right *in rem*. The subject property, for example, is insulated from the reach of the obligor's personal creditors and may be followed or traced by the third-party obligees in the face of an unauthorized alienation to a non-BFP. Under the Code, an owner of property may also enter into such a contract for his or her own benefit.

Scotland's dual patrimony trust analog (the "Tartan trust"). A Tartan trust is not a true trust. "Although Scottish trust law has been influenced by the law of England and Wales over the years and the two may now appear very similar, its roots developed in the 17th century, on Roman civil-law principles."[121] Thus, Scottish law does not recognize the legal-equitable ownership dichotomy that is at the heart of the Anglo-American trust concept. Instead, the trustee of a Tartan trust fully owns both his personal assets and the assets that have been "entrusted" to his care, but holds each category in a separate, segregated "patrimony." The beneficiary of a Tartan trust is vested with a

---

[117] Gretton, *Trusts Without Equity*, 49 Intl. & Comp. L.Q. 599, 609.

[118] Gretton, *Trusts Without Equity*, 49 Intl. & Comp. L.Q. 599, 609.

[119] Gretton, *Trusts Without Equity*, 49 Intl. & Comp. L.Q. at 610.

[120] *See generally* Charles E. Rounds, Jr. and István Illés, *Is a Hungarian Trust a Clone of the Anglo-American Trust, or Just a Type of Contract?: Parsing the Asset-Management Provisions of the New Hungarian Civil Code*, 6 Geo. Mason J. Int'l Com. L. 153 (2015).

[121] Debbie King, *Tartan trusts*, 23 STEP J. 27 (Issue 3/Apr. 2015).

personal right of enforcement against the Tartan trustee, a right that falls short of an equitable/beneficial property interest in the subject property itself.

Power of attorney (civil law). The civil law power of attorney is another trust analog.[122] "[T]he reader should be forewarned . . . [however] . . . that the common law concept of a general power of attorney simply is not comparable to the remarkably broad and versatile general power found in civil law countries."[123]

§8.12.2 The Hague Convention on the Law Applicable to Trusts and on Their Recognition

As a comparison to Italy, Dr. Christian Von Oertzen presented the reception of trusts in Germany, another civil law country. If the trust in Italy could be characterized as largely unknown but being considered, in Germany, the reception is more hostile. The German Federal Supreme Court even ruled in 1985 that a legal trust relationship is incompatible with German public policy for structural reasons. Germany has not signed the Hague Convention on Trusts and probably won't in the near future.[124]

[A] major challenge in achieving a single financial market in Europe is a lack of a domestic law of trusts in the civil jurisdictions making up all of Europe other than England and Ireland.[125]

The Hague Convention on the Law Applicable to Trusts and on Their Recognition (the "Hague Convention") (concluded July 1, 1985), available at <http://www.hcch.net/index_en.php?act=conventions.text&cid=59>,[126] states that its purpose is to deal with the most important issues concerning the recognition in civil law jurisdictions of trusts established in common law jurisdictions. The Hague Convention has entered into force in seven civil law jurisdictions: Italy, Liechtenstein, Luxembourg, the Netherlands, Malta, San Marino, and Switzerland. It has been ratified in the following common law jurisdictions: Australia, Canada (with the exception of Quebec), and the United Kingdom. China has ratified the Convention for the Hong Kong Special Administrative Region only.

---

[122] Jeffrey A. Schoenblum, 1 Multistate and Multinational Estate Planning 1260–1262 (1999).

[123] Schoenblum, 1 Multistate and Multinational Estate Planning at 1260.

[124] Howard S. Simmons reporting on STEP Conference held at the Villa D'Este, Milan, on 27–29 October 2002. *See* STEP J. (Dec. 2002) at 21.

[125] Excerpt from an email (Oct. 9, 2002) from Dr. Joanna Benjamin, member of Bank of England's Financial Markets Law Committee to Steven L. Schwarcz. The excerpt is reprinted in footnote 17 of Steven L. Schwarcz, *Commercial Trusts as Business Organizations: An Invitation to Comparatists*, Duke Law School Public Law and Legal Theory Research Paper Series, Research Paper No. 39 (Apr. 2003).

[126] *See generally* Hein Kotz, *The Hague Convention on the Law Applicable to Trusts and Their Recognition*, in Trusts in Prime Jurisdictions 3 (Alon Kaplan ed., 2000). The Hague Convention is also reproduced in footnote 55 of §9 of Bogert.

The United States, however, has yet to ratify the Convention. Some in the United States, most notably Professor Jeffrey A. Schoenblum of Vanderbilt Law School, while applauding the goal of gaining wider acceptance for the trust in non-common law jurisdictions, have suggested that ratification by the U.S. Congress of the Hague Convention in its current form would have adverse "inbound effects" in that it would cause foreign law to apply to transfers of U.S. real property, unsettle U.S. choice of law rules regarding trusts, and interfere with the jurisdiction of U.S. courts over U.S. trusts.[127] In Louisiana, concern has been expressed that ratification "would lead to problems in its domestic property law caused by interference of foreign trust law with domestic rights of inheritance and forced heirship."[128]

Others in and outside the United States, most notably Professor Luc Thévenoz of the University of Geneva Faculty of Law, see no adverse "inbound effects."[129] In his opinion, "the Convention deals with the law applicable to trusts, not with the law applicable to transfers of property to or from the trustee."[130]

§8.13   In Litigation Pertaining to a Trust, When Is the Beneficiary Entitled to Reimbursement from the Trust Estate for Legal Fees?

In a judicial proceeding involving the administration of a trust, the court, as justice and equity may require, may award costs and expenses, including reasonable attorney's fees, to any party, to be paid by another party or from the trust that is the subject of the controversy.[1]

In litigation pertaining to a trust, the court has discretion to order the trustee to reimburse the beneficiary from the trust estate for the beneficiary's reasonable legal fees and other litigation costs.[2] The litigation, however, must be indispensable to the proper administration of the trust or confer a benefit on

---

[127] *See generally* Jeffrey A. Schoenblum, 1 Multistate and Multinational Estate Planning 1334–1357 (1999).

[128] Henry Christensen, III, *Foreign Trusts and Alternative Vehicles*, SH032 ALI-ABA 81, 92 (2002).

[129] Letter from Luc Thévenoz, Professor, University of Geneva Faculty of Law, to Charles E. Rounds, Jr., Professor, Suffolk University Law School (May 23, 2000) (on file with the author). *See generally* Pietro Supino and Andreas C. Limburg, *A Swiss Perspective on Trusts*, in Prime Jurisdictions 383 (Alon Kaplan ed., 2000).

[130] Letter from Luc Thévenoz, Professor, University of Geneva Faculty of Law, to Charles E. Rounds, Jr., Professor, Suffolk University Law School (May 23, 2000) at 1 (on file with the author).

§8.13 [1] UTC §1004 (available at <http://www.uniformlaws.org/Act.aspx?title=Trust%20 Code>). *See also* Mass. Gen. Laws ch. 215, §§39A, 39B, & 45.

[2] Restatement (Third) of Trusts §88 cmt. d. "A trustee cannot properly pay costs incurred by a beneficiary in a judicial or other proceeding involving the administration of the trust or the beneficiary's interests in the trust, except pursuant to a court order." Restatement (Third) of Trusts §88 cmt. d. *See generally* 3 Scott & Ascher §18.1.2.4.

the beneficiary class.[3] The Restatement (Third) of Restitution and Unjust Enrichment is generally in accord.[4] Thus, allowance of reasonable costs and attorneys' fees is proper if the trust instrument is sufficiently ambiguous to warrant a judicial complaint for instructions and if the beneficiary is not responsible for the ambiguity.[5] After all, the beneficiary must be a party to the proceedings if there is to be a binding resolution of the issue. Of course, when litigation involves a breach of trust, ultimate liability may well attach to the trustee himself.[6] In other words, the trustee may have to reimburse the trust for the beneficiary's litigation costs.[7]

Things, however, are not quite so simple. In Delaware, for example, a beneficiary successfully sued a corporate trustee for certain breaches of trust including "failing to inform...[him]...of his current beneficiary status in a timely fashion, showing partiality...[to the other beneficiaries,]...and

---

[3] *See generally* Restatement (Third) of Trusts §88 cmt. d; Bogert §871; 3 Scott & Ascher §18.1.2.4; §8.15.13 of this handbook (common fund doctrine); Lowery v. Evonuk, 95 Or. App. 98, 767 P. 2d 489 (1989) (awarding attorneys' fees to plaintiffs where litigation was necessary and benefited all beneficiaries).

[4] *See* Restatement (Third) of Restitution and Unjust Enrichment §26 ("If the claimant incurs necessary expense to protect an interest in property and in so doing confers an economic benefit on another person in consequence of the other's interest in the same property, the claimant is entitled to restitution from the other as necessary to prevent unjust enrichment."); Restatement (Third) of Restitution and Unjust Enrichment §29, illus. 4 (the common fund doctrine).

[5] *See generally* Bogert §871; 76 Am. Jur. 2d *Trusts* §§731–741 (1992); Allan E. Korpela, LL.B., Annot., *Amount of attorney's compensation in matters involving guardianships and trusts*, 57 A.L.R.3d 550 (1974); §8.15.13 of this handbook (common fund doctrine); Annot., *Costs and fees—Trust Litigation*, 9 A.L.R.2d 1132 (1950). *See* Boeing Co. v. Van Gemert, 444 U.S. 472 (1980) (holding that common fund doctrine is entirely consistent with the American rule against taxing the losing party with the victor's attorneys' fees). *See, e.g.,* Hall v. Cole, 412 U.S. 1 (1973) (noting that counsel fees may be awarded to plaintiff out of trust estate when litigation confers benefit on beneficiary class).

[6] *See generally* §7.1 of this handbook (trustee's liabilities generally). *See, e.g.,* Hughes v. Cafferty, 495 Utah Adv. Rep. 5, 89 P.3d 148 (2004) (two cotrustees who disregarded plain language of all the trust documents and who failed to regularly account to the trust beneficiaries must pay out of their own pockets the legal fees of a beneficiary who had sued the cotrustees for breach of trust, the court having found that the litigation had resulted in a recapture of substantial funds for the trust estate, which benefited all of the beneficiaries); Murphy v. Murphy, 1997 Me. 103, 694 A.2d 932 (1997) (court having found trustee in breach of trust for borrowing trust funds for his own personal use, ordered trustee to pay beneficiaries' legal fees); Feinberg v. Feinberg Hotel Trust, 922 S.W.2d 21, 34–35 (Mo. App. Ct. 1996) (holding trustees who engaged in self-dealing personally liable for attorneys' fees); In re Estate of Stowell, 595 A.2d 1022 (Me. 1991) (awarding beneficiaries attorneys' fees out of trust estate and ordering trustee to reimburse the trust estate where trustee had breached his fiduciary duties).

[7] *See, e.g.,* Davis v. Davis, 889 N.E.2d 374, 388 (Ind. Ct. App. 2008) ("...[W]e reverse the trial court's attorney fee award in the amount of $4,000.00 and remand this issue to the trial court to determine what attorney fees were reasonably incurred by...[the beneficiary]...in securing from the Trust a proper and timely accounting, in uncovering the need for the Trustee to repay loans made to him from Trust funds, and in ensuring that the Trust received the appropriate interest on money loaned from the Trust. We order the Trust to pay...[the beneficiary]...such reasonable attorney fees as the court shall determine, and order the Trustee to reimburse the Trust for such sums"). *See generally* §7.2.3.7 (assessment of attorneys' fees as equitable relief for a breach of trust).

allowing the trust to operate on 'autopilot.'"[8] The trustee was surcharged and removed. Nevertheless, the court ordered the beneficiary to pay his own legal costs while it permitted the trustee to be reimbursed for its legal fees from the trust estate. The beneficiary had to absorb his own litigation costs because "the suit did not benefit the trust, only him."[9] In other words, the common fund doctrine was inapplicable.[10] The Restatement (Third) of Restitution and Unjust Enrichment would seem generally supportive of that conclusion.[11] As for the trustee, "success is not the test"[12] when it comes to the recovery of counsel fees. "Although the extent of the breach was serious (and extended), the Court of Chancery specifically concluded that the . . . trustee's . . . actions were ill considered and wrong, but not in bad faith."[13] The trustee's conduct did not warrant departure from "the usual rule that trustees who defend litigation against the trust are entitled to look to the trust for reimbursement."[14]

In another case out of Delaware, beneficiaries who had unsuccessfully sought removal of a trustee were awarded their counsel fees from the trust estate. The court found that the litigation had "conferred a benefit on the Trust, both by reducing its administrative costs and by reconfiguring its governance structure."[15] The trustee was awarded his legal fees from the trust estate as well as his conduct, though possibly negligent, did not rise to the level of gross negligence.

Under certain circumstances a beneficiary may be ordered to pay out of personal funds the fees of the *trustee's* attorneys, a topic we take up in Section 5.6 of this handbook. In one case, a nuisance beneficiary and his counsel were held jointly and severally liable for the trustee's litigation defense costs.[16]

§8.14 When a Guardian ad Litem (or Special Representative) Is Needed: Virtual Representation Issues

As a practical matter, however, the necessary consents . . . [to a trust termination or modification] . . . may not be obtainable in many situations. This is not only because some beneficiaries may dissent from a termination or modification plan but also because of fiduciary inhibitions on the part of those called upon to represent the interests of others. The

---

[8] McNeil v. McNeil, 798 A.2d 503, 508 (Del. 2002).

[9] McNeil v. McNeil, 798 A.2d at 514.

[10] *See generally* §8.15.13 of this handbook (common fund doctrine).

[11] *See* Restatement (Third) of Restitution and Unjust Enrichment §29, illus. 18.

[12] McNeil v. McNeil, 798 A.2d 503, 515 (Del. 2002).

[13] McNeil v. McNeil, 798 A.2d at 514–515.

[14] McNeil v. McNeil, 798 A.2d at 515. *See generally* §3.5.2.3 of this handbook (right in equity to exoneration and reimbursement).

[15] Unfunded Insurance Trust Agreement of Capaldi, 870 A.2d 493, 498 (Del. 2005).

[16] *See* Pederson Trust, 757 N.W.2d 740 (N.D. 2008).

technical and practical problems of representing others are particularly challenging when-ever more is involved than mutually beneficial modification of administrative provisions.[1]

Trustee represents beneficiaries in external matters. Assuming no breach of trust, the trustee represents the interests of the beneficiaries in an action by a third party against the "trust."[2] Likewise, in the situation where the "trust" (actually the trustee) has received a pour-over from a probate estate, the trust beneficiaries are represented by the trustee.[3] Notice of the petition for the allowance of *the executor's accounts* is given to the trustee.[4] Absent special facts, notice need not also be given to the trust beneficiaries. "There is no conflict of interest between the trustee and the beneficiaries."[5] Both trustee and beneficiaries "are equally interested in acquiring all property belonging to the trust."[6] Now if the trustee and the executor are one and the same, or if there is some other conflict of interest between the trustee and the trust beneficiaries that relates in some way to the pour-over, then the situation would be different. Notice of the petition for the allowance *of the executor's accounts* then would have to be given to the trust beneficiaries, unless possibly if there were an independent cotrustee in the picture.[7] A guardian ad litem might well also have to be appointed to represent any unborn and unascertained among them.

Necessary parties in an internal trust dispute. All beneficiaries are necessary parties, however, to an internal dispute involving an irrevocable trust.[8] In this context, even an action brought by the trustee for instructions or declaratory judgment would likely qualify as a "dispute." So also would an uncontested proceeding to reform, modify, rectify, rescind, revoke, or terminate the trust.[9] Having said that, a beneficiary whose equitable interests would be unaffected or "unprejudiced" whatever the outcome of a particular dispute might well not be a necessary party, such as in the case of a petition or complaint to terminate a segregated trust share that is being administered exclusively for

---

§8.14 [1] Restatement (Third) of Trusts §65 cmt. b.

[2] UTC   §303(4)   (available   at   <http://www.uniformlaws.org/Act.aspx?title=Trust%20Code>); UPC §1-403(2)(B)(iii).

[3] UPC §1-403(2)(B)(iii).

[4] UPC §1-403(2)(B)(iii).

[5] In re Claflin, 336 Mass. 578, 581, 146 N.E.2d 914, 916 (1958).

[6] In re Claflin, 336 Mass. 578, 581, 146 N.E.2d 914, 916 (1958).

[7] *See* Azarian v. First Nat'l Bank of Boston, 383 Mass. 492, 495, 423 N.E.2d 749, 751 (1981) ("Unless the cotrustee is financially responsible and is represented by independent counsel, the representation may well be far less adequate than self-representation by a competent adult beneficiary.").

[8] Bogert §871. *See generally* §5.7 of this handbook (the necessary parties to a suit brought by a beneficiary). *Cf.* In re Claflin, 336 Mass. 578, 581, 146 N.E.2d 914, 916 (1958) ("The ordinary rule is that in relations between a trust and the outside world, where internal administration of the trust is not involved, the trustee represents the cestuis que trust."). *See also* UPC §7-201 (defining proceedings involving the "internal affairs" of trusts as "those concerning the administration and distribution of trusts, the declaration of rights and the determination of other matters involving trustees and beneficiaries of trusts").

[9] *See generally* 5 Scott & Ascher §34.4 (When Some of the Beneficiaries Do Not or Cannot Give Binding Consent); §8.2.2.1 of this handbook (terminating trusts mid-course).

the benefit of other beneficiaries,[10] or a complaint to reform a trust to remedy faulty tax planning, provided the proposed reformation "cannot harm the interests of any beneficiary."[11]

Beneficiary representing self in internal trust matters, or delegating the task to agents. A beneficiary of full age and legal capacity may represent himself or herself in the internal matter, or appoint an agent to handle things.[12] The agent, if duly authorized, may represent and bind the principal, who in this case is the beneficiary.[13] A beneficiary may be represented by his or her conservator[14] and, if there is no conservator, then by his or her guardian.[15] A minor child who has neither a conservator nor a guardian or an unborn child may be represented by his or her parent.[16] Those having an interest in a deceased trust beneficiary's probate estate may be represented in matters pertaining to the trust by the deceased beneficiary's personal representative (executor or administrator).[17] In the case of a trust-to-trust distribution, the recipient trustee may represent and bind the beneficiaries of his trust.[18] All this assumes that the interests of the representative are not in conflict with the represented.[19]

As noted above, the trustee of a trust entitled to a pour-over devise under someone's will has authority to approve the personal representative's (executor's or administrator's) account on behalf of the trust beneficiaries.[20] Such consent, however, would not be binding on a trust beneficiary who registers an objection.[21] In a suit by the beneficiary of an irrevocable trust against a trustee

---

[10] *See generally* 5 Scott & Ascher §34.4 (When the Interests of the Nonconsenting Beneficiaries Are Not Affected).

[11] Schultz v. Shultz, 451 Mass. 1014 n.3, 888 N.E.2d 950 n.3 (2008) (upholding the decision of the lower court to dispense with the appointment of a guardian ad litem to represent the unborn and unascertained beneficiaries, this because their interests would not be harmed by reforming the trust as proposed). *See generally* §8.17 of this handbook (trust reformation to remedy mistakes that have adverse tax consequences).

[12] *See generally* 5 Scott & Ascher §34.4.

[13] UTC §303(3) (available at <http://www.uniformlaws.org/Act.aspx?title=Trust%20 Code>). The agent must have the authority to act with respect to the particular question or dispute. UTC §303(3). *See also* 5 Scott & Ascher §34.4.

[14] UTC §303(1) (available at <http://www.uniformlaws.org/Act.aspx?title=Trust%20 Code>); 5 Scott & Ascher §34.4; UPC §1-403(2)(B)(i).

[15] UTC §303(2) (available at <http://www.uniformlaws.org/Act.aspx?title=Trust%20 Code>; 5 Scott & Ascher §34.4; UPC §1-403(2)(B)(ii).

[16] UTC §303(6) (available at <http://www.uniformlaws.org/Act.aspx?title=Trust%20 Code>); 5 Scott & Ascher §34.4; UPC §1-403(3).

[17] UTC §303(5) (available at <http://www.uniformlaws.org/Act.aspx?title=Trust%20 Code>); 5 Scott & Ascher §34.4; UPC §1-403(2)(B)(iv).

[18] UTC §303(4) (available at <http://www.uniformlaws.org/Act.aspx?title=Trust%20 Code>); 5 Scott & Ascher §34.4.; UPC §1-403(2)(B)(iii).

[19] UTC §303 (available at <http://www.uniformlaws.org/Act.aspx?title=Trust%20Code>); 5 Scott & Ascher §34.4.

[20] UTC §301 cmt. (available at <http://www.uniformlaws.org/Act.aspx?title=Trust%20 Code>); 5 Scott & Ascher §34.4; UPC §1-403(2)(B)(iii).

[21] UTC §301 cmt. (available at <http://www.uniformlaws.org/Act.aspx?title=Trust%20 Code>); 5 Scott & Ascher §34.4.

for breach of trust, it is unlikely that the interests of the unborn and unascertained remaindermen can be adequately represented by the cotrustee. Why? Because there may be cofiduciary liability.[22] "A consent by a representative is invalid to the extent there is a conflict of interest between the representative and the person represented."[23] Nor is the cotrustee in the position to represent their interests in an action for instructions or declaratory judgment. Why? Because of the duty of impartiality.[24]

Virtual representation. The unborn and unascertained remaindermen and others who, for whatever reason, are unrepresented in the dispute are a problem.[25] Who is to look after their interests? If the facts are right, the doctrine of virtual representation may offer a solution, at least in those jurisdictions in which it is recognized.[26] The doctrine of virtual representation, as enunciated in the Uniform Trust Code, is as follows: Unless otherwise represented, a minor, incapacitated or unborn individual, or a person whose identity or location is unknown and not reasonably ascertainable may be represented by and bound by another having a substantially identical interest with respect to the particular question or dispute but only to the extent there is no conflict of interest between the representative and the person represented.[27] The Uniform Probate Code is generally in accord, except that it has no express conflict-of-interest exception.[28]

To illustrate the doctrine, let us take a trust with the following provisions: *A* to *B* for *C* for life, then to John Jones outright and free of trust if he is then living; but if John Jones is not then living, to his then-living issue from a first marriage.[29] Absent special facts, it is likely that either *C* or John Jones could represent the other beneficiaries in an action to remove the trustee, that is *B*, and appoint a suitable successor to *B*.[30]

Now let us assume that *C* wishes a distribution of principal but the governing instrument is silent on the matter. Under the doctrine of "virtual representation," if applicable, the assent of John Jones to the distribution may or may not be binding on the aforementioned issue of John Jones who are

---

[22] *See* §7.2.4 of this handbook (cofiduciary and predecessor liability and contribution).

[23] UTC §411 cmt. (available at <http://www.uniformlaws.org/Act.aspx?title=Trust%20 Code>); UPC §1-403(2)(B).

[24] *See* §6.2.5 of this handbook (duty of impartiality).

[25] *See generally* 4 Scott & Ascher §20.1 (Impartiality Between Successive Beneficiaries).

[26] Bogert §871; 5 Scott & Ascher §34.4. *See also* UPC §1-403(2)(C) (providing that unless otherwise represented, a minor or an incapacitated, unborn, or unascertained person is bound by an order to the extent the person's interest is adequately represented by another party having a substantially identical interest in the proceeding). *See generally* §8.15.34 of this handbook (virtual representation doctrine).

[27] UTC §304 (available at <http://www.uniformlaws.org/Act.aspx?title=Trust%20Code>). *See generally* 5 Scott & Ascher §34.4.

[28] UPC §1-403(2)(C). *See also* Mass. Gen. Laws ch. 190B, §1-403(2)(iii) (no express conflict-of-interest exception).

[29] *See* §8.30 of this handbook (the difference between a vested equitable remainder subject to divestment and a vested (transmissible) contingent equitable remainder).

[30] *See, e.g.*, Davis v. U.S. Bank Nat'l Ass'n, 243 S.W.3d 425 (Mo. Ct. App. 2007).

unborn and unascertained, depending upon the actual facts and circumstances. There is the argument that the economic interests of John Jones and his issue are not in conflict: If he survives C, he is entitled to the remainder interest; if he does not, then they are.

Of course, the argument against applying the doctrine is that John Jones may be swayed by external considerations (*e.g.*, C might be his second wife) that would not sway the unborn grandchildren, that is to say he has a conflict of interest.[31] After all, C would not be their grandmother.

Virtual representation may not be appropriate for another reason as well, namely, that a distribution of principal is a form of partial termination. As a general rule, a presumptive remainderman may not represent alternative remaindermen when it comes to trust termination issues.[32] Insuring against John Jones predeceasing C might be a practical way around the impasse.[33] Another option might be for John Jones to agree to indemnify the trustee for any liability occasioned by the trustee's making principal distributions to C.[34] "In short, where the rights of infants and incompetents are concerned, virtual representation never assures the same finality in decree as does representation by a guardian ad litem."[35]

Many states now have statutes that have codified and "greatly expanded" the common law virtual representation doctrine.[36] A number of them are modeled on the virtual representation provisions of the Uniform Trust Code, but a significant number are not. For a 50-state-plus-D.C. survey of virtual representation statutes as of March 5, 2010, the reader is referred to Susan T. Bart and Lyman W. Welch.[37]

---

[31] For a case in which such "external considerations" foreclosed virtual representation of minor children, see Mennen v. Wilmington Trust Co., George Mennen and Owen Roberts as Trustees, C.A. No. 8432-ML, Master LeGrow (Del. Ch. Apr. 24, 2015) (Master's Final Report), at pages 76 & 77: "The evidence at trial removed any doubt that, with respect to the transactions challenged in this section, John . . . [,a beneficiary of the trust,] . . . has a material conflict with his . . . [minor] . . . children because (1) he placed nearly complete emphasis on the present income of the Trust, without any apparent regard for the capital growth or long-term stability of the Trust, and (2) he was beholden to Jeff . . . [the individual co-trustee] . . . to the point that John could not himself take action to remedy Jeff's bad faith conduct." *See generally* UTC §304 cmt. (available at <http://www.uniformlaws.org/Act.aspx?title=Trust%20Code>); 5 Scott & Ascher §34.4.

[32] UTC §304 cmt. (available at <http://www.uniformlaws.org/Act.aspx?title=Trust%20 Code>). *See generally* §8.2.2.1 of this handbook (trust terminations by consent); 5 Scott & Ascher §34.4 (When Some of the Beneficiaries Do Not or Cannot Give Binding Consent).

[33] *See* Restatement (Third) of Trusts, Reporter's Notes on §65 cmts. b, c.

[34] Restatement (Third) of Trusts, Reporter's Notes on §65 cmts. b, c.

[35] In re Estate of Putignano, 82 Misc. 2d 389, 395, 368 N.Y.S.2d 420, 428 (1975).

[36] Susan T. Bart & Lyman W. Welch, *State Statutes on Virtual Representation—A New State Survey*, 35 ACTEC Journal 368 (2009). *See generally* §8.15.34 of this handbook (the common law virtual representation doctrine).

[37] Susan T. Bart & Lyman W. Welch, *State Statutes on Virtual Representation—A New State Survey*, 35 ACTEC L.J. 368, 376–406 (2009).

Time will tell, but we suspect that virtual representation will not live up to the expectations of the codifiers. This is because the terms of the modern noncommercial trust typically bestow on the trustee discretionary authority to invade principal for the benefit of fewer than all the equitable interests, thus putting all those interests in at least technical conflict with one another. Abuse of trustee discretion cases are particularly prone to conflict-infestation. Moreover, there is always the preliminary question of whether a prospective virtual representative has a disqualifying conflict. It is hard to see how he or she could possibly adequately represent the unborn and unascertained in the litigation of that critical preliminary issue, at least without the involvement of . . . an independent guardian ad litem. The doctrine of virtual representation should not be oversold.

Holders of powers of appointment. *The general inter vivos power of appointment.* In the case of a revocable inter vivos trust, the current holder of the power of revocation, if competent, is deemed, for all intents and purposes, to be the only beneficiary of the trust.[38] Thus, "[a]n order binding the sole holder or coholders of a power of revocation or a presently exercisable general power of appointment, including one in the form of a power of amendment, binds other persons to the extent their interests are objects, takers in default, or otherwise subject to the power."[39] It follows that the holder of a presently exercisable general inter vivos power of appointment may excuse breaches of trust and in so doing bind all the other equitable interests. In Massachusetts, the holder of a presently exercisable *special or limited inter vivos power of appointment* (nongeneral inter vivos power of appointment) may do the same, as well, provided the holder may "appoint among a class of appointees which is broader than the class of those persons who would take in default of the exercise of such power."[40]

General testamentary powers. The holder (donee) of a general testamentary power of appointment may not virtually represent the takers in default of exercise.[41] The interest of the powerholder and those of the takers in default are inherently in conflict in that the powerholder postmortem may extinguish the interests of the takers in default.

Under the Uniform Trust Code, however, the holder of a general testamentary power of appointment may *represent* and bind persons whose interests, as permissible appointees, takers in default, or otherwise are subject to the power.[42] There is a critical qualification, however. "Such representation is allowed except to the extent there is a conflict of interest with respect to the

---

[38] *See generally* §§8.11 of this handbook (duties of trustee of revocable trust) and 8.1.1 of this handbook (defining the general power of appointment).

[39] UPC §1-403(2)(A). *See also* UPC §1-108 (the power of holder of right of revocation to bind other beneficiaries and takers in default).

[40] Mass. Gen. Laws ch. 190B, §1-108 (acts of holder of certain powers); Mass. Gen. Laws ch. 190B, §1-403(2)(i) (when parties bound by others). *See generally* §8.1.1 of this handbook (defining the nongeneral power of appointment).

[41] *See, e.g.*, Brams Trust #2 v. Haydon, 266 S.W.3d 307 (Mo. Ct. App. 2008).

[42] UTC §302 (available at <http://www.uniformlaws.org/Act.aspx?title=Trust%20Code>). *See generally* 4 Scott & Ascher §24.21.2 (Several Beneficiaries); 5 Scott & Ascher §34.4 (When Some of the Beneficiaries Do Not or Cannot Give Binding Consent).

particular matter or dispute."[43] The Uniform Probate Code is generally in accord.[44]

The Uniform Trust Code, specifically Section 302, speaks in terms of the holder of a general testamentary power of appointment "representing" other interests under the trust, unless there is a conflict of interest between the holder and the other interests. As the holder may exercise the power postmortem unimpeded by fiduciary constraints, and in so doing lawfully eradicate altogether those other interests, it is hard to see when there would not be a conflict. When it comes to the testamentary power of appointment, the more precise question, it would seem, is the extent to which the powerholder may authorize or ratify breaches of trust and in so doing eradicate altogether the other interests during the powerholder's lifetime. Section 302 may well have been misfiled in UTC Article 3, which is devoted to "representation" matters.

---

[43] UTC §302 cmt. (available at <http://www.uniformlaws.org/Act.aspx?title=Trust%20 Code>). "Without the exception for conflict of interest, the holder of the power could act in a way that could enhance the holder's income interests to the detriment of the appointees or takers in default, whoever they may be." UTC §302 cmt. A trustee's investing for income generation at the expense of principal growth is a "matter or dispute" that involves conflicting equitable interests. Accordingly, any consent the income beneficiary might attempt to give to the breach would not bind takers in default and appointees, notwithstanding the fact that the income beneficiary also holds a general testamentary power of appointment. On the other hand, if the trustee were breaching his trust by investing for growth at the expense of income generation, the consent of the holder of the testamentary power would be effective. This is because the powerholder's consent would be in derogation of the income account. Under the UPC, only the consent of the holder of a general inter vivos power of appointment to a breach of trust may bind the appointee and taker in default. *See* UPC §1-108. The UPC rejects the proposition that the holder of a testamentary power can as well. 3 Scott on Trusts §216.2 n.11. Many of the cases are in accord. *See, e.g.*, Atwood v. First Nat'l Bank of Boston, 366 Mass. 519, 320 N.E.2d 873 (1974) (holding that wishes of the holder of a testamentary power of appointment may not override the intentions of the settlor). The Restatement (Third) of Trusts seems to endorse the UTC's approach, namely that the holder of a limited power or a general testamentary power of appointment may not speak for those with conflicting interests. *See* Restatement (Third) of Trusts §74, Reporter's Notes (Comments b–e and g) (suggesting that Fla. Stat. §731-303, which provides for representation of conflicting interests by holders of powers of appointment, whether "general, special, or limited," is problematic in terms of fairness, or even due process). In 1948, Professor Scott had introduced into the Restatement of Trusts a provision endorsing his long-held opinion that a life beneficiary who was also the holder of a general testamentary power of appointment should be able to consent to a breach of trust and in so doing bind the appointees and takers in default. Restatement of Trusts §216 cmt. g. *See also* 3 Scott on Trust §216.2. "In such a case the life beneficiary is in substance the equitable owner of the fee." 3 Scott on Trust §216.2. "Accordingly it would seem that his consent to a deviation from the terms of the trust is binding not only on himself but also on those in whose favor he exercises the power of appointment." 3 Scott on Trust §216.2. *See also* Restatement (Second) of Trusts §216 cmt. h (1959). *See also* 4 Scott & Ascher §24.21.2 (Multiple Beneficiaries); 5 Scott & Ascher §34.4 (When Some of the Beneficiaries Do Not or Cannot Give Binding Consent). *But see* that in New York, by statute, a holder of a general testamentary power of appointment may represent takers in default and prospective appointees, although discretion is bestowed on the court to direct their joinder when their interests cannot be adequately represented by the power-holder. N.Y. Surr./Ct. Proc. Act §315. "SCPA 315 is not blind either to the frailties of human nature or to any other possibility that can arise in a given case to negate the assumption of virtual representation upon which it initially depends." N.Y. Surr./Ct. Proc. Act §315. David D. Siegel & Patrick M. Connors, Practice Commentaries, 1994 Main Volume.

[44] *See* UPC §1-403(2)(B)(v).

What may be going on here is that UTC Section 302 is conflating two questions. The first question is whether and the extent to which the holder of a general testamentary power of appointment may approve or ratify breaches of trust and, in so doing, cut back or eradicate altogether during the powerholder's lifetime the interests of the takers in default of exercise. In 1948, Professor Scott had introduced into the Restatement of Trusts a provision endorsing his long-held view that a life beneficiary who was also the holder of a general testamentary power of appointment should be able to consent to a breach of trust and, in so doing, bind the appointees and taker in default. If that is what UTC Section 302 is all about, then it belongs somewhere else, perhaps in UTC Article 6. One cannot help but hear the echoes of Prof. Scott's voice in the last 17 or so words of UTC Section 302.[45]

The second and very different question is whether the holder of a general testamentary power of appointment may represent in a quasi-fiduciary sense the takers in default. (It is not at all clear what "represent" actually means in the context of UTC Section 302.) The express conflict of interest qualification suggests that it must mean something.

As noted, in the *general* sense the holder of a testamentary power of appointment has a *per se* conflict of interest because of his ability postmortem to eradicate altogether the interests of the takers in default. As to a *particular* question, one can conjure up fact patterns where the interests of the powerholder and those of the takers in default are not in conflict, as we shall do next. But what constitutes a conflict in this context? Must it be a patent one, or can it also be a fact-based latent one? And, in any case, wouldn't the services of a guardian ad litem still be required to represent the unborn and unascertained takers in default when it come to litigating the critical threshold question of whether the powerholder has a disqualifying conflict? How can the powerholder virtually represent them in the litigation of that issue without putting in jeopardy the finality of the court's decrees?

In Massachusetts, there is no express conflict-of-interest exception. In addition, the holder of a *limited or special testamentary power of appointment* (nongeneral) also may excuse breaches of trust and in so doing bind the other equitable interests, provided the holder may "appoint among a class of appointees which is broader than the class of those persons who would take in default of the exercise of such power."[46] Should Massachusetts enact into law UTC Section 302, presumably all this preexisting legislation will have to be repealed.

To illustrate what is meant by a particular conflict of interest in the context of the relationship between the holder of a general testamentary power of appointment and the takers in default, take a standard trust, *A* to *B* for *C* for life. Upon *C*'s death, the property passes outright and free of trust to the *D*s. *A* is the settlor, *B* is the trustee, *C* is the current beneficiary, and the *D*s are the remaindermen. They, the *D*s, are unborn and unascertained issue of *C*. *C* also is given a general testamentary power of appointment, in this case a power by will

---

[45] " . . . [T]he holder may represent *and bind* persons whose interests, as permissible appointees, takers in default, or otherwise, are subject to the power."

[46] Mass. Gen. Laws ch. 190B, §1-108.

to appoint the trust property to C's estate.[47] The trust is income-only, *i.e.,* the trustee must distribute all net trust accounting income to C, but may not touch the principal. The Ds are the takers in default of the power's exercise. Were C to request an allowance from principal on the grounds that her support is not sufficiently provided for by the income stream, the Ds, being unborn and unascertained, could not give their consent to the invasion.[48] Because the trustee's invasion of principal would adversely affect the interests of the Ds, C, though she holds a general testamentary power of appointment, may not "virtually represent" them. Accordingly, C's consent to, or ratification of, B's invasion of principal would not be binding on the Ds. Otherwise we would have the fox guarding the chicken coop.

In a similar vein, "in most states, the fact that the settlor [A] has retained a testamentary general power of appointment is not sufficient to allow the settlor to revoke the trust without the consent of all of the beneficiaries [the Cs & the Ds]."[49] The problem is that others as well as the settlor (A) now have equitable property rights in the subject property. The settlor's interests are adverse to the interests of the other beneficiaries, whose equitable property rights would extinguish were the settlor to revoke the trust and take back title to the subject property outright and free of trust. The settlor of an irrevocable trust is in no position to represent anyone but himself or herself in any proceeding to effect its mid-course termination, except when the settlor also is the sole beneficiary.[50]

In one case, the current beneficiary (C) of a testamentary spendthrift trust petitioned to have the court terminate the trust in mid-course and to distribute the trust property outright and free of trust to him. The remaindermen (D) were the current beneficiary's issue, and in default of issue, his heirs at law.[51] The current beneficiary (C) possessed a general testamentary power of appointment. The trustee (B) had broad discretionary authority to invade principal for the current beneficiary's benefit.[52] The current beneficiary (C) had no children and medical examinations indicated that he was sterile. The court declined to order termination of the trust, notwithstanding the fact that the current beneficiary (C) possessed a general testamentary power of appointment, on the grounds that to terminate the trust would contravene the settlor's intent:

---

[47] *See generally* §8.1 of this handbook (powers of appointment).

[48] *See generally* 5 Scott & Ascher §34.4 (noting that in the absence of a statute to the contrary, such as, perhaps, N.Y Est. Powers & Trusts Law §7-1-9, the traditional view has been that C—whether C is the settlor or a designated current beneficiary—may not revoke a trust that was established for C's benefit *and* for the benefit of C's issue, even though C has yet to have children). *See also* 5 Scott & Ascher §34.4.1 (noting that one incapable of having biological children might still be capable of acquiring children by adoption).

[49] 5 Scott & Ascher §34.4.

[50] *See generally* 5 Scott & Ascher §34.3 (When Settlor Is Sole Beneficiary).

[51] *See generally* §5.2 of this handbook (class designation: "children," "issue," "heirs," and "relatives" (some rules of construction)).

[52] *See generally* §3.5.3.2(a) of this handbook (the power to make discretionary payments of income and principal (the discretionary trust)).

On the other hand, the testatrix did not provide for a termination of the trust in favor of . . . [the current beneficiary] . . . on the death of his father. She did not name him sole trustee to exercise discretion whether to pay over principal. She did not give . . . [the current beneficiary] . . . the right during his life to appoint to anyone, including himself, but limited his absolute right to control the distribution of the principal to a testamentary direction. Additionally, it is significant that even the more broadly expressed discretion of the trustees or their successors to pay principal "if they deem wise" applies only to one-half of the trust property. This limitation suggests that the testatrix intended the trust to continue throughout . . . [the current beneficiary's] . . . life. Thus, we believe that all purposes of the trust have not been achieved so as to compel its termination.[53]

Before proceeding, we should remind ourselves again that the holder of a general inter vivos power of appointment, which would include a reserved right of revocation, who is of full age and legal capacity may give an informed approval of the acts of the trustee and in so doing bind the takers in default of the power's exercise.[54] The holder also may unilaterally modify or terminate the trust at any time.[55] The doctrine of virtual representation would not be applicable, nor would the appointment of a guardian ad litem be appropriate, absent special facts.

The guardian ad litem. *Representing the unrepresented.* Moving on. When the doctrine of "virtual representation" is unavailable, the services of a court-appointed guardian ad litem (or special representative)[56] may be required to look after the interests of unrepresented parties.[57] When the situation warrants, the prudent trustee will insist that a guardian ad litem be appointed so that decrees issuing from the court shall be final and binding on all beneficiaries present and future, whether their interests are vested or contingent, including minors, the unborn, and the unascertained.[58] Having said that, decrees may

---

[53] Atwood v. First Nat'l Bank of Boston, 366 Mass. 519, 524, 320 N.E.2d 873, 876 (1974).

[54] UPC §1-108. *See, e.g.,* Mass. Gen. Laws ch. 190B, §1-108.

[55] 5 Scott & Ascher §34.4 (When Some of the Beneficiaries Do Not or Cannot Give Binding Consent).

[56] In Oregon, a "special representative" may be appointed by the court to represent the interests of a person with a beneficial interest in a trust who is otherwise unrepresented, *e.g.,* a minor, an incompetent or someone who is unborn or unascertained. The special representative is authorized to sign on behalf of that person an agreement that resolves disputes arising out of the administration of the trust. *See* Or. Rev. Stat. §128.179. For the Massachusetts guardian ad litem statute, *see* Mass. Gen. Laws ch. 190B, §1-404.

[57] *See* Bogert §871; 5 Scott & Ascher §34.4; UTC §305(a) cmt. (available at <http://www.uniformlaws.org/Act.aspx?title=Trust%20Code>) (distinguishing the UTC's concept of the "representative" from the traditional concept of the "guardian ad litem"). "Unlike a guardian ad litem, . . . a representative can be appointed to act with respect to a nonjudicial settlement or to receive a notice on a beneficiary's behalf." Bogert §871. Furthermore, in making decisions, a representative may consider the general benefit accruing to living members of the beneficiary's family. Bogert §871. For other such "general benefit" statutes, *see* 5 Scott & Ascher §34.4 n.33.

[58] *See generally* 5 Scott & Ascher §34.4 (When Some of the Beneficiaries Do Not or Cannot Give Binding Consent).

well be final and binding on those interested parties who are competent to receive and do receive advance notice of the proceeding.[59]

Conflicting interests. In one case, a victim of the terrorist attack on the World Trade Center on September 11, 2001, was survived by his wife and two children, one of whom was a minor. The core of his estate plan was two trusts, a standard combination of credit shelter trust and marital deduction trust.[60] The two children were remainder beneficiaries under each trust. There were three cotrustees: the widow and the victim's two brothers. The two brothers took the position that the credit shelter allocation was governed by the Victims of Terrorism Tax Relief Act of 2001, and that the Act effectively raised the amount that was allocable to the credit shelter trust beyond the exclusion amount of $675,000 applicable in 2001 to the point where there would be nothing allocable to the marital deduction trust.

The widow and her adult son took the position that the Act was inapplicable. The son's position was against his own economic interests: "After all, if the marital deduction trust is funded by limiting the credit shelter trust to the exclusion amount of $675,000, then the remainder interest of the two children in the marital deduction trust may be reduced by virtue of the taxability of the remainder of the marital deduction trust, the standard 'five and five' limited right to principal of the marital deduction trust of the mother, and the standard of living component of the marital deduction trust, not to mention the tax-free quality of the remainder of the credit shelter trust."[61]

Could the brother virtually represent the sister? The New York courts have traditionally looked to three criteria when asked to resolve such issues:

- Similarity of economic interest between the representor and the representee;
- The absence of any conflict of interest between them; and
- The adequacy of the representation by the representor of the representee.[62]

While there may have been technical compliance with all three criteria in this case, the court, "mindful of its obligation to guard the finality of its decrees" and to be "vigilant in the protection of the interests of persons suffering from a disability," exercised its discretionary authority to order the appointment of a guardian ad litem to represent the minor daughter. While the adult son's position against his own economic interests may have been "reasonable and even laudable," the court was simply not comfortable allowing him to speak for

---

[59] UPC §7-206.

[60] *See generally* §8.9 of this handbook (why more than one trust: the estate and generation-skipping tax).

[61] Estate of Dickey, 76 N.Y.S.2d 473, 474 (2003). *See generally* §8.9 of this handbook (why more than one trust: the estate and generation-skipping tax) and §9.18 of this handbook (the Crummey trust) (discussing in part the "5 and 5" limitation).

[62] Matter of Holland, 84 Misc. 2d 922, 377 N.Y.S.2d 854; Matter of Putignano, 82 Misc. 2d 389, 368 N.Y.S.2d 420. *Cf.* 5 Scott & Ascher §34.4 (noting that under New York law the settlor may revoke the trust upon the written consent of all persons "beneficially interested").

his minor sister, his position being adverse to his sister's economic interests as well.[63] The court noted that it was not convinced that even an independent guardian ad litem acting on behalf of the minor daughter could or should adopt the widow's position that the marital deduction trust was entitled to an allocation at the expense of the credit shelter trust.

The Uniform Trust Code. So also would the Uniform Probate Code grant judges broad discretion to appoint guardians ad litem, even in cases where virtual representation would technically be an option: "At any point in a proceeding, a court may appoint a guardian ad litem to represent the interest of a minor, an incapacitated, unborn, or unascertained person, . . . if the court determines that representation of the interest otherwise would be inadequate."[64]

Under the Uniform Trust Code, notice to a person who may represent and bind another person has the same effect as if notice were given to the other person.[65] And the consent of a person who may represent and bind another person is binding on the person represented unless the person represented objects to the representation before the consent would otherwise have become effective.[66]

The Uniform Trust Code would divide the GAL's loyalties. Uniform Trust Code's §305(c) provides that a guardian ad litem may "consider in making decisions" the "general benefit" accruing to the living members of the "family" of the unborn or unascertained individual whose equitable property interests the guardian ad litem has been charged with representing. The term "family" in this context is not defined, a glaring and unfortunate oversight. Moreover, when the economic interests of the individual and those of "the family" diverge, as we suspect they usually will, how is the guardian ad litem expected to square the circle? No guidance is provided. Sorting out the conflicting and competing equitable property interests, we suggest, is best be left to the court. A court that is endeavoring to effect a fair, efficient, and lawful resolution of a contested trust matter needs the benefit of robust advocacy on behalf of the economic interests of the unrepresented, not advocacy distracted and diluted by nebulous, speculative, and open-ended collateral "family" considerations. Whether an express trust provision negating the guardian ad litem's §305(c) discretionary authority is enforceable remains to be seen. If settlor intent is the lodestar that should guide a court in sorting out the rights, duties, and obligations of the parties to a trust relationship, then it ought to be.

---

[63] *See generally* 5 Scott & Ascher §34.4 (Absence of a Conflict of Interest Is Critical When It Comes to Virtual Representation).

[64] UPC §1-403(5).

[65] UTC §301(a) (available at <http://www.uniformlaws.org/Act.aspx?title=Trust%20Code>); 5 Scott & Ascher §34.4.

[66] UTC §301(b) (available at <http://www.uniformlaws.org/Act.aspx?title=Trust%20Code>).

Charitable trusts. In Massachusetts, the court has authority to appoint a guardian ad litem to represent those who possess contingent equitable interests under charitable trusts.[67] The court, however, must notify the attorney general of its intent to make the appointment and the reasons for doing so.[68] In Oregon, a written agreement that relates to the administration of a charitable trust would be ineffective without the signature of the attorney general.[69]

Laches and statutes of limitation. The highest Massachusetts court took a radical and unprecedented departure from traditional trust law principles when it held that a statute of limitations had begun to run *against the beneficiaries* of a trust whose former trustees had never properly accounted to them when the *successor trustee* knew or should have known of the predecessors' breaches.[70] At the time the successor was deemed to know of the predecessor's breach, one beneficiary was a minor and the other was missing. No guardian ad litem had ever been duly and formally appointed by the court to represent their interests. It appears that the court had confused and conflated the limitation rules applicable to external *legal* actions by third-party tort and contract claimants against trustees with the rules applicable to internal breach of fiduciary *equitable* actions by beneficiaries against their trustees.[71] There also was a suggestion in the opinion that the court might not be the only entity empowered to appoint an "independent counsel" for a minor or missing trust beneficiary, that the appointment of such an agent for two "principals" each under a disability could be effected by language in the terms of a trust or by an adverse party. That surely would be a radical and unprecedented departure from fundamental principles of agency law.

§8.15   Doctrines Ancient and Modern

Nor is this the end. Desecrated as the body is, a vengeful ghost survives and hovers over it to scare. Espied by some timid man-of-war or blundering discovery-vessel from afar, when the distance obscuring the swarming fowls, nevertheless still shows the white mass floating in the sun, and the white spray heaving high against it; straightway the whale's unharming corpse, with trembling fingers is set down in the log—shoals, rocks, and breakers hereabouts: beware! And for years afterwards, perhaps, ships shun the place; leaping over it as silly sheep leap over a vacuum, because their leader originally leaped when a stick was held. There's

---

[67] In the Matter of the Trusts Under the Will of Lotta M. Crabtree, 2003 WL 22119871 (Mass.).

[68] In the Matter of the Trusts Under the Will of Lotta M. Crabtree, 2003 WL 22119871 (Mass.). *See generally* §9.4.2 of this handbook (standing to enforce charitable trusts).

[69] Or. Stat. Rev. §128.177(2)(d).

[70] O'Connor v. Redstone, 452 Mass. 537, 896 N.E.2d 595 (2008). *See generally* §7.1.3 of this handbook (the laches doctrine as partially codified by a statute of limitations).

[71] *See generally* §7.3 of this handbook (trustee's external liability to third parties in contract and tort); §8.25 of this handbook (few American law schools still require instruction in Agency, Trusts and Equity).

your law of precedents; there's your utility of traditions; there's the story of your obstinate survival of old beliefs never bottomed on the earth, and now even hovering in the air! There's orthodoxy!—Ishmael[1]

Common law is an anomaly, a beautiful, miraculous anomaly. In the rest of the world, laws are written down from first principles and then applied to specific disputes, but the common law grows like a coral, case by case, each judgment serving as the starting point for the next dispute. In consequence, it is an ally of freedom rather than an instrument of state control. It implicitly assumes residual rights.—Daniel Hannan[2]

Sprinkled throughout the trust literature are references to doctrines, some quite ancient, some quite recent in origin, and some in between. What follows are brief explanations of a few of them. The focus of this section is on what implications, if any, each may have for trustees operating in the United States and elsewhere today. As to the Statute of Uses, the Doctrine of Worthier Title, and the Rule in Shelley's Case, the trustee would be well advised to have near at hand Professor Moynihan's compact Introduction to the Law of Real Property.[3]

In that the trust evolved in England and not in France,[4] one might ask how it is that a good deal of trust-related terminology appears to be French-like, *e.g.*,

---

§8.15 [1] Herman Melville, Moby-Dick, Ch. 69. *See also* Charles Dickens, Bleak House, Ch. 1 (In Chancery) ("On such an afternoon, some score of members of the High Court of Chancery bar ought to be—as here they are—mistily engaged in one of the ten thousand stages of an endless cause, tripping one another up on slippery precedents, groping knee-deep in technicalities, running their goat-hair and horsehair warded heads against walls of words and making a pretence of equity with serious faces, as players might"). Certainly Professor Leach is Ishmael's counterpart in the trust world:

> Since 1787 these Fertile Octogenarian cases have bedevilled estate planners and destroyed perfectly sensible wills and trusts with the remorselessness of a guillotine. The acme of silliness was achieved when an English court ruled that it was conclusively presumed that a widow of 67 could have a child and that the child could in turn have a child before the age of five! . . . In all the Anglo-American world only one Irish judge, Gavan Duffy, J., rejected this nonsense. W. Barton Leach, Perpetuities in the Atomic Age: The Sperm Bank and the Fertile Decedent, 48 A.B.A. J 942 (1962) (referring to Judge Duffy's decision in Exham v. Beamish, [1939] I.R. 336 and reacting to In Re Gaite's Will Trusts, [1949] 1 All E. R. 459).

The authors of this handbook do not necessarily share the intensity of Prof. Leach's (and Ishmael's) impatience with traditions and doctrines of earlier times and other eras. The fertile octogenarian doctrine, "law French" and other such curiosities remind us that the law of trusts has been a work-in-progress for centuries. If nothing else, they provide valuable clues as to its evolution. There is nothing "efficient" about repeating some failed experiment or reinventing some wheel.

[2] Daniel Hannan, *Eight Centuries of Liberty*, Wall St. J., May 30-31, 2015, at C2. Mr. Hannan is a British member of the European Parliament for the Conservative Party, a columnist for the Washington Examiner, and the author of "Inventing Freedom: How the English-speaking Peoples Made the Modern World."

[3] C. J. Moynihan, Introduction to the Law of Real Property (2d ed. 1988) (hereinafter "Moynihan").

[4] *See generally* §8.37 of this handbook (the origin of the Anglo-American trust).

cestuy que trust (beneficiary)[5] and *cestuy en remainder* (remainderman).[6] For Rule against Perpetuities analysis purposes, one may qualify as a life in being though *en ventre sa mere*[7] when the contingent interest was created. These Norman French terms and expressions are the last vestiges of what was once a customary practice of English lawyers, namely, to write their reports and professional notes in French.

One would expect that this practice began sometime around 1066. That, however, appears not to be the case. Recent scholarship suggests "that French may not have been used in the law courts until about the middle of the thirteenth century, by which time it had become known to some of the English gentry and perhaps to some of the 'common people' as well."[8] In any case, it was not until sometime around the reign of Charles II that "law French" began to fall out of general usage in the English court system.

While Norman French probably ceased to be spoken at the bar by English lawyers somewhere around 1362, the use of "law French" continued on as a kind of legal shorthand. "Sir Edward Coke said of Littleton's French that it was 'most commonly written and read, and very rarely spoken, and therefore cannot be either pure or well pronounced'; but it could not be abolished without danger, because 'so many ancient terms and words drawn from that Legall French are grown to be *vocabula artis*, vocables of art, so apt and significant to express the truest sense of the law, and so woven into laws themselves, as it is in a manner impossible to change them.'"[9] It was even said that English lawyers took perverse delight in mispronouncing the French.

In 1731, Parliament finally put an end to the use of law French in official legal pleadings and reports. "The only French heard in the courts thereafter was the *oyez* of the crier."[10] But the use of law French did not disappear from the halls of Parliament. We refer to the following passage on Parliament's website:

> Although English is the language used in Parliament some of the formalities of a Bill's passage through Parliament are written in Norman French. This is because these traditions date back to a time just after the Norman Conquest when Norman French was the official language of Government. Many of the words and phrases used are similar to modern day French. Some examples of the use of Norman French are:
>
> i)   'A ceste Bille les Seigneurs sont assentus'—used to signify that the House of Lords agrees with a House of Commons Bill

---

[5] One also sees the term spelled *cesui que trust*. *See generally* Sweet, *Cestui Que Use: Cestui Que Trust*, 26 L.Q. Rev. 196 (1910).

[6] Other terms from the law French include *surcharge, lien,* and *laches*. For a contemporary definition of the term *laches, see* §7.1.3 of this handbook (defense of failure of beneficiary to take timely action against trustee).

[7] In its mother's womb.

[8] J. H. Baker, Manual of Law French 1 (2d ed. 1989).

[9] Baker, Manual of Law French at 3–4.

[10] Baker, Manual of Law French at 6.

ii) 'Ceste Bille est remise aux Seigneurs avecque des raisons'—used when the House of Lords lists the reasons why it does not agree with a House of Commons Bill. The reasons themselves are written in English

iii) 'La Reine le veult'—used to show the Royal Assent.[11]

And thanks to Professor Leach, it will be some time before the law French phenomenon passes altogether from the collective memory of those who practice in the common law jurisdictions. We refer to his 1962 article.[12] With tongue firmly planted in cheek and due credit given to one of his "young lady" students, he introduced a new term into the law French lexicon, namely the child *en ventre sa frigidaire*.[13] Though freshly minted, at least by law French standards, the term has already gained some currency in the halls of academia, both here[14] and abroad.[15]

§8.15.1 Statute of Uses

Prior to the seventeenth century the typical form of conveyance of a present freehold estate in land was the feoffment with livery of seisin. A feoffment was the grant of a fief or feudal tenement and livery of seisin was the means by which the grant was effected.[16]

The term cestui que use is a corruption of the law French phrase cestui a que use le feoffment fuit fait (he to whose use the feoffment was made).[17]

An important milestone on the road to the modern trust was reached in the early 15th century when the English chancery courts began *enforcing* "uses."[18] A "use" was a transfer of an interest in real estate from *A* to *B* for the benefit of *C*.[19] In other words, it was a transfer "to his use" (*a son oes*). A landholder, in order to prevent the property from descending to his heirs at law[20] or to deprive an overlord of his feudal rights[21] or to avoid Crown

---

[11] *See* <http://www.parliament.uk/site-information/glossary/norman-french/#!>.

[12] *Perpetuities in the Atomic Age: The Sperm Bank and the Fertile Decedent*, 48 A.B.A. J. 942 (1962).

[13] Leach, *Perpetuities in the Atomic Age: The Sperm Bank and the Fertile Decedent*, 48 A.B.A. J. at 943, n.3.

[14] *See, e.g.*, Paul Coelus, *Inheritance Problems of Frozen Embryos (The Child* En Ventre Sa Frigidaire), 7 Prob. L.J. 119 (1986) (U.S.).

[15] Rosalind Atherton, *En ventre sa Frigidaire*: Posthumous children in the succession context, 19 Legal Studies 139 (1999) (U.K.); Rosalind Atherton, *Between a Fridge and a Hard Place: The Case of the Frozen Embryos or Children* en Ventre Sa Frigidaire, 6 Austl. Prop. L.J. 53 (1998) (Australia).

[16] Cornelius J. Moynihan, Introduction to the Law of Real Property 162 (2d ed. 1988).

[17] Moynihan at 172, n.2.

[18] Moynihan, chs. 8 & 9; 1 Scott on Trusts §§1, 1.1–1.11; Restatement (Second) of Trusts §§67–73 (1959); 1A Scott on Trusts §§67–73; Bogert §3. For the Roman, Germanic, and Islamic theories as to the origin of the English use, *see* §8.37 of this handbook (the origin of the Anglo-American trust); Bogert §2.

[19] *See* Maitland, *The Origin of Uses*, 8 Harv. L. Rev. 127 (1894); Bogert §2.

[20] 1 Scott on Trusts §1.5; Bogert §2.

[21] 1 Scott on Trusts §1.5; Bogert §2.

taxes,[22] would transfer his interest in the land to a *feoffee* (a sort of paleo-trustee) for the benefit of the *cestui que use* (a sort of paleo-beneficiary).[23] Now that uses could be enforced, either the *feoffor* (*A*) or the *cestui que use* (*C*) had a cause of action against a "faithless *feoffee*" (*B*).[24] "The process by which the chancellor acted was known as a *subpoena*."[25] Prof. Maitland explains why it was customary to have more than one *feoffee*:

> If there were a single owner, a single *feoffatus*, he might die, and then the lord would claim the ordinary rights of a lord; *relevium, custodia haeredis, maritagium haeredis, escaeta*, all would follow as a matter of course. But here the Germanic *Gesammthandschaft* comes to our help. Enfeoff five or perhaps ten friends *zu gesammter Hand* ("as joint tenants"). When one of them dies there is no inheritance; there is merely accrescence. The lord can claim nothing. If the number of the *feoffati* is running low, then indeed it will be prudent to introduce some new ones, and this can be done by some transferring and retransferring.[26]

Already by the time of the Wars of the Roses (1455–1485), most of the land in England was held to uses.[27] In an attempt to "put a stop to the drainage of royal revenues by the evasion of feudal dues through the practice of conveying to uses," Parliament, in 1536, enacted the Statute of Uses.[28] The statute provided that title to land held upon a use would now lodge with the *cestui que use* (the beneficiary).[29] In other words, the interest of the *cestui que use* was converted into a legal estate or, as they say, "executed."[30] The intention was that the title-holding *feoffee* (trustee) would then be out of the picture.[31] Now the *cestui que use* (the beneficiary) would have *both* the legal title and the entire

---

[22] 1 Scott on Trusts §1.5; Bogert §2.

[23] 1 Scott on Trusts §1.3; Bogert §2.

[24] 1 Scott on Trusts §1.4; Bogert §2.

[25] Bogert §3 ("It commanded the defendant to do or refrain from doing a certain act. The relief was personal and specific, not merely money damages. Hence historians say that the cestui que use had a remedy only by subpoena.").

[26] *Frederic William Maitland, Selected Essays (1936)* 158. *See also* Bogert §2 ("In order to avoid the feudal burdens which would ensue upon the death of a single feofee, several feofees could be used as joint tenants and their number renewed from time to time."); §3.4.4.1 of this handbook (multiple trustees (cotrustees)) (noting that today both at common law and by statute trustees take title to trust property jointly).

[27] 1 Scott & Ascher §1.5 (noting the extreme damage that the use had done to the feudal system); Bogert §2 ("Indeed, by the time of Henry V (1413–1422) . . . [uses] . . . were the rule rather than the exception in landholding.").

[28] Moynihan at 203; *see generally* Bogert §4 n.4 (containing the full text of the preamble to the statute of uses, which is essentially a catalog of the various nefarious purposes to which the use was allegedly being put). The citation to the statute of uses is 27 Hen. VIII, c. 10. (1536). *See also* Attorney-Gen. v. Sands, Hardres, 488, 491 per Atkyns, arguendo (1669) ("A trust is altogether the same that an use was before . . . [the Statute of Uses] . . . , and they have the same parents, fraud and fear; and the same nurse, a court of conscience."); Bogert §2 ("The reasons for the introduction of uses were in some instances dishonorable.").

[29] 1 Scott on Trusts §1.5.

[30] Moynihan at 180; 1 Scott & Ascher §3.4.1; Bogert §2.

[31] Moynihan at 180; 1 Scott on Trusts §§1.5, 1.6; 1 Scott & Ascher §3.4.1; Bogert §2.

equitable interest.[32] Now the beneficial owner would have no "use" (trust) to hide behind for the purpose of avoiding taxes and feudal obligations.[33] At least that was how things were supposed to work. In practice, however, the common law judges quickly set about defanging the statute's provisions to the point where about the only equitable arrangement that did not manage to escape its snare was the passive trust.[34] Those equitable arrangements, those uses, that did escape are referred to today as *trusts*.[35] They constitute the basis of modern trust law.[36]

The statute was subsequently held inapplicable by the courts to trusts where the trustee had *active responsibilities*.[37] (Those responsibilities might be as minimal as collecting and disbursing rents.[38]) And of course it did not apply to *trusts of personal property*.[39] Most trusts today fall into one or both of these categories. The statute of uses also was held not to apply to a so-called *use upon a use*[40] a concept much loved by academics[41] but beyond the scope of this handbook and of little or no practical concern for today's trustee[42]—and not to apply to a use *raised on a term for years*,[43] to be distinguished from "a use for a

---

[32] Moynihan at 180; 1 Scott on Trusts §§1.5, 1.6; 1 Scott & Ascher §3.4.1; Bogert §2.

[33] 1 Scott & Ascher §3.4.1; Bogert §2.

[34] 1 Scott & Ascher §3.4.1; Bogert §5 ("The three-fold task of construing the Statute of Uses, determining when the Statute executed the use, and when it gave to the cestui que use the legal estate fell to the common law judges who had to deal with legal estates.").

[35] Bogert §5.

[36] Bogert §5.

[37] 1 Scott & Ascher §§1.6, 1.7; Bogert §5 ("Duties of administration required the legal title in the trustee.").

[38] 1 Scott & Ascher §§1.6, 1.7; Moynihan at 203; 1 Scott & Ascher §3.4.2 (noting that under the Restatement (Third) of Trusts, a trust is active if the trustee has *any* affirmative duties to perform).

[39] 1 Scott on Trusts §1.6; Restatement (Second) of Trusts §70; Bogert §5 ("The express words of the Statute made clear that uses in personalty were excluded."). *See, however*, 1 Scott & Ascher §3.4.4 (noting that more recent cases tend to hold that a passive trust of personal property is subject to execution or terminable by the beneficiary, by analogy to the Statute of Uses or under a counterpart rule).

[40] 1 Scott on Trusts §1.6; Restatement (Second) of Trusts §71; Bogert §5 ("Thus if lands were conveyed to A, and his heirs, to the use of B and his heirs, to the use of C and his heirs, the Statute was held to transfer the use of B into possession and give him the legal estate but not to convert the use of C into possession and destroy B's legal estate. . . . About 100 years after the passage of the Statute of Uses, chancery recognized the second use in the case of the use upon a use and held it enforceable as a trust against the person in whom the court of law had vested the legal estate.").

[41] 1 Scott on Trusts §1.6; Restatement (Second) of Trusts §71; 1 Scott & Ascher §1.7.

[42] *See generally* 1 Scott & Ascher §3.4.5 (suggesting that "it is doubtful whether a court today would be willing to decide a case by reference to such an odd and hoary principle"). In any case, today it is quite permissible to fund a trust with an equitable interest in another trust. *See* 2 Scott & Ascher §10.7.

[43] 1 Scott & Ascher §1.7; 1 Scott on Trusts §1.6; Restatement (Second) of Trusts §70 cmt. b; Bogert §5 ("Furthermore . . . [the Statute] . . . referred only to instances in which the feoffee to uses was 'seized,' so it was readily held that the Statute had no application to interests in real property other than freehold estates. Therefore a gift to A of a term for five years, to the use of B, was not affected by the Statute.").

term of years raised on a freehold estate."[44] Oral trusts, resulting trusts,[45] and constructive trusts[46] also managed to slip through thenet.[47] In 1924 Parliament repealed the statute.[48]

The Statute of Uses also spawned the *legal* executory interest, which is "a legal future interest created by means of an executed springing or shifting use."[49] Shifting and springing interests in land are covered in Section 8.15.80 of this handbook.

The statute of uses was a critical component of a global compromise that had been struck after extensive negotiations between the Crown and the common law lawyers on behalf of their clients, the realm's equitable landowners. "Part of this negotiation also included *The Statute of Enrolments* (1536), 27 Hen. VIII, c. 16, which provided for registration of most executed uses that affected land and, after a great outcry from gentry concerned about their lost ability to leave land by will, *The Statute of Wills* (1540), 32 Hen. VIII, c. 16, which permitted free devise of all fee simple socage interests in land, and two-thirds of the land held by knight service. The result was more legal freedoms for landowners, subject to the enrolment of land interests to protect the fiscal interests of the Crown."[50] The land registration system of the typical common law jurisdiction to this day, however, remains something of a sieve. In twenty-first-century Massachusetts, shares of beneficial interest in a nominee trust of land still need not be recorded, a topic we take up in Section 9.6 of this handbook.

We close with a discussion of the status of the statute of uses generally on this side of the Atlantic. "Prior to the Revolution, the Statute of Uses was deemed to be in force in the American colonies and upon the formation of the states it was incorporated into their legal systems as part of the common law."[51] Today, there are remnants of the statute scattered throughout the United States,[52] although in England, the statute of uses itself was repealed in 1925 by the Law of Property Act.[53] What are the practical implications for the modern trustee? Simply this: In the unlikely event that a trust of real estate is truly passive, if the trustee's responsibilities are little more than to refrain from interfering with the beneficiary's enjoyment of the property,[54] there may be no trust. The beneficiary would have the entire legal and equitable interest. "In the modern trust context, the sometimes archaic concepts of these statutes and

---

[44] *See* 1 Scott & Ascher §1.7.

[45] 1 Scott & Ascher §3.4.6.

[46] 1 Scott & Ascher §3.4.7.

[47] 1 Scott & Ascher §3.4.1. *See generally* §§3.3 of this handbook (the constructive trust) and 4.1.1.1 of this handbook (the resulting trust).

[48] *See* Percy Bordwell, *The Repeal of the Statute of Uses*, 39 Harv. L. Rev. 466 (1926).

[49] Cornelius J. Moynihan, Introduction to the Law of Real Property 187 (2d ed. 1988).

[50] Daniel R. Coquillette, Francis Bacon 51 (1992).

[51] Moynihan at 204; *see generally* Bogert §6.

[52] Moynihan at 204.

[53] 15 Geo. V, c.20, §1.

[54] Restatement (Second) of Trusts §69 cmt. a.

decisions are strictly interpreted and narrowly applied to avoid interfering with the proper implementation of trust provisions and purposes."[55] Thus, for example, it is the "prevailing view" that the statute of uses did not execute resulting trusts.[56]

Today, however, a trustee is unlikely to find himself involved in such a "passive" arrangement.[57] But in the rare case when the statute of uses or a counterpart rule is applicable, *e.g.*, a simple "to *B* in trust for *C*" without more,[58] the rights of creditors, bona fide purchasers, and others may be affected, as well as the duties of the purported trustee (*e.g.*, there may be no obligation or need to make conveyance upon the death of the purported beneficiary).[59]

§8.15.2   *Doctrine of Worthier Title*

In England, the doctrine of worthier title was once a rule of law, not merely a rule of construction, but in England the doctrine was abolished in 1833. Its ghost nonetheless continued to haunt the American courts. Fortunately, most states have now either demoted it to a rule of construction or, better yet, followed England in abolishing it.[60]

Prior Trusts Restatements recognized and discussed worthier title as a rule of construction . . . ; and they recognized and discussed Shelley's rule as a rule of law, except in the many states that had then abolished it.[61]

In Section 5.2 of this handbook we considered those trusts whose remaindermen are to be determined by reference to formulas set forth in

---

[55] Restatement (Third) of Trusts §6 cmt. b(1).

[56] 6 Scott & Ascher §43.1.4.

[57] It should be noted, however, that "[a]s a result of the Statute of Uses, . . . [the words 'to the use of'] . . . have long been used in some conveyancing practices, and sometimes continue to be used even if unnecessarily, in order that the transferee might retain *legal* title." Restatement (Third) of Trusts §21 cmt. c.

[58] 1 Scott & Ascher §3.4.2.

[59] Restatement (Second) of Trusts §69 cmt. a. *See generally* §3.5.1 of this handbook (nature and extent of the trustee's estate). *See* In re Estate of Richards, Territories Court of the Virgin Islands, St. Thomas and St. John, Probate No. 3/1979, 1996 V.I. Lexis 14 (because trust was passive, it was executed by the statute of uses with the result that legal title was in purported "Beneficiaries"). Even if the statute of uses were to eliminate any obligation or need on the part of the trustee to make conveyance to a beneficiary, the beneficiary's title would still be subject to the trustee's powers and duties so far as necessary to satisfy obligations and wind up administration. *See* Restatement (Third) of Trusts §89 cmt. g. "The trustee's duty of distribution is performed by surrendering possession of the subject matter of the trust within a reasonable time and taking steps that may be necessary to enable the beneficiaries readily to establish ownership." Restatement (Third) of Trusts §89 cmt. g. *See also* 1 Scott & Ascher §3.4.3 (suggesting that a conveyance may not be necessary at the point when an active trust goes passive, but cautioning that a trust in the process of terminating is unlikely to be a passive one, the trustee having residual affirmative duties to wind-up the affairs of the trust).

[60] 2 Scott & Ascher §12.14.1.

[61] Restatement (Third) of Trusts, Reporter's Notes on §49. The Restatement (Third) of Trusts recognizes neither the worthier title rule of construction nor Shelley's rule of law. Restatement (Third) of Trusts cmt. a(1).

intestacy statutes, provisions such as "upon the death of the life beneficiary, the property passes to those who *would be* the settlor's heirs," or words to that effect. But what if "heirs" actually means *the estate* of the settlor? Here, the doctrine of worthier title may come into play. The doctrine of worthier title, a remnant of Anglo-Norman feudal law,[62] may apply to the following type of trust: *A* (settlor) to *B* (trustee) for *A* for life, then to the "heirs of *A*." If the "heirs of *A*" actually means the estate of *A*, then the only beneficiary of the trust is *A*.[63] Upon the death of *A*, the property goes back to the estate of *A* upon a resulting trust.[64] *A*'s presumptive heirs *do not* take title from *B*, the trustee, as "purchasers."[65] If they take at all, they take as beneficiaries of *A*'s estate, "by descent" as it were.[66] But they may in fact not take at all because *A*, having possessed a vested reversionary interest, could have transferred out that interest to a third party before he died, or by will.[67]

Today, the doctrine of worthier title has evolved into a rule of construction.[68] In other words, what did the settlor intend? Does "heirs" mean his estate or is it an abbreviated formula for ascertaining remaindermen along the lines of Professor Casner's more elaborate formula set forth in Section 5.2?[69] Some states have addressed the issue by creating statutory presumptions.[70] Massachusetts has abolished the doctrine both as a rule of law and a rule of construction.[71]

What is the practical concern for today's trustee? Simply this: If the doctrine of worthier title is applicable to a given situation, *A* is the sole beneficiary. There are no other interests to be accommodated. Thus, *A may* be able to revoke the trust, his creditors *may* be able to reach the principal, and *A* will be able to defeat the interests of his presumptive heirs at law by transferring the reversionary interest inter vivos or by will. If *A* is also the sole trustee, then there is no trust at all because all interests are "merged" in *A*.[72] It should be noted that Section 2-710 of the Uniform Probate Code would abolish the doctrine altogether, both as a rule of law and as a rule of construction.[73] The Restatement (Third) of Trusts recognizes no such rule of construction.[74]

---

[62] Moynihan at 151–161; 2 Scott on Trusts §§12.14.1, 127.1; 5 Scott & Ascher §34.4.

[63] Moynihan at 151–161; 2 Scott on Trusts §§12.14.1, 127.1; 5 Scott & Ascher §34.4.

[64] Moynihan at 151–161; 2 Scott on Trusts §§12.14.1, 127.1; 5 Scott & Ascher §34.4.

[65] Moynihan at 151, 152; 2 Scott on Trusts §127.1; 5 Scott & Ascher §34.4.

[66] Moynihan at 151, 152; 2 Scott on Trusts §127.1; 5 Scott & Ascher §34.4.

[67] Moynihan at 151, 152; 2 Scott on Trusts §127.1; 5 Scott & Ascher §34.4.

[68] Moynihan at 155; 2 Scott on Trusts §127.1; 5 Scott & Ascher §34.4.

[69] *See generally* 2 Scott & Ascher §12.14.1.

[70] 2 Scott on Trusts §127.1; Moynihan at 161.

[71] Mass. Gen. Laws ch. 190B, §2-710 (providing that "language in a governing instrument describing the beneficiaries of a donative disposition as the transferor's 'heirs', 'heirs at law', 'next of kin', 'distributes', 'relatives,' or 'family', or language of similar import, does not create or presumptively create a reversionary interest in the transferor").

[72] *See generally* §8.7 of this handbook (merger).

[73] UPC §2-710 (providing that language in a governing instrument describing the beneficiaries of a disposition as the transferor "heirs," "heirs at law," "next of kin," "distributees," "relatives," or "family," or language of similar import, does not create or presumptively create a reversionary interest in the transferor). *See generally* §5.2 of this handbook (class designations such as "children," "issue," "heirs," and "relatives").

[74] Restatement (Third) of Trusts §49 cmt. a(1).

§8.15.3 Rule in Shelley's Case

In the Harleian mss. (530) is an account of Peter Bales, a clerk of the Court of Chancery about 1590, who wrote a bible so small that he enclosed it in a walnut shell of English growth.[75]

But it is one thing to put a case like Shelley's in a nutshell and another thing to keep it there.[76]

No such rules of law or construction are recognized by this Restatement.[77]

The doctrine of worthier title is about the heirs of the settlor. The *Rule in Shelley's Case*,[78] another remnant of Anglo-Norman late feudal law,[79] is about the *heirs of someone other than the settlor*[80] and has been limited for the most part to legal and equitable interests in real property.[81] To the extent it has been applied to entrusted personalty, it has been applied only "indirectly."[82]

Let us take the following trust: *A* (settlor) to *B* (trustee) for the benefit of *C* for life; and, upon the death of *C*, *B* shall convey the trust property to *C*'s "heirs." If the Rule is applicable, *C* takes a fully vested equitable interest that is referred to in some places as an "equitable fee simple."[83] There are no other beneficiaries.[84] (If *C* were the sole trustee, there would be a merger.[85]) The "heirs" of *C* are cut out regardless of the intentions of the settlor,[86] that is *C* may gift inter vivos or devise postmortem the underlying property to persons other than the "heirs." For the Rule to apply, however, "the life estate in the ancestor and the remainder to the heirs or heirs of the body must both be legal or both equitable."[87] Also, "heirs of *C*" must essentially mean the actual probate estate of *C*, not those who might be entitled to it, which is the approach the Uniform Probate Code takes for dispositions of both realty and personalty. The Code provides that the property would pass "to those persons, including the state, and in such shares as would succeed to . . . [*C*'s] . . . intestate estate under the

---

[75] Ivor H. Evans, Brewer's Dictionary of Phrase and Fable 788 (14th ed.). For the Lord Chancellor in office at the time, *see* Chapter 1 of this handbook.

[76] Van Grutten v. Foxwell, [1897] A.C. 658, 671.

[77] Restatement (Third) of Trusts §49 cmt. a(1) (referring in part to the Rule in Shelley's Case).

[78] 1 Co. Rep. 93b (1581).

[79] *See generally* Lewin ¶6-43 & ¶6-44.

[80] 2 Scott & Ascher §12.14.2.

[81] Moynihan at 141–150; 2 Scott on Trusts §127.2.

[82] *See* Note, Application of the Rule in Shelley's Case to Gifts of Personal Property, 23 Harv. L. Rev. 51 (1909).

[83] 2 Scott on Trusts §127.2; 2 Scott & Ascher §12.14.2.

[84] 2 Scott on Trusts §127.2; 2 Scott & Ascher §12.14.2.

[85] Moynihan at 145.

[86] 2 Scott on Trusts §127.2.

[87] Cornelius J. Moynihan, Introduction to the Law of Real Property 149 (2d ed. 1988). *See generally* §2.1 of this handbook (the trust's property requirement).

intestate succession law of ... [*C's*] ... domicile if ... [*C*] ... died when the disposition is to take effect in possession or enjoyment."[88]

In a number of states, the Rule has been abolished by statute.[89] "Where the rule has been abolished or where it is not applicable because the trust property is personalty, the inference is that the settlor intends to give the first taker only a life estate, and there is a contingent interest limited to the persons who may be his heirs or next of kin at his death."[90] Even in those states where the Rule has been abolished, however, it may well be that the spendthrift clause of a trust under which the underlying trust property is to be paid to the actual *probate estate* of *C* upon the death of *C* is ineffective.[91] In other words, trust principal, notwithstanding the express restraint on its future involuntary alienation, would be currently accessible to *C*'s creditors during *C*'s lifetime.[92]

§8.15.4 Charitable Purpose Doctrine (Statute of Elizabeth/Charitable Uses)

The captives principally contemplated in the St. of 43 Eliz. were doubtless Englishmen taken and held as slaves in Turkey and Barbary.[93]

In Section 9.4.1 of this handbook we discuss the Statute of Elizabeth, also known as the statute of charitable uses.[94] The statute, which had been drafted by Sir Francis Moore,[95] was enacted by Parliament in 1601 to provide for a more orderly administration and supervision of charitable trusts extant in the realm.[96] While it created an administrative infrastructure for enforcing charitable trusts, it in no way clipped the Chancellor's wings.[97] Its preamble catalogs those purposes that qualify as charitable and thus, by implication, are exempt from the durational constraints of the Rule against Perpetuities.[98] In 1792, the

---

[88] UPC §2-711.

[89] 2 Scott on Trusts §127.2. Massachusetts abolished the Rule in Shelley's Case in 1791. *See* M.G.L.A. c. 184 §5.

[90] 2 Scott on Trusts §127.2. *See generally* Restatement (Second) of Property (Wills and Other Donative Transfers) §30.1 (including comments and illustrations).

[91] *See generally* 3 Scott & Ascher §15.2.7.

[92] *See generally* 3 Scott & Ascher §15.2.7. *See also* §5.3.3.3 (c) of this handbook (non-self-settled spendthrift trusts).

[93] Jackson v. Phillips, 96 Mass. (14 Allen) 539, 558 (1867).

[94] Stat. 43 Eliz. I, c.4 (1601).

[95] *See* 6 Scott & Ascher §38.4.

[96] 4A Scott on Trusts §368.1; 5 Scott & Ascher §37.1.2; 6 Scott & Ascher §38.1.1.

[97] 5 Scott & Ascher §37.1.2.

[98] 4A Scott on Trusts §365. The Restatement (Second) of Trusts "concluded" that a trust was charitable if it was "sufficiently beneficial to the community to justify permitting property to be devoted forever to [its] accomplishment." Restatement (Second) of Trusts §374. One learned commentator, however, has noted that "[g]iven the fact that in a number of states it is now possible to devote property forever to the accomplishment of purely private purposes, ... even this definition is suspect." 6 Scott & Ascher §38.1. *See generally* §8.2.1.9 of this handbook (abolition of the Rule against Perpetuities).

legislature of Virginia passed an act repealing all English statutes including the Statute of Elizabeth. Other states took similar action after the Revolution. In Massachusetts, the Statute, "in substance and principle, has always been considered as part of . . . [her] . . . common law."[99] In 1888 the body of the statute itself was repealed by Parliament.[100] By then the administrative infrastructure that the statute had created had fallen into disuse.[101]

To this day, however, courts in both England and the United States[102] still look to the preamble for guidance in determining whether a particular trust purpose is charitable, bearing in mind, however, that the "enumeration is not and was not intended to be exhaustive":

> some for relief of aged, impotent and poor people, some for maintenance of sick and maimed soldiers and mariners, schools of learning, free schools, and scholars in universities, some for repair of bridges, ports, havens, causeways, churches, sea-banks and highways, some for education and preferment of orphans, some for or towards relief, stock or maintenance for houses of correction, some for marriages of poor maids, some for supportation, aid and help of young tradesmen, handicraftsmen and persons decayed, and others for relief or redemption of prisoners or captives, and for aid or ease of any poor inhabitants concerning payments of fifteens, setting out of soldiers and other taxes.[103]

There are two U.S. Supreme Court opinions that examine in remarkable depth the state of the law of charities before and after Parliament enacted the Statute of Elizabeth, *i.e.*, the statute of charitable uses. They are *Trustees of the Philadelphia Baptist Association v. Hart's Executors*[104] and *Vidal v. Girard's Executors*.[105] The issue that prompted these tours de force of legal scholarship by lawyers and justices alike was a narrow one: whether a charitable trust was

---

[99] Jackson v. Phillips, 96 Mass. (14 Allen) 539, 591 (1867).

[100] 4A Scott on Trusts §348.2.

[101] 5 Scott & Ascher §37.1.2; 6 Scott & Ascher §38.1.1 (The statute provided that "the chancellor might from time to time award commissions to the bishop of every diocese and to others, authorizing them to inquire into abuses and breaches of trust involving property that had been given for charitable purposes, and that these orders would remain valid until the chancellor altered them.").

[102] *See, e.g.*, Jackson v. Phillips, 96 Mass. (14 Allen) 539, 551 (1867) (noting that it has been well settled in Massachusetts that any purpose is charitable in the "legal sense" of the word which is within the "principle and reason" of the statute of charitable uses, *i.e.*, Statute of Elizabeth, even though the particular purpose is not expressly set forth in the statute).

[103] Stat. 43 Eliz. I, c.4 (1601). *See generally* 4A Scott on Trusts §368.1 at 138, 139. Although Sir Francis Moore had intentionally omitted religious purposes from the statute's preamble, that is other than making a narrow reference to the "repair of churches," by 1639 English courts were enforcing perpetual trusts for the advancement of religion. *See* 6 Scott & Ascher §38.4.

[104] 17 U.S. 1 (1819).

[105] 43 U.S. 127 (1844). *See* 6 Scott & Ascher §38.1 (criticizing from a legal perspective defendant counsel's definition of a charitable purpose as being motive-based rather than purpose-based).

enforceable at common law before enactment of the Statute of Elizabeth.[106] An answer was needed because, as we noted above, in some states the statute was not in force.[107] By 1844, the Court was confident that the charitable trust was embedded in the common law, that it was not a creature of the 1601 English statute.[108] In fact, when Parliament in 1818 initiated an investigation into how charities were being administered in England and Wales, there were at least 5,000 charitable trusts that had come into existence before 1601 that were still in operation.[109]

It is also likely that even the Preamble's catalog of charitable uses itself had been woven into the fabric of English common law by the time of the statute's enactment in 1601. Certainly something remarkably similar was well ensconced in the general culture by then, as evidenced by *The Vision of Piers the Plowman*, a fourteenth-century poem by William Langland "wherein anxious (and rich) merchants are counseled by Truth to obtain remission of sins and a happy death by using their fortunes"[110] to:

> . . . repair hospitals,
> help sick people,
> mend bad roads,
> build up bridges that had been broken down,
> help maidens to marry or to make them nuns,
> find food for prisoners and poor people,
> put scholars to school or to some other craft,
> help religious orders, and
> ameliorate rents or taxes.[111]

While it was in the early part of the fifteenth century that the proto-charitable trust known as the charitable use became enforceable, enforceability being a critical characteristic of the modern trust, Prof. Maitland has suggested that the gestation of the modern trust actually commenced back in the early thirteenth century when the faithful began conveying land to third parties for the use of the Franciscan friars, who had arrived in England about that time.[112] Neither an individual friar nor the order collectively could own land.[113] A conveyance to a third party was a way around the letter if not the spirit of the

---

[106] *See generally* 6 Scott & Ascher §38.1.1.

[107] *See generally* 5 Scott & Ascher §37.1.3 (Charitable Trusts in the United States).

[108] *See generally* 5 Scott & Ascher §37.1.3 ("Yet the law of charitable trusts did not originate in, nor was it dependent upon, the enactment of the Statute of Charitable Uses"); Craig Kaufman, *Sympathy for the Devil's Advocate: Assisting the Attorney General When Charitable Matters Reach the Courtroom*, 40 Real Prop, Prob. & Tr. J. 706, 711 (Winter 2006).

[109] 5 Scott & Ascher §37.1.2.

[110] Marion R. Fremont-Smith, Governing Nonprofit Organizations 29 (2004).

[111] William Langland, The Vision of Piers the Plowman 114 (W. W. Skeat et al. trans., London: Chatto and Windus, 1931).

[112] 5 Scott & Ascher §37.1.2 (History of Charitable Trusts in England).

[113] 5 Scott & Ascher §37.1.2.

vow of poverty.[114] While these arrangements had some of the characteristics of the modern trust, they were not trusts. This is because they were "honorary," *i.e.,* they were not enforceable in some court.[115] Back in those early days, however, there was a vehicle for making a gift for religious purposes that did "receive . . . certain protections in the courts of law."[116] In 1290, however, the Statute Quia Emptores, for all intents and purposes, rendered it irrelevant, or at least of "slight importance," by mandating the personal acquiescence of the Crown in its employment.[117] The vehicle was a category of free land tenure known as frankalmoign or frankalmoin. "[M]eaning free alms, . . . [it] . . . was a tenure arising from a gift of lands to a church, religious body or ecclesiastical official in return for services of a religious nature, such as saying Masses or prayers, but with no secular obligation."[118] Anyone in search of the origins of the charitable trust, however, will find this particular form of land tenure to be a dead end, notwithstanding the fact that at the beginning of the twentieth century a small portion of the land of England was still being held in frankalmoign.[119] While the tenure's nonsecular character may serve to buttress an argument that England's culture of private charity is of ancient origin, it is elsewhere that we must look for the origins of the modern charitable trust.

Today, the charitable trust is enforceable in every state of the United States.[120] Moreover, deathbed and family protection statutory restrictions on one's ability to create a charitable trust have "all but disappeared."[121] So have statutory restrictions that were designed to prevent large aggregations of wealth from being taken out of commerce and entrusted for charitable purposes.[122]

§8.15.5 Statute of Frauds

A trust in personal property may be established by parol evidence. . . . [W]hile no particular form of words or conduct is necessary for the creation of a trust, language or conduct and a

---

[114] 5 Scott & Ascher §37.1.2.

[115] 5 Scott & Ascher §37.1.2.

[116] 5 Scott & Ascher §37.1.2.

[117] Moynihan at 11–12. *See also* 5 Scott & Ascher §37.1.2.

[118] Moynihan at 11–12.

[119] Moynihan at 21 (noting in footnote 5 that in 1922 Parliament began the process of abolishing the frankalmoign tenure altogether).

[120] 5 Scott & Ascher §37.1.3.

[121] 5 Scott & Ascher §§37.2.6 (Restrictions on the Creation of Charitable Trusts), 37.2.6.3 (Restrictions in England on Devises for Charitable Purposes), 37.2.6.4 (Statutory Restrictions in the United States), 37.2.6.6 (suggesting that to the extent any statutory restrictions on one's ability to devise to a charity still remain in place, on policy grounds they should apply as well to dispositions by will substitute, particularly the revocable inter vivos trust). *See generally* §8.11 of this handbook (the revocable inter vivos trust as a will substitute). In England, the Georgian Statute of Mortmain, which was enacted by Parliament in 1736, lumped testamentary dispositions and revocable inter vivos dispositions together in imposing restrictions on one's ability to make dispositions for charitable purposes. *See* Stat. 9 Geo. II, c. 36 (1736).

[122] 5 Scott & Ascher §37.2.6 (Restrictions on the Creation of Charitable Trusts).

manifestation of an intention to create the same must be proven by evidence which is sufficiently clear, precise and unambiguous....[123]

The Statute of Frauds required not only that the declaration or creation of a trust of land be manifested and proven by a writing, but also that all grants and assignments of any trust or confidence shall likewise be in writing, signed by the party granting or assigning the same, or by such last will or devise, or else shall likewise be wholly void and of none effect.[124]

Creation of the trust. To this day, oral trusts of personal property are generally enforceable.[125] In England before 1676, a trust of real or personal property, with some exceptions, was "averable," *i.e.*, it could be declared by word of mouth.[126] In that year, however, Parliament enacted a statute commonly known as the statute of frauds.[127] Section 7 provided that "all declarations or creations of trusts or confidences of any *lands*, tenements, or hereditaments shall be manifested and proved by some *writing* signed by the party who is by law enabled to declare such trust, or by his last will in writing, or else they shall be utterly void and of none effect."[128]

The statute did not require that a trust of land be created by a written instrument, merely that it be proved by one.[129] Thus, a writing—perhaps even an oral admission in open court or a revoked will—whose purpose is to assert the unenforceability of an oral trust of land may itself constitute a writing that satisfies the statute's requirements, provided it contains a direct or indirect acknowledgment or admission of the trust's existence.[130] Moreover, if lost or destroyed, the writing itself may be proved by parol (oral) evidence.[131]

Either by case law or by statute, some form of Section 7 has found its way into the law of most U.S. jurisdictions.[132] As a general rule, then, with the exception of the resulting trust[133] and the constructive

---

[123] Wolff v. Calla, 288 F. Supp. 891, 893 (1968). *See* Snuggs v. Snuggs, 571 S.E.2d 800 (2002) (involving an oral trust of personal property established by a grandfather to fund the advanced educations of his four grandchildren).

[124] 3 Scott & Ascher §14.7 (referring to Stat. 29 Car. II, c. 3).

[125] *See, e.g.*, In re Estate of Fournier, 902 A.2d 852 (Me. 2006).

[126] 1 Scott & Ascher §6.1.

[127] Stat. 29 Chas. II, c.3 (1676).

[128] 1 Scott on Trusts §40 at 413, 414.

[129] 1 Scott & Ascher §6.3.2.

[130] 1 Scott & Ascher §6.6.

[131] 1 Scott & Ascher §6.8.

[132] 1 Scott & Ascher §6.2.1; 1 Scott on Trusts §§40, 40.1; Restatement (Second) of Trusts §40. *See also* UTC §407 cmt. (available at <http://www.uniformlaws.org/Act.aspx?title=Trust%20Code>). "The term 'statute of frauds' is used in . . . [the Restatement (Third) of Trusts] . . . to refer to all of these rules requiring that inter vivos trusts be created or proved in writing, including those rules that are based on judicial decisions finding the requirement in the common law, and those rules that apply to some or all inter vivos trusts of personal property." Restatement (Third) of Trusts §22 cmt. a.

[133] Restatement (Second) of Trusts §40 cmt. d; 1 Scott & Ascher §6.12 (a written conveyance of land "in trust" that does not specify the trust beneficiaries or its purposes will trigger a resulting trust in favor of the transferor notwithstanding the Statute of Frauds). *See generally* §§3.3 of this handbook (the purchase money resulting trust) and 4.1.1.1 of this handbook (the resulting trust);

trust,[134] a trust concerning an interest in land requires a writing if it is to be enforceable.[135] The writing must show with reasonable definiteness the trust property.[136] It also must show the trust beneficiaries and the extent of their interests or the purposes of the trust.[137] While a resulting trust of land may be exempt from the writing requirements of the statute of frauds, an oral *assignment* of the nonpossessory equitable reversionary interest to the trustee most likely would not be.[138] "Just as parol evidence is ordinarily inadmissible to rebut a resulting trust, such evidence should also ordinarily be inadmissible to extinguish a resulting trust."[139]

The writing may consist of several writings[140] and, again, need not be intended as the expression of a trust.[141] Take, for example, a prospective settlor who writes and signs a letter explaining that he or she intends at some time *in the future* to impress a trust by oral declaration on a certain parcel of land. The letter sets forth what the terms of the trust will be. If at some time in the future the trust is declared, the letter will satisfy the writing requirement of the statute of frauds.[142] Also, a corroborating letter written *after* an oral trust of land has been declared will satisfy the writing requirement.[143]

In the case of nondeclarations of trust, the statute of frauds does not require that delivery of the deed or conveyance of the real property to the trustee and the creation of the trust occur simultaneously so long as ultimately there is documentation connecting the property to the trust.[144] For declarations of trust, the writing must be signed by the declarant, *i.e.*, the settlor/trustee.[145] While perhaps desirable, "there is no requirement that the settlor/trustee execute a separate writing conveying the property to the trust."[146] For inter

---

6 Scott & Ascher §§40.1 (When a Resulting Trust Arises), 40.2 (The Statute of Frauds and the Resulting *Use*), 40.3 (the Statute of Frauds and the Resulting Trust), 43.1 (The Purchase Money Resulting Trust).

[134] Restatement (Second) of Trusts §40 cmt. d. *See generally* §3.3 of this handbook (involuntary trustees); 6 Scott & Ascher §40.1 (When a Resulting Trust Arises).

[135] *See generally* 6 Scott & Ascher §43.1 (The Purchase Money Resulting Trust).

[136] 1 Scott & Ascher §6.5.

[137] 1 Scott & Ascher §6.5.

[138] *See generally* 6 Scott & Ascher §§41.2 (Rebutting the Resulting Trust), 41.20 (Failure of Express Trust), 42.10 (Trust Fully Performed without Exhausting the Trust Estate).

[139] 6 Scott & Ascher §41.20 (Parol Extinguishment). "A different result has been reached, however, when the resulting trust arose wholly by parol, as in the case in which one person paid the purchase price for a conveyance of land to another." 6 Scott & Ascher §41.20 (Parol Extinguishment). *See generally* §3.3 of this handbook (the purchase money resulting trust).

[140] 1 Scott & Ascher §6.7.

[141] Restatement (Third) of Trusts §22(2).

[142] 1 Scott & Ascher §6.3.1. *See, e.g.*, Orud v. Groth, 708 N.W.2d 72 (Iowa 2006).

[143] 1 Scott & Ascher §6.3.2.

[144] *See, e.g.*, Tretola v. Tretola, 2004 WL 1586999 (Mass. App. Ct. 2004) (holding that statute of frauds not violated though trust may not come have come into existence until after the real estate had been transferred to the trustee).

[145] Restatement (Third) of Trusts §23(1).

[146] Heggstad v. Heggstad, 16 Cal. App. 4th 943, 948 (1993).

vivos transfers in trust from *A* to *B*, either *A* (the settlor)[147] or *B* (the trustee)[148] must sign.[149]

For purposes of the statute, "interests in land" would include leaseholds and condominiums but would not include mortgage notes and stock in cooperative apartments.[150] On the other hand, if the inception assets of an oral trust are personal property, the trustee may subsequently convert them to real property without running afoul of the statute of frauds.[151] The trust would still be enforceable.

If a trustee in reliance upon the statute of frauds refuses to perform an oral trust of land, a constructive trust may arise in favor *of the settlor*, a topic we take up in Section 3.3 of this handbook.[152] The Restatement (Third) of Restitution and Unjust Enrichment suggests that alternatively a constructive trust could arise in favor not of the settlor but *of the designated beneficiaries of the oral trust*. Unjust enrichment principles ought to extend to intended third-party beneficiaries of unenforceable promises is the thinking.[153] Also, courts have enforced oral trusts of land when there has been part performance.[154] A trustee who elects to perform an oral trust of land may do so over the objections of his personal creditors, but not his trustee in bankruptcy.[155]

Also in Section 3.3 of this handbook we discuss the purchase money resulting trust, an express trust/resulting trust hybrid which, like the constructive trust, is exempt from the statute of frauds writing requirement, even when land is involved.[156] "Six years after enactment of the Statute of Frauds, it was decided that 'When a man buys Land in another name, and pays Mony, it will be a Trust for him that pays the Mony, tho' no Deed declaring the Trust; for the Statute of 29 Car. 2, called Statute of Frauds, doth not extend to Trusts, raised by Operation of the Law.'"[157] So too a purchase money resulting trust of land may be *rebutted* by parol evidence that a gift to the grantee was actually intended.[158] Or if a gift to the grantee was not intended *at the time of purchase*, the

---

[147] 1 Scott & Ascher §6.4.1 (noting, however, that a writing signed by the settlor after the transfer would not satisfy the statute of frauds as the settlor would not then have been in a position to declare a trust).

[148] 1 Scott & Ascher §§6.4.2 (Trustee Signs Prior to or at the Time of Transfer), 6.4.3 (Trustee Signs after Transfer).

[149] Restatement (Third) of Trusts §23(2).

[150] Restatement (Third) of Trusts §22 cmt. b; 1 Scott & Ascher §6.2.2.

[151] 1 Scott & Ascher §6.15.1.

[152] 1 Scott & Ascher §6.9.

[153] Restatement (Third) of Restitution and Unjust Enrichment §31 cmt. g.

[154] 1 Scott & Ascher §6.13.

[155] 1 Scott & Ascher §6.14. *See generally* §7.4 of this handbook (trustee's discharge in bankruptcy).

[156] *Cf.* 6 Scott & Ascher §43.2.2 (Unenforceable Express Agreement by Grantee to Hold in Trust).

[157] 6 Scott & Ascher §43.1.1 (quoting Anonymous, 2 Vent. 361 (1683)).

[158] 6 Scott & Ascher §43.2. "In contrast, a resulting trust that arises because of the failure of an express trust declared in a will or other written instrument ordinarily cannot be rebutted by the settlor's oral statements." 6 Scott & Ascher §43.2. *See generally* §3.3 of this handbook (the purchase money resulting trust).

weight of authority is that the payor subsequently may orally surrender his or her equitable interest in the land in favor of the grantee, *i.e.*, in favor of the trustee of the purchase money resulting trust.[159] An oral assignment of the beneficial interest *to a third person*, however, would be invalid under the statute of frauds.[160]

The ERISA statute of frauds is all-inclusive: Section 402(a)(1) of ERISA requires that "every employee benefit plan shall be maintained pursuant to a written instrument."[161] On the other hand, under the Uniform Trust Code, the creation of an oral trust even of land can be established by clear and convincing evidence.[162]

Still, unless an interest in land is involved, an inter vivos trust can arise orally: "Except as required by a statute of frauds, a writing is not necessary to create an enforceable inter vivos trust, whether by declaration, by transfer to another as trustee, or by contract."[163] Some jurisdictions, however, most notably Florida,[164] now have statutes requiring that certain inter vivos trust instruments be executed with testamentary formalities, even when the subject matter is personal property.[165] It remains to be seen what effect such statutes will have on the enforceability of informal trusts, particularly in cases where the manifestation of intention to impose equitable duties is merely the conduct of the parties.[166] If such trusts have been rendered unenforceable by this legislation, then we await to see how the courts will deal with the inevitable unjust enrichment issues.

Transfer of equitable interest. As noted above, the original Statute of Frauds enacted by Parliament in 1676 required that the creation of an express trust of land by declaration or otherwise must be manifested and proven by a writing to be effective. The statute, in addition, however, provided that the transfer of an equitable or beneficial interest in a trust of land also would no longer be effective without a writing.[167] In a number of, but not all, states (U.S.), the statute of frauds likewise also covers *transfers of equitable interests* under trusts,[168] including most likely equitable reversionary interests.[169] "In some states a writing is required for a transfer of the beneficiary's interest in a trust of land only; in some a writing is required for the transfer of a beneficial interest in any trust."[170] In either case, there is no dispute that it is the assigning beneficiary who must sign the writing:

---

[159] *See generally* 6 Scott & Ascher §43.14 (Parol Extinguishment).

[160] *See generally* 6 Scott & Ascher §43.14 (Parol Extinguishment).

[161] *See* Frahm v. Equitable Life Assurance Soc., 137 F.3d 955, 958 (7th Cir. 1998) (suggesting that §402(a)(1) of ERISA is "a long way toward a statute of frauds").

[162] UTC §407 (available at <http://www.uniformlaws.org/Act.aspx?title=Trust%20Code>).

[163] Restatement (Third) of Trusts §20.

[164] Fla. Stat. Ann. §737.111.

[165] 1 Scott & Ascher §6.15.

[166] *See generally* 1 Scott & Ascher §4.1.

[167] 3 Scott & Ascher §14.7.

[168] 3 Scott & Ascher §14.7, n.6 & n.7.

[169] *See generally* 6 Scott & Ascher §41.20.

[170] Restatement (Third) of Trusts §53 cmt. a.

We have seen that difficult questions may arise as to who is the proper party to sign the writing that evidences the creation of a trust. No similar difficulty arises in the case of the assignment of a beneficial interest. It is the beneficiary who makes the assignment, and that beneficiary alone, who may sign the memorandum, whether at the time of the assignment or thereafter. Whether the beneficiary's agent may sign depends on both the language of the statute and the scope of the agent's authority.[171]

§8.15.6   Parol Evidence and Plain Meaning Rules

The plain meaning rule appears simple: courts shall not admit extrinsic evidence to contradict or add to the plain meaning of the words in a will. In his famous treatise on evidence, Wigmore explained that the rule arose from the English society's reverence for the power and legal effect of written words.[172]

Furthermore, to be influenced by and draw meaning from subtle details of wording may well ignore the realities of how drafting is done, not to mention that the words were those of one whose work product suggests inattention to the particular issue or circumstances for which it has become necessary to discover, or attribute, an intention.[173]

The plain meaning rule. In the trust context, the plain meaning rule, when applicable, excludes extrinsic evidence of the settlor's intent. Instead, in construing the terms of a trust the court is bound by the plain meaning of words employed in the governing instrument. Implicit in the rule is the fiction that a word has one universal or absolute meaning. "In truth there can be only *some person's* meaning; and that person, whose meaning the law is seeking, is the writer of the document."[174] Still, the policy rationale for honoring the fiction, at least in the context of testamentary trusts, is compelling: "Modern justifications of the rule include (1) a fear of evidence fabrication, (2) the possibility of fraud, (3) a concern that a decedent had relied on the language used, and (4) that such extrinsic evidence is unattested and therefore violates the will statutes."[175]

The plain meaning rule and the parol evidence rule distinguished. The parol evidence rule would restrict the introduction of extrinsic evidence of settlor intent only if the terms of the governing instrument are all inclusive. "Once reduced to a writing embodying the complete expression of such settlor intent, there is no need for any other evidence of such intent; all earlier expressions of intent have become integrated into the final document."[176]

---

[171] 3 Scott & Ascher §14.7.

[172] Andrea W. Cornelison, *Dead Man Talking: Are Courts Ready to Listen? The Erosion of the Plain Meaning Rule*, 35(4) Real Prop. Prob. & Tr. J. 813 (Winter 2001).

[173] Restatement (Third) of Trusts §50 cmt. g.

[174] Fred Franke & Anna Katherine Moody, *The Terms of the Trust: Extrinsic Evidence of Settlor Intent*, 40 ACTEC L.J. 1, 4 (2014) (citing John Henry Wigmore, Evidence in Trials at Common Law §2462 (1981)).

[175] Fred Franke & Anna Katherine Moody, *The Terms of the Trust: Extrinsic Evidence of Settlor Intent*, 40 ACTEC L.J. 1, 5 (2014).

[176] Fred Franke & Anna Katherine Moody, *The Terms of the Trust: Extrinsic Evidence of Settlor Intent*, 40 ACTEC L.J. 1, 6 (2014).

The plain meaning rule's surrounding circumstances exception. There is a long-standing surrounding-circumstances exception to the plain meaning rule. "The document is meant to be understood as...[the settlor]...understood it—against the backdrop of his or her occupation, property holdings, and relationships with family and others."[177] The surrounding-circumstances exception to the plain meaning rule "pays tribute to the importance of context."[178]

Ambiguous dispositions. Under the parol evidence rule, "if the manifestation of intention of the settlor is integrated in a writing, that is, if a written instrument is adopted by him as the complete expression of his intention, extrinsic evidence, in the absence of fraud, duress, mistake, or other ground for reformation or rescission, is not admissible to contradict or vary it."[179] The Rule applies even when the law does not require that there be a writing.[180] Only when the trust instrument is ambiguous may extrinsic evidence be considered in ascertaining the intentions of the settlor.[181] An example might be a conveyance "to the use of" X. Extrinsic evidence would be allowed in to clarify whether such words evidence an intention to establish a trust relationship.[182] Or consider the ambiguity inherent in a provision that calls for a termination distribution to "X and the children of Y." The introduction of extrinsic evidence would be warranted to ascertain whether the settlor intended that X take half or share equally with the children of Y. At least one court has so held.[183] For more on the drafting pitfalls of "coupling an individual with a class," the reader is referred to Section 5.2 of this handbook.

The plain meaning rule's latent ambiguity exception. It has been a general rule of evidence that "latent ambiguities permit extrinsic evidence, whereas patent ambiguities do not."[184] A latent ambiguity is not apparent from the naked language of the governing instrument. Only in the carrying out of its terms is

---

[177] Fred Franke & Anna Katherine Moody, *The Terms of the Trust: Extrinsic Evidence of Settlor Intent*, 40 ACTEC L.J. 1, 13 (2014).

[178] Fred Franke & Anna Katherine Moody, *The Terms of the Trust: Extrinsic Evidence of Settlor Intent*, 40 ACTEC L.J. 1, 13 (2014).

[179] 1 Scott on Trusts §38 at 403; Restatement (Second) of Trusts §38; 1 Scott & Ascher §4.5. *See generally* Lewin ¶6-03 through ¶6-13 (England).

[180] 1 Scott on Trusts §38.

[181] Dennis v. Kline, 120 So. 3d 11, 38 Fla. L. Weekly D1337 (Fla. Dist. Ct. App. 2013); 1 Scott on Trusts §38. *See also* Restatement (Third) of Trusts §21(2); 1 Scott & Ascher §4.5. *But see* UTC §103(17) (available at <http://www.uniformlaws.org/Act.aspx?title=Trust%20Code>) (defining "Terms of Trust" as the manifestation of the settlor's intent regarding a trust's provisions as expressed in the trust instrument or as may be established by other evidence that would be admissible in a judicial proceeding); UTC §414 cmt. (noting that in determining the settlor's original intent, the court may consider evidence relevant to the settlor's intention even though it contradicts an apparent plain meaning of the text). "The objective of the plain meaning rule, to protect against fraudulent testimony, is satisfied by the requirement of clear and convincing proof." UTC §414 cmt.

[182] Restatement (Third) of Trusts §21 cmt. c.

[183] Will of Schaffner, 557 N.Y.S.2d 198 (App. Div. 1990).

[184] Fred Franke & Anna Katherine Moody, *The Terms of the Trust: Extrinsic Evidence of Settlor Intent*, 40 ACTEC L.J. 1, 10 (2014).

the ambiguity revealed. "A patent ambiguity, on the other hand, is one arising from an apparent contradiction within the document itself or where a term that is used in the document could yield several meanings."[185] For more on patent and latent ambiguities, see Section 5.2 of this handbook.

The UTC is extrinsic-evidence friendly. The Uniform Trust Code via its reformation sections sweeps away such time-honored checks on the introduction of extrinsic evidence, a topic we take up in Section 8.15.22 of this handbook.[186] Even unambiguous provisions are no longer are safe in the typical Code jurisdiction.

Words with multiple meanings. Words that cause confusion are not necessarily ambiguous.[187] The word *family* is a good example. A provision for the benefit of *X*'s family may mean *X*'spouse and children.[188] Or it may be more expansive in scope encompassing perhaps *X*'s siblings and parents as well. In any case, the word has only one intended meaning within the particular context. It may take a court, however, to divine its contextualized plain meaning.[189] Ordinarily the court does so without the benefit of parol evidence.

Still, there is the case that involved whether a class of trust beneficiary characterized as "spouses" of certain designated individuals included their surviving spouses, *i.e.*, their widows and widowers.[190] While the trial court found the word *spouses* to be "unambiguous on its face," the appellate courts disagreed.[191] They saw the term *spouses* as contextually ambiguous. The trial court, in holding that "spouses" included surviving spouses, was guided by the plain meaning rule.[192] The appellate courts in upholding the decision of the trial court saw themselves as resolving a contextual ambiguity. All three courts took into consideration extrinsic evidence, particularly the testimony of the scrivener as to the settlor's probable intent.[193]

Consider a trust established in contemplation of divorce for the benefit of the settlor's ex-wife until such times as she "remarries." Did her status as a beneficiary terminate upon her remarriage *to the settlor*? One court has held that it did not.[194] Notwithstanding the confusion that was caused by the particular

---

[185] Fred Franke & Anna Katherine Moody, *The Terms of the Trust: Extrinsic Evidence of Settlor Intent*, 40 ACTEC L.J. 10, 5 (2014).

[186] *See, e.g.*, Frakes v. Nay, 247 Or. App. 95, 273 P.3d 137 (2010) (applying Oregon's UTC trust reformation provisions).

[187] *See, e.g.*, Citizens Bus. Bank v. Carrano, 117 Cal. Rptr. 3d 119, 126 (2010) (there being no latent ambiguity attached to the term *issue* as employed in the governing trust instrument, "Christopher's issue" included his illegitimate biological son, even though the biological mother was married to someone other than Christopher).

[188] 2 Scott & Ascher §12.14.3.

[189] *See generally* Andrea W. Cornelison, *Dead Man Talking: Are Courts Ready to Listen? The Erosion of the Plain Meaning Rule*, 35(4) Real Prop. Prob. & Tr. J. 813 (Winter 2001). *See also* the quotations that introduce this section.

[190] *See* Trust Agreement of Johnson, 194 N.J. 276, 944 A.2d 588 (2008).

[191] *See* Trust Agreement of Johnson, 194 N.J. 276 n.1, 944 A.2d 588 n.1 (2008).

[192] *See* Trust Agreement of Johnson, 194 N.J. 276 n.1, 944 A.2d 588 n.1 (2008).

[193] *See* Trust Agreement of Johnson, 194 N.J. 276, 281, 944 A.2d 588, 591 (2008).

[194] Bank of N.Y. v. Hiss, 27 N.Y.S.2d 646 (Sup. Ct. 1941).

fact pattern, it cannot be said that the word "remarriage" itself was somehow inherently ambiguous.

The word *widow* is another example of an unambiguous word that can nonetheless cause confusion in the hands of the unskilled draftsperson.[195] One learned commentator has observed:

> Where the settlor makes a gift in trust for his "widow" the instrument and the surrounding circumstances may indicate that the settlor meant only the woman to whom he was married at the time of his death should take. . . . In other cases the intent is inferred that he meant only the woman to whom he was married at the time of the creation of the trust.[196]

A poorly drafted provision for someone's "education" is another example of where the context in which a word is used, not necessarily the meaning of the word itself, is what causes the confusion, at least in the minds of some. Take the case of a trust that was established in part for the education of the settlor's grandson. The trust provided as follows: "for the purposes of this trust, . . . [my grandson] . . . shall not be deemed to have 'completed his education' so long as he is under thirty-five (35) years of age and shall be continuing his formal education at a recognized academic college or university which meets the approval of the trustee." The trust was to terminate when the grandson had "completed his education" and the trust property as it then existed was to pass outright and free of trust to the settlor's children. When the grandson was 20 years of age, he dropped out of college, telling the trust officer that he did not want to continue his education. Approximately eighteen months later, he returned to college. At the time the grandson dropped out of college, had the trust terminated and the trust property vested in the settlor's children? The trustee brought an action for declaratory judgment. The appellate court held as follows:

> The Bank argued at trial and argues on appeal that the provision in the trust giving Nathan until he is 35 years old to complete his education is an indication that the settlor did not intend that Nathan be required to be enrolled in a college or university every semester without break. . . . We agree. The purpose of the trust was to provide an education for Nathan, and the trust allowed Nathan up to the age of 35 to complete his education. . . . Considering the will and trust language as a whole, we hold that the terms of the trust are not ambiguous. We further hold that the trial court did nor err in determining that the trust did not . . . [at the time Nathan dropped out of college] . . . terminate by its own terms.[197]

---

[195] *See, e.g.,* Offerman v. Rosile, 31 Kan. App. 2d 1055, 1061, 77 P.3d 504, 508 (2003) (while it was unclear to the litigants whether the former wife of the settlor of a revocable trust who had died unmarried qualified as his "widow" thus entitling her to an equitable interest under the trust, the trust instrument by the way having been drafted by a stockbroker who was not an attorney, the court saw "absolutely nothing ambiguous in the use of the term 'widow,'" ruling that because the settlor had died unmarried, he had died without a "widow").

[196] Bogert §182. *Cf.* In re Lynch, [1943] 1 All E. R. 168 (Ch.) (involving a dispute over the meaning of the word *widowhood*).

[197] Hurley v. Moody Nat'l Bank of Galveston, 98 S.W.3d 307, 311 (Tex. 2003).

The terms *minority* and *majority* become problematic when their ages are changed by statute during the life of a trust:

> Where the age of majority has been changed by statute from 21 to 18, a question may arise as to when a trust beneficiary is entitled to receive the trust property. This depends on the manifestation of the settlor's intention. If the governing instrument provides that the beneficiary is to receive the trust property on reaching his or her "majority," it would seem that the beneficiary is entitled to receive the property at age 18, regardless of when the governing instrument was executed. If the governing instrument provides that the beneficiary is to receive the trust property at age 21, however, he or she is not entitled to it until he or she reaches that age.[198]

Is the concept of a property's *market value* inherently ambiguous? Perhaps not inherently, but in the context of a particular governing trust instrument one court has found it actually to mean the property's net value, *i.e.*, its fair market value net of encumbrances.[199]

The Uniform Probate Code for its purposes defines the word *child* as "an individual entitled to take as a child under . . . [the] . . . Code by intestate succession from the parent whose relationship is involved and excludes a person who is only a stepchild, a foster child, a grandchild, or any more remote descendant."[200] A well-drafted trust instrument should have its own definition of child, one that explicitly and unambiguously addresses the issues of adoption and illegitimacy, as well as keeps to a minimum incorporations by reference.[201] Not all trustees are lawyers and not all lawyers have taken trusts.[202] The topics of adoption and illegitimacy are covered in Section 5.2 of this handbook as part of our discussion of class designations.

The Uniform Trust Code's generous reformation sections, whether for good or for ill, have gutted the plain meaning rule and in so doing opened the floodgates to extrinsic evidence, a topic we take up in Section 8.15.20 of this handbook and in Section 8.15.22 of this handbook.[203] At least one Florida court, however, appears to be bucking the trend.[204] Indiana would seem not to be fully on board as well.[205]

---

[198] 5 Scott & Ascher §33.1 n.3.

[199] *See* Trupp v. Naughton, No. 320843 (Mich. App. Ct. May 26, 2015).

[200] UPC §1-201(5).

[201] *See generally* §8.15.17 of this handbook (doctrine of incorporation by reference).

[202] *See generally* §8.25 of this handbook (few American law schools still require Agency, Trusts and Equity).

[203] *See, e.g.*, Frakes v. Nay, 247 Or. App. 95, 273 P.3d 137 (2010) (the court applying Oregon's UTC trust reformation provisions).

[204] *See* Miami Children's Hosp. Found., Inc. v. Estate of Hillman, 101 So. 3d 861 (2012) ("We find that the trust documents are clearly not ambiguous and that the trial court erred in concluding that MCHF was not the intended beneficiary of the . . . trust.").

[205] *See* Kristoff v. Centier Bank, 985 N.E.2d 20 (2013) (the court declining to order termination of a trust under Indiana's version of UTC §412 as such an order would be in

Resulting trusts. When an express trust fails, or is fully performed and there is property still remaining in the trust estate, a resulting trust is generally imposed on the surplus, a topic we take up in Section 4.1.1.1 of this handbook.[206] In other words, the trustee may not walk away with the property, unless the terms of the express trust provide otherwise.[207] "Whether the trust is inter vivos or testamentary, the traditional view is that extrinsic evidence of the settlor's declarations that the trustee is to be permitted to keep the property if the trust is fully accomplished without exhausting the trust estate is ordinarily inadmissible."[208] So also when an express trust fails.[209]

In Section 3.3 of this handbook, we discuss the purchase money resulting trust, an express trust/resulting trust hybrid that can arise orally even when the subject property is land.[210] A purchase money resulting trust may be *rebutted* as well by parol evidence that an outright gift to the transferee was actually intended.[211] Courts, however, are generally reluctant to engraft an express trust upon an absolute conveyance of land.[212] This is not because of the parol evidence rule but because of the statute of frauds, a topic that is covered in Section 8.15.5 of this handbook.

§8.15.7 *The Claflin Doctrine (Material Purpose Doctrine)*

In the recent decision of Buschau v. Rogers Communications, Inc. (No. 2) [2002], the Supreme Court of British Columbia revisited, in the context of a pension dispute, the application of the rule in Saunders v. Vautier [1841]. The principle of Saunders . . . , an English case, . . . allows a . . . [settlor's] . . . intentions to be frustrated completely unexpectedly. It applies in circumstances where a gift is made to a person who is not to receive it until they [sic] attain an age greater than that of majority and, where there is no gift over, the person may call for the gift on reaching the age of majority.[213]

The American cases espouse the view that the owner of property can do with it as he or she pleases, as long as the resulting disposition does not run afoul of any rule of law or principle

---

contravention of the dispositive intentions of the settlor as those intentions had been clearly and unambiguously articulated within the four corners of the governing trust instrument).

[206] *See generally* 6 Scott & Ascher §41.2 (Failure); §42.2 (Surplus); §4.1.1.1 of this handbook (the resulting trust).

[207] *See generally* 6 Scott & Ascher §§41.2 (Failure), 42.2 (Surplus); §4.1.1.1 of this handbook (the resulting trust).

[208] *See generally* 6 Scott & Ascher §§41.2 (Failure), 42.2 (Surplus); §4.1.1.1 of this handbook (the resulting trust).

[209] 6 Scott & Ascher §41.2.

[210] *See generally* 6 Scott & Ascher §43.1. *Cf.* 6 Scott & Ascher §43.2.2 (Unenforceable Express Agreement by Grantee to Hold in Trust).

[211] 6 Scott & Ascher §43.2.

[212] 1 Scott & Ascher §4.5.

[213] Ian M. Hull, A Fresh Look at *Saunders*, Trusts and Estates, A Legalese Special Report (2003) at 23 (in association with STEP). For more commentary on *Saunders v. Vautier*, 4 Beav. 115, 49 E.R. 282 (1841), *see* 5 Scott & Ascher §34.1.3 (Postponement of Enjoyment).

of public policy. The American cases also state that it is the duty of the court to carry out the settlor's directions. Of course, the English courts can also claim refuge in maxims.[214]

The English are not in accord. Let us take the following type of trust: *A* (settlor) to *B* (trustee) for ten years, then to *C* outright and free of trust; but if *C* dies during the ten-year period, the trust property shall be distributed to *C*'s estate.[215] There is no spendthrift clause. It is not a support trust.[216] Actually, *B* has no discretion whatsoever to invade principal.[217] *C* is the sole beneficiary.[218] In other words, during the lifetime of the trust, *C* possesses unconditionally a fully vested equitable interest.[219] Were the corpus a parcel of real estate, the beneficiary might even be said to possess an equitable fee simple.[220] In England, *C* may compel termination of the trust in his or her favor before the term of years has expired, even though to do so would contravene the wishes of the settlor.[221] This is an application of the so-called rule in *Saunders v. Vautier*, which is covered in Section 8.15.92 of this handbook.[222]

---

[214] 5 Scott & Ascher §34.1.3. The origins of the American material purpose doctrine can be traced to the landmark case, Claflin v. Claflin, 149 Mass. 19, 20 N.E. 454 (Mass. 1889), which rejected the English position that to deny the sole beneficiary of a trust the right to terminate it is to impose an impermissible restraint on the beneficiary's right to alienate his or her property, even in a case where the property is an equitable interest under a trust.

[215] If, instead, all the trust property were to pass to the probate estate of *C* should *C* die before attaining a certain age, *C* would still be the sole beneficiary. *See* 5 Scott & Ascher §34.1.3 (Postponement of Enjoyment).

[216] 5 Scott & Ascher §34.1.4 (the applicability of the *Claflin* or material purpose doctrine to support and discretionary trusts).

[217] 5 Scott & Ascher §34.1.4.

[218] *See* 3 Scott & Ascher §13.2.2 (defining sole beneficiary as follows: "If the terms of a trust require the payment to one person of both the income for a period of time, and, thereafter, the principal, that person is the trust's sole beneficiary, unless there is a contingent gift to another or a resulting trust upon the designated person's failure to survive the stated period"). A sole beneficiary possesses the entire equitable or beneficial interest if the underlying trust property passes to the beneficiary's probate estate in lieu of the imposition of a resulting trust. *See also* 4 Scott & Ascher §24.1.2 (Multiple Beneficiaries) (defining sole beneficiary); 5 Scott & Ascher §§34.1.3 (Postponement of Enjoyment) (defining sole beneficiary), 34.1.1 (Successive Beneficiaries and the *Claflin* or Material Purpose Doctrine).

[219] *See generally* §5.4.1.7 of this handbook (right to conveyance).

[220] *See* 3 Scott & Ascher §13.2.1 (noting also that words of inheritance such as "to X and his heirs" are no longer required to create by deed an equitable fee simple in land).

[221] *See generally* 5 Scott & Ascher §34.1.3; 4 Scott on Trusts §337.3; Lewin ¶ 24-06 through ¶ 24-07 (England). *Saunders v. Vautier*, 49 Eng. Rep. 282, 4 Beav. 115 (1841) (England), allows for termination of a trust if all its beneficiaries consent and are of full age and legal capacity. *See generally* Ian M. Hull, A Fresh Look at *Saunders*, Trusts and Estates, A Legalese Special Report 2003 at 23 (in association with STEP) (concluding that "[w]hile the rule in *Saunders* has been around . . . [in Canada and England] . . . for many years and its application in the context of wills and trusts has been firmly established, the basic concepts have, again, been revisited in Canada, [*see* Buschau v. Rogers Communications, Inc. (1998) 54 BCLR (3d) 125; Buschau v. Rogers Communications, Inc. (2002). BCJ No. 865; and Buschau v. Rogers Communications, Inc. (2003) BCJ No. 1025] and its use in the context of . . . pension law has added another twist for the courts to consider when reviewing this important rule and its application").

[222] Saunders v. Vautier, [1841] EWHC Ch J82 (1841) Cr & Ph 240, (1841) 4 Beav. 115 8; 41 ER 482 (England) (in the High Court of Chancery).

The material purpose doctrine is the brainchild of Massachusetts equity. In the United States, most courts will look to the 1889 Massachusetts case of *Claflin v. Claflin*[223] and hold that *C* must wait out the term specified: "It cannot be said that these restrictions upon [*C*'s] possession and control of the property are altogether useless, for there is not the same danger that he will spend the property while it is in the hands of the trustees as there would be if it were in his own."[224] On the other hand, if the trustee does transfer the underlying trust property to the beneficiary before the end of the ten-year period, "the trust ends and the trustee is under no liability to the beneficiary for making the transfer."[225]

The Restatement (Third) of Trusts generally recognizes the *Claflin* doctrine.[226] Again, the *Claflin* doctrine would not be invoked with respect to a trust that had no purpose whatsoever.[227] Thus, it is sometimes referred to as the "material purpose doctrine."[228] The doctrine does not apply just to trusts for a term of years. It would apply, as well, to the single-beneficiary trust whose sole purpose is to manage the underlying property while the beneficiary is under a legal, physical, or mental incapacity.[229] In this case, the trust would be terminable in favor of the beneficiary upon the beneficiary's attaining or regaining capacity, absent special additional facts.[230] Or take a trust for the care, maintenance, and welfare of *X* and *Y* so that they may live in the style and manner to which they are accustomed, *for and during the remainder of their natural lives.* The trustee must use all of the income and such part of the principal as is necessary for this purpose. To assure *X* and *Y* "life-long income" is a material purpose that would be thwarted were the trust to be ordered terminated in mid-course and

---

[223] 149 Mass. 19, 23, 20 N.E. 454 (1889). *See generally* 5 Scott & Ascher §34.1.3 (Postponement of Enjoyment).

[224] 149 Mass. 19, 23, 20 N.E. 454 (1889). *See also* Restatement (Second) of Trusts §337; §5.4.1.7 of this handbook (right to conveyance); 5 Scott & Ascher §34.1.3 (Postponement of Enjoyment); John Chipman Gray, The Rule Against Perpetuities §121.2 (4th ed. 1942). *But see* Johnson v. First Nat'l Bank of Jackson, 386 So. 2d 1112 (Miss. 1980) (allowing for termination of a trust even in the face of a spendthrift clause if the settlor as well as all the beneficiaries consent).

[225] 5 Scott & Ascher §32.1. So also "if a claim against a third person is held in trust and the third person pays the amount of the claim to the sole beneficiary, who is under no incapacity, the third person is discharged, even if, under the terms of the trust, the beneficiary is not yet entitled to terminate the trust." 5 Scott & Ascher §32.1. In other words, the third person need not pay twice. 5 Scott & Ascher §32.1.

[226] Restatement (Third) of Trusts §65(2). *See generally* 5 Scott & Ascher §§34.1 (Consent of Beneficiaries), 34.1.3 (Postponement of Enjoyment).

[227] 5 Scott & Ascher §§34.1(Consent of Beneficiaries), 34.1.3 (Postponement of Enjoyment).

[228] As to those purposes that would be deemed sufficiently material to satisfy the *Claflin* doctrine, *see* Bogert §§1007–1008; 4 Scott on Trusts §§337–337.8. *See also* UTC §402(a)(4) (available at <http://www.uniformlaws.org/Act.aspx?title=Trust%20Code>) (reciting standard doctrine that a trust is created only if the trustee had duties to perform). *See also* 5 Scott & Ascher §34.1 (noting that "if all of the beneficiaries wish to terminate a trust, it will not be continued merely to enable the trustee to earn additional compensation").

[229] *See generally* 5 Scott & Ascher §34.1.5 (When Beneficiary Is Under Disability That Subsequently Ceases).

[230] 5 Scott & Ascher §34.1.5.

the principal distributed outright and free of trust to them, at least one court has so held.[231]

The *Claflin* or material purpose doctrine generally allows for severability. By that we mean that "[w]hen continuance of the trust, as to the entire trust property, is not necessary to carry out a material purpose, and all of the beneficiaries agree, they can compel a partial termination of the trust."[232]

The *Claflin* doctrine applies notwithstanding the absence of a spendthrift clause: "It is true that [C's] interest is alienable by him, and can be taken by his creditors to pay his debts, but it does not follow that, because [the settlor] has not imposed all possible restrictions, the restrictions which he has imposed should not be carried into effect."[233] It also applies even though the beneficiary may consent to or ratify *the trustee's* acts of self-dealing, a situation that is not without its irony.[234] This, of course, assumes that the beneficiary is of full age and legal capacity and that any consents are informed.[235] Thus, it is said that the English approach the matter from the perspective of the beneficiary, while the American approach, as embodied in the *Claflin* doctrine, is from the perspective of the settlor.[236]

It should be noted that the Uniform Trust Code negates any presumption that the presence of a spendthrift clause evidences a material purpose that would bar the judicial termination or modification of a trust that has only one beneficiary.[237] The Restatement (Third) of Trusts is in accord.[238] There is much case law, however, that is not.[239] Under the Restatement, authority in the trustee to invade principal for the beneficiary's support, or otherwise for the beneficiary's benefit, does raise a strong material purpose presumption, but only a

---

[231] In re Estate of Brown, 528 A.2d 752 (Vt. 1987).

[232] 5 Scott & Ascher §34.1.7.

[233] Claflin v. Claflin, 149 Mass. 19, 23, 20 N.E. 454 (1889).

[234] 4 Scott & Ascher §24.21.2 (Several Beneficiaries).

[235] *See generally* §7.1.2 of this handbook (defenses to allegations that the trustee breached the duty of loyalty); 5 Scott & Ascher §§34.1 (Consent of Beneficiaries), 34.1.1 (Successive Beneficiaries).

[236] 4 Scott on Trusts §337.3; 5 Scott & Ascher §34.1.3.

[237] UTC §411(c) (available at <http://www.uniformlaws.org/Act.aspx?title=Trust%20 Code>). *See, e.g.,* In re the Pike Family Trusts, 38 A.3d 329, 331, 2012 Me. 8 (2012) (confirming that after enactment of its version of the Uniform Trust Code, Maine no longer recognized the common law presumption "that a spendthrift clause, simply by virtue of its presence, was a material purpose of . . . [a] . . . trust."). The version of UTC §411 that Massachusetts has adopted does not repudiate the common law presumption. This was intentional, as per the section's accompanying commentary: "The Committee changed the Uniform Code section to retain current Massachusetts law that a spendthrift provision is a material purpose of a trust." *See generally* §8.15.7 of this handbook (the *Claflin* doctrine (material purpose doctrine)); 5 Scott & Ascher §§34.1.2 (Spendthrift Trusts), 34.1.4 (Support Trusts and Discretionary Trusts).

[238] Restatement (Third) of Trusts §65 cmt. e. *See generally* 5 Scott & Ascher §34.1.2 (Spendthrift Trusts). Likewise, a discretionary provision may or may not evidence a material purpose that would bar termination or modification. Restatement (Third) of Trusts §65 cmt. e.

[239] 5 Scott & Ascher §34.1.2 n.1.

presumption.[240] The case law is less equivocal.[241] "In England, in contrast, the sole beneficiary of the trust can terminate the trust at any time, even if the trust is for the beneficiary's support or the trustee has discretion over distributions or when to terminate the trust."[242]

Under the Uniform Trust Code, a noncharitable irrevocable trust may be modified or terminated upon consent of the settlor and all beneficiaries, even if the modification or termination is inconsistent with a material purpose of the trust.[243] This merely reflects what has been the state of the case law.[244] On the other hand, after the settlor's death, the settlor's personal representative or heirs may not step into the shoes of the settlor and, along with all the beneficiaries, effect a termination of the trust, at least to the extent that that it continues to have a material purpose.[245] This is because "the settlor's ability to consent to the termination of the trust is personal to the settlor."[246]

Merely tracking what has been the case law, primarily *Claflin* and its progeny, the Code expressly provides that a noncharitable irrevocable trust may be terminated upon consent of all of the beneficiaries if the court concludes that continuance of the trust is not necessary to achieve any material purpose of the trust.[247] There is nothing new here.[248] The Code further provides that a noncharitable irrevocable trust may be modified upon consent of all of the beneficiaries if the court concludes that modification is not inconsistent with a material purpose of the trust.[249] Again, the Restatement (Third) of Trusts is generally in accord.[250]

The TEDRA factor. In recent years, reformers of trust law have been hard at work defanging the plain meaning rule, primarily by liberalizing the doctrines of reformation and deviation. The rule is discussed generally in Section 8.15.6 of this handbook; the doctrines, generally in Section 8.15.22. We also have the decanting statutes and decanting court decisions, which are covered in Section 3.5.3.2(a) of this handbook. That having been said, the reformers have generally been quick to caution that these liberalizations are intended to buttress

---

[240] Restatement (Third) of Trusts §65 cmt. e. *See generally* §8.15.7 of this handbook (the *Claflin* doctrine (material purpose doctrine)); 5 Scott & Ascher §34.1.4 (Support Trusts and Discretionary Trusts); §3.5.3.2(a) of this handbook (the discretionary trust, including the support invasion standard).

[241] 5 Scott & Ascher §34.1.4 n.1.

[242] 5 Scott & Ascher §34.1.4. *See generally* §3.5.3.2(a) of this handbook (the discretionary trust, including the support invasion standard).

[243] UTC §411(a) (available at <http://www.uniformlaws.org/Act.aspx?title=Trust%20 Code>). *See generally* 5 Scott & Ascher §34.1.3 (Postponement of Enjoyment).

[244] 5 Scott & Ascher §34.2 n.4.

[245] 5 Scott & Ascher §34.2 (Consent of Beneficiaries and Settlor).

[246] 5 Scott & Ascher §34.2.

[247] UTC §411(b) (available at <http://www.uniformlaws.org/Act.aspx?title=Trust%20 Code>).

[248] *See generally* 5 Scott & Ascher §34.1 (Consent of Beneficiaries).

[249] UTC §411(b) (available at <http://www.uniformlaws.org/Act.aspx?title=Trust%20 Code>).

[250] Restatement (Third) of Trusts §65.

settlor-intent, not subvert it. At minimum, lip service is being paid to settlor-intent. There is one notable exception: Prof. Langbein's "intent-defeating" (his words) benefit-the-beneficiaries rule, which has been incorporated into the Uniform Trust Code. This is a topic that is taken up in Section 6.1.2 of this handbook. This radical intent-defeating policy reform embedded in the UTC has met with considerable push-back. Both the Massachusetts and the New Hampshire legislatures, for example, have said "no thanks." Even some denizens of the ivory tower have declined to fall in line.[251]

Now, while all this has been going on, in Washington State the material purpose doctrine may well have been effectively defanged by an obscure piece of legislation, namely, the Trust and Estate Dispute Resolution Act, or TEDRA.[252] The legislation in part provides that a trust may be reformed nonjudicially by agreement of the trustee and beneficiaries without regard to the trust's material purposes, at least that is what its drafters intended. The agreement is final and binding on all parties. Idaho is, so far at least, the only other TEDRA state. These developments, isolated though they may be, have national implications. Here is why: There have already been decantings from other states into trusts sited in the Washington State to facilitate subversion of their material purposes. Assuming this practice takes on a head of steam, which is likely, the trust instrument scrivener should consider advising his or her settlor-client that the material purpose doctrine may well be TEDRA-vulnerable, unless effective countermeasures can be taken at the drafting stage to defang TEDRA, or forestall a decanting to a TEDRA state. In theory, a decanting from a non-TEDRA state to a TEDRA state in order to subvert a trust's material purposes would be subject to equitable reversal by the courts of the non-TEDRA state. As a practical matter, however, the pursuit by a beneficiary (presumably someone who had not been a party to the TEDRA agreement) of such an equitable multi-jurisdictional action would not be a realistic option, absent special facts, if only because of the numerous and substantial personal expenditures of time and treasure that likely would be required to maintain the action.

§8.15.8   Rule Against Accumulations

An interesting story from Dutch television reported by the Associated Press from Haarlem, The Netherlands, January 6, 1999, describes a bequest in 1805 to aid the poor, but to accumulate and to be expended until 140 years after the death of the last of the testator's servants. The fund first became distributable on January 5, 1999, and was then worth nearly $5,000,000.[253]

---

[251] *See generally* §6.1.2 of this handbook.

[252] Ch. 11.96A.220 RCW.

[253] Restatement (Third) of Trusts §29, Reporter's Notes (Tentative Draft No. 2, Mar. 10, 1999). *See generally* §8.12.1 of this handbook (civil law alternatives to the trust).

It seems settled—at least in the United States[254]—that if a noncharitable trust terminates *within* the period of the Rule against Perpetuities, the terms of the trust may direct the accumulation of income *for the duration of the trust*.[255] In the case of an invalid accumulation directive, "the income is ordinarily payable to the presumptive remainder beneficiaries or, if this is inconsistent with the testator's probable intention, there is a resulting trust of the income for the testator's estate."[256]

The *Claflin* doctrine[257] raises the question of whether income may accumulate beyond the period of the Rule against Perpetuities in cases where remainder interests vest but do not become possessory within the period of the Rule.[258] By way of illustration, let us take the following trust: *A* (settlor) to *B* (trustee) for *C1* for life, then for *C2* for life. Upon the death of *C2*, the principal shall be distributed outright and free of trust *to C2's estate*. *C1* is a life in being. Income shall accumulate until the death of *C2* and then be payable *to C2's estate*. As to the principal, there is no violation of the Rule against Perpetuities. The principal vests in *C2* upon the death of *C1*, the life in being.[259] The interest simply is not possessory during *C2*'s lifetime.[260] The income, however, could accumulate for more than twenty-one years after the death of *C1*, the life in being. "In such a trust, the trustee may continue to have and exercise administrative powers (to sell, lease, invest and the like), but the trustee no longer may have discretion with respect to distributions to beneficiaries; discretionary interests must not be subject to a condition precedent of the trustee's exercise of discretion beyond the perpetuities period."[261] Nor would a spendthrift be

---

[254] For a discussion of the current state of the law against accumulations in England, *see* John Ross Martyn, *Setting Trustees Free?*, Tr. & Est. L.J., No. 42, (Dec. 2002), at 4.

[255] *See generally* 2 Scott & Ascher §9.3.10. *See* White v. Fleet Bank of Me., 1999 Me. 148, 739 A.2d 373 (Me. 1999) (holding that there being no statute in Maine comparable to the Thellusson Act 39 and 40 Géo. 3, c. 98 which provides in derogation of the common law that an accumulation period extending beyond 21 years without reference to lives in being may nonetheless run for 21 years, a trust for a gross number of years in excess of 21 is void *ab initio* under Maine law); Thellusson v. Woodford, 11 Ves. Jr. 112 (Ch. 1805) (allowing for accumulations within the period of the Rule against Perpetuities). For more on the Thellusson Act, Parliament's response to Thellusson v. Woodford, *see* 1A Scott on Trusts §62.11. *See generally* Note, *Accumulations of Income at Common Law*, 54 Harv. L. Rev. 839, 840–841 (1941); 1A Scott on Trusts §62.11. As to income accumulations in the context of charitable trusts, *see* Franklin Found. v. Attorney Gen., 416 Mass. 483, 623 N.E.2d 1109 (1993). *But see* Bogert §341.

[256] 6 Scott & Ascher §41.2.1. A number of states the disposition of income in the face of an invalid income accumulation directive is now governed by statute. 6 Scott & Ascher §41.2.1.

[257] *See generally* §8.15.7 of this handbook (the *Claflin* doctrine (material purpose doctrine)).

[258] Note, *Accumulations of Income at Common Law*, 54 Harv. L. Rev. 839, 841 (1941); 1A Scott on Trusts §62.11. *See* Restatement (Third) of Trusts §29 cmt. h (confirming that a trust is not invalid, either in whole or in part, merely because its duration may exceed the period of the Rule against Perpetuities, providing the vesting requirement of the applicable rule is satisfied).

[259] *See generally* §§8.2.1 of this handbook (the Rule against Perpetuities) and 8.2.1.3 of this handbook (the vesting of interests under trusts).

[260] *See generally* §§8.2.1 of this handbook (the Rule against Perpetuities) and 8.2.1.3 of this handbook (the vesting of interests under trusts).

[261] Restatement (Third) of Trusts §29 cmt. h.

effective beyond the period.[262] Finally, as to a noncharitable trust, all beneficiaries may agree to its termination.[263]

There is a sense in some jurisdictions that this direction to accumulate violates a "'common-law rule' limiting the permissible duration of private accumulations."[264] The matter has been the subject of some legislation.[265] The Thellusson Act, enacted by Parliament in 1800, is one example. This statute against accumulation is discussed in Section 8.15.23 of this handbook.

As to charitable trusts, it is generally held in the United States that income may accumulate for a reasonable[266] period beyond the period of the Rule.[267] A court, however, may "prevent, by appropriate reformation, directed accumulations that are capricious."[268] Strictly speaking, in cases where the equitable interest is unconditionally dedicated to a charitable purpose, *i.e.*, when the interest is vested in the charity, the Rule itself is inapplicable, the Rule being about when contingent interests must vest.[269] Income accumulations in the charitable context merely pose a generalized a public policy issue.[270] In the case of an accumulation period that is determined by the court to be unreasonably long, either the direction to accumulate is disregarded or the trust itself fails, depending upon whether the settlor intended that the benefaction be subject to the condition precedent that income be accumulated for the period stated.[271] In Section 8.31 of this handbook, we discuss the fate of a charitable trust that was established under the will of Benjamin Franklin which was to accumulate income, and which did accumulate income, for 200 years.

Jurisdictions outside the United States are not in accord when it comes to the accumulation of trust income. Take the Isle of Man and the United Kingdom, where "the courts have held that no direction to accumulate is binding, and that the court may direct an immediate application of the property to the designated charitable purpose"[272]:

---

[262] Restatement (Third) of Trusts §29 cmt. h.

[263] Restatement (Third) of Trusts §65 cmt. a.

[264] Note, *Accumulations of Income at Common Law*, 54 Harv. L. Rev. 839, 840 (1941).

[265] 1A Scott on Trusts §62.11, n.10.

[266] "The rule which has met with the most favor is that whether a particular direction for the accumulation of income for the benefit of charity is valid is to be decided by the court, upon consideration of the reasonableness of the provision in view of the value of the trust principal and the amount of its income, the proportion of the income to be accumulated and the length of time during which the accumulation is to occur, the status of the trust, the purpose for which the accumulation is to be made, and any other relevant circumstances." In re Estes Estate, 207 Mich. App. 194, 523 N.W.2d 863 (1994) (citing to Bogert §352).

[267] 1A Scott on Trusts §62.11, n.10. *See, e.g.*, Franklin Found. v. Attorney Gen., 416 Mass. 483, 623 N.E.2d 1109 (1993) (involving a 200-year accumulation trust established under the will of Benjamin Franklin). *See also* Bogert §341. *See generally* Annot., *Validity, construction, and effect of provisions of charitable trust providing for accumulation of income*, 6 A.L.R.4th 903; Bogert §§351, 352.

[268] Restatement (Third) of Trusts §29 cmt. h(2).

[269] *See generally* 6 Scott & Ascher §39.7.9 (Provisions for Accumulation).

[270] *See generally* 6 Scott & Ascher §39.7.9 (Provisions for Accumulation).

[271] *See generally* 6 Scott & Ascher §39.7.9 (Provisions for Accumulation).

[272] 6 Scott & Ascher §39.7.9 (Provisions for Accumulation).

In Isle of Man trust law, in the absence of contrary provision in the trust deed there is no restriction on the accumulation of income of the trust for the whole of the perpetuity period. Caution is necessary where trust property includes real property situate in the United Kingdom. An English court may claim jurisdiction over such property and, on the basis that accumulations beyond the 21-year period permitted under English law are contrary to public policy, it may rule the trust void. In order to avoid the possibility of such an outcome, it is common for real property situate in a jurisdiction other than the Isle of Man to be owned by an underlying company instead of directly by a trust governed by Manx law.[273]

§8.15.9 Doctrine of [Facts of, Acts of, Events of] Independent Legal Significance

Where the inter vivos trust is created by an instrument in which the settlor has reserved no power to modify or revoke the trust, and the settlor in his or her will identifies that trust and leaves property to its trustee or to be held upon the trust stated in that instrument, the disposition made by the will is valid on two grounds. . . . First, the instrument, being in existence at the time of the execution of the will that manifests the intention to incorporate, is validly identified and incorporated by reference. . . . Second, the inter vivos trust is a fact of independent significance.[274]

The common law doctrine of [facts of, acts of, or events of] independent legal significance in its most common manifestation is a gloss on the statute of wills.[275] Most wills statutes provide in part that for a will to be valid it must be in writing and signed by the testator and two witnesses. What if a will contains a bequest to "those in my employ at the time of my death"? Would an employee who was hired after the will was signed and witnessed be entitled to take? Under the common law doctrine of independent legal significance he would.[276] This is because the acts of hiring and firing are acts whose significance are independent of the will.[277] The preparation of a postexecution unattested writing purporting to set forth additional takers under the will, however, would not be such an act as its sole purpose would be to "complement" the will.[278] An early invocation of

---

[273] Paul Dougherty, *Focus: Trust Law in the Isle of Man*, 11(2) STEP J. 12 (May 2003). For an in-depth discussion of the current state of the law in England relating to accumulation trusts, the reader is referred to ¶5-81 through ¶5-108 of Lewin.

[274] Restatement (Third) of Trusts §19 cmt. c. *See generally* §8.15.17 of this handbook (the doctrine of incorporation by reference).

[275] 1A Scott on Trusts §54.2.

[276] 1A Scott on Trusts §54.2.

[277] 1 Scott & Ascher §7.1.2.

[278] 1A Scott on Trusts §54.2. "A devise to the persons named or of the property identified in an unattested writing to be prepared by the testator in the future has no independent significance, and is invalid unless authorized by statute or unless enforceable as a secret trust." Restatement (Third) of Property (Wills and Other Donative Transfers) §3.7 cmt. e. Secret trusts are taken up in §9.9.6 of this handbook.

the doctrine may be found in an 1838 decision of the Chancellor in the case of *Stubbs v. Sargon*.[279]

The Restatement (Third) of Property, which gathers "facts of, or acts of, or events of" under the umbrella term "external circumstances," confirms that the doctrine is not about motive: "An external circumstance has independent legal significance if it is one that would naturally occur or be done for some reason other than the effect it would have on the testamentary disposition, *notwithstanding that it might occur or be done, or did occur or was done, for the purpose of affecting the testamentary disposition*."[280]

The Uniform Probate Code codifies the doctrine's application in the wills context:

> A will may dispose of property by reference to acts and events that have significance apart from their effect upon the dispositions made by the will, whether they occur before or after the execution of the will or after the testator's death. The execution or revocation of another individual's will is such an event.[281]

The trustee needs to be concerned about the doctrine primarily in the context of testamentary pour-overs to *revocable* inter vivos trusts.[282] Let us take the following situation: A will provides that the residue of the testator's estate shall be distributed to the trustee of a certain revocable inter vivos trust to be held in accordance with the terms of said trust, "as from time to time amended."[283] Would the statute of wills permit the residue to be administered in accordance with the terms of a trust that had been amended *by a writing* of the testator *after* the will had been signed and witnessed? Under the doctrine of independent legal significance, it would.[284] Because the revocable inter vivos trust is an arrangement of independent legal significance, *i.e.*, independent of the will, it follows that trust amendments, like hirings and firings, are the product of acts of independent legal significance.[285] In many states the doctrine has been adopted or codified through legislation.[286]

---

[279] Stubbs v. Sargon, 3 My. & Cr. 507, 40 Eng. Rep. 1022 (Ch. 1838) [England].

[280] Restatement (Third) of Property (Wills and Other Donative Transfers) §3.7 cmt. a.

[281] UPC §2-512 (events of independent significance).

[282] 1A Scott on Trusts §54.3.

[283] *See generally* Restatement (Third) of Trusts §19 cmt. e.

[284] 1A Scott on Trusts §54.3.

[285] 1A Scott on Trusts §54.3. *See generally* Second Bank-State St. Trust Co. v. Pinion, 341 Mass. 366, 170 N.E.2d 350 (1960). Massachusetts has since codified its doctrine of independent legal significance. *See* Mass. Gen. Laws ch. 190B, §2-512.

[286] *See* 1A Scott on Trusts §54.3. For a compilation of state statutes codifying the doctrine of independent legal significance in the context of inter vivos trusts and associated pour-over wills, *see* Jeffrey A. Schoenblum, 2000 Multistate Guide to Estate Planning 5-45 through 5-59 (Table 5.02) (2000). *See generally* §2.2.1 of this handbook (the pour-over statute). The Restatement (Third) of Property describes the Doctrine of Independent [legal] Significance as follows: "The meaning of a dispositive or other provision in a will may be supplied or affected by an external circumstance referred to in the will, unless the external circumstance has no significance apart from its effect upon the will." Restatement (Third) of Property (Wills and Other Donative Transfers) §3.7 (1998). The Reporter's Note to §3.7 discusses the doctrine's history, beginning

The doctrine of independent legal significance also can rear its head in the estate tax context. Say a settlor establishes an irrevocable inter vivos trust for the benefit of his children, including children conceived or adopted after the trust is funded. The settlor dies. Is the subject property part of his federal gross estate for tax purposes? The argument for inclusion is that he retained a power to change the beneficial interests of the trust by conceiving or adopting children.[287] The argument against inclusion, which is the argument that is likely to carry the day, is that "the act of bearing or adopting children is an act of independent significance, the incidental and collateral consequence of which is to add the child as beneficiary to the trust."[288]

To the extent an exercise of an inter vivos power of appointment created under the terms of a power-grantor's will is enforceable, it is not on account of the doctrine of independent legal significance. Rather, the exercise would be enforceable "on the theory that the exercise relates back and becomes part of the . . . [power-grantor's] . . . will, even if the writing exercising the power is not executed in accordance with the statutory formalities for wills."[289] The power of appointment is discussed generally in Section 8.1.1 of this handbook.

§8.15.10   The Loring Exemption

In all events, it is the conduct of the trustee and the trustee's staff, not their intentions, which governs the applicability of Loring and the statutory exemptions. Basically, any conduct that indicates that the lawyer is acting beyond the scope of the law practice in dealing with client investments, and particularly any holding out or advertising as investment adviser, would risk the loss of entitlement to exemption from registration. . . . The organization of an affiliated entity . . . , which is essentially a law firm's private trust company, has recently become a trend among law firms seeking to relieve themselves of regulatory involvement while maintaining trustee relationships with their clients.[290]

---

with the English case of Stubbs v. Sargon, 3 My. & Cr. 507, 40 Eng. Rep. 1022 (Ch. 1838), which upheld a testamentary disposition to those who were copartners of the life beneficiary at the time of her death. *See also* §8.15.17 of this handbook (the doctrine of incorporation by reference).

[287] *See* I.R.C. §2036(a)(2) (providing that the value of the gross estate shall include the value of any interest in property transferred by a decedent if the decedent has retained for life the right, alone or in conjunction with any person, to designate the persons who shall possess or enjoy the property or the income therefrom); I.R.C. §2038(a)(1) (providing that the value of the gross estate shall include the value of all property transferred by the decedent if the enjoyment of the property was subject to change at his death through the exercise of a power by the decedent, alone or in conjunction with any person, to alter, amend, revoke, or terminate). *See generally* §8.9.3 of this handbook (tax-sensitive powers).

[288] Rev. Rul. 80-255.

[289] Restatement (Third) of Property (Wills and Other Donative Transfers) §3.7 cmt. e.

[290] ACTEC Practice Committee, Fiduciary Matters Subcommittee, *Guide for ACTEC Fellows Serving as Trustees,* 26 ACTEC Notes 313, 320–321 (2001).

The Investment Advisers Act of 1940[291] requires that an investment advisor, as defined by the Act, register with the SEC (Form ADV), make annual reports to the SEC (Form ADV-S), and conduct his or her business activities in certain specified ways.[292] Filing with the SEC also may bring with it state filing obligations.[293] For purposes of the Act, an investment advisor is:

> any person who, for compensation, engages in the business of advising others, either directly or through publication or writings, as to the value of securities or as to the advisability of investing in, purchasing, or selling securities, or who, for compensation and as part of a regular business, issues or promulgates analysis or reports concerning securities.[294]

In 1942, Augustus P. Loring, Jr., an individual professional trustee, by SEC administrative order, was held *not* to be an investment advisor within the meaning of the Act.[295] The Loring exemption was based in part on the fact that Mr. Loring, as trustee, had legal title to trust assets and thus was acting for himself.[296] He was not "in the business of advising others."[297]

A warning: One learned commentator has written that "[i]n recent years the SEC staff, in public statements and in response to requests for no-action, has distanced itself from the *Loring* decision and limited the reach of that case to its special facts and circumstances, and it probably would decide *Loring* differently today."[298] The staff, for example, is now construing the Loring exemption as

---

[291] *See generally* George T. Shaw, *The Trusts and Estates Lawyer, the Investment Process, and Selected Securities Law Issues*, SC85 ALI-ABA 35 (June 25, 1998); George T. Shaw, *The Probate Lawyer, The Investment Process, and Selected Law Issues*, 18 ACTEC Notes 91 (1992).

[292] *See generally* Audrey C. Talley, *Family Offices: Securities and Commodities Law Issues*, 34 ACTEC L.J. 284 (2009); George T. Shaw, *The Probate Lawyer, The Investment Process and Selected Law Issues*, 18 ACTEC Notes 91 (1992).

[293] George T. Shaw, *The Probate Lawyer, The Investment Process and Selected Law Issues*, 18 ACTEC Notes 91 (1992).

[294] Shaw, *The Probate Lawyer, The Investment Process and Selected Law Issues*, 18 ACTEC Notes at 91.

[295] In the Matter of Loring, [1942 Transfer Binder] Fed. Sec. L. Rep. (CCH) 75, 299.

[296] *See generally* §3.5.1 of this handbook (nature and extent of the trustee's estate).

[297] In the Matter of Loring, [1942 Transfer Binder] Fed. Sec. L. Rep. (CCH) 75, 299. Note, however, that a trustee who is neither a lawyer nor a beneficiary may not be permitted to represent himself *pro se* on behalf of his trusts in the federal courts. *See* C. E. Pope Equity Trust v. United States, 818 F.2d 696 (9th Cir. 1987) (citing the language of the Judiciary Act of 1789, now found in 28 U.S.C. §1654, as indirect authority for the proposition that a trustee who is neither a beneficiary nor a lawyer must retain a lawyer to represent the trust in any federal court litigation).

[298] George T. Shaw, *The Probate Lawyer, The Investment Process, and Selected Law Issues*, 18 ACTEC Notes 91, 92 (1992). *But see* Selzer v. Bank of Bermuda, Ltd., 385 F. Supp. 415 (S.D.N.Y. 1974) (holding the Investment Adviser Act inapplicable in a suit against a trustee and noting that "while there may be public policy reasons for holding a trustee who deals in securities for its trust to the standards of the Investment Advisers Act, neither the common sense meaning of the word 'adviser' nor a comparison with other situations to which the 1940 Act has been held applicable militates in favor of doing so"). *See generally* Harold S. Bloomenthal, Securities Law Series, Securities Law Handbook §20.03 (2002 ed.); Melanie L. Fein, Securities Activities of Banks §7.03.

limited to trustees acting as "court-appointed fiduciaries."[299] Even when the exemption in unavailable, however, there may be other status and registration exemptions available to a trustee with investment discretion. A bank acting as trustee, for example, is exempt from the definition of investment advisor.[300] Also, a trustee with fewer than fifteen clients—the SEC deems each trust a "client"—or a trustee who exclusively advises charitable organizations would not have to register as an investment advisor, at least under federal law.[301]

§8.15.11   Rule in Clayton's Case

Those who believe that the rule in Devaynes v. Noble applies to determine creditors' rights to a deficient bank account cannot have read the case in its entirety. It is an example of error in the comprehension of a case that is still noticed only because of its persistence.[302]

The Rule in Clayton's Case,[303] as it has been commonly understood, applies to funds that are wrongfully commingled in a bank account. It is a "first in, first out" presumption.[304]

Assume that the trustee wrongfully deposits $1,000 from Trust *X*, $1,000 from Trust *Y*, and $1,000 from Trust *Z* in his own personal bank account. He then withdraws $1,000 from the account and dissipates it so that the $1,000 is untraceable. Applying the Rule in Clayton's Case, that $1,000 is presumed to have belonged to Trust *X* such that the beneficiaries of Trust *X* are now out of luck as to that account.[305] Only Trust *Y* and Trust *Z* are entitled to the remaining $2,000. The Rule as it applies to trusts has been criticized as "irrational," "arbitrary," and "unfair" by Judge Learned Hand and Professor Scott.[306] They would have all three trusts share equally, that is, in proportion to what each, relative to one another, had contributed to the fund.[307] Nowadays, the "equality is equity" maxim generally informs tracing doctrine in cases where the assets of multiple trusts are wrongly commingled in a single fund, not the Rule in

---

[299] Claire H. Springs, SEC No-action Letter (pub. avail. Sept. 13, 1990); Joseph J. Nameth, SEC No-action Letter (pub. avail. Jan. 31, 1983); Philip Eiseman, SEC No-action Letter (pub. avail. July 22, 1976).

[300] Investment Advisers Act §202(a)(11)(A), 15 U.S.C. §80b-2(a)(11)(A).

[301] Investment Advisers Act §203(b)(3), (b)(4); 15 U.S.C. §80b-3(b)(3) & (4).

[302] W. A. Lee, *Purifying the Dialect of Equity*, 7 Trust Quarterly Review, Issue 2, pg. 13, May 2009 [a STEP publication]. *See also* Restatement of Restitution §211 cmt. a.

[303] Devaynes v. Noble; Clayton's Case (1816) 1 Mer. 572; 35 ER 781. Not to be confused with Estate of Clayton v. Comm'r, 976 F.2d 1486 (5th Cir. 1992), *rev'g* 97 T.C. 327 (1991) (allowing a marital deduction for the value of the elected portion of a QTIP trust whose terms provided for a "pour over" of the unelected portion to a nonmarital trust). *See generally* Pennell, 843 T.M., Estate Tax Marital Deduction A-64 through A-68.

[304] 5 Scott on Trusts §519.

[305] 5 Scott on Trusts §519.

[306] 5 Scott on Trusts §519.

[307] 5 Scott on Trusts §519.

Clayton's Case.[308] Numerous courts have rejected the Rule in Clayton's Case in favor of the "pro rata" approach,[309] as does the Restatement of Restitution.[310] One learned commentator has gone so far as to suggest that the much-maligned Rule is actually based on a profound misreading of *Devaynes v. Noble; Clayton's Case*:

> To put it simply, if creditors A, B and C have claims against funds X and Y and creditors E, F, and G have claims against only fund Y then A, B, and C must exhaust fund X before proceeding against fund Y. This ensures that all the creditors receive the maximum possible shareout. Devaynes v. Noble was a simple case of asset marshalling and nothing else. It is a well-known principle of banking law.[311]

§8.15.12   Doctrine of Capture

Under the doctrine of capture, where the donee of a general power attempts to make an appointment that fails, but where, nevertheless, the donee has manifested an intent wholly to withdraw the appointive property from the operation of the instrument creating the power for all purposes and not merely for the purposes of the invalid appointment, the attempted appointment will commonly be effective to the extent of causing the appointive property to be taken out of the original instrument and to become in effect part of the estate of the donee of the power. . . . The application of this doctrine captures the property that is the subject of the power and makes it part of the donee's estate.[312]

Traditional capture doctrine. Let us assume that a settlor of a testamentary trust bestows on Mr. Jones a general testamentary power of appointment.[313] Let us also assume that Mr. Jones effectively exercises the power in further trust by appointing the legal title to the property to another trustee upon a trust that fails immediately or sometime thereafter,[314] or upon a trust that becomes fully performed without the trust estate having been exhausted.[315]

If the doctrine of capture is applicable, at the time of the failure or full performance the property reverts upon a resulting trust to *Mr. Jones' estate.*[316] In other words, it is "captured" by the donee's estate, the exercise in favor of the

---

[308] *See generally* Matter of Mich. Boiler & Eng'g Co., 171 B.R. 565 (Bankr. E.D. Mich. 1993). The equity maxims are discussed generally in §8.12 of this handbook.

[309] 5 Scott on Trusts §519 n.4.

[310] Restatement of Restitution §213 cmt. c.

[311] W. A. Lee, *Purifying the dialect of equity*, 7(2) Tr. Q. Rev. 13 (May 2009) [a STEP publication].

[312] Hochberg v. Proctor, 441 Mass. 403, 417, 805 N.E.2d 979, 991 (2004).

[313] *See generally* §8.1 of this handbook (powers of appointment).

[314] *See generally* 6 Scott & Ascher §41.17 (Failure).

[315] *See generally* 6 Scott & Ascher §42.7 (Surplus).

[316] 5 Scott on Trusts §426; 6 Scott & Ascher §41.17 (Trust Created by Exercise of General Power of Appointment). *See, e.g.,* Fiduciary Trust Co. v. Mishou, 75 N.E.2d 3, 9 (1947) (noting that

"new" trustee technically having been consummated.[317] The property does not revert back to the settlor's estate upon a resulting trust, and then pass to the takers in default of exercise. The doctrine would apply equally well to general inter vivos powers.[318]

The doctrine of capture has generally been *per se* applicable to failed exercises of general powers in further trust. Here is the rationale:

> When a donee of a general power appoints the appointive assets to a trustee upon specified trusts, the appointment to the trustee is not ineffective even though some or all of the beneficial interests under the trust are ineffective because they violate the rule against perpetuities or for some other reason. Normally when the beneficial interests under a trust fail for some reason or other, there is a resulting trust to the person who created the trust or such person's estate, unless such person manifests a different intention. When the donee of the general power appoints to a trustee, the donee is regarded as the creator of the trust for the purpose of applying the resulting trust rules unless the donor or the donee manifest an inconsistent intent.[319]

This marriage of resulting trust and power of appointment doctrine was a rare union of the logical and the practical: The longer an estate is closed the more difficult is the task of reopening it. Better to have to reopen the donee's estate than the donor's, absent special facts. As to appointments outright and free of trust that failed, "the ineffectively appointed property passed to the donee or the donee's estate, but only if the donee's ineffective appointment manifested an intent to assume control of the appointive property 'for all purposes' and not merely for the limited purpose of giving effect to the attempted appointment."[320]

The Restatement (Third) of Property would alter the law applicable to ineffective exercises of general powers. *Exercises in further trust.* It appears the Restatement (Third) of Property (Wills and Other Donative Transfers), specifically Section 19.21, would change the rules applicable to successful testamentary exercises in further trust that ultimately fail, but how, as a practical matter? Take the trust instrument that grants an equitable general testamentary power of appointment (Trust #1). The instrument designates persons to take outright and free of trust in default of the power's effective exercise. The Restatement (Third) provides that the subject property passes not to the donee or to the

---

the doctrine of capture originated in a series of decisions of the English courts and citing Old Colony Trust Co. v. Allen, 307 Mass. 40, 29 N.E.2d 310, where many of those decisions are collected).

[317] *See generally* John Chipman Gray, The Rule Against Perpetuities §540.1 (making fund part of donee's estate) (4th ed. 1942).

[318] 5 Scott on Trusts §426; 6 Scott & Ascher §41.17 (Trust Created by Exercise of General Power of Appointment). A failed exercise of a general *inter vivos* power of appointment in further trust could cause the property to pass to the *donee if then living*, and otherwise to the estate of the donee.

[319] Restatement (Second) of Property (Wills and Other Donative Transfers) §23.2 cmt. b.

[320] Restatement (Third) of Property (Wills and Other Donative Transfers) §19.21 cmt. b.

donee's estate by capture but to those takers in default.[321] But how does it get to them? What is the chain of legal title? Assume, for example, an exercise in further trust of the general testamentary power of appointment. A new trust is effectively created (Trust #2), but it fails years later for want of an equitable quasi remainderman. Does the Restatement (Third) contemplate that the appointed property pass once the failure has occurred somehow directly to the designated takers in default under Trust #1 without an actual resulting trust having to be imposed? Or is the route to them legally more circuitous? Does title to the subject property in the first instance pass upon an actual resulting trust from the trustee of Trust #2 to the express trustee of Trust #1, and then from the express trustee of Trust #1 to the takers in default under Trust #1?

The only explanation offered is found in comment c of section 19.21: "To the extent that the donee of a general power to *appoint* a future interest makes an ineffective appointment, the ineffective appointed property passes *under the gift-in-default clause.*" At least when it comes to an equitable power of appointment created incident to a trust relationship, it is the failure to effectively create an equitable future interest, and not the failure to *appoint* it, that causes the dominoes to fall. Again, one needs to keep in mind that not all such failed exercises in further trust fail at the outset. An exercise in further trust may be effective for the life of the beneficiary designated in the exercise but then fail upon the beneficiary's death. The failure is likely to come about because there is no designated equitable quasi remainderman then capable of taking the legal title to the subject property from the trustee upon the beneficiary's death. Upon such failure, the property to which the trustee had the legal title ends up with the takers in default. But how does it procedurally get to them? A few illustrations would have been helpful.

Appointments outright and free of trust. As to exercises of general powers outright and free of trust, the doctrine's applicability has traditionally depended upon the particular facts and circumstances. Specifically there needs to have been a "blending" of the property with the property of the donee,[322] or the donee needs to have somehow otherwise manifested an intent to assume control of the appointive property for all purposes, as noted above.

If, for example, Mr. Jones ineffectively attempted to exercise the general power outright and free of trust to his daughter, the doctrine generally would not apply. The property would pass to the takers in default of the power's exercise. Blending, however, might occur if Mr. Jones's estate and the appointive assets had been disposed of together by the whole will, or by the residuary

---

[321] Restatement (Third) of Property (Wills and Other Donative Transfers) §19.21.

[322] 5 Scott on Trusts §426; 6 Scott & Ascher §41.17 (Trust Created by Exercise of General Power of Appointment). A "blending" could occur should the general residuary clause in the donee's will exercise the donee's general testamentary power in favor of someone who predeceases the donee. In the event of a lapse, both the trust property and the donee's estate residue would "blend" and pass by intestacy. *See, e.g.,* Old Colony Trust Co. v. Allen, 307 Mass. 40, 29 N.E.2d 310 (1940) (*Caution:* Under Massachusetts law (Mass. Gen. Laws ch. 191, §1A), a general residue clause will no longer in and of itself exercise a general testamentary power of appointment). *See generally* §§8.1.1 of this handbook (powers of appointment) and 8.26 of this handbook (why trustees need to know about will residue clauses).

clause of his will, or "by a single fund that was neither the whole will nor a residuary clause."[323] Blending might trigger capture under English law as well.[324]

The Restatement (Third) of Property would strip the doctrine of its facts and circumstances nuances. It provides that "[t]to the extent that the donee of a general power makes an ineffective appointment, the gift-in-default clause controls the disposition of the ineffectively appointed property to the extent that the gift-in-default clause is effective."[325] End of story. Were it only that simple, as we explain next.

Ineffective exercise of a right of revocation, amendment, or withdrawal will not trigger capture. The Restatement (Third) of Property, specifically Comment f to Section 19.21, breaks new ground by drawing a distinction between rights of revocation, amendment, and withdrawal on the one hand and other "types" of general power on the other when it comes to applying capture doctrine: "To the extent that the donee of this type of general power makes an ineffective appointment, the ineffectively appointed property remains in the trust as originally written." Presumably what is meant by *in the trust as originally written* is that legal title to the ineffectively appointed property remains in the express trustee. In other words, there is no capture in the face of an ineffective exercise of a right to revoke, amend, or withdraw. What is concerning is the implication that there are "types" of *general inter vivos powers of appointment* other than rights of revocation, amendment, and withdrawal. Otherwise, presumably, a blanket capture exemption for all general inter vivos powers of appointment of whatever "type" would have been proposed.

The Restatement (Third)'s limited-purpose taxonomy of equitable general inter vivos powers in the capture context makes no sense conceptually for the simple reason that (1) every general inter vivos power of appointment in substance encompasses the right to revoke, amend, or withdraw, even when appointment may only be to one's creditors; and (2) every equitable inter vivos right to revoke, amend, or withdraw in substance encompasses the right to appoint to third parties.[326] Anyone who processes trust-revocation instruments in the real world operates under these assumptions. A nonfiduciary untrammeled right to *direct* or *demand* is a general inter vivos power of appointment for all purposes, not some "type" of general inter vivos power that needs to be fathomed by trust counsel. This was new ground that the Restatement (Second) had declined to break, and for good reason.[327] Trusts that are revocable and amendable by settlors, beneficiaries, and other nonfiduciaries are covered generally in Section 8.2.2.2 of this handbook.

---

[323] Restatement (Second) of Property (Wills and Other Donative Transfers) §23.2 cmt. d.

[324] Lewin ¶ 8-28 (England); 6 Scott & Ascher §41.17 (U.S.).

[325] Restatement (Third) of Property (Wills and Other Donative Transfers) §19.21(a).

[326] *See* Restatement (Third) of Property (Wills and Other Donative Transfers) §17.1 cmt. e.

[327] *See* Restatement (Second) of Property (Donative Transfers) §23.2.

In summary. When it comes to all failed appointments under general powers, outright and otherwise, the Restatement (Third) of Property purports to alter traditional capture doctrine in two principal ways: "(1) the gift-in-default clause takes precedence over any implied alternative appointment to the donee or the donee's estate deduced from the use of the blending clause or otherwise; and (2) the ineffectively appointed property passes to the donee or the donee's estate only if there is no gift-in-default clause or the gift-in-default clause is ineffective."[328]

These alterations make some practical sense in the context of appointments outright and free of trust and appointments in further trust that fail at the outset. But in the case of appointments in further trust that are effective at the outset but fail at a later time, there was traditionally no "implied alternative appointment to the donee or the donee's estate." Instead, there was the imposition of a resulting trust in favor of the donee, the deemed settlor of the second trust, or his estate.[329] In other words, there was an actual ripening into possession of the donee's vested equitable reversion, not a deemed creation in the donee of some kind of an equitable remainder-by-appointment.[330] The Restatement (Third) not only fails to address the mechanics of capture that would prevail under what would be a new regime, it also manages to misdescribe the mechanics that currently prevail under the old.

The Restatement (Third) of Property would inject some quasi-capture doctrine into the law applicable to expired general powers of appointment. If the donee of a general inter vivos power of appointment dies without having effectively exercised the power, the power expires.[331] Likewise, if the donee of an equitable general testamentary power of appointment fails to effectively exercise the power by will, the power expires at the donee's death. In either case, the gift-in-default clause in the granting instrument, if there is such a clause, controls the disposition of the unappointed property.[332] (So also if a power expires by inter vivos disclaimer or release.[333]) The time when a power expires "is almost invariably the death of the donee,"[334] although one could certainly fashion a grant of a general power that would be capable of expiring before its donee had, such as upon the exhaustion of an intervening equitable estate *pur autre vie*. The concept of the estate *pur autre vie* is discussed generally in Section 8.15.64 of this handbook.

---

[328] Restatement (Third) of Property (Wills and Other Donative Transfers) §19.21 cmt. b.

[329] *See generally* §4.1.1.1 of this handbook (the resulting trust).

[330] *See generally* §4.1.1 of this handbook [the introductory quotation] (Blackstone comparing reversions and remainders). *See also* Restatement (Third) of Property (Wills and Other Donative Transfers) §25.2 ("A future interest is either a reversion or a remainder. A future interest is a reversion if it was retained by the transferor. A future interest is a remainder if it was created in a transferee.").

[331] As we note in §8.1.1 of this handbook, a power of appointment is exercisable; it is never directly transferable.

[332] Restatement (Third) of Property (Wills and Other Donative Transfers) §19.22(a).

[333] Restatement (Third) of Property (Wills and Other Donative Transfers) §19.22(a).

[334] Restatement (First) of Property §367 cmt. d.

The Restatement (Third) of Property speaks in terms of a general power "lapsing," an unfortunate innovation.[335] Its predecessors spoke in terms of a power "expiring,"[336] which is less ambiguous in that the term lapse can mean "to pass to another through neglect or omission."[337] As we note in Section 8.1.1 of this handbook, a power of appointment itself is never directly transmissible.

But what has been the rule if the donor of an expired equitable power neglected in the granting trust instrument to provide for takers-in-default, or the instrument's gift-in-default clause is ineffective when the power expires? In that case the black-letter law was that unappointed property passed upon a resulting trust back to the donor if the donor was then living, or into the probate estate of the donor if the donor was not then living, but, again, not until all valid intervening equitable interests have themselves expired.[338] Resulting trusts are covered generally in Section 4.1.1.1 of this handbook.

In a radical departure from settled doctrine, the Restatement (Third) of Property provides that if the donee "merely failed to exercise the power" the unappointed property, in the absence of a taker in default, is captured by the donee or the donee's estate.[339] There is no resulting trust. There is no antilapse. A resulting trust in favor of the donor or the donor's estate, however, would still be imposed in the case of (1) expiration by disclaimer or release;[340] (2) expiration by any means of a power of revocation, amendment, or withdrawal;[341] and (3) the donee expressly refraining from exercising the power. Pity the poor trustee on the front line who has to sort out all these nuances.

Again, as we did in more detail in our discussion above of ineffective exercises of general powers, we question the logic of treating a power of "revocation, amendment, or withdrawal" differently from other "types" of general inter vivos power of appointment, whether for capture purposes generally or for any other purpose. A resulting trust also would be imposed if the donee "expressly refrained from exercising the power."[342] Of course, this discussion is entirely academic if the donor is also the donee of the expired general power. The unappointed property would then end up in the probate estate of the donee in any case, whether by imposition of a resulting trust under traditional doctrine or by quasi-capture.

The Restatement (Third) of Property exhibits a curious and tenacious aversion to invoking applicable resulting trust doctrine,[343] particularly in the

---

[335] *See* Restatement (Third) of Property (Wills and Other Donative Transfers) §19.22 (term lapse employed even in the section's title).

[336] *See, e.g.*, Restatement (First) of Property §367 cmt. d.

[337] The American Heritage Dictionary 1014 (3d ed. 1996).

[338] *See, e.g.*, Restatement (First) of Property §367(1).

[339] Restatement (Third) of Property (Wills and Other Donative Transfers) §19.22(b).

[340] Restatement (Third) of Property (Wills and Other Donative Transfers) §19.22(b).

[341] Restatement (Third) of Property (Wills and Other Donative Transfers) §19.22 cmt. f.

[342] Restatement (Third) of Property (Wills and Other Donative Transfers) §19.22(b).

[343] *See, e.g.*, Restatement (Third) of Property (Wills and Other Donative Transfers) §25.2 (although the title to the sections is *Reversion or Remainder*, the resulting trust is mentioned once, and only in passing).

sections devoted to unexercised or ineffectively exercised general powers of appointment. The result is an unhelpful dearth of context, particularly when it comes to following chains of title, as well as a fair amount of general incoherence. Take, for example, Section 19.22(b), which in part reads: "... but if the donee released the power or expressly refrained from exercising the power, the unappointed property passes under a reversionary interest to the donor or to the donor's transferees or successors in interest." The phrase "passes under a reversionary interest" is nonsensical in the trust context. What actually happens is that the legal title to the unappointed property passes from the trustee to the donor or his personal representative upon a resulting trust such that the equitable reversion, which had vested *ab initio*, becomes possessory. Nothing is passing from the trustee under, over, or in a reversionary interest.

We also quibble with the failure of all of the Restatements to expressly confirm that in the face of an expired power of appointment, title to property unappointed does not leave the hands of the trustee until such time as all valid intervening equitable estates have themselves expired, unless the terms of the trust so provide. An intervening equitable estate typically would be an equitable life estate.[344]

Capture is default doctrine. Capture being default doctrine is avoidable with the help of the knowledgeable scrivener.[345] If the settlor or the donee has expressed the clear intention that the doctrine shall not apply, it need not. The property will then revert to the settlor (or his estate) *or* pass to an alternate taker that has been designated either in the governing instrument or by the donee *or* be administered as if the power had not been exercised.[346]

The capture doctrine's inapplicability to exercises of nongeneral powers of appointment. The doctrine of capture does not apply to limited powers of appointment.[347]

§8.15.13   Common Fund Doctrine

We will proceed with the hearing on Wednesday fortnight, says the Chancellor. For the question at issue is only a question of costs, a mere bud on the forest tree of the parent suit, and really will come to a settlement one of these days.—Charles Dickens[348]

Not to be confused with the common trust fund[349] or the practice of commingling in a "common fund" for investment purposes the assets of a

---

[344] *See generally* §8.27 of this handbook (the equitable life estate).

[345] 6 Scott & Ascher §41.17 (Trust Created by Exercise of General Power of Appointment).

[346] 5 Scott on Trusts §426; 6 Scott & Ascher §41.17 (Trust Created by Exercise of General Power of Appointment).

[347] 5 Scott on Trusts §426; 6 Scott & Ascher §41.18 (Trust Created by Exercise of General Power of Appointment).

[348] Bleak House, Chapter 1 (In Chancery).

[349] *See generally* §9.7.1 of this handbook (the common trust fund and the proprietary mutual fund).

number of trusts created under the same instrument,[350] the "common fund doctrine" relates to whether a beneficiary who brings an action involving the trust may be reimbursed from the trust estate for his or her attorneys' fees.[351] In other words, must those beneficiaries who did not bring the case indirectly shoulder some of the economic burden of the litigation? Under the common fund doctrine, the answer is yes, provided the litigation "successfully created, increased, or preserved a fund in which the non-litigants were entitled to share,"[352] or "clarified a significant uncertainty in the terms of the trust."[353] Otherwise the nonparticipants would be unjustly enriched.[354] The Restatement (Third) of Restitution and Unjust Enrichment is generally in accord.[355] Of course, the trustee, if found culpable in his individual capacity, ultimately may be required to reimburse the trust for any attorneys' fees paid to the litigating beneficiary out of the trust estate.[356] It should be noted that the common fund doctrine is an exception to the "American rule" that litigants, win or lose, absorb their own legal costs.[357] The beneficiary who pursues "vexatious and burdensome litigation" can expect to have the litigation costs of all parties paid from his or her equitable interest under the trust, to the extent the interest is

---

[350] See generally §3.5.3.2(d) of this handbook (the trustee's power to invest in mutual funds and common trust funds; to administer common funds; and to combine trusts).

[351] See generally §8.13 of this handbook (in litigation pertaining to a trust, when the beneficiary is entitled to reimbursement from the trust estate for his or her attorneys' fees). See also Boeing Co. v. Van Gemert, 444 U.S. 472 (1980) (upholding judgment of lower court assessing attorneys' fees against common fund created by successful litigation).

[352] Feinberg v. Feinberg Hotel Trust, 922 S.W.2d 21, 26 (Mo. App. E. Dist. 1996). See In re Estate of Pfoertner, 298 Ill. App. 3d 1134, 233 Ill. Dec. 133, 700 N.E.2d 438 (1998) (allowing attorney to be compensated from estate where attorney prevented a fraud on the estate and by doing so preserved its value). It is well established that "a litigant or a lawyer who recovers a common fund for the benefit of persons other than himself or his client is entitled to a reasonable attorney's fee from the fund as a whole." Boeing Co. v. Van Gemert, 444 U.S. 472, 478 (1980). See also UTC §1004 cmt. (available at <http://www.uniformlaws.org/Act.aspx?title=Trust%20Code>); Fla. Stat. §737.2035. For a common fund case in which the beneficiaries were denied their attorneys' fees from the trust estate, see In re Trust of Papuk, 2002 WL 366519 (Ohio Ct. App.) (involving beneficiaries who won a decree of outright distribution at the trial level but on appeal had to settle for only an income interest). For a case in which the beneficiaries unsuccessfully sought the removal of the trustee but nonetheless were awarded their counsel fees from the trust estate, the litigation conferring "a benefit on the Trust, both by reducing its administrative costs and by reconfiguring its governance structure," see Unfunded Insurance Trust Agreement of Capaldi, 870 A.2d 493 (Del. 2005). See generally 3 Scott & Ascher §18.1.2.4.

[353] Restatement (Third) of Trusts §88 cmt. d.

[354] See generally §8.15.78 of this handbook (unjust enrichment).

[355] See Restatement (Third) of Restitution and Unjust Enrichment §29, illus. 4.

[356] See Feinberg v. Feinberg Hotel Trust, 922 S.W.2d 21, 34–35 (Mo. Ct. App. 1996) (holding trustees who engaged in self-dealing personally liable for attorneys' fees); In re Estate of Stowell, 595 A.2d 1022 (Me. 1991) (awarding beneficiaries attorneys' fees from the estate but requiring the trustee, who breached his fiduciary duties, to reimburse the estate); Heller v. First Nat'l Bank, N.A., 657 P.2d 992 (Colo. App. 1982) (awarding attorneys' fees against a corporate trustee for breach of trust). But see McNeely v. Hiatt, 138 Or. App. 434, 909 P.2d 191 (1996) (holding that trustee who was not sued personally by beneficiaries could not be ordered to pay beneficiaries' attorneys' fees).

[357] Feinberg v. Feinberg Hotel Trust, 922 S.W.2d 21, 31(Mo. Ct. App. 1996); Boeing Co. v. Van Gemert, 444 U.S. 472, 478 (1980).

susceptible of being identified and segregated out.[358] For more on the vexatious trust litigant, see Section 5.6 of this handbook.

A variant on the common fund doctrine is the principle that "[t]he trustee is entitled to indemnity for expenses *improperly* incurred if and to the extent they have benefitted the trust estate."[359] This is a topic that is covered in more detail in Section 3.5.2.3 of this handbook.

Under certain circumstances a beneficiary may be ordered to pay *out of personal funds* the fees of the *trustee's* attorneys, a topic we take up in Section 5.6 of this handbook. In one case, a nuisance beneficiary and his counsel were held jointly and severally liable for the trustee's litigation defense costs.[360]

§8.15.14   The Massachusetts Rule of Allocation versus the Pennsylvania Rule of Apportionment

Roughly speaking, under the Pennsylvania rule, extraordinary dividends were income if declared out of earnings that accrued to the corporation during the term of the trust but were principal if declared out of earnings that accrued prior to the creation of the trust. Another way of stating the Pennsylvania rule was that extraordinary dividends were income to the extent that they did not impair the intact value of the shares at the time of the creation of the trust.[361]

The Massachusetts rule of allocation is a rule of convenience that regulates the allocation of *extraordinary dividends*.[362] Let us assume that we have a traditional trust: *A* to *B*, for *C* for life, then to *D*. Let us assume that a share of stock in a certain corporation is an asset of the trust. Upon receipt of an extraordinary dividend issued by the directors of the corporation, the trustee (*B*), pursuant to the Massachusetts rule, merely allocates it to the income account (*C*) if it is a cash dividend or to the principal account (*D*) if it is a stock dividend.[363] The Massachusetts rule is a reaction to the cumbersome Pennsylvania rule of apportionment described above in the introductory quote to this section, which requires that the trustee pick apart and analyze the extraordinary dividend to determine what portion of it has been derived from income earned by the corporation during the term of the trust.[364] That portion is then allocated to the income account (*C*) and the balance to the principal account (*D*):

---

[358] *See, e.g.,* Larkin v. Wells Fargo Bank, N.A., A13-1839 (Minn. Ct. App. Oct. 6, 2014).

[359] 4 Scott & Ascher §22.2.1 (Benefit to Trust Estate).

[360] *See* Pederson Trust, 757 N.W.2d 740 (N.D. 2008).

[361] 4 Scott & Ascher §20.6.2.

[362] *See generally* 4 Scott & Ascher §20.6.2.

[363] *See generally* 4 Scott & Ascher §20.6.2; 3A Scott on Trusts §236.3. *See also* §6.2.4.2 of this handbook (receipts that are entirely allocated to principal for trust accounting purposes).

[364] *See generally* 4 Scott & Ascher §20.6.2; 3A Scott on Trusts §236.3. For a detailed discussion of the history and inefficiencies of the Pennsylvania Rule, *see* In re Trust of Catherwood, 405 Pa. 61, 173 A.2d 86 (1961).

Perhaps the strongest argument in favor of the Massachusetts rule is simplicity. Regardless of whether it would be more just to apportion extraordinary dividends, doing so is extremely difficult.[365]

§8.15.15   The Ascertainable Standard

Despite the breadth of discretion purportedly granted by the wording of a trust, no grant of discretion to a trustee, whether with respect to management or distribution, is ever absolute. A grant of discretion establishes a range within which the trustee may act.[366]

With all due respect, these cases say much less about the actual state of the law relating to the settlor's ability, under the terms of a trust, to grant the trustee discretion to allocate receipts and expenses between income and principal than they say about the willingness of the courts to extricate taxpayers from adverse tax consequences that their advisors have failed to anticipate.[367]

The term *ascertainable standard* is found in Internal Revenue Code Sections 2041 and 2514.[368] In the former section, a general power of appointment is defined for estate tax purposes.[369] In the latter, a general power of appointment is defined for gift tax purposes.[370] Each definition has its exceptions. A common exception is that a trustee-beneficiary shall not be deemed to have a general power of appointment merely by the virtue of the fact that the trustee-beneficiary can invade, or could have invaded, principal for purposes limited by an ascertainable standard relating to the trustee-beneficiary's own *health, education, support, or maintenance.*[371] For tax purposes, these limitations on the trustee's authority are deemed to be "ascertainable standards."[372] The regulations elaborate somewhat on what qualifies as an ascertainable standard:

[T]he words "support" and "maintenance" are synonymous and their meaning is not limited to the bare necessities of life. A power to use property for the comfort,

---

[365] 4 Scott & Ascher §20.6.2.

[366] UTC §814 cmt. (available at <http://www.uniformlaws.org/Act.aspx?title=Trust%20Code>). *See also* Restatement (Third) of Trusts §50 cmt. c.

[367] 4 Scott & Ascher §20.2.3.

[368] *See generally* Cline, 825-2d T.M., Powers of Appointment—Estate, Gift, and Income Tax Considerations A-10 to A-16.

[369] The term *general power of appointment* means a power that is exercisable in favor of the decedent, his estate, his creditors, or the creditors of his estate. I.R.C. §2041(b)(1). *See also* §8.9.3 of this handbook (tax-sensitive powers).

[370] The term *general power of appointment* means a power that is exercisable in favor of the individual possessing the power, his estate, his creditors, or the creditors of his estate. I.R.C. §2514(c). *See also* §8.9.3 of this handbook (tax-sensitive powers).

[371] I.R.C. §2041(b)(1)(A) (The Estate Tax); I.R.C. §2514(c) (1) (The Gift Tax). *See, e.g.,* Dana v. Gring, 374 Mass. 109, 371 N.E.2d 755 (1977) (finding the following an ascertainable standard for estate tax purposes: "as said trustees . . . deem necessary or desirable for the purpose of contributing to the reasonable welfare or happiness of . . . [decedent]").

[372] *See generally* 3 Scott & Ascher §18.2.5 (Trustee with Discretionary Power to Distribute to Self).

welfare, or happiness of the holder of the power is not limited by the requisite standard. Examples of powers which are limited by the requisite standard are powers exercisable for the holder's "support," "support in reasonable comfort," "maintenance in health and reasonable comfort," "support in his accustomed manner of living," "education, including college and professional education," "health," and "medical, dental, hospital and nursing expenses and expenses of invalidism."[373]

It should be noted that the Uniform Trust Code would make the concept of an ascertainable standard for estate and gift tax purposes a general default rule.[374] It provides that a person other than a settlor who is a beneficiary and trustee of a trust that confers on the trustee a power to make discretionary distributions to or for the trustee's personal benefit may exercise the power only in accordance with an ascertainable standard relating to the trustee's health, education, support, or maintenance within the meaning of Section 204(b)(1)(A) or 2514(c)(1) of the Internal Revenue Code.[375] In addition, to the extent the fiduciary power is limited by such an ascertainable standard, the subject property will not be vulnerable to attack by the personal creditors of the nonsettlor trustee-beneficiary.[376] Under New York default law, by legislation, a trustee may not make discretionary distributions of income or principal to himself or herself unless the power is limited by an ascertainable standard for tax purposes.[377]

Let the reader, however, not confuse tax law with common law when it comes to the question of whether the limits on a particular trustee's discretionary powers are "ascertainable." Under the common law, they are always ascertainable.[378] "It is contrary to sound public policy, and a contradiction in terms, to permit the settlor to relieve a 'trustee' of all accountability."[379] While a trustee's authority may be so expansive that it meets the definition of a general

---

[373] Reg. §§20.2041-1(c)(2) (The Estate Tax), 25.2514-1(c)(2) (The Gift Tax). On the matter of whether a beneficiary's power to remove and replace a trustee is a general power of appointment as defined in I.R.C. §2041, *see* Ltr. Ruls. 9735023 (May 30, 1997), 9741009 (July 8, 1997), and 9746007 (Aug. 11, 1997).

[374] *See generally* 3 Scott & Ascher §18.2.5 (Trustee with Discretionary Power to Distribute to Self).

[375] UTC §814(b)(1) (available at <http://www.uniformlaws.org/Act.aspx?title=Trust%20 Code>). *See generally* 3 Scott & Ascher §18.2.5 (Trustee with Discretionary Power to Distribute to Self).

[376] *See* UTC §103(10) (available at <http://www.uniformlaws.org/Act.aspx?title=Trust%20 Code>). *See generally* Alan Newman, *Spendthrift and Discretionary Trusts: Alive and Well Under the Uniform Trust Code*, 40 Real Prop. Prob. & Tr. J. 567, 592–593 (Fall 2005).

[377] N.Y. Est. Powers & Trusts Law §10-10.1. *See generally* §3.5.3.2(a) of this handbook (the power to make discretionary payments of income and principal (the discretionary trust)); 3 Scott & Ascher §18.2.5 (Trustee with Discretionary Power to Distribute to Self).

[378] Frederick R. Franke, Jr., *Resisting the Contractarian Insurgency: The Uniform Trust Code, Fiduciary Duty, and Good Faith in Contract*, 36 ACTEC L.J. 517, 528–530 (2010) (noting that in practice the courts impose on trustees duties to act reasonably and in good faith even when their discretions are ostensibly absolute).

[379] Restatement (Third) of Trusts §50 cmt. c. *See generally* §6.1.5 of this handbook (duty to account to the beneficiary).

power of appointment for estate and gift tax or creditor accessibility purposes, its limits cannot be "unascertainable" by a court of equity.[380] "No matter how broad the language of the trust instrument, the court will never permit the trustee to act dishonestly or in bad faith."[381] Otherwise, we would not have a trust; we would have a gift to the "trustee."[382] At minimum, a trustee of a valid trust is constrained by his duty "to exercise a discretionary power in good faith and in accordance with the terms and purposes of the trust and the interests of the beneficiaries."[383]

§8.15.16   Incidents of Ownership

Incidents of ownership are personal rights that, taken together, constitute "property."[384] In the tax context, however, the term has taken on a narrower,

---

[380] *See* 3 Scott & Ascher §13.2.3 (noting that even when the trustee ostensibly has "uncontrolled" discretion, the court still will interfere "if the trustee acts dishonestly or from an improper motive or fails to exercise its judgment"); Frederick R. Franke, Jr., *Resisting the Contractarian Insurgency: The Uniform Trust Code, Fiduciary Duty, and Good Faith in Contract*, 36 ACTEC L.J. 517, 528–530 (2010) (noting that in practice the courts impose on trustees duties to act reasonably and in good faith even when their discretions are ostensibly absolute).

[381] 3 Scott & Ascher §18.2.3.

[382] Restatement (Third) of Trusts §87 cmt. d; 3 Scott & Ascher §18.2.3; Frederick R. Franke, Jr., *Resisting the Contractarian Insurgency: The Uniform Trust Code, Fiduciary Duty, and Good Faith in Contract*, 36 ACTEC L.J. 517, 530 (2010) (noting that where there is no binding legal obligation on the purported trustee, we have not a trust but an arrangement in the nature of an absolute estate in the title holder or fee simple grant of property to the title holder).

[383] UTC §814(a) (available at <http://www.uniformlaws.org/Act.aspx?title=Trust%20 Code>). *See* Farkas v. Williams, 5 Ill. 2d 417, 125 N.E.2d 600 (1955) (suggesting that even the settlor-trustee of a revocable inter vivos trust is bound by its terms.); Old Colony Trust Co. v. Silliman, 352 Mass. 6, 9, 223 N.E.2d 504, 506 (1967) ("A fair reading of the whole of most trust instruments will reveal a 'judicially enforceable, external, and ascertainable standard' for the exercise of even broadly expressed fiduciary powers."); United States v. O'Shaughnessy, 517 N.W.2d 574, 577 (Minn. 1994) ("Even where trustees have absolute, unlimited, or uncontrolled discretion, any attempt to violate the settlor's intent or the trust's purpose is considered an abuse of that discretion. Restatement (Second) of Trusts, §187 cmt. j"); UTC §801 (providing that upon acceptance of a trusteeship, the trustee shall administer the trust in good faith, in accordance with its terms and purposes and the interests of the beneficiaries, and in accordance with the UTC); UTC §814 (providing that notwithstanding the breadth of discretion granted to a trustee in the terms of the trust, including the use of such terms as "absolute," "sole," or "uncontrolled," the trustee shall exercise a discretionary power in good faith and in accordance with the terms and purposes of the trust and the interests of the beneficiaries); Restatement (Third) of Trusts §50 cmt. c ("It is contrary to sound policy, and a contradiction in terms, to permit the settlor to relieve a 'trustee' of all accountability. . . . Once it is determined that the authority over trust distributions is held in the role of trustee . . . , words such as 'absolute' or 'unlimited' or 'sole and uncontrolled' are not interpreted literally."); Frederick R. Franke, Jr., *Resisting the Contractarian Insurgency: The Uniform Trust Code, Fiduciary Duty, and Good Faith in Contract*, 36 ACTEC L.J. 517, 528–530 (2010) (noting that in practice the courts impose on trustees duties to act reasonably and in good faith even when their discretions are ostensibly absolute).

[384] *See* Restatement of Property §6 cmt. a.

more technical meaning: "Incidents of ownership" are the rights in an insurance contract (policy) that the insured must relinquish if the insurance proceeds are *not* to be subject to the federal estate tax upon the insured's death.[385]

If a decedent during the three-year period ending on the date of death had owned a life insurance contract on his or her life, the proceeds thereof would be included in the insured's federal gross estate for estate tax purposes, whether payable to the insured's executor or to a third party.[386] If, on the other hand, the insured had transferred the contract more than three years before death to a third party such as a trustee of a trust under which the insured possessed no beneficial interest,[387] the value of the proceeds would not be factored into the calculation of the federal gross estate, provided, of course, that someone other than the insured's executor were the recipient of the proceeds.[388] There would be inclusion, however, if the insured had failed to make a completed transfer of the contract.[389]

Under Code Section 2042 and the regulations, a transfer would not be deemed completed if the insured had retained within the three-year period one or more of the following "incidents of ownership" in the contract (policy):

- The power to change the beneficiary.
- The power to surrender or cancel the policy.
- The power to assign the policy.
- The power to revoke an assignment.
- The power to pledge the policy for a loan.
- The power to obtain from the insurer a loan against surrender value.[390]

Other incidents of ownership for Code Section 2042 purposes include a reversionary interest in the policy of more than 5 percent of the value of the contract (policy) immediately before the death of the insured;[391] the retained right to select payment options;[392] the right to veto beneficiary designations or further assignments;[393] and the right to convert a contract (policy) from group to individual status.[394]

---

[385] I.R.C. §2042(2).

[386] I.R.C. §2035(a)(2). *See* Mitchell Gans & Jonathan G. Blattmachr, *Life Insurance and Some Common 2035/2036 Problems: A Suggested Remedy*, 26 ACTEC Notes 39 (2000) (suggesting that a sale rather than a gift of the contract's incidents of ownership may be a way around the transfer-within-three-years-of-death rule).

[387] *See* §9.2 of this handbook (the irrevocable life insurance trust).

[388] I.R.C. §2042.

[389] I.R.C. §2042.

[390] Reg. §20.2042-1(c)(2).

[391] I.R.C. §2042(2).

[392] Estate of Lumpkin v. Comm'r, 474 F.2d 1092 (5th Cir. 1973).

[393] Rev. Rul. 75-70, 1975-1 C.B. 301.

[394] Priv. Ltr. Rul. 80-46-110.

§8.15.17 The Doctrine of Incorporation by Reference

And in a jurisdiction that does recognize incorporation by reference but in terms that recite highly technical requirements for the doctrine's application, the disposition should not fail merely because the will is construed as referring also to possible future instruments of revocation or modification . . . [of the inter vivos trust instrument] . . . (an objection sometimes expressed in terms of words of futurity).[395]

In most cases, the doctrine of incorporation by reference sets forth the conditions that must be met for an unattested writing to complete the terms of a will.[396] An unattested writing is a writing that has not been signed and witnessed in accordance with the requirements of the statute of wills. The conditions are generally three: (1) the writing must be in existence when the will is executed, *i.e.*, signed, witnessed, etc.; (2) the will must manifest an intention to incorporate the unattested writing; and (3) the unattested writing must be identified with reasonable certainty.[397] The Uniform Probate Code would do away with a fourth condition which some courts have imposed, namely, that the will expressly refer to the extrinsic writing as being in existence at the time of execution.[398] The Restatement (Third) of Property (Wills and Other Donative Transfers) is in accord.[399]

Thus, the common law doctrine of incorporation by reference cannot validate the transfer of probate property to the trustee of an amendable inter vivos trust. This is because the final writing that ultimately governs the administration of the property might not come into existence until after the will is executed.[400] Such words of futurity as "from time to time amended" are fatal. It took another common law doctrine, the doctrine of independent legal significance,[401] to validate testamentary additions to trusts that are amendable by the settlor between the time when the settlor executes his or her will and the time the settlor dies.

The Restatement (Third) of Trusts, however, is somewhat ambivalent as to whether we have one or two trusts when a pour-over is rescued by the doctrine of incorporation by reference. If the inter vivos trust was funded during the lifetime of the settlor, the Restatement would have as the default rule that the property is administered in that trust without the establishment of a second

---

[395] Restatement (Third) of Trusts §19 cmt. d.

[396] There a few cases where the terms of a will have been incorporated into a trust in order to supply the terms of the trust. *See generally* 5 Scott & Ascher §35.1.7.

[397] Restatement (Third) of Property (Wills and Other Donative Transfers) §3.6 cmt. For a compilation of state statutes that codify the Doctrine of Incorporation by Reference as it applies to testamentary dispositions, *see* Jeffrey A. Schoenblum, 2000 Multistate Guide to Estate Planning 5-46 to 5-49 (Table 5.02) (2000).

[398] UPC §2-510 cmt. Massachusetts has also done away with the fourth condition. *See* Mass. Gen. Laws ch. 190B, §2-510.

[399] Restatement (Third) of Property (Wills and Other Donative Transfers) §3.6 cmt. a.

[400] Lewin Trusts ¶3-71.

[401] *See generally* §8.15.9 of this handbook (doctrine of [facts or acts of] independent legal significance).

testamentary trust to administer the pour-over.[402] Things get murky, however, if there was no funding during the lifetime of the settlor:

> If, however, the testamentary disposition is to a trustee pursuant to the terms of an inter vivos instrument of trust that is not funded from any other source during life or at the death of the testator, the matter is at least theoretically somewhat different. In such a case, the single trust that is thereby created may be either an inter vivos trust or a testamentary trust, where the distinction may matter, depending on the intention of the settlor. Still, however, unless the testator expresses an intent on this matter, the question is one of interpretation, with the inference being that the trust is intended to be nontestamentary.[403]

The Restatement (Third) of Property, on the other hand, is quite dogmatic on the subject: "Even when the pour-over devise supplies the initial funding of and thus creates the trust, the trust it creates is an inter vivos trust, unless the testator's will clearly manifests a contrary intent."[404] This would be the case even in the rare case of the pour-over devise (to the trustee of an inter vivos trust) that has been somehow validated by the doctrine of incorporation by reference.[405]

Notwithstanding the general acceptance and codification[406] of the common law doctrine of independent legal significance, four important reasons remain why the trustee may not ignore the doctrine of incorporation by reference.

The first reason is that the provisions of an extrinsic unattested writing may incorporated by reference into a will for the purpose of supplying the terms of a testamentary trust. The incorporation rules applicable in the nontrust context would be applicable here as well, *e.g.*, the need to avoid words of futurity.[407]

The second reason is that some estate planners employ the doctrine as a fall-back to cover the contingency of the inter vivos trust's being unavailable to receive the pour-over from the probate estate due to intentional revocation, inadvertent defunding, or some other reason. It works this way: The will provides that in the event the inter vivos trust is not in existence at the time of death, the terms of the inter vivos trust (not the trust itself) are incorporated by reference into the will as those terms exist at the time the will is executed.[408] These unattested writings then become the terms of a testamentary trust that is

---

[402] Restatement (Third) of Trusts §19 cmt. i.

[403] Restatement (Third) of Trusts §19 cmt. i.

[404] Restatement (Third) of Property (Wills and Other Donative Transfers) §3.8 cmt. e.

[405] Restatement (Third) of Property (Wills and Other Donative Transfers) §3.8 cmt. e.

[406] UPC §2-511 (Testamentary Additions to Trusts). *See generally* §2.2.1 of this handbook (the pour-over statute).

[407] 1 Scott & Ascher §7.1.1.

[408] *But see* UPC §2-513 (providing that items of tangible personal property may be disposed of by reference in a will to a future writing having no independent legal significance). *See also* Restatement (Third) of Property (Wills and Other Donative Transfers) §3.9 (1998) (Testamentary Disposition by Unattested Writing).

funded with the property that would have poured over to the inter vivos trust. Although such unattested writings are treated as part of the will for purposes of distribution, construction, and administration of the estate, the Restatement (Third) of Property (Wills and Other Donative Transfers) would not afford them the status of a "physical part" of the will such that they would have to be offered for probate or otherwise made part of the public record.[409]

In the context of pour-overs, it needs to be kept in mind that the doctrine of incorporation by reference should only be employed as a fall-back should the doctrine of independent legal significance be unavailable in a given situation:

> Prior to the widespread enactment of statutes validating pour-over devises, the doctrine of incorporation by reference was initially the only theory for validating such devises, but it applied in limited circumstances. In order for that doctrine to be applicable, the inter vivos trust instrument had to be in existence when the will was executed. If this requirement was met, some courts would still only incorporate the terms of an *irrevocable* trust. Other courts would incorporate the terms of a revocable and amendable trust, but not if the trust had been amended *after* the will was executed. Because the post-execution amendment could not be incorporated, the court was left with the choice of incorporating only the terms of the original trust or invalidating the devise altogether. The usual choice was to invalidate the devise altogether because incorporating the original terms of the trust, ignoring the amendment, would be intent-defeating.[410]

The third reason why the trustee may not ignore the doctrine of incorporation by reference is that the Uniform Testamentary Additions Trust Act, which has been adopted in one form or another by a number of states, specifically provides that there shall be no incorporation by reference in the event that, for whatever reason, the inter vivos trust is not in existence at the time of death, unless the will specifically provides otherwise.[411] If the will makes no express provision for an "incorporation by reference fall-back," the pour-over bequest or devise lapses. If it is the residue that is the subject of a failed pour-over, an intestacy may result.

Is having one's property pass in accordance with the terms of a revoked inter vivos trust preferable to having one's property pass by intestacy? It depends. It depends upon why and how the inter vivos trust comes to be revoked and who the testamentary trust beneficiaries, as opposed to the intestate takers, would be. Because it is hazardous to predict the future, it is probably appropriate that the "incorporation by reference fall-back" is not the default rule.

The fourth reason why the trustee needs to be attentive to the doctrine of incorporation by reference is that it is theoretically possible for the terms of an inter vivos trust to incorporate by reference the terms of an executed will, this in

---

[409] Restatement (Third) of Property (Wills and Other Donative Transfers) §3.6 cmt. h.

[410] Restatement (Third) of Property (Wills and Other Donative Transfers) §3.8 cmt. c. The doctrine of independent legal significance is covered in §8.15.9 of this handbook.

[411] UPC §2-511(c).

order to supply the inter vivos trust with missing dispositive terms.[412] In fact, this has happened at least once.[413] The subsequent revocation of the will did not effect a revocation of the trust as the terms of the trust contained no express reserved power of revocation.[414] The physical pages of the will, not the will itself, were locked like a fly in amber into the inter vivos trust instrument.[415]

The doctrine of incorporation by reference is not to be confused with the doctrine of integration applicable to wills. "A writing that is integrated into the will must be present when the will was executed, and therefore by definition must exist when the will was executed. A writing to be incorporated by reference must also exist, but need not be present, when the will was executed."[416]

§8.15.18   The Delaware Tax Trap

When we worked on our statute in Florida, we chose not to guess on the outcome of the Delaware tax trap issue—that is, is it a problem or not? Is infinity really a number for purposes of section 2041(a)(3)? We concluded that it would be more than sufficient to allow trusts to last for a very long period of time set by a fixed number of years. Our draft of the statute provided for a 1,000 year maximum duration. Why would anyone care for a longer term? What client cares about infinity? A fixed term of years avoided the problem. . . . One Senator wanted a term that was divisible by 90 years (the basic USRAP period), and another Senator did not want to go beyond 350 years. The compromise was 360 years.[417]

Let us assume that the holder of a limited/special/nongeneral power of appointment exercises it in further trust and in so doing creates a contingent equitable remainder in someone not yet conceived. If the common law version of the rule against perpetuities were applicable, the future interest would be void if it could possibly vest more than twenty-one years after the death of some life in being *at the time the power was created*.[418] In 1933, Delaware enacted a statute providing that the measuring lives need only be in being *at the time of exercise*.[419] In theory, the way was now open in Delaware for nongeneral powers

---

[412] 5 Scott & Ascher §35.1.7.

[413] 5 Scott & Ascher §35.1.7.

[414] 5 Scott & Ascher §35.1.7. *See generally* §8.2.2.2 of this handbook (reserved rights of revocation).

[415] 5 Scott & Ascher §35.1.7.

[416] Restatement (Third) of Property (Wills and Other Donative Transfers) §3.6 cmt. a.

[417] Bruce Stone, Esq., Goldman, Felcoski & Stone, P. A., Coral Gables, FL (Sept. 19, 2003) (excerpt of e-mail to author). *See generally* §8.2.1.7 of this handbook (perpetuities legislation) (discussing the Uniform Statutory Rule Against Perpetuities (USRAP)).

[418] 6 American Law of Property §§24.30–24.36 (A. James Casner ed., 1952); Lewis M. Simes & Allan F. Smith, The Law of Future Interests §§1271–1277 (2d ed. 1956); Marx v. Rice, 3 N.J. Super. 581, 67 A.2d 918 (1949). *See generally* §8.2.1.8 of this handbook (perpetuities and powers of appointment).

[419] 38 Del. L. Ch. 198 (now 25 Del. Ch. §501). Professor Leach noted that Delaware's enactment of this statute had two consequences: "(1) Property . . . [could] . . . thus be tied up in a family *forever*—a result which . . . [had] . . . not been possible in Anglo-American law since Taltarum's Case, Y.B. 12 Edw. IV, pl. 25 (1472), emasculated the Statute De Donis; (2) No federal

of appointment over trust property to constructively pass from generation to generation ad infinitum without a federal estate tax ever being assessed against the subject property.

Congress responded with what is now Section 2041(a)(3), the so-called Delaware tax trap. It provides in part that the creation of a second power of appointment through the exercise of a nongeneral power of appointment will subject the trust property to the federal estate tax at the time *the first power* is exercised, provided that the first power is exercised in a way that enables the trust under applicable state law[420] to continue for more than twenty-one years after the death of some life in being at the time the first power is created.[421]

The trap, however, can also serve as a tax-avoidance vehicle under the right circumstances. This is because property caught in it receives a basis step-up for federal income tax purpose.[422] For the trap to spring, however, the decedent must have exercised a limited/special/nongeneral power of appointment (first power) in further trust such that another power of appointment is created "which under the applicable local law can be validly exercised so as to postpone the vesting of any estate or interest in such property, or suspend the absolute ownership or power of alienation of such property, for a period ascertainable without regard to the date of the creation of the first power."[423] Thus, the exercise of a limited/special/nongeneral power of appointment (first power) in further trust such that someone is granted a presently exercisable general inter vivos power of appointment (second power) should serve to spring the trap at the time of the exercise of the first power *not just in Delaware*.[424] At least it should spring it in states that have not abolished the RAP altogether. As we note in Section 8.2.1.8 of this handbook, the granting of a presently exercisable general inter vivos power of appointment is tantamount to the granting of a vested property interest. This means that any exercise of the presently exercisable general inter vivos power (the second power) in further trust would commence the running of a new perpetuities period.[425] Bottom

---

estate tax . . . [was] . . . payable after such tax had been paid in the estate of . . . [the settlor]. . . ." W. Barton Leach, *Perpetuities in a Nutshell*, 51 Harv. L. Rev. 638, 653 n.37 (1938).

[420] *See* Estate of Mary Margaret Murphy, 71 T.C. 671 (1979), *acq.* 1979-2 C.B. 2 (holding that the exercise of a limited testamentary power of appointment so as to create a second limited power of appointment did not spring the Delaware Tax Trap because, under Wisconsin law, to be a measuring life for Rule against Perpetuities computation purposes, one still needed to have been in being when the first power was created).

[421] *See, e.g.,* James P. Spica, *A Practical Look at Springing the Delaware Tax Trap to Avert Generation Skipping Transfer Tax*, 41 Real Prop. Prob. & Tr. J. 165 (Spring 2006) (springing the Delaware Tax trap by exercising a limited power of appointment in a way that creates in someone a general inter vivos power of appointment).

[422] *See generally* Chapter 11 of this handbook (tax basis/cost of trust property).

[423] I.R.C. §2041(a)(3).

[424] Exercising a nongeneral power of appointment in favor of a permissible appointee by appointing the subject property to the trustee of a trust under which the appointee has reserved or been granted a presently exercisable general inter vivos power of appointment should spring the Delaware tax trap.

[425] In other words, the lives-in-being are determined for RAP-analysis purposes at the time of the second exercise.

line: The trap would be sprung at the time the first power is exercised in further trust. What if a general *testamentary* power of appointment were the second power? An exercise of a general testamentary power of appointment in further trust may or may not commence the running of a new perpetuities period, a topic that is also taken up in Section 8.2.1.8 of this handbook.

Thus, some states are refraining from abolishing altogether the rule against perpetuities as it applies to trusts so as to preserve for tax-avoidance purposes the availability of the Delaware tax trap. Alaska, for example, has enacted a statute that provides that if a nongeneral power of appointment is exercised to create another such power, all property interests subject to the second power are invalid unless within 1,000 years from *the time when the first power was created* the interests subject to the second power either vest or terminate.[426] If the Rule were abolished altogether, a trust could last forever, which arguably is not a finite period beyond which there could be a vesting. In other words, the trap may well have a finite-period requirement. No finite period, no trap; no trap, no springing of the trap. Florida's rationale for settling on a period of 360 years is explained in the quotation that introduces this subsection.

Caveat: One should think long and hard before springing the Delaware tax trap in a dynasty trust[427] that is GST exempt.[428]

Cross referencing. For the federal gift tax regime's Delaware tax trap, see 26 U.S.C. §2514.

§8.15.19   The Probate Exception (to Federal Diversity Jurisdiction)

The . . . [federal] . . . district court shall have original jurisdiction of all civil actions where the matter in controversy exceeds the sum of value of $10,000, exclusive of interest and costs, and is between . . . citizens of different states.[429]

The probate exception to federal diversity jurisdiction does not apply to trusts,[430] except perhaps to trusts employed as will substitutes.[431]

---

[426] *See generally* David G. Shaftel, *Alaska Refines Abolishment of Rule Against Perpetuities to Avoid Delaware Tax Trap*, 2000 STT (State Tax Today) 100-1 (May 23, 2000).

[427] *See* §8.2.1.10 of this handbook (the dynasty trust).

[428] *See generally* Jonathan G. Blattmachr & Jeffrey N. Pennell, *Adventures in Generation-Skipping, or How We Learned to Love the Delaware Tax Trap*, 24 Real Prop. Prob. & Tr. J. 75 (1989).

[429] 28 U.S.C. §1332(a).

[430] Weingarten v. Warren, 753 F. Supp. 491, 494 (S.D.N.Y. 1990); Curtis v. Brunsting, 704 F.3d 406 (5th Cir. 2013).

[431] *See, e.g.*, In re Marshall, 392 F.3d 1118, 1133–1135 (9th Cir. 2004); Golden ex rel. Golden v. Golden, 382 F.3d 348, 359 (3d Cir. 2004); Macken ex rel. Macken v. Jensen, 333 F.3d 797, 799 (7th Cir. 2003); Salis v. Jensen, 294 F.3d 994, 999 (8th Cir. 2002).

As far back as 1827,[432] the U.S. Supreme Court recognized that there were certain limits to federal jurisdiction over probate matters. In 1972, a court finally gave this aggregation of limits a name: the probate exception.[433] In 2006, the U.S. Supreme Court attempted once and for all to define its limits:

> Thus, the probate exception reserves to state probate courts the probate or annulment of a will and the administration of a decedent's estate; it also precludes federal courts from endeavoring to dispose of property that is in the custody of a state probate court. But it does not bar federal courts from adjudicating matters outside those confines and otherwise within federal jurisdiction.[434]

Why has the jurisdiction of state courts over strictly probate proceedings historically been considered exclusive? Because the equity power conferred on federal courts by the Judiciary Act of 1789 included only those powers held by the English Chancery Court in 1789. The probate of wills and the granting of letters of administration were not among them. Those activities were the domain of the English ecclesiastical courts.[435]

In England in 1789, on the other hand, controversies concerning trusts were not the exclusive jurisdiction of the ecclesiastical courts. "And 'it was early established that as to controversies that were not then [in 1789] regarded as probate matters federal jurisdiction could not be ousted by the mere internal arrangement of the state courts.'"[436] Accordingly, while there may be other doctrines that from time to time constrain a federal court from asserting jurisdiction over a local trust matter,[437] the probate exception is not one of them.

As early as 1808, the U.S. Supreme Court stated that trustees of an express trust are entitled to bring diversity actions in their own names and upon the basis of their own citizenship.[438] The residence of those who may have the equitable interest is "irrelevant," for example, in an action by the trustee against a third party for breach of contract.[439] Note, however, that "[i]n a number of representative cases it has been held or recognized that for the purpose of

---

[432] Armstrong v. Lear, 25 U.S. (12 Wheat.) 169, 176 (1827) (involving the unsuccessful efforts of one claiming to be a legatee under the will of Continental Army General Thaddeus Kosciuszko to have the matter heard in federal court).

[433] Magaziner v. Montemuro, 468 F.2d 782, 787 (3d Cir. 1972). *See also* Estate of Masters, 361 F. Supp. 2d 1303 (E.D. Okla. 2005); Peter Nicolas, *Fighting the Probate Mafia: A Dissection of the Probate Exception to Federal Court Jurisdiction*, 74 S. Cal. L. Rev. 1479, 1493–1494 & n.70 (2001); John F. Winkler, *The Probate Jurisdiction of the Federal Courts*, 14 Probate L.J. 77 (1997).

[434] Marshall v. Marshall, 126 S. Ct. 1735, 1748 (2006) (the court suggesting that the probate exception in part is rooted in the general principle that, when one court is exercising *in rem* jurisdiction over a *res*, a second court will not assume *in rem* jurisdiction over the same *res*.).

[435] Barnes v. Brandrup, 506 F. Supp. 396, 398–399 (1981).

[436] Barnes v. Brandrup, 506 F. Supp. at 399 (quoting Beach v. Rome Trust Co., 269 F.2d 367, 373 (2d Cir. 1959)).

[437] *See generally* Barnes v. Brandrup, 506 F. Supp. 396 (1981).

[438] Navarro Sav. Ass'n v. Lee, 446 U.S. 458, 462–463 (1980).

[439] Navarro Sav. Ass'n v. Lee, 446 U.S. 458, 462–463 (1980). *See generally* 5 Scott & Ascher §28.1.

determining federal jurisdiction based on diversity of citizenship, the citizenship of a business trust is that of the owners of beneficial interest."[440] The general topic of judicial jurisdiction over trustees is covered in Section 8.40 of this handbook.

§8.15.20   *Doctrine of Equitable Deviation*

The rationale for modifying a donative document is that the donor would have desired the modification to be made if he or she had realized that the desired tax objectives would not be achieved. A similar rationale underlies the cy pres doctrine for charitable trusts, the deviation doctrine for private trusts, and the special-purpose reformation doctrine for curing perpetuity violations.[441]

The traditional doctrine. Under the doctrine of equitable deviation, a court may effect a change in the express administrative provisions of a trust in order to accomplish the trust's express purpose.[442] Courts generally require both an unforeseen and unforeseeable change in circumstances[443] and a "frustration of ... [the] ... settlor's main objective if the trust conditions are strictly followed"[444] before the doctrine is applied.[445] The test is not the "best interests" of the beneficiaries; rather the petitioners must establish that the settlor's presumed intent is incapable of fulfillment.[446] "In the case of a private [*i.e.,* noncharitable] trust, ... the court ordinarily does not substitute new beneficiaries for those designated in the terms of the trust; nor does it ordinarily enlarge the interest of one beneficiary at the expense of another."[447]

---

[440] Herbert B. Chermside, Jr., *Modern Status of the Massachusetts or Business Trust*, 88 A.L.R.3d 704, §63 (2006).

[441] Restatement (Third) of Property (Donative Transfers) §12.2 (Tentative Draft No. 1, 1995).

[442] *See* 4A Scott on Trusts §381; Restatement (Second) of Trusts §381; 6 Scott & Ascher §39.5.

[443] *See, e.g.,* Church of the Little Flower v. U.S. Bank, 979 N.E.2d 106 (Ill. App. 2012) ("Plaintiff contends equitable deviation is justified because ... [the settlor] ... could not have foreseen the amendment of the ... [charitable] ... trust to comply with the private foundation- ... [tax] ... rules. The trust agreement, which directs the trustee to maintain compliance with those rules, plainly refutes that premise."); Matter of Trust Under Will of Nobbe, 831 N.E.2d 835 (Ind. Ct. App. 2005) (the court declining to grant the "extraordinary" relief of equitable deviation, the events that occasioned the litigation having been "anticipated" by the settlor). *See generally Power of court to authorize modification of trust instrument because of changes in tax law*, 57 A.L.R.3d 1044.

[444] First Nat'l Bank & Trust Co. of Wyo. v. Brimmer, 504 P.2d 1367, 1370 (Wyo. 1973).

[445] *See generally* 6 Scott & Ascher §39.5. *See, e.g.,* Church of the Little Flower v. U.S. Bank, 979 N.E.2d 106 (Ill. App. 2012) (holding that the trial court's granting of an equitable deviation petition to terminate a split-interest trust upon a finding that the substantial fees that the trustee had been collecting from the trust estate had been interfering with the trust's charitable purposes was unwarranted in light of the trust's particular terms).

[446] In re JP Morgan Chase Bank, N.A., 19 Misc.3d 337, 342, 852 N.Y.S.2d 718, 722 (2008).

[447] 6 Scott & Ascher §39.5.

On the other hand, a *cy pres* judgment in the charitable context generally does effect a shifting of equitable or beneficial interests.[448] Thus, in the charitable context, "courts apply equitable deviation to make changes in the manner in which a charitable trust is carried out while courts apply cy pres in situations where trustees seek to modify or redefine the settlor's specific charitable purpose."[449] In the few states that do not recognize *cy pres*, the courts are inclined to apply a "somewhat more robust than usual notion of equitable deviation" to charitable trusts that would otherwise by *cy pres*-eligible.[450]

One court has outlined the general differences between the *cy pres* doctrine[451] and the doctrine of equitable deviation:

> The cy pres doctrine is a rule of judicial construction under which the court is required to first find a general charitable intent in the instrument creating the trust; the general charitable purpose of the settlor moves the court to substitute a different charitable purpose for the one which has failed. Cy pres is applied only in the field of charitable trusts, whereas, *a court of equity may order a deviation in private as well as charitable trusts*. In ordering a deviation a court of equity is merely exercising its general power over the administration of trusts; it is an essential element of equity jurisdiction. In ordering a deviation the court does not touch the question of the purpose or object of the trust, nor vary the class of beneficiaries, nor divert the fund from the charitable purpose designated.[452]

In order to avoid a "defeat or substantial impairment" of a trust's purposes due to a change of circumstances that was unanticipated by the settlor, a court, for example, may in a given situation allow or direct the trustee to sell, mortgage, pledge, or lease the trust property even though the terms of the trust have directed the trustee not to.[453] In cases where the settlor has limited the investment options of the trustee to bonds, some courts have been willing, nonetheless, to expand the trustee's investment options to include common stocks: "Typically, the reason for such a departure is that the proposed investments will act as a hedge against inflation, diversify the trust's portfolio, or improve the trust's overall return."[454]

---

[448] *See generally* 6 Scott & Ascher §39.5.

[449] Niemann v. Vaughn Cmty. Church, 154 Wash. 2d 365, 378, 113 P.3d 463, 469 (2005).

[450] 6 Scott & Ascher §39.5.2.

[451] *See generally* §9.4.3 of this handbook (*cy pres*).

[452] Craft v. Shroyer, 74 N.E.2d 589, 598 (1947). *See also* Plummer Memorial Loan Fund Trust v. Nebraska, 661 N.W.2d 307 (Neb. 2003) (strictly construing the doctrine of *cy pres* and the doctrine of equitable or administrative deviation and finding neither applicable). *Cf.* UTC §412(b) (available at <http://www.uniformlaws.org/Act.aspx?title=Trust%20Code>) (providing that the court may modify the administrative terms of a trust if continuation of the trust on its existing terms would be impracticable or wasteful or impair the trust's administration). *See generally* 6 Scott & Ascher §39.5.

[453] *See generally* 3 Scott & Ascher §16.4 (Change of Circumstances). *See, e.g.*, Niemann v. Vaughn Cmty. Church, 154 Wash. 2d 365, 113 P.3d 463 (2005) (an equitable deviation action in which the court, overriding express retention language in the governing trust instrument, authorized the sale of certain entrusted church property, the court finding the property alienation restriction to be administrative rather than integral to the trust's dominant charitable purpose).

[454] *See generally* 3 Scott & Ascher §16.4 (Change of Circumstances).

Equitable deviation is not just for tweaking a trust's investment provisions, as one appellate court has confirmed. In lieu of the eventual outright distribution of the assets of an ongoing trust to the victim of schizophrenia affective disorder and bipolar disorder, which was the mode of terminating distribution called for by the trust's terms, the court, invoking the doctrine of equitable deviation, let it be known that it would uphold a diversion of the distribution to the trustee of a third-party special needs trust established down the road for the benefit of the victim.[455] Circumstances had changed.[456] The deceased settlors had been unaware of their granddaughter's disability and would not have wanted trust assets squandered to no avail, or unnecessarily diverted into the coffers of the state.[457] Third-party special needs trusts are covered in Section 9.3 of this handbook.

Substantive equitable deviation under the Uniform Trust Code. The Uniform Trust Code would broaden the court's ability to modify the administrative terms of a trust.[458] The standard is similar to the standard for applying *cy pres* to a charitable trust.[459] "Just as a charitable trust may be modified if its particular charitable purpose becomes impracticable or wasteful, so can the administrative terms of any trust, charitable or noncharitable."[460]

The UTC, specifically Section 412, also would broaden the court's ability to apply equitable deviation to encompass a trust's termination or modification: The court may modify the administrative or dispositive terms of a trust or terminate the trust if, because of circumstances not anticipated by the settlor, modification or termination will further the purposes of the trust.[461] "For example, modification of the dispositive provisions to increase support of a beneficiary might be appropriate if the beneficiary has become unable to provide for support due to poor health or serious injury."[462] The Restatement (Third) of Trusts is generally in accord.[463] The Uniform Prudent Management of Institutional Funds Act (UPMIFA)—which applies to charitable corporations as well as charitable trusts—takes a similarly expansive approach to equitable

---

[455] In re Riddell, 138 Wash. App. 485, 157 P.3d 888 (2007).

[456] In re Riddell, 138 Wash. App. 485, 157 P.3d 888 (2007).

[457] In re Riddell, 138 Wash. App. 485, 157 P.3d 888 (2007).

[458] UTC §412 cmt. (available at <http://www.uniformlaws.org/Act.aspx?title=Trust%20 Code>).

[459] UTC §412 cmt. (available at <http://www.uniformlaws.org/Act.aspx?title=Trust%20 Code>).

[460] UTC §412 cmt. (available at <http://www.uniformlaws.org/Act.aspx?title=Trust%20 Code>). "Although the settlor is granted considerable latitude in defining the purposes of the trust, the principle that a trust have a purpose which is for the benefit of its beneficiaries precludes unreasonable restrictions on the use of trust property." UTC §412 cmt. "An owner's freedom to be capricious about the use of the owner's own property ends when the property is impressed with a trust for the benefit of others." UTC §412 cmt.

[461] UTC §412(a) (available at <http://www.uniformlaws.org/Act.aspx?title=Trust%20 Code>).

[462] UTC §412 cmt. §412 cmt. (available at <http://www.uniformlaws.org/Act.aspx? title=Trust%20Code>).

[463] Restatement (Third) of Trusts §66(1).

deviation, but in the charitable context.[464] Invoking the modern doctrine of equitable deviation, one court has authorized the conversion of a preexisting non–self-settled trust to a special/supplemental needs trust.[465]

Under Oregon's version of Section 412 of the UTC, the court lacks the power to grant equitable deviation relief *sua sponte*.[466] This is an exception to the general rule that "a court in equity has broad discretion in crafting relief, and the parties in equity are not necessarily limited to the relief that they seek in their complaint."[467]

The plain meaning rule. Has Uniform Trust Code's Section 412 defanged the plain meaning rule? Not, at least, in Indiana. In *Kristoff v. Centier Bank*, a trust beneficiary, invoking Indiana's version of Section 412, sought a judicial termination of the trust in mid-course.[468] Circumstances had made it impossible for the trust to function as a GST-avoidance vehicle. The requested termination, however, would have contravened the intentions of the settlor as they had been clearly and unambiguously articulated in the governing instrument. Her request was denied. The denial was upheld on appeal. The instrument's dispositive provisions being clear and unambiguous, namely that tax avoidance was not the trust's only purpose, the court declined to consider extrinsic evidence that might have suggested that the settlor's dispositive wishes were something other than what had been expressed in the writing. That others as well as the petitioner had contingent equitable interests under the trust did not help her case. The plain meaning rule is covered generally in Section 8.15.6 of this handbook.

The role of the courts. If the circumstances are such that the court would authorize an equitable deviation from the terms of the trust, then the trustee would seem to have the inherent authority to do so without court approval.[469] The problem is that the only way for the trustee to know for sure what a court would actually do when presented with a given set of facts is to ask it, which would likely entail initiating some type of judicial proceeding, be it a complaint for instructions,[470] a complaint for declaratory judgment,[471] or perhaps a petition to have his accounts allowed.[472] This can generally be done at trust expense.[473] A trustee who proceeds to deviate from the terms of the trust without first seeking judicial approval to do so assumes the risk that some court

---

[464] Unif. Prudent Management of Institutional Funds Act §6(b).

[465] *See* In re Riddell, 157 P.3d 888 (Wash. Ct. App. 2007). *Cf.* §9.3 of this handbook (the self-settled "special needs"/"supplemental needs" trust).

[466] *See* Head v. Head, 323 P.3d 505 (Or. Ct. App. 2014).

[467] Head v. Head, 323 P.3d 505, 510 (Or. Ct. App. 2014).

[468] Kristoff v. Centier Bank, 985 N.E.2d 20 (Ind. App. 2013).

[469] *See generally* 3 Scott & Ascher §16.4.1.

[470] *See generally* §8.42 of this handbook (what is the difference between a complaint (petition) for instructions and a complaint (petition) for declaratory judgment?).

[471] *See generally* §8.42 of this handbook (what is the difference between a complaint (petition) for instructions and a complaint (petition) for declaratory judgment?).

[472] *See generally* §6.1.5.2 of this handbook (duty to keep and render accounts).

[473] *See generally* §3.5.2.3 of this handbook (discussing the trustee's right in equity to exoneration and reimbursement).

down the road will determine that deviation was not warranted, that the trust was somehow harmed as a result of the trustee's actions, and that the trustee must use his personal funds to remedy the situation.[474] In lieu of seeking judicial permission, the trustee might attempt to attain the consent of all beneficiaries. If there are unborn and unascertained remaindermen, however, as is likely to be the case, then the nonjudicial approach is probably not an option.[475] Nor in some cases is inaction: "If there has been such a change of circumstances that compliance with the terms of the trust would defeat or substantially impair the trust purposes, the trustee cannot sit idly by and do nothing to prevent the loss."[476]

The posture of the trustee in a contested substantive equitable deviation action. In the face of the trustee's duty to defend his trust, a topic we take up generally in Section 6.2.6 of this handbook, it is hard to see how a trustee can properly maintain a neutral posture in a contested substantive equitable deviation action, particularly if some but not all of the beneficiaries are seeking to reorder and/or diminish the ostensible equitable property rights of their cobeneficiaries, and even more so if the terms of the trust are patently and latently unambiguous. At trust expense the trustee should mount a vigorous opposition to the action, unless to do so would be unreasonable; and the trustee certainly should not initiate it, as to do so would most assuredly implicate the trustee's duty of impartiality, a topic we take up generally in Section 6.2.5 of this handbook.

Doctrinal analogues. The doctrines of *cy pres*[477] and equitable deviation should not be confused with the variance power granted the trustees of a charitable foundation in its governing documentation.[478]

It is not entirely clear what the practical difference is between UTC substantive equitable deviation and UTC substantive equitable reformation. The latter topic we take up in Section 8.15.22 of this handbook.

Is it possible to alter a trust term via a trust-to-trust decanting? Decanting as an alternative to the reformation or deviation action in the trust context is taken up in Section 3.5.3.2(a) of this handbook.

§8.15.21   Doctrine of Clobberie's Case versus the Divide-and-Pay-Over Rule

The rule was known as the divide-and-pay-over rule. It seems clear, however, that the mere fact that there is no direct gift of the remainder, but only a direction to divide and pay over, is a wholly insufficient basis for reading in a survival requirement.[479]

---

[474] *See generally* 3 Scott & Ascher §16.4.1.

[475] *See generally* §8.14 of this handbook (when a guardian ad litem (or special representative) is needed: virtual representation issues).

[476] 3 Scott & Ascher §16.4.2.

[477] *See generally* 6 Scott & Ascher §39.5 (*cy pres*); §9.4.3 of this handbook (*cy pres*).

[478] The concept of a variance power is discussed in §8.15.37 of this handbook.

[479] 3 Scott & Ascher §13.2.9.

Let's assume the following three trusts:

Trust #1: A to *B* to John Jones at (or when he attains) age 21.
Trust #2: A to *B* to be paid to John Jones at age 21.
Trust #3: A to *B*, income to John Jones and then to him at age 21.

Clobberie's case. Assuming the contingency is not addressed by express language in the governing instrument,[480] what would happen to the trust property were John Jones to die before attaining the age of 21? If one were to apply the *Doctrine of Clobberie's Case* (1677),[481] the property of *Trust #1* would pass to *A* or *A*'s estate upon a resulting trust, and the property of *Trust #2* and of *Trust #3* would be turned over to John Jones' executor or administrator, *i.e.*, to his estate.[482] In other words, a condition precedent of survivorship would be inferred with respect to John Jones' interest under *Trust #1*, whereas it would be inferred that John Jones possessed a vested equitable remainder under each of the other two trusts.

While the rules of the *Clobberie's Case* may be arbitrary, they do have the advantage of taking the guesswork out of parsing the language of a grant of a future interest that is distributable upon the grantee reaching a specified age, particularly when the language fails to specify what happens should the grantee die before attaining the specified age. The Restatement (Third) of Property would sacrifice certainty upon the altar of unexpressed donor intent. Thus, "[l]anguage providing that the share is 'to be paid at' a specified age [our Trust # 2] is treated as a factor but not necessarily a controlling factor suggesting that there is no condition of survival to the specified age."[483] In other words, there is a likelihood that the future interest vested *ab initio*, but we can't be sure. We need to get the court involved. The Restatement (Third) sows other such litigation-fostering uncertainties about the landscape: "If requiring survival to the specified age would have adverse tax consequence to the donor, that is a factor weighing against a requirement of survival."[484] The absence of a gift over might suggest the absence of a condition of survival.[485] As would a remainderman who leaves descendants who survive the termination of the preceding estate.[486] If that were not enough confusion for one day, the Restatement (Third) adds an additional layer for good measure: It calls for the application of antilapse principles to future interests that are distributable at a specified age.[487] Antilapse is discussed generally in Section 8.15.55 of this handbook.

---

[480] *See generally* §5.2 of this handbook (class designation: "children," "issue," "heirs," and "relatives" (some rules of construction)).

[481] 2 Vent. 342 (1677). *See generally* 5 American Law of Property §§21.17, 21.18 (1952).

[482] *See, e.g.*, Smith v. Morgan, 2004 WL 345503 (Mich. Ct. App.) (noting that "the common law in Michigan provides that future interests should be treated as vested where there is any present interest in the income of the property").

[483] Restatement (Third) of Property (Wills and Other Donative Transfers) §26.6 cmt. e.

[484] Restatement (Third) of Property (Wills and Other Donative Transfers) §26.6 cmt. g.

[485] Restatement (Third) of Property (Wills and Other Donative Transfers) §26.6 cmt. h.

[486] Restatement (Third) of Property (Wills and Other Donative Transfers) §26.6 cmt. i.

[487] Restatement (Third) of Property (Wills and Other Donative Transfers) §26.6 cmt. j.

The divide-and-pay-over rule. There is another default doctrine, however, the so-called divide-and-pay-over rule, that to some extent conflicts with *Clobberie*. The reader's attention is called particularly to the Trust #2 hypothetical above. Take a trust with the following terms: "*A* to *B* for *C* for life, and then upon the death of *C* the property shall be *divided and paid over* to *X*, *Y*, & *Z*, three named individuals."[488] Under the divide-and-pay-over rule, in the event that *X* dies before *C*, nothing passes to *X*'s estate. In other words, the import of the divide-and-pay-over language is that *X's* interest is subject to the condition precedent of *X* surviving *C*. The divide-and-pay-over rule was essentially declared obsolete by Section 260 of the Restatement (First) of Property (1940), although as late as 1987 it was still being applied in the courts.[489] The Restatement (Third) of Property also "rejects" the rule.[490]

§8.15.22 Doctrines of Reformation, Modification, and Rectification

Reformation or modification of inter vivos trusts for mistake. A court will reform the terms of a trust upon clear and convincing evidence that a material *mistake* has caused the terms not to reflect the settlor's intent, or that but for the mistake the settlor would have used different terms.[491] This is known as the doctrine of reformation.[492] Unless the trust was established for consideration,[493] a material unilateral mistake on the part of the settlor would ordinarily be enough to warrant reformation.[494] Otherwise someone could be unjustly enriched by the mistake.[495] The Restatement of Restitution is in accord: "Where there has been an error in the legal effect of the language used in a conveyance, the normal proceeding for restitution is by a bill in equity to reform the instrument to accord with the donor's intent...."[496]

The doctrine of reformation corrects mistakes that go to the very purpose of the trust.[497] The doctrine of deviation, on the other hand, deals with administrative provisions that stand in the way of accomplishing that purpose,[498] a topic we cover in Section 8.15.20 of this handbook.

---

[488] *See generally* Scott & Ascher §13.2.9.

[489] *See, e.g.,* Harris Trust & Sav. Bank v. Beach, 513 N.E.2d 833 (Ill. 1987).

[490] *See* Restatement (Third) of Property (Wills and Other Donative Transfers) §26.3 cmt. i.

[491] *See generally* 4A Scott on Trusts §333.4; Restatement (Second) of Trusts §333.4. *See, e.g.,* Bilafar v. Bilafar, 73 Cal. Rptr. 3d 880 (Ct. App. 2008) (granting the nonbeneficiary settlor of a non–self-settled irrevocable inter vivos trust standing to bring a mistake-based reformation action).

[492] *See generally* Barry F. Spivey, *Completed Transactions, Qualified Reformation and Bosch: When Does the IRS Care about State Law of Trust Reformation?*, 26 ACTEC Notes 345 (2001).

[493] Restatement of Restitution §12 (unilateral mistake in bargains).

[494] 5 Scott & Ascher §33.4.

[495] *See generally* §8.15.78 of this handbook (unjust enrichment).

[496] Restatement of Restitution §49 cmt. a (gratuitous transactions).

[497] Matter of Trusts of Hicks, 10 Misc. 3d 1078(A) (N.Y. Surr. Ct. 2006) (2006 Westlaw 250508).

[498] *See also* §8.17 of this handbook (trust reformation to remedy mistakes; trust modification; tax objectives). *See generally* §8.15.20 of this handbook (doctrine of [equitable] deviation).

Under the Uniform Trust Code, the court may reform the terms of a trust, even if unambiguous, to conform the terms to the settlor's intention if it is proved by clear and convincing evidence that both the settlor's intent and the terms of the trust were affected by a mistake of fact or law, whether in expression or inducement.[499] "A mistake of expression occurs when the terms of the trust misstate the settlor's intention, fail to include a term that was intended to be included, or include a term that was intended to be excluded."[500] Thus the Uniform Trust Code would sweep away time-honored restraints on the introduction of extrinsic evidence, such as the plain meaning rule.[501] Even the unambiguous trust term is no longer safe.[502] The plain meaning rule is taken up in Section 8.15.6 of this handbook.

Clear and convincing evidence has been defined as evidence leading to a firm belief or conviction that the allegations are true. "Although it is a higher standard of proof than proof by the greater weight of the evidence, the evidence presented need not be undisputed to be clear and convincing."[503] This "higher" standard is likely to prove a paper tiger when it comes to trust- reformation litigation deterrence. In fact, there is already some evidence that the standard is not being taken seriously in the real world, not even by the bench.[504]

In the Restatement (Third) of Trusts, "reformation" and "modification" are not synonymous: Reformation involves "the use of interpretation (including evidence of mistake, etc.) in order to ascertain—and properly restate—the true, legally effective intent of settlors with respect to the original terms of trusts they have created,"[505] while modification "involves a change in—a departure from—the true, original terms of the trust, whether the modification is done by a court . . . or a power holder. . . ."[506] The execution-focused harmless-error rule is discussed in Section 8.15.53 of this handbook as it applies to the requisite formalities for creating, revoking, and amending self-settled revocable trusts.

---

[499] UTC §415 (available at <http://www.uniformlaws.org/Act.aspx?title=Trust%20Code>); *see, e.g.*, In re Matthew Larson Trust Agreement Dated May 1, 1996, 2013 ND 85, 831 N.W.2d 388 (2013) (petition to reform terms of trust due to mistake of law granted).

[500] UTC §415 cmt. (available at <http://www.uniformlaws.org/Act.aspx?title=Trust%20Code>).

[501] *See, e.g.*, Frakes v. Nay, 247 Or. App. 95, 273 P.3d 137 (2010) (applying Oregon's UTC trust reformation provisions).

[502] *See, e.g.*, Frakes v. Nay, 247 Or. App. 95, 273 P.3d 137 (2010) (applying Oregon's UTC trust reformation provisions).

[503] In re Matthew Larson Trust Agreement Dated May 1, 1996, 2013 ND 85, 831 N.W.2d 388 (2013).

[504] *See, e.g.*, Justice Mary Muehlen Maring's dissent in In re Matthew Larson Trust Agreement Dated May 1, 1996, 2013 ND 85, 831 N.W.2d 388 (2013), in which the Supreme Court of North Dakota cleared the way for the reformation of the unambiguous terms of an inter vivos trust although the trial court had never made a finding under the clear and convincing standard as to the settlors' intent.

[505] Restatement (Third) of Trusts, Reporter's Notes to §62.

[506] Restatement (Third) of Trusts, Reporter's Notes to §62.

A scrivener's material mistake is grounds for reformation of a trust, provided the extrinsic evidence of the intended disposition is clear and convincing.[507] As a general rule, when a settlor creates a trust in *exchange for consideration*, the fact that the settlor did so by mistake is not grounds for reformation of the terms of the trust.[508] If, however, consideration is not involved, a material mistake as to the law or the facts that induced the settlor to create the trust is grounds for reformation,[509] whether or not the governing instrument is ambiguous.[510] This would include a material mistake as to the tax consequences of establishing the trust, a topic we cover in Section 8.17 of this handbook.[511] The settlor's undue delay in seeking reformation or the settlor's subsequent ratification by word or deed of the trust's terms, however, may preclude reformation.[512] In such cases, and even in the case of a successful mistake-driven reformation suit, which is likely to have been expensive for all concerned, a scrivener who has failed to shoulder the burden of the attendant costs should expect that at least some aggrieved parties will be entertaining the idea of bringing a drafting malpractice tort action against him or her.[513] Whether the privity defense would be available to the scrivener is discussed in Section 8.15.61 of this handbook.

Legal title to the property of a trust being in the trustee, it is likely that the trustee would have standing to bring a mistake-based reformation action.[514] Whether under equitable principles the trustee should do so is another matter.

---

[507] Restatement (Third) of Trusts §62 cmt. b; UTC §415 (available at <http://www.uniformlaws.org/Act.aspx?title=Trust%20Code>). *See, e.g.*, In re Estate of Tuthill, 754 A.2d 272 (D.C. 2000) (confirming that a scrivener's mistake is a valid ground for reformation provided the mistake is proved by full, clear, and decisive evidence). *See also* Wennett v. Ross, 439 Mass. 1003, 786 N.E.2d 336 (2003) (reforming an irrevocable life insurance trust to correct an alleged scrivener's error); Colt v. Colt, 438 Mass. 1001, 777 N.E.2d 1235 (2002) (in part reforming a trust so that certain transfers will qualify for the generation-skipping transfer tax exemption, the court deeming the insertion of a general power of appointment to be a scrivener's error).

[508] Restatement (Third) of Trusts §62 cmt. a; 4 Scott on Trusts §333.4; Restatement (Second) of Trusts §333; Restatement of Restitution §12.

[509] *See* Restatement (Third) of Trusts §62; 1 Scott & Ascher §4.6.3; UTC §414 cmt. (available at <http://www.uniformlaws.org/Act.aspx?title=Trust%20Code>) (suggesting that "[i]n determining the settlor's original intent, the court may consider evidence relevant to the settlor's intention even though it contradicts an apparent plain meaning of the text" and that the "objective of the plain meaning rule, to protect against fraudulent testimony, is satisfied by the requirement of clean and convincing proof"); Restatement of Restitution §49 cmt. a (mistake of law warranting reformation of instrument of gratuitous conveyance). *See, however*, §8.15.6 of this handbook (parol evidence rule). *See generally* §9.4.3 of this handbook (*cy pres*).

[510] Restatement (Third) of Trusts §62 cmt. b.

[511] *See, e.g.*, UTC §416 (available at <http://www.uniformlaws.org/Act.aspx?title=Trust%20Code>) (providing that to achieve the settlor's tax objectives, the court may modify the terms of a trust in a manner that is not contrary to the settlor's probable intention). *See also* Restatement (Third) of Property (Wills and Other Donative Transfers) §12.2.

[512] *See generally* 1 Scott & Ascher §4.6.4. *See also* §§7.1.3 of this handbook (discussing the concept of laches) and 8.12 of this handbook (containing a catalog of equity maxims including the "Delay defeats equities" maxim).

[513] *See, e.g.*, Estate of Carlson, 895 N.E.2d 1191 (Ind. 2008).

[514] *See, e.g.*, Reid v. Temple Judea & Hebrew Union Coll. Jewish Inst. of Religion, 994 So. 2d 1146 (Fla. Ct. App. 2008).

If the trustee is seeking to bring about a reordering of the equitable property interests at the expense of one or more of the beneficiaries designated within the four corners of the governing instrument, then his initiating the reformation action, and certainly his appealing of any lower court decision not to reform, would be difficult to square with his fiduciary duties of loyalty and impartiality, not to mention his duty to defend the trust, a topic we take up in Section 6.2.6 of this handbook.[515] Even as a nominal defendant in a mistake-based reformation action brought by someone else, the trustee should be wary of taking a position that is adverse to any designated beneficiary.

Reformation of testamentary trusts for mistake. The terms of a testamentary trust are generally found within the four corners of some will. It is traditional wills doctrine that a provision in a will that is neither patently nor latently ambiguous may not be reformed to remedy a mistake of fact or law.[516] It matters not whether the mistake was in the expression or the inducement. The Supreme Judicial Court of Massachusetts, in *Flannery v. McNamara* (2000), emphatically articulated the public policy/practical reasons for maintaining the traditional proscription:

> To allow for reformation in this case would open the floodgates of litigation and lead to untold confusion in the probate of wills. It would essentially invite disgruntled individuals excluded from a will to demonstrate extrinsic evidence of the decedent's "intent" to include them. The number of groundless will contests could soar. We disagree that employing "full, clear and decisive proof" as the standard for reformation would suffice to remedy such problems. Judicial resources are simply too scarce to squander on such consequences.[517]

The academics who authored the Uniform Trust Code were apparently unmoved by such practical concerns. Section 415 of the Uniform Trust Code provides that the court may reform the terms of a testamentary trust, even if unambiguous, to conform to the testator's/settlor's intention, provided it is proved by clear and convincing evidence what the testator's/settlor's intention was and that the terms of the trust were created by mistake of fact or law, whether in expression or inducement.[518] As authority for upending the long-standing proscription against the mistake-based reformation of unambiguous wills, the commentary to UTC §415 cites as authority the Restatement (Third) of Property (Wills and Other Donative Transfers), specifically §12.1. A perusal of §12.1 and its commentary reveals that the Code and the Restatement are cross-tracking, and cross-citing to, one another.

---

[515] *See* §§6.1.3.6 of this handbook (breaches of the trustee's duty of loyalty that do not involve self-dealing) and 6.2.5 of this handbook (the trustee's duty of impartiality).

[516] *See generally* Flannery v. McNamara, 432 Mass. 665, 668–671, 738 N.E.2d 739, 742–744 (2000); §5.2 of this handbook.

[517] Flannery v. McNamara, 432 Mass. 665, 674, 738 N.E.2d 739, 746 (2000).

[518] UTC §415 cmt. (available at <http://www.uniformlaws.org/Act.aspx?title=Trust%20 Code>).

The policy that implicitly underpins the discarding of the ancient reformation proscription is this: The need to prevent unintended devisees, and unintended beneficiaries of testamentary trusts, from being "unjustly" enriched outweighs any need to control the litigation floodgates.[519] And as to distributions already made, there is always the procedural equitable remedy of the constructive trust.[520] No problem. Perhaps. But we cannot help but recall the words of Francis Bacon: "As for the philosophers . . . [of the law,] . . . they make imaginary law for imaginary commonwealths; and their discourses are as the stars, which give little light because they are so high."[521] Effective July 1, 2011, Florida abolished its proscription against the postmortem mistake-based reformation of unambiguous wills.[522]

In 2012, a Nebraska court reformed the unambiguous terms of two operating testamentary trusts such that the equitable property interests of those who would have benefited economically from the imposition of a resulting trust were nullified. Applying Nebraska's version of Section 415 of the Uniform Trust Code, the trial court found clear and convincing extrinsic evidence to the effect that the testator/settlor's failure to expressly designate a remainderman had been occasioned by "a mistake of fact or law." The judicial reformation was upheld on appeal.[523]

Reformation to correct a violation of the Rule against Perpetuities. The Uniform Statutory Rule Against Perpetuities (USRAP) expressly provides for the reformation of trusts that violate its provisions.[524] "Upon the petition of an interested person, the court is directed to reform a disposition within the limits of the allowable 90-year period, in the manner deemed by the court most closely to approximate the transferor's manifested plan of distribution. . . ."[525] Apparently in deference to the vested equitable property rights (reversionary interests) of those who would take upon imposition of a resulting trust should an express trust fail,[526] USRAP would only interfere with certain problematic nonvested equitable interests under express trusts, namely, those interests that are created on or after the effective date of the legislation.[527] The authors of the Uniform Probate Code, however, have suggested that a court might have the equitable power to reform a problematic contingent disposition under an

---

[519] This is a distortion of classic unjust enrichment doctrine. *See* §8.15.78 of this handbook.

[520] Restatement (Third) of Property (Wills and Other Donative Transfers) §12.1 cmt. f (nature of reformation and constructive trust). For a general discussion of the constructive trust, *see* §3.3 of this handbook and §7.2.3.1.6 of this handbook.

[521] Daniel R. Coquillette, Francis Bacon 84 (Stanford Univ. Press 1992). Francis Bacon held the position as Lord Chancellor from 1617 to 1621. A list of all of the Lord Chancellors who served from 1066 to 2010, including the present encumbant, may be found in Chapter 1 of this handbook.

[522] Fla. Stat. §732.615.

[523] *See* In re Trust of O'Donnell, 815 N.W.2d 640 (Neb. Ct. App. 2012).

[524] UPC §2-903. *See generally* §8.2.1.7 of this handbook (USRAP).

[525] UPC §2-903 cmt.

[526] *See generally* §4.1.1.1 of this handbook (the vested equitable reversionary interest and the resulting trust).

[527] UPC §2-905 (USRAP's prospective application). *See generally* §8.15.71 of this handbook (retroactive application of new trust law).

express trust created before enactment by judicially inserting a perpetuity saving clause, "because a perpetuity saving clause would probably have been used at the drafting stage of the disposition had it been drafted competently."[528] Those who would take upon imposition of a resulting trust could be expected to oppose any reformation initiative that seeks to extinguish their equitable reversionary property interests. The authors of the Code also have suggested that it would be appropriate if the trustee brought the reformation suit.[529] How this would comport with the trustee's fiduciary duty to the reversionary interests, as well as his duty of impartiality generally, is not entirely clear.[530]

Reformation in response to an unanticipated change of circumstances. Until relatively recently, the application of the doctrine of reformation in the context of a change of circumstances that had been unanticipated by a settlor was a narrow one. Judicial reformation of the dispositive terms of a trust was generally only considered warranted if not to do so would defeat the trust's purposes, or at least substantially impair their accomplishment.[531] "Under neither of the first two Restatements was termination or modification available on any sort of widespread basis, such as in response to unanticipated circumstances generally, to *further* the trust purposes, or to serve the best interests of the beneficiaries."[532] The third Restatement, on the other hand, would permit a change-of-circumstances judicial reformation of the dispositive terms of a trust merely to *further* its purposes.[533] The Uniform Trust Code, specifically Section 412, would as well.[534] Also, there are now statutes on the books in a number of jurisdictions that purport to authorize courts under certain circumstance to vary the dispositive provisions even of multibeneficiary trusts.[535] Still, a simple misunderstanding about the effect of a legal instrument, in and of itself, is not an unanticipated *future* circumstance.[536]

Has Uniform Trust Code's Section 412 defanged the plain meaning rule? Not, at least, in Indiana. In *Kristoff v. Centier Bank*, a trust beneficiary, invoking Indiana's version of Section 412, sought a judicial termination of the trust in mid-course.[537] Circumstances had made it impossible for the trust to function as a GST-avoidance vehicle. The requested termination, however, would have contravened the intentions of the settlor as they had been clearly and unambiguously articulated in the governing instrument. Her request was denied. The denial was upheld on appeal. The instrument's dispositive provisions being clear and unambiguous, namely that tax avoidance was not the trust's

---

[528] UPC §2-905 cmt. *See generally* §8.2.1.6 of this handbook (the perpetuities saving clause).

[529] UTC §2-903 cmt.

[530] *See generally* §6.2.5 of this handbook (trustee's duty of impartiality).

[531] 5 Scott & Ascher §33.4.

[532] 5 Scott & Ascher §33.4.

[533] Restatement (Third) of Trusts §66(1).

[534] Uniform Trust Code §412(a).

[535] 5 Scott & Ascher §33.4 nn 39–44.

[536] Purcella v. Olive Kathryn Purcella Trust, 325 P.3d 987 (Alaska 2014).

[537] Kristoff v. Centier Bank, 985 N.E.2d 20 (Ind. App. 2013).

only purpose, the court declined to consider extrinsic evidence that might have suggested that the settlor's dispositive wishes were something other than what had been expressed in the writing. That others as well as the petitioner had contingent equitable interests under the trust did not help her case. The plain meaning rule is covered generally in Section 8.15.6 of this handbook.

Certainly, a change-of-circumstances judicial reformation of the dispositive terms of a trust is less problematic from a policy perspective, and also less likely to encroach upon someone's preexisting equitable property rights, when only one person is in possession of the entire equitable interest, that is when there is only one beneficiary.[538] While the third Restatement may have opened the door a crack when it comes to re-arranging multiple equitable interests pursuant to a reformation action, it is still just a crack: "[I]t is appropriate that courts act with particular caution in considering a modification or deviation that can be expected to diminish the interest(s) of one or more of the beneficiaries in favor of one or more others."[539]

And we cannot forget the settlor in all of this. The lodestar that should guide a court in determining whether and how to reform the dispositive terms of a noncharitable trust is and should remain first and foremost what the settlor would have wanted as divined from the terms of the trust, not what the beneficiaries would like.[540]

Posture of the trustee in a trust reformation action. In the face of the trustee's duty to defend his trust, a topic we take up generally in Section 6.2.6 of this handbook, it is hard to see how a trustee can properly maintain a neutral posture in a contested substantive trust reformation action, particularly if some but not all of the beneficiaries are seeking to reorder and/or diminish the ostensible equitable property rights of their cobeneficiaries, and even more so if the terms of the trust are patently and latently unambiguous. At trust expense the trustee should mount a vigorous opposition to the action, unless to do so would be unreasonable; and the trustee certainly should not initiate it, as to do so would most assuredly implicate the trustee's duty of impartiality, a topic we take up generally in Section 6.2.5 of this handbook.

Rectification. It is said that "Courts of Equity do not rectify contracts; they may and do rectify instruments purporting to have been made in pursuance of the terms of contracts."[541] When a trust is incident to a contract, that is to say when consideration is involved,[542] the doctrine of rectification may be available to correct a mistake, provided the mistake is one of expression that is common to all parties:[543]

---

[538] *See generally* 5 Scott & Ascher §33.4; *but see* §8.15.7 of this handbook (the *Claflin* doctrine (material purpose doctrine)).
[539] Restatement (Third) of Trusts §66 cmt. b.
[540] 5 Scott & Ascher §33.4.
[541] Mackenzie v. Coulson (1869) L.R. 8 Eq. 368 at 375, *per* James V.C.
[542] *See generally* Lewin ¶4-58.
[543] Snell's Equity ¶14-14(a).

There will be cases where the terms of the instrument do not accord with the agreement between the parties: a term may have been omitted, or an unwanted term included, or a term may be expressed in the wrong way. In such cases, equity has power to reform, or rectify, that instrument so as to make it accord with the true agreement. What is rectified is not a mistake in the transaction itself, but a mistake in the way in which that transaction has been expressed in writing.[544]

Reformation and resolving ambiguities distinguished. There is a difference between reformation and resolving an ambiguity. The latter involves the interpretation of language already in the instrument.[545] The former, on the other hand, "may involve the addition of language not originally in the instrument, or the deletion of language originally included by mistake. . . ."[546] The extrinsic evidence, however, needs to meet the higher, *i.e.*, intermediate, clear and convincing standard. A lower standard and we could have a wholesale destabilization of trust settlements. "In determining the settlor's original intent, the court may consider evidence relevant to the settlor's intention even though it contradicts an apparent plain meaning of the text."[547]

Harmless-error rule. The more technically focused harmless-error rule is discussed in Section 8.15.53 of this handbook as it applies to the creation, revocation, and amendment of self-settled revocable trusts.

Substantive equitable deviation. It is not entirely clear what the practical difference is between UTC substantive equitable reformation and UTC substantive equitable deviation. The latter topic we take up in Section 8.15.20 of this handbook.

The decanting alternative. Is it possible to reform a trust term via a trust-to-trust decanting? Decanting as an alternative to the trust reformation action is taken up in Section 3.5.3.2(a) of this handbook.

§8.15.23   *The Thellusson Act*

Finally, in 1798, came the great case of Thellusson v. Woodford. . . . *The eccentricity of the will and the large amount involved excited great interest in the case. The arguments were of the most elaborate character, and the judges did not conceal their dislike of the will, but no one of the many eminent lawyers who took part in the decision seems to have felt any doubt in the case—*John Chipman Gray[548]

In 1800, Parliament enacted the Thellusson Act.[549] "It prohibited accumulations for a longer term than any one of the following: (1) the life of the grantor; (2) 21 years from the death of the grantor or testator; (3) during the

---

[544] Snell's Equity ¶ 14-02.

[545] Snell's Equity ¶ 14-02.

[546] Snell's Equity ¶ 14-02.

[547] Snell's Equity ¶ 14-02.

[548] John Chipman Gray, The Rule Against Perpetuities §190 (4th ed. 1942).

[549] Stat. 39 & 40 Geo. III, c. 98 (1800). *See generally* John Chipman Gray, The Rule Against Perpetuities, Appendix B (4th ed. 1942).

minority or respective minorities of any person or persons who shall be living or in *ventre sa mere*" "at the death of the grantor or testator; or (4) during the minority or respective minorities of any person or persons who under the instrument directing accumulations would, for the time being, if of full age, be entitled to the income so directed to be accumulated."[550] The Act was a political reaction to the decision of the Lord Chancellor in *Thellusson v. Woodford*[551] upholding a trust that provided for income to accumulate until the death of the last survivor of the settlor's issue who were alive at his death.[552] The trust did not violate the rule against perpetuities.[553]

Cross references. As to how accumulation trusts are dealt with in the United States, the reader is referred to Section 8.15.8 of this handbook (rule against accumulations). As to how England is currently dealing with accumulation trusts, the reader is referred to ¶5-81 through ¶5-108 of Lewin on Trusts. Scotland's trust analog (the Tartan trust) is discussed generally in Section 8.12.1 of this handbook. While not subject to a rule against perpetuities, the Tartan trust is subject to the rule against accumulations. "Like the English and Welsh . . . [accumulations] . . . rule, the Scottish rule originated in the *Thellusson Act* and is now enshrined in legislation."[554]

§8.15.24   Reciprocal Trust Doctrine

It is a fundamental principle of trust law that if a person furnishes consideration for the creation of a trust, that person is the settlor.[555] Thus, if *A1* establishes a trust for the benefit of *A2 in consideration of A2* establishing a similar trust for the benefit of A1, then under the reciprocal trust doctrine, *A1* is deemed the settlor of the trust for *A1*'s benefit and *A2* is deemed the settlor of the trust for *A2*'s benefit.[556] In other words, each trust is deemed self-settled.[557] Accordingly, upon the death of *A1*, the property of the trust that was ostensibly created by *A2* for *A1*'s benefit "is included in . . . *[A1's]* . . . gross estate . . . [for federal estate tax purposes] . . . because of one or more 'retained' powers, interests or control under Sections 2036-2038."[558] Note, however, that in the tax context, there need not be an enforceable contract for the doctrine to be

---

[550] Lewis M. Simes, *Statutory Restrictions on the Accumulation of Income*, 7 U. Chi. L. Rev. 409 (1940). *See also* John Chipman Gray, The Rule Against Perpetuities, Appendix B (4th ed. 1942).

[551] 4 Ves. Jr. 227 (Ch. 1798), *aff'd*, 11 Ves. Jr. 112 (H.L. 1805). *See generally* John Chipman Gray, The Rule Against Perpetuities, Appendix B (4th ed. 1942).

[552] 2 Scott & Ascher §9.3.10; John Chipman Gray, The Rule Against Perpetuities, Appendix B (4th ed. 1942).

[553] 4 Ves. Jr. 227 (Ch. 1798), *aff'd*, 11 Ves. Jr. 112 (H.L. 1805). *See generally* 1A Scott on Trusts §62.11; John Chipman Gray, The Rule Against Perpetuities, Appendix B (4th ed. 1942).

[554] Debbie King, *Tartan trusts*, 23 STEP J. 27 (Issue 3/Apr. 2015).

[555] 3 Scott & Ascher §15.4.4; 2A Scott on Trusts §156.3.

[556] 3 Scott & Ascher §15.4.4; 2A Scott on Trusts §156.3.

[557] *See generally* §8.43 of this handbook (who is the settlor of the trust?).

[558] Bogert §273.45 at 333.

implicated. "Instead, its application requires 'only that the trusts be interrelated, and that the arrangement, to the extent of mutual value, leaves the settlors in approximately the same economic position as they would have been in had they created trusts naming themselves as life beneficiaries.'"[559] In the creditors' rights context, however, the settlors must have been in an actual agency and/or contractual relationship for the reciprocal trust doctrine to be implicated such that the trusts are deemed self-settled.[560]

§8.15.25 Doctrine of Undisclosed Principal

The inscrutable thing is chiefly what I hate; and be the white whale agent, or be the white whale principal, I will wreak that hate upon him.—Ahab[561]

Under the common law of agency, if an agent who has not disclosed the agency's existence enters into a contract with *X* on behalf of the principal, *X* may enforce the contract against the principal upon the principal's coming forth or being discovered.[562] This is the doctrine of undisclosed principal. "Much can be explained in terms of trust law."[563] The agent holds the legal title to the contractual rights, *i.e.*, the property, as trustee for the benefit of the principal. The principal holds the equitable interest. The agent-trustee is subject to the control of the principal-beneficiary in the same way that the trustee of a nominee trust is subject to the control of those with the shares of beneficial interests, or that the trustee of a revocable inter vivos trust is subject to the control of the settlor.[564]

§8.15.26 Fraud on a Special Power Doctrine

The case law relating to fraud on a power stretches back as far as Aleyn v. Belcher in 1758, but the most recent leading case is the decision of the Privy Council in Vatcher v. Paull [1915].[565]

---

[559] 3 Scott & Ascher §15.4.4 (citing to United States v. Estate of Grace, 395 U.S. 316, 324 (1969)).

[560] *See generally* §5.3.3.1 of this handbook (reaching settlor's reserved beneficial interest) and §8.43 of this handbook (who is the settlor of the trust?); 3 Scott & Ascher §15.4.4 (Determining Who Is the Settlor).

[561] Herman Melville, Moby-Dick, Ch. 36.

[562] Floyd R. Mechem, Outlines of the Law of Agency 96–99 (1952).

[563] Mechem, Outlines of the Law of Agency at 97.

[564] Mechem, Outlines of the Law of Agency at 97–98. *See generally* §8.11 of this handbook (what are the duties of the trustee of a revocable inter vivos trust?) and §9.6 of this handbook (trusts that resemble corporations or agencies) (discussing the nominee trust).

[565] Ryan Myint, *Trustee Powers: Honest Fraud?*, Tr. & Est. L. & Tax J. (Jan./Feb. 2005), No. 63, at 8 (citing to Aleyn v. Belcher (1758) 1 Eden 132 (England) and Vatcher v. Paull, [1915] AC 372 (England)). *See also* Kerry Ayers, *Fraud on a power revisited*, 16(10) STEP J. 54–55 (Nov. 2008).

Fiduciary discretionary powers in the trustee. "The notion of a fraud on a power itself rests on the fundamental juristic principle that any form of authority may only be exercised for the purpose conferred, and in accordance with its terms."[566] In this context, the term *fraud* has a particular meaning, namely, "it denotes an improper motive in which a power given for one purpose is improperly used for another purpose."[567] Where there has been a fraud on a power, the exercise that gave rise to the fraud is invalidated:

> Public policy does not permit the creator of a trust to deprive the court of all control. Thus, the court will interpose if a trustee takes a bribe for making an investment. So also, the court will set aside a payment to a beneficiary if the trustee receives consideration for making the payment, even if the terms of the trust give the trustee broad discretion in distributing the trust property among various beneficiaries.[568]

The motive to benefit a nonobject of a power can be benign, *e.g.*, compassion. An example of a compassionate fraud on a power might be discretionary distributions made by a trustee for the direct or indirect benefit of orphaned children, the governing instrument having made provision only for their deceased parents.[569] We have already given an example of a not-so-benign fraud on a power, namely, a discretionary distribution to a permissible beneficiary that is conditioned on a bribe. A kickback of a certain percentage to the trustee also would not be a good idea.[570] Unauthorized social investing would be an example of a fraud on a discretionary administrative power.[571] Another example would be the trustee of a discretionary support trust who makes a distribution to a beneficiary while on actual or constructive notice that the beneficiary intends to gift away the property to a nonbeneficiary, a fact pattern that is discussed in Section 3.5.3.2(a). of this handbook. A discretionary fiduciary decanting to a new trust for the benefit of nonbeneficiaries, that is for the benefit of nonobjects of the trustee's discretionary power under the old trust, also may implicate the fraud on a power doctrine.[572] Such discretionary fiduciary distributions in further trust (decanting) are discussed generally in Section 3.5.3.2(a) of this handbook as well.

Nonfiduciary special/limited/nongeneral powers of appointment. The expression *fraud on a power* applies not only to trustee discretions but also to nonfiduciary special/limited/nongeneral powers of appointment. "If, in making

---

[566] Wong & ors v. Burt & ors., [2004] NZCA 174 (New Zealand).

[567] Wong & ors v. Burt & ors., [2004] NZCA 174 (New Zealand).

[568] 3 Scott & Ascher §18.2.3 (When Trustee Acts Dishonestly). *See also* §6.1.3.4 of this handbook (unauthorized social investing having some of the characteristics of a fraud on an administrative power).

[569] *See, e.g.*, Wong & ors v. Burt & ors., [2004] NZCA 174 (New Zealand).

[570] *See generally* Restatement (Third) of Trusts §87 cmt. c.

[571] *See generally* §6.1.3.4 of this handbook (indirect benefit accruing to the trustee).

[572] *See, e.g.*, Kain v. Hutton [2008] 3NZLR589 (New Zealand) (finding that a particular exercise of a fiduciary power in further trust (decanting) was not a fraud on the power as the trustee and primary beneficiary of the new trust was a permissible beneficiary under the old trust).

an appointment to a permissible appointee, the donee's purpose was to circumvent the donee's scope of authority by benefitting an impermissible appointee (a nonobject), the donee has acted impermissibly."[573] An appointment under such a power to a person who is not a permissible object of the power, *i.e.*, to an impermissible appointee or nonobject,[574] is invalid, unless there has been an equitable election.[575] That having been said, a valid appointment to a trustee who is nominally not a permissible object of the power does not implicate the fraud on a special power doctrine absent special facts, the trustee receiving no beneficial interest incident to the exercise in further trust.[576]

Contracts to appoint. The donee of a presently exercisable nongeneral power of appointment may not enter into an enforceable contract to exercise the power if the promised appointment confers a benefit on an impermissible appointee.[577] "A contract confers a benefit on an impermissible appointee if the consideration given by the promisee for the contract inures to the benefit of an impermissible appointee. The promised appointment inures to the benefit of an impermissible appointee whenever the property appointed pursuant to the terms of the contract would be an appointment in fraud of the power."[578] It should be noted that the section of the Restatement (Third) of Property (Wills and Other Donative Transfers) that is devoted to the intersection of powers of appointment and contract, namely Section 21.1, is miscaptioned. The caption reads "Enforceability of Contract to *Appoint* a Presently Exercisable Power." It should read contract to *exercise*, not to appoint. A power is exercised. It is the subject property that is appointed. In the trust context, that would generally be the property to which the trustee has the legal title. The identical error is repeated in the captioning of Section 21.2, which deals with contracts to exercise powers that are not presently exercisable.

Cross-references. The doctrine of equitable election is taken up in Section 8.15.82 of this handbook, powers of appointment generally in Section 8.1.1 of this handbook. The fraud on a special power doctrine is not to be confused with the rule that equity will aid the defective exercise of a power of appointment, a topic that is covered in Section 8.15.88 of this handbook. Usually worth exploring is whether a timely application of the doctrine of selective allocation (marshalling), which is discussed in Section 8.15.79 of this handbook, might serve to mitigate the adverse consequences of an impermissible appointment. The failure altogether to exercise a nongeneral *nonfiduciary* power of appointment as a violation *by the donee* of the power-in-trust doctrine is taken up in Section 8.15.90 of this handbook.

---

[573] Restatement (Third) of Property (Wills and Other Donative Transfers) §19.16 cmt. a.

[574] *See* Restatement (Third) of Property (Wills and Other Donative Transfers) §17.2(d) (defining an impermissible appointee or nonobject as anyone who is not a permissible appointee).

[575] Restatement (Third) of Property (Wills and Other Donative Transfers) §19.15 ("An appointment that benefits an impermissible appointee is ineffective.").

[576] Restatement (Third) of Property (Wills and Other Donative Transfers) §19.15 cmt. e. *See generally* §8.1.2 of this handbook (exercises of powers of appointment in further trust).

[577] *See* Restatement (Third) of Property (Wills and Other Donative Transfers) §21.1.

[578] Restatement (Third) of Property (Wills and Other Donative Transfers) §21.1 cmt. f.

Some common applications of the fraud on a special power doctrine. Here are some common applications of the fraud on a special power doctrine:

- "Appointment to permissible appointee conditioned on permissible appointee conferring benefit on impermissible appointee.
- Appointment to permissible appointee subject to a charge in favor of impermissible appointee.
- Appointment to permissible appointee in trust for the benefit of an impermissible appointee.
- Appointment to permissible appointee in consideration of benefit conferred upon or promised to impermissible appointee.
- Appointment primarily for the benefit of impermissible appointee-creditor of a permissible appointee."[579]

A hypothetical. An appointment the purpose of which is to circumvent the terms of the power, such as incident to an agreement between the donee and appointee that the appointee shall divert some or all of the appointed property to a nonobject of the power, is void.[580] Let us assume that under a trust *C* is given a limited/special/nongeneral power to appoint the trust property to one or more of a class of people consisting of *X*, *Y*, and *Z*. Let us assume that *C* appoints the property to *X* in consideration of *X*'s bestowing benefits on *C* or a third party. Under the fraud on a power doctrine, the exercise would be ineffective.[581] The reason? "[A]n element is injected into the motivation of the exercise of the power which is foreign to the intent of the donor in creating the power for the benefit of the objects."[582]

Quasi-antilapse. In the future, however, there may be some appointments to nonobjects that are enforceable. We have in mind the radical departure from the settled law proposed by the Restatement (Third) of Property (Wills and Other Donative Transfers), specifically Section 19.12(c).[583] In a triumph of faux logic over common sense, it would afford the donee of a nongeneral power of appointment default authority to exercise the power directly in favor of a descendant of a predeceasing permissible appointee, *even though the descendant himself was not a permissible appointee under the express terms of the power grant.*[584] The predeceasing appointee apparently need not even be a relative protected by some antilapse statute. Here is the logic: "If an antilapse statute can substitute the descendants of a deceased appointee, the donee of the power should be allowed to make a direct appointment to one or more descendants of

---

[579] Restatement (Third) of Property (Wills and Other Donative Transfers) §19.16, Comments b through f.

[580] *See, e.g.,* In re Carroll's Will, 8 N.E.2d 864 (N.Y. 1937).

[581] Restatement (Second) of Property (Wills and Other Donative Transfers) §20.2.

[582] Restatement (Second) of Property (Wills and Other Donative Transfers) §20.2 cmt. f.

[583] California has had such a statute since 1982. *See* Cal. Prob. Code §674 (Death of permissible appointee before exercise of special power).

[584] The deceased permissible appointee, however, would have to have survived the execution of the instrument that created the power.

a deceased permissible appointee."[585] It should be noted that the Restatement (Third) proposes that even when an antilapse statute fails to expressly address an appointment to a deceased appointee, its "purpose and policy" should still apply to such an appointment *as if the appointed property were owned by either the donor or the donee*.[586] For the policy debate over whether antilapse should be applied to equitable interests under trusts generally, the reader is referred to Section 8.15.55 of this handbook.

Certain exercises of nongeneral powers in further trust may be exempt from the doctrine's application. In the case of a nongeneral equitable power that may be exercised in further trust (Special Power #1), any grant of *another nongeneral power of appointment* incident to the exercise in further trust (Special Power #2) must be for the benefit of the permissible appointees of Special Power #1.[587] Under the Restatement (First) of Property, only a permissible appointee of Special Power #1 could be a grantee of Special Power #2.[588] The topic of exercising powers of appointment in further trust is taken up in Section 8.1.2 of this handbook.

Under the Restatement (Third) of Property (Wills and Other Donative Transfers), specifically Section 19.14, however, an impermissible appointee of Special Power #1 may be a grantee as well.[589] The impermissible appointee, however, holds Special Power #2 in "confidence" for the benefit of the permissible appointees of Special Power #1. Unexplained in the commentary and Reporter's Notes to Section 19.14 is whether the impermissible appointee assumes any fiduciary duties incident to his stewardship of Special Power #2. Here is the only guidance proffered, guidance that is fraught with ambiguity: "Because the donor has imposed confidence in the donee to select which permissible appointees to benefit by an appointment, the donee is authorized to grant the selection power to any other person."[590]

By definition, the original donee of an equitable nonfiduciary nongeneral power is unconstrained by the fiduciary principle. The status of the donee's surrogate, however, is another matter. Loaded words like "confidence" and "benefit" suggest that the donee's surrogate may well be holding the Special Power #2 itself in trust for the benefit of the Special Power #1's permissible appointees. If what we have here is essentially the conversion of an equitable nonfiduciary power into some kind of a fiduciary one, then there is nothing in the Restatement (Third) of Property about how the fiduciary duties of the surrogate are to be coordinated with those of the express trustee in whom the title to the trust property resides, or even what the scope of those duties might be. Recall the discussion in Section 3.2.6 of this handbook of the ambiguous

---

[585] Restatement (Third) of Property (Wills and Other Donative Transfers) §19.12 cmt. f.

[586] Restatement (Third) of Property (Wills and Other Donative Transfers) §19.12(b).

[587] Restatement (Third) of Property (Wills and Other Donative Transfers) §19.14.

[588] Restatement (First) of Property §359(2) ("The donee of a special power can effectively exercise it by creating in an object an interest for life and a special power to appoint among persons all of whom are objects of the original power, unless the donor manifests a contrary intent.").

[589] Restatement (Third) of Property (Wills and Other Donative Transfers) §19.14 cmt. g(4).

[590] Restatement (Third) of Property (Wills and Other Donative Transfers) §19.14 cmt. g(4).

status of the trust protector vis-à-vis the express trustee, at least in certain situations. In any case, presumably a breach of the surrogate's duty of confidence would constitute in the first instance and at minimum a fraud on Special Power #1.

Constructive receipt and assignment versus fraud. Assume a *permissible appointee* constructively receives appointive property incident to the exercise of a non-general power of appointment. Possession, however, remains back with the trustee. The permissible appointee is free to turn around and assign the legal property interest to an impermissible appointee without running afoul of the fraud on a special power doctrine. The express trustee is merely acting as the ministerial agent of the permissible appointee/assignor in honoring the assignment. The Restatement (Third) of Property is in accord, although its explanation is flawed: "The appointment directly to the impermissible appointee in this situation is effective, being treated for all purposes as an appointment first to the permissible appointee, followed by a transfer by the permissible appointee to the impermissible appointee."[591] The appointment itself is not to the impermissible appointee. Not even indirectly. The appointment of the legal title is to the permissible appointee. It is only mere possession that is the subject of a direct transfer from the express trustee to the impermissible appointee.

The fraud on a special power doctrine, however, would be implicated if, in making an appointment to a permissible appointee, the *donee's* purpose is "to circumvent the donee's scope of authority by benefiting an impermissible appointee (a nonobject)."[592] Admittedly, the distinction between a constructive receipt followed by assignment and a fraud on a special power is a subtle one.[593] Ultimately, it hinges on the subjective intent of the donee of the power, not the final destination of the appointive property itself.[594]

Postreceipt expenditures benefiting impermissible appointees. It is unlikely that the postreceipt expenditure of appointed property by a permissible appointee for the benefit of an impermissible appointee would trigger a retroactive invalidation of the power exercise. This would even be the case had the donee been given advance notice of the permissible appointee's postreceipt plans for the appointed property. Take a permissible appointee's application of appointed property towards the purchase price of a house in which his

---

[591] Restatement (Third) of Property (Wills and Other Donative Transfers) §19.15 cmt. f.

[592] Restatement (Third) of Property (Wills and Other Donative Transfers) §19.16 cmt. a.

[593] Ascertaining the motive of the donee involves a subjective test. *See* Restatement (Third) of Property (Wills and Other Donative Transfers) §19.16 cmt. g. "Hence, only factors known to the donee can be considered in determining whether the donee was motivated in making the appointment to a permissible appointee to confer a benefit on an impermissible appointee." *Id.*

[594] The Restatement (Third) of Property (Wills and Other Donative Transfers) §19.16 cmt. g would seem to be in accord with this assertion:

Fulfillment of the intent of the donor that the property be devoted exclusively to the benefit of permissible appointees requires that an appointment be ineffective so far as it is motivated by the purpose of benefiting an impermissible appointee. That policy does not require the entire appointment to be invalidated in all cases. Circumstances may indicate that the desire to benefit impermissible appointees was the predominant motive for the appointment, that such desire affected only the amount of the appointment, or that such desire had no substantial effect. Ineffectiveness ensues only so far as necessary to overcome the impropriety of motive.

impermissible-appointee-grandchildren will be residing. Such an expenditure is unlikely to implicate the doctrine, absent special facts.[595] Most donees (and donors, as well) would subjectively view such a postreceipt application as benefiting the permissible appointee first and foremost.[596] "It is only when the evidence establishes that the donee's essential purpose was to confer direct benefits on impermissible appointees that the appointment fails...."[597]

The liability of a trustee who honors a fraudulent appointment. A trustee who transfers trust property to a permissible appointee for the benefit of an impermissible appointee such that the fraud on a special power doctrine is implicated incurs no liability as a consequence, unless the trustee knew or should have known of the *donee's* (powerholder's) fraud.[598] If the trustee knew or had reason to know of the donee's fraud, then the transfer would constitute a breach of trust.[599] In the case of such a breach of trust, the person entitled to the appointive assets may seek recovery from the trustee personally, as well as from the impermissible appointee who has been unjustly enriched.[600] Otherwise, the trustee would still have an obligation upon learning of the fraud "to notify the persons entitled to the appointive assets of their rights and to initiate action against the mistaken payee to recover the wrongfully dispensed assets."[601] When there is reasonable doubt as to whether there actually has been a fraud perpetrated on the special power, the trustee should petition the court for instructions and/or a declaratory judgment.[602]

Whether an impermissible appointee of a special power of appointment may transfer good title to a BFP. The rights of the good faith purchaser for value (BFP) of entrusted property is taken up generally in Section 8.15.63 of this handbook. As a general rule, an impermissible appointee of a special power of appointment may transfer to a BFP good title to the appointed property. The Restatement (Third) of Property's explanation of how the rule actually works in practice is inaccurate. Here is the description: "If an appointee of an ineffective appointment transfers the appointive assets to a purchaser for value, the purchaser is protected from liability, unless the purchaser knows or has reason to know that the appointment was a violation of the donee's scope of authority."[603] Absent special facts, the issue is not whether the purchaser incurs liability by taking the legal title from an impermissible appointee but whether equity will compel the purchaser to disgorge the property by means of a conveyance of title back to the trustee. This is particularly so in the case of a good faith transferee who furnishes no value in return. All he or she would need do is relinquish the title.

---

[595] Restatement (Third) of Property (Wills and Other Donative Transfers) §19.16 cmt. g.

[596] Restatement (Third) of Property (Wills and Other Donative Transfers) §19.16 cmt. g.

[597] Restatement (Third) of Property (Wills and Other Donative Transfers) §19.16 cmt. g.

[598] Restatement (Third) of Property (Wills and Other Donative Transfers) §19.17(b).

[599] Restatement (Third) of Property (Wills and Other Donative Transfers) §19.17 cmt. b.

[600] Restatement (Third) of Property (Wills and Other Donative Transfers) §19.17 cmt. b; §8.15.78 of this handbook (unjust enrichment).

[601] Restatement (Third) of Property (Wills and Other Donative Transfers) §19.17 cmt. b.

[602] Restatement (Third) of Property (Wills and Other Donative Transfers) §19.17 cmt. b; §8.42 of this handbook (actions for instructions and/or declaratory judgment).

[603] Restatement (Third) of Property (Wills and Other Donative Transfers) §19.18.

The Restatement (Second) of Property had it right: The transfer to a BFP of title to impermissibly appointed property is generally *effective*.[604] "The equitable right to upset the transfer, like other equitable interests, cannot be asserted against a bona fide purchaser."[605]

Now, it is possible that the phrase "protected from liability" is an oblique and fragmentary reference to the unfortunate concept of "liability in restitution," which underpins the newly minted Restatement (Third) of Restitution and Unjust Enrichment: "A person who is unjustly enriched at the expense of another is subject to liability in restitution."[606] But where is the commentary linking the two Restatement (Third)s? The Restatement (First) of Restitution quite sensibly refrained from characterizing the generic obligation to make restitution as a liability.[607]

If the purchaser of the impermissibly appointed property may keep it, what then? The answer is that the person otherwise entitled to the appointive assets may recover from the impermissible appointee the greater of the following two amounts: (1) the consideration received for the property; (2) the value of such property.[608] Otherwise the impermissible appointee would be unjustly enriched.[609]

A general power to appoint only to the donee's creditors. "A general power under which the donee is free to appoint to himself or herself or to his or her estate has no impermissible appointee."[610] The Restatement (Third) of Property (Wills and Other Donative Transfers), however, proposes that a power to appoint only to the donee's creditors permits only such an appointment, *even though the power is general*.[611] Powers of appointment are covered generally in Section 8.1.1 of this handbook. The Restatement (Second) of Property adopted a similar posture.[612] In neither Restatement, however, is, or was, any light shed on the policy behind the proposition, in the Reporter's Notes, or anywhere else for that matter. The proposition just hangs there.

As the *primary* subjective motive behind most such creditor-focused general grants has to be to benefit the donee by indirection, not to bestow some gratuitous benefit on the donee's creditors, it is hard to see how a deviation from the express terms of the typical grant could somehow implicate the fraud on a power doctrine, particularly in light of the maxim: Equity looks to the intent rather than to the form.[613] On the other hand, in a given situation, an appointment other than to the creditors of the donee might well have been duly

---

[604] Restatement (Second) of Property (Wills and Other Donative Transfers) §20.4.

[605] Restatement (Second) of Property (Wills and Other Donative Transfers) §20.4 cmt. a.

[606] Restatement (Third) of Restitution and Unjust Enrichment §1.

[607] Restatement (First) of Restitution §1 ("A person who has been unjustly enriched at the expense of another is required to make restitution to the other.").

[608] Restatement (Third) of Property (Wills and Other Donative Transfers) §19.18 cmt. b.

[609] *See generally* §8.15.78 of this handbook (unjust enrichment).

[610] Restatement (Third) of Property (Wills and Other Donative Transfers) §19.15 cmt. b.

[611] Restatement (Third) of Property (Wills and Other Donative Transfers) §19.13(b) and §19.15 cmt. b.

[612] Restatement (Second) of Property (Wills and Other Donative Transfers) §19.1 cmt. b.

[613] *See generally* §8.12 of this handbook (equity's maxims).

considered by the donor *not* to be in the best interests of the donee. The donee straitjacketed by education loans comes to mind. In that case, equity ought to honor the narrow focus and intent of the power grant. To do otherwise would be to abet a fraud on a *general* power.

§8.15.27   The Bosch Decision

There is no federal property law. As a result, the federal transfer tax system looks to state law to determine whether property has been transferred in a manner that is subject to tax under the federal estate, gift, or generation-skipping transfer tax.[614]

Bosch is a 1967 decision of the U.S. Supreme Court that arose out of a controversy involving the validity of the purported release of a general inter vivos power of appointment under an inter vivos trust created by a husband for the benefit of his wife.[615] The husband had died. If the widow had validly released the power during his lifetime, then the corpus of the trust would not have qualified for the marital deduction. The executor claimed the marital deduction, taking the position that the release was invalid as a matter of state property law. The executor was supported by certain probate court rulings.

Federal tax litigation ensued over whether the corpus of the trust qualified for the marital deduction, the IRS having issued a tax-deficiency notice. The issue that the U.S. Supreme Court ultimately was asked to decide was a narrow one: Is a federal court or agency in a federal estate tax controversy conclusively bound by a state trial court adjudication of property rights or characterization of property interests when the United States is not made a party to the proceeding?

The holding, which has come to be known as the *Bosch* decision, was that a trial court adjudication is insufficient to bind federal authorities when an estate tax liability turns upon the character of a property interest. What is needed is an adjudication by the state's highest court. It should be noted that "four circuits, and certain other courts, notwithstanding . . . [*Bosch*'s] . . . rejection of the adversity test . . . , have focused on the presence or absence of adversity in the lower court proceedings."[616]

Why would making the United States a party to the state court proceeding not be a simple solution to the *Bosch* problem? The simple answer is the doctrine of sovereign immunity. "The government will be dismissed as a party in a state court action unless Congress has specifically waived sovereign immunity, which it has done in very limited instances in the tax arena (none of which involve trust reformation)."[617]

---

[614] Shirley L. Kovar, *Adversity After* Bosch, 28 ACTEC L.J. 88, 89 (2002).

[615] Comm'r v. Bosch's Estate, 387 U.S. 456, 87 S. Ct. 1776 (1967).

[616] Shirley L. Kovar, *Adversity After* Bosch, 28 ACTEC L.J. 88, 94 (2002).

[617] Barry F. Spivey, *Completed Transactions, Qualified Reformation and* Bosch: *When Does the IRS Care about State Law of Trust Reformation?*, 26 ACTEC Notes 345, 346 (2001).

One more thing: *Bosch* involves prospective state court determinations of state property rights. As a general rule, "[t]he Internal Revenue Service, supported by decisions of the U.S. Tax Court and other federal courts, will not recognize as effective for tax purposes a judicial reformation or other action that would retroactively change the tax consequences of a completed transaction."[618] This has come to be known as the completed transaction rule.[619]

§8.15.28   The Cy Pres Doctrine Applicable to Charities

[A] liberal construction is to be given to charitable donations, with a view to promote and accomplish the general charitable intent of the donor, . . . and when this cannot be strictly and literally done, this court will cause it to be fulfilled, as nearly in conformity with the intent of the donor as practicable.[620]

The Uniform Trust Code provides that "if a particular charitable purpose becomes unlawful, impracticable, impossible to achieve, or wasteful . . . the court may . . . modify or terminate the trust by directing that the trust property be applied or distributed, in whole or in part, in a manner consistent with the settlor's charitable purposes."[621] This is a codification of the court's inherent power to apply the doctrine of *cy pres*, or what one court has referred to as the doctrine of approximation.[622] Application of the *cy pres* doctrine, an alternative to the imposition of a resulting trust,[623] is discussed in some detail in Section 9.4.3 of this handbook. The Restatement (Third) of Trusts touches on the origins of the doctrine:

> At common law in England, a prerogative power of cy pres, exercisable by the Crown in certain circumstances and without regard to the settlor's intent, developed in addition to the judicial power in the Chancellor. The prerogative power (or legislative counterpart) has not been recognized in the United States, although legislation may reasonably regulate the extent and exercise of the cy pres power of courts. The judicial power of cy pres has evolved in this country along lines generally similar to the equity power under English common law.[624]

---

[618] Spivey, *Completed Transactions, Qualified Reformation and* Bosch: *When Does the IRS Care about State Law of Trust Reformation?*, 26 ACTEC Notes at 346–347. "The only trust reformations that will be retroactively effective when there is a completed transaction for tax purposes—the exceptions to the general rule—are the 'qualified reformations' permitted under federal law." Spivey, *Completed Transactions, Qualified Reformation and* Bosch: *When Does the IRS Care about State Law of Trust Reformation?*, 26 ACTEC Notes at 347. "Qualified reformations" would include charitable split-interest trusts, qualified domestic trusts, and qualified personal residence trusts.

[619] Barry F. Spivey, *Completed Transactions, Qualified Reformation and* Bosch: *When Does the IRS Care about State Law of Trust Reformation?*, 26 ACTEC Notes 346–347 (2001).

[620] American Acad. of Arts & Sci. v. Harvard Coll., 12 Gray (78 Mass.) 582, 596 (1832).

[621] UTC §413 (available at <http://www.uniformlaws.org/Act.aspx?title=Trust%20Code>).

[622] Tincher v. Arnold, 147 F. 665 (7th Cir. 1906).

[623] UTC §413 (available at <http://www.uniformlaws.org/Act.aspx?title=Trust%20Code>).

[624] Restatement (Third) of Trusts §67 cmt. a. For more on the difference between judicial *cy pres* and prerogative *cy pres*, prerogative *cy pres* possibly being "derived from the power exercised by

As noted, judicial *cy pres* power was vested in the chancellor and prerogative *cy pres* power in the king. "Dispositions under the prerogative power seem to have occurred primarily in two classes of cases: first, those in which property was given for a purpose that was illegal but that, except for the illegality, would have been charitable; and, second, those in which property was given directly to charity, but without any indication of a specific charitable purpose and without any indication that a trustee was to administer the charity."[625] For more on the nonrecognition in the United States of prerogative or legislative *cy pres*, see Section 9.4.4 of this handbook. Suffice it to say, "the prerogative power has no place in American jurisprudence."[626]

The doctrines of *cy pres* and deviation[627] should not be confused with the variance power granted the trustees of a charitable foundation in its governing documentation.[628] The *cy pres* doctrine applicable to charities also should not be confused with an ancient exception to the rule that the question of remoteness will not affect the construction of limitations expressed in unambiguous language.[629]

§8.15.29 The Public Trust Doctrine (Coastlines)

The colonial charters of 1641 and 1647 reserved to the public the right to fish, fowl, and boat in the area between high and low water, but the Massachusetts Supreme Judicial Court has refused to extend these meager rights to walking along the beach, let alone sunbathing or picnicking. All along our coastline, landowners are free to put up fences, post No Trespassing signs, and close their beaches to public access.[630]

"Throughout history, the shores of the sea have been recognized as a special form of property of unusual value; and therefore subject to different legal rules from those which apply to inland property."[631] At Roman law, the

---

the Roman emperor, who was sovereign legislator as well as supreme interpreter of the laws," the reader is referred to Jackson v. Phillips, 96 Mass. (14 Allen) 539, 575 (1867). *See also* 6 Scott & Ascher §39.5.1 (Judicial and Prerogative *Cy Pres*). In England, the king would exercise his prerogative *cy pres* power by indicating over his sign manual, that is over his signature, "the disposition that he wished to be made of the property, and the chancellor would order that the disposition be made." 6 Scott & Ascher §39.5.1.

[625] 6 Scott & Ascher §39.5.1.

[626] 6 Scott & Ascher §39.5.1.

[627] *See generally* §8.15.20 of this handbook (doctrine of [equitable] deviation).

[628] The concept of a variance power is discussed in §8.15.37 of this handbook.

[629] Here is the exception: "When land is devised to an unborn person for life, remainder to his children in tail, either successively or as tenants in common with cross-remainders, the unborn person takes an estate tail; and when land is devised to an unborn person for life, remainder to his sons in tail male, either successively or as tenants in common with cross-remainders, the unborn person takes an estate tail male." Unfortunately, this is also called the doctrine of *cy pres*. John Chipman Gray, The Rule Against Perpetuities §643 (4th ed. 1942) (*cy pres* construction).

[630] Alexandra Dawson, *George III Never Heard of Sunbathing*, Boston Sunday Globe, July 13, 2003, at H12.

[631] Boston Waterfront Dev. Corp. v. Commonwealth, 378 Mass. 629, 631, 393 N.E.2d 356, 358 (1979).

shores could not be said to belong to anyone.[632] So too the common law has afforded special status to lands lying between the high and low water marks. After the Magna Charta, a legal theory evolved that "divided the Crown's rights to shore land below high water mark into two categories: a proprietary jus privatum, or ownership interest, and a governmental jus publicum, by which the king held the land in his sovereign capacity as a representative of all the people."[633]

On this side of the Atlantic, the so-called public trust doctrine has its roots in the latter category. A version of the doctrine is recognized in Massachusetts whose Supreme Judicial Court "has frequently referred in its opinions to the notion that the Crown's ownership of shoreland, from which all Massachusetts titles historically derived, was 'in trust, for public uses.' "[634] Massachusetts is not alone. In 1842, Chief Justice Taney concluded that the grant of tidal lands from the king to the founders of New Jersey was intended to be a trust for the common use of the new community.[635] "On the California coast, abutting landowners own only the 'dry sand' areas in front of their homes, while the public has the right to use the tidal lands."[636]

§8.15.30   No-Further-Inquiry Rule

Viewed from the beneficiaries' perspective, especially that of remainder beneficiaries, efforts to prevent or detect actual improprieties can be expected to be inefficient if not ineffective.[637]

The no-further-inquiry rule addresses what facts are and are not relevant when the subject of litigation is a direct act of self-dealing on the part of a trustee.[638] The rule goes something like this: When a trustee without authority enters into a contract to acquire trust property, the beneficiaries may void the transaction even if the trustee had acted fairly with respect to the transaction.[639] The rule applies as well to sales to the trust. The rule and its policy underpinnings are covered in much greater detail in Section 6.1.3 of this handbook.

---

[632] Boston Waterfront Dev. Corp. v. Commonwealth, 378 Mass. 629, 631, 393 N.E.2d 356, 358 (1979).

[633] Boston Waterfront Dev. Corp. v. Commonwealth, 378 Mass. at 632, 393 N.E.2d at 358.

[634] Boston Waterfront Dev. Corp. v. Commonwealth, 378 Mass. at 633, 393 N.E.2d at 359.

[635] Martin v. Waddell, 41 U.S. (16 Pet.) 367, 10 L. Ed. 997 (1842).

[636] Alexandra Dawson, *Who Owns the Beach?*, Boston Sunday Globe, July 13, 2003, at H12. Hawaii has the most liberal beach access laws in the nation. Boston Sunday Globe, July 13, 2003, at H12.

[637] Restatement (Third) of Trusts §78 cmt. b.

[638] *See generally* 3 Scott & Ascher §17.2 (Duty of Loyalty).

[639] *See also* §6.1.3 of this handbook (duty to be loyal to the trust) and §8.24 of this handbook (who has the burden of proof in an action for breach of trust brought by the beneficiary against the trustee?).

§8.15.31 The Fertile Octogenarian Principle

At common law, a man or woman was treated as capable of having children, however old he or she might be. Thus a bequest to the children of the testator's brothers and sisters was held void on the ground that his parents might have further children, though they were both 66 years old.[640]

Since 1787 these Fertile Octogenarian cases have bedevilled estate planners and destroyed perfectly sensible wills and trusts with the remorselessness of a guillotine. The acme of silliness was achieved when an English court ruled that it was conclusively presumed that a widow of 67 could have a child and that the child thus born could in turn have a child before the age of five! . . . In all the Anglo-American world only one Irish judge, Gavan Duffy, J., rejected this nonsense.[641]

Under a classic application of the common law Rule against Perpetuities, a woman of any age is deemed capable of bearing children naturally up to the moment of her death.[642] This is the fertile octogenarian rule and it works like this: Assume a trust is established for the benefit of an 80-year-old woman. The terms of the trust further provide that upon her death, the trust property is to be held for the benefit of "her children," with the property to pass outright and free of trust to her then-living issue upon the death of the last child. "By the traditional English view the gift of the principal is bad; for the children . . . [of the woman] . . . include after-born children and . . . [the woman] . . . is conclusively presumed to be capable of having children until death."[643]

In other words, the woman, a life in being, could produce a child after the trust is established.[644] Those of her children who were alive at the time the trust was established could die the next day.[645] She could then die two days later. The "after-born" child could then die more than twenty-one years after the woman's death. That would trigger an impermissible vesting in the issue more than twenty-one years after the death of the last life in being, namely, the woman. The wait-and-see and reformation features of the Uniform Statutory Rule Against Perpetuities (USRAP) would essentially do away with the fertile octogenarian principle.[646]

---

[640] Lewin ¶ 5-41.

[641] W. Barton Leach, *Perpetuities in the Atomic Age: The Sperm Bank and the Fertile Decedent*, 48 A.B.A. J. 942 (1962) (referring to Judge Duffy's decision in Exham v. Beamish, [1939] I.R. 336 and reacting to In re Gaite's Will Trusts, [1949] 1 All E. R. 459).

[642] John Chipman Gray, The Rule Against Perpetuities §215 (4th ed. 1942).

[643] W. Barton Leach, *Perpetuities in a Nutshell*, 51 Harv. L. Rev. 638, 643 (1938). *See also* John Chipman Gray, The Rule Against Perpetuities §215 (4th ed. 1942).

[644] *See* John Chipman Gray, The Rule Against Perpetuities §215 (4th ed. 1942).

[645] *See* John Chipman Gray, The Rule Against Perpetuities §215 (4th ed. 1942).

[646] UPC §§2-901 (wait-and-see), 2-903 (reformation); §8.2.1.7 of this handbook (USRAP generally).

As to the related fertile decedent doctrine, the reader is referred to Professor Leach's somewhat tongue-in-cheek 1962 article.[647] For a discussion of the Rule against Perpetuities generally, the reader is referred to Section 8.2.1 of this handbook. The unborn widow principle is covered in Section 8.15.32 of this handbook; the doctrine of infectious invalidity in Section 8.15.72 of this handbook; and the "all-or-nothing" rule in Section 8.15.73 of this handbook, along with its two exceptions.

§8.15.32 The Unborn Widow Principle

The common law set a trap for the draftsman, in that a gift to vest on the death of the widow of a life in being was void because he might marry someone who was born after the date of the gift.[648]

Let us assume the following facts: A testamentary trust is established for the benefit of *C* and "his widow."[649] The terms of the trust further provide that upon the death of the survivor of the two, the property passes outright and free of trust to the settlor's then-living issue.[650] At the time the trust is created, *C*, who is 45 years old, has a spouse and a grown child. Under a classic application of the common law Rule against Perpetuities, the trust would have an unborn widow problem with the result that the provision for the benefit of the issue would be invalid at the time the trust was established regardless of the ultimate facts and circumstances.[651] This is because *C* "may marry again and his second wife may be a person who was unborn at the settlor's death."[652]

The analysis would go something like this: The first wife, the grown child, and *C* could die in that order and the "unborn widow" could then die more than 21 years after the death of *C*, her death triggering an impermissible vesting in certain non-life-in-being issue more than twenty-one years after the death of *C*, the last life in being.[653] That the equitable property interest of each member of the issue class is contingent upon the member outliving the unborn widow is a critical drafting defect.[654] The wait-and-see and reformation features of the USRAP would essentially do away with the unborn widow principle.[655]

---

[647] *Perpetuities in the Atomic Age: The Sperm Bank and the Fertile Decedent*, 48 A.B.A. J. 942 (1962). *See also* §8.15 of this handbook (welcoming a new addition to the law French lexicon, namely the term child *en ventre sa frigidaire*).

[648] Lewin ¶ 5-55 (noting that in 1964 England by statute "sprung" the unborn widow trap).

[649] *See generally* John Chipman Gray, The Rule Against Perpetuities §214 (4th ed. 1942) (the immateriality of probabilities).

[650] *See* John Chipman Gray, The Rule Against Perpetuities §214 (4th ed. 1942).

[651] *See* John Chipman Gray, The Rule Against Perpetuities §214 (4th ed. 1942).

[652] W. Barton Leach, *Perpetuities in a Nutshell*, 51 Harv. L. Rev. 638, 644 (1938).

[653] For a general discussion of the Rule against Perpetuities, the reader is referred to §8.2.1 of this handbook (the Rule against Perpetuities).

[654] *See* John Chipman Gray, The Rule Against Perpetuities §214 (4th ed. 1942).

[655] UPC §§2-901 (wait-and-see), 2-903 (reformation); §8.2.1.7 of this handbook (USRAP generally).

For a discussion of the Rule against Perpetuities generally, the reader is referred to Section 8.2.1 of this handbook. The fertile octogenarian principle is covered in Section 8.15.31 of this handbook; the doctrine of infectious invalidity in Section 8.15.72 of this handbook; and the "all-or-nothing" rule in Section 8.15.73 of this handbook, along with its two exceptions.

§8.15.33   The Anti-Netting Rule for Multiple Breaches

A misapplied anti-netting rule would make portfolio theory impossible to use, for the very essence of a portfolio strategy is diversification such that losses will be balanced out by gains in a way that makes the overall portfolio less risky and overall returns more dependable. A riskless portfolio would be one in which two securities had a negative covariance of minus one (-1). Any loss would be balanced out by a gain. It is a rational portfolio strategy to include some securities whose expected returns are negative, if, for example, in unusually difficult economic times their returns are positive and will balance out losses on the rest of the portfolio.[656]

It is black-letter law that "[a] trustee who is liable for a loss caused by a breach of trust may not reduce the amount of the liability by deducting the amount of profit that accrued through another and distinct breach of trust. . . ."[657] This is known as the anti-netting rule.[658] (If the breaches of trust, however, are not separate and distinct, the trustee is accountable only for the net gain or chargeable only with the net loss resulting therefrom.[659]) Without the anti-netting rule, a trustee under certain circumstances might be inclined to commit multiple breaches of trust. "For example, the trustee whose misconduct has caused a loss may take improper risks in pursuit of extra profits if those profits may serve to eliminate or reduce the amount of expected surcharge."[660] In Section 7.2.3.2 of this handbook we consider various possible methodologies for computing equitable damages against a trustee who, with respect to the

---

[656] Jeffrey N. Gordon, *The Puzzling Persistence of the Constrained Prudent Man Rule*, 62 N.Y.U. L. Rev. 52, 97 (1987).

[657] Restatement (Third) of Trusts §213 (balancing losses against profits) [provisional and superseded by §101 (offsetting profit against loss), which reads as follows: "The amount of a trustee's liability for breach of trust may not be reduced by a profit resulting from other misconduct unless the acts of misconduct causing the loss and the profit constitute a single breach."]. *See also* Restatement (Second) of Trusts §213 (balancing losses against gains).

[658] Loren C. Ipsen, *Trends in the Liability of Corporate Fiduciaries*, 24 Idaho L. Rev. 443, 450 (1989).

[659] Restatement (Third) of Trusts §213 (balancing losses against profits) [provisional and superseded by §101 (offsetting profit against loss)]. *See also* Restatement (Second) of Trusts §213 (balancing losses against gains). For factors determining whether breaches of trust are distinct, *see* Restatement (Third) of Trusts §213 cmt. f. [provisional and superseded by §101 cmt. c]; Restatement (Second) of Trusts §213 cmt. e.

[660] Restatement (Third) of Trusts §213 cmt. f. [provisional and superseded by §101 cmt. a]. "Similarly, but without the same degree of motivation to benefit personally, a trustee whose breach of trust has resulted in exceptional profits might be tempted later to take excessive risks if the prior success provided a degree of insulation from surcharge." Restatement (Third) of Trusts §213 cmt. f [provisional and superseded by §100 cmt. a]. *See generally* §7.2.3.2 of this handbook (damages).

same part of the trust property or its proceeds, has engaged in more than one breach of trust.[661]

§8.15.34   Virtual Representation Doctrine

"Often the doctrine of 'virtual representation' is employed so that some members of a class of beneficiaries are allowed to represent, as defendants, other beneficiaries who have similar or identical interests or may acquire them later."[662]

Assume a trust under which members of X class take a vested remainder interest subject to divestment upon the fulfillment of a condition subsequent.[663] If the condition is fulfilled, the property passes outright and free of trust to the then living members of Y class, Y class being the issue of the members of X class.

If there were litigation over whether the trustee had invested the principal prudently, the X class could represent the members of Y class in a jurisdiction that recognized the doctrine of virtual representation. Why? Because each class would have an identical interest in the subject of the litigation, namely, the well-being of the principal account.[664] On the other hand, if the litigation were over whether or not the condition subsequent had been fulfilled, the members of X class could not represent the members of Y class because the interests of each class in the litigation would be in conflict: It is in the interests of the members of X class that the status quo be preserved, that the condition subsequent had not been fulfilled; it is in the interests of the members of Y class that the members of X class be divested of their equitable interests, that the condition had been fulfilled.[665]

"If necessary parties, such as unborns, unascertained persons, minors or otherwise incompetent beneficiaries, are not served and cannot be represented under the doctrine of virtual representation, the appointment of a guardian or guardians ad litem may be necessary to protect the interests of such parties in the proceedings."[666] In any case, "virtual representation never assures the same finality in decree as does representation by a guardian ad litem."[667] For more on

---

[661] See generally Restatement (Second) of Trusts §212 cmt. a.

[662] Bogert §871. See also §8.14 of this handbook (when a guardian ad litem (or special representative) is needed; virtual representation issues).

[663] See, e.g., Robertson v. Hert's Admr. 312 Ky. 405, 227 S.W.2d 899 (1950) (involving virtual representation of a class of remaindermen who would take the equitable interest should another class be divested of its interest). See generally §8.30 of this handbook (the difference between a vested equitable remainder subject to divestment and a vested (transmissible) contingent equitable remainder).

[664] See generally UTC §304 cmt. (suggesting that whether identity of interest is present may depend upon the nature and subject of the litigation).

[665] For actual decisions in which the virtual representation doctrine has been applied, see Bogert §871, footnote 42. For a discussion of the UPC's approach to virtual representation, see §8.14 of this handbook.

[666] Bogert §871.

[667] In re Estate of Putignano, 82 Misc.2d 389, 395, 368 N.Y.S.2d 420, 428 (1975).

the virtual representation doctrine, the reader is referred to Section 8.14 of this handbook.

§8.15.35 Trustees de Son Tort; de Facto Trustees; Officious Intermeddlers

The direct connection between trustees de son tort and executors de son tort is ... not difficult to infer. The executor de son tort can be traced back to at least the 13th century, but there seems no reason to doubt that the institution and the problems which created it went back for some time before that. On the other hand the term trustee de son tort seems not to have been used until the mid-19th century, indeed it appears first to have been devised by Sir John Romilly MR in Hope v. Liddell (No 1). ...[668]

Trustees *de son tort; de facto* trustees. A person who intermeddles[669] with, and assumes the management of, trust property becomes a trustee by construction. The person is said to be a trustee *de son tort*.[670] A *de facto* trustee differs from a trustee *de son tort* in that the former assumes the office of trustee under a color of right or title.[671] "Where one without authority undertakes to execute a trust requiring the investment of a fund, he must carry all the risks, and make good all the losses, and have none of the profits. ..."[672] Trustees *de son tort* are "subject to the same rules and remedies"[673] as trustees who have been duly appointed. This goes for *de facto* trustees as well.[674]

A trusteeship *de son tort* has been described by English commentators as a type of institutional constructive trust.[675] "Institutional constructive trusts are trusts which arise from some preexisting fiduciary relationship before and apart from any breach of trust or duty, whereas remedial constructive trusts are imposed where no fiduciary relationship previously existed."[676]

---

[668] Nolan v. Nolan & ors, [2004] VSCA 109 (citing to Hope v. Liddell (No. 1), (1856) 21 Beav. 183 at 205.

[669] "If the word 'intermeddle' be used, it tends to confuse the issue to the extent that it suggests wrongful intermeddling, which frequently gives rise to cases where the question of liability is in issue, rather than circumstances in which the original intention is merely to act in the role of trustee in relation to certain property." Nolan v. Nolan & ors, [2004] VSCA 109.

[670] *See generally* Lewin ¶ 42-60 through ¶ 42-63 (England).

[671] Allen Trust Co. v. Cowlitz Bank, 210 Or. App. 648, 152 P.3d 974 (2006). *See also* In the Matter of the Estate of Max Sakow, 146 Misc. 2d 672, 676 (N.Y. 1990).

[672] Stephan v. Equitable Sav. & Loan Ass'n, 268 Or. 544, 559, 522 P.2d 478, 486 (1974).

[673] Stephan v. Equitable Sav. & Loan Ass'n, 268 Or. 544, 559, 522 P.2d 478, 486 (1974).

[674] Allen Trust Co. v. Cowlitz Bank, 210 Or. App. 648, 152 P.3d 974 (2006).

[675] *See, e.g.,* Lewin ¶ 7-11 (England). *See generally* §3.3 of this handbook (involuntary trustees) (in part discussing the constructive trust).

[676] Lewin ¶ 7-11 (England). "The proposition that constructive trusts are imposed on the holder of property against his intention is, however, one that needs to be approached with some caution since there are some trusts, often classified as constructive trusts, where the intention of the holder of property is critical to the creation of the trust, for example the case of a 'trustee' 'de son tort' or common intention trusts." Lewin ¶ 7-02.

Officious intermeddlers. Assume a trustee in breach of trust transfers an entrusted parcel of real estate to a third party who knows of the breach. Assume, also, that the third party then voluntarily proceeds to make improvements on the property, *e.g.*, by landscaping the front yard. Is the third party entitled to be reimbursed from the trust estate for the costs of those improvements? Probably not: "As is true in the law of contracts, a person is not entitled to recover for a benefit conferred if in conferring the benefit the person acted as an officious intermeddler."[677] The third party knew the parcel belonged to others. On the other hand, payments made in satisfaction of obligations that run with the property, *e.g.*, real estate taxes, probably are reimbursable.[678] For a general discussion of the rights of the beneficiary as against BFPs and non-BFPs of the trust property, the reader is referred to Section 5.4.2 of this handbook.

§8.15.36   Merger

Problems may arise when a thing belonging to one person is united to or mixed with that of another, as, for example, if I pour your oil into the same vat as my oil, or if I paint a picture on your canvas with my paints, or weld your silver handle on to my silver cup.[679]

The doctrine of merger applies to equitable interests under trusts. But the concept of merger is not of recent origin. We know this from the Digest of Justinian, a Roman emperor who was crowned in Constantinople in 527 A.D. At the end of 530, he constituted a commission to review and revise the books "on Roman law of the ancient jurists to whom the emperors gave authority to write and interpret the laws."[680] On December 16, 533, the Commission published a fifty-book digest of the law. The Digest itself received the force of law on December 30 of that year.

At Digest 8.4.10 is the doctrine *nulli res sua servit, i.e.*, no one can have a servitude over one's own property. If *X* had a right of way over *Y*'s land and then proceeded to purchase the land from *Y*, the right of way would be extinguished, the servitude having been swallowed up[681] by *X*'s full ownership interest. There was said to be a merger, or in Latin a *confusio* (a pouring or melting together). A merger or *confusio* could have practical consequences. If *X* then sold the land to *Z*, the right of way was not revived; and had there been no new reservation of a right of way, *X* would have lost his right of way over the land.

---

[677] 5 Scott & Ascher §29.1.8.6 9 (Credit for Expenditures to Improve Trust Property). *See also* Hawley v. Tesch, 88 Wis. 213, 59 N.W. 670, 677 (1894).

[678] 5 Scott & Ascher §29.1.8.6 9 (Credit for Expenditures to Improve Trust Property). *See also* Hawley v. Tesch, 88 Wis. 213, 59 N.W. 670, 677 (1894).

[679] Barry Nichols, An Introduction to Roman Law 133–136 (1962).

[680] R. W. Lee, The Elements of Roman Law 26 (1956).

[681] *See generally* Cornelius J. Moynihan, Introduction to the Law of Real Property 136 (2d ed. 1988) (discussing destructibility by merger).

As noted, the doctrine of merger applies to equitable interests under trusts. When *B*, the ostensible trustee, possesses not only the entire legal interest but also the entire equitable interest, then there is no trust. *B* is the full owner of the subject property and owes no fiduciary duties to himself, all rights being "merged" in him. "The equitable interest is said to merge into the legal title."[682] It is analogous to the principle that one may not enter into an enforceable contract with oneself, or otherwise owe duties to oneself that are enforceable in law or equity.[683]

The doctrine of merger as applied in the trust context is addressed in much more detail in Section 8.7 of this handbook.

§8.15.37   *The Variance Power*

Since the creation of the Cleveland Foundation in 1914, community foundations or community trusts have proliferated. In fact, in recent years, they have become one of the fastest growing areas of philanthropy, there now being approximately 500 such foundations worldwide, mostly in the United States.[684]

A donor who wishes to make a charitable gift may employ the medium of a community foundation, which can be organized as a trust, a corporation, or a hybrid of the two.[685] The distinguishing feature of a community foundation is the variance power that is granted to the fiduciary in the *governing documentation*. In the case of a community trust, the instrument might grant the trustees broad authority to "modify any restriction or condition on the distribution of funds for any specified charitable purposes or to specified organizations if in [its] ... sole judgment ... such restriction or condition becomes, in effect, unnecessary, incapable of fulfillment, or inconsistent with the charitable needs of the community. ..."[686]

Such broad grants of authority in part are intended to obviate the need for *cy pres* proceedings when and as circumstances change.[687] While the traditional focus of the *cy pres* doctrine has been on donor intent, even at the expense of the perceived needs of the community,[688] the focus of the variance power has been

---

[682] 5 Scott & Ascher §34.5 (a merger that triggers termination is not to be confused with the coalescing of the entire beneficial interest only in a single person, *e.g.*, when the sole remainder beneficiary of a trust acquires the trust's entire income interest).

[683] 5 Scott & Ascher §34.5.

[684] John Clymer, *Community Foundations and the Variance Power*, 26 ACTEC Notes, 217 (Winter 2000).

[685] *See generally* §9.8.1 of this handbook (the charitable corporation) (comparing the charitable trust and the charitable corporation).

[686] Treas. Reg. §1.170A-9(e)(11)(v)(B)(1).

[687] *See generally* §9.4.3 of this handbook (*cy pres*).

[688] *See, e.g.*, American Acad. of Arts & Sci. v. Harvard Coll., 12 Gray (78 Mass.) 582, 596 (1832).

on the evolving needs of the community, although one court invoking donor intent has second guessed a fiduciary's exercise of the variance power.[689]

§8.15.38   The Charitable Immunity Doctrine (The Trust Application)

To give damages out of a trust fund would not be to apply it to those objects whom the author of the fund had in view, but would be to divert it to a completely different purpose.[690]

The institution should be just before it is generous.[691]

Embedded in the common law is the principal that the funds of a charitable trust may not be diverted to those who have been tortiously injured by the trust. This is the trust application of the charitable immunity doctrine. The leading case for the proposition that the funds of a charitable trust are not available to tort claimants is the 1846 English case of *Feoffees of Heriot's Hospital v. Ross*.[692] The doctrine, which surfaced in the United States in 1876,[693] has at least three policy rationales, whether the charity operates as a corporation or a trust:[694]

- Charitable assets should not be diverted to noncharitable purposes, the so-called "trust fund theory,"
- He who avails himself of a charity's largesse agrees by implication to waive any right to sue the charity in tort,
- Because the charity (the master) derives no personal or private benefit from the actions of its employees (its servants), the doctrine of *respondeat superior* is inapplicable when it comes to the torts that its servants commit while on the job against third parties, a rationale that essentially leaves the charity on the hook for the torts of its governing board.[695]

Most of the charitable immunity cases have involved charitable corporations.[696] "Ordinarily where property is left to individual trustees or to a trust

---

[689] Community Serv. Soc'y v. New York Cmty. Trust, 713 N.Y.S.2d 712 (App. Div. 2000), *aff'd*, 751 N.E.2d 940 (N.Y. 2001).

[690] Feofees of Heriot's Hosp. v. Ross, 12 Clark & Fin. 507, 513, 8 Eng. Rep. 1508, 1510 (1846).

[691] Scott on Trusts §402 (1939).

[692] 12 Cl. & F. 507 (1846).

[693] MacDonald v. Massachusetts Gen. Hosp., 120 Mass. 432 (1876).

[694] *See generally* §9.4.2 of this handbook (standing to enforce charitable trusts).

[695] *See generally* 5 Scott & Ascher §37.3.13 (The Charitable Corporation); 5 Scott & Ascher §37.3.13.2 (the charitable trust).

[696] *See generally* 5 Scott & Ascher §§37.3.13 (The Charitable Corporation), 37.3.13.2 (The Charitable Trust). *See also* §9.8.1 of this handbook (the charitable corporation) (comparing the charitable trust and the charitable corporation).

company in trust for charitable purposes, the duty of the trustee is merely to invest the trust funds and apply the income for charitable purposes; and in such a case the question of liability in tort seldom arises."[697] Operating charities, particularly hospitals, tend to be incorporated.[698] In any case, a court under fundamental principles of trust law was traditionally reluctant to entertain a direct action by a third-party tort claimant against a trust estate, whether the trust was private or charitable. The action had to be against the trustee personally, a topic we cover in Section 7.3.3 of this handbook. It is the current state of the common law that the trustee of a charitable trust would be subject to personal liability to third persons for torts committed in the course of the administration of the trust, provided the trustee is personally at fault.[699] "When there are several trustees of a charitable trust, and tort liability arises out of the administration of the trust, and some of the trustees are at fault and others are not, the former, but not the latter, are personally liable to the person injured."[700]

The trend of the law has long been in the direction of repudiating the doctrine of charitable immunity.[701] The Restatement of Trusts is in support.[702] Though Massachusetts has abolished the doctrine of charitable immunity, it does limit a charity's liability to $20,000.[703] The liability cap is a creature of legislation.[704]

§8.15.39 The Rule Against Capricious [Trust] Purposes (Noncharitable Trusts)

The rule that the trust must be for the benefit of the beneficiaries reworks an older doctrine, the rule against capricious purposes.[705]

When a transferee holds property, purportedly in trust, for a noncharitable purpose that is purely capricious such that there is no one who can derive a benefit from the arrangement, the transferee must hold the property upon a

---

[697] Scott on Trusts §402; 5 Scott & Ascher §§37.3.13 (The Charitable Corporation), 37.3.13.2 (The Charitable Trust).

[698] *See generally* 5 Scott & Ascher §§37.3.13 (The Charitable Corporation), 37.3.13.2 (The Charitable Trust).

[699] Restatement (Second) of Trusts §402(1). *See generally* 5 Scott & Ascher §37.3.13.2; §7.3.3 of this handbook (liability [of trustee] as legal owner in tort to nonbeneficiaries).

[700] 5 Scott & Ascher §37.3.13.2.

[701] Restatement (Second) of Trusts §402(2) cmt. d. *See generally* 5 Scott & Ascher §§37.3.13 (The Charitable Corporation), 37.3.13.2 (The Charitable Trust).

[702] Restatement (Second) of Trusts §402(2).

[703] Mass. Gen. Laws ch. 231, §85K.

[704] Mass. Gen. Laws ch. 231, §85K. For a discussion of the events leading up to the enactment of §85k, *see* Connors v. Northeast Corp., 439 Mass. 469, 473, 789 N.E.2d 129, 132–133 (2003).

[705] John H. Langbein, *Mandatory Rules in the Law of Trusts*, 98 Nw. U. L. Rev. 1105, 1107 (2004).

resulting trust for the transferor or for the transferor's estate.[706] In other words, he must reconvey the property. He may not perform the trust.[707] That, in a nutshell, is the rule against capricious purposes in the noncharitable trust context.[708] The following trust purposes have been deemed capricious by courts: bricking up the windows and doors of a house for twenty years, laying waste the trust estate, throwing trust income into the sea, and expending trust income on monthly funeral services in memory of the settlor. Likewise, discharging salvoes of artillery upon the settlor's birthday has been deemed a capricious purpose. So also has keeping a clock or a portrait in repair. Again, we are in the noncharitable realm.

The rule against capricious purposes and the rule that a trust purpose may not violate public policy, which is addressed in Section 9.24 of this handbook, are easily conflated. In one case, for example, a testator impressed a trust upon two parcels of real estate. Its terms provided that no leases could be given for a period exceeding one year and that buildings erected on the properties could not exceed three stories in height. The court invalidated the restrictions:

> The restrictions militate too strongly against the interests of the beneficiaries and the public welfare to be sustained, particularly when it is remembered that they are designed to benefit no one, and are harmful to all persons interested, and we hold them invalid as against public policy.[709]

§8.15.40   The Rule Against Direct Restraints on Alienation: The Trust Exception

The rule against perpetuities and that against restraints upon alienation are in reality entirely distinct, the former being concerned only with the vesting of estates in right, and the latter with the limitation which may be imposed upon the enjoyment of the property.[710]

There are, however, many legal devices which may indirectly restrain alienation. Most important among these are the contingent future interest and the trust. But these devices are prevented from removing property from commerce to too great an extent, not by the rules as to direct restraints . . . , but by other rules such as the rule against perpetuities.[711]

The law has traditionally disfavored restrictions placed upon a property owner's right to alienate, *i.e.*, transfer, the property.[712] A restriction can be a

---

[706] 2 Scott & Ascher §12.11.7.

[707] 1 Scott & Ascher §9.3.13.

[708] *See generally* Restatement (Third) of Trusts §29 cmt. h (2003); Scott on Trusts §124.7.

[709] Colonial Trust Co. v. Brown, 105 Conn. 261, 135 A. 555, 564 (1926).

[710] Colonial Trust Co. v. Brown, 105 Conn. 261, 135 A. 555 (1926).

[711] Lewis M. Simes, Cases and Materials on the Law of Future Interests 508 (2d ed. 1951).

[712] *See generally* 6 American Law of Property, §§26.1–26.47 (A. J. Casner ed. 1952); 6 R. Powell, The Law of Real Property §§839–843 (P. Rohan rev. 1981); Restatement (Second) of Property (Wills and Other Donative Transfers) §§3.1–4.5. Note, however, that "[a]t common law lands were not devisable except by special custom in certain localities in England." Cornelius J.

blanket one or it can take the form of divestment upon an attempt to alienate.[713] If, for example, *A* were to devise a parcel of real estate to John Jones outright and free of trust but attempt by a provision in the will to restrict Jones's right to sell the property for a period of years, the restriction at common law might well be unenforceable. On the other hand, had the transfer been to *B* in trust for John Jones, the restriction might well be valid, though applicable to *both B* and John Jones. " . . . [T]here would be some party besides . . . [the devisee] . . . interested in the observance of the condition, with a right to take advantage of the breach, viz.: the heirs of the devisor. . . ."[714] This is an example of the trust exception to the doctrine that restraints on the alienability of property are void as against public policy. The trust, however, would still be subject to the durational requirements of the common law Rule against Perpetuities, even in those jurisdictions that have abolished the rule's application to certain trusts.[715]

§8.15.41 The Illusory Trust Doctrine

The fact that it . . . [the defendant] . . . desired to evade the law, as it is called, is immaterial, because the very meaning of a line in the law is that you intentionally may go as close to it as you can if you do not pass it.—Oliver Wendell Holmes, Jr.[716]

As a general rule, a self-settled revocable inter vivos trust is indeed a trust.[717] There is a line of cases, however, that have held that such a trust would be "illusory" if it were established for the purpose of depriving the surviving spouse of his or her postmortem spousal election rights.[718] Thus, upon the settlor's death, the property that is the subject of the "trust" would pass to the

---

Moynihan, Introduction to the Law of Real Property 32 (2d ed. 1988). "It was not until the first Statute of Wills was enacted in 1540 that a limited power to devise was granted to land owners." Moynihan, Introduction to the Law of Real Property 32 (2d ed. 1988).

[713] "At common law, however, prior to the statute *quia emptores*, a condition against alienation . . . [of a fee simple estate] . . . would in England have been good, because prior to that statute the feoffor or grantor of such an estate was entitled to the escheat on failure of heirs of the grantee, which was properly a possibility of reverter, and was treated as a reversion; so that the vendor did not, by the feoffment or conveyance part with the entire estate; but this reversion, dependent on this contingency, remained in him and his heirs, which gave them an interest to insist upon the condition and take the benefit accruing to them upon the breach." Mandelbaum v. McDonell, 29 Mich. 78, 18 Am. Rep. 61 (1874). The Statute *Quia Emptores* was enacted in 1290. It provided that "from henceforth it shall be lawful to every free man to sell at his own pleasure his lands and tenements or part of them, to that the feoffee shall hold the same lands or tenements of the chief lord of the same fee, by such service and customs as his feoffor held before." 18 Edw. I, c.1. The statute's name is derived from the two Latin words, *quia* (because or since) and *emptores* (purchasers), that open the statute.

[714] Mandlebaum v. McDonell, 29 Mich. 78, 18 Am. Rep. 61 (1874).

[715] *See generally* §8.2.1.9 of this handbook (abolition of the Rule against Perpetuities).

[716] Superior Oil Co. v. Mississippi, 280 U.S. 390, 395 (1930).

[717] *See, e.g.*, National Shawmut Bank v. Joy, 315 Mass. 457, 53 N.E.2d 113 (1944).

[718] *See, e.g.*, Newman v. Dore, 275 N.Y. 371, 9 N.E.2d 966 (1937); Seifert v. Southern Nat'l Bank of S.C., 305 S.C. 353, 409 S.E.2d 337 (1991). *See generally* §5.3.4 of this handbook (rights of beneficiary's spouse and children to trust property or equitable interest).

personal representative of the settlor's probate estate, not to the successor beneficiaries designated in the trust instrument. This is the so-called illusory trust doctrine. Some jurisdictions have repudiated the doctrine by case law.[719] Others have done so by legislation.[720] The Jersey Channel Islands had an analogous doctrine, embodied in the maxim *donner et retenir ne vaut (rien).* The Jersey maxim is covered in Section 8.15.45 of this handbook.

§8.15.42　*The Potential Possession Doctrine*

There is virtually no relevant caselaw.[721]

A trust is a fiduciary relationship with respect to property.[722] The doctrine of potential possession in the context of trusts may address whether a trust can be impressed upon future crops or on the unborn young of animals.[723] In other words, are such items property or mere expectancies? There is some analogous authority in contract law to the effect that they are assignable property interests, provided that at the time of an assignment—such as to the trustee of an inter vivos trust—the crops were planted or the young conceived. There appear to be no cases on point involving gratuitous transfers in trust, although title to crops not planted at adjudication of bankruptcy would probably not pass to the bankruptcy trustee.[724] Assignments in trust of future crops if for consideration, *i.e.,* if pursuant to the terms of a contract, have been upheld.[725]

§8.15.43　*The Diplock Principle*

The House of Lords was of the view that the . . . [trustees under the will of Caleb Diplock-] . . . were liable even though they did not know the trust was invalid, because its invalidity sufficiently appeared on the face of the will.[726] *The Restatement (Second) of Trusts, however, suggested a more liberal approach . . .* [727]

---

[719] *See, e.g.,* Sullivan v. Burkin, 390 Mass. 864, 872–873, 460 N.E.2d 572, 677 (1984) (prospectively affording a surviving spouse access to property in his or her deceased spouse's self-settled trust while declining to invoke the illusory trust doctrine).

[720] *See, e.g.,* S.C. Code §62-7-112.

[721] 2 Scott & Ascher §10.10.3.

[722] *See generally* §2.1.1 of this handbook (the inter vivos trust).

[723] *See generally* Scott on Trusts §86.3.

[724] *See generally* Restatement (Third) of Trusts, Reporter's Notes on §41, specifically on Comment b thereto. *See generally* §9.11 of this handbook (the bankruptcy trustee).

[725] *See, e.g.,* the English case of Petch v. Tutin, 15 M. & W. 110 (1846).

[726] *See generally* Restatement (Third) of Trusts, Reporter's Notes on §47.

[727] 4 Scott & Ascher §24.31.1 (Liability for Distributions Under Invalid, Amended, Revoked, or Ineffective Instruments) (referring to Restatement (Second) of Trusts §226A cmt. e).

Under the so-called Diplock principle,[728] a trust for "charitable or benevolent" purposes of the trustee's selection will fail notwithstanding the use of the word "or" and even if the trustee were to select only charitable objects. The subject property must revert to the settlor or the settlor estate upon a resulting trust.[729] Even distributions already made to actual charities must be disgorged. The trust fails because a benevolent trust purpose is neither limited to charitable purposes[730] nor definite beneficiaries.[731] For a discussion of the difference between a charitable trust and a benevolent trust, see Section 9.4.1 of this handbook. For a discussion of the so-called purpose trust, see Section 9.27 of this handbook.

§8.15.44   The Equitable Conversion Doctrine

It is sometimes said that a court of equity regards land as personalty if the trustees have been directed to sell it. This, however, is a fictitious form of expression. It is also sometimes said that equity regards that as done which ought to be done. This again is a fictitious form of expression. Where something ought to be done but has not been done, a court of equity, so far from regarding it as having been done, proceeds to order it to be done.[732]

Where real property is the subject of a trust and the trustee by the terms of the trust is directed to sell it, the interest of the beneficiaries is personal property, not real property, whether or not the trustee has sold the property.[733] This is the doctrine of equitable conversion as applied in the trust context.[734] In other words, if the beneficiary has the *right* to receive the proceeds from the sale of land, rather than the land itself, his or her equitable interest is considered personal property. If all beneficiaries, notwithstanding the express direction to sell, elect to take the real estate in kind, an "equitable reconversion" is said to occur.[735] The doctrine of equitable conversion in the nontrust context is discussed in Section 9.9.11 of this handbook (a contract to convey land is not a trust).

---

[728] *See* Ministry of Health v. Simpson, [1951] A.C. 251, *affirming* Re Diplock [1948] Ch. 465, CA (taken from a House of Lords decision involving the will of a one Caleb Diplock).

[729] *See generally* §4.1.1.1 of this handbook (resulting trust defined).

[730] *See* Restatement (Third) of Trusts §27. *See generally* §9.4.1 of this handbook (charitable purposes).

[731] *See* Restatement (Third) of Trusts §45.

[732] 1 Scott on Trusts §131 (1939). *See also* 3 Scott & Ascher §13.1.1 (suggesting that the equity maxim "equity regards as done that which ought to be done" is a "fictitious notion," at least as a rationale for the equitable conversion doctrine). *See generally* §8.12 of this handbook (in part containing a list of equity maxims).

[733] *See* 3 Scott & Ascher §13.1.1.

[734] At the point when the owner of land contracts to sell it, there is said to be an equitable conversion though the actual conveyance is to happen later.

[735] 3 Scott & Ascher §13.1.1.

Whether a beneficiary's equitable interest is realty or personalty[736] could make a difference in the following situations:

- If, upon the beneficiary's death, title to his or her personal property would pass to the personal representative while title to the beneficiary's real property would descend directly to the devisee, bypassing the personal representative;[737]
- If the beneficiary is an alien and in the applicable jurisdiction there are legal restrictions on the right of an alien to own land;
- If the surviving spouse of the beneficiary is electing to take a forced share of the beneficiary's estate;[738]
- If a creditor of the beneficiary wishes to attach or otherwise reach the equitable interest;[739]
- If a state wishes to levy a tax with respect to the equitable interest during the beneficiary's lifetime,[740] or at his or her death;[741] and
- If a testamentary trust of land would be invalid under the law of the situs of the land but not under the law of the place of trust administration, which is a conflict of laws question that is considered generally in Section 8.5 of this handbook.

In the trust context, the equitable conversion of land that the trustees have been directed to sell is an application of the maxim "Equity sees as done that which ought to be done." The word "ought" is employed not in the moral sense but in the legal/equitable sense. The rights to the land having already been re-ordered by the terms of the trust, equity sees to it that "the land will devolve as personalty irrespective of the precise time at which the sale takes place, thus preventing the devolution of beneficial interests from being altered by failure or delay on the part of the trustees in executing this duty to sell."[742] A direction to purchase could also implicate equitable conversion doctrine.

§8.15.45   *Donner et Retenir Ne Vaut Rien (a Jersey Channel Islands Law Maxim)*

The maxim thus applied to trusts wherever the gift into trust (don) was incomplete. The fact that it derived from the Coutume de Normandie, to which the trust concept was unknown, cast no doubt on this because the need for the settlor irrevocably to have dispossessed himself

---

[736] *See generally* §5.3.1 of this handbook (nature and extent of [beneficiary's] property interest).

[737] 3 Scott & Ascher §13.1.1.

[738] 3 Scott & Ascher §13.1.1, n.1.

[739] 3 Scott & Ascher §13.1.1, n.1.

[740] *See generally* §5.3.1 of this handbook (nature and extent of [beneficiary's] property interest).

[741] 3 Scott & Ascher §13.1.1, n.1 (Inheritance Tax); 1 Scott on Trusts §131 (discussing the state rather than federal tax implications of the character of a property interest).

[742] Hanbury & Maudsley, *Modern Equity* 277 (10th ed. 1976).

of the object of the gift and to have vested ownership and possession of it in the trustee was maintained in order to distinguish gifts into trust from those by will, in the same way as it was with regard to the French substitution fidéicommissaire and other gifts inter vivos.[743]

A rough English translation of the Jersey Channel Islands maxim of law *donner et retenir ne vaut rien*[744] is "giving and retaining is not worth anything."[745] The maxim, whose purpose was to "protect the rights of succession of heirs, to protect creditors and to prevent frauds,"[746] applied "wherever the donor retained the power freely to dispose of that which had purportedly been gifted or where the gifted property, whether movable or immovable, remained in his possession, rendering the gift invalid."[747] Its application to trusts was as follows: If one purported to establish a trust of one's property retaining, however, the power to control the "destination of the gifted assets," the settlement offended against the maxim and was wholly invalid.[748] *Donner et retenir ne vaut rien* is somewhat analogous to our illusory trust doctrine, which is covered in Section 8.15.41 of this handbook.

§8.15.46 *Bona Vacantia Doctrine*

Indeed, in many states there are now statutes that deal explicitly with abandoned property.[749]

Under the English common law doctrine of *bona vacantia* (ownerless personal property), the Crown, by virtue of the royal prerogative, could claim title to personal property that was deemed to have no owner.[750] "It was thought that the Crown's claim was more equitable than that of a stranger, and that possession by the Crown would eliminate conflicting claims of private parties."[751] The doctrine of common law escheat, on the other hand, related to the Crown's quasi-reversionary interest in realty.[752] There are echoes of both doctrines in modern escheat statutes, which generally apply to both personal and real property.[753]

---

[743] Abdel Rahman v. Chase Bank (C.I.) Trust Co. Ltd., & Five Others, [1991 JLR 103]. *See generally* §8.12.1 of this handbook (Civil Law Alternatives to the Trust) (in part discussing the civil law *fideicommissum*).

[744] "[T]he incorporation of the additional word 'rien' adding nothing of substance to the meaning." Abdel Rahman v. Chase Bank (C.I.) Trust Co. Ltd., & Five Others, [1991 JLR 103].

[745] In re Portnoy, 201 B.R. 685, 699 (1996).

[746] In re Portnoy, 201 B.R. 685, 699 (1996).

[747] Abdel Rahman v. Chase Bank (C.I.) Trust Co. Ltd., & Five Others, [1991] JLR 103.

[748] Abdel Rahman v. Chase Bank (C.I.) Trust Co. Ltd., & Five Others, [1991] JLR 103.

[749] 3 Scott & Ascher §14.10.3.

[750] *See generally* 3 Scott & Ascher §14.10.3.

[751] Note, *Origins and Development of Modern Escheat*, 61 Colum. L. Rev. 1319, 1326–1327 (1961).

[752] *See* Burgess v. Wheate, 1 Ed. 177, 96 Eng. Rep. 67 (Ch. 1759).

[753] *See generally* 3 Scott & Ascher §14.10.3.

In the trust context, the doctrine of *bona vacantia* could have relevance in two situations: The first is the imposition of a resulting trust[754] where the settlor dies intestate without heirs at law and the trust is comprised of personal property.[755] The second is where a beneficiary of a trust of personal property dies intestate without heirs at law and the terms of the trust make no provision for an alternate disposition of the beneficial interest, the interest being vested and transmissible.[756] In such cases, courts, invoking the doctrine of *bona vacantia*, have directed these orphaned equitable interests into the hands of the Crown or the state.[757]

The doctrine of *bona vacantia* also might have relevance in a third situation, namely, myriad small "street" donations for a purpose that has been accomplished, assuming the doctrine of *cy pres* is inapplicable.[758] For practical reasons, a court might be inclined to direct the property remaining after accomplishment of the trust purpose to the Crown or the state, rather than attempt to impose a resulting trust in favor of numerous anonymous donors.[759] Or, take a trust for the benefit of a noncharitable association that has been in existence for many years but is now in dissolution. If the imposition of a resulting trust on the subject property is not warranted, if the current members of the association have no beneficial interest in the property, and if the trustee may not walk away with the property, then there is no one who has a claim to it.[760] The property passes to the Crown or the state as *bona vacantia*.[761]

§8.15.47   Acceleration [of Vested and Contingent Equitable Interests] Doctrine

Clearly the intellectual climate is unfavourable to the high technique of the common law to say nothing of strict logic. It is certainly not a time when many minds can be found to respond with lively animation to an encounter with a tolled entry upon a descent cast, or with a demurrer to a plea giving express colour on the ground that lacking a protestando, the plea confesses but does not avoid a count in trespass; or even with the acceleration of a legal contingent remainder by the destruction of a prior contingent remainder interest. We have

---

[754] *See generally* §4.1.1.1 of this handbook (the resulting trust).

[755] *See generally* Scott on Trusts §411.4 (1939 ed.) (discussing the resulting trust where the settlor dies without heirs). *See, e.g.*, Taylor v. Haygarth, 14 Sim. 8 (1844).

[756] *See generally* Scott on Trusts §142.2 (1939 ed.) (discussing death of beneficiary without heirs).

[757] *See generally* 3 Scott & Ascher §14.10.3.

[758] *See* §§4.1.1.1 of this handbook (the resulting trust) and 8.15.28 of this handbook (cy pres); 6 Scott & Ascher §41.1.5 (Several Donors and the Resulting Trust).

[759] *See, e.g.*, Re West Sussex Constabulary's Widows, Children and Benevolent (1930) Fund Trustees [1971] Ch. 1, [1970] 1 All ER 544. *See generally* §4.1.1.1 of this handbook (the resulting trust).

[760] *See generally* 6 Scott & Ascher §42.1.4 (Trust for Noncharitable Association); §4.1.1.1 of this handbook (the resulting trust).

[761] *See* 6 Scott & Ascher §42.1.4.

turned in other directions.—Sir Owen Dixon—Concerning Judicial Method Address at Yale University, September 19, 1955[762]

Acceleration of remainder interests. Let us assume the designated life beneficiary of a trust to be established under Mr. Jones's will predeceases Mr. Jones. The trust is to be impressed upon the residue of the probate estate. There are remaindermen specified in the will, perhaps generically as "issue," who are to take upon the death of the life beneficiary and who are designated as "then living." Mr. Jones dies without changing his will. What about the remaindermen? Are they out of luck? There are several possibilities. One is that the interest the remaindermen were supposed to take fails as it was in part conditioned upon the life beneficiary surviving Mr. Jones and they surviving the life beneficiary; a resulting trust is therefore imposed; and the probate residue passes as intestate property to Mr. Jones's heirs at law.

Another is that the doctrine of acceleration applies and the property passes outright and free of trust upon Mr. Jones's death to the presumptive remaindermen. Absent a clear indication in the will that the consequences of acceleration would contravene the intentions of Mr. Jones, it is likely that an acceleration will be ordered.[763] "English and Australian courts... [as well-]... have accepted for many years the concept that interests, whether for life or in remainder, may be accelerated by removal, destruction, disclaimer, surrender or failure of a prior interest or even power."[764]

The doctrine of acceleration also might have application if the life beneficiary of either a testamentary trust or an inter vivos trust disclaims or renounces (releases) his or her equitable property interest. This is the case even if the property disclaimed is a current contingent equitable interest under a discretionary trust where the applicable condition precedent is that the trustee exercise his discretionary authority to make distributions of income and/or principal.[765] At the time of the disclaimer or renunciation, the successor equitable interests are likely accelerated,[766] unless the terms of the trust make provision for alternate takers.[767] There almost certainly would be an acceleration if the interests of the remaindermen were indefeasibly vested.[768] According to the Restatement (Third) of Trusts, a release "is treated for many purposes... as a transfer of the renounced interest to those who benefit from the

---

[762] *See generally* §8.25 of this handbook (few American law schools still require Agency, Trusts, and Equity); Charles E. Rounds, Jr., *The Common Law Is Not Just About Contracts: How Legal Education Has Been Short-Changing Feminism*, 43 U. Rich. L. Rev. 1185 (2009).

[763] *See, e.g.*, Thompson v. Thornton, 197 Mass. 273; 83 N.E. 880 (1908) (involving the acceleration of contingent equitable remainders).

[764] Bassett & ors v. Bassett & ors, [2003] NSWSC 691 (Australia) (involving the acceleration of vested equitable remainders). *See generally* Lewin on Trusts ¶8-32 through ¶8-37 (England).

[765] *See, e.g.*, In re Estate of Gilbert, 592 N.Y.S.2d 224 (N.Y. Surr. Ct. 1992).

[766] *See, e.g.*, UPC §2-1106(b)(3)(A) (Disclaimers).

[767] *See, e.g.*, UPC §2-1106(b)(2) (Disclaimers).

[768] 6 Scott & Ascher §41.2.1 (Acceleration).

release, generally to be determined as if the beneficiary had died at the time of the release."[769]

Acceleration of income interests. There also can be an acceleration of equitable income interests. Take, for example, a trust for the benefit of *C1* for life, and, upon the death of *C1*, to *C2* for life. The remainder is to *D*. Should *C1* disclaim or renounce his or her income interest, there is an immediate acceleration of the income interest to *C2*.[770]

Presumption of acceleration. Baked into the doctrine of acceleration is a presumption that the settlor intended for the next equitable estate to take upon the extinguishment of the prior estate however that might happen, "rather than from and after the death of the particular tenant."[771] The English cases are generally in accord.[772] This presumption, however, is rebuttable.[773] In the case of an equitable remainder interest that is distributable at the death of the life beneficiary to members of a class,[774] *e.g.*, to someone's issue, an acceleration of the equitable interest that is triggered by the life beneficiary's renunciation or disclaimer will not necessarily result in a closing of the class and a termination of the trust. It is possible that the class remains open and the trust continues until the time when the life beneficiary actually does die.[775] It all depends upon the intention of the settlor as divined from the terms of the trust.[776]

But settlor intent trumps the presumption of acceleration. Note that if the identity of the remaindermen cannot be ascertained until the death of the equitable life tenant who has renounced or disclaimed, particularly if the remainder interests are subject to a condition precedent such as survivorship, then the trustee may have no choice but to hold the trust property upon a resulting trust for the benefit of the settlor or his or her estate (which would mean paying net income to the settlor or his or her estate) until such time as the life tenant actually does die;[777] accumulate and/or to add to principal the income as earned for ultimate distribution to the actual remaindermen; or distribute income to the presumptive remaindermen until the named life tenant actually does die.[778] In such a situation the trustee should ask the court for guidance by means of a complaint for instructions and/or declaratory

---

[769] Restatement (Third) of Trusts §51 cmt. f.

[770] *See generally* 6 Scott & Ascher §41.2.1 (Acceleration).

[771] 24 Am. Jur. 2d *Estates* §305 at 497.

[772] Lewin ¶ 8-34.

[773] *See, e.g.*, Wetherbee v. First State Bank & Trust Co., 266 Ga. 364, 466 S.E.2d 835 (1996).

[774] *See generally* §5.2 of this handbook (class designation: "children," "issue," "heirs," and "relatives," (some rules of construction)).

[775] Lewin ¶ 5-50.

[776] In England, it is now accepted that the doctrine of acceleration applies to inter vivos trusts, though, as one learned commentator has noted, it is not all that easy "to collect the intention necessary to bring the doctrine into play." Lewin ¶ 8-32.

[777] Restatement (Second) of Trusts §412 cmt. c. *See generally* 6 Scott & Ascher §41.1.2 (Partial Failure of Trust).

[778] *See generally* 6 Scott & Ascher §41.2.1 (Acceleration).

judgment as to which course of action is the appropriate one.[779] In England, an interest of an unborn person cannot be accelerated.[780] For more on the possible consequences of a disclaimer or mid-course renunciation by a life beneficiary of his or her equitable interest, see Section 4.1.1.1 of this handbook, particularly the discussion surrounding Situation #2. For a general discussion of what is to be done with income when there is no current beneficiary for whatever reason, see Section 8.41 of this handbook.

§8.15.48 The Two-Party Rule

It is a traditional rule of contract law that one cannot enter into an enforceable contract with oneself. This is known as the two-party rule.[781] In other words, it takes two to make a contract. The rule has relevance in the trust context when, for example, a trustee wishes to purchase an asset comprising a portion or all of the trust estate. Apart from the equitable issue of whether he would be in breach of trust for so doing,[782] there is the legal issue of whether it is mechanically even possible to do it, the trustee being on one side of the purported contract in his individual capacity and on the other in his fiduciary capacity. In England, the rule may well pose a problem for the trustee.[783] "In the United States, however, identity of parties may not prevent a contract being made if the capacities are different."[784]

§8.15.49 The Genuine Transaction Rule

The two party rule is easily circumvented because it has no application to a sale to a nominee of the trustee. . . .[785]

It is the default law that a trustee with a power to sell trust property may only sell to independent third parties in arm's-length transactions.[786] This is known as the genuine transaction rule.[787] The rule is incident to the trustee's duty of loyalty.[788] Thus, if a trustee in his fiduciary capacity sells the trust property to a straw, or as the English say to a "nominee," who in turn sells the

---

[779] *See generally* §8.42 of this handbook (the difference between a complaint for instructions and a complaint for declaratory judgment).

[780] Lewin ¶8-36.

[781] Lewin ¶20-56.

[782] *See generally* §6.1.3.3 of this handbook (trustee benefiting as buyer and seller).

[783] *See generally* Lewin ¶20-56 (suggesting that while the rule prevents a trustee from contracting with himself through his own agent, it may not prevent him from contracting with a nominee for himself).

[784] Lewin ¶20-56, n.43 (citing to Restatement (2d) Contracts §9 comment (b)).

[785] Lewin ¶20-59.

[786] Lewin ¶20-59.

[787] Lewin ¶20-59.

[788] *See generally* §6.1.3.3 of this handbook (trustee benefiting as buyer and seller).

property to the trustee in his individual capacity,[789] the transactions are ineffective in equity, unless they were authorized by statute; court order; the beneficiaries, provided all are of full age and legal capacity and have given their informed consents; or the terms of the trust, either expressly or by implication.[790] The rule also would apply to the sale of a trust asset by an outgoing trustee to a straw with the understanding that the trustee, after leaving office, is to purchase the asset for himself.[791]

§8.15.50   Equitable Subrogation Doctrine

The word subrogation is an "antique synonym" for substitution.[792] It can function as an asset-based procedural equitable remedy for a "claimant who can establish both (i) unjust enrichment at the expense of the claimant, and (ii) a transactional nexus making it appropriate that the claimant obtain restitution via rights in identifiable property of the defendant."[793] The other asset-based procedural equitable remedies are constructive trust, which is taken up in Section 7.2.3.1.6 of this handbook, and equitable lien, which is taken up in Section 7.2.3.1.4 of this handbook.

Subrogation is commonly employed as a remedy for the legally unjustifiable satisfaction of a secured obligation. John Jones, for example, is enriched if X transfers to him free of trust and without encumbrance title to, say, a marble sculpture worth $10,000. But John Jones is also similarly enriched economically by X if X pays off John Jones's $10,000 obligation to County Bank, an obligation that is secured, say, by an oil painting that John Jones lawfully owns. In each case the enrichment involves an identifiable asset. In each case the enrichment would be unjust if there were no legal basis for it, such as if John Jones had procured the enrichment from X by fraud, duress, or undue influence. The constructive trust is tailor-made to procedurally remedy unjust enrichments that are occasioned by the transfer of title to identifiable property. Subrogation, on the other hand, is tailor-made to remedy unjust enrichments that are occasioned by the payment of a debt that is secured by identifiable property. This is because subrogation puts the claimant (in our case X) in the shoes of the lender (in our case County Bank) vis-à-vis the security (in our case John Jones's lawfully owned oil painting). "Subrogation becomes a meaningful remedy principally when the restitution claimant is in competition with general creditors of the defendant, and when the obligation that was satisfied with the claimant's money enjoyed some form of priority over the claims of general creditors."[794]

---

[789] *See generally* Lewin ¶ 20-69.

[790] *See generally* §6.1.3.3 of this handbook (trustee benefiting as buyer and seller).

[791] *See generally* Lewin ¶ 20-71.

[792] Restatement (Third) of Restitution and Unjust Enrichment §57 cmt. a.

[793] Restatement (Third) of Restitution and Unjust Enrichment §57 cmt. a.

[794] Restatement (Third) of Restitution and Unjust Enrichment §57 cmt. a.

In Section 9.9.23 of this handbook, we discuss why an equitable right of subrogation is not a trust. In this section, we provide some examples of how the doctrine of equitable subrogation and the law of trusts can nevertheless intersect.

The trustee's right of indemnity. Subrogation is the substitution of one creditor for another. A corporation is a juristic entity. Under classic principles of trust law, however, a trust is not a juristic entity.[795] As to the world, the trustee owns the subject property. When a trustee contracts with a third party on behalf of the "trust" for goods and services, it is the trustee, not the "trust," who is a party to the contract. In an action on the contract brought by the third party, it is the trustee whom the third party sues:

> The third party creditor of a trust is subject to capricious contractual risks that have been done away with for those dealing with companies . . . The distinction seems to stem from the historical separation of the Courts of Law and Equity. The contracting trustee was liable for the contracted debt at law in a Court which ignored or would not recognise any trust. This separation continues to cast a long shadow.[796]

Now in equity, a trustee may have a right of indemnity, either through exoneration or reimbursement, from the trust estate for his contractual liability.[797] In other words, he may be a creditor of the "trust" to the extent of his right to be made whole from the trust estate. The doctrine of subrogation would allow the third-party creditor to stand in the shoes of the trustee and to seek satisfaction directly from the trust estate.[798] The creditor's recovery, however, would be limited by what the trustee could have obtained from the trust estate by way of exoneration or reimbursement. For the current state of the doctrine of subrogation in the context of a trustee's contractual liability to third parties, the reader is referred to Section 7.3.1 of this handbook.

Trustee wrongfully uses trust funds to release mortgage on his personal realty. Assume that an innocent third party owns a mortgage on the personal realty of a trustee. The trustee wrongfully pays off the debt to the mortgagee with trust funds such that the mortgage is released. As the third party is a good faith purchaser for value (BFP) of those funds, the beneficiaries of the trust will have no recourse against him. The doctrine of bona fide purchase is taken up in Section 8.15.63 of this handbook. "The beneficiary cannot trace the trust property into the fee-simple title to the realty because that was held by the trustee before the misappropriation and as a result of a deed to him, nor can the beneficiary show that his trust money was gone into a mortgage, because the mortgage is discharged, as is the note or bond to which it was an incident."[799]

---

[795] *See generally* §3.5.1 of this handbook (nature and extent of the trustee's estate).

[796] Keith Wallace, *Recourse Revisited—What Are the Risks for Trustees' Counterparties?* 8 Trust Quarterly Review, Issue 1, 2010, at 9 [a STEP publication].

[797] *See generally* §3.5.2.3 of this handbook (right in equity to indemnity (exoneration and reimbursement)).

[798] *See generally* Lewin ¶21-31 through ¶21-36.

[799] Bogert §930.

The procedural equitable remedy of tracing is taken up in Section 7.2.3.1.3 of this handbook. Assuming the trustee is insolvent, do the beneficiaries have a claim to the realty that is in any way superior to the claims of the trustee's personal general creditors? Under the doctrine of equitable subrogation, they do:

> The beneficiary's funds have freed this property from a burden, without his knowledge or consent and it is fair and equitable that the beneficiary should have a lien upon the realty to the extent that his funds have removed the mortgage encumbrance. Equity sanctions this result, and calls the process "subrogating" the beneficiary to the rights of the mortgagee whose debt was paid and whose encumbrance was removed by the use of the beneficiary's funds. The same principle should be applied if the encumbrance removed was a tax or other lien, or the right of a pledgee.[800]

The Restatement (Third) of Restitution and Unjust Enrichment is generally in accord, except that it takes an entity approach to the trust relationship: "If restitution from property would be more advantageous than restitution via money judgment, Trust is entitled to be subrogated to the mortgage that its funds were used to discharge."[801]

Equitable rights of surety when debt secured by entrusted funds. Assume a debtor entrusts certain items of intangible personal property to the creditor in order to secure the payment of the debt. If the surety on the debt pays off the creditor, the surety is subrogated to the creditor's security interest in the entrusted property.[802] In other words, the surety is entitled in equity to be reimbursed from the entrusted property.[803] "This right of subrogation is independent of contract, and extends to securities of which the surety had no knowledge at the time he guaranteed the debt, and even to securities which were taken by the creditor after the date of the guarantee."[804] A corollary is that a release of the property by the trustee-creditor from its entrustment releases also the surety from his suretyship obligations.[805]

§8.15.51 Hotchpot

Hotchpot. From the French hocher, to shake and pot, a pot. Littleton, Tenures sec. 267, wrote, Et il semble que cest parol 'hochepot' est en english a puddyng. See too Baker, Manuel of Law

---

[800] Bogert §930.

[801] Restatement (Third) of Restitution and Unjust Enrichment §57, illus. 1. *See generally* §8.15.77 of this handbook (the trust entity doctrine).

[802] Bogert §33.

[803] Bogert §33.

[804] Snell's Equity ¶ 43-20.

[805] Bogert §33.

French, tit. hochepot, a stew. Sed quaere: the Oxford English Dictionary records earlier legal than culinary uses.[806]

In its usual application to trusts, hotchpot is an equitable device for calculating what the recipients of a final distribution are to receive when the trustee has made prior partial distributions or advancements to one or more of the recipients pursuant to the trustee's fiduciary power of appointment. The device is employed only when the terms of the trust call for offsetting prior partial distributions and advancements.[807] The Restatement (Second) of Property, which incorrectly suggests that a hotchpot contribution is actual, not notional,[808] contains a somewhat ungrammatical example of such a trust term:

> A by will transfers property to B in trust. B is given discretion to pay the income and principal from time to time "to such one or more of A's issue living from time to time as B in B's uncontrolled discretion may determine until the death of A's surviving [sic] child, at which time B shall distribute the trust property to A's issue then living, such issue to take per stirpes as though the trust property included all the amounts previous distributed by B to A's issue, the issue in each per stirpes line being charged with having received their [sic] share [sic] of the previous distributions."[809]

The Restatement (Third) of Property, specifically comment k to Section 17.5, sets the record straight: A hotchpot contribution is notional, that is to say hotchpot is a calculation exercise only. The comment, however, contains no illustrations of hotchpot applications. What is worse, the section's Reporter's Notes skip over the topic of hotchpot altogether.

The key to unlocking the gist of comment k is an appreciation that it is addressing hotchpot applications in the context of partial exercises of *fiduciary* (as well as nonfiduciary) nongeneral powers of appointment: "To minimize unintended inequalities of distribution among permissible appointees, the language creating a power sometimes provides that no appointee shall receive any share in default of appointment, unless the appointee consents to allow the mount of the appointment to be taken into account in calculating the fund to be distributed in default of appointment." Recall that the trustee of a discretionary trust possesses a nongeneral fiduciary power of appointment over the trust property, with the designated remaindermen being the takers in default of its

---

[806] Lewin ¶ 28-01, n.1. *See generally* §8.15 of this handbook (doctrines ancient and modern) in part containing a discussion of the phenomenon known as law French).

[807] Lewin ¶ 28-02.

[808] *See* Restatement (Second) of Property (Wills and Other Donative Transfers) §21.2 cmt. f.

[809] Restatement (Second) of Property (Wills and Other Donative Transfers) §21.2 cmt. f, illus. 12.

exercise.[810] A hotchpot clause, by the way, "does not make the power nonexclusionary, because the terms do not prevent the donee from making an appointment that excludes a permissible appointee."[811] Nonexclusionary powers of appointment are covered in Section 8.1.1 of this handbook.

The Restatement (Third) of Property endorses the following intent-based default assumption: "If the donee of a power of appointment makes a valid partial appointment to a taker in default, the taker in default-appointee also takes his or her share of any unappointed property as taker in default. . . ."[812] As noted, the donor of a power of appointment may expressly provide in the terms of the grant that, to the extent the donee makes an appointment to a taker in default, the appointee must elect either to take by appointment or to take in default thereof.[813] The donor though might provide that in the case of an actual partial appointment to a taker in default, the appointee may elect to take in default as well, provided the appointee's share of the fund to be divided up among all the takers in default is determined by hotchpot calculation.[814] As the English say, the appointed property notionally needs to be "brought into hotchpot."[815]

A hotchpot calculation works like this. The value of the fund to be distributed is augmented for computation purposes only by the cash[816] values of prior partial distributions and advancements. It is said that "[e]ach beneficiary who has already had a distribution notionally brings its value into the common pot with the fund which is actually to be distributed."[817] Even in the case when someone has received more than what a hotchpot calculation would allow, there is no actual contribution of funds.[818] Again, the augmentation is notional only.

The amount that is notionally augmented is then notionally allocated among those who are to receive shares of the final distribution. Each then receives an actual share of the final distribution equal to the value of what has been allocated to him or to her for computation purposes minus the aggregate value of what he or she actually received in the way of prior distributions and advancements, if any. "A beneficiary who has had an advance often has to bring interest on the advance into hotchpot, as well as the capital."[819]

---

[810] *See generally* §8.1.1 of this handbook.

[811] Restatement (Third) of Property (Wills and Other Donative Transfers) §17.5 cmt. k.

[812] Restatement (Third) of Property (Wills and Other Donative Transfers) §19.24.

[813] Restatement (Third) of Property (Wills and Other Donative Transfers) §19.24 cmt. b.

[814] Restatement (Third) of Property (Wills and Other Donative Transfers) §19.24 cmt. b

[815] Lewin ¶28-02.

[816] Lewin ¶28-04.

[817] Lewin ¶28-03.

[818] Lewin ¶28-03.

[819] Lewin ¶28-11.

§8.15.52 Rule of Convenience (Class Gifts)

The rule of convenience[820] is a default rule of construction that applies to both legal property interests[821] and equitable interests under trusts. In the trust context, it governs when the membership of a class closes when the membership is capable of increasing over time.[822] Simply stated, unless the terms of the trust provide otherwise, a class closes at the time of first distribution.[823]

Take, for example, a testamentary trust established for the settlor's widow for life, and on her death the "remainder to the settlor's grandchildren in equal shares." If the terms of the trust had provided that upon the death of the widow the property was to pass outright and free of trust in equal shares to the "then living grandchildren," then the express terms of the trust would have dictated when the class closed. It would have closed at the death of the widow with the result that those grandchildren alive and in existence at the time of the widow's death would take in equal shares. Any grandchildren subsequently born would be out of luck, as would, by the way, the estates of any grandchildren who had predeceased the widow. But the terms did not expressly so provide. So what then?

There are at least two approaches when there is no clear indication when a class closes. The approach that complies with the rule of convenience is that it closes at the time of first distribution, in this case, upon the widow's death. Distribution is then made to those grandchildren who are then living and to the estates[824] of those grandchildren who are not but who had survived the settlor. Grandchildren who are conceived after the widow's death are out of luck.

The other approach, the one that runs afoul of the rule of convenience, is that the trustee must continue to administer the trust property until such time as all children of the settlor have died. It is at that time that the class of grandchildren closes, there no longer being a possibility that additional grandchildren can be conceived into the class. Distribution is then made to the settlor's grandchildren or their estates, excluding the estates of grandchildren who have predeceased the settlor.[825] As noted, a prospective settlor can always disable the rule of convenience by express language in the governing instrument.[826] In this case, all the settlor need have done is make express provision for the class of grandchildren to be kept open until all the settlor's children had died. Nor would the Rule against Perpetuities have been an impediment to his

---

[820] *See generally* 2 Scott & Ascher §12.14.4.

[821] *See generally* §8.27 of this handbook (what is the difference between a legal life estate and an equitable life estate under a trust?).

[822] *See generally* §5.2 of this handbook (class designation: "children," "issue," "heirs," and "relatives" (some rules of construction)).

[823] *See generally* 2 Scott on Trusts §127.4.

[824] *See generally* §8.2.1 of this handbook (the Rule against Perpetuities) (in part discussing the concept of vesting).

[825] *See generally* §8.2.1 of this handbook (the Rule against Perpetuities).

[826] 2 Scott & Ascher §12.14.4.

doing this, his children in this case being lives in being for perpetuities analysis purposes.[827]

The justification for the rule of convenience is that "otherwise the distribution that was directed to take effect at . . . [the widow's] . . . death would have to be postponed, since it would be impossible to ascertain how many persons might become members of the class thereafter."[828] In the case of our hypothetical testamentary trust, which calls for a first distribution at the death of the widow, the trustee cannot know how much to distribute to those grandchildren who survived the settlor (or their estates), as well as to those grandchildren who were conceived after the settlor died but before the widow died (or their estates) unless the class of grandchildren closes at the time of her death. As long as there are children of the settlor alive, there is a possibility, however remote, of more grandchildren coming into existence who would be entitled to take pro rata shares of the fixed pot of assets.

§8.15.53   Harmless-Error Rule [The Trust Application]

The trend towards excusing harmless errors is based on a growing acceptance of the broader principle that mistake, whether in execution or in expression, should not be allowed to defeat intention nor to work unjust enrichment—Restatement (Third) of Property (Wills and Donative Transfers)[829]

American courts have traditionally required that there be strict compliance with statutory formalities *for a will to be valid.* That a will must be signed by the testator is a common formality. Another is the two-witness requirement. It is said that will execution formalities serve evidentiary, cautionary, protective, and channeling purposes.[830] "Modern authority . . . [however] . . . is moving away from insistence on strict compliance with statutory formalities, recognizing that the statutory formalities are not ends in themselves but rather the means of determining whether their underlying purpose has been met."[831]

The Restatement (Third) of Property (Wills and Donative Transfers) is fully in accord with the drift of the law away from strict compliance and in the direction of substantial compliance, to wit: "A harmless error in executing a will may be excused if the proponent establishes by clear and convincing evidence that the decedent adopted the document as his or her will."[832] This is a version of the so-called harmless-error rule. The Restatement expressly extends the reach of the rule's application beyond will execution formalities to the will

---

[827] *See generally* §8.2.1.2 of this handbook (validating life or worst-case life in being) (the worst-case life in being).

[828] 2 Scott on Trusts §127.4.

[829] Restatement (Third) of Property (Wills and Other Donative Transfers) §3.3 cmt. b.

[830] Restatement (Third) of Property (Wills and Other Donative Transfers) §3.3 cmt. a.

[831] Restatement (Third) of Property (Wills and Other Donative Transfers) §3.3 cmt. b.

[832] Restatement (Third) of Property (Wills and Other Donative Transfers) §3.3.

revocation and revival process.[833] But what should be of particular interest to the readers of this handbook, the rule's reach also has been extended to efforts to create, revoke, and amend will substitutes such as trusts under which the settlor has reserved a right of revocation.[834] For a discussion of the related topic of reforming trusts to remedy mistakes, the reader is referred to Section 8.15.22 of this handbook.

§8.15.54 Ademption by Extinction [The Trust Application]

A specific devise is a testamentary disposition of a specifically identified asset . . . A general devise is a testamentary disposition, usually of a specified amount of money or quantity of property, that is payable from the general assets of the estate.—Restatement (Third) of Property (Wills & Donative Transfers)[835]

The doctrine of ademption by extinction has its origin in the law of wills and its primary application in the failure of specific testamentary bequests and devises.[836] The scope of the doctrine, however, may be expanding to encompass the functional equivalent of specific bequests and devises under will substitutes such as self-settled revocable inter vivos trusts.[837]

In the wills context ademption-by-extinction works this way. If a specifically bequeathed or devised item of property is not in the probate estate at the time of the testator's death, with certain exceptions[838] the bequest or devise adeems.[839] That means that the designated legatee or devisee is out of luck. He or she is not entitled to something of comparable economic value from the general assets of the estate. An example of a specific bequest would be "I bequeath 'two-thirds of the X-Y-Z Mutual Fund shares owned by me at my death' to my mother if she survives me."[840] On the other hand, a general bequest or devise would not work an ademption. An example of a general bequest would be "I bequeath 1000 shares of the X-Y-Z Mutual Fund to my mother if she survives me."[841] If, for example, there are no such shares in the probate estate at the time

---

[833] Restatement (Third) of Property (Wills and Other Donative Transfers) §3.3 cmt. c.

[834] Restatement (Third) of Property (Wills and Other Donative Transfers) §7.2 cmt. d. *See generally* §8.2.2.2 of this handbook (the revocable trust).

[835] Restatement (Third) of Property (Wills and Other Donative Transfers) §5.1.

[836] Restatement (Third) of Property (Wills and Other Donative Transfers) §5.2.

[837] Restatement (Third) of Property (Wills and Other Donative Transfers) §§5.2 cmt. I, 7.2 cmt. f.; 5 Scott & Ascher §35.1.6 (Partial Revocation of a Trust Due to Ademption by Extinction). *See generally* §8.2.4 of this handbook (trust termination checklist), §8.2.2.2 of this handbook (the revocable trust), and §8.11 of this handbook (what are the duties of the trustee of a revocable inter vivos trust).

[838] *See, e.g.*, Restatement (Third) of Property (Wills and Other Donative Transfers) §5.2 cmts. d (change in form), f (unpaid proceeds at death), g (disposition by a guardian, conservator, or agent), & h (failure inconsistent with testator's intent).

[839] Restatement (Third) of Property (Wills and Other Donative Transfers) §5.2(c).

[840] Restatement (Third) of Property (Wills and Other Donative Transfers) §5.1 cmt. b.

[841] Restatement (Third) of Property (Wills and Other Donative Transfers) §5.1 cmt. c.

of death and the testator is survived by his mother, then the personal representative may well be obliged to go out and purchase the shares for her, tapping for that purpose the estate's general assets.

The Restatement (Third) of Property (Wills and Other Donative Transfers) would apply the rules of ademption by extinction that have developed over time in the wills context to comparable dispositions under self-settled revocable inter vivos trusts.[842] The terms of a self-settled revocable inter vivos trust, for example, might provide that upon the death of the settlor, the trustee "shall segregate and distribute outright and free of trust to the settlor's mother if she is then living all shares of the X-Y-Z Mutual Fund then comprising the trust estate." If there are no such shares in the trust at the death of the settlor, then the mother is out of luck. She would not be entitled to a trust distribution of comparable economic value.

Over the centuries from Byzantium[843] to Massachusetts,[844] a vast body of testamentary law and lore has developed around the ademption doctrine. For the most part, it speaks to how the doctrine should be applied in particular fact situations. Assume, for example, that the testator specifically bequeathed all his shares of the X-Y-Z Mutual Fund but the fund merged with another fund during the testator's lifetime and in so doing lost its legal identity. In exchange for shares of the X-Y-Z Mutual Fund, the testator received shares of the other fund. Has the merger worked an ademption? The answer may hinge on whether we are in an "intent" or "identity" jurisdiction:

> The common law developed two conflicting theories of ademption, the "identity" theory and the "intent" theory. Under the "identity" theory, which predominates in the case law, a specific devise completely fails—i.e., the devisee is entitled to nothing—if the specifically devised property is not in the estate at death. Like any doctrine that treats the testator's intent as irrelevant, the identity theory sometimes operates to defeat intent, sometimes not, but then only by coincidence. Under the "intent" theory, however, the testator's intent is central to the inquiry. Under that theory, the devise fails unless the evidence establishes that failure would be inconsistent with the testator's intent.[845]

---

[842] Restatement (Third) of Property (Wills and Other Donative Transfers) §§5.2 cmt. I, 7.2 cmt. f.

[843] *See* Newbury v. McCammant, 182 N.W.2d 147, 149 (Iowa 1970 (suggesting that historically the courts of this country, and England, in early times followed the dictates of Justinian holding that a testator's intention was crucial to the operation of the ademption-by-extinction doctrine).

[844] *See* Wasserman v. Cohen, 414 Mass. 172, 174, 606 N.E.2d 901, 903 (1993) (noting that Massachusetts courts have been taking a strict identity approach to ademption-by-extinction issues for nearly 160 years).

[845] Restatement (Third) of Property (Wills and Other Donative Transfers) §5.2 cmt. b. Note that under the change-in-form principle, the merger of the two mutual funds would probably not work an ademption. Restatement (Third) of Property (Wills and Other Donative Transfers) §5.2 cmt. d. "By well-established authority, the change-in-form principle applies if the change in form is insubstantial." Restatement (Third) of Property (Wills and Other Donative Transfers) §5.2 cmt. d.

In 1993, the Supreme Judicial Court of Massachusetts applied ademption principles to the inter vivos sale to a third party of a parcel of real estate that had been specifically referenced in the seller's revocable inter vivos trust.[846] The terms of the trust directed the trustee upon the death of the settlor to segregate and distribute out the real estate to a trust beneficiary. Strictly applying the intent theory of ademption, which had been its practice in the testamentary context for nearly 160 years, the Court held that the designated trust beneficiary was not entitled to the sale proceeds, the sale having worked an ademption: "We have held that a trust, particularly when executed as part of a comprehensive estate plan, should be construed according to the same rules traditionally applied to wills."[847]

§8.15.55   Lapse; Antilapse [The Trust Application]

Antilapse statutes typically provide, as a rebuttable rule of construction, that devises to certain relatives who predecease the testator pass to specified substitute takers, usually the descendants of the predeceased legatee who survive the testator— Restatement (Third) of Property (Wills & Don. Trans.)[848]

If the inter vivos donative document of transfer is a substitute for a will, by analogy to the case of a will, the result that would obtain if a will is involved may justifiably be adopted because of the similarity of the two situations—Restatement (Third) of Property (Wills & Don. Trans.)[849]

Lapse defined. Lapse is the failure of any testamentary gift for want of a taker; ademption is the failure of a specific testamentary gift for want of the property designated. "[T]he common-law rule of lapse is predicated on the principle that a will transfers property at the testator's death, not when the will was executed, and on the principle that property cannot be transferred to a deceased individual. Under the rule of lapse, all devises are automatically and by law conditioned on survivorship of the testator. A devise to a devisee who predeceases the testator fails (lapses); the devised property does *not* pass to the devisee's estate, to be distributed according to the devisee's will or pass by intestate succession from the devisee."[850]

Antilapse in the wills context. In the event that a named legatee *under a will* predeceases the testator, there may well be an antilapse statute that applies which redirects the bequest directly to the legatee's issue, provided the legatee

---

[846] Wasserman v. Cohen, 414 Mass. 172, 606 N.E.2d 901 (1993).

[847] Wasserman v. Cohen, 414 Mass. at 175, 606 N.E.2d at 903.

[848] Restatement (Third) of Property (Wills and Other Donative Transfers) §5.5.

[849] Restatement (Third) of Property (Wills and Other Donative Transfers) §5.5, Reporter's Notes on cmt. p.

[850] UPC §2-603 cmt.

was related to the testator and provided the will contains no alternate disposition.[851] (The statute would most likely apply to devises of real property as well[852]). Were there no such statute, the bequest or devise would fail, *i.e.*, it would "lapse."[853] The property then would pass to the residuary takers under the will, or to the testator's heirs at law if the residuary bequest itself had lapsed. In 1783, Massachusetts enacted the first antilapse statute.[854] Maryland enacted one in 1810.[855] England's antilapse statute was enacted in 1837.[856] Today, every U.S. state has some form of antilapse statute, except Louisiana.[857]

As noted, whether property bequeathed under a will lapses or is redirected pursuant to the terms of an antilapse statute, the property which is the subject of the lapsed bequest generally does *not* pass from the probate estate of the testator to the probate estate of the deceased legatee, regardless of what the will may say.[858] This is because a will speaks only at the death of the testator.[859] In other words, a legatee designation under a living person's will gives rise to, with a few contract-related exceptions, no property rights, only an expectancy. Accordingly, as a will cannot effect the passage of a property interest during the lifetime of the testator to a named legatee, all the more it cannot effect the passage of a property interest to a predeceased named legatee's executor, administrator, or personal representative, the one who merely stands in the shoes of the predeceased legatee.

Antilapse in the trust context. Some courts by analogy are applying antilapse principles to will substitutes such as the revocable inter vivos trust.[860] The Restatement (Third) of Property (Wills and Other Donative Transfers) is fully in accord with these decisions.[861] The Uniform Probate Code, specifically Section 2-707, is as well, and actually goes farther, applying the antilapse concept to future interests in irrevocable as well as revocable trusts.[862] In the case of a revocable trust, the predeceased beneficiary must be related to the settlor; in the case of the irrevocable trust, he or she need not be. "In addition, the UPC provides that the share of a deceased class member passes to his or her surviving descendants (if any), unless the settlor has provided *unmistakably* to the contrary *and* provided for an effective alternate disposition of the share in question."[863] Mere words of survivorship would not be enough to defeat the

---

[851] Restatement (Third) of Property (Wills and Other Donative Transfers) §5.5. *See, e.g.*, UPC §2-603 (antilapse; deceased devisee; class gifts).

[852] Restatement (Third) of Property (Wills and Other Donative Transfers) §3.1 cmt. d.

[853] Restatement (Third) of Property (Wills and Other Donative Transfers) §5.5 cmt. a.

[854] Ruotolo v. Tietjen, 93 Conn. App. 432, 437, 890 A.2d 166, 170 (2006).

[855] Ruotolo v. Tietjen, 93 Conn. App. 432, 437, 890 A.2d 166, 170 (2006).

[856] Ruotolo v. Tietjen, 93 Conn. App. 432, 437, 890 A.2d 166, 170 (2006).

[857] Ruotolo v. Tietjen, 93 Conn. App. 432, 437, 890 A.2d 166, 170 (2006).

[858] Restatement (Third) of Property (Wills and Other Donative Transfers) §5.5 cmts. a, b.

[859] UPC §2-603 cmt.

[860] *See, e.g.*, In re Estate of Button, 490 P.2d 731 (Wash. 1971).

[861] Restatement (Third) of Property (Wills and Other Donative Transfers) §§5.5 cmt. p., 7.2 cmt. f.

[862] UPC §2-707. *See, e.g.*, Mass. Gen. Laws ch. 190B, §2-707.

[863] 2 Scott & Ascher §12.14.4.

antilapse statute.[864] Thus, if the terms of an irrevocable trust were *A to B, for C for life, and upon the death of C, the trust property shall pass outright and free of trust to the then living children of A*, the death with issue of a child of *A* after the trust was established but before the death of *C* might well trigger application of the Uniform Probate Code (UPC) antilapse provisions upon the death of *C*.

The UPC's presumption against early vesting. Assume instead that upon the death of *C*, the property passes outright and free of trust not to the members of a class but to a named individual, say *X*. Assume, also, that *X* had been in existence at the time of entrustment but died before *C* (the equitable life beneficiary). Consistent with traditional early-vesting doctrine, title to the entrusted property passes at termination from *B* (the trustee) to the personal representative of the deceased *X*, *X* having taken a vested equitable remainder *ab initio*.[865] The subject of vested equitable interests incident to the trust relationship is discussed generally in Section 8.2.1 of this handbook.

UPC Section 2-707 replaces the classic early-vesting presumption with a late-vesting presumption, namely that "a future interest under the terms of a trust is contingent on the beneficiary's surviving the distribution date."[866] It then couples the late-vesting presumption with an ultra-complicated and hyper-technical antilapse regime. Under the regime, title to the entrusted property would pass at trust termination not to *X*'s personal representative but directly to *X*'s issue then alive.[867]

The Restatement (Third) of Property (Wills and Other Donative Transfers) shies away from endorsing some kind of equitable presumption comparable to the UPC's statutory one. The traditional "rule of construction is the rule best suited within the confines of the common-law tradition to approximate the likely preference of the transferor, and is supported by the constructional preference for the construction that does not disinherit a line of descent."[868] The Restatement (Third), however, does call upon the state legislatures to enact UPC Section 2-707, suggesting that it "provide[s] a more direct and efficient means of protecting equality among different lines of descent" than having the trust property augment the probate estate of a beneficiary who predeceases the distribution date, as did Mrs. Jones.[869]

Likely preferences? Protecting equality among different lines of descent? One learned commentator was struck by the fact that Section 2-707 had made it to promulgation unsupported by any credible "empirical evidence indicating

---

[864] *See generally* Ruotolo v. Tietjen, 93 Conn. App. 432, 448, 890 A.2d 166, 176 (2006) (citing to holdings from various jurisdictions to the effect that words of survivorship alone are insufficient to defeat an antilapse statute).

[865] For another example of the application of traditional early-vesting doctrine, see Estate of Woodworth, 22 Cal. Rptr. 2d 676 (Cal. Ct. App. 1993).

[866] UPC §2-707(b).

[867] UPC §2-707(b)(1).

[868] Restatement (Third) of Property (Wills and Other Donative Transfers) §26.3 cmt. c.

[869] Restatement (Third) of Property (Wills and Other Donative Transfers) §26.3 cmt. h. *But see* Mark L. Ascher, *The 1990 Uniform Probate Code: Older and Better, Or More Like the Internal Revenue Code?*, 77 Minn. L. Rev. 639, 640 (1993) ("To be blunt, the 1990 version . . . [of the UPC] . . . is also quite pretentious.").

that most trust settlors want a remainderman to lose the remainder if he does not survive the life tenant, substituting his descendants for him if he leaves descendants."[870] In other words, the drafters appear to have been "proceeding purely on their own speculation."[871] The same might be said for the authors of the Restatement (Third) of Property.

The notional resulting trust. But what if there were no issue then living? Under the UPC antilapse regime, essentially those who *would have taken* the trust property had a resulting trust been imposed are deemed to be alternate remaindermen.[872] In other words, the resulting trust is only notional. There would be no actual imposition of a resulting trust, no actual passage of legal title to the trust property from *B* (the trustee) to *A*'s (the settlor's) personal representative. What traditionally would have been an equitable reversion has been constructively converted by statute into an equitable remainder. Time will tell whether the prevention of "cumbersome and costly distributions to and through the estate of deceased beneficiaries of future interests, who may have died long before the distribution date,"[873] is worth the inevitable unintended consequences of all this cumbersome, that is to say all this hyper-technical and convoluted, "law reform." That the evolution of the trust relationship over the centuries has been gradual rather than precipitous, and principles-based rather than code-based, in large part accounts for the relationship's protean genius.

The resulting trust is covered generally in Section 4.1.1.1 of this handbook. For an explanation of the vested equitable property interest, the reader is referred to Section 8.2.1.3 of this handbook.

The policy debate over applying antilapse principles to equitable interests under trusts. Professor Ascher has observed that these aspects of the UPC have proven more controversial than influential, although a Connecticut court has acknowledged the influence of the UPC in deciding that mere words of survivorship *in a will* are insufficient to avoid application of Connecticut's antilapse statute, which has seen only minor substantive statutory changes since its enactment in 1821.[874] In 2008, Massachusetts enacted a substantially reworked version of UPC Section 2-707. It provides that "[i]f an instrument is silent on the requirement of survivorship, a future interest under the terms of a trust is contingent on the beneficiary's surviving the distribution date."[875]

Under the model UPC antilapse default provisions applicable to trusts certain equitable future interests that had traditionally been construed as vested would become subject to the condition precedent of survivorship.[876] This could, for example, cause the contingent equitable interests of some takers in default of survivorship to violate the Rule against Perpetuities, at least in jurisdictions

---

[870] Jesse Dukeminier, *The Uniform Probate Code Upends the Law of Remainders*, 94 Mich. L. Rev. 148, 149–150 (1995).

[871] Jesse Dukeminier, *The Uniform Probate Code Upends the Law of Remainders*, 94 Mich. L. Rev. 148, 149–150 (1995).

[872] UPC §2-707(d).

[873] UPC §2-707 cmt. (common-law background).

[874] Ruotolo v. Tietjen, 93 Conn. App. 432, 449–450, 890 A.2d 166, 177 (2006).

[875] Mass. Gen. Laws ch. 190B, §2-707(b).

[876] *See generally* §8.2.1.3 of this handbook (vested and contingent equitable interests).

where the rule is still enforced.[877] What had once been safely vested would no longer be.[878] "To prevent an injustice from resulting because of this, the Uniform Statutory Rule Against Perpetuities, which has a wait-and-see element, is incorporated into the Code as part 9."[879] Still, the legislative conversion of one's vested equitable interest into an interest that is nontransmissible post-mortem in the absence of an overt expression of intent on the part of the settlor that the interest be vested would seem to pose a problem under the U.S. Constitution.[880] The U.S. Supreme Court in *Hodel v. Irving* has confirmed that the right to pass property postmortem is a property right that is covered by the Takings Clause.[881] The topic of the retroactive application of new trust law to preexisting irrevocable trusts is covered generally in Section 8.15.71 of this handbook.

One must concede that it makes some sense to treat the will and the funded revocable trust similarly for antilapse purposes. Each, after all, is a device commonly employed to effect a gratuitous transfer of property. There is, however, a fundamental difference between the will and the funded revocable trust that suggests that one can go only so far in analogizing such trusts to wills. A will speaks at death. Its execution, *i.e.*, its signing, witnessing, etc., is a nonevent for property law purposes. No property interest passes to anyone at that time. In the case of a funded revocable inter vivos trusts, however, property rights do accrue at the point of execution to persons other than the settlor, assuming there is funding at that time and assuming the property is not to pass to the settlor's probate estate at his death.[882] Consider a revocable inter vivos trust for the benefit of the settlor for his or her lifetime. The terms of the trust provide that upon the death of the settlor, the property passes outright and free of trust to John Jones. Under traditional default law, John Jones receives at the time of funding either a vested remainder subject to divestment[883] or a vested

---

[877] *See generally* §8.2.1 of this handbook (the Rule against Perpetuities) and §8.2.1.9 of this handbook (abolishing the Rule against Perpetuities).

[878] *See generally* §8.2.1 of this handbook (the vesting concept).

[879] UPC §2-707 cmt. *See generally* §8.2.1.7 of this handbook (perpetuities legislation).

[880] The UPC's §2- 707 antilapse regime is still merely a rule of construction. *See* UPC §2-701. In trusts like "income to . . . [C] . . . for life, remainder in corpuso . . . [D] . . . whether or not . . . [D]. . . . survives . . . [C] . . . ," or "income to . . . [C] . . . for life, remainder in corpus to . . . [D] . . . or [D's] . . . estate," this section [§2-707] would not apply and, "should . . . [D] . . . predecease . . . [C] . . . , . . . [D's] . . . future interest would pass through . . . [D's] . . . estate to . . . [D's] . . . successors in interest, who would be entitled to posses-sion or enjoyment at . . . [C's] . . . death." UPC §2-707 cmt. In other words, D's future equitable interest would be validly vested *ab initio*. *See generally* §8.2.1 of this handbook (the concept of vesting).

[881] 481 U.S. 704, 104 S. Ct. 2076 (1987).

[882] *See generally* §8.30 of this handbook (the difference between a vested equitable remainder subject to divestment and a vested (transmissible) contingent equitable remainder).

[883] *See, e.g.*, Baldwin v. Branch, 2004 WL 407157(Ala.) (categorizing the future interest as vested subject to divestment upon the settlor's exercising his right of revocation). *See also* Restatement (Second) of Property (Wills and Other Donative Transfers) §34.6, illus. 3.

(transmissible) contingent remainder.[884] These are transmissible property interests.[885] If John Jones dies before the settlor, these vested property rights would pass to John Jones's estate for disposition in accordance with the terms of his will. This has been the law for some time, the inheritability of vested remainders having been recognized in the time of Edward I, and their devisability having been recognized with the Statute of Wills in 1540.[886]

To be sure, all of this is default law that can be drafted around by knowledgeable counsel.[887] Still, extending the concept of antilapse to revocable trusts such that property is automatically redirected to the issue of certain predeceased remaindermen runs somewhat counter to the principle that property should be as freely alienable as possible.[888]

While the benefits of synchronizing the will with the revocable trust, a type of will substitute, may well outweigh the attendant costs of eroding somewhat a predeceased remainderman's rights of alienation, that rationale cannot be applied to the *irrevocable* trust, the irrevocable trust not being a will substitute. It would seem then that a compelling case for the wholesale "projection of the antilapse idea into the area of . . . [equitable] . . . future interests"[889] has yet to be made. For the case against extending the "antilapse idea" to irrevocable trusts, the reader is referred to Jesse Dukeminier.[890]

Applying antilapse to the exercise and nonexercise of powers of appointment. *The common law.* It has been traditional black-letter law that the exercise of an equitable testamentary power of appointment in favor of a permissible appointee who has predeceased the donee of the power is ineffective.[891] As the appointee's interest in the property subject to the unexercised power was a mere expectancy *at the time of the appointee's death*, no property interest in the subject property, whether vested or contingent, passed at that time to the appointee's executor or administrator. It is only later when the donee of the power of appointment dies that the donee's will, the instrument of power exercise, speaks. When that time comes, it is too late for the predeceasing designated appointee to benefit economically from the power exercise, and thus too late as well for those who stand in his shoes. To recapitulate: One may not effectively exercise a testamentary power of appointment in favor of

---

[884] *See, e.g.*, First Nat'l Bank of Bar Harbor v. Anthony, 557 A.2d 957 (Me. 1989) (categorizing the future interest as a vested contingent/transmissible equitable remainder, the condition precedent being the nonexercise of the settlor's right of revocation).

[885] *See generally* Jesse Dukeminier, *The Uniform Probate Code Upends the Law of Remainders*, 94 Mich. L. Rev. 148 (1995).

[886] Jesse Dukeminier, *The Uniform Probate Code Upends the Law of Remainders*, 94 Mich. L. Rev. 148 (1995).

[887] Restatement (Third) of Property (Wills and Other Donative Transfers) §5.5 cmt. g.

[888] *See generally* §8.15.40 of this handbook (the rule against direct restraints on alienation; the trust exception).

[889] UPC §2-707 cmt.

[890] *The Uniform Probate Code Upends the Law of Remainders*, 94 Mich. L. Rev. 148 (1995).

[891] *See, e.g.*, MacBryde v. Burnett, 45 F. Supp. 451, 453–454 (D. Md. 1942) ("But it seems reasonable to suppose that the donor who did not permit the donee to make an effective appointment until the donee's death intended the donee to make an appointment only to persons who survived him.").

someone who is dead at the time of exercise. This has been the rule at least since 1748 when it was enunciated by Lord Hardwicke in the English case of *Oke v. Heath*.[892]

Antilapse statutes that are applicable to exercises of powers of appointment. The model Uniform Probate Code's antilapse section, Section 2-603, cheered on by the Restatement (Third) of Property (Wills and Other Donative Transfers), "rescues" not only devises to predeceasing devisees but also exercises of testamentary powers of appointment in favor of certain predeceasing appointees.[893] If the predeceasing appointee is a grandparent, a descendant of a grandparent, or a stepchild *of the donor of the power of appointment*, there is a substitute appointment in favor of that person's descendants. "Unless the language creating … [the] … power of appointment expressly excludes the substitution of the descendants of an appointee for the appointee, a surviving descendant of a deceased appointee of a power of appointment can be substituted for the appointee under this section, *whether or not the descendant is an object of the power*."[894] Apparently, a provision in default of exercise alone would not suffice as an expression of intent to negate the default substitution. The section's Comment asserts without explanation that this radical departure from settled law is "a step long overdue."[895]

The Restatement (Third) of Property is in full accord, and then some. It provides, for example, that even when a particular antilapse statute fails to expressly address appointments to deceased appointees, its "purpose and policy" should apply to such an appointment "as if the appointed property were owned by *either the donor or the donee*."[896] But what if a deemed ownership by the donor of the power would bring about a result that is different from a deemed ownership by a donee of the power? Which assumption is applied? The Restatement fails to address such a conflict.

The Restatement would have the substituted takers "treated" as permissible appointees of the power.[897] Such "treatment" could render the fraud on a special power doctrine inapplicable to an antilapse substitution who happened not to be a permissible appointee under the express terms of the power grant.[898] The fraud on a special power doctrine is taken up generally in Section 8.15.26 of this handbook. For the public policy case against applying antilapse principles in the context of power of appointment exercises, the reader is referred to Rounds, Old Doctrine Misunderstood, New Doctrine Misconceived:

---

[892] Oke v. Heath, 1 Ves. Sen. 136, 27 Eng. Rep. 940 (Ch. 1748) (England).

[893] *See generally* Restatement (Third) of Property (Wills and Other Donative Transfers) §19.12 (appointment to deceased appointee or permissible appointee's descendants; application of antilapse statute).

[894] UPC §2-603(b)(5).

[895] Massachusetts quite sensibly declined to enact this later version of UPC Section 2-603 with all its pretentious complexities and convolutions. Instead it dropped into the slot a pre-1990 version of the section that made no mention of exercises of powers of appointment.

[896] Restatement (Third) of Property (Wills and Other Donative Transfers) §19.12(b).

[897] Restatement (Third) of Property (Wills and Other Donative Transfers) §19.12(b).

[898] *See* Restatement (Third) of Property (Wills and Other Donative Transfers) §19.12(c).

Deconstructing the Newly-Minted Restatement (Third) of Property's Power of Appointment Sections.[899]

The expired general power of appointment: The Restatement (Third) of Property muddles the interplay of lapse, resulting trust, and capture doctrine. If the holder of a general inter vivos power of appointment dies without having effectively exercised the power, the power expires.[900] Likewise, if the holder of a general testamentary power of appointment fails to effectively exercise the power by will, the power expires at the holder's death. In either case, the gift-in-default clause in the granting instrument, if there is such a clause, controls the disposition of the unappointed property.[901] (So also if a power expires by inter vivos disclaimer or release.[902]) The time when a power expires "is almost invariably the death of the donee,"[903] although one could certainly fashion a grant of a general power that would be capable of expiring before its donee had, such as upon the exhaustion of an intervening equitable estate *pur autre vie*. The concept of the estate *pur autre vie* is discussed generally in Section 8.15.64 of this handbook.

The Restatement (Third) of Property speaks in terms of a general power "lapsing," an unfortunate innovation.[904] Its predecessors spoke in terms of a power "expiring,"[905] which is less ambiguous in that the term lapse can mean "to pass to another through neglect or omission."[906] As we note in Section 8.1.1 of this handbook, a power of appointment itself is never directly transmissible.

But what if the donor of an expired power had neglected in the granting instrument to provide for takers-in-default, or the instrument's gift-in-default clause was ineffective when the power expired? In that case, the unappointed property passes upon a resulting trust back to the donor if the donor is then living, or into the probate estate of the donor if the donor is not then living, but, again, not until all valid intervening equitable interests have themselves expired.[907] Resulting trusts are covered generally in Section 4.1.1.1 of this handbook. *In a radical departure from settled doctrine, the Restatement (Third) of Property provides that if the donee "merely failed to exercise the power" the unappointed property is captured by the donee or the donee's estate.*[908] There is no resulting trust. There is no antilapse.

A resulting trust, however, would still be imposed in the case of expiration by disclaimer or release,[909] or upon the expiration by any means of a power of

---

[899] 26 Quinnipiac Prob. L.J. 240, 275–279 (2013).

[900] As we note in §8.1.1 of this handbook, a power of appointment is exercisable; it is never directly transferable.

[901] Restatement (Third) of Property (Wills and Other Donative Transfers) §19.22(a).

[902] Restatement (Third) of Property (Wills and Other Donative Transfers) §19.22(a).

[903] Restatement (First) of Property §367 cmt. d.

[904] *See* Restatement (Third) of Property (Wills and Other Donative Transfers) §19.22 (term lapse employed even in the section's title).

[905] *See, e.g.,* Restatement (First) of Property §367 cmt. d.

[906] The American Heritage Dictionary 1014 (3d ed. 1996).

[907] *See, e.g.,* Restatement (First) of Property §367(1).

[908] Restatement (Third) of Property (Wills and Other Donative Transfers) §19.22(b).

[909] Restatement (Third) of Property (Wills and Other Donative Transfers) §19.22(b).

revocation, amendment, or withdrawal.[910] Again, as we did in more detail in our discussion of ineffective exercises of general powers in Section 8.15.12 of this handbook, we question the logic of treating a power of "revocation, amendment, or withdrawal" differently from other "types" of general inter vivos power of appointment, whether for capture purposes generally or for any other purpose. A resulting trust also would be imposed if the donee "expressly refrained from exercising the power."[911] Of course, this discussion is entirely academic if the donor is also the donee of the expired general power. The unappointed property would then end up in the probate estate of the donee in any case, whether by imposition of a resulting trust under traditional doctrine or by quasi-capture.[912]

The Restatement (Third) of Property exhibits a curious and tenacious aversion to invoking applicable resulting trust doctrine,[913] particularly in the sections devoted to unexercised or ineffectively exercised general powers of appointment.[914] The result is an unhelpful dearth of context, particularly when it comes to following chains of title, as well as a fair amount of general incoherence. Take, for example, Section 19.22(b), which in part reads: " . . . but if the donee released the power or expressly refrained from exercising the power, the unappointed property passes under a reversionary interest to the donor or to the donor's transferees or successors in interest." The phrase "passes under a reversionary interest" is nonsensical in the trust context. What actually happens is that the legal title to the unappointed property passes from the trustee to the donor or his personal representative upon a resulting trust such that the equitable reversion, which had vested *ab initio*, becomes possessory. Nothing is passing from the trustee under, over, or in a reversionary interest.

We also quibble with the failure of all of the Restatements to expressly confirm that in the face of an expired power of appointment, title to property unappointed does not leave the hands of the trustee until such time as all valid intervening equitable estates have themselves expired, unless the terms of the trust so provide. An intervening equitable estate typically would be an equitable life estate.[915]

The expired unexercised nongeneral power in the absence of a taker-in-default provision. We take up in Section 8.15.90 of this handbook the disposition of property subject to an expired unexercised nongeneral power of appointment when there is no taker-in-default provision in the instrument that granted the power. As we explain in the section, under the power-in-trust and the implied-gift-in-default doctrines, title to the appointive property passes outright and

---

[910] Restatement (Third) of Property (Wills and Other Donative Transfers) §19.22 cmt. f.

[911] Restatement (Third) of Property (Wills and Other Donative Transfers) §19.22(b).

[912] The traditional capture doctrine is discussed generally in Section 8.15.12 of this handbook.

[913] *See, e.g.,* Restatement (Third) of Property (Wills and Other Donative Transfers) §25.2 (although the title to the sections is *Reversion or Remainder,* the resulting trust is mentioned once, and only in passing).

[914] *See generally* §8.1.1 of this handbook (the power of appointment).

[915] *See generally* §8.27 of this handbook (the equitable life estate).

free of trust to the permissible appointees in lieu of the imposition of a resulting trust. In Section 8.1.1 of this handbook we discuss how the property Restatements have been pushing the implied-gift-in-default approach. Breaking with tradition, the Restatement (Third) of Property would apply antilapse principles to the situation where a permissible appointee has predeceased a power's expiration.[916] Antilapse, of course, would still not be an option in the face of an operative taker-in-default provision in the granting instrument, or when the class of permissible appointees has not been sufficiently defined and limited.[917]

§8.15.56   120-Hour Survival Requirement [The Trust Application]

. . . [F]or purposes of a provision of a governing instrument that relates to an individual surviving an event, including the death of another individual, an individual who is not established by clear and convincing evidence to have survived the event by 120 hours is deemed to have predeceased the event.—Uniform Probate Code[918]

The requirement. Let us take an equitable interest under an irrevocable trust that is subject to the condition precedent of survivorship. *A* (the settlor), for example, establishes a trust for the benefit of *C* (the current beneficiary) for *C*'s lifetime. Upon the death of *C*, the property passes outright and free of trust to *D* (the remainderman), provided *D* is then living. If *D* is not then living, the property passes to the Red Cross for its purposes.

At common law, if *D* survived *C* even for a second, *D* met the survivorship requirement.[919] If *D* then died before distribution was effected, the property having vested in *D* would pass to *D*'s probate estate.[920] Under the Uniform Probate Code's 120 hours survival requirement, on the other hand, the property would pass either to *D*'s issue under the Code's antilapse provision or divert to the Red Cross.[921]

At common law, if *C* and *D* were to die together in an automobile accident, it would fall to the competing parties, in this case the executor of *D*'s probate estate and the Red Cross, to prove the order of deaths.[922] Such litigation was expensive and time-consuming, requiring on occasion the introduction of "gruesome" facts into evidence.[923] Outcomes often turned on "minor and fortuitous differences in timing."[924] The Uniform Probate Code's 120 hours

---

[916] Restatement (Third) of Property (Wills and Other Donative Transfers) §19.23(b).

[917] Restatement (Third) of Property (Wills and Other Donative Transfers) §19.23(b).

[918] UPC §2-702(b).

[919] Uniform Simultaneous Death Act (1993), Prefatory Note.

[920] *See generally* §8.2.1.3 of this handbook (the vesting of interests under trusts).

[921] UPC §2-702 (Requirement of Survival by 120 Hours). *See generally* §8.15.55 of this handbook (antilapse [the trust application]).

[922] Uniform Simultaneous Death Act (1993), Prefatory Note.

[923] Uniform Simultaneous Death Act (1993), Prefatory Note.

[924] Edward C. Halbach, Jr. & Lawrence W. Waggoner, *The UPC's New Survivorship and Antilapse Provisions*, 55 Alb. L. Rev. 1091, 1095 (1992).

survivorship requirement in cases (1) where there is no evidence that the order of deaths was other than simultaneous and (2) where the period of survival is insubstantial is intended to more or less render moot for property devolution purposes the factual question of who survived whom.[925]

To be sure one may draft around the 120-hour survival requirement in jurisdictions that have adopted the Uniform Probate Code (or the Uniform Simultaneous Death Act (1993)), but doing so takes some skill: The governing instrument must expressly indicate that an individual is not required to survive an event, including the death of another individual, by a specified period or expressly require the individual to survive the event by any specified period.[926] Survival of the event or the specified period, however, must be established by clear and convincing evidence.[927] Language in the governing instrument dealing explicitly with simultaneous death or deaths in a common disaster will also trump the default law, provided the "language is operable under the facts of the case."[928] Finally, there are some technical exceptions to the 120-hour survival requirement. One example is when its application to multiple governing instruments would result in an unintended failure or duplication of a disposition.[929] Another exception is when imposition of the requirement would cause a nonvested property interest or a power of appointment to violate the Rule against Perpetuities.[930] Massachusetts has elected not to include the 120-hour survivorship requirement in its version of the Uniform Probate Code.

Evidentiary matters. Under the Uniform Probate Code, a certified or authenticated copy of a death certificate purportedly issued by an official or agency of the place where the death purportedly occurred is prima facie evidence of the identity of the decedent and the fact of his or her death.[931] It also is prima facie evidence of the place, date, and time of death.[932] A certified or authenticated copy of any record or report of a governmental agency, domestic or foreign, that an individual has died is prima facie evidence of that fact, as well as of any circumstances surrounding the event that are disclosed by the record or report.[933] Otherwise, the fact of death must be established by clear and convincing evidence, which may include circumstantial evidence.[934] An undisputed entry on one of the aforementioned official documents of a time of death that is 120 hours or more after the time when another person was purported to have died establishes clear and convincing that there has been compliance with the Code's 120-hour survivorship requirement, no matter how

[925] Uniform Simultaneous Death Act (1993), Prefatory Note.
[926] UPC §2-702(d)(2).
[927] UPC §2-702(d)(2).
[928] UPC §2-702(d)(1).
[929] UPC §2-702(d)(4).
[930] UPC §2-702(d)(3).
[931] UPC §1-107(2).
[932] UPC §1-107(2).
[933] UPC §1-107(3).
[934] UPC §1-107(4).

the other person's time of death was determined.[935] A beneficiary who has been missing without a trace and for no apparent reason for a continuous period of five years is *presumed* dead, providing there has been a diligent good faith inquiry into the circumstances surrounding the beneficiary's absence that has turned up nothing.[936]

§8.15.57   Novation

In the civil law, there are three kinds of novation: Where the debtor and creditor remain the same, but a new debt takes the place of the old one; where the debt remains the same, but a new debtor is substituted; where the debt and debtor remain, but a new creditor is substituted.[937]

A novation is the substitution of one enforceable obligation for another with full consent of all parties. At law, it can take the form of the substitution of one contractual obligation for another.[938] In equity it can take the form of the substitution of a debt for a trust, or the substitution of a trust for a debt.[939]

Here is an example of a trust-to-debt novation: A trustee, which happens to be a bank, at the beneficiary's request credits the beneficiary's checking account at the bank with a trust income payment. The trust is a spendthrift trust. At the time the payment is credited, there is a trust-to-debt novation, *i.e.*, the relationship between the parties with respect to the payment changes from one of trustee-beneficiary to one of debtor-creditor. As a consequence, the payment—unlike the trust principal and any undistributed or uncredited trust income—is commingled with the general assets of the bank and becomes accessible to *the bank's general creditors* in the event of the bank's insolvency. Moreover, the debt is reachable by *the beneficiary's creditors*, notwithstanding the trust's spendthrift clause.[940]

A debt-to-trust novation would work like this: A borrower owes the lender $1 million. The borrower impresses a trust upon property valued at $1 million for the benefit of the lender. It the lender consents, the debt is discharged, with the result that the lender's contractual rights are replaced by an equitable interest in the trust property.[941] There is, in other words, a debt-to-trust novation.[942] Absent the lender's consent, however, the creditor may elect to enforce either the debt or the trust. One practical consequence of a novation

---

[935] UPC §1-107(6).

[936] UPC §1-107(5). "His [or her] death is presumed to have occurred at the end of the period unless there is sufficient evidence for determining that death occurred earlier." UPC §1-107(5).

[937] Black's Law Dictionary (4th ed.) (citing to Wheeler v. Wardell, 173 Va. 168, 3 S.E.2d 377, 380 (1939).

[938] Wheeler v. Wardell, 173 Va. 168, 3 S.E.2d 377, 380 (1939).

[939] *See generally* 1 Scott on Trusts §§12.11 (Trust-to-Debt), 12.12 (Debt-to-Trust); 1 Scott & Ascher §§2.3.8.8 (Trust-to-Debt) & 2.3.8.9 (Debt-to-Trust).

[940] *See generally* §5.3.3.3(c) of this handbook (the non–self-settled spendthrift trust).

[941] *See generally* 5 Scott & Ascher §35.1.9 (Trust for Particular Creditor).

[942] 5 Scott & Ascher §35.1.9 (Trust for Particular Creditor).

may be that the lender is out from under the statute of limitations applicable to contract actions.[943]

For a discussion of the fundamental differences between a debt and a trust, the reader is referred to Section 9.9.4 of this handbook.

§8.15.58 Precatory Words

precatory adj. Relating to or expressing entreaty or supplication. [Late Latin precatorius, from Latin precari, to entreat]—The American Heritage Dictionary of the English Language.

As the Third Restatement puts it, It is no longer the case, as it once appeared to be in England, that the wish of the testator, like that of a sovereign, is to be taken as a command.[944]

Giving rise to an express trust. Precatory words are words of entreaty, request, desire, wish, or recommendation, rather than command. Today, courts are less inclined to read into precatory words a polite manifestation of intention to create a trust than was the case in earlier times.[945] In earlier times, a devise from *A* to *B* coupled with an expression of desire that *B* at his death pass the property on to *A*'s issue might well be construed as the manifestation of an intention to impress a trust upon the devised property.[946] Today, courts would be less inclined to find a trust under these facts. Instead, *B* would take the property outright and free of trust and would be free to do whatever he wanted with it. "...[U]nder the modern view, the question is whether the...[settlor]...intended to impose an enforceable obligation to carry out the stated desire."[947]

Giving rise to a power of appointment. Comment e of Section 18.1 of the Restatement (Third) of Property (Wills and Other Donative Transfers) begins with an endorsement of the presumption that precatory words alone are unlikely to give rise to an enforceable trust. It then suggests that such words might, however, "be a sufficient indication of intent to give the transferee a power of appointment over an interest not given to the transferee." The comment's precatory words discussion, however, does not get into the equitable power of appointment, such as when certain precatory words might suggest that the trustee, the transferee of the legal title, possesses a nonfiduciary equitable power of appointment over the beneficiary's equitable property interest. The only supportive illustration (Illustration 9) involves precatory words that might evidence an intention to grant someone a legal power of appointment over

---

[943] *See generally* §7.2.10 of this handbook (limitation of action by beneficiary against trustee (laches and statutes of limitation)).

[944] 1 Scott & Ascher §4.3.2 (citing to Restatement (Third) of Trusts §13 cmt. d).

[945] 1 Scott & Ascher §4.3.2.

[946] 1 Scott & Ascher §4.3.1.

[947] 1 Scott & Ascher §4.3.2. *See generally* Frank L. Schiavo, *Does the Use of "Request," "Wish," or "Desire," Create a Precatory Trust or Not?*, 40 Real Prop. Prob. & Tr. J. 647 (Winter 2006) (concluding that there is no bright-line test for determining whether a wish is actually a command).

someone else's property. The Reporter's Notes are not particularly helpful either. For the most part, they address when precatory expressions might indicate that a power is nongeneral rather than general, an issue that the comment itself addresses only obliquely, and not in the trust context.

§8.15.59   The Tontine

The concept of the tontine surely predates its namesake, Neapolitan banker Lorenzo de Tonti (c.1602–c.1684).[948] In its crassest form, investors pay into a pool with the understanding that the principal will pass to the last survivor, a form of "death gamble" that one U.S. court suggested as recently as 1981 "ought not to be encouraged or expanded beyond limits of tontine insurance which has hitherto been recognized by law."[949] The court, of course, was alluding to the age-old societal concern that the tontine might tempt its investors to kill one another off. In the tontine's traditional and more benign form, the investors receive an ever-increasing share of the pool's income stream as their numbers die off, with the principal ultimately passing to the state or to the scheme sponsor, perhaps the developer of a building or a block of houses. (One court has referred to a frozen underfunded pension plan under which older participants receive full benefits and younger participants receive reduced benefits as a "reverse tontine."[950])

Today, the spirit of the tontine lives on, and not just in the works of Robert Louis Stevenson[951] and P. G. Wodehouse.[952] There are insurance products with tontine features. A premium-payer's property interest, however, is not in a segregated pool but in the form of contractual rights against the insurance company.[953] A joint bank account with right of survivorship, to be sure, is a poor man's will; but it is also a poor man's tontine. One commentator has suggested that the traditional tontine is a financial product that is tailor-made for investors concerned about outliving their nest eggs.[954]

As we write, there are personal trusts being administered with tontine-like features, e.g., income in equal shares to a class of individuals, with the principal passing outright and free of trust to those members of the class alive at the expiration of the trust's term. One court, in upholding such a provision in a testamentary trust, addressed the public policy considerations:

---

[948] It is said that Lorenzo de Tonti proposed to Louis XIV that a national tontine income scheme would be a way of financing his military campaigns without levying new taxes, with the principal passing to the state upon the death of the last investor.

[949] Quinn v. Stuart Lakes Club, Inc., 80 A.D.2d 350, 354, 439 N.Y.S.2d 30, 33 (1981).

[950] Aon Trust Corp. v. KPMG (a firm) and others, [2005] EWCA Civ. 1004 (England).

[951] *The Wrong Box* (1889).

[952] *Something Fishy* (*The Butler Did It* in the United States) (1957).

[953] Pierce v. Equitable Life Assurance Soc'y, 145 Mass. 56, 12 N.E. 858 (1887); Uhlman v. New York Life Ins. Co., 109 N.Y. 421, 17 N.E. 363 (1888).

[954] *See* Moshe A. Milevsky, *Want Financial Security? Look to the Renaissance*, Wall St. J, Apr. 22, 2013, at R4.

A court may not distribute the testator's estate according to the court's sense of equity and justice rather than the testator's intention as expressed in the will. After all, except as limited by statute or contract, a testator has the right to distribute his property as he wishes. He can only do this through the words he employs in his will. Accordingly he must be able to rely on the fact that the court cannot and will not distort the clear language to achieve a result it prefers to the result the testator desired. It may be true, as appellants contend, that the quasi-tontine arrangement in the will is not equitable but it is not illegal. Being legal and not contrary to public policy, it must be given effect.[955]

§8.15.60 Constructive Fraud

Constructive fraud has all the elements of fraud, except the element of intent to defraud or deceive: "The principle is well settled, that if a person makes a representation of a fact, as of his own knowledge, in relation to a subject matter susceptible of knowledge, and such representation is not true; if the party to whom it is made relies and acts upon it, as true, and sustains damage by it, it is fraud for which the party making it is responsible."[956] The negligent misrepresentation must be incident to some legal or equitable relationship.[957] Parties in a contractual relationship generally have a legal duty to deal fairly and in good faith.[958] The fiduciary in an equitable relationship, *e.g.*, an agent or a trustee, has a panoply of duties incident to that relationship, duties that are enumerated and discussed in Chapter 6 of this handbook.

In the trust context, the doctrine of constructive fraud and the *Cambridge Trust Case*[959] will be forever linked in the minds of trust professionals on this side of the Atlantic. The case involved a testamentary trust for the benefit of the settlor's widow. Upon her remarriage, the trust was to continue for the benefit of a charity. The trust was funded in 1932. In 1945 the widow remarried but through the employment of elaborate ruses she managed to hide the fact of her remarriage from the trustee until her death in 1967. Thus, the trustee in violation of the terms of the trust and to the detriment of the charity continued to pay the net trust accounting income to the widow until her death, when at last it discovered its mistake.

The charity sought to have the court reopen a number of the trustee's previously allowed accounts and order the trustee to make the trust whole out of its own pocket, if necessary, for the amounts that it had misdelivered. By statute,

---

[955] Continental Ill. Nat'l Bank & Trust Co. of Chicago v. Bailey, 104 Ill. App. 3d 1131, 1139, 433 N.E.2d 1098, 1103 (1982).

[956] Page v. Bent, 2 Met. 371, 374 (Mass. 1841) (Chief Justice Lemuel Shaw rendering the opinion).

[957] *Cf.* Estate of Draper v. Bank of Am., N.A., 288 Kan. 510, 205 P.3d 698 (2009) ("Constructive fraud is a 'breach of a legal or equitable duty which, irrespective of moral guilt, the law declares fraudulent because of its tendency to deceive others or violate a confidence, and neither actual dishonesty [n]or purpose or intent to deceive is necessary.'").

[958] Wells v. Stone City Bank, 691 N.E.2d 1246 (Ind. Ct. App. 1998).

[959] National Acad. of Sci. v. Cambridge Trust Co., trustee, 370 Mass. 303, 346 N.E.2d 879 (1976).

allowed trustee accounts generally cannot be reopened, except for fraud or manifest error.[960] While it was clear that the trustee had not intended to misrepresent the widow's marital status on the accountings, it was also clear that the trustee's inattention, in the words of even the dissent, was "pathetic."[961] In fact, the trial court found that the trustee had exerted no effort whatsoever to ascertain the widow's marital status, not even going so far as to solicit from her periodic affidavits. Accordingly, the court found that the trustee's negligent misrepresentation of the widow's marital status on the face of the accountings, a misrepresentation that was occasioned by the absence of even a halfhearted effort to ascertain the critical fact of the widow's marital status, constituted a constructive fraud perpetrated by the trustee against the charity warranting a reopening of the trustee's previously allowed accounts.

One court, this time in New York, has ruled that misrepresentations of law and fact made by a corporate cotrustee's counsel to a beneficiary, *i.e.*, by an agent of the corporate cotrustee, were grounds for opening and vacating a decree that had judicially settled the intermediate accounts of the cotrustees, notwithstanding the fact that the beneficiary had signed a general waiver and release running to the cotrustees.[962] The time for appeal had long passed. As it happened, the testamentary trust during the period covered by the intermediate account had sustained substantial realized losses from the sale of stock in the corporate cotrustee.[963] Granted the stock was an inception asset; but the will contained no language expressly authorizing its retention. All things being equal, the presence of such language would have been a defense to allegations that the corporate cotrustee had breached its duty of loyalty to the beneficiary in retaining its own stock in the trust.[964] Trust counsel's statements to the beneficiary to induce the beneficiary to execute the waiver and release, namely, "that nothing could be done about . . . [the shrinkage in value of the trust estate] . . . and that the signing of the release would save time and money," constituted at least constructive fraud such that a reopening of the accounts was warranted.[965] The fraud having been perpetrated by an agent of the corporate cotrustee, the court imputed it to the cotrustee.

A trustee seeking a waiver or release who fails to disclose to the beneficiary all material facts, including those facts that are not in the interest of the trustee to disclose, perpetrates a fraud against the beneficiary.[966] If the failure to disclose is *not* coupled with an intent to deceive, then the fraud is constructive.[967] To the extent trust counsel is involved in a continuing deliberate effort to defeat the rights of the beneficiary through the withholding of material

---

[960] *See generally* §6.1.5.2 of this handbook (duty to keep and render accounts).

[961] National Acad. of Sci. v. Cambridge Trust Co., trustee, 370 Mass. 303, 313, 346 N.E.2d 879, 885 (1976).

[962] In re Gillies' Will, 98 N.YS.2d 853 (1950).

[963] *See generally* §6.1.3.2 of this handbook (trustee invests in its own stock).

[964] *See generally* §7.1.2 of this handbook (defenses to allegations that the trustee breached the duty of loyalty).

[965] In re Gillies' Will, 98 N.YS.2d 853, 856 (1950).

[966] First Union Nat'l Bank v. Turney, 824 So. 2d 172, 188–189 (Fla. 2002).

[967] First Union Nat'l Bank v. Turney, 824 So. 2d 172, 191 (Fla. 2002).

information, communications between the trustee and trust counsel made in the course of that effort may not be privileged.[968] They are said to come within the crime-fraud exception to the attorney-client privilege.

§8.15.61   The Privity Barrier (Scrivener Malpractice)

Trust litigation usually involves an adjudication of the rights of the beneficiaries and the duties of the trustee, followed by the granting of equitable relief when appropriate. Often, however, the root cause of the conflict is the governing instrument itself. Terms may be ambiguous or contingencies may not have been addressed. Those whom the settlor intended to share the equitable interest may have been left out. Or there may be tax liabilities that could have been avoided. Inevitably, the question will come up whether someone should be thinking about filing a separate legal malpractice tort action against the drafting attorney, *i.e.*, against the scrivener.[969] If the settlor is deceased, there may be a privity barrier to doing this. Over the last fifty years, we have seen it reinforced in some jurisdictions,[970] afforded reluctant deference in others,[971] and dismantled in still others.[972]

Here is the privity doctrine and its rationale: The settlor was in an agency relationship with the drafting attorney,[973] not the beneficiaries. The settlor and attorney also were in a contractual relationship incident to the agency relationship. The duties of the lawyer-agent ran solely to the client-principal.[974] The beneficiaries, and those who would be beneficiaries but for the malpractice, therefore, lack the standing to bring the malpractice action. "Absent fraud, collusion, malicious acts, or other special circumstances, an attorney is not liable

---

[968] First Union Nat'l Bank v. Turney, 824 So. 2d 172, 191 (Fla. 2002).

[969] *See, e.g.*, Estate of Carlson, 895 N.E.2d 1191 (Ind. 2008).

[970] *See, e.g.*, Fredriksen v. Fredriksen, 817 N.Y.S.2d 320 (2006).

[971] *See, e.g.*, Peleg v. Spitz, 2007 WL 4200611 (Ohio App. 8th Dist.).

[972] *See, e.g.*, Lucas v. Hamm, 56 Cal. 2d 583, 364 P.2d 685 (1961); Bucquet v. Livingston, 129 Cal. Rptr. 514 (Ct. App. 1976). *But see* Radovich v. Locke-Paddon, 41 Cal. Rptr. 2d 573 (Ct. App. 1995) (attorney owed no duty to potential testamentary trust beneficiary of a will that was never executed); Chang v. Lederman, 90 Cal. Rptr. 3d 758 (Ct. App. 2009) ("Accordingly, we conclude a testator's attorney owes no duty to a person in the position of Chang, an expressly named beneficiary who attempts to assert a legal malpractice claim not on the ground her actual bequest (here, the $15,000 gift) was improperly perfected but based on an allegation the testator intended to revise his or her estate plan to increase that bequest and would have done so but for the attorney's negligence. Expanding the attorney's duty of care to include actual beneficiaries who could have been, but were not, named in a revised estate plan, just like including third parties who could have been, but were not, named in a bequest, would expose attorneys to impossible duties and limitless liability because the interests of such potential beneficiaries are always in conflict").

[973] *See generally* Charles E. Rounds, Jr., *Lawyer Codes Are Just About Licensure, the Lawyer's Relationship with the State: Recalling the Common Law Agency, Contract, Tort, Trust, and Property Principles the Regulate the Lawyer-Client Fiduciary Relationship*, 60 Baylor L. Rev. 771 (2008).

[974] *See generally* Charles E. Rounds, Jr., *Lawyer Codes Are Just About Licensure, the Lawyer's Relationship with the State: Recalling the Common Law Agency, Contract, Tort, Trust, and Property Principles the Regulate the Lawyer-Client Fiduciary Relationship*, 60 Baylor L. Rev. 771 (2008).

to third parties not in privity or near-privity for harm caused by professional negligence."[975] This is as good an example as any of a wrong without a remedy.[976]

And as to the trustee, his fiduciary duties run to those who, rightly or wrongly, are the beneficiaries, not to those who would be but for the scrivener's malpractice. For more on whom counsel represents when a trust is involved, the reader is referred to Section 8.8 of this handbook.

§8.15.62 Equitable Apportionment Doctrine

No more just doctrine is found in the entire range of equity; although it is now a familiar rule of the law, it should not be forgotten that its conception and origin are wholly due to the creative functions of the chancellor.[977]

The doctrine of equitable apportionment is an application of the equitable maxim: Equality is equity.[978] In the contract context, it requires that each cocontractor share in the liabilities incident to the contract in proportion to the benefits he or she receives under the contract. It is, of course, a default law principle. Express provisions in the contract may provide otherwise. "This doctrine is evidently based upon the notion that the burden in all such cases should be equally borne by all persons upon whom it is imposed, and its necessary effect is to equalize that burden whenever one of the parties has, in pursuance of his mere *legal* liability, paid or been compelled to pay the whole amount, or any amount greater than his proportionate share."[979]

In the trust context, the doctrine's most common application is in the apportionment of tax obligations between and among classes of beneficiaries of a trust, between and among trusts, and between a probate estate and one or more trusts.[980] The residue of a probate estate, for example, might have a statutory or legal obligation to bear the burden of all estate taxes occasioned by the death of the testator, in the absence of provisions to the contrary in the governing estate planning documentation. Under the doctrine of equitable apportionment, the testator's revocable inter vivos trust or the QTIP trust of his

---

[975] *See, e.g.*, Fredriksen v. Fredriksen, 817 N.Y.S.2d 320, 321 (2006).

[976] *See, e.g.*, Peleg v. Spitz, 2007 WL 4200611 (Ohio App. 8th Dist.) (confirming that under Ohio law, as of 2007, intended or potential trust beneficiaries has no legal remedy for damages suffered as a result of scrivener malpractice).

[977] Roe v. Estate of Farrell, 372 N.E.2d 662, 665–666 (Ill. 1978) (citing 2 John N. Pomeroy, Jr., Equity Jurisprudence §411 (5th ed. 1941). All the Lord Chancellors who have held office from 1066 A.D. to the present are listed in Chapter 1 of this handbook.

[978] *See generally* §8.12 of this handbook (containing a catalog of equity maxims).

[979] Roe v. Estate of Farrell, 372 N.E.2d 662, 665–666 (Ill. 1978) (citing 2 John N. Pomeroy, Jr., Equity Jurisprudence §411 (5th ed. 1941).

[980] *See, e.g.*, Estate of Williams, 853 N.E.2d 79 (Ill. Ct. App. 2006) (the court equitably apportioning the estate tax obligation occasioned by the death of the surviving spouse between her probate estate and the assets of her late husband's marital deduction trust for her benefit, although her will expressly provided for the payment of estate taxes from her probate residue and his trust lacked a tax clause).

or her predeceased spouse might be called upon to bear an appropriate share of the tax liability. The topic of the apportionment of tax liabilities within a trust and between a trust and other entities is discussed in Section 8.20 of this handbook.

§8.15.63   Doctrine of Bona Fide Purchase; the BFP

If my trustee conveys the land to a third person who well knows that the trustee holds for my use, I shall have a remedy in the Chancery against both of them: as well against the buyer as against the trustee; for in conscience he buys my land.—1471 English decision[981]

The rule of purchase for value without notice or bona fide purchase is an affirmative defense to a claim for restitution, a topic that is taken up in Section 7.2.3.3 of this handbook. "One who purchases an asset for value, without notice of competing claims, takes the asset subject to prior legal interests, but free of equitable interests to which the asset was subject in the hands of the grantor."[982] In the trust context that simply means that a trustee generally may transfer his or her title to the trust property to a BFP, who will take the property free of trust. The Restatement (Third) of Trusts is fully in accord.[983] The trustee, however, cannot convey to the purchaser a more extensive *legal title* than the trustee had to begin with.[984]

The BFP concept's legal backdrop. When a trustee sells trust property to a third person and the transaction is not in breach of trust, the third person holds the property free of trust.[985] On the other hand, when a trustee *in breach of trust* transfers to a third person title to an item of trust property, the transferee takes it subject to the trust and to the beneficiary's equitable interests thereunder. Otherwise, the transferee would be unjustly enriched.[986] This is the case even if the transfer is a breach of trust occasioned by the death of the trustee.[987] In other words, the transferee, if innocent, is a resulting trustee of the subject property, and if not innocent, then a constructive trustee of it.[988] As such, he may be ordered by the court in the exercise of its equitable powers to reconvey

---

[981] Anonymous, Y.B. 11 Edw. 4, Trin., fol. 8, pl. 13 (1471), translated in Maitland, Selected Essays 166 (1936).

[982] Restatement (Third) of Restitution and Unjust Enrichment §66 cmt. a.

[983] *See* Restatement (Third) of Trusts §108(2).

[984] Restatement (Third) of Restitution and Unjust Enrichment §66 cmt. a.

[985] 5 Scott & Ascher §29.1.

[986] *See* §8.15.78 of this handbook (unjust enrichment).

[987] *See generally* 5 Scott & Ascher §29.1.6.1 (Devolution on Death of Trustee); §3.4.3 of this handbook (death of trustee).

[988] *See generally* §§3.3 of this handbook (the constructive trust); 7.2.3.1.6 of this handbook (the constructive trust as a procedural equitable remedy); 4.1.1.1 of this handbook (the resulting trust).

the title back to the trustee or to his successor in office.[989] The doctrine of bona fide purchase is an exception to this general rule.[990]

The equitable rights of the good-faith purchaser for value (BFP). If the transferee is a bona fide or good-faith purchaser for full value (BFP) of the item of property, the transferee may keep the item,[991] or transfer it on to a fourth party free of the trust and its attendant equities, *notwithstanding the fact that the initial transfer was occasioned by a breach of trust*.[992] The rights of the trust beneficiary to that property are subordinated to those of the BFP, and to those who take lawfully from the BFP, as the BFP has not been unjustly enriched.[993] The transfer of a specific item of trust property by the trustee to a BFP also cuts off any nonpossessory vested equitable reversionary interest which the settlor may have in that property that could have become possessory upon imposition of a resulting trust.[994] It also would cut off the rights of anyone who had succeeded to that interest by assignment, on account of the settlor's death, or otherwise.[995] The rights of the beneficiary of a purchase money resulting trust are similarly cut off by a transfer to a BFP.[996]

Critical elements of the BFP doctrine. For the transferee to be a BFP of property held in an express trust, the transferee must neither have had notice,[997] actual or constructive,[998] of the trustee's breach of trust and must have

---

[989] *See generally* §7.2.3.1 of this handbook (tracing and accounting for proceeds and profits).

[990] *See generally* Restatement of Restitution §172 (the defense of bona fide purchase).

[991] *See generally* Scott & Ascher §13.1; Restatement of Restitution §172 (the defense of bona fide purchase).

[992] *See generally* 5 Scott & Ascher §29.6.1 (Transferee from Bona Fide Purchaser); Restatement of Restitution §172 (the defense of bona fide purchase). Should the trustee reacquire the property from a BFP, the property will again become subject to the terms of the trust. 5 Scott & Ascher §29.6.2 (Retransfer by Bona Fide Purchaser to Trustee); Restatement of Restitution §176 (retransfer by bona fide purchaser). So too if a prior transferee with notice reacquires the property from a BFP. *See generally* 5 Scott & Ascher §29.6.3 (Retransfer by Bona Fide Purchaser to Transferee with Notice).

[993] Restatement of Restitution §172 (the defense of bona fide purchase); §8.15.78 of this handbook (unjust enrichment).

[994] *See generally* 6 Scott & Ascher §40.5 (Transfer by Trustee); §4.1.1.1 of this handbook (the resulting trust and the equitable reversionary interest).

[995] Restatement of Restitution §172 (the defense of bona fide purchase).

[996] *See generally* 6 Scott & Ascher §43.13 (Rights of Creditors of Trustee When Beneficiary of Purchase-Money Resulting Trust Is Estopped); §3.3 of this handbook (the purchase-money resulting trust generally); Restatement of Restitution §172 (the defense of bona fide purchase).

[997] *See generally* 5 Scott & Ascher §29.1.5 (Transferee with Notice); §8.3.6 of this handbook (negotiable instruments and the duty of third parties to inquire into the trustee's authority); Restatement of Restitution §174 (notice); Restatement (Third) of Restitution and Unjust Enrichment §69 (notice).

[998] "A broad definition of notice for these and similar purposes is widely accepted. 'Notice' is a legal category that combines actual knowledge with imputed knowledge. While imputed knowledge is described in practice under such various headings as 'statutory notice,' 'record notice,' 'constructive notice,' and 'inquiry notice,' or by reference to a person's 'duty of inquiry,' the different labels attach to what is essentially a common idea. In particular circumstances, and for a variety of reasons, the law will treat a person as knowing a fact without requiring that such knowledge be proven directly." Restatement (Third) of Restitution and Unjust Enrichments §69 cmt. a., illus. 7 & illus.13.

paid value[999] for the item. And title must have passed.[1000] Even the indenture trustee of a corporate trust may pass good title to a BFP.[1001] Moreover, nowadays a BFP would have no duty to the trust beneficiaries to see to it that the trustee properly applies the purchase price.[1002] Since time immemorial, however, it has been the case that if the transferee pays no consideration, he or she takes subject to the express trust. Innocence is no defense. Justice Holmes explained in an 1897 Massachusetts case:

> A person to whose hands a trust fund comes by conveyance from the original trustee is chargeable as a trustee in his turn if he takes it without consideration, whether he has notice of the trust or not. This has been settled for 300 years,—since the time of uses. "If the feoffees enfeoff one without consideration it is to the first use although it be without notice." Y.B. 14 Hen. VIII. p. 9, pl. 5: Chudleigh's Case, 1 Coke, 120, 122b.[1003]

The restitutionary claimant versus the judicial lien creditor. Assume the trustee wrongfully makes off with an identifiable asset of the trust estate, say, an oil painting. A personal creditor of the trustee obtains a judicial lien on the painting. Who prevails, the restitutionary claimant, *i.e.*, the trust beneficiary (the trust) or the judicial lien creditor? "When the question is adjudicated as a matter of common law and equity, unmodified by statute, the answer uniformly given is that a judicial lien creditor is not a purchaser for value; so that whereas a bona fide purchaser would indeed take the contested asset free of the 'equities' of . . . restitutionary claimants . . . , a creditor's judicial lien can reach only the 'actual estate' of the debtor, subject to any adverse claim to which it was subject in the debtor's hands."[1004] In other words, the beneficiary (the trust) prevails. The general topic of equitable restitution is taken up in Section 7.2.3.3 of this handbook.

Trustee takes title to the sale proceeds from the BFP subject to the terms of the trust. In the case of a transfer of entrusted assets to a BFP incident to a breach of trust, the trustee, of course, takes title to the sale proceeds subject to the terms of the trust. Thus, all is not lost as far as the beneficiary is concerned. Moreover, the beneficiary would still have recourse *against the trustee personally* for any residual harm to the equitable interest that had been occasioned by the

---

[999] 5 Scott & Ascher §29.1.6; Restatement of Restitution §173 (value).

[1000] *See generally* §5.4.2 of this handbook (rights of the beneficiary as against transferees of the underlying property, including BFPs); Restatement of Restitution §172 (a BFP must have acquired title); Restatement of Restitution §175 (transfer after notice). The trustee also could cut off the rights of the beneficiaries to the item by transferring title to a non-BFP in breach of trust who then transfers the item on to a BFP. The beneficiaries would then have recourse against the non-BFP for the sales proceeds. *See generally* 5 Scott & Ascher §29.1.4.

[1001] *See generally* §9.31 of this handbook (corporate trusts; trusts to secure creditors; the Trust Indenture Act of 1939; protecting bondholders).

[1002] *See generally* §8.15.69 of this handbook (third-party liability for trustee's misapplication of payments to trustee; the purchaser's duty to monitor the trustee's application of the purchase price).

[1003] Otis v. Otis, 167 Mass. 245, 246, 45 N.E. 737 (1897).

[1004] Restatement of Restitution and Unjust Enrichment §60 cmt. b.

breach. For coverage of the practical applications of the bona fide purchase doctrine, the reader is referred to Sections 5.4.2 and 8.3.2 of this handbook.

The BFP doctrine is a gloss on an equity maxim. The BFP doctrine is actually incident to an equity maxim: Where there is equal equity, the law shall prevail.[1005] Why are the equities between the beneficiary and the BFP equal such that equity will decline to wrest the legal title from the transferee and return it to the trustee or his successor? They are equal because each party is innocent.[1006] It is self-evident that the trust beneficiary is innocent.[1007] The reason the BFP is innocent is because the BFP neither knowingly participated with the trustee in a breach of trust (recall the lack-of-notice requirement) nor was unjustly enriched (recall the payment-of-full-value requirement).[1008] The beneficiary's recourse, if any, is a complaint in equity against the trustee-transferor for breach of trust.[1009]

Whether moneys paid under a mistake of law to an innocent non-BFP need to be returned. At common law, moneys paid under a *mistake of law* to an innocent non-BFP also were not recoverable.[1010] In the trust context, when an insolvent trustee of an express trust misdelivered trust property to an innocent non-BFP, the beneficiary was out of luck,[1011] though the non-BFP had been unjustly enriched.[1012] The Restatement of Restitution has never been in accord.[1013] The injured beneficiary had no recourse against the transferee, although it is not entirely clear why the innocent transferee would not have held the property upon a resulting trust for the benefit of the beneficiary, or, if not innocent, upon a constructive trust.[1014] "In one of the most significant changes of direction in private law in the twentieth century the . . . [general] . . . rule was overturned in the House of Lords . . . by way of a lengthy deconstruction of the

---

[1005] *See generally* §8.12 of this handbook (in part containing a catalog of equity maxims); Restatement of Restitution §172 cmt. a ("The question in such cases is which of two innocent persons should suffer a loss which must be borne by one of them. . . . The principle which is applied by courts of equity is that they will not throw the loss upon a person who has innocently acquired title to property for value.").

[1006] Restatement of Restitution §172 cmt. a.

[1007] Recall that the trustee, not the beneficiary, has the legal title to the underlying trust property, and thus the power to convey. *See generally* §3.5.2.2 of this handbook (right at law to transfer title).

[1008] *See generally* 5 Scott & Ascher §§29.1.1 (Bona Fide Purchaser), 29.1.6 (Donee); Restatement of Restitution §172 (the BFP not having been unjustly enriched, there would be no grounds for the court to issue a restitution order against the BFP); §8.15.78 of this handbook (unjust enrichment). *See generally* §8.15.78 of this handbook (unjust enrichment).

[1009] 5 Scott & Ascher §29.1.1 (Bona Fide Purchaser).

[1010] *See generally* W.A. Lee, *Purifying the Dialect of Equity*, 7(2) Tr. Q. Rev. 16–23 (May 2009) [a STEP publication].

[1011] *See, e.g.*, Re Diplock [1948] Ch. 465 (England).

[1012] *See generally* §8.15.78 of this handbook (unjust enrichment).

[1013] Restatement of Restitution §44.

[1014] *See generally* §3.3 of this handbook (the constructive trust); §7.2.3.1.6 of this handbook (the constructive trust as a procedural equitable remedy); §4.1.1.1 of this handbook (the resulting trust).

precedents and academic literature by Lord Goff of Chieveley."[1015] In the trust context the rule is being nibbled away by particular exceptions.[1016] But back to the BFP.

A naked promise of the purchaser or the cancellation of an antecedent debt of the trustee will generally fall short of the BFP doctrine's value requirement. While the naked promise of a purchaser of property to pay the purchase price or the satisfaction (cancellation) of an antecedent (preexisting) debt the transferor owes to the purchaser may be sufficient consideration for an enforceable contract, neither would satisfy the BFP value requirement.[1017] This holds true in the case of the promise, absent a statute to the contrary or a sufficient change of position on the part of the transferee.[1018] In the case of the antecedent debt, it holds true as well, with some exceptions.

Exceptions to the antecedent-debt-cancellation impediment. Here are some of the exceptions: There was a release of security by the transferee; or the property transferred was a negotiable instrument or money; or there was a sufficient change of position on the part of the transferee.[1019] When it is trust money that transfers in satisfaction of an antecedent personal debt of the trustee, the innocent personal creditor of the trustee is said to be a bona fide payee.[1020] The

---

[1015] W.A. Lee, *Purifying the Dialect of Equity*, 7(2) Tr. Q. Rev. 19 (May 2009) [a STEP publication] (referring to Kleinwort Benson v. Lincoln CC, [1999] 2 AC 349 (England)).

[1016] *See, e.g.*, Re Hastings-Bass, [1975] Ch. 25; [1974] 2 WLR 904 (England).

[1017] 5 Scott & Ascher §§29.3 (Value), 29.3.5 (Promise as Value) ("For this purpose, then, it would appear that it is not the making but the performance of the promise that constitutes value"). In this regard, *see* 5 Scott & Ascher §§29.3.2 (Payment of Value Prior to Transfer) ("Since the purchaser has paid value for the property and has already received it, a court of equity will not deprive him or her of it merely because the payment of the purchase price and the transfer of title did not occur simultaneously"), 29.3.3 (Payment of Value After Transfer) ("A transferee of trust property who pays value for the transfer is a bona fide purchaser although he or she pays for the property subsequent to the transfer as long as both the transfer and the payment occur before the transferee has notice that the transfer is in breach of trust"), 29.3.7 (Satisfaction of Antecedent Debt as Value) ("Although the general rule in a majority of the states is that a creditor who receives property in satisfaction of the debt is not a purchaser for value, the rule does not apply to . . . negotiable instruments or money"). Under general equitable principles, the trust beneficiaries may not compel the innocent transferee to perform in lieu of surrendering the subject property. *See generally* 5 Scott & Ascher §29.3.5. Were the beneficiaries entitled to elect between performance and surrender, any decline in the value of the subject property would be borne by the innocent transferee and any gain would accrue to the trust beneficiaries. If the value of the subject property were to decline, for example, the beneficiaries would surely elect performance over surrender if permitted to do so, thus enriching themselves at the expense of the innocent transferee.

[1018] *See* Restatement of Restitution §173 cmt. e (promise as value); 5 Scott & Ascher §29.3.5 (noting that a land recording statute may provide that a promise to pay for property in the future satisfies the BFP value requirement with respect to a transaction covered by the statute). The Uniform Commercial Code §3-303(a)(4) provides that the purchaser's own negotiable instrument, *i.e.*, a negotiable instrument under which the purchaser is the promisor, would satisfy the BFP value requirement. *See also* 5 Scott & Ascher §29.3.5 (promise in form of negotiable instrument). A negotiable instrument held by the purchaser under which a third party is the promisor "unquestionably" would. 5 Scott & Ascher §29.3.5.

[1019] 5 Scott & Ascher §29.3.7.

[1020] *See* Restatement (Third) of Restitution and Unjust Enrichment §67, illus. 3.

creditor is not "liable in restitution" to the trust beneficiaries, provided the creditor received payment without notice of their equitable claim.[1021] The beneficiaries' (the trust's) recourse is only against the trustee.

Thus, if a trustee in breach of trust transfers trust property to an innocent third party who then cancels a debt that the trustee personally owes the third party,[1022] the third party is unlikely to be a BFP, unless one of the exceptions enumerated in the prior paragraph applies. This would certainly be the case if the entrusted property were transferred in breach of trust merely as security for the debt, although there are some commercial paper and other statutory exceptions even here.[1023] There are also some equitable exceptions, *e.g.*, if the innocent transferee releases other security or there is a substantial change of the transferee's position.[1024] Also, if an innocent third party were to make a secured personal loan to the trustee, the third party might well be a BFP, even if the trustee in breach of trust eventually secures the loan with trust property.[1025] In other words, the third party may hold the subject property as security, provided the third party had no notice of the breach prior to the transfer of the security.[1026] The key here is that we do not have an antecedent or preexisting debt.[1027]

What generally qualifies as value in the BFP context. On the other hand, a present assignment to the trustee of enforceable contractual rights which the transferee has against a third person could satisfy the BFP value requirement.[1028] So, too, could the passage of cash, real estate, or tangible personal property, or the rendering of personal services.[1029] If the purchaser makes an enforceable promise to pay a third person in exchange for the entrusted property, that too may satisfy the BFP value requirement: "The purchaser is also protected if he or she has made a promise to a third person on which the

---

[1021] *See* Restatement (Third) of Restitution and Unjust Enrichment §67, illus. 3.

[1022] *See generally* §8.3.1 of this handbook (the trustee's personal creditors and the trustee's spouse). *See also* 5 Scott & Ascher §§29.3.9 (Assignee for Creditors) ("When a debtor makes an assignment for the benefit of creditors, the assignee is not a purchaser for value"), 29.3.10 (Trustee in Bankruptcy) ("Indeed, numerous cases have held that the trustee in bankruptcy is not for this purpose a bona fide purchaser and does not take the property of the bankrupt free of equities").

[1023] 5 Scott & Ascher §29.3.8 (Security for Antecedent Debt as Value).

[1024] 5 Scott & Ascher §29.3.8.

[1025] 5 Scott & Ascher §29.3.8.

[1026] 5 Scott & Ascher §29.3.8.

[1027] 5 Scott & Ascher §29.3.8.

[1028] 5 Scott & Ascher §29.3.1 (Present Value). Assume the transferee owns a bond that has been issued by a corporation. A transfer of the bond to the transferor-trustee is an example of an assignment of contractual rights against a third party, namely the bond issuer. Such an assignment would satisfy the BFP value requirement. *See generally* §9.31 of this handbook (corporate trusts; trusts to secure creditors; the Trust Indenture Act of 1939; protecting bondholders).

[1029] 5 Scott & Ascher §29.3.1 (Present Value). If in exchange for some entrusted property, say an engagement ring and a wedding ring, the innocent transferee marries the trustee, could the transferee be a BFP such that the equitable rights of the trust beneficiaries to the rings are cut off? Possibly so! *See* 5 Scott & Ascher §29.3.5. Their recourse then would be just against the trustee. A mere promise to marry, however, would not satisfy the BFP value requirement. 5 Scott & Ascher §29.3.5. Thus, if the fiancée acquired actual or constructive knowledge of the breach of trust before the wedding, the rings would have to be returned to the trust estate.

purchaser would be liable even if the purchaser were compelled to surrender the property purchased."[1030]

On the other hand, if a transferee has made only partial payment of the purchase price before acquiring notice of the breach of trust, then all the subject property may well have to be returned to the trust estate upon the transferee's getting back the partial payment.[1031] Finally, "... [I]f a third person lends money to the trustee personally; and, subsequently, the trustee lends trust funds to the same person, who has no notice that the borrowed funds are trust funds, the third person can set off the two claims."[1032]

Whether in the BFP context value means fair market value. Value does not necessarily mean fair market value.[1033] A BFP is generally entitled to the benefit of the bargain.[1034] A great disparity in value between what the transferee paid for the subject property and what it is actually worth, on the other hand, "may indicate that the purchaser knew or should have known that the transferor was committing a breach of trust or other wrong in making the transfer," or that that the transferee was actually a donee rather than a purchaser.[1035]

Consideration versus value. What qualifies as consideration in the contract context will not necessarily qualify as value in the BFP context. Take an innocent transferee's executory or unperformed promise to a trustee that is made in exchange for wrongfully transferred trust property. "[T]he uniform rule at common law is that an executory promise (secured or unsecured) is not value for purposes of bona fide purchase."[1036] On the other hand, the making of an executory or unperformed promise can give rise to an enforceable contract.

Burdens of proof as between the transferee of entrusted property (the BFP candidate) and the beneficiary. In litigation over whether a transferee of trust property is entitled to BFP status, there is a split of authority on the question of whether the burden of proof is on the transferee to prove that the transferee is a BFP or on the beneficiary to prove that the transferee is not.[1037]

Whether the transferee of an entrusted chose in action may be a BFP. One can certainly be a BFP of entrusted real property, and of entrusted tangible personal property, as well. As to an entrusted chose in action, the law is not entirely settled. "If the chose in action takes the form of a negotiable instrument, it is, of course, well settled that a holder in due course takes free and clear not only of any trust on which the instrument was previously held, but also of

---

[1030] 5 Scott & Ascher §29.3.5 (When Purchaser's Promise Is Enforceable).

[1031] 5 Scott & Ascher §29.3.6 (Partial Payment) (citing a few cases where the transferee could keep the property provided the balance of the purchase price was paid into the trust estate).

[1032] 5 Scott & Ascher §30.3 (Set-Off of Claim of Third Person Against Trustee). *See generally* §6.2.1.2 of this handbook (duty [of trustee] to segregate and earmark trust property (duty not to commingle)).

[1033] Restatement of Restitution §173 cmt. b ("The transfer is for value although the consideration is of less value than the property transferred").

[1034] 5 Scott & Ascher §29.3.1 (Present Value).

[1035] 5 Scott & Ascher §29.3.1 (Present Value); Restatement of Restitution §172 cmt. b (present value).

[1036] Restatement (Third) of Restitution and Unjust Enrichment §68 cmt. e.

[1037] 5 Scott & Ascher §29.1.1.

any defense of any party to the instrument,"[1038] unless we have an assignment for the benefit of creditors.[1039] If the entrusted chose of action is not a negotiable instrument, New York apparently takes the position that *as between the trust beneficiary and the transferee*, the interests of the beneficiary trump those of the transferee, even if the transferee would otherwise qualify as a BFP. Neither the Restatement of Trusts nor the Restatement of Contracts is in accord.[1040]

BFPs of transferable equitable interests. It seems reasonably settled that equity is as deferential to BFPs of equitable interests as it is to BFPs of legal interests. Thus, the trustee of shares of beneficial interest in a mutual fund, which are essentially equitable interests in another trust, has the power to irrevocably convey the shares to a BFP.[1041]

Equity will not enforce a contract that is the product of a breach of trust if title has yet to pass to a BFP. On the other hand, if a trustee *in breach of trust* enters into a contract with someone who would be a BFP were title to pass, equity will not enforce the contract.[1042] "A court will not compel a trustee to complete a breach of trust."[1043] The Restatement (Third) of Restitution and Unjust Enrichment is generally in accord.[1044] So too if a trustee obtains nonnegotiable contractual rights fraudulently and purports to transfer them on to a BFP, the BFP may not seek the aid of equity in enforcing those rights.[1045] "This is . . . [also] . . . an application of the principle that an assignee of a nonnegotiable chose in action takes subject to equitable defenses of the obligor."[1046]

Decanting trust property in breach of trust for the benefit of a third party who would otherwise be a BFP. Equity will not permit a trustee in breach of trust to declare himself trustee of the subject property for the benefit of a third party who would otherwise qualify as a BFP. The equitable rights of the trust beneficiaries will trump those of the third party, no matter how innocent the third party may be, unless the beneficiaries by words or conduct have somehow misled the third party into believing that the trustee possessed the

---

[1038] 5 Scott & Ascher §29.1.1. *See generally* §8.3.6 of this handbook (negotiable instruments and the duty of third parties to inquire into the trustee's authority) and §8.15.68 of this handbook (holder in due course (trust application)).

[1039] *See generally* 5 Scott & Ascher §29.3.9 (Assignee for Creditors).

[1040] Restatement (Second) of Trusts §284 cmt. b & illus. 1; Restatement (Second) of Contracts §343. *See generally* 5 Scott & Ascher §29.1.1 (noting also that "[e]ven in states in which assignees of other choses in action take subject to latent equities, the purchaser of a chose in action represented by a specialty takes free of any trust on which it is held, even if it is not negotiable, if the purchaser gives value and has no notice of the equity").

[1041] *See generally* 5 Scott & Ascher §29.1.2 (Conveyance of Equitable Interest).

[1042] 5 Scott & Ascher §29.1.2 (Conveyance of Equitable Interest); Restatement of Restitution §175 cmt. a & cmt. b.

[1043] 5 Scott & Ascher §29.1.2 (Conveyance of Equitable Interest). *See generally* §5.4.2 of this handbook (rights of the beneficiary as against transferees of the underlying property, including BFPs).

[1044] Restatement (Third) of Restitution and Unjust Enrichment §66, illus. 13.

[1045] 5 Scott & Ascher §29.1.2 (Conveyance of Equitable Interest).

[1046] 5 Scott & Ascher §29.1.2.

authority to bestow on the third party an equitable interest in the subject property.[1047] Such behavior on the parts of the beneficiaries would in equity "estop" them from asserting their superior equitable claims.[1048] Should the equitable rights of the innocent third party be "cut off" because they are not prior in time, the third party still might be able to recoup from the beneficiaries any expenditures that the third party made to the property to the extent they inured to the benefit of the beneficiaries.[1049] If the beneficiaries were not unjustly enriched, only the trustee, then the third party's only recourse would be to seek indemnity from the trustee personally.[1050]

Multiple assignments of the same trust property. If a *trust beneficiary* first assigns the beneficiary's equitable interest to X, a BFP, and then subsequently purports to assign the very same interest to Y, who would otherwise qualify as a BFP, X being first in time prevails over Y.[1051] "Where the equities are equal, the first in time shall prevail: *qui prior est tempore, potior est jure.*"[1052] Multiple assignments of an equitable interest are not to be confused with the following situation: A trustee not in breach of trust contracts to sell an item of trust property to X, who would be a BFP were title to pass, and then subsequently actually does transfer title to the item to Y, a BFP. In that case, X, though first in time, loses.[1053] Granted, had title not passed, equity would specifically enforce X's contract, it being first in time.[1054]

When the transfer by the trustee is incident to an illegal transaction. What if the trustee in breach of trust transfers trust funds to a third party incident to an illegal transaction, *e.g.*, to pay off a personal illegal gambling debt? Can the third party ever be a BFP? Yes. If the third party pays full value, is unaware of the trust, and is unaware "of the circumstances that make the transaction illegal."[1055] Otherwise, the third party takes the funds subject to the trust.[1056]

Passage of title to entrusted property incident to murder or divorce. Even one who succeeds to property held in a revocable trust by feloniously and intentionally killing its settlor may pass good title to a BFP, although he or she

---

[1047] 5 Scott & Ascher §29.1.3.

[1048] 5 Scott & Ascher §29.1.3.

[1049] 5 Scott & Ascher §29.1.3.

[1050] 5 Scott & Ascher §29.1.3. The trustee in breach of trust might contract with a third party to sell a parcel of entrusted land. The third party pays the full purchase price to the trustee, who then misappropriates the funds. Title has yet to pass. The contract is unenforceable in equity as it was entered into in breach of trust. Nor is the third party entitled to a lien on the property itself. This is because no benefit accrued to the beneficiaries as a result of the transaction.

[1051] 5 Scott & Ascher §29.1.2 (Conveyance of Equitable Interest). *See generally* §5.3.2 of this handbook (voluntary transfers of the equitable (beneficial) interest).

[1052] *See generally* §8.12 of this handbook (containing a catalog of equity maxims).

[1053] 5 Scott & Ascher §29.1.3.

[1054] 5 Scott & Ascher §29.1.3.

[1055] 5 Scott & Ascher §29.1.7 (Transferee in an Illegal Transaction).

[1056] 5 Scott & Ascher §§29.1.7 (Transferee in an Illegal Transaction), 29.1.10 (Extent of Liability of Transferee in an Illegal Transaction).

is deemed to have disclaimed the property.[1057] Likewise, one who divorces the settlor of a revocable trust and in so doing forfeits any interest he or she may have in the subject property may still pass good title to it to a BFP.[1058]

The public policy underpinnings of the BFP doctrine. The doctrine of bona fide purchase is not just "commercially expedient."[1059] Without it, the institution of the trust itself would be a very different one. The ability of a trustee to convey in breach of trust to a BFP is what allows us to say: "The trustee is the owner of the underlying trust property."[1060] The inability of the trustee, with some procedural exceptions, to get away with conveying in breach of trust to a non-BFP is what allows us to say: "The beneficiary as well has a proprietary interest in the underlying trust property."[1061] It is these overlapping interests in the underlying property of a trust that distinguishes the trust from its contract-based civil law trust analogs on the European continent, South America, and elsewhere.[1062]

Cross-references. For coverage of the practical applications of the bona fide purchase doctrine, the reader is referred to Sections 5.4.2 and 8.3.2 of this handbook. For a discussion of the differences between the BFP, a creature of equity, and the holder in due course, a creature of law, the reader is referred to Sections 8.3.6 of this handbook and 8.15.68 of this handbook. The impermissible appointee of a special power of appointment may pass good title to a BFP, a topic we take up in Section 8.15.26 of this handbook. At one time even a good faith purchaser for value might have had an affirmative obligation to see to it that the funds paid to the trustee as consideration for the entrusted asset were properly applied as per the terms of the trust. This is a topic that is taken up in Section 8.15.69 of this handbook.

§8.15.64   The Special Occupant (Equitable Estates pur Autre Vie)

In England, however, the Administration of Estates Act, 1925 . . . abolished devolution by special occupancy.[1063]

An estate *pur autre vie* is an estate the duration of which is determined by the life of someone other than the holder of the estate.[1064] The law French term for the other person, the measuring life, is the *cestui que vie*. In the nontrust context, one creates a legal estate in land *pur autre vie* by transferring the land

---

[1057] UPC §2-803(i).

[1058] UPC §2-804(h).

[1059] Scott & Ascher §13.1.

[1060] *See generally* §3.5.2.2 of this handbook (right at law to transfer title).

[1061] Scott & Ascher §13.1.

[1062] *See generally* §8.12.1 of this handbook (civil law alternatives to the trust).

[1063] 3 Scott & Ascher §14.10.2, n.1 (citing to 15 Geo. V., c. 23, §45).

[1064] *See generally* Restatement (Third) of Property (Wills and Other Donative Transfers) §24.5 cmt. c (providing examples of estates *pur autre vie*).

to "*Y* and his heirs" for the life of *Z*.[1065] In the trust context, one creates an equitable estate *pur autre vie* in land by transferring the land to *B* as trustee for the benefit of "*C* and his heirs" for the life of *Z*, remainder to *D*. In each case, *Z* is the measuring life.[1066]

At one time, if the holder of either a legal or an equitable estate *pur autre vie* died before the measuring life, the "heir" was entitled to the estate *pur autre vie* up until the time the measuring life died. The "heir," however, took the interest for the balance of its duration not as an actual heir, *i.e.*, not by descent, but as a so-called special occupant. This was because an estate *pur autre vie* at common law was not an estate of inheritance. The taker was actually the person who *would have been* the heir, an heir being someone who takes by an actual intestacy.[1067]

Today, upon the death of the holder of an estate *pur autre vie*, be it legal or equitable, the interest generally passes to the deceased holder's probate estate and follows the fortunes thereof, unless the governing instrument provides otherwise.[1068] Ultimately, upon the subsequent death of the measuring life, the *pur autre vie* interest itself extinguishes. For a discussion of the strange happenings at common law when there was an equitable estate *pur autre vie* in land not for the benefit of the holder "and his heirs" but just for the benefit of the holder, and the holder died before the measuring life, the reader is referred to Section 4.1.1 of this handbook.

§8.15.65 *Destructibility of Contingent Remainders Rule (The Trust Exemption)*

Here is a simple statement of the rule of destructibility of contingent remainders: A remainder in land is destroyed if it does not vest at or before the termination of the preceding freehold estate. If the remainder is still subject to a condition precedent when the preceding estate terminates, the remainder is wiped out, and the right of possession moves on to the next vested interest.[1069]

Take a conveyance of land *not in trust* from *A* to *C* for life, remainder to *D*, the eldest son of *X*. *X* at the time of the conveyance is without issue alive or dead. *C* possesses a legal life estate.[1070] The currently nonexistent eldest son, *i.e.*, *D*, possesses a legal contingent remainder. The condition precedent that makes the interest contingent is that the eldest son be conceived. If, at the death of *C*,

---

[1065] *See generally* Cornelius J. Moynihan, Introduction to the Law of Real Property §10 (2d ed. 1988).

[1066] *See generally* 3 Scott & Ascher §14.10.2.

[1067] *See generally* §5.2 of this handbook (class designation: "children," "issue," "heirs," and "relatives" (some rules of construction)).

[1068] *See generally* 3 Scott & Ascher §14.10.2.

[1069] Dukeminier, Krier, Alexander & Schill, Property 241 (6th ed. 2006). Note that the next vested interest could well be the holder of the reversionary interest.

[1070] *See generally* §8.27 of this handbook (what is the difference between a legal life estate and an equitable life estate under a trust).

there is no eldest son of *X* dead or alive, then the contingent remainder extinguishes, *i.e.*, is "destroyed," and the property reverts back to *A*, the grantor, whose legal reversionary interest was vested *ab initio*.[1071] A legal reversion is triggered because the seisin cannot be suspended or put in abeyance until such time as *X* produces a son.

This is an application of the classic common law destructibility of contingent remainders rule. "Although this rule apparently grew out of the feudal need for continuity of seisin, another policy came to support it: Destroying contingent remainders enhanced the alienability of land."[1072] On the other hand, had the remainder vested *ab initio*, or even at the death of *C*, there would not have been a continuity of seisin problem:

> It became a fundamental rule of common law conveyancing that there can be no livery of seisin to take effect in futuro. Livery of seisin is a present act and A cannot convey a freehold estate to . . . [C] . . . today to take effect next month. From the nature of livery of seisin the rule was derived that there could be no conveyance, by feoffment or otherwise, of a freehold estate to commence in futuro. *The limitation of a remainder . . . [qua remainder] . . . did not violate this rule since a remainder follows after the present, particular estate created by the same conveyance.*[1073]

While the destructibility of contingent remainders rule applied to legal remainders, it did not apply to equitable remainders, *i.e.*, to situations where the land was entrusted. The reason: Legal title from beginning to end was in the trustee. Thus, *A* could avoid application of the rule simply by transferring the parcel of land to *B as trustee*, for *C* for life, with the land passing outright and free of trust to the eldest son of *X*. If at the death of *C*, *X* was still childless, the trustee if the terms of the conveyance so permitted could continue to retain the land in trust until the earlier of such time as *X* produced a child or died, provided, of course, there was no violation of the dreaded other rule, namely, the Rule against Perpetuities.[1074] This is yet another example of why the trust has always been an indispensable tool in the kit of the creative common law lawyer.[1075] For why the trust continues to be, the reader is referred to Charles E. Rounds, Jr. and Andreas Dehio.[1076]

The destructibility of contingent remainders rule also did not apply to legal executory interests.[1077] Here is an example of such a shifting executory interest: *A* devises *not in trust* a parcel of land to *D* and his heirs, but if *D* dies

---

[1071] Lewin ¶ 5-66; J. Gray, The Rule Against Perpetuities, §§113, 603.9 (4th ed. 1942). *See generally* §4.1.1 of this handbook (the reversionary interest).

[1072] Dukeminier, Krier, Alexander & Schill, Property 241 (6th ed. 2006).

[1073] Cornelius J. Moynihan, Introduction to the Law of Real Property 133 (2d ed. 1988).

[1074] *See generally* §8.2.1 of this handbook (the Rule against Perpetuities).

[1075] *See generally* Charles E. Rounds, Jr., *The Case for a Return to Mandatory Instruction in the Fiduciary Aspects of Agency and Trusts in the American Law School*, 18 Regent L. Rev. 251 (2005-2006).

[1076] *Publicly-Traded Open End Mutual Funds in Common Law and Civil Law Jurisdictions: A Comparison of Legal Structures*, 3 N.Y.U. J.L. & Bus. 473.

[1077] Dukeminier, Krier, Alexander & Schill, Property 242 (6th ed. 2006).

leaving no surviving children then to Z and his heirs.[1078] Z's interest is executory.[1079] "An executory interest, like a remainder, can be created only in a transferee, never in the transferor."[1080] An executory interest, however, is a divesting interest, whereas a remainder is a successive interest.[1081] By the way, a provision *in a trust* that the trustee periodically distribute income in equal shares only to the members of the class of income beneficiaries who are alive when a particular income distribution is made, that is not to the probate estates of any deceased members of the class, is actually a collection of executory equitable income interests.[1082] They are executory because the death of a class member triggers a divestment of his or her pro rata share of the income stream in favor of those class members who are alive at the time of the next income distribution. For a general discussion of springing and shifting executory interests in land, both of the legal and the equitable varieties, the reader is referred to Section 8.15.80 of this handbook.

It is said that the exemption of legal executory interests from application of the destructibility rule "was a main reason why judges developed the Rule Against Perpetuities."[1083] By the nineteenth century, the Rule against Perpetuities, which was and is applicable to both legal and equitable interests, had essentially rendered the more narrowly focused destructibility rule redundant, at least from a public policy perspective. This accounts for why the destructibility rule has now been abolished judicially or legislatively in a number of states (U.S.). In fact, by 1936, it could be said that the destructibility rule was no longer a part of American law.[1084]

[1078] *See generally* §8.30 of this handbook (the difference between a vested equitable remainder subject to divestment and a vested (transmissible) contingent equitable remainder).

[1079] Cornelius J. Moynihan, Introduction to the Law of Real Property 191 (2d ed. 1988).

[1080] Cornelius J. Moynihan, Introduction to the Law of Real Property 191 (2d ed. 1988). "In some respects, an executory interest that divests an estate in a prior grantee resembles a common law right of entry but a right of entry could be created only in favor of the transferor." Moynihan, Introduction to the Law of Real Property 191 (2d ed. 1988).

[1081] Cornelius J. Moynihan, Introduction to the Law of Real Property 191–192 (2d ed. 1988) ("A remainder can take effect in possession only at the expiration of the preceding estate in another grantee, not by divesting it. By contrast, an executory interest can take effect only by divesting a preceding estate in another grantee (except where the preceding estate is a fee simple determinable), or by divesting a freehold estate in the transferor or his successors in interest. Put another way, a remainder is a successive interest; an executory interest is, normally, a divesting interest.").

[1082] *See, e.g.*, Warner v. Whitman, 353 Mass. 468, 233 N.E.2d 14 (Mass. 1968) (involving the shifting of equitable interests in the income stream of a trust).

[1083] Dukeminier, Krier, Alexander & Schill, Property 242 (6th ed. 2006); *see also* John Chipman Gray, The Rule Against Perpetuities §285 (4th ed. 1942) ("It is true that the indestructibility of executory devises led to the establishment of the Rule against Perpetuities, while the ease with which . . . [legal] . . . contingent remainders might be destroyed prevented or postponed the starting of any question as to their remoteness."). *See generally* §8.2.1 of this handbook (the Rule against Perpetuities).

[1084] Restatement of Property §240.

§8.15.66   Rule Against Perpetuities

The Rule against Perpetuities is covered in Section 8.2.1 of this handbook and its ten sub-sections.

§8.15.67   Implied Warranty of Authority (Trust Application)

As we have noted in Section 7.3.1 of this handbook, a third party *to the trust*, *i.e.*, a nonbeneficiary, who enters into a contract with a trustee involving the trust estate ordinarily may not reach the trust estate if the transaction was outside the scope of a proper trust administration. The third party, however, may be able to hold the trustee personally liable on the contract under an implied warranty of authority to bind the trust estate.[1085] This is analogous to the agent who enters into a contract on behalf of the principal without actual or apparent authority to do so.[1086] If the contract is enforceable, it is against the agent personally, not the principal.

§8.15.68   Holder in Due Course (Trust Application)

A negotiable instrument is a special kind of formal contract, including bills of exchange and promissory notes drawn in a required form. The rules applicable to this form and to the legal effects of transfer are the result of centuries of commercial usage. The evolution of these rules was long quite independent of the English common law and equity, being referred to as law merchant to indicate that independence. It fell to the lot of Lord Mansfield to incorporate most of that law into the common law of England, by his judicial action; but the usage of merchants was becoming the usage of Englishmen, so as to make the judicial incorporation inevitable.[1087]

A negotiable instrument is a special type of contract, namely, "a written promise, or order, to pay to the order of a named payee, or to bearer, a specified sum of money" that on its face is unilateral and unconditional.[1088] An individual promissory note in bearer form and a check made payable to "cash" are examples of negotiable instruments.[1089] An assignment is a transfer of one's rights under a contract to a third party; a negotiation is a transfer of one's rights under a negotiable instrument.[1090] Generally the assignee of contract rights

---

[1085] *See generally* 4 Scott & Ascher §26.2.2 (Implied Warranty).

[1086] *See generally* §9.9.2 of this handbook (agency arrangements).

[1087] Arthur Linton Corbin, Corbin on Contracts §863 (1952).

[1088] Arthur Linton Corbin, Corbin on Contracts §863 (1952).

[1089] U.C.C. §3-102 cmt.

[1090] Arthur Linton Corbin, Corbin on Contracts §863 (1952) ("In so far as the rules applicable to negotiable instruments differ from those applicable to the assignment of other contract rights, they are due to the commercial advantages accruing from the use of a readily transferable credit instrument").

takes only the rights that the assignor possessed, unless the assignee is a BFP.[1091] The transferee of rights under a negotiable instrument takes only the rights that the transferor possessed, unless the transferee is a holder in due course.[1092] Thus if X transfers to Y a check made out to cash in the amount of $50 in exchange for Y's promise to mow X's lawn, and Y does not mow the lawn, then X is entitled to get the check back from Y. But if Y in the interim has negotiated the check to a holder in due course, the holder in due course may keep the check and enforce its terms against X.[1093] Any recourse X may have is against Y alone.[1094]

A holder in due course is like a BFP[1095] in the following respects:

- Each has to have paid value.[1096]
- Each has to have had lack of notice that the transfer might be in derogation of the legal or equitable property rights of others.[1097]

There are some critical differences, however:

- The BFP is an equitable concept while the holder in due course is a legal one that is now generally codified, at least in the United States.[1098] See Article 3 of the Uniform Commercial Code, versions of which have been enacted into law in most if not all the states.
- Cancellation of an antecedent (preexisting) debt owed by the transferor to the transferee can satisfy the holder-in-due-course value requirement but, with some exceptions, not the BFP value requirement.[1099]
- In a case where trust property is transferred for value to a third party in breach of trust and the third party is to pay the funds *to the trustee personally*, it is unlikely that the third party would qualify as a BFP,[1100] whereas, if the property were a negotiable instrument, a third party who

---

[1091] *See generally* §8.15.63 of this handbook (doctrine of bona fide purchase; the BFP).

[1092] U.C.C. §3-302 (Holder in Due Course); Bogert §883 (The Rule of Negotiability).

[1093] U.C.C. §3-302 cmt.

[1094] U.C.C. §3-302 cmt.

[1095] *See generally* §§5.4.2 of this handbook (rights of the beneficiary as against transferees of the underlying property, including BFPs), 8.3.2 of this handbook (bona fide purchaser for value of trust property: what constitutes notice that transfer in breach of trust), and 8.15.63 of this handbook (doctrine of bona fide purchase; the BFP).

[1096] *See generally* §8.15.63 of this handbook (doctrine of bona fide purchase; the BFP); U.C.C. §3-302 (Holder in Due Course).

[1097] *See generally* §8.15.63 of this handbook (doctrine of bona fide purchase; the BFP); U.C.C. §3-302 (Holder in Due Course). *See also* U.C.C. §3-307 (Notice of Breach of Fiduciary Duty).

[1098] *See* Dearman v. Trimmier, 26 S.C. 506, 2 S.E. 501, 504 (1887).

[1099] 5 Scott & Ascher §29.3.7 (Satisfaction of Antecedent Debt as Value). *See, e.g.*, Dearman v. Trimmier, 26 S.C. 506, 2 S.E. 501, 504 (1887).

[1100] *See generally* §8.15.63 of this handbook (doctrine of bona fide purchase; the BFP).

pays value and who has no actual knowledge of the breach would likely qualify as a holder in due course.[1101]

If a trustee in breach of trust transfers an entrusted negotiable instrument to a third party for value who has actual notice of the breach, the third party is not a holder in due course.[1102] Moreover, under Section 3-307 of the Uniform Commercial Code, the party has notice of a possible breach of trust if the third party has actual knowledge that the transferor is a fiduciary[1103] and that (1) the payment is in satisfaction of the trustee's personal obligation; (2) the payment is otherwise to be applied for the trustee's personal benefit; or (3) the payment is not to be deposited into an account of the trust.[1104] No such inference is raised, however, if the payment is made to the trustee personally.[1105] The Uniform Fiduciaries Act is generally in accord.[1106]

For a general discussion of whether a third party who transacts with the trustee has a duty to ascertain the trustee's authority in equity to enter into the transaction and to ascertain whether the authority is being properly exercised, the reader is referred to Section 8.21 of this handbook.

§8.15.69   Third-Party Liability for Trustee's Misapplication of Payments to Trustee; The Purchaser's Duty to Monitor the Trustee's Application of the Purchase Price

Professor Ames found this rule indefensible on any principle.[1107]

I do not think it is for the good of cestuis que trust, or the good of the world, that those cases should be extended—William Milburne James.[1108]

As we have noted elsewhere, a third party who knowingly participates with a trustee in a breach of trust shares with the trustee liability for any loss caused by the breach.[1109] Thus, if the trustee transfers trust property in breach of trust to a third-party purchaser who is aware of the breach, the third-party purchaser holds the trust property subject to the terms of the trust.[1110] Otherwise, "such a

---

[1101] U.C.C. §3-307 (Notice of Breach of Fiduciary Duty).

[1102] U.C.C. §3-307 (Notice of Breach of Fiduciary Duty).

[1103] *See generally* 5 Scott & Ascher §29.2.6 (Negotiable Instruments).

[1104] *See generally* 5 Scott & Ascher §29.2.6 (Negotiable Instruments).

[1105] U.C.C. §3-307 (Notice of Breach of Fiduciary Duty).

[1106] Unif. Fiduciaries Act §§4 & 6.

[1107] 5 Scott & Ascher §30.1 (referring to Ames, Cases on Trusts 269n (2d ed. 1893).

[1108] These observation of William Milburne James, Lord Justice of Appeal in Chancery, may be found in Barnes v. Addy, L.R. 9 Ch. App. 244 (1874) (England). *See* 5 Scott & Ascher §30.6.6 for more excerpts from the opinion.

[1109] *See* §7.2.9 of this handbook (personal liability of third parties to the beneficiary).

[1110] *See* §5.4.2 of this handbook (rights of the beneficiary as against transferees of the underlying property).

purchaser is liable only if the trustee commits a breach of trust in making the transfer and the purchaser has notice that the trustee is doing so."[1111]

At common law, however, it was doctrine that even the innocent third-party purchaser had a continuing obligation running to the trust beneficiaries to see to it that the trustee properly applied the purchase price.[1112] In the United States, such an innocent third party either by case law or by statute has been relieved of such an obligation.[1113] The Restatements have endeavored to nudge the blackletter law into conformance with this reality.[1114] "In England, the old rule has been repudiated by statute."[1115] Even a good faith purchaser for value (BFP) of entrusted property was not necessarily relieved of the equitable obligation to see to the proper application of funds paid. The BFP is discussed generally in Section 8.15.63 of this handbook.

Still, we continue to see vestigial allusions to the old default rule in the boilerplate, such as the following: "*No person dealing with the trustee hereunder shall be required to see to the application of any money or property delivered to the trustee or to see that the terms and conditions of this trust have been complied with*" and "*No insurance company issuing any policy or policies which are or shall become subject to this declaration of trust shall be responsible for the application of any money or thing of value paid to the trustee hereunder or for the carrying out of the provisions of this instrument or any of them.*" The introductory quotation from Moby-Dick in Section 8.15 of this handbook comes to mind. In any case, any such exonerating boilerplate would be ineffective if a third party purchaser were to be on actual notice *at the time of the transfer of the entrusted property* of the trustee's intention to misapply the purchase price.[1116] If the trustee in fact were to do so, the purchaser would be liable for participating in the commission of a breach of trust.[1117] It would not be the receipt of the entrusted property so much as the fate of the purchase price that would give rise to the third party's liability.[1118] Also, even today paying the purchase price to a cotrustee without the consent of the other cotrustees would not be without its risks.[1119] If the cotrustee were then to misapply the purchase price, there is the remote chance that the purchaser might have to pay up a second time.[1120]

[1111] 5 Scott & Ascher §30.1 (Misapplication of Payments Made to Trustee).

[1112] 5 Scott & Ascher §30.1.

[1113] 5 Scott & Ascher §30.1, n.5 (Case Law) & n.7 (Statutes).

[1114] *See, e.g.*, Restatement (Third) of Trusts §108(3)(b) ("In dealing with a trustee, a third party need not ensure that assets transferred to the trustee are properly applied to trust purposes.").

[1115] 5 Scott & Ascher §30.1 (referring to Trustee Act, 1925, 15 Geo. V., c. 19, §14).

[1116] 5 Scott & Ascher §30.1.1 (Payment with Notice).

[1117] 5 Scott & Ascher §30.1.1 (Payment with Notice).

[1118] 5 Scott & Ascher §30.1.1 (Payment with Notice).

[1119] 5 Scott & Ascher §30.1.2 (Payment to One of Several Trustees). *See generally* §3.4.4.1 of this handbook (multiple trustees (cotrustees)).

[1120] 5 Scott & Ascher §30.1.2 (Payment to One of Several Trustees).

§8.15.70   Laches, Doctrine of

Delay defeats equities, or, equity aids the vigilant and not the indolent: vigilantibus, non dormientibus, jura subveniunt.[1121]

Laches is a delay that is sufficient to prevent a party from obtaining an equitable remedy, a remedy to which the party but for the delay would otherwise be entitled.[1122] In order to be fair to both sides, a court of equity is loath to entertain stale demands brought forth by those who have slept on their rights.[1123] "Delay will accordingly be fatal to a claim for equitable relief if there is evidence of an agreement by the claimant to abandon or release his right, or if it has resulted in the destruction or loss of evidence by which the claim might have been rebutted, or if the claim is to a business (for the claimant should not be allowed to wait and see if it prospers), or if the claimant has so acted as to induce the defendant to alter his position on the reasonable faith that the claim has been released or abandoned."[1124] In order to abandon an equitable claim, such as a claim by a trust beneficiary against the trustee for breach of trust, one or one's authorized surrogate must be of full age and legal capacity and have "full knowledge" of the claim.[1125] In equity's eyes, lack of notice, legal disability, or undue influence can be a "satisfactory explanation" for why a party has delayed in seeking enforcement of the claim.[1126] In equity, even ignorance of the law, *i.e.*, of one's legal or equitable rights, can be a "satisfactory explanation."[1127]

It is classic laches doctrine that a competent trust beneficiary would have a reasonable time after receiving actual notice of the trustee's breach of fiduciary duty to bring an equitable action against the trustee to remedy the breach.[1128] By actual notice we mean that the trustee must openly "repudiate" the trust, a concept that is discussed in Section 7.1.3 of this handbook.

An unreasonable delay is a delay that would make the granting of equitable relief unjust, that would unfairly prejudice the trustee.[1129] Classic laches

---

[1121] Snell's Equity ¶ 5-16.

[1122] Snell's Equity ¶ 5-19.

[1123] Snell's Equity ¶ 5-16 (England); Restatement (Third) of Trusts §98 cmt. b (U.S.).

[1124] Snell's Equity ¶ 5-19.

[1125] Snell's Equity ¶ 5-19. *See also* §7.1.2 of this handbook (discussing what constitutes informed consent to a breach of trust).

[1126] Snell's Equity ¶ 5-19 (England); Restatement (Third) of Trusts §98 cmt. b(1) (excuses for delay) (U.S.).

[1127] Snell's Equity ¶ 5-19. *See also* §7.2.7 of this handbook (beneficiary consent, release, or ratification).

[1128] Restatement (Third) of Trusts §98 cmt. b.

[1129] *See, e.g.*, Lindsay Petroleum Co. v. Hurd (1874) L.R. 5 P.C. 221 at 239, 240, *per* Lord Selborne L.C. (England). *See generally* Restatement (Third) of Trusts §98 cmt. b(2) (delay prejudicial to trustee); §7.2.10 of this handbook (limitation of action by beneficiary against trustee (laches

doctrine has no fixed time periods.[1130] In many jurisdictions, however, there are now statutes of limitation in effect that do fix a time in which a competent beneficiary with actual notice of a breach of trust may bring an action against the trustee to compel the trustee to remedy the breach.[1131] These statutes tweak traditional laches doctrine; they do not do away with the applicability of its general principles, such as the actual-knowledge-of-legal-rights requirement.[1132] Again, the laches doctrine itself is not a creature of statute.[1133] An ancient invention of the English court of chancery,[1134] it is still honed and applied today in common law jurisdictions, both here and abroad.[1135] The reader who is interested in the doctrine's modern-day practical applications is referred to Sections 3.6 of this handbook, 7.1.3 of this handbook, and 7.2.10 of this handbook.

It should be noted that the state attorney general is not bound by the doctrine of laches when it comes to the enforcement of charitable trusts.[1136] Neither is the court. "The mere fact that the trustees of a charitable trust have long applied the trust property to purposes other than those designated by the settlor does not preclude the court from directing that the trust be administered according to its terms."[1137]

---

and statutes of limitation)); §7.1.3 of this handbook (defense of failure of beneficiary to take timely action against trustee).

[1130] *See* Restatement (Third) of Trusts §98 cmt. b.

[1131] *See generally* §7.2.10 of this handbook (limitation of action by beneficiary against trustee (laches and statutes of limitation) and §7.1.3 of this handbook (defense of failure of beneficiary to take timely action against trustee).

[1132] *See generally* Restatement (Third) of Restitution and Unjust Enrichment §70 cmt. f (discovery rule).

[1133] Restatement (Third) of Trusts §98 cmt. a.

[1134] *See generally* Chapter 1 of this handbook (containing a list of all those who have occupied the office of Lord Chancellor from 1068 to the present).

[1135] *See generally* Restatement (Third) of Trusts §98 cmt. a ("The doctrine of laches evolved in English and American jurisdictions during times in which statutes of limitations did not apply to equitable causes of action. The doctrine ordinarily remains applicable today along with modern statutes of limitations. . . ."); §8.12 of this handbook (listing some of the more common equity maxims, including in the footnoting examples of their present-day applications). In litigation in a New York court over the ownership of a medieval prayer book containing within its pages the partially obliterated but recoverable text of the long-lost Codex C of Archimedes (287 B.C.–212 B.C.), the "greatest mathematician of antiquity," the trial judge in her August 18, 1999 dismissal noted that had New York law rather than the French law of adverse possession applied, the case would still have been dismissed as the claimant would have been found guilty of laches. Reviel Netz & William Noel, The Archimedes Codex 135–136 (2007).

[1136] *See* Restatement (Third) of Trusts §98 cmt. a(2) (immunity of attorneys general).

[1137] 5 Scott & Ascher §37.3.10.

§8.15.71   The Constitutional Impediment to Retroactively Applying New Trust Law

While expediency can furnish no reason or basis upon which to determine the constitutionality of the retroactive operation of the Act, we cannot refrain from noting the unworkability of the Rule under present day economic conditions.[1138]

Taking by redefinition. A model codification of some aspect of state trust law is likely to provide that its rules of construction and presumptions shall apply retroactively upon enactment. Section 8-101(b)(5) of the Uniform Probate Code[1139] and Section 1106(a)(4) of the Uniform Trust Code[1140] do just that. While the application of new substantive law to a trust that is fully revocable on the date a statute becomes effective, or a court decision is handed down, is unlikely to violate the Takings Clause of the Fifth Amendment to the U.S. Constitution (which has been made applicable to the states by the Fourteenth Amendment), there would be a violation if the trust were irrevocable, particularly if the equitable property rights of its beneficiaries, whether vested or contingent, would be diminished or eliminated as a consequence.[1141]

To illustrate, let us assume that in 1900 an irrevocable trust was created. Its terms provide that, upon its termination at the death of the last survivor of the settlor's children, the property passes outright and free of trust to the "then living issue" of the settlor. Let us assume further that the term *issue* as understood in 1900 did *not* include persons who were adopted. At the time the trust was created, members of the class of the settlor's grandchildren and more remote descendants, whether born or unborn, acquired property rights in the form of equitable contingent remainders. It is a popular misconception that contingent interests under trusts are not property interests—nothing could be further from the truth.[1142] The office of the guardian ad litem itself has evolved to represent just such property interests on behalf of minors, the unborn, and the unascertained.[1143] Thus, when the state, effective retroactively, redefines a class designation in an irrevocable trust to capture persons not encompassed in the designation's plain meaning at the time the trust became irrevocable, the state dilutes the property interests, contingent or otherwise, of the persons who

---

[1138] In re Trust of Catherwood, 405 Pa. 61, 74, 173 A.2d 86, 92 (1961) (referring to the Pennsylvania rule of apportionment, which is discussed in §8.15.14 of this handbook).

[1139] "...(5) any rule of construction or presumption provided in this Code applies to governing instruments executed before the effective date unless there is a clear indication of a contrary intent..."

[1140] "...(4) any rule of construction or presumption provided in this[Code] applies to trust instruments executed before [the effective date of the [Code]] unless there is a clear indication of a contrary intent in the terms of the trust..."

[1141] *See generally* §8.11 of this handbook (the agency-like nature of the revocable inter vivos trust) and §8.2.2.2 of this handbook (the will-like nature of the revocable inter vivos trust).

[1142] *See generally* §2.1 of this handbook (types of property interests).

[1143] *See* §3.5.3.2(h) of this handbook (the power to exclude the remainderman from the accounting process), §5.1 of this handbook (who can be a beneficiary?), and §8.14 of this handbook (representing contingent remainder interests); and Restatement (Second) of Trusts §214 cmt. a.

were contemplated, whether those persons are born or unborn.[1144] In other words, we have a taking by redefinition. Likewise, the property rights of "adopted outs" ought to be determined by the settlor, not by the retroactive application of statutes and/or case law.[1145]

Not everyone sees it that way. New Jersey courts now seem relatively comfortable applying adoption-related rules of construction retroactively, at least in most cases.[1146] As mentioned, Section 1106(a)(4) of the Uniform Trust Code, available on the Internet at <http://www.uniformlaws.org/Act.aspx?title =Trust%20Code>, provides that unless there is a clear intention of a contrary intent, its rules of construction and presumptions apply to trust instruments executed before its effective date. The Uniform Probate Code has similar language.[1147]

In one case, however, a court *declined* to apply a double-damages provision of Kansas's Uniform Trust Code retroactively *against a trustee* who had misappropriated trust funds. Its rationale was as follows: "Because substantive laws affect vested rights, they are not subject to retroactive legislation because doing so would constitute the taking of property without due process."[1148] Why the constitutional rights of trust beneficiaries should be entitled to less deference than the constitutional rights of their trustees merely because the means of

---

[1144] McGehee v. Edwards, 268 Va. 15, 597 S.E.2d 99 (2004) (to protect the property interests of beneficiaries, their interests having accrued at the time the trust was created, the court construed the terms of the trust as of that time); Wachovia Bank & Trust Co. v. Andrews, 264 N.C. 531, 142 S.E.2d 182 (1965) (holding that the state may not retroactively redefine a class to include adopteds and thus dilute the property interests of nonadopted members); Continental Bank, N.A. v. Herguth, 248 Ill. App. 3d 292, 187 Ill. Dec. 395, 617 N.E.2d 852 (1993) ("Because the settlor is presumed to have known these legal principles when he executed the trust, the terms 'descendant' and 'per stirpes' unmistakably evidenced his . . . intent to limit the class of beneficiaries to his natural born progeny."). *See, however*, Anderson v. BNY Mellon, 463 Mass. 299, 974 N.E.2d 21 (Mass. 2012) (the retroactive application to a preexisting irrevocable trust of a statutory presumption that the term issue encompasses adopteds is unconstitutional on substantive due process grounds rather than on the grounds that there has been an uncompensated partial taking by the state). *See generally* §8.15.6 of this handbook (plain meaning rule).

[1145] One court that was asked to construe the terms of a testamentary trust determined that when the testator/settlor employed the word issue, he meant biological issue including adopted-out biological issue. Lockwood v. Adamson, 409 Mass. 325, 566 N.E.2d 96 (1996). Another, finding no guidance within the four corners of the governing instrument, looked to the intestacy statute in effect at the time the will was executed. The result: adopted-outs were out. "A testator is presumed to be aware of the public policy reflected in the statutory definitions of the terms used in a will at the time the will is executed and to intend that those definitions be followed in construction of the will unless a contrary intent is expressed in the will." Newman v. Wells Fargo Bank, 59 Cal. Rptr. 2d 2, 14 Cal. 4th 126, 926 P.2d 969 (1996).

[1146] *See* In re Trust under Agreement of Vander Poel, 396 N.J. Super. 218, 227–230, 933 A.2d 628, 633–636 (2007).

[1147] *See* UPC §2-705 ("Adopted individuals and individuals born out of wedlock, and their respective descendants if appropriate to the class, are included in class gifts and other terms of relationship in accordance with the rules of intestate succession."); UPC §8-101(b)(5) (providing that "any rule of construction or presumption provided in this Code applies to governing instruments executed before the effective date unless there is a clear indication of a contrary intent").

[1148] McCabe v. Duran, 180 P.3d 1098, 1100 (Kan. App. 2008).

divestment, or partial divestment, of their equitable property rights is the retroactive application of a rule of construction is not entirely clear to these authors. Nor presumably would it be to the justices of the Supreme Judicial Court of Massachusetts, who, in 1987, changed the default presumption that the term *issue* shall be construed to mean "lawful issue" to the default presumption that the term shall be construed to include all biological issue, including those born out of wedlock. It did so, however, prospectively. The court ordered that the new rule of construction shall apply only to instruments executed after the date of its opinion.[1149] In 1984, the same court had prospectively construed the Massachusetts spousal election statute as applying not only to probate assets but also to assets in *revocable* trusts.[1150] This departure from past law was made applicable only to inter vivos trusts created or amended after the date of the opinion.[1151] Similarly, when the Florida legislature revised the Florida spousal election statute, it provided that the changes were to be applied prospectively.[1152]

In 1991, the Court of Appeals for the Eighth Circuit in *Whirlpool Corp. v. Ritter*[1153] held the retroactive default application of a statute that would nullify a revocable life insurance beneficiary designation in favor of the spouse of the policy owner should the couple divorce to be an unconstitutional violation of the Contracts Clause. The decision unsettled the probate codification community. In response, the Joint Editorial Board of the Uniform Probate Code fired off a statement to the effect that "[t]he Contracts Clause has never been read to pose any obstacle to the application of legislatively altered constructional rules to preexisting donative documents such as revocable trusts that have no contractual component."[1154] The statement is even referenced in the General Comment to Part 7 of the Uniform Probate Code. What needs to be kept in mind here is that the subject of the case and the statement in response to it was a *revocable* beneficiary designation. Diluting or eliminating fixed vested or contingent equitable property rights under irrevocable trusts by state action without just compensation would be quite a different matter. That would or should implicate not so much the Contracts Clause as the Takings Clause.

In 2012, the Massachusetts Supreme Judicial Court in *Anderson v. BNY Mellon*[1155] ruled that the dilution of a beneficiary's equitable interest under a testamentary trust occasioned by the retroactive application of a default statutory rule of construction, namely that the term issue shall include adopted issue as well as blood issue, was in violation of *substantive due process* under the

---

[1149] *See* Powers v. Wilkinson, 399 Mass. 650, 506 N.E.2d 842 (1987).

[1150] Sullivan v. Burkin, 390 Mass. 864, 460 N.E.2d 572 (1984).

[1151] Sullivan v. Burkin, 390 Mass. 864, 871, 460 N.E.2d 572, 577 (1984).

[1152] *See* Estate of Magee, 988 So. 2d 1 (Fla. Ct. App. 2008) (involving a trust that was amended after the effective date of the statutory amendments).

[1153] 929 F.2d 1318 (8th Cir. 1991).

[1154] *See Joint Editorial Board Statement Regarding the Constitutionality of Changes in Default Rules as Applied to Pre-Existing Documents*, 17 ACTEC Notes 184 (1991).

[1155] 463 Mass. 299, 974 N.E.2d 21 (Mass. 2012).

Commonwealth's constitution.[1156] The court seems not to have fully appreciated the fact that an equitable interest under a trust, even one that is contingent, is a true property interest.[1157] Rather than deciding the case on federal taking principles, which would have been the simplest and most direct route, the court decided it on state substantive due process principles. It found the constitutional question not to be whether the statute's retroactive application "results in deprivation of property" (which we suggest it clearly did) but whether the retroactive application was "unreasonable."[1158] Thus, the decision may not necessarily stand for the proposition that such enactments are *per se* unconstitutional.

Taking by antilapse. Under the model Uniform Probate Code's antilapse default provisions applicable to trusts certain equitable future interests *that had traditionally been construed as vested* would become subject to the condition precedent of survivorship.[1159] This could, for example, cause the contingent equitable interests of some takers in default of survivorship to violate the Rule against Perpetuities, at least in jurisdictions where the rule is still enforced.[1160] What had once been safely vested would no longer be.[1161] "To prevent an injustice from resulting because of this, the Uniform Statutory Rule Against Perpetuities, which has a wait-and-see element, is incorporated into the Code as part 9."[1162] Still, the legislative conversion of one's vested equitable interest into an interest that is nontransmissible postmortem in the absence of an overt expression of intent on the part of the settlor that the interest be vested would seem to pose a problem under the U.S. Constitution.[1163] The U.S. Supreme Court in *Hodel v. Irving* has confirmed that the right to pass property postmortem is a property right that is covered by the Takings Clause.[1164]

Taking by changing the rules of the income allocation and apportionment game. We now turn to the matter of altering the economic interests of trust beneficiaries by redefining, either by statute, regulation, or court decision, trust accounting income and principal, specifically by applying new definitions retroactively to preexisting irrevocable trusts. The general subject of allocating and apportioning receipts to income and principal is covered in Section 6.2.4 of this handbook. One's point of departure when analyzing the constitutionality of

---

[1156] Article 10 of the Massachusetts Declaration of Rights provides, in pertinent part: "Each individual of the society has a right to be protected by it in the enjoyment of his life, liberty and property, according to standing law . . . [N]o part of the property of any individual can, with justice, be taken from him, or applied to public uses, without his own consent, or that of the representative body of the people."

[1157] *See generally* §5.1 of this handbook (equitable property interests).

[1158] Anderson v. BNY Mellon, 463 Mass. 299, 974 N.E.2d 21 (Mass. 2012).

[1159] *See generally* UPC §2-707; §8.2.1.3 of this handbook (vested and contingent equitable interests) and §8.15.55 of this handbook (lapse and antilapse).

[1160] *See generally* §8.2.1 of this handbook (the Rule against Perpetuities) and §8.2.1.9 of this handbook (abolishing the Rule against Perpetuities).

[1161] *See generally* §8.2.1 of this handbook (the vesting concept).

[1162] UPC §2-707 cmt. *See generally* §8.2.1.7 of this handbook (perpetuities legislation).

[1163] *See* UPC §2-707 cmt. (some examples of overt expressions of the intent to vest).

[1164] 481 U.S. 704, 104 S. Ct. 2076 (1987).

retroactive application of new allocation and apportionment rules would seem to be the U.S. Supreme Court case of *Webb's Fabulous Pharmacies, Inc. v. Beckwith*, which involved a state taking of the income generated by an interpleader fund administered in the registry of a county court.[1165] As is the case with most such escrow-trust arrangements, the long-standing rule had been that any interest on an interpleaded and deposited fund followed the principal and was allocated to those who were ultimately to be the owners of the principal.[1166] The Court held that the state could not take the income for itself. "Neither the Florida Legislature by statute, not the Florida courts by judicial decree, may accomplish the result the county seeks simply by recharacterizing the principal as 'public money' because it is held temporarily by the court."[1167]

Webb's involved a state taking by redefinition for a public purpose of the income that had accrued on entrusted funds. When new apportionment and allocation default rules are made applicable to re-existing irrevocable trusts, the issue is not whether there has been an uncompensated taking by the state for a public purpose but whether there has been an uncompensated taking by the state for a private purpose. The private purpose is the reordering of the respective equitable interests of the income and principal beneficiaries, in this case by redefining what is trust accounting income. The victims of the taking would be any beneficiaries who were adversely affected economically by a change of the rules in the middle of the game. Thus, when an irrevocable traditional trust is judicially reformed into a unitrust, a topic we take up in Section 6.2.2.4 of this handbook, care should be taken that one class of beneficiary not be advantaged at the expense of another, unless the terms of the trust so permit.[1168]

In the 1961 Pennsylvania case of *In re Trust of Catherwood*, the Court had no problem upholding the application of the income apportionment rules that were set forth in an updated version of the Uniform Principal and Income Act to preexisting irrevocable trusts.[1169] The majority's rationale was that while one may have a vested equitable right to trust accounting income, in the case where an interest in a corporation is a trust asset, a beneficiary can have no vested right in the default rule as to how internal corporate income must be apportioned between the life tenant and the remaindermen in order to arrive at trust accounting income. "A vested property right cannot exist in a rule of law, although a rule of law may establish a vested property right."[1170] We are not convinced that the *Webb's* court would necessarily have agreed with the logic of that aphorism, or that its sentiments would pass constitutional muster. The

---

[1165] 449 U.S. 155, 101 S. Ct. 446 (1980).

[1166] Webb's Fabulous Pharmacies, Inc. v. Beckwith, 449 U.S. 155, 162, 101 S. Ct. 446, 451 (1980). *See generally* §9.9.2 of this handbook (agency arrangements).

[1167] Webb's Fabulous Pharmacies, Inc. v. Beckwith, 449 U.S. 155, 164, 101 S. Ct. 446, 452 (1980).

[1168] *See, e.g.*, In re Moore, 41 Misc. 3d 687, 971 N.Y.S.2d 419 (Sur. Ct. N.Y. Cty. 2013) (the court justifying its granting of a unitrust conversion application on the grounds that conversion is consistent with settlor intent and will not result in a "rapid depletion" of corpus).

[1169] 405 Pa. 61, 173 A.2d 86 (1961).

[1170] In re Trust of Catherwood, 405 Pa. 61, 72, 173 A.2d 86, 91 (1961).

Catherwood dissenters certainly did not buy it. Justice Bell wrote in dissent: "The majority not only repudiated the 100 year old Pennsylvania rule of apportionment which was unanimously reaffirmed approximately one year ago, but they further declare that what this Court repeatedly said was unconstitutional, was constitutional and vice versa ... Once again I plaintively ask: Stare Decisis –' Quo Vadis?' "[1171]

Taking by retroactively applying a modified Rule against Perpetuities. Apparently in deference to the vested equitable property rights (reversionary interests) of those who would take upon imposition of a resulting trust should an express trust fail,[1172] the Uniform Statutory Rule Against Perpetuities (USRAP) would only interfere with certain problematic nonvested equitable interests under express trusts, namely those interest that would come into existence on or after the effective date of the legislation.[1173] The authors of the Uniform Probate Code, however, have suggested that a court might have the equitable power to reform a problematic contingent disposition under an irrevocable express trust created before enactment. This would be done by judicially inserting a perpetuity saving clause, "because a perpetuity saving clause would probably have been used at the drafting stage of the disposition had it been drafted competently."[1174] Those who would take upon imposition of a resulting trust could be expected to oppose such a reformation initiative, which, after all, would seek to have the state extinguish their equitable property interests. In any case, in light of the trustee's duty of impartiality, it difficult to see why the trustee would or should be afforded the standing to bring such an action.[1175]

§8.15.72 *Doctrine of Infectious Invalidity*

The rule against perpetuities. The doctrine of infectious invalidity is a rarely applied exception to the severability principle that "[w]hen an interest is void under the Rule against Perpetuities, it is stricken out; and ... the other interests created in the will or trust instrument take effect as if the void interest had never been written."[1176] Under the doctrine of infectious invalidity, if severing and saving the others interests would so disrupt the settlor's dispositive scheme that the settlor would have wanted the other interests to fail as well,

---

[1171] In re Trust of Catherwood, 405 Pa. 61, 72, 173 A.2d 86, 91 (1961). *See generally* §8.15.14 of this handbook (the Massachusetts rule of allocation and the Pennsylvania rule of apportionment).

[1172] *See generally* §4.1.1.1 of this handbook (the vested equitable reversionary interest and the resulting trust).

[1173] UPC §2-905 (USRAP's prospective application).

[1174] UPC §2-905 cmt. *See generally* §§8.2.1.6 of this handbook (the perpetuities saving clause) and 8.15.22 of this handbook (reformation proceedings).

[1175] *But see* UPC §2-903 cmt. ("The 'interested person' who would frequently bring the reformation suit would be the trustee."). *See generally* §6.2.5 of this handbook (trustee's duty of impartiality).

[1176] W. Barton Leach, *Perpetuities in a Nutshell*, 51 Harv. L. Rev. 638, 656 (1938).

then all the interests are voided.[1177] The doctrine is more a rule of construction than an "inexorable rule of law."[1178]

The following illustration of the doctrine's application is taken from an actual case. *A* transfers property in irrevocable trust to *B* for the benefit of *C* for life. Upon the death of *C*, income shall be distributed quarterly to *C*'s issue *per stirpes* until there is no longer a child of *C* alive. Fearing that the provisions for the benefit of *C*'s issue could violate the common law Rule against Perpetuities, as *C* could conceive a nonlife-in-being child after the creation of the trust,[1179] *A* proceeds to transfer irrevocably his vested equitable reversionary property interest, an interest that could become possessory upon the imposition of resulting trust, to *B* upon a new express trust for the benefit of the issue of *C*, until the death of the last child of *C* who is *alive at the time the new trust is created.*[1180]

Now how should the first trust be administered? Should the court sever and save the income interests of the children of *C*, which vested upon the death of *C*, a life in being, and invalidate piecemeal over time all the other equitable interests, or should the court invalidate all equitable interests at *C*'s death and in so doing cause all property immediately thereafter to become subject to the new trust? Invoking the doctrine of infectious invalidity, the court did the latter:

> As the case now stands, all interests after the gift of income to the children for their lives are invalid, and after the death of each child his or her one-third share of the trust will be governed by the . . . [new trust. . . . This, we think, does not accord with the settlor's intent, which was to benefit each line of descendants equally. . . . This inequality can be eliminated and full effect can be given to the settlor's original plan if all the interests in the . . . [original trust] . . . following the gift of income to . . . [*C*] . . . are declared invalid under the principle sometimes called 'infectious invalidity.' [n.3] . . . This would eliminate the transition period during which the two trusts would concurrently operate under overlapping plans. . . .[1181]

Section 3 of the Uniform Statutory Rule Against Perpetuities (USRAP) supersedes the doctrine of infectious invalidity but retains the common law severability doctrine. Under USRAP, a topic we take up in Section 8.2.1.7 of this handbook, invalid severed interests are to be reformed "in the manner that most closely approximates the transferor's manifested plan of distribution."[1182]

[1177] New England Trust Co. v. Sanger, 337 Mass. 342, 354, 149 N.E.2d 598, 605 (1958).

[1178] New England Trust Co. v. Sanger, 337 Mass. 342, 353, 149 N.E.2d 598, 605 (1958).

[1179] The fertile octogenarian principle illustrates how the possibility of conception and birth after at trust has become irrevocable can cause an inartfully drafted class gift to violate the common law Rule against Perpetuities. *See* §8.15.31 of this handbook (the fertile octogenarian principle).

[1180] New Eng. Trust Co. v. Sanger, 337 Mass. 342, 348–349, 149 N.E.2d 598, 602–603 (1958). *See* §4.1.1 of this handbook (the reversionary interest), particularly the introductory quotation, and §4.1.1.1 of this handbook (the resulting trust).

[1181] New Eng. Trust Co. v. Sanger, 337 Mass. 342, 351–352, 149 N.E.2d 598, 603–604 (1958).

[1182] UPC §2-903 (reformation).

The Rule against Perpetuities is covered generally in Section 8.2.1 of this handbook. The fertile octogenarian principle is discussed in Section 8.15.31 of this handbook; the unborn widow principle in Section 8.15.32 of this handbook; and the "all-or-nothing" rule in Section 8.15.73 of this handbook, along with its two exceptions.

Partially ineffective exercises of powers of appointment. *Appointees.* The doctrine of infectious invalidity is also implicated if the donee of a power of appointment exercises it in favor of both permissible and impermissible appointees in a common disposition.[1183] Powers of appointment are covered generally in Section 8.1.1 of this handbook. While the appointment to the impermissible appointees is ineffective, what about the permissible ones? Can the appointment to them be salvaged?

> Whether the ineffective part of an appointment renders otherwise effective parts ineffective depends upon whether the donee's general dispositive scheme is more nearly approximated by treating as effective some or all of the remaining parts or by allowing some or all of the remaining parts to pass to those persons who would receive it if no appointment had been attempted.[1184]

Take the following situation: *X* is the donee of a nongeneral power of appointment whose permissible appointees are *X*'s issue. Charities are the takers in default. The power may be exercised in further trust. *X* proceeds to do just that by appointing the subject property to a trustee for the benefit of *X*'s spouse for life. Upon the death of *X*'s spouse, per the terms of the exercise, the trust property is to pass outright and free of trust to *X*'s issue. While the equitable life estate in *X*'s spouse is patently invalid, the spouse being an impermissible appointee, what about the so-called equitable remainders? Have they been fatally infected by the invalidity of the prior equitable life estate? Probably not. A judicial validation of the equitable remainders would tend to further the donee's general dispositive scheme, which is to benefit the donor's issue, not certain charities. Thus, pending the death of the spouse, trust accounting income flows upon a resulting trust into the coffers of the takers in default of the appointment, namely the charities.[1185] Then, upon the death of the spouse, the trust property passes outright and free of trust from the trustee to *X*'s issue pursuant to the express terms of the exercise. Exercising powers of appointment in further trust is covered generally in Section 8.1.2 of this handbook.

Appointive property. A donee in a common disposition purports to exercise a power of appointment over both appointive and nonappointive property, or over a sum of money greater than that which is covered by the power grant. Absent special facts, the exercise is effective as to the portion of the trust

---

[1183] Restatement (Third) of Property (Wills and Other Donative Transfers) §19.20 cmt. a.

[1184] Restatement (Third) of Property (Wills and Other Donative Transfers) §19.20 cmt. a.

[1185] *See generally* §8.41 of this handbook (resulting trusts of income).

property that is covered by the power grant and ineffective as to the portion that is not.[1186]

§8.15.73   *"All-or-Nothing" Rule with Respect to Class Gifts and Its "Specific Sum" and "Subclass" Exceptions [The Rule Against Perpetuities]*

In the context of determining whether a particular class gift violates the common law Rule against Perpetuities, which we take up generally in Section 8.2.1 of this handbook, the "all-or-nothing" rule requires that a class gift stand or fall as a whole.[1187] A class gift does not vest as a collective until the interest of each member has vested.[1188] If it is possible that the interest of one class member can vest too remotely, all the interests, including the interests of any lives in being, fail.[1189] Here is how one can run afoul of the common law "all-or-nothing" rule: A transfers property to B in an irrevocable discretionary trust for C's issue. When no child of C is alive and under the age of 25, the trust terminates and what is left over of the trust property passes outright and free of trust in equal shares to C's children who shall have reached the age of 25.[1190] Four of C's five children are alive at the time the trust is settled.[1191] The fifth is conceived and born later.[1192] Under the "all-or-nothing" rule, all equitable interests are invalid, including those of the four life-in-being children.[1193] The wait-and-see and reformation features of the USRAP would substantially mitigate the "all-or-nothing" rule's harshness.[1194]

The common law has two limitations on or exceptions to the "all-or-nothing" rule. One is the specific-sum limitation and the other is the sub-class limitation. As to the former, if a specified sum of money is to be paid to each member of a class, the interest of each class member is entitled to separate treatment and stands on his or her own with respect to the rule's application.[1195] Thus lives in being at least would be entitled to take.[1196] As to the latter,

---

[1186] Restatement (Third) of Property (Wills and Other Donative Transfers) §19.20 cmt. f.

[1187] *See* Leake v. Robinson, 2 Mer. 363, 35 Eng. Rep. 979 (Ch. 1817) ("all-or-nothing" rule). *See generally* §8.2.1 of this handbook (the Rule against Perpetuities) and §5.2 of this handbook (class gifts).

[1188] W. Barton Leach, Perpetuities in a Nutshell, 51 Harv. L. Rev. 638, 648–649 (1938). *See generally* §8.2.1.3 of this handbook (the vesting concept).

[1189] W. Barton Leach, Perpetuities in a Nutshell, 51 Harv. L. Rev. 638, 648–649 (1938).

[1190] For a similar hypothetical, complete with a timeline, *see* §8.2.1 of this handbook.

[1191] *See generally* §8.2.1.2 of this handbook (the life in being).

[1192] *See generally* §8.2.1 of this handbook (gestation and the Rule against Perpetuities).

[1193] W. Barton Leach, Perpetuities in a Nutshell, 51 Harv. L. Rev. 638, 649 (1938). *See generally* §8.2.1.5 of this handbook (consequences of a violation of the common law Rule against Perpetuities).

[1194] UPC §§2-901 (wait-and-see), 2-903 (reformation). *See generally* §§8.2.1.7 of this handbook (perpetuities legislation) and 8.15.22 of this handbook (reformation generally).

[1195] W. Barton Leach, *Perpetuities in a Nutshell*, 51 Harv. L. Rev. 638, 649–650 (1938).

[1196] *See generally* §8.2.1.2 of this handbook (the life in being).

if the ultimate takers are not described as a single class but rather as a group of sub-classes, "the gift to a particular sub-class can be valid even though the gift to another sub-class is too remote."[1197] Sub-class severability is an application of the so-called doctrine of vertical severability.[1198] USRAP's wait-and-see and reformation features should take care of any interests that are not rescued by these two exceptions to the "all-or-nothing" rule.

We take up the related doctrine of infectious invalidity in Section 8.15.72 of this handbook. The fertile octogenarian principle is covered in Section 8.15.31 of this handbook and the unborn widow principle in Section 8.15.32 of this handbook.

§8.15.74 The Principle That Money Paid to an Innocent Non-BFP Under a Mistake of Law Is Not Recoverable

Moneys paid to a good-faith purchaser for value (BFP) are not recoverable by the transferor.[1199] At common law, moneys paid under a *mistake of law* to an innocent non-BFP also were not recoverable.[1200] In the trust context, when a an insolvent trustee of an express trust misdelivered trust property to an innocent non-BFP, the beneficiary was out of luck.[1201] The injured beneficiary had no recourse against the transferee, although it is not entirely clear why the innocent transferee would not have held the property upon a resulting trust for the benefit of the beneficiary, or, if not innocent, upon a constructive trust.[1202] "In one of the most significant changes of direction in private law in the twentieth century the . . . [general] . . . rule was overturned in the House of Lords . . . by way of a lengthy deconstruction of the precedents and academic literature by Lord Goff of Chieveley."[1203] In the trust context the rule is being nibbled away by particular exceptions.[1204]

[1197] W. Barton Leach, *Perpetuities in a Nutshell*, 51 Harv. L. Rev. 638, 649–651 (1938). *See also* Kern's Estate, 296 Pa. 348, 145 A. 824 (1929) (the doctrine of vertical severability).

[1198] *See generally* Murphy, *Separability and the Rule Against Perpetuities*, 77 Dick. L. Rev. 277 (1973). A decree of vertical separation, however, may not thwart a material purpose of the trust. *Id.*

[1199] *See* §8.15.63 of this handbook (the BFP).

[1200] *See generally* W.A. Lee, *Purifying the dialect of equity*, 7(2) Tr. Q. Rev. 16–23 (May 2009) [a STEP publication].

[1201] *See, e.g.*, Re Diplock, [1948] Ch 465 (England).

[1202] *See generally* §3.3 of this handbook (the constructive trust) and §4.1.1.1 of this handbook (the resulting trust).

[1203] W.A. Lee, *Purifying the dialect of equity*, 7(2) Tr. Q. Rev. 19 (May 2009) [a STEP publication] (referring to Kleinwort Benson v. Lincoln CC, [1999] 2 AC 349 (England)).

[1204] *See, e.g.*, Re Hastings-Bass, [1975] Ch 25; [1974] 2 WLR 904 (England).

§8.15.75   The Nonassignability of a Debt at Early Common Law

We begin with a minor concession. Prior to the 17th century, English law would not have authorized a suit like this one—Justice Stephen Breyer, U.S. Supreme Court.[1205]

Prior to the seventeenth century, English common law generally did not recognize the assignment of contractual rights incident to a debt.[1206] The law courts feared a multiplication of "contentions and suits" and the promotion of "maintenance," which was the officious intermeddling with litigation.[1207] Equity, however, would recognize the assignment and the common law deferred.[1208] Equity deemed the assignor to hold the contractual rights for the assignee. Blackstone explains: "But this nicety is now disregarded: though, in compliance with the ancient principle, the form of assignment of a chose of action is in the nature of a declaration of trust, and an agreement to permit the assignee to make use of the name of the assignor, in order to recover the possession."[1209] Equity still refrained from disturbing the legal title to the contractual rights, which remanded back with the assignor.

Assuming the title-holding assignor was an actual trustee of the chose in action postassignment, his residual duties were nominal,[1210] at least as nominal as those of the trustee of a nominee trust today. Even the trustee of a nominee trust is a full-blown fiduciary, whereas, "the relationship between assignor and assignee . . . [was] . . . not a fiduciary relationship involving any especially high standards of honesty, any duty to exclude selfish interest, or any special intimacy."[1211] Nominee trusts are covered in Section 9.6 of this handbook.

Time and the procedural blendings of law and equity have washed away the ancient assignability proscription.[1212] Equity's end-run around this doctrine of nonassignability, however, supports the proposition that law and equity have been intertwined since time immemorial, that it would be inaccurate to say that the common law never recognized that creature of equity we now call the trust. As late as 2008, the U.S. Supreme Court had occasion to review the ancient assignability proscription in deciding whether an assignee of a legal claim for money owed had standing to pursue that claim in federal court, even

---

[1205] Sprint Commc'ns Co., L.P. v. APCC Servs., Inc., 128 S. Ct. 2531, 2536 (2008).

[1206] *See, e.g.*, Lampet's Case, 10 Co. Rep. 46b, 48a, 77 Eng. Rep 994, 997 (K.B. 1612) (stating that "no possibility, right, title, nor thing in action, shall be granted or assigned to strangers"). *See also* Winch v. Keeley, (1787) 1 TR 619 at 622–623; 99 ER 1284 at 1286 (England). *See generally* §9.9.4 of this handbook (though the contractual rights incident to a debtor-creditor relationship may be made the subject of a trust, the debt itself is not a trust).

[1207] Sprint Commc'ns Co., L.P. v. APCC Servs., Inc., 128 S. Ct. 2531, 2536 (2008) (U.S.).

[1208] Winch v. Keeley, (1787) 1 TR 619 at 622–623; 99 ER 1284 at 1286 (England).

[1209] William Blackstone, Commentaries on the Laws of England, Book II, §442 (1765–1769).

[1210] *See generally* Bogert §25 (assignments of nonnegotiable choses in action).

[1211] Bogert §25.

[1212] *See generally* Sprint Commc'ns Co., L.P. v. APCC Servs., Inc., 128 S. Ct. 2531 (2008) (U.S.).

when the assignor had promised to remit the proceeds of the litigation to the assignor.[1213] "We have often said that history and tradition offer a meaningful guide to the types of cases that Article III empowers federal courts to consider."[1214] The assignor was a consortium of coinless payphone operators. The assignee was a consortium of billing and collection firms called aggregators. The defendants were long-distance carriers.

§8.15.76   Forum Non Conveniens Doctrine

The judicial doctrine of *forum non conveniens* is an equitable doctrine that may have been applied for the first time in this country in 1801 when a federal district court in Pennsylvania deferred to the Danish courts in a dispute between a Danish sea captain and a Danish seaman over back wages.[1215] Under the doctrine, if a plaintiff could have brought an action in more than one forum, the court of one forum may for reasons convenience decline jurisdiction in deference to the court of another forum. The judicial power is discretionary. It is the convenience of the litigants and the public generally that the doctrine accommodates. Trust litigation is fertile ground for the doctrine's application as the trust relationship, at least at its inception, involves three parties, the settlor, the trustee, and the beneficiary, not to mention the subject property itself. One court may have *in personam* jurisdiction over the trustee while another may have *in rem* jurisdiction over the property. Or both courts may have *in personam* jurisdiction over the trustee, as would be the case if a testamentary trustee moved himself and the trust property to a state other than the state where the will was probated. In these and other such situations, the doctrine of *forum non conveniens* is implicated, a topic we take up in Section 8.40 of this handbook as part of our discussion of jurisdiction in the context of trust litigation.

§8.15.77   The Trust Entity Doctrine

The whole bundle of property, persons, rights, and duties makes up the trust.[1216]

The trust is being deemed an entity for certain purposes. Under classic principles of trust law, a trust is a fiduciary relationship with respect to property, not a juristic person.[1217] As to the world, the trustee is the legal owner of the

---

[1213] Sprint Commc'ns Co., L.P. v. APCC Servs., Inc., 128 S. Ct. 2531 (2008).

[1214] Sprint Commc'ns Co., L.P. v. APCC Servs., Inc., 128 S. Ct. 2531, 2535 (2008).

[1215] Willendson v. Forsoket, 29 Fed. Cas. 1283 (D.C. Pa 1801) (No. 17,682). *See* Leet v. Union Pac. R. Co., 25 Cal. 2d 605, 609, 155 P.2d 42, 44 (1945) (the doctrine's equitable nature).

[1216] Bogert §1, n.29.

[1217] *See* Portico Mgmt. Grp., LLC v. Harrison, 202 Cal. App. 4th 464 (2011); Jimenez v. Corr, 764 S.E.2d 115 (Va. 2014) ("In contrast, an inter vivos trust is inseparable from the parties related to it, and the trust does not have a separate legal status.").

property.[1218] The beneficiaries, however, have equitable property rights incident to the relationship. In other words, trusts are not corporate-like entities.[1219] Having said that, for some purposes legislatures and courts are treating trusts as if they were. "Under the 'trust entity' theory ... [, for example,] ... a testamentary trust is established and remains at the testator's domicile, thereby giving the domiciliary court in rem jurisdiction independent and apart from the presence of the trustee, the trust assets or the trust beneficiaries."[1220] For years the tax laws have deemed certain trusts to be entities for purposes of the income tax, a topic we take up in Chapter 10 of this handbook. In Section 7.3.1 of this handbook, we consider the trust entity doctrine in the context of contracts between the trustee and third parties. The trust entity doctrine in the context of the trustee's liability in tort to third parties is considered in Section 7.3.3 of this handbook. A trust created under the Uniform Statutory Trust Entity Act is intended to be a juridical entity, "separate from its trustees and beneficial owners, that has the capacity to sue and be sued, own property, and transact in its own name."[1221] In some jurisdictions, a formal conveyance to, or registration in the name of, "the trust" rather than the trustee will nonetheless have the effect of lodging legal title to the subject property in the trustee. See generally Section 2.1.1 of this handbook.

To fundamentally transmogrify the trust into an entity, however, would be ill-advised. While it may be convenient to *deem* a trust an entity *for certain purposes*, such as when it comes to the formal titling of entrusted assets, it would be ill-advised, legislatively or otherwise, to altogether revise the default law of trusts such that the trust is no longer fundamentally a relationship; rather, it is now fundamentally a juristic entity/person. The two classic fiduciary relationships are the agency and the trust. Just as a conversion of the agency into a juristic entity/person would self-evidently destroy the agency's practical utility, so also would such a conversion of the trust into a juristic entity/person destroy the trust's practical utility, particularly in the case of the informal trust. The corporation has already been invented. There is no need to reinvent it. That the legal title to the trust property is in the trustee, that the trustee as to the world is the owner of the property, that the entrusted assets are segregated from the trustee's personal asset, and that the trustee assumes direct burdensome fiduciary duties to identifiable individuals or charitable purposes is what has made the trust such an attractive alternative to the corporation in certain settings, particularly in the informal, noncommercial setting. Even in the commercial context, the trust's protean nature can make it an attractive alternative to the standardized corporation, particularly when structural flexibility and operational nimbleness are a priority. And then there are the inevitable unanticipated/unintended consequences were the trust to be fundamentally transmogrified into a juristic entity/person. What, for example, would now be the legal/equitable status of the "trustee"? Would the "trustee" be an agent/

[1218] *See* Portico Mgmt. Grp., LLC v. Harrison, 202 Cal. App. 4th 464 (2011).

[1219] *See* Portico Mgmt. Grp., LLC v. Harrison, 202 Cal. App. 4th 464 (2011).

[1220] Bogert §292.

[1221] Uniform Statutory Trust Entity Act, Prefatory Note.

employee of "the trust"? Where would the legal title to the underlying property now be lodged? Still in the "trustee" or now in "the trust"? The rights, duties, and obligations of the "parties" to "the trust," once a long-seasoned legal/ equitable relationship, now a fledgling juristic entity/person, would take decades, if not centuries, to sort out.

Cross-reference. See generally Section 3.5.1 of this handbook (nature and extent of the trustee's estate).

§8.15.78   Unjust Enrichment

In 1997, Gummow, J, a justice of the High Court of Australia, . . . signaled in Hill v. Van Erp . . . his unhappiness with the exorbitant claims of those who sought to pack down the whole of restitution into a tight unjust enrichment box.[1222]

Lord Mansfield (William Murray, 1st Earl of Mansfield), via the 1750 English case of *Moses v. Macferlan*, had injected unjust enrichment doctrine into the English legal tradition.[1223] Long before 1937, which was when the United States Supreme Court expressly applied the doctrine in *Stone v. White*, the doctrine also had been a thread in the fabric of America's (U.S.) legal tradition.[1224]

Unjust enrichment can be either an equitable or a legal wrong.[1225] Whether in equity or at law, unjust enrichment is the basic principle, on this side of the Atlantic, at least, that underlies the substantive equitable remedy of restitution.[1226] Restitution as a remedy for a trustee's unauthorized self-dealing is covered in Section 7.2.3.3 of this handbook. One who is unjustly enriched is unjustifiably enriched, that is to say there is no legal or equitable basis for the enrichment, such as what might be supplied by the law of gifts or the law of contracts.[1227] "Restitution is accordingly subordinate to contract as an organizing principle of private relationships, and the terms of an enforceable agreement normally displace any claim of unjust enrichment within their reach."[1228] Likewise, absent special facts, gift doctrine trumps considerations of unjust enrichment. Thus the term *unjustified enrichment* better captures the essence of traditional unjust enrichment doctrine in the Anglo-American legal tradition. It also better approximates the gist of comparable doctrine in the civil law tradition. "One reason is that 'unjustified enrichment' makes an approximate

---

[1222] Justice Keith Mason, Chancery Bar Assoc., Inner Temple, *What Has Equity to Do with Restitution? Does It Matter?* (Nov. 27, 2006).

[1223] Moses v. Macferlan, 2 Burr. 1005 (K.B. 1750).

[1224] Stone v. White, 301 U.S. 532, 534–535 (1937).

[1225] Andrew Kull, James Barr Ames and the *Early Modern History of Unjust Enrichment*, 25 Oxford J. Legal Stud. 297 (2005).

[1226] Edwin W. Patterson, Book Review, 47 Yale L.J. 1420, 1421 (1938) (reviewing Restatement of Restitution).

[1227] Restatement (Third) of Restitution and Unjust Enrichment §2, cmts. b (gift) and c (contract).

[1228] Restatement (Third) of Restitution and Unjust Enrichment §2 cmt. c.

translation of both the German *ungerechtfertige Bereicherung* (BGB §812) and the French *enrichissement sans cause*."[1229]

At law, the concept of unjust enrichment incubated in the corner of the common law we now refer to as quasi contracts or "contracts implied in law."[1230] "That heading includes a wide variety of situations . . . , as where a person by mistake pays a debt a second time, or is coerced into conferring a benefit upon another, or renders aid to another in an emergency or is wrongfully deprived of his chattels by another who has used them for his own benefit."[1231] The legal remedy is generally limited to the payment of money.[1232] In equity, the concept of unjust enrichment evolved as a corollary to both the fiduciary principle and constructive trust jurisprudence.[1233] The constructive trust is covered in Section 3.3 of this handbook and in Section 7.2.3.1 of this handbook. By the end of the nineteenth century American legal scholars were busy developing a unified theory of unjust enrichment that straddled and transcended the traditional law/equity divide of the Anglo-American legal tradition.[1234] The Restatement of Restitution (1937) is the culmination of those efforts. It purported to sever the concept of restitution for unjust enrichment from its various cultural roots and placed it in its own vase on the shelf of the constructs of the common law as it has been enhanced by Equity: "The task of 'restatement,' in this instance, took the form of a radical reconception of an important area of the law that antiquated formal categories had previously obscured, following exactly in this regard the prescriptions of some noted realists."[1235] One such realist was Harvard's Prof. James Barr Ames.[1236]

And yet it is also said that the concept of unjustified enrichment is actually of exceedingly ancient origin. In the writings of Sextus Pomponius, a Roman jurist of the mid-second century A.D., appears this maxim: *Jure naturae aequum est, neminem cum alterius detrimento et injuria fieri locupletiorerm* ("It is a principle of natural justice and equity, that no one should be enriched through loss or injury to another").[1237]

[1229] Restatement (Third) of Restitution and Unjust Enrichment §1, Reporter's Note. "In the statute law of Louisiana, the source of what is here called a liability in restitution is described as an 'enrichment without cause.' La. Civ. Code art. 2298. As expressed in Canadian law, a claim in restitution requires that the plaintiff establish an enrichment, a corresponding deprivation, and 'the absence of any juristic reason . . . for the enrichment.' Rathwell v. Rathwell, [1978] 2 S.C.R. 436, 455." Restatement (Third) of Restitution and Unjust Enrichment §1, Reporter's Note.

[1230] Restatement of Restitution, Part I, Introductory Note.

[1231] Restatement of Restitution 1 (General Scope Note).

[1232] Restatement of Restitution 1 (General Scope Note).

[1233] Harold Greville Hanbury & Ronald Harling Maudsley, Modern Equity, Chap. 14 (10th ed. 1976).

[1234] Restatement (Third) of Restitution and Unjust Enrichment §4 cmt. b.

[1235] Andrew Kull, *Restitution and Reform*, 32 S. Ill. U. L.J. 83, 86 (2007).

[1236] *See generally* Restatement (Third) of Restitution and Unjust Enrichment §4, Reporter's Note.

[1237] Restatement (Third) of Restitution and Unjust Enrichment §4 cmt. b. and Reporter's Note.

The English and the Australians, however, have yet to fully buy into the American idea of a freestanding law of restitution for unjust enrichment.[1238] In any case, on this side of the Atlantic there are now few left who are equipped, by formal legal training at least, to appreciate the boldness of the efforts of the realists, via the Restatement of Restitution (1937), to colonize the "vast *terra incognita* occupied by the set of legal actions grouped under the impenetrable name of 'quasi-contract' and a miscellaneous set of equitable remedies (principally constructive trust)" in that "many American lawyers would be hard pressed even to say what equity is (or was)."[1239] For more on the marginalization of Equity in the curriculum of the American law school, the reader is referred to Section 8.25 of this handbook.

As to unjust enrichment as a principle of substantive liability, all that critical doctrine fell through the cracks years ago with the introduction of the traditional Remedies course into the American law school curriculum.[1240] The course was a pedagogical contraption of selected elements of the traditional Damages, Equity, and Restitution required courses.[1241] Now even Remedies is elective, or no longer offered at all. It is no wonder that unjust enrichment doctrine is generally a mystery to contemporary American lawyers, and to contemporary law professors even more so.[1242] "Much of the substantive law of equity—in particular, the law describing equitable interests in property held by another—suffered the same fate."[1243]

§8.15.79 Doctrine of Selective Allocation (Marshalling)

Here may be mentioned a question somewhat related to equitable election, which has arisen in the United States.—John Chipman Gray on the subject of marshalling[1244]

John Chipman Gray. In Section 8.2.1.8 of this handbook we discuss how the exercise of a general testamentary power of appointment in further trust could violate the rule against perpetuities if the exercise is intended for the benefit of persons not in being at the time the power was created. If the vehicle for the exercise were a single provision in the will of the donee blending property that had been owned by the donee with property that was subject to the power, all may not be lost, however, provided some portion of the blended fund is to pass outright and free of trust.

Assume, for example, that 50 percent of the fund is to pass in further trust for the benefit of Mr. X, with a remainder to those of his children who survive

---

[1238] *See* Charles E. Rounds, Jr., *Relief for IP Rights Infringement Is Primarily Equitable: How American Legal Education Is Short-Changing the 21st Century Corporate Litigator*, 26 Santa Clara Computer & High Tech. L.J. 313, 333–335 (2010).

[1239] Andrew Kull, *Restitution and Reform*, 32 S. Ill. U. L.J. 83, 87 (2007).

[1240] Restatement (Third) of Restitution and Unjust Enrichment §1, Reporter's Note.

[1241] Restatement (Third) of Restitution and Unjust Enrichment §1, Reporter's Note.

[1242] Restatement (Third) of Restitution and Unjust Enrichment §1, Reporter's Note.

[1243] Restatement (Third) of Restitution and Unjust Enrichment §1, Reporter's Note.

[1244] John Chipman Gray, The Rule Against Perpetuities §561.7 (4th ed. 1942).

him. The other 50 percent of the blended fund is to pass outright and free of trust. Mr. X was not in being when the power was created. Assume also that the trust property and the probate property are each worth $100. Under the doctrine of selective allocation (marshalling), a new trust is impressed upon the probate property and the property that had been subject to the power passes outright and free of trust to the probate devisees.[1245] By allocating selectively rather than ratably, a violation of the rule against perpetuities is avoided.[1246] This is because Mr. X, *as to the new trust,* is a life in being for rule against perpetuities analysis purposes.[1247] "An intention is presumed that the whole mass of property should be applied for the purposes of the will in such a matter as to make the will effective, as far as possible, with respect to the property subject to the power as well as with respect to the testator's own property."[1248] The somewhat related doctrine of equitable election is taken up in Section 8.15.82 of this handbook.

The Restatement (Third) of Property. The Restatement (Third) of Property would deem the donee's will, any codicils to the donee's will, and any revocable trust created by the donee that did not become irrevocable before the donee's death a single document for purposes of applying the doctrine of selective allocation (marshalling) in a given situation.[1249] It also departs from traditional doctrine and from the previous Restatements, as well, "by providing for selective allocation even though the donee . . . [of a power of appointment] . . . has not blended owned and appointive assets in a common disposition."[1250] Thus, the doctrine is extended to the exercise of a powers of appointment either by nonblending specific exercise clause or nonblending blanket-exercise clause.[1251] Powers of appointment are covered generally in Section 8.1.1 of this handbook. While the doctrine may be employed as an administrative mechanism for avoiding violations of the rule against perpetuities, it has other such administrative uses as well. Avoidance of impermissible appointments particularly comes to mind.[1252]

The mechanics of selective allocation. Selective allocation does not necessarily require a physical allocation. "Selective allocation simply means that the allocation is treated as if it were made selectively . . . [, rather than ratably,] . . . for purposes of furthering the donee's intent." Ultimately the doctrine of selective allocation (marshalling) it is all about effectuating donee intent. The Restatement (Third) of Property is fully in accord, and then some: "If the donee of a power of appointment exercises the power in a document that also disposes

---

[1245] Restatement (First) of Property §363 cmt. f; John Chipman Gray, The Rule Against Perpetuities §561.7 (4th ed. 1942).

[1246] Restatement (First) of Property §363 cmt. f; John Chipman Gray, The Rule Against Perpetuities §561.7 (4th ed. 1942).

[1247] Restatement (First) of Property §363,cmt. f; John Chipman Gray, The Rule Against Perpetuities §561.7 (4th ed. 1942).

[1248] John Chipman Gray, The Rule Against Perpetuities §561.7 (4th ed. 1942).

[1249] Restatement (Third) of Property (Wills and Other Donative Transfers) §19.19 cmt. a.

[1250] Restatement (Third) of Property (Wills and Other Donative Transfers) §19.19 cmt. b.

[1251] Restatement (Third) of Property (Wills and Other Donative Transfers) §19.19 cmt. b.

[1252] Restatement (Third) of Property (Wills and Other Donative Transfers) §19.19 cmt. i.

of owned property, the owned and appointive property are deemed to be allocated in the manner that best carries out the donee's intent."[1253]

§8.15.80   Springing and Shifting Interests in Land

A springing property interest cuts short an interest that is in the hands of the original transferor.[1254] A shifting property interest cuts short an interest in a person other than the original transferor.[1255] More about that later.

The modern trust evolved from the use, an equitable relationship that is covered in Section 8.15.1 of this handbook. Already by the time of the Wars of the Roses (1455-1485) most of the land in England was held to uses. The seeds of the modern trust were sown in 1536 when Parliament enacted the Statute of Uses. Before 1536, only *equitable* springing and shifting property interests in land were enforced.[1256] After its enactment, *legal* springing and shifting interests in land also became enforceable.[1257] Still, an equitable property interest in land incident to a trust will likely have a greater range of practical applications than its less scrivener-friendly and more administratively problematic legal counterpart. In Section 8.27 of this handbook, we discuss some of these applications.

Interests that spring. *Equitable interests.* Today, a springing equitable interest incident to a trust relationship might look like this: On July 1, *A* (the settlor) transfers Blackacre to *B* in trust for *C* for life, *C*'s interest to commence on August 1. During the month of July, there is a resulting trust of the equitable interest in favor of *A* (the settlor), the mechanics of which we touch upon in Section 8.41 of this handbook. On August 1, however, the equitable interest springs up in favor of *C*. Before 1536, it was likewise possible to create a use of land that commenced in futuro. It was called unsurprisingly a *springing use*.[1258]

Legal interests. On the other hand, before 1536 no freehold estate could be created to commence *in futuro*.[1259] Thus a *legal* enfeoffment of land outright to *X* and his heirs, said enfeoffment to go into effect sometime the following year, would result in *X* taking nothing.[1260] One consequence of the enactment of the Statute of Uses was that it became possible for a legal freehold estate to

---

[1253] Restatement (Third) of Property (Wills and Other Donative Transfers) §19.19.

[1254] Cornelius J. Moynihan, Introduction to the Law of Real Property 176 (2d ed. 1988); John Chipman Gray, The Rule Against Perpetuities §54 (4th ed. 1942).

[1255] Cornelius J. Moynihan, Introduction to the Law of Real Property 175–176 (2d ed. 1988); John Chipman Gray, The Rule Against Perpetuities §52 (4th ed. 1942).

[1256] Cornelius J. Moynihan, Introduction to the Law of Real Property 187 (2d ed. 1988); John Chipman Gray, The Rule Against Perpetuities §69 (4th ed. 1942).

[1257] Cornelius J. Moynihan, Introduction to the Law of Real Property 187–188 (2d ed. 1988); John Chipman Gray, The Rule Against Perpetuities §52 (4th ed. 1942).

[1258] Cornelius J. Moynihan, Introduction to the Law of Real Property 187 (2d ed. 1988).

[1259] Cornelius J. Moynihan, Introduction to the Law of Real Property 175 (2d ed. 1988).

[1260] Cornelius J. Moynihan, Introduction to the Law of Real Property 175 (2d ed. 1988).

commence *in futuro*.[1261] A grantor might, for example, bargain and sell land to *X* and his heirs to have and to hold from and after the impending marriage of *X*. The state of the title would be as follows: estate in fee simple in the grantor subject to an executory interest in *X* in fee simple to take effect in possession on *X*'s marriage.[1262]

Interests that shift. *Equitable interests*. Today, a shifting equitable interest in land incident to a trust relationship might look like this: *A* (the settlor) transfers Blackacre to *B* in trust for *C* for life, remainder to *D*, an ascertained individual; but if Susan marries Tom during *C*'s lifetime, then the property passes outright and free of trust to *X*. *D* possesses a vested equitable interest that is subject to complete divestment, a topic that is covered in Section 8.30 of this handbook. The equitable interest would shift to *X* should the condition subsequent ever happen.[1263]

Legal interests. Before 1536, shifting uses were likewise enforceable in equity.[1264] Shifting legal interests, however, were not.[1265] Thus, an enfeoffment to *X* and his heirs but if *X* dies childless then to *Y* and his heirs would result in *Y* taking nothing.[1266] After enactment of the Statute of Uses, there could be "a valid limitation of a . . . [legal] . . . future interest taking effect by cutting short a prior estate in another grantee."[1267] A grantor might, for example, bargain and sell land to *X* for life but if *X* becomes bankrupt then to *Y* and his heirs. The state of the title would be as follows: life estate in *X* subject to an executory interest in fee simple in *Y*, reversion in the grantor.[1268] The interest of *Y* is said to be executory.[1269] Should there be a shifting, *Y*'s interest would then become possessory.[1270] Because there is no trustee in the picture to hold legal title and monitor *Y*'s financial situation, the legal executory interest is no match for the trust, at least when it comes to the practicalities of administering property interests that can shift.

§8.15.81   *Good-Faith Doctrine*

Historically, the common law of trusts and the principles of equity did not look to contract law when applying a good faith standard to trustees. Instead, courts have consistently applied a

---

[1261] Cornelius J. Moynihan, Introduction to the Law of Real Property 187–188 (2d ed. 1988).

[1262] Cornelius J. Moynihan, Introduction to the Law of Real Property 187 (2d ed. 1988).

[1263] *Cf.* John Chipman Gray, The Rule Against Perpetuities §78 (4th ed. 1942) ("Therefore, in settling property, chattels personal, like leaseholds, are settled in trust, the equitable interest shifting on the death of a *cestui que trust* or other future event.").

[1264] Cornelius J. Moynihan, Introduction to the Law of Real Property 175–176 (2d ed. 1988).

[1265] Cornelius J. Moynihan, Introduction to the Law of Real Property 175 (2d ed. 1988).

[1266] Cornelius J. Moynihan, Introduction to the Law of Real Property 175 (2d ed. 1988).

[1267] Cornelius J. Moynihan, Introduction to the Law of Real Property 188 (2d ed. 1988).

[1268] Cornelius J. Moynihan, Introduction to the Law of Real Property 188 (2d ed. 1988).

[1269] Cornelius J. Moynihan, Introduction to the Law of Real Property 188 (2d ed. 1988).

[1270] Cornelius J. Moynihan, Introduction to the Law of Real Property 188 (2d ed. 1988).

good faith standard within the context of a broad fiduciary duty of loyalty.—Frederick R. Franke, Jr.[1271]

The contract is a legal relationship, while the trust is an equitable one. Each relationship, however, brings with it a nonwaivable duty of good faith.[1272] The parties to a contract owe each other a legal duty of good faith, while the trustee owes the beneficiaries an equitable duty of good faith. In the contract context, good faith is generally viewed as little more than the absence of bad faith.[1273] "Thus, good faith merely polices subjective bad conduct in the performance of the contract."[1274]

The Restatement (Third) of Trusts provides that a cotrustee who commits a breach of trust in bad faith is not entitled to contribution from his fellow cotrustees, absent special facts. Bad faith, in this context at least, includes fraud, embezzlement, "and other misconduct involving a dishonest motive or conscious disregard for the interests of the beneficiaries or the purposes of the trust."[1275] The Restatement sets a particularly high bar for what constitutes bad faith behavior on the part of a breaching trustee and, by implication, a low one for what constitutes good faith behavior, at least when it comes to adjudicating a breaching cotrustee's right to contribution: "Intentional participation in a known breach of trust . . . does not necessarily entail bad faith. Thus, if trustees join in what they know to be a breach of trust, even one involving self-dealing, they do not act in bad faith if their objective is to advance the interests of the beneficiaries."[1276]

The good faith principle in the trust context generally may be synonymous with the fiduciary principle. In the trust context, the trustee is obliged to exercise his discretionary powers in good faith. It is arguable that this equitable duty of good faith is generally broader and more intense than its legal counterpart. It is a duty of "good faith in reasonably implementing the settlor's intent for the benefit of the beneficiary."[1277] This definition of the trustee's equitable duty of good faith is essentially a compressed compilation of the general fiduciary duties of a trustee.[1278]

Or perhaps the good faith principle in the trust context generally sets a lower bar than the fiduciary principle. Prof. Frances H. Foster has chronicled the contractarians' incursion into the law of trusts: "Under the influence of law

---

[1271] *See generally* Frederick R. Franke, Jr., *Resisting the Contractarian Insurgency: The Uniform Trust Code, Fiduciary Duty, and Good Faith in Contract*, 36 ACTEC L.J. 517, 544 (2010).

[1272] *See generally* Frederick R. Franke, Jr., *Resisting the Contractarian Insurgency: The Uniform Trust Code, Fiduciary Duty, and Good Faith in Contract*, 36 ACTEC L.J. 517 (2010).

[1273] *See generally* Frederick R. Franke, Jr., *Resisting the Contractarian Insurgency: The Uniform Trust Code, Fiduciary Duty, and Good Faith in Contract*, 36 ACTEC L.J. 517, 533 (2010).

[1274] *See generally* Frederick R. Franke, Jr., *Resisting the Contractarian Insurgency: The Uniform Trust Code, Fiduciary Duty, and Good Faith in Contract*, 36 ACTEC L.J. 517, 535 (2010).

[1275] Restatement (Third) of Trusts §102 cmt. d.

[1276] Restatement (Third) of Trusts §102 cmt. d.

[1277] *See generally* Frederick R. Franke, Jr., *Resisting the Contractarian Insurgency: The Uniform Trust Code, Fiduciary Duty, and Good Faith in Contract*, 36 ACTEC L.J. 517, 531 (2010).

[1278] *See generally* §6.1 of this handbook (the trustee's general duties).

and economics theory, prominent scholars and reformers are rapidly dismantling the traditional legal and moral constraints on trustees. Trusts are becoming mere 'contracts,' and trust law nothing more than 'default rules.'"[1279] Prof.
John H. Langbein, one of the godfathers on this side of the Atlantic of the
movement to codify bold swaths of the law of trusts, dismisses as "pulpit-
thumpers" those who display their reverence for the fiduciary principle on their
sleeves. His "theme" is that "despite decades of pulpit-thumping rhetoric about
the sanctity of fiduciary obligations, fiduciary duties in trust law are unambiguously contractarian."[1280] Can it then really be just a coincidence that the facially
contractarian good faith principle is mentioned numerous times in the Uniform Trust Code while equity's fiduciary principle is rarely alluded to, and only
obliquely at that? We are not so sure. In any case, the failure of the UTC to lay
down a working definition of good faith renders the principle an empty vessel
in the trust context. Thus, we should not be surprised if courts pour into that
vessel a contractarian brew that is not in the long-term interests of the Anglo-
American institution of the trust, an institution which, at its core, is *sui generis*,
not merely an aspect of the law of contracts.

One practitioner-scholar has expressed the concern that the good faith
principle will be "imported" from the law of contracts into the law of trusts and
become the "gold standard." But it would be "fool's gold" in that "the standard
of good faith in the law of contracts is functionally weaker than in the trust law,
and it should be because the commercial context of contractual bargaining is
quite different."[1281]

It may already be too late to rescue the default law of trusts from such
degradation. The good faith infection seems to have taken hold. For example,
French v. Wachovia Bank, N.A.[1282] is a federal Wisconsin case involving a corporate trustee who invested trust assets in a life insurance contract that was
purchased through the trustee's insurance affiliate. The affiliate's sizeable
commission, $512,000, was paid from trust assets, not waived. The trust instru-
ment contained a general boilerplate provision authorizing the trustee "to deal
with any trust hereunder without regard to conflicts of interest." It has been a
traditional principle of trust law that a trustee in breach of trust may not seek
refuge in such boilerplate. In other words, good faith reliance on such boilerplate has generally been an ineffective defense to a breach-of-trust allegation.
There needs to be more specificity in the authorizing language.[1283] The French
court would have none of these fiduciary paternalistics. Just as long as there is
an absence of bad faith: "That Wachovia's insurance affiliate earned a substantial commission does not amount to bad faith; the trust instrument permitted
this kind of self-dealing, and the insurance exchange was a 'win-win' for both

---

[1279] *See* Frances H. Foster, *American Trust Law in a Chinese Mirror*, 94 Minn. L. Rev. 602, 651 (2010).

[1280] *See* John H. Langbein, *The Contractarian Basis of the Law of Trusts*, 105 Yale L.J. 625, 629 (1995).

[1281] Excerpted from a blog comment authored by Donald Kozusko, Esq., a transcript of which is on file with the authors of this handbook.

[1282] 722 F.3d 1079 (7th Cir. 2013).

[1283] *See generally* §3.5.3.2 of this handbook (boilerplate).

the trust and the bank. See John H. Langbein, Questioning the Trust Law Duty of Loyalty: Sole Interest or Best Interest?, 114 Yale L.J. 929, 980-89 (2005)."[1284]

§8.15.82 Doctrine of Equitable Election

The doctrine of equitable election is as follows: "A person who accepts a benefit under a deed or will must conform to the instrument in all respects, by giving effect to all its provisions, and renouncing every right inconsistent with it."[1285] Assume the donee of a special/limited testamentary power of appointment under a trust exercises by will the power in favor of persons who are not permissible objects of the power, but devises in the same will his *own* property to the permissible objects.[1286] Assume also that the permissible objects would take *under the trust* in default of a proper exercise of the power. Under the doctrine of equitable election, the devises are impliedly conditioned upon the devisees not challenging the validity of the exercise.[1287] In other words, the devisees are "put to an election."[1288] They can either accept the devises or take in default of the power's proper exercise.[1289] They cannot, however, double dip. The somewhat related doctrine of selective allocation (marshalling) is taken up in Section 8.15.79 of this handbook.

§8.15.83 The Adverse Party (Powers of Appointment)

In the case of a power of appointment created under the terms of a trust, an adverse party is one whose economic interests would be adversely affected in a substantial way by the power's exercise.[1290] Typically, it is someone who is enjoying the equitable interest as per the express terms of the trust and who would lose that interest were the power exercised. If the donee of a power of appointment may only, pursuant to the terms of the power, exercise it in favor of the donee, the donee's estate (or the creditors of either) *with the joinder of another person*, then whether the power is deemed general or nongeneral will hinge on whether that other person is an adverse party. If he or she is, then the power is nongeneral.[1291] Otherwise, the power is general. The topic of powers

---

[1284] The court also cited as its authority the Restatement (Third) of Trusts, Wisconsin's version of the UTC not yet having been enacted. In December 2013, a few months later, it was enacted. A perusal of the Langbein article, a contractarian manifesto if there ever was one, however, suggests that the academics who authored the UTC would not consider the *French* decision an unintended and/or undesired consequence of its enactment.

[1285] John Chipman Gray, The Rule Against Perpetuities §541 (4th ed. 1942).

[1286] *See generally* §8.1 of this handbook (powers of appointment).

[1287] John Chipman Gray, The Rule Against Perpetuities §541 (4th ed. 1942).

[1288] John Chipman Gray, The Rule Against Perpetuities §541 (4th ed. 1942).

[1289] John Chipman Gray, The Rule Against Perpetuities §541 (4th ed. 1942).

[1290] *See* Restatement (Third) of Property (Wills and Other Donative Transfers) §17.3 cmt. e.

[1291] *See* Restatement (Third) of Property (Wills and Other Donative Transfers) §17.3 cmt. e.

of appointment is taken up in Section 8.1.1 of this handbook. The tax-sensitivity of powers that are exercisable with the joinder of adverse and nonadverse parties is taken up in Section 8.9.3 of this handbook.

§8.15.84   Classifying Powers of Appointment as Either "In Gross" or "Collateral"

That is to say, if a power is simply collateral, the donee has no interest in the land or personalty which is the subject matter of the power, other than the power itself. If a power is in gross, the donee has an interest in the land or personalty which is the subject matter of the power, but this interest is not subject to the power, and will not be affected by its exercise.—Lewis M. Simes[1292]

Section 17.3, comment f, of the Restatement (Third) of Property (Wills and Other Donative Transfers) explains the difference between a collateral power of appointment and a power of appointment in gross: "In traditional terminology, a power of appointment is 'collateral' if the donee has no owned interest in the appointive assets. A power of appointment is 'in gross' if the donee has an owned interest in the appointive assets separate from the donee's power of appointment, such as when the income beneficiary of a trust has a power of appointment over the remainder interest." So far so good, although the term remainder in this context is not entirely accurate.[1293]

But the comment concludes with an assertion that is neither explained nor buttressed by supporting authority in the Reporter's Notes: "The terms collateral power and power in gross are descriptive only, and carry no legal consequences." There is a 1990 English pension trust chancery case in which the judge sort of said the same thing. He described the dual-classification as "of antiquarian interest only."[1294] We are not so sure. Consider the following four examples of where it might well be "legally consequential," even today, if a donee holds a power of appointment in gross rather than collaterally.

First, a donee/holder of an equitable general testamentary power of appointment in gross may be able to ratify breaches of trust and in so doing, eradicate the interests of the takers in default. This possibility is considered in Section 8.14 of this handbook.

Second, it may still be the case in some jurisdictions that property subject to a reserved collateral equitable general inter vivos power of appointment is not subject to the claims of the powerholder's creditors, whereas if the power were held in gross, the property would be subject to such claims. This possibility is considered in Section 5.3.3.1(a) of this handbook.

[1292] Lewis M. Simes, Cases and Materials on the Law of Future Interests 208 (2d ed. 1951).

[1293] *See* John Chipman Gray, The Rule Against Perpetuities §324 (4th ed. 1942) (as an equitable future interest under a trust lacks a previous estate to support it, legal title being in the trustee, it is analogyzing to refer to such an interest as a remainder).

[1294] Mettoy Pension Trustees Ltd. v. Evans, [1990] 1 W.L.R. 1587, at 1613.

Third, take an equitable collateral power of appointment. The donee of the power is *X*. The trustee is *Y*. Both the equitable life estate and the equitable quasi remainder are in *Z*. If *Y* were to transfer legal title to *Z*, there would be a merger in *Z*. One consequence of the merger would be that *X*'s collateral power of appointment would extinguish. Now assume that *X*'s power is in gross. *X* is, say, both the donee of the power and owner of the quasi remainder. *Z* is the current equitable beneficiary. Were *Y* to transfer the legal title to *Z*, there would be no merger and thus no extinguishment of *X*'s power of appointment in gross. The topic of merger is discussed generally in Section 8.7 of this handbook and in Section 8.15.36 of this handbook.

Fourth, assume *Y* possesses a *legal* fee simple in property that is not entrusted. A *legal* naked collateral power of appointment in *X* would be void as being repugnant to *Y*'s fee.[1295] This would not necessarily be the case if the *legal* power, instead, were in gross. Note that an *equitable* naked collateral power of appointment incident to a trust relationship should not run afoul of the doctrine of repugnancy, absent a merger of the legal and equitable property interests.[1296]

Powers of appointment are covered generally in Section 8.1 of this handbook. The power appendant (or appurtenant) is covered in Section 8.15.85 of this handbook.

§8.15.85 The Appendant (or Appurtenant) Power of Appointment

I am attracted by his submission that the classification of powers into powers simply collateral, powers in gross, and powers appendant or appurtenant . . . is now of antiquarian interest only.[1297]

The United States has generally not been receptive to the appendant (or appurtenant) power of appointment.[1298] The Restatement (Second) of Property (Wills and Other Donative Transfers) had endeavored to close the door once and for all on such powers.[1299] The Restatement (Third) of Property (Wills and Other Donative Transfers) has now thrown the door wide open.[1300] Its rationale for doing so, however, could be better explained.

An appendant power of appointment is a power of appointment over property that the holder/donee of the power beneficially owns.[1301] In the context of legal interests, not equitable interests under trusts, here is an

---

[1295] *See* Doan v. Vestry of Parish of Ascension of Carroll Cnty., 103 Md. 662, 64 A. 314, 317 (1906).

[1296] The doctrine of merger is covered generally in §8.7 and §8.15.36 of this handbook.

[1297] Mettoy Pension Trustees Ltd. v. Evans, [1990] 1 W.L.R. 1587, 1613 (England).

[1298] *See generally* William B. Stoebuck, *Infants' Exercise of Powers of Appointment*, 43 Denv. L.J. 255, 260 (1966).

[1299] Restatement (Second) of Property (Wills and Other Donative Transfers) §12.3.

[1300] *See* Restatement (Third) of Property (Wills and Other Donative Transfers) §17.3 cmt. g.

[1301] Lewis B. Simes, Cases and Materials on the Law of Future Interests 208 (2d ed. 1951).

example of an appendant power: *A* devises Blackacre to such persons as *X* shall appoint, and in default of appointment to *X* in fee simple. *X*'s power is said to be appendant.[1302] In the United States, *X*'s power was deemed invalid for two reasons: (1) the power had merged into the fee, and (2) the power to appoint was a superfluous addition to the power to convey that is incident to the fee. "When the holder of a life estate has a power presently exercisable, the result should be that he has a power in gross as to the remainder but no power to appoint the life estate. So if he purports to make an inter vivos appointment of the fee, we could analyze this as being a conveyance of his life estate and an appointment of the remainder."[1303]

In the trust context, however, an equitable "quasi remainder" is not supported by the intervening equitable income interest.[1304] Thus, an equitable general inter vivos power of appointment would be over the subject trust property, the property to which the trustee holds the legal title, not over the quasi remainder.

The Restatement (Second) provided that in both contexts, the legal and the equitable, an appendant power would never come into existence because of the donee's/holder's beneficial interest. The Restatement (Third) would have the power come into existence, but extinguish upon a transfer of the beneficial interest. So far so good. It seems to address the fraud issue, namely by making it impossible for a donee/holder of a power appendant to first transfer the beneficial interest for value and then divest the transferee's interest by exercising the power in favor of the donee/holder himself, or another.

But further on in the Reporter's Notes, the following reason is given for resurrecting the power appendant: "The logical conclusion of treating a power appendant as invalid . . . would be that a power of revocation, amendment, or withdrawal held by the income beneficiary of a trust would be invalid to the extent of the donee's owned income interest."[1305] In the trust context, this assertion is incompatible with basic property doctrine. If legal title to trust principal passes from a trustee to the donee free of trust pursuant to the exercise of an equitable power of appointment, the income subsequently thrown off from the detached principal must follow that principal. This has been the case in the Anglo-American legal tradition since time immemorial.[1306] A flame must follow its candle, or extinguish. It cannot exist on its own. Thus, a power to withdraw trust principal perforce brings with it a constructive power of appointment over future income no matter what.

The Reporter's explanation might have made more sense if the example had featured an equitable quasi remainderman under a trust who happened also to possess a general inter vivos power of appointment over the subject

---

[1302] Lewis B. Simes, Cases and Materials on the Law of Future Interests 208 (2d ed. 1951).

[1303] William B. Stoebuck, *Infants' Exercise of Powers of Appointment*, 43 Denv. L.J. 255, 260 (1966).

[1304] *See* John Chipman Gray, The Rule Against Perpetuities §324 (4th ed. 1942).

[1305] Restatement (Third) of Property (Wills and Other Donative Transfers) §17.3, Reporter's Note.

[1306] *See* Webb's Fabulous Pharmacies, Inc. v. Beckwith, 449 U.S. 155, 162, 101 S. Ct. 446, 451 (1980).

property, a not inconceivable scenario in the real world. A literal reading of the Restatement (Second), for example, might suggest that in the case of a garden-variety nominee trust, the beneficiaries' collective power of revocation would be a nullity, which would not be good.[1307] The Restatement (Third) appears to be on to something, but that is about all one can say.

Powers of appointment are covered generally in Section 8.1 of this handbook. Powers collateral and in gross are covered in Section 8.15.84 of this handbook. The nominee trust is taken up generally in Section 9.6 of this handbook.

§8.15.86   The Illusory Appointments Doctrine [Powers of Appointment]

The donee/holder of a nonexclusionary/nonexclusive power of appointment may not exercise the power in a way that excludes one or more of the permissible appointees from a share of the appointive property. Powers of appointment are covered generally in Section 8.1.1 of this handbook.

Should the donee/holder nonetheless attempt to exercise the power exclusively, such as by selectively appointing token or "illusory" shares of the appointive property, then the doctrine of illusory appointments might well be implicated. The doctrine is traceable back to the 1682 English Chancery case of *Gibson v. Kinven*,[1308] which held that if a donor of a nonexclusive power fails to give a *substantial* share of the appointive property to each permissible appointee, the appointment is void. To enforce the appointment would thwart the express intentions of the settlor-donor. To judicially reform an exclusive exercise into a nonexclusive one would thwart the intentions of the donee/holder of the power. As to what makes one appointment illusory and another substantial, that is for equity to sort out incrementally over time.

To make equity's task even more difficult, the Restatement (Third) of Property (Wills and Other Donative Transfers) would drop into the equation an "inference" that the donor of a nonexclusive power intends that any exercise confer a *reasonable* benefit upon each permissible appointee.[1309] Presumably, the reasonable benefit inference would supplant the substantial benefit inference, which was the centerpiece of the old doctrine of illusory appointments. As the very terms of a particular valid nonexclusive power may be patently unreasonable, the reasonable benefit inference applicable to its exercise would seem to be a fish out of water. The illusory appointments doctrine should not be confused with the fraud on a special power doctrine, which is taken up in Section 8.15.26 of this handbook.

The prospective donor of a nonexclusionary/nonexclusive power of appointment should give serious consideration to expressly requiring that there be strict compliance with the dispositive terms of the power grant. Keep it

---

[1307] *See generally* §9.6 of this handbook (the nominee trust).

[1308] 1 Vern. 66, 23 Eng. Rep. 315 (Ch. 1682).

[1309] Restatement (Third) of Property (Wills and Other Donative Transfers) §17.5 cmt. j.

simple and unambiguous so as to minimize the chances of expensive complaints for instruction and/or declaratory litigation down the road. On the other hand, if the prospective donor is comfortable with reasonable deviations from the nonexclusivity requirement, then he or she might just as well make the power exclusionary/exclusive to begin with, or instead grant a fiduciary power of appointment to the trustee. The fiduciary power of appointment is discussed generally in Section 8.1.1 of this handbook.

§8.15.87   The Irrevocability of Appointments Rule [Powers of Appointment]

Here is the black-letter law: "The donee of a power of appointment lacks the authority to revoke or amend an exercise of the power, except to the extent that the donee reserved a power of revocation or amendment when exercising the power, and the terms of the power do not prohibit the reservation."[1310] The rule of irrevocability of appointments has its origins in the 1717 English case of *Hele v. Bond*.[1311] "When an appointment presently and unreservedly transfers appointive property to an object, the rule of irrevocability derived from *Hele v. Bond* . . . is recognized by American authorities without exception."[1312] For more on the rule of irrevocability of appointments, particularly as it applies to the exercise of inter vivos powers, the reader is referred to Section 8.1.1 of this handbook.

§8.15.88   Equity Will Aid the Defective Execution of a Power

It was a rule of the English Courts of Chancery that equity will aid the defective exercise of a power of appointment if doing so would benefit certain favored permissible appointees; specifically, certain individuals who were regarded as having provided good "consideration," such as "a purchaser (including a mortgagee or a lessee), a creditor, a wife, a legitimate child, and a charity."[1313] The rule was a specific application of the general maxim that equity looks to substance (intent) rather than to form.[1314]

The defect in execution had to have been formal, as opposed to substantive, and occasioned by accident or mistake. Thus, "[t]he court . . . [would grant] . . . relief against the execution by will of a power which should have been executed by deed because the defect . . . [was] . . . purely one of form. But no relief . . . [could be] . . . granted where . . . [the donee purported] . . . to exercise a

---

[1310] Restatement (Third) of Property (Wills and Other Donative Transfers) §19.7.

[1311] Hele v. Bond, [1717] Prec. Ch. 474, 24 Eng. Rep. 213. *See also* Saunders v. Evans, [1861] 8 H.L. Cas. 721, 11 Eng. Rep. 611; Shirley v. Fisher, [1882] 43 Ch. Div. 290.

[1312] Restatement (Second) of Property (Wills and Other Donative Transfers) §15.2, Reporter's Notes.

[1313] Snell's Equity ¶9-07.

[1314] Snell's Equity ¶9-07.

power by will before the age of 25 and the power must be exercised by deed before he attains that age."[1315] A defect in execution was substantive if it undermined the accomplishment of a significant purpose of the power grant.[1316]

The exercise formalities had to have been donor-imposed for equitable relief to be granted.[1317] "Formal requirements imposed by law with reference to instruments of appointment . . . [were] . . . always regarded as fulfilling a significant purpose."[1318] Consequently, consistent with the maxim that equity follows the law, see Section 8.12 of this handbook, substantial compliance was never sufficient grounds in equity to effectuate an exercise impermissible at law.

The rule that equity will aid the defective execution of a power is not to be confused with the fraud on a special power doctrine; a topic we take up in Section 8.15.26 of this handbook. Powers of appointment are covered generally in Section 8.1.1 of this handbook, as are equity's maxims in Section 8.12 of this handbook.

The Restatement (Second) of Property. The Restatement (Second) of Property (Wills and Other Donative Transfers) essentially tracked the English rule, although the favored class of appointees became more expansive, and decidedly more amorphous:

- A natural object of the donee's affection
- A person with whom the donee has had a relationship akin to that with one who would be a natural object of the donee's bounty
- A creditor of the donee
- A charity
- A person who has paid value for the appointment
- Some other person favored by a court applying equitable principles.[1319]

The Restatement (Third) of Property. The Restatement (Third) of Property (Wills and Other Donative Transfers) sweeps away the limitations on who is entitled to benefit from application of the English rule, as the rule had been tweaked by the Restatement (Second). What remains is essentially a garden-variety substantial compliance regime:

Substantial compliance with formal requirements of an appointment imposed by the donor, including a requirement that the instrument of exercise make reference or specific reference to the power, is sufficient if: (i) the donee knew of and intended to exercise the power; and (ii) the donee's manner of attempted exercise did not impair a material purpose of the donor in imposing the requirement.[1320]

[1315] Snell's Equity ¶ 9-08.

[1316] Restatement (Second) of Property (Wills and Other Donative Transfers) §18.3 cmt. c.

[1317] Restatement (Second) of Property (Wills and Other Donative Transfers) §18.3 cmt. c

[1318] Restatement (Second) of Property (Wills and Other Donative Transfers) §18.3 cmt. b.

[1319] Restatement (Second) of Property (Wills and Other Donative Transfers) §18.3(2).

[1320] Restatement (Third) of Property (Wills and Other Donative Transfers) §19.10.

In the world of substantial compliance, certainty and finality are not high priorities—nor is litigation prevention. What did the powerholder subjectively know and subjectively intend? So many facts to assert and rebut, prove and disprove, find and not find. Of course, this is all default law. The scrivener of a power-of-appointment grant is always free to specify whether or not there may be substantial compliance with prescribed power-exercise formalities.

UPC §2-704 Power of Appointment; Meaning of Specific Reference Requirement. Section 2-704 of the model Uniform Probate Code also adopts a substantial compliance approach to the donor-imposed specific reference requirement. It does so by creating a "presumption" that such a requirement is to prevent inadvertent exercises of the power of appointment. Thus, a power whose terms specify that any exercise be by an instrument making specific reference to the power might still have been exercised by a "blanket-exercise" clause in, say, the powerholder's will. Those who would benefit from an effective exercise, however, would still have to prove by extrinsic evidence that the powerholder "had knowledge of and intended to exercise the power."[1321] Massachusetts has sensibly declined to enact the model UPC's Section 2-704. Instead, however, it has dropped into the slot some totally unrelated content dealing with taxes on QTIP property.

§8.15.89   *Pretermission*

Pretermission, n.1. The action of overlooking or disregarding something; the omission of something from a speech, narrative, etc.; omission of or neglect to do something ... 4. Roman Law. The omission by a testator to mention in his or her will one of his or her children or natural heirs.—Oxford English Dictionary

A pretermission statute in a common law jurisdiction is designed to prevent *unintentional* disinheritance by will of the members of a designated class of individuals. The typical protected class is comprised of some cohort of the testator's descendants/issue. The Uniform Probate Code's omitted child or "pretermitted-heir" section, Section 2-302, protects the children of a testator who were born or adopted after the will's execution. Some statutes cover not only afterborn children, but also children alive when the will was executed. A minority of states have expansive pretermission statutes that operate in favor of a testator's other issue as well.

While the focus of a pretermission statute is unintentional disinheritance by will, pretermission via the trusteed will substitute, namely the revocable inter vivos trust, can come about in two ways. One could have a technical pretermission if a will which makes no reference to any of the testator's children pours a portion or all of the probate estate over into a preexisting inter vivos trust for the benefit of those very children. One could have a full-blown substantive pretermission if the terms of the revocable trust make no provision whatsoever

---

[1321] UPC §2-704 cmt.

for those children and the trust was fully funded inter vivos such that there is no probate estate to pour over into the trust.

Technical pretermission by pour-over. The pour-over to a trust for the benefit of persons covered by a pretermission statute is omission in form only. Thus, the Restatement (Third) of Property (Wills and Other Donative Transfers) provides that: "[i]f the testator's will contains a pour-over devise..., a child who is a beneficiary of the trust into which the devise pours over is not entitled to an omitted-child share."[1322] Certainly such a principle comports with the spirit if not the letter of most pretermission statutes. Pour-over devises are covered generally in Section 2.1.1 of this handbook and in Section 2.2.1 of this handbook.

Substantive pretermission by funding the revocable inter vivos trust predeath. Those who advocate expanding either by legislation or judicial fiat the reach of the generic pretermission statute to the will substitute, particularly to the revocable inter vivos trust, have little to show for their advocacy.[1323] "No cases have been found in which the protections by statute or case law afforded to a child omitted from a will have been extended to a child omitted from a will substitute used as a comprehensive dispositive plan. Courts that have addressed the issue have decided against expanding the policy."[1324] The Restatement (Second) of Property (Donative Transfers) had proposed that the policy be so expanded.[1325] Its successor, the Restatement (Third) of Property (Wills and Other Donative Transfers), has declined to take up the torch.[1326]

§8.15.90   The Power-in-Trust Doctrine [Expired Nongeneral Powers of Appointment]

The power-in-trust concept. *The generic power-in-trust doctrine.* The generic power-in-trust doctrine works like this: Assume a nongeneral equitable power of appointment over a defined and limited class of permissible appointees has expired without the donee of the power having exercised it. For whatever reason, there is no provision-in-default-of-exercise in the instrument that granted the power. Under the power-in-trust doctrine, the donee of the power is deemed to have held the power itself in trust for the benefit of the permissible appointees with an attendant quasi-fiduciary obligation to exercise it.[1327] If the power is not exercised, upon expiration of the power, title to the appointive property passes upon a resulting trust from the express trustee back down the line to the settlor-donor of the power, or to the probate estate of the

---

[1322] Restatement (Third) of Property (Wills and Other Donative Transfers) §9.6 cmt. h.

[1323] *See, e.g.,* Kidwell v. Rhew, 268 S.W.3d 309 (Ark. 2007).

[1324] Restatement (Third) of Property (Wills and Other Donative Transfers) §9.6, Reporter's Note, No. 17.

[1325] Restatement (Second) of Property (Donative Transfers) §34.2(2).

[1326] Restatement (Third) of Property (Wills and Other Donative Transfers) §9.6.

[1327] *See* Restatement (First) of Property §367 cmt. c.

settlor-donor if the settlor-donor is not then living.[1328] The settlor-donor or the settlor-donor's estate, as the case may be, then holds the appointive property upon a constructive trust for the benefit of the permissible appointees back up the line. The constructive trustee is then compelled by equity to transfer legal title to them, usually per capita.[1329] Otherwise, the holders of the equitable reversion would be unjustly enriched by the donee's nonfeasance.

The mandatory-power-in-trust doctrine. The mandatory-power-in-trust doctrine is a variation on the entrusted-power theme. In the absence of a taker-in-default provision in the power-granting trust instrument, an equitable nongeneral power is considered mandatory such that "upon the donee's wrongful failure to exercise it the court will make an appointment in the donee's place by ordering a distribution among the defined limited class of objects."[1330] No resulting trust is imposed. The title to the appointive property passes directly from the express trustee to the permissible appointees.

Fraud-on-a-special-power distinguished. Note here that the fraud-on-a-special-power doctrine generally addresses wrongful affirmative exercises of nongeneral powers, not the wrongful failure to exercise. The fraud-on-a-special-power doctrine is taken up in Section 8.15.26 of this handbook.

The Restatements' muddled explanations of the power-in-trust concept. The Restatement (Second) of Property and the Restatement (Third) of Property could each do a better job of explaining the mechanics of the power-in-trust concept in its various manifestations. We explain why in Rounds, *Old Doctrine Misunderstood, New Doctrine Misconceived: Deconstructing the Newly-Minted Restatement (Third) of Property's Power of Appointment Sections*.[1331] This failure to adequately explain how the power-in-trust concept works in large part accounts for the profound incoherence of the Restatement (Third)'s explanation of the context in which the implied-gift-in-default rationale has evolved, an alternative rationale that the Restatements have been pushing.[1332] For more on the implied-gift-in-default concept in the context of expired nongeneral powers of appointment, the reader is referred to Section 8.15.93 of this handbook.

§8.15.91   *The Direct-Benefits Estoppel Doctrine [Trust Arbitration Clauses]*

The direct-benefits estoppel doctrine, a category of general equitable estoppel doctrine, is an invention of contract law. Under the doctrine a nonsignatory to a contract who accepts its benefits is estopped from attempting to avoid its burdens. The Supreme Court of Texas has applied the doctrine in

---

[1328] *See* Restatement (Second) of Property (Donative Transfers) §24.2 cmt. b.

[1329] *See* Restatement (Second) of Property (Donative Transfers) §24.2 cmt. b.

[1330] Restatement (Third) of Property (Wills and Other Donative Transfers) §24.2 cmt. b.

[1331] 26 Quinnipiac Prob. L.J. 240, 251–253 (2013).

[1332] *See* Restatement (First) of Property §367 cmt. b; Restatement (Second) of Property (Wills and Other Donative Transfers) §24.2 cmt. a; Restatement (Third) of Property (Wills and Other Donative Transfers) 19.23(b).

the trust context. In 2013, it ordered the enforcement of a trust arbitration clause over the objection of the settlor's two sons, whom the court characterized as the trust's "sole beneficiaries."[1333] The court based its ruling on two grounds: (1) Enforcement is in conformance with the intentions of the settlor, and (2) the applicability of the doctrine of direct benefits estoppel satisfies the agreement requirement of the Texas Arbitration Act. The Act provides that a written agreement to arbitrate is enforceable if it provides for arbitration of either an existing controversy or one that arises between the parties after the date of the agreement. The court explained its application of a contract-based doctrine to a trust, a relationship that most serious scholars have concluded is not per se contract-based: " . . . [A] beneficiary who attempts to enforce rights that would not exist without the trust manifests her assent to the trust's arbitration clause. For example, a beneficiary who brings a claim for breach of fiduciary duty seeks to hold the trustee to her obligations under the instrument and thus has acquiesced to its provisions, including the arbitration clause. In such circumstances, it would be incongruent to allow a beneficiary to hold a trustee to the terms of the trust but not to hold the beneficiary to those same terms."[1334] If, by implication, a trust arbitration clause would not be enforceable against someone incapable of granting such an assent, such as an unborn or unascertained equitable quasi remainderman, then the court, as a practical matter, may have neutered most Texas trust arbitration clauses, except those in commercial trust instruments. Trust arbitration clauses are covered generally in Section 8.44 of this Handbook.

§8.15.92 The Rule in Saunders v. Vautier

Saunders v. Vautier is the 1841 English case which laid down the rule that if the entire equitable interest incident to a trust is concentrated in a beneficiary who is of full age and legal capacity, then that beneficiary, notwithstanding any terms of the trust that might provide otherwise, may have the trust judicially terminated and the title to the subject property transferred outright and free of trust from the trustee to the beneficiary.[1335] The Rule in *Saunders v. Vautier* generally conflicts with the Rule in *Claflin v. Claflin*, an 1889 Massachusetts case.[1336] The *Claflin* Doctrine, otherwise known as the Material Purpose Doctrine, is taken up in Section 8.15.7 of this handbook.

[1333] Hal Rachal, Jr. v. John W. Reitz, No. 11-0708 (Tex. May 3, 2013).

[1334] Hal Rachal, Jr. v. John W. Reitz, No. 11-0708 (Tex. May 3, 2013), at 11. For a discussion of why the trust relationship per se is not contract-based, see §8.22 of this Handbook.

[1335] Saunders v. Vautier, [1841] EWHC Ch J82 (1841) Cr & Ph 240, (1841) 4 Beav. 115 8; 41 ER 482 (England) (in the High Court of Chancery).

[1336] Claflin v. Claflin, 149 Mass. 19, 20 N.E. 454 (Mass. 1889).

§8.15.93   The Implied-Gift-In-Default Doctrine [Expired Nongeneral Powers of Appointment]

The Restatements for some time now have been pushing an alternative to the power-in-trust concept discussed in Section 8.15.90 of this handbook, namely the implied-gift-in-default concept.[1337] Either concept supplies a rationale for getting appointive property into the hands of permissible appointees of an expired nongeneral power of appointment, provided there is no express taker-in-default provision in the instrument that granted the power and provided the class of permissible takers is sufficiently defined and limited.[1338] The logic of the implied-gift-in-default is not derived from the fiction that someone, somehow, holds a nongeneral power in trust. Rather, it is derived from the inference that the grantor intended the permissible appointees to benefit from the appointive property come what may. "His [the donor's] mind is focused on having them receive the property through an appointment by the donee, but if this particular method of transfer fails, there is apparent a fundamental intent of the donor to pass the property to the objects. . . ."[1339]

§8.15.94   Trust Repudiation Doctrine (Open Repudiation Doctrine)

In the case of a breach of trust, it is a principle of equity that the laches period, or the applicable statute of limitations period, as the case may be, does not commence to run against the beneficiary until the trustee "openly" makes the beneficiary aware that he is "repudiating" his fiduciary duty not to be in breach of trust.[1340] For either period to commence to run, it is not necessary that the trustee openly deny the very existence of, or abandon altogether, the trust. Repudiation is taken up in Section 7.1.3 of this handbook.

[1337] *See* Restatement (First) of Property §367 cmt. b; Restatement (Second) of Property (Wills and Other Donative Transfers) §24.2 cmt. a; Restatement (Third) of Property (Wills and Other Donative Transfers) 19.23(b).

[1338] *See* Restatement (First) of Property §367 cmt. b; Restatement (Second) of Property (Wills and Other Donative Transfers) §24.2 cmt. a; Restatement (Third) of Property (Wills and Other Donative Transfers) §19.23(b).

[1339] Restatement (First) of Property §367 cmt. b.

[1340] *See, e.g.,* Matter of JPMorgan Chase Bank, N.A., 2014 N.Y. Slip Op. 07799 (Nov. 14, 2014) (trust for benefit of Mary Gill Roby, et al.) (the court confirming that the "open repudiation rule" requires "either an *open repudiation of the fiduciary's obligation* or a judicial settlement of the fiduciary's account.").

§8.16 The Trustee of Revocable Trust as "Inadvertent Executor": When There Is a Duty to Prepare the Estate Tax Return

By choosing to convey the bulk of her assets through a trust, . . . [the decedent] . . . limited the amount of her property that was transferred in her estate and consequently limited the estate's tax deduction for administration expenses.[1]

As a general rule, the value of property in a revocable inter vivos trust will generate an estate tax upon the death of the settlor.[2] There are some exceptions. The property, for example, could be subject to a marital[3] or charitable deduction.[4] Any tax liability could be absorbed by the unified credit.[5] The fact remains, however, that the federal estate tax, though it is a transfer tax, cannot be avoided merely because title to the property at the time of the settlor's death is in the trustee. The settlor's executor has the responsibility for preparing the federal estate tax return and paying the tax.[6]

What if no executor has been appointed? What if all the settlor's property, for example, had been transferred inter vivos to the trustee of a revocable trust so that there is no probate estate? In that case, the Internal Revenue Code places the responsibility for preparing and filing the federal estate tax return on the trustee.[7] The trustee is responsible for satisfying (out of assets of the trust) the trust's tax liability.[8] The liability of the trustee as "inadvertent executor" is generally limited to the property that is the subject of the trust.[9] A warning, however: The trustee will be personally liable for any shortfall in estate taxes owed should he pay the debts of the settlor, or make distributions in accordance with the terms of the trust, and in so doing not leave enough in the trust to satisfy the trust's tax liability.[10] When in doubt, the prudent trustee will want to make written application to the IRS for a determination of the amount of the

---

§8.16   [1] Grant v. Comm'r, 294 F.3d 352, 354 (2002).

[2] *See generally* §8.9.1 of this handbook (the federal estate tax).

[3] *See generally* §8.9.1.3 of this handbook (the marital deduction).

[4] *See generally* §9.4.1 of this handbook (charitable purposes).

[5] *See generally* §8.9.1.1 of this handbook (the unified credit).

[6] I.R.C. §2203.

[7] I.R.C. §2203.

[8] I.R.C. §2203.

[9] I.R.C. §2203. *See* New York Trust Co. v. Comm'r, 26 T.C. 257, 262. Much of the information contained in this section is taken from Hanna, *The Inadvertent Executor Under Section 2203 of the Internal Revenue Code*, 22 ACTEC Notes 196 (1996). The term *inadvertent executor* was employed in the article "to refer to those persons that are treated as executors or administrators under §2203, for federal estate tax purposes, due to their actual or constructive possession of property of the decedent and the absence of a named or appointed representative of the decedent's estate." Hanna, *The Inadvertent Executor Under Section 2203 of the Internal Revenue Code*, 22 ACTEC Notes at 197 n.8.

[10] 31 U.S.C. §3713(b).

tax and for a discharge from *personal liability* therefor.[11] The Uniform Probate Code would authorize a trustee concerned about being saddled with an estate tax liability to do one or more of the following:

- Defer a distribution until the trustee is satisfied that adequate provision for payment of the estate tax has been made.
- Withhold from a distributee an amount equal to the amount of estate tax apportioned to an interest of the distributee.
- As a condition to a distribution, require the distributee to provide a bond or other security for the portion of the estate tax apportioned to the distributee.[12]

The inadvertent executor's duty to the *state* is limited to filing the return, paying the tax owed, and responding to any notice of deficiency. As a fiduciary, his duty to *the beneficiaries* of the trust is to see to it that only that which is lawfully owed is paid out of trust assets. If there has been an estate tax overpayment, for example, the trustee must file a timely application for a refund. If the tax obligation is shared with third parties, the trustee has a fiduciary duty to the trust beneficiaries to collect from the third parties the tax apportioned to and the tax required to be advanced by the third parties.[13] The trustee as inadvertent executor would also have a duty to make appropriate and timely tax elections (*e.g.*, the QTIP election and the special use valuation election).

The trustee should consider whether legal fees incurred by the trustee in the course of his inadvertent executorship duties, to the extent they benefit the trust estate, should be taken as a deduction for estate tax purposes.[14]

Frayda L. Bruton has prepared an exhaustive checklist of tasks that trustees serving as inadvertent executors are required to perform.[15] The so-called administrative trust is discussed in Section 9.9.14 of this handbook.

§8.17   Mistake-Based Trust Reformation or Modification Actions to Achieve Tax-Efficiency; Trust Reformation to Remedy Mistakes; Trust Modification; Tax Objectives

Indeed, many of the cases pretty plainly boil down to nothing more than an attempt to obtain, through post-mortem litigation, the benefits of better, or more sophisticated, estate planning

---

[11] I.R.C. §2204.

[12] UPC §3-9A-108 (securing payment of estate tax from property in possession of fiduciary).

[13] UPC §3-9A-109 (mechanics of collecting the estate tax).

[14] *See generally* Hanna, *The Inadvertent Executor Under Section 2203 of the Internal Revenue Code*, 22 ACTEC Notes 196, 204 (1996).

[15] Frayda L. Bruton, *Post Mortem Trust Administration Checklist*, 25 ACTEC Notes 331 (2000). *See also* §8.2.4 of this handbook (trust termination checklist).

than the settlor was able or willing to procure while alive. So, though it is possible to rationalize each of these cases as merely correcting mistakes, in many, the petitioner is plainly asking the court to rewrite a document whose dispositive terms are exactly the way the settlor intended them to be, simply to improve tax efficiency.[1]

[Certain tax curative provisions of the Uniform Trust Code] . . . , by interpreting the original language of the trust instrument in a way that qualifies for intended tax benefits, obviates the need to seek a later modification of the trust.[2]

A court will reform the terms of a trust upon clear and convincing evidence that a material mistake has caused the terms not to reflect the settlor's intent, or that but for the mistake the settlor would have used different terms. For a general discussion of this topic, the reader is referred to Section 8.15.22 of this handbook (doctrines of reformation, modification, and rectification).

A trust modification action to achieve a settlor's tax objectives tends to be nonadversarial, and generally may be.[3] It is an exception to the general rule that a court may only entertain cases that have adverse parties.[4] The usual vehicle for bringing a trust modification matter into the judicial system is a complaint for declaratory judgment, a topic we cover in Section 8.42 of this handbook.[5] Because of the U.S. Supreme Court's *Bosch* decision, which is covered in Section 8.15.27 of this handbook, a trial court adjudication is likely to be insufficient to bind federal authorities, particularly the IRS, when a federal estate tax liability turns upon the character of a property interest. What is needed is an adjudication by the state's highest court. Thus, even an uncontested tax-driven trust modification case generally needs to get by appeal, or by some other "reporting up" process, before the highest court of the state for final adjudication of the property rights of the parties.[6] Whether to notify the IRS in the state court proceeding is a question of litigation strategy. As a matter of pure law, if the taxing event is yet to occur, the IRS may well lack the requisite standing,[7] in which case the pros and cons of "*Bosch*ing the Service" without giving it an opportunity need to be considered.[8]

---

§8.17 [1] 5 Scott & Ascher §33.5.

[2] UTC §814 cmt. (available at <http://www.uniformlaws.org/Act.aspx?title=Trust%20 Code>).

[3] *See, e.g.*, In re Paul F. Suhr Trust, 222 P.3d 506, 2010 WL 198467 (Kan. 2010); O'Connell v. Houser, 470 Mass. 1004 (2014).

[4] *See* In re Paul F. Suhr Trust, 222 P.3d 506, 2010 WL 198467 (Kan. 2010).

[5] *See, e.g.*, In re Paul F. Suhr Trust, 222 P.3d 506, 2010 WL 198467 (Kan. 2010) (in this case, the court had jurisdiction under Kansas' Declaratory Judgments Act to review the propriety of the trustee's reformation of the trust at issue).

[6] *See, e.g.*, In re Paul F. Suhr Trust, 222 P.3d 506, 2010 WL 198467 (Kan. 2010) (in this case, the appeal process was employed).

[7] *See, e.g.*, In re Paul F. Suhr Trust, 222 P.3d 506, 2010 WL 198467 (Kan. 2010).

[8] *See* 22 Probate Practice Report, No. 2, at 7 (Feb. 2010) (noting also that "[i]n many cases, it may be preferable to obtain a reformation rather than a modification for purposes of dealing with the Service").

In the interest of achieving "tax efficiency"[9] in the administration of trusts, "the courts have seemed especially ready, perhaps sometimes overly so, to rectify 'mistakes,' " so long as equitable property interests are not materially rearranged in the process.[10] As one learned commentator has noted, "the only real losers in such litigation are the tax collector and, hence, the tax-paying public, neither of which, typically, is before the court."[11] Having said that, one court, with the approval of the guardian ad litem,[12] has shifted the equitable interests under a Qualified Personal Residence Trust (QPRT) from grandchildren to children in order to avoid eventual application of a federal generation-skipping transfer tax that would have been in the range of $1,375,000.[13] Because tax reduction was the overriding purpose in creating the QPRT, the court held that a misunderstanding of the generation-skipping tax implications of including the grandchildren was the type of mistake that warranted reformation.[14] This decision is probably an aberration. Courts generally are loathe to sacrifice someone's equitable property rights on the altar of tax efficiency, or they should be.[15] Thus, the same court has declined to reform a charitable trust in a way that would have saved some income taxes, because to do so would have conflicted with the settlor's intention that the trust last in perpetuity.[16]

The same Massachusetts court has reformed a trust so that it would qualify for the marital deduction.[17] This was not the first time that the court had

---

[9] *See generally* Barry F. Spivey, *Completed Transactions, Qualified Reformation and Bosch: When Does the IRS Care about State Law of Trust Reformation?*, 26 ACTEC Notes 345 (2001); Boyle, *When It's Broke—Fix It: Reforming Irrevocable Trusts to Change Tax Consequences*, 53 The Tax Lawyer 835 (Summer 2000); §§8.15.22 of this handbook (doctrines of reformation, modification, and rectification) and 8.15.20 of this handbook (doctrine of [equitable] deviation). *See also* §8.2.2.1 of this handbook (mid-course reformation, modification, termination, or rescission of the irrevocable trust).

[10] 5 Scott & Ascher §33.5.

[11] 5 Scott & Ascher §33.5 n.5 (noting, however, that the U.S. Supreme Court in the *Bosch* decision "has imposed substantial limitations on the effectiveness, for federal tax purposes, of state court decrees reforming trust instruments"). *See generally* §8.15.27 of this handbook (the *Bosch* decision).

[12] *But see* Alcott v. Union Planters Nat'l Bank, 686 S.W.2d 79 (Tenn. Ct. App. 1984) (suggesting that a guardian ad litem cannot or should not consent to the extinguishment of the equitable interests of those whom he represents).

[13] Simches v. Simches, 423 Mass. 683, 671 N.E.2d 1226 (Mass. 1996). *See also* Diwadkar v. Daial, 439 Mass. 1011, 790 N.E.2d 221 (2003) (granting settlor's request to reform trust due to a scrivener's error by removing settlor and his wife as beneficiaries, the settlor having stated in an affidavit that he had established trust for the benefit of his issue after both had died and that the intent was that the trust funds would not be subject to the estate tax at the times of their respective deaths).

[14] Simches v. Simches, 671 N.E.2d 1226, 1230 (Mass. 1996).

[15] In Matter of Estate of Branigan, 609 A.2d 431 (N.J. 1992); *see also* Schultz v. Shultz, 451 Mass. 1014, 888 N.E.2d 950 (2008) (the court noting that the proposed reformation "cannot harm the interests of any beneficiary"); *see generally* 5 Scott & Ascher §33.5 (Termination or Modification to Save Taxes).

[16] U.S. Trust Co. v. Attorney Gen., 854 N.E.2d 1231 (Mass. 2006).

[17] *See* DiCarlo v. Mazzarella, 717 N.E.2d 257 (Mass. 1999).

reformed a trust to remedy faulty tax planning involving the marital deduction.[18] The same court also has reformed a trust, which had not been expressly drafted as a charitable remainder annuity trust (CRAT), so that it would qualify as a CRAT and receive the associated estate tax deduction.[19] The mistake that warranted the reformation was a miscommunication between the settlor and his attorney concerning the legal consequences of the size of the estate. The same court also has reformed a trust to accommodate an unanticipated change in the estate tax laws of the state in order to effectuate the settlor's intent to minimize or eliminate estate taxes generally.[20] For the same reasons, it also has reformed a defective qualified personal residence trust (QPRT).[21] On the other hand, the same court has declined to reform a charitable trust in a way that would have saved some income taxes, because to do so would have conflicted with the settlor's intention that the trust last in perpetuity.[22] As we shall see, the Uniform Trust Code employs a concept of "modification" rather than "reformation" when it comes to tax-driven judicial alteration of a trust's terms.[23]

The Massachusetts court also has authorized a trustee to divide the trust into exempt and nonexempt shares in order to minimize federal generation-skipping transfer taxes.[24] The terms of the trust did not prohibit the division. Moreover, the general language of the trust instrument suggested that the settlor was "tax conscious." While the court characterized what it was doing as reforming the trust, in Uniform Trust Code parlance it was actually modifying the trust. The court reasoned that "[t]his type of trust reform is relatively minimal and represents a mere 'fine tuning of the administration of the trust[] . . . in order to reduce, if not eliminate, the applications of the GST tax' "[25] This is by no means an isolated case: In recent years there have been numerous other such decisions, that is decisions driven by GST tax avoidance

---

[18] DiCarlo v. Mazzarella, 717 N.E.2d at 259. *See also* Schultz v. Shultz, 451 Mass. 1014, 888 N.E.2d 950 (2008) (reforming discretionary trust to make it QTIP-eligible); In Matter of Substitute Indenture of Trust, 439 Mass. 1009, 789 N.E.2d 1051 (2003) (reforming the dispositive provisions of a trust so that it qualifies for the marital deduction, the court having found a general intent that the trust qualify for the marital deduction in the boilerplate marital deduction savings clause).

[19] Ratchin v. Ratchin, 792 N.E.2d 116 (Mass. 2003). *See generally* §9.4.5.1(b) of this handbook (charitable remainder annuity trust (CRAT)).

[20] Grassian v. Grassian, 835 N.E.2d 607 (Mass. 2005).

[21] Van Riper v. Van Riper, 834 N.E.2d 239 (Mass. 2005).

[22] U.S. Trust Co., N.A. v. Attorney Gen., 854 N.E.2d 1231 (Mass. 2006).

[23] Modification is similar in concept to the *cy pres* doctrine for charitable trusts and the deviation doctrine for unanticipated circumstances. UTC §416 cmt. (available at <http://www.uniformlaws.org/Act.aspx?title=Trust%20Code>). *See also* Restatement (Third) of Property (Wills and Other Donative Transfers) §12.2 cmt. (Tentative Draft No. 1, 1995) (noting that modification to achieve the settlor's tax objectives requires that the settlor's tax objectives be established by a preponderance of the evidence).

[24] Fleet Nat'l Bank v. Kahn, 438 Mass. 1004, 779 N.E.2d 126 (2002).

[25] Fleet Nat'l Bank v. Kahn, 779 N.E.2d at 126 (citing to Fleet Nat'l Bank v. Mackey, 433 Mass. 1009, 1010 n.11, 745 N.E.2d 943 (2001), quoting BankBoston v. Marlow, 428 Mass. 283, 286, 701 N.E.2d 304 (1998), and First Agric. Bank v. Coxe, 406 Mass. 879, 883 n.6, 550 N.E.2d 875 (1990)).

considerations, some out of other jurisdictions.[26] "In addition, there are now statutes in many states that permit the combination or division of trusts, under a variety of circumstances."[27] The taxing authorities, as well as the courts, have a role to play in all of this: "Among the specific modifications authorized by the Internal Revenue Code or Service include the revision of split-interest trusts to qualify for the charitable deduction, modification of a trust for a noncitizen spouse . . . [so that the trust may] . . . become eligible as a qualified domestic trust (QDOT), and the splitting of a trust to utilize better the exemption from generation-skipping tax."[28]

Since our involvement in the Loring Project, the number of these tax-driven reformation cases has sky-rocketed, not just in Massachusetts.[29] There also has been a flurry of tax-driven trust reformation legislation: There are statutes authorizing reformation "to save the marital deduction, to save the charitable deduction generally, to save the charitable deduction in the context of the split-interest charitable trust, or to avoid the GST tax."[30]

Under the Uniform Trust Code, the court may "modify" the terms of a trust, retroactively if necessary, in a manner that is not contrary to the settlor's probable intention in order to achieve the settlor's taxobjectives.[31] Reformation and modification are not the same. Reformation is available when the terms of the trust fail to reflect the settlor's "original, particularized intention."[32] Modification, on the other hand, "allows the terms of the trust to be changed to meet the settlor's tax-saving objective as long as the resulting terms, particularly the dispositive provisions, are not inconsistent with the settlor's probable intent."[33] One court has reformed the *disclaimer* of an equitable interest under a trust: "We determine that a disclaimer may be reformed in circumstances like those presented here, where there is decisive evidence of the . . . [disclaimant's] . . . intent to minimize tax consequences and where that intent was clearly frustrated."[34] In this case, the disclaimant had been unaware

---

[26] *See* 5 Scott & Ascher §33.5 n.17.

[27] *See* 5 Scott & Ascher §33.5 n.18.

[28] UTC §416 cmt. (available at <http://www.uniformlaws.org/Act.aspx?title=Trust%20 Code>). "Absent specific statutory or regulatory authority, binding recognition is normally given only to modifications made prior to the taxing event, for example, the death of the testator or settlor in the case of the federal estate tax." UTC §416 cmt.

[29] 5 Scott & Ascher §33.5 n.6.

[30] 5 Scott & Ascher §33.5. *See also* 5 Scott & Ascher §§33.5 nn.19 (Saving Marital Deduction), 20 (Saving Charitable Deduction), 21 (Saving Charitable Deduction in the Context of a Split-Interest Charitable Trust), 22 (Avoiding GST Tax).

[31] UTC §416 cmt. (available at <http://www.uniformlaws.org/Act.aspx?title=Trust%20 Code>). *See, e.g.*, In re Paul F. Suhr Trust, 222 P.3d 506, 2010 WL 198467 (Kan. 2010) (modifying a trust under §416 of the Kansas UTC to accomplish the settlor's original intent, which was to put in place an estate plan that would minimize or eliminate federal estate taxes upon the subsequent death of his wife).

[32] UTC §416 cmt. (available at <http://www.uniformlaws.org/Act.aspx?title=Trust%20 Code>).

[33] UTC §416 cmt. (available at <http://www.uniformlaws.org/Act.aspx?title=Trust%20 Code>).

[34] Kaufman v. Richmond, 811 N.E.2d 987 (Mass. 2004).

of the adverse federal generation-skipping transfer tax consequences of her disclaimer at the time it was made.[35]

There is a difference between reformation and *resolving an ambiguity*. The latter involves the interpretation of language already in the instrument.[36] The former, on the other hand, "may involve the addition of language not originally in the instrument, or the deletion of language originally included by mistake. . . ."[37] The extrinsic evidence, however, needs to meet the higher, *i.e.*, intermediate, clear and convincing standard. A lower standard and we could have a wholesale destabilization of trust settlements. Thus, reformation and modification are not the only ways to skin the tax cat. There is also creative judicial interpretation, such as that which the Massachusetts Supreme Judicial Court occasionally engages in. The Court, by its own admission, "tend[s] to disfavor interpretations that would resolve ambiguities 'by attributing to the [settlor] an intention which as a practical matter is likely to benefit the taxing authorities and no one else.'"[38, 39]

The reader is referred to Section §8.15.20 of this handbook for a discussion of the doctrine of *equitable deviation*. The doctrine of equitable deviation would permit judicial modification of the administrative terms of a trust in the face of a change of circumstances that was unforeseen or unforeseeable by the settlor in order to further the purposes of the trust. A subsequent change in the tax laws might qualify as such a circumstance.[40]

Counsel advocating for the tax-efficient judicial reformation or modification of a trust should not forget that the trustee has a fiduciary duty not to attempt to comply with a trust provision if compliance would incur unreasonable expense, a duty we explore in Section 6.2.13 of this handbook. Thus, a court may modify the terms of a trust "[i]f it appears to the court that compliance with a trust provision is not possible, or that it would be wasteful to attempt to comply, and if the impossibility or impracticability is a result of unanticipated circumstances."[41] The trust reformation or modification advocate actually has a number of arrows in his or her quiver.

---

[35] *See generally* §5.5 of this handbook (voluntary or involuntary loss of the beneficiary's rights) (containing in part a general discussion of disclaiming equitable interests under trusts).

[36] UTC §414 cmt. (available at <http://www.uniformlaws.org/Act.aspx?title=Trust%20 Code>).

[37] UTC §416 cmt. (available at <http://www.uniformlaws.org/Act.aspx?title=Trust%20 Code>).

[38] Hillman v. Hillman, 433 Mass. 590, 593, 744 N.E.2d 1078, 1080 (2001) (citing in part Putnam v. Putnam, 366 Mass. 261, 271, 316 N.E.2d 729 (1974)).

[39] Restatement (Third) of Trusts §73 cmt. c. *See generally* §6.2.13 of this handbook (duty not to attempt to comply with a trust provision if compliance would be impossible or incur unreasonable expense).

[40] *See also Power of court to authorize modification of trust instrument because of changes in tax laws*, 57 A.L.R.3d 1044.

[41] Restatement (Third) of Trusts §73 cmt. c. *See generally* §6.2.13 of this handbook (duty not to attempt to comply with a trust provision if compliance would be impossible or incur unreasonable expense).

§8.18   Regulation 9 Revised

Regulation 9 governs *the fiduciary activities of national banks*.[1] The Office of
the Comptroller of the Currency ("OCC") has completed the first comprehensive revision of the regulation since 1963. Regulation 9, as revised, *became
effective January 29, 1997* and is available at <www.gpoaccess.gov/cfr/
index.html>. The regulation has been "streamlined" in part to accommodate
changes in the banking industry since 1963, particularly the rise of multistate
fiduciary banking organizations.

It is important to understand that Regulation 9, in and of itself, is not
about creating substantive fiduciary law. Nor is it about resolving conflicts
among competing bodies of local law or between local law and federal law. For
the most part, it defers to the body of state law and federal law (*e.g.*, ERISA) that
is the subject of this handbook. The regulation, for example, will not resolve a
conflict between the terms of a trust instrument and a state statute or a federal
regulation. The former Regulation 9 employed the term *local law*. Revised
Regulation 9 instead employs the term *applicable law*. The new term acknowledges that federal law is one of many sources of law that may govern a fiduciary
relationship; however, it does not preempt state law or resolve conflicts of law.

By express language, the regulation is made applicable to a national bank
that is serving in certain specified capacities, *e.g.*, trustee, executor, guardian,
and compensated investment advisor.[2] Revised Regulation 9 introduces the
simple test of *investment discretion*[3] for determining what other national banking
"fiduciary" activities are subject to oversight by the Comptroller of the Currency. Revised Regulation 9 requires a national bank "to adopt and follow
written policies and procedures adequate to maintain its fiduciary activities in
compliance with applicable law."[4] The bank's policies and procedures, "among
other relevant matters,"[5] should cover:

---

§8.18 [1] 12 C.F.R. Part 9 (Fiduciary Activities of National Banks) (available at
<www.gpoaccess.gov/cfr/index.html>). The Office of Thrift Supervision (OTS) is charged with the
supervision of federal savings associations. 12 U.S.C. §1463(a) ("Home Owners' Loan
Act"—HOLA). The regulation governing fiduciary activities of federal savings bank (FSBs) is 12
C.F.R. Part 550, which is promulgated under Section 5(n) of the Home Owners' Loan Act (HOLA).
12 U.S.C. §1463(a). Part 550 was designed to closely parallel 12 U.S.C. §92a, which authorizes the
Comptroller of the Currency to grant fiduciary powers to national banks. Thus, OTS regulations
closely parallel Regulation 9. A federal savings bank may have fewer limits on its ability to market
and render fiduciary services nationwide if it possesses trust powers, is owned by a unitary thrift
holding company, and if the holding company was in existence May 4, 1999 (or had an application
pending as of that date). *See also* Gramm-Leach-Bliley Act §401 (grandfathering preexisting
unitary thrift holding companies from the Act's restrictions on offering trust products on a
nationwide basis, said restrictions in part having been aimed at keeping Wal-Mart from chartering
a thrift or from conducting Wal-Mart brand banking operations in its stores).

[2] 12 C.F.R. §9.2(e).

[3] 12 C.F.R. §9.2(i).

[4] 12 C.F.R. §9.5 (Policies and procedures).

[5] 12 C.F.R. §9.5 (Policies and procedures).

1. Brokerage placement practices;[6]
2. Methods for ensuring that fiduciary officers and employees do not use material inside information in connection with any decision or recommendation to purchase or sell any security;[7]
3. Methods for preventing self-dealing and conflicts of interest;[8]
4. Selection and retention of legal counsel who is readily available to advise the bank and its fiduciary officers and employees on fiduciary matters;[9] and
5. Investment of funds held as fiduciary, including short-term investments and the treatment of fiduciary funds awaiting investment or distribution.[10]

In litigation against a national bank trustee, plaintiff's counsel will want to obtain as soon as possible, through the discovery process if necessary, the bank's Regulation 9-mandated written policies and procedures. It should be noted that most of the items on the above list were derived from specific requirements in the former regulation.

The former regulation required national banks to perform two types of written reviews of their fiduciary accounts. One was an "account by account" review. The other was an "asset by asset" review to determine what assets are generally appropriate for the bank's fiduciary accounts. In a tip of the hat to modern portfolio and the prudent investor rule,[11] Revised Regulation 9 has done away with the "asset by asset" review requirement.

Because so much of trust operations is now automated, the "account by account" review need no longer be "written." Finally, Revised Regulation 9 has done away with the requirement that a review be conducted "within 15 months after the last review." There need only be a review of the assets of each account for which the bank has investment discretion once during each calendar year.[12] The purpose of the review is to "evaluate whether the assets are appropriate, individually and collectively, for the account."[13]

The former regulation had a "10% Rule" for collective investment funds: No trust or other participating account could have more than a 10 percent participation in any one fund and no single asset could comprise more than 10 percent of the value of a fund.[14] Revised Regulation 9 does away with the "10% Rule" in both its applications on the grounds that the concerns underlying the

---

[6] *See generally* §6.1.3.4 of this handbook (indirect benefit accruing to the trustee).

[7] *See generally* §6.1.3.4 of this handbook (indirect benefit accruing to the trustee).

[8] *See generally* §6.1.3 of this handbook (duty to be loyal to the trust).

[9] *See generally* §8.8 of this handbook (whom does counsel represent?).

[10] *See generally* §6.1.3.1 of this handbook (trustee benefiting as borrower and lender; bank deposits on commercial side of trustee bank).

[11] *See generally* §6.2.2.1 of this handbook (the *Harvard College* Prudent Man Rule and its progeny).

[12] *See* 12 C.F.R. §9.6(c) (Review of Fiduciary Accounts—Annual Review).

[13] *See* 12 C.F.R. §9.6(c) (Review of Fiduciary Accounts—Annual Review).

[14] 12 C.F.R. §9.18(b)(9) (**NOTE:** Superseded effective Jan. 29, 1997).

Rule are adequately addressed by the principles of state fiduciary law that are the subject of this handbook.

The OCC answers the following 18 questions regarding the reach and content of Revised Regulation 9 at <www.gpoaccess.gov/cfr/index.html>.

1. What does "investment advice" for a fee mean?
2. Do full-service brokerage activities fall under the scope of investment advice for a fee?
3. What activities are outside the scope of "investment advice" for a fee?
4. Does a national bank have "investment discretion" when it administers asset allocation accounts or sweep accounts?
5. Are the five policies listed in 12 CFR 9.5 the only "required" policies under the revised regulation?
6. Do the reviews required by 12 CFR 9.6 need to be documented?
7. What does the preacceptance review need to include? How detailed does it need to be?
8. Are annual reviews by issuer still required?
9. What is the definition of "significant fiduciary activities"?
10. What is the "interval" that should be used in a continuous audit system? Is there a requirement that all fiduciary activities be audited within a certain maximum time period?
11. Can a risk-based approach be used for the annual audit approach in [Reg.] 9.9(a)?
12. Is custody with a broker allowed?
13. What are "adequate safeguards and controls"?
14. Do banks need to amend their collective investment fund plans?
15. If a bank delegates collective investment fund (CIF) investment responsibilities under the new prudent delegation standard, will the CIF lose its exemption from federal securities laws (Section 3(a)(2) of the 1933 Act) and from federal taxation (Code Section 584, for common trust funds)?
16. Why were the short-term investment fund provisions changed?
17. What constitutes a summary of purchases and sales for purposes of the collective investment fund financial reports?
18. What happens to the Fiduciary Precedents and Trust Interpretive Letters?

§8.19   When the Bank Trustee Merges or Consolidates

What happens when a bank that is serving as trustee of an ongoing trust merges into, or consolidates with, another bank? May the successor by merger or consolidation serve as the trustee without court appointment? Today, because of federal and state legislation, the answer is generally yes, absent language in the governing instrument to the contrary.[1]

In the absence of legislation, one would first look to the governing instrument for guidance.[2] It may well contain a provision for the automatic transfer of power and authority from the named trustee to its successor entity. In the absence of legislation or express language in the governing instrument, the state of the common law is probably a presumption that the settlor intends for power and authority automatically to pass to the successor by merger or consolidation.[3] Ultimately, however, it would come down to the inferred or expressed intention of the settlor. One court has denied automatic transmission of power and authority because the successor institution had acquired the assets of the named trustee other than by merger or consolidation.[4]

Under the Uniform Trust Code, the court may remove a trustee if there has been a "substantial change of circumstances," *e.g.*, a substantial change in the character of the service or location of the trustee.[5] "A corporate reorganization of an institutional trustee is not itself a change of circumstances if it does not affect the service provided the individual trust account."[6]

§8.20 Tax Apportionment Within and Without Trust

Indeed, in Swallen, the court found that the will seemed full of that impossible dream of exonerating all of the beneficiaries: "The will thus seems to evince an intent to burden no one with taxes—a feat that many aspire to, but few achieve legally."[1]

Within trust. Property in a revocable inter vivos trust is subject to the federal estate tax upon the death of the settlor.[2] While the settlor may not relieve the trustee of his legal obligation to pay what taxes are owed, the settlor may specify in the governing instrument which equitable interests are to

---

§8.19 [1] *See* 2 Scott & Ascher §11.1.6.4: 2 Scott on Trusts §96.7 n.3 (each cataloging the federal and state statutes that authorize the automatic transmission of the fiduciary powers of named bank trustees to their successors by merger and consolidation). For related issues, *see* §3.4.4.3 of this handbook (successor trustees).

[2] 2 Scott & Ascher §11.1.6.4.

[3] *See generally* 2 Scott on Trusts §96.7.

[4] In re De Coppet, 10 Misc. 2d 748, 173 N.Y.S.2d 443 (1958).

[5] UTC §706 cmt. (available at <http://www.uniformlaws.org/Act.aspx?title=Trust%20Code>).

[6] UTC §706 cmt. (available at <http://www.uniformlaws.org/Act.aspx?title=Trust%20Code>).

§8.20 [1] Wendy C. Gerzog, *Equitable Apportionment: Recent Cases and Continuing Trends*, 41 Real Prop. Prob. & Tr. J. 671, 687 (2007) (citing to Estate of Swallen v. Comm'r, 98 F.3d 919, 924 (6th Cir. 1996).

[2] *See generally* §8.9.1 of this handbook (the federal estate tax).

shoulder the economic burden of satisfying the tax obligation.[3] The prospective trustee of a *revocable* inter vivos trust that contains charitable and noncharitable equitable interests, or dispositions that qualify for the marital deduction,[4] will want to pay particular attention to the trust's "tax clause."[5]

Let us take a revocable inter vivos trust that divides into two equal shares upon the death of the settlor. One share is held for the benefit of a charity and the other for the benefit of the settlor's children. Let us also assume that the settlor intends to fund the trust with all of his or her property before death. If there is no provision in the governing instrument explaining which class of beneficiaries is to bear the economic burden of the estate taxes, just a general direction that the trust estate is to bear the tax burden, then the trustee will have to fall back on a tax apportionment statute, if any. Such statutes are not always models of clarity.[6] Unless there is some statute that clearly addresses the issue,[7] the question will be whether the taxes must be paid "off the top" *or* paid out of the children's share after division.[8] The policy argument for charging estate taxes to the children's share is that the children's share is generating the tax, the charity being entitled to a charitable deduction.[9] In other words, the doctrine of equitable apportionment applies.[10] The Uniform Probate Code would dock the children's share for the full amount.[11]

On the other hand, the children are likely to put forth the argument that the governing instrument, taken in its totality, reveals an intention to put the interests of family members at least on a par with the charity. Accordingly, taxes should be paid "off the top."[12] If the taxes are paid "off the top," then the

---

[3] *Cf.* Estate of Miller v. Comm'r, 209 F.3d 720 (5th Cir. 2000), *aff'g per curiam* T.C. Memo 1998-416 (resolving apparently conflicting tax provisions in will and revocable inter vivos trust).

[4] *See generally* §8.9.1.3 of this handbook (the marital deduction).

[5] *See, e.g.,* In re Estate of Baltic, 946 N.E.2d 244, 247 (Ohio App. 2010) ("Moreover, although the trust agreement is unclear as to how estate taxes are to be paid, it provides language directing how estate taxes are not to be paid, *i.e.*, they are not to be paid from the property of the estate that 'would be excluded' from the estate 'for federal estate tax purposes.' Thus, the trust prohibits taxes from being paid out of . . . [distributions] . . . to charitable institutions.").

[6] *See, e.g.,* The First Nat'l Bank of Boston v. Judge Baker Guidance Ctr., 13 Mass. App. 144, 431 N.E.2d 243 (1982). For a complete citation catalog of state estate tax apportionment statutes and cases, *see* Jeffrey N. Pennell, *Apportionment of Death Taxes*, ACTEC Studies, Study 5 (all verified as of June 11, 2002).

[7] The 2003 Revised Uniform Estate Tax Apportionment Act specifically calls for an equitable apportionment in such a situation. *See* 2003 Uniform Act §3 cmt.

[8] *See, e.g.,* In re Menchhofer Family Trust, 765 N.W.2d 607 (2009) (Table) 2009 WL 398268 (Iowa Ct. App.) (court ordering inheritance taxes to be paid "off the top" of a trust with charitable and noncharitable beneficiaries).

[9] *See, however,* Estate of Boder, 850 S.W.2d 76 (Mo. 1993) (calling for taxes to be paid "off the top" before division, thus causing the charitable interests to bear a portion of the tax burden).

[10] *See generally* §8.15.62 of this handbook (doctrine of equitable apportionment). *See also* Uniform Estate Tax Apportionment Statute §2 cmt. *Cf.* In re Estate of Pyle, 570 A.2d 1074 (Pa. Super. Ct. 1990) (a case involving charitable and noncharitable residuary takers under a will, where the noncharitable taker was saddled with the entire burden of the estate taxes).

[11] UPC §3-9A-103(b)(2).

[12] *See, e.g.,* Estate of Bradford v. Comm'r, T.C. Memo 2002-238, 84 T.C.M. (CCH) 337, 346 (the court ordering that taxes be paid "off the top," the trust agreement having directed that "any

charity of course gets less than it would otherwise get if the noncharitable interests alone were to bear the tax burden. This is because the charity is sharing some of the burden of the tax: But there is an added twist: An "off the top" payment will require a circular tax computation to accommodate the corresponding reduction in the charitable deduction occasioned by the reduced amount passing to the charity.[13] "Section 2055 . . . [of the Internal Revenue Code] . . . provides an estate tax deduction for charitable contributions, but section 2055(c) reduces the deduction by the amount of death taxes payable from . . . [what passes to the charity] . . ."[14] Had there been no general direction in the trust instrument that the trust estate shall bear the tax burden, the Uniform Probate Code would seem to call for the taxes to be paid "off the top."[15]

The point is that the settlor's intentions with respect to the apportionment of estate taxes between charitable and noncharitable interests should be fully and unambiguously addressed in the tax clause of the governing instrument. Internal tax apportionment questions can arise not only when there are successive charitable and noncharitable equitable interests but also when there are classes of noncharitable interests.[16]

Let us take a funded revocable inter vivos trust that calls for the trustee, upon the death of the settlor, to carve out $1 million for the settlor's children by the first marriage and to distribute the "residue" to the children of the second marriage. Who bears the burden of the estate taxes when the governing instrument is silent on the subject? If this were a will, the common law default rule is that the estate tax liability would be borne by the portion passing to the children of the second marriage, with the children of the first marriage receiving the full $1 million undiminished by estate taxes. "If a state does not have a statutory apportionment law, the burden of the estate taxes generally will fall on residuary beneficiaries of the probate estate."[17] But this is not a will. Thus it is likely that the doctrine of equitable apportionment would be applicable, with each class of beneficiary bearing its share of the economic burden of the taxes.[18]

On the other hand, if the "residue" were to pass to the second wife outright or into a marital deduction trust, QTIP or otherwise, for her benefit, would

---

death taxes . . . are to be paid before the trust property is allocated to the two trust beneficiaries and, thus, before the share of the charitable beneficiary is determined").

[13] *See* Treas. Reg. §20.2055-3(a)(2) (providing that the charitable deduction amount can be calculated either "by a series of trial-and-error computations, or by a formula" and noting that "[i]f, in addition, interdependent State and Federal taxes are involved, the computation becomes highly complicated").

[14] Wendy C. Gerzog, *Equitable Apportionment: Recent Cases and Continuing Trends*, 41 Real Prop. Prob. & Tr. J. 671, 689 (2007).

[15] UPC §3-9A-104(1).

[16] *See, e.g.*, Folger v. Hillier, 2003 WL 21916367 (Cal. App.) (holding an internal trust tax apportionment provision bestowing discretion on the trustee to pay estate taxes "without proration" to be ambiguous, the result being that the tax burden must be shared pro rata by all beneficiaries—none of whom were charities—as required by the applicable default law).

[17] Uniform Estate Tax Apportionment Statute, pref. n.

[18] *See generally* §8.15.62 of this handbook (doctrine of equitable apportionment).

there still be an apportionment of the tax burden? Probably not. "As a general rule, equitable apportionment statutes do not apportion taxes to the marital share because that share does not generate any estate tax liability."[19] If the governing documentation had explicitly called for an apportionment, calculating the marital deduction would then require a "circular tax computation." Why? Because "[u]nder Section 2056(b)(4) . . . [of the Internal Revenue Code-,] . . . the marital deduction must reflect the effect of any death taxes on the net value of property passing to the surviving spouse."[20]

Rather than having to grapple with some tax apportionment statute after the settlor's death, the prudent prospective trustee will insist that the settlor's intentions with respect to the apportionment of estate taxes be fully and unambiguously spelled out in the governing instrument.

Without trust. The prudent prospective trustee will make sure that the estate and generation-skipping tax apportionment clause of the revocable inter vivos trust[21] and the corresponding tax apportionment clause of the pour-over will dovetail.[22] Under no circumstances should they be in conflict, or appear to be in conflict,[23] for the trustee can never be sure that the trust will contain all the settlor's property at the time of his or her death.[24] Nor should the scrivener mechanically insert into a pour-over will, or into any will for that matter, a provision allocating all taxes occasioned by the testator's death to the probate

---

[19] Wendy C. Gerzog, *Equitable Apportionment: Recent Cases and Continuing Trends*, 41 Real Prop. Prob. & Tr. J. 671, 681 (2007).

[20] Wendy C. Gerzog, *Equitable Apportionment: Recent Cases and Continuing Trends*, 41 Real Prop. Prob. & Tr. J. 671, 681–682 (2007).

[21] *See, e.g.*, Estate of Lurie v. Comm'r, T.C. Memo. 2004-19 (Jan. 28, 2004) (as trust tax clause caused marital trust to bear some of the burden of the estate tax liability, the marital deduction must be reduced to reflect the diversion of assets from the marital trust to the taxing authorities).

[22] *See* Patterson v. United States, 181 F.3d 927, 83 A.F.T.R.2d 99-2476 (8th Cir. 1999) (applying Kansas law, which requires that the will and the trust instrument be considered and construed together in determining which document shall govern the apportionment of death taxes, the court found that a mandatory tax payment provision in the will and a discretionary tax payment provision in the trust instrument, taken together, express the decedent's intent that the trust provision preempt the will provision).

[23] *See, e.g.*, In re Estate of Brownlee, 654 N.W.2d 206, 212 (S.D. 2002), *remanded on another issue sub nom.*, Wagner v. Brownlee, 713 N.W.2d 592 (S.D. 2006) (in the face of "two thoroughly conflicting clauses within the testator's estate plan, the Will and the Trust," the court fell back on a codified version of the doctrine of equitable apportionment). *See generally* §8.15.62 of this handbook (doctrine of equitable apportionment).

[24] The Uniform Estate Tax Apportionment Act (Revised 1964) addresses the apportionment of the federal and state wealth transfer tax burden between and among the probate estate and the will substitutes (including the revocable inter vivos trust) when the governing instruments are silent on the subject. In other words, it is limited to external allocations. It has little to say about internal allocations, *i.e.*, the sub-parceling of the burden among the recipients of the probate estate and among the recipients of property passing pursuant to the substitutes. For an analysis of the state laws governing internal allocations and external allocations, *see* Jeffrey N. Pennell, Tax Payment Provisions and Equitable Apportionment, SC28 ALI-ABA 1835 (1997). A state-by-state synopsis of tax apportionment laws is set forth in the Appendix to Prof. Pennell's materials. The Act was revised in 2003. Under the revised Act, equitable apportionment default rules now apply to certain internal allocations, specifically in cases where the estate tax marital or charitable deduction is implicated. *See* 2003 Uniform Act §3 cmt. *See generally* Douglas A Kahn, *The 2003*

residue, particularly as in some jurisdictions such a provision could well trump language to the contrary in the recipient revocable trust:[25]

> With respect to competing taxable shares, the questions is . . . . : Did the inclusion of what is often boilerplate language mean that the testator or settlor intended the residuary beneficiary to bear the brunt of the tax liability, even if it completely consumes all benefit to him?[26]

The tax clause of the will[27] or the revocable trust[28] also should be coordinated with the tax clauses of trusts whose assets might be subject to taxation upon the death of the settlor.[29] A QTIP trust, for example, can create external tax apportionment uncertainties upon the death of its beneficiary, unless there is adequate coordination among the governing instruments.[30] Let us take a revocable living trust. Assume the wife of the settlor of the revocable trust predeceases the settlor. A QTIP trust was established under her estate planning documents for his benefit. His revocable trust makes general provision for the payment of "all estate taxes occasioned by his death." Ordinarily, the portion of the estate tax liability occasioned by his subsequent death that is allocable to her QTIP trust would be absorbed by the QTIP trust itself, unless

---

Revised Uniform Estate Tax Apportionment Act, 38 Real Prop. Prob. & Tr. J. 613, 625 (2004); Wendy C. Gerzog, *Equitable Apportionment: Recent Cases and Continuing Trends*, 41 Real Prop. Prob. & Tr. J. 671 (2007).

[25] *See generally* Ira Mark Bloom, *Unifying the Rules for Wills and Revocable Trusts in the Federal Estate Tax Apportionment Arena: Suggestions for Reform*, 62 U. Miami L. Rev. 767, 773 (2008) (noting that 2003 Uniform Estate Tax Apportionment Act provides that "if a will unambiguously provides the method for apportionment then the will provision will control without regard to any inconsistent provision in a revocable trust").

[26] Wendy C. Gerzog, *Equitable Apportionment: Recent Cases and Continuing Trends*, 41 Real Prop. Prob. & Tr. J. 671, 675–676 (2007). *Cf.* Estate of Williams, 853 N.E.2d 79 (Ill. Ct. App. 2006) (the court equitably apportioning the estate tax obligation occasioned by the death of the surviving spouse between her probate estate and the assets of her late husband's marital deduction trust for her benefit, although her will expressly provided for the payment of estate taxes from her probate residue and his trust lacked a tax clause).

[27] *See, e.g.,* Estate of Cord, 58 N.Y.2d 539, 449 N.E.2d 402, 462 N.Y.S.2d 622 (1983) (involving conflicting tax clauses, one in a self-settled irrevocable trust with a retained life estate and the other in the deceased settlor's will).

[28] In re Estate of Klarner, 98 P.3d 892 (Colo. Ct. App. 2003); In re Estate of Klarner, 113 P.3d 150 (Colo. 2005) (involving conflicting tax clauses, one in a QTIP trust and the other in the revocable trust of the surviving spouse of settlor of QTIP trust, the surviving spouse now having died).

[29] *See, e.g.,* Lurie v. Comm'r, 425 F.3d 1021 (7th Cir. 2005), *aff'g* T.C. Memo. 2004-14.

[30] *See, e.g.,* In re Blauhorn Revocable Trust, 275 Neb. 256, 746 N.W.2d 136 (2008) (tax clause in husband's revocable inter vivos trust, which made no specific reference to his predeceased wife's QTIP trust, though generally expansive, held not to impose on those who took under the husband's trust [which had one set of remainder beneficiaries] the burden of the estate taxes attributable to his wife's trust [which had a different set of remainder beneficiaries], this because of the lack of such a specific reference).

his will or revocable trust by *specific* provision were to shift that burden else-where, such as onto his probate estate.[31] Massachusetts has a statute to that effect.[32] In Colorado, a general tax payment provision in a revocable trust was held to cover *state* estate taxes attributable to QTIP property, but, because of its lack of specificity, not the federal estate tax liability attributable thereto.[33] That burden, pursuant to the applicable state default law, remained on the QTIP property. On appeal, however, the federal specificity requirement was held applicable to the *state* estate tax liability as well.[34] Who is to bear the burden of the QTIP tax liability can become an unpleasant pocketbook issue, for example, when the QTIP remaindermen are the children of a first marriage and those who take under the revocable trust are the children of a second marriage.[35]

Four sections of the Internal Revenue Code, Sections 2206, 2207, 2207A and 2207B, functionally deal with the allocation of the burden of the federal estate tax among those who take by will and will substitute. For a discussion of the interaction of those sections and the apportionment statutes of the various states, the reader is referred to Ira Mark Bloom.[36]

Tax apportionment rules also can differ from state to state.[37] Thus, if the settlor of a funded revocable trust dies domiciled in a state other than the one in which the trust is being administered, which jurisdiction's default tax appor-tionment rules are applicable? There is not a lot of helpful law out there.[38] One learned commentator proffers the following advice:

> Proper resolution of cases of this sort, however, is not to be achieved by mechani-cally applying either the law of the situs of the nonprobate assets or that of the decedent's domicil, but instead by trying to ascertain what the decedent, in view of all the circumstances, would probably have preferred. In this inquiry, any number of factors may prove relevant. As we have seen, the fact that the tax attributable to nonprobate assets is very large in comparison with the fund out of which it might under the law of one of the relevant states be payable seems almost undeniably relevant in determining what the decedent actually or presumably intended. This

---

[31] I.R.C. §2207A(a)(2) provides that a QTIP trust established by the first-to-die-spouse shall bear its pro rata share of estate taxes owed at the death of the surviving spouse, unless the surviving spouse in his or her will or revocable trust has "specifically indicated an intent" that the QTIP trust be relieved of that burden.

[32] Mass. Gen. Laws ch. 190B, §2-704.

[33] In re Estate of Klarner, 98 P.3d 892 (Colo. App. 2003).

[34] In re Estate of Klarner, 113 P.3d 150 (Colo. 2005).

[35] *Cf.* Estate of Cord, 58 N.Y.2d 539, 449 N.E.2d 402, 462 N.Y.S.2d 622 (1983) (involving conflicting tax apportionment clauses, one in a non-QTIP *irrevocable* trust whose beneficiaries were decedent-settlor's children by a prior marriage and the other in decedent's will of which decedent's surviving husband was the executor and a beneficiary, the corpus of the trust having been included in the decedent's gross estate for tax purposes due to her retained life interest in the trust income).

[36] *Unifying the Rules for Wills and Revocable Trusts in the Federal Estate Tax Apportionment Arena: Suggestions for Reform*, 60 U. Miami L. Rev. 786–806 (2008).

[37] *See generally* 7 Scott & Ascher §45.3.11 (Allocation of Estate Taxes/Conflict of Laws); §8.5 of this handbook (conflict of laws).

[38] *See* 7 Scott & Ascher §45.3.11.

is especially so when it appears that the decedent did not realize how large the taxes were, or that the nonprobate assets would be part of the gross estate.[39]

§8.21 Duty of Third Parties to Investigate Whether Trustee Has Power to Act or Is Properly Exercising the Power

After this unfortunate decision . . . [King v. Richardson, 136 F.2d 849 (4th Cir.), cert. denied. 320 U.S. 777 (1943)] . . . , it would have been understandable if corporations generally had demanded a judicial decree binding on the beneficiaries before registering a trustee's stock transfer. They did not do this, but they often required a copy of the trust instrument for review by counsel. This delayed and complicated fiduciary stock transfers.[1]

Generally. Under the common law, a third party who transacted with the trustee had a duty to ascertain the trustee's authority in equity to enter into the transaction and to ascertain whether the authority was being properly exercised.[2] As between the beneficiaries and the third party, the risk of the trustee's acting without authority fell on the third party,[3] unless the third party was a good-faith purchaser for value (*i.e.*, a BFP).[4] And a third party who knew of the trust would not be acting in good faith if the third party failed to make reasonable investigation of the trustee's authority.[5] Thus, the third party (*e.g.*, a prospective purchaser of trust real estate) at minimum would need to see a copy of the governing instrument to ascertain whether the trustee had authority in equity to sell the property. If the inspection raised questions regarding the trustee's authority, or the propriety of its exercise, then the third party would be obliged to expand the inquiry.

Apart from whether or not a trust instrument should be recorded in some registry when the subject property is real estate,[6] a tension has always existed between the need of third parties to ascertain a trustee's authority to enter into a particular transaction and the desire of the beneficiaries for privacy.[7] A number of states have harmonized these competing public policy considerations by affording certain statutory protections to third parties who rely on a

---

[39] 7 Scott & Ascher §45.3.11.

§8.21 [1] 3 Scott & Ascher §17.11.4.

[2] *See generally* 3 Scott & Ascher §17.11.4.

[3] *See generally* 3 Scott & Ascher §17.11.4.

[4] *See generally* §5.4.2 of this handbook (rights of the beneficiary as against transferees, including BFPs) and §8.15.63 of this handbook (doctrine of bona fide purchase); 5 Scott & Ascher §29.1.1 (Bona Fide Purchaser).

[5] *See generally* 3 Scott & Ascher §17.11.4; 4 Scott on Trusts §297.4.

[6] *See generally* §9.6 of this handbook.

[7] *See generally* Frances H. Foster, Privacy *and the Elusive Quest for Uniformity in the Law of Trusts*, 38 Ariz. St. L J. 713 (2006).

trustee's "certification of trust."[8] The third parties need not, and in some cases may not, scrutinize the trust instrument itself.[9] More about the Uniform Trust Code's certification of trust compromise appears at the end of this subsection. The trustees of testamentary trusts, of course, are on the sidelines in this particular clash of interests, as a probated will is generally a public record.

In order to facilitate the flow of commerce, the laws addressing commercial paper, investment securities, and banking transactions, in any case, have downgraded somewhat the third party's duty to investigate the trustee's authority to what is essentially an "actual notice" standard.[10] Even at common law, the duty of inquiry of a depository of trust funds was less onerous than that of a purchaser, mortgagee, or pledgee of trust property.[11] The same could be said for the trustee's stockbroker.[12] Similarly, a third party who sold property *to a trustee* probably had little or no duty to inquire into the trustee's authority to make the purchase, absent actual knowledge that the purchase would be a breach of trust.[13] Many trust instruments now contain express language relieving third parties of the duty to inquire into the trustee's actual authority to transact.

The result of all of this is to shift the economic risk occasioned by a breach of the trustee's fiduciary duty from the third party to the beneficiaries (up to the value of the trust estate), to turn the trust into a quasi-entity that has some of the characteristics of a corporation. Section 7 of the Uniform Trustees' Powers Act has done nothing to stem the tide.[14] In fact, it has taken the lower "actual

---

[8] *See generally* Frances H. Foster, *Privacy and the Elusive Quest for Uniformity in the Law of Trusts*, 38 Ariz. St. L.J. 713 (2006); 5 Scott & Ascher §29.2 (Notice to Transferee of Trust Property).

[9] *See generally* Frances H. Foster, *Privacy and the Elusive Quest for Uniformity in the Law of Trusts*, 38 Ariz. St. L.J. 713 (2006).

[10] U.C.C. §§3-307, (b), (1), (2), and (4) (1990) (establishing the commercial paper standard as actual notice unless the paper runs to the trustee personally); U.C.C. §§8-302, 8-304 (investment securities); Unif. Fiduciaries Act §§3-10 (banking transactions). *See also* §§8.3.6 of this handbook (negotiable instruments and the duty of third parties to inquire into the trustee's authority) and 8.3.7 of this handbook (the duty of stockbrokers to inquire into the trustee's authority to transact).

See generally 3 Scott & Ascher §17.11.4 (Nominee Registration of Investment Securities Held by Fiduciaries and the Duty of Third Parties to Inquire into the Authority of the Fiduciaries and Their Nominees).

[11] For more on a bank's duty of inquiry when it comes to deposits and withdrawals of trust funds, *see* §8.3.4 of this handbook. *See also* 5 Scott & Ascher §30.4 (Depositories of Trust Funds); §8.3.2 of this handbook (bona fide purchaser for value of trust property: what constitutes notice that transfer in breach of trust?), §8.3.3 of this handbook (pledgees of trust property and the bona fide purchase doctrine), and §8.15.63 of this handbook (doctrine of bona fide purchase; the BFP).

[12] *See generally* §8.3.7 of this handbook (the duty of stockbrokers to inquire into the trustee's authority to transact).

[13] 5 Scott & Ascher §30.6.1 (Sales to Trust Estate).

[14] *See, e.g.*, Wetherill v. Bank IV of Kansas, N.A., 145 F.3d 1187 (10th Cir. 1998) (depository bank not liable for defalcations of depositor-trustee as had no actual knowledge). *See* UTC §1012 (available at <http://www.uniformlaws.org/Act.aspx?title=Trust%20Code>) (affording expansive protections to third parties who deal with a trustee, protections that are similar to those afforded by §7 of the Uniform Trustees' Powers Act).

notice" standard of inquiry beyond the specialized world of commercial, investment, and banking "paper" to encompass transactions involving tangible personal property and real estate.

The reader should understand, however, that while a beneficiary's right of recourse against a third party may be eroding, these commerce-facilitating measures in no way foreclose the beneficiary from moving *against the trustee personally* for acting beyond the scope of his authority. To be sure, this may be small consolation to the beneficiary faced with an insolvent trustee. The Uniform Trust Code takes its cue from the Uniform Trustees' Powers Act.[15] The Code also would authorize a trustee to furnish third parties a certification of trust in lieu of the copy of the trust instrument.[16] Still, while under the Code "it is no longer necessary, as a matter of course, for a third person dealing with a trustee to inquire the trustee's powers and the propriety of their exercise, a third person continues, as under common law, to be bound to inquire into the underlying facts if the third person has notice that the trustee is exceeding the trustee's powers or otherwise engaging in a breach of trust, or if facts and circumstances give the third person reason to know that the trustee is doing so."[17]

It is still good practice, however, for the third party who is contemplating entering into a nonroutine transaction with a "trust" to ascertain beforehand whether the trustee possesses the requisite authority. A knowing participation in a breach of trust would not be covered by these commerce-facilitating statutes.[18] Nor would they protect the third party from the inconvenience of being called as a witness in litigation between the beneficiary and the trustee.

There are levels of due diligence. If the stakes are not particularly high, the third person might request a copy of the governing instrument and have it reviewed by counsel. For transactions of a more serious nature, particularly those involving land, the third person also might require a written opinion of the trustee's counsel that the trustee has the requisite authority. In questionable cases where the stakes are high, it may be appropriate for the third person to require that the trustee obtain a court order.

Liability of a third party who fails to honor a Uniform Trust Code Section 1013 certification. Again, the trustee of the typical trust will have numerous occasions to transact with third parties in furtherance of the trust's lawful purposes. This is appropriate as the trustee holds the legal title to the trust property and, thus, "as to the world" is its owner. A third party might be selling an asset to, or purchasing an entrusted asset from, the trustee. A third party might be loaning funds to the trustee in his fiduciary capacity or borrowing entrusted property from the trustee. A third party might be selling goods

---

[15] UTC §1012 (available at <http://www.uniformlaws.org/Act.aspx?title=Trust%20Code>).

[16] UTC §1013 (available at <http://www.uniformlaws.org/Act.aspx?title=Trust%20Code>). *See generally* Frances H. Foster, *Privacy and the Elusive Quest for Uniformity in the Law of Trusts*, 38 Ariz. St. L.J. 713 (2006).

[17] 5 Scott & Ascher §29.2 (referring to UTC §104(a)).

[18] *See, e.g.*, 3 Scott & Ascher §17.11.4 n.7 (containing a list of citations to state statutes regarding fiduciary registration of securities in the name of a nominee).

and services to the trustee or purchasing goods and services from the trustee, all in furtherance of the trust's lawful purposes. The trustee also may properly retain third-party agents in furtherance of the trust's lawful purposes, such as attorneys-at-law and investment managers.

Section 1013(h) of the Uniform Trust Code provides as follows: "A person . . . [other than a beneficiary] . . . making a demand for the trust instrument in addition to a certification of trust or excerpts is liable for damages if the court determines that the person did not act in good faith in demanding the instrument."

The information in a trustee's UTC Section 1013 certification is limited to the following bits of information:

- That the trust exists and its date of execution
- The identity of the settlors
- The powers of the trustee
- The revocability or irrevocability of the trust and the identity of any persons holding a power to revoke
- The authority of cotrustees to sign or otherwise authenticate and whether all or less than all are required in order to exercise the powers of the trustee
- The trust's taxpayer identification number
- The manner of taking title to trust property
- A statement that the trust has not been revoked, modified, or amended in any manner that would cause the representations contained in the certification to be incorrect

A UTC Section 1013 certification, however, "need not contain the dispositive terms of a trust." Unexplained are the nature of the "liability" and "damages" that are being contemplated by subsection (h). Nor is a definition of "good faith" even supplied in this context. Presumably, the third party is subject to some type of tort liability, but what duty of care is implicated by the "making of a demand for a trust instrument"? According to the section's official commentary, left to "other law" is the issue of "how damages for a bad faith refusal are to be computed." Also unspecified is to whom this demanding "person" would be liable in the face of a judicial determination of liability.

A third party contemplating dealing with a trustee should be able contractually to defang UTC Section 1013(h), assuming it actually has fangs. Time will tell whether it actually does in the face of all this statutory vagueness.

May UTC Section 1013's general applicability be negated effectively *ab initio* by the trust's terms? In the face of subsection (g) of UTC Section 1013, some settlors may want to consider doing just that so as to better protect the equitable property rights of the beneficiaries of their trusts. Subsection (g) provides as follows: "A person who in good faith enters into a transaction in reliance upon a certification of trust may enforce the transaction *against the trust property* [emphasis supplied] as if the representations contained in the certification were correct." The problem is that the third party who is not furnished a copy of the trust instrument, only a cryptic trustee certification, will not be privy to the UTC Section 1013 negation provision and therefore may well not be bound by its terms.

The third party's duty to see to it that trustee properly applies the purchase price. As we have noted elsewhere, a third party who knowingly participates with a trustee in a breach of trust shares with the trustee liability for any loss caused by the breach.[19] Thus, if the trustee transfers trust property in breach of trust to a third-party purchaser who is aware of the breach, the third-party purchaser holds the trust property subject to the terms of the trust.[20] Otherwise, "such a purchaser is liable only if the trustee commits a breach of trust in making the transfer and the purchaser has notice that the trustee is doing so."[21] At common law, however, it was doctrine that even the innocent third-party purchaser had a continuing obligation running to the trust beneficiaries to see to it that the trustee properly applied the purchase price.[22] In the United States, such an innocent third party either by case law or statute has been relieved of such an obligation.[23] "In England, the old rule has been repudiated by statute."[24]

§8.22 Why Do We Need the Trust When We Have the Corporation and the Third-Party Beneficiary Contract?

[T]he slogan of modern comparative law—compare function rather than form—does not work for the trust. One cannot identify the function of the trust because there is no such function. The trust is functionally protean. Trusts are quasi-entails, quasi-usufructs, quasi-wills, quasi-corporations, quasi-securities over assets, schemes for collective investment, vehicles for the administration of bankruptcy, vehicles for bond issues, and so on and so forth. In software terminology, trusts are emulators.[1]

The corporation.[2] While a trust, in theory, can be designed to do what a corporation can do and more,[3] the corporation has for some time been an

---

[19] *See* §7.2.9 of this handbook (personal liability of third parties to the beneficiary).

[20] *See* §5.4.2 of this handbook (rights of the beneficiary as against transferees of the underlying property).

[21] 5 Scott & Ascher §30.1 (Misapplication of Payments Made to Trustee).

[22] 5 Scott & Ascher §30.1. *See also* §8.15.69 of this handbook (third-party liability for trustee's misapplication of payments to trustee; the purchaser's duty to monitor the trustee's application of the purchase price).

[23] 5 Scott & Ascher §30.1, n.5 (Case Law) & n.7 (Statutes).

[24] 5 Scott & Ascher §30.1 (referring to Trustee Act, 1925, 15 Geo. V., c. 19, §14).

§8.22 [1] George L. Gretton, *Trusts Without Equity*, 49 Int'l & Comp. L.Q. 599 (2000).

[2] C. Bishop & D. Kleinberger, Limited Liability Companies ¶ 1.01[1] (1998). For a discussion of the advantages of the LLC for a wide variety of business ventures, *see* ¶ 1.02[1].

[3] *See generally* H. Hansmann & U. Mattei, *The Functions of Trust Law: A Comparative Legal and Economic Analysis*, 73 N.Y.U. L. Rev. 434 (1998).

important instrument of commerce. This is, in part, because of the efficiencies attendant to a standardized form of doing business that can vary in format only within narrow limits. There are a number of advantages to standardization: "These include: reducing the burden of drafting; reducing information costs of various actors—lawyers, judges, and businesspeople—by inducing them to use the same form; making it easier for actors to bond themselves credibly to certain structures or forms of conduct; and facilitating an accretion of clarifying legal precedent."[4]

In the eighteenth and first half of the nineteenth centuries things were different. Incorporation was conferred either by the Crown issuing a charter or Letters Patent, or by private Act of Parliament, each a cumbersome, time-consuming, and sometimes even futile process.[5] Thus the unincorporated joint stock company operating under deed of trust was the preferred instrument of commerce, and it remained so until 1844 when Parliament authorized incorporation by registration.[6] While one era in the commercial life of the Anglo-American trust had come to an end, another was just beginning on the other side of the Atlantic, namely, that of the great American industrial trust. It too would fall victim to legislation, but not until 1890 when Congress passed and the President signed the Sherman Antitrust Act.

Notwithstanding the many modern-day advantages of the corporation,[7] there are still commercial tasks that only a trust, a child of equity and creature of the common law, can perform—or perform well. The reason: its flexibility.[8] By way of example, the nominee trust will continue to prove a useful instrument of commerce and estate planning in situations where minimal property management is called for. In the investment management industry, the trust has become a popular form of doing business in part because of the common law principle that a trustee need not be controlled by the beneficiary. In fact, roughly 40 percent of U.S. equities and 30 percent of corporate and foreign bonds are now held in pension funds and mutual funds, most of which are trusts or trusts in substance if not in form.[9] In Section 9.31 of this handbook, we

---

[4] Hansmann & Mattei, *The Functions of Trust Law: A Comparative Legal and Economic Analysis*, 73 N.Y.U. L. Rev. at 476.

[5] *See* Kevin Lindgren QC, *The Birth of the Trading Trust*, 9(2) Tr. Q. Rev. 5 (2011) [a STEP publication].

[6] *See* Kevin Lindgren QC, *The Birth of the Trading Trust*, 9(2) Tr. Q. Rev. 5 (2011) [a STEP publication] (referring to the Joint Stock Companies Act 1844 [7 & 8 Vict c 110]).

[7] *See* Tamar Frankel, *The Delaware Business Trust Act Failure as the New Corporate Law*, 23 Cardozo L. Rev. 325, 327, 330 (2001) (suggesting that while the trust is an ideal vehicle for "managing other people's money and real estate," it is "inconvenient" as a vehicle for operating commercial and manufacturing enterprises).

[8] "Next to contract, the universal tool, and incorporation, the standard instrument of organization, . . . [the trust] . . . takes its place wherever the relations to be established are too delicate or too novel for these courser devices." Isaacs, *Trusteeship in Modern Business*, 42 Harv. L. Rev. 1048, 1060 (1929).

[9] H. Hansmann & U. Mattei, *The Functions of Trust Law: A Comparative Legal and Economic Analysis*, 73 N.Y.U. L. Rev. 434, 436, 437 (1998). According to the Investment Company Institute, as of July 2000, the aggregate value of property held in U.S. mutual funds was $7.077 trillion. "The mutual funds controlled by the 75 largest fund managers alone own $2.9 trillion of U.S. equities,

discuss how the trust is particularly suited for managing property that has been segregated to secure the contractual rights of a class of bondholders. These trusts are known in the trade as "corporate trusts" and their trustees as "indenture trustees."

Let us take the nominee trust. Both trustees and corporations can hold title to real estate. However, *in cases where active management of that real estate is not called for*, it is generally more practical and cost-effective for a trustee to hold the bare legal title than it is for a corporation. This is because the typical incorporation statute calls for an internal governance structure and a paper trail that is ill suited to a mission that is fundamentally passive. If all one is looking for is divisibility and transferability,[10] and perhaps an element of privacy, the simple device of the nominee trust may well be the way to go.

As mentioned, there are also advantages to operating pension and mutual funds through trustees. To be sure, both trustees and corporations can hold title to portfolios of securities. But *when the beneficial ownership of a portfolio is lodged with a fluid and potentially expanding class of anonymous investors*, as is the case with most mutual funds, the trust model offers an important advantage over the corporate model: the trustee need not be subject to beneficiary direction.[11] A corporate board of directors, on the other hand, must answer to shareholders in matters of internal governance. The corporate model, while appropriate perhaps for a manufacturing concern, is generally not appropriate for the mutual fund, provided the underlying assets, as well as the fund participations themselves, are reasonably liquid. If the investor does not like how the fund is being managed, he can easily cash out and invest his property elsewhere.

The administrative "efficiencies" attendant to employing the trust model in the investment context is generally perceived to be worth the loss of investor control over the inner workings of the enterprise. It is no coincidence that most mutual funds in the United States operate as trusts even when their trappings are corporate.[12]

---

equal to 20 percent of the $14.4 trillion market capitalization of the stock market at the beginning of 2001." John C. Bogle, *The 800-Pound Gorilla: Shareholders Arise!* The American Spectator, Mar./Apr. 2002, at 40.

[10] *See generally* §9.6 of this handbook (discussing the nominee trust).

[11] *See, e.g.*, Aaron Lucchetti, *Vanguard Moves to Alter Indexes*, Wall St. J., Aug. 27, 2002, at D7, col. 2 (reporting that Vanguard Group, the nation's No. 2 mutual-fund firm, plans to make it easier for some of its large index funds to change the indexes the fund portfolios are designed to mimic: "The proposal, announced in a preliminary proxy statement filed by the Malvern, Pa., company yesterday, would allow trustees for eight large Vanguard index funds to authorize changes in their target indexes without having to call for shareholder votes.").

[12] *See generally* Charles E. Rounds, Jr. & Andreas Dehio, *Publicly-Traded Open End Mutual Funds in Common Law and Civil Law Jurisdictions: A Comparison of Legal Structures*, 3 N.Y.U.J.L & Bus. 473 (2007). For an explanation of the advantages of the Massachusetts business trust as an investment vehicle, the reader is referred to the Fidelity Magellan Fund, Inc. Notice of Special Meeting In Lieu of the Annual Meeting of Shareholders (held Aug. 15, 1984). The purpose of the meeting was in part to obtain approval to reorganize the Fund as a Massachusetts business trust. The Notice is reprinted in Mary Ann Tynan, *Form of Investment Company Organization: Corporation vs. Massachusetts Business Trust*, 515 PLI/Corp 55, 65 (Appendix A) (1986). For an explanation of the Delaware Business Trust and its advantages, the reader is referred to James A. Florack & Martin I. Lubaroff, *Delaware Business Trusts*, 937 PLI/Corp 371 (1996). A Form of Delaware Business Trust

The trust, however, takes center stage in the personal (noncommercial) context. The trust makes an excellent *will substitute*.[13] It is also about the only practical way to provide for the *administration* of interests in property that are contingent and/or subject to shifting. Moreover, it can "create and protect future interests in property for persons who are not presently ascertainable and who may be conceived in the future."[14] The corporation as a practical matter can perform none of these tasks.[15] While the trustee's role as a facilitator of wealth management over time and intrafamily wealth transfers may seem trivial as set against his ever-expanding role as a commercial facilitator,[16] on a personal level his contribution to the well-being and peace of mind of individuals can be incalculable.

As noted, a trust can serve as a will substitute. Upon the death of a beneficiary, neither the legal interest nor the equitable interest need be subject to probate. The corporation, on the other hand, in and of itself, cannot serve as a vehicle for transmitting property postmortem. When a shareholder dies, under most enabling statutes, his economic interest in the corporation will pass to his estate for disposition pursuant to the terms of his will or the laws of intestate succession, unless the interest had been held jointly or had been made the subject of a trust during the decedent's lifetime. A trust is a fiduciary relationship *with respect to property* to which the trustee has the title.[17] A corporation, on the other hand, is *itself property*. Although it may internally involve

---

Agreement is reprinted at 938 PLI/Corp 393. *See generally* §8.10 of this handbook (fiduciary principles applicable to the mutual fund).

[13] The life insurance policy, a third-party beneficiary contract, is also a will substitute. As a practical matter, however, it is difficult, if not impossible, through contractual means alone, without the participation of a trustee, to create shifting and/or contingent interests in insurance proceeds, and to do so in a way that will make adequate provision for the ongoing administration of those interests. That problem is best addressed by designating a trustee as the recipient of the proceeds. This would be the case whether the payout is lump sum or periodic. *See generally* §9.3 of this handbook (the self-settled "special needs"/"supplemental needs" trust); John Langbein, *The Nonprobate Revolution and the Future of the Law of Succession*, 97 Harv. L. Rev. 1108 (1984).

[14] W. F. Fratcher, Trust §101, in Intl. Encyclopedia of Comp. Law, Vol. VI, ch. 11 (F. H. Lawson ed., 1973). The civil law tradition offers no trust analog that can "create and protect future interests in property for persons who are not presently ascertainable and who may be conceived in the future." W. F. Fratcher, Trust §101, in Intl. Encyclopedia of Comp. Law, Vol. VI, ch. 11. *See generally* §8.12.1 of this handbook (civil law alternatives to the trust).

[15] "As has been noted, a trust may be used to collect ownership of various assets and continue management after the underlying owner's death, while bypassing probate and administration. . . . In the case of ownership through other forms such as corporations, partnerships, and individual ownership, no such avoidance of probate and administration is possible." Jeffrey A. Schoenblum, 1 Multistate and Multinational Estate Planning 42–43 (1999).

[16] *See* H. Hansmann & U. Mattei, *The Functions of Trust Law: A Comparative Legal and Economic Analysis*, 73 N.Y.U. L. Rev. 434, 437 (1998) ("Similarly, turning from the demand side to the supply side of the securities markets, asset securitization trusts are now the issuers of a large fraction of all outstanding American debt securities—more than $2 trillion worth.").

[17] *See generally* Chapter 1 of this handbook.

fiduciary relationships, it is not itself a fiduciary relationship with respect to property.[18]

As also noted, the corporation is unsuited to the administration of multiple, successive, shifting, and contingent[19] property interests. Something more is needed, be it a guardianship coupled with a will, a durable power of attorney coupled with a will, or a trust. Again, the reason is grounded in first principles: A corporation is not a fiduciary relationship with respect to property, externally it is itself property. Absent substantial legislative retrofitting, the corporate model cannot serve as a trust substitute.

The contract.[20] The academic community is revisiting the question of whether the trust is a branch of contract law or a branch of property law.[21] This debate—essentially a continuation of what was begun by Frederick W. Maitland, who argued the former, and Austin W. Scott, who argued the latter—presupposes only two private fundamental legal relationships: contract and property.[22] Note, however, that while Maitland may have come down on the side of contract, he did so with some ambivalence:

> For my own part if a foreign friend asked me to tell him in one word whether the right of the English Destinatär (the person for whom property is held in trust) is *dinglich* [a property interest] or *obligatorisch* [a personal claim], I should be inclined to say: "No, I cannot do that. If I said *dinglich*, that would be untrue. If I said *obligatorisch*, I should suggest what is false. In ultimate analysis the right may be *obligatorisch*; but for many practical purposes of great importance it has been treated as though it were *dinglich*, and indeed people habitually speak and think of it as a kind of *Eigenthum* [property]."[23]

---

[18] What about the partnership that, with certain statutory exceptions, operates on the basis of agency principles? The partnership, like the trust, involves fiduciary relationships with respect to property. However, a partnership, like the corporation, alone cannot serve as a vehicle for the postmortem transmission of property interests. The reason: An agency terminates at the death of either the principal or the agent. Upon death, the deceased partner's economic interest passes to his estate, unless a trust or trust-like will substitute is somehow involved. *See generally* Restatement (Second) of Agency §14A cmt. a, §14B cmt. i.

[19] An interest is contingent if it is subject to a condition precedent such as the exercise of someone's discretion or survivorship. *See generally* §8.2.1 of this handbook (the Rule against Perpetuities).

[20] "Although the trustee by accepting the office of trustee subjects himself to the duties of administration, his duties are not contractual in nature." Restatement (Second) of Trusts §169 cmt. c.

[21] *See generally* George L. Gretton, *Trusts Without Equity*, 49 Int'l & Comp. L.Q. 599, 603–608 (2000).

[22] For the recent articulation of the contract argument, *see* J. Langbein, *The Contractarian Basis of the Law of Trusts*, 105 Yale L.J. 625 (1995); for the recent articulation of the property argument, *see* H. Hansmann & U. Mattei, *The Functions of Trust Law: A Comparative Legal and Economic Analysis*, 73 N.Y.U. L. Rev. 434 (1998). *See also* 7 Scott & Ascher §46.4.2 ("In any event, the creation of a trust is not a contract but a disposition of the beneficial interest in the trust property"). *Cf.* 3 Scott & Ascher §13.1 (coming down on the side of those who argue that a trust beneficiary has a proprietary interest in the underlying trust property, not just a chose in action or claim against the trustee, but acknowledging that "the scholarly debate continues").

[23] Maitland, Selected Essays (1936) 146.

The issue as framed, however, can never be resolved because the premise, it is suggested, is false. Our legal system does *not* have two private fundamental legal relationships of the consensual variety.[24] It has four, notwithstanding what the scholars may say: They are the agency, the contract, the bundle of legal rights and correlative duties known as property, and the trust. There are four because four are needed. No one is sufficiently elastic to encompass another without turning into the other.[25] The Cayman Islands STAR trust, a contract-trust hybrid discussed in Section 9.8.10 of this handbook, endeavors to walk the tightrope. How successful it will be in doing this over the long term remains to be seen. These relationships are facets, however, of the single gem we loosely call the common law.[26]

The four private fundamental consensual legal relationships are profoundly different and profoundly interrelated.[27] The trust exhibits agency, property, contractual, and even corporate attributes, but is *sui generis*.[28] Contractual rights are themselves property rights. Contractual rights may be the subject of a trust.[29] The equitable interest in one trust may constitute the property of another. An agency may be gratuitous or associated with contractual obligations. The corporation, internally a statutory tangle of agencies, externally is merely property (a legal interest). And in the case of an incorporated mutual fund, it may actually be a trust.[30]

One commentator has focused not on the profound dearth of nuance of academia's efforts to demote the trust to a sub-set of the law of contracts but on the unsavory subversiveness of it all:

---

[24] There are also nonconsensual legal duties which, when breached, can constitute torts.

[25] Attempting to squeeze a trust into the third-party beneficiary contract slot inevitably leaves too much hanging out, *e.g.*, the charitable trust or the private discretionary trust that calls for the shifting of property interests between and among generations of persons who at the time the contract is struck are unborn and unascertained. To doctor a third-party beneficiary contract into something that would be a satisfactory substitute for such high maintenance arrangements would merely transmogrify it into a trust. While a trust has the attributes of a contract, of property, of agency, and even of a corporation, it is now sui generis, regardless of its evolutionary origins. As one learned commentator versed in the taxonomies of both the common law and the civil law has noted: "Trusts do, indeed, impinge deeply upon the law of obligations and the law of property, but they do not belong essentially to either." George L. Gretton, *Trusts Without Equity*, 49 Int'l & Comp. L.Q. 599, 614 (July 2000).

[26] For purposes of this section, the term *common law* encompasses the law of equity.

[27] *See generally* Charles E. Rounds, Jr., *The Case For a Return to Mandatory Instruction in the Fiduciary Aspects of Agency and Trusts in the American Law School, Together with a Model Fiduciary Relations Course Syllabus*, 18 Regent U. L. Rev. 251 (2005-2006); Charles E. Rounds, Jr. & Andreas Dehio, *Publicly-Traded Open End Mutual Funds in Common Law and Civil Law Jurisdictions: A Comparison of Legal Structures*, 3 N.Y.U.J.L, & Bus. 473 (2007).

[28] *See* Schoneberger v. Oelze, 208 Ariz. 591, 595, 96 P.3d 1078, 1082 (2004) (confirming that a trust is not a contract). *See generally* Frederick R. Franke, Jr., *Resisting the Contractarian Insurgency: The Uniform Trust Code, Fiduciary Duty, and Good Faith in Contract*, 36 ACTEC L.J. 517 (2010).

[29] *See, e.g.*, §9.8.7 of this handbook (the Quistclose trust).

[30] *See generally* Charles E. Rounds, Jr. & Andreas Dehio, *Publicly-Traded Open End Mutual Funds in Common Law and Civil Law Jurisdictions: A Comparison of Legal Structures*, 3 N.Y.U.J.L. & Bus. 473 (2007).

Under the influence of law and economics theory, prominent scholars and reformers are rapidly dismantling the traditional legal and moral constraints on trustees. Trusts are becoming mere "contracts," and trust law nothing more than "default rules." "Efficiency" is triumphing over morality. In the law and economics universe of foresighted settlors, loyal trustees, informed beneficiaries, and sophisticated family and commercial creditors, trusting trustees may make sense. In the real world, however, it does not. A trust system that exalts trustee autonomy over accountability can and increasingly does impose significant human costs on all affected by trusts.[31]

At least one prominent jurist, Dame Sonia Proudman, of the High Court of Justice of England and Wales (Chancery Division), also not in accord that the trust relationship is contract-based was tasked with sorting out whether a certain deed of trust imposes certain unenforceable contract-based obligations on the University of London vis-à-vis the assets of the Warburg Library/Institute or whether those obligations are trust-based and therefore "enforceable" by the Attorney General.[32] She decided the latter. There is an implicit assumption in the decision that the trust relationship is *sui generis*. The Warburg case's backstory was the subject of an article in The New Yorker.[33]

Conclusion. Neither the corporation nor the contract can replace the trust as the foundation of an estate plan because neither can administer multiple, successive, shifting, and contingent property interests. For those functions, we must still look to the trust. *To be sure, in the years to come we will be seeing more and more trusts containing interests in LLCs*[34] *and more and more LLCs containing interests in trusts.*[35] But it will be many years, if ever, before we see the corporation or the third party beneficiary contract transmogrified into something capable of functioning as a satisfactory substitute for the common law trust that is the subject of this handbook.[36] While the civil law foundation nowadays can be fitted out to perform some of the functions of a common law trust, the entity still has a long way to evolve before it could be said to be as

---

[31] Frances H. Foster, *American Trust Law in a Chinese Mirror*, 94 Minn. L. Rev. 602, 651 (2010). *See also* Frederick R. Franke, Jr., *Resisting the Contractarian Insurgency: The Uniform Trust Code, Fiduciary Duty, and Good Faith in Contract*, 36 ACTEC L.J. 517, 526 (2010) ("The law governing fiduciary duty, however, came by its 'pulpit-thumping' roots honestly and those roots serve the 'institutional integrity' of the trust and its progeny.").

[32] *See* University of London v. Prag, [2014] EWHC 3564 (Ch).

[33] *See* Adam Gopnik, *In the Memory Ward: The Warburg is Britain's most eccentric and original library. Can it survive?*, The New Yorker, Mar. 16, 2015.

[34] *See generally* UTC §1011 cmt. (available at <http://www.uniformlaws.org/Act.aspx?title=Trust%20Code>).

[35] Massachusetts courts, for example, have imposed liability on the owners of the shares of beneficial interests in nominee trusts, particularly when real estate is involved. In response, the owner of shares of beneficial interest in a nominee trust that contains Massachusetts business real estate may want to transfer those shares into a LLP or LLC in exchange for legal interests in the limited liability entity of equivalent economic value.

[36] *Cf.* Charles E. Rounds, Jr. & István Illés, *Is a Hungarian Trust a Clone of the Anglo-American Trust, or Just a Type of Contract?: Parsing the Asset-Management Provisions of the New Hungarian Civil Code*, 6 Geo. Mason J. Int'l Com. L. 153 (2015).

protean as the trust relationship. For the reasons why, the reader is referred to Section 8.12.1 of this handbook.

As a means of facilitating investment management services in the commercial context, the trust also is superior to the other fundamental legal relationships. Having full decision-making power over the trust property, the trustee can exclude from it anybody in the world including the beneficiary.[37] "This is particularly important in the business world where quick, reliable, unimpaired decision making is per se an important asset that an agent, in principle, does not enjoy but that the trustee does."[38] On the other hand, the U.S. and U.K. trust-based mutual fund models are more investor-friendly than their civil law counterparts on the Continent, in large part due to the expansive and free-ranging nature of the common law fiduciary relationship.[39]

Also important is that whereas the creditors of a contract promisor, *e.g.*, the creditors of an insurance company, will have access to the economic interest which is the subject of the contract, the creditors of the trustee, *e.g.*, the creditors of a mutual fund trustee, will not have access to the subject matter of the trust.[40] Nothing beats the trust when it comes to *securitizing* a collection of assets or *securing* a collection of assets against the claims of certain classes of creditors. For more on such commercial applications of the Anglo-American trust relationship, the reader is referred to Charles E. Rounds, Jr.[41]

§8.23   How a Trust Can Facilitate Gifts to Minors

An outright and substantial gift of property to someone under the age of 18 might well bring with it a need for the judicial appointment of a guardian to administer the property. This is first and foremost because the minor lacks the capacity to contract and thus is prevented from transacting with others (*e.g.*, bankers and brokers) with respect to the property. The younger the minor, the

---

[37] Ugo Mattei, *Basic Issues of Private Law Codification in Europe: Trust*, 1 Global Jurist Frontiers, Issue 1, Article 5 (2001).

[38] Ugo Mattei, *Basic Issues of Private Law Codification in Europe: Trust*, 1 Global Jurist Frontiers, Issue 1, Article 5 (2001).

[39] *See generally* Charles E. Rounds, Jr. & Andreas Dehio, *Publicly-Traded Open End Mutual Funds in Common Law and Civil Law Jurisdictions: A Comparison of Legal Structures*, 3 N.Y.U.J.L. & Bus. 473 (2007).

[40] Ugo Mattei, *Basic Issues of Private Law Codification in Europe: Trust*, 1(1) Global Jurist Frontiers, Article 5 (2001). *See generally* Charles E. Rounds, Jr. & Andreas Dehio, *Publicly-Traded Open End Mutual Funds in Common Law and Civil Law Jurisdictions: A Comparison of Legal Structures*, 3 N.Y.U.J.L. & Bus. 473 (2007).

[41] *State Common Law Aspects of the Global Unwindings of the Madoff Ponzi Scheme and the Sub-Prime Mortgage Securitization Debacle*, 27 Wis. Int'l L.J. 99 (2009).

more he or she will lack as well the physical and mental capacity to properly handle the property.[1]

The trust can be a way around the property administration problem. A gift in trust allows legal title to pass to someone of full age and legal capacity who then can administer the property for the benefit of the minor in accordance with the wishes of the donor. The intervention of a trustee into the process, however, can bring with it gift tax complications: if the trust is designed in such a way that the minor does not receive a "present" interest in the property, *e.g.*, if the trust is a discretionary one,[2] then the donor runs a risk of losing the $14,000 per donee annual gift tax exclusion found in Code Section 2503(b).[3]

One way for a donor to "tie up" gifted property and still preserve the annual exclusion is to employ a "2503(c) Minor's Trust," the requirements of which are set forth in Section 9.17 of this handbook. Another way is to employ a "Crummey Trust," the requirements of which are set forth in Section 9.18 of this handbook. Neither trust, however, is without its drawbacks. The former requires that the "minor" possess at least a general inter vivos power of appointment over the trust property, *i.e.*, a termination right, upon obtaining age 21.[4] The latter requires that the minor possess a general inter vivos power of appointment over some portion of the annual gift (*i.e.*, withdrawal rights) for at least several weeks after title to the gifted property is transferred to the trustee.[5]

§8.24   Burdens of Proof; Standards of Proof

Where a trustee co-mingles funds of a cestui que trust with those of his own, the court will hold such trustee to a strict accountability and any doubt will be resolved against the trustee.[1]

Burdens of proof. *Proving the trust.* In an action for breach of an *express trust* brought by a beneficiary against the trustee, the beneficiary has the burden of proof.[2] That is the general rule. A titleholder, be it a trustee or someone else, is

---

§8.23   [1] *See generally* William H. Soskin, *Gifts to Minors After 2001: Minors' Trusts, Qualified Tuition Programs, Education IRAs and Custodial Accounts Compared*, 27 ACTEC L.J. 344 (2002); Bradley E.S. Fogel, *Billion Dollar Babies: Annual Exclusion Gifts to Minors*, 12 Prob. & Prop. 6 (No. 5, Sept./Oct. 1998).

[2] *See generally* §3.5.3.2(a) of this handbook (the discretionary trust).

[3] *See generally* §9.17 of this handbook (I.R.C. §2503(c) trusts for minors) and §9.18 of this handbook (the Crummey trust and the "5 and 5" limitation).

[4] Rev. Rul. 74-43, 1974-1 C.B. 285.

[5] *See* Estate of Cristofani v. Comm'r, 97 T.C. 74 (1991) (IRS declined to challenge a fifteen-day withdrawal period).

§8.24   [1] Kirby v. Frank, 132 N.J. Eq. 378, 379, 28 A.2d 267 (1942). *See generally* §6.2.1.2 of this handbook (duty to segregate and earmark trust property (duty not to commingle)).

[2] Neel v. Barnard, 24 Cal. 2d 406, 150 P.2d 177 (1944); Cleary v. Cleary, 427 Mass. 286, 692 N.E.2d 955 (1998).

entitled to the presumption of regularity and good faith.[3] The general rule, however, is moderated somewhat in two important situations: when the trustee of an express trust self-deals and when the trustee of an express trust fails to properly account.

The general rule is essentially turned on its head when it comes to the *resulting trust*.[4] In the case of the resulting trust, "there is an inference, which arises from the character of the transaction, that the person taking title to the property is not to have the beneficial interest."[5]

Unauthorized self-dealing (express trusts). In an action brought by the beneficiary against a trustee of an express trust for *unauthorized self-dealing*, the plaintiff still has the burden of proving the existence of the trust, the plaintiff's equitable or beneficial interest thereunder, and that the trustee has in fact engaged in unauthorized acts of self-dealing with the trust property.[6] In some jurisdictions, satisfaction of this burden alone is sufficient to establish liability.[7] This is an application of the so-called no-further-inquiry rule, an application which the Restatement (Third) of Trusts endorses.[8] In other jurisdictions, the burden of proof will then fall on the trustee to demonstrate that his actions were fair and reasonable under the circumstances.[9] In other words, the burden of

---

[3] Neel v. Barnard, 24 Cal. 2d 406, 150 P.2d 177 (1944); Cleary v. Cleary, 427 Mass. 286, 692 N.E.2d 955 (1998). *Cf.* Restatement (Third) of Property (Wills and Other Donative Transfers) §8.1 cmt. f (Tentative Draft No. 3, Apr. 4, 2001) (providing that the party contesting the validity of a trust has the burden of persuasion in establishing that the settlor lacked mental capacity to create the trust).

[4] *See generally* 6 Scott & Ascher §43.1. *See also* §3.3 of this handbook (the purchase money resulting trust) and §4.1.1.1 of this handbook (the resulting trust).

[5] 6 Scott & Ascher §40.1.1. *See also* §8.15.6 of this handbook (parol evidence rule) and §8.15.5 of this handbook (statute of frauds).

[6] *See generally* Bogert §50; §6.1.3 of this handbook (duty to be loyal to the trust).

[7] *See generally* Bogert §543.

[8] *See generally* Estate of Rothko, 43 N.Y.2d 305, 372 N.E.2d 291 (1977) (involving an application of the no-further-inquiry rule). *See also* UTC §802(b) (available at <http://www.uniformlaws.org/Act.aspx?title=Trust%20Code>) (adopting no-further-inquiry rule for substantial conflicts of interest); Restatement (Third) of Trusts §100 cmt. f (the Reporter's Notes to cmt. f listing this handbook as an authority on the burden of proof in trust litigation).

[9] *See, e.g.,* Zink v. Carlile, 248 P.3d 306 (Colo. 1952). *See generally* Bogert §543; Restatement of Restitution §191 cmt. a (burden of proof as to informed consent to fiduciary self-dealing) & cmt. e (where transaction is not fair and reasonable). *See also* UTC §802(c) (available at <http://www.uniformlaws.org/Act.aspx?title=Trust%20Code>) (providing that a transaction involving the investment or management of trust property is *presumed* to be affected by a conflict between personal and fiduciary interests if it involves a sale, encumbrance, or other transaction concerning the trust property entered into by the trustee with the spouse of the trustee; the trustee's descendants, siblings, parents, or their spouses; an agent or attorney of the trustee; or a corporation or other person or enterprise in which the trustee, or a person that owns a significant interest in the trustee, has an interest that might affect the trustee's best judgment); UTC §1008(b) (providing that the burden of proof rests with attorney-trustee to show insertion of exculpatory clause not an abuse of confidential relationship). An agent who benefits from a transaction with his principal also has the burden of proving that the transaction was not the result of fraud or undue influence. *See* Cleary v. Cleary, 427 Mass. 286, 692 N.E.2d 955 (1998).

proof is on the trustee "to show that he . . . has not taken advantage of the fiduciary relationship."[10]

In cases where the beneficiary has conveyed his or her equitable interest to the trustee, the burden is on the trustee to prove that the trustee acted in good faith; that the transaction was fair and reasonable;[11] and that the beneficiary having been apprised of all relevant and material facts[12] gave his or her informed consent to the fiduciary self-dealing.[13] The subject of beneficiary consent to trustee self-dealing is generally taken up in Section 7.1 of this handbook.

The Uniform Trust Code embraces the no-further-inquiry rule by making transactions involving trust property entered into by a trustee for the trustee's own personal account voidable without further proof.[14] "The rule is less severe with respect to transactions involving trust property entered into with persons who have close business or personal ties with the trustee."[15] A transaction between a trustee and business associate is presumptively voidable, not void.[16]

It should be kept in mind, however, that there is such a thing as an authorized act of self-dealing. "[N]o breach of the duty of loyalty occurs if the transaction was authorized by the terms of the trust or approved by the court, of if the beneficiary failed to commence a judicial proceeding within the time allowed or chose to ratify the transaction, either prior to or subsequent to its occurrence."[17]

The failure to account (express trusts). All doubts are resolved against a trustee who maintains an inadequate accounting system.[18] In an action brought by the beneficiary against a trustee of an express trust for *failure to properly account*, it is true that the plaintiff has the burden of proving the existence of the trust and

---

[10] 3 Scott & Ascher §17.2.1; Restatement of Restitution §191 cmt. b ("Thus, if a trustee purchases for himself trust property with the consent of the beneficiary who has just come of age, or who is an aged person who has lost his capacity for exercising judgment, or a person wholly unfamiliar with business affairs, the transaction may be set aside") and cmt. d ("Thus, the transaction can be set aside where the fiduciary over-persuades the beneficiary, even though he is not guilty of fraud, duress, or of conduct which would justify setting aside the transaction for undue influence if he were not a fiduciary").

[11] Restatement of Restitution §191 cmt. e (where transaction is not fair and reasonable).

[12] *See generally* Bogert §188; Restatement of Restitution §191(2)(b).

[13] Restatement of Restitution §191 cmt. a (trustee has burden of proving informed consent).

[14] UTC§802 cmt. (available at <http://www.uniformlaws.org/Act.aspx?title=Trust%20 Code>). "The right of a beneficiary to void a transaction affected by a conflict of interest is optional." UTC §802 cmt. "If the transaction proves profitable to the trust and unprofitable to the trustee, the beneficiary will likely allow the transaction to stand." UTC §802 cmt.

[15] UTC §802 cmt. (available at <http://www.uniformlaws.org/Act.aspx?title=Trust%20 Code>). *See generally* 12 C.F.R. §9.12(a) ("Reg. 9") (available at <www.gpoaccess.gov/cfr/ index.html>) (requiring national banks to avoid self-dealing and conflicts of interest when investing the funds of their fiduciary accounts).

[16] UTC §802 cmt. (available at <http://www.uniformlaws.org/Act.aspx?title=Trust%20 Code>).

[17] UTC §802 cmt. (available at <http://www.uniformlaws.org/Act.aspx?title=Trust%20 Code>). *See generally* 3 Scott & Ascher §17.2.

[18] *See* Jimenez v. Lee, 547 P.2d 126 (Or. 1976).

that the plaintiff has an interest thereunder that would entitle him to an accounting.[19] The burden, however, then falls on the trustee to prove that the information in the accountings is sufficiently accurate and complete to enable the beneficiary to protect and defend the equitable or beneficial interest.[20] After all, "[t]he trustee alone is in a position to know all the facts concerning the administration of the trust, and obviously he cannot be permitted to gain any possible advantage from his failure to keep proper records."[21] Thus, a trustee who fails to keep a regular account of his legitimate expenses puts at risk his right to be indemnified from the trust estate.[22] Still, for a trustee in a given situation to be surcharged for failing to properly account, the beneficiary's equitable interests somehow must have been harmed by the actions of the trustee *and* there must have been some direct or indirect nexus between the harm and the failure to properly account.[23]

It is the substance of the information, however, not the format in which it is presented, that is critical. Once the trustee makes out a prima facie case that the beneficiary has been furnished with all the information needed to protect the equitable or beneficial interest, the burden then falls on the beneficiary to supply contradictory evidence.[24] All doubts, however, should be resolved in the beneficiary's favor.[25] The Restatement (Third) of Trusts is in accord in this regard.[26]

Take as an example a beneficiary who files an action against the trustee in which it is alleged that a particular accounting of the trustee is incorrect: The market value of the trust estate should be reflected as $10.5 million, not $10 million. The trustee answers that $10 million is the correct value, that $500,000 was used to satisfy a federal tax obligation. During the discovery phase, the trustee furnishes the beneficiary through counsel a copy of the tax return with

---

[19] *See generally* Bogert §970. *See also* §7.2 of this handbook (trustee's liability as fiduciary to the beneficiary).

[20] *See* §6.1.5.1 of this handbook (trustee's duty to provide information); UTC §810 cmt. (available at <http://www.uniformlaws.org/Act.aspx?title=Trust%20Code>) (noting that implicit in the duty to report to beneficiaries is the duty to keep adequate records).

[21] 2A Scott on Trusts §172.

[22] Lewin ¶ 21-29; 3 Scott & Ascher §17.4 (noting that "[a]ny expenses and costs that arise as a result of the trustee's failure to keep proper accounts are chargeable against the trustee personally, rather than against the trust estate"). *See generally* §3.5.2.3 of this handbook (Right in Equity to Indemnity (Exoneration and Reimbursement)).

[23] *See, e.g.,* O'Riley v. U.S. Bank, N.A., 412 S.W.3d 400, 412 (Mo. Ct. App. 2013) ("In fact, Beneficiaries' own trust expert, Professor David English, conceded that he could not identify damages from the failure to provide account statements.").

[24] *See generally* Bogert §970; Restatement (Third) of Trusts §100 cmt. f (Reporter's Notes thereto).

[25] 3 Scott & Ascher §17.4; 2A Scott on Trusts §172. *See, e.g.,* In re Testamentary Trust of Flynn, Slip Copy, 2005 WL 1846520 (Ohio App. 2 Dist.), 2005-Ohio-4028 (in affirming the lower court's decision to reduce for excessiveness the attorney-trustee's compensation, the appellate court resolved its doubts against the attorney-trustee observing that it should be the responsibility of the attorney-trustee, not the Court or the trial court, to sort out what services she had been performing as a trustee and what services as attorney).

[26] Restatement (Third) of Trusts §100 cmt. f (the Reporter's Notes to cmt. f listing this handbook as an authority on the burden of proof in trust litigation).

all schedules. By so doing, the trustee has made out a prima facie case that the accounting is accurate and complete as supplemented. The burden then shifts to the beneficiary to prove that the tax was miscalculated, or not owed.

It should be noted that while it may turn out that the trustee was not in breach of trust in the payment of the tax and the preparation of the accounting, the trustee could still be held in breach of trust for allowing things to get out of hand, and held personally liable for the associated costs. A beneficiary should not have to commence litigation to extract from the trustee a tax return that pertains to the beneficiary's equitable interest.

Trustee-drafted exculpatory clauses. The Restatement (Third) of Trusts provides as follows: "[A]n exculpatory clause drafted (or caused to be included in the trust instrument) by the trustee is presumptively unenforceable, with the trustee having the burden of rebutting the presumption."[27] Exculpatory clauses in trust instruments are covered generally in Section 7.2.6 of this handbook.

The inadequately diversified trust portfolio. The Restatement (Third) of Trusts places the burden on the beneficiary to prove that the trust portfolio has suffered a loss in economic value and that the loss was occasioned by a failure on the part of the trustee to diversify the portfolio. No new ground is broken here. According to Comment f. of Section 100 of the Restatement, however, the burden of proof then shifts onto the shoulders of the trustee to prove "the existence of an exception to the normal duty to diversify." As authority for this burden-shifting, the comment cites to Section 90 of the Restatement, the section that sets forth the Prudent Investor Rule, specifically Section 90(b). Here is the text: "In making and implementing investment decisions, the trustee has a duty to diversify the investments of the trust unless, under the circumstances, it is prudent not to do so." It is not self-evident that Section 90(b) is speaking to burdens of proof. That having been said, if an exception to the duty to diversify is functionally a defense to a failure-to-diversify allegation, then perhaps it is doing so implicitly.

Absence of causation. The beneficiary generally has the burden of proving that there has been a breach of trust and that a "related" loss has occurred.[28] The burden of proof then shifts to the trustee to prove "that the loss would have occurred in the absence of the breach."[29]

The resulting trust (failed trusts and fully performed trusts with outstanding account balances). As we have noted, in the case of an express trust the burden is on the beneficiary who is alleging a breach of trust to prove that there had been an intention to impress a trust upon the subject property in the first place. On the other hand, "[w]hen the circumstances are such as to give rise to a resulting trust, it is unnecessary for the person seeking to recover the property to prove that a trust was intended, since the inference that arises from the circumstances,

---

[27] Restatement (Third) of Trusts §100 cmt. f (referring to Restatement (Third) of Trusts §96 cmt. d).

[28] Restatement (Third) of Trusts §100 cmt. f.

[29] Restatement (Third) of Trusts §100 cmt. f.

until rebutted, suffices to justify recovery."[30] We cover the resulting trust in Section 4.1.1.1 of this handbook.

The purchase money resulting trust. So also with the purchase money resulting trust, a sort of express trust/resulting trust hybrid, which we take up in Section 3.3 of this handbook.[31] A transferee of property for which a third party rather than the transferor has paid the purchase price is presumed to hold it upon a purchase money-resulting trust for the third party.[32] Thus the payor's only initial burden is to prove that he or she has actually paid the purchase price.[33] The evidence must be clear and convincing.[34] It then falls to the transferee, assuming the transferee wishes to retain the property, to prove that the payor intended to make an outright gift of the property to the transferee.[35] If that burden cannot be met, then the court will order the transferee to convey the legal title to the payor outright and free of trust, unless, in reliance on what was ostensibly a gift, the transferee has so changed position that it would be inequitable to compel the transferee to surrender the property.[36] "But if there is evidence that tends to show that the payor intended to make a gift or loan, the ultimate burden of proof is on the payor to establish a claim to a resulting trust, by showing that the payor intended to obtain the beneficial interest in the property, and not to make a gift or a loan to the grantee."[37] Again, the evidence must be clear and convincing.[38] When the grantee pays the purchase price as a loan to a third party, a purchase money resulting trust may be imposed on the property for the benefit of the third party. The burden, however, is on the third party to prove that a loan was intended.[39]

A conveyance to a close relative of the payor raises an inference that an outright gift was intended, particularly if the transferee is a natural object of the payor's bounty.[40] If one spouse buys a home and takes title in the name of the other, or in both jointly as tenants by the entireties or otherwise, then there is a rebuttable presumption that a gift has been made of all or a portion of the property such that no purchase-money resulting trust arises in favor of the payor spouse.[41]

---

[30] 6 Scott & Ascher §40.3. *See generally* §4.1.1.1 of this handbook (defining and discussing the resulting trust). *See also* 6 Scott & Ascher §43.1.

[31] *See also* 6 Scott & Ascher §43.1.

[32] 6 Scott & Ascher §43.1. In this case, the transferor is merely a vendor. 6 Scott & Ascher §43.1.

[33] 6 Scott & Ascher §§43.1, 43.12 (Burden of Proof).

[34] 6 Scott & Ascher §43.12 (Burden of Proof).

[35] 6 Scott & Ascher §§43.1, 43.2 (Rebutting the Purchase Money Resulting Trust), 43.12 (Burden of Proof).

[36] 6 Scott & Ascher §43.1.

[37] 6 Scott & Ascher §43.12 (Burden of Proof).

[38] *See generally* 6 Scott & Ascher §43.12 (Burden of Proof). *But see* Restatement (Third) of Trusts §9 cmt. f(1) (preponderance of evidence).

[39] 6 Scott & Ascher §43.12 (Burden of Proof).

[40] 6 Scott & Ascher §§34.12 (Burden of Proof), 43.2 (Rebutting the Purchase Money Resulting Trust).

[41] *See generally* 6 Scott & Ascher §43.11(Marital Home and Family Assets).

The good-faith purchaser for value (BFP). In litigation over whether one who takes trust property from a trustee is entitled to BFP status, there is a split of authority on the question of whether the burden of proof is on the transferee to prove that the transferee is a BFP, or on the beneficiary to prove that the transferee is not.[42]

Standards of proof. *Generally.* The Uniform Probate Code has no blanket standard of proof for contested trust matters. Massachusetts, however, has added a section to its version of the Code which provides that in contested matters generally, the standard of proof is a preponderance of evidence.[43] Under Ohio law, on the other hand, the standard of proof for breach of fiduciary duty claims in the trust context is clear and convincing evidence.[44]

Exercise of powers of appointment. Under the Uniform Probate Code, a blanket-exercise clause in the will of the donee (holder) of a testamentary power of appointment, whether the power is general or nongeneral, will effect its exercise.[45] "If a governing instrument creating a power of appointment expressly requires that the power be exercised by a reference, an express reference, or a specific reference, to the power or its source, it is presumed that the donor's intention, in requiring that the donee exercise the power by making reference to the particular power or to the creating instrument, was to prevent an inadvertent exercise of the power."[46] Thus, if there is clear and convincing extrinsic evidence that the purpose of a blanket-exercise clause, at least in part, was to exercise a particular power that has a specific-reference requirement associated with it, then the blanket-exercise clause might well serve to exercise the power, unless the presumption as to the limited purpose of the requirement, namely, just to avoid inadvertent exercise, is overcome.[47] The subject of powers of appointment is generally covered in Section 8.1.1 of this handbook.

Proving fact of death. Under the Uniform Probate Code, a certified or authenticated copy of a death certificate purportedly issued by an official or agency of the place where the death purportedly occurred is prima facie evidence of the identity of the decedent and the fact of his or her death.[48] It also is prima facie evidence of the place, date, and time of death.[49] A certified or authenticated copy of any record or report of a governmental agency, domestic or foreign, that an individual has died is prima facie evidence of that fact, as well as of any circumstances surrounding the event that are disclosed by the record or report.[50] Otherwise, the fact of death must be established by clear and

---

[42] 5 Scott & Ascher §29.1.1.

[43] Mass. Gen. Laws ch. 190B, §1-109.

[44] *See* Newcomer v. National City Bank, 19 N.E.3d 492, 503 (Ohio 2014).

[45] UPC §2-608 cmt.

[46] UPC §2-704.

[47] UPC §2-704 cmt.

[48] UPC §1-107(2).

[49] UPC §1-107(2).

[50] UPC §1-107(3).

convincing evidence, which may include circumstantial evidence.[51] An undisputed entry on one of the aforementioned official documents of a time of death that is 120 hours or more after the time when another person was purported to have died establishes clear and convincing that there has been compliance with the Code's 120-hour survivorship requirement, no matter how the other person's time of death was determined.[52] A beneficiary who has been missing without a trace and for no apparent reason for a continuous period of five years is *presumed* dead, providing there has been a diligent good faith inquiry into the circumstances surrounding the beneficiary's absence that has turned up nothing.[53]

Homicide. The Restatement of Property provides that a remainder beneficiary whose interest is contingent upon surviving the current beneficiary forfeits the equitable interest if he or she murders the current beneficiary.[54] So too would the beneficiary who murders the holder of a right of revocation.[55] The Uniform Probate Code is in accord. It provides that the felonious and intentional killing of the settlor of a *revocable* trust, whether or not the killing results in a criminal conviction, extinguishes any provisions in the trust for the benefit of the killer, any powers of appointment granted to the killer, and any present or future role fiduciary role the killer might have in the administration of the trust.[56] Likewise for any testamentary trust created under the victim's will.[57] The killer is deemed to have disclaimed all beneficial interests and powers, and, in the case of any fiduciary roles, to have predeceased the settlor.[58] The equitable principle that a wrongdoer may not profit by his or her own wrong is a civil one,[59] although the killer may pass good title to a good-faith purchaser for value (BFP).[60] Thus a court of equity, such as the probate court, is perfectly competent to adjudicate whether a killer may be allowed to succeed to the property of his or her victim.[61] "In the absence of a conviction, the court, upon the petition of an interested person, must determine whether, under the preponderance of evidence standard, the individual would be found criminally accountable for the felonious and intentional killing of the decedent."[62]

---

[51] UPC §1-107(4).

[52] UPC §1-107(6). *See generally* §8.15.56 (the 120-hour survivorship requirement).

[53] UPC §1-107(5). "His [or her] death is presumed to have occurred at the end of the period unless there is sufficient evidence for determining that death occurred earlier." UPC §1-107(5). *See generally* §5.5 of this handbook (missing beneficiaries).

[54] Restatement (Third) of Property (Wills and Other Donative Transfers) §8.4 cmt. n, illus. 9.

[55] Restatement (Third) of Property (Wills and Other Donative Transfers) cmt. k, illus. 2.

[56] UPC §2-803(c)(1).

[57] UPC §2-803(c)(1).

[58] UPC §2-803(e). *See generally* §8.15.55 of this handbook (lapse and antilapse).

[59] UPC §2-803 cmt.

[60] UPC §2-803(i). *See generally* §8.15.63 of this handbook (the BFP).

[61] UPC §2-803 cmt.

[62] UPC §2-803(g).

Trust reformation actions. A scrivener's material mistake is grounds for reformation of a trust, provided the extrinsic evidence of the intended disposition is clear and convincing.[63] As a general rule, when a settlor creates a trust in *exchange for consideration*, the fact that the settlor did so by mistake is not grounds for reformation of the terms of the trust.[64] If, however, consideration is not involved, a material mistake as to the law or the facts that induced the settlor to create the trust is grounds for reformation,[65] whether or not the governing instrument is ambiguous.[66] This would include a material mistake as to the tax consequences of establishing the trust, a topic we cover in Section 8.17 of this handbook.[67]

§8.25 Few American Law Schools Still Require Agency, Trusts, and Equity

The common law of agency has not always attracted the degree of academic interest that's warranted by its ubiquity, as well as its theoretical interest and practical significance.[1]

In other words, do we still know what a trust is and will we still have trusts as we know them in the twenty-first century?[2]

---

[63] Restatement (Third) of Trusts §62 cmt. b; UTC §415 (available at <http://www.uniformlaws.org/Act.aspx?title=Trust%20Code>). *See, e.g.*, In re Estate of Tuthill, 754 A.2d 272 (D.C. 2000) (confirming that a scrivener's mistake is a valid ground for reformation provided the mistake is proved by full, clear, and decisive evidence). *See also* Wennett v. Ross, 439 Mass. 1003, 786 N.E.2d 336 (2003) (reforming an irrevocable life insurance trust to correct an alleged scrivener's error); Colt v. Colt, 438 Mass. 1001, 777 N.E.2d 1235 (2002) (in part reforming a trust so that certain transfers will qualify for the generation-skipping transfer tax exemption, the court deeming the insertion of a general power of appointment to be a scrivener's error).

[64] Restatement (Third) of Trusts §62 cmt. a; 4 Scott on Trusts §333.4; Restatement (Second) of Trusts §333.

[65] *See* Restatement (Third) of Trusts §62; 1 Scott & Ascher §4.6.3; UTC §414 cmt. (available at <http://www.uniformlaws.org/Act.aspx?title=Trust%20Code>) (suggesting that "[i]n determining the settlor's original intent, the court may consider evidence relevant to the settlor's intention even though it contradicts an apparent plain meaning of the text"). "The objective of the plain meaning rule, to protect against fraudulent testimony, is satisfied by the requirement of clean and convincing proof." UTC §414 cmt. *See, however,* §8.15.6 of this handbook (parol evidence rule). *See generally* §9.4.3 of this handbook (*Cy Pres*).

[66] Restatement (Third) of Trusts §62 cmt. b.

[67] *See, e.g.*, UTC §416 (available at <http://www.uniformlaws.org/Act.aspx?title=Trust%20Code>) (providing that to achieve the settlor's tax objectives, the court may modify the terms of a trust in a manner that is not contrary to the settlor's probable intention). *See also* Restatement (Third) of Property (Wills and Other Donative Transfers) §12.2.

§8.25 [1] Deborah A. DeMott, Disloyal Agents, 58 Ala. L. Rev. 1049, 1067 (2007).

[2] Joel C. Dobris, *Changes in the Role and the Form of the Trust at the New Millennium, or, We Don't Have to Think of England Anymore*, 62 Alb. L. Rev. 543, 544 (1998).

Many major law schools have stopped teaching estate planning. Few law students find the field interesting anymore, says [Prof.] Langbein.[3]

Agency, contracts, torts, property (legal interests), and trusts are facets of the same gem. Each offers a perspective of the Anglo-American common law, *as broadly defined to include equity's substantive embellishments.*[4] Together, they make up the law's periodic table. Statutes either fill gaps in the common law (*e.g.*, the will and the corporation), modify the common law (*e.g.*, the health care proxy), or embellish the common law (*e.g.*, the tax-qualified employee benefit plan). The Investment Company Act of 1940, for example, was written by lawyers who were clearly well versed in the common law and who presumed that their successors would be as well.[5]

The civil law jurisdictions generally have not developed a trust regime of the type that is the subject of this handbook, a trust being a creature of equity.[6] This occasioned Prof. Maitland to muse on how a complete English lawyer would likely react upon first encountering the Civil Code of Germany:

> "This," he would say, "seems a very admirable piece of work, worthy in every way of the high reputation of German jurists. But surely it is not a complete statement of German private law. Surely there is a large gap in it. I have looked for the Trust, but I cannot find it; and to omit the Trust is, I should have thought, almost as bad as to omit Contract."[7]

The common law trustee who retains a lawyer with no formal instruction in some of these fundamental legal relationships (*e.g.*, the equity-focused relationships of agency and trust) needs to be extra vigilant. If the trustee's imprudent selection of counsel should cause economic harm to the trust, it is the trustee who first and foremost would be on the hook.[8] On the other hand, "if a trustee has selected trust counsel prudently and in good faith, and has relied on plausible advice on a matter within counsel's expertise, the trustee's conduct is significantly probative of prudence."[9]

As noted, the common law legal relationships cannot be viewed in isolation. By way of example, contractual rights, such as incident to a life insurance policy, are property rights that may be the subject of a trust. Likewise, some

---

[3] John J. Fialka, Wall St. J., July 9, 2004, at A1.

[4] "Equity without common law would have been a castle in the air, an impossibility." Frederic William Maitland, Equity: Also the Forms of Action at Common Law 19 (Cambridge University Press, 1909).

[5] *See generally* Charles E. Rounds, Jr. & Andreas Dehio, *Publicly-Traded Open End Mutual Funds in Common Law and Civil Law Jurisdictions: A Comparison of Legal Structures*, 3 N.Y.U.J.L. & Bus. 473 (2007).

[6] *See generally* Charles E. Rounds, Jr. & Andreas Dehio, *Publicly-Traded Open End Mutual Funds in Common Law and Civil Law Jurisdictions: A Comparison of Legal Structures*, 3 N.Y.U.J.L. & Bus. 473 (2007); §8.12.1 of this handbook (civil law alternatives to the trust).

[7] Maitland, Selected Essays 142–143 (1936).

[8] *See generally* §8.32 of this handbook (whether the trustee can escape liability for making a mistake of law if he acted in good faith on advice of counsel).

[9] Restatement (Third) of Trusts §77 cmt. b(2).

equitable interests under trusts, such as shares of a mutual fund, are interests in property that may be the subject of a contract or an agency. Even the legal structure of the modern American mutual fund we owe to the trial and error of creative common law lawyers practicing in the first half of the twentieth century, particularly in Massachusetts.[10] Their media were common law legal relationships, namely the agency, the contract, the trust, and to some extent the statutory corporation.[11] Or take a transfer for the benefit of creditors. Professors Scott and Ascher remind us that "[w]hen a debtor delivers money or other property to a third person with instructions to pay a particular creditor, the relationship that arises may be a contract for the benefit of the creditor, an agency for the debtor, or a trust."[12] The opportunities for flexible and advantageous interplays between law and equity are limitless. In any case, most matters, whether transactional or adversarial, will implicate equity in some way.[13] A course in contracts does not a complete lawyer make.[14]

To avoid a legal misdiagnosis, trust counsel needs to know the common law, not about the common law. "One need only consider the term 'corporation' in the . . . [Investment Company Act of 1940's] . . . short title, a choice of words guaranteed to confuse lawyers on both sides of the Atlantic who are not well versed in the common law."[15] This is because in the United States, as well as in the United Kingdom, an incorporated mutual fund is actually a trust.[16]

Although trust concepts are marbled throughout the common law, Stanford and Harvard in the early 1960s each made an institutional determination that to be a lawyer it was no longer *necessary* that one know the law of Trusts—to pass the bar, perhaps, but not to be a complete lawyer.[17] Since then, most of the other 186 or so ABA-approved law schools have followed suit. Current reform initiatives aimed at "globalizing" the American law school curriculum are only

---

[10] *See generally* Charles E. Rounds, Jr. & Andreas Dehio, *Publicly-Traded Open End Mutual Funds in Common Law and Civil Law Jurisdictions: A Comparison of Legal Structures*, 3 N.Y.U.J.L. & Bus. 473 (2007).

[11] *See generally* Charles E. Rounds, Jr. & Andreas Dehio, *Publicly-Traded Open End Mutual Funds in Common Law and Civil Law Jurisdictions: A Comparison of Legal Structures*, 3 N.Y.U.J.L. & Bus. 473 (2007).

[12] 5 Scott & Ascher §35.1.9 (Trust for Particular Creditor).

[13] *See, e.g.,* Charles E. Rounds, Jr., *Proponents of Extracting Slavery Reparations from Private Interests Must Contend with Equity's Maxims*, 42 U. Tol. L. Rev. 673 (2011).

[14] *See generally* Charles E. Rounds, Jr., *The Common Law Is Not Just About Contracts: How Legal Education Has Been Short-Changing Feminism*, 43 U. Rich. L. Rev. 1185 (2009).

[15] *See generally* Charles E. Rounds, Jr. & Andreas Dehio, *Publicly-Traded Open End Mutual Funds in Common Law and Civil Law Jurisdictions: A Comparison of Legal Structures*, 3 N.Y.U.J.L. & Bus. 473 (2007).

[16] *See generally* Charles E. Rounds, Jr. & Andreas Dehio, *Publicly-Traded Open End Mutual Funds in Common Law and Civil Law Jurisdictions: A Comparison of Legal Structures*, 3 N.Y.U.J.L. & Bus. 473 (2007).

[17] *See generally* E. Gordon Gee & Donald W. Jackson, Following the Leader? The Unexamined Consensus in Law School Curricula 6, 14–15, 22–25, 47–48 (1975) (examining the "follow the leader" behavior of law school faculties and comparing core law school curricula in the 1950s, 1960s, and 1970s); William B. Powers, A.B.A., A Study of Contemporary Law School Curricula 12 (1986) (providing a catalog of courses that were typically required in law schools in the 1970s, which does not include discrete courses in the agency and the trust).

accelerating the process of marginalizing the core fiduciary relationships within the confines of the ivory tower,[18] notwithstanding the fact that the society without "is evolving into one based predominantly on fiduciary relations."[19] In 1964, Professor Warren A. Seavey speculated on why it was that agency was being marginalized in the American law schools:

> Agency has attracted very few writers. There are few law review articles and, aside from the Restatement, no very recent texts. Perhaps for this reason, it has been given diminishing attention in law schools; the time given to it now is far less than its intrinsic importance warrants, since practically all of the world's business involves agents and in most important transactions, an agent on each side. This in turn results in a poor understanding of its characteristic features.[20]

As to unjust enrichment as a principle of substantive liability, a topic that is covered in Section 8.15.78 of this handbook, all that critical doctrine fell through the cracks years ago with the introduction of the traditional Remedies course into the American law school curriculum.[21] The course was a pedagogical contraption of selected elements of the traditional Damages, Equity, and Restitution required courses.[22] Now even Remedies is elective, or no longer offered at all. It is no wonder that unjust enrichment doctrine is generally a mystery to contemporary American lawyers, and to contemporary law professors even more so.[23] "Much of the substantive law of equity—in particular, the law describing equitable interests in property held by another—suffered the same fate."[24]

Even the traditional required Property course has undergone some "shrinkage," although it is unlikely to suffer the same fate as the equity-based core courses.[25] Recall that a trust is a fiduciary relationship with respect to property. "For many decades, Property received six credits in most law schools—typically three in the Fall and three in the Winter semester of the first year. Now, few schools give the course more than four or five credits, and some have cut it to three."[26]

The trust is not just an estate planning vehicle for the rich. The role that the private trust plays in lubricating the American capital markets has come to eclipse in significance the traditional role it has played in facilitating intrafamily

---

[18] *See generally* Charles E. Rounds, Jr., *State Common Law Aspects of the Global Unwindings of the Madoff Ponzi Scheme and the Sub-Prime Mortgage Securitization Debacle: Buttressing the Thesis that Globalizing the American Law School Curriculum at the Expense of Instruction in Core Common Law Doctrine Will Only Further Provincialize It*, 27 Wis. Int'l L.J. 101 (2009).

[19] Tamar Frankel, *Fiduciary Law*, 71 Cal. L. Rev. 795, 798 (1983).

[20] Warren A. Seavey, Handbook of the Law of Agency IX (1964).

[21] Restatement (Third) of Restitution and Unjust Enrichment §1, Reporter's Note.

[22] Restatement (Third) of Restitution and Unjust Enrichment §1, Reporter's Note.

[23] Restatement (Third) of Restitution and Unjust Enrichment §1, Reporter's Note.

[24] Restatement (Third) of Restitution and Unjust Enrichment §1, Reporter's Note.

[25] *See generally* Dale A. Whitman, *Teaching Property—A Conceptual Approach*, 72 Mo. L. Rev. 1353 (2007).

[26] *See generally* Dale A. Whitman, *Teaching Property—A Conceptual Approach*, 72 Mo. L. Rev. 1353 (2007).

wealth transfers.[27] On April 28, 2001, even the Peoples' Republic of China jumped on the global trust bandwagon:[28] "According to Chinese drafters and scholars, the initial impetus for the legislation was the urgent need to promote China's accession to the World Trade Organization and to address China's financial sector by adopting 'an important pillar of the modern financing industry in developed countries,' the trust."[29]

In 2006, the Suffolk University Law School faculty voted 27–20, over the strenuous objections of the senior author, to downgrade formal instruction in the fiduciary aspects of agency and the fiduciary and property aspects of trusts from required to fully elective status.[30] The Equity course had already been purged from the required curriculum a decade or so before. That the core business of a law school is to turn out agent-fiduciaries carried little weight.

Back in 1908 when the American Bar Association adopted the original Canons of Professional Ethics, instruction in the core equity-based relationships of agency and trust, as well as the core law-based relationships of contract, tort, and property, was mandatory in most if not all the law schools. It most certainly never occurred to those who had been encouraging the bench and bar to endorse and adopt a lawyer code that by the end of the century instruction in the two private fiduciary relationships would no longer be required in most American law schools. Back then lawyer codes presumed a bench and bar that were thoroughly grounded in the common law, as the focus of such codifications was on licensure, the lawyer's relationship with the state. Licensure is still the focus of the typical lawyer code.[31] There has been no appreciable expansion in the scope and coverage of the Canons of Professional Ethics, or its successor codifications.[32] On the other hand, we have seen a considerable pedagogical undermining over time of the common law foundations upon which those regulatory edifices were and are constructed.

---

[27] *See* Henry Hansmann & Ugo Mattei, *The Functions of Trust Law: A Comparative Legal and Economic Analysis*, 73 N.Y.U.L. Rev., 434, 436 (1998).

[28] Xintuo Fa [Trust Law] (promulgated by the Standing Comm. Nat'l People's Cong., Apr. 28, 2001, effective Oct. 1, 2001).

[29] Frances H. Foster, *American Trust Law in a Chinese Mirror*, 94 Minn. L. Rev. 602, 639–640 (2010).

[30] For the various reasons that American law faculties have put forth for not requiring that their students take courses dedicated to the agency and trust relationships, particularly the fiduciary aspects of those relationships, the reader is referred to Charles E. Rounds, Jr., *The Case for a Return to Mandatory Instruction in the Fiduciary Aspects of Agency and Trusts in the American Law School, Together With a Model Fiduciary Relations Course Syllabus*, 18 Regent U. L. Rev. 251 (2005–2006).

[31] *See generally* Charles E. Rounds, Jr., *Lawyer Codes Are Just About Licensure, the Lawyer's Relationship with the State: Recalling the Common Law Agency, Contract, Tort, Trust,* and *Property Principles the Regulate the Lawyer-Client Fiduciary Relationship*, 60 Baylor L. Rev. 771 (2008).

[32] *See, e.g.*, In re Karavidas, 2013 IL 115767, 999 N.E.2d 296, 317 (Ill. 2013) ("Personal misconduct that falls outside the scope of the Rules of Professional Conduct may be the basis for civil liability or other adverse consequences, but will not result in professional discipline.").

For more on the marginalization of the fiduciary in the American legal academy, the reader is referred to Charles E. Rounds, Jr.[33]

§8.26 Why Trustees Need to Know About Will Residue Clauses

Now, Ahab and his three mates formed what may be called the first table in the Pequod's cabin. After their departure, taking place in inverted order to their arrival, the canvas cloth was cleared, or rather was restored to some hurried order by the pallid steward. And then the three harpooners were bidden to the feast, they being its residuary legatees. They made a sort of temporary servants' hall of the high and mighty cabin.—Ishmael[1]

"A residuary devise is a testamentary disposition of property of the testator's net probate estate not disposed of by a specific, general, or demonstrative devise."[2] In other words, it is a provision, usually of the *all the rest, residue and remainder of my estate* variety, that picks up probate property not otherwise dealt with in the will, including failed (lapsed) specific bequests and devises. Were it not for a residue clause, at least some portion of the testator's probate estate most likely would pass by intestacy. Why then is it necessary for the trustee to know about residue clauses?

The first reason is that a revocable inter vivos trust, together with an associated pour-over will, forms the core of most modern estate plans. The subject of pour-overs is covered elsewhere in this handbook.[3]

The second reason is that when a trust fails, the property to which the trustee has title could pass to the executor or administrator of the settlor's estate upon a resulting trust. Assuming the settlor's will provides that the residue of his or her probate estate shall be distributed to an individual or corporation other than the trustee of the failed trust, then most likely the property of the failed trust will follow the fortunes of the estate residue that went out at the time the will was probated. If the will provides that the residue shall pass to the trustee of the failed trust, then the property coming from the failed trust into the probate estate could pass by intestacy in the absence of an express alternate disposition. The subject of resulting trusts is covered elsewhere in this handbook.[4]

The third reason is that in a few jurisdictions, a general residue clause in the will of the holder of a general testamentary power of appointment can serve

---

[33] *The Case for a Return to Mandatory Instruction in the Fiduciary Aspects of Agency and Trusts in the American Law School, Together with a Model Fiduciary Relations Course Syllabus,* 18 Regent U. L. Rev. 251 (2005–2006).

§8.26 [1] Herman Melville, Moby-Dick, Ch. 34.

[2] Restatement (Third) of Property (Wills and Other Donative Transfers) §5.1 cmt. e.

[3] *See* §2.1.1 of this handbook (the inter vivos trust); §2.2.1 of this handbook (the pour-over statute); §8.15.9 of this handbook (doctrine of [facts or acts of] independent legal significance); and §8.15.17 of this handbook (the doctrine of incorporation by reference).

[4] *See* §4.1.1 of this handbook (the equitable reversionary interest).

to exercise the power in favor of the residuary takers, even when there is no express reference in the will to the power or how it is to be exercised, a topic we take up in Section 8.1.1 of this handbook.[5] This rule of construction at one time prevailed in Massachusetts.[6] Of course, the terms of the power itself can negate this result. They can provide that an exercise may only be effected by a provision in the will that makes specific reference to the power. At one time, Section 2-608 of the Uniform Probate Code provided that a general residuary clause in a will or a will making a general disposition of all of the testator's property did *not* exercise a power of appointment held by the testator, unless specific reference was made to the power or there was some other indication of intention to include the property subject to the power.[7] In 1990 the negative rule was made subject to several exceptions. One is that if a power is a general one and there is no gift over in default of its exercise, a general residuary clause or general disposition in the will of the donee (holder) of the power will serve to exercise it.[8]

The fourth reason is that in cases where the residue of the probate estate is made the subject of a trust, either by its transfer to the trustee of a testamentary trust or by a pour-over (*i.e.*, a transfer to the trustee of an inter vivos trust), the trustee must deal with the question of who is entitled to the income generated by the residue from the date of death to the date of funding. Should it be distributed to the trust's income beneficiaries or should it be credited to the trust's principal account? The matter of what to do with the income thrown off by the residue during the period of estate administration is covered elsewhere in this handbook.[9]

§8.27 The Difference Between a Legal and an Equitable Life Estate, Between a Legal and an Equitable Reversion, Between a Legal and an Equitable Springing Interest, and Between a Legal and an Equitable Shifting Interest

Where property is transferred for the benefit of two or more persons in succession, it is a question of the intention of the transferor whether the property is to be held in trust for them

---

[5] Of course, the testamentary power of appointment must have come into existence by the time the testator dies, which is the time when the will speaks. "An attempted exercise of a nonexistent power or a nonexercisable power cannot produce an appointment." Restatement (Second) of Property (Wills and Other Donative Transfers) §18.4 cmt. a.

[6] *See* Beals v. State St. Bank & Trust Co., 326 N.E.2d 896 (Mass. 1975).

[7] UPC §2-608 cmt.

[8] UPC §2-608 cmt.

[9] *See* §6.2.4.5 of this handbook (when does income begin and what happens to accrued but undistributed income when the trust's term expires or the beneficiary dies?).

or whether they take successive legal estates . . . Where a trust is created, the trustee may be the life beneficiary, or the remainderman, or a third person.[1]

An executory interest, therefore, may be defined, in the primary sense of the term, as a legal future interest created by means of an executed springing or shifting use.[2]

The life estate. A *legal* life estate arises when A, who owns Blackacre[3] in fee simple, transfers it to C for life and then to D and his heirs.[4] C's interest is called a possessory life estate.[5] D's interest is called a remainder in fee simple.[6] A trust is not involved in this hypothetical.[7]

An *equitable* life estate, on the other hand, arises when A transfers Blackacre to B in trust for C for life and then to D outright and free of trust.[8] Here a trust is involved. What, then, is the critical difference between the two life estates? In two words: legal title (to Blackacre). In the legal life estate situation, legal title is in C and D, those with the beneficial interests. In the equitable life estate situation, legal title is in B, the trustee. From this fundamental difference flow a number of consequences.

The owner of a legal life estate, for example, has a right to the undisturbed possession of Blackacre and to the income and profits therefrom.[9] He or she also owes certain duties to D, the remainderman, such as the duty to "preserve the land and structures in a reasonable state of repair."[10] Nor is D without recourse should the legal life tenant be in dereliction of his duties: "If the legal life tenant violates obligations to the remainder beneficiaries and thereby acquires a benefit or injures the remainder beneficiaries, the life tenant can be held liable in damages, can be required to permit the remainder beneficiaries to share in the benefits of the transaction, or can be made the trustee of a constructive trust for the benefit of the remainder beneficiaries."[11] The subject of constructive trusts is taken up in Section 3.3 of this handbook. On the other

---

§8.27 [1] Restatement (Second) of Trusts §16 C. *See also* Restatement (Third) of Trusts §5 cmt. b; Bogert §27.

[2] Cornelius J. Moynihan, Introduction to the Law of Real Property 187 (2d ed. 1988).

[3] Personal property as well as real property may be made the subject of a legal life estate, although such an arrangement has its impracticalities. *See, e.g.,* In the Matter of the Estate of Smith, 87 Misc. 2d 868, 386 N.Y.S.2d 755 (1976) (involving a legal life estate in General Electric stock which had never come into the possession of the life tenant, the certificates having been kept with the County Treasurer).

[4] For a discussion of the similarities and differences between the concept of the usufruct and the concept of the life estate, *see* Jeffrey A. Schoenblum, 1 Multistate and Multinational Estate Planning 1256–1257 (1999). *See generally* §8.12 of this handbook (where the trust is recognized outside the United States) (discussing civil law trust analogues, including the usufruct).

[5] Cornelius J. Moynihan, Introduction to the Law of Real Property 118 (2d ed. 1988).

[6] Cornelius J. Moynihan, Introduction to the Law of Real Property 118 (2d ed. 1988).

[7] *See generally* Bogert §27.

[8] *See generally* §8.15.65 of this handbook (destructibility of contingent remainders [the trust exemption]).

[9] Cornelius J. Moynihan, Introduction to the Law of Real Property 52 (2d ed. 1988).

[10] Moynihan, Introduction to the Law of Real Property at 54. *See also* Bogert §27.

[11] Bogert §27.

hand, the owner of a legal life estate who elects to improve the subject property cannot compel the legal remainderman to pay for the residual benefit the improvement confers, unless the legal life tenant had been obliged to improve the property "under circumstances not of his own choosing, or compelled to do so by government authority."[12]

To confuse matters, one court has indicated in some of its older decisions that he who possesses a legal life estate is in effect a trustee of the subject property.[13] That cannot be, however. "A legal life tenant and a legal remainder beneficiary have successive several interests in the same property. Trustee and beneficiary have simultaneous interests in the same property."[14] Thus, it cannot be said that a legal life tenant owes the remainderman any fiduciary duties.[15]

In our equitable hypothetical, it is said that while *B*, the trustee, has legal title to Blackacre itself, *C* has title to an equitable interest in Blackacre.[16] The rights, duties, and obligations of the life beneficiary under a trust are a central theme of this handbook.[17] Suffice it to say here that they are quite different from those of the owner of a legal life estate. The life or current beneficiary of a trust, for example, incurs no liabilities arising inherently out of ownership of the equitable interest, except for certain personal derivative income tax liabilities, and except of course in situations in which the beneficiary controls the trustee.[18] A personal trust under which the beneficiary is entitled to reside in an entrusted residence is a possible exception.[19] "It depends on the terms of the trust whether the trustee is under a duty, when the beneficiary is entitled to occupy trust property, to repair the premises and pay the taxes and other carrying charges."[20]

The legal life estate lacks a third party administrator. The legal life estate is not particularly well suited to situations where the parties are required to *do something* upon the happening of certain events. Take the devise of a legal life estate in Blackacre to *C* so that *C* may "live in" and "enjoy" the property. The remaindermen are *D1*, *D2*, and *D3*. *C* at any time prior to *C*'s death may sell the property and distribute the proceeds in equal shares among the three remaindermen. What if *C* chose not to live in the property but rent it out and pocket the proceeds? One court, faced with similar facts, found the terms of the legal life estate ambiguous such that extrinsic (parol) evidence on the grantor's intent was allowed in.[21] It held that *C*'s legal interest extinguished in favor of the

---

[12] Restatement (Third) of Restitution and Unjust Enrichment §30 cmt. b.

[13] In the Matter of Smith, 87 Misc. 2d 868, 877, 386 N.Y.S.2d 755, 761 (1976).

[14] Bogert §27.

[15] *See generally* Alford v. Thibault, 83 Mass. App. Ct. 822 (2013).

[16] Restatement (Second) of Trusts §2 cmt. d.

[17] *See, e.g.*, §3.5.1 of this handbook (nature and extent of the trustee's estate), §5.3.1 of this handbook (nature and extent of property interest), §5.4 of this handbook (rights of the beneficiary), and 5.6 of this handbook (duties and liabilities of the beneficiary).

[18] *See* §5.6 of this handbook (duties and liabilities of the beneficiary).

[19] *See* Chapter 1 of this handbook for a definition of the personal trust.

[20] 3 Scott & Ascher §13.2.6.

[21] *See* Garcia v. Celestron, 2 So. 3d 1061 (Fla. Ct. App. 3d Dist; 2009). *See generally* §8.15.6 of this handbook (the parol evidence rule).

designated remaindermen. Had Blackacre been put in the charge of a trustee and had there been a few well-chosen words of generalized guidance in the governing trust instrument as to how Blackacre should be administered for the benefit of the parties, including *C*, the equitable life tenant, then there would have been no need for a cumbersome spelling out of everyone's legal rights, duties, and obligations in every conceivable situation. The default law of trusts would have filled in the gaps. Of course, this all assumes that the trust would have had access to sufficient liquidity such that the real estate could be properly serviced and the fiduciary properly compensated.

The common law of waste is a poor substitute for equity's trust. The common law action for waste has evolved over time to protect the property interests of the legal remainderman as against the legal life tenant in possession, or at least to deter the life tenant from injuring the interest. Its origins can be traced as far back as 1278, the year the Statute of Gloucester was enacted.[22] That it falls to someone not in possession to somehow monitor the actions of someone who is makes the common law of waste somewhat of a paper tiger. If the legal remainderman has yet even to be conceived, there is virtually no deterrence value. Thus, the law of waste "has largely been supplanted by a more efficient method of administering property: the trust . . ."

> By placing property in trust, the grantor can split the beneficial interest as many ways as he pleases without worrying about the inefficiencies of divided ownership. The trustee will manage the property as a unit, maximizing its value and allocating the value among the trust's beneficiaries in the proportions desired by the grantor. Of course, the trustee has to be given the proper incentives to do this. Both carrot and stick are employed to this end. The trustee is compensated, but he is also placed under a duty (a "fiduciary" duty, as it is called) to administer the trust as if it were his own property and he had the same preferences, including attitude toward risk, as the beneficiaries of the trust are known or can be assumed to have.[23]

Adverse possession of the subject property by third parties. Whether a life estate is legal or equitable also has practical consequences when it comes to adverse possession. Take the third party who adversely takes possession of a parcel of real estate that is subject to an outstanding life estate. If the life estate is a legal

---

[22] *See generally* Sackett v. Sackett, 8 Pick. 309, 25 Mass. 309, 1829 WL 1865 (Mass. 1829) (containing a historical overview of the common law action for waste). The leading U.S. waste cases are Melms v. Pabst Brewing Co., 104 Wis. 7, 79 N.W. 738 (1899) (the legal life tenant held not liable for demolishing subject property, a mansion), and Brokaw v. Fairchild, 135 Misc. 70, 237 N.Y.S. 6 (1929), *aff'd* 231 App. Div. 704, 245 N.Y.S. 402 (1930), *aff'd* 256 N.Y. 670, 177 N.E. 186 (1931) (life tenant may not demolish subject property, a mansion). While few actions for waste are apparently being filed nowadays, the action by no means has gone extinct. *See, e.g.*, Matteson v. Walsh, 79 Mass. App. 402, 947 N.E.2d 44 (2011) (in part involving a failure on the part of the legal life tenant to pay real estate taxes). For a discussion of the particular jurisprudence of the American common law of waste, *see* Thomas W. Merrill, Melms v. Pabst Brewing Co.: *The Doctrine of Waste in American Property Law*, Marq. Law. 8 (Summer 2011).

[23] Richard A. Posner, *Comment on Merrill On the Law of Waste*, Marq. Law. 23 (Summer 2011) (suggesting at page 24 that the trust is a "more efficient way of dealing with the problem of conflicting interests in the same piece of property than the law of waste" in that the trust "establishes a neutral third party—the trustee—to arbitrate the parties' competing claims").

one, then the adverse possession statute of limitations will not begin to run against the remaindermen until the life tenant dies.[24] If the life estate is an equitable one, then the statute will begin to run directly against the title-holding trustee and indirectly against the trust beneficiaries, including any unborn or unascertained remaindermen, at the time possession is taken adversely by the third party.[25] Should the trustee be foreclosed by the running of the statute from ejecting the third party, the beneficiaries would likely be as well.[26] On the other hand, the beneficiaries would be entitled to obtain redress from the trustee personally in an equitable action, provided the loss of the property to the third party were attributable to a breach of trust.[27] Had the third party knowingly participated with the trustee in the breach of trust, then the adverse possessing third party might not be in the clear after all,[28] unless the trust beneficiaries themselves were guilty of laches.[29]

The reversion. The settlor of a trust retains a *legal reversion* if the transfer of legal title to the trustee is subject to a condition subsequent.[30] The settlor would then have a legal right of entry for condition broken.[31] A legal reversion also could be triggered if the trustee's legal title is subject to a contingency-based limitation, such as "until a designated event occurs or so long as a certain state of affairs continues," and the event occurs or the state of affairs ceases.[32]

The settlor retains an *equitable reversion* if the transfer of legal title to the trustee is in fee simple absolute but the equitable interest is subject to a condition subsequent.[33] In the event the condition is breached, the settlor, or the settlor's personal representative if the settlor is then deceased, could then seek to have the court impose a resulting trust upon the property for the benefit of the settlor or the settlor's probate estate.[34] So also if the equitable interest is subject to a contingency-based limitation that has matured.[35] For more on the vested equitable reversionary interest and the resulting trust, see Section 4.1.1.1 of this handbook.

Springing and shifting interests in land. Generally speaking, a springing property interest in land is one which cuts short an estate in the creator of the

---

[24] 5 Scott & Ascher §31.1.1.

[25] *See generally* 5 Scott & Ascher §31.1.1 (Persons Acting Adversely to Trustee); §3.6 of this handbook (external in-bound liabilities of third parties to the trustee and the beneficiaries).

[26] *See* 5 Scott & Ascher §31.1.1.

[27] *See generally* §6.2.1.3 of this handbook (trustee's duty to protect and preserve the trust property). *See also* §7.1.3 of this handbook ([trustee's] defense of failure of beneficiary to take timely action against trustee) and §7.1.4 of this handbook ([trustee's] defense of consent, release, ratification, or affirmance by the beneficiary).

[28] 5 Scott & Ascher §31.1 (Rights of Beneficiaries When Trustee Is Barred by Laches or Statute of Limitations).

[29] 5 Scott & Ascher §31.1.2.

[30] 6 Scott & Ascher §39.7.2 (Conditions Subsequent).

[31] 6 Scott & Ascher §39.7.2 (Conditions Subsequent).

[32] 6 Scott & Ascher §39.7.3 (Limitations).

[33] 6 Scott & Ascher §39.7.2 (Conditions Subsequent).

[34] 6 Scott & Ascher §39.7.2 (Conditions Subsequent).

[35] 6 Scott & Ascher §39.7.3 (Limitations).

springing interest. A shifting property interest in land, on the other hand, cuts short an estate in a person other than the creator of the shifting interest. There are legal springing and shifting interests and there are equitable springing and shifting interests. How legal springing and equitable interests differ from their equitable counterparts is taken up in Section 8.15.80 of this handbook.

Estates in personalty. The trust is particularly suited to creating life estates, remainders, and other such limitations in personal property (chattels personal). In Appendix F of his treatise, The Rule Against Perpetuities,[36] Prof. John Chipman Gray discusses the profound obscurity of that corner of the common law that is reserved for legal future interests in chattels personal. There is also the perplexing practical issue of how to safeguard a legal remainder interest in a movable chattel personal while physical possession is in the legal life tenant. Both as a legal matter and as a practical matter, vesting the full legal title to the chattel personal in a trustee, who in equity is bound to prudently look after, administer, and balance the equitable property interests of all parties, is generally the only way to go.

§8.28   The Bishop Estate Controversy

According to Jones, the closest comparison to Kamehameha was the Milton Hershey School in Pennsylvania.[1] Members of its board served without compensation.[2]

In 1884, a charitable trust was established under the will of Hawaiian Princess Bernice Pauahi Bishop, the great-granddaughter and last descendant of King Kamehameha the Great. The trust was initially funded with Waikiki and other real estate (approximately 10 percent of the Kingdom of Hawaii's land mass). Today, the value of the trust corpus is in the range of $10 billion, which at one point included a 10 percent interest in Goldman Sachs.

Under the terms of the will, five trustees are directed "to erect and maintain in the Hawaiian Islands two schools, each for boarding and day scholars, one for boys and one for girls, to be known as, and called the Kamehameha Schools." Up to one-half of the corpus is for "the purchase of suitable premises, the erection of school buildings, and in furnishing the same with the necessary and appropriate fixtures, furniture and apparatus." Annual income generated by the remaining corpus is to be expended "in the maintenance of said schools; meaning thereby the salaries of teachers, the repairing

---

[36] John Chipman Gray, The Rule Against Perpetuities, Appendix F (4th ed. 1942).

§8.28 [1] Much of the information contained herein is taken from Randall W. Roth, *Overview of the Bishop Estate Controversy*, I Int'l J. Not-for-Profit L. (Issue 3). The rest is taken from communications between the authors and Prof. Roth. The authors wish to thank Prof. Roth for his assistance with this section.

[2] Samuel P. King & Randall W. Roth, Broken Trust 272 (2006) (University of Hawaii Press). *See generally* §8.35 of this handbook (the Hershey Trust).

[of] buildings and other incident expenses" and in the "support and education of orphans, and others in indigent circumstances, giving the preference to Hawaiians of pure or part aboriginal blood." The proportions in which the annual income is to be allocated to these various purposes are to be determined solely by the trustees.

The will requires that teachers and trustees be "persons of the Protestant religion." For many years, admission to Kamehameha Schools has been limited to children of pure or part aboriginal blood, most of whom are neither orphans nor indigents.

The two schools were established relatively soon after the testatrix's death. They have since merged. Today, competition for admission to the Kamehameha Schools is intense, with about ten applications for each slot. One of the trustees, the so-called Lead Trustee for Education, has been delegated responsibility for overseeing the day-to-day operations of the school.

The will directed that the justices of the Supreme Court of the Kingdom of Hawaii select the trustees. When Hawaii became a state, its supreme court justices took over trustee selection responsibilities. In recent times, the trustees have been accused, among other things, of breaching the duty of loyalty, failing to properly account, imprudently investing trust assets, improper delegation, and failing to carry out the terms of the trust. These allegations have triggered investigations by the IRS and the Hawaii Attorney General; the empanelling of two grand juries, one federal and the other state; and an inquiry by the state Campaign Spending Commission.

The trustees have included a Speaker of the House (Hawaii), a President of the Senate (Hawaii), and a Chief Justice of the Supreme Court (Hawaii), all of whom are charged with selecting the members of Hawaii's Judicial Selection Commission. One trustee was the best friend and political confidant of the governor, who was also responsible for appointing commission members. Trustees have paid themselves annual fees averaging about $900,000 each. The law firm of a recent Commission chairman received $15 million in fees from the trustees while on the Commission. The law firm of a former governor received millions in fees soon after he left office in 1995. It was reported that among other questionable expenditures, the trustees were paying nearly $100,000 of trust funds each month to a law firm that the attorney general believed was working for the protection and benefit of the individual trustees and not the estate or its beneficiaries.[3]

On August 9, 1997, the *Honolulu State Bulletin* published an article entitled "Broken Trust." The 6,400-word essay sparked a public outcry for reform. Since the article was published, much has happened besides the various investigations, including the suicide of a female attorney for the trust who was reported in the press to have been caught by a hotel security guard "in a tryst" with one of the trustees.[4] Thanks primarily to the vigorous interventions of the IRS and the state attorney general, the situation is better than it was. Successor trustees are now in place, although it cannot be said that the break with the past has been

---

[3] Samuel P. King & Randall W. Roth, Broken Trust 272 (2006) (University of Hawaii Press).

[4] Bruce Dunford, *Rich Hawaii Trust Mired in Scandal*, AP-NY-03-28-99 2006 EST.

a totally clean one. Moreover, it certainly cannot be said that the trust was afforded the panoply of equitable remedies to which it was clearly entitled, essentially almost all the remedies discussed in Section 7.2.3 of this handbook. In 2006, the entire saga was fleshed out and recounted by Judge Samuel P. King and Professor Randall W. Roth in *Broken Trust*,[5] the book. It remains to be seen, however, whether any new lessons have been learned. Perhaps all we really can take away from the saga is further confirmation of the principle that account-ability, not trust, is the glue that holds a trust together, human nature being what it is. It is no coincidence that trustee accountability is the dominant theme of this handbook. According to Prof. Roth the Bishop Trust Controversy has raised—though certainly not resolved—some important public policy questions:

1. When and to what extent can one trustee safely and appropriately delegate an important function to a cotrustee?[6]
2. How should trustee compensation be determined?[7]
3. What is the best way to provide for the appointment of replacement trustees?[8]
4. How should trustees be required, or allowed, to report financial results?
5. What does impartiality really mean in the context of charitable trusts?[9]
6. How might trustees of charitable trusts best be held accountable?[10]
7. When and why should trustees be removed?[11]
8. Is it possible for an attorney to represent a trust, as opposed to a trustee?[12]
9. To what extent should discriminatory provisions or practices be allowed or enforced?[13]
10. When defending a lawsuit alleging breach of trust, should defendant trustees pay their own attorneys' fees?[14]

---

[5] Samuel P. King & Randall W. Roth, Broken Trust (2006) (University of Hawai'i Press).

[6] *See generally* §6.1.4 of this handbook (duty to give personal attention (not to delegate)).

[7] *See generally* §8.4 of this handbook (the trustee's compensation).

[8] *See generally* §3.2.6 of this handbook (considerations in the selection of a trustee) (in discussing the office of trust protector).

[9] *See generally* §6.2.5 of this handbook (duty of impartiality).

[10] *See generally* §9.4.2 of this handbook (standing to enforce charitable trusts).

[11] *See generally* §7.2.3.6 of this handbook (removal).

[12] *See generally* §3.5 of this handbook (trustee's relationship to the trust estate) and §8.8 of this handbook (whom does counsel represent?).

[13] *See generally* §9.4.3 of this handbook (*cy pres*).

[14] *See generally* §3.5.2.3 of this handbook (right in equity to exoneration and reimburse-ment).

§8.29 Is a Custodial Parent the Trustee of Child Support Payments?

It is clear that a court may expressly order the custodial parent (or a third party for that matter) to take title as trustee to child support payments made by the noncustodial parent pursuant to a divorce decree.[1] The custodial parent holds the property for the benefit of the child and is accountable for how it is administered and expended. Subject to any equitable rights of reimbursement in the custodial parent,[2] the property is off limits to the custodial parent's creditors.

The law, however, is sparse, murky, and unsettled when a court fails to specify in advance the capacity in which a custodial parent shall take title to child support payments. Is it in his or her individual capacity or as trustee? Applying the law of Indiana, one appellate court has held that " '[t]he custodial parent becomes a trustee of the funds for the use and benefit of the child" and the noncustodial parent " becomes a debtor to the [custodial parent] trustee as the installments accrue[.]' "[3] Applying the law of Oregon, another court has held that there is no trust, "that ... [a child support] ... payment is an amount which the custodial parent may recover from the non-custodial parent to assist in providing for the care of the child."[4]

§8.30 The Difference Between a Vested Equitable Remainder Subject to Divestment and a Vested (Transmissible) Contingent Equitable Remainder

I am quite aware that this is all largely matter of words, but so is much of the law of property; and unless we treat such formal distinctions as real, that law will melt away and leave not a rack behind.—Learned Hand[1]

---

§8.29 [1] *See, e.g.*, Miller v. Miller, 29 Or. App. 723, 732, 565 P.2d 382, 387 (1977) (Johnson, J., specially concurring).

[2] Henady, 165 B.R. 887, 892 (1994) (Indiana).

[3] Henady, 165 B.R. at 889 (quoting Grace v. Quigg, 150 Ind. App. 371, 378, 276 N.E.2d 594, 598 (1971)). Indiana is not the only state in which a court has ruled that a custodial parent is the trustee of child support payments. *See, e.g.*, Department of Health & Rehabilitative Servs. v. Holland, 602 So. 2d 652 (Fla. Dist. Ct. App. 1992); Cumberland v. Cumberland, 564 So. 2d 839, 847 (Miss. 1990); Thompson v. Korupp, 440 So. 2d 68 (Fla. Dist. Ct. App. 1983); Armour v. Allen, 377 So. 2d 798 (Fla. Dist. Ct. App. 1979); Kimble v. Kimble, 341 S.E.2d 420 (W. Va. 1986); Ditmar v. Ditmar, 293 P.2d 759 (Wash. 1956).

[4] Miller v. Miller, 29 Or. App. 723, 731, 565 P.2d 382, 386 (1977).

§8.30 [1] Comm'r v. City Bank Farmers' Trust Co., 74 F.2d 242, 247 (2d Cir. 1934).

A *legal* future interest requires a previous estate to support it.[2] Because no *equitable* future interest incident to a trust relationship requires a previous supporting estate, legal title being in the trustee, there is technically no such thing as an equitable remainder.[3] Thus, Prof. John Chipman Gray, exhibiting his characteristic scholarly precision, has labeled the equitable equivalent of a legal remainder a quasi remainder.[4] The Restatement (Third) of Property (Wills and Other Donative Transfers) has no patience with such scholarly precision as evidenced in its coverage of remainder doctrine. We explain in *Old Doctrine Misunderstood, New Doctrine Misconceived: Deconstructing the Newly-Minted Restatement (Third) of Property's Power of Appointment Sections*.[5]

The vested equitable remainder subject to divestment. A *vested equitable remainder subject to complete* divestment[6] would look something like this: *A* (settlor) transfers property to *B* (trustee) for *C* (life beneficiary) for life, remainder to *D*, an ascertained individual (remainderman); but if Susan marries Tom during *C*'s lifetime (condition subsequent), then the trust property passes outright and free of trust to *X* (alternate remainderman). At the time the property is transferred from *A* to *B*, *D* receives a vested equitable remainder subject to complete divestment during the period that *C*, Susan and Tom are all alive and Susan and Tom are unmarried to one another. Should *D* die during that period, *D*'s equitable remainder interest passes to his estate.

If the condition subsequent, *i.e.*, the marriage of Susan to Tom, is still unfulfilled at *C*'s death, the underlying trust property passes to the executor of *D*'s estate at *C*'s death. If, on the other hand, Susan and Tom end up marrying during *C*'s lifetime, *D*'s equitable remainder extinguishes at the time of the marriage because the condition subsequent has been fulfilled. The practical consequence is that the underlying trust property passes to *X* upon the death of *C*. Unlike a remainder which is a successive interest, an executory interest is a divesting interest.[7] *X*'s interest is an example of an equitable shifting executory interest. Springing and shifting executory property interests, both of the legal and the equitable varieties, are covered generally in Section 8.15.80 of this handbook.

One court has found the equitable interest of a remainderman vested subject to divestment where the trust was revocable and the remainderman was named and alive at the trust's inception.[8] In this case, the condition subsequent was the settlor exercising her right of revocation. The remainderman having predeceased the settlor, the property subject to the unrevoked trust passed to the estate of the remainderman upon the settlor's death. Another court,

---

[2] *See generally* §8.27 of this handbook (the difference between a legal estate and an equitable one).

[3] *See* John Chipman Gray, The Rule Against Perpetuities §324 (4th ed. 1942).

[4] *See* John Chipman Gray, The Rule Against Perpetuities §324 (4th ed. 1942).

[5] Charles E. Rounds, Jr, *Old Doctrine Misunderstood, New Doctrine Misconceived: Deconstructing the Newly-Minted Restatement (Third) of Property's Power of Appointment Sections*, 26 Quinnipiac Prob. L.J. 240, 247–248 (2013).

[6] *See generally* John Chipman Gray, The Rule Against Perpetuities §108 (4th ed. 1942).

[7] Cornelius J. Moynihan, Introduction to the Law of Real Property 191–192 (2d ed. 1988).

[8] First Nat'l Bank v. Tenney, 165 Ohio St. 513, 138 N.E.2d 15 (1956).

however, sees such arrangements very differently, as do the authors of this handbook: "...[T]rusts in which the settlor retains the right to amend or revoke the instrument [sic] do not convey 'presently vested rights' to beneficiaries because their interests are contingent upon the settlor not amending or revoking the trust."[9]

If enforcement of a condition subsequent is illegal or violates public policy,[10] there are at least two possibilities: The interest subject to the condition becomes absolute[11] or the condition is deemed not to have been imposed, not to have been satisfied actually.[12] The Restatement (Third) of Trusts generally favors the second approach so as to accommodate provisions in default of the condition's fulfillment.[13]

We would note here that vested equitable *reversionary* interests also can be rendered subject to a divestment. In response to "concerns about the clogging of title and other administrative problems caused by remote default provisions upon failure of a charitable purpose,"[14] for example, the Uniform Trust Code would sharply curtail the ability of a settlor to create a charitable trust whose property would revert to the settlor's personal representative, *i.e.*, the settlor's probate estate, upon the accomplishment of that purpose (or upon the impossibility of its fulfillment), even when the purpose is a limited one.[15] This is a topic we cover in some detail in Section 9.4.3 of this handbook as part of our discussion of the *cy pres* doctrine. In England, on the other hand, a reversion upon the happening of a condition subsequent now implicates the Rule against Perpetuities.[16] The Rule is also implicated when the duration of an English charitable trust is subject to a contingency-based limitation, such as so long as a certain state of affairs continues.[17] Thus, an equitable reversion upon the failure of an English charitable trust would be unenforceable if the interest were to become possessory beyond the period of the rule.[18] *Cy pres* would then have to be applied.

The vested (transmissible) contingent equitable remainder. *A vested (transmissible) contingent equitable remainder,*[19] on the other hand, would look something like this: *A* (settlor) transfers property to *B* (trustee) for *C* (beneficiary) for life, remainder to *D*, an ascertained individual (remainderman), if

---

[9] Patterson v. Patterson, 266 P.3d 828, 836 (Utah 2011).

[10] *See generally* §9.24 of this handbook (the incentive trust (and the public policy considerations); marriage restraints).

[11] 1 Scott & Ascher §9.6.2.

[12] 1 Scott & Ascher §9.6.2. *See also* 1 Scott & Ascher §§9.7 (When Performance Is Impossible) and 9.8 (When the Terms of the Trust Are Indefinite).

[13] Restatement (Third) of Trusts §29 cmt. i(1).

[14] UTC §413 cmt. (available at <http://www.uniformlaws.org/Act.aspx?title=Trust%20 Code>).

[15] UTC §413 (available at <http://www.uniformlaws.org/Act.aspx?title=Trust%20Code>). *See generally* 6 Scott & Ascher §39.5.2.

[16] *See generally* 6 Scott & Ascher §39.7.2.

[17] 6 Scott & Ascher §39.7.3 (Limitations).

[18] *See generally* 6 Scott & Ascher §39.7.2.

[19] *See generally* John Chipman Gray, The Rule Against Perpetuities §118 (4th ed. 1942).

Susan marries Tom during *C*'s lifetime; if Susan is not married to Tom at the death of *C*, then to *X* (alternate remainderman). At the time the property is transferred from *A* to *B*, *D* takes a vested (in the sense of transmissible) contingent equitable remainder.[20]

Why transmissible? Because *D*, at the trust's inception, is an ascertained individual whose interest is not conditioned upon his surviving *C*.

Why contingent? Because *D*'s interest is subject to a condition precedent, namely Susan's marrying Tom by the time *C* dies. As an aside, if the condition precedent were illegal or violated public policy, *e.g.*, if the interest instead were subject to the precondition of *D* divorcing his own wife,[21] then a court might well deem the interest to be fully vested in *ab initio*, with enjoyment to await the expiration of *C*'s prior estate.[22]

And what are the practical consequences of *D*'s possessing what is sometimes called a vested contingent remainder? If *D* dies after the trust's inception but before *C* dies and if Susan marries Tom during that period as well, then the trust property passes to *D*'s estate upon the death of *C*.[23] If Susan and Tom are not married at *C*'s death, the property passes to *X*. That having been said, for rule against perpetuities analysis purposes, *D*'s interest is deemed to be fully contingent.[24]

How can one tell the difference between a *vested equitable remainder subject to complete divestment* and a *vested (transmissible) contingent remainder*? Ultimately it hinges on the words used, as Professor Gray has explained: "If the conditional element is incorporated into the description of, or into the gift to, the remainderman, then the remainder is contingent; but if, after words giving a vested interest, a clause is added divesting it, the remainder is vested."[25] Professor Moynihan has found the test to be helpful, but not always that easy to apply in a given situation, noting that "it may be difficult to determine in some cases whether the conditional element is 'incorporated into the gift to the remainderman.' "[26] He suggests that "[i]t may first be necessary to resort to rules of

---

[20] *See also* §8.15.65 of this handbook (destructibility of contingent remainders rule [the trust exemption]).

[21] *See generally* §9.24 of this handbook (the incentive trust (and the public policy considerations); marriage restraints).

[22] 2 Scott & Ascher §9.6.3. *See also* 2 Scott & Ascher §§9.7 (When Performance Is Impossible) and 9.8 (When the Terms of the Trust Are Indefinite).

[23] *See, e.g.*, Hills v. Barnard, 152 Mass. 67, 25 N.E. 96 (1890).

[24] *See* John Chipman Gray, The Rule Against Perpetuities §118 (4th ed. 1942).

[25] John Chipman Gray, The Rule Against Perpetuities 95 (4th ed. 1942). Some courts have found a reserved right of revocation to be a condition precedent, others to be a condition subsequent. *See, e.g.*, Baldwin v. Branch, 2004 WL 407157 (Ala.) (involving a vested interest subject to divestment upon the settlor's exercising his right of revocation); First Nat'l Bank of Bar Harbor v. Anthony, 557 A.2d. 957 (Me. 1989) (involving a vested contingent/transmissible equitable remainder that was conditioned on the settlor not exercising his right to revoke). It should be noted that a transmissible equitable remainder whether vested or contingent is an interest in property which itself may be the subject of a trust. *See generally* §2.1.1 of this handbook (the inter vivos trust).

[26] Cornelius J. Moynihan, Introduction to the Law of Real Property 128 (2d ed. 1988).

construction to determine the meaning of the language."[27] He elaborates with some examples in his *Introduction to the Law of Real Property*.[28]

The Restatement (Third) of Property intentionally conflates the two types of future interest. The Restatement (Third) of Property further complicates matters by pretzeling the traditional vested equitable future interest that is subject to a condition subsequent into an interest that is subject to a condition precedent.[29] "A condition subsequent is a condition that is expressed as a condition that, if satisfied on or before the distribution date, extinguishes the possibility that the future interest will take effect in possession or enjoyment."[30] This intentional conflation is unfortunate as the transmissibility of the vested remainder subject to divestment is easier to grasp conceptually than the transmissibility of the contingent remainder. Moreover, while all such vested remainders are transmissible, the same cannot be said for all versions of the contingent remainder.[31]

The holder of a *legal* right of entry for condition broken is not a trust beneficiary. This is a topic we take up in Section 9.9.24 of this handbook. For a discussion of the differences between a legal property interest and an equitable one, the reader is referred to Section 8.27 of this handbook.

§8.31 The Franklin Trust (Boston)

Benjamin Franklin died on April 17, 1790. Two trusts were established under his will, one sited in Pennsylvania and the other in Massachusetts. The latter, at its inception, was funded with 1,000 pounds sterling. The City of Boston came to be its trustee. The Franklin Foundation, pursuant to a statute enacted in the early 1900s, came to be agent for the trustee with exclusive authority over the trust's administration.

Under the terms of the trust, income was to accumulate for 200 years. At the end of the first 100 years, three-quarters of the principal was to be carved out for "public" works "which may be judged of most utility" to the inhabitants of Boston. At the end of the second 100-year period (June 30, 1991), Boston was to have a right of disposition over one-fourth of the balance of the trust estate and the Commonwealth of Massachusetts over three-fourths. The will provided that trust assets were to be invested in low interest loans to "young married artificers . . . as have served an Apprenticeship" in Boston.

---

[27] Cornelius J. Moynihan, Introduction to the Law of Real Property 128 (2d ed. 1988).

[28] Cornelius J. Moynihan, Introduction to the Law of Real Property 128 (2d ed. 1988).

[29] Restatement (Third) of Property (Wills and Other Donative Transfers) §26.2 cmt. c ("This Restatement declines to perpetuate a difference in classification between a condition precedent and a condition subsequent.").

[30] Restatement (Third) of Property (Wills and Other Donative Transfers) §26.2 cmt. b.

[31] *See generally* §8.30 of this handbook.

When the first 100 years were up, the time came for the fund managers to carve out the portion specified under the terms of the will, about $400,000 worth of property. There were many suggestions as to what should be done with the distribution, including the following: that it should be applied to reduce Boston's debt, that it should go toward the construction of a public bath house, and that it should be used to build a recreation hall in the Boston Public Gardens. In 1904, Andrew Carnegie intervened at the request of Henry S. Pritchett, president of MIT. Carnegie offered to match the distribution on two conditions: (1) that the amount, together with his contribution, be used for "the establishment of a school for the industrial training of men and women along the lines of The Mechanics and Tradesmen's School of New York and the Cooper Union" and (2) that Boston furnish the land on which the school would be built.

In October 1904, Carnegie wrote to the fund managers: I am trustee of both schools mentioned [The Mechanics' and Tradesmen's School of New York and Cooper Union] and do not hesitate to say that to the best of my knowledge no money has produced more valuable results. I think it is from the class who not only spend laborious days but also spend laborious nights fitting themselves for hard work that the most valuable citizens are to come. We are here helping only those who show an intense desire, and strong determination, to help themselves—the only class worth helping, the only class that it is possible to help to any great extent.

There was initially some resistance to Carnegie's condition that Boston supply the land. In 1904, however, just before Christmas, Mr. Carnegie dashed off the following note to Mayor Patrick Collins:

> Now then, my idea was that the city of Boston should cooperate with The Franklin Fund and with my contribution. Frankly, I should not like to give aid to a city that would remain apart and do nothing. If the growing city of Boston, with such a mayor, cannot give a site for The Franklin School, it must fall somewhat from the pinnacle I have it upon. We expect great things from Boston . . . you may have noticed that I rarely give anything for nothing . . . think it all over, and I believe you will see that on no consideration must Boston be left out.

In July 1905, Mayor Collins wrote to Mr. Carnegie, who was vacationing in Scotland:

> On behalf of the managers of The Franklin Fund, I have the honor to report that all the conditions governing your proposed contribution have been complied with.

Shortly thereafter, the city treasurer received, as promised, Carnegie's matching gift in the form of $408,000 in U.S steel bonds and a personal check for $398.48. The Franklin Institute of Boston was born. In 1958, the legislature passed and the Governor signed into law a statute that purported to exercise the Commonwealth's right of disposition over the balance of the fund for the benefit of the Institute. There was a comparable section covering Boston's portion that had the approval of the mayor and the city council.

In 1959, the Institute filed in state court an equity petition seeking acceleration of the trust's termination date. The court denied the request but in so doing, left the fate of the statute up in the air.[1] Thirty or so years later, on the eve of the expiration of the 200-year period, The Franklin Foundation filed a complaint for instructions seeking a judicial determination as to whether the statute would be operative were it not repealed before June 30, 1991.

The Massachusetts Attorney General declined to defend the statute and his division of public charities declined to represent the Institute (itself a public charity). The Foundation, which had management responsibilities not only for the trust fund but also for the Institute, took it upon itself to retain independent counsel to represent the interests of the Institute in the matter. Boston, which was trustee of the Institute as well as the trust fund, also declined to defend the interests of the Institute.

In 1993, the court rendered its decision: The statute was inoperative. Additional legislation would be required if Boston and the Commonwealth were effectively to exercise their respective rights of disposition over the trust property, which by then had grown in value to $5 million.[2] Immediately, the governor, members of the legislature, and a number of others outside the Massachusetts state government rallied to the cause of the Institute. A bill was filed that were it to become law would effect an exercise of the Commonwealth's right of disposition in favor of the Institute. In January 1994, the Institute won the war when the governor signed into law legislation impressing a further trust on its portion of the fund for the benefit of the Institute. Shortly thereafter, the city council and the mayor followed suit with respect to Boston's portion.

§8.32 Can the Trustee Escape Liability for Making a Mistake of Law If He Acted in Good Faith on Advice of Counsel?

What protection does a cestui que trust have when a finding that the trustee acted in good faith need only be based on advice of counsel?[1]

Reliance on advice of counsel, however, is not a complete defense to an alleged breach of trust, because that would reward a trustee who shopped for legal advice that would support the trustee's desired course of conduct or who otherwise acted unreasonably in procuring or following legal advice.[2]

The general default law. As a general rule, the trustee is liable for any breaches of trust that are occasioned by a misunderstanding of the applicable

---

§8.31 [1] The Franklin Inst. v. Attorney Gen., 340 Mass. 197, 163 N.E.2d 662 (1961).
[2] Franklin Found. v. Attorney Gen., 416 Mass. 483, 623 N.E.2d 1109 (1993).
§8.32 [1] Bolton v. Stillwagon, 410 Pa. 618, 626, 190 A.2d 105, 109 (1963).
[2] Restatement (Third) of Trusts §77 cmt. b(2).

law.[3] Moreover, unless the terms of the trust provide otherwise,[4] as between the beneficiary and the trustee, the trustee, in the first instance, must bear the burden of an injury to the trust occasioned by trust counsel's legal malpractice,[5] except, perhaps, when selection of counsel was prudent[6] and the trustee's reliance on counsel's advice was reasonable.[7] Misdelivery occasioned by counsel's misidentification of the remainderman would be an example of such an injury.[8] "The extent of the duties and powers of a trustee is determined by the rules of law that are applicable to the situation, and not the rules that the trustee or his attorney believes to be applicable, and by the terms of the trust as the court may interpret them, and not as they may be interpreted by the trustee himself or by his attorney."[9] English law is generally in accord.[10] Of course, this does not foreclose the trustee in a separate action from instituting a legal malpractice action against the attorney. Trust officers too are admonished not to rely upon bank or trust counsel, whether internal or external, for nonlegal trust decisions.[11] When in reasonable doubt as to the applicable law, the trustee is always entitled at trust expense to seek instructions from the court.[12] The bottom line is this: While reliance on the advice of counsel is not necessarily an absolute defense to a breach of fiduciary duty claim, it can be evidence that the trustee acted reasonably and in good faith, which, as one commentator has noted, is surely a "plus."[13]

The Uniform Prudent Investor Act. It remains to be seen whether the widespread adoption of the Uniform Prudent Investor Act, at least in some jurisdictions, has shifted *all* liability for good-faith mistakes of law off the

---

[3] *See generally* 3 Scott & Ascher §16.8 (Application for Instructions); 4 Scott & Ascher §24.5 (What Constitutes a Breach of Trust); 4 Scott & Ascher §24.31 (Liability for Incorrect Distributions).

[4] 4 Scott & Ascher §24.5.

[5] 4 Scott & Ascher §24.5; 3A Scott on Trusts §201.

[6] *See generally* §8.25 of this handbook (which American law schools still require Trusts).

[7] *See, e.g.,* 4 Scott & Ascher §24.5 n.20; Dardovitch v. Haltzman, 190 F.3d 125, 151 (3d Cir. 1999); 4 Scott & Ascher §24.31 (Liability for Incorrect Distributions).

[8] 4 Scott & Ascher §§24.5 (What Constitutes a Breach of Trust), 24.31 (Liability for Incorrect Distributions). The trustee, however, would still be entitled to seek restitution from the transferee, the transferee having been unjustly enriched by the misdelivery of the trust property. *See* Restatement (Third) of Restitution and Unjust Enrichment §6. It is questionable though whether the trustee would be entitled to indemnification from the trust estate for the costs of bringing the action, the trustee having been at fault. *See generally* §3.5.2.3 of this handbook (the trustee's right in equity to exoneration and reimbursement).

[9] 3A Scott on Trusts §221. *See also* 4 Scott & Ascher §§24.5 (What Constitutes a Breach of Trust), 24.31 (Liability for Incorrect Distributions).

[10] *See, e.g.,* Futter v. Comm'r, [2013] UKSC 26 (paragraph 80) ("Trustees may be liable, even if they have obtained apparently competent professional advice, if they act outside the scope of their powers (excessive execution), or contrary to the general law (for example, in the Australian case, the law regulating entitlement on intestacy). . . . That can be seen as a form of strict liability in that it is imposed regardless of personal fault.").

[11] *See* Krug v. Krug, 838 S.W.2d 197, 203 (Tenn. Ct. App. 1992).

[12] *See generally* 3 Scott & Ascher §16.8 (Application for Instructions); 4 Scott & Ascher §§24.5 (What Constitutes a Breach of Trust), 24.31 (Liability for Incorrect Distributions).

[13] 4 Scott & Ascher §24.5.

shoulders of the trustee and on to the shoulders of the attorney who had rendered the defective legal advice, provided the trustee had exercised reasonable care in selecting the attorney. Here is the situation: Section 9 of the Uniform Prudent Investor Act provides that if a trustee exercises reasonable care, skill, and caution in selecting an agent, he will not be liable to the beneficiaries or to the trust for the decisions or actions of the agent to whom a particular function was delegated.[14] Now as a general rule, counsel represents the trustee, not the beneficiaries.[15] In some jurisdictions, however, trust counsel has duties that run to the beneficiaries as well, at least as to routine matters.[16] Thus, in a jurisdiction that sees trust counsel as having some duties that run to the beneficiaries and that has also has adopted the Uniform Prudent Investor Act, the *primary and sole* liability for any injury to a trust that is occasioned by the trustee's good-faith reliance on improper advice of counsel may well now be on the shoulders of counsel himself or herself.

Express exculpation. What if the terms of the trust purport to relieve the trustee of liability for a breach of trust that is occasioned by the good faith reliance on the advice of counsel? Would such exculpation be void on public policy grounds? Not in New York necessarily, unless the trust were testamentary.[17]

§8.33   Is the Level of an Uncompensated Trustee's Duty of Care Lower Than That of a Compensated Trustee?

Indeed, a trustee who has not yet accepted can disclaim the trusteeship and, upon doing so, has no liability. But a trustee who has accepted the trusteeship cannot thereafter disclaim it. Generally, a trustee can resign only with the court's permission, unless all the beneficiaries are adult and competent and give their consent, or unless the terms of the trust provide otherwise.[1]

The level of a trustee's duty of care is not affected by whether the trustee receives compensation or acts gratuitously.[2] "There is no room in the field of trusts for the distinctions which have been applied in the law of bailments, namely, that bailees for the sole benefit of the bailor are held to slight care, bailees for mutual benefit to ordinary care, and bailees for the sole benefit of the bailee to great care."[3] What is the trustee's duty of care? The trustee shall

---

[14] *See* §6.1.4 of this handbook (duty to give personal attention (not to delegate)).

[15] *See generally* §8.8 of this handbook (whom does counsel represent?).

[16] *See generally* §8.8 of this handbook (whom does counsel represent?).

[17] *See* In re HSBC Bank USA, N.A., 947 N.Y.S.2d 292 (N.Y. App. Div. 2012).

§8.33   [1] 3 Scott & Ascher §17.1.

[2] Bogert   §541;   UTC   §804   cmt.   (available   at   <http://www.uniformlaws.org/Act.aspx?title=Trust%20Code>); 3 Scott & Ascher §§17.1, 17.6.

[3] Bogert §541.

administer the trust as a prudent person would, by considering the purposes, terms, distributional requirements, and other circumstances of the trust.[4] In satisfying this standard, the trustee shall exercise reasonable care, skill, and caution.[5] For more on the trustee's duty to be generally prudent, that is to exercise reasonable care and skill, the reader is referred to Section 6.1.1 of this handbook.

§8.34   When an Employer Identification Number (EIN) Is Not Required

TIN (taxpayer identification number) is an umbrella term for the EIN (employer identification number), ITIN (individual taxpayer identification number), and ATIN (adoption taxpayer identification number). The EIN is used to identify taxpayers who are not individuals, *e.g.*, corporations, partnerships, estates, and trusts. An EIN may be issued to a trust whether or not the trust has employees. An EIN consists of nine digits and is formatted as follows: 00-0000000.[1] It can be obtained electronically on the IRS website.[2]

"Generally, all trusts with gross income of at least $600 during the taxable year or that have one or more nonresident alien beneficiaries must obtain an EIN and file an annual income tax return within three and one-half months of the end of their taxable years."[3] An EIN, however, is not required for most grantor-type trusts.[4] The social security number of either the grantor or the grantor's spouse will suffice. A grantor-type trust that satisfies the following criteria may even enjoy a blanket tax filing and reporting exemption: (1) the trust is a domestic trust; (2) the trust is taxed as owned entirely by the grantor or the grantor and the grantor's spouse because it is revocable by the grantor or a nonadverse party under Section 676; and (3) the grantor, the grantor's spouse, or both are trustees or cotrustees.[5] In the case of a self-settled revocable inter vivos trust, a new TIN, in this case an EIN, must be obtained when the grantor-settlor dies. Thus the trustee of an administrative trust will need to obtain a separate EIN.[6]

---

[4] UTC §804 (available at <http://www.uniformlaws.org/Act.aspx?title=Trust%20Code>); 3 Scott & Ascher §17.6 (Duty to Exercise Reasonable Care and Skill).

[5] UTC §804 (available at <http://www.uniformlaws.org/Act.aspx?title=Trust%20Code>); 3 Scott & Ascher §17.6 (Duty to Exercise Reasonable Care and Skill).

§8.34 [1] Treas. Reg. §301.7701-12.

[2] http://www.irs.gov/businesses.

[3] Zaritsky, 858-2d T.M., Grantor Trusts: Sections 671-679 A-17.

[4] Zaritsky, 858-2d T.M., Grantor Trusts: Sections 671-679 A-17. *See also* §9.1 of this handbook (The Grantor Trust); Chapter 10 of this handbook (the income taxation of trusts).

[5] Zaritsky, 858-2d T.M., Grantor Trusts: Sections 671-679 A-17.

[6] *See generally* §9.9.14 of this handbook (the administrative trust).

§8.35 The Hershey Trust

But the Hershey School Trust started to grow concerned more than a year ago about its fiduciary duty to beneficiaries as it watched the technology bubble burst, says someone familiar with the matter.[1] The meltdown of Enron and telecom stars such as WorldCom Inc. added to concerns. The trustees felt they had a responsibility to the beneficiaries, and exploring a possible sale was the best option, this person says.[2]

A spokesman for the . . . [Pennsylvania attorney general's] . . . office declined to comment on whether anyone there had talked to the Hershey School Trust about diversifying. Mark Pacella, the chief deputy attorney general charged with overseeing charitable trusts, said that in general, there has been no new push on our part to force diversification as a policy matter. But he said current market conditions have underlined the age-old proposition that diversification is almost always a hallmark of prudent portfolio management.[3]

In 1909 chocolate industrialist Milton S. Hershey and his wife Catherine S. Hershey executed a deed of trust to endow a school for "white orphan boys," which is now called the Milton Hershey School. Over his lifetime and at his death in 1945, Mr. Hershey transferred blocks of stock in the Hershey chocolate manufacturing operations to the trustee. The trustee is a trust company. A board of managers administers both the trust company and the school. The school is a nonprofit corporation. The Dauphin County (Pennsylvania) Orphans Court has exercised its *cy pres* powers to enable females and nonwhites to attend the school.

The Hershey Trust Company, as trustee, owns 31 percent of the outstanding common shares of Hershey Foods Corp. and roughly 76 percent of its voting stock.[4] The market value of the trust's ownership interest is in the range of $10 billion.[5] Approximately 50 percent of the trust's portfolio is in Hershey stock.[6] In July 2002, the board of managers of the Hershey Trust Company voted to "pursue the sale of its majority-controlled Hershey Foods Corp."[7] In September 2002, the board, "succumbing to intense public opposition to . . . [a] . . . sale,"

---

§8.35 [1] *See generally* §6.2.2.1 of this handbook (the *Harvard College* Prudent Man Rule and its progeny) and §9.4 of this handbook (the charitable trust).

[2] Shelley Branch, Sarah Ellison, & Gordon Fairclough, *Hershey Foods Is Considering a Plan to Put Itself Up for Sale*, Wall St. J., July 25, 2002, at A6, col. 2.

[3] Branch, Ellison, & Fairclough, *Hershey Foods Is Considering a Plan to Put Itself Up for Sale*, Wall St. J., July 25, 2002, at col. 3. *See also* §6.2.2.1 of this handbook (the *Harvard College* prudent man rule and its progeny) (in part discussing investment diversification issues).

[4] Branch, Ellison, & Fairclough, *Hershey Foods Is Considering a Plan to Put Itself Up for Sale*, Wall St. J., July 25, 2002,. at 1, col. 5.

[5] Branch, Ellison, & Fairclough, *Hershey Foods Is Considering a Plan to Put Itself Up for Sale*, Wall St. J., July 25, 2002.

[6] Branch, Ellison, & Fairclough, *Hershey Foods Is Considering a Plan to Put Itself Up for Sale*, Wall St. J., July 25, 2002,at A6, col. 3.

[7] Shelley Branch, *Trust Pushing Sale of Hershey Faces Rising Level of Criticism*, Wall St. J., Aug. 1, 2002, at B6, col. 4.

took the company "off the auction block."[8] The Hershey saga was a case study in the intersection of charity and politics:

> The attorney general, who at the time was running for Governor of Pennsylvania, sought and was granted a preliminary injunction to stop the sale, and participated in a shakeup of Hershey's board of directors shortly after losing the gubernatorial election. Consequently, critics attacked the attorney general for essentially treating the Hershey assets as his election campaign funds.[9]

The Hershey Trust is not the only charity whose portfolio is perhaps underdiversified. "The endowment of the David and Lucile Packard Foundation, which holds stock only in H-P and a spinoff, Agilent Technologies Inc., soared to a peak of more than \$18 billion in 2000, only to plummet to \$6.2 billion at the end of . . . 2001. . . ."[10]

§8.36 May the Trustee Represent the Trust in the Courts Without Counsel?

Federal. The trustee has the legal title to the trust property.[1] As the owner of the trust property, it is he who contracts with third parties, *i.e.*, nonbeneficiaries, on behalf of the trust.[2] If he may represent himself in personal litigation without counsel, *i.e.*, represent himself *pro se*,[3] one would think he also could handle litigation between the trust and third parties without counsel. (Whether he would be in breach of trust for doing so is another matter.)[4] Citing as indirect authority the language of the Judiciary Act of 1789, now found in 28 U.S.C. Section 1654, one court, however, has ruled that a trustee who is neither a beneficiary nor a lawyer may not represent the trust in federal court litigation.[5]

State. A nonattorney trustee who brings suit in his fiduciary capacity only against a third party with the intention to prosecute the suit *pro se* runs the risk

---

[8] Robert Frank & Sarah Ellison, *Meltdown in Chocolatetown*, Wall St. J., Sept. 10, 2002, at B1, col. 2.

[9] Craig Kaufman, *Sympathy for the Devil's Advocate: Assisting the Attorney General When Charitable Matters Reach the Courtroom*, 40 Real Prop. Prob. & Tr. J. 705, 728 (Winter 2006).

[10] David Bank, *Loading Up: Should Foundations Rely on One Stock or Diversify?*, Wall St. J., Feb. 14, 2002, at C1, col. 3.

§8.36 [1] *See generally* §3.5.1 of this handbook (nature and extent of the trustee's estate).

[2] *See generally* §7.3.1 of this handbook (liability as legal owner in contract to nonbeneficiaries).

[3] The Judiciary Act of 1789 §35, 1 Stat. 73, 92 (1789), for example, provides that "in all the courts of the United States, the parties may plead and manage their own causes personally. . . ." There is similar language in 28 U.S.C. §1654.

[4] *See generally* §6.1.1 of this handbook (duty to be generally prudent) and §6.1.4 of this handbook (duty to give personal attention (not to delegate)) (noting that a trustee has an affirmative fiduciary obligation to seek out the advice of experts if it is prudent to do so).

[5] C. E. Pope Equity Trust v. United States, 818 F.2d 696 (9th Cir. 1987).

of having the action dismissed. One court has done just that, interpreting a statute authorizing parties to "prosecute their own suits personally" as depriving nonattorney trustees of the right to represent themselves in their fiduciary capacities in trust litigation.[6] That a trust is not a legal entity was either not appreciated by the court or not taken seriously in this context. In any case, dismissal presumably could have been avoided had the trustees simply brought the action in their individual capacities as well.

§8.37 The Origin of the English Trust

The trust has had no such success with respect to another system of law—Islam. Legal historians have long recognized that the origins of the trust may actually be traceable to an Islamic legal construct, the waqf. However, whereas the trust has expanded its domain in the modern economy, the waqf has experienced a precipitous decline throughout the Islamic world. To some degree, this has been attributable to factors that point less to inefficiencies with respect to waqf legal doctrine itself than to consolidation of power by political movements intent on gaining control of private capital. To a large degree, however, it is ascribable to the legal doctrine associated with the waqf.[1]

Introduction. The English trust is a unique legal device[2] whose origin has been the source of much debate among legal scholars.[3] There are three theories concerning the origin of the English trust:[4] the Roman,[5] Germanic,[6] and Islamic.[7] Until the nineteenth century, it was believed the trust was modeled on the Roman *fideicommissum*.[8] By the nineteenth century, the accepted theory was

---

[6] *See* Staten v. O'Neill, 83 Mass. App. Ct. 1105, 980 N.E.2d 471 (2013).

§8.37 [1] Jeffrey A. Schoenblum, *The Role of Legal Doctrine in the Decline of the Islamic Waqf: A Comparison with the Trust*, 32 Vand. J. Transnatl. L. 1191 (1999).

[2] Frederick W. Maitland, Equity: Also the Forms of Action at Common Law 23 (A. H. Chaytor & W. J. Whittaker eds. 1984) (stating that the trust "perhaps forms the most distinctive achievement of English lawyers. . . . There is nothing quite like it in foreign law.").

[3] Avisheh Avini, Comment, *The Origins of the Modern English Trust Revisited*, 70 Tul. L. Rev. 1139, 1140 (1996).

[4] There is actually a fourth theory advanced by Frederick W. Maitland called the Romano-Germanic theory. Frederick Pollock & Frederick W. Maitland, The History of English Law 228–255 (2d ed. 1968) (theorizing that the use was modeled on both Roman and German law). However, this theory has received the same criticisms as the Roman and Germanic theories. Avisheh Avini, Comment, *The Origins of the Modern English Trust Revisited*, 70 Tul. L. Rev. 1139, 1152 (1996).

[5] *See* 2 William Blackstone, Commentaries 328 (suggesting that the English use was modeled on the Roman *fideicommissum*).

[6] *See* Oliver W. Holmes, *Law in Science and Science in Law*, 12 Harv. L. Rev. 443 (1899) (suggesting that the Salic Salmannus was the ancestor of the English use).

[7] George Makdisi, The Rise of Colleges 227–240 (1981) (suggesting that the English trust emerged from the Islamic law of the waqf).

[8] *See generally* §8.12.1 of this handbook (civil law alternatives to the trust).

that the trust was modeled on the Salic law of the Salmannus.[9] The latest theory is that the trust is based on the Islamic example of the *waqf*.[10]

The English Use. Until the passage of the Statute of Uses in 1535, the English trust was known by its predecessor, the *use*.[11] The trust's antecedent, the use emerged in equity in order to circumvent to narrowness and rigidity of English common law restrictions on ownership and transfer of property.[12] The *use* "entailed the transfer of legal title (enfeoffment) to a person who was to hold the property (the feoffee to uses) for the benefit of another (the cestui que use)."[13] Through this device, feudal landowners could transfer property and circumvent the feudal incidents of tenancy (*e.g.*, ward, heriot, and escheat).[14] The *use* had other purposes as well. "Probably, as Maitland suggests, the first general employment of uses was in the thirteenth century, for conveying lands to the use of the Franciscan friars, who by the laws of their order could neither individually or as a community own property."[15]

Henry VII enacted the statute of uses to counteract the negative revenue effects of the employment of the use, by attributing ownership of the "legal title" to the *cestui que* use for taxation purposes.[16] Exceptions to the statute of uses, however, were recognized, such as "active trusts," in which the "feoffee to uses" retained certain incidents of ownership.[17] It is from these exceptions that the English trust emerged.[18]

The *fideicommissum* and the Roman theory. The *fideicommissum* was created in order to circumvent the strict regime of the *ius civile*.[19] Under the law of *ius civile*, certain classes of people, *e.g.*, infants and non-Romans, were prohibited from becoming beneficiaries of a legal testament.[20] A testator could nevertheless entrust his property to an intermediary person who was allowed to be an heir by law.[21] The testator would then instruct the intermediary third

---

[9] *See generally* Oliver W. Holmes, *Law in Science and Science in Law*, 12 Harv. L. Rev. 443 (1899) (suggesting that the trust is based on the Salic Salmannus).

[10] Ann Van Wynen Thomas, *Note on the Origin of Uses and Trusts, Waqfs*, 3 S. L.J. 162, 163–166; Henry Cattan, *The Law of Waqf*, 1 Law in The Middle East 213–218 (Majid Khadduri & Herbert H. Liebesny eds., 1955); Monica M. Gaudiosi, Comment, *The Influence of the Islamic Law of Waqf on the Development of the Trust in England*, 136 U. Pa. L. Rev. 1231, 1232 (1988).

[11] *See generally* §8.15.1 of this handbook (statute of uses).

[12] Avisheh Avini, Comment, *The Origins of the Modern English Trust Revisited*, 70 Tul. L. Rev. 1139, 1143 (1996).

[13] Avisheh Avini, Comment, *The Origins of the Modern English Trust Revisited*, 70 Tul. L. Rev. 1139, 1143 (1996).

[14] Paul G. Haskell, Preface to the Law of Trusts 5 (1975); 1 Scott on Trusts §1.5.

[15] 1 Scott & Ascher §1.4 (The First Period); 5 Scott & Ascher §37.1.2 (History of Charitable Trusts in England).

[16] 1 Scott on Trusts §1.5.

[17] 1 Scott on Trusts §1.5 (stating that the "feoffee to uses" had the right to take profits and hold seisin).

[18] Bogert §5.

[19] The *ius civile* was the law of the Roman Empire applicable to Roman citizens. Barry Nicholas, An Introduction to Roman Law 57–59 (1962).

[20] J. Inst. 2.23.1.

[21] J. Inst. 2.23.1.

party to transfer the entrusted property to the intended beneficiary, who was not allowed to be an heir by law.[22] This informal testamentary trust was known as the *fideicommissum*, a legal device by which property was "entrusted" to one person (the *haeres* fiduciaries) for the benefit of another (the *fideicommissarius*).[23] The *fideicommissum* was eventually recognized and adopted by Roman law.[24]

The Roman theory traces the origins of the English *use* to the *fideicommissum* by pointing to the similarities between both institutions.[25] Both the *use* and the *fideicommissum* share a "common fiduciary nature: property is entrusted to one person for the benefit of another."[26] Both legal institutions "developed in independent jurisdictions, the trust in equity, outside the common law; the fideicommissum outside the Roman formulary system in a new official procedure."[27]

The Roman theory suggests that ecclesiastics introduced the *fideicommissum* into England as the *use* in order to circumvent the restrictions on the transfer of property imposed by the Mortmain Statute.[28] Further, proponents of the Roman theory theorize that because the law of the Church was founded on Roman law, logic dictates that the ecclesiastics would turn to Roman law for guidance.[29] Finally, the Roman theory's position was most recently revived by a letter Saint Jerome wrote in 393 A.D. condemning the ecclesiastics' usage of the *fideicommissum* to circumvent restrictions on the transfer of property to the clergy.[30]

The Roman theory has, however, been criticized by several scholars who point out that any similarities between the *fideicommissum* and the English *use* are merely superficial.[31] The fundamental criticism remains that the *fideicommissum* was a testamentary bequest, while the English *use* seldom arose by will.[32]

---

[22] J. Inst. 2.23.1.

[23] David Johnston, The Roman Law of Trusts 1 (1988).

[24] Barry Nicholas, An Introduction to Roman Law 27–28 (1962).

[25] 2 William Blackstone, Commentaries 328 (suggesting that the Roman fideicommissum was the direct ancestor of the English use). *See generally* Bogert, Trusts and Trustees §2.

[26] David Johnston, The Roman Law of Trusts 1 (1988).

[27] David Johnston, The Roman Law of Trusts 1 (1988). The reader of this handbook may find amusing the first paragraph of the Roman Law of Trusts: Trusts did not exist in Roman law; nor do they exist in the civil systems which derive from it. They are rightly regarded as one of the hallmarks of legal systems of the common law family. Since this is the case, a book on the Roman law of trusts might well be expected to be short. David Johnston, The Roman Law of Trusts 1 (1988).

[28] Avisheh Avini, Comment, *The Origins of the Modern English Trust Revisited*, 70 Tul. L. Rev. 1139, 1143–1444 (1996). The Mortmain Statute of the late fourteenth century prohibited the clergy from receiving donations of land. Avini, Comment, *The Origins of the Modern English Trust Revisited*, 70 Tul. L. Rev. 1139 at n.26.

[29] Avini, Comment, *The Origins of the Modern English Trust Revisited*, 70 Tul. L. Rev. at 1148–1149 (citing Brendan F. Brown, *The Ecclesiastical Origin of the Use*, 10 Notre Dame L. Rev. 357, 365–366 (1935)).

[30] Avini, Comment, *The Origins of the Modern English Trust Revisited*, 70 Tul. L. Rev. 1139, 1143 (1996).

[31] Avini, Comment, *The Origins of the Modern English Trust Revisited*, 70 Tul. L. Rev. at 1149.

[32] Avini, Comment, *The Origins of the Modern English Trust Revisited*, 70 Tul. L. Rev. at 1149.

Further, another critical difference is that for the fideicommissum, the beneficiary (the *fideicommissarius*) was considered the real owner of the transferred property, while for the English *use*, the third party intermediary (the feoffee to uses) held legal title to the transferred property.[33]

The Salmannus and the Germanic theory. The *Salmannus* was predominantly used to aid in the disposition of a transferor's property upon his death.[34] This institution dates back to the fifth-century legal code of the German tribe of the Salian Franks, the Lex Salica.[35] The term *Salmannus* is derived from "sala," which means "to transfer."[36] The *Salmannus* entailed the transfer of the transferor's property during his lifetime to a *Salmannus*, a person trusted to transfer the property to a designated beneficiary upon the death of the original transferor.[37] Thus, the use of the *Salmannus* permitted the transferor to adopt or appoint an heir.[38] The *Salmannus* held the property "on account of or to the use of another" and was "bound to fulfill his trust."[39] The *Salmannus* is "the 'person through whom effect is given to a transfer,' and hence, the anglicized 'saleman.' "[40]

The Germanic theory on the origin of the English trust was propounded by Oliver Wendell Holmes and Frederick William Maitland.[41] Holmes and Maitland traced the origin of the English trust to the Salic *Salmannus*[42] and propounded that "the saleman became in England the better known feoffee to uses."[43] After the withdrawal of the Roman legions in the fifth century, Germanic tribes migrated to England, and the *Salmannus* was introduced with the Norman conquest of the eleventh century.[44] The Germanic theory that the

---

[33] Avini, Comment, *The Origins of the Modern English Trust Revisited*, 70 Tul. L. Rev. at 1149.

[34] J. L. Barton, *The Medieval Use*, 81 Law. Q. Rev. 562, 562 (1962).

[35] John H. Wigmore, A Panorama of the World's Legal Systems 834–835 (1928). The Lex Salica was the earliest code of laws promulgated in the early sixth century. Wigmore, A Panorama of the World's Legal Systems.

[36] William S. Holdsworth, A History of English Law 410 (3d ed. 1945).

[37] Brendan F. Brown, *The Ecclesiastical Origin of the Use*, 10 Notre Dame L. Rev. 357 (1935). The Salmannus was a third party, distinct from the original transferor and designated beneficiary, who agreed to carry out the specific instructions of a transferor of property, either as an inter vivos transfer or as a postmortem transfer. Frederick Pollock & Frederick W. Maitland, The History of the English Law 226–259 (2d ed. 1968).

[38] William S. Holdsworth, A History of English Law 410–411 (3d ed. 1945).

[39] Monica M. Gaudiosi, Comment, *The Influence of the Islamic Law of Waqf on the Development of the Trust in England*, 136 U. Pa. L. Rev. 1231, 1243 (1988) (quoting Holdsworth at 412).

[40] Monica M. Gaudiosi, Comment, *The Influence of the Islamic Law of Waqf on the Development of the Trust in England*, 136 U. Pa. L. Rev. 1231, 1243 (1988) (quoting Holdsworth at 411 & n.1).

[41] *See* Oliver W. Holmes, *Law in Science and Science in Law*, 12 Harv. L. Rev. 443, 445 (1899). *See also* Frederick W. Maitland, *The Origin of Uses*, 8 Harv. L. Rev. 127 (1894). *See generally* Bogert §2.

[42] Oliver W. Holmes, *Law in Science and Science in Law*, 12 Harv. L. Rev. 443, 445–446 (1899); Frederick W. Maitland, *The Origin of Uses*, 8 Harv. L. Rev. 127, 129 (1894).

[43] Monica M. Gaudiosi, Comment, *The Influence of the Islamic Law of Waqf on the Development of the Trust in England*, 136 U. Pa. L. Rev. 1231 (1988) (citing to Oliver W. Holmes, *Law in Science and Science in Law*, 12 Harv. L. Rev. 443, 446 (1899)).

[44] Brendan F. Brown, *The Ecclesiastical Origin of the Use*, 10 Notre Dame L. Rev. 357, 365 (1935).

Salmannus developed into the feoffee to uses is supported by "evidence of use of the salmannus in postmortem transfers of land in twelfth century England."[45] The theory further suggests that shortly after the Norman conquest, a series of cases emerged in England in which a transferor would convey his land to a third party "to the use" of another.[46]

Critics of the Germanic theory, like critics of the Roman theory, point to the superficiality of the similarities between the Salic *Salmannus* and the English *use*.[47] Critics further suggest that there is no concrete evidence that the *Salmannus* was used by the Normans during the eleventh century.[48]

The Waqf and the Islamic theory. The Islamic *waqf* was created by Muslim jurists during the first three centuries of Islam.[49] This legal institution was, and still is, used as a charitable device.[50] The Islamic *waqf* (plural: *awqaf*) entails the "detention of the corpus from the ownership of any person and the gift of its income or usufruct either presently or in the future, to some charitable purpose."[51] Islamic *awqaf* are of two types: family endowments (*waqf ahli* or *dhurri*) [also known as family *awqaf*] and charitable endowments (*waqf khairi*) [also known as welfare *awqaf*].[52] A family endowment is created for the security and

---

[45] Avini, Comment, *The Origins of the Modern English Trust Revisited*, 70 Tul. L. Rev. 1139, 1150 (1996) (citing to Brendan F. Brown, *The Ecclesiastical Origin of the Use*, 10 Notre Dame L. Rev. 357, 358 (1935)).

[46] Frederick Pollock & Frederick W. Maitland, The History of English Law 231 (2d ed. 1968).

[47] Henry Cattan, *The Law of Waqf*, 1 Law in the Middle East 216 (Majid Khadduri & Herbert H. Liebesny eds. 1955). The Salmannus merely adopted the role of a testamentary executor or of an intermediary for a conveyance, while the feoffee to uses adopted the role of a trustee. Henry Cattan, *The Law of Waqf*, 1 Law in the Middle East 216.

[48] J. L. Barton, *The Medieval Use*, 81 Law Q. Rev. 562 (1962).

[49] Henry Cattan, *The Law of Waqf*, 1 Law in the Middle East 205 (Majid Khadduri & Herbert H. Liebesny eds. 1955).

[50] Avini, Comment, *The Origins of the Modern English Trust Revisited*, 70 Tul. L. Rev. 1139, 1154–1155 (1996). Avini has suggested the following: Although the ostensible purpose of the waqf was always charitable, the waqifs of awqaf also had many undeclared motives in creating a waqf. Because the waqf is the only form of perpetuity in Islamic law, it was bound to fulfill many other functions. Some of these secular uses included evasion of taxation, control over the excesses of heirs, accession of power over the masses by paying their religious leaders, and most prominently, immunity from government confiscation. There is also evidence that conquered peoples forced to convert to Islam used the *waqf* to circumvent the constraints of the Islamic law of inheritance. Avini, Comment, *The Origins of the Modern English Trust Revisited*, 70 Tul. L. Rev. at 1154–1155.

[51] Avini, Comment, *The Origins of the Modern English Trust Revisited*, 70 Tul. L. Rev. 1139, 1152–1153 (1996) (quoting Henry Cattan, *The Law of Waqf*, 1 Law in the Middle East 203 (Majid Khadduri & Herbert H. Liebesny eds. 1955)). The ultimate purpose of the endowment must be pleasing to God and be in accordance with the laws of Islam. Heffening, *Waqf*, 8 Encyclopedia of Islam 1096 (1928).

[52] Henry Cattan, *The Law of Waqf*, 1 Law in the Middle East 213–218 (Majid Khadduri & Herbert H. Liebesny eds. 1955). The *waqf ahli* or *dhurri* (family endowment) entailed the dedication of property with an ultimate charitable purpose. Avisheh Avini, Comment, *The Origins of the Modern English Trust Revisited*, 70 Tul. L. Rev. 1139, 1153 (1996). The owner of the property could reserve the income of the property for his children and descendants in perpetuity. Avini, Comment, *The Origins of the Modern English Trust Revisited*, 70 Tul. L. Rev. 1139. Upon extinction of his descendants, the income would be transferred to the charitable purpose. Avini, Comment, *The Origins of the Modern English Trust Revisited*, 70 Tul. L. Rev. 1139. On the other hand, the *waqf khairi*

welfare of the near relatives of the one who contributes the subject property. Once the private objectives have been achieved, it converts to a charitable endowment. *Waqf* property always belongs to Allah; no human being may alienate the beneficial interest.

The *waqf* is created upon the declaration by the owner of the property (the *waqif*) that the income of the subject property (the property to be dedicated as waqf) is reserved for a specific purpose.[53] The *waqif* is responsible for appointing a trustee (*mutawalli*), designating beneficiaries (*mustahiqqun*), and providing for the manner of distribution of *waqf* income.[54] The *mutawalli* then administers the *waqf* according to the instructions of the *waqif*, under the supervision of the judge (*qadi*) within whose jurisdiction the *waqf* property is located.[55]

A *waqf* has custody of Jerusalem's Temple Mount, on which now sits the Dome of the Rock and Al-Aqsa Mosque:

> This is the holiest site in the world to Jews, where the deeply religious fear to tread lest they step on the Holy of Holies: Solomon's Temple and the Second Temple built by Herod the Great once stood on this site. The site is sacred to Muslims as well: Known in Arabic as the Haram al-Sharif, the Noble Sanctuary.[56]

Just as there is a "plausible" argument that the Gothic style was the result of "European encounters with Islamic architecture,"[57] so also there is a plausible argument that the trust was the result of European encounters with Islamic legal institutions. The Islamic theory traces the origin of the English *use* to the Islamic *waqf*.[58] Proponents of this theory advance that the *waqf* was introduced to England by Franciscan Friars returning from the thirteenth-century crusades.[59] Under the laws of their Order, the Friars were not allowed to own property because of their strict interpretation of religious poverty.[60] Because the Friars still needed property for their religious activities, they used the

---

(the charitable endowment) entailed the immediate and irrevocable dedication of property to a charitable purpose. Avini, Comment, *The Origins of the Modern English Trust Revisited*, 70 Tul. L. Rev. 1139.

[53] Heffening, *Waqf*, 8 Encyclopedia of Islam 1096. The *waqif* must clearly and unequivocally express his intentions to declare a property as waqf with the phrase, "it must neither be sold nor given away nor bequeathed." Heffening, *Waqf*, 8 Encyclopedia of Islam 1096.

[54] George Makdisi, The Rise of Colleges 35–36 (1981).

[55] Makdisi, The Rise of Colleges at 55.

[56] Hershel Shanks, *Biblical Destruction*, Wall St. J., July 18, 2007, at A14.

[57] Michael J. Lewis, *How Chartres Reached for the Divine*, Wall St. J, July 5–6, 2008, at W9 (noting that Philip Ball in his Universe of Stone "shows how Crusaders took home not only a knowledge of Islamic architecture's forms but also, in at least one case . . . and perhaps more, the architects themselves," the one recorded case being "a hapless prisoner named Lalys").

[58] Monica M. Gaudiosi, Comment, *The Influence of the Islamic Law of Waqf on the Development of the Trust in England*, 136 U. Pa. L. Rev. 1231, 1244 (1988).

[59] Gaudiosi, Comment, *The Influence of the Islamic Law of Waqf on the Development of the Trust in England*, 136 U. Pa. L. Rev. 1231, 1244 (1988).

[60] M. D. Lambert, Franciscan Poverty 84 (1961).

concept behind the *waqf* to circumvent the Order's vow of poverty.[61] Accordingly, benefactors would transfer property to a trustee "ad opus franciscanorum," *i.e.*, "for the use of the Franciscans."[62]

The Islamic theory on the origin of the English trust has received the least amount of criticism.[63] The *waqf* and the English *use* are almost identical institutions in purpose and structure.[64] Both have a settlor, a trustee, and a beneficiary, and both were used to circumvent restrictions of ownership and transfer of property.[65] The only significant difference between the *waqf* and the English *use* is that the *waqf* requires that the corpus of the trust be applied exclusively to a charitable purpose, whether immediately, as in the case of the charitable endowment, or as a reversion, as is the case of the family endowment.[66] As an aside, a charitable "reversion" under a family *waqf* regime is actually more analogous to an equitable charitable remainder than it is to an equitable reversion upon the imposition of a resulting trust.[67]

Conclusion. The exact institution from which the modern Anglo-American trust originated remains to date the source of much debate and speculation.[68] At a time when land was the principal form of wealth, the English use, the Roman *fideicommissum*, the Salic Salmannus, and the Islamic *waqf*, "all emerged as a result of positive-law deficiencies and restrictions concerning the ownership and devolution of property."[69]

§8.38 The Warren Trust (a.k.a. The Mills Trust)

The key player in this saga of sexual politics and family greed is Edward Perry Ned Warren. He is a zealous, sophisticated collector of Greek antiquities and an avowed homosexual, indeed an avid admirer of the idealized homoerotic tradition of classical Greece. His mores, in a word, are anathema to staid, turn-of-the-century Boston. Ned's quarrel over the estate with elder brother Sam eventually leads to the latter's suicide, a scandal that overshadows the

---

[61] Marianne Guerin-McManus, *Conservation Trust Funds*, 20 UCLA J. Envtl. L. & Poly. 1, 5 (2001/2002).

[62] M. D. Lambert, Franciscan Poverty 84 (1961).

[63] Monica M. Gaudiosi, Comment, *The Influence of the Islamic Law of Waqf on the Development of the Trust in England*, 136 U. Pa. L. Rev. 1231, 1244 (1988).

[64] Avini, Comment, *The Origins of the Modern English Trust Revisited*, 70 Tul. L. Rev. 1139, 1161 (1996).

[65] Avini, Comment, *The Origins of the Modern English Trust Revisited*, 70 Tul. L. Rev. 1139, 1161 (1996).

[66] Henry Cattan, *The Law of Waqf*, 1 Law in the Middle East 214 (Majid Khadduri & Herbert H. Liebesny eds. 1955).

[67] *See* the quotation introducing §4.1.1 of this handbook. *See also* §4.1.1.1 of this handbook (the resulting trust).

[68] Marianne Guerin-McManus, *Conservation Trust Funds*, 20 UCLA J. Envtl. L. & Poly. 1, 4–5 (2001/2002).

[69] Guerin-McManus, *Conservation Trust Funds*, 20 UCLA J. Envtl. L. & Poly. at 5 (quoting Avisheh Avini, Comment, *The Origins of the Modern English Trust Revisited*, 70 Tul. L. Rev. 1139 (1996)).

family's important contributions to and impact on the city of Boston and Harvard University. It was the Warren fortune that funded the Boston Museum of Fine Arts with its classical antiquities collection, Dennison House, Harvard Yard, Harvard's great oriental book series, the restoration of Shakerton, and the Tahanto commune in Harvard township—all reflections of the Warren children's diverse interests. . . . The Warren children's deep but individualistic engagement in the arts and politics as well as their social standing involved them with the notable figures of their day: Oscar Wilde, Louis Brandeis, Henry Adams, Bernard Berenson, Rudyard Kipling, the Cabots, the Lowells, Oliver Wendell Holmes —directly or indirectly, all integral characters in Green's account.[1]

Samuel D. Warren, Sr., owned and operated S. D. Warren & Co. The company, which he acquired in the 1850s, owned paper mills and Maine real estate. He died in 1888, leaving one-third of the enterprise outright to his widow and two-thirds outright to his five children: Sam, Jr., Henry, Ned, Fiske, and Cornelia. Louis Brandeis—later to become a member of the U.S. Supreme Court—was a law partner of Sam, Jr., in Boston.

The widow and the five children elected in 1889 to transfer the mills and the real estate to Sam, Jr., the widow, and one Mortimer Mason, as trustees, for the benefit of the widow and the five children (the Trust). "It was also understood at the time the Mills property was conveyed to the Trust that the Trust would in turn lease the Mills Property to a firm also to be called S. D. Warren & Co . . . , that the Firm would operate the manufacturing facility and share profits therefrom with the Trust, and that the principals of the Firm would be Sam, Fiske, and Mortimer Mason."[2] Brandeis represented all parties to the series of transactions.

The Trust, which was irrevocable, was to last for thirty-three years. The compensation of the principals of the firm was tied to the firm's profits. The principals controlled whether profits were distributed to the Trust or ploughed back into the firm. Capital improvements were chargeable to the Trust while repairs were chargeable to the firm. The principals controlled the characterization and allocation of these expenditures.

In 1909, Ned filed suit against Sam, Jr., and others alleging certain breaches of the duty of loyalty in their stewardship of the properties of the Trust. In 1910, the matter became a local cause célèbre when Sam, Jr., shot himself. The case was settled shortly thereafter when Ned's interest was bought out by the other family members.

The matter became a national cause célèbre when opponents of Brandeis suggested in his 1916 confirmation hearings for the U. S. Supreme Court that he had engaged in unethical conduct in simultaneously representing persons with conflicting interests, namely, the trust beneficiaries and the principals of the firm.

Today, legal ethicists use the Warren Trust as a case study when debating such issues as whom trust counsel represents,[3] whether one ethically can be a

---

§8.38 [1] Martin Green, The Mount Vernon Street Warrens: A Boston Story, 1860–1910 (dust jacket blurb) (1989).

[2] Richard W. Painter, *Contracting Around Conflicts in a Family Representation: Louis Brandeis and the Warren Trust*, 8 U. Chi. L. Sch. Roundtable 353, 360 (2001).

[3] *See* §8.8 of this handbook (whom does counsel represent?).

lawyer for a "family" or a "situation,"[4] and what constitutes adequate informed consent to a lawyer's representation of persons whose interests are in conflict.[5]

§8.39 Settlor's Choice of Law as to Meaning and Effect of Terms of Trust

[C]hoice of law involves a decision by the forum to proceed with an analytical process resulting in the application of rules of either the forum or some other state.[1]

If the settlor in the governing instrument designates what state's law will govern the meaning and effect of the terms of the trust, the court, as a general rule, will honor the designation. There are exceptions. The designated law may not be contrary to the "public policy" of the "jurisdiction having the most significant relationship to the matter at issue,"[2] particularly the jurisdiction's laws relating to postmortem spousal rights, restrictions on testamentary gifts to charities, and qualifications of trustees.[3] For a more detailed discussion of the general rule and its exceptions, the reader is referred to Section 8.5 of this handbook.

§8.40 Judicial Jurisdiction over Trustee, Beneficiary, and/or the Trust Property; Venue Issues; Subject Matter Jurisdiction

Distinctions between actions in rem and those in personam are ancient and originally expressed in procedural terms what seems really to have been a distinction in the substantive law of property under . . . [Roman law,] . . . a system quite unlike our own. The legal recognition and rise in economic importance of incorporeal or intangible forms of property have upset the ancient simplicity of property law and the clarity of its distinctions, while new forms of proceedings have confused the old procedural classification. American courts have sometimes classed certain actions as in rem because personal service of process was not required, and at other times have held personal service of process not required because the action was in rem. —Justice Robert H. Jackson[1]

---

[4] *See, e.g.*, Clyde Spillenger, *Elusive Advocate: Reconsidering Brandeis as People's Lawyer*, 105 Yale L.J. 1445 (1996); John P. Frank, *The Legal Ethics of Louis D. Brandeis*, 17 Stan. L. Rev. 683 (1965).

[5] *See, e.g.*, Richard W. Painter, *Contracting Around Conflicts in a Family Representation: Louis Brandeis and the Warren Trust*, 8 U. Chi. L. Sch. Roundtable 353, 373–377 (2001).

§8.39 [1] Jeffrey A. Schoenblum, 1 Multistate and Multinational Estate Planning 1216 (1999).

[2] UTC §107(1) (available at <http://www.uniformlaws.org/Act.aspx?title=Trust%20 Code>).

[3] Bogert §301. *See generally* §8.5 of this handbook (conflict of laws).

§8.40 [1] Mullane v. Central Hanover Bank & Trust Co., 339 U.S. 306, 311 (1950).

I have said this because, so it seems to me, the Trust could hardly have been evolved among a people who had clearly formulated the distinction between a right in personam and a right in rem, and had made that distinction one of the main outlines of their legal system—Frederic William Maitland[2]

The dichotomy between personal liberties and property rights is a false one. Property does not have rights. People have rights. . . . —Justice Potter Stewart[3]

Summary. Leaving aside questions of federal jurisdiction, a topic we take up in Section 8.15.19 of this handbook,[4] when we say that a court has jurisdiction over a "trust," we mean that the court has the power to sort out the rights, duties, and obligations of the parties to the particular trust relationship.[5] A state court that is in a position to exercise its power over either the trustee or over the trust property would have the power to sort out the equitable rights of the beneficiaries, even when the beneficiaries themselves are physically beyond the reach of the court. The beneficiaries, however, must be given due notice of any proceeding that could affect their equitable property rights, as well as a fair opportunity to be heard in the proceeding.[6] "The requirement of notice may be met by personal or constructive service of process (by publication or otherwise) depending upon the nature of the proceeding and the type of relief sought."[7] As a general rule, however, when it comes to entrusted land, only the courts of the state where the land is situated have the jurisdiction to adjudicate the rights, duties, and obligations of the parties with respect to that land. "Land and some things intimately connected with land are immovables. Other things, such as chattels, rights embodied in a document, and choses in action not so embodied, are movables."[8] In Section 8.5 of this handbook (conflict of laws), we discuss not competing jurisdictions but the law of what state is to be *applied* by a court that is exercising jurisdiction over a trust.

NOTICE: Article VII of the Uniform Probate Code addressed selected issues of trust administration, including trust registration, the jurisdiction of the courts concerning trusts, and the duties and liabilities of trustee. ARTICLE VII of the UPC was superseded by the Uniform Trust Code, which was approved in 2000. In 2010, UPC ARTCLE VII was repealed/ withdrawn following the widespread enactment of the UTC.

---

[2] Maitland, Selected Essays (1936) 144–145.

[3] Lynch v. Household Fin. Corp., 405 U.S. 538, 552 (1972).

[4] *See also* Bogert §292 ("Though a federal court is reluctant to exercise jurisdiction in cases where probate and trust questions are before a state court, a federal court has equitable jurisdiction over trusts and estates which it will exercise where not in conflict with state court proceedings.").

[5] *See* Bogert §292.

[6] *See* Bogert §292 (citing as authority Mullane v. Central Hanover Bank & Trust Co., 339 U.S. 306 (1950)).

[7] Bogert §292.

[8] 7 Scott & Ascher §46.1.

Judicial versus regulatory trustee qualification. It may or may not be a requirement in a given situation that a trustee's appointment must be confirmed by the court if it is to be effective. A trustee whose appointment has been so confirmed is said to be judicially qualified.[9] Judicial qualification is not to be confused with regulatory qualification, such as when a state banking regulator, an agent of the executive branch of the state's government, authorizes an out-of-state trust company to conduct trust business in the state. The judicial qualification of a trustee and the regulatory qualification of a trustee are easily confused and/or conflated.[10]

A jurisdiction primer. A personal judgment, that is to say a judgment *in personam*, "imposes a personal liability or obligation on the defendant or extinguishes the plaintiff's claim against the defendant."[11] Traditional due process notions of fair play and substantial justice require that for a court to render a binding judgment *in personam*, the defendant must have had at least some minimum contacts within the territory of the forum.[12] "It is sufficient, ... [for example] ... that the defendant has done acts or owns things in the state, at least as to causes of action arising out of such acts or ownership."[13] When a judgment issues *in personam*, the original claim is extinguished.[14] Prospectively the plaintiff owns the judgment and may maintain an action on the judgment. It is said that the original claim has "merged" into the judgment such that the parties are collaterally estopped from relitigating the claim in any subsequent actions between or among them.[15] An *in personam* judgment rendered against someone with insufficient contacts in the forum state is not entitled to recognition and enforcement under the full faith and credit clause of the federal constitution in the other states.[16] This is because the constitution "does not require a State to apply another State's law in violation of its own legitimate public policy."[17]

A judgment *in rem* does not create a personal liability or obligation.[18] Instead, it clarifies, orders, and otherwise sorts out the rights that are incident to the ownership of an item of property.[19] The judgment binds not only the

---

[9] *See generally* Scott & Ascher §45.2.1.

[10] *See, e.g.*, Mass. Gen. Laws ch. 203E, §113 (qualification of foreign trustee).

[11] 7 Scott & Ascher §45.2.2 (Jurisdiction Over Trusts of Movables). *See also* Bogert, Trusts and Trustees §292.

[12] International Shoe Co. v. Washington, 326 U.S. 310 (1945); McGee v. International Life Ins. Co., 355 U.S. 220 (1957). *See generally* Bogert §292.

[13] 7 Scott & Ascher §45.2.2. *See also* Bogert, Trusts and Trustees §292 ("Personal jurisdiction over a party defendant may be based upon his residence, domicile or mere physical presence within the state; by his voluntary appearance or consent in the proceedings; or by his performance of one or more acts within the state constituting a sufficient 'business' or fiduciary contact to give the court judicial jurisdiction over him").

[14] 7 Scott & Ascher §45.2.2.

[15] 7 Scott & Ascher §45.2.2.

[16] *See generally* Bogert §292.

[17] Nevada v. Hall, 440 U.S. 410, 422 (1978).

[18] 7 Scott & Ascher §45.2.2.

[19] 7 Scott & Ascher §45.2.2.

parties to the litigation but also all others.[20] For example, a proceeding to register title to land is *in rem*.[21] "When land is held in trust, a court of the state in which the land is situated has jurisdiction in rem or quasi in rem."[22] If a court has jurisdiction over a disputed item of property but not over those who own the rights to that property, the court may issue a judgment *quasi in rem* that is binding only on them.[23] "If the judgment affects only the interests of particular persons in the thing, as in the case of actions to partition land, to quiet title, for the foreclosure of a mortgage, or to establish the interests of the beneficiaries of a trust, and the court has jurisdiction over the property but not over the persons whose interests are to be affected, it is a proceeding quasi in rem."[24] For an *in rem* decree, quasi or otherwise, to be final and binding, however, the affected parties must have been given notice and an opportunity to be heard sufficient to have satisfied the due process requirements of the federal Constitution.[25]

In the context of trusts, jurisdiction *in personam* and jurisdiction *in rem* are not mutually exclusive. They can overlap; they can even partially overlap, such as when the court lacks *in personam* jurisdiction over the beneficiaries: "The forum court may have jurisdiction over the trustee and the trust property so that its decree can have an in rem effect on all interests in the trust property and an *in personam* effect on the trustee."[26]

An introduction to jurisdiction in the trust context. Let us assume that a trust beneficiary wishes to sue the trustee for breach of trust. The beneficiary files suit against the trustee in the court of a state other than where the trustee, is domiciled. The trust property, however, is located in the state where the suit is being brought. Will the court have the power to adjudicate the rights, duties, and obligations of the trustee and to issue binding decrees relating to the status of the trust property.[27] For the court to have jurisdiction, it must either have *in personam* jurisdiction over the trustee or *in rem* jurisdiction over the trust property.[28] In the case of a trust under a will that had been probated in the state, the court by statute may have retained continuing or supervisory jurisdiction, in particular if the trustee had been required to be qualified by the court.[29] Should the testamentary trustee subsequently move himself, and even the subject

---

[20] 7 Scott & Ascher §45.2.2.

[21] 7 Scott & Ascher §45.2.2.

[22] 7 Scott & Ascher §46.2.2.1.

[23] 7 Scott & Ascher §45.2.2.

[24] 7 Scott & Ascher §45.2.2.

[25] 7 Scott & Ascher §45.2.2; Bogert §292 (each citing as authority Mullane v. Central Hanover Bank & Trust Co., 339 U.S. 306 (1950), a case involving the settlement of the accounts of a trustee of a common trust fund). Common trust funds are discussed in §9.7.1 of this handbook.

[26] Bogert §292.

[27] " . . . [J]urisdiction to decide a particular issue turns on the adequacy of a state's contacts with the matter in dispute and on the adequacy of the steps taken to bring the litigants under the court's control." Jeffrey A. Schoenblum, 1 Multistate and Multinational Estate Planning 1216 (1999).

[28] *See generally* Jurisdiction of suit involving trust as affected by location of res, residence of parties to trust, and appearance, 15 A.L.R.2d 610; 7 Scott & Ascher §45.2.2.

[29] *See generally* Bogert §292.

property, out-of-state, the court would still be in a position to exercise primary supervision over the affairs of the trust.[30]

The probate process in and of itself should not give the court jurisdiction over trusts that a decedent had funded *inter vivos*:

> [A] State acquires no *in rem* jurisdiction to adjudicate the validity of *inter vivos* dispositions simply because its decisions might augment an estate passing under a will probated in its courts. If such a basis of jurisdiction were sustained, probate courts would enjoy nationwide service of process to adjudicate interests in property with which neither the State nor the decedent could claim any affiliation. The settlor-decedent's Florida domicile is equally unavailing as a basis for jurisdiction over the trust assets. For the purpose of jurisdiction *in rem* the maxim that personalty has its situs at the domicile of its owner is a fiction of limited utility. The maxim is no less suspect when the domicile is that of a decedent. In analogous cases, this Court has rejected the suggestion that the probate decree of the State where decedent was domiciled has an *in rem* effect on personalty outside the forum State that could render it conclusive on the interests of nonresidents over whom there was no personal jurisdiction.[31]

In the case of an inter vivos trust, the trustee generally need not be judicially qualified.[32] Thus, in the case of an inter vivos trust of movables, some court in the state where the trust is primarily being administered ordinarily exercises primary jurisdiction over it.[33]

In the case of a testamentary trust of land, if the land is located in the state where the will was probated, the courts of that state "can determine the interests of the beneficiaries in the land, even if it lacks jurisdiction over the trustee and some or all of the beneficiaries. It can determine the construction, validity, and effect of the will or trust instrument insofar as interests in the land are concerned."[34] If the land is located in a state other than the state where the will was probated, the testamentary trustee may have to have his appointment confirmed by a court in the state where the land is located.[35] Otherwise the court of the situs will appoint a substitute trustee to administer the land.[36] It depends upon the jurisdiction.[37] In the case of an inter vivos trust of land, the

---

[30] *See* Bogert §292 ("Under the 'trust entity' theory a testamentary trust is established and remains at the testator's domicile, thereby giving the domiciliary court in rem jurisdiction independent and apart from the presence of the trustee, the trust assets or the trust beneficiaries"); 7 Scott & Ascher §45.2.2.5 ("The court in which the trustee has qualified as trustee may remove the trustee and appoint another, even if the trustee has left the state and relocated the trust property"). *See generally* §7.2.3.6 of this handbook (removing the trustee).

[31] Hanson v. Denckla, 357 U.S. 235, 248–249 (1958). *See generally* 7 Scott & Ascher §45.2.1.6 (Pouring Over by Will into Inter Vivos Trust).

[32] *See* 7 Scott & Ascher §45.2.2.4.2 (Inter Vivos Trusts).

[33] *See* 7 Scott & Ascher §45.2.2.4.2 (Inter Vivos Trusts).

[34] 7 Scott & Ascher §46.2.2.1.

[35] *See generally* 7 Scott & Ascher §46.2.1.

[36] *See generally* 7 Scott & Ascher §46.2.1.

[37] *See generally* 7 Scott & Ascher §46.2.1.

courts of the situs have primary jurisdiction over at least those aspects of the trust's administration that relate to the land.[38]

That the court has jurisdiction over the trustee is critical not just in actions by beneficiaries against trustees but also in actions by creditors against trust beneficiaries who owe them money. When a creditor seeks to reach in satisfaction of a debt the debtor's equitable interest under a trust, or perhaps even the underlying trust property itself, it is generally not necessary that the court have personal jurisdiction over the beneficiary, just over the trustee, "at least when the court also has jurisdiction over the administration of the trust."[39]

It was at one time problematic if a court with primary supervision of a trust of land lacked *in personam* jurisdiction over the trustee. The court, for example, incident to an action to remove the trustee might have lacked the authority to compel a transfer of title to, or to vest title in, a successor trustee.[40] "At common law, indeed, the rule was that a court of equity acted in personam, and only in personam; thus although the property was within the state, a court of equity could not by its decree affect interests in the property."[41] Today, in an equitable action to remove a trustee, the court may effect a vesting of legal title in the successor trustee if it has jurisdiction over the trust property.[42] A number of states now have statutes requiring a nonresident trustee of land to appoint a resident or an in-state public official as agent for service of process.[43]

If a state court has *in rem* jurisdiction only over the property of a trust, it nonetheless may determine the interests of the parties in that property though it lacks the authority to issue judgments and decrees that personally bind the parties.[44] Such judgments and decrees are entitled to be recognized and enforced by the courts of all the other states, provided proper notice and an opportunity to be heard has been given to the beneficiaries and the trustee.[45] It is said that the judgments and decrees are entitled to be given "full faith and

---

[38] *See generally* 7 Scott & Ascher §46.2.2.1 (Courts of the Situs).

[39] 3 Scott & Ascher §14.11.2. *See generally* §5.3.3 of this handbook (rights of beneficiary's creditors and others to the equitable interest and/or the underlying trust property).

[40] 2 Scott & Ascher §11.12.

[41] 7 Scott & Ascher §45.2.2.

[42] *See* 7 Scott & Ascher §45.2.2.

[43] 2 Scott & Ascher §11.12. *See generally* §3.1 of this handbook (who can be a trustee).

[44] Bogert §292.

[45] *See* 7 Scott & Ascher §45.2.2.5. "When the trustee has not qualified as trustee in a court, but trust administration is fixed in a particular state, as when the settlor names a trust company as trustee, the courts of that state have primary supervision over the administration of the trust- . . . The situs of the trust is in that state . . . Because the court has jurisdiction over both the trustee and the trust property, its judgment is binding upon the courts of other states as to all matters involving the validity, construction, or administration of the trust." 7 Scott & Ascher §45.2.2.5. If a testamentary trustee has qualified as such in the court where the will was probated, the judgments of the court in matters pertaining to the trust are entitled to recognition and enforcement in all the states. 7 Scott & Ascher §45.2.2.5.

credit"[46] in the other states. "If therefore, on a trustee's accounting, the court determines that the trustee is not subject to surcharge and that the beneficiaries have had proper notice and an opportunity to be heard, the court's judgment complies with the requirements of due process and is entitled to full faith and credit throughout the country."[47] This is the case even if some or all of the beneficiaries are beyond the jurisdiction of the court in which the trust's administration is fixed or the trustee has qualified.[48] "Clearly any attempt to render a judgment where there has been improper notice violates due process of law; the judgment is void in the state where rendered and is not entitled to recognition in other states."[49]

There are several ways for courts to give effect under the full faith and credit clause to a foreign judgment issued by a court that has been exercising jurisdiction over a trust. "They may do this by entertaining a suit to enforce the judgment, holding that the original cause of action has been merged in or barred by the judgment, or holding that the matters litigated and determined by the judgment are res judicata under the doctrine of collateral estoppel. If the proceeding was in rem or quasi in rem, the courts of other states may give effect to the judgment by recognizing the interests in the property affected by the judgment."[50]

***In personam* jurisdiction in the trust context.** For the court to have *in personam*, *i.e.*, personal, jurisdiction over the trustee, the trustee must have had "minimal contacts" within the state. "Personal jurisdiction over . . . [the trustee] . . . may be based upon his residence, domicile or mere physical presence within the state; by his voluntary appearance or consent in the proceedings; or by his performance of one or more acts within the state constituting a sufficient 'business' or fiduciary contact to give the court judicial jurisdiction over him."[51] Thus, a state court acquires *in personam* jurisdiction over a willing testamentary trustee by confirming his appointment as such, and will retain it even if the trustee subsequently becomes a resident of and removes the trust property to another state.[52] Some court in the other state, though, would then be in a position to exercise concurrent jurisdiction over the affairs of the trust, although it might well decline to do so if it would be more convenient for all concerned if matters were litigated in the court where the will had been probated and the trustee's appointment confirmed.[53] "There may, indeed, be circumstances under which the exercise of jurisdiction by a court that does not have primary supervision over the administration of the trust would so interfere with the exercise of jurisdiction by the court that has primary supervision, that

---

[46] U.S. Const. Art. IV, Sec. 1. *See generally* 7 Scott & Ascher §45.2.2.5 (Effect in Other States of a Judgment of a Court of Primary Supervision).

[47] 4 Scott & Ascher §24.25 (Judicial Discharge).

[48] 7 Scott & Ascher §45.2.2.5.

[49] Bogert §292.

[50] 7 Scott & Ascher §45.2.2.5.

[51] Bogert §292.

[52] 7 Scott & Ascher §45.2.2.1.

[53] 7 Scott & Ascher §45.2.2.2.

the judgment would not be entitled to full faith and credit, or even be void, as a denial of due process."[54]

If the court has *in personam* jurisdiction, the trustee will be personally bound by the court's judgment and decrees. This would be the case even if the court lacked jurisdiction over the subject property.[55] While the court might be entitled to assert personal jurisdiction, it would normally be inclined not to do so if some other state were primarily responsible for supervising the trust and the trust property were located out of state.[56] "The presence of the trustee within the state, without more, will limit the court in granting relief to entering such orders as may be necessary to protect the trust assets, but unless the court also has jurisdiction over trust assets, or over the trust itself under the trust entity theory giving continuing jurisdiction, further relief with respect to administration of the trust may be declined."[57] For more on the trust entity theory, the reader is referred to Section 8.15.77 of this handbook. A court lacking *in rem* jurisdiction over the property of a trust with multiple trustees, *in personam* jurisdiction over its beneficiaries, and *in personam* jurisdiction over some of the cotrustees may lack jurisdiction that is "sufficient" to effectively sort out the rights, duties and obligations of the parties.[58]

What about *in personam* jurisdiction over the beneficiaries only of a trust? Their interests should normally be determined by a court that has jurisdiction over the trust property, or at least over the trustee.[59]

***In rem* jurisdiction in the trust context (when personal jurisdiction over the trustee and/or the beneficiaries is lacking).** For the court to have *in rem* jurisdiction, *i.e.*, jurisdiction over the trust property, the property would have to be located in-state. "A state's in rem jurisdiction over trust property will give a court of that state power to affect the interests of all persons in the trust property even though the court lacks personal jurisdiction over any trust party."[60]

When jurisdiction over the trustee is lacking. If the court possesses *in rem* jurisdiction only, its judgments and decrees will affect the rights, duties, and obligations of the trustee *with respect to the property*. If the property is land situated in-state, the court will be inclined to take jurisdiction even though it lacks *in personam* jurisdiction over the trustee. The court would have *in rem* jurisdiction over an uncertificated item of tangible personal property located in-state. "Largely for reasons of commercial convenience, competing interests in an intangible asset embodied in a document, such as a stock, bond or promissory note, are subject to adjudicatory jurisdiction in the state where the document is located."[61]

---

[54] 7 Scott & Ascher §45.2.2.2.
[55] 7 Scott & Ascher §45.2.2 (Jurisdiction Over Trusts of Movables).
[56] Bogert §292.
[57] Bogert §292.
[58] Bogert §292.
[59] Bogert §292.
[60] Bogert §292.
[61] Bogert §292.

When jurisdiction over the beneficiaries is lacking. The court of the place where a trust is being administered may instruct the trustee as to his rights, duties, and obligations though some or all of the beneficiaries are not subject to the court's jurisdiction, particularly if they were given due notice and an adequate opportunity to be heard.[62] The court may even remove the trustee and appoint a successor.[63] If jurisdiction is based on the court's power over property within its territory, it could be *in rem* or *quasi in rem*. "A judgment *in rem* affects the interests of all persons in designated property . . . [while] . . . [a] judgment *quasi in rem* affects the interests of particular persons in designated property."[64] If there is jurisdiction over a trustee and/or the property but not over the beneficiaries, a court will still be able to determine the interests of the beneficiaries, provided there had been fair notice to them and an opportunity for them to be heard.[65] This would include a proceeding to establish the validity of the trust itself.[66] Any judgment would not operate personally against those presumptive beneficiaries who are beyond the jurisdiction of the court. It would, however, "operate on the property to the extent that they had or claimed an interest in it."[67] A court with mere *quasi in rem* jurisdiction also may entertain a proceeding to determine who are and are not the beneficiaries[68] Under the Uniform Trust Code, the nonresident beneficiaries of a trust having its principal place of administration in a state are subject to the jurisdiction of the courts of that state as to all matters involving the trust.[69] Under the Uniform Probate Code the courts of the state where the trust is registered would have had similarly broad jurisdiction.[70]

Accounting actions.[71] Proceedings to settle trustee accounts, a topic we take up in Section 6.1.5.2 of this handbook, have been characterized by some courts as *in rem*, as *quasi in rem* by others, and "more vaguely still as 'in the nature of a proceeding *in rem*' "[72] by still others.[73] The Uniform Probate Code at one time provided that in a proceeding involving the internal affairs of a properly

---

[62] 7 Scott & Ascher §45.2.2.3.

[63] 7 Scott & Ascher §45.2.2.3.

[64] Shaffer v. Heitner, 433 U.S. 186, 97 S. Ct. 2569, n.17 (1977).

[65] Mullane v. Central Hanover Bank & Trust Co., 339 U.S. 306 (1950). *See generally* 7 Scott & Ascher §45.2,2.3 (When a Court Does Not Have Jurisdiction Over Some or All of the Beneficiaries).

[66] 7 Scott & Ascher §45.2.2.3.

[67] 7 Scott & Ascher §45.2.2.3.

[68] 7 Scott & Ascher §45.2.2.3.

[69] UTC §202.

[70] UPC §7-103 (repealed/withdrawn 2010).

[71] *See generally* §6.1.5 of this handbook (the trustee's duty to account to the beneficiaries).

[72] Mullane v. Central Hanover Bank & Trust Co., 339 U.S. at 311.

[73] "When a party is beyond the court's personal jurisdiction, *quasi in rem* jurisdiction may attach." Jeffrey A. Schoenblum, 1 Multistate and Multinational Estate Planning 1219, n.323 (1999). "In this situation, property of the defendant within the forum state is used as something of a hostage to assure satisfaction of the judgment in the event the defendant refuses to submit to the court's jurisdiction . . . , [though] . . . the property must have some connection with the subject matter of the lawsuit." Schoenblum, 1 Multistate and Multinational Estate Planning 1219, n.323 (1999).

registered trust, such as an action to review and settle the trustee's accounts,[74] all beneficiaries of the trust would be subject to the jurisdiction of the court of registration *to the extent of their interests in the trust*, provided they had been given proper advance notice of the proceeding.[75] In other words, all beneficiaries need not be personally served for a decree of allowance to be final and binding on all interested parties.[76] This was not new law.[77] "It is perhaps less clear, however, if the court has no other basis of jurisdiction over a beneficiary, whether, in the absence of a statute permitting it to do so, it can impose liability upon the beneficiary, as for example, when the beneficiary has been over-paid."[78] Under the Uniform Trust Code, an out-of-stater who accepts a trust distribution submits personally to the jurisdiction of the local court as to any matter involving the trust.[79]

When courts of two or more states have concurrent jurisdiction over the affairs of the trust. In Section 8.15.76 of this handbook there is a general discussion of the equitable doctrine of *forum non conveniens*. What follows is a discussion of how the doctrine is applied when more than one court has jurisdiction over the administration of a trust.

A testamentary trust of movables. If the place of administration of a testamentary trust of movables is "fixed" in a state other than the state where the will was probated, the courts of either state will be in a position to exercise jurisdiction over the affairs of the trust, no matter where the beneficiaries may be domiciled, particularly if the court where the will was probated has "qualified" the trustee and is actively supervising the trust's administration.[80] The appointment of a foreign trust company is an example of how the place of administration can be "fixed" out of state.[81] In such a case, the less convenient forum is likely to defer to the more convenient forum, an application of the equitable doctrine of *forum non conveniens*.[82] The court where the will was probated is likely to be the more convenient forum if the trustee has been filing regular accountings there.[83] And certainly if a court of the state where the will was probated has already assumed jurisdiction, "the courts of another state with jurisdiction based upon the situs of trust property or upon the trustee's domicile generally will decline to entertain a proceeding relating to the construction, validity or administration of the trust."[84] Still, if litigation relating to the testamentary trust is already ongoing in the other forum, then the forum of the state where the will was

---

[74] *See* UPC §7-201(a)(2) (repealed/withdrawn 2010).
[75] UPC §7-103(b) (repealed/withdrawn 2010).
[76] 7 Scott & Ascher §45.2.2.3.
[77] *See* Mullane v. Central Hanover Bank & Trust Co., 339 U.S. 306, 313 (1950).
[78] 7 Scott & Ascher §45.2.2.3.
[79] UTC §202(b).
[80] 7 Scott & Ascher §45.2.2.4.1; Bogert §292.
[81] 7 Scott & Ascher §45.2.2.4.1; Bogert §292.
[82] 7 Scott & Ascher §45.2.2.4.1; Bogert §292. *See, e.g.,* Matter of Cary, 313 N.W.2d 625 (Minn. 1981).
[83] 7 Scott & Ascher §45.2.2.4.1.
[84] Bogert §292.

probated may choose to defer, provided the litigation has not been interfering with its prerogatives.[85]

On the other hand, "[w]hen the trustee is not required to qualify and has not qualified in the court of the state in which the testator died domiciled, and trust administration is fixed elsewhere, the courts of the latter state ordinarily have primary supervision over trust administration."[86]

In the case of a testamentary charitable trust of movables that is administered in a state other than the deceased settlor's last domicil, a *cy pres* petition may be brought, and probably should be brought, in an appropriate court of the state where the trust is being administered.[87] This is particularly the case if the trustee has been filing periodic reports with the attorney general of the administration state.[88] We cover the *cy pres* doctrine in Section 9.4.3 of this handbook and Section 8.15.28 of this handbook. The role of the state attorney general in the supervision and enforcement of a charitable trust is taken up in Section 9.4.2 of this handbook.

Under the Uniform Trust Code, the courts of the state where a testamentary trust is principally being administered has broad jurisdiction to sort out the rights, duties, and obligations of the parties to the trust relationship.[89] The Uniform Probate Code was generally in accord.[90]

An inter vivos trust of movables. Absent special facts, one may assume the trusteeship of an inter vivos trust of movables without court involvement.[91] The courts of the state where the inter vivos trust is being administered ordinarily will exercise jurisdiction over controversies arising out of its creation and administration, rather than the courts of the state where the settlor is or was domiciled.[92]

If the administration of an inter vivos trust of movables is fixed in a particular state, it is the courts of that state that will have jurisdiction over the trustee and the trust property, even if they lack jurisdiction over some or all of the beneficiaries.[93] "In contrast, when the settlor has not definitely fixed trust administration in any particular state, the courts of the state that has the most important contacts with the administration of the trust may exercise such jurisdiction."[94] Though the settlor has fixed the administration of a trust in a particular state, such as by appointing a local corporate trustee, the courts of

---

[85] 7 Scott & Ascher §45.2.2.4.1. *See, e.g.,* Marsh v. Marsh's Executors, 67 A. 706 (N.J. Ch. 1907).

[86] 7 Scott & Ascher §45.2.2.4.1.

[87] 7 Scott & Ascher §45.2.2.4.1. *See generally* §8.15.28 of this handbook (the *cy pres* doctrine) and §9.4.3 of this handbook (the *cy pres* doctrine).

[88] *See generally* §9.4.2 of this handbook (the state attorney general's standing to enforce charitable trusts).

[89] UTC §202.

[90] UPC §7-203 (repealed/withdrawn 2010). *See generally* Bogert §292.

[91] 7 Scott & Ascher §45.2.2.4.2.

[92] 7 Scott & Ascher §45.2.2.4.2.

[93] 7 Scott & Ascher §45.2.2.4.2.

[94] 7 Scott & Ascher §45.2.2.4.2.

that state may not necessarily have exclusive jurisdiction over the administration of the trust.[95] "If a court has jurisdiction over the parties or over the trust property, it may exercise jurisdiction, if doing so would not unduly interfere with control of administration by the courts of the place of administration."[96] It may chose not to, however, if an appropriate court in the place of administration would be a more convenient forum.[97] "When a suit is brought to compel the trustee to account in a court of a state that has jurisdiction over the trustee, but the court finds that it is not a convenient forum and that the proceeding should be entertained in a court of another state that does not have jurisdiction over the trustee, it may simply dismiss the suit; it may dismiss the suit if, but only if, the trustee submits to the jurisdiction of the other court; or it may direct the trustee to submit to the jurisdiction of the other court."[98]

At one time, the Uniform Probate Code had a principal-place-of-administration registration requirement that applied to both testamentary and inter vivos trusts of movables, unless registration would be inconsistent with the retained jurisdiction of a foreign court from which the trustee could not obtain release.[99] It expressly authorized the release of a registration in appropriate circumstances,[100] such as to effect a change in the place of administration in furtherance of the trust's efficient administration and the interests of the beneficiaries.[101] The courts of the state where the inter vivos trust was registered were entitled to jurisdictional deference.[102] The exception was when all appropriate parties could not be bound by the courts of that state or the interests of justice would otherwise be seriously impaired.[103]

Under the Uniform Trust Code, the courts of the state that is the principal place of administration of a trust of movables have jurisdiction to determine essentially all matters relating to the trust.[104] The UTC would confer on the courts of the trust's principal place of administration *in personam* jurisdiction over the trustee,[105] and over the beneficiaries as well.[106] Anyone who received a

---

[95] 7 Scott & Ascher §45.2.2.4.2.

[96] 7 Scott & Ascher §45.2.2.4.2.

[97] 7 Scott & Ascher §45.2.2.4.2; Bogert §292 ("The court may decline to exercise jurisdiction if proceedings involving the same matter are pending in another state, or if the question has already been decided by another state, or if, by reason of state law limitations or by some lack of adequate power over the trustee or trust assets, the forum court is unable to grant appropriate relief in the matter.").

[98] 7 Scott & Ascher §45.2.2.4.2.

[99] UPC §7-101 (repealed/withdrawn 2010). *See generally* Bogert §292.

[100] UPC §7-102 (repealed/withdrawn 2010).

[101] UPC §7-305 (repealed/withdrawn 2010). *See generally* 7 Scott & Ascher §45.2.2.7.

[102] UPC §§7-103, 7-201(a) (repealed/withdrawn 2010) (under the UTC, jurisdiction is not tied to registration, the UTC not having a trust registration requirement). *See generally* Bogert §292.

[103] UPC §7-203 (repealed/withdrawn 2010). *See generally* 7 Scott & Ascher §45.2.2.7.

[104] UTC §202 (available at <http://www.uniformlaws.org/Act.aspx?title=Trust%20Code>). *See generally* 7 Scott & Ascher §45.2.2.8.

[105] UTC §202(a) (available at <http://www.uniformlaws.org/Act.aspx?title=Trust%20 Code>).

[106] UTC §202(b) (available at <http://www.uniformlaws.org/Act.aspx?title=Trust%20 Code>).

distribution in the mistaken belief that he or she was a proper beneficiary would also be captured in the UTC jurisdictional net.[107] "These provisions apply regardless of whether the trust is inter vivos or testamentary, and regardless of whether the trust assets consist exclusively of movables or also include land."[108] Having said that, the UTC does not rule out more than one state having jurisdiction over the administration of a trust.[109]

Whether a court of primary supervision of a testamentary or inter vivos trust of movables should give full faith and credit to an out-of-state judgment. In the case of a testamentary or inter vivos trust of movables, the court of primary supervision is generally the court where the trustee has qualified, or where administration has been fixed by the trust's terms. Still it is possible that the court of another state could acquire jurisdiction over the trustee, the beneficiaries, or the property and render a judgment in a proceeding involving the trust. Is the court of primary supervision obliged to honor the judgment, to give it full faith and credit? In other words, is the judgment binding on the courts of all the other states? "This depends upon whether and to what extent the judgment unduly interferes with the exercise of jurisdiction by the court of primary supervision." A judgment surcharging the trustee for breach of trust or a judgment removing the trustee and replacing him with a successor or a judgment terminating the trust is likely not to constitute such an interference. On the other hand, an out-of-state judgment as to whether a power of appointment has been properly exercised or a judgment instructing the trustee as to the trustee's powers and duties or a judgment authorizing (or directing) the trustee to deviate from the terms of the trust might well. "Thus, in the case of a power of appointment created by will, the validity of the exercise of a power is generally governed by the law of the donor's domicil, rather than by the law of the donee's domicil."[110]

A trust of land. As noted, when it comes to entrusted land, the courts of the state where the land is located have jurisdiction *in rem* or *quasi in rem*. What about the courts of another state? Could another state's court, though it lacked jurisdiction over the property, nonetheless have the power to sort out the rights and duties of the trustee and the beneficiaries?[111] Possibly, although "[i]n general, a court other than a court of the situs will exercise jurisdiction only when doing so will not unduly interfere with the exercise of jurisdiction by the court of the situs that has the primary supervision over the administration of the trust."[112] Provided the out-of-state court has personal jurisdiction over the trustee, it in theory can entertain an accounting and surcharge action brought by the beneficiaries against the trustee; or sort out the rights and duties of the

---

[107] UTC §202 (available at <http://www.uniformlaws.org/Act.aspx?title=Trust%20Code>).

[108] 7 Scott & Ascher §45.2.2.8.

[109] UTC §202(c) (available at <http://www.uniformlaws.org/Act.aspx?title=Trust%20 Code>).

[110] 7 Scott & Ascher §45.2.2.6.

[111] Under the UTC, the courts of the principal place of administration of a testamentary or inter vivos trust of land would have *in personam* jurisdiction over the trustee and the beneficiaries. *See generally* 7 Scott & Ascher §45.2.2.8.

[112] 7 Scott & Ascher §46.2.2.2 (Courts Other Than Those of the Situs).

parties with respect to the proceeds generated by a sale of the land; or enforce a resulting or constructive trust arising out of the purchase of the land with the plaintiff's money; or remove the trustee, name a new trustee, and direct the former trustee to convey the trust property to the successor trustee.[113] The out-of-state court, however, "will not entertain jurisdiction to determine the construction, validity, or effect of a will or trust instrument insofar as it relates to land situated elsewhere, even if it has jurisdiction over the trustee and all of the beneficiaries."[114] Only a court of the situs can make such determinations with finality.[115]

Judgments of the courts of the state where entrusted land is sited are binding on the courts of the other states.[116] A judgment of a court of a state *other than the situs state* cannot "directly" affect interests in the land, although it may indirectly do so if it has personal jurisdiction over the claimants, such as by "imposing personal obligations on the parties over whom it has jurisdiction, enforceable by suit in the state of the situs, or by application at the situs of the doctrine of *res judicata* or the doctrine of collateral estoppel."[117] An out-of-state decree ordering a conveyance of entrusted land, particularly in the context of a divorce or contract enforcement action, "is enforceable in the state of the situs by entertaining a suit thereon, unless the courts of the situs determine that doing so would unduly interfere with their control of the land or otherwise run counter to the policy of the situs."[118] On policy grounds, for example, an out-of-state court with *in personam* jurisdiction only over the parties has no jurisdiction to determine who are the beneficiaries of an entrusted parcel of land.[119] Thus, the courts of the state where the land is located need not give such a determination by an out-of-state court full faith and credit.[120] It is a fundamental principle that a sovereignty, in this case each of the 50 states, has exclusive jurisdiction over the land within its borders:[121]

> ... [T]he state in which land is situated has a special interest in the land. The reasons for this are partly historical, partly practical, and partly sentimental. A state has sovereign power over all of the land within its boundaries. It alone has control over the land, and this control is permanent, not merely ephemeral, as in the case of movables. A state has obvious concerns as to the ownership of the land, both legal and equitable, and as to its use. Moreover, as a matter of convenience,

---

[113] 7 Scott & Ascher §46.2.2.2 (Courts Other Than Those of the Situs). *See generally* §3.3 of this handbook (the constructive trust and the purchase money resulting trust).

[114] 7 Scott & Ascher §46.2.2.2 (Courts Other Than Those of the Situs).

[115] 7 Scott & Ascher §46.2.2.2.

[116] 7 Scott & Ascher §46.2.3.1 (Judgment of a Court of the Situs).

[117] 7 Scott & Ascher §46.2.3.2. "Under collateral estoppel, when a question of fact essential to the judgment is actually litigated and determined by a valid and final judgment, the determination is ordinarily conclusive between the parties in a subsequent action on a different cause of action. The determination of a question of law may also be conclusive as between the parties, but not if injustice would result." 7 Scott & Ascher §46.2.3.2.

[118] 7 Scott & Ascher §46.2.3.2.

[119] 7 Scott & Ascher §46.2.3.2.

[120] 7 Scott & Ascher §46.2.3.2.

[121] 7 Scott & Ascher §46.2.3.2.

one who does a title search as to a parcel of land should not be required to delve into the law of any other state.[122]

Relocating the administration of a trust's movables to another jurisdiction. If doing so would be consistent with the settlor's expressed or implied intentions, the court may permit the relocation of a trust's place of administration to another state.[123] The matter is covered by statute in many states.[124] Thus, if the terms of the trust designate an out-of-state trust company as the custodial successor trustee, the court will be inclined to honor the designation should the office of trustee become vacant.[125] This assumes court permission is even required.[126] The court also may, in furtherance of the interests of the beneficiaries or the trust's charitable purposes as the case may be, relinquish jurisdiction by ordering or authorizing a relocation of the trust's place of administration to another state.[127] The Uniform Trust Code is in accord.[128] As was the Uniform Probate Code.[129] "In a number of cases, however, the court has held that under the circumstance the convenience of the parties did not justify changing the place of administration."[130] In Section 6.2.15 of this handbook, we consider when the *trustee* may have a *duty* to attempt to relocate the trust's place of administration to another state.[131] In Section 8.5 of this handbook, we discuss how such a relocation might result in different law governing the trust's administration going forward.

Venues within the state (trust-related proceedings). Under the Uniform Probate Code, where a proceeding concerning a trust can be maintained in more than one place in a state, "the Court in which the proceeding is first commenced has the exclusive right to proceed."[132] If proceedings are commenced in more than one court, "the Court in which the proceeding was first commenced shall continue to hear the matter and the other courts shall hold the matter in abeyance until the question of venue is decided."[133] If the "ruling court" determines that the venue is properly in another court, the ruling court

---

[122] 7 Scott & Ascher §46.1.

[123] 7 Scott & Ascher §45.5.3.1 (Permitting Change of Place of Administration).

[124] 7 Scott & Ascher §45.5.3.1 n.28 (the accompanying text noting that some statutes speak merely of the transfer of trust assets to a trustee in another state, others by their terms apply only when some or all of the beneficiaries reside in another state, and many "require that the foreign trustee qualify in a court of the trustee's own state").

[125] 7 Scott & Ascher §45.5.3.1.

[126] 7 Scott & Ascher §45.5.3.1 (suggesting that §108(c) of the model UTC "unequivocally authorizes the trustee, under certain circumstances, to remove the trust to another jurisdiction without prior judicial approval").

[127] 7 Scott & Ascher §45.5.3.1.

[128] UTC §108(c) (available at <http://www.uniformlaws.org/Act.aspx?title=Trust%20 Code>).

[129] UPC §7-305 (repealed/withdrawn 2010) (relocation also could have been effected in furtherance of the trust's "efficient" administration).

[130] 7 Scott & Ascher §45.5.3.1.

[131] *See also* 7 Scott & Ascher §45.5.3.1.

[132] UPC §1-303(a).

[133] UPC §1-303(b).

shall transfer the proceeding to the other court.[134] If in the course of a proceeding the presiding judge finds that it is "in the interest of justice" that the proceeding be transferred to another court, he or she may endeavor to effect such a transfer.[135]

    Subject matter jurisdiction. While there may be no issue as to the forum and venue in which a particular trust-related matter should be tried, there may still be an issue as to whether a particular court within the venue has the statutory authority to hear the matter. In other words, is the court "competent" to do so. "A court may not try a case beyond the scope of its statutory jurisdiction, and any judgment entered by the court lacking competence will be void and not entitled to recognition elsewhere."[136]

    Federal jurisdiction. For a discussion of federal jurisdictional issues, the reader is referred to Section 8.15.19 of this handbook.

§8.41   What Is to Be Done with Net Income When There Is No Current Beneficiary Due to a Gap in the Dispositive Terms of the Trust?

On July 1, A enfeoffs B and his heirs to the use of C and his heirs beginning on August 1. The legal estate is in B before and after August 1. There is a resulting use in A in fee for the period of a month and on August 1 the use springs up in favor of C. Thus, a use could be created to commence in futuro. Such a use was called a springing use.[1]

    Assume that, for whatever reason, there is no express provision in a trust's governing instrument for the disposition of a portion or all of the net income earned on the trust property. Assume also that terminating the trust by acceleration[2] would not comport with the settlor's intent. Perhaps a member of the class of current income beneficiaries has just died, each member being entitled to a pro rata share of the net income stream.[3] Or perhaps there is no current beneficiary at all because of scrivener error. Maybe the only designated current beneficiary has disclaimed his or her equitable interest and there is no alternate provision for the disposition of net income. In any event, the trustee is in a quandary as to how to handle a portion or all of the net income that is being and will be generated during the remainder of the trust's duration. Here are the possibilities:

---

[134] UPC §1-303(b).

[135] UPC §1-303(c).

[136] Bogert §292.

§8.41 [1] Cornelius J. Moynihan, Introduction to the Law of Real Property 175 (2d ed. 1988).

[2] *See generally* §8.15.47 of this handbook (acceleration [of vested and contingent equitable remainders] doctrine).

[3] *See generally* 3 Scott & Ascher §14.10.

- In the case of the death of a member of a class of current beneficiaries, that member's share of the net income stream going forward is distributed to his or her probate estate[4] (or to his or her issue pursuant to an applicable antilapse statute[5]), until such time as the trust terminates; or in the alternative, there is a reallocation going forward, each member living from time to time receiving pro rata shares of the entire net income stream, until the trust terminates.[6] One court in the absence of express direction has inferred from the particular trust's general dispositive scheme that the settlor upon the death of a class member would have wanted that member's share of the income stream to pass to the member's issue rather than accumulate or shift to the surviving class members.[7]
- In the case of the death of the last survivor of a class of current beneficiaries that may in the future receive additions by birth or otherwise, net income is accumulated for distribution to any new members who may materialize.
- The net income as earned is accelerated to the remaindermen, if their interests are vested; or to the presumptive remaindermen, if their interests are contingent.[8]
- The net income is accumulated and/or added to principal for ultimate distribution to the actual remaindermen at the time the trust terminates.[9]
- The net income as earned reverts upon a resulting trust[10] to the settlor, or the settlor's probate estate.[11] Once the trust terminates, the equitable interest springs up in favor of the remaindermen. The subject of springing equitable executory interests is taken up in Section 8.15.80 of this handbook.

"In these various situations the result is to be determined in accordance with what would presumably have been the intention of the . . . [settlor] . . ."[12] A court will attempt to divine his or her intention from the terms of the trust considered in their totality, taking into account such factors as whether the interests of the remaindermen are indefeasibly vested and whether the remaindermen, presumptive or otherwise, are relatives of the settlor. In the case of the death of a member of a class of current beneficiaries, there is probably a default

---

[4] *See generally* 3 Scott & Ascher §14.10.

[5] *See generally* §8.15.55 of this handbook (antilapse [the trust application]).

[6] *See generally* 3 Scott & Ascher §14.10.

[7] *See* Dewire v. Haveles, 534 N.E.2d 782 (Mass. 1989).

[8] *See generally* 3 Scott & Ascher §14.10; 6 Scott & Ascher §41.2.1. *See also* §4.1.1.1 of this handbook.

[9] *See generally* 3 Scott & Ascher §14.10; 6 Scott & Ascher §41.2.1. *See also* §4.1.1.1 of this handbook.

[10] *See* §4.1.1.1 of this handbook (the resulting trust and the vested equitable reversionary interest); 6 Scott & Ascher §41.2.1.

[11] *See generally* 3 Scott & Ascher §14.10; 6 Scott & Ascher §41.2.

[12] 4 Scott on Trusts §412; 6 Scott & Ascher §41.2.1.

presumption that the net income going forward is reallocated among the members, if any, who are living from time to time:

> This is clear enough when the settlor has given the income to a "floating" class of beneficiaries, membership of which is to be determined each time there is a payment of income. The same result obtains, however, even if the settlor has not treated the beneficiaries as a class, since the ordinary inference is that the settlor intends to create cross remainders among income beneficiaries. It is immaterial whether the settlor has named the income beneficiaries as a group or individually. It is also immaterial whether they are to take "in equal shares."[13]

The Restatement (Third) of Property (Wills and Other Donative Transfers) whenever possible would have the terms of a trust construed against its settlor and his successors should there be a gap in the provisions governing the disposition of the trust's income stream.[14] "Nevertheless, when the disposition is more complex, and it appears the gap was not anticipated by the transferor, there is a basis for implying a future interest by construction if doing so furthers the transferor's overall dispositive plan."[15] This "implying a future interest by construction" is in keeping with the Restatement (Third)'s general unmindfulness of the resulting trust and the vested equitable reversionary property interest that it procedurally supports. The resulting trust is nowhere to be found in the Restatement (Third)'s index, and all but ignored in the main text. Still, the owner of a vested equitable reversionary interest incident to a trust relationship has property rights that are as deserving of constitutional protection as are any legal property rights he may possess.[16] Accordingly, a court should eschew the retroactive "implication" of a future interest via the novel rule of construction.

§8.42 What Is the Difference Between a Complaint (Petition) for Instructions and a Complaint (Petition) for Declaratory Judgment?

Courts of equity, in the exercise of their jurisdiction over the administration of trusts, have long been willing to provide trustees instructions, upon request, as to their duties and powers . . . Thus, a trustee need not act at his or her peril in administering a trust. Nor need a trustee act first and discover later whether a particular act was in breach of trust.[1]

---

[13] 3 Scott & Ascher §14.10.

[14] *See* Restatement (Third) of Property (Wills and Other Donative Transfers) §26.9.

[15] Restatement (Third) of Property (Wills and Other Donative Transfers) §26.9 cmt. a.

[16] *See generally* §8.15.71 (the constitutional implications of retroactively applying new trust law).

§8.42 [1] 3 Scott & Ascher §16.8.

In the past, a trustee or beneficiary[2] would bring a petition for instructions in a court having equity jurisdiction over the trust when there was a question as to his current rights, duties, and obligations that called for judicial determination.[3] Ordinarily, the trustee would take a neutral position, leaving it to the beneficiaries and the guardian ad litem, if any, to advocate on one side or the other of the issue. Beyond, say, clarifying the meaning of an ambiguous term or otherwise instructing the trustee as to what he should be doing, "there was no method of having the instrument construed and the rights of parties determined until the declaratory judgment procedure was introduced."[4]

The Uniform Declaratory Judgments Act, which in one form or another has been adopted in a number of states, has served to fill the gap. It provides a beneficiary with a means of obtaining a determination of his or her equitable rights, even when the duties of the trustee are not immediately implicated.

A court, however, will be inclined to dismiss a beneficiary's complaint if his or her equitable rights are subject to the happening of some future event.[5] A remainder beneficiary's interest under a testamentary trust, for example, might be subject to the condition precedent of there being no descendants of the settlor alive when the current income beneficiary dies. If the income beneficiary and numerous descendants are all very much alive when the complaint is filed, the court will likely want to wait until at least the death of the current beneficiary before committing time and resources to adjudicating the issue. If it turns out that there are descendants alive at that time, then events themselves will have resolved the matter without the need for court involvement.

Because of the ambulatory nature of a revocable inter vivos trust (or will), it has been the general rule that the validity of either may not be determined in a declaratory judgment action during the lifetime of the settlor (or testator).[6] This is no longer the case in New Hampshire. In New Hampshire, by statute, a settlor during his or her life may commence a judicial proceeding to determine the validity of a trust, whether revocable or irrevocable, that he or she has created.[7]

Under Section 4(c) of the Uniform Declaratory Judgments Act, it would appear that a complaint for declaratory judgment also may do what a traditional equitable complaint for instructions can do, thus obviating the need for the latter in many instances:

---

[2] *See generally* 3 Scott & Ascher §16.8 (confirming that beneficiaries as well as trustees may apply to the court for instructions).

[3] *See generally* 3 Scott & Ascher §16.8 (Application for Instructions); Chapter 1 of this handbook (in part discussing the right of trustees and beneficiaries to apply to the court for instructions); §8.32 of this handbook (can the trustee escape liability for making a mistake of law if he acted in good faith on advice of counsel?).

[4] 1 Belknap, Newhall's Settlement of Estates and Fiduciary Law in Massachusetts §2:16 (5th ed. 1994).

[5] *Cf.* 3 Scott & Ascher §16.8 (Application for Instructions).

[6] *See* Ullman v. Garcia, 645 So. 2d 168 (Fla. Ct. App. 3d Dist 1994).

[7] *See* RSA 564-B:4-406 (N.H.).

Any person interested as or through an executor, administrator, trustee, guardian or other fiduciary, creditor, devisee, legatee, heir, next of kin, or cestui que trust, in the administration of a trust, or of the estate of a decedent, an infant, lunatic, or insolvent, may have a declaration of rights or legal relations in respect thereto:

(a) To ascertain any class of creditors, devisees, legatees, heirs, next of kin or others; or

(b) To direct the executors, administrators, or trustees to do or abstain from doing any particular act in their fiduciary capacity; or

(c) To determine any question arising in the administration of the estate or trust, including questions of construction of wills and other writings.

§8.43   Who Is the Settlor of the Trust?

A somewhat different question may arise when a will fails to provide for one or more heirs, who contest or threaten to contest the will and obtain a compromise, under which there is a spendthrift trust for the heirs' benefit. It has been held in such a case that the heirs are settlors of the trust, and that their creditors can reach their interests.[1]

One would be hard pressed to sort out whether the creditors of the beneficiary of a trust can reach the equitable interest and/or the underlying trust property,[2] or even the tax liabilities of the parties to the trust relationship,[3] without knowing who the settlor is.[4] If, for example, the trust is self-settled, that is, if income and/or principal, initially at least, is to be administered solely for the benefit of the settlor, then for purposes of fixing the rights of creditors and the tax liabilities of the parties, it is as if the settlor-beneficiary owned the underlying trust property outright and free of trust.[5] Usually who is the settlor is self-evident; but not always. The settlor is the one whose property has been entrusted. It is not necessarily the one who has been designated as settlor in the governing trust documentation.[6] Nor is it necessarily the one who conveyed legal title to the trustee.[7] And in cases where there have been multiple transfers

---

§8.43   [1] 3 Scott & Ascher §15.4.4.

[2] *See generally* §5.3.3.1 of this handbook (reaching settlor's reserved beneficial interest).

[3] *See generally* §8.9.3 of this handbook (tax-sensitive powers); Chapter 10 of this handbook (the income taxation of trusts).

[4] Bogert §41 ("The identity of the settlor may be of practical importance in applying certain rules governing trusts; examples are the rule that a spendthrift provision is not valid to protect the interest of the settlor of a trust [*see generally* §5.3.3.1 of this handbook]; the rule permitting a settlor to revoke a voluntary trust with the consent of all persons beneficially interested [*see generally* §8.2.2.1 of this handbook]; the statutes and regulations that enumerate available resources for purposes of determining eligibility for certain public assistance programs [*see, e.g.,* §5.3.5 of this handbook (Medicaid eligibility)]; or for other reasons.").

[5] *See generally* §5.3.3.1 of this handbook (reaching settlor's reserved beneficial interest).

[6] *See generally* 3 Scott & Ascher §15.4.4.

[7] *See generally* 3 Scott & Ascher §15.4.4.

of property to the trustee over time by different settlors, as to each transferor the trust can be said to be partially self-settled. But which part?

First, it borders on the self-evident that if X, as authorized agent of A, transfers A's property to B, as trustee, A is the settlor, not X.[8] This is the case even if X happens to have had the legal title.[9] A, for example, might purchase some stock from a broker and direct the broker to transfer the stock to B, as trustee, for the benefit of whomever. A is the settlor, not the broker.

A participant in a company-sponsored defined benefit or defined contribution employee benefit plan is the settlor of his or her allocable portion of any entrusted assets, even that which is attributable to employer contributions.[10] Essentially, it the employee's own property rights incident to the employment contract that are being entrusted.[11] It would be nonsensical to suggest that the employer is making gratuitous transfers in trust of its own property for the benefit of its employees.

Or take a civil award of damages for some personal injury done to an infant that by court order is being held in trust for the benefit of the infant, even an infant who is severely brain damaged. It is the infant, not the court,[12] not the infant's guardian, who is the settlor of the trust, whatever the governing documentation may say.[13] Neither the court nor the guardian owned the subject property. At all times, the property was owned by the infant. Accordingly, any income generated by the entrusted property is taxable to the infant, not to the court or to the guardian personally, and potentially reachable by the infant's creditors, unless there is some statute to the contrary.

Assume that $A1$ and $A2$ simultaneously establish identical inter vivos trusts purporting to be for one another's benefit. A compelling equitable argument, however, can be made that the trusts are actually self-settled. The argument is that $A1$, as settlor, has in equity established for his own benefit a trust the property of which is a collection of rights incident to a contract with $A2$, and vice versa. The contract is to impress trusts upon the subject properties. In creating the trusts, each is acting as an agent of the other in fulfillment of his or her contractual obligations. This substance over form analysis is at the heart of the reciprocal trust doctrine.[14] In the estate tax context, however, there need not be a contract for the doctrine to be implicated. "Instead, its application requires

---

[8] *See generally* 3 Scott & Ascher §15.4.4.

[9] *See generally* §9.9.2 of this handbook (agency arrangements) (noting in a footnote that an agent-trustee takes legal title to the property that is the subject of the agency).

[10] *See generally* 3 Scott & Ascher §15.4.4.

[11] *See generally* §9.5.1 of this handbook (the employee benefit trust (tax qualified)).

[12] One commentator, however, has suggested that the settlor of an express trust established by court decree can be the court itself. *See* Bogert §41. That one is deemed to be the settlor of an express trust by statute or by its terms does not make one the actual settlor. The actual settlor of an express trust is the one whose property is entrusted. Thus, for a "court" to qualify as the actual settlor of an express trust, the "court" would have to have been the owner of the subject property in its own right and to have had the authority to impress a trust upon it, a most unlikely set of facts.

[13] *See generally* 3 Scott & Ascher §15.4.4; §9.3 of this handbook (the self-settled "special needs"/"supplemental needs" trust).

[14] *See generally* §8.15.24 of this handbook (reciprocal trust doctrine).

'only that the trusts be interrelated, and that the arrangement, to the extent of mutual value, leaves the settlors in approximately the same economic position as they would have been in had they created trusts naming themselves as life beneficiaries.' "[15]

    When there have been incremental self-settled transfers of property into trust over time by different transferors, each transferor is deemed the settlor of that portion of the trust that is attributable to his or her contribution.[16] (This would be the case even if the transfers were not for the benefit of the transferors.) But equitably determining what that portion is may not be all that easy if, for example, some of the transfers were in kind and others in cash; or if over time there have been unequal discretionary distributions of principal to some but not all the beneficiaries; or if a beneficiary has used his or her own funds to make substantial improvements on the trust property; or if a beneficiary has used his or her own funds to pay off a mortgage on the trust property.[17] If *A1* transfers a parcel of real estate to the trustee of a discretionary trust that has multiple settlors, then *A1*'s creditors may well have access at least to that parcel, provided it is still in the trust. At least one court has so held.[18]

§8.44   Mediation and Arbitration Have Their Limitations When It Comes to Trust Disputes

In drawing attention to the benefits of mediation, it would be simplistic to suggest it is a cure-all for all trust and probate disputes. Some disputes will not be appropriate for mediation, in particular those that turn on technical construction of trust deeds or wills, cases in which injunctions are sought and claims involving allegations of fraud.[1]

    Certainly no harm can come from endeavoring to mediate or arbitrate a contract dispute, particularly if all parties are of full age and legal capacity. A trust, however, is not a contract,[2] and, except in the case of a trust that is an

---

[15] 3 Scott & Ascher §15.4.4 (citing to United States v. Estate of Grace, 395 U.S. 316, 324 (1969).

[16] *See generally* 3 Scott & Ascher §15.4.4. *See also* Bogert §46 (but also leaving the impression that a third party who takes trust property from the trustee in fair market exchange or substitution for other property would be a settlor as to that other property, which is not the law).

[17] *See generally* 3 Scott & Ascher §15.4.4.

[18] In re Shurley, 115 F.3d 333 (5th Cir.), *cert denied*, 522 U.S. 982 (1997).

§8.44 [1] Jeremy Gordon, *More talk*, 15(7) STEP J. 29 (July/Aug. 2007) (a publication of The Society of Trust and Estate Practitioners (STEP)).

[2] *See* Schoneberger v. Oelze, 208 Ariz. 591, 595, 96 P.3d 1078, 1082 (2004) (" . . . [D]efendants face a fundamental problem that defeats their demand for arbitration . . . [, namely that] . . . the trusts at issue here . . . [are] . . . not contracts."). *See also* Rachal v. Reitz, 347 S.W.3d 305 (Tex. Sup. Ct. 2011). *See generally* §9.9.1 of this handbook (life insurance and third party beneficiary contracts generally).

instrument of commerce, *e.g.*, a mutual fund,[3] it is generally not incident to one. A trust is a fiduciary relationship with respect to property, in which the trustee generally will have numerous ongoing duties that run to the beneficiaries,[4] but in which the beneficiaries will have few if any duties that run to the trustee.[5] The parties to a contract, on the other hand, generally are not in a fiduciary relationship,[6] unless the same parties happen simultaneously also to be in an agency or trust relationship.[7]

Many trusts bestow equitable property rights on unborn or unascertained individuals, or on individuals under some legal disability, *e.g.*, minority. Thus, unless the fiduciary issues and the representation issues are properly sorted out before hand, there is the very real risk that an ill-considered rush to mediate or arbitrate, at best, will be an expensive and time-consuming diversion to no-where, and, at worst, will actually exacerbate the situation:

> One area that can cause serious complications in negotiation and drafting of nonjudicial agreements is failing to identify all of the parties interested in the matter. There are any number of individuals or entities who may have an interest in a matter and each interested party must be properly identified and given an opportunity to be heard. The failure to properly identify all of the parties interested in a matter can result in a nonjudicial agreement being deemed ineffective or a court determining that it does not have jurisdiction or that venue is improper in a judicial proceeding. In addition, the practitioner must make sure that in situations where a conflict exists or may exist, a virtual representative or special representative (or in the event of court proceedings, a guardian ad litem) is appointed to represent the interest of minor, incapacitated, unborn, or unascertained beneficiaries.[8]

Again, for a mediation or arbitration to bear fruit, all interested parties need to be a part of the process.[9] In the case of the typical trust dispute, that will generally mean that someone is going to have to go into court and seek to have it appoint a disinterested guardian ad litem who can represent the interests of the unborn and unascertained beneficiaries who are not virtually represented.[10]

---

[3] *See generally* Charles E. Rounds, Jr. & Andreas Dehio, *Publicly-Traded Open End Mutual Funds in Common Law and Civil Law Jurisdictions: A Comparison of Legal Structures*, 3 N.Y.U.J.L. & Bus. 473 (2007).

[4] *See generally* Chapter 1 of this handbook (defining the trust).

[5] *See generally* §5.6 of this handbook (duties and liabilities of the beneficiary).

[6] *See* Schoneberger v. Oelze, 208 Ariz. 591, 595, 96 P.3d 1078, 1082 (2004) (" . . . [A] fiduciary relationship exists between a trustee and a trust beneficiary while no such relationship generally exists between parties to a contract.").

[7] *See generally* Charles E. Rounds, Jr., *Lawyer Codes Are Just About Licensure, the Lawyer's Relationship with the State: Recalling the Common Law Agency, Contract, Tort, Trust and Property Principles that Regulate the Lawyer-Client Fiduciary Relationship*, 60 Baylor L. Rev. 771 (2008).

[8] Gail E. Mautner & Heidi L. G. Orr, *A Brave New World: Nonjudicial Dispute Resolution Procedures Under the Uniform Trust Code and Washington's and Idaho's Trust and Estate Dispute Resolution Acts*, 35 ACTEC J. 159, 180 (2009).

[9] *See generally* §5.7 of this handbook (the necessary parties to a suit brought by a beneficiary).

[10] *See, e.g.*, Mass. Gen. Laws ch. 190B, §§1-401, 3-1101, & 3-1102 (judicial approval of arbitrations and compromises involving Massachusetts trusts); Mark S. Poker & Amy S. Kiiskila,

Otherwise, any agreement that is ultimately forged among the other parties will not be binding on the unborn and unascertained, at least to the extent that their equitable property rights may have been adversely affected.[11] Once the matter of a guardian ad litem is in the hands of the court, the dispute, like it or not, is for all intents and purposes in formal litigation, and the court may well have its own views on whether and how to mediate or arbitrate. Moreover, it is not unusual for a knowledgeable guardian ad litem, once appointed, to settle into the role of a quasi-mediator. If that happens, any plans for formal mediation or arbitration should probably be put on hold until such time, if ever, as it becomes clear that the involvement of the guardian ad litem is either failing to break the logjam or actually exacerbating it.

A nonjudicial mediation or arbitration of a *breach-of-fiduciary-duty trust dispute* of which the actions of an incumbent trustee are the focus is at best awkward and at worst problematic and costly.[12] The trustee continues to have an affirmative duty to act solely in the interest of the beneficiaries in matters pertaining to the trust.[13] Thus, any agreement that is the product of a mediation or arbitration between the trustee and the beneficiaries is not binding on a beneficiary who does not subjectively understand the applicable law and facts, unless, perhaps, if the beneficiary is being represented by independent counsel.[14] This is particularly the case when the duty of loyalty is implicated.[15] The principle applies even in the case of a beneficiary who is of full age and legal

---

Prevention and Resolution of Trust and Estate Controversies, 33 ACTEC 262, 266 (2008). *See generally* §8.14 of this handbook (when a guardian ad litem (or special representative) is needed; virtual representation issues).

[11] *See, e.g.,* Mass. Gen. Laws ch. 190B, §3-1102.

[12] *See* Michael Heise, *"Why ADR Programs Aren't More Appealing: An Empirical Perspective,"* paper presentation, Research Symposium on Empirical Studies of Civil Liability, Northwestern University School of Law, Chicago, IL (Oct. 9, 2008) (Abstract: "Standard law and economic theory suggests that litigating parties seeking to maximize welfare will participate in alternative dispute resolution (ADR) programs if they generate a surplus. ADR programs claim to generate social surplus partly through promoting settlements and reducing case disposition time. Although most associate ADR programs with trial courts, a relatively recent trend involves appellate courts' use of ADR programs. The emergence of court-annexed ADR programs raises a question. Specifically, if ADR programs achieve their goals of promoting settlements and reducing disposition time, why do some courts find it necessary to impose ADR participation? Attention to ADR's ability to achieve its goals provides one clue. Most empirical assessments of ADR programs' efficacy have been mixed. This study exploits a uniquely comprehensive database of state civil court trials and appeals and tests hypotheses germane to questions about whether court-annexed appellate ADR programs stimulate settlement and reduce disposition time. Using data from 46 large counties consisting of 8,038 trials that generated 965 filed appeals, with 166 appeals participating in ADR programs, findings from this study provide mixed support for ADR programs. Specifically, results from this study indicate that participation in an ADR program correlates with an increased likelihood of settlement but not reduced disposition time. ADR programs' mixed efficacy diminishes its appeal to litigants. Institutional interests help explain why appellate courts impose ADR participation notwithstanding mixed results on ADR efficacy.").

[13] *See generally* §6.1.3 of this handbook (duty of loyalty).

[14] *See generally* §7.2.7 of this handbook (informed consent).

[15] *See generally* §7.1.2 of this handbook (defenses to allegations that the trustee breached the duty of loyalty); Restatement of Restitution §191 (acquisition by a fiduciary/effect of consent of beneficiary).

capacity. Moreover any nonjudicial resolution of a breach-of-fiduciary-duty trust dispute must be fair to the beneficiaries and reasonable: "A transaction between the fiduciary and the beneficiary in which the fiduciary is dealing on his own account in regard to a matter within the scope of the relation can be set aside if the transaction is not fair and reasonable. Thus, if a trustee purchases for himself property with the consent of the beneficiary, the beneficiary can set aside the sale if the price paid by the trustee was not in fact an adequate price, even though at the time of the sale the parties believed that it was adequate."[16]

Certainly the chances of having an agreement that is forged in a nonjudicial mediation or arbitration "stick" are enhanced if the trustee who is the subject of the dispute resigns before the nonjudicial process commences, if the successor trustee becomes a party to the mediation or arbitration, and if all parties are represented by independent counsel.[17] The problem is that if all that occurs, then the professional mediator or arbitrator risks becoming an expensive fifth wheel, and will certainly be one, in any case, if he or she is not at least as well versed in trust law as are the mediation or arbitration participants.[18] When it comes to trust disputes, retaining the services of an experienced and impartial trust lawyer to assist the parties collectively in framing the issues and ferreting out the applicable law is likely to be more efficient and cost-effective in the long run than going the formal mediation or arbitration route.

If it is best that the trustee step aside at least until such time as the arbitration process has run its course, a court of equity would have the inherent equitable power to appoint a receiver, special fiduciary, or trustee ad litem to administer the trust in the interim. These fiduciary offices, essentially tools in the court's box of procedural equitable remedies, are discussed generally in Section 7.2.3.8 of this handbook. A trustee ad litem might be appropriate if the trustee's ongoing conflict of interest is limited to a claim that ought to be asserted on behalf of the trust against a third party. *Getty v. Getty* comes to mind in this regard.[19] A trustee ad litem would be appointed for the limited purpose of handling the prosecution of that claim.

In any case, particularly if there is a guardian ad litem in the picture, the court has the last word, as no mediated settlement—and certainly no settlement that is inequitable—can relieve the court of its inherent and overarching equitable authority to supervise the administration of trusts.[20] The court is an

---

[16] Restatement of Restitution §191 cmt. e.

[17] *See generally* §7.1.4 of this handbook (defense of consent, release, or ratification by the beneficiary).

[18] *See generally* §8.25 of this handbook (few American law schools still require Trusts).

[19] 205 Cal. App. 3d 134, 252 Cal. Rptr. 342 (1988).

[20] *See, e.g.,* Mass. Gen. Laws ch. 190B, §3-1102(3) (providing that if the court finds a particular contest or controversy "is in good faith and that the effect of the agreement upon the interests of persons represented by fiduciaries or other representatives is just and reasonable, shall make an order approving the agreement and directing all fiduciaries subject to its jurisdiction to execute the agreement"). *Cf.* Mark S. Poker & Amy S. Kiiskila, *Prevention and Resolution of Trust and Estate Controversies*, 33 ACTEC 262, 266 (2008) ("If a dispute involves trust beneficiaries, however, it is not clear whether an arbitration provision can require the beneficiaries to participate or relinquish their rights to litigate in the court system.").

agent neither of the fiduciaries nor of the beneficiaries. Not even a trust term that purports to oust the court of its traditional equitable jurisdiction over trust matters is enforceable, *e.g.*, one that purports to bestow on a member of the executive branch of a state's government the authority to make binding determinations as to whether the trustee is complying with the other trust terms.[21] Nor can the court be "ousted" by an expansive grant of discretion to the trustee. "It is submitted . . . that, even as to matters thus firmly committed to the trustee's discretion, judicial review should remain available if the trustee acts in bad faith, contrary to the terms of the trust, or with an improper motive."[22]

The Supreme Court of Texas has ordered the enforcement of a trust arbitration clause over the objection of the settlor's two sons, whom the court characterized as the trust's "sole beneficiaries."[23] The court based its ruling on two grounds: (1) Enforcement is in conformance with the intentions of the settlor, and (2) the applicability of the doctrine of direct benefits estoppel, a category of general equitable estoppel doctrine, satisfies the agreement requirement of the Texas Arbitration Act. The Act provides that a written agreement to arbitrate is enforceable if it provides for arbitration of either an existing controversy or one that arises between the parties after the date of the agreement. The court explains its application of a contract-based doctrine to a trust, a relationship that most serious scholars have concluded is not *per se* contract-based: " . . . [A] beneficiary who attempts to enforce rights that would not exist without the trust manifests her assent to the trust's arbitration clause. For example, a beneficiary who brings a claim for breach of fiduciary duty seeks to hold the trustee to her obligations under the instrument and thus has acquiesced to its provisions, including the arbitration clause. In such circumstances, it would be incongruent to allow a beneficiary to hold a trustee to the terms of the trust but not to hold the beneficiary to those same terms."[24] If, by implication, a trust arbitration clause would not be enforceable against someone incapable of granting such an assent, such as an unborn or unascertained equitable quasi remainderman, then the court, as a practical matter, may have neutered most Texas trust arbitration clauses, except those in commercial trust instruments. Mandatory arbitration clauses in trust instruments are covered generally in Section 3.5.3.3 of this handbook.

---

[21] *See generally* 3 Scott & Ascher §18.2 (Executive Branch Encroachment on Court's Equitable Prerogatives). *Cf.* §9.4.4 of this handbook (legislative branch encroachment on court's equitable prerogatives).

[22] 3 Scott & Ascher §18.2 (Control of Discretionary Powers).

[23] Hal Rachal, Jr. v. John W. Reitz, No. 11-0708 (Tex. May 3, 2013).

[24] Hal Rachal, Jr. v. John W. Reitz, No. 11-0708 (Tex. May 3, 2013), at 11. For a discussion of why the trust relationship *per se* is not contract-based, see Section 8.22 of this handbook.

§8.45 What Is the Difference Between a Good-Faith Purchaser for Value (BFP) and a Holder in Due Course?

As one learned commentator has noted: "The doctrine that an innocent taker of money for value acquires a perfect title, and that a holder in due course of a negotiable instrument obtains a title free of all equities, is a separate rule which often affects trustees in the administration of trusts but it should be kept distinct from the bona fide purchaser rule in equity."[1] A holder in due course is like a BFP in that each has to have paid value[2] and each has to have had lack of notice that the transfer might be in derogation of the legal or equitable property rights of others.[3] There are some critical differences, however:

- The BFP is an equitable concept while the holder in due course is a legal one that is now generally codified, at least in the United States.[4] See Article 3 of the Uniform Commercial Code, versions of which have been enacted into law in most if not all the states.
- Cancellation of an antecedent (preexisting) debt owed by the transferor to the transferee can satisfy the holder in due course value requirement but not, with some exceptions, the BFP value requirement.[5]
- In a case where trust property is transferred for value to a third party in breach of trust and the third party is to pay the funds *to the trustee personally*, it is unlikely that the third party would qualify as a BFP,[6] whereas, if the property were a negotiable instrument, a third party who pays value and who has no actual knowledge of the breach would likely qualify as a holder in due course.[7]

For more on the concept of the holder in due course and how it differs from the BFP, the reader is referred to Section 8.3.6 of this handbook. Section 8.15.63 of this handbook is devoted to a general discussion of the concept of the BFP.

---

§8.45 [1] Bogert §883 (The Rule of Negotiability). *See generally* §8.3.6 of this handbook (negotiable instruments and the duty of third parties to inquire into the trustee's authority) (the holder in due course is a legal construct while the BFP is a creature of equity). *See generally* §8.15.63 (doctrine of bona fide purchase; the BFP).

[2] *See generally* §8.15.63 of this handbook (doctrine of bona fide purchase; the BFP); U.C.C. §3-302 (Holder in Due Course).

[3] *See generally* §8.15.63 of this handbook (doctrine of bona fide purchase; the BFP); U.C.C. §3-302 (Holder in Due Course). *See also* U.C.C. §3-307 (Notice of Breach of Fiduciary Duty).

[4] *See* Dearman v. Trimmier, 26 S.C. 506, 2 S.E. 501, 504 (1887).

[5] 5 Scott & Ascher §29.3.7 (Satisfaction of Antecedent Debt as Value). *See, e.g.*, Dearman v. Trimmier, 26 S.C. 506, 2 S.E. 501, 504 (1887).

[6] *See generally* §8.15.63 of this handbook (doctrine of bona fide purchase; the BFP).

[7] U.C.C. §3-307 (Notice of Breach of Fiduciary Duty).

§8.46   Proof of Facts in Trust Litigation

I suppose that when one sees a perfect stranger on a mortuary slab and a policeman tells one that his name is Dimitrios Makropoulos, one assumes, if one has your respect for the police, that one has the truth of the matter. I knew that it was not Dimitrios you saw . . . "There was a French carte d'identité, issued in Lyons a year ago to Dimitrios Makropoulos, sewn inside the lining of this coat." Latimer spoke mechanically . . . Mr. Peters smiled tolerantly. 'I could get you a dozen genuine French cartes d'identité, Mr. Latimer, each in the name of Dimitrios Makropoulos and each with a different photograph.'[1]

Fact and time of death. Under the Uniform Probate Code, a certified or authenticated copy of a death certificate purportedly issued by an official or agency of the place where the death purportedly occurred is prima facie evidence of the identity of the decedent and the fact of his or her death.[2] It also is prima facie evidence of the place, date, and time of death.[3] A certified or authenticated copy of any record or report of a governmental agency, domestic or foreign, that an individual has died is prima facie evidence of that fact, as well as of any circumstances surrounding the event that are disclosed by the record or report.[4] Otherwise, the fact of death must be established by clear and convincing evidence, which may include circumstantial evidence.[5] An undisputed entry on one of the aforementioned official documents of a time of death that is 120 hours or more after the time when another person was purported to have died establishes clear and convincing that there has been compliance with the Code's 120-hour survivorship requirement, no matter how the other person's time of death was determined.[6] A beneficiary who has been missing without a trace and for no apparent reason for a continuous period of five years is *presumed* dead, providing there has been a diligent good faith inquiry into the circumstances surrounding the beneficiary's absence that has turned up nothing definitive.[7]

Purchase money resulting trust. As to burdens of proof, a transferee of property for which a third party rather than the transferor has paid the purchase price is presumed to hold it upon a purchase money resulting trust for the third party.[8] Thus the third party's only initial burden is to prove that the

---

§8.46 [1] Eric Ambler, A Coffin for Dimitrios 226–227 (First Vintage Crime/Black Lizard ed., Oct. 2001).

[2] UPC §1-107(2).

[3] UPC §1-107(2).

[4] UPC §1-107(3).

[5] UPC §1-107(4).

[6] UPC §1-107(6). *See generally* §8.15.56 of this handbook (120-hour survival requirement [the trust application]).

[7] UPC §1-107(5). "His [or her] death is presumed to have occurred at the end of the period unless there is sufficient evidence for determining that death occurred earlier." UPC §1-107(5).

[8] 6 Scott & Ascher §43.1. *See generally* §3.3 of this handbook (the purchase money resulting trust).

purchase price had actually been paid by the third party.[9] It then falls to the transferee, assuming the transferee wishes to retain the property, to prove that the third party intended to make an outright gift of the property to the transferee.[10] If that burden cannot be met, then the court will order the transferee to convey the legal title to the property to the third party outright and free of trust, unless, in reliance on what was ostensibly a gift the transferee has so changed position that it would be inequitable to compel the transferee to surrender the property.[11] A conveyance to a close relative of the third party will raise an inference that an outright gift was intended, particularly if the relative is a natural object of the third party's bounty.[12]

A purchase money resulting trust of land need not comply with the memorandum requirements of statute of fraud to be enforceable.[13] In other words oral purchase money resulting trusts are enforceable, as they are said to arise by "operation" or "implication" of law; although, as we have seen, such trusts are actually more express-like than resulting-like. "The real reason, it would seem, that such trusts are valid without a writing is that, although they arise out of the parties' intention, the evidence of those intentions lies in the circumstances of the transaction rather than in testimony of the parties' discussions."[14] So also a purchase money resulting trust may be *rebutted* by parol evidence that a gift to the transferee was actually intended.[15] The statute of frauds applicable to trusts is covered in Section 8.15.5 of this handbook.

§8.47   The President John Adams Trust for the Benefit of The Woodward School for Girls

The President John Adams Trust was established in 1822 by the former U.S. President. In 1886, its assets were supplemented by a bequest from his grandson. The City of Quincy served as trustee of the Trust, known as the Adams Temple and School Fund and the Charles Francis Adams Fund, through two boards. The Woodward School for Girls, Inc., the income beneficiary of the trust since 1953, filed suit in July of 2007 against the City of Quincy, as trustee, initially seeking an equitable accounting and later asserting that the trustee had

---

[9] 6 Scott & Ascher §43.1.

[10] 6 Scott & Ascher §§43.1, 43.2 (Rebutting the Purchase Money Resulting Trust), 43.2.3 (Rebutting Resulting Trust in Part), 43.2.4 (Purchase in Name of Payor and Another), 43.3 (Purchase in the Name of a Relative), 43.4 (Rebutting Presumption of Gift to Relative).

[11] 6 Scott & Ascher §43.1. *See generally* §8.15.5 of this handbook (statute of frauds).

[12] 6 Scott & Ascher §43.2 (Rebutting the Purchase Money Resulting Trust).

[13] 6 Scott & Ascher §43.1.

[14] 6 Scott & Ascher §43.1. "There is not, therefore, the same danger of perjured testimony." 6 Scott & Ascher §43.1.

[15] 6 Scott & Ascher §43.2 (Rebutting the Resulting Trust). "In contrast, a resulting trust that arises because of the failure of an express trust declared in a will or other written instrument ordinarily cannot be rebutted by the settlor's oral statements." 6 Scott & Ascher §43.2.

committed multiple breaches of trust, specifically by failing to keep adequate records, imprudently investing the Trust's assets, failing to exercise reasonable prudence in the sales of entrusted real estate, and incurring unreasonable expenses managing the assets of the Trust. The case, which is captioned *The Woodward School for Girls, Inc. v. City of Quincy, trustee*, ultimately made its way to the Supreme Judicial Court of Massachusetts (SJC), which rendered its decision in July 2014.[1] The Trust is essentially an income-only perpetual charitable trust that had been invested almost exclusively for income generation. The SJC criticized Quincy, as had the trial judge, for failing to pursue a trust-investment strategy that had an appropriate capital-appreciation component to it as required by the Massachusetts Prudent Investor Act and the common law as enhanced by equity. The SJC, however, disagreed with the trial judge as to what specific strategy would have been appropriate and, in particular, how the foregone capital appreciation should be calculated for damages-computation purposes. Among other things, the SJC confirmed that there is a modern-portfolio-theory gloss on the Massachusetts prudent investor rule.[2]

---

§8.47 [1] *See* The Woodward School for Girls, Inc. v. City of Quincy, trustee, SJC-11390, 2013 WL 8923423 (Mass. July 23, 2014).

[2] *See generally* §6.2.2.1 of this handbook (modern portfolio theory and the prudent investor rule).

Special Types of Trusts

§9.1   The Grantor Trust

The term *grantor trust* appears in the income tax sections of the Internal Revenue Code (I.R.C.).[1] It is not a common law trust term. It simply means any trust over which someone, referred to as the "grantor," has such control that he or she is deemed to be the owner of the trust property or a portion of the trust property *for income tax purposes*.[2] Thus, a noncontributor of property to a trust can be considered its "owner" for income tax purposes.[3]

When a trust qualifies as a grantor trust, *e.g.*, a rabbi trust,[4] any income tax liability or benefit associated with the trust property does not affix to the trust. Rather, income, deductions, and credits enter into the computation of the *personal* income tax liability of the grantor.[5] This is pursuant to the Code's so-called grantor trust rules.[6] "The tax returns for trusts that are owned entirely by the grantor or third person need be only skeleton forms."[7] As to the tax basis/cost of an asset held in a grantor trust, the reader is referred to Section 11.3 of this handbook.

---

§9.1 [1] *See* I.R.C. §§671–679; Fiore et al., Modern Estate Planning §6A.02 (1990). For a detailed analysis of the grantor rules, *see* Zaritsky, 858-2nd T.M., Grantor Trusts: Sections 671–679; Schwartz, *Grantor and Non Grantor Trusts: Asking the Right Questions*, 11 Prac. Tax Law. 31 (1997). *See also* §8.9.3 of this handbook (tax-sensitive powers), §9.4.5 of this handbook (tax-oriented trusts that mix charitable and noncharitable interests (split-interest trusts)), and §10.1 of this handbook (introduction to the fiduciary income tax).

[2] Zaritsky, 858-2nd T.M., Grantor Trusts: Sections 671–679.

[3] *See generally* Jonathan G. Blattmachr, Mitchell M. Gans, Alvina H. Lo, *A Beneficiary as Trust Owner: Decoding Section 678*, 35 ACTEC J. 106 (2009) (examining "whether a non-grantor holding a power to distribute trust property to himself or herself, subject to an 'ascertainable standard,' is properly treated as the trust's owner for income tax purposes and the extent to which a non-grantor who held an unrestricted power of withdrawal that has lapsed may continue to be treated, for income tax purposes, as the owner of the portion of the trust with respect to which the power lapsed").

[4] *See generally* §9.5.3 of this handbook (the rabbi trust (nonqualified executive deferred compensation)).

[5] Zaritsky, 858-2nd T.M., Grantor Trusts: Sections 671–679.

[6] Zaritsky, 858-2nd T.M., Grantor Trusts: Sections 671–679. For the grantor rules applicable to foreign trusts, *see* I.R.C. §§679, 672. *See also* §6.3.1 of this handbook (tax filings) and §10.1 of this handbook (introduction to the fiduciary income tax).

[7] Zaritsky, 858-2nd T.M., Grantor Trusts: Sections 671–679 A-17. A grantor trust return "may merely indicate that the trust is a grantor-type trust and identify the person to whom the trust income32. . . is taxable." Zaritsky, 858-2nd T.M., Grantor Trusts: Sections 671–678 A-17.

For a discussion of the income taxation of business trusts, see Section 10.7 of this handbook.

It should be noted here that if a U.S. citizen or resident transfers property to the trustee of a foreign trust,[8] the trust is deemed a grantor trust for income tax purposes under Section 679 of the Internal Revenue Code.

§9.1.1   Intentionally Defective Grantor Trust (IDGT)

The key to the IDGT . . . [pronounced "I dig it"] . . . tax-planning strategy is the misalign-ment between the grantor trust rules' and the estate tax's treatment of transfers to trusts. Not all retained powers listed in the grantor trust rules will cause trust assets to be included in the grantor's estate at death under §§2036-2038. An IDGT, therefore, is an irrevocable trust which is structured to be a grantor trust for income tax purposes, a transfer to which, however, is deemed a complete transfer for estate and gift tax purposes.[9]

There is some lack of coordination between the Code's grantor trust sections and the Code's estate and gift tax sections.[10] The result: It is possible for a trust to be structured in such a way that a transfer of property to the trustee is a completed gift for tax purposes while the income that is subsequently generated by the property is taxable to the settlor, not to the trust or the beneficiaries. (The settlor, for example, might retain only the limited right to substitute assets of equivalent value.)[11] Thus, someone could be taxed on the fruits of appreciating property, property that is itself not subject to the estate tax upon his or her death.[12]

From the settlor's perspective, this residual income tax liability may actually be a good thing. He or she, for example, would be entitled to take advantage of any income tax deductions and credits associated with the trust's income stream. Because the income tax liability is a personal obligation *of the settlor*, its satisfaction by the settlor is not a taxable gift to the trust or to its beneficiaries.[13] In other words, within the trust itself, income can accumulate tax-free.

There are potential advantages in the charitable giving area as well. When a settlor transfers property to the trustee of a charitable lead trust that is also a grantor trust, the settlor is entitled to an up-front income tax deduction for the

---

[8] A foreign trust is any trust in which one or more substantial decisions is or are made by non-U.S. persons. I.R.C. §§7701(a)30(E)(ii), 7701(a)31(B). *See generally* §6.3.1(b) of this handbook (outlining foreign trust reporting requirements).

[9] Daniel L. Ricks, *I Dig It, But Congress Shouldn't Let Me: Closing the IDGT Loophole*, 36 ACTEC L.J. 641, 644–645 (2010).

[10] *See generally* Jerold I. Horn, *Avoiding and Attracting Grantor Trust Treatment*, 24 ACTEC Notes 204 (1998).

[11] I.R.C. §675(4).

[12] Note, however, that a mandatory reimbursement clause for the settlor's income tax liability could have adverse estate tax consequences upon the settlor's death under I.R.C. §2036(a)(1). *See* Rev. Rul. 2004-64.

[13] Rev. Rul. 2004-64.

amount of the actuarial value on the date of transfer of the charity's equitable interest.

Finally, because for income tax purposes the settlor is deemed the owner of property held in a grantor trust, he or she may be able to effect a bona fide sale of appreciated property to the trustee free of income and gift tax consequences.[14] Nontaxable fair market exchanges between the settlor and the trustee may also be possible. For an exhaustive discussion of the potential risks and rewards of so-called *intentionally defective grantor trusts*, the reader is referred to BNA's Tax Management Portfolio, *Grantor Trusts: Sections 671–679*.[15]

§9.1.2   Tax Qualified Noncharitable Split-Interest Grantor Trusts

"The grantor retained annuity trust (GRAT) or grantor retained unitrust (GRUT) is often used to transfer large assets at a substantially reduced gift tax cost."[16] Specifically, a GRAT or a GRUT "is an irrevocable gift of a remainder interest in a trust, in which the grantor (or an applicable family member) reserves for a term of years either a fixed annuity or a fixed percentage of the annual value of the trust fund (a unitrust amount)."[17] GRATs and GRUTs are exempt from the reach of Code Section 2702, which deems a grantor retained interest to have a $0 offset value for gift tax computation purposes. The qualified personal residence trust (QPRT) is another type of tax-qualified noncharitable split-interest grantor trust. The QPRT is explained in Section 9.15 of this handbook.

§9.1.2.1   Grantor Retained Annuity Trusts (GRAT)

When setting up the trust, a savvy grantor will select the combination of annuity payment and trust term that will result in the present value of all future payments exactly equaling the amount contributed. That way, the IRS calculates that the GRAT will have zero assets by the time the trust expires and therefore no gift tax is levied—not then, not ever. But fortunately for investors, reality can be drastically different from IRS expectations. In the event that the actual rate of return exceeds the IRS hurdle rate, the additional value of the trust will be gifted free of tax.[18]

Under a GRAT, the grantor, *i.e.*, the settlor, receives a fixed amount from the trust each year for the term of the trust. The settlor's interest can be structured to qualify for the marital deduction if the settlor dies before the end of the annuity payment period. For gift tax computation purposes, the value of

---

[14] *See generally* Michael D. Mulligan, *Fifteen Years of Sales to IDITs—Where Are We Now?*, 35 ACTEC L.J. 227 (2009).

[15] Zaritsky, 858-2nd T.M., Grantor Trusts: Sections 671–679.

[16] Howard M. Zaritsky, *A GRAT (or GRUT) Checklist*, 12(8) Prob. Prac. 1 (Aug. 2000).

[17] Zaritsky, *A GRAT (or GRUT) Checklist*, 12(8) Prob. Prac. 1 (Aug. 2000).

[18] The Bernstein J., Spring 2004, at 2.

the property transferred into the GRAT is reduced by the value of the retained interest. If the grantor outlives the term of the trust, the date of death value of the trust property is not included in his or her gross estate for estate tax computation purposes.[19] A GRAT, however, must meet the rigid design requirements of Code Section 2702. Moreover, it is critical that the trustee make the annual annuity payments to the grantor in a timely fashion. It can be useful for the estate planning attorney to send out GRAT reminder emails using Outlook or other software. If the GRAT is not properly designed, the value of the gift to the trust for gift tax computation purposes will not be reduced by the value of the retained interest.[20] While a third-party loan to the GRAT to meet the annuity payments is probably acceptable, a loan from the grantor or even the grantor's spouse will likely be scrutinized by the IRS, The trustee should be aware of the advantages and disadvantages of employing a short-term rolling GRAT as opposed to a long-term GRAT (*e.g.*, the longer the trust term, the more likely the settlor's death will occur and the less chance to capture volatility in the actual rate of return).

The Uniform Probate Code provides that if the settlor should die before the trust's term expires and leave a surviving spouse, the value of some portion or all of the corpus might well be included in the UPC "augmented estate" for spousal election purposes.[21] The topic of spousal election is taken up in Section 5.3.4.1 of this handbook.

§9.1.2.2 Grantor Retained Unitrust (GRUT)

Under a GRUT, the grantor, *i.e.*, the settlor, receives *a fixed percentage of the net fair market value of the trust property* each year for the term of the trust. For gift tax computation purposes, the value of the property transferred into the GRUT is reduced by the value of the retained interest. If the grantor outlives the term of the trust, the date of death value of the trust property is not included in his or her gross estate for estate tax computation purposes.[22] A GRUT, however, must meet the rigid design requirements of Code Section 2702. If it does not, the value of the gift to the trust for gift tax purposes will not be reduced by the value of the retained interest.

The Uniform Probate Code (UPC) provides that if the settlor should die before the trust's term expires and leave a surviving spouse, the full value of the corpus would be included in the UPC "augmented estate" for spousal election

---

[19] If the grantor dies before the trust terminates, the trust assets will be included in the grantor's estate at their date of death value under I.R.C. §2036. *See generally* Michael D. Whitty, *GRAT Expectations: Questioning, Challenging, and Litigating the Service Position on Estate Tax Inclusion of Grantor Retained Annuity Trusts*, 36 ACTEC J. 87 (2010).

[20] Failure to satisfy §2702 causes the retained interest to be valued at zero. This has been referred to as the zero valuation rule.

[21] UPC §2-205 cmt. (Example 12).

[22] If the grantor dies before the trust terminates, the trust assets will be included in the grantor's estate at their date of death value under I.R.C. §2036.

purposes.[23] The topic of spousal election is taken up in Section 5.3.4.1 of this handbook.

§9.1.3 Availability of I.R.C. §121 Exclusion for Sale of Principal Residence by Trustee of Grantor Trust

An individual may exclude from tax up to $250,000 of capital gains realized on the sale of a personal residence. For most joint returns, the number is $500,000. The residence must have been owned by the taxpayer two years out of the five years preceding the sale, it must have been occupied by the taxpayer as a personal residence for an aggregate of two years out of the five years preceding the sale, and the taxpayer must not have applied the exclusion from capital gains to a previous sale within the prior two years. As a general rule, a taxpayer who transfers his or her personal residence to the trustee of a grantor trust is entitled to the Code Section 121 exclusion, provided the taxpayer has reserved the right to revoke the trust and get back the property.[24]

§9.2 The Irrevocable Life Insurance Trust

The American common law incorporates the principles of the English Life Assurance Act of 1774, providing that a life insurance policy is void unless it is issued to someone who has an insurable interest in the life of the insured. . . . Generally, a person has an insurable interest in the life of the insured if that person can reasonably expect to receive a pecuniary benefit from the insured's continued longevity or suffer a loss from the insured's death.[1]

Be cognizant of the Generation-Skipping Tax (GST) risk. Except when the ILIT is an IRC section 2642(c) or IRC section 2503(c) generation-skipping trust, every ILIT has potential GST exposure. Therefore, every time a transfer is made, a decision must be made whether GST exemption will be allocated to the ILIT on a timely-filed gift tax return via the required Notice of Allocation attachment.[2]

A life insurance contract (or policy) is an item of property even during the lifetime of the insured.[3] The proceeds are another form of that property interest, just as the butterfly is another form of the caterpillar, or a flower

---

[23] UPC §2-205 cmt. (Example 10).

[24] Ltr. Rul. 200018021.

§9.2 [1] Howard M. Zaritsky, *Irrevocable Life Insurance Trusts and Insurable Interests: Chawla Raises Some Nasty Issues for Estate Planners*, 18(4) Prob. Prac. Rep. 1-2 (Apr. 2006).

[2] Sebastian V. Grassi, Jr., *Checklist for Drafting the Irrevocable Life Insurance Trust—Part II*, 14(9) Prob. Pract. Rep. 1 (Sept. 2002).

[3] *See generally* 4 Scott & Ascher §19.1.8.

another form of the seed.[4] Because the estate tax system imposes a tax on property transfers occasioned by death, life insurance proceeds will generate an estate tax.[5] One way to avoid this is for the insured, during his or her lifetime, to transfer title to the contract to the trustee of an irrevocable trust. If the insured retains no beneficial interest in the contract, then, upon death, the proceeds may not generate an estate tax liability, provided the "three-year" rule is satisfied.[6] Avoidance of estate taxes is what the irrevocable life insurance trust is all about.[7] A way around the "three-year" rule might be for the trustee to purchase from an insurance company an insurance contract on the life of the settlor after the irrevocable trust has been established, provided the trust has an insurable economic interest in the continued life of the settlor[8] or is somehow exempt from the need for such an interest.[9] The contract would be purchased with trust funds. The Uniform Trust Code, specifically Section 113, purports to clarify the circumstances under which a trustee, *qua* trustee, has an insurable interest in the life of another. The section and accompanying commentary are lengthy and hyper-technical.

In the typical irrevocable life insurance trust, the trustee pays the life insurance premium from cash contributions periodically made to the trust by someone, usually the settlor. These contributions are gifts to the trust. To ensure that the contributions qualify for the annual gift tax exclusion, the beneficiaries are given a limited withdrawal power.[10] This power gives the beneficiaries the right to withdraw the amount contributed to the trust within a specified number

---

[4] *See* Sebastian V. Grassi, Jr., *Drafting a Flexible Irrevocable Life Insurance Trust*, 31 ACTEC J. 208 (2005). *See generally* 4 Scott & Ascher §19.1.8 (discussing how insurance payout options implicate the prudent investor rule).

[5] *See* §8.9 of this handbook (why more than one trust: the estate and generation-skipping tax).

[6] It should be noted, however, that the settlor must survive for a period of three years following the transfer. I.R.C. §§2035(a), 2035(d)(2). This "three-year" rule can be avoided if the trustee purchases the policy rather than the insured. *See* TAM 93-23002; Estate of Perry v. Comm'r, 927 F.2d 209 (5th Cir. 1991). *See generally* §8.15.16 of this handbook (incidents of ownership). Also, insurance proceeds will be subject to the estate tax upon the death of the settlor-insured if, under the terms of the irrevocable insurance trust instrument, the trustee is *required* to pay the settlor's debts and/or estate taxes. *Discretionary* powers in the trustee to *buy* for fair market value assets from the estate and to *lend* funds to the estate to pay estate taxes, however, probably are not, in and of themselves, tax-sensitive powers.

[7] *See generally* Slade, 807 T.M., Personal Life Insurance Trusts.

[8] *See, e.g.*, Del. Code Ann. tit. 18, §2704(c)(5); Va. Code §38.2-301(b)(5); Wash. Rev. Code Ann. §48.18.030(3)(c).

[9] *See generally* Chawla, ex rel. Geisinger v. Transamerica Occidental Life Ins. Co. (E.D. Va. 2005), *aff'd in part, vacated in part*, 440 F.3d 639 (4th Cir. 2006) (a case that has rekindled concerns that an irrevocable life insurance trust may not be exempt from the insurable interest rule); Mary Ann Mancini & Howard M. Zaritsky, *Insurable Interests: Après* Chawla, *le Deluge?* 32 ACTEC J. 194 (2006).

[10] To qualify for the annual exclusion, the transfer must be a gift of a "present" interest. I.R.C. §2503(b). A gift to a trust must be subject to withdrawal by the beneficiary in the calendar year during which the gift was made to be considered a "present" interest. For an exception to the present interest requirement, *See generally* §9.17 of this handbook (I.R.C. §2503(c) trusts for minors).

of days. The power lapses if it is not exercised. These limited withdrawal provisions are often referred to as "Crummey" powers and trusts containing such provisions are called "Crummey" trusts.[11] It is the trustee's responsibility to notify the beneficiaries that a contribution has been made. Failure to do so is a breach of trust.[12]

Of course, the settlor does not want a beneficiary to withdraw his or her portion of the contribution. Explaining to beneficiaries that it is not in their best interests for them to exercise their withdrawal rights will usually deter them from doing so. If the beneficiaries were to exercise their rights of withdrawal, there usually would be no money with which to pay the insurance premium and the policy would eventually lapse. In the case of minor beneficiaries, the terms of the trust should vest the powers of withdrawal in "cooperative" adult individuals.

An insurance policy or contract held in a trust is an investment.[13] Thus, the Prudent Man Rule or Prudent Investor Rule must guide the trustee with respect to its retention, absent language in the governing instrument to the contrary.[14] There are unique considerations in managing this type of financial asset.[15] The trustee should review and monitor the financial health of the life insurance company and the policy's performance. A. M. Best, Moody's, Standard & Poor's, and Duff & Phelps are in the business of rating insurance companies.

The trustee must be familiar with the terms of the trust. The terms will usually give the trustee the power to turn in the policy for its cash surrender value, to exchange the policy for another, and to borrow against its cash value. These powers become particularly important in situations where the financial health of the insurance company is questionable, the policy itself is not performing as anticipated, or the settlor has ceased making cash contributions to the trust. When considering whether to exercise these powers, the trustee may want to seek the advice of an insurance specialist and should keep the beneficiaries and the settlor informed. On the other hand, the trustee would be ill-advised to rely on the advice and counsel of the insurance broker as to his fiduciary duties with respect to the acquisition and administration of the

---

[11] Crummey v. Comm'r, 397 F.2d 82 (9th Cir. 1968). *See generally* §9.18 of this handbook (the Crummey trust).

[12] Karpf v. Karpf, 240 Neb. 302, 309–311, 481 N.W.2d 891, 896–897 (1992); Bogert §961.

[13] *See generally* 4 Scott & Ascher §19.1.8.

[14] *See generally* 4 Scott & Ascher §19.1.8; William B. Davis, *Life Insurance: A Fiduciary Time Bomb*, 131(5) Tr. & Est. 35 (May 1992). *But see* S.C. Code §62-7-302(e) (1994) (providing that the duties of a trustee with respect to acquiring or retaining a contract of insurance upon the life of the trustor, or upon the lives of the trustor and the trustor's spouse, children, or parents, *do not* include a duty to (1) determine whether any such contract is or remains a proper investment, (2) exercise policy options available under any such contract, or (3) diversify any such contract).

[15] *See generally* Kathryn A. Ballsun, Patrick J. Collins, & Dieter Jurkat, *Trust Administration of Life Insurance (Part 1 of 4)*, 31 ACTEC J. 280 (2006); Kathryn A. Ballsun, Patrick J. Collins, & Dieter Jurkat, *Standards of Prudence and Management of the Insurance Portfolio (Part 2 of 4)*, 32 ACTEC J. 66 (2006); Kathryn A. Ballsun, Patrick J. Collins, & Dieter Jurkat, *Evidencing Care, Skill and Caution in The Management of ILITs (Part 3 of 4)*, 32 ACTEC J. 145 (2006); Kathryn A. Ballsun, Patrick J. Collins, & Dieter Jurkat, *ILIT Asset Management: The Written Investment Policy Statement (Part 4 of 4)*, 32 ACTEC J. 229 (2006).

insurance contract, and does so at his peril.[16] That function should be performed by independent legal counsel.[17] If the trustee opts for a life settlement on the policy, the issue then becomes whether the proceeds are taxed as capital gain or ordinary income.

For trust accounting purposes, the acquisition value of a life insurance contract (policy) is generally its net cash surrender value (plus any unexpired premium) as of the time the trustee acquired, or was deemed to have acquired, the contract. Going forward, absent special facts, the contract's market values for trust accounting purposes are its net cash surrender value (plus any unexpired premium) as of the beginning and end of each accounting period.[18] This all assumes that any mid-administration sale of the contract on the open market by the trustee—to the extent such a sale would even be legally permissible and a practical option—would not command a price that is greater than its net cash surrender value. For more on the general mechanics of trust accounting, the reader is referred to Section 6.1.5.2 of this handbook.

Irrevocable Life Insurance Trust Setup Checklist[19]

Instrument Review[20]

(1) Are there Crummey powers?[21]
(2) Is the trustee authorized, but not directed, to invest in a life insurance contract?[22]

---

[16] *Cf.* §8.32 of this handbook (can the trustee escape liability for making a mistake of law if he acted in good faith on advice of counsel?).

[17] *See generally* §8.8 of this handbook (whom does counsel represent?).

[18] Special circumstances may call for a different valuation method, *e.g.*, the ratable charge method, the interest-adjusted ratable charge method, the deferred-premium asset method, the accrual basis (policy reserve) method, or the economic benefit method.

[19] *See also* Sebastian V. Grassi, Jr., *Selected Issues in Drafting the Irrevocable Life Insurance Trust After the 2001 Tax Act*, 28 ACTEC J. 277 (2003) (containing ILIT drafting and administration checklists as well as a discussion of how to draft an ILIT in a way that accommodates changed circumstances).

[20] *See generally* Sebastian V. Grassi, Jr., *Checklist for Drafting the Irrevocable Life Insurance Trust—Part I*, 14(7) Prob. Prac. Rep. 1 (July 2002).

[21] *See generally* §9.18 of this handbook (the Crummey trust).

[22] Language specifically directing the trustee to purchase a life insurance policy has been held to "convert" the trustee into an agent of the donor/settlor, resulting in inclusion of the policy in the donor/settlor's gross estate. *See* Estate of Kurihara v. Comm'r, 82 T.C. 51 (1984); Detroit Bank & Trust Co. v. United States, 467 F.2d 964 (6th Cir. 1972).

Setting Up the Trust

(1) Has the trustee filed on behalf of the trust an application for a taxpayer identification number (TIN) with the Internal Revenue Service (IRS)?[23]

(2) Have the insurance companies whose contracts are to be held by the trustee been furnished the TIN?

(3) Has the donor/settlor written a check to the trustee to cover the amount of the first year's premium, as well as any other agreed upon costs of trust administration?[24]

(4) Has the trustee taken the check to a bank or other financial institution and opened an account in the trust's name, indicating the TIN?

(5) Has the trustee taken title to the insurance policy?

[If the insurance policy was in existence pre-setup,

(a) *Did the donor/settlor, trustee, and insurance company execute an assignment contract effecting a transfer of the policy's title to the trustee?*[25]

(b) *Did the donor/settlor relinquish all incidents of ownership in the policy?*[26]

(c) *Did a gift tax return get filed (assuming a gift tax was owed as a result of the policy assignment)?*[27]

---

[23] TIN forms may be obtained by contacting an IRS Service Center. If the application is faxed to the IRS, the TIN should be faxed out in five to seven days. The IRS will eventually deactivate and reassign the trust's TIN number, unless income tax returns are being filed under it. If the ILIT will not be generating enough income to warrant the filing of income tax returns, the trustee may want to discuss with the IRS what steps need to be taken to keep the TIN in force.

[24] If the policy funding the trust is being provided by the donor/settlor's employer with no contribution toward the premiums being made by the donor/settlor, the employer may pay premiums directly to the insurance company, bypassing the trustee. If, on the other hand, the policy is being provided by the employer but the donor/settlor is paying some portion of the premium obligations, a portion equal to the donor/settlor's portion of the premium obligation should be paid to the trustee, who in turn will make the actual premium payments directly to the insurance company or through the employer, depending upon the terms of the contract. While having the trustee pay the premiums is probably the better practice, nowadays having the donor/settlor pay the premiums directly to the insurance company is unlikely, in and of itself, to be construed as an incident of ownership such that the proceeds will be subject to estate taxation upon the donor/settlor's death. *See* Estate of Perry v. Comm'r, 927 F.2d 209 (5th Cir. 1991), *aff'g* 59 T.C.M. 1990-123; Estate of Headrick v. Comm'r, 918 F.2d 1263 (6th Cir. 1990), *aff'g* 93 T.C. 171 (1989); Estate of Leder v. Comm'r, 893 F.2d 237 (10th Cir. 1989), *aff'g* 89 T.C. 235 (1987). *See generally* §8.15.16 of this handbook (incidents of ownership).

[25] An insurance contract assignment form is obtainable from the insurance company. It should name the trustee as both the sole owner of the policy and the sole beneficiary of the proceeds.

[26] *See* §8.15.16 of this handbook (incidents of ownership).

[27] A gift tax on the transfer value, if any, of the policy, *i.e.*, the interpolated terminal reserve value, may be payable by the donor/settlor, unless the value is covered by the beneficiaries' Crummey withdrawal rights. It should be noted that the "face value" of a life insurance policy is not the same as the interpolated terminal reserve value, which is calculated using several factors, one of which is face value.

    (d) *Did the trustee take physical possession of the assignment contract and the policy itself?]*

[If the policy was not in existence at the time of setup,

    (e) *Did the trustee make the first premium payment from trust funds?*
    (f) *Did the check have on it the TIN number?]*

(6) Has the trustee mailed out "Crummey notices" in a timely fashion to all beneficiaries informing them of their withdrawal rights?[28]

(7) Has the trustee mailed a check (bearing the trust's name and TIN) to the insurance company following lapse of the Crummey period to ensure timely payment of the policy's premium?

For a comprehensive irrevocable life insurance trust drafting checklist, the reader is referred to Sebastian V. Grassi, Jr.[29] The Guide also contains a useful administration checklist for trustees of such trusts. Once an ILIT becomes operational, the trustee should keep *How to Fix a "Broken" Life Insurance Trust* near at hand.[30]

§9.3 The Disability[1]/Special Needs/Supplemental Needs[2] Trust

Despite the apparent good intent of Congress to provide this safe harbor trust for disabled clients who acquire assets, they missed at least one very important point., As noted, the law states that an Under 65 SNT must be established by a parent, grandparent, guardian or court; it does not state that the client himself may establish it, or that it may be established by the client's conservator. Most commentators and some courts, however, believe the restrictions on who may establish an Under 65 SNT was an oversight and have not bound themselves by the bald statutory terms.[3]

---

[28] *See generally* §9.18 of this handbook (the Crummey trust).

[29] A Practical Guide to Drafting Irrevocable Life Insurance Trusts, ALI-ABA (1st ed. 2003; 2d ed. 2007).

[30] Sebastian V. Grassi, Jr., 35 *Tax Mgm't Est., Gifts, & Trusts J.*, No. 1 (Jan. 14, 2010).

§9.3 [1] In contrast to a self-settled SNT, "[a] Third Party SNT is a special needs trust created and funded with the assets of a person other than the disabled beneficiary." Andrew H. Hook, *What the Trust and Estates Lawyer Needs to Know About d(4)(A) Special Needs Trusts*, 29 ACTEC J. 192, 193 (2003).

[2] Also known as an "Under 65 trust," an "Under 65 special needs trust," or a "(d)(4)(A) trust." *See generally* Clifton B. Kruse, Jr., Third Party and Self-Created Trusts (3d ed. ABA Publications, Chicago, Ill. 2002). The third-party SNT need not have a payback provision. The terms "Under 65 trust," "Under 65 special needs trust," and "(d)(4)(A) trust" are also employed in this context. *See generally* Clifton B. Kruse, Jr., Third Party and Self-Created Trusts (3d ed. ABA Publications, Chicago, Ill. 2002).

[3] Alexander A. Bove, Jr. & Melissa Langa, *Protecting Personal-Injury Awards With SNTs*, 30 Mass. Law. Wkly. 4357, Mar. 11, 2002 (citing to In re Moretti, 606 N.Y.S.2d 543 (Sup. Ct. Kings

The self-settled disability trust. We now turn to a version of the self-settled trust that need not jeopardize a disabled settlor's eligibility for public assistance. The safe harbor was carved out by federal legislation for that type of self-settled trust whose purpose is to pay for critical goods and services not covered by Medicaid, that is to say to address a disabled person's special or supplemental needs. A disabled person has needs over and above basic medical care, food, clothing, and shelter. They include the following:

- Recreation
- Transportation
- Dental care
- Telephone and television services
- Hair and nail care
- Differentials in cost of housing and shelter
- Supplemental nursing care
- Private case management, and
- Mobility aids, including electric wheelchairs[4]

Property held in a self-settled "d(4)(A)"[5] special/supplemental[6] needs trust (SNT) created for the sole benefit of a disabled individual under the age of 65 will not jeopardize that individual's eligibility for SSI or Medicaid benefits.[7] The terms of the SNT, however, must provide that the state shall receive the balance in the SNT upon the individual's death up to the aggregate amount paid under the Medicaid program for services to the individual.[8] This is known as the "payback" requirement. Under Code Section 677(a), such an SNT is a grantor trust for income tax purposes.[9] Moreover, the maximum amount that could be expended for the benefit of the settlor-beneficiary under the terms of the SNT,

---

County 1993) where an Under 65 SNT established by a conservator was approved and suggesting that "an Under 65 SNT may be 'established' by, say, a parent as settlor, with a transfer of the client's funds to the trust by the client's attorney-in-fact acting under a durable power of attorney").

[4] Andrew H. Hook, *What the Trust and Estates Lawyer Needs to Know About d(4)(A) Special Needs Trusts*, 29 ACTEC J. 192, 193 (2003).

[5] 42 U.S.C. §1396p(d)(4)(A).

[6] "While the terms are sometimes used interchangeably, many refer to trusts that are funded with the beneficiary's own assets, including those to which the beneficiary is entitled under a personal injury award, as 'special needs trusts,' and to trusts that are funded by third parties for a disabled beneficiary as 'supplemental needs trusts.'" Alan Newman, *Spendthrift and Discretionary Trusts: Alive and Well Under the Uniform Trust Code*, 40 Real Prop. Prob. & Tr. J. 567, 618–619 (Fall 2005).

[7] *See generally* 3 Scott & Ascher §15.3. An "Under 65 trust," an "Under 65 special needs trust," an "Under 65 SNT," a "(d)(4)(A) trust," an individual disability trust, and a disability payback trust are essentially synonymous terms. *See generally* Clifton B. Kruse, Jr., Third Party and Self-Created Trusts (3d ed. ABA Publications, Chicago, Ill. 2002).

[8] Andrew H. Hook, *What the Trust and Estates Lawyer Needs to Know About d(4)(A) Special Needs Trusts*, 29 ACTEC J. 192, 193 (2003) (referring to 42 U.S.C. §1396p(d)(4)(A)). *See also* 3 Scott & Ascher §15.4.3.

[9] *See generally* §9.1 of this handbook (the grantor trust).

which is likely to be the entire corpus, would be accessible to his or her general creditors.[10]

The corpus of a self-settled SNT might be an unprotected inheritance, or perhaps a personal injury award or settlement.[11] In the latter case, the corpus can take the form of a lump sum or the contractual right to receive periodic payments under an annuity issued by an insurance company. Whether an inheritance or litigation award, the disabled person is both the beneficiary and the settlor of the SNT.[12] Notwithstanding the fact that the SNT may have been set in motion by a court[13] or by a guardian, the inception assets still belonged to the disabled beneficiary.[14] As neither the court nor the guardian owned the inception assets, neither could qualify under fundamental principles of property and trust law as the trust's settlor, even constructively.[15]

Again, because the disabled beneficiary is the settlor, income and principal may be reachable by the disabled beneficiary's private creditors,[16] income subsequently generated by the trust property may be taxable to the beneficiary,[17] and the subsequent death of the disabled beneficiary may give rise to an estate tax liability with respect to the trust property.[18] For a discussion of how creditor accessibility can give rise to a constructive general inter vivos power of appointment for income, estate, and gift tax purposes, see Section 4.1.3 of this handbook.[19] The nonpunitive component of any insurance recovery paid into the SNT as compensation for personal injury or sickness, however, would

---

[10] *See generally* §5.3.3.1 of this handbook (creditor accessibility).

[11] *See generally* Jo-Anne Herina Jeffreys, *What Every Elder Law Attorney Should Know About Structured Settlements*, XIV The ElderLaw Rep., No. 10, at 1 (May 2003).

[12] *See generally* 3 Scott & Ascher §15.4.4 (Determining Who Is the Settlor); §8.43 of this handbook (the settlor of a trust must have legally or equitably owned the inception assets).

[13] "If a trust established by order of court is to be administered as an express trust, the terms of the trust are determined from the court order as interpreted in light of the general rules governing interpretation of judgments." UTC §103 cmt. (available at <http://www.uniformlaws.org/Act.aspx?title=Trust%20Code>).

[14] *See, e.g.*, Hertsberg v. Department of Mental Health, 457 Mich. 430, 578 N.W.2d 289 (1998) (beneficiary of trust funded by Social Security benefits received by her mother on her behalf was the settlor of the trust, not the mother). *See also* UTC §103 cmt. (available at <http://www.uniformlaws.org/Act.aspx?title=Trust%20Code>) (noting that the fact that a person is designated in the governing instrument as "settlor" is not necessarily determinative).

[15] *See, e.g.*, Strand v. Rasmussen, 2002 WL 1558529, 648 N.W.2d 95 (Iowa 2002).

[16] *See generally* §5.3.3.1 of this handbook (reaching settlor's reserved beneficial interest).

[17] *Cf.* Rev. Rul. 83-25, 1983-1 C.B. 116 (IRS ruling that a minor beneficiary of a trust established to hold a litigation recovery is the grantor for income tax purposes). *See generally* §8.34 of this handbook (when an employer identification number (EIN) is not required) and §9.1 of this handbook (the grantor trust). *See generally* §9.1 of this handbook (the grantor trust).

[18] Priv. Ltr. Rul. 95-020-19 (Jan. 13, 1995) (income tax); TAM 95-060-04 (Feb. 10, 1995) (estate tax); Rev. Rul. 83-25, 1983-1 C.B. 116. *See* Arrington v. United States, 34 Fed. Cl. 144, 149–150 (1995) (affirming estate tax liability). *See generally* Restatement (Third) of Trusts §10, Reporter's Note to Comment g, re: Clause (e).

[19] *See* particularly the quotation that introduces §4.1.3 of this handbook.

escape income taxation at the time it was constructively received by the disabled plaintiff.[20]

It is thanks to the Omnibus Budget Reconciliation Act of 1993 (OBRA '93)[21] that a disabled beneficiary's *eligibility*[22] for Medicaid is no longer jeopardized merely because his or her SNT is self-settled. All that is required is that the terms of the SNT call for the trustee to reimburse the state postmortem for any lifetime Medicaid assistance that had been furnished to the disabled beneficiary.[23] Thus, the arrangement is referred to in some circles as a disability payback trust. As noted above, this payback obligation extends only to amounts, if any, remaining in the SNT upon the disabled settlor-beneficiary's death.[24]

While the absence of such a payback provision could render *ab initio* the underlying property of a "(d)(4)(A)" SNT countable for purposes of determining whether the disabled settlor-beneficiary would be eligible for Medicaid,[25] not so with the self-settled "pooled" SNT,[26] which a qualifying nonprofit association may administer for the benefit of disabled individuals and which has many of the characteristics and safe harbor attributes of the "(d)(4)(A)" SNT. In lieu of a payback provision, the terms of a pooled SNT may call for the balance, if any, remaining in the disabled individual's separate account at death to be retained in the SNT for the benefit of the other beneficiaries of the pooled trust.[27]

The non–self-settled disability trust. The non–self-settled SNT also has its advantages. Such a trust, for example, under certain circumstances need not

---

[20] I.R.C. §104(a)(2) (exempting damages for "personal injuries or sickness"). Punitive damages and damages for emotional distress, however, are generally taxable. Neither the disabled SNT nor the SNT trust itself would incur an income tax liability on the nonpunitive component of the insurance recovery.

[21] Omnibus Budget Reconciliation Act of 1993, Pub. L. No. 103-66, §13611(a)(1), 107 Stat. 312, 622-23 (codified as amended at 42 U.S.C. §1396p(c)(1)).

[22] For a discussion of some of the other advantages of a supplemental needs trust in the Medicaid context, *see* Alexander A. Bove, Jr. and Melissa Langa, *Protecting Personal-Injury Awards with SNTs*, 30 Mass. Law. Wkly. 4357, Mar. 11, 2002.

[23] *See* 42 U.S.C. §1396p(d)(4)(A). *See generally* Kruse, *OBRA '93 Disability Trusts—A Status Report*, 10 Prob. & Prop. 15 (May–June 1996). *But see* Cohen v. Comm'r of the Div. of Med. Assistance, 423 Mass. 399, 420–424, 668 N.E.2d 769, 781–783 (1996) (denying Medicaid benefits to beneficiary of supplemental needs trust).

[24] *See* 42 U.S.C. §1396p(d)(4)(A) (1994 & Supp. 1998). *See generally* Kruse, *OBRA '93 Disability Trusts—A Status Report*, 10 Prob. & Prop. 15 (May–June 1996). *But see* Sullivan v. County of Suffolk, 1 F. Supp. 2d 186, 196 (E.D.N.Y. 1998) (requiring payment of Medicaid lien prior to placement of Medicaid recipient's funds in supplemental needs trusts); Norwest Bank of N.D., N.A. v. Doth, 969 F. Supp. 532, 535 (D. Minn. 1997) (prohibiting evasion of existing state lien through placement of Medicaid recipient's funds in supplemental needs trust); Cricchio v. Pennisi, 90 N.Y.2d 296, 683 N.E.2d 301, 660 N.Y.S.2d 679 (1997).

[25] 42 U.S.C. §1396p(d)(4)(A) (the individual disability trust).

[26] 42 U.S.C. §1396p(d)(4)(C) (the pooled disability trust).

[27] 42 U.S.C. §1396p(d)(4)(C). Also unlike the individual "(d)(4)(A)" trust, the pooled disability trust may be funded directly by the disabled individual, that is without the involvement of the court or some third party, such as a parent or guardian.

have a payback provision.[28] For a discussion of the circumstances under which beneficiaries of non–self-settled special/supplemental needs trusts may qualify for public benefits, the reader is referred to an article by Alan Newman.[29] Invoking the modern doctrine of equitable deviation, one court has authorized the conversion of a preexisting non–self-settled trust to an SNT.[30] For a response to those who assert that the Uniform Trust Code weakens the effectiveness of supplemental needs trusts and special needs trusts, see an article by Kevin D. Millard.[31]

Sebastian V. Grassi, Jr., has authored an article reminding us that the financial plight of a special needs child cannot be adequately addressed in isolation.[32] In this regard, the reader is also referred to his *Special Needs Requires Special Attention*,[33] *Special Planning Is Needed for Retirement Benefits Payable to a Disabled Special-Needs Child*,[34] and *A Practical Guide to Estate Planning for a Family with a Special Needs Child*.[35]

§9.4   The Charitable Trust

The most important distinction between charities and other trusts is in the time of duration allowed and the degree of definiteness required. . . .   [A] public or charitable trust may be

---

[28] In contrast to a self-settled SNT, "[a] Third Party SNT is a special needs trust created and funded with the assets of a person other than the disabled beneficiary." Andrew H. Hook, *What the Trust and Estates Lawyer Needs to Know About d(4)(A) Special Needs Trusts*, 29 ACTEC J. 192, 193 (2003). The third-party SNT need not have a payback provision. The terms "Under 65 trust," "Under 65 special needs trust," and "(d)(4)(A) trust" are also employed in this context. *See generally* Clifton B. Kruse, Jr., Third Party and Self-Created Trusts (3d ed. ABA Publications, Chicago, Ill. 2002).

[29] *Spendthrift and Discretionary Trusts: Alive and Well Under the Uniform Trust Code* 40 Real Prop. Prob. & Tr. J. 567, 619–625 (Fall 2005).

[30] *See* In re Riddell, 157 P.3d 888 (Wash. Ct. App. 2007). *See generally* §8.15.20 of this handbook (equitable deviation). The *Riddell* case is also discussed in §8.2.3 of this handbook, which is devoted to a general discussion of trust termination and distribution issues.

[31] *Rights of a Trust Beneficiary's Creditors Under the Uniform Trust Code* 34 ACTEC J. 58, 73–74 (2008).

[32] *Estate Planning for Families with a Special Needs Child* 32 Tax Mgm't Est. Gifts & Trusts J. 209 (July 12, 2007).

[33] Sebastian V. Grassi, Jr., *Special Needs Requires Special Attention: Estate Planning for a Family With a Special Needs Child*, Proceedings of the 43rd Annual Heckerling Institute on Estate Planning, Chap. 9, Univ. of Miami (2009). *See also* Sebastian V. Grassi, Jr. & Nancy H. Welber, *Estate Planning with Retirement Benefits for a Special Needs Child: Part 2—Trusts as Beneficiaries of Retirement Plan Benefits*, 24 Prob. & Prop. 60 (Sept./Oct. 2009).

[34] Sebastian V. Grassi, Jr., & Nancy H. Welber, Journal of Practical Estate Planning 51 (June–July 2010).

[35] Sebastian V. Grassi, Jr., A Practical Guide to Estate Planning for a Family with a Special Needs Child, ALI ABA (2009).

perpetual in its duration and may leave the mode of application and selection of particular objects to the discretion of the trustees.[1]

It was once held in half a dozen states, including New York, that, although property might be left to a charitable corporation, charitable trusts were invalid because there were no definite beneficiaries to enforce them, or because they involved a perpetuity.[2]

Mechanics of creating a charitable trust. A charitable trust may be created by will, inter vivos transfer, declaration, or the exercise of a power of appointment.[3] "Most of the principles that apply in connection with the creation of a private trust apply as well in connection with the creation of a charitable trust."[4] First and foremost, the settlor of a charitable trust must intend to (and, of course, must have the legal right to) impress a trust for charitable purposes upon the subject property.[5] There is no "particular language" that has to be employed in order to manifest that intention.[6] As long as at least the general purpose of a trust is charitable, it may be left to the trustee's discretion to determine the specific charitable purpose or purposes to which the subject property is to be devoted.[7] A charitable trust is a public trust:

> Every charitable trust is a public trust, as distinguished from a private trust. The term "public charity" is plainly not limited to trusts for governmental or municipal purposes, such as those for public schools and hospitals, and parks and public buildings. Indeed, when the word "public" appears in a statute or a trust instrument, it generally neither adds to nor subtracts from the word "charitable."[8]

In the case of a transfer in trust, as in the case of a common law gift, there must be a completed delivery. On the other hand, just because the transferee is incapable by death or otherwise of taking the legal title, or just because the instruments of conveyance are defective, does not necessarily mean that a valid trust has not been impressed upon the subject property.[9] "It is possible to create a charitable trust without notice to or acceptance by the trustee."[10] A charitable trust does not fail merely because the named trustee is unable[11] or unwilling to serve, or continue to serve, unless it appears that the named trustee was

---

§9.4 [1] Jackson v. Phillips, 96 Mass. (14 Allen) 539, 550 (1867).

[2] 7 Scott & Ascher §45.4.1.6. Not until 1893 with the passage of the Tilden Act did charitable trusts become enforceable in New York. *See* N.Y. Est. Powers & Trusts Law §8-1.1.

[3] 5 Scott & Ascher §37.2.1 (Methods of Creating a Charitable Trust).

[4] 5 Scott & Ascher §37.2 (The Creation of a Charitable Trust).

[5] 5 Scott & Ascher §37.2.2 (Intention to Create a Trust).

[6] 5 Scott & Ascher §37.2.2.

[7] 6 Scott & Ascher §38.1.2.

[8] 6 Scott & Ascher §38.1.2.

[9] 5 Scott & Ascher §37.2.3 (Necessity of Transfer).

[10] 5 Scott & Ascher §37.2.3.

[11] Such as a transfer in trust to an unincorporated charitable association that lacks the authority to take legal title to the property. *See generally* 6 Scott & Ascher §39.3.2.

essential to the settlor's scheme.[12] The court will step in and appoint an individual or a corporation to fill the vacancy,[13] or replace a trustee who has been unable or unwilling to exercise his discretionary authority to select particular charitable purposes.[14] Just as the settlor of a private trust may reserve a right to modify or revoke it, so too may the settlor of a charitable trust.[15]

In the case of a provision in a will devising certain property to a trustee for a charitable purpose the precise nature of which is not discernable from a reading of the will itself, the trust does not necessarily fail for noncompliance with the statute of wills. It may still be salvageable, provided one or more of the following is applicable:

- The doctrine of incorporation by reference[16]
- The doctrine of facts or acts of independent legal significance[17]
- The terms of a pour-over statute[18]
- The charitable purpose is actually a general one[19]
- The imposition of a constructive trust is warranted due to an inter vivos agreement between the testator and the devisee[20]

As we note in Section 8.2.2.1 of this handbook, for the trust to be valid, the settlor, at the time it was created, must have been of full age and legal capacity and free from undue influence. Fraud would be grounds for the trust's rescission, and quite possibly mistake as well.

In the case of a discretionary trust that has been established for charitable purposes and for purposes for which a trust may not be validly created, the court has a full range of options. The court can:

- "... [A]llocate the property equally among all the purposes, uphold the trust as to any shares allocated to the charitable or otherwise valid purposes, and hold that the trust fails as to the remaining shares..."[21]
- "... [R]equire application of all the property to the charitable purposes..."[22]

---

[12] A trust shall not fail for want of a trustee. *See generally* 6 Scott & Ascher §39.3 (Failure of Trustee); §3.4 of this handbook (avoiding, assuming, and vacating the office of trustee).

[13] 6 Scott & Ascher §39.3.1.

[14] 6 Scott & Ascher §39.3.1.

[15] 5 Scott & Ascher §37.2.5 (When Settlor Reserves Power to Revoke, Modify, or Control Inter Vivos Charitable Trust). *See generally* §8.2.2.2 of this handbook (the revocable trust).

[16] 5 Scott & Ascher §37.2.4. *See generally* §8.15.17 of this handbook (doctrine of incorporation by reference).

[17] 5 Scott & Ascher §37.2.4. *See generally* §8.15.9 of this handbook (doctrine of facts or acts of independent legal significance).

[18] 5 Scott & Ascher §37.2.4. *See generally* §2.2.1 of this handbook (the pour-over statute).

[19] 5 Scott & Ascher §37.2.4. *See generally* §9.4.3 of this handbook (general charitable intent).

[20] 5 Scott & Ascher §37.2.4. *See generally* §9.9.6 of this handbook (secret and semi-secret trusts).

[21] 6 Scott & Ascher 39.4.2.

[22] 6 Scott & Ascher 39.4.2.

- "... [R]equire application of all the property to the charitable purposes, except such amounts as are necessary for the invalid purposes, as to which the trust fails..."[23]
- "... [H]old that the trust fails altogether."[24]

Indefinite beneficiaries. The beneficial interest of a charitable trust generally may not be vested in individual beneficiaries as would be the case with beneficial interests under private trusts.[25] "Indeed, the trust property is devoted to the accomplishment of purposes that are or are supposed to be beneficial to the community, and the persons who are to receive these benefits need not be designated."[26] College fraternities and sororities are generally not charitable, nor are trade unions.[27] YMCAs and YWCAs, however, are now generally held to be public charities.[28]

Though a charitable trust generally may have "no defined *cestui que trust*,"[29] there is some law to the effect that a trust for the benefit of needy employees of a particular trade or profession, or even of a particular proprietary corporation, would qualify as having a charitable purpose.[30] Provided the class of beneficiaries of a charitable trust is sufficiently indefinite, the number of possible recipients can be narrow both horizontally and vertically.[31] By horizontally narrow, we mean those eligible to take at any given time are few in number.[32] By vertically narrow, we mean that the trust's duration is limited in time.[33] Equity, however, "which looks to the intent rather than the form,"[34] would not tolerate a trust that is ostensibly charitable but actually a subterfuge to effect the conferring of gratuitous benefits on named individuals, unless the arrangement meets the durational requirements of the rule against perpetuities,[35] or is otherwise exempt from those requirements.[36]

Unincorporated societies and clubs. "... [W]hen property is transferred in trust for an unincorporated association for a period in excess of the rule

---

[23] 6 Scott & Ascher 39.4.2.

[24] 6 Scott & Ascher 39.4.2. *See also* §9.4.1 of this handbook (the possible invalidity of a "benevolent" trust); Morice v. Bishop of Durham, 10 Ves. 522, 32 Eng. Rep. 947 (L.C. 1805), *aff'g* 9 Ves. 399, 32 Eng. Rep. 656 (Ch. 1804) (a case involving a trust for charitable *and* benevolent purposes where the court held that the trust had totally failed, the court having rejected the attorney general's request that there be an apportionment of some portion of the trust property to the charitable purposes).

[25] 6 Scott & Ascher §38.8.

[26] 6 Scott & Ascher §38.8.

[27] *See generally* 6 Scott & Ascher §38.9.2.

[28] *See generally* 6 Scott & Ascher §38.9.2.

[29] John Chipman Gray, The Rule Against Perpetuities §328 (4th ed. 1942).

[30] *See generally* 6 Scott & Ascher §38.9.2.

[31] 6 Scott & Ascher §38.9.1.

[32] 6 Scott & Ascher §38.9.1.

[33] 6 Scott & Ascher §38.9.1.

[34] *See generally* §8.12 of this handbook (in part discussing equity's maxims).

[35] *See generally* §8.2.1 of this handbook (the rule against perpetuities).

[36] *See generally* §8.2.1.9 of this handbook (abolition of the rule against perpetuities) and §8.2.1.10 of this handbook (the dynasty trust).

against perpetuities, the trust's validity may depend on whether the association is charitable, or merely for the benefit of its members."[37] If the entrustment is for the benefit of the present members, such that "they have the entire beneficial use of the property, and can, if they please alienate it and put the proceeds in their own pockets," then the rule is not implicated.[38] "The Rule against Perpetuities is not concerned with their relations to each other as co-owners."[39] If the entrustment is for the benefit of future members, then the gift is good only if it is confined within the limits of the rule.[40]

Enforcement. It generally falls to the state attorney general to seek judicial enforcement of charitable trusts, a topic we take up in Section 9.4.2 of this handbook. In special circumstances, others may have standing to seek enforcement as well.

Duration. Ignoring for the moment the fact that "in a number of states it is now possible to devote property forever to the accomplishment of purely private purposes,"[41] the main nontax advantage that a charitable trust has enjoyed over a private trust is this: A trust for a charitable purpose is exempt from the durational requirements of the Rule against Perpetuities.[42] The equitable interest, however, must, in all events, become devoted to some charitable purpose within the period of the Rule.[43] Still, contingent charitable interests created under such trusts may remain contingent forever.[44]

A charitable trust, however, need not continue indefinitely.[45] The transfer of property to the trustee of a charitable trust may be subject to a *condition subsequent*, or it may be for a duration that is contingency-based, such as "until the happening of a certain event, or for so long as a certain state of affairs continues."[46] The latter provision is known as a *limitation*.[47] In the event the charitable trust terminates on its own terms and the gift over fails, whether because the gift over violates the Rule against Perpetuities or for some other reason, there is a divergence. In the case of the limitation there is likely to be a

---

[37] 6 Scott & Ascher §38.9.2.

[38] John Chipman Gray, The Rule Against Perpetuities §896 (4th ed. 1942).

[39] John Chipman Gray, The Rule Against Perpetuities §896 (4th ed. 1942).

[40] John Chipman Gray, The Rule Against Perpetuities §896.2 (4th ed. 1942).

[41] 6 Scott & Ascher §38.1.

[42] *See generally* §8.2.1 of this handbook (the Rule against Perpetuities). Regarding the Rule's application to income accumulations, *see* §8.15.8 of this handbook (rule against accumulations) and §8.15.23 of this handbook (the Thelluson Act); 4A Scott on Trusts §§365, 401.9; Franklin Found. v. Attorney Gen., 416 Mass. 483, 623 N.E.2d 1109 (1993) (involving a 200-year accumulation trust established under the will of Benjamin Franklin); Bogert §341.

[43] W. Barton Leach, *Perpetuities in a Nutshell*, 51 Harv. L. Rev. 638, 668–669 (1938). *See generally* 5 Scott & Ascher §37.4.1.

[44] 5 Scott & Ascher §37.4.1.

[45] 5 Scott & Ascher §37.4.1.

[46] 6 Scott & Ascher §39.7 (Conditions and Limitations); 6 Scott & Ascher §39.7.2 (Conditions Subsequent); 6 Scott & Ascher §39.7.3 (Limitations).

[47] *See generally* 6 Scott & Ascher §39.7.6 (Gift Over from Charity to Noncharity).

resulting trust.[48] In the case of the condition subsequent, the charitable trust might well be allowed to continue.[49]

A breach of trust generally does not trigger a resulting trust.[50] Nor does a condition precedent that is illegal in the sense that it violates public policy, unless it is determined that that is what the settlor would have wanted.[51] The usual inference is that the settlor would want the illegal condition judicially voided so that the trust could operate.[52] In any case, "[t]he courts strictly construe any provision that would require the termination of a charitable trust and reversion of its property to the donor or the donor's estate."[53] Having said that, a court would be more amendable to enforcing a resulting trust in lieu of applying *cy pres* were the trust were to fail at the outset than were it to fail in mid-course.[54] The court will not enforce a termination provision in a charitable trust if to do so would be "inequitable."[55] For a discussion of the doctrine of *cy pres* as an alternative to the imposition of a resulting trust, see Section 9.4.3 of this handbook.

Tax status irrelevant. That a trust is charitable for trust and property law purposes does not necessarily mean that it is also tax-exempt.[56] In 1936, for example, it was held that the Boston Symphony Orchestra, a public charitable trust,[57] was subject to a property tax on its hall because it charged admission and permitted renewable season ticket privileges.[58] On the other hand, that a trust is tax-exempt does not necessarily make it a public charity. The common trust fund comes to mind in this regard.[59]

Charitable immunity. As to a charitable trust's immunity from the attacks of third-party tort claimants, the reader is referred to Section 8.15.38 of this handbook.[60]

---

[48] *See generally* 6 Scott & Ascher §39.7.6 (Gift Over from Charity to Noncharity). "In cases like this, it is said that charity takes only a limited interest, which is not enlarged merely because of the failure of the gift over." 6 Scott & Ascher §39.7.6 (Gift Over from Charity to Noncharity).

[49] *See generally* 6 Scott & Ascher §39.7.6 (Gift Over from Charity to Noncharity).

[50] 6 Scott & Ascher §39.7.1 (No Reverter for Breach of Trust). *See generally* §4.1.1.1 of this handbook (defining the resulting trust).

[51] 6 Scott & Ascher §39.7.10 (Illegal Condition Precedent).

[52] 6 Scott & Ascher §39.7.10 (Illegal Condition Precedent). The settlor, of course, could have specified an alternate disposition, that is to say a charitable "gift-over," in the event that the condition were held unenforceable. 6 Scott & Ascher §39.7.10. A valid gift over would likely be honored by the court. 6 Scott & Ascher §39.7.10.

[53] *See generally* 6 Scott & Ascher §39.7.4; §9.4.3 of this handbook (*cy pres* versus the vested equitable reversionary interest and the resulting trust).

[54] *See generally* 6 Scott & Ascher §41.3 (Failure of Charitable Trusts).

[55] 6 Scott & Ascher §39.7.4.

[56] 6 Scott & Ascher §§38.9, 38.9.2.

[57] *See generally* 6 Scott & Ascher §38.9.2.

[58] Boston Symphony Orchestra v. Board of Assessors, 1 N.E.2d 6 (Mass. 1936).

[59] *See generally* §9.7.1 of this handbook (in part discussing the tax aspects of the common trust fund).

[60] As to the current status of a charitable trust's traditional immunity against the claims of third-party tort claimants, the reader is referred to §8.15.38 of this handbook (the charitable immunity doctrine).

Split-interest trusts. A trust may be partly for charitable purposes and partly for private beneficiaries.[61] "Under the Uniform Trust Code, when a trust has both charitable and noncharitable beneficiaries, only the charitable portion qualifies as a charitable trust."[62]

Charitable purposes. Although charitable trusts have been around for a long time,[63] the law of trusts has yet to develop a truly satisfactory definition of the term *charitable*.[64] In Section 9.4.1 of this handbook we explain why.

§9.4.1 Charitable Purposes

In the leading case of Jackson v. Phillips, 96 Mass. (12 Allen) 539 (1867), a trust to create a public sentiment that will put an end to negro slavery was upheld along with a trust for the benefit of fugitive slaves that may escape from the slave-holding states. That very case, however, held invalid another intended trust to promote women's suffrage because the purpose was to change the laws.[65]

In England until 1934, and in some early cases in the United States, trusts for masses were held not to be charitable. . . .   Now, by a considerable weight of authority in this country, trusts for masses are charitable as benefiting living members of the church and possibly, according to the Roman Catholic church doctrine, the world as a whole.[66]

Profits must be deployed for charitable purposes. A trust for private profit or to maintain an institution for private profit is noncharitable.[67] The question is not whether profits are generated but how those profits are deployed.[68] Thus, a school may charge tuition, or a hospital fees, provided all payments inure to the benefit of the institution's charitable purposes.[69] The taking of *reasonable* compensation by trustees, managers, officers, and employees generally does not render an otherwise charitable undertaking noncharitable.[70]

The charitable exemption from the rule against perpetuities. In determining whether or not equity has before it a charitable trust, equity looks to the purposes of a trust, not to the subjective motive or motives of the settlor in creating it.[71] A charitable trust has traditionally enjoyed a critical exemption that has nothing to do with tax avoidance, namely, an exemption from the

---

[61] 6 Scott & Ascher §38.8.

[62] UTC §103 cmt. (available at <http://www.uniformlaws.org/Act.aspx?title=Trust%20 Code>).

[63] *See generally* §8.15.4 of this handbook (Statute of Elizabeth/charitable uses).

[64] *See generally* 6 Scott & Ascher §38.1.1.

[65] Restatement (Third) of Trusts §28 cmt. l.

[66] Restatement (Third) of Trusts §28 cmt. h.

[67] 6 Scott & Ascher §38.10.

[68] 6 Scott & Ascher §38.10.

[69] 6 Scott & Ascher §38.10.

[70] 6 Scott & Ascher §38.10.

[71] 5 Scott & Ascher §37.1 (The Definition of a Charitable Trust); 6 Scott & Ascher §38.1.

durational requirements of the Rule against Perpetuities:[72] A trust involving contingent interests may continue in perpetuity for a charitable purpose but not for a private or a political purpose.[73] Even to this day, for a particular trust purpose to be construed as charitable, it needs to conform to the spirit of the Preamble to the now-repealed English statute of charitable uses (Statute of Elizabeth), which we took up in Section 8.15.5 of this handbook, unless some statute currently in force and effect dictates otherwise.

Political purposes. "It is necessary . . . to distinguish between objects that are merely political and those that have a broader social significance."[74] Unfortunately, distinguishing political trusts from private and charitable trusts is not as easy as it sounds.[75] In a breathtaking tour de force of judicial scholarship that takes the reader from the age of Justinian to the American Civil War, Justice Gray took up that challenge in the 1867 Massachusetts case of *Jackson v. Phillips*, which in part involved a trust to promote women's rights.[76] The court held that the trust had a political and not a charitable purpose.[77]

Preamble to the Statute of Charitable Uses. As noted, judges have traditionally looked to the purposes enumerated in the preamble of the English statute of charitable uses[78] for examples of purposes qualifying for the charitable exemption from the time limitations of the Rule against Perpetuities.[79] Justice Gray was no exception. These purposes include relief for the poor, maintenance of nonprofit hospitals and schools, and repair of bridges and roads.[80] As is the case with the American Uniform Prudent Management of Institutional Funds Act (UPMIFA),[81] a model statute whose provisions would apply to charitable corporations as well as charitable trusts,[82] the list of charitable uses set forth in the American Restatement (Third) of Trusts differs from

---

[72] *See generally* 6 Scott & Ascher §38.8. "So also, a charitable institution may be exempt from liability in tort, whereas a noncharitable institution has no such exemption." 6 Scott & Ascher §38.9. *See also* §8.15.38 of this handbook (the charitable immunity doctrine applicable to trusts).

[73] *See generally* 4A Scott on Trusts §§368, 374.6; J. A. Bryant, Jr., J.D., LL.M., Annot., *Application of Cy Pres Doctrine to Trust for Promulgation of Particular Political or Philosophical Doctrines*, 67 A.L.R.3d 417 (1975). *See, e.g.,* Marsh v. Frost Nat'l Bank, 129 S.W.3d 174 (Tex. 2004) (ruling that an accumulation trust to provide a million-dollar trust fund for every American 18 years or older upon the expiration of 346 years was a noncharitable trust that violated the rule against perpetuities). *See generally* §8.2.1 of this handbook (the Rule against Perpetuities).

[74] 6 Scott & Ascher §38.7.8.

[75] *See generally* 6 Scott & Ascher §38.1; Rounds, *Social Investing, IOLTA, and the Law of Trusts,* 22 Loy. U. Chi. L.J. 163, 178–181 (1990).

[76] 96 Mass. (14 Allen) 539 (1867).

[77] *See generally* 6 Scott & Ascher §38.7.9.

[78] *See generally* §8.15.4 of this handbook (Charitable Purpose Doctrine (Statute of Elizabeth/ Charitable Uses)).

[79] *See generally* 4A Scott on Trusts §368.1.

[80] 4A Scott on Trusts §368.1; Bogert §§321, 362. *See* UTC §405(a) (available at <http://www.uniformlaws.org/Act.aspx?title=Trust%20Code>) (providing that a charitable trust may be created for the relief of poverty, the advancement of education or religion, the promotion of health, governmental or municipal purposes, or other purposes the achievement of which is beneficial to the community).

[81] Unif. Prudent Management Inst. Funds Act §2(1).

[82] Unif. Prudent Management Inst. Funds Act §2 cmt.

that of the English statute of charitable uses in style, language, and detail, but not in substance:

- The relief of poverty;[83]
- The advancement of knowledge or education;[84]
- The advancement of religion;[85]
- The promotion of health;[86]
- Governmental or municipal purposes;[87] and
- Other purposes that are beneficial to the community.[88]

Generalizing from the preamble's list, or the Restatement's, or UPMIFA's, for that matter, however, is easier said than done. A trust to keep the settlor's children off the welfare rolls is a private trust, although its purpose is the relief

---

[83] Restatement (Third) of Trusts §28 cmt. g; 6 Scott & Ascher §38.2. "A trust for the relief of the poor is charitable although it is not limited to those who are destitute." 6 Scott & Ascher §38.2.3. "It is sufficient that those who are to benefit from the trust are in needy circumstances, even if they have a certain amount of property." 6 Scott & Ascher §38.2.3.

[84] Restatement (Third) of Trusts §28 cmt. h; 6 Scott & Ascher §38.3. A trust "to educate a particular person or a narrow class of persons is ordinarily not charitable" 6 Scott & Ascher §38.3.6. "A trust for educational purposes need not be limited to the training of the mind, but may include the training of the body." 6 Scott & Ascher §38.3.2. On the other hand, "trusts that serve merely to promote a sport, as such, have generally been held not to be charitable." 6 Scott & Ascher §38.2.3. A trust to support a public educational institution or a nonproprietary private educational institution, even one that charges tuition, would qualify as charitable. 6 Scott & Ascher §38.3.5. The support of an educational institution conducted for private profit, however, would not qualify as a charitable purpose. 6 Scott & Ascher §38.2.3.

[85] Restatement (Third) of Trusts §28 cmt. i; 6 Scott & Ascher §38.4. Although the statute of charitable uses made only a passing reference to religion, specifically in the context of the repair of churches, and although the statute's author, Sir Francis Moore, had intentionally omitted religious purposes from the statute's preamble, nonetheless by 1639 courts in England had begun enforcing perpetual trusts for the advancement of religion. 6 Scott & Ascher §38.4. "In England today and in the United States a trust for the promotion of religion is a valid trust even if the religion has few adherents or seems foolish to most people." 6 Scott & Ascher §38.4.4. On the other hand, "[w]hen a trust is for the religious benefit of only one or a few persons, it is not charitable." 6 Scott & Ascher §38.4.6.

[86] Restatement (Third) of Trusts §28 cmt. j. "A nonprofit hospital is charitable, even if it requires all of its patients to pay and provides no free or reduced-cost services for those who cannot pay." 6 Scott & Ascher §38.5. "An institution for the promotion of health is not charitable if it is privately owned and run for a profit." 6 Scott & Ascher §38.5.1. A charitable institution for the promotion of health must apply any profits to charitable purposes. 6 Scott & Ascher §38.5.1. "The fact that an institution pays salaries to those rendering services to it does not prevent it from being charitable, but if the payment of salaries is merely a device for passing its profits along to its owners, the institution is not charitable." 6 Scott & Ascher §38.5.1.

[87] Restatement (Third) of Trusts §28 cmt. k; 6 Scott & Ascher §38.6.

[88] Restatement (Third) of Trusts §28 cmt. l; 6 Scott & Ascher §38.7. *See also* 6 Scott & Ascher §§38.7.1 (Promotion of Temperance), 38.7.2 (Relief of Animals), 38.7.3 (Trusts for Persons of Limited Opportunities), 38.7.4 (Humanitarian Purposes), 38.7.5 (Patriotic Purposes), 38.7.6 (Unpopular Causes), 38.7.7 (Improving Government), 38.7.8 (Political Objects), 38.7.9 (Changes in Existing Law), 38.7.10 (Monuments and Tombs), 38.7.11 (Community Purposes), 38.7.12 (Promotion of Sports), 38.7.13 (Housing and Services for the Elderly and Handicapped).

of poverty.[89] "In other words, in the case of a private trust, the trust property is devoted to the use of designated beneficiaries."[90] On the other hand, "[a] trust may well be charitable notwithstanding the fact that the donor's motive was to glorify himself or herself or to spite his or her relatives."[91] In England, a *perpetual* trust for the purpose of supporting and/or educating the settlor's needy descendants is generally enforceable.[92] In the United States, this is not the case, except in those jurisdictions that have done away with the rule against perpetuities for certain types of trust.[93] It goes without saying that charitable trusts whose particular purposes are illegal or otherwise violate public policy are unenforceable.[94]

A trust for the saying of masses for the soul of a particular deceased individual has a private flavor to it but is now generally held to be charitable.[95] A trust for the maintenance of a building is charitable "if the building is of such historic or other public interest that its preservation benefits the community."[96] A trust for the perpetual maintenance of the grave or tomb of someone who is not a public figure,[97] however, would be noncharitable and thus fail, absent authorizing legislation.[98] In most states such trusts are now exempt by statute from the Rule against Perpetuities.[99] "A trust for the benefit of poor members, or the widows and orphan children of members, of a particular club or fraternal organization is also charitable, although a gift to the organization itself would not be."[100] For a purpose to qualify as charitable, it "must go beyond merely providing financial enrichment to the individual members of . . . [a] . . . community, . . . [it] . . . must promote the social interest of the community as

---

[89] 4A Scott on Trusts §369.5; *see, e.g.,* Hardage v. Hardage, 211 Ga. 80, 84 S.E.2d 54 (1954). *See also* 6 Scott & Ascher §38.2.5.

[90] 5 Scott & Ascher §37.1.

[91] 6 Scott & Ascher §38.1.

[92] 6 Scott & Ascher §38.9.3.

[93] *See generally* 6 Scott & Ascher §38.9.3 (Trusts for Relatives); §8.2.1.9 of this handbook (abolition of the rule against perpetuities). "On the other hand, in the United States as well as in England, a trust for the relief of poverty or the promotion of knowledge or education is ordinarily charitable, though the terms of the trust provide that in selecting beneficiaries the trustees are to give preference to the relatives or descendants of the settlor or one or more other designated persons." 6 Scott & Ascher §38.9.3.

[94] 6 Scott & Ascher §38.11 (Illegal Purposes); *cf.* §9.24 of this handbook (public policy considerations).

[95] 2 Scott & Ascher §12.11.4. "In 1919, the House of Lords held that a bequest for the saying of masses was not illegal . . . Finally, in 1934, it was held that such a bequest was charitable." 6 Scott & Ascher §38.4.4. *See also* 6 Scott & Ascher §38.4.5 (Masses).

[96] 2 Scott & Ascher §12.11.5.

[97] *See generally* §9.4.2 of this handbook.

[98] *See* 6 Scott & Ascher §39.7.5. *See, e.g.,* Lucker v. Bayside Cemetery, 114 A.D.3d 162, 979 N.Y.S.2d 8 (2013) (in New York by statute, a trust for the perpetual care of a gravesite is deemed to be a charitable trust, the State Attorney General thus being the only one with the requisite standing to seek its judicial enforcement, absent special facts).

[99] *See generally* §5.1 of this handbook (whether a deceased person can be a trust beneficiary); §9.9.5 of this handbook (the honorary trust).

[100] 6 Scott & Ascher §38.2.5.

a whole."[101] The community to be benefited, however, need not be of the state in which the trust is created.[102]

A trust for the dissemination of literature to bring about legislatively, or bring an end legislatively, to rent control risks being construed as a political trust, although, as far as the settlor may be concerned, its purpose is the relief of poverty and the advancement of education.[103] Having said that, "[i]n the United States...[,as opposed to England,]...the notion that a trust for a purpose otherwise charitable is not charitable if accomplishment of its purposes involves a change in existing laws has been pretty thoroughly rejected."[104] A trust to support a hostel for the homeless, of course, would fall well within the letter and spirit of the statute of charitable uses;[105] so would a trust "for the purpose of providing training in the duties and responsibilities of citizenship,"[106] or for the dissemination of general beliefs and doctrines, unless they are so irrational or absurd as to be of no benefit to the community.[107] When it comes to the intersection of charity and politics, trustees would benefit from criteria that are patently objective.[108]

A trustee who is unsure whether a particular activity is charitable should consider whether the activity is private or political before consulting the statute of charitable uses.[109] If it is clearly neither then the chances are good that it is charitable. As a rule of thumb, a trust for the benefit of a named individual or of a class of beneficiaries ascertainable by their relationship to a named individual is a *private* trust (*e.g.*, a trust for the settlor's issue);[110] a trust whose purpose is to influence the exercise of state power is a political trust[111] (*e.g.*, a trust for the

---

[101] *See, e.g.*, Marsh v. Frost Nat'l Bank, 129 S.W.3d 174 (Tex. 2004) (ruling that an accumulation trust to provide a million-dollar trust fund for every American 18 years or older upon the expiration of 346 years was a noncharitable trust that violated the rule against perpetuities).

[102] 6 Scott & Ascher §38.7.14.

[103] *See* Rounds, *Social Investing, IOLTA, and the Law of Trusts*, 22 Loy. U. Chi. L.J. 163, 179 (1990). *But see* Jackson v. Phillips, 96 Mass. (14 Allen) 539 (1867). *See also* Russell G. Donaldson, J.D., Annot., *Validity, as for a charitable purpose, or [sic] trust for publication or distribution of particular books or writings*, 34 A.L.R.4th 419 (1984).

[104] 6 Scott & Ascher §38.7.9.

[105] *See* Rounds, *Social Investing, IOLTA, and the Law of Trusts*, 22 Loy. U. Chi. L.J. 163, 179 n.75 and accompanying text (1990); 4A Scott on Trusts §369.3.

[106] 6 Scott & Ascher §38.3.3.

[107] 6 Scott & Ascher §38.3.4.

[108] *Cf.* 6 Scott & Ascher §38.1 ("So too what one community regards as beneficial may in another community be regarded as useless or illegal.").

[109] *See also* Restatement (Third) of Trusts §28 (furnishing a list of charitable purposes that is similar in substance to that found in the Statute of Charitable Uses, the two listings differing only in "style, language and detail").

[110] 6 Scott & Ascher §38.2.5.

[111] Rounds, *Social Investing, IOLTA, and the Law of Trusts*, 22 Loy. U. Chi. L.J. 163, 179–180 (1990). *But see* Restatement (Second) of Trusts §374 cmt. j (suggesting that a trust to support *legal* lobbying activity is a charitable purpose). Section 374 formally adds most political purposes to the catalog of charitable purposes set forth in the preamble to the Statute of Charitable Uses. For all intents and purposes, we are now at the base of the slippery slope. *See generally* §8.15.4 of this handbook (charitable purpose doctrine (Statute of Elizabeth/charitable uses)).

purpose of influencing tax policy through lobbying activity).[112] It is settled law that a trust to support a political party is noncharitable.[113] In most states, so is a trust created to maintain individual burial lots, absent special facts.[114]

The charitable tax exemption. Above all, the trustee should not confuse Code Section 501(c) criteria for tax exemption[115] with the criteria that have evolved over the years in a particular state for the charitable exemption from the time limitations of the Rule against Perpetuities.[116] A trust may not be exempt for income tax purposes[117] but may still be a common law charitable trust, and a trust may be exempt from income tax but not qualify as a charitable trust.[118]

The modern trend is to blend politics and charity. "Gifts for purposes prohibited by or opposed to the existing laws cannot be upheld as charitable, even if for objects which would otherwise be deemed such."[119] Again, that has been the tradition. Moreover, it has been expected of trustees of charitable trusts that they will indulge their politics with their own funds, not with the funds of others, and that they will resist pressures from whatever quarter to exploit for their own political purposes the enormous economic power that they control as stewards of the benefactions of others.

Today, however, for good or for ill, much political activity is being directly or indirectly fueled by charitable funds. Perhaps in recognition of a *fait accompli*, the Restatement (Third) of Trusts would allow for some crossing of the traditional bright line between the charitable and the political:

> The mere fact . . . that the purpose of a trust is to advocate and bring about a particular change of law does not prevent the purpose from being charitable. This is so whether the change is pursued indirectly through the education and persuasion of the electorate, so as to bring about a public sentiment favorable to the change, or through more direct but lawful influences, such as by proper lobbying and other persuasion brought to bear upon legislators.[120]

Ultimately, however, all politics are subjective, local, relative, and situational.[121] In England in 1851, a bequest "towards the political restoration of the Jews to Jerusalem and to their own land" was voided as "tending to create a

---

[112] *But see* Register of Wills of Baltimore City v. Cook, 241 Md. 264, 216 A.2d 542 (1966).

[113] Restatement (Second) of Trusts §374 cmt. k; 6 Scott & Ascher §38.7.8. *See generally* Note, *Charitable Trusts for Political Purposes*, 37 Va. L. Rev. 988 (1951).

[114] *See generally* In re Mary R. Latimer Trust, 2013 WL 4463388 (Del. Ch. Aug. 9, 2013).

[115] *See generally* Bogert §362.

[116] *See generally* 5 Scott & Ascher §37.1.4 (Collateral Consequences of Charitable Dispositions); Restatement (Third) of Trusts §28, General Comment (citing to §9.4.1 of the 1997 edition of this handbook in Reporter's Notes on §28); 6 Scott & Ascher §38.7.9.

[117] *See, e.g.,* Crisp Area YMCA v. Nationsbank, N.A., 272 Ga. 182, 526 S.E.2d 63 (2000) (upholding a bequest to a YMCA that had lost its tax-exempt status due to inactivity).

[118] *See generally* Scott on Trusts §§348.4, 374.4, 374.5; 5 Scott & Ascher §37.1.4.

[119] Jackson v. Phillips, 96 Mass. (14 Allen) 539, 555 (1867).

[120] Restatement (Third) of Trusts §28, Comment on Clause f.

[121] *See generally* 6 Scott & Ascher §38.1.

political revolution in a friendly country."[122] About that time, across the Atlantic in Mississippi, a testamentary trust for paying the expenses of transporting the settlor's slaves to Africa and maintaining them there was being enforced.[123] In a 1925 New York case, the court held that a trust to "further the development of the Irish Republic" was for a political rather than a charitable purpose.[124]

The benevolent trust. It has been the law that a benevolent trust would fail as being unenforceable, and, depending upon its term, as violating the Rule against Perpetuities.[125] A benevolent trust is a trust whose general purposes are not limited to the charitable,[126] *e.g.*, to such objects of benevolence and liberality as the Bishop of Durham and his successors in their own discretion shall most approve of.[127] Our sample language of benevolence is too broad to qualify the trust as a charitable trust subject to an enforcement action by the attorney general,[128] nor is there a designated individual with standing to seek its enforcement.[129] And an intention that the Bishop should take the title outright and free of trust is lacking. Accordingly, the trust fails and returns to the settlor or his estate upon a resulting trust.[130] Had the phrase "and his successors" been absent from our sample language, there probably would not have been a perpetuities violation as the Bishop would have been a life in being.[131]

When a settlor intends that a trust's purposes be *both* charitable *and* benevolent, then we have a trust that conforms to the spirit of the preamble to statute of charitable uses.[132] The problem comes when the trust's purposes may be *either* charitable *or* benevolent, the latter purpose having a broader

---

[122] Jackson v. Phillips, 96 Mass. (14 Allen) 539, 555 (1867) (referring to Habershon v. Vardon, 4 De Gex & Sm. 467 (1851)).

[123] Wade v. American Colonization Soc'y, 7 Sm. & Marsh. 663 (1846).

[124] Matter of Killen, 209 N.Y.S. 206 (Surr. Ct. 1925).

[125] Shenandoah Valley Nat'l Bank v. Taylor, 192 Va. 135, 139, 63 S.E.2d 786, 789 (1951).

[126] *See generally* 2 Scott & Ascher §12.10 (discussing the similarities between a benevolent trust and a power of appointment); 6 Scott & Ascher §38.1.2 ("The better view is that . . . [the adjective 'benevolent'] . . . was not intended to go beyond 'charitable,' although when a settler uses the word, it has sometimes been held in both England and the United States not to be limited to charity, and to cause the intended trust to fail.").

[127] Sample language was taken from an English case, Morice v. Bishop of Durham, 9 Ves. 399 (1804), 10 Ves. 521 (1805), but with the addition of the phrase "and his successors." *See generally* John Chipman Gray, The Rule Against Perpetuities §895 (4th ed. 1942).

[128] *See generally* §9.4.2 of this handbook (standing to enforce charitable trusts); John Chipman Gray, The Rule Against Perpetuities §895.1 (4th ed. 1942) ("In the majority of these and similar cases, the trust is said to be invalid because indefinite, uncertain, or incapable of being executed by the court.").

[129] John Chipman Gray, The Rule Against Perpetuities §894 (4th ed. 1942) (no trust without a beneficiary).

[130] *See generally* §4.1.1.1 of this handbook (the noncharitable trust; resulting trust defined).

[131] *See generally* §8.2.1.2 of this handbook (validating life or worst-case life in being).

[132] 6 Scott & Ascher §39.4.1.

connotation than the former.[133] Coming up with an example of a purpose that is benevolent but not charitable, however, is easier said than done:

> Considerable ingenuity has been expended in imagining purposes that are benevolent but not charitable. It was once suggested that a trust to provide music on the village green was for a benevolent but not charitable purpose, but it is now clear that such a purpose is charitable. It was once suggested that a trust to provide oysters for the Benchers of the Inns of Court was benevolent but not charitable, although Lord Wright said that he would not be disposed to regard such a fund as either benevolent or charitable. In England, it has been held that neither a trust to provide a pennyworth of sweets for all boys and girls under the age of fourteen in a certain parish, nor a trust to apply the income to provide knickers for boys, not necessarily poor, between the ages of ten and fifteen in a particular district, was charitable. All these are perhaps illustrations of purposes that might be called "benevolent," though not "charitable."[134]

In the future, benevolent or mixed trusts[135] are likely to be given the benefit of the doubt if at all possible.[136] "If the charitable and other purposes are distinctly divided either by time or into separate and independent shares, the period or share devoted to charity will be treated as a charitable trust just as if separate trust has been created for the different purposes."[137] Moreover, the noncharitable portion may well be upheld as a purpose adapted trust.[138] The topic of purpose trusts is covered in Section 9.27 of this handbook. Adapted trusts are covered in Section 9.29 of this handbook. In Section 9.8.10 of this handbook we take up the Cayman Islands STAR trust, which has some of the attributes of the benevolent trust. If the equitable charitable and noncharitable interests are blended, the benevolent trust will still be subject to the Rule against Perpetuities.[139]

---

[133] 6 Scott & Ascher §39.4.1. Although some courts have founds the words "charitable" and "benevolent" to be synonymous. 6 Scott & Ascher §39.4.1. "Indeed there are now in many states statutes relating to charitable trusts, a number of which use the word 'benevolent.'" 6 Scott & Ascher §39.4.1.

[134] 6 Scott & Ascher §39.4.1.

[135] *See generally* §9.4.5 of this handbook (tax-oriented trusts that mix charitable and noncharitable interests (split-interest trusts)).

[136] *See, e.g.,* Hight v. United States, 256 F.2d 795 (2d Cir. 1958) (applying the principle of *ejusdem generis,* the court held that a trust for the benefit of "charitable, benevolent, religious or education institutions" was a charitable trust). *See generally* 6 Scott & Ascher §38.1.2 (The Law Relating to Charitable Purposes in America); 6 Scott & Ascher §39.4.1 (Indefinite Purposes Not Limited to Charity).

[137] Restatement (Third) of Trusts §28, General Comment e. *See generally* 6 Scott & Ascher §39.4.1.

[138] *See generally* 2 Scott & Ascher §12.10.

[139] Restatement (Third) of Trusts §28, General Comment e.

§9.4.2   Standing to Enforce Charitable Trusts

Several commentators have noted that foreclosing the donor from enforcing the terms of his or her gift is an inefficient method of ensuring that charitable organizations comply with the donor's stated intent. They assert that the resources available to attorneys general are insufficient to adequately monitor and protect the wishes of donors. Further, these commentators state that attorneys general interpose public policy considerations that often do not coincide with the donor's stated interests.[140]

In the United States, a suit for the enforcement of a charitable trust may be maintained by the attorney general (or the official charged with overseeing the administration of charitable trusts if the attorney general is not so charged) of the state in which the trust is to be administered, or is being administered.[141] As we shall see, others may as well. When, however, suit to enforce a charitable trust is brought by a person other than the state attorney general, the attorney general must be joined as a party.[142] If the state official charged with overseeing public charities is someone other than the attorney general, then it is that official who must be joined as a party.

The noncharitable beneficiary of a split interest trust and the nontrustee holder of a power under a charitable trust. *The split-interest trust.* A split-interest trust is a trust that has charitable and noncharitable components. See generally Section 9.4.5 of this handbook. "If an otherwise charitable trust has one or more noncharitable beneficiaries, such as potential takers by gift over or resulting trust, those beneficiaries have standing to protect or assert their interests in the trust."[143] It should be noted that the doctrine of *cy pres* is being so buttressed by legislation that there is now an ever "diminishing likelihood" that the settlor of a charitable trust will be able to demonstrate to a court's satisfaction that he holds a vested equitable reversionary property interest under it.[144] Recall that the holder of an equitable reversion takes title to the underlying property of a failed express trust from its trustee via the judicial

---

[140] Michael M. Schmidt & Taylor T. Pollock, *Modern Tomb Raiders: Nonprofit Organizations' Impermissible Use of Restricted Funds*, 31-SEP Colo. Law. 57, 59 (Sept. 2002). In one case involving a charitable education trust with gender, race, and religious restrictions, the scholarship selection committee filed a *cy pres* action seeking removal of the gender and race restrictions. The state attorney general sought the removal of the religious restrictions as well, citing public policy considerations. His efforts to interpose his policy predilections were rebuffed by the court. *See* Lockwood v. Killian, 172 Conn. 496, 375 A.2d 998 (1977). In the United States the courts have had no difficulty in upholding trusts for the promotion of any form of religion. 4A Scott on Trusts §371. "[A]s early as 1639 [in England] it was held that a trust to maintain a preaching minister was a valid charitable trust." 4A Scott on Trusts §371. *See also* Jackson v. Phillips, 96 Mass. (14 Allen) 539, 553 (1867) (noting that from very soon after the passage of the statute of charitable uses or Statute of Elizabeth "gifts for the support of a minister, the preaching of an annual sermon, or other uses connected with public worship and the advancement of religion, have been constantly upheld and carried out as charities in the English courts of chancery").

[141] Restatement (Third) of Trusts §94(2).

[142] Restatement (Third) of Trusts §94 cmt. e.

[143] Restatement (Third) of Trusts §94 cmt. g(2).

[144] *See generally* §9.4.3 of this handbook (*cy pres*).

imposition of a resulting trust.[145] The resulting trust is one of a number of equity's procedural remedies.[146]

A nontrustee power holder. The terms of a charitable trust may reserve to the settlor, or grant to someone other than the trustee, certain powers, such as a power to control/advise the trustee, enforce the trust, or modify its terms.[147] "Express powers of these types give the power holder a special interest in enforcing the charitable trust, and therefore standing, essentially . . . to the same extent that similar powers provide standing to sue trustees of private trusts. . . ."[148]

The state attorney general or other designated public official. As a general rule, the court does not act on its own initiative in enforcing trusts, charitable or otherwise.[149] "It is the duty of the king, as parens patriae, to protect property devoted to charitable use; and that duty is executed by the officer who represents the crown for all forensic purposes."[150] This is the foundation of the state attorney general's authority to seek enforcement of charitable trusts in the courts.[151] Even in the case of trusts that mix charitable and noncharitable interests, *e.g.*, charitable lead trusts, charitable remainder unitrusts (CRUTs), and charitable remainder annuity trusts (CRATs), the state attorney general has an oversight function.[152] "In some . . . [U.S.] . . . states, the local district or county attorney, or other public official, can maintain such a suit; as appropriate, references to the 'Attorney General' . . . [in the Restatement (third) of Trusts] . . . include such officials."[153]

It is in the nature of the typical charitable trust that its beneficiaries are so numerous and their interests under it so contingent and tangential that, as a practical matter, no beneficiary possesses a sufficient interest to seek its enforcement.[154] While each of us, for example, is a direct and indirect contingent

---

[145] *See generally* §4.1.1.1 of this handbook (resulting trust).

[146] *See generally* §7.2.3 of this handbook (the procedural versus the substantive equitable remedy).

[147] *See generally* §3.2.6 of this handbook.

[148] Restatement (Third) of Trusts §94 cmt. g(2).

[149] 4 Scott & Ascher §24.4.4 (Court Acting on Its Own Motion).

[150] Jackson v. Phillips, 96 Mass. (14 Allen) 539, 579 (1867).

[151] *See generally*, Craig Kaufman, *Sympathy for the Devil's Advocate: Assisting the Attorney General When Charitable Matters Reach the Courtroom*, 40 Real Prop. Prob. & Tr. J. 705, 706–709 (Winter 2006); 5 Scott & Ascher §37.3.10.

[152] *See, e.g.*, Fifth Third Bank v. Firstar Bank, Slip Copy, 2006 WL 2520329, Ohio App. 1 Dist., 2006, Sept. 01, 2006 (involving a CRUT). *See generally* §9.4.5 of this handbook (tax-oriented trusts that mix charitable and noncharitable interests (split-interest trusts)).

[153] Restatement (Third) of Trusts §94 cmt. e.

[154] *See generally* 5 Scott & Ascher §37.3.10; 4A Scott on Trusts §391; Bogert §§411–417; Jackson v. Phillips, 96 Mass. (14 Allen) 539, 579 (1867). In the noncharitable context, *cf.* E.F. Hutton Sw. Props. II, Ltd. v. Union Planters Nat'l Bank, 953 F.2d 963, 970 (1992) (". . . a trust for the benefit of a numerous and changing body of bondholders appears to us to be preeminently an occasion for a scruple even greater than ordinary; for such beneficiaries often have too small a stake to follow the fate of their investment and protect their rights"). *See generally* §9.31 of this handbook (corporate trusts; trusts to secure creditors; the Trust Indenture Act of 1939; protecting bondholders).

beneficiary of endowed medical research, in essence it is all of us *collectively*—the *public*, the *community* as it were—who is the beneficiary.[155] As one learned commentator has observed: "It is difficult, if not impossible, in dealing with charitable trusts to employ the terminology of the late Professor Hohfeld, who insisted that all legal relations are relations between persons, and that, when one person is under a duty, another person always has a correlative right."[156] Be that as it may, the trustee of a charitable trust is a fiduciary whose equitable duties with respect to the subject property run not to the attorney general, not to the state, but to the public, to the community.[157]

Still, for hundreds of years both in the United States and in England[158] the "duty of maintaining the rights of the public, and of a number of persons too indefinite to vindicate their own, has vested in the [state] and is exercised here, as in England through the attorney general."[159] In fact, records show that in the sixteenth century, suits to enforce charitable trusts were being brought in England by the Crown's Attorney General. This is a practical solution to the enforceability dilemma inherent in the charitable trust.[160] The alternative—vesting everyone with standing to seek enforcement—would be intolerably chaotic and impractical.[161]

---

[155] *See generally* 5 Scott & Ascher §37.1.

[156] 5 Scott & Ascher §37.1 (The Definition of a Charitable Trust).

[157] 5 Scott & Ascher §37.1. Only in rare cases is the state itself actually a beneficiary of a charitable trust, as was the case in The Franklin Trust. *See* §8.31 of this handbook (the Franklin Trust (Boston)). As to split-interest trusts, see Fifth Third Bank v. Firstar Bank, Slip Copy, 2006 WL 2520329 (Ohio Ct. App. Sept. 1, 2006) (involving a CRUT) and §9.4.5 of this handbook (tax-oriented trusts that mix charitable and noncharitable interests (split-interest trusts)).

[158] *See* David Hayton, *The Uses of Trusts in the Commercial Context*, in Trusts in Prime Jurisdictions 431 (Alon Kaplan ed., 2000) (noting that in England the Attorney General, the government's law officer representing the legal interest of the Crown, or some statutory body like the English Charity Commissioners has rights to enforce the terms of charitable trusts against the trustees).

[159] Jackson v. Phillips, 96 Mass. (14 Allen) 539, 579 (1867). In a few states, the district or county attorney is charged with the responsibility of overseeing public charities. *See* Warren v. Board of Regents, 527 S.E.2d 563, 564 (Ga. 2000); Collins v. Citizens & S. Trust Co., 373 S.E.2d 612, 613 (Ga. 1988). In England, a permanent Charity Commission was established in the nineteenth century to oversee public charities, this in response to a parliamentary commission's findings that England's charitable sector was in a "sorry state of affairs" due to a lack of any meaningful supervision. *See generally* 5 Scott & Ascher §§37.1.2 (History of Charitable Trusts in England), 37.3.10 (Who Can Enforce a Charitable Trust).

[160] *See, e.g.*, §8.35 of this handbook (the Hershey trust) (discussing a charitable trust portfolio with a 50 percent concentration in a single enterprise and quoting the Pennsylvania deputy chief attorney general charged with overseeing charitable trusts on the subject of prudent investment diversification).

[161] *See generally* Craig Kaufman, *Sympathy for the Devil's Advocate: Assisting the Attorney General When Charitable Matters Reach the Courtroom*, 40 Real Prop. Prob. & Tr. J. 705, 720 (Winter 2006) (noting that a traditional justification for limiting those who have standing to seek enforcement of charitable trusts is to "ensure that charities are not constantly harassed by suits brought by individuals with no substantial stake in the charity"); 5 Scott & Ascher §37.3.10 ("If everyone were entitled, as a matter of right, to seek to enforce charitable trusts, charitable trusts would be subject to repetitious and harassing, and perhaps often baseless, litigation").

Here is how the process generally works. "In most states, as in England, . . . suit is brought in the name of the Attorney General, although in some states the Attorney General prosecutes the case in the name of the people of the state."[162] When it comes to enforcing charitable trusts, the attorney general is vested with prosecutorial discretion that is virtually limitless, as we shall see further on in this section when we consider a possible role for the guardian ad litem in the enforcement of charitable trusts. ". . . [I]ndeed, there is authority to the effect that a person who has no special interest in the performance of a charitable trust cannot maintain a proceeding, by mandamus or otherwise, to compel the Attorney General to bring an action to enforce a charitable trust."[163]

Certainly one drawback to giving the state attorney general a central role in the enforcement of charitable trusts is that he or she is first and foremost a politician,[164] with responsibilities that go well beyond the enforcement of charitable trusts.[165] Moreover, when there is tension between the "public interest" and donor intent, there is not much law on the extent to which the state attorney general must give deference to the latter in his or her advocacy. The Uniform Prudent Management of Institutional Funds Act (UPMIFA), which would regulate the investment activities of charitable corporations as well as charitable trusts, does little more than acknowledge that "the attorney general protects donor intent as well as the public's interest."[166] One learned commentator "is astonished that there has been no in-depth consideration of the parameters of the attorney general's enforcement duty."[167]

Under the Uniform Trust Code, the attorney general of a state has the rights of a qualified beneficiary with respect to charitable trusts whose principal place of administration is in the state.[168] So also does a charitable organization

---

[162] 5 Scott & Ascher §37.3.10. *See also* Restatement (Third) of Trusts §94(2).

[163] 5 Scott & Ascher §37.3.10.

[164] An attorney general is first and foremost a political animal. *See generally* Craig Kaufman, *Sympathy for the Devil's Advocate: Assisting the Attorney General When Charitable Matters Reach the Courtroom*, 40 Real Prop. Prob. & Tr. J. 705, 727 (Winter 2006) (suggesting that the "understandable political desire of the attorney general to emphasize the interest of the public at large can conflict with and work to the detriment of the interest of the smaller public that the donor intended to benefit or that the charity was established to serve"). *See, e.g.,* Sarah Ellison, *Sale of Hershey Foods Runs Into Opposition*, Wall St. J., Aug. 26, 2002, at A3, col. 1 (suggesting that the Pennsylvania attorney general who had at one time called for diversifying The Hershey Trust investment portfolio has since reversed his position out of personal political considerations: "While the recent opposition by Mr. Fisher is viewed by many as political posturing, it could complicate the sale. . . [of the trust's 77 percent stake in Hershey Foods Corp]. . . by scaring off bidders and giving some board members of the trust, already being criticized from local officials and employees, the cover they need to scrap the sale, say takeover experts"). *See generally* §8.35 of this handbook (the Hershey trust).

[165] *See* 5 Scott & Ascher §37.3.10 (confirming that "[i]n both England and the United States, . . . the Attorney General has a great many duties that have nothing to do with the enforcement of charitable trusts").

[166] Unif. Prudent Management Inst. Funds Act §6 cmt.

[167] Craig Kaufman, *Sympathy for the Devil's Advocate: Assisting the Attorney General When Charitable Matters Reach the Courtroom*, 40 Real Prop. Prob. & Tr. J. 705, 708 (Winter 2006).

[168] UTC §110(c) (available at <http://www.uniformlaws.org/Act.aspx?title=Trust%20Code>).

expressly entitled to receive benefits under the terms of a charitable trust.[169] "Under UPMIFA, as under trust law, the court will determine whether and how to apply cy pres or deviation and the attorney general will receive notice and have the opportunity to participate in the proceeding."[170]

To say, however, that a state attorney general "oversees" public charities is not to suggest that he or she "audits" charitable trusts.[171] In fact, until relatively recently most overworked and understaffed attorneys general had no idea even how many charitable trusts they were supposed to be "overseeing."[172] Many a charitable trust was going unperformed for one reason or another, including indifference, neglect, or death of the trustee. In an effort to get an accurate running head count of how many charitable trusts are running or supposed to be running at any given time, and to maintain as well a depository of basic information regarding them, many states have enacted statutes requiring that charitable trustees make certain periodic filings with their respective attorneys general.[173] In some states, the reporting and licensing function is handled by a separate agency altogether, *e.g.*, the office of the secretary of state or some consumer protection bureaucracy. In ten states, there is no general system of registration and reporting whatsoever.

These reforms have enhanced somewhat the oversight of charitable trusts if only because the informational filings are generally available for public inspection.[174] Still, most state attorneys general lack the staffing, resources, and organization, and often the inclination, to properly oversee charities,[175] except, perhaps, when it comes to charitable trusts that have been established by celebrities.[176] There are only eleven offices that have designated sections staffed by three or more full-time attorneys. "Staffing problems and a relative lack of interest in monitoring nonprofits make attorney general oversight more theoretical than deterrent."[177] Today, England has a permanent Charity Commission that is charged with overseeing, along with the Attorney General, most of her charitable trusts.[178] It was put in place in

---

[169] UTC §110(b) (available at <http://www.uniformlaws.org/Act.aspx?title=Trust%20 Code>).

[170] Unif. Prudent Management Inst. Funds Act, Prefatory Note.

[171] *See generally* 5 Scott & Ascher §37.3.10.

[172] *See generally* 5 Scott & Ascher §37.3.10.

[173] *See generally* 5 Scott & Ascher §37.3.10.

[174] *See generally* 5 Scott & Ascher §37.3.10.

[175] *See generally* Craig Kaufman, *Sympathy for the Devil's Advocate: Assisting the Attorney General When Charitable Matters Reach the Courtroom*, 40 Real Prop. Prob. & Tr. J. 705, 726–727 (Winter 2006).

[176] *See, e.g.*, Wilson v. Dallas, 403 S.C. 411, 743 S.E.2d 746 (2013) (the court criticizing the state attorney general for usurping the administration of a constellation of charitable and noncharitable trusts established by James Brown a/k/a "The Godfather of Soul").

[177] James J. Fishman, *Improving Charitable Accountability*, 62 Md. L. Rev. 218, 262 (2003).

[178] *See generally* 5 Scott & Ascher §37.1.2.

1853.[179] "The United States, . . . [on the other hand] . . . has been slower than England to supervise the administration of charitable trusts."[180]

We now consider who else besides the state attorney general might have standing to seek the judicial enforcement of a charitable trust. As we do so, the reader should keep in mind that the court always has the last word, whether or not it is the attorney general who brings the action.[181] In any litigation involving a charitable trust, except in the rare case "[w]hen the interests of the community would not be affected by the suit," the state attorney general will be a necessary party.[182] The attorney general would be entitled to a citation in any one of the following actions involving *the internal affairs* of the trust,[183] again bearing in mind that the consent or nonconsent of the attorney general can never bind the court:

- Complaint for deviating from the terms of a trust
- Complaint to apply the doctrine of *cy pres*
- Complaint to terminate a trust
- Complaint to compromise the terms of a trust[184]

Relator. A relator action in the trust context is an action brought by and in the name of the attorney general "on the relation," *i.e.*, at the suggestion of, a third party who does not necessarily have any interest in the trust.[185] If it turns out that the suit is without merit, the relator may be personally liable for the litigation costs.[186] Even if the suit is successful, the relator could be saddled with the litigation costs.[187] "The Attorney General, however, cannot be compelled to sue (or to allow suit) by the relator; and the Attorney General may exercise control of the conduct of the suit, and may terminate the suit and the authorization granted to the relator."[188]

A cotrustee or successor trustee. The standing of a trustee of a charitable trust to seek its enforcement in the courts "is not dependent on authorization, or subject to control, by the Attorney General. (Contrast the role of 'realtor' . . .)."[189]

---

[179] *See* 5 Scott & Ascher §37.3.10 (outlining the various changes that Parliament has made since 1853 to the Commission's structure and mission, to include in 2006 an expansion of its writ to include Wales and the creation of a Charity Tribunal "to hear appeals and applications in respect of the decisions, orders, and directions of the Commission").

[180] 5 Scott & Ascher §37.3.10.

[181] *See generally* 5 Scott & Ascher §37.3.10.

[182] *See generally* 5 Scott & Ascher §37.3.10 (who can enforce a charitable trust).

[183] Absent special facts, the attorney general need not be brought into an action in contract or tort brought by a trustee of a charitable trust against a third party. *See generally* 5 Scott & Ascher §37.3.11 (Actions against Third Persons).

[184] *See generally* 5 Scott & Ascher §37.3.10.

[185] Snell's Equity ¶ 16-09.

[186] *See, e.g.*, Attorney Gen. v. Butler, 123 Mass. 304, 308–309 (1879).

[187] *See generally* Restatement (Third) of Trusts §94 cmt. e.

[188] Restatement (Third) of Trusts §94 cmt. e.

[189] Restatement (Third) of Trusts §94 cmt. f.

Cotrustees. If only because a cotrustee of a charitable trust has a duty to defend the trust and protect its assets, he will have the necessary standing to bring an action against his cotrustee to remedy the cotrustee's breach of trust, or to otherwise seek enforcement of the trust.[190] For a discussion of the duties and rights of cotrustees generally, the reader is referred to Section 3.4.4.1 of this handbook.

Successor trustees. The Restatement (Third) of Trusts confirms that "[i]f a trustee . . . [of a charitable trust] . . . who has committed a breach of trust is thereafter removed or otherwise ceases to serve as trustee, a successor trustee can maintain a suit against that former trustee to redress the breach of trust."[191] For a discussion of the duties and rights of successor trustees generally, the reader is referred to Section 3.4.4.3 of this handbook.

Cross-reference. The topics of cofiduciary and successor-fiduciary liability in the trust context are covered generally in Section 7.2.4 of this handbook.

Citizens and taxpayers. But just because a member of the universe of contingent beneficiaries of a charitable trust would lack the standing to seek its enforcement, the universe essentially being everyone, it does not necessarily follow that the member of a somewhat smaller class of individuals, such as taxpayers, would, as well. To be sure, "a person ordinarily does not have a special interest in the enforcement of a charitable trust merely because he or she is a citizen or a taxpayer, even in the case of a trust administered by the state or a local municipality."[192] In one case involving a charitable corporation formed to maintain a hospital in a particular municipality, however, the municipality itself and two individual residents and taxpayers of the municipality brought an action in the court to prevent the corporation from proceeding with a plan to move the hospital facilities to an adjacent municipality. Although the court ruled that the corporation could carry through with its plan, it went out of its way to say that the plaintiffs had had the standing to bring the action: "While public supervision of the administration of charities remains inadequate, a liberal rule as to the standing of a plaintiff to complain about the administration of a charitable trust or charitable corporation seems decidedly in the public interest."[193]

Institutions and individuals with special interests. *Institutions*. It is not uncommon for a charitable trust to be established for the purpose of supporting other charities, whether incorporated or unincorporated.[194] "Thus, if the terms of a charitable trust require that its income be paid periodically to a particular

---

[190] *See generally* 5 Scott & Ascher §37.3.10 k (who can enforce a charitable trust); Restatement (Third) of Trusts §94 cmt. f.

[191] Restatement (Third) of Trusts §94 cmt. f.

[192] *See generally* 5 Scott & Ascher §37.3.10.

[193] City of Paterson v. Paterson Gen. Hosp., 97 N.J. Super. 514, 235 A.2d 487 (1967). *See generally* 5 Scott & Ascher §37.3.10.

[194] *See, e.g.*, The Woodward School for Girls, Inc. v. City of Quincy, trustee, SJC-11390, 2013 WL 8923423 (Mass. July 23, 2014) (involving an income-only charitable trust established in 1822 by former U.S. President John Adams, which, since 1953, has been for the benefit of The Woodward School for Girls, Inc., a charitable corporation). For more details on the President John Adams Trust, see §8.47 of this handbook.

incorporated church, hospital, school, or the like, the corporation can maintain a suit against the trustee (with notice to the Attorney General) for enforcement of the trust."[195] In the case of an unincorporated charitable association, the suit would be maintained in the name of the association by "the appropriate officer."[196] That having been said, a charitable institution that is "merely a possible beneficiary of a charitable trust, or a member of a class of possible beneficiaries, is not entitled to sue for enforcement of the trust."[197]

Individuals. Let us assume that many years ago a number of grateful citizens contributed sums of money to a city for the purpose of erecting and maintaining a tomb and museum to house the remains and papers of a famous general. The tomb was built and the museum established. Now the tomb is in disrepair and the museum has been all but abandoned by the mayor, whose thoughts are on other matters. What about the currently living relatives of the general? Would they have standing to enjoin the city from neglecting its stewardship of the tomb and museum? Would those who contributed to the complex have standing in their capacities as settlors to seek enforcement of the trust? Must the welfare of the tomb and museum be dependent solely on the enforcement discretion of the attorney general who perhaps does not want to embarrass the mayor?[198]

According to Professor Scott, persons having a special interest in the performance of a charitable trust can maintain a suit for its enforcement.[199] The Restatement (Third) of Trusts is in accord.[200] Such persons, however, must show that their interest is not merely derived from their status as members of the general public. In the case of a trust established for the purpose of contributing to the medical care of the "needy residents" of a specified small town, for example, "any reasonably qualified member of the community" would have standing to seek its enforcement in the courts.[201] "Indeed, a study of the Calendars in Chancery, listing numerous cases brought prior to the enactment of the Statute of Charitable Uses in 1601, shows that although in many instances the Attorney General brought the suit, in many others, the suit was brought by a third person." Professor Bogert has found cases that are in accord with Professor Scott's assertion:

---

[195] Restatement (Third) of Trusts §94 cmt. g(1). *See, e.g.,* The Woodward School for Girls, Inc. v. City of Quincy, trustee, SJC-11390, 2013 WL 8923423 (Mass. July 23, 2014) (a case in which a charitable corporation that was the beneficiary of a charitable trust filed suit against the trustee and the state attorney general as a "nominal" party-defendant).

[196] Restatement (Third) of Trusts §94 cmt. g(1).

[197] *See* Sagtikos Manor Historical Soc'y, Inc. v. Robert David Lion Gardiner Found., 9 N.Y.S.3d 80 (App. Div. 2015).

[198] *See generally* Hochman v. Babbitt, 94 Civ. 3000 (wk) (S.D.C.N.Y. 1994) (the "Grant's Tomb Case"); 6 Scott & Ascher §38.7.10 (Monuments and Tombs).

[199] 4A Scott on Trusts §391; 5 Scott & Ascher §37.3.10. *See also* UTC §405 cmt. (available at <http://www.uniformlaws.org/Act.aspx?title=Trust%20Code>) (noting that the grant of standing to the settlor does not negate the right of the state attorney general or persons with special interests to enforce either the trust or their interests).

[200] Restatement (Third) of Trusts §94 cmt. g(1).

[201] Restatement (Third) of Trusts §94 cmt. g(1).

Thus where a trust was established for the sick and destitute members of a National Guard regiment, the president of the board of officers of the regiment has been allowed to sue to have the trustee removed and to compel him to pay damages for improper investment. In the case of a trust for the orphans and widows of deceased members of the brotherhood of locomotive engineers, several of the officers of the brotherhood were permitted to sue to enforce the trust on behalf of themselves and others similarly situated.[202]

One also may have standing if one is entitled to a preference under the terms of the trust, is a member of a small class of identifiable beneficiaries, or is certain to receive trust benefits.[203] Here is an example of a small class that would most likely meet either of the first two standing-eligibility criteria: "[I]f a college is trustee of a trust the terms of which direct that its income be used to provide graduate-study scholarships each year to selected students graduating from the college, based on prescribed procedures and criteria, the trust purpose may be enforced by one or more of the current students who might reasonably expect to meet the criteria."[204] The incumbent of an endowed chair at a medical research facility is an example of one who is certain to receive trust benefits and thus would have standing to seek enforcement of the endowment trust in the courts.[205]

Rights of enforcement also would accrue to a minister entitled to income distributions from a clergy support trust.[206] Likewise, a respectable argument could be made that the general's proximate relatives who are currently living would have an interest in the proper maintenance of their ancestor's museum and that this interest is sufficiently "special" to vest them with standing to seek enjoinment of its neglect.[207]

Assume the owner of a parcel of real property grants a conservation easement to the trustee of a charitable trust for purposes that are beneficial to the community. "Owners of adjoining land have special-interest standing to enforce adherence to the easement's charitable purpose, as in many circumstances do others (such as nearby or downstream landowners) who benefit significantly more than the public in general."[208]

For gifts to charitable trusts that are subject to conditions subsequent or conditions precedent, see Bogert.[209]

---

[202] Bogert §412.

[203] *See generally* 5 Scott & Ascher §37.3.10. *See, e.g.*, State v. Hutcherson, 96 S.W.3d 81, 84 (Mo. 2003) (denying standing to putative class representatives in class-action lawsuit to enforce certain provisions of a charitable trust, the representatives having failed to show a clear, identifiable, and present claim to any benefits sufficient to establish that they had had a "special interest" in the trust).

[204] Restatement (Third) of Trusts §94 cmt. g(2).

[205] 4A Scott on Trusts §391; 5 Scott & Ascher §37.3.10.

[206] 4A Scott on Trusts §391; 5 Scott & Ascher §37.3.10; Restatement (Third) of Trusts §94 cmt. g(1).

[207] *Cf.* §5.1 of this handbook (the common law right of the relatives of a deceased person to visit, honor, and protect his gravesite).

[208] Restatement (Third) of Trusts §94 cmt. g(1).

[209] Bogert §420. *See also* Bogert §419 (Possibility of Reverter May Be Expressly Reserved).

The guardian ad litem. In a Massachusetts case involving a charitable trust for the purpose of making interest-free educational loans, the court appointed a *guardian ad litem* "to represent the interests of potential student charitable beneficiaries." The state attorney general had failed to file an appearance after having been notified of the court proceeding. On appeal, the Supreme Judicial Court of Massachusetts confirmed that the judge had properly exercised his authority to appoint a guardian ad litem,[210] but expressed some concern that the guardian ad litem's fees would be paid from trust assets:

> But it may be, as the judge noted, that for reasons of resource allocation or otherwise, the Attorney General did not undertake a detailed review of the activities of these trustees, sufficient to satisfy the concerns of the judge. In the future, before a guardian ad litem is appointed to review the activities of the trustees of a charitable trust, the Attorney General should be informed of a judge's intent to make the appointment, and of his reasons for doing so. The Attorney General should be provided with a reasonable date by which to register an objection, if any, to such appointment. If the Attorney General does not respond within the designated period, the judge may conclude that there is, in fact, no opposition to the appointment of a guardian ad litem, and that the Attorney General has no objection to the expenditure of charitable trust resources to pay such services.[211]

The trustee ad litem. One learned commentator would have the court appoint a *trustee ad litem* for purposes of ascertaining what the *donor* would have wanted in a given situation, provided the donor is no longer alive or there is no one with a special interest in the administration of the charitable trust. "Under certain circumstances, . . . courts should use their equitable powers to allow other interested persons—not just the attorney general and the trustees—into the courtroom to ensure that charitable trusts are properly administered."[212]

The settlor or those with an interest as fiduciary or otherwise in a deceased settlor's probate estate. That the settlor of a *noncharitable* trust, *qua* settlor, lacks the requisite standing to seek its enforcement in the courts has generally been assumed, at least with respect to the default law. The Restatement (Third) of Trusts breaks no new ground in this regard, although the principle has never been as ironclad as some would suggest, neither in concept nor in practice. We explain in Section 4.1.2 of this handbook.

Across the board, however, much new ground is being broken when it comes to settlor standing to seek the enforcement of charitable trusts. The Uniform Trust Code, for example, expressly bestows on the settlor standing to maintain an action to enforce or modify a charitable trust.[213] The Restatement

---

[210] *See generally* §8.14 of this handbook (when a guardian ad litem (or special representative) is needed; virtual representation issues).

[211] In the Matter of the Trusts Under the Will of Lotta M. Crabtree, 440 Mass. 177, 795 N.E.2d 1157 (2003).

[212] Craig Kaufman, *Sympathy for the Devil's Advocate: Assisting the Attorney General When Charitable Matters Reach the Courtroom*, 40 Real Prop. Prob. & Tr. J. 705, 731 (Winter 2006).

[213] UTC §405(c)9 (available at <http://www.uniformlaws.org/Act.aspx?title=Trust%20 Code>).

(Third) of Trusts, unlike its predecessors, is generally in accord.[214] The public policy case for affording the settlor of a charitable trust such standing has been made for centuries.[215] Today, the case for standing—*i.e.*, standing coexistent with that of the state attorney general—is still being made:

> [T]he traditional position has been that the settlor lacks standing to enforce a charitable trust. There is, however, impressive and growing authority, including under the Uniform Trust Code, for the contrary proposition, i.e., that the settlor can enforce a charitable trust. Given the historical under-enforcement of charitable trusts in both England and the United States, it would seem that allowing the settlor to enforce his or her own trust might well be a step in the right direction. In any event, settlor standing is a small price to pay for the settlor's generosity.[216]

The traditional public policy argument against affording the settlor of a charitable trust standing, *qua* settlor, has been that keeping the settlor in the picture would constitute an unnecessary, unwarranted, and distracting ongoing intrusion into the affairs of the charitable community. If the settlor were an institution, such a right to seek enforcement could theoretically be of unlimited duration. The Restatement (Third) of Trusts responds to some of these concerns by subjecting settlor standing in the charitable context to certain qualifications:

- A duly completed unrestricted gift of property to a charitable corporation severs once and for all the donor's relationship to the property; a restricted gift in trust to the corporation entitles the donor/settlor only "to enforce the restriction."[217]
- When numerous donors (settlors) contribute to the funding of a charitable trust, only a donor (settlor) who is a "major contributor" relative to the trust's total funding would have standing to seek the trust's enforcement in the courts.[218]
- Settlor standing attaches to the settlor "personally," meaning that it is transferable neither during his life nor by his will or intestate succession.[219]

Another way for the default law to address the intrusiveness issue is to keep the central grant of settlor standing narrow in scope. California, for example,

---

[214] Restatement (Third) of Trusts §94 cmt g(3).

[215] One can trace the concept of a transferor's standing to seek enforcement of the obligations of the transferee at least as far back as the Anglo-Normans. In the fourteenth century, if the *feoffee to uses* failed to perform his duties, the *feoffor* could seek enforcement in the Court of Common Pleas. Later, the *cestui que use* also gained a right to seek enforcement, but in the Court of Chancery. *See generally* W. F. Fratcher, 6 Intl. Encyclopedia of Comp. Law 14 (F.H. Lawson ed., 1973). *See generally* Restatement (Second) of Trusts §25 cmts. c, a.

[216] 5 Scott & Ascher §37.3.10.

[217] Restatement (Third) of Trusts §94 cmt. g(3). *See also* §9.8.1 of this handbook (whether the charitable corporation is a trust).

[218] Restatement (Third) of Trusts §94 cmt. g(3).

[219] Restatement (Third) of Trusts §94 cmt. g(3).

has enacted a statute affirmatively granting settlors of irrevocable living trusts standing to petition for trustee removal.[220] California also provides for settlor involvement in the modification or termination of an irrevocable trust.[221]

UPMIFA provides for the release or modification of a restriction on the management, investment, or charitable purpose of an institutional fund with donor consent.[222] On the other hand, UPMIFA does not require that the donor even be notified of an equitable deviation or *cy pres* proceeding.[223] Here is the rationale: "The trust law rules of equitable deviation and cy pres do not require donor notification and instead depend on the court and the attorney general to protect donor intent and the public's interest in charitable assets."[224] When, in a given situation, donor intent and the public interest cannot be reconciled, presumably the attorney general would have an ethical obligation to retain special outside counsel to advocate on behalf of donor intent.

In the absence of a statutory grant of standing, however, the settlor of a charitable trust will have an uphill battle obtaining it from the court, at least for now. Certainly the settlor's chances for a grant of standing are enhanced if it can be demonstrated that the settlor "has a special interest in the performance of the trust," such as a reserved power to nominate the candidates for a faculty chair that the trust is supporting financially.[225] A few courts might even grant the settlor's executor or administrator, or even the settlor's heirs at law, standing to seek the trust's enforcement.[226] If standing is denied, the settlor might explore "petition[ing] . . . in mandamus seeking an order requiring the Attorney General to act."[227] If that is not a practical option, and it is likely not to be,[228] then the settlor's only recourse would be to attempt to exert some kind of nonjudicial pressure on the state attorney general, whether by mounting a press campaign or by exploiting political contacts.[229] Most settlors, however, will not have the financial resources and/or political clout needed to persuade a dilatory or reluctant attorney general to do the right thing.

In one case, the Connecticut attorney general actually stood on the sidelines and watched a grantor charity and grantee charity battle it out in the courts over whether the grantor charity had standing to seek enforcement of certain grant restrictions.[230] The Carl J. Herzog Foundation had filed an action against the University of Bridgeport, the foundation in 1987 and 1988 having made various restricted grants to the University "to provide need-based merit scholarship aid to disadvantaged students for medical related education." The

---

[220] Cal. Prob. Code §15642 (West 1991).
[221] Cal. Prob. Code §15404 (West 1991).
[222] Unif. Prudent Management Inst. Funds Act §6(a).
[223] Unif. Prudent Management Inst. Funds Act §6 cmt.
[224] Unif. Prudent Management Inst. Funds Act §6 cmt.
[225] 5 Scott & Ascher §37.3.10.
[226] 5 Scott & Ascher §37.3.10 n.61.
[227] Estate of Leitner, 2004 WL 440202 n.3 (2004).
[228] *See generally* 5 Scott & Ascher §37.3.10.
[229] *See generally* 5 Scott & Ascher §37.3.10.
[230] *See* Carl J. Herzog Found., Inc. v. University of Bridgeport, 243 Conn. 1, 699 A.2d 995 (1997).

grants were used to provide scholarship aid to students in the university's nursing program. On November 21, 1991, however, the foundation was informed that the university had closed its nursing school on June 20, 1991. It was alleged by the foundation that the grant money had then been commingled with the general funds of the university and used for its general purposes. The foundation requested that the university be ordered to segregate from its general funds the $250,000 in grant money and begin to administer those funds in accordance with the restrictions.[231]

The trial court determined that the Connecticut attorney general, not the foundation, was vested with standing to seek enforcement of the restrictions in the courts. The attorney general had chosen for whatever reason not to get involved. And with that, the case was dismissed. The actions of the trial court were upheld on appeal. One commentator has referred to the saga of the Carl J. Herzog Foundation as "perhaps the most shocking example of a court's unwillingness to enforce contractual rights in charitable entities."[232] Whether or not contractual rights are involved, the court's unwillingness to vindicate the equitable expectation interests of donor charities is certainly troubling.

In 2001, however, a New York court actually granted standing to the wife of a deceased settlor of a charitable trust (in her capacity as court-appointed special administratrix of his estate) so that she might seek judicial enforcement of the trust's charitable provisions. "The donor of a charitable gift is in a better position than the Attorney General to be vigilant and, if he or she is so inclined, to enforce his or her own intent,"[233] opined the court. The court went on to say that the circumstances of the case "demonstrate the need for co-existent standing for the Attorney General and the donor."[234] Whether the decision of the New York court is an aberration or the start of a trend remains to be seen.

Again, public oversight of charitable trusts is generally more apparent than actual.[235] As a practical matter, there may be no one looking over the trustee's shoulder. Still, the ethical trustee conscientiously carries out the intentions of the settlor-benefactor.

Faced with the stark reality that public oversight of charitable trusts is often illusory, sometimes even subversive of donor intent, more and more prospective settlors are taking matters into their own hands by including express "donor control" provisions in their governing instruments, such as by reserving the right to receive and object to trustee accountings.[236] "What better way to see that the gift is delivered than to have an accounting?"[237] For more on such countermeasures, the reader is referred to Section 4.1.1.2 of this handbook. While a donor control provision should take care of the standing problem, it

---

[231] *See generally* §9.8.1 of this handbook (the charitable corporation) (discussing the segregation of restricted gifts to charitable corporations).

[232] Craig Kaufman, *Sympathy for the Devil's Advocate: Assisting the Attorney General When Charitable Matters Reach the Courtroom*, 40 Real Prop. Prob. & Tr. J. 705, 721 (Winter 2006).

[233] Smithers v. St. Luke's-Roosevelt Hosp. Ctr., 723 N.Y.S.2d 426, 434 (2001).

[234] Smithers v. St. Luke's-Roosevelt Hosp. Ctr., 723 N.Y.S.2d at 435.

[235] *See generally* 4A Scott on Trusts §391.

[236] *See, e.g.*, Patton v. Sherwood, 152 Cal. App. 4th 339, 61 Cal. Rptr. 3d 289 (2007).

[237] Patton v. Sherwood, 152 Cal. App. 4th 339, 347, 61 Cal. Rptr. 3d 289, 295 (2007).

needs to be carefully drawn so as not to cause another problem, namely a tax problem. For more on the tax implications of donor control provisions, the reader is referred to Alan F. Rothschild, Jr.[238]

The visitor. In England one may create and fund a charitable corporation that provides in its governing documentation that a third party, known as a visitor, shall have the power to "elect and remove the members of the corporation, to regulate the management of its property, to decide the construction of the statutes of the foundation, and to adjudicate all claims and complaints concerning the internal affairs of the corporation."[239] Such a provision is generally enforceable.[240] In 1946, the Massachusetts Supreme Judicial Court rendered a decision that lends the impression at least that under the right facts and circumstance it would recognize visitor oversight in the charitable trust context.[241] The visitor would seem to have many of the attributes of the protector, a creature we endeavored to corral in Section 3.2.6 of this handbook, albeit with limited success.

§9.4.3 Cy Pres

It is. . . well settled by decisions of the highest authority, that when a gift is made to trustees for a charitable purpose, the general nature of which is pointed out, and which is lawful and valid at the time [the transfer is made], and no intention is expressed to limit it to a particular institution or mode of application, and afterwards, either by change of circumstances the scheme of the [settlor] becomes impracticable, or by change of law becomes illegal, the fund, having once vested in the charity, does not go to the heirs at law as a resulting trust, but is to be applied by the court of chancery, in the exercise of its jurisdiction in equity, as near the [settlor's] particular directions as possible, to carry out his general charitable intent.[242]

Cy pres **described.** In the event that circumstances make it unlawful, impossible, or impracticable to carry out the specified purpose of a charitable trust,[243] or "to the extent it is or becomes wasteful to apply all of the property to

---

[238] *The Do's and Don'ts of Donor Control*, 30 ACTEC J. 261 (2005).

[239] *See generally* 5 Scott & Ascher §37.3.10.

[240] *See generally* 5 Scott & Ascher §37.3.10.

[241] *See* Trustees of Putnam Free Sch. v. Attorney Gen., 320 Mass. 94, 100, 67 N.E.2d 658, 661 (1946).

[242] Jackson v. Phillips, 96 Mass. (14 Allen) 539, 580 (1867). *See also* American Acad. of Arts & Sci. v. Harvard Coll., 78 Mass. (12 Gray) 582, 596 (1832). *See* §8.15.20 of this handbook (doctrine of [equitable] deviation) (in part outlining the differences between the *cy pres* doctrine explaining the doctrine of deviation).

[243] *See generally* 6 Scott & Ascher §39.5.2. For an example of an "impracticable" specified charitable purpose, see Matter of Noble Hospital Gouverneur, 39 Misc. 3d 279, 959 N.Y.S.2d 623 (2013). The court in the exercise of its equitable *cy pres* powers modified the terms of three separate charitable trusts established for the benefit of the Hospital so as to enable the trustees to collateralize the trust corpus, this in furtherance of the trusts' general charitable purposes. The income-only restrictions in the governing trust instruments were "impracticable" in that combined net trust accounting income was being totally consumed by trustees' fees. The collateral would enable the Hospital to gain access to much-needed operating cash.

the designated purpose,"[244] the doctrine of *cy pres*[245] may be available as an alternative to the imposition of a resulting trust in favor of the settlor or the settlor's estate.[246] In other words, the doctrine of *cy pres* may provide an alternative to the trust's termination.[247] "The theory is that the settlor would have wanted the property to be devoted to an alternate charitable purpose if the settlor had realized that it would be impossible to carry out the stated purpose."[248] The concept of *cy pres* involves the textual search for general charitable intent, for any generalized intent on the part of the settlor that is independent of the specific circumstances of a given moment.[249] There are many ways that a charitable purpose can "fail" such that a *cy pres* action is triggered. Here are some of them:

- Insufficient funds to carry out specified charitable purpose[250]
- Charitable purpose already accomplished[251]
- Specified charitable purpose impossible to accomplish, or refusal of trustee or third person to cooperate[252]
- Nonexistent charitable corporation or association is the intended beneficiary[253]

---

[244] Restatement (Third) of Trusts §67. The codifications are generally in accord, namely, that *cy pres* may be applied if to carry out a stated charitable purpose would be wasteful or impractical. *See, e.g.*, UTC §413(a) (available at <http://www.uniformlaws.org/Act.aspx?title= Trust%20Code>); Unif. Prudent Mgmt. of Inst. Funds Act §6(b). *See generally* 6 Scott & Ascher §39.5.4 (advocating that the courts apply *cy pres* to charitable purposes that are no longer "useful to mankind"). *Cf.* Restatement (Second) of Trusts §399; Unif. Mgmt. of Inst. Funds Act §7(b).

[245] *Cy pres* is an Anglo-French phrase equivalent to the modern French *si pres*, meaning "so near" or "as near." 4A Scott on Trusts §399; 6 Scott & Ascher §39.5. This abbreviated phrase was taken from *si pres comme possible*, which means "as near as possible." Bogert §431; 6 Scott & Ascher §39.5. For a discussion of the "law French" phenomenon, *see* §8.15 of this handbook. *See generally* UTC §412(a) (available at <http://www.uniformlaws.org/Act.aspx?title=Trust%20Code>) (authorizing a court to apply *cy pres* if a particular charitable purpose becomes unlawful, impracticable, impossible to achieve, or wasteful).

[246] *See generally* Bogert §§431–442.

[247] Of course, "[i]f the terms of the trust expressly provide for disposition of the property in case a particular charitable purpose fails, the terms of the trust ordinarily control." 6 Scott & Ascher §39.5.2.

[248] 6 Scott & Ascher §39.5. The concept of a variance power is discussed in §8.15.37 of this handbook.

[249] *See, e.g.*, American Acad. of Arts & Sci. v. Harvard Coll., 12 Gray (78 Mass.) 582, 596 (1832); In re Neher's Will, 18 N.E.2d 625 (N.Y. 1939).

[250] 6 Scott & Ascher §39.5.2. *See, e.g.*, In re Neher's Will, 18 N.E.2d 625 (N.Y. 1939) ("In March, 1937, the village presented to the Surrogate's Court its petition asserting that it was without the resources necessary to establish and maintain a hospital on the property devised to it by the testatrix. . . .").

[251] 6 Scott & Ascher §39.5.2. *See, e.g.*, Jackson v. Phillips, 96 Mass (14 Allen) 539 (1867) (involving a trust to create a public sentiment that would put an end to slavery in the United States that became operational after slavery had been abolished by the Thirteenth Amendment).

[252] 6 Scott & Ascher §39.5.2.

[253] 6 Scott & Ascher §39.5.2.

- Unsuitability of donated premises for the particular charitable institution[254]
- Excess or surplus funds[255]

***Cy pres* requires judicial involvement.** *Cy pres* is applied by the court, not the trustee, although in most cases it is the trustee who, at trust expense, brings the *cy pres* petition.[256] Generally the state attorney general is a necessary party to the proceeding.[257] The court may well refer the matter to a master to fashion an appropriate alternate scheme of disposition, which the court is free to accept or reject.[258] It is within the equitable powers of the court to allow a third party, such as a potential alternate charity, to intervene in the *cy pres* proceeding, although the charity's standing to appeal the court's ruling is uncertain.[259] Trustees, on the other hand, generally do have standing to appeal *cy pres* judgments.[260] If the court finds that a particular trust is *cy pres*-eligible, it will fashion an alternative scheme of disposition that closely approximates the specified unfeasible one.[261] "In such a case, all the court can do is make an educated guess, not as to what the settlor actually intended, but as to what the settlor would have intended, if the settlor had thought about the matter."[262]

***Cy pres* can fill in gaps.** What if the settlor has enunciated a general charitable purpose but neglected to specify a particular charitable purpose or organization to receive distributions or has neglected to delegate that function to the trustee? Under the Uniform Trust Code, the court may validate the trust by specifying particular charitable purposes or recipients or delegate to the trustee the framing of an appropriate scheme.[263] The court, however, must apply the trust property in a manner consistent with the settlor's charitable purposes to the extent they can be ascertained.[264] In a state that has yet to enact the Code, one court has done just that.[265] "On the other hand, when a testator

---

[254] 6 Scott & Ascher §39.5.2.

[255] 6 Scott & Ascher §39.5.2. *See also* 6 Scott & Ascher §39.6 (noting that when there are more funds in a charitable trust than needed to accommodate its stated charitable purpose, the court may (1) apply *cy* pres to the surplus, (2) impose a resulting trust upon the surplus, (2) or, if the trustee is a charitable corporation, allow the trustee to apply the surplus to its own general purposes). ". . . [T]he longer the period between the creation of the trust and the generation of the surplus, the less likely the court is to impose a resulting trust." 6 Scott & Ascher §39.6.

[256] 6 Scott & Ascher §39.5.

[257] 6 Scott & Ascher §39.5. *See generally* §9.4.2 of this handbook (standing to enforce charitable trusts).

[258] 6 Scott & Ascher §39.5.

[259] 6 Scott & Ascher §39.5.

[260] 6 Scott & Ascher §39.5.

[261] 6 Scott & Ascher §39.5.

[262] 6 Scott & Ascher §39.5.2.

[263] UTC §405 cmt. (available at <http://www.uniformlaws.org/Act.aspx?title=Trust%20 Code>).

[264] UTC §405 cmt. (available at <http://www.uniformlaws.org/Act.aspx?title=Trust%20 Code>).

[265] *See* Morton v. Potts, 57 Mass. App. Ct. 55, 781 N.E.2d 43 (2003). *See generally* 6 Scott & Ascher §39.5.

leaves property for such charitable purposes as a named trustee selects, and the trustee is willing and able to make selections, the trustee may dispose of the property for such charitable purposes as the trustee selects."[266] The Uniform Trust Code broadens the court's ability to modify the administrative terms of trusts generally.[267] "Just as a charitable trust may be modified if its particular charitable purpose becomes impracticable or wasteful, so can the administrative terms of any trust, charitable or noncharitable."[268]

Powers of Appointment. Powers of appointment are covered generally in Section 8.1.1 of this handbook. The Restatement (Third) of Property proposes, as did the Restatement (Second), that the doctrine of *cy pres* be extended to exercises of nongeneral powers of appointment whose objects are charities. "If the donee of the power appoints to one or more designated charities, and the donee appoints to a charity not designated as a permissible appointee of the power, the appointment to the impermissible appointee-charity is ineffective. The court, however, may apply *cy pres* in such situations and will select from among the charities that are the permissible appointees of the power the one or more that have charitable purposes similar to the charity selected by the donee as recipient of the appointive assets."[269] Neither restatement, however, proffers or proffered any judicial authority or public policy rationale in support of the proposition.

Related doctrines. *Cy pres* should not be confused with a court's inherent equitable power to order adjustments in how any trust is being administered, which might even include the power to countermand an express direction in the terms of the trust not to sell a particular parcel of entrusted real estate.[270] *Cy pres* relates to the core purposes of a charitable trust, not how it is administered, unless there is a clear nexus between the two.[271] The doctrines of *cy pres* and equitable deviation,[272] equitable deviation being the judicial negation of a trust's administrative provisions in furtherance of its purposes,[273] should not be confused with the variance power granted to the trustees of a charitable foundation in its governing documentation.[274] We take up the doctrine of

---

[266] 6 Scott & Ascher §39.5. "If, however, the named trustee is unable or unwilling to make the selection, and selection by the named trustee is not an essential part of the testator's scheme, the court will either direct the framing of a scheme or name a successor trustee to make the selection." 6 Scott & Ascher §39.5.

[267] UTC §412(b) (available at <http://www.uniformlaws.org/Act.aspx?title=Trust%20 Code>). *See generally* 6 Scott & Ascher §39.5; §8.15.20 of this handbook (doctrine of equitable deviation).

[268] UTC §412 cmt. (available at <http://www.uniformlaws.org/Act.aspx?title=Trust%20 Code>). *See generally* §8.15.20 of this handbook (doctrine of equitable deviation).

[269] Restatement (Third) of Property (Wills and Other Donative Transfers) §19.15 cmt. h; Restatement (Second) of Property (Wills and Other Donative Transfers) §20.1 cmt. h.

[270] 5 Scott & Ascher §37.3.3 (Deviating from Terms of a Charitable Trust).

[271] 5 Scott & Ascher §37.3.3.

[272] *See generally* §8.15.20 of this handbook (doctrine of [equitable] deviation).

[273] Craig Kaufman, *Sympathy for the Devil's Advocate: Assisting the Attorney General When Charitable Matters Reach the Courtroom*, 40 Real Prop. Prob. & Tr. J. 705, 715 (Winter 2006).

[274] The concept of a variance power is discussed in §8.15.37 of this handbook.

equitable deviation as it relates to the administrative provisions of trusts generally in Section 8.15.20 of this handbook.[275]

The charitable corporation. The UPMIFA would have the doctrines of *cy pres* and deviation apply not only to charitable trusts but also to charitable corporations,[276] a topic we take up in Section 9.8.1 of this handbook.

General charitable intent. For a trust to be *cy pres*-eligible, however, the settlor must have manifested a "general charitable intent."[277] The fact that property is entrusted upon the "condition" that it be applied for a particular charitable purpose does not necessarily preclude a finding of general charitable intent.[278] The Uniform Trust Code presumes such an intention when a particular charitable purpose becomes impossible or impracticable to achieve.[279] The Restatement (Third) of Trusts would do so as well.[280] "Traditional doctrine did not supply that presumption, leaving it to the courts to determine whether the settlor had general charitable intent."[281] One learned commentator suggests that in the face of such a presumption, "it would rarely, if ever, be appropriate . . . [for a court] . . . to conclude that a trust created to accomplish a particular charitable purpose fails merely because it is impossible to ascertain the particular purpose that the settlor may have had in mind."[282] In England such liberal applications of the *cy pres* doctrine have been the norm since at least 1702.[283] In the case of a trust with a general charitable purpose, the settlor may leave it to the trustees to select the actual charitable purposes to be furthered.[284] There is no need to bring a *cy pres* action.

General charitable intent and the tax code. For a trust to be treated for federal *income tax purposes* as an exempt private charitable foundation, its charitable purposes must be general rather than specific,[285] a topic beyond the scope of this handbook.

***Cy pres* versus the resulting trust and the vested equitable reversionary interest.** As many charitable trusts are designed to continue forever, specific

---

[275] *See also* 6 Scott & Ascher §39.5.

[276] Unif. Prudent Management Inst. Funds Act, Prefatory Note.

[277] *See generally* 4A Scott on Trusts §399; Bogert §436; Restatement (Second) of Trusts §399.

[278] 6 Scott & Ascher §39.5.2. "Similarly, when a trust is for a particular purpose 'and no other purpose' or for 'only' one purpose, inclusion of the additional word or words in the terms of the trust does not necessarily preclude the court from applying the property to other purposes if the particular purpose fails." 6 Scott & Ascher §39.5.2. "So also, a direction that property be applied 'forever' to a particular purpose does not prevent the application of cy pres if the particular purpose fails." 6 Scott & Ascher §39.5.2.

[279] UTC §413 cmt. (available at <http://www.uniformlaws.org/Act.aspx?title=Trust%20 Code>). *See generally* 6 Scott & Ascher §§39.1, 39.5.

[280] Restatement (Third) of Trusts §67 cmt. b.

[281] UTC §413 cmt. (available at <http://www.uniformlaws.org/Act.aspx?title=Trust%20 Code>).

[282] 6 Scott & Ascher §39.1.

[283] 6 Scott & Ascher §39.1.

[284] 6 Scott & Ascher §39.2.

[285] *See generally* Rockland Trust Co. v. Attorney Gen., 463 Mass. 1004, 976 N.E.2d 801 (2012) (a tax-driven judicial confirmation by reformation that the purposes of a certain charitable trust are general).

circumstances are bound to change. Institutions come and go; what was legal becomes illegal; problems are solved and new ones surface.[286] Even if courts had not articulated the doctrine, a trustee, in the face of changed circumstances, would always have an obligation to ascertain from the court whether the settlor's charitable intent was general or specific and then to act accordingly.[287] Thus a prospective trustee of a charitable trust would do well to insist that the settlor-benefactor spell out unambiguously whether the charitable intent is general or specific.

Having said that, the total failure of a trust with a specific charitable purpose can present expensive and time-consuming administrative problems, particularly if the settlor is deceased at the time of failure and the administration of his or her probate estate has been long closed.[288] Recall that *ab initio* the settlor of such a trust has traditionally retained a vested reversionary interest, an interest that in the United States, unlike England,[289] has generally not been subject to the Rule against Perpetuities.[290] Thus the administration of the deceased settlor's probate estate might well have to be reopened so that a personal representative of the deceased settlor can be appointed by the court to take title to the underlying property of the failed trust.[291] The longer a trust has been in existence, the more likely it is that the settlor's residuary takers or heirs at law, as well as a number of *their* successors in interest, also will have died, thus necessitating the reopening of numerous probate estates that pour into one another.[292] In Section 8.2.1.9 of this handbook we provide several illustrations of how a decedent's class of descendants can relentlessly expand over time. After twelve generations, for example, the number of descendants of those who came over on the Mayflower was in the range of 25 million. Even if the court should manage to devise a process for getting the underlying property of a failed charitable trust to its rightful owners without the reopening of probate

---

[286] *See generally* 5 Scott & Ascher §37.3.3 (Deviating from Terms of a Charitable Trust).

[287] UTC §412(a) (available at <http://www.uniformlaws.org/Act.aspx?title=Trust%20 Code>) would permit modification or termination of a *noncharitable* trust because of "unanticipated circumstances."

[288] 6 Scott & Ascher §39.5.3.

[289] "In the United States, a legal right of entry for condition broken or a possibility of reverter is not subject to the rule against perpetuities, nor is a resulting trust on termination of a charitable trust, though in England the rule is otherwise." 6 Scott & Ascher §39.7.2.

[290] *See generally* §4.1.1.2 of this handbook (equitable reversions under charitable trusts); 6 Scott & Ascher §39.7.2 (Conditions Subsequent); §8.30 of this handbook (vested equitable interests subject to divestment).

[291] 6 Scott & Ascher §39.5.3.

[292] *See generally* 6 Scott & Ascher §39.5.3. The entrusted property generally will revert upon a resulting trust to the residuary takers under the deceased settlor's will, or to their successors in interest, unless the probate residue was what had funded the charitable trust (or unless the will contains no residuary provision), in which case the property will pass to the settlor's heirs under the laws of intestacy, or to their successors in interest. 6 Scott & Ascher §39.5.3. Things can get fiendishly complicated should the property revert to trustees of other trusts, particularly other trusts that have terminated. On the other hand, reversionary interests being always vested, it may be of some consolation to the trustee charged with winding up the affairs of a failed charitable trust that running afoul of the rule against perpetuities at least should not be an issue. *See generally* J. C. Gray, The Rule Against Perpetuities §327.1 (4th ed. 1942).

estates, the task of ascertaining and locating the individuals, trusts and charities entitled to the property upon the reversion will likely prove daunting.[293] The legal and genealogical research costs alone are likely to be hefty.[294]

It is no wonder that American courts with great reluctance find limited charitable intent, especially when it comes to charitable trusts whose settlors are long dead.[295] A charitable trust that has been funded by the small contributions of many mostly anonymous individual donors (settlors) poses a similar logistical nightmare should the trust fail or its purposes be fulfilled without the trust estate having been fully exhausted.[296] In England a resulting trust almost never arises upon the failure of a charitable trust, once the trust has taken effect.[297] "Responding to concerns about the clogging of title and other administrative problems caused by remote default provisions upon failure of a charitable purpose,"[298] the Uniform Trust Code would sharply curtail the ability of a settlor to create a charitable trust whose property would revert to the settlor's personal representative, i.e., the settlor's probate estate, upon the accomplishment of that purpose, or upon the impossibility of its fulfillment.[299] Section 413 provides that the settlor's vested equitable reversionary interest would remain outstanding only until the later to occur of the following events, at which point the interest would divest:[300]

- The settlor dies
- The elapse of 21 years since the date of the trust's creation[301]

Thereafter, the court, notwithstanding the terms of the trust,[302] must apply *cy pres* in the event the specified charitable purpose ever fails.[303] "To the extent that the UTC thus disregards even the plainest of statements of the settlor's alternate plans for disposition of the trust assets upon failure of the original charitable purpose, it abruptly breaks with the traditional notion of cy pres."[304] Some states have enacted the Uniform Probate Code without this

---

[293] *See generally* 6 Scott & Ascher §39.5.3.

[294] 6 Scott & Ascher §39.5.3.

[295] *See generally* 6 Scott & Ascher §§39.5.3 (noting that it is "rare" that a court will allow a charitable trust to fail altogether once it has become operational), 41.3 (noting that "when an intended charitable trust fails at the outset and cy pres does not apply, there is ordinarily no difficulty in enforcing a resulting trust").

[296] *See generally* §8.15.46 of this handbook (the *bona vacantia* doctrine). *See also* 6 Scott & Ascher §41.3 (Failure of Charitable Trusts).

[297] 6 Scott & Ascher §39.5.3.

[298] UTC §413 cmt. (available at <http://www.uniformlaws.org/Act.aspx?title=Trust%20Code>).

[299] *See generally* 6 Scott & Ascher §39.5.2.

[300] *Cf.* §8.30 of this handbook (vested equitable interests that are subject to divestment).

[301] *See generally* 6 Scott & Ascher §39.5.3.

[302] Even when the terms articulate only a limited charitable purpose and expressly confirm the equitable reversion.

[303] *See generally* 6 Scott & Ascher §39.5.2.

[304] 6 Scott & Ascher §39.5.2.

Section 413 divestment provision.[305] Others have done so, but with periods that are longer than 21 years.[306]

Unless a charitable trust's continuance is conditioned upon the designated trustee and only the designated trustee carrying out its terms, a breach of trust generally does not warrant the imposition of a resulting trust in favor of the settlor or the settlor's probate estate.[307] "In such a case, if it is not unlawful, impossible, impracticable, or wasteful to carry out the designated purposes, the remedy is by a suit by the attorney general to compel the trustees to perform the trust, and not by a suit by the settlor or the settlor's estate to enforce a resulting trust."[308] The court also would have the equitable discretionary authority to remove the trustee and install a suitable successor.[309] A trust shall not fail for want of a trustee, or for want of a suitable trustee for that matter.

Racial, sexual, and religious restrictions: The political aspects of the *cy pres* doctrine. As a general rule, the trustee of a charitable trust may abide by a racial, sexual, or religious restriction in its terms, provided the trustee is not a governmental entity.[310] It may now be the law in some quarters, however, that even when the trustee and his agents are not state actors, such restrictions may not entail discrimination that is "invidious."[311] It has long been the case that such restrictions may not be unlawful or otherwise violate public policy.[312] Suffice to say that "invidiousness" and "public policy" are unruly horses not easily corralled.[313]

In the case of a restriction that is not enforceable, courts generally apply the *cy pres* doctrine or the equitable deviation doctrine to reform the terms of the trust to remove the restriction.[314] Rarely do the courts allow such trusts to fail altogether.[315] Once in a while, the court will reform the terms of a trust in a way that saves the discriminatory restriction.[316] In the case of a restriction that is not enforceable, a court's refusal to apply *cy pres* or equitable deviation to save the trust is likely to be the type of state action or inaction that is permissible.[317] The law, however, is far from clear as to whether the court may affirmatively remove the impediment in order to save the discriminatory restriction.[318] In the case of an enforceable restriction that the named trustee refuses to carry out, courts have been known to apply *cy pres* to remove the restriction.[319]

---

[305] 6 Scott & Ascher §39.5.2.

[306] 6 Scott & Ascher §39.5.2.

[307] 6 Scott & Ascher §39.7.1.

[308] 6 Scott & Ascher §39.7.1.

[309] *See generally* §7.2.3.6 of this handbook (removal).

[310] 6 Scott & Ascher §39.5.5.

[311] *See generally* 6 Scott & Ascher §39.5.5; Restatement (Third) of Trusts §28 cmt. f.

[312] *Cf.* §9.24 of this handbook (incentive trusts and the public policy considerations).

[313] 6 Scott & Ascher §39.5.5.

[314] 6 Scott & Ascher §39.5.5.

[315] 6 Scott & Ascher §39.5.5.

[316] 6 Scott & Ascher §39.5.5.

[317] 6 Scott & Ascher §39.5.5.

[318] 6 Scott & Ascher §39.5.5.

[319] 6 Scott & Ascher §39.5.5.

Some case studies. An example of judicial deference to reversionary interests[320] is illustrated in the events that gave rise to the Supreme Court case of *Evans v. Abney*.[321] The Court was asked to consider the constitutional implications of the administration and termination of a trust created under the 1911 will of U.S. Senator A. O. Bacon of Georgia. Pursuant to the terms of the will, property had been transferred in trust to the Senator's home city of Macon, Georgia for the creation of a whites-only public park.[322]

Following the Court's earlier decision in *Evans v. Newton*[323] (holding that the park could not continue to be operated on a racially discriminatory basis), a state court had ruled that the senator's intention to provide a park for whites only was not of a general charitable nature. Accordingly, it was held that the trust had failed and that the parkland and other trust property associated with it must revert upon a resulting trust[324] to the senator's estate. If, on the other hand, there had been a finding of general charitable intent, presumably the state court, invoking the *cy pres* doctrine, would have ordered the continued operation of the park on an integrated basis. Such a finding would have, for all intents and purposes, voided the equitable reversionary interests of those entitled to the senator's estate.

As to the actual holding of *Abney*, the Court found that the state court's failure to find general charitable intent in the establishment of the trust did not constitute "state action" under Fourteenth Amendment analysis. Thus, no federal constitutional grounds were found for extinguishing the private reversionary interests in favor of continued public operation of the park.[325]

In *Ebitz v. Pioneer National Bank*,[326] the Massachusetts court applied the doctrine of *cy pres* in substance, though not in form. At issue was the provision of a testamentary trust established "to aid and assist worthy and ambitious young men to acquire a legal education."[327] The will was executed in 1963 and allowed in 1970. The plaintiffs were female law students who made timely applications to the trustee for assistance from the fund. Their applications were rejected on the ground that the testator had intended males, not females, to be beneficiaries of his largess.

The trial judge held that "[t]o exclude females as possible recipients of financial assistance from a trust fund established for the purpose of assisting

---

[320] *See, e.g.*, J. Gray, The Rule Against Perpetuities §§34, 41.1, 113, 113.1, 113.3, 327.1 (4th ed. 1942) (settlor of limited charitable purpose trust retains vested reversionary interest in trust property); National Shawmut Bank v. Joy, 315 Mass. 457, 462–469, 53 N.E.2d 113, 117–121 (1944) (failure of trust triggers resulting trust in favor of settlor or settlor's estate).

[321] 396 U.S. 435 (1970).

[322] *See generally* 6 Scott & Ascher §38.6.

[323] 382 U.S. 296 (1966).

[324] *See generally* §4.1.1 of this handbook and §8.2.1.5 of this handbook (consequences of a violation of the common law rule) (each discussing the resulting trust).

[325] *See generally* 6 Scott & Ascher §38.6.

[326] 372 Mass. 207, 361 N.E.2d 225 (1977).

[327] Ebitz v. Pioneer Nat'l Bank, 372 Mass. 207 at 209, 361 N.E.2d at 226. *See generally* Tracy A. Bateman, J.D., Annot., *Validity of charitable gift or trust containing gender restrictions on beneficiaries*, 90 A.L.R.4th 836 (1992).

qualified students interested in the pursuit of a legal education would constitute an unreasonable and arbitrary exclusion."[328] He then speculated that the enforcement of such a provision might be unconstitutional. With that he ruled that the term "young men" meant "young men and young women." The trustee appealed. The trial judge was upheld on appeal by the Massachusetts Supreme Judicial Court, which found the reference to "young men" ambiguous in the context of the entire instrument. One would be hard pressed to conjure up a more blatant example of constructive or informal *cy pres*. Also, one cannot help but wonder what would qualify as an expression of limited charitable intent in Massachusetts after *Ebitz*. "When I say young men, I mean young men, M-E-N"?

In dissent, Justice Quirico wrote: "Surely it is not the law that a testator or donor may not bestow the benefit of his own funds on a class or persons of one sex to the exclusion of persons of a similar class but of the opposite sex, if that is his stated intention."[329] Citing *Abney*, he suggested that the case was not "clouded" by any constitutional question.[330]

In 2002, a Maryland court took an *Ebitz* approach to a charitable bequest to a private nonprofit hospital for the benefit of "white patients who need physical rehabilitation."[331] The will provided that if the bequest was not "acceptable" to the primary beneficiary, there would be a gift over to an alternate beneficiary.[332] Instead of ruling in favor of the alternate beneficiary, the court found general charitable intent and ordered the bequest administered for the benefit of the primary beneficiary "without giving effect to the word 'white.'"[333] The court concluded that "where the gift over is also to a charity, it would seem that the testator's general charitable intent is confirmed."[334] It should be noted here that absent "invidious discrimination," charitable trusts to alleviate the poverty of those of a particular race or gender are generally enforceable.[335]

The expansive approach to general charitable intent exemplified by the Maryland case is contrasted by the approach taken by the Montana court in *In re*

---

[328] Ebitz v. Pioneer Nat'l Bank, 372 Mass. at 212, 361 N.E.2d at 228 (Quirico, J., dissenting) (quoting trial court's holding).

[329] Ebitz v. Pioneer Nat'l Bank, 372 Mass. at 213, 361 N.E.2d at 228.

[330] *Cf.* Shapira v. Union Nat'l Bank, 39 Ohio Misc. 28, 315 N.E.2d 825 (1974) (cautioning that seeking judicial enforcement of a testamentary trust provision conditioning one's enjoyment of the decedent's property on one marrying within a particular faith not be confused with what would be clouded by a constitutional question, namely seeking to have a state court actually enjoin one from marrying outside one's faith). "It is a fundamental rule of law in Ohio that a testator may legally entirely disinherit his children." Shapira v. Union Nat'l Bank, 39 Ohio Misc. 28, 315 N.E.2d 825 (1974). *See generally* §9.24 of this handbook (the incentive trust (and the public policy considerations); marriage restraints)).

[331] Home for Incurables of Baltimore City v. University of Md. Med. Sys. Corp., 369 Md. 67, 797 A.2d 746 (2002).

[332] Home for Incurables of Baltimore City v. University of Md. Med. Sys. Corp., 369 Md. 67, 797 A.2d 746 (2002).

[333] Home for Incurables of Baltimore City v. University of Md. Med. Sys. Corp., 369 Md. 67, 797 A.2d 746 (2002).

[334] Home for Incurables of Baltimore City v. University of Md. Med. Sys. Corp., 369 Md. at 83–84, 797 A.2d at 756.

[335] *See generally* 6 Scott & Ascher §38.2.5.

Will of Cram.[336] At issue was a testamentary trust that provided for cash stipends to young males certified by the Future Farmers of America of Montana and the 4-H Club of Montana to be of good character, in need of financial assistance, and interested in the sheep raising business. The two organizations had links to the state educational system. In response to an equal protection challenge to those provisions of the trust that were gender exclusive, the Montana lower court modified the trust to remove any state involvement in the mechanics of the grantee selection process. On appeal, the actions of the lower court were affirmed.

The settlor clearly intended to discriminate, that is, to benefit young males to the exclusion of young females. However, the trust as modified involved no state action.

> A private person has the right to dispose of his money or property as he wishes and in so doing may lawfully discriminate in regard to the beneficiaries of his largess without offending the Equal Protection Clause as long as the State and its instrumentalities are not involved, and unless the trust is unlawful, private trusts are to be encouraged.[337]

As *Abney, Ebitz, Cram,* and the Maryland case suggest, there is yet no judicial consensus as to the elasticity and limits of general charitable intent. Thus the trustee, when faced with a charitable trust whose purposes cannot be carried out, ought not to be surprised if the court uses the *cy pres* process to indulge its own collective social or political predilections.[338] The prospective settlor with definite ideas, therefore, will want to do some jurisdiction shopping. He or she also needs to choose his or her trustees and their successors carefully. And still there can be no guarantees. As one commentator has noted:

> Yesterday's news that the trustees of the Barnes Foundation have petitioned the court to move its collection of art from its home in Merion, Pa., to Philadelphia, should give pause to anyone who is considering a philanthropic bequest. Most people believe that, with due diligence, they can have a considerable say over how their property will be disposed after their death. Having engaged expensive legal talent, they place a high degree of trust in Trusts. How justified is their faith? The case of the Barnes Foundation provides grounds for concern. . . . But let the donor beware. "Perpetuity" no longer means "forever." It means "until lawyers representing powerful interests get to work."[339]

---

[336] 186 Mont. 37, 606 P.2d 145 (Mont. 1980).

[337] In re Will of Cram, 186 Mont. at 45, 606 P.2d at 150. *See also* Estate of Wilson, 452 N.E.2d 1228, 1235, 465 N.Y.S.2d 900, 907 (1983) ("The Fourteenth Amendment, however, 'erects no shield against merely private conduct, however discriminatory or wrongful.' Shelley v. Kraemer, 334 U.S. 1, 13 . . .").

[338] *See, e.g.,* Home for Incurables of Baltimore City v. University of Md. Med. Sys. Corp., 797 A.2d 746 (Md. 2002) (faced with a charitable trust for the benefit of the white patients of a hospital with a charitable gift over to a university, the court excised the racial restriction rather than enforce the gift over).

[339] Roger Kimball, *Donor Beware: Art May Be Long, But Trusts Aren't,* Wall St. J., Sept. 25, 2002, at D8, col. 1 (discussing a pending *cy pres* petition in a Pennsylvania court which if granted might effectively alter the terms of a charitable trust created by Albert C. Barnes in 1922 for the purpose of establishing a museum/art school to administer his priceless art collection, the terms of the trust

Safeguarding donor intent. What is a prospective settlor of a charitable trust to do, particularly one with very definite ideas? At minimum, the limited charitable purpose needs to be unambiguously labeled as such in the governing instrument.[340] He or she also may want to look into appointing a trust protector.[341] In Section 4.1.1.1 of this handbook we catalogued some countermeasures that might be taken at the drafting stage to help safeguard a donor's charitable intentions. Mergers of colleges and universities and withdrawals of local churches from their parent organizations will generally implicate the law of trusts, particularly when such events frustrate the charitable intentions of past donors.[342]

§9.4.4 In the United States Neither the Legislative nor the Executive Branches May Apply Prerogative Cy Pres to a Charitable Trust

The Court has exclusive jurisdiction of proceedings initiated by interested parties concerning the internal affairs of trusts.[343]

At common law in England, a prerogative power of cy pres, exercisable by the Crown in certain circumstances and without regard to the settlor's intent, developed in addition to the judicial power in the Chancellor. The prerogative power (or legislative counterpart) has not been recognized in the United States, although legislation may reasonably regulate the extent and exercise of the cy pres power of courts. The judicial power of cy pres has evolved in this country along lines generally similar to the equity power under English common law.[344]

---

providing that there be no loaning and reproducing of the art works). "On December 13, 2004, the Court issued its Opinion, approving the Trustee's petition, breaking the Trust and permitting the gallery to move to the City of Philadelphia." Terrance A. Kline, *Comment on the Barnes Foundation,* 31 ACTEC J., 245, 248 (2005) (concluding that the decision is "disturbing" in that the Court failed "to enforce less drastic deviations to the Trust that would have preserved the Trust consistent with Dr. Barnes' intent"). *See generally* Chris Abbinante, Comment, *Protecting Donor Intent in Charitable Foundations: Wayward Trusteeship and the Barnes Foundation,* 145 U. Pa. L. Rev. 665 (1997). *See also* John Anderson, The Battle Over the Barnes Collection (New York, W.W. Norton & Co. 2003).

[340] *See* Wendy A. Lee, *Charitable Foundations and the Argument for Efficiency: Balancing Donor Intent with Practicable Solutions Through Expanded Use of Cy Pres,* 34 Suffolk Univ. L. Rev. 173, 201 (2000) (advising that donors "must take proactive steps to clearly articulate and mandate their philanthropic intentions, lest their words become prey to easy manipulation" and noting that "violations of donor intent have occurred in numerous situations throughout the last two centuries, even where the intent was explicit and binding").

[341] *See generally* §3.2.6 of this handbook (considerations in the selection of a trustee).

[342] *See generally* 6 Scott & Ascher §9.3.3.

[343] UPC §7-201(a).

[344] Restatement (Third) of Trusts §67 cmt. a. For more on the difference between judicial *cy pres* and prerogative *cy pres*, prerogative *cy pres* possibly being "derived from the power exercised by the Roman emperor, who was sovereign legislator as well as supreme interpreter of the laws," the reader is referred to Jackson v. Phillips, 96 Mass. (14 Allen) 539, 575 (1867). *See also* 6 Scott & Ascher §39.5.1 (Judicial and Prerogative *Cy Pres*). In England, the king would exercise his prerogative *cy pres* power by indicating over his sign manual, *i.e.,* over his signature, "the disposition that he wished to be made of the property, and the chancellor would order that the disposition be made." 6 Scott & Ascher §39.5.1.

The *cy pres* doctrine is covered generally in Sections 8.15.28 of this handbook and 9.4.3 of this handbook. In England judicial *cy pres* power was vested in the chancellor and prerogative *cy pres* power in the king.[345] "Dispositions under the prerogative power seem to have occurred primarily in two classes of cases: first, those in which property was given for a purpose that was illegal but that, except for the illegality, would have been charitable; and, second, those in which property was given directly to charity, but without any indication of a specific charitable purpose and without any indication that a trustee was to administer the charity."[346] The king had no legal or equitable duty to consider donor intent in the exercise of his power to apply prerogative *cy pres*.[347] Thus, "[t]he exercise of the prerogative power by a biased, cynical, or whimsical king sometimes resulted in the devotion of property to purposes the settlor never would have approved and sometimes, indeed, to purposes contrary to the settlor's wishes."[348]

Suffice it to say, "the prerogative power has no place in American jurisprudence."[349] Only the judiciary may apply the doctrine of *cy pres* to charitable trusts,[350] "[a]lthough the legislature can, of course, properly lay down rules governing charitable trusts."[351] Application of the *cy pres* doctrine is a function neither of the executive branch nor of the legislative.[352] Except pursuant to its right to take by eminent domain for just compensation, a legislature may not alter the terms of an *ongoing charitable corporation or trust with a lawful purpose that is capable of being carried out*. As to charitable corporations, the U.S. Supreme Court so held in the 1816 Dartmouth College case.[353] The principles of the Dartmouth College case have been held applicable to charitable trusts as well.[354] The New Hampshire legislature had attempted by statute to amend the charter of the charitable corporation known as Dartmouth College.[355] The Court found that the statute violated Article I, Section 10, of the U.S.

---

[345] *See* Chapter 1 of this handbook (containing a list of all the Lord Chancellors since 1066).

[346] 6 Scott & Ascher §39.5.1.

[347] 6 Scott & Ascher §39.5.1.

[348] 6 Scott & Ascher §39.5.1.

[349] 6 Scott & Ascher §39.5.1. *See also* 6 Scott & Ascher §39.5.6.

[350] *See* Opinion of the Justices to the House of Representatives, 374 Mass. 843, 371 N.E.2d 1349 (1978) (providing that the Massachusetts legislature does not have the power to alter the terms of a trust established under the will of Benjamin Franklin). *See also* Franklin Found. v. Attorney Gen., 416 Mass. 483, 623 N.E.2d 1109 (1993) (addressing how the Massachusetts legislature must exercise its right to dispose of a portion of the trust property upon expiration of the trust's 200-year term, Benjamin Franklin, *by express language in his will*, having given to the Commonwealth of Massachusetts a right of disposition over a portion of the trust corpus).

[351] 6 Scott & Ascher §39.5.6.

[352] *See generally* 4A Scott on Trusts §399.1.

[353] Trustees of Dartmouth Coll. v. Woodward, 17 U.S. 518, 4 L. Ed. 629, 4 Wheat. 518 (1819). *See generally* 6 Scott & Ascher §39.5.6.

[354] 4A Scott on Trusts §399.5, n.7, and accompanying text; 5 Scott & Ascher §37.4.2.3; 6 Scott & Ascher §39.5.6.

[355] *See generally* 6 Scott & Ascher §39.5.6.

Constitution providing that no state shall pass any law impairing the obligations of contracts.[356]

The Court found two contracts: the implied contract between the Crown which had granted the charter and benefactors that the Crown would not alter the terms of the charter and the implied contract between the benefactors and the corporation that gifts would be administered in accordance with the terms of the charter.[357] For a charter amendment to be effective, it must be consented to by the corporation and approved by a court in the exercise of its *cy pres* power.[358] Again, the principles of the *Dartmouth College* case have been held applicable to charitable trusts.[359]

§9.4.5   Tax-Oriented Trusts That Mix Charitable and Noncharitable Interests (Split-Interest Trusts)

[A] trust may be created for charitable purposes . . . or for private purposes, or for a combination of charitable and private purposes.[360]

The equitable interests of a trust may be divided between charitable and noncharitable beneficiaries.[361] Let us take our standard formula: *A* to *B* for *C*, then to *D*. A trust where *C* is a noncharitable beneficiary (*e.g.*, a member of the settlor's family) and *D* is a charity is a charitable remainder trust. A trust where *C* is a charity and *D* is a noncharitable beneficiary is a charitable lead trust. The incentive for establishing these split-interest arrangements is usually tax avoidance.[362] In fact, "[m]ost of our recent learning and practices on the use and drafting of unitrusts and annuity interests . . . arise from the 1969 enactment of the split-interest (specifically the charitable lead-and-remainder-interest) rules of I.R.C. §2055(e)(2)(A) and (B)."[363] In the case of an inter vivos charitable remainder trust, the settlor is looking for an income and gift tax charitable deduction at the time the *D* interest is deemed created for tax purposes (and for an estate tax deduction in the case of a revocable inter vivos trust or testamentary trust).[364] In the case of the *C* interest under a charitable lead trust, the

---

[356] *See generally* 6 Scott & Ascher §39.5.6.

[357] *See generally* 6 Scott & Ascher §39.5.6.

[358] *See generally* 4A Scott on Trusts §399.5; 6 Scott & Ascher §39.5.6.

[359] 4A Scott on Trusts §399.5, n.7, and accompanying text; 5 Scott & Ascher §37.4.2.3; 6 Scott & Ascher §39.5.6.

[360] For more on split-interest trusts in general, see Bogert §264.25.
   Restatement (Third) of Trusts §27(1).

[361] *See, e.g.*, 6 Scott & Ascher §39.3.5 (Power of Trustee to Distribute among Charitable and Other Valid Objects).

[362] *See generally* Beckwith, 261-3rd T.M., Estate and Gift Tax Charitable Deductions.

[363] Restatement (Third) of Trusts, Reporter's Notes on §49.

[364] I.R.C. §§170(f)(2)(A) (income tax deduction), 2522(c)(2)(A) (gift tax deduction), 2055(e)(2)(A) (estate tax deduction).

settlor is looking for a gift or estate tax deduction[365] and an income tax charitable deduction to the extent the lead trust qualifies as a grantor trust.[366]

In the case of a charitable remainder trust or a charitable lead trust, the present values of the equitable interests that pass to the charitable and non-charitable entities, assuming there are no outstanding unfulfilled conditions precedent that render valuation impossible, are determined for tax purposes by reference to IRS-prepared tables that take into account a range of interest rates and the most recent mortality experience.[367] The applicable interest rate is 120 percent of the federal midterm rate prevailing at the time the interest in the charity is created for tax purposes.

The tables are prepared by the IRS pursuant to Section 7520 of the Internal Revenue Code. Each month, the IRS publishes a revenue ruling setting forth the currently applicable interest rate. From time to time, the actuarial tables are revised to accommodate changes in mortality experience. For an explanation of how to work with the tables in a given situation, the reader is referred to BNA's Tax Management Portfolio.[368]

§9.4.5.1   IRS-Approved Charitable Remainder Trusts

In order for the settlor to receive a gift tax charitable deduction, or for his estate to receive an estate tax charitable deduction, the IRS requires that the remainder interest be susceptible to valuation *at the time the deduction is being taken*.[369] For a testamentary trust, that would occur when the settlor dies. For an irrevocable inter vivos trust, that would occur at the time of funding. For a revocable inter vivos trust, that would usually occur at the death of the settlor. Beware of the appearance of self-dealing in cases in which there is joint ownership of assets by the charitable remainder trust and the settlor. In such a case, the settlor must not directly or indirectly use the joint asset. Also, a charitable remainder trust cannot own S corporation shares.[370] For a charitable deduction with respect to a remainder interest to survive audit, the trust's design must conform to IRS requirements:

(a) **Charitable remainder unitrust (CRUT).**[371] The IRS has authorized a charitable deduction in connection with the creation of a charitable remainder unitrust that meets the following specifications:[372] Each year, at least 5 percent but not more than 50 percent of the net fair market value of all the assets, valued

---

[365] I.R.C. §§2055(e)(2)(B) (estate tax deduction), 2522(c)(2)(B) (gift tax deduction).

[366] I.R.C. §170(f)(2)(B). *See also* §9.1 of this handbook (the grantor trust).

[367] Bogert §§264.25, 506.

[368] Beausang, 830 T.M., Valuation: General and Real Estate.

[369] I.R.C. §664(d).

[370] *See generally* §9.23 of this handbook (S corporations; qualified Subchapter S trusts (QSSTs); electing small business trusts (ESBTs).

[371] *See generally* §9.13 of this handbook (the unitrust).

[372] I.R.C. §664(d)(2).

annually, shall be distributed to the noncharitable beneficiary either for life or for a period not greater than twenty years; and upon the death of the noncharitable beneficiary, the equitable interest passes to a designated charity. *For percentage computation purposes, the trust estate is revalued each year but the percentage is fixed.* The value of the trust estate includes net income applied and principal appreciation. The IRS has issued sample CRUT forms.[373] If investment performance is poor, however, it is possible that when the trust's term ends, there are no assets remaining to transfer to the designated charity.

The IRS also permits a so-called NIMCRUT (or net income with make-up unitrust).[374] Under a NIMCRUT, only the net income *up to the stated percentage* is paid out. Shortfalls in income distributions are made up in later years when and if net income exceeds the stated percentage. A net income *up to the stated percentage* with no make up unitrust will also pass IRS muster.

(b) Charitable remainder annuity trust (CRAT). The IRS has authorized a charitable deduction in connection with the creation of a charitable remainder annuity trust that meets the following specifications:[375] *A fixed sum*, which must be at least 5 percent but not more that 50 percent of the initial net fair market value of the trust estate, shall be distributed yearly to the noncharitable beneficiary for either not greater than twenty years or life. The charity receives the remainder. Unlike the unitrust, there is no yearly reevaluation of the net trust estate and the value of the actual amount received each year is static. The IRS has issued sample CRAT forms.[376]

§9.4.5.2 IRS-Approved Charitable Lead Trust

With respect to those split-interest arrangements where the *remainder* is in a noncharity,[377] the IRS has authorized a charitable deduction for the charitable "C" interest if the "charitable lead trust" meets the following specifications:[378] The charity receives a fixed sum (that may be satisfied out of income and/or principal) for a specified period (CLAT) *or* the charity yearly receives a fixed unitrust percentage of the net fair market value of the trust estate (CLUT). The

---

[373] Rev. Procs. 2005-52–2005-59, 2005-34 I.R.B. 326 *et seq.* (Aug. 22, 2005).

[374] I.R.C. §664(d)(3). *See generally* Peter J. Brevorka & Robert B. Lloyd, Jr., *Reforming NIMCRUTS*, 25 ACTEC Notes 271 (1999) (discussing final treasury regulations that authorize "reformation" of a NIMCRUT into a standard CRUT). *See generally* §8.15.22 of this handbook (doctrines of reformation and rectification).

[375] I.R.C. §664(d)(1).

[376] Rev. Proc. 2003-54, 2003-31 I.R.B. 236 (Aug. 4, 2003); Rev. Proc. 2003-55, 2003-31 I.R.B. 242 (Aug. 4, 2003); Rev. Proc. 2003-56, 2003-31 I.R.B. 249 (Aug. 4, 2003); Rev. Proc. 2003-57, 2003-31 I.R.B. 257 (Aug. 4, 2003); Rev. Proc. 2003-58, 2003-31 I.R.B. 262 (Aug. 4, 2003); Rev. Proc. 2003-59, 2003-31 I.R.B. 268 (Aug. 4, 2003); Rev. Proc. 2003-60, 2003-31 I.R.B. 274 (Aug. 4, 2003).

[377] *See* UTC §413 cmt. (available at <http://www.uniformlaws.org/Act.aspx?title=Trust%20 Code>) (noting that the UTC's restrictions on noncharitable gift overs in the *cy pres* context are inapplicable to charitable lead trusts).

[378] I.R.C. §§2055(e)(2)(B) (estate tax), 2522(c)(2)(B) (gift tax).

value of the net trust estate must be recomputed yearly. Unlike the charitable remainder trusts, there is no minimum percentage requirement. The settlor who reserves a power to direct who or what gets the benefit of the amounts going to the charity risks subjecting all the trust property to the federal estate tax upon the settlor's death.[379] For a more detailed discussion of the inner-workings of the charitable lead trust, the reader is referred to *Innovative CLAT Structures: Providing Economic Efficiencies to a Wealth Transfer Workhorse*.[380]

§9.4.5.3 Pooled Income Fund

An estate tax deduction is allowed for the value of a charitable remainder interest in property transferred to a pooled income fund, as defined in Code Section 642(c)(5).[381]

§9.5 Trusts for Deferring Taxation of Income

In Germany, pensions are essentially unfunded; instead, employers make a balance sheet entry and receive a tax credit for it. But it does operate an insurance fund, the PSV, which covers accrued pension obligations of an insolvent employer and insures benefits up to 82,000.[1]

In the United States, private employee benefit plans essentially are funded schemes for deferring the taxation of income. Unless an insurance company[2] is in the picture, a plan will be linked to a segregated pool of assets, with title to the assets themselves being in a trustee. An IRA is also a funded arrangement. More often than not, however, the assets of an IRA will be held by a custodian for the taxpayer rather than in the name of a trustee.

§9.5.1 The Employee Benefit Trust (Tax Qualified)

It is to be hoped that the federal courts will continue to show sensitivity to the primary role of state law in the field of probate and non-probate transfers. To the extent that the federal courts think themselves unable to craft exceptions to ERISA's preemption language, it is open to

---

[379] *See* Rev. Proc. 2007-45. *See generally* §8.9.3 of this handbook (tax-sensitive powers).

[380] Paul S. Lee, Turney P. Berry, & Martin Hall, *Innovative CLAT Structures: Providing Economic Efficiencies to a Wealth Transfer Workhorse*, 37 ACTEC L.J. 93 (Summer 2011).

[381] I.R.C. §642(c)5. *See generally* Beckwith, 261-3rd T.M., Estate and Gift Tax Charitable Deductions A-13, A-14. For more on pooled income funds, the reader is referred to §9.7.3 of this handbook.

§9.5 [1] Financial Times Weekly Review of the Investment Industry, Issue No. 70, June 23, 2003, at 3.

[2] *See generally* §9.9.1 of this handbook (Life Insurance and Third Party Beneficiary Contracts Generally).

them to apply state law concepts as federal common law. Because the Uniform Probate Code contemplates multistate applicability, it is well suited to be the model for federal common law absorption.[3]

When an employer in the United States establishes a retirement "plan" for its employees it is usually of the "qualified" variety.[4] If it is a qualified plan, the employer can take its contributions to the plan as a tax deduction.[5] Under certain circumstances, contributions by or on behalf of an employee are not taxed as income to the employee at the time the contributions are made.[6] Taxation on income generated by plan assets may also be deferred.[7] Plan distributions at retirement or at some other time, on the other hand, may have tax consequences.[8] The reader interested in a comprehensive and practical discussion of those consequences is referred to Natalie B. Choate.[9] For a discussion of the complex and time-sensitive mechanics of funding a trust with distributions from a qualified defined contribution plan account or IRA after the account owner's death, the reader is referred to Grassi and Welber.[10]

For a plan to be qualified it must meet certain requirements set forth in the Internal Revenue Code and elsewhere.[11] Congress, by means of the Employee Retirement Income Security Act of 1974 (ERISA), articulated a comprehensive federal statutory framework for the design and administration of qualified plans.[12]

With the exception of so-called *insured plans*, for a plan to be qualified it must have associated with it a trust that serves as a receptacle for the plan's assets. Unfortunately, the establishment of a plan often requires a consortium of actuaries, pension lawyers, tax lawyers, labor lawyers, human resource lawyers, and SEC lawyers in order to determine what property may enter the trust. The common law trust lawyers, that is, those who are familiar with the common law rules applicable once property finds its way into the hands of a trustee, are left out of the process altogether. Moreover, most if asked would prefer not to get involved.

---

[3] UPC §2-804 cmt. (discussing in part ERISA preemption of state law).

[4] For a discussion of a plan of the nonqualified variety, *see* §9.5.3 of this handbook (the rabbi trust (nonqualified executive deferred compensation)).

[5] *See generally* Bogert §§255, 270.20.

[6] *See generally* Bogert §§255, 270.20.

[7] *See generally* Bogert §§255, 270.20.

[8] *See generally* Bogert §264.7.

[9] Life and Death Planning for Retirement Benefits (published by Ataxplan Publications, P.O. Box 51371, Boston, MA 02205-1371). Information on how to obtain text and updates is available at <www.ataxplan.com>.

[10] Sebastian V. Grassi, Jr. & Nancy H. Welber, *Special Planning Is Needed for Retirement Benefits Payable to a Disabled Special-Needs Child*, J. Prac. Est. Plan. 51 (June–July 2010) ("Many of the concepts discussed in this article are also applicable where the beneficiary child is not a special-needs child").

[11] *See generally* Bogert §255.

[12] *See generally* Bogert §255.

When confronted with an employee benefit trust, the trustee should first examine it from a common law perspective.[13] Most likely, it will be a trust with several trustees. Depending upon the type of plan, it could have many settlors (the employees and, to the extent of any overfunding, the employer),[14] many beneficiaries (perhaps retirees entitled to annuitized payments), and many remaindermen (employees and retirees). To the extent a particular benefit is actually consideration for services rendered, in equity it is the employee, not the employer, who is the trust settlor.[15] In many instances, a plan participant will have obtained from human resources and filled out a form designating who is to take at death whatever remains of the participant's equitable interest. A participant's right to so direct the equitable interest is tantamount to a power of appointment.[16] "When federalizing the administration of pension and employee benefit plans in ERISA, Congress made a deliberate choice to subject these plans to the pre-existing regime of trust law rather than to invent a new regulatory structure."[17]

Some beneficiaries and remaindermen are likely to have vested interests and some to have interests that are partially vested and partially contingent upon length of time with the employer.[18] Depending upon the type of plan, some beneficiaries and remaindermen (perhaps certain retirees) may well have rights of withdrawal in the nature of general inter vivos powers of appointment.

The employer may have either an equitable contingent remainder or a vested reversionary interest in trust assets to the extent they are not needed to fund benefits.[19] Each employee is probably entitled to complete the dispositive terms with respect to that employee's interest in the trust.[20] (As noted, this is

---

[13] Tittle v. Enron, 284 F. Supp. 2d 511, 546 (2003) (noting that the common law of trusts offers a "starting point" for analysis of ERISA unless it is inconsistent with the language of the statute, its structure, or its purposes).

[14] *See generally* 3 Scott & Ascher §15.4.4 (Determining Who Is the Settlor) (U.S.); §8.43 of this handbook (who is the settlor of the trust?); Lewin ¶ 5-75 (England) (noting that ". . . with a defined benefit scheme, . . . the trusts can properly be regarded as comprising a series of separate settlements, created when individual employees join the scheme, comprising the contributions made by the employee or the company in respect of the employee, and with the employee as a life in being" for purposes of the Rule against Perpetuities).

[15] 6 Scott & Ascher §§41.13 (noting that "[i]f a third person gives consideration for a transfer in trust, the third person is the trust's creator, and if the trust fails, a resulting trust ordinarily arises in the third person's favor"), 41.15 (when third person provides consideration for transfer in trust).

[16] "In essence, the power to appoint the 'death-in-employment benefit' is no different from any other power of appointment." Baird v. Baird, [1990] 2 A.C. 548 at 557, PC (England). *See generally* 1 Scott & Ascher §8.2.4 (Compliance with Testamentary Formalities Not Required); §8.1 of this handbook (powers of appointment).

[17] John H. Langbein, *What ERISA Means by Equitable: The Supreme Court's Trail of Error in Russell, Mertens, and Great-West*, 103 Colum. L. Rev. 1317 (2003).

[18] Bogert §255.

[19] *See, e.g.*, Davis v. Richards & Wallington Indus. Ltd., [1991] 2 All ER 563 (an English case adjudicating the disposition of surplus pension funds where the court imposed a resulting trust and considered but did not apply the doctrine of *bona vacantia*). *See generally* §4.1.1.1 of this handbook (the noncharitable trust; resulting trust defined) and §8.15.46 of this handbook (*bona vacantia* doctrine).

[20] 1 Scott & Ascher §8.2.4.

accomplished by the filling out of a beneficiary designation form supplied by the employer's human resources department.) The governing instrument is likely to provide that income generated by the trust assets be periodically added to principal.

Once the trust is looked at in common law terms (*i.e.*, once the governing trust document is analyzed to determine in what respects it requires a *deviation* from the common law regime), the trustee and trust counsel should then turn to ERISA to determine in what respects federal trust law alters and embellishes the common law trust principles discussed in this handbook.[21] They will be surprised to discover that ERISA has codified some long-standing common law trust principles; but, contrary to what they may have heard, the federal gloss has added little that would alarm the conscientious and ethical trustee of an old-fashioned private trust.[22]

Insofar as the trustee is concerned, ERISA has codified and embellished the duty of loyalty by creating a thicket of prohibited transactions.[23] Still, it amounts to little more than an elaborate codification of the common law prohibition against self-dealing by trust fiduciaries.[24] The "Prudent Man Rule" of investment as it applies to employee benefit trusts has been altered by ERISA so that it might better be called the *Federal Prudent Expert Rule*.[25] Again, this is not a particularly radical development as it is unlikely that the common law would have long tolerated an amateur standard for investing the massive aggregation of wealth lodged in the nation's employee benefit trusts.[26] ERISA also has limited the common law rights of a beneficiary's creditors to reach employee benefit trust assets.[27] It has put certain nontrustees on the hot

---

[21] They will find, for example, that ERISA has rendered exculpatory clauses in the employee benefit context unenforceable (*see* §7.2.6 of this handbook) and that employee benefit plan and trust documents may not relieve fiduciaries of those fiduciary duties set forth, expressly or by implication, in ERISA.

[22] *See, e.g.*, Bixler v. Central Pa. Teamsters Health & Welfare Fund, 12 F.3d 1292 (1993) (noting that fiduciary duties articulated in ERISA are not exhaustive and that Congress relied on the common law of trusts to define the general scope of the ERISA trustee's authority and responsibility). *See also* Martin v. Walton, 773 F. Supp. 1524 (S.D. Fla. 1991); Marshall v. Teamsters Local 282 Pension Trust Fund, 458 F. Supp. 986 (E.D.N.Y. 1978). *See* Pegram v. Herdrich, 120 S. Ct. 2143, 68 U.S.L.W. 4501 (2000) (discussing the meaning of the word "fiduciary" as that term is employed in ERISA and distinguishing the duties of a common law trustee from those of an HMO physician). *See generally* Chapter 1 of this handbook (in part discussing the meaning of the word *fiduciary*).

[23] *See* Wade & Loebl, *Individual Prohibited Transaction Exemptions: The Common Law*, 29 Real Prop. Prob. & Tr. J. 185 (1994).

[24] *See* Wade & Loebl, *Individual Prohibited Transaction Exemptions: The Common Law*, 29 Real Prop. Prob. & Tr. J. 185 (1994).

[25] *See* Wade & Loebl, *Individual Prohibited Transaction Exemptions: The Common Law*, 29 Real Prop. Prob. & Tr. J. 185 (1994).

[26] *Compare* §6.1.4 of this handbook (duty to give personal attention (not to delegate)) (noting that there has been evolving for some time in the common law of trusts a principle that the professional or corporate trustee should be held to a higher standard than that to which an amateur should be held).

[27] ERISA §1056(d)(1); I.R.C. §401(a)(13): For an employee benefit plan to be qualified, an employee's interest in its associated trust may not be assigned or alienated.

seat—particularly investment managers—by imposing on them fiduciary status. Finally, the area of allocation of fiduciary responsibilities has been elaborated and codified.[28]

Of all ERISA's codifications, the allocation of fiduciary responsibility may be perhaps the most perplexing.[29] Many troubling common law questions lurk behind the codification. For example, if the governing instrument allocates investment responsibility to an investment manager, what common law oversight obligations remain back with the trustee?[30] To what extent has the allocation of responsibility provisions of ERISA altered the common law principles of cofiduciary liability?[31]

The beneficiary designation form is completed by an employee usually without legal advice and usually at the human resources office. It is by means of the form that the terms of the employee benefit trust applicable to that employee are completed and that the link is made between the employee benefit trust and the employee's own estate plan. More wealth is likely to transfer pursuant to the terms of the form than pursuant to the terms of the employee's will,[32] yet much more attention and thought are likely to have gone into the drawing of the will than into the filling out of the form. In any case it is in the interests of all parties that the terms of the beneficiary designation form cover all contingencies and be unambiguous. Unaddressed contingencies and ambiguities, however, are inevitable in a less than perfect world. Accordingly, ERISA trustees and plan administrators would be well advised to review the rules set forth in the official comment to Section 7.2 of the Restatement (Third) of Property (Wills and Other Donative Transfers), the section that extends certain will doctrines to will substitutes. These are rules that are intended among other things to "inform the federal common law of will substitutes under the Employee Retirement Income Security Act (ERISA)."[33]

§9.5.2   The IRA Trust

An individual retirement plan[34] (commonly known as an IRA) may offer some income tax deferral opportunities for individuals. Associated with a particular IRA may be a trust that serves as a receptacle for an individual's

---

[28] *See generally* Bogert §255.

[29] *See, e.g.*, Tittle v. Enron, 284 F. Supp. 2d 511 (S.D. Tex. 2003).

[30] *See generally* §6.1.4 of this handbook (duty to give personal attention (not to delegate)).

[31] *See generally* Tittle v. Enron, 284 F. Supp. 2d 511 (S.D. Tex. 2003).

[32] *See generally* Langbein, *The Nonprobate Revolution and the Future of the Law of Succession*, 97 Harv. L. Rev. 1108 (1984).

[33] Restatement (Third) of Property (Wills and Other Donative Transfers) §7.2 cmt. k.

[34] *See generally* I.R.C. §408.

contributions.[35] With the possible exception of a simplified employee pension (SEP) IRA,[36] the trust is essentially a common law revocable inter vivos trust.

In order for an IRA to qualify as such, the Internal Revenue Code requires that the trustee of any associated trust be a bank, a thrift institution, an insurance company, a brokerage firm, or any other person who demonstrates to the IRS that he or she will administer the account in a manner consistent with the requirements of the law.[37] It should be noted that by these provisions the Internal Revenue Code is not bestowing trust powers on such institutions or otherwise preempting state law[38]—it is merely laying down requirements that must be met if an individual is to enjoy the tax deferral advantages of an IRA.

One requirement for tax deferral is that the IRA trustee may not invest trust assets in works of art, rugs, antiques, metals, gems, stamps, coins, or other items of tangible personal property specified by the IRS.[39] Amounts invested in such "collectibles" are treated for tax purposes as distributions to the individual.[40] However, gold or silver coins issued by the U.S. government or any type of coin issued under the laws of any state will not be considered collectibles.[41] An interest in a portion of a gold coin portfolio is not considered a collectible.[42]

It is a common misconception that under federal law, an IRA trust affords the same protection from creditors as a trust associated with a qualified employee benefit plan. A qualified plan is established under Section 401 of the Code. To be sure, that section has an anti-alienation requirement that appears to preempt state property law. An IRA on the other hand is established under Section 408 of the Code, a section that contains no such anti-alienation provision.

Thus, the trustee should first look to see if an applicable state statute speaks to the rights of creditors in the IRA context. If there is no such statute, then, unless the taxpayer has filed for bankruptcy,[43] the assets in an IRA trust likely would be reachable by the taxpayer's creditors. This is because in an ever-increasing number of jurisdictions, assets held in a common law inter vivos trust, are reachable by creditors of the settlor-beneficiary.[44]

---

[35] *See generally* I.R.C. §408.

[36] In a SEP IRA, the employee establishes the arrangement and the employer participates in its funding and administration. I.R.C. §408(k).

[37] *See* I.R.C. §408(a)(2).

[38] *See* I.R.C. §408(h).

[39] *See* I.R.C. §408(m).

[40] I.R.C. §408(m)(3).

[41] I.R.C. §408(m)(3).

[42] I.R.C. §408(m)(3)(A). *See also* Priv. Ltr. Rul. 89-40-067 (July 12, 1989).

[43] *See* Rousey v. Jacoway, 125 S. Ct. 1561 (2005) (exempting IRA assets from the bankruptcy estate under 11 U.S.C. §522(d)(10)(E)).

[44] *See* §5.3.3.3(d) of this handbook (trusteed employee benefit plans and IRAs).

§9.5.3 The Rabbi Trust (Nonqualified Executive Deferred Compensation)

Taxpayers can use a number of strategies to avoid application of the economic benefit doctrine. . . . [O]ne strategy is to ensure . . . that the employer's promise to pay is subject to the claims of the employer's creditors. One variation of such a promise is the rabbi trust, so called because the first ruling on such a trust was issued to a synagogue that created a trust as a deferred compensation arrangement for its rabbi.[45]

A rabbi trust is a trust established incident to a contract between an employer and an employee to defer taxable compensation until the happening of some future event, such as the employee's death, disability, retirement, or termination of employment. The primary difference between a rabbi trust and a trust associated with a tax-qualified employee benefit plan[46] is that the assets in the rabbi trust are subject to the claims of the employer's creditors in the event of the employer's insolvency. To the extent funds are transferred irrevocably to the trustee of a rabbi trust, the employee-beneficiary has a contingent equitable interest in the trust property, the condition precedent being that the employer not become insolvent before all the deferred compensation is paid out. Though the trust is not administered solely for the benefit of the employee-beneficiary, the contingent equitable interest is nonetheless an equitable property right. That being the case, the employee-beneficiary is afforded some measure of security against a breach of the deferred compensation contract.

A rabbi trust is deemed a grantor trust for tax purposes.[47] This means that the income generated by the trust property while in the hands of the trustee is taxable to the employer-settlor. If the governing instrument meets IRS specifications,[48] the transfer of funds to the trustee is not a taxable event. In other words, the employee-beneficiary will not be deemed to have "constructively received" the funds for income tax purposes. The other side of the coin is that the employer-settlor at the time of transfer will not be entitled to a tax deduction. When funds are ultimately paid out to the employee-beneficiary, however, the employer-settlor receives an income tax deduction as they are paid and the employee receives taxable income.

The Department of Labor has ruled that rabbi trusts, while certainly funded for trust law purposes, are not "funded" employee benefit plans for ERISA purposes. That takes them out from under Title 1 of ERISA with its participation, vesting, and funding requirements. Likewise such trusts are not

---

[45] Robert B. Chapman, *A Matter of Trust, or Why ERISA-Qualified Is Nonsense Upon Stilts: The Tax and Bankruptcy Treatment of Section 457 Deferred Compensation Plans as Exemplar*, 40 Willamette L. Rev. 1, 18 (2004) (referring to Priv. Ltr. Rul. 81-13-107, 1980 WL 137740 (IRS PLR)).

[46] *See generally* §9.5.1 of this handbook (the tax-qualified employee benefit trust).

[47] *See* §9.1 of this handbook (the grantor trust). Note also that the trustee of a rabbi trust must file a fiduciary income tax return. *See* Chapter 10 of this handbook (the income taxation of trusts).

[48] *See* Rev. Proc. 92-64.

deemed "funded" for tax purposes such that an employee-beneficiary would realize taxable income at the time property is transferred to the trustee.

§9.6   Business Trusts; Trusts That Generally Function Like Corporations or Agencies

The arrangement at which the Sherman Antitrust Act was directed was a business application of the trust form. The Standard Oil Company, for example, induced stockholders in various enterprises to assign their stock to a board of trustees and to receive dividend-bearing trust certificates in return. The board was thus able to manage simultaneously enterprises that many believed should have been in active competition. Soon most business combinations in restraint of trade came to be called trusts, whether in the legal form of a trust or otherwise.[1]

The Massachusetts or business trust, which is also called a common-law trust, is essentially a business organization cast in the trust form. It is said to have originated in Massachusetts to circumvent a prohibition in that state against the organization of corporations to deal in real estate.[2]

Introduction. A trust can be employed to facilitate the management of certain property and to make it readily divisible and transferable.[3] Let us assume, for example, that the owner of an apartment building wishes over a period of time to give it and the land on which it sits to his grandchildren. He might transfer the land and building to a trustee and take back 100 certificates, each representing a 1 percent fully vested beneficial interest in the trust. As time goes by he parcels out the certificates to his grandchildren.[4] "These certificates, which resemble certificates for shares of stock in a corporation and are issued and transferred in like manner, entitle the holders to share ratably in the

---

§9.6   [1] Columbia Encyclopedia (5th ed. 1993) at 2793. *See generally* 1 Scott & Ascher §9.1. *See* Hecht v. Malley, 265 U.S. 144, 146–147 (1924) (the U.S. Supreme Court defining a business trust as "an arrangement whereby property is conveyed to trustees, in accordance with the terms of an instrument of trust, to be held and managed for the benefit of such persons as may from time to time be the holders of transferable certificates issued by the trustees showing the shares into which the beneficial interest in the property is divided").

[2] Herbert B. Chermside, Jr., Modern Status of the Massachusetts or Business Trust, 88 A.L.R.3d 704 (2006). *See also* Am. Jur. 2d *Business Trusts* §§1–107; Charles E. Rounds, Jr. & Andreas Dehio, *Publicly-Traded Open End Mutual Funds in Common Law and Civil Law Jurisdictions: A Comparison of Legal Structures*, 3 N.Y.U.J.L. & Bus. 473 (2007).

[3] *See generally* Bogert §§247–252.

[4] *See generally* Jason M. Scally, *Practitioners Needn't File Entire Trust Document*, 31 Mass. Law. Wkly., Jan. 13, 2003, at 905, 939 col. 4 (although the establishment of a nominee trust to take title to Massachusetts real estate may no longer be necessary to keep the personally sensitive provisions of one's revocable inter vivos trust instrument and other such private documentation off the public record, there now being legislation authorizing the filing in the registry deeds of a trust "certificate" in lieu of the entire trust instrument, the nominee trust "will still probably be used. . . [in Massachusetts]. . . in the business context or for making installment gifts of real estate").

income of the property, and upon termination of the trust, in the proceeds."[5] Sometimes, in lieu of certificates, the proportional ownership of the equitable interest, to include changes of ownership, are memorialized by notations on a separate schedule. Upon the transfer of a beneficial interest, it is generally the responsibility of the transferee-beneficiary to inform the trustee of the transfer. A trustee who does not have actual or constructive knowledge of the transfer of a share of beneficial interest ought not to be held liable for any misdelivery of income and/or principal to the transferor.[6] The nominee trust, the realty trust, the Massachusetts business trust,[7] the voting trust,[8] the investment trust (trusteed mutual fund),[9] the real estate investment trust (a type of mutual fund),[10] the Delaware business trust,[11] and the Illinois land trust[12] are some of the types of trusts that have these corporate attributes.[13] While these arrangements are particularly suited to administering real estate, there is no reason why they may not serve as vehicles for administering other types of

---

[5] Herbert B. Chermside, Jr., *Modern Status of the Massachusetts or Business Trust*, 88 A.L.R.3d 704 (2006).

[6] *See generally* Baar v. Fidelity & Columbia Trust Co., 302 KY 91, 193 S.W.2d 1011 (1946) (holding the trustee of a business trust with actual, though not formal, knowledge of the transfer of certain shares of beneficial interest liable to the transferee for misdelivery of dividends to the transferor).

[7] Many mutual funds are structured as Massachusetts business trusts. *See generally* Bogert §247; Jones, Moret, & Storey, *The Massachusetts Business Trust and Registered Investment Companies*, 13 Del. J. Corp. L. 421 (1988); Herbert B. Chermside, Jr., J.D., Annot., *Modern status of the Massachusetts or business trust*, 88 A.L.R.3d 704 (1978). *See also* Mary Ann Tynan, *Form of Investment Company Organization: Corporation vs. Massachusetts Business Trust*, 515 PLI/Corp 55 (1986) (containing in Appendix A therein a copy of the notice to shareholders of a special meeting to approve the reorganization of Fidelity Magellan Fund, Inc., as a Massachusetts Business Trust).

"A . . . 'Massachusetts . . . [business] . . . trust' is a form of business organization consisting essentially of an arrangement whereby property is conveyed to trustees, in accordance with the terms of an instrument of trust, to be held and managed for the benefit of such persons as may from time to time be holders of transferable certificates issued by trustees showing the shares into which the beneficial interest is divided, which certificates entitled the holders to share ratably in the income of the property, and, on termination of the trust, in the proceeds thereof. . . ." 12A C.J.S. *Business Trusts* §2 (Definitions).

[8] *See generally* Bogert §252; E. Le Fevre, Annot., *Removal of trustees of voting Trust*, 34 A.L.R.2d 1136 (1954).

[9] *See generally* Bogert §248; §8.10 of this handbook (fiduciary principles applicable to the mutual fund).

[10] *See generally* Bogert §248.

[11] *See generally* Tamar Frankel, *The Delaware Business Trust Act Failure as the New Corporate Law*, 23 Cardozo L. Rev. 325 (2002); Florack & Lubaroff, *Delaware Business Trusts*, 937 PLI/Corp 371 (1996). *See also* Martin I. Lubaroff, *Form of Delaware Business Trust Agreement*, 938 PLI/Corp 393 (1996).

[12] *See generally* Bogert §249. *See also* Taylor v. Richmond's New Approach Ass'n, Inc., 351 So. 2d 1094 (Fla.1977) (defining an Illinois land trust as a trust whereby title to real property is taken in the name of the trustee under a recorded deed of trust while a second unrecorded agreement between the trustee and the beneficiaries declares the trustee to be vested with full legal and equitable title subject to certain specified rights of the beneficiaries, which are declared to be the personal property of the beneficiaries).

[13] *See generally* Langbein, *The Secret Life of the Trust: The Trust as an Instrument of Commerce*, 107 Yale L.J. 165 (1997).

property.[14] In fact, most trusteed mutual funds, are either Massachusetts business trusts or Delaware statutory trusts.[15]

The nominee & business trust. The key characteristic of these corporation-like and/or partnership-like trust arrangements is that the trustee has the legal title[16] and the beneficiaries have fully vested transferable shares of beneficial interest.[17] Thus, in theory, the inter vivos or postmortem transfer of a share of beneficial interest ought not to trigger public filings at the registry of deeds or a cumbersome subdividing of the underlying asset.[18] The arrangement, as well, may offer a measure of confidentiality and convenience of management in the face of fractured ownership.[19] Under the governing instrument, the management responsibilities of the trustee, the one with the legal title, may be intense (*e.g.*, the mutual fund) or virtually nonexistent (*e.g.*, the nominee trust).[20] When the trustee's role is a passive one, as is the case with most nominee trusts, "[s]uch a trustee is entitled to compensation only if it appears from all of the circumstances that this was the intention of the parties."[21] In other words, the nominee trustee's compensation is essentially contract-based.

Generally not a vehicle for limiting tort liability in a noncommercial setting. If the owner of an automobile, for example, transfers legal title to it to the trustee of a nominee trust in exchange for fully vested transferable shares of beneficial/ equitable interest, is the trustee or the owner of the shares, or neither, primarily

---

[14] *See, e.g.*, Nathaniel Popper, *Restyled as Real Estate Trusts, Varied Businesses Avoid Taxes*, N.Y. Times (Apr. 21, 2013) ("It is not a far stretch to envision REITs concentrated in railroads, highways, mines, landfills, vineyards, farmland or any other 'immovable' structure that generates revenues."). *Cf.* Charles E. Rounds, Jr. & Andreas Dehio, *Publicly-Traded Open End Mutual Funds in Common Law and Civil Law Jurisdictions: A Comparison of Legal Structures*, 3 N.Y.U.J.L. & Bus. 473, 498–500 (2007). (In Germany, in order to avoid some of the red tape of real estate title registration, the sponsor of a real estate mutual fund will typically employ the *Treuhand*, a civil law contractual relationship that has some of the attributes of a common law trust.)

[15] *See generally* Charles E. Rounds, Jr. & Andreas Dehio, *Publicly-Traded Open End Mutual Funds in Common Law and Civil Law Jurisdictions: A Comparison of Legal Structures*, 3 N.Y.U.J.L. & Bus. 473 (2007).

[16] Note, however, that in the case of a statutory trust created under the Uniform Statutory Trust Entity Act, legal title to the subject property can be in the trust "entity" itself. *See* Uniform Statutory Trust Entity Act §307.

[17] "The feature of transferable certificates of beneficial interest is regarded as an essential component of a true Massachusetts or business trust, and in the absence of the right to issue transferable shares, it has been held that the organization is not a business trust." Herbert B. Chermside, Jr., *Modern Status of the Massachusetts or Business Trust*, 88 A.L.R.3d 704 (2006).

[18] *Cf.* Charles E. Rounds, Jr. & Andreas Dehio, *Publicly-Traded Open End Mutual Funds in Common Law and Civil Law Jurisdictions: A Comparison of Legal Structures*, 3 N.Y.U.J.L & Bus. 473, 498–500 (2007). (In Germany, in order to avoid some of the red tape of real estate title registration, the sponsor of a real estate mutual fund will typically employ the *Treuhand*, a civil law contractual relationship that has some of the attributes of a common law trust.)

[19] *See generally* Charles E. Rounds, Jr., *State Common Law Aspects of the Global Unwindings of the Madoff Ponzi Scheme and the Sub-Prime Mortgage Securitization Debacle*, 27 Wis. Int'l L.J. 99 (2009).

[20] There is no such thing as a passive trustee of a troubled collection of assets. *See generally* Charles E. Rounds, Jr., *State Common Law Aspects of the Global Unwindings of the Madoff Ponzi Scheme and the Sub-Prime Mortgage Securitization Debacle*, 27 Wis. Int'l L.J. 99 (2009).

[21] 4 Scott & Ascher §21.1.4 (Passive and Informal Trusts).

liable in tort should there be an accident due to the beneficial/equitable owner's negligent operation of the vehicle? Or are they perhaps jointly liable? Or is only the trust estate at risk? It seems settled that the shareowner is the one primarily and personally exposed, absent special facts or a statute to the contrary.[22] Had title to the vehicle been transferred to the trustee of a garden-variety self-settled trust under which the transferor had reserved a general inter vivos power of appointment (such as a right to revoke the trust and get back title to the vehicle), it is suggested that the result would be the same.[23] The transferor would be the one exposed to primary and personal liability, absent special facts. Certainly for purposes of applying the rule against perpetuities, the holder of a general inter vivos power of appointment incident to a trust relationship is deemed to own the entrusted property outright and free of trust.[24] So also for taxation,[25] welfare-eligibility,[26] and creditor-accessibility purposes.[27] There is no discernible policy reason why this should not also be the case for tort liability purposes.

Equity's creative commercial applications have ancient roots. It is worth a mention here that the seeds of the equitable property interest's current "elasticity"—the U.S. real estate investment trust (U.S.-REIT) particularly comes to mind—were sown long ago:

> One of the principal purposes in creating uses was to avoid the application of rules of law. The chancellors felt at liberty to select the rules of law that they viewed as equitable and to reject those they felt were harsh, arbitrary, or obsolete. They refused to apply legal rules that rested on the technical doctrine of seisin or other feudal ideas that had already become antiquated. For example, they refused to follow the legal rules requiring continuity in seisin and permitted springing and shifting uses. They did not subject the cestui que use to the feudal burdens imposed on the owners of legal estates. They permitted devises of uses long before the Statute of Wills permitted devises of legal estates. Although the chancellors often treated the interest of the cestui que use as an estate of land, they introduced an elasticity into the law of equitable estates that was lacking in the law of legal estates.[28]

The trust had become an unruly creature as the nineteenth century was drawing to a close on this side of the Atlantic. On this side of the Atlantic, the dramatic focusing of economic power in the hands of a few trustees as the nineteenth century drew to a close was just another manifestation of the trust's elasticity, dynamism,

---

[22] *See, e.g.,* Morrison v. Lennett, 415 Mass. 857, 616 N.E. 2d 92 (1993) ("In prior decisions, involving nominee provisions in trust instruments, the court has disregarded the trustees' record ownership of the property and liability has been imposed directly on the beneficiaries.").

[23] *See* Restatement (Third) of Property (Wills and Other Donative Transfers) §17.4, cmt. f(1) ("A presently exercisable general power of appointment is an ownership-equivalent power."). *See also* Restatement (Third) of Trusts §74.

[24] *See generally* §8.2.1.1 of this handbook.

[25] *See generally* §8.9.3 of this handbook.

[26] *See generally* §5.3.5 of this handbook.

[27] *See generally* §5.3.3.1 of this handbook.

[28] 3 Scott & Ascher §13.1.

adaptability, and general staying power as an instrument of commerce.[29] At the close of the nineteenth century, Henry Adams found the huge business trusts charged with "vigorous and unscrupulous energy."[30] He saw them as "revolutionary, troubling all the old conventions and values, as the screws of ocean steamers must trouble a school of herring."[31] The trust is tamer today, but only somewhat. In July 2009 the private trustee of the SPDR Gold Trust (GLD), an ETF mutual fund, was holding legal title to more gold than any sovereign entity, with the exception of the United States, Germany, the International Monetary Fund (IMF), France, and Italy; and the major U.S. institutional trustees were holding in their portfolios billions of dollars worth of toxic assets, mostly sub-prime mortgages, for the benefit of the global investing public.[32] For good and for ill, those at the commercial cutting edge are still exploiting the trust's protean nature, as one Bermuda lawyer has noted:

> Many of the new and exciting innovations in trust law have been developed by non-trust lawyers seeking to achieve results that are not available using traditional tools. For example, commercial . . . [lawyers,] . . . funds . . . or tax lawyers may find that they cannot achieve a desired result by using a corporation, partnership, contract, agency or bailment. In some cases a trust is the ideal tool, as it is a relationship governed by a body of legal principles, subject to modification by legislation. Business lawyers are coming to appreciate the appeal of a trust—it is incredibly flexible.[33]

Commercial trusts have agency and corporate attributes. As noted, trusts that are instruments of commerce tend to behave somewhat like agencies[34] or corporations.[35] The shares of vested beneficial interests, for example, are generally alienable like shares of corporate stock.[36] A share of beneficial interest being an item of intangible personal property, it generally may be pledged or sold by the holder.[37] Should the holder die without having alienated the interest, it is likely to end up either in the holder's estate or in a marital deduction or family trust established under an instrument that the holder executed while alive. A share of

---

[29] *See* this section's introductory quote.

[30] Henry Adams, The Education of Henry Adams Ch. XXXV (1918).

[31] Henry Adams, The Education of Henry Adams Ch. XXXV (1918).

[32] *See generally* Charles E. Rounds, Jr., *State Common Law Aspects of the Global Unwindings of the Madoff Ponzi Scheme and the Sub-Prime Mortgage Securitization Debacle*, 27 Wis. Int'l L.J. 99 (2009).

[33] Randall Krebs, *Flexible friend*, 16(2) STEP J. 15 (Feb. 2008). (discussing the commercial uses of trusts in Bermuda).

[34] *See generally* Roberts v. Roberts, 419 Mass. 685, 646 N.E.2d 1061 (1995). *See also* Moscatiello v. Board of Assessors of Boston, 36 Mass. App. Ct. 622, 626, 634 N.E.2d 147, 149 (1994) ("We recognize that, for many purposes, nominee trusts are regarded as creating a principal-agent, rather than a true trustee-beneficiary, relationship. . . . Taxing authorities sometimes disregard nominee trust arrangements altogether.").

[35] *See generally* Charles E. Rounds, Jr. & Andreas Dehio, *Publicly-Traded Open End Mutual Funds in Common Law and Civil Law Jurisdictions: A Comparison of Legal Structures*, 3 N.Y.U.J.L. & Bus. 473 (2007).

[36] *See, e.g.*, Uniform Statutory Trust Entity Act §601(a) ("A beneficial interest in a statutory trust is freely transferable.").

[37] *See, e.g.*, Lawn Sav. & Loan Ass'n v. Quinn, 81 Ill. App. 2d 304, 225 N.E.2d 683 (1967).

beneficial interest in a Dutch *stichting administratiekantoor*, a civil law nominee-trust analog, would likely suffer a similar fate, that is to say, the share of beneficial interest (depository receipt) would likely pass to the deceased holder's heirs-at-law.

A trustee is first and foremost a principal. Still, the trustee of a nominee or business trust is a principal.[38] Thus, absent special facts, it cannot be said that legally he is an employee or an agent of the trust.[39] Nor can it be said that that the holders from time to time of the shares of beneficial are constructive general partners owing fiduciary duties to one another. At least one court has so held.[40]

The commercial advantages of the trust's hybrid nature. The hybrid nature of these arrangements offers practical advantages, particularly in the real estate conveyancing area. Let us take the common law nominee trust, which is permitted in every state except Louisiana[41] and operates somewhat like a realty trust under which those with the beneficial interests jointly possess a general inter vivos power of appointment. Because the arrangement is a trust, the trustee's power to transfer the underlying property is "autonomous."[42] In other words, as noted, the trustee's legal function is that of a principal, particularly when it comes to transacting with third parties on behalf of the trust. On the other hand, in equity the trustee is, for all intents and purposes, an agent of the beneficiaries:

> The terms of the trust may provide that the trustee is merely to hold title to the trust property and that management and control are to be in the hands of the settlor, the beneficiaries, or a third party. In such a case, the trustee is not guilty of improper delegation for permitting the appropriate person to administer the trust.[43]

The terms of such a hybrid trust may bestow on the trustee the power to pass good title and may relieve purchasers for value of any need to look behind that express authority, unless such purchasers are in possession of actual

---

[38] *See generally* Charles E. Rounds, Jr. & Andreas Dehio, *Publicly-Traded Open End Mutual Funds in Common Law and Civil Law Jurisdictions: A Comparison of Legal Structures*, 3 N.Y.U.J.L. & Bus. 473 (2007).

[39] *See, e.g.*, Loring v. United States, 80 F. Supp. 781 (D. Mass. 1948).

[40] *See* Krensky v. DeSwarte, 335 Ill. App. 435, 82 N.E.2d 168 (1948) (holders of shares of beneficial interest in a business trust not having fiduciary duties that run to one another, one holder may enter into a contract with the trustees for the purchase of the trust property, even though the holder had already in place an arrangement to turn around and sell the property to a third party at a profit).

[41] *See* Louis H. Hamel, Jr., *Keeping a Vacation Home in the Family for Younger Generations*, 23(3) Est. Plan. 123, 126 (Mar./Apr. 1996). *See also* §3.5.2.2 of this handbook (right at law to transfer title). Although it must be admitted that in a number of states, most notably New York, the nominee trust is not widely used.

[42] Louis H. Hamel, Jr., *Keeping a Vacation Home in the Family for Younger Generations*, 23(3) Est. Plan. 123, 127 (Mar./Apr. 1996).

[43] 3 Scott & Ascher §17.3.1.

knowledge that something is awry.[44] If a conveyance is in defiance of the beneficiaries' off-record instructions, then it is an equitable matter between the beneficiaries and the trustee. If the beneficiaries are at loggerheads, that is their problem. The legal title of the good-faith purchaser for value (*i.e.*, the BFP)[45] is secure.

It should be noted that in the case of real estate, a signed purchase and sale agreement would not be enough to qualify as a BFP.[46] There would have to have been an actual conveyance.[47] One learned commentator offers some practical observations that are grounded in a subtle appreciation of the nominee trust's common law underpinnings:

> However sound the legal theory may be, a conveyancing agreement is nearly useless if it does not feel comfortable to the local conveyancing bar. The nominee trust would be a novelty in many places (New Hampshire, for example, found it necessary to soothe conveyancers by statute when they worried about the Statute of Uses),[48] but it is merely a new combination of old common law components.... The nominee trust and the deed of conveyance are the only recorded instruments. The others [*e.g.*, the schedule of beneficial interests] can be recorded in a pinch, but no one would record them unless the scheme to blind the purchaser to backstage activities has failed. The deliberate purpose is to split the known world into two parts—the world of the purchaser and the world of relationships among the trustees and beneficiaries. A third world . . . is the world of relationships among the beneficiaries (which may not involve the trustees).[49]

Whether there is a need to record the shares of beneficial interest. The commentator makes reference to a Massachusetts requirement that the nominee trust instrument be recorded in the registry of deeds. A number of jurisdictions, however, including Arkansas, Connecticut, Delaware, Florida, Georgia, Hawaii, Illinois, Indiana, Iowa, Michigan, Missouri, Nevada, New York, North Carolina, Oregon, Tennessee, Texas, and Vermont, have no such recording requirement.

---

[44] *See* Louis H. Hamel, Jr., *Keeping a Vacation Home in the Family for Younger Generations*, 23(3) Est. Plan. 123, 126 (Mar./Apr. 1996). *See also* §3.5.2.2 of this handbook (trustee's right at law to transfer title). Although it must be admitted that in a number of states, most notably New York, the nominee trust is not widely used. *See also* §8.21 of this handbook (duty of third parties to investigate whether trustee has power to act or is properly exercising the power).

[45] *See* 5 Scott & Ascher §29.1.1 (Bona Fide Purchaser). *See generally* §5.4.2 of this handbook (rights of the beneficiary as against transferees of the underlying property, including BFPs), §8.3.2 of this handbook (bona fide purchase for value of trust property: what constitutes notice that a transfer is in breach of trust), and §8.15.63 of this handbook (doctrine of bona fide purchase; the BFP). *See also* §8.3.6 of this handbook (negotiable instruments and the duty of third parties to inquire into the trustee's authority). For a comparison of the BFP, a creature of equity, with the holder in due course, a creature of law, *see* §8.15.68 of this handbook (holders in due course in the trust context).

[46] *See generally* §8.15.63 of this handbook (doctrine of bona fide purchase); 5 Scott & Ascher §29.1.1 (Bona Fide Purchaser).

[47] *See generally* 4 Scott on Trusts §311.

[48] *See* §8.15.1 of this handbook (statute of uses).

[49] *See* Louis H. Hamel, Jr., *Keeping a Vacation Home in the Family for Younger Generations*, 23(3) Est. Plan. 123, 127 (Mar./Apr. 1996).

Even Massachusetts now has a statute that allows for the recording or registering of a certificate that sets forth information about the trust in lieu of recording or registering a copy of the trust instrument itself.[50]

> The recorded or registered certificate constitutes conclusive evidence of the facts recited in the certificate and the authority of the trustee or trustees to act with respect to real estate held in the trust. Third parties can rely on the information contained in the certificate. Successor trustees would subsequently record or register a certificate to indicate their succession to the trusteeship. The most recently recorded certificate in the registry for the county or district in which the real estate is located shall control. The Act precludes having to record or register trusts that hold an interest in real estate in order to convey good title or provide record evidence of the holder of a mortgage for the purpose of recording a discharge or partial release. This puts Massachusetts practice in this regard in line with the vast majority of, if not all, other states.[51]

Apart from whether or not a trust instrument should be recorded in some registry when the subject property is real estate, a tension has always existed between the need of third parties to ascertain a trustee's authority to enter into a particular transaction[52] and the desire of the beneficiaries for privacy.[53] A number of states have harmonized these competing public policy considerations by affording certain statutory protections to third parties who rely on a trustee's "certification of trust."[54] The third parties need not, and in some cases may not, scrutinize the trust instrument itself.[55] The trustees of testamentary trusts, of course, are on the sidelines in this particular clash of interests as a probated will is generally a public record.

Liability of a third party who fails to honor a Uniform Trust Code §1013 certification. The trustee of the typical trust will have numerous occasions to transact with third parties in furtherance of the trust's lawful purposes. This is appropriate as the trustee holds the legal title to the trust property, and thus, "as to the world," is its owner. A third party might be selling an asset to, or

---

[50] Mass. Gen. Laws ch. 184, §35; Mass. Gen. Laws ch. 203, §2. The certificate should contain (1) the identity of the trustees or the beneficiaries of the trust; (2) the authority of the trustees to act with respect to real estate owned by the trust; and (3) the existence or nonexistence of any facts that constitute conditions precedent to acts by the trustees or that are in any other way germane to the affairs of the trust.

[51] Mass. Gen. Laws ch. 184, §35; Mass. Gen. Laws ch. 203, §2. The certificate should contain (1) the identity of the trustees or the beneficiaries of the trust; (2) the authority of the trustees to act with respect to real estate owned by the trust; and (3) the noted, existence or nonexistence of any facts that constitute conditions precedent to acts by the trustees or that are in any other way germane to the affairs of the trust.

[52] *See generally* §8.21 of this handbook (duty of third parties to investigate whether trustee has power to act or is properly exercising the power).

[53] *See generally* Frances H. Foster, *Privacy and the Elusive Quest for Uniformity in the Law of Trusts*, 38 Ariz. St. L.J. 713 (2006).

[54] *See generally* Frances H. Foster, *Privacy and the Elusive Quest for Uniformity in the Law of Trusts*, 38 Ariz. St. L.J. 713 (2006).

[55] *See generally* Frances H. Foster, *Privacy and the Elusive Quest for Uniformity in the Law of Trusts*, 38 Ariz. St. L.J. 713 (2006).

purchasing an entrusted asset from, the trustee. A third party might be loaning funds to the trustee in his fiduciary capacity or borrowing entrusted property from the trustee. A third party might be selling goods and services to the trustee or purchasing goods and services from the trustee, all in furtherance of the trust's lawful purposes. The trustee also may properly retain third-party agents in furtherance of the trust's lawful purposes, such as attorneys-at-law and investment managers.

Section 1013(h) of the Uniform Trust Code provides as follows: "A person . . . [other than a beneficiary] . . . making a demand for the trust instrument in addition to a certification of trust or excerpts is liable for damages if the court determines that the person did not act in good faith in demanding the instrument."

The information in a trustee's UTC §1013 certification is limited to the following bits of information:

- That the trust exists and its date of execution
- The identity of the settlors
- The powers of the trustee
- The revocability or irrevocability of the trust and the identity of any persons holding a power to revoke
- The authority of cotrustees to sign or otherwise authenticate and whether all or less than all are required in order to exercise the powers of the trustee
- The trust's taxpayer identification number
- The manner of taking title to trust property
- A statement that the trust has not been revoked, modified, or amended in any manner that would cause the representations contained in the certification to be incorrect

A UTC §1013 certification, however, "need not contain the dispositive terms of a trust." Unexplained are the nature of the "liability" and "damages" that are being contemplated by subsection (h). Nor is a definition of "good faith" even supplied in this context. Presumably, the third party is subject to some type of tort liability, but what duty of care is implicated by the "making of a demand for a trust instrument"? According to the section's official commentary, left to "other law" is the issue of "how damages for a bad faith refusal are to be computed." Also unspecified is to whom this demanding "person" would be liable in the face of a judicial determination of liability.

A third party contemplating dealing with a trustee should be able contractually to defang UTC Section 1013(h), assuming it actually has fangs. Time will tell whether it actually does in the face of all this statutory vagueness.

May UTC Section 1013's general applicability be negated effectively *ab initio* by the trust's terms? In the face of subsection (g) of UTC Section 1013, some settlors may want to consider doing just that so as to better protect the equitable property rights of the beneficiaries of their trusts. Subsection (g) provides as follows: "A person who in good faith enters into a transaction in reliance upon a certification of trust may enforce the transaction *against the trust property* [emphasis supplied] as if the representations contained in the certification were correct." The problem is that the third party who is not furnished a copy of the trust instrument, only a cryptic trustee certification, will not be privy to the UTC Section 1013 negation provision and therefore may well not be bound by its terms.

When the beneficiary is granted a power to control the trustee. As noted, it will often be the case that the holders of the shares of beneficial interest in a nominee trust or business trust collectively will possess the power to control and direct the trustee. Even so, fiduciary duties run from the trustee to the holders, not the other way around. When disagreements between and among the shareholders of such a trust frustrate the trustee's ability to administer properly the trust or otherwise carry out its purposes, then the trustee has an affirmative duty to bring the matter before the court. The court is empowered to order a liquidation of the underlying property and a pro rata distribution of the proceeds outright and free of trust to the shareholders,[56] or to effect such other equitable resolution of the matter as it may deem appropriate.

Trustee and beneficiary liability considerations. These corporate-like/agency-like trust arrangements also raise a number of tax and securities regulation issues which are well beyond the scope of this handbook.[57] There is also, however, the issue of limited liability, which deserves at least a mention here. It is a matter of paramount concern to all parties, trustees and beneficiaries alike. Do the certificate owners as the equitable owners and the trustee as the legal owner of the land and building enjoy limited liability as they might if the land and building were inside a corporation?[58] What about the general rule that the beneficiary incurs no liabilities arising inherently out of his beneficial ownership, except for taxes?[59] Would such a rule apply to these corporate-like/agency-like trust arrangements? Unfortunately, it is impossible to generalize with respect to these issues. It depends upon the facts and circumstances and the jurisdiction.[60]

---

[56] *See, e.g.,* Regas v. Danigeles, 54 Ill. App. 2d 271, 203 N.E.2d 730 (1964).

[57] For a brief summary of the federal income tax treatment of corporate-like trusts, *see* Bogert §§270.30–270.40; for matters relating to securities regulation, *see generally* L. Loss & J. Seligman, Securities Regulation (3d ed. 1993). *See also Problems of Fiduciaries Under the Securities Laws,* 20 Real Prop. Prob. & Tr. J. 503 (1985).

[58] *See generally* Bogert §247. *See* §7.3 of this handbook (trustee's liability as legal owner to nonbeneficiaries) and §8.22 of this handbook (whether we need the trust when we have the corporation and the third party beneficiary contract).

[59] *See generally* Bogert §247. *See* §5.6 of this handbook (duties and liabilities of the beneficiary).

[60] *See* Bogert §247 E-G, K (outlining jurisdictional differences). In many states, beneficiaries avoid personal liability unless they have substantial control over the trustees or the management of the trust business. *See, e.g.,* Minkin v. Commissioner of Revenue, 40 Mass. App. Ct. 345, 347, 664 N.E.2d 851, 853 (1996), *rev'd on other grounds,* 425 Mass. 174, 680 N.E.2d 27 (1997); Just Pants v. Bank of Ravenswood, 136 Ill. App. 3d 543, 483 N.E.2d 331 (1985); Pennsylvania Co. for Insurances [sic] on Lives and Granting Annuities v. Wallace, 346 Pa. 532, 31 A.2d 71 (1943). *But see* Sylvia v. Johnson, 44 Mass. App. Ct. 483, 691 N.E.2d 608 (1998) (holding beneficiaries were not personally liable on contract with third party even though beneficiaries were also trustees and controlled the trust because third party had knowledge of nonrecourse clause in trust); Del. Laws

In Massachusetts, for example, a trustee is personally liable for torts committed in the course of administering a trust the purpose of which is to develop real estate.[61] Moreover, in Massachusetts it is likely that both the trustee and the beneficiaries of a nominee trust would be subject to liability to third parties for torts committed in the course of administering the trust property.[62] This is likely to be the case in Illinois as well, particularly if the wrongful acts were done at the instigation of the beneficiaries.[63] Under Massachusetts law, the holders of the shares of beneficial interest in a Massachusetts business trust, like the limited partners of a limited partnership, enjoy limited liability only so long as they do not participate in the management of the business. In the case of a mutual fund operating as a Massachusetts business trust, the investors "face the remote possibility of being subjected to personal liability for the liabilities of the trust,"[64] this due to their theoretical collective power to control the trustees.[65] Investor exposure, however, as a practical matter, is virtually nonexistent:

> . . . [T]he mutual fund industry and most lawyers conversant with the 1940 Act consider the issue non-material for the following reasons: (i) a mutual fund has substantial assets and virtually no liabilities, thus there should never be an occasion when a mutual fund cannot pay its debts; and (ii) appropriate provisions exonerating shareholders from liability for debts of the trust may be included in the trust instrument and in all contracts with creditors and other third parties dealing with the trust.[66]

---

c. 335 (1998) (amending Del. Code Ann. tit. 12, §3806 to preclude personal liability for persons who control trust or trustee). There are some states, however, that follow the rule that beneficiaries of a business trust are partners and do not enjoy limited liability. *See* Thompson v. Schmitt, 115 Tex. 53, 274 S.W. 554 (1925). Trustees at common law are generally held personally liable unless the third party has knowledge when contracting with the trust that recourse can only be had from the trust. *See* Sylvia v. Johnson, 44 Mass. App. Ct. 483, 691 N.E.2d 608 (1998) (holding trustees not personally liable on contract because third party had knowledge of nonrecourse clause in trust agreement). Some states have enacted statutes that exempt the trustee from personal liability and require the third party to seek recovery from the trust assets only. *See, e.g.,* Del. Code Ann. tit. 12, §§3803 (West 1997); Ky. Rev. Stat. Ann. §386.390 (Banks-Baldwin 1997); Miss. Code Ann. §79-15-9 (West 1997). The Delaware Business Trust Statute is favorable to both trustees and beneficiaries because it provides limited liability for trustees and beneficiaries irrespective of the beneficiaries' level of control. *See* Del. Code Ann. tit. 12, §§3803, 3806 (1997); Del. Laws c. 335 (1998) (amending §3806); Henry Hansmann & Ugo Mattei, *The Functions of Trust Law: A Comparative Legal And Economic Analysis*, 73 N.Y.U. L. Rev. 434, 475 (1998) (discussing limited liability benefits of Delaware Business Trust).

[61] First E. Bank, N.A. v. Jones, 413 Mass. 654, 602 N.E.2d 211 (1992).

[62] *See, e.g.,* Morrison v. Lennett, 415 Mass. 857, 860 (1993) (quoting Johnson v. Holiday Inns, Inc., 595 F.2d 890, 893 (1st. Cir. 1979)).

[63] *See* Piff v. Berresheim, 405 Ill. 617, 92 N.E.2d 113 (1950) (involving an Illinois land trust).

[64] Edward T. O'Dell & Philip H. Newman, *Legal Considerations in Selecting the Form and Jurisdiction of Organization of a Mutual Fund*, C628 ALI-ABA 247, 250 (1991).

[65] *See generally* Sheldon A. Jones, Laura M. Moret, & James M. Storey, *The Massachusetts Business Trust and Registered Investment Companies*, 13 Del. J. Corp. L. 421, 439–441 (1988).

[66] Edward T. O'Dell & Philip H. Newman, *Legal Considerations in Selecting the Form and Jurisdiction of Organization of a Mutual Fund*, C628 ALI-ABA 247, 250 (1991).

Nevertheless, the first thing that the prospective trustee of a corporate-like/agency-like trust arrangement should do is ascertain to what extent (if at all) the liability of the parties is limited.[67] In the case of a statutory trust created under the Uniform Statutory Trust Entity Act, for example, legal liability in contract and/or tort *to third parties* is expressly limited to trust assets.[68] "A beneficial owner, trustee, agent of the trust, or agent of the trustee is not personally liable, directly or indirectly, by way of contribution or otherwise, for a debt, obligation, or other liability of the trust or series thereof solely by reason of being or acting as a trustee, beneficial owner, agent of the trust, or agent of the trustee."[69] This would be the case even if the beneficiaries had the legal and equitable power and authority to control the trustee.[70] (That is not to say that the trustee of a statutory trust could not be held personally liable in equity to the trust "entity," and thus indirectly to the beneficiaries, for a breach of trust.)[71] A general discussion of the alternatives and countermeasures, contractual[72] and otherwise, available to prospective trustees and shareholders in the face of potential unlimited liability to third parties is beyond the scope of this handbook.[73]

It is better that the nominee trust not have contingent equitable interests. It should be noted that the authors over the years have encountered a number of instances where attorneys, particularly conveyancers, have attempted to fashion a nominee or realty trust form into a viable private revocable inter vivos trust instrument. They do this by making the interest of beneficiaries contingent upon such events as survivorship.

Usually the modified instruments are awash in ambiguities and gaps, *i.e.,* contingencies not provided for.[74] The best approach is to keep the corporate-like trust instrument separate from the private inter vivos trust instrument. It is the latter that should contain the contingent provisions, such as those that relate to generational succession and the unborn and unascertained. Moreover, there is no reason why the latter vehicle may not contain as an asset beneficial

---

[67] *See generally* Herbert B. Chermside, Jr., J.D., Annot., *Modern status of the Massachusetts Business Trust,* 88 A.L.R.3d 704 (1978) (in part discussing beneficiary liability issues).

[68] Uniform Statutory Trust Entity Act §304(a).

[69] Uniform Statutory Trust Entity Act §304(a).

[70] Uniform Statutory Trust Entity Act §304 cmt.

[71] Uniform Statutory Trust Entity Act §304 cmt. ("However, nothing in this section limits the personal liability of a trustee to the statutory trust for breach of duty under Section 505.")

[72] *See, e.g.,* Loomis Land & Cattle Co. v. Diversified Mortgage Investors, 533 S.W.2d 420 (1976) (upholding provision in business trust limiting recourse of third parties transacting with the trust to the trust property itself).

[73] *See, however,* Sheldon A. Jones, Laura M. Moret, & James M. Storey, *The Massachusetts Business Trust and Registered Investment Companies,* 13 Del. J. Corp. L. 421, 433–446 (1988) (suggesting practical counter measures that may be taken at the drafting stage and later administratively to reduce or eliminate the personal liabilities of mutual fund trustees and investors).

[74] Joint trusts pose similar problems. *See* UTC §601 cmt. (available at <http://www.uniformlaws.org/Act.aspx?title=Trust%20Code>).

interests in the former.[75] Recall, a share of beneficial interest in a trust, particularly one that is fully vested and transferable, is an item of intangible personal property.

The Uniform Statutory Trust Entity Act. It has long been a principle of law and equity that the trust relationship is fundamentally not a juridical entity/person.[76] In July 2009, the National Conference of Commissioners on Uniform State Laws approved the model Uniform Statutory Trust Entity Act. A trust created under the Act is intended to be a juridical entity, "separate from its trustees and beneficial owners, that has capacity to sue and be sued, own property, and transact in its own name."[77] A statutory trust created under the Act may not have "a predominantly donative purpose."[78] For whatever reason, the critical phrase *predominantly donative purpose* is not defined in the Act, although there is some murky and oblique commentary about excluding trusts established in an "estate planning or other donative context,"[79] commentary that is undermined by the fact that a statutory trust may have a charitable purpose,[80] and by the Reporter's own musings:

> Although the drafting committee contemplated that a statutory trust under this act will be used primarily as a mode of business organization, Section 603(a) confirms that a person may become a beneficial owner of a statutory trust without an exchange of consideration. It is therefore possible that a statutory trust could be used as a substitute for the common-law trust in noncommercial contexts.[81]

The incorporated mutual fund (U.S. and U.K.). A standard U.S. open-end incorporated mutual fund is actually a trust.[82] Title to fund assets is in the corporation, which is governed by directors. The directors are trustees with fiduciary duties that run directly to the investors.[83] The manager, which is typically the sponsor and public face of the fund, is in a contractual and agency

---

[75] *Cf.* Papale-Keefe v. Altomare, 38 Mass. App. Ct. 308 (1995) (involving an uncompleted transfer of shares of beneficial interest in a nominee trust to the trustee of an inter vivos trust). For a brief discussion of the trust issues associated with investment companies (mutual funds), *see* §8.10 of this handbook (fiduciary principles applicable to the mutual fund). *See also* §7.3.3.3 of this handbook (registration and sale of securities). For a discussion of the income taxation of business trusts, *see* §10.7 of this handbook.

[76] *See, e.g.,* Jimenez v. Corr, 764 S.E.2d 115 (Va. 2014) ("In contrast, an inter vivos trust is inseparable from the parties related to it, and the trust does not have a separate legal status.").

[77] Uniform Statutory Trust Entity Act, Prefatory Note.

[78] Uniform Statutory Trust Entity Act §303.

[79] Uniform Statutory Trust Entity Act §303 cmt.

[80] Uniform Statutory Trust Entity Act §303 cmt.

[81] Uniform Statutory Trust Entity Act, Prefatory Note.

[82] *See generally* Charles E. Rounds, Jr. & Andreas Dehio, *Publicly-Traded Open End Mutual Funds in Common Law and Civil Law Jurisdictions: A Comparison of Legal Structures,* 3 N.Y.U. J. L. & Bus. 473 (2007).

[83] *See generally* Charles E. Rounds, Jr. & Andreas Dehio, *Publicly-Traded Open End Mutual Funds in Common Law and Civil Law Jurisdictions: A Comparison of Legal Structures,* 3 N.Y.U. J. L. & Bus. 473 (2007).

relationship with the corporation. The manager provides investment management and other services to the corporation. The investors are the stockholders of the corporation. They are in a contractual relationship with the corporation, the holder of the title to the underlying assets. In equity, the corporate package or shell is actually the trustee of a nominee trust, the underlying trust assets of which are held for the benefit of the director-trustees in their fiduciary capacities.[84] They in turn hold the equitable interest for the benefit of the investor-beneficiaries.[85]

A standard U.K. incorporated open-end mutual fund or open-end investment company (OEIC) is trusteed as well.[86] An OEIC typically has only one director, the fund's sponsor and public face. The director, in most cases a corporation, manages the investing of the underlying assets. An independent depository bank, however, holds the legal title to the underlying fund assets.[87] It also has certain oversight responsibilities. These roles make the depository the functional equivalent of the trustee of a U.S. mutual fund.[88] As well as being in a contractual and agency relationship with the OEIC, the depositary has fiduciary duties that run directly to the investors.[89] The investors are shareholders of the OEIC, which is also known as an "investment company with variable capital."

§9.7   Commingled Trust Funds

MFS Massachusetts Investors Trust began operation in 1924, making it America's first mutual fund. Also started that year was State Street Research Investment Fund. And the other three possible answers listed certainly aren't spring chickens: Pioneer Fund, Vanguard Wellington Fund and Fidelity Fund all opened for business in 1930 or earlier.[1]

---

[84] *See generally* Charles E. Rounds, Jr. & Andreas Dehio, *Publicly-Traded Open End Mutual Funds in Common Law and Civil Law Jurisdictions: A Comparison of Legal Structures*, 3 N.Y.U. J. L. & Bus. 473 (2007).

[85] *See generally* Charles E. Rounds, Jr. & Andreas Dehio, *Publicly-Traded Open End Mutual Funds in Common Law and Civil Law Jurisdictions: A Comparison of Legal Structures*, 3 N.Y.U. J. L. & Bus. 473 (2007).

[86] *See generally* Charles E. Rounds, Jr. & Andreas Dehio, *Publicly-Traded Open End Mutual Funds in Common Law and Civil Law Jurisdictions: A Comparison of Legal Structures*, 3 N.Y.U. J. L. & Bus. 473 (2007).

[87] *See generally* Charles E. Rounds, Jr. & Andreas Dehio, *Publicly-Traded Open End Mutual Funds in Common Law and Civil Law Jurisdictions: A Comparison of Legal Structures*, 3 N.Y.U. J. L. & Bus. 473 (2007).

[88] *See generally* Charles E. Rounds, Jr. & Andreas Dehio, *Publicly-Traded Open End Mutual Funds in Common Law and Civil Law Jurisdictions: A Comparison of Legal Structures*, 3 N.Y.U. J. L. & Bus. 473 (2007).

[89] *See generally* Charles E. Rounds, Jr. & Andreas Dehio, *Publicly-Traded Open End Mutual Funds in Common Law and Civil Law Jurisdictions: A Comparison of Legal Structures*, 3 N.Y.U. J. L. & Bus. 473 (2007).

§9.7 [1] *Quiz Results: Did You Know It All?*, Wall St. J., Apr. 7, 2003, at R33.

As a general rule, the trustee may not commingle the assets of one trust with the assets of other trusts, absent express authority in the governing instrument and/or statutory authority. The IOLTA concept is an exception, the typical IOLTA program having been established by judicial fiat and without the knowledge and consent of those who possess the equitable interests.[2]

§9.7.1 The Common Trust Fund and the Proprietary Mutual Fund

Since about 1928 or 1929, trustmen have been increasingly interested in the idea of improving investment methods for small trusts by means of the common trust fund.[3]

[L]ast year, Bank One Corp.—which has since merged with J.P. Morgan Chase—settled a . . . class-action suit for $9 million in credits towards bank fees. In that case, plaintiffs alleged that their trustee—once First Chicago, subsequently absorbed by Bank One—violated its fiduciary duty by using clients' trust funds to jump start its mutual-fund business.[4]

Background. The common trust fund is a special type of corporate-like trust arrangement that, because of Section 584 of the Internal Revenue Code, is available as a practical matter only to banks and their fiduciary customers. In theory, it allows for cost-efficient, diversified administration of small accounts.[5] It works this way: The bank executes a declaration of trust or plan for the purpose of serving as trustee of a common trust fund. The specifications are set forth in a state statute and in federal regulations, particularly "Regulation 9."[6] The arrangement is then available exclusively for the collective investment and reinvestment of moneys contributed to the fund by the bank in its capacity as trustee of other trusts and as executor and administrator of estates. The bank's guardianships may also participate. Essentially a participating entity, such as a trust, purchases a beneficial interest in a trusteed basket of securities—a piece of another trust. One can see the similarity between the common trust fund and the corporate-like trust arrangements mentioned in Section 9.6 of this handbook (trusts that resemble corporations or agencies).

In the 1930s there had been concern that a common trust fund would be taxed as an association.[7] If that were the case, the common trust fund would

---

[2] *See generally* §9.7.2 of this handbook (IOLTA trusts).

[3] American Bankers Association, *Common Trust Funds* 9 (2d ed. 1948).

[4] Rachel Emma Silverman & Carrick Mollenkamp, *As Financial Services Consolidate, Trust Managers Come Under Fire*, Wall St. J., July 20, 2004, at A4, col. 4.

[5] *See generally* 4 Scott & Ascher §19.1.9 (Combining Trust Funds in Making Investments).

[6] 12 C.F.R. §9.18 (1997) (where consistent with applicable law, a national bank may invest in a common trust fund that meets the requirements of §9.18). *See generally* Bogert §677. Revised Regulation 9 is available at <www.gpoaccess.gov/cfr/index.html>.

[7] *See* Brooklyn Trust Co. v. Comm'r, 80 F.2d 865 (2d Cir. 1936), *cert. denied*, 298 U.S. 659 (1936) (composite fund taxable as an association); Bogert §677.

have no economic utility, because with each participating fiduciary account being subject in any case to tax on income attributable to its participations in the fund, participation in a common trust fund would have effectively generated a double tax. Beginning in 1936 these roadblocks were removed. In that year the precursor to Section 584[8] was enacted into law removing the threat of federal income taxation at the fund level.

In recent years the hot issue associated with the common trust fund has been whether banks should be allowed to commingle their investment management agency accounts. This would effectively give banks the authority to market participations in their common trust funds to the public in competition with mutual fund participations. So far, banks have been unsuccessful in acquiring this authority.[9]

To reiterate, because of Section 584 there is no economic advantage for anyone other than a bank to operate a common trust fund. A nonbank trustee who wishes to afford his small trusts the diversification that comes with commingling must look to the mutual fund.[10] While the default common law has generally prohibited the commingling of the assets of multiple trusts and the delegation by fiduciaries of investment discretion,[11] already by the late 1940s in the United States, a consensus was developing among trust professionals that trustees wishing to prudently invest in mutual funds ought not to be prevented from doing so, at least by such common law proscriptions:

> At one time, there was some doubt whether a trustee could properly invest in mutual funds. The chief objections were that the trustee, in making such an investment, was delegating the duty to select trust investments, and that commissions would thus become payable to both the trustee and the operators of the mutual fund. Over time, these objections have faded.[12]

Not only is the common trust fund exempt from federal taxation, it also enjoys an exemption from federal securities laws under Section 3(a)(2) of the 1933 Act. It is the position of the Comptroller of the Currency that a bank may delegate collective investment fund responsibilities under the new "Prudent Investor" delegation standard without losing either exemption, provided the delegation is prudent.[13]

---

[8] Federal Revenue Act of 1936 §169, 26 U.S.C.A. §169 (1936). *See generally* Bogert §677.

[9] *See* Investment Co. Inst. v. Camp, 401 U.S. 617 (1971). *See generally* Bogert §677; Melanie L. Fein, Securities Activities of Banks §§11.04[A][9] (advertising restriction) and 11.03[F] (Glass-Steagall Act).

[10] 4 Scott & Ascher §19.1.10.

[11] *See* §6.1.4 of this handbook (duty to give personal attention (not to delegate)) and §6.2.1 of this handbook (duty to take active control of, segregate, earmark, and protect trust property).

[12] 4 Scott & Ascher §19.1.10.

[13] *See generally* §8.18 of this handbook (Regulation 9 revised).

Conversion of Common Trust Funds into Mutual Funds. By preemptive legislation and regulation at both the federal and state level, many of the legal obstacles that had prevented banks from folding their common trust funds into their proprietary mutual funds have been removed.[14] A major obstacle was removed in 1996 when Congress amended Code Section 584 to permit tax-free conversions.

Since then, conversion activity has increased substantially.[15] There is one outstanding legal impediment, however, that can only be addressed on a conversion by conversion basis, namely *the trustee's duty of undivided loyalty*.[16] A bank trustee, for example, still may not convert common trust fund participations into *proprietary* mutual fund participations at beneficiary expense,[17] nor may it do so as a subterfuge for raising fees, double-dipping, or making its *proprietary* mutual funds attractive to nontrust customers.[18]

And going forward, "[t]he trustee, in deciding whether to invest in a mutual fund, must not place its own interests ahead of those of the beneficiaries."[19] For a general discussion of the duties of loyalty and prudence in the context of a corporate trustee's investing in its proprietary mutual funds, see Section 6.1.3.4 of this handbook.

Having said all that, mutual funds are not without their advantages:

> By comparison with common trust funds, mutual fund shares may be distributed in-kind when trust interests terminate, avoiding liquidation and the associated recognition of gain for tax purposes. Mutual funds commonly offer daily pricing,

---

[14] I.R.C. §584, OCC Interpretive Letter 722, May 12, 1996, Fed. Banking L. Rep. (CCH) ¶81-037. A trustee, however, would be well advised to ascertain whether conversion would generate a capital gains tax liability at the state level. *See also* UTC §802(f) (available at <http://www.uniformlaws.org/Act.aspx?title=Trust%20Code>) (creating an exception to the "no further inquiry rule" for trustee investment in mutual funds). *See generally* 4 Scott & Ascher §19.1.10 (Mutual Funds).

[15] Board of Governors of the Federal Reserve System. SR-97-3 (SPE), Feb. 26, 1997. Fed. Banking L. Rep. (CCH) ¶37-052.

[16] *See generally* §6.1.3 of this handbook (duty to be loyal to the trust).

[17] 12 C.F.R. §9.18(b)(10) (1997) (known as Reg. 9) (available at <www.gpoaccess.gov/cfr/index.html>). *See also* §8.4 of this handbook (the trustee's compensation). *But cf.* Texas Commerce Bank v. Grizzle, 46 Tex. Sup. Ct. J. 318, 96 S.W.3d 240 (2002) (a corporate trustee having liquidated common trust fund participations incident to its merger with another bank and in so doing having caused economic harm to the trust containing the participations was held not to be liable for its acts of "self-dealing" because of the trust's exculpatory clause). *See generally* §7.2.6 of this handbook (exculpatory (also exemption or indemnity) provisions covering breach of fiduciary duty to the beneficiary).

[18] It cannot be said that a transfer of assets from a bank common trust fund to its proprietary retail mutual fund is a transaction between unrelated parties. *See* Board of Governors of the Federal Reserve System, SR-97-3 (SPE), Feb. 26, 1997, Fed. Banking L. Rep. (CCH) ¶37-052; Melanie L. Fein, Securities Activities of Banks §11.05[E][2]. *See also* Supervisory Letter (SR 99-7 Mar. 26, 1999) (Federal Reserve Board, Division of Banking Supervision) (raising concerns that banks that invest their fiduciary funds in their proprietary mutual funds may be subject to suit for breach of the common law duty of undivided loyalty notwithstanding general statutory authority to do so).

[19] UTC §802 cmt. (available at <http://www.uniformlaws.org/Act.aspx?title=Trust%20Code>).

which gives trustees and beneficiaries better information about performance. Because mutual funds can combine fiduciary and nonfiduciary accounts, they can achieve larger size, which can enhance diversification and produce economies that can lower investment costs.[20]

§9.7.2   IOLTA Trusts

By raising the analogy of a tax or user fee the Court does, however, usefully call attention to one of the more offensive features of the takings scheme devised by the Washington Supreme Court: A tax or user fee would be enacted by a democratically elected legislature. The IOLTA scheme, by contrast, circumvents politically accountable decision making, and effects a taking of clients' funds through application of a rule purportedly regulating professional ethics, promulgated by the Washington Supreme Court. (The taking has nothing to do with ethics, of course)—Justice Scalia, dissenting.[21]

At Suffolk University, after giving a lecture on his book Active Liberty, Justice Breyer was pressed by two students in Q&A about his decision on the IOLTA case. In response to their questions he stated that IOLTA may be bad policy (he remained agnostic on this question but the students' questions clearly indicated they did think it was bad policy) but that legislatures must be given wide discretion to promote public goals and it was beyond the judge's job to decide it was in fact bad policy.[22]

All states and the District of Columbia are administering either by judicial fiat or in a few cases by statute IOLTA programs.[23] IOLTA stands for Interest on Lawyers Trust Accounts. Under an IOLTA scheme, a lawyer is compelled under threat of license suspension to commingle or pool unproductive nominal and short-term client funds that the lawyer holds in trust. The income generated by the pool is then remitted to designated charitable and professional entities. For IOLTA administration purposes, what would otherwise be an equitable duty on the part of the lawyer to obtain from the client an informed consent to the diversion is generally suspended, also by judicial fiat.

The aggregate amount of income generated by IOLTA nationwide and collectively taken from clients since 1978 is in the many billions of dollars. As we shall see, the U.S. Supreme Court has confirmed that the diversion does constitute a taking by the state.[24]

One court has ruled that common law trust principles are not applicable to IOLTA.[25] The Federal Court of Appeals for the Fifth Circuit, however, has held

---

[20] UTC §802 cmt. (available at <http://www.uniformlaws.org/Act.aspx?title=Trust%20 Code>).

[21] Brown v. Legal Found. of Wash., 538 U.S. 216 n.2 (2003) (Justice Scalia dissent).

[22] E-mail from Benjamin Powell, Assist. Prof. of Economics, to Charles E. Rounds, Jr. (Mar. 10, 2008) (on file with the authors).

[23] *See* Rounds, *Social Investing, IOLTA, and the Law of Trusts*, 22 Loy. U. Chi. L.J. 163, 173–174 (1990).

[24] *See* Brown v. Legal Found. of Wash., 123 S. Ct. 1406 (2003).

[25] "We are not convinced that the deposit of clients' funds into IOLTA accounts transforms a lawyer's fiduciary obligation to clients into a formal trust with the reserved right to control the

that IOLTA income is the property of the client; and, on appeal, the U.S. Supreme Court affirmed, holding that, "for purposes of the Takings Clause of the Fifth Amendment," IOLTA income is the property of the client.[26] Since then, the United States Court of Appeals for the Ninth Circuit has ruled that the government appropriation of interest generated by IOLTA pooled trust accounts is not an uncompensated taking in violation of the Fifth Amendment.[27] A decision of the U.S. Court of Appeals for the Fifth Circuit, however, has held that it is.[28] The U.S. Supreme Court granted certiorari June 10, 2002, to hear an appeal of the Ninth Circuit decision that IOLTA does not effect an unconstitutional taking in violation of the Fifth Amendment. Oral arguments were heard December 9, 2002.

In 2003, the U.S. Supreme Court ruled that though gross IOLTA income constitutes the property of clients and though the gross income has been taken from them by the state, there is no compensation due them.[29] This is because, under a properly administered program, principal sums that could generate net income for a client may not be deposited in an IOLTA account.[30] Query: Would the lawyer-trustee still have a common law duty to inform the client in advance that the client's property, *i.e.*, the equitable interest, is being taken by the state under the auspices of an IOLTA program?[31] "Despite their widespread acceptance, these programs have always been controversial, in large part because they appear to deprive clients of the interest on their funds."[32] Moreover, "[t]here seem no longer to be any practical impediments to making trust funds productive, even on a temporary basis, while retaining a very high level of liquidity, whether by bank deposits or investment in money-market funds or other short-term funds."[33]

---

beneficial use of the funds as claimed by the plaintiffs." Washington Legal Found. v. Massachusetts Bar Found., 993 F.2d 962, 974 (1st Cir. 1993). *But see* Ritchie et al., Decedents' Estates and Trusts 1318 (8th ed. 1993) ("funds received by a lawyer on behalf of a client are held in trust for the client").

[26] Washington Legal Found. v. Texas Equal Access to Justice Found., 94 F.3d 996 (5th Cir. 1996); Phillips v. Washington Legal Found., 118 S. Ct. 1925 (1998). *See also* Schneider v. California Dep't of Corr., 151 F.3d 1194 (9th Cir. 1998); Bockman v. Vail, 161 F.3d 11 (9th Cir. 1998) (each holding that interest on entrusted funds belonging to a prisoner is the property of the prisoner).

[27] Washington Legal Found. v. Legal Found. of Wash., 271 F.3d 835 (9th Cir. 2001).

[28] Washington Legal Found. v. Texas Equal Access to Justice Found., 2001 WL 1222105 (5th Cir.).

[29] Brown v. Legal Found. of Wash., 123 S. Ct. 1406 (2003).

[30] *See* Schneider v. California Dep't of Corr., 345 F.3d 716 (9th Cir. 2003) (remanding for a determination of whether an individual inmate was unconstitutionally deprived of any net interest earned on funds held in his state prison inmate trust account).

[31] *See* §6.1.5.1 of this handbook (duty to provide information).

[32] 1 Scott & Ascher §2.3.8.1.

[33] 3 Scott & Ascher §17.13.

§9.7.3   Pooled Income Fund

A qualifying charitable organization may establish a pooled income fund for the purpose of receiving and administering split-interest tax-deductible charitable gifts.[34] The charity and the commingled trust fund must meet the requirements of Code Section 642(c)(5). A donor may retain an income interest for life in the transferred property. In addition, he or she may bestow concurrent or successive life income interests on other individuals, provided they are alive at the time the gift is made. Once all income interests are extinguished, the portion of the pooled income fund that was allocable to the noncharitable interests is segregated from the fund and distributed to the designated charity. For more on pooled income funds, the reader is referred to BNA's Tax Management Portfolio.[35]

§9.7.4   Pre-need Funeral Trusts (Collective Investments)

States have statutes that enable one to put aside before death funds to pay for one's funeral expenses. To the extent these arrangements call for the commingling of investments, the question arises as to whether a participating national bank must operate the pool of assets as a common trust fund that complies with the design and administrative provisions of Regulation 9 of the Comptroller of the Currency.[36] The short answer is no. The bank may defer to local law.[37]

§9.7.5   The Mutual Fund

In the U.S., the common law informs the Investment Company Act of 1940, not the other way around... Unlike the...[Act,]...whose codifications are selective and narrowly-focused, the common law as it relates to mutual funds is all-encompassing and self-contained. The common law does not need the help of the Act when it comes to protecting investors, but the Act would be gibberish without the common law. The Act does not create the concept of the fiduciary, it invokes it, and does so with minimal Federal preemption.[38]

A mutual fund is a pool of items of property—whether tangible, intangible or real, and whether fractional or whole—that is legally structured so that beneficial ownership of the pool itself, as contrasted with the property interests

---

[34] *See generally* §9.4.5 of this handbook (tax-oriented trusts that mix charitable and noncharitable interests (split-interest trusts)).

[35] Brier & Knauer, 435-2d T.M., Charitable Remainder Trusts and Pooled Income Funds.

[36] *See generally* §8.18 of this handbook (Regulation 9 revised) and §9.7.1 of this handbook (the common trust fund and the proprietary mutual fund).

[37] 12 C.F.R. §9.18(c)(4).

[38] Charles E. Rounds, Jr. & Andreas Dehio, *Publicly-Traded Open End Mutual Funds in Common Law and Civil Law Jurisdictions: A Comparison of Legal Structures*, 3 N.Y.U. J. L. & Bus. 473, 502–503 (2007).

that comprise the pool, is divisible and transferable.[39] An open-end fund is a fund whose shares may be exchanged by their owners for fund cash.[40] In other words, the shares are "redeemable."[41] The shares of a closed-end fund generally are not.[42]

Closed-end investment trusts were operating in England as far back as the 1830s. "Throughout the 1920s, the closed-end funds with debt and preferred stock in their capital structure dominated in the U.S., with over 98% of the assets. In Great Britain it was nearly 100%."[43] Whether State Street Investment Corporation or Massachusetts Investors Trust managed the first "Boston-type" open-end trusteed mutual fund on this side of the Atlantic continues to be debated. "State Street began operating early in 1924 but did not incorporate until July. Massachusetts Investors Trust incorporated in March but did not operate until July."[44]

§9.7.5.1   The Trusteed Mutual Fund (U.S. and U.K.)

A standard U.S. trusteed mutual fund or U.K. unit trust (open end) is first and foremost a trust.[45] Title to the underlying assets is in the fund trustees, who hold the underlying assets for the sole benefit of the investor-beneficiaries.[46] The trustees are in a contractual and agency relationship with the investment manager, which typically is the fund's sponsor and public face.[47] It is the sponsor who designed and launched the fund. The sponsor selects the fund

---

[39] Charles E. Rounds, Jr. & Andreas Dehio, *Publicly-Traded Open End Mutual Funds in Common Law and Civil Law Jurisdictions: A Comparison of Legal Structures*, 3 N.Y.U. J. L. & Bus. 473, 477 (2007).

[40] Charles E. Rounds, Jr. & Andreas Dehio, *Publicly-Traded Open End Mutual Funds in Common Law and Civil Law Jurisdictions: A Comparison of Legal Structures*, 3 N.Y.U. J. L. & Bus. 473, 477 (2007).

[41] Charles E. Rounds, Jr. & Andreas Dehio, *Publicly-Traded Open End Mutual Funds in Common Law and Civil Law Jurisdictions: A Comparison of Legal Structures*, 3 N.Y.U. J. L. & Bus. 473, 477 (2007).

[42] 15 U.S.C.A. §80a-5(a) (2005).

[43] Michael R. Yogg, *Passion for Reality: The Extraordinary Life of the Investing Pioneer Paul Cabot* 38 (Columbia Business School Publishing 2014).

[44] Michael R. Yogg, *Passion for Reality: The Extraordinary Life of the Investing Pioneer Paul Cabot* 39 (Columbia Business School Publishing 2014).

[45] *See generally* Charles E. Rounds, Jr. & Andreas Dehio, *Publicly-Traded Open End Mutual Funds in Common Law and Civil Law Jurisdictions: A Comparison of Legal Structures*, 3 N.Y.U.J.L & Bus. 473 (2007).

[46] *See generally* Charles E. Rounds, Jr. & Andreas Dehio, *Publicly-Traded Open End Mutual Funds in Common Law and Civil Law Jurisdictions: A Comparison of Legal Structures*, 3 N.Y.U. J. L. & Bus. 473 (2007).

[47] *See generally* Charles E. Rounds, Jr. & Andreas Dehio, *Publicly-Traded Open End Mutual Funds in Common Law and Civil Law Jurisdictions: A Comparison of Legal Structures*, 3 N.Y.U. J. L. & Bus. 473 (2007).

trustees, subject to investor approval. The manager has fiduciary duties that run directly to the investor.[48] A UK-REIT, however, is not a trust.[49]

§9.7.5.2   The Incorporated U.S. or U.K. Mutual Fund Is Trusteed

A standard U.S. open-end incorporated mutual fund is actually a trust.[50] Title to fund assets is in the corporation, which is governed by directors. The directors are trustees with fiduciary duties that run directly to the investors.[51] The manager, which is typically the sponsor and public face of the fund, is in a contractual and agency relationship with the corporation. The manager provides investment management and other services to the corporation. The investors are the stockholders of the corporation. They are in a contractual relationship with the corporation, the holder of the title to the underlying assets. In equity, the corporate package or shell is actually the trustee of a nominee trust, the underlying trust assets of which are held for the benefit of the director-trustees in their fiduciary capacities.[52] They in turn hold the equitable interest for the benefit of the investor-beneficiaries.[53]

A standard U.K. incorporated open end mutual fund or OEIC is trusteed as well.[54] An OEIC typically has only one director, the fund's sponsor and public face. The director, in most cases a corporation, manages the investing of the underlying assets. An independent depository bank, however, holds the legal title to the underlying fund assets.[55] It also has certain oversight responsibilities. These roles make the depository the functional equivalent of the trustee of

---

[48] *See generally* Charles E. Rounds, Jr. & Andreas Dehio, *Publicly-Traded Open End Mutual Funds in Common Law and Civil Law Jurisdictions: A Comparison of Legal Structures*, 3 N.Y.U. J. L. & Bus. 473 (2007).

[49] *See generally* §9.9.12 of this handbook (U.K.-REITs and G-REITS are not trusts).

[50] *See generally* Charles E. Rounds, Jr. & Andreas Dehio, *Publicly-Traded Open End Mutual Funds in Common Law and Civil Law Jurisdictions: A Comparison of Legal Structures*, 3 N.Y.U. J. L. & Bus. 473 (2007).

[51] *See generally* Charles E. Rounds, Jr. & Andreas Dehio, *Publicly-Traded Open End Mutual Funds in Common Law and Civil Law Jurisdictions: A Comparison of Legal Structures*, 3 N.Y.U. J. L. & Bus. 473 (2007).

[52] *See generally* Charles E. Rounds, Jr. & Andreas Dehio, *Publicly-Traded Open End Mutual Funds in Common Law and Civil Law Jurisdictions: A Comparison of Legal Structures*, 3 N.Y.U. J. L. & Bus. 473 (2007).

[53] *See generally* Charles E. Rounds, Jr. & Andreas Dehio, *Publicly-Traded Open End Mutual Funds in Common Law and Civil Law Jurisdictions: A Comparison of Legal Structures*, 3 N.Y.U. J. L. & Bus. 473 (2007).

[54] *See generally* Charles E. Rounds, Jr. & Andreas Dehio, *Publicly-Traded Open End Mutual Funds in Common Law and Civil Law Jurisdictions: A Comparison of Legal Structures*, 3 N.Y.U. J. L. & Bus. 473 (2007).

[55] *See generally* Charles E. Rounds, Jr. & Andreas Dehio, *Publicly-Traded Open End Mutual Funds in Common Law and Civil Law Jurisdictions: A Comparison of Legal Structures*, 3 N.Y.U. J. L. & Bus. 473 (2007).

a U.S. mutual fund.[56] As well as being in a contractual and agency relationship with the OEIC, the depositary has fiduciary duties that run directly to the investors.[57] The investors are shareholders of the OEIC, which is also known as an "investment company with variable capital."

§9.7.5.3   Civil Law Trust Analogs[58] in the Mutual Fund Context

A standard German open end mutual fund of the *Miteigentumslösung* variety is not a trust.[59] The fund's assets are collected in a segregated fund, or *Sondervermögen*, title to which is held collectively by the investors themselves.[60] The *Sondervermögen* is managed by a *Kapitalanlagegesellschaft* (KAG), which is typically a daughter company of the sponsor and the fund's public face.[61] The *Depotbank* is a custodian of the underlying assets of the *Sondervermögen* and oversees some of the activities of the KAG.[62] The KAG, the *Depotbank*, and the investors are in contractual and agency relationships with one another. A Luxembourgian *fonds communs de placement* or FCP has almost the same legal structure. In the case of a FCP, however, there is no segregated *Sondervermögen*.

A standard German open-end mutual fund of the *Treuhandlösung* variety has some attributes of a common law trust.[63] The fund's underlying assets are collected in a segregated fund, or *Sondervermögen*, title to which is in the KAG, typically a daughter company of the sponsor and the fund's public face. The KAG is a *Treuhänder* with a duty to act solely in the interests of the investors. A *Treuhänder* has some, but not all, of the attributes of a common law trustee. Unlike the beneficiaries of a common law trust, for example, the investors have no beneficial interest in the underlying assets, the relationship between the

---

[56] *See generally* Charles E. Rounds, Jr. & Andreas Dehio, *Publicly-Traded Open End Mutual Funds in Common Law and Civil Law Jurisdictions: A Comparison of Legal Structures*, 3 N.Y.U. J. L. & Bus. 473 (2007).

[57] *See generally* Charles E. Rounds, Jr. & Andreas Dehio, *Publicly-Traded Open End Mutual Funds in Common Law and Civil Law Jurisdictions: A Comparison of Legal Structures*, 3 N.Y.U. J. L. & Bus. 473 (2007).

[58] *See generally* §8.12.1 of this handbook (civil law alternatives to the trust).

[59] *See generally* Charles E. Rounds, Jr. & Andreas Dehio, *Publicly-Traded Open End Mutual Funds in Common Law and Civil Law Jurisdictions: A Comparison of Legal Structures*, 3 N.Y.U. J. L. & Bus. 473 (2007).

[60] *See generally* Charles E. Rounds, Jr. & Andreas Dehio, *Publicly-Traded Open End Mutual Funds in Common Law and Civil Law Jurisdictions: A Comparison of Legal Structures*, 3 N.Y.U. J. L. & Bus. 473 (2007).

[61] *See generally* Charles E. Rounds, Jr. & Andreas Dehio, *Publicly-Traded Open End Mutual Funds in Common Law and Civil Law Jurisdictions: A Comparison of Legal Structures*, 3 N.Y.U. J. L. & Bus. 473 (2007).

[62] *See generally* Charles E. Rounds, Jr. & Andreas Dehio, *Publicly-Traded Open End Mutual Funds in Common Law and Civil Law Jurisdictions: A Comparison of Legal Structures*, 3 N.Y.U. J. L. & Bus. 473 (2007).

[63] *See generally* Charles E. Rounds, Jr. & Andreas Dehio, *Publicly-Traded Open End Mutual Funds in Common Law and Civil Law Jurisdictions: A Comparison of Legal Structures*, 3 N.Y.U. J. L. & Bus. 473 (2007).

KAG-*Treuhänder* and the investors being merely contractual. The *Depotbank* is custodian of the *Sondervermögen*. The KAG, the *Depotbank* and the investors are in contractual and agency relationships with one another.

A standard German/Luxembourgian incorporated mutual fund (open end) is not a trust.[64] Title to the underlying fund assets is in the investment company (*Investmentaktiengesellschaft*) which is governed by a board of directors (*Vorstand*).[65] The manager is not a KAG, though it is typically a daughter company of the sponsor and the fund's public face. The manager is in a contractual relationship with the investment company. The investors are the stockholders of the investment company. They do not have title to the fund's underlying assets.[66] There is a requirement under Luxembourg law that a bank custodian (*dépositaire*) hold the underlying assets of a SICAV.[67] German law has no such requirement.

§9.7.5.4 Substantive Differences Between the Common Law and Civil Law Mutual Fund Structural Models

While there are adequate safeguards in place on both sides of the Atlantic to protect mutual fund assets from the creditors of the intermediaries who have title to or control of those assets, the Anglo-American equitable concept of the fiduciary brings with it more proactivity and less respect for the corporate package than does its civil law statutory analogs when it comes to looking out for the investor.[68] Also, more of the parties in a mutual fund's tangle of legal relationships are likely to be tagged with the fiduciary or "fiduciary-like" label in a common law jurisdiction than in a civil law one.[69] Thus, the common law model affords the investor more nonregulatory protection in the form of private rights of action than the civil law model.[70] Moreover, in a multifiduciary

---

[64] *See generally* Charles E. Rounds, Jr. & Andreas Dehio, *Publicly-Traded Open End Mutual Funds in Common Law and Civil Law Jurisdictions: A Comparison of Legal Structures*, 3 N.Y.U. J. L. & Bus. 473 (2007).

[65] *See generally* Charles E. Rounds, Jr. & Andreas Dehio, *Publicly-Traded Open End Mutual Funds in Common Law and Civil Law Jurisdictions: A Comparison of Legal Structures*, 3 N.Y.U.J.L. & Bus. 473, 477 (2007).

[66] *See generally* Charles E. Rounds, Jr. & Andreas Dehio, *Publicly-Traded Open End Mutual Funds in Common Law and Civil Law Jurisdictions: A Comparison of Legal Structures*, 3 N.Y.U.J.L. & Bus. 473 (2007).

[67] *See generally* Charles E. Rounds, Jr. & Andreas Dehio, *Publicly-Traded Open End Mutual Funds in Common Law and Civil Law Jurisdictions: A Comparison of Legal Structures*, 3 N.Y.U.J.L. & Bus. 473 (2007).

[68] *See generally* Charles E. Rounds, Jr. & Andreas Dehio, *Publicly-Traded Open End Mutual Funds in Common Law and Civil Law Jurisdictions: A Comparison of Legal Structures*, 3 N.Y.U.J.L. & Bus. 473 (2007).

[69] *See generally* Charles E. Rounds, Jr. & Andreas Dehio, *Publicly-Traded Open End Mutual Funds in Common Law and Civil Law Jurisdictions: A Comparison of Legal Structures*, 3 N.Y.U.J.L. & Bus. 473 (2007).

[70] *See generally* Charles E. Rounds, Jr. & Andreas Dehio, *Publicly-Traded Open End Mutual Funds in Common Law and Civil Law Jurisdictions: A Comparison of Legal Structures*, 3 N.Y.U.J.L. & Bus. 473 (2007).

environment, the common law principle of cofiduciary liability[71] causes to be put in place, at least in theory, a private system of checks and balances and cross-fiduciary oversight that can only inure to the benefit of the investor-beneficiary. For more information, the reader is referred to Rounds and Dehio.[72]

§9.7.6 The Corporate Trust [As a Vehicle to Secure the Contractual Rights of a Class of Bondholders]

It is common practice for a bond issuer to transfer some of its property to a trustee for the purpose of securing the bondholders' contractual rights. Such trusts are known in the trade as "corporate trusts." The trustees themselves are generally referred to as "indenture trustees." These security arrangements are generally regulated by the federal Trust Indenture Act of 1939. For a discussion of the rights, duties, and obligations of indenture trustees, see Section 9.31 of this handbook.

§9.8 Quasi-Trusts, Hybrids, and Virtual Trusts

Certain arrangements are trusts in substance but not in form. The charitable corporation is a classic example. Some hybrid arrangements, such as the custodial IRA, have the characteristics of both the trust and the agency. The Massachusetts Supreme Judicial Court has ruled that the Boston Common is held by the City of Boston upon a quasi-trust.[1] One English commentator has referred to the directors of a for-profit corporation as quasi trustees of its assets.[2] The Restatement (Third) of Trusts refers to Uniform Transfers to Minors Act custodianships as virtual trusts.[3]

---

[71] See generally §7.2.4 of this handbook (cofiduciary and predecessor liability and contribution).

[72] Charles E. Rounds, Jr. & Andreas Dehio, *Publicly-Traded Open End Mutual Funds in Common Law and Civil Law Jurisdictions: A Comparison of Legal Structures*, 3 N.Y.U.Y.J.L & Bus. 473 (2007).

§9.8 [1] Codman v. Crocker, 203 Mass. 146, 150, 89 N.E. 177, 178 (1909). *See also* Lowell v. City of Boston, 322 Mass. 709, 79 N.E.2d 713, 725 (1948) (holding that title to the Boston Common, vested in fee simple in the Town of Boston, is owned free from any trust but holding also that title is not held by the City of Boston free of restriction, the Town of Boston having dedicated the Common and the Public Garden to the use of the public as a public park).

[2] Lewin ¶ 7-16.

[3] Restatement (Third) of Trusts §5 cmt. a(1).

§9.8.1   The Charitable Corporation: Is It a Trust?

Princeton is under the impression that this is their money, says Mr. Robertson. If my parents intended Princeton to have the money, they would have just given it to them instead of having a separate foundation.[4]

The Robertsons have spent about $20 million in pursuing the lawsuit, and Princeton has spent $22 million defending itself. No trial date has been set.[5]

The charitable corporation: a quasi-trust that also may serve as a trustee. To be sure, under *the tax laws* of the United States, a so-called charitable foundation can be structured as either a charitable trust or a charitable corporation.[6] Likewise, the doctrine of charitable immunity draws no distinction between the charitable trust and the charitable corporation.[7] But under a particular state's common law of trusts and property, is a gift of property to a charitable corporation a transfer in trust? Is a charitable trust and a charitable corporation essentially one and the same?

In the case of a charitable trust, the state attorney general may maintain a suit to prevent the subject property from being squandered or misapplied.[8] The attorney general also has standing to maintain a suit to prevent the squandering or misapplication of the assets of a charitable corporation.[9] "Likewise, in both cases, cy pres may be available."[10] But is the charitable corporation *a trustee* of its own property such that its governing body is subject to all the common law duties and obligations of a trustee?[11]

Professor Scott, while acknowledging some technical differences between the charitable trust and the charitable corporation, on balance found them more similar than dissimilar.[12] In the noncharitable context it is not uncommon

---

[4] Editorial (Review & Outlook), *Follow the Money*, Wall St. J., July 19, 2002, at A15.

[5] John Hechinger, *Ruling May Cost Princeton Millions if Heirs Win Case*, Wall St. J., Oct. 26, 2007, at B6 ("the lawsuit is the biggest dispute over donor intent in higher education"). It is worth noting here that a prospective charitable donor can structure his or her benefaction in a way that the charity will have little choice but to carry out the donor's charitable intentions, a topic we cover in §4.1.1.2 of this handbook. In other words, there are some steps that the Robertson family perhaps could have taken *before* the gift to Princeton was made that would have, for all intents and purposes, put them in the driver's seat.

[6] *See generally* Bogert §330.

[7] *See generally* 5 Scott & Ascher §37.3.13.2.

[8] 5 Scott & Ascher §37.1.1.

[9] 5 Scott & Ascher §37.1.1.

[10] 5 Scott & Ascher §37.1.1. *See generally* §9.4.3 of this handbook (*cy pres*).

[11] *Cf.* Charles E. Rounds, Jr. & Andreas Dehio, *Publicly-Traded Open End Mutual Funds in Common Law and Civil Law Jurisdictions: A Comparison of Legal Structures*, 3 N.Y.U.J.L. & Bus. 473, 479 (2007). (an incorporated U.S. or U.K. mutual fund is actually a trust).

[12] 4A Scott on Trusts §348.1; 5 Scott & Ascher §37.1.1. *See also* Paterson v. Paterson Gen. Hosp., 235 A.2d 487, 489 (N.J. Super. Ct. 1967) (suggesting that a charitable corporation is not strictly speaking a charitable trust but that the law of charitable corporations has its roots in the law of trusts). *But see* Stegemeier v. Magness, 728 A.2d 557, 562 (Del. Super. 1999) (noting that the absolute prohibition under common law against self-dealing by a trustee has been modified in the corporate setting to offer a safe harbor for the directors of a charitable corporation if the

to see trusts masquerading as corporations.[13] Certainly if the gift is restricted, the directors of the corporation should segregate the gift from the corporation's other assets and act as if they were the trustees of the gift, even though it is in the entity that the legal title to the gift resides. Above all, they should carry out the lawful intentions of the transferor, and the attorney general, and the courts should see to it that they do.

The better view, at least from the donor's perspective, is that a restricted gift to a charitable corporation is a gift to the charitable corporation as trustee of a charitable trust, the subject of which is the restricted gift.[14] This should certainly apply to an endowment fund, which is a fund that under the terms of a gift instrument is not wholly expendable by the charitable corporation on a current basis.[15] In California, a charitable corporation formed in California has general statutory authority to serve as a trustee.[16] When property is left to a charitable corporation upon a charitable trust and the corporation either declines to accept the trust, or accepts the trust and then proceeds to violate it, the court has inherent equitable powers to order a transfer of the legal title to the property to a charitable corporation that is ready, willing, and able to properly carry out the terms of the trust.[17]

There is no question that a gratuitous transfer of property to a third party, *e.g.*, a bank or trust company, in trust for the benefit of a charitable corporation gives rise to a charitable trust.[18] Moreover, "[w]hen the settlor creates a trust of unlimited duration to pay the income to a charitable corporation, the court will neither compel nor permit the termination of the trust by a transfer of the principal to the corporation, even if the corporation is the sole beneficiary and wants to terminate the trust."[19] Nor will the court permit an early termination of the trust in favor of the corporation if acceleration would be contrary to a material purpose of the trust.[20]

It is when the initial transfer of legal title is to the charitable corporation itself that things can get ambiguous, particularly if the gift is unrestricted.[21] Do we have a trust or don't we? One court has referred to the arrangement as a

---

transaction is approved by a majority of disinterested directors). *See generally* Bogert §361 (also discussing the differences between a charitable trust and a charitable corporation).

[13] *See, e.g.*, §9.7.5.2 of this handbook (the incorporated U.S. or U.K. mutual fund is trusteed).

[14] 5 Scott & Ascher §37.1.1. *See, e.g.*, In re Estate of Lind, 314 Ill. App. 3d 1055, 248 Ill. Dec. 339, 734 N.E.2d 47 (2000); University of London v. Prag, [2014] EWHC 3564 (Ch) (England). *See generally* §8.6 of this handbook (the trustee who is not a human being). Because the "community" has a beneficial interest in the charitable corporation, not the corporation, the doctrine of merger would not apply in the case of a restricted gift to a charitable corporation. *See generally* §8.7 of this handbook (merger).

[15] Unif. Prudent Management of Institutional Funds Act §2(2) (defining the term *endowment fund*).

[16] Cal. Prob. Code §15604.

[17] *See generally* 5 Scott & Ascher §37.3.7.

[18] 5 Scott & Ascher §37.1.1.

[19] 5 Scott & Ascher §37.4.2.4.

[20] 5 Scott & Ascher §37.4.2.4.

[21] *See generally* 5 Scott & Ascher §37.1.1.

quasi trust.[22] Presumably most of the corporation's donors intend that their gifts be used only for the legitimate expressed charitable purposes of the corporation, and expect that those purposes will not change materially after the gifts have been made.[23] As a practical matter, however, especially if it is the practice of management to commingle unrestricted gifts with the general assets of the charitable corporation, a donor will find it difficult, if not impossible, establishing a link between his or her particular gift and any particular expenditure.[24] Money is fungible. The governing body certainly has a moral obligation to the donors of unrestricted gifts to see to it that the corporation cleaves to the letter and spirit of the corporation's stated charitable purposes, and, at minimum, that it gives them advance warning of any material deviation from those purposes. Whether that obligation is, as a practical matter, enforceable is another matter.[25] If management expects to materially deviate from the charitable corporation's stated mission, in theory it should, at least for accounting purposes,[26] segregate benefactions already in hand and conduct its deviations with future funds. This is, of course, all much easier said than done, and almost impossible to effectively monitor privately from the outside. Moreover, in at least one jurisdiction, namely, Virginia, the directors of a nonstock charitable corporation would likely have no such duty to segregate, her Supreme Court having in no uncertain terms rejected any notion that such corporations are governed by the law of trusts.[27]

Qualifying the foreign charitable corporation. In Section 8.6 of this handbook, we take up the topic of qualifying foreign corporations to service as testamentary trustees of local trusts. In the case of the charitable corporation, "[i]t has been held that even though a bequest to a foreign charitable corporation is to be applied to a specific charitable purpose, the corporation is entitled to the legacy without qualifying in a court of the testator's domicil."[28] Local qualification may be required, however, if the property is for the benefit of

---

[22] American Inst. of Architects v. Attorney Gen., 332 Mass. 619, 624, 127 N.E.2d 161, 164 (1955).

[23] *See, e.g.*, Dodge v. Trustees of Randolph-Macon Woman's Coll., 661 S.E.2d 805 (Va. 2008).

[24] *See, e.g.*, Jose Cabranes, University Trusteeship in the Enron Era <http://www.nacua.org/documents/Enron_Speech_07-23-02.pdf> (suggesting that bad feelings between donor families and universities are almost guaranteed these days: While donors expect more from a university in the way of transparency and accountability, universities generally give less).

[25] *See, e.g.*, Morris v. E. A. Morris Charitable Corp., 358 N.C. 235, 593 S.E.2d 592 (2004) (court declining to apply *cy pres* though remainder beneficiary of a charitable remainder trust, a charitable corporation, made various changes to its administration, management, and pattern of charitable giving). *See generally* Fishman, *The Development of Nonprofit Corporation Law and an Agenda for Reform*, 34 Emory L.J. 617, 668–671 (1985).

[26] *But see* 5 Scott & Ascher §37.3.8 (suggesting that even restricted gifts to a charitable corporation may be "mingled" in a "common pool"). *See generally* §3.5.3.2(d) of this handbook (common funds or pools).

[27] *See, e.g.*, Dodge v. Trustees of Randolph-Macon Woman's Coll., 661 S.E.2d 805 (Va. 2008) (involving benefactors to Randolph-Macon Woman's College who objected to its conversion from a single-sex educational institution to one that educates both men and women).

[28] 7 Scott & Ascher §45.2.1.3.

persons in the state of the testator's domicil.[29] Qualification might entail the execution by the foreign charitable corporation of a power of attorney appointing an in-state official to accept service of process in proceedings relating to the administration of the local charitable trust, quasi trust, or what have you.[30]

Donor intent. The Uniform Prudent Management of Institutional Funds Act (UPMIFA), which would regulate the activities of fiduciaries charged with administering the endowment funds of charitable trusts and charitable corporations, endeavors to shore up the principle that donor intent is generally paramount. It provides that "[u]nless stated otherwise in the gift instrument, the assets in an endowment fund are donor-restricted assets until appropriated for expenditure by the institution."[31] Unfortunately, its efforts are largely toothless, as it still falls to the state attorney general, a politician, to protect both "the public interest in charitable assets" as he or she perceives it and donor intent.[32] As dead donors generally don't vote, the game in most cases can be expected to be rigged in favor of the "public interest" which, like public policy, is an unruly horse that is not easily corralled.

One influential academic journal, however, has been cited by a court in support of the proposition that donors really should have no say when it comes to changing the mission of a charitable corporation:

> With respect to the right to modify the charter powers of a charitable corporation it has been said, "Where there is general statutory authority allowing amendment of the corporate charter, the corporation and its board of trustees are the proper parties to institute the amendment process. Donors, who are generally considered to have surrendered all their rights, and beneficiaries, who are of necessity an indefinite group without ability to act effectively, lack this power. Allowing amendment at the instigation of the corporation alone has been justified on the ground that the charity in effect represents the interest of the donors, and that the interest of the beneficiaries is protected by the consent of either the corporation or the state. However, such reasoning seems unnecessary to justify changes which are actually allowed because of society's interest in the efficient utilization of property held for charitable purposes. . . ."[33]

Failed dispositions and the *cy pres* doctrine. Enforceability and fiduciary obligation are key elements of the trust. With respect to an unrestricted gift to a charitable corporation, the former element may well be lacking as a practical matter, as we have alluded to above. Thus benefactors interested in enforceability may want to shun the charitable corporation in favor of making gifts to a charitable trust for the benefit of the corporation where the parties are more

---

[29] 7 Scott & Ascher §45.2.1.3.

[30] 7 Scott & Ascher §45.2.1.3.

[31] Unif. Prudent Management Inst. Funds Act §4(a).

[32] Unif. Prudent Management Inst. Funds Act §6 cmt.

[33] City of Paterson v. Paterson Gen. Hosp., 97 N.J. Super. 514, 520, 235 A.2d 487, 490 (1967) (citing to Note, *The Charitable Corporation*, 64 Harv. L. Rev. 1168, 1178–1179 (1951) but noting that when a charitable corporation's charter provides for third-party supervision of the trustees by "visitors" or others, then their consent to a mission change would probably have to be obtained).

legally defined and where their rights and obligations more legally settled.[34] The *cy pres* sections of the Uniform Trust Code would *not* control failed dispositions made through charitable corporations.[35] As the common law doctrine of *cy pres*, however, does apply to such dispositions,[36] presumably there is nothing to prevent courts wrestling with the doctrine in the corporate context from looking to the Code for guidance.[37] In jurisdictions that have enacted the UPMIFA, which has replaced the Uniform Management of Institutional Funds Act (UMIFA), the *cy pres* doctrine applicable to trusts has been made expressly applicable to charitable corporations as well.[38]

When a charitable corporation takes property as trustee for a "particular charitable purpose" and subsequently the purpose fails, there is the question of whether the corporation can then apply the property to its own general purposes.[39] If the settlor so intended, the answer is yes.[40] Otherwise it will be up to the court to determine what is to be done with the subject property, whether by the application of *cy pres* or by the invocation of a resulting trust.[41] The *cy pres* doctrine is covered in Section 9.4.3 of this handbook.[42] The resulting trust is covered in Section 4.1.1.1 of this handbook.

When a *restricted gift* to a charitable corporation fails *ab initio* because the charitable corporation has disclaimed the gift or because the corporation does not exist, then it falls to the court to consider whether it should apply the property *cy pres*.[43] One solution might be for the court to appoint a suitable trustee to receive the gift and carry out its intended charitable purposes, provided the particular corporation was not the very "essence of the gift."[44] The same also applies to a gift to a charitable corporation that subsequently goes out of existence.[45] In such cases, it is probably more accurate to say that the court is

---

[34] *See* Karst, *The Efficiency of the Charitable Dollar: An Unfulfilled State Responsibility*, 73 Harv. L. Rev. 433, 435 (1960).

[35] UTC §413 cmt. (available at <http://www.uniformlaws.org/Act.aspx?title=Trust%20 Code>).

[36] *See generally* 5 Scott & Ascher §37.1.1 (confirming that the directors of a charitable corporation may bring a *cy pres* petition); 6 Scott & Ascher §39.3.3 (Gift to Charitable Corporation).

[37] UTC §413 cmt. (available at <http://www.uniformlaws.org/Act.aspx?title=Trust%20 Code>).

[38] Unif. Prudent Management Inst. Funds Act §6(d).

[39] 6 Scott & Ascher §39.5.2.

[40] 6 Scott & Ascher §39.5.2.

[41] 6 Scott & Ascher §39.5.2.

[42] We also briefly discuss the *cy pres* doctrine in §8.15.28 of this handbook.

[43] 6 Scott & Ascher §39.3.3. A disposition to or for the benefit of a named charitable corporation generally will not fail though no entity precisely fits the description, or though two or more do. When the ambiguity is patent, that is apparent from the face of the instrument, extrinsic evidence as to the settlor's intent is generally not admissible. When the ambiguity is latent, which is likely to be the case with there is a misnomer, extrinsic evidence generally will be. *See generally* 6 Scott & Ascher §39.3.3 (Misnomer).

[44] 6 Scott & Ascher §39.3.3.

[45] 6 Scott & Ascher §39.3.3. Note also that "[w]hen there is a disposition to a charitable corporation that is consolidated with, or merged into, another, the surviving corporation is entitled to the property, unless the settlor has manifested a contrary intention." 6 Scott & Ascher

invoking the doctrine that "a trust shall not fail for want of a trustee" than it is to say that it is invoking the *cy pres* doctrine. On the other hand, in the case of *unrestricted gifts* to such charitable corporations, there could be vested equitable reversionary interests that need to be accommodated:

> Some cases have held that the property reverts to the donor, either because the corporation takes only a determinable fee or by resulting trust. It would seem, however, that cy pres should apply, and that the property should not revert to the donor unless he or she has manifested a contrary intention. In many states there are now statutes dealing with the dissolution of nonprofit corporations.[46]

We should note here that in response to concerns "about the clogging of title and other administrative problems caused by remote default provisions upon failure of a charitable purpose,"[47] the Uniform Trust Code would sharply curtail the ability of a settlor to create a charitable *trust* whose property would revert to the settlor's personal representative, *i.e.*, the settlor's probate estate, upon the accomplishment of that purpose (or upon the impossibility of its fulfillment), even when the purpose is a limited one.[48] This is a topic we cover in some detail in Section 9.4.3 of this handbook as part of our coverage of the *cy pres* doctrine.

Investments. When it comes to investing, it is probably safe to say that charitable trusts and charitable corporations are now regulated by the same default rules, or soon will be, namely, those embodied in the Uniform Prudent Investor Act applicable to trusts.[49] "UPMIFA reflects the fact that standards for managing and investing institutional funds are and should be the same, regardless of whether a charitable organization is organized as a trust, a nonprofit corporation, or some other entity."[50] Lawyers with a corporate focus, however, need not fear: "The standard is consistent with the business judgment standard under corporate law, *as applied to charitable institutions*."[51]

It may well still be that there remain outstanding some residual differences between the default standards of loyalty applicable to directors of charitable corporations and trustees of charitable trusts. It has been said that directors are subject to a "best interest" standard, whereas trustees are subject to a "sole

---

§39.3.3. The merger or consolidation of charitable corporations is now dealt with by statute in many states. 6 Scott & Ascher §39.3.3. The merger of colleges and universities and the withdrawal of local churches from their parent organizations raise troubling issues of donor intent. 6 Scott & Ascher §39.3.3. *See generally* §4.1.1.2 (measures that can be taken at the drafting intent to protect a donor's charitable intentions).

[46] 6 Scott & Ascher §39.3.3. *See generally* §4.1.1.1 (discussing the vested equitable reversionary interest and how it can become possessory through the imposition of a resulting trust).

[47] UTC §413 cmt. (available at <http://www.uniformlaws.org/Act.aspx?title=Trust%20 Code>).

[48] UTC §413 (available at <http://www.uniformlaws.org/Act.aspx?title=Trust%20Code>). *See generally* 6 Scott & Ascher §39.5.2.

[49] *See generally* 5 Scott & Ascher §37.3.8.

[50] Unif. Prudent Management Inst. Funds Act, Prefatory Note. *See generally* 5 Scott & Ascher §37.3.8.

[51] Unif. Prudent Management Inst. Funds Act §3 cmt.

interest" standard.[52] How this subtle difference might play itself out in a given set of facts and circumstances is at present not entirely clear to these authors. Suffice it to say that UPMIFA makes no effort to fashion an overarching loyalty standard applicable to both directors and trustees in the charitable context.[53]

Creditor access. Creditor access is another area where the charitable trust and the charitable corporation are more and more coming to be subject to the same rules.[54] "It has long been the case that, when a charitable corporation incurs a liability in contract or in tort, a . . . [direct] . . . action at law lies against the corporation itself."[55] As we discuss in Section 7.3 of this handbook and the sub-sections thereto, under classic principles of trust law the recourse of a third-party contract or tort creditor of a "trust" was limited to an action at law against the trustee personally.[56] Under certain circumstances, the creditor might have been able to reach the underlying trust assets, but only derivatively in an equitable action to reach and apply whatever rights that the trustee might have had against the trust estate.[57] Today, either by contract or by statute a creditor of the "trust" is likely to be afforded direct access to the trust estate incident to an action at law against the trustee.[58]

Fiduciary liability. While we have touched on some important similarities, and some relatively minor differences, between the charitable trust and the charitable corporation,[59] limiting fiduciary liability is one area where there is fundamental divergence: ". . . [A]n exculpatory provision relieves or exempts a party from liability for his or her prospective acts, while an indemnity agreement obligates one party to make good a loss or damage that another party has already incurred."[60] *Settlors* of charitable trusts generally control the insertion of exculpatory provisions into trust instruments, not the trustees.[61] When it comes

---

[52] Unif. Prudent Management Inst. Funds Act §3 cmt.

[53] Unif. Prudent Management Inst. Funds Act §3 cmt.

[54] *See generally* 5 Scott & Ascher §37.1.1.

[55] 5 Scott & Ascher §37.1.1 n.9.

[56] *See generally* §7.3.1 of this handbook (trustee's external liability as legal owner in contract to third-party creditors), §7.3.2 of this handbook (trustee's agreement with creditors to limit external contractual liability), and §7.3.3 of this handbook (trustee's external liability as legal owner in tort to third parties).

[57] *See generally* §7.3.1 of this handbook (trustee's external liability as legal owner in contract to third party creditors), §7.3.2 of this handbook (trustee's agreement with creditors to limit external contractual liability), and §7.3.3 of this handbook (trustee's external liability as legal owner in tort to third parties).

[58] *See generally* §7.3.1 of this handbook (trustee's external liability as legal owner in contract to third-party creditors), §7.3.2 of this handbook (trustee's agreement with creditors to limit external contractual liability), and §7.3.3 of this handbook (trustee's external liability as legal owner in tort to third parties).

[59] 4A Scott on Trusts §348.1 ("In both cases the Attorney General can maintain a suit to prevent a diversion of the property to purposes other than those for which it was given; and in both cases the doctrine of cy pres is applicable.").

[60] 86 Ops. Cal. Atty. Gen. 95, 2003 WL 21672836 (Cal. A.G.).

[61] *See generally* §7.2.6 of this handbook (exculpatory (also exemption or indemnity) provisions covering breach of fiduciary duties to the beneficiary). It should be noted that under §410(a) of ERISA, an ERISA trustee may not be relieved from responsibility by the plan documentation and by the instrument governing the associated trust.

to charitable corporations, however, it is the *directors*, the fiduciaries themselves, who generally have statutory authority[62] to determine whether they are entitled to be indemnified by the corporation for their negligent acts.[63]

Such self-indemnification authority, however, is not without its limitations. In California, for example, indemnification for amounts paid in settlement of a threatened or pending derivative action is not permitted.[64] On the other hand, most states would permit a director who prevailed on the merits of a contested matter to be indemnified by the entity. Some state statutes provide for automatic indemnification or certain specified liabilities; others require as well that there be express authority in the instruments that govern the entity. Accordingly, the director of a charitable corporation interested in ascertaining the limits of his or her liability needs to examine both the applicable statutes and the organization's governing instruments. Note that an attorney who drafts an indemnity provision into the bylaws of a private foundation should be careful not to run afoul of the provisions of the Internal Revenue Code's Section 4941.[65]

The Revised Model Nonprofit Corporation Act provides that a director shall not be deemed to be a trustee with respect to the corporation or with respect to any property held or administered by the corporation, including without limit, property that may be subject to restrictions imposed by the donor or transferor of such property.[66] The Restatement (Third) of Trusts is in accord, the director not holding title to either the corporation or its property.[67]

Principal invasion. Another fundamental divergence in the law of charitable trusts and charitable corporations relates to principal invasion. An unrestricted gift to a charitable corporation carries with it the presumption that principal as well as income may be devoted to its charitable purpose; a charitable trust is presumed to be income only, absent an expression of contrary intent in the governing instrument.[68]

Standards of care. A third fundamental difference between the charitable trust and the charitable corporation relates to the fiduciary's standard of care. "As nonprofits gradually came to be organized as corporations, many courts began to apply the corporate standard of care to nonprofit directors, a level of care that, at least in the for-profit world, goes hand-in-hand with the business judgment rule."[69]

---

[62] *See* Revised Model Nonprofit Corporation Act Subchapter E, cmt. 1 (Directors and Officers) (1987); *see also* Moody, *State Statutes Governing Directors of Charitable Corporations*, 18 U.S.F. L. Rev. 749, 782–783 (1984) (presenting a table of state indemnification statutes applicable to nonprofit corporations).

[63] *See generally* T. G. Lynch & M. K. Fallon, *A Primer on Suing Charitable Corporations*, 27 Mass. Law. Wkly. 539, Nov. 16, 1998, at 11, col. 1 (focusing on Massachusetts, the authors suggest that plaintiffs may avoid statutory caps by suing compensated employees and officers directly).

[64] Cal. Corp. Code §5238.

[65] *See generally* Berry, 879-2nd T.M., Private Foundations—Self Dealing [I.R.C. §4941].

[66] Model Revised Nonprofit Corporation Act §8.30(e).

[67] Restatement (Third) of Trusts §5 cmt. g.

[68] *See generally* §5.4.1.3 of this handbook (right to income or possession).

[69] Denise Ping Lee, *The Business Judgment Rule: Should It Protect Nonprofit Directors?*, 103 Colum. L. Rev. 925 (2003). *See also* §9.12 of this handbook (the condominium trustee) (noting that

Ancient restrictions on the right to take and hold land. What was once a fourth difference between the charitable corporation and the charitable trust related to ancient statutory restrictions on the right *to take and hold* land in England.[70] Early on, Parliament took to placing certain restrictions on the ability of a corporation, which in most cases would be the church, to take and hold land, this so as not to "deprive the overlord, including the king as lord paramount, of the benefits accruing from human tenants, who would live, marry, have children, and die" and so as not "to undermine the defense of the realm, which was based on the relationship between land-lord and tenant."[71] The process of imposing such restrictions began with the signing of the Magna Carta.[72] In 1960, they were removed once and for all by an act of Parliament.[73]

Mortmain. What was once a fifth difference between the charitable corporation and the charitable trust related to one's ability to *devise* one's land by will. Prior to the enactment of the statute of wills in 1540, a land owner at common law could not devise his land to anyone, "except, by local custom, in London and certain other towns."[74] With enactment of the statute of wills, land could now be devised, but not to corporations.[75] As discussed in Section 8.15.1 of this handbook, landowners in the latter part of the fifteenth century and early part of the sixteenth century employed the feoffment to use in part as a will substitute.[76] The statute of charitable uses, which Parliament enacted in 1601 and which we cover in Section 8.15.4 of this handbook, came to be construed by the English courts as validating devises to charitable corporations.[77] In 1736, however, Parliament enacted the Georgian Statute of Mortmain, "which forbade devises of land to any person or corporation for charitable uses."[78] In 1891, this statute was repealed.[79] In England, by 1960, most statutory restrictions on one's ability to devise land to a charitable corporation had been lifted.[80] In the United States, there are now only a few states that still place some restriction on one's ability to bequeath or devise property to a charitable corporation,[81] or on the amount or type of property that may be so transferred.[82]

---

a condominium trustee is generally held to a corporate-like business judgment standard rather than to the prudent man standard of a trustee).

[70] *See generally* 5 Scott & Ascher §37.2.6.1 (Restrictions in England on the Holding of Land by Corporations).

[71] *See generally* 5 Scott & Ascher §37.2.6.1.

[72] *See generally* 5 Scott & Ascher §37.2.6.1.

[73] *See generally* 5 Scott & Ascher §37.2.6.1.

[74] *See generally* 5 Scott & Ascher §37.2.6.2 (Restrictions in England on Devises of Land to Corporations).

[75] *See generally* 5 Scott & Ascher §37.2.6.2.

[76] *See also* 5 Scott & Ascher §37.2.6.2.

[77] *See generally* 5 Scott & Ascher §37.2.6.2.

[78] 5 Scott & Ascher §37.2.6.2 (referring to Stat. 9 Geo. II, c. 36 (1736)).

[79] *See* Stat. 54 & 55 Vict. C. 73 (1891).

[80] *See* Charities Act, 1960, 8 & 9 Eliz. II, c. 58, §38.

[81] 5 Scott & Ascher §37.2.6.4 n.6.

[82] 5 Scott & Ascher §37.2.6.4 n.7.

§9.8.2   *The City, the State, or the United States as Trustee*[83]

At common law it was held that a use . . . could not be enforced against the Crown.[84]

Jurisdiction over any suit against the Government requires a clear statement from the United States waiving sovereign immunity, together with a claim falling within the terms of the waiver.[85]

While the United States and the states, counties, and municipalities within it in theory may have common law or statutory authority to hold property in trust, the absence of the key element of credible enforceability makes such trusteeship, for all intents and purposes, illusory.[86] It is true that in the case of

---

[83] *See generally* Bogert §330.

[84] United States v. Mitchell, 463 U.S. 206 n.8 (1983) (Powell, J., dissenting) (citing 2A Scott, Law of Trusts §95, at 772 (3d ed. 1967)).

[85] United States v. White Mountain Apache Tribe, 123 S. Ct. 1126, 1131–1132 (2003) (holding that a federal statute providing that Fort Apache shall be held by the United States in trust for the White Mountain Apache Tribe imposed certain fiduciary obligations on the United States to include keeping the property from falling into disrepair).

[86] 2 Scott & Ascher §11.1.5 (suggesting that when either the United States or a state holds land in trust, sovereign immunity may complicate enforcement). *See, e.g.,* Kelly Patricia O'Meara, *Digging for Gold in L.A.'s Courts,* 16(33) Insight on the News 20 (Sept. 4, 2000) (reporting that millions of dollars are hidden in a trust fund overseen by Los Angeles County's Superior Court, which a pair of insiders have plundered in a major bribery scandal); *Probe Hits US Funding of Indian Trust Funds,* Boston Globe, Apr. 4, 1992, at 5 (Bureau of Indian Affairs accused of decades of mismanagement of trusts); John J. Fialka, *Indians Demand Money in U.S. Trust-Fund Labyrinth,* Wall St. J., July 9, 1998, at A20, col. 1 ("Under U.S. law, banks and others that manage trusts must make good on losses, but Ed Cohen, The Interior Department's deputy solicitor, argues that the law 'doesn't necessarily mean we have the same burden as the private-sector trustee.'"); Kelly Patricia O'Meara, *Total Lack of Trust,* 17(35) Insight on the News 10 (Sept. 17, 2001) (suggesting that "unscrupulous politicians and bureaucrats have mislaid $10 billion-plus from a century-old trust fund established to aid Native Americans"); Kelly Patricia O'Meara, *Bureaucrats Circle Their Wagons,* 17 Insight on the News 16 (Dec. 31, 2001) (reporting that Interior officials facing civil contempt-of-court proceedings for their department's role in "looting" the Indian trust fund "add another layer to the bureaucracy"); John J. Fialka, *House Panel Narrows Search Into Payments Made to Indians,* Wall St. J., July 15, 2002, at B8, col. 5 (a federal judge having ordered the Interior Department to do an accounting of trust funds it had been administering for individual Indians back to the nineteenth century, the House Appropriations Committee says it will provide funds for only a search of computer records back to 1985); John J. Fialka, *Judge Holds Interior Secretary In Contempt Over Indian Trust,* Wall St. J., Sept. 18, 2002, at A6, col. 4 (Judge Royce C. Lamberth indicating that his next action may be to take over the Indian trust accounts by putting them in the hands of a court-appointed receiver); John J. Fialka, *Panel Removes Federal Judge From Indian Trust-Fund Case,* Wall St. J., July 12, 2006, at A6 (the court of appeals panel determining that while the Department of the Interior record in the matter was "deplorable," the trial judge had essentially lost his objectivity); Associated Press, *U.S. Owes Indians Award, Judge Rules,* Wall St. J, Aug. 8, 2008, at A12 ("A federal judge ruled American Indian plaintiffs are entitled to $455 million in a long-running trust case, a fraction of the $47 billion they wanted"). "The lead plaintiff in the suit, Elouise Cobell, a Blackfeet Indian, said she is 'disappointed, to say the least.'" Associated Press, *U.S. Owes Indians Award, Judge Rules,* Wall St. J, Aug. 8, 2008, at A12 "The Interior Department praised the ruling." Associated Press, *U.S. Owes Indians Award, Judge Rules,* Wall St. J, Aug. 8, 2008, at A12. *See* United States v. Mitchell, 463 U.S. 206, 225 (1983) ("Moreover, a fiduciary relationship necessarily arises when the government assumes such elaborate control over forests and property belonging to

land entrusted to a municipal corporation, the state attorney general would
have standing to seek enforcement of the trust in the courts.[87] The practical,
political, and legal realities are, however, that an attorney general, even if so
inclined, would find it difficult, if not impossible, to effect a judicial removal of
any governmental entity as trustee, at least of the type of trust that is the subject
of this handbook.[88] There is only so much that the courts can do when the
government is involved in the administration of trusts, as we have seen with the
Indian trust accounting litigation.[89] As political influence and press oversight[90]
are generally the only viable means of enforcing governmental "trusteeships,"
such arrangements generally fall outside the scope of this handbook. That
having been said, the Restatement (Third) of Restitution and Unjust Enrichment proffers an optimistic illustration of a municipality successfully being
compelled by a court to honor its fiduciary responsibilities as a charitable
trustee of some real estate:

> City holds Blackacre under a perpetual charitable trust for public park purposes.
> Acting with the consent of the mayor and city council, as subsequently ratified by
> the State legislature, City conveys Blackacre to Developer for use as a parking lot.
> Taxpayers (as trust beneficiaries) sue City and Developer to compel rescission of
> the conveyance. City argues that (i) the original conveyance to City did not create
> a public trust, (ii) if a trust was created it has since become impossible to carry out,
> (iii) using Blackacre as a parking lot is justified under the doctrine of cy pres, and
> (iv) any breach of trust was eliminated when the State legislature enacted a statute

---

Indians. . . . All of the necessary elements of a common-law trust are present: a trustee (the United
States), a beneficiary (the Indian allottees), and a trust corpus (Indian timber, lands and funds)");
Cobell v. Babbit, 30 F. Supp. 2d 24 (D.D.C. 1998) (confirming that the United States as a matter of
law can be a common law trustee).

[87] 5 Scott & Ascher §37.1.1 (noting that under certain circumstances owners of adjoining
properties, taxpayers, and residents of the municipality also might have standing to seek enforcement of the trust, or of any use restrictions to which the land may lawfully be subject in the absence
of a trust).

[88] *See* Karst, *The Efficiency of the Charitable Dollar: An Unfulfilled State Responsibility*, 73 Harv. L.
Rev. 433, 478–479 (1960).

[89] *See* Mary Clare Jalonick, *Federal Judge Says Interior Dept. Delayed Indian Trust Accounting*,
Boston Globe, Jan. 31, 2008, at A16 ("The federal agency 'has not, and cannot, remedy . . . [its
breach of fiduciary duty] . . . to account for the Indian money, US District Judge James Robertson
said in a 165-page decision . . . ,'" the judge also blaming Congress for failing to appropriate
enough money for a proper forensic accounting).

[90] The contempt orders against Interior Secretary Bruce Babbitt and Treasury Secretary
Robert Rubin grew out of a class-action law suit over the government's mishandling of 300,000
trust fund accounts totaling $2.5 billion that it managed on behalf of American Indians. Senator
John McCain said that if anyone in the private sector had operated the way the government
had "they would be in jail today." Indeed, the bottom line of U.S. District Court Judge Royce
Lamberth's ruling is that Washington isn't exempt from the standards it sets for private
trustees . . . that the government has a fiduciary obligation to properly manage accounts it controls
(Social Security trustees take note). He noted that the Bureau of Indian Affairs lacked records for
$2 billion of tribal account transactions over a twenty-year period. Editorial, *Indian Takers*, Wall St.
J., Feb. 23, 1999, at A22, col. 1. *See also* John J. Fialka, *Babbitt Misled Judge About New System for
Indian Funds in '99, Report Alleges*, Wall St. J., Aug. 10, 2001, at A10, col. 1.

authorizing the conveyance to Developer. The court rejects each of these arguments, concluding that the conveyance was made in breach of trust and that Developer had notice of the relevant facts. Taxpayers are entitled to an order rescinding the conveyance and to injunctive relief enforcing City's duties as trustee.[91]

Enforcing a trust against a municipality as trustee is one thing, but against a sovereign state (or its agents) as trustee is quite another. Take Calpers. Calpers is an acronym for California's Public Employees' Retirement System. Unlike Congress when it created the phantom social security trust fund,[92] the California legislature created the Public Employees Retirement Fund "solely for the benefit of the members and retired members of . . . [the] . . . system and their survivors and beneficiaries."[93] Moreover, by law the pension rights of a California public employee "may not be destroyed, once vested, without impairing a contractual obligation of the employing public entity."[94] Unlike a participant in Social Security, which is legally a welfare program that creates no private property rights,[95] a California public employee would have a property right in his accrued pension benefits that would warrant the protections of the taking clause of the Fifth Amendment to the U.S. Constitution, the U.S. Constitution under its Article I, Section 10(1) having prohibited a state from passing a law impairing the obligations of contracts. Moreover, unlike the Social Security welfare recipient,[96] he would have standing to seek redress in the courts should California interfere with those contractual property rights.[97]

Accordingly, if it is discovered that the assets in the Calpers fund are being improperly or imprudently invested, the worker, a private citizen, in theory would have standing to go into court and seek to enjoin the Calpers board from continuing to abuse its trust. His or her counsel would argue that "the interest of the employee at issue is in the security and integrity of the funds to pay future benefits."[98] Moreover, the California cases suggest that a Calpers beneficiary would also have a cause of action against the state were the Calpers board's investment practices actually to interfere with his or her defined benefit. In

---

[91] Restatement (Third) of Restitution and Unjust Enrichment §17, illus. 1. The illustration is based on Cohen v. City of Lynn, 33 Mass. App. Ct. 271, 598 N.E.2d 682 (1992). *See also* The Woodward School for Girls, Inc. v. City of Quincy, trustee, SJC-11390, 2013 WL 8923423 (Mass. July 23, 2014) ("[W]hen Quincy agreed to serve as trustee, it assumed the fiduciary duties of that role, including the consequences for not fulfilling these duties. The policy purposes of sovereign immunity are not served where, as here, a municipality takes on a responsibility beyond its inherent or core government functions and therefore serves in a capacity that could just as easily be accomplished by a nongovernmental entity.").

[92] *See* §9.9.3 of this handbook (social security and other legislative budget items couched in trust terminology).

[93] Cal. Gov. Code Ann. §20170 (West).

[94] Valdes v. Cory, 139 Cal. App. 3d 773, 783–784, 189 Cal. Rptr. 212, 221 (1983).

[95] Helvering v. Davis, 301 U.S. 619 (1937).

[96] *See* Flemming v. Nestor, 363 U.S. 603 (1960).

[97] *See* Valdes v. Cory, 139 Cal. App. 3d 773, 189 Cal. Rptr. 212 (1983).

[98] *See* Valdes v. Cory, 139 Cal. App. 3d 773, 189 Cal. Rptr. 212 (1983).

other words, the beneficiary could sue the State of California for breach of contract. But the victory could well be a pyrrhic one:

> It does not necessarily follow, however, that the pensioner possesses the ability to compel the payment of benefits as they mature. If the Legislature fails to appropriate sums from the general fund for the purpose of funding the special retirement account or otherwise paying the state's indebtedness to pensioners, a court of this state is powerless to compel the Legislature to appropriate such sums or to order payment of the indebtedness.[99]

The problem is that it is hugely expensive and time consuming for a member of the public to take on the full might of the state in an action for breach of fiduciary duty. In California, the cards are particularly stacked against the petitioner. On June 5, 2003, for example, California's attorney general rendered a legal opinion that Calpers may allow its fiduciaries to purchase "waivers of recourse" coverage from its own self-insurance program, thus effectively enabling them to socially invest with impunity.[100] Bottom line: When the government gets involved in investing the property of others, the law talks loudly but carries a very small stick. As a practical matter, the beneficiary is left with either waiting until election day or going to the press.

Those charged with administering the Calpers fund are politicians, political appointees, agents of politicians, and agents of political appointees.[101] "Calpers is a political entity in every sense of the word."[102] The state attorney general, of course, is a politician as well. When a governmental entity gets into the business of investing, whether the portfolio is prudently invested in the last analysis depends upon the inclinations of the politicians in office from time to time.

And as to the press option, mounting a citizens' campaign to interest the fourth estate in shining a spotlight on a public retirement board's improper or imprudent investing practices can be time consuming; and in the few instances when the press has gotten involved, successes have been modest, fleeting, and generally at the margins:

> Despite Calpers' frequent calls for full disclosure by companies, it can be a little reticent itself. Two years ago the fund refused to release details on the returns racked up by its private equity investments, which total some $7.8 billion. The San Jose Mercury has to go to court to get hold of the data. Calpers argued it wanted to disclose the data but was prevented by a confidentiality agreement with Grove Street Advisors, a firm it hired to assemble private equity funds. A judge disagreed. A year ago the Mercury News disclosed that one director, Angelides, had received political contributions from some Grove Street-related funds.[103]

---

[99] *See* Valdes v. Cory, 139 Cal. App. 3d 773, 189 Cal. Rptr. 212 (1983).
[100] 86 Ops. Cal. Atty. Gen. 95, 2003 WL 21672836 (Cal. A.G. 2003).
[101] Cal. Gov. Code Ann. §20090 (West).
[102] Benn Steil, *California's Sovereign Wealth Fund*, Wall St. J., Mar. 7, 2008, at A14.
[103] Neil Weinberg, *Sanctimonious in Sacramento*, Forbes, May 10, 2004, at 52, 54.

Unless funds are entrusted to an independent private trustee, *e.g.*, a bank or trust company, such that the entity assumes the actual legal title, "explicit . . . [statutory] . . . organizational mandates to maximize return on contributors' investment," "independent boards of trustees," and "contracting out portfolio management on a competitive basis,"[104] are safeguards in form only. There is no legal substance to them as the Calpers experience so amply demonstrates.

§9.8.3   Cemeteries, Parks, Roads, and Shorelines

Cemeteries. Cemetery land is usually held by a municipality or other governmental entity, a cemetery corporation, or a religious organization. Occasionally one will come across a cemetery situated within the borders of a privately owned parcel. Is a trust impressed upon such land? It would seem that some kind of trust is associated with cemetery land and there are some cases to that effect.[105] In the face of the common law rights of persons to visit, honor, and protect the graves of their deceased relatives, it is clear that those in control of cemetery land do not have untrammeled rights to exploit and alienate the land.[106]

On the other hand, as a matter of classic trust law it is not always clear to whom the burden of responsibility runs. In the case of a cemetery corporation it is clear that an affirmative burden runs to the governing body; with respect to a cemetery situated on private property, the fiduciary responsibilities of the owner of the property may be passive, such as merely to leave the cemetery undisturbed and to allow others on to the land at reasonable times to visit, honor, and protect the gravesites.[107] The law of trusts has been an underutilized weapon in the battle to protect cemeteries, particularly historic cemeteries.[108]

Parks. The legal status of parkland is also somewhat ambiguous.[109] Much depends upon how the land came to be a park. "While many cases and statutes describe the municipality as holding the dedicated land in trust, often the word 'trust' is used in a nontechnical sense, as denoting merely an obligation arising out of the acceptance of the dedicated property, and not as meaning that the city became a trustee for charitable purposes."[110] If the land was set aside

---

[104] *See generally* Alicia H. Munnell & R. Kent Weaver, *Hot to Privatize Social Security*, Wash. Post, July 9, 2001, at A17 [opinion editorial].

[105] *See* Rounds, *Protections Afforded to Massachusetts' Ancient Burial Grounds*, 73 Mass. L. Rev. 176, 180 n.118 (1988). *See, e.g.*, Sanford v. Vinal, 28 Mass. App. Ct. 476, 552 N.E.2d 579 (1990).

[106] *See* Rounds, *Protections Afforded to Massachusetts' Ancient Burial Grounds*, 73 Mass. L. Rev. 176, 180–182 (1988).

[107] Rounds, *Protections Afforded to Massachusetts' Ancient Burial Grounds*, 73 Mass. L. Rev. at 183–184, 188.

[108] *See* In the Matter of the Trusts Under the Will of Lotta M. Crabtree, 2003 WL 22119871 (Mass. 2003) (perhaps serving as precedent for the judicial appointment of a guardian ad litem to represent those who may have an interest in a historic burial ground that is being encroached upon).

[109] *See generally* Bogert §34.

[110] Bogert §34.

pursuant to the terms of someone's will, it may well be held upon a charitable trust,[111] although, as in the case of governmental trusts in general, the trust's enforceability may exist more in theory than in reality. If the governmental entity had carved out the parkland from public land or had taken the land by eminent domain, the arrangement looks less like a trust. One court, however, has held that the Boston Common is held by the City of Boston upon a quasi-trust.[112] The law of trusts has been an underutilized weapon not only in historic preservation battles but also in battles for open space.

Roads. If a landowner *dedicates* a strip of land of land for a public street, the municipality in which the land is located is not a trustee of the land.[113] Rather the public receives a legal interest in the land in the nature of an easement.[114] Legal title to the fee remains back with the "dedicator."[115] "Many of the suits against municipalities to compel the application of dedicated land to the special purpose for which it was dedicated are brought by taxpayers as such, on the usual theory of improper use of public property and consequent financial loss to the taxpayers. Equity takes jurisdiction because of the inadequacy of the remedy at law, and not because of any trust."[116] That is not to say that the owner of a strip of land could not *impress a public charitable trust* upon it or *donate* it unconditionally to the municipality. In the case of a charitable trust, the state attorney general would be charged with its enforcement, a topic we generally take up in Section 9.4.2 of this handbook.

Shorelines. The Commonwealth of Massachusetts holds "in trust" the rights of the public to navigate, fish, and fowl the area of its shoreline between the high and low water lines.[117] This is known as the public trust doctrine.[118] This, however, is not a trust of the type that is the subject of this handbook. Why? Because the government can and has from time to time interfered with those rights since 1647.[119]

---

[111] *See generally* Bogert §322.

[112] Codman v. Crocker, 203 Mass. 146, 150, 89 N.E. 177, 178 (1909). *See generally* Bogert §34 ("Where states hold land for special public purposes courts or legislatures sometimes state that the land is held in trust, but this usually is not true in a strict sense. A state may have a duty to use the property for a limited or general purpose but it arises from the acquisition of the property under special circumstances and from the duties of the state under its constitution and statutes.").

[113] Bogert §34.

[114] Bogert §34.

[115] Bogert §34.

[116] Bogert §34.

[117] *See* Donald D. Cooper, *In Recreation We Trust: The Public Trust Doctrine After* Fafard, 45(4) Boston B.J. 8, 23 (Sept./Oct. 2001).

[118] *See* Donald D. Cooper, *In Recreation We Trust: The Public Trust Doctrine After* Fafard, 45(4) Boston B.J. 8, 23 (Sept./Oct. 2001).

[119] *See* Donald D. Cooper, *In Recreation We Trust: The Public Trust Doctrine After* Fafard, 45(4) Boston B.J. 8, 23 (Sept./Oct. 2001).

§9.8.4 Custodial IRAs

In form a custodial IRA administered by a bank or mutual fund is an investment management agency relationship between the custodian and the person establishing the IRA.[120] If the arrangement were in substance a common law agency, it would terminate upon the death of the customer. The result then would be that all funds subject to the arrangement would pass to the customer's estate, notwithstanding any provisions of a beneficiary form to the contrary.

Most states, however, now have statutes on their books anticipating this problem.[121] The statutes provide that the terms of custodial IRA beneficiary designation forms shall be honored notwithstanding the failure of such forms to comply with the statute of wills.[122] Thus, by virtue of these statutes an IRA custodian begins to look very much like a common law trustee, particularly during the period between when the taxpayer dies and when the balance in the account is distributed.

§9.8.5 The Totten or Tentative Trust

Even though a settlor who creates a tentative trust reserves complete control over the deposit during life, the disposition is not invalid as an illusory or testamentary disposition. To the contrary, it is upheld as a convenient and permissible method of disposing of money at death. The tentative trust is an accepted form of will substitute that need not comply with the requirements of the Statute of wills and, ordinarily at least, . . . will be implemented without involvement in estate administration.[123]

In New York, and in many other jurisdictions as well, it has long been settled "that tentative trusts of bank accounts, or, as they are frequently called, 'Totten trusts,' are not subject to the statute of wills."[124] When *A* opens a savings account in the name of *C* and retains control of the account, courts are inclined to find that the arrangement is essentially a revocable living trust with *A* being both the trustee and the holder of a reserved right of revocation.[125] Some jurisdictions require that upon the death of *A* the money be paid to *A*'s estate, unless notice of the arrangement is given to *C* during *A*'s lifetime.[126] The validity of the standard revocable inter vivos trust, however, is not contingent upon notice being given to postmortem beneficiaries. "[The American Law] . . . Institute's position on Totten trusts, set forth in Restatement Third,

---

[120] *See* I.R.C. §408(h).

[121] *See* Bogert §255 n.11 (second n.11 of section) and accompanying text.

[122] *See* Bogert §255 n.11.

[123] Restatement (Third) of Trusts §26 cmt. b.

[124] 1 Scott & Ascher §8.3.3. *See also* 1 Scott & Ascher §§8.3.4 (Revocation of Tentative Trusts), 8.3.5 (Spousal and Creditor Access to Tentative Trusts).

[125] *See* 1A Scott on Trusts §58.1 n.3. *See also* In re Totten, 179 N.Y. 112, 71 N.E. 748 (1904).

[126] *See* L.S. Tellier, Annot., *Gift or trust by deposit in bank in another's name or in depositor's own name in trust for another, as affected by lack of knowledge on part of such other person*, 157 A.L.R. 925 (1945).

Trusts §26 . . . is that such trusts are valid without being executed in compliance with the formalities required for a will, and that, unless revoked, the balance on hand at the depositor's death passes outside probate to the beneficiary."[127] When the depositor is domiciled in one state and the bank is organized and doing business in another, the laws governing the validity of the Totten trust, not to mention the relevant administrative and dispositive default rules of construction, may be in conflict. This is a topic we take up in Section 8.5 of this handbook.

§9.8.6   Executor or Administrator of a Probate Estate

An executor is often called a trustee, and in the broad sense of the term so he is.— Scott on Trusts.[128]

In a stricter sense of the word trustee, however, it does not apply to personal representatives. . . .   —Lewin on Trusts.[129]

The executorship and the trusteeship have similarities. At common law, a personal representative, *i.e.*, an executor or administrator,[130] was like a trustee in that title to the personal property of the probate estate[131] was in the personal representative[132] and, the relation between the personal representative and the takers under the will was a fiduciary one.[133] "Traditionally, both executors and administrators on the one hand, and trustees on the other, have been personally liable on contracts they make and for torts they commit, in the absence of

---

[127] Restatement (Third) of Property (Wills and Other Donative Transfers) §7.1 cmt. i (Tentative Draft No. 3, Apr. 4, 2001).

[128] 1 Scott on Trusts §6. *See, e.g.*, Hartlove v. Maryland Sch. for the Blind, 111 Md. App. 310, 681 A.2d 584 (1996) (citing to Hon. Albert W. Northrop & Robert A. Schmuhl, Decedents' Estates in Maryland §6-4(e) at 242 (1994), for the proposition that the personal representative's "office is in the nature of a trustee for the creditors, legatees and next-of-kin of the deceased").

[129] Lewin ¶1-12.

[130] *See, e.g.*, Welch v. Flory, 294 Mass. 138, 200 N.E. 900 (1936) (holding that an administrator acts in a trust capacity in respect to his conduct in making distribution of an intestate estate).

[131] "A decedent's 'probate estate' is the estate subject to administration under applicable laws relating to decedents' estates." Restatement (Third) of Property (Wills and Other Donative Transfers) §1.1(a). For its purposes, the UPC defines estate as "the property of the decedent, trust, or other person whose affairs are subject to this Code as originally constituted and as it exists from time to time during administration." UPC §1-201(13).

[132] 1 Scott on Trusts §6; Bogert §12.

[133] 1 Scott on Trusts §6. *See also* UPC §1-201(15) (confirming that it is still the case that a personal representative, like a trustee, is a fiduciary). For a discussion of the concept of the fiduciary, *see* Chapter 1 of this handbook. In Bogert §12, it is noted that many decisions state that personal representatives are not trustees, but are "probate fiduciaries." As a fiduciary is either an agent or a trustee, or some statutory variant of an agent or trustee, by process of elimination the term *probate fiduciary* must be a statutory variant of a trustee, assuming he is not an actual trustee. A decedent's personal representative cannot be an agent of the decedent because an agency terminates upon the death of the principal. In the case of probate personalty, the personal representative cannot be an agent of the legatees with respect to the personalty until such time as

special circumstances. In this regard, and in the consequent right to indemnity or reimbursement from the estate and the freedom from personal liability on the part of the legatee and beneficiary, the two relationships are alike."[134] There is symmetry when it comes to set-offs, as well: "An executor has a right to set off a debt from a legatee to the testator against the legacy, as a trustee can set off a claim of the trust against the beneficiary."

Just as the beneficiary of a trust has an equitable property interest in the entrusted property so also does a legatee under a will have an equitable property interest in the probate estate. One commentator, however, is not in accord, suggesting that the legatee has merely "a claim that the executor shall set off something in satisfaction of the legacy."[135] If the legatee's claim is not a contractual property right assertable against the executor, and it is not, then it would seem that by process of elimination the "claim" would have to be an equitable property interest in the probate property itself.

The differences. At common law, a personal representative was *unlike* a trustee in that the duties of a personal representative were temporary in character, being limited to the "winding up" of the probate estate.[136] Also, the personal representative ordinarily did not have a duty to invest probate estate assets.[137] Today, in the case of realty, "title passes directly to the devisees or heirs, although the executor or administrator may have a power to sell to pay debts of the deceased; hence no trust arises merely from the appointment of the personal representative."[138] This was the case at common law as well.

The common historical root of the executorship and the trusteeship. The notion that an executorship in many respects is like a trusteeship is not a new one.[139] After all, each was an invention of the English chancery court.[140] By the fourteenth century, the English will with executors, "an offshoot of the ancient Germanic *Treuhandschaft*," was well established.[141] It had evolved from a *donatio post obitum* or inter vivos contract to convey postmortem into something that was testamentary, that spoke at death.[142] The executor was becoming the personal representative of the deceased in all matters other than the disposition of real estate. "In later days when the Trust, strictly so called, had been

---

legal title passes from the personal representative to them. As a general rule, title to property that is the subject of an agency is in the principal, not the agent. *See generally* §9.9.2 of this handbook (agencies).

[134] Bogert §12. *See generally* §7.3 of this handbook (trustee's external liability as legal owner to nonbeneficiaries); §3.5.2.3 of this handbook (trustee's right to indemnity and reimbursement); §5.6 of this handbook (liabilities of the trust beneficiary).

[135] Bogert §12.

[136] 1 Scott on Trusts §6; Bogert §12.

[137] 1 Scott on Trusts §6; Bogert §12. *But see* 1 Scott & Ascher §2.3.2 (suggesting that nowadays, the executor may have a duty to make estate funds productive).

[138] Bogert §12.

[139] *See* 1 Scott on Trusts §6; 1 Scott & Ascher §2.3.2.

[140] Bogert §12 ("Both executorship and trust are therefore originally institutions of chancery, but this does not mean that they are equivalent or that executorship is merely one form of trust.").

[141] Maitland, Selected Essays (1936) 155.

[142] Maitland, Selected Essays (1936) 155.

developed, these two institutes, which indeed had a common root, began to influence one another."[143]

The Uniform Probate Code conflates the executorship and the trusteeship. The Uniform Probate Code conflates the executorship and the trusteeship in its definition of the word *estate*: " 'Estate' includes the property of the decedent, trust, or other person whose affairs are subject to this Code as originally constituted and as it exists from time to time during administration."[144] The Code further provides that "[u]ntil termination of his appointment a personal representative has the same power over the title to property of the estate that an absolute owner would have, in trust however, for the benefit of the creditors and others interested in the estate."[145] Those "others" would include the decedent's heirs and devisees. In Uniform Probate Code jurisdictions the relationship of the personal representative to the estate *is* that of a trustee.[146] Accordingly, a personal representative is a fiduciary who shall observe the standards of care applicable to trustees.[147] The Restatement (Third) of Trusts is in accord, although it rejects the notion that the personal representative is a trustee.[148]

Duties to creditors. As noted, a personal representative has fiduciary duties that run to the creditors of the probate estate as well as to the devisees or heirs at law as the case may be.[149] As a general rule, however, the trustee of a trust, be it revocable or irrevocable, owes no fiduciary duties to the creditors of the settlor's probate estate,[150] or to the creditors of the beneficiaries of the trust.[151]

When the executor is also the testamentary trustee. Sometimes the provisions of a will, when read together, suggest that the testator may have intended that the personal representative morph, at some point, into a trustee of certain property passing under the will. Failure of the executor to expressly designate the trustee is not determinative.[152] Rather, it is the nature and duration of the duties to be performed.[153] "If the direction concerns realty, courts often find a trust intent, because an executor ordinarily would have no title to the real estate, although he might have powers over it."[154]

When the same person is both executor of the probate estate and the expressly designated trustee of a trust established under the terms of the will, it is not always clear when the person ceases being an executor and assumes the

---

[143] Maitland, Selected Essays (1936) 155.

[144] UPC §1-201(13).

[145] UPC §3-711. *See also* Bogert §12.

[146] UPC §3-703(a) cmt.

[147] UPC §3-703(a).

[148] Restatement (Third) of Trusts §5 cmt. c.

[149] Rounds, 853 T.M., Fiduciary Liability of Trustees and Personal Representatives at A-2.

[150] Rounds, 853 T.M., Fiduciary Liability of Trustees and Personal Representatives at A-2.

[151] Rounds, 853 T.M., Fiduciary Liability of Trustees and Personal Representatives at A-2.

[152] Bogert §12.

[153] Bogert §12.

[154] Bogert §12.

role of trustee with respect to a particular investment.[155] "This determination depends on the evidence of possession of the res, disposition of its income, and bookkeeping records."[156] The exact status and function of the fiduciary at a given point in time, however, may have a bearing on the rights, duties, and obligations of the parties, including those with an equitable interest in the subject property, a topic that is covered in Section 2.1.2 of this handbook.

Wrongful death actions. In the case of an action for wrongful death, by statute the decedent's executor or administrator holds the action "in an entirely distinct capacity" as trustee for the benefit of the testator's spouse and certain blood relations.[157] The cause of action is not an asset of the probate estate, nor is any recovery, and thus neither is typically subject to the claims of the decedent's creditors.[158]

Disposition of surplus fiduciaried property. When an express trust is fully performed and there is property still remaining in the trust estate, a resulting trust is generally imposed on the surplus.[159] In other words, the trustee may not walk away with the trust property, unless the terms of the express trust provide otherwise.[160] "Whether the trust is inter vivos or testamentary, the traditional view is that extrinsic evidence of the settlor's declarations that the trustee is to be permitted to keep the property if the trust is fully accomplished without exhausting the trust estate is ordinarily inadmissible."[161] At English common law, however, the default presumption was otherwise when it came to executors of probate estates. "The usual inference was that the testator intended that the executor would keep any surplus that remained after payment of debts and legacies, if there was no residuary disposition."[162] The inference, however, is now the opposite both in England and in the United States.[163]

§9.8.7 The Quistclose Trust

I can appreciate no reason why the flexible interplay of law and equity cannot let in these practical arrangements, and other variations if desired: it would be to the discredit of both

---

[155] Bogert §12.

[156] Bogert §12.

[157] Bogert §12.

[158] Bogert §12.

[159] *See generally* 6 Scott & Ascher §42.2 (Rebutting the Resulting Trust); §4.1.1.1 of this handbook (the resulting trust).

[160] *See generally* 6 Scott & Ascher §42.2 (Rebutting the Resulting Trust); §4.1.1.1 of this handbook (the resulting trust).

[161] *See generally* 6 Scott & Ascher §42.2 (Rebutting the Resulting Trust); §4.1.1.1 of this handbook (the resulting trust).

[162] 6 Scott & Ascher §42.2. "This inference, however, was overcome if from the whole will there could be gathered an intention not to give the executor the surplus." 6 Scott & Ascher §42.2. Evidence that the executor was *not* to take the surplus could be rebutted by parol evidence. 6 Scott & Ascher §42.2.

[163] 6 Scott & Ascher §42.2.

systems if they could not. In the present case the intention to create a secondary trust for the benefit of the lender, to arise if the primary trust, to pay the dividend, could not be carried out, is clear and I can find no reason why the law would not give effect to it.[164]

"[T]he common law rules of tracing are not available where money is paid into and through a mixed fund, unlike the equitable rules."[165] Equity, however, traditionally has required proof of a fiduciary relationship.

The Quistclose trust, which some commentators have labeled a "quasi-trust,"[166] derives its name from the 1970 English case of *Barclays Bank Ltd. v. Quistclose Investments Ltd.*[167] In that case, the court held that if *X* (a lender) lends funds to *Y* (a borrower) with the understanding that *Y* (the borrower) will use the funds to pay down a debt that *Y* (the borrower) owes to *Z* (a third party), then *Y* (the borrower) will be deemed a trustee of the funds for the benefit of *Z* (the third party). If the debt cannot be paid, the funds return to *X* (the lender) upon a resulting trust.[168] It is not an express purpose trust, which we cover in Section 9.27 of this handbook, although some would disagree.[169]

In the *Quistclose* case, the debt that *Y* (the borrower) had owed to *Z* (the third party) was a dividend that *Y* (the borrower) had declared. *Y* (the borrower) had gone bankrupt before it could pay down its debt to *Z* (the third party).

The issue was whether the relationship between the parties with respect to the funds had been one of trust or contract. If *X* (the lender) and *Y* (the borrower) had been in only a contractual relationship, *X* (the lender) would have been a mere creditor of *Y* (the borrower), one of many, with only a legal claim to the funds. If *X*, *Y*, and *Z* had been parties to a trust relationship as well, the funds would have been segregated in equity from *Y*'s (the borrower's) personal assets and would now be returnable to *X* (the lender) upon a resulting trust.[170] *X*'s (the lender's) claim being equitable as well as legal, the creditors of *Y* (the borrower) would have no access to the funds.

The court held that a trust had been established and that *X* (the lender) was entitled to the funds, not the general creditors of *Y* (the borrower). The creditors had argued that a legal action of debt and a claim in equity were mutually exclusive, that "a transaction may attract one action or the other, it could not admit of both."[171] The court rejected such a "conceptualist" approach to the interaction of law and equity.

---

[164] Barclays Bank Ltd. v. Quistclose Invs. Ltd., [1970] A.C. 567, 582.

[165] Angus Ross & Michael Godden, *Robbing Peter to Pay Paul*, 1(4) Tr. Q. Rev. 11 (2004).

[166] *See, e.g.*, Simon Baughen, *Quistclose Trusts and Knowing Receipt*, Conv. & Prop. Law. 351–357 (July/Aug. 2000).

[167] [1970] A.C. 567, HL. *See generally* Lewin ¶ 8-38 through ¶ 8-48.

[168] Twinsecta v. Yardley [2002] 2 WLR 8002 [England] (judgment rendered by Lord Millet).

[169] *See* Stuart Pryke, *Protectors and Enforcers: Duties and Considerations*, 8 Trust Quarterly Review, Issue 1 (2010), footnote 22, at 12 [a STEP publication] ("Glasson, however, argues that a *Quistclose* trust is not a resulting trust; it is an express trust in favour of the lender, with a power vested in the borrower to pay the funds for the agreed purpose . . ."). *See generally* §4.1.1.1 of this handbook (the resulting trust).

[170] *See generally* §4.1.1.1 of this handbook (the noncharitable trust; resulting trust defined) (in which the resulting trust is defined).

[171] Barclays Bank Ltd. v. Quistclose Invs. Ltd., [1970] A.C. 567.

In the United States, whether a nondonative transfer of money from *X* to *Y* would give rise to something akin to a Quistclose trust (with an attendant duty on the part of the transferee to segregate the funds) or whether it would give rise to a mere third party beneficiary contract (with no attendant duty on the part of the transferee to segregate) would depend upon the intentions of the parties:

> If the intention is that the money shall be kept or used as a separate fund for the benefit of the payor or one or more third persons, a trust is created. If it is intended, however, that the person receiving the money shall have the unrestricted use of it, being liable to pay a similar amount to the payor or a third person, whether with or without interest, a debt is created.[172]

For a discussion of the fundamental differences between a debt and a trust, the reader is referred to Section 9.9.4 of this handbook.

§9.8.8   Custodianships for Minors

An account established for a minor in a state pursuant to its Uniform Transfers to Minors Act or Uniform Gifts to Minors Act will have all the attributes of a common law trust with one technical exception: The beneficiary, not the trustee, will have the legal title.[173] Because equity looks to the substance rather than the form of an arrangement, it will deem the custodian to be a trustee of the account property and subject to the equitable duties and obligations that are the subject of this handbook.[174] The Restatement (Third) of Trusts is in accord. In it, such custodial arrangements are referred to as "virtual trusts."[175]

§9.8.9   The Uniform Custodial Trust Act

Its purpose is to provide a statutory standby inter vivos trust for use by persons who are of modest means or who are relatively unsophisticated in estate plan matters.[176]

The Uniform Custodial Trust Act allows one to establish a trust for oneself or another adult by registering securities or other property in the name of a custodial trustee and invoking the Act's provisions. This can be done by filling out and signing a form. The provisions of the statute spell out the rights, duties and obligations of the parties to what is essentially a standardized trust. Although the adjective "custodial" is used, title is in the custodial trustee.[177]

---

[172] Restatement (Third) of Trusts §5 cmt. k. *See also* 1 Scott & Ascher §2.3.8.1.

[173] *See generally* 1 Scott & Ascher §2.3.12.

[174] *See generally* Restatement (Third) of Trusts §5 cmt. a(1).

[175] *See generally* Restatement (Third) of Trusts §5 cmt. a(1).

[176] Bogert §15.

[177] Unif. Custodial Trust Act §2(c).

"This statutory trust is intended to avoid the problems of court appointment and accountings, bonds and sureties, and other complexities that are involved in most states under a guardianship or conservatorship."[178]

§9.8.10   The STAR Trust [Cayman Islands]

STAR is the acronym for Special Trusts (Alternate Regime), a creature of Cayman Island legislation.[179] A STAR trust is a contract-trust hybrid.[180] It differs from the common law trust in that equitable ownership is not a necessary element of the legal relationship, although some argue that equitable ownership is essentially lacking in the common law charitable trust as well.[181] If the administration of an item of property may be ordered by contract, so, too, it may be ordered pursuant to a STAR trust arrangement.[182] A STAR trust may exist in perpetuity and need not be for a charitable purpose.[183] It is not enforceable at the petition of the attorney general.[184] In this respect, it appears to have some of the attributes of the benevolent trust, which is discussed in Section 3.4.1 of this handbook. In the absence of equitable ownership, the terms of the STAR trust should address to whom the trustee will be accountable.[185] Otherwise, it is not entirely clear what the default law would be in this regard. Perhaps the trustee has full ownership subject to fiduciary duties.[186] Perhaps the settlor possesses some kind of contractual reversion.[187] If that is the case, then the STAR trust would have some of the attributes of the purpose trust, a topic we take up in Section 9.27 of this handbook. Why the STAR trust? One local commentator has explained it this way:

> But we did see the need for a way to enable certain perfectly legitimate property arrangements to be made that for technical reasons could not be made under the inherited regime. I think all of us who practice Cayman law advise clients that, if there is no particular reason to have a STAR trust, they should have an ordinary trust, and take the full benefit of all the refinements and adjustments that judges have made over the centuries, and the full benefit of all the learned treatises analysing and discussing the law—even if that does give lawyers a great deal of material to disagree about. But if the client's wishes cannot be achieved with an ordinary trust, he may prefer to use STAR rather than change or abandon his project.[188]

---

[178] Bogert §15.

[179] For a discussion of the civil law trust analogues, see §8.12.1 of this handbook.

[180] See generally §8.22 of this handbook (comparing the trust and contract relationships).

[181] See generally §9.4.2 of this handbook (standing to enforce charitable trusts).

[182] Anthony Duckworth, STAR trusts, 7(2) Tr. Q. Rev. 37 (May 2009) [a STEP publication].

[183] See generally §8.2.1 of this handbook (the Rule against Perpetuities).

[184] See generally §9.4.2 of this handbook (standing to enforce charitable trusts).

[185] See generally §6.1.5 of this handbook (the trustee's duty to account).

[186] For a discussion of the civil law contract-based trust analogues, see §8.12.1 of this handbook

[187] See generally §4.1.1 of this hand book (reversionary interests).

[188] Anthony Duckworth, STAR trusts, 7(2) Tr. Q. Rev. 41–42 (May 2009) [a STEP publication].

§9.8.11   The Quasi Trustee [The Corporate Director]

In Section 9.9.8 of this handbook we explain why it cannot be said that the directors of a noncharitable corporation are either trustees of the corporation itself or its assets. That being said, their duties are trustee-like and thus, in some quarters at least, they are referred to as quasi trustees: "Such fiduciaries are not true trustees, because the property is not vested in them, but are in an analogous position, as they claim no personal interest in it, and are treated in many ways as if they were true trustees, including their accountability for abusing the trust and confidence reposed in them, and for the purpose of imposing proprietary and personal liability in equity in respect of unauthorized profits they make from their position or the property, or by reason of self-dealing, or in respect of property transferred in breach of trust."[189]

§9.9   False Trusts

The public should be aware that just because an arrangement is described in trust-like terms, it does not necessarily have the requisite elements of a trust. Phrases such as *cash surrender value* or *internal build-up* do not make an insurance contract a trust. Nor is the Social Security trust fund a trust fund. Though a mortgagee may take title to the mortgagor's real estate, the mortgagee, absent special facts, is not a trustee of the real estate.

§9.9.1   Contracts Generally; Life Insurance and Third-Party Beneficiary Contracts in Particular

To appreciate why trusts are used in various contexts it is necessary to appreciate the nature and strengths of the trust concept. This concept straddles the law of property and the law of personal obligations and allows circumvention of the English privity of contract doctrine that prevents third parties from enforcing a contract for their benefit made by others.[1]

The debtor is not a steward for the creditor.[2]

A contract is not a trust. The trust relationship is *sui generis*.[3] It is not some sub-category of the contractual relationship, although the occasional judge or

---

[189] Lewin ¶ 7-16 (England).

§9.9 [1] David Hayton, *The Uses of Trusts in the Commercial Context*, in Trusts in Prime Jurisdictions 431 (Alon Kaplan ed., 2000).

[2] Bogert §17.

[3] *Cf.* Charles E. Rounds, Jr. & István Illés, *Is a Hungarian Trust a Clone of the Anglo-American Trust, or Just a Type of Contract?: Parsing the Asset-Management Provisions of the New Hungarian Civil Code*, 6 Geo. Mason J. Int'l Com. L. 153 (2015).

academic will confuse the two.[4] A trust beneficiary possesses an equitable property interest in the subject property incident to a declaration or conveyance that need not involve the exchange of consideration.[5] "Contracts are still dependent on consideration for their enforceability. This is a marked distinction between a trust and a contract."[6] A contract requires the mutual assent of the parties. A trust, on the other hand, can come into existence without the knowledge, let alone the consent, of either the designated trustee or the beneficiary.[7]

It is said that the interest of a creditor is a chose in action while the interest of a trust beneficiary amounts to equitable ownership of the subject property.[8] Contractual rights, however, may be the subject of a trust.[9] So may equitable interests in other trusts.[10]

The property of a trust is not commingled with the trustee's personal assets and thus is insulated from the reach of the trustee's personal creditors and spouse.[11] Absent special facts, an unsecured contract creditor has no equitable property interest in the personal assets of the debtor.[12] In other words there is no segregation of a portion or all of the debtor's personal assets for the purpose of securing the creditor's contractual rights.[13] "A debtor ordinarily may freely dispose of all property interests. A debtor has no positive duty to use property for the benefit of the creditors. Rather, debtors have a negative duty not to employ their assets in ways that might be detrimental to the creditors."[14] It is said that the debtor owns his own property absolutely.[15] There is no divided ownership.[16] That having been said, a debtor's personal assets may be reached by the debtor's unsecured contract creditors in satisfaction of the debtor's contractual obligations to them.[17] That a debtor owes certain duties to creditors that may be enforceable in equity, however, does not somehow transform the

---

[4] *See* Bogert §17 n.2.

[5] *See generally* §5.3.1 of this handbook (nature and extent of beneficiary's property interest).

[6] Bogert §17.

[7] *See generally* §3.4.2 of this handbook (a trust shall not fail for want of a trustee).

[8] "Because a beneficiary has equitable ownership in the ordinary case, the beneficiary receives the net income of the trust property rather than any fixed rate of income or return on the value of that property. The creditor, however, is not the owner of the money or other property which he has transferred to the debtor, and has no rights to the actual income which it produces in the absence of special contract." Bogert §17.

[9] *See generally* §2.1.1 of this handbook (entrusted contractual rights generally) and §2.2.2 of this handbook (entrusted third-party beneficiary contractual rights).

[10] *See generally* §2.1.1 of this handbook (entrusted equitable property rights generally).

[11] *See generally* §8.3.1 of this handbook (the trustee's personal creditors and the trustee's spouse). "Because a trustee's duties apply to specific assets in which a beneficiary has an equitable interest, a trustee may be excused from all liability if the trust res is lost through no fault of the trustee. This is because none of the trustee's other assets are affected by trust duties." Bogert §17.

[12] Bogert §17.

[13] "The loss or destruction of any particular property of a debtor, on the other hand, even though wholly without the debtor's fault, will not discharge a debt." Bogert §17.

[14] Bogert §17.

[15] Bogert §17.

[16] Bogert §17.

[17] Bogert §17.

contract into a trust, or make those duties fiduciary in nature.[18] The only duty that comes to mind is to not fraudulently convey.[19]

Third-party beneficiary contracts are not trusts. At one time, only the promisor and the promisee of a third-party beneficiary contract had standing to seek its enforcement.[20] By the middle of the twentieth century, however, it had become settled law that a third-party beneficiary of the contract would have the requisite standing as well.[21] English law is now in accord. In England, The Contracts (Rights of Third Parties) Act 1999 "provides that a contract may confer the right to enforce a term of the contract on a person who is not a party to it."[22] In the United States today, the third-party contract beneficiary can sue the promisor at law, or sue the promisor and promisee in equity.[23]

Back when it was questionable whether a third-party contract beneficiary would have standing to seek the contract's enforcement in a court of law, there was always the trust argument, which was that the promisee was contracting as a trustee for the benefit of the third party.[24] "If the contract...[was]...not performed, the trustee...[could]...take proceedings in his own name to enforce it for the benefit of the third party and, if he refuse...[d]...to do so, the third party...[could]...sue, joining the trustee as a defendant."[25] Essentially the promisee held the chose in action in trust for the benefit of the third party.[26] *The fact that the promisee was a trustee, however, did not somehow transmogrify the third-party beneficiary contract itself into a trust.*[27] Had the core arrangement been a trust, there would have been no question that the beneficiary would have had standing to seek its enforcement, even if the beneficiary had not been a party to the trust's creation.[28]

In the case of an equitable breach-of-trust action by a trust beneficiary against the trustee, laches principles may well govern when the applicable statute of limitations began to run against the beneficiary, a topic we take up in Section 7.1.3 of this handbook. Had it instead been a legal breach-of-contract action brought by a third-party contract beneficiary against the promisor, laches principles likely would not have governed.[29]

---

[18] Bogert §17.

[19] Bogert §17.

[20] Bogert §17.

[21] Bogert §17.

[22] Snell's Equity ¶ 19-21.

[23] Bogert §17. "The right of a third party contract beneficiary to sue in equity, joining the promisor and promisee, may seem to support the view that the beneficiary is in fact a beneficiary of a trust. More likely, however, chancery takes jurisdiction in this contract case, not because any trust is involved, but because more than two parties are interested in the same transaction, and hence equity is capable of administering full justice where law could not." Bogert §17.

[24] Bogert §17.

[25] Snell's Equity ¶ 19-21. *See also* §5.4.1.8 of this handbook (beneficiary's standing to proceed in stead of trustee against those with whom the trustee has contracted).

[26] Bogert §17.

[27] Bogert §17.

[28] *See generally* §7.1 of this handbook (trust beneficiary's standing to seek the trust's enforcement).

[29] Bogert §17.

A life insurance policy is a third-party beneficiary contract, not a trust.[30] The insurance company does not segregate the policy premium as a trustee would;[31] rather the premium is commingled with the general assets of an insurance company and in exchange the insurance customer receives the company's promise to pay a certain amount, at a certain time, subject to the happening of certain events.[32]

On the other hand, an interest in a variable life or annuity product may be an interest in a fund that is segregated from the general assets of the insurance company and thus insulated from the reach of the insurance company's general creditors in the event of insolvency.[33] Because such an interest is more in the nature of a trust participation than "insurance," the fund itself may be subject to registration as an investment company under the Investment Company Act of 1940.[34]

What about the situation where the insured under a standard life insurance contract dies and the proceeds are to be paid out over time in increments to the designated beneficiary? Is the insurance company a trustee of the proceeds? Unless the proceeds are to be segregated from the general assets of

---

[30] *See generally* 1 Scott on Trusts §14; Bogert §17. *See also* Uhlman v. New York Life Ins. Co., 109 N.Y. 421, 17 N.E. 363 (1888). *Cf.* Schoneberger v. Oelze, 208 Ariz. 591, 96 P.3d 1078 (2004) (confirming that a trust is not a contract).

[31] *See generally* 1A Scott on Trusts §87.1 (Life Insurance Companies Not Trustees); Bogert Trusts and Trustees §17(contract and trust). A trust is not to be confused with insurance company reserves, which are sums of money an insurer is required to set aside to insure the solvency of the company. *See* Arrow Trucking Co. v. Continental Ins. Co., 465 So. 2d 691, 696 (La. 1985).

[32] 1 Scott & Ascher §2.3.10.

[33] *See* Stephen E. Roth, *Separate Account/General Account Products: Insulation Issues and Developments in Conference on Life Insurance Company Products: Current Securities, Tax, ERISA, and State Regulatory Issues 1992*, at 105, 107–112 (ALI-ABA Course of Study No. C783, 1992); Rohm & Haas Co. v. Continental Assurance Co., 58 Ill. App. 3d 378, 374 N.E.2d 727 (1978) (holding assets held in "properly maintained and administered" separate accounts not chargeable with general liabilities of insolvent insurance company); *Variable Annuity Separate Accounts*, in Investment Company Regulation and Compliance 1993, at 277, 279 (ALI-ABA Course of Study No. C850, 1993) (noting that most "registered separate accounts [as that term is defined in Section 2(a)(37) of the 1940 Act] are formed as unit investment trusts"). For a general discussion of separate accounts, *see* Thomas J. Finnegan, Jr. and Joseph P. Garner, *The Separate Account as an Investment Company: The Structural Problems of the Ectoplasmic Theory*, 3 Conn. L. Rev. 107 (1970).

[34] *See* Stephen E. Roth, *Separate Account/General Account Products: Insulation Issues and Developments in Conference on Life Insurance Company Products: Current Securities, Tax, ERISA, and State Regulatory Issues 1992*, at 105, 107–112 (ALI-ABA Course of Study No. C783, 1992); Rohm & Haas Co. v. Continental Assurance Co., 58 Ill. App. 3d 378, 374 N.E.2d 727 (1978) (holding assets held in "properly maintained and administered" separate accounts not chargeable with general liabilities of insolvent insurance company); *Variable Annuity Separate Accounts*, in Investment Company Regulation and Compliance 1993, at 277, 279 (ALI-ABA Course of Study No. C850, 1993) (noting that most "registered separate accounts [as that term is defined in Section 2(a)(37) of the 1940 Act] are formed as unit investment trusts"). For a general discussion of separate accounts, *see* Thomas J. Finnegan, Jr. and Joseph P. Garner, *The Separate Account as an Investment Company: The Structural Problems of the Ectoplasmic Theory*, 3 Conn. L. Rev. 107 (1970).

the insurance company, the answer is probably no.[35] The beneficiary is merely a creditor of the insurance company.[36]

Every third-party beneficiary contract does not necessarily involve insurance. If the owner of an item of property, for example, transfers it to X in consideration of X's promise to pay a third party a certain sum out of X's general assets, then we have a third-party beneficiary contract.[37] The arrangement is not a trust, in part because (1) X is not obliged to segregate the property from his own property and (2) X may use the property for his own purposes.[38]

Whether one's rights are categorized as equitable under a trust or legal under a third party beneficiary contract can have practical consequences.[39] A contractual claim, for example, may be barred by a statute of limitations not applicable to beneficiary claims in equity against trustees.[40] A trustee's insolvency generally will not affect the equitable interests of the trust beneficiaries, the assets of the trust being segregated from the personal assets of the trustee.[41] In the event of the insolvency of an insurance company, however, its policy holders and third party beneficiaries would generally have to stand in line with the company's other general creditors.[42]

A contract in and of itself is not a fiduciary relationship,[43] nor is a fiduciary relationship with its "generous, zeal-requiring, benefit-conferring aspects" a contract.[44] A trustee is a fiduciary with a duty of full disclosure.[45] Promisors under third-party beneficiary contracts, *e.g.*, insurance companies, generally have no such fiduciary obligations.[46]

§9.9.2 Simple Agencies, Such as Powers of Attorney, and Complex Agencies, Such as Partnerships, Are Not Trusts

A trustee holds legal title for the welfare of the beneficiary, who holds equitable title. An escrow agent, on the other hand, is not vested with title to the property, though he may be entrusted with possession and he may have power to pass title.[47]

---

[35] 1 Scott & Ascher §10.11.1.

[36] 1 Scott & Ascher §2.3.8.1.

[37] 1 Scott on Trusts §14.1; 1 Scott & Ascher §2.3.10.1.

[38] 2 Scott & Ascher §12.13.1; Bogert §17.

[39] *See generally* Bogert §17.

[40] *See generally* §7.2.10 of this handbook (laches and statutes of limitation); Bogert §17.

[41] *See generally* §7.4 of this handbook (trustee's discharge in bankruptcy).

[42] 1 Scott & Ascher §2.3.10.3.

[43] Schoneberger v. Oelze, 208 Ariz. 591, 596, 96 P.3d 1078, 1082 (2004) ("... [A] fiduciary relationship exists between a trustee and a trust beneficiary while no such relationship generally exists between parties to a contract"). *See also* Bogert §17.

[44] *See* Scott Fitzgibbon, *Fiduciary Relationships Are Not Contracts*, 82 Marq. L. Rev. 303, 325 (1999).

[45] *See generally* §6.1.5.1 of this handbook (trustee's duty to provide information).

[46] 1 Scott & Ascher §2.3.10.3; Bogert §17.

[47] Albrecht v. Brais, 324 Ill. App. 3d 188, 191, 754 N.E.2d 396, 399 (2001).

When a debtor delivers money or other property to a third person with instructions to pay a particular creditor, the relationship that arises may be a contract for the benefit of the creditor, an agency for the debtor, or a trust.[48]

The simple agency is not a trust. Powers of attorney involving property (including "durable" powers of attorney (U.S.), "enduring" powers of attorney (U.K.) and "lasting" powers attorney (U.K.)),[49] investment management agency accounts, and escrow agency accounts are not trusts.[50] And they certainly are not powers of appointment.[51] They are all agencies. So are custodial accounts.[52] With some common law and statutory exceptions,[53] under none of these arrangements does title to the subject property pass to the agent.[54]

One important exception is when money is involved. "When an agent receives money for a principal, the agent acquires title to the money according to the view that title to money passes with possession, but he or she remains an agent, and the principles of agency apply."[55] That is not to say that the agent might not also be a trustee of the funds for the benefit of the principal.[56] A lawyer who deposits funds belonging to his client in an IOLTA account, for example, is separately acting as trustee incident to the lawyer-client agency relationship.[57] Likewise, an agent who undertakes to collect the proceeds from the sale of the principal's property is a trustee of those proceeds, absent special facts.[58] Absent special facts, an insurance agent who undertakes to collect

---

[48] 5 Scott & Ascher §35.1.9 (Trust for Particular Creditor).

[49] 1 Scott on Trusts §§8–8.1.

[50] *See generally* 1 Scott & Ascher §2.3.4; Bogert §15. *See, however,* §8.15.25 of this handbook (doctrine of undisclosed principal) (suggesting that if the agent of an undisclosed principal contracts on behalf of the undisclosed principal with a third party, the contractual rights are held in trust by the agent for the benefit of the undisclosed principal); Bogert §15 (noting that "Dean Ames argued that an agent for an undisclosed principal is a trustee of rights which he acquires in such capacity" and citing to James Barr Ames, *Undisclosed Principal—His Rights and Liabilities*, 18 Yale L.J. 443 (1909)).

[51] Restatement (Third) of Property (Wills and Other Donative Transfers) §17.1 cmt. j. *See generally* §8.1 of this handbook (the power of appointment).

[52] *See generally* Bogert §15. "Although the . . . [Uniform Transfers to Minors Act] . . . has become a widely used method for making gifts to minors and can be regarded as a 'trust substitute,' a custodian is not a trustee because both legal title and equitable ownership of the gift property are vested in the minor." *Id.*

[53] *See* 1 Scott on Trusts §8 n.6. *See also* Restatement (Second) of Agency §14B (one who has title to property that he agrees to hold for the benefit and subject to the control of another is an agent-trustee and is subject to the rules of agency). An agent-trustee "is not, however, entitled to the compensation to which trustees are ordinarily entitled, but only to such compensation as was agreed on or as is reasonable under the circumstances." 4 Scott & Ascher §21.1.4. Here are the citations to the sections of the Massachusetts durable power of attorney statute: Mass. Gen. Laws ch. 190B, §§5-501, 5-502, 5-503, 5-504, 5-505, 5-506, and 5-507.

[54] 1 Scott on Trusts §8.

[55] 1 Scott & Ascher §2.3.4.

[56] Bogert §§15 & 22.

[57] Bogert §22 (confirming that in cases in which an attorney collects a judgment for a client, the attorney is acting as a trustee of the collected funds). *See generally* §6.1.3.4 of this handbook and §9.7.2 of this handbook (IOLTA accounts).

[58] Bogert §22.

insurance premiums on behalf of the home office is a trustee of those premiums.[59] So also is a property management agent who undertakes to collect the rents on behalf of the property owner a trustee of the funds collected.[60] One who solicits and receives cash contributions on behalf of a charity takes title to the funds, but as a trustee.[61]

Nor is an agency relationship in and of itself a contractual relationship, though the consent of the parties is a critical element of each.[62] Gratuitous agencies, *i.e.*, agencies that do not involve the exchange of consideration, are perhaps the most common type of agency—*e.g.*, powers of attorney that spouses grant one another. That is not to say that two parties, such as a client and a lawyer, may not contract to enter into an agency relationship. In such a situation, the agency and the contractual relationships are separate but incident to one another. The contract, for example, will fix the terms of the lawyer's compensation for acting as the client's agent in legal matters. Thus, a breach of the lawyer's fiduciary duty to the client may or may not warrant a rescission of the associated but separate compensation contract. One commentator on the law of trusts, however, has asserted without authority or elaboration that "[a]n agency is a contractual relationship."[63]

The element of control is a critical difference between the agency and the trust. An agent is subject to the control and direction of the principal. A trust is enforceable even if the trustee is subject to the control of neither the settlor nor the beneficiaries.

An agency is terminable at the will of either the principal or the agent. In the case of a trust, its terms will determine whether it is revocable, and if so, by whom.[64]

Upon the death of a principal, any property that is a subject of the agency will likely belong to the principal's probate estate, the agency having terminated.[65] An exception would be if *the principal* were a trustee. In the case of a trust, the death of the settlor, the trustee, or a beneficiary need not trigger its termination.[66] Thus while an agency may not function as a will substitute absent statutory authority,[67] a revocable inter vivos trust may.[68]

---

[59] Bogert §22.

[60] Bogert §22.

[61] Bogert §22.

[62] "[A] trust . . . [,however,] . . . is in the nature of a conveyance and consent of the trustee or beneficiary is not necessary to its origin, although either may decline the trust." Bogert §15.

[63] Bogert §15.

[64] *See generally* §8.2.2.2 of this handbook (trusts that are revocable).

[65] The death of either the principal or the agent will terminate the agency. *See generally* 2 Scott & Ascher §12.13.1; Bogert §15. *See, e.g.*, Albrecht v. Brais, 324 Ill. App. 3d 188, 754 N.E.2d 396 (2001). Note, however, that the typical durable power of attorney statute provides that acts taken by the agent during any period when doubt exists as to whether the principal is deceased or alive are binding upon the principal's successors and personal representatives. Bogert §15.

[66] *See generally* 1 Scott & Ascher §2.3.4.

[67] The typical custodial IRAs by state statute is an effective will substitute.

[68] *See generally* National Shawmut Bank of Boston v. Joy, 315 Mass. 457, 53 N.E.2d 113 (1944).

Another difference between agency and trust relationships relates to the duty to act. Once one accepts the office of trustee, one assumes an affirmative duty to act. An agent, on the other hand, is authorized to act but assumes no duty to do so.

An agent may subject the principal to personal liability to third persons, whereas a trustee as such cannot subject the beneficiary to such liability.[69] The trustee in his dealings with third parties with respect to the trust property is a principal.[70] He is not acting as an agent of the beneficiaries.[71]

An agent with discretion is a fiduciary, a topic we take up in Chapter 1 of this handbook. All trustees are fiduciaries. Thus, the core fiduciary relationships of agency and trust can overlap functionally at times. "The duties of an agent who has authority to make and to manage investments...[, for example,]...can be quite similar to those of the trustee of a formal trust, except in so far as they are affected by the fact that the principal has control and may modify or determine the investments at any time."[72] Still, unless the parties agree otherwise, the investment manager or agent should make the investments in the name of the principal.[73] On the other hand, a trustee in some situations can, for all intents and purposes, be an agent of the settlor. This is a topic we take up in Section 8.11 of this handbook in our discussion of the duties of the trustee of a revocable trust.[74] Bernard Madoff's Ponzi scheme victims were principals in an investment management agency relationship with him; he was generally not acting as a trustee of their trusts. For fiduciary liability purposes, however, this was a distinction without a difference.[75]

Such functional overlaps have implications as well when it comes to remedies, a topic we take up generally in Section 7.2.3 of this handbook. As one commentator has noted:

> The remedies of the principal lie ordinarily in a court of law; those of the beneficiary usually lie in a court of equity. The fiduciary nature of agency causes equity to take jurisdiction of a suit for accounting by an agent, but this is an illustration of the special ground for equitable cognizance. In the law of trusts the beneficiary is at home in equity without regard to legal remedies that may be available.[76]

If, following execution of a durable power of attorney, a court of the principal's domicile appoints a trustee to manage the principal's property, the attorney in fact is accountable to the trustee as well as to the principal, at least

---

[69] Restatement (Third) of Trusts §5 cmt. e.

[70] Bogert §15.

[71] Bogert §15.

[72] Restatement (Second) of Agency §425 cmt. a.

[73] Restatement (Second) of Agency §425 cmt. e.

[74] *See also* §9.27 of this handbook (the inter vivos purpose trust) and §9.29 of this handbook (the inter vivos adapted trust).

[75] *See generally* Charles E. Rounds, Jr., *State Common Law Aspects of the Global Unwindings of the Madoff Ponzi Scheme and the Sub-Prime Mortgage Securitization Debacle*, 27 Wis. Int'l L.J. 99 (2009).

[76] Bogert §15.

under the Uniform Probate Code.[77] The trustee would have "the same power to revoke or amend the power of attorney that the principal would have had if he were not disabled or incapacitated."[78]

A breach of fiduciary duty in the agency context can give rise to a constructive trust.[79] Take, for example, the situation in which *X* asks *Y* to purchase on *X*'s behalf a certain parcel of land from an *independent vendor*.[80] *Y* orally agrees to do so. *Y* (the agent), however, in violation of his *fiduciary duty* to *X* (the principal), proceeds instead to purchase *with his own money*, not *X*'s, the land for himself. A court may order *Y* to hold the land upon a constructive trust for *X*, with an appropriate offset for what *Y* had paid.[81] Were the parties in neither a confidential nor a fiduciary relationship, *Y* might well be allowed to keep the land, unless the arrangement had somehow been incident to an enforceable contract.[82] Had *X* even indirectly furnished the consideration for the land transaction, then *Y* might be ordered to hold the land upon a purchase money resulting trust for *X*'s benefit, a topic we take up in Section 3.3 of this handbook.[83] One has to be nimble at the intersection of agency law and trust law. It is no place for the literal minded. The ancillary trusteeship also can be found at the intersection, a topic we take up in Section 9.32 of this handbook.

Officers of a corporation, such as its president and its secretary, are not trustees of the corporate assets.[84] They are agents of the entity who have undertaken contractual obligations.[85] "A suit in equity against them must be justified . . . on the ground of inadequacy of remedies available at law, and not on the basis of the enforcement of an express trust."[86]

It is said that majority stockholders of a corporation owe certain fiduciary duties to the minority stockholders.[87] They are not, however, trustees of corporate assets, nor are they, absent special facts, agents of either the corporation or the minority stockholders.[88] Still, if the majority stockholders are unjustly enriched at the expense of the minority stockholders, whether through

---

[77] UPC §5-503(a).

[78] UPC §5-503(a).

[79] *See* §3.3 of this handbook (the constructive trust generally); §7.2.3.1.6 of this handbook (the constructive trust as a procedural equitable remedy); 6 Scott & Ascher §43.1.1.

[80] *See generally* §9.9.11 of this handbook (a contract to convey land).

[81] 6 Scott & Ascher §43.1.1. *See* §3.3 of this handbook (the constructive trust generally); §7.2.3.1.6 of this handbook (the constructive trust as a procedural equitable remedy).

[82] *See generally* 6 Scott & Ascher §43.1.1; §3.3 of this handbook (the constructive trust). *See also* §9.9.11 of this handbook (contracts to convey land).

[83] *See also* 6 Scott & Ascher §43.1.1.

[84] Bogert §16.

[85] Bogert §16.

[86] Bogert §16.

[87] Bogert §16.

[88] Bogert §16 ("A shareholder's property interest is absolute and subject to no equitable interest in another").

a breach of fiduciary duty or otherwise, the minority stockholders may be entitled to restitution.[89]

Though each is a fiduciary relationship, a partnership is not a trust. A partnership is a contract of mutual agency, not a trust. "Persons associated together as co-owners for the purpose of doing business, and hence are partners, are agents and also principals for each other. Each partner is a general agent for the other."[90]

In the case of a tenancy in partnership, each partner has full co-ownership of the subject property. In the case of a trust relationship, the trustee and the beneficiary simultaneously share different interests in the subject property, a phenomenon we take up in Section 5.3.1 of this handbook. Whereas the legal title is in the trustee, the equitable interest is in the beneficiary.

Absent statute, each general partner is personally liable for the contracts and torts of the collective.[91] With some exceptions, which are discussed in Section 9.6 of this handbook, a trust beneficiary is not personally liable for the contracts that the trustee enters into with third parties on behalf of the trust, nor is the beneficiary personally liable for any torts that the trustee may commit against third parties.[92]

As explained in Section 3.4.2 of this handbook, a trust shall not fail for want of a trustee. A partnership is different. "Ordinarily a partnership may be destroyed by the death or bankruptcy of a partner."[93]

The statute of frauds, which is covered in Section 8.15.5 of this handbook, requires that a trust of land be proved by a writing. "A partnership agreement is not subject to the statute of frauds merely because it relates to realty."[94]

That a partnership, in and of itself, is not a trust, however, does not mean that a partner might not, in a given situation, hold partnership assets upon a resulting or constructive trust for the benefit of the other partners.[95] The resulting trust and the constructive trust are covered in Section 3.3 of this handbook. Under certain circumstances, the partner might even hold partnership assets upon an express trust: "Under the Uniform Partnership Act (1997), . . . [for example,] . . . a partner has a duty to account to the partnership and hold as trustee for it any property, profit, or benefit derived by the partner in the conduct and winding up of the partnership business or derived from a use by the partner of partnership property, including the appropriation of partnership opportunity."[96]

---

[89] *See* Restatement of Restitution §131 ("A person who by the sale or surrender of land, chattels, or choses in action, has tortiously terminated the interests of another therein, is under a duty of restitution to the other for the amount received from the sale or surrender of such interest").

[90] Warren A. Seavey, Handbook of the Law of Agency 18 (1964).

[91] Bogert §36.

[92] *See generally* §5.6 of this handbook (liabilities of the trust beneficiary).

[93] Bogert §36.

[94] Bogert §36.

[95] *See generally* Bogert §36.

[96] Section 3.3 of this handbook.

There is no better example of the intersection of agency and trust law than the doctrine of undisclosed principal, which is covered in Section 8.15.25 of this handbook.

§9.9.3 Social Security and Other Legislative Budget Items Couched in Trust Terminology

A deep root of this predicament is a crucial but under-examined aspect of Social Security: the misleading manner in which the program has been depicted to the public from 1935 on. Specifically, Social Security is retirement insurance under which taxpayers pay insurance premiums or contributions to buy protection from destitution in old age, with their contributions being held in a trust fund which will pay guaranteed benefits which, being paid for, will be theirs as a matter of earned right, as America keeps its compact (or contract) between generations. The entire previous sentence is demonstrably, documentably false.[97]

It has become a practice of politicians to employ trust terminology to promote various governmental programs.[98] The so-called social security trust fund is a good example. The social security trust fund is a budget item; it is not a common law trust of the type that is the subject of this handbook. Nor is a "trustee" of the social security "trust fund" a fiduciary.[99] If a "trustee" is not a fiduciary, then he is not a real trustee; the trust, by definition, being a fiduciary relationship. Nor are the social security "bonds" in the social security "trust fund" property, property being another key element in any trust relationship. This is because they are not real bonds. A real bond creates enforceable contractual rights in someone. These "bonds" do not. They are in the nature of internal memoranda to the file,[100] nothing more. A taxpayer thus could not successfully in a judicial forum invoke principles of trust law to prevent a congressional raid on the fund.

---

[97] John Attarian, Social Security: False Consciousness and Crisis (2002).

[98] *See* I.R.C. §§9501 ("Black Lung Disability Trust Fund"), 9502 ("Airport and Airway Trust Fund"), 9504 ("Aquatic Resources Trust Fund"), 9505 ("Harbor Maintenance Trust Fund"), 9506 ("Inland Waterways Trust Fund"), 9507 ("Hazardous Substance Superfund"), 9508 ("Leaking Underground Storage Tank Trust Fund"), 9509 ("Oil Spill Liability Trust Fund"), and 9510 ("Vaccine Injury Compensation Trust Fund"); Exec. Order No. 12858 ("Deficit Reduction Fund," more commonly referred to as the Clinton Deficit Reduction Trust Fund). With respect to the Clinton Deficit Reduction Trust Fund, *see generally* Mitchell, . . . *and Marred by Trust Fund Gimmick*, Wall St. J., Aug. 5, 1993, at A12.

[99] *See* 42 U.S.C.A. §401(c) (providing that a person serving on the Board of Trustees shall not be considered to be a fiduciary and shall not be personally liable for actions taken in such capacity with respect to the "Trust Funds").

[100] They are not real bonds because they are unissued. *See* 41 U.S.C.A. §401(e). And even if they were, they would constitute economic value to the purchasers, not to the United States or the phantom trust fund. Because they may not be issued, these "bonds" are a legal nullity: The United States may not contract with itself and, by so doing, bind future congresses. *See* Fletcher v. Peck, 6 Cranch 87, 135 (1810) (in which Chief Justice Marshall enunciated the constitutional principle that one legislature cannot abridge the powers of a succeeding legislature). *See also* Marbury v. Madison, 1 Cranch 137, 177 (1803) (unlike the Constitution, a legislative Act is "alterable when the legislature shall please to alter it").

For some time it has been settled law that the Social Security Act is constitutional and that employees have no property rights in their FICA payments. *Helvering v. Davis,*[101] decided in 1937, stands for the proposition that Social Security does not violate Article I, Section 8 of the U.S. Constitution, which provides that Congress may spend money in aid of the "general welfare." "When money is spent to promote the general welfare, the concept of welfare or the opposite is shaped by Congress, not the states,"[102] and not the courts. FICA receipts are tax receipts. Congress may expend such receipts for the general welfare. Congress has determined that Social Security is a scheme that promotes the general welfare. Ergo, Social Security is constitutional.

Flemming v. Nestor,[103] decided in 1960, stands for the proposition that Social Security is an umbrella term for two schemes that, for all intents and purposes, are legally unrelated. One is a taxation scheme and the other is a welfare scheme. Ergo, workers and their families have no legal claim on the tax payments that they make into the U.S. Treasury or that are made on their behalf. Those funds are gone, commingled with the general assets of the U.S. government. For more on the inappropriate use of trust and contract terminology by those making the case for and against the privatization of Social Security, the reader is referred to Property Rights: The Hidden Issue of Social Security Reform, by the author.[104]

§9.9.4 Bank Accounts and Other Such Debtor-Creditor Contractual Arrangements Are Not Trusts

There is a fiduciary relationship between trustee and beneficiary, but not between debtors and creditor as such.[105]

Bank accounts generally. It is a popular misconception that a bank account is a trust. It is not.[106] A bank account is a contract, the bank being the debtor and the depositor being the creditor.[107] In other words, a contract debt is not a trust.[108] A debt is a personal obligation *of the debtor.*[109] When one places money in an ATM, the money is commingled with the general assets of the

---

[101] 301 U.S. 619 (1937).

[102] Helvering v. Davis, 301 U.S. at 645.

[103] 363 U.S. 603 (1960).

[104] Charles E. Rounds, Jr., *Property Rights: The Hidden Issue of Social Security Reform*, SSP No. 19, Apr. 19, 2000, Cato Institute. *See also* Karl J. Borden & Charles E. Rounds, Jr., *A Proposed Legal, Regulatory, and Operational Structure for an Investment-Based Social Security System*, SSP No. 25, Feb. 19, 2002, Cato Institute.

[105] 1 Scott & Ascher §2.3.8.

[106] *See* Bogert §21.

[107] *See* Bogert §21. As a general rule, the owner of property can create a trust of the property by declaring himself trustee of it, although he receives no consideration for the declaration of trust. Restatement (Second) of Trusts §28. On the other hand, a gratuitous promise to pay a sum of money is generally insufficient to create an enforceable debt. *See generally* 1 Scott & Ascher §2.3.8.5.

[108] *See generally* 1 Scott on Trusts §§12, 12.9.

[109] Bogert §21.

bank.[110] "The bank can use the money as it pleases and the customer acquires no interest in or charge over any asset of the bank."[111] Should the bank become insolvent, the depositor would then be no more than a general creditor of the bank.[112] The depositor would have no special right to a particular item of property or to a dedicated account.[113] "If the payee of a check or draft presents a claim against the bank before or after its failure, the claim should be based on third party beneficiary contract principles rather than trust principles."[114] There should be no exception for cashier's checks, although a few courts have held otherwise: "Where a bank gives a customer a cashier's check or draft for value, courts should not hold that it is a trustee of any of its assets until the draft is paid, and they should give no preference from the bank's assets if the bank fails before paying the check or draft."[115] Likewise, one who purchases from a domestic bank a letter of credit against a foreign bank is typically a mere unsecured contract creditor.[116] The purchase money is not entrusted.[117]

Assume that Mr. Jones, who has a checking account with Bank X, deposits into the checking account for collection a third party's check that is drawn on another bank. Before collection, Bank X becomes insolvent. Under the Uniform Commercial Code, Mr. Jones is a statutory preferred creditor vis-à-vis Bank X's general depositors.[118] The Code, however, "abandons the fictional theory that a trust was intended as to the proceeds of the collection."[119]

While a debt is not a trust, it is property. Thus, *as to the depositor*, the contract debt (the bank account) is an item of intangible personal property.[120] As such, the contractual rights associated therewith may be made the subject of a trust.[121] But the debt itself is not a trust.[122] Prior to the seventeenth century, however, such contractual rights would not have been *legally* assignable to a trustee—a topic we take up in Section 8.15.75 of this handbook—although they would have been assignable in equity. *As to the bank*, however, the contract debt (the bank account) is an obligation, not an interest in property.

If, however, the owner of the funds had *intended* to *entrust* the property to the bank, as evidenced perhaps by his or her bringing the funds upstairs to the bank's trust department, then the bank would be obliged to segregate the

---

[110] Lewin ¶ 20-58 (England); Bogert §21 (U.S.).
[111] Lewin ¶ 1-16 (England). *See also* Bogert §21 (U.S.).
[112] *See* Bogert §21. *See also* §9.8.7 of this handbook (the Quistclose trust).
[113] *See* Bogert §21.
[114] Bogert §21.
[115] Bogert §21.
[116] Bogert §21.
[117] Bogert §21.
[118] Bogert §23.
[119] Bogert §23.
[120] 1 Scott & Ascher §3.1.3.
[121] 1 Scott on Trusts §14.2; 1 Scott & Ascher §2.3.10. 2. *See, e.g.*, §9.8.7 of this handbook (the Quistclose trust).
[122] Bogert §21.

property.[123] The property would then be insulated from the bank's creditors in the event of insolvency to the extent the funds were not on deposit on the commercial side of the bank.[124]

Public funds on deposit. A *rightful deposit* of funds belonging to a governmental entity in a bank creates a debtor-creditor contractual relationship between the governmental entity and the bank.[125] In the event of the bank's insolvency, the governmental entity is a mere general creditor of the bank.[126] In the case of an *unlawful deposit* of public funds, however, the entity may enjoy the status of a preferred creditor, but not because the bank is an express trustee of the public funds in any way.[127] "A more accurate analysis is that, while title to the money and paper that the public treasurer left at the bank passed to the bank, because the parties so intended and the treasurer had power to pass it, still the bank either knew actually of the wrongful nature of the deposit or was charged with knowledge of it, and hence acquired title by participating in a wrongful act of the treasurer, and should be charged as a constructive trustee because of its inequitable acquisition."[128] The subject of constructive trustees is taken up generally in Section 3.3 of this handbook. Beyond the scope of this handbook are situations in which the governmental entity by statute is a "superior kind of creditor."[129]

Trust funds on deposit. Absent special facts, when a trustee deposits trust funds in a bank, a debtor-creditor contractual relationship is established.[130] The bank is a debtor of the trustee, not, itself, a trustee of the deposited funds.[131] The subject of whether the bank had a duty to inquire into the trustee's authority to make such a deposit is taken up in Section 8.3.4 of this handbook.

Creditors of a corporation. Absent special facts, a corporation is not a trustee of its assets for the benefit of its creditors.[132] "The corporation occupies merely a contract or debt relationship to the creditor, with no special intimacy or duty of degree of good faith."[133] On the other hand, a separate trust may be employed by the corporation to secure the contractual rights of certain of the corporation's creditors, such as its bondholders. This is a topic we take up in our discussion of the Trust Indenture Act of 1939, which can be found at Section 9.31 of this handbook.

An unpaid dividend may be made the subject of a trust as well: "If a corporation declares a dividend and deposits funds in a bank account to pay the dividend, courts generally have held that the corporation makes itself trustee of the claim against the bank for the persons entitled to the dividend, and such

---

[123] *See generally* Lewin ¶1-15 (England); 1 Scott & Ascher §2.3.8.6 (U.S.); Bogert §21 (U.S.).
[124] 1 Scott & Ascher §2.3.8.1; Bogert §21.
[125] Bogert §21.
[126] Bogert §21.
[127] Bogert §21.
[128] Bogert §21.
[129] *See* Bogert §21.
[130] Bogert §21.
[131] Bogert §21.
[132] Bogert §16.
[133] Bogert §16.

persons are entitled to the proceeds of the claim against the bank, even though the corporation may fail before the dividend actually is paid."[134] Having said that, should the bank itself fail before the entrusted dividend is paid, the corporation remains on the hook. "The corporation does not discharge its debt to the stockholders by setting up the dividend account trust, but merely provides an auxiliary means of paying the debt."[135]

Debtor promises to satisfy debt from a specified source. When a debtor makes it known to the creditor that he intends to satisfy the debt from specified property, such as from the dividends from the debtor's personal stock portfolio, whether the specified property, in this case the stock, is to be the subject of a trust depends upon the actions and intentions of the parties. "Often the allegation that a trust was created fails because, although the debtor had a duty to create a trust for his creditor, he set apart no subject matter for the trust, or the subject-matter mentioned was nonexistent or future in its nature. In other instances, the reason that a court held that no trust had been proven was that, while the debtor mentioned a specific source from which he expected to pay his debt, he did not manifest an intent to charge himself as trustee of that source for the creditor, but rather declared a mere expectation or hope."[136]

Borrower promises lender to use borrowed funds to satisfy borrower's contract debt to a third party. Assume a borrower promises a lender that the borrower will use the borrowed funds to satisfy the borrower's contract debt to a third party. Whether a trust is impressed upon the borrowed funds for the benefit of the third party, or whether the arrangement is essentially a third-party beneficiary contract, is taken up in Section 9.8.7 of this handbook. If we have a trust, the borrowed funds are segregated from the personal assets of the borrower. If we have a third- party beneficiary contract, the borrowed funds are not. That would make them subject to the claims of the borrower's general creditors. In the event of the borrower's bankruptcy, these ambiguities are likely to put the bankruptcy trustee at loggerheads with either the third party or the lender, or both, over the fate of the borrowed funds. One American commentator, however, is skeptical of the trust argument:

> If a creditor directs a debtor to pay a third person, and the debtor agrees, courts sometimes say that the debtor thereupon becomes a trustee "of the money" for the third party. Because debtors cannot be trustees of their own obligation to pay, and because they almost certainly never set apart any assets to be delivered to the third party, any trust is fictitious. It lacks subject-matter. In the English cases, where the doctrine has been put forth, the courts probably felt the pressure of the rules of the law of contracts preventing recovery by a third party contract beneficiary. In many American cases, the problem can be solved to the satisfaction of the third party using contract principles regarding third-party beneficiaries and novations.[137]

---

[134] Bogert §20.

[135] Bogert §20.

[136] Bogert §19.

[137] Bogert §19; §8.15.57 of this handbook (novation).

Property in exchange for support. Assume an elderly gentleman transfers title to his residence to his niece with the expectation that she will reciprocate by caring for him in his dotage. The nature of the legal or equitable relationship that was established with respect to the property will dictate the type of relief that is available to him should the expected services not be forthcoming.[138] If the elderly gentleman intended that the property be segregated from the niece's personal assets and dedicated to subsidizing his care, then the niece would be a trustee of the property.[139] Once she has breached the terms of the trust, he would then be entitled to equitable relief, a topic that is taken up generally in Section 7.2.3 of this handbook. Another possibility is that a trust was impressed upon the property to secure the niece's contractual obligation to support her elderly uncle.[140] If she upholds her end of the bargain, then upon his death she takes title to the property outright and free of trust.

If the niece is not a trustee of the property, then there are at least four possibilities. One is that she was the donee of a valid completed gift that carried with it no attendant legal obligation to care for her uncle. In that case, she may keep the property and he is out of luck. This is an unlikely scenario.

A second possibility is that she, through fraud, duress, or undue influence, procured the property from him.[141] In that case, she has been unjustly enriched and he is entitled to full restitution.[142] She would then be a constructive trustee of the property. Constructive trusts are taken up in Section 3.3 of this handbook.

A third is that uncle and niece were parties to an enforceable contract. The property was the consideration that the uncle had furnished.[143] The property would then be owned by the niece outright and free of trust. The niece having failed to uphold her end of the bargain, the uncle would be entitled to a return of the consideration, in kind, if feasible.[144] A minority of courts would limit the relief to damages or specific performance.[145]

A fourth is that the land conveyance was subject to a *legal* condition subsequent, a topic that is well beyond the scope of this handbook.[146]

---

[138] Bogert §19.

[139] Bogert §19.

[140] "If the grantor intends the transferred property to be security for the grantee's promise, the deed conveying the property to the grantee should include a clause making this clear. If the deed contains such a provision, its recordation will prevent the grantee from terminating the grantor's rights by conveying the property to a bona fide purchaser." Bogert §19. *See generally* §8.15.63 of this handbook (doctrine of bona fide purchase).

[141] *See generally* Bogert §19.

[142] *See generally* Restatement of Restitution §130 ("A person who has tortiously acquired or retained a title to land, chattels, or choses in action, is under a duty of restitution to the person entitled thereto.").

[143] Bogert §19.

[144] Bogert §19.

[145] Bogert §19.

[146] Bogert §19. "Alternatively, if the conveyance is construed as creating an estate on condition subsequent, the grantor may take back the property by exercising the power of termination." *Id. Cf.* §8.30 of this handbook (equitable conditions subsequent).

Debtor delivers specific property to creditor to be liquidated and applied in partial or full satisfaction of debt. Assume a debtor delivers specific property to the creditor in full satisfaction of the contract debt. Before the specific property can be liquidated and applied in satisfaction of the debt, *the creditor* becomes insolvent and files for bankruptcy. Is the specific property an asset of the bankruptcy estate such that it is unrecoverable by the debtor? If so, the trustee in bankruptcy will deem the debt itself a separate asset of the bankruptcy estate and decline to offset its value by the value of the specific property. Besides being unable to get back the specific property, the unfortunate debtor will still be on the hook for the full amount of the debt. Had the specific property been transferred to the now-bankrupt creditor in trust pending its liquidation, then the debtor might well be entitled to get the specific property back. Most likely, however, the parties intended to enter into a second contractual relationship, with the creditor-deliveree taking full ownership of the specific property in exchange for a mere promise to convert it into cash or credit and apply the proceeds in satisfaction of the original debt. The now-bankrupt creditor was neither an agent nor trustee of the debtor with respect to the specific property. One should not take away from this that the parties can never have been in a trust relationship when there has been a failure to liquidate specific property prebankruptcy. Everything hinges on the intentions of the parties in light of the particular facts and circumstances.

When a debtor delivers property to a third person with instructions to pay a particular creditor. As noted above, the intentions of the parties will generally determine the nature of the core legal relationship in a given situation.[147] Take a transfer to facilitate paying a creditor:

> When a debtor delivers money or other property to a third person with instructions to pay a particular creditor, the relationship that arises may be a contract for the benefit of the creditor, an agency for the debtor, or a trust. If the understanding is that the third person is to have unrestricted use of the money or other property and agrees merely to pay the creditor the amount the debtor owes, the transaction is a contract for the benefit of the creditor.[148]

In ambiguous situations generally, the fact that someone in return for receiving money agrees to pay interest is strong evidence that the parties intend to create a contract debt and not a trust.[149] "It is not natural for anyone to agree to pay interest on money unless he or she can use it as his or her own."[150] The

---

[147] There are exceptions, of course, such as when the parties endeavor to impress an inter vivos trust on a mere hope or expectancy. In such a case, a trust will not arise, regardless of the intentions of the parties, a trust being a fiduciary relationship with respect to property. Neither a hope nor an expectancy is property. Expectancies should not be confused with future interests, such as remainders, which are property. One who possesses a vested legal remainder or a vested equitable remainder under a trust that lacks a spendthrift clause may well be entitled to assign that interest to a trustee.

[148] 5 Scott & Ascher §35.1.9. *See also* §9.8.7 of this handbook (the Quistclose trust) and §9.9.2 of this handbook (agency arrangements).

[149] 1 Scott & Ascher §2.3.8.1.

[150] 1 Scott & Ascher §2.3.8.1.

evidence is even stronger if the interest to be paid is at a fixed rate.[151] On the other hand, if the funds are to be segregated and/or invested, and only what interest is actually earned is to be paid over, then in all likelihood we have a trust.[152]

One who collects money as agent for another is a trustee of the collected funds in the absence of evidence that the parties intended the agent during the collection process to have the use of the funds.[153] Insurance agents, real estate agents, attorneys, and stockbrokers[154] take note.[155] Building contractors are probably in a different position. Absent statute[156] or agreement by the parties to the contrary, a building contractor who receives a payment from the customer does not hold that payment in trust for the subcontractors, laborers, and suppliers.[157] They are mere creditors of the contractor,[158] and thus would not have a favored position in the event of the contractor's insolvency. Absent a statute to the contrary, an employer who agrees incident to an employee benefit arrangement to deduct certain sums from an employee's wages is most likely not a trustee of those sums until such time as there has been a physical segregation.[159]

Security deposits. Unless addressed by statute[160] or spelled out unambiguously in the terms of the governing documentation, whether a security deposit incident to a rental agreement is a debt or the subject of a trust will hinge on the inferred intentions of the parties.[161] If the landlord is to have the personal use of the funds during the term of the lease, then we probably have a mere debt.[162] If the funds are to be segregated from the landlord's own assets, then the arrangement looks more like a trust,[163] with the attendant protections in the event of the landlord-trustee's insolvency.[164] Likewise in the case of the mortgagor who places funds with the mortgagee for the purpose of paying real

---

[151] 1 Scott & Ascher §2.3.8.1.

[152] 1 Scott & Ascher §2.3.8.1. *See generally* §9.8.7 of this handbook (the Quistclose trust).

[153] 1 Scott & Ascher §2.3.8.1.

[154] *See generally* 1 Scott & Ascher §2.3.8.7.

[155] 1 Scott & Ascher §2.3.8.1.

[156] 1 Scott & Ascher §2.3.8.1.

[157] 1 Scott & Ascher §2.3.8.1.

[158] 1 Scott & Ascher §2.3.8.1.

[159] 1 Scott & Ascher §2.3.8.1.

[160] 1 Scott & Ascher §2.3.8.1.

[161] Bogert §19. (asserting that "[o]rdinarily the parties do not expect that the amount deposited is to be earmarked and segregated so as to constitute a trust fund, but rather intend the recipient of the deposit to be free to use it as a personal asset and to make bookkeeping entries showing an obligation to apply personal assets toward satisfaction of the depositor's obligation or to return an amount equal to the deposit of the depositor"). "This lack of subject-matter should be fatal to a trust claim, but some statutes have created a trust for the depositor and some decisions support this view." *Id.*

[162] 1 Scott & Ascher §2.3.8.1.

[163] 1 Scott & Ascher §2.3.8.1.

[164] 1 Scott & Ascher §2.3.8.4.

estate taxes and insurance premiums. Whether or not the funds are entrusted will depend on what the parties intended.[165]

In the case of a security deposit or a tax escrow account, there also is the question of whether income earned on funds which have yet to be returned or paid out accrues to the payor or payee, regardless of whether the particular arrangement is one of debtor-creditor or trustee-beneficiary.[166] If the answer cannot be found in a statute or the express terms of the governing documentation, then the intentions of the parties will have to be inferred. "A few cases have determined that mortgagors are entitled to interest on such funds, but most have held otherwise."[167] For a discussion of the trustee's general default duty to make trust property productive, the reader is referred to Section 6.2.2 of this handbook.

Deductions from wages and accrued but unpaid wages. Ordinarily, an employer is not the trustee of deductions it lawfully takes from its employee's wages, *unless some statute provides otherwise*.[168] Nor is the employer a trustee with respect to the employee's accrued but unpaid wages. In each case, it is unlikely, absent special facts, that the parties intended that any specific property be segregated, either to provide a source for the payment of the claims or as a way of securing their payment.[169] The employee is merely an unsecured contract creditor of the employer.[170] Having said that, a "corporation might make itself trustee for its employees by setting up a *payroll* account, the res of the trust being the claim against the bank."[171] As to the bank, it would merely be a contract debtor *of the corporation*.[172] The bank itself would owe fiduciary duties neither to the corporation nor to the corporation's employees.[173]

Parking trust cash on the commercial side of the bank trustee. As a general rule, the corporate trustee of a trust who lawfully parks trust cash on its commercial side need not remit to the trust any profits that accrue to the trustee in loaning the property out to third parties.[174] "[A] trustee is not accountable for profits earned outside of trust administration."[175] Again, the contractual rights incident to the debtor-creditor relationship constitute the trust property. That is what replaced the cash. The cash is now the individual property of the trustee.[176] So too will be any fruits of that property. Interest generally follows

---

[165] 1 Scott & Ascher §2.3.8.1.

[166] 1 Scott & Ascher §2.3.8.1.

[167] 1 Scott & Ascher §2.3.8.1.

[168] Bogert §19.

[169] Bogert §19.

[170] Bogert §19.

[171] Bogert §20.

[172] Bogert §20.

[173] Bogert §20.

[174] 4 Scott & Ascher §24.7. *See generally* §6.1.3.1 of this handbook (trustee benefiting as borrower and lender; bank deposits on commercial side of trustee bank).

[175] 4 Scott & Ascher §24.7.

[176] 4 Scott & Ascher §24.7.

principal. "The earnings of a fund are incidents of ownership of the fund itself and are property just as the fund itself is property."[177]

When the borrower loses the loan proceeds. Whether we have a debt or a trust also makes a difference when there has been an accidental loss of funds. If the borrower (debtor) loses the loan proceeds, he or she is still on the hook to the lender (creditor). It is the borrower who bears the burden of the loss. On the other hand, if the funds were the subject of a trust *and the trustee is without fault*, it is the beneficiary, the one who had the equitable property interest in the funds, who is out of luck.

Cross-reference. For a discussion of trust-to-debt and debt-to-trust *novations*, the reader is referred to Section 8.15.57 of this handbook. There are statutory *limitation periods* for the recovery of contract debts that do not apply to breaches of trust. This is a topic that is taken up in Section 7.2.10 of this handbook. In earlier times, the *assignor of a chose in action*, such as a debt, retained the legal title to the associated contractual rights. The property interest that the assignee took was equitable. Did that mean that the assignor was an actual trustee of those rights for the benefit of the assignee? This is a topic we take up in Section 8.15.75 of this handbook.[178]

§9.9.5 Honorary Trusts

The most common situation is where clients don't have any children and their pets really are their children, she said. When a pet trust is used, the amount of money put into it is typically about $25,000 per animal, according to lawyers.[179]

Generally. Where the owner of property transfers it in trust for a specific noncharitable purpose, and there is no definite or definitely ascertainable beneficiary designated, no enforceable trust is created.[180] This nontrust is sometimes referred to as an "honorary trust."[181] The terms are unenforceable by a beneficiary because there is none[182] and by the attorney general because

---

[177] Webb's Fabulous Pharmacies, Inc. v. Beckwith, 449 U.S. 155, 164, 101 S. Ct. 446, 452 (1980).

[178] *See also* Bogert §25 (assignments of nonnegotiable choses in action).

[179] James L. Dam, *Trusts to Care for Pets After-Death Catching On*, Law. Wkly. USA, July 22, 2002, at 483 (listing the following states as having laws allowing trusts to name pets as beneficiaries and providing for enforcement by someone acting on the pet's behalf: Alaska (§13.12.907); Arizona (§14-2907); Colorado (§15-11-901); Florida (§737.116); Iowa (§633.2105); Michigan (700.2722); Montana (72-2-1017); New Mexico (§45-2-907); New Jersey (3B:11-38); New York (§7-6.1); North Carolina (§36A-147); Oregon (§128.308); and Utah (§75-2-1001)).

[180] Restatement (Second) of Trusts §124. The transferee, however, would have the power to apply the property to the designated purpose, unless such application is authorized or directed to be made at a time beyond the period of the rule against perpetuities, or the purpose is capricious. Restatement (Second) of Trusts §124.

[181] Restatement (Second) of Trusts §124 cmt. c; 2 Scott & Ascher §12.11; John Chipman Gray, The Rule Against Perpetuities, Appendix H §909.1 (4th ed. 1942).

[182] Restatement (Second) of Trusts §124 cmt. a. *See also* §5.1 of this handbook (who can be a beneficiary?).

the purposes are noncharitable.[183] The transferee has two choices: to voluntarily carry out the terms of the unenforceable arrangement or to return the property to the transferor or his estate upon a resulting trust.[184] In no event will he be permitted to keep the property. Legislatures, of course, are free to carve out exceptions to the common law principle that dispositions for noncharitable purposes are unenforceable, and they have done so. Gravesite perpetual care statutes come to mind.[185]

The Uniform Trust Code,[186] as well as the Uniform Probate Code,[187] would allow for the enforcement of two types of honorary dispositions: those for general but noncharitable purposes such as "a bequest of money to be distributed to such objects of benevolence as the trustee might select" and those for specific noncharitable purposes such as the care of a cemetery plot,[188] or perhaps even for the purpose of promoting fox hunting.[189] Who would enforce these trusts? A person appointed in the terms of the trust or, if no person is so appointed, a person selected by the court.[190] Property not required for the intended use must be distributed to the settlor, if then living, otherwise to the settlor's successors in interest.[191] An honorary trust authorized by either code, however, could not be enforced for more than twenty-one years.[192] Again, legislatures would be free to carve out exceptions. Most perpetual care trusts, for example, have been exempted by statute from the durational requirements of the rule against perpetuities.

The Restatement (Third) of Trusts would enforce certain honorary trusts[193] as purpose adapted trusts. The topic of purpose trusts is covered in Section 9.27 of this handbook. The adapted trust is covered in Section 9.29 of this handbook.

---

[183] Restatement (Second) of Trusts §124 cmt. a.

[184] Restatement (Second) of Trusts §124 cmt. b.

[185] *See generally* 2 Scott & Ascher §12.11.2; Rounds, *Protections Afforded to Massachusetts' Ancient Burial Grounds*, 73 Mass. L. Rev. 176 (1988).

[186] UTC §§408 (Trust for Care of Animal), 409 (Noncharitable Trust Without Ascertainable Beneficiary) (available at <http://www.uniformlaws.org/Act.aspx?title=Trust%20Code>).

[187] UPC §2-907 (Honorary Trusts; Trusts for Pets).

[188] UTC §409 cmt. (available at <http://www.uniformlaws.org/Act.aspx?title=Trust%20 Code>). *See also* 6 Scott & Ascher §39.7.5 (confirming that a trust for the perpetual maintenance of a grave or a tomb is generally considered noncharitable, unless the deceased was a well-known public figure such as perhaps a president or a general).

[189] *See* 2 Scott & Ascher §12.11.6.

[190] UTC §409(2) (available at <http://www.uniformlaws.org/Act.aspx?title=Trust%20 Code>).

[191] UTC §409(3) (available at <http://www.uniformlaws.org/Act.aspx?title=Trust%20 Code>). The property may be applied only to its intended use, except to the extent the court determines that the value of the trust property exceeds the amount required for the intended us. UTC §409(3).

[192] UTC §409(3) §409(1) (available at <http://www.uniformlaws.org/Act.aspx?title=Trust %20Code>). *See* 2 Scott & Ascher §12.11.1 (discussing the applicability of various manifestations of the rule against perpetuities, statutory and otherwise, to honorary trusts); John Chipman Gray, The Rule Against Perpetuities, Appendix H §909.1 (4th ed. 1942) (application of the rule against perpetuities to honorary trusts).

[193] Restatement (Third) of Trusts §47 cmt. a.

Trusts for Pets. In one case, a testator bequeathed in trust his horses and dogs for their maintenance as long as any of them should live. Though unenforceable, the trust was held not to violate the rule against perpetuities.[194] Prof. John Chipman Gray was not so sure: "Can a gift over be made to take effect upon the death of any animal however longevous—an elephant, a crow, a carp, a crocodile, or a toad?"[195]

At common law, an honorary trust for the care of an animal was unenforceable because there was no person authorized to enforce the trustee's obligations.[196] That having been said, a resulting trust did not necessarily arise, provided there was someone ready and willing to carry out its terms.[197]

The Uniform Trust Code provides that a trust may be created to provide for the care of an animal alive during the settlor's lifetime.[198] "The trust terminates upon the death of the animal or, if the trust was created to provide for the care of more than one animal alive during the settlor's lifetime, upon the death of the last surviving animal."[199] The trust may be enforced by a person appointed in the terms of the trust or, if no person is so appointed, by a person appointed by the court.[200] "A person having an interest in the welfare of the animal may request the court to appoint a person to enforce the trust or to remove a person appointed."[201] Property not required for the intended use must be distributed to the settlor, if then living, otherwise to the settlor's successors in interest.[202] The Uniform Probate Code also provides for the enforcement of trusts for pets,[203] as does the Restatement (Third) of Trusts.[204] As to the tax considerations, the reader is referred to Gerry W. Beyer and Jonathan P. Wilkerson.[205]

When it comes to caring for a pet after its owner has died, the honorary trust may not be the only option that involves a trust.[206] One might, for example, create a garden-variety express trust *for the benefit of human beings* that

---

[194] In re Dean, 41 Ch. D. 552.

[195] John Chipman Gray, The Rule Against Perpetuities §896.3 (4th ed. 1942).

[196] 2 Scott & Ascher §12.11.3; Uniform Trust Code §408 cmt.

[197] *See, e.g.*, In re Searight's Estate, 95 N.E.2d 779 (Ohio App. 1950).

[198] UTC §408(a) (available at <http://www.uniformlaws.org/Act.aspx?title=Trust%20Code>).

[199] UTC §408(a) (available at <http://www.uniformlaws.org/Act.aspx?title=Trust%20Code>).

[200] UTC §408(b) (available at <http://www.uniformlaws.org/Act.aspx?title=Trust%20Code>).

[201] UTC §408(b) (available at <http://www.uniformlaws.org/Act.aspx?title=Trust%20Code>).

[202] UTC §408(c) (available at <http://www.uniformlaws.org/Act.aspx?title=Trust%20Code>). Property of a trust for the care of an animal may be applied only to its intended use, except to the extent the court determines that the value of the trust property exceeds the amount required for the intended use. UTC §408(c).

[203] UPC §2-907(b).

[204] Restatement (Third) of Trusts §47 cmt. f.

[205] *Max's Taxes: A Tax-Based Analysis of Pet Trusts*, 43 U. Rich. L. Rev. 1219 (2009).

[206] Or, as one wag has phrased it, the honorary trust may not be only way to "skin the cat" when it comes to caring for a pet after its owner has died.

does not violate the Rule Against Perpetuities. The trust would *in part* be funded with the subject pet, the pet being property and a trust being a fiduciary relationship with respect thereto.[207] The governing instrument would have appropriately strong pet retention language. The trustee also might be relieved of the duty to make the pet productive. The equitable interests of the human beneficiaries would be subject to the condition precedent that at least one of them assumes custody of the pet and cares for it. Title to the pet, however, would remain in the trustee.[208]

§9.9.6   Secret and Semi-Secret Testamentary Trusts

The equitable rules . . . [regarding secret trusts] . . . seem originally to have been based on a fraudulent encouragement of the testator but are now a normal exercise of general equitable jurisdiction, fastening a trust on the primary donee under the will where his conscience is bound by the extraneous arrangement. Though the facts commonly involve immoral and selfish conduct on the part of the primary donee, that is not a necessary element.[209]

Testate dispositions. Where a testator devises property to a person in reliance upon his agreement to hold the property in trust, no express trust is created.[210] Where the will is silent as to the agreement, *i.e.*, where it appears from a reading of the will that the transferee takes outright and free of trust, the property is said to be held upon a secret trust.[211] Ordinarily such an arrangement would be unenforceable as violating the doctrine of independent legal significance, a topic we take up in Section 8.15.9 of this handbook.[212] Where the will reveals an intention that the transferee be a trustee of the property, the property is said to be held upon a semi-secret trust.[213] In either case, what happens to the subject property?

The secret trust. In the case of the secret trust, the transferee holds the property upon a constructive trust for the purposes and persons per the agreement.[214] Similarly, the trustee of a secret charitable trust holds the property upon a constructive trust in furtherance of "the charitable purposes for

---

[207] *See generally* Chapter 1 of this handbook.

[208] *But see* Wesley J. Smith, *So Three Cows Walk into Court . . .* , 14(41) The Weekly Standard, at 14, 15 ("But animal standing would do more than just plunge the entire animal industry into chaos. In one fell swoop, it would both undermine the status of animals as property and elevate them with the force of law toward legal personhood").

[209] Lewin ¶ 3-74 (England). *See also* Restatement of Restitution §186 cmt. b (U.S.).

[210] Restatement (Second) of Trusts §55(1); Restatement (Third) of Trusts §18(1). *See generally* 5 Scott & Ascher §37.2.4.1 (Secret Charitable Trusts).

[211] 1 Scott & Ascher §7.2 (Secret Trusts); 5 Scott & Ascher §37.2.4.1 (Secret Charitable Trusts).

[212] *See* Restatement (Third) of Property (Wills and Other Donative Transfers) §3.7 cmt. e.

[213] *See generally* 1 Scott & Ascher §7.2.6 (Secret Trusts); 5 Scott & Ascher §37.2.4.1 (Secret Charitable Trusts).

[214] Restatement (Second) of Trusts §55(1); Restatement (Third) of Trusts §18(1); 5 Scott & Ascher §37.2.4.1 (Secret Charitable Trusts); §3.3 of this handbook (involuntary trustees); Restatement of Restitution §186.

which the devisee agreed to hold it,"[215] unless "a testamentary disposition in favor of charity is forbidden by statute," in which case the devisee holds the subject property upon a resulting trust pending transfer of the legal title to the executor or administrator of the testator's probate estate.[216]

The semi-secret trust. In the case of a semi-secret trust, there are two possibilities.[217] The Restatement of Trusts and a number of decisions would have the property held upon a constructive trust for the purposes and persons per the agreement.[218]

The current weight of authority, however, would have the property return to the estate of the testator upon a resulting trust.[219] In fact, this has been the weight of authority on this side of the Atlantic since well before the first edition of this handbook was published, which was in 1898.[220]

The Restatement (Third) of Restitution and Unjust Enrichment, which finds the semi-secret trust to be just another example of a wrongful interference with a donative transfer, would authorize restitution in favor of the intended beneficiaries: "If the problem is approached from the perspective of unjust enrichment, . . . it is impossible to draw a persuasive distinction between the 'secret trust' . . . and the 'semi-secret' trust whose intended beneficiary is known."[221]

England. In England, the "difficult question of whether fully and semi-secret trusts are express or constructive remains unsettled."[222]

Intestacy. "Where a person dies intestate in reliance upon an agreement by his heir or next of kind to hold the property which he acquires by such intestacy upon a trust, the heir or next of kind holds the property upon a constructive trust for the person for whom he agreed to hold."[223] In other words, an intestate disposition as well as a testate disposition can give rise to a

---

[215] 5 Scott & Ascher §37.2.4.1 (Secret Charitable Trusts).

[216] 5 Scott & Ascher §37.2.6.5 (Agreement by Devisee or Heir to Hold upon Charitable Trust).

[217] *See generally* 5 Scott & Ascher §37.2.4.1 (Secret Charitable Trusts).

[218] Restatement (Second) of Trusts §55(1); Restatement (Third) of Trusts §18(1); 5 Scott & Ascher §37.2.4.1 (Secret Charitable Trusts); §3.3 of this handbook (involuntary trustees); *cf.* Restatement of Restitution §186 cmt. b.

[219] *See, e.g.,* Olliffe v. Wells, 130 Mass. 221 (1881). *See generally* 5 Scott & Ascher §37.2.4.1 (Secret Charitable Trusts). *See also* §8.26 of this handbook (why trustees need to know about will residue clauses). *But cf.* Restatement of Restitution §186 cmt. b.

[220] *See* Olliffe v. Wells, 130 Mass. 221 (1881) (This decision of Chief Justice Horace Gray is said to be the source of the distinction between the secret and semi-secret trust (U.S.)). Horace Gray would later serve as an Associate Justice of the U.S. Supreme Court. His half-brother, Prof. John Chipman Gray, authored the classic formulation of the Rule Against Perpetuities, which is set out verbatim in §8.2.1 of this handbook.

[221] Restatement (Third) of Restitution and Unjust Enrichment §46 cmt. g.

[222] Lewin ¶3-76 (England).

[223] Restatement (Second) of Trusts §55(2); Restatement (Third) of Trusts §18(2); Restatement of Restitution §186(2).

secret trust. The English cases are in accord.[224] As is the Restatement (Third) of Restitution and Unjust Enrichment.[225]

§9.9.7 The Corporation Is Not a Trustee of Corporate Assets

Not to be confused with a trust company that takes title as trustee to the property of others,[226] a private corporation is not a trustee of its own assets, although some courts have suggested otherwise.[227] Shareholders, being in a mere contractual relationship with the corporation, have no equitable or beneficial interest in its underlying assets.[228] Thus, there is no fiduciary relation between the corporation and its shareholders as there is between a trustee and the beneficiaries of the trust.[229] Accordingly, the remedies of a trust beneficiary as against the trustee are equitable, while those of a shareholder as against the corporation are legal.[230] In the absence of a legal remedy, however, the shareholders, under certain circumstances, would have the right to bring an equitable action against the corporation.[231] That a corporation's contractual duty to act for the benefit of its shareholder is often enforced in equity is probably the reason why some courts have fallen into the trap of mischaracterizing a corporation as the trustee of its own assets.[232]

§9.9.8 Directors of a Corporation Are Not Trustees of Corporate Assets

As in so many cases of so-called trusts, the fiduciary feature is present, but the dual property ownership is absent. The directors have no legal interest and the stockholders no equitable interest.—Bogert's Trusts and Trustees §16

Directors of a corporation are not the trustees of the corporation's assets, although some courts and commentators have suggested otherwise.[233] As to the world, a trustee of a trust is the owner of the underlying trust property.[234] Legal title is in the trustee. The corporation, on the other hand, is the owner and legal

---

[224] Lewin ¶ 3-82.

[225] Restatement (Third) of Restitution and Unjust Enrichment §46 cmt. g.

[226] *See generally* §8.6 of this handbook (the trustee who is not a human being).

[227] *See generally* Bogert §16.

[228] *See* Bogert §16 ("The relationship of shareholder to corporation is contractual.").

[229] Bogert §16.

[230] Bogert §16.

[231] Bogert §16.

[232] Bogert §16.

[233] *See generally* Bogert §16 ("Often one finds the phrase that the 'relation of the directors to the stockholders is essentially that of trustee and cestui que trust.' This statement, however, is far from accurate technically.") *See also* Lewin ¶ 7-16 (England) (referring to company directors as *quasi* trustees).

[234] *See generally* §3.5.1 of this handbook (nature and extent of the trustee's estate).

titleholder of corporate assets, not its directors.[235] The directors neither have title to nor an equitable interest in the corporation's underlying property.[236] "The directors or other members of the managing board of the corporation sometimes are called 'trustees' in the charter or articles of incorporation. Their legal position is the same no matter by what name they are called, whether directors, trustees, or governors."[237]

Directors of a corporation, however, are in a fiduciary relationship with the corporation.[238] They also are in a fiduciary relationship with its shareholders incident to some sort of agency relationship. Who the principal is in that relationship is beyond the scope of this handbook. While it is settled law that the shareholders are not the principals, it is not settled who, then, is the principal. Some commentators have suggested that the corporation itself is the principal.[239] One learned commentator has suggested that it is actually the state:

> The model behind corporate law's treatment of authority is one of a unilaterally controlled flow of authority from a single wellspring of power rather than a bubbling up and flowing together of many individual sources of personal power. The state has power; it chooses to delegate it to the board of directors of a corporation. They in turn may choose to delegate it to the officers and even to employees at a much lower level.[240]

§9.9.9   *A Mortgagee Is Not a Trustee of the Mortgaged Property*

The great jurist Sir Edward Coke, who lived from 1552 to 1634, has explained why the term mortgage comes from the Old French words mort, dead, and gage, pledge. It seemed to him to have to do with the doubtfulness of whether or not the mortgagor will pay the debt. If the mortgagor does not, then the land pledged to the mortgagee as security for the debt is taken from him for ever, and so dead to him upon condition, . . . And if he doth pay the money, then the pledge is dead as to the [mortgagee].[241]

A lender whose loan is secured by the borrower's real estate is a mortgagee.[242] The borrower is the mortgagor. In some states, legal title to the real estate is in the mortgagee until such time as the loan is paid off. A mortgagee has a security interest in the subject property. "Although a mortgagee owes the mortgagor equitable duties with respect to foreclosure, possession of mortgaged property, and recognition of the mortgagor's equity of redemption, such

---

[235] *See generally* 1 Scott & Ascher §2.3.12.
[236] Bogert §16.
[237] Bogert §16.
[238] 1 Scott & Ascher §2.3.12.
[239] *See, e.g.*, Bogert §16.
[240] Robert Charles Clark, Corporate Law 22 (1986).
[241] American Heritage Dictionary 1176 (3d ed. 1992).
[242] The UPC defines a mortgage as "any conveyance, agreement, or arrangement in which property is encumbered or used as security." UPC §1-201(29).

duties arise under the law of mortgages . . ."[243] The mortgagee is not a trustee of the real estate for the following reasons:

- The mortgagee holds the property for his own benefit; a trustee, absent special facts, holds the property for someone else's benefit.[244]
- The mortgagee, absent special facts, owes no fiduciary duties to the mortgagor;[245] a trustee owes fiduciary duties to the beneficiaries.[246]
- The mortgagee has inherent authority to transfer his interest in the mortgaged property to a third party; a trustee may not delegate away all his fiduciary duties to a third party, nor transfer the underlying property to a third party, unless authorized to do so by the terms of the trust, the court, or under certain circumstances by the beneficiaries.[247]
- The mortgagee may purchase for its own account prior mortgages; a trustee may not profit from purchasing an encumbrance on the trust property.[248]
- "The claim of a mortgagor against the mortgagee to recover the mortgaged property may be barred by a statute of limitations when the claim of the beneficiary of a trust against the trustee would not be barred."[249]

The principle that a mortgagee is not *per se* a trustee of the mortgaged property does not mean that one cannot be trustee of a mortgage. A trustee, for example, could lend trust funds to *X* and take back a mortgage on *X*'s real estate. In that situation, the trustee would hold the mortgage in trust for the benefit of the trust's beneficiaries. The trustee, however, would not hold the property in trust for the mortgagor, nor would the trustee owe the mortgagor any fiduciary duties.[250]

§9.9.10   An Equitable Charge Is Not a Trust

An equitable charge, unlike a trust, does not entail a fiduciary relationship.[251]

If the owner of property bequeaths funds to someone for the purpose of, say, paying someone's debt, then chances are we have a trust. If there are still

---

[243] Bogert §29.

[244] 1 Scott on Trusts §9; Bogert §29.

[245] Note, however, that "[a] mortgagee who takes possession of the mortgaged premises is accountable to the mortgagor for what he receives while he is in possession and is under a fiduciary duty to pay due regard to the rights of the mortgagor, but he is not a trustee." Restatement (Second) of Trusts §9 cmt. c. *See generally* Bogert §29.

[246] 1 Scott & Ascher §2.3.4.1; Bogert §29.

[247] 1 Scott on Trusts §9.

[248] 1 Scott on Trusts §9.

[249] Restatement (Second) of Trusts §9 cmt. d.

[250] Restatement (Second) of Trusts §9 cmt. e.

[251] 1 Scott & Ascher §2.3.6.4.

funds remaining after the debt has been paid, the remaining property returns to the estate of the owner-settlor upon a resulting trust,[252] there having been no intention on the part of the owner-settlor that the transferee, *i.e.*, the trustee, should enjoy any beneficial interest in the underlying property.[253]

On the other hand, if the testator's intention was that the transferee acquire a beneficial interest in the property in addition to the legal title thereto, *subject only to* an obligation that the debt be satisfied from that property, then we have a mere equitable charge.[254] To the extent there are funds remaining after the debt has been satisfied, there is no resulting trust.[255] The transferee gets to keep what is left,[256] as well as any rents or profits that have been thrown off by the charged property.[257] An equitable charge then is essentially a naked equitable security interest that attaches to the subject property.[258] The creditor's remedy if the charge is not met is generally limited to a petition in equity for a sale of the charged property, followed by a payment of the debt out of the proceeds thereof.[259] The more generous selection of equitable remedies that may be available to a trust beneficiary in the event the trustee breaches his trust is covered in Section 7.2.3 of this handbook. As with all things equitable,[260] substance trumps form when it comes to sorting out whether one is faced with a trust or a charge:

> This distinction is not dependent upon whether the word "trust" or "charge" is used in the will, *and is not confined to cases involving the dispositions for the payment of debts* [emphasis added]. If an intention can be found in the will to confer the beneficial ownership on the devisee or legatee concerned, he will take beneficially, subject to complying with the relevant injunction, notwithstanding the use of the word "trust."[261]

---

[252] *See* §4.1.1.1 of this handbook (the noncharitable trust; resulting trust defined) (in part defining the resulting trust).

[253] *See generally* Bogert §31.

[254] The equitable charge is not confined to dispositions for the payment of debts. *See generally* Lewin ¶ 8-40 (England); Bogert §30 (U.S.) (noting that "[a]lthough no particular term is required to create a charge, use of the words 'subject to' generally is held to show that the transferor intends to create a charge"); Harold Greville Hanbury & Ronald Harling Maudsley, Modern Equity 121–122 (10th ed. 1976) (charge and trust distinguished).

[255] Lewin ¶ 8-39 (England); Bogert §30 (U.S.).

[256] Bogert §30.

[257] David Hayton, Paul Matthews, & Charles Mitchell, Underhill and Hayton: Law of Trusts and Trustees ¶ 1.93 (17th ed. 2007) (noting that during the subsistence of an equitable charge, the transferee, unlike a trustee, is not accountable for rents and profits arising from the subject property).

[258] *See generally* David Hayton, Paul Matthews, & Charles Mitchell, Underhill and Hayton: Law of Trusts and Trustees ¶ 1.93 (17th ed. 2007) (confirming that an equitable charge is an equitable security interest that imposes no personal fiduciary obligations on the transferee of the charged property).

[259] David Hayton, Paul Matthews, & Charles Mitchell, Underhill and Hayton: Law of Trusts and Trustees ¶ 1.93 (17th ed. 2007).

[260] *See generally* §8.12 of this handbook (Equity's maxims).

[261] Lewin ¶ 8-40.

An equitable charge resembles a trust in that title is in the transferee while someone else has an equitable interest.[262] The difference is that while the trust beneficiary has a property interest in the underlying property,[263] the person with the equitable charge, *i.e.*, the equitable encumbrancer, has only a security interest.[264] "If a devisee subject to an equitable charge fails to pay the equitable encumbrancer the sum to which he is entitled, the latter's remedy is a suit in equity to obtain a decree for the sale of the land to pay the charge; if a trustee fails to perform his duties under the trust, the remedy of the beneficiary is a suit in equity to compel specific performance or redress of the breach of trust."[265] One who takes property subject to an equitable charge has only a negative duty: He may not deal with the property in a way that compromises the equitable charge, such as transferring the property to a BFP, which, like a trustee, he would have the naked power to do.[266] "Arguably, the absence of a fiduciary duty in the equitable charge is the most important distinction between a charge and trust."[267]

The defense that the beneficiary has failed to take timely action against the trustee to remedy a particular breach of trust is taken up in Section 7.1.3 of this handbook, and in Section 8.15.70 of this handbook in our discussion of the equitable doctrine of laches. "The statute of limitations normally runs against a charge beneficiary at the time performance is due under the charge; if a trustee refuses to perform required duties, on the other hand, repudiation and notice of the repudiation must occur for the statute of limitation to begin to run."[268] In other words, a statute of limitations that is applicable to an action for breach of trust is little more than a partial codification of the equitable doctrine of laches.

While an equitable charge is not a trust, an owner of a transferable property interest may transfer it to a trustee and in the process subject it to an equitable charge for the benefit of a third party, who need not be a beneficiary of the trust. Conversely, the beneficiary of an equitable charge may transfer his property rights incident thereto to a trustee, said rights to be held for the benefit of the trust beneficiaries. The topic of trust funding generally is taken up in Section 2.1.1 of this handbook.

---

[262] 1 Scott & Ascher §2.3.6; Bogert §30.

[263] Scott on Trusts §10 (1939 ed.).

[264] 1 Scott & Ascher §2.3.6; Bogert §30.

[265] Scott on Trusts §10 (1939 ed.). *See also* Bogert §30.

[266] Bogert §30. *See generally* §5.4.2 of this handbook (rights of the beneficiary as against transferees, including BFPs).

[267] Bogert §30.

[268] Bogert §30.

§9.9.11   A Specifically Enforceable Contract to Convey Land Is Not a Trust

It is still more inaccurate to speak of the purchaser as trustee for the vendor of the purchase money, since the purchaser is not bound to hold any specific money for the vendor, but is merely under a personal obligation to pay the amount of the purchase price.[269]

Two parties enter into a contact for the purchase and sale of a parcel of land. Under the doctrine of equitable conversion, at the time the contract is struck, the purchaser acquires an equitable interest in the land, even though there has yet to be an actual conveyance or deeding of the land.[270] This is because the contract is specifically enforceable in equity.[271] In other words, "equity looks on that as done which ought to be done."[272] The purchaser has a personal obligation to pay the purchase price.[273] The seller (vendor) retains the legal title to the land, essentially as security for the purchase price.[274] The seller's status thus is analogous to that of a mortgagee.[275] In order to secure the seller's interest, "the legal interest is held back until the purchaser completes performance of the obligations under the contract."[276] For a discussion of the mortgagor-mortgagee relationship, the reader is referred to Section 9.9.9 of this handbook.

Although between the time the contract is struck and the time of conveyance legal tile is in the seller, it cannot be said that the seller is a trustee of the property for the buyer because (1) the seller is not in a fiduciary relationship with the buyer[277] and (2) the seller may unilaterally transfer title and otherwise

---

[269] 1 Scott on Trusts §13.

[270] 1 Scott & Ascher §2.3.9.

[271] *See, e.g.*, Gilles v. Sprout, 293 Minn. 53, 196 N.W.2d 612 (1972). *See also* Bogert §18 (noting that "[i]n contracts of sale that are not specifically enforceable the purchaser generally has no equitable rights and therefore cannot legally be considered a beneficiary.").

[272] *See generally* §8.12 of this handbook (in which there is a catalog of equity maxims).

[273] Bogert §18 (noting that "a party cannot be a trustee of indefinite property and as the proceeds to pay the purchase price are not usually specified in the purchase agreement, the purchaser cannot be considered a trustee.").

[274] Bogert §18.

[275] 1 Scott on Trusts §13; 1 Scott & Ascher §2.3.9; Bogert §18 ("The relationship of the seller and the purchaser in a specifically enforceable contract is entitled to its own place in the law. It should not be pushed into an existing category. However, this relationship most closely resembles a mortgage."). In the case of a vendor's lien to secure full payment of the purchase price, which has many of the attributes mortgage, the purchaser's legal interest in the subject property is *not* held in trust to secure the seller's contractual rights. Bogert §18. "The purchaser has full and complete and uncontrolled enjoyment of the res, subject to no obligations to the seller." *Id.*

[276] Bogert §18 (suggesting that though performance is often delayed in order for the purchaser to investigate the seller's title and to permit the seller to prove ownership of the full interest in the subject property, the primary purpose of the seller's retention of the legal title is still to secure collection of the purchase price).

[277] "The vendor in entering into further transactions with the purchaser . . . [, for example,] . . . is under no duty to make full disclosure to him." 1 Scott on Trusts §13. *See also* Bogert §18 ("A seller who acquires an outstanding interest in the property the seller contracted to sell holds this interest for the benefit of the buyer. This is the case for reasons similar to those of

alienate what remains of his interest in the land to third parties.[278] Thus, "[w]hen sellers purchase insurance on the property that is payable to themselves, a loss occurs on the property, and the purchaser subsequently fulfills the contract and pays the purchase price in full, the weight of authority suggests that the sellers do not hold the collected insurance proceeds in trust for the purchaser."[279] The proceeds belong to them. Had the sellers held the property as trustees for the benefit of the purchaser pending conveyance, then the proceeds also would have been held for the benefit of the purchaser, the proceeds having been an item of trust accounting principal.[280] Having said all that, a seller who wrongfully refuses to convey after having received the full purchase price does run the risk of being declared by some court a *constructive trustee* of the property for the benefit of the buyer, this in order to keep the seller from being unjustly enriched by his nonfeasance.[281] The constructive trust is taken up generally in Section 3.3 of this handbook.

A word of caution to the reader. In Section 8.15.44 of this handbook, the doctrine of equitable conversion is addressed in another and quite different context, namely, when land *is* the subject of a trust, in this case an express trust, and the trustee by the terms of the trust is directed to sell it. The focus in Section 8.15.44 is on whether *the beneficiary's* equitable interest is deemed realty or personalty.

§9.9.12 U.K.-REITs and G-REITs Are Not Trusts

REIT is an acronym for real estate investment trust.[282] In the United States, a REIT is a trusteed mutual fund.[283] In England, however, a REIT is actually neither a trust nor a mutual fund.[284] Rather, the UK-REIT in many respects resembles a U.S. Subchapter S corporation, both in form and in

---

estoppel by deed rather than on the basis of a fiduciary relationship."). *See generally* §6.1.5.1 of this handbook (trustee's duty to furnish the beneficiaries with critical information regarding the trust).

[278] "Although a trustee cannot properly transfer trust property to another person subject to the trust, since he is under a duty not to delegate, a vendor can properly sell his interest subject to the contract with the purchaser." 1 Scott on Trusts §13. *See generally* §6.1.4 of this handbook (trustee's duty to give personal attention to the affairs of the trust); Bogert §18.

[279] Bogert §18.

[280] Bogert §18. *See generally* §6.2.4.2 of this handbook (receipts that are entirely allocated to principal).

[281] Bogert §18.

[282] Charles E. Rounds, Jr. & Andreas Dehio, *Publicly-Traded Open End Mutual Funds in Common Law and Civil Law Jurisdictions: A Comparison of Legal Structures*, 3 N.Y.U.J.L. & Bus. 473, 479 (2007).

[283] Charles E. Rounds, Jr. & Andreas Dehio, *Publicly-Traded Open End Mutual Funds in Common Law and Civil Law Jurisdictions: A Comparison of Legal Structures*, 3 N.Y.U.J.L. & Bus. 473, 479 (2007).

[284] Charles E. Rounds, Jr. & Andreas Dehio, *Publicly-Traded Open End Mutual Funds in Common Law and Civil Law Jurisdictions: A Comparison of Legal Structures*, 3 N.Y.U.J.L. & Bus. 473, 479 (2007).

function.[285] Germany's REIT does so as well.[286] The UK-REIT is a creature of
the Finance Act 2006.[287] Germany's G-REIT is a creature of a statute that was
enacted by the German parliament (Bundestag) in 2007.[288]

§9.9.13 A Bailment Is Not a Trust

*Bailment arose in the common law courts before the use was recognized in chancery. Detinue
was allowed to the bailor in courts of law before the subpoena in chancery was made available
to the trust beneficiary. The law courts have attached certain incidents to the bailment, as it
developed under their tutelage, and the courts of chancery have separately shaped the use
and the trust. The two might have been developed equally logically by the same court as
merely two phases of the same institution.[289]*

A trust is an equitable relationship whereas a bailment is a legal one.[290] A
bailment, though sometimes confused with a trust,[291] is not a trust.[292] While a
trustee generally takes the legal title to the subject property, a bailee generally
does not.[293] Thus, a bailee may not transfer the property in his possession to a
BFP (good-faith purchaser for value).[294] A trustee, on the other hand, can pass
good title to a BFP.[295] "Bailments must concern personal property only, but
trusts may affect either realty or personalty."[296]

There are differences related to procedure as well: The remedies against a
recalcitrant bailee are generally legal, unless the subject property is unique,

---

[285] Charles E. Rounds, Jr. & Andreas Dehio, *Publicly-Traded Open End Mutual Funds in Common Law and Civil Law Jurisdictions: A Comparison of Legal Structures*, 3 N.Y.U.J.L. & Bus. 473, 479 (2007).

[286] Charles E. Rounds, Jr. & Andreas Dehio, *Publicly-Traded Open End Mutual Funds in Common Law and Civil Law Jurisdictions: A Comparison of Legal Structures*, 3 N.Y.U.J.L. & Bus. 473, 479 (2007).

[287] Charles E. Rounds, Jr. & Andreas Dehio, *Publicly-Traded Open End Mutual Funds in Common Law and Civil Law Jurisdictions: A Comparison of Legal Structures*, 3 N.Y.U.J.L. & Bus. 473, 479 (2007).

[288] Charles E. Rounds, Jr. & Andreas Dehio, *Publicly-Traded Open End Mutual Funds in Common Law and Civil Law Jurisdictions: A Comparison of Legal Structures*, 3 N.Y.U.J.L. & Bus. 473, 479 (2007).

[289] Bogert §11. The "use," a precursor of the modern trust, is covered in §8.15.1 of this handbook. For more on the now obsolete common law tort action of detinue, the reader is referred to Restatement of Restitution §4 cmt. c.

[290] Restatement (Second) of Trusts §5 cmt. e; Bogert §11.

[291] *See* Doyle v. Burns, 123 Iowa 488, 497, 99 N.W. 195 (1904) (musing that the likes of Story and Kent have failed to sort out the differences between a trust and bailment); Bogert §11 ("Occasionally, a court treats a bailee as a strict trustee. . . . A bailment, however, is different from a trust in several legally significant ways.").

[292] 1 Scott & Ascher §1.8; Bogert §11.

[293] Bogert §11.

[294] Bogert §11. *See generally* §5.4.2 of this handbook (rights of the beneficiary as against transferees of trust property, including BFPs).

[295] Bogert §11.

[296] Bogert §11.

while those against a recalcitrant trustee are generally equitable.[297] Unless the bailment is coupled with an agency or trust, it is not a fiduciary relationship.[298] "Although a few cases outside of the United States treat bailments as fiduciary relationships, that characterization has not been adopted by U.S. Courts."[299]

§9.9.14   The Administrative Trust (U.S.)

The terms of the typical revocable inter vivos trust provide that upon the death of the settlor the trust shall divide or fracture into two or more separate sub-trusts,[300] or terminate altogether, with the remaindermen taking outright and free of trust shares of the underlying trust property. As we have noted elsewhere in this handbook, for trust and property law purposes, these sub-trusts or shares are deemed to be funded as of the time when the settlor dies.[301] "Equity looks on that as done which ought to be done."[302]

The typical revocable inter vivos trust, however, is seldom more than token-funded or partially funded while the settlor is alive.[303] The trustee can expect that the lion's share of the physical funding will take place well after the settlor's death and will take the form of pour-overs from the settlor's probate estate, proceeds from insurance on the settlor's life,[304] distributions from employee benefit plans,[305] and the like.[306] In other words, it will not be until many months after the settlor's death that all assets due the trust are marshaled and valued and there is a full physical funding of the sub-trusts or outright distribution of the remainder shares, as the case may be.

This delay poses some practical problems for the trustee, particularly if it extends beyond twelve months or straddles more than one income tax reporting year.[307] As of the time of the settlor's death, the beneficiaries of the sub-trusts or the remaindermen will have received equitable property rights,

---

[297] *See* Bogert §11; §7.2.3 of this handbook (types of equitable relief for breaches of trust).

[298] 1 Scott & Ascher §2.3.1; Bogert §11.

[299] D. Gordon Smith, *The Critical Resource Theory of Fiduciary Duty*, 55 Vand. L. Rev. 1399, n.61 (2002). *See also* Bogert §11.

[300] *See generally* §8.9 of this handbook (why more than one trust: the estate and generation-skipping tax). *See also* §3.5.3.2(d) of this handbook (an express power in the trustee to combine the property of multiple sub-trusts in a common fund for investment purposes).

[301] *See generally* §6.2.4.5 of this handbook (when a beneficiary's entitlement to income begins) and §8.2.3 of this handbook (trust termination and distribution issues).

[302] *See* §8.12 of this handbook (containing a catalogue of critical equity maxims).

[303] *See generally* §2.1.1 of this handbook (token-funding, partially funding and fully funding revocable inter vivos trusts). *See also* §2.2.1 of this handbook (the pour-over statute).

[304] *See generally* §2.2.2 of this handbook (life insurance beneficiary designations).

[305] *See generally* §9.5 of this handbook (trusts for deferring taxation of income).

[306] *See, e.g.,* §2.2.3 of this handbook (the custodial IRA).

[307] *See generally* John A. Hartog & George R. Dirkes, Assisting the Nonprofessional Trustee in Implementing the Administrative Trust (visited Sept. 10, 2014) <http://www.hartogbaer.com/forms/USCArticle.pdf>.

either vested or contingent, or both.[308] Also, the items of property that ultimately find their way into the hands of the trustee of the sub-trusts or the
remaindermen are likely to have been throwing off taxable income since the
time when the settlor died. Taxes are likely to be owed on that income.[309] In
other words, the trustee during this asset-marshaling limbo period needs to
keep track of and protect the equitable property rights of the beneficiaries of
the phantom sub-trusts or the remaindermen,[310] as well as see to it that
whatever income taxes are owed with respect to the property items are paid.
Also, obligations for debts and expenses attributable to the phantom sub-trusts
or undistributed remainder shares need to be properly allocated.[311]

During this limbo period, *i.e.*, during the period from the time when the
settlor dies to the time when all the sub-trusts are fully funded or the remainder
shares are distributed, the trustee may want to administer the property that was
in the revocable inter vivos trust as if it were the subject of what has been referred
to as an "administrative trust." The reserved right of revocation having
extinguished with the death of the settlor, the "administrative trust" would need
its own separate tax identification number.[312] The trustee also would need to file
with the IRS a separate Form 56.[313] Still, as a matter of trust and property law, the
administrative trust would be more a probate estate analog than a true trust:

> At the outset, the attorney should understand that there is a common
> misconception that professional services are unnecessary in the administration of
> living trusts after death. In fact, even though most successor trustees do not know
> it, probate and trust administration require the same three administrative func-
> tions: (1) Making an inventory of assets; (2) Paying debts and taxes; and (3) Dis-
> tributing the remaining assets to the designated beneficiaries.[314]

---

[308] *See generally* §6.2.4.5 of this handbook (when a beneficiary's entitlement to trust accounting income begins) and §8.2.3 of this handbook (when the trustee, for whatever reason, fails, in
contravention of the terms of the trust, to effect the termination and division of a one-pot trust, or
unduly delays in doing so).

[309] *See generally* John A. Hartog & George R. Dirkes, Assisting the Nonprofessional Trustee
in Implementing the Administrative Trust (visited Sept. 10, 2014) <http://www.hartogbaer.com/
forms/USCArticle.pdf>.

[310] *See generally* §6.2.4.5 of this handbook (when a beneficiary's entitlement to trust accounting income begins).

[311] *See generally* §6.2.4.4 of this handbook.

[312] *See generally* John A. Hartog & George R. Dirkes, Assisting the Nonprofessional Trustee
in Implementing the Administrative Trust (visited Sept. 10, 2014) <http://www.hartogbaer.com/
forms/USCArticle.pdf>. *See also* §8.34 of this handbook (when an employer identification number
(EIN) is not required).

[313] Notice Concerning Fiduciary Relationship. *See generally* John A. Hartog & George R.
Dirkes, Assisting the Nonprofessional Trustee in Implementing the Administrative Trust (visited
Sept. 10, 2014) <http://www.hartogbaer.com/forms/USCArticle.pdf> (noting also that a "successor trustee should attach to the Form 56 an Affidavit of Successor Trustee, declaring that the
successor is the duly constitute successor trustee"). *See generally* §3.4.2 of this handbook (acceptance of trusteeship).

[314] 2 California Trust Administration §13.1 (2d ed. 2002).

For a general discussion of the mechanics of implementing an administrative trust, the reader is referred to an article by two practitioners, John A. Hartog and George R. Dirkes.[315] For an in-depth detailed step-by-step explanation of the procedures that the trustee should follow in establishing, administering, and terminating an administrative trust, the reader is referred to California Trust Administration.[316] Two chapters therein contain numerous forms and checklists.

Joel Bernstein, Esq., a Massachusetts-based trusts and estates practitioner, has modified his trust administration software to accommodate the idiosyncrasies of the administrative trust.[317]

For a discussion of how the trustee of a revocable trust could find himself functioning as an "inadvertent executor," the reader is referred to Section 8.16 of this handbook.

§9.9.15 The Civil Law Foundation Is Not a Trust

The private civil law foundation, unlike the trust, is a creature of statute.[318] Also, unlike the trust, the civil law foundation is a separate juristic entity or legal person.[319] It resembles a corporation, only without shareholders, in that the entity itself owns the managed assets. A noncharitable civil law foundation may have individual beneficiaries, although it is a principle of foundation law that the members of the foundation's board or council owe their primary allegiance to the entity itself rather than to the beneficiaries.[320] This is a critical difference between the civil law noncharitable foundation and the noncharitable trust.[321] A discretionary permissible beneficiary of a civil law foundation has no enforceable legal or quasi-equitable property rights in foundation assets,[322] which can pose a problem for the beneficiary's creditors;[323] nor would the

---

[315] John A. Hartog & George R. Dirkes, Assisting the Nonprofessional Trustee in Implementing the Administrative Trust (visited Sept. 10, 2014) <http://www.hartogbaer.com/forms/USCArticle.pdf>.

[316] 2 California Trust Administration Chs. 13, 14 (2d ed. 2002).

[317] See http://www.livingtrustma.com/. Mr. Bernstein may be reached at **Joel@jbernsteinlaw.com.**

[318] Unlike a statutory civil law noncharitable foundation, a trust may change its situs without having to be dissolved and reconstituted, the trustee being the legal "owner" of the subject property.

[319] The trust is a legal relationship between the trustee and the beneficiaries rather than an entity.

[320] A civil law private noncharitable foundation also may exist to carry out a noncharitable purpose, such as the furtherance of a family business.

[321] See generally §6.1.3 of this handbook (the trustee's duty of loyalty to the beneficiaries).

[322] See generally §5.3.1 of this handbook (the trust beneficiary's property interest).

[323] See generally §5.3.3.3 of this handbook (the creditors of a trust beneficiary).

beneficiary have a default right to scrutinize the foundation's books or otherwise demand an accounting from the foundation's board or council,[324] which could pose a problem for the beneficiary himself.

Another critical difference between the noncharitable civil law foundation and the common law trust is that the duties of the members of the foundation's board or council, who do not hold legal title to the foundation's assets, are contractual in nature, rather than fiducial. Their duties are set forth in the foundation's bylaws or regulations. A noncharitable civil law foundation may have a perpetual duration.[325] In the United States, there is no such thing as a noncharitable foundation, or a charitable foundation for that matter. Under the U.S. tax laws, a "charitable foundation" is defined as either a charitable trust or a charitable corporation, each being a creature of state law.[326] A trustee of a common law trust, however, would likely have the *legal authority* to establish with trust assets a noncharitable foundation in a civil law jurisdiction.[327] Whether under equitable principles the trustee would be violating the terms of that particular trust in so doing is a separate issue. For more on the civil law foundation and other such civil law trust analogues, the reader is referred to Section 8.12.1 of this handbook.

§9.9.16   The Property Guardianship Is Not a Trust

The guardians have only a naked power, not coupled with an interest.[328]

A guardianship of the property of a minor or someone otherwise incapacitated is not a trust, principally because legal title to the ward's property remains with the ward.[329] In the case of a trust, legal title to the subject property is in the trustee. "A guardian's position resembles much more closely that of an agent for the ward, rather than that of one owning property for the benefit of another."[330] The fact that a guardian may serve without the ward's consent, however, keeps the relationship from being a true common law agency. A guardianship is a creature of statute; the trust relationship is not. Guardians and trustees, however, are fiduciaries.[331]

---

[324] *See generally* §6.1.5 of this handbook (the trustee's duty to account to the beneficiary) and §5.4.1.1 of this handbook (the trust beneficiary's right to information).

[325] *See generally* §8.2.1 of this handbook (the rule against perpetuities)

[326] *See generally* §9.4 of this handbook (the charitable trust) and §9.8.1 of this handbook (the charitable corporation).

[327] *Cf.* §3.5.3.1(a) of this handbook (incorporating the trust estate).

[328] Rollins v. Marsh, 128 Mass. 116, 118, 1880 WL 10618 (1880).

[329] Bogert §13.

[330] Bogert §13.

[331] Bogert §13.

§9.9.17   The Chancery Receiver Is Not a Trustee

"By the time of Elizabeth the jurisdiction of the Court of Chancery to appoint a receiver had become well-established; indeed, such an appointment 'is one of the oldest remedies in this court.'"[332]

Absent statute or court decree, the judicial appointment of a receiver to manage the property of a debtor for the benefit of his creditors does not result in the passage of legal title to the receiver as trustee, or otherwise.[333] The preexisting property interests of the parties remain undisturbed by the appointment.[334] "Property in his possession is *in custodia legis*, his possession being that of the court which appointed him."[335] A receiver is neither a trustee nor an agent for any of the parties.[336] He is said to be an officer of the court.[337]

The judicial appointment of a receiver as an equitable remedy for breaches of trust is taken up in Section 7.2.3.8 of this handbook. "Ordinarily, the court simply removes a trustee who is not properly administering the trust. While removal proceedings are pending, however, the court may appoint a receiver."[338]

§9.9.18   Community Property Is Not Entrusted

A brief explanation of the concept of community property may be found in Section 5.3.4 of this handbook. "The community property system involves a unique relationship created by statute, possibly resembling partnership or tenancy in common, but not modeled after any method of property holding developed by the courts of law or chancery under Anglo-American law, and which cannot, in any strict sense, be said to be a form of express trusteeship."[339]

§9.9.19   A Legal Life Tenant Is Not a Trustee of the Subject Property

In Section 8.27 of this handbook, we discuss the differences between a legal life estate and an equitable life estate under a trust. Absent special facts,

---

[332] Snell's Equity ¶ 17-01.

[333] 1 Scott & Ascher §2.3.12.

[334] Bogert §14.

[335] Nevitt v. Woodburn, 190 Ill. 283, 289–290, 60 N.E. 500, 503 (1901).

[336] Snell's Equity ¶ 17-07.

[337] Snell's Equity ¶ 17-07.

[338] 4 Scott & Ascher §24.3.4; *see also* Lewin ¶ 38-23 (England) ("Receivers are seldom sought for ordinary trusts nowadays, a judicial trustee being generally preferred, or in less serious cases, the appointment of a new trustee under section 41 of the Trustee Act of 1925"); Snell's Equity ¶ 17-21 (England) ("But the modern practice in appropriate cases is to apply for the appointment of a judicial trustee . . . rather than a receiver").

[339] Bogert §26.

the holder of a legal life estate is not a trustee of the subject property, either for the benefit of the remainderman or for anyone else.[340] "A legal life tenant and a legal remainder beneficiary have successive several interests in the same property. Trustee and beneficiary have simultaneous interests in the same property."[341]

§9.9.20   Legal Tenancies in Common and Legal Joint Tenancies Are Not Trusts

A legal tenancy in common, *per se*, is not a trust.[342] "In co-tenancy each owns something different, namely a share of a particular item of realty or personalty. In a trust both trustee and beneficiary own the same thing, the former owning it in law and the latter in equity."[343] Cotenants owe one another no fiduciary duties.[344] On the other hand, if one cotenant comes into possession of property belonging to the collective, such as rents thrown off by the subject property, then the cotenant is under a duty to the other cotenants to account for it.[345] If the cotenant fails to do so, the others are entitled to restitution,[346] which may entail some court declaring the cotenant a constructive trustee of the funds that do not belong to him.[347] Constructive trusts are discussed in Section 3.3 of this handbook. While a legal tenancy in common is not a trust, a cotenant may impress a trust upon his transferable property rights in the cotenancy.[348] Or, to put it another way, a trust may be funded with a transferable interest in a legal tenancy in common.[349] Legal joint tenancies and legal tenancies by the entirety, also, are not, *per se*, trusts.[350]

§9.9.21   Pledges Are Not Trusts

A pledge *per se* is neither a mortgage nor a trust. "... [A] mortgage is essentially a transfer of ownership of the property or an interest in the property to the mortgagee by way of security; and the mortgagor usually retains possession of the property. A pledge, on the other hand, is essentially a transfer of the

---

[340] Bogert §27.
[341] Bogert §27.
[342] Bogert §28.
[343] Bogert §28.
[344] Bogert §28.
[345] Restatement of Restitution §125 cmt. b.
[346] *See generally* §7.2.3.3 of this handbook (restitution and specific reparation).
[347] Restatement of Restitution §125(2); Bogert §28.
[348] *See generally* §2.1 of this handbook.
[349] *See generally* §2.1 of this handbook.
[350] Bogert §28.

possession of personal chattels to the pledgee by way of security; the ownership remains in the pledgor. . . ."[351]

That title to the pledged property remains back with the pledgor is key.[352] Recall from Chapter 1 of this handbook that in the case of a trust, legal title is in the trustee. This eliminates any chance that the pledgee could cut off the pledgor's interest by transferring the pledged property to a good-faith purchaser for value (BFP), as a trustee could do to the beneficiary's interest in an item of entrusted property.[353] On the other hand, while the title-holding trustee may pass clear title to a BFP, the title-holding pledgor may not.[354] "A bona fide purchaser takes subject to the pledgee's special, legal property interest."[355] For a general discussion of the doctrine of bona fide purchase, the reader is referred to Section 8.15.63 of this handbook.

A pledge being a legal relationship rather than an equitable one, in the ordinary course of things a pledgee owes the pledgor no fiduciary duties.[356] The pledgee's legal duties are limited to retaining possession, using ordinary care in protecting the pledged property, accounting for income thrown off by the pledged property, exercising any power of sale for the pledgor's benefit, and accounting for any surplus from the sale.[357]

A pledgee in violation of a legal duty to the pledgor is generally subject to the legal remedies of recovery of possession and damages.[358] In some cases, however, the pledgor also may be entitled to equitable relief, which might entail the judicial imposition of a constructive trust on the pledged property.[359] "Although a pledgor may file a bill in equity to redeem and may demand an accounting, the availability of these remedies does not make the pledgor's property interest equitable."[360] Constructive trusts are covered generally in Section 3.3 of this handbook.

§9.9.22 An Equitable Lienee Is Not a Trustee

The judicially imposed equitable lien, discussed in Section 7.2.3.1.4 of this handbook, is not a trust.[361] It differs from the equitable charge "only in that it arises by operation of equity from the relationship between the parties rather than by any act of theirs."[362] What an equitable charge is and why it is not a trust

---

[351] Snell's Equity ¶ 34-04.
[352] Bogert §30.
[353] Bogert §30.
[354] Bogert §30.
[355] Bogert §30.
[356] Bogert §30.
[357] Bogert §30.
[358] Bogert §30.
[359] Restatement of Restitution §160 cmt. c; Bogert §30.
[360] Bogert §30.
[361] Bogert §32.
[362] Snell's Equity ¶ 42-03.

is covered in Section 9.9.10 of this handbook. Unlike a trustee, one whose property is subject to an equitable lien or charge owes no fiduciary duties incident to holding legal title to the subject property.[363] Like a trustee, however, both the equitable lienee and the equitable chargee have the raw power to pass good title to the subject property to a BFP.[364] The doctrine of bona fide purchase is taken up in Section 8.15.63 of this handbook.

§9.9.23   An Equitable Right of Subrogation Is Not a Trust

In Section 8.15.50 of this handbook, we offer some examples of how the equitable doctrine of subrogation can intersect with the law of trusts. In this section, we explain why an equitable subrogation does not, in and of itself, put the parties to the subrogation into some kind of trust relationship.

Defining subrogation. Subrogation is essentially a procedural equitable remedy that supports the substantive equitable remedy of restitution for unjust enrichment.[365] It is one alternative to the imposition of a constructive trust or equitable lien.[366] Here is the Restatement of Restitution's definition of subrogation: "Where property of one person is used in discharging an obligation owed by another or a lien upon the property of another, under such circumstances that the other would be unjustly enriched by the retention of the benefit thus conferred, the former is entitled to be subrogated to the position of the obligee or lien-holder."[367] Thus, in the case of an insurance contract, if the insurer pays the loss, the insurer is entitled "to stand in the shoes of the insured in respect of his action against the party responsible for the loss."[368] Or in the case of a contract of suretyship, if the debtor's surety makes payment to the creditor, the surety is entitled to be subrogated to the position of the creditor.[369] So also if someone is induced by fraud or some other wrong to pay the debt of another.[370] "However, it is held that an officious payment of another's debt does not entitle the payor to sue the other in quasi-contractual action for the money paid or to maintain a proceeding in equity to be subrogated to the claim of the creditor."[371]

---

[363] Bogert §32.

[364] Bogert §32.

[365] William E. Fratcher, 5 Scott on Trusts §464 (1989). *See also* §7.2.3 (the procedural equitable remedy).

[366] William E. Fratcher, 5 Scott on Trusts §464 (1989). *See also* §7.2.3 (the procedural equitable remedy). *See also* §7.2.3.1.6 of this handbook (the constructive trust) and §7.2.3.1.4 of this handbook (the equitable line).

[367] Restatement of Restitution §162.

[368] Harold Greville Hanbury & Ronald Harling Maudsley, Modern Equity 574 (10th ed. 1976).

[369] Harold Greville Hanbury & Ronald Harling Maudsley, Modern Equity 574 (10th ed. 1976).

[370] William E. Fratcher, 5 Scott on Trusts §464 (1989).

[371] William E. Fratcher, 5 Scott on Trusts §464 (1989). *Cf. generally* §8.15.35 of this handbook (officious intermeddling in the trust context).

Subrogation does not put the parties into a trust relationship. Assume that a residence is consumed by fire due to a neighbor's negligent act. The homeowner's insurance company pays up. Under the doctrine of equitable subrogation, the insurance company is entitled to stand in the shoes of the homeowner and bring an action in tort against the neighbor. Does the homeowner hold the cause of action upon an express or constructive trust for the benefit of the insurance company? The answer is neither.[372] The imposition of a constructive trust would not lie because the home owner acquired the cause of action through no fault of his own.[373] There is no express trust because, both before and after an equitable subrogation order issues, there is no division of ownership of the cause of action.[374] Before, the entire interest is in the homeowner; after, it is in the insurance company.[375]

Both constructive trusts and subrogation by operation of law "have as their fundamental purpose the shifting of property interests to accomplish justice. But their theories of origin and operation are different, and one may apply where the other would not be appropriate."[376] Only if the homeowner defies the court order "could one conceivably say that any inequitable holding of a property interest had occurred that could be made the basis for a constructive trust."[377] Again, subrogation is merely a procedural equitable remedy that may be available in a given situation to support the substantive equitable remedy of restitution for unjust enrichment. The constructive trust is covered in Section 7.2.3.1.6 of this handbook.

§9.9.24 The Holder of a Legal Right of Entry for Condition Broken or a Legal Future Executory Interest Is Not a Trust Beneficiary: Legal Conditions Subsequent

In the case of a vested *equitable* interest subject to divestment,[378] there is the trust beneficiary with the vested equitable interest and the trust beneficiary with the contingent equitable interest, namely the one who would take upon the divestment.[379] This is a topic we take up in Section 8.30 of this handbook.

---

[372] *See generally* Bogert §33.

[373] Bogert §33.

[374] Bogert §33.

[375] Bogert §33.

[376] Bogert §33.

[377] Bogert §33.

[378] *See generally* Restatement (Second) of Trusts §11 cmt. h ("By the terms of the trust the interest of a beneficiary may be subject to a condition").

[379] "In the absence of other evidence a transfer of property 'upon condition' that it be dealt with in a manner beneficial to a third person indicates an intention to create a trust rather than an intention to make a transfer upon condition." Restatement (Second) of Trusts §11 cmt. c. *See generally* §5.1 of this handbook (one whose equitable interest under a trust is contingent is nonetheless considered a beneficiary of that trust).

The holder of a *legal* right of entry for condition broken, on the other hand, is not a trust beneficiary.[380] "A right of entry for condition broken is a future interest created in a transferor who conveys an estate on condition subsequent."[381] If the legal future interest is in a third person, the interest is technically not a right of entry but an executory interest; but here too, the holder of the executory interest would not be a trust beneficiary.[382] "On breach of the condition, the transferor or his successors in interest or a designated person will be entitled to recover the property from the transferee."[383]

In the case of a trust, the beneficiary possesses an equitable interest in the subject property.[384] In the case of the holder of a legal right of entry, the holder has merely a power of termination, "enforceable under older law by self-help and under modern law by an action of ejectment or other action to recover possession."[385] The one who has the legal title to the subject property owes no fiduciary duties to the holder of the conditional right of entry, whether the holder is the transferor himself or a third party, nor does he owe any fiduciary duties to anyone who would benefit from a continued performance of the core condition.

While a trustee of a trust may pass good title to the entrusted property to a BFP, a topic we take up in Section 8.15.63 of this handbook, once a legal condition subsequent attaches, "it will continue to burden the property interest in the hands of all successive owners, whether bona fide purchasers or not."[386] In recent years, however, "legislation has been enacted in many states limiting the duration of rights of entry arising from the creation of fees simple on condition subsequent."[387]

In the case of a breach of trust, the beneficiary may compel performance by a suit in equity.[388] In the case of a legal right of entry for condition broken, "[n]either the transferor nor the person, if any, who would be benefited by the performance of the condition can compel performance."[389]

While it is true that a transfer of property "upon condition" is likely to give rise to either a trust or a cocktail of legal interests and powers, at least one of which would be a right of entry for condition broken, there is a third possibility: The transferor intended merely to impress an equitable charge upon the subject

---

[380] Restatement (Second) of Trusts §11.

[381] Cornelius J. Moynihan, Introduction to the Law of Real Property 112 (2d ed. 1988).

[382] Cornelius J. Moynihan, Introduction to the Law of Real Property 112 n.1 (2d ed. 1988).

[383] Restatement (Second) of Trusts §11 cmt. a.

[384] *See generally* §5.3.1 of this handbook (nature and extent of beneficiary's property interest).

[385] Bogert §35. *See also* Cornelius J. Moynihan, Introduction to the Law of Real Property 112–113 (2d ed. 1988) ("This right of entry is not, strictly speaking, a 'right' in the sense of being a present legally enforceable claim. It is rather a power to terminate the granted estate on breach of a specified condition.").

[386] Bogert §35.

[387] Cornelius J. Moynihan, Introduction to the Law of Real Property 117 (2d ed. 1988).

[388] Restatement (Second) of Trusts §11 cmt. b.

[389] Restatement (Second) of Trusts §11 cmt. b.

property.[390] What an equitable charge is and why it is not a trust is discussed in Section 9.9.10 of this handbook.

For a discussion of the differences between a legal property interest and an equitable one, the reader is referred to Section 8.27 of this handbook.

§9.9.25   The Quiet or Silent Trust May Not Be a True Trust

Is a quiet or silent trust illusory? The question is intentionally ambiguous. Is the question whether the trust itself is illusory, or just its quietness? A quiet or silent trust has been defined as "an irrevocable trust that, by its terms, directs the trustee not to inform the beneficiaries of the existence of the trust, its terms and the details of the administration of the trust."[391] South Dakota, for example, would seem to authorize such trusts by statute. See S.D. Codified Laws §55-2-13, which provides that "[t]he settlor, trust advisor, or trust protector, may, by the terms of the governing instrument, or in writing delivered to the trustee, expand, restrict, eliminate, or otherwise modify the rights of beneficiaries to information relating to the trust." It seems there are two possibilities:

The first is that Section 55-2-13 means what it says, in which case a quiet or silent trust is something other than the legal/equitable relationship that is the subject of this handbook. Perhaps it is just a constructive principal/agency relationship, the "settlor" being the principal and the "trustee" being the agent. Or perhaps it is just a fancy completed common law gift to the "trustee."

The second is that a quiet or silent trust is a true trust. If that is the case, then how, as a practical matter, is the trustee to hide the existence of the trust from the beneficiary and comply with applicable tax laws?[392] Assuming that that is possible, then how is the trustee to handle a request for information from the curious beneficiary about the terms of the trust should the beneficiary somehow otherwise get wind of its existence? If the trustee lies to the beneficiary, or intentionally obfuscates, is he not committing an act of actual, or constructive, fraud against the beneficiary, such that any applicable statute of ultimate repose is tolled?[393] Finally, the trustee's duty to account is a two-edged sword. Yes, it is burdensome for the trustee. But rendering accounts to the beneficiary is also the tried-and-true vehicle for limiting the trustee's liability.

The trustee's duty to provide critical information to the beneficiary is covered generally in Section 6.1.5.1 of this handbook. The quiet or silent trust is not to be confused with the secret (or semi-secret) trust, which is the subject of Section 9.9.6 of this handbook.

---

[390] Restatement (Second) of Trusts §11 cmt. g.

[391] Joyce Crivellari, Trust & Estate Insights, May 2013 [A UBS Private Wealth Management Newsletter].

[392] *See generally* Alan Newman, *The Intention of the Settlor Under the Uniform Trust Code: Whose Property Is It, Anyway?*, 38 Akron L. Rev. 659, 679 (2005) (taxation and the quiet/silent trust).

[393] *See generally* §7.1.3 of this handbook (the Uniform Trust Code's statute of ultimate repose).

9.9.26   The Hungarian Trust Is Not a True Trust

On March 15, 2014, the Hungarian Parliament enacted into law the New Hungarian Civil Code (NHCC). The NHCC creates out of whole cloth a civil law fiduciary asset-management vehicle that in form and function bears some resemblance to the Anglo-American trust but is not a true trust.[394] This is a topic that is taken up in §8.12.1 of this handbook.

§9.10   The Offshore Asset Protection Trust

This has to be one of the biggest myths in the offshore trust world. The fact of the matter is that the typical flee clause is cumbersome and extremely time consuming to effectuate. It should be called the molasses clause. By the time the flee clause gets even close to fruition, the creditor has likely obtained a Mareva injunction in the original jurisdiction, freezing the trust's assets and rendering the flee clause a flop.[1]

With the exception of Alaska, possibly Colorado, Delaware, Hawaii, Missouri, Nevada, New Hampshire, Oklahoma, Rhode Island, South Dakota, Tennessee, Utah, and Wyoming,[2] it is public policy in the United States that a settlor cannot place property in trust for the settlor's own benefit and keep it beyond the reach of creditors.[3] On the other hand, some jurisdictions outside the United States, such as the Bahamas;[4] Belize; Bermuda; The Cayman Islands;[5] The Cook Islands; Cyprus; Gibraltar;[6] Guernsey,[7] Channel Islands;

---

[394] *See generally* Charles E. Rounds, Jr. & István Illés, *Is a Hungarian Trust a Clone of the Anglo-American Trust, or Just a Type of Contract?: Parsing the Asset-Management Provisions of the New Hungarian Civil Code*, 6 Geo. Mason J. Int'l Com. L. 153 (2015).

§9.10 [1] Alexander A. Bove, Jr. & Melissa Langa, *Drafting Considerations for Asset Protection Trusts*, 33 Mass. Law. Wkly. 87, Sept. 6, 2004. "Originating in English courts, the 'Mareva' injunction is designed to prevent a defendant from transferring assets, that, in the court's opinion, the defendant is likely to move outside the court's jurisdiction. *Mareva Compania Naviera SA v. International Bulkcarriers SA*, [1975] 2 Lloyd's Rep. 509." Bove, Jr. & Langa, *Drafting Considerations for Asset Protection Trusts*, 33 Mass. Law. Wkly. 87, Sept. 6, 2004.

[2] *See generally* §5.3.3.1(c) of this handbook (reaching the settlor's reserved beneficial interest: domestic asset protection havens); Gideon Rothschild, *Asset Protection Trusts, in* Trusts in Prime Jurisdictions 424–426 (Alon Kaplan ed., 2000).

[3] *See generally* §5.3.3.1 of this handbook (whether the settlor's creditors may reach the settlor's reserved beneficial interest). *See also* Marty-Nelson, *Offshore Asset Protection Trusts: Having Your Cake and Eating It Too*, 47 Rutgers L. Rev. 11 (1994).

[4] *See generally* Peter D. Maynard, *Trusts in the Bahamas, in* Trusts in Prime Jurisdictions 187 (Alon Kaplan ed., 2000).

[5] *See generally* Anthony Travers & Justin Appleyard, *Trusts in the Cayman Islands, in* Trusts in Prime Jurisdictions 239 (Alon Kaplan ed., 2000).

[6] *See generally* James Levy & Louise Kentish, *Trusts in Gibraltar, in* Trusts in Prime Jurisdictions 261 (Alon Kaplan ed., 2000).

[7] *See generally* St. John A. Robilliard, *Trusts in Guernsey, in* Trusts in Prime Jurisdictions 283 (Alon Kaplan ed., 2000).

Jersey, Channel Islands; Liechtenstein;[8] Niue; Nevis; St. Vincent and the Grenadines; and The Turks and Caicos Islands have adopted an opposite policy.[9] This has caused U.S. citizens, concerned about exposure to attack from tort and contract creditors, to transfer their property to trustees operating in these settlor-friendly havens.[10] These trusts are known as offshore asset protection trusts.[11]

At minimum, such trusts will slow the major creditors down and deter the minor ones altogether. This is because of the inevitable costs, both in time and treasure, of litigating in a foreign jurisdiction whose laws are settlor-friendly.[12] As a starter, a creditor will need to retain a brace of lawyers, one domestic, and one local.[13] Moreover, in some jurisdictions, the so-called English System prevails under which the loser must pay the winner's legal fees.[14] For a discussion of the nontax advantages and reservations concerning the use of offshore trusts as well as some tips for U.S. lawyers on drafting foreign trust instruments, the reader is referred to Jeffrey A. Schoenblum.[15]

To be successful, an offshore trust center needs "an adequate legal system, an adequate judicial system, political stability, adequate professional services, good communications, and an absence of significant taxation, exchange controls, or excessive regulation."[16] A center that had once been an English colony by settlement, e.g., Bermuda, the Bahamas, and the Cayman Islands, would always have had the trust as part of its jurisprudence. A center with a preexisting body of law that came under British administration, e.g., Cyprus, Mauritius, and Nauru, would have acquired the trust concept by "osmosis" and legislation. The Channel Islands, never a colony of England or a part of the United Kingdom, are a unique and interesting case. They had been part of Normandy when the

---

[8] Guido Meier, *The Trust in the Liechtenstein Law on Person and Companies,* in Trusts in Prime Jurisdictions 349 (Alon Kaplan ed., 2000).

[9] Gideon Rothschild, *Asset Protection Trusts,* in Trusts in Prime Jurisdictions 413–414 (Alon Kaplan ed., 2000); Rothschild, *Establishing and Drafting Offshore Asset Protection Trusts,* 23 Est. Plan. 65 n.1 (Feb. 1996). *See also* Richard J. Hay, *Offshore Centres under Attack,* in Trusts in Prime Jurisdictions 493 (Alon Kaplan ed., 2000).

[10] *See generally* Gideon Rothschild, *Asset Protection Trusts, in* Trusts in Prime Jurisdictions 405 (Alon Kaplan ed., 2000).

[11] Gideon Rothschild, *Asset Protection Trusts, in Trusts in Prime Jurisdictions* 405 (Alon Kaplan ed., 2009). *See also* Lorenzetti, *The Offshore Trust: A Contemporary Asset Protection Scheme,* 102 Com. L. J. 138 (1997); Joseph W. Malka, *Internet Pathfinder: Learning About Offshore Asset Protection Trusts (OAPT),* <www.oocities.com/Heartland/4994/OAPTpage.html> (visited Oct. 27, 2015) (offering helpful links to government legislation, the IRS, and U.S. Treaties); *Trusts and Trustees,* <http://tandt.oxfordjournals.org/> (visited Oct. 27, 2015) (offering articles on and links to offshore jurisdictions and their laws).

[12] *See generally* John E. Sullivan, III, *Gutting the Rule Against Self Settled Trusts: How the New Delaware Trust Law Competes with Offshore Trusts,* 23 Del. J. Corp. L. 423 (1998).

[13] *See generally* John E. Sullivan, III, *Gutting the Rule Against Self Settled Trusts: How the New Delaware Trust Law Competes with Offshore Trusts,* 23 Del. J. Corp. L. 423 (1998).

[14] *See generally* John E. Sullivan, III, *Gutting the Rule Against Self Settled Trusts: How the New Delaware Trust Law Competes with Offshore Trusts,* 23 Del. J. Corp. L. 423 (1998).

[15] 1 Multistate and Multinational Estate Planning 1375-97 (1999).

[16] Anthony G.D. Duckworth, *The Trust Offshore,* 32 Vand. J. Transnatl. L., 879, 883 (1999).

Normans took control of England in 1066.[17] Until recently, their concept of the trust was somewhat amorphous:

> There is no doubt that the Channel Island has acquired a "trust" concept by osmosis through long association with England and the English, but the nature and effect of this "trust" has not been defined by the courts. Given the fundamental differences between Norman customary law and English law, particularly in relation to property, it was plain that this "trust" was not the same as that of England. Trust rules were equally undefined, though it was generally expected that the local courts would try to follow English practice insofar as that was consistent with local law and procedure. This may seem to be a rather shaky foundation upon which to build a trust center, but apparently it caused little concern among the London lawyers who helped their clients to choose a trust domicile. Eventually, in 1984, Jersey did adopt comprehensive trust legislation, and five years later Guernsey followed suit.[18]

Offshore trusts created by U.S. citizens are of questionable utility, however, when it comes to avoiding U.S. income and estate taxes.[19] One learned commentator offers a warning:

> A U.S. person who establishes a foreign trust is subject to the grantor trust rules if any beneficiary is a U.S. person. Such trusts may also be deemed grantor trusts by virtue of certain retained powers or interests. Furthermore, existing reporting requirements mandate filing returns upon the creation of a foreign trust or transfer of assets to such a trust. The advisor should ascertain that the client's intentions for creating a trust are not tax motivated because Sections 7206 and 7212 may provide grounds for imposing criminal liability on one who assists a taxpayer in avoiding the tax collection efforts of the Service.[20]

In 1999, the U.S. Court of Appeals for the Ninth Circuit affirmed the judgment of the U.S. District Court for the District of Nevada holding a married couple in contempt of court for refusing to repatriate assets held in a self-settled Cook Islands trust.[21]

---

[17] *See generally* §8.37 of this handbook (the origins of the English trust).

[18] Anthony G.D. Duckworth, *The Trust Offshore*, 32 Vand. J. Transnatl. L., 879, 884 (1999).

[19] *But see* Marty-Nelson, *Taxing Offshore Asset Protection Trusts: Icing on the Cake*, 15 Va. Tax Rev. 399 (1996).

[20] Gideon Rothschild, Esq., *Establishing and Drafting Offshore Asset Protection Trusts*, 23 Est. Plan. 65 (1996). *See also* §6.3.1(b) of this handbook (foreign trusts) and §9.1 of this handbook (the grantor trust).

[21] Federal Trade Comm'n v. Affordable Media, LLC, 179 F.3d 1228 (9th Cir. 1999) (The "*Anderson* Case"). It should be noted that the settlors remained as trust protectors after the court issued its repatriation order.

§9.11   The Bankruptcy Trustee

This was a strict trusteeship, not one of those quasi-trusteeships in which self-interest and representative interests are combined. A reorganization trustee is the representative of the court and it is not contended and would not be arguable that if he had engaged for his own advantage in the same transactions that he authorized on the part of his subordinates he should not be surcharged. Equity tolerates in bankruptcy no interest adverse to the trust. This is not because such interests are always corrupt but because they are always corrupting.[1]

One should not confuse the trustee in bankruptcy, which is the subject of this section, with the personal bankruptcy of a trustee,[2] which is covered in Section 8.3.1 of this handbook. A trustee appointed by the bankruptcy court to take title to the property of a debtor is a trustee in bankruptcy. Being a trustee, he has fiduciary duties.[3] He owes a primary duty to the creditors of the bankrupt and a residual duty to the bankrupt.[4] Because the trustee in bankruptcy is required by statute to "collect and reduce to money the property of the estate" his responsibilities deviate somewhat from those of the common law trustee.[5] There may be no duty to invest, for example. Unlike a common law trustee, "[a] . . . trustee in bankruptcy . . . is not personally liable on a contract made by him in the performance of his duties . . . , even though there is no provision in the contract relieving him of personal liability."[6] A full discussion of the law of bankruptcy and the duties of the trustee in bankruptcy, however, is beyond the scope of this handbook. For that, the trustee is referred to Professor D. B. Bogart.[7]

Note that an insolvent debtor's common law assignment to a trustee for the benefit of creditors can give rise to a "true trust" under state law.[8] The creditors are the beneficiaries. Any surplus reverts to the debtor upon a resulting trust. The problem, however, is that under federal law, the assignment may be reversible:

---

§9.11   [1] Mosser v. Darrow, 341 U.S. 267, 271 (1951).

[2] *See* Restatement (Third) of Trusts §42 cmt. c (providing that the trustee's personal creditors or trustee in bankruptcy may not reach either the trust property or the trustee's nonbeneficial interest therein).

[3] *See generally* D. B. Bogart, *Liability of Directors of Chapter 11 Debtors in Possession: Don't Look Back—Something May Be Gaining on You*, 68 Am. Bankr. L.J. 155 (1994).

[4] Bogart, *Liability of Directors of Chapter 11 Debtors in Possession: Don't Look Back—Something May Be Gaining on You*, 68 Am. Bankr. L.J. at 187.

[5] Bogart, *Liability of Directors of Chapter 11 Debtors in Possession: Don't Look Back—Something May Be Gaining on You*, 68 Am. Bankr. L.J. at 186–212.

[6] 3A Scott on Trusts §262 at 122. *See generally* §7.3.1 of this handbook (trustee's liability as legal owner in contract to nonbeneficiaries) and §7.3.2 of this handbook (trustee's agreements with nonbeneficiaries to limit his contractual liability).

[7] *Liability of Directors of Chapter 11 Debtors in Possession: Don't Look Back—Something May Be Gaining on You*, 68 Am. Bankr. L.J. 155 (1994).

[8] Bogert §250.

It is not necessary to secure the consent of the creditors, but . . . they may invalidate the assignment by putting the debtor into bankruptcy. It is a lawful transaction, though seldom used since the adoption of the federal Bankruptcy Act (Bankruptcy Code, since 1979) which supersedes state statutes covering similar matters. That Code makes a general assignment for the benefit of creditors an act of bankruptcy, thus giving a small number of creditors the power to throw the debtor into bankruptcy and set aside the assignment.[9]

A trustee in bankruptcy of another trustee's personal estate is not a good-faith purchaser for value (BFP) of the property which the other trustee has been holding trust.[10] That property the trustee in bankruptcy holds "subject to the trust or other equity."[11] Note, however, that "although the beneficiary retains his or her equitable interest in the trust property, some claims for damages against a trustee or one who has assisted or participated in a breach of trust may be discharged in bankruptcy."[12]

§9.12   The Condominium Trustee

The directors of an ordinary business corporation often have been called trustees and their relation to the corporation is at least fiduciary. They are bound to act with absolute fidelity and must place their duties to the corporation above every other financial or business obligation. They must act, also, with reasonable intelligence, although they cannot be held responsible for mere errors of judgment or want of prudence.[1]

The condominium is a property interest that is structured either as an interest in a corporation or as an interest in a trust. When a trust is employed, the condominium trustee takes title to the property and the "owners" of the units take the beneficial interests. Holding title to the underlying property in trust facilitates divisibility and transferability. Despite the trust form, however, the rights, duties, and obligations of the condominium trustee are more corporate-like than trust-like.

This is in part because much of the "default" law that forms the basis of this handbook has been preempted by condominium legislation and standardized condominium documentation that are "corporate" in orientation. But the courts also have contributed to moving things into the corporate category. Take, for example, the standard for judicial review of decisions by condominium

---

[9] Bogert §250.

[10] 5 Scott & Ascher §29.3.10 (Trustee in Bankruptcy). *See generally* §8.3.1 of this handbook (the trustee's personal creditors and the trustee's spouse) and §8.15.63 of this handbook (doctrine of bona fide purchase; the BFP).

[11] 5 Scott & Ascher §29.3.10 (Trustee in Bankruptcy).

[12] 5 Scott & Ascher §29.3.10.

§9.12 [1] Spiegel v. Beacon Participations, 297 Mass. 398, 410–411, 8 N.E.2d 895, 904 (1937) (enunciating the Massachusetts business judgment rule).

trustees. Courts generally have found that the standard of judicial review should be along the lines of the business judgment rule, *i.e.*, the standard courts apply when considering challenges to the actions of corporate directors.[2]

The business judgment rule would prohibit judicial inquiry into the actions of condominium trustees that are taken in good faith and in the exercise of honest judgment in the lawful and legitimate furtherance of the purposes of the condominium enterprise.[3] The point is that the actions of the condominium trustee will not be subject to judicial sanction simply because the actions were unwise, imprudent, or inexpedient.[4] On the other hand, a court will review the actions of a common law trustee not only to determine whether he exercised undivided loyalty in carrying out the terms of the trust, but whether his actions were "reasonable" or "prudent."[5]

§9.13   The Unitrust

Under traditional principles of trust law, income is segregated from principal and then distributed to someone other than the remainderman. Under a typical "unitrust," income is added to principal and the beneficiary yearly receives a fixed percentage of the net market value of the trust estate for a predetermined term of years or for life. The distribution for a given year is typically determined by applying the percentage (usually 5 percent) against the value of the net trust estate computed as of the end of the preceding year. The remainderman then receives the trust estate outright and free of trust when the term of years expires or the unitrust beneficiary dies. There are many variations on the theme.[1]

Generally the terms of the trust specify whether unitrust amounts are to come in whole or in part from net trust accounting income, in whole or in part from the principal account, or whether the settlor has left it to the trustee to make the call. Absent such guidance, the better view is that the trustee has default authority to make the unitrust distributions from the general funds of the trust without regard to distinction between income and principal.[2]

In the noncharitable context, the unitrust is considered by some to be more accommodating to total return investment strategies than the traditional

---

[2] Levandusky v. One Fifth Ave. Apt. Corp., 75 N.Y.2d 530, 553 N.E.2d 1317, 554 N.Y.S.2d 807 (1990).

[3] Levandusky v. One Fifth Ave. Apt. Corp., 75 N.Y.2d 530, 553 N.E.2d 1317, 554 N.Y.S.2d 807 (1990).

[4] Levandusky v. One Fifth Ave. Apt. Corp., 75 N.Y.2d 530, 553 N.E.2d 1317, 554 N.Y.S.2d 807 (1990).

[5] *See generally* §6.1.1 of this handbook (trustee's duty to be generally prudent).

§9.13 [1] *See generally* John H. Langbein, *The Uniform Investor Act and the Future of Trust Investing*, 81 Iowa L. Rev. 641 (1996).

[2] 3 Scott & Ascher §13.2.8.

"net income to *C*, remainder to *D*" format.[3] In the charitable context, a unitrust meeting rigid IRS specifications can offer the settlor tax avoidance opportunities.[4]

§9.14   The Qualified Domestic Trust (QDOT)

When a spouse dies, not all property that passes to the surviving spouse who is a U.S. citizen qualifies for the federal estate tax marital deduction.[1] To qualify, the property must pass either outright and unconditionally to the surviving spouse or to the trustee of a trust for the sole benefit of the surviving spouse. The trust, however, must meet certain design specifications if the deduction is to be allowed. The trust must be eligible for the QTIP election[2] *or* the surviving spouse must be given a general power of appointment over the property coupled with a life interest[3] *or* the property and any income not distributed to the surviving spouse must pass upon the death of the surviving spouse to the surviving spouse's estate.[4] Congress imposed these design requirements so that whatever is left over of the property that escaped the transfer tax upon the death of the first spouse to die ultimately gets taxed to the extent not consumed.

If, however, the surviving spouse is *not* a U.S. citizen (or does not become one before the estate tax return of the first to die is filed),[5] the federal estate tax marital deduction will not be available to the estate of the first to die, unless the property passes to the trustee of a trust for the benefit of the surviving spouse.[6] Furthermore, the trust must not only meet one of the marital deduction design specifications mentioned above but the trust must *also* qualify as a qualified domestic trust or "QDOT," this in order to secure the ultimate payment of the deferred transfer tax.

A QDOT whose assets reach a value in excess of $2 million, and each QDOT whose holdings of foreign real property reach a value that exceeds 35 percent of the value of the trust estate, must have a U.S. bank as a trustee *or* post an appropriate bond to secure at least 65 percent of the liability *or* take out a letter of credit to secure at least 65 percent of the liability.[7] For computation

---

[3] *See generally* §6.2.2.4 of this handbook (the noncharitable unitrust (total return trust) and the investment considerations).

[4] *See generally* §9.4.5 of this handbook (tax-oriented trusts that mix charitable and noncharitable interests (split-interest trusts)).

§9.14 [1] *See generally* Pennell, 843 T.M., Estate Tax Marital Deduction A-77 through A-84.

[2] *See generally* §8.9.1.3 of this handbook (the marital deduction).

[3] I.R.C. §2056(b)(5).

[4] Rev. Rul. 68-554, 1968-2 C.B. 412.

[5] I.R.C. §2056(d)(4).

[6] I.R.C. §2056(d)(2)(A).

[7] Treas. Reg. §20.2056A-2(d)(1).

purposes, indebtedness may not be taken into account; but there is a $600,000 exclusion for up to two personal residences that are used by the surviving spouse and that are assets of the QDOT.[8]

For the definitive treatment of the tax implications of designating a QDOT as the recipient of distributions from qualified plans and IRAs, the reader is referred to Natalie B. Choate.[9]

As a general rule, any *principal* distributions from a QDOT to the surviving spouse (other than for hardship) will be subject to an estate tax at the marginal estate tax rate applicable to the estate of the deceased spouse whose property funded the QDOT.[10] Any property remaining in the QDOT upon the death of the surviving spouse will also be so taxed.[11] Each trustee is personally liable for payment of the tax.[12] The trustee must report a taxable QDOT distribution on IRS Form 706-QDT. The return must be filed April 15 of the year following the year in which the distribution was made.[13] Any QDOT tax owed on account of the death of the surviving spouse is owed nine months after the death of the surviving spouse.[14]

§9.15 The Qualified Personal Residence Trust (QPRT)

The[1] qualified personal residence trust or "QPRT" is a device for avoiding gift and estate taxes on the future appreciation of the settlor's personal residence.[2] It works like this: The settlor transfers his or her personal residence to a trustee, retaining a beneficial interest in the property for a term of years, usually ten. Upon the expiration of the term, the property passes outright and free of trust to the remaindermen, usually the settlor's children. There is no step-up in basis for capital gains tax purposes. If the settlor dies before the expiration of the term, the governing instrument might provide that the property either reverts to the settlor's estate or passes to the remaindermen. If the trust is to continue after expiration of the fixed term of years, having the trust retain its grantor trust tax status postexpiration may present some general tax avoidance opportunities.[3]

---

[8] Treas. Reg. §20.2056A-2(d)(1)(iv).

[9] *Life and Death Planning for Retirement Benefits,* published by Ataxplan Publications, P. O. Box 1093-K, Boston, MA 02103-1093. Information on how to obtain text and updates is available at <www.ataxplan.com>.

[10] I.R.C. §2056A(b).

[11] I.R.C. §2056A(b).

[12] I.R.C. §2056A(b)(6).

[13] I.R.C. §2056A(b)(5)(A).

[14] I.R.C. §2056A(b)(5)(B).

§9.15 [1] *See generally* Blattmachr and Slade, 836 T.M., Partial Interests GRATs, GRUTs, QPRTs (Section 2702).

[2] I.R.C. §2702(a)(3).

[3] *See generally* §9.1 of this handbook (the grantor trust).

Whichever is the case, if the settlor dies during the term, the full value of the property, *including any subsequent appreciation,* is included in the settlor's estate *for tax purposes.*[4] But if the settlor survives the term, the property is out of his or her estate for tax purposes. The price? The remaindermen may order the settlor to leave the residence. It now belongs to them.

At the time the residence is transferred to the trustee, a gift tax must be calculated. The gift of the remainder interests is not a present interest and thus will not qualify for the annual gift tax exclusion.[5] The gift tax liability, however, will be offset by the unified credit to the extent that it has not been drawn down by other donative transfers[6] and it will *not* be computed on the then full value of the residence. This is because the value of the remainder interest is discounted for the delay in possession occasioned by the settlor's retained beneficial interest.[7] If the property is to revert to the settlor's estate in the event that he or she does not outlive the term, the value of the gift will be further discounted to take into account that possibility.

For a personal residence trust to be "qualified," it must meet the design requirements of Treasury Regulations Section 25.2702-5(c).[8] If "qualified," the settlor is entitled to a gift tax discount and the trust may include certain features such as the conversion of the QPRT into another arrangement should the residence be liquidated in midterm. While a QPRT may offer some potential gift and estate tax avoidance opportunities, it does not offer much else. There is always the risk, for example, that the creditors of the settlor could attach the retained interest and force a sale and division of the proceeds. The prospective trustee will want to think long and hard before getting involved in such an arrangement. The asset is illiquid. There is the matter of how taxes; insurance premiums; costs of maintenance, repairs, and renovations; counsel fees; and trustee fees are to be paid. The trustee should understand that if the settlor becomes insolvent or incapacitated before the QPRT term has expired, the trustee's responsibilities could substantially escalate in intensity and complexity.

The Uniform Probate Code provides that if the settlor should die before the trust's term expires and leave a surviving spouse, the full value of the corpus would be included in the Uniform Probate Code "augmented estate" for spousal election purposes.[9] The topic of spousal election is taken up in Section 5.3.4.1 of this handbook.

For more on the QPRT, the reader is referred to Natalie B. Choate.[10]

---

[4] I.R.C. §2036(a). The property will then receive a step-up in basis for capital gains income tax purposes.

[5] I.R.C. §2503(b).

[6] *See* §8.9.1.1 of this handbook (the unified credit).

[7] I.R.C. §2702.

[8] For a QPRT planning and drafting checklist, *see* Howard M. Zaritsky, *A QPRT Checklist,* 12(5) Prob. Prac. Rep. 1 (May 2000).

[9] UPC §2-205 cmt. (Example 11).

[10] The QPRT Manual, <www.ataxplan.com>.

§9.16   Statutory Trusts

In Mitchell II, the Court held that a network of . . . statutes and regulations did impose judicially enforceable fiduciary duties upon the United States in its management of forested allotted lands. . . .   Although the undisputed existence of a general trust relationship between the United States and the Indian people can reinforce the conclusion that the relevant statute or regulation imposes fiduciary duties, that relationship is insufficient to support jurisdiction under the Indian Tucker Act. Instead, the analysis must train on specific rights-creating or duty-imposing statutory or regulatory prescriptions.[1]

As a general rule, for an express trust to arise, the owner of the property must intend that the property become the subject of a trust.[2] The statutory trust is an exception to this rule.[3] A legislature, by statute, may impose a trust upon someone else's property.[4] Under the Social Security Law, for example, an employee's wages for social security taxes are held in trust for the United States.[5]

The United States or one of its constituent states may also impose a trust upon its own property.[6] A state, for example, may take a tract of land by eminent domain for just compensation and then impress a trust on it for recreation or conservation purposes. In this case, it cannot be said that the element of intent is absent. The citizens, through their legislators, are manifesting a collective intent that an item of public property be made the subject of a trust.[7] When the sovereign declares itself the trustee of the item, however, the trust as a practical matter may well be illusory.[8]

---

§9.16   [1] United States v. Navajo Nation, 123 S. Ct. 1079, 1082 (2003).

[2] *See generally* Introduction to this handbook.

[3] *See generally* 1 Scott on Trusts §17.5.

[4] *See generally* Bogert §246. *See also* UTC §401 cmt. (available at <http://www.uniformlaws.org/Act.aspx?title=Trust%20Code>) (confirming that trusts can also be created by special statute).

[5] In re Carl's Estate, 94 N.E.2d 239 (Ohio 1950). *See also* §9.9.3 of this handbook (social security "trust fund" *not* a trust).

[6] In 1993, for example, the Massachusetts legislature impressed a common law trust upon property over which it had a right of disposition pursuant to the terms of the will of Benjamin Franklin. *See* §127 of the Special Acts of the Massachusetts Legislature (1993 Session Laws). *See also* Franklin Found. v. Attorney Gen., 416 Mass. 483, 623 N.E.2d 1109 (1993) (providing in part that the Commonwealth of Massachusetts must exercise its right of disposition *after* the trust has terminated).

[7] *But see* 1 Scott & Ascher §3.1.5 (suggesting that no one manifests an intention to create a statutory trust).

[8] *See* §9.8.2 of this handbook.

§9.17   I.R.C. §2503(c) Trusts for Minors

In 1998,[1] the first $12,000 of gifts that a donor made to any individual was not subject to the federal gift tax.[2] In calendar years after 1998, the amount became subject to upward inflation adjustments.[3] The gift tax exclusion increased to $13,000 for 2009 and $14,000 for 2013, 2014, 2015, and 2016. Gifts of future property interests, however, do not qualify for the gift tax exclusion.[4] To be eligible, gifts must be of "present" interests.[5] This present interest requirement poses a practical problem for those wishing to make gifts to minors. How can one make a nontaxable gift to a minor and still have the beneficial interest "tied up" until that minor comes of age? The "2503(c) trust" is an option.[6]

Under Code Section 2503(c), a donor may make a yearly nontaxable $14,000 transfer to a trustee for the benefit of a minor if all of the following requirements are met:

- The "minor"[7] is under 21 years of age at the time of the transfer.
- The net income and principal is available in the untrammeled discretion of the trustee for the benefit of the "minor" and no other.[8]
- Upon attaining the age of 21, the "minor" has a present right to withdraw the trust property.[9]
- If the "minor" dies before attaining the age of 21, the property becomes a part of his or her probate estate or is subject to a general testamentary power of appointment.[10]

A trust that satisfies the requirements of Code Section 2503(c) does have its drawbacks, however:

---

§9.17   [1] *See generally* Lischer, 846 T.M., Gifts to Minors A-21; William H. Soskin, *Gifts to Minors After 2001: Minors' Trusts, Qualified Tuition Programs, Education IRAs and Custodial Accounts Compared*, 27 ACTEC J. 344 (2002).

[2] *See* I.R.C. §2503(b).

[3] *See* I.R.C. §2503(b)(2).

[4] I.R.C. §2503(b)(2).

[5] I.R.C. §2503(b)(2).

[6] In Illinois, the custodian of a Uniform Transfer to Minors account for the benefit of a minor may transfer account funds to a qualified minor's trust established by the custodian for the sole benefit of the minor. *See* 760 Ill. Comp. Stat. §§20/2 (13.5) & 20/15(a-5).

[7] For purposes of I.R.C. §2503(c), a person under the age of 21 is deemed a "minor" even if, as a matter of state law, he has attained the age of majority. Rev. Rul. 73-287, 1973-2 C.B. 321.

[8] Treas. Reg. §25.2503-4(a)(2).

[9] I.R.C. §25.2503-4(b)(2). Some instruments provide a time limitation, perhaps 30 days, in which the right of withdrawal may be exercised. Once the window closes, assuming the right has not been exercised, the trust then becomes a grantor trust for income tax purposes. *See* I.R.C. §§677, 678. *See generally* §9.1 of this handbook (the grantor trust).

[10] *See* I.R.C. §2503(c)(2)(b); Treas. Reg. §25.2503-4(b).

- The *settlor/donor* may not restrict the "minor's" right to gain access to the trust property beyond the "minor's" 21st birthday.[11]
- Income accumulated within the trust is subject to a trust income tax rate that is likely to be higher than the personal rate.[12]
- Trust income distributed to a "minor" under the age of 14 is likely to be taxed at the parents' marginal rate under the so-called kiddie tax.[13]
- If the *settlor/donor* is the trustee, the trustee's untrammeled discretion is likely to subject the trust property to the federal estate tax upon the death of the *settlor/trustee* under Code Sections 2036 and 2038.[14]
- If a *parent* of the minor is the trustee, the trust property may become subject to the federal estate tax in the event of the parent's death if distributions can be made that would discharge the parent's support obligation.[15]

§9.18 The Crummey Trust

The annual gift tax exclusion.[1] In 1998, X could make gifts with a combined value of $12,000 or less to Y without having to file a federal gift tax return.[2] This $12,000-per-donee annual exclusion from taxable gifts was subject to upward cost-of-living adjustments for gifts made after 1998.[3] The exclusion increased to $13,000 for 2009, and $14,000 for 2013, 2014, 2015, and 2016.

For a gift to be "nontaxable," however, it must be of a "present" interest.[4] A donative transfer of property to the trustee of an irrevocable discretionary trust with multiple permissible beneficiaries, for example, would not qualify either in whole or in part for the exclusion.[5] Either the donor's credit

---

[11] *See* I.R.C. §2503(c)(2)(b); Treas. Reg. §25.2503-4(b). *See also* Rev. Rul. 74-43, 1974-1 C.B. 285 (holding that a trust still qualifies for I.R.C. §2503(c) treatment where the settlor limited the time in which the beneficiary upon attaining the age of 21 could terminate the trust). *See generally* Bradley E.S. Fogel, *Billion Dollar Babies: Annual Exclusion Gifts to Minors*, 12(5) Prob. & Prop. 6 (Sept./Oct. 1998).

[12] *See* §10.4 of this handbook (fiduciary income tax and payments).

[13] *See* I.R.C. §1(g).

[14] *See* §7.3.4.3 of this handbook (when death of a trustee who possessed no beneficial interest in the trust will subject the trust property to federal estate tax liability).

[15] I.R.C. §2041 and Treas. Reg. §20.2041-1(c)(1). *See also* UTC §814(d)(3) & cmt. (available at <http://www.uniformlaws.org/Act.aspx?title=Trust%20Code>).

§9.18 [1] *See generally* Lischer, 845 T.M., Gifts A-115.

[2] I.R.C. §2503(b) (the annual exclusion); I.R.C. §6019(1) (a gift tax return need not be filed).

[3] I.R.C. §2503(b)(2).

[4] I.R.C. §2503(b)(2); Treas. Reg. §25.2503-3(a).

[5] Treas. Reg. §25.2503-3(c).

equivalent/applicable exclusion amount[6] would be tapped or a gift tax would be owed with respect to the entire amount.[7] What if the present permissible beneficiaries—let us say adult and minor issue of the transferor—had the right to withdraw pro rata portions of the gift for a limited period of time after the transfer to the trustee and were given a timely notice of that right? What if, at the expiration of the period, withdrawal rights would then cease? Would the annual exclusion be available then?

In a similar case, *Crummey v. Commissioner*,[8] the Federal Court of Appeals for the Ninth Circuit held that it would. These limited rights of withdrawal would be enough to qualify the gift as a "present" interest transfer for purposes of the annual exclusion. Hence the term *Crummey* trust.

Since the Ninth Circuit case, the IRS has ceased challenging the concept of the Crummey trust.[9] It has, however, tussled with taxpayers over such issues as what constitutes adequate notice of withdrawal rights;[10] what is a reasonable time in which those rights may be exercised;[11] how notice is to be given to minors;[12] whether the gift tax annual exclusion is available to the transferor when those with the withdrawal rights otherwise have only remote successive, contingent,[13] or even nonexistent beneficial interests under the trust itself;[14] and whether the presence of an in terrorem clause in the governing trust instrument renders the right of withdrawal illusory.[15]

A typical Crummey trust is funded with an insurance contract on the life of the settlor.[16] The idea is that holders of withdrawal rights will decline to exercise

---

[6] *See* §8.9.1.1 of this handbook (the unified credit).

[7] Treas. Reg. §25.2502-1(a).

[8] 397 F.2d 82 (9th Cir. 1968).

[9] Rev. Rul. 73-405, 1973-2 C.B. 321; Rev. Rul. 75-415, 1975-2 C.B. 374.

[10] *See, e.g.*, Priv. Ltr. Rul. 8008040. *See generally* Sebastian V. Grassi, Jr., A Practical Guide to Drafting Irrevocable Life Insurance Trusts (2d ed., 2007, ALI-ABA); Sebastian V. Grassi, Jr., *Selected Issues in Drafting the Irrevocable Life Insurance Trust After the 2001 Tax Act*, 28 ACTEC J. 277, 291–292 (2003) (advising against having beneficiaries waive being notified each year of their Crummey withdrawal rights). *See also* TAM 9532001 (Apr. 12, 1995) (discouraging the use of "once for all time" Crummey notifications).

[11] Priv. Ltr. Rul. 8004172 (withdrawal periods in the range of thirty, forty-five, or sixty days would seem to be the norm). *See* TAM 9141008 (suggesting that a twenty-day withdrawal period was unreasonable).

[12] *See, e.g.*, Priv. Ltr. Rul. 8133070 (suggesting that notice to parent of minor donee may be sufficient notice). *See also* Priv. Ltr. Rul. 9030005 (providing that trustee and guardian of minor Crummey power-holder need not give notice to self).

[13] *See, e.g.*, Cristofani v. Comm'r, 97 T.C. 74 (1991) (allowing the present interest exclusion in the context of a Crummey trust, though some beneficiaries with present withdrawal rights possessed, in addition to those rights, mere contingent future interests under the trust itself).

[14] *See, e.g.*, TAM 9141008, TAM 9045002, TAM 9628004 (suggesting that the IRS will challenge annual exclusion eligibility when those with withdrawal rights otherwise have remote or nonexistent equitable interests).

[15] *See* Mikel v. Comm'r, T.C.Memo. 2015-64 ("Assuming arguendo that the beneficiaries' withdrawal rights must be enforceable in State court, we conclude that this remedy, which respondent concedes was literally available, was also practically available because the in terrorem provision, properly construed, would not deter beneficiaries from pursuing judicial relief.").

[16] *See generally* §9.2 of this handbook (the irrevocable life insurance trust).

those rights, thus freeing up the trustee to apply the gift toward payment of the insurance policy's annual premium.

The $5,000 or 5 percent exception.[17] While the person who is making the gift to a Crummey trust is affected by the $14,000 gift tax exclusion limitation of Code Section 2503(b), those beneficiaries with rights of withdrawal are affected by the "5 and 5" limitation of Code Section 2514(e). There is a tension here. Section 2514(e) provides as follows: The lapse of a power of appointment created after October 21, 1942, during the life of the individual possessing the power shall be considered a release of such power. The rule of the preceding sentence shall apply with respect to the lapse of powers during any calendar year only to the extent that the property, which could have been appointed by exercise of such lapsed powers, exceeds in value the greater of the following amounts:

(1) $5,000, or
(2) 5 percent of the aggregate value at the time of the lapse[18] of the assets out of which, or the proceeds of which, the exercise of the lapsed powers could be satisfied.

The problem is that when a power-holder through nonexercise (lapse) or otherwise *releases* a general inter vivos power of appointment (and that is what a Crummey withdrawal right is) the *power-holder* could be making a taxable gift to the extent the property subject to the power exceeds in value that which is subject to the "5 and 5" exception. Therefore, in order to avoid adverse gift tax consequences *for the power-holder* at the time of lapse, the typical Crummey Trust will provide that in any given year, there is a $5,000/5 percent limitation on what a power-holder may release. Excess withdrawal rights, referred to as "hanging" powers, are then carried over to later years. On the other hand, if someone releases a withdrawal right but retains some beneficial interest under the trust, the release may not be deemed a completed gift for tax purposes.

To the extent a Crummey Trust contains income-producing assets, both the settlor/donor and the one with the withdrawal rights, *i.e.*, the power-holder, may be liable for some portion of the resulting income tax liability.[19] If the settlor has retained at least one of the powers specified in Sections 671 through 679 of the Internal Revenue Code such that the trust is a grantor trust for income tax purposes and if a beneficiary at the same time possesses a Crummey

---

[17] *See generally* Cline, 825-2nd T.M., Powers of Appointment—Estate, Gift, and Income Tax Considerations.

[18] Treas. Reg. §25.2514-3.

[19] As to the potential income tax liability of the power-holder, *see* I.R.C. §678. *See also* §9.1 of this handbook (The Grantor Trust) and §10.1 of this handbook (Introduction to the Fiduciary Income Tax). If trust income is used to pay premiums for insurance on the life of the settlor/donor or the settlor/donor's wife, then such income is taxable to the settlor/donor under the grantor trust rules (I.R.C. §677(a)(3)).

withdrawal right over the same income, it is the settlor, not the beneficiary, who is taxed as the owner of the trust income.[20]

While a Crummey Trust may facilitate the avoidance of estate taxes upon the settlor/donor's death, it is certain that property subject to withdrawal at the time of the power-holder's death will be subject to the federal estate tax.[21] Prior taxable releases can also result in estate tax liability at the power-holder's death.[22] Finally, annual exclusion gifts to a Crummey Trust under which there are multiple permissible beneficiaries can have generation-skipping tax implications if one or more of those with withdrawal rights are skip persons.[23]

Creditor-access issues. When it comes to Crummey Trusts, potential tax traps are not the only concern. So also is creditor accessibility. Under the Uniform Trust Code, see Section 505(b)(2), a lapse, release, or waiver of a power of withdrawal will cause the holder to be treated as the settlor of the trust for creditor accessibility purposes to the extent the value of the property affected by the lapse, release, or waiver exceeds the Crummey or "5 and 5" power.[24] In Section 5.3.3.1 of this handbook, we explain why being deemed the settlor of a trust under which one is, say, a discretionary beneficiary of principal will likely render the principal reachable by the deemed settlor's creditors. The following states have either fallen in line with the UTC or are even less creditor friendly when it comes to the lapse, release, or waiver of general powers: Alabama, Alaska, Arizona, Arkansas, Colorado, Delaware, D.C., Florida, Idaho, Illinois, Indiana, Kansas, Kentucky, Louisiana, Maryland, Michigan, Missouri, Nebraska, Nevada, New Hampshire, North Carolina, Ohio, Oregon, Pennsylvania, Tennessee, Texas, Utah, Vermont, Virginia, Washington, and Wisconsin. It is significant that California and New York are not on this list. Massachusetts case law, arguably, suggests that a lapse, release, or waiver of a general inter vivos power incident to a non–self-settled trust relationship does *not* in and of itself render the former holder a deemed settlor of the trust to the extent of the value of the affected property.[25]

---

[20] *See generally* Sebastian V. Grassi, Jr., A Practical Guide to Drafting Irrevocable Life Insurance Trusts (2d ed., 2007, ALI-ABA).

[21] *See* I.R.C. §2041(a)(2). *See also* Treas. Reg. §20.2041-3(d)(3).

[22] *See* I.R.C. §2041(a)(2).

[23] *See* I.R.C. §2642(c)(2). *See generally* §8.9.2 of this handbook (the generation-skipping transfer tax).

[24] UTC §505(b)(2) (available at <http://www.uniformlaws.org/Act.aspx?title=Trust%20 Code>).

[25] *Cf.* State St. Trust Co. v. Kissel, 302 Mass. 328, 19 N.E.2d 25 (1939) (Property subject to a general *testamentary* power of appointment is accessible to the postmortem creditors of the power-holder *only to the extent the power is actually exercised.*). Of course, all bets are off if it turns out that under Massachusetts common law as enhanced by equity, the lapse, release, or waiver of a general inter vivos power of appointment is a constructive exercise of the power. The Massachusetts legislature enacted subsection (a) of §505 of the UTC but expressly declined to enact subsection (b), leaving the "current law" in place. No explanation was furnished in the commentary accompanying the MUTC, specifically the commentary accompanying Mass. Gen. Laws ch. 190B, §505(a), as to what that "current law" might be or how that "current law" would have been changed by the enactment of §505(b). All the commentary does is confirm that the omission of §505(b) from the MUTC was intentional.

Colorado case law would seem more or less in accord,[26] as would Indiana's case law.[27]

§9.19 Blind Trusts in the Public and Private Sectors

Unlike the public sector where qualified blind trusts are statutorily defined, there is no universally prescriptive definition of blind trusts in the private sector. Nevertheless, blind trusts in the private space typically contain the same core features: an independent trustee, independent management of the trust, and a gag order or mutual blindness provisions.[1]

It is one thing for the settlor to make himself blind, another for the settlor to make another beneficiary blind. . . .[2]

Public sector. "At least 37 states, the District of Columbia, and the Virgin Islands have statutes or regulations recognizing blind trusts, and the majority of them relate to ethical conduct of public officials."[3] On the federal level, we have the statutory qualified blind trust, a creature of the Ethics in Government Act of 1978 (the Act).[4] Major presidential candidates and high-ranking personnel of the three branches of the federal government are required to file financial disclosure reports pursuant to the Act.[5] There is an important exception: A reporting individual need not disclose the nature of the property that he or she transfers to the trustee of a *qualified blind trust* as that term is defined in the Act. Only values need be reported. This exception applies even in cases where the settlor, *i.e.*, the reporting individual, retains the entire beneficial interest and reserves a right of revocation.

For a self-settled trust to be a qualified blind trust, the settlor and the trustee must agree to abide by the Act's restrictions. Before execution, for example, the final draft of the governing instrument (and the prospective trustee himself) must be approved by the settlor's supervising ethics office. The trustee must be an institution that is not under the direct or indirect control of the settlor. This would rule out the settlor, his or her close relatives, and the

---

[26] *See* University Nat'l Bank v. Rhoadarmer, 827 P.2d 561 (Colo. App. 1991).

[27] *See* Irwin Union Bank & Trust Co. v. Long, 312 N.E.2d 908 (Ind. App. 1st Dist. 1974).

§9.19 [1] Edmond M. Ianni, *Blind Trusts Offer Clients Customized Wealth Planning*, 30 Est. Plan. 319—324 (2003).

[2] Lewin ¶ 23-14. *See generally* §5.4.1.1 of this handbook (trust beneficiary's equitable right to information and confidentiality) and §6.1.5 of this handbook (trustee's duty to account to the beneficiary).

[3] Edmond M. Ianni, *Blind Trusts Offer Clients Customized Wealth Planning*, 30 Est. Plan. 320 (2003) (providing in footnote 3 the following examples of state blind trust legislation: Conn. Gen. Stat. §§1-79 to 1-89; Md. Regs. Code tit. 19A, §§19A.06.01.03, 19A.06.02.04, 19A.06.02.05, 19A.06.03.02; Iowa Code §507.6; Alaska Stat. §§39.50.040, 39.52.410).

[4] 15 U.S.C.A. App. 4.

[5] *See generally* Mark A. Adams, Jeremy W. Barber, & Hildy Herrera, *Ethics in Government*, 30 Am. Crim. L. Rev. 617 (1993).

settlor's business associates. The underlying trust property must be freely alienable by the trustee. The trustee must agree not to consult with the settlor on matters that relate to the trustee's authority and discretion to manage and control trust assets. After-the-fact notifications are forbidden as well. The trustee, however, is required to notify the settlor and the supervising ethics office of the sale or other disposition of an asset that the settlor had transferred to the trustee.

A qualified blind trust may not contain assets that the settlor is prohibited by law or regulation from owning in his or her individual capacity. Only the income portions of the trust tax return may be disclosed to the settlor. Quarterly statements furnished the settlor may not identify particular assets. Direct communications between the settlor and the trustee are generally forbidden, except for purposes of disclosing to the trustee the settlor's cash requirements or of heading off an ethics violation.

Within 30 days of the dissolution of a qualified blind trust, the settlor shall notify his or her supervising ethics office of the dissolution and file with such office a list of the trust assets as of the time of dissolution. The trustee who knowingly and willfully violates the nondisclosure provisions of the Act is subject to civil penalties. The settlor is also subject to civil penalties for soliciting or receiving information relating to the administration and disposition of trust assets. In most cases, if the Act's restrictions apply to the settlor, they will apply as well to his or her spouse and dependent children.

Congress has assigned to the following agencies the overall responsibility for administering the Act's provisions to include overseeing the qualified blind trust reporting exception:

Executive Branch:	Office of Government Ethics
Legislative Branch:	Select Committee on Ethics of the Senate Committee on Standards of Official Conduct
Judicial Branch:	Judicial Conference

Private sector. A private sector blind trust may afford a business insider a way to have his or her personal investment portfolio freed of burdensome restrictions that could impair the portfolio's diversification and liquidity. "As an insider, the executive is subject to insider trading restrictions and possibly other constraints that prohibit him from selling his company stock except during open 'window periods' (usually a limited period of time following an earnings release)."[6]

---

[6] Edmond M. Ianni, *Blind Trusts Offer Clients Customized Wealth Planning*, 30 Est. Plan. 319, 322–323 (2003). *See, e.g.*, S.E.C. Rule 10b5-1(c)(1) (suggesting that someone in possession of material nonpublic information regarding a company may trade company securities that he or she personally owns, provided they are traded pursuant to a preestablished trading plan (PTP) by the trustee of a properly established and administered blind trust).

A private sector blind trust also may limit the opportunities for a company insider who personally owns company stock or debt to breach his or her fiduciary duties to the other company stockholders, particularly the duty of undivided loyalty. As the corporate insider is subject to conflict of interest proscriptions that are embedded in the common law of agency, however, it is critical how his or her blind trust is actually administered. The terms of the trust instrument, while important, are secondary. Equity looks past the form of the arrangement to its substance.

Blind trust samples. For samples of public sector and private sector blind trust instruments, the reader is referred to Edmond M. Ianni's *Fiduciary Firewalls: A Look at Blind Trusts.*[7]

Israel. The Israeli counterpart to the U.S. Ethics in Government Act of 1978 is the *Notice of Rules to Prevent Conflicts of Interest by Ministers and Deputy Ministers of 2003*. The Notice requires that within 60 days of a minister's appointment the minister shall transfer custody of his or her investment assets to a public and independent trust company, which shall manage them in a "blind trust." It is the opinion of Alon Kaplan, Israel's resident trust expert, that the fiduciary relationship contemplated by the Notice is one of agency, not trust. In Hebrew "the terms 'fiduciary' and 'trust' are both translated as *'ne'emanut'*."[8] This may be why there is confusion.

§9.20 The Gallo Trust

Once in a while, one encounters someone who says he or she is the trustee or beneficiary of a Gallo trust.[1] What is being referred to is a trust that was created to take advantage of a special direct generation-skipping tax exemption for transfers to grandchildren made possible by the Tax Reform Act of 1986.[2] The Act provided a generation-skipping tax exemption for transfers outright or in trust to the extent that the aggregate transfers from a transferor to a grandchild did not exceed $2 million. A husband and wife could pass up to $4 million to a grandchild by split-gifting. Whether outright or in trust, or both, the transfers had to be made before January 1, 1990. For a transfer in trust to be eligible for the exemption, the trust had to be designed in such a way that income and principal could not be diverted to anyone other than the grandchild; that the trust property would be includable in the grandchild's gross estate should the grandchild die before the trust terminated; and that after the grandchild turned 21, all net income would be paid to the grandchild at least annually.

---

[7] 37 U. Miami Heckerling Institute on Estate Planning (2003).

[8] Alon Kaplan, *The blind trust*, 21(1) STEP J. 77 (Feb. 2013).

§9.20 [1] *See generally* Harrington & Acker, 850 T.M., Generation-Skipping Tax A-80 (discussing grandchild (Gallo) exclusion for direct skips).

[2] I.R.C. §1433(b)(3).

§9.21 Alaska's "Community Property Trust"

Alaska's opt-in community property system for non-residents is a brazen attempt to entice non-residents to create community property trusts to obtain income tax benefits which are derived from the estate tax system.[1]

In Alaska, a husband and wife, whether or not domiciled in Alaska, may convert their property (or some of it) into community property by transferring it to the trustee of a so-called Alaska Community Property Trust.[2] Each spouse will then own an undivided one-half interest in the community property. At least one trustee must be an Alaska bank or trust company or an individual permanently residing in Alaska. The possible favorable tax consequences of all of this? Upon the first death, the basis of the undivided one-half community property interest of the surviving spouse gets stepped up along with the basis of the decedent's one-half interest for capital gains calculations on future fiduciary or beneficiary income tax returns.[3] A prospective settlor who is not from Alaska may want to seek an opinion of counsel on the extent to which the community property status of the entrusted property is likely to be recognized outside of Alaska, especially in the state where the settlor is domiciled.

§9.22 Medicaid Qualifying Trust

Pursuant to federal law, assets held in a self-settled discretionary trust[1] are now, with a few exceptions,[2] countable for purposes of determining the settlor's

---

§9.21 [1] Ira Mark Bloom, *How Federal Transfer Taxes Affect Property Laws*, 48 Clev. St. L. Rev. 661, 672 (2000).

[2] *See generally* Jeffrey A. Schoenblum, 1 Multistate and Multinational Estate Planning §18.16 (1999). *See also* §5.3.4 of this handbook (rights of beneficiary's spouse and children to trust property and/or equitable interest).

[3] "A quirk in the income tax law provides that the basis in both halves of the community property on the death of the first spouse will be determined by reference to federal estate tax value of the community property." Ira Mark Bloom, *How Federal Transfer Taxes Affect Property Laws*, 48 Clev. St. L. Rev. 661, 672 (2000). *See* I.R.C. §1014(b)(6).

§9.22 [1] For purposes of determining Medicaid eligibility, a trust established by an individual's legal conservator, guardian, or spouse on behalf of the individual with the individual's assets would be deemed a self-settled trust, *i.e.*, a trust established by the individual himself for his or her own benefit. *See* Strand v. Rasmussen, 648 N.W.2d 95 (Iowa 2002). "A contrary interpretation would create an absurd result by permitting guardians and others acting on behalf of an individual to do what the law prevents the actual individual from doing himself or herself." Strand v. Rasmussen, 648 N.W.2d at 105.

[2] For some exceptions, *see* §9.3 of this handbook (the self-settled "special needs"/ "supplemental needs" trust).

eligibility for Medicaid.[3] How much is countable? The maximum amount that the trustee could expend for the settlor's benefit.[4] For whatever reason, Congress chose to label these trusts "Medicaid *qualifying* trusts."[5] It would have been more appropriate and less confusing had the label "Medicaid *disqualifying* trust" been employed.[6] For a general discussion of Medicaid including issues of eligibility and recoupment, see Section 5.3.5 of this handbook.

§9.23   S Corporations; Qualified Subchapter S Trusts (QSSTs); Electing Small Business Trusts (ESBTs)

In 1958, Congress added the Subchapter S corporations provisions to the Code. Under these special rules, the income of a corporation that qualifies and makes an election is attributed directly to the shareholders and is not taxed to the corporation. In 1984, the name for these corporations was changed to S corporations.[1]

The income of a Subchapter S corporation (S corporation) is not taxed at the corporate level and then again at the shareholder level. It is taxed directly to the corporate shareholder. Under Code Section 1361(b)(1), an S corporation may not have more than 100 shareholders at any time.[2] However, members of a family can be treated as one shareholder if an election is made.[3] Only certain trusts are eligible to hold S corporation stock. They include grantor trusts, qualified Subchapter S trusts (QSSTs), and electing small business trusts (ES-BTs). As we have noted throughout this handbook, it is not entirely accurate to say that a trust "holds" a block of stock. In trust law parlance, the trustee holds the legal title to the block of stock in a fiduciary capacity. The trustee, not the "trust," is actually the shareholder, *i.e.*, the legal owner of the stock.

The grantor trust is discussed in Sections 9.1 and 10.1 of this handbook. "A QSST is a type of qualifying trust that owns stock in an S corporation, and all of

---

[3] 42 U.S.C. §1396p(d). *See generally* §5.3.5 of this handbook (Medicaid eligibility and recoupment).

[4] 42 U.S.C. §1396p(d).

[5] *See* Guerriero v. Commissioner of the Div. of Med. Assistance, 433 Mass. 628, 629–631, 745 N.E.2d 324, 326–328 (2001).

[6] *See, e.g.*, Victor v. Massachusetts Executive Office of Health & Human Servs., 77 Mass. App. Ct. 1111, 2010 WL 2835747 (Mass. App. Ct. 2010) ("For trusts created before August 11, 1993, an MQT [Medicaid Qualifying Trust] is defined as one 'created or funded by the individual or spouse, other than by will'. . . . The assets of such a trust, if available to a beneficiary applying for Medicaid benefits, *must be counted* in determining eligibility for those benefits").

§9.23 [1] Jonathan G. Blattmacher & F. Ladson Boyle, *The ESBT: Making S Corporations More Available for Estate Planning—Part 1*, 19(6) Prob. Prac. Rep. 1 (June 2007).

[2] Jonathan G. Blattmacher & F. Ladson Boyle, *The ESBT: Making S Corporations More Available for Estate Planning—Part 1*, 19(6) Prob. Prac. Rep. 1 (June 2007); Jonathan G. Blattmacher & F. Ladson Boyle, *The ESBT: Making S Corporations More Available for Estate Planning—Part 11*, 19(7) Prob. Prac. Rep.1 (July 2007).

[3] I.R.C. §1361(c)(1).

the accounting income is distributed or is required to be distributed currently to one individual who is a citizen or resident of the United States."[4] A QTIP marital deduction trust, for example, would be QSST-eligible. An ESBT is any trust (other than a qualified subchapter S trust (QSST)), all of the beneficiaries of which are individuals or estates eligible to be S corporation shareholders, and no interest in which was acquired by purchase.[5] ESBT status, however, is not automatic. It requires an election by the trustee.[6] In the case of an ESBT, the S corporation income is taxed first at the trust level.[7] "ESBTs specifically differ from QSSTs in that an ESBT can have multiple beneficiaries and is not required to distribute all of its income annually."[8] It is also possible to convert a QSST to an ESBT.[9]

§9.24 The Incentive Trust (and the Public Policy Considerations); Marriage Restraints; Provisions Encouraging Anti-Social Behavior

The nature of the behavior the donor seeks to influence and the nature of the incentive used, however, are as varied as the human imagination.[1]

As an English judge once said, public policy is an unruly horse.[2]

Public policy. Public policy is a horse that truly is difficult to corral. According to one court, it "concerns what is right and just and what affects the citizens of the State collectively,"[3] hardly a helpful definition. In any case, the public policy that the owner of property may freely dispose of it, *cujus est dare, ejus est disponere*, has its limitations. Certain gifts in trust, for example, may run afoul of competing public policy considerations.

Incentive trusts. An incentive trust is a trust with incentive provisions. Incentive provisions "are provisions that seek to affect a beneficiary's behavior

---

[4] Jonathan G. Blattmacher & F. Ladson Boyle, *The ESBT: Making S Corporations More Available for Estate Planning—Part 1*, 19(6) Prob. Prac. Rep. 2 (June 2007).

[5] I.R.C. §1361(e).

[6] I.R.C. §1361(e).

[7] Jonathan G. Blattmacher & F. Ladson Boyle, *The ESBT: Making S Corporations More Available for Estate Planning—Part 1*, 19(6) Prob. Prac. Rep. 2 (June 2007).

[8] Jonathan G. Blattmacher & F. Ladson Boyle, *The ESBT: Making S Corporations More Available for Estate Planning—Part 1*, 19(6) Prob. Prac. Rep. 2 (June 2007).

[9] Treas. Reg. 1.1361-1(j)(12).

§9.24 [1] David R. Hodgman & Debra L. Stetter, *Can Incentive Trusts Encourage Children to Behave Responsibly?* 27(10) Est. Plan. 459 (Dec. 2000) (containing sample incentive provisions).

[2] 1A Scott on Trusts §62 (citing to Richardson v. Mellish, 2 Bing. 229, 252 (1824)). *See also* Egerton v. Earl Brownlow, 4 H.L.C. 1, 68, 70, *per* Crompton, L.J. (opining that it is "extremely dangerous to limit the power of disposition on any general notion of impolicy, without some definite rule or principle being shown to apply to the case").

[3] Palmateer v. Int'l Harvester Co., 421 N.E.2d 876, 878 (1981).

by conditioning a benefit—such as the distribution of property—on the beneficiary's displaying desired behavior."[4] The targets of the typical incentive trust are the settlor's children, *e.g.*, a trust under which the trustee is authorized to make distributions of income and principal only during periods when a child is gainfully employed on a full-time basis.[5] A court will generally not second-guess the trustee of an incentive trust who has exercised reasonable judgment in exercising his discretionary powers:

> If the trustee refuses to pay the trust fund to a beneficiary who has clearly fulfilled the conditions specified in the terms of the trust, the court will compel the trustee to do so. But if there is room for doubt whether the beneficiary has fulfilled the conditions, so that a reasonable person might believe, and the trustee honestly believes, that the beneficiary has not complied, the court will not interfere with the trustee's judgment.[6]

Marriage restraints. An incentive trust provision, the purpose of which is to totally restrain marriage, is generally unenforceable on public policy grounds.[7] There is an important exception: a condition terminating the equitable interest of a surviving spouse of a deceased settlor upon the spouse's remarriage.[8] At least one court, however, has found even this exception to be an unacceptable restraint on marriage.[9] Another exception is a provision designed to discourage one from marrying a particular person.[10] "So too, the courts have upheld provisions tending to restrain marriage with particular classes of persons, as, for example, Roman Catholics, domestic servants, Scotsmen, persons other than Jews or Protestants or Quakers."[11] A third exception is reasonable restraints on marriage, *e.g.*, a provision inducing someone to wait until reaching a reasonable age, perhaps 21, before marrying.[12]

Certainly, one of the more controversial provisions, conditions a person's equitable interest on the person's marrying within a particular religious faith. The argument in favor of this partial restraint on marriage is that the settlor while alive can condition an outright gift on whom the donee does or does not

---

[4] David R. Hodgman & Debra L. Stetter, *Can Incentive Trusts Encourage Children to Behave Responsibly?* 27(10) Est. Plan. 459 (Dec. 2000).

[5] *See generally* 1 Scott & Ascher §9.3.8.

[6] 3 Scott & Ascher §18.2.6 (Reasonableness of Trustee's Exercise of a Power).

[7] 1A Scott on Trusts §62.6; 1 Scott & Ascher §9.3.5; Restatement (Third) of Trusts §29(c). *Cf.* Restatement Second, Property (Wills and Other Donative Transfers) §§6.1, 6.2; Restatement Second, Contracts §189.

[8] 1A Scott on Trusts §62.6; 1 Scott & Ascher §9.3.5; Restatement (Third) of Trusts §29(c). *Cf.* Restatement Second, Property (Wills and Other Donative Transfers) §§6.1, 6.2; Restatement Second, Contracts §189.

[9] *See* Estate of Robertson, 859 N.E.2d 772 (Ind. Ct. App. 2007).

[10] 1 Scott & Ascher §9.3.5.

[11] 1A Scott on Trusts §62.6; 1 Scott & Ascher §9.3.5. *See, e.g.*, James H. Cundiff & Andrew D. Copans, *In re Estate of Feinberg: When Legal Fees Consume an Estate—Restrictive Clauses Are Moot*, 35 ACTEC J. 255 (2009) (discussing the marriage restraint at issue in In re Estate of Feinberg, 235 Ill. 2d 256, 919 N.E. 2d 888 (2009), which has become widely known as the "Jewish Clause").

[12] 1 Scott & Ascher §9.3.5.

marry. Why should a gift in trust be any different? The counterargument is that "[t]he living donor can always change his or her mind, as he or she observes the consequences of an unwise course of conduct, or as other circumstances change, but the settlor who is deceased or who, though living, occupies a decedent-like relationship to the trust by having the trust's terms irrevocable cannot."[13]

Provisions that encourage anti-social behavior. An incentive provision is invalid if it encourages criminal or tortious conduct on the part of the beneficiary.[14] Though an incentive provision does not encourage unlawful behavior, as we have seen, it may still be contrary to public policy, *e.g.*, provisions that tend to induce the commission of immoral acts[15] or provisions that would "tend to encourage disruption of a family relationship or to discourage formation or resumption of such a relationship"[16] or "tend to restrain the religious freedom of the beneficiary by offering a financial inducement to embrace or reject a particular faith or set of beliefs concerning religion"[17] or tend to restrain performance of public duties.[18]

It should be kept in mind that while an incentive provision that seeks to influence a beneficiary's sexual or reproductive behavior may be invalid on public policy grounds, *e.g.*, a provision that would tend to encourage a beneficiary not to undergo an abortion, the provision is not "unconstitutional." Why? Because of the absence of state action.[19]

Finally, the trustee of a trust with an incentive provision is more likely to incur the wrath of the beneficiaries than the trustee of a trust with no such provision. Accordingly, the prospective trustee will want to pay particular attention to the quality and scope of the trust's exculpatory, exoneration, and indemnification provisions.[20]

For more on the incentive trust, the reader is referred to an article by Marjorie J. Stephens.[21] A related public policy doctrine, the rule against capricious trust purposes, is discussed in Section 8.15.39 of this handbook.

It goes without saying that charitable trusts whose particular purposes are illegal or otherwise violate public policy are unenforceable.[22]

---

[13] John H. Langbein, *Mandatory Rules in the Law of Trusts*, 98 Nw. U. L. Rev. 1105, 1111 (2004).

[14] Restatement (Third) of Trusts §29(c) (comment on Clause (c)); 1 Scott & Ascher §9.3.1.

[15] 1 Scott & Ascher §9.3.2.

[16] Restatement (Third) of Trusts §29(c) cmt. j; 1 Scott & Ascher §§9.3.3 (Tendency to Encourage Divorce or Separation), 9.3.4 (Tendency to Encourage Neglect of Parental Duties).

[17] Restatement (Third) of Trusts §29(c) cmt. k. *See also* 1 Scott & Ascher §9.3.6.

[18] 1 Scott & Ascher §9.3.7.

[19] *See, e.g.*, Evans v. Abney, 396 U.S. 435 (1970) (holding enforcement of a resulting trust not to have Fourteenth Amendment implications because of the absence of state action).

[20] *See* David R. Hodgman & Debra L. Stetter, *Can Incentive Trusts Encourage Children to Behave Responsibly?* 27(10) Est. Plan. 459, 464–465 (Dec. 2000) (containing sample incentive trust exculpatory, exoneration, and indemnification provisions).

[21] *Incentive Trusts: Considerations, Uses and Alternatives*, 29 ACTEC J. 5 (2003).

[22] *See generally* §9.4.1 of this handbook (charitable purposes); 6 Scott & Ascher §38.11 (Illegal Purposes).

§9.25   The Joint Trust

Credit shelter preservation (joint) revocable trust. A husband and wife with substantial joint property wishing to avoid estate taxes upon the death of the survivor could disjoint that property and establish separate revocable trusts.[1] They, however, are comfortable with the concept of joint ownership. Moreover, they see two trusts as involving too much redundancy, too much expensive documentation.[2] For them, establishing a joint revocable trust may be more palatable. The joint trust approach would entail disjointing[3] their property and transferring it to the trustee of a single revocable trust, *with each spouse reserving a sole right of withdrawal over the trust estate.* Then upon the death of the predeceasing spouse, the trust would become irrevocable and the trust estate would be divided into two trusts: a marital deduction trust and a credit shelter trust.[4] (To the extent the credit shelter trust is funded, property passing to the trust would be treated for tax purposes as if passing from the predeceasing spouse.)[5]

Tax basis revocable (joint) trust. A key difference between the joint trust described in the previous paragraph and the so-called tax basis revocable joint trust (TBRT) is that the TBRT contains a provision subjecting all trust assets to the federal estate tax upon the death of the surviving spouse, as well as a provision extinguishing the surviving spouse's right of revocation. Some commentators[6] are of the opinion that *all* the property would then be entitled to a basis step-up for income tax purposes upon the first death. The IRS, however, disagrees, taking the position that as to the property contributed by the surviving spouse to the joint trust there can be no basis step-up. Why? Because Code Section 1014(e) disallows a step-up for property transferred to a decedent within one year before death; and in the case of TBRT, it is not until the predeceasing spouse dies that the surviving spouse relinquishes dominion and

---

§9.25 [1] *See generally* §8.9 of this handbook (why more than one trust: the estate and generation-skipping tax).

[2] It may be necessary, for example, to establish a nominee trust so that shares of beneficial interests in the family residence can be allocated between the two trusts. *See generally* §9.6 of this handbook (trusts that resemble corporations or agencies).

[3] Unless the property is disjointed, the trustee would not be able to take title to the property. *See generally* §2.1.1 of this handbook (discussing in part the inability of a nontrustee settlor to hold property jointly with a trustee).

[4] *See generally* §8.9.1.1 of this handbook (the unified credit) and §8.9.1.3 of this handbook (the marital deduction).

[5] Priv. Ltr. Rul. 200604028 (Jan. 27, 2006); Priv. Ltr. Rul. 200403094 (Jan. 16, 2004); Priv. Ltr. Rul. 200210051 (Mar. 8, 2002); TAM 9308002 (Nov. 16, 1992); Priv. Ltr. Rul. 200101021 (Jan. 8, 2001). For a discussion of how after the issuance of the PLR having a deceased spouse die with a general power of appointment over the survivor's share might prevent underutilization of the deceased spouse's unified credit, *see* Jonathan G. Blattmacher & Mitchell M. Gans, *Possible Strategy to Make Fuller Use of Each Spouse's Exemption*, 16(7) Prob. Prac. Rep. 1 (July 2004); James L. Dam, *Creditor Shelter Trust Technique Catching On*, Law. Wkly. USA 141, Feb. 18, 2002.

[6] *See, e.g.,* Paul M. Fletcher, *Drafting Revocable Trusts to Facilitate a Stepped-Up Basis*, 22 Est. Plan. 100 (Mar./Apr. 1995).

control over the property that the surviving spouse has contributed to the joint trust.[7]

For more on the tax aspects of joint trusts, the reader is referred to John H.[8] Mr. Martin provides prototype language for a basic joint trust, a disclaimer joint trust, two different tax plan joint trusts, and a joint trust for a second marriage.

§9.26   The Marital Deduction Trust (Including the QTIP Trust)

The marital deduction trust, including the qualified terminable interest property (QTIP) trust,[1] is addressed in Section 8.9.1.3 of this handbook. For coverage of the qualified domestic trust (QDOT), see Section 9.14 of this handbook.

§9.27   The Purpose Trust

From the offshore jurisdictions that are sometimes credited with giving us a number of other unique ideas for creative trust provisions (the flee clause, the anti-duress clause and the change in governing law clause) comes the purpose trust, which, although definitely not faster than a speeding bullet, can in fact leap over age-old trust laws in a single bound.[1]

Charitable trusts and trusts for individuals have long been recognized, the attorney general having standing to seek enforcement of the former and beneficiaries having standing to seek enforcement of the latter.[2] The Restatement (Third) of Trusts provides that a noncharitable "purpose" trust is not necessarily invalid *ab initio*, though it has no beneficiaries, other than the reversionary interests which it refers to as "reversionary beneficiaries,"[3] that are ascertainable within the period of the rule against perpetuities, and though it

---

[7] Priv. Ltr. Rul. 200604028 (Jan. 27, 2006); Priv. Ltr. Rul. 200403094 (Jan. 16, 2004); Priv. Ltr. Rul. 200210051 (Mar. 8, 2002); TAM 9308002 (Nov. 16, 1992); Priv. Ltr. Rul. 200101021 (Jan. 8, 2001).

[8] *The Joint Trust: Estate Planning in a New Environment*, 39 Real Prop. Prob. & Tr. J. 275 (Summer 2004).

§9.26 [1] *See generally* Sebastian V. Grassi, Jr., *Estate Planning with QTIP Trusts after the 2001 Tax Act*, 30 ACTEC J. 111 (2004).

§9.27 [1] Alexander A. Bove, Jr. & Melissa Langa, *The Purpose of Purpose Trusts*, 32 Mass. Law. Wkly. 1407, Mar. 1, 2004.

[2] *See generally* §9.4.2 of this handbook (standing to enforce charitable trusts).

[3] 2 Scott & Ascher §12.10.

has no charitable purpose.[4] It could be administered as an adapted trust[5] in lieu of imposition of a resulting trust.[6] Thus, "[i]n the case of an inter vivos transfer for a specific noncharitable purpose, the settlor may be thought of as a beneficiary."[7] The trustee of a viable purpose trust holds the trust property for the benefit of the reversionary interests;[8] subject, however, to a *nonmandatory power* in the trustee, pursuant to the terms of the trust, to apply the property for the benefit of definite or indefinite noncharitable purposes of his selection.[9] During the settlor's lifetime, the trust would be revocable.[10] Thus principles of agency law would more or less govern the inter vivos purpose trust, the trustee being a constructive agent of the settlor under such an arrangement.[11] In the case of a testamentary purpose trust, however, even agency principles are inapplicable as a will speaks at death. Since at least 1917, courts have been sustaining such imperfect trusts as powers.[12]

As suggested above, courts have traditionally looked askance at such "benevolent"[13] trusts because it has been thought that there is no one who could maintain proceedings to enforce them.[14] This is because a noncharitable purpose trust has no definite or ascertainable beneficiaries, other than those who would take upon the imposition of a resulting trust, and the attorney general's writ covers only charitable trusts.[15] The Restatement would sustain such arrangements, other than those intended to be created by declaration,[16] as adapted trusts,[17] bestowing standing on one or more of the following to bring an action to prevent or redress a breach of trust:

---

[4] *See also* 6 Scott & Ascher §41.8 (Testamentary Disposition for Specific Noncharitable Purposes).

[5] *See* §9.29 of this handbook (adapted trusts).

[6] *See* 6 Scott & Ascher §41.8 (Testamentary Disposition for Specific Noncharitable Purposes); §4.1.1.1 of this handbook (the resulting trust).

[7] 2 Scott & Ascher §12.11.8.

[8] *See generally* §4.1.1 of this handbook (the reversionary interest).

[9] Restatement (Third) of Trusts §47; 6 Scott & Ascher §41.8 (Testamentary Disposition for Specific Noncharitable Purposes).

[10] Restatement (Third) of Trusts §47 cmt. g.

[11] *See generally* 6 Scott & Ascher §41.9.

[12] John Chipman Gray, The Rule Against Perpetuities, Appendix H §909 n.1 (4th ed. 1942) (*see, e.g., Re Gibbons*, [1917] 1 I.R. 448).

[13] *See* §9.4.1 of this handbook (Charitable Purposes) (discussing in part the benevolent trust).

[14] *See generally* 6 Scott & Ascher §41.8 (Testamentary Disposition for Specific Noncharitable Purposes).

[15] *See generally* §9.4.1 of this handbook (charitable purposes).

[16] Restatement (Third) of Trusts §47 cmt. g. "If, however, the . . . declarant dies believing that a trust has been created that will be continued by a successor trustee, an adapted trust will then be given effect by constructive trust." Restatement (Third) of Trusts §47 cmt. g. *See generally* §3.3 of this handbook (Involuntary Trustees).

[17] Restatement (Third) of Trusts §47 cmt. a.

- "the personal representative of the settlor or of a trustee who dies while in office,"[18]
- "any of the settlor's successors in interest,"[19] and
- "a person identifiably interested in the purpose of the power, such as the person caring for a pet or a member of the immediate family of a decedent for whom masses, grave care, or a monument is provided."[20]

While trusts for the care of graves, the erection and maintenance of monuments, and the care and support of animals would be recognized,[21] trusts whose purposes are capricious would not.[22] They would fail *ab initio*.[23] The Restatement advocates a flexible approach to duration when it comes to viable purpose adapted trusts:

> The 21-year period is neither sacred nor necessarily suitable to all cases of adapted trust powers. If an adapted trust for the care of a pet is worth allowing at all . . . , it makes sense to allow it to continue for the life of the pet, although not a human "life in being" for perpetuities purposes. . . . Also, a trust power to maintain a grave should be allowed for the lifetime of the decedent's spouse and children, or of other concerned individuals designated in the will. . . , all lives in being at the testator's death.[24]

The related topic of honorary trusts, including trusts for pets,[25] is covered in Section 9.9.5 of this handbook. Benevolent trusts are covered in more detail in Section 9.4.1 of this handbook. In Section 9.8.10 of this handbook we take up the Cayman Islands STAR trust, which has some of the attributes of the purpose trust.

§9.28   The Domestic Asset Protection Trust (DAPT)

Domestic asset protection trusts are covered in Section 5.3.3.1(c) of this handbook.

---

[18] Restatement (Third) of Trusts §47 cmt. f.

[19] Restatement (Third) of Trusts §47 cmt. f.

[20] Restatement (Third) of Trusts §47 cmt. f.

[21] Restatement (Third) of Trusts §47 cmt. d(1).

[22] *See generally* 6 Scott & Ascher §41.8 (Testamentary Disposition for Specific Noncharitable Purposes).

[23] Restatement (Third) of Trusts §47 cmt. e. *See generally* §8.15.39 of this handbook (rule against capricious [trust] purposes).

[24] Restatement (Third) of Trusts §47 cmt. d(2).

[25] *See generally* 2 Scott & Ascher §12.11.3.

§9.29 The Adapted Trust

In brief, if a devisee can properly make distributions where merely authorized to do so, there is no reason why a devisee should be precluded from doing so where directed to do so.[1]

An adapted trust arises when a settlor intends to impress a trust upon property other than by declaration[2] and directs the trustee to distribute the trust property to an indefinite class of beneficiaries.[3] Ordinarily, a resulting trust would immediately be triggered because "where the owner of property transfers it upon intended trust for the members of an indefinite class of persons, no trust is created."[4] Rather than the trust failing *ab initio*, however, the trustee is deemed to hold the trust property in trust for the settlor or the settlor's estate, *i.e.*, for the reversionary interests; subject, however, to the trustee's voluntary exercise of his power to distribute the trustee property to such class members as he shall select.[5]

The concept of the adapted trust is endorsed in the Restatement (Third) of Trusts. American case law, however, has so far not supported the concept.[6] One might ask why we do not have here some kind of power of appointment in the trustee.[7] "Under well-established doctrine, the objects of powers of appointment may properly consist of classes that are either definite or indefinite."[8] The answer is that a traditional power of appointment is permissive. The holder has no duty, fiduciary or otherwise, to exercise the power.[9] In the adapted trust situation, the trustee, though he may not be compelled to do so, has been directed by the settlor to select who shall take the trust property. It is said that the trustee holds a power in trust.[10] It should be noted that until "the earlier of the settlor's death . . . [and] . . . the exercise of the power of selection and distribution," an adapted trust is revocable.[11] Thus principles of agency law more or less govern the inter vivos adapted trust, at least at the outset, the trustee being a constructive agent of the settlor under such an arrangement.[12] In the case of a testamentary adapted or purpose trust, however, even agency principles are inapplicable as a will speaks at death.

---

§9.29 [1] Restatement (Third) of Trusts §46 cmt. d(2).

[2] Restatement (Third) of Trusts §46 cmt. f. *See also* 6 Scott & Ascher §41.7 (Testamentary Disposition for Indefinite or General Purposes).

[3] Restatement (Third) of Trusts §46 cmt. d(2).

[4] Restatement (Third) of Trusts §46(1).

[5] Restatement (Third) of Trusts §46(2); 6 Scott & Ascher §41.7.

[6] Restatement (Third) of Trusts, Reporter's Notes on §46; *but see* 6 Scott & Ascher §41.7 (Testamentary Disposition for Indefinite or General Purposes).

[7] *See generally* §8.1 of this handbook (powers of appointment).

[8] Restatement (Third) of Trusts §46 cmt. c.

[9] *See generally* §8.1 of this handbook (powers of appointment).

[10] 1 Scott on Trusts §27 (1939).

[11] Restatement (Third) of Trusts §46 cmt. f. *See generally* §9.29 of this handbook (the adapted trust).

[12] *See generally* 6 Scott & Ascher §41.9.

It will not always be that easy to distinguish an adapted trust from a transfer that is outright and free of trust, particularly when a transferor's language is ambiguous and purposes are broadly articulated.[13] When there is reasonable doubt, the court will have to somehow divine the transferor's intentions.[14]

A purpose trust is also an adapted trust. Purpose trusts are covered in Section 9.27 of this handbook.

§9.30   Marriage Settlements (England)

Although, except as otherwise provided by statute, a married woman has no capacity to hold legal title to chattels since they pass to her husband, she has capacity to be the beneficiary of a trust of chattels for her separate use. A trust of interests in land and choses in action may also be created for the separate use of a married woman. By statute, a married woman has generally been given capacity to hold and deal with property separate from her husband.—
The First Restatement of Trusts, §118, adopted and promulgated May 11, 1935

The old gentleman is rusty to look at, but is reputed to have made good thrift out of aristocratic marriage settlements and aristocratic wills, and to be very rich. He is surrounded by a mysterious halo of family confidence; of which he is known to be the silent depository.—Charles Dickens[1]

In England, from the latter part of the eighteenth century until the enactment of legislation in the nineteenth century providing that a husband upon marriage would no longer automatically acquire an interest in his wife's property, it was common practice to create a trust upon marriage. "By the marriage settlement the parents or other relatives of the persons who . . . [were] . . . to marry, or those persons themselves, transfer[red] property to trustees in trust for the parties to the marriage and for their prospective issue."[2] *If a settlor had so provided*, a wife's equitable interest under a marriage settlement had the status of separate property. According to Professor Scott, "[t]his was a most remarkable piece of judicial legislation, since it effected a revolution in the economic position of married women by making it possible for a married woman to be economically independent of her husband."[3]

---

[13] *See generally* 6 Scott & Ascher §41.7 (Testamentary Disposition for Indefinite or General Purposes).

[14] 2 Scott & Ascher §12.12.

§9.30 [1] *Bleak House*, Ch. 2 (In Fashion).

[2] Scott on Trusts §17 (1939 ed.).

[3] Scott on Trusts §146.1 (1939 ed.). *See also* Charles E. Rounds, Jr., *The Common Law is Not Just About Contracts: How Legal Education Has Been Short-Changing Feminism*, 43 U. Rich L. Rev. 1185 (2009).

§9.31   Corporate Trusts; Trusts to Secure Creditors; The Trust Indenture Act of 1939; Protecting Bondholders

Use of the indenture vehicle in connection with the issuance of corporate debt dates back to the early nineteenth century when the largest enterprises of the day, the railroads, issued debt secured by mortgages. These issuers found it impractical to name all of the original bondholders as mortgagees, since the public records would have to be amended frequently as title to the bonds passed from person to person. Moreover, an 1873 case held that in the absence of a trustee, every single holder had to be a party to a foreclosure action.[1]

One way for an entity, usually a corporation, to borrow money is through the sale of bonds. In this context, a bond is essentially a contractual IOU.[2] The issuing entity is the debtor. The bondholders are the creditors. Each bondholder is in a contractual relationship with the entity. If the debt is secured by some property belonging to the entity, perhaps a parcel of real estate, then the trust is tailor-made for managing the security, particularly when a class of bondholders is large and its composition ever changing. The process works this way: The entity transfers title to the security to a trustee who holds it as a fiduciary for the benefit of the bondholders. If there is a default, the trustee liquidates the security and pays off the bondholders with the proceeds. Anything left over reverts upon a resulting trust to the entity.[3] The interposition of a trustee makes the process far more efficient than would be the case were each bondholder left to deal one-on-one with the entity in matters relating to the administration and disposition of the security. In the absence of fraud, segregating and impressing a trust upon the security for the benefit of the bondholders, of course, insulates the security not only from the entity's other creditors but also from the trustee's own creditors.[4] A corporate trust of intangible personal property can actually be quite labor-intensive:

A collateral trust indenture securing a bond issue or a note issue usually contemplates a continuous substitution of collateral, and in this connection imposes especially serious responsibilities upon the trustee. For example, if the collateral which is the security for the bond issue is to be many individual mortgages, with a power of substitution of other mortgages coming within a certain description, the trustee can release the original collateral only if the substituted collateral comes within the limitations of the indenture. The same rule applies in the case of

---

§9.31   [1] E.F. Hutton Sw. Props. II, Ltd. v. Union Planters Nat'l Bank, 953 F.2d 963, 967 (5th Cir. 1992).

[2] *See generally* §9.9.4 (noting that a debt obligation in and of itself is not a trust). For the unrelated topic of fiduciary bonds and sureties, *see* §3.5.4.3 of this handbook.

[3] *See generally* Bogert §250, n.56 and accompanying text. Were the indenture trustee and the debtor the same entity, then there would simply be a merger in the entity. *See* 5 Scott & Ascher §34.5 (Merger). *See generally* §8.7 of this handbook (merger).

[4] *See generally* §8.3.1 of this handbook (the trustee's personal creditors and the trustee's spouse).

substitutions where the collateral is conditional sales contracts, chattel mortgages, or negotiable securities.[5]

Such trusts for the benefit of bondholders are known in the trade as "corporate trusts" and their trustees as "indenture trustees." A word of caution: A corporate trust is not to be confused with a trust that happens to contain a corporation.[6] Nor is the trustee of a corporate trust to be confused with a trustee that happens to be a corporation.[7] This is easy to do as at least one trustee of a corporate trust generally must either be a bank or a trust company.[8] The typical corporate trustee, of course, will be authorized to administer all kinds of trusts, not just corporate trusts.[9]

A corporate trust is first and foremost a creature of state law.[10] Its terms, however, must comply with the provisions of the federal Trust Indenture Act of 1939[11] and its operations will generally be subject to regulation by the SEC,[12] at least to the extent the bonds are marketed through the mails or in interstate commerce. In derogation of the common law of trusts, the Act requires that the trustee of a corporate trust be independent of the bond issuer and may not be exculpated for negligent breaches of trust. Otherwise, common law principles are generally applicable: "This may be seen in cases involving the duty of loyalty, a right to reimbursement for advances, the duty to preserve the trust property, and the duty to bid and act for the bondholders on foreclosure"[13] An indenture trustee, for example, would have a common law fiduciary duty not to compete with the beneficiary-bondholders,[14] and in equity could be declared a constructive trustee for their benefit of any fruits of that disloyalty.[15] Unless the terms of the trust indenture provide otherwise, there is a duty on the part of the

---

[5] Bogert §250.

[6] *See generally* §9.6 of this handbook (trusts that resemble corporations or agencies, specifically the introductory quote discussing the entrustment of entire industries).

[7] *See generally* §8.6 of this handbook (the trustee who is not a human being; corporate trustees; bank trustees).

[8] 15 U.S.C.A. §77jjj.

[9] *See generally* §8.6 of this handbook (the trustee who is not a human being; corporate trustees; bank trustees).

[10] *See, e.g.,* E.F. Hutton Sw. Props. II, Ltd. v. Union Planters Nat'l Bank, 953 F.2d 963, 970 (1992) (". . . [the federal Trust Indenture Act] . . . did not supplant state law, and debenture holders under the TIA would certainly have *at least* as much protection under the TIA as they would in an action, such as the one before us, governed strictly by state law").

[11] The Barkley Trust Indenture Act of 1939, 15 U.S.C.A. §§77aaa to 77bbb, as amended 15 U.S.C.A. §77ddd.

[12] 15 U.S.C.A. §§77sss to 77vvv.

[13] Bogert §250. *See generally* §3.5.2.3 of this handbook (trustee's right in equity to exoneration and reimbursement), §6.1.3 of this handbook (trustee's duty to be loyal to the trust), and §6.2.1.3 of this handbook (trustee's duty to preserve the trust property).

[14] Bogert §250, n.43 and accompanying text. *See generally* §6.1.3 of this handbook (discussing the nature and scope of a trustee's duty not to compete with the beneficiaries).

[15] Bogert §250, n.43 and accompanying text. *See generally* §3.3 of this handbook (the remedial constructive trust).

trustee to treat all bondholders equally.[16] As would be the case with any trustee, an indenture trustee may pass good title to a BFP.[17] At common law, if a trustee refuses to enforce a claim against a third party on behalf of the trust, the beneficiary may step into the shoes of the trustee and do so.[18] "Likewise, when property is conveyed by deed of trust to . . . [an indenture trustee] . . . to secure an issue of bonds, and the trustee, upon default, refuses to bring a proceeding for foreclosure, one or more of the bondholders can maintain a suit for foreclosure, joining the trustee and the obligor as defendants."[19]

As most trust portfolios will contain at least some bonds, all trustees, not just indenture trustees, need some familiarity with corporate trust terminology. The corporate trust indenture, for example, may call for the establishment and administration of a "sinking fund." Generically, a "sinking fund" is "the aggregate of sums of money (as those arising from particular taxes or sources of revenue) set apart and invested, usually at fixed intervals, for the extinguishment of the debt of a government or corporation, by the accumulation of interest."[20] A sinking fund established incident to a bond issue is generally held in trust by the indenture trustee for the benefit of the bondholders.[21]

A "closed end" trust indenture calls for the issuance of a fixed number of bonds. "Where the amount of bonds which may be outstanding is determined by reference to the amount of security transferred to the trustee, it is termed an 'open end' indenture."[22] The reader is cautioned not to confuse an open-end trust indenture with an open-end mutual fund trust instrument. An open-end trusteed mutual fund is a mutual fund whose trustees offer for sale or have outstanding *redeemable securities in the fund itself.*[23]

A "debenture" bond obligation is generally not secured by a mortgage or collateral. The bond issue, however, is often made payable to a trustee in order that the "powers of enforcement may be centralized."[24]

Finally, we offer the following for those who are curious about the origin of the term *indenture*: An indenture is actually a type of deed, a deed being a formal writing that either memorializes a contract or effects a conveyance of property, or does both. At one time, for a writing to qualify as a deed, it needed, among

---

[16] Bogert §250, n.74 and accompanying text. *See generally* §6.2.5 of this handbook (trustee's duty of impartiality).

[17] Bogert §250, n.43 and accompanying text *See generally* §8.15.63 of this handbook (doctrine of bona fide purchase).

[18] 5 Scott & Ascher §28.2.1 (When the Trustee Fails to Sue).

[19] 5 Scott & Ascher §28.2.1.

[20] Black's Law Dictionary 803 (4th ed.).

[21] *See, e.g.*, Warder v. Brady, 115 F.2d 89 (C.A. 4, 1940).

[22] Bogert §250.

[23] 15 U.S.C.A. §80a-5(a) (2005). *See generally* Charles E. Rounds, Jr. & Andreas Dehio, *Publicly-Traded Open End Mutual Funds in Common Law and Civil Law Jurisdictions: A Comparison of Legal Structures*, 3 N.Y.U.J.L. & Bus. 473 (2007).

[24] Bogert §250. *See also* E.F. Hutton Sw. Props. II, Ltd. v. Union Planters Nat'l Bank, 953 F.2d 963, 968 (1992) (noting that "although the debts created by debentures run directly from the issuer to the holders, the contractual rights conferred by the indenture run from the issuer to the trustee for the benefit of the holders of the debentures").

other things, to be under seal. A deed that imposed continuing obligations on
one or more of the parties, fiduciary obligations, perhaps, was known as an
indenture. Here is why: Long, long ago, "[i]n the days before typewriters and
carbon paper, and centuries before Xerox," it was English custom and practice
for an indenture to be written out twice on a single sheet of parchment
("sheepskin stretched, scraped, and scoured"), with each rendition being signed
by the parties.[25] "The parchment was then cut into two pieces in an irregular
line, leaving a sawtooth or indented edge."[26] One party received half, and the
other party the other half. This enabled the "genuineness" of the indenture to
be demonstrated by a fitting of the two halves together.[27] By contrast, a deed
that imposed no continuing obligations on one or more of the parties was
known as a *deed poll*. "It was called a deed poll because the top was not indented
but polled or shaved even."[28] As to how many sheep had to be sacrificed to make
all this happen, we defer to Charles Dickens: "In dirty upper casements, here
and there, hazy little patches of candlelight reveal where some wise draughtsman and conveyancer yet toils for the entanglement of real estate in meshes of
sheep-skin, in the average ratio of about a dozen of sheep to an acre of land."[29]

§9.32   The Ancillary Trusteeship

Under Section 816(20) of the Uniform Trust Code, a trustee would have
the default power to appoint an ancillary trustee to act in another jurisdiction
with respect to trust property located in the other jurisdiction, confer upon the
ancillary trustee all of the powers and duties of the appointing trustee, require
that the ancillary trustee furnish security, and remove the ancillary trustee so
appointed. Such authority would be useful, for example, in a situation where the
appointing trustee is not qualified to administer a particular parcel of land
situated out-of-state, that is to say situated in a jurisdiction other than the trust's
principal place of administration. The topic of trustee qualification generally is
taken up in Section 3.1 of this handbook.

An ancillary trustee is both a full-blown trustee of the out-of-state property,
with a fiduciary duty to act solely in the interests of the trust beneficiaries,[1] and

---

[25] Dukeminier, Krier, Alexander, & Schill, Property 517 (6th ed. 2006). *See also* Reviel Netz
& William Noel, The Archimedes Codex 81 (2007): "Parchment was invented at Pergamum in Asia
Minor—or so legend has it . . . King Eumenes II wanted his library to match that of Alexandria, so
the Ptolemies put an embargo on the export of papyrus from Egypt at the beginning of the second
century BC . . . Parchment was Eumenes' home-grown substitute."

[26] Dukeminier, Krier, Alexander, & Schill, Property 517 (6th ed. 2006).

[27] Dukeminier, Krier, Alexander, & Schill, Property 517 (6th ed. 2006).

[28] Dukeminier, Krier, Alexander, & Schill, Property 517 (6th ed. 2006).

[29] Charles Dickens, *Bleak House*, Ch. 32 (The Appointed Time).

§9.32 [1] *See generally* §6.1.3 of this handbook (the trustee's duty of loyalty to the
beneficiaries).

an agent-fiduciary of the appointing trustee.[2] Analogizing to the law of sub-agency, it is suggested that in the face of a clash between the interests of the appointing trustee and the legitimate interests of the trust beneficiaries, the interests of the beneficiaries are paramount.[3] The ancillary trustee must side with the beneficiaries. While neither the appointing trustee nor the ancillary trustee is an agent of the beneficiaries,[4] each owes the beneficiaries a fiduciary duty of undivided loyalty, just as the sub-agent owes the principal a duty of undivided loyalty. And as the ancillary trustee must be proactive in carrying out that duty,[5] he would be ill advised to blindly or passively follow the directions of the appointing trustee, even a direction to step down from the ancillary trusteeship. Again, the interests of the trust beneficiaries are paramount.

---

[2] *Cf.* Restatement (Third) Of Agency §3.15 cmt. d ("A subagent owes duties of loyalty to the principal as well as to the appointing agent").

[3] *Cf.* Restatement (Third) Of Agency §3.15 cmt. d ("Though an appointing agent is responsible for the subagent's action and has the right and duty to control the subagent, the principal's interests . . . are nonetheless paramount").

[4] *See generally* §5.6 of this handbook (trustee not an agent of the beneficiary).

[5] *See generally* §6.1.2 of this handbook (the trustee's duty to be proactive).

CHAPTER *10*

The Income Taxation of Trusts

§10.1   Introduction to the Fiduciary Income Tax

Although it is not widely known, the law appears to be relatively well settled: The rent-free use of property owned by a trust by its beneficiary does not result in imputed income to either the trust or the beneficiary. Acquiring property (such as a home, recreational property, or works of art, for example) for beneficiaries and allowing them to use it for free means the assets continue to be owned by the trust. As such they are not subject to claims arising in the event of divorce or bankruptcy, [and] generation skipping transfer and income taxes are minimized.[1]

---

§10.1 [1] *See generally* Alan S. Acker, 852-2nd T.M., Income Taxation of Trusts and Estates; Jeffrey G. Sherman, *All You Really Need to Know About Subchapter J You Learned from This Article*, 63 Mo. L. Rev. 1 (1998).

> ... *In some ways, therefore, a trust can be used to allow beneficiaries to live like millionaires but not have to face the potential adverse effects of being millionaires.*[2]

A trust is a fiduciary relationship with respect to property. For federal income tax purposes, however, the trust is treated as a separate legal entity. The exception is the grantor trust.[3]

While a thorough discussion of the grantor trust rules is beyond the scope of this handbook, suffice it to say that if someone during a particular tax year possesses certain powers, the most common being a general inter vivos power of appointment (be it reserved or in the hands of someone other than the settlor), the chances are we have a grantor trust.[4] If that is the case, the property subject to the power will be treated for federal income tax purposes, as if it were owned by the holder of the power. (Under the grantor trust rules, the settlor also will be treated as the owner of the trust property for federal income tax purposes if he or she reserves the income interest or the settlor's spouse is the income beneficiary.)[5] "The particular type of grantor power or interest, however, determines whether income only, principal only, or both income and principal items are treated as owned by the grantor or third person and the grantor trust regulations refer to the general income taxation of trust and estate regulations to determine whether a particular item of trust accounting income is properly allocable to trust principal or trust income."[6] Chapter 11 of this handbook is devoted entirely to the subject of the tax cost/basis of entrusted property, including property held in a grantor trust.

In the case of a grantor trust, the payment of the tax on trust income out of the grantor's own assets should allow trust assets to appreciate at a faster rate than would be the case if the tax liability had to be shouldered by the trust itself. Conveniently, the payment of the tax on trust income by the grantor is considered a nontaxable gift to the trust by the grantor.[7]

The trustee only needs to obtain a separate employer identification number (EIN) once the grantor dies,[8] unless he or she wants the IRS statute of limitations to begin running if there are doubts about the grantor trust status. Thus the trustee of an administrative trust will need to obtain a separate EIN.[9] However, Section 645 of the Taxpayer Relief Act of 1997 does allow a trustee of an irrevocable inter vivos trust and the executor of the grantor's estate to make

---

[2] Jonathan G. Blattmachr, Put It In Trust D-4–JGB (1999).

[3] For a discussion of the income taxation of business trusts, *see* §10.7 of this handbook.

[4] I.R.C. §678. *See also* §8.9.3 of this handbook (tax-sensitive powers) and §9.1 of this handbook (the grantor trust). *See generally* Jay A. Soled, *Reforming the Grantor Trust Rules*, 76 Notre Dame L. Rev. 375 (2001).

[5] I.R.C. §677(a).

[6] Howard M. Zaritsky, 858-2nd T.M., Grantor Trusts: Sections 671–679 A-9. *See generally* §8.34 of this handbook (when an employer identification number (EIN) is not required) (focusing on the grantor trust).

[7] Rev. Rul. 2004-64, 2004-2 C.B. 7.

[8] *See generally* §8.34 of this handbook (when an employer identification number (EIN) is required).

[9] *See generally* §9.32 of this handbook (the administrative trust).

an irrevocable election to treat the trust as part of the estate for federal income tax purposes. Potential advantages to this election include the adoption of a fiscal tax year and administrative cost savings.[10]

If a trust is not a grantor trust, it is either a simple trust or a complex trust. (Again, the income taxation of business trusts is addressed in Section 10.7 of this handbook.) This, by the way, is tax parlance. These terms do not appear anywhere else in this handbook. In either case, be it simple or complex, the trust will have to file its own Form 1041 and will be treated for tax purposes as its own entity, separate and apart from the settlor, the trustee, and the beneficiaries.[11]

A simple trust is essentially your traditional "*A* to *B* for *C* for life then to *D*"-type of trust. The trustee does not invade principal or accumulate income. All net trust accounting income is paid out to *C*.[12] A complex trust is any trust that is not a grantor trust or a simple trust.[13] When one thinks of a complex trust one thinks of the discretionary trust.

The key thing to remember is that a simple or complex trust gets a deduction for distributable net income (DNI) that is paid out to the beneficiary. DNI is discussed in the next section. The beneficiary then includes the payment on his or her own individual tax return. As we will see, particularly when we look at income in respect of a decedent (IRD) and the "throwback rules," the past tax affairs of the beneficiary and the past tax affairs of the trust may have to be taken into account in the preparation of the various tax returns. Thanks, however, to the Taxpayer Relief Act of 1997, trustees of most domestic trusts need no longer concern themselves with the throwback rules, beginning with calendar tax year 1998.[14]

§10.2   Trust Income[1]

The Internal Revenue Code nowhere defines a trust.[2]

For federal income tax purposes, someone (*i.e.*, either the beneficiary or the trust) will have to pay an income tax on the taxable portion of trust accounting income plus capital gains,[3] less certain deductions. We will call this

---

[10] *See generally* §9.32 of this handbook (the administrative trust).

[11] For a discussion of the trustee's liability for the failure to file trust tax returns, *see* §7.3.4.1 of this handbook (liability for taxes; liability for shareholder calls and assessments).

[12] I.R.C. §651.

[13] I.R.C. §661(a).

[14] Pub. L. No. 105-134, Aug. 5, 1997, 111 Stat. 788, §507.

§10.2   [1] *See generally* Jeffrey G. Sherman, *All You Really Need to Know About Subchapter J You Learned from This Article*, 63 Mo. L. Rev. 1 (1998).

[2] Henry Christensen, III, *Foreign Trusts and Alternative Vehicles*, SH032 ALI-ABA 81, 85 (2002).

[3] As far as capital gains are concerned, Chapter 11 of this handbook is devoted entirely to the subject of the tax basis/cost of entrusted property.

the total taxable amount. To determine what is taxable to the beneficiary, we need to calculate DNI.[4] We start with taxable trust accounting income (and, in the case of a complex trust, tax-exempt income as well). That is covered in Section 6.2.4 of the handbook, where the duty to separate income from principal and the right to income is discussed. There is nothing new here. An ordinary dividend or interest on a savings account, for example, would be trust accounting income. We then add to the trust accounting income amount capital gains that are distributable to current beneficiaries[5] and, in the case of a simple trust, add back for computation purposes the trust's $300 deduction or personal exemption.[6]

If the trust is simple, it is *required* to distribute all of its fiduciary accounting income to the income beneficiaries, but no other amounts of any kind.[7] The amount required to be distributed may, but also may not equal DNI because of adjustments, *e.g.*, generally capital gains are excluded from the calculation of DNI.[8] DNI serves as an upper limit both on the amount the beneficiaries will have to include in their gross income from the simple trust and on the amount of the distribution deduction that can be claimed by the simple trust.[9] The simple trust is taxed on the remaining balance of the trust's taxable income.

For purposes of computing the total taxable amount, one cannot forget IRD. IRD is essentially income that a decedent was entitled to receive but that was not properly captured in the decedent's final Form 1040.[10] A common example of IRD is a taxable distribution from a qualified pension or profit-sharing plan. Other examples of IRD are a dividend declared before death but paid after death and a binding contract to sell an item when the sale does not close until after death. Thus, IRD that enters a trust on account of the death of the settlor may be subject in whole or in part to the federal income tax, though it is carried on the books of the trust as accounting principal.[11]

---

[4] I.R.C. §643(a). *See generally* Alan S. Acker, 852-2nd T.M., Income Taxation of Trusts and Estates A-59.

[5] I.R.C. §661(a). As far as capital gains are concerned, Chapter 11 of this handbook is devoted entirely to the subject of the tax basis/cost of entrusted property.

[6] I.R.C. §§642(b)(2)(B), 643(a)(1), (2).

[7] PPC's 1041 Deskbook (16th ed., Thomson Tax & Accounting, 2007) at 17-11.

[8] Jeffrey G. Sherman, *All You Really Need to Know About Subchapter 3 You Learned from this Article*, 63 Mo. L. Rev. 1, 13 (1998). As far as capital gains are concerned, Chapter 11 of this handbook is devoted entirely to the subject of the tax basis/cost of entrusted property.

[9] PPC's 1041 Deskbook (16th ed., Thomson Tax & Accounting, 2007) at 17-7: Sherman, *All You Really Need to Know About Subchapter 3 You Learned from this Article*, 63 Mo. L. Rev. 1, 13 (1998).

[10] I.R.C. §691. *See generally* Alan S. Acker, 862 T.M., Income in Respect of a Decedent.

[11] *See generally* Natalie B. Choate, Life and Death Planning for Retirement Benefits. For a thorough treatment of the subject of IRD, the reader is referred to Alan S. Acker's Estate Planners' Guide to Income in Respect of a Decedent (CCH, Inc.).

§10.3 Deductions (Fiduciary Income Tax)[1]

A simple trust is allowed a $300 deduction or personal exemption.[2] A complex trust is allowed a $100 deduction or personal exemption.[3] The total taxable amount may also be reduced by income payments made pursuant to the terms of the governing instrument to a qualified charity.[4] One court has explained the law as to the deductibility of trust expenses for federal income tax purposes this way:

> I.R.C. §67(a) allows individuals to deduct "miscellaneous itemized deductions" only to the extent that the aggregate of the deductions exceeds two percent of the taxpayer's adjusted gross income. This is referred to as the "two percent floor." Section 67(e) requires the adjusted gross income for a trust to be computed in the same manner as in the case of an individual. Therefore, the two percent floor rule generally applies to deductions from trust income. However, section 67(e)(1) allows deductions below the two percent floor if the claimed expenditures are "paid or incurred in connection with the administration of the estate or trust and . . . would not have been incurred if the property were not held in such trust or estate."[5]

"It is undisputed that trustee fees are fully deductible."[6] The Court of Appeals for the Federal Circuit, however, has ruled that investment advice and management fees incurred by a trustee on behalf of the trust are subject to the 2 percent floor.[7] The matter of "whether the expenses incurred by a trust for investment advice required under state fiduciary responsibility rules can be deducted under section 67(e), without regard to the two percent floor on miscellaneous itemized deductions," has been decided by the U.S. Supreme Court.[8] The Court held that for federal income tax purposes trust investment advisory fees are subject to the 2 percent floor of Internal Revenue Code Section 67(a) because they do not fall under the category of costs which are uncommon

---

§10.3 [1] 13 Prob. Prac. Reporter No. 10 at 12–13 (Oct. 2001).

[2] I.R.C. §642(b)(2)(B).

[3] I.R.C. §642(b)(2)(B).

[4] I.R.C. §642(c)(1).

[5] Mellon Bank, N.A. v. United States, 265 F.3d 1275, 1277 (Fed. Cir. 2001).

[6] Mellon Bank, N.A. v. United States, 265 F.3d 1275, 1279 (Fed. Cir. 2001).

[7] Mellon Bank, N.A. v. United States, 265 F.3d 1275, 1281 (Fed. Cir. 2001). *But see* O'Neill Irrevocable Trust v. Comm'r, 994 F.2d 302 (6th Cir. 1993) (holding investment advice and management fees incurred by trustee on behalf of trust not subject to 2 percent floor because "fiduciaries uniquely occupy a position of trust for others and have an obligation to the beneficiaries to exercise proper skill and care with the assets of the trust," whereas individual investors are "not required to consult advisors and suffer no penalties or potential liability if they act negligently for themselves").

[8] Michael J. Knight, Trustee v. Comm'r (128 S. Ct. 782, No. 06-1286, Jan. 16, 2008).

or unusual for an individual to incur.[9] Unresolved is the issue of unbundling trustees' fees and other costs.

In February 2008, the IRS issued interim guidance via Notice 2008-32 on how fiduciaries should handle issues under Code Section 67. Specifically, it exempted taxpayers from determining the portion of a bundled fiduciary fee that is subject to the 2 percent floor under Section 67 for any taxable year beginning before January 1, 2008. Taxpayers could deduct the full bundled fiduciary fee without regard to the 2 percent floor for tax years beginning before 2008. "In Notice 2008-116, the IRS extended the reprieve from unbundling fiduciary fees to tax years beginning before 2009 as regulations on the subject had not yet been issued. In Notice 2010-32, the IRS again extended the interim guidance provided in Notices 2008-32 and 2008-116 to tax years beginning before January 1, 2010."[10]

It is worth remembering that if expenditures are not deductible by an individual, they probably are not deductible by a trust. With respect to interest expense on a mortgage, a grantor trust is subject to the investment interest limitation of Code Section 163(d) and the disallowance of deductions for personal interest under Code Section 163(d), as an individual is.

Some deductions may be taken either on the settlor's federal estate tax return or on the trust's Form 1041[11] (e.g., executor's commissions and attorneys' fees). If the trust includes IRD that generated an estate tax or generation-skipping tax, then the trust is entitled to an income tax deduction for that portion of estate tax allocable to the IRD.[12] In the case of a simple trust, the entity then gets a deduction for trust accounting income credited out to the beneficiary in a given tax year. The deduction, however, may not exceed the DNI computation[13] and does not include the tax-exempt component, if any.[14]

In the case of a complex trust, the entity gets a deduction up to its DNI ceiling[15] for the trust accounting income required to be distributed currently plus other taxable amounts[16] paid out to the beneficiary, less the tax-exempt portion if any.[17] A beneficiary's share of the taxable distribution, as well as the deductions and credits allocable to it, are recorded on Schedule K-1 of Form 1041.[18] The important thing to note is that not only does the beneficiary get the income distribution, but the beneficiary also gets the benefit of the distribution's pro rata share of certain deductions and credits. Because estate and trust

---

[9] See generally Ronald D. Aucutt, The "2% Floor" Grows Up—A Biography of Legislation, Litigation, and Regulations, 33 ACTEC J. 214 (2008).

[10] Domingo P. Such, III & Thomas P. Ward, Deductibility of Investment Advisory Expenses by Individuals, Estates and Non-Grantor Trusts, 35 ACTEC J. 407, 412 (2009).

[11] I.R.C. §642(g).

[12] I.R.C. §691(c)(1).

[13] I.R.C. §651(b).

[14] Treas. Reg. §1.651(b)-1.

[15] I.R.C. §§651(b) (simple trust), 661(a) (complex trust).

[16] I.R.C. §661(a).

[17] I.R.C. §661(c).

[18] Forms and Instructions can be downloaded from <http://www.irs.gov/Forms-&-Pubs>.

tax brackets are compressed, the executor or trustee has tax planning opportunities by passing out DNI to beneficiaries.

With respect to a particular tax year, the trustee of a complex trust may elect, by checking a box on the Form 1041 return for that year, to treat certain distributions made or credited within the first 65 days of the next year as having been made in the year covered by the return.[19] There is an issue of what the definition of "credited" is for purposes of meeting the "65-day rule." This "65-day rule" gives the trustee time to assess the trust's income picture for the year covered by the return and respond by making deductions that can be attributed to that year.

§10.4   Fiduciary Income Tax and Payments

Income taxed to the trust is taxed at the following rates:[1]

2015 Tax Rate Schedule for Trusts[2]

If Taxable Income Is:	The Tax Is:
Not over $2,500	15% of the taxable income not over $2,500
Over $2,500 but not over $5,900	$375 plus 25% on taxable income over $2,500 but not over $5,900
Over $5,900 but not over $9,050	$1,225 plus 28% on taxable income over $5,8900 but not over $9,050
Over $9,050 but not over $12,300	$2,107 plus 33% on taxable income over $9,050 but not over $12,300
Over $12,300	$3,179.50 plus 39.6% on taxable income over $12,300

---

[19] I.R.C. §663(b).

§10.4 [1] I.R.C. §1(e). For the income taxation of business trusts, *see* §10.7 of this handbook (income taxation of business trusts). *See also* Rev. Proc. 2009-50.

[2] This was the most up-to-date information at the time that the 2016 Edition of this handbook went to press. Check with www.irs.gov for possible updates.

2016 Projected Tax Rate Schedule for Trusts[3]

If Taxable Income Is:	The Tax Is:
Not over $2,550	15% of the taxable income not over $2,500
Over $2,550 but not over $5,950	$382.50 plus 25% on taxable income over $2,550 but not over $5,950
Over $5,950 but not over $9,050	$1,232.50 plus 28% on taxable income over $5,950 but not over $9,050
Over $9,050 but not over $12,400	$2,100.50 plus 33% on taxable income over $9,050 but not over $12,400
Over $12,400	$3,206 plus 39.6% on taxable income over $12,400

In the case of a simple trust, a distribution of current income up to the amount of its allocable DNI is taxed as if received by the beneficiary directly.

The Taxpayer Relief Act of 1997,[4] enacted into law August 5, 1997, has done away with the throwback rules for distributions, made in any taxable year beginning after the date of enactment, from most domestic complex trusts.[5] In other words, such distributions will be computed without regard to any undistributed net income. The following is a brief introduction to the throwback rules for those trustees who still must deal with them:

In the case of a complex trust subject to the throwback rules, current distributable income, known as "Tier 1" income, is taxed up to the DNI ceiling whether distributed to the beneficiary or not.[6] The tax rate for a distribution of DNI accumulated from prior years in a complex trust, "Tier 2" income, is determined by a complicated set of computations required by the so-called accumulation distribution and throwback rules.[7] These computations are designed to approximate the rate at which a prior year's income accumulation would have been taxed had it been distributed to the beneficiary in the year of accumulation. The throwback rules are applicable in a given year only if that year's distribution of Tier 1 and Tier 2 income exceeds net trust accounting income.[8] This is because any current unexpended DNI, to the extent not

---

[3] *See* <http://news.cchgroup.com/index.php/tax-headlines/federal-tax-headlines/wolters-kluwer-projects-inflation-adjusted-tax-brackets-and-other-amounts-for-2016/>.

[4] Pub. L. No. 105-134, Aug. 5, 1997, 111 Stat. 788.

[5] Trusts still subject to the throwback rules are foreign trusts, certain domestic trusts that were once treated as foreign trusts, and any trust created before March 1, 1984, unless it is established that the trust would not be aggregated with other trusts under I.R.C. §643(f) if such section applied to such trust. *See* I.R.C. §665 (as amended).

[6] I.R.C. §662(a)(1).

[7] Treas. Reg. §1.665(a)-0A(a)(1).

[8] I.R.C. §662(a)(2).

used up in distributions to Tier 1 beneficiaries, gets assigned to the Tier 2 beneficiaries.[9]

To determine the tax on an accumulation distribution, one essentially computes the number of prior years in which there has been an accumulation of DNI that has not been made up by an earlier throwback.[10] We call these "open years." Only those years, starting from the earliest, that can absorb the distribution are counted.[11] Years during which accumulations have been "de minimis" are excluded.[12] For computation purposes, the taxes *paid by the trust* allocable to the accumulation are added to the value of the accumulation distribution.[13] The grossed up accumulation is then divided by the number of open years to arrive at an average yearly accumulation distribution.[14] An average yearly "deemed" increase in the beneficiary's tax is then computed.[15] This is done by ascertaining the beneficiary's taxable income for the five years immediately preceding the year of distribution.[16] The high year and the low year are excluded.[17] An averaged yearly accumulation is then deemed added to the taxable income of the beneficiary in each of the three middle years.[18] The deemed additional tax that would have been owed in each of the three middle years is then computed and divided by 3 to obtain an average yearly increase in tax that would have been owed had there been no accumulation.[19] The average yearly increase is then multiplied by the number of open years.[20] A credit is then applied for the tax that was *paid by the trust* on the accumulation.[21] A credit is also applied for any estate or generation-skipping taxes that may have been paid with respect to the accumulation.[22] *No refund, however, is available if it turns out that the trust paid more in taxes on the accumulation distribution than the beneficiary would have paid had there been no accumulation.*[23]

Income accumulated before a beneficiary was born or before the beneficiary turned 21 is exempt from the throwback rules.[24] This exception does not apply to distributions from foreign trusts.[25]

---

[9] I.R.C. §662(a)(2).

[10] *See generally* Carlyn S. McCaffrey, Ellen K. Harrison & Elyse G. Kirschner, *U.S. Taxation of Foreign Trusts, Trusts with Non-U.S. Grantors and Their U.S. Beneficiaries*, SJ027 ALI-ABA 137, 178 (2003) (in part explaining the calculation of the throwback tax on an accumulation distribution).

[11] I.R.C. §666(a).

[12] I.R.C. §667(b)(3).

[13] I.R.C. §§666(b), (c).

[14] I.R.C. §667(b)(1)(C).

[15] I.R.C. §667(b)(1)(D).

[16] I.R.C. §667(b)(1)(B).

[17] I.R.C. §667(b)(1)(B).

[18] I.R.C. §667(b)(1)(C).

[19] I.R.C. §667(b)(1)(D).

[20] I.R.C. §667(b)(1).

[21] I.R.C. §667(b)(1).

[22] I.R.C. §667(b)(6).

[23] I.R.C. §§666(e), 667(b)(1).

[24] I.R.C. §665(b).

[25] I.R.C. §665(b).

The trustee computes the accumulation distribution on Schedule J of Form 1041.[26] The beneficiary uses Form 4970 to compute the tax he or she must pay on the distribution.

§10.5 Practical Information Relating to the Fiduciary Income Tax

Form 1041 with schedules and instructions can be downloaded from <http://www.irs.gov/Forms-&-Pubs>.

The trustee or one of the cotrustees of a domestic trust must file Form 1041 (a) if the trust has any taxable income for the tax year or gross income of $600 (regardless of taxable income) or (b) has a beneficiary who is a nonresident alien. Form 1041 is used to report (1) the income, deductions, gains, and losses of the trust; (2) the income that is either accumulated or held for future distribution or distributed currently to the beneficiaries; (3) any income tax liability of the trust; and (4) employment taxes on wages paid to household employees.

The trustee, or an authorized representative, must sign the Form 1041. Anyone who is paid to prepare the tax return must also sign it. A financial institution that submitted estimated tax payments for trusts for which it is the trustee must enter its Employer Identification Number (EIN) in the space provided for the EIN of the fiduciary. Do not enter the EIN of the trust. An attorney or other individual functioning in a fiduciary capacity should leave the space blank. That person's social security number should not be entered.

For calendar year trusts, the trustee files Form 1041 and Schedule K-1 on or before April 15. (For fiscal years, it is the 15th day of the 4th month following the close of the tax year.) Trusts other than of the charitable, tax exempt under Section 501(a), and grantor variety must use the calendar year. If the due date falls on a Saturday, Sunday, or legal holiday, then the deadline is the next business day. Form 8736 is used to apply for an automatic three-month extension of time to file, but any tax due still must be paid by the original filing date. If more time is needed, Form 8800 must be used.

Schedule D of Form 1041 deals with capital gains and losses. The step-up basis of assets to decedent's date of death value is an important concept for the tax preparer to grasp. It can lead to significant income tax savings when the decedent's assets are sold. If partnership interests are involved, the election for step-up basis on the partnership's internal assets needs to be kept in mind on the partnership's income tax return.[1]

On June 17, 2008, the Heroes Earning Assistance and Relief Tax (HEART) Act was enacted into law. It imposes an immediate tax penalty on wealthy U.S.

---

[26] Forms and Instructions can be downloaded from <http://www.irs.gov/Forms-&-Pubs>.
§10.5 [1] I.R.C. §754.

residents who permanently leave the country, relinquishing their citizenship or residence. Ignoring thresholds and exceptions, a "mark-to-market" tax is now imposed on the net unrealized gains on an expatriate's worldwide assets as if he or she had just sold them. Also, in the nongrantor trust context, any trustee who distributes to an expatriate-beneficiary will be required to withhold U.S. tax of 30 percent of the portion of the distribution that would have been taxable to the expatriate had he or she not expatriated. If dealing with expatriated beneficiaries, trustees are advised to become familiar with the new withholding requirements or face potential personal liability for unpaid U.S. taxes.[2]

The accumulation distribution for a complex trust is computed on Schedule J. The alternative minimum tax (AMT) is computed on Schedule I. The trustee reports the beneficiary's share of income, deductions, and credits to the IRS on Schedule K-1 and furnishes the beneficiary with a copy. The beneficiary uses the information to complete his or her own Form 1040. The beneficiary, however, does *not* file the K-1. The social security number of the beneficiary is required on the Schedule K-1 so it is prudent, if possible, for the trustee to obtain the social security number of each beneficiary well in advance of preparing the Form 1041.

As to grantor trusts, Form 1041 is used only to report any income that is taxable to the trust. Income that is taxable to the "grantor" under the grantor rules is reported to the "grantor" (usually the settlor if he or she holds a reserved right of revocation *or* the holder of a general inter vivos power of appointment if it is someone other than the settlor or the settlor, if the settlor has either reserved an income interest or a 5 percent reversionary interest at the trust's inception) in a grantor "letter" that details the item of taxable income, deductions, and credits. The income taxable to the "grantor" and the deductions and credits applied to the income must be reported on the "grantor's" income tax return.[3] For situations in which an EIN is not required, see Section 8.34 of this handbook. Again, Chapter 11 of this handbook is devoted entirely to the subject of the tax basis/cost of entrusted property.

Interest is charged on taxes not paid by the due date, even if an extension of time to file is granted. Interest is also charged on the failure to-file penalty, the accuracy-related penalty, and the fraud penalty. The interest charge is figured at a rate determined under Internal Revenue Code Section 6621.

There are penalties for filing late without reasonable cause. These penalties are paid out of the trust estate. Of course, to the extent the penalties are occasioned by a breach of trust on the part of the trustee, the trustee ultimately may have to make the trust whole out of his or her own pocket. There are also late-payment penalties. There are penalties for failure to furnish beneficiaries with K-1s. Penalties for underpaying estimated taxes are figured on Form 2210.

If Form 1041 is filed electronically or on magnetic media, Form 9041, Application for Electronic/Magnetic Media Filing of Business and Employee Benefit Plan Returns, and Form 8453-F, U.S. Estate or Income Tax Declaration

[2] *See generally* Jay Rubinstein, Eril Wallace, Kurt Rademacher & Chris McLemore, *Fleece the Fleeing*, Tr. & Est., July 2008, at 361.

[3] Howard M. Zaritsky, 858-2nd T.M., Grantor Trusts: Sections 671–679 A-17.

and Signature for Electronic and Magnetic Media Filing, must be filed. For more details, see IRS Pub. 1437, Procedures for Electronic and Magnetic Media Filing of U.S. Income Tax Returns for Estates and Trusts, Form 1041, and Pub. 1438, File Specifications, Validation Criteria, and Record Layouts for Electronic and Magnetic Media Filing of Estate and Trust Returns, Form 1041. To order these forms and publications, or for more information on electronic and magnetic media filing of Form 1041, call 1-800-829-3676, or write to:

> Internal Revenue Service Center
> Attention: ELF Processing Support Section-DP 2720
> 11601 Roosevelt Blvd.
> Philadelphia, PA 19154

IRS forms and publications may be obtained by personal computer, by CD-ROM, by phone, or in person. The details are set forth near the beginning of the *Instructions for Form 1041 and Schedules A, B, D, G, I, J, and K-1*, which can be downloaded from <http://www.irs.gov/Forms-&-Pubs>.

§10.6 Final Word on the Fiduciary Income Tax

This chapter should be taken as nothing more than a broad-brush introduction to the trustee's world of fiduciary income tax, as little more than a collection of some of the more important "red flags." When it comes to actually doing a return, the best way to start is by studying the Form 1041 itself, including the accompanying schedules and instructions. These items can be downloaded from <http://www.irs.gov/Forms-&-Pubs>. Any other IRS publications on the subject, such as Publication 559, Survivors, Executors, and Administrators, should then be perused.

The trustee should have near at hand a good treatise on the subject of fiduciary income taxation. *Federal Income Taxation of Estates, Trusts, and Beneficiaries*, by Ferguson, Freeland, and Ascher comes to mind. The volume is both practical and scholarly. For something more portable, the reader is referred to Tax Management's "Income Taxation of Trusts and Estates,"[1] "All You Really Need to Know About Subchapter J You Learned from This Article,"[2] the federal materials in the introduction to "ACTEC Study 6: State Taxation on Income of Trusts with Multi-State Contacts,"[3] or PPC's 1041 Deskbook (Thomson Reuters Tax & Accounting).

---

§10.6 [1] Alan S. Acker, 852-2nd T.M., Income Taxation of Trusts and Estates.

[2] Jeffrey G. Sherman, *All You Really Need to Know About Subchapter J You Learned from This Article*, 63 Mo. L. Rev. 1 (1998).

[3] American College of Trust and Estate Counsel.

The trustee cannot forget that a *state* fiduciary income tax return also may be due. In this regard, the reader is referred to Richard W. Nenno.[4] The taxing state will be determined by the *situs* of the trust; however, more than one *state* return may be due depending on the source of income and the residence of the trustees and beneficiaries. The subject of the trustee's state tax filing obligations is beyond the scope of this edition of the handbook.[5] Finally, the trustee should not fall behind when it comes to paying the trust's quarterly estimated taxes. Although, an estate and or a revocable trust which holds or will receive the decedent's residuary estate is only required to pay estimated income taxes after the second taxable year of administration.[6] Also, it should be noted that estimated tax payments are not required to be made with respect to an individual after the date of death.

Trust decanting is discussed generally in Section 3.5.3.2(a) of this handbook. "While the tax treatment of F . . . [corporate] . . . reorganizations is well settled, with case law going back to the 1920s and statutes providing nonrecognition treatment, the tax treatment of decantings is surprisingly unsettled."[7]

§10.7 Income Taxation of Business Trusts

Ordinary trusts established for the exclusive purpose of protecting or conserving property for trust beneficiaries are taxed under the traditional rules found in Subchapter J of the Internal Revenue Code.[1] However, the federal taxation of "other trusts" is governed by tax rules applicable to business organizations such as partnerships and corporations rather than ordinary trusts because, while organized as trusts, they more closely resemble these entities than ordinary trusts.[2] Moreover, the federal tax regime for classifying other trusts as partnerships or corporations changed radically in 1997 with the adoption of the check-the-box regulations.[3]

---

[4] *Planning to Minimize or Avoid State Income Tax on Trusts*, 34 ACTEC J. 131 (2008) (following the article is a comprehensive appendix summarizing each state's maximum trust income tax rate and the standards that each state uses when determining whether a trust will be subject to its tax).

[5] *See generally* ACTEC Study 6: State Taxation on Income of Trusts with Multi-State Contacts (American College of Trust and Estate Counsel).

[6] *See* I.R.C. §6654.

[7] Jason Kleinman, *Trust Decanting: A Sale Without Gain Realization*, 49 Prop., Trust & Estate L.J. 453, 458 (2015).

§10.7 [1] *See generally* Treas. Reg. §301.7701-4(a). While state income taxation of trusts as well as other business entities normally mirrors the federal treatment, every state system should be separately considered as exceptions and variations are common.

[2] *See generally* §9.6 of this handbook (trusts that resemble corporations or agencies).

[3] *See generally* Treas. Reg. §§301.7701-1 to -4. The rules are generally applicable to investment and business trusts formed after January 1, 1997. Trusts formed before January 1, 1997, continue their claimed classification provided there was a reasonable basis for the claim under the old rules.

Prior to 1997, business trusts were routinely classified as corporations for federal tax purposes and hence taxed as corporations. Investment trusts were routinely classified as partnerships for federal tax purposes. To characterize a trust as an investment or business rather than an ordinary trust, the trust declaration is characteristically examined to determine the breadth of applicable trustee powers. For example, the presence of a common broad power to conduct a business will cause the trust to be a business trust rather than an ordinary trust (regardless of whether this was a settlor intent and regardless of whether the trustee intends to so engage or has actually so engaged). Likewise, the presence of a common broad power to vary the investment of the certificate holders will cause the trust to be classified as an investment trust rather than an ordinary trust.

The check-the-box regulations unified the treatment of other trusts by classifying them as unincorporated[4] business entities.[5] The result is that investment and business trusts are now classified as either partnerships[6] or disregarded entities[7] (depending on the number of beneficiaries). An investment or business trust with a single beneficiary will be classified as a disregarded entity while one with two or more beneficiaries will be classified as a partnership. When a particular trust acquires or loses beneficiaries, its classification will likewise change provided there is a crossover of the applicable one member threshold.

An investment or business trust may alter its default classification under these rules by filing an affirmative election to be taxed as a corporation—even though organized as a trust.[8] If such an election is made, the trust is treated as a corporation for all purposes under the Internal Revenue Code and may therefore engage in a tax-free reorganization with another corporation or file a Subchapter S election.[9] As with the case of an investment or business trust's acquiring or losing beneficiaries, an existing trust filing an election to change its default classification after formation and operation will suffer a classification change—generally to or from a partnership to a corporation. Consequently, elections of existing trusts should be cautiously undertaken, whereas elections of newly formed trusts are less sensitive.

---

[4] Treas. Reg. §301.7701-2(b)(1).

[5] Treas. Reg. §301.7701-2(a).

[6] Treas. Reg. §301.7701-2(c)(1).

[7] Treas. Reg. §301.7701-2(c)(2).

[8] Generally, an election may be made and filed on any date (and a copy must be attached to the first trust income tax return filed after the election) but is effective on the date made, an earlier specified date provided that date does not exceed seventy-five days from the date the election is made, or a later specified date provided that date does not exceed twelve months from the date the election is made.

[9] State law will often play an important role in the elective process. For example, while Massachusetts state income taxation mirrors federal taxation applicable to Subchapter S corporations, Massachusetts imposes a special "gross receipts" tax on Subchapter S corporations with more than $6 million in gross receipts. This tax does not apply to a Massachusetts Business Trust—even one generally taxed as a corporation—thus favoring such entities operating as a Massachusetts Business Trust rather than a Subchapter S corporation.

CHAPTER *11*

Tax Basis/Cost of Trust Property

§11.1   Tax Basis/Cost of Trust Property—A General Introduction

In general, the basis of property is its cost. Basis includes all costs which enter into the creation of the property and give it value; what has been paid for the property; and what has been engaged to be paid. In other words, basis is not limited to the taxpayer's equity in the property, but includes all liabilities assumed. Indeed, it may include liabilities encumbering the property acquired even though not assumed.[1]

If a trustee, in transactions that are expense-free, purchases for the trust an item for $5 with principal cash and later sells the item for $10, the entire

---

§11.1   [1] 47A C.J.S. Internal Revenue §114.

proceeds are typically principal for trust accounting purposes.[2] For income taxation purposes, however, the $5 of realized appreciation is a capital gain, which is computed by subtracting the tax basis of the item, in this case the $5 purchase price, from the sales proceeds.[3]

As one can see, it is critical that the trustee knows and keeps track of the tax basis of each entrusted item, as each will eventually be sold, either by the trustee or by someone whose title to the asset can be traced back to the trustee, such as a remainderman. And once the item is sold, someone will likely have to disclose the item's tax basis on an income tax return. To be sure, trustees of qualified employee benefit plan assets and charitable funds generally need not concern themselves with all of this. And there is always the remote chance that an item of entrusted property will work its way gratuitously into the hands of a charity. But for the typical trustee of the typical noncharitable trust, knowing and keeping track of the tax basis of each entrusted item is both a legal and an equitable duty.[4] Moreover, computing tax basis is generally trickier, both conceptually and administratively, than the above hypothetical would suggest.[5]

§11.2   Tax Basis of Trust Inception Assets

For purposes of this chapter, an inception asset is an asset that comes into the hands of the trustee by gratuitous assignment (gift), or by devise (will pour-over), or by trust distribution (trust to trust transfer).[1] In other words, the trustee did not purchase the asset with trust funds for full consideration. Inception assets can enter a trust incrementally over its life. They need not necessarily enter the trust at the time when it receives its first funding, token or otherwise.[2]

---

[2] *See generally* §6.2.4.2 of this handbook (defining trust accounting principal and noting that the proceeds from the sale of trust property are considered principal, unless the property was taken from the income account).

[3] *See generally* §10.2 of this handbook (trust income for tax purposes may not be income for trust accounting purposes).

[4] *See generally* §6.2.9 of this handbook (duty to keep precise, complete, and accurate records); §6.3.1 of this handbook (tax filings); §8.2.4 of this handbook (trust termination checklist).

[5] *See generally* 47A C.J.S. Internal Revenue §114.

§11.2   [1] *See* §6.1.3.2 of this handbook (containing a reference to inception assets).

[2] *See generally* §6.2.1.2 of this handbook (whether to administer additions to a trust fund as separate trusts); §2.1.1 of this handbook (the concept of token funding).

§11.2.1   Basis Carried Over

A gratuitous assignment (gift). A gratuitous assignment in trust of an item of property (a gift in trust) will generally not alter the tax basis of the item.[3] The tax basis of the item in the hands of the trustee-donee will generally be what it was when the donor parted with the title to and the beneficial interest in the item. The basis is said to be "carried over."

Acquired from a decedent who dies after December 31, 2009 and before January 1, 2011 (will or will substitute). Each asset that passes to a trustee in trust via the will or will substitute[4] of a decedent who dies after December 31, 2009 and before January 1, 2011 is subject to a modified carryover basis regime,[5] unless the executor of the decedent's estate elects to have the estate be subject to the estate tax regime.[6] The tax basis of the asset in the hands of the trustee is the lesser of:

- the decedent's adjusted basis
- the fair market value of the property as of the date of the decedent's death[7]

There is an aggregate general basis increase of $1.3 million.[8] The surviving spouse is entitled to an aggregate basis increase of $3 million,[9] plus the $1.3 million general basis increase, for a total permissible increase of $4.3 million.[10] The decedent's executor is charged with parceling out the basis increases asset by asset in accordance with the decedent's wishes and subject to fiduciary constraints.[11] The allocations are memorialized in a tax return required to be prepared and filed by the executor pursuant to I.R.C. §6018.

§11.2.2   Basis Stepped Up (or Down)

Acquired from a decedent by will and will substitute other than in 2010. If an asset passes to the trustee in trust via will or will substitute, the tax basis of the asset in the hands of the trustee is its value for estate tax purposes, which will either

---

[3] 33A Am. Jur. 2d Federal Taxation ¶ 11584.

[4] 33A Am. Jur. 2d Federal Taxation ¶ 11595.

[5] 33A Am. Jur. 2d Federal Taxation ¶ 11594.

[6] On December 17, 2010, the Tax Relief Unemployment Insurance Reauthorization, and Job Creation Act of 2010 became law. Instead of repealing carryover basis, the Act gives the executor of the estate of a 2010 decedent the power to opt out of carryover basis. There is a price, however. The 2010 estate would then become subject to the estate tax regime, with its basis step-up and a $5 million basic exclusion amount.

[7] 33A Am. Jur. 2d Federal Taxation ¶ 11594.

[8] 33A Am. Jur. 2d Federal Taxation ¶ 11596.

[9] 33A Am. Jur. 2d Federal Taxation ¶ 11597.

[10] Frank S. Berall, Ellen K. Harrison, Jonathan G. Blattmachr, Lauren Y. Detzel, Planning for Carryover Basis That Can Be/Should Be/Must Be Done Now, 29 ESTPLAN 99 (Mar. 2002), 2002 WL 239157.

[11] 33A Am. Jur. 2d Federal Taxation ¶ 11601.

be its value as of the date of death or the six-month alternate valuation date.[12] In other words, there is a basis "step-up" for appreciated assets, or a "step-down" for depreciated assets.[13] This may not necessarily be the case for decedents dying in 2010, a topic we take up in Sections 11.2.1 and 11.5 of this handbook.

§11.3 Tax Basis of Trust Property While in Trust

The tax basis for internal capital gains income tax calculation purposes of an item of property held in a nongrantor trust depends on whether the item is an inception asset or had been purchased by the trustee for the trust with entrusted assets. Recall that an inception asset is an asset that the trustee acquired in his fiduciary capacity by gift, devise, or trust-to-trust transfer, such as by the exercise of a power of appointment in further trust.[1] By internal capital gains, we mean capital gains that are incurred by the sale or constructive sale of entrusted assets, provided the gains are taxable at the "entity level."[2] An asset is entrusted if title to it is in the trustee in his fiduciary capacity.[3] In the case of an entrusted share of corporate stock, for example, the trustee would hold the legal title.[4] In the case of an entrusted participation in a trusteed mutual fund, the trustee would hold the equitable title.[5]

If the item is an *inception asset*, its tax basis is either what it was in the hands of the settlor-donor (gift in trust); or its tax basis while it was an asset of another trust (trust to trust transfer); or its fair market value[6] at the date of the settlor-decedent's death (postmortem addition); or possibly its modified carry-over basis (2010 postmortem addition). For more on the tax basis of trust inception assets, the reader is referred to Section 11.2 of this handbook. If the item had been *purchased by the trustee with entrusted assets*, its tax basis would be the item's purchase price.[7] The same applies to the tax basis of a principal item held

---

[12] 33A Am. Jur. 2d Federal Taxation ¶ 11582.

[13] 33A Am. Jur. 2d Federal Taxation ¶ 11582.

§11.3 [1] *See generally* §8.1.2 of this handbook (exercising powers of appointment in further trust); §11.2 of this handbook (defining inception asset).

[2] *See* §10.1 of this handbook (though at law and in equity a trust is a relationship rather than an entity, nongrantor trusts are generally deemed entities for tax purposes). For some nontax situations in which a trust is deemed to be an entity, *see* §7.3.3 of this handbook.

[3] *See generally* §3.5.1 of this handbook (nature and extent of the trustee's estate).

[4] *See generally* §3.5.1 of this handbook (legal title to trust property is in the trustee).

[5] *See generally* §3.5.1 of this handbook (legal title to equitable interests) and §9.6 of this handbook (equitable participations in a business trust such as a mutual fund).

[6] "The fair market value of property is the price at which the property would be sold by a knowledgeable seller to a knowledgeable buyer with each party under no compulsion to act." 47A C.J.S. Internal Revenue §114.

[7] *See generally* 47A C.J.S. Internal Revenue §114.

in a grantor trust,[8] except of the type under which the grantor or deemed grantor holds substantial control over and/or substantial rights in the principal item.[9] In that case, the tax basis of the principal item is what it would be if the principal item were owned outright and free of trust by the grantor, or deemed grantor as the case may be.[10] A grantor, for example, "is treated as the owner of any portion of a trust with respect of which the beneficial enjoyment of the corpus or the income therefrom is subject to a power of disposition, exercisable by the grantor or a nonadverse party, or both, without the approval or consent of the adverse party."[11]

§11.4 Tax Basis of Trust Distributions Out of Trusts

As a general rule, when a trust beneficiary receives a distribution in kind, his or her tax basis in the asset will be the adjusted basis of such property in the hands of the trustee immediately before the distribution, increased by any gain recognized by the trust on the distribution and decreased by any loss.[1] This applies whether or not the beneficiary has gross income from the distribution.[2]

§11.5 Recent Developments in the Law (Tax Basis Determination)

The Economic Growth and Tax Relief Reconciliation Act of 2001 (EGTRRA 2001) repealed the federal estate and generation-skipping tax regime for estates of decedents dying in 2010 and replaced it with the modified carryover basis regime that is described in Section 11.2.1 of this handbook. This is not the first time that Congress has flirted with carryover basis. Under The Tax Reform Act of 1976 (TRA '76), the tax basis of certain property acquired from a decedent was to be the same as the decedent's basis in the property immediately before death, with certain adjustments.[1] Implementation, however, proved so impractical that Congress repealed carryover basis, which had

---

[8] *See generally* §9.1 of this handbook (the grantor trust).

[9] *See* 26 U.S.C. §§672–679.

[10] Regs. §1.671-3(a).

[11] 47B C.J.S. Internal Revenue §454 (citing to 26 U.S.C. §674(a)).

§11.4 [1] *See, e.g.,* 26 U.S.C. §1012.

[2] *See, e.g.,* 26 U.S.C. §1012.

§11.5 [1] 33A Am. Jur. 2d Federal Taxation ¶11593 (carryover basis election—decedents dying after '76 and before Nov. 7, '78).

been scheduled to take effect for estates of decedents dying after 1976.[2] "However, the executor or administrator of the estate of a decedent who died after '76 and before Nov. 7, '78 could have irrevocably elected by July 31, '80 to have the basis of all property acquired from or passing from the decedent determined for all purposes as though the carryover basis rules applied to that property. If this election was made, the basis of all carryover basis property acquired or passing from the decedent had to be determined under the carryover basis rules."[3]

Now Congress again, this time via EGTRRA 2001, has ventured into the land of carryover basis.[4] As the typical decedent will have kept incomplete records, if any were kept at all, of his or her lifetime property acquisitions, executors will confront "almost insurmountable obstacles" in making basis determinations and filing the necessary returns with the IRS.[5] There will be situations where the executor's duty to allocate basis adjustments among conflicting beneficial interests will patently conflict with the executor's fiduciary duty of impartiality.[6] Resolving such conflicts will further complicate the estate administration process.[7] Finally, it is expected that the IRS itself will find the implementation of carryover basis a monumental regulatory challenge.[8] Since 2001, the hope had been that EGTRRA's modified version of carryover basis would go the way of the TRA '76 version and be repealed:

> In view of the unfortunate experience with the carryover basis provisions of TRA '76, it is surprising that an attempt has been made to reenact it. Even more surprising is that there was little or no opposition to these provisions in either the 1999 and 2000 bills (both vetoed by President Clinton) or during enactment of the 2001 Act. Opponents of the concept may have muted their opposition, both to facilitate repeal of the estate and GST taxes and because there will be a number of opportunities to repeal carryover basis before it ever comes into effect in 2010.[9]

---

[2] 33A Am. Jur. 2d Federal Taxation ¶ 11593 (carryover basis election—decedents dying after '76 and before Nov. 7, '78).

[3] 33A Am. Jur. 2d Federal Taxation ¶ 11593 (carryover basis election—decedents dying after '76 and before Nov. 7, '78).

[4] *See generally* Frank S. Berall, et al., Planning for Carryover Basis That Can Be/Should Be/Must Be Done Now, 29 ESTPLAN 99 (Mar. 2002), 2002 WL 239157.

[5] Frank S. Berall, et al., Planning for Carryover Basis That Can Be/Should Be/Must Be Done Now, 29 ESTPLAN 99 (Mar. 2002), 2002 WL 239157.

[6] Frank S. Berall, et al., Planning for Carryover Basis That Can Be/Should Be/Must Be Done Now, 29 ESTPLAN 99 (Mar. 2002), 2002 WL 239157.

[7] Frank S. Berall, et al., Planning for Carryover Basis That Can Be/Should Be/Must Be Done Now, 29 ESTPLAN 99 (Mar. 2002), 2002 WL 239157.

[8] Frank S. Berall, et al., Planning for Carryover Basis That Can Be/Should Be/Must Be Done Now, 29 ESTPLAN 99 (Mar. 2002), 2002 WL 239157.

[9] Frank S. Berall, et al., Planning for Carryover Basis That Can Be/Should Be/Must Be Done Now, 29 ESTPLAN 99 (Mar. 2002), 2002 WL 239157.

On December 17, 2010, the Tax Relief Unemployment Insurance Reauthorization, and Job Creation Act of 2010 became law. Instead of repealing carryover basis, the Act gives the executor of the estate of a 2010 decedent the power to opt out of carryover basis. There is a price, however: The 2010 estate would then become subject to the estate tax regime, with its basis step-up and a $5 million basic exclusion amount.

TABLE OF CASES

Table of Cases

Table of Cases

Table of Cases

TABLE OF RESTATEMENTS

References are to sections.

Table of Restatements

RESTATEMENT (SECOND) OF TORTS

RESTATEMENT (SECOND) OF TRUSTS

Table of Restatements

Table of Restatements

RESTATEMENT (THIRD) OF TRUSTS (PRUDENT INVESTOR RULE)

§170, comment g	6.1.3.1	§206, comment j	7.2.3.2
§170, comment h	6.1.3.3	§206, comment l	7.2.3.2
§170, comment i	6.1.3.3	§208	7.2.3.2
§170, comment k	6.1.3.3	§208, comment c	7.2.3.2
§170, comment l	6.1.3	§209	7.2.3.2, 7.2.8
§170, comment o	6.1.3.3	§§209–211	7.2.8
§170, comment p	6.1.3	§209(1)	7.2.3.2
§170, comment q	6.1.3.3	§209, comment b	7.2.3.2
§170, comment r	6.1.3, 6.1.3.3	§210	7.2.3.2, 7.2.8
§170, comment s	6.2.3	§210(1)(a)	7.2.3.2
§170, comment w	6.1.3	§210(1)(b)	7.2.3.2
§171	6.1.4, 6.2.2.2, 7.2.4	§210(2)	7.2.3.2
§171, comment a	6.1.4	§210, comment b	7.2.3.2
§171, comment e	6.1.4	§211	7.2.3.2, 7.2.8
§171, comment f	6.1.4	§211(2)	7.2.3.2
§171, comment h	6.1.4	§211, comment d	7.2.3.2
§171, comment j	6.1.4	§211, comment e	7.2.3.2
§171, comment k	6.1.4	§211, comment f	7.2.3.2
§181, comment a	6.2.2	§211, comment g	7.2.3.2
§183	6.1.3.5, 6.2.5	§212, comment b	7.2.3.2
§184	6.1.4	§212, comment c	7.2.3.2
§184, comment a	6.2.1	§212, comment d	7.2.3.2
§184, comment c	6.1.4	§213	7.2.3.2, 8.15.33
§185, comment b	4.2	§213, comment c	7.2.3.2
§185, comment c	4.2	§213, comment e	7.2.3.2
§185, comment d	4.2	§213, comment f	7.2.3.2, 8.15.33
§185, comment e	4.2	§213, comment j	7.2.3.2
§185, comment f	4.2	§227	3.5.3.2(a), 6.1.1, 6.2.5,
§185, comment g	4.2		7.2.4, 6.2.2.1, 6.2.2.2
§185, comment h	4.2	§227, comment a	6.2.2
§190	3.5.3.1	§227, comment b	6.2.2, 6.2.2.1
§190, comment b	3.5.3.1	§227, comment c	6.1.3.4
§190, comment d	3.5.3.1	§227, comment d	6.1.4
§190, comment i	3.5.3.1	§227, comment e	6.2.1.3, 6.2.2.1, 6.2.2.2,
§190, comment j	3.5.3.1		6.2.5
§190, comment m	3.5.3.1	§227, comment f	6.2.2.1
§191	3.5.3.2	§227, comment g	6.2.2.1
§193	5.3.3	§227, comment h	6.2.2.1
§204	6.1.1	§227, comment i	6.2.2, 6.2.2.1, 6.2.5
§205	7.2.3.2, 7.2.8	§227, comment j	6.1.4
§205, comment a	7.2.3.2, 7.2.3.3	§227, comment k	6.2.2.1
§205, comment e	7.2.3.2	§227, comment l	6.2.2.1
§205, comment f	7.1, 7.2.3.2	§227, comment m	3.5.3.2(d), 6.1.4, 6.2.2.1
§206	6.1.3	§227, comment n	6.2.2.1
§206, comment a	7.2.3.2	§227, Reporter's Notes	6.2.2.1
§206, comment b	7.2.3.2	§228, comment g	3.5.3.2(i)
§206, comment c	7.2.3.2	§229, comment d	3.5.3, 3.5.3.1(a)
§206, comment d	7.2.3.2	§229, comment e	3.5.3.2(i)
§206, comment e	7.2.3.2	§232, comment b	6.2.5
§206, comment f	7.2.3.2	§232, comment c	6.2.5
§206, comment g	7.2.3.2	§240	6.2.2.1, 6.2.4.3
§206, comment h	7.2.3.2	§241	6.2.4.3
§206, comment i	7.2.3.2	§241, comment b	6.2.4.3

TABLE OF UNIFORM ACTS*

References are to sections.

---

* Cornell Law School has a web site where one can view the text of all the Uniform Acts listed here. Within each Act is a list of states where one can link to a particular state's codification of that Act. See <https://www.law.cornell.edu/uniform/vol7> and <https://www.law.cornell.edu/ucc>.

The web address for the Uniform Prudent Investor Act, The Uniform Statutory Rule Against Perpetuities, and the Uniform Transfers to Minors Act is <http://www.uniformlaws.org>. The web address for the Uniform Probate Code is <https://www.law.cornell.edu/uniform/probate>.

Table of Uniform Acts

UNIFORM PRUDENT INVESTOR ACT

UNIFORM PRUDENT MANAGEMENT OF INSTITUTIONAL FUNDS ACT

UNIFORM REAL PROPERTY TRANSFER ON DEATH ACT

UNIFORM SECURITIES ACT OF 1956

UNIFORM SECURITIES ACT OF 1985

UNIFORM STATUTORY RULE AGAINST PERPETUITIES

UNIFORM STATUTORY TRUST ENTITY ACT

INDEX

Index

Agent (*continued*)
power of trustee to hire agents at trust expense, 3.5.3.2(p)
revocation of trust by agent of holder of right of revocation, 8.2.2.2
standing of beneficiary to sue agent of trustee, 3.6, 5.4.1.8
trustee
agents of
delegation issues (trustee's duty to give personal attention), 6.1.4
hiring of agents, trustee power in, 3.5.3.1(d), 3.5.3.2(p)
liability of directors and officers of trust company, 7.2.9
liability of trust officers and other agents of trustee, 3.5.4.2, 7.2.9
liability of trustee for improper acts of agents, 6.1.4. *See also* liability of trustee for
improper acts of agents, this heading
liability of trustee for torts of agents, 7.3.1
participation in breach of trust, 3.6, 5.4.1.8
power of trustee to hire agents, 3.5.3.1(d), 3.5.3.2(p)
standing of beneficiary to sue agents, 3.6, 5.4.1.8
trustee not beneficiary's agent, 7.3
undisclosed principal, doctrine of, 8.15.25
Alaska
beneficiary notification requirement, 3.4.2, 3.4.4.3
community property trust, 5.3.4
domestic asset protection trust, 4.1.3, 5.3.3.1
legislation to end-run Delaware tax trap, 8.2.1.8
as strong spendthrift jurisdiction, 5.3.3.3(c)
trust protector's legal status in, 3.2.6
Aliens
enemy alien's interest in spendthrift trust subject to governmental seizure, 5.3.3.3(c)
limitations on capacity to serve as trustee in certain states, 3.1
settlor's alien spouse as beneficiary (QDOT), 9.14
as trustee, 3.1
Alienability. *See also* Assignment of equitable interest
of beneficial interests
in nominee trusts, 9.6
in realty trusts, 9.6
of contingent equitable interests, 5.3.2
of equitable interest by beneficiary under certain circumstances, 5.3.3.3
of legal remainders, 5.3.2
rule against direct restraints on alienation (the trust exception), 8.15.40
of trust property by trustee, 3.5.2, 3.5.2.2
Alienation restraints
generally, 5.3.3.3(c), 8.15.40
abolition of rule against perpetuities (trustee's power of sale), 8.2.1.9
public policy considerations, 8.15.40
rule against direct restraints on alienation, 8.15.40
rule against perpetuities not aimed at alienation restraints, 8.2.1
spendthrift trusts, 5.3.3.3(c)
trust exception, 8.15.40
Alimony
access of beneficiary's spouse to trust property, 5.3.4
property division compared, 5.3.4
All-or-nothing rule
generally, 8.15.73
specific sum exception, 8.15.73
sub-class exception, 8.15.73
Allocation
of fiduciary responsibilities, 6.1.4
of receipts and expenses
generally, 6.2.4.1–6.2.4.4, 6.2.4.7
constitutional considerations when allocation rules made retroactive, 8.15.71

Index

Index

Index

damages as result of sale to BFP, 7.2.3.2
death of trustee
    trustee's devisee not BFP of trust property, 3.4.3, 5.4.2
    trustee's heir not BFP of trust property, 5.4.2
    trustee's legatee not BFP of trust property, 5.4.2
    trustee's personal representative not BFP of trust property, 5.4.2
    trustee's surviving spouse not BFP of trust property, 3.5.1, 5.4.2, 8.3.1
defalcating trustee makes one trust whole with property misappropriated from another,
    3.5.4.3
divorce, receipt by BFP of title to trust property forfeited upon, 8.15.63
donee of trust property
    donee who pays value after notice of breach still not BFP, 5.4.2
    not a BFP, 5.4.2
    unjust enrichment, 5.4.2
duty of BFP to *see* to application of purchase price, 5.4.2, 8.15.69, 8.21
enforcement of contract incident to breach of trust
    violation of equitable principles, 8.15.63
entrusted property wrongfully held by trustee for innocent third party, 8.15.63
estoppel, doctrine of (when beneficiary estopped from challenging transfer to non-BFP),
    7.1.3
equity maxim underlying BFP concept, 8.15.63
fraud on a special power of appointment,
    impermissible appointee may pass good title to a BFP, 8.15.26
    recourse of permissible appointees in face of transfer to a BFP, 8.15.26
heir of trustee cannot be BFP of trust property, 3.4.3
holder in due course (negotiable instruments) and BFP compared, 8.3.6, 8.45
illegality of transaction does not necessarily preclude BFP status, 5.4.2, 8.15.63
indenture trustee's conveyance to BFP, 8.15.63
judicial lien creditor generally not a BFP, 8.15.63
legal condition subsequent not cut off by transfer of subject property to a BFP, 9.9.24
legatee of trustee cannot be BFP of trust property, 3.4.3
lessees as BFPs, 3.5.3.1(b)
mistake of law causing transfer of trust property to an innocent non-BFP, 8.15.63
monies paid under mistake of law to innocent non-BFP, nonrecoverability of, 8.15.63, 8.15.74
multiple assignments of same equitable interest, BFP issues regarding, 8.15.63
murder, receipt by BFP of title to trust property acquired by, 8.15.63
mutual fund equitable participations held in trust
    transfer to BFP, 8.15.63
nature of trustee's title, effect on rights of BFP, 2.1
negation of alienation restraint by transfer of legal title to BFP (charitable trusts), 5.3.3.3(c)
no duty of BFP to *see* to application of purchase price, 3.6, 8.21
nominee trusts and sales to BFPs, 9.6
notice of breach of trust precludes transferee's BFP status
    generally, 8.3.2, 8.15.63
    constructive notice of breach, 8.3.2
    deed of land to grantee "as trustee," 8.3.2
    duty of transferee to *see* to application of purchase price, 8.15.69, 8.21
    judgment creditors of trustee, 8.3.2
    land recording statutes (trustee's personal creditors versus the beneficiaries), 8.3.2
    notice to transferee's agent, 8.3.2
    notice to transferee's straw, 8.3.2
    personal creditor of trustee not BFP even though has no notice of breach, 8.3.2
    purchaser of trustee's assets at judicial sale might qualify as BFP, 8.3.2
    securities whose certificates disclose trust's existence, 8.3.2
    transfer in breach of trust to innocent trustee for benefit of person with notice, 8.3.2
    unrecorded trust instruments, 8.3.2
one acquiring trust property by murder may pass good title to BFP, 8.15.63
one who has forfeited trust property due to divorce may pass good title to BFP, 8.15.63
parties to suit against non-BFP of trust property, 5.4.2

Index

Index

income taxation of, 10.7
trustee as principal but not agent, 9.6
when beneficiary controls trustee, 9.6

Bypass trust
generation-skipping transfer tax, 8.9.2
marital deduction, 8.9.1.3, 8.9.2

Byzantium
ademption by extinction, 8.15.54
perpetuities, 8.2.1

California
A long-time trust code state, Chap. 1
Public Employees' Retirement System (Calpers)
fiduciary capitalism, Chap. 1
hedge fund investments of, 6.2.2.1
mismanagement of, 9.8.2
oversight of illusory, 9.8.2
politicization of, 9.8.2
as a quasi-trust, 9.8.2
Rules of Court on trustee compensation, 8.4

Calpers. *See* California, Public Employees' Retirement System (Calpers)

Cambridge Trust Case. *See* Constructive Fraud

Canada Index, 6.2.2.1

Canon law, 3.5.1

Canons of Professional Ethics (lawyers), 8.25

Capacity
to establish a trust, Chap. 1, 3.1, 8.2.2.1
to exercise power of appointment, Chap. 1
lack of, Chap. 1
as grounds for voidance of trust, 8.2.2.1

Capital
capital gains
apportionment of, 6.2.4.2
internal, defined, 11.3
taxation of, Chap. 10
corporate trustee, capital requirements of, 8.6
principal, as synonym for, Chap. 1, 3.5.3.2(g), 6.2.4
requirements of corporate trustee, 8.6
as synonym for principal, res, and subject matter of trust, Chap. 1, 3.5.3.2(g), 6.2.4

Capricious trust purposes, rule against
generally, 8.15.39
public policy considerations, 9.24

Capture
doctrine of capture, 4.1.1.1, 8.15.12
exercise of power of appointment in further trust, 4.1.1.1, 8.1.2, 8.2.1.8, 8.15.12
expired powers of appointment, 8.2.2.2, 8.15.12
failed exercises of powers of appointment, 8.15.12
failures to exercise, 8.15.12
ineffective exercises, 8.15.12
lapsed powers, 8.15.12
outright exercises, 8.15.12
released powers, 8.15.12
resulting trust, capture incident to imposition of, 4.1.1.1, 8.1.1
reversions, 8.15.12

Carnegie, Andrew (Franklin Trust), 8.31

Carryover basis. *See* Tax basis of trust property

Cashier's check, 9.9.4
Casner, A. James
  doctrine of worthier title and rules of construction, 8.15.2
  issue and other class designations (rules of construction), 5.2, 8.15.2
Cayman Islands
  offshore asset protection trusts, 9.10
  STAR trusts, 9.8.10
Cede & Co.
  DTC nominee, 6.2.1.4
Cemeteries. *See* Gravesites
CERCLA
  environmental protection, 7.3.4.2(b)
Certificates of beneficial interest
  bank collective funds, 7.3.3.3
  title in trustee, 2.1
  trusts resembling corporations, 9.6
Certification of trust
  furnished third parties in lieu of trust instrument, 8.21, 9.6
  liability of third parties (UTC §1013 certification), 3.6, 7.2.9, 8.21, 9.6
  public filings, 9.6
  real estate, 9.6
Cestui que trust (*cestui que* **trustent)**
  how pronounced, Chap. 1
  term for beneficiary, generally, Chap. 1, 5.3.1, 5.6
Cestui que **use**
  law French, 8.15
  term for beneficiary, 5.3.1
  translated, 8.15.1
Chancellor. *See also* Chancery court
  acted by subpoena, 8.15.1
  Bacon, Sir Francis, Chap. 1
  Brougham, Henry Peter, Chap. 1
  chancellors since 1066, Chap. 1
  cy pres power, 8.15.28
  functions of, Chap. 1
  Governor of New York, Chap. 1
  More, Sir Thomas, Chap. 1
Chancery court (England)
  afforded minors access to equitable interest, 5.4.1.3
  Bacon, Sir Francis, Chap. 1
  Brougham, Henry Peter, Chap. 1
  Calendars of Chancery, 9.4.2
  chancery receiver not a trustee, 9.9.17
  function of, Chap. 1
  history of, Chap. 1
  jurisdiction of, Chap. 1, 5.3.1
  More, Sir Thomas, Chap. 1
  origins of, Chap. 1
  standing of *cestui que* use to seek enforcement of use in, 4.1.2, 5.3.1
Chancery receiver
  is not a trustee, 9.9.17
Change of circumstances warranting reformation
  generally, 8.15.22
  doctrine of reformation, 8.15.22
Channel Islands
  donner et retenir ne vaut rien (the maxim), 8.15.45
  Guernsey trust legislation (1989), 9.10
  Jersey trust legislation (1984), 9.10
  offshore asset protection haven, 9.10
  as part of Normandy in 1066, making its trust jurisprudence unique, 9.10

Index

Index

Index

Contingent equitable interests
generally, 5.3.1, 8.30
antilapse, 8.15.55
creditor access to beneficiary's contingent equitable interest depends on whether trust is
    self-settled, 4.1.3, 5.3.3.1
domestic asset protection trusts involving contingent interests, 4.1.3, 5.3.3.1(c)
employee benefit trusts involving contingent interests, 9.5.1
equitable interests defined, 3.5.1
interests subject to exercise of trustee's discretion, 5.3.1
LLC ill suited to administer contingent interests, 8.22
Medicaid eligibility and recoupment when equitable interests of applicant/recipient are
    contingent, 5.3.5
rule against perpetuities limits duration of contingent interests, 8.2.1, 8.2.1.1, 8.2.1.3
spouse's access to contingent equitable interest of other spouse, 5.3.4
vested (transmissible) contingent equitable remainder defined, 8.30
Contingent remainder interests
defined, 8.2
destructibility of contingent remainders, 8.15.65
vested (transmissible) contingent equitable remainder defined, 8.30
Contract
alteration of trust terms by, 6.1.2
arbitration provision in inter vivos trust as, 3.5.3.3
Art. 1, §10, U.S. Const. and altering charitable corporation charters by legislation, 9.4.4
bank account as contract, not trust, 9.9.4
of beneficiary
    to indemnify trustee, 5.6
    to pay property into trust, 5.6
beneficiary's contract action against trustee as recourse when court lacks equity jurisdiction,
    Chap. 1
bond as, 9.31
borrower promises lender to use borrowed funds to satisfy borrower's contract debt to a third
    party, 9.9.4
capacity of settlor to enter into trust and contract, Chap. 1, 3.1
consideration for establishing trust,
    failure of consideration grounds for rescission by settlor, 8.2.2.1
    precludes reformation of trust for mistake, 8.17
of constructive trustee in breach of trust not specifically enforceable, 3.3
contract to assign interest in spendthrift trust not specifically enforceable, 5.3.3.3(c)
contract to convey land as not a trust, 9.9.11
contract to exercise a power of appointment a certain way, 8.15.26
Contract (Rights of Third Parties) Act 1999 (England), 9.9.1
Dartmouth College Case and charitable entities, 9.4.4
debenture as, 9.31
debt as, 9.9.4
distinguished from trust, 3.5.1, 9.9.1
exoneration
    for trustee's breaching contract with third party to benefit trust estate, 3.5.2.3
    for trustee's contractual obligations to third parties incurred on behalf of trust, 3.5.2.3
external in-bound contractual liabilities of third parties to trust relationship, 3.6, 5.4.1.8
indenture defined, 8.31
intention of parties dictates whether contract, agency, or trust, 8.25
life insurance as, 8.22, 9.9.1
limiting trustee's contractual liability to third parties, 7.3.2, 9.6
mediation, 8.44
nonrecourse clause in trust limiting trustee's personal contractual liability to third parties,
    7.3.2
parties to typical contract not in fiduciary relationship, 8.44
partnership as contract of mutual agency, Chap. 1
party to contract with trustee, BFP issues
    generally, 8.15.63
    contract incident to breach of trust unenforceable, 8.15.63

Index

Index

Index

Index

Due diligence on part of trustee required (*continued*)
  in investments, 6.2.2.2
  irrevocable trust, assuming trusteeship of, 8.2.2.1
  Reg. 9, pre-acceptance review pursuant to, 8.18, 8.2.3
  tax-sensitive powers, recognition, acceptance, exercise, and relinquishment of, 8.9.3
Due process,
  accountability of trustee, 6.1.5
  burdens of proof in trust litigtion, 8.24
  conflict of laws in trust conext, 8.5
  guardians ad litem, 8.14
  jurisdiction issues, 8.40
  laches doctrine, 8.15.70
  litigation involving trust (notice requirements), 5.7
  proof of facts in trust litigation, 8.46
  retroactive application of new trust law, 5.2, 8.15.71
  statutes of limitation, 7.1.3
  trustee entitled to due process in a removal action, 7.2.3.6
  virtual representation, 8.14
Duff & Phelps
  rating insurance companies, 9.2
Duke of Norfolk's Case (perpetuities), 8.2.1
Durable Power of Attorney (DPA). *See also* Agency; Agent
  agent under
    establishing trust of principal's property, 2.1.1
    no duty to act, 6.1.2
    postmortem additions of settlor's property to trust not allowed, 2.1.1
    postmortem transfers of settlor's property, 2.1.1
    trustee compared, 6.1.2
  appointment of trustee by agent acting under a DPA, 3.4.1
  attorney-in-fact a fiduciary, Chap. 1
  enduring power of attorney (England), 9.9.2
  holder may establish a revocable trust for principal, 2.1.1
  lasting power of attorney (England), 9.9.2
  liability of third party for failing to honor DPA, 8.2.2.2
  postmortem additions to a trust cannot be effected by agent acting under a DPA, 2.1.1
  revocation of revocable trust by settlor's agent acting under a DPA, 8.2.2.2
  terminates as death of principal, 2.1.1
  not a trust, 9.9.2
Duress
  constructive trust a procedural equitable remedy for, 3.3, 7.2.3.1.6
  defined, 8.2.2.1
  trust void if induced by, Chap. 1, 8.2.2.1
  undue influence and duress compared, 8.2.2.1
Dutch law
  be wind, 8.12.1
  doelvermogen, 8.12.1
  stichting, 8.12.1
Duties
  of agents, 6.1.2
  of beneficiary
    generally, 5.6
    of beneficiaries to one another, 5.6
    to disgorge misdelivered trust property, 5.6
    England, 5.6
    to indemnify trustee, 5.6
  of donee of expired nongeneral power of appointment, 8.15.90
  of transfer agent to inquire into the trustee's authority to transfer entrusted securities, 8.3.5, 8.21
  of transferee of entrusted property to *see* to application of purchase price, 8.15.69, 8.21
  of trustee
    generally, 6.1

Index

Index

Fiduciary (*continued*)
  broker as fiduciary, Chap. 1
  capacity, 3.1
  confidential and fiduciary relationships compared, Chap. 1
  defined, Chap. 1
  duties. *See* Fiduciary duties
  fiduciary capitalism, Chap. 1
  holder of expired nongeneral power of appointment as, 8.15.90
  impermissible appointee of nongeneral powers as, 3.2.6
  income tax return filed by fiduciary, 6.3.1, Chap. 10
  lawyer as fiduciary, Chap. 1, 3.2.6
  liability insurance for fiduciaries, 3.5.4.2
  liability of fiduciary under CERCLA (environmental), 7.3.4.2(b)
  negligence on part of trustee not a *per se* breach of fiduciary duty, 7.2.2
  one with duty of care not necessarily a fiduciary, Chap. 1
  person with power to direct trustee may be a fiduciary, 3.2.6, 4.2
  powers. *See* Fiduciary powers
  precedents and trust interpretive letters (OCC), 8.18
  principles applicable to mutual fund, 8.10
  protector as fiduciary, 3.2.6
  relationship (fiduciary)
    defined, Chap. 1
    confidential relationship not a fiduciary relationship, Chap. 1
    contract incident to a fiduciary relationship, Chap. 1
    equitable charge not a fiduciary relationship, Chap. 1
    fiduciary relationship incident to a contract, Chap. 1
    informal fiduciary relationship synonym for confidential relationship, Chap. 1
    one with duty of care not necessarily a fiduciary, Chap. 1
    relationship between trustee and settlor may arise before trust created, 6.2.3
  special fiduciary, appointment of, 7.2.3.8
  trustee as, 6.1.3
  whether protector is a fiduciary is unsettled, 3.2.6, 4.2
Fiduciary abuse, 7.1.2, 8.2.3
Fiduciary bonds and sureties, 3.5.4.3
Fiduciary capacity,
  defined (Reg. 9), 3.1
  of done of expired nongeneral powers of appointment, 8.15.90
Fiduciary duties
  of agent of trustee to beneficiaries, 6.1.4, 7.2.9
  of agents generally to their principals, Chap. 1
  of corporate directors of trust company to beneficiaries, 6.1.1
  of directed trustee to beneficiaries, 6.1.4
  of directors of trust company to beneficiaries, 7.2.9
  duty of care, Chap. 1
  of trust counsel to beneficiaries, 8.8
  of trust protector to beneficiaries, 3.2.6
  of trustee
    to the beneficiaries generally, Chap. 6
    to advance personal funds, 3.5.2.3
    in possession of a nonfiduciary general inter vivos power of appointment, 6.1
Fiduciary powers
  power to appoint trustees as fiduciary power under English law, 3.4.1
  of donee (power-in-trust doctrine), 8.15.90
  of trustee
    generally, 3.5.3
    implied powers, 3.5.3.1
    specified powers, 3.5.3.2
Fifth Amendment (takings clause)
  IOLTA, 6.1.3.4, 9.7.2

Index

Index

Index

Index

equity aids the vigilant and not the indolent, 8.15.70
equity looks as done which ought to be done, 8.12
following the law, 8.12
form must give way to intent, 8.12
imputing an intention to fulfill an obligation, 8.12
not suffering advantage to be taken of a penalty forfeiture, 8.12
seeking and doing equity, 3.3, 3.5.2.3, 5.6, 8.12
suffering wrongs without remedies, 8.12
Mayflower descendants (dynasty trust), 8.2.1.9
McCain, John (Indian trust accounts), 9.8.2
MDP (multidisciplinary practice), 6.1.3.3, 6.1.3.5
Measuring life (rule against perpetuities). *See* Life in being
Mechanics and Tradesmen's School of New York (the Franklin Trust), 8.31
Mediation (mediating trust disputes). *See also* Arbitration
   generally, 8.44
   court involvement probably unavoidable, 8.44
   external disputes between trustees and third parties, 3.5.3.2(f)
   guardian ad litem
      as a necessary party, 8.44
      as a quasi-mediator, 8.44
   independence of counsel is critical, 8.44
   internal trust disputes, 3.5.3.3
   the matter of the unborn and unascertained, 8.44
   mediation's limitations, 8.44
   a trust is not a contract, 8.44
   a trustee who remains in office during mediation in awkward position, 8.44
   trust terms purporting to oust court of its equitable jurisdiction unenforceable, 8.44
Medicaid
   generally, 5.3.5
   boilerplate trust termination clauses, 3.5.3.2(k)
   discretionary trust created by third party for applicant's benefit, 5.3.5
   general inter vivos power of appointment, 4.1.3
   look-back proof, 5.3.5
   means testing, 5.3.5
   permanently disabled applicants, 5.3.5
   qualifying trust, 5.3.5, 9.22
   structured settlement trust, 9.3
   transfer by applicant of property to trust for benefit of third party who is not the spouse,
      5.3.5
Medical care (invasion standard), 3.5.3.2(a)
Megarry Judgment (social investing), 6.1.3.4
Mental capacity of settlor, Chap. 1
Mental incapacity of trustee, 3.2
Merger
   alienation restraint, negation of, by merger, 5.3.3.3(c)
   of bank trustee with another bank
      generally, 8.19
      when it results in bank's becoming trustee of its own stock
         generally, 6.1.3.2
         loyalty considerations, 6.1.3.2
Merger doctrine
   generally, 8.7
   all beneficial interests pass to sole trustee, 8.7
   confusio, 8.15.36
   equitable interest "swallowed up," 8.7
   extinguishing a spendthrift restraint by merger, 5.3.3.3(c), 8.7
   involuntary merger
      generally, 8.7
      title-holder as constructive trustee, 8.7
   Justinian, 8.15.36

Index

formal execution requirements for trust instruments, Chap. 1

once a legal list jurisdiction, 6.2.2.1

nonsettlor donee of unexercised general inter vivos power of appointment (creditor accessibility), 5.3.3.2

rule against perpetuities, 8.2.1, 8.2.1.7

spendthrift trusts (income not needed to maintain beneficiary's station in life), 5.3.3.3(c)

transferee of an entrusted chose in action may not be a BFP, 8.15.63

trusts presumed to be spendthrift absent language in instrument to contrary, 5.3.3.3(c)

unitrust conversion legislation, 6.2.2.4

virtual representation, 8.14

NIMCRUT, 9.4.5.1

No-contest clauses in trusts

generally, 5.5

contest defined, 5.5

enforceable in England, 5.5

No further inquiry rule

generally, 6.1.3, 7.2.3.2, 8.15.30, 8.24

endorsed in Restatement (Third) of Trusts, 6.1.3

loans of trustee's personal funds to trust an exception, 6.1.3.1

proof of self-dealing shifts burden of proof to trustee, 6.1.3, 8.24

proprietary mutual funds, 6.1.3.4

trustee borrowing from trust estate, 6.1.3.1

Nobel Prize Committee, 6.2.2.1

Nominee partnership, securities held in, 3.5.3.2(e)

Nominee trust

generally, 9.6

the certification of trust, 9.6

as an instrument of commerce, 8.22

liability

of beneficiary, 5.6, 9.6

Illinois, 9.6

Massachusetts, 9.6

trustee, 5.6, 9.6

recording requirement (Massachusetts), 9.6

the sub-trust, 6.2.1.4

trustee compensation, 9.6

trustee a principal, 9.6

when beneficiary controls the trustee, 9.6

Nonbeneficiaries, trustee's liability to

liability in contract, 7.3.1, 7.3.2

liability to sovereign, 7.3.4

liability in tort, 7.3.3

Noncash exchange inherent in trustee's power to sell, 3.5.3.1(a)

Non-exclusive limited power defined, 8.1.1. *See also* Limited power of appointment; Powers of appointment

Nongeneral power of appointment. *See* Limited power of appointment

Nonqualified executive deferred compensation

generally, 9.5.3

economic benefit doctrine, 9.5.3

Non-recourse clause in trust (limiting trustee's contractual liability), 7.3.2

Nonresident trustee

nonresidency not necessarily grounds for trustee removal, 7.2.3.6

who can be a trustee, 3.1

who is fit to be trustee, 3.2

Non-U.S. citizen spouse of settlor

marital deduction generally, 8.9.1.3

qualified domestic trust (QDOT), 9.14

North Dakota

Rule Against Perpetuities, abolition of, 8.2.1.9

Index

Origin of the English trust (*continued*)
waqf and the Islamic theory, 8.37
OTS (Office of Thrift Supervision), 8.6, 8.18
Ousting court. *See* Jurisdiction
Out-of-state property
ancillary trusteeship, 3.5.3.1(i), 9.32
Out-of-state trustee. *See* Foreign trustee
Overpayment to beneficiary. *See also* Misdelivery
liabilities of beneficiary, 5.6
reopening accounts only to correct fraud, 6.1.5.2
Overseas branch of U.S. bank (American Depository Receipts), 6.2.1.4

Packard Foundation (David & Lucile), 4.1, 9.4.1
Parchment
described, 9.31
history of, 9.31
indentures, 9.31
Parens patriae **(the state as)**
Blackstone on, 7.1
enforcement of charitable trusts, 9.4.2
Parent-child relationship
as not a fiduciary relationship (confidential relationship), Chap. 1
Parks and parkland, 9.8.3
Parliament
Georgian Statute of Mortmain enacted in 1736, 8.11
law French
parliamentary terms and expressions still in use, 8.15
usage outlawed by Parliament in 1731, 8.15
lifting by Parliament of final restrictions on corporation's right to own land in 1960, 8.6, 9.8.1
Statute of Charitable Uses (Statute of Elizabeth) enacted in 1601, 8.15.14
Statute Quia Emptores enacted in 1290, 8.15.4
Statute of Uses enacted in 1536, 8.15.1
Parol evidence rule
generally, 8.15.6
plain meaning rule, 8.15.6
trust reformation, 8.17
Participation in breach of trust
assignees of negotiable instruments, 8.3.6
banks as depositories of trust cash, 8.3.4
beneficiary standing to sue, 3.6
duty of transferee of entrusted property to *see* to application of purchase price, 8.15.69, 8.21
external in-bound liabilities of third parties to trust relationship, 3.6
laches, 3.6
non-BFPs, 8.3.1, 8.3.2
officious intermeddlers, 8.15.35
pledgees of trust property, 8.3.3
safe deposit box lessors, 8.3.8
statutes of limitation, 3.6
stock transfer agents and issuing corporations, 8.3.5
stockbrokers, 8.3.7
third parties to trust relationship, external in-bound liabilities of, 3.6
transferees of trust property, 3.6, 8.3.2
Partner
as trustee, 3.3
Partnership
agencies are not trusts, 9.9.2
as contract of mutual agency, Chap. 1
is not a trust, Chap. 1, 9.9.2
post-mortem transfers

Index

Power of appointment (*continued*)
 joinder of adverse party can be required for exercise, 8.1.1
 by last unrevoked instrument, 8.1.1
 mechanics of exercising a power of appointment, 8.1.1
 must be in good faith, 3.5.3.2(a)
 partially ineffective exercises (doctrine of infectious invalidity), 8.15.72
 when the product of wrongdoing, 8.1.1
 by proxy, 8.2.2.2
 by revocable inter vivos trust, 8.1.1
 revocation/amendment of an exercise, 8.1.1
 specific exercise clause, 8.1.1
 by unprobated will, 8.1.1
 by will residue clause, 4.1.1.1, 8.1.1
 expired powers of appointment, 4.1.1.1, 8.1.1
  generally, 4.1.1.1, 8.1.1, 8.15.93
  implied-gift-in-default doctrine, 8.15.93
 fraud on a special power doctrine
  generally, 8.15.26
  abuse of discretionary power, 3.5.3.2(a), 8.15.26
 hotchpot clauses, 8.1.1, 8.15.51
 illusory appointments doctrine, 8.1.1, 8.15.86
 impermissible appointees defined, 8.1.1
 jointly held powers, 8.1.1
 negating a power of appointment, 8.1.1
 objects of power of appointment defined, 8.1.1
 permissible appointees defined, 8.1.1
 partial exercises
  defined, 8.1.1
  distinguished from power of appointment over only part of trust property, 8.1.1
 power-in-trust doctrine, 3.3, 8.15.90
 releasing powers, 8.1.1
 spendthrift restrictions, 5.3.3.3(c)
 status of property subject to unexercised power, 5.3.3
 remoteness, 8.2.1.8
 takers in default,
  defined, 8.1.1
  disclaimer by, 8.1.1
  when lacking, 8.1.1
 toggling authority in trustee, 8.1.1
Power of attorney. *See also* Agency; Agent; Durable Power of Attorney
 agencies are not trusts, 9.9.2
 attorney-in-fact acting under durable power of attorney as a fiduciary, Chap. 1
 wrongful transfer of principal's property to a trustee, 3.4.1
Powers of trustee
 generally, 3.5.3, 3.5.3.1, 3.5.3.2, 3.5.3.2(c)
 to abandon
  claims, 3.5.3.2(f)
  trust property, 3.5.3.1(h)
 to administer distributions to minors, 3.5.3.2(l)
 administrative powers generally, 3.5.3
 to appoint own cotrustee or successor, 3.4.1
 arbitration, to submit disputes to, 3.5.3.3
 to bind trust in contract, 3.5.3.1(d)
 to borrow on behalf of the trust, 3.5.3.2(c)
 to combine trusts, 3.5.3.2(d)
 to compromise claims, 3.5.3.2(f)
 to cooperate with others (protective committees and representative suits), 3.5.3.2(o)
 cotrustee's powers, 3.4.4.1
 to deduct compensation from trust estate, 3.5.2.4

Powers of trustee (*continued*)
to incur expenses, 3.5.3.1(g)
to invest, 3.5.3.1(a)
to lease trust property, 3.5.3.1(b)
to pay expenses, 3.5.3.1(g)
to sell trust property, 3.5.3.1(a)
to sue third parties, 3.5.3.1(c)
to vote proxies with respect to shares comprising trust estate, 3.5.3.1(e)
to impress a different trust upon trust property, 6.1
to incur and pay expenses, 3.5.3.1(g)
to invest in common trust funds and mutual funds, 3.5.3.2(d)
to lease property beyond term of trust, 3.5.3.1(b)
as that of legally competent and unmarried individual (Restatement (Third) of Trusts), 3.5.3, 3.5.3.1
leveraging trust assets, 3.5.3.2(c), 6.2.2.1
to litigate on behalf of trust, 3.5.3.1(c)
to make gifts of trust property generally lacking, 3.5.3.2(f)
to make loans of own funds to trust, 3.5.3.2(j), 5.4.1.7, 6.1.3.1
to make loans of trust property to remainderman, 5.4.1.7, 5.4.1.3
to manage trust estate, 3.5.3
to mortgage trust property, 3.5.3.2(c)
to negotiate with third parties on behalf of trust, 3.5.3.2(f)
to pledge trust property, 3.5.3.2(c)
to prudently make property productive, 6.2.2
releasability of discretionary powers, 8.1.1
to resign, 3.5.3.2(n)
to resolve income and principal apportionment questions, 3.5.3.2(g)
to retain specified property, 3.5.3
to retain un-conflicted counsel notwithstanding terms of trust, 3.5.3
redeem at par entrusted flower bonds, 3.5.3.5
to sell trust property, 3.5.3.1(a), 8.2.1.9
special investment powers, 3.5.3.2(i)
statutory powers of trustee, 3.5.3.2(l)
to submit disputes to arbitration, 3.5.3.3
of successor, 3.4.4.3
to sue third parties on behalf of trust, 3.5.3.1(c)
of surviving cotrustee, 3.4.4.2
to terminate trust, 3.5.3.2(k)
to transfer property to a BFP, 3.5.2.2, 5.4.2, 8.21
to vote proxies, 3.5.3.1(e)
Pre-acceptance review (Reg. 9), 8.18
Precatory words,
evidence of intention to impress a trust on property, 8.15.58
powers of appointment, 8.15.58
Predecessor trustee
attorney-client privilege of, as against successor trustee, 3.4.4.3, 8.8
contribution of, to damage award, 7.2.4
duty of successor trustee to examine accounts of predecessor, 6.2.2.2
liability of, 7.2.4
Preemption, federal
ERISA, 5.3.3.3(d)
soft dollar, 6.1.3.4
Preliminary injunction to preserve trust property, 7.2.3.1.5
Premiums as a trust expense, insurance, 3.5.4.2
Preponderance of evidence of homicide, 8.24
Present interest (annual gift tax exclusion)
generally, 9.18
Crummey trust, 9.18
gifts to minors, 8.23, 9.17, 9.18

Index

Principal place of administration
administrative matters, 8.5
charitable trust, 9.4.2
conflict of laws, 8.5
construction of dispositive terms, 8.5
Hague Convention of the Law Applicable to Trusts, 8.5
notice of change in, 6.1.5.1
relocation of, 6.2.15
Principal residence, sale of
§121 exclusion, 9.1.3
Pritchett, Henry S. (The Franklin Trust), 8.31
Privacy of beneficiary fostered by title being in trustee
generally, Chap. 1
UPC trust registration requirement, 2.1.1
Private trust companies
generally, 8.6
Investment Advisors Act of 1940, 8.6
proper organizational structure, 6.2.11
Privatstiftung **(Austrian foundation),** 8.2.1
Privilege, attorney-client
whom trust counsel represents, 8.8
Privileges and immunities clause, 3.1
Privity of contract doctrine
bar to scrivener malpractice action, 8.15.61
circumvention by trust, 9.9.1
legal malpractice, 8.8
Probate
administrative trust as probate substitute, 9.9.14
avoidance of, by means of a trust, Chap. 1, 8.22
defined, Chap. 1
disposition of surplus fiduciaried property, 9.8.6
duties to creditors, 9.8.6
federal diversity jurisdiction, probate exception to, 8.15.19
generation skipping in Israel not possible without probate, 8.9.2
lifetime (probate), 8.42
probate court, registration of trust in, Chap. 1
probate estate
disposed of, by residue clause, 8.26
distributions to closed probate estate, 8.2.1
personal representative (executor) quasi-trustee of, 9.8.6
trust compared and contrasted, 9.8.6
registration of trust in probate court, Chap. 1
testamentary power of appointment, and exercise of, 8.1.1
Uniform Probate Code conflates executorship and trusteeship, 9.8.6
Procedure, principle of, 7.1.3
Professional liability insurance, 3.5.4.2
Professional trustee
need for working capital, 3.2.2
Professor-student relationship
as not a fiduciary relationship, Chap. 1
Profit rule
trustee's unauthorized profit held upon constructive trust, 6.1.3
trustees may not profit from trusteeship, 6.1.3
Promissory note
indebtedness as an investment, 6.2.2.1
Proof
of beneficiary's death, 5.5
of BFP status, 8.24
burdens of, 8.24
clear and convincing evidence standard,
generally, 8.24

Index

Index

Receiver
    appointment of, 7.2.3.8
    chancery receiver,
        an officer of the court, 9.9.17
        not a trustee, 9.9.17
        subject property *in custodia legis*, 9.9.17
    as fiduciary, 7.2.3.8
    judicial appointment of, as remedy for breach of trust, 7.2.3.4, 7.2.3.8
    not a trustee because does not have legal title, 7.2.3.8
Reciprocal trust doctrine, 8.15.24
Recording of trust instrument
    foreclosure of claims as effect of
        non-BFPs of real estate, claims of, 8.3.2
        trustee's personal creditors, claims of, against real estate in trust, 8.3.1
    instruments limiting trustee's liability to nonbeneficiaries in contract, 7.3.2
    registry of deeds filing requirements, 9.6
    shares of beneficial interest in nominee trust need not be recorded, 9.6
    Smith, Janet M., 9.6
Record-keeping
    asset custody and transfer, 6.2.1.4
Rectification, doctrine of
    generally, 8.15.22
    when a trust is incident to a contract, 8.15.22
Reformation
    generally, 8.15.22
    converting a trust into a CRAT by judicial reformation, 8.17
    to cure a perpetuities violation, 8.15.22
    defined, 8.17
    difference between reformation and deviation murky, 8.15.20
    doctrine of, 8.15.22
    evidence of mistake warranting reformation must be clear and convincing, 8.15.22, 8.17
    mistake-based reformation actions
        generally, 8.15.22
        to achieve tax efficiency, 8.17
        loyalty implications when brought by trustee, 6.2.6
        to remedy faulty tax planning, 8.17
        testamentary trusts, 8.15.22
    modification and reformation distinguished, 8.17
    plain meaning rule may constrain reformation doctrine, 8.15.22
    posture of trustee in light of the duty to defend, 8.15.22
    rectification, 8.15.22
    to remedy faulty tax planning involving mistake, 8.17
    resolving ambiguity and reformation distinguished, 8.17
    of terms of testamentary trust, 8.15.22
Registration
    of deeds. *See* Recording
    of securities (SEC), 7.3.3.3, 7.3.4.2(a), 8.18
    of trusts. *See* Registration of trusts
Registration of trusts
    generally, Chap. 1
    UPC trust registration requirement
        generally, 2.1.1, 3.4.1, 6.1.5.1, 7.2.3.6
        failure to register, consequences of, 7.2.3.5(c), 7.3.4.2(d)
Regulation 9 (Reg. 9)
    collective investment funds, and prudent investor rule, 6.2.2.1
    common trust funds, 6.2.1.2, 9.7.1
    compensation, 8.4
    conflicts of interest, 6.1.3, 6.1.3.4
    directors of national bank, self-dealing, 6.1.3.4
    duty of institutional trustee to have an effective organizational structure, 6.2.11

Regulation 9 (Reg. 9) (*continued*)
    employees of national bank, self-dealing, 6.1.3.4
    full-service brokerage, 8.18
    insider trading by national bank personnel, 6.1.3.4
    national banks
        brokerage placement practices, 6.1.3.4
        fiduciary activities, 3.1
        officers, self-dealing by, 6.1.3.4
    OTS regulations parallel Reg. 9, 8.6
    participation certificates in bank collective funds may not be issued, 7.3.3.3
    Q & As regarding revised Reg. 9, 8.18
    revisions to (1997), 8.18
    self-dealing, 6.1.3
    short-term investments, 6.1.3.1
    summary of, 8.18
    written policies and procedures, 6.1.3, 6.1.3.1, 6.1.3.4, 8.18
Regulation D (SEC), 7.3.3.3
Reich, Robert
    ETIs, 6.1.3.4
Reimbursement from trust estate
    attorneys' fees of trustee
        generally, 3.5.2.3, 5.6
        whether reimbursable in discretion of court, 3.5.2.3
    beneficiaries' right to legal fees from trust estate, 8.13
    loyalty duty exception, trustee's right of reimbursement as, 6.1.3
    outgoing trustee's right of, 3.5.2.3
    trustee's right to, 3.5.2.3, 6.1.3, 7.3, 7.3.1, 7.3.3, 7.3.4.1, 7.3.4.2(b)
REIT (real estate investment trust)
    G-REIT (Germany) is not a trust, 9.9.12
    as instrument of commerce, Chap. 1
    U.K.-REIT is not a trust, 9.9.12
    U.S. REIT
        mutual fund, as type of, 9.6
        as a trust, 9.9.12
    use as proto-REIT, 9.6
Relatives. *See* Class designations
Relator actions, 9.4.2
Release
    beneficiary's
        disclaimer and release compared, 5.5
        ineffective if procured by improper conduct of trustee, 7.2.7
        informed, requirement that release be, 8.2.3
        of power of appointment, 5.3.3.3(c), 8.1.1
        spendthrift provision not foreclosing release of power of appointment, 5.3.3.3(c)
    of trustee from liability
        for breach of trust, 7.1.4, 7.2.7
        in lieu of judicial settlement of accountings, 8.2.4
        under seal, 8.2.3
    donee's release of his nonfiduciary power of appointment, 8.1.1
    trustee's release or disclaimer of fiduciary power
        generally, 3.5.3.4
        discretionary fiduciary power may not be releasable by trustee, 3.5.3.4
Reliance on part of beneficiary
    fiduciary relationship, existence of, without reliance, Chap. 1
Relief for breaches of trust
    generally, 7.2.3
    assessment of attorneys' fees, 7.2.3.7
    denial of compensation, 7.2.3.7
    liability without economic injury, 7.2.8
    reduction of compensation, 7.2.3.7

Index

Index

Index

Index

Index

Standing (trust enforcement) (*continued*)
  appointee pursuant to exercise of power of appointment, 7.1
  assignee of beneficial interest, 7.1, 7.2
  attorney general, for charitable trusts, 9.4.2, 9.4.3
  beneficiary's standing to seek enforcement of trust in the courts
    generally, Chap. 1, 5.1
    declaratory judgment, complaints for, 5.4.1.9, 8.42
    discretionary trusts, 5.3.1
    instructions, complaints for, 5.4.1.9, 8.42
  beneficiary's standing to sue third party in derivative action when trustee fails to do so
    generally, 3.6, 5.4.1.8
    agents of trustee who participate in breach of trust, 5.4.1.8, 8.21
    assignment of cause of action to beneficiary, 3.6
    beneficiary entitled to immediate possession, 3.6
    external in-bound liabilities of third parties to trust relationship, 3.6, 8.21
    knowing participation of third party in breach of trust, 3.6
    passive trusts, 3.6
  charitable trusts, standing to seek enforcement of
    attorney general of state, 9.4.2
    citizens, 9.4.2
    guardian ad litem, 9.4.2
    co-trustees, 9.4.2
    institutions and individuals special interests, 9.4.2
    other designated public official of state, 9.4.2
    personal representative of settlor, 9.4.2
    settlor, 9.4.2
    split-interest trust, 9.4.2
    successor trustees, 9.4.2
    taxpayers, 9.4.2
    trustee ad litem, 9.4.2
    visitor, 9.4.2
  cotrustee seeking trust's enforcement, 3.4.4.1
  creditor of beneficiary, 7.1, 7.2
  donee of power of appointment, 7.1
  relatives of someone interred in cemetery plot, 5.1
  revocable trust, enforcement of terms of, 7.1
  settlor
    generally, 4.1–4.2, 6.1.2, 8.2.2.1
    of charitable trust, 9.4.2
  successor trustee, 7.1
  takers pursuant to terms of antilapse statute, 7.1
  takers upon a resulting trust, 7.1
  when trust revocable, 7.1
  third parties' external in-bound liabilities to trust relationship, 3.6
    standing of beneficiaries to sue third parties
      generally, 3.6, 5.4.1.8
      bondholders when indenture trustee fails to foreclose, 5.4.1.8
    standing of trustee to sue third parties, 3.6, 5.4.1.8
Stanford Law School
  one of first to downgrade course on trusts to elective status, 8.25
STAR trusts
  in Cayman Islands, 9.8.10
Stare decisis
  principles foster both stability and flexibility in the law, Chap. 1
State action. *See Cy pres*; IOLTA
State-imposed ownership restrictions
  involuntary trustees, 3.3

Index

Index

Taxation (*continued*)
    no longer applicable to gifts out of revocable trusts, 8.9.1
  throwback, income tax, 10.4
  tier 1 income, 10.4
  tier 2 income, 10.4
  TIN (taxpayer identification number), 6.3.1, 8.34, 9.2
  TPT (tax on prior transfers), 8.9.1.2
  treaties (estate and gift taxes), 8.9
  trusts, clauses in, 8.2.1.10, 8.20
  U.S. Treasury, 9.9.3
  valuing split interests, 9.4.5
  Victims of Terrorism Tax Relief Act of 2001
    credit shelter allocation, 8.14
  when an EIN is not required, 8.34
  wills, clauses in, 8.2.1.10, 8.20
Taxpayer identification number (TIN), 6.3.1, 9.2, Chap. 10
TEDRA (Trust Dispute Resolution Act)
  decanting opportunities afforded by, 3.5.3.2(a)
  described, 3.5.3.2(a)
  material purpose doctrine (Claflin doctrine) undermined by, 3.5.3.2(a), 8.15.11
Temporary injunction
  to preserve trust property, 7.2.3.1.5
Tenancy in common
  conveyance to two trustees as tenants in common creates two trusts, 3.4.3
  of equitable interests, 5.3.1
  legal tenancy in common not a trust, 9.9.20
Tentative trust. *See* Totten trust
Termination of trust. *See also* Remainderman; Revocability
  generally, 8.2
  abolition of rule against perpetuities, 8.2.1.9
  administrative trusts, 9.9.14
  beneficiaries who do not consent to termination, 8.2.3
  by beneficiary, 5.4.4, 8.2.2.1, 8.2.2.2
  beneficiary's income interest at termination, 6.2.4.5
  charitable trust, 9.4.3
  checklist, 8.2.4
  conveyance upon, 5.4.1.7
  date of termination date, defined, 8.2
  defunding does not necessarily result in termination, 8.2.2.1
  destination of trust property upon termination, 5.4.4
  duty to expeditiously distribute upon termination, 8.2.3
  events triggering termination, 3.4.2
  fees, 8.2.3
  form of terminating distributions
    generally, 8.2.3
    annuity contracts, 8.2.3
    in cash, 8.2.3
    in kind, 8.2.3
    valuation issues, 8.2.3
  internal procedures for flagging terminating events, desirability of, 3.4.2
  lease beyond, 3.5.3.2(b)
  loans of principal to remainderman, 5.4.1.7
  through merger, 8.7
  method of final distribution
    cash, 8.2.3
    in kind, 8.2.3
  in mid-course
    generally, 5.4.1.7, 8.2.2, 8.2.2.1
    absence of trust purpose, 8.2.2.1
    charitable trusts, 8.2.2.1

Index

Testamentary trust, Chap. 1
  acceptance of trusteeship, 3.4.2
  appointment of trustee, 3.4.1
  bond, trustee's, 3.4.1, 3.5.4.3
  conflict of laws, 8.5
  court involvement, 3.4.4.3
  defined, Chap. 1, 2.1.2
  established by spouse of Medicaid applicant, 5.3.5
  execution requirements, 2.1.2
  foreign trustee, qualification in court of deceased settlor's domicile, 2.11, 2.1.2
  funding of, 2.1.2
  general inter vivos power of appointment may be created under, 8.1.1
  inter vivos trust compared, 2.1.1
  inventory, trustee's, 6.1.5.2
  reformation of, 8.15.22
  replacement of trustee of, 3.4.4.3
  split interest trusts, 9.4.5
  UPC trust registration requirement, 3.4.1, 3.4.2
  when it arises when executor and trustee one and same, 2.1.2
Texas
  spendthrift trust, access to, by beneficiary's spouse and children, 5.3.3.3(c)
Thellusson Act
  generally, 8.15.23
  rule against accumulations, 8.15.8
Third parties (rights, duties, and obligations of those not party to trust relationship)
  external in-bound liabilities of third parties, 3.6
    generally, 3.6, 5.4.1.8
    adverse possession by third parties, 3.6
    beneficiary suit against culpable third party allowed if
      cause of action has been assigned to beneficiary, 3.6
      participation in any breach of trust was knowing, 3.6, 5.4.1.8
      recovery accrues immediately to beneficiary, 3.6
      trust is passive, 3.6
      trustee fails to do so, 3.6
    BFP has no duty to *see* to application of purchase price, 3.6, 7.2.9, 8.45
    duty of transferee of entrusted property to *see* to application of purchase price, 8.15.69, 8.21
    feoffee to uses, 3.6
    interest of trustee and beneficiaries not joint, 3.6
    laches defense, 3.6
    participation of third party in breach of trust, 3.6, 7.2.9
    res judicata, 3.6
    standing of beneficiary to sue third party, 3.6, 5.4.1.8
    statutes of limitation, 3.6
    successor trustees, 3.6
    third party generally ill-advised to directly deal with beneficiary
      generally, 3.6, 7.2.9
      beneficiary may have validly assigned equitable interest
      generally, 5.3.2, 7.2.9
      third party may have to pay twice, 5.3.3.3(c), 7.2.9
      trustee's duty to compel second payment, 5.3.3.3(c), 7.2.9
    tortfeasors, 3.6
    transferees of trust property, 3.6, 7.2.9, 8.21
    trustee contracting with third parties for goods and services, 3.6
    trustee's responsibility in first instance to sue culpable third party
      generally, 3.6
      beneficiaries need to be made parties to suit, when, 3.6
      trustee legal owner of underlying trust property, 3.6
  liability of trustee to nonbeneficiaries, 7.3

Index

Index

Trustee (*continued*)
relationship to trust estate, 3.5
release by beneficiary of trustee's liability, 5.5
reliance on terms of trust, 3.5.2.4
reorganization, 9.11
resignation of, 3.4.3
rights of
generally, 3.5.2
to attorneys' fees, 3.5.2.3
to compensation, 3.5.2.4, 8.4
to exoneration, 3.5.2.3
to indemnity, 3.5.2.3
to interest on personal funds advanced, 3.5.2.3
to possession of trust property, 3.5.2.1
to reimbursement, 3.5.2.3
to rely on trust instrument, 3.5.2.5
to seek instructions from court, 3.5.2.6
to transfer title to trust property, 3.5.2.2
security interest of trustee in trust property (for compensation), 6.1.3
selection of, 3.2.6
settlor of trust, 3.1
single-purpose trust corporation, 3.2.1
of spendthrift trust as still entitled to indemnified from trust estate, 5.3.3.3(c)
state trust charter, 8.6
statement of authority, 2.1.1
status of, 3.5.2.3
stockbrokers as, 3.2.3
successor trustee, 3.4.4.3
third parties' external in-bound liabilities to, 3.6
title, legal capacity to take, 3.1
title of, 2.1
torts of, 9.6
trust counsel, 8.8
trustee *de son tort*, 8.15.35
unauthorized practice of law. *See* Unauthorized practice of law by trustee
unincorporated association as, 3.1
U.S. as, 9.8.2
vacating office, 3.4
vacations, permissibility for trustee to take, 6.1.4
who may serve as
generally, 3.1
non-humans
corporations, 8.6
federal savings banks, 8.5
foreign charitable corporations, 8.6
foreign trust companies, 8.6
limited liability companies, 8.6
national banks, 8.6
partnerships, 8.6
private trust companies, 8.6
unincorporated associations, 8.6
windfall accruing to trustee in lieu of imposition of resulting trust, 4.1.1.1
Trustee ad Litem, 7.2.3.8
Trustee *de son tort*
generally, 8.15.35
de facto trustee, 8.15.35
executor *de son tort* concept predates trustee *de son tort* concept, 8.15.35
indemnity, entitlement to, 3.3
as institutional constructive trusteeship, 3.3, 8.15.35

Index

Index

Index

Index